Famous Passage

p. 315 – Whittier

Property of Jean Sentz
Tobelmann

6.50

The Literature of the United States

Revised edition

Volume two

The Literature of the United States

Revised edition

An anthology and a history

From the Civil War to the present

Walter Blair, University of Chicago

Theodore Hornberger, University of Minnesota

Randall Stewart, Brown University

Scott, Foresman and Company

Chicago   Atlanta   Dallas   Palo Alto   Fair Lawn, N.J.

Acknowledgment is made on pages 1182-1183 for the use of copyrighted selections and pictures

Preface

For an explanation of the objectives and procedures of *The Literature of the United States,* the reader is referred to the Preface for Volume I.

To indicate their individual responsibility in Volume II, the editors have initialed the interchapters; the division of labor in the preparation of biographies, texts, headnotes, footnotes, and bibliographies is shown in the following list:

W. B. (Walter Blair): George L. Aiken, Civil War Singers, Abraham Lincoln, "I Hear America Singing," David Crockett, William Tappan Thompson, George Washington Harris, Thomas Bangs Thorpe, Charles Farrar Browne, Henry Wheeler Shaw, Charles Heber Clark, John Greenleaf Whittier (regional poetry), Harriet Beecher Stowe, Bret Harte, Samuel Clemens, Edgar Watson Howe, Joseph Kirkland, Harold Frederic, Frank Norris, Edward Rowland Sill, Emily Dickinson, Finley Peter Dunne, Henry Adams, Herbert Clark Hoover, Franklin Delano Roosevelt, Henry Louis Mencken, Irving Babbitt, Robert Frost, Carl Sandburg, Vachel Lindsay, Wallace Stevens, Clarence Shepard Day, Jr.,

James Thurber, Stephen Vincent Benét, Ernest Hemingway.

T. H. (Theodore Hornberger): William J. Grayson, Hamlin Garland, William Vaughn Moody, Henry George, Edward Bellamy, Lincoln Steffens, Upton Sinclair, Woodrow Wilson, Kenneth Burke, William Van O'Connor, Robinson Jeffers, Karl Shapiro, Gwendolyn Brooks, Willa Cather, Sinclair Lewis, William Faulkner, John Steinbeck.

R. S. (Randall Stewart): John C. Calhoun, Daniel Webster, John Greenleaf Whittier (abolitionist poetry), Henry Timrod, Walt Whitman, Edward Eggleston, George Washington Cable, Mary Noailles Murfree, Joel Chandler Harris, Sarah Orne Jewett, Mary E. Wilkins Freeman, William Sydney Porter, William Dean Howells, Henry James, Stephen Crane, Theodore Dreiser, Paul Hamilton Hayne, Sidney Lanier, Dwight D. Eisenhower, Thomas Stearns Eliot, Allen Tate, Edwin Arlington Robinson, Hart Crane, Eugene O'Neill, Sherwood Anderson, Katherine Anne Porter, F. Scott Fitzgerald, John Dos Passos, Thomas Wolfe, Robert Penn Warren.

WALTER BLAIR
THEODORE HORNBERGER
RANDALL STEWART

Chapter **4**

The Civil War

1850-1865

Table of Contents

Volume II

The Literature of the United States

Chapter **5**

The Rise of Modern America
1865-1914

"I Hear America Singing"

Southwestern Yarnspinners

Literary Comedians

Local Colorists

JOHN GREENLEAF WHITTIER 307
The Barefoot Boy 308
Skipper Ireson's Ride 309
Telling the Bees 311
Snow-Bound 312
Among the Hills 322
The Meeting 329

HARRIET BEECHER STOWE 332
from • Oldtown Fireside Stories
Captain Kidd's Money 333

BRET HARTE 338
The Luck of Roaring Camp 339
Tennessee's Partner 344
Plain Language from Truthful James 348

EDWARD EGGLESTON 350
from • The Circuit Rider
Chapter XX 351

GEORGE WASHINGTON CABLE 355
Belles Demoiselles Plantation 356

MARY NOAILLES MURFREE (Charles E. Craddock) 364
Over on the T'other Mounting 365

JOEL CHANDLER HARRIS 375
from • Uncle Remus: His Songs and Sayings
Uncle Remus Initiates the Little Boy 376
How Mr. Rabbit Saved His Meat 377
Mr. Rabbit Meets His Match Again 377
from • Nights with Uncle Remus
Mr. Benjamin Ram and His Wonderful Fiddle 380

SARAH ORNE JEWETT 382
The Courting of Sister Wisby 383

MARY E. WILKINS FREEMAN 391
The Revolt of 'Mother' 392

WILLIAM SYDNEY PORTER (O. Henry) 400
from • The Four Million
The Furnished Room 400

Clemens

SAMUEL L. CLEMENS (Mark Twain) 404
The Celebrated Jumping Frog of Calaveras County. 406
from • The Innocents Abroad
Chapter XIX, The Old Masters 410
Chapter LIII, The Tomb of Adam 412
from • Roughing It
Chapter III, Jackass Rabbits and Sagebrush 413
from • The Gilded Age
Chapter VII, Colonel Sellers's Schemes for Money-Making 416
Chapter VIII, Colonel Sellers Entertains Washington Hawkins 419
from • Old Times on the Mississippi
A Daring Deed 423
Continued Perplexities 426
from • A Tramp Abroad
Baker's Blue-Jay Yarn 429
from • Life on the Mississippi
Chapter III, Frescoes from the Past 432
Chapter XXXVIII, The House Beautiful 439
from • Huckleberry Finn
The Grangerfords Take Me In 442
An Arkansaw Difficulty 453
from • Mark Twain's Autobiography
The Character of Man 457

Howells

WILLIAM DEAN HOWELLS 459
from • Criticism and Fiction 461
from • A Hazard of New Fortunes 467

James

HENRY JAMES 495
from • Hawthorne
The House of the Seven Gables 497
The Art of Fiction 501
Daisy Miller 512
The Middle Years 540
The Beast in the Jungle 551

Realists and Naturalists

EDGAR WATSON HOWE 573
from • The Story of a Country Town
Chapter XVI, More of the Village of Twin Mounds 575

JOSEPH KIRKLAND 579
from • Zury: The Meanest Man in Spring County
Chapter V, How the Meanest Man Got So Mean, and How Mean He Got 580

HAMLIN GARLAND 585
Mrs. Ripley's Trip 586
from • Crumbling Idols
Local Color in Art 592
The Local Novel 595

HAROLD FREDERIC 597
from • The Damnation of Theron Ware
The Trustees and the Rev. Mr. Ware 598

STEPHEN CRANE 603
The Open Boat 604

FRANK NORRIS 616
from • The Octopus 618
A Neglected Epic 640

Chapter **6**
U.S.A.

1914 to the present

The Political Struggle

Eugene O'Neill, Dramatist

Humorists

Main Currents in Contemporary Fiction

Two details in editorial procedure should be mentioned: (1) The text of each selection is, in the judgment of the editors, the best available. The text has been specified, however, only when there has been some problem about the version to be adopted. (2) The first date following each selection is that of composition; the second date is that of publication.

Chapter 4

The Civil War *1850 · 1865*

"Over the carnage rose prophetic a voice,
Be not disheorten'd, affection shall solve the problems
    of freedom yet,
Those who love each other shall become invincible,
They shall yet make Columbia victorious."

Whitman

I. Intellectual Currents

The Irrepressible Conflict

The Civil War was the bloodiest conflict which the world had seen up to that time, and it struck a blow which was almost fatal to the American Union. The issues were complex and confused. On the Northern side, the primary objective of the abolitionists was the destruction of slavery as an institution, while the aim of the nationalists was the preservation of the Union. On the Southern side, many fought to defend slavery—an institution whose rights had been guaranteed by the Constitution—while others believed that the basic issue was the vindication of the sovereignty of the individual state. Beneath these immediate issues lay the conflict between two radically different forms of society: the democratic, industrial economy of the North and the aristocratic, agrarian economy of the South. Although the causes of conflict were deeply imbedded in the American past, a series of dramatic events in the 1850's precipitated the outbreak of war in 1861.

The Fugitive Slave Law of 1850, which compelled the return of runaway slaves to their owners, fanned the fires of abolitionism. Emerson declared that he would not obey it; Thoreau actually helped at least one fugitive slave to escape into Canada; and the gentle-souled Whitman implied in one of his poems that he would aid all such fugitives with his "firelock" if the occasion should arise. A decisive incident occurred in Boston in 1854, when an infuriated mob attempted to rescue Anthony Burns, a fugitive slave, from the police, and United States troops intervened to enforce the law.

The rival efforts of Northerners and Southerners to control Kansas, where the issue of slavery was to be decided by popular vote, resulted in bloody strife in that territory in 1855. In a speech called "The Crime Against Kansas," Senator Charles Sumner of Massachusetts spoke too harshly of Senator Butler of South Carolina; whereupon Butler's young kinsman, Preston Brooks, assaulted

Sumner on the floor of the Senate and inflicted an injury from which Sumner never fully recovered. The controversy over Kansas hastened the organization, in 1856, of the Republican party, with a platform opposing the extension of slavery.

Sectional bitterness was increased still further in 1857 by the Dred Scott decision of Chief Justice Taney. Having been taken by his owner into a free state and then brought back into a slave state, Dred sued for his freedom. The Supreme Court denied his petition, declaring that since a Negro was not a citizen, he did not have access to the courts. The decision was attacked by Lincoln in his famous debates with Stephen A. Douglas. Still more dramatic and more far-reaching in its effects was the attempt of John Brown, a fanatical abolitionist, to foment an insurrection of slaves in Virginia. After having captured the federal arsenal at Harper's Ferry in October 1859, he was arrested by a company of marines under Colonel Robert E. Lee, and was later tried and executed. Emerson and Thoreau spoke out in Brown's defense, while Southerners were horrified by the threat of a black uprising. The "martyrdom" of Brown contributed enormously to the rise of sectional feeling. He became the subject of a stirring battle song (p. 121) which Northern soldiers were to sing during the war: "John Brown's body lies a-moldering in the grave,/His soul is marching on!"

The election to the Presidency in 1860 of the Republican nominee, Abraham Lincoln, precipitated the secession movement in the South. The new party was exclusively the party of the North; political lines were more completely sectional than ever before. Since Lincoln had declared that "this government cannot endure permanently half slave and half free," and the Republican party vigorously opposed the extension of slavery, Southern extremists believed that they were forced to choose between abolition and secession. South Carolina seceded from the Union in December 1860, and by February 1861, Georgia, Alabama, Florida, Mississippi, Louisiana, and Texas had followed her example. Shortly thereafter, the Confederate States of America was organized in Montgomery, Alabama, with Jefferson Davis as president. On April 12, 1861, the Confederate batteries in Charleston harbor fired on the federal garrison in Fort Sumter, which surrendered the next day. Soon after this decisive event marking the opening of the war,

Virginia, Arkansas, Tennessee, and North Carolina joined the Confederacy.

The choice between state and nation was a difficult one for many Southerners to make. The old constitutional argument that the states were older than the Union (true of course of only the original thirteen) and that the Union consequently derived its authority from the states was no doubt intellectually convincing to some. But loyalty is based in the emotions rather than in the intellect. The most distinguished officer of the Confederate army, Robert E. Lee, resigned his commission in the United States army when Virginia seceded because, as he put it, "I have been unable to make up my mind to raise my hand against my native state, my relatives, my children, and my home." A New England writer, Hawthorne, expressed sympathy with Lee's view when he said, with a touch of irony: "If a man loves his own State and is content to be ruined with her, let us shoot him if we can, but allow him an honorable burial in the soil he fights for."

At the outset of the war, the South believed that cotton alone was a guarantee of victory; that if deprived of cotton, the textile industry—and therefore the entire economy—of the North and of England would collapse. The Southern expectation was not realized. England, though on the point of doing so in 1862, never recognized the Confederacy. The issue was to be decided by arms alone, and the overwhelming superiority of the North in population and resources permitted little doubt of the eventual outcome. It is hardly necessary here to recount the shifting tides of battle during the four years of war. The turning point came in July 1863, when Lee was defeated at Gettysburg and Vicksburg capitulated after a long siege. The surrender of Lee to Grant at Appomattox on April 9, 1865, in effect terminated the war. The assassination of Lincoln five days later plunged the nation into the turmoil of reconstruction, which for the South proved to be more trying in many ways than the war itself.

Attackers and Defenders of Slavery

From the foregoing brief survey it is clear that slavery was the great issue before the American people, and it is not surprising that slavery was the subject of much of the literature, both Northern and Southern, during the decade which preceded the Civil War.

In the North, the two chief representatives of antislavery literature were John Greenleaf Whittier (p. 55) and Mrs. Harriet Beecher Stowe (p. 332). Both writers were motivated by a sincere devotion to the cause of human freedom. Whittier's poems were characterized by a fiery intensity rarely equalled even in polemical verse. His "Ichabod" (p. 59) was a scorching condemnation of Webster for his support of the Fugitive Slave Law:

> Let not the land once proud of him
>   Insult him now,
> Nor brand with deeper shame his dim,
>   Dishonored brow.

A better, though equally partisan, poem was his "Massachusetts to Virginia" (p. 57), with its swinging rhythm and its impressive roll call of the Massachusetts counties. If the author's zeal caused him to forget that New Englanders had once been actively engaged in the slave trade—as when he said to Virginia,

But that one dark loathsome burden ye must stagger
    with alone,
And reap the bitter harvest which ye yourselves have
    sown!—

the poem was none the less effective both as an indictment of the South and as a summons to action at home. Mrs. Stowe's *Uncle Tom's Cabin* (p. 332), published in 1852, reached a larger number of readers than did all of Whittier's poems combined; indeed, the novel immediately became, and remained for many years, a best seller. It was dramatized and was long successful on the stage. Mrs. Stowe's appeal was more sentimental than Whittier's; her book emphasized the pathos of the traffic in Christian souls.

Among the early defenders of slavery was John Pendleton Kennedy, the Baltimore novelist. Although he has already been considered as a creator of romantic fiction, it should be recalled here that in *Swallow Barn*, published in 1832, he presented a reassuring picture of the friendly relations which existed between master and slaves on a Virginia plantation.

The abolitionist attacks of the 1840's and 1850's called forth a more elaborate and more vigorous defense. Calhoun pointed out that slavery was a necessary part of

"Twenty-eight fugitives escaping from the eastern shore of M[...]
Rail Road, 1879

the Southern economy and that its abolition would destroy the South:

> The Southern States are an aggregate, in fact, of communities, not of individuals. Every plantation is a little community, with the master at its head, who concentrates in himself the united interests of capital and labor, of which he is the common representative. These small communities aggregated make the State in all, whose action, labor, and capital is equally represented and perfectly harmonized. Hence the harmony, the union, the stability of that section.

With the rising tide of sectional feeling, Southern apologists carried the argument to still greater extremes. William Gilmore Simms doubtless spoke for a substantial body of Southern opinion when he declared in 1852 that "slavery is a wisely devised institution of heaven devised for the benefit, improvement, and safety, morally, socially, and physically, of a barbarous and inferior

the "Myself" of his longest poem was Everyman. The experiences related in his poems were partly actual and partly imaginary. So great was his family of empathy that he could project himself into the personalities of others in a very real sense and thus become "the hounded slave" or "the mashed fireman." He took his stand for absolute equality; he desired nothing for himself which others could not have in the same measure. It was natural that such a complete democrat should oppose slavery, and equally natural that such a sensitive sympathizer with all men should not bear arms against the slave owner. The war wrought no change in Whitman's basic ideas and attitudes. He was still "the caresser of life," still "a Southerner soon as a Northerner." His war poems reveal no partisan rage like Whittier's or Timrod's, nor were they concerned with the issues of the war. He felt a profound compassion for all soldiers and the mothers of soldiers, whether Yankee or Rebel.

Aside from polemics and sectional rancor, with which he was not at all concerned, Whitman's *Drum-Taps* (p. 92) affords the richest account of the war to be found in our poetry. One group of poems conveys the excitement of the early enlistments—the scholar is torn from his school; the bridegroom, from his bride. Another

[fro]m Harper's Weekly, *August 1, 1863*

group pictures military scenes as sharply as a camera, and more suggestively—the cavalrymen slumping in their saddles while the horses drink from a stream, the shadowy forms of men and horses around the campfire on a mountainside. Other poems describe hospital scenes with modern realism or reveal the poignant suffering of a mother just notified of her son's death.

Though the war contributed nothing to Whitman's ideas, and changed not at all his fundamental attitudes, it stimulated the poet and clarified and spiritualized his poetry. He was never again to sing so lustily (and as some thought, sensually) of the "jolly bodily phase." His poetry became more mystical. His greatest poem, "When Lilacs Last in the Dooryard Bloom'd" (p. 197), reflects these changes. In this poem, written as an elegy on the death of Lincoln, due emphasis is given to the grief of the poet, memorialized by "lilac and star and bird"; due emphasis is given also to the sorrow of the nation, the funeral procession, and the tolling of bells. But these details are the background of the poet's mystical exaltation in the hymn to death. In the poem's burning core, America and the war and Lincoln are forgotten.

Except in such moments of mystical release, Whitman never forgot America. "Thou Mother with Thy Equal Brood" (p. 208) celebrated the restoration of the Union and the new solidarity of "these states." "Democratic Vistas" (p. 212) revealed an acute concern for the evils, more and more apparent, in our rapidly developing industrialism. But in the poems after the Civil War, Whitman recurred with an increasing frequency and a growing intensity to the mood of the Lincoln poem in his ultimate quest of a "passage to more than India."

R. S.

II. *Literary Trends*

Varied though they are, the selections in this chapter are alike in being works intended to persuade. The appeals made during the bitter controversy about slavery and kindred matters, and during the consequent war, urged moderation or fierce opposition. And the poems of Walt Whitman, though they did not deal with slavery, eloquently preached the poet's doctrines about the individual and society. It was only natural that all such writings, since they were meant to influence opinions and beliefs, not only conformed to ways of thinking and feeling then current, but also took forms particularly likely to appeal to the tastes of the day. Some of the authors, nevertheless, created literature which was to have other than historical interest long after the controversy had ended.

Works dealing with the slavery controversy, naturally, were quite likely to reflect the spirit of the times by being intemperate. Objective historians have made it clear that neither side was blameless—that neither North nor South had a monopoly upon virtue. As was all too human, however, a majority of people on each side felt that they were wholly right and their opponents wholly wrong. "Both [parties]," Lincoln observed in his *Second Inaugural,* "read the same Bible, and pray to the same God; and each invokes his aid against the other." Each party asked such aid with superb confidence that God and right were on its side and the forces of evil on the other. This belief often found expression in literary productions strongly tinged with elements of melodrama—one group of characters was pictured as too villainous, another group too innocent, to remain quite believable to readers of later, less impassioned times. The acrimony and the anger which then seemed inevitable were to appear extreme to readers far in time from the contest.

Modern readers are likely, also, to perceive a rather quaint quality in the two extremes of literary style which the taste of the day obviously approved. One extreme sort was literary, learned, allusive, usually solemn, often highly ornate and figurative. Such a style is represented in the passage in Grayson's *The Hireling and the Slave* which portrays child laborers in the North:

There, unconcerned, the philanthropic eye
Beholds each phase of human misery;
Sees the worn child compelled in mines to slave
Through narrow seams of coal, a living grave,
Driven from the breezy hill, the sunny glade,
By ruthless hearts, the drudge of labor made,
Unknown the boyish sport, the hours of play,

Stripped of the common boon, the light of day,
Harnessed like brutes, like brutes to tug, and strain,
And drag, on hands and knees, the loaded wain . . . .

Such ink-stained phrases as "the philanthropic eye," "the breezy hill, the sunny glade," "unknown the boyish sport," "the common boon," and "the loaded wain" give the verse a tone which would be disastrous to a poem written to sway readers today. At the other extreme was a vernacular style, unlearned, earthy, humorous, homely in any figures of speech which it happened to employ. This style is represented by a passage expressing ideas somewhat similar to those of Grayson—the comment of W. T. Thompson's homespun character, Major Jones (see p. 276), upon the sad plight of the charwoman of Philadelphia:

> The servant galls was scrubbin the doresteps of the houses and washin off the pavements in front of 'em. I looked at 'em as I rode along in the hack, and I couldn't help feelin sorry to see such butiful, rosy-cheeked white galls, down in the dirt and slop in the streets, doin work that is only fit for niggers. They say here they aint nothin but slewers—but I seed sum that I would tuck for respectable white galls if I had seed 'em in Georgia.

Here, in a style which was the Southern counterpart of Hosea Biglow's Yankee versifying, the author used ungrammatical phrases, misspellings, and words which, if they were found in argumentative writings today, would prejudice many against the author. Modern readers tend to prefer writings which, like those of Emerson and Thoreau—or of Lincoln—avoided both extremes.

Whether moderns like the two styles or not, they should have little trouble understanding the attitudes to which the two ways of writing appealed—attitudes which have coexisted for a long time. One attitude was that bookish learning provided the best clues to truth and virtue, the other that experience and common sense taught men best what was true and virtuous. As far back as the 1720's and 1730's, two kinds of appeal had been illustrated by Cotton Mather and Benjamin Franklin. The ideal author, Mather said, "could not have writ as he does if he had not read very much in his time."

"And his composures," Mather went on, "are not only a cloth of gold but stuck with as many jewels as the gown of a Russian ambassador." Franklin's Widow Silence Dogood and Poor Richard, by contrast, depended upon the teachings of experience rather than the teachings of books, and used the simple language of farm folk and mechanics. Later, the Jeffersonian aristocrat and the Jacksonian common man provided a similar contrast. In recent times, the opposing attitudes have again been exemplified—on the one hand by "brain trusters" and theorists in government, and on the other by "practical" men who have been chiefly schooled by experience. Thus, these contrasting styles dramatically represent two continuing American attitudes.

Oratory

The chief instrument for dispute in the period, by general agreement at the time, was oratory. Rightly or wrongly, it was still assumed that nothing so swayed public opinion as speeches. The function now jointly performed by books, the newspapers, moving pictures, television, and the radio was then chiefly performed by speakers addressing public meetings or legislative bodies.

To be sure, all oratory is likely to lose much of its force when, instead of being spoken, it is translated into print. The excitement of the occasion and the reactions of the audience are lost, as are any impressions made by the physical appearance of the speaker and by the sound of his voice. Those who saw massive, dark-browed Daniel Webster and heard his thunderous voice always were tremendously impressed (there was a saying that no human being was ever really so great as Webster appeared to be), and all who wrote of him in retrospect were sure that his great presence had much to do with his forensic power. Similarly, speeches delivered by even lesser men lost much of their power when they became printed instead of uttered words.

But modern readers find that there are barriers above and beyond the usual ones to appreciation of the oratory of the midcentury. The most formidable barrier is the style—or styles—of spoken discourse. In this field of literature, as in others, there were at the time two extremes. One was discoverable in the talks of local politicians delivered to neighbors and, at times, in the speeches of national figures. This extreme was parodied in an unsigned skit which went the rounds of the newspapers in the 1840's; it purported to be a speech of Candidate Earth, who wanted his backwoods neighbors to elect him sheriff. Said he:

> Now, gentlemen, don't you think they ought to make me sheriff? I say, if Bob Black has floated farther on a log, killed more Injuns, or stayed longer under water than I have, elect him; if not, I say what has he done to qualify him for the office of sheriff? Did any of you ever know him to call for a quart? I never did; I have known him to call for several half-pints in the course of a day, but I never did know him to step forward manfully and say, "Give us a quart of your best." Then I say again, what has Bob Black done to qualify him for sheriff?

In similar (though probably even less literate) language, Davy Crockett and other backwoods candidates regularly appealed for votes. And the very simplicity of the diction, its very freedom from adornment, recommended the speakers to constituents who believed they prized horse sense above "book larnin'." The other extreme was represented not only in the orations of men still remembered for their eloquence—Daniel Webster (p. 34), Wendell Phillips, Henry Clay—but also of a number who have been pretty well forgotten: John Randolph, George McDuffie, Seargent S. Prentiss, William C. Preston, Thomas Corwin, and others. Often the style used by these men was to the style of Candidate Earth as the style of Grayson was to that of Major Jones.

At the time, even when their words were not heard but read, these orators were extraordinarily effective. Time after time, they moved audiences to scornful laughter, to tears, to cheers, and constantly they molded public opinion both in the centers of learning and in the backwoods territory of Candidate Earth. (Whether they admitted it or not, backwoods folk were awed by learning.) The usually calm Professor George Ticknor of Harvard supplied an instance when, the evening after he had heard a speech by Webster, he wrote an account of his reactions in a letter: "Three or four times I thought my temples would burst with the gush of blood . . . . When I came out I was almost afraid to come near him [Webster]. It seemed to me as if he was like the mount that might not be touched and that burned with fire. I was beside myself, and am so still." The implication was that Webster was inspired as he spoke, and the scholar was, therefore, awed by the almost superhuman result. As one reads other comments upon orations of the period, one sees that this picture of the transported speaker and awe-struck listeners is quite common.

Eloquence, many believed, was essentially like poetry. Irresistibly it mastered the speaker. "True eloquence," said Webster in 1826, in his speech on Adams and Jefferson, "comes, if it come at all, like the outbreaking of a fountain from the earth, or the bursting forth of volcanic fires, with spontaneous, original, native

Bombardment of Fort Sumter as viewed from Charleston—from Harper's Weekly, *May 1861*

force." And the inspiration which so mastered the speaker communicated itself to the audience. "By eloquence," said Bryant in his *Lectures on Poetry*—also in 1826, "I understand those appeals to our moral perceptions that produce emotion as soon as they are uttered. It is in these that the orator is himself affected with the feelings he would communicate, that his eyes glisten, and his frame seems to dilate, and his voice acquires an unwonted melody, and his sentences arrange themselves into a sort of measure and harmony, and the listener is chained in involuntary and breathless attention."

Some of the most admired passages in the oratory of the day, in consequence, were remarkably figurative and rhythmic. Particularly admired, for instance, was the conclusion of Webster's most celebrated speech in the Senate, the "Reply to Hayne" of 1830:

> When my eyes shall be turned to behold for the last time the sun in heaven, may I not see him shining on the broken and dishonored fragments of a once glorious Union; on States dissevered, discordant, belligerent; on a land rent with civil feuds, or drenched, it may be, in fraternal blood! Let their last feeble and lingering glance rather behold the gorgeous ensign of the republic, now known and honored throughout the earth, still full high advanced, its arms and trophies streaming in their original lustre, not a stripe erased or polluted, nor a single star obscured, bearing for its motto, no such miserable interrogatory as "What is all this worth?" nor those other words of delusion and folly, "Liberty first and Union afterwards"; but everywhere, spread all over it in characters of living light, blazing on all its ample folds, as they float over the sea and the land, and in every wind under the whole heavens, that other sentiment, dear to every true American heart,—Liberty *and* Union, now and for ever, one and inseparable!

Customarily many who commended the great oratory of the day cited this passage or similar ones. Our appreciation for such flights is tepid. The reason is that there has been a change in taste during the last century.

In the years before the Civil War, there were already some portents of the change in taste which eventually

was to take place. In 1857, Edward G. Parker, in his book *The Golden Age of American Oratory,* indicated that the age which he had in mind was then, after exactly a hundred years, about to end. He saw two reasons for its conclusion. First, what he called "the age of chivalry" was closing and, said he, "A brazen age, anti-sentimental, succeeds; an age when sordid, calculating interest rather than conscious merit dares to run after reason." Secondly, "the growing taste of our people for reading" was bringing into prominence a new kind of persuasive composition—"accurate rhetorical composition, rather than the dashing vigor and vivacious sparkle of spontaneous oratory."

Whether for the reasons he suggested or not, Parker's prophecy about the changes in American taste was, in general, to come true. Even as he wrote, some had begun to lose their liking for what Parker characterized as "the oratory of America . . . bursting from the lips of Prophets" and to prefer, as he feared they might, "the less contagious influences of logic, and figures and facts." The addresses of Calhoun and of Webster included in this chapter (pp. 24 and 35) were delivered in 1850 and represent, in style, the transitional period.

By 1850, Webster had developed what students of his work call his "mature style"—a style which, compared with his earliest efforts, had greatly gained in simplicity. Edwin P. Whipple, in "Daniel Webster as a Master of English Style" (1879), wrote: "The mature style of Webster is perfect of its kind, being in words the express image of his mind and character,—plain, terse, clear, forcible; and rising to the level of lucid statement and argument into passages of superlative eloquence only when his whole nature is stirred by some grand sentiment. . . ." Modern readers, of course, will shy away from the passages of "superlative eloquence" which Whipple obviously admired. But they will be pleased to find that Webster does not indulge in such eloquence too often and that the bulk of his oratory is concerned with expressing thoughts clearly. They will be pleased to find that most of the speech of March 7, 1850, is devoted to Webster's version of history, to arguments justifying his attitude, set forth massively to be sure, but for the most part simply and moderately—at least for the times—and that the address is excellently organized. Only when they reach the most famous passage in the speech—that on "peaceable secession" (p. 53)—will they be painfully aware of Webster's eminence in the florid school of oratory. John C. Calhoun (p. 23), generally ranked below Webster at the time, may be preferred by readers today. The reason was suggested by a comment made upon his style by a critic of oratory in 1849. "Mr. Calhoun," E. L. Magoon wrote in *Living Orators in America,* "flaunts in no gaudy rhetorical robes of scarlet and gold, but comes into the forum clothed in the simplest garb, with firm hands grasping the reins of fancy, and intent only on giving a reason for the faith that is in him." Readers today will admire the relatively simple dress and the tight grip upon the reins, will find Calhoun's logic and his clarity admirable.

Lincoln

Although modern readers can endure the reading of Webster and Calhoun, they will probably find more moving the one speaker of the Golden Age of Oratory who, by general consent, has become a classic author—Abraham Lincoln. At least four of Lincoln's speeches—*Farewell to Springfield, First Inaugural, Gettysburg Address,* and *Second Inaugural Address* (see pp. 124-134)—whether one agrees or disagrees with their interpretation of history, were great utterances.

A student of Lincoln's collected speeches will find that a surprising amount of his work is far below these masterpieces in excellence. His first speech, delivered in 1832 when, as a gangling, ill-dressed youth of twenty-three, he was running for the state legislature, went this way:

> I presume you-all know who I am. I am humble Abe Lincoln. I have been solicited by many friends to become a candidate for the legislature. My politics are short and sweet like the old woman's dance. I am in favor of a national bank. I am in favor of the internal improvements system, and a high protective tariff. These are my sentiments and political principles. If elected I shall be thankful. If not it will be all the same.

The speech, to be sure, is somewhat better than that of Candidate Earth, but clearly its eloquence is in a similar style. And many of Lincoln's later speeches, among them the historic debates with Douglas, now appear to have

"Long Abraham Lincoln a little longer"—from Harper's Weekly, November 1864. Having been re-elected Lincoln was to serve "a little longer." Harper's was generally in sympathy with the President and his aims during his period in office. Its usual generous treatment of him was opposed to the frequent malicious attacks in many of the Northern newspapers and magazines.

little more than a certain homespun straightforwardness, well adapted to public debate, to recommend them. At times, by contrast, especially during his early career, Lincoln indulged in spread-eagle melodramatic oratory as tawdry as any produced at the time. There was, for instance, a campaign speech of 1840, in which he said:

> I know that the great volcano at Washington, aroused and directed by the spirit that reigns there, is belching forth the lava of political corruption in a current broad and deep, which is sweeping with frightful velocity over the whole length and breadth of the land, bidding fair to leave unscathed no green spot or living thing; while on its bosom are riding, like demons on the wave of hell, the imps of the evil spirit, and fiendishly taunting all who dare to resist its destroying course with the hopelessness of their efforts; and knowing this, I cannot deny that all may be swept away. Broken by it, I, too, may be; bow to it, I never will. The probability that we may fall in the struggle ought not to deter us from the support of a cause we believe to be just. It shall not deter me. If ever I feel the soul within me elevate and expand to those dimensions not wholly unworthy of its Almighty Architect, it is when I contemplate the cause of my country, deserted by all the world beside, and I standing up boldly alone, hurling defiance at her victorious oppressors.

Clearly the figurative language here used was meant to appeal to the current taste. But although many contemporaries did not sufficiently appreciate him, Lincoln did manage, at least in his later years, to achieve greatness as a composer of speeches.

Just why Lincoln managed to steer away, as he did, from both the crude utterances of a small-town politician and the fustian elegance of the popular orator is something of a problem. The very fact that he, unlike many of the leaders of the day, was self-schooled probably was important. While others among his contemporaries had studied the classical rules and examples of oratory in college, Lincoln had learned his art chiefly in frontier political debates and in clashes in law courts. Because he relied upon the teachings of experience, he shared the democratic belief in common sense and its direct expression, and that fact, too, was significant. Literary influences upon Lincoln, nevertheless, were important, and fortunately some of the most notable were those of authors who achieved forceful expression by means of simplicity and restraint—Robert Burns, William Shakespeare, and the translators of the Bible into the King James version. Finally, Lincoln's own character and feeling, as they developed during the trying years of his Presidency, were strongly reflected in his thought and the form of its expression. As Edgar Dewitt Jones remarks, somewhat flossily, in his study of orators, *Lords of Speech,* "The graces of an orator's presence, the charm of his voice and manner, are ephemeral; while the grandeur of his thoughts, the magnanimity of his soul and the soundness of his reasoning live after him. It is the substance of his speeches, together with the chaste beauty of a style which matches the sheer beauty of his spirit, that lifts Abraham Lincoln into the small and elect company of the world's supreme masters of public speech." Lincoln, despite the intemperance of the times in which he lived, was a temperate man, and he was an extremely sincere man. He was also something of a poet. His utterances, therefore, could outlast both the crude mouthings of the folksy politicians and the highly ornate orations of less temperate, less sincere, and less poetic speakers.

Two Styles in the Drama

In drama as in oratory there were, between 1829 and 1865, two styles—the romantic literary style and the realistic vernacular style. These were utilized to portray characters to whom they were appropriate in dramas of two sorts—poetic plays usually of foreign scenes and of past times and comedies of native American types. In some plays, *Uncle Tom's Cabin* for instance, the two styles and the two types of character were brought together.

A famous actor, Edwin Forrest (1806-1872), was active in stimulating authors to produce some of the most notable romantic plays of the period. After making his debut at fourteen in the Chestnut Street Theater of Philadelphia, his home city, Forrest served an apprenticeship in frontier theaters. Upon returning to the East, he was sensationally successful. He was a great figure of a man with a voice of extraordinary melody and volume, whose style of delivery reflected that of such impassioned orators as Clay and Webster. His favorite rôles were those of intense characters who, every few scenes, gave thunderous utterance to passionate feelings.

Forrest offered prizes and other inducements to native playwrights in order to secure dramas suitable for his robust acting. In 1829, for example, he awarded a prize to John Augustus Stone (1800-1834) for a drama entitled *Metamora, or the Last of the Wampanoags.* The part of an Indian chief in this drama gave Forrest such fine chances to rant and swagger about the stage that he continued to play it, at intervals, to the end of his long career. Equally successful was one of several plays written for the actor by Robert Montgomery Bird (1806-1854), a Philadelphia doctor who had turned to writing. *The Gladiator* (1831) was based upon Plutarch; in unfolding the story of the insurrection of the gladiators, it provided Forrest, in the rôle of Spartacus, their leader, with several excellent scenes and many sonorous blank verse lines. The close of Act II, one of several climaxes in the play, invariably brought the house to its feet wildly cheering. When Spartacus found that his opponent in the arena was his own brother, he stood, stripped to the waist, his deep chest heaving, and issued the call to rebellion in these words:

Death to the Roman fiends, that make their mirth
Out of the groans of bleeding misery!
Ho, slaves, arise! it is your hour to kill!
Kill and spare not—for wrath and liberty!
Freedom for bondsmen—freedom and revenge!

The Gladiator was given hundreds of successful performances. This play and *Metamora* were typical of many written for other actors as well as for Forrest. Dramatic scenes and poetic lines combined to tell romantic stories of distant lands or of the America of the past. Robert T. Conrad's *Jack Cade, the Captain of the Commons* (1835), N. P. Willis' *Bianca Visconti* (1837) and *Tortesa the Usurer* (1839), Epes Sargent's *Velasco* (1837), and George H. Miles' *Mohammed* (1850) were some with foreign settings. Charlotte Barnes Conner, *The Indian Princess* (1830), Cornelius Mathews, *Witchcraft, or the Martyrs of Salem* (1846), George H. Miles, *Her-*

nando de Soto (1852), and Oliver Bell Bunce, *Love in '76* (1857) offer a sampling of many dealing poetically with American history. The best among all plays of both sorts, by general consent, was *Francesca da Rimini* (1855) by George Henry Boker (1823-1890), a play which has been successfully revived several times. Like other dramas of the era, this transports its audience to a distant time and place; it tells a romantic story—the medieval tale of Paolo and Francesca—in five acts, numerous scenes, and blank verse, a form modeled after Elizabethan dramas. Boker's ability for characterization and his real talent as a poet made this play outstanding, but inevitably it suffers when compared with the great British dramas.

Crude by comparison but nevertheless more instinct with the life and spirit of our country were a vast number of plays of a quite different sort which were being produced during the period—plays which appealed to audiences because, instead of poetically portraying the past, they realistically set before the public recognizable native types. Some, continuing the tradition of *The Contrast* (1787), made capital of the stage Yankee; some represented frontiersmen; some portrayed still other types. Yankees such as Lot Sap Sago in *Yankee Land* (1834) by Cornelius A. Logan, Solon Shingle in *The People's Lawyer* (1839) by Joseph Stevens Jones, and Calvin Cartwheel in *The Brazen Drum* (1841) by Silas S. Steele, played by character actors, delighted thousands of playgoers. Frontier characters who were similarly prominent were rather infrequent, but one such figure who made a hit was boastful Nimrod Wildfire, a backwoodsman patently modeled after Davy Crockett (see p. 270), in J. K. Paulding's *The Lion of the West* (1831).

Beginning in the 1840's the city as well as the farm and the frontier was the source of numerous character representations on the stage. The political connivers of New York were comically drawn in *The Politicians,* by Cornelius Mathews, in 1840; those of the capital city in *Fashions and Follies of Washington Life,* by Henry Clay Preuss, in 1857. A gallery of New York types was offered by an outstanding play comparable with *The Contrast,* Anna Cora Mowatt's *Fashion,* in 1845—the social climber, the coquette, the poet, and the important merchant. Probably the most popular (and often the crudest) dramas of city types were those in which a

Poster advertising Uncle Tom's Cabin—*Culver Service*

swashbuckling figure of the New York Bowery, the volunteer fireman, and his fellow Manhattanites appeared. Mose, as this comic figure was called, was a leading attraction in B. A. Baker's *A Glance at New York* (1848), W. B. Chapman's *Mose in California* (1849), and more than a dozen others. As Richard M. Dorson remarks in "Mose the Far-Famed and World-Renowned" (*American Literature,* November 1943), Mose was a "unique compound of East Side swell, gutter bum, and volunteer fire laddie," and his queer ways, queer talk, and heroic deeds caught the fancy not only of New Yorkers familiar with his living prototype but also of theatergoers in every part of the country.

Aiken's dramatization, *Uncle Tom's Cabin* (1852; p. 64), undoubtedly was popular (and therefore important in the slavery controversy) because it combined

so many details of plot and character found in both kinds of plays. Like Aiken, of course, other authors in this period saw no reason for separating the romantic characters and their flowery speeches from the earthy native types. As a result, just as racy "low" characters mingled with stiff heroes and heroines in the fiction of the time, numerous localized comedy figures often appeared on the same stage as did romantic heroes and heroines. Prominent in S. E. Glover's *The Cradle of Liberty; or Boston in 1775,* produced in 1832, is Yankee Seth Sage, whose nature and style of talk is suggested by his remark, "I calculate we shall give the reg'lars a considerable damned smart drubbing." Again, in J. G. Burnett's *Blanche of Brandywine* (1858), we encounter both heroic characters (including Generals Washington and Greene) and two native types, Seth Hope, a Yankee, and Krout, a Pennsylvania Dutchman. Several of the plays about Indians showed aborigines who indulged in highly poetic orations mingling with frontier character types whose talk was spiced with racy backwoods phrases. But *Uncle Tom's Cabin* goes about as far as a play could in alternating hilarious scenes with thrilling or pathetic ones and in drawing together ideal characters and a variety of realistic ones.

In Aiken's long-lived play, we have the type hero and heroine; we have also the saintly little Eva and the pious Uncle Tom. We have a bloodcurdling villain, Simon Legree, and a minor villain or two for good measure. There is, too, a varied collection of low comedy types—the frontiersman, the Yankee bumpkin (Gumption Cute), the Yankee spinster (Ophelia), and the Negro comic straight from the minstrel shows of the day (Topsy). Scenes are arranged so that audiences may indulge alternately in the two favorite pastimes of theatergoers in this country—laughing and weeping—time after time. The speeches in the play range between the realistic echoes of everyday speech and the grandiloquent orations of romanticized characters. Consider the extremes in style in two speeches of Act I. The first is a shout of the comic frontiersman, Phineas:

Halloa, thar! bring us a jug of whiskey instantaneously, or expect to be teetotally chawed up! Squat yourself, stranger, and go in for enjoyment.

The second is a prayer and soliloquy uttered by Eliza as she prepares to make her hazardous journey across the ice-filled river:

Powers of mercy, protect me! How shall I escape these human bloodhounds? Ah! the window—the river of ice! That dark stream lies between me and liberty! Surely the ice will bear my trifling weight. It is my only chance of escape—better sink beneath the cold waters, with my child locked in my arms, than have him torn from me and sold into bondage. He sleeps upon my breast—Heaven, I put my trust in thee!

No better summary of the taste of the day could be found than *Uncle Tom's Cabin,* and no play of the past can teach us more about the sure-fire devices of melodrama

which have to be modernized only slightly to enthrall moving-picture audiences in our own time.

Poetry

Two passages of verse by James Russell Lowell, one published in 1845, the other in 1846, show how one author active in this period could use both the high style and the low style of poetry in persuasive compositions. Lines in "The Present Crisis" (1845) read:

Slavery, the earth-born Cyclops, fellest of the giant
  brood,
Son of brutish Force and Darkness, who have
  drenched the earth with blood,
Famished in his self-made desert, blinded by our
  purer day,
Gropes in yet unblasted regions for his miserable
  prey;—
Shall we guide his gory fingers where our helpless
  children play?

The first of the *Biglow Papers,* the next year, had this stanza:

Aint it cute to see a Yankee
  Take sech everlastin' pains,
All to git the Devil's thankee
  Helpin' on 'em weld their chains?
Wy, it's jest ez clear ez figgers,
  Clear ez one an' one make two,
Chaps that make black slaves o' niggers
  Want to make wite slaves o' you.

Few other authors could switch at will, as their contemporary Lowell could, from one extreme of style to the other, and in general the writers of the period tended toward one or the other of the two styles of popular appeal.

Some of the popular songs show how both styles might be adapted to a single tune, "John Brown's Body" and "The Battle Hymn of the Republic" (p. 120), for instance, as well as the two versions of "Dixie" (p. 118). Grayson and Timrod, although they heatedly disagreed about the definition of poetry, both followed the literary rather than the illiterate tradition in their verse. Grayson modeled his versification after what he called the "School of Dryden and Pope," writing his most representative

poetry in heroic couplets. "I have faith," he wrote in his unpublished "Autobiography," "in the ancient classical models, the masters directly or indirectly of all the great poets of modern times." Timrod, by contrast, frankly acknowledged indebtedness to such authors as Milton, Wordsworth, and Tennyson. In some poems (see "Charleston," p. 115, and "Ode," p. 117), he used the simple ballad stanza or a slight adaptation; in more, perhaps—notably "Ethnogenesis" and "The Cotton Boll"—he employed the irregular ode form which had been employed by Wordsworth and Tennyson with marked success. But Grayson, disciple of Neoclassical poets, and Timrod, disciple of nineteenth-century poets and the seventeenth-century poet, Milton, were alike in using diction of a highly literary nature.

Whittier (p. 307) tried at times to write formidably literary verse, and his use of dialect in poetry was infrequent. Nevertheless, at his most effective he was a writer of songs which were relatively simple—almost in the manner of folk songs—both in metrical form and in the kind of words used. The Quaker poet's country rearing, his brief schooling, and his particular admiration for the seemingly artless songs of Robert Burns all led him to write unpretentious poems. Never, it appears, did he give much consideration to matters of technique. His aim, as he stated it, was

> To paint, forgetful of the tricks of art,
> With pencil dipped alone in colors of the heart.

As a rule, therefore, no sign appeared of his striving for novelty of effect. All his life, his favorite measures were ballad measure, octosyllabics, and iambic pentameter—quite conventional forms of verse; and he used a vocabulary and figures of speech which were far from complex. His were "journalistic" poems which, because of their almost rustic directness and simplicity, appealed greatly to many untutored readers.

Whittier's songs resemble most other poems of the period, both literary and unliterary, proslavery and antislavery, in their depiction of the friends and the foes of the poet. Sure that his Quaker Inner Light had shown him what attitudes to take, Whittier conceived of the abolitionists as engaged in a "moral warfare," girded "in God's own might" and "in conflict with unholy powers," and he constantly pictured the struggle in such terms. Vouchsafed similar visions, as they believed, other poets

on both sides were similarly intemperate. The author of a famous version of "Dixie" urged Southerners to battle "Till the spoilers are defeated,/Till the Lord's work is completed." Julia Ward Howe saw the Northern army clothed in righteousness and proclaimed that "God was marching on." Timrod saw the enemy as "the Goth," and confidently expected the Lord to release the Con-

Extra edition of the Charleston Mercury *for December 20, 1860, announcing secession*

Britannia joins with Columbia and the Negro in mourning the death of Lincoln—from Punch, *May 1865. This was Sir John Tenniel's apology for the tone of his cartoons which had ridiculed and slandered Lincoln throughout the war.*

federacy from "the great burthen of our country's wrong." For both North and South, the issue was as clear-cut as that. Such were the signs of bitter partisanship in many melodramatic poems.

Walt Whitman, War-Born Poet

Although, like other poets, he was a controversialist, Walt Whitman made no contribution worth noting to the argument about slavery. His poems about the Civil War are concerned with the experiences and the sufferings shared by men and women of both sides. However, Whitman found himself as a poet in the years when the nation was deeply engaged in the controversy about slavery, and he himself saw his own wartime experiences as the "final reasons-for-being" of his mature songs. Hence, despite the fact that he lived and wrote for many years after Appomattox, Whitman was in a very real sense a war-born poet. His poetry, though it seemed strange to readers when it first appeared, was, we now can see, molded by the literature being produced at the

time he began to write. Emerson's poetry, for example, obviously left its mark. Perhaps even more important, the oratory and the styles of the 1840's and 1850's left their imprint upon the form of Whitman's poetry.

Whitman was like the orators of the day in that he wanted to preach to men the ways of righteous thinking and living. In notebooks which he filled when he was working toward the writing of *Leaves of Grass,* he voiced his determination to "elevate, enlarge, purify, deepen and make happy the attributes of the body and soul of man." Furthermore, as he considered how he would deliver this message to his countrymen, evidently he was not sure, for some time, whether his medium was to be oratory or poetry. His considering oratory was hardly surprising, since the accepted medium for social or religious preachments was the oration or the sermon, and he was fascinated all his life by public speaking and public speakers. Possibly Whitman's inability to succeed as an orator was an important factor leading to his final decision to become a poet. In his early New York days, so he said, he "haunted the courts to witness notable trials, and . . . heard all the famous actors and

actresses." Over the years, he listened to Webster, Garrison, Beecher, Clay, Everett, and Phillips, as well as less famous orators. His "Poem of Joys" contains an interesting description of the great speaker swaying his audience.

O the orator's joys!
To inflate the chest—to roll the thunder of the voice
    out from the ribs and throat,
To make the people rage, weep, hate, desire, with
    yourself,
To lead America—to quell America with a great tongue.

He enjoyed the declamatory interpretations of Shakespeare by Booth and Forrest which were then fashionable, and he himself loved to intone sonorous lines from the dramas while riding Broadway omnibuses, tramping with friends, and strolling by the seashore. He knew and greatly admired, too, literature which approximated the oratorical effect he wanted—the lecture-essays of Emerson, the songs of Ossian, translations of Greek and Latin dramas and epics, the exhortatory parts of the Bible and their adaptations and paraphrases in sermons.

In the notes that Whitman wrote for his early works, there were passages which might have done for either lectures or poems. One scrap of paper bears the caption "Poem—Religious," and then, underneath this title is written "or lecture on Religion"; and one note, though it was headed "lecture," eventually was utilized as part of a poem. As a reciter of his own poetry, he attempted (though unfortunately with questionable success) to use the resonant tones, the modulations, the gesticulations of an old-school public speaker. As late as 1888, in his final Preface, he spoke of his art as a "new and national declamatory expression." There can be little question that the methods of oratory were important in shaping Whitman's style. In a note on "style" for his projected lectures he wrote: "besides direct addressing to You another leading trait of Lectures may well be —strong assertion—('I say') it is so?)—launched out with fire, or emphasis, or enthusiasm, or anger." This oratorical device occurs frequently in the poems, as in the line, "And I say to any man or woman, Let your soul stand cool and composed before a million universes." Other oratorical devices which are used time after time include apostrophes, rhetorical questions, aphorisms, exclamations, alliterative phrases, and parenthetical asides. Often the phrasal order is that of oratory

—lines which loosely balance on both sides of a pause, or series of parallel structures all of which contribute to a periodic sentence. (See, for example, the opening stanza of "Out of the Cradle Endlessly Rocking," p. 188.) Such devices, in Whitman's poems, pretty regularly perform functions of rhymes and stanzas in more conventional poems: they hold lines together and set off units of thought.

The scheme of Leaves of Grass as a whole and the schemes of individual poems, moreover, have noteworthy resemblances to oratory. Whitman evidently hoped that the impact of the book would be comparable to that of dynamic presence of a great orator—that it would, as he said, "possess, more than any other known book, the magnetism of living flesh and blood, sitting near the reader, & looking & talking." Like the collected works of a great orator, it would convey, in addition to the personality of the speaker, his gospel, developed and modulated in a number of individual compositions on varied topics. There is evidence, in the whole book, that Whitman attempted to unfold his beliefs in this fashion. In quite a few of the poems, too, there are organizations typically used by orators as well as by some poets—ideas developed by analogy, by passages of narrative, by comparison and contrast, and quite a number which are developed in the style of Emerson's lectures and poems.

But although eventually Whitman's poems, in their form, thus resembled oratory, even as he conceived of them they differed from oratory. In one of his self-criticisms the poet found fault with his method of composing and delivering lectures. "The trouble," he said, "is often the endeavor (from the habit of forming the rhythmic style of Leaves of Grass) involuntarily to preserve a sort of rhythm in the Lecture sentences,—It seems to me this rhythm, for them, is not only not necessary, but is often dangerous to their character-requirements—which, for speaking purposes, need to be abrupt. . . ." Whitman conceived of his free verse poems as "chants" more rhythmical than spoken discourses and corresponding, in some ways, to the arias or recitatives of operas. Toward his free verse, after starting as a quite conventional poet, he worked his way slowly. According to Emory Holloway, in his Introduction to The Uncollected Prose and Poetry of Walt Whitman, "he began versifying with the simplest of forms . . . then made use of more difficult stanza forms . . . ; next he wrote a little blank verse . . . ; then he made private experiments with some of the very material he was to work over, through several years, for the 1855 edition of *Leaves of Grass*. . . ." When this first edition appeared, concludes Holloway, his verse was disciplined, "poise and sweeping rhythm were added, and a standard of line length was adopted which would fit the bold but delicate burden of his song." What he evolved was a form blending prose and poetry, which carried still further liberating tendencies in poetry which had been initiated by a number of his predecessors including, notably, Emerson and Thoreau. His lines, characteristically, corresponded to the grammatical-phrasings or at least the thought-phrasings of speech. His rhythms were, as he put it, "in a loose and free metre of his own, of an irregular length of lines, apparently lawless at first perusal, although on closer examination a certain regularity appears, like the recurrence of lesser and larger waves on the sea-shore, rolling in without intermission, and fitfully rising and falling." And he found, as later poets were to find, that patterns of repeated vowel and consonant sounds could do much to unify parts and wholes.

Whitman not only broke away from some of the conventions of versification; he also broke away from some of the conventions of style. He was distressed by "stock poetical touches" and by ornamentation as such in poetry. *"No ornaments,"* he sternly enjoined himself, "especially no ornamental adjectives, unless they have come molten hot, and imperiously prove themselves. No ornamental similes at all—not one: *perfect transparent clearness. . . ."* His dislike for what he called "drawing room poetry" led him, in general, to use relatively simple words and to avoid an excess of figurative language. His feelings about common speech led him to interject it into a style not then thought hospitable to it. Most orators who employed the more literary style, as we have seen, tended to disdain the use of words in the vernacular. Whitman, however, from the early days of his career, appreciated the force of humble speech, and praised such speech as growing out of human life. In his youth, he was an avid searcher after colloquial and slang phrases with life to them, and his early prose is dotted with expressions such as "loaded down to the guards," "they do say," "some pumpkins," and "a great place and *no* mistake." "Slang," he wrote, "profoundly consider'd, is the lawless germinal element,

below all words and sentences, and behind all poetry, and proves a certain perennial rankness and protestantism in speech . . . an attempt of common humanity to escape from bald literalism, and express itself illimitably, which in highest walks produces poets and poems." He reveled in nicknames for men of different states (Kentucky Corn Crackers, Michigan Wolverines, Connecticut Wooden Nutmegs, etc.); in original place-names (Hog-eye, Lick-skillet, Rake-pocket, and Steal-easy, Texas, for instance); in the racy and imaginative phrases of bus drivers, laborers, railroad men, and boatmen. The result was that with the rolling periods and some of the more elegant diction characteristic of oratory, Whitman intermingled localisms, bits of slang, common talk. In Section 6 of "Song of Myself" (p. 148), for instance, along with sonorous and dignified lines comparable to those of oratory, occur lines like these:

Or I guess it [the grass] is the handkerchief of the Lord.
A scented gift and remembrancer designedly dropt. . .

* * *

Kanuck, Tuckahoe, Congressman, Cuff. . . .

* * *

And now it seems to me the beautiful uncut hair of
    graves.

* * *

The smallest sprout shows there is really no death. . . .

To mingle such homely phrasings, as Whitman typically did, with the highfalutin style of heightened oratory represented a daring experiment.

These details about the form of Whitman's poetry suggest that in several ways he was a culmination of some important literary tendencies of his period. They may, perhaps, also suggest to modern readers ways of approach to him. They imply that he should be read differently from most poets—as a man with a message, as a chanting orator, as an experimenter with a form which blends poetry with prose and mingles the words of everyday talk with those of more formal literature. He should be read not only as a wartime poet of the past but also as a pioneer breaking a trail toward modern poetic achievements.

W. B.

Chronological Table
of Literature and History

This chronological table carries back to the year 1838 in order to give a more complete background of the events leading up to the Civil War

1838 John P. Kennedy's **Rob of the Bowl**
Atherton resolutions in Congress, a second "gag" on discussions of slavery

1839 William G. Simms' **Border Beagles**

1840 1200 cotton factories in the United States, two thirds being in New England • United States census: population 17,000,000, including 400,000 free Negroes and 2,500,000 slaves • William Henry Harrison elected ninth President

1841 Thomas B. Thorpe's "Big Bear of Arkansas"
Death of Harrison; succeeded by John Tyler as tenth President

1842 Henry W. Longfellow's **Poems on Slavery**

1843 William T. Thompson's **Major Jones's Courtship**

1844 Repeal of "gag" rule against slavery discussions in Congress • James K. Polk elected eleventh President

1845 Florida and Texas, the twenty-seventh and twenty-eighth states, annexed to the Union with slavery, making fifteen slave states to thirteen free

1846 John G. Whittier's **Voices of Freedom** • Thorpe's **Mysteries of the Backwoods**
Treaty with Great Britain determined the Oregon boundary line • War with Mexico, "by act of Mexico" • Wilmot Proviso, prohibiting slavery in any territory to be acquired from Mexico, passed the House but was defeated in the Senate • Iowa, the twenty-ninth state, admitted as a free state

1848 Mexican cession of what is now California, Nevada, Utah, and Arizona • Gold discovered in California, resulting in the famous "rush" • Wisconsin, the thirtieth state, admitted as a free state, restoring the balance of free and slave states • Zachary Taylor elected twelfth President

1850 Nathaniel Hawthorne's **The Scarlet Letter** • John C. Calhoun's **Speech on the Slavery Question** • Daniel Webster's **Seventh of March Speech**
Death of President Taylor; succeeded by Millard Fillmore as thirteenth President • Compromise of 1850: admission of California, the thirty-first state, as free state • A drastic Fugitive Slave Law • First act of Congress making land grants to aid in construction of railroads—in this case, the Illinois Central • United States census: population 23,000,000

1851 Hawthorne's **House of the Seven Gables** • Herman Melville's **Moby Dick**
Slavery prohibited in the District of Columbia

1852 Mrs. Stowe's **Uncle Tom's Cabin**, greatest literary stimulus to the antislavery movement
Franklin Pierce elected fourteenth President

1853 Joseph G. Baldwin's **Flush Times of Alabama and Mississippi**

1854 Henry D. Thoreau's **Walden**
Kansas-Nebraska Act establishing "squatter sovereignty" in those territories; bloody conflicts between free-state and slave-state settlers; emergence of John Brown • Republican party organized as protest against the Kansas-Nebraska Act • Anthony Burns, fugitive slave, captured in Boston and returned to his owner despite the efforts of

a Boston mob to rescue him from the police • Preston Brooks of South Carolina assaulted Senator Charles Sumner of Massachusetts in the Senate chamber

1855   Simms' **Forayers** • Whittier's "Barefoot Boy" • Whitman's **Leaves of Grass**

1856   Simms' **Eutaw** • Whitman's **Leaves of Grass** (second edition, containing Emerson's letter) James Buchanan elected fifteenth President

1857   Founding of the **Atlantic Monthly** in Boston, with Lowell as editor • Founding of **Russell's Magazine** (1857-1861) in Charleston, with Paul Hamilton Hayne as editor
Chief Justice Taney's Dred Scott decision: a Negro was not a citizen and therefore had no right to bring suit in a federal court • Financial panic

1858   The Lincoln-Douglas debates in Illinois on the questions arising from the slavery issue • Minnesota admitted as thirty-second state

1859   Oregon admitted as thirty-third state • Silver discovered in the Comstock lode, Nevada • First oil well, Oil Creek, Pennsylvania • John Brown's raid on Harper's Ferry

1860   Thoreau's "Plea for John Brown" • Whitman's **Leaves of Grass** (third edition) • William D. Howells' campaign biography of Lincoln
United States census: population 31,500,000 including 450,000 free Negroes and 4,000,000 slaves • South Carolina seceded from the Union • Abraham Lincoln elected sixteenth President

1861   Henry Timrod's "Ethnogenesis," "The Cotton Boll"
Kansas, thirty-fourth state, admitted as a free state • Mississippi, Florida, Alabama, Georgia, Louisiana, and Texas seceded from the Union • Confederate States of America organized at Montgomery with Jefferson Davis president • The Civil War began when the Confederates fired on Fort Sumter, 12 April • Virginia, Arkansas, Tennessee, and North Carolina joined the Confederacy • Great Britain and France recognized the belligerency of the Confederate States • The First Battle of Bull Run

1862   **Merrimac-Monitor** engagement in Hampton Roads, first battle of ironclads • The Battles of Shiloh, Seven Days, Second Bull Run, Antietam, Murfreesboro • Slavery abolished in the territories • The Lancashire cotton famine in England • Pacific Railway Act to promote by land grants the construction of a railroad between Missouri points and California

1863   Whittier's "Barbara Frietchie" • Lincoln's "Emancipation Proclamation" and **Gettysburg Address**
West Virginia admitted as thirty-fifth state; formed by secession from Virginia • Death of Stonewall Jackson, great Confederate general, at Battle of Chancellorsville • Battle of Gettysburg (1-3 July) and surrender of Vicksburg (4 July) the turning point of the war

1864   William C. Bryant's **Thirty Poems**
Battles of the Wilderness, Spottsylvania Courthouse, Cold Harbor • Grant versus Lee in Virginia • Farragut at Mobile Bay • Sherman's March to the Sea • Nevada admitted as thirty-sixth state • Lincoln reëlected President

1865   Lincoln's **Second Inaugural** • Whittier's **Snow-Bound** • Whitman's **Drum-Taps** • Mark Twain's "Celebrated Jumping Frog of Calaveras County"
Surrender of Lee to Grant at Appomattox, 9 April • Assassination of Lincoln, 14 April; succeeded by Andrew Johnson as seventeenth President • Thirteenth Amendment, abolishing slavery, ratified by 27 states

John C. Calhoun

1782 · 1850

John C. Calhoun was born in South Carolina and educated at Yale. His was a distinguished career in public life. He was a member of the House of Representatives (1811-1817), secretary of war (1817-1825), vice-president (1825-1832), senator from South Carolina (1833-1844), secretary of state (1844-1845), and again senator until his death in 1850. The chief opponent of the centralization of power in the federal government and the chief advocate of the sovereignty of the individual state under the constitution, Calhoun, for more than twenty years, fought a brilliant but losing fight against what seems now to have been an inevitable course of events. As early as 1828, when South Carolina rebelled against a tariff measure designed to protect Northern manufacturers, Calhoun advanced in the famous "South Carolina Exposition" his doctrine of nullification: the right of the individual state to veto an act of the federal government. When slavery supplanted the tariff as the main question of controversy, he sought to protect Southern interests by opposing the principle of majority rule (the population of the North greatly exceeded that of the South) and by developing his doctrine of "concurrent majority": "the concurring assent of all the great and distinct interests of the community to the measures of the Government." Without such "concurring assent," he argued, there could be no check upon the tyranny of the numerical majority.

Illustration: John C. Calhoun—portrait from **United States Magazine and Democratic Review**, 1838

Calhoun deserves a place in the history of American literature not only for his contribution to political thought but also for the literary merits of his writings. He developed his subject systematically, with perfect clarity and inexorable logic. His style, when compared with Webster's, is plain, straightforward, unencumbered by poetic embellishment or rhetorical flourish.

W. E. Dodd, Life of Calhoun, New York, 1911 • V. L. Parrington, Main Currents in American Thought, New York, 1930, II • C. M. Wiltse, John C. Calhoun, Nationalist, Indianapolis, 1944

Speech on the Slavery Question Delivered in the Senate, March 4, 1850

The controversy over slavery had been made acute again by the question whether slavery should be permitted in the new territories acquired as a result of the Mexican War. Calhoun's speech, which he was too ill to deliver and which was read by Senator Mason of Virginia, came in the course of the debate on Clay's compromise proposals. Webster replied three days later with his "Seventh of March Speech" (p. 35). The Compromise of 1850, as finally adopted, included the following measures: the admission of California as a free state; the organization of New Mexico and Utah as territories with the provision that the territories themselves, when ready for statehood, should decide the question of slavery; and the Fugitive Slave Law, which provided that slaves who escaped to the North should be compelled to return to their owners.

Calhoun's discourse is a comprehensive survey, from a Southern point of view, of developments leading up to 1850, and was designed to show that the compromise measures of Clay did not meet the radical demands of the crisis.

I have, Senators, believed from the first that the agitation of the subject of slavery would, if not prevented by some timely and effective measure, end in disunion. Entertaining this opinion, I have, on all proper occasions, endeavored to call the attention of both the two great parties which divide the country to adopt some measure to prevent so great a disaster, but without success. The agitation has been permitted to proceed with almost no attempt to resist it, until it has reached a point when it can no longer be disguised or denied that the Union is in danger. You have thus had forced upon you the greatest and the gravest question that can ever come under your consideration—How can the Union be preserved?

To give a satisfactory answer to this mighty question, it is indispensable to have an accurate and thorough knowledge of the nature and the character of the cause by which the Union is endangered. Without such knowledge it is impossible to pronounce, with any certainty, by what measure it can be saved; just as it would be impossible for a physician to pronounce, in the case of some dangerous disease, with any certainty, by what remedy the patient could be saved, without similar knowledge of the nature and character of the cause which produced it. The first question, then, presented for consideration, in the investigation I propose to make in order to obtain such knowledge, is—What is it that has endangered the Union?

To this question there can be but one answer,—that the immediate cause is the almost universal discontent which pervades all the States composing the Southern section of the Union. This widely-extended discontent is not of recent origin. It commenced with the agitation of the slavery question, and has been increasing ever since. The next question, going one step further back, is—What has caused this widely diffused and almost universal discontent?

It is a great mistake to suppose, as is by some, that it originated with demagogues, who excited the discontent with the intention of aiding their personal advancement, or with the disappointed ambition of certain politicians, who resorted to it as the means of retrieving their fortunes. On the contrary, all the great political influences of the section were arrayed against excitement, and exerted to the utmost to keep the people quiet. The great mass of the people of the South were divided, as in the other section, into Whigs and Democrats. The leaders and the presses of both parties in the South were very solicitous to prevent excitement and to preserve quiet; because it was seen that the effects of the former would necessarily tend to weaken, if not destroy, the political ties which united them with their respective parties in the other section. Those who know the strength of party ties will readily appreciate the immense force which this cause exerted against agitation, and in favor of preserving quiet. But, great as it was, it was not sufficient to prevent the widespread discontent which now pervades the section. No; some cause, far deeper and more powerful than the one supposed, must exist, to account for discontent so wide and deep. The question then recurs—What is the cause of this discontent? It will be found in the belief of the people of the Southern States, as prevalent as the discontent itself, that they cannot remain, as things now are, consistently with honor and safety, in the Union. The next question to be considered, is—What has caused this belief?

One of the causes is, undoubtedly, to be traced to the long-continued agitation of the slave question on the part of the North, and the many aggressions which they have made on the rights of the South during the time. I will not enumerate them at present, as it will be done hereafter in its proper place.

There is another lying back of it—with which this is intimately connected—that may be regarded as the great and primary cause. This is to be found in the fact that the equilibrium between the two sections, in the Government as it stood when the constitution was ratified and the Government put in action, has been destroyed. At that time there was nearly a perfect equilibrium between the two, which afforded ample means to each to protect itself against the aggression of the other; but, as it now stands, one section has the exclusive power of controlling the Government, which leaves the other without any adequate means of protecting itself against its encroachment and oppression. To place this subject distinctly before you, I have, Senators, prepared a brief statistical statement, showing the relative weight of the two sections in the Government under the first census of 1790 and the last census of 1840.

According to the former, the population of the United States, including Vermont, Kentucky, and Tennessee, which then were in their incipient condition of becoming States, but were not actually admitted, amounted to 3,929,827. Of this number the Northern States had 1,997,899, and the Southern 1,952,072, making a difference of only 45,827 in favor of the former States. The number of States, including Vermont, Kentucky, and Tennessee, were sixteen; of which eight, including Vermont, belonged to the Northern section, and eight, including Kentucky and Tennessee, to the Southern,— making an equal division of the States between the two sections under the first census. There was a small preponderance in the House of Representatives, and in the Electoral College, in favor of the Northern, owing to the fact that, according to the provisions of the constitution, in estimating federal numbers five slaves count but three; but it was too small to affect sensibly the perfect equilibrium which, with that exception, existed at the time. Such was the equality of the two sections when the States composing them agreed to enter into a Federal Union. Since then the equilibrium between them has been greatly disturbed.

According to the last census the aggregate population of the United States amounted to 17,063,357, of which the Northern section contained 9,728,920, and the Southern 7,334,437, making a difference, in round numbers, of 2,400,000. The number of States had increased from sixteen to twenty-six, making an addition of ten States. In the mean time the position of Delaware had become doubtful as to which section she properly belonged. Considering her as neutral, the Northern States will have thirteen and the Southern States twelve, making a difference in the Senate of two Senators in favor of the former. According to the apportionment under the census of 1840, there were two hundred and twenty-three members of the House of Representatives, of which the Northern States had one hundred and thirty-five, and the Southern States (considering Delaware as neutral) eighty-seven, making a difference in favor of the former in the House of Representatives of forty-eight. The difference in the Senate of two members, added to this, gives to the North in the electoral college, a majority of fifty. Since the census of 1840, four States have been added to the Union—Iowa, Wisconsin, Florida, and Texas. They leave the difference in the Senate as it stood when the census was taken; but add two to the side of the North in the House, making the present majority in the House in its favor fifty, and in the electoral college fifty-two.

The result of the whole is to give the Northern section a predominance in every department of the Government, and thereby concentrate in it the two elements which constitute the Federal Government,—majority of States, and a majority of their population, estimated in federal numbers. Whatever section concentrates
10 the two in itself possesses the control of the entire Government.

But we are just at the close of the sixth decade, and the commencement of the seventh. The census is to be taken this year, which must add greatly to the decided preponderance of the North in the House of Representatives and in the electoral college. The prospect is, also, that a great increase will be added to its present preponderance in the Senate, during the period of the decade, by the addition of new States. Two territories, Oregon
20 and Minnesota, are already in progress, and strenuous efforts are making to bring in three additional States from the territory recently conquered from Mexico; which, if successful, will add three other States in a short time to the Northern section, making five States; and increasing the present number of its States from fifteen to twenty, and of its Senators from thirty to forty. On the contrary, there is not a single territory in progress in the Southern section, and no certainty that any additional States will be added to it during the decade. The
30 prospect then is, that the two sections in the Senate, should the efforts now made to exclude the South from the newly acquired territories succeed, will stand, before the end of the decade, twenty Northern States to fourteen Southern (considering Delaware as neutral), and forty Northern Senators to twenty-eight Southern. This great increase of Senators, added to the great increase of members of the House of Representatives and the electoral college on the part of the north, which must take place under the next decade, will effectively and ir-
40 retrievably destroy the equilibrium which existed when the Government commenced.

Had this destruction been the operation of time, without the interference of Government, the South would have had no reason to complain; but such was not the fact. It was caused by the legislation of this Govern-

ment, which was appointed, as the common agent of all, and charged with the protection of the interests and security of all. The legislation by which it has been effected, may be classed under three heads. The first, is
50 that series of acts by which the South has been excluded from the common territory belonging to all the States as members of the Federal Union—which have had the effect of extending vastly the portion allotted to the Northern section, and restricting within narrow limits the portion left the South. The next consists in adopting a system of revenue and disbursements, by which an undue proportion of the burden of taxation has been imposed upon the South, and an undue proportion of its proceeds appropriated to the North; and the last is a
60 system of political measures, by which the original character of the Government has been radically changed. I propose to bestow upon each of these, in the order they stand, a few remarks, with the view of showing that it is owing to the action of this Government that the equilibrium between the two sections has been destroyed, and the whole powers of the system centered in a sectional majority.

The first of the series of acts by which the South was deprived of its due share of the territories, originated with the confederacy which preceded the existence of
70 this Government. It is to be found in the provision of the Ordinance of 1787. Its effect was to exclude the South entirely from that vast and fertile region which lies between the Ohio and the Mississippi rivers, now embracing five States and one territory. The next of the series is the Missouri compromise, which excluded the South from that large portion of Louisiana which lies north of 36° 30′, excepting what is included in the State of Missouri. The last of the series excluded the South from the whole of the Oregon Territory. All
80 these, in the slang of the day, were what are called slave territories, and not free soil; that is, territories belonging to slaveholding powers and open to the emigration of masters with their slaves. By these several acts, the South was excluded from 1,238,025 square miles—an extent of country considerably exceeding the entire

---

31 **exclude the South.** The phrase here, as elsewhere in the speech, means to exclude slavery

valley of the Mississippi. To the South was left the portion of the Territory of Louisiana lying south of 36° 30′, and the portion north of it included in the State of Missouri, with the portion lying south of 36° 30′, including the States of Louisiana and Arkansas, and the territory lying west of the latter, and south of 36° 30′, called the Indian country. These, with the Territory of Florida, now the State, make, in the whole, 238,503 square miles. To this must be added the territory ac- quired with Texas. If the whole should be added to the Southern section, it would make an increase of 325,520, which would make the whole left to the South, 609,023. But a large part of Texas is still in contest between the two sections, which leaves it uncertain what will be the real extent of the portion of territory that may be left to the South.

I have not included the territory recently acquired by the treaty with Mexico. The North is making the most strenuous efforts to appropriate the whole to herself, by excluding the South from every foot of it. If she should succeed, it will add to that from which the South has already been excluded, 526,078 square miles, and would increase the whole which the North has appropriated to herself, to 1,764,023, not including the portion that she may succeed in excluding us from in Texas. To sum up the whole, the United States, since they declared their independence, have acquired 2,373,046 square miles of territory, from which the North will have excluded the South, if she should succeed in monopolizing the newly acquired territories, about three-fourths of the whole, leaving to the South but about one-fourth.

Such is the first and great cause that has destroyed the equilibrium between the two sections in the Government.

The next is the system of revenue and disbursements which has been adopted by the Government. It is well known that the Government has derived its revenue mainly from duties on imports. I shall not undertake to show that such duties must necessarily fall mainly on the exporting States, and that the South, as the great exporting portion of the Union, has in reality paid vastly more than her due proportion of the revenue; because I deem it unnecessary, as the subject has on so many occasions been fully discussed. Nor shall I, for the same reason, undertake to show that a far greater

portion of the revenue has been disbursed at the North, than its due share; and that the joint effect of these causes has been, to transfer a vast amount from South to North, which, under an equal system of revenue and disbursements, would not have been lost to her. If to this be added, that many of the duties were imposed, not for revenue, but for protection,—that is, intended to put money, not in the treasury, but directly into the pocket of the manufacturers,—some conception may be formed of the immense amount which, in the long course of sixty years, has been transferred from South to North. There are no data by which it can be estimated with any certainty; but it is safe to say, that it amounts to hundreds of millions of dollars. Under the most moderate estimate, it would be sufficient to add greatly to the wealth of the North, and thus greatly increase her population by attracting emigration from all quarters to that section.

This, combined with the great primary cause, amply explains why the North has acquired a preponderance in every department of the Government by its disproportionate increase of population and States. The former, as has been shown, has increased, in fifty years, 2,400,000 over that of the South. This increase of population, during so long a period, is satisfactorily accounted for, by the number of emigrants, and the increase of their descendants, which have been attracted to the Northern section from Europe and the South, in consequence of the advantages derived from the causes assigned. If they had not existed—if the South had retained all the capital which has been extracted from her by the fiscal action of the Government; and, if it had not been excluded by the ordinance of 1787 and the Missouri compromise, from the region lying between the Ohio and the Mississippi rivers, and between the Mississippi and the Rocky Mountains north of 36° 30′— it scarcely admits of a doubt, that it would have divided the emigration with the North, and by retaining her own people would have at least equalled the North in population under the census of 1840, and probably under that about to be taken. She would also, if she had retained her equal rights in those territories, have maintained an equality in the number of States with the North, and have preserved the equilibrium between the two sections that existed at the commencement of the

Government. The loss, then, of the equilibrium is to be attributed to the action of this Government.

But while these measures were destroying the equilibrium between the two sections, the action of the Government was leading to a radical change in its character, by concentrating all the power of the system in itself. The occasion will not permit me to trace the measures by which this great change has been consummated. If it did, it would not be difficult to show that the process com-
10 menced at an early period of the Government; and that it proceeded, almost without interruption, step by step, until it absorbed virtually its entire powers; but without going through the whole process to establish the fact, it may be done satisfactorily by a very short statement.

That the Government claims, and practically maintains, the right to decide in the last resort, as to the extent of its powers, will scarcely be denied by any one conversant with the political history of the country.
20 That it also claims the right to resort to force to maintain whatever power it claims, against all opposition, is equally certain. Indeed it is apparent, from what we daily hear, that this has become the prevailing and fixed opinion of a great majority of the community. Now, I ask, what limitation can possibly be placed upon the powers of a government claiming and exercising such rights? And, if none can be, how can the separate governments of the States maintain and protect the powers reserved to them by the constitution—or the people of
30 the several States maintain those which are reserved to them, and among others, the sovereign powers by which they ordained and established, not only their separate State Constitutions and Governments, but also the Constitution and Government of the United States? But, if they have no constitutional means of maintaining them against the right claimed by this Government, it necessarily follows that they hold them at° its pleasure and discretion, and that all the powers of the system are in reality concentrated in it. It also follows that the
40 character of the Government has been changed, in consequence, from a federal republic, as it originally came from the hands of its framers, into a great national consolidated democracy. It has indeed, at present, all the characteristics of the latter, and not one of the former, although it still retains its outward form.

The result of the whole of these causes combined is—

that the North has acquired a decided ascendancy over every department of this Government, and through it a control over all the powers of the system. A single section governed by the will of the numerical majority, has 50 now, in fact, the control of the Government and the entire powers of the system. What was once a constitutional federal republic, is now converted, in reality, into one as absolute as that of the Autocrat of Russia, and as despotic in its tendency as any absolute government that ever existed.

As, then, the North has the absolute control over the Government, it is manifest that on all questions between it and the South, where there is a diversity of interests, the interest of the latter will be sacrificed to the former, 60 however oppressive the effects may be; as the South possesses no means by which it can resist, through the action of the Government. But if there was no question of vital importance to the South, in reference to which there was a diversity of views between the two sections, this state of things might be endured, without the hazard of destruction to the South. But such is not the fact. There is a question of vital importance to the Southern section, in reference to which the views and feelings of the two sections are as opposite and hostile as they can pos- 70 sibly be.

I refer to the relation between the two races in the Southern section, which constitutes a vital portion of her social organization. Every portion of the North entertains views and feelings more or less hostile to it. Those most opposed and hostile, regard it as a sin, and consider themselves under the most sacred obligation to use every effort to destroy it. Indeed, to the extent that they conceive that they have power, they regard themselves as implicated in the sin, and responsible for not 80 suppressing it by the use of all and every means. Those less opposed and hostile, regard it as a crime—an offence against humanity, as they call it; and although not so fanatical, feel themselves bound to use all efforts to effect the same object; while those who are least opposed and hostile, regard it as a blot and a stain on the character of what they call the Nation, and feel themselves accordingly bound to give it no countenance or support. On the contrary, the Southern section regards the relation as one which cannot be destroyed without 90 subjecting the two races to the greatest calamity, and the section to poverty, desolation, and wretchedness; and accordingly they feel bound, by every consideration of interest and safety, to defend it.

This hostile feeling on the part of the North towards the social organization of the South long lay dormant; but it only required some cause to act on those who felt most intensely that they were responsible for its continuance, to call it into action. The increasing power of this Government, and of the control of the Northern section over all its departments, furnished the cause. It was this which made an impression on the minds of many, that there was little or no restraint to prevent the Government from doing whatever it might choose to do. This was sufficient of itself to put the most fanatical portion of the North in action, for the purpose of destroying the existing relation between the two races in the South.

The first organized movement towards it commenced in 1835. Then, for the first time, societies were organized, presses established, lecturers sent forth to excite the people of the North, and incendiary publications scattered over the whole South through the mail. The South was thoroughly aroused. Meetings were held everywhere, and resolutions adopted, calling upon the North to apply a remedy to arrest the threatened evil, and pledging themselves to adopt measures for their own protection if it was not arrested. At the meeting of Congress, petitions poured in from the North, calling upon Congress to abolish slavery in the District of Columbia, and to prohibit what they called internal slave trade between the States—announcing at the same time, that their ultimate object was to abolish slavery, not only in the District, but in the States and throughout the Union. At this period, the number engaged in the agitation was small, and possessed little or no personal influence.

Neither party in Congress had, at that time, any sympathy with them or their cause. The members of each party presented their petitions with great reluctance. Nevertheless, small and contemptible as the party then was, both of the great parties of the North dreaded them. They felt that though small, they were organized in reference to a subject which had a great and a commanding influence over the Northern mind. Each party, on that account, feared to oppose their petitions, lest the opposite party should take advantage of the one who might do so, by favoring them. The effect was that both united in insisting that the petitions should be received, and that Congress should take jurisdiction over the subject. To justify their course, they took the extraordinary ground that Congress was bound to receive petitions on every subject, however objectionable they might be, and whether they had or had not jurisdiction over the subject. These views prevailed in the House of Representatives, and partially in the Senate; and thus the party succeeded, in their first movements, in gaining what they proposed—a position in Congress from which agitation could be extended over the whole Union. This was the commencement of the agitation, which has ever since continued, and which, as is now acknowledged, has endangered the Union itself.

As for myself, I believed at that early period, if the party who got up the petitions should succeed in getting Congress to take jurisdiction, that agitation would follow; and that it would in the end, if not arrested, destroy the Union. I then so expressed myself in debate, and called upon both parties to take grounds against assuming jurisdiction; but in vain. Had my voice been heeded, and had Congress refused to take jurisdiction, by the united votes of all parties, the agitation which followed would have been prevented; and the fanatical zeal that gives impulse to the agitation, and which has brought us to our present perilous condition, would have become extinguished from the want of fuel to feed the flame. That was the time for the North to have shown her devotion to the Union; but, unfortunately, both of the great parties of that section were so intent on obtaining or retaining party ascendancy, that all other considerations were overlooked or forgotten.

What has since followed are but natural consequences. With the success of their first movement, this small fanatical party began to acquire strength; and with that, to become an object of courtship to both the great parties. The necessary consequence was a further increase of power, and a gradual tainting of the opinions of both of the other parties with their doctrines, until the infection has extended over both; and the great mass of the population of the North, who, whatever may be their opinion of the original abolition party, which still preserves its distinctive organization, hardly ever fail, when it comes to acting, to co-operate in carrying out their measures. With the increase of their influence, they extended the sphere of their action. In a short time after the commencement of their first movement, they had acquired sufficient influence to induce the legislatures of most of the Northern States to pass acts which in effect abrogated the clause of the constitution that provides for the delivery up of fugitive slaves. Not long after, petitions followed to abolish slavery in forts, magazines, and dockyards, and all other places where Congress had exclusive power of legislation. This was followed by petitions and resolutions of legislatures of the Northern States, and popular meetings, to exclude the Southern States from all territories acquired, or to be acquired; and to prevent the admission of any State hereafter into the Union, which, by its constitution, does not prohibit slavery. And Congress is invoked to do all this, expressly with the view to the final abolition of slavery in the States. That has been avowed to be the ultimate object from the beginning of the agitation until the present time; and yet the great body of both parties of the North, with the full knowledge of the fact, although disavowing the abolitionists, have co-operated with them in almost all their measures.

Such is a brief history of the agitation, as far as it has yet advanced. Now I ask, Senators, what is there to prevent its further progress, until it fulfils the ultimate end proposed, unless some decisive measure should be adopted to prevent it? Has any one of the causes, which had added to its increase from its original small and contemptible beginning until it has attained its present magnitude, diminished in force? Is the original cause of the movement—that slavery is a sin, and ought to be suppressed—weaker now than at the commencement? Or is the abolition party less numerous or influential, or have they less influence with, or control over, the two great parties of the North in elections? Or has the South greater means of influencing or controlling the movements of this Government now, than it had when the agitation commenced? To all these questions but one answer can be given: No—no—no. The very reverse is true. Instead of being weaker, all the elements in favor of agitation are stronger now than they were in 1835, when it first commenced; while all the elements of influence on the part of the South are weaker. Unless something decisive is done, I again ask, what is to stop this agitation, before the great and final object at which it aims—the abolition of slavery in the States—is consummated? Is it, then, not certain, that if something

is not done to arrest it, the South will be forced to choose between abolition and secession? Indeed, as events are now moving, it will not require the South to secede, in order to dissolve the Union. Agitation will of itself effect it, of which its past history furnishes abundant proof—as I shall next proceed to show.

It is a great mistake to suppose that disunion can be effected by a single blow. The cords which bind these States together in one common Union, are far too numerous and powerful for that. Disunion must be the work of time. It is only through a long process, and successively, that the cords can be snapped, until the whole fabric falls asunder. Already the agitation of the slavery question has snapped some of the most important, and has greatly weakened all the others, as I shall proceed to show.

The cords that bind the States together are not only many, but various in character. Some are spiritual or ecclesiastical; some political; others social. Some appertain to the benefit conferred by the Union, and others to the feeling of duty and obligation.

The strongest of those of a spiritual and ecclesiastical nature, consisted in the unity of the great religious denominations, all of which originally embraced the whole Union. All these denominations, with the exception, perhaps, of the Catholics, were organized very much upon the principle of our political institutions. Beginning with smaller meetings, corresponding with the political divisions of the country, their organization terminated in one great central assemblage, corresponding very much with the character of Congress. At these meetings the principal clergymen and lay members of the respective denominations, from all parts of the Union, met to transact business relating to their common concerns. It was not confined to what appertained to the doctrines and discipline of the respective denominations, but extended to plans for disseminating the Bible—establishing missions, distributing tracts—and of establishing presses for the publication of tracts, newspapers, and periodicals, with a view of diffusing

---

4 clause . . . slaves. "No Person held to Service or Labour in one State, under the Laws thereof, escaping into another, shall, in Consequence of any Law or Regulation therein, be discharged from such Service or Labour, but shall be delivered up on Claim of the Party to whom such Service or Labour may be due." Article IV, Section 2 of the Constitution

religious information—and for the support of their respective doctrines and creeds. All this combined contributed greatly to strengthen the bonds of the Union. The ties which held each denomination together formed a strong cord to hold the whole Union together; but, powerful as they were, they have not been able to resist the explosive effect of slavery agitation.

The first of these cords which snapped, under its explosive force, was that of the powerful Methodist Episcopal Church. The numerous and strong ties which held it together are all broken, and its unity gone. They now form separate churches; and, instead of that feeling of attachment and devotion to the interests of the whole church which was formerly felt, they are now arrayed into two hostile bodies, engaged in litigation about what was formerly their common property.

The next cord that snapped was that of the Baptists— one of the largest and most respectable of the denominations. That of the Presbyterians is not entirely snapped, but some of its strands have given way. That of the Episcopal Church is the only one of the four great Protestant denominations which remains unbroken and entire.

The strongest cord of a political character, consists of the many and powerful ties that have held together the two great parties which have, with some modifications, existed from the beginning of the Government. They both extended to every portion of the Union, and strongly contributed to hold all its parts together. But this powerful cord has fared no better than the spiritual. It resisted, for a long time, the explosive tendency of the agitation, but has finally snapped under its force—if not entirely, in a great measure. Nor is there one of the remaining cords which has not been greatly weakened. To this extent the Union has already been destroyed by agitation, in the only way it can be, by sundering and weakening the cords which bind it together.

If the agitation goes on, the same force, acting with increased intensity, as has been shown, will finally snap every cord, when nothing will be left to hold the States together except force. But, surely that can with no propriety of language be called a Union, when the only means by which the weaker is held connected with the stronger portion is *force*. It may, indeed, keep them connected; but the connection will partake much more of the character of subjugation, on the part of the weaker

to the stronger, than the union of free, independent, and sovereign States, in one confederation, as they stood in the early stages of the Government, and which only is worthy of the sacred name of Union.

Having now, Senators, explained what it is that endangers the Union, and traced it to its cause, and explained its nature and character, the question again recurs—How can the Union be saved? To this I answer, there is but one way by which it can be; and that is, by adopting such measures as will satisfy the States belonging to the Southern section, that they can remain in the Union consistently with their honor and their safety. There is, again, only one way by which this can be effected; and that is, by removing the causes by which this belief has been produced. Do this, and discontent will cease, harmony and kind feelings between the sections be restored, and every apprehension of danger to the Union removed. The question then is—How can this be done? But before I undertake to answer this question, I propose to show by what the Union cannot be saved.

It cannot, then, be saved by eulogies on the Union, however splendid or numerous. The cry of "Union, Union—the glorious Union!" can no more prevent disunion than the cry of "Health, health—glorious health!" on the part of the physician, can save a patient lying dangerously ill. So long as the Union, instead of being regarded as a protector, is regarded in the opposite character, by not much less than a majority of the States, it will be in vain to attempt to conciliate them by pronouncing eulogies on it.

Besides, this cry of Union comes commonly from those whom we cannot believe to be sincere. It usually comes from our assailants. But we cannot believe them to be sincere; for, if they loved the Union, they would necessarily be devoted to the constitution. It made the Union; and to destroy the constitution would be to destroy the Union. But the only reliable and certain evidence of devotion to the constitution is to abstain, on the one hand, from violating it; and to repel, on the other, all attempts to violate it. It is only by faithfully performing these high duties that the constitution can be preserved, and with it the Union.

But how stands the profession of devotion to the

67 eulogies . . . Union. The reference is specifically to Webster

Union by our assailants, when brought to this test? Have they abstained from violating the constitution? Let the many acts passed by the Northern States to set aside and annul the clause of the constitution providing for the delivery up of fugitive slaves answer. I cite this, not that it is the only instance (for there are many others), but because the violation in this particular is too notorious and palpable to be denied. Again: have they stood forth faithfully to repel violations of the constitu-
10 tion? Let their course in reference to the agitation of the slavery question, which was commenced and has been carried on for fifteen years, avowedly for the purpose of abolishing slavery in the States—an object all acknowledged to be unconstitutional—answer. Let them show a single instance, during this long period, in which they have denounced the agitators or their attempts to effect what is admitted to be unconstitutional, or a single measure which they have brought forward for that purpose. How can we, with all these facts before
20 us, believe that they are sincere in their profession of devotion to the Union, or avoid believing their profession is but intended to increase the vigor of their assaults and to weaken the force of our resistance?

Nor can we regard the profession of devotion to the Union, on the part of those who are not our assailants, as sincere, when they pronounce eulogies upon the Union, evidently with the intent of charging us with disunion, without uttering one word of denunciation against our assailants. If friends of the Union, their
30 course should be to unite with us in repelling these assaults, and denouncing the authors as enemies of the Union. Why they avoid this, and pursue the course they do, it is for them to explain.

Nor can the Union be saved by invoking the name of the illustrious Southerner whose mortal remains repose on the western bank of the Potomac. He was one of us—a slaveholder and a planter. We have studied his history, and find nothing in it to justify submission to wrong. On the contrary, his great fame rests on the
40 solid foundation that, while he was careful to avoid doing wrong to others, he was prompt and decided in repelling wrong. I trust that, in this respect, we profited by his example.

Nor can we find any thing in his history to deter us from seceding from the Union, should it fail to fulfil the objects for which it was instituted, by being permanent-

ly and hopelessly converted into the means of oppressing instead of protecting us. On the contrary, we find much in his example to encourage us, should we be forced to the extremity of deciding between submission 50 and disunion.

There existed then, as well as now, a union: that between the parent country and her then colonies. It was a union that had much to endear it to the people of the colonies. Under its protecting and superintending care, the colonies were planted, and grew up, and prospered, through a long course of years, until they became populous and wealthy. Its benefits were not limited to them. Their extensive agricultural and other productions gave birth to a flourishing commerce, which 60 richly rewarded the parent country for the trouble and expense of establishing and protecting them. Washington was born and grew up to manhood under that union. He acquired his early distinction in its service, and there is every reason to believe that he was devotedly attached to it. But his devotion was a rational one. He was attached to it not as an end, but as a means to an end. When it failed to fulfil its end, and instead of affording protection, was converted into the means of oppressing the colonies, he did not hesitate to draw his 70 sword, and head the great movement by which that union was forever severed, and the independence of these States established. This was the great and crowning glory of his life, which has spread his fame over the whole globe, and will transmit it to the latest posterity.

Nor can the plan proposed by the distinguished Senator from Kentucky, nor that of the administration, save the Union. I shall pass by, without remark, the plan proposed by the Senator, and proceed directly to the 80 consideration of that of the administration. I however assure the distinguished and able Senator, that, in taking this course, no disrespect whatever is intended to him or his plan. I have adopted it, because so many Senators of distinguished abilities, who were present when he delivered his speech, and explained his plan, and who were fully capable to do justice to the side they support, have replied to him.

The plan of the administration cannot save the Union,

---

35 illustrious Southerner, George Washington • 77 Senator, Henry Clay, chief sponsor of the Compromise of 1850

because it can have no effect whatever towards satisfying the States composing the Southern section of the Union, that they can, consistently with safety and honor, remain in the Union. It is, in fact, but a modification of the Wilmot Proviso. It proposes to effect the same object,—to exclude the South from all territory acquired by the Mexican treaty. It is well known that the South is united against the Wilmot Proviso, and has committed itself by solemn resolutions, to resist, should it be adopted. Its opposition *is not the name,* but that which it *proposes to effect.* That, the Southern States hold to be unconstitutional, unjust, inconsistent with their equality as members of the common Union, and calculated to destroy irretrievably the equilibrium between the two sections. These objections equally apply to what, for brevity, I will call the Executive Proviso. There is no difference between it and the Wilmot, except in the mode of effecting the object; and in that respect, I must say, that the latter is much the least objectionable. It goes to its object openly, boldly, and distinctly. It claims for Congress unlimited power over the territories, and proposes to assert it over the territories acquired from Mexico, by a positive prohibition of slavery. Not so the Executive Proviso. It takes an indirect course, and in order to elude the Wilmot Proviso, and thereby avoid encountering the united and determined resistance of the South, it denies, by implication, the authority of Congress to legislate for the territories, and claims the right as belonging exclusively to the inhabitants of the territories. But to effect the object of excluding the South, it takes care, in the mean time, to let in emigrants freely from the Northern States and all other quarters, except from the South, which it takes special care to exclude by holding up to them the danger of having their slaves liberated under the Mexican laws. The necessary consequence is to exclude the South from the territory, just as effectually as would the Wilmot Proviso. The only difference in this respect is, that what one proposes to effect directly and openly, the other proposes to effect indirectly and covertly.

Having now shown what cannot save the Union, I return to the question with which I commenced, How can the Union be saved? There is but one way by which it can with any certainty; and that is, by a full and final settlement, on the principle of justice, of all the questions at issue between the two sections. The South asks for justice, simple justice; and less she ought not to take. She has no compromise to offer but the constitution; and no concession or surrender to make. She has already surrendered so much that she has little left to surrender. Such a settlement would go to the root of the evil, and remove all cause of discontent, by satisfying the South that she could remain honorably and safely in the Union, and thereby restore the harmony and fraternal feelings between the sections, which existed anterior to the Missouri agitation. Nothing else can, with any certainty, finally and for ever settle the questions at issue, terminate agitation, and save the Union.

But can this be done? Yes, easily; not by the weaker party, for it can of itself do nothing—not even protect itself—but by the stronger. The North has only to will it to accomplish it, to do justice by conceding to the South an equal right in the acquired territory, and to do her duty by causing the stipulations relative to fugitive slaves to be faithfuly fulfilled; to cease the agitation of the slave question, and to provide for the insertion of a provision in the constitution, by an amendment, which will restore to the South, in substance, the power she possessed of protecting herself, before the equilibrium between the sections was destroyed by the action of this Government. There will be no difficulty in devising such a provision: one that will protect the South, and which, at the same time, will improve and strengthen the Government, instead of impairing and weakening it.

But will the North agree to this? It is for her to answer the question. But, I will say, she cannot refuse, if she has half the love of the Union which she professes to have, or without justly exposing herself to the charge that her love of power and aggrandizement is far greater than her love of the Union. At all events, the responsibility of saving the Union rests on the North, and not on the South. The South cannot save it by any act of hers, and the North may save it without any sacrifice whatever, unless to do justice, and to perform her duties under the constitution, should be regarded by her as a sacrifice.

It is time, Senators, that there should be an open and

---

5 **Wilmot Proviso,** which did not pass, prohibited slavery in any territory acquired from Mexico • 57 **Missouri agitation,** the Missouri Compromise of 1820

manly avowal on all sides, as to what is intended to be done. If the question is not now settled, it is uncertain whether it ever can hereafter be; and we, as the representatives of the States of this Union, regarded as governments, should come to a distinct understanding as to our respective views, in order to ascertain whether the great questions at issue can be settled or not. If you, who represent the stronger portion, cannot agree to settle them on the broad principle of justice and duty, say so;

10 and let the States we both represent agree to separate and part in peace. If you are unwilling we should part in peace, tell us so; and we shall know what to do, when you reduce the question to submission or resistance. If you remain silent, you will compel us to infer by your acts what you intend. In that case, California will become the test question. If you admit her, under all the difficulties that oppose her admission, you compel us to infer that you intend to exclude us from the whole of the acquired territories; with the intention of destroy-

20 ing, irretrievably, the equilibrium between the two sec-

tions. We would be blind not to perceive in that case, that your real objects are power and aggrandizement, and infatuated not to act accordingly.

I have now, Senators, done my duty in expressing my opinions fully, freely, and candidly, on this solemn occasion. In doing so, I have been governed by the motives which have governed me in all stages of the agitation of the slavery question since its commencement. I have exerted myself, during the whole period, to arrest it, with the intention of saving the Union, if it 30 could be done; and if it could not, to save the section where it has pleased Providence to cast my lot, and which I sincerely believe has justice and the constitution on its side. Having faithfully done my duty to the best of my ability, both to the Union and my section, throughout this agitation, I shall have the consolation, let what will come, that I am free from all responsibility.

1850

15 **California** was admitted as a free state on September **9, 1850**

Daniel Webster

1782 · 1852

Daniel Webster was possibly the greatest political orator America has ever produced. He was born in New Hampshire and was graduated from Dartmouth College. Beginning in 1813 and continuing with few interruptions until 1850, his long career in the national Congress, first as a Federalist and later as a Whig member from Massachusetts, was one of the most brilliant in the annals of that body. He was secretary of state under President Tyler and negotiated with England in 1842 the Webster-Ashburton Treaty, which permanently

settled the boundary between the United States and Canada as far west as the Rocky Mountains.

Always a staunch advocate of the supremacy of the Federal Union, Webster made his first famous pronouncement on the subject in 1830 in his reply to Robert Y. Hayne of South Carolina, who argued for the right of the individual state to nullify an act of Congress. It was this speech which concluded with the memorable words, "Liberty and Union, now and forever, one and inseparable." Webster's last great oratorical effort to preserve the Union came on March 7, 1850, when he replied to the speech made three days earlier by Calhoun. In this "Seventh of March Speech," Webster gave his full support to Henry Clay's "Compromise" (see p. 24). Thanks largely to Webster's support, the Compromise was adopted; but like all compromises, it pleased the extremists of neither side. The New England abolitionists, many of whom had been admirers of Webster up to this time, were especially bitter in their attacks (see,

for example, Whittier's "Ichabod," p. 59). Saddened by the defection of many friends and the rising tide of sectional conflict, he did not live to see the outbreak of the war which, by his mighty efforts, he had been able to postpone, but not to prevent.

The Writings and Speeches of Daniel Webster, 18 vols., National Edition, Boston, 1903 • C. M. Fuess, Daniel Webster, Boston, 1930

Speech on the Constitution and the Union, March 7, 1850

If Webster lacked the inexorable logic of Calhoun, he was at once more realistic and more imaginative. The portion of the following speech dealing with the question of slavery in New Mexico and California illustrates his use of a realistic argument; his glowing peroration on the Union— like other similar passages in his works—shows the largeness and vigor of his imagination. His style was classical, modeled on that of Demosthenes and Cicero, and despite the modern preference for naturalness and simplicity, it is still impressive.

M_{r.} President,—I wish to speak to-day, not as a Massachusetts man, nor as a Northern man, but as an American, and a member of the Senate of the United States. It is fortunate that there is a Senate of the United States; a body not yet moved from its propriety, not lost to a just sense of its own dignity and its own high responsibilities, and a body to which the country looks, with confidence, for wise, moderate, patriotic, and healing counsels. It is not to be denied that we live in the
10 midst of strong agitations, and are surrounded by very

considerable dangers to our institutions and government. The imprisoned winds are let loose. The East, the North, and the stormy South combine to throw the whole sea into commotion, to toss its billows to the skies, and disclose its profoundest depths. I do not affect to regard myself, Mr. President, as holding, or as fit to hold, the helm in this combat with the political elements; but I have a duty to perform, and I mean to perform it with fidelity, not without a sense of existing dangers, but not without hope. I have a part to act, not for my own 20 security or safety, for I am looking out for no fragment upon which to float away from the wreck, if wreck there must be, but for the good of the whole, and the preservation of all; and there is that which will keep me to my duty during this struggle, whether the sun and the stars shall appear, or shall not appear for many days. I speak to-day for the preservation of the Union. "Hear me for my cause." I speak to-day, out of a solicitous and anxious heart, for the restoration to the country of that quiet and that harmony which make the blessing of this Union 30 so rich, and so dear to us all. These are the topics that I propose to myself to discuss; these are the motives, and the sole motives, that influence me in the wish to communicate my opinions to the Senate and the country; and if I can do any thing, however little, for the promotion of these ends, I shall have accomplished all that I expect.

Mr. President, it may not be amiss to recur very briefly to the events which, equally sudden and extraordinary, have brought the country into its present political con- 40

27 Hear . . . cause, from the speech of Brutus in Julius Caesar, Act III, sc. ii, l. 13

dition. In May, 1846, the United States declared War against Mexico. Our armies, then on the frontiers, entered the provinces of that republic, met and defeated all her troops, penetrated her mountain passes, and occupied her capital. The marine force of the United States took possession of her forts and her towns, on the Atlantic and on the Pacific. In less than two years a treaty was negotiated, by which Mexico ceded to the United States a vast territory, extending seven or eight
10 hundred miles along the shores of the Pacific, and reaching back over the mountains, and across the desert, until it joins the frontier of the State of Texas. It so happened, in the distracted and feeble state of the Mexican government, that before the declaration of war by the United States against Mexico had become known in California, the people of California, under the lead of American officers, overthrew the existing Mexican provincial government, and raised an independent flag. When the news arrived at San Francisco that war had been
20 declared by the United States against Mexico, this independent flag was pulled down, and the stars and stripes of this Union hoisted in its stead. So, Sir, before the war was over, the forces of the United States, military and naval, had possession of San Francisco and Upper California, and a great rush of emigrants from various parts of the world took place into California in 1846 and 1847. But now behold another wonder.

In January of 1848, a party of Mormons made a discovery of an extraordinarily rich mine of gold, or rather
30 of a great quantity of gold, hardly proper to be called a mine, for it spread near the surface, on the lower part of the south, or American branch of the Sacramento. They attempted to conceal their discovery for some time; but soon another discovery of gold, perhaps of greater importance, was made, on another part of the American branch of the Sacramento, and near Sutter's Fort, as it is called. The fame of these discoveries spread far and wide. They inflamed more and more the spirit of emigration towards California, which had already been
40 excited; and adventurers crowded into the country by hundreds, and flocked towards the Bay of San Francisco. This, as I have said, took place in the winter and spring of 1848. The digging commenced in the spring of that year, and from that time to this the work of searching for gold has been prosecuted with a success not heretofore known in the history of this globe. You

recollect, Sir, how incredulous at first the American public was at the accounts which reached us of these discoveries; but we all know, now, that these accounts received, and continue to receive, daily confirmation, and 50 down to the present moment I suppose the assurance is as strong, after the experience of these several months, of the existence of deposits of gold apparently inexhaustible in the regions near San Francisco, in California, as it was at any period of the earlier dates of the accounts.

It so happened, Sir, that although, after the return of peace, it became a very important subject for legislative consideration and legislative decision to provide a proper territorial government for California, yet differences of opinion between the two houses of Congress prevented 60 the establishment of any such territorial government at the last session. Under this state of things, the inhabitants of California, already amounting to a considerable number, thought it to be their duty, in the summer of last year, to establish a local government. Under the proclamation of General Riley, the people chose delegates to a convention; and that convention met at Monterey. It formed a constitution for the State of California, which, being referred to the people, was adopted by them in their primary assemblages. Desirous 70 of immediate connection with the United States, its Senators were appointed and representatives chosen, who have come hither, bringing with them the authentic constitution of the State of California; and they now present themselves, asking, in behalf of their constituents, that it may be admitted into this Union as one of the United States. This constitution, Sir, contains an express prohibition of slavery, or involuntary servitude, in the State of California. It is said, and I suppose truly, that, of the members who composed that 80 convention, some sixteen were natives of, and had been residents in, the slave-holding States, about twenty-two were from the non-slave-holding States, and the remaining ten members were either native Californians or old settlers in that country. This prohibition of slavery, it is said, was inserted with entire unanimity.

It is this circumstance, Sir, the prohibition of slavery, which has contributed to raise, I do not say it has wholly raised, the dispute as to the propriety of the admission of California into the Union under this constitution. It 90 is not to be denied, Mr. President, nobody thinks of denying, that, whatever reasons were assigned at the commencement of the late war with Mexico, it was prosecuted for the purpose of the acquisition of territory, and under the alleged argument that the cession of territory was the only form in which proper compensation could be obtained by the United States from Mexico, for the various claims and demands which the people of this country had against that government. At any rate, it will be found that President Polk's message, at the commencement of the session of December, 1847, avowed that the war was to be prosecuted until some acquisition of territory should be made. As the acquisition was to be south of the line of the United States, in warm climates and countries, it was naturally, I suppose, expected by the South, that whatever acquisitions were made in that region would be added to the slave-holding portion of the United States. Very little of accurate information was possessed of the real physical character, either of California or New Mexico, and events have not turned out as was expected. Both California and New Mexico are likely to come in as free States; and therefore some degree of disappointment and surprise has resulted. In other words, it is obvious that the question which has so long harassed the country, and at times very seriously alarmed the minds of wise and good men, has come upon us for a fresh discussion; the question of slavery in these United States.

Now, Sir, I propose, perhaps at the expense of some detail and consequent detention of the Senate, to review historically this question, which, partly in consequence of its own importance, and partly, perhaps mostly, in consequence of the manner in which it has been discussed in different portions of the country, has been a source of so much alienation and unkind feeling between them.

We all know, Sir, that slavery has existed in the world from time immemorial. There was slavery, in the earliest periods of history, among the Oriental nations. There was slavery among the Jews; the theocratic government of that people issued no injunction against it. There was slavery among the Greeks; and the ingenious philosophy of the Greeks found, or sought to find, a justification for it exactly upon the grounds which have been assumed for such a justification in this country; that is, a natural and original difference among the races of mankind, and the inferiority of the black or colored race to the white. The Greeks justified their system of slavery upon that idea, precisely. They held the African and some of the Asiatic tribes to be inferior to the white race; but they did not show, I think, by any close process of logic, that if this were true, the more intelligent and the stronger had therefore a right to subjugate the weaker.

The more manly philosophy and jurisprudence of the Romans placed the justification of slavery on entirely different grounds. The Roman jurists, from the first and down to the fall of the empire, admitted that slavery was against the natural law, by which, as they maintain, all men, of whatsoever clime, color, or capacity, were equal; but they justified slavery, first upon the ground and authority of the law of nations, arguing, and arguing truly, that at that day the conventional law of nations admitted that captives in war, whose lives, according to the notions of the times, were at the absolute disposal of the captors, might, in exchange for exemption from death, be made slaves for life, and that such servitude might descend to their posterity. The jurists of Rome also maintained, that, by the civil law, there might be servitude or slavery, personal and hereditary; first, by the voluntary act of an individual, who might sell himself into slavery; secondly, by his being reduced into a state of slavery by his creditors, in satisfaction of his debts; and, thirdly, by being placed in a state of servitude or slavery for crime. At the introduction of Christianity, the Roman world was full of slaves, and I suppose there is to be found no injunction against that relation between man and man in the teachings of the Gospel of Jesus Christ or of any of his Apostles. The object of the instruction imparted to mankind by the founder of Christianity was to touch the heart, purify the soul, and improve the lives of individual men. That object went directly to the first fountain of all the political and all social relations of the human race, as well as of all true religious feeling, the individual heart and mind of man.

Now, Sir, upon the general nature and influence of slavery there exists a wide difference of opinion between the northern portion of this country and the southern. It is said on the one side, that, although not the subject of any injunction or direct prohibition in the New Testament, slavery is a wrong; that it is founded merely in the right of the strongest; and that it is an oppression, like unjust wars, like all those conflicts by which a powerful nation subjects a weaker to its will; and that, in its nature, whatever may be said of it in the modifications which have taken place, it is not according to the meek spirit of the Gospel. It is not "kindly affectioned"; it does not "seek another's, and not its own"; it does not "let the oppressed go free." These are sentiments that are cherished, and of late with greatly augmented force, among the people of the Northern States. They have taken hold of the religious sentiment of that part of the country, as they have, more or less, taken hold of the religious feelings of a considerable portion of mankind. The South, upon the other side, having been accustomed to this relation between the two races all their lives, from their birth, having been taught, in general, to treat the subjects of this bondage with care and kindness, and I believe, in general, feeling great kindness for them, have not taken the view of the subject which I have mentioned. There are thousands of religious men, with consciences as tender as any of their brethren at the North, who do not see the unlawfulness of slavery; and there are more thousands, perhaps, that, whatsoever they may think of it in its origin, and as a matter depending upon natural right, yet take things as they are, and, finding slavery to be an established relation of the society in which they live, can see no way in which, let their opinions on the abstract question be what they may, it is in the power of the present generation to relieve themselves from this relation. And candor obliges me to say, that I believe they are just as conscientious, many of them, and the religious people, all of them, as they are at the North who hold different opinions.

The honorable Senator from South Carolina the other day alluded to the separation of that great religious community, the Methodist Episcopal Church. That separation was brought about by differences of opinion upon this particular subject of slavery. I felt great concern, as that dispute went on, about the result. I was in hopes that the difference of opinion might be adjusted, because I looked upon that religious denomination as one of the great props of religion and morals throughout the whole country, from Maine to Georgia, and westward to our utmost western boundary. The result was against my wishes and against my hopes. I have read all their proceedings and all their arguments; but I have never yet been able to come to the conclusion that there was any real ground for that separation; in other words, that any good could be produced by that separation. I must say I think there was some want of candor and charity. Sir, when a question of this kind seizes on the religious sentiments of mankind, and comes to be discussed in religious assemblies of the clergy and laity, there is always to be expected, or always to be feared, a great degree of excitement. It is in the nature of man, manifested by his whole history, that religious disputes are apt to become warm in proportion to the strength of the convictions which men entertain of the magnitude of the questions at issue. In all such disputes, there will sometimes be found men with whom every thing is absolute; absolutely wrong, or absolutely right. They see the right clearly; they think others ought so to see it, and they are disposed to establish a broad line of distinction between what is right and what is wrong. They are not seldom willing to establish that line upon their own convictions of truth and justice, and are ready to mark and guard it by placing along it a series of dogmas, as lines of boundary on the earth's surface are marked by posts and stones. There are men who, with clear perceptions, as they think, of their own duty, do not see how too eager a pursuit of one duty may involve them in the violation of others, or how too warm an embracement of one truth may lead to a disregard of other truths equally important. As I heard it stated strongly, not many days ago, these persons are disposed to mount upon some particular duty, as upon a war-horse, and to drive furiously on and upon and over all other duties that may stand in the way. There are men who, in reference to disputes of that sort, are of opinion that human duties may be ascertained with the exactness of mathematics. They deal with morals as with mathematics; and they think what is right may be distinguished from what is wrong with the precision of an algebraic equation. They have, therefore, none too much charity towards others who differ from them. They are apt, too, to think that nothing is good but what is perfect, and that there are no compromises or modifications to be made in consideration of difference of opinion or in deference to other men's judgment. If their perspicacious

---

4 kindly affectioned. Compare Romans 12:10: "Be kindly affectioned one to another..." • 5 seek...own. Compare I Corinthians 13:5: "Charity... seeketh not her own..." • 6 let...free. Compare Isaiah 58:6: "...let the oppressed go free" • 32 Senator, Calhoun.

vision enables them to detect a spot on the face of the sun, they think that a good reason why the sun should be struck down from heaven. They prefer the chance of running into utter darkness to living in heavenly light, if that heavenly light be not absolutely without any imperfection. There are impatient men; too impatient always to give heed to the admonition of St. Paul, that we are not to "do evil that good may come"; too impatient to wait for the slow progress of moral

10 causes in the improvement of mankind. They do not remember that the doctrines and the miracles of Jesus Christ have, in eighteen hundred years, converted only a small portion of the human race; and among the nations that are converted to Christianity, they forget how many vices and crimes, public and private, still prevail, and that many of them, public crimes especially, which are so clearly offences against the Christian religion, pass without exciting particular indignation. Thus wars are waged, and unjust wars. I do not deny that there may

20 be just wars. There certainly are; but it was the remark of an eminent person, not many years ago, on the other side of the Atlantic, that it is one of the greatest reproaches to human nature that wars are sometimes just. The defence of nations sometimes causes a just war against the injustice of other nations. In this state of sentiment upon the general nature of slavery lies the cause of a great part of those unhappy divisions, exasperations, and reproaches which find vent and support in different parts of the Union.

30 But we must view things as they are. Slavery does exist in the United States. It did exist in the States before the adoption of this Constitution, and at that time. Let us, therefore, consider for a moment what was the state of sentiment, North and South, in regard to slavery, at the time this Constitution was adopted. A remarkable change has taken place since; but what did the wise and great men of all parts of the country think of slavery then? In what estimation did they hold it at the time when this Constitution was adopted? It will

40 be found, Sir, if we will carry ourselves by historical research back to that day, and ascertain men's opinions by authentic records still existing among us, that there was then no diversity of opinion between the North and the South upon the subject of slavery. It will be found that both parts of the country held it equally an evil, a moral and political evil. It will not be found

that, either at the North or at the South, there was much, though there was some, invective against slavery as inhuman and cruel. The great ground of objection to it was political; that it weakened the social fabric; that, 50 taking the place of free labor, society became less strong and labor less productive; and therefore we find from all the eminent men of the time the clearest expression of their opinion that slavery is an evil. They ascribed its existence here, not without truth, and not without some acerbity of temper and force of language, to the injurious policy of the mother country, who, to favor the navigator, had entailed these evils upon the Colonies. I need hardly refer, Sir, particularly to the publications of the day. They are matters of history on the record. 60 The eminent men, the most eminent men, and nearly all the conspicuous politicians of the South, held the same sentiments; that slavery was an evil, a blight, a scourge, and a curse. There are no terms of reprobation of slavery so vehement in the North at that day as in the South. The North was not so much excited against it as the South; and the reason is, I suppose, that there was much less of it at the North, and the people did not see, or think they saw, the evils so prominently as they were seen, or thought to be seen, at the South. 70

Then, Sir, when this Constitution was framed, this was the light in which the Federal Convention viewed it. That body reflected the judgment and sentiments of the great men of the South. A member of the other house, whom I have not the honor to know, has, in a recent speech, collected extracts from these public documents. They prove the truth of what I am saying, and the question then was, how to deal with it, and how to deal with it as an evil. They came to this general result. They thought that slavery could not be continued in the 80 country if the importation of slaves were made to cease, and therefore they provided that, after a certain period, the importation might be prevented by the act of the new government. The period of twenty years was proposed by some gentleman from the North, I think, and many members of the Convention from the South opposed it as being too long. Mr. Madison especially was somewhat warm against it. He said it would bring

8 do . . . come. Compare Romans 3:8 • 87 Mr. Madison, James Madison (1751-1836), fourth President of the United States (1809-1817)

too much of this mischief into the country to allow the importation of slaves for such a period. Because we must take along with us, in the whole of this discussion, when we are considering the sentiments and opinions in which the constitutional provision originated, that the conviction of all men was, that, if the importation of slaves ceased, the white race would multiply faster than the black race, and that slavery would therefore gradually wear out and expire. It may not be improper here to allude to that, I had almost said, celebrated opinion of Mr. Madison. You observe, Sir, that the term *slave,* or *slavery,* is not used in the Constitution. The Constitution does not require that "fugitive slaves" shall be delivered up. It requires that persons held to service in one State, and escaping into another, shall be delivered up. Mr. Madison opposed the introduction of the term *slave,* or *slavery,* into the Constitution; for he said that he did not wish to see it recognized by the Constitution of the United States of America that there could be property in men.

Now, Sir, all this took place in the Convention in 1787; but connected with this, concurrent and contemporaneous, is another important transaction, not sufficiently attended to. The Convention for framing this Constitution assembled in Philadelphia in May, and sat until September, 1787. During all that time the Congress of the United States was in session at New York. It was a matter of design, as we know, that the Convention should not assemble in the same city where Congress was holding its sessions. Almost all the public men of the country, therefore, of distinction and eminence, were in one or the other of these two assemblies; and I think it happened, in some instances, that the same gentlemen were members of both bodies. If I mistake not, such was the case with Mr. Rufus King, then a member of Congress from Massachusetts. Now, at the very time when the Convention in Philadelphia was framing this Constitution, the Congress in New York was framing the Ordinance of 1787, for the organization and government of the territory northwest of the Ohio. They passed that Ordinance on the 13th of July, 1787, at New York, the very month, perhaps the very day, on which these questions about the importation of slaves and the character of slavery were debated in the Convention at Philadelphia. So far as we can now learn, there was a perfect concurrence of opinion between

these two bodies; and it resulted in this Ordinance of 1787, excluding slavery from all the territory over which the Congress of the United States had jurisdiction, and that was all the territory northwest of the Ohio. Three years before, Virginia and other States had made a cession of that great territory to the United States; and a most munificent act it was. I never reflect upon it without a disposition to do honor and justice, and justice would be the highest honor, to Virginia, for the cession of her northwestern territory. I will say, Sir, it is one of her fairest claims to the respect and gratitude of the country, and that, perhaps, it is only second to that other claim which belongs to her, that from her counsels, and from the intelligence and patriotism of her leading statesmen, proceeded the first idea put into practice of the formation of a general constitution of the United States. The Ordinance of 1787 applied to the whole territory over which the Congress of the United States had jurisdiction. It was adopted two years before the Constitution of the United States went into operation; because the Ordinance took effect immediately on its passage, while the Constitution of the United States, having been framed, was to be sent to the States to be adopted by their Conventions; and then a government was to be organized under it. This Ordinance, then, was in operation and force when the Constitution was adopted, and the government put in motion, in April, 1789.

Mr. President, three things are quite clear as historical truths. One is, that there was an expectation that, on the ceasing of the importation of slaves from Africa, slavery would begin to run out here. That was hoped and expected. Another is, that, as far as there was any power in Congress to prevent the spread of slavery in the United States, that power was executed in the most absolute manner, and to the fullest extent. An honorable member, whose health does not allow him to be here to-day—

A SENATOR. He is here.

I am very happy to hear that he is; may he long be here, and in the enjoyment of health to serve his country! The honorable member said, the other day, that he con-

---

82 honorable member, Calhoun

sidered this Ordinance as the first in the series of measures calculated to enfeeble the South, and deprive them of their just participation in the benefits and privileges of this government. He says, very properly, that it was enacted under the old Confederation, and before this Constitution went into effect; but, my present purpose is only to say, Mr. President, that it was established with the entire and unanimous concurrence of the whole South. Why, there it stands! The vote of every State in the Union was unanimous in favor of the Ordinance, with the exception of a single individual vote, and that individual vote was given by a Northern man. This Ordinance prohibiting slavery for ever northwest of the Ohio has the hand and seal of every Southern member in Congress. It was therefore no aggression of the North on the South. The other and third clear historical truth is, that the Convention meant to leave slavery in the States as they found it, entirely under the authority and control of the States themselves.

This was the state of things, Sir, and this the state of opinion, under which those very important matters were arranged, and those three important things done; that is, the establishment of the Constitution of the United States with a recognition of slavery as it existed in the States; the establishment of the ordinance for the government of the Northwestern Territory, prohibiting, to the full extent of all territory owned by the United States, the introduction of slavery into that territory, while leaving to the States all power over slavery in their own limits; and creating a power, in the new government, to put an end to the importation of slaves, after a limited period. There was entire coincidence and concurrence of sentiment between the North and the South, upon all these questions, at the period of the adoption of the Constitution. But opinions, Sir, have changed, greatly changed; changed North and changed South. Slavery is not regarded in the South now as it was then. I see an honorable member of this body paying me the honor of listening to my remarks; he brings to my mind, Sir, freshly and vividly, what I have learned of his great ancestor, so much distinguished in his day and generation, so worthy to be succeeded by so worthy a grandson, and of the sentiments he expressed in the Convention in Philadelphia.

Here we may pause. There was, if not an entire unanimity, a general concurrence of sentiment running through the whole community, and especially entertained by the eminent men of all parts of the country. But soon a change began, at the North and the South and a difference of opinion showed itself; the North growing much more warm and strong against slavery, and the South growing much more warm and strong in its support. Sir, there is no generation of mankind whose opinions are not subject to be influenced by what appear to them to be their present emergent and exigent interests. I impute to the South no particularly selfish view in the change which has come over her. I impute to her certainly no dishonest view. All that has happened has been natural. It has followed those causes which always influence the human mind and operate upon it. What, then, have been the causes which have created so new a feeling in favor of slavery in the South, which have changed the whole nomenclature of the South on that subject, so that, from being thought of and described in the terms I have mentioned and will not repeat, it has now become an institution, a cherished institution, in that quarter; no evil, no scourge, but a great religious, social, and moral blessing, as I think I have heard it latterly spoken of? I suppose this, Sir, is owing to the rapid growth and sudden extension of the COTTON plantations of the South. So far as any motive consistent with honor, justice, and general judgment could act, it was the COTTON interest that gave a new desire to promote slavery, to spread it, and to use its labor. I again say that this change was produced by causes which must always produce like effects. The whole interest of the South became connected, more or less, with the extension of slavery. If we look back to the history of the commerce of this country in the early years of this government, what were our exports? Cotton was hardly, or but to a very limited extent, known. In 1791 the first parcel of cotton of the growth of the United States was exported, and amounted only to 19,200 pounds. It has gone on increasing rapidly, until the whole crop may now, perhaps, in a season of great product and high prices, amount to a hundred millions of dollars. In the years I have mentioned, there was more of wax, more of indigo, more of rice, more of almost every article of export from

---

38 honorable member, James M. Mason of Virginia, whose grandfather, George Mason, was a member of the Constitutional Convention

the South, than of cotton. When Mr. Jay negotiated the treaty of 1794 with England, it is evident from the twelfth article of the treaty, which was suspended by the Senate, that he did not know that cotton was exported at all from the United States.

Well, Sir, we know what followed. The age of cotton became the golden age of our Southern brethren. It gratified their desire for improvement and accumulation, at the same time that it excited it. The desire grew
10 by what it fed upon, and there soon came to be an eagerness for other territory, a new area or new areas for the cultivation of the cotton crop; and measures leading to this result were brought about rapidly, one after another, under the lead of Southern men at the head of the government, they having a majority in both branches of Congress to accomplish their ends. The honorable member from South Carolina observed that there has been a majority all along in favor of the North. If that be true, Sir, the North has acted either very liberally and
20 kindly, or very weakly; for they never exercised that majority efficiently five times in the history of the government, when a division or trial of strength arose. Never. Whether they were out-generalled or whether it was owing to other causes, I shall not stop to consider; but no man acquainted with the history of the Union can deny that the general lead in the politics of the country, for three fourths of the period that has elapsed since the adoption of the Constitution, has been a Southern lead.
30 In 1802, in pursuit of the idea of opening a new cotton region, the United States obtained a cession from Georgia of the whole of her western territory, now embracing the rich and growing States of Alabama and Mississippi. In 1803 Louisiana was purchased from France, out of which the States of Louisiana, Arkansas, and Missouri have been framed, as slave-holding States. In 1819 the cession of Florida was made, bringing in another region adapted to cultivation by slaves. Sir, the honorable member from South Carolina thought he
40 saw in certain operations of the government, such as the manner of collecting the revenue, and the tendency of measures calculated to promote emigration into the country, what accounts for the more rapid growth of the North than the South. He ascribes that more rapid growth, not to the operation of time, but to the system of government and administration established under

this Constitution. That is matter of opinion. To a certain extent it may be true; but it does seem to be that, if any operation of the government can be shown in any degree to have promoted the population, and growth, 50 and wealth of the North, it is much more sure that there are sundry important and distinct operations of the government, about which no man can doubt, tending to promote, and which absolutely have promoted, the increase of the slave interest and the slave territory of the South. It was not time that brought in Louisiana; it was the act of men. It was not time that brought in Florida; it was the act of men. And lastly, Sir, to complete those acts of legislation which have contributed so much to enlarge the area of the institution of slavery, 60 Texas, great and vast and illimitable Texas, was added to the Union as a slave State in 1845; and that, Sir, pretty much closed the whole chapter, and settled the whole account.

That closed the whole chapter and settled the whole account, because the annexation of Texas, upon the conditions and under the guaranties upon which she was admitted, did not leave within the control of this government an acre of land, capable of being cultivated by slave labor, between this Capitol and the Rio Grande 70 or the Nueces, or whatever is the proper boundary of Texas; not an acre. From that moment, the whole country, from this place to the western boundary of Texas, was fixed, pledged, fastened, decided, to be slave territory for ever, by the solemn guaranties of law. And I now say, Sir, as the proposition upon which I stand this day, and upon the truth and firmness of which I intend to act until it is overthrown, that there is not at this moment within the United States, or any territory of the United States, a single foot of land, the character of 80 which, in regard to its being free territory or slave territory, is not fixed by some law, and some irrepealable law, beyond the power of the action of the government. Is it not so with respect to Texas? It is most manifestly

---

1 **Mr. Jay.** John Jay (1745-1829) was one of the authors of **The Federalist** and first chief justice of the United States. The treaty negotiated by him settled a variety of disputes between the United States and England. Article XII, which was struck out by the Senate, prohibited export of sugar, coffee, cocoa, and cotton from the United States in American vessels • **9 desire . . . upon.** Compare **Hamlet,** Act I, sc. ii, l. 145: "As if increase of appetite had grown/By what it fed on"

so. The honorable member from South Carolina, at the time of the admission of Texas, held an important post in the executive department of the government; he was Secretary of State. Another eminent person of great activity and adroitness in affairs, I mean the late Secretary of the Treasury, was a conspicuous member of this body, and took the lead in the business of annexation, in cooperation with the Secretary of State; and I must say that they did their business faithfully and thoroughly; there was no botch left in it. They rounded it off, and made as close joiner-work as ever was exhibited. Resolutions of annexation were brought into Congress, fitly joined together, compact, efficient, conclusive upon the great object which they had in view, and those resolutions passed.

Allow me to read a part of these resolutions. It is the third clause of the second section of the resolution of the 1st of March, 1845, for the admission of Texas, which applies to this part of the case. That clause is as follows:—

"New States, of convenient size, not exceeding four in number, in addition to said State of Texas, and having sufficient population, may hereafter, by the consent of said State, be formed out of the territory thereof, which shall be entitled to admission under the provisions of the Federal Constitution. And such States as may be formed out of that portion of said territory lying south of thirty-six degrees thirty minutes north latitude, commonly known as the Missouri Compromise line, shall be admitted into the Union with or without slavery, as the people of each State asking admission may desire; and in such State or States as shall be formed out of said territory north of said Missouri Compromise line, slavery or involuntary servitude (except for crime) shall be prohibited."

Now, what is here stipulated, enacted, and secured? It is, that all Texas south of 36° 30', which is nearly the whole of it, shall be admitted into the Union as a slave State. It was a slave State, and therefore came in as a slave State; and the guaranty is, that new States shall be made out of it, to the number of four, in addition to the State then in existence and admitted at that time by these resolutions, and that such States as are formed out of that portion of Texas lying south of 36° 30' may

come in as slave States. I know no form of legislation which can strengthen this. I know no mode of recognition that can add a tittle of weight to it. I listened respectfully to the resolutions of my honorable friend from Tennessee. He proposed to recognize that stipulation with Texas. But any additional recognition would weaken the force of it; because it stands here on the ground of a contract, a thing done for a consideration. It is a law founded on a contract with Texas, and designed to carry that contract into effect. A recognition now, founded not on any consideration or any contract, would not be so strong as it now stands on the face of the resolution. I know no way, I candidly confess, in which this government, acting in good faith, as I trust it always will, can relieve itself from that stipulation and pledge, by any honest course of legislation whatever. And therefore, I say again, that, so far as Texas is concerned, in the whole of that State south of 36° 30', which, I suppose, embraces all the territory capable of slave cultivation, there is no land, not an acre, the character of which is not established by law; a law which cannot be repealed without the violation of a contract, and plain disregard of the public faith.

I hope, Sir, it is now apparent that my proposition, so far as it respects Texas, has been maintained, and that the provision in this article is clear and absolute; and it has been well suggested by my friend from Rhode Island, that that part of Texas which lies north of 36° 30' of north latitude, and which may be formed into free States, is dependent, in like manner, upon the consent of Texas, herself a slave State.

Now, Sir, how came this? How came it to pass that within these walls, where it is said by the honorable member from South Carolina that the free States have always had a majority, this resolution of annexation, such as I have described it, obtained a majority in both houses of Congress? Sir, it obtained that majority by the great number of Northern votes added to the entire Southern vote, or, at least nearly the whole of the Southern vote. The aggregate was made up of North-

1 honorable member, Calhoun, who was secretary of state under Tyler • 4 eminent person. Robert J. Walker was secretary of the treasury under President Polk and senator from Mississippi when the Texas question was before Congress • 14 resolutions passed. The joint resolution for the annexation of Texas was passed March 1, 1845

ern and Southern votes. In the House of Representatives there were about eighty Southern votes and about fifty Northern votes for the admission of Texas. In the Senate the vote for the admission of Texas was twenty-seven, and twenty-five against it; and of those twenty-seven votes, constituting the majority, no less than thirteen came from the free States, and four of them were from New England. The whole of these thirteen Senators, constituting within a fraction, you see, one half of all the votes in this body for the admission of this im-measurable extent of slave territory, were sent here by free States.

Sir, there is not so remarkable a chapter in our history of political events, political parties, and political men as is afforded by this admission of a new slave-holding territory, so vast that a bird cannot fly over it in a week. New England, as I have said, with some of her own votes, supported this measure. Three fourths of the votes of liberty-loving Connecticut were given for it in the other house, and one half here. There was one vote for it from Maine, but, I am happy to say, not the vote of the honorable member who addressed the Senate the day before yesterday, and who was then a Representative from Maine in the House of Representatives; but there was one vote from Maine, ay, and there was one vote for it from Massachusetts, given by a gentleman then representing, and now living in, the district in which the prevalence of Free Soil sentiment for a couple of years or so has defeated the choice of any member to represent it in Congress. Sir, that body of Northern and Eastern men who gave those votes at that time are now seen taking upon themselves, in the nomenclature of politics, the appellation of the Northern Democracy. They undertook to wield the destinies of this empire, if I may give that name to a republic, and their policy was, and they persisted in it, to bring into this country and under this government all the territory they could. They did it, in the case of Texas, under pledges, absolute pledges, to the slave interest, and they afterwards lent their aid in bringing in these new conquests, to take their chance for slavery or freedom. My honorable friend from Georgia, in March, 1847, moved the Senate to de-clare that the war ought not to be prosecuted for the conquest of territory, or for the dismemberment of Mexico. The whole of the Northern Democracy voted against it. He did not get a vote from them. It suited the patriotic and elevated sentiments of the Northern

Democracy to bring in a world from among the moun-tains and valleys of California and New Mexico, or any other part of Mexico, and then quarrel about it; to bring it in, and then endeavor to put upon it the saving grace of the Wilmot Proviso. There were two eminent and highly respectable gentlemen from the North, and East, then leading gentlemen in the Senate, (I refer, and I do so with entire respect, for I entertain for both of those gentlemen, in general, high regard, to Mr. Dix of New York and Mr. Niles of Connecticut,) who both voted for the admission of Texas. They would not have that vote any other way than as it stood; and they would have it as it did stand. I speak of the vote upon the annexation of Texas. Those two gentlemen would have the resolution of annexation just as it is, without amend-ment; and they voted for it just as it is, and their eyes were all open to its true character. The honorable mem-ber from South Carolina who addressed us the other day was then Secretary of State. His correspondence with Mr. Murphy, the Chargé d'Affaires of the United States in Texas, had been published. That correspondence was all before those gentlemen, and the Secretary had the bold-ness and candor to avow in that correspondence, that the great object sought by the annexation of Texas was to strengthen the slave interest of the South. Why, Sir, he said so in so many words—

MR. CALHOUN. Will the honorable Senator permit me to interrupt him for a moment?

Certainly.

MR. CALHOUN. I am very reluctant to interrupt the honorable gentleman; but, upon a point of so much im-portance, I deem it right to put myself *rectus in curia*. I did not put it upon the ground assumed by the Senator. I put it upon this ground: that Great Britain had an-nounced to this country, in so many words, that her object was to abolish slavery in Texas, and, through Texas, to accomplish the abolition of slavery in the United States and the world. The ground I put it on was, that it would make an exposed frontier, and, if Great Britain succeeded in her object, it would be im-possible that that frontier could be secured against the aggressions of the Abolitionists; and that this govern-

---

52 **Wilmot Proviso.** See note, p. 33 • 79 **rectus in curia,** right in the court

ment was bound, under the guaranties of the Constitution, to protect us against such a state of things.

That comes, I suppose, Sir, to exactly the same thing. It was that Texas must be obtained for the security of the slave interest of the South.

MR. CALHOUN. Another view is very distinctly given.

That was the object set forth in the correspondence of a worthy gentleman not now living, who preceded the honorable member from South Carolina in the Department of State. There repose on the files of the Department, as I have occasion to know, strong letters from Mr. Upshur to the United States minister in England, and I believe there are some to the same minister from the honorable Senator himself, asserting to this effect the sentiments of this government; namely, that Great Britain was expected not to interfere to take Texas out of the hands of its then existing government and make it a free country. But my argument, my suggestion, is this; that those gentlemen who composed the Northern Democracy, when Texas was brought into the Union, saw clearly that it was brought in as a slave country, and brought in for the purpose of being maintained as slave territory, to the Greek Kalends. I rather think the honorable gentleman who was then Secretary of State might, in some of his correspondence with Mr. Murphy, have suggested that it was not expedient to say too much about this object, lest it should create some alarm. At any rate, Mr. Murphy wrote to him that England was anxious to get rid of the constitution of Texas, because it was a constitution establishing slavery; and that what the United States had to do was to aid the people of Texas in upholding their constitution; but that nothing should be said which should offend the fanatical men of the North. But, Sir, the honorable member did avow this object himself, openly, boldly, and manfully; he did not disguise his conduct or his motives.

MR. CALHOUN. Never, never.

What he means he is very apt to say.

MR. CALHOUN. Always, always.

And I honor him for it.

This admission of Texas was in 1845. Then, in 1847, *flagrante bello* between the United States and Mexico, the proposition I have mentioned was brought forward **by my** friend from Georgia, and the Northern Democ-

racy voted steadily against it. Their remedy was to apply to the acquisitions, after they should come in, the Wilmot Proviso. What follows? These two gentlemen, worthy and honorable and influential men, (and if they had not been they could not have carried the measure,) these two gentlemen, members of this body, brought in Texas, and by their votes they also prevented the passage of the resolution of the honorable member from Georgia, and then they went home and took the lead in the Free Soil party. And there they stand, Sir! They leave us here, bound in honor and conscience by the resolutions of annexation; they leave us here, to take the odium of fulfilling the obligations in favor of slavery which they voted us into, or else the greater odium of violating those obligations, while they are at home making capital and rousing speeches for free soil and no slavery. And therefore I say, Sir, that there is not a chapter in our history, respecting public measures and public men, more full of what would create surprise, more full of what does create, in my mind, extreme mortification, than that of the conduct of the Northern Democracy on this subject.

Mr. President, sometimes, when a man is found in a new relation to things around him and to other men, he says the world has changed and that he has not changed. I believe, Sir, that our self-respect leads us often to make this declaration in regard to ourselves when it is not exactly true. An individual is more apt to change, perhaps, than all the world around him. But, under the present circumstances, and under the responsibility which I know I incur by what I am now stating here, I feel at liberty to recur to the various expressions and statements, made at various times, of my own opinions and resolutions respecting the admission of Texas, and all that has followed. Sir, as early as 1836, or in the early part of 1837, there was conversation and correspondence between myself and some private friends on this project of annexing Texas to the United States; and an honorable gentleman with whom I have had a long acquaintance, a friend of mine, now perhaps in this chamber, I mean General Hamilton, of South Carolina, was privy to that correspondence. I had voted for the recognition of Texan independence, because I

---

23 to . . . Kalends, an expression meaning "forever"; the Kalends, the first day of the Roman month, had no counterpart in the Greek calendar • **43 flagrante bello,** while war was being waged

believed it to be an existing fact, surprising and astonishing as it was, and I wished well to the new republic; but I manifested from the first utter opposition to bringing her, with her slave territory, into the Union. I happened, in 1837, to make a public address to political friends in New York, and I then stated my sentiments upon the subject. It was the first time that I had occasion to advert to it; and I will ask a friend near me to have the kindness to read an extract from the speech made by me on that occasion. It was delivered in Niblo's Garden, in 1837.

Mr. Greene then read the following extract from the speech of Mr. Webster, to which he referred:

"Gentlemen, we all see that, by whomsoever possessed, Texas is likely to be a slave-holding country; and I frankly avow my entire unwillingness to do any thing which shall extend the slavery of the African race on this continent, or add other slave-holding States to the Union. When I say that I regard slavery in itself as a great moral, social, and political evil, I only use language which has been adopted by distinguished men, themselves citizens of slave-holding States. I shall do nothing, therefore, to favor or encourage its further extension. We have slavery already amongst us. The Constitution found it in the Union; it recognized it, and gave it solemn guaranties. To the full extent of these guaranties we are all bound, in honor, in justice, and by the Constitution. All the stipulations contained in the Constitution in favor of the slave-holding States which are already in the Union ought to be fulfilled, and, so far as depends on me, shall be fulfilled, in the fulness of their spirit, and to the exactness of their letter. Slavery, as it exists in the States, is beyond the reach of Congress. It is a concern of the States themselves; they have never submitted it to Congress, and Congress has no rightful power over it. I shall concur, therefore, in no act, no measure, no menace, no indication of purpose, which shall interfere or threaten to interfere with the exclusive authority of the several States over the subject of slavery as it exists within their respective limits. All this appears to me to be matter of plain and imperative duty.

"But when we come to speak of admitting new States, the subject assumes an entirely different aspect. Our rights and our duties are then both different.

"I see, therefore, no political necessity for the annexation of Texas to the Union; no advantages to be derived from it; and objections to it of a strong, and, in my judgment, decisive character."

I have nothing, Sir, to add to, or to take from, those sentiments. That speech, the Senate will perceive, was made in 1837. The purpose of immediately annexing Texas at that time was abandoned or postponed; and it was not revived with any vigor for some years. In the mean time it happened that I had become a member of the executive administration, and was for a short period in the Department of State. The annexation of Texas was a subject of conversation, not confidential, with the President and heads of departments, as well as with other public men. No serious attempt was then made, however, to bring it about. I left the Department of State in May, 1843, and shortly after I learned, though by means which were no way connected with official information, that a design had been taken up of bringing Texas, with her slave territory and population, into this Union. I was in Washington at the time, and persons are now here who will remember that we had an arranged meeting for conversation upon it. I went home to Massachusetts and proclaimed the existence of that purpose, but I could get no audience and but little attention. Some did not believe it, and some were too much engaged in their own pursuits to give it any heed. They had gone to their farms or to their merchandise, and it was impossible to arouse any feeling in New England, or in Massachusetts, that should combine the two great political parties against this annexation; and, indeed, there was no hope of bringing the Northern Democracy into that view, for their leaning was all the other way. But Sir, even with Whigs, and leading Whigs, I am ashamed to say, there was a great indifference towards the admission of Texas, with slave territory, into this Union.

The project went on. I was then out of Congress. The annexation resolutions passed on the 1st of March, 1845; the legislature of Texas complied with the conditions and accepted the guaranties; for the language of the resolution is, that Texas is to come in "upon the conditions and under the guaranties herein prescribed."

---

11 Niblo's Garden, a saloon in New York City

I was returned to the Senate in March, 1845, and was here in December following, when the acceptance by Texas of the conditions proposed by Congress was communicated to us by the President, and an act for the consummation of the union was laid before the two houses. The connection was then not completed. A final law, doing the deed of annexation ultimately, had not been passed; and when it was put upon its final passage here, I expressed my opposition to it, and recorded my vote in the negative; and there that vote stands, with the observations that I made upon that occasion. Nor is this the only occasion on which I have expressed myself to the same effect. It has happened that, between 1837 and this time, on various occasions, I have expressed my entire opposition to the admission of slave States, or the acquisition of new slave territories, to be added to the United States. I know, Sir, no change in my own sentiments, or my own purposes, in that respect. I will now ask my friend from Rhode Island to read another extract from a speech of mine made at a Whig Convention in Springfield, Massachusetts, in the month of September, 1847.

Mr. Greene here read the following extract:

"We hear much just now of a *panacea* for the dangers and evils of slavery and slave annexation, which they call the 'Wilmot Proviso.' That certainly is a just sentiment, but it is not a sentiment to found any new party upon. It is not a sentiment on which Massachusetts Whigs differ. There is not a man in this hall who holds to it more firmly than I do, nor one who adheres to it more than another.

"I feel some little interest in this matter, Sir. Did not I commit myself in 1837 to the whole doctrine, fully, entirely? And I must be permitted to say that I cannot quite consent that more recent discoverers should claim the merit and take out a patent.

"I deny the priority of their invention. Allow me to say, Sir, it is not their thunder.

"We are to use the first and the last and every occasion which offers to oppose the extension of slave power.

"But I speak of it here, as in Congress, as a political question, a question for statesmen to act upon. We must so regard it. I certainly do not mean to say that it is less important in a moral point of view, that it is not more important in many other points of view, but as

a legislator, or in any official capacity, I must look at it, consider it, and decide it as a matter of political action."

On other occasions, in debates here, I have expressed my determination to vote for no acquisition, or cession, or annexation, north or south, east or west. My opinion has been, that we have territory enough, and that we should follow the Spartan maxim, "Improve, adorn what you have," seek no further. I think that it was in some observations that I made on the three-million loan bill that I avowed this sentiment. In short, Sir, it has been avowed quite as often, in as many places, and before as many assemblies, as any humble opinions of mine ought to be avowed.

But now that, under certain conditions, Texas is in the Union, with all her territory, as a slave State, with a solemn pledge, also, that, if she shall be divided into many States, those States may come in as slave States south of 36° 30′, how are we to deal with this subject? I know no way of honest legislation, when the proper time comes for the enactment, but to carry into effect all that we have stipulated to do. I do not entirely agree with my honorable friend from Tennessee, that, as soon as the time comes when she is entitled to another representative, we should create a new State. On former occasions, in creating new States out of territories, we have generally gone upon the idea that, when the population of the territory amounts to about sixty thousand, we would consent to its admission as a State. But it is quite a different thing when a State is divided, and two or more States made out of it. It does not follow in such a case that the same rule of apportionment should be applied. That, however, is a matter for the consideration of Congress, when the proper time arrives. I may not then be here; I may have no vote to give on the occasion; but I wish it to be distinctly understood, that, according to my view of the matter, this government is solemnly pledged, by law and contract, to create new States out of Texas, with her consent, when her population shall justify and call for such a proceeding, and, so far as such States are formed out of Texan territory lying south of 36° 30′, to let them come in as slave States. That is the meaning of the contract which our friends, the Northern Democracy, have left us to fulfil; and I, for one, mean to fulfil it, because I will not violate the faith of the government. What I mean to say is, that the time for the admission of new States formed out of Texas, the number of such States, their boundaries, the requisite amount of population, and all other things connected with the admission, are in the free discretion of Congress, except this; to wit, that, when new States formed out of Texas are to be admitted, they have a right by legal stipulation and contract, to come in as slave States.

10 Now, as to California and New Mexico, I hold slavery to be excluded from those territories by a law even superior to that which admits and sanctions it in Texas. I mean the law of nature, of physical geography, the law of the formation of the earth. That law settles for ever, with a strength beyond all terms of human enactment, that slavery cannot exist in California or New Mexico. Understand me, Sir; I mean slavery as we regard it; the slavery of the colored race as it exists in the Southern States. I shall not discuss the point, but 20 leave it to the learned gentlemen who have undertaken to discuss it; but I suppose there is no slavery of that description in California now. I understand that *peonism,* a sort of penal servitude, exists there, or rather a sort of voluntary sale of a man and his offspring for debt, an arrangement of a peculiar nature known to the law of Mexico. But what I mean to say is, that it is as impossible that African slavery, as we see it among us, should find its way, or be introduced, into California and New Mexico, as any other natural impossibility. 30 California and New Mexico are Asiatic in their formation and scenery. They are composed of vast ridges of mountains of great height, with broken ridges and deep valleys. The sides of these mountains are entirely barren; their tops capped by perennial snow. There may be in California, now made free by its constitution, and no doubt there are, some tracts of valuable land. But it is not so in New Mexico. Pray, what is the evidence which every gentleman must have obtained on this subject, from information sought by himself or communicated 40 by others? I have inquired and read all I could find, in order to acquire information on this important subject. What is there in New Mexico that could, by any possibility, induce any body to go there with slaves? There are some narrow strips of tillable land on the borders of the rivers; but the rivers themselves dry up before midsummer is gone. All that the people can do

in that region is to raise some little articles, some little wheat for their *tortillas,* and that by irrigation. And who expects to see a hundred black men cultivating tobacco, corn, cotton, rice, or any thing else on lands in 50 New Mexico, made fertile only by irrigation?

I look upon it, therefore, as a fixed fact, to use the current expression of the day, that both California and New Mexico are destined to be free, so far as they are settled at all, which I believe, in regard to New Mexico, will be but partially for a great length of time; free by the arrangement of things ordained by the Power above us. I have therefore to say, in this respect also, that this country is fixed for freedom, to as many persons as shall ever live in it, by a less repealable law than that which 60 attaches to the right of holding slaves in Texas; and I will say further, that, if a resolution or a bill were now before us, to provide a territorial government for New Mexico, I would not vote to put any prohibition into it whatever. Such a prohibition would be idle, as it respects any effect it would have upon the territory; and I would not take pains uselessly to reaffirm an ordinance of nature, nor to reënact the will of God. I would put in no Wilmot Proviso for the mere purpose of a taunt or a reproach. I would put into it no evidence of the 70 votes of superior power, exercised for no purpose but to wound the pride, whether a just and a rational pride, or an irrational pride, of the citizens of the Southern States. I have no such object, no such purpose. They would think it a taunt, an indignity; they would think it to be an act taking away from them what they regard as a proper equality of privilege. Whether they expect to realize any benefit from it or not, they would think it at least a plain theoretic wrong; that something more or less derogatory to their character and their rights had taken 80 place. I propose to inflict no such wound upon any body, unless something essentially important to the country, and efficient to the preservation of liberty and freedom, is to be effected. I repeat, therefore, Sir, and, as I do not propose to address the Senate often on this subject, I repeat it because I wish it to be distinctly understood, that, for the reasons stated, if a proposition were now here to establish a government for New Mexico, and it was moved to insert a provision for a prohibition of slavery, I would not vote for it. 90

Sir, if we were now making a government for New Mexico, and any body should propose a Wilmot Proviso,

I should treat it exactly as Mr. Polk treated that provision for excluding slavery from Oregon. Mr. Polk was known to be in opinion decidedly averse to the Wilmot Proviso; but he felt the necessity of establishing a government for the territory of Oregon. The proviso was in the bill, but he knew it would be entirely nugatory; and, since it must be entirely nugatory, since it took away no right, no describable, no tangible, no appreciable right of the South, he said he would sign the bill for the sake of enacting a law to form a government in that Territory, and let that entirely useless, and, in that connection, entirely senseless, proviso remain. Sir, we hear occasionally of the annexation of Canada; and if there be any man, any of the Northern Democracy, or any one of the Free Soil party, who supposes it necessary to insert a Wilmot Proviso in a territorial government for New Mexico, that man would of course be of opinion that it is necessary to protect the everlasting snows of Canada from the foot of slavery by the same overspreading wing of an act of Congress. Sir, wherever there is a substantive good to be done, wherever there is a foot of land to be prevented from becoming slave territory, I am ready to assert the principle of the exclusion of slavery. I am pledged to it from the year 1837; I have been pledged to it again and again; and I will perform those pledges; but I will not do a thing unnecessarily that wounds the feelings of others, or that does discredit to my own understanding.

Now, Mr. President, I have established, so far as I proposed to do so, the proposition with which I set out, and upon which I intend to stand or fall; and that is, that the whole territory within the former United States, or in the newly acquired Mexican provinces, has a fixed and settled character, now fixed and settled by law which cannot be repealed; in the case of Texas without a violation of public faith, and by no human power in regard to California or New Mexico; that, therefore, under one or other of these laws, every foot of land in the States or in the Territories has already received a fixed and decided character.

Mr. President, in the excited times in which we live, there is found to exist a state of crimination and recrimination between the North and South. There are lists of grievances produced by each; and those grievances, real or supposed, alienate the minds of one portion of the country from the other, exasperate the feelings, and subdue the sense of fraternal affection, patriotic love, and mutual regard. I shall bestow a little attention, Sir, upon these various grievances existing on the one side and on the other. I begin with complaints of the South. I will not answer, further than I have, the general statements of the honorable Senator from South Carolina, that the North has prospered at the expense of the South in consequence of the manner of administering this government, in the collecting of its revenues, and so forth. These are disputed topics, and I have no inclination to enter into them. But I will allude to other complaints of the South, and especially to one which has in my opinion just foundation; and that is, that there has been found at the North, among individuals and among legislators, a disinclination to perform fully their constitutional duties in regard to the return of persons bound to service who have escaped into the free States. In that respect, the South, in my judgment, is right, and the North is wrong. Every member of every Northern legislature is bound by oath, like every other officer in the country, to support the Constitution of the United States; and the article of the Constitution which says to these States that they shall deliver up fugitives from service is as binding in honor and conscience as any other article. No man fulfils his duty in any legislature who sets himself to find excuses, evasions, escapes from this constitutional obligation. I have always thought that the Constitution addressed itself to the legislatures of the States or to the States themselves. It says that those persons escaping to other States "shall be delivered up," and I confess I have always been of the opinion that it was an injunction upon the States themselves. When it is said that a person escaping into another State, and coming therefore within the jurisdiction of that State, shall be delivered up, it seems to me the import of the clause is, that the State itself, in obedience to the Constitution, shall cause him to be delivered up. That is my judgment. I have always entertained that opinion, and I entertain it now. But when the subject, some years ago, was before the Supreme Court of the United States, the majority of the judges held that the power to cause fugitives from service to be delivered up was a power to be exercised under the authority of this government. I do not know, on the whole, that it may not have been a fortunate decision. My habit is to respect the result of judicial deliberations and the solemnity of judicial decisions. As it now stands, the business of seeing that these fugitives are delivered up resides in the power of Congress and the national judicature, and my friend at the head of the Judiciary Committee has a bill on the subject now before the Senate, which, with some amendments to it, I propose to support, with all its provisions, to the fullest extent. And I desire to call the attention of all sober-minded men at the North, of all conscientious men, of all men who are not carried away by some fanatical idea or some false impression, to their constitutional obligations. I put it to all the sober and sound minds at the North as a question of morals and a question of conscience. What right have they, in their legislative capacity or any other capacity, to endeavor to get round this Constitution, or to embarrass the free exercise of the rights secured by the Constitution to the persons whose slaves escape from them? None at all; none at all. Neither in the forum of conscience, nor before the face of the Constitution, are they, in my opinion, justified in such an attempt. Of course it is a matter for their consideration. They probably, in the excitement of the times, have not stopped to consider of this. They have followed what seemed to be the current of thought and of motives, as the occasion arose, and they have neglected to investigate fully the real question, and to consider their constitutional obligations; which, I am sure, if they did consider, they would fulfil with alacrity. I repeat, therefore, Sir, that here is a well-founded ground of complaint against the North, which ought to be removed, which it is now in the power of the different departments of this government to remove; which calls for the enactment of proper laws authorizing the judicature of this government, in the several States, to do all that is necessary for the recapture of fugitive slaves and for their restoration to those who claim them. Wherever I go, and whenever I speak on the subject, and when I speak here I desire to speak to the whole North, I say that the South has been injured in this respect, and has a right to complain; and the North has been too careless of what I think the Constitution peremptorily and emphatically enjoins upon her as a duty.

Complaint has been made against certain resolutions that emanate from legislatures at the North, and are sent here to us, not only on the subject of slavery in this District, but sometimes recommending Congress to consider the means of abolishing slavery in the States. I should be sorry to be called upon to present any resolutions here which could not be referable to any committee or any power in Congress; and therefore I should be unwilling to receive from the legislature of Massachusetts any instructions to present resolutions expressive of any opinion whatever on the subject of slavery, as it exists at the present moment in the States, for two reasons: first, because I do not consider that the legislature of Massachusetts has any thing to do with it; and next, because I do not consider that I, as her representative here, have anything to do with it. It has become, in my opinion, quite too common; and if the legislatures of the States do not like that opinion, they have a great deal more power to put it down than I have to uphold it; it has become, in my opinion, quite too common a practice for the State legislatures to present resolutions here on all subjects and to instruct us on all subjects. There is no public man that requires instruction more than I do, or who requires information more than I do, or desires it more heartily; but I do not like to have it in too imperative a shape. I took notice, with pleasure, of some remarks made upon this subject, the other day, in the Senate of Massachusetts, by a young man of talent and character, of whom the best hopes may be entertained. I mean Mr. Hillard. He told the Senate of Massachusetts that he would vote for no instructions whatever to be forwarded to members of Congress, nor for any resolutions to be offered expressive of the sense of Massachusetts as to what her members of Congress ought to do. He said that he saw no propriety in one set of public servants giving instructions and reading lectures to another set of public servants. To his own master each of them must stand or fall, and that master is his constituents. I wish these sentiments could become more common. I have never entered into the question, and never shall, as to the binding force of instructions. I will, however, simply say this: if there be any matter pending in this body, while I am a member of it, in which Massachusetts has an interest of her own not adverse to the general interests of the country, I shall pursue her instructions with gladness of heart and with all the efficiency which I can bring to the occasion. But if the question be one which affects her interest, and at the same time equally affects the interests of all the other States, I shall no more regard her particular wishes or instructions than I should regard the wishes of a man who might appoint me an arbitrator or referee to decide some question of important private right between him and his neighbor, and then *instruct* me to decide in his favor. If ever there was a government upon earth it is this government, if ever there was a body upon earth it is this body, which should consider itself as composed by agreement of all, each member appointed by some, but organized by the general consent of all, sitting here, under the solemn obligations of oath and conscience, to do that which they think to be best for the good of the whole.

Then, Sir, there are the Abolition societies, of which I am unwilling to speak, but in regard to which I have very clear notions and opinions. I do not think them useful. I think their operations for the last twenty years have produced nothing good or valuable. At the same time, I believe thousands of their members to be honest and good men, perfectly well-meaning men. They have excited feelings; they think they must do something for the cause of liberty; and, in their sphere of action, they do not see what else they can do than to contribute to an Abolition press, or an Abolition society, or to pay an Abolition lecturer. I do not mean to impute gross motives even to the leaders of these societies, but I am not blind to the consequences of their proceedings. I cannot but see what mischiefs their interference with the South has produced. And is it not plain to every man? Let any gentleman who entertains doubts on this point recur to the debates in the Virginia House of Delegates in 1832, and he will see with what freedom a proposition made by Mr. Jefferson Randolph for the gradual abolition of slavery was discussed in that body. Every one spoke of slavery as he thought; very ignominious and disparaging names and epithets were applied to it. The debates in the House of Delegates on that occasion, I believe, were all published. They were read by every colored man who could read, and to those who could not read, those debates were read by others. At that time Virginia was not unwilling or afraid to discuss this question, and to let that part of her population know as much of the discussion as they could learn. That was in 1832. As has been said by the honorable member from South Carolina, these Abolition societies commenced their course of action in 1835. It is said, I do not know how true it may be, that they sent incendiary publications into the

slave States; at any rate, they attempted to arouse, and did arouse, a very strong feeling; in other words, they created great agitation in the North against Southern slavery. Well, what was the result? The bonds of the slaves were bound more firmly than before, their rivets were more strongly fastened. Public opinion, which in Virginia had begun to be exhibited against slavery, and was opening out for the discussion of the question, drew back and shut itself up in its castle. I wish to know whether any body in Virginia can now talk openly as Mr. Randolph, Governor McDowell, and others talked in 1832, and sent their remarks to the press? We all know the fact, and we all know the cause; and every thing that these agitating people have done has been, not to enlarge, but to restrain, not to set free, but to bind faster, the slave population of the South.

Again, Sir, the violence of the Northern press is complained of. The press violent! Why, Sir, the press is violent everywhere. There are outrageous reproaches in the North against the South, and there are reproaches as vehement in the South against the North. Sir, the extremists of both parts of this country are violent; they mistake loud and violent talk for eloquence and for reason. They think that he who talks loudest reasons best. And this we must expect, when the press is free, as it is here, and I trust always will be; for, with all its licentiousness and all its evil, the entire and absolute freedom of the press is essential to the preservation of government on the basis of a free constitution. Wherever it exists there will be foolish and violent paragraphs in the newspapers, as there are, I am sorry to say, foolish and violent speeches in both houses of Congress. In truth, Sir, I must say that, in my opinion, the vernacular tongue of the country has become greatly vitiated, depraved, and corrupted by the style of our Congressional debates. And if it were possible for those debates to vitiate the principles of the people as much as they have depraved their tastes, I should cry out, "God save the Republic!"

Well, in all this I see no solid grievance, no grievance presented by the South, within the redress of the government, but the single one to which I have referred; and that is, the want of a proper regard to the injunction of the Constitution for the delivery of fugitive slaves.

There are also complaints of the North against the South. I need not go over them particularly. The first and gravest is, that the North adopted the Constitution, recognizing the existence of slavery in the States, and recognizing the right, to a certain extent, of the representation of slaves in Congress, under a state of sentiment and expectation which does not now exist; and that, by events, by circumstances, by the eagerness of the South to acquire territory and extend her slave population, the North finds itself, in regard to the relative influence of the South and the North, of the free States and the slave States, where it never did expect to find itself when they agreed to the compact of the Constitution. They complain, therefore, that instead of slavery being regarded as an evil, as it was then, an evil which all hoped would be extinguished gradually, it is now regarded by the South as an institution to be cherished, and preserved, and extended; an institution which the South has already extended to the utmost of her power by the acquisition of new territory.

Well, then, passing from that, every body in the North reads and every body reads whatsoever the newspapers contain; and the newspapers, some of them, especially those presses to which I have alluded, are careful to spread about among the people every reproachful sentiment uttered by any Southern man bearing at all against the North; every thing that is calculated to exasperate and to alienate; and there are many such things, as every body will admit, from the South, or some portion of it, which are disseminated among the reading people; and they do exasperate, and alienate, and produce a most mischievous effect upon the public mind at the North. Sir, I would not notice things of this sort appearing in obscure quarters; but one thing has occurred in this debate which struck me very forcibly. An honorable member from Louisiana addressed us the other day on this subject. I suppose there is not a more amiable and worthy gentleman in this chamber, nor a gentleman who would be more slow to give offence to any body, and he did not mean in his remarks to give offence. But what did he say? Why, Sir, he took pains to run a contrast between the slaves of the South and the laboring people of the North, giving the preference, in all points of condition, and comfort, and happiness, to the slaves of the South. The honorable member, doubtless, did not suppose that he gave any offence, or did any injustice. He was merely expressing his opinion. But does he know how remarks of that sort will be received by the laboring people of the North? Why, who are the labor-

ing people of the North? They are the whole North. They are the people who till their own farms with their own hands; freeholders, educated men, independent men. Let me say, Sir, that five sixths of the whole property of the North is in the hands of the laborers of the North; they cultivate their farms, they educate their children, they provide the means of independence. If they are not freeholders, they earn wages; these wages accumulate, are turned into capital, into new freeholds, and small capitalists are created. Such is the case, and such the course of things, among the industrious and frugal. And what can these people think when so respectable and worthy a gentleman as the member from Louisiana undertakes to prove that the absolute ignorance and the abject slavery of the South are more in conformity with the high purposes and destiny of immortal, rational human beings, than the educated, the independent free labor of the North?

There is a more tangible and irritating cause of grievance at the North. Free blacks are constantly employed in the vessels of the North, generally as cooks or stewards. When the vessel arrives at a Southern port, these free colored men are taken on shore, by the police or municipal authority, imprisoned, and kept in prison till the vessel is again ready to sail. This is not only irritating, but exceedingly unjustifiable and oppressive. Mr. Hoar's mission, some time ago, to South Carolina, was a well-intended effort to remove this cause of complaint. The North thinks such imprisonments illegal and unconstitutional; and as the cases occur constantly and frequently, they regard it as a great grievance.

Now, Sir, so far as any of these grievances have their foundation in matters of law, they can be redressed, and ought to be redressed; and so far as they have their foundation in matters of opinion, in sentiment, in mutual crimination and recrimination, all that we can do is to endeavor to allay the agitation, and cultivate a better feeling and more fraternal sentiments between the South and the North.

Mr. President, I should much prefer to have heard from every member on this floor declarations of opinion that this Union could never be dissolved, than the declaration of opinion by any body, that, in any case, under

73 **Mr. Hoar,** Judge E. Rockwood Hoar of Concord, Massachusetts, a friend of Emerson's

the pressure of any circumstances, such a dissolution was possible. I hear with distress and anguish the word "secession," especially when it falls from the lips of those who are patriotic, and known to the country, and known all over the world, for their political services. Secession! Peaceable secession! Sir, your eyes and mine are never destined to see that miracle. The dismemberment of this vast country without convulsion! The breaking up of the fountains of the great deep without ruffling the surface! Who is so foolish, I beg every body's pardon, as to expect to see any such thing? Sir, he who sees these States, now revolving in harmony around a common centre, and expects to see them quit their places and fly off without convulsion, may look the next hour to see the heavenly bodies rush from their spheres, and jostle against each other in the realms of space, without causing the wreck of the universe. There can be no such thing as a peaceable secession. Peaceable secession is an utter impossibility. Is the great Constitution under which we live, covering this whole country, is it to be thawed and melted away by secession, as the snows on the mountain melt under the influence of a vernal sun, disappear almost unobserved, and run off? No, Sir! No, Sir! I will not state what might produce the disruption of the Union; but, Sir, I see as plainly as I see the sun in heaven what that disruption itself must produce; I see that it must produce war, and such a war as I will not describe, *in its twofold character.*

Peaceable secession! Peaceable secession! The concurrent agreement of all the members of this great republic to separate! A voluntary separation, with alimony on one side and on the other. Why, what would be the result? Where is the line to be drawn? What States are to secede? What is to remain American? What am I to be? An American no longer? Am I to become a sectional man, a local man, a separatist, with no country in common with the gentlemen who sit around me here, or who fill the other house of Congress? Heaven forbid! Where is the flag of the republic to remain? Where is the eagle still to tower? or is he to cower, and shrink, and fall to the ground? Why, Sir, our ancestors, our fathers and our grandfathers, those of them that are yet living amongst us with prolonged lives, would rebuke and reproach us; and our children and our grand-children would cry out shame upon us, if we of this generation should dishonor these ensigns of the power of the government and the harmony of that Union

which is every day felt among us with so much joy and gratitude. What is to become of the army? What is to become of the navy? What is to become of the public lands? How is each of the thirty States to defend itself? I know, although the idea has not been stated distinctly, there is to be, or it is supposed possible that there will be, a Southern Confederacy. I do not mean, when I allude to this statement, that any one seriously contemplates such a state of things. I do not mean to say that it is true, but I have heard it suggested elsewhere, that the idea has been entertained, that, after the dissolution of this Union, a Southern Confederacy might be formed. I am sorry, Sir, that it has ever been thought of, talked of, or dreamed of, in the wildest flights of human imagination. But the idea, so far as it exists, must be of a separation, assigning the slave States to one side and the free States to the other. Sir, I may express myself too strongly perhaps, but there are impossibilities in the natural as well as in the physical world, and I hold the idea of a separation of these States, those that are free to form one government, and those that are slave-holding to form another, as such an impossibility. We could not separate the States by any such line, if we were to draw it. We could not sit down here to-day and draw a line of separation that would satisfy any five men in the country. There are natural causes that would keep and tie us together, and there are social and domestic relations which we could not break if we would, and which we should not if we could.

Sir, nobody can look over the face of this country at the present moment, nobody can see where its population is the most dense and growing, without being ready to admit, and compelled to admit, that ere long the strength of America will be in the Valley of the Mississippi. Well, now, Sir, I beg to inquire what the wildest enthusiast has to say on the possibility of cutting that river in two, and leaving free States at its source and on its branches, and slave States down near its mouth, each forming a separate government? Pray, Sir, let me say to the people of this country, that these things are worthy of their pondering and of their consideration. Here, Sir, are five millions of freemen in the free States north of the river Ohio. Can any body suppose that this population can be severed, by a line that divides them from the territory of a foreign and an alien government, down somewhere, the Lord knows where, upon the lower banks of the Mississippi? What would become of Mis-

souri? Will she join the *arrondissement* of the slave States? Shall the man from the Yellow Stone and the Platte be connected, in the new republic, with the man who lives on the southern extremity of the Cape of Florida? Sir, I am ashamed to pursue this line of remark. I dislike it, I have an utter disgust for it. I would rather hear of natural blasts and mildews, war, pestilence, and famine, than to hear gentlemen talk of secession. To break up this great government! to dismember this glori-
10 ous country! to astonish Europe with an act of folly such as Europe for two centuries has never beheld in any government or any people!! No, Sir, no, Sir! There will be no secession! Gentlemen are not serious when they talk of secession.

Sir, I hear there is to be a convention held at Nashville. I am bound to believe that, if worthy gentlemen meet at Nashville in convention, their object will be to adopt conciliatory counsels; to advise the South to forbearance and moderation, and to advise the North to forbearance and
20 moderation; and to inculcate principles of brotherly love and affection, and attachment to the Constitution of the country as it now is. I believe, if the convention meet at all, it will be for this purpose; for certainly, if they meet for any purpose hostile to the Union, they have been singularly inappropriate in their selection of a place. I remember, Sir, that, when the treaty of Amiens was concluded between France and England, a sturdy Englishman and a distinguished orator, who regarded the conditions of the peace as ignominious to England,
30 said in the House of Commons, that, if King William could know the terms of that treaty, he would turn in his coffin! Let me commend this saying of Mr. Windham, in all its emphasis and in all its force, to any persons who shall meet at Nashville for the purpose of concerting measures for the overthrow of this Union over the bones of Andrew Jackson!

Sir, I wish now to make two remarks, and hasten to a conclusion. I wish to say, in regard to Texas, that if it should be hereafter, at any time, the pleasure of the gov-
40 ernment of Texas to cede to the United States a portion, larger or smaller, of her territory which lies adjacent to New Mexico, and north of 36° 30′ of north latitude, to be formed into free States, for a fair equivalent in money or in the payment of her debt, I think it an object well worthy the consideration of Congress, and I shall be happy to concur in it myself, if I should have a connection with the government at that time.

I have one other remark to make. In my observations upon slavery as it has existed in this country, and as it now exists, I have expressed no opinion of the mode of 50 its extinguishment or melioration. I will say, however, though I have nothing to propose, because I do not deem myself so competent as other gentlemen to take any lead on this subject, that if any gentleman from the South shall propose a scheme, to be carried on by this government upon a large scale, for the transportation of free colored people to any colony or any place in the world, I should be quite disposed to incur almost any degree of expense to accomplish that object. Nay, Sir, following an example set more than twenty years ago 60 by a great man, then a Senator from New York, I would return to Virginia, and through her to the whole South, the money received from the lands and territories ceded by her to this government, for any such purpose as to remove, in whole or in part, or in any way to diminish or deal beneficially with, the free colored population of the Southern States. I have said that I honor Virginia for her cession of this territory. There have been received into the treasury of the United States eighty millions of dollars, the proceeds of the sales of the public 70 lands ceded by her. If the residue should be sold at the same rate, the whole aggregate will exceed two hundred millions of dollars. If Virginia and the South see fit to adopt any proposition to relieve themselves from the free people of color among them, or such as may be made free, they have my full consent that the government shall pay them any sum of money out of the proceeds of that cession which may be adequate to the purpose.

And now, Mr. President, I draw these observations to a close. I have spoken freely, and I meant to do so. 80 I have sought to make no display. I have sought to enliven the occasion by no animated discussion nor have I attempted any train of elaborate argument. I have wished only to speak my sentiments, fully and at length, being desirous, once and for all, to let the country know the opinions and sentiments which I entertain on all these subjects. These opinions are not likely to be suddenly changed. If there be any future service that I can render to the country, consistently with these sentiments and opinions, I shall cheerfully render it. If there be not, I shall still be glad to have had an opportunity to disburden myself from the bottom of my heart, and to make known every political sentiment that therein exists.

And now, Mr. President, instead of speaking of the possibility or utility of secession, instead of dwelling in those caverns of darkness, instead of groping with those ideas so full of all that is horrid and horrible, let us come out into the light of day; let us enjoy the fresh air of Liberty and Union; let us cherish those hopes which belong to us; let us devote ourselves to those great objects that are fit for our consideration and our action; let us raise our conceptions to the magnitude and the importance of the duties that devolve upon us; let our comprehension be as broad as the country for which we act, our aspirations as high as its certain destiny; let us not be pigmies in a case that calls for men. Never did there devolve on any generation of men higher trusts than now devolve upon us, for the preservation of this Constitution and the harmony and peace of all who are destined to live under it. Let us make our generation one of the strongest and brightest links in that golden chain which is destined, I fondly believe, to grapple the people of all the states to this Constitution for ages to come. We have a great, popular, constitutional government, guarded by law and by judicature, and defended by the affections of the whole people. No monarchical throne presses these States together, no iron chain of military power encircles them; they live and stand under a government popular in its form, representative in its character, founded upon principles of equality, and so constructed, we hope, as to last for ever. In all its history it has been beneficent; it has trodden down no man's liberty; it has crushed no State. Its daily respiration is liberty and patriotism; its yet youthful veins are full of enterprise, courage, and honorable love of glory and renown. Large before, the country has now, by recent events, become vastly larger. This republic now extends, with a vast breadth, across the whole continent. The two great seas of the world wash the one and the other shore. We realize, on a mighty scale, the beautiful description of the ornamental border of the buckler of Achilles:

"Now, the broad shield complete, the artist crown'd
With his last band, and poured the ocean round;
In living silver seem'd the waves to roll,
And beat the buckler's verge, and bound the whole."

1850

---

48 Now . . . whole, from Pope's translation of the Iliad, Bk. XVIII, II. 701-704

---

written during civil war!

abolition

John Greenleaf Whittier

a quaker – reformer!

1807 · 1892

The background of John Greenleaf Whittier in more than one way helped make him one of the most effective battlers for abolition. Born on a farm near Haverhill, Massachusetts, educated in country schools, long a worker on his father's farm and at the cobbler's bench, he saw things through the eyes of a common man and his words were drawn from nature rather than art. From Robert Burns, his first and most important model, he learned a simple style of versifying which pleased ordinary readers. A member of a religious sect which had contributed

Illustration above Whittier's poem, "Our Countrymen in Chains," in an early broadside, 1834

For several decades Whittier devoted a large share of his energy to the antislavery cause. He was successful in practical politics, winning his own election to the Massachusetts legislature in 1835, acting as a lobbyist at the State House, and giving assistance to political leaders who were helpful to abolitionism. As a pamphleteer and as an editor of various periodicals, notably of the *National Era* (1845-1860), he attacked slavery ferociously. Finally, as a poet he composed fiery or touching songs which spoke directly to hosts of readers. His propagandistic verse, though far from great as poetry, was admirable as rhetoric. After broadside or newspaper publication, this work was brought together chiefly in *Poems Written During the Progress of the Abolition Question* . . . (1837), *Voices of Freedom* (1846), *Songs of Labor and Other Poems* (1850), and *In War Time and Other Poems* (1863).

After the war, Whittier turned to a field of work in which he had already shown proficiency—the portrayal of the rural New England life which he knew so well. It was as a local colorist that he did his most distinguished writing. (See Chapter 5 for this phase of his career.)

many great opponents of the slave system, Whittier followed the promptings of his Quaker Inner Light to work zealously for reform.

The Complete Poetical and Prose Works, 7 vols., Boston, 1888-1889 • Whitman Bennett, *Whittier, Bard of Freedom*, Chapel Hill, 1941 • J. A. Pollard, *Whittier, Friend of Man*, Boston, 1949

The abolition cause is a moral warfare

The Moral Warfare

abolitionists' cause

war against wrong

When Freedom, on her natal day,
Within her war-rocked cradle lay,
An iron race around her stood,
Baptized her infant brow in blood;
And, through the storm which round her swept,
Their constant ward and watching kept.

Then, where our quiet herds repose
The roar of baleful battle rose,
And brethren of a common tongue

To mortal strife as tigers sprung,   10
And every gift on Freedom's shrine
Was man for beast, and blood for wine!

Our fathers to their graves have gone;
Their strife is past, their triumph won;
But sterner trials wait the race
Which rises in their honored place;
A moral warfare with the crime
And folly of an evil time.

So let it be. In God's own might
We gird us for the coming fight,   20
And, strong in Him whose cause is ours

In conflict with unholy powers,
We grasp the weapons He has given,—
The Light, and Truth, and Love of Heaven.

1838

against slavery!

Massachusetts to Virginia

Whittier printed the following explanatory note with a later edition of the poem: "Written on reading an account of the proceedings of the citizens of Norfolk, Virginia, in reference to George Latimer, the alleged fugitive slave, who was seized in Boston without warrant at the request of James B. Grey, of Norfolk, claiming to be his master. The case caused great excitement North and South, and led to the presentation of a petition to Congress, signed by more than fifty thousand citizens of Massachusetts, calling for such laws and proposed amendments to the Constitution as should relieve the Commonwealth from all further participation in the crime of oppression. George Latimer himself was finally given free papers for the sum of four hundred dollars."

"Massachusetts to Virginia" is one of the most stirring of Whittier's poems against slavery. The use of place names, rich in association, is particularly effective.

The blast from Freedom's Northern hills, upon its South-
ern way,
Bears greeting to Virginia from Massachusetts Bay;
No word of haughty challenging, nor battle bugle's peal,
Nor steady tread of marching files, nor clang of horse-
men's steel.

No trains of deep-mouthed cannon along our highways go;
Around our silent arsenals untrodden lies the snow;
And to the land-breeze of our ports, upon their errands far,
A thousand sails of commerce swell, but none are spread
for war.

We hear thy threats, Virginia! thy stormy words and high
Swell harshly on the Southern winds which melt along
our sky;   10
Yet, not one brown, hard hand foregoes its honest
labor here,
No hewer of our mountain oaks suspends his axe in fear.

Wild are the waves which lash the reefs along St.
George's bank;
Cold on the shores of Labrador the fog lies white
and dank;
Through storm, and wave, and blinding mist, stout are
the hearts which man
The fishing-smacks of Marblehead, the sea-boats of
Cape Ann.

The cold north light and wintry sun glare on their
icy forms.
Bent grimly o'er their straining lines or wrestling with
the storms;
Free as the winds they drive before, rough as the waves
they roam,
They laugh to scorn the slaver's threat against their
rocky home.   20

What means the Old Dominion? Hath she forgot the day
When o'er her conquered valleys swept the Briton's
steel array?
How side by side, with sons of hers, the Massachusetts men
Encountered Tarleton's charge of fire, and stout Corn-
wallis, then?

Forgets she how the Bay State, in answer to the call
Of her old House of Burgesses, spoke out from Faneuil
Hall?
When, echoing back her Henry's cry, came pulsing in
each breath
Of Northern winds the thrilling sounds of "Liberty or
Death!"

---

13 **St. George's bank**, off Newfoundland • 16 **Marblehead . . .
Cape Ann**, on the Massachusetts coast • 24 **Tarleton . . . Cornwallis**,
commanders of the British army in Virginia in the American Revolution
• 26 **Faneuil Hall**, in Boston, is famous as the scene of patriotic
meetings • 27 **Henry's cry**, an allusion to Patrick Henry's "Speech in
the Virginia Convention of Delegates," March 23, 1775

What asks the Old Dominion? If now her sons have proved
False to their fathers' memory, false to the faith they
    loved;   30
If she can scoff at Freedom, and its great charter spurn,
Must we of Massachusetts from truth and duty turn?

We hunt your bondmen, flying from Slavery's hateful
    hell;
Our voices, at your bidding, take up the bloodhound's
    yell;
We gather, at your summons, above our fathers' graves,
From Freedom's holy altar-horns to tear your wretched
    slaves!

Thank God! not yet so vilely can Massachusetts bow;
The spirit of her early time is with her even now;
Dream not because her Pilgrim blood moves slow and
    calm and cool,
She thus can stoop her chainless neck, a sister's slave
    and tool!   40

All that a sister State should do, all that a free State may,
Heart, hand, and purse we proffer, as in our early day;
But that one dark loathsome burden ye must stagger
    with alone,
And reap the bitter harvest which ye yourselves have
    sown!

Hold, while ye may, your struggling slaves, and burden
    God's free air
With woman's shriek beneath the lash, and manhood's
    wild despair;
Cling closer to the "cleaving curse" that writes upon
    your plains
The blasting of Almighty wrath against a land of chains.

Still shame your gallant ancestry, the cavaliers of old,
By watching round the shambles where human flesh
    is sold;   50
Gloat o'er the newborn child, and count his market
    value, when
The maddened mother's cry of woe shall pierce the
    slaver's den!

Lower than plummet soundeth, sink the Virginia name;
Plant, if ye will, your fathers' graves with rankest weeds
    of shame;
Be, if ye will, the scandal of God's fair universe;

We wash our hands forever of your sin and shame
    and curse.

A voice from lips whereon the coal from Freedom's
    shrine hath been,
Thrilled, as but yesterday, the hearts of Berkshire's moun-
    tain men:
The echoes of that solemn voice are sadly lingering still
In all our sunny valleys, on every wind-swept hill.   60

And when the prowling man-thief came hunting for
    his prey
Beneath the very shadow of Bunker's shaft of gray,
How, through the free lips of the son, the father's warn-
    ing spoke;
How, from its bonds of trade and sect, the Pilgrim
    city broke!

A hundred thousand right arms were lifted up on high,
A hundred thousand voices sent back their loud reply;
Through the thronged towns of Essex the startling
    summons rang,
And up from bench and loom and wheel her young me-
    chanics sprang!

The voice of free, broad Middlesex, of thousands as
    of one,
The shaft of Bunker calling to that of Lexington;   70
From Norfolk's ancient villages, from Plymouth's rocky
    bound

---

31 **great charter,** translating England's Magna Charta, refers here
to the Declaration of Independence • 36 **altar-horns,** an allusion
to I Kings 1:50-53, where Adonijah, fearing King Solomon, "caught
hold on the horns of the altar," and was spared • 44 **which . . .
sown** seems less than fair in view of Massachusetts' and New
England's participation in the slave trade in colonial times •
47 **cleaving curse,** a reference to Deuteronomy 13:17: "And there
shall cleave nought of the cursed thing to thine hand" • 50 **shambles,**
strictly, a place where butcher's meat is sold or animals are
slaughtered for meat • 53 **Lower . . . soundeth** echoes The Tempest, Act III, sc. iii, ll. 101-102: "I'll seek him deeper than e'er
plummet sounded/And with him there lie mudded" • 57 **lips . . .
coal.** Compare Isaiah 6:6-7: "Then flew one of the seraphims unto
me, having a live coal in his hand, which he had taken with the
tongs from off the altar: And he laid it upon my mouth, and said, Lo,
this hath touched thy lips; and thine iniquity is taken away, and
thy sin purged" • 58 **Berkshire . . . Essex . . . Middlesex . . .
Norfolk . . . Plymouth . . . Worcester . . . Barnstable . . .
Bristol . . . Hampden . . . Hampshire,** counties in Massachusetts •
62 **Bunker's shaft,** the monument on Bunker Hill, near Boston

To where Nantucket feels the arms of ocean close her
    round;

From rich and rural Worcester, where through the calm
    repose
Of cultured vales and fringing woods the gentle Nashua
    flows,
To where Wachuset's wintry blasts the mountain
    larches stir,
Swelled up to Heaven the thrilling cry of "God save
    Latimer!"

And sandy Barnstable rose up, wet with the salt sea spray;
And Bristol sent her answering shout down Narragansett
    Bay!
Along the broad Connecticut old Hampden felt the thrill,
And the cheer of Hampshire's woodmen swept down
    from Holyoke Hill.   80

The voice of Massachusetts! Of her free sons and
    daughters,
Deep calling unto deep aloud, the sound of many waters!
Against the burden of that voice what tyrant power
    shall stand?
No fetters in the Bay State! No slave upon her land!

Look to it well, Virginians! In calmness we have borne,
In answer to our faith and trust, your insult and your
    scorn;
You've spurned our kindest counsels; you've hunted for
    our lives;
And shaken round our hearths and homes your mana-
    cles and gyves!

We wage no war, we lift no arm, we fling no torch within
The fire-damps of the quaking mine beneath your
    soil of sin;   90
We leave ye with your bondmen, to wrestle, while ye can,
With the strong upward tendencies and god-like soul
    of man!

But for us and for our children, the vow which we have
    given
For freedom and humanity is registered in heaven;
No slave-hunt in our borders,—no pirate on our strand!
No fetters in the Bay State,—no slave upon our land!
    1843

Ichabod

Means — The Glory has departed

"Ichabod" first appeared, May 2, 1850, in the National
Era, the organ of the "American and Foreign Anti-Slavery
Society," which was published in Washington and of
which Whittier was an editor. In his collected poems
Whittier supplied the following note: "This poem was the
outcome of the surprise and grief and forecast of evil
consequences which I felt on reading the seventh of March
speech of Daniel Webster in support of the 'compromise'
and the Fugitive Slave Bill. No partisan or personal enmity
dictated it. On the contrary my admiration of the splendid
personality and intellectual power of the great senator
was never stronger than when I laid down his speech, and,
in one of the saddest moments of my life, penned my
protest . . . in tones of stern and sorrowful rebuke."

    The title is taken from I Samuel 4:21: "And she named
the child Ichabod, saying, the glory is departed from
Israel."

Whittier is complaining of Daniel Webster for giving a speech in which he compromised with the South!

So fallen! so lost! the light withdrawn
    Which once he wore!
The glory from his gray hairs gone
    Forevermore!

Revile him not,—the Tempter hath
    A snare for all;
And pitying tears, not scorn and wrath,
    Befit his fall!

Oh, dumb be passion's stormy rage,
    When he who might   10
Have lighted up and led his age,
    Falls back in night.

---

72 **Nantucket**, an island south of Cape Cod • 75 **Wachuset**, a
mountain near Fitchburg, Massachusetts • 79 **Connecticut**, river
which flows through Massachusetts • 82 **Deep . . . waters.** Compare
Psalms 42:7: "Deep calleth unto deep at the noise of thy waterspouts"
• 90 **fire-damps**, properly fire damp, a combustible gas formed by
the decomposition of coal, or the explosive mixture of this gas with air

Scorn! would the angels laugh, to mark
    A bright soul driven,
Fiend-goaded, down the endless dark,
    From hope and heaven!

Let not the land once proud of him
    Insult him now,
Nor brand with deeper shame his dim,
    Dishonored brow.   20

But let its humbled sons, instead,
    From sea to lake,
A long lament, as for the dead,
    In sadness make.

Of all we loved and honored, naught
    Save power remains,—
A fallen angel's pride of thought,
    Still strong in chains.

All else is gone; from those great eyes
    The soul has fled: 30
When faith is lost, when honor dies,
    The man is dead!

Then, pay the reverence of old days
    To his dead fame;
Walk backward, with averted gaze,
    And hide the shame!

        1850

meaning

Barbara Frietchie

The story of "Barbara Frietchie" was told to Whittier in a letter by a Mrs. Southworth of Georgetown, D. C. For Mrs. Southworth's account, which Whittier regarded as authentic and which he followed closely in the poem, see S. T. Pickard, **Life and Letters of John Greenleaf Whittier**, II, 454-456. The historical authenticity of the narrative has been denied by Allen Tate, who remarks in his **Stonewall Jackson**: "Among the women . . . whom General Jackson never saw, was an old woman named Barbara Frietchie." But whether fact or myth, the story

became in Whittier's hands one of the most successful ballads of the Civil War.

    "Barbara Frietchie" was first printed in the **Atlantic Monthly**, October 1863.

Up from the meadows rich with corn,
Clear in the cool September morn,

The clustered spires of Frederick stand
Green-walled by the hills of Maryland.

Round about them orchards sweep,
Apple and peach tree fruited deep,

Fair as the garden of the Lord
To the eyes of the famished rebel horde,

On that pleasant morn of the early fall
When Lee marched over the mountain-wall;   10

Over the mountains winding down,
Horse and foot, into Frederick town.

Forty flags with their silver stars,
Forty flags with their crimson bars,

Flapped in the morning wind: the sun
Of noon looked down, and saw not one.

Up rose old Barbara Frietchie then,
Bowed with her fourscore years and ten;

Bravest of all in Frederick town
She took up the flag the men hauled down;   20

In her attic window the staff she set,
To show that one heart was loyal yet.

Up the street came the rebel tread,
Stonewall Jackson riding ahead.

Under his slouched hat left and right
He glanced; the old flag met his sight.

"Halt!"—the dust-brown ranks stood fast.
"Fire!"—out blazed the rifle-blast.

It shivered the window, pane and sash;
It rent the banner with seam and gash.   30

Quick, as it fell, from the broken staff
Dame Barbara snatched the silken scarf.

She leaned far out on the window-sill,
And shook it forth with a royal will.

"Shoot, if you must, this old gray head,
But spare your country's flag," she said.

A shade of sadness, a blush of shame,
Over the face of the leader came;

The nobler nature within him stirred
To life at that woman's deed and word;   40

"Who touches a hair of yon gray head
Dies like a dog! March on!" he said.

All day long through Frederick street
Sounded the tread of marching feet:

All day long that free flag tost
Over the heads of the rebel host.

Ever its torn folds rose and fell
On the loyal winds that loved it well;

And through the hill-gaps sunset light
Shone over it with a warm good-night.   50

Barbara Frietchie's work is o'er,
And the Rebel rides on his raids no more.

Honor to her! and let a tear
Fall, for her sake, on Stonewall's bier.

Over Barbara Frietchie's grave,
Flag of Freedom and Union, wave!

Peace and order and beauty draw
Round thy symbol of light and law;

And ever the stars above look down
On thy stars below in Frederick town!   60

1863

Laus Deo

Whittier supplied the following note to this poem: "On
hearing the bells ring on the passage of the constitutional
amendment abolishing slavery. The resolution was adopted
by Congress, January 31, 1865. The ratification by the
requisite number of states was announced December 18,
1865."

The Latin title means "Praise be to God." Writing with
Hebraic fervor, Whittier drew extensively (as the footnotes will point out) upon the imagery and phraseology of
the Old Testament.

It is done!
    Clang of bell and roar of gun
Send the tidings up and down.
    How the belfries rock and reel!
    How the great guns, peal on peal,
Fling the joy from town to town!

    Ring, O Bells!
    Every stroke exulting tells
Of the burial hour of crime.
    Loud and long, that all may hear,   10
    Ring for every listening ear
Of Eternity and Time!

    Let us kneel:
    God's own voice is in that peal,
And this spot is holy ground.
    Lord, forgive us! What are we,
    That our eyes this glory see,
That our ears have heard the sound!

    For the Lord
    On the whirlwind is abroad;   20
In the earthquake He has spoken;
    He has smitten with His thunder

---

19 Lord . . . whirlwind. Compare Job 38:1: "Then the Lord answered
Job out of the whirlwind"

The iron walls asunder,
And the gates of brass are broken!

    Loud and long
    Lift the old exulting song;
Sing with Miriam by the sea,
    He has cast the mighty down;
    Horse and rider sink and drown;
"He hath triumphed gloriously!"   30

    Did we dare,
    In our agony of prayer,
Ask for more than He has done?
    When was ever His right hand
    Over any time or land
Stretched as now beneath the sun?

    How they pale,
    Ancient myth and song and tale,
In this wonder of our days,
    When the cruel rod of war   40
    Blossoms white with righteous law,
And the wrath of man is praise!

    Blotted out!
    All within and all about
Shall a fresher life begin;

Freer breathe the universe
    As it rolls its heavy curse
On the dead and buried sin!

    It is done!
    In the circuit of the sun   50
Shall the sound thereof go forth.
    It shall bid the sad rejoice,
    It shall give the dumb a voice,
It shall belt with joy the earth!

    Ring and swing,
    Bells of joy! On morning's wing
Send the song of praise abroad!
    With a sound of broken chains
    Tell the nations that He reigns,
Who alone is Lord and God!   60
                                        1865

24 gates . . . broken. Compare Psalms 107:16: "For he hath broken the gates of brass" • 27 Sing . . . gloriously. Compare Exodus 15:21: "And Miriam answered them, Sing ye to the Lord, for he hath triumphed gloriously; the horse and his rider hath he thrown into the sea" • 34 His . . . Stretched. Compare Isaiah 23:11: "He [the Lord] stretched out his hand over the sea, he shook the kingdoms" • 40 rod . . . Blossoms. Compare Numbers 17:8: " . . . the rod of Aaron for the house of Levi was budded, and brought forth buds, and bloomed blossoms"

George L. Aiken

1830 · 1876

Although obscure as both an actor and a playwright, George L. Aiken in 1852 wrote, in *Uncle Tom's Cabin,* a drama destined to have an almost continuous stage history from its first production down to the present day. It is a drama with notable faults, to be sure; but by and large it has stirred more Americans than any other native play. Somewhere, this very year, some little theater groups and several showboat or traveling companies are doubtless acting out this drama. Because it appeals to something very basic in popular taste, one may learn a great deal about Americans by studying this old play.

Few details are known about Aiken's life. He was born in Boston on December 19, 1830. How much education he had is not known. Eventually, however, he was attracted to the stage, and in 1848 he made his debut in Providence, Rhode Island. By 1851 he had begun to write for the stage: his *Orion,* based upon a novel, was produced that year. In 1852 G. C. Howard, manager of the Museum in Troy, New York, decided that a play based upon Mrs. Harriet Beecher Stowe's famous novel, *Uncle Tom's Cabin* (1852), would provide excellent rôles for his daughter and his wife, and he commissioned Aiken to write such a dramatization. The play opened in September 1852, with Cordelia Howard playing Eva, her mother playing Topsy, and with Aiken assuming two rôles—those of George Shelby and George Harris. The play ran a hundred nights in Troy, moved on to Albany, and then to New York. In New York it ran for 325 consecutive performances. Given by other companies in various cities—Philadelphia, Detroit, Chicago, and elsewhere—it was also notably successful. It became one of the great stand-bys for itinerant companies and has continued to be popular down to the present.

Aiken's later work was undistinguished. He continued to act and to write plays, most of them evanescent melodramas. After retiring from the stage in 1867, Aiken wrote dramas and fictional works until his death, April 27, 1876.

Much of the early appeal of the play doubtless derived from the fact that it treated a subject of contemporary controversy—slavery. There were additional and more lasting appeals, however, which Aiken managed to preserve when, with relatively few changes, he turned Mrs. Stowe's sensationally popular novel into a play. The daughter of one preacher and the wife of another, Mrs. Stowe had exalted the piety of Little Eva and the slaves in a way certain to touch the hearts of religious Americans. Moreover, her pictures "of slave families broken up for sale, ailing and dying children, Negro women at the mercy of their masters, white households which at best are slovenly and extravagant . . . and at worst are abodes of brutality and license" were certain, as Mr. Carl Van Doren has pointed out, to deeply move readers and theatergoers who idolized the family. Finally, the stark melodrama of Negroes battling for their freedom—the race of Eliza across the ice, the underground railway, physical skirmishes—offered primitive elements of excitement.

Aiken's chief contribution was to work in most of the more interesting scenes in the novel and to point up the comic elements. In addition, as did many of the other producers of the play, he took certain liberties with Mrs. Stowe's plot. Chief among these was his alteration of the circumstances of St. Clare's and Legree's deaths. In the novel, St. Clare, shortly after Little Eva's death, was killed accidentally while trying to separate two unidentified brawlers in a café; Legree came to a timely end, a victim of delirium tremens and remorse. The stabbing of St. Clare apparently served no other purpose in Mrs. Stowe's plot than to bring about the selling of Uncle Tom and the other slaves. Aiken's version heightened the drama and perhaps provided a certain poetic justice by having it revealed in Act V that the tavern brawlers had been Gumption Cute and Legree, and that it had been Legree's bowie knife—aimed at Cute—which had struck the fatal blow at the innocent St. Clare. Armed with the knowledge that Legree was a murderer, Cute and the lawyer Marks planned to confront him at his plantation and to blackmail him, demanding a thousand dollars for their silence. Legree resisted, however, and was shot by Marks.

Comedy looms large in the drama, much of it the most popular kind—that of type characters. Phineas is a typical Kentuckian of the period, incongruously turned Quaker. Topsy exploits the comic vein of minstrel show caricatures of Negroes. Ophelia is a Yankee spinster comparable to those limned by the popular humorist Miriam Whitcher in the 1850's. Gumption Cute, played for a long while by the famous character actor, Joseph Jefferson, is a pawky Yankee comparable to Smith's Jack Downing or Lowell's Birdofredum Sawin.

Tears, excitement, and laughter are thus combined in a play which, despite its lumbering construction and rather crude characterization, is a great document in our social and political history. America has, strictly speaking, no real folk plays. But *Uncle Tom's Cabin* comes closer to being one than any other.

G. L. Aiken, Uncle Tom's Cabin: or, Life among the Lowly, New York, 1852 • Harry Birdoff, The World's Greatest Hit: Uncle Tom's Cabin, New York, 1947 • A. H. Quinn, A History of the American Drama from the Beginning to the Civil War, New York, 1923 • T. A. Brown, A History of the New York Stage . . . , New York, 1903, I

Uncle Tom's Cabin

or, Life Among the Lowly

Dramatis Personae

Uncle Tom	Sambo
George Harris	Quimbo
George Shelby	Doctor
St. Clare	Waiter
Phineas Fletcher	Harry, a child
Gumption Cute	Eva
Mr. Wilson	Eliza
Deacon Perry	Cassy
Shelby	Marie
Haley	Ophelia
Legree	Chloe
Tom Loker	Topsy
Marks	

ACT I

SCENE I. Plain Chamber. Enter **Eliza**, meeting **George**.

ELIZA. Ah! George, is it you? Well, I am so glad you've come! [GEORGE *regards her mournfully.*] Why don't you smile, and ask after Harry?

GEORGE. [*Bitterly.*] I wish he'd never been born! I wish I'd never been born myself!

ELIZA. [*Sinking her head upon his breast and weeping.*] Oh, George!

GEORGE. There, now, Eliza; it's too bad for me to make you feel so. Oh! how I wish you had never seen
10 me—you might have been happy!

ELIZA. George! George! how can you talk so? What dreadful thing has happened, or is going to happen? I'm sure we've been very happy till lately.

GEORGE. So we have, dear. But oh! I wish I'd never seen you, nor you me.

ELIZA. Oh, George! how can you?

GEORGE. Yes, Eliza, it's all misery! misery! The very life is burning out of me! I'm a poor, miserable, forlorn drudge! I shall only drag you down with me, that's all! What's the use of our trying to do anything—try- 20 ing to know anything—trying to be anything? I wish I was dead!

ELIZA. Oh! now, dear George, that is really wicked. I know how you feel about losing your place in the factory, and you have a hard master; but pray be patient—

GEORGE. Patient! Haven't I been patient? Did I say a word when he came and took me away—for no earthly reason—from the place where everybody was kind to me? I'd paid him truly every cent of my earnings, and they all say I worked well. 30

ELIZA. Well, it *is* dreadful; but, after all, he is your master, you know.

GEORGE. My master! And who made him my master? That's what I think of! What right has he to me? I'm as much a man as he is! What right has he to make a dray-horse of me?—to take me from things I can do better than he can, and put me to work that any horse can do? He tries to do it; he says he'll bring me down and humble me, and he puts me to just the hardest, meanest and dirtiest work, on purpose. 40

ELIZA. Oh, George! George! you frighten me. Why, I never heard you talk so. I'm afraid you'll do something dreadful. I don't wonder at your feelings at all; but oh! do be careful—for my sake, for Harry's.

GEORGE. I have been careful, and I have been patient, but it's growing worse and worse—flesh and blood can't bear it any longer. Every chance he can get to insult and torment me he takes. He says that though I don't say anything, he sees that I've got the devil in me, and he means to bring it out; and one of these days it will 50 come out, in a way that he won't like, or I'm mistaken.

ELIZA. Well, I always thought that I must obey my master and mistress, or I couldn't be a Christian.

GEORGE. There is some sense in it in your case. They have brought you up like a child—fed you, clothed you and taught you, so that you have a good education—that is some reason why they should claim you. But I have been kicked and cuffed and sworn at, and what do I owe? I've paid for all my keeping a hundred times over. I won't bear it!—no, I *won't!* Master will find out that I'm one whipping won't tame. My day will come yet, if he don't look out!

ELIZA. What are you going to do? Oh! George, don't do anything wicked; if you only trust in heaven and try to do right, it will deliver you.

GEORGE. Eliza, my heart's full of bitterness. I can't trust in heaven. Why does it let things be so?

ELIZA. Oh, George! we must all have faith. Mistress says that when all things go wrong to us, we must believe that heaven is doing the very best.

GEORGE. That's easy for people to say who are sitting on their sofas and riding in their carriages; but let them be where I am—I guess it would come some harder. I wish I could be good; but my heart burns and can't be reconciled. You couldn't, in my place, you can't now, if I tell you all I've got to say; you don't know the whole yet.

ELIZA. What do you mean?

GEORGE. Well, lately my master has been saying that he was a fool to let me marry off the place—that he hates Mr. Shelby and all his tribe—and he says he won't let me come here any more, and that I shall take a wife and settle down on his place.

ELIZA. But you were married to *me* by the minister, as much as if you had been a white man.

GEORGE. Don't you know I can't hold you for my wife if he chooses to part us? That is why I wish I'd never seen you—it would have been better for us both —it would have been better for our poor child if he had never been born.

ELIZA. Oh! but my master is so kind.

GEORGE. Yes, but who knows?—he may die, and then Harry may be sold to nobody knows who. What pleasure is it that he is handsome and smart and bright? I tell you, Eliza, that a sword will pierce through your soul for every good and pleasant thing your child is or has. It will make him worth too much for you to keep.

ELIZA. Heaven forbid!

GEORGE. So, Eliza, my girl, bear up now, and good-by, for I'm going.

ELIZA. Going, George! Going where?

GEORGE. To Canada; and when I'm there I'll buy you—that's all the hope that's left us. You have a kind master, that won't refuse to sell you. I'll buy you and the boy—heaven helping me, I will!

ELIZA. Oh, dreadful! If you should be taken?

GEORGE. I won't be taken, Eliza—I'll *die* first! I'll be free, or I'll die!

ELIZA. You will not kill yourself?

GEORGE. No need of that; they will kill me, fast enough. I will never go down the river alive.

ELIZA. Oh, George! for my sake, do be careful. Don't lay hands on yourself, or anybody else. You are tempted too much, but don't. Go, if you must, but go carefully, prudently, and pray heaven to help you!

GEORGE. Well, then, Eliza, hear my plan. I'm going home quite resigned, you understand, as if all was over. I've got some preparations made, and there are those that will help me; and in the course of a few days I shall be among the missing. Well, now, good-by.

ELIZA. A moment—our boy.

GEORGE. [*Choked with emotion.*] True, I had forgotten him; one last look, and then farewell!

ELIZA. And heaven grant it be not forever! [*Exeunt.*]

SCENE II. A dining-room. Table and chairs. Dessert, wine, etc., on table. **Shelby** and **Haley** discovered at table.

SHELBY. That is the way I should arrange the matter.

HALEY. I can't make trade that way—I positively can't, Mr. Shelby. [*Drinks.*]

SHELBY. Why, the fact is, Haley, Tom is an uncommon fellow! He is certainly worth that sum anywhere—steady, honest, capable, manages my whole farm like a clock!

HALEY. You mean honest, as niggers go. [*Fills glass.*]

SHELBY. No; I mean, really, Tom is a good, steady, sensible, pious fellow. He got religion at a camp-meeting, four years ago, and I believe he really *did* get it. I've trusted him since then, with everything I have— money, house, horses, and let him come and go round the country, and I always found him true and square in everything!

HALEY. Some folks don't believe there is pious niggers, Shelby, but *I* do. I had a fellow, now, in this yer last lot I took to Orleans—'twas as good as a meetin' now, really, to hear that critter pray; and he was quite gentle and quiet like. He fetched me a good sum, too, for I bought him cheap of a man that was 'bliged to sell out, so I realized six hundred on him. Yes, I consider religion a valeyable thing in a nigger, when it's the genuine article and no mistake.

SHELBY. Well, Tom's got the real article, if ever a fellow had. Why, last fall I let him go to Cincinnati alone, to do business for me and bring home five hundred dollars.

"Tom," says I to him, "I trust you, because I think you are a Christian—I know you wouldn't cheat." Tom comes back sure enough; I knew he would. Some low fellows, they say, said to him—"Tom, why don't you make tracks for Canada?"

"Ah, master trusted me, and I couldn't," was his answer. They told me all about it. I am sorry to part with Tom, I must say. You ought to let him cover the whole balance of the debt, and you would, Haley, if you had any conscience.

HALEY. Well, I've got just as much conscience as any man in business can afford to keep, just a little, you know, to swear by, as 'twere; and then I'm ready to do anything in reason to 'blige friends, but this yer, you see, is a leetle too hard on a fellow—a leetle too hard! [Fills glass again.]

SHELBY. Well, then, Haley, how will you trade?

HALEY. Well, haven't you a boy or a girl that you could throw in with Tom?

SHELBY. Hum! none that I could well spare; to tell the truth, it's only hard necessity makes me willing to sell at all. I don't like parting with any of my hands, that's a fact. [HARRY runs in.] Hulloa! Jim Crow! [Throws a bunch of raisins towards him.] Pick that up now. [HARRY does so.]

HALEY. Bravo, little 'un! [Throws an orange, which HARRY catches. He sings and dances around the stage.] Hurrah! Bravo! What a young 'un! That chap's a case, I'll promise. Tell you what, Shelby, fling in that chap, and I'll settle the business. Come, now, if that ain't doing the thing up about the rightest!

[ELIZA enters. Starts on beholding HALEY, and gazes fearfully at HARRY, who runs and clings to her dress, showing the orange, etc.]

SHELBY. Well, Eliza?

ELIZA. I was looking for Harry, please, sir.

SHELBY. Well, take him away, then.

[ELIZA grasps the child eagerly in her arms, and casting another glance of apprehension at HALEY, exits hastily.]

HALEY. By Jupiter! There's an article, now. You might make your fortune on that ar gal in Orleans any day. I've seen over a thousand in my day, paid down for gals not a bit handsomer.

SHELBY. I don't want to make my fortune on her. Another glass of wine. [Fills the glasses.]

HALEY. [Drinks and smacks his lips.] Capital wine —first chop! Come, how will you trade about the gal? What shall I say for her? What'll you take?

SHELBY. Mr. Haley, she is not to be sold. My wife wouldn't part with her for her weight in gold.

HALEY. Ay, ay! women always say such things, 'cause they hain't no sort of calculation. Just show 'em how many watches, feathers and trinkets one's weight in gold would buy, and that alters the case, I reckon.

SHELBY. I tell you, Haley, this must not be spoken of—I say no, and I mean no.

HALEY. Well, you'll let me have the boy tho'; you must own that I have come down pretty handsomely for him.

SHELBY. What on earth can you want with the child?

HALEY. Why, I've got a friend that's going into this yer branch of the business—wants to buy up handsome boys to raise for the market. Well, what do you say?

SHELBY. I'll think the matter over and talk with my wife.

HALEY. Oh, certainly, by all means; but I'm in a devil of a hurry, and shall want to know as soon as possible, what I may depend on. [Rises and puts on his overcoat, which hangs on a chair. Takes hat and whip.]

SHELBY. Well, call up this evening, between six and seven, and you shall have my answer.

HALEY. All right. Take care of yourself, old boy! [Exit.]

SHELBY. If anybody had ever told me that I should sell Tom to those rascally traders, I should never have believed it. Now it must come for aught I see, and Eliza's child too. So much for being in debt, heigho! The fellow sees his advantage and means to push it. [Exit.]

Scene III. Snowy Landscape. **Uncle Tom's Cabin.** Snow on roof. Practicable door and window. Dark Stage. Music. Enter **Eliza** hastily, with **Harry** in her arms.

ELIZA. My poor boy; they have sold you, but your mother will save you yet! [Goes to Cabin and taps on *window.* AUNT CHLOE *appears at window with a large white night-cap on.*]

CHLOE. Good Lord! what's that? My sakes alive if it ain't Lizy! get on your clothes, old man, quick! I'm gwine to open the door. [*The door opens and* CHLOE *enters, followed by* UNCLE TOM, *in his shirt sleeves, holding a tallow candle.*]

TOM. [*Holding the light towards* ELIZA.] Lord bless you! I'm skeered to look at ye, Lizy! Are ye tuck
10 sick, or what's come over ye?

ELIZA. I'm running way, Uncle Tom and Aunt Chloe, carrying off my child! Master sold him!

TOM and CHLOE. Sold him!

ELIZA. Yes, sold him! I crept into the closet by mistress' door to-night and heard master tell mistress that he had sold my Harry, and you, Uncle Tom, both, to a trader, and that the man was to take possession to-morrow.

CHLOE. The good Lord have pity on us! Oh! it don't
20 seem as if it was true. What has he done that master should sell *him?*

ELIZA. He hasn't done anything—it isn't for that. Master don't want to sell, and mistress—she's always good. I heard her plead and beg for us, but he told her 'twas no use—that he was in this man's debt, and he had got the power over him, and that if he did not pay him off clear, it would end in his having to sell the place and all the people and move off.

CHLOE. Well, old man, why don't you run away, too?
30 Will you wait to be toted down the river, where they kill niggers with hard work and starving? I'd a heap rather die than go there, any day! There's time for ye; be off with Lizy—you've got a pass to come and go any time. Come, bustle up, and I'll get your things together.

TOM. No, no—I ain't going. Let Eliza go—it's her right. I wouldn't be the one to say no—'tain't in natur for her to stay; but you heard what she said? If I must be sold, or all the people on the place, and everything
40 go to rack, why, let me be sold. I s'pose I can bar it as well as any one. Mas'r always found me on the spot—he always will. I never have broken trust, nor used my pass no ways contrary to my word, and I never will. It's better for me to go alone, than to break up the place and sell all. Mas'r ain't to blame, and he'll take care of you and the poor little 'uns! [*Overcome.*]

CHLOE. Now, old man, what is you gwine to cry for? Does you want to break this old woman's heart? [*Crying.*]

ELIZA. I saw my husband only this afternoon, and I 50 little knew then what was to come. He told me he was going to run away. Do try, if you can, to get word to him. Tell him how I went and why I went, and tell him I'm going to try and find Canada. You must give my love to him, and tell him if I never see him again on earth, I trust we shall meet in heaven!

TOM. Dat is right, Lizy, trust in the Lord—He is our best friend—our only comforter.

ELIZA. You won't go with me, Uncle Tom?

TOM. No; time was when I would, but the Lord's 60 given me a work among these yer poor souls, and I'll stay with 'em and bear my cross with 'em till the end. It's different with you—it's more'n you could stand, and you'd better go if you can.

ELIZA. Uncle Tom, I'll try it!

TOM. Amen! The Lord help ye! [*Exit* ELIZA *and* HARRY.]

CHLOE. What is you gwine to do, old man? What's to become of you?

TOM. [*Solemnly.*] Him that saved Daniel in the den 70 of lions—that saved the children in the fiery furnace—Him that walked on the sea and bade the winds be still—He's alive yet! and I've faith to believe He can deliver me!

CHLOE. You is right, old man.

TOM. The Lord is good unto all that trust Him, Chloe. [*Exeunt into Cabin.*]

SCENE IV. Room in Tavern by the river side. A large window, through which the river is seen, filled with floating ice. Moonlight. Table and chairs brought on. Enter Phineas.

PHINEAS. Chaw me up into tobaccy ends! how in the name of all that's onpossible am I to get across that yer pesky river? It's a reg'lar blockade of ice! I prom- 80 ised Ruth to meet her to-night, and she'll be into my har if I don't come. [*Goes to window.*] Thar's a conglomerated prospect for a loveyer! What in creation's to be done? That thar river looks like a permiscuous ice-cream shop come to an awful state of friz. If I war on the adjacent bank, I wouldn't care a teetotal atom.

Rile up, you old varmint, and shake the ice off your back!

[*Enter* ELIZA *and* HARRY.]

ELIZA. Courage, my boy—we have reached the river. Let it but roll between us and our pursuers, and we are safe! [*Goes to window.*] Gracious powers! the river is choked with cakes of ice!

PHINEAS. Holloa, gal!—what's the matter? You look kind of streaked.

ELIZA. Is there any ferry or boat that takes people
10 over now?

PHINEAS. Well, I guess not; the boats have stopped running.

ELIZA. [*In dismay.*] Stopped running?

PHINEAS. Maybe you're wanting to get over—anybody sick? Ye seem mighty anxious.

ELIZA. I—I—I've got a child that's very dangerous. I never heard of it till last night, and I've walked quite a distance to-day, in hopes to get to the ferry.

PHINEAS. Well, now, that's onlucky; I'm re'lly con-
20 sarned for ye. Thar's a man, a piece down here, that's going over with some truck this evening, if he duss to, he'll be in here to supper to-night, so you'd better set down and wait. That's a smart little chap. Say, young 'un, have a chaw tobacky? [*Takes out a large plug and a bowie-knife.*]

ELIZA. No, no! not any for him.

PHINEAS. Oh! he don't use it, eh? Hain't come to it yet? Well, I have. [*Cuts off a large piece, and returns the plug and knife to pocket.*] What's the matter with
30 the young 'un? He looks kind of white in the gills!

ELIZA. Poor fellow! he is not used to walking, and I've hurried him on so.

PHINEAS. Tuckered, eh? Well, there's a little room there, with a fire in it. Take the babby in there, make yourself comfortable till that thar ferryman shows his countenance—I'll stand the damage.

ELIZA. How shall I thank you for such kindness to a stranger?

PHINEAS. Well, if you don't know how, why, don't
40 try; that's the teetotal. Come, vamoose! [*Exit* ELIZA *and* HARRY.] Chaw me into sassage meat, if that ain't a perpendicular fine gal! she's a reg'lar A No. 1. sort of female! How'n thunder am I to get across this refrigerated stream of water? I can't wait for that ferryman. [*Enter* MARKS.] Halloa! what sort of a critter's

this? [*Advances.*] Say, stranger, will you have something to drink?

MARKS. You are excessively kind: I don't care if I do.

PHINEAS. Ah! he's a human. Halloa, thar! bring us a jug of whisky instantaneously, or expect to be teetotal- 50 ly chawed up! Squat yourself, stranger, and go in for enjoyment. [*They sit at table.*] Who are you, and what's your name?

MARKS. I am a lawyer, and my name is Marks.

PHINEAS. A land shark, eh? Well, I don't think no worse on you for that. The law is a kind of necessary evil; and it breeds lawyers just as an old stump does fungus. Ah! here's the whisky. [*Enter* WAITER, *with jug and tumblers. Places them on table.*] Here, you—take that shin-plaster. [*Gives bill.*] I don't want any change 60 —thar's a gal stopping in that room—the balance will pay for her—d'ye hear?—vamoose! [*Exit* WAITER.— *Fills glass.*] Take hold, neighbour Marks—don't shirk the critter. Here's hoping your path of true love may never have an ice-choked river to cross! [*They drink.*]

MARKS. Want to cross the river, eh?

PHINEAS. Well, I do, stranger. Fact is, I'm in love with the teetotalist pretty girl, over on the Ohio side, that ever wore a Quaker bonnet. Take another swig, 70 neighbour. [*Fills glasses, and they drink.*]

MARKS. A Quaker, eh?

PHINEAS. Yes—kind of strange, ain't it? The way of it was this:—I used to own a grist of niggers—had 'em to work on my plantation, just below here. Well, stranger, do you know I fell in with that gal—of course I was considerably smashed—knocked into a pretty conglomerated heap—and I told her so. She said she wouldn't hear a word from me so long as I owned a nigger! 80

MARKS. You sold them, I suppose?

PHINEAS. You're teetotally wrong, neighbour. I gave them all their freedom, and told 'em to vamoose!

MARKS. Ah! yes—very noble, I dare say, but rather expensive. This act won you your lady-love, eh?

PHINEAS. You're off the track again, neighbour. She felt kind of pleased about it, and smiled, and all that; but she said she could never be mine unless I turned Quaker! Thunder and earth! what do you think of that? You're a lawyer—come, now, what's your opinion? 90 Don't you call it a knotty point?

MARKS. Most decidedly. Of course you refused.

PHINEAS. Teetotally; but she told me to think better of it, and come to-night and give her my final conclusion. Chaw me into mincemeat, if I haven't made up my mind to do it!

MARKS. You astonish me!

PHINEAS. Well, you see, I can't get along without that gal;—she's sort of fixed my flint, and I'm sure to hang fire without her. I know I shall make a queer sort of Quaker, because you see, neighbour, I ain't precisely the kind of material to make a Quaker out of.

MARKS. No, not exactly.

PHINEAS. Well, I can't stop no longer. I must try to get across that candaverous river some way. It's getting late—take care of yourself, neighbour lawyer. I'm a teetotal victim to a pair of black eyes. Chaw me up to feed hogs if I'm not in a ruinatious state! [*Exit.*]

MARKS. Queer genius, that, very! [*Enter* TOM LOKER.] So you've come at last.

LOKER. Yes. [*Looks into jug.*] Empty! Waiter! more whisky! [WAITER *enters with jug, and removes the empty one.*]

[*Enter* HALEY.]

HALEY. By the land! if this yer ain't the nearest, now, to what I've heard people call Providence! Why, Loker, how are ye?

LOKER. The devil! What brought you here, Haley?

HALEY. [*Sitting at table.*] I say, Tom, this yer's the luckiest thing in the world. I'm in a devil of a hobble, and you must help me out!

LOKER. Ugh! aw! like enough. A body may be pretty sure of that when you're glad to see 'em, or can make something off of 'em. What's the blow now?

HALEY. You've got a friend here—partner, perhaps?

LOKER. Yes, I have. Here, Marks—here's that ar fellow that I was with in Natchez.

MARKS. [*Grasping* HALEY'S *hand.*] Shall be pleased with his acquaintance. Mr. Haley, I believe?

HALEY. The same, sir. The fact is, gentlemen, this morning I bought a young 'un of Shelby up above here. His mother got wind of it, and what does she do but cut her lucky with him; and I'm afraid by this time that she has crossed the river, for I tracked her to this very place.

MARKS. So, then, ye're fairly sewed up, ain't ye? He! he! he! he! It's neatly done, too.

HALEY. This young 'un business makes lots of trouble in the trade.

MARKS. Now, Mr. Haley, what is it? Do you want us to undertake to catch this gal?

HALEY. The gal's no matter of mine—she's Shelby's—it's only the boy. I was a fool for buying the monkey.

LOKER. You're generally a fool!

MARKS. Come now, Loker, none of your huffs; you see, Mr. Haley's a-puttin' us in a way of a good job, I reckon; just hold still—these yer arrangements are my forte. This yer gal, Mr. Haley—how is she?—what is she?

[ELIZA *appears, with* HARRY, *listening.*]

HALEY. Well, white and handsome—well brought up. I'd have given Shelby eight hundred or a thousand, and then made well on her.

MARKS. White and handsome—well brought up! Look here, now, Loker, a beautiful opening. We'll do a business here on our own account. We does the catchin'; the boy, of course, goes to Mr. Haley—we takes the gal to Orleans to speculate on. Ain't it beautiful?

[*They confer together.*]

ELIZA. Powers of mercy, protect me! How shall I escape these human bloodhounds? Ah! the window—the river of ice! That dark stream lies between me and liberty! Surely the ice will bear my trifling weight. It is my only chance of escape—better sink beneath the cold waters, with my child locked in my arms, than have him torn from me and sold into bondage. He sleeps upon my breast—Heaven, I put my trust in thee! [*Gets out of window.*]

MARKS. Well, Tom Loker, what do you say?

LOKER. It'll do! [*Strikes his hand violently on the table.—*ELIZA *screams.—They all start to their feet.——*ELIZA *disappears.*]

HALEY. By the land, there she is now!

[*They all rush to the window.*]

MARKS. She's making for the river!

LOKER. Let's after her!

[*They all leap through the window.—Change.*]

SCENE V. Snowy Landscape. Enter **Eliza**, with **Harry**, hurriedly.

ELIZA. They press upon my footsteps—the river is my only hope! Heaven grant me strength to reach it, ere they overtake me! Courage, my child!—we will be free —*or perish!* [*Rushes off.*]

[*Enter* LOKER, HALEY *and* MARKS.]

HALEY. We'll catch her yet; the river will stop her!

MARKS. No, it won't, for look! she has jumped upon the ice! She's a brave gal, anyhow!

LOKER. She'll be drowned.

HALEY. Curse that young 'un. I shall lose him, after all.

LOKER. Come on, Marks, to the ferry!

HALEY. Aye, to the ferry!—a hundred dollars for a boat! [*They rush off.*]

SCENE VI. The entire depth of stage, representing the Ohio River filled with Floating Ice. Bank on right hand. **Eliza** appears, with **Harry**, on a cake of ice, and floats slowly across. **Haley, Loker** and **Marks**, on bank, right hand, observing. **Phineas** on opposite shore.

ACT II

SCENE I. A Handsome Parlour. **Marie** discovered reclining on a sofa.

MARIE. [*Looking at a note.*] What can possibly detain St. Clare? According to this note, he should have been here a fortnight ago. [*Noise of carriage without.*] I do believe he has come at last.

[EVA *runs in.*]

EVA. Mamma! [*Throws her arms around* MARIE'S *neck, and kisses her.*]

MARIE. That will do—take care, child—don't you make my head ache! [*Kisses her languidly.*]

[*Enter* ST. CLARE, OPHELIA, *and* TOM, *nicely dressed.*]

ST. CLARE. Well, my dear Marie, here we are at last. The wanderers have arrived, you see. Allow me to present my cousin, Miss Ophelia, who is about to undertake the office of our housekeeper.

MARIE. [*Rising to a sitting posture.*] I am delighted to see you. How do you like the appearance of our city?

EVA. [*Running to* OPHELIA.] Oh! is it not beautiful? My own darling home!—is it not beautiful?

OPHELIA. Yes, it is a pretty place, though it looks rather old and heathenish to me.

ST. CLARE. Tom, my boy, this seems to suit you?

TOM. Yes, mas'r, it looks about the right thing.

ST. CLARE. See here, Marie, I've brought you a coach-man, at last, to order. I tell you, he's a regular hearse for blackness and sobriety, and will drive you like a funeral, if you wish. Open your eyes, now, and look at him. Now, don't say I never think about you when I'm gone.

MARIE. I know he'll get drunk.

ST. CLARE. Oh! no he won't. He's warranted a pious and sober article.

MARIE. Well, I hope he may turn out well; it's more than I expect, though.

ST. CLARE. Have you no curiosity to learn how and where I picked up Tom?

EVA. *Uncle* Tom, papa; that's his name.

ST. CLARE. Right, my little sunbeam!

TOM. Please, mas'r, that ain't no 'casion to say nothing 'bout me.

ST. CLARE. You are too modest, my modern Hannibal. Do you know, Marie, that our little Eva took a fancy to Uncle Tom—whom we met on board the steamboat—and persuaded me to buy him?

MARIE. Ah! she is so odd!

ST. CLARE. As we approached the landing, a sudden rush of the passengers precipitated Eva into the water—

MARIE. Gracious heavens!

ST. CLARE. A man leaped into the river, and, as she rose to the surface of the water, grasped her in his arms, and held her up until she could be drawn on the boat again. Who was that man, Eva?

EVA. Uncle Tom! [*Runs to him.—He lifts her in his arms.—She kisses him.*]

TOM. The dear soul!

OPHELIA. [*Astonished.*] How shiftless!

ST. CLARE. [*Overhearing her.*] What's the matter now, pray?

OPHELIA. Well, I want to be kind to everybody, and I wouldn't have anything hurt, but as to kissing—

ST. CLARE. Niggers! that you're not up to, hey?

OPHELIA. Yes, that's it—how can she?

ST. CLARE. Oh! bless you, it's nothing when you are used to it!

OPHELIA. I could never be so shiftless!

EVA. Come with me, Uncle Tom, and I will show you about the house. [*Crosses with Tom.*]

TOM. Can I go, mas'r?

ST. CLARE. Yes, Tom; she is your little mistress—your only duty will be to attend to her!

[TOM *bows and exits.*]

MARIE. Eva, my dear!

EVA. Well, mamma?

MARIE. Do not exert yourself too much!

EVA. No, mamma! [*Runs out.*]

OPHELIA. [*Lifting up her hands.*] How shiftless!

[ST. CLARE *sits next to* MARIE *on sofa.*—OPHELIA *next to* ST. CLARE.]

ST. CLARE. Well, what do you think of Uncle Tom, Marie?

MARIE. He is a perfect behemoth!

ST. CLARE. Come, now, Marie, be gracious, and say
10 something pretty to a fellow!

MARIE. You've been gone a fortnight beyond the time!

ST. CLARE. Well, you know I wrote you the reason.

MARIE. Such a short, cold letter!

ST. CLARE. Dear me! the mail was just going, and it had to be that or nothing.

MARIE. That's just the way; always something to make your journeys long and letters short!

ST. CLARE. Look at this. [*Takes an elegant velvet case from his pocket.*] Here's a present I got for you in
20 New York—a daguerreotype of Eva and myself.

MARIE. [*Looks at it with a dissatisfied air.*] What made you sit in such an awkward position?

ST. CLARE. Well, the position may be a matter of opinion, but what do you think of the likeness?

MARIE. [*Closing the case snappishly.*] If you don't think anything of my opinion in one case, I suppose you wouldn't in another.

OPHELIA. [*Sententiously, aside.*] How shiftless!

ST. CLARE. Hang the woman! Come, Marie, what do
30 you think of the likeness? Don't be nonsensical now.

MARIE. It's very inconsiderate of you, St. Clare, to insist on my talking and looking at things. You know I've been lying all day with the sick headache, and there's been such a tumult made ever since you came, I'm half dead!

OPHELIA. You're subject to the sick headache, ma'am?

MARIE. Yes, I'm a perfect martyr to it!

OPHELIA. Juniper-berry tea is good for sick headache; at least, Molly, Deacon Abraham Perry's wife,
40 used to say so; and she was a great nurse.

ST. CLARE. I'll have the first juniper-berries that get ripe in our garden by the lake brought in for that especial purpose. Come, cousin, let us take a stroll in the garden Will you join us, Marie?

MARIE. I wonder how you can ask such a question, when you know how fragile I am. I shall retire to my chamber and repose till dinner time. [*Exit.*]

OPHELIA. [*Looking after her.*] How shiftless!

ST. CLARE. Come, cousin! [*As he goes out.*] Look out for the babies! If I step upon anybody, let them 50 mention it.

OPHELIA. Babies under foot! How shiftless!

[*Exeunt.*]

SCENE II. A Garden. **Tom** discovered, seated on a bank, with **Eva** on his knee, his button-holes are filled with flowers, and **Eva** is hanging a wreath around his neck. Enter **St. Clare** and **Ophelia**, observing.

EVA. Oh, Tom; you look so funny.

TOM. [*Sees* ST. CLARE, *and puts* EVA *down.*] I begs pardon, mas'r, but the young missis would do it. Look yer, I'm like the ox, mentioned in the Good Book, dressed for the sacrifice.

ST. CLARE. I say, what do you think, Pussy? Which do you like the best—to live as they do at your uncle's, up in Vermont, or to have a house full of servants, as 60 we do?

EVA. Oh! of course our way is the pleasantest.

ST. CLARE. [*Patting her head.*] Why so?

EVA. Because it makes so many more round you to love, you know.

OPHELIA. Now, that's just like Eva—just one of her odd speeches.

EVA. Is it an odd speech, papa?

ST. CLARE. Rather, as this world goes, Pussy. But where has my little Eva been? 70

EVA. Oh! I've been up in Tom's room, hearing him sing.

ST. CLARE. Hearing Tom sing, hey?

EVA. Oh, yes! he sings such beautiful things about the new Jerusalem, and bright angels, and the land of Canaan.

ST. CLARE. I dare say; it's better than the opera, isn't it?

EVA. Yes; and he's going to teach them to me. 80

ST. CLARE. Singing lessons, hey? You are coming on.

EVA. Yes, he sings for me, and I read to him in my Bible, and he explains what it means. Come, Tom. [*She takes his hand and they exit.*]

ST. CLARE. [*Aside.*] Oh, Evangeline! Rightly named; hath not heaven made thee an evangel to me?

OPHELIA. How shiftless! How can you let her?

ST. CLARE. Why not?

OPHELIA. Why, I don't know; it seems so dreadful.

ST. CLARE. You would think no harm in a child's caressing a large dog, even if he was black; but a creature that can think, reason and feel, and is immortal, you shudder at. Confess it, cousin. I know the feeling among some of you Northerners well enough. Not that there is a particle of virtue in our not having it, but custom with us does what Christianity ought to do: obliterates the feeling of personal prejudice. You loathe them as you would a snake or a toad, yet you are indignant at their wrongs. You would not have them abused, but you don't want to have anything to do with them yourselves. Isn't that it?

OPHELIA. Well, cousin, there may be some truth in this.

ST. CLARE. What would the poor and lowly do without children? Your little child is your only true democrat. Tom, now, is a hero to Eva; his stories are wonders in her eyes; his songs and Methodist hymns are better than an opera, and the traps and little bits of trash in his pockets a mine of jewels, and he the most wonderful Tom that ever wore a black skin. This is one of the roses of Eden that the Lord has dropped down expressly for the poor and lowly, who get few enough of any other kind.

OPHELIA. It's strange, cousin; one might almost think you was a *professor,* to hear you talk.

ST. CLARE. A professor?

OPHELIA. Yes, a professor of religion.

ST. CLARE. Not at all; not a professor as you town folks have it, and, what is worse, I'm afraid, not a *practicer,* either.

OPHELIA. What makes you talk so, then?

ST. CLARE. Nothing is easier than talking. My forte lies in talking, and yours, cousin, lies in doing. And speaking of that puts me in mind that I have made a purchase for your department. There's the article now. Here, Topsy! [*Whistles.* TOPSY *runs on.*]

OPHELIA. Good gracious! what a heathenish, shiftless looking object! St. Clare, what in the world have you brought that thing here for?

ST. CLARE. For you to educate, to be sure, and train in the way she should go. I thought she was a rather funny specimen in the Jim Crow line. Here, Topsy, give us a song, and show us some of your dancing.

[TOPSY *sings a verse and dances a breakdown.*]

OPHELIA [*Paralyzed.*] Well, of all things! If I ever saw the like!

ST. CLARE. [*Smothering a laugh.*] Topsy, this is your new mistress—I'm going to give you up to her. See now that you behave yourself.

TOPSY. Yes, mas'r.

ST. CLARE. You're going to be good, Topsy, you understand?

TOPSY. Oh, yes, mas'r.

OPHELIA. Now, St. Clare, what upon earth is this for? Your house is so full of these plagues now, that a body can't set down their foot without treading on 'em. I get up in the morning and find one asleep behind the door, and see one black head poking out from under the table—one lying on the door mat, and they are moping and mowing and grinning between all the railings, and tumbling over the kitchen floor! What on earth did you want to bring this one for?

ST. CLARE. For you to educate—didn't I tell you? You're always preaching about educating; I thought I would make you a present of a fresh caught specimen, and let you try your hand on her and bring her up in the way she should go.

OPHELIA. I don't want her, I am sure; I have more to do with 'em now than I want to.

ST. CLARE. That's you Christians, all over. You'll get up a society, and get some poor missionary to spend all his days among just such heathens; but let me see one of you that would take one into your house with you, and take the labour of their conversion upon yourselves.

OPHELIA. Well, I didn't think of it in that light. It might be real missionary work. Well, I'll do what I can. [*Advances to* TOPSY.] She's dreadful dirty and shiftless! How old are you, Topsy?

TOPSY. Dunno, missis.

OPHELIA. How shiftless! Don't know how old you are? Didn't anybody ever tell you? Who was your mother?

TOPSY. [*Grinning.*] Never had none.

OPHELIA. Never had any mother? What do you mean? Where was you born?

TOPSY. Never was born.

OPHELIA. You mustn't answer me in that way. I'm not playing with you. Tell me where you was born, and who your father and mother were?

TOPSY. Never was born, tell you; never had no father, nor mother, nor nothin'. I war raised by a speculator, with lots of others. Old Aunt Sue used to take care on us.

ST. CLARE. She speaks the truth, cousin. Speculators buy them up cheap, when they are little, and get them raised for the market.

OPHELIA. How long have you lived with your master and mistress?

TOPSY. Dunno, missis.

OPHELIA. How shiftless! Is it a year, or more, or less?

TOPSY. Dunno, missis.

ST. CLARE. She does not know what a year is; she don't even know her own age.

OPHELIA. Have you ever heard anything about heaven, Topsy? [TOPSY *looks bewildered and grins.*] Do you know who made you?

TOPSY. Nobody, as I knows on, he, he, he! I 'spect I growed. Don't think nobody never made me.

OPHELIA. The shiftless heathen! What can you do? What did you do for your master and mistress?

TOPSY. Fetch water—and wash dishes—and rub knives—and wait on folks—and dance breakdowns.

OPHELIA. I shall break down, I'm afraid, in trying to make anything of you, you shiftless mortal!

ST. CLARE. You find virgin soil there, cousin; put in your own ideas—you won't find many to pull up. [*Exit laughing.*]

OPHELIA. [*Takes out her handkerchief—a pair of gloves falls.* TOPSY *picks them up slyly and puts them in her sleeve.*] Follow me, you benighted innocent!

TOPSY. Yes, missis. [*As* OPHELIA *turns her back to her, she seizes the end of the ribbon she wears around her waist, and twitches it off.—*OPHELIA *turns and sees her as she is putting it in her other sleeve.—*OPHELIA *takes ribbon from her.*]

OPHELIA. What's this? You naughty, wicked girl, you've been stealing this?

TOPSY. Laws! why, that ar's missis' ribbon, ain't it? How could it got caught in my sleeve?

OPHELIA. Topsy, you naughty girl, don't you tell me a lie—you stole that ribbon!

TOPSY. Missis, I declare for't, I didn't—never seed it till dis yer blessed minnit.

OPHELIA. Topsy, don't you know it's wicked to tell lies?

TOPSY. I never tells no lies, missis; it's just de truth I've been telling now, and nothing else.

OPHELIA. Topsy, I shall have to whip you, if you tell lies so.

TOPSY. Laws, missis, if you's to whip all day, couldn't say no other way. I never seed dat ar—it must a got caught in my sleeve. [*Blubbers.*]

OPHELIA. [*Seizes her by the shoulders.*] Don't you tell me that again, you barefaced fibber! [*Shakes her.—The gloves fall on stage.*] There you, my gloves too—you outrageous young heathen! [*Picks them up.*] Will you tell me, now, you didn't steal the ribbon?

TOPSY. No, missis; stole de gloves, but didn't steal de ribbon. It was permiskus.

OPHELIA. Why, you young reprobate!

TOPSY. Yes—I's knows I's wicked!

OPHELIA. Then you know you ought to be punished. [*Boxes her ears.*] What do you think of that?

TOPSY. He, he, he! De Lord, missis; dat wouldn't kill a 'skeeter! [*Runs off laughing.—*OPHELIA *follows indignantly.*]

SCENE III. The Tavern by the River. Table and chairs. Jug and glasses on table. On flat is a printed placard, headed: "Four Hundred Dollars Reward—Runaway—George Harris!" **Phineas** is discovered, seated at table.

PHINEAS. So yer I am; and a pretty business I've undertook to do. Find the husband of the gal that crossed the river on the ice two or three days ago. Ruth said I must do it, and I'll be teetotally chawed up if I don't do it. I see they've offered a reward for him, dead or alive. How in creation am I to find the varmint? He isn't likely to go round looking natural, with a full description of his hide and figure staring him in the face. [*Enter* MR. WILSON.] I say, stranger, how are ye? [*Rises and comes forward.*]

WILSON. Well, I reckon.

PHINEAS. Any news? [*Takes out plug and knife.*]

WILSON. Not that I know of.

PHINEAS. [*Cutting a piece of tobacco and offering it.*] Chaw?

WILSON. No, thank ye—it don't agree with me.

PHINEAS. Don't, eh? [*Putting it in his own mouth.*] I never felt any the worse for it.

WILSON. [*Sees placard.*] What's that?

PHINEAS. Nigger advertised. [*Advances towards it and spits on it.*] There's my mind upon that.

WILSON. Why, now stranger, what's that for?

PHINEAS. I'd do it all the same to the writer of that ar paper, if he was here. Any man that owns a boy like that and can't find any better way of treating him than 10 branding him on the hand with the letter H, as that paper states, *deserves* to lose him. Such papers as this ar' a shame to old Kaintuck! that's my mind right out, if anybody wants to know.

WILSON. Well, now, that's a fact.

PHINEAS. I used to have a gang of boys, sir—that was before I fell in love—and I just told 'em:—"Boys," says I, "run now! Dig! put! jest when you want to. I never shall come to look after you!" That's the way I kept mine. Let 'em know they are free to run any time, and it jest 20 stops their wanting to. It stands to reason it should. Treat 'em like men, and you'll have men's work.

WILSON. I think you are altogether right, friend, and this man described here is a fine fellow—no mistake about that. He worked for me some half dozen years in my bagging factory, and he was my best hand, sir. He is an ingenious fellow, too; he invented a machine for the cleaning of hemp—a really valuable affair; it's gone into use in several factories. His master holds the patent of it.

PHINEAS. I'll warrant ye; holds it, and makes money 30 out of it, and then turns round and brands the boy in his right hand! If I had a fair chance, I'd mark him, I reckon, so that he'd carry it *one* while!

[*Enter* GEORGE HARRIS, *disguised.*]

GEORGE. [*Speaking as he enters.*] Jim, see to the trunks. [*Sees* WILSON.] Ah! Mr. Wilson here?

WILSON. Bless my soul, can it be?

GEORGE. [*Advances and grasps his hand.*] Mr. Wilson, I see you remember me, Mr. Butler, of Oaklands, Shelby county.

WILSON. Ye—yes—yes—sir.

40 PHINEAS. Halloa! there's a screw loose here somewhere. That old gentleman seems to be struck into a pretty considerable heap of astonishment. May I be teetotally chawed up! if I don't believe that's the identical man I'm arter. [*Crosses to* GEORGE.] How are ye, George Harris?

GEORGE. [*Starting back and thrusting his hands into his breast.*] You know me?

PHINEAS. Ha, ha, ha! I rather conclude I do; but don't get riled, I ain't a bloodhound in disguise.

GEORGE. How did you discover me? 50

PHINEAS. By a teetotal smart guess. You're the very man I want to see. Do you know I was sent after you?

GEORGE. Ah! by my master?

PHINEAS. No; by your wife.

GEORGE. My wife! Where is she?

PHINEAS. She's stopping with a Quaker family over on the Ohio side.

GEORGE. Then she is safe?

PHINEAS. Teetotally!

GEORGE. Conduct me to her. 60

PHINEAS. Just wait a brace of shakes and I'll do it. I've got to go and get the boat ready. 'Twon't take me but a minute—make yourself comfortable till I get back. Chaw me up! but this is what I call doing things in short order. [*Exit.*]

WILSON. George!

GEORGE. Yes, George!

WILSON. I couldn't have thought it!

GEORGE. I am pretty well disguised, I fancy; you see I don't answer to the advertisement at all. 70

WILSON. George, this is a dangerous game you are playing; I could not have advised you to it.

GEORGE. I can do it on my own responsibility.

WILSON. Well, George, I suppose you're running away—leaving your lawful master, George (I don't wonder at it), at the same time, I'm sorry, George, yes, decidedly. I think I must say that it's my duty to tell you so.

GEORGE. Why are you sorry, sir?

WILSON. Why, to see you, as it were, setting yourself 80 in opposition to the laws of your country.

GEORGE. *My* country! What country have *I,* but the grave? And I would to heaven that I was laid there!

WILSON. George, you've got a hard master, in fact he is—well, he conducts himself reprehensibly—I can't pretend to defend him. I'm sorry for you, now; it's a bad case—very bad; but we must all sudmit to the indications of Providence, George, don't you see?

GEORGE. I wonder, Mr. Wilson, if the Indians should come and take you a prisoner away from your wife and 90 children, and want to keep you all your life hoeing corn for them, if you'd think it your duty to abide in the condition in which you were called? I rather imagine that you'd think the first stray horse you could find an indication of Providence, shouldn't you?

WILSON. Really, George, putting the case in the somewhat peculiar light—I don't know—under those circumstances—but what I might. But it seems to me you are running an awful risk. You can't hope to carry it out. If you're taken it will be worse with you than ever;
10 they'll only abuse you, and half kill you, and sell you down river.

GEORGE. Mr. Wilson, I know all this. I *do* run a risk, but—[*Throws open coat and shows pistols and knife in his belt.*] There! I'm ready for them. Down South I never *will* go! no, if it comes to that, I can earn myself at least six feet of free soil—the first and last I shall ever own in Kentucky!

WILSON. Why, George, this state of mind is awful—it's getting really desperate. I'm concerned. Going to
20 break the laws of your country?

GEORGE. My country again! Sir, I haven't any country any more than I have any father. I don't want anything of *your* country, except to be left alone—to go peaceably out of it; but if any man tries to stop me, let him take care, for I am desperate. I'll fight for my liberty, to the last breath I breathe! You say your fathers did it; if it was right for them, it is right for me!

WILSON. [*Walking up and down, and fanning his face with a large yellow silk handkerchief.*] Blast 'em all!
30 Haven't I always said so—the infernal old cusses! Bless me! I hope I ain't swearing now! Well, go ahead, George, go ahead. But be careful, my boy; don't shoot anybody, unless—well, you'd *better* not shoot—at least I wouldn't *hit* anybody, you know.

GEORGE. Only in self-defense.

WILSON. Well, well. [*Fumbling in his pocket.*] I suppose, perhaps, I ain't following my judgment—hang it, I won't follow my judgment. So here, George. [*Takes out a pocket-book and offers* GEORGE *a roll of*
40 *bills.*]

GEORGE. No, my kind, good sir, you've done a great deal for me, and this might get you into trouble. I have money, enough, I hope to take me as far as I need it.

WILSON. No; but you must, George. Money is a great help everywhere; can't have too much, if you get it honestly. Take it, do take it, *now* do, my boy!

GEORGE. [*Taking the money.*] On condition, sir, that I may repay it at some future time, I will.

WILSON. And now, George, how long are you going to travel in this way? Not long or far, I hope? It's well 50 carried on, but too bold.

GEORGE. Mr. Wilson, it is *so bold,* and this tavern is so near, that they will never think of it; they will look for me on ahead, and you yourself wouldn't know me.

WILSON. But the mark on your hand?

GEORGE. [*Draws off his glove and shows scar.*] That is a parting mark of Mr. Harris' regard. Looks interesting, doesn't it? [*Puts on glove again.*]

WILSON. I declare, my very blood runs cold when I think of it—your condition and your risks! 60

GEORGE. Mine has run cold a good many years; at present, it's about up to the boiling point.

WILSON. George, something has brought you out wonderfully. You hold up your head, and move and speak like another man.

GEORGE. [*Proudly.*] Because I'm a *freeman.* Yes, sir; I've said "master" for the last time to any man. *I'm free!*

WILSON. Take care! You are not sure; you may be taken. 70

GEORGE. All men are free and equal *in the grave,* if it comes to that, Mr. Wilson.

[*Enter* PHINEAS.]

PHINEAS. Them's my sentiments, to a teetotal atom, and I don't care who knows it! Neighbour, the boat is ready, and the sooner we make tracks the better. I've seen some mysterious strangers lurking about these diggings, so we'd better put.

GEORGE. Farewell, Mr. Wilson, and heaven reward you for the many kindnesses you have shown the poor fugitive! 80

WILSON. [*Grasping his hand.*] You're a brave fellow, George. I wish in my heart you were safe through, though—that's what I do.

PHINEAS. And ain't I the man of all creation to put him through, stranger? Chaw me up if I don't take him to his dear little wife, in the smallest possible quantity of time. Come, neighbour, let's vamoose.

GEORGE. Farewell, Mr. Wilson.

WILSON. My best wishes go with you, George. [*Exit.*]

PHINEAS. You're a trump, old Slow-and-Easy. 90

GEORGE. [*Looking off.*] Look! Look!

PHINEAS. Consarn their picters, here they come! We can't get out of the house without their seeing us. We're teetotally treed!

GEORGE. Let us fight our way through them!

PHINEAS. No, that won't do; there are too many of them for a fair fight—we should be chawed up in no time. [*Looks round and sees trap door.*] Holloa! here's a cellar door. Just you step down here a few minutes, while I parley with them. [*Lifts trap.*]

10   GEORGE. I am resolved to perish sooner than surrender! [*Goes down trap.*]

PHINEAS. That's your sort! [*Closes trap and stands on it.*] Here they are!

[*Enter* HALEY, MARKS, LOKER *and three* MEN.]

HALEY. Say, stranger, you haven't seen a runaway darkey about these parts, eh?

PHINEAS. What kind of a darkey?

HALEY. A mulatto chap, almost as light-complexioned as a white man.

PHINEAS. Was he a pretty good-looking chap?

20   HALEY. Yes.

PHINEAS. Kind of tall?

HALEY. Yes.

PHINEAS. With brown hair?

HALEY. Yes.

PHINEAS. And dark eyes?

HALEY. Yes.

PHINEAS. Pretty well dressed?

HALEY. Yes.

PHINEAS. Scar on his right hand?

30   HALEY. Yes, yes.

PHINEAS. Well, I ain't seen him.

HALEY. Oh, bother! Come, boys, let's search the house. [*Exeunt.*]

PHINEAS. [*Raises trap.*] Now, then, neighbour George. [GEORGE *enters, up trap.*] Now's the time to cut your lucky.

GEORGE. Follow me, Phineas. [*Exit.*]

PHINEAS. In a brace of shakes. [*Is closing trap as* HALEY, MARKS, LOKER, *etc., re-enter.*]

40   HALEY. Ah! he's down in the cellar. Follow me, boys! [*Thrusts* PHINEAS *aside, and rushes down trap, followed by the others.* PHINEAS *closes trap and stands on it.*]

PHINEAS. Chaw me up! but I've got 'em all in a trap. [*Knocking below.*] Be quiet, you pesky varmints! [*Knocking.*] They're getting mighty oneasy. [*Knock-*

ing.] Will you be quiet, you savagerous critters! [*The trap is forced open.* HALEY *and* MARKS *appear.* PHINEAS *seizes a chair and stands over trap.*] Down with you or I'll smash you into apple-fritters! [*Tableau.*]

SCENE IV. A Plain Chamber.

TOPSY. [*Without.*] You go 'long. No more nigger   50 dan you be! [*Enters—shouts and laughter without—looks off.*] You seem to think yourself white folks. You ain't nerry one—black *nor* white. I'd like to be one or turrer. Law! you niggers, does you know you's all sinners? Well, you is—everybody is. White folks is sinners too—Miss Feely says so—but I 'spects niggers is the biggest ones. But Lor'! ye ain't any on ye up to me. I's so awful wicked there can't nobody do nothin' with me. I used to keep old missis a-swarin' at me half de time. I 'spects I's de wickedest critter in de world. [*Song*   60 *and dance introduced.*]

[*Enter* EVA.]

EVA. Oh, Topsy! Topsy! you have been very wrong again.

TOPSY. Well, I 'spects I have.

EVA. What makes you do so?

TOPSY. I dunno; I 'spects it's cause I's so wicked.

EVA. Why did you spoil Jane's earrings?

TOPSY. 'Cause she's so proud. She called me a little black imp, and turned up her pretty nose at me 'cause she is whiter than I am. I was gwine by her room, and   70 I seed her coral earrings lying on de table, so I threw dem on de floor, and put my foot on 'em, and scrunched 'em all to little bits—he! he! he! I's so wicked.

EVA. Don't you know that was very wrong?

TOPSY. I don't car'. I despises dem what sets up for fine ladies, when dey ain't nothin' but cream-coloured niggers! Dere's Miss Rosa—she gives me lots of 'pertinent remarks. T'other night she was gwine to ball. She put on a beau'ful dress that missis give her—wid her har curled, all nice and pretty. She hab to go down de back   80 stairs—dey am dark—and I puts a pail of hot water on dem, and she puts her foot into it, and den she go tumblin' to de bottom of de stairs, and de water go all ober her, and spile her dress, and scald her dreadful bad! He! he! he! I's so wicked!

EVA. Oh! how could you!

TOPSY. Don't dey despise me 'cause I don't know

nothin'? Don't dey laugh at me 'cause I'm brack, and dey ain't?

EVA. But you shouldn't mind them.

TOPSY. Well, I don't mind dem; but when dey are passing under my winder, I trows dirty water on 'em, and dat spiles der complexions.

EVA. What does make you so bad, Topsy? Why don't you try and be good? Don't you love anybody, Topsy?

TOPSY. Can't recommember.

EVA. But you love your father and mother?

TOPSY. Never had none; ye know, I telled ye that, Miss Eva.

EVA. Oh! I know; but hadn't you any brother, or sister, or aunt, or—

TOPSY. No, none on 'em—never had nothin' nor nobody. I's brack—no one loves me!

EVA. Oh! Topsy, I love you! [*Laying her hand on* TOPSY'S *shoulder.*] I love you because you haven't had any father, or mother, or friends. I love you, and I want you to be good. I wish you would try to be good for my sake. [TOPSY *looks astonished for a moment, and then bursts into tears.*] Only think of it, Topsy—*you* can be one of those spirits bright Uncle Tom sings about!

TOPSY. Oh! dear Miss Eva—dear Miss Eva! I will try —I will try! I never did care nothin' about it before.

EVA. If you try, you will succeed. Come with me. [*Takes* TOPSY'S *hand.*]

TOPSY. I will try; but den I's so wicked!

[*Exit* EVA, *followed by* TOPSY, *crying.*]

SCENE V. Chamber. Enter **George, Eliza and Harry.**

GEORGE. At length, Eliza, after many wanderings, we are again united.

ELIZA. Thanks to these generous Quakers, who have so kindly sheltered us.

GEORGE. Not forgetting our friend Phineas.

ELIZA. I do indeed owe him much. 'Twas he I met upon the icy river's bank, after that fearful but successful attempt, when I fled from the slave-trader with my child in my arms.

GEORGE. It seems almost incredible that you could have crossed the river on the ice.

ELIZA. Yes, I did. Heaven helping me, I crossed on the ice, for they were behind me—right behind me—and there was no other way.

GEORGE. But the ice was all in broken-up blocks, swinging and heaving up and down in the water.

ELIZA. I know it was—I know it; I did not think I should get over, but I did not care—I could but die if I did not! I leaped on the ice, but how I got across I don't know; the first I remember, a man was helping me up the bank—that man was Phineas.

GEORGE. My brave girl! you deserve your freedom— you have richly earned it!

ELIZA. And when we get to Canada I can help you to work, and between us we can find something to live on.

GEORGE. Yes, Eliza, so long as we have each other, and our boy. Oh, Eliza, if these people only knew what a blessing it is for a man to feel that his wife and child belong to *him!* I've often wondered to see men that could call their wives and children *their own,* fretting and worrying about anything else. Why, I feel rich and strong, though we have nothing but our bare hands. If they will only let me alone now, I will be satisfied— thankful!

ELIZA. But we are not quite out of danger; we are not yet in Canada.

GEORGE. True; but it seems as if I smelt the free air, and it makes me strong.

[*Enter* PHINEAS, *dressed as a Quaker.*]

PHINEAS. [*With a snuffle.*] Verily, friends, how is it with thee?—hum!

GEORGE. Why, Phineas, what means this metamorphosis?

PHINEAS. I've become a Quaker! that's the meaning on't.

GEORGE. What—you?

PHINEAS. Teetotally! I was driven to it by a strong argument, composed of a pair of sparkling eyes, rosy cheeks, and pouting lips. Them lips would persuade a man to assassinate his grandmother! [*Assumes the Quaker tone again.*] Verily, George, I have discovered something of importance to the interests of thee and thy party, and it were well for thee to hear it.

GEORGE. Keep us not in suspense!

PHINEAS. Well, after I left you on the road, I stopped at a little, lone tavern, just below here. Well, I was tired with hard driving, and, after my supper, I stretched myself down on a pile of bags in the corner, and pulled a buffalo hide over me—and what does I do but get fast asleep.

Uncle Tom's Cabin **77**

GEORGE. With one ear open, Phineas?

PHINEAS. No, I slept ears and all for an hour or two, for I was pretty well tired; but when I came to myself a little, I found that there were some men in the room, sitting round a table, drinking and talking; and I thought, before I made much muster, I'd just see what they were up to, especially as I heard them say something about the Quakers. Then I listened with both ears and found they were talking about you. So I kept quiet, and
10 heard them lay off all their plans. They've got a right notion of the track we are going to-night, and they'll be down after us, six or eight strong. So, now, what's to be done?

ELIZA. What *shall* we do, George?

GEORGE. I know what I shall do! [*Takes out pistols.*]

PHINEAS. Ay—ay, thou seest, Eliza, how it will work—pistols—phitz—poppers!

ELIZA. I see; but I pray it come not to that!

GEORGE. I don't want to involve anyone with or for
20 me. If you will lend me your vehicle, and direct me, I will drive alone to the next stand.

PHINEAS. Ah! well, friend, but thee'll need a driver for all that. Thee's quite welcome to do all the fighting thee knows; but I know a thing or two about the road that thee doesn't.

GEORGE. But I don't want to involve you.

PHINEAS. Involve me! Why, chaw me—that is to say —when thee does involve me, please to let me know.

ELIZA. Phineas is a wise and skillful man. You will
30 do well, George, to abide by his judgment. And, oh! George, be not hasty with these—young blood is hot! [*Laying her hand on pistols.*]

GEORGE. I will attack no man. All I ask of this country is to be left alone, and I will go out peaceably. But I'll fight to the last breath before they shall take from me my wife and son! Can you blame me?

PHINEAS. Mortal man cannot blame thee, neighbour George! Flesh and blood could not do otherwise. Woe unto the world because of offenses, but woe unto them
40 through whom the offense cometh! That's gospel, teetotally!

GEORGE. Would not even you, sir, do the same, in my place?

PHINEAS. I pray that I be not tried; the flesh is weak —but I think my flesh would be pretty tolerably strong in such a case; I ain't sure, friend George, that I shouldn't

hold a fellow for thee, if thee had any accounts to settle with him.

ELIZA. Heaven grant we be not tempted.

PHINEAS. But if we are tempted too much, why, con-50 sarn 'em! let them look out, that's all.

GEORGE. It's quite plain you was not born for a Quaker. The old nature has its way in you pretty strong yet.

PHINEAS. Well, I reckon you are pretty teetotally right.

GEORGE. Had we not better hasten our flight?

PHINEAS. Well, I rather conclude we had; we're full two hours ahead of them, if they start at the time they planned; so let's vamoose. [*Exeunt.*]

SCENE VI. A Rocky Pass in the Hills. Large set rock and platform.

PHINEAS. [*Without.*] Out with you in a twinkling, 60 every one, and up into those rocks with me! run *now*, if you *ever* did run!

[PHINEAS *enters, with* HARRY *in his arms.*—GEORGE *supporting* ELIZA.]

Come up here; this is one of our old hunting dens. Come up. [*They ascend the rock.*] Well, here we are. Let 'em get us if they can. Whoever comes here has to walk single file between those two rocks, in fair range of your pistols—d'ye see?

GEORGE. I do see. And now, as this affair is mine, let me take all the risk, and do all the fighting.

PHINEAS. Thee's quite welcome to do the fighting, 70 George; but I may have the fun of looking on, I suppose. But see, these fellows are kind of debating down there, and looking up, like hens when they are going to fly up onto the roost. Hadn't thee better give 'em a word of advice, before they come up, jest to tell 'em handsomely they'll be shot if they do.

[LOKER, MARKS, *and three* MEN *enter.*]

MARKS. Well, Tom, your coons are fairly treed.

LOKER. Yes, I see 'em go up right here; and here's a path—I'm for going right up. They can't jump down in a hurry, and it won't take long to ferret 'em out. 80

MARKS. But, Tom, they might fire at us from behind the rocks. That would be ugly, you know.

LOKER. Ugh! always for saving your skin, Marks. No danger; niggers are too plaguy scared!

MARKS. I don't know why I shouldn't save my skin;

it's the best I've got; and niggers do fight like the devil sometimes.

GEORGE. [*Rising on the rock.*] Gentlemen, who are you down there, and what do you want?

LOKER. We want a party of runaway niggers. One George and Eliza Harris, and their son. We've got the officers here, and a warrant to take 'em too. D'ye hear? Ain't you George Harris, that belonged to Mr. Harris, of Shelby county, Kentucky?

10 GEORGE. I am George Harris. A Mr. Harris, of Kentucky, did call me his property. But now I'm a freeman, standing on Heaven's free soil! My wife and child I claim as mine. We have arms to defend ourselves, and we mean to do it. You can come up if you like, but the first one that comes within range of our bullets is a dead man.

MARKS. Oh, come—come, young man, this ain't no kind of talk at all for you. You see we're officers of justice. We've got the law on our side, and the power
20 and so forth; so you'd better give up peaceably, you see —for you'll certainly have to give up at last.

GEORGE. I know very well that you've got the law on your side, and the power; but you haven't got us. We are standing here as free as you are, and by the great power that made us, we'll fight for our liberty till we die!

[*During this,* MARKS *draws a pistol, and when he concludes fires at him.*—ELIZA *screams.*]

GEORGE. It's nothing, Eliza; I am unhurt.

PHINEAS. [*Drawing* GEORGE *down.*] Thee'd better keep out of sight with thy speechifying; they're teetotal mean scamps.

30 LOKER. What did you do that for, Marks?

MARKS. You see, you get jist as much for him dead as alive in Kentucky.

GEORGE. Now, Phineas, the first man that advances I fire at; you take the second, and so on. It won't do to waste two shots on one.

PHINEAS. But what if you don't hit?

GEORGE. I'll try my best.

PHINEAS. Creation! chaw me up if there ain't stuff in you!

40 MARKS. I think I must have hit some on 'em. I heard a squeal.

LOKER. I'm going right up for one. I never was afraid of niggers, and I ain't a going to be now. Who goes after me?

[LOKER *dashes up the rock.*—GEORGE *fires.*—He staggers for a moment, then springs to the top.*—PHINEAS *seizes him.*—A struggle.*]

PHINEAS. Friend, thee is not wanted here! [*Throws* LOKER *over the rock.*]

MARKS. [*Retreating.*] Lord help us—they're perfect devils! [MARKS *and* PARTY *run off.* GEORGE *and* ELIZA *kneel in an attitude of thanksgiving, with the* CHILD *between them.*—PHINEAS *stands over them exulting.*] 50

ACT III

SCENE I. Chamber. Enter **St. Clare**, followed by **Tom**.

ST. CLARE. [*Giving money and papers to* TOM.] There, Tom, are the bills, and the money to liquidate them.

TOM. Yes, mas'r.

ST. CLARE. Well, Tom, what are you waiting for? Isn't all right there?

TOM. I'm 'fraid not, mas'r.

ST. CLARE. Why, Tom, what's the matter? You look as solemn as a coffin.

TOM. I feel very bad, mas'r. I allays have thought that 60 mas'r would be good to everybody.

ST. CLARE. Well, Tom, haven't I been? Come, now, what do you want? There's something you haven't got, I suppose, and this is the preface.

TOM. Mas'r allays been good to me. I haven't nothing to complain of on that head; but there is one that mas'r isn't good to.

ST. CLARE. Why, Tom, what's got into you? Speak out —what do you mean?

TOM. Last night, between one and two, I thought so. I 70 studied upon the matter then—mas'r isn't good to *himself.*

ST. CLARE. Ah! now I understand; you allude to the state in which I came home last night. Well, to tell the truth, I *was* slightly elevated—a little more champagne on board than I could comfortably carry. That's all, isn't it?

TOM. [*Deeply affected—clasping his hands and weeping.*] All! Oh! my dear young mas'r, I'm 'fraid it will be *loss of all—all,* body and soul. The Good Book says, "It biteth like a serpent and stingeth like an adder," 80 my dear mas'r.

ST. CLARE. You poor, silly fool! I'm not worth crying over.

TOM. Oh, mas'r! I implore you to think of it before it gets too late.

ST. CLARE. Well, I won't go to any more of their cursed nonsense, Tom—on my honour, I won't. I don't know why I haven't stopped long ago; I've always despised *it,* and myself for it. So now, Tom, wipe up your eyes and go about your errands.

TOM. Bless you, mas'r. I feel much better now. You have taken a load from poor Tom's heart. Bless you!

ST. CLARE. Come, come, no blessings! I'm not **so** wonderfully good, now. There, I'll pledge my honour to you, Tom, you don't see me so again. [*Exit* TOM.] I'll keep my faith with him, too.

OPHELIA. [*Without.*] Come along, you shiftless mortal!

ST. CLARE. What new witchcraft has Topsy been brewing? That commotion is of her raising, I'll be bound.

[*Enter* OPHELIA, *dragging in* TOPSY.]

OPHELIA. Come here now; I will tell your master.

ST. CLARE. What's the matter now?

OPHELIA. The matter is that I cannot be plagued with this girl any longer. It's past all bearing; flesh and blood cannot endure it. Here I locked her up and gave her a hymn to study; and what does she do but spy out where I put my key, and has gone to my bureau, and got a bonnet-trimming and cut it all to pieces to make dolls' jackets! I never saw anything like it in my life!

ST. CLARE. What have you done to her?

OPHELIA. What have I done? What haven't I done? Your wife says I ought to have her whipped till she couldn't stand.

ST. CLARE. I don't doubt it. Tell me of the lovely rule of woman. I never saw above a dozen women that wouldn't half kill a horse, or a servant, either, if they had their own way with them—let alone a man.

OPHELIA. I am sure, St. Clare, I don't know what to do. I've taught and taught—I've talked till I'm tired; I've whipped her, I've punished her in every way I could think of, and still she's just what she was at first.

ST. CLARE. Come here, Tops, you monkey! [TOPSY *crosses to* ST. CLARE, *grinning.*] What makes you behave so?

TOPSY. 'Spects it's my wicked heart—Miss Feely says so.

ST. CLARE. Don't you see how much Miss Ophelia has done for you? She says she has done everything she can think of.

TOPSY. Lor', yes, mas'r! Old missis used to say so, too. She whipped me a heap harder, and used to pull my ha'r, and knock my head agin the door; but it didn't do me no good. I 'spects if they's to pull every spear of ha'r out o' my head, it wouldn't do no good neither—I's so wicked! Laws! I's nothin' but a nigger, no ways! [*Goes up.*]

OPHELIA. Well, I shall have to give her up; I can't have that trouble any longer.

ST. CLARE. I'd like to ask you one question.

OPHELIA. What is it?

ST. CLARE. Why, if your doctrine is not strong enough to save one heathen child, that you can have at home here, all to yourself, what's the use of sending one or two poor missionaries off with it among thousands of just such? I suppose this girl is a fair sample of what thousands of your heathen are.

OPHELIA. I'm sure I don't know; I never saw such a girl as this.

ST. CLARE. What makes you so bad, Tops? Why won't you try and be good? Don't you love any one, Topsy?

TOPSY. Dunno nothing 'bout love! I loves candy and sich, that's all.

OPHELIA. But, Topsy, if you'd only try to be good, you might.

TOPSY. Couldn't never be nothing but a nigger, if I was ever so good. If I could be skinned and come white, I'd try then.

ST. CLARE. People can love you, if you are black, Topsy. Miss Ophelia would love you, if you were good. [TOPSY *laughs.*] Don't you think so?

TOPSY. No, she can't b'ar me 'cause I'm a nigger—she'd's soon have a toad touch her. There can't nobody love niggers, and niggers can't do nothin'! I don't car'! [*Whistles.*]

ST. CLARE. Silence, you incorrigible imp, and begone!

TOPSY. He! he! he! didn't get much out of dis chile! [*Exit.*]

OPHELIA. I've always had a prejudice against Negroes, and it's a fact—I never could bear to have that child touch me, but I didn't think she knew it.

ST. CLARE. Trust any child to find that out; there's no keeping it from them. But I believe all the trying in the world to benefit a child, and all the substantial favours you can do them, will never excite one emotion of gratitude, while that feeling of repugnance remains in the heart. It's a queer kind of fact, but so it is.

OPHELIA. I don't know how I can help it—they are disagreeable to me, this girl in particular. How can I help feeling so?

ST. CLARE. Eva does, it seems.

OPHELIA. Well, she's so loving. I wish I was like her. She might teach me a lesson.

ST. CLARE. It would not be the first time a little child had been used to instruct an old disciple, if it were so. Come, let us seek Eva, in her favourite bower by the lake.

OPHELIA. Why, the dew is falling; she mustn't be out there. She is unwell, I know.

ST. CLARE. Don't be croaking cousin—I hate it.

OPHELIA. But she has that cough.

ST. CLARE. Oh, nonsense, of that cough—it is not anything. She has taken a little cold, perhaps.

OPHELIA. Well, that was just the way Eliza Jane was taken—and Ellen.

ST. CLARE. Oh, stop these hobgoblin, nurse legends. You old hands get so wise, that a child cannot cough or sneeze, but you see desperation and ruin at hand. Only take care of the child, keep her from the night air, and don't let her play too hard, and she'll do well enough. [Exeunt.]

SCENE II. The flat represents the lake. The rays of the setting sun tinge the waters with gold. A large tree.— Beneath this a grassy bank on which **Eva** and **Tom** are seated side by side. **Eva** has a Bible open on her lap.

TOM. Read dat passage again, please, Miss Eva?

EVA. [Reading.] "And I saw a sea of glass, mingled with fire." [Stopping suddenly and pointing to lake.] Tom, there it is!

TOM. What, Miss Eva?

EVA. Don't you see there? There's a "sea of glass, mingled with fire."

TOM. True enough, Miss Eva [Sings.]

Oh, had I the wings of the morning,
I'd fly away to Canaan's shore;
Bright angels should convey me home,
To the New Jerusalem.

EVA. Where do you suppose New Jerusalem is, Uncle Tom?

Engraving by "Baker-Smith" for the first edition

TOM. Oh, up in the clouds, Miss Eva.

EVA. Then I think I see it. Look in those clouds; they look like great gates of pearl; and you can see beyond them—far, far off—it's all gold! Tom, sing about "spirits bright."

TOM. [Sings.]

I see a band of spirits bright,
That taste the glories there;
They are all robed in spotless white,
And conquering palms they bear.

EVA. Uncle Tom, I've seen *them.*

TOM. To be sure you have; you are one of them yourself. You are the brightest spirit I ever saw.

EVA. They come to me sometimes in my sleep— those spirits bright—

They are all robed in spotless white,
And conquering palms they bear.

Uncle Tom, I'm going there.

TOM. Where, Miss Eva?

EVA. [Pointing to the sky.] I'm going *there,* to the spirits bright, Tom; I'm going before long.

TOM. It's jest no use trying to keep Miss Eva here; I've allays said so. She's got the Lord's mark in her forehead. She wasn't never like a child that's to live— there was always something deep in her eyes. [Rises and comes forward.—EVA also comes forward, leaving Bible on bank.]

[Enter ST. CLARE.]

ST. CLARE. Ah! my little pussy, you look as blooming as a rose! You are better now-a-days, are you not?

EVA. Papa, I've had things I wanted to say to you a great while. I want to say them now, before I get weaker.

ST. CLARE. Nay, this is an idle fear, Eva; you know you grow stronger every day.

EVA. It's all no use, papa, to keep it to myself any longer. The time is coming that I am going to leave you; I am going, and never to come back.

ST. CLARE. Oh, now, my dear little Eva! you've got nervous and low-spirited; you mustn't indulge such gloomy thoughts.

EVA. No, papa, don't deceive yourself, I am *not* any better; I know it perfectly well, and I am going before long. I am not nervous—I am not low-spirited. If it were not for you, papa, and my friends, I should be perfectly happy. I want to go—I long to go!

ST. CLARE. Why, dear child, what has made your poor little heart so sad? You have everything to make you happy that could be given you.

EVA. I had rather be in heaven! There are a great many things here that make me sad—that seem dreadful to me; I had rather be there; but I don't want to leave you—it almost breaks my heart!

ST. CLARE. What makes you sad, and what seems dreadful, Eva?

EVA. I feel sad for our poor people; they love me dearly, and they are all good and kind to me. I wish, papa, they were all *free!*

ST. CLARE. Why, Eva, child, don't you think they are well enough off, now?

EVA. [*Not heeding the question.*] Papa, isn't there a way to have slaves made free? When I am dead, papa, then you will think of me, and do it for my sake?

ST. CLARE. When you are dead, Eva? Oh, child, don't talk to me so! You are all I have on earth!

EVA. Papa, these poor creatures love their children as much as you do me. Tom loves his children. Oh, do something for them!

ST. CLARE. There, there darling; only don't distress yourself, and don't talk of dying, and I will do anything you wish.

EVA. And promise me, dear father, that Tom shall have his freedom as soon as—[*hesitating*]—I am gone!

ST. CLARE. Yes, dear, I will do anything in the world—anything you could ask me to. There, Tom, take her to

her chamber; this evening air is too chill for her. [*Kisses her.*]

[TOM *takes* EVA *in his arms, and exit.*]

ST. CLARE. [*Gazing mournfully after* EVA.] Has there ever been a child like Eva? Yes, there has been; but their names are always on grave-stones, and their sweet smiles, their heavenly eyes, their singular words and ways, are among the buried treasures of yearning hearts. It is as if heaven had an especial band of angels, whose office it is to sojourn for a season here, and endear to them the wayward human heart, that they might bear it upward with them in their homeward flight. When you see that deep, spiritual light in the eye, when the little soul reveals itself in words sweeter and wiser than the ordinary words of children, hope not to retain that child; for the seal of heaven is on it, and the light of immortality looks out from its eyes! [*Exit.*]

SCENE III. A corridor. Enter **Tom**; he listens at door and then lies down. Enter **Ophelia**, with candle.

OPHELIA. Uncle Tom, what alive have you taken to sleeping anywhere and everywhere, like a dog, for? I thought you were one of the orderly sort, that liked to lie in bed in a Christian way.

TOM. [*Rises.—Mysteriously.*] I do, Miss Feely, I do, but now—

OPHELIA. Well, what now?

TOM. We mustn't speak loud; Mas'r St. Clare won't hear on't; but Miss Feely, you know there must be somebody watchin' for the bridegroom.

OPHELIA. What do you mean, Tom?

TOM. You know it says in Scripture, "At midnight there was a great cry made, behold the bridegroom cometh!" That's what I'm 'spectin' now, every night, Miss Feely, and I couldn't sleep out of hearing, noways.

OPHELIA. Why, Uncle Tom, what makes you think so?

TOM. Miss Eva, she talks to me. The Lord, he sends his messenger in the soul. I must be thar, Miss Feely; for when that ar blessed child goes into the kingdom, they'll open the door so wide, we'll all get a look in at the glory!

OPHELIA. Uncle Tom, did Miss Eva say she felt more unwell than usual to-night?

TOM. No; but she told me she was coming nearer—

thar's them that tells it to the child, Miss Feely. It's the angels—it's the trumpet sound afore the break o' day!

OPHELIA. Heaven grant your fears be in vain! Come in, Tom. [*Exeunt.*]

SCENE IV. Eva's Chamber. **Eva** discovered on a couch. A table stands near the couch, with a lamp on it. The light shines upon **Eva's** face, which is very pale. Scene half dark. **Uncle Tom** is kneeling near the foot of the couch. **Ophelia** stands at the head. **St. Clare** at back. Scene opens to plaintive music. Enter **Marie**, hastily.

MARIE. St. Clare! Cousin! Oh! what is the matter now?

ST. CLARE [*Hoarsely.*] Hush! she is dying!

MARIE. [*Sinking on her knees, beside* TOM.] Dying!

ST. CLARE. Oh! if she would only wake and speak
10 once more. [*Bending over* EVA.] Eva, darling!

EVA. [*Uncloses her eyes, smiles, raises her head and tries to speak.*]

ST. CLARE. Do you know me, Eva?

EVA. [*Throwing her arms feebly about his neck.*] Dear papa! [*Her arms drop and she sinks back.*]

ST. CLARE. Oh, heaven! this is dreadful! Oh! Tom, my boy, it is killing me!

TOM. Look at her, mas'r. [*Points to* EVA.]

ST. CLARE. Eva! [*A pause.*] She does not hear. Oh,
20 Eva! tell us what you see. What is it?

EVA. [*Feebly smiling.*] Oh! love! joy! peace! [*Dies.*]

TOM. Oh! bless the Lord! it's over, dear mas'r, it's over.

ST. CLARE. [*Sinking on his knees.*] Farewell, beloved child! the bright eternal doors have closed after thee. We shall see thy sweet face no more. Oh! wo for them who watched thy entrance into heaven, when they shall wake and find only the cold, gray sky of daily life, and thou gone forever.

[*Solemn music, slow curtain.*]

ACT IV

SCENE I. A street in New Orleans. Enter **Gumption Cute**, meeting **Marks**.

30 CUTE. How do ye dew?

MARKS. How are you?

CUTE. Well, now, squire, it's a fact that I am dead broke and busted up.

MARKS. You have been speculating, I suppose?

CUTE. That's just it and nothing shorter.

MARKS. You have had poor success, you say?

CUTE. Tarnation bad, now I tell you. You see I came to this part of the country to make my fortune.

MARKS. And you did not do it?

CUTE. Scarcely. The first thing I tried my hand at 40 was keeping school. I opened an academy for the instruction of youth in the various branches of orthography, geography, and other graphies.

MARKS. Did you succeed in getting any pupils?

CUTE. Oh, lots on 'em! and a pretty set of dunces they were, too. After the first quarter, I called on the respectable parents of the juveniles, and requested them to fork over. To which they politely answered—don't you wish you may get it?

MARKS. What did you do then? 50

CUTE. Well, I kind of pulled up stakes and left those diggin's. Well, then I went into Spiritual Rappings for a living. That paid pretty well for a short time, till I met with an accident.

MARKS. An accident?

CUTE. Yes; a tall Yahoo called on me one day, and wanted me to summon the spirit of his mother—which, of course, I did. He asked me about a dozen questions which I answered to his satisfaction. At last he wanted to know what she died of—I said, Cholera. You never 60 did see a critter so riled as he was. "Look yere, stranger," said he, "It's my opinion that you're a pesky humbug! for my mother was blown up in a *Steamboat!*" With that he left the premises. The next day the people furnished me with a conveyance, and I rode out of town.

MARKS. Rode out of town?

CUTE. Yes; on a rail!

MARKS. I suppose you gave up the spirits, after that?

CUTE. Well, I reckon I did; it had such an effect on my spirits. 70

MARKS. It's a wonder they didn't tar and feather you.

CUTE. There was some mention made of that, but when they said *feathers,* I felt as if I had wings, and flew away.

MARKS. You cut and run?

CUTE. Yes; I didn't like their company and I cut it. Well, after that I let myself out as an overseer on a cotton plantation. I made a pretty good thing of that, though it was dreadful trying to my feelings to flog the darkies; but I got used to it after a while, and then I 80 used to lather 'em like Jehu. Well, the proprietor got the fever and ague and shook himself out of town. The place and all the fixings were sold at auction, and I found myself adrift once more.

MARKS. What are you doing at present?

CUTE. I'm in search of a rich relation of mine.

MARKS. A rich relation?

CUTE. Yes, a Miss Ophelia St. Clare. You see, a niece of hers married one of my second cousins—that's how I came to be a relation of hers. She came on here from Vermont to be housekeeper to a cousin of hers, of the same name.

MARKS. I know him well.

CUTE. The deuce you do!—well, that's lucky.

MARKS. Yes, he lives in this city.

CUTE. Say, you just point out the locality, and I'll give him a call.

MARKS. Stop a bit. Suppose you shouldn't be able to raise the wind in that quarter, what have you thought of doing?

CUTE. Well, nothing particular.

MARKS. How should you like to enter into a nice, profitable business—one that pays well?

CUTE. That's just about my measure—it would suit me to a hair. What is it?

MARKS. Nigger catching.

CUTE. Catching niggers! What on airth do you mean?

MARKS. Why, when there's a large reward offered for a runaway darkey, we goes after him, catches him, and gets the reward.

CUTE. Yes, that's all right so far—but s'pose there ain't no reward offered?

MARKS. Why, then we catches the darkey on our own account, sells him, and pockets the proceeds.

CUTE. By chowder, that ain't a bad speculation!

MARKS. What do you say? I want a partner. You see, I lost my partner last year, up in Ohio—he was a powerful fellow.

CUTE. Lost him! How did you lose him?

MARKS. Well, you see, Tom and I—his name was Tom Loker—Tom and I were after a mulatto chap, called George Harris, that run away from Kentucky. We traced him through the greater part of Ohio, and came up with him near the Pennsylvania line. He took refuge among some rocks, and showed fight.

CUTE. Oh! then runaway darkies show fight, do they?

MARKS. Sometimes. Well, Tom—like a headstrong fool as he was—rushed up the rocks, and a Quaker chap, who was helping this George Harris, threw him over the cliff.

CUTE. Was he killed?

MARKS. Well, I didn't stop to find out. Seeing that the darkies were stronger than I thought, I made tracks for a safe place.

CUTE. And what became of this George Harris?

MARKS. Oh! he and his wife and child got away safe into Canada. You see, they will get away sometimes, though it isn't very often. Now what do you say? You are just the figure for a fighting partner. Is it a bargain?

CUTE. Well, I rather calculate our teams won't hitch, no how. By chowder, I hain't no idea of setting myself up, as a target for darkies to fire at—that's a speculation that don't suit my constitution.

MARKS. You're afraid, then?

CUTE. No, I ain't; it's against my principles.

MARKS. Your principles—how so?

CUTE. Because my principles are to keep a sharp look-out for No. I. I shouldn't feel wholesome if a darkey was to throw me over that cliff to look after Tom Loker. [*Exeunt, arm-in-arm.*]

SCENE II. Gothic Chamber. **St. Clare** discovered, seated on sofa. **Tom** to the left.

ST. CLARE. Oh! Tom, my boy, the whole world is as empty as an egg-shell.

TOM. I know it, mas'r, I know it. But oh! if mas'r could look up—up where our dear Miss Eva is—

ST. CLARE. Ah, Tom! I do look up; but the trouble is, I don't see anything when I do. I wish I could. It seems to be given to children and poor, honest fellows like you, to see what we cannot. How comes it?

TOM. "Thou hast hid from the wise and prudent, and revealed unto babes; even so, Father, for so it seemed good in thy sight."

ST. CLARE. Tom, I don't believe—I've got the habit of doubting—I want to believe and I cannot.

TOM. Dear mas'r, pray to the good Lord: "Lord, I believe; help thou my unbelief."

ST. CLARE. Who knows anything about anything? Was all that beautiful love and faith only one of the ever-shifting phases of human feeling, having nothing real to rest on, passing away with the little breath? And is there no more Eva—nothing?

TOM. Oh! dear mas'r, there is. I know it; I'm sure of it. Do, do, dear mas'r, believe it!

ST. CLARE. How do you know there is, Tom? You never saw the Lord.

TOM. Felt Him in my soul, mas'r—feel Him now! Oh, mas'r, when I was sold away from my old woman
10 and the children, I was jest a'most broken up—I felt as if there warn't nothing left—and then the Lord stood by me, and He says, "Fear not, Tom," and He brings light and joy into a poor fellow's soul—makes all peace; and I's so happy, and loves everybody, and feels willin' to be jest where the Lord wants to put me. I know it couldn't come from me, 'cause I's a poor, complaining creature—it comes from above, and I know He's willin' to do for mas'r.

ST. CLARE. [Grasping TOM's hand.] Tom, you love
20 me!

TOM. I's willing to lay down my life this blessed day for you.

ST. CLARE. [Sadly.] Poor, foolish fellow! I'm not worth the love of one good, honest heart like yours.

TOM. Oh, mas'r! there's more than me loves you—the blessed Saviour loves you.

ST. CLARE. How do you know that, Tom?

TOM. The love of the Saviour passeth knowledge.

ST. CLARE. [Turns away.] Singular! that the story of
30 a man who lived and died eighteen hundred years ago, can affect people so yet. But He was no man. [Rises.] No man ever had such long and living power. Oh! that I could believe what my mother taught me, and pray as I did when I was a boy! But, Tom, all this time I have forgotten why I sent for you. I'm going to make a freeman of you; so have your trunk packed, and get ready to set out for Kentuck.

TOM. [Joyfully.] Bless the Lord!

ST. CLARE. [Dryly.] You haven't had such very bad
40 times here, that you need be in such a rapture, Tom.

TOM. No, no, mas'r, 'tain't that; it's being a freeman—that's what I'm joyin' for.

ST. CLARE. Why, Tom, don't you think, for your own part, you've been better off than to be free?

TOM. No, indeed, Mas'r St. Clare—no, indeed!

ST. CLARE. Why, Tom, you couldn't possibly have

earned, by your work, such clothes and such living as I have given you.

TOM. I know all that, Mas'r St. Clare—mas'r's been too good; but I'd rather have poor clothes, poor house, 50 poor every thing, and have 'em mine, than have the best, if they belonged to somebody else. I had so, mas'r; I think it's natur', mas'r.

ST. CLARE. I suppose so, Tom; and you'll be going off and leaving me in a month or so—though why you shouldn't no mortal knows.

TOM. Not while mas'r is in trouble. I'll stay with mas'r as long as he wants me, so as I can be any use.

ST. CLARE. [Sadly.] Not while I'm in trouble, Tom? And when will my trouble be over? 60

TOM. When you are a believer.

ST. CLARE. And you really mean to stay by me till that day comes? [Smiling and laying his hand on TOM'S shoulder.] Ah, Tom! I won't keep you till that day. Go home to your wife and children, and give my love to all.

TOM. I's faith to think that day will come—the Lord has a work for mas'r.

ST. CLARE. A work, hey? Well, now, Tom, give me your views on what sort of a work it is—let's hear.

TOM. Why, even a poor fellow like me has a work; 70 and Mas'r St. Clare, that has larnin', and riches, and friends, how much he might do for the Lord.

ST. CLARE. Tom, you seem to think the Lord needs a great deal done for him.

TOM. We does for him when we does for his creatures.

ST. CLARE. Good theology, Tom. Thank you, my boy; I like to hear you talk. But go now, Tom, and leave me alone. [Exit TOM.] That faithful fellow's words have excited a train of thoughts that almost bear me, on the strong tide of faith and feeling, to the gates of that 80 heaven I so vividly conceive. They seem to bring me nearer to Eva.

OPHELIA. [Outside.] What are you doing there, you limb of Satan? You've been stealing something, I'll be bound. [OPHELIA drags in TOPSY.]

TOPSY. You go 'long, Miss Feely, 'tain't none o' your business.

ST. CLARE. Heyday! what is all this commotion?

OPHELIA. She's been stealing.

TOPSY. [Sobbing.] I hain't neither. 90

OPHELIA. What have you got in your bosom?

TOPSY. I've got my hand dar.

OPHELIA. But what have you got in your hand?

TOPSY. Nuffin'.

OPHELIA. That's a fib, Topsy.

TOPSY. Well, I 'spects it is.

OPHELIA. Give it to me, whatever it is.

TOPSY. It's mine—I hope I may die this bressed minute, if it don't b'long to me.

OPHELIA. Topsy, I order you to give me that article; don't let me have to ask you again. [TOPSY *reluctantly*
10 *takes the foot of an old stocking from her bosom and hands it to* OPHELIA.] Sakes alive! what is all this? [*Takes from it a lock of hair, and a small book, with a bit of crape twisted around it.*]

TOPSY. Dat's a lock of ha'r dat Miss Eva give me— she cut it from her own beau'ful head herself.

ST. CLARE. [*Takes book.*] Why did you wrap *this* [*Pointing to crape*] around the book?

TOPSY. 'Cause—'cause—'cause 'twas Miss Eva's. Oh! don't take 'em away, please! [*Sits down on stage, and,*
20 *putting her apron over her head, begins to sob vehemently.*]

OPHELIA. Come, come, don't cry; you shall have them.

TOPSY. [*Jumps up joyfully and takes them.*] I wants to keep 'em 'cause dey makes me good; I ain't half so wicked as I used to was. [*Runs off.*]

ST. CLARE. I really think you can make something of that girl. Any mind that is capable of a *real sorrow* is capable of good. You must try and do something
30 with her.

OPHELIA. The child has improved very much; I have great hopes of her.

ST. CLARE. I believe I'll go down the street, a few moments, and hear the news.

OPHELIA. Shall I call Tom to attend you?

ST. CLARE. No, I shall be back in an hour. [*Exit.*]

OPHELIA. He's got an excellent heart, but then he's so dreadful shiftless! [*Exit.*]

SCENE III. Front chamber. Enter **Topsy**.

TOPSY. Dar's somethin' de matter wid me—I isn't a
40 bit like myself. I haven't done anything wrong since poor Miss Eva went up in de skies and left us. When I's gwine to do anything wicked, I tinks of her, and somehow I can't do it. I's getting to be good, dat's a fact. I 'spects when I's dead I shall be turned into a little brack angel.

[*Enter* OPHELIA.]

OPHELIA. Topsy, I've been looking for you; I've got something very particular to say to you.

TOPSY. Does you want me to say the catechism?

OPHELIA. No, not now.

TOPSY. [*Aside.*] Golly! dat's one comfort.   50

OPHELIA. Now, Topsy, I want you to try and understand what I am going to say to you.

TOPSY. Yes, missis, I'll open my ears dreful wide.

OPHELIA. Mr. St. Clare has given you to me, Topsy.

TOPSY. Den I b'longs to you, don't I? Golly! I thought I always belong to you.

OPHELIA. Not till to-day have I received any authority to call you my property.

TOPSY. I's your property, am I? Well, if you say so, I 'spects I am.   60

OPHELIA. Topsy, I can give you your liberty.

TOPSY. My liberty?

OPHELIA. Yes, Topsy.

TOPSY. Has you got 'um with you?

OPHELIA. I have, Topsy.

TOPSY. Is it clothes or wittles?

OPHELIA. How shiftless! Don't you know what your liberty is, Topsy?

TOPSY. How should I know when I never seed 'um?

OPHELIA. Topsy, I am going to leave this place; I am   70
going many miles away—to my own home in Vermont.

TOPSY. Den what's to become of dis chile?

OPHELIA. If you wish to go, I will take you with me.

TOPSY. Miss Feely, I doesn't want to leave you no how, I loves you, I does.

OPHELIA. Then you shall share my home for the rest of your days. Come, Topsy.

TOPSY. Stop, Miss Feely; does dey hab any oberseers in Varmount?

OPHELIA. No, Topsy.   80

TOPSY. Nor cotton plantations, nor sugar factories, nor darkies, nor whipping, nor nothing?

OPHELIA. No, Topsy.

TOPSY. By golly! de quicker you is gwine de better den. [*Enter* TOM, *hastily.*]

TOM. Oh, Miss Feely! Miss Feely!

OPHELIA. Gracious me, Tom! what's the matter?

TOM. Oh, Mas'r St. Clare! Mas'r St. Clare!

OPHELIA. Well, Tom, well?

TOM. They've just brought him home and I do believe he's killed.

OPHELIA. Killed?

TOPSY. Oh, dear! what's to become of de poor darkies now?

TOM. He's dreadful weak. It's just as much as he can do to speak. He wanted me to call you.

OPHELIA. My poor cousin! Who would have thought of it? Don't say a word to his wife, Tom; the danger may not be so great as you think; it would only distress her. Come with me; you may be able to afford some assistance. [Exeunt.]

SCENE IV. Handsome Chamber. **St. Clare** discovered seated on sofa. **Ophelia, Tom** and **Topsy** are clustered around him. **Doctor** back of sofa, feeling his pulse.

ST. CLARE. [Raising himself feebly.] Tom—poor fellow!

TOM. Well, mas'r?

ST. CLARE. I have received my death wound.

TOM. Oh, no, no, mas'r!

ST. CLARE. I feel that I am dying—Tom, pray!

TOM. [Sinking on his knees.] I do pray, mas'r! I do pray!

ST. CLARE. [After a pause.] Tom, one thing preys upon my mind.—I have forgotten to sign your freedom papers. What will become of you when I am gone?

TOM. Don't think of that, mas'r.

ST. CLARE. I was wrong, Tom, very wrong, to neglect it. I may be the cause of much suffering to you hereafter. Marie, my wife—she—oh!—

OPHELIA. His mind is wandering.

ST. CLARE. [Energetically.] No! it is coming home at last! [Sinks back.] at last! at last! Eva, I come! [Dies.]

ACT V

SCENE I. An Auction Mart. **Uncle Tom** and **Emmeline** at back. **Adolf, Skeggs, Marks, Mann,** and various spectators discovered. **Marks** and **Mann** come forward.

MARKS. Hulloa, Alf! what brings you here?

MANN. Well, I was wanting a valet, and I heard that St. Clare's lot was going; I thought I'd just look at them.

MARKS. Catch me ever buying any of St. Clare's people. Spoilt niggers, every one—impudent as the devil.

MANN. Never fear that; if I get 'em, I'll soon have their airs out of them—they'll soon find that they've another kind of master to deal with than St. Clare. 'Pon my word, I'll buy that fellow—I like the shape of him. [Pointing to ADOLF.]

MARKS. You'll find it'll take all you've got to keep him —he's deucedly extravagant.

MANN. Yes, but my lord will find that he can't be extravagant with me. Just let him be sent to the calaboose a few times, and thoroughly dressed down, I'll tell you if it don't bring him to a sense of his ways. Oh! I'll reform him, up hill and down, you'll see. I'll buy him, that's flat.

[Enter LEGREE; he goes up and looks at ADOLF, whose boots are nicely blacked.]

LEGREE. A nigger with his boots blacked—bah! [Spits on them.] Holloa, you! [To TOM.] Let's see your teeth. [Seizes TOM by the jaw and opens his mouth.] Strip up your sleeve and show your muscle. [TOM does so.] Where was you raised?

TOM. In Kentuck, mas'r.

LEGREE. What have you done?

TOM. Had care of mas'r's farm.

LEGREE. That's a likely story. [Turns to EMMELINE.] You're a nice looking girl enough. How old are you? [Grasps her arm.]

EMMELINE. [Shrieking.] Ah! you hurt me.

SKEGGS. Stop that, you minx! No whimpering here. The sale is going to begin. [Mounts the rostrum.] Gentlemen, the next article I shall offer you to-day is Adolf, late valet to Mr. St. Clare. How much am I offered? [Various bids are made. ADOLF is knocked down to MANN for eight hundred dollars.] Gentlemen, I now offer a prime article—the quadroon girl, Emmeline, only fifteen years of age, warranted in every respect. [Business as before. EMMELINE is sold to LEGREE for one thousand dollars.] Now, I shall close to-day's sale by offering you the valuable article known as Uncle Tom, the most useful nigger ever raised. Gentlemen in want of an overseer, now is the time to bid.

[Business as before. TOM is sold to LEGREE for twelve hundred dollars.]

LEGREE. Now look here, you two belong to me.

[TOM *and* EMMELINE *sink on their knees.*]

TOM. Heaven help us, then!

[*Music*—LEGREE *stands over them exulting. Picture.*]

SCENE II. The Garden of **Miss Ophelia's** House in Vermont. Enter **Ophelia** and **Deacon Perry.**

DEACON. Miss Ophelia, allow me to offer you my congratulations upon your safe arrival in your native place. I hope it is your intention to pass the remainder of your days with us?

OPHELIA. Well, Deacon, I have come here with that express purpose.

DEACON. I presume you were not over pleased with the South?

OPHELIA. Well, to tell the truth, Deacon, I wasn't; I liked the country very well, but the people there are so dreadful shiftless.

DEACON. The result, I presume, of living in a warm climate.

OPHELIA. Well, Deacon, what is the news among you all here?

DEACON. Well, we live on in the same even jog-trot pace. Nothing of any consequence has happened.—Oh! I forgot. [*Takes out handkerchief.*] I've lost my wife; my Molly has left me. [*Wipes his eyes.*]

OPHELIA. Poor soul! I pity you, Deacon.

DEACON. Thank you. You perceive I bear my loss with resignation.

OPHELIA. How you must miss her tongue!

DEACON. Molly certainly was fond of talking. She always would have the last word—heigho!

OPHELIA. What was her complaint, Deacon?

DEACON. A very mild and soothing one, Miss Ophelia; she had a severe attack of the lockjaw.

OPHELIA. Dreadful!

DEACON. Wasn't it? When she found she couldn't use her tongue, she took it so much to heart that it struck to her stomach and killed her. Poor dear! Excuse my handkerchief; she's been dead only eighteen months.

OPHELIA. Why, Deacon, by this time you ought to be setting your cap for another wife.

DEACON. Do you think so, Miss Ophelia?

OPHELIA. I don't see why you shouldn't—you are still a good-looking man, Deacon.

DEACON. Ah! well, I think I do wear well—in fact, I may say remarkably well. It has been observed to me before.

OPHELIA. And you are not much over fifty?

DEACON. Just turned of forty, I assure you.

OPHELIA. Hale and hearty?

DEACON. Health excellent—look at my eye! Strong as a lion—look at my arm! A No. 1 constitution—look at my leg!!!

OPHELIA. Have you no thoughts of choosing another partner?

DEACON. Well, to tell you the truth, I have.

OPHELIA. Who is she?

DEACON. She is not far distant. [*Looks at* OPHELIA *in a languishing manner.*] I have her in my eye at this present moment.

OPHELIA. [*Aside.*] Really, I believe he's going to pop. Why, surely, Deacon, you don't mean to—

DEACON. Yes, Miss Ophelia, I do mean; and believe me, when I say—[*Looking off.*] The Lord be good to us, but I believe there is the devil coming!

[TOPSY *runs on with bouquet. She is now dressed very neatly.*]

TOPSY. Miss Feely, here is some flowers dat I hab been gathering for you. [*Gives bouquet.*]

OPHELIA. That's a good child.

DEACON. Miss Ophelia, who is this young person?

OPHELIA. She is my daughter.

DEACON. [*Aside.*] Her daughter! Then she must have married a colored man off South. I was not aware that you had been married, Miss Ophelia?

OPHELIA. Married? Sakes alive! what made you think I had been married?

DEACON. Good gracious! I'm getting confused. Didn't I understand you to say that this—somewhat tanned—young lady was your daughter?

OPHELIA. Only by adoption. She is my adopted daughter.

DEACON. O—oh! [*Aside.*] I breathe again.

TOPSY. [*Aside.*] By golly! dat old man's eyes stick out of 'um head dre'ful. Guess he never seed anything like me afore.

OPHELIA. Deacon, won't you step into the house and refresh yourself after your walk?

DEACON. I accept your polite invitation. [*Offers his arm.*] Allow me.

OPHELIA. As gallant as ever, Deacon. I declare, you grow younger every day.

DEACON. You can never grow old, madam.

OPHELIA. Ah, you flatterer! [*Exeunt.*]

TOPSY. Dar dey go, like an old goose and gander. Guess dat ole gemblemun feels kind of confectionary—rather sweet on my old missis. By golly! she's been dre'ful kind to me ever since I come away from de South; and I loves her, I does, 'cause she takes such car' on me and gives me dese fine clothes. I tries to be good, too, and I's getting 'long 'mazin' fast. I'se not so wicked as I used to was. [*Looks out.*] Hulloa! dar's someone comin' here. I wonder what he wants now. [*Retires, observing.*]

[*Enter* GUMPTION CUTE, *very shabby—a small bundle, on a stick, over his shoulder.*]

CUTE. By chowder, here I am again. Phew! it's a pretty considerable tall piece of walking between here and New Orleans, not to mention the wear of shoe-leather. I guess I'm about done up. If this streak of bad luck lasts much longer, I'll borrow sixpence to buy a rope, and hang myself right straight up! When I went to call on Miss Ophelia, I swow if I didn't find out that she had left for Vermont; so I kind of concluded to make tracks in that direction myself, and as I didn't have any money left, why I had to foot it, and here I am in old Varmount once more. They told me Miss Ophelia lived up here. I wonder if she will remember the relationship. [*Sees* TOPSY.] By chowder, there's a darkey. Look here, Charcoal!

TOPSY. [*Comes forward.*] My name isn't Charcoal—it's Topsy.

CUTE. Oh! your name is Topsy, is it, you juvenile specimen of Day & Martin?

TOPSY. Tell you I don't know nothin' 'bout Day & Martin. I's Topsy and I belong to Miss Feely St. Clare.

CUTE. I'm much obleeged to you, you small extract of Japan, for your information. So Miss Ophelia lives up there in the white house, does she?

TOPSY. Well, she don't do nothin' else.

CUTE. Well, then, just locomote your pins.

TOPSY. What—what's dat?

CUTE. Walk your chalks!

TOPSY. By golly! dere ain't no chalk 'bout me.

CUTE. Move your trotters.

TOPSY. How you does spoke! What you mean by trotters?

CUTE. Why, your feet, Stove Polish.

TOPSY. What does you want me to move my feet for?

CUTE. To tell your mistress, you ebony angel, that a gentleman wishes to see her.

TOPSY. Does you call yourself a gentleman? By golly! you look more like a scar'-crow.

CUTE. Now look here, you Charcoal, don't you be sassy. I'm a gentleman in distress; a done-up speculator; one that has seen better days—long time ago—and better clothes too, by chowder! My creditors are like my boots—they've no soles. I'm a victim to circumstances. I've been through much and survived it. I've taken walking exercise for the benefit of my health; but as I was trying to live on air at the same time, it was a losing speculation, 'cause it gave me such a dreadful appetite.

TOPSY. Golly! you look as if you could eat an ox, horns and all.

CUTE. Well, I calculate I could if he was roasted—it's a speculation I should like to engage in. I have returned like the fellow that run away in Scripture; and if anybody's got a fatted calf they want to kill, all they got to do is to fetch him along. Do you know, Charcoal, that your mistress is a relation of mine?

TOPSY. Is she your uncle?

CUTE. No, no, not quite so near as that. My second cousin married her niece.

TOPSY. And does you want to see Miss Feely?

CUTE. I do. I have come to seek a home beneath her roof, and take care of all the spare change she don't want to use.

TOPSY. Den just yo' follow me, mas'r.

CUTE. Stop! By chowder, I've got a great idee. Say, you Day & Martin, how should you like to enter into a speculation?

TOPSY. Golly! I doesn't know what a spec—spec—cu—what-do-you-call-'um am.

CUTE. Well, now, I calculate I've hit upon about the right thing. Why should I degrade the manly dignity of the Cutes by becoming a beggar—expose myself to the chance of receiving the cold shoulder as a poor relation? By chowder, my blood biles as I think of it! Topsy, you can make my fortune, and your own, too. I've an idee in my head that is worth a million of dollars.

TOPSY. Golly! is your head worth dat? Guess you wouldn't bring dat out South for de whole of you.

CUTE. Don't you be too severe, now, Charcoal; I'm a man of genius. Did you ever hear of Barnum?

TOPSY. Barnum! Barnum! does he live out South?

CUTE. No, he lives in New York. Do you know how he made his fortin?

TOPSY. What is him fortin, hey? Is it something he wears?

CUTE. Chowder, how green you are!

TOPSY. [*Indignantly.*] Sar, I hab you to know I's not green; I's brack.

CUTE. To be sure you are, Day & Martin. I calculate, when a person says another has a fortune, he means he's got plenty of money, Charcoal.

TOPSY. And did he make the money?

CUTE. Sartin sure, and no mistake.

TOPSY. Golly! now I thought money always growed.

CUTE. Oh, git out! You are too cute—you are cuter than I am; and I'm Cute by name and cute by nature. Well, as I was saying, Barnum made his money by exhibiting a *woolly* horse; now wouldn't it be an all-fired speculation to show you as the woolly gal?

TOPSY. You want to make a sight of me?

CUTE. I'll give you half the receipts, by chowder!

TOPSY. Should I have to leave Miss Feely?

CUTE. To be sure you would.

TOPSY. Den you hab to get a woolly gal somewhere else, Mas'r Cute. [*Runs off.*]

CUTE. There's another speculation gone to smash, by chowder! [*Exit.*]

SCENE III. A Rude Chamber. **Tom** is discovered, in old clothes, seated on a stool; he holds in his hand a paper containing a curl of **Eva's** hair. The scene opens to the symphony of "Old Folks at Home."

TOM. I have come to de dark places; I's going through de vale of shadows. My heart sinks at times and feels just like a big lump of lead. Den it gits up in my throat and chokes me till de tears roll out of my eyes; den I take out dis curl of little Miss Eva's hair, and the sight of it brings calm to my mind and I feels strong again. [*Kisses the curl and puts it in his breast—takes out a silver dollar, which is suspended around his neck by a string.*] Dere's de bright silver dollar dat Mas'r George Shelby gave me the day I was sold away from old Kentuck, and I've kept it ever since. Mas'r George must have grown to be a man by this time. I wonder if I shall ever see him again.

SONG.—"*Old Folks at Home.*"

[*Enter* LEGREE, EMMELINE, SAMBO *and* QUIMBO.]

LEGREE. Shut up, you black cuss! Did you think I wanted any of your infernal howling? [*Turns to* EMMELINE.] We're home. [EMMELINE *shrinks from him. He takes hold of her ear.*] You didn't ever wear earrings?

EMMELINE. [*Trembling.*] No, master.

LEGREE. Well, I'll give you a pair, if you're a good girl. You needn't be so frightened; I don't mean to make you work very hard. You'll have fine times with me and live like a lady; only be a good girl.

EMMELINE. My soul sickens as his eyes gaze upon me. His touch makes my very flesh creep.

LEGREE. [*Turns to* TOM, *and points to* SAMBO *and* QUIMBO.] Ye see what ye'd get if ye'd try to run off. These yer boys have been raised to track niggers, and they'd just as soon chaw one on ye up as eat their suppers; so mind yourself. [*To* EMMELINE.] Come, mistress, you go in here with me. [*Taking* EMMELINE'S *hand, and leading her away.*]

EMMELINE. [*Withdrawing her hand, and shrinking back.*] No, no! let me work in the fields; I don't want to be a lady.

LEGREE. Oh! you're going to be contrary, are you? I'll soon take all that out of you.

EMMELINE. Kill me, if you will.

LEGREE. Oh! you want to be killed, do you? Now, come here, you Tom—you see I told you I didn't buy you just for the common work; I mean to promote you and make a driver of you, and to-night ye may jest as well begin to get yer hand in. Now, ye jest take this yer gal, and flog her; ye've seen enough on't to know how.

TOM. I beg mas'r's pardon—hopes mas'r won't set me at that. It's what I ain't used to—never did, and can't do —no way possible.

LEGREE. Ye'll larn a pretty smart chance of things ye never did know before I've done with ye. [*Strikes* TOM *with whip, three blows.—Music chord each blow.*] There! now will ye tell me ye can't do it?

TOM. Yes, mas'r! I'm willing to work night and day, and work while there's life and breath in me; but this yer thing I can't feel it right to do, and, mas'r, I *never* shall do it, *never!*

LEGREE. What! ye black beast! tell *me* ye don't think it right to do what I tell ye! What have any of you cussed cattle to do with thinking what's right? I'll put a stop to it. Why, what do ye think ye are? Maybe ye think yer a gentleman, master Tom, to be telling your master what's right and what ain't! So you pretend it's wrong to flog the gal?

TOM. I think so, mas'r; 'twould be downright cruel, and it's what I never will do, mas'r. If you mean to kill
10 me, kill me; but as to raising my hand agin any one here, I never shall—I'll die first!

LEGREE. Well, here's a pious dog at last, let down among us sinners—powerful holy critter he must be. Here, you rascal! you make believe to be so pious, didn't you never read out of your Bible, "Servants, obey your masters?" Ain't I your master? Didn't I pay twelve hundred dollars, cash, for all there is inside your cussed old black shell? Ain't you mine, body and soul?

TOM. No, no! My soul ain't yours, mas'r; you haven't
20 bought it—ye can't buy it; it's been bought and paid for by one that is able to keep it, and you can't harm it!

LEGREE. I can't? we'll see, we'll see! Here, Sambo! Quimbo! give this dog such a breaking in as he won't get over this month!

EMMELINE. Oh, no! you will not be so cruel—have some mercy! [*Clings to* TOM.]

LEGREE. Mercy? you won't find any in this shop! Away with the black cuss! Flog him within an inch of his life!

[SAMBO *and* QUIMBO *seize* TOM *and drag him up stage.*]

[LEGREE *seizes* EMMELINE, *and throws her. She falls on her knees, with her hands lifted in supplication.—* LEGREE *raises his whip, as if to strike* TOM.—*Picture.*]

SCENE IV. Plain Chamber. Enter **Ophelia**, followed by **Topsy.**

30 OPHELIA. A person inquiring for me, did you say, Topsy?

TOPSY. Yes, missis.

OPHELIA. What kind of a looking man is he?

TOPSY. By golly! he's very queer looking man, anyway; and den he talks so dre'ful funny. What does you think?—yah! yah! he wanted to 'xibite me as de woolly gal! yah! yah!

OPHELIA. Oh! I understand. Some cute Yankee, who wants to purchase you, to make a show of—the heartless
40 wretch!

TOPSY. Dat's just him, missis; dat's just his name. He tole me dat it was Cute—Mr. Cute Speculashum—dat's him.

OPHELIA. What did you say to him, Topsy?

TOPSY. Well, I didn't say much; it was brief and to the point—I tole him I wouldn't leave you, Miss Feely, no how.

OPHELIA. That's right, Topsy; you know you are very comfortable here—you wouldn't fare quite so well if
50 you went away among strangers.

TOPSY. By golly! I know dat; you takes care on me, and makes me good. I don't steal any now, and I don't swar, and I don't dance breakdowns. Oh! I isn't so wicked as I used to was.

OPHELIA. That's right, Topsy; now show the gentleman, or whatever he is, up.

TOPSY. By golly! I guess he won't make much out of Miss Feely. [*Exit.*]

OPHELIA. I wonder who this person can be? Perhaps it is some old acquaintance, who has heard of my arrival,
60 and who comes on a social visit.

[*Enter* CUTE.]

CUTE. Aunt, how do ye do? Well, I swan, the sight of you is good for weak eyes. [*Offers his hand.*]

OPHELIA. [*Coldly drawing back.*] Really, sir, I can't say that I ever had the pleasure of seeing you before.

CUTE. Well, it's a fact that you never did. You see I never happened to be in your neighbourhood afore now. Of course you've heard of me? I'm one of the Cutes—Gumption Cute, the first and only son of Josiah and Maria Cute, of Oniontown, on the Onion river, in
70 the north part of this ere State of Varmount.

OPHELIA. Can't say I ever heard the name before.

CUTE. Well then, I calculate your memory must be a little ricketty. I'm a relation of yours.

OPHELIA. A relation of mine! Why, I never heard of any Cutes in our family.

CUTE. Well, I shouldn't wonder if you never did. Don't you remember your niece, Mary?

OPHELIA. Of course I do. What a shiftless question!

CUTE. Well, you see, my second cousin, Abijah Blake,
80 married her; so you see that makes me a relation of yours.

OPHELIA. Rather a distant one, I should say.

CUTE. By chowder! I'm *near* enough, just at the present.

OPHELIA. Well, you certainly are a sort of connection of mine.

CUTE. Yes, kind of sort of.

OPHELIA. And of course you are welcome to my house, as long as you choose to make it your home.

CUTE. By chowder! I'm booked for the next six months—this isn't a bad speculation.

OPHELIA. I hope you left all your folks well at home?

CUTE. Well, yes, they're pretty comfortably disposed of. Father and mother's dead, and Uncle Josh has gone to California. I am the only representative of the Cutes left.

OPHELIA. There doesn't seem to be a great deal of *you* left. I declare, you are positively in rags.

CUTE. Well, you see, the fact is, I've been speculating —trying to get bank-notes—specie-rags, as they say— but I calculate I've turned out rags of another sort.

OPHELIA. I'm sorry for your ill luck, but I am afraid you have been shiftless.

CUTE. By chowder! I've done all that a fellow could do. You see, somehow, everything I take hold of kind of bursts up.

OPHELIA. Well, well, perhaps you'll do better for the future; make yourself at home. I have got to see to some household matters, so excuse me for a short time. [*Aside.*] Impudent and shiftless! [*Exit.*]

CUTE. By chowder! I rather guess that this speculation will hitch. She's a good-natured old critter; I reckon I'll be a son to her while she lives, and take care of her valuables after she's a defunct departed. I wonder if they keep the vittles in this ere room? Guess not. I've got extensive accommodations for all sorts of eatables. I'm a regular vacuum, throughout—pockets and all. I'm chuck full of emptiness. [*Looks out.*] Holloa! who's this elderly individual coming upstairs? He looks like a compound essence of starch and dignity. I wonder if he isn't another relation of mine. I should like a rich old fellow now for an uncle.

[*Enter* DEACON PERRY.]

DEACON. Ha! a stranger here!

CUTE. How d'ye do?

DEACON. You are a friend to Miss Ophelia, I presume?

CUTE. Well, I rather calculate that I am a leetle more than a friend.

DEACON. [*Aside.*] Bless me! what can he mean by those mysterious words? Can he be her—no, I don't think he can. She said she wasn't—well, at all events, it's very suspicious.

CUTE. The old fellow seems kind of stuck up.

DEACON. You are a particular friend to Miss Ophelia, you say?

CUTE. Well, I calculate I am.

DEACON. Bound to her by any tender tie?

CUTE. It's something more than a tie—it's a regular double-twisted knot.

DEACON. Ah! Just as I suspected. [*Aside.*] Might I inquire the nature of that tie?

CUTE. Well, it's the natural tie of relationship.

DEACON. A relation—what relation!

CUTE. Why, you see, my second cousin, Abijah Blake, married her niece, Mary.

DEACON. Oh! is that all?

CUTE. By chowder, ain't that enough?

DEACON. Then you are not her husband?

CUTE. To be sure I ain't. What put that 'ere idee into your cranium?

DEACON. [*Shaking him vigorously by the hand.*] My dear sir, I'm delighted to see you.

CUTE. Holloa! you ain't going slightly insane, are you?

DEACON. No, no fear of that; I'm only happy, that's all.

CUTE. I wonder if he's been taking a nipper?

DEACON. As you are a relation of Miss Ophelia's, I think it proper that I should make you my confidant; in fact, let you into a little scheme that I have lately conceived.

CUTE. Is it a speculation?

DEACON. Well, it is, just at present; but I trust before many hours to make it a surety.

CUTE. By chowder! I hope it won't serve you the way my speculations have served me. But fire away, old boy, and give us the prospectus.

DEACON. Well, then, my young friend, I have been thinking, ever since Miss Ophelia returned to Vermont, that she was just the person to fill the place of my lamented Molly.

CUTE. Say, you couldn't tell us who your lamented Molly was, could you?

DEACON. Why, the late Mrs. Perry, to be sure.

CUTE. Oh! then the lamented Molly was your wife?

DEACON. She was.

CUTE. And now you wish to marry Miss Ophelia?

DEACON. Exactly.

CUTE. [*Aside.*] Consarn this old porpoise! if I let him do that he'll Jew me out of my living. By chowder! I'll put a spoke in his wheel.

DEACON. Well, what do you say? Will you intercede for me with your aunt?

CUTE. No! bust me up, if I do!

DEACON. No?

CUTE. No, I tell you. I forbid the bans. Now, ain't you a purty individual, to talk about getting married, you old superannuated Methuselah specimen of humanity! Why, you've got one foot in etarnity already, and t'other ain't fit to stand on. Go home and go to bed! have your head shaved, and send for a lawyer to make your will; leave your property to your heirs—if you hain't got any, why leave it to me—I'll take care of it, and charge nothing for the trouble.

DEACON. Really, sir, this language, to one of my standing, is highly indecorous—it's more, sir, than I feel willing to endure, sir. I shall expect an explanation, sir.

CUTE. Now, you see, old gouty toes, you're losing your temper.

DEACON. Sir, I'm a deacon; I never lost my temper in all my life, sir.

CUTE. Now, you see, you're getting excited; you had better go; we can't have a disturbance here!

DEACON. No, sir! I shall not go, sir! I shall not go until I have seen Miss Ophelia. I wish to know if she will countenance this insult.

CUTE. Now keep cool, old stick-in-the-mud! Draw it mild, old timber-toes!

DEACON. Damn it all, sir, what—

CUTE. Oh! only think, now, what would people say to hear a deacon swearing like a trooper?

DEACON. Sir—I—you—this is too much, sir.

CUTE. Well, now, I calculate that's just about my opinion, so we'll have no more of it. Get out of this! start your boots, or by chowder! I'll pitch you from one end of the stairs to the other.

[*Enter* OPHELIA.]

OPHELIA. Hoity toity! What's the meaning of all these loud words.

[*Together.*]

CUTE. Well, you see, Aunt—

DEACON. Miss Ophelia, I beg—

CUTE. Now, look here, you just hush your yap! How can I fix up matters if you keep jabbering?

OPHELIA. Silence! for shame, Mr. Cute. Is that the way you speak to the deacon?

CUTE. Darn the deacon!

OPHELIA. Deacon Perry, what is all this?

DEACON. Madam, a few words will explain everything. Hearing from this person that he was your nephew, I ventured to tell him that I cherished hopes of making you my wife, whereupon he flew into a violent passion, and ordered me out of the house.

OPHELIA. Does this house belong to you or me, Mr. Cute?

CUTE. Well, to you, I reckon.

OPHELIA. Then how dare you give orders in it?

CUTE. Well, I calculated you wouldn't care about marrying old half-a-century there.

OPHELIA. That's enough; I will marry him; and as for you, [*points to the right*] get out.

CUTE. Get out?

OPHELIA. Yes; the sooner the better.

CUTE. Darned if I don't serve him out first though.

[CUTE *makes a dash at* DEACON *who gets behind* OPHELIA. TOPSY *enters with a broom and beats* CUTE *around stage.*—OPHELIA *faints in* DEACON'S *arms.*—CUTE *falls, and* TOPSY *butts him, keeling over him.*—*Quick drop.*]

ACT VI

SCENE I. Dark Landscape. An old, roofless shed. **Tom** is discovered in shed, lying on some old cotton bagging. **Cassy** kneels by his side, holding a cup to his lips.

CASSY. Drink all ye want. I knew how it would be. It isn't the first time I've been out in the night, carrying water to such as you.

TOM. [*Returning cup.*] Thank you, missis.

CASSY. Don't call me missis. I'm a miserable slave like yourself—a lower one than you can ever be! It's no use, my poor fellow, this you've been trying to do. You were a brave fellow. You had the right on your side; but it's all in vain for you to struggle. You are in the Devil's hands: he is the strongest, and you must give up.

TOM. Oh! how can I give up?

CASSY. You see *you* don't know anything about it; I do. Here you are, on a lone plantation, ten miles from any other, in the swamps; not a white person here who could testify, if you were burned alive. There's no law here that can do you, or any of us, the least good; and this man! there's no earthly thing that he is not bad 10 enough to do. I could make one's hair rise, and their teeth chatter, if I should only tell what I've seen and been knowing to here; and it's no use resisting! Did I *want* to live with him? Wasn't I a woman delicately bred? and he!—Father in Heaven! what was he and is he? And yet I've lived with him these five years, and cursed every moment of my life, night and day.

TOM. Oh, heaven! have you quite forgot us poor critters?

CASSY. And what are these miserable low dogs you 20 work with, that you should suffer on their account? Everyone of them would turn against you the first time they get a chance. They are all of them as low and cruel to each other as they can be; there's no use in your suffering to keep from hurting them!

TOM. What made 'em cruel? If I give out, I shall get used to it and grow, little by little, just like 'em. No, no, missis, I've lost everything, wife, and children, and home, and a kind master, and he would have set me free if he'd only lived a day longer—I've lost everything 30 in *this* world, and now I can't lose heaven, too; no, I can't get to be wicked besides all.

CASSY. But it can't be that He will lay sin to our account; he won't charge it to us when we are forced to it; he'll charge it to them that drove us to it. Can I do anything more for you? Shall I give you some more water?

TOM. Oh missis! I wish you'd go to Him who can give you living waters!

CASSY. Go to Him! Where is He? Who is He?

40 TOM. Our Heavenly Father!

CASSY. I used to see the picture of Him, over the altar, when I was a girl; but *he isn't here!* There's nothing here but sin, and long, long despair! There, there, don't talk any more, my poor fellow. Try to sleep, if you can. I must hasten back, lest my absence be noted. Think of me when I am gone, Uncle Tom, and pray, pray for me. [*Exit* CASSY. TOM *sinks back to sleep.*]

94 *Aiken*

SCENE II. Street in New Orleans. Enter **George Shelby**.

GEORGE. At length my mission of mercy is nearly finished; I have reached my journey's end. I have now but to find the house of Mr. St. Clare, re-purchase old 5 Uncle Tom, and convey him back to his wife and children, in old Kentucky. Some one approaches; he may, perhaps, be able to give me the information I require. I will accost him. [*Enter* MARKS.] Pray, sir, can you tell me where Mr. St. Clare dwells?

MARKS. Where I don't think you'll be in a hurry to seek him.

GEORGE. And where is that?

MARKS. In the grave!

GEORGE. Stay, sir! you may be able to give me some 60 information concerning Mr. St. Clare.

MARKS. I beg pardon, sir, I am a lawyer; I can't afford to *give* anything.

GEORGE. But you would have no objections to selling it?

MARKS. Not the slightest.

GEORGE. What do you value it at?

MARKS. Well, say five dollars, that's reasonable.

GEORGE. There they are. [*Gives money.*] Now answer me to the best of your ability. Has the death of 70 St. Clare caused his slaves to be sold?

MARKS. It has.

GEORGE. How were they sold?

MARKS. At auction—they went dirt cheap.

GEORGE. How were they bought—all in one lot?

MARKS. No, they went to different bidders.

GEORGE. Was you present at the sale?

MARKS. I was.

GEORGE. Do you remember seeing a Negro among them called Tom?
80
MARKS. What, Uncle Tom?

GEORGE. The same—who bought him?

MARKS. A Mr. Legree.

GEORGE. Where is his plantation?

MARKS. Up in Louisiana, on the Red River; but a man never could find it unless he had been there before.

GEORGE. Who could I get to direct me there?

MARKS. Well, stranger, I don't know of any one just at present, 'cept myself, could find it for you; it's such an out-of-the-way sort of hole; and if you are a mind to 90 come down handsomely, why, I'll do it.

GEORGE. The reward shall be ample.

MARKS. Enough said, stranger; let's take the steam-boat at once. [Exeunt.]

SCENE III. A Rough Chamber. Enter **Legree**. Sits.

LEGREE. Plague on that Sambo, to kick up this yer row between me and the new hands. [CASSY steals on, and stands behind him.] The fellow won't be fit to work for a week now, right in the press of the season.

CASSY. Yes, just like you.

LEGREE. Hah! you she-devil! you've come back, have you? [Rises.]

CASSY. Yes, I have; come to have my own way, too.

LEGREE. You lie, you jade! I'll be up to my word. Either behave yourself, or stay down in the quarters and fare and work with the rest.

CASSY. I'd rather, ten thousand times, live in the dirtiest hole in the quarters, than be under your hoof!

LEGREE. But you are under my hoof, for all that, that's one comfort; so sit down here and listen to reason. [Grasps her wrists.]

CASSY. Simon Legree, take care! [LEGREE lets go his hold.] You're afraid of me, Simon, and you've reason to be; for I've got the Devil in me!

LEGREE. I believe to my soul you have. After all, Cassy, why can't you be friends with me, as you used to?

CASSY. [Bitterly.] Used to!

LEGREE. I wish, Cassy, you'd behave yourself decently.

CASSY. You talk about behaving decently! and what have you been doing? You haven't even sense enough to keep from spoiling one of your best hands, right in the most pressing season, just for your devilish temper.

LEGREE. I was a fool, it's a fact, to let any such brangle come up; but when Tom set up his will he had to be broke in.

CASSY. You'll never break him in.

LEGREE. Won't I? I'd like to know if I won't! He'll be the first nigger that ever come it round me! I'll break every bone in his body but he shall give up.

[Enter SAMBO with a paper in his hand; he stands bowing.]

LEGREE. What's that, you dog?

SAMBO. It's a witch thing, mas'r.

LEGREE. A what?

SAMBO. Something that niggers gets from witches. Keep 'em from feeling when they's flogged. He had it tied round his neck with a black string.

[LEGREE takes the paper and opens it.—A silver dollar drops on the stage, and a long curl of light hair twines around his finger.]

LEGREE. Damnation. [Stamping and writhing, as if the hair burned him.] Where did this come from? Take it off! burn it up! burn it up! [Throws the curl away.] What did you bring it to me for?

SAMBO. [Trembling.] I beg pardon, mas'r; I thought you would like to see 'um.

LEGREE. Don't you bring me any more of your devilish things. [Shakes his fist at SAMBO who runs off. LEGREE kicks the dollar after him.] Blast it! where did he get that? If it didn't look just like—whoo! I thought I'd forgot that. Curse me if I think there's any such thing as forgetting anything, any how.

CASSY. What is the matter with you, Legree? What is there in a simple curl of fair hair to appal a man like you—you who are familiar with every form of cruelty!

LEGREE. Cassy, to-night the past has been recalled to me—the past that I have so long and vainly striven to forget.

CASSY. Hast aught on this earth power to move a soul like thine?

LEGREE. Yes, for hard and reprobate as I now seem, there has been a time when I have been rocked on the bosom of a mother, cradled with prayers and pious hymns, my now seared brow bedewed with the waters of holy baptism.

CASSY. [Aside.] What sweet memories of childhood can thus soften down that heart of iron.

LEGREE. In early childhood a fair-haired woman has led me, at the sound of Sabbath bells, to worship and to pray. Born of a hard-tempered sire, on whom that gentle woman had wasted a world of unvalued love, I followed in the steps of my father. Boisterous, unruly and tyrannical, I despised all her counsel, and would have none of her reproof, and, at an early age, broke from her to seek my fortunes on the sea. I never came home but once after that; and then my mother, with the yearning of a heart that must love something, and had nothing else to love, clung to me, and sought with passionate prayers and entreaties to win me from a life of sin.

CASSY. That was your day of grace, Legree; then good angels called you, and mercy held you by the hand.

LEGREE. My heart inly relented; there was a conflict, but sin got the victory, and I set all the force of my rough nature against the conviction of my conscience. I drank and swore, was wilder and more brutal than ever. And one night, when my mother, in the last agony of her despair, knelt at my feet, I spurned her from me, threw her senseless on the floor, and with brutal curses fled to my ship.

CASSY. Then the fiend took thee for his own!

LEGREE. The next I heard of my mother was one night while I was carousing among drunken companions. A letter was put in my hands. I opened it, and a lock of long, curling hair fell from it, and twined about my fingers, even as that lock twined but now. The letter told me that my mother was dead, and that dying she blest and forgave me! [Buries his face in his hands.]

CASSY. Why did you not even then renounce your evil ways?

LEGREE. There is a dread, unhallowed necromancy of evil, that turns things sweetest and holiest to phantoms of horror and affright. That pale, loving mother,—her dying prayers, her forgiving love,—wrought in my demoniac heart of sin only as a damning sentence, bringing with it a fearful looking for judgment and fiery indignation.

CASSY. And yet you would not strive to avert the doom that threatened you.

LEGREE. I burned the lock of hair and I burned the letter; and when I saw them hissing and crackling in the flame, inly shuddered as I thought of everlasting fires! I tried to drink and revel, and swear away the memory; but often in the deep night, whose solemn stillness arraigns the soul in forced communion with itself, I have seen that pale mother rising by my bedside, and felt the soft twining of that hair around my fingers, 'till the cold sweat would roll down my face, and I would spring from my bed in horror—horror! [Falls in chair.—After a pause.] What the devil ails me? Large drops of sweat stand on my forehead, and my heart beats heavy and thick with fear. I thought I saw something white rising and glimmering in the gloom before me, and it seemed to bear my mother's face! I know one thing; I'll let that fellow Tom alone, after this. What did I want with his cussed paper? I believe I am bewitched sure enough! I've been shivering and sweating ever since! Where did he get that hair? It couldn't have been that! I burn'd that up, I know I did! It would be a joke if hair could rise from the dead! I'll have Sambo and Quimbo up here to sing and dance one of their dances, and keep off these horrid notions. Here, Sambo! Quimbo! [Exit.]

CASSY. Yes, Legree, that golden tress was charmed; each hair had in it a spell of terror and remorse for thee, and was used by a mightier power to bind thy cruel hands from inflicting uttermost evil on the helpless! [Exit.]

SCENE IV. Street. Enter Marks, meeting Cute, who enters, dressed in an old faded uniform.

MARKS. By the land, stranger, but it strikes me that I've seen you somewhere before.

CUTE. By chowder! do you know now, that's just what I was a going to say?

MARKS. Isn't your name Cute?

CUTE. You're right, I calculate. Yours is Marks, I reckon.

MARKS. Just so.

CUTE. Well, I swow, I'm glad to see you. [They shake hands.] How's your wholesome?

MARKS. Hearty as ever. Well, who would have thought of ever seeing you again. Why, I thought you was in Vermont?

CUTE. Well, so I was. You see I went there after that rich relation of mine—but the speculation didn't turn out well.

MARKS. How so?

CUTE. Why, you see, she took a shine to an old fellow —Deacon Abraham Perry—and married him.

MARKS. Oh, that rather put your nose out of joint in that quarter.

CUTE. Busted me right up, I tell you. The deacon did the handsome thing though; he said if I would leave the neighbourhood and go out South again, he'd stand the damage. I calculate I didn't give him much time to change his mind, and so, you see, here I am again.

MARKS. What are you doing in that soldier rig?

CUTE. Oh, this is my sign.

MARKS. Your sign?

CUTE. Yes; you see, I'm engaged just at present in an all-fired good speculation; I'm a Fillibusterow.

MARKS. A what?

CUTE. A Fillibusterow! Don't you know what that is? It's Spanish for Cuban Volunteer; and means a chap that goes the whole porker for glory and all that ere sort of thing.

MARKS. Oh! you've joined the order of the Lone Star!

CUTE. You've hit it. You see I bought this uniform at a second-hand clothing store; I puts it on and goes to a benevolent individual and I says to him,—appealing to his feelings,—I'm one of the fellows that went to Cuba and got massacred by the bloody Spaniards. I'm in a destitute condition—give me a trifle to pay my passage back, so I can whop the tyrannical cusses and avenge my brave fellow soger what got slewed there.

MARKS. How pathetic!

CUTE. I tell you it works up the feelings of benevolent individuals dreadfully. It draws tears from their eyes and money from their pockets. By chowder! one old chap gave me a hundred dollars to help on the cause.

MARKS. I admire a genius like yours.

CUTE. But I say, what are you up to?

MARKS. I am the travelling companion of a young gentleman by the name of Shelby, who is going to the plantation of a Mr. Legree, on the Red River, to buy an old darky who used to belong to his father.

CUTE. Legree—Legree? Well, now, I calculate I've heard that ere name afore.

MARKS. Do you remember that man who drew a bowie knife on you in New Orleans?

CUTE. By chowder! I remember the circumstance just as well as if it was yesterday; but I can't say that I recollect much about the man, for you see I was in something of a hurry about that time and didn't stop to take a good look at him.

MARKS. Well, that man was this same Mr. Legree.

CUTE. Do you know, now, I should like to pay that critter off?

MARKS. Then I'll give you an opportunity.

CUTE. Chowder! how will you do that?

MARKS. Do you remember the gentleman that interfered between you and Legree?

CUTE. Yes—well?

MARKS. He received the blow that was intended for you, and died from the effects of it. So, you see, Legree is a murderer, and we are the only witnesses of the deed. His life is in our hands.

CUTE. Let's have him right up and make him dance on nothing to the tune of Yankee Doodle!

MARKS. Stop a bit. Don't you see a chance for a profitable speculation?

CUTE. A speculation! Fire away, don't be bashful; I'm the man for a speculation.

MARKS. I have made a deposition to the Governor of the State of all the particulars of that affair at Orleans.

CUTE. What did you do that for?

MARKS. To get a warrant for his arrest.

CUTE. Oh! and have you got it?

MARKS. Yes; here it is. [*Takes out paper.*]

CUTE. Well, now, I don't see how you are going to make anything by that bit of paper?

MARKS. But I do. I shall say to Legree, I have got a warrant against you for murder; my friend, Mr. Cute, and myself are the only witnesses who can appear against you. Give us a thousand dollars, and we will tear up the warrant and be silent.

CUTE. Then Mr. Legree forks over a thousand dollars, and your friend Cute pockets five hundred of it. Is that the calculation?

MARKS. If you will join me in the undertaking.

CUTE. I'll do it, by chowder!

MARKS. Your hand to bind the bargain.

CUTE. I'll stick by you thro' thick and thin.

MARKS. Enough said.

CUTE. Then shake. [*They shake hands.*]

MARKS. But I say, Cute, he may be contrary and show fight.

CUTE. Never mind, we've got the law on our side, and we're bound to stir him up. If he don't come down handsomely, we'll present him with a neck-tie made of hemp!

MARKS. I declare you're getting spunky.

CUTE. Well, I reckon I am. Let's go and have something to drink. Tell you what, Marks, if we don't get *him,* we'll have his hide, by chowder! [*Exeunt, arm in arm.*]

SCENE V. Rough Chamber. Enter **Legree**, followed by **Sambo.**

LEGREE. Go and send Cassy to me.

SAMBO. Yes, mas'r. [*Exit.*]

LEGREE. Curse the woman! she's got a temper worse than the devil! I shall do her an injury one of these days, if she isn't careful. [*Re-enter* SAMBO, *frightened.*] What's the matter with you, you black scoundrel?

SAMBO. S'help me, mas'r, she isn't dere.

LEGREE. I suppose she's about the house somewhere?

SAMBO. No, she isn't, mas'r; I's been all over de house and I can't find nothing of her nor Emmeline.

LEGREE. Bolted, by the Lord! Call out the dogs! saddle my horse! Stop! are you sure they really have gone?

SAMBO. Yes, mas'r; I's been in every room 'cept the haunted garret, and dey wouldn't go dere.

LEGREE. I have it! Now, Sambo, you jest go and walk that Tom up here, right away! [*Exit* SAMBO.] The old cuss is at the bottom of this yer whole matter; and I'll have it out of his infernal black hide, or I'll know the reason why! I *hate* him—I *hate* him! And isn't he *mine*? 10 Can't I do what I like with him? Who's to hinder, I wonder?

[TOM *is dragged on by* SAMBO *and* QUIMBO.]

LEGREE. [*Grimly confronting* TOM.] Well, Tom, do you know I've made up my mind to *kill* you?

TOM. It's very likely, mas'r.

LEGREE. I—have—done—just—that—thing, Tom, unless you tell me what do you know about these yer gals? [TOM *is silent.*] D'ye hear? Speak!

TOM. I hain't got anything to tell, mas'r.

LEGREE. Do you dare to tell me, you old black rascal, 20 you don't know? Speak! Do you know anything?

TOM. I know, mas'r; but I can't tell anything. *I can die!*

LEGREE. Hark ye, Tom! ye think, 'cause I have let you off before, I don't mean what I say; but, this time, I have made *up my mind,* and counted the cost. You've always stood it out agin me; now, *I'll conquer ye or kill ye!* one or t'other. I'll count every drop of blood there is in you, and take 'em, one by one 'till ye give up!

TOM. Mas'r, if you was sick, or in trouble, or dying, and I could save, I'd *give* you my heart's blood; and, if 30 taking every drop of blood in this poor old body would save your precious soul, I'd give 'em freely. Do the worst you can, my troubles will be over soon; but if you don't repent, yours won't never end.

[LEGREE *strikes* TOM *down with the butt of his whip.*]

LEGREE. How do you like that?

SAMBO. He's most gone, mas'r!

TOM. [*Rises feebly on his hands.*] There ain't no more you can do! I forgive you with all my soul. [*Sinks back, and is carried off by* SAMBO *and* QUIMBO.]

LEGREE. I believe he's done for finally. Well, his 40 mouth is shut up at last—that's one comfort.

[*Enter* GEORGE SHELBY, MARKS *and* CUTE.]
Strangers! Well, what do you want?

GEORGE. I understand that you bought in New Orleans a Negro named Tom?

LEGREE. Yes, I did buy such a fellow, and a devil of a bargain I had of it, too! I believe he's trying to die, but I don't know as he'll make it out.

GEORGE. Where is he? Let me see him!

SAMBO. Dere he is! [*Points to* TOM.]

LEGREE. How dare you speak? [*Drives* SAMBO *and* QUIMBO *off.*—GEORGE *exits.*]

CUTE. Now's the time to nab him.

MARKS. How are you, Mr. Legree?

LEGREE. What the devil brought you here?

MARKS. This little bit of paper. I arrest you for the murder of Mr. St. Clare. What do you say to that?

LEGREE. This is my answer! [*Makes a blow at* MARKS, *who dodges, and* CUTE *receives the blow—he*

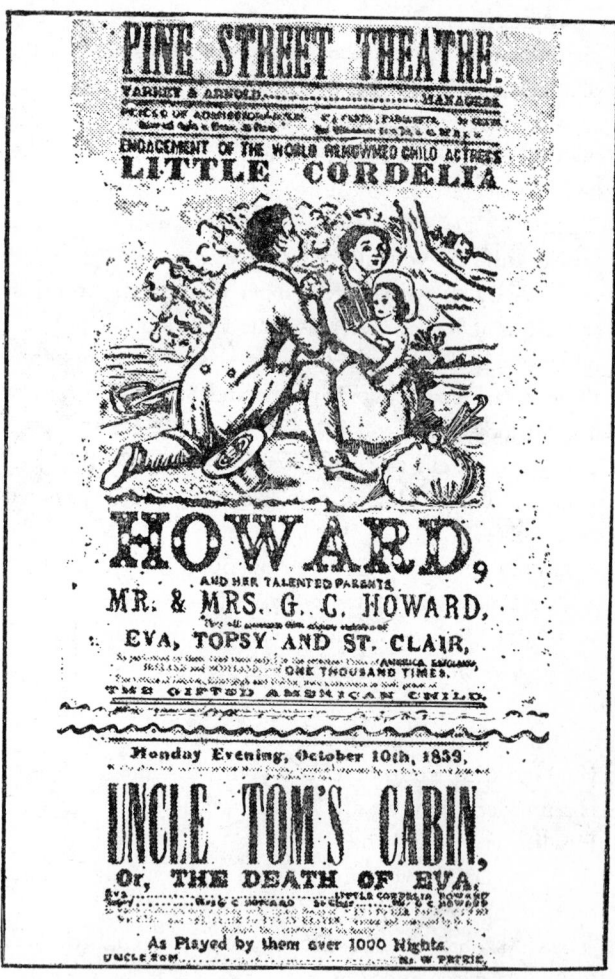

Poster advertising a performance of Uncle Tom's Cabin *by the Howards. From the Harvard Theatre Collection*

cries out and runs off. MARKS *fires at* LEGREE *and follows* CUTE.] I am hit!—the game's up! [*Falls dead.* QUIMBO *and* SAMBO *return and carry him off laughing.*]

[GEORGE SHELBY *enters, supporting* TOM—*Music. They advance and* TOM *falls, centre.*]

GEORGE. Oh! dear Uncle Tom! do wake—do speak once more! look up! Here's Master George—your own little Master George. Don't you know me?

TOM. [*Opening his eyes and speaking in a feeble tone.*] Mas'r George! Bless de Lord! It's all I wanted! They hav'n't forgot me! It warms my soul; it does my
10 old heart good! Now I shall die content!

GEORGE. You sha'n't die! you mustn't die, nor think of it. I have come to buy you, and take you home.

TOM. Oh, Mas'r George, you're too late. The Lord has bought me, and is going to take me home.

GEORGE. Oh! don't die. It will kill me—it will break my heart to think what you have suffered, poor, poor fellow!

TOM. Don't call me poor fellow. I *have* been poor fellow; but that's all past and gone now, I'm right in the door, going into glory! Oh, Mas'r George! *Heaven* 20 *has come!* I've got the victory! the Lord has given it to me! Glory be to His name! [*Dies.*]

[*Solemn music*—GEORGE *covers* UNCLE TOM *with his cloak, and kneels over him. Clouds work on and conceal them, and then work off.*]

SCENE VII. Gorgeous clouds, tinted with sunlight. **Eva**, robed in white, is discovered on the back of a milk-white dove, with expanded wings, as if just soaring upward. Her hands are extended in benediction over **St. Clare** and **Uncle Tom**, who are kneeling and gazing up to her. Impressive music. Slow curtain.

1852

William J. Grayson

1788 · 1863

William Sumner Jenkins, in his *Pro-Slavery Thought in the Old South,* has shown that the defense of slavery, always roused by attack, developed gradually from apology to militance. Before 1820 Southerners tended to argue either that they were not responsible for the institution, and should be given time to work out in their own way the problem forced upon them by English and Yankee slave-traders, or that the Negro race was so inferior that slavery was its natural condition. A second stage of Southern opinion shows a more positive appeal to the authoritative sanctions of Scripture and history. Finally, and chiefly after 1835, as the abolition movement gained in fervor, Southerners came to study their "peculiar institution" and to glorify it as the best of all possible solutions to the economic and moral puzzles of a biracial and agricultural society.

Of the hundreds of books and pamphlets which make up proslavery literature the most readable today are probably those by William J. Grayson. As one of his biographers has said, Grayson "was a very temperate advocate of state rights, and a very amiable defender of Southern institutions." Calhoun doubtless had a sharper mind when it came to political analysis, and other Southern leaders loomed larger than Grayson in their day: William Harper (*Memoir on Slavery,* 1838), Thomas R. Dew (*Essay on Slavery,* 1849), George Fitzhugh (*Sociology for the South,* 1854), and Albert Taylor Bledsoe (*Essay on Liberty and Slavery,* 1856), to name a few examples. Grayson, however, succeeded in condensing most of the favorite Southern arguments into short space and reasonably attractive form, so that he provides perhaps the most convenient view of the defense of the institution which nearly split the Union.

Grayson was a down-state South Carolinian, born in Beaufort District in 1788. From Columbia College, later the University of South Carolina, where he was graduated in 1809, he proceeded to law and politics. He sat in the state legislature, served two terms in the national House of Representatives, and from 1841 until 1853 was Collector of the Port of Charleston. In the conservative literary circles of Charleston he had a leading place as a contributor to the newspapers and to such magazines as *DeBow's Review* and the *Southern Literary Messenger.* Unlike Calhoun he rejected secession as an instrument to obtain what the South wanted, and a letter to Governor Seabrook, published in 1850, helped to halt a strong movement for separation. His Unionist sentiment, however, did not keep him from defending slavery, first in a series of essays published in the Charleston *Courier* and reprinted as *Letters to Curtius* (1851) and then in the poem for which he is best known today, *The Hireling and the Slave* (1854). He was also the author of a number of pamphlets and a biography of his friend and college classmate, James Louis Petigru. The last-named book appeared in 1866, three years after Grayson's death; he who reads it now can find between the lines its author's deep grief at the tragedy of the Civil War.

Like most of his Charleston contemporaries Grayson was somewhat old-fashioned in his literary tastes, happier with Dryden and Pope than with most of the poets of his own time. For reasons which he gives in his Preface he chose to write his best-remembered poem in heroic couplets. As a poet he can scarcely merit much attention. His ideas, however, were those of a class and a time which the serious student, observing the South of the present day, cannot afford to ignore. As Parrington has said, Grayson was "an intelligent and humane writer who might be blind to certain evils in slavery but whose eyes were open to the social ills that grew rankly in the muck of industrialism." Southern agrarianism still has its force as one of the recurrent protests against mechanization in American life. Its roots are to be found in the views of the planter aristocracy which Grayson ably represented.

Selected Poems by William J. Grayson, selected and compiled by Mrs. W. H. Armstrong, with introd. by J. J. Dickinson, New York and Washington, 1907 • V. L. Parrington, The Romantic Revolution in America, 1800-1860, New York, 1927 • G. A. Wauchope, "William John Grayson," Library of Southern Literature, ed. E. A. Alderman and others, Atlanta, 1907, V, 2011-2073 • W. S. Jenkins, Pro-Slavery Thought in the Old South, Chapel Hill, 1935

From

The Hireling and the Slave

Grayson's most ambitious poem consists of nearly sixteen hundred lines in heroic couplets, together with the Preface reprinted here and more than twenty pages of explanatory notes (of which the longest have been omitted). He argues that the state of the slave is essentially the same as that of the pauperized workman of England; both are forced to labor hard for their subsistence. The hireling, however, does not always obtain his reward, being subject to starvation, vice, brutality, military service, and expulsion from his home—evils which the slave ordinarily escapes. Part I describes the miserable condition of the free laborer and attacks the meddling of abolitionists. The portion here reprinted is that directed at Harriet Beecher Stowe, together with the concluding summary of the advantages of the slave system of economy. Part II is largely an account of the pleasures of plantation life, of which the first portion is selected here. Its pictures of cabin life, Christmas pleasures, dancing, and church worship are the type of thing which Southern writers of the postwar era recalled with nostalgia. Note that Grayson appealed strongly to nationalistic, anti-British feeling. In lines 743-758 of Part I he effectively presents the ruling-class philosophy, with its emphasis upon order and industry. The vitriolic treatment of Mrs. Stowe and the contemptuous allusions to "Utopian" reformers are significant revelations of the Southern mind in the 1850's.

The malignant abuse lavished on the slaveholders of America by writers in this country and England can be accounted for but in one way consistently with any degree of charitable consideration for the slanderers. They have no knowledge of the thing abused. They substitute an ideal of their own contriving for the reality. They regard slavery as a system of chains, whips, and tortures. They consider its abuses as its necessary condition, and a cruel master its fair representative. Mr. Clarkson took up the subject, originally, as a fit one for a college exercise in rhetoric, and it became a rhetorical exercise for life to himself and his followers. With these people the cruelty of slavery is an affair of tropes and figures. But they have dealt so long in metaphorical fetters and prisons, that they have brought themselves to believe that the Negroes work in chains and live in dungeons.

To prove the evils of slavery, they collect, from all quarters, its abuses, and show the same regard for fairness and common sense as they would do to gather all the atrocities of their own country committed by husbands and wives, parents and children, masters and servants, priest and people, and denounce these several relations in life in consequence of their abuses.

The laborer suffers wrong and cruelty in England, but they say it is against the law, against public opinion; he may apply to the courts for redress; these are open to him. Cruelty to the slave is equally against the law. It is equally condemned by public opinion; and as to the courts of law being open to the pauper hireling, we may remember the reply of Sheridan to a similar remark, Yes, and so are the London hotels: justice and a good dinner at a public house are equally within his reach. If, in consequence of the evils incident to hireling labor—because there are severe, heartless, grinding employers, and miserable, starving hirelings, it were proposed to abolish hireling labor, it would be quite as just and logical as the argument to abolish slavery because there are sufferings among slaves, and hard hearts among masters. The cruelty or suffering is no more a necessary part of the one system than of the other. Notwithstanding its abuses and miseries, the hireling system works beneficially with white laborers; and so also, notwithstanding hard masters, slavery, among a Christian people, is advantageous to the Negro. But to establish the

This pro-slavery cartoon is one of a pair entitled "Black and White Slaves." The companion picture appears on page 107. Courtesy of The New-York Historical Society, New York City

hireling system with Africans would be as wise as to endeavor to bestow the constitutional government of England on Ashantee or Dahomey. In both cases there would be an equal amount of abstract truth and practical absurdity.

Slavery is that system of labor which exchanges subsistence for work, which secures a life-maintenance from the master to the slave, and gives a life-labor from the slave to the master. The slave is an apprentice for life, and owes his labor to his master; the master owes support, during life, to the slave. Slavery is the Negro system of labor. He is lazy and improvident. Slavery makes all work, and it insures homes, food, and clothing for all. It permits no idleness, and it provides for sickness, infancy, and old age. It allows no tramping or skulking, and it knows no pauperism.

This is the whole system substantially. All cruelty is an abuse; does not belong to the institution; is now pun-

Text: The Hireling and Slave, Chicora, and Other Poems, Charleston, 1856, the second edition of the title poem • 10 Clarkson, Thomas Clarkson (1760-1846), English abolitionist, whose interest in slavery was roused by the subject set for a Latin essay competition at Cambridge, 1785 • 31 Sheridan, Richard Brinsley Sheridan (1751-1816), English dramatist and statesman, famous for his championship of the poor • 48 Ashantee or Dahomey, Negro kingdoms in West Africa, now colonial dependencies of Great Britain and France, respectively

The Hireling and the Slave 101

ished, and may be in time prevented. The abuses of slavery are as open to all reforming influences as those of any other civil, social, or political condition. The improvement in the treatment of the slave is as marked as in that of any other laboring class in the world. If it be true of the English soldier or sailor that his condition has been ameliorated in the last fifty years, it is quite as true of the Negro.

If slavery is subject to abuses, it has its advantages also. It establishes more permanent, and, therefore, kinder relations between capital and labor. It removes what Stuart Mill calls "the widening and imbittering feud between the class of labor and the class of capital." It draws the relation closer between master and servant. It is not an engagement for days or weeks, but for life. There is no such thing with slavery as a laborer for whom nobody cares or provides. The most wretched feature in hireling labor is the isolated, miserable creature who has no home, no work, no food, and in whom no one is particularly interested. *This is seen among hirelings only.*

The sale of slaves is thought to be a great evil to the slave. But what is it substantially more than a transfer of labor from one employer to another? Is this an evil to the laborer? Would it be considered an evil by the European hireling if the laws required every master, before he dismissed his workmen, to secure to them another employer? Would it be an evil to the hireling to be certain of obtaining work—to be safe from the misery of having no employer, no work, while he is starving for bread? The sale of the slave is the form in which the laws secure the slave from this misery of the hireling—secure to him a certainty of employment and a certainty of subsistence. The hireling has neither.

I do not say that slavery is the best system of labor, but only that it is the best for the Negro in this country. In a nation composed of the same race or similar races, where the laborer is intelligent, industrious, and provident, money-wages may be better than subsistence. Even under all advantages there are great defects in the hireling system, for which, hitherto, no statesman has discovered an adequate remedy. In hireling states there are thousands of idlers, trampers, poachers, smugglers, drunkards, and thieves, who make theft a profession. There are thousands who suffer for want of food and clothing, from inability to obtain them. For these two classes—those who will not work, and those who cannot—there is no sufficient provision. Among slaves there are no trampers, idlers, smugglers, poachers, and none suffer from want. Every one is made to work, and no one is permitted to starve. Slavery does for the Negro what European schemers in vain attempt to do for the hireling. It secures work and subsistence for all. It secures more order and subordination also. The master is a Commissioner of the Poor on every plantation, to provide food, clothing, medicine, houses, for his people. He is a police-officer to prevent idleness, drunkeness, theft, or disorder. I do not mean by formal appointment of law, but by virtue of his relation to his slaves. There is, therefore, no starvation among slaves. There are, comparatively, few crimes. If there are paupers in slave states, they are the hirelings of other countries, who have run away from their homes. Pauperism began with them when serfage was abolished.

But you must confess, it is said, that slavery is an evil. True enough; in the same sense in which the hireling's hard labor is an evil. But the poet tells us that there are worse things in the world than hard labor, "withouten that would come a heavier bale;" and so there are worse things for the Negro than slavery in a Christian land. Archbishop Hughes, in his late visit to Cuba, asked the Africans if they wished to return to their native country; the answer was always *no.* If the African is happier here than in his own country, can we say that, for him, the establishment of slavery is an evil? If the master is contented with his part in the system, with what reason can we regard it as an evil, so far as he is concerned? Slaves and masters are equally satisfied. The discontented are those who are neither.

What more can be required of slavery, in reference to the Negro, than has been done? It has made him, from

---

12 **Mill,** John Stuart Mill (1806-1873), English writer on politics and economics. His Principles of Political Economy (1848) contains numerous comments to this effect, but the editors have not located the exact sentence quoted • 54 **order and subordination.** "One of the best arrangements for the relief of the hireling laborer is the provision made in France of houses where the children of laborers are taken in when the laborers go to work in the morning, are carefully attended during the day, and restored to the parents on their return at night. A similar provision for the care of children is found on every plantation."—Grayson • 67 **the poet,** James Thomson (1700-1748), in The Castle of Indolence (1748) • 71 **Hughes,** John Hughes (1797-1864), first archbishop of the Roman Catholic archdiocese of New York

a savage, an orderly and efficient laborer; it supports him in comfort and peace; it restrains his vices; it improves his mind, morals, and manners; it instructs him in Christian knowledge.

But the quarrel is with the master, and the design is to calumniate and injure him. And why this attack on the master? Who, among its pretended friends, will dare to say that they have done for the African race what the slaveholders of North America have done and are doing? What Abolitionist has bestowed on the Negro the same enduring patience, the same useful education, the same care and attendance? Who among them has done, or given, or sacrificed as much? Under the master's care, the miserable black savage has been fed, clothed, instructed in useful arts, and made an important contributor to the business and enjoyments of the world. What have the Abolitionists done, what have they given, for the Negro race? They use the slave for the purposes of self-glorification only, indifferent about his present or future condition. They are ambitious to bring about a great social revolution—what its effects may be they do not care to inquire.

All Christians believe that the affairs of the world are directed by Providence for wise and good purposes. The coming of the Negro to North America makes no exception to the rule. His transportation was a rude mode of emigration; the only practicable one in his case; not attended with more wretchedness than the emigrant ship often exhibits even now, notwithstanding the passenger law. What the purpose of his coming is we may not presume to judge. But we can see much good already resulting from it—good to the Negro in his improved condition; to the country whose rich fields he has cleared of the forest, and made productive in climates unfit for the labor of the white man; to the Continent of Africa in furnishing, as it may ultimately, the only means for civilizing its people.

The end of slavery, then, would seem to be, present good to the slave himself, to the country in which he labors and the world at large, and future good to his race. Whether Mr. Clarkson or Lord Carlisle approve or disapprove of the mode in which it has pleased divine Providence to bring all this about, the event will probably be the same. It may be doubted whether these gentlemen and their friends could have administered the affairs of the world more wisely, whatever our opinion may be of their wisdom or benevolence. As they will never have the power to try, this must remain among the other unsettled questions that perplex the ingenuity of mankind.

There is, however, a plain, practicable mode in which these anti-slavery zealots may confer freedom on thousands, year after year, without offense to any party. The plan is simple and easy. Let them show their sympathy for the Negro, not by eloquent speeches, but more eloquent acts; not with sentiment, but with sovereigns. They can buy any number of Negroes and carry them where they please. For such a purpose the government would not object. Efficient laborers are wanted in the West Indies. Here is a ready way to procure them. They may, in this manner, bestow freedom on many of the slaves of America, confer a benefit on their colonies, and gratify their own excited sensibilities with something more profound than unprofitable words. They feel profoundly for the Negro; let them feel to the amount of a million a year. This would be better than bringing Coolies from Asia and Negroes from Africa by a system of very doubtful character. It would convince the world that their sympathy is an honest one, and not the offspring of vanity or arrogance.

An ingenious lady of South Carolina, in a very admirable letter, has made a similar proposal to the Duchess of Sutherland. But Her Grace is a near relation of the priest in the fable, who refused a half crown to a suppliant, but was ready enough to give him a blessing. The Abolitionists all belong to this benevolent class of world-menders, who are willing at all times to help every body, if it cost them no more than pretty phrases.

In the remarks made in reference to the condition of the hireling in Europe—of England especially—I have no feeling but compassion for the unfortunate paupers, and intend no reproach to their country. I venerate

41 Lord Carlisle, G. W. F. Howard (1802-1864), seventh Earl of Carlisle. He was one of the philanthropists to whom Mrs. Stowe sent copies of Uncle Tom's Cabin and who entertained her when she visited England in 1853 • 73 Duchess of Sutherland, Harriet Elizabeth Georgiana Leveson-Gower (1806-1868), wife of the second Duke of Sutherland. After reading Uncle Tom's Cabin she led a group of prominent Englishwomen in the framing of An Affectionate and Christian Address (1853), a petition signed by over 500,000 women urging their American sisters to work for the abolition of slavery

England as the great mother of nations, as our teacher in law, literature, civil and political liberty. The facts relating to the poverty, vice, brutality, and ignorance of the British laborer are taken, as may be seen from the notes attached, from English authorities; they can be multiplied a hundred fold. In adverting to them, I have merely desired to show that there is a poor and suffering class in all countries, the richest and most civilized not excepted—laborers who get their daily bread by 10 daily work, and that the slave is as well provided for as any other. The poor we shall have with us always; and whether the poor hireling or the poor slave is most the object of pity or subject of distress, is the only question proposed, and the true one at issue.

In comparing their several conditions, no contempt is implied, certainly none intended for the situation of the hireling poor. All honest labor is worthy of honor, that of the faithful slave not less so than any other. Moralists are accustomed to weigh the advantages and 20 evils of the highest and lowest, the palace and cottage; what forbids us to do so with the good and ill of the two humblest stations of civilized life?

It may be thought unnecessary to invite public attention again to the subject of slavery. But if the subject be trite, it is also of incalculable and unceasing interest. I have endeavored to diversify the mode, if not the matter of the argument, by throwing the remarks offered into verse. I have done so, not only for the reason assigned, but with the additional purpose of of- 30 fering some variety to the poetic forms that are almost universally prevalent. The poetry of the day is, for the most part, subtile and transcendental in its character. Every sentiment, reflection, or description is wrought into elaborate modes of expression from remote and fanciful analogies. The responses of the Muses have become as mystical and sometimes as obscure as those of more ancient oracles, and disdain the older and homelier forms of English verse.

It has occurred to me that a return to the more sober 40 style of an earlier period may not be an unreasonable experiment on the public taste. The fashion in dress and furniture now and then goes back a century or two; why not the fashion of verse? The school of Dryden and Pope is not entirely forgotten. May we not imitate the poetry of Queen Anne's time as well as the tables and chairs? The common measure of that period, applied to a didactic subject, may diversify the dishes pre-

sented to the public, and provide for its appetite the same kind of relief that bread and butter or beef and pudding would offer after a long indulgence in more 50 refined and elaborate dishes. The most fastidious appetite may tolerate an occasional change of diet, and exchange dainties now and then for plainer fare.

FROM PART FIRST

There Stowe, with prostituted pen, assails
One half her country in malignant tales;
Careless, like Trollope, whether truth she tells,
And anxious only how the libel sells,
To slander's mart she furnishes supplies,
And feeds its morbid appetite for lies
On fictions fashioned with malicious art,
The venal pencil, and malignant heart,
With fact distorted, inference unsound,
Creatures in fancy, not in nature found—   610
Chaste Quadroon virgins, saints of sable hue,
Martyrs, than zealous Paul more tried and true,
Demoniac masters, sentimental slaves,
Mulatto cavaliers, and Creole knaves—
Monsters each portrait drawn, each story told!
What then? The book may bring its weight in gold;
Enough! upon the crafty rule she leans,
That makes the purpose justify the means,
Concocts the venom, and, with eager gaze,
To Glasgow flies for patron, pence, and praise,   620
And for a slandered country finds rewards
In smiles or sneers of duchesses and lords.

For profits and applauses poor as these,
To the false tale she adds its falser Keys

---

603 **Trollope,** Mrs. Frances M. Trollope (1780-1863), English writer, author of **Domestic Manners of the Americans** (1832), a book much resented in the United States • 620 **To Glasgow . . . praise.** "Among her profits for Uncle Tom, Mrs. Stowe received a penny apiece subscription in Scotland from the laboring people, who starve sometimes for the want of potatoes."—Grayson • 622 **In smiles . . . lords.** In a long note Grayson suggests that Mrs. Stowe has overlooked cannibalism as a charge against the slaveholders. "It will be as authentic as the rest of her facts, and as readily believed by her Northern and European readers" • 624 **Keys.** "Mrs. Stowe has published what she calls a Key to her tale. It is a compilation of all the slanders and crimes among slaveholders; just as she would write a story denouncing matrimony, and make a Key, from the courts or gossiping chronicles, of all the cruelties, murders, and adulteries of husbands and wives, representing the crimes as the normal condition of the relation."—Grayson

Of gathered slanders—her ignoble aim,
With foes to traffic in her country's shame.

Strange power of nature, from whose efforts flow
Such diverse forms as Nightingale and Stowe!
One glares a torch of discord; one a star
Of blessing shines amid the wrecks of war;   630
One prone to libel; one to deeds of love;
The vulture-spirit one, and one the dove;
In various joys their various natures deal,
One leaves her home to wound it, one to heal;
That to expose its sorrows, not deplore;
To help and cheer, this seeks a foreign shore.

Far from her country, where Marmora flows,
On Mercy's errand England's daughter goes,
To tend the suffering sick with woman's care,
To snatch the bleeding soldier from despair;   640
Bend o'er his couch, his languid head sustain,
With tender hand assuage the pangs of pain,
Watch o'er the dying moments of the brave,
And smooth, at least, his passage to the grave;
Love's labor this, and—her's no common fame!
With the heart's homage millions bless her name.

Not such with Stowe, the wish or power to please,
She finds no joys in gentle deeds like these;
A moral scavenger, with greedy eye,
In social ills her coarser labors lie;   650
On fields where vice eludes the light of day,
She hunts up crimes as beagles hunt their prey;
Gleans every dirty nook—the felon's jail,
And hangman's mem'ry, for detraction's tale,
Snuffs up pollution with a pious air,
Collects a rumor here, a slander there;
With hatred's ardor gathers Newgate spoils,
And trades for gold the garbage of her toils.

In sink and sewer thus, with searching eye,
Through mud and slime unhappy wretches pry;   660
In fetid puddles dabble with delight,
Search every filthy gathering of the night;
Fish from its depths, and to the spacious bag
Convey with care the black, polluted rag;
With reeking waifs secure the nightly bed,
And turn their noisome stores to daily bread.

These use the Negro, a convenient tool,
That yields substantial gain or party rule,
Gives what without it they could never know,
To Chase distinction, courtly friends to Stowe,   670
To Parker, themes for miracles of rant,
And Beecher, blesses with new gifts of cant.
The master's task has been the black to train,
To form his mind, his passions to restrain;
With anxious care and patience to impart
The knowledge that subdues the savage heart,
To give the Gospel lessons that control
The rudest breast, and renovate the soul—
Who does, or gives as much, of all who raise
Their sland'rous cry for foreign pence or praise;   680
Of all the knaves who clamor and declaim
For party power or philanthropic fame,
Or use the Negro's fancied wrongs and woes
As pretty themes for maudlin verse or prose?

Taught by the master's efforts, by his care
Fed, clothed, protected many a patient year,
From trivial numbers now to millions grown,
With all the white man's useful arts their own,
Industrious, docile, skilled in wood and field,
To guide the plow, the sturdy axe to wield,   690
The Negroes schooled by slavery embrace
The highest portion of the Negro race;
And none the savage native will compare,
Of barbarous Guinea, with its offspring here.

If bound to daily labor while he lives,
His is the daily bread that labor gives;
Guarded from want, from beggary secure,
He never feels what hireling crowds endure,
Nor knows, like them, in hopeless want to crave,
For wife and child, the comforts of the slave,   700
Or the sad thought that, when about to die,
He leaves them to the cold world's charity,

---

628 Nightingale, Florence Nightingale (1820-1910), who attained
world-wide renown by organizing the British military hospital system
in the Crimean War (1854-1856) • 637 Marmora, the inland sea on
which Istanbul is situated, between the Dardanelles and the Bosporus •
670 Chase, Salmon P. Chase (1808-1873), antislavery leader who was
governor of Ohio at the time Grayson wrote • 671 Parker, Theodore
Parker (1810-1860), Boston clergyman, an active agent in assisting
slaves to escape from the South • 672 Beecher, Henry Ward Beecher
(1813-1887), Brooklyn clergyman, brother of Mrs. Stowe, and long
active in the antislavery crusade

And sees them slowly seek the poor-house door—
The last, vile, hated refuge of the poor.

Still Europe's saints, that mark the motes alone
In other's eyes, yet never see their own,
Grieve that the slave is never taught to write,
And reads no better than the hireling white;
Do their own plowmen no instruction lack,
Have whiter clowns more knowledge than the black? 710
Has the French peasant, or the German boor,
Of learning's treasure any larger store;
Have Ireland's millions, flying from the rule
Of those who censure, ever known a school?
A thousand years and Europe's wealth impart
No means to mend the hireling's head or heart;
They build no schools to teach the pauper white,
Their toiling millions neither read nor write;
Whence, then, the idle clamor when they rave
Of schools and teachers for the distant slave? 720

And why the soft regret, the coarse attack,
If Justice punish the offending black?
Are whites not punished? When Utopian times
Shall drive from earth all miseries and crimes,
And teach the world the art to do without
The cat, the gauntlet, and the brutal knout,
Banish the halter, galley, jails, and chains,
And strip the law of penalties and pains;
Here, too, offense and wrong they may prevent,
And slaves, with hirelings, need no punishment: 730
Till then, what lash of slavery will compare
With the dread scourge that British soldiers bear?
What gentle rule, in Britain's Isle, prevails,
How rare her use of gibbets, stocks, and jails!
How much humaner than a master's whip,
Her penal colony and convict ship!
Whose code of law can darker pages show,
Where blood for smaller misdemeanors flow?
The trifling theft or trespass, that demands
For slaves light penance from a master's hands, 740
Where Europe's milder punishments are known,
Incurs the penalty of death alone.

And yet the master's lighter rule insures
More order than the sternest code secures;
No mobs of factious workmen gather here,
No strikes we dread, no lawless riots fear;
Nuns, from their convent driven, at midnight fly,

Churches, in flames, ask vengeance from the sky,
Seditious schemes in bloody tumults end,
Parsons incite, and senators defend, 750
But not where slaves their easy labors ply,
Safe from the snare, beneath a master's eye;
In useful tasks engaged, employed their time,
Untempted by the demagogue to crime,
Secure they toil, uncursed their peaceful life,
With labor's hungry broils and wasteful strife.
No want to goad, no faction to deplore,
The slave escapes the perils of the poor.

FROM PART SECOND

Where hireling millions toil, in doubt and fear,
For food and clothing all the weary year, 760
Content and grateful if their masters give
The boon they beg—to labor and to live;
While dreamers task their idle wits to find
A short-hand method to enrich mankind,
And Fourier's scheme or Owen's plans entice
Expectant thousands with some deep device
For raising wages, for abating toil,
And reaping crops from ill-attended soil:
If, while the anxious multitudes appear,
Now glad with hope, now yielding to despair, 770
A seraph form, descending from the skies,
In mercy sent, should meet their wond'ring eyes,

---

704 refuge . . . poor. "None submit to entering the poor-house except in extreme want. Some are hardly able to walk before they will apply.— London Labor, etc."—Grayson • 720 schools . . . slave. Grayson cites some statements regarding illiteracy in Great Britain and France and insists that slaves learn to read if they wish and are able to do so • 730 punishment. In 1846, says Grayson, 2468 persons were whipped in England. His note compares such punishment with that of slaves • 747 Nuns . . . fly. "A convent was destroyed by the mob near Boston. Churches, there and elsewhere have been burned by rioters. Violence and outrage are increasing yearly at the North. In Boston, lately, an officer of the federal government was murdered, while in the discharge of his duty, by a gang of white and black ruffians, instigated by men of wealth and by clergymen."—Grayson. The allusions are to the burning of an Ursuline convent in Charlestown in 1834 and to the Anthony Burns affair of 1854. Anti-Catholic feeling was strong at the time Grayson wrote, and violent interference with the enforcement of the Fugitive Slave Law was common • 756 strife. "The late Preston strike lost to the parties—masters and workmen—over two millions of dollars, and ended where it began."—Grayson. A seven months' lockout of the cotton-spinners at Preston, in Lancashire, England, in 1853-1854, is here referred to • 765 Fourier's . . . plans, allusions to the socialism of F. M. C. Fourier (1772-1837), whose ideas were adopted at Brook Farm and elsewhere in the 1840's, and of Robert Owen (1771-1858), who in 1824-1828 had attempted to found an ideal community at New Harmony, Indiana

And, smiling, offer to each suppliant there
The promised good that fills the laborer's prayer—
Food, clothing, freedom from the wants, the cares,
The pauper hireling ever feels or fears;
And, at their death, these blessings to renew,
That wives and children may enjoy them too,
That, when disease or age their strength impairs,
Subsistence and a home should still be theirs—   780
What wonder would the gracious boon impart,
What grateful rapture swell the peasant's heart!
How freely would the hungry list'ners give
A life-long labor thus secure to live!

And yet the life, so unassailed by care,
So blessed with moderate work, with ample fare,
With all the good the starving pauper needs,
The happier slave on each plantation leads;
Safe from harassing doubts and annual fears,
He dreads no famine in unfruitful years;   790
If harvests fail from inauspicious skies,
The master's providence his food supplies;
No paupers perish here for want of bread,
Or lingering live, by foreign bounty fed;
No exiled trains of homeless peasants go,
In distant climes, to tell their tales of woe:
Far other fortune, free from care and strife,
For work, or bread, attends the Negro's life,
And Christian slaves may challenge as their own,
The blessings claimed in fabled states alone—   800
The cabin home, not comfortless, though rude,
Light daily labor, and abundant food,
The sturdy health that temperate habits yield,
The cheerful song that rings in every field,
The long, loud laugh, that freemen seldom share,
Heaven's boon to bosoms unapproached by care,
And boisterous jest and humor unrefined,
That leave, though rough, no painful sting behind;
While, nestling near, to bless their humble lot,
Warm social joys surround the Negro's cot,   810
The evening dance its merriment imparts,
Love, with his rapture, fills their youthful hearts,
And placid age, the task of labor done,
Enjoys the summer shade, the winter sun,
And, as through life no pauper want he knows,
Laments no poor-house penance at its close.

Safe in Ambition's trumpet call to strife,
No conscript fears harass his quiet life,

Courtesy of The New-York Historical Society, New York City. See companion picture, page 101

While the crushed peasant bleeds—a worthless thing,
The broken toy of emperor or king;   820
Calm in his peaceful home, the slave prepares
His garden-spot, and plies his rustic cares;
The comb and honey that his bees afford,
The eggs in ample gourd compactly stored,
The pig, the poultry, with a chapman's art,
He sells or barters at the village mart,
Or, at the master's mansion, never fails
An ampler price to find and readier sales.

There, when December's welcome frosts recall
The friends and inmates of the crowded hall,   830
To each glad nursling of the master's race
He brings his present, with a cheerful face
And offered hand—of warm, unfeigning heart,
In all his master's joys he claims a part,
And, true as clansman to the Highland chief,
Mourns every loss, and grieves in all his grief;
When Christmas now, with its abundant cheer
And thornless pleasure, speeds the parting year,
He shares the common joy—the early morn
Wakes hunter, clamorous hound, and echoing horn,   840
Quick steps are heard, the merry season named,
The loiterers caught, the wonted forfeit claimed,
In feasts maturing busy hands appear,
And jest and laugh assail the ready ear;
Whose voice, than his, more gayly greets the dawn,

Whose foot so lightly treads the frosty lawn,
Whose heart as merrily, where mirth prevails,
On every side the joyous season hails?
Around the slaughtered ox—a Christmas prize,
The slaves assembling stand with eager eyes,   850
Rouse, with their dogs, the porker's piercing cry,
Or drag its squealing tenant from the sty;
With smile and bow receive their winter dues,
The strong, warm clothing and substantial shoes,
Blankets adorned with stripes of border red,
And caps of wool that warm the woollier head;
Then clear the barn, the ample area fill,
In the gay jig display their vigorous skill;
No dainty steps, no mincing measures here—
Ellsler's trained graces—seem to float in air,   860
But hearts of joy and nerves of living steel,
On floors that spring beneath the bounding reel;
Proud on his chair, with magisterial glance
And stamping foot, the fiddler rules the dance;
Draws, if he nods, the still unwearied bow,
And gives a joy no bearded bands bestow;
The triple holiday, on angel wings,
With every fleeting hour a pleasure brings;
No ennui clouds, no coming cares annoy,
Nor wants nor sorrows check the Negro's joy.   870

His, too, the Christian privilege to share
The weekly festival of praise and prayer;
For him the Sabbath shines with holier light,
The air grows balmier, and the sky more bright;
Winter's brief suns with warmer radiance glow,
With softer breath the gales of autumn blow,
Spring with new flowers more richly strews the ground,
And summer spreads a fresher verdure round;
The early shower is past; the joyous breeze
Shakes patt'ring rain-drops from the rustling trees,   880
And with the sun, the fragrant offerings rise
From Nature's censers to the bounteous skies;
With cheerful aspect, in his best array,
To the far forest church he takes his way;
With kind salute the passing neighbor meets,
With awkward grace the morning traveler greets,
And joined by crowds, that gather as he goes,
Seeks the calm joy the Sabbath morn bestows.
There no proud temples to devotion rise,
With marble domes that emulate the skies,   890
But bosomed deep in ancient trees, that spread

Their limbs o'er mouldering mansions of the dead,
Moss-cinctured oaks and solemn pines between,
Of modest wood, the house of God is seen,
By shaded springs, that from the sloping land
Bubble and sparkle through the silver sand,
Where high o'er arching laurel blossoms blow,
Where fragrant bays breathe kindred sweets below,
And elm and ash their blended arms entwine
With the bright foliage of the mantling vine: 900
In quiet chat, before the hour of prayer,
Masters and slaves in scattered groups appear;
Loosed from the carriage, in the shades around,
Impatient horses neigh and paw the ground;
No city discords break the silence here,
No sounds unmeet offend the listener's ear;
But rural melodies of flocks and birds,
The lowing, far and faint, of distant herds,
The mocking-bird, with minstrel pride elate,
The partridge whistling for its absent mate,   910
The thrush's solitary notes prolong,
Bold, merry blackbirds swell the general song;
The crested cardinal, of scarlet hue,
The jay, with restless wing of softer blue,
The cawing crow—upon the loftiest pine
Cautious and safe—their various voices join.

When now the pastor lifts his earnest eyes,
And hands outstretched, a suppliant to the skies,
No rights of pomp or pride beguile the soul,
No organs peal, no clouds of incense roll,   920
But, line by line, untutored voices raise,
Like the wild birds, their simple notes of praise,
And hearts of love, with true devotion, bring
Incense more pure to Heaven's eternal King;
On glorious themes their humble thoughts employ,
And rise transported with no earthly joy;
The blessing said, the service o'er, again
Their swelling voices raise the sacred strain;
Lingering, they love to sing of Jordan's shore,
Where sorrows cease, and toil is known no more. . . . 930
1853?•1854

860 Ellsler, Fanny Elssler (1810-1884), Austrian dancer who toured the
United States in 1841 • 929 Jordan's shore. "In these country churches,
where sometimes three or four hundred slaves assemble with a dozen
whites, the delight of the Negroes is in their spiritual songs and hymns.
. . . The Sunday service is a source of infinite enjoyment to them and
they conduct themselves with perfect decorum and attention."—Grayson

Henry Timrod

1828 · 1867

"No writer of equal stature in this country," Professor E. W. Parks observes, "has received so little attention" as Henry Timrod, the "Laureate of the Confederacy."

Timrod attended the Coates School in Charleston, South Carolina—his birthplace—and studied for a year and a half at the University of Georgia. After trying the law, he turned to tutoring in planters' families. Later he was a contributor to *Russell's Magazine* (1857-1860), a journal of literary promise published in Charleston and edited by his friend Paul Hamilton Hayne. In 1861 Timrod enlisted in the Confederate army, but because of ill health was able to serve less than a year. Undertaking the work of a war correspondent, he observed at close range the battle of Shiloh. In 1864 he edited a newspaper in Columbia, South Carolina; this position ended abruptly when Columbia was taken by Sherman's army. The three last years of his life were a losing struggle against poverty and disease. His poems were collected, with a memoir, by Paul Hamilton Hayne in 1873.

Timrod's early verses were imitative of Wordsworth. The war called forth his latent originality and inspired his best poems. These poems, though romantic in their ardor, are remarkable for certain classical qualities; indeed, it is the fusion of romantic and classical elements that gives to Timrod's poetry a special distinction. To quote Professor Parks again: "Although sincerity and throbbing emotion beat through his words in passionate undertones, the passion never carries the verse into formlessness of thought or reference. Instead an almost classic coolness and restraint appears, from first to last, in his war poems. . . . He saw a poem as a whole, yet as composed of lines, and his best poems combine a clear distinction of line with a sense of rounded completeness." Other noteworthy merits of Timrod's verse are the mastery of the sustained, or epic, simile and the classic purity of his diction.

Henry Timrod—from Century Magazine, *April 1898*

Poems of Henry Timrod, ed. P. H. Hayne, New York, 1873 • J. B. Hubbell, The Last Years of Henry Timrod, Durham, North Carolina, 1941 • E. W. Parks, Southern Poets, Cincinnati, 1936 • E. W. Parks, "Southern Poetry," Segments of Southern Thought, Athens, Georgia, 1938

Ethnogenesis

Written During the Meeting of the First Southern Congress, at Montgomery, February, 1861

The following poem was first printed, with the title "Ode, on the Meeting of the Southern Congress," in the **Charleston Mercury,** September 26, 1861. The title "Ethnogenesis," which was substituted when the poem was reprinted in the Charleston **Courier,** January 31, 1862, is a Greek coinage meaning "the birth of a nation." At once ardent and restrained, the poem expresses the patriotic spirit of the newly formed Confederate States of America.

I

Hath not the morning dawned with added light?
And shall not evening call another star
Out of the infinite regions of the night,
To mark this day in Heaven? At last, we are
A nation among nations; and the world
Shall soon behold in many a distant port
  Another flag unfurled!
Now, come what may, whose favor need we court?
And, under God, whose thunder need we fear?
  Thank him who placed us here   10
Beneath so kind a sky—the very sun
Takes part with us; and on our errands run
All breezes of the ocean; dew and rain
Do noiseless battle for us; and the Year,
And all the gentle daughters in her train,
March in our ranks, and in our service wield
Long spears of golden grain!
A yellow blossom as her fairy shield,
June flings her azure banner to the wind,
  While in the order of their birth   20
Her sisters pass, and many an ample field
Grows white beneath their steps, till now, behold,
  Its endless sheets unfold
THE SNOW OF SOUTHERN SUMMERS! Let the earth
Rejoice! beneath those fleeces soft and warm
  Our happy land shall sleep
  In a repose as deep
As if we lay intrenched behind
Whole leagues of Russian ice and Arctic storm!

II

And what if, mad with wrongs themselves have wrought, 30
  In their own treachery caught,
  By their own fears made bold,
  And leagued with him of old,
Who long since in the limits of the North
Set up his evil throne, and warred with God—
What if, both mad and blinded in their rage,
Our foes should fling us down their mortal gage,
And with a hostile step profane our sod!
We shall not shrink, my brothers, but go forth
To meet them, marshaled by the Lord of Hosts,   40
And overshadowed by the mighty ghosts
Of Moultrie and Eutaw—who shall foil
Auxiliars such as these? Nor these alone,
  But every stock and stone
  Shall help us; but the very soil,
And all the generous wealth it gives to toil,
And all for which we love our noble land,
Shall fight beside, and through us; sea and strand,
  The heart of woman, and her hand,
Tree, fruit, and flower, and every influence,   50
  Gentle, or grave, or grand;
  The winds in our defence
Shall seem to blow; to us the hills shall lend
  Their firmness and their calm;
And in our stiffened sinews we shall blend
  The strength of pine and palm!

III

Nor would we shun the battle-ground,
  Though weak as we are strong;
Call up the clashing elements around,
  And test the right and wrong!   60

---

24 Snow refers to cotton, of the importance of which to the South Timrod had an exaggerated conception. Contrast Lanier's later protest in "Corn" against the tyranny of "coquette cotton" • 34 **limits . . . North.** When Satan (according to Milton) revolted in Heaven against God, he withdrew with his followers to the North. See particularly **Paradise Lost,** Bk. **V, l.** 755: "At length into the limits of the North/They came . . ." • 42 **Moultrie and Eutaw.** The repulse of the British at Sullivan's Island, June 28, 1776, was led by General William Moultrie, for whom the fort on the island was later named. Eutaw Springs was the scene of an American attack on a British outpost, September 8, 1781. Hence, the "mighty ghosts" are the ghosts of Revolutionary patriots who fought at these places • 44 **stock and stone,** every senseless thing

On one side, creeds that dare to teach
What Christ and Paul refrained to preach;
Codes built upon a broken pledge,
And Charity that whets a poniard's edge;
Fair schemes that leave the neighboring poor
To starve and shiver at the schemer's door,
While in the world's most liberal ranks enrolled,
He turns some vast philanthropy to gold;
Religion, taking every mortal form
But that a pure and Christian faith makes warm,   70
Where not to vile fanatic passion urged,
Or not in vague philosophies submerged,
Repulsive with all Pharisaic leaven,
And making laws to stay the laws of Heaven!
And on the other, scorn of sordid gain,
Unblemished honor, truth without a stain,
Faith, justice, reverence, charitable wealth,
And, for the poor and humble, laws which give,
Not the mean right to buy the right to live,
    But life, and home, and health!   80
To doubt the end were want of trust in God,
    Who, if he has decreed
    That we must pass a redder sea
Than that which rang to Miriam's holy glee,
    Will surely raise at need
    A Moses with his rod!

IV

But let our fears—if fears we have—be still,
And turn us to the future! Could we climb
Some mighty Alp, and view the coming time,
The rapturous sight would fill   90
    Our eyes with happy tears!
Not only for the glories which the years
Shall bring us; not for lands from sea to sea,
And wealth, and power, and peace, though these shall be;
But for the distant peoples we shall bless,
And the hushed murmurs of a world's distress:
For, to give labor to the poor,
    The whole sad planet o'er,
And save from want and crime the humblest door,
Is one among the many ends for which   100
    God makes us great and rich!
The hour perchance is not yet wholly ripe
When all shall own it, but the type

Whereby we shall be known in every land
Is that vast gulf which lips our Southern strand,
And through the cold, untempered ocean pours
Its genial streams, that far off Arctic shores
May sometimes catch upon the softened breeze
Strange tropic warmth and hints of summer seas.

                                                    1861

The Cotton Boll

First printed in the **Charleston Mercury,** September 3, 1861, "The Cotton Boll" is Timrod's most successful poem. It is remarkable, among other things, for its fluency and precision, its eloquence and restraint, and its mastery of the expanded or epic simile and a varied, flexible meter.

While I recline
At ease beneath
This immemorial pine,
Small sphere!
(By dusky fingers brought this morning here
And shown with boastful smiles),
I turn thy cloven sheath,
Through which the soft white fibres peer,
That, with their gossamer bands,
Unite, like love, the sea-divided lands,   10
And slowly, thread by thread,
Draw forth the folded strands,
Than which the trembling line,
By whose frail help yon startled spider fled
Down the tall spear-grass from his swinging bed,

Ethnogenesis • 61 **creeds . . . preach.** Timrod asserts that the creed of the abolitionists has no Biblical authority • 63 **pledge** refers to the protection of slavery under the Constitution • 65 **neighboring poor,** the underpaid workers in Northern factories • 75 **the other,** the other side, meaning the South • 83 **redder sea.** The reference is to the crossing of the Red Sea by the Israelites and their subsequent rejoicing, recorded in Exodus 14:15. It is interesting to note that Whittier, speaking for the North, used the same Biblical story in "Laus Deo" (p. 61) • 95 **distant . . . bless,** presumably through the exportation of cotton • 105 **gulf,** the Gulf Stream **The Cotton Boll** • 5 **dusky fingers,** of a Negro slave

Is scarce more fine;
And as the tangled skein
Unravels in my hands,
Betwixt me and the noonday light,
A veil seems lifted, and for miles and miles   20
The landscape broadens on my sight,
As, in the little boll, there lurked a spell
Like that which, in the ocean shell,
With mystic sound,
Breaks down the narrow walls that hem us round,
And turns some city lane
Into the restless main,
With all his capes and isles!

Yonder bird,
Which floats, as if at rest,   30
In those blue tracts above the thunder, where
No vapors cloud the stainless air,
And never sound is heard,
Unless at such rare time
When, from the City of the Blest,
Rings down some golden chime,
Sees not from his high place
So vast a cirque of summer space
As widens round me in one mighty field,
Which, rimmed by seas and sands,   40
Doth hail its earliest daylight in the beams
Of gray Atlantic dawns;
And, broad as realms made up of many lands,
Is lost afar
Behind the crimson hills and purple lawns
Of sunset, among plains which roll their streams
Against the Evening Star!
And lo!
To the remotest point of sight,
Although I gaze upon no waste of snow,   50
The endless field is white;
And the whole landscape glows,
For many a shining league away,
With such accumulated light
As Polar lands would flash beneath a tropic day!
Nor lack there (for the vision grows,
And the small charm within my hands—
More potent even than the fabled one,
Which oped whatever golden mystery
Lay hid in fairy wood or magic vale,   60

The curious ointment of the Arabian tale—
Beyond all mortal sense
Doth stretch my sight's horizon, and I see,
Beneath its simple influence,
As if with Uriel's crown,
I stood in some great temple of the Sun,
And looked, as Uriel, down!)
Nor lack there pastures rich and fields all green
With all the common gifts of God,
For temperate airs and torrid sheen   70
Weave Edens of the sod;
Through lands which look one sea of billowy gold
Broad rivers wind their devious ways;
A hundred isles in their embraces fold
A hundred luminous bays;
And through yon purple haze
Vast mountains lift their plumèd peaks cloud-crowned;
And, save where up their sides the ploughman creeps,
An unhewn forest girds them grandly round,
In whose dark shades a future navy sleeps!   80
Ye Stars, which, though unseen, yet with me gaze
Upon this loveliest fragment of the earth!
Thou Sun, that kindlest all thy gentlest rays
Above it, as to light a favorite hearth!
Ye Clouds, that in your temples in the West
See nothing brighter than its humblest flowers!
And you, ye Winds, that on the ocean's breast
Are kissed to coolness ere ye reach its bowers!
Bear witness with me in my song of praise,
And tell the world that, since the world began   90
No fairer land hath fired a poet's lays,
Or given a home to man!

But these are charms already widely blown!
His be the meed whose pencil's trace
Hath touched our very swamps with grace,
And round whose tuneful way
All Southern laurels bloom;
The Poet of "The Woodlands," unto whom

---

22 As, as if • 61 ointment . . . tale, in the story describing the
adventures of Haroun Al Raschid in the **Arabian Nights** • 65 Uriel,
regent of the Sun, described in Milton's **Paradise Lost**, Bk. III •
98 **Poet . . . Woodlands**, a reference to William Gilmore Simms
(1806-1870) and his country estate near Charleston. Simms wrote a
good many poems (including a poem entitled ''The Edge of the
Swamp''), though he is best known for his prose romances

Alike are known
The flute's low breathing and the trumpet's tone,   100
And the soft west wind's sighs;
But who shall utter all the debt,
O Land wherein all powers are met
That bind a people's heart,
The world doth owe thee at this day,
And which it never can repay,
Yet scarcely deigns to own!
Where sleeps the poet who shall fitly sing
The source wherefrom doth spring
That mighty commerce which, confined   110
To the mean channels of no selfish mart,
Goes out to every shore
Of this broad earth, and throngs the sea with ships
That bear no thunders; hushes hungry lips
In alien lands;
Joins with a delicate web remotest strands;
And gladdening rich and poor,
Doth gild Parisian domes,
Or feed the cottage-smoke of English homes,
And only bounds its blessings by mankind!   120
In offices like these, thy mission lies,
My Country! and it shall not end
As long as rain shall fall and Heaven bend
In blue above thee; though thy foes be hard
And cruel as their weapons, it shall guard
Thy hearth-stones as a bulwark; make thee great
In white and bloodless state;
And haply, as the years increase—
Still working through its humbler reach
With that large wisdom which the ages teach—   130
Revive the half-dead dream of universal peace!
As men who labor in that mine
Of Cornwall, hollowed out beneath the bed
Of ocean, when a storm rolls overhead,
Hear the dull booming of the world of brine
Above them, and a mighty muffled roar
Of winds and waters, yet toil calmly on,
And split the rock, and pile the massive ore,
Or carve a niche, or shape the archèd roof;
So I, as calmly, weave my woof   140
Of song, chanting the days to come,
Unsilenced, though the quiet summer air
Stirs with the bruit of battles, and each dawn
Wakes from its starry silence to the hum

Of many gathering armies. Still,
In that we sometimes hear,
Upon the Northern winds, the voice of woe
Not wholly drowned in triumph, though I know
The end must crown us, and a few brief years
Dry all our tears,   150
I may not sing too gladly. To Thy will
Resigned, O Lord! we cannot all forget
That there is much even Victory must regret.
And, therefore, not too long
From the great burthen of our country's wrong
Delay our just release!
And, if it may be, save
These sacred fields of peace
From stain of patriot or of hostile blood!
Oh, help us, Lord! to roll the crimson flood   160
Back on its course, and while our banners wing
Northward, strike with us! till the Goth shall cling
To his own blasted altar-stones, and crave
Mercy; and we shall grant it, and dictate
The lenient future of his fate
There, where some rotting ships and crumbling quays
Shall one day mark the Port which ruled the Western seas.
                                                        1861

Carolina

First printed in the Charleston Courier, March 8, 1862, and reprinted there, November 12 of the same year, "Carolina" is perhaps the most fervid of all the patriotic lyrics written during the Civil War.

I

The despot treads thy sacred sands,
Thy pines give shelter to his bands,
Thy sons stand by with idle hands,
                Carolina!

---

133 **Cornwall**, on the southwest coast of England • 162 **Goth.**
Timrod uses this uncomplimentary name to refer to the people of the **North** • 167 **Port**, New York

He breathes at ease thy airs of balm,
He scorns the lances of thy palm;
Oh! who shall break thy craven calm,
        Carolina!
Thy ancient fame is growing dim,
A spot is on thy garment's rim;   10
Give to the winds thy battle hymn,
        Carolina!

II

Call on thy children of the hill,
Wake swamp and river, coast and rill,
Rouse all thy strength and all thy skill,
        Carolina!
Cite wealth and science, trade and art,
Touch with thy fire the cautious mart,
And pour thee through the people's heart,
        Carolina!   20
Till even the coward spurns his fears,
And all thy fields and fens and meres
Shall bristle like thy palm with spears,
        Carolina!

III

Hold up the glories of thy dead;
Say how thy elder children bled,
And point to Eutaw's battle-bed,
        Carolina!
Tell how the patriot's soul was tried,
And what his dauntless breast defied;   30
How Rutledge ruled and Laurens died,
        Carolina!
Cry! till thy summons, heard at last,
Shall fall like Marion's bugle-blast
Re-echoed from the haunted Past,
        Carolina!

IV

I hear a murmur as of waves
That grope their way through sunless caves,
Like bodies struggling in their graves,
        Carolina!   40
And now it deepens; slow and grand
It swells, as, rolling to the land,
An ocean broke upon thy strand,
        Carolina!

Shout! let it reach the startled Huns!
And roar with all thy festal guns!
It is the answer of thy sons,
        Carolina!

V

They will not wait to hear thee call;
From Sachem's Head to Sumter's wall   50
Resounds the voice of hut and hall,
        Carolina!
No! thou hast not a stain, they say,
Or none save what the battle-day
Shall wash in seas of blood away,
        Carolina!
Thy skirts indeed the foe may part,
Thy robe be pierced with sword and dart,
They shall not touch thy noble heart,
        Carolina!   60

VI

Ere thou shalt own the tyrant's thrall
Ten times ten thousand men must fall;
Thy corpse may hearken to his call,
        Carolina!
When, by thy bier, in mournful throngs
The women chant thy mortal wrongs,
'Twill be their own funereal songs,
        Carolina!
From thy dead breast by ruffians trod
No helpless child shall look to God;   70
All shall be safe beneath thy sod,
        Carolina!

VII

Girt with such wills to do and bear,
Assured in right, and mailed in prayer,
Thou wilt not bow thee to despair,
        Carolina!

---

17 Cite, summon or call • 27 Eutaw's battle-bed. See note, p. 110 •
31 Rutledge, John Rutledge (1739-1800), governor of South Carolina
• 31 Laurens, John Laurens (1754-1782), Revolutionary soldier and
South Carolinian, killed in battle • 34 Marion, Francis Marion
(1732-1795), Revolutionary general and South Carolinian • 45 Huns,
here applied to the soldiers of the North • 50 Sachem's . . . wall,
that is, from the mountains to the sea • 74 mailed . . . prayer,
reminiscent of St. Paul's Christian armor, described in Ephesians 6

Throw thy bold banner to the breeze!
Front with thy ranks the threatening seas
Like thine own proud armorial trees,
                    Carolina!   80
Fling down thy gauntlet to the Huns,
And roar the challenge from thy guns;
Then leave the future to thy sons,
                    Carolina!

                                                        1862

Charleston

"Charleston" was first printed in the **Charleston Mercury,**
December 13, 1862.

Calm as that second summer which precedes
    The first fall of the snow,
In the broad sunlight of heroic deeds
    The City bides the foe.

As yet, behind their ramparts stern and proud,
    Her bolted thunders sleep—
Dark Sumter, like a battlemented cloud,
    Looms o'er the solemn deep.

No Calpe frowns from lofty cliff or scar
    To guard the holy strand;   10
But Moultrie holds in leash her dogs of war
    Above the level sand.

And down the dunes a thousand guns lie couched
    Unseen beside the flood—
Like tigers in some Orient jungle crouched
    That wait and watch for blood.

Meanwhile, through streets still echoing with trade,
    Walk grave and thoughtful men
Whose hands may one day wield the patriot's blade
    As lightly as the pen.   20

And maidens with such eyes as would grow dim
    Over a bleeding hound

Fort Sumter, 1863—frontispiece from Q. A. Gillmore,
Engineer and Artillery Operations Against the Defences
of Charleston Harbor, 1865

Seem each one to have caught the strength of him
    Whose sword she sadly bound.

Thus girt without and garrisoned at home,
    Day patient following day,
Old Charleston looks from roof and spire and dome
    Across her tranquil bay.

Ships, through a hundred foes, from Saxon lands
    And spicy Indian ports   30
Bring Saxon steel and iron to her hands
    And Summer to her courts.

But still, along yon dim Atlantic line,
    The only hostile smoke
Creeps like a harmless mist above the brine
    From some frail, floating oak.

Shall the Spring dawn, and she, still clad in smiles
    And with an unscathed brow,
Rest in the strong arms of her palm-crowned isles
    As fair and free as now?   40

We know not; in the temple of the Fates
    God has inscribed her doom;
And, all untroubled in her faith, she waits
    The triumph or the tomb.

                                                        1862

---

7 **Sumter,** a fort on an island at the entrance of Charleston harbor,
the firing upon which by the Confederates in April 1861 precipitated
the Civil War • 9 **Calpe,** Gibraltar • 11 **Moultrie.** See note, p.
110 • 29 **foes,** the Federal blockade

Spring

"Spring" was first printed in the Charleston Southern Illustrated News, April 4, 1863.

Spring, with that nameless pathos in the air
Which dwells with all things fair,
Spring, with her golden suns and silver rain,
Is with us once again.

Out in the lonely woods the jasmine burns
Its fragrant lamps, and turns
Into a royal court with green festoons
The banks of dark lagoons.

In the deep heart of every forest tree
The blood is all aglee,   10
And there's a look about the leafless bowers
As if they dreamed of flowers.

Yet still on every side we trace the hand
Of Winter in the land,
Save where the maple reddens on the lawn,
Flushed by the season's dawn;

Or where, like those strange semblances we find
That age to childhood bind,
The elm puts on, as if in Nature's scorn,
The brown of Autumn corn.   20

As yet the turf is dark, although you know
That, not a span below,
A thousand germs are groping through the gloom,
And soon will burst their tomb.

Already, here and there, on frailest stems
Appear some azure gems,
Small as might deck, upon a gala day,
The forehead of a fay.

In gardens you may note amid the dearth
The crocus breaking earth;   30

And near the snowdrop's tender white and green,
The violet in its screen.

But many gleams and shadows need must pass
Along the budding grass,
And weeks go by, before the enamored South
Shall kiss the rose's mouth.

Still there's a sense of blossoms yet unborn
In the sweet airs of morn;
One almost looks to see the very street
Grow purple at his feet.   40

At times a fragrant breeze comes floating by,
And brings, you know not why,
A feeling as when eager crowds await
Before a palace gate

Some wondrous pageant; and you scarce would start,
If from a beech's heart,
A blue-eyed Dryad, stepping forth, should say,
"Behold me! I am May!"

Ah! who would couple thoughts of war and crime
With such a blessèd time!   50
Who in the west wind's aromatic breath
Could hear the call of Death!

Yet not more surely shall the Spring awake
The voice of wood and brake,
Then she shall rouse, for all her tranquil charms,
A million men to arms.

There shall be deeper hues upon her plains
Than all her sunlit rains,
And every gladdening influence around,
Can summon from the ground.   60

Oh! standing on this desecrated mould,
Methinks that I behold,
Lifting her bloody daisies up to God,
Spring kneeling on the sod,

And calling, with the voice of all her rills,
Upon the ancient hills
To fall and crush the tyrants and the slaves
Who turn her meads to graves.

1863

Ode

Mr. Parks says of the poem: "Timrod's 'Ode' has the supreme artistic merit of throbbing with vibrant emotion in its effect upon the reader, yet of possessing a classic coolness of phrase which might have been carved from stone. The poet indulges in no histrionic exhibitionism, but this controlled and inevitable verse leaves nothing to be said." The poem has been often compared with William Collins' "How Sleep the Brave."

The "Ode" was first printed in the Charleston **Courier** as "Ode Sung on the Occasion of Decorating the Graves of the Confederate Dead, at Magnolia Cemetery, Charleston, S. C."

Sleep sweetly in your humble graves,
  Sleep, martyrs of a fallen cause;
Though yet no marble column craves
  The pilgrim here to pause.

In seeds of laurel in the earth,
  The blossom of your fame is blown,
And somewhere, waiting for its birth,
  The shaft is in the stone!

Meanwhile, behalf the tardy years
  Which keep in trust your storied tombs,   10
Behold! your sisters bring their tears,
  And these memorial blooms.

Small tributes! but your shades will smile
  More proudly on these wreaths today,
Than when some cannon-moulded pile
  Shall overlook this Bay.

Stoop, angels, hither from the skies!
  There is no holier spot of ground
Than where defeated valor lies,
  By mourning beauty crowned!   20
                       1866

Civil War Singers

Compared with Revolutionary War songs, those chanted by soldiers and civilians during the Civil War had somewhat less courtliness, less of the British manner about them. The colloquial language, however, which had begun to influence much popular literature, was an element in remarkably few: words and phrases were still likely to be oratorical. The meters of many were determined by the older tunes for which they were written—"The Star-Spangled Banner," "The Campbells Are Coming," "Hearts of Oak," and so on. Although there were exceptions—"The Battle Hymn of the Republic" and "Maryland," for instance—those best remembered were distinguished less for their sentiment and phrasing than for their rhythms and their tunes. Quite a large number continued to be popular down into modern times.

F. F. Browne, Bugle Echoes, a Collection of Poems of the Civil War, Northern and Southern, New York, 1886 • G. E. Eggleston, American War Ballads and Lyrics, 2 vols., New York, 1889 • E. A. Dolph, Sound Off! Soldier Songs, New York, 1929

Dixie

Daniel Decatur Emmett 1815 • 1904

On Broadway, in 1859, "Dixie," the most stirring tune associated with the war, had its first public performance. The author and composer of the first of many versions was Daniel Decatur Emmett, who was born, the son of an Irish blacksmith of Southern origin, in Mt. Vernon, Ohio, in 1815. Emmett had the most elementary sort of education before, at seventeen, he entered the United States army. He served for three years as a fifer. Discharged, he traveled with circus bands and in time became a composer and singer in minstrel troupes. It was for Bryant's Minstrels that he composed his famous song, a "walk-around," rendered by the whole company. The composition was introduced to the South by a chorus in John Brougham's New Orleans production of **Pocahontas** shortly before the war began. The Confederate regiments of Louisiana marched to a military version of the song, and soon its use in Southern armies was widespread. The nonsense words as well as the lively tune evidently had great appeal.

I wish I was in de land ob cotton,
Old times dar am not forgotten;
  Look away! Look away! Look away! Dixie Land!
In Dixie Land whar I was born in,
Early on one frosty mornin',
  Look away! Look away! Look away! Dixie Land!

Chorus

    Den I wish I was in Dixie! Hooray! Hooray!
    In Dixie's Land we'll take our stand, to lib an'
      die in Dixie.
    Away! away! away down South in Dixie.
    Away! away! away down South in Dixie.   10

Ole missus marry "Will-de-weaber";
Willum was a gay deceaber;
  Look away, look away, look away, Dixie Land!

But when he put his arm around her,
He smiled as fierce as a forty-pounder;
  Look away, look away, look away, Dixie Land!

His face was sharp as a butcher's cleaber;
But dat did not seem to greab her;
  Look away, look away, look away, Dixie Land!
Ole missus acted de foolish part,   20
And died for a man dat broke her heart;
  Look away, look away, look away, Dixie Land!

Now here's a health to de next ole missus,
An' all the gals dat want to kiss us;
  Look away, look away, look away, Dixie Land!
But if you want to drive 'way sorrow,
Come hear dis song tomorrow;
  Look away, look away, look away, Dixie Land!

Dar's buckwheat cakes and Injin batter,
Makes you fat or a little fatter;   30
  Look away, look away, look away, Dixie Land!
Den hoe it down an' scratch your grabble,
To Dixie's land I'm bound to trabble;
  Look away, look away, look away, Dixie Land!

                     1859

Dixie

Albert Pike 1809 • 1891

The best-known "literary" version of "Dixie" was written by Albert Pike, born and educated in Massachusetts but transplanted to the South as a young man. Pike was a newspaper editor and a lawyer who had a commission in the Confederate army. His words for the song were popular during the war, but in time they dropped from general memory in favor of Emmett's humbler version written to the same tune.

Southrons, hear your country call you!
Up! lest worse than death befall you!
  To arms! to arms! to arms! in Dixie!

Lo! all beacon fires are lighted,
Let our hearts be now united!
  To arms! to arms! to arms! in Dixie!

Chorus
    Advance the flag of Dixie!
      Hurrah! Hurrah!
    For Dixie's land we'll take our stand,
      To live or die for Dixie!   10
    To arms! To arms!
      And conquer peace for Dixie!
    To arms! To arms!
      And conquer peace for Dixie!

Hear the Northern thunders mutter!
Northern flags in South winds flutter!
  To arms! to arms! to arms! in Dixie!
Send them back your fierce defiance!
Stamp upon the cursed alliance!
  To arms! to arms! to arms! in Dixie!   20

Fear no danger! shun no labor!
Lift up rifle, pike and sabre!
  To arms! to arms! to arms! in Dixie!
Shoulder pressing close to shoulder,
Let the odds make each heart bolder!
  To arms! to arms! to arms! in Dixie!

How the South's great heart rejoices,
At your cannon's ringing voices;
  To arms! to arms! to arms! in Dixie!
For faith betrayed and pledges broken,   50
Wrongs inflicted, insults spoken!
  To arms! to arms! to arms! in Dixie!

Strong as lions, swift as eagles,
Back to their kennels hunt these beagles!
  To arms! to arms! to arms! in Dixie!
Cut the unequal bonds asunder!
Let them hence each other plunder!
  To arms! to arms! to arms! in Dixie!

Swear upon your country's altar,
Never to give up or falter;   30
  To arms! to arms! to arms! in Dixie!
Till the spoilers are defeated,

Till the Lord's work is completed.
  To arms! to arms! to arms! in Dixie!

Halt not till our Federation,
Secures among earth's Powers its station!
  To arms! to arms! to arms! in Dixie!
Then at peace and crowned with glory,
Hear your children tell the story!
  To arms! to arms! to arms! in Dixie!   40

If the loved ones weep in sadness,
Victory soon shall bring them gladness.
  To arms! to arms! to arms! in Dixie!
Exultant pride soon banish sorrow;
Smiles chase tears away tomorrow.
  To arms! to arms! to arms! in Dixie!

1861

My Maryland

James Ryder Randall 1839 • 1908

Upon hearing of the attack by the Massachusetts troops on his native city, Baltimore, James Ryder Randall wrote "My Maryland." At the time he composed the poem, Randall was a teacher in Louisiana, unacceptable for military duty because of poor health. He turned from teaching to journalism, and was in newspaper work until his death in 1908.

"My Maryland" appeared first in the New Orleans *Delta*, but shortly it was reprinted in newspapers throughout the South. The tune for which the verses were designed was the German song "Tannenbaum, O Tannenbaum."

The despot's heel is on thy shore,
    Maryland!
His torch is at thy temple door,
    Maryland!
Avenge the patriotic gore
That flecked the streets of Baltimore,
And be the battle-queen of yore,
    Maryland! My Maryland!

Hark, to an exiled son's appeal,
   Maryland!
My Mother-State, to thee I kneel,
   Maryland!
For life and death, for woe and weal,
Thy peerless chivalry reveal,
And gird thy beautious limbs with steel!
   Maryland! My Maryland!

Thou wilt not cower in the dust,
   Maryland!
Thy beaming sword shall never rust,
   Maryland!
Remember Carroll's sacred trust,
Remember Howard's warlike thrust,
And all thy slumberers with the just,
   Maryland! My Maryland!

Come! 'tis the red dawn of the day,
   Maryland!
Come! with thy panoplied array,
   Maryland!
With Ringgold's spirit for the fray,
With Watson's blood at Monterey,
With fearless Lowe and dashing May,
   Maryland! My Maryland!

Dear Mother! burst the tyrant's chain,
   Maryland!
Virginia should not call in vain,
   Maryland!
She meets her sisters on the plain—
"Sic semper," 'tis the proud refrain
That baffles minions back amain,
   Maryland!
Arise, in majesty again,
   Maryland! My Maryland!

Come! for thy shield is bright and strong,
   Maryland!
Come! for thy dalliance does thee wrong,
   Maryland!
Come! to thine own heroic throng,
That stalks with Liberty along,
And ring thy dauntless Slogan-song,
   Maryland! My Maryland!

I see the blush upon thy cheek,
   Maryland!
For thou wast ever bravely meek,
   Maryland!
But lo! there surges forth a shriek
From hill to hill, from creek to creek—
Potomac calls to Chesapeake,
   Maryland! My Maryland!

Thou wilt not yield the Vandal toll,
   Maryland!
Thou wilt not crook to his control,
   Maryland!
Better the fire upon thee roll,
Better the shot, the blade, the bowl,
Than crucifixion of the soul,
   Maryland! My Maryland!

I hear the distant thunder-hum,
   Maryland!
The Old Line's bugle, fife, and drum,
   Maryland!
She is not dead, nor deaf, nor dumb—
   Huzza! she spurns the Northern scum!
She breathes—she burns! she'll come! she'll come!
   Maryland! My Maryland!

1861

Battle Hymn of the Republic

Julia Ward Howe 1819 · 1910

This poem was written by Mrs. Howe to accompany a well-established tune, that of the doggerel song, "John Brown's Body." Interestingly, this latter song had fitted its words to a Southern revival hymn, "Say, Brothers, Will

21 **Carroll,** Charles Carroll, a citizen of Maryland, the last surviving signer of the Declaration of Independence • 22 **Howard,** John Eager Howard, a military leader in the Revolution • 29 **Ringgold . . . Watson . . . Lowe . . . May,** Marylanders who fought with distinction in the Mexican War • 38 **Sic semper,** the opening words of the motto of Virginia, **Sic semper tyrannis** — Thus always to tyrants • 57 **Potomac . . . Chesapeake,** extreme boundaries of Maryland

You Meet Us?'' popular throughout the United States in the 1850's. Soldiers of a Massachusetts regiment stationed in Boston worked out the words for "John Brown's Body" in 1861; when they sang them while marching through New York in July of the same year, the song began to have wide currency. The opening lines of the song were:

John Brown's body lies a-mold'ring in the grave,
John Brown's body lies a-mold'ring in the grave,
John Brown's body lies a-mold'ring in the grave,
   His soul is marching on!
Chorus
   Glory! Glory Hallelujah!
   Glory! Glory Hallelujah!
   Glory! Glory Hallelujah!
      His soul is marching on.

Mrs. Howe, a Bostonian and descendant of a distinguished colonial family, had won distinction before the war as a supporter of women's suffrage and other reforms, including abolition. She wrote her poem one night after she had been stirred by a visit to an army camp near Washington, D. C. Unlike Pike's "improvement" on the words of "Dixie," her words replaced the initial ones in popular memory. "The Battle Hymn of the Republic" first was published in the **Atlantic Monthly**, February 1862.

Mine eyes have seen the glory of the coming of the Lord:
He is trampling out the vintage where the grapes of
   wrath are stored;
He hath loosed the fateful lightning of his terrible swift
   sword;
   His truth is marching on.

Chorus
   Glory! glory! Hallelujah!
   Glory! glory! Hallelujah!
   Glory! glory! Hallelujah!
      His truth is marching on!

I have seen him in the watch-fires of a hundred circling
   camps;
They have builded him an altar in the evening dews
   and damps;   10
I can read his righteous sentence by the dim and flaring
   lamps:
   His day is marching on.

I have read a fiery gospel, writ in burnished rows of
   steel:
"As ye deal with my contemners, so with you my grace
   shall deal;
Let the Hero, born of woman, crush the serpent with
   his heel,
   Since God is marching on."

He has sounded forth the trumpet that shall never call
   retreat;
He is sifting out the hearts of men before his judgment-
   seat;
Oh, be swift, my soul, to answer him! be jubilant, my
   feet!
   Our God is marching on.   20

In the beauty of the lilies Christ was born across the sea,
With a glory in his bosom that transfigures you and me:
As he died to make men holy, let us die to make men
   free,
   While God is marching on.

                                                  1861·1862

Three Hundred Thousand More

James Sloan Gibbons 1810 • 1892

On July 16, 1862, shortly after Lincoln had issued a call for three hundred thousand additional volunteers, this poem was published anonymously in the New York **Evening Post**. William Cullen Bryant was credited with its authorship, but eventually it was attributed to Gibbons, a Quaker editor and abolitionist. Stephen Collins Foster wrote a musical setting, the most successful of his war songs.

We are coming, Father Abraham, three hundred thou-
   sand more,
From Mississippi's winding stream and from New
   England's shore;
We leave our plows and workshops, our wives and
   children dear,

We are coming Father A-braam, Three hun-dred thou-sand more, From Mis-sis-sip-pi's wind-ing stream and from New Eng-land's shore, We leave our plows and work-shops, our wives and chil-dren dear, With hearts too full for ut-ter-ance, with but a si-lent tear; We — dare not look be-hind us, but stead-fast-ly be-fore, We are com-ing Fa-ther A-braam, three hun-dred thou-sand more

Chorus

We are com-ing, com-ing our un-ion to re-store, We are com-ing, Fa-ther A-braam with three hun-dred thou-sand more.

With hearts too full for utterance, with but a silent tear;
We dare not look behind us, but steadfastly before:
We are coming, Father Abraham, three hundred thousand more!

If you look across the hill-tops that meet the northern sky,
Long moving lines of rising dust your vision may descry;
And now the wind, an instant, tears the cloudy veil aside,
And floats aloft our spangled flag in glory and in pride, 10
And bayonets in the sunlight gleam, and bands brave music pour:

We are coming, Father Abraham, three hundred thousand more!

If you look all up our valleys where the growing harvests shine,
You may see our sturdy farmer boys fast forming into line;
And children from their mother's knees are pulling at the weeds,
And learning how to reap and sow against their country's needs;
And a farewell group stands weeping at every cottage door:

We are coming, Father Abraham, three hundred thousand more!

You have called us, and we're coming, by Richmond's
    bloody tide
To lay us down, for Freedom's sake, our brothers' bones
    beside,   20
Or from foul treason's savage grasp to wrench the
    murderous blade,

And in the face of foreign foes its fragments to parade.
Six hundred thousand loyal men and true have gone
    before:
We are coming, Father Abraham, three hundred thou-
    sand more!

                        1862

Abraham Lincoln

1809 · 1865

An autobiography which Lincoln wrote in 1859 tells the main details of his early life in his characteristic style. It reads, in part:

"I was born February 12, 1809, in Hardin County, Kentucky. My parents were both born in Virginia, of undistinguished families. . . . My mother, who died in my tenth year, was of a family of the name of Hanks. . . . My father, at the death of his father, was but six years of age, and he grew up literally without education. He removed from Kentucky to what is now Spencer County, Indiana, in my eighth year. . . . It was a wild region, with many bears and other wild animals still in the woods. There I grew up. There were some schools, so called, but no qualification was ever required of a teacher beyond 'readin', writin', and cipherin',' to the rule of three. . . . There was absolutely nothing to excite ambition for education. Of course, when I came of age, I did not know much. Still, somehow, I could read, write, and cipher to the rule of three, but that was all. I have not been to school since. The little advance I now have upon this store of education, I have picked up from time to time under the pressure of necessity.

"I was raised to farm work, which I continued till I was twenty-two. At twenty-one I came to Illinois, Macon County. Then I got to New Salem . . . where I remained a year as a sort of clerk in a store. Then came The Black Hawk War; and I was elected a captain of volunteers, a success which gave me more pleasure than any I have had since. I went the campaign, was elected, ran for the legislature the same year (1832), and was beaten—the only time I ever have been beaten by the people. The next and three succeeding biennial elections I was elected to the legislature. I was not a candidate afterward. During this legislative period I had studied law, and removed to Springfield to practice it. In 1846 I was once elected to the lower House of Congress. Was not a candidate for reelection. From 1849 to 1854, both inclusive, practised law more as-siduously than ever before. . . . I was losing interest in politics when the repeal of the Missouri Compromise aroused me again. What I have done since then is pretty well known.

"If any personal description of me is thought desir-able, it may be said I am, in height, six feet four inches, nearly; lean in flesh, weighing on an average one hundred and eighty pounds; dark complexion, with coarse black hair and gray eyes. No other marks or brands recollected."

Lincoln's account breaks off at the time of the repeal of the Missouri Compromise (1854), a political move which caused him to return to public life when the Republican party was founded. In 1858 the Lincoln-Douglas debates, on the subject of popular sovereignty, attracted nation-wide attention and led to Lincoln's becoming a dark-horse candidate for the Presidential nomination. He was nominated in 1860, subsequently elected, and began to serve in 1861, as the Civil War was starting. His wartime leadership was rewarded by his reëlection in 1864. He was shot to death by John Wilkes Booth, in a Washington theater, about a month after his second inaugural.

One reason for his countrymen's idolizing Lincoln as they have is suggested in his claim, in his autobiography, that he had little book learning. Americans loved to think of him as a typical practical citizen. Joe Gillespie, an old friend, praised him in these words: "He had passed through all the grades of society when he reached the Presidency, and he had found common sense a sure reliance and he put it into practice. He acted all through his career upon just such principles as every man of good sense would approve. . . . Lincoln

was a great common man." His ways of thinking were, indeed, much like those of ordinary Americans who distrust abstractions and rely upon experience and sound logic to help solve problems.

Yet Lincoln and many of his friends and worshipers probably underestimated the extent of his education. From boyhood, he was passionately fond of reading. He read the Bible, *Pilgrim's Progress,* and such fine writers as Milton, Gibbon, Voltaire, Paine, Hawthorne, and others with great appreciation. He knew much of Shakespeare and could recite long passages from the great plays. Finally, he had the urge to write well. As a young man, he wrote quite a number of poems. Of one poem which he read in 1846, he said, "I would give all I am worth and go in debt to be able to write so fine a piece. . . ." He took great pains with his writing. Mentor Graham, his teacher, said, "I have known him . . . to study for hours the best way of three to express an idea." Such care is evident in his most famous utterances—most of them masterpieces of American oratory.

The Collected Works of Abraham Lincoln, ed. R. P. Basler, 9 vols., New Brunswick, 1953 • Carl Sandburg, Abraham Lincoln: the Prairie Years, New York, 1926 • Carl Sandburg, Abraham Lincoln: the War Years, New York, 1939 • Nathaniel Stephenson, "Lincoln," Cambridge History of American Literature, New York, 1931

Farewell Address at Springfield, Illinois

Lincoln had been elected President in November 1860. The following month, South Carolina had seceded. By February 8, 1861, five additional states had seceded, and the Confederate government had been formed. Because it had been rumored that Lincoln would never be allowed to

reach Washington alive, precautions had been taken to ensure his safety on the journey.

Such was the situation when, on February 11, the Presidential party went to the railroad station in Springfield to depart for Washington. There were dense clouds overhead, and a chilly drizzle of rain fell through the gray mist. From the platform of a car on the train, Lincoln spoke to the thousand townspeople who stood in the rain.

My Friends: No one, not in my situation, can appreciate my feeling of sadness at this parting. To this place, and the kindness of these people, I owe everything. Here I have lived a quarter of a century, and have passed from a young to an old man. Here my children have been born, and one is buried. I now leave, not knowing when or whether ever I may return, with a task before me greater than that which rested upon Washington. Without the assistance of that Divine Being who ever attended him, I cannot succeed. With that assistance, I cannot fail. Trusting in Him who can go with me, and remain with you, and be everywhere for good, let us confidently hope that all will yet be well. To His care commending you, as I hope in your prayers you will commend me, I bid you an affectionate farewell.

1861

First Inaugural Address

"The 4th of March has come and gone," wrote a Washington clerk, "and we have a live, Republican President. And, what is perhaps more singular, during the whole day we saw no one who appeared to manifest the least dislike to his living." The account reflects the general fear in Washington on the day of the inauguration in 1861. During the parade and during the address, riflemen on rooftops along the Avenue and in windows of the Capitol Building watched the crowd for signs of violence. In addition to the fear for Lincoln's life, there was the tense feeling of a nation on the verge of war.

The speech, like most inaugurals, was addressed not only to the audience at Washington but also to a wider one. For the North, which half feared that he might be a waverer like his predecessor, Lincoln clearly stated his belief that the Union could not be dissolved and firmly defined the duty of the government in the face of a threat of dissolution. For the South, he made his account of the controversy dispassionate and offered in the closing lines the appeal for a continuance of peace. The address was revised in accordance with suggestions made by his advisers Browning and Seward, who chiefly urged more temperance of tone. The most notable indication of Lincoln's artistry is his rephrasing of the final paragraph from the form originally written out by Secretary of State Seward. (See footnote, p. 130.)

Fellow Citizens of the United States: In compliance with a custom as old as the government itself, I appear before you to address you briefly, and to take in your presence the oath prescribed by the Constitution of the United States to be taken by the President "before he enters on the execution of his office."

I do not consider it necessary at present for me to discuss those matters of administration about which there is no special anxiety or excitement.

Apprehension seems to exist among the people of the 10 Southern states that by the accession of a Republican administration their property and their peace and personal security are to be endangered. There has never been any reasonable cause for such apprehension. Indeed, the most ample evidence to the contrary has all the while existed and been open to their inspection. It is found in nearly all the published speeches of him who now addresses you. I do but quote from one of those speeches when I declare that "I have no purpose, directly or indirectly, to interfere with the institution of 20 slavery in the states where it exists. I believe I have no lawful right to do so, and I have no inclination to do so." Those who nominated and elected me did so with full knowledge that I had made this and many similar declarations, and had never recanted them. And, more than this, they placed in the platform for my acceptance, and as a law to themselves and to me, the clear and emphatic resolution which I now read:

"*Resolved*, That the maintenance inviolate of the rights of the states, and especially the right of each state 30 to order and control its own domestic institutions ac-

---

7 **I do not consider . . . .** This paragraph was written and inserted after the main part of the address had been composed • 10 **Apprehension seems . . . .** Marginal marks indicated that this paragraph was to receive special emphasis in reading

cording to its own judgment exclusively, is essential to that balance of power on which the perfection and endurance of our political fabric depend, and we denounce the lawless invasion by armed force of the soil of any state or territory, no matter under what pretext, as among the gravest of crimes."

I now reiterate these sentiments; and, in doing so, I only press upon the public attention the most conclusive evidence of which the case is susceptible, that 10 the property, peace, and security of no section are to be in any wise endangered by the now incoming administration. I add, too, that all the protection which, consistently with the Constitution and the laws, can be given, will be cheerfully given to all the states when lawfully demanded, for whatever cause—as cheerfully to one section as to another.

There is much controversy about the delivering up of fugitives from service or labor. The clause I now read is as plainly written in the Constitution as any other 20 of its provisions:

"No person held to service or labor in one state, under the laws thereof, escaping into another, shall in consequence of any law or regulation therein be discharged from such service or labor, but shall be delivered up on claim of the party to whom such service or labor may be due."

It is scarcely questioned that this provision was intended by those who made it for the reclaiming of what we call fugitive slaves; and the intention of the 30 lawgiver is the law. All members of Congress swear their support to the whole Constitution—to this provision as much as to any other. To the proposition, then, that slaves whose cases come within the terms of this clause "shall be delivered up," their oaths are unanimous. Now, if they would make the effort in good temper, could they not with nearly equal unanimity frame and pass a law by means of which to keep good that unanimous oath?

There is some difference of opinion whether this 40 clause should be enforced by national or by state authority; but surely that difference is not a very material one. If the slave is to be surrendered, it can be of but little consequence to him or to others by which authority it is done. And should anyone in any case be content that his oath shall go unkept on a merely unsubstantial controversy as to how it shall be kept?

Again, in any law upon this subject, ought not all the safeguards of liberty known in civilized and humane jurisprudence to be introduced, so that a free man be not, in any case, surrendered as a slave? And might it 50 not be well at the same time to provide by law for the enforcement of that clause in the Constitution which guarantees that "the citizen of each state shall be entitled to all privileges and immunities of citizens in the several states"?

I take the official oath today with no mental reservations, and with no purpose to construe the Constitution or laws by any hypercritical rules. And while I do not choose now to specify particular acts of Congress as proper to be enforced, I do suggest that it will be much 60 safer for all, both in official and private stations, to conform to and abide by all those acts which stand unrepealed, than to violate any of them, trusting to find impunity in having them held to be unconstitutional.

It is seventy-two years since the first inauguration of a president under our national Constitution. During that period fifteen different and greatly distinguished citizens have, in succession, administered the executive branch of the government. They have conducted it 70 through many perils, and generally with great success. Yet, with all this scope of precedent, I now enter upon the same task for the brief constitutional term of four years under great and peculiar difficulty. A disruption of the federal Union, heretofore only menaced, is now formidably attempted.

I hold that, in contemplation of universal law and of the Constitution, the union of these states is perpetual. Perpetuity is implied, if not expressed, in the fundamental law of all national governments. It is safe to 80 assert that no government proper ever had a provision in its organic law for its own termination. Continue to execute all the express provisions of our national Constitution, and the Union will endure forever—it being

---

17 **There is much controversy** . . . . Marginal marks show that this was another paragraph to be given emphasis • 50 **And might . . . states.** This sentence was added after the first draft • 56 **I take the official oath** . . . . This paragraph was originally marked for emphatic delivery, but the mark was crossed out • 59 **choose,** originally, "think proper" • 66 **It . . . years** . . . . This was marked for oral emphasis, but the mark was deleted • 75 **heretofore only menaced** . . . and the rest of the sentence, replaced an earlier, longer phrasing

impossible to destroy it except by some action not provided for in the instrument itself.

Again, if the United States be not a government proper, but an association of states in the nature of contract merely, can it, as a contract, be peaceably unmade by less than all the parties who made it? One party to a contract may violate it—break it, so to speak; but does it not require all to lawfully rescind it?

Descending from these general principles, we find the proposition that, in legal contemplation the Union is perpetual confirmed by the history of the Union itself. The Union is much older than the Constitution. It was formed, in fact, by the Articles of Association in 1774. It was matured and continued by the Declaration of Independence in 1776. It was further matured, and the faith of all the then thirteen states expressly plighted and engaged that it should be perpetual, by the Articles of Confederation in 1778. And, finally, in 1787 one of the declared objects for ordaining and establishing the Constitution was "to form a more perfect Union."

But if the destruction of the Union by one or by a part only of the states be lawfully possible, the Union is less perfect than before the Constitution, having lost the vital element of perpetuity.

It follows from these views that no state upon its own mere motion can lawfully get out of the Union; that resolves and ordinances to that effect are legally void; and that acts of violence, within any state or states, against the authority of the United States, are insurrectionary or revolutionary, according to circumstances.

I therefore consider that, in view of the Constitution and the laws, the Union is unbroken and to the extent of my ability I shall take care, as the Constitution itself expressly enjoins upon me, that the laws of the Union be faithfully executed in all the states. Doing this I deem to be only a simple duty on my part; and I shall perform it so far as practicable, unless my rightful masters, the American people, shall withhold the requisite means, or in some authoritative manner direct the contrary. I trust this will not be regarded as a menace, but only as the declared purpose of the Union that it will constitutionally defend and maintain itself.

In doing this there needs to be no bloodshed or violence; and there shall be none, unless it be forced upon the national authority. The power confided to me will be used to hold, occupy, and possess the property and places belonging to the government, and to collect the duties and imposts; but beyond what may be necessary for these objects, there will be no invasion, no using of force against or among the people anywhere. Where hostility to the United States, in any interior locality, shall be so great and universal as to prevent competent resident citizens from holding the federal offices, there will be no attempt to force obnoxious strangers among the people for that object. While the strict legal right may exist in the government to enforce the exercise of these offices, the attempt to do so would be so irritating, and so nearly impracticable withal, that I deem it better to forego for the time the uses of such offices.

The mails, unless repelled, will continue to be furnished in all parts of the Union. So far as possible, the people everywhere shall have that sense of perfect security which is most favorable to calm thought and reflection. The course here indicated will be followed unless current events and experience shall show a modification or change to be proper, and in every case and exigency my best discretion will be exercised according to circumstances actually existing, and with a view and a hope of a peaceful solution of the national troubles and the restoration of fraternal sympathies and affections.

That there are persons in one section or another who seek to destroy the Union at all events, and are glad of any pretext to do it, I will neither affirm nor deny; but if there be such, I need address no word to them. To those, however, who really love the Union may I not speak?

Before entering upon so grave a matter as the destruction of our national fabric, with all its benefits, its memories, and its hopes, would it not be wise to ascertain precisely why we do it? Will you hazard so desperate a step while there is any possibility that any portion of the ills you fly from have no real existence? Will you,

---

31 **I therefore consider** . . . . This paragraph was added to the original draft • 45 **The power confided** . . . . An earlier version read: "All the power at my disposal will be used to reclaim the public property and places which have fallen; to hold, occupy and possess these and all other properties and places belonging to the government." Browning suggested the use of the less threatening version. The sentence nevertheless was considered by contemporaries the most warlike utterance in the speech • 72 **That there are persons** . . . . Marginal marks indicated that Lincoln was to emphasize this paragraph

while the certain ills you fly to are greater than all the real ones you fly from—will you risk the commission of so fearful a mistake?

All profess to be content in the Union if all constitutional rights can be maintained. Is it true, then, that any right, plainly written in the Constitution, has been denied? I think not. Happily the human mind is so constituted that no party can reach to the audacity of doing this. Think, if you can, of a single instance in which a plainly written provision of the Constitution has ever been denied. If by the mere force of numbers a majority should deprive a minority of any clearly written constitutional right, it might, in a moral point of view, justify revolution—certainly would if such a right were a vital one. But such is not our case. All the vital rights of minorities and of individuals are so plainly assured to them by affirmations and negations, guarantees and prohibitions, in the Constitution, that controversies never arise concerning them. But no organic law can ever be framed with a provision specifically applicable to every question which may occur in practical administration. No foresight can anticipate, nor any document of reasonable length contain, express provisions for all possible questions. Shall fugitives from labor be surrendered by national or by state authority? The Constitution does not expressly say. *May* Congress prohibit slavery in the territories? The Constitution does not expressly say. *Must* Congress protect slavery in the territories? The Constitution does not expressly say.

From questions of this class spring all our constitutional controversies, and we divide upon them into majorities and minorities. If the minority will not acquiesce, the majority must, or the government must cease. There is no other alternative; for continuing the government is acquiescence on one side or the other.

If a minority in such case will secede rather than acquiesce, they make a precedent which in turn will divide and ruin them; for a minority of their own will secede from them whenever a majority refuses to be controlled by such minority. For instance, why may not any portion of a new confederacy a year or two hence arbitrarily secede again, precisely as portions of the present Union now claim to secede from it? All who cherish disunion sentiments are now being educated to the exact temper of doing this.

Is there such perfect identity of interests among the states to compose a new Union, as to produce harmony only, and prevent renewed secession?

Plainly, the central idea of secession is the essence of anarchy. A majority held in restraint by constitutional checks and limitations, and always changing easily with deliberate changes of popular opinions and sentiments, is the only true sovereign of a free people. Whoever rejects it does, of necessity, fly to anarchy or to despotism. Unanimity is impossible; the rule of a minority, as a permanent arrangement, is wholly inadmissible; so that, rejecting the majority principle, anarchy or despotism in some form is all that is left.

I do not forget the position, assumed by some, that constitutional questions are to be decided by the Supreme Court; nor do I deny that such decisions must be binding, in any case, upon the parties to a suit, as to the object of that suit, while they are also entitled to very high respect and consideration in all parallel cases by all other departments of the government. And while it is obviously possible that such decisions may be erroneous in any given case, still the evil effect following it, being limited to that particular case, with the chance that it may be overruled and never become a precedent for other cases, can better be borne than could the evils of a different practice. At the same time, the candid citizen must confess that if the policy of the government, upon vital questions affecting the whole people, is to be irrevocably fixed by decisions of the Supreme Court, the instant they are made, in ordinary litigation between parties in personal actions, the people will have ceased to be their own rulers, having to that extent practically resigned their government into the hands of that eminent tribunal. Nor is there in this view any assault upon the court or the judges. It is a duty from which they may not shrink to decide cases properly brought before them, and it is no fault of theirs if others seek to turn their decisions to political purposes.

One section of our country believes slavery is right, and ought to be extended, while the other believes it is wrong, and ought not be extended. This is the only substantial dispute. The fugitive-slave clause of the Constitution, and the law for the suppression of the foreign slave-trade, are each as well enforced, perhaps, as any law can ever be in a community where the moral sense of the people imperfectly supports the law itself. The great body of the people abide by the dry legal obligation in both cases, and a few break over in each. This, I think, cannot be perfectly cured; and it would be worse in both cases after the separation of the sections than before. The foreign slave-trade, now imperfectly suppressed, would be ultimately revived, without restriction, in one section, while fugitive slaves, now only partially surrendered, would not be surrendered at all by the other.

Physically speaking, we cannot separate. We cannot remove our respective sections from each other, nor build
10 an impassable wall between them. A husband and wife may be divorced, and go out of the presence and beyond the reach of each other; but the different parts of our country cannot do this. They cannot but remain face to face, and intercourse, either amicable or hostile, must continue between them. Is it possible, then, to make that intercourse more advantageous or more satisfactory after separation than before? Can aliens make treaties easier than friends can make laws? Can treaties be more faithfully enforced between aliens than laws can among
20 friends? Suppose you go to war, you cannot fight always; and when, after much loss on both sides, and no gain on either, you cease fighting, the identical old questions as to terms of intercourse are again upon you.

This country, with its institutions, belongs to the people who inhabit it. Whenever they shall grow weary of the existing government, they can exercise their constitutional right of amending it, or their revolutionary right to dismember or overthrow it. I cannot be ignorant of the fact that many worthy and patriotic citizens are de-
30 sirous of having the national Constitution amended. While I make no recommendation of amendments, I fully recognize the rightful authority of the people over the whole subject, to be exercised in either of the modes prescribed in the instrument itself; and I should, under existing circumstances, favor rather than oppose a fair opportunity being afforded the people to act upon it. I will venture to add that to me the convention mode seems preferable, in that it allows amendments to originate with the people themselves, instead of only permitting them
40 to take or reject propositions originated by others not especially chosen for the purpose, and which might not be precisely such as they would wish to either accept or refuse. I understand a proposed amendment to the Constitution—which amendment, however, I have not seen— has passed Congress, to the effect that the federal government shall never interfere with the domestic institutions

A silhouette of Lincoln, which appeared on many emblems after his death

of the states, including that of persons held to service. To avoid misconstruction of what I have said, I depart from my purpose not to speak of particular amendments so far as to say that, holding such a provision to now 50 be implied constitutional law, I have no objections to its being made express and irrevocable.

The chief magistrate derives all his authority from the people, and they have conferred none upon him to fix terms for the separation of the states. The people themselves can do this also if they choose; but the executive, as such, has nothing to do with it. His duty is to administer the present government, as it came to his hands, and to transmit it, unimpaired by him, to his successor.

Why should there not be a patient confidence in the 60 ultimate justice of the people? Is there any better or equal hope in the world? In our present differences is either party without faith of being in the right? If the Almighty Ruler of Nations, with His eternal truth and justice, be on your side of the North, or on yours of the South, that truth and that justice will surely prevail by the judgment of this great tribunal of the American people.

By the frame of the government under which we live, this same people have wisely given their public servants 70 but little power for mischief; and have, with equal wisdom, provided for the return of that little to their own hands at very short intervals. While the people retain their virtue and vigilance, no administration, by any extreme of wickedness or folly, can very seriously injure the government in the short space of four years.

My countrymen, one and all, think calmly and well upon this whole subject. Nothing valuable can be lost by taking time. If there be an object to hurry any of you in hot haste to a step which you would never take 80

---

77 **My countrymen** . . . . The paragraph was marked for oral emphasis

deliberately, that object will be frustrated by taking time; but no good object can be frustrated by it. Such of you as are now dissatisfied, still have the old Constitution unimpaired, and, on the sensitive point, the laws of your own framing under it; while the new administration will have no immediate power, if it would, to change either. If it were admitted that you who are dissatisfied hold the right side in the dispute, there still is no single good reason for precipitate action. Intelligence, patriotism, Christianity, and a firm reliance on Him who has never yet forsaken this favored land, are still competent to adjust in the best way all our present difficulty.

In your hands, my dissatisfied fellow-countrymen, and not in mine, is the momentous issue of civil war. The government will not assail you. You can have no conflict without being yourselves the aggressors. You have no oath registered in heaven to destroy the government, while I shall have the most solemn one to "preserve, protect, and defend it."

I am loath to close. We are not enemies, but friends. We must not be enemies. Though passion may have strained, it must not break our bonds of affection. The mystic chords of memory, stretching from every battlefield and patriot grave to every living heart and hearthstone all over this broad land, will yet swell the chorus of the Union when again touched, as surely they will be, by the better angels of our nature.

---

21 **I am loath** . . . . This, at Seward's suggestion, replaced a more aggressive conclusion: "You can forbear the assault upon it [the Government]; I cannot shrink from the defense of it. With you, and not with me, is the solemn question of 'shall it be peace, or a sword?'" Seward, wanting "some words of affection, some of calm and cheerful confidence," suggested: "I close. We are not we must not be aliens or enemies but fellow countrymen and brethren. Although passion has strained our bonds of affection too hardly they must not, I am sure they will not be broken. The mystic chords which proceeding from so many battle fields and so many patriot graves pass through all the hearts and all the hearths in this broad continent of ours will yet again harmonize in their ancient music when breathed upon by the guardian angel of the nation"

Open Letter to Horace Greeley

Horace Greeley, famous and influential editor of the New York **Tribune**, in the issue of August 19, 1862, published an editorial—"The Prayer of 20,000,000 People." It urged complete emancipation of the slaves and indicated doubt concerning Lincoln's policies. Actually, the "Emancipation Proclamation" had already been written, and Lincoln was only waiting for a Union victory which would make politic its publication. The letter which Lincoln wrote in answer to Greeley's attack contains a clear and eloquent statement of the President's policy.

Executive Mansion, Washington,
August 22, 1862

Hon. Horace Greeley.

Dear Sir: I have just read yours of the 19th, addressed to myself through the New York *Tribune.* If there be in it any statements or assumptions of fact which I may know to be erroneous, I do not, now and here, controvert them. If there be in it any inferences which I may believe to be falsely drawn, I do not, now and here, argue against them. If there be perceptible in it an impatient and dictatorial tone, I waive it in deference to an old friend whose heart I have always supposed to be right.

As to the policy I "seem to be pursuing," as you say, I have not meant to leave any one in doubt.

I would save the Union. I would save it the shortest way under the Constitution. The sooner the national authority can be restored, the nearer the Union will be "the Union as it was." If there be those who would not save the Union unless they could at the same time save slavery, I do not agree with them. If there be those who would not save the Union unless they could at the same

time destroy slavery, I do not agree with them. My paramount object in this struggle is to save the Union, and is not either to save or to destroy slavery. If I could save the Union without freeing any slave, I would do it; and if I could save it by freeing all the slaves, I would do it; and if I could save it by freeing some and leaving others alone, I would also do that. What I do about slavery and the coloured race, I do because I believe it helps to save the Union; and what I forbear, I forbear because I do
10 not believe it would help to save the Union. I shall do less whenever I shall believe what I am doing hurts the

cause, and I shall do more whenever I shall believe doing more will help the cause. I shall try to correct errors when shown to be errors, and I shall adopt new views so fast as they shall appear to be true views.

I have here stated my purpose according to my view of official duty; and I intend no modification of my oft-expressed personal wish that all men everywhere could be free.

Yours,

A. LINCOLN
1862

The Gettysburg Address

In September 1863, the dedication of the Gettysburg National Cemetery was planned for the following October 23, but when Edward Everett, a renowned orator of the day, wrote that he could not prepare his oration in so short a time, the date was moved along to November 19. The request that Lincoln speak was an afterthought: the committee asked him, "as Chief Executive," to set apart the grounds "by a few appropriate remarks."

Busy with military and civil duties, the President found little time for composing his brief speech and actually did some work on it the night before its delivery. Lincoln, many of his friends, and most newsmen at the ceremonies thought it was not much of an address; but Everett wrote on November 20: "I should be glad if I could flatter myself that I came as near to the central idea of the occasion in two hours as you did in two minutes." Later, Americans were to come to regard the address as one of the noblest utterances in American history.

The simplicity of the diction, the impressive rhythm, and the majesty of the thought of the address account for much of its appeal. Important, too, is an ordering of the material more complex than at first evident. The treat-

ment of the past, then the present, and, finally, the future is strengthened throughout by a subtle analogy of birth, death, and rebirth. In mentioning the continent, then the nation, then the battlefield, then a portion of the battlefield, Lincoln parallels in a sense the movement which begins with the great accomplishment of the founding fathers, then narrows down to the futile ceremonies at Gettysburg. He thus prepares for a triumphant conclusion which from another view enlarges the true significance of the occasion by noting the vast accomplishment of the heroic dead for the nation and for all the earth.

Four score and seven years ago our fathers brought forth on this continent a new nation, conceived in liberty, and dedicated to the proposition that all men are created equal.

Now we are engaged in a great civil war, testing whether that nation, or any nation so conceived and so dedicated, can long endure. We are met on a great battlefield of that war. We have come to dedicate a portion of that field as a final resting-place for those who here

---

1 **Four score and seven years ago** . . . . Scholars have noted that Robert Toombs of Georgia in 1850 began a speech: "Sixty years ago our fathers joined together to form a more perfect Union and establish justice . . . . We have now met to put that government on trial . . . . In my judgment the verdict is such as to give hope to the friends of liberty throughout the world." Lincoln, speaking to a crowd of serenaders, four and a half months before the dedication, had mentioned the founding of the republic "eighty odd years since" • 8 **We have come** . . . originally read, "We are met . . ."

gave their lives that that nation might live. It is altogether fitting and proper that we should do this.

But in a larger sense we cannot dedicate, we cannot consecrate, we cannot hallow this ground. The brave men, living and dead, who struggled here have consecrated it, far above our poor power to add or detract. The world will little note, nor long remember what we say here, but it can never forget what they did here. It is for us, the living, rather, to be dedicated here to the
10 unfinished work which they who fought here have thus far so nobly advanced. It is rather for us to be here dedicated to the great task remaining before us,—that from these honored dead we take increased devotion to that cause for which they gave the last full measure of

devotion; that we here highly resolve that these dead shall not have died in vain; that this nation, under God, shall have a new birth of freedom; and that government of the people, by the people, and for the people, shall not perish from the earth.

1863

1 **It is altogether fitting** .... The sentence replaced an earlier phrasing, "This we may, in all propriety do" • 16 **under God.** The phrase was not in the copy from which Lincoln read; he apparently inserted it orally while reading • 17 **a new birth of freedom.** The **Chicago Times** criticized this phrase as a misrepresentation of "the motives of men who were slain at Gettysburg." "They gave their lives," said the paper, "to maintain the old government, and the only Constitution and Union." Thus some, at least, saw Lincoln voicing in this phrase his "odious abolition doctrines"

Letter to Mrs. Bixby

This letter was written to a woman who purportedly had heard news of the death of five of her sons on the battlefield. James Bryce, a great English scholar and an admirer of Lincoln, called it "perhaps the most impressive" of Lincoln's letters, and added, "It is short, and it deals with a theme on which hundreds of letters were written daily. But I do not know where the nobility of self-sacrifice for a great cause, and of the consolation which the thought of a sacrifice so made may bring, is set forth with such simple and pathetic beauty."

Executive Mansion
Washington, Nov. 21, 1864

To Mrs. Bixby, Boston, Mass.

Dear Madam. I have been shown in the files of the War Department a statement of the Adjutant-General of Massachusetts that you are the mother of five sons who have died gloriously on the field of battle. I feel how weak and fruitless must be any word of mine which

should attempt to beguile you from the grief of a loss so overwhelming. But I cannot refrain from tendering you the consolation that may be found in the thanks of the republic they died to save. I pray that our Heav- 10 enly Father may assuage the anguish of your bereavement, and leave you only the cherished memory of the loved and lost, and the solemn pride that must be yours to have laid so costly a sacrifice upon the altar of freedom.

Yours very sincerely and respectfully,

A. LINCOLN
1864

Second Inaugural Address

"What think you of the inaugural?" wrote Charles Francis Adams, Jr., to his father, shortly after its delivery, March 4, 1865. "That rail-splitting lawyer is one of the wonders of the day. Once at Gettysburg and now again on a greater occasion he has shown a capacity for rising to the demands of the hour. . . . This inaugural strikes me in its grand simplicity and directness as being for all time the historical keynote of this war. . . ."

Mr. Carl Sandburg indicated the situation at the time the address was delivered when he said in his biography of Lincoln: "On Grant now menacing Lee before Richmond, on Sherman thrusting agony into the vitals of South Carolina—on these final struggles depended the length of the storm not yet spent. And on what the Chief Magistrate might have to say, on his words now, such had become his stature and place, depended much of the face of events and the character of what was to happen when the war was over. This no one understood more deeply and sensitively than Lincoln as he wrote his second inaugural address."

Fellow-Countrymen: At this second appearing to take the oath of the presidential office, there is less occasion for an extended address than there was at the first. Then a statement, somewhat in detail, of a course to be pursued, seemed fitting and proper. Now, at the expiration of four years, during which public declarations have been constantly called forth on every point and phase of the great contest which still absorbs the attention and engrosses the energies of the nation, little that is new
10 could be presented. The progress of our arms, upon which all else chiefly depends, is as well known to the public as to myself; and it is, I trust, reasonably satis-factory and encouraging to all. With high hope for the future, no prediction in regard to it is ventured.

On the occasion corresponding to this four years ago, all thoughts were anxiously directed to an impending civil war. All dreaded it—all sought to avert it. While the inaugural address was being delivered from this place, devoted altogether to saving the Union without war, insurgent agents were in the city seeking to destroy it 20 without war—seeking to dissolve the Union, and divide effects, by negotiation. Both parties deprecated war; but one of them would make war rather than let the nation survive; and the other would accept war rather than let it perish. And the war came.

One eighth of the whole population were colored slaves, not distributed generally over the Union, but localized in the southern part of it. These slaves constituted a peculiar and powerful interest. All knew that this interest was, somehow, the cause of the war. To 30 strengthen, perpetuate, and extend this interest was the object for which the insurgents would rend the Union, even by war; while the government claimed no right to do more than to restrict the territorial enlargement of it.

Neither party expected for the war the magnitude or the duration which it has already attained. Neither anticipated that the cause of the conflict might cease with, or even before, the conflict itself should cease. Each looked for an easier triumph and a result less fundamental and astounding. Both read the same Bible, and 40 pray to the same God; and each invokes his aid against the other. It may seem strange that any man should dare to ask a just God's assistance in wringing their bread from the sweat of other men's faces; but let us judge not, that we be not judged. The prayers of both could not be answered—that of neither has been answered fully.

The Almighty has his own purposes. "Woe unto the world because of offenses! for it must needs be that offenses come; but woe to that man by whom the offense cometh." If we shall suppose that American slavery is 50 one of those offenses which in the providence of God, must needs come, but which, having continued through his appointed time, he now wills to remove, and that he gives to both North and South this terrible war, as the woe due to those by whom the offense came, shall we discern therein any departure from those divine attributes which the believers in a living God always ascribe to him? Fondly do we hope—fervently do we pray—that this mighty scourge of war may speedily pass away. Yet, if God wills that it continue until all the wealth piled by the bondman's two hundred and fifty years of unrequited toil shall be sunk, and until every drop of blood drawn with the lash shall be paid by another drawn with the sword, as was said three thousand years ago, so still it must be said, "The judgments of the Lord are true and righteous altogether."

With malice toward none; with charity for all; with firmness in the right, as God gives us to see the right, let us strive on to finish the work we are in; to bind up the nation's wounds; to care for him who shall have borne the battle, and for his widow and his orphan—to do all which may achieve and cherish a just and lasting peace among ourselves, and with all nations.

1865

"Specimen Days" autobiographical prose work!

1855

Walt Whitman

" Poet of the body + of the soul "

1819 · 1892

Eighteen fifty-five was a year of epoch-making importance in the history of American literature, for in that year appeared the first edition of Walt Whitman's *Leaves of Grass*. Emerson read the book, and wrote enthusiastically to its author: "I greet you at the beginning of a great career, which yet must have had a long foreground somewhere for such a start." Whitman was thirty-six when the *Leaves* first appeared; there had

been a long foreground of preparation, the best record of which is found in his autobiographical prose work, *Specimen Days*.

The son of a carpenter, Whitman was born on Long Island (which he preferred to call by its Indian name,

Illustration: Walt Whitman—frontispiece from the original edition of **Leaves of Grass**

Paumanok), and spent his early life on Long Island and in Brooklyn and New York. "All along the island and its shores," he tells us in *Specimen Days,* "I spent intervals many years, all seasons, sometimes riding, sometimes boating, but generally afoot, absorbing fields, shores, marine incidents, characters, the bay-men, farmers, pilots. . . ." He went frequently to Coney Island, "at that time, a long, bare, unfrequented shore, which I had all to myself, and where I loved, after bathing, to race up and down the hard sand, and declaim Homer or Shakespeare to the surf and sea-gulls by the hour." He attended the public schools of Brooklyn, read omnivorously, listened to Elias Hicks, a Quaker preacher (the Quaker influence is important in Whitman; his mother's family were Quakers). Other early experiences included participating in a debating society, working in printing offices, and teaching country schools on Long Island and "boarding round." "This latter," he said, "I consider one of my best experiences and deepest lessons in human nature behind the scenes." He enjoyed the ferry boats and their pilots, the Broadway omnibuses and their drivers. He had an enormous enthusiasm, moreover, for the theater; he lists in *Specimen Days* the names of plays and actors, of operas and singers, familiar to him in those formative years. In the 1840's he was connected with various newspapers, including the Brooklyn *Daily Eagle,* which he edited in 1846-1847. His knowledge of American life was further enlarged in 1848 by a leisurely journey down the Ohio and Mississippi to New Orleans, a stay of two or three months in that city, and the return journey by way of Chicago and the Great Lakes. (Some biographers have believed—the evidence is not convincing—that while in New Orleans, Whitman had a passionate and transforming love affair.) Upon his return to Brooklyn, he resumed journalistic work and assisted his father in the building of houses. All of these experiences, and many more, in Whitman's expressive phrase, "entered into the gestation of *Leaves of Grass.*" What the decisive influence was which made of Whitman the poet of the *Leaves*—if, indeed, any such influence can ever be posited—no one knows, though it seems reasonable to believe that his reading of Emerson (the essay "The Poet," for example) must have had a quickening effect.

Whitman was not a soldier in the Civil War, but he was none the less one of the war's real heroes. He served indefatigably as a volunteer nurse in the Washington hospitals, distributing knickknacks among the soldiers, writing letters home, radiating cheerfulness and the will to live. He records typical cases in *Specimen Days:* "J.G. lies in bed 52, Ward I; is of Company B, 7th Pennsylvania. I gave him a small sum of money, some tobacco and envelopes. . . . Bed 3, Ward E, Armory, has a great hankering for pickles, something pungent. After consulting the doctor, I gave him a small bottle of horse-radish; also some apples; also a book. . . . Marcus Small, Company K, 7th Maine, sick with dysentery and typhoid fever. . . . I write a letter for him home to East Livermore, Maine." He was supplied with funds, he tells us, "by good women and men in Boston, Salem, Providence, Brooklyn, and New York." He also visited the camp hospitals of the Army of the Potomac in Virginia. Some of his best poems (*Drum-Taps,* 1865) came out of these war experiences. His hitherto magnificent health, however, suffered under the strain and exposure. In the summer of 1864 he was ill with "hospital malaria," from the effects of which he never fully recovered. In 1873 he had a paralytic stroke, and he continued a partial invalid during the remaining nineteen years of his life.

Some ten editions of *Leaves of Grass* were published during Whitman's lifetime. In each succeeding edition, new poems were added and the old poems were considerably revised. His poems were strenuously objected to because of their "formlessness," and still more because of their frank treatment of sex. Emerson tried to persuade Whitman, before the publication of the third edition of the *Leaves* in 1860, to omit the more offensive passages; but Whitman was too well grounded in the Emersonian doctrine of "self-reliance" to heed Emerson's advice. In 1865 Whitman was dismissed by Secretary Harlan from a clerkship in the Department of the Interior on the charge that he was the author of an "indecent book," and W. D. O'Connor wrote his famous defense, *The Good Gray Poet.* The objections to Whitman's "formlessness" and "sensuality" have, no doubt, a measure of validity even today. It is to be noted, however, that his later work is less open to these objections. A study of Whitman's poetic development reveals an increasing mastery of form. Moreover, the later verses are less physical. "I am the poet of the Body and I am the poet of the Soul," he proclaimed in the "Song of Myself" (1855), and he was always both. But the emphasis in the earlier work is upon the flesh, "the jolly bodily phase," and in the later, upon the spirit. In "When Lilacs Last in the Dooryard Bloom'd" (1865), this lover of the body wrote a lyrical hymn to Death, "the strong deliveress." In "Passage to India" (1871), the soul is mystically released from the prison house of the flesh.

Whitman was the poet of America and American democracy. He attempted to embrace the whole of America—an impossible task for a poet. But Whitman succeeded as well in that direction, perhaps, as it is poetically possible to do. He celebrated the westward course of empire. He found his subjects among all sorts and conditions: his catalogues symbolize the equalizing processes of democracy. He asserted "the majesty and reality of the American people *en masse.*" He envisaged, in "Thou Mother with Thy Equal Brood" (1872), an artistic and moral growth:

> Thee in thy own musicians, singers, artists,
>   unborn yet, but certain,
> Thee in thy moral wealth and civilization
>   (until which thy proudest material civili-
>   zation must remain in vain) . . .
> I prophesy.

Above all, he saw America as a nation of free individuals. Newton Arvin's view that Whitman desired a "socialist" state is difficult to accept. Despite his fondness for the phrase *en masse*, his poetry everywhere exalts the individual. To Whitman as to Emerson, the individual was supreme:

> All forces have been steadily employed to com-
>   plete and delight me;
> Now on this spot I stand with my robust soul.

Whitman's poetry was original and revolutionary and indisputably American. He broke with the conventions and traditions of English verse. Of the composition of his poems he said, "I had great trouble in leaving out the stock 'poetical' touches, but succeeded at last." He employed free rhythms which are comparable with those of the Old Testament. There have been, and are still, sharp differences of opinion as to the absolute merit of his work as poetry. Intellectual critics object to his emotionalism and vagueness; formal critics, to his lack of close structure; academic critics, to his apotheosis of the uncultivated. But there can be no question of his power and influence. Even if one reads his poems with certain critical reservations, one responds, as did Thoreau, to Whitman's "alarum or trumpet-note ringing through the American camp" and feels the peculiar magnetic force of

> Camerado, this is no book;
> Who touches this, touches a man.

Leaves of Grass, ed. Emory Holloway, Inclusive Edition, Garden City, 1925 • **Complete Prose Works,** Philadelphia, 1892 • Bliss Perry, **Walt Whitman,** Boston, 1906 • Emory Holloway, **Whitman: An Interpretation in Narrative,** New York, 1926 • Norman Foerster, "Whitman," **American Criticism,** Boston, 1928 • Newton Arvin, **Whitman,** New York, 1938 • H. S. Canby, **Walt Whitman, an American,** Boston, 1943 • G. W. Allen, **Walt Whitman Handbook,** Chicago, 1946 • C. B. Willard, **Whitman's American Fame,** Providence, 1950

Preface to 1855 Edition of "Leaves of Grass"

his ideas of what Poetry should consist of + what should the qualities of a poet be.

The following Preface epitomizes better than any other single selection Whitman's philosophy and his aims in literature. Parts of the Preface were later incorporated, with only minor changes, in the poem "By Blue Ontario's Shore."

America does not repel the past or what it has produced under its forms or amid other politics or the idea of castes or the old religions . . . accepts the lesson with calmness . . . is not so impatient as has been supposed that the slough still sticks to opinions and manners and literature while the life which served its requirements has passed into the new life of the new forms . . . perceives that the corpse is slowly borne from the eating and sleeping rooms of the house . . . perceives that it

3 religions. . . . The dots are Whitman's throughout and do not indicate omissions

His aims in Poetry:
(1) To show Common man —
(2) to show his own country — America
in a new way. No imitation.

waits a little while in the door . . . that it was fittest for its days . . . that its action has descended to the stalwart and wellshaped heir who approaches . . . and that he shall be fittest for his days.

The Americans of all nations at any time upon the earth have probably the fullest poetical nature. The United States themselves are essentially the greatest poem. In the history of the earth hitherto the largest and most stirring appear tame and orderly to their ampler 10 largeness and stir. Here at last is something in the doings of man that corresponds with the broadcast doings of the day and night. Here is not merely a nation but a teeming nation of nations. Here is action untied from strings necessarily blind to particulars and details magnificently moving in vast masses. Here is the hospitality which forever indicates heroes. . . . Here are the roughs and beards and space and ruggedness and nonchalance that the soul loves. Here the performance disdaining the trivial unapproached in the tremendous audacity of its 20 crowds and groupings and the push of its perspective spreads with crampless and flowing breadth and showers its prolific and splendid extravagance. One sees it must indeed own the riches of the summer and winter, and need never be bankrupt while corn grows from the ground or the orchards drop apples or the bays contain fish or men beget children upon women.

Other states indicate themselves in their deputies . . . but the genius of the United States is not best or most in its executives or legislatures, nor in its ambassadors 30 or authors or colleges or churches or parlors, nor even in its newspapers or inventors . . . but always most in the common people. Their manners speech dress friendships —the freshness and candor of their physiognomy—the picturesque looseness of their carriage . . . their deathless attachment to freedom—their aversion to anything indecorous or soft or mean—the practical acknowledgment of the citizens of one state by the citizens of all other states—the fierceness of their roused resentment— their curiosity and welcome of novelty—their self-esteem 40 and wonderful sympathy—their susceptibility to a slight —the air they have of persons who never knew how it felt to stand in the presence of superiors—the fluency of their speech—their delight in music, the sure symptom of manly tenderness and native elegance of soul . . . their good temper and open-handedness—the terrible significance of their elections—the President's taking off his

hat to them not they to him—these too are unrhymed poetry. It awaits the gigantic and generous treatment worthy of it.

The largeness of nature or the nation were monstrous 50 without a corresponding largeness and generosity of the spirit of the citizen. Not nature nor swarming states nor streets and steamships nor prosperous business nor farms nor capital nor learning may suffice for the ideal of man . . . nor suffice the poet. No reminiscences may suffice either. A live nation can always cut a deep mark and can have the best authority the cheapest . . . namely from its own soul. This is the sum of the profitable uses of individuals or states and of present action and grandeur and of the subjects of poets.—As if it were necessary to 60 trot back generation after generation to the eastern records! As if the beauty and sacredness of the demonstrable must fall behind that of the mythical! As if men do not make their mark out of any times! As if the opening of the western continent by discovery and what has transpired since in North and South America were less than the small theatre of the antique or the aimless sleepwalking of the middle ages! The pride of the United States leaves the wealth and finesse of the cities and all returns of commerce and agriculture and all the magni- 70 tude of geography or shows of exterior victory to enjoy the breed of full sized men or one full sized man unconquerable and simple.

The American poets are to enclose old and new for America is the race of races. Of them a bard is to be commensurate with a people. To him the other continents arrive as contributions . . . he gives them reception for their sake and his own sake. His spirit responds to his country's spirit . . . he incarnates its geography and natural life and rivers and lakes. Mississippi with annual 80 freshets and changing chutes, Missouri and Columbia and Ohio and Saint Lawrence with the falls and beautiful masculine Hudson, do not embouchure where they spend themselves more than they embouchure into him. The blue breadth over the inland sea of Virginia and Maryland and the sea off Massachusetts and Maine and over Manhattan bay and over Champlain and Erie and over Ontario and Huron and Michigan and Superior, and over

---

83 **embouchure,** used here as a verb meaning to pour or empty. The word is properly a noun meaning "mouth"

America is a great
poem in itself!
all people have poetical nature

the Texan and Mexican and Floridian and Cuban seas and over the seas off California and Oregon, is not tallied by the blue breadth of the waters below more than the breadth of above and below is tallied by him. When the long Atlantic coast stretches longer and the Pacific coast stretches longer he easily stretches with them north or south. He spans between them also from east to west and reflects what is between them. On him rise solid growths that offset the growths of pine and cedar and 10 hemlock and liveoak and locust and chestnut and cypress and hickory and limetree and cottonwood and tuliptree and cactus and wildvine and tamarind and persimmon . . . and tangles as tangled as any canebreak or swamp . . . and forests coated with transparent ice and icicles hanging from the boughs and crackling in the wind . . . and sides and peaks of mountains . . . and pasturage sweet and free as savannah or upland or prairie . . . with flights and songs and screams that answer those of the wild-pigeon and highhold and orchard-oriole and coot and 20 surf-duck and redshouldered-hawk and fish-hawk and white-ibis and indianhen and cat-owl and water-pheasant and qua-bird and pied-sheldrake and blackbird and mockingbird and buzzard and condor and night-heron and eagle. To him the hereditary countenance descends both mother's and father's. To him enter the essences of the real things and past and present events—of the enormous diversity of temperature and agriculture and mines—the tribes of red aborigines—the weather-beaten vessels entering new ports or making landings on rocky coasts— 30 the first settlements north or south—the rapid stature and muscle—the haughty defiance of '76, and the war and peace and formation of the constitution . . . the union always surrounded by blatherers and always calm and impregnable—the perpetual coming of immigrants —the wharf-hem'd cities and superior marine—the unsurveyed interior—the loghouses and clearings and wild animals and hunters and trappers . . . the free commerce —the fisheries and whaling and gold-digging—the endless gestation of new states—the convening of Congress 40 every December, the members duly coming up from all climates and the uttermost parts . . . the noble character of the young mechanics and of all free American workmen and workwomen . . . the general ardor and friendliness and enterprise—the perfect equality of the female with the male . . . the large amativeness—the fluid movement of the population—the factories and mercan-

tile life and laborsaving machinery—the Yankee swap— the New-York firemen and the target excursion—the southern plantation life—the character of the northeast and of the northwest and southwest—slavery and the 50 tremulous spreading of hands to protect it, and the stern opposition to it which shall never cease till it ceases or the speaking of tongues and the moving of lips cease. For such the expression of the American poet is to be transcendant and new. It is to be indirect and not direct or descriptive or epic. Its quality goes through these to much more. Let the age and wars of other nations be chanted and their eras and characters be illustrated and that finish the verse. Not so the great psalms of the republic. Here the theme is creative and has vista. Here 60 comes one among the well-beloved stonecutters and plans with decision and science and sees the solid and beautiful forms of the future where there are now no solid forms.

Of all nations the United States with veins full of poetical stuff most need poets and will doubtless have the greatest and use them the greatest. Their Presidents shall not be their common referee so much as their poets shall. Of all mankind the great poet is the equable man. Not in him but off from him things are grotesque or eccen- 70 tric or fail of their sanity. Nothing out of its place is good and nothing in its place is bad. He bestows on every object or quality its fit proportions neither more nor less. He is the arbiter of the diverse and he is the key. He is the equalizer of his age and land . . . he supplies what wants supplying and checks what wants checking. If peace is the routine out of him speaks the spirit of peace, large, rich, thrifty, building vast and populous cities, encouraging agriculture and the arts and commerce—lighting the study of man, the soul, immortal- 80 ity—federal, state or municipal government, marriage, health, free trade, inter-travel by land and sea . . . nothing too close, nothing too far off . . . the stars not too far off. In war he is the most deadly force of the war. Who recruits him recruits horse and foot . . . he fetches parks of

---

19 **highhold**, woodpecker • 19 **coot**, a ducklike bird • 22 **qua-bird**, the heron • 45 **amativeness**, the capacity for physical love, a term from phrenology. For Whitman's interest in phrenology, see Edward Hungerford, "Walt Whitman and his Chart of Bumps," **American Literature** (January 1931)

artillery the best that engineer ever knew. If the time becomes slothful and heavy he knows how to arouse it . . . he can make every word he speaks draw blood. Whatever stagnates in the flat of custom or obedience or legislation he never stagnates. Obedience does not master him, he masters it. High up out of reach he stands turning a concentrated light . . . he turns the pivot with his finger . . . he baffles the swiftest runners as he stands and easily overtakes and envelops them. The time straying toward infidelity and confections and persiflage he withholds by his steady faith . . . he spreads out his dishes . . . he offers the sweet firmfibred meat that grows men and women. His brain is the ultimate brain. He is no arguer . . . he is judgment. He judges not as the judge judges but as the sun falling around a helpless thing. As he sees the farthest he has the most faith. His thoughts are the hymns of the praise of things. In the talk on the soul and eternity and God off of his equal plane he is silent. He sees eternity less like a play with a prologue and denouement . . . he sees eternity in men and women . . . he does not see men and women as dreams or dots. Faith is the antiseptic of the soul . . . it pervades the common people and preserves them . . . they never give up believing and expecting and trusting. There is that indescribable freshness and unconsciousness about an illiterate person that humbles and mocks the power of the noblest expressive genius. The poet sees for a certainty how one not a great artist may be just as sacred as the greatest artist. . . . The power to destroy or remould is freely used by him but never the power of attack. What is past is past. If he does not expose superior models and prove himself by every step he takes he is not what is wanted. The presence of the greatest poet conquers . . . not parleying or struggling or any prepared attempts. Now he has passed that way see after him! there is not left any vestige of despair or misanthropy or cunning or exclusiveness or the ignominy of a nativity or color or delusion of hell or the necessity of hell . . . and no man thenceforward shall be degraded for ignorance or weakness or sin.

The greatest poet hardly knows pettiness or triviality. If he breathes into any thing that was before thought small it dilates with the grandeur and life of the universe. He is a seer . . . he is individual . . . he is complete in himself . . . the others are as good as he, only he sees it and they do not. He is not one of the chorus . . . he does not stop for any regulations . . . he is the president of regulation. What the eyesight does to the rest he does to the rest. Who knows the curious mystery of the eyesight? The other senses corroborate themselves, but this is removed from any proof but its own and foreruns the identities of the spiritual world. A single glance of it mocks all the investigations of man and all the instruments and books of the earth and all reasoning. What is marvelous? what is unlikely? what is impossible or baseless or vague? after you have once just opened the space of a peachpit and given audience to far and near and to the sunset and had all things enter with electric swiftness softly and duly without confusion or jostling or jam.

The land and sea, the animals fishes and birds, the sky of heaven and the orbs, the forests mountains and rivers, are not small themes . . . but folks expect of the poet to indicate more than the beauty and dignity which always attach to dumb real objects . . . they expect him to indicate the path between reality and their souls. Men and women perceive the beauty well enough . . probably as well as he. The passionate tenacity of hunters, woodmen, early risers, cultivators of gardens and orchards and fields, the love of healthy women for the manly form, seafaring persons, drivers of horses, the passion for light and the open air, all is an old varied sign of the unfailing perception of beauty and of a residence of the poetic in outdoor people. They can never be assisted by poets to perceive . . . some may but they never can. The poetic quality is not marshalled in rhyme or uniformity or abstract addresses to things nor in melancholy complaints or good precepts, but is the life of these and much else and is in the soul. The profit of rhyme is that it drops seeds of a sweeter and more luxuriant rhyme, and of uniformity that it conveys itself into its own roots in the ground out of sight. The rhyme and uniformity of perfect poems show the free growth of metrical laws and bud from them as unerringly and loosely as lilacs or roses on a bush, and take shapes as compact as the shapes of chestnuts and oranges and melons and pears, and shed the perfume impalpable to form. The fluency and ornaments of the finest poems or music or orations or recitations are not independent but dependent. All beauty comes from beautiful blood and a beautiful brain. If the greatnesses are in conjunction in a man or woman it is enough . . . the fact will prevail through the universe . . . but the gaggery and gilt of a million years will not prevail. Who troubles himself about his ornaments or fluency is lost. This is what you shall do: Love the earth and sun and the animals, despise riches, give alms to every one that asks, stand up for the stupid and crazy, devote your income and labor to others, hate tyrants, argue not concerning God, have patience and indulgence toward the people, take off your hat to nothing known or unknown or to any man or number of men, go freely with powerful uneducated persons and with the young and with the mothers of families, read these leaves in the open air every season of every year of your life, re-examine all you have been told at school or church or in any book, dismiss whatever insults your own soul, and your very flesh shall be a great poem and have the richest fluency not only in its words but in the silent lines of its lips and face and between the lashes of your eyes and in every motion and joint of your body. . . . The poet shall not spend his time in unneeded work. He shall know that the ground is always ready plowed and manured . . . others may not know it but he shall. He shall go directly to the creation. His trust shall master the trust of everything he touches . . . and shall master all attachment.

The known universe has one complete lover and that is the greatest poet. He consumes an eternal passion and is indifferent which chance happens and which possible contingency of fortune or misfortune and persuades daily and hourly his delicious pay. What balks or breaks others is fuel for his burning progress to contact and amorous joy. Other proportions of the reception of pleasure dwindle to nothing to his proportions. All expected from heaven or from the highest he is rapport with in the sight of the daybreak or a scene of the winterwoods or the presence of children playing or with his arm round the neck of a man or woman. His love above all love has leisure and expanse . . . he leaves room ahead of himself. He is no irresolute or susspicious lover . . . he is sure . . . he scorns intervals. His experience and the showers and thrills are not for nothing. Nothing can jar him . . . suffering and darkness cannot—death and fear cannot. To him complaint and jealousy and envy are corpses buried and rotten in the earth . . . he saw them buried. The sea is not surer of the shore or the shore of the sea than he is of the fruition of his love and of all perfection and beauty.

The fruition of beauty is no chance of hit or miss . . . it is inevitable as life . . . it is exact and plumb as gravitation. From the eyesight proceeds another eyesight and from the hearing proceeds another hearing and from the voice proceeds another voice eternally curious of the harmony of things with man. To these respond perfections not only in the committees that were supposed to stand for the rest but in the rest themselves just the same. These understand the law of perfection in masses and floods . . . that its finish is to each for itself and onward from itself . . . that it is profuse and impartial . . . that there is not a minute of the light or dark nor an acre of the earth or sea without it—nor any direction of the sky nor any trade or employment nor any turn of events. This is the reason that about the proper expression of beauty there is precision and balance . . . one part does not need to be thrust above another. The best singer is not the one who has the most lithe and powerful organ . . . the pleasure of poems is not in them that take the handsomest measure and similes and sound.

Without effort and without exposing in the least how it is done the greatest poet brings the spirit of any or all events and passions and scenes and persons some more and some less to bear on your individual character as you hear or read. To do this well is to compete with the laws that pursue and follow time. What is the purpose must surely be there and the clue of it must be there . . . and the faintest indication is the indication of the best and then becomes the clearest indication. Past and present and future are not disjoined but joined. The greatest poet forms the consistence of what is to be from what has been and is. He drags the dead out of their coffins and stands them again on their feet . . . he says to the past, Rise and walk before me that I may realize you. He learns the lesson . . . he places himself where the future becomes present. The greatest poet does not only dazzle his rays over character and scenes and passions . . . he finally ascends and finishes all . . . he exhibits the pinnacles that no man can tell what they are for or what is beyond . . . he glows a moment on the extremest verge. He is most wonderful in his last half-hidden smile or frown . . . by that flash of the moment of parting the one that sees it shall be encouraged or terrified after-

1 gaggery, joking ridicule

His Poetry can disguess anything & It's free.

Nothing can hinder or effect his individuality

wards for many years. The greatest poet does not moralize or make applications of morals . . . he knows the soul. The soul has that measureless pride which consists in never acknowledging any lessons but its own. But it has sympathy as measureless as its pride and the one balances the other and neither can stretch too far while it stretches in company with the other. The inmost secrets of art sleep with the twain. The greatest poet has lain close betwixt both and they are vital in his style and thoughts.

The art of art, the glory of expression and the sunshine of the light of letters is simplicity. Nothing is better than simplicity . . . nothing can make up for excess or for the lack of definiteness. To carry on the heave of impulse and pierce intellectual depths and give all subjects their articulations are powers neither common nor very uncommon. But to speak in literature with the perfect rectitude and insouciance of the movements of animals and the unimpeachableness of the sentiment of trees in the woods and grass by the roadside is the flawless triumph of art. If you have looked on him who has achieved it you have looked on one of the masters of the artists of all nations and times. You shall not contemplate the flight of the graygull over the bay or the mettlesome action of the blood horse or the tall leaning of sunflowers on their stalk or the appearance of the sun journeying through heaven or the appearance of the moon afterward with any more satisfaction than you shall contemplate him. The greatest poet has less a marked style and is more the channel of thoughts and things without increase or diminution, and is the free channel of himself. He swears to his art, I will not be meddlesome, I will not have in my writing any elegance or effect or originality to hang in the way between me and the rest like curtains. I will have nothing hang in the way, not the richest curtains. What I tell I tell for precisely what it is. Let who may exalt or startle or fascinate or soothe I will have purposes as health or heat or snow has and be as regardless of observation. What I experience or portray shall go from my composition without a shred of my composition. You shall stand by my side and look in the mirror with me.

The old red blood and stainless gentility of great poets will be proved by their unconstraint. A heroic person walks at his ease through and out of that custom or precedent or authority that suits him not. Of the

traits of the brotherhood of writers savans musicians inventors and artists nothing is finer than silent defiance advancing from new free forms. In the need of poems philosophy politics mechanism science behaviour, the craft of art, an appropriate native grand-opera, shipcraft, or any craft, he is greatest forever and forever who contributes the greatest original practical example. The cleanest expression is that which finds no sphere worthy of itself and makes one.

The messages of great poets to each man and woman are, Come to us on equal terms, Only then can you understand us, We are no better than you, What we enclose you enclose, What we enjoy you may enjoy. Did you suppose there could be only one Supreme? We affirm there can be unnumbered Supremes, and that one does not countervail another any more than one eyesight countervails another . . . and that men can be good or grand only of the consciousness of their supremacy within them. What do you think is the grandeur of storms and dismemberments and the deadliest battles and wrecks and the wildest fury of the elements and the power of the sea and the motion of nature and of the throes of human desires and dignity and hate and love? It is that something in the soul which says, Rage on, Whirl on, I tread master here and everywhere, Master of the spasms of the sky and of the shatter of the sea, Master of nature and passion and death, And of all terror and all pain.

The American bards shall be marked for generosity and affection and for encouraging competitors. . . . They shall be kosmos . . . without monopoly or secrecy . . glad to pass any thing to any one . . . hungry for equals night and day. They shall not be careful of riches and privilege they shall be riches and privilege . . . they shall perceive who the most affluent man is. The most affluent man is he that confronts all the shows he sees by equivalents out of the stronger wealth of himself. The American bard shall delineate no class of persons nor one or two out of the strata of interests nor love most nor truth most nor the soul most nor the body most . . . and not be for the eastern states more than the western or the northern states more than the southern.

Exact science and its practical movements are no checks on the greatest poet but always his encouragement and support. The outset and remembrance are there . . . there are the arms that lifted him first and

brace him best . . . there he returns after all his goings and comings. The sailor and traveler . . . the atomist chemist astronomer geologist phrenologist spiritualist mathematician historian and lexicographer are not poets, but they are the lawgivers of poets and their construction underlies the structure of every perfect poem. No matter what rises or is uttered they sent the seed of the conception of it . . . of them and by them stand the visible proofs of souls . . . always of their father-
10 stuff must be begotten the sinewy races of bards. If there shall be love and content between the father and the son and if the greatness of the son is the exuding of the greatness of the father there shall be love between the poet and the man of demonstrable science. In the beauty of poems are the tuft and final applause of science.

Great is the faith of the flush of knowledge and of the investigation of the depths of qualities and things. Cleaving and circling here swells the soul of the poet yet is president of itself always. The depths are fath-
20 omless and therefore calm. The innocence and nakedness are resumed . . . they are neither modest not immodest. The whole theory of the special and supernatural and all that was twined with it or educed out of it departs as a dream. What has ever happened . . . what happens and whatever may or shall happen, the vital laws enclose all . . . they are sufficient for any case and for all cases . . . none to be hurried or retarded . . . any miracle of affairs or persons inadmissible in the vast clear scheme where every motion and every spear
30 of grass and the frames and spirits of men and women and all that concerns them are unspeakably perfect miracles all referring to all and each distinct and in its place. It is also not consistent with the reality of the soul to admit that there is anything in the known universe more divine than men and women.

Men and women and the earth and all upon it are simply to be taken as they are, and the investigation of their past and present and future shall be unintermitted and shall be done with perfect candor. Upon this basis
40 philosophy speculates ever looking toward the poet, ever regarding the eternal tendencies of all toward happiness never inconsistent with what is clear to the senses and to the soul. For the eternal tendencies of all toward happiness make the only point of sane philosophy. Whatever comprehends less than that . . . whatever is less than the laws of light and of astronomical motion

. . . or less than the laws that follow the thief the liar the glutton and the drunkard through this life and doubtless afterward . . . or less than vast stretches of time or the slow formation of density or the patient upheaving of 50 strata—is of no account. Whatever would put God in a poem or system of philosophy as contending against some being or influence, is also of no account. Sanity and ensemble characterise the great master . . . spoilt in one principle all is spoilt. The great master has nothing to do with miracles. He sees health for himself in being one of the mass . . . he sees the hiatus in singular eminence. To the perfect shape comes common ground. To be under the general law is great for that is to correspond with it. The master knows that he is unspeakably great and 60 that all are unspeakably great . . . that nothing for instance is greater than to conceive children and bring them up well . . . that to be is just as great as to perceive or tell.

In the make of the great masters the idea of political liberty is indispensable. Liberty takes the adherence of heroes wherever men and women exist . . . but never takes any adherence or welcome from the rest more than from poets. They are the voice and exposition of liberty. They out of ages are worthy the grand idea . . . to them it is confided and they must sustain it. Nothing has 70 precedence of it and nothing can warp or degrade it. The attitude of great poets is to cheer up slaves and horrify despots. The turn of their necks, the sound of their feet, the motions of their wrists, are full of hazard to the one and hope to the other. Come nigh them awhile and though they neither speak or advise you shall learn the faithful American lesson. Liberty is poorly served by men whose good intent is quelled from one failure or two failures or any number of failures, or from the casual indifference or ingratitude of the 80 people, or from the sharp show of the tushes of power, or the bringing to bear soldiers and cannon or any penal statutes. Liberty relies upon itself, invites no one, promises nothing, sits in calmness and light, is positive and composed, and knows no discouragement. The battle rages with many a loud alarm and frequent advance and retreat . . . the enemy triumphs . . . the prison, the handcuffs, the iron necklace and anklet, the scaffold, garrote and leadballs do their work . . . the cause is asleep . . . the strong throats are choked with their own 90 blood . . . the young men drop their eyelashes toward the ground when they pass each other . . . and is liberty gone out of that place? No never. When liberty goes it is not the first to go nor the second nor third to go . . . it waits for all the rest to go . . . it is the last . . . When the memories of the old martyrs are faded utterly away . . . when the large names of patriots are laughed at in the public halls from the lips of the orators . . . when the boys are no more christened after the same but christened after tyrants and traitors instead . . . when the laws of the free are grudgingly permitted and laws for informers and blood-money are sweet to the taste of the people . . . when I and you walk abroad upon the earth stung with compassion at the sight of numberless brothers answering our equal friendship and calling no man master—and when we are elated with noble joy at the sight of slaves . . . when the soul retires in the cool communion of the night and surveys its experience and has much extasy over the word and deed that put back a helpless innocent person into the gripe of the gripers or into any cruel inferiority . . . when those in all parts of these states who could easier realize the true American character but do not yet—when the swarms of cringers, suckers, doughfaces, lice of politics, planners of sly involutions for their own preferment to city offices or state legislatures or the judiciary or congress or the presidency, obtain a response of love and natural deference from the people whether they get the offices or no . . . when it is better to be a bound booby and rogue in office at a high salary than the poorest free mechanic or farmer with his hat unmoved from his head and firm eyes and a candid and generous heart . . . and when servility by town or state or the federal government or any oppression on a large scale or small scale can be tried on without its own punishment following duly after in exact proportion against the smallest chance of escape . . . or rather when all life and all the souls of men and women are discharged from any part of the earth—then only shall the instinct of liberty be discharged from that part of the earth.

As the attributes of the poets of the kosmos concentre in the real body and soul and in the pleasure of things they possess the superiority of genuineness over all fiction and romance. As they emit themselves facts are showered over with light . . . the daylight is lit with more volatile light . . . also the deep between the setting and rising sun goes deeper many fold. Each precise object or condition or combination or process exhibits

a beauty . . . the multiplication table its—old age its— the carpenter's trade its—the grand-opera its . . . the hugehulled cleanshaped New-York clipper at sea under steam or full sail gleams with unmatched beauty . . . the American circles and large harmonies of government gleam with theirs . . . and the commonest definite intentions and actions with theirs. The poets of the kosmos advance through all interpositions and coverings and turmoils and stratagems to first principles. They are of use . . . they dissolve poverty from its need and riches from its conceit. You large proprietor they say shall not realize or perceive more than any one else. The owner of the library is not he who holds a legal title to it having bought and paid for it. Any one and every one is owner of the library who can read the same through all the varieties of tongues and subjects and styles, and in whom they enter with ease and take residence and force toward paternity and maternity, and make supple and powerful and rich and large. . . . These American states strong and healthy and accomplished shall receive no pleasure from violations of natural models and must not permit them. In paintings or mouldings or carvings in mineral or wood, or in the illustrations of books or newspapers, or in any comic or tragic prints, or in the patterns of woven stuffs or anything to beautify rooms or furniture or costumes, or to put upon cornices or monuments or on the prows or sterns of ships, or to put anywhere before the human eye indoors or out, that which distorts honest shapes or which creates unearthly beings or places or contingencies is a nuisance and revolt. Of the human form especially it is so great it must never be made ridiculous. Of ornaments to a work nothing outre can be allowed . . . but those ornaments can be allowed that conform to the perfect facts of the open air and that flow out of the nature of the work and come irrepressibly from it and are necessary to the completion of the work. Most works are most beautiful without ornament. . . . Exaggerations will be revenged in human physiology. Clean and vigorous children are jetted and conceived only in those communities where the models of natural forms are public every day. . . .

---

22 suckers . . . doughfaces, an interesting example of Whitman's use of slang. Doughfaces were Northern Congressmen who did not oppose Negro slavery in the South, or its extension into the Southwest (see Dictionary of American English) • 47 its, exhibits its beauty • 79 outre, or outré, uncommon, bizarre

Great genius and the people of these states must never be demeaned to romances. As soon as histories are properly told there is no more need of romances.

The great poets are also to be known by the absence in them of tricks and by the justification of perfect personal candor. Then folks echo a new cheap joy and a divine voice leaping from their brains: How beautiful is candor! All faults may be forgiven of him who has perfect candor. Henceforth let no man of us lie, for we have seen that openness wins the inner and outer world and that there is no single exception, and that never since our earth gathered itself in a mass have deceit or subterfuge or prevarication attracted its smallest particle or the faintest tinge of a shade—and that through the enveloping wealth and rank of a state or the whole republic of states a sneak or sly person shall be discovered and despised . . . and that the soul has never been once fooled and never can be fooled . . . and thrift without the loving nod of the soul is only a fœtid puff . . . and there never grew up in any of the continents of the globe nor upon any planet or satellite or star, nor upon the asteroids, nor in any part of ethereal space, nor in the midst of density, nor under the fluid wet of the sea, nor in the condition which precedes the birth of babes, nor at any time during the changes of life, nor in that condition that follows what we term death, nor in any stretch of abeyance or action afterward of vitality, nor in any process of formation or reformation anywhere, a being whose instinct hated the truth.

Extreme caution or prudence, the soundest organic health, large hope and comparison and fondness for women and children, large alimentiveness and destructiveness and causality, with a perfect sense of the oneness of nature and the propriety of the same spirit applied to human affairs . . . these are called up of the float of the brain of the world to be parts of the greatest poet from his birth out of his mother's womb and from her birth out of her mother's. Caution seldom goes far enough. It has been thought that the prudent citizen was the citizen who applied himself to solid gains and did well for himself and his family and completed a lawful life without debt or crime. The greatest poet sees and admits these economies as he sees the economies of food and sleep, but has higher notions of prudence than to think he gives much when he gives a few slight attentions at the latch of the gate. The premises of the prudence of life are not the hospitality of it or the ripeness and harvest of it. Beyond the independence of a little sum laid aside for burial-money, and of a few clap-boards around and shingles overhead on a lot of American soil owned, and the easy dollars that supply the year's plain clothing and meals, the melancholy prudence of the abandonment of such a great being as a man is to the toss and pallor of years of moneymaking with all their scorching days and icy nights and all their stifling deceits and underhanded dodgings, or infinitesimals of parlors, or shameless stuffing while others starve . . . and all the loss of the bloom and odor of the earth and of the flowers and atmosphere and of the sea and of the true taste of the women and men you pass or have to do with in youth or middle age, and the issuing sickness and desperate revolt at the close of a life without elevation or naivete, and the ghastly chatter of a death without serenity or majesty, is the great fraud upon modern civilization and forethought, blotching the surface and system which civilization undeniably drafts, and moistening with tears the immense features it spreads and spreads with such velocity before the reached kisses of the soul. . . . Still the right explanation remains to be made about prudence. The prudence of the mere wealth and respectability of the most esteemed life appears too faint for the eye to observe at all when little and large alike drop quietly aside at the thought of the prudence suitable for immortality. What is wisdom that fills the thinness of a year or seventy or eighty years to wisdom spaced out by ages and coming back at a certain time with strong reinforcements and rich presents and the clear faces of wedding-guests as far as you can look in every direction running gaily toward you? Only the soul is of itself . . . all else has reference to what ensues. All that a person does or thinks is of consequence. Not a move can a man or woman make that affects him or her in a day or a month or any part of the direct lifetime or the hour of death but the same affects him or her onward afterward

---

2 **demeaned to romances**, debased to the standard of conduct set forth in romantic fiction • 32 **alimentiveness**, capacity for eating and drinking; a term from phrenology • 32 **destructiveness and causality**, also phrenological terms. Destructiveness means a capacity for excited interest in scenes of destructive violence such as storms, fires, and battles; causality, a sense of cause and effect

through the indirect lifetime. The indirect is always as great and real as the direct. The spirit receives from the body just as much as it gives to the body. Not one name of word or deed . . . not of venereal sores or discolorations . . . not the privacy of the onanist . . . not of the putrid veins of gluttons or rum drinkers . . . not peculation or cunning or betrayal or murder . . . no serpentine poison of those that seduce women . . . not the foolish yielding of women . . . not prostitution . . . not

10 any depravity of young men . . . not of the attainment of gain by discreditable means . . . not any nastiness of appetite . . . not any harshness of officers to men or judges to prisoners or fathers to sons or sons to fathers or husbands to wives or bosses to their boys . . . not of greedy looks or malignant wishes . . . nor any of the wiles practised by people upon themselves . . . ever is or ever can be stamped on the programme but it is duly realized and returned, and that returned in further per-

formances . . . and they returned again. Nor can the

20 push of charity or personal force ever be any thing else than the profoundest reason, whether it brings arguments to hand or no. No specification is necessary . . . to add or subtract or divide is in vain. Little or big, learned or unlearned, white or black, legal or illegal, sick or well, from the first inspiration down the windpipe to the last expiration out of it, all that a male or female does that is vigorous and benevolent and clean is so much sure profit to him or her in the unshakable order of the universe and through the whole scope of it

30 forever. If the savage or felon is wise it is well . . . if the greatest poet or savan is wise it is simply the same . . . if the President or chief justice is wise it is the same . . . if the young mechanic or farmer is wise it is no more or less . . . if the prostitute is wise it is no more nor less. The interest will come round . . . all will come round. All the best actions of war and peace . . . all help given to relatives and strangers and the poor and old and sorrowful and young children and widows and the sick, and to all shunned persons . . . all furtherance

40 of fugitives and of the escape of slaves . . . all the self-denial that stood steady and aloof on wrecks and saw others take the seats of the boats . . . all offering of substance or life for the good old cause, or for a friend's sake or opinion's sake . . . all pains of enthusiasts scoffed at by their neighbors . . . all the vast sweet love and precious suffering of mothers . . . all honest men baffled

in strifes recorded or unrecorded . . . all the grandeur and good of the few ancient nations whose fragments of annals we inherit . . . and all the good of the hundreds of far mightier and more ancient nations unknown to us 50 by name or date or location . . . all that was ever manfully begun, whether it succeeded or not . . . all that has at any time been well suggested out of the divine heart of man or by the divinity of his mouth or by the shaping of his great hands . . . and all that is well thought or done this day on any part of the surface of the globe . . . or on any of the wandering stars or fixed stars by those there as we are here . . . or that is henceforth to be well thought or done by you whoever you are, or by any one—these singly and wholly inured at their 60 time and inure now and will inure always to the identities from which they sprung or shall spring. . . . Did you guess any of them lived only its moment? The world does not so exist . . . no parts palpable or impalpable so exist . . . no result exists now without being from its long antecedent result, and that from its antecedent, and so backward without the farthest mentionable spot coming a bit nearer to the beginning than any other spot. . . . Whatever satisfies the soul is truth. The prudence of the greatest poet answers 70 at last the craving and glut of the soul, is not contemptuous of less ways of prudence if they conform to its ways, puts off nothing, permits no let-up for its own case or any case, has no particular sabbath or judgment-day, divides not the living from the dead or the righteous from the unrighteous, is satisfied with the present, matches every thought or act by its correlative, knows no possible forgiveness or deputed atonement . . . knows that the young man who composedly periled his life and lost it has done exceeding well for 80 himself, while the man who has not periled his life and retains it to old age in riches and ease has perhaps achieved nothing for himself worth mentioning . . . and that only that person has no great prudence to learn who has learnt to prefer real longlived things, and favors body and soul the same, and perceives the indirect assuredly following the direct, and what evil or good he does leaping onward and waiting to meet him again—and who in his spirit in any emergency whatever neither hurries or avoids death. 90

The direct trial of him who would be the greatest poet is to-day. If he does not flood himself with the immediate age as with vast oceanic tides . . . and if he does not attract his own loud body and soul to himself and hang on its neck with incomparable love and plunge his semitic muscle into its merits and demerits . . . and if he be not himself the age transfigured . . . and if to him is not opened the eternity which gives similitude to all periods and locations and processes and animate and inanimate forms, and which is the bond of time, and rises up from its inconceivable vagueness and infiniteness in the swimming shape of to-day, and is held by the ductile anchors of life, and makes the present spot the passage from what was to what shall be, and commits itself to the representation of this wave of an hour and this one of the sixty beautiful children of the wave—let him merge in the general run and wait his developement. . . . Still the final test of poems or any character or work remains. The prescient poet projects himself centuries ahead and judges performer or performance after the changes of time. Does it live through them? Does it still hold on untired? Will the same style and the direction of genius to similar points be satisfactory now? Has no new discovery in science or arrival at superior planes of thought and judgment and behaviour fixed him or his so that either can be looked down upon? Have the marches of tens and hundreds and thousands of years made willing detours to the right hand and the left hand for his sake? Is he beloved long and long after he is buried? Does the young man think often of him? and the young woman think often of him? and do the middle-aged and the old think of him?

A great poem is for ages and ages in common and for all degrees and complexions and all departments and sects and for a woman as much as a man and a man as much as a woman. A great poem is no finish to a man or woman but rather a beginning. Has anyone fancied he could sit at last under some due authority and rest satisfied with explanations and realize and be content and full? To no such terminus does the greatest poet bring . . . he brings neither cessation or sheltered fatness and ease. The touch of him tells in action. Whom he takes he takes with firm sure grasp into live regions previously unattained . . . thenceforward is no rest . . . they see the space and ineffable sheen that turn the old spots and lights into dead vacuums. The companion of him beholds the birth and progress of stars and learns one of the meanings. Now there

shall be a man cohered out of tumult and chaos . . . the elder encourages the younger and shows him how . . . they two shall launch off fearlessly together till the new world fits an orbit for itself and looks unabashed on the lesser orbits of the stars and sweeps through the ceaseless rings and shall never be quiet again.

There will soon be no more priests. Their work is done. They may wait awhile . . . perhaps a generation or two . . . dropping off by degrees. A superior breed shall take their place . . . the gangs of kosmos and prophets en masse shall take their place. A new order shall arise and they shall be the priests of man, and every man shall be his own priest. The churches built under their umbrage shall be the churches of men and women. Through the divinity of themselves shall the kosmos and the new breed of poets be interpreters of men and women and of all events and things. They shall find their inspiration in real objects to-day, symptoms of the past and future . . . They shall not deign to defend immortality or God or the perfection of things or liberty or the exquisite beauty and reality of the soul. They shall arise in America and be responded to from the remainder of the earth.

The English language befriends the grand American expression . . . it is brawny enough and limber and full enough. On the tough stock of a race who through all change of circumstances was never without the idea of political liberty, which is the animus of all liberty, it has attracted the terms of daintier and gayer and subtler and more elegant tongues. It is the powerful language of resistance . . . it is the dialect of common sense. It is the speech of the proud and melancholy races and of all who aspire. It is the chosen tongue to express growth faith self-esteem freedom justice equality friendliness amplitude prudence decision and courage. It is the medium that shall well nigh express the inexpressible.

No great literature nor any like style of behaviour or oratory or social intercourse or household arrangements or public institutions or the treatment by bosses of employed people, nor executive detail or detail of the army or navy, nor spirit of legislation or courts or police or tuition or architecture or songs or amuse-

---

56 **gangs,** without the usual unfavorable connotation

ments or the costumes of young men, can long elude the jealous and passionate instinct of American standards. Whether or no the sign appears from the mouths of the people, it throbs a live interrogation in every freeman's and freewoman's heart after that which passes by or this built to remain. Is it uniform with my country? Are its disposals without ignominious distinctions? Is it for the evergrowing communes of brothers and lovers, large, well-united, proud beyond the old models, generous beyond all models? Is it something grown fresh out of the fields or drawn from the sea for use to me to-day here? I know that what answers for me an American must answer for any individual or nation that serves for a part of my materials. Does this answer? or is it without reference to universal needs? or sprung of the needs of the less developed society of special ranks? or old needs of pleasure overlaid by modern science and forms? Does this acknowledge liberty with audible and absolute acknowledgement, and set slavery at naught for life and death? Will it help breed one goodshaped and wellhung man, and a woman to be his perfect and independent mate? Does it improve manners? Is it for the nursing of the young of the republic? Does it solve readily with the sweet milk of the nipples of the breasts of the mother of many children? Has it too the old ever-fresh forbearance and impartiality? Does it look with the same love on the last born and those hardening toward stature, and on the errant, and on those who disdain all strength of assault outside of their own?

The poems distilled from other poems will probably pass away. The coward will surely pass away. The expectation of the vital and great can only be satisfied by the demeanor of the vital and great. The swarms of the polished deprecating and reflectors and the polite float off and leave no remembrance. America prepares with composure and goodwill for the visitors that have sent word. It is not intellect that is to be their warrant and welcome. The talented, the artist, the ingenious, the editor, the statesman, the erudite . . . they are not unappreciated . . . they fall in their place and do their work. The soul of the nation also does its work. No disguise can pass on it . . . no disguise can conceal from it. It rejects none, it permits all. Only toward as good as itself and toward the like of itself will it advance half-way. An individual is as superb as a nation when he has the qualities which make a superb nation. The soul of the largest and wealthiest and proudest nation may well go half-way to meet that of its poets. The signs are effectual. There is no fear of mistake. If the one is true the other is true. The proof of a poet is that his country absorbs him as affectionately as he has absorbed it.

1855

One's-Self I Sing

"One's-Self I Sing" is the first poem in the standard edition of **Leaves of Grass** issued in 1902 by Whitman's literary executors, Richard Maurice Bucke, Thomas B. Harned, and Horace L. Traubel, and the sequence of poems in the following selections follows the sequence of that edition. The first date appended to this and other poems by Whitman is that of earliest publication. The second date is that of the poem's first appearance in final form. It should be noted that Whitman constantly revised his work, that most of his poems exist in several intermediary stages, and that the versions presented here show the poems as they were finally revised by the poet.

"One's-Self I Sing" strikes at once the keynote of much of Whitman's poetry: his democratic society is composed of "simple separate persons."

One's-Self I sing, a simple separate person,
Yet utter the word Democratic, the word En-Masse.

Of physiology from top to toe I sing,
Not physiognomy alone nor brain alone is worthy for
   the Muse,
   I say the Form complete is worthier far,
The Female equally with the Male I sing.

Of Life immense in passion, pulse, and power,
Cheerful, for freest action form'd under the laws divine,
The Modern Man I sing.

1867·1871

Song of Myself

Strictly speaking, Whitman is not writing about himself. Many, perhaps most, of the experiences recorded in the poem are purely imaginary. His aim is to embrace the whole of human experience by means of imaginative sympathy. This power of imaginative sympathy, which Whitman possessed to an extraordinary degree, enables him to identify himself with all sorts and conditions of men. "Of every hue and caste am I, of every rank and religion," he declared; he becomes "the hounded slave," "the mashed fireman," and the scores of others described in the poem. He fraternizes with all; their interests are his ("Whatever interests the rest interests me"). All men and women, moreover, are potentially equal in the sight of Whitman—"size is only development." "Song of Myself" is perhaps the most thoroughly democratic poem in the literature of the world.

Structurally, it is the loosest of compositions, held together chiefly by the all-pervading personality of the author.

The present form of "Song of Myself" is the result of many revisions, deletions, and additions made between 1855, the date of its first appearance, and 1881. The student can trace these changes by consulting the "Variorum Readings" in Emory Holloway's "Inclusive Edition" of **Leaves of Grass**.

1

I celebrate myself, and sing myself,
And what I assume you shall assume,
For every atom belonging to me as good belongs to you.

I loafe and invite my soul,
I lean and loafe at my ease observing a spear of summer grass. *The individual —*

My tongue, every atom of my blood, form'd from this
    soil, this air,
Born here of parents born here from parents the same,
    and their parents the same,
I, now thirty-seven years old in perfect health begin,
Hoping to cease not till death.

Creeds and schools in abeyance,   10
Retiring back a while sufficed at what they are, but
    never forgotten,
I harbor for good or bad, I permit to speak at every
    hazard,
Nature without check with original energy.

2

Houses and rooms are full of perfumes, the shelves are
    crowded with perfumes,
I breathe the fragrance myself and know it and like it,
The distillation would intoxicate me also, but I shall not
    let it.

The atmosphere is not a perfume, it has no taste of the
    distillation, it is odorless,
It is for my mouth forever, I am in love with it,
I will go to the bank by the wood and become undis-
    guised and naked,
I am mad for it to be in contact with me.   20

The smoke of my own breath,
Echoes, ripples, buzz'd whispers, love-root, silk-thread,
    crotch and vine,
My respiration and inspiration, the beating of my heart,
    the passing of blood and air through my lungs,
The sniff of green leaves and dry leaves, and of the shore
    and dark-color'd sea-rocks, and of hay in the barn,
The sound of the belch'd words of my voice loos'd to
    the eddies of the wind,
A few light kisses, a few embraces, a reaching around
    of arms,
The play of shine and shade on the trees as the supple
    boughs wag,
The delight alone or in the rush of the streets, or along
    the fields and hill-sides,
The feeling of health, the full-noon trill, the song of me
    rising from bed and meeting the sun.

Have you reckon'd a thousand acres much? have you
    reckon'd the earth much?   30
Have you practis'd so long to learn to read?
Have you felt so proud to get at the meaning of poems?

Stop this day and night with me and you shall possess
    the origin of all poems,

divinity of body.

You shall possess the good of the earth and sun, (there are millions of suns left,)
You shall no longer take things at second or third hand, nor look through the eyes of the dead, nor feed on the spectres in books,
You shall not look through my eyes either, nor take things from me,
You shall listen to all sides and filter them from your self.

3

I have heard what the talkers were talking, the talk of the beginning and the end,
But I do not talk of the beginning or the end.

There was never any more inception than there is now,   40
Nor any more youth or age than there is now,
And will never be any more perfection than there is now,
Nor any more heaven or hell than there is now.

Urge and urge and urge,
Always the procreant urge of the world.
Out of the dimness opposite equals advance, always substance and increase, always sex,
Always a knit of identity, always distinction, always a breed of life.

To elaborate is no avail, learn'd and unlearn'd feel that it is so.

Sure as the most certain sure, plumb in the uprights, well entretied, braced in the beams,
Stout as a horse, affectionate, haughty, electrical,   50
I and this mystery here we stand.

Clear and sweet is my soul, and clear and sweet is all that is not my soul.

Lack one lacks both, and the unseen is proved by the seen,
Till that becomes unseen and receives proof in its turn.

Showing the best and dividing it from the worst age vexes age,
Knowing the perfect fitness and equanimity of things, while they discuss I am silent, and go bathe and admire myself.

Welcome is every organ and attribute of me, and of any man hearty and clean,
Not an inch nor a particle of an inch is vile, and none shall be less familiar than the rest.

I am satisfied—I see, dance, laugh, sing;
As the hugging and loving bed-fellow sleeps at my side through the night, and withdraws at the peep of the day with stealthy tread,   60
Leaving me baskets cover'd with white towels swelling the house with their plenty,
Shall I postpone my acceptation and realization and scream at my eyes,
That they turn from gazing after and down the road,
And forthwith cipher and show me to a cent,
Exactly the value of one and exactly the value of two, and which is ahead?

4

Trippers and askers surround me,
People I meet, the effect upon me of my early life or the ward and city I live in, or the nation,
The latest dates, discoveries, inventions, societies, authors old and new,
My dinner, dress, associates, looks, compliments, dues,
The real or fancied indifference of some man or woman I love,   70
The sickness of one of my folks or of myself, or ill-doing or loss or lack of money, or depressions or exaltations,
Battles, the horrors of fratricidal war, the fever of doubtful news, the fitful events;
These come to me days and nights and go from me again,
But they are not the Me myself.

Apart from the pulling and hauling stands what I am,
Stands amused, complacent, compassionating, idle, unitary,
Looks down, is erect, or bends an arm on an impalpable certain rest,
Looking with side-curved head curious what will come next,

---

49 entretied, tied together

Both in and out of the game and watching and wonder-
    ing at it.

Backward I see in my own days where I sweated through
    fog with linguists and contenders,   80
I have no mockings or arguments, I witness and wait.

5

I believe in you my soul, the other I am must not abase
    itself to you,
And you must not be abased to the other.

Loafe with me on the grass, loose the stop from your
    throat,
Not words, not music or rhyme I want, not custom or
    lecture, not even the best,
Only the lull I like, the hum of your valvèd voice.

I mind how once we lay such a transparent summer
    morning,
How you settled your head athwart my hips and gently
    turn'd over upon me,
And parted the shirt from my bosom-bone, and plunged
    your tongue to my bare-stript heart,
And reach'd till you felt my beard, and reach'd till you
    held my feet.   90

Swiftly arose and spread around me the peace and
    knowledge that pass all the argument of the earth,
And I know that the hand of God is the promise of my
    own,
And I know that the spirit of God is the brother of my
    own,
And that all the men ever born are also my brothers,
    and the women my sisters and lovers,
And that a kelson of the creation is love,
And limitless are leaves stiff or drooping in the fields,
And brown ants in the little wells beneath them,
And mossy scabs of the worm fence, heap'd stones, elder,
    mullein and poke-weed.

6

A child said *What is the grass?* fetching it to me with
    full hands,
How could I answer the child? I do not know what it is
    any more than he.   100

I guess it must be the flag of my disposition, out of
    hopeful green stuff woven.

★ Or I guess it is the handkerchief of the Lord,   *match*
A scented gift and remembrancer designedly dropt,
Bearing the owner's name someway in the corners, that
    we may see and remark, and say *Whose?*

Or I guess the grass is itself a child, the produced babe
    of the vegetation.   *man — a projection of God —*

Or I guess it is a uniform hieroglyphic,
And it means, Sprouting alike in broad zones, and nar-
    row zones,
Growing among black folks as among white,
Kanuck, Tuckahoe, Congressman, Cuff, I give them the
    same, I receive them the same.

And now it seems to me the beautiful uncut hair of
    graves.   110

Tenderly will I use you curling grass,
It may be you transpire from the breasts of young
    men,
It may be if I had known them I would have loved
    them,
It may be you are from old people, or from offspring
    taken soon out of their mothers' laps,
And here you are the mothers' laps.

This grass is very dark to be from the white heads of old
    mothers,
Darker than the colorless beards of old men,
Dark to come from under the faint red roofs of mouths.
O I perceive after all so many uttering tongues,
And I perceive they do not come from the roofs of
    mouths for nothing.   120

I wish I could translate the hints about the dead young
    men and women,
And the hints about old men and mothers, and the off-
    spring taken soon out of their laps.

---

109 **Kanuck**, a French Canadian • 109 **Tuckahoe**, an inhabitant of
the lowlands of Virginia • 109 **Cuff**, a Negro • 112 **transpire**,
in the literal sense of "breathe through"

What do you think has become of the young and old men?
And what do you think has become of the women and
    children?

They are alive and well somewhere,
The smallest sprout shows there is really no death,
And if ever there was it led forward life, and does not
    wait at the end to arrest it,
And ceas'd the moment life appear'd.

All goes onward and outward, nothing collapses,
And to die is different from what any one supposed,
    and luckier.   130

7

Has any one supposed it lucky to be born?
I hasten to inform him or her it is just as lucky to die,
    and I know it.

I pass death with the dying and birth with the new-
    wash'd babe, and am not contain'd between my
    hat and boots,
And peruse manifold objects, no two alike and every
    one good,
The earth good and the stars good, and their adjuncts
    all good.

I am not an earth nor an adjunct of an earth,
I am the mate and companion of people, all just as im-
    mortal and fathomless as myself,
(They do not know how immortal, but I know.)

Every kind for itself and its own, for me mine male and
    female,
For me those that have been boys and that love
    women,   140
For me the man that is proud and feels how it stings to
    be slighted,
For me the sweet-heart and the old maid, for me mothers
    and the mothers of mothers,
For me lips that have smiled, eyes that have shed tears,
For me children and the begetters of children.

Undrape! you are not guilty to me, nor stale nor dis-
    carded,
I see through the broadcloth and gingham whether or no,

And am around, tenacious, acquisitive, tireless, and can-
    not be shaken away.

8

The little one sleeps in its cradle,
I lift the gauze and look a long time, and silently brush
    away flies with my hand.

The youngster and the red-faced girl turn aside up the
    bushy hill,   150
I peeringly view them from the top.

The suicide sprawls on the bloody floor of the bedroom,
I witness the corpse with its dabbled hair, I note where
    the pistol has fallen.

The blab of the pave, tires of carts, sluff of boot-soles,
    talk of the promenaders,
The heavy omnibus, the driver with his interrogating
    thumb, the clank of the shod horses on the granite
    floor,
The snow-sleighs, clinking, shouted jokes, pelts of snow-
    balls,
The hurrahs for popular favorites, the fury of rous'd
    mobs,
The flap of the curtain'd litter, a sick man inside borne
    to the hospital,
The meeting of enemies, the sudden oath, the blows and
    fall,
The excited crowd, the policeman with his star quickly
    working his passage to the centre of the crowd,   160
The impassive stones that receive and return so many
    echoes,
What groans of over-fed or half-starv'd who fall sun-
    struck or in fits,
What exclamations of women taken suddenly who hurry
    home and give birth to babes,
What living and buried speech is always vibrating here,
    what howls restrain'd by decorum,
Arrests of criminals, slights, adulterous offers made, ac-
    ceptances, rejections with convex lips,
I mind them or the show or resonance of them—I come
    and I depart.

---

154 **blab . . . pave,** idle talk of the street or pavement

The big doors of the country barn stand open and ready,
The dried grass of the harvest-time loads the slow-drawn
    wagon,
The clear light plays on the brown gray and green in-
    tertinged,
The armfuls are pack'd to the sagging mow.   170

I am there, I help, I came stretch'd atop of the load,
I felt its soft jolts, one leg reclined on the other,
I jump from the cross-beams and seize the clover and
    timothy,
And roll head over heels and tangle my hair full of wisps.

10

Alone far in the wilds and mountains I hunt,
Wandering amazed at my own lightness and glee,
In the late afternoon choosing a safe spot to pass the
    night,
Kindling a fire and broiling the fresh-kill'd game,
Falling asleep on the gather'd leaves with my dog and
    gun by my side.

The Yankee clipper is under her sky-sails, she cuts the
    sparkle and scud,   180
My eyes settle the land, I bend at her prow or shout joy-
    ously from the deck.
The boatmen and clam-diggers arose early and stopt for
    me,
I tuck'd my trowser-ends in my boots and went and had
    a good time;
You should have been with us that day round the
    chowder-kettle.

I saw the marriage of the trapper in the open air in the
    far west, the bride was a red girl,
Her father and his friends sat near cross-legged and
    dumbly smoking, they had moccasins to their feet
    and large thick blankets hanging from their
    shoulders,
On a bank lounged the trapper, he was drest mostly in
    skins, his luxuriant beard and curls protected his
    neck, he held his bride by the hand,
She had long eyelashes, her coarse straight locks de-
    scended upon her voluptuous limbs and reach'd to
    her feet.

The runaway slave came to my house and stopt outside,
I heard his motions crackling the twigs of the
    woodpile,   190
Through the swung half-door of the kitchen I saw him
    limpsy and weak,
And went where he sat on a log and led him in and
    assured him,
And brought water and fill'd a tub for his sweated body
    and bruis'd feet,
And gave him a room that enter'd from my own, and
    gave him some coarse clean clothes,
And remember perfectly well his revolving eyes and his
    awkwardness,
And remember putting plasters on the galls of his neck
    and ankles;
He staid with me a week before he was recuperated and
    pass'd north,
I had him sit next me at table, my fire-lock lean'd in the
    corner.

11

Twenty-eight young men bathe by the shore,
Twenty-eight young men and all so friendly;   200
Twenty-eight years of womanly life and all so lonesome.

She owns the fine house by the rise of the bank,
She hides handsome and richly drest aft the blinds of the
    window.

Which of the young men does she like the best?
Ah the homeliest of them is beautiful to her.

Where are you off to, lady? for I see you,
You splash in the water there, yet stay stock still in your
    room.

Dancing and laughing along the beach came the twenty-
    ninth bather,
The rest did not see her, but she saw them and loved
    them.

The beards of the young men glisten'd with wet, it ran
    from their long hair,   210
Little streams pass'd all over their bodies.

---

191 limpsy, limp

An unseen hand also pass'd over their bodies,
It descended tremblingly from their temples and ribs.

The young men float on their backs, their white bellies
    bulge to the sun, they do not ask who seizes fast to
    them,
They do not know who puffs and declines with
    pendant and bending arch,
They do not think whom they souse with spray.

12

The butcher-boy puts off his killing-clothes, or sharpens
    his knife at the stall in the market,
I loiter enjoying his repartee and his shuffle and break-
    down.
Blacksmiths with grimed and hairy chests environ the
    anvil,
Each has his main-sledge, they are all out, there is a great
    heat in the fire.   220

From the cinder-strew'd threshold I follow their move-
    ments,
The lithe sheer of their waists plays even with their
    massive arms,
Overhand the hammers swing, overhand so slow, over-
    hand so sure,
They do not hasten, each man hits in his place.

13

The Negro holds firmly the reins of his four horses, the
    block swags underneath on its tied-over chain,
The Negro that drives the long dray of the stone-yard,
    steady and tall he stands pois'd on one leg on the
    string-piece,
His blue shirt exposes his ample neck and breast and
    loosens over his hip-band,
His glance is calm and commanding, he tosses the
    slouch of his hat away from his forehead,
The sun falls on his crispy hair and mustache, falls on
    the black of his polish'd and perfect limbs.

I behold the picturesque giant and love him, and I do
    not stop there,   230
I go with the team also.

In me the caresser of life wherever moving, backward as
    well as forward sluing,

To niches aside and junior bending, not a person or ob-
    ject missing,
Absorbing all to myself and for this song.

Oxen that rattle the yoke and chain or halt in the leafy
    shade, what is that you express in your eyes?
It seems to me more than all the print I have read in my
    life.

My tread scares the wood-drake and wood-duck on my
    distant and day-long ramble,
They rise together, they slowly circle around.

I believe in those wing'd purposes,
And acknowledge red, yellow, white, playing within
    me,   240
And consider green and violet and the tufted crown
    intentional,
And do not call the tortoise unworthy because she is not
    something else,
And the jay in the woods never studied the gamut, yet
    trills pretty well to me,
And the look of the bay mare shames silliness out of me.

14

The wild gander leads his flock through the cool
    night,
Ya-honk he says, and sounds it down to me like an
    invitation,
The pert may suppose it meaningless, but I listening
    close,
Find its purpose and place up there toward the wintry
    sky.

The sharp-hoof'd moose of the north, the cat on the
    house-sill, the chickadee, the prairie-dog,
The litter of the grunting sow as they tug at her
    teats,   250
The brood of the turkey-hen and she with her half-
    spread wings,
I see in them and myself the same old law.

---

218 **shuffle and break-down**, a noisy, rapid, shuffling dance • 222
sheer, upward curvature (applied to the lines of a ship when viewed
from the side) • 226 **string-piece**, a long piece of timber serving to
connect and support a framework • 232 **sluing**, turning or twisting

The press of my foot to the earth springs a hundred affections,
They scorn the best I can do to relate them.

I am enamour'd of growing out-doors,
Of men that live among cattle or taste of the ocean or
woods,
Of the builders and steerers of ships and the wielders of
axes and mauls, and the drivers of horses,
I can eat and sleep with them week in and week out.

What is commonest, cheapest, nearest, easiest, is Me,
Me going in for my chances, spending for vast
returns,   260
Adorning myself to bestow myself on the first that will
take me,
Not asking the sky to come down to my good will,
Scattering it freely forever.

15

The pure contralto sings in the organ loft,
The carpenter dresses his plank, the tongue of his fore-
plane whistles its wild ascending lisp,
The married and unmarried children ride home to their
Thanksgiving dinner,
The pilot seizes the king-pin, he heaves down with a
strong arm,
The mate stands braced in the whale-boat, lance and
harpoon are ready,
The duck-shooter walks by silent and cautious stretches,
The deacons are ordain'd with cross'd hands at the
altar,   270
The spinning-girl retreats and advances to the hum of
the big wheel,
The farmer stops by the bars as he walks on a First-day
loafe and looks at the oats and rye,
The lunatic is carried at last to the asylum a confirm'd
case,
(He will never sleep any more as he did in the cot in his
mother's bed-room;)
The jour printer with gray head and gaunt jaws works
at his case,
He turns his quid of tobacco while his eyes blurr with
the manuscript;
The malform'd limbs are tied to the surgeon's table,
What is removed drops horribly in a pail;

The quadroon girl is sold at the auction-stand, the
drunkard nods by the bar-room stove,
The machinist rolls up his sleeves, the policeman travels
his beat, the gate-keeper marks who pass,   280
The young fellow drives the express-wagon, (I love him,
though I do not know him;)
The half-breed straps on his light boots to compete in
the race,
The western turkey-shooting draws old and young, some
lean on their rifles, some sit on logs,
Out from the crowd steps the marksman, takes his posi-
tion, levels his piece;
The groups of newly-come immigrants cover the wharf
or levee,
As the woolly-pates hoe in the sugar-field, the overseer
views them from his saddle,
The bugle calls in the ball-room, the gentlemen run for
their partners, the dancers bow to each other,
The youth lies awake in the cedar-roof'd garret and
harks to the musical rain,
The Wolverine sets traps on the creek that helps fill the
Huron,
The squaw wrapt in her yellow-hemm'd cloth is offering
moccasins and bead-bags for sale,   290
The connoisseur peers along the exhibition-gallery with
half-shut eyes bent sideways.
As the deck-hands make fast the steamboat the plank is
thrown for the shore-going passengers,
The young sister holds out the skein while the elder
sister winds it off in a ball, and stops now and then
for the knots,
The one-year wife is recovering and happy having a
week ago borne her first child,
The clean-hair'd Yankee girl works with her sewing-
machine or in the factory or mill,
The paving-man leans on his two-handed rammer, the
reporter's lead flies swiftly over the note-book, the
sign painter is lettering with blue and gold,
The canal boy trots on the tow-path, the book-keeper
counts at his desk, the shoemaker waxes his
thread,
The conductor beats time for the band and all the performers follow him,

275 jour, journeyman • 289 Wolverine, an inhabitant of Michigan

The child is baptized, the convert is making his first professions,

The regatta is spread on the bay, the race is begun, (how the white sails sparkle!) 300

The drover watching his drove sings out to them that would stray,

The pedler sweats with his pack on his back, (the purchaser higgling about the odd cent;)

The bride unrumples her white dress, the minute-hand of the clock moves slowly,

The opium-eater reclines with rigid head and just-open'd lips,

The prostitute draggles her shawl, her bonnet bobs on her tipsy and pimpled neck,

The crowd laugh at her blackguard oaths, the men jeer and wink to each other,

(Miserable! I do not laugh at your oaths nor jeer you;)

The President holding a cabinet council is surrounded by the great Secretaries,

On the piazza walk three matrons stately and friendly with twined arms,

The crew of the fish-smack pack repeated layers of halibut in the hold, 310

The Missourian crosses the plains toting his wares and his cattle,

As the fare-collector goes through the train he gives notice by the jingling of loose change,

The floor-men are laying the floor, the tinners are tinning the roof, the masons are calling for mortar,

In single file each shouldering his hod pass onward the laborers;

Seasons pursuing each other the indescribable crowd is gather'd, it is the fourth of Seventh-month, (what salutes of cannon and small arms!)

Seasons pursuing each other the plougher ploughs, the mower mows, and the winter-grain falls in the ground;

Off on the lakes the pike-fisher watches and waits by the hole in the frozen surface,

The stumps stand thick round the clearing, the squatter strikes deep with his axe,

Flatboatmen make fast towards dusk near the cottonwood or pecan-trees,

Coon-seekers go through the regions of the Red river or through those drain'd by the Tennessee, or through those of the Arkansas, 320

Torches shine in the dark that hangs on the Chattahooche or Altamahaw,

Patriarchs sit at supper with sons and grandsons and great grandsons around them,

In walls of adobie, in canvas tents, rest hunters and trappers after their day's sport,

The city sleeps and the country sleeps,

The living sleep for their time, the dead sleep for their time,

The old husband sleeps by his wife and the young husband sleeps by his wife;

And these tend inward to me, and I tend outward to them,

And such as it is to be of these more or less I am,

And of these one and all I weave the song of myself.

I am of old and young, of the foolish as much as the wise, 330

Regardless of others, ever regardful of others,

Maternal as well as paternal, a child as well as a man,

Stuff'd with the stuff that is coarse and stuff'd with the stuff that is fine,

One of the Nation of many nations, the smallest the same and the largest the same,

A Southerner soon as a Northerner, a planter nonchalant and hospitable down by the Oconee I live,

A Yankee bound my own way ready for trade, my joints the limberest joints on earth and the sternest joints on earth,

A Kentuckian walking the vale of the Elkhorn in my deer-skin leggings, a Louisianian or Georgian,

A boatman over lakes or bays or along coasts, a Hoosier, Badger, Buckeye;

At home on Kanadian snow-shoes or up in the bush, or with fishermen off Newfoundland,

At home in the fleet of ice-boats, sailing with the rest and tacking, 340

At home on the hills of Vermont or in the woods of Maine, or the Texan ranch,

Comrade of Californians, comrade of free North-Westerners, (loving their big proportions,)

---

320 **Coon,** raccoon • 321 **Chattahooche or Altamahaw,** rivers in Georgia • 335 **Oconee,** a river in Georgia • 337 **Elkhorn,** a river in Nebraska • 338 **Hoosier,** an inhabitant of Indiana • 338 **Badger,** an inhabitant of Wisconsin • 338 **Buckeye,** an inhabitant of Ohio

Comrade of raftsmen and coalmen, comrade of all who
    shake hands and welcome to drink and meat,
A learner with the simplest, a teacher of the thought-
    fullest,
A novice beginning yet experient of myriads of seasons,
Of every hue and caste am I, of every rank and religion,
A farmer, mechanic, artist, gentleman, sailor, quaker,
Prisoner, fancy-man, rowdy, lawyer, physician, priest.

I resist any thing better than my own diversity,
Breathe the air but leave plenty after me,   350
And am not stuck up, and am in my place.

(The moth and the fish-eggs are in their place,
The bright suns I see and the dark suns I cannot see
    are in their place,
The palpable is in its place and the impalpable is in
    its place.)

17

These are really the thoughts of all men in all ages
    and lands, they are not original with me,
If they are not yours as much as mine they are noth-
    ing, or next to nothing,
If they are not the riddle and the untying of the
    riddle they are nothing,
If they are not just as close as they are distant they are
    nothing.

This is the grass that grows wherever the land is and
    the water is,
This the common air that bathes the globe.   360

18

With music strong I come, with my cornets and my
    drums,
I play not marches for accepted victors only, I play
    marches for conquer'd and slain persons.

Have you heard that it was good to gain the day?
I also say it is good to fall, battles are lost in the same
    spirit in which they are won.

I beat and pound for the dead,
I blow through my embouchures my loudest and
    gayest for them.

Vivas to those who have fail'd!
And to those whose war-vessels sank in the sea!
And to those themselves who sank in the sea!
And to all generals that lost engagements, and all
    overcome heroes!   370
And the numberless unknown heroes equal to the
    greatest heroes known!

19

This is the meal equally set, this the meat for natural
    hunger,
It is for the wicked just the same as the righteous, I
    make appointments with all,
I will not have a single person slighted or left away,
The kept-woman, sponger, thief, are hereby invited,
The heavy-lipp'd slave is invited, the venerealee is
    invited;
There shall be no difference between them and the
    rest.

This is the press of a bashful hand, this the float and
    odor of hair,
This the touch of my lips to yours, this the murmur
    of yearning,
This the far-off depth and height reflecting my own
    face,   380
This the thoughtful merge of myself, and the outlet
    again.

Do you guess I have some intricate purpose?
Well I have, for the Fourth-month showers have, and
    the mica on the side of a rock has.

Do you take it I would astonish?
Does the daylight astonish? does the early redstart
    twittering through the woods?
Do I astonish more than they?
This hour I tell things in confidence,
I might not tell everybody, but I will tell you.

20

Who goes there? hankering, gross, mystical, nude;
How is it I extract strength from the beef I eat?   390

---

348 **fancy-man,** a man who lives on the gains of a prostitute • 367
Vivas, literally "long live"; shouts expressing good will

famous

What is a man anyhow? what am I? what are you?

All I mark as my own you shall offset it with your own,
Else it were time lost listening to me.

I do not snivel that snivel the world over,
That months are vacuums and the ground but wallow
    and filth.

Whimpering and truckling fold with powders for in-
    valids, conformity goes to the fourth-remov'd,
I wear my hat as I please indoors or out.

Why should I pray? why should I venerate and be
    ceremonious?

Having pried through the strata, analyzed to a hair,
    counsel'd with doctors and calculated close,
I find no sweeter fat than sticks to my own bones.   400

In all people I see myself, none more and not one a
    barley-corn less,
And the good or bad I say of myself I say of them.

I know I am solid and sound,
To me the converging objects of the universe perpetually
    flow,
All are written to me, and I must get what the writing
    means.

I know I am deathless,
I know this orbit of mine cannot be swept by a car-
    penter's compass,
I know I shall not pass like a child's carlacue cut with a
    burnt stick at night.

I know I am august,
I do not trouble my spirit to vindicate itself or be under-
    stood,   410
I see that the elementary laws never apologize,
(I reckon I behave no prouder than the level I plant my
    house by, after all.)

I exist as I am, that is enough,
If no other in the world be aware I sit content,
And if each and all be aware I sit content.

One world is aware and by far the largest to me, and
    that is myself,
And whether I come to my own to-day or in ten thousand
    or ten million years,
I can cheerfully take it now, or with equal cheerfulness
    I can wait.

My foothold is tenon'd and mortis'd in granite,
I laugh at what you call dissolution,   420
And I know the amplitude of time.

I am the poet of the Body and I am the poet of the Soul,
The pleasures of heaven are with me and the pains of
    hell are with me,
The first I graft and increase upon myself, the latter I
    translate into a new tongue.

I am the poet of the woman the same as the man,
And I say it is as great to be a woman as to be a man,
And I say there is nothing greater than the mother of men.

I chant the chant of dilation or pride,
We have had ducking and deprecating about enough,
I show that size is only development.   430

Have you outstript the rest? are you the President?
It is a trifle, they will more than arrive there every one,
    and still pass on.

I am he that walks with the tender and growing night,
I call to the earth and sea half-held by the night.

Press close bare-bosom'd night—press close magnetic
    nourishing night!
Night of south winds—night of the large few stars!
Still nodding night—mad naked summer night.

Smile O voluptuous cool-breath'd earth!
Earth of the slumbering and liquid trees!

---

408 **carlacue . . . stick,** a curlicue or flourish made (cut) by waving
the glowing end of a stick in the darkness • 412 **level,** carpenter's
spirit level • 419 **tenon'd and mortis'd,** terms from the carpenter's
trade, which Whitman followed. A mortise is a cavity into which
the piece to be joined (tenon) fits

Earth of departed sunset—earth of the mountains misty-
    topt!   440
Earth of the vitreous pour of the full moon just tinged
    with blue!
Earth of shine and dark mottling the tide of the river!
Earth of the limpid gray of clouds brighter and clearer
    for my sake!
Far-swooping elbow'd earth—rich apple-blossom'd earth!
Smile, for your lover comes.

Prodigal, you have given me love—therefore I to you
    give love!
O unspeakable passionate love.

22

You sea! I resign myself to you also—I guess what you
    mean,
I behold from the beach your crooked inviting fingers,
I believe you refuse to go back without feeling of me, 450
We must have a turn together, I undress, hurry me out of
    sight of the land,
Cushion me soft, rock me in billowy drowse,
Dash me with amorous wet, I can repay you.

Sea of stretch'd ground-swells,
Sea breathing broad and convulsive breaths,
Sea of the brine of life and of unshovell'd yet always-
    ready graves,
Howler and scooper of storms, capricious and dainty
    sea,
I am integral with you, I too am of one phase and of all
    phases.

Partaker of influx and efflux, I, extoller of hate and con-
    ciliation,
Extoller of amies and those that sleep in each others'
    arms,   460

I am he attesting sympathy,
(Shall I make my list of things in the house and skip the
    house that supports them?)

I am not the poet of goodness only, I do not decline to be
    the poet of wickedness also.

What blurt is this about virtue and about vice?

*Evil propels me and reform of evil propels me, I stand
    indifferent,
My gait is no fault-finder's or rejecter's gait,
I moisten the roots of all that has grown.

Did you fear some scrofula out of the unflagging preg-
    nancy?
Did you guess the celestial laws are yet to be work'd over
    and rectified?

I find one side a balance and the antipodal side a bal-
    ance,   470
Soft doctrine as steady help as stable doctrine,
Thoughts and deeds of the present our rouse and early
    start.

This minute that comes to me over the past deciillions,
There is no better than it and now.

What behaved well in the past or behaves well to-day is
    not such a wonder,
The wonder is always and always how there can be a
    mean man or an infidel.

23

Endless unfolding of words of ages!
And mine a word of the modern, the word En-Masse.

A word of the faith that never balks,
Here or henceforward it is all the same to me, I accept
    Time absolutely.   480

It alone is without flaw, it alone rounds and completes
    all,
That mystic baffling wonder alone completes all.

I accept Reality and dare not question it,
Materialism first and last imbuing.

Hurrah for positive science! long live exact demonstra-
    tion!
Fetch stonecrop mixt with cedar and branches of lilac,

---

460 amies, friends or lovers • 486 stonecrop, a mosslike plant, so
called because it grows on rocks and walls.

Pagan blasphemy!

This is the lexicographer, this the chemist, this made a
    grammar of the old cartouches,
These mariners put the ship through dangerous unknown
    seas,
This is the geologist, this works with the scalpel, and this
    is a mathematician.

Gentlemen, to you the first honors always!   490
Your facts are useful, and yet they are not my dwelling,
I but enter by them to an area of my dwelling.

Less the reminders of properties told my words,
And more the reminders they of life untold, and of free-
    dom and extrication,
And make short account of neuters and geldings, and
    favor men and women fully equipt.
And beat the gong of revolt, and stop with fugitives and
    them that plot and conspire.

24

Walt Whitman, a kosmos, of Manhattan the son,
Turbulent, fleshy, sensual, eating, drinking and breeding,
No sentimentalist, no stander above men and women or
    apart from them,
No more modest than immodest.   500

Unscrew the locks from the doors!
Unscrew the doors themselves from their jambs!
Whoever degrades another degrades me,
And whatever is done or said returns at last to me.

Through me the afflatus surging and surging, through
    me the current and index.

I speak the pass-word primeval, I give the sign of de-
    mocracy,
By God! I will accept nothing which all cannot have their
    counterpart of on the same terms.
Through me many long dumb voices,
Voices of the interminable generations of prisoners and
    slaves,
Voices of the diseas'd and despairing and of thieves and
    dwarfs,   510
Voices of cycles of preparation and accretion,
And of the threads that connect the stars, and of wombs
    and of the father-stuff,

And of the rights of them the others are down upon,
Of the deform'd, trivial, flat, foolish, despised,
Fog in the air, beetles rolling balls of dung.

Through me forbidden voices,
Voices of sexes and lusts, voices veil'd and I remove the
    veil,
Voices indecent by me clarified and transfigur'd.

I do not press my fingers across my mouth,
I keep as delicate around the bowels as around the head
    and heart,   520
Copulation is no more rank to me than death is.

I believe in the flesh and the appetites,   *Whitman the Sensualist*
Seeing, hearing, feeling, are miracles, and each part and
    tag of me is a miracle.

Whitman's divinity
Divine am I inside and out, and I make holy whatever I
    touch or am touch'd from,   *sacreligious*
The scent of these arm-pits aroma finer than prayer,
This head more than churches, bibles, and all the creeds.

If I worship one thing more than another it shall be the
    spread of my own body, or any part of it,
Translucent mould of me it shall be you!
Shaded ledges and rests it shall be you!
Firm masculine colter it shall be you!   530
Whatever goes to the tilth of me it shall be you!
You my rich blood! your milky stream pale strippings of
    my life!
Breast that presses against other breasts it shall be you!
My brain it shall be your occult convolutions!
Root of wash'd sweet-flag! timorous pond-snipe! nest of
    guarded duplicate eggs! it shall be you!
Mix'd tussled hay of head, beard, brawn, it shall be you!
Trickling sap of maple, fibre of manly wheat, it shall be
    you!
Sun so generous it shall be you!
Vapors lighting and shading my face it shall be you!
You sweaty brooks and dews it shall be you!   540
Winds whose soft-tickling genitals rub against me it
    shall be you!

---

487 **cartouches,** figures on ancient monuments; for example, Egyptian
hieroglyphics

Broad muscular fields, branches of live oak, loving loung-
er in my winding paths, it shall be you!
Hands I have taken, face I have kiss'd, mortal I have ever
touch'd, it shall be you.

Divinity of human body

I dote on myself, there is that lot of me and all so luscious,
Each moment and whatever happens thrills me with joy,
I cannot tell how my ankles bend, nor whence the cause
of my faintest wish,
Nor the cause of the friendship I emit, nor the cause of
the friendship I take again.

That I walk up my stoop, I pause to consider if it really be,
A morning-glory at my window satisfies me more than
the metaphysics of books.

To behold the day-break!   550
The little light fades the immense and diaphanous
shadows,
The air tastes good to my palate.

Hefts of the moving world at innocent gambols silently
rising, freshly exuding,
Scooting obliquely high and low.

Something I cannot see puts upward libidinous prongs,
Seas of bright juice suffuse heaven.

The earth by the sky staid with, the daily close of their
junction,
The heav'd challenge from the east that moment over my
head,
The mocking taunt, See then whether you shall be master!

26

Now I will do nothing but listen,
To accrue what I hear into this song, to let sounds contribute toward it.

I hear bravuras of birds, bustle of growing wheat, gossip
of flames, clack of sticks cooking my meals.
I hear the sound I love, the sound of the human voice,
I hear all sounds running together, combined, fused or
following,
Sounds of the city and sounds out of the city, sounds of
the day and night,
Talkative young ones to those that like them, the loud
laugh of work-people at their meals,
The angry base of disjointed friendship, the faint tones
of the sick,

Speech is the twin of my vision, it is unequal to measure
itself,
It provokes me forever, it says sarcastically,
Walt you contain enough, why don't you let it out then?

Come now I will not be tantalized, you conceive too
much of articulation,
Do you not know O speech how the buds beneath you
are folded?   570
Waiting in gloom, protected by frost,
The dirt receding before my prophetical screams,
I underlying causes to balance them at last,
My knowledge my live parts, it keeping tally with the
meaning of all things,
Happiness, (which whoever hears me let him or her set
out in search of this day.)

My final merit I refuse you, I refuse putting from me
what I really am,
Encompass worlds, but never try to encompass me,
I crowd your sleekest and best by simply looking toward
you.

Writing and talk do not prove me,
I carry the plenum of proof and every thing else in my
face,   580
With the hush of my lips I wholly confound the skeptic.

25

Dazzling and tremendous how quick the sun-rise would
kill me,   560
If I could not now and always send sun-rise out of me.

We also ascend dazzling and tremendous as the sun,
We found our own O my soul in the calm and cool of
the daybreak.

My voice goes after what my eyes cannot reach,
With the twirl of my tongue I encompass worlds and
volumes of worlds.

---

589 base, bass

The judge with hands tight to the desk, his pallid lips pronouncing a death-sentence,   590

The heave'e'yo of stevedores unlading ships by the wharves, the refrain of the anchor-lifters,

The ring of alarm-bells, the cry of fire, the whirr of swift-streaking engines and hose-carts with premonitory tinkles and color'd lights,

The steam-whistle, the solid roll of the train of approaching cars,

The slow march play'd at the head of the association marching two and two,

(They go to guard some corpse, the flag-tops are draped with black muslin.)

I hear the violoncello, ('tis the young man's heart's complaint,)

I hear the key'd cornet, it glides quickly in through my ears,

It shakes mad-sweet pangs through my belly and breast.

I hear the chorus, it is a grand opera,

Ah this indeed is music—this suits me.   600

A tenor large and fresh as the creation fills me,

The orbic flex of his mouth is pouring and filling me full.

I hear the train'd soprano (what work with hers is this?)

The orchestra whirls me wider than Uranus flies,

It wrenches such ardors from me I did not know I possess'd them,

It sails me, I dab with bare feet, they are lick'd by the indolent waves,

I am cut by bitter and angry hail, I lose my breath,

Steep'd amid honey'd morphine, my windpipe throttled in fakes of death,

At length let up again to feel the puzzle of puzzles,

And what we call Being.   610

27

To be in any form, what is that?

(Round and round we go, all of us, and ever come back thither,)

If nothing lay more develop'd the quahaug in its callous shell were enough.

Mine is no callous shell,

I have instant conductors all over me whether I pass or stop,

They seize every object and lead it harmlessly through me.

I merely stir, press, feel with my fingers, and am happy,

To touch my person to some one else's is about as much as I can stand.

28

Is this then a touch? quivering me to a new identity,

Flames and ether making a rush for my veins,   620

Treacherous tip of me reaching and crowding to help them,

My flesh and blood playing out lightning to strike what is hardly different from myself,

On all sides prurient provokers stiffening my limbs,

Straining the udder of my heart for its withheld drip,

Behaving licentious toward me, taking no denial,

Depriving me of my best as for a purpose,

Unbuttoning my clothes, holding me by the bare waist,

Deluding my confusion with the calm of the sunlight and pasture-fields,

Immodestly sliding the fellow-senses away,

They bribed to swap off with touch and go and graze at the edges of me,   630

No consideration, no regard for my draining strength or my anger,

Fetching the rest of the herd around to enjoy them a while,

Then all uniting to stand on a headland and worry me.

The sentries desert every other part of me,

They have left me helpless to a red marauder,

They all come to the headland to witness and assist against me.

I am given up by traitors,

I talk wildly, I have lost my wits, I and nobody else am the greatest traitor,

I went myself first to the headland, my own hands carried me there.

604 **Uranus,** one of the remotest of the planets, with an extraordinarily large orbit • 608 **fakes,** circles or coils of a cable

You villain touch! what are you doing? my breath is tight
 in its throat,   640
Unclench your floodgates, you are too much for me.

29

Blind loving wrestling touch, sheath'd hooded sharp-
 tooth'd touch!
Did it make you ache so, leaving me?

Parting track'd by arriving, perpetual payment of perpetual loan,
Rich showering rain, and recompense richer afterward.

Sprouts take and accumulate, stand by the curb prolific
 and vital,
Landscapes projected masculine, full-sized and golden.

30

All truths wait in all things,
They neither hasten their own delivery nor resist it,
They do not need the obstetric forceps of the surgeon, 650
The insignificant is as big to me as any,
(What is less or more than a touch?)

Logic and sermons never convince,
The damp of the night drives deeper into my soul.

(Only what proves itself to every man and woman is so,
Only what nobody denies is so.)

A minute and a drop of me settle my brain,
I believe the soggy clods shall become lovers and lamps,
And a compend of compends is the meat of a man or
 woman,
And a summit and flower there is the feeling they have
 for each other,   660
And they are to branch boundlessly out of that lesson
 until it becomes omnific,
And until one and all shall delight us, and we them.

31

I believe a leaf of grass is no less than the journey-work
 of the stars,
And the pismire is equally perfect, and a grain of sand,
 and the egg of the wren,
And the tree-toad is a chef-d'œuvre for the highest,

All that is beautiful on earth can compare with anything in heaven!

And the running blackberry would adorn the parlors of
 heaven,
And the narrowest hinge in my hand puts to scorn all
 machinery,
And the cow crunching with depress'd head surpasses
 any statue,
And a mouse is miracle enough to stagger sextillions of
 infidels.

I find I incorporate gneiss, coal, long-threaded moss,
 fruits, grains, esculent roots,   670
And am stucco'd with quadrupeds and birds all over,
And have distanced what is behind me for good reasons,
But call any thing back again when I desire it.

In vain the speeding or shyness,
In vain the plutonic rocks send their old heat against my
 approach,
In vain the mastodon retreats beneath its own powder'd
 bones,
In vain objects stand leagues off and assume manifold
 shapes,
In vain the ocean settling in hollows and the great mon-
 sters lying low,
In vain the buzzard houses herself with the sky,
In vain the snake slides through the creepers and logs, 680
In vain the elk takes to the inner passes of the woods,
In vain the razor-bill'd auk sails far north to Labrador,
I follow quickly, I ascend to the nest in the fissure of the
 cliff.

32 *a comment on business, rush, worrys anxiety, of people!*

I think I could turn and live with animals, they're so
 placid and self-contain'd,   *he desires*
I stand and look at them long and long.

They do not sweat and whine about their condition,
They do not lie awake in the dark and weep for their
 sins,
They do not make me sick discussing their duty to God,
Not one is dissatisfied, not one is demented with the
 mania of owning things,

663 **journey-work**, work done by a journeyman at his trade; hence,
routine or mechanical work • 665 **chef-d'œuvre**, a masterpiece • 675
plutonic rocks are formed from molten rock which is forced from
deep in the earth to the surface by intense heat

animals have to worry!

Not one kneels to another, nor to his kind that lived
  thousands of years ago,   690
Not one is respectable or unhappy over the whole earth.

So they show their relations to me and I accept them,
They bring me tokens of myself, they evince them plainly
  in their possession.

I wonder where they get those tokens,
Did I pass that way huge times ago and negligently drop
  them?

Myself moving forward then and now and forever,
Gathering and showing more always and with velocity,
Infinite and omnigenous, and the like of these among
  them,
Not too exclusive toward the reachers of my remem-
  brancers,
Picking out here one that I love, and now go with him
  on brotherly terms.   700

A gigantic beauty of a stallion, fresh and responsive to
  my caresses,
Head high in the forehead, wide between the ears,
Limbs glossy and supple, tail dusting the ground,
Eyes full of sparkling wickedness, ears finely cut, flexibly
  moving.

His nostrils dilate as my heels embrace him,
His well-built limbs tremble with pleasure as we race
  around and return.

I but use you a minute, then I resign you, stallion,
Why do I need your paces when I myself out-gallop
  them?
Even as I stand or sit passing faster than you.

33

Space and Time! now I see it is true, what I guess'd at, 710
What I guess'd when I loaf'd on the grass,
What I guess'd while I lay alone in my bed,
And again as I walk'd the beach under the paling stars
  of the morning.
My ties and ballasts leave me, my elbows rest in sea-gaps,
I skirt sierras, my palms cover continents,
I am afoot with my vision.

By the city's quadrangular houses—in log huts, camping
  with lumbermen,
Along the ruts of the turnpike, along the dry gulch and
  rivulet bed,
Weeding my onion-patch or hoeing rows of carrots and
  parsnips, crossing savannas, trailing in forests,
Prospecting, gold-digging, girdling the trees of a new
  purchase,   720
Scorch'd ankle-deep by the hot sand, hauling my boat
  down the shallow river,
Where the panther walks to and fro on a limb overhead,
  where the buck turns furiously at the hunter,
Where the rattlesnake suns his flabby length on a rock,
  where the otter is feeding on fish,
Where the alligator in his tough pimples sleeps by the
  bayou,
Where the black bear is searching for roots or honey,
  where the beaver pats the mud with his paddle-
  shaped tail;
Over the growing sugar, over the yellow-flower'd cotton
  plant, over the rice in its low moist field,
Over the sharp-peak'd farm house, with its scallop'd scum
  and slender shoots from the gutters,
Over the western persimmon, over the long-leav'd corn,
  over the delicate blue-flower flax,
Over the white and brown buckwheat, a hummer and
  buzzer there with the rest,
Over the dusky green of the rye as it ripples and shades
  in the breeze;   730
Scaling mountains, pulling myself cautiously up, holding
  on by low scragged limbs,
Walking the path worn in the grass and beat through
  the leaves of the brush,
Where the quail is whistling betwixt the woods and the
  wheat-lot,
Where the bat flies in the Seventh-month eve, where the
  great gold-bug drops through the dark,
Where the brook puts out of the roots of the old tree
  and flows to the meadow,
Where cattle stand and shake away flies with the tremulous shuddering of their hides,
Where the cheese-cloth hangs in the kitchen, where
  andirons straddle the hearth-slab, where cobwebs
  fall in festoons from the rafters;

---

720 **girdling,** removing a ring of outer bark and thus killing the tree

Places man comes in contact with

Where trip-hammers crash, where the press is whirling its cylinders,

Where the human heart beats with terrible throes under its ribs,

Where the pear-shaped balloon is floating aloft, (floating in it myself and looking composedly down,) 740

Where the life-car is drawn on the slip-noose, where the heat hatches pale-green eggs in the dented sand,

Where the she-whale swims with her calf and never forsakes it,

Where the steam-ship trails hind-ways its long pennant of smoke,

Where the fin of the shark cuts like a black chip out of the water,

Where the half-burn'd brig is riding on unknown currents,

Where shells grow to her slimy deck, where the dead are corrupting below;

Where the dense-starr'd flag is borne at the head of the regiments,

Approaching Manhattan up by the long-stretching island,

Under Niagara, the cataract falling like a veil over my countenance,

Upon a door-step, upon the horse-block of hard wood outside, 750

Upon the race-course, or enjoying picnics or jigs or a good game of base-ball,

At he-festivals, with blackguard jibes, ironical license, bull-dances, drinking, laughter,

At the cider-mill tasting the sweets of the brown mash, sucking the juice through a straw,

At apple-peelings wanting kisses for all the red fruit I find,

At musters, beach-parties, friendly bees, huskings, house-raisings;

Where the mocking-bird sounds his delicious gurgles, cackles, screams, weeps,

Where the hay-rick stands in the barn-yard, where the dry-stalks are scatter'd, where the brood-cow waits in the hovel,

Where the bull advances to do his masculine work, where the stud to the mare, where the cock is treading the hen,

Where the heifers browse, where geese nip their food with short jerks,

Where sun-down shadows lengthen over the limitless and lonesome prairie, 760

Where herds of buffalo make a crawling spread of the square miles far and near,

Where the humming-bird shimmers, where the neck of the long-lived swan is curving and winding,

Where the laughing-gull scoots by the shore, where she laughs her near-human laugh,

Where bee-hives range on a gray bench in the garden half hid by the high weeds,

Where band-neck'd partridges roost in a ring on the ground with their heads out,

Where burial coaches enter the arch'd gates of a cemetery,

Where winter wolves bark amidst wastes of snow and icicled trees,

Where the yellow-crown'd heron comes to the edge of the marsh at night and feeds upon small crabs,

Where the splash of swimmers and divers cools the warm noon,

Where the katy-did works her chromatic reed on the walnut-tree over the well, 770

Through patches of citrons and cucumbers with silver-wired leaves,

Through the salt-lick or orange glade, or under conical firs,

Through the gymnasium, through the curtain'd saloon, through the office or public hall;

Pleas'd with the native and pleas'd with the foreign, pleas'd with the new and old,

Pleas'd with the homely woman as well as the handsome,

Pleas'd with the quakeress as she puts off her bonnet and talks melodiously,

Pleas'd with the tune of the choir of the whitewash'd church,

Pleas'd with the earnest words of the sweating Methodist preacher, impress'd seriously at the camp-meeting;

Looking in at the shop-windows of Broadway the whole forenoon, flatting the flesh of my nose on the thick plate glass,

Wandering the same afternoon with my face turn'd up to the clouds, or down a lane or along the beach, 780

My right and left arms round the sides of two friends, and I in the middle;

---

741 life-car, a watertight conveyance traveling on a rope from a wrecked vessel to the shore

Coming home with the silent and dark-cheek'd bush-
     boy, (behind me he rides at the drape of the day,)
Far from the settlements studying the print of animals'
     feet, or the moccasin print,
By the cot in the hospital reaching lemonade to a fever-
     ish patient,
Nigh the coffin'd corpse when all is still, examining
     with a candle;
Voyaging to every port to dicker and adventure,
Hurrying with the modern crowd as eager and fickle as
     any,
Hot toward one I hate, ready in my madness to knife
     him,
Solitary at midnight in my back yard, my thoughts
     gone from me a long while,
Walking the old hills of Judæa with the beautiful
     gentle God by my side,   790
Speeding through space, speeding through heaven and
     the stars,
Speeding amid the seven satellites and the broad ring,
     and the diameter of eighty thousand miles,
Speeding with tail'd meteors, throwing fire-balls like
     the rest,
Carrying the crescent child that carries its own full
     mother in its belly,
Storming, enjoying, planning, loving, cautioning,
Backing and filling, appearing and disappearing,
I tread day and night such roads.

I visit the orchards of spheres and look at the product,
And look at quintillions ripen'd and look at quintillions
     green.

I fly those flights of a fluid and swallowing soul,   800
My course runs below the soundings of plummets.

I help myself to material and immaterial,
No guard can shut me off, no law prevent me.

I anchor my ship for a little while only,
My messengers continually cruise away or bring their
     returns to me.

I go hunting polar furs and the seal, leaping chasms with
     a pike-pointed staff, clinging to topples of brittle
     and blue.

I ascend to the foretruck,
I take my place late at night in the crow's nest,
We sail the arctic sea, it is plenty light enough,
Through the clear atmosphere I stretch around on the
     wonderful beauty,   810
The enormous masses of ice pass me and I pass them, the
     scenery is plain in all directions,
The white-topt mountains show in the distance, I fling
     out my fancies toward them,
We are approaching some great battle-field in which we
     are soon to be engaged,
We pass the colossal outposts of the encampment, we
     pass with still feet and caution,
Or we are entering by the suburbs some vast and ruin'd
     city,
The blocks and fallen architecture more than all the liv-
     ing cities of the globe.

I am a free companion, I bivouac by invading watchfires,
I turn the bridegroom out of bed and stay with the bride
     myself,
I tighten her all night to my thighs and lips.

My voice is the wife's voice, the screech by the rail of the
     stairs,   820
They fetch my man's body up dripping and drown'd.

I understand the large hearts of heroes,
The courage of present times and all times,
How the skipper saw the crowded and rudderless wreck
     of the steamship, and Death chasing it up and down
     the storm,
How he knuckled tight and gave not back an inch, and
     was faithful of days and faithful of nights,
And chalk'd in large letters on a board, *Be of good cheer,
     we will not desert you;*
How he follow'd with them and tack'd with them three
     days and would not give it up,
How he saved the drifting company at last,
How the lank loose-gown'd women look'd when boated
     from the side of their prepared graves,

---

790 **Judæa,** southern Palestine, the scene of part of the ministry
of Christ • 792 **ring . . . miles.** The reference is to the planet
Saturn • 794 **crescent . . . belly.** The reference is to the new
moon • 806 **topples,** surfaces about to topple over

Leaves

of

Grass.

Brooklyn, New York:
1855.

* * *

Title page designed by Whitman for the first edition

How the silent old-faced infants and the lifted sick, and
    the sharp-lipp'd unshaven men;   830
All this I swallow, it tastes good, I like it well, it becomes
    mine,
I am the man, I suffer'd, I was there.

The disdain and calmness of martyrs,
The mother of old, condemn'd for a witch, burnt with
    dry wood, her children gazing on,
The hounded slave that flags in the race, leans by the
    fence, blowing, cover'd with sweat,
The twinges that sting like needles his legs and neck, the
    murderous buckshot and the bullets,
All these I feel or am.

I am the hounded slave, I wince at the bite of the dogs,
Hell and despair are upon me, crack and again crack the
    marksmen,
I clutch the rails of the fence, my gore dribs, thinn'd with
    the ooze of my skin,   840

I fall on the weeds and stones,
The riders spur their unwilling horses, haul close,
Taunt my dizzy ears and beat me violently over the head
    with whip-stocks.
Agonies are one of my changes of garments.
I do not ask the wounded person how he feels, I myself
    become the wounded person,
My hurts turn livid upon me as I lean on a cane and
    observe.

I am the mash'd fireman with breast-bone broken,
Tumbling walls buried me in their debris,
Heat and smoke I inspired, I heard the yelling shouts of
    my comrades,
I heard the distant click of their picks and shovels,   850
They have clear'd the beams away, they tenderly lift me
    forth.
I lie in the night air in my red shirt, the pervading hush
    is for my sake,
Painless after all I lie exhausted but not so unhappy,
White and beautiful are the faces around me, the heads
    are bared of their fire-caps,
The kneeling crowd fades with the light of the torches.

Distant and dead resuscitate,
They show as the dial or move as the hands of me, I am
    the clock myself.

I am an old artillerist, I tell of my fort's bombardment,
I am there again.

Again the long roll of the drummers,   860
Again the attacking cannon, mortars,
Again to my listening ears the cannon responsive.

I take part, I see and hear the whole,
The cries, curses, roar, the plaudits for well-aim'd
    shots,
The ambulanza slowly passing trailing its red drip,
Workmen searching after damages, making indispensable
    repairs,
The fall of grenades through the rent roof, the fan-
    shaped explosion,
The whizz of limbs, heads, stone, wood, iron, high in the
    air.

* * *

840 **dribs,** drips

I am part or suffer with those that suffer — slaves — poor — hurt firemen etc.

Again gurgles the mouth of my dying general, he furiously waves with his hand,
He gasps through the clot *Mind not me—mind—the
entrenchments.*   870

34

he relates a war story

Now I tell what I knew in Texas in my early youth,
(I tell not the fall of Alamo,
Not one escaped to tell the fall of Alamo,
The hundred and fifty are dumb yet at Alamo,)
'Tis the tale of the murder in cold blood of four hundred
and twelve young men.

Retreating they had form'd in a hollow square with their
baggage for breastworks,
Nine hundred lives out of the surrounding enemy's, nine
times their number, was the price they took in advance,
Their colonel was wounded and their ammunition gone,
They treated for an honorable capitulation, receiv'd writing and seal, gave up their arms and march'd back
prisoners of war.

They were the glory of the race of rangers,   880
Matchless with horse, rifle, song, supper, courtship,
Large, turbulent, generous, handsome, proud, and affec-
tionate,
Bearded, sunburnt, drest in the free costume of hunters,
Not a single one over thirty years of age.

The second First-day morning they were brought out in
squads and massacred, it was beautiful early summer,
The work commenced about five o'clock and was over by
eight.

None obey'd the command to kneel,
Some made a mad and helpless rush, some stood stark and
straight,
A few fell at once, shot in the temple or heart, the living
and dead lay together,
The maim'd and mangled dug in the dirt, the new-comers
saw them there,   890
Some half-kill'd attempted to crawl away,
These were despatch'd with bayonets or batter'd with the
blunts of muskets.
A youth not seventeen years old seiz'd his assassin till
two more came to release him,

The three were all torn and cover'd with the boy's
blood.

At eleven o'clock began the burning of the bodies;
That is the tale of the murder of the four hundred and
twelve young men.

35

a sea story

Would you hear of an old-time sea-fight?
Would you learn who won by the light of the moon and
stars?
List to the yarn, as my grandmother's father the sailor
told it to me.

Our foe was no skulk in his ship I tell you, (said he,) 900
His was the surly English pluck, and there is no tougher
or truer, and never was, and never will be;
Along the lower'd eve he came horribly raking us.

We closed with him, the yards entangled, the cannon
touch'd,
My captain lash'd fast with his own hands.

We had receiv'd some eighteen pound shots under the
water,
On our lower-gun-deck two large pieces had burst at the
first fire, killing all around and blowing up overhead.

Fighting at sun-down, fighting at dark,
Ten o'clock at night, the full moon well up, our leaks on
the gain, and five feet of water reported,
The master-at-arms loosing the prisoners confined in the
after-hold to give them a chance for themselves.

---

871 **Texas . . . youth.** Whitman was never in Texas. Many of the
experiences described in the poem are imaginary • 872 **Alamo.**
On March 6, 1836, a Mexican army under Santa Anna attacked the
Alamo, a fortified mission at San Antonio, Texas, and killed the
entire garrison. Texas won her independence from Mexico a month
later, when an army of Texans, shouting "Remember the Alamo,"
defeated the Mexicans at the battle of San Jacinto • 875 **tale . . .
murder,** the battle of Coleto and the massacre of Goliad during
the Texas Revolution of 1836 • 897 **old-time sea-fight.** While many
details are supplied by the author's imagination, Whitman had in
mind the historic battle between the **Bonhomme Richard,** commanded
by John Paul Jones, and the English warship **Serapis** in 1778. Jones'
famous words, "We have just begun to fight," are quoted with a
slight alteration in l. 916

The transit to and from the magazine is now stopt by
  the sentinels,   910
They see so many strange faces they do not know whom
  to trust.

Our frigate takes fire,
The other asks if we demand quarter?
If our colors are struck and the fighting done?

Now I laugh content, for I hear the voice of my little
  captain,
We have not struck, he composedly cries, *we have just
  begun our part of the fighting.*

Only three guns are in use,
One is directed by the captain himself against the enemy's
  main-mast,
Two well serv'd with grape and canister silence his
  musketry and clear his decks.

The tops alone second the fire of this little battery,
  especially the main-top,   920
They hold out bravely during the whole of the action.

Not a moment's cease,
The leaks gain fast on the pumps, the fire eats toward
  the powder-magazine.

One of the pumps has been shot away, it is generally
  thought we are sinking.

Serene stands the little captain,
He is not hurried, his voice is neither high nor low,
His eyes give more light to us than our battle-lanterns.

Toward twelve there in the beams of the moon they
  surrender to us.

36

Stretch'd and still lies the midnight,
Two great hulls motionless on the breast of the dark-
  ness,   930
Our vessel riddled and slowly sinking, preparations to
  pass to the one we have conquer'd,
The captain on the quarter-deck coldly giving his orders
  through a countenance white as a sheet,
Near by the corpse of the child that serv'd in the cabin,

The dead face of an old salt with long white hair and
  carefully curl'd whiskers,
The flames spite of all that can be done flickering aloft
  and below,
The husky voices of the two or three officers yet fit for
  duty,
Formless stacks of bodies and bodies by themselves, dabs
  of flesh upon the masts and spars,
Cut of cordage, dangle of rigging, slight shock of the
  soothe of waves,
Black and impassive guns, litter of powder-parcels, strong
  scent,
A few large stars overhead, silent and mournful shining,   940
Delicate sniffs of sea-breeze, smells of sedgy grass and
  fields by the shore, death-messages given in charge
  to survivors,
The hiss of the surgeon's knife, the gnawing teeth of his
  saw,
Wheeze, cluck, swash of falling blood, short wild scream,
  and long, dull, tapering groan,
These so, these irretrievable.

37 *I feel with the prisoner*

You laggards there on guard! look to your arms!
In at the conquer'd doors they crowd! I am possess'd!
Embody all presences outlaw'd or suffering,
See myself in prison shaped like another man,
And feel the dull unintermitted pain,

For me the keepers of convicts shoulder their carbines
  and keep watch,   950
It is I let out in the morning and barr'd at night.

Not a mutineer walks handcuff'd to jail but I am handcuff'd to him and walk by his side,
(I am less the jolly one there, and more the silent one
  with sweat on my twitching lips.)

Not a youngster is taken for larceny but I go up too, and
  am tried and sentenced.

Not a cholera patient lies at the last gasp but I also lie
  at the last gasp,
My face is ash-color'd, my sinews gnarl, away from me
  people retreat.

*I suffer with the
sick*

168 *Whitman*

I feel with beggars

Askers embody themselves in me and I am embodied in them,
I project my hat, sit shame-faced, and beg.

38

Enough! enough! enough!
Somehow I have been stunn'd. Stand back!　　960
Give me a little time beyond my cuff'd head, slumbers, dreams, gaping,
I discover myself on the verge of a usual mistake.

That I could forget the mockers and insults!
That I could forget the trickling tears and the blows of the bludgeons and hammers!
That I could look with a separate look on my own crucifixion and bloody crowning!

I remember now,
I resume the overstaid fraction,
The grave of rock multiplies what has been confided to it, or to any graves,
Corpses rise, gashes heal, fastenings roll from me.

I troop forth replenish'd with supreme power, one of an average unending procession,　　970
Inland and sea-coast we go, and pass all boundary lines,
Our swift ordinances on their way over the whole earth,
The blossoms we wear in our hats the growth of thousands of years.

Eleves, I salute you! come forward!
Continue your annotations, continue your questionings.

39

Indians

The friendly and flowing savage, who is he?
Is he waiting for civilization, or past it and mastering it?

Is he some Southwesterner rais'd out-doors? is he Kanadian?
Is he from the Mississippi country? Iowa, Oregon, California?
The mountains? prairie-life, bush-life? or sailor from the sea?　　980

Wherever he goes men and women accept and desire him,

They desire he should like them, touch them, speak to them, stay with them.

Behavior lawless as snow-flakes, words simple as grass, uncomb'd head, laughter, and naivetè,
Slow-stepping feet, common features, common modes and emanations,
They descend in new forms from the tips of his fingers,
They are wafted with the odor of his body or breath, they fly out of the glance of his eyes.

40

Flaunt of the sunshine I need not your bask—lie over!
You light surfaces only, I force surfaces and depths also.

Earth! you seem to look for something at my hands,
Say, old top-knot, what do you want?　　990

Man or woman, I might tell how I like you, but cannot,
And might tell what it is in me and what it is in you, but cannot,
And might tell that pining I have, that pulse of my nights and days.

Behold, I do not give lectures or a little charity,
When I give I give myself.

You there, impotent, loose in the knees,
Open your scarf'd chops till I blow grit within you,
Spread your palms and lift the flaps of your pockets,
I am not to be denied, I compel, I have stores plenty and to spare,
And any thing I have I bestow.　　1000

I do not ask who you are, that is not important to me,
You can do nothing and be nothing but what I will infold you.

To cotton-field drudge or cleaner of privies I lean,
On his right cheek I put the family kiss,
And in my soul I swear I never will deny him.

---

965 crucifixion . . . crowning. Whitman identifies himself, and all other human sufferers, with Christ • 974 Eleves, pupils • 997 chops, jaws or mouth

On women fit for conception I start bigger and nimbler
babes,

(This day I am jetting the stuff of far more arrogant
republics.)

To any one dying, thither I speed and twist the knob of
the door,
Turn the bed-clothes toward the foot of the bed,
Let the physician and the priest go home.   1010

I seize the descending man and raise him with resistless
will,
O despairer, here is my neck,
By God, you shall not go down! hang your whole weight
upon me.

I dilate you with tremendous breath, I buoy you up,
Every room of the house do I fill with an arm'd force,
Lovers of me, bafflers of graves.

Sleep—I and they keep guard all night,
Not doubt, not disease shall dare to lay finger upon you,
I have embraced you, and henceforth possess you to my-
self,
And when you rise in the morning you will find what I
tell you is so.   1020

41

I am he bringing help for the sick as they pant on their
backs,
And for strong upright men I bring yet more needed
help.

I heard what was said of the universe,
Heard it and heard it of several thousand years;
It is middling well as far as it goes—but is that all?

Magnifying and applying come I,
Outbidding at the start the old cautious hucksters,
Taking myself the exact dimensions of Jehovah,
Lithographing Kronos, Zeus his son, and Hercules his
grandson,
Buying drafts of Osiris, Isis, Belus, Brahma, Buddha, 1030
In my portfolio placing Manito loose, Allah on a leaf,
the crucifix engraved,
With Odin and the hideous-faced Mexitli and every idol
and image,

Taking them all for what they are worth and not a cent
more,
Admitting they were alive and did the work of their
days,
(They bore mites as for unfledg'd birds who have now to
rise and fly and sing for themselves,)
Accepting the rough deific sketches to fill out better in
myself, bestowing them freely on each man and
woman I see,
Discovering as much or more in a framer framing a
house,
Putting higher claims for him there with his roll'd-up
sleeves driving the mallet and chisel,
Not objecting to special revelations, considering a curl
of smoke or a hair on the back of my hand just as
curious as any revelation,
Lads ahold of fire-engines and hook-and-ladder ropes no
less to me than the gods of the antique wars,   1040
Minding their voices peal through the crash of destruction,
Their brawny limbs passing safe over charr'd laths, their
white foreheads whole and unhurt out of the flames;
By the mechanic's wife with her babe at her nipple inter-
ceding for every person born,
Three scythes at harvest whizzing in a row from three
lusty angels with shirts bagg'd out at their waists,
The snag-tooth'd hostler with red hair redeeming sins
past and to come,
Selling all he possesses, traveling on foot to fee lawyers
for his brother and sit by him while he is tried for
forgery;
What was strewn in the amplest strewing the square rod
about me, and not filling the square rod then,
The bull and the bug never worshipp'd half enough,
Dung and dirt more admirable than was dream'd,

1029 **Kronos, Zeus . . . Hercules.** In Greek mythology, Kronos, the
Titan, was dethroned by his son Zeus, the chief of the Olympian gods.
Hercules, son of Zeus, was celebrated for his strength and especially
for his twelve great "labors" • 1030 **Osiris, Isis.** In Egyptian
mythology, Osiris was the god of the underworld and judge of the
dead; Isis was a goddess of fecundity • 1030 **Belus.** In classical
mythology, Belus was king of Tyre and father of Dido and Pygmalion
• 1030 **Brahma,** or the creator of the world, the first member of the
trinity in the Hindu religion • 1030 **Buddha,** the founder of the
Buddhist religion • 1031 **Manito.** Among the Algonquian Indians,
one of the spirits which dominate the forces of nature • 1031 **Allah,**
the name used by the Mohammedans for the Supreme Being • 1032
Odin, the supreme deity of Norse mythology • 1032 **Mexitli,** war
god of the Aztecs

170   *Whitman*

The supernatural of no account, myself waiting my time to be one of the supremes,   1050
The day getting ready for me when I shall do as much good as the best, and be as prodigious;
By my life-lumps! becoming already a creator,
Putting myself here and now to the ambush'd womb of the shadows.

42

A call in the midst of the crowd,
My own voice, orotund sweeping and final.

Come my children,
Come my boys and girls, my women, household and intimates,
Now the performer launches his nerve, he has pass'd his prelude on the reeds within.

Easily written loose-finger'd chords—I feel the thrum of your climax and close.

My head slues round on my neck,   1060
Music rolls, but not from the organ,
Folks are around me, but they are no household of mine.

Ever the hard unsunk ground,
Ever the eaters and drinkers, ever the upward and downward sun, ever the air and the ceaseless tides,
Ever myself and my neighbors, refreshing, wicked, real,
Ever the old inexplicable query, ever that thorn'd thumb, that breath of itches and thirsts,
Ever the vexer's *hoot! hoot!* till we find where the sly one hides and bring him forth,
Ever love, ever the sobbing liquid of life,
Ever the bandage under the chin, ever the trestles of death.

Here and there with dimes on the eyes walking,   1070
To feed the greed of the belly the brains liberally spooning,
Tickets buying, taking, selling, but in to the feast never once going,
Many sweating, ploughing, thrashing, and then the chaff for payment receiving,
A few idly owning, and they the wheat continually claiming.

This is the city and I am one of the citizens,
Whatever interests the rest interests me, politics, wars, markets, newspapers, schools,
The mayor and councils, banks, tariffs, steamships, factories, stocks, stores, real estate and personal estate.

The little plentiful manikins skipping around in collars and tail'd coats,
I am aware who they are, (they are positively not worms or fleas,)
I acknowledge the duplicates of myself, the weakest and shallowest is deathless with me,   1080
What I do and say the same waits for them,
Every thought that flounders in me the same flounders in them.

I know perfectly well my own egotism,
Know my omnivorous lines and must not write any less,
And would fetch you whoever you are flush with myself.

Not words of routine this song of mine,
But abruptly to question, to leap beyond yet nearer bring;
This printed and bound book—but the printer and the printing-office boy?
The well-taken photographs—but your wife or friend close and solid in your arms?
The black ship mail'd with iron, her mighty guns in her turrets—but the pluck of the captain and engineers?   1090
In the houses the dishes and fare and furniture—but the host and hostess, and the look out of their eyes?
The sky up there—yet here or next door, or across the way?
The saints and sages in history—but you yourself?
Sermons, creeds, theology—but the fathomless human brain,
And what is reason? and what is love? and what is life?

43   *exponents of religion*

I do not despise you priests, all time, the world over,
My faith is the greatest of faiths and the least of faiths,

1069 **trestles,** used as supports for the coffin • 1093 **saints . . . yourself.** Compare Emerson's "Thank God for these good men, but say, 'I also am a man,' " in **The Divinity School Address.** Here, as often in **Leaves of Grass,** Whitman repeats Emerson

He believes
all worship

Enclosing worship ancient and modern and all between ancient and modern,
Believing I shall come again upon the earth after five thousand years,
Waiting responses from oracles, honoring the gods, saluting the sun,   1100
Making a fetich of the first rock or stump, powowing with sticks in the circle of obis,
Helping the llama or brahmin as he trims the lamps of the idols,
Dancing yet through the streets in a phallic procession, rapt and austere in the woods a gymnosophist,
Drinking mead from the skull-cup, to Shastas and Vedas admirant, minding the Koran,
Walking the teokallis, spotted with gore from the stone and knife, beating the serpent-skin drum,
Accepting the Gospels, accepting him that was crucified, knowing assuredly that he is divine,
To the mass kneeling or the puritan's prayer rising, or sitting patiently in a pew,
Ranting and frothing in my insane crisis, or waiting dead-like till my spirit arouses me,
Looking forth on pavement and land, or outside of pavement and land,
Belonging to the winders of the circuit of circuits.   1110

One of that centripetal and centrifugal gang I turn and talk like a man leaving charges before a journey.

Down-hearted doubters dull and excluded,
Frivolous, sullen, moping, angry, affected, dishearten'd, atheistical,
I know every one of you, I know the sea of torment, doubt, despair and unbelief.

How the flukes splash!
How they contort rapid as lightning, with spasms and spouts of blood!

Be at peace bloody flukes of doubters and sullen mopers,
I take my place among you as much as among any,
The past is the push of you, me, all, precisely the same,
And what is yet untried and afterward is for you, me, all precisely the same.   1120

I do not know what is untried and afterward,
But I know it will in its turn prove sufficient, and cannot fail.
Each who passes is consider'd, each who stops is consider'd, not a single one can it fail.

It cannot fail the young man who died and was buried,
Nor the young woman who died and was put by his side,
Nor the little child that peep'd in at the door and then drew back and was never seen again,
Nor the old man who has lived without purpose, and feels it with bitterness worse than gall,
Nor him in the poor house tubercled by rum and the bad disorder,
Nor the numberless slaughter'd and wreck'd, nor the brutish koboo call'd the ordure of humanity,
Nor the sacs merely floating with open mouths for food to slip in,   1130
Nor any thing in the earth, or down in the oldest graves of the earth,
Nor any thing in the myriads of spheres, nor the myriads of myriads that inhabit them,
Nor the present, nor the least wisp that is known.

44

It is time to explain myself—let us stand up.

What is known I strip away,
I launch all men and women forward with me into the Unknown.

The clock indicates the moment—but what does eternity indicate?

We have thus far exhausted trillions of winters and summers,
There are trillions ahead, and trillions ahead of them.

1101 **obis, obi,** a kind of sorcery practiced among West Indian Negroes • 1102 **llama, lama,** a high priest of Tibet and Mongolia • 1104 **Shastas,** sastra or shastra, a treatise explaining the Vedas, the most ancient sacred literature of the Hindus • 1105 **teokallis,** ancient Mexican temples • 1111 **centripetal . . . gang,** apparently a reference to the Methodist circuit-riders • 1115 **flukes,** the lobes of a whale's tail • 1128 **tubercled,** made tubercular • 1129 **koboo,** a savage of the Ladrone Islands

Births have brought us richness and variety, 1140
And other births will bring us richness and variety.

I do not call one greater and one smaller,
That which fills its period and place is equal to any.

Were mankind murderous or jealous upon you, my
brother, my sister?
I am sorry for you, they are not murderous or jealous
upon me,
All has been gentle with me, I keep no account with
lamentation,
(What have I to do with lamentation?)

I am an acme of things accomplish'd, and I an encloser
of things to be.

My feet strike an apex of the apices of the stairs,
On every step bunches of ages, and larger bunches be-
tween the steps, 1150
All below duly travel'd, and still I mount and mount.

Rise after rise bow the phantoms behind me,
Afar down I see the huge first Nothing, I know I was
even there,

I waited unseen and always, and slept through the le-
thargic mist,
And took my time, and took no hurt from the fetid carbon.

Long I was hugg'd close—long and long.

Immense have been the preparations for me,
Faithful and friendly the arms that have help'd me.

Cycles ferried my cradle, rowing and rowing like cheer-
ful boatmen,
For room to me stars kept aside in their own rings, 1160
They sent influences to look after what was to hold me.

Before I was born out of my mother generations guided
me,
My embryo has never been torpid, nothing could over-
lay it.

For it the nebula cohered to an orb,
The long slow strata piled to rest it on,

Vast vegetables gave it sustenance,
Monstrous sauroids transported it in their mouths and
deposited it with care.

All forces have been steadily employ'd to complete and
delight me,
Now on this spot I stand with my robust soul.

45

O span of youth! ever-push'd elasticity. 1170
O manhood, balanced, florid and full.

My lovers suffocate me,
Crowding my lips, thick in the pores of my skin,
Jostling me through streets and public halls, coming
naked to me at night,
Crying by day *Ahoy!* from the rocks of the river, swing-
ing and chirping over my head,
Calling my name from flower-beds, vines, tangled under-
brush,
Lighting on every moment of my life,
Bussing my body with soft balsamic busses,
Noiselessly passing handfuls out of their hearts and giv-
ing them to be mine.

Old age superbly rising! O welcome, ineffable grace of
dying days! 1180

Every condition promulges not only itself, it promulges
what grows after and out of itself,
And the dark hush promulges as much as any.

I open my scuttle at night and see the far-sprinkled systems,
And all I see multiplied as high as I can cipher edge but
the rim of the farther systems.

Wider and wider they spread, expanding, always expanding,
Outward and outward and forever outward.

My sun has his sun and round him obediently wheels,

1167 **sauroids**, prehistoric lizards • 1169 **soul**. Section 44 is a notable
expression of the evolutionary theory. Whitman's conception of the
process stemmed from Lamarck rather than from Darwin • 1181
promulges, promulgates

He joins with his partners a group of superior circuit,
And greater sets follow, making specks of the greatest
inside them.

There is no stoppage and never can be stoppage,   1190
If I, you, and the worlds, and all beneath or upon their
surfaces, were this moment reduced back to a pallid
float, it would not avail in the long run,
We should surely bring up again where we now stand,
And surely go as much farther, and then farther and
farther.

A few quadrillions of eras, a few octillions of cubic
leagues, do not hazard the span or make it impatient,
They are but parts, any thing is but a part.

See ever so far, there is limitless space outside of that,
Count ever so much, there is limitless time around that.

life after death — some belief in immortality

My rendezvous is appointed, it is certain,
The Lord will be there and wait till I come on perfect
terms,
The great Camerado, the lover true for whom I pine
will be there.   1200

46

I know I have the best of time and space, and was never
measured and never will be measured.

I tramp a perpetual journey, (come listen all!)
My signs are a rain-proof coat, good shoes, and a staff
cut from the woods,
No friend of mine takes his ease in my chair,
I have no chair, no church, no philosophy,
I lead no man to a dinner-table, library, exchange,
But each man and each woman of you I lead upon a
knoll,
My left hand hooking you around the waist,
My right hand pointing to landscapes of continents and
the public road.

Not I, not any one else can travel that road for you,   1210
You must travel it for yourself.

It is not far, it is within reach,

Perhaps you have been on it since you were born and
did not know,
Perhaps it is everywhere on water and on land.

Shoulder your duds dear son, and I will mine, and let
us hasten forth,
Wonderful cities and free nations we shall fetch as
we go.

If you tire, give me both burdens, and rest the chuff of
your hand on my hip,
And in due time you shall repay the same service to me,
For after we start we never lie by again.

This day before dawn I ascended a hill and look'd at the
crowded heaven,   1220
And I said to my spirit *When we become the enfolders
of those orbs, and the pleasure and knowledge of
every thing in them, shall we be fill'd and satisfied
then?*
And my spirit said *No, we but level that lift to pass and
continue beyond.*

You are also asking me questions and I hear you,
I answer that I cannot answer, you must find out for
yourself.

Sit a while dear son,
Here are biscuits to eat and here is milk to drink,
But as soon as you sleep and renew yourself in sweet
clothes, I kiss you with a good-by kiss and open the
gate for your egress hence.

Long enough have you dream'd contemptible dreams,
Now I wash the gum from your eyes,
You must habit yourself to the dazzle of the light and
of every moment of your life.   1230

Long have you timidly waded holding a plank by the
shore,
Now I will you to be a bold swimmer,
To jump off in the midst of the sea, rise again, nod to
me, shout, and laughingly dash with your hair.

1217 chuff, fat part

*lonesome
valley*

very good quote for teachers !

47

I am the teacher of athletes,
He that by me spreads a wider breast than my own
    proves the width of my own,
He most honors my style who learns under it to destroy
    the teacher.

The boy I love, the same becomes a man not through
    derived power, but in his own right,
Wicked rather than virtuous out of conformity or
    fear,
Fond of his sweetheart, relishing well his steak,
Unrequited love or a slight cutting him worse than
    sharp steel cuts,   1240
First-rate to ride, to fight, to hit the bull's eye, to sail a
    skiff, to sing a song, or play on the banjo,
Preferring scars and the beard and faces pitted with
    small-pox over all latherers,
And those well-tann'd to those that keep out of the
    sun.

I teach straying from me, yet who can stray from me?
I follow you whoever you are from the present hour,
My words itch at your ears till you understand them.

I do not say these things for a dollar or to fill up the
    time while I wait for a boat,
(It is you talking just as much as myself, I act as the
    tongue of you,
Tied in your mouth, in mine it begins to be loos-
    en'd.)

I swear I will never again mention love or death inside
    a house,   1250
And I swear I will never translate myself at all, only to
    him or her who privately stays with me in the
    open air.

If you would understand me go to the heights or water-
    shore,
The nearest gnat is an explanation, and a drop or motion
    of waves a key,
The maul, the oar, the hand-saw, second my words.

No shutter'd room or school can commune with me,
But roughs and little children better than they.

The young mechanic is closest to me, he knows me
    well,
The woodman that takes his axe and jug with him
    shall take me with him all day,
The farm-boy ploughing in the field feels good at the
    sound of my voice,
In vessels that sail my words sail, I go with fishermen
    and seamen and love them.   1260

The soldier camp'd or upon the march is mine,
On the night ere the pending battle many seek me, and
    I do not fail them,
On that solemn night (it may be their last) those that
    know me seek me.

My face rubs to the hunter's face when he lies down alone
    in his blanket,
The driver thinking of me does not mind the jolt of his
    wagon,
The young mother and old mother comprehend me,
The girl and the wife rest the needle a moment and for-
    get where they are,
They and all would resume what I have told them.

48

I have said that the soul is not more than the body,
And I have said that the body is not more than the
    soul,   1270
And nothing, not God, is greater to one than one's
    self is,
And whoever walks a furlong without sympathy walks
    to his own funeral drest in his shroud,
And I or you pocketless of a dime may purchase the
    pick of the earth,
And to glance with an eye or show a bean in its pod
    confounds the learning of all times,
And there is no trade or employment but the young
    man following it may become a hero,
And there is no object so soft but it makes a hub for
    the wheel'd universe,
And I say to any man or woman, Let your soul stand
    cool and composed before a million universes.

1268 **resume,** review, summarize, make a résumé of

transcendental concept!

And I say to mankind, Be not curious about God,
For I who am curious about each am not curious
about God,
(No array of terms can say how much I am at peace
about God and about death.)   1280

I hear and behold God in every object, yet understand
God not in the least,
Nor do I understand who there can be more wonderful
than myself.

more than I would this day

Why should I wish to see God better than this day?
I see something of God each hour of the twenty-four,
and each moment then,
In the faces of men and women I see God, and in my
own face in the glass,
I find letters from God dropt in the street, and every
one is sign'd by God's name,
And I leave them where they are, for I know that
wheresoe'er I go,
Others will punctually come for ever and ever.

*everything - since our soul penetrates
letter from God - so many objects, it's just as a
God is in everything!*

49
And as to you Death, and you bitter hug of mortality,
it is idle to try to alarm me.

To his work without flinching the accoucheur comes, 1290
I see the elder-hand pressing receiving supporting,
I recline by the sills of the exquisite flexible doors,
And mark the outlet, and mark the relief and escape.

And as to you Corpse I think you are good manure,
but that does not offend me,
I smell the white roses sweet-scented and growing,
I reach to the leafy lips, I reach to the polish'd breasts
of melons.

And as to you Life I reckon you are the leavings of
many deaths,
(No doubt I have died myself ten thousand times
before.)

I hear you whispering there O stars of heaven,
O suns—O grass of graves—O perpetual transfers and
promotions,
                                        1300
If you do not say any thing how can I say any thing?

Of the turbid pool that lies in the autumn forest,
Of the moon that descends the steeps of the soughing
twilight,
Toss, sparkles of day and dusk—toss on the black
stems that decay in the muck,
Toss to the moaning gibberish of the dry limbs.

I ascend from the moon, I ascend from the night,
I perceive that the ghastly glimmer is noonday sun-
beams reflected,
And debouch to the steady and central from the offspring great or small.

50

There is that in me—I do not know what it is—but I
know it is in me.

Wrench'd and sweaty—calm and cool then my body
becomes,
                                        1310
I sleep—I sleep long.

I do not know it—it is without name—it is a word
unsaid,
It is not in any dictionary, utterance, symbol.

Something it swings on more than the earth I swing
on,
To it the creation is the friend whose embracing
awakes me.

Perhaps I might tell more. Outlines! I plead for my
brothers and sisters.
Do you see O my brothers and sisters?

It is not chaos or death—it is form, union, plan—it is
eternal life—it is Happiness.

51

The past and present wilt—I have fill'd them, emptied
them,
And proceed to fill my next fold of the future.   1320

Listener up there! what have you to confide to me?

1290 accoucheur, obstetrician • 1291 elder-hand, left hand • 1308
debouch, emerge, issue

Look in my face while I snuff the sidle of evening,
(Talk honestly, no one else hears you, and I stay only
a minute longer.)

Do I contradict myself?
Very well then I contradict myself,
(I am large, I contain multitudes.)

I concentrate toward them that are nigh, I wait on
the door-slab.

Who has done his day's work? who will soonest be
through with his supper?
Who wishes to walk with me?

Will you speak before I am gone? will you prove
already too late?   1330

52

The spotted hawk swoops by and accuses me, he complains of my gab and my loitering.

I too am not a bit tamed, I too am untranslatable,
I sound my barbaric yawp over the roofs of the world.

The last scud of day holds back for me,
It flings my likeness after the rest and true as any on
the shadow'd wilds,
It coaxes me to the vapor and the dusk.

I depart as air, I shake my white locks at the runaway sun,
I effuse my flesh in eddies, and drift it in lacy jags.

I bequeath myself to the dirt to grow from the grass
I love,
If you want me again look for me under your boot-
soles.   1340

You will hardly know who I am or what I mean,
But I shall be good health to you nevertheless,
And filter and fibre your blood.

Failing to fetch me at first keep encouraged,
Missing me one place search another,
I stop somewhere waiting for you.

                                              1855·1881

*a concept that
after death he might be in another life,
something else - transformed!*

Once I Pass'd Through a Populous City

It has been often supposed that the following poem refers
to a love affair in New Orleans in 1848. Whitman's
poems, however, can never be safely taken as literal
autobiography, and the evidence in support of such a
romance is far from conclusive. For the best account of the
subject, see Emory Holloway's **Whitman**, pp. 39-71.

Once I pass'd through a populous city imprinting my
brain for future use with its shows, architecture,
customs, traditions,
Yet now of all that city I remember only a woman
I casually met there who detain'd me for love of me,
Day by day and night by night we were together—
all else has long been forgotten by me,
I remember I say only that woman who passionately
clung to me,
Again she holds me by the hand, I must not go,
I see her close beside me with silent lips sad and
tremulous.

                                              1860·1867

For You O Democracy

Better than any other single phrase, perhaps, "the love
of comrades" expresses Whitman's concept of the true
basis of a democratic society.

Song of Myself • 1322 sidle, properly a verb meaning to move
sidewise • 1324 **I contradict myself.** Compare Emerson's **Self-
Reliance:** "Speak what you think now in hard words and to-
morrow speak what to-morrow thinks in hard words again, though
it contradict everything you said to-day" • 1334 scud, clouds driven
swiftly by the wind
Once I Passed . . . City • 2 a woman. In an early manuscript
version of this poem, the lover was a man. See Emory Holloway,
Uncollected Poetry and Prose of Walt Whitman, II, 102

Come, I will make the continent indissoluble,
I will make the most splendid race the sun ever shone
    upon,
I will make divine magnetic lands,
    With the love of comrades,
      With the life-long love of comrades.

I will plant companionship thick as trees along all the
    rivers of America, and along the shores of the
    great lakes, and all over the prairies,
I will make inseparable cities with their arms about
    each other's necks,
    By the love of comrades,
      By the manly love of comrades.

For you these from me, O Democracy, to serve you
    ma femme!   10
For you, for you I am trilling these songs.

                    1860·1881

Song of the Open Road

Later poets were to take up Whitman's call to the open
road. Among these, Richard Hovey and Bliss Carman,
in **Songs from Vagabondia** (1900), and Vachel Lindsay,
in "The Santa-Fé Trail" (1912), are interesting examples.

1

Afoot and light-hearted I take to the open road,
Healthy, free, the world before me,
The long brown path before me leading wherever I
    choose.

Henceforth I ask not good-fortune, I myself am good-
    fortune,
Henceforth I whimper no more, postpone no more, need
    nothing,
Done with indoor complaints, libraries, querulous criti-
    cisms,
Strong and content I travel the open road.

The earth, that is sufficient,
I do not want the constellations any nearer,
I know they are very well where they are,   10

I know they suffice for those who belong to them.
(Still here I carry my old delicious burdens,
I carry them, men and women, I carry them with me
    wherever I go,
I swear it is impossible for me to get rid of them,
I am fill'd with them; and I will fill them in return.)

2

You road I enter upon and look around, I believe you
    are not all that is here,
I believe that much unseen is also here.

Here the profound lesson of reception, nor preference
    nor denial,
The black with his woolly head, the felon, the diseas'd,
    the illiterate person, are not denied;
The birth, the hasting after the physician, the beggar's
    tramp, the drunkard's stagger, the laughing party
    of mechanics,   20
The escaped youth, the rich person's carriage, the fop,
    the eloping couple,
The early market-man, the hearse, the moving of
    furniture into the town, the return back from the
    town,
They pass, I also pass, any thing passes, none can be
    interdicted,
None but are accepted, none but shall be dear to me.

3

You air that serves me with breath to speak!
You objects that call from diffusion my meanings
    and give them shape!
You light that wraps me and all things in delicate
    equable showers!
You paths worn in the irregular hollows by the
    roadsides!
I believe you are latent with unseen existences, you
    are so dear to me.

You flagg'd walks of the cities! you strong curbs
    at the edges!   30
You ferries! you planks and posts of wharves! you
    timberlined sides! you distant ships!
You rows of houses! you window-pierc'd facades!
    you roofs!
You porches and entrances! you copings and iron
    guards!

Open Road — teaches lessons —
gives all manning people — all are accepted by the
Open Road —
Cheer + sentiment on Open Road

You windows whose transparent shells might expose so much!

You doors and ascending steps! you arches!

You gray stones of interminable pavements! you
trodden crossings!

From all that has touch'd you I believe you have imparted to yourselves, and now would impart the
same secretly to me,

From the living and the dead you have peopled your
impassive surfaces, and the spirits thereof would
be evident and amicable with me.

4

liked music!

The earth expanding right hand and left hand,

The picture alive, every part in its best light,   40

The music falling in where it is wanted, and stopping
where it is not wanted,

The cheerful voice of the public road, the gay fresh
sentiment of the road.

O highway I travel, do you say to me *Do not leave
me?*

Do you say *Venture not—if you leave me you are
lost?*

Do you say *I am already prepared, I am well-beaten and
undenied, adhere to me?*

O public road, I say back I am not afraid to leave you,
yet I love you,

You express me better than I can express myself,
You shall be more to me than my poem.

I think heroic deeds were all conceiv'd in the open air,
and all free poems also,

I think I could stop here myself and do miracles,   50

I think whatever I shall meet on the road I shall like,
and whoever beholds me shall like me,

I think whoever I see must be happy.

5

From this hour I ordain myself loos'd of limits and
imaginary lines,

Going where I list, my own master total and absolute,

Listening to others, considering well what they say,

Pausing, searching, receiving, contemplating,

Gently, but with undeniable will, divesting myself of the
holds that would hold me.

I inhale great draughts of space,

The east and the west are mine, and the north and the
south are mine.

I am larger, better than I thought,   60

I did not know I held so much goodness.

transcendental icon

All seems beautiful to me,

I can repeat over to men and women You have done such
good to me I would do the same to you,

I will recruit for myself and you as I go,

I will scatter myself among men and women as I go,

I will toss a new gladness and roughness among them,

Whoever denies me it shall not trouble me,

Whoever accepts me he or she shall be blessed and
shall bless me.

6

Now if a thousand perfect men were to appear it would
not amaze me,

Now if a thousand beautiful forms of women appear'd
it would not astonish me.   70

Now I see the secret of the making of the best persons,

It is to grow in the open air and to eat and sleep with
the earth.

Here a great personal deed has room,

(Such a deed seizes upon the hearts of the whole race of
men,

Its effusion of strength and will overwhelms law and
mocks all authority and all argument against it.)

Here is the test of wisdom,

Wisdom is not finally tested in schools,

Wisdom cannot be pass'd from one having it to another
not having it,

Wisdom is of the soul, is not susceptible of proof, is its
own proof,

Applies to all stages and objects and qualities and is
content,   80

Is the certainty of the reality and immortality of things,
and the excellence of things;

Something there is in the float of the sight of things
that provokes it out of the soul.

Now I re-examine philosophies and religions,

in your many people + vocations

(4) light —
(5) paths

wisdom is not just by books
It must be applied to everyday life + used!

They may prove well in lecture-rooms, yet not prove at
all under the spacious clouds and along the landscape and flowing currents.

Here is realization,
Here is a man tallied—he realizes here what he has in him,
The past, the future, majesty, love—if they are vacant of
you, you are vacant of them.

*man sees what
he is or can do*

Only the kernel of every object nourishes;
Where is he who tears off the husks for you and me?
Where is he that undoes stratagems and envelopes for
you and me?

90

Here is adhesiveness, it is not previously fashion'd, it is
apropos;

closeness @ men & women
*desire
to be
with
them*

Do you know what it is as you pass to be loved by
strangers?
Do you know the talk of those turning eye-balls?

7

Here is the efflux of the soul,
The efflux of the soul comes from within through em-
bower'd gates, ever provoking questions,
These yearnings why are they? these thoughts in the
darkness why are they?
Why are there men and women that while they are
nigh me the sunlight expands my blood?
Why when they leave me do my pennants of joy sink
flat and lank?
Why are there trees I never walk under but large and
melodious thoughts descend upon me?
(I think they hang there winter and summer on those
trees and always drop fruit as I pass;)
100
What is it I interchange so suddenly with strangers?
What with some driver as I ride on the seat by his side?
What with some fisherman drawing his seine by the
shore as I walk by and pause?
What gives me to be free to a woman's and man's
good-will? what gives them to be free to mine?

8

The efflux of the soul is happiness, here is happiness,
I think it pervades the open air, waiting at all times,
Now it flows unto us, we are rightly charged.
Here rises the fluid and attaching character,

The fluid and attaching character is the freshness and
sweetness of man and woman,
(The herbs of the morning sprout no fresher and
sweeter every day out of the roots of themselves,
than it sprouts fresh and sweet continually out of
itself.)
110
Toward the fluid and attaching character exudes the
sweat of the love of young and old,
From it falls distill'd the charm that mocks beauty and
attainments,
Toward it heaves the shuddering longing ache of contact.

Allons! whoever you are come travel with me!
Traveling with me you find what never tires.

The earth never tires,
The earth is rude, silent, incomprehensible at first,
Nature is rude and incomprehensible at first,
Be not discouraged, keep on, there are divine things
well envelop'd,
I swear to you there are divine things more beautiful
than words can tell.

Allons! we must not stop here,
120
However sweet these laid-up stores, however convenient this dwelling we cannot remain here,
However shelter'd this port and however calm these
waters we must not anchor here,
However welcome the hospitality that surrounds us we
are permitted to receive it but a little while.

10

Allons! the inducements shall be greater,
We will sail pathless and wild seas,
We will go where winds blow, waves dash, and the
Yankee clipper speeds by under full sail.
Allons! with power, liberty, the earth, the elements,
Health, defiance, gayety, self-esteem, curiosity;

---

91 adhesiveness, the capacity for friendship and social attraction, a
term from phrenology. Specifically, in Whitman, the term ordinarily
refers to what he calls in "For You O Democracy" "the manly love
of comrades," and is to be distinguished from "amativeness," which
is the love for the opposite sex • 114 Allons! Let's go!

On the Open Road — is real life [man what he is & can do!] It shows

Allons! from all formules!

From your formules, O bat-eyed and materialistic priests.
130

The stale cadaver blocks up the passage—the burial waits
no longer.

Allons! yet take warning!

He traveling with me needs the best blood, thews, endurance,

None may come to the trial till he or she bring courage
and health,

Come not here if you have already spent the best of
yourself,

Only those may come who come in sweet and determin'd
bodies,

No diseas'd person, no rum-drinker or venereal taint is
permitted here.

(I and mine do not convince by arguments, similes,
rhymes, We convince by our presence.)

11

Listen! I will be honest with you,

I do not offer the old smooth prizes, but offer rough
new prizes,
140

These are the days that must happen to you:

You shall not heap up what is call'd riches,

You shall scatter with lavish hand all that you earn or
achieve,

You but arrive at the city to which you are destin'd, you
hardly settle yourself to satisfaction before you are
call'd by an irresistible call to depart,

You shall be treated to the ironical smiles and mockings
of those who remain behind you,

What beckonings of love you receive you shall only
answer with passionate kisses of parting,

You shall not allow the hold of those who spread their
reach'd hands toward you.

12   Companions on the Road

Allons! after the great Companions, and to belong to
them!

They too are on the road—they are the swift and
majestic men—they are the greatest women,

Enjoyers of calms of seas and storms of seas,
150

Sailors of many a ship, walkers of many a mile of land,

"Walt Whitman inciting the bird of freedom to soar"—
drawing by Max Beerbohm, Bookman, 1904

catalogue

Habitués of many distant countries, habitués of far-
distant dwellings,

Trusters of men and women, observers of cities, solitary
toilers,

Pausers and contemplators of tufts, blossoms, shells of
the shore,

Dancers at wedding-dances, kissers of brides, tender
helpers of children, bearers of children,

Soldiers of revolts, standers by gaping graves, lowerers-
down of coffins,

Journeyers over consecutive seasons, over the years, the
curious years each emerging from that which
preceded it,

Journeyers as with companions, namely their own
diverse phases,

Forth-steppers from the latent unrealized baby-days,

Journeyers gayly with their own youth, journeyers with
their bearded and well-grain'd manhood,
160

Journeyers with their womanhood, ample, unsurpass'd,
content,

Journeyers with their own sublime old age of manhood
or womanhood,

Old age, calm, expanded, broad with the haughty breadth
of the universe,
Old age, flowing free with the delicious near-by freedom
of death.

13

Allons! to that which is endless as it was beginningless,
To undergo much, tramps of days, rests of nights,
To merge all in the travel they tend to, and the days and
nights they tend to,
Again to merge them in the start of superior journeys,
To see nothing anywhere but what you may reach it
and pass it,
To conceive no time, however distant, but what you may
reach it and pass it,   170
To look up or down no road but it stretches and waits
for you, however long but it stretches and waits for
you,
To see no being, not God's or any, but you also go
thither,
To see no possession but you may possess it, enjoying all
without labor or purchase, abstracting the feast yet
not abstracting one particle of it,
To take the best of the farmer's farm and the rich man's
elegant villa, and the chaste blessings of the well-
married couple, and the fruits of orchards and
flowers of gardens,
To take to your use out of the compact cities as you pass
through,
To carry buildings and streets with you afterward
wherever you go,
To gather the minds of men out of their brains as you
encounter them, to gather the love out of their hearts,
To take your lovers on the road with you, for all that you
leave them behind you.
To know the universe itself as a road, as many roads, as
roads for traveling souls.

All parts away for the progress of souls,   180
All religion, all solid things, arts, governments—all that
was or is apparent upon this globe or any globe,
falls into niches and corners before the procession
of souls along the grand roads of the universe.
Of the progress of the souls of men and women along
the grand roads of the universe, all other progress
is the needed emblem and sustenance.

Forever alive, forever forward,
Stately, solemn, sad, withdrawn, baffled, mad, turbulent,
feeble, dissatisfied,
Desperate, proud, fond, sick, accepted by men, rejected
by men,
They go! they go! I know that they go, but I know not
where they go,
But I know that they go toward the best—toward something great. *trials — in becoming better on the Road!*
Whoever you are, come forth! or man or woman come
forth!
You must not stay sleeping and dallying there in the
house, though you built it, or though it has been
built for you.
despair in those who need not the open Road
Out of the dark confinement! out from behind the
screen!   190
It is useless to protest, I know all and expose it.

Behold through you as bad as the rest,
Through the laughter, dancing, dining, supping, of
people,
Inside of dresses and ornaments, inside of those wash'd
and trimm'd faces,
Behold a secret silent loathing and despair.

No husband, no wife, no friend, trusted to hear the confession,
Another self, a duplicate of every one, skulking and hiding it goes,
Formless and wordless through the streets of the cities,
polite and bland in the parlors,
In the cars of railroads, in steamboats, in the public
assembly,
Home to the houses of men and women, at the table, in
the bedroom, everywhere,   200
Smartly attired, countenance smiling, form upright,
death under the breast-bones, hell under the skull-
bones,
Under the broadcloth and gloves, under the ribbons and
artificial flowers,
Keeping fair with the customs, speaking not a syllable
of itself,
Speaking of any thing else but never of itself.

[handwritten: he becomes wise →]

[handwritten: → men in Conventionality of Past of life — are artificial not themselves as those on Open Road.]

Allons! through struggles and wars!
The goal that was named cannot be countermanded.

Have the past struggles succeeded?
What has succeeded? yourself? your nation? Nature?
Now understand me well—it is provided in the essence
　　of things that from any fruition of success, no mat-
　　ter what, shall come forth something to make a
　　greater struggle necessary.

My call is the call of battle, I nourish active rebellion, 210
He going with me must go well arm'd,
He going with me goes often with spare diet, poverty,
　　angry enemies, desertions.

15

Allons! the road is before us!
It is safe—I have tried it—my own feet have tried it
　　well—be not detain'd!
Let the paper remain on the desk unwritten, and the book
　　on the shelf unopen'd!
Let the tools remain in the workshop! let the money re-
　　main unearn'd!
Let the school stand! mind not the cry of the teacher!
Let the preacher preach in his pulpit! let the lawyer plead
　　in the court, and the judge expound the law.

Camerado, I give you my hand!
I give you my love more precious than money, 　　　220
I give you myself before preaching or law;
Will you give me yourself? will you come travel with me?
Shall we stick by each other as long as we live?

　　　　　　　　　　　　　　　　　　　1856·1881

Crossing Brooklyn Ferry

Whitman wrote in **Specimen Days:** "Living in Brooklyn
or New York city . . . my life . . . was curiously identified
with Fulton ferry, already becoming the greatest of its
sort in the world for general importance, volume, variety,
rapidity, and picturesqueness. Almost daily ('50 to '60) I
cross'd on the boats, often up in the pilot-houses where I
could get a full sweep, absorbing shows, accompaniments,
surroundings. What oceanic currents, eddies, underneath—
the great tides of humanity also, with ever-shifting movements! Indeed, I have always had a passion for ferries;
to me they afford inimitable, streaming, never-failing, living poems. The river and bay scenery, all about New York
island, any time of a fine day—the hurrying, splashing
sea-tides—the changing panorama of steamers, all sizes,
often a string of big ones outward bound to distant ports
—the myriads of white sail'd schooners, sloops, skiffs, and
the marvellously beautiful yachts—the majestic Sound
boats as they rounded the Battery and came along towards
5, afternoon, eastward bound—the prospect off toward
Staten Island, or down the Narrows, or the other way up
the Hudson—what refreshment of spirit such sights and
experiences gave me years ago (and many a time since)!
My old pilot friends, the Balsirs, Johnny Cole, Ira Smith,
William White, and my young ferry friend, Tom Gere—
how well I remember them all!"

1

Flood-tide below me! I see you face to face!
Clouds of the west—sun there half an hour high—I see
　　you also face to face.

Crowds of men and women attired in the usual cos-
　　tumes, how curious you are to me!
On the ferry-boats the hundreds and hundreds that cross,
　　returning home, are more curious to me than you
　　suppose,
And you that shall cross from shore to shore years hence
　　are more to me, and more in my meditations, than
　　you might suppose.

2

The impalpable sustenance of me from all things at all
　　hours of the day,
The simple, compact, well-join'd scheme, myself disinte-
　　grated, every one disintegrated yet part of the
　　scheme,
The similitudes of the past and those of the future,
The glories strung like beads on my smallest sights and
　　hearings, on the walk in the street and the passage
　　over the river,
The current rushing so swiftly and swimming with me
　　far away,　　　　　　　　　　　　　　　　　　10

all in future will enjoy what I see on the ferry —

The others that are to follow me, the ties between me
    and them,
The certainty of others, the life, love, sight, hearing of
    others.
Others will enter the gates of the ferry and cross from
    shore to shore,
Others will watch the run of the flood-tide,
Others will see the shipping of Manhattan north and west,
    and the heights of Brooklyn to the south and east,
Others will see the islands large and small;
Fifty years hence, others will see them as they cross, the
    sun half an hour high,
A hundred years hence, or ever so many hundred years
    hence, others will see them,
Will enjoy the sunset, the pouring-in of the flood-tide,
    the falling-back to the sea of the ebb-tide.

Poet of the people!

It avails not, time nor place—distance avails not,   20
I am with you, you men and women of a generation, or
    ever so many generations hence,
Just as you feel when you look on the river and sky, so
    I felt,
Just as any of you is one of a living crowd, I was one of
    a crowd,
Just as you are refresh'd by the gladness of the river and
    the bright flow, I was refresh'd,
Just as you stand and lean on the rail, yet hurry with the
    swift current, I stood yet was hurried,
Just as you look on the numberless masts of ships and the
    thick-stemm'd pipes of steamboats, I look'd.

I too many and many a time cross'd the river of old,
Watched the Twelfth-month sea-gulls, saw them high in
    the air floating with motionless wings, oscillating
    their bodies,
Saw how the glistening yellow lit up parts of their bodies
    and left the rest in strong shadow,
Saw the slow-wheeling circles and the gradual edging
    toward the south,   30
Saw the reflection of the summer sky in the water,
Had my eyes dazzled by the shimmering track of beams,
Look'd at the fine centrifugal spokes of light round the
    shape of my head in the sunlit water,
Look'd on the haze on the hills southward and south-
    westward,

Look'd on the vapor as it flew in fleeces tinged with
    violet,
Look'd toward the lower bay to notice the vessels arriv-
    ing,
Saw their approach, saw aboard those that were near
    me,
Saw the white sails of schooners and sloops, saw the ships
    at anchor,
The sailors at work in the rigging or out astride the
    spars,
The round masts, the swinging motion of the hulls, the
    slender serpentine pennants,   40
The large and small steamers in motion, the pilots in
    their pilot-houses,
The white wake left by the passage, the quick tremulous
    whirl of the wheels,
The flags of all nations, the falling of them at sunset,
The scallop-edged waves in the twilight, the ladled cups,
    the frolicsome crests and glistening,
The stretch afar growing dimmer and dimmer, the gray
    walls of the granite storehouses by the docks,
On the river the shadowy group, the big steam-tug closely
    flank'd on each side by the barges, the hay-boat, the
    belated lighter,
On the neighboring shore the fires from the foundry
    chimneys burning high and glaringly into the night,
Casting their flicker of black contrasted with wild red
    and yellow light over the tops of houses, and down
    into the clefts of streets.

4   *theme*

These and all else were to me the same as they are to
    you,
I loved well those cities, loved well the stately and rapid
    river,   50
The men and women I saw were all near to me,
Others the same—others who look back on me because
    I look'd forward to them,
(The time will come, though I stop here to-day and
    to-night.)

---

28 **Twelfth-month.** In the 1856 edition, Whitman wrote "December";
he substituted "Twelfth-month" in the edition of 1860 and retained it
in subsequent editions. His preference for so naming the months is
usually attributed to the Quaker influence • 46 **hay-boat**, boat for
transporting hay (see **Dictionary of American English**)

5

What is it then between us?

What is the count of the scores or hundreds of years between us?

Whatever it is, it avails not—distance avails not, and
place avails not,

I too lived, Brooklyn of ample hills was mine,

I too walk'd the streets of Manhattan island, and bathed
in the waters around it,

I too felt the curious abrupt questionings stir within me.

In the day among crowds of people sometimes they came
upon me,   60

In my walks home late at night or as I lay in my bed
they came upon me,

I too had been struck from the float forever held in
solution,

I too had receiv'd identity by my body,

That I was I knew was of my body, and what I should be
I knew I should be of my body.

6

It is not upon you alone the dark patches fall,

The dark threw its patches down upon me also,

The best I had done seem'd to me blank and suspicious,

My great thoughts as I supposed them, were they not in
reality meagre?

Nor is it you alone who know what it is to be evil,

I am he who knew what it was to be evil,   70

I too knitted the old knot of contrariety,

Blabb'd, blush'd, resented, lied, stole, grudg'd,

Had guile, anger, lust, hot wishes I dared not speak,

Was wayward, vain, greedy, shallow, sly, cowardly,
malignant,

The wolf, the snake, the hog, not wanting in me,

The cheating look, the frivolous word, the adulterous
wish, not wanting,

Refusals, hates, postponements, meanness, laziness, none
of these wanting,

Was one with the rest, the days and haps of the rest,

Was call'd by my nighest name by clear loud voices of
young men as they saw me approaching or passing,

Felt their arms on my neck as I stood, or the negligent
leaning of their flesh against me as I sat,   80

Saw many I loved in the street or ferry-boat or public
assembly, yet never told them a word,

Lived the same life with the rest, the same old laughing,
gnawing, sleeping,

Play'd the part that still looks back on the actor or actress,

The same old role, the role that is what we make it, as
great as we like,

Or as small as we like, or both great and small.

7

Closer yet I approach you,

What thought you have of me now, I had as much of you
—I laid in my stores in advance,

I consider'd long and seriously of you before you were born.

Who was to know what should come home to me?

Who knows but I am enjoying this?   90

Who knows, for all the distance, but I am as good as
looking at you now, for all you cannot see me?

8

Ah, what can ever be more stately and admirable to me
than mast-hemm'd Manhattan?

River and sunset and scallop-edg'd waves of flood-tide?

The sea-gulls oscillating their bodies, the hay-boat in the
twilight, and the belated lighter?

What gods can exceed these that clasp me by the hand,
and with voices I love call me promptly and loudly
by my nighest name as I approach?

What is more subtle than this which ties me to the
woman or man that looks in my face?

Which fuses me into you now, and pours my meaning
into you?

We understand then do we not?

What I promis'd without mentioning it, have you not
accepted?

What the study could not teach—what the preaching
could not accomplish is accomplish'd, is it not?   100

9

Flow on, river! flow with the flood-tide, and ebb with the
ebb-tide!

Frolic on, crested and scallop-edg'd waves!

---

79 **nighest,** shortest

Gorgeous clouds of the sunset! drench with your splendor
    me, or the men and women generations after me!
Cross from shore to shore, countless crowds of passengers!
Stand up, tall masts of Mannahatta! stand up, beautiful
    hills of Brooklyn!
Throb, baffled and curious brain! throw out questions
    and answers!
Suspend here and everywhere, eternal float of solution!
Gaze, loving and thirsting eyes, in the house or street or
    public assembly!
Sound out, voices of young men! loudly and musically
    call me by my nighest name!
Live, old life! play the part that looks back on the actor
    or actress!   110
Play the old role, the role that is great or small according
    as one makes it!
Consider, you who peruse me, whether I may not in un-
    known ways be looking upon you;
Be firm, rail over the river, to support those who lean
    idly, yet haste with the hasting current;
Fly on, sea-birds! fly sideways, or wheel in large circles
    high in the air;
Receive the summer sky, you water, and faithfully hold
    it till all downcast eyes have time to take it from
    you!
Diverge, fine spokes of light, from the shape of my head,
    or any one's head, in the sunlit water!
Come on, ships from the lower bay! pass up or down,
    white-sail'd schooners, sloops, lighters!
Flaunt away, flags of all nations! be duly lower'd at
    sunset!
Burn high your fires, foundry chimneys! cast black
    shadows at nightfall! cast red and yellow light over
    the tops of the houses!
Appearances, now or henceforth, indicate what you are, 120
You necessary film, continue to envelop the soul,
About my body for me, and your body for you, be hung
    our divinest aromas,
Thrive, cities—bring your freight, bring your shows,
    ample and sufficient rivers,
Expand, being than which none else is perhaps more
    spiritual,
Keep your places, objects than which none else is more
    lasting.
You have waited, you always wait, you dumb, beautiful
    ministers,

We receive you with free sense at last, and are insatiate
    henceforward,
Not you any more shall be able to foil us, or withhold
    yourselves from us,
We use you, and do not cast you aside—we plant you
    permanently within us,
We fathom you not—we love you—there is perfection in
    you also,   130
You furnish your parts toward eternity,
Great or small, you furnish your parts toward the soul.
                    1856·1881

Pioneers! O Pioneers!

"Pioneers! O Pioneers!" is the chief celebration in American poetry of the Westward movement. From the stand-
point of sober fact, the poem romanticizes its subject
too much: those who remained in the older settlements
were not necessarily more "gluttonous" (l. 93) than those
who moved forward, the pioneers seem now to have
felled too many of the "primeval forests" (l. 25), and mere
"restlessness" (l. 37) is not always a virtue. But Whitman's
purpose was to celebrate, not criticize, and he caught
admirably, in "Pioneers! O Pioneers!" the spirit and
momentum of a mass movement which embraced large
sections of Europe as well as the entire American continent.

    The student should read, in conjunction with Whitman's
poem, Frederick Jackson Turner's "The Significance of the
Frontier in American History" (1893).

      Come my tan-faced children,
Follow well in order, get your weapons ready,
Have you your pistols? have you your sharp-edged
    axes?
      Pioneers! O pioneers!

      For we cannot tarry here,
We must march my darlings, we must bear the brunt of
    danger,
We the youthful sinewy races, all the rest on us
    depend,
      Pioneers! O pioneers!

O you youths, Western youths,
So impatient, full of action, full of manly pride and
    friendship, 10
Plain I see you Western youths, see you tramping with
    the foremost,
        Pioneers! O pioneers!

Have the elder races halted?
Do they droop and end their lesson, wearied over there
    beyond the seas?
We take up the task eternal, and the burden and the lesson,
        Pioneers! O pioneers!

All the past we leave behind,
We debouch upon a newer mightier world, varied world,
Fresh and strong the world we seize, world of labor and
    the march,
        Pioneers! O pioneers! 20

We detachments steady throwing,
Down the edges, through the passes, up the mountains
    steep,
Conquering, holding, daring, venturing as we go the un-
    known ways,
        Pioneers! O pioneers!

We primeval forests felling,
We the rivers stemming, vexing we and piercing deep
    the mines within,
We the surface broad surveying, we the virgin soil up-
    heaving,
        Pioneers! O pioneers!

Colorado men are we,
From the peaks gigantic, from the great sierras and the
    high plateaus, 30
From the mine and from the gully, from the hunting
    trail we come,
        Pioneers! O pioneers!

From Nebraska, from Arkansas,
Central inland race are we, from Missouri, with the con-
    tinental blood intervein'd,
All the hands of comrades clasping, all the Southern, all
    the Northern,
        Pioneers! O pioneers!

O resistless restless race!
O beloved race in all! O my breast aches with tender love
    for all!
O I mourn and yet exult, I am rapt with love for all,
        Pioneers! O pioneers! 40

Raise the mighty mother mistress,
Waving high the delicate mistress, over all the starry
    mistress, (bend your heads all,)
Raise the fang'd and warlike mistress, stern, impassive,
    weapon'd mistress,
        Pioneers! O pioneers!

See my children, resolute children,
By those swarms upon our rear we must never yield or
    falter,
Ages back in ghostly millions frowning there behind us
    urging,
        Pioneers! O pioneers!

On and on the compact ranks,
With accessions ever waiting, with the places of the dead
    quickly fill'd, 50
Through the battle, through defeat, moving yet and never
    stopping,
        Pioneers! O pioneers!

O to die advancing on!
Are there some of us to droop and die? has the hour
    come?
Then upon the march we fittest die, soon and sure the
    gap is fill'd,
        Pioneers! O pioneers!

All the pulses of the world,
Falling in they beat for us, with the Western movement
    beat,
Holding single or together, steady moving to the front,
    all for us,
        Pioneers! O pioneers! 60

Life's involv'd and varied pageants,
All the forms and shows, all the workmen at their work,

26 stemming, damming up • 26 vexing, shaking, disturbing

Pioneers! O Pioneers! 187

All the seamen and the landsmen, all the masters with
    their slaves,
      Pioneers! O pioneers!

All the hapless silent lovers,
All the prisoners in the prisons, all the righteous and the
    wicked,
All the joyous, all the sorrowing, all the living, all the
    dying,
      Pioneers! O pioneers!

I too with my soul and body,
We, a curious trio, picking, wandering on our way,   70
Through these shores amid the shadows, with the appari-
    tions pressing,
      Pioneers! O pioneers!

Lo, the darting bowling orb!
Lo, the brother orbs around, all the clustering suns and
    planets,
All the dazzling days, all the mystic nights with dreams,
      Pioneers! O pioneers!

These are of us, they are with us,
All for primal needed work, while the followers there in
    embryo wait behind,
We to-day's procession heading, we the route for travel
    clearing,
      Pioneers! O pioneers!   80

O you daughters of the West!
O you young and elder daughters! O you mothers and
    you wives!
Never must you be divided, in our ranks you move united,
      Pioneers! O pioneers!

Minstrels latent on the prairies!
(Shrouded bards of other lands, you may rest, you have
    done your work,)
Soon I hear you coming warbling, soon you rise and
    tramp amid us,
      Pioneers! O pioneers!

Not for delectations sweet,
Not the cushion and the slipper, not the peaceful and
    the studious,   90

Not the riches safe and palling, not for us the tame en-
    joyment,
      Pioneers! O pioneers!

Do the feasters gluttonous feast?
Do the corpulent sleepers sleep? have they lock'd and
    bolted doors?
Still be ours the diet hard, and the blanket on the ground,
      Pioneers! O pioneers!

Has the night descended?
Was the road of late so toilsome? did we stop discouraged
    nodding on our way?
Yet a passing hour I yield you in your tracks to pause
    oblivious,
      Pioneers! O pioneers!   100

Till with sound of trumpet,
Far, far off the daybreak call—hark! how loud and clear
    I hear it wind,
Swift! to the head of the army!—swift! spring to your
    places,
      Pioneers! O pioneers!

      1865·1881

Death of a bird

Out of the Cradle Endlessly Rocking

Whose mate is sorrowful!

" 'Out of the Cradle Endlessly Rocking' is certainly among
the half-dozen finest of Whitman's longer poems, and one
of the finest lyrics of the nineteenth century. The sea always
moved Whitman, and more than any other physical fact
lifted him above the world of assertions and opinions into
that of imagination and vision" (John Bailey, **Whitman**,
p. 165).

nearly symbolically about Lincoln

Out of the cradle endlessly rocking,
Out of the mocking-bird's throat, the musical shuttle,
Out of the Ninth-month midnight,
Over the sterile sands and the fields beyond, where the
    child leaving his bed wander'd alone, bareheaded,
    barefoot,
Down from the shower'd halo,

Up from the mystic play of shadows twining and twisting
    as if they were alive,
Out from the patches of briers and blackberries,
From the memories of the bird that chanted to me,
From your memories sad brother, from the fitful risings
    and fallings I heard,
From under that yellow half-moon late-risen and swollen
    as if with tears,   10
From those beginning notes of yearning and love there
    in the mist,
From the thousand responses of my heart never to
    cease,
From the myriad thence-arous'd words,
From the word stronger and more delicious than any,
From such as now they start the scene revisiting,
As a flock, twittering, rising, or overhead passing,
Borne hither, ere all eludes me, hurriedly,
A man, yet by these tears a little boy again,
Throwing myself on the sand, confronting the waves,
I, chanter of pains and joys, uniter of here and here-
    after,   20
Taking all hints to use them, but swiftly leaping beyond
    them,
A reminiscence sing.
Once Paumanok,
When the lilac-scent was in the air and Fifth-month grass
    was growing,
Up this seashore in some briers,
Two feather'd guests from Alabama, two together,
And their nest, and four light-green eggs spotted with
    brown,
And every day the he-bird to and fro near at hand,
And every day the she-bird crouch'd on her nest, silent,
    with bright eyes,
And every day I, a curious boy, never too close, never
    disturbing them,   30
Cautiously peering, absorbing, translating.

Shine! shine! shine!
Pour down your warmth, great sun!
While we bask, we two together.

Two together!
Winds blow south, or winds blow north,
Day come white, or night come black,
Home, or rivers and mountains from home,

Singing all time, minding no time,
While we two keep together.   40

Till of a sudden,
May-be kill'd, unknown to her mate,
One forenoon the she-bird crouch'd not on the nest,
Nor return'd that afternoon, nor the next,
Nor ever appear'd again.

And thenceforward all summer in the sound of the sea,
And at night under the full of the moon in calmer weather,
Over the hoarse surging of the sea,
Or flitting from brier to brier by day,
I saw, I heard at intervals the remaining one the he-bird, 50
The solitary guest from Alabama.

Blow! blow! blow!
Blow up sea-winds along Paumanok's shore;
I wait and I wait till you blow my mate to me.

Yes, when the stars glisten'd,
All night long on the prong of a moss-scallop'd stake,
Down almost amid the slapping waves,
Sat the lone singer wonderful causing tears.
He call'd on his mate,
He pour'd forth the meanings which I of all men know. 60

Yes my brother I know,
The rest might not, but I have treasur'd every note,
For more than once dimly down to the beach gliding,
Silent, avoiding the moonbeams, blending myself with
    the shadows,
Recalling now the obscure shapes, the echoes, the sounds
    and sights after their sorts,
The white arms out in the breakers tirelessly tossing,
I, with bare feet, a child, the wind wafting my hair,
Listen'd long and long.

Listen'd to keep, to sing, now translating the notes,
Following you my brother.   70

Soothe! soothe! soothe!
Close on its wave soothes the wave behind,

---

23 Paumanok. Whitman preferred to call Long Island by its Indian name

Out of the Cradle Endlessly Rocking   189

And again another behind embracing and lapping, every
    one close,
But my love soothes not me, not me.

Low hangs the moon, it rose late,
It is lagging—O I think it is heavy with love, with love.

O madly the sea pushes upon the land,
With love, with love.

O night! do I not see my love fluttering out among the
    breakers?
What is that little black thing I see there in the white? 80

Loud! loud! loud!
Loud I call to you, my love!
High and clear I shoot my voice over the waves,
Surely you must know who is here, is here,
You must know who I am, my love.

Low-hanging moon!
What is that dusky spot in your brown yellow?
O it is the shape, the shape of my mate!
O moon do not keep her from me any longer.

Land! land! O land!   90
Whichever way I turn, O I think you could give me my
    mate back again if you only would,
For I am almost sure I see her dimly whichever way I look.

O rising stars!
Perhaps the one I want so much will rise, will rise with
    some of you.

O throat! O trembling throat!
Sound clearer through the atmosphere!
Pierce the woods, the earth,
Somewhere listening to catch you must be the one I want.

Shake out carols!
Solitary here, the night's carols!   100
Carols of lonesome love! death's carols!
Carols under that lagging, yellow, waning moon!
O under that moon where she droops almost down into
    the sea!
O reckless despairing carols.

But soft! sink low!
Soft! let me just murmur,
And do you wait a moment you husky-nois'd sea,
For somewhere I believe I heard my mate responding
    to me,
So faint, I must be still, be still to listen,
But not altogether still, for then she might not come
    immediately to me.   110

Hither my love!
Here I am! here!
With this just-sustain'd note I announce myself to you,
This gentle call is for you my love, for you.

Do not be decoy'd elsewhere,
That is the whistle of the wind, it is not my voice,
That is the fluttering, the fluttering of the spray,
Those are the shadows of leaves.

O darkness! O in vain!
O I am very sick and sorrowful.   120
O brown halo in the sky near the moon, drooping upon
    the sea!
O troubled reflection in the sea!
O throat! O throbbing heart!
And I singing uselessly, uselessly all the night.

O past! O happy life! O songs of joy!
In the air, in the woods, over fields,
Loved! loved! loved! loved! loved!
But my mate no more, no more with me!
We two together no more.

The aria sinking,   130
All else continuing, the stars shining,
The winds blowing, the notes of the bird continuous
    echoing.
With angry moans the fierce old mother incessantly
    moaning,
On the sands of Paumanok's shore gray and rustling,
The yellow half-moon enlarged, sagging down, drooping,
    the face of the sea almost touching,
The boy ecstatic, with his bare feet the waves, with his
    hair the atmosphere dallying,
The love in the heart long pent, now loose, now at last
    tumultuously bursting,

The aria's meaning, the ears, the soul, swiftly depositing,

The strange tears down the cheeks coursing,

The colloquy there, the trio, each uttering,   140

The undertone, the savage old mother incessantly crying,

To the boy's soul's questions sullenly timing, some drown'd secret hissing,

To the outsetting bard.

Demon or bird! (said the boy's soul,)

Is it indeed toward your mate you sing? or is it really to me?

For I, that was a child, my tongue's use sleeping, now I have heard you,

Now in a moment I know what I am for, I awake,

And already a thousand singers, a thousand songs, clearer, louder and more sorrowful than yours,

A thousand warbling echoes have started to life within me, never to die.

O you singer solitary, singing by yourself, projecting me,   150

O solitary me listening, never more shall I cease perpetuating you,

Never more shall I escape, never more the reverberations,

Never more the cries of unsatisfied love be absent from me,

Never again leave me to be the peaceful child I was before what there in the night,

By the sea under the yellow and sagging moon,

The messenger there arous'd, the fire, the sweet hell within,

The unknown want, the destiny of me.

O give me the clew! (it lurks in the night here somewhere,)

O if I am to have so much, let me have more!

A word then, (for I will conquer it,)   160

The word final, superior to all,

Subtle, sent up—what is it?—I listen;

Are you whispering it, and have been all the time, you sea waves?

Is that it from your liquid rims and wet sands?

Whereto answering, the sea,

Delaying not, hurrying not,

Whisper'd me through the night, and very plainly before daybreak,

Lisp'd to me the low and delicious word death,

And again death, death, death, death,

Hissing melodious, neither like the bird nor like my arous'd child's heart,   170

But edging near as privately for me rustling at my feet,

Creeping thence steadily up to my ears and laving me softly all over,

Death, death, death, death, death.

Which I do not forget,

But fuse the song of my dusky demon and brother,

That he sang to me in the moonlight on Paumanok's gray beach,

With the thousand responsive songs at random,

My own songs awakened from that hour,

And with them the key, the word up from the waves,

The word of the sweetest song and all songs,   180

That strong and delicious word which, creeping to my feet,

(Or like some old crone rocking the cradle, swathed in sweet garments, bending aside,)

The sea whisper'd me.

1859·1881

When I Heard the Learn'd Astronomer

When I heard the learn'd astronomer,

When the proofs, the figures, were ranged in columns before me,

When I was shown the charts and diagrams, to add, divide, and measure them,

When I sitting heard the astronomer where he lectured with much applause in the lecture-room,

How soon unaccountable I became tired and sick,

Till rising and gliding out I wander'd off by myself,

In the mystical moist night-air, and from time to time,

Look'd up in perfect silence at the stars.

1865·1867

First O Songs for a Prelude

This poem and seven poems which follow ("Beat! Beat! Drums!" "Cavalry Crossing a Ford," "Bivouac on a Mountain Side," "By the Bivouac's Fitful Flame," "Come Up from the Fields Father," "The Wound-Dresser," "Give Me the Splendid Silent Sun") were among those which first appeared in Drum-Taps in 1865. The poems of Drum-Taps were later incorporated in the inclusive work **Leaves of Grass.**

First O songs for a prelude,
Lightly strike on the stretch'd tympanum pride and joy in my city,
How she led the rest to arms, how she gave the cue,
How at once with lithe limbs unwaiting a moment she sprang,
(O superb! O Manhattan, my own, my peerless!
O strongest you in the hour of danger, in crisis! O truer than steel!)
How you sprang—how you threw off the costumes of peace with indifferent hand,
How your soft opera-music changed, and the drum and fife were heard in their stead,
How you led to the war, (that shall serve for our prelude, songs of soldiers,)
How Manhattan drum-taps led.   10

Forty years had I in my city seen soldiers parading,
Forty years as a pageant, till unawares the lady of this teeming and turbulent city,
Sleepless amid her ships, her houses, her incalculable wealth,
With her million children around her, suddenly,
At dead of night, at news from the south,
Incens'd struck with clinch'd hand the pavement.

A shock electric, the night sustain'd it,
Till with ominous hum our hive at daybreak pour'd out its myriads.
From the houses then and the workshops, and through all the doorways,
Leapt they tumultuous, and lo! Manhattan arming.   20

To the drum-taps prompt,
The young men falling in and arming,
The mechanics arming, (the trowel, the jack-plane, the blacksmith's hammer, tost aside with precipitation,)
The lawyer leaving his office and arming, the judge leaving the court,
The driver deserting his wagon in the street, jumping down, throwing the reins abruptly down on the horses' backs,
The salesman leaving the store, the boss, book-keeper, porter, all leaving;
Squads gather everywhere by common consent and arm,
The new recruits, even boys, the old men show them how to wear their accoutrements, they buckle the straps carefully,
Outdoors arming, indoors arming, the flash of the musket-barrels,
The white tents cluster in camps, the arm'd sentries around, the sunrise cannon and again at sunset,   30
Arm'd regiments arrive every day, pass through the city, and embark from the wharves,
(How good they look as they tramp down to the river, sweaty, with their guns on their shoulders!
How I love them! how I could hug them, with their brown faces and their clothes and knapsacks cover'd with dust!)
The blood of the city up—arm'd! arm'd! the cry everywhere,
The flags flung out from the steeples of churches and from all the public buildings and stores,
The tearful parting, the mother kisses her son, the son kisses his mother,
(Loth is the mother to part, yet not a word does she speak to detain him,)
The tumultuous escort, the ranks of policemen preceding, clearing the way,
The unpent enthusiasm, the wild cheers of the crowd for their favorites,
The artillery, the silent cannons bright as gold, drawn along, rumble lightly over the stones,   40
(Silent cannons, soon to cease your silence,
Soon unlimber'd to begin the red business;)
All the mutter of preparation, all the determin'd arming,

---

42 unlimber'd, detached from the limber or forepart of a gun carriage, and so made ready for firing

The hospital service, the lint, bandages and medicines,
The women volunteering for nurses, the work begun for in earnest, no mere parade now;
War! an arm'd race is advancing! the welcome for battle, no turning away;
War! be it weeks, months, or years, an arm'd race is advancing to welcome it.

Mannahatta a-march—and it's O to sing it well!
It's O for a manly life in the camp.

And the sturdy artillery,   50
The guns bright as gold, the work for giants, to serve well the guns,
Unlimber them! (no more as the past forty years for salute or courtesies merely,
Put in something now besides powder and wadding.)
And you lady of ships, you Mannahatta,
Old matron of this proud, friendly, turbulent city,
Often in peace and wealth you were pensive or covertly frown'd amid all your children,
But now you smile with joy exulting old Mannahatta.

1865·1867

Beat! Beat! Drums!

Beat! beat! drums!—blow! bugles! blow!
Through the windows—through doors—burst like a ruthless force,
Into the solemn church, and scatter the congregation,
Into the school where the scholar is studying;
Leave not the bridegroom quiet—no happiness must he have now with his bride,

Nor the peaceful farmer any peace, ploughing his field or gathering his grain,
So fierce you whirr and pound you drums—so shrill you bugles blow.

Beat! beat! drums!—blow! bugles! blow!
Over the traffic of cities—over the rumble of wheels in the streets;
Are beds prepared for sleepers at night in the houses? no sleepers must sleep in those beds,   10

No bargainers' bargains by day—no brokers or specu- lators—would they continue?
Would the talkers be talking? would the singer attempt to sing?
Would the lawyer rise in the court to state his case before the judge?
Then rattle quicker, heavier drums—you bugles wilder blow.

Beat! beat! drums!—blow! bugles! blow!
Make no parley—stop for no expostulation,
Mind not the timid—mind not the weeper or prayer,
Mind not the old man beseeching the young man,
Let not the child's voice be heard, nor the mother's entreaties,
Make even the trestles to shake the dead where they lie awaiting hearses,   20
So strong you thump O terrible drums—so loud you bugles blow.

1865·1867

Cavalry Crossing a Ford

A line in long array where they wind betwixt green islands,
They take a serpentine course, their arms flash in the sun—hark to the musical clank,
Behold the silvery river, in it the splashing horses loitering stop to drink,
Behold the brown-faced men, each group, each person a picture, the negligent rest on the saddles,
Some emerge on the opposite bank, others are just en- tering the ford—while,
Scarlet and blue and snowy white,
The guidon flags flutter gayly in the wind.

1865·1871

Bivouac on a Mountain Side

I see before me now a traveling army halting,
Below a fertile valley spread, with barns and the orchards of summer,

Behind, the terraced sides of a mountain, abrupt, in places rising high,
Broken, with rocks, with clinging cedars, with tall shapes dingily seen,
The numerous camp-fires scatter'd near and far, some away up on the mountain,
The shadowy forms of men and horses, looming, large-sized, flickering,
And over all the sky—the sky! far, far out of reach, studded, breaking out, the eternal stars.

1865·1871

By the Bivouac's Fitful Flame

By the bivouac's fitful flame,
A procession winding around me, solemn and sweet and slow—but first I note,
The tents of the sleeping army, the fields' and woods' dim outline,
The darkness lit by spots of kindled fire, the silence,
Like a phantom far or near an occasional figure moving,
The shrubs and trees, (as I lift my eyes they seem to be stealthily watching me,)
While wind in procession thoughts, O tender and wondrous thoughts,
Of life and death, of home and the past and loved, and of those that are far away;
A solemn and slow procession there as I sit on the ground,
By the bivouac's fitful flame.   10

1865·1867

Come Up from the Fields Father

Come up from the fields father, here's a letter from our Pete,
And come to the front door mother, here's a letter from thy dear son.

Lo, 'tis autumn,
Lo, where the trees, deeper green, yellower and redder,

Cool and sweeten Ohio's villages with leaves fluttering in the moderate wind,
Where apples ripe in the orchards hang and grapes on the trellis'd vines,
(Smell you the smell of the grapes on the vines?
Smell you the buckwheat where the bees were lately buzzing?)
Above all, lo, the sky so calm, so transparent after the rain, and with wondrous clouds,
Below too, all calm, all vital and beautiful, and the farm prospers well.   10

Down in the fields all prospers well,
But now from the fields come father, come at the daughter's call,
And come to the entry mother, to the front door come right away.

Fast as she can she hurries, something ominous, her steps trembling,
She does not tarry to smooth her hair nor adjust her cap.
Open the envelope quickly,
O this is not our son's writing, yet his name is sign'd,
O a strange hand writes for our dear son, O stricken mother's soul!
All swims before her eyes, flashes with black, she catches the main words only,
Sentences broken, *gunshot wound in the breast, cavalry skirmish, taken to hospital,*   20
At present low, but will soon be better.

Ah now the single figure to me,
Amid all teeming and wealthy Ohio with all its cities and farms,
Sickly white in the face and dull in the head, very faint,
By the jamb of a door leans.

Grieve not so, dear mother, (the just-grown daughter speaks through her sobs,
The little sisters huddle around speechless and dismay'd,)
See, dearest mother, the letter says Pete will soon be better.

Alas poor boy, he will never be better, (nor may-be
    needs to be better, that brave and simple soul,)
While they stand at home at the door he is dead
    already, 30
The only son is dead.

But the mother needs to be better,
She with thin form presently drest in black,
By day her meals untouch'd, then at night fitfully
    sleeping, often waking,
In the midnight waking, weeping, longing with one
    deep longing,
O that she might withdraw unnoticed, silent from life
    escape and withdraw,
To follow, to seek, to be with her dear dead son.

1865·1867

The Wound-Dresser

An old man bending I come among new faces,
Years looking backward resuming in answer to
    children,
Come tell us old man, as from young men and maidens
    that love me,
(Arous'd and angry, I'd thought to beat the alarum,
    and urge relentless war,
But soon my fingers fail'd me, my face droop'd and I
    resign'd myself,
To sit by the wounded and soothe them, or silently
    watch the dead;)
Years hence of these scenes, of these furious passions,
    these chances,
Of unsurpass'd heroes, (was one side so brave? the
    other was equally brave;)
Now be witness again, paint the mightiest armies of
    earth,
Of those armies so rapid so wondrous what saw you
    to tell us? 10
What stays with you latest and deepest? of curious
    panics,
Of hard-fought engagements or sieges tremendous what
    deepest remains?

2

O maidens and young men I love and that love me,
What you ask of my days those the strangest and
    sudden your talking recalls,
Soldier alert I arrive after a long march cover'd with
    sweat and dust,
In the nick of time I come, plunge in the fight, loudly
    shout in the rush of successful charge,
Enter the captur'd works—yet lo, like a swift-running
    river they fade,
Pass and are gone they fade—I dwell not on soldiers'
    perils or soldiers' joys,
(Both I remember well—many of the hardships, few
    the joys, yet I was content.)
But in silence, in dreams' projections, 20
While the world of gain and appearance and mirth
    goes on,
So soon what is over forgotten, and waves wash the
    imprints off the sand,
With hinged knees returning I enter the doors, (while
    for you up there,
Whoever you are, follow without noise and be of
    strong heart.)

Bearing the bandages, water and sponge,
Straight and swift to my wounded I go,
Where they lie on the ground after the battle brought
    in,
Where their priceless blood reddens the grass the
    ground,
Or to the rows of the hospital tent, or under the roof'd
    hospital,
To the long rows of cots up and down each side I
    return, 30
To each and all one after another I draw near, not one
    do I miss,
An attendant follows holding a tray, he carries a refuse
    pail,
Soon to be fill'd with clotted rags and blood, emptied,
    and fill'd again.

I onward go, I stop,
With hinged knees and steady hand to dress wounds,
I am firm with each, the pangs are sharp yet unavoid-
    able,

One turns to me his appealing eyes—poor boy! I never
   knew you,
Yet I think I could not refuse this moment to die for
   you, if that would save you.

3

On, on I go, (open doors of time! open hospital doors!)
The crush'd head I dress, (poor crazed hand tear not
   the bandage away,)   40
The neck of the cavalry-man with the bullet through and
   through I examine,
Hard the breathing rattles, quite glazed already the eye,
   yet life struggles hard,
(Come sweet death! be persuaded O beautiful death!
In mercy come quickly.)
From the stump of the arm, the amputated hand,
I undo the clotted lint, remove the slough, wash off the
   matter and blood,
Back on his pillow the soldier bends with curv'd neck
   and side falling head,
His eyes are closed, his face is pale, he dares not look on
   the bloody stump,
And has not yet look'd on it.

I dress a wound in the side, deep, deep,   50
But a day or two more, for see the frame all wasted and
   sinking,
And the yellow-blue countenance see.

I dress the perforated shoulder, the foot with the
   bullet-wound,
Cleanse the one with a gnawing and putrid gangrene,
   so sickening, so offensive,
While the attendant stands behind aside me holding
   the tray and pail.

I am faithful, I do not give out,
The fractur'd thigh, the knee, the wound in the
   abdomen,
These and more I dress with impassive hand, (yet deep
   in my breast a fire, a burning flame.)

4

Thus in silence in dreams' projections,
Returning, resuming, I thread my way through the
   hospitals,   60

The hurt and wounded I pacify with soothing hand,
I sit by the restless all the dark night, some are so
   young,
Some suffer so much, I recall the experience sweet and
   sad,
(Many a soldier's loving arms about this neck have
   cross'd and rested,
Many a soldier's kiss dwells on these bearded lips.)
                                            1865·1881

Give Me the Splendid Silent Sun

1

Give me the splendid silent sun with all his beams
   full-dazzling,
Give me juicy autumnal fruit ripe and red from the
   orchard,
Give me a field where the unmow'd grass grows,
Give me an arbor, give me the trellis'd grape,
Give me fresh corn and wheat, give me serene-
   moving animals teaching content,
Give me nights perfectly quiet as on high plateaus west
   of the Mississippi, and I looking up at the stars,
Give me odorous at sunrise a garden of beautiful
   flowers where I can walk undisturb'd,
Give me for marriage a sweet-breath'd woman of
   whom I should never tire,
Give me a perfect child, give me away aside from
   the noise of the world a rural domestic life,
Give me to warble spontaneous songs recluse by
   myself, for my own ears only,   10
Give me solitude, give me Nature, give me again O
   Nature your primal sanities!

These demanding to have them, (tired with ceaseless
   excitement, and rack'd by the war-strife,)
These to procure incessantly asking, rising in cries from
   my heart,
While yet incessantly asking still I adhere to my city.
Day upon day and year upon year O city, walking your
   streets,
Where you hold me enchain'd a certain time refusing
   to give me up,

With loaded arms I come, pouring for you,
For you and the coffins all of you O death.)

8

O western orb sailing the heaven,
Now I know what you must have meant as a month
　　since I walk'd,
As I walk'd in silence the transparent shadowy night,
As I saw you had something to tell as you bent to me
　　night after night,
As you droop'd from the sky low down as if to my side,
　　(while the other stars all look'd on,)
As we wander'd together the solemn night, (for some-
　　thing I know not what kept me from sleep,)
As the night advanced, and I saw on the rim of the west
　　how full you were of woe,
As I stood on the rising ground in the breeze in the
　　cool transparent night,
As I watch'd where you pass'd and was lost in the nether-
　　ward black of the night,
As my soul in its trouble dissatisfied sank, as where you
　　sad orb,
Concluded, dropt in the night, and was gone.

9

Sing on there in the swamp,
O singer bashful and tender, I hear your notes, I hear
　　your call,
I hear, I come presently, I understand you,
But a moment I linger, for the lustrous star has detain'd
　　me,
The star my departing comrade holds and detains me.

10

O how shall I warble myself for the dead one there
　　I loved?
And how shall I deck my song for the large sweet soul
　　that has gone?
And what shall my perfume be for the grave of him I
　　love?

Sea-winds blown from east and west,
Blown from the Eastern sea and blown from the Western
　　sea, till there on the prairies meeting,
These and with these and the breath of my chant,
I'll perfume the grave of him I love.

11

O what shall I hang on the chamber walls?
And what shall the pictures be that I hang on the
　　walls,
To adorn the burial-house of him I love?

Pictures of growing spring and farms and homes,
With the Fourth-month eve at sundown, and the gray
　　smoke lucid and bright,
With floods of the yellow gold of the gorgeous, in-
　　dolent, sinking sun, burning, expanding the air,
With the fresh sweet herbage under foot, and the pale
　　green leaves of the trees prolific,
In the distance the flowing glaze, the breast of the river,
　　with a wind-dapple here and there,
With ranging hills on the banks, with many a line
　　against the sky, and shadows,
And the city at hand with dwellings so dense, and stacks
　　of chimneys,
And all the scenes of life and the workshops, and the
　　workmen homeward returning.

12

Lo, body and soul—this land,
My own Manhattan with spires, and the sparkling and
　　hurrying tides, and the ships,
The varied and ample land, the South and the North in
　　the light, Ohio's shores and flashing Missouri,
And ever the far-spreading prairies cover'd with grass
　　and corn.
Lo, the most excellent sun so calm and haughty,
The violet and purple morn with just-felt breezes,
The gentle soft-born measureless light,
The miracle spreading bathing all, the fulfill'd noon,
The coming eve delicious, the welcome night and the
　　stars,
Over my cities shining all, enveloping man and land.

13

Sing on, sing on you gray-brown bird,
Sing from the swamps, the recesses, pour your chant
　　from the bushes,
Limitless out of the dusk, out of the cedars and pines.

Sing on dearest brother, warble your reedy song,
Loud human song, with voice of uttermost woe.

When Lilacs Last 199

O liquid and free and tender!
O wild and loose to my soul—O wondrous singer!
You only I hear—yet the star holds me, (but will soon
    depart,)
Yet the lilac with mastering odor holds me.

14

Now while I sat in the day and look'd forth,
In the close of the day with its light and the fields of
    spring, and the farmers preparing their crops,   110
In the large unconscious scenery of my land with its
    lakes and forests,
In the heavenly aerial beauty, (after the perturb'd winds
    and the storms,)
Under the arching heavens of the afternoon swift pass-
    ing, and the voices of children and women,
The many-moving sea-tides, and I saw the ships how
    they sail'd,
And the summer approaching with richness, and the
    fields all busy with labor,
And the infinite separate houses, how they all went on,
    each with its meals and minutia of daily usages,
And the streets how their throbbings throbb'd, and the
    cities pent—lo, then and there,
Falling upon them all and among them all, enveloping
    me with the rest,
Appear'd the cloud, appear'd the long black trail,
And I knew death, its thought, and the sacred knowledge
    of death.   120

Then with the knowledge of death as walking one side
    of me,
And the thought of death close-walking the other side
    of me,
And I in the middle as with companions, and as holding
    the hands of companions,
I fled forth to the hiding receiving night that talks not,
Down to the shores of the water, the path by the swamp
    in the dimness,
To the solemn shadowy cedars and ghostly pines so still.

And the singer so shy to the rest receiv'd me,
The gray-brown bird I know receiv'd us comrades three,
And he sang the carol of death, and a verse for him I
    love.
From deep secluded recesses,   130

From the fragrant cedars and the ghostly pines so still,
Came the carol of the bird.

And the charm of the carol rapt me,
As I held as if by their hands my comrades in the night,
And the voice of my spirit tallied the song of the bird.

Come lovely and soothing death,
Undulate round the world, serenely arriving, arriving,
In the day, in the night, to all, to each,
Sooner or later delicate death.

Prais'd be the fathomless universe,   140
For life and joy, and for objects and knowledge curious,
And for love, sweet love—but praise! praise! praise!
For the sure-enwinding arms of cool-enfolding death.

Dark mother always gliding near with soft feet,
Have none chanted for thee a chant of fullest welcome?
Then I chant it for thee, I glorify thee above all,
I bring thee a song that when thou must indeed come,
    come unfalteringly.

Approach strong deliveress,
When it is so, when thou hast taken them I joyously
    sing the dead,
Lost in the loving floating ocean of thee,   150
Laved in the flood of thy bliss O death.

From me to thee glad serenades,
Dances for thee I propose saluting thee, adornments and
    feastings for thee,
And the sights of the open landscape and the high-spread
    sky are fitting,
And life and the fields, and the huge and thoughtful
    night.

The night in silence under many a star,
The ocean shore and the husky whispering wave whose
    voice I know,
And the soul turning to thee O vast and well-veil'd death,
And the body gratefully nestling close to thee.

Over the tree-tops I float thee a song,   160
Over the rising and sinking waves, over the myriad fields
    and the prairies wide,

Over the dense-pack'd cities all and the teeming wharves
  and ways,
I float this carol with joy, with joy to thee O death.

15

To the tally of my soul,
Loud and strong kept up the gray-brown bird,
With pure deliberate notes spreading filling the night.

Loud in the pines and cedars dim,
Clear in the freshness moist and the swamp-perfume,
And I with my comrades there in the night.

While my sight that was bound in my eyes unclosed,   170
As to long panoramas of visions.   *visions of Civil War*

And I saw askant the armies,
I saw as in noiseless dreams hundreds of battle-flags,
Borne through the smoke of the battles and pierc'd with
  missiles I saw them,
And carried hither and yon through the smoke, and
  torn and bloody,
And at last but a few shreds left on the staffs, (and all
  in silence,)
And the staffs all splinter'd and broken.

I saw battle-corpses, myriads of them,
And the white skeletons of young men, I saw them,
I saw the debris and debris of all the slain soldiers of the
  war,   180
But I saw they were not as was thought,
They themselves were fully at rest, they suffer'd not,
The living remain'd and suffer'd, the mother suffer'd,
And the wife and the child and the musing comrade
  suffer'd,
And the armies that remain'd suffer'd.

16

Passing the visions, passing the night,
Passing, unloosing the hold of my comrades' hands,
Passing the song of the hermit bird and the tallying
  song of my soul,
Victorious song, death's outlet song, yet varying ever-
  altering song,
As low and wailing, yet clear the notes, rising and
  falling, flooding the night,   190

Sadly sinking and fainting, as warning and warning, and
  yet again bursting with joy,
Covering the earth and filling the spread of the heaven,
As that powerful psalm in the night I heard from
  recesses,
Passing, I leave thee lilac with heart-shaped leaves,
I leave thee there in the door-yard, blooming, returning
  with spring.

I cease from my song for thee,
From my gaze on thee in the west, fronting the west,
  communing with thee,
O comrade lustrous with silver face in the night.   *star*

Yet each to keep and all, retrievements out of the night,
The song, the wondrous chant of the gray-brown
  bird,   200
And the tallying chant, the echo arous'd in my soul,
With the lustrous and drooping star with the counte-
  nance full of woe,
With the holders holding my hand nearing the call of
  the bird,
Comrades mine and I in the midst, and their memory
  ever to keep, for the dead I loved so well,
For the sweetest, wisest soul of all my days and lands—
  and this for his dear sake,
Lilac and star and bird twined with the chant of my
  soul,
There in the fragrant pines and the cedars dusk and dim.

1865·1881

poet
devotion
Lincoln

There Was a Child Went Forth

*he became a part of the things he saw —
+ the experiences he met with.*

There was a child went forth every day,
And the first object he look'd upon, that object he be-
  came,   *imitation make-believe*
And that object became part of him for the day or a
  certain part of the day,
Or for many years or stretching cycles of years.

The early lilacs became part of this child,
And grass and white and red morning-glories, and white
  and red clover, and the song of the phœbe-bird,

And the Third-month lambs and the sow's pink-faint litter, and the mare's foal and the cow's calf,

And the noisy brood of the barnyard or by the mire of the pond-side,

And the fish suspending themselves so curiously below there, and the beautiful curious liquid,

And the water-plants with their graceful flat heads, all became part of him.   10

The field-sprouts of Fourth-month and Fifth-month became part of him,

Winter-grain sprouts and those of the light-yellow corn, and the esculent roots of the garden,

And the apple-trees cover'd with blossoms and the fruit afterward, and wood-berries, and the commonest weeds by the road,

And the old drunkard staggering home from the out-house of the tavern whence he had lately risen,

And the schoolmistress that pass'd on her way to the school,

And the friendly boys that pass'd, and the quarrelsome boys,

And the tidy and fresh-cheek'd girls, and the barefoot Negro boy and girl,

And all the changes of city and country wherever he went.

His own parents, he that had father'd him and she that had conceiv'd him in her womb and birth'd him,

They gave this child more of themselves than that,   20

They gave him afterward every day, they became part of him.

The mother at home quietly placing the dishes on the supper-table,

The mother with mild words, clean her cap and gown, a wholesome odor falling off her person and clothes as she walks by,

The father, strong, self-sufficient, manly, mean, anger'd, unjust,

The blow, the quick loud word, the tight bargain, the crafty lure,

The family usages, the language, the company, the furniture, the yearning and swelling heart,

Affection that will not be gainsay'd, the sense of what is real, the thought if after all it should prove unreal,

The doubts of day-time and the doubts of night-time, the curious whether and how,

Whether that which appears so is so, or is it all flashes and specks?

Men and women crowding fast in the streets, if they are not flashes and specks what are they?   30

The streets themselves and the façades of houses, and goods in the windows,

Vehicles, teams, the heavy-plank'd wharves, the huge crossing at the ferries,

The village on the highland seen from afar at sunset, the river between,

Shadows, aureola and mist, the light falling on roofs and gables of white or brown two miles off,

The schooner near by sleepily dropping down the tide, the little boat slack-tow'd astern,

The hurrying tumbling waves, quick-broken crests, slapping,

The strata of color'd clouds, the long bar of maroon-tint away solitary by itself, the spread of purity it lies motionless in,

The horizon's edge, the flying sea-crow, the fragrance of salt marsh and shore mud,

These became part of that child who went forth every day, and who now goes, and will always go forth every day.

1855·1871

Miracles

"Romanticism" is many-sided, but one of its chief aspects in nineteenth-century poetry was described by Theodore Watts-Dunton, the friend of Swinburne, as "the renascence of wonder." Wordsworth's purpose, according to Coleridge, was to direct the attention to "the loveliness and the wonders of the world before us; an inexhaustible treasure, but for which, in consequence of the film of familiarity and selfish solicitude, we have eyes, yet see not, ears that hear not, and hearts that neither feel nor understand." Similarly, Emerson (in "Woodnotes") char-

---

7 Third-month. The 1855 version had "March-born"; "Third-month" was substituted in the version of 1860 • **19 he . . . father'd.** The 1855 version read "he that had propelled the fatherstuff at night, and fathered him"; the present reading dates from the 1860 edition. The student should consult Holloway's "Inclusive Edition" of **Leaves of Grass** for a complete list of Whitman's many revisions

acterized the poet as "Wonderer at all he meets." In "Miracles" and in countless other places in his writings Whitman expresses this distinctively romantic view of the world.

Why, who makes much of a miracle?
As to me I know of nothing else but miracles,
Whether I walk the streets of Manhattan,
Or dart my sight over the roofs of houses toward the sky,
Or wade with naked feet along the beach just in the
    edge of the water,
Or stand under trees in the woods,
Or talk by day with any one I love, or sleep in the bed
    at night with any one I love,
Or sit at table at dinner with the rest,
Or look at strangers opposite me riding in the car,
Or watch honey-bees busy around the hive of a summer
    forenoon,   10
Or animals feeding in the fields,
Or birds, or the wonderfulness of insects in the air,
Or the wonderfulness of the sundown, or of stars shining
    so quiet and bright,
Or the exquisite delicate thin curve of the new moon in
    spring;
These with the rest, one and all, are to me miracles,
The whole referring, yet each distinct and in its place.

To me every hour of the light and dark is a miracle,
Every cubic inch of space is a miracle,
Every square yard of the surface of the earth is spread
    with the same,
Every foot of the interior swarms with the same.   20

To me the sea is a continual miracle,
The fishes that swim—the rocks—the motion of the
    waves—the ships with men in them,
What stranger miracles are there?

                  1856·1881

Passage to India

"Passage to India" is the most transcendental of Whitman's poems, the most notable expression of mysticism in his writings. He begins by celebrating the physical explora-

tions of man. Columbus, in discovering America, was seeking a water-route to India. The completion of the American transcontinental railroad, the Atlantic cable, and the Suez Canal had accomplished the "rondure" of the earth and brought India nearer to the Western world. But these physical voyages and explorations are mere symbols, in man's development, of spiritual voyages and explorations. Since Oriental religious thought, preëminently, has been concerned with the problem of spiritual reality, "Passage to India" suggests the soul's confronting of the "aged fierce enigmas." The solution of these enigmas becomes possible only in the mystic union of the soul with God:

        . . . the Elder Brother found,
    The Younger melts in fondness in his arms.

In the end the soul achieves "passage to more than India," perhaps in a double sense: to more than a physical India, and to a spiritual realization which transcends even the highest teachings of the Brahmins.

    The poem recalls Emerson's and Thoreau's interest in the Oriental scriptures.

1

Singing my days,
Singing the great achievements of the present,
Singing the strong light works of engineers,
Our modern wonders, (the antique ponderous Seven
    outvied,)
In the Old World the east the Suez canal,
The New by its mighty railroad spann'd,
The seas inlaid with eloquent gentle wires;
Yet first to sound, and ever sound, the cry with thee O
    soul,
The Past! the Past! the Past!

The Past—the dark unfathom'd retrospect!   10
The teeming gulf—the sleepers and the shadows!

Passage to India • **4 Seven.** The Seven Wonders of the ancient world were: the pyramids of Egypt, the Pharos (lighthouse on the island of Pharos) of Alexandria, the walls and hanging gardens of Babylon, the temple of Diana at Ephesus, the statue of Jupiter by Phidias, the mausoleum erected by Artemisia at Halicarnassus, the Colossus of Rhodes • **5 Suez canal**, completed in 1867, formally opened in 1869 • **6 railroad.** The Union Pacific Railroad was completed in 1869 • **7 wires.** The laying of the first permanently successful Atlantic cable was completed in 1866

The past—the infinite greatness of the past!

For what is the present after all but a growth out of the past?

(As a projectile form'd, impell'd, passing a certain line, still keeps on,

So the present, utterly form'd, impell'd by the past.)

2

Passage O soul to India!

Eclaircise the myths Asiatic, the primitive fables.

Not you alone proud truths of the world,

Nor you alone ye facts of modern science,

But myths and fables of eld, Asia's, Africa's fables,   20

The far-darting beams of the spirit, the unloos'd dreams,

The deep diving bibles and legends,

The daring plots of the poets, the elder religions;

O you temples fairer than lilies pour'd over by the rising sun!

O you fables spurning the known, eluding the hold of the known, mounting to heaven!

You lofty and dazzling towers, pinnacled, red as roses, burnish'd with gold!

Towers of fables immortal fashion'd from mortal dreams!

You too I welcome and fully the same as the rest!

You too with joy I sing.

Passage to India!   30

Lo, soul, seest thou not God's purpose from the first?

The earth to be spann'd, connected by network,

The races, neighbors, to marry and be given in marriage,

The oceans to be cross'd, the distant brought near,

The lands to be welded together.

A worship new I sing,

You captains, voyagers, explorers, yours,

You engineers, you architects, machinists, yours,

You, not for trade or transportation only,

But in God's name, and for thy sake O soul.   40

3

Passage to India!

Lo soul for thee of tableaus twain.

I see in one the Suez canal initiated, open'd,

I see the procession of steamships, the Empress Euge-nie's leading the van,

I mark from on deck the strange landscape, the pure sky, the level sand in the distance,

I pass swiftly the picturesque groups, the workmen gather'd,

The gigantic dredging machines.

In one again, different, (yet thine, all thine, O soul, the same,)

I see over my own continent the Pacific railroad sur-mounting every barrier,

I see continual trains of cars winding along the Platte carrying freight and passengers,   50

I hear the locomotives rushing and roaring, and the shrill steam-whistle,

I hear the echoes reverberate through the grandest scenery in the world,

I cross the Laramie plains, I note the rocks in grotesque shapes, the buttes,

I see the plentiful larkspur and wild onions, the barren, colorless, sage-deserts,

I see in glimpses afar or towering immediately above me the great mountains, I see the Wind river and the Wahsatch mountains,

I see the Monument mountain and the Eagle's Nest, I pass the Promontory, I ascend the Nevadas,

I scan the noble Elk mountain and wind around its base,

I see the Humboldt range, I thread the valley and cross the river,

I see the clear waters of lake Tahoe, I see forests of majestic pines,

Or crossing the great desert, the alkaline plains, I behold enchanting mirages of waters and meadows,   60

Marking through these and after all, in duplicate slender lines,

Bridging the three or four thousand miles of land travel,

Tying the Eastern to the Western sea,

The road between Europe and Asia.

---

17 Eclaircise, explain, clarify • 44 Eugenie, wife of Napoleon III and the empress of the French, who was on board the ship at the head of a procession whose passage marked the formal opening of the canal in November 1869 • 50 Platte. The Platte River flows through Nebraska into the Missouri River • 53 Laramie plains, in Wyoming • 53 buttes, isolated small mountains or hills, with steep sides and turretlike formations • 55 Wind river, a river in central Wyoming • 55 Wahsatch mountains. The Wasatch Range is in Utah • 56 Eagle's Nest, in Colorado • 57 Elk mountain, in Wyoming • 58 Humboldt range, in Nevada • 59 lake Tahoe, in Nevada and California

(Ah Genoese thy dream! thy dream!
Centuries after thou art laid in thy grave,
The shore thou foundest verifies thy dream.)

4

Passage to India!
Struggles of many a captain, tales of many a sailor dead,
Over my mood stealing and spreading they come,   70
Like clouds and cloudlets in the unreach'd sky.

Along all history, down the slopes,
As a rivulet running, sinking now, and now again to the
    surface rising,
A ceaseless thought, a varied train—lo, soul, to thee, thy
    sight, they rise,
The plans, the voyages again, the expeditions;
Again Vasco de Gama sails forth,
Again the knowledge gain'd, the mariner's compass,
Lands found and nations born, thou born America.
For purpose vast, man's long probation fill'd,
Thou rondure of the world at last accomplish'd.   80

5

O vast Rondure, swimming in space,
Cover'd all over with visible power and beauty,
Alternate light and day and the teeming spiritual
    darkness,
Unspeakable high processions of sun and moon and
    countless stars above,
Below, the manifold grass and waters, animals, moun-
    tains, trees,
With inscrutable purpose, some hidden prophetic in-
    tention,
Now first it seems my thought begins to span thee.

Down from the gardens of Asia descending radiating,
Adam and Eve appear, then their myriad progeny after
    them,
Wandering, yearning, curious, with restless explora-
    tions,   90
With questionings, baffled, formless, feverish, with
    never-happy hearts,
With that sad incessant refrain, *Wherefore unsatisfied
    soul?* and *Whither O mocking life?*

Ah who shall soothe these feverish children?
Who justify these restless explorations?

Who speak the secret of impassive earth?
Who bind it to us? what is this separate Nature so **un-**
natural?
What is this earth to our affections? (unloving **earth,**
    without a throb to answer ours,
Cold earth, the place of graves.)

Yet soul be sure the first intent remains, and shall **be**
    carried out,
Perhaps even now the time has arrived.   100
After the seas are all cross'd, (as they seem already
    cross'd,)
After the great captains and engineers have accomplish'd
    their work,
After the noble inventors, after the scientists, **the**
    chemist, the geologist, ethnologist,
Finally shall come the poet worthy that name,
The true son of God shall come singing his songs.

Then not your deeds only O voyagers, O scientists **and**
    inventors, shall be justified,
All these hearts as of fretted children shall be sooth'd,
All affection shall be fully responded to, the secret **shall**
    be told,
All these separations and gaps shall be taken up and
    hook'd and link'd together,
The whole earth, this cold, impassive, voiceless earth,
    shall be completely justified,   110
Trinitas divine shall be gloriously accomplish'd and com-
    pacted by the true son of God, the poet,
(He shall indeed pass the straits and conquer **the**
    mountains,
He shall double the cape of Good Hope to some
    purpose,)
Nature and Man shall be disjoin'd and diffused no **more,**
The true son of God shall absolutely fuse them.

6

Year at whose wide-flung door I sing!
Year of the purpose accomplish'd!
Year of the marriage of continents, climates and
    oceans!

(No mere doge of Venice now wedding the Adriatic,)
I see O year in you the vast terraqueous globe given and
    giving all,   120
Europe to Asia, Africa join'd, and they to the New
    World,
The lands, geographies, dancing before you, holding a
    festival garland,
As brides and bridegrooms hand in hand.

Passage to India!
Cooling airs from Caucasus, far, soothing cradle of man,
The river Euphrates flowing, the past lit up again.
Lo soul, the retrospect brought forward,
The old, most populous, wealthiest of earth's lands,
The streams of the Indus and the Ganges and their
    many affluents,
(I my shores of America walking to-day behold, resum-
    ing all,)   130
The tale of Alexander on his warlike marches suddenly
    dying,
On one side China and on the other side Persia and
    Arabia,
To the south the great seas and the bay of Bengal,
The flowing literatures, tremendous epics, religions, castes,
Old occult Brahma interminably far back, the tender
    and junior Buddha,
Central and southern empires and all their belongings,
    possessors,
The wars of Tamerlane, the reign of Aurungzebe,
The traders, rulers, explorers, Moslems, Venetians,
    Byzantium, the Arabs, Portuguese,
The first travelers famous yet, Marco Polo, Batouta the
    Moor,
Doubts to be solv'd, the map incognita, blanks to be
    fill'd,   140
The foot of man unstay'd, the hands never at rest,
Thyself O soul that will not brook a challenge.
The mediæval navigators rise before me,
The world of 1492, with its awaken'd enterprise,
Something swelling in humanity now like the sap of the
    earth in spring,
The sunset splendor of chivalry declining.

And who art thou sad shade?
Gigantic, visionary, thyself a visionary,
With majestic limbs and pious beaming eyes,

Spreading around with every look of thine a golden
    world,   150
Enhuing it with gorgeous hues.

As the chief histrion,
Down to the footlights walks in some great scena,
Dominating the rest I see the Admiral himself,
(History's type of courage, action, faith,)
Behold him sail from Palos leading his little fleet,
His voyage behold, his return, his great fame,
His misfortunes, calumniators, behold him a prisoner,
    chain'd,
Behold his dejection, poverty, death.
(Curious in time I stand, noting the efforts of heroes, 160
Is the deferment long? bitter the slander, poverty, death?
Lies the seed unreck'd for centuries in the ground? lo, to
    God's due occasion,
Uprising in the night, it sprouts, blooms,
And fills the earth with use and beauty.)

7

Passage indeed O soul to primal thought,
Not lands and seas alone, thy own clear freshness,
The young maturity of brood and bloom,
To realms of budding bibles.

O soul, repressless, I with thee and thou with me,
Thy circumnavigation of the world begin,   170
Of man, the voyage of his mind's return,
To reason's early paradise,
Back, back to wisdom's birth, to innocent intuitions,
Again with fair creation.

8

O we can wait no longer,
We too take ship O soul,

119 doge . . . Adriatic. When Venice was a city-state, the doge or
chief magistrate annually symbolized the "marriage" of Venice to
the sea, and her dependence on sea-borne commerce, by tossing
a gold ring into the Adriatic • 126 Euphrates, river in southwest Asia
• 129 Indus . . . Ganges, rivers in India • 130 resuming. See note,
p. 175 • 137 Tamerlane (1333-1405), Mongol conquerer • 137
Aurungzebe (1619-1707), emperor of Hindustan • 139 Marco Polo
(1254-1323), Venetian traveler in China • 139 Batouta the Moor
(1303-1377), traveler in Asia and Africa • 140 incognita, unknown
• 152 histrion, actor • 153 scena, a scene in opera (of which
Whitman was very fond) • 154 Admiral, Columbus • 156 Palos,
Spanish seaport • 162 unreck'd, unheeded, made no account of

Joyous we too launch out on trackless seas,
Fearless for unknown shores on waves of ecstasy to sail,
Amid the wafting winds, (thou pressing me to thee, I
    thee to me, O soul,)
Caroling free, singing our song of God,   180
Chanting our chant of pleasant exploration.

With laugh and many a kiss,
(Let others deprecate, let others weep for sin, remorse,
    humiliation,)
O soul thou pleasest me, I thee.

Ah more than any priest O soul we too believe in God,
But with the mystery of God we dare not dally.
O soul thou pleasest me, I thee,
Sailing these seas or on the hills, or waking in the night,
Thoughts, silent thoughts, of Time and Space and
    Death, like waters flowing,
Bear me indeed as through the regions infinite,   190
Whose air I breathe, whose ripples hear, lave me all over,
Bathe me O God in thee, mounting to thee,
I and my soul to range in range of thee.

O Thou transcendent,
Nameless, the fibre and the breath,
Light of the light, shedding forth universes, thou centre
    of them,
Thou mightier centre of the true, the good, the loving,
Thou moral, spiritual fountain—affection's source—thou
    reservoir,
(O pensive soul of me—O thirst unsatisfied—waitest
    not there?
Waitest not haply for us somewhere there the Com-
    rade perfect?)   200
Thou pulse—thou motive of the stars, suns, systems,
That, circling, move in order, safe, harmonious,
Athwart the shapeless vastnesses of space,
How should I think, how breathe a single breath, how
    speak, if, out of myself,
I could not launch, to those, superior universes?

Swiftly I shrivel at the thought of God,
At Nature and its wonders, Time and Space and Death,
But that I, turning, call to thee O soul, thou actual Me,
And lo, thou gently masterest the orbs,
Thou matest Time, smilest content at Death,   210

And fillest, swellest full the vastnesses of Space.

Greater than stars or suns,
Bounding O soul thou journeyest forth;
What love than thine and ours could wider amplify?
What aspirations, wishes, outvie thine and ours O soul?
What dreams of the ideal? what plans of purity, perfec-
    tion, strength,
What cheerful willingness for others' sake to give up all?
For others' sake to suffer all?

Reckoning ahead O soul, when thou, the time achiev'd,
The seas all cross'd, weather'd the capes, the voyage
    done,   220
Surrounded, copest, frontest God, yieldest, the aim attain'd,
As fill'd with friendship, love complete, the Elder
    Brother found,
The Younger melts in fondness in his arms.

9

Passage to more than India!
Are thy wings plumed indeed for such far flights?
O soul, voyagest thou indeed on voyages like those?
Disportest thou on waters such as those?
Soundest below the Sanscrit and the Vedas?
Then have thy bent unleash'd.

Passage to you, your shores, ye aged fierce enigmas! 230
Passage to you, to mastership of you, ye strangling
    problems!
You, strew'd with the wrecks of skeletons, that, living,
    never reach'd you.

Passage to more than India!
O secret of the earth and sky!
Of you O waters of the sea! O winding creeks and rivers!
Of you O woods and fields! of you strong mountains of
    my land!
Of you O prairies! of you gray rocks!
O morning red! O clouds! O rain and snows!
O day and night, passage to you!

---

183 deprecate, pray to be delivered from • 221 copest, meets,
encounters • 228 Sanscrit . . . Vedas. Sanskrit is the ancient
language in which the Vedas, the sacred books of the Hindus, were
written

O sun and moon and all you stars! Sirius and Jupiter! 240
Passage to you!

Passage, immediate passage! the blood burns in my
    veins!
Away O soul! hoist instantly the anchor!
Cut the hawsers—haul out—shake out every sail!
Have we not stood here like trees in the ground long
    enough?
Have we not grovel'd here long enough, eating and
    drinking like mere brutes?
Have we not darken'd and dazed ourselves with books
    long enough?

Sail forth—steer for the deep waters only,
Reckless O soul, exploring, I with thee, and thou with
    me,
For we are bound where mariner has not yet dared
    to go,   250
And we will risk the ship, ourselves and all.

O my brave soul!
O farther farther sail!
O daring joy, but safe! are they not all the seas of God?
O farther, farther, farther sail!

                                            1871

Thou Mother with Thy Equal Brood

This poem was read by Whitman at the commencement
of Dartmouth College, June 26, 1872. As read on that
occasion, the poem began with what is now Section 2
and was known by the title "As a Strong Bird on Pinions
Free." Section 1 was added in the 1881 edition.

In a Preface to the poem, Whitman wrote: "The Four
Years' War is over—and in the peaceful, strong, exciting,
fresh occasions of today, and of the future, that strange,
sad war is hurrying even now to be forgotten. The camp,
the drill, the lines of sentries, the prisons, the hospitals—
(ah! the hospitals!)—all have passed away—all seem now
like a dream. A new race, a young and lusty generation,
already sweeps in with oceanic currents, obliterating the
war, and all its scars, its mounded graves, and all its
reminiscences of hatred, conflict, death. So let it be obliterated. I say the life of the present and the future makes

undeniable demands upon us each and all, south, north,
east, west. To help put the United States (even if only in
imagination) hand in hand, in one unbroken circle in a
chant—to rouse them to the unprecedented grandeur
of the part they are to play, and are even now playing—
to the thought of their great future, and the attitude conform'd to it—especially their great esthetic, moral, scientific future (of which their vulgar material and political
present is but as the preparatory tuning of instruments
by an orchestra), these, as hitherto, are still, for me,
among my hopes, ambitions."

1

Thou Mother with thy equal brood,
Thou varied chain of different States, yet one identity
    only,
A special song before I go I'd sing o'er all the rest,
For thee, the future.

I'd sow a seed for thee of endless Nationality,
I'd fashion thy ensemble including body and soul,
I'd show away ahead thy real Union, and how
    it may be accomplish'd.

The paths to the house I seek to make,
But leave to those to come the house itself.

Belief I sing, and preparation;   10
As Life and Nature are not great with reference to the
    present only,
But greater still from what is yet to come,
Out of that formula for thee I sing.

2

As a strong bird on pinions free,
Joyous, the amplest spaces heavenward cleaving,
Such be the thought I'd think of thee America,
Such be the recitative I'd bring for thee.

The conceits of the poets of other lands I'd bring thee
    not,
Nor the compliments that have served their turn so long,

Passage to India • 240 Sirius, the brightest star • 240 Jupiter, the
largest planet

Nor rhyme, nor the classics, nor perfume of foreign
    court or indoor library;   20
But an odor I'd bring as from forests of pine in Maine,
    or breath of an Illinois prairie,
With open airs of Virginia or Georgia or Tennessee, or
    from Texas uplands, or Florida's glades,
Or the Saguenay's black stream, or the wide blue spread
    of Huron,
With presentment of Yellowstone's scenes, or Yosem-
    ite,
And murmuring under, pervading all, I'd bring the
    rustling sea-sound,
That endlessly sounds from the two Great Seas of the
    world.

And for thy subtler sense subtler refrains dread Mother,
Preludes of intellect tallying these and thee, mind-
    formulas fitted for thee, real and sane and large as
    these and thee,
Thou! mounting higher, diving deeper than we knew,
    thou transcendental Union!
By thee fact to be justified, blended with thought,   30
Thought of man justified, blended with God,
Through thy idea, lo, the immortal reality!
Through thy reality, lo, the immortal idea!

3

Brain of the New World, what a task is thine,
To formulate the Modern—out of the peerless grandeur
    of the modern,
Out of thyself, comprising science, to recast poems,
    churches, art,
(Recast, maybe discard them, end them—maybe their
    work is done, who knows?)
By vision, hand, conception, on the background of the
    mighty past, the dead,
To limn with absolute faith the mighty living present.

And yet thou living present brain, heir of the dead, the
    Old World brain,   40
Thou that lay folded like an unborn babe within its folds
    so long,
Thou carefully prepared by it so long—haply thou but
    unfoldest it, only maturest it,
It to eventuate in thee—the essence of the by-gone time
    contain'd in thee,

Its poems, churches, arts, unwitting to themselves,
    destined with reference to thee;
Thou but the apples, long, long, long a-growing,
The fruit of all the Old ripening to-day in thee.

4

Sail, sail thy best, ship of Democracy,
Of value is thy freight, 'tis not the Present only,
The Past is also stored in thee,
Thou holdest not the venture of thyself alone, not of the
    Western continent alone,   50
Earth's *résumé* entire floats on thy keel O ship, is steadied
    by thy spars,
With thee Time voyages in trust, the antecedent nations
    sink or swim with thee,
With all their ancient struggles, martyrs, heroes, epics,
    wars, thou bear'st the other continents,
Theirs, theirs as much as thine, the destination-port
    triumphant;
Steer then with good strong hand and wary eye O helms-
    man, thou carriest great companions,
Venerable priestly Asia sails this day with thee,
And royal feudal Europe sails with thee.

5

Beautiful world of new superber birth that rises to my
    eyes,
Like a limitless golden cloud filling the western sky,
Emblem of general maternity lifted above all,   60
Sacred shape of the bearer of daughters and sons,
Out of thy teeming womb thy giant babes in ceaseless
    procession issuing,
Acceding from such gestation, taking and giving con-
    tinual strength and life,
World of the real—world of the twain in one,
World of the soul, born by the world of the real alone,
    led to identity, body, by it alone,
Yet in beginning only, incalculable masses of composite
    precious materials,
By history's cycles forwarded, by every nation, language,
    hither sent,
Ready, collected here, a freer, vast, electric world, to be
    constructed here,

---

23 **Saguenay,** a river which flows through the province of Quebec
into the St. Lawrence

(The true New World, the world of orbic science, morals, literatures to come,)

Thou wonder world yet undefined, unform'd, neither do I define thee, 70

How can I pierce the impenetrable blank of the future?

I feel thy ominous greatness evil as well as good,

I watch thee advancing, absorbing the present, transcending the past,

I see thy light lighting, and thy shadow shadowing, as if the entire globe,

But I do not undertake to define thee, hardly to comprehend thee,

I but thee name, thee prophesy, as now,

I merely thee ejaculate!

Thee in thy future,

Thee in thy only permanent life, career, thy own unloosen'd mind, thy soaring spirit,

Thee as another equally needed sun, radiant, ablaze, swift-moving, fructifying all, 80

Thee risen in potent cheerfulness and joy, in endless great hilarity,

Scattering for good the cloud that hung so long, that weigh'd so long upon the mind of man,

The doubt, suspicion, dread, of gradual, certain decadence of man;

Thee in thy larger, saner brood of female, male—thee in thy athletes, moral, spiritual, South, North, West, East,

(To thy immortal breasts, Mother of All, thy every daughter, son, endear'd alike, forever equal,)

Thee in thy own musicians, singers, artists, unborn yet, but certain,

Thee in thy moral wealth and civilization, (until which thy proudest material civilization must remain in vain,)

Thee in thy all-supplying, all-enclosing worship—thee in no single bible, saviour, merely,

Thy saviours countless, latent within thyself, thy bibles incessant within thyself, equal to any, divine as any,

(Thy soaring course thee formulating, not in thy two great wars, nor in thy century's visible growth, 90

But far more in these leaves and chants, thy chants, great Mother!)

Thee in an education grown of thee, in teachers, studies, students, born of thee,

Thee in thy democratic fêtes en-masse, thy high original festivals, operas, lecturers, preachers,

Thee in thy ultimata, (the preparations only now completed, the edifice on sure foundations tied,)

Thee in thy pinnacles, intellect, thought, thy topmost rational joys, thy love and godlike aspiration,

In thy resplendent coming literati, thy full-lung'd orators, thy sacerdotal bards, kosmic savans,

These! these in thee, (certain to come,) to-day I prophesy.

6

Land tolerating all, accepting all, not for the good alone, all good for thee,

Land in the realms of God to be a realm unto thyself,

Under the rule of God to be a rule unto thyself. 100

(Lo, where arise three peerless stars,

To be thy natal stars my country, Ensemble, Evolution, Freedom,

Set in the sky of Law.)

Land of unprecedented faith, God's faith,

Thy soil, thy very subsoil, all upheav'd,

The general inner earth so long so sedulously draped over, now hence for what it is boldly laid bare,

Open'd by thee to heaven's light for benefit or bale.

Not for success alone,

Not to fair-sail unintermitted always,

The storm shall dash thy face, the murk of war and worse than war shall cover thee all over, 110

(Wert capable of war, its tugs and trials? be capable of peace, its trials,

---

89 **thy bibles.** Whitman's prophecy recalls Emerson's in the concluding paragraph of **The Divinity School Address**: ''I look for the hour when that supreme Beauty which ravished the souls of those Eastern men, and chiefly of those Hebrews, and through their lips spoke oracles to all time, shall speak in the West also'' • 91 **these . . . chants.** Whitman was never modest about his poems • 96 **orators.** Whitman had an old-fashioned fondness for oratory. For the influence of oratory and oratorical considerations upon his poetry, see ''Three Analogies for a Poem,'' in F. O. Matthiessen's **American Renaissance** • 96 **sacerdotal bards** echoes Emerson's statement in his essay on Shakespeare (in **Representative Men**): ''The world still wants its poet-priest . . .''

For the tug and mortal strain of nations come at last in
    prosperous peace, not war;)
In many a smiling mask death shall approach beguiling
    thee, thou in disease shalt swelter,
The livid cancer spread its hideous claws, clinging upon
    thy breasts, seeking to strike thee deep within,
Consumption of the worst, moral consumption, shall
    rouge thy face with hectic,
But thou shalt face thy fortunes, thy diseases, and
    surmount them all,
Whatever they are to-day and whatever through time
    they may be,
They each and all shall lift and pass away and cease
    from thee,
While thou, Time's spirals rounding, out of thyself,
    thyself still extricating, fusing,
Equable, natural, mystical Union thou, (the mortal with
    immortal blent,)   120
Shalt soar toward the fulfilment of the future, the spirit
    of the body and the mind,
The soul, its destinies.

The soul, its destinies, the real real,
(Purport of all these apparitions of the real;)
In thee America, the soul, its destinies,
Thou globe of globes! thou wonder nebulous!
By many a throe of heat and cold convuls'd, (by these
    thyself solidifying,)
Thou mental, moral orb—thou New, indeed new,
    Spiritual World!
The Present holds thee not—for such vast growth as
    thine,
For such unparallel'd flight as thine, such brood as
    thine,   130
The FUTURE only holds thee and can hold thee.

1872·1881

To a Locomotive in Winter

Whitman's treatment of the locomotive may be profitably
contrasted with Emily Dickinson's in "I Like to See It Lap
the Miles" (p. 678) and compared with Thomas Wolfe's in
many passages in his novels.

Thee for my recitative,
Thee in the driving storm even as now, the snow, the
    winterday declining.
Thee in thy panoply, thy measur'd dual throbbing and
    thy beat convulsive,
Thy black cylinder body, golden brass and silvery
    steel,
Thy ponderous side-bars, parallel and connecting rods,
    gyrating, shuttling at thy sides,
Thy metrical, now swelling pant and roar, now tapering
    in the distance,
Thy great protruding head-light fix'd in front,
Thy long, pale, floating vapor-pennants, tinged with
    delicate purple,
The dense and murky clouds out-belching from thy
    smokestack,
Thy knitted frame, thy springs and valves, the tremulous
    twinkle of thy wheels,   10
Thy train of cars behind, obedient, merrily following,
Through gale or calm, now swift, now slack, yet steadily
    careering;
Type of the modern—emblem of motion and power—
    pulse of the continent,
For once come serve the Muse and merge in verse, even
    as here I see thee,
With storm and buffeting gusts of wind and falling
    snow,
By day thy warning ringing bell to sound its notes,
By night thy silent signal lamps to swing.

Fierce-throated beauty!
Roll through my chant with all thy lawless music, thy
    swinging lamps at night,
Thy madly-whistled laughter, echoing, rumbling like an
    earthquake, rousing all,   20
Law of thyself complete, thine own track firmly holding,
(No sweetness debonair of tearful harp or glib piano
    thine,)
Thy trills of shrieks by rocks and hills return'd,
Launch'd o'er the prairies wide, across the lakes,
To the free skies unpent and glad and strong.

1876·1881

Thou Mother . . . Brood • 124 apparitions, outward appearances
To a Locomotive . . . • 3 panoply, full suit of plane armor

From

Democratic Vistas

Unlike the poems, **Democratic Vistas** is censorious of America. Two reasons for the difference may be suggested. One reason is doubtless Whitman's conception of the proper functions of poetry and prose. Prose may be critical in tone, while poetry should be affirmative and expansive. Accordingly, in **Leaves of Grass** Whitman consistently celebrates American democracy; in **Democratic Vistas**, he is free to point out its faults. Another reason is to be found in the changing times. The Gilded Age (particularly, the administrations of Grant, 1869-1877) was notorious for its corruption in business and politics. Whitman might well have believed that America had failed to fulfill its earlier promise.

While holding to his faith in democracy, he warned of disaster unless certain radical changes were made. He was disappointed in Americans as individuals. He called for the appearance in America of healthier, more robust, and more spiritual personalities and (repeating Emerson's **The American Scholar** and his own 1855 Preface) the production of a literature indigenous to America and embodying truly democratic ideals.

. . . I say we had best look our times and lands searchingly in the face, like a physician diagnosing some deep disease. Never was there, perhaps, more hollowness at heart than at present, and here in the United States. Genuine belief seems to have left us. The underlying principles of the States are not honestly believ'd in, (for all this hectic glow, and these melo-dramatic screamings) nor is humanity itself believ'd in. What penetrating eye does not everywhere see through the mask? 10 The spectacle is appaling. We live in an atmosphere of hypocrisy throughout. The men believe not in the women, nor the women in the men. A scornful superciliousness rules in literature. The aim of all the *littérateurs* is to find something to make fun of. A lot of churches, sects, &c., the most dismal phantasms I know, usurp the name of religion. Conversation is a mass of badinage. From deceit in the spirit, the mother of all false deeds, the offspring is already incalculable. An acute and candid person, in the revenue department in Washington, who is led by the course of his employ- 20 ment to regularly visit the cities, North, South and West, to investigate frauds, has talk'd much with me about his discoveries. The depravity of the business classes of our country is not less than has been supposed, but infinitely greater. The official services of America, national, state, and municipal, in all their branches and departments, except the judiciary, are saturated in corruption, bribery, falsehood, mal-administration; and the judiciary is tainted. The great cities reek with respectable as much as non-respectable robbery and scoundrel- 30 ism. In fashionable life, flippancy, tepid amours, weak infidelism, small aims, or no aims at all, only to kill time. In business, (this all-devouring modern word, business), the one sole object is, by any means, pecuniary gain. The magician's serpent in the fable ate up all the other serpents; and money-making is our magician's serpent, remaining to-day sole master of the field. The best class we show, is but a mob of fashionably dress'd speculators and vulgarians. True, indeed, behind this fantastic farce, enacted on the visible stage of society, solid things and 40 stupendous labors are to be discover'd, existing crudely and going on in the background, to advance and tell themselves in time. Yet the truths are none the less terrible. I say that our New World democracy, however great a success in uplifting the masses out of their sloughs, in materialistic development, products, and in a certain highly-deceptive superficial popular intellectuality, is, so far, an almost complete failure in its social aspects, and in really grand religious, moral, literary, and esthetic results. In vain do we march with 50 unprecedented strides to empire so colossal, outvying the antique, beyond Alexander's, beyond the proudest sway of Rome. In vain have we annex'd Texas, California, Alaska, and reach north for Canada and south

35 fable. See Exodus 7: 9-12

for Cuba. It is as if we were somehow being endow'd with a vast and more and more thoroughly-appointed body, and then left with little or no soul.

Let me illustrate further, as I write, with current observations, localities, &c. The subject is important, and will bear repetition. After an absence, I am now again (September, 1870) in New York City and Brooklyn, on a few weeks' vacation. The splendor, picturesqueness, and oceanic amplitude and rush of these great cities, the unsurpass'd situation, rivers and bay, sparkling seatides, costly and lofty new buildings, facades of marble and iron, of original grandeur and elegance of design, with the masses of gay color, the preponderance of white and blue, the flags flying, the endless ships, the tumultuous streets, Broadway, the heavy, low, musical roar, hardly ever intermitted, even at night; the jobbers' houses, the rich shops, the wharves, the great Central Park, and the Brooklyn Park of hills, (as I wander among them this beautiful fall weather, musing, watching, absorbing)—the assemblages of the citizens in their groups, conversations, trades, evening amusements, or along the by-quarters—these, I say, and the like of these, completely satisfy my senses of power, fulness, motion, &c., and give me, through such senses and appetites, and through my esthetic conscience, a continued exaltation and absolute fulfilment. Always and more and more, as I cross the East and North rivers, the ferries, or with the pilots in their pilot-houses, or pass an hour in Wall Street, or the gold exchange, I realize, (if we must admit such partialisms) that not Nature alone is great in her fields of freedom and the open air, in her storms, the shows of night and day, the mountains, forests, seas—but in the artificial, the work of man too is equally great—in this profusion of teeming humanity —in these ingenuities, streets, goods, houses, ships— these hurrying, feverish, electric crowds of men, their complicated business genius (not least among the geniuses) and all this mighty, many-threaded wealth and industry concentrated here.

But sternly discarding, shutting our eyes to the glow and grandeur of the general superficial effect, coming down to what is of the only real importance, Personalities, and examining minutely, we question, we ask, Are there, indeed, *men* here worthy the name? Are there athletes? Are there perfect women, to match the generous material luxuriance? Is there a pervading at-

"A Grafter's Monument"—cartoon by C. Grey-Parker, *satirizing the political corruption of the notorious Tweed machine in New York, from* Harper's Weekly, *October 7, 1871.*

mosphere of beautiful manners? Are there crops of fine youths, and majestic old persons? Are there arts worthy freedom and a rich people? Is there a great moral and religious civilization—the only justification of a great material one? Confess that to severe eyes, using the moral microscope upon humanity, a sort of dry and flat Sahara appears, these cities, crowded with petty grotesques, malformations, phantoms, playing meaningless antics. Confess that everywhere, in shop, street, church, theatre, bar-room, official chair, are pervading flippancy and vulgarity, low cunning, infidelity—everywhere the youth puny, impudent, foppish, prematurely ripe— everywhere an abnormal libidinousness, unhealthy forms, male, female, painted, padded, dyed, chignon'd, muddy complexions, bad blood, the capacity for good motherhood deceasing or deceas'd, shallow notions of beauty, with a range of manners, or rather lack of manners, (considering the advantages enjoy'd), probably the meanest to be seen in the world.

Of all this, and these lamentable conditions, to breathe into them the breath recuperative of sane and heroic life, I say a new founded literature, not merely to copy and reflect existing surfaces, or pander to what is called taste—not only to amuse, pass away time, celebrate the beautiful, the refined, the past, or exhibit technical, rhythmic, or grammatical dexterity—but a literature underlying life, religious, consistent with science, handling the elements and forces with competent power, teaching and training men—and, as perhaps the most precious of its results, achieving the entire redemption of woman out of these incredible holds and webs of silliness, millinery, and every kind of dyspeptic depletion—and thus insuring to the States a strong and sweet Female Race, a race of perfect Mothers—is what is needed. . . .

Assuming Democracy to be at present in its embryo condition, and that the only large and satisfactory justification of it resides in the future, mainly through the copious production of perfect characters among the people, and through the advent of a sane and pervading religiousness, it is with regard to the atmosphere and spaciousness fit for such characters, and of certain nutriment and cartoon-draftings proper for them, and indicating them for New-World purposes, that I continue the present statement—an exploration, as of new ground, wherein, like other primitive surveyors, I must do the best I can, leaving it to those who come after me to do much better. (The service, in fact, if any, must be to break a sort of first path or track, no matter how rude and ungeometrical.)

We have frequently printed the word Democracy. Yet I cannot too often repeat that it is a word the real gist of which still sleeps, quite unawaken'd, notwithstanding the resonance and the many angry tempests out of which its syllables have come, from pen or tongue. It is a great word, whose history, I suppose, remains unwritten, because that history has yet to be enacted. It is, in some sort, younger brother of another great and often-used word, Nature, whose history also waits unwritten. As I perceive, the tendencies of our day, in the States, (and I entirely respect them), are toward those vast and sweeping movements, influences, moral and physical, of

humanity, now and always current over the planet, on the scale of the impulses of the elements. Then it is also good to reduce the whole matter to the consideration of a single self, a man, a woman, on permanent grounds. Even for the treatment of the universal, in politics, metaphysics, or anything, sooner or later we come down to one single, solitary soul.

There is, in sanest hours, a consciousness, a thought that rises, independent, lifted out from all else, calm, like the stars, shining eternal. This is the thought of identity—yours for you, whoever you are, as mine for me. Miracle of miracles, beyond statement, most spiritual and vaguest of earth's dreams, yet hardest basic fact, and only entrance to all facts. In such devout hours, in the midst of the significant wonders of heaven and earth (significant only because of the Me in the centre), creeds, conventions, fall away and become of no account before this simple idea. Under the luminousness of real vision, it alone takes possession, takes value. Like the shadowy dwarf in the fable, once liberated and look'd upon, it expands over the whole earth, and spreads to the roof of heaven.

The quality of BEING, in the object's self, according to its own central idea and purpose, and of growing therefrom and thereto—not criticism by other standards, and adjustments thereto—is the lesson of Nature. True, the full man wisely gathers, culls, absorbs; but if, engaged disproportionately in that, he slights or overlays the precious idiocrasy and special nativity and intention that he is, the man's self, the main thing, is a failure, however wide his general cultivation. Thus, in our times, refinement and delicatesse are not only attended to sufficiently, but threaten to eat us up, like a cancer. Already, the democratic genius watches, ill-pleased, these tendencies. Provision for a little healthy rudeness, savage virtue, justification of what one has in one's self, whatever it is, is demanded. Negative qualities, even deficiencies, would be a relief. Singleness and normal simplicity and separation, amid this more and more complex, more and more artificialized state of society— how pensively we yearn for them! how we would welcome their return!

---

27 cartoon-draftings, models to be copied • 75 idiocrasy, idiosyncrasy • 78 delicatesse, exaggerated delicacy • 82 savage virtue. Whitman recalls Thoreau at this point

In some such direction, then—at any rate enough to preserve the balance—we feel called upon to throw what weight we can, not for absolute reasons, but current ones. To prune, gather, trim, conform, and ever cram and stuff, and be genteel and proper, is the pressure of our days. While aware that much can be said even in behalf of all this, we perceive that we have not now to consider the question of what is demanded to serve a half-starved and barbarous nation, or set of 10 nations, but what is most applicable, most pertinent, for numerous congeries of conventional, over-corpulent societies, already becoming stifled and rotten with flatulent, infidelistic literature, and polite conformity and art. In addition to establish'd sciences, we suggest a science as it were of healthy average personalism, on original-universal grounds, the object of which should be to raise up and supply through the States a copious race of superb American men and women, cheerful, religious, ahead of any yet known.

20 America has yet morally and artistically originated nothing. She seems singularly unaware that the models of persons, books, manners, &c., appropriate for former conditions and for European lands, are but exiles and exotics here. No current of her life, as shown on the surfaces of what is authoritatively called her society, accepts or runs into social or esthetic democracy; but all the currents set squarely against it. Never, in the Old World, was thoroughly upholster'd exterior appearance and show, mental and other, built entirely on the idea 30 of caste, and on the sufficiency of mere outside acquisition—never were glibness, verbal intellect, more the test, the emulation—more loftily elevated as head and sample—than they are on the surface of our republican States this day. The writers of a time hint the mottoes of its gods. The word of the modern, say these voices, is the word Culture.

We find ourselves abruptly in close quarters with the enemy. This word Culture, or what it has come to represent, involves, by contrast, our whole theme, and has 40 been, indeed, the spur, urging us to engagement. Certain questions arise. As now taught, accepted and carried out, are not the processes of culture rapidly creating a class of supercilious infidels, who believe in nothing? Shall a man lose himself in countless masses of adjustments, and be so shaped with reference to this, that, and the other, that the simply good and healthy and brave parts of him are reduced and clipp'd away, like the bordering of box in a garden? You can cultivate corn and roses and orchards—but who shall cultivate the mountain peaks, the ocean, and the tumbling gor- 50 geousness of the clouds? Lastly—is the readily-given reply that culture only seeks to help, systematize, and put in attitude, the elements of fertility and power, a conclusive reply?

I do not so much object to the name, or word, but I should certainly insist, for the purposes of these States, on a radical change of category, in the distribution of precedence. I should demand a programme of culture, drawn out, not for a single class alone, or for the parlors or lecture-rooms, but with an eye to practical life, the 60 West, the working-men, the facts of farms and jack-planes and engineers, and of the broad range of the women also of the middle and working strata, and with reference to the perfect equality of women, and of a grand and powerful motherhood. I should demand of this programme or theory a scope generous enough to include the widest human area. It must have for its spinal meaning the formation of a typical personality of character, eligible to the uses of the high average of men —and *not* restricted by conditions ineligible to the 70 masses. The best culture will always be that of the manly and courageous instincts, and loving perceptions, and of self-respect—aiming to form, over this continent, an idiocrasy of universalism, which, true child of America, will bring joy to its mother, returning to her own spirit, recruiting myriads of offspring, able, natural, perceptive, tolerant, devout believers in her, America, and with some definite instinct why and for what she has arisen, most vast, most formidable of historic births, and is, now and here, with wonderful step, journeying through Time. 80

The problem, as it seems to me, presented to the New World, is, under permanent law and order, and after preserving cohesion (ensemble-Individuality), at all hazards, to vitalize man's free play of special Personalism, recognizing in it something that calls ever more to be consider'd, fed, and adopted as the substratum for the best that belongs to us, (government indeed is for it), including the new esthetics of our future.

To formulate beyond this present vagueness—to help

---

61 jack-planes, carpenter's plane

line and put before us the species, or a specimen of the species, of the democratic ethnology of the future, is a work toward which the genius of our land, with peculiar encouragement, invites her well-wishers. Already certain limnings, more or less grotesque, more or less fading and watery, have appear'd. We too (repressing doubts and qualms), will try our hand.

Attempting, then, however crudely, a basic model or portrait of personality for general use for the manliness
10 of the States (and doubtless that is most useful which is most simple and comprehensive for all, and toned low enough), we should prepare the canvas well beforehand. Parentage must consider itself in advance. (Will the time hasten when fatherhood and motherhood shall become a science—and the noblest science?) To our model, a clear-blooded, strong-fibred physique, is indispensable; the questions of food, drink, air, exercise, assimilation, digestion, can never be intermitted. Out of these we descry a well-begotten selfhood—in youth,
20 fresh, ardent, emotional, aspiring, full of adventure; at maturity, brave, perceptive, under control, neither too talkative nor too reticent, neither flippant nor sombre; of the bodily figure, the movements easy, the complexion showing the best blood, somewhat flush'd, breast expanded, an erect attitude, a voice whose sound outvies music, eyes of calm and steady gaze, yet capable also of flashing—and a general presence that holds its own in the company of the highest. (For it is native personality, and that alone, that endows a man to stand
30 before presidents or generals, or in any distinguish'd collection, with *aplomb*—and *not* culture, or any knowledge or intellect whatever.)

With regard to the mental-educational part of our model, enlargement of intellect, stores of cephalic knowledge, &c., the concentration thitherward of all the customs of our age, especially in America, is so overweening, and provides so fully for that part, that, important and necessary as it is, it really needs nothing from us here—except, indeed, a phrase of warning and
40 restraint. Manners, costumes, too, though important, we need not dwell upon here. Like beauty, grace of motion, &c., they are results. Causes, original things, being attended to, the right manners unerringly follow. Much is said, among artists, of "the grand style," as if it were a thing by itself. When a man, artist or whoever, has

health, pride, acuteness, noble aspirations, he has the motive-elements of the grandest style. The rest is but manipulation (yet that is no small matter).

Leaving still unspecified several sterling parts of any model fit for the future personality of America, I must 50 not fail, again and ever, to pronounce myself on one, probably the least attended to in modern times—a hiatus, indeed, threatening its gloomiest consequences after us. I mean the simple, unsophisticated Conscience, the primary moral element. If I were asked to specify in what quarter lie the grounds of darkest dread, respecting the America of our hopes, I should have to point to this particular. I should demand the invariable application to individuality, this day and any day, of that old, ever-true plumb-rule of persons, eras, nations. Our 60 triumphant modern civilizee, with his all-schooling and his wondrous appliances, will still show himself but an amputation while this deficiency remains. Beyond (assuming a more hopeful tone), the vertebration of the manly and womanly personalism of our Western world, can only be, and is, indeed, to be (I hope) its all penetrating Religiousness.

The ripeness of Religion is doubtless to be looked for in this field of individuality, and is a result that no organization or church can ever achieve. As history is 7 poorly retain'd by what the technists call history, and is not given out from their pages, except the learner has in himself the sense of the well-wrapt, never yet written, perhaps impossible to be written, history—so Religion, although casually arrested, and, after a fashion, preserv'd in the churches and creeds, does not depend at all upon them, but is a part of the identified soul, which, when greatest, knows not bibles in the old way, but in new ways—the identified soul, which can really confront Religion when it extricates itself entirely from the 80 churches, and not before.

Personalism fuses this, and favors it. I should say, indeed, that only in the perfect uncontamination and solitariness of individuality may the spirituality of religion positively come forth at all. Only here, and on such terms, the meditation, the devout ecstasy, the soaring flight. Only here, communion with the mysteries,

---

61 **civilizee,** one who passes for civilized • 71 **technists,** specialists

the eternal problems, whence? whither? Alone, and identity, and the mood—and the soul emerges, and all statements, churches, sermons, melt away like vapors. Alone, and silent thought and awe, and aspiration—and then the interior consciousness, like a hitherto unseen inscription, in magic ink, beams out its wondrous lines to the sense. Bibles may convey, and priests expound, but it is exclusively for the noiseless operation of one's isolated Self, to enter the pure ether of venera-
10 tion, reach the divine levels, and commune with the unutterable.

To practically enter into politics is an important part of American personalism. To every young man, North and South, earnestly studying these things, I should here, as an offset to what I have said in former pages, now also say, that may-be to views of very largest scope, after all, perhaps the political (perhaps the literary and sociological), America goes best about its development its own way—sometimes, to temporary sight, appaling
20 enough. It is the fashion among dillettants and fops (perhaps I myself am not guiltless) to decry the whole formulation of the active politics of America, as beyond redemption, and to be carefully kept away from. See you that you do not fall into this error. America, it may be, is doing very well upon the whole, notwithstanding these antics of the parties and their leaders, these half-brain'd nominees, the many ignorant ballots, and many elected failures and blatherers. It is the dillettants, and all who shirk their duty, who are not doing well. As
30 for you, I advise you to enter more strongly yet into politics. I advise every young man to do so. Always inform yourself; always do the best you can; always vote. Disengage yourself from parties. They have been useful, and to some extent remain so; but the floating, uncommitted electors, farmers, clerks, mechanics, the masters of parties—watching aloof, inclining victory this side or that side—such are the ones most needed, present and future. For America, if eligible at all to downfall and

ruin, is eligible within herself, not without; for I see clearly that the combined foreign world could not beat her down. But these savage, wolfish parties alarm me. Owning no law but their own will, more and more combative, less and less tolerant of the idea of ensemble and of equal brotherhood, the perfect equality of the States, the ever-over-arching American ideas, it behooves you to convey yourself implicitly to no party, nor submit blindly to their dictators, but steadily hold yourself judge and master over all of them. . . .

I hail with joy the oceanic, variegated, intense practical energy, the demand for facts, even the business materialism of the current age, our States But wo to the age or land in which these things, movements, stopping at themselves, do not tend to ideas. As fuel to flame, and flame to the heavens, so must wealth, science, materialism—even this democracy of which we make so much—unerringly feed the highest mind, the soul. Infinitude the flight: fathomless the mystery. Man, so diminutive, dilates beyond the sensible universe, competes with, outcopes space and time, meditating even one great idea. Thus, and thus only, does a human being, his spirit, ascend above, and justify, objective Nature, which, probably nothing in itself, is incredibly and divinely serviceable, indispensable, real, here. And as the purport of objective Nature is doubtless folded, hidden, somewhere here—as somewhere here is what this globe and its manifold forms, and the light of day, and night's darkness, and life itself, with all its experiences, are for—it is here the great literature, especially verse, must get its inspiration and throbbing blood. Then may we attain to a poetry worthy the immortal soul of man, and which, while absorbing materials, and, in their own sense, the shows of Nature, will, above all, have, both directly and indirectly, a freeing, fluidizing, expanding, religious character, exulting with science, fructifying the moral elements, and stimulating aspirations, and meditations on the unknown. . . .

1871

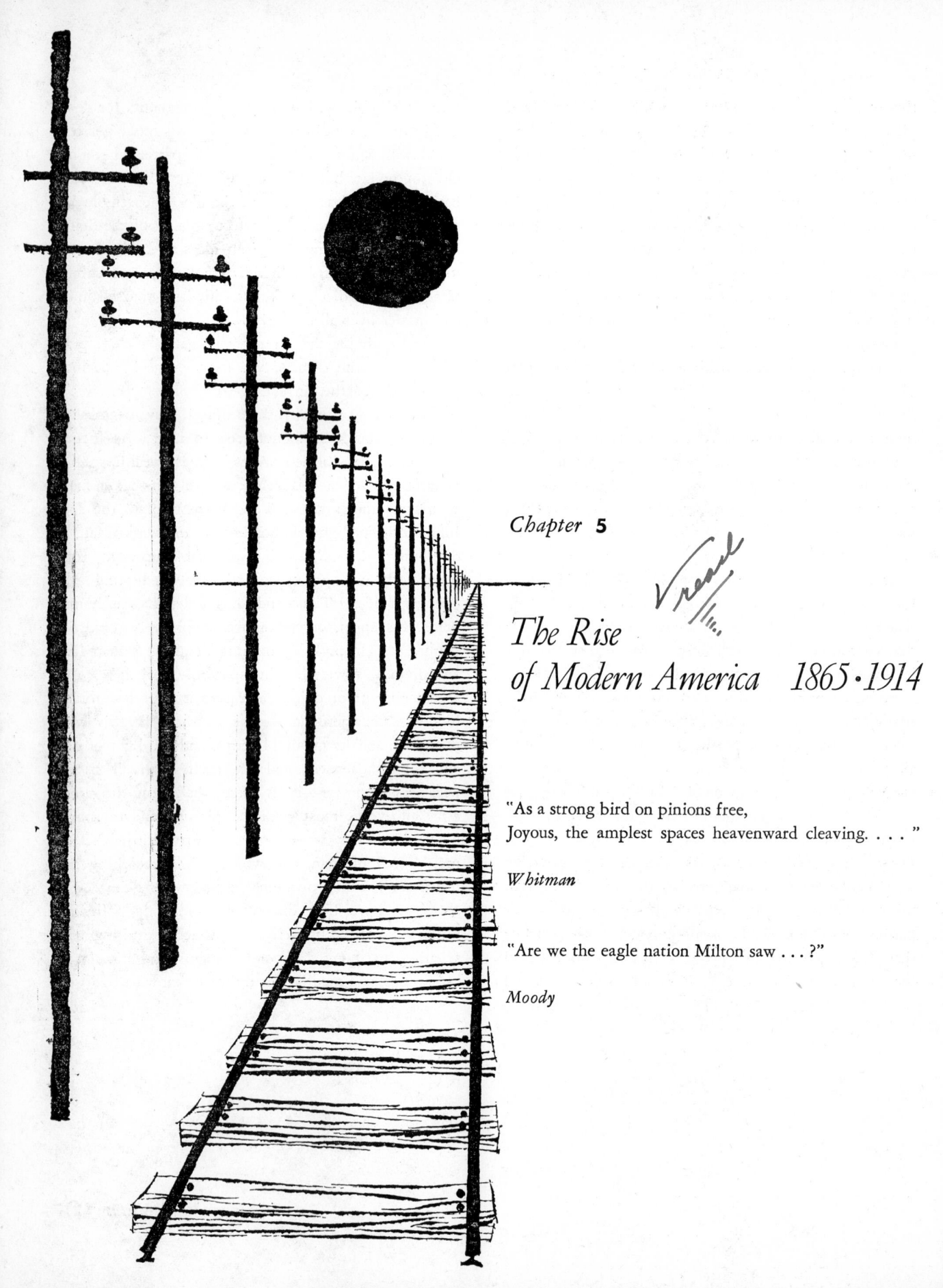

Chapter **5**

*The Rise
of Modern America   1865·1914*

"As a strong bird on pinions free,
Joyous, the amplest spaces heavenward cleaving. . . . "

Whitman

"Are we the eagle nation Milton saw . . . ?"

Moody

I. Intellectual Currents

Reunion

The Civil War, which terminated when Lee surrendered to Grant at Appomattox in April 1865, left the nation sadly disrupted. The restoration of unity—at best a long and difficult process—was made longer and more difficult by the Era of Reconstruction, which imposed the rule of ill-qualified Negroes and of carpetbaggers and scalawags upon the Southern states and maintained this rule by the presence of federal troops. When President Hayes withdrew the troops in 1877, reconstruction governments collapsed and the "tragic era" ended.

Much ill feeling was engendered on both sides by sectional controversy, civil war, and tyrannical misrule. On the other hand, many forces were working inexorably for the restoration of national unity. The states were bound together by a common language, common traditions, and a close interdependence of economic interests. The establishment of schools and colleges in the South by Northern philanthropy contributed much to the growing unity of feeling; the abandonment by the national government after 1883 of the attempt to control race relations in the South contributed still more. Not the least of the unifying influences was our postwar literature. Some writers preached the gospel of union, while others contributed less directly to the same end by exemplifying in the local color story the admirable qualities to be found in the rank and file of people in various regions.

Among those who celebrated unity and reunion, three writers stand out above the others: Lowell in New England, Whitman in the Middle Atlantic States, and Lanier in the South. On July 3, 1875, Lowell read in Cambridge his poem "Under the Old Elm," which celebrated the hundredth anniversary of Washington's taking command of the Colonial army. After paying eloquent tribute to the greatness of Washington, the poet held out the hand of reconciliation and friendship to Virginia.

> Virginia gave us this imperial man . . .
> She gave us this unblemished gentleman:
> What shall we give her back but love and praise
> As in the dear old unestrangèd days
> Before the inevitable wrong began?
> Mother of states and undiminished men,
> Thou gavest us a country, giving him,
> And we owe alway what we owed thee then . . .
> A great man's memory is the only thing
> With influence to outlast the present whim
> And bind us as when here he knit our golden ring.

A great man's memory. Lowell was right. The common memory of Washington helped to restore national unity after the schismatic years. Mount Vernon soon became a national shrine. So important to a nation's well-being is the principle enunciated by Lowell that in the years to follow, other great Americans, such as Jefferson, Lincoln, and Lee, irrespective of sectional differences, were to become national heroes.

Whitman's plea for reunion took the characteristic form of an inspiring prophecy of the future greatness of the United States. This greatness would be the achievement of states which are "varied" and "different" and at the same time united in "one identity." In the famous poem ("As a Strong Bird on Pinions Free," later changed to "Thou Mother with Thy Equal Brood," p. 208) read at Dartmouth College in 1872, Whitman expressed unbounded confidence in the future progress of America—a progress which would be not only political and material, but scientific, aesthetic, and moral as well:

> Thee in an education grown of thee, in teachers, studies,
> students, born of thee,
> Thee in thy democratic fêtes en-masse, thy high original
> festivals, operas, lecturers, preachers . . .
> Thee in thy pinnacles, intellect, thought, thy topmost
> rational joys, thy love and godlike aspiration,
> In thy resplendent coming literati, thy full-lung'd orators,
> thy sacerdotal bards, kosmic savans,
> These! these in thee, (certain to come,) to-day I prophesy.

It was a vision calculated to make men forget the quarrels of the past and unite in the achievement of a splendid civilization.

Although Sidney Lanier (p. 658) fought through the Civil War and spent several months as a federal prisoner, there was no bitterness in his soul. He saw clearly that the South could not attain well-being in isolation and estrangement from the North. In the centennial year of 1876, he attempted in two poems to draw the sections together in loving harmony: "The Psalm of the West" and "The Centennial Meditation of Columbia," the second of which was sung at the Philadelphia Exposition by a great chorus with orchestral accompaniment. Both poems employ the historical approach: a backward glance over the events which have brought us to this good hour should awaken a new sense of pride and responsibility. In "The Psalm of the West" Lanier surveyed the early voyages to the New World (the eight sonnets on Columbus are especially notable), the settling of New England, the progress of the Revolutionary War from Lexington to Yorktown, and the Civil War between "Heart-strong South" and "Head-strong North." The "Psalm" concluded with a prophecy of America's future glory as ardent as Whitman's. The "Centennial Meditation" suggested more briefly the same historical evolution and concluded likewise with a prophecy which was also a prayer for America's future:

> Long as thine Art shall love true love,
> > Long as thy Science truth shall know,
> Long as thine Eagle harms no Dove,
> > Long as thy Law by law shall grow,
> Long as thy God is God above,
> > Thy brother every man below,
> So long, dear Land of all my love,
> > Thy name shall shine, thy fame shall glow.

If the three writers just considered aided the process of reunion by emphasizing the solidarity of a new and glorious America, the fictionists of the local color school contributed to the same end with perhaps even greater effectiveness by drawing attention to the innate virtues of Americans everywhere and by adding to their understanding of one another. During the two or three decades following the Civil War, our most popular form of literature was the regional short story. Bret Harte (p. 338) and Hamlin Garland (p. 585) in the West, George Washington Cable (p. 355), Joel Chandler Harris (p. 375), and Mary Noailles Murfree (p. 364) in the South, Sarah Orne Jewett (p. 382) and Mary E. Wilkins Free-

man (p. 391) in New England—all portrayed with tender sympathy the lives of the inhabitants of their respective regions. One effect of this body of literature was to reassure Southern readers that there was much natural goodness in the North, and Northern readers that there was much natural goodness in the South. Only the most stubborn of hard feelings could persist under such an emollient.

Consider, for example, the reputedly flinty New England character as seen in the soft light of Miss Jewett's tales. Describing a family reunion on the Maine coast, Miss Jewett wrote in *The Country of the Pointed Firs:* "Each heart is warm and every face shines with the ancient light. Such a day as this has transfiguring powers, and easily makes friends of those who have been cold-hearted, and gives to those who are dumb their chance to speak, and lends some beauty to the plainest face." Miss Jewett assured her readers that beneath the plain, taciturn, and cold exterior of the New England character could be discovered, on propitious occasions, beauty, ampleness of speech, and warmth of heart. These were the points on which non-New Englanders were likely to entertain serious doubts. It is reasonable to suppose that Miss Jewett's stories substantially increased the amount of good feeling in America toward New England.

Or take the character of the Southern highlander—reputedly wild and lawless—as seen through the sympathetic eyes of Miss Murfree. She saw that friendliness, charity, the domestic virtues can be found in abundance in the hill and mountain country of the South. It is a natural goodness, produced not by schools and the higher civilization, but by Nature herself, and therefore the more worthy of recognition and admiration. "The grace of culture is, in its way, a fine thing," Miss Murfree said in one of the stories in *In the Tennessee Mountains,* "but the best that art can do—the polish of a gentleman— is hardly equal to the best that Nature can do in her higher moods."

Or look (to mention only one more example) at the Southern planter—by report brutal and tyrannical—as he is reflected in the genial pages of *Uncle Remus* (p. 376). More effectively than any other single writer, Joel Chandler Harris reassured the world of the essential kindliness which had existed between master and slave on the ante-bellum plantation and implied that not even emancipation and reconstruction could destroy the friendly relations of the two races. Harris' stories had an effect similar to that produced in one of his tales by Mr. Benjermun Ram's fiddling:

> W'en ole man Benjermun Ram sorter let up wid he fiddlin', he don't see no Brer Wolf, en he don't year no ole Miss Wolf. Den he look in de back room; no Wolf dar. Den he look in de back po'ch; no Wolf dar. Den he look in de closet en de cubbard; no Wolf ain't dar yit.

The infectious laughter of Uncle Remus and the pervasive good humor and kindliness expressed by Harris did much toward putting to flight (as Benjermun Ram put to flight Brer Wolf and Miss Wolf) the ill will which persisted in partisans both North and South in the postwar years.

It is not too much to say that the writers of the period contributed greatly to the reëstablishment of national unity. The local color stories, in particular, were for many readers a fresh and exciting discovery of America, and the writers of this school might have taken for their motto the words spoken by Senator Lamar of Mississippi in his eulogy of Charles Sumner: "My countrymen, know one another and you will love one another."

The remarkable extent to which reunion had been achieved by the end of the century was dramatically demonstrated in the war with Spain, in which Northerners and Southerners fought side by side and ex-Confederate generals held positions of command. World War I and World War II were to afford even more impressive evidence of the growing solidarity of the American nation.

Social and Economic Problems

Industry and Agriculture Expand

American social and economic life changed radically and rapidly during the years between 1865 and 1914. The railroad was a typical achievement of the age, and powerful in its influence on economic and social life. In 1865 there were only thirty-five thousand miles of track in the United States; by 1900 this mileage increased to nearly two hundred thousand. The Westinghouse air brake and other inventions improved the efficiency of railroad transportation. Enormous land grants by the government financed the building of the transcontinental lines: the Union Pacific, the Northern Pacific, and the Santa Fe, all of which had reached the Pacific Coast by 1884. If the cost in land grants was high, the railroads made substantial returns by peopling and developing the vast region west of the Mississippi. The roads, however, often abused their great power, and the Interstate Commerce Act of 1887 marked the beginning of federal regulation.

The railroad was only one factor in the economic revolution which followed the Civil War. A great transportation system presupposed commodities to transport, and these were supplied by an expanding industry and an expanding agriculture.

Industrial expansion was stimulated by a variety of factors: the exploitation of our resources in iron, coal, and oil; the development of improved machinery; the procurement of cheap labor through immigration; and the government's policy of protecting infant industries by high tariffs and allowing a free hand to business. There were many marvels of scientific invention: Andrew Carnegie was using the improved Bessemer process in the manufacture of steel by 1875; Alexander Graham Bell demonstrated the telephone at the Philadelphia Centennial Exposition in 1876; Thomas A. Edison and others made possible the dynamo, which was exhibited at the World's Columbian Exposition in Chicago in 1893 and which, as Henry Adams declared, "gave to history a new phase." Expanding industry required an abundance of labor, and this was supplied by a growing stream of immigrants, who, at the turn of the century, came in larger proportions from the southern and eastern than (as they had done previously) from the northern and western European countries. They were motivated in part by hardships at home, but even more by inducements proffered by agents of American factories and transportation lines. Immigration continued without drastic reduction until 1921.

Under these favorable conditions, our rapidly expanding industry soon got out of hand, and toward the end of the century it became increasingly apparent that some form of government regulation was necessary. Trusts and monopolies exceeded reasonable bounds. The railroads of the entire country were controlled by only a half-dozen small groups of men. A disproportionate

The new subway planned for New York—from Harper's Weekly, *vol.* XXVIII, *1884*

part of the wealth of the nation became concentrated in the pockets of a relatively few people. Big business had formed a corrupt alliance with politics. Abuses were rampant. Attempts at regulation and reform—at first ineffective—began with the Sherman Anti-Trust Act of 1890, and in response to growing social criticism became more effective after the turn of the century: among other things, the powers of the Interstate Commerce Commission were increased, and in 1906 a Pure Food and Drugs Act heralded a new era in the responsibilities of business to society.

Agriculture also underwent a revolution during the post-Civil War years. Vast new lands in the West were opened to farming. New machines—reapers, binders, threshers—and new scientific devices—fertilizers, insecticides, improved strains—greatly increased the yield of the land. The methods of big business invaded the farm: the cash crop supplanted subsistence farming.

But fewer people were needed to do the work, thanks to the improved machinery; the financial returns were precarious; and migration from the farms to the cities grew steadily.

Growth of Cities

Perhaps the most conspicuous change of all during these years was the rapid growth of cities, fed by immigrants from abroad and by farm and village folk from the American countryside. In 1860 one sixth of our population was urban; in 1900, one third. Between 1880 and 1900 the population of Chicago grew from a half million to a million and a half, and the number of American cities with a population of one hundred thousand or more increased from nineteen to thirty-six. City life gained, while country life suffered, in prestige. It was supposed by thousands of young Americans that a better life, somehow, could be lived in the city than in the country, and the bigger the city, the better the life. Many novels of the time—especially those of Theodore Dreiser (p. 644)—show the error of this supposition. The sudden growth of great urban centers created new social and economic problems, and municipal government broke down under the strain. The evils of the slums appeared for the first time in American life.

Labor Organizes

The new industry exploited labor, and it was inevitable that labor should organize to combat the exploitation. A beginning was made by the Knights of Labor, founded in 1869; but the movement did not gain appreciable strength until 1886, when the American Federation of Labor was organized under the leadership of Samuel Gompers. The A. F. of L. continued to gain steadily until 1920, when it reached a peak of more than four million members. As organized labor grew in strength, industrial conflicts increased in number and intensity. The first of these was the railroad strike of 1877. Others worthy of note are the Pullman strike of 1894 and the strike in the Pennsylvania coal fields in 1902. Strikes have often been an effective weapon, and much has been accomplished to improve the lot of labor by social legislation. Since the Massachusetts "Ten Hour Act for Women and Children in Factories" in 1874, much progress has been made in the working conditions, hours, and wages of labor. Early reform legislation was often declared unconstitutional on the disingenuous principle that "a person has the right to sell his labor upon such terms as he deems proper." But after 1900, more liberal judges, like Louis D. Brandeis, were instrumental in reversing many of the decisions which had blocked social reform.

The Literature of Social Criticism

St. Paul said that "the love of money is the root of all evil," and the history of America after the Civil War exhibits the truth or near-truth of that statement. Perhaps never before was a nation so engrossed in the business of making money. Perhaps never before was materialism so rampant, or so much pride taken in material achievements.

The writers of the period pointed out forcefully the evils of this crass materialism. In *Democratic Vistas* (p. 212) Walt Whitman warned his readers that material wealth alone would not make a nation great:

> I hail with joy the oceanic, variegated, intense practical energy, the demand for facts, even the business materialism of the current age, our States. But wo to the age or land in which these things, movements, stopping at themselves, do not tend to ideas. As fuel to flame, and flame to the heavens, so must wealth, science, materialism—even this democracy of which we make so much—unerringly feed the highest mind, the soul.

Lanier in "The Symphony" (p. 662) pleaded eloquently for a Christian and chivalric code in place of the unfeeling relations between employer and employed:

> 'Thou Trade! thou king of the modern days!
>   Change thy ways,
>   Change thy ways;
> Let the sweaty laborers file
>   A little while,
>   A little while,
> Where Art and Nature sing and smile.
> Trade! is thy heart all dead, all dead?
> And hast thou nothing but a head?
> I'm all for heart,' the flute-voice said.

In "these cold, merchantable days," the poet declared, even the love of the sexes is tainted by mercenary motives:

> Now, comes a suitor with sharp prying eye—
> Says *Here, you Lady, if you'll sell, I'll buy:*
> *Come, heart for heart—a trade? What! weeping? why?*
> Shame on such wooers' dapper mercery!

While Whitman and Lanier were voicing their spiritual protests, Mark Twain (p. 404) was ridiculing mercilessly the get-rich-quick schemes of his money-mad countrymen. In *The Gilded Age* (p. 416)—a book whose name has been given to the Grant era (1869-1877) and by extension to the twenty or thirty years following the Civil War—the author presented at once hilariously and devastatingly Colonel Sellers' designs for money-making. At one and the same time, Sellers was scheming to corner the corn and hog crops, buy up the wildcat banks, and market an "Optic Liniment" (his own concoction) throughout the world. He and his associates attempted to sell a large tract of worthless land ("the Tennessee land") to the government. Despite skillful lobbying in Washington, they failed, though by a narrow margin, and the book ends with the moral that sober industry and contentment with a modest income honestly earned are infinitely preferable to frantic schemes to get rich quick. It was a good moral, but one which the author himself never learned, and one which millions of Americans had not learned as late as 1929.

The Gilded Age also exposed political corruption in the national capital, where votes were bought and sold. Henry Adams (p. 739) in his novel *Democracy* (1880) turned a censorious eye on similar political phenomena. He portrays a distinguished United States senator, the leader of his party, who accepted a bribe of $100,000. His reasons were good "political" ones, but they did not satisfy Adams' heroine, whose break with the senator parallels Adams' own withdrawal from the corrupt politics of the Gilded Age. But Adams remained a fascinated observer and refused to surrender his belief in democracy despite its current evil manifestations. "I grant it is an experiment," he said through one of the characters in the novel, "but it is the only direction society can take that is worth its taking. . . . Every other possible step is backward."

Our writers were not long content with a general censure of materialism and political corruption. Growing ills awakened the social conscience and called forth specific indictments which became increasingly prominent in the literature of the late nineteenth and early twentieth centuries. Prepared by his own experience on an Iowa farm and indoctrinated in the economic theories of Henry George (p. 695), Hamlin Garland in *Main-Travelled Roads* (p. 585) exposed, with strong emotional appeal, the hardships and injustices suffered by the farmers in the Iowa-Wisconsin country. An angry and anger-arousing book, *Main-Travelled Roads* suggests the gathering strength of the Populist Movement and helps explain the spectacular rise of William Jennings Bryan in 1896. An important phase in the history of the railroad's exploitation of the farmer is presented in Frank Norris' *The Octopus* (p. 618), which powerfully portrays the struggle between the Southern Pacific Railroad (the "octopus") and the wheat farmers of California. The triumphant force is neither the railroad nor the farmers, but the wheat, which Norris represents in both *The Octopus* (1901) and *The Pit* (1903) as more powerful than any man or combination of men.

Criticisms of Industrialism

With the opening of the new century, the exposure of injustices and abuses in our national life became the most popular of literary subjects. In politics, the 1900's were the era of Theodore Roosevelt's progressivism and "trust-busting"; in literature, the era of the "muckrakers." Literature was dedicated to the exposé, and scores of books revealed all sorts of malpractices to an indignant public. Perhaps the greatest of the muckraking books was Upton Sinclair's *The Jungle* (p. 732), which dealt graphically with the life of a Lithuanian immigrant employed in the Chicago stockyards. This sturdy young man is gradually broken, and his family completely ruined, by the inhuman cruelties of the stockyards. The book's exposure of unsanitary practices in the processing of meat undoubtedly hastened the enactment of the Pure Food and Drugs Act.

The leader among the muckrakers was Lincoln Steffens, whose *The Shame of the Cities* (p. 715) brought to focus the problems created by the sudden emergence of great urban communities and contributed to the movement for municipal reform. Steffens' book drew attention to the corruption in city government and attempted to fix the blame on certain prominent citizens. The growing problems of the Big City had been noticed before Steffens and were to be further exposed after his notable book. As early as 1890 William Dean Howells (p. 459) had exhibited, somewhat conservatively, the grime and squalor of New York City in *A Hazard of New Fortunes* (p. 467). Less conservatively, Stephen Crane's *Maggie: A Girl of the Streets* (1893) exposed the ugly life of New York's Bowery. In *Sister Carrie* (1900) and *Jennie Gerhardt* (1911) Theodore Dreiser told affectingly of the hard lot of the underpaid working girl in the big cities of the Middle West. Henry Blake Fuller in *The Cliff-Dwellers* (1893) and Robert Herrick in *The Common Lot* (1904) underscored the degrading effect on Chicago's social life of greed and cutthroat competition. Possibly the apogee of the literary attack on the Big City as a monster of corruption and vice was reached in David Graham Phillips' *Susan Lenox* (1917), whose heroine encounters (and miraculously survives) nearly all the evils of our modern Babylons.

The most prominent and commanding figure in the new industrial scene was the captain of industry. The years following the Civil War saw the amassing of unprecedented private fortunes. Financiers like Jay Cooke, the first great American banker; John D. Rockefeller, the Oil King; Andrew Carnegie, monopolist of iron and steel; and Jay Gould, Commodore Vanderbilt, and Collis P. Huntington, railroad magnates, became the real rulers of America. The reputations of these great entrepreneurs are now tarnished; their money was often acquired unethically; they have been called, with a good deal of justice, the "robber barons."

The type early attracted the attention of our novelists, but the literary treatment was for a good many years comparatively gentle. In Howells' *The Rise of Silas Lapham* (1885), Lapham, a wealthy Boston paint manufacturer, is crude but honest. At the great crisis of his career, he loses his business rather than accept a price for properties which is greater than he knows them to be worth. Howells would have defended his portrait of Lapham by saying that the great majority of American financiers were honest, that robber barons were the exception, not the rule. In *A Hazard of New Fortunes*, Dryfoos, the millionaire, is less amiable in his domestic and social relations than Lapham, and less honorable in business, though we are told that he never "wrecked a railroad" or belonged to a "swindling company or grinding monopoly."

Living abroad, Henry James (p. 495) had the opportunity of knowing only those prosperous and emancipated Americans who took a vacation in Europe. His Christopher Newman (*The American*, 1877) and

Union stock yards in Chicago, 1866—courtesy of The New-York Historical Society, New York City

The Literature of Social Criticism 225

Adam Verver (*The Golden Bowl,* 1904) are men of integrity and charm. Although James does not enter at all into their business careers—a subject on which he is always vague—we see Newman and Verver behaving decently and even magnanimously. Newman is devoted to culture in a limited way; Verver has built in "American City" a museum of art which he has filled with priceless treasures. Both are men of honor as well as of cultural aspirations.

The balance has never been struck between the portraits drawn by Howells and James and the authentic careers of the "robber barons." Were all successful businessmen in the Gilded Age boors and scoundrels? Some social historians have implied as much. But the modern reader—unless he is a cynic—is still free to believe that the Gilded Age produced Laphams and Newmans as well as Cookes and Goulds.

The emphasis of the muckrakers on the exposé resulted in much less flattering portrayals of the American businessman after the turn of the century. The most elaborate study of the type was made by Dreiser in two voluminously documented novels, *The Financier* (1912) and *The Titan* (1914), in both of which the business career of Frank Cowperwood more closely approximates the unsavory records of the barons. The literary pendulum was to swing back to a more favorable picture of the American millionaire in *Dodsworth* (1929), where Sinclair Lewis' hero (recalling James' Newman in many ways) is an admirable person despite his wealth.

The Reformers

While emphasizing the blight of materialism upon the soul, and the injustices and abuses of the new industrial order, the literature of social criticism was not entirely destructive; there were constructive elements as well. Specific utopias were proposed. The greatest and most influential of these was Edward Bellamy's *Looking Backward* (p. 706): "Not since *Uncle Tom's Cabin*," declares V. L. Parrington, "had an American novel reached so many readers." Believing that economic inequality was the cause of all social ills, Bellamy described a Socialist utopia in which the wealth was distributed with exact equality among its members. A benevolent state controlled public and private economy in the minutest detail; it assigned members to tasks according to their aptitudes; it provided incentives through special recognition of public service. A planned and coöperative society produced sufficient wealth to permit the early retirement of its members and the free enjoyment of cultural pursuits. *Looking Backward* has made many converts to Socialism. Other writers of the period also proposed the Socialist solution: among them, Howells in *A Traveler from Altruria* (1894) and Upton Sinclair in *The Jungle*—after the incredible woes of the stockyards, Sinclair's hero embraces Socialism and becomes an active worker for the cause.

The great body of the literature dealing with social problems, however, proposes not a radical alteration of the American system of free enterprise, but reforms and ameliorations. If men would be honest and fair, if they would be satisfied with a modest income, if they would spend their money unselfishly, if they would be Christians imbued with the spirit of the Sermon on the Mount—then all would be well: this is the burden of many writers who have concerned themselves with the subject. Charles M. Sheldon's *In His Steps* (1896), which had an amazing sale of more than fifteen million copies, recommended that everyone when confronted by a problem should ask himself, "What would Jesus do?" Less popular and better writers also emphasized the importance of the Christian attitude. Robert Herrick advised in *The Common Lot* a quiet withdrawal from the market place into a Wordsworthian simplicity. William Vaughn Moody (p. 688), the first of our poets to examine the new social problems with critical insight, urged in "Gloucester Moors" (1900) the necessity of a social conscience among the more fortunate members of society. The results of the Machine Age, he pointed out in "The Brute" (1900), had been disappointing: contrary to expectations, the Machine (the "brute") had not brought prosperity and leisure to all, but only to "the strong and cunning few." The solution lay, Moody thought, not in the rejection of the Machine (as some nineteenth-century Romantics had believed), but in a better control of the Machine and a fairer distribution of the wealth which it produces:

For the Brute must bring the good time on . . .
He must loose the curse of Adam from the worn neck
of the race.

He must give each man his portion, each his pride and
  worthy place.

Substantial progress was to be made in the new century
toward the realization of these aims.

The Frontier Versus Europe: A Question of Values

The Freedom of the Frontier

"Westward the course of empire takes its way," wrote
Bishop Berkeley in his "Verses on the Prospect of Planting Arts and Learning in America" published in 1752.
The Westward movement in America was a fulfillment
of the prophecy beyond anything which the good bishop
could have foreseen. Before the end of the eighteenth
century, pioneers had crossed the Alleghenies; by the
middle of the nineteenth century, they had settled the
Mississippi Valley as far as Texas and the upper reaches
of the Missouri and had invaded California and Oregon;
by the end of the century, only the Rocky Mountains and
the arid tracts of Arizona and Nevada remained unsettled;
and by the beginning of World War I, there was no more
frontier. The "epic of America" before 1914 was in no
small part the epic of the ever advancing frontier. The
treatment of the frontier in literature has been of two
kinds: romantic, and realistic and critical. In the nineteenth century the romantic treatment predominated;
the realistic and critical treatment did not prevail until
after World War I.

Whitman sounded the dominant nineteenth-century
note in "Pioneers! O Pioneers!" (p. 186). Whitman's
pioneers were heroes—"tan-faced children," "youthful
and sinewy," armed with "pistols and sharp-edged axes."

We primeval forests felling,
We the rivers stemming, vexing we and piercing deep
  the mines within,
We the surface broad surveying, we the virgin soil
  upheaving,
  Pioneers! O Pioneers!

(A century later it was to appear that the pioneers had
done too thorough a job in upheaving the soil and felling the forests.) They were "impatient" and "full of
action"—a "resistless, restless race." Such was Whitman's
glorification of the Westward movement. Other poets
of the nineteenth century—Emerson and Lowell in New
England, Lanier in the South, and Joaquin Miller in the
West—echoed Whitman's praise and admiration.

The distinguished historian Frederick Jackson Turner
was almost as romantic as the poets in his treatment of
the subject in "The Significance of the Frontier in American History" written in 1893. "Stand at Cumberland
Gap," he wrote, "and watch the procession of civilization, marching single file—the buffalo following the trail
to the salt springs, the Indian, the fur trader and hunter,
the cattle raiser, the pioneer farmer—and the frontier
has passed by. Stand at South Pass in the Rockies a
century later and see the same procession with wider
intervals between." Turner defined the frontier as "the
line of most rapid and effective Americanization." The
American character was largely formed by the frontier;
frontier traits became the traits most distinctive of
America:

> To the frontier the American intellect owes its
> striking characteristics. That coarseness and
> strength combined with acuteness and inquisitive-
> ness; that practical, inventive turn of mind, quick
> to find expedients; that masterful grasp of material
> things, lacking in the artistic but powerful to
> effect great ends; that restless, nervous energy, that
> dominant individualism, working for good and for
> evil, and withal that buoyancy and exuberance
> which comes with freedom—these are the traits
> of the frontier, or traits called out elsewhere be-
> cause of the existence of the frontier.

Turner's sentences are almost a prose paraphrase of Whitman.

When we come to the literature written by frontiersmen, we find much that is sordid and unattractive in the
life described, but the total effect is still romantic. Frontier life was vital, expansive, exuberant; it was in the
full tide of growth; here was no Indian summer, no sere
and yellow leaf.

The life portrayed in the books by Mark Twain's pre-
cursors—Davy Crockett's *Autobiography* (1834, p. 271),

Sketch by J. C. Beard from A. D. Richardson, Beyond the Mississippi: 1857-1867, *1867*

A. B. Longstreet's *Georgia Scenes* (1835), W. T. Thompson's *Major Jones's Courtship* (1843, p. 276), Johnson J. Hooper's *Some Adventures of Captain Simon Suggs* (1846), J. G. Baldwin's *The Flush Times of Alabama and Mississippi* (1853), G. W. Harris' *Sut Lovingood Yarns* (1867, p. 281)—contains much that is vulgar, brutal, and unprincipled. The bloody athletic contests described by Longstreet, the low chicanery of Simon Suggs, the rough practical jokes of Sut Lovingood may repel the delicate reader. But there is no denying the vitality, the sturdy strength and individualism, and, above all, the high spirits and love of fun. Life on the frontier must have been good to produce so much solid enjoyment; perhaps no other early settlements in the world's history have been enlivened by such hilarity. The literary apex of the hilarity was *Sut Lovingood;* nowhere else, even in our own literature, will one find quite so much of that quality, or the qualities it connotes—good health and an inexhaustible enjoyment of physical living. Sut Lovingood and his fellows were a remarkably healthy and uninhibited race.

Lincoln liked to read the Southwestern Yarnspinners, for he was one of them; and from their writings runs a straight line of genealogical descent to the great works of Mark Twain: *Roughing It* (p. 413), in which he told with gusto the tall tales of his sojourn in the Far West, and *Life on the Mississippi* (p. 432), *The Adventures of Tom Sawyer,* and *The Adventures of Huckleberry Finn* (p. 442), in which he immortalized the Mississippi from Hannibal to New Orleans. Mark Twain did not omit the seamy side of the Mississippi River region in the 1850's—the squalor, the vulgarity, the lawlessness; but this aspect is not too depressing because there was so much that was splendid and exhilarating. The splendor was symbolized for Mark Twain in the steamboat, and "the boat *was* rather a handsome sight!" The exhilaration was owing to the freedom symbolized by Huck and Jim on the raft:

> I never felt easy till the raft was two miles below there and out in the middle of the Mississippi. Then we hung up our signal lantern, and judged that we was free and safe once more. I hadn't had a bite to eat since yesterday, so Jim he got out some corn-dodgers and buttermilk, and pork and cabbage and greens—there ain't nothing in the world so good when it's cooked right—and whilst I eat my supper we talked and had a good time. I was powerful glad to get away from the feuds, and so was Jim to get away from the swamp. We said there warn't no home like a raft, after all. Other places do seem so cramped up and smothery, but a raft don't. You feel mighty free and easy and comfortable on a raft.

It is important to note, however, that the freedom symbolized by Huck and his raft is social as well as individual. Despite his revolt against Miss Watson's "civilization," Huck's behavior is not irresponsible. The freedom of *Huckleberry Finn* turns out to be, paradoxically, a qualified freedom, a freedom complicated by responsibilities and social ties. As Lionel Trilling has acutely observed, "Huck is always 'in a sweat' over the predicament of someone else." It was with good reason that William Dean Howells called Mark Twain "the Lincoln of our literature."

The European Tradition

The Westward movement was a powerful driving force which settled the American continent. But there has been another, a counter-force, less powerful but insistent, which has operated throughout our history. As Ferner Nuhn pointed out in *The Wind Blew from the East,* there has been in American life and literature from the beginning "the everpresent pullback toward modes of culture that lie in our past . . . the desire to retrace the racial steps . . . the nostalgic tradition." The Atlantic seaboard has felt drawn constantly to Europe; the Middle West and the Far West, to the Atlantic seaboard. In colonial times, Increase Mather and William Byrd— each in his own way—enjoyed London. In the nineteenth century, Irving and Longfellow and Lowell assimilated the culture of Europe, and Hawthorne felt acutely the ancestral ties to "our old home." Among our major writers, only Thoreau and Whitman—those staunch Americans—never traveled abroad. In the latter half of the century, the Eastward pull began to be felt in the newly settled West: Howells and Garland were drawn from their Western habitats to Boston by the lodestone of the East; Mark Twain settled in Hartford. Some Westerners even today confess to a feeling of "isolation."

The counter-pull has produced two kinds of literary subjects: comparisons of the Eastern and the Western parts of the United States, and comparisons of Europe and America. Although the first subject may be found here and there in our literature (*A Hazard of New Fortunes* transplants several Midwesterners to the East and suggests some comparisons of the two sections; Moody's *The Great Divide* studies the contrasting moralities of New England and the West), it does not attain the importance of the second: Europe versus America is one of the more significant themes in American literature.

Mark Twain treated Europe with unorthodox scorn in *The Innocents Abroad* (p. 410). He had a frontiersman's hatred of tyranny, and Europe to him meant the twofold tyranny of church and state, of priests and kings. The best thing that had ever happened in Europe, he thought, was the French Revolution, and he regretted that it had not done its work more thoroughly. He could not enjoy the great art of Florence when he recalled the sycophantic attitude of the artists toward the Medicis. Not only in *Innocents Abroad* but in other works as well (*A Connecticut Yankee at King Arthur's Court, Life on the Mississippi, Huckleberry Finn*) he lashed out against feudalism and its survivals wherever he found them, whether in Europe or in Walter Scott's

novels or in the ante-bellum South. It was primarily Mark Twain's love of freedom and his sense of the dignity of the common man which blinded him to the glories of Europe.

Two great contemporaries of Mark Twain were not so blinded: Henry James spent most of his life in England because he felt that "it takes an old civilization to set a novelist in motion"; Henry Adams, the historian, was drawn to medieval France as an example of "unity," against which he set the "multiplicity" of the modern world.

Though James admired the "items of high civilization" which he professed to find in Europe and failed to find in America, he wrote in large part about Americans—Americans in Europe. In novel after novel (*The American, The Portrait of a Lady, The Ambassadors, The Golden Bowl*) he shows us Americans, admirable though unsophisticated, in the process of exposure to European influences. These influences make for social and aesthetic enrichment; they are, at the same time, often questionable morally. James' innocent Americans —Christopher Newman, Isabel Archer, Lambert Strether, Maggie Verver, in, respectively, the four novels just named—are shocked by the evil which they discover in Europe. But they do not succumb to the evil; indeed, they are triumphant over it. Lesser Americans in James' stories may be corrupted by Europe or may remain impervious to its culture, but his American heroes and heroines, though not always happy or successful, emerge from their European experiences culturally enriched and strong of soul. Perhaps James meant to suggest that the ideal civilization would combine the freshness and moral strength of America with the rich culture of the Old World.

Henry Adams was not interested in the richness of contemporary Europe so much as in the richness of its medieval past. In his attempt to establish historical lines of force—his "dynamic theory of history"—by which he might explain the modern world and perhaps predict its future course, Adams centered his interest in twelfth-century France and in the Cathedral of Chartres as the epitome of that time and place. In Chartres he found the perfect symbol of unity. In that distant age, the Virgin, in whose worship Chartres was built, exerted a dominating influence over all men. She was the greatest force of the age—energizing, controlling, comforting, beatifying.

The Frontier Versus Europe

If the Virgin was the symbol of medieval unity, the dynamo, Adams thought, was the symbol of modern multiplicity. The Virgin was a unifying spiritual force; the dynamo was obviously a force, but neither spiritual nor unifying. As religion decayed, enormous, incalculable forces unleashed by science—steam power, electricity, radioactivity—threatened to destroy mankind. It was a serious question, Adams thought in the *Education,* whether there was enough intelligence and moral character in the world to control these new forces and use them for man's welfare. The release of atomic energy makes the question an even more serious one today. *The Education of Henry Adams* (p. 741) is perhaps the best statement in our literature of the background of our present problems.

In *Mont-Saint-Michel and Chartres* (1904) Adams, the disillusioned intellectual, almost surrendered to the spell of Chartres and the Virgin:

> One sees her personal presence on every side. Anyone can feel it who will only consent to feel like a child. Sitting here any Sunday afternoon, while the voices of the children are chanting in the choir—your mind held in the grasp of the strong lines and shadows of the architecture; your eyes flooded with the autumn tones of the glass; your ears drowned with the purity of the voices; one sense reacting upon another until sensation reaches the limit of its range—you, or any other lost soul, could, if you cared to look and listen, feel a sense beyond the human ready to reveal a sense divine that would make that world once more intelligible, and would bring the Virgin to life again, in all the depths of feeling which she shows here—in lines, vaults, chapels, colours, legends, chants—more eloquent than the prayerbook, more beautiful than the autumn sunlight.

Europe to Adams was a bright symbol of something eminently valuable—possibly essential to man's prosperity and happiness—which the modern world has lost.

Europe retained a good deal of prestige throughout the nineteenth century and after, despite *Innocents Abroad* and the frontier school; but European prestige lost ground steadily as the twentieth century advanced, despite a growing disposition of Americans to be critical of frontier values.

Science and Religion

The march of science in the nineteenth century profoundly affected religious thought. Geology established the antiquity of the earth, thus discrediting the chronology of Genesis. Evolution, as set forth in Darwin's *The Origin of Species* in 1859, saw man as the result of a slow development from simpler forms of animal life, thus challenging the Christian belief in his special creation. Astronomical science seemed to point to an infinite universe, in the face of which man appeared insignificant. Before the end of the period 1865-1914, sociological, biological, and psychological investigations still further reduced man's importance and autonomy. William Graham Sumner argued that human behavior was largely determined by "folkways," the mores of one's environment. Biology emphasized the determining influence of physical inheritance, of glandular secretions; psychology, the determining influence of automatic responses to stimuli. So effective was the combined onslaught of the sciences that by the end of the period, man appeared to be—from the scientific point of view—little more than an ingenious mechanism. Modern science seemed to leave no room for the soul, or God, or the transcendental perception of truth—for those religious beliefs, in short, which had motivated most Americans for nearly three centuries and which had found eloquent expression in the writings of Edwards, Emerson, and Whitman. The inspired view of the psalmist—"What is man that thou art mindful of him? . . . For thou hast made him a little lower than the angels, and hast crowned him with glory and honor"—became little short of absurd to the scientific mind. All phenomena, we were to suppose, were naturalistic phenomena, and were explicable on purely naturalistic, as opposed to spiritual or transcendental, grounds.

Early Resistance to Science

The scientific movement did not capture our literature immediately, and, as one might expect, the poets offered a sturdier resistance than other writers. Although Whitman accepted the evolutionary idea, it was the Emersonian (which was in turn the Lamarckian) concept, rather than the concept of Darwin, which emphasized the struggle for survival. For Whitman, as for Emerson, the evolutionary idea exalted man by enlarging his future possibilities:

My feet strike an apex of the apices of the stairs,
On every step bunches of ages, and larger bunches between the steps,
All below duly travel'd, and still I mount and mount.

As the scientific movement advanced in the post-Civil War years, Whitman became not less but more Transcendental. His Transcendentalism reached its highest points in the late poems, "Passage to India" (p. 203):

O my brave soul!
O farther farther sail!

and the "Prayer of Columbus" (1876):

Shadowy vast shapes smile through the air and sky,
And on the distant waves sail countless ships,
And anthems in new tongues I hear saluting me.

Lanier was a spiritually minded person who had no intention of surrendering his Christian faith to the new science. But partly as a natural reaction against his strict Calvinistic upbringing in Macon, partly through the influence of his professor of science, James Woodrow, at Oglethorpe, and partly because of the liberal atmosphere at Johns Hopkins, he welcomed science with an open mind. His copy of Darwin, we are told, was copiously annotated. He made a special study of the physics of sound in connection with his investigation of prosody in *The Science of English Verse*. Science, then, was an unmixed good. An intelligent man, he thought, must be, above all else, "catholic" ("The Marshes of Glynn," p. 669): he must eschew the narrowness of creed and cultivate breadth. The ideal soul is characterized by its "loves," its points of receptivity, and excludes neither science nor any other good thing ("My Springs"):

And home-loves and high glory-loves,
And science-loves and story-loves.

He was aware (in "The Mocking Bird") that science might have its limitations:

Sweet Science, this large riddle read me plain:
How may the death of that dull insect be
The life of yon trim Shakspere in the tree?

He admitted (in "Acknowledgement") that possibly his age was dazzled by the new science: "blinking at o'er bright science." These, however, were small reservations in Lanier's mind; no writer of the period was more hospitable to science. Lanier's eager search for truth was thoroughly admirable. But one cannot avoid a suspicion of indiscrimination and naïveté. Lanier did not recognize the contradictions involved; like more able thinkers than himself in the 1870's, he advocated the reconciliation of religion and science. Unlike some other reconcilers, he was apparently unaware that such a reconciliation would entail a diminution of Christian doctrine.

The breadth which Lanier extolled and exemplified seemed vicious to the greatest of the New England poets of the time, Emily Dickinson (p. 675). In liberalism, she thought, lurked an insidious and fatal danger to religion. Religion was being watered down to the point of insipidity. Her satire of the liberal clergyman—and she must have had in mind the popular advocates of reconciliation between the old religion and the new science—is a telling indictment: "He preached upon 'breadth' till it argued him narrow. . . ." Miss Dickinson was scarcely touched by the scientific movement. Her religion was the older Puritanism, modified somewhat by Emersonian Transcendentalism. For her, the things of religion still lay beyond the realm of scientific demonstration; they were still the objects of faith:

I never spoke with God,
Nor visited in heaven;
Yet certain am I of the spot
As if the chart were given.

If religious faith transcends the world of science, so does the individual life, on occasion, transcend the mechanisms with which science strives to hem it in:

We never know how high we are
Till we are called to rise;
And then, if we are true to plan,
Our statures touch the skies.

The "plan" Miss Dickinson refers to is not the scientist's but God's.

The Spread of Mechanistic Philosophy

Lanier died in 1881; Emily Dickinson, in 1886; Whitman, in 1892; and with them died in American literature a religious faith untroubled by science. By the end of the century, our poets and prose writers were feeling the full impact of the scientific movement.

Stephen Crane (p. 603) inferred from the biological struggle for survival and the astronomical immensity of the universe that man is unimportant:

> A man said to the universe
> "Sir, I exist!"
> "However," replied the universe,
> "The fact has not created in me
> A sense of obligation."

"A high cold star on a winter's night" ("The Open Boat," p. 604) is the symbol of the indifference of Nature and Nature's God. It seemed ironical to Crane, who found intense irony everywhere in human experience, that the discoverer of the universe should be dwarfed by his discovery, that the chief spiritual result of man's scientific achievements should be the conviction of his own insignificance.

Mark Twain, late in life, became a convert to the mechanistic philosophy. Partly through the influence of the new agnosticism as expounded by Robert G. Ingersoll and others, and partly, perhaps, in the attempt to stifle the deep-seated feeling that his literary performance had not been in keeping with his creative powers, he declared and attempted to prove that "man is a machine." In *What Is Man?* (1906) he summarized his argument as follows:

> To me, Man is a machine, made up of many mechanisms, the moral and mental ones acting automatically in accordance with the impulses of an interior Master who is built out of born-temperament and an accumulation of multitudinous outside influences and trainings; a machine whose one function is to secure the spiritual contentment of the Master, be his desires good or be they evil; a machine whose will is absolute and must be obeyed; and always *is* obeyed.

If to Henry Adams man himself was something more than a machine, man at least seemed to be impelled along lines of force. "Modern politics," he said in the *Education,* "is a struggle not of men but of forces. The men become every year more and more creatures of force, massed about central power-houses." He began to "see lines of force all about him, where he had always seen lines of will," and thus "before knowing it," he confessed, "the mind stepped into the mechanical theory of the universe." The future which Adams envisioned for the race was not too hopeful. There was a fair possibility of man's being engulfed in the new forces: "In the earlier stages of progress, the forces to be assimilated were simple and easy to absorb, but, as the mind of man enlarged its range, it enlarged the field of complexity, and must continue to do so, even into chaos, until the reservoirs of sensuous or supersensuous energies are exhausted, or cease to affect him, or until he succumbs to their excess."

Like Adams, Theodore Dreiser believed that men were creatures of force. With the turn of the century, the mechanistic philosophy began to appear in the naturalistic novel, which soon became its chief literary vehicle. Many naturalistic novelists felt a profound sympathy with the unfortunate members of modern society, who appeared to be the helpless and blameless victims of forces beyond their control. The mechanistic philosophy afforded a means of complete exoneration: if a person was dominated by chemical forces from within and social forces from without, he was not morally responsible for his acts or culpable for his misdeeds. In accordance with this view Dreiser wrote his great naturalistic novels: *Sister Carrie, Jennie Gerhardt, The Financier, The Titan,* and *An American Tragedy.* "All of us," declared Lester Kane in *Jennie Gerhardt,* "are more or less pawns. We're moved about like chessmen by circumstances over which we have no control." The world seemed utterly without purpose to Dreiser:

> In distant ages a queer thing had come to pass. There had started on its way in the form of evolution a minute cellular organism which had apparently reproduced itself by division, had early learned to combine itself with others, to organize itself into bodies, strange forms of fish, animals and birds, and had finally learned to organize itself into man.

Man, on his part, composed as he was of self-organizing cells, was pushing himself forward into comfort and different aspects of existence by means of union and organization with other men. Why? Heaven only knew.

The obvious tendency through Crane, Mark Twain, Adams, and Dreiser was a growing pessimism.

Mechanistic materialism, so prominent in the literature of the 1900's, was not unchallenged after its apparent triumph. Josiah Royce expounded at Harvard an idealism reminiscent of Emerson's. William James, another Harvard professor, brother of the novelist and America's first great authority in the new science of psychology, emphasized in *The Varieties of Religious Experience* (1902) the energizing power of religious faith. This power could hardly be accounted for, he thought, in terms of a mechanistic universe. The creative individual need not succumb to Adams' lines of force or Dreiser's weight of circumstance. James set up the pragmatic test of truth: "The ultimate test for us of what a truth means is the conduct it dictates or inspires." And, finally, Herrick among the novelists and Moody among the poets in the first decade of the century presented the religious view of life. But despite these dissenting voices, it appeared likely that the determinism of mechanistic science would continue to gain in popular and literary acceptance.

The New Imperialism

Throughout the nineteenth century, expansionist doctrines had been urged sporadically. Certain prominent Americans had advocated in the name of "manifest destiny" the desirability of annexing the entire North American continent. Out of this agitation had come the war with Mexico and the acquisition of large territories in the Southwest in 1845-1853 and the purchase of Alaska in 1867. But this expansion could hardly be called flagrantly imperialistic since, Alaska excepted, the new territory seemed necessary to round out our natural boundaries.

The Cuban Revolution of 1895 afforded a plausible excuse for American intervention, and the quick victory over Spain in 1898 stimulated imperialistic sentiments. The spectacular and exciting events of the war—Dewey's victory in Manila Bay, the crushing defeat of Cevera's squadron as it attempted to escape from Santiago, the charge of Roosevelt's Rough Riders up San Juan Hill—evoked a dubious mixture of patriotism and jingoism. After the defeat of Spain, the Filipinos resisted our rule and General Miles' army put down the insurrection. Many thoughtful Americans were alarmed at the new imperialistic policy upon which our nation seemed to be embarking. The crisis called forth protests from persons as various as William Jennings Bryan, Jane Addams, Charles W. Eliot, Finley Peter Dunne, and William Vaughn Moody.

Through the inimitable "Observations of Mr. Dooley," Dunne (p. 727) satirized the whole American imperialistic policy:

> "An there ye ar-re, Hinnissy. I hope this here lucid story will quite the waggin tongues iv scandal an' that people will let th' Ph'lippeens stew in their own happiness."
>
> "But sure they might do something f'r thim," said Mr. Hennessy.
>
> "They will," said Mr. Dooley. "They'll give thim a measure iv freedom."
>
> "But whin?"
>
> "Whin they'll stand still long enough to be measured. . . ."

Moody lashed out against the conquest of the Philippines in one of the most impassioned poems of our literature, "An Ode in Time of Hesitation" (p. 689):

Are we the eagle nation Milton saw
Mewing its mighty youth,
Soon to possess the mountain winds of truth,
And be a swift familiar of the sun . . .
Or have we but the talons and the maw,
And for the abject likeness of our heart
Shall some less lordly bird be set apart?—
Some gross-billed wader where the swamps are fat?
Some gorger in the sun? Some prowler with the bat!

But neither the humor of Dunne nor the Miltonic fervor

of Moody could stem the tide—we took the Philippines. The immediate outcome notwithstanding, the protests need not be regarded as futile: they may very well have had the effect of making our rulers more careful, for our record in administering the Islands proved to be creditable.

Secretary of State Hay made partial amends to the anti-imperialists by his Chinese policy, and Moody's tone changed from condemnation in the "Ode" to pride in "The Quarry." Having declared the policy of the "Open Door," Hay backed it up by thwarting the obvious intention of the European powers to use the Boxer Rebellion as a favorable opportunity for the dismemberment of China. The American eagle—no longer a "gross-billed wader"—now appeared in a heroic rôle. When China—backward, helpless, unaware (the description of China in the poem is extraordinarily fine)—was about to be pounced upon by the "brutes of prey," the "grand circler," uttering a cry of warning, drove them away:

> . . . stiller-tongued, with eyes somewhat askance,
> They settled to the slot and disappeared.

A distinguished historian has recently declared that " 'The Quarry' is worth all of the literature of imperialism together."

The United States emerged from the war with Spain a world power. National pride centered to an unprecedented degree (except possibly during the War of 1812) in the Navy. Alfred T. Mahan's *Influence of Sea Power upon History,* whose doctrine was espoused by Theodore Roosevelt, helped to make us navy-minded; the victories over Spain raised naval patriotism to a high pitch; Theodore Roosevelt dramatized the rôle of the "big stick" by sending the fleet around the world in 1907. But the great majority of Americans were not imperialists at heart, and by 1910 pacifism seemed to be gathering strength: Bryan, thrice Democratic candidate for the Presidency, advocated disarmament; David Starr Jordan, president of Stanford, argued that war was the reversal of evolution—the survival of the unfit; William James attempted to discover "a moral equivalent of war." Not deeply affected by the flare-up of 1898-1900, the national temperament preferred peace with isolation.

R.S.

II. Literary Trends

"The eight years in America from 1860 to 1868," wrote Charles Dudley Warner and his collaborator, Mark Twain, in *The Gilded Age* (1873), "uprooted institutions that were centuries old, changed the politics of a people, transformed the social life of half the country, and wrought so profoundly upon the entire national character that the influence cannot be measured short of two or three generations." Although many writers continued to follow older patterns, these changes in American life brought changes in at least some forms of the literature. Some changes adapted forms to the tastes of the growing middle-class reading public. Others helped in the expression of the nostalgia, the puzzlement, or the distress of people living in a transitional period.

Authors continued to write old-fashioned essays, but this form began to date as it was crowded from magazines by journalistic articles. By the end of the period, muckraking reports by Lincoln Steffens (see p. 714) and others had become much more typical. A great deal of poetry—some of it weak and imitative, some redeemed by individual qualities of its creators—was poured into prewar molds. But the period saw the rise to prominence of much popular poetry, some created by the people for the people, some written by more literate poets who consciously tried to please the growing group of readers who enjoyed poetry in dialect. Preëminently, though, this was an age of fiction, and fiction changed more than any other type of literature. There were some developments in the drama, too, which paralleled developments in fiction and which foreshadowed some achievements of the modern period.

Older Patterns of Poetry

Much poetry—"literary" poetry as contrasted with folk songs and folk poetry—showed remarkably few effects of the changing intellectual climate. Poetry in general somehow lost its vitality for many intelligent readers; it

fiction – most productive
drama – least productive
poetry – produced, only two – well known poets!

awaited a rebirth, portents of which began to appear in the final years of the period. This was partly because many poets—Bryant, Longfellow, Holmes, Lowell, Emerson, and Whittier—whose careers had begun in an earlier period continued to satisfy and to determine tastes after the war. It was partly because these established artisans and their British contemporaries were imitated in innocuous, genteel poems by hosts of inferior poets—Richard Henry Stoddard (1825-1903), Bayard Taylor (1825-1878), Edmund Clarence Stedman (1833-1908), Thomas Bailey Aldrich (1836-1907), and Richard Watson Gilder (1844-1909), to name but a few. Even on a higher level, Sill, Hayne, and Moody—all of whom had important things to say and said them with real eloquence—were well satisfied with established verse forms. Crane was a minor, though arresting, exception in his use of free verse. With the exception of Whitman, who was generally ignored, even the leading poets of the period—Sidney Lanier and Emily Dickinson—usually shaped their poetry to conform with accepted schemes. Each, however, sang with a noteworthy difference.

Sidney Lanier: Musician and Poet

Sidney Lanier, in his conception of poetry, was much closer to prewar New England poets than he was to Walt Whitman. "Whitman," he charged, "is poetry's butcher. Huge raw collops slashed from the rump of poetry, and never mind gristle—is what Whitman feeds our souls with." In his lectures on *The English Novel* Lanier devoted a good deal of time, a bit irrelevantly, to attacks upon Whitman's heresies. And when Lanier himself wrote free verse, as he frequently did, he did not think of publishing it. Instead, he conceived of himself as writing not poems but outlines for poems which awaited more conventional artistic clothing before they were fit to appear in public. Whitman, he held, had been at his best when writing "O Captain, My Captain" because in it he had "abandoned his theory of formlessness and written in form." Like the Brahmins, Lanier saw the poet achieving greatness when he used his supreme artistry to fuse beauty and truth. "Art, to be free," he wrote, "is not to be independent of form but to be master of many forms."

Lanier's departures from conventional versification came, therefore, less because he disagreed with the older poets than because he had individual tastes and talents. Because, even better than Emerson, he knew and loved the Elizabethans, he tended to use many images and conceits which were Elizabethan in their daring. Because he was a musician and a lover of the forms of music, in several poems, notably "The Symphony," he employed organizations analogous to those of musical compositions. And also because he was a musician, he tended, as he showed in his *Science of English Verse,* to think of poetic rhythms as essentially the same as musical rhythms. The result of this belief was that, though he kept within the limits which he had defined, he was a master of more complex modulations of meter, of more artful handlings of vowels and consonants for melody, than any of his predecessors, save Poe.

Emily Dickinson: Meaning in Miniatures

Emily Dickinson, despite the fact that only a few of her poems were published before 1890, actually was almost contemporaneous, as a writer, with her idol, Ralph Waldo Emerson (1803-1882): she began to write poetry, it appears, in the mid-fifties and continued until her death. She was probably as innocent of theories about technique as any poet could possibly be, as her test for poetry shows —"If I read a book and it makes my body so cold no fire can ever warm me, I know that is poetry. If I feel physically as if the top of my head were taken off, I know that is poetry." In all probability when such an impressionistic critic conceived of what she was doing, she did not self-consciously consider herself a rebel against established forms. Like Lanier, therefore, when she diverged from conventional procedures, she did so less because she had new theories than because, even for a poet, she was an unusual personality.

One belief of Emerson which his admirer in Amherst did share and enunciate was that a task for the poet was, as Emerson put it, to "embrace the common, . . . explore and sit at the feet of the familiar, the low." "Give me," said Emerson, "insight into to-day, and you may have the antique and future worlds." Miss Dickinson saw the poet as one who distills attars "from the familiar species that perished by the door." So in stanzas ordinarily like those of Emerson and, incidentally, like those of church hymns, she tried to tell (again as Emerson phrased it) the "meaning" of "the meal in the firkin; the milk in the pan; . . .

the glance of the eye . . . every trifle bristling with the polarity that ranges it instantly on an eternal law. . . ."

The common, for her, included a household group of men, women, and children; New England nature in the small range of nearby fields; and the rooms of a house as they were known to a housekeeper. She saw these with eyes focused to minute details—with intimate knowledge comparable to a nun's knowledge of each stone and lichen in her narrow cell. And when she announced what the details in her world of miniatures meant, the revelations were very personal ones—the discoveries of a mind which was both serious and playful, both mystical and whimsical. Novel imagery was the result, much of it predicted by nothing else in literature so well as by the poem "Huswifery" by seventeenth-century Edward Taylor, which had told of faith by employing conceits derived from household tasks.

"I'll Tell You How the Sun Rose" (p. 682) is in some ways typical. Like a large share of the poems by this introspective recluse, it begins with the first personal pronoun, and goes on to record highly individual insights into a common experience. In the second line she playfully interprets the sunrise in terms of feminine fineries —"A ribbon at a time"—a conceit paralleled, in the next stanza, by the image of ladylike hills "untying their bonnets." A comparison of the light with darting squirrels, two details of the commonplace scene—steeples "swimming" in "amethyst" and bobolinks bursting into song— then the soft soliloquy of the watcher, give the effect of the dawn. The end of the day is impressionistically represented, in the next two stanzas, by figures which involve children climbing a stile and a "dominie" putting up pasture bars and leading away his flock. All the details come from ordinary observations, and their very commonplaceness gives the interpretation a unique appeal.

Though this poem is less intense in thought and feeling than many by Miss Dickinson, its imagery is fairly representative. As Henry W. Wells remarks in *The American Way of Poetry,* "Children playing in the garret or asleep in their beds at dawn, New England customs at Thanksgiving, apples snug in the cellar through the winter, the loud ticking of the clock at night, signs on chimneys and doors, needle and thread, the little girl shut in the closet and told to be still—such images

take on the most piquant and unexpected emotional meanings. . . . Her microscope requires only one clover and one bee to make a prairie; one flake of snow debating whether it will cross a rut suffices her to create at once a mood and a winter's day." The fusion of such homespun imagery with the thoughts and whimsies of a poet made Emily Dickinson's work a new thing.

Folk Songs and Folk Poetry

One of the glories of the period 1865-1914 was the discovery, by many, of one aspect in particular of our rich native folklore—the folk songs. The scholars active before and after 1914 did not, to be sure, create the songs. The ballads had been made by humble, uneducated folk, and the scholars merely collected them and made them known. Even before the war there had been some interest in such lore, indicated by sporadic studies. Notably, young Francis James Child (1825-1896), newly appointed to the Harvard faculty, had been inspired, by study in Germany in the 1840's, to carry on research in British balladry. His lifelong work, climaxed by his five-volume collection, *English and Scottish Popular Ballads* (1882-1898), made such work "respectable" and aroused the interest of many scholars in the subject. Postwar interest in sectional life and in national history stimulated new enthusiasm. By the end of the period, therefore, knowledge about folk songs had increased tremendously.

During the war and the years after it, the songs which had been chanted by soldiers were collected in such volumes as *Songs of Soldiers* (1864), *Poetry of the Civil War* (1866), and *Southern Poems of the War* (1867). At least some of the verses drawn together in such volumes were of folk origin. Concurrently, several writers began to introduce the public to Negro spirituals in magazine articles such as "Negro Spirituals" (*Atlantic Monthly,* 1867) and in books such as *Slave Songs of the United States* (1867), *Jubilee Songs* (1872), and *Cabin and Plantation Songs* (1875). The last two volumes contained versions of folk songs as sung by the students of two newly founded institutions, Fisk and Hampton.

In the following decades, more songs of the people came slowly to light. In 1880, for example, when Joel

Chandler Harris issued his first collection of Uncle Remus stories, themselves valuable as folklore, he included a number of plantation songs as he had heard them sung in Georgia. In 1883 a fine study, *Games and Songs of American Children,* was published by W. W. Newell. The American Folk-Lore Society began in 1888 the regular publication of its *Journal,* which from time to time published, along with other lore, folk songs as they were sung by the Negroes, the folk of New England, or the Southern mountaineers. Other learned journals printed occasional articles. Stedman and Hutchinson included several sections of folk songs in their anthology, *A Library of American Literature* (1889-1890). In 1894, Alfred M. Williams included in his *Studies in Folk-Song and Popular Poetry* not only the ballads of other nations but also Civil War songs and American sea-chanteys. In 1908 a new vein was opened when N. Howard Thorp, Southwestern cowhand and himself a maker of ballads, published a little pamphlet, *Songs of the Cowboys,* a collection in which he stated, whenever possible, exactly where, when, and from whom he had picked up each. Two years later John Lomax, who had learned at Harvard to prize the ballads he had heard as a boy and a youth in Texas, published a better-known collection, *Cowboy Songs and Other Frontier Ballads.*

During the year between these two collections, a folk song very different from cowboy ballads swept the country, carried from coast to coast by vaudeville singers and gramophone records. This was "Casey Jones" (p. 263), a railroad song which had been composed years before by some anonymous lyricist to celebrate "a brave engineer," and which was published, in a somewhat refined version, by T. L. Siebert and E. Newton. During 1909, too, a writer in the *Journal of American Folk-Lore,* Louise Rand Bascom, published the opening lines of another railroad song, as heard in North Carolina:

Johnie Henry was a hard-workin' man,
He died with his hammer in his hand.

These, she said, were all the words of the song she had heard. A few years later (1913) in "Songs and Rhymes from the South," an article in the same publication, E. C. Perrow printed fragments or complete versions of songs about this same John Henry which he had collected in east Tennessee, Indiana, Mississippi, and Kentucky.

UNCLE REMUS

HIS SONGS AND HIS SAYINGS

THE FOLK-LORE OF THE OLD PLANTATION

By JOEL CHANDLER HARRIS

WITH ILLUSTRATIONS BY FREDERICK S. CHURCH AND JAMES H. MOSER

NEW YORK
D. APPLETON AND COMPANY
1, 3, AND 5 BOND STREET
1881

Title page from the first edition

All these, as well as others to be recorded later, were apparently based upon the exploits of a giant Negro who had driven steel for the Chesapeake and Ohio Big Bend Tunnel in West Virginia in the early 1870's.

This record of a few milestones tells only the beginnings of the American study of folk songs which, in the modern period, was to engage the attention of both careful scholars and lovers of poetry and music. Two rather different reasons for the awakened interest in such lore may be suggested. The study of folklore, thanks largely to the efforts of Child and his students, had become both respectable and scientific. For another thing, in those days when life was beginning to show its present pace and complexity, there was an attraction in the arts and cultures of the primitive, unlearned folk who sang such songs. Their traditional creations, at least, were not marred by the harassing problems of a transitional period.

The makers of the songs, naturally, plied their art for reasons which had nothing to do with either the science of ballad collecting or the distress of city folk during a time of change. Their songs came directly from their own experiences, their way of living, their feelings. To express what they had to say, they fitted poetic words of the only kind they knew to music of the only sort with which they were familiar. Thus the Negroes amalgamated the old-time hymns which whites had taught them with African rhythms which had been passed along to them by their enslaved forebears; and the isolated whites of the mountains or the prairies fashioned their compositions after the example of current songs or of ballads which had been brought to America from England or Scotland by early settlers.

These folk songs probably had few appeals to a sizable group which thought that poetry had to be elegant, genteel, and ornamental. Appreciation of balladry was usually confined to a pair of audiences differing greatly from one another. One audience, like the makers of the songs, was, in some ways, naïve—shy on book knowledge, although probably learned in the emotions and behavior of real men and women. Such an audience appreciated the songs much as had their original audiences. The other audience was highly sophisticated—one which could perceive the historical value of balladry as a cultural expression, and one which could appreciate simplicity of style, suggestiveness of detail, and music which, though it differed from the music currently fashionable, had a beauty of its own.

Some poets who were not folk poets took hints about writing from the ballad makers and wrote what might be called not folk songs but "folk poetry." Some of these —Whittier, for instance—used ballad verse or metrical forms resembling it, and employed language with ballad-like simplicity. Others, in various parts of the country, wrote dialect verse.

In the South a number of poets continued the tradition which had been started before the war by Stephen Collins Foster, and wrote poetry echoing Negro melodies and employing Negro dialect. Irwin Russell (1853-

1879) of Mississippi, in his *Christmas Night in the Quarters* (1878), produced a masterpiece of this genre, a sympathetic mingling of the Negroes' religion and humor in authentic dialect. Hayne and Lanier, as well as other less famous Southerners, also wrote poetry using Negro dialect. During the period, too, Paul Laurence Dunbar (1872-1906) in *Lyrics of Lowly Life* (1896) showed himself to be, as Howells held, the first writer of pure African descent "to feel the Negro life aesthetically and to express it lyrically."

The most popular dialect poetry, however, was written in the Far West and the Middle West. Outstanding were John Hay (1838-1905), author of *Pike County Ballads*; Bret Harte, whose most famous poem in this style was the popular "Plain Language from Truthful James" (p. 348), and James Whitcomb Riley (1849-1916), whose first book was *The Old Swimmin' Hole and 'Leven More Poems* (1883). At their best, such poems caught some of the flavor of rural life and some of the tang of American speech; they had wholesome humor and sentiment. At their worst, they were maudlin in their sentimental nostalgia for the "olden times." At both their best and their worst, however, they were interesting reflections of the tastes and the expressions of the feelings of the period. The extraordinary success of such writings showed that a large class of readers had come into being who were happy to buy the writings of even "humbler poets" than those Longfellow had praised —poets whose "simple and heartfelt lays" were, indeed, extraordinarily simple.

Humor

The period 1865-1914 is noteworthy as one during which humor perceptibly contributed to the development of fiction and merged with that type of literature. Thus our most admired humorist to date, Mark Twain, whose works were written in this period, was praised not only for making people laugh but also for writing great fiction. His mingling, in some of his work, of the techniques of comedy with the techniques of the short story and the novel was typical: many authors found the procedures of some of the humorists useful in creating postwar fiction. Some humor, by contrast, moved further and further from fiction, in the end becoming almost divorced from it.

In the years before the Civil War, magazines and newspapers—"exchanges"—came from all over the country to the office of the little Hannibal, Missouri, newspaper run by Mark's brother, Orion Clemens. Young Samuel Clemens, in the days when he was learning the printer's trade, read humorous writings in these publications and set some of them up in type. Some of the humor was that of New England—sketches and stories of Yankee characters like Jack Downing. More often it was the fine brand of humor then being produced in the part of the country with which he was familiar, the old Southwest—Tennessee, Georgia, Alabama, Louisiana, Mississippi, Arkansas, and Missouri.

One important thing about much of this Southwestern humor was its relationship to a favorite frontier pastime, yarnspinning. Traveling across country, moving down river, resting at night by campfires, household firesides, or by glowing stoves, the people of the section (like rural folk elsewhere in the country) found that good stories helped pass the time pleasantly. Able storytellers were greatly admired, and political figures like Davy Crockett and Abe Lincoln, who were masters of the art, could win votes by spinning yarns for their constituents. So the art of oral narration flourished on the frontier.

The stories ranged all the way from wild fantasy to fairly straightforward accounts of everyday happenings. Some fireside yarns were playful lies comparable to their modern survivors, "fish stories" or Walt Disney animated cartoons. Their tellers, like Ovid Bolus, described in Baldwin's *The Flush Times of Alabama and Mississippi,* "lied with a relish . . . lied with a coming appetite, growing with what it fed on . . . lied from the delight of invention and the charm of fictitious narrative." They lied about the astonishing fertility of the soil, about encounters with huge beasts, as did Jim Doggett in "The Big Bear of Arkansas" (p. 290). Almost as often, in some parts of the country, they imaginatively exaggerated the poverty of the soil, telling of land so poor that birds flying across it had to carry rations, so poor that if a buyer couldn't read he was likely to learn to his sorrow that the seller had got rid of two sections instead of the one contracted for.

Such lies about land, climate, and beasts were inventive and fantastic, and so were those about certain mythical heroes—gigantic comic demigods capable, so the stories asserted, of superhuman deeds. Among these were Mike Fink, keelboat king on Western rivers; Davy Crockett, hunter, congressman, and warrior; John Henry, the Negro steeldriver; Pecos Bill, the rootin-tootin Texas cowboy; Paul Bunyan, mighty logger of the whole north country from Maine to Washington. Some of the tall tales which gifted truth-stretchers recounted about a few of these worthies began to get into print as early as the 1820's. Mike Fink, for instance, was introduced in a short story in the *Western Souvenir* in 1828, and between that date and 1914 stories about him were told in a hundred varied publications—books, magazines, almanacs, and newspapers. Davy Crockett, who became prominent about the same time, was yarned about in even more publications. As the period ended, Paul Bunyan stories began to appear, and after 1914 all three heroes were to be celebrated by a number of authors.

The printed yarns about these men and others of their ilk were definitely influenced by the forms of the oral tales. Many details were products of the soaring frontier imagination; some of them were indeed fantastic (see the almanac stories of Davy Crockett, p. 273). But the incongruity which made the tales comic was the incongruity between the actual and the impossible. Thus though whole sequences of events were completely impossible, happening was made to arise from happening in an elaborately logical fashion. An earthy dialect style rather than the majestic language of inspired poetry matter-of-factly recounted astonishing feats. Details painstakingly rendered—highly authentic details—gave added verisimilitude. Sometimes, even touches which were quite vulgar heightened contrasts between the earthy and the unearthly. A few lines after Jim Doggett had poetically evoked a giant bear of Arkansas which "loomed like a black mist," Jim was shamefacedly telling about losing his pants. And frequently, though the tale was impossible by any sane standards, the character of the teller, and his motives for inventing his lie, were most plausibly rendered. The playfulness of tall tales was underlined, in short, by the constant reminders of actuality.

Even more of actuality entered into stories of another sort told by Western firesides and eventually translated into print—comic tales about more commonplace frontier characters and happenings. Several reasons for authenticity in such narratives may be cited. There was a desire on the part of some sophisticated storytellers and writers to show that they, like eighteenth-century British humorists, could detachedly perceive and appreciate "originals" and "eccentrics." Again, there was a wish, on the part of many, to write history—as A. B. Longstreet put it, in his pioneer book, *Georgia Scenes,* ". . . to supply a chasm in history which has always been overlooked —the manners, customs, amusements, wit, dialect, as they appear in all grades of society to an eye and ear witness. . . ." Finally, of course, there was a desire to entertain one's fellows. Lawyers, for instance, riding the circuits, said Samuel A. Hammett, in 1853, "living as they do in the thinly inhabited portion of our land, and among a class of persons generally their inferiors in point of education . . . are apt to seek for amusement in listening to the droll stories and odd things always to be heard at the country store or bar-room."

Whatever their motivation, authors who wrote such tales managed among them to record in extraordinary detail many aspects of frontier life. Franklin J. Meine, in his excellent anthology, *Tall Tales of the Southwest,* lists a group of subjects that is strikingly inclusive— local customs, games, courtships, weddings, law circuits, political life, hunting, travel, medicine, gambling, religion, fights, and oddities in character. As Bernard De Voto claims, in *Mark Twain's America,* "No aspect of the life in the simpler America is missing from this literature." The details about backgrounds, costumes, mores, and dialect are plentiful and vivid. Regardless of their crudities and exaggerations, such authors as Crockett, Thorpe, Thompson, and G. W. Harris represent the first American achievement of what later was called "realism."

Although some humorists, for instance Finley Peter Dunne, continued the older style, humor in general after the Civil War followed two channels. That which was generally classified as "humor" lost much of its prewar localized quality—tended in fact to become divorced from fiction. Professional humorists such as Josh Billings (p. 300) and Artemus Ward (p. 297) managed to appeal to larger audiences than ante-bellum humorists had by replacing much of the humor of regional scene

and individualized characters with humor which depended almost exclusively upon expression; and background, character, and plot became unimportant. Characters became generalized so that it was practically impossible for readers to tell where they lived (except somewhere on the North American continent) and whether they were good or bad, wise or foolish. The source of laughter, rather, was the style—ludicrously assembled sentences, words badly spelled, malapropisms, puns, and the like. This, then, was the first type of humor that developed after the war. The second type merged with a kind of fiction which flourished between about 1868 and 1900—local color.

Local Color

In the decade following the end of the Civil War, Whittier and Harriet Beecher Stowe of New England, Bret Harte of the Far West, Edward Eggleston and Mark Twain of the Middle West, and George Washington Cable of the Deep South all won enthusiastic praise for their depictions of life and character in their particular corners of the country. This was the beginning of a great movement in fiction in the United States. In 1894, critic Edward E. Hale, Jr., could write, in *The Dial,* "Everybody writes 'local' stories nowadays; it is as natural as whooping cough." There was a slight exaggeration in this statement, but certainly at least a vast number of authors were so engaged. Mary Noailles Murfree of Tennessee, Joel Chandler Harris of Georgia, Sarah Orne Jewett of Maine, Mary E. Wilkins Freeman of Massachusetts, and O. Henry of Texas and New York City are only a few of scores who wrote such fiction.

Directly or indirectly, much of this writing was influenced by the prewar humor of New England or the old Southwest. Mrs. Stowe's best work took the form of fireside yarns, many of them humorous, spun by a quaint Yankee character, Sam Lawson. It seems probable that Edward Eggleston learned much of his art from such dialect humorists as Jack Downing, Hosea Biglow, and various Southwestern practitioners. Miss Murfree admittedly was indebted to Sut Lovingood. Joel Chandler Harris, too, and O. Henry knew American humor well, and actually wrote a good deal of it themselves, before they began to write fiction. And it is noteworthy that Bret Harte, who was so successful that many fictionists paid him the tribute of imitation, definitely believed that the humorous story of "bar-rooms, gatherings in the 'country store,' and . . . public meetings" was "the parent of the American 'short story.'"

Naturally, it was not so simple as that. Many influences which had shaped our fiction in the past continued to shape it. The genial essays of Irving, sentimental novels, the writings of Scott, Cooper, Dickens, and others left their imprint. Yet the prewar humorous story was influential in ways which Harte suggested when he described it: "It was concise and condensed, yet suggestive . . . delightfully extravagant—or a miracle of understatement. It voiced not only the dialect, but the habits of thought of a people or locality. . . . It went directly to the point." Many details in this formula applied to representative local color stories.

So far as the local colorists, in their narratives, lived up to this description, they tended to be recorders of actuality. Several thought of themselves as merely reflectors of life. Typical was Mrs. Stowe's claim that in her New England fiction she tried to "make her mind as still and passive as a looking-glass, or a mountain lake," in order that she might reflect "New England life and character." "My studies for this object," she said, "have been . . . taken from real characters, real scenes, and real incidents." But perhaps because of the example set by romantic fictionists, perhaps, also, because of the nostalgia which most writers felt for the past, local colorists tended to write not of the scene of the day but of a day that was ended. So Mrs. Stowe wrote of the New England of her childhood, Eggleston of the Indiana of frontier days, Harte of the California of the Gold Rush, and others of happy ante-bellum plantations. The mists of time blurred the mirrors somewhat, and the local colorists as a rule avoided the sordid and the tragic in favor of geniality, sentiment, and pathos.

Mark Twain: Humorist and Local Colorist

Reared on the frontier and instructed in writing by prewar Yankee and Southwestern humorists, Mark Twain came into national prominence in the years when postwar professional humorists and local colorists were flourishing. In his varied writings the student of humor may see evidence of the influences of all these schools. But since Samuel L. Clemens happened to be a genius, he frequently managed to surpass his teachers.

Most of Twain's ephemeral works and passages are the creations of a "Funny Man" who was working rather too hard to get laughs. At their worst such creations were typified by the "Thomas Jefferson Snodgrass Letters," which he wrote in the late fifties, newspaper screeds soon forgotten and not reprinted until they were dug up by scholars as specimens of his youthful efforts. The style was like that of Artemus Ward and his cohorts of the postwar period—a style notable for cacography and for outlandish expressions. Later, Clemens, like other humorists of the school, refined this style somewhat—dropping bad spelling, for instance—in various sketches and in parts of his travel books. Often, in using the later style, he was quite funny. At its best, nevertheless, this type of humor never marked his highest reaches. And now and then—as in some later chapters of *Huckleberry Finn*—burlesque and buffoonery struck discordant notes.

The artistry of the frontier oral story, by contrast, was one of Twain's most important assets. Having lived in the frontier town of Hannibal, traveled around the whole country, and worked on river boats and in mining camps, he had, by 1865, heard as well as read a great number of humorous stories told by master storytellers. He knew, as he said in "How to Tell a Story," that ". . . the humorous story is strictly a work of art, high and delicate art—and only an artist can tell it." He knew important aspects of the technique: "The humorous story is told gravely; the teller does his best to conceal the fact that there is anything funny about it. . . ." Again, "To string incongruities and absurdities together in a wandering and sometimes purposeless way, and seem innocently unaware that they are absurdities, is the basis of the American art. . . ." Finally, he knew how the introductory framework of an enclosed narrative, as well as the language and thoughts of the yarnspinner, might be made to reveal the narrator as an appealing or amusing character. When, therefore, Clemens heard the "Jumping Frog" story unfolded by a mining-camp fireside in 1865, he was able to write it out in a masterly

Virginia City—from Harper's Weekly, *June 1865*

form (p. 406). And when later, in "Baker's Blue-Jay Yarn" (p. 429) and elsewhere, he created tall tales in the style of "A Coon Hunt in a Fency Country" (p. 279) and "The Big Bear of Arkansas," his were even better than those ante-bellum masterpieces.

Twain's travel books and to some extent his novels were combinations of similar brief narratives with longer chronological accounts. As Mr. De Voto remarks, in *Mark Twain's America*:

> He took the humorous anecdote, combined it with autobiographical reminiscence, and so achieved the narrative form best adapted to his mind. . . . *The Innocents Abroad* is structurally an autobiographical narrative. Descriptive passages . . . interrupt the narrative from time to time but its steady progress is accomplished by means of stories. Some of them are brief, unelaborated anecdotes, in no way different from the type out of which they proceed, but others already show Mark's perception that this form can be utilized for more intricate effects.

. . . The same framework produces *Roughing It, A Tramp Abroad, Life on the Mississippi,* and *Following the Equator.*

Similarly in novels such as *The Gilded Age* and *Huckleberry Finn,* Twain constructed mosaics made up of anecdotal units.

Just as anyone familiar with humor sees these resemblances, so anyone familiar with local color writing notices resemblances to writings of that type. The material for all of Twain's best narratives was his boyhood home, Hannibal, or the great river which rolled before it. More accurately, the stuff of his best works was not the actuality but his memory of the scenes and of the life he had known in childhood and youth. Memory, somehow, had blurred away most sordid and unlovely details, leaving an idyll to be set forth in nostalgic fiction. The localized details and the longing for times past were completely typical of local color fiction.

Two skills in particular give Twain's best fiction, long or short, much of its distinction: ability to characterize and ability to use words in a masterly fashion. Other humorists in America before Twain had managed, at best, to create only a few memorable characters. Twain dotted his pages with them with a prodigality comparable to that of Chaucer or Dickens. And he had such descriptive skill, such a knack for portraying actions, such an accurate ear for speech that he could make both characters who appeared for a few lines and characters whose stories occupied many pages come alive for readers. As a stylist, also, he was outstanding. He took great pains with style; it is remarkable that a large share of his remarks about literature touch knowingly upon this aspect of writing. Some of his reasons for praising a sentence which he quotes are illuminating: "For compactness, simplicity, and vigor of expression, I will 'back' that sentence against any in literature." He praises a letter from his daughter Susan for "clearness of statement, directness, felicity of expression, photographic ability in setting forth an incident—style—good style— no barnacles on it in the way of unnecessary, retarding words." He came close to living up to the ideal implied by these comments. He wrote very much as he talked, transferring to the printed page the natural rhythms of characters. His words were simple; almost always they were distinctly American; and he used them economically. Perhaps even more important, without any appearance of being "literary," he was able to find words which gave full scope to his exuberant, poetic imagination. It makes some sense, therefore, to claim, as some critics do, that Mark Twain was the first great stylist who wrote purely in the American language.

Varied Types of Realism

Comic tall tales, by juxtaposing the workaday world with the world of fantasy, made fun of imaginative excesses, and even the most extravagant American humor was in some ways anti-romantic. Since funny character sketches drew many details directly from actuality, some of the humor led the way toward fiction which was concerned with ordinary characters and scenes. Local color writing, which had a similar concern, also departed to some extent from the romantic fiction of the ante-bellum period. Scholars, therefore, see in both humorous writ-

ing and local color writing a trend toward "realism" which culminated, toward the end of the century, in numerous realistic and naturalistic fictional works.

The term "realism," like its counterpart "romanticism," is a vague term which has been variously defined. The group pursuing it in this period differed in theory and practice. They generally agreed, probably, that realistic fiction truly presented "actuality"—"real life"—and that it was concerned with the near, rather than the distant, in time and place. Most realists, therefore, believed that the probability of happenings in novels might properly be tested, not by rules set up by the inventor of an imaginative world but by what was likely in the actions of living men and women. Alice might properly dwindle to a minute size in Wonderland, but not in a realistic novel, since there the laws of physics and of biology as well as the stern limitations of heredity and environment were constantly operative. So far there was agreement; but disagreement naturally arose when authors tried to define "actuality." Where was the "real" to be found—in the world itself, in the inductively discovered scientific truths about the nature of the world, in the impression which the world made upon the observer's mind, or in a combination of these? The methods of authors depended upon their answer to this question and upon their ability to portray what they considered to be reality.

Clemens clearly indicated how he thought art should portray actuality when, in a newspaper letter of 1867, he thus criticized a painting by Bierstadt: "Now, to sum up the picture's merits, those snow-peaks are correct—they look natural; the valley is correct and natural; the pine trees clinging to the bluff on the right, and the grove on the left, and the boulders, are all like nature. . . . But when I got around to the atmosphere, I was obliged to say 'This man has imported this atmosphere . . . from some foreign country, because nothing like it was ever seen in California.'" Steadfastly Twain believed that the artist in colors or in words did his work best when he was "true to nature," accurately and honestly recording what he saw. "There is nothing," he wrote in a personal letter of 1868, "that makes me prouder than to be regarded by intelligent people as 'authentic.'" So far as he could, therefore, he made his fiction an exact transcript of life. Only because his memory changed things,

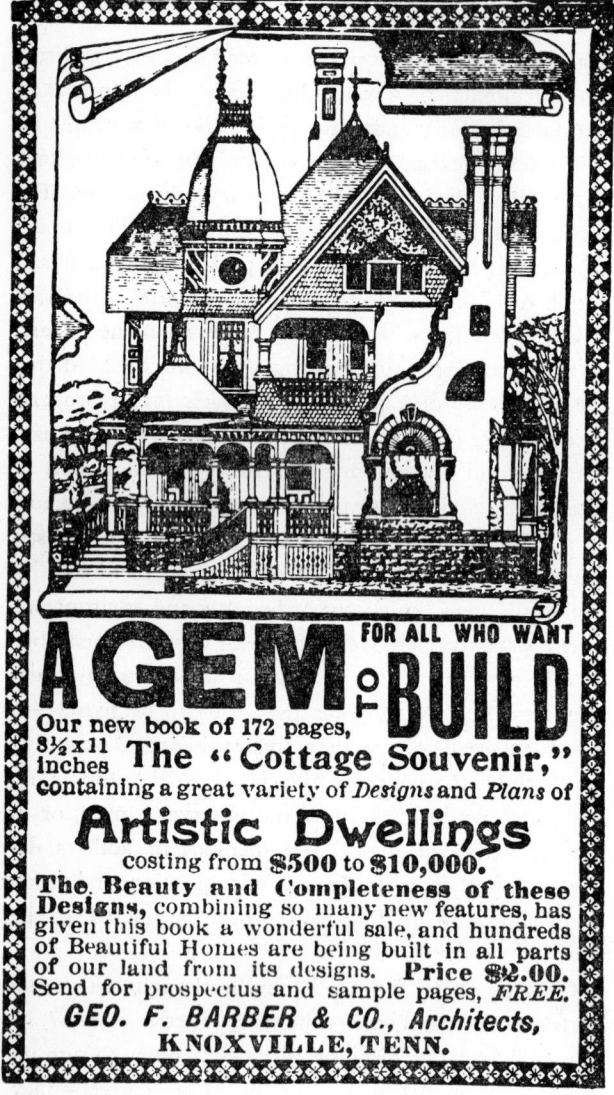

Advertisement appearing in Harper's Weekly, *vol. XXXVI, 1892*

because his notions of propriety changed things, and because he was something of a poet did he (to use his own terms) "import" the "atmosphere" in his best narratives.

William Dean Howells, Twain's close friend, had at the start of his career a similar conception of the task of the fictionist. Fiction, Howells also thought, should be lifelike. Moreover, it should concern itself only with the most ordinary facets of life. A passage in *Their Wedding Journey* (1872) concerning the people in a railway car suggests the attitude: "It was in all respects

an ordinary carful of human beings, and it was perhaps the more worthy to be studied on that account. As in literature the true artist will shun the use even of real events if they are of an improbable character, so the sincere observer of man will not desire to look upon his heroic or occasional phases, but will seek him in his habitual moods of vacancy and tiresomeness. To me, at any rate, he is at such times very precious. . . ." Since he followed this formula, the literalness of Howells' transcripts in his early writings was significant. But he recognized certain limitations—limitations which kept his literalness from being complete. It is important to recall that he first glimpsed the possibilities of realism while reading the comedies of Carlo Goldoni and that he was extremely fond, all his life, of the witty novels of Jane Austen. Like these two writers, he tended to concern himself, at the start of his career, more with the comedies of human experience than with the tragedies. In addition, because he believed that American life, typically, was relatively pure, and because he held that, even if it were not, it was wrong for an American novelist "to deal with certain facts of life which are not usually talked of before young people, and especially young ladies," he rather prudishly limited his treatment of sex.

An admirer of Howells, Harold Frederic (p. 597), and Joseph Kirkland (p. 579) as well, had much the general attitude Howells had about the fiction writer: his task was to serve up "a slice of life." Kirkland's *Zury: The Meanest Man in Spring County* (p. 580), he told an acquaintance, was authentic: "I know farm life. All the characters in *Zury* have their prototypes in my down-state acquaintances. The book is as true as I could make it. Many of its incidents are literally exact." But both Frederic and Kirkland were less convinced of the need for limitations upon subject matter than Howells was. Frederic, as he demonstrated clearly in *Seth's Brother's Wife* (1887) and *The Lawton Girl* (1890), was not averse to treating sex in a fashion which might distress young ladies; *The Damnation of Theron Ware* (1896) dealt in an equally frank way with religion. And Kirkland admitted his indebtedness to an English novelist who was in those days considered quite daring. "This novel," he wrote of *Zury,* "is a palpable imitation of Thomas Hardy's *Far from the Madding Crowd;* an attempt to reproduce on American soil the unflinching realism given by that remarkable work of English low life down in actual contact with the soil itself." The word "unflinching" as well as Kirkland's uninhibited treatment of moral problems in *Zury* showed that he had an attitude toward frankness in the novel closer to that of Hardy than to that of Howells.

When Hamlin Garland met Howells in Cambridge, Massachusetts, in 1885, Garland had, so Howells said later, "convictions flatteringly like mine." As Garland made clear in *Crumbling Idols* (1894, p. 592), he believed in what a French critic had dubbed "veritism." The true artist, he held, "must consciously stand alone before nature and before life" and must sincerely set down "the drama of the average type of character." In two ways, however, he departed from the early Howells. In the first place, Garland was moderately frank in his consideration of sex. ("I am old-fashioned," wrote Howells of this tendency in 1912, "and I have moments when I could wish that the author had not been of such unsparing conscience.") In the second place, Garland, under the tutelage of a group of assorted nineteenth-century thinkers, acquired the belief that "to fiction is given the task of subtilely embodying the splendid creed" of improvement—social, moral, and philosophical. "It is safe to say," he prophesied in *Crumbling Idols,* "that the fiction of the future will grow more democratic in outlook and more individualistic in method. . . . The higher art would seem to be the art that perceives and states the relations of things, giving atmosphere and relative values as they appear to the sight." Hence, *Main-Travelled Roads* not only pictured some of the harsher aspects of Middlewestern farm life; it also crusaded against conditions and suggested remedies.

By the time this first collection of Garland's stories appeared, Howells, too, had come to believe that fiction should have an element—one of great importance—which had been lacking in his early fiction. His first encounter—at fifty—with Tolstoy's writings had, as Howells indicated in *My Literary Passions,* brought about a change in his thinking. "He," wrote Howells, "has been to me that final consciousness which he speaks of so easily in his essay on Life. I came in it to the knowledge of myself in ways that I had not dreamt before, and began at last to discern my relations to the race, without which we are nothing. The supreme art in literature had its highest effect in making me set art forever below humanity. . . ." What this meant was that

Howells, in *Annie Kilburn* (1889), *A Hazard of New Fortunes* (1890, p. 467), *The World of Chance* (1893), and his other mature novels became a novelist of social purpose—selecting characters not only because they were typical but also because their characteristics and their stories preached sermons about society and economics.

Naturalism

Just as the line between some local color fiction and some realism is hard to draw, it is difficult to distinguish clearly and surely between realism and some "naturalism," another "ism" about which there was, in this period, a great deal of discussion. In general, the American naturalists—Crane, Norris, Dreiser, and others—took at least some of their cues from a group of authors, led by Émile Zola (1840-1902), who were important in France after 1880. The characteristics of the French group have been admirably summarized by Professors Nitze and Dargan in their *History of French Literature:*

> Naturalism . . . is an excessive form of Realism and is usually considered as possessing the following characteristics. First, it allows a still larger variety of subjects, emphasizing the lower and coarser forms of life; it presents this material in a form which is often revolting; it rejects ideality, it minimizes heart-interest and plot interest in favor of "facts" and notations; it magnifies the study of the industries and seeks to apply to fiction the processes of the natural sciences; from these, taken in their application to heredity and environment, it draws its conception of life—deterministic, fatalistic, essentially pessimistic. The laws of brute Nature are viewed as grimly controlling the destinies of helpless and hopeless men.

An interesting fact about this accurate description of a literary method is that it deals more with the philosophical views of novelists than with their fictional technique. The reason may well be that, for the naturalistic writers, "actuality" is located not merely in life itself but also in the philosophical interpretation of life. For Zola, art was nature, yes, but nature as it was interpreted by the artist. In a fashion comparable to that of the scientist, theoretically, the naturalist exposed his sensibility to life and then "scientifically" worked with characters and actions known through his experience. But the vast difference between the artist and the scientist whom he thought he was imitating was that the artist, unable really to prove his hypotheses in the laboratory, took them for granted and merely illustrated them from his experience.

American naturalists resembled their French prototypes in treating subjects barred even from realistic writings, in treating lower forms of life—thus differing from realists in their details. Also each American naturalist, on the basis of his own reading and his own thinking, created characters and plots illustrative of his own peculiar "scientific" convictions. Thus Dreiser, believing that men's actions were "chemical compulsions," pictured situations and happenings which made clear that characters had no control over their actions. Believing, further, that "the race was to the swift and the battle to the strong," he devised plots which showed weak characters conquered by ruthless and mighty opponents. Norris, excitedly perceiving both unconquerable forces of Nature and the relentless man-made power of the soulless railroad, devised in *The Octopus* a plot which showed Force at work:

> Men were mere nothings, mere animalculae, mere ephemerides that fluttered and fell and were forgotten between dawn and dusk. . . . Men were nought, death was nought, life was nought. Force only existed—Force that brought men into the world—Force that crowded them out to make way for the succeeding generation—Force that made the wheat grow—Force that garnered it from the soil to give place to the succeeding crop.

And Stephen Crane showed the hero of *The Red Badge of Courage* discovering naturalistic truths on the blood-drenched field of battle, or showed the correspondent in "The Open Boat" becoming aware of the complete indifference of Nature to puny men.

Dreiser, unlike some of the French naturalists, had a good deal of contempt for niceties of style. Not so Norris and Crane. Norris used a great deal of symbolism,

some of it rather explicit—readers may feel a bit obvious. (The slaughter of the sheep, p. 618, is an example.) Crane, rather more subtle as a poet, was sometimes less labored in his handling of symbolism, but much of it came into his work—usually in the form of images seen through the eyes and interpreted by the minds of his characters. Such images both pictured and interpreted details. The correspondent in "The Open Boat," for instance, thus saw a wind-tower on the tantalizing beach: "This tower was a giant, standing with its back to the plight of the ants. It represented in a degree, to the correspondent, the serenity of nature amid the struggle of the individual—nature in the wind, and nature in the vision of men. She did not seem cruel to him then, nor beneficent, nor treacherous, nor wise. But she was indifferent, flatly indifferent." Touches similar to this were to give significance, later, to backgrounds and actions in the writings of such diverse authors as Willa Cather, Ernest Hemingway, and John Steinbeck.

Henry James

To Stephen Crane, one of the most intuitive fictional artists of the period, thoughts and feelings of characters, then, were important. To Henry James, probably the most conscious artist, they were even more important. As his "The Art of Fiction" (p. 501) shows, James was a careful thinker about the nature of reality, the nature of art, and the relationship between the two. His belief was that "reality," as a story presented it, was twice translated, once through the author's experiencing of it, again through the artistic representation of it. Both the initial impression and the execution were important.

For him a novel "in its broadest definition" was "a personal, a direct impression of life: that, to begin with, constitutes its value, which is greater or less according to the intensity of the impression." For a person with the kind of sensitivity needed in writing great fiction, he went on, "Experience is never limited, and it is never complete; it is an immense sensibility, a kind of huge spider-web of the finest silken threads suspended in the chamber of consciousness, and catching every air-borne particle in its tissue." Since "impressions were experience," James did not hesitate to advise the novice,

"Try to be one of the people on whom nothing is lost!"

But having gained such a sensitive and complete impression of life, the artist, James contended, also had the problem of giving his fiction "that air of reality (solidity of specification)" which he felt was "the supreme virtue of the novel—the merit on which all its other merits . . . helplessly and submissively depend." James was aware throughout his career that to achieve this end through artistry was a highly complicated and delicate business. A brilliant series of Prefaces which he wrote, in his maturity, for the volumes of his collected works showed in detail how, during his artistic lifetime, he struggled with problems of form to give his writings exactly the intended "effects."

Such a conception of fiction clearly sets James off from those practitioners who believed that the best fiction was the exact reproduction of life as well as from those who believed that it was an embodiment of naturalistic generalizations about life. Since he saw reality—even generalizations about reality—as a series of impressions, and since he saw fiction as the artistic rendition of such impressions, his sort of realism was essentially a complicated psychological process. In his writings, more than others, therefore, one sees the impact of the newer psychology upon which his brother, William James, was a leading authority. One sees, too, progress in the development of a technique which had been notably advanced even before James by George Eliot in England and Gustave Flaubert in France—the technique of making new psychological insights a vital part of fiction.

How James' notions led him to shape the form of a narrative is shown in some of the details in his 1907 Preface to *Roderick Hudson* (1876), wherein he told how that book had been written. After a "story idea" had come to him, the chief difficulty, he suggested, was to decide exactly how to limit "developments" so as to interrelate them. "Up to what point," he asked himself, "is such and such a development *indispensable* to interest? . . . When, for the complete expression of one's subject, does a particular relation stop—giving way to some other not concerned in that expression?" The complexity of experience made this problem difficult: "Really, universally, relations stop nowhere, and the exquisite problem of the artist is eternally but to draw, by a geometry of his own, the circle within which they shall happily *appear* to do so." Selection and arrangement therefore were absolutely necessary. He needed to hit upon exactly the right details of background; he needed (though later he felt he had failed, in this particular book) to devise an adequate time scheme; he needed—and this was very important—to find a "centre, the point of command of all the rest." In this story, such a center was the impression of the whole action received by someone other than Hudson.

> From this centre the subject has been treated, from this centre the interest has spread, and so, whatever else it may do or may not do, the thing has acknowledged a principle of composition and continues at least to hang together. . . . The centre of interest throughout . . . is Rowland Mallet's consciousness—which I had of course to make sufficiently acute to enable it, like a set and lighted scene, to hold the play.

James believed that what Mallet saw, felt, or guessed could, if properly rendered, be made to give the story unity, movement, and meaning. Though James gave details about a number of additional procedures, this summary traces a main line of his typical thought about his artistry.

An author with such concerns obviously was bound to write narratives which differed greatly from those by most of James' contemporaries. James, naturally, was horrified by what he saw as the formlessness of many fictional works. He believed, as he said in "The Art of Fiction," that ". . . a novel is a living thing, all one and continuous, like any other organism, and in proportion as it lives it will be found, I think, that in each of the parts is something of the other parts." And he learned that quite often his most useful step in achieving the selectivity and the arrangement necessary for such an organic entity was the location of the story in the mind of some character—a consciousness, like Rowland's, say, "connected intimately with the general human exposure, and thereby bedimmed and befooled and bewildered, anxious, restless, fallible," in short "not *too* acute," but endowed, nevertheless, "with such intelligence that the appearances reflected in it, and constituting together there the situation and the 'story,' should become by that fact

The kitchen set for the last act of Shore Acres—*from the Theatre Collection, The New York Public Library*

intelligible." Thus the sensitive author had, in the story, a sensitive counterpart whose limitations and perceptions both bounded and filled in the pattern. Working in such a fashion, James became a leader in calling attention to the importance of the "fictional point of view"—to the values to be derived from letting a narrative unfold as it was experienced by some character. Psychology thus became of central importance in his fiction, and its hither-to unexploited potentialities for writers were suggested to a great number of authors who followed James.

The Drama

In general, the period between the Civil War and 1914 was one of depression in the history of American drama. Hundreds of plays, to be sure, were produced, and many were admired; but few have proved to be worthy of memory. As Barrett Clark says of the plays of the period in *An Hour of American Drama:* "It is not the quaint-ness of the language and the labored style of these plays that has caused them to be forgotten, it is the funda-mental fact that they are the products of superficial writers, of men who could believe that 'plays are not written but rewritten,' an epigram appropriately attrib-uted to [such popular playwrights of the period as] Boucicault, Bronson Howard, Augustin Daly, Augustus Thomas, and a dozen other able playmakers. The kind of plays these men wrote were indeed rewritten: they

had to be. But here 'rewritten' means picked apart, built up, 'lifted,' like a dowager's face, put on a diet, painted, and rouged." During this comparatively arid period, pro-ductive chiefly of melodramas and slick plays cunningly designed to lure cash customers, there were three tenden-cies of some significance, each comparable to some con-temporary development in fiction: toward realism, toward the more intelligent consideration of serious problems, and toward symbolism.

Hamlin Garland, lecturing on "Local Color in Fiction and Drama," was able, so he said later, to consider quite a few playwrights who, like his favorite fiction writers, were moving toward realism via stage representations of the life and character of certain regions. Examples—typical, though in some ways superior—were Bronson Howard (1842-1908), who in *Shenandoah* (1888) vividly pictured the valley of the title as it had been during the war; James A. Herne (1839-1901), who made a noteworthy effort to draw true-to-life characters against a homely background in *Margaret Fleming* (1890) and *Shore Acres* (1892); and Augustus Thomas (1857-1934), who dramatized the life of varied sections in plays such as *Alabama* (1891), *In Mizzouri* (1893), *The Capitol* (1895), and *Arizona* (1899).

These same authors serve as well as others to show how the drama, like the novel of purpose, began to con-sider various problems. Here, Americans were particu-larly influenced by the Norwegian Henrik Ibsen (1828-1906), who became world-famous during this period as an author of problem plays. Herne's *Shore Acres* was much discussed not only because it was realistic but also because it contained references to advanced scientific and social ideas, and *Margaret Fleming* dealt with family relationships in a fashion then considered quite daring. Bronson Howard's *The Henrietta* (1887) satirized the fever and the greed of financial and social life. And Thomas treated pseudo-scientific topics such as hypnotism, psychological domination, and mental healing in plays including *The Witching Hour* (1907) and *As a Man Thinks* (1911).

Toward the end of the period, many critics of the day found in Clyde Fitch (1865-1909) a man who could fuse sincerity and artistry with good theater. Fitch's creed, as he expressed it in "The Play and the Public," sounded like one of the definitions of realism then current in writings about fiction:

> In the modern play, I feel myself very strongly the particular value—a value I can't help feeling inestimable—of reflecting absolutely and truthfully the life and environment about us. Be truthful, and then nothing can be too big, nothing should be too small, so long as it is here, and there. Every class, every kind, every emotion, every motive, every occupation, every business, every idleness. . . . Apart from the question of literalism, apart from the question of art, reflect the real thing with true observation and with sincere feeling for what it is and what it represents, and that is art and literature.

Fitch tried to follow this formula in a varied group of plays, dramas which not only tried to be "true to life" but which also commented upon various problems. *The Climbers* (1901) and *The City* (1909) were serious portrayals of various aspects—political, financial, and social—of New York life. *The Girl with the Green Eyes* (1902) and *The Truth* (1907) were interesting psychological studies, the first of a character abnormally jealous, the second of a congenital liar. The feeling of a reader today is likely to be that these plays have fine stuff in them—as fine as anything to be found in the theater of the era—but that they suffer because Fitch, like other dramatists, had to shape his work to make it appeal to theatergoers who were a little too fond of broad effects.

Two authors were ranked with Fitch, or even above him: Langdon Mitchell and William Vaughn Moody. In *The New York Idea* (1906), Mitchell, active contemporaneously with Fitch, showed rather more of a tendency to deal with problems than a tendency toward realism. Nevertheless, since this drama, like Royall Tyler's *The Contrast* and a host of other plays, was a social comedy, it was essentially realistic in a good many of its details. And its deft construction and witty dialogue made it more memorable than many dramas of its day which were heavily serious.

William Vaughn Moody, a poet and a professor, started his career as a "practical dramatist" after having written poetic dramas which were profound in their ideas and impressive as poetry, but which had no chance of professional presentation. When he tried his hand at writing plays which might be produced, his very aloofness from the commercial theater helped him avoid some of its bad tendencies. As Walter Prichard Eaton remarks in *The Drama in English:* "The superficial traits of modern drama meant little to him, one way or the other. It was its deeper spirit he was after." Having such an attitude, and having, moreover, a real flair for dramatizing the psychologies of characters and for representing ideas by action, he wrote for the stage *The Great Divide,* a surprisingly successful play. This drama had in it, to be sure, elements of sensationalism and melodrama; but these were means to an end rather than ends themselves. Actually *The Great Divide* was a symbolic representation of the conflict between the Puritanical tradition of New England on the one hand and, on the other, the frontier's impulsive gusto for life. It showed the approach of a poet. "Poetry," Moody believed, "is the salvation of the stage. . . . It is the poetry in a play that makes it great." A play written in such a spirit, although in retrospect it might seem a bit crude, pointed to a better period in the American theater. As Mr. Eaton asserts, "With a play like this the modern drama in America was coming of age." It was not to come fully of age, however, until after 1914. The greatest achievements of the era between the Civil War and World War I were decidedly not in drama or (except in a few instances) in poetry, but in fiction.

W. B.

Chronological Table
of Literature and History

1866 Whittier's **Snow-Bound** • Charles H. Smith's **Bill Arp, So Called** • John W. DeForest's **Miss Ravenel's Conversion**
Civil Rights Bill passed, designed to assure equal treatment of Southern Negroes • Ku Klux Klan organized

1867 Henry Timrod's "Ode" • George W. Harris' **Sut Lovingood Yarns** • Lowell's **The Biglow Papers, Second Series** • Bret Harte's **Condensed Novels**
Alaska purchased from Russia • Nebraska admitted as the thirty-seventh state • Reconstruction Act passed, providing conditions of the return of the Confederate States to the Union

1868 **The Overland Monthly** (1868-1933) established in California • Harte's "The Luck of Roaring Camp" Fourteenth Amendment, guaranteeing fair trial for all persons, ratified • President Johnson impeached, acquitted • Ulysses S. Grant elected eighteenth President

1869 Harte's "Tennessee's Partner," "The Outcasts of Poker Flat" • Mark Twain's **The Innocents Abroad** Fifteenth Amendment, ensuring Negro suffrage, ratified • Union Pacific Railway completed first transcontinental line, 10 May • "Black Friday" in New York, caused by gold corner, 24 September • Opening of the Suez Canal, 15 November

1870 Lowell's **Among My Books** • Bronson Howard's **Saratoga** • Harte's "Plain Language from Truthful James" • Joaquin Miller's **Songs of the Sierras** • Emerson's **Society and Solitude**
United States census: population 38,558,371

1871 Edward Eggleston's **The Hoosier Schoolmaster** • Walt Whitman's **Democratic Vistas** • Harriet Beecher Stowe's **Oldtown Fireside Stories**

1872 Mark Twain's **Roughing It** • Holmes' **The Poet at the Breakfast-Table** • William D. Howells' **Their Wedding Journey**
Grant reëlected

1873 Mark Twain and Charles Dudley Warner's **The Gilded Age** • Howells' **A Chance Acquaintance**
Financial panic began, 19 September

1875 Sidney Lanier's "Corn," "The Symphony" • Howells' **A Foregone Conclusion** • Mary Baker Eddy's **Science and Health**

1876 Twain's **The Adventures of Tom Sawyer** • Henry James' **Roderick Hudson**
Rutherford B. Hayes elected nineteenth President Colorado admitted as the thirty-eighth state

1877 James' **The American** • Lanier's **Poems** • Sarah Orne Jewett's **Deephaven**

1878 James' **Daisy Miller** • Lanier's "The Marshes of Glynn," "The Revenge of Hamish"

1879 James' **Hawthorne** • George W. Cable's **Old Creole Days** • James A. Herne's **Hearts of Oak** • Frank R. Stockton's **Rudder Grange** • Howells' **The Lady of the Aroostook** • Henry George's **Progress and Poverty**

1880 Twain's **A Tramp Abroad** • Henry Adams' **Democracy** • Lew Wallace's **Ben Hur** • Lanier's **The Science of English Verse** • Joel Chandler Harris' **Uncle Remus: His Songs and Sayings** • Steele MacKaye's **Hazel Kirke**

United States census: population 50,155,783 • James A. Garfield elected twentieth President

1881 James' **The Portrait of a Lady**
Garfield shot, 2 July; died, 19 September; succeeded by Chester A. Arthur as twenty-first President • Tuskegee Institute founded • Federation of Organized Trades and Labor Unions, forerunner of the American Federation of Labor, founded

1882 Stockton's "The Lady or the Tiger?" • Twain's **The Prince and the Pauper** • Howells' **A Modern Instance**

1883 Edgar Watson Howe's **The Story of a Country Town** • Harris' **Nights with Uncle Remus** • Twain's **Life on the Mississippi**

1884 Twain's **Huckleberry Finn** • Lanier's **Poems** • Mary Noailles Murfree's **In the Tennessee Mountains** • Lowell's "Democracy" • Helen Hunt Jackson's **Ramona**
Grover Cleveland elected twenty-second President

1885 Murfree's **The Prophet of the Great Smoky Mountains** • Howells' **The Rise of Silas Lapham**

1886 James' **The Princess Casamassima**
Haymarket Riot in Chicago turned public opinion against labor organizations • American Federation of Labor organized under the leadership of Samuel Gompers

1887 Harold Frederic's **Seth's Brother's Wife** • Joseph Kirkland's **Zury** • Mary E. Wilkins Freeman's **A Humble Romance** • Thomas Nelson Page's **In Ole Virginia**

1888 Edward Bellamy's **Looking Backward** • Howard's **Shenandoah** • Whitman's **November Boughs** and **Complete Poems and Prose** (1888-1889)
Benjamin Harrison elected twenty-third President

1889 Twain's **A Connecticut Yankee**
North Dakota and South Dakota admitted as thirty-ninth and fortieth states, Montana as forty-first, Washington as forty-second

1890 Emily Dickinson's **Poems** • James' **The Tragic Muse** • Howells' **A Hazard of New Fortunes**
United States census: population 62,979,766 • Sherman Anti-Trust Act • Idaho admitted as forty-third state, Wyoming as forty-fourth

1891 Hamlin Garland's **Main-Travelled Roads** • Howells' **Criticism and Fiction** • Freeman's **A New England Nun and Other Stories** • Ambrose Bierce's **Tales of Soldiers and Civilians**

1892 Herne's **Shore Acres**
Grover Cleveland reëlected

1893 Frederick J. Turner's "The Significance of the Frontier in American History" • Stephen Crane's **Maggie: A Girl of the Streets**

1894 Twain's **Pudd'nhead Wilson** • James Lane Allen's **A Kentucky Cardinal** • Howells' **A Traveler from Altruria**
Pullman strike; widespread sympathetic strikes called by American Railway Union; Federal troops called out and Sherman Anti-Trust Act invoked in settlement of Pullman dispute

1895 Crane's **The Black Riders, and Other Lines** and **The Red Badge of Courage** • Garland's **Rose of Dutcher's Coolly**

1896 Jewett's **The Country of the Pointed Firs** • Edwin A. Robinson's **The Torrent and the Night Before** • Twain's **Joan of Arc** • Frederic's **The Damnation of Theron Ware**
William McKinley elected twenty-fifth President

1897 Henry James' **What Maisie Knew** and **The Spoils of Poynton** • Robinson's **The Children of the Night** • William James' **The Will to Believe** • Twain's **Following the Equator**

1898 Crane's "The Open Boat" • Finley Peter Dunne's **Mr. Dooley in Peace and in War** • Henry James' **The Turn of the Screw**
Destruction of the battleship **Maine** precipitated Spanish-American War, which resulted in United States' acquisition of Puerto Rico, Guam, and the Philippines

1899   Frank Norris' **McTeague** • James' **The Awkward Age** • Crane's **War Is Kind** and **The Monster and Other Stories** • Dunne's **Mr. Dooley in the Hearts of His Countrymen** • Edwin Markham's "The Man with the Hoe" • Thorstein Veblen's **The Theory of the Leisure Class**

1900   Theodore Dreiser's **Sister Carrie** • Crane's **Whilomville Stories** • Howells' **Literary Friends and Acquaintance** • Ellen Glasgow's **The Voice of the People** • William V. Moody's "An Ode in Time of Hesitation"
United States census: population 76,303,387 • President McKinley reëlected

1901   Norris' **The Octopus** • Moody's **Poems** • Clyde Fitch's **The Climbers** • Booker T. Washington's **Up from Slavery**
McKinley shot, 6 September; died, 14 September; succeeded by Theodore Roosevelt as twenty-sixth President

1902   Robinson's **Captain Craig** • Owen Wister's **The Virginian** • James' **The Wings of the Dove** • Fitch's **Girl with the Green Eyes** • Glasgow's **The Battleground** • Edith Wharton's **The Valley of Decision**

1903   Norris' **The Pit** • James' **The Ambassadors** • Jack London's **The Call of the Wild**

1904   Lincoln Steffens' **The Shame of the Cities** • Ida Tarbell's **History of the Standard Oil Company** • Paul Elmer More's **Shelburne Essays** (1904-1935) • Adams' **Mont-Saint-Michel and Chartres** • O. Henry's **Cabbages and Kings** • James' **The Golden Bowl**
Theodore Roosevelt elected President

1905   Howells' **The Kentons** • Wharton's **The House of Mirth** • David Belasco's **The Girl of the Golden West**

1906   Adams' **The Education of Henry Adams** • Upton Sinclair's **The Jungle** • Langdon E. Mitchell's **The New York Idea** • Moody's **The Great Divide** • O. Henry's **The Four Million**

1907   Augustus Thomas' **The Witching Hour**

1908   William Howard Taft elected twenty-seventh President

1909   William Allen White's **A Certain Rich Man** • Gertrude Stein's **Three Lives** • Moody's **The Faith Healer** • Percy MacKaye's **The Scarecrow**

1910   Robinson's **The Town Down the River** • John A. Lomax' **Cowboy Songs** • Irving Babbitt's **The New Laokoön**
United States census: population 93,402,151

1911   Dreiser's **Jennie Gerhardt** • Wharton's **Ethan Frome**

1912   Dreiser's **The Financier** • Amy Lowell's **A Dome of Many-Coloured Glass** • Robinson Jeffers' **Flagons and Apples** • **Poetry: A Magazine of Verse** founded
Woodrow Wilson elected twenty-eighth President • New Mexico admitted as forty-seventh state, Arizona as forty-eighth

1913   Robert Frost's **A Boy's Will** • Vachel Lindsay's **General William Booth Enters into Heaven and Other Poems** • Willa Cather's **O Pioneers!**
Sixteenth (income tax) and Seventeenth (direct senatorial election) Amendments ratified

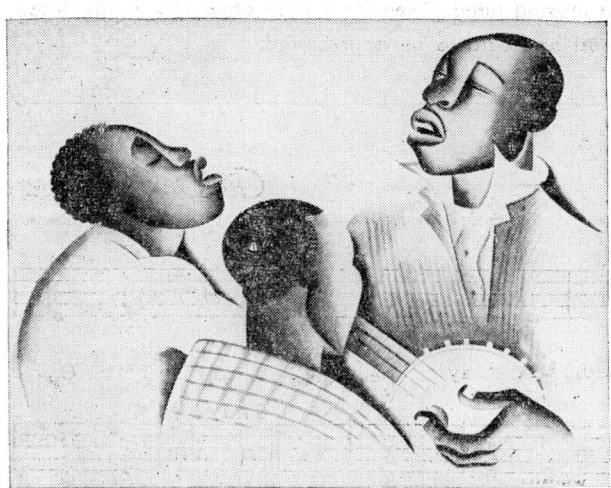

The many ways of living in America between the Civil War and 1914 influenced various makers of folk songs. Groups had their own individual favorites, and they kept these anonymous creations alive by singing them again and again. Since the forms of these works were not frozen in print, what typically happens to folk songs happened to them: words or even lines were changed, and sometimes whole stanzas disappeared. Early settlers had brought to America a number of Scotch and English ballads which were still being sung and admired by their descendants. The American songs had many qualities of these older ballads: intriguing uses of incremental repetitions and refrains, dramatic ways of unfolding happenings, ways of leaping over some details and of presenting others with minute care.

Whittier and Bryant, among the famous literary men, and four or five scholars were about the only Americans who paid much heed to these American songs until the 1860's. But in the period following the war, and in the twentieth century the growing interest of Americans in our social and literary history caused many literary men and scholars to become active as students of the folklore.

Illustration: by Miguel Covarrubias from A Treasury of the Blues, ed. W. C. Handy with Abbe Niles, 1949, published by Charles Boni
J. A. Lomax and Alan Lomax, American Ballads and Folk Songs, New York, 1934 • Louise Pound, American Ballads and Songs, New York, 1922 • Carl Sandburg, The American Songbag, New York, 1930 • F. H. Hubbard, Railroad Avenue, New York, 1945 • (In addition to these books, a number of recordings of folk songs will be of great value—those made by such singers as Burl Ives, Paul Robeson, Marian Anderson, Carl Sandburg, and John Jacob Niles, as well as the recordings of nonprofessional folk singers issued by the Archive of American Folk Song of the Library of Congress)

Spirituals

The Negroes were the makers of the spirituals—religious songs which, as a rule, translated Biblical tales or Christian sentiments into the idiom of the race. Details about the origins of the songs are not known, but two things seem likely: that the camp meetings of Southern whites in pre-Civil War days suggested both words and ways of singing, and that both the sense of rhythm and the racial experiences of the Negroes molded the songs. Unable to express their feelings directly, the Negroes often interpreted their own experiences in Biblical stories and lyrics.

"Go Down, Moses," for example—used as Harriet Tubman's signal of safety as she, a former slave, helped many other Negroes escape to freedom—translated the bondage of Israel into a parallel of their own enslavement. Hundreds of spirituals were composed, and most of them have noble themes simply and sincerely developed and fitted to moving tunes. Even more than other folk songs, these must be heard to be appreciated.

Go Down, Moses

When Is - rael was in E - gypt's land, Let my peo - ple go! Op-press'd so hard dev could not stand, Let my peo - ple go! Go down, Mo - ses, Way down in E-gypt's land; Tell old Pha - roah ___ Let my peo - ple go!

When Israel was in Egypt's land,
    Let my people go!
Oppress'd so hard dey could not stand,
    Let my people go!

Chorus
    Go down, Moses,
        Way down in Egypt's land.
    Tell ole Pha-roah,
        Let my people go!

Thus say de Lawd, bold Moses said,
    Let my people go!
If not I'll smite your first-born dead,
    Let my people go!

No more shall dey in bondage toil,
    Let my people go!
Let dem come out wid Egypt's spoil,
    Let my people go!

Lay Dis Body Down

I know moon-rise, I know star-rise,
    Lay dis body down;
I walk in de moonlight, I walk in de starlight,
    To lay dis body down.

I walk in de graveyard, I walk troo de graveyard,
    To lay dis body down.

I'll lie in de grass and stretch out my arms—
    Lay dis body down.

I go to de judgment in de evenin' of de day,
    When I lay dis body down;
And my soul and your soul will meet in de day
    When I lay dis body down.

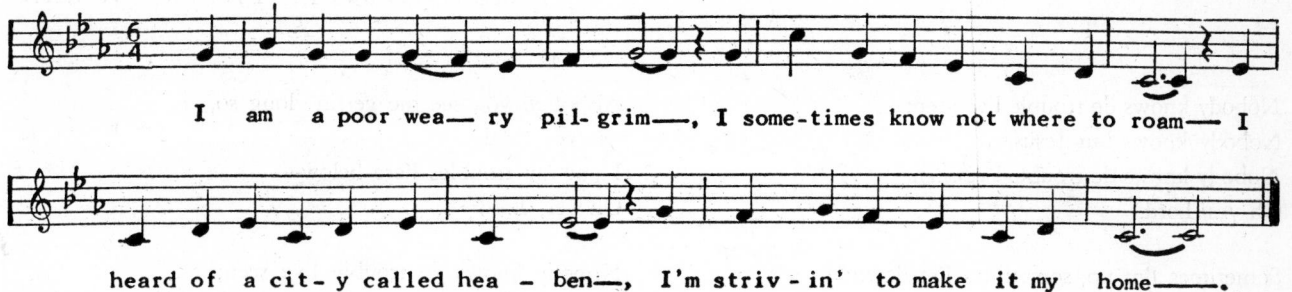

I am a poor wea— ry pil- grim—, I some-times know not where to roam— I

heard of a cit- y called hea – ben—, I'm striv- in' to make it my home——.

I am a poor weary pilgrim,
    I sometimes know not where to roam—
I heard of a city called heaben,
    I'm strivin' to make it my home.

Sometimes I'm both tossed and driven,
    I sometimes know not where to roam,

I heard of a city called heaben,
    I'm strivin' to make it my home.

My friends and relations forsake me,
    And troubles roll round me so high,   10
I thought ob de kind voice of Jesus
    Sayin' "Poor pilgrim, I'm always nigh."

Joshua Fit de Battle ob Jerico

Joshua fit de battle ob Jerico—Jerico—Jerico—
Joshua fit de battle ob Jerico,
And de walls came a-tumblin' down.

"Good mornin', Brudder Pilgrim,
Pray tell me where you boun';
O tell me where you travelin' to
'Cause dis enchanted groun'."

"My name it is Poor Pilgrim,
To Canaan I am boun';
Travelin' through dis wilderness   10
'Cause dis enchanted groun'."

You may talk about yo' King ob Gideon,
You may talk about yo' man ob Saul,

Dere's none like good ole Joshua,
At de battle ob Jerico.

Up to de walls ob Jerico
He marched wid spear in han',
"Go blow dem ram horns," Joshua cried,
"Kase de battle am in my han'."

Den de lam' ram sheep-horns begin to blow,   20
Trumpets begin to soun',
Joshua commanded de chillun to shout,
An' de walls came a-tumblin' down.

Dat mornin'—
Joshua fit de battle ob Jerico—Jerico—Jerico,
Joshua fit de battle ob Jerico,
An' de walls came a-tumblin' down.

Nobody knows de trouble I've seen;
Nobody knows but Jesus.
Nobody knows de trouble I've seen;
Oh yes, Lord.

Sometimes I'm up, sometimes I'm down:
Oh yes, Lord.
Sometimes I'm almost to de groun',
Oh yes, Lord.

Although you see me gettin' 'long so,
Oh, yes, Lord.
I got my troubles here below—
Oh yes, Lord.

10

Nobody knows de trouble I've seen;
Nobody knows but Jesus.
Nobody knows de trouble I've seen;
Oh yes, Lord.

Cowboy Songs

Rich in ballad lore, the cowboys of the plains in some of their songs told of the work of the cowboy—caring for cattle in the wintertime, rounding them up in the spring, driving them up the trail to market. Many songs were used for practical purposes, to stir up the cattle or to quiet them when they were nervous at night. Others told stories of adventures or of love affairs, and the old stuff of balladry took on new coloring because of the way men lived in the cow country. Since many of the cowhands came from the Southern uplands, where old British ballads were preserved by singing, many cowboy tunes are reminiscent of the older ones. But since Americans had developed tunes of a different sort, several mutations—

modifications of the older tunes—were frequent. "Oh Bury Me Not on the Lone Prairie" offers an example of such a modified old melody, in this case a parody of a sentimental ballad entitled "The Ocean Burial." The simple guitar accompaniment to many of these songs accentuates the distinctive rhythm of cowboy ballads.

Of the songs that follow, "Whoopee Ti Yi Yo" tells of the spring roundup; "Good-by, Old Paint" is addressed to a good pony; "The Old Chisholm Trail" recounts the hardships of a drive up the trail; "Sam Bass" unfolds the history of a Western bad man; and "Blood on the Saddle" tells of the gory death of a cowboy killed when a bronco rolled on him in a rodeo.

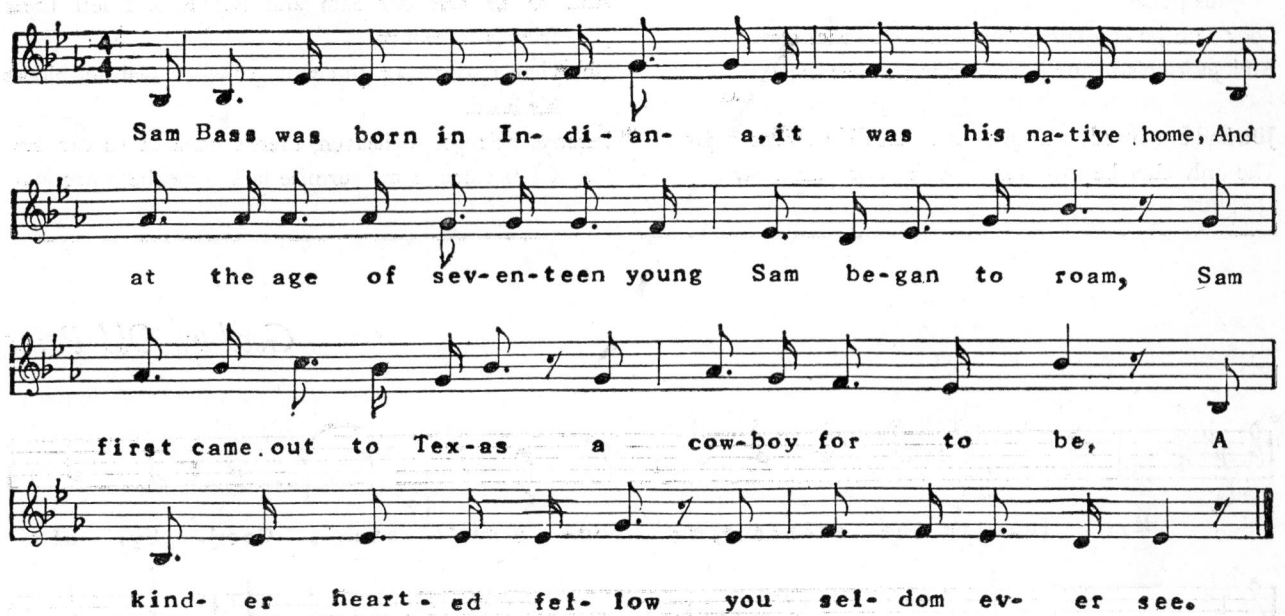

Sam Bass was born in In- di- an- a, it was his na- tive home, And

at the age of sev- en- teen young Sam be- gan to roam, Sam

first came out to Tex- as a cow- boy for to be, A

kind- er heart- ed fel- low you sel- dom ev- er see.

Sam Bass was born in Indiana, it was his native home,
And at the age of seventeen young Sam began to roam,
Sam first came out to Texas a cowboy for to be,—
A kinder-hearted fellow you seldom ever see.

Sam used to deal in race stock, one called the Denton
    mare,
He matched her in scrub races, and took her to the fair.
Sam used to coin the money and spent it just as free,
He always drank good whiskey wherever he might be.

Sam left the Collins ranch in the merry month of May
With a herd of Texas cattle the Black Hills
        for to see,   10
Sold out in Custer City and then got on a spree,—
A harder set of cowboys you seldom ever see.

On their way back to Texas they robbed the U.P. train,
And then split up in couples and started out again.
Joe Collins and his partner were overtaken soon,
With all their hard-earned money they had to meet
        their doom.

Sam made it back to Texas all right side up with care;
Rode into the town of Denton with all his friends to
        share.
Sam's life was short in Texas; three robberies did he do,
He robbed all the passenger, mail, and express
        cars too.   20

Sam had four companions—four bold and daring lads—
They were Richardson, Jackson, Joe Collins, and Old Dad;
Four more bold and daring cowboys the rangers never
        knew,
They whipped the Texas rangers and ran the boys in blue.

Sam had another companion, called Arkansas for short,
Was shot by a Texas ranger by the name of Thomas
        Floyd;
Oh, Tom is a big six-footer and thinks he's mighty fly,
But I can tell you his racket,—he's a deadbeat on the sly.

Jim Murphy was arrested, and then released on bail;
He jumped his bond at Tyler and took the train for
        Terrell;   30

But Mayor Jones had posted Jim and that was all a stall,
'Twas only a plan to capture Sam before the coming fall.

Sam met his fate at Round Rock, July the twenty-first,
They pierced poor Sam with rifle balls and then emptied
    his purse.
Poor Sam he is a corpse and six foot under clay,
And Jackson's in the bushes trying to get away.

Jim had borrowed Sam's good gold and didn't want to pay,
The only shot he saw was to give poor Sam away.

He sold out Sam and Barnes and left their friends to
    mourn,—
Oh, what a scorching Jim will get when Gabriel blows
    his horn.
               40

And so he sold out Sam and Barnes and left their
    friends to mourn,
Oh, what a scorching Jim will get when Gabriel blows
    his horn.
Perhaps he's got to heaven, there's none of us can say,
But if I'm right in my surmise he's gone the other way.

Good-by, Old Paint

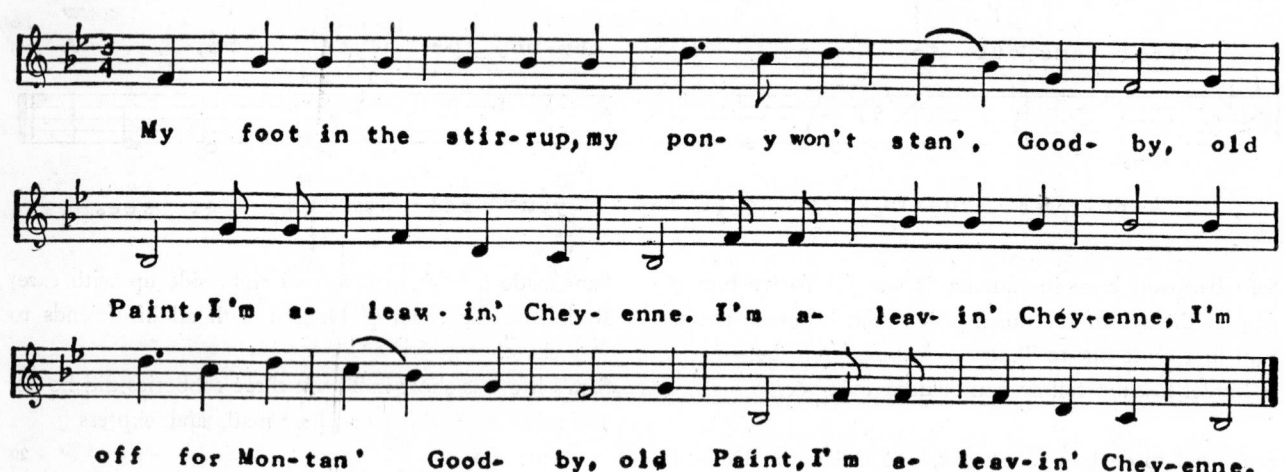

My foot in the stir-rup, my pon-y won't stan', Good-by, old Paint, I'm a-leav-in' Chey-enne. I'm a-leav-in' Chéy-enne, I'm off for Mon-tan' Good-by, old Paint, I'm a-leav-in' Chey-enne.

My foot in the stirrup, my pony won't stan',
Good-by, old Paint, I'm a-leavin' Cheyenne.
I'm a-leavin' Cheyenne, I'm off for Montan';
Good-by, old Paint, I'm a-leavin' Cheyenne.

I'm a-ridin' old Paint, I'm a-leadin' old Dan;
Good-by, old Paint, I'm a-leavin' Cheyenne.
With my feet in the stirrups, my bridle in my hand;
Good-by, old Paint, I'm a-leavin' Cheyenne.

Old Paint's a good pony, he paces when he can;
Good-by, little Annie, I'm off for Cheyenne.   10
Oh, hitch up your horses and feed 'em some hay,
And seat yourself by me as long as you stay.

My hosses ain't hungry, they won't eat your hay;
My wagon is loaded and rollin' away.
I'm a-ridin', old Paint, I'm a-leadin' old Dan,
I'm a-goin' to Montan' to throw the hoolihan.

They feed in the coulees, they water in the draw,
Their tails are all matted, their backs are all raw.
Old Bill Jones had two daughters and a song;
One went to Denver, the other went wrong.   20

Good-by, Old Paint • 2 Paint is a corruption of pinto, meaning a
piebald or mottled pony • 16 **throw the hoolihan,** to knock a steer
down by leaping on his horns

His wife died in a pool-room fight,
And still he sings from morning till night.
I'm a rambler and a gambler and far from my home,
And those that don't like me can leave me alone.

Oh, whiskey and beer, they are nothing to me,
They killed my old Dad, now they can try me.

I'll tell you the truth, not lyin' or jokin',
I'd rather be in jail than to be heart-broken.

Oh, when I die take my saddle from the wall,
Put it on my pony, lead him from the stall,
Tie my bones to his back, turn our faces to the west,
And we'll ride the prairie that we love the best.

30

Whoopee Ti Yi Yo, Git Along, Little Dogies

As I was a-walking one morning for pleasure, I
spied a cow-punch-er a-rid-ing a-long; His hat was throwed back and his
spurs were a-jin-glin', As he ap-proached me a-sing-in' this song:

Chorus
Whoopee ti yi yo,___ git a-long,___ lit-tle do-gies, It's
your mis-for-tune and none of my own; Whoopee ti yi yo,___ git a-
long,___ lit-tle do-gies, For you know___ Wy-o-ming will be your new home.

As I was a-walking one morning for pleasure,
I spied a cow-puncher a-riding along;
His hat was throwed back and his spurs were a-jin-glin',
As he approached me a-singin' this song:

Chorus

Whoopee ti yi yo, git along, little dogies,
It's your misfortune and none of my own;
Whoopee ti yi yo, git along, little dogies,
For you know Wyoming will be your new home.

Early in the springtime we'll round up the dogies,
Slap on their brands, and bob off their tails; 10
Round up our horses, load up the chuck wagon,
Then throw those dogies upon the trail.

It's whooping and yelling and driving the dogies,
Oh, how I wish you would go on;
It's whooping and punching and go on, little dogies,
For you know Wyoming will be your new home.

Some of the boys goes up the trail for pleasure,
But that's where they git it most awfully wrong;
For you haven't any idea the trouble they give us
When we go driving them dogies along. 20

When the night comes on and we hold them on the
    bed-ground,
These little dogies that roll on so slow;
Roll up the herd and cut out the strays,
And roll the little dogies that never rolled before.

Your mother she was raised way down in Texas,
Where the jimson weed and sand-burrs grow;
Now we'll fill you up on prickly pear and cholla
Till you are ready for the trail to Idaho.

Oh, you'll be soup for Uncle Sam's Injuns;
"It's beef, heap beef," I hear them cry. 30
Git along, git along, git along, little dogies,
You're going to be beef steers by and by.

The Old Chisholm Trail

Come along, boys, and listen to my tale,
I'll tell you of my troubles on the old Chisholm trail.

Chorus
> Come ti yi youpy, youpy yea, youpy yea,
> Coma ti yi youpy, youpy yea.

I started up the trail October twenty-third,
I started up the trail with the 2-U herd.

Oh, a ten-dollar hoss and a forty-dollar saddle,
And I'm goin' to punchin' Texas cattle.

I woke up one morning on the old Chisholm trail,
Rope in my hand and a cow by the tail. 10

I'm up in the mornin' afore daylight
And afore I sleep the moon shines bright.

My hoss throwed me off at the creek called Mud,
My hoss throwed me off round the 2-U herd.

Last time I saw him he was going 'cross the level
A-kicking up his heels and a-running like the devil.

It's cloudy in the west, a-looking like rain,
And my damned old slicker's in the wagon again.

No chaps, no slicker, and it's pouring down rain,
And I swear, by God, I'll never night-herd again. 20

Last night I was on guard and the leader broke the
    ranks,
I hit my horse down the shoulders and I spurred him
    in the flanks.

The wind commenced to blow, and the rain began to
    fall,
Hit looked, by grab, like we was goin' to lose 'em all.

My slicker's in the wagon and I'm gittin' mighty cold,
And these longhorn sons-o'-guns are gittin' hard to hold.

Saddle up, boys, and saddle up well,
For I think these cattle have scattered to hell.

With my blanket and my gun and my rawhide rope,
I'm a-slidin' down the trail in a long, keen lope. 30

I don't give a damn if they never do stop;
I'll ride as long as an eight-day clock.

We rounded 'em up and put 'em on the cars,
And that was the last of the old Two Bars.

Oh, it's bacon and beans most every day—
I'd as soon be a-eatin' prairie hay.

I went to the boss to draw my roll,
He had it figgered out I was nine dollars in the hole.

I'll sell my outfit just as soon as I can,
I won't punch cattle for no damned man.   40

With my knees in the saddle and my seat in the sky,
I'll quit punching cows in the sweet by-and-by.

Fare you well, old trail-boss, I don't wish you any harm,
I'm quittin' this business to go on the farm.

Blood on the Saddle

There was bul-lud on the saddle—
And bul-lud all araound,
An' a great big puddle
Of bul-lud on the graound.

Oh, a cowboy lay in it,
All covered with gore,
An' he never will ride on
Any broncos no more.

Oh, pity the cowboy,
All bul-luddy and red;   10

Oh, a bronco fell on him,
An' mashed in his head.

There was bul-lud on the saddle—
And bul-lud all araound,
An' a great big puddle
Of bul-lud on the graound.

---

1 **bul-lud,** the lingering pronunciation of "blood." The ballad mocks the distressing but widespread habit of savoring sanguinary details in an accident

---

On the Railroad

For city and country people alike, in the days before widespread automobile travel, the railroads were routes to adventure, lines of communication with the rest of the world. In a small town the most exciting daily event was the arrival of the limited. Among the people along the tracks there was much railroad lore, and naturally the hobos, the construction gangs, and the roundhouse workers had their own songs. In **American Ballads and** d by John A. Lomax and Alan Lomax, "Working on the Railroad" included ... songs. Some of these are "Steel Laying Holler," "Tie Tamping Chant," and "The Wreck of the C. & O." The first song given here celebrates a mythically strong Negro steel-driving man, and "Casey Jones" tells the story of an engineer who was brave but had a fickle helpmate.

John Henry

John Henry was a li'l baby, uh-huh,
Sittin' on his mama's knee, oh, yeah,
Said: "De Big Bend Tunnel on de C. & O. road
Gonna cause de death of me,
Lawd, Lawd, gonna cause de death of me."

John Henry, he had a woman,
Her name was Mary Magdalene,
She would go to de tunnel and sing for John,
Jes' to hear John Henry's hammer ring,
Lawd, Lawd, jes' to hear John Henry's hammer ring.   10

John Henry had a li'l woman,
Her name was Lucy Ann,
John Henry took sick an' had to go to bed,
Lucy Ann drove steel like a man,
Lawd, Lawd, Lucy Ann drove steel like a man.

Cap'n says to John Henry,
"Gonna bring me a steam drill 'round,
Gonna take dat steam drill out on de job,
Gonna whop dat steel on down,
Lawd, Lawd, gonna whop dat steel on down."   20

John Henry tol' his cap'n,
Lightnin' was in his eye:
"Cap'n, bet yo' las' red cent on me,
Fo' I'll beat it to de bottom or I'll die,
Lawd, Lawd, I'll beat it to de bottom or I'll die."

Sun shine hot an' burnin',
Wer'n't no breeze a-tall,
Sweat ran down like water down a hill,
Dat day John Henry let his hammer fall,
Lawd, Lawd, dat day John Henry let his hammer fall.   30

John Henry went to de tunnel,
An' dey put him in de lead to drive;
De rock so tall an' John Henry so small,
Dat he lied down his hammer an' he cried,
Lawd, Lawd, dat he lied down his hammer an' he cried.

John Henry started on de right hand,
De steam drill started on de lef'—
"Before I'd let dis steam drill beat me down,
I'd hammer my fool self to death,
Lawd, Lawd, I'd hammer my fool self to death."   40

White man tol' John Henry,
"Nigger, damn yo' soul,
You might beat dis steam an' drill of mine,
When de rocks in dis mountain turn to gol',
Lawd, Lawd, when de rocks in dis mountain turn to gol'."

John Henry said to his shaker,
"Nigger, why don' you sing?
I'm throwin' twelve poun's from my hips on down,
Jes' listen to de col' steel ring,
Lawd, Lawd, jes' listen to de col' steel ring."   50

Oh, de captain said to John Henry,
"I b'lieve this mountain's sinkin' in."
John Henry said to his captain, oh my!
"Ain' nothin' but my hammer suckin' win',
Lawd, Lawd, ain' nothin' but my hammer suckin' win'."

John Henry tol' his shaker,
"Shaker, you better pray,

3 **Big Bend Tunnel,** the largest tunnel on the Chesapeake and Ohio Railroad, constructed in West Virginia, 1870-1873   • 46 **shaker,** drill holder

For, if I miss dis six-foot steel,
Tomorrow'll be yo' buryin' day,
Lawd, Lawd, tomorrow'll be yo' buryin' day."   60

John Henry tol' his captain,
"Looka yonder what I see—
Yo' drill's done broke an' yo' hole's done choke,
An' you cain' drive steel like me,
Lawd, Lawd, an' you cain' drive steel like me."

De man dat invented de steam drill,
Thought he was mighty fine.
John Henry drove his fifteen feet,
An' de steam drill only made nine,
Lawd, Lawd, an' de steam drill only made nine.   70

De hammer dat John Henry swung,
It weighed over nine pound;
He broke a rib in his lef'-han' side,
An' his intrels fell on de groun',
Lawd, Lawd, an' his intrels fell on de groun'.

John Henry was hammerin' on de mountain,
An' his hammer was strikin' fire,
He drove so hard till he broke his pore heart,
An' he lied down his hammer an' he died,
Lawd, Lawd, he lied down his hammer an' he died.   80

All de womens in de Wes',
When dey heared of John Henry's death,
Stood in de rain, flagged de eas'-boun' train,

Goin' where John Henry fell dead,
Lawd, Lawd, goin' where John Henry fell dead.

John Henry's lil mother,
She was all dressed in red,
She jumped in bed, covered up her head,
Said she didn' know her son was dead,
Lawd, Lawd, didn' know her son was dead.   90

John Henry had a pretty lil woman,
An' de dress she wo' was blue,
An' de las' words she said to him:
"John Henry, I've been true to you,
Lawd, Lawd, John Henry, I've been true to you."

"Oh, who's gonna shoe yo' lil feetses,
An' who's gonna glub yo' han's,
An' who's gonna kiss yo' rosy, rosy lips,
An' who's gonna be yo' man,
Lawd, Lawd, an' who's gonna be yo' man?"   100

"Oh, my mama's gonna shoe my lil feetses,
An' my papa's gonna glub my lil han's,
An' my sister's gonna kiss my rosy, rosy lips,
An' I don' need no man,
Lawd, Lawd, an' I don' need no man."

Dey took John Henry to de graveyard,
An' dey buried him in de san',
An' every locomotive come roarin' by,
Says, "Dere lays a steel-drivin' man,
Lawd, Lawd, dere lays a steel-drivin' man."   110

Casey Jones

Come all you rounders if you want to hear
The story of a brave engineer.
Casey Jones was the rounder's name,
On the six-eight wheeler he won his fame.

The caller called Casey at half-past four;
He kissed his wife at the station door;
He mounted to the cabin with his orders in his hand,
And took a farewell trip to that promised land.

Chorus

    Casey Jones! Mounted to the cabin,
    Casey Jones! With his orders in his hand,   10
    Casey Jones! Mounted to the cabin
    And took that farewell trip to the promised land.

"Put in your water and shovel in your coal;
Put your head out the window, watch them drivers roll.
I'll run her till she leaves the rail,
'Cause I'm eight hours late with that western mail."

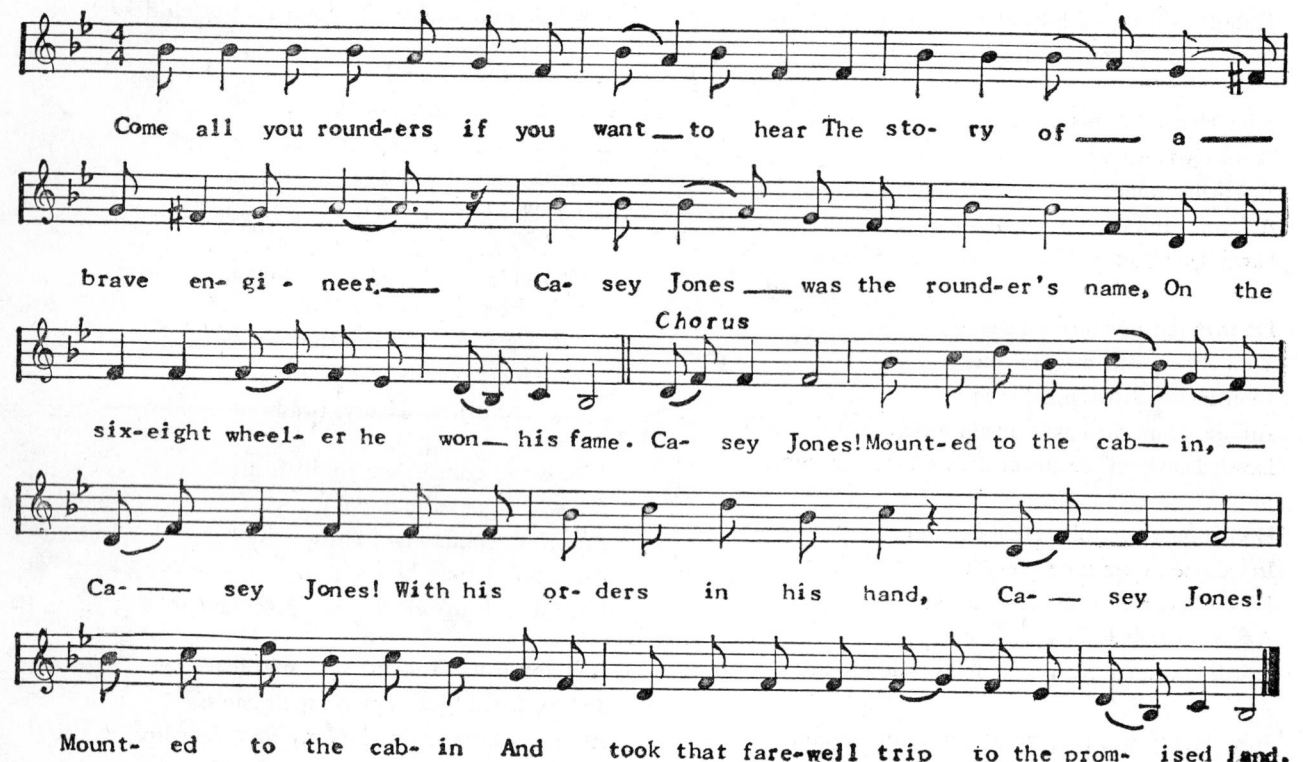

Come all you round-ers if you want to hear The sto-ry of a brave en-gi-neer. Ca-sey Jones was the round-er's name, On the six-eight wheel-er he won his fame.

Chorus

Ca-sey Jones! Mount-ed to the cab-in, Ca-sey Jones! With his or-ders in his hand, Ca-sey Jones! Mount-ed to the cab-in And took that fare-well trip to the prom-ised land.

He looked at his watch and his watch was slow;
He looked at the water and the water was low;
He turned to the fireman and then he said,
"We're going to reach Frisco, if we'll all be dead."   20

Chorus

    Casey Jones! Going to reach Frisco,
    Casey Jones! If we'll all be dead.
    Casey Jones! Going to reach Frisco,
    We're going to reach Frisco, but we'll all be dead.

Casey pulled up that Reno hill,
He tooted for the crossing; it was awful shrill.
The switchman knew by the engine's moans
That the man at the throttle was Casey Jones.

He pulled up within two miles of the place;
Number Four stared him right in the face;   30
Turned to the fireman, said, "Boy, you'd better jump,
'Cause there's two locomotives that's going to bump."

Chorus

    Casey Jones! Two locomotives!
    Casey Jones! That's a-going to bump!
    Casey Jones! Two locomotives!
    There's two locomotives that's a-going to bump.

Casey mumbled just before he died,
"There's two more railroads that I'd like to ride."
Fireman said, "What can they be?"
"The Southern Pacific and the Santa Fe."   40

Mrs. Jones sat on her bed a-sighing,
Just received a message that poor Casey was dying,
Said, "Go to bed, children, and hush your crying,
'Cause you got another papa on the Salt Lake Line."

Chorus

    Mrs. Casey Jones! Got another papa!
    Mrs. Casey Jones! On the Salt Lake Line!
    Mrs. Casey Jones! Got another papa!
    You've got another papa on the Salt Lake Line.

Hallelujah, I'm a Hobo

The hobos of the United States have contributed to American folk music several fine songs, ranging from the carefree "Hallelujah, Bum Again" and "We Are Four Bums" to the rather wistful "Wanderin'." Some of these songs were set to modifications of popular tunes and ballads. Others were mockingly sung to the music of the revival hymns which the hobos heard in mission shelters. Among these were "Hallelujah, Bum Again," which employs the tune of "Hallelujah, Thine the Glory," and "Pie in the Sky," which is based on "In the Sweet Bye and Bye."

In "The Big Rock Candy Mountain," an imaginative singer describes his vision of a far-off land where fine weather, abundant food and drink, and an absence of policemen combine to make a hobo's paradise.

The Big Rock Candy Mountain

One ev'ning as the sun went down
And the jungle fire was burning,
Down the track came a hobo, humming,
And he said, "Boys, I'm not turning.
I'm headed for a land that's far away,
Beside the crystal fountain.
I'll see you all this coming fall
On the Big Rock Candy Mountain."

Chorus

    In the Big Rock Candy Mountain,
    There's a land that's fair and bright,   10
    Where the handouts grow on bushes
    And you sleep out ev'ry night,
    Where the boxcars all are empty
    And the sun shines ev'ry day—
    Oh, the birds and the bees and the cigaret trees,
    The rock-and-rye springs where the whang-
        doodle sings,
    On the Big Rock Candy Mountain.

On the Big Rock Candy Mountain,
All the cops have wooden legs,
And the bulldogs all have rubber teeth,   20
And the hens lay softboiled eggs.
The farmers' trees are full of fruit,
And the barns are full of hay.
Oh, I'm bound to go where there ain't no snow,
Where the sleet don't fall and the wind don't blow,
On the Big Rock Candy Mountain.

On the Big Rock Candy Mountain,
You never change your socks,
And the little streams of alkyhol
Come trickling down the rocks.   30
The shacks all have to tip their hats
And the railroad bulls are blind,
There's a lake of stew and of whisky, too,
You can paddle all around in a big canoe,
On the Big Rock Candy Mountain.

On the Big Rock Candy Mountain,
The jails are made of tin,
And you can bust right out again
As soon as they put you in.
There ain't no shorthandled shovels,
No axes, saws or picks—

I'm a-going to stay where you sleep all day—
Oh, they boiled in oil the inventor of toil
On the Big Rock Candy Mountain.

40

Oh, come with me, and we'll go see
The Big Rock Candy Mountain.

In the Slums

Like many such songs, this one is sung in many versions and has an origin about which there is much dispute. One authority claims that the song originated as early as 1840, and another places it in 1850. In 1942, however, a Mrs. Frankie Baker claimed during the course of a suit that she was the original Frankie and that the incident upon which the song was founded had taken place in 1900. In spite of her claim, Mrs. Baker lost the suit when various scholars testified that "Frankie and Johnny" certain-ly had been sung before the end of the nineteenth century.

Regardless of its origin, this ballad about a tragedy in the Negro slums of St. Louis, by what it takes for granted and by what it casually mentions, reveals a notion of etiquette, a concept of elegance, and a moral code which represent a way of life. Note, for instance, Frankie's pious grief for the man she has murdered. The variations in the refrain are admirable examples of an old artistic device of the folk song.

Frankie and Johnny

Frank-ie and John-ny were lov-ers, O how that cou-ple could love. They swore to be true to each oth-er, true as the stars a-bove;___ He was ___ her man, but he done her wrong.

Frankie and Johnny were lovers, O, how that couple
    could love.
Swore to be true to each other, true as the stars above.
He was her man, but he done her wrong.

Frankie she was his woman, everybody knows.
She spent one hundred dollars for a suit of Johnny's
    clothes.
He was her man, but he done her wrong.

Frankie and Johnny went walking, Johnny in his bran'
    new suit,
"O good Lawd," says Frankie, "but don't my Johnny look
    cute?"
He was her man, but he done her wrong.

Frankie went down to Memphis; she went on the
    evening train.   10
She paid one hundred dollars for Johnny a watch and
    chain.
He was her man, but he done her wrong.

Frankie went down to the corner, to buy a glass of beer;
She says to the fat bartender, "Has my loving man been
    here?
He was my man, but he done me wrong."

"Ain't going to tell you no story, ain't going to tell you
    no lie,
I seen your man 'bout an hour ago with a girl named
    Alice Fry.
If he's your man, he's doing you wrong."

Frankie went back to the hotel, she didn't go there for fun,
Under her long red kimono she toted a forty-four gun.   20
He was her man, but he done her wrong.

Frankie went down to the hotel, looked in the window
    so high,
There was her lovin' Johnny a-lovin' up Alice Fry;
He was her man, but he done her wrong.

Frankie threw back her kimono; took out the old forty-
    four;
Roota-toot-toot, three times she shot, right through
    that hotel door.
She shot her man, 'cause he done her wrong.

Johnny grabbed off his Stetson. "O good Lawd, Frankie,
    don't shoot."
But Frankie put her finger on the trigger, and the gun
    went roota-toot-toot.
He was her man, but she shot him down.   30

"Roll me over easy, roll me over slow,
Roll me over easy, boys, 'cause my wounds are hurting
    me so,
I was her man, but I done her wrong."

With the first shot Johnny staggered; with the second
    shot he fell;
When the third bullet hit him, there was a new man's
    face in hell.
He was her man, but he done her wrong.

Frankie heard a rumbling away down under the ground.
Maybe it was Johnny where she had shot him down.
He was her man, and she done him wrong.

"Oh, bring on your rubber-tired hearses, bring on your
    rubber-tired hacks,   40
They're takin' my Johnny to the buryin' groun' but
    they'll never bring him back.
He was my man, but he done me wrong."

The judge he said to the jury, "It's plain as plain can be.
This woman shot her man, so it's murder in the second
    degree.
He was her man, though he done her wrong."

Now it wasn't murder in the second degree, it wasn't
    murder in the third.
Frankie simply dropped her man, like a hunter drops
    a bird.
He was her man, but he done her wrong.

"Oh, put me in that dungeon. Oh, put me in that cell.
Put me where the northeast wind blows from the south-
    east corner of hell.   50
I shot my man 'cause he done me wrong."

Frankie walked up to the scaffold, as calm as a girl
    could be,
She turned her eyes to heaven and said, "Good Lord, I'm
    coming to thee.
He was my man, and I done him wrong."

Homesteadin'

According to a Nebraskan, the following song was an adaptation by Emery Miller of a popular song—"The Little Old Log Cabin in the Lane"—written by one Will S. Hays. Miller was a Nebraska settler of the 1880's. "Early settlers," writes Carl Sandburg, "noticed log cabins were scarcer as timber land thinned out going further west.

On the windy, open prairies of the Great Plains, the best house to be had on short order was of sod. A cellar was dug first; long slices of turf were piled around the cellar lines; wooden crosspoles held the sod roof." This song is typical of several which jocosely and lugubriously lament the hardships of pioneer life. It is still current.

The Little Old Sod Shanty on the Claim

I am looking rather seedy now while holding down my
    claim,
And my victuals are not always of the best;
And the mice play shyly round me as I nestle down to
    rest,
In my little old sod shanty in the West.
Yet I rather like the novelty of living in this way,
Though my bill of fare is always rather tame,
But I'm happy as a clam on the land of Uncle Sam,
In my little old sod shanty on my claim.

Chorus
    The hinges are of leather and the windows have
        no glass,
    While the board roof lets the howling blizzards
        in,   10

    And I hear the hungry kiyote as he slinks up
        through the grass,
    Round my little old sod shanty on my claim.

O when I left my eastern home, a bachelor so gay,
To try and win my way to wealth and fame,
I little thought that I'd come down to burning twisted
    hay
In the little old sod shanty on my claim.
My clothes are plastered o'er with dough, I'm looking
    like a fright,
And everything is scattered round the room,
But I wouldn't give the freedom that I have out in
    the West
For the table of the Eastern man's old home.   20

I am look-ing rath-er seed-y now while hold-ing down my
Yet I rath-er like the no-vel-ty of liv-ing in this

claim, And my vict-uals are not al-ways of the best; And the
way, Though my bill of fare is al-ways rath-er tame, But I'm

mice play shy-ly round me as I nes-tle down to rest, In my
hap-py as a clam on the land of Un-cle Sam, In my

1.
lit-tle old sod shan-ty in the West.
2.
lit-tle old sod shan-ty on my claim.

Chorus

The hing-es are of leath-er and the win-dows have no glass, While the

board roof lets the howl-ing bliz-zards in, And I hear the hun-gry ki-yote as he

slinks up through the grass, Round my lit-tle old sod shan-ty on my claim.

Still I wish that some kind-hearted girl would pity on
me take,
And relieve me from the mess that I am in;
The angel, how I'd bless her if this her home she'd
make
In the little old sod shanty on my claim.
And we would make our fortunes on the prairies of the
West,
Just as happy as two lovers we'd remain;
We'd forget the trials and troubles we endured at the
first,
In the little old sod shanty on our claim.

And if kindly fate should bless us with now and then
an heir,
To cheer our hearts with honest pride of fame,
O then we'd be contented for the toil that we had
spent
In the little old sod shanty on our claim.
When time enough had lapsed and all of those little
brats
To noble man- and womanhood had grown,
It wouldn't seem half so lonely as around us we should
look,
And see the little old sod shanty on our claim.

Homesteadin' 269

David Crockett

1786 · 1836

In the days when Tennessee was still part of the Far West, David Crockett was born and reared in a Tennessee frontier log cabin. His schooling was meager, totaling altogether about one hundred days; but his lack of book learning did not keep him from becoming, in time, a United States congressman and a hero of the folk. Davy won followers in the period of coonskin democracy because, as a hunter, an Indian fighter, and a commoner who relied on good horse sense, he had abilities and ways particularly admired by his neighbors. His motto—"Be sure you're right, and then go ahead"—caught in a few words the spirit of the times.

Davy learned to farm and to hunt in boyhood. After fighting in the Creek War under Jackson (1813-1814), he was twice elected to the state legislature (1821-1823) and twice to Congress (1827-1831, 1833-1835). Newspapers of the day made much of his rough, homespun humor, and books about him—some by others, some by Davy himself—swelled his fame. When a Western critic read Crockett's autobiography, *Narrative of the Life of David Crockett of West Tennessee* (1834), he noticed that "the events are such . . . as we have seen acted over and over, and heard repeatedly recited by the firesides of our hardy backwoodsmen." The comment suggests Crockett's importance in literary history. His accounts did much to bring in the fireside yarn, with its authentic rendering of Western ways of living, thinking, talking, and narrating, as an eventual literary influence upon authors such as Harte (p. 338) and Clemens (p. 404).

Furthermore, during Crockett's lifetime, and particularly after his heroic death in the Alamo in 1836,

tall tales about him circulated in yarnspinning sessions and in print. He was pictured in such tales as a comic demigod, doing superhuman deeds imagined by exuberant storytellers. These tales combined imagination of the sort one finds in poetry with enough robust humor to make them palatable to ordinary men. They are related to the earlier whoppers of Samuel Peters, the later yarns of Mark Twain, and the present-day fantastic moving pictures of Walt Disney.

An Autobiography of Davy Crockett (containing Crockett's **Narrative**, A Tour of the North and Down East, 1834, and most of **Colonel Crockett's Exploits and Adventures in Texas**, 1836), ed. Hamlin Garland, New York, 1923 • **Davy Crockett: American Comic Legend**, ed. R. M. Dorson, New York, 1939 • Constance Rourke, **Davy Crockett**, New York, 1934

Davy Crockett—woodcut from one of the Crockett Almanacs

From • Narrative of the Life of David Crockett of West Tennessee

Bear Hunting

In the morning I left my son at the camp, and we started on towards the harricane; and when we had went about a mile, we started a very large bear, but we got along mighty slow on account of the cracks in the earth occasioned by the earthquakes. We, however, made out to keep in hearing of the dogs for about three miles, and then we come to the harricane. Here we had to quit our horses, as old Nick himself couldn't have got through it without sneaking it along in the form
10 that he put on, to make a fool of our old grandmother Eve. By this time several of my dogs had got tired and come back; but we went ahead on foot for some little time in the harricane, when we met a bear coming straight to us, and not more than twenty or thirty yards off. I started my tired dogs after him, and McDaniel pursued them, and I went on to where my other dogs were. I had seen the track of the bear they were after, and I knowed he was a screamer. I followed on to about the middle of the harricane, but my dogs pursued
20 him so close, that they made him climb an old stump about twenty feet high. I got in shooting distance of him and fired, but I was all over in such a flutter from fatigue and running, that I couldn't hold steady; but, however, I broke his shoulder, and he fell. I run up and loaded my gun as quick as possible, and shot him again and killed him. When I went to take out my knife to butcher him, I found I had lost it in coming through the harricane. The vines and briers was so thick that I would sometimes have to get down and crawl like a
30 varment to get through at all; and a vine had, as I supposed, caught in the handle and pulled it out. While I was standing and studying what to do, my friend came to me. He had followed my trail through the harricane, and had found my knife, which was mighty

good news to me; as a hunter hates the worst ____ world to lose a good dog, or any part of his hunting-tools. I now left McDaniel to butcher the bear, and I went after our horses, and brought them as near as the nature of case would allow. I then took our bags, and went back to where he was; and when we had 40 skin'd the bear, we fleeced off the fat and carried it to our horses at several loads. We then packed it up on our horses, and had a heavy pack of it on each one. We now started and went on till about sunset, when I concluded we must be near our camp; so I hollered and my son answered me, and we moved on in the direction to the camp. We had gone but a little way when I heard my dogs make a warm start again; and I jumped down from my horse and gave him up to my friend, and told him I would follow them. He went on to the camp, and 50 I went ahead after my dogs with all my might for a considerable distance, till at last night came on. The woods were very rough and hilly, and all covered over with cane.

I now was compel'd to move on more slowly; and was frequently falling over logs, and into the cracks made by the earthquakes, so that I was very much afraid I would break my gun. However I went on about three miles, when I came to a good big creek, which I waded. It was very cold, and the creek was 60 about knee-deep; but I felt no great inconvenience from it just then, as I was all over wet with sweat from running, and I felt hot enough. After I got over the creek and out of the cane, which was very thick on all our creeks, I listened for my dogs. I found they had either treed or brought the bear to a stop, as they continued barking in the same place. I pushed on as near in the direction to the noise as I could, till I found the hill was too steep for me to climb, and so I backed and went down the creek some distance till I came to a hollow, 70 and then took up that, till I come to a place where I could climb up the hill. It was mighty dark, and was difficult to see my way or any thing else. When I got up the hill, I found I had passed the dogs; and so I turned and went to them. I found, when I got there, they had treed the bear in a large forked poplar, and it was setting in the fork.

I could see the lump, but not plain enough to shoot with any certainty, as there was no moonlight; and so I set in to hunting for some dry brush to make me a 80 light; but I could find none, though I could find that the ground was torn mightily to pieces by the cracks.

At last I thought I could shoot by guess, and kill him; so I pointed as near the lump as I could, and fired away. But the bear didn't come; he only clomb up higher and got out on a limb, which helped me to see him better. I now loaded up again and fired, but this time he didn't move at all. I commenced loading for a third fire, but the first thing I knowed, the bear was down among the dogs, and they were fighting all around me. I had my big butcher in my belt, and I had a pair of dressed buckskin breeches on. So I took out my knife, and stood, determined, if he should get hold of me, to defend myself in the best way I could. I stood there for some time, and could now and then see a white dog I had, but the rest of them, and the bear, which were dark coloured, I couldn't see at all, it was so miserable dark. They still fought around me, and sometimes within three feet of me; but, at last, the bear got down into one of the cracks, that the earthquakes had made in the ground, about four feet deep, and I could tell the biting end of him by the hollering of my dogs. So I took my gun and pushed the muzzle of it about, till I thought I had it against the main part of his body, and fired; but it happened to be only the fleshy part of his foreleg. With this, he jumped out of the crack, and he and the dogs had another hard fight around me, as before. At last, however, they forced him back into the crack again, as he was when I had shot.

I had laid down my gun in the dark, and I now began to hunt for it; and while hunting, I got hold of a pole, and I concluded I would punch him awhile with that. I did so, and when I would punch him, the dogs would jump in on him, when he would bite them badly, and they would jump out again. I concluded, as he would take punching so patiently, it might be that he would lie still enough for me to get down in the crack, and feel slowly along till I could find the right place to give him a dig with my butcher. So I got down, and my dogs got in before him and kept his head towards them, till I got along easily up to him; and placing my hand on his rump, felt for his shoulder, just behind which I intended to stick him. I made a lounge with my long knife, and fortunately stuck him right through the heart; at which he just sank down, and I crawled out in a hurry. In a little time my dogs all come out too, and

seemed satisfied, which was the way they always had of telling me that they had finished him.

I suffered very much that night with cold, as my leather breeches, and every thing else I had on, was wet and frozen. But I managed to get my bear out of this crack after several hard trials, and so I butchered him, and laid down to try to sleep. But my fire was very bad, and I couldn't find any thing that would burn well to make it any better; and I concluded I should freeze, if I didn't warm myself in some way by exercise. So I got up, and hollered a while, and then I would just jump up and down with all my might, and throw myself into all sorts of motions. But all this wouldn't do; for my blood was now getting cold, and the chills coming all over me. I was so tired, too, that I could hardly walk; but I thought I would do the best I could to save my life, and then, if I died, nobody would be to blame. So I went to a tree about two feet through, and not a limb on it for thirty feet, and I would climb up it to the limbs, and then lock my arms together around it, and slide down to the bottom again. This would make the insides of my legs and arms feel mighty warm and good. I continued this till daylight in the morning, and how often I clomb up my tree and slid down I don't know, but I reckon at least a hundred times.

In the morning I got my bear hung up so as to be safe, and then set out to hunt for my camp. I found it after a while, and McDaniel and my son were very much rejoiced to see me get back, for they were about to give me up for lost. We got our breakfasts, and then secured our meat by building a high scaffold, and covering it over. We had no fear of its spoiling, for the weather was so cold that it couldn't.

We now started after my other bear, which had caused me so much trouble and suffering; and before we got him, we got a start after another, and took him also. We went on to the creek I had crossed the night before and camped, and then went to where my bear was, that I had killed in the crack. When we examined the place, McDaniel said he wouldn't have gone into it, as I did, for all the bears in the woods.

We took the meat down to our camp and salted it and also the last one we had killed; intending, in the morning, to make a hunt in the harricane again.

We prepared for resting that night, and I can assure the reader I was in need of it. We had laid down by our fire, and about ten o'clock there came a most terrible earthquake, which shook the earth so, that we were rocked about like we had been in a cradle. We were very much alarmed; for though we were accustomed to feel earthquakes, we were now right in the region which had been torn to pieces by them in 1812, and we thought it might take a notion and swallow us up, like the big fish did Jonah.

In the morning we packed up and moved to the harricane, where we made another camp, and turned out that evening and killed a very large bear, which made *eight* we had now killed in this hunt.

The next morning we entered the harricane again, and in little or no time my dogs were in full cry. We pursued them, and soon came to a thick cane-brake, in which they had stop'd their bear. We got up close to him, as the cane was so thick that we couldn't see more than a few feet. Here I made my friend hold the cane a little open with his gun till I shot the bear, which was a mighty large one. I killed him dead in his tracks. We got him out and butchered him, and in a little time started another and killed him, which now made *ten* we had killed; and we know'd we couldn't pack any more home, as we had only five horses along; therefore we returned to the camp and salted up all our meat, to be ready for a start homeward next morning.

The morning came, and we packed our horses with the meat, and had as much as they could possibly carry, and sure enough cut out for home. It was about thirty miles, and we reached home the second day. I had now accommodated my neighbour with meat enough to do him, and had killed in all, up to that time, fifty-eight bears, during the fall and winter.

As soon as the time come for them to quit their houses and come out again in the spring, I took a notion to hunt a little more, and in about one month I killed forty-seven more, which made one hundred and five bears I had killed in less than one year from that time.

1834

From

The Crockett Almanacs

Between 1835 and 1856 there appeared in various cities—Nashville, New York, Boston, Philadelphia, and others—almanacs put out by various publishers and called the **Crockett Almanacs**. Like others, these almanacs contained data about the calendar year; unlike most others, they contained many tall tales, usually written as if in the language of Crockett or his unlearned frontier neighbors.

Whether Crockett had anything to do with the earliest almanacs is not known, and certainly before long the tales were concocted by journalists, some of whom knew a good deal about frontier life and some of whom knew very little. The stories in the periodicals, however, all were purportedly told by the famous frontiersman. At their best these almanac humorists, whoever they were, **caught the qualities of good** yarnspinning sessions. The style was that of lively fireside talk, homely, relatively simple, but concrete, vigorous, full of conceits. The materials were typical combinations of earthy, even vulgar, reality with the unearthly inventions of soaring imaginations. The sort of literature in the almanacs, in other words, foreshadowed the widespread use of the American language of informal talk in print and the fantastic inventions of T. B. Thorpe, Joel Chandler Harris, Mark Twain, and Walt Disney. "A Sensible Varmint" and "Death of Crockett" are from Turner and Fisher almanacs, "Crockett's Morning Hunt" from a Cozans almanac; all appeared in New York.

A SENSIBLE VARMINT

Almost every body that knows the forest, understands parfectly well that Davy Crockett never loses powder and ball, havin' ben brought up to believe it a sin to throw away amminition, and that is the benefit of a vartuous eddikation. I war out in the forest one arternoon, and had jist got to a place called the Great Gap, when I seed a rackkoon setting all alone upon a tree.

I clapped the breech of Brown Betty to my shoulder, and war jist going to put a piece of lead between his shoulders, when he lifted one paw, and sez he, "Is your name Crockett?"

Sez I, "You are rite for wonst, my name is Davy Crockett."

Davy and the sensible varmint—woodcut from one of the Crockett Almanacs

"Then," sez he, "you needn't take no further trouble, for I may as well come down without another word." And the cretur walked rite down from the tree, for he considered himself shot.

I stoops down and pats him on the head, and sez I, "I hope I may be shot myself before I hurt a hair of your head, for I never had sich a compliment in my life."

"Seeing as how you say that," sez he, "I'll jist walk off for the present, not doubting your word a bit, d'ye see, but lest you should kinder happen to change your mind."   1841

DEATH OF CROCKETT

Thar's a great rejoicin' among the bears of Kaintuck, and the alligators of the Massissippi rolls up thar shining ribs to the sun, and has grown so fat and lazy that they will hardly move out of the way for a steamboat. The rattlesnakes come up out of thar holes and frolic within ten foot of the clearings, and the foxes goes to sleep in the goose-pens. It is bekase the rifle of Crockett is silent forever, and the print of his moccasins is found no more in our woods. His old fox-skin cap hangs up in the cabin, and every hunter, whether he are a Puke, a Wolverine, or a Sucker, never looks at it without turnin' away his head and droppin' a salt tear.

Luke Wing entered the cabin the other day and took down old Killdevil to look at it. The muzzle was half stopped up with rust, and a great green spider run out of it and made his escape in the cracks of the wall. The varmints of the forest will fear it no more. His last act to defend it, war when the poor gallant Kurnill drew a bead on a pesky Mexican and brought him down. Crockett went to put "Big Butcher" into another, and the feller on the ground turned half over, and stuck a knife into him. Another come up behind and run his bayonet into Crockett's back, for the cretur would as soon have faced a hindred live mammoths as to have faced Crockett at any time.

Down fell the Kurnill like a lion struck by thunder and lightning. He never spoke again. It war a great loss to the country, and the world, and to ole Kaintuck in particklar. Thar were never known such a member of Congress as Crockett, and never will be agin. The painters and bears will miss him, for he never missed them.

He died like a member o' Congress ought to die. While he war about to do his country some sarvice, and raise her name as high as her mountains, he war cut down in the prime o' life, and at a time when he war most wanted. His screams and yells are heard no more, and the whole country are clouded with a darkness for the gallant Kurnill. He war an ornament to the forest, and war never known to refuse his whiskey to a stranger. When he war alive, it war most beautiful to hear his scream coming through the forest; it would turn and twist itself into some of the most splendifferous knots, and then untie itself and keep on till it got clar into nowhere.

---

27 Puke, Wolverine, Sucker, natives, respectively, of Missouri, Michigan, and Illinois

But he are a dead man now, and if you want to see old Kaintuck's tears, go thar, and speak o' her gallant Kurnill, and thar's not a human but what will turn away and go behind some tree and dry up thar tears. He are dead now, and may he rest forever and a day arter.

1847

CROCKETT'S MORNING HUNT

One January morning it was so all-screwen-up cold that the forest trees war so stiff that they couldn't shake, and the very day-break froze fast as it war tryin' to dawn. The tinder-box in my cabin would no more ketch fire than a sunk raft at the bottom o' the sea. Seein' that daylight war so far behind time, I thought creation war in a fair way for freezin' fast.

"So," thinks I, "I must strike a leetle fire from my fingers, light my pipe, travel out a few leagues, and see about it."

Then I brought my knuckles together like two thunder clouds, but the sparks froze up afore I could begin to collect 'em—so out I walked, and endeavored to keep myself unfriz by goin' at a hop, step and jump gait, and whistlin' the tune of "fire in the mountains!" as I went along in three double quick time. Well, arter I had walked about twenty-five miles up the peak o' Daybreak Hill, I soon discovered what war the matter. The airth had actually friz fast in her axis, and couldn't turn round; the sun had got jammed between two cakes o' ice under the wheels, an' thar he had bin shinin' and workin' to get loose, till he friz fast in his cold sweat.

"C-r-e-a-t-i-o-n!" thought I, "this are the toughest sort o' suspension, and it mustn't be endured—somethin' must be done, or human creation is done for."

It war then so antedeluvian and premature cold that my upper and lower teeth an' tongue war all collapsed together as tight as a friz oyster. I took a fresh twenty pound bear off o' my back that I'd picked up on the road, an' beat the animal agin the ice till the hot ile began to walk out on him at all sides. I then took an' held him over the airth's axes, an' squeezed him till I thaw'd 'em loose, poured about a ton on it over the sun's face, give the airth's cog-wheel one kick backward, till I got the sun loose—whistled "Push along, keep movin'!" an' in about fifteen seconds the airth gin a grunt, and begun movin'—the sun walked up beautiful, salutin' me with sich a wind o' gratitude that it made me sneeze. I lit my pipe by the blaze o' his top-knot, shouldered my bear, an' walked home, introducin' the people to fresh daylight with a piece of sunrise in my pocket, with which I cooked my bear steaks, an' enjoyed one o' the best breakfasts I had tasted for some time. If I didn't, jist wake some mornin' and go with me to the office o' sunrise!

1853

William Tappan Thompson

1812 · 1882

In 1842 William Tappan Thompson was an editor of a weekly newspaper, *The Southern Miscellany,* published in Madison, Georgia. Born in Ohio in 1812, orphaned at fourteen, Thompson had been prepared for editorship by work as a printer's devil, by political executive work in Tallahassee, Florida, and by newspaper, magazine, and printing work in Augusta. The readers to whom the *Miscellany* was intended to appeal, the citizens of surrounding Morgan County, were Scotch-Irish farmers who owned few or no slaves. Moderately educated, rustic, thrifty, rather stern in their Protestant morality, they were aptly nicknamed at the time "the Yankees of the South."

It was for such readers that Thompson prepared his most famous humorous pieces—the Major Jones letters. Major Jones, a Georgia prototype of Smith's Jack Downing, was much like the people who enjoyed his writings—a semi-educated, highly moral farmer who derived his income from a small plantation worked by a few slaves. His letters to the editor of the *Miscellany* told of his homely thoughts and adventures—his experiences as a major in the militia, his humble courtship, his marriage and family life. Published as *Major Jones's Courtship* in 1843, this set of letters had huge sales, both in the South and in the North, going through more than twenty editions scattered over a period of fifty years.

Major Jones, who also appeared in *The Chronicles of Pineville* (1845) and a series of pro-Southern letters —*Major Jones's Sketches of Travel* (1848)—published first in a Baltimore paper, differed a great deal from most of the other leading Southwestern humorous characters of the time. A fellow of great naïveté, he nevertheless was blessed with so much horse sense that he, as a rule, had sounder ideas and sentiments about most subjects than did other contemporary Southwestern humorous characters. More than most such figures of the period and the section, too, he recorded the day-by-day domestic life of his class and others. And rough vulgarity often typical of other humorous writings did not get into the works of Major Jones. Such qualities were partly the result of Thompson's attempt to make the Major's letters appeal to a particular group of readers, partly the result, of course, of his skill in seeing keenly and recording authentically the life he knew.

The letters, with their accurate use of the vernacular speech of Georgia, were clearly related to the humor, based on the oral tale, so popular in the Southwest at the time. Even closer to this prevalent sort of humor were a number of mock oral tales represented by "A Coon Hunt in a Fency Country." These short, direct narratives, told in dialect, usually followed a formula thus described by Professor Henry Prentice Miller: "A single paragraph of general moralizing or crackerbox philosophizing; a quick, phrased sketching of the characters; a few statements about background; a single incident, and finally the point or nub, which ties up with the initial paragraph." Some of these economically told yarns deserve high rank among short humorous masterpieces.

H. P. Miller, **The Life and Works of William Tappan Thompson** (an unpublished doctoral dissertation done at the University of Chicago), 1941 • J. H. Nelson, "William Tappan Thompson," **Dictionary of American Biography**, New York, 1935

From

Major Jones's Courtship

LETTER XII

Pineville, December 27, 1842

To Mr. Thompson:—Dear Sir—Crismus is over, and the thing is done did! You know I told you in my last letter I was gwine to bring Miss Mary up to the chalk on Crismus. Well, I done it, slick as a whistle, though it come mighty nigh bein a serious bisness. But I'll tell you all about the whole circumstance.

The fact is, I's made my mind up more'n twenty times to jest go and come right out with the whole bisness; but whenever I got whar she was, and whenever she looked at me with her witchin eyes, and kind o' blushed at me, I always felt sort o' skeered and fainty, and all what I made up to tell her was forgot, so I couldn't think of it to save me. But you's a married man, Mr. Thompson, so I couldn't tell you nothin about popin the question, as they call it. It's a mighty grate favour to ax of a pretty gall, and to people what aint used to it, it goes monstrous hard, don't it? They say widders don't mind it no more'n nothin. But I'm makin a transgression, as the preacher ses.

Crismus eve I put on my new suit, and shaved my face as slick as a smoothin iron, and after tea went over to old Miss Stallinses. As soon as I went into the parler whar they was all settin round the fire, Miss Carline and Miss Kesiah both laughed right out.

"There! there!" ses they, "I told you so! I know'd it would be Joseph."

"What's I done, Miss Carline?" ses I.

"You come under little sister's chicken bone, and I do believe she know'd you was comin when she put it over the dore."

"No I didn't—I didn't no such thing, now," ses Miss Mary, and her face blushed red all over.

"Oh, you needn't deny it," ses Miss Kesiah, "you belong to Joseph now, jest as sure as ther's any charm in chicken bones."

I know'd that was a first rate chance to say something, but the dear little creeter looked so sorry and kep blushin so, I couldn't say nothin zactly to the pint! so I tuck a chair and reached up and tuck down the bone and put it in my pocket.

"What are you gwine to do with that old chicken bone now, Majer?" ses Miss Mary.

"I'm gwine to keep it as long as I live," ses I, "as a Crismus present from the handsomest gall in Georgia."

When I sed that, she blushed worse and worse.

"Aint you shamed, Majer?" ses she.

"Now you ought to give *her* a Crismus gift, Joseph, to keep all *her* life," sed Miss Carline.

"Ah," ses old Miss Stallins, "when I was a gall we used to hang up our stockins——"

"Why, mother!" ses all of 'em, "to say stockins right before——"

Then I felt a little streaked too, cause they was all blushin as hard as they could.

"Highty-tity!" ses the old lady—"what monstrous 'finement to be shore! I'd like to know what harm ther is in stockins. People now-a-days is gittin so mealy-mouthed they can't call nothin by its right name, and I don't see as they's any better than the old time people was. When I was a gall like you, child, I use to hang up my stockins and git 'em full of presents."

The galls kep laughin and blushin.

"Never mind," ses Miss Mary, "Majer's got to give me a Crismus gift—won't you, Majer?"

"Oh, yes," ses I, "you know I promised you one."

"But I didn't mean *that,*" ses she.

"I've got one for you, what I want you to keep all your life, but it would take a two bushel bag to hold it," ses I.

"Oh, that's the kind," ses she.

"But will you promise to keep it as long as you live?" ses I.

"Certainly I will, Majer."

"—monstrous 'finement now-a-days—old people don't know nothin about perliteness," said old Miss Stallins, jest gwine to sleep with her nittin in her lap.

"Now you hear that, Miss Carline," ses I. "She ses she'll keep it all her life."

"Yes, I will," ses Miss Mary—"but what is it?"

"Never mind," ses I, "you hang up a bag big enough to hold it and you'll find out what it is, when you see it in the mornin."

Miss Carline winked at Miss Kesiah, and then whispered to her—then they both laughed and looked at me as mischievous as they could. They 'spicioned something.

"You'll be shore to give it to me now, if I hang up a bag," ses Miss Mary.

"And promise to keep it," ses I.

"Well, I will, cause I know that you wouldn't give me nothin that wasn't worth keepin."

They all agreed they would hang up a bag for me to put Miss Mary's Crismus present in, on the back porch, and about ten o'clock I told 'em good evenin and went home.

I sot up till mid-night, and when they was all gone to bed I went softly into the back gate, and went up to the porch, and thar, shore enough, was a great big meal-bag hangin to the jice. It was monstrous unhandy to git to it, but I was termined not to back out. So I sot some chairs on top of a bench and got hold of the rope and let myself down into the bag; but jest as I was gittin in, it swung agin the chairs, and down they went with a terrible racket; but nobody din't wake up but Miss Stallinses old cur dog, and here he come rippin and tearin through the yard like rath, and round and round he went tryin to find what was the matter. I scrooch'd down in the bag and didn't breathe louder nor a kitten, for fear he'd find me out, and after a while he quit barkin.

The wind begun to blow bominable cold, and the old bag kep turnin round and swingin so it made me sea-sick as the mischief. I was afraid to move for fear the rope would break and let me fall, and thar I sot with my teeth rattlin like I had a ager. It seemed like it would never come daylight, and I do believe if I didn't love Miss Mary so powerful I would froze to death; for my heart was the only spot that felt warm, and it didn't beat more'n two licks a minit, only when I thought how she would be supprised in the mornin, and then it went in a canter. Bimeby the cussed old dog come up on the porch and begun to smell about the bag, and then he barked like he thought he'd treed something. "Bow! wow! wow!" ses he. Then he'd smell agin, and try to git up to the bag. "Git out!" ses I, very low, for fear the galls mought hear me. "Bow! wow!" ses he. "Be gone! you bominable fool," ses I, and I felt all over in spots, for I spected every minit he'd nip me, and what made it worse, I didn't know whar abouts he'd take hold. "Bow! wow! wow!" Then I tried coaxin——"Come here, good feller," ses I, and whistled a little to him, but it wasn't no use. Thar he stood and kep up his everlastin whinin and barkin, all night. I couldn't tell when daylight was breakin, only by the chickens crowin, and I was monstrous glad to hear 'em, for if I'd had to stay thar one hour more, I don't believe I'd ever got out of that bag alive.

Old Miss Stallins come out fust, and as soon as she seed the bag, ses she,

"What upon yeath has Joseph went and put in that bag for Mary? I'll lay its a yearlin or some live animal, or Bruin wouldn't bark at it so."

She went in to call the galls, and I sot thar, shiverin all over so I couldn't hardly speak if I tried to—but I didn't say nothin. Bimeby they all come running out on the porch.

"My goodness! what is it?" ses Miss Mary.

"Oh, it's alive!" ses Miss Kesiah, "I seed it move."

"Call Cato, and make him cut the rope," ses Miss Carline, "and let's see what it is. Come here, Cato, and git this bag down."

"Don't hurt it for the world," ses Miss Mary.

Cato untied the rope that was round the jice, and let the bag down easy on the floor, and I tumbled out all covered with corn meal, from head to foot.

"Goodness gracious!" ses Miss Mary, "if it aint the Majer himself!"

"Yes," ses I, "and you know you promised to keep my Crismus present as long as you lived."

The galls laughed themselves almost to death, and went to brushin off the meal as fast as they could, sayin they was gwine to hang that bag up every Crismus till they got husbands too. Miss Mary—bless her bright eyes—she blushed as beautiful as a morning-glory, and sed she'd stick to her word. She was right out of bed, and her hair wasn't komed, and her dress wasn't fix'd at all, but the way she looked pretty was real distractin. I do believe if I was froze stiff, one look at her sweet face, as she stood thar lookin down to the floor with her roguish eyes, and her bright curls fallin all over her snowy neck, would have fotched me too. I tell you what, it was worth hangin in a meal bag from one Crismus to another to feel as happy as I have ever sense.

I went home after we had the laugh out, and sot by the fire till I got thawed. In the forenoon all the Stallinses come over to our house and we had one of the greatest Crismus dinners that ever was seed in Georgia, and I don't believe a happier company ever sot down to the same table. Old Miss Stallins and mother settled the match, and talked over every thing that ever happened in ther families, and laughed at me and Mary, and cried about ther dead husbands, cause they wasn't alive to see ther children married.

It's all settled now, 'cept we haint sot the weddin day. I'd like to have it all over at once, but young galls always like to be engaged a while, you know, so I spose I must wait a month or so. Mary (she ses I mustn't call her Miss Mary now) has been a good deal of trouble and botheration to me; but if you could see her you wouldn't think I ought to grudge a little sufferin to git sich a sweet little wife.

You must come to the weddin if you possibly kin. I'll let you know when. No more from

Your friend, till death,   Jos. Jones

N. B. I like to forgot to tell you about cousin Pete. He got snapt on egnog when he heard of my ingagement, and he's been as meller as hoss-apple ever sense.

1843·1872

Major Jones—illustration by Felix O. C. Darley for Major Jones's Sketches of Travel, *1847*

A Coon Hunt in a
Fency Country

It is really astonishin what a monstrous sight of mischief ther is in a bottle of rum. If one of 'em was to be submitted to a analization as the doctors calls it, it would be found to contain all manner of devilment that ever entered the head of man, from cussin and stealin up to murder and whippin his own mother, and nonsense enough to turn all the men in the world out of ther senses. If a man's got any badness in him, let him drink whiskey, and it will bring it out jest as sassafras tea does the measles; and if he's a good-for-nothin sort of a feller, without no bad traits in partickeler, it'll bring out all his foolishness. It affects different people in different ways—it makes some men monstrous brave and full of fight, and some it makes cowards—some it makes rich and happy and some pore and miserable. And it has different effects on different people's eyes—some it makes see double, and some it makes so blind that they can't tell themselves from a side of bacon. One of the worst cases of rum-foolery that I've heard of for a long time tuck place in Pineville last fall.

Bill Sweeney and Tom Culpepper is the two greatest old conveys in our settlement for coon-huntin. The fact is, they don't do much of any thing else, and when *they* can't catch coons, it's a shore sign that coons is scarce. Well, one night they had every thing ready for a reglar hunt, but owin to some extra good fortin, Tom had got a pocket-pistol, as he called it, of genewine old Jimmaky rum. After takin a good startin horn, they went out on ther hunt, with ther lightwood torch a blazin, and the dogs a barkin and yelpin like they was crazy. They struck out into the woods, gwine in the direction of old Starlin Jones's new ground, a great place for coons. Every now and then they would stop to wait for the

dogs, and then they would drink one another's health, until they begun to feel first-rate. On they went, chattin away about one thing and another, takin a nip now and then from Tom's bottle, not mindin much whar they was gwine. Bimeby they come to a fence. Well, over they got without much difficulty.

"Who's fence is this?" ses Bill.

"Taint no matter," ses Tom, "let's take a drink."

After takin a pull at the bottle, they went on agin, wonderin what upon yeath had come of the dogs. The next thing they come to was a terrible muddy branch. After gropin ther way through the bushes and briers and gittin on t'other side, they tuck another drink. Fixin up ther torch and startin on agin, they didn't go but a little ways before they come to another branch, as bad as the first one, and a little further they come to another fence—a monstrous high one this time.

"Whar upon yeath is we got to, Culpepper?" ses Bill; "I never seed sich a heap of fences and branches in these parts."

"Why," ses Tom, "it's old Starlin's doins; you know he's alway bildin fences and makin infernal improvements, as he calls 'em. But never mind; we's through 'em now."

"The devil we is," ses Bill; "why, here's the alfiredest high fence yit."

Shore enough, thar they was right agin another fence. By this time they begun to be considerable tired and limber in ther jints; and it was sich a terrible high fence. Tom drapped the last piece of the torch, and thar they was in the dark.

"Now you *is* done it!" ses Bill.

Tom knowd he had, but he thought it was no use to grieve over what couldn't be helped, so, ses he,

"Never mind, old hoss—come ahead, and I'll take you out," and the next minit, kerslash! he went into the water up to his neck.

Bill heard the splash, and he clung to the fence with both hands like he thought it was slewin round to throw him off.

"Hellow, Tom!" ses he, "whar in creation has you got to?"

"Here I is!" ses Tom, spittin the water out of his mouth, and coughin like he'd swallered something. "Look out, ther's another dratted branch here."

"Name o' sense, whar is we?" ses Bill. "If this isn't a fency country, dad fetch my buttons!"

"Yes, and a branchy one, too!" ses Tom, "and they is the thickest and the highest and the deepest that I ever seed in all my born days."

After a good deal of cussin and gruntin Bill got himself loose from the fence.

"Which way is you?" ses he.

"Here, right over the branch," ses Tom.

The next minit in Bill went, up to his middle in branch.

10 "Come ahead," ses Tom, "and let's go home."

"Come thunder!" ses Bill, "in sich a place as this, whar a feller hain't more'n got his coat-tail unhitched from a fence before he's over head and ears in a cussed branch."

Bill made a terrible job of gittin across the branch, which he swore was the deepest one yit. They managed to git together agin after feelin about in the dark a while, and, takin another drink, they sot out for home, cussin the fences and the branches, and helpin one 20 another up now and then when they got ther legs tangled in the brush; but they hadn't gone more'n twenty yards before they found themselves in the middle of another branch. After gittin through the branch and gwine about twenty yards they was brung up all standin agin by another everlastin fence.

"Dad blame my picter," ses Bill, "if I don't think we's bewitched. Who upon yeath would go and build fences all over outdoors this way?"

It tuck 'em a long time to climb this fence, but when they got on top of it they found the ground on tother 30 side without much trouble. This time the bottle was broke, and they come monstrous nigh havin a fight about the catastrofy. But it was a very good thing the licker was spilt, for after crossin three or four more branches and climbin as many more fences, it got to be daylight, when to ther great astonishment they found out that they had been climbin the same fence and wadin the same branch all night, not more'n a hundred yards from the place whar they first come to 'em.

Bill Sweeney ses he can't account for it no other way 40 but that the licker sort o' turned ther heads; and he ses he really does believe if it hadn't gin out, they'd been climbin that same fence and wadin that same branch till now.

1847·1872

George Washington Harris

1814 · 1869

At the age of five, George Washington Harris was taken from his birthplace in Allegheny City, Pennsylvania, to Knoxville, Tennessee. For forty years he lived in this sleepy village, coming to know intimately the life of its peaceful valley. He left its "Knobs" and mountains only when the economic stirrings preceding the Civil War forced him away.

Harris' wide and varied experience included an apprenticeship in a jewelry shop, the captaincy of a steamboat, farming, the operation of a metalworking shop, glass factory, and sawmill, service as postmaster, and, finally, work on a railroad. During his whole career, Harris had a deep interest in politics, and from 1839 until his death, whenever the political situation became crucial, he boisterously attacked forces which threatened the "good old days."

For a number of years Harris wrote humorous sketches for the New York *Spirit of the Times*. After 1854 his stories couched in the quaint language of his comic character, Sut Lovingood, obtained, according to one discerning critic of that period, "a circulation and popularity, throughout the country, which no similar productions, in modern times, have enjoyed." Sut, as a self-confessed "nat'ral born durn'd fool," delivered blows at the foibles of mankind from the vantage point of this "unassailable position." For his victims he reached as high as Abraham Lincoln and as low as a "durn'd, infurnel, hiperkritical, pot-bellied, scaley-hided, whisky-wastin'" circuit rider. In fact, most of humanity in some form or other can find itself "sloshin' about" in his cal-

dron of comic situation. In a typical Lovingood story, the characters whom Sut disliked were comically portrayed and then, in all probability, physically maltreated. Sut's notion of the height of humor was a man whom he disliked surrounded by a knot of angry hornets and trying vainly to get away in a hurry. What Harris is admired for by modern enthusiasts about his yarns is his ability to put oral tales with all the art of their comic movement and all the poetry of their style onto the printed page.

Sut Lovingood Yarns, New York, 1867 • Walter Blair, **Native American Humor (1800-1900),** Cincinnati, 1937 • F. J. Meine, **Tall Tales of the Southwest,** New York, 1938 • (Numerous tales published only in newspapers have been found recently by Donald Day and F. J. Meine, who plan to bring them all together in a book)

Bart Davis's Dance

Du yu know that bow-laiged boy on the fence thar?" said Sut.

"No; who is he?"

"That's Bart Davis's yungest son, name Obed. Jis' obsarve how his snout's skin'd an' his year slit an' so forth."

"Yes, I see; how did it happen?"

"Happen? hit didn't happen et all, hit wer dun a-pupos, permeditated a-pupos. Ther wer a dance et his dad's, las' Sat'day nite wer two weeks ago, what hed like tu bred a berryin ur two; the corpses wer mos' redy, an' nuffin but acksidint kep em frum bein finished. I wer thar mysef, an' kin say an' swar that the chances run mity even, a-tween mirth an' mournin. Fur a spell hit wer the exhitenest time I ever seed on sich a ocashun, not tu hev no more whisky nur we hed. Thar warn't but 'bout half a barril when we

begun, an' when we quit, we burnt the hoops an' staves tu dance the las' reel by.

"Everybody knows Bart is a durn'd no-count, jug-kerryin, slow-thinkin, flea-hurtin, herrin-eatin, Noth Calinian, plays a three-string fiddil wif a grasshopper jirk, while his wife totes the wood. He hes but two gifs wuf a durn: wun is, he'll vide his whisky wif yu down tu the las' half pint; thar he stops, fur that's jis' a horn yu know; an' tuther is, he ain't feard ove enything a-livin, sept ole Peg. I don't wunder et that, fur hit mus' take a man wif a onnatrally big melt, not tu be fear'd ove his wife, onless she's blind ur hes a sweethart. Peg (she's his ole quilt, yu know) is a regular steel-trap ove an 'oman; she goes wif wun side ove her frock tucked up at the hips, her har down her back, an' a roasted hickory onder her arm tu scold the brats wif, an' tu skeer Bart. They's bof great on dancin ove Sat'day nites et home, an' sumwhar else on tuther nites. Ef thar's a frolic enywhar in five mile, Bart is sure tu be thar, an' Peg, too, ef she's in travilin fix, which ain't more nur five months in the year. She goes fur two reasons: wun is, tu eat an' dance, an' tuther tu watch Bart. He hes two reasons also: wun is tu suck in all the whisky floatin roun, an' tu du a heap ove things what needs watchin. They giner'lly hes a dermestic dis-cussun arter they gets home, in which, teeth, claws, an' beggin am the argymints, an' 'I won't du so no more,' the aind ove hit. They am a lively an' even yok'd par.

Nobody else on the green yeath orter be tied tu either ove em.

"Well they mounted that par ove hames yu see on the fence thar, the boy name Obed ontu a muel, an' sent him tu the still-hous, tu narrate hit that thar wud be a dance et home the nex nite, an' fur every feller what warn't married tu fetch a gal, an' them what wer married tu fetch two. Now this rangement show'd Bart's good sence, fur he know'd that hit takes more gals tu du married fellers then single wuns. Caze people what hes but one kind ove vittils et home, hit allers takes more tu du em abroad.

"When the nite cum they wer all thar, a hous' plum full, an' amung em a lot ove counter-hoppers wif strip'd sugar candy in their pockets, an' young lawyers wif cinamint ile ontu ther har; all on em frum town, an' jis' ole enuf tu begin tu strut an' gobble. Thunder and litnin, an' sun-flower pattrin calliker, mixed wif check an' stripe, homspun swept all about thar, wif one, jis' one black silk. They laid off two reels, wun call'd the leather shoe reel, an' tuther, the barfoot reel. I danced in the wun I nam'd las'."

Sut Lovingood—illustration from the first edition

"Why did they divide that way, Sut?"

"Why, durn hit, don't yu know that the dancin wud turn intu fitin afore the fust set got ofen the flure, ef they mix'd em? The shoes wud scronch the bar toes in dancin, an' rite then an' thar they'd mix fur a fite. A hard-shell preacher wif his mouf mortised intu his face in shape like a muel's shoe, heels down, fotch hissef thar soon arter dark, an' made moshuns like he ment tu stay all nite. He got intu a corner, an' commenced a'tchunin up his sighin an' groanin aperatus, a-shakin ove his head, an' lookin like he hed the belly-ake. He cudn't hev look'd more solemcoly, ef his mam hed died that mornin a-owin him two dullars an' a 'alf. All these wimin an' luvely souns an' moshuns wer made on count ove the dancin, an' p'raps the cussin an' kissin. The whisky part ove that inturtainment he'd nuffin against. I *know'd* that, fur every time he roll'd his eyes to'ards the barril, he'd lick his lips sorter sloppy like, jis' es ef he'd been dippin his bill intu a crock ove chicken gravy, an' wer tryin tu save the stray draps, what hung outside his face. Oh! he wer jis' a-honin arter that ball-face whisky; he'd a jis' kiss'd hit es sweet, an' es long, es ef hit hed been a willin gal. I sorter aidged up a-side him, an' sez I—

"'Mister, will yu hev a few draps ove camfire, ur laudamy? Yu seems tu be pow'ful ailin in yer innards. Yu hesent swallered a live rat, ur a mole, hes yu?'

"He shook his head, an' fotch a sigh, what ainded in a groan. Sez I—

"'Rats ur moles am onhelthy things tu swaller afore they'se departed this life.'

"He blow'd out a orful sigh, part outen his nose, but mos' ove hit out whar the toe ove the muel-shoe wer, an' sez he—

"'This am a wicked an' a parvarse generashun ove vipurs, yung man.'

"'An' gin up tu hardness ove hart, an' deviltry, an' belevin thunderin lies,' said I; an' I puff'd out a big sigh, wif a little groan fur a tail. Sez he—

"'Thar am no-o-o-o dancin in hell,' an sot intu shakin ove his head, till I thot he'd keep on fur everlastin, an' ever more. Sez I—

"'Haint yu *slitely* mistaken'd in that las' re-mark ove yourn? Ef thar's es much hot truck, an' brimstone, an'

14 **counter-hoppers,** store clerks

cinders, an' hickory smoke, an' big hurtin, in hell es yu folks sez thar am, thar mus' be *sum* dancin, purtickelerly jigs an' quick-steps; they don't lack fur music, I reckon, fur I'se allers hearn hell wer full ove fiddlers, an' thar's Yankees enuf thar tu invent fire-proof fiddils fur em, so they don't want fur tchunes. All on yeath that bothers me is the rosim.'

" 'Ah, yung onregenerit man,' sez he, 'thar's more rosim in hell than thar's in all Noth Caliny.'

10   " 'But hit ain't quite hard enuf tu rub ontu fiddil bows, is hit?' sez I.

"He groan'd an' shook his head, an' sent one ove his eyes to'ards the whisky corner. I went an' fotch 'im a big slug intu a gourd. That shovel-shaped onder lip ove his'n jis' fell out'ards like ontu the fallin door ove a stone coal stove, an' he upsot the gourd inside ove his teef. I seed the mark ove the truck gwine down his froat jis' like a snake travelin thru a wet sassidge gut. He smelt intu the gourd a good long smell, turned up

20   his eyes, an' sed 'Barlm ove life.'

"Thinks I, ole Sock, I know what fotch yu tu this frolic besides yu're hoss an' our whisky. Bart now cum up, an' Hardshell tole him he'd cum tu stay all nite, ef he suited all roun.

" 'Sartinly, oh yas, an' welcum,' sed Bart.

"The ole Sock, never alterin the shape ove the hole tore in his face, sed, mity sneerin like, 'Yu is hosspitabil.' I seed Bart sorter start, an' look at him, an' go off a-winkin at me tu foller him. We went outside the hous',

30   intu a chimbly corner, an' thar wer two fellers, wun ove em a she, a-whisperin. We went tu tuther corner, an' thar wer two more; then we went tu the stabil, an' hearn whisperin thar; hit mout been rats a-runnin in straw. So Bart cud hold in no longer. Sez he—

" 'Never mine, I don't keer a durn who hears me. I b'leve I'se been 'sulted in my own hous'; didn't that durn'd preachin mersheen call me a hoss?'

" 'That's jis' what he sed. He call'd yu a hoss-pitabil,' sez I.

40   " 'Pitabil, pitabil,' sez Bart, 'dam ef I don't b'leve that's wus nur the hoss.'

" 'Sartinly,' sez I, 'pitabil is a sorter Latin tail stuck tu hit so yu moutn't onderstand; hit means pitiful hoss in Inglish, an' ef I wer yu, I'd see that his stumack wer spiled fur Peg's fried chicken an' biskit. I'd go rite in an' show him how a hoss ken kick an' sich like.' He jis'

gritted his teef, like he wer a-chompin aigshells, ur paragorick phials, an' put fur the hous', a-rollin up his shut-sleeves es he went, plum up to his arm-pit.

"The durn'd, hiperkritikil, groanin ole Hardshell raskil   50
hed dun got the dancin stop't; he'd tuck the fiddil away frum the nigger, an' wer a-holdin hit by the naik in wun han, an' a-makin gesters wif the bow in tuther. He wer mounted ontu a cheer, clost by the meal barril, an' wer exortin em orfully 'bout thar sins ove omishun an' cummishun, purtickerly the cummishun wuns, wif the dancin sins at the head, warin sunflower caliker wuns nex'; an' then cum thar smaller sins, sich es ridin a-hine fellers on the same hoss, whisperin outen doors, an' a-winkin a-hine fans, tuckey-tails an' hankerchers, an'   60
sed that black silk wer plenty in hell, that hit wer used fur mournin thar, an' not tu dance in. The *he* sins, ove the small sort, wer cumin frum town ove nites, a-warin store clothes, smellin ove cinamint ile, an' a-totin striped sugar candy in thar pockets, tu turn the minds ove the weak gals, instead ove a flask ove that good holesum ole truck, what they'se got in towns, name 'coniack.'

"The wimmen folks wer backed up in bunches, in the corners, an' agin the beds, wif thar fingers in thar   70
moufs, an' wun ur two ove em saftest ove em wer gettin up a quiet sort ove dry cryin.

"The he fellers all looked like they'd mos' es leave fite es not, ef they knew how tu start the thing, when in bounced Bart; he looked like a catamount; wun jump an' he stood a-top ove the meal barril, squar in frunt ove Hardshell, his har a-swayin about wif pure mad, like a patch ove ripe rye in a wind, an' his eyes wer es roun an' es red as a bull's when he's a-jinin in battil wif anuther bull frum Bashan. He struck wun fistes away   80
out a-hine, an' wif tuther reachin at arm's laingth, he cummenc'd borin, like he hed a gimblit in his shot fis', rite onder the snout ove the thunderin Hardshell, like he wer tryin tu bore his mouf inter a better shape, an' a-narratin thru his teef these facs, in words what sounded like grittin hard co'n.

" '*Yu* durn'd infunel, incumpassabil warter-dorg! *yu* cuss'd hiperkritikal, ongrateful ole mus-rat! *yu* h-ll fir'd, divin, splatterin, pond-makin, iron-jacket'd ole son ove a mud-turtil, yu hes 'sulted me in my own hous',   90
an' in Latin et that, an' then yu've tuck the imperdent liberty tu skare these yere children outen thar innersent

mucement, (still borin away frum left tu right, wif that horny fis' ove his'n, an' the Hardshell's head gwine furder back every twist.) Call'd me a hoss——Git ofen that cheer!'

"Es he sed 'git,' he loaned the passun a mos' tremenjus contushun, rite in the bull curl. I seed his shoe-soles a-gwine up each side ove Bart's fis' afore he hed time tu muve hit, arter he struck. Hit wer a lick, George, that hed hit been a kick, a four year ole muel wud hev been pow'ful proud ove. I seed ni ontu a gallon ove sparks ove fire fly outen the passun's eyes mysef (he mus hev seed a bushel) when hit reached his curl. He let the fiddil go when he wer in the highes part ove his back-ward summerset, an' the nigger what hed been watchin up at hit all this time, wis'ful like, es a dorg watches a meat-skin when yu holds hit too high fur him tu grab, cotch his fiddil in bof hans afore hit toch the yeath.

"'Dar by golly, you no git tu smash dis fiddil, wid yu durn fool fitin an' preachin.'

"An' holdin it wavinly abuv his head, he dodged outen the surkil ove imejut danger. The old Shell lit ontu his all fours, hit bein that much more nur a full summerset, an' *the* black silk lit a-stradil ove him. I know'd hit wer the black silk, bekase I seed the white stockins an' grey garters. Hev I mention'd that thar wer one hundred an' twenty-five pouns ove live, black-eyed gal in under that black silk?"

"No, Sut."

"Well, thar wer, an' that she wer bof live an' willin, ole Dipper wer soon redy tu swar. 'Black silk in hell is thar,' scream'd she, a-hissin like ontu a cat, an' cummenced a-pullin up by the roots his long har, like hit wer flax, wif bof hans, an' a-shakin the bunches ofen her fingers, an' then gwine fur more, the hissin gittin a littil louder every pull. George, that wer the fust spessamin ove a smokin mad gal I've seed in a hen's age; she kerried out my idear ove a fust-rate flax-puller, pullin agin two, fur a bet. I think she gin the ole Shell the idear that sum strong man body wer a-holden his head ni ontu the saws ove a activ cotton gin.

"Now the boy name Obed, with the hame laigs, hevin a sorter jestis' ove the peace turn ove mine, run in tu pull her off, an' cudn't du hit afore she made a rake fur his har, an' got hit. She jis' mixed the hanful wif the pile on the flure, an' gin hersef back tu the job ove preparin the passun fur a wig. A hawk-billed, weazel-eyed, rat-mouthed feller, what hed been a-struttin roun Black Silk all nite, a-trailin wun wing, an' a-lickin his lips, seed the fool boy name Obed, a-tryin tu git her tu lite ofen the old Sock, so he jis' growl'd low, an' barked once, an' kiver'd him, an' afore his mam Peg, an' me, an' five uther gals, cud git him loose, he hed made her cub the speckterkil yu sees roostin on that ar fence, an' he's hed ni ontu three weeks tu mend his looks in, by Jew David's plarster, sweet ile, an' the keer ove his mam.

"The fitin now got tu be gineral on mos' parts ove the field, an' es the cuppils cum in frum outen doors, lookin sorter sneakin, an' pale, (frum the nise ove the rumpus, I speck,) wun at leas', outen every par, got jump't on by sumbody. P'raps a gal wud kiver a cumin in gal, anuther gal wud go fur the har an' skin ove a cumin in he feller; then, agin, the fis' ove a he wud meet anuther cumin in he, right atween the eyes, an' so on till the thing got tu be durn'dably mix'd up an' lively. Peg boun up the boy name Obed's wouns, bruises, an' petrifyin sores, an' then went on wif supper cookin, like all wer quiet on the Pertomack.

"Es soon es ole Shell begun to cum to, frum Bart's dubbil distill'd thunder-bolt, the hurtin all over his head begun tu attrack his 'tenshun, an' soaked thru his skull, an' in thar tuck the shape ove an idear; the idear shaped hitsef intu spoken wurds, an' they wer, 'Gird up yer loins an' *git*.' I seed the wurkin ove his mind, so I jis' shouted es loud es I could beller, 'The Pherlistshuns be upon yu Sampsin.' He hearn hit, an' wer struck wif the force ove the remark, an' started fur the back door, still on his all fours, in a single foot rack. Es soon es Black Silk felt him movin, she cummenced spurrin him wif her heels; while she hilt tu his har wif wun han, she tuck a pin outen her collar wif tuther, an' made a cushion fur hit in the hill, ontu the north side ove the pint ove his back-bone; he kicked up an' snorted, an' changed the single foot rack intu a tarin pace, loped outen the door intu outer darkness, an' his heel-tops wer the last I seed ove him. He stumbled an' fell down the log-steps, an' flung Black Silk like onto a full balloon over his head, (I seed a heap ove white shinin es she went.) He felt his way in the dark, thru the woods, fur more pleasant places, an' she cum in larfin, 'Black silk in hell, hey?' wer every word she sed."

"Go on, Sut."

"That's all. I ain't like ole Glabbergab; when I'se spoke off what I knows, I stops talkin."

"Well, what became of Hardshell?"

"Oh! es tu that, he made his 'pearance las' Sunday, in the pulpit, es bald es a jug, wif a black spot aidged wif green an' yaller, 'bout the size ove a prickly par, on his forehead, an' preach't bout the orful konsekenses ove Absalom's hevin long har, human depravity, an' the Salt Lake; sed he wer gwine thar right off, an' *he'll du hit.*"

1845·1867

Mrs. Yardley's Quilting

Thar's one durn'd nasty muddy job, an' I is jis' glad enuf tu take a ho'n ur two, on the straingth ove hit."

"What have you been doing, Sut?"

"Helpin tu salt ole Missis Yardley down."

"What do you mean by that?"

"Fixin her fur rotten cumfurtably, kiverin her up wif sile, tu keep the buzzards frum cheatin the wurms."

"Oh, you have been helping to bury a woman."

"That's hit, by golly! Now why the devil can't I
10 'splain mysef like yu? I ladles out my words at randum, like a calf kickin at yaller-jackids; yu jis' rolls em out tu the pint, like a feller a-layin bricks—every one fits. How is it that bricks fits so clost enyhow? Rocks won't ni du hit."

"Becaze they'se all ove a size," ventured a man with a wen over his eye.

"The devil yu say, hon'ey-head! haint reapin-mersheens ove a size? I'd like to see two ove em fit clost. Yu wait ontil yu sprouts tuther ho'n, afore yu venters tu
20 'splain mix'd questions. George, did yu know ole Missis Yardley?"

"No."

"Well, she wer a curious 'oman in her way, an' she wore shiney specks. Now jis' listen: Whenever yu see a ole 'oman ahine a par ove *shiney* specks, yu keep yer eye skinn'd: they am dang'rus in the extreme. Thar is jis' no knowin what they ken du. I hed one a-stradil ove me onst, fur kissin her gal. She went fur my har, an' she went fur my skin, ontil I tho't she ment tu kill me, an' wud a-dun hit, ef my hollerin hadent fotch ole Dave 30 Jordan, a *bacheler,* tu my aid. He, like a durn'd fool, cotch her by the laig, an' drug her back'ards ofen me. She jis' kivered him, an' I run, by golly! The nex time I seed him he wer bald headed, an' his face looked like he'd been a-fitin wildcats.

"Ole Missis Yardley wer a great noticer ove littil things, that nobody else ever seed. She'd say right in the middil ove sumbody's serious talk: 'Law sakes! thar goes that yaller slut ove a hen, a-flingin straws over her shoulder; she's arter settin now, an' haint laid but seven 40 aigs. I'll disapint *her,* see ef I don't; I'll put a punkin in her ne's, an' a feather in her nose. An' bless my soul! jis' look at that cow wif the wilted ho'n, a-flingin up dirt an' a-smellin the place whar hit cum frum, wif the rale ginuine still-wurim twis' in her tail, too; what upon the face ove the yeath kin she be arter now, the ole fool? watch her, Sally. An' sakes alive! jis' look at that ole sow; she's a-gwine in a fas' trot, wif her empty bag a-floppin agin her sides. Thar, she hes stop't, an's a-listenin! massy on us! what a long yearnis grunt she gin; 50 hit cum frum way back ove her kidneys. Thar she goes agin; she's arter no good, sich kerryin on means no good.'

"An' so she wud gabble, no odds who wer a-listenin. She looked like she mout been made at fust 'bout four foot long, an' the common thickness ove wimen when they's at tharsefs, an' then had her har tied tu a stump, a par ove steers hitched to her heels, an' then straiched out a-mos' two foot more—mos' ove the straichin cumin outen her laigs an' naik. Her stockins, a-hangin on the clothes-line tu dry, looked like a par ove sabre scab- 60 bards, an' her naik looked like a dry beef shank smoked, an' mout been ni ontu es tough. I never felt hit mysef, I didn't, I jis' jedges by looks. Her darter Sal wer bilt at fust 'bout the laingth ove her mam, but wer never straiched eny by a par ove steers an' she wer fat enuf tu kill; she wer taller lyin down than she wer a-standin up. Hit wer her who gin me the 'hump shoulder.' Jis' look at me; haint I'se got a tech ove the dromedary back thar bad? haint I humpy? Well, a-stoopin tu kiss that squatty lardstan ove a gal is what dun hit tu me. She wer the fairest-lookin gal I ever seed. She allers wore thick woolin stockins 'bout six inches too long fur her laig; they rolled down over her garters, lookin like a par ove life-presarvers up thar. I tell yu she wer a tarin gal enyhow. Luved kissin, wrastlin, an' biled cabbige, an' hated tite clothes, hot weather, an' suckit-riders. B'leved strong in married folk's ways, cradles, an' the remishun ove sins, an' didn't b'leve in corsets, fleas, peaners, nur the fashun plates."

"What caused the death of Mrs. Yardley, Sut?"

"Nuffin, only her heart stop't beatin 'bout losin a nine dimunt quilt. True, she got a skeer'd hoss tu run over her, but she'd a-got over that ef a quilt hadn't been mix'd up in the catastrophy. Yu see quilts wer wun ove her speshul gifts; she run strong on the bed-kiver question. Irish chain, star ove Texas, sun-flower, nine dimunt, saw teeth, checker board, an' shell quilts; blue, an' white, an' yaller an' black coverlids, an' callickercum-furts reigned triumphan' 'bout her hous'. They wer packed in drawers, layin in shelfs full, wer hung four dubbil on lines in the lof, packed in chists, piled on cheers, an' wer everywhar, even ontu the beds, an' wer changed every bed-makin. She told everybody she cud git tu listen tu hit that she ment tu give every durn'd one ove them tu Sal when she got married. Oh, lordy! what es fat a gal es Sal Yardley cud ever du wif half ove em, an' sleepin wif a husbun at that, is more nor I ever cud see through. Jis' think ove her onder twenty layer ove quilts in July, an' yu in thar too. Gewhillikins! George, look how I is sweatin' now, an' this is December. I'd 'bout es lief be shet up in a steam biler wif a three hundred pound bag ove lard, es tu make a bisiness ove sleepin wif that gal—'twould kill a glass-blower.

"Well, tu cum tu the serious part ove this conversashun, that is how the old quilt-mersheen an' coverlid-loom cum tu stop operashuns on this yeath. She hed narrated hit thru the neighborhood that nex Saterday she'd gin a quiltin—three quilts an' one cumfurt tu tie. 'Goblers, fiddils, gals, an' whisky,' wer the words she sent tu the men-folk, an' more tetchin ur wakenin words never drap't ofen an 'oman's tongue. She sed tu the gals, 'Sweet toddy, huggin, dancin, an' huggers in 'bun-

dunce.' Them words struck the gals rite in the pit ove the stumick, an' spread a ticklin sensashun bof ways, ontil they scratched thar heads wif one han, an' thar heels wif tuther.

"Everybody, he an' she, what wer baptized b'levers in the righteousnes ove quiltins wer thar, an' hit jis' so happen'd that everybody in them parts, frum fifteen summers tu fifty winters, wer unannamus b'levers. Strange, warn't hit? Hit wer the bigges' quiltin ever Missis Yardley hilt, an' she hed hilt hundreds; everybody wer thar, 'scept the constibil an' suckit-rider, two dam easily-spared pussons; the numbers ni ontu even too; jis' a few more boys nur gals; that made hit more exhitin, fur hit gin the gals a chance tu kick an' squeal a littil, wifout runnin eny risk ove not gittin kissed at all, an' hit gin reasonabil grouns fur a few scrimmages amung the he's. Now es kissin an' fitin am the pepper an' salt ove all soshul getherins, so hit wer more espishully wif this ove ours. Es I swung my eyes over the crowd, George, I thought quiltins, managed in a morril an' sensibil way, truly am good things—good fur free drinkin, good fur free eatin, good fur free huggin, good fur free dancin, good fur free fitin, an' goodest ove all fur poperlatin a country fas'.

"Thar am a fur-seein wisdum in quiltins, ef they hes proper trimmins: 'vittils, fiddils, an' sperrits in 'bun-dunce.' One holesum quiltin am wuf three old pray'r-meetins on the poperlashun pint, purtickerly ef hits hilt in the dark ove the moon, an' runs intu the night a few hours, an' April ur May am the time chosen. The moon don't suit quiltins whar everybody is well acquainted an' already fur along in courtin. She dus help pow'ful tu begin a courtin match onder, but when hit draws ni ontu a head, nobody wants a moon but the ole mammys.

"The mornin cum, still, saft, sunshiney; cocks crowin, hens singin, birds chirpin, tuckeys gobblin—jis' the day tu sun quilts, kick, kiss, squeal, an' make love.

"All the plow-lines an' clothes-lines wer straiched tu every post an' tree. Quilts purvailed. Durn my giz-zard ef two acres roun that ar house warn't jis' one solid quilt, all out a-sunnin, an' tu be seed. They dazzled the eyes, skeered the hosses, gin wimen the heart-burn, an' perdominated.

"To'ards sundown the he's begun tu drap in. Yearnis' needil-drivin cummenced tu lose groun; threads broke ofen, thimbils got los', an' quilts needed anuther roll.

Gigglin, winkin, whisperin, smoofin ove har, an' gals a-ticklin one anuther, wer a-gainin every inch ove groun what the needils los'. Did yu ever notis, George, at all sushul getherins, when the he's begin tu gather, that the young she's begin tu tickil one anuther an' the ole maids swell thar tails, roach up thar backs, an' sharpen thar nails ontu the bed-posts an' door jams, an' spit an' groan sorter like cats a-courtin? Dus hit mean *rale* rath, ur is hit a dare tu the he's, sorter kivered up wif
10 the outside signs ove danger? I honestly b'leve that the young shes' ticklin means, 'Cum an' take this job ofen our hans.' But that swellin I jis' don't onderstan; dus yu? Hit looks skeery, an' I never tetch one ove em when they am in the swellin way. I may be mistaken'd 'bout the ticklin bisiness too; hit may be dun like a feller chaws poplar bark when he haint got eny terbacker, a-sorter better nur nun make-shif. I dus know one thing tu a certainty: that is, when the he's take hold the ticklin quits, an' ef yu gits one ove the ole maids out tu herself,
20 then she subsides an' is the smoofes, sleekes, saft thing yu ever seed, an' dam ef yu can't hear her purr, jis' es plain!

"But then, George, gals an' ole maids haint the things tu fool time away on. Hits widders, by golly, what am the rale sensibil, steady-goin, never-skeerin, never-kickin, willin, sperrited, smoof pacers. They cum clost up tu the hoss-block, standin still wif thar purty silky years playin, an' the naik-veins a-throbbin, an' waits fur the word, which ove course yu gives, arter yu finds yer
30 feet well in the stirrup, an' away they moves like a cradil on cushioned rockers, ur a spring buggy runnin in damp san'. A tetch ove the bridil, an' they knows yu wants em tu turn, an' they dus hit es willin es ef the idear wer thar own. I be dod rabbited ef a man can't 'propriate happiness by the skinful ef he is in contack wif sumbody's widder, an' is smart. Gin me a willin widder, the yeath over: what they don't know, haint worth larnin. They hes all been tu Jamakey an' larnt how sugar's made, an' knows how tu sweeten wif hit;
40 an' by golly, they is always ready tu use hit. All yu hes tu du is tu find the spoon, an' then drink cumfort till yer blind. Nex tu good sperrits an' my laigs, I likes a twenty-five year ole widder, wif roun ankils, an' bright eyes, honestly an' squarly lookin intu yurn, an' sayin es plainly es a partrige sez 'Bob White,' 'Don't be afraid ove me; I hes been thar; yu know hit ef yu hes eny sense, an' thar's no use in eny humbug, ole feller—cum ahead!'"

"Ef yu onderstans widder nater, they ken save yu a power ove troubil, onsartinty, an' time, an' ef yu is inter-prisin yu gits mons'rous well paid fur hit. The very soun 50 ove thar littil shoe-heels speak full trainin, an' hes a knowin click as they tap the floor; an' the rustil ove thar dress sez, 'I dar yu tu ax me.'

"When yu hes made up yer mind tu court one, jis' go at hit like hit wer a job ove rail-maulin. Ware yer workin close, use yer common, every-day moshuns an' words, an' abuv all, fling away yer cinamint ile vial an' burn all yer love songs. No use in tryin tu fool em, fur they sees plum thru yu, a durn'd sight plainer than they dus thru thar veils. No use in a pasted shut; she's been 60 thar. No use in borrowin a cavortin fat hoss; she's been thar. No use in har-dye; she's been thar. No use in cloves, tu kill whisky breff; she's been thar. No use in buyin clost curtains fur yer bed, fur she has been thar. Widders am a speshul means, George, fur ripenin green men, killin off weak ones, an makin 'ternally happy the soun ones.

"Well, es I sed afore I flew the track an' got ontu the widders. The fellers begun tu ride up an' walk up, sorter slow, like they warn't in a hurry, the durn'd 'saitful 70 raskils, hitchin thar critters tu enything they cud find. One red-comb'd, long-spurr'd, dominecker feller, frum town, in a red an' white gridiron jackid an' patent leather gaiters, hitched his hoss, a wild, skeery, wall-eyed devil, inside the yard palins, tu a cherry tree lim'. Thinks I, that hoss hes a skeer intu him big enuf tu run intu town, an' perhaps beyant hit, ef I kin only tetch hit off; so I sot intu thinkin.

"One aind ove a long clothes-line, wif nine dimunt quilts ontu hit, wer tied tu the same cherry tree that the 80 hoss wer. I tuck my knife and socked hit thru every quilt, 'bout the middil, an' jis' below the rope, an' tied them thar wif bark, so they cudent slip. Then I went tu the back aind, an' ontied hit frum the pos', knottin in a hoe-handil, by the middil, tu keep the quilts frum slippin off ef my bark strings failed, an' laid hit on the groun. Then I went tu the tuther aind: thar wer 'bout ten foot tu spar, a-lyin on the groun arter tyin tu the tree. I tuck hit atwix Wall-eye's hine laigs, an' tied hit fas' tu bof stirrups, an' then cut the cherry tree lim' 90

---

72 dominecker, an uncomplimentary allusion to the youth's resem-blance to a rooster of the American breed called Dominickers

betwix his bridil an' the tree, almos' off. Now, mine yu thar wer two ur three uther ropes full ove quilts atween me an' the hous', so I wer purty well hid frum thar. I jis' tore off a palin frum the fence, an' tuck hit in bof hans, an' arter raisin hit 'way up yander, I fotch hit down, es hard es I cud, flatsided to'ards the groun, an' hit acksidentally happen'd tu hit Wall-eye, 'bout nine inches ahead ove the root ove his tail. Hit landed so hard that hit made my hans tingle, an' then busted intu splinters.
10 The first thing I did, wer tu feel ove mysef, on the same spot whar hit hed hit the hoss. I cudent help duin hit tu save my life, an' I swar I felt sum ove Wall-eye's sensashun, jis' es plain. The fust thing he did, wer tu tare down the lim' wif a twenty foot jump, his head to'ards the hous'. Thinks I, now yu hev dun hit, yu durn'd wall-eyed fool! tarin down that lim' wer the beginin ove all the troubil, an' the hoss did hit hissef; my conshuns felt clar es a mountin spring, an' I wer in a frame ove mine tu obsarve things es they happen'd,
20 an' they soon begun tu happen purty clost arter one another rite then, an' thar, an' tharabouts, clean ontu town, thru hit, an' still wer a-happenin, in the woods beyant thar ni ontu eleven mile frum ole man Yardley's gate, an' four beyant town.

"The fust line ove quilts he tried tu jump, but broke hit down; the nex one he ran onder; the rope cotch ontu the ho'n ove the saddil, broke at bof ainds, an' went along wif the hoss, the cherry tree lim' an' the fust line ove quilts, what I hed proverdensally tied fas' tu the
30 rope. That's what I calls foresight, George. Right furnint the frunt door he cum in contack wif ole Missis Yardley hersef, an' anuther ole 'oman; they wer a-holdin a nine dimunt quilt spread out, a-'zaminin hit, an' a-praisin hits purfeckshuns. The durn'd onmanerly, wall-eyed fool run plum over Missis Yardley, frum ahine, stompt one hine foot through the quilt, takin hit along, a-kickin ontil he made hits corners snap like a whip. The gals screamed, the men hollered wo! an' the ole 'oman wer toted intu the hous' limber es a wet
40 string, an' every word she sed wer, 'Oh, my preshus nine dimunt quilt!'

"Wall-eye busted thru the palins, an' Dominicker sed 'im, made a mortal rush fur his bitts, wer too late fur them, but in good time fur the strings ove flyin quilts, got tangled amung em, an' the gridiron jackid patren wer los' tu my sight amung star an' Irish chain quilts;

he went frum that quiltin at the rate ove thuty miles tu the hour. Nuffin lef on the lot ove the hole consarn, but a nine biler hat, a par ove gloves, an' the jack ove hearts.

"What a onmanerly, suddin way ove leavin places 50 sum folks hev got, enyhow.

"Thinks I, well, that fool hoss, tarin down that cherry tree lim', hes dun sum good, enyhow; hit hes put the ole 'oman outen the way fur the balance ove the quiltin, an' tuck Dominicker outen the way an' outen danger, fur that gridiron jackid wud a-bred a scab on his nose afore midnite; hit wer morrily boun tu du hit.

"Two months arterwards, I tracked the route that hoss tuck in his kalamatus skeer, by quilt rags, tufts ove cotton, bunches ove har, (human an' hoss,) an' scraps 60 ove a gridiron jackid stickin ontu the bushes, an' plum at the aind ove hit, whar all sign gin out, I foun a piece ove watch chain an' a hosses head. The places what know'd Dominicker, know'd 'im no more.

"Well, arter they'd tuck the ole 'oman up stairs an' camfired her tu sleep, things begun tu work agin. The widders broke the ice, an' arter a littil gigilin, goblin, an' gabblin, the kissin begun. *Smack!*—'Thar, now,' a widder sed that. *Pop!*—'Oh, don't!' *Pfip!*—'Oh, yu quit!' *Plosh!*—'Go *way* yu awkerd critter, yu kissed me 70 in the eye!' anuther widder sed that. *Bop!* 'Now yu ar satisfied, I recon, big mouf!' *Vip!*—'That haint fair!' *Spat!*—'Oh, lordy! May, cum pull Bill away; he's a-tanglin my har.' *Thut!*—'I jis' d-a-r-e yu tu du that agin!' a widder sed that, too. Hit sounded all 'roun that room like poppin co'n in a hot skillet, an' wer pow'ful sujestif.

"Hit kep on ontil I be durn'd ef *my* bristils didn't begin tu rise, an' sumthin like a cold buckshot wud run down the marrow in my back-bone 'bout every ten 80 secons, an' then run up agin, tolerabil hot. I kep a swallerin wif nuthin tu swaller, an' my face felt swell'd; an' yet I wer fear'd tu make a bulge. Thinks I, I'll ketch one out tu hersef torreckly, an' then I guess we'll rastil. Purty soon Sal Yardley started fur the smoke-'ous, so I jis' gin my head a few short shakes, let down one ove my wings a-trailin, an' sirkiled roun her wif a side twis' in my naik, steppin sidewise, an' a-fetchin up my hinmos' foot wif a sorter jerkin slide at every step. Sez I, 'Too coo-took a-too.' She onderstood hit, an stopt, 90 sorter spreadin her shoulders. An' jis' es I hed pouch'd out my mouf, an' wer a-reachin forrid wif hit, for the article hitsef, sunthin interfared wif me, hit did. George, wer yu ever ontu yer hans an' knees, an' let a hell-tarin big, mad ram, wif a ten-yard run, but yu yearnis'ly, jis' onst, right squar ontu the pint ove yer back-bone?"

"No, you fool; why do you ask?"

"Kaze I wanted tu know ef yu cud hev a realizin' noshun ove my shock. Hits scarcely worth while tu try tu make yu onderstan the case by words only, onless yu hev been tetched in that way. Gr-eat golly! the fust thing I felt, I tuck hit tu be a back-ackshun yeathquake; an' the fust thing I seed wer my chaw'r terbacker a-flyin over Sal's head like a skeer'd bat. My mouf wer pouch'd out, ready fur the article hitsef, yu know, an' hit went outen the roun hole like the wad outen a pop-gun—thug! an' the fust thing I know'd, I wer a flyin over Sal's head too, an' a-gainin on the chaw'r terbacker fast. I wer straitened out strait, toes hinemos', middil finger-nails foremos', an' the fust thing I hearn wer, 'Yu dam Shanghi!' Great Jerus-a-lam! I lit ontu my all fours jis' in time tu but the yard gate ofen hits hinges, an' skeer loose sum more hosses—kep on in a four-footed gallop,

clean acrost the lane afore I cud straiten up, an' yere I cotch up wif my chaw'r terbacker, stickin flat agin a fence-rail. I hed got so good a start that I thot hit a pity tu spile hit, so I jis' jump'd the fence an' tuck thru the orchurd. I tell yu I dusted these yere close, fur I tho't hit wer arter me.

"Arter runnin a spell, I ventered tu feel roun back thar, fur sum signs ove what hed happened tu me. George, arter two pow'ful hard tugs, I pull'd out the vamp an' sole ove one ove ole man Yardley's big bro-gans, what he hed los' amung my coat-tails. Dre'ful, dre'-ful! Arter I got hit away frum thar, my flesh went fas' asleep, frum abuv my kidneys tu my knees; about now, fur the fust time, the idear struck me, what hit wer that hed interfar'd wif me, an' los' me the kiss. Hit wer ole Yardley hed kicked me. I walked fur a month like I wer straddlin a thorn hedge. Sich a shock, at sich a time, an' on sich a place—jis' think ove hit! hit am tremenjus, haint hit? The place feels num, right now."

"Well, Sut, how did the quilting come out?"

"How the hell du yu 'speck me tu know? I warn't thar eny more."

1867

Thomas Bangs Thorpe

1815 · 1878

Although he was the author of the most famous tall tale of the pre-Civil War Southwest, "The Big Bear of Arkansas," Thomas Bangs Thorpe was born in the East—in Westfield, Massachusetts, in 1815. He left Wesleyan University, in Middletown, Connecticut, in 1836, when ill health made it necessary for him to move to a milder climate, and settled down in Baton Rouge, Louisiana. In Louisiana and other parts of what was then the Far West, Thorpe gathered material for both paint-ings and writings which won a fine reputation for him.

Thorpe had a varied career. He painted various frontier scenes and numerous portraits, among the most admired of which were one of Jenny Lind and one of his friend, Zachary Taylor. He edited several newspapers and wrote a number of sketches which were widely reprinted. He was in the army during the Mexican War. After the

Thorpe 289

war, he returned to the East—to New York, where he was an editor until his death in 1878.

The Mysteries of the Backwoods; or Sketches of the Southwest including Character, Scenery and Rural Sports (1846) and *The Hive of the Bee Hunter* (1854) were Thorpe's best books—both of them collections of sketches detailing life in the backwoods. "The Big Bear of Arkansas," this author's masterpiece, first appeared in a great publication of masculine humor of the day, *The Spirit of the Times,* in 1841. Like many other pieces published in that journal, this narrative shows how the art of the oral tale gave shape and substance to narrative in print.

F. J. Meine, "Thomas Bangs Thorpe," **Dictionary of American Biography**, New York, 1935 • Walter Blair, **Native American Humor (1800-1900)**, Cincinnati, 1937

The Big Bear of Arkansas

In 1839 John Neal, an Eastern critic and fiction writer quite prominent at the time, published the article "Story-Telling" in the **New York Mirror**. "Of all the stories I meet with," he testified, "none are so delightful to me as those I **over**-hear on board a steam-boat or a stage-coach . . . **live** stories, brimful of energy and vivacity." Thorpe's "Big Bear," published a couple of years later, conveyed much of the life and the gusto of a good yarn spun in the social hall of a steamboat.

If, as many good critics agree, the essence of humor is incongruity, Thorpe's narrative contains that essence. One notes the disparity, for instance, between the various worlds in the story—worlds which are identified with various groups and various scenes. Contrasted are the heterogeneous world of the steamboat, realistically portrayed in the "literary" words of the author; the fashionable world of New Orleans, satirically described in the homely words of Jim Doggett; and the comic, wildly fantastic world of Shirt-tail Bend in Arkansas, imaginatively revealed by Jim's poetical invention. Each of these worlds has its own elements of amusement, and the juxtaposition underlines and contrasts these elements.

As Jim—a fascinating character in his own right—tells his tall tale, he becomes more and more imaginative. The "creation state" of Arkansas, as he pictures it, is astonishing compared with any other part of America, and Shirt-tail Bend is astonishing even for Arkansas. Ordinary bear hunts in Jim's section are truly extraordinary, but the great hunt here described is even more wonderful. And as the account of the Big Bear proceeds, even that monster takes on more and more of a supernatural aspect.

Just at the moment Jim's fancy soars into the empyrean, a homely detail—the loss of the valiant hunter's "inexpressibles"—contrasts his imaginative flight with mundane reality. But Jim, having started to soar, is carried along by his imaginings. At the end his yarn, which has started as a jest, has become so real to its creator that he is tremendously impressed by it.

A steamboat on the Mississippi frequently, in making her regular trips, carries between places varying from one to two thousand miles apart; and as these boats advertise to land passengers and freight at "all intermediate landings," the heterogeneous character of the passengers of one of these up-country boats can scarcely be imagined by one who has never seen it with his own eyes. Starting from New Orleans in one of these boats, you will find yourself associated with men from every state in the Union, and from every portion of the globe; and a man of observation need not lack for amusement or instruction in such a crowd, if he will take the trouble to read the great book of character so favourably opened before him. Here may be seen jostling together the wealthy Southern planter, and the pedlar of tin-ware from New England—the Northern merchant, and the Southern jockey—a venerable bishop, and a desperate gambler,—the land speculator, and the honest farmer—professional men of all creeds and characters—Wolvereens, Suckers, Hoosiers, Buckeyes, and Corn-crackers, beside a "plentiful sprinkling" of the half-horse and half-alligator species of men, who are peculiar to "old Mississippi," and who appear to gain a livelihood simply by going up and down the river. In the pursuit of pleasure or business, I have frequently found myself in such a crowd.

On one occasion, when in New Orleans, I had occasion to take a trip of a few miles up the Mississippi, and I hurried on board the well-known "high-pressure-and-beat-everything" steamboat *Invincible,* just as the last note of the last bell was sounding; and when the confusion and bustle that is natural to a boat's getting under way had subsided, I discovered that I was associated in as heterogeneous a crowd as was ever got together. As my trip was to be of a few hours' duration only, I made no endeavours to become acquainted with my fellow passengers, most of whom would be together many days. Instead of this, I took out of my pocket the "latest paper," and more critically than usual examined its contents; my fellow passengers at the same time disposed themselves in little groups. While I was thus busily employed in reading, and my companions were more busily employed in discussing such subjects as suited their humours best, we were startled most unexpectedly by a loud Indian whoop, uttered in the "social hall," that part of the cabin fitted off for a bar; then was to be heard a loud crowing, which would not have continued to have interested us—such sounds being quite common in that place of spirits—had not the hero of these windy accomplishments stuck his head into the cabin and hallooed out, "Hurra for the Big Bar of Arkansaw!" and then might be heard a confused hum of voices, unintelligible, save in such broken sentences as "horse," "screamer," "lightning is slow" etc. As might have been expected, this continued interruption attracted the attention of every one in the cabin; all conversation dropped, and in the midst of this surprise the "Big Bar" walked into the cabin, took a chair, put his feet on the stove, and looking back over his shoulder, passed the general and familiar salute of "Strangers, how are you?" He then expressed himself as much at home as if he had been at "the Forks of Cypress," and "perhaps a little more so." Some of the company at this familiarity looked a little angry, and

some astonished; but in a moment every face was wreathed in a smile. There was something about the intruder that won the heart on sight. He appeared to be a man enjoying perfect health and contentment: his eyes were as sparkling as diamonds, and good-natured to simplicity. Then his perfect confidence in himself was irresistibly droll. "Perhaps," said he, "gentlemen," running on without a person speaking, "perhaps you have been to New Orleans often; I never made *the first visit before,* and I don't intend to make another in a crow's life. I am thrown away in that ar place, and useless, that ar a fact. Some of the gentlemen thar called me *green*—well, perhaps I am, said I, *but I arn't so at home;* and if I ain't off my trail much, the heads of them perlite chaps themselves wern't much the hardest; for according to my notion, they were real *know-nothings,* green as a pumpkin-vine—couldn't, in farming, I'll bet, raise a crop of turnips; and as for shooting, they'd miss a barn if the door was swinging, and that, too, with the best rifle in the country. And then they talked to me 'bout hunting, and laughed at my calling the principal game in Arkansaw poker, and high-low-jack. 'Perhaps,' said I, 'you prefer chickens and rolette'; at this they laughed harder than ever, and asked me if I lived in the woods, and didn't know what *game* was? At this I rather think I laughed. 'Yes,' I roared, and says, 'Strangers, if you'd asked me *how we got our meat* in Arkansaw, I'd a told you at once, and given you a list of varmints that would make a caravan, beginning with the bar, and ending off with the cat; that's *meat* though, not game.' Game, indeed, that's what city folks call it; and with them it means chippen-birds and shite-pokes; maybe such trash live in my diggens, but I arn't noticed them yet; a bird any way is too trifling. I never did shoot at but one, and I'd never forgiven myself for that, had it weighed less than forty pounds. I wouldn't draw a rifle on any thing less than that; and when I meet with another wild turkey of the same weight I will drap him."

"A wild turkey weighing forty pounds!" exclaimed twenty voices in the cabin at once.

"Yes, strangers, and wasn't it a whopper? You see,

---

2 Wolvereens, Suckers. See note, p. 274 • 2 Hoosiers, Buckeyes, Corn-crackers, natives, respectively, of Indiana, Ohio, and Kentucky • 78 chippen-birds and shite-pokes, chipping sparrows and green herons

The Big Bear of Arkansas 291

the thing was so fat that it couldn't fly far; and when he fell out of the tree, after I shot him, on striking the ground he bust open behind, and the way the pound gobs of tallow rolled out of the opening was perfectly beautiful."

"Where did all that happen?" asked a cynical-looking Hoosier.

"Happen! happened in Arkansaw: where else could it have happened, but in the creation state, the finishing-up country—a state where the *sile* runs down to the centre of the 'arth, and government gives you a title to every inch of it? Then its airs—just breathe them, and they will make you snort like a horse. It's a state without a fault, it is."

"Excepting mosquitoes," cried the Hoosier.

"Well, stranger, except them; for it ar a fact that they are rather *enormous,* and do push themselves in somewhat troublesome. But, stranger, they never stick twice in the same place; and give them a fair chance for a few months, and you will get as much above noticing them as an alligator. They can't hurt my feelings, for they lay under the skin; and I never knew but one case of injury resulting from them, and that was to a Yankee; and they take worse to foreigners, anyhow, than they do to natives. But the way they used that fellow up! first they punched him until he swelled up and busted; then he su-per-a-ted, as the doctor called it, until he was as raw as beef; then he took the ager, owing to the warm weather, and finally he took a steamboat and left the country. He was the only man that ever took mosquitoes to heart that I know of. But mosquitoes is natur, and I never find fault with her. If they ar large, Arkansaw is large, her varmints ar large, her trees ar large, her rivers ar large, and a small mosquito would be of no more use in Arkansaw than preaching in a canebrake."

This knock-down argument in favour of big mosquitoes used the Hoosier up, and the logician started on a new track, to explain how numerous bear were in his "diggins," where he represented them to be "about as plenty as blackberries, and a little plentifuler."

Upon the utterance of this assertion, a timid little man near me inquired if the bear in Arkansaw ever attacked the settlers in numbers.

"No," said our hero, warming with the subject, "no, stranger, for you see it ain't the natur of bar to go in droves; but the way they squander about in pairs and single ones is edifying. And then the way I hunt them the old black rascals know the crack of my gun as well as they know a pig's squealing. They grow thin in our parts, it frightens them so, and they do take the noise dreadfully, poor things. That gun of mine is perfect *epidemic among bar;* if not watched closely, it will go off as quick on a warm scent as my dog Bowie-knife will: and then that dog—whew! why the fellow thinks that the world is full of bar, he find them so easy. It's lucky he don't talk as well as think; for with his natural modesty, if he should suddenly learn how much he is acknowledged to be ahead of all other dogs in the universe, he would be astonished to death in two minutes. Strangers, the dog knows a bar's way as well as a horse-jockey knows a woman's; he always barks at the right time, bites at the exact place, and whips without getting a scratch. I never could tell whether he was made expressly to hunt bar, or whether bar was made expressly for him to hunt; any way, I believe they were ordained to go together as naturally as Squire Jones says a man and woman is, when he moralizes in marrying a couple. In fact, Jones once said, said he, 'Marriage according to law is a civil contract of divine origin; it's common to all countries as well as Arkansaw, and people take to it as naturally as Jim Doggett's Bowie-knife takes to bar.'"

"What season of the year do your hunts take place?" inquired a gentlemanly foreigner, who, from some peculiarities of his baggage, I suspected to be an Englishman, on some hunting expedition, probably at the foot of the Rocky Mountains.

"The season for bar hunting, stranger," said the man of Arkansaw, "is generally all the year round, and the hunts take place about as regular. I read in history that varmints have their fat season, and their lean season. That is not the case in Arkansaw, feeding as they do upon the *spontenacious* productions of the sile, they have one continued fat season the year round; though in winter things in this way is rather more greasy than in summer, I must admit. For that reason bar with us run in warm weather, but in winter, they only waddle. Fat, fat! it's an enemy to speed; it tames everything that has plenty of it. I have seen wild turkeys, from its influence, as gentle as chickens. Run a bar in this fat condition, and the way it improves the critter for eating is amazing; it sort of mixes the ile up with the meat, until you can't tell t'other from which. I've done this often. I recollect one perty morning in particular, of putting an old fellow on the stretch, and considering the weight he carried, he run well. But the dogs soon tired him down, and when I came up with him wasn't he in a beautiful sweat—I might say fever; and then to see his tongue sticking out of his mouth a feet, and his sides sinking and opening like bellows, and his cheeks so fat he couldn't look cross. In this fix I blazed at him, and pitch me naked into a briar path if the steam didn't come out of the bullet-hole ten foot in a straight line. The fellow, I reckon, was made on the high-pressure system, and the lead sort of bust his biler."

"That column of steam was rather curious, or else the bear must have been *warm*," observed the foreigner, with a laugh.

"Stranger, as you observe, that bar was WARM, and the blowing off of the steam show'd it, and also how hard the varmint had been run. I have no doubt if he had kept on two miles farther his insides would have been stewed; and I expect to meet with a varmint yet of extra bottom, who will run himself into a skinful of bar's grease: it is possible, much onlikelier things have happened."

"Whereabouts are these bears so abundant?" inquired the foreigner, with increasing interest.

"Why, stranger, they inhabit the neighbourhood of my settlement, one of the prettiest places on old Mississippi—a perfect location, and no mistake; a place that had some defects until the river made the 'cut-off' at 'Shirt-tail bend,' and that remedied the evil, as it brought my cabin on the edge of the river—a great advantage in wet weather, I assure you, as you can now roll a barrel of whiskey into my yard in high water from a boat, as easy as falling off a log. It's a great improvement, as toting it by land in a jug, as I used to do, *evaporated* it too fast, and it became expensive. Just stop with me, stranger, a month or two, or a year if you like, and you will appreciate my place. I can give you plenty to eat; for beside hog and hominy, you can have bar-ham, and bar-sausages, and a mattrass of bar-skins to sleep on, and a wildcatskin, pulled off hull, stuffed with corn-shucks for a pillow. That bed would put you to sleep if you had the rheumatics in every joint in your body. I call that ar bed a *quietus*. Then look at my land—the government ain't got another such a piece to dispose of. Such timber, and such bottom land, why you can't preserve

any thing natural you plant in it unless you pick it young, things thar will grow out of shape so quick. I once planted in those diggins a few potatoes and beets; they took a fine start, and after that an ox team couldn't have kept them from growing. About that time I went off to old Kentuck on bisiness, and did not hear from them things in three months, when I accidentally stumbled on a fellow who had stopped at my place, with an idea of buying me out. 'How did you like things?' said I. 'Pretty well,' said he; 'the cabin is convenient, and the timber land is good; but that bottom land ain't worth the first red cent.' 'Why?' said I. ' 'Cause,' said he. ' 'Cause what?' said I. ' 'Cause it's full of cedar stumps and Indian mounds,' said he, *and it can't be cleared.*' 'Lord,' said I, 'Them ar "cedar stumps" is beets, and them ar "Indian mounds" ar tater hills.' As I expected, the crop was overgrown and useless; the sile is too rich, *and planting in Arkansaw is dangerous.* I had a good-sized sow killed in that same bottom land. The old thief stole an ear of corn, and took it down where she slept at night to eat. Well, she left a grain or two on the ground, and lay down on them; before morning the corn shot up, and the percussion killed her dead. I don't plant any more; natur intended Arkansaw for a hunting ground, and I go according to natur."

The questioner who thus elicited the description of our hero's settlement, seemed to be perfectly satisfied and said no more; but the "Big Bar of Arkansaw" rambled on from one thing to another with a volubility perfectly astonishing, occasionally disputing with those around him, particularly with a "live Sucker" from Illinois, who had the daring to say that our Arkansaw friend's stories "smelt rather tall."

In this manner the evening was spent; but conscious that my own association with so singular a personage would probably end before morning, I asked him if he would not give me a description of some particular bear hunt; adding that I took great interest in such things, though I was no sportsman. The desire seemed to please him, and he squared himself round towards me, saying, that he could give me an idea of a bar hunt that was never beat in this world, or in any other. His manner was so singular, that half of his story consisted in his excellent way of telling it, the great peculiarity of which was the happy manner he had of emphasizing the prominent parts of his conversation. As near as I can

" ' . . . the dogs . . . pulled him about. . . . ' "—illustration by Darley for "The Big Bear of Arkansas"

recollect, I have italicized them, and given the story in his own words.

"Stranger," said he, "in bar hunts *I am numerous,* and which particular one, as you say, I shall tell, puzzles me. There was the old she devil I shot at the Hurricane last fall—then there was the old hog thief I popped over at the Bloody Crossing, and then—Yes, I have it! I will give you an idea of a hunt, in which the greatest bar was killed that ever lived, *none excepted;* about an old
10 fellow that I hunted more or less for two or three years; and if that ain't a particular bar hunt, I ain't got one to tell. But in the first place, stranger, let me say, I am pleased with you, because you ain't ashamed to gain information by asking, and listening, and that's what I say to Countess's pups every day when I'm home; and I have got great hopes of them ar pups, because they are continually *nosing* about; and though they stick it sometimes in the wrong place, they gain experience any how, and may learn something useful to boot. Well,
20 as I was saying about this big bar, you see when I and some more first settled in our region, we were drivin to hunting naturally; we soon liked it, and after that we

found it an easy matter to make the thing our business. One old chap who had pioneered 'afore us, gave us to understand that we had settled in the right place. He dwelt upon its merits until it was affecting, and showed us, to prove his assertions, more marks on the sassafras trees than I ever saw on a tavern door 'lection time. 'Who keeps that ar reckoning?' said I. 'The bar,' said he. 'What for?' said I. 'Can't tell,' said he; 'but so it is; 30 the bar bite the bark and wood too, at the highest point from the ground they can reach, and you can tell, by the marks,' said he, 'the length of the bar to an inch.' 'Enough,' said I; 'I've learned something here a'ready, and I'll put it in practice.'

"Well, stranger, just one month from that time I killed a bar, and told its exact length before I measured it, by those very marks; and when I did that, I swelled up considerable—I've been a prouder man ever since. So I went on, larning something every day, until I was 40 reckoned a buster, and allowed to be decidedly the best bar hunter in my district; and that is a reputation as much harder to earn than to be reckoned first man in Congress, as an iron ramrod is harder than a toadstool. Did the varmints grow over-cunning by being fooled with by green-horn hunters, and by this means get troublesome, they send for me as a matter of course; and thus I do my own hunting, and most of my neighbours'. I walk into the varmints though, and it has become about as much the same to me as drinking. It is 50 told in two sentences—a bar is started, and he is killed. The thing is somewhat monotonous now—I know just how much they will run, where they will tire, how much they will growl, and what a thundering time I will have in getting them home. I could give you this history of the chase with all particulars at the commencement, I know the signs so well—*Stranger, I'm certain.* Once I met with a match though, and I will tell you about it; for a common hunt would not be worth relating.

"On a fine fall day, long time ago, I was trailing about 60 for bar, and what should I see but fresh marks on the sassafras trees, about eight inches above any in the forests that I knew of. Says I, 'them marks is a hoax, or it indicates the d———t bar that was ever grown.' In fact, stranger, I couldn't believe it was real, and I went on. Again I saw the same marks, at the same height, and *I knew the thing lived.* That conviction came home to my soul like an earthquake. Says I, 'here is something a-purpose for me: that bar is mine, or I give up the hunting business.' The very next morning what should I see but a number of buzzards hovering over my cornfield. 'The rascal has been there,' said I, 'for that sign is certain:' and, sure enough, on examining, I found the bones of what had been as beautiful a hog the day before, as was ever raised by a Buckeye. Then I tracked the critter out of the field to the woods, and all the marks he left behind, showed me that he was *the bar.*

"Well, stranger, the first fair chase I ever had with that big critter, I saw him no less than three distinct times at a distance: the dogs run him over eighteen miles and broke down, my horse gave out, and I was as nearly used up as a man can be, made on *my* principle, *which is patent.* Before this adventure, such things were unknown to me as possible; but, strange as it was, that bar got me used to it before I was done with him; for he got so at last, that he would leave me on a long chase *quite easy.* How he did it, I never could understand. That a bar runs at all, is puzzling; but how this one could tire down and bust up a pack of hounds and a horse, that were used to overhauling everything they started after in no time, was past my understanding. Well, stranger, that bar finally got so sassy, that he used to help himself to a hog off my premises whenever he wanted one; the buzzards followed after what he left, and so between *bar and buzzard,* I rather think I was *out of pork.*

"Well, missing that bar so often took hold of my vitals, and I wasted away. The thing had been carried too far, and it reduced me in flesh faster than an ager. I would see that bar in every thing I did; *he hunted me,* and that, too, like a devil, which I began to think he was. While in this fix, I made preparations to give him a last brush, and be done with it. Having completed every thing to my satisfaction, I started at sunrise, and to my great joy, I discovered from the way the dogs run, that they were near him; finding his trail was nothing, for that had become as plain to the pack as a turnpike road. On we went, and coming to an open country, what should I see but the bar very leisurely ascending a hill, and the dogs close at his heels, either a match for him in speed, or else he did not care to get out of their way— I don't know which. But wasn't he a beauty, though? I loved him like a brother.

"On he went, until he came to a tree, the limbs of which formed a crotch about six feet from the ground. Into this crotch he got and seated himself, the dogs yelling all around it; and there he sat eyeing them as quiet as a pond in low water. A green-horn friend of mine, in company, reached shooting distance before me, and blazed away, hitting the critter in the centre of his forehead. The bar shook his head as the ball struck it, and then walked down from that tree as gently as a lady would from a carriage. 'Twas a beautiful sight to see him do that—he was in such a rage that he seemed to be as little afraid of the dogs as if they had been sucking pigs; and the dogs warn't slow in making a ring around him at a respectful distance, I tell you; even Bowie-knife, himself, stood off. Then the way his eyes flashed—why the fire of them would have singed a cat's hair; in fact that bar was in a *wrath all over.* Only one pup came near him, and he was brushed out so totally with the bar's left paw, that he entirely disappeared; and that made the old dogs more cautious still. In the meantime, I came up, and taking deliberate aim as a man should do, at his side, just back of his foreleg, *if my gun did not snap,* call me a coward, and I won't take it personal. Yes, stranger, *it snapped,* and I could not find a cap about my person. While in this predicament, I turned round to my fool friend—says I, 'Bill,' says I, 'you're an ass—you're a fool—you might as well have tried to kill that bar by barking the tree under his belly, as to have done it by hitting him in the head. Your shot has made a tiger of him, and blast me, if a dog gets killed or wounded when they come to blows, I will stick my knife into your liver, I will—' my wrath was up. I had lost my caps, my gun had snapped, the fellow with me had fired at the bar's head, and I expected every moment to see him close in with the dogs, and kill a dozen of them at least. In this thing I was mistaken, for the bar leaped over the ring formed by the dogs, and giving a fierce growl, was off—the pack, of course, in full cry after him. The run this time was short, for coming to the edge of a lake the varmint jumped in, and swam to a little island in the lake, which it reached just a moment before the dogs. 'I'll have him now,' said I, for I had found my caps in the *lining of my coat*—so, rolling a log into the lake, I paddled myself across to the island, just as the dogs had cornered the bar in a thicket. I rushed up and fired—

at the same time the critter leaped over the dogs and came within three feet of me, running like mad; he jumped into the lake, and tried to mount the log I had just deserted, but every time he got half his body on it, it would roll over and send him under; the dogs, too, got around him, and pulled him about, and finally Bowie-knife clenched with him, and they sunk into the lake together. Stranger, about this time, I was excited, and I stripped off my coat, drew my knife, and intended to have taken a part with Bowie-knife myself, when the bar rose to the surface. But the varmint staid under— Bowie-knife came up alone, more dead than alive, and with the pack came ashore. 'Thank God,' said I, 'the old villain has got his deserts at last.' Determined to have the body, I cut a grape-vine for a rope, and dove down where I could see the bar in the water, fastened my queer rope to his leg, and fished him, with great difficulty, ashore. Stranger, may I be chawed to death by young alligators, if the thing I looked at wasn't a *she bar, and not the old critter after all.* The way matters got mixed on that island was onaccountably curious, and thinking of it made me more than ever convinced that I was hunting the devil himself. I went home that night and took to my bed—the thing was killing me. The entire team of Arkansaw in barhunting, acknowledged himself used up, and the fact sunk into my feelings like a snagged boat will in the Mississippi. I grew as cross as a bar with two cubs and a sore tail. The thing got out 'mong my neighbours, and I was asked how come on that individu-al that never lost a bar when once started? and if that same individ-u-al didn't wear telescopes when he turned a she bar, of ordinary size, into an old he one, a little larger than a horse? 'Perhaps,' said I, 'friends'—getting wrathy—'perhaps you want to call somebody a liar.' 'Oh, no,' said they, 'we only heard such things as being *rather common* of late, but we don't believe one word of it; oh, no,'—and then they would ride off and laugh like so many hyenas over a dead nigger. It was too much, and I determined to catch that bar, go to Texas, or die,—and I made my preparations accordin'. I had the pack shut up and rested. I took my rifle to pieces and iled it. I put caps in every pocket about my person, *for fear of the lining.* I then told my neighbours, that on Monday morning— naming the day—I would start THAT BAR, and bring him home with me, or they might divide my settlement

among them, the owner having disappeared. Well, stranger, on the morning previous to the great day of my hunting expedition, I went into the woods near my house, taking my gun and Bowie-knife along, just *from habit,* and there sitting down also from habit, what should I see, getting over my fence, but *the bar!* Yes, the old varmint was within a hundred yards of me, and the way he walked *over that fence*—stranger, he loomed up like a *black mist,* he seemed so large, and he walked right towards me. I raised myself, took deliberate aim, and fired. Instantly the varmint wheeled, gave a yell, and *walked through the fence* like a falling tree would through a cobweb. I started after, but was tripped up by my inexpressibles, which either from habit, or the excitement of the moment, were about my heels, and before I had really gathered myself up, I heard the old varmint groaning in a thicket near by, like a thousand sinners, and by the time I reached him he was a corpse. Stranger, it took five niggers and myself to put that carcase on a mule's back, and old long-ears waddled under the load, as if he was foundered in every leg of his body, and with a common whopper of a bar, he would have trotted off, and enjoyed himself. 'Twould astonish you to know how big he was: I made a *bedspread of his skin* and the way it used to cover my bar mattress, and leave several feet on each side to tuck up, would have delighted you. It was in fact a creation bar, and if it had lived in Samson's time, and had met him, in a fair fight, it would have licked him in the twinkling of a dice-box. But, strangers, I never like the way I hunted, and *missed him.* There is something curious about it, I could never understand,—and I never was satisfied at his giving in so easy at last. Perhaps, he had heard of my preparations to hunt him the next day, so he jist come in, like Capt. Scott's coon, to save his wind to grunt with in dying; but that ain't likely. My private opinion is, that that bar was an *unhuntable bar, and died when his time come."*

When the story was ended, our hero sat some minutes with his auditors in a grave silence; I saw there was a mystery to him connected with the bear whose death

---

81 **Capt. Scott's coon.** Oral lore pictured Captain Scott as such a great hunter that when he approached a raccoon, the animal shouted down to him, "Don't shoot! I'm a-comin' down." The same tall story was told about Davy Crockett (see p. 273)

he had just related, that had evidently made a strong impression on his mind. It was also evident that there was some superstitious awe connected with the affair,—a feeling common with all "children of the wood," when they meet with any thing out of their everyday experience. He was the first one, however, to break the silence, and jumping up, he asked all present to "liquor" before going to bed,—a thing which he did, with a number of companions, evidently to his heart's content.

Long before day, I was put ashore at my place of destination, and I can only follow with the reader, in imagination, our Arkansas friend, in his adventures at the "Forks of Cypress" on the Mississippi.

1841

LITERARY COMEDIANS:

Browne Shaw Clark

Charles Farrar Browne (Artemus Ward)

1834 · 1867

Beginning as a printer's devil, Charles Farrar Browne, like Samuel L. Clemens, drifted into humorous writing and lecturing and was, at the end of his life, fabulously well known. He was born in Waterford, Maine, in 1834. As a young man, he was apprenticed to a printer in Lancaster, New Hampshire. From there he went to other printing shops, first in New England, later in the Middle West. In time he moved from his printer's case to the editorial desks of various newspapers.

Browne was an editor of the Cleveland, Ohio, *Plain Dealer* in 1858 when some playful letters he composed started him on his way to fame. Artemus Ward, the purported author of the letters, introduced himself as the illiterate, humorless owner of an itinerant waxworks and menagerie. From various towns he wrote requests for publicity or accounts of his adventures while traveling. After these pieces had won a large following for him, Browne went to New York to work on the comic magazine *Vanity Fair*. In 1861 he embarked on a highly remunerative career as a comic lecturer, and during the next several years he attracted large audiences in lecture halls everywhere in this country and, eventually, in Egyptian Hall in London. He died in England in 1867.

Browne, in contrast with such earlier comic authors as Seba Smith and William Tappan Thompson, became a full-time humorist. To keep his readers and his lecture audiences laughing, he perfected all sorts of tricks which amused—bad spellings and queer sentences, phrases, and words. Since the emphasis on laughable diction was so great, Browne tried less and less to depict a clear-cut character, and in time Artemus Ward was hard to distinguish from his creator. They stood for the same things and got laughs by employing the same devices. Browne was typical of a majority of the humorists of his day—professional funnymen, literary comedians who exploited the humor of diction rather than the humor of character. Although these humorists have lost some of their appeal because the taste for poor grammar and distorted spelling in humor has largely abated, their writings are interesting as social documents and as works foreshadowing much of the "free association humor" of such twentieth-century authors as Benchley, Thurber, and Perelman.

Artemus Ward: His Book, New York, 1862 • *Artemus Ward: His Travels*, New York, 1865 • *Artemus Ward in London*, London, 1867 • D. C. Seitz, *Artemus Ward*, New York, 1919

Browne 297

Artemus Ward, His Book

ONE OF MR. WARD'S BUSINESS LETTERS

To the Editor of the———

Sir—I'm movin along—slowly along—down tords your place. I want you should rite me a letter, sayin how is the show bizniss in your place. My show at present consists of three moral Bares, a Kangaroo (a amoozin little Raskal—t' would make you larf yerself to deth to see the little cuss jump up and squeal) wax figgers of G. Washington Gen. Tayler John Bunyan Capt. Kidd and Dr. Webster in the act of killin Dr. Park-
man, besides several miscellanyus moral wax statoots of celebrated piruts & murderers, &c., ekalled by few & exceld by none. Now Mr. Editor, scratch orf a few lines sayin how is the show bizniss down to your place. I shall hav my hanbills dun at your offiss. Depend upon it. I want you should git my hanbills up in flamin stile. Also git up a tremenjus excitemunt in yr. paper 'bowt my onparaleld Show. We must fetch the public sumhow. We must wurk on their feelins. Cum the moral on 'em strong. If it's a temprance community tell 'em I sined the pledge fifteen minits arter Ise born, but on the contery ef your peple take their tods, say Mister Ward is as Jenial a feller as we ever met, full of conwiviality, & the life an sole of the Soshul Bored. Take, don't you? If you say anythin abowt my show say my snaiks is as harmliss as the new born Babe. What a interestin study it is to see a zewological animil like a snaik under perfeck subjecshun! My kangaroo is the most larfable little cuss I ever saw. All for 15 cents. I am anxyus to skewer your infloounce. I repeet in regard to them hanbills that I shall git 'em struck orf up to your printin office. My perlitercal sentiments agree with yourn exactly. I know thay do, becawz I never saw a man whoos didn't.

Respectively yures,

A. Ward.

P.S.—You scratch my back & Ile scratch your back.

1858·1862

I hav no politics. Nary a one. I'm not in the bisiness. If I was I spose I should holler versiffrusly in the streets at nite and go home to Betsy Jane smellen of coal ile and gin, in the mornin. I should go to the Poles arly. I should stay there all day. I should see to it that my nabers was thar. I should git carriges to take the kripples, the infirm and the indignant thar. I should be on guard agin frauds and sich. I should be on the look out for the infamus lise of the enemy, got up jest be4 elecshun for perlitical effeck. When all was over and my candydate was elected, I should move heving & arth—so to speak—until I got orfice, which if I didn't git a orfice I should turn round and abooze the Administration with all my mite and maine. But I'm not in the bisness. I'm in a far more respectful bisniss nor what pollertics is. I wouldn't giv two cents to be a Congresser. The wuss insult I ever received was when sertin citizens of Baldinsville axed me to run fur the Legislater. Sez I, "My friends, dostest think I'd stoop to that there?" They turned as white as a sheet. I spoke in my most orfullest tones, & they knowd I wasn't to be trifled with. They slunked out of site to onct.

There4, havin no politics, I made bold to visit Old Abe at his humstid in Springfield. I found the old feller in his parler, surrounded by a perfeck swarm of orfice seekers. Knowin he had been capting of a flat boat on the roarin Mississippy I thought I'd address him in sailor lingo, so sez I "Old Abe, ohoy! Let out yer mainsuls, reef hum the forecastle & throw yer jib-poop overboard! Shiver my timbers, my harty!" [N. B. This is ginuine mariner langwidge. I know, becawz I've seen sailor plays acted out by them New York theater fellers.] Old Abe lookt up quite cross & sez, "Send in yer petition by & by. I can't possibly look at it now. Indeed, I can't. It's onpossible sir."

"Mr. Linkin, who do you spect I air?" sed I.

"A orfice-seeker, to be sure?" sed he.

"Wall, sir," sed I, "yous never more mistaken in your life. You hain't gut a orfiss I'd take under no circumstances. I'm A. Ward. Wax figgers is my perfeshun. I'm the father of Twins, and they look like me—*both of them*. I cum to pay a frendly visit to the President eleck of the United States. If so be you wants to see me say so—if not, say so, & I'm orf like a jug handle."

"Mr. Ward, sit down. I am glad to see you, Sir."

"Repose in Abraham's Buzzum!" sed one of the orfice seekers, his idee bein to git orf a goak at my expense.

"Wall," sez I, "ef all you fellers repose in that there Buzzum thare'll be mity poor nussin for sum of you!" whereupon Old Abe buttoned his weskit clear up and blusht like a maidin of sweet 16. Jest at this pint of the conversation another swarm of the orfice-seekers arrove & cum pilin into the parler. Sum wanted post orfices, sum wanted collectorships, sum wantid furrin missions, and all wanted sumthin. I thought Old Abe would go crazy. He hadn't more than had time to shake hands with 'em, before another tremenjis crowd cum porein onto his premises. His house and dooryard was now perfeckly overflowed with orfice seekers, all clameruss for a immejit interview with Old Abe. One man from Ohio, who had about seven inches of corn whisky into him, mistook me for Old Abe and addrest me as "The Prahayrie Flower of the West!" Thinks I *you* want a offiss putty bad. Another man with a gold heded cane and a red nose told Old Abe he was "a seckind Washington & the Pride of the Boundliss West."

Sez I, "Square, you wouldn't take a small postoffis if you could git it, would you?"

Sez he, "A patrit is abuv them things, sir!"

"There's a putty big crop of patrits this season, ain't there Squire?" sez I, when *another* crowd of offiss seekers pored in. The house, door-yard, barn & woodshed was now all full, and when another crowd cum I told 'em not to go away for wan't of room as the hog-pen was still empty. One patrit from a small town in Michygan went up on top the house, got into the chimney and slid down into the parler where Old Abe was endeverin to keep the hungry pack of orfice-seekers from chawin him up alive without benefit of clergy. The minit he reached the fire-place he jumpt up, brusht the soot out of his eyes, and yelled: "Don't make eny pintment at the Spunkville postoffiss till you've read my papers. All the respectful men in our town is signers to that there dockyment!"

"Good God!" cride Old Abe, "they cum upon me from the skize—down the chimneys, and from the bowels of the yearth!" He hadn't more'n got them words out of his delikit mouth before two fat offissseekers from Wisconsin, in endeverin to crawl atween his legs for the purpuss of applyin for the toll-gateship at Milwawky, upsot the President eleck & he would hev gone sprawlin into the fire-place if I hadn't caught him in these arms. But I hadn't more'n stood him up strate before another man cum crashin down the chimney, his head strikin me vilently agin the inards and prostratin my voluptoous form onto the floor. "Mr. Linkin," shoutid the infatooated being, "my papers is signed by every clergyman in our town, and likewise the skoolmaster!"

Artemus Ward interviews President Lincoln—cartoon in Vanity Fair, *December 9, 1860*

Sez I, "you egrejis ass," gittin up & brushin the dust from my eyes, "I'll sign your papers with this bunch of bones, if you don't be a little more keerful how you make my bread basket a depot in the futer. How do you like that air perfumery?" sez I, shuving my fist under his nose. "Them's the kind of papers I'll giv you! Them's the paper's you want!"

"But I workt hard for the ticket; I toiled night and day! The patrit should be rewarded!"

"Virtoo," sed I, holdin' the infatooated man by the coat-collar, "Virtoo, sir, is its own reward. Look at me!" He did look at me, and qualed be4 my gase. "The fact is," I continued, lookin' round on the hungry crowd, "there is scacely a offiss for every ile lamp carrid round durin' this campane. I wish thare was. I wish thare was furrin missions to be filled on varis lonely Islands where eppydemics rage incessantly, and if I was in Old Abe's place I'd send every mother's son of you to them. What air you here for?" I continnered, warmin up considerable, "can't you giv Abe a minit's peace? Don't you see he's worrid most to death! Go home, you miserable men, go home & till the sile! Go to peddlin tinware—go to choppin wood—go to bilin' sope—stuff sassengers— black boots—git a clerkship on sum respectable manure

10 cart—go round as original Swiss Bell Ringers—becum 'origenal and only' Campbell Minstrels—go to lecturin at 50 dollars a nite—imbark in the peanut bizniss— *write for the Ledger*—saw off your legs and go round givin concerts, with techin appeals to a charitable public, printed on your handbills—anything for a honest living, but don't come round here drivin Old Abe crazy by your outrajis cuttings up! Go home. Stand not upon the order of your goin' but go to onct! If in five minits from this time," sez I pullin' out my new sixteen dollar

20 huntin cased watch, and brandishin' it before their eyes, "Ef in five minits from this time a single sole of you remains on these here premises, I'll go out to my cage near by, and let my Boy Constructor loose! & ef he gits amung you, you'll think old Solferino has cum again and no mistake!" You ought to hev seen them scamper, Mr. Fair. They run orf as tho Satun his self was arter them with a red hot ten pronged pitchfork. In five minits the premises was clear.

"How kin I ever repay you, Mr. Ward, for your kindness?" sed Old Abe, advancin and shakin me warmly 30 by the hand. "How kin I ever repay you, sir?"

"By givin the whole country a good, sound administration. By poerin' ile upon the troubled waturs, North and South. By pursooin' a patriotic, firm, and just course, and then if any State wants to secede, let 'em Sesesh!"

"How 'bout my Cabinit, Mister Ward?" sed Abe.

"Fill it up with Showmen sir! Showmen is devoid of politics. They hain't got any principles! They know how to cater for the public. They know what the public 40 wants, North & South Showmen, sir, is honest men. Ef you doubt their literary ability, look at their posters, and see small bills! Ef you want a Cabinit as is a Cabinit fill it up with showmen, but don't call on me. The moral wax figger perfeshun musn't be permitted to go down while there's a drop of blood in these vains! A. Linkin, I wish you well! Ef Powers or Walcutt wus to pick out a model for a beautiful man, I scarcely think they'd sculp you; but ef you do the fair thing by your country you'll make as putty a angel as any of us! A. Linkin, use the 50 talents which Nature has put into you judishusly and firmly, and all will be well. A. Linkin, adoo!"

He shook me cordyully by the hand—we exchanged picters, so we could gaze upon each others' liniments when far away from one another—he at the hellum of the ship of State, and I at the hellum of the show bizniss—admittance only 15 cents.

1861·1862

Henry Wheeler Shaw (Josh Billings)

1818 · 1885

"He was Aesop and Ben Franklin, condensed and abridged." So Bill Arp, a contemporary of Henry Wheeler Shaw, described Shaw's creation, Josh Billings. Believing that "you have got to be wise before you can be witty," Shaw adapted to the days of the literary comedian the materials and techniques of earlier aphorists and moralizers. Americans, long fond of horse sense spiced with humor, naturally found such a writer most appealing.

Shaw was born in Lanesboro, Massachusetts, April 21, 1818. He prepared for college at Lenox Academy, and then attended Hamilton College for about two years before he was expelled for a prank. At seventeen he migrated to the West, where he traveled widely, stopping off now and then to do odd jobs. He was, at various times, a farmer, a coal operator, and a proprietor of an Ohio River steamboat before he returned to the East and settled down to be a real estate operator and an auctioneer in Poughkeepsie, New York. In the late 1850's, when some of his comic writings for newspapers were widely reprinted, he got off to a start as a successful funnyman. He moved to New York City and remained there the rest of his life.

Lectures and the publication of his work in newspapers, magazines, and books—*Josh Billings, His Sayings* (1865), *Josh Billings on Ice and Other Things* (1868) —added to his fame. Beginning in 1869, he published an annual series titled *Josh Billings' Farmer's Allminax*

which sold more than a hundred thousand copies almost every year for a decade.

Billings was famous not for stories but for essays or single sentences packed with amusingly phrased common sense. His kinship with Poor Richard was obvious, but his cacography showed that his writing was also related to that of such a contemporary as Artemus Ward. In his hayfield cogitations on beasts and men, in addition to a flair for comic and well-ordered sentences, he had, as Max Eastman has observed, a gift for setting down "a series of verbal pictures" expressing his ideas. This talent for concreteness is evident in such a sentence as "Pride lives on itself, it is like a raccoon in the winter, kept fat by sucking its claws." It is also evident in the selections which follow.

Josh Billings, His Works Complete, New York, 1888 • Cyril Clemens, Josh Billings, Yankee Humorist, Webster Groves, Missouri, 1932

Essa on the Muel

The muel iz haf hoss and haf Jackass, and then kums tu a full stop, natur diskovering her mistake.

Tha weigh more, akordin tu their heft, than enny other kreetur, except a crowbar.

Tha kant hear enny quicker, nor further than the hoss, yet their ears are big enuff for snow shoes.

You kan trust them with enny one whose life aint worth enny more than the muels. The only wa tu keep them in a paster, is tu turn them into a medder jineing, and let them jump out.

Tha are reddy for use, just as soon as they will du tu abuse.

Tha haint got enny friends, and will live on huckle berry brush, with an ocksional chanse at Kanada thistels.

Honesty haz a short kreed, and branes haz no pedigree at all.—J. B.

Its better to kno less, than to kno so much that aint so.—JOSH BILLINGS.

If you want to git there quick, go slow—Josh.

JOSH BILLINGS
Struggling with his Great Serio-Comic Lecture
THE PROBABILITIES OF LIFE
Perhaps rain—Perhaps not.

Advertisement of a lecture by Josh Billings

Tha are a modern invenshun, i dont think the Bible deludes tu them at tall.

Tha sel for more money than enny other domestik animile. Yu kant tell their age by looking into their mouth, enny more than you kould a Mexican kannons. Tha never hav no dissease that a good club wont heal.

If tha ever die tha must kum rite tu life agin, for i never herd noboddy sa "ded muel."

Tha are like sum men, verry korrupt at harte; ive known them tu be good muels for 6 months, just tu git a good chanse to kick sumbody.

I never owned one, nor never mean to, unless thare is a United Staits law passed, requiring it.

The only reason why tha are pashunt, is bekause tha are ashamed ov themselfs.

I have seen eddikated muels in a sirkus.

Tha kould kick, and bite, tremenjis. I would not sa what I am forced tu sa again the muel, if his birth want an outrage, and man want tu blame for it.

Enny man who is willing tu drive a muel, ought to be exempt by law from running for the legislatur.

Tha are the strongest creeturs on earth, and heaviest ackording tu their sise; I herd tell ov one who fell oph from the tow path, on the Eri kanawl, and sunk as soon as he touched bottom, but he kept rite on towing the boat tu the nex stashun, breathing thru his ears, which stuck out ov the water about 2 feet 6 inches; i didn't see this did, but an auctioneer told me ov it, and i never knew an auctioneer tu lie unless it was absolutely convenient.

1860

Hoss Sense

There is nothing that has bin diskovered yet, that iz as skarse as good Hoss sense, about 28 hoss power.

I don't mean race hoss, nor trotting hoss sense, that kan run a mile in 1:28 and then brake down; nor trot in 2:13, and good for nothing afterwards, only to brag on; but I mean the all-day hoss sense, that iz good for 8 miles an hour, from rooster crowing in the morning, until the cows cum home at night, klean tew the end ov the road.

I hav seen fast sense, that was like sum hosses, who could git so far in one day that it would take them two days tew git back, on a litter. I don't mean this kind nuther.

Good hard-pan sense iz the thing that will wash well, wear well, iron out without wrinkling, and take starch without kracking.

Menny people are hunting after uncommon sense, but they never find it a good deal; uncommon sense iz ov the nature of genius, and all genius iz the gift of God, and kant be had, like hens eggs, for the hunting.

Good, old-fashioned common sense iz one ov the hardest things in the world to out-wit, out-argy, or beat in enny way, it iz az honest az a loaf ov good domestik bread, alwus in tune either hot from the oven or 8 days old.

Common sense kan be improved upon by edukashun —genius kan be too, sum, but not much.

Edukashun gauls genius like a bad setting harness.

Common sense iz like biled vittles, it is good right from the pot, and it is good nex day warmed up.

If every man waz a genius, mankind would be az bad oph az the heavens would be, with every star a comet, things would git hurt badly, and noboddy tew blame.

Common sense iz instinkt, and instinkt don't make enny blunders mutch, no more than a rat duz, in coming out, or going intew a hole, he hits the hole the fust time, and just fills it.

Genius iz always in advance ov the times, and makes sum magnificent hits, but the world owes most ov its tributes to good hoss sense.

1873?

Charles Heber Clark
(Max Adeler)

1847 · 1915

William H. Clark was an Episcopalian clergyman in Maryland when, in 1847, his son Charles Heber Clark, was born. During the author's youth, the family did not prosper, because the father was an abolitionist and a Northern sympathizer preaching in the South. Schooled at Georgetown, Washington, D. C., at fifteen Charles became an office boy in a Philadelphia commission house. In 1863, at eighteen, he joined the Union army to serve during the final two years of the Civil War. After the war, Clark returned to Philadelphia and became a reporter on the *Philadelphia Inquirer.* He did well as a journalist, and spent the rest of his life working for various Philadelphia newspapers and magazines.

His literary fame was chiefly as a humorist—the portrayer of life in the suburbs. Under the pen name Max Adeler, he wrote *Out of the Hurly-Burly* (1874), *Elbow Room* (1876), *Random Shots* (1879), and several rather negligible works of serious fiction. In his final years. having turned to what he considered higher pursuits, he did what he could to live down his reputation as a comic writer.

Like others of his period, Clark was a transitional figure between the old humor and the humor of today. His pictures of home life in some ways forecast Clarence Day's *Life with Father* (p. 999), and on occasion in his associative, self-deprecatory humor he foreshadowed such modern humorists as Robert Benchley and James Thurber. Yet in his writings there are touches of narrative, bits of diction, methods of getting laughs, which show his relationship to the earlier humorists.

G. H. Genzmer, "Charles Heber Clark," **Dictionary of American Biography,** New York, 1930

From

Out of the Hurly-Burly

TROUBLE WITH COOLEY

I hardly think I shall get along so well with my neighbor on the other side, Cooley, as I do with Pitman. He is not only exceedingly ill-natured, but he inclines to be impertinent. Several times he has volunteered advice respecting the management of my garden and grounds, and has displayed a disposition to be somewhat sarcastic when his plans did not meet with my approval. I contrived, however, to avoid a breach of our amicable relations until the other day, when his conduct became absolutely unendurable.

I observed in the last number of Ball's *Journal of Health* some suggestions concerning a good method of exercising the lungs and expanding the chest. They were to this effect:

"Training for a prize-fight, Adeler?"—illustration by
A. B. Frost for the first edition

"Step out into the purest air you can find;
stand perfectly erect with the head up and the
shoulders back, and then, fixing the lips as though
you were going to whistle, draw the air, not
through the nostrils, but through the lips, into
the lungs. When the chest is about half full,
gradually raise the arms, keeping them extended
with the palms of the hands down, as you suck in
the air, so as to bring them over the head just as
10 the lungs are quite full. Then drop the thumbs
inward, and after gently forcing the arms backward and the chest open, reverse the process by
which you draw your breath till the lungs are
empty. This process should be repeated three or
four times immediately after bathing, and also
several times through the day."

This seemed reasonable, and I determined to give it
a trial. For that purpose I went out into the yard; and

pinning the directions to a tree, I stood in front of them
where I could see them. Just as I began, Cooley came 20
out; and perceiving me, he placed his elbows upon the
fence, rested his chin upon his arms and watched me
with a very peculiar smile upon his face. I was exceedingly annoyed and somewhat embarrassed, but I
was determined that he should not have the gratification of driving me away from my own ground. I made
up my mind that I would continue the exercise without
appearing to notice him. In a few moments, however,
he remarked:

"Training for a prize-fight, Adeler?" 30

I made no reply, but continued the exercise. When I
had gone through the programme once, I began again.
As I arrived at that portion of it where the instructions
direct the arrangement of the lips, Mr. Cooley, by this
time somewhat incensed at my silence, observed,

"Whistle us a tune, Adeler. Give us something lively!"

As I paid no attention to this invitation, Cooley
embraced the opportunity afforded by the upward motion of my arms, in accordance with the directions, to
ask me if I was going to dive, and to offer to bring me 40
out a tub in case I cherished such a design.

Then I completed the exercise and went into the house
without giving Cooley any reason to suppose that I was
aware of his presence. The next day I performed the
ceremony at the same place, at the same hour. On the
third day Cooley evidently expected me, for as soon as
I appeared he came up to the fence and assumed his old
position. He had with him a couple of friends, whom
he must have summoned for the express purpose of
tormenting me. When I had gone through the move- 50
ments once, Cooley said:

"See here, Adeler, I don't want to do you any harm,
but let me advise you as a friend to go to an asylum. I
have known much worse cases than yours to be cured.
It isn't kind to your family for you to remain at large.
You're afflicted with only a mild form now; but if you
don't do something, you'll have a violent paroxysm
some day, and smash things. Now, take my advice, and
put yourself under treatment."

Silence upon my part. 60

"How would you take it now," inquired Cooley, in
a tone indicative of yearning tenderness, "if I should get
over the fence and chain you to the pump while I go
for the doctor? I really think you are getting dangerous."

"Mr. Cooley," I said, "I wish you would attend to your own business. I do not wish to quarrel with you, sir, but I will not have any interference on your part with my affairs. If it will make you any happier to learn what I am doing, I will tell you, seeing that you are so much interested in the matter, that I am exercising, under medical direction, for the benefit of my lungs."

"Exercising for the benefit of his lungs!" moaned Cooley. "His mind is entirely gone."

"Yes, sir," I said, angrily, "I am exercising for the benefit of my lungs, according to the directions of Dr. Ball, and I will thank you to keep your tongue quiet about it."

"He has them awfully bad," exclaimed Cooley, with a pathetic look. "There is no such man as Dr. Ball, you know," he remarked, in a confidential tone, to one of his companions.

"I wish you distinctly to understand that I will not tolerate this impertinence much longer, sir," I exclaimed, indignantly. "What right have you to interfere with me upon my own ground, you ruffian?"

"His intellect's completely shattered," said Cooley, with a mournful shake of his head, to his companions. "Poor Mrs. Adeler! It will be a terrible blow for her and for the children. My heart bleeds for them."

"Mr. Cooley," I said, "I want no more of this. I shall discontinue Dr. Ball's exercise at this place for the present, but I will tell you before I go that I consider you an insolent, unendurable idiot, and I will repay you some day or other for your outrageous behavior to me."

"Sad, sad, indeed!" said Cooley to his friends. "Strange how he clings to that fancy about a man named Ball, isn't it?"

One of Cooley's companions observed that the deranged were apt to get such notions in their heads, and he supplemented this statement with the remark, "This is a very interesting case—very."

Then I went into the house, and from the window saw Cooley and his companions walk away laughing. Not even the unpardonable insolence of Cooley can disguise the fact that the affair has a certain comic aspect; and when I became calmer, I confess that I appreciated this phase of the occurrence with some keenness, even though I happened to occupy an exceedingly unpleasant position as the victim of the joke. But I shall be even

with Cooley for this. I will devise a scheme for tormenting him which will cause him to rue the day that he interfered with my pulmonary gymnastics. Dr. Ball's recipe, however, I think I will toss into the fire. I will expand my lungs by learning to sing or to play upon the flute. My family can then participate in my enjoyment. A married man has no right to be selfish in his pleasures.

1874

PITMAN AS A POLITICIAN

Some of the friends of Judge Pitman induced him, just before the last election, to permit himself to be nominated for the State Legislature, and accordingly he was presented to the people of this community as a candidate. Of course he was not selected because of his fitness for the position. The party managers knew him to be a very popular man; and as the success of the party is the only thing they care for, they chose Pitman as the person most likely to secure that result. I cannot say that I disapproved of the selection. For some reason, it appears to be entirely impossible for American citizens who live in any of the Middle States to find educated and intelligent men who are willing to represent them in the Legislatures. Those bodies are composed for the most part of men whose solitary purpose is plunder. They are legislators simply because it pays better to blackmail railroad companies and to accept bribes from people who want votes for rascally measures than it does to pick pockets. They have the instincts and the principles of a pickpocket, but their ambition is greater. They do not steal handkerchiefs and watches, because they can filch fabulous sums of money from the public treasury and from villains who want to do dirty work under the color of the law. They know enough to enable them, with the assistance of party rings, to have themselves counted in at election-time, and to devise new and dexterous schemes of dishonesty; but in other and rather more desirable of the qualifications of lawmakers they are deficient. They occupy the most important place in republican governments without knowing what republicanism means, and they create laws for the communities without having any knowledge of the science of law or the slightest acquaintance with the needs and requirements of the people for whom they act. The average American legislator is both ignorant and dishonest. Judge Pitman is ignorant, but he is honest; and as his election would secure at least a very important half of a fitting legislator, I supported him.

My other neighbor, Cooley, was the chairman of the committee to whose care was consigned the management of the campaign in which Judge Pitman played so prominent a part; and Cooley conducted the business with even an excess of enthusiasm. Just after the nomination of Pitman, Cooley called on him to say that a number of his friends had declared their intention to offer him a serenade. Cooley informed the judge that some refreshment must be given to the serenaders, but he, as the chairman of the committee, would attend to that; the judge need not make preparations of any kind. Accordingly, on the following evening a brass band, accompanied by a score or two politicians, entered Pitman's front yard, and for half an hour there was some very good music. Then the judge came out upon the porch and made a better speech than I had expected to hear from him. He concluded by asking the company to enter his house. Cooley was there with a wagon-load of meat and drink, including, of course, a large quantity of rum of the most impressive kinds. The judge, with the fear of the temperance society present in his mind, protested against the liquor; but Cooley demonstrated to him that he would be defeated and the party ruined if it was excluded, and so Pitman reluctantly permitted it to be placed upon his table. Besides, as Cooley had been so very liberal in undertaking to make this provision at his own cost, the judge disliked to hurt his feelings by refusing to permit the use of that which Cooley evidently considered the most important portion of it.

The guests remained at the banquet until four o'clock the next morning, the politicians meanwhile making speeches and the band playing occasionally in the dining-room in a most uproarious manner. We could hear the noise at my house during the night, and sleep was possible only with the windows closed.

At four o'clock my door-bell rang violently; and upon descending to ascertain the cause of a visit at such an unseemly hour, I encountered Judge Pitman. He was nearly frantic with indignation.

"Adeler," he said, "them fellers is a-carryin' on scan-

d'lous over yer at my house. They're all drunk as owls; an' when I want 'em to go home, they laugh an' swear an' cheer an' smash the furniture an' bu'st things generally. Mrs. Pitman's 'bout skeered to death. Can't you come over an' help me clear them out?"

"Why don't you call a couple of policemen? You hunt up two or three officers while I dress myself, and we will see if we can't adjourn the meeting."

By the time I was ready Pitman arrived with one policeman, and we proceeded to his house. As we entered, the leader of the band was sitting upon the stairs, infamously drunk, with the handle of his umbrella in his mouth, vainly endeavoring to play a tune by fumbling his fingers among the ribs. Mr. Cooley was in a corner of the parlor supporting himself by the wall while he endeavored to discuss the question of the tariff with Pitman's plaster bust of Daniel Webster, and to correct Daniel's view of the local option law. Another politician was sitting upon the carpet crying because, so he informed us, his wife's maiden name was McCarthy, and just as the policeman was removing him a combat occurred between the bass drummer and a man from Wilmington, during which the drummer was hurled against the pier glass and then dragged out to bleed upon the rug. The house was finally cleared of the company just as the church clock struck six, and then Pitman went to bed with sentiments of complete disgust for politics and politicians.

But he remained a candidate of the party. He had promised to run, and he determined to go through with the business.

"That serenade was rough enough without anythin' wuss," said the judge to me a day or two afterward; "but I did think Cooley was a-rubbin' it in 'most too hard when he come over yesterday with a bill for the refreshments which he wanted me to pay."

"Why, I thought he agreed to supply the supper?"

"So he did. But now he says that of course he was only actin' for me. 'The candidate,' he says, 'always foots all the bills.' I'll foot this one, an' then I'll foot Cooley if he ever brings them ruffians to my house again. I expect nothin' else but the temperance society will shut down on me for that riot we had t'other night."

"I hope not; but I should think that affair would have made you sorry that you ever undertook this business."

"So it does," replied the judge, "but I never back down when I go into a thing. I'm goin' to run for the Legislatur'; and if I'm elected, I'm goin' to serve my country honestly until my time's up. Then I'm comin' home, an' goin' to stay home. And what's more, I'll stir up that Legislatur' while I'm in it. You mind me!"

The result of the contest was that the judge was elected by a large majority, and he will sit in the next Assembly.

1874

LOCAL COLORISTS:

Whittier   Stowe   Harte   Eggleston   Cable   Murfree

Harris   Jewett   Freeman   Porter

Quaker

Local Colorists of new England

John Greenleaf Whittier

abolitionist

1807 · 1892

Even during the years when he had been active as an abolitionist (see pp. 55-62), Whittier had written a good deal of verse and prose portraying the life and lore of his native district, Essex County in Massachusetts. "His mind," as Van Wyck Brooks has said, "was steeped in local associations, tales of witches, tales of the Indian wars, the gossip of wandering farm hands and gypsies." He had used such materials in *Legends of New England* (1831), *Mogg Megone* (1836), *Lays of My Home and Other Poems* (1843), *Margaret Smith's Journals* (1849), and *Home Ballads, Poems and Lyrics* (1860).

After the end of the Civil War, Whittier devoted more of his energies to writing regional poetry, publishing his most admired poem, *Snow-Bound* (1866) as well as *The Tent of the Beach and Other Poems*

Illustration: the old covered bridge—reproduced from a drawing by Emmett Owen in Everyday Things in American Life: 1776-1876 by W. C. Langdon, copyright 1930, 1941 by Charles Scribner's Sons, used by permission of the publishers

(1867), *Among the Hills and Other Poems* (1869), *Ballads of New England* (1870), and other less notable volumes. The extraordinary success of *Snow-Bound* both puzzled and delighted its author.

In his poetic local color writing, Whittier belonged to the tradition represented before his birth by the poet of Scottish rural life, Robert Burns, and carried on today by Robert Frost. His achievement was to record in simple verse the sort of life lived in New England before his day and during his lifetime. At times—particularly in his idyllic reminiscence, "The Barefoot Boy"—he was sentimental; but on many occasions he created authentic and detailed, though relatively uncomplicated, depictions of Yankee life which were and still are greatly enjoyed by many readers. The Prelude to "Among the Hills" and *Snow-Bound*, each with its own particular emphasis, complement one another to present an admirably rounded picture. Seemingly, these are artless creations, yet the selection and ordering of details as well as the simple phrasings are more artful than they may at first appear to be. (For bibliographical note, see p. 56.)

The Barefoot Boy

Blessings on thee, little man,
Barefoot boy, with cheek of tan!
With thy turned-up pantaloons,
And thy merry whistled tunes;
With thy red lip, redder still
Kissed by strawberries on the hill;
With the sunshine on thy face,
Through thy torn brim's jaunty grace,
From my heart I give thee joy,—
I was once a barefoot boy!   10
Prince thou art,—the grown-up man
Only is republican.
Let the million-dollared ride!
Barefoot, trudging at his side,
Thou hast more than he can buy
In the reach of ear and eye,—
Outward sunshine, inward joy:
Blessings on thee, barefoot boy!

O for boyhood's painless play,
Sleep that wakes in laughing day,   20
Health that mocks the doctor's rules,
Knowledge never learned of schools,
Of the wild bee's morning chase,
Of the wild-flower's time and place,
Flight of fowl and habitude
Of the tenants of the wood;
How the tortoise bears his shell,
How the woodchuck digs his cell,
And the ground-mole sinks his well;
How the robin feeds her young,   30
How the oriole's nest is hung;
Where the whitest lilies blow,
Where the freshest berries grow,
Where the groundnut trails its vine,
Where the wood-grape's clusters shine;
Of the black wasp's cunning way,
Mason of his walls of clay,
And the architectural plans
Of gray hornet artisans!—
For, eschewing books and tasks,   40
Nature answers all he asks;
Hand in hand with her he walks,
Face to face with her he talks,
Part and parcel of her joy,—
Blessings on the barefoot boy!

O for boyhood's time of June,
Crowding years in one brief moon,
When all things I heard or saw,
Me, their master, waited for.
I was rich in flowers and trees,   50
Humming-birds and honey-bees;
For my sport the squirrel played,
Plied the snouted mole his spade;
For my taste the blackberry cone
Purpled over hedge and stone;
Laughed the brook for my delight
Through the day and through the night,
Whispering at the garden wall,

Talked with me from fall to fall;
Mine the sand-rimmed pickerel pond,   60
Mine the walnut slopes beyond,
Mine, on bending orchard trees,
Apples of Hesperides!
Still as my horizon grew,
Larger grew my riches too,
All the world I saw or knew
Seemed a complex Chinese toy,
Fashioned for a barefoot boy!

O for festal dainties spread,
Like my bowl of milk and bread,—   70
Pewter spoon and bowl of wood,
On the door-stone, gray and rude!
O'er me, like a regal tent,
Cloudy-ribbed, the sunset bent,
Purple-curtained, fringed with gold,
Looped in many a wind-swung fold;
While for music came the play
Of the pied frog's orchestra;
And, to light the noisy choir,
Lit the fly his lamp of fire.   80
I was monarch: pomp and joy
Waited on the barefoot boy!

Cheerily, then, my little man,
Live and laugh, as boyhood can!
Though the flinty slopes be hard,
Stubble-speared the new-mown sward,
Every morn shall lead thee through
Fresh baptisms of the dew;
Every evening from thy feet
Shall the cool wind kiss the heat: 90
All too soon these feet must hide
In the prison cells of pride,
Lose the freedom of the sod,
Like a colt's for work be shod,
Made to tread the mills of toil,
Up and down in ceaseless moil:
Happy if their track be found
Never on forbidden ground;
Happy if they sink not in
Quick and treacherous sands of sin,   100
Ah! that thou couldst know thy joy,
Ere it passes, barefoot boy!

1856

This poem, Whittier said in a letter of 1880, twenty-three years after its publication, "was founded solely on a fragment of rhyme which I heard from one of my early schoolmasters, a native of Marblehead. I supposed the story to which it referred dated back at least a century. I knew nothing of the participators, and the narrative of the ballad was pure fancy." The letter was addressed to Samuel Roads, Jr., who, in his **History of Marblehead**, had stated that Ireson's crew, rather than the Captain, actually had been responsible for the abandonment of the vessel. Whittier was indebted to James Russell Lowell, then editor of the **Atlantic**, for the suggestion that the quoted refrain be phrased in Cape Ann dialect.

Of all the rides since the birth of time,
Told in story or sung in rhyme,—
On Apuleius's Golden Ass,
Or one-eyed Calendar's horse of brass,
Witch astride of a human back,
Islam's prophet on Al-Borák,—
The strangest ride that ever was sped
Was Ireson's, out from Marblehead!
Old Floyd Ireson, for his hard heart,
Tarred and feathered and carried in a cart   10
By the women of Marblehead!

Body of turkey, head of owl,
Wings a-droop like a rained-on fowl,
Feathered and ruffled in every part,
Skipper Ireson stood in the cart.
Scores of women, old and young,
Strong of muscle, and glib of tongue,
Pushed and pulled up the rocky lane,
Shouting and singing the shrill refrain:

---

3 **Apuleius's Golden Ass,** the ass into which a young man was transformed in Lucius Apuleius' Roman satire, **Metamorphoses** (155 A.D.?) • 4 **Calendar,** the story of "The Third Calendar" in **The Arabian Nights** • 6 **Islam's . . . Al-Borák.** Mohammed, the prophet of Islam, was carried to the seventh heaven on a winged white animal called Al-Borák

"Here's Flud Oirson, fur his horrd horrt,   20
Torr'd an' futherr'd an' corr'd in a corrt
    By the women o' Morble'ead!"

Wrinkled scolds with hands on hips,
Girls in bloom of cheek and lips,
Wild-eyed, free-limbed, such as chase
Bacchus round some antique vase,
Brief of skirt, with ankles bare,
Loose of kerchief and loose of hair,
With conch-shells blowing and fish-horns' twang,
Over and over the Maenads sang: 30
    "Here's Flud Oirson, fur his horrd horrt,
    Torr'd an' futherr'd an' corr'd in a corrt
        By the women o' Morble'ead!"

Small pity for him!—He sailed away
From a leaking ship, in Chaleur Bay,—
Sailed away from a sinking wreck,
With his own town's-people on her deck!
"Lay by! lay by!" they called to him.
Back he answered, "Sink or swim!
Brag of your catch of fish again!"
And off he sailed through the fog and rain!
    Old Floyd Ireson, for his hard heart,
    Tarred and feathered and carried in a cart
        By the women of Marblehead!

Fathoms deep in dark Chaleur
That wreck shall lie forevermore.
Mother and sister, wife and maid,
Looked from the rocks of Marblehead
Over the moaning and rainy sea,—
Looked for the coming that might not be!
What did the winds and the sea-birds say   50
Of the cruel captain who sailed away?—
    Old Floyd Ireson, for his hard heart,
    Tarred and feathered and carried in a cart
        By the women of Marblehead!

Through the street, on either side,
Up flew windows, doors swung wide;
Sharp-tongued spinsters, old wives gray,
Treble lent the fish-horn's bray.
Sea-worn grandsires, cripple-bound,   60
Hulks of old sailors run aground,

Shook head, and fist, and hat, and cane,
And cracked with curses the hoarse refrain:
    "Here's Flud Oirson, fur his horrd horrt,
    Torr'd an' futherr'd an' corr'd in a corrt
        By the women o' Morble'ead!"

Sweetly along the Salem road
Bloom of orchard and lilac showed.
Little the wicked skipper knew
Of the fields so green and the sky so blue.   70
Riding there in his sorry trim,
Like an Indian idol glum and grim,
Scarcely he seemed the sound to hear
Of voices shouting, far and near:
    "Here's Flud Oirson, fur his horrd horrt,
    Torr'd an' futherr'd an' corr'd in a corrt
        By the women o' Morble'ead!"

Hear me, neighbors!" at last he cried,—
"What to me is this noisy ride?
What is the shame that clothes the skin
To the nameless horror that lives within?
Waking or sleeping, I see a wreck,   80
And hear a cry from a reeling deck!
Hate me and curse me,—I only dread
The hand of God and the face of the dead!"
    Said old Floyd Ireson, for his hard heart,
    Tarred and feathered and carried in a cart
        By the women of Marblehead!

Then the wife of the skipper lost at sea
Said, "God has touched him!—why should we?"   90
Said an old wife mourning her only son,
"Cut the rogue's tether and let him run!"
So with soft relentings and rude excuse,
Half scorn, half pity, they cut him loose,
And gave him a cloak to hide him in,
And left him alone with his shame and sin.
    Poor Floyd Ireson, for his hard heart,
    Tarred and feathered and carried in a cart
        By the women of Marblehead!

1857

26 Bacchus, god of wine, is frequently portrayed on antique vases •
30 Maenads, also called Bacchantes, the feminine followers of the
god • 35 Chaleur Bay, inlet of the Gulf of St. Lawrence

Telling the Bees

Samuel T. Pickard, Whittier's biographer, notes that the description at the beginning of this poem contains many details concerning the poet's own birthplace. The approach, the "gap in the old wall," "the stepping-stones," the garden and its daffodils, the red-barred gate, the poplars, the cattle-yard were all parts of the scene. But the story is wholly imaginative: Whittier's sister Mary was still living when the poem was written. The tale unfolded is of the returning lover who hears the chore-girl performing the Yankee ceremony of chanting to the bees the news of a death in the house. Only in the final lines does the lover discover that the one who has died is his beloved.

Here is the place; right over the hill
   Runs the path I took:
You can see the gap in the old wall still,
   And the stepping-stones in the shallow brook.

There is the house, with the gate red-barred,
   And the poplars tall;
And the barn's brown length, and the cattle-yard,
   And the white horns tossing above the wall.

There are the beehives ranged in the sun;
   And down by the brink   10
Of the brook are her poor flowers, weed o'errun,
   Pansy and daffodil, rose and pink.

A year has gone, as the tortoise goes,
   Heavy and slow;
And the same rose blows, and the same sun glows,
   And the same brook sings of a year ago.

There's the same sweet clover-smell in the breeze;
   And the June sun warm
Tangles his wings of fire in the trees,
   Setting, as then, over Fernside farm.   20

I mind me how with a lover's care
   From my Sunday coat
I brushed off the burrs, and smoothed my hair,
   And cooled at the brookside my brow and throat.

Since we parted, a month had passed,—
   To love, a year;
Down through the beeches I looked at last
   On the little red gate and the well-sweep near.

I can see it all now,—the slantwise rain
   Of light through the leaves,   30
The sundown's blaze on her window-pane,
   The bloom of her roses under the eaves.

Just the same as a month before,—
   The house and the trees,
The barn's brown gable, the vine by the door,—
   Nothing changed but the hives of bees.

Before them, under the garden wall,
   Forward and back,
Went drearily singing the chore-girl small,
   Draping each hive with a shred of black.   40

Trembling, I listened: the summer sun
   Had the chill of snow;
For I knew she was telling the bees of one
   Gone on the journey we all must go!

Then I said to myself, "My Mary weeps
   For the dead to-day:
Haply her blind old grandsire sleeps
   The fret and the pain of his age away."

But her dog whined low; on the doorway sill,
   With his cane to his chin,   50
The old man sat; and the chore-girl still
   Sung to the bees stealing out and in.

And the song she was singing ever since
   In my ear sounds on:—
"Stay at home, pretty bees, fly not hence!
   Mistress Mary is dead and gone!"

1857

(handwritten annotations) Written after death of his sister & mother • memorial poem • Old-fashioned farmer's fireside in winter —

Snow-Bound
A Winter Idyl

Of this poem, Whittier wrote a friend, "It is a winter idyl —a picture of an old-fashioned farmer's fireside in winter— and if it were not mine I should call it pretty good." This memorial poem, written shortly after the death of two persons—his sister and his mother—whom the poet had loved very much, was a loving re-creation of the scenes and personalities of the poet's boyhood.

The manuscript was completed and sent to the publisher October 3, 1865, but before it reached print in 1866, the poet had made a number of careful revisions. Despite this care and his faith in the excellence of the poem, Whittier was astonished at the public reception. Because it was a poem which all could understand and because it expressed sentiments shared by many Americans, it sold widely. Whittier's first royalty check was for $10,000, and the poem continued to be popular for a number of years. It is still generally considered the best poem of its kind ever written in America.

Whittier wrote this note on the poem: "The inmates of the family at the Whittier homestead who are referred to . . . were my father, mother, my brother and two sisters, and my uncle and aunt, both unmarried. In addition, there was the district school-master, who boarded with us. The 'not unfeared, half-welcome guest' was Harriet Livermore . . . a young woman of fine natural ability, enthusiastic, eccentric, with slight control over her violent temper, which sometimes made her religious profession doubtful. . . . She early embraced the doctrine of the Second Advent, and felt it her duty to proclaim the Lord's speedy coming."

(handwritten) to his own family

To the Memory of the Household It Describes,
This Poem Is Dedicated by the Author

"*As the Spirits of Darkness be stronger in the dark, so Good Spirits which be Angels of Light are augmented not only by the Divine light of the Sun, but also by our common VVood Fire: and as the Celestial Fire drives away dark spirits, so also this our Fire of VVood doth the same.*"—

COR. AGRIPPA, Occult Philosophy, Book I. ch. v.

"*Announced by all the trumpets of the sky,
Arrives the snow; and, driving o'er the fields,
Seems nowhere to alight; the whited air
Hides hills and woods, the river and the heaven,
And veils the farm-house at the garden's end.
The sled and traveller stopped, the courier's feet
Delayed, all friends shut out, the housemates sit
Around the radiant fireplace, enclosed
In a tumultuous privacy of storm.*"—

EMERSON, The Snow-Storm.

The sun that brief December day
Rose cheerless over hills of gray,
And, darkly circled, gave at noon
A sadder light than waning moon.
Slow tracing down the thickening sky
Its mute and ominous prophecy,
A portent seeming less than threat,
It sank from sight before it set.
A chill no coat, however stout,
Of homespun stuff could quite shut out,   10
A hard, dull bitterness of cold,
That checked, mid-vein, the circling race
Of life-blood in the sharpened face,
The coming of the snow-storm told.
The wind blew east; we heard the roar
Of Ocean on his wintry shore,
And felt the strong pulse throbbing there
Beat with low rhythm our inland air.

Meanwhile we did our nightly chores,—
Brought in the wood from out of doors,   20
Littered the stalls, and from the mows
Raked down the herd's-grass for the cows:
Heard the horse whinnying for his corn;
And, sharply clashing horn on horn,
Impatient down the stanchion rows
The cattle shake their walnut bows;

---

15 wind blew east, from the east. The home was about fifteen miles west of the ocean • 22 herd's-grass, timothy • 26 walnut bows were fastened around the necks of the cows and affixed to the stanchions

While, peering from his early perch
Upon the scaffold's pole of birch,
The cock his crested helmet bent
And down his querulous challenge sent.   30

Unwarmed by any sunset light
The gray day darkened into night,
A night made hoary with the swarm
And whirl-dance of the blinding storm,
As zigzag wavering to and fro
Crossed and recrossed the wingéd snow:
And ere the early bedtime came
The white drift piled the window-frame,
And through the glass the clothes-line posts
Looked in like tall and sheeted ghosts.   40

So all night long the storm roared on:
The morning broke without a sun;
In tiny spherule traced with lines
Of Nature's geometric signs,
In starry flake, and pellicle,
All day the hoary meteor fell;
And, when the second morning shone,   *2 nites*
We looked upon a world unknown,
On nothing we could call our own.
Around the glistening wonder bent   50
The blue walls of the firmament,
No cloud above, no earth below,—
A universe of sky and snow!
The old familiar sights of ours
Took marvellous shapes; strange domes and towers
Rose up where sty or corn-crib stood,
Or garden-wall, or belt of wood;
A smooth white mound the brush-pile showed,
A fenceless drift what once was road;
The bridle-post an old man sat   60
With loose-flung coat and high cocked hat;
The well-curb had a Chinese roof;
And even the long sweep, high aloof,
In its slant splendor, seemed to tell
Of Pisa's leaning miracle.

A prompt, decisive man, no breath
Our father wasted: "Boys, a path!"
Well pleased, (for when did farmer boy
Count such a summons less than joy?)

Our buskins on our feet we drew;   70
With mittened hands, and caps drawn low,
To guard our necks and ears from snow,
We cut the solid whiteness through.
And, where the drift was deepest, made
A tunnel walled and overlaid
With dazzling crystal: we had read
Of rare Aladdin's wondrous cave,
And to our own his name we gave,
With many a wish the luck were ours
To test his lamp's supernal powers.   80
We reached the barn with merry din,
And roused the prisoned brutes within.
The old horse thrust his long head out,
And grave with wonder gazed about;
The cock his lusty greeting said,
And forth his speckled harem led;
The oxen lashed their tails, and hooked,
And mild reproach of hunger looked;
The hornéd patriarch of the sheep,
Like Egypt's Amun roused from sleep,   90
Shook his sage head with gesture mute,
And emphasized with stamp of foot.

All day the gusty north-wind bore
The loosening drift its breath before;
Low circling round its southern zone,
The sun through dazzling snow-mist shone.
No church-bell lent its Christian tone
To the savage air, no social smoke
Curled over woods of snow-hung oak.
A solitude made more intense   100
By dreary-voicéd elements,
The shrieking of the mindless wind,
The moaning tree-boughs swaying blind,
And on the glass the unmeaning beat
Of ghostly finger-tips of sleet.
Beyond the circle of our hearth
No welcome sound of toil or mirth
Unbound the spell, and testified
Of human life and thought outside.
We minded that the sharpest ear   110

65 **Pisa's . . . miracle,** the leaning tower of Pisa • 77 **Aladdin's . . . cave** refers to the story in *The Arabian Nights* of Aladdin and his magic lamp • 90 **Amun,** or **Ammon,** an Egyptian god who had the head of a ram

Snow-Bound   **313**

The buried brooklet could not hear,
The music of whose liquid lip
Had been to us companionship,
And, in our lonely life, had grown
To have an almost human tone.

As night drew on, and, from the crest
Of wooded knolls that ridged the west,
The sun, a snow-blown traveller, sank
From sight beneath the smothering bank,
We piled, with care, our nightly stack   120
Of wood against the chimney-back,—
The oaken log, green, huge, and thick,
And on its top the stout back-stick;
The knotty forestick laid apart,
And filled between with curious art
The ragged brush; then, hovering near,
We watched the first red blaze appear,
Heard the sharp crackle, caught the gleam
On whitewashed wall and sagging beam,
Until the old, rude-furnished room   130
Burst, flower-like, into rosy bloom;
While radiant with a mimic flame
Outside the sparkling drift became,
And through the bare-boughed lilac-tree
Our own warm hearth seemed blazing free.
The crane and pendent trammels showed,
The Turks' heads on the andirons glowed;
While childish fancy, prompt to tell
The meaning of the miracle,
Whispered the old rhyme: *"Under the tree,*   140
When fire outdoors burns merrily,
There the witches are making tea."

The moon above the eastern wood
Shone at its full; the hill-range stood
Transfigured in the silver flood,
Its blown snows flashing cold and keen,
Dead white, save where some sharp ravine
Took shadow, or the sombre green
Of hemlocks turned to pitchy black
Against the whiteness at their back.   150
For such a world and such a night
Most fitting that unwarming light,
Which only seemed where'er it fell
To make the coldness visible.

Shut in from all the world without,
We sat the clean-winged hearth about,
Content to let the north-wind roar
In baffled rage at pane and door,
While the red logs before us beat
The frost-line back with tropic heat;   160
And ever, when a louder blast
Shook beam and rafter as it passed,
The merrier up its roaring draught
The great throat of the chimney laughed,
The house-dog on his paws outspread
Laid to the fire his drowsy head,
The cat's dark silhouette on the wall
A couchant tiger's seemed to fall;
And, for the winter fireside meet,
Between the andirons' straddling feet,   170
The mug of cider simmered slow,
The apples sputtered in a row,
And, close at hand, the basket stood
With nuts from brown October's wood.

What matter how the night behaved?
What matter how the north-wind raved?
Blow high, blow low, not all its snow
Could quench our hearth-fire's ruddy glow.
O Time and Change!—with hair as gray
As was my sire's that winter day,   180
How strange it seems, with so much gone
Of life and love, to still live on!
Ah, brother! only I and thou
Are left of all that circle now,—
The dear home faces whereupon
That fitful firelight paled and shone.
Henceforward, listen as we will,
The voices of that hearth are still;
Look where we may, the wide earth o'er
Those lighted faces smile no more.   190
We tread the paths their feet have worn,
  We sit beneath their orchard trees,
  We hear, like them, the hum of bees
And rustle of the bladed corn;
We turn the pages that they read,

---

137 **The Turks' heads.** The ornamented tops of the uprights resembled
Turkish fezzes • 160 **frost-line,** the cold point at which the radiation
of heat from the fire ended • 183 **brother,** Matthew Franklin
Whittier (1812-1883)

Their written words we linger o'er,
But in the sun they cast no shade,
No voice is heard, no sign is made,
   No step is on the conscious floor!
Yet Love will dream, and Faith will trust,
(Since He who knows our need is just,)
That somehow, somewhere, meet we must.
Alas for him who never sees
The stars shine through his cypress-trees!
Who, hopeless, lays his dead away,
Nor looks to see the breaking day
Across the mournful marbles play!
Who hath not learned in hours of faith
   The truth to flesh and sense unknown,
That Life is ever lord of Death,
   And Love can never lose its own!

We sped the time with stories old,
Wrought puzzles out, and riddles told,
Or stammered from our school-book lore
"The Chief of Gambia's golden shore."
How often since, when all the land
Was clay in Slavery's shaping hand,
As if a trumpet called, I've heard
Dame Mercy Warren's rousing word:
"Does not the voice of reason cry,
   Claim the first right which Nature gave
From the red scourge of bondage fly,
   Nor deign to live a burdened slave!"
Our father rode again his ride   220
On Memphremagog's wooded side;
Sat down again to moose and samp
In trapper's hut and Indian camp;
Lived o'er the old idyllic ease
Beneath St. François' hemlock-trees;
Again for him the moonlight shone
On Norman cap and bodiced zone;   230
Again he heard the violin play
Which led the village dance away,
And mingled in its merry whirl
The grandam and the laughing girl.
Or, nearer home, our steps he led
Where Salisbury's level marshes spread
   Mile-wide as flies the laden bee;
Where merry mowers, hale and strong,
Swept, scythe on scythe, their swaths along   240

The low green prairies of the sea.
We shared the fishing off Boar's Head,
   And round the rocky Isles of Shoals
   The hake-broil on the drift-wood coals;   200
The chowder on the sand-beach made,
Dipped by the hungry, steaming hot,
With spoons of clam-shell from the pot.
We heard the tales of witchcraft old,
And dream and sign and marvel told
To sleepy listeners as they lay   250
Stretched idly on the salted hay,
Adrift along the winding shores,
When favoring breezes deigned to blow
The square sail of the gundalow
And idle lay the useless oars.

Our mother, while she turned her wheel
Or run the new-knit stocking-heel,
Told how the Indian hordes came down
At midnight on Cocheco town,
And how her own great-uncle bore
His cruel scalp-mark to fourscore.   260
Recalling, in her fitting phrase,
   So rich and picturesque and free,
   (The common unrhymed poetry
Of simple life and country ways,)
The story of her early days,—
She made us welcome to her home;
Old hearths grew wide to give us room;
We stole with her a frightened look
At the gray wizard's conjuring-book,   270

215 **The Chief . . . shore.** This line and ll. 220-223 are from "The African Chief" by Sarah Wentworth Morton. Whittier incorrectly attributed them • 224 **father,** John Whittier (1760-1830). As a young man, he had made the trip which he recalls here • 225 **Memphremagog,** a lake in Canada and Vermont • 226 **samp,** corn-meal mush • 229 **St. François,** a river north of Lake Memphremagog • 237 **Salisbury,** a town in northern Massachusetts near the Whittier farm • 242 **Boar's Head,** a promontory on the New England coast between Salisbury and Portsmouth • 243 **Isles of Shoals,** a group of islands near the Boar's Head • 244 **hake,** a fish • 254 **gundalow,** a large, flat-bottomed scow • 256 **mother,** Abigail Hussey Whittier (1781-1857) • 259 **Cocheco,** or Cochecho, a town near Dover, New Hampshire • 270 **conjuring-book.** Whittier's mother, the poet said, "described strange people who lived on the Piscataqua and Cocheco, among whom was Bantam the sorcerer. I have in my possession the wizard's 'conjuring book,' which he solemnly opened when consulted. It is a copy of Cornelius Agrippa's **Magic** printed in 1651." A quotation from this tome precedes the poem

The fame whereof went far and wide
Through all the simple country side;
We heard the hawks at twilight play,
The boat-horn on Piscataqua,
The loon's weird laughter far away;
We fished her little trout-brook, knew
What flowers in wood and meadow grew,
What sunny hillsides autumn-brown
She climbed to shake the ripe nuts down,
Saw where in sheltered cove and bay   280
The ducks' black squadron anchored lay,
And heard the wild geese calling loud
Beneath the gray November cloud.

Then, haply, with a look more grave,
And soberer tone, some tale she gave
From painful Sewel's ancient tome,
Beloved in every Quaker home,
Of faith fire-winged by martyrdom,
Or Chalkley's Journal old and quaint,—
Gentlest of skippers, rare sea-saint!—
Who, when the dreary calms prevailed,   290
And water-butt and bread-cask failed,
And cruel, hungry eyes pursued
His portly presence mad for food,
With dark hints muttered under breath
Of casting lots for life or death,
Offered, if Heaven withheld supplies,
To be himself the sacrifice.
Then, suddenly, as if to save
The good man from his living grave,
A ripple on the water grew,   300
A school of porpoise flashed in view.
"Take, eat," he said, "and be content;
These fishes in my stead are sent
By Him who gave the tangled ram
To spare the child of Abraham."

Our uncle, innocent of books,
Was rich in lore of fields and brooks,
The ancient teachers never dumb
Of Nature's unhoused lyceum.
In moons and tides and weather wise,   310
He read the clouds as prophecies,
And foul or fair could well divine,
By many an occult hint and sign,

Holding the cunning-warded keys
To all the woodcraft mysteries;
Himself to Nature's heart so near
That all her voices in his ear
Of beast or bird had meanings clear,
Like Apollonius of old,   320
Who knew the tales the sparrows told,
Or Hermes who interpreted
What the sage cranes of Nilus said;
A simple, guileless, childlike man,
Content to live where life began;
Strong only on his native grounds,
The little world of sights and sounds
Whose girdle was the parish bounds,
Whereof his fondly partial pride
The common features magnified,   330
As Surrey hills to mountains grew
In White of Selborne's loving view,—
He told how teal and loon he shot,
And how the eagle's eggs he got,
The feats on pond and river done,
The prodigies of rod and gun;
Till, warming with the tales he told,
Forgotten was the outside cold,
The bitter wind unheeded blew,
From ripening corn the pigeons flew,   340
The partridge drummed i' the wood, the mink
Went fishing down the river-brink.
In fields with bean or clover gay,
The woodchuck, like a hermit gray,
    Peered from the doorway of his cell;
The muskrat plied the mason's trade,
And tier by tier his mud-walls laid;

---

274 **Piscataqua,** a New England river which runs its course chiefly in Maine and New Hampshire • 286 **Sewel's . . . tome.** Willem Sewel (1650-1725) wrote the **History of the Christian People Called Quakers.** Whittier read an American edition published in Philadelphia in 1823 • 289 **Chalkley's Journal,** published in 1747, was by the Quaker preacher Thomas Chalkley (1675-1741) • 305 **the tangled ram.** See Genesis 22:13: "And Abraham lifted up his eyes, and looked, and behold behind him a ram caught in a thicket by his horns: and Abraham went and took the ram, and offered him up for a burnt offering in the stead of his son" • 307 **uncle,** Moses Whittier • 320 **Apollonius,** Greek mystic of Tyana, first century A.D. • 322 **Hermes,** Hermes Trismegistus, an Egyptian god to whom were attributed third-century books on medicine, ritual, and mystic subjects • 332 **White,** Gilbert White (1720-1793), an English naturalist, author of the **Natural History and Antiquities of Selborne**

And from the shagbark overhead
  The grizzled squirrel dropped his shell.

Next, the dear aunt, whose smile of cheer   350
And voice in dreams I see and hear,—
The sweetest woman ever Fate
Perverse denied a household mate,
Who, lonely, homeless, not the less
Found peace in love's unselfishness,
And welcome wheresoe'er she went,
A calm and gracious element,
Whose presence seemed the sweet income
And womanly atmosphere of home,—
Called up her girlhood memories,
The huskings and the apple-bees,   360
The sleigh-rides and the summer sails,
Weaving through all the poor details
And homespun warp of circumstance
A golden woof-thread of romance.
For well she kept her genial mood
And simple faith of maidenhood;
Before her still a cloud-land lay,
The mirage loomed across her way;
The morning dew, that dried so soon   370
With others, glistened at her noon;
Through years of toil and soil and care,
From glossy tress to thin gray hair,
All unprofaned she held apart
The virgin fancies of the heart.
Be shame to him of woman born
Who hath for such but thought of scorn.

There, too, our elder sister plied
Her evening task the stand beside;
A full, rich nature, free to trust,   380
Truthful and almost sternly just,
Impulsive, earnest, prompt to act,
And make her generous thought a fact,
Keeping with many a light disguise
The secret of self-sacrifice.
O heart sore-tried! thou hast the best
That Heaven itself could give thee,—rest,
Rest from all bitter thoughts and things!
  How many a poor one's blessing went
  With thee beneath the low green tent
Whose curtain never outward swings!   390

As one who held herself a part
Of all she saw, and let her heart
Against the household bosom lean,
Upon the motley-braided mat
Our youngest and our dearest sat,
Lifting her large, sweet, asking eyes,
  Now bathed within the fadeless green
And holy peace of Paradise.
Oh, looking from some heavenly hill,   400
  Or from the shade of saintly palms,
  Or silver reach of river calms,
Do those large eyes behold me still?
With me one little year ago:—
The chill weight of the winter snow
  For months upon her grave has lain;
And now, when summer south-winds blow
  And brier and harebell bloom again,
I tread the pleasant paths we trod,
I see the violet-sprinkled sod   410
Whereon she leaned, too frail and weak
The hillside flowers she loved to seek,
Yet following me where'er I went
With dark eyes full of love's content.
The birds are glad; the brier-rose fills
The air with sweetness; all the hills
Stretch green to June's unclouded sky;
But still I wait with ear and eye
For something gone which should be nigh,
A loss in all familiar things,   420
In flower that blooms, and bird that sings.
And yet, dear heart! remembering thee,
  Am I not richer than of old?
Safe in thy immortality,
  What change can reach the wealth I hold?
  What chance can mar the pearl and gold
Thy love hath left in trust with me?
And while in life's late afternoon,
  Where cool and long the shadows grow,
I walk to meet the night that soon   430
  Shall shape and shadow overflow,
I cannot feel that thou art far,

---

350 **aunt,** Mercy Evans Hussey, who died in 1846 • 378 **elder sister,** Mary Whittier Caldwell (1806-1860) • 396 **Our youngest,** Elizabeth Whittier, who was the poet's closest companion until her death in 1864

Since near at need the angels are;
And when the sunset gates unbar,
   Shall I not see thee waiting stand,
And, white against the evening star,
   The welcome of thy beckoning hand?

Brisk wielder of the birch and rule,
The master of the district school
Held at the fire his favored place,
Its warm glow lit a laughing face
Fresh-hued and fair, where scarce appeared
The uncertain prophecy of beard.
He teased the mitten-blinded cat,
Played cross-pins on my uncle's hat,
Sang songs, and told us what befalls
In classic Dartmouth's college halls.
Born the wild Northern hills among,
From whence his yeoman father wrung
By patient toil subsistence scant,
Not competence and yet not want,
He early gained the power to pay
His cheerful, self-reliant way;
Could doff at ease his scholar's gown
To peddle wares from town to town;
Or through the long vacation's reach
In lonely lowland districts teach,
Where all the droll experience found
At stranger hearths in boarding round,
The moonlit skater's keen delight,
The sleigh-drive through the frosty night,
The rustic party, with its rough
Accompaniment of blind-man's-buff,
And whirling plate, and forfeits paid,
His winter task a pastime made.
Happy the snow-locked homes wherein
He tuned his merry violin,
Or played the athlete in the barn,
Or held the good dame's winding yarn,
Or mirth-provoking versions told
Of classic legends rare and old,
Wherein the scenes of Greece and Rome
Had all the commonplace of home,
And little seemed at best the odds
'Twixt Yankee pedlers and old gods;
Where Pindus-born Araxes took
The guise of any grist-mill brook,

And dread Olympus at his will
Became a huckleberry hill.

A careless boy that night he seemed;
   But at his desk he had the look
And air of one who wisely schemed,
   And hostage from the future took
   In trained thought and lore of book.
Large-brained, clear-eyed,—of such as he
Shall Freedom's young apostles be,
Who, following in War's bloody trail,
Shall every lingering wrong assail;
All chains from limb and spirit strike,
Uplift the black and white alike;
Scatter before their swift advance
The darkness and the Ignorance,
The pride, the lust, the squalid sloth,
Which nurtured Treason's monstrous growth,
Made murder pastime, and the hell
Of prison-torture possible;
The cruel lie of caste refute,
Old forms remould, and substitute
For Slavery's lash the freeman's will,
For blind routine, wise-handed skill;
A school-house plant on every hill,
Stretching in radiate nerve-lines thence
The quick wires of intelligence;
Till North and South together brought
Shall own the same electric thought,
In peace a common flag salute,
And, side by side in labor's free
And unresentful rivalry,
Harvest the fields wherein they fought.

Another guest that winter night
Flashed back from lustrous eyes the light.
Unmarked by time, and yet not young,
The honeyed music of her tongue
And words of meekness scarcely told
A nature passionate and bold,
Strong, self-concentred, spurning guide,
Its milder features dwarfed beside

439 **master,** George Haskell (1799–1876) • 445 **cross-pins,** a game in
which the object was to cause pins lying in a hat to cross by tapping
the hat • 476 **Araxes,** or Arakthos, a river in Greece which originates
in the Pindus mountain range • 510 **Another guest,** Harriet Livermore

Her unbent will's majestic pride.
She sat among us, at the best,
A not unfeared, half-welcome guest,
Rebuking with her cultured phrase   520
Our homeliness of words and ways.
A certain pard-like, treacherous grace
  Swayed the lithe limbs and dropped the lash,
  Lent the white teeth their dazzling flash;
  And under low brows, black with night,
  Rayed out at times a dangerous light;
The sharp heat-lightnings of her face
Presaging ill to him whom Fate
Condemned to share her love or hate.   530
A woman tropical, intense
In thought and act, in soul and sense,
She blended in a like degree
The vixen and the devotee,
Revealing with each freak or feint
  The temper of Petruchio's Kate,
The raptures of Siena's saint.
Her tapering hand and rounded wrist
Had facile power to form a fist;
The warm, dark languish of her eyes   540
Was never safe from wrath's surprise.
Brows saintly calm and lips devout
Knew every change of scowl and pout;
And the sweet voice had notes more high
And shrill for social battle-cry.

Since then what old cathedral town
Has missed her pilgrim staff and gown,
What convent-gate has held its lock
Against the challenge of her knock!
Through Smyrna's plague-hushed thoroughfares,   550
Up sea-set Malta's rocky stairs,
Gray olive slopes of hills that hem
Thy tombs and shrines, Jerusalem,
Or startling on her desert throne
The crazy Queen of Lebanon
With claims fantastic as her own,
Her tireless feet have held their way;
And still, unrestful, bowed, and gray,
She watches under Eastern skies,
  With hope each day renewed and fresh,   560
  The Lord's quick coming in the flesh,
Whereof she dreams and prophesies!

Where'er her troubled path may be,
  The Lord's sweet pity with her go!
The outward wayward life we see,
  The hidden springs we may not know.
Nor is it given us to discern
  What threads the fatal sisters spun,
  Through what ancestral years has run
The sorrow with the woman born,   570
What forged her cruel chain of moods,
What set her feet in solitudes,
  And held the love within her mute,
What mingled madness in the blood,
  A life-long discord and annoy,
  Water of tears with oil of joy,
And hid within the folded bud
  Perversities of flower and fruit.
It is not ours to separate
The tangled skein of will and fate,   580
To show what metes and bounds should stand
Upon the soul's debatable land,
And between choice and Providence
Divide the circle of events;
  But He who knows our frame is just,
Merciful and compassionate,
And full of sweet assurances
And hope for all the language is,
  That He remembereth we are dust!

At last the great logs, crumbling low,   590
Sent out a dull and duller glow,
The bull's-eye watch that hung in view
Ticking its weary circuit through,
Pointed with mutely warning sign
Its black hand to the hour of nine.
That sign the pleasant circle broke:
My uncle ceased his pipe to smoke,
Knocked from its bowl the refuse gray,
And laid it tenderly away,
Then roused himself to safely cover   600
The dull red brands with ashes over.
And while, with care, our mother laid

536 **Petruchio's Kate**, in Shakespeare's **The Taming of the Shrew,**
the violent-tempered heroine, Kate, who was subdued by Petruchio
568 **fatal sisters**, the three Fates of Greek mythology who **spun**
the thread of life, measured it, and snapped it off

The work aside, her steps she stayed
One moment, seeking to express *prayer*
Her grateful sense of happiness
For food and shelter, warmth and health,
And love's contentment more than wealth,
With simple wishes (not the weak,
Vain prayers which no fulfilment seek,
But such as warm the generous heart,   610
O'er-prompt to do with Heaven its part)
That none might lack, that bitter night,
For bread and clothing, warmth and light.

SNOW·BOUND.

A WINTER IDYL.

BY

JOHN GREENLEAF WHITTIER.

BOSTON:
TICKNOR AND FIELDS.
1866.

Title page of the first edition, 1866

Within our beds awhile we heard
The wind that round the gables roared,
With now and then a ruder shock,
Which made our very bedsteads rock.
We heard the loosened clapboards tost,

The board-nails snapping in the frost;
And on us, through the unplastered wall,   620
Felt the light sifted snow-flakes fall.
But sleep stole on, as sleep will do
When hearts are light and life is new;
Faint and more faint the murmurs grew,
Till in the summer-land of dreams
They softened to the sound of streams,
Low stir of leaves, and dip of oars,
And lapsing waves on quiet shores.

Next morn we wakened with the shout
Of merry voices high and clear;   630
And saw the teamsters drawing near
To break the drifted highways out.
Down the long hillside treading slow
We saw the half-buried oxen go,
Shaking the snow from heads uptost,
Their straining nostrils white with frost.
Before our door the straggling train
Drew up, an added team to gain.
The elders threshed their hands a-cold,
    Passed, with the cider-mug, their jokes   640
    From lip to lip; the younger folks
Down the loose snow-banks, wrestling, rolled,
Then toiled again the cavalcade
    O'er windy hill, through clogged ravine,
    And woodland paths that wound between
Low drooping pine-boughs winter-weighed.
From every barn a team afoot,
At every house a new recruit,
Where, drawn by Nature's subtlest law
Haply the watchful young men saw
Sweet doorway pictures of the curls
And curious eyes of merry girls,   *realistic*   650
Lifting their hands in mock defence
Against the snow-ball's compliments,
And reading in each missive tost
The charm with Eden never lost.

We heard once more the sleigh-bells' sound;
    And, following where the teamsters led,
The wise old Doctor went his round,
Just pausing at our door to say,   660
In the brief autocratic way
Of one who, prompt at Duty's call,
Was free to urge her claim on all,

That some poor neighbor sick abed
At night our mother's aid would need.
For, one in generous thought and deed,
  What mattered in the sufferer's sight
  The Quaker matron's inward light,
The Doctor's mail of Calvin's creed?
All hearts confess the saints elect   670
  Who, twain in faith, in love agree,
And melt not in an acid sect
  The Christian pearl of charity!

So days went on: a week had passed
Since the great world was heard from last.
The Almanac we studied o'er,
Read and reread our little store
Of books and pamphlets, scarce a score;
One harmless novel, mostly hid
From younger eyes, a book forbid,   680
And poetry, (or good or bad,
A single book was all we had,)
Where Ellwood's meek, drab-skirted Muse,
  A stranger to the heathen Nine,
  Sang, with a somewhat nasal whine,
The wars of David and the Jews.
At last the floundering carrier bore
The village paper to our door.
Lo! broadening outward as we read,
To warmer zones the horizon spread;   690
In panoramic length unrolled
We saw the marvels that it told.
Before us passed the painted Creeks,
  And daft McGregor on his raids
  In Costa Rica's everglades.
And up Taygetos winding slow
Rode Ypsilanti's Mainote Greeks,
A Turk's head at each saddle-bow!
Welcome to us its week-old news,
Its corner for the rustic Muse,   700
  Its monthly gauge of snow and rain,
Its record, mingling in a breath
The wedding knell and dirge of death;
Jest, anecdote, and love-lorn tale,
The latest culprit sent to jail;
Its hue and cry of stolen and lost,
Its vendue sales and goods at cost,
  And traffic calling loud for gain.

We felt the stir of hall and street,
The pulse of life that round us beat;   710
The chill embargo of the snow
Was melted in the genial glow;
Wide swung again our ice-locked door,
And all the world was ours once more!

Clasp, Angel of the backward look
  And folded wings of ashen gray
  And voice of echoes far away,
The brazen covers of thy book;
The weird palimpsest old and vast,
Wherein thou hid'st the spectral past;   720
Where, closely mingling, pale and glow
The characters of joy and woe;
The monographs of outlived years,
Or smile-illumed or dim with tears,
  Green hills of life that slope to death,
And haunts of home, whose vistaed trees
Shade off to mournful cypresses
  With the white amaranths underneath.
Even while I look, I can but heed
  The restless sands' incessant fall,   730
Importunate hours that hours succeed,
Each clamorous with its own sharp need,
  And duty keeping pace with all.
Shut down and clasp the heavy lids;
I hear again the voice that bids
The dreamer leave his dream midway
For larger hopes and graver fears:
Life greatens in these later years,
The century's aloe flowers to-day!

Yet, haply, in some lull of life,   740
Some Truce of God which breaks its strife,
The worldling's eyes shall gather dew,
  Dreaming in throngful city ways

---

realistic
newspaper
Contents

683 **Ellwood,** Thomas Ellwood (1639-1714), who wrote **Davideis,** a
pedestrian poem of King David's life • 693 **Creeks,** an Indian tribe.
Probably the story told of their removal to an Indian reservation in 1821
694 **daft McGregor,** Sir Gregor McGregor, who in the 1820's tried
to establish a colony in Costa Rica • 696 **Taygetos . . . Greeks.**
Taygetos is a mountain in Greece near Maina, a district which was
noted for its robbers and pirates. During the Greek struggle for independence from Turkey (1821-1833), the Greek General Ypsilanti sent a
force of these mountaineers up Mount Taygetos against the Turks

Of winter joys his boyhood knew;
And dear and early friends—the few
Who yet remain—shall pause to view
　These Flemish pictures of old days;
Sit with me by the homestead hearth,
And stretch the hands of memory forth
　To warm them at the wood-fire's blaze!　　750
And thanks untraced to lips unknown
Shall greet me like the odors blown
From unseen meadows newly mown,
Or lilies floating in some pond,
Wood-fringed, the wayside gaze beyond;
The traveller owns the grateful sense
Of sweetness near, he knows not whence,
And, pausing, takes with forehead bare
The benediction of the air.

　　　　　　　　　　　　　　　1866

Among the Hills

In its first form, entitled "The Wife: an Idyl of Bearcamp Water," this poem appeared in the **Atlantic**, January 1868. Before the volume **Among the Hills and Other Poems** appeared in December of the same year, Whittier made numerous changes. Says Pickard: "The inspiration . . . came to him in the summer of 1867. It is a tender and romantic love-story in verse, idealizing New England farm life; with a prelude which furnishes the darker shades needed to make the picture a faithful reproduction of the rural scenes he intended to portray. . . . In its original form there were sixty-four lines in the Prelude, and it did not deal with the prosaic and disagreeable side of farm life, as does the Prelude in its present form, which consists of one hundred and fifty-six lines. . . . The whole tenor of the Prelude is changed, so as to make it a new poem . . . The ballad proper enlarges upon the sweet story originally told, making three hundred and forty-four lines instead of one hundred and sixty-eight, as at first."

Modern readers may find the poem itself rather too sweet for their taste. The Prelude, however, is clearly a forerunner of modern poems and stories which emphasize the drabness and the flinty quality of life on New England farms.

Along the roadside, like the flowers of gold
That tawny Incas for their gardens wrought,
Heavy with sunshine droops the golden-rod,
And the red pennons of the cardinal-flowers
Hang motionless upon their upright staves.
The sky is hot and hazy, and the wind,
Wing-weary with its long flight from the south,
Unfelt; yet, closely scanned, yon maple leaf
With faintest motion, as one stirs in dreams,
Confesses it.　The locust by the wall　　10
Stabs the noon-silence with his sharp alarm.
A single hay-cart down the dusty road
Creaks slowly, with its driver fast asleep
On the load's top.　Against the neighboring hill,
Huddled along the stone wall's shady side,
The sheep show white, as if a snowdrift still
Defied the dog-star.　Through the open door
A drowsy smell of flowers—gray heliotrope,
And white sweet clover, and shy mignonette—
Comes faintly in, and silent chorus lends　　20
To the pervading symphony of peace.

No time is this for hands long overworn
To task their strength: and (unto Him be praise
Who giveth quietness!) the stress and strain
Of years that did the work of centuries
Have ceased, and we can draw our breath once more
Freely and full.　So, as yon harvesters
Make glad their nooning underneath the elms
With tale and riddle and old snatch of song,
I lay aside grave themes, and idly turn　　30
The leaves of memory's sketch-book, dreaming o'er
Old summer pictures of the quiet hills,
And human life, as quiet, at their feet.

And yet not idly all.　A farmer's son,
Proud of field-lore and harvest craft, and feeling
All their fine possibilities, how rich
And restful even poverty and toil

Snow-Bound • **747 Flemish pictures.** The Flemish School (the van Eycks, Rubens, Van Dyck, and others) was noted for its detailed depiction of domestic scenes

Among the Hills • **2 tawny Incas,** a Peruvian tribe of Indians noted for their handiwork in gold

Become when beauty, harmony, and love
Sit at their humble hearth as angels sat
At evening in the patriarch's tent, when man   40
Makes labor noble, and his farmer's frock
The symbol of a Christian chivalry
Tender and just and generous to her
Who clothes with grace all duty; still, I know
Too well the picture has another side,—
How wearily the grind of toil goes on
Where love is wanting, how the eye and ear
And heart are starved amidst the plenitude
Of nature, and how hard and colorless
Is life without an atmosphere. I look   50
Across the lapse of half a century,
And call to mind old homesteads, where no flower
Told that the spring had come, but evil weeds,
Nightshade and rough-leaved burdock in the place
Of the sweet doorway greeting of the rose
And honeysuckle, where the house walls seemed
Blistering in sun, without a tree or vine
To cast the tremulous shadow of its leaves
Across the curtainless windows from whose panes
Fluttered the signal rags of shiftlessness;   60
Within, the cluttered kitchen-floor, unwashed
(Broom-clean I think they called it); the best room
Stifling with cellar damp, shut from the air
In hot midsummer, bookless, pictureless
Save the inevitable sampler hung
Over the fireplace, or a mourning piece,
A green-haired woman, peony-cheeked, beneath
Impossible willows; the wide-throated hearth
Bristling with faded pine-boughs half concealing
The piled-up rubbish at the chimney's back;   70
And, in sad keeping with all things about them,
Shrill, querulous women, sour and sullen men,
Untidy, loveless, old before their time,
With scarce a human interest save their own
Monotonous round of small economies,
Or the poor scandal of the neighborhood;
Blind to the beauty everywhere revealed,
Treading the May-flowers with regardless feet;
For them the song-sparrow and the bobolink
Sang not, nor winds made music in the leaves;   80
For them in vain October's holocaust
Burned, gold and crimson, over all the hills,
The sacramental mystery of the woods.
Church-goers, fearful of the unseen Powers,

But grumbling over pulpit-tax and pew-rent,
Saving, as shrewd economists, their souls
And winter pork with the least possible outlay
Of salt and sanctity; in daily life
Showing as little actual comprehension
Of Christian charity and love and duty,   90
As if the Sermon on the Mount had been
Out dated like a last year's almanac:
Rich in broad woodlands and in half-tilled fields,
And yet so pinched and bare and comfortless,
The veriest straggler limping on his rounds,
The sun and air his sole inheritance,
Laughed at a poverty that paid its taxes,
And hugged his rags in self-complacency!

Not such should be the homesteads of a land
Where whoso wisely wills and acts may dwell   100
As king and lawgiver, in broad-acred state,
With beauty, art, taste, culture, books, to make
His hours of leisure richer than a life
Of fourscore to the barons of old time,
Our yeoman should be equal to his home
Set in the fair, green valleys, purple walled,
A man to match his mountains, not to creep
Dwarfed and abased below them. I would fain
In this light way (of which I needs must own
With the knife-grinder of whom Canning sings,   110
"Story, God bless you! I have none to tell you!")
Invite the eye to see and the heart to feel
The beauty and the joy within their reach,—
Home, and home loves, and the beatitudes
Of nature free to all. Haply in years
That wait to take the places of our own,
Heard where some breezy balcony looks down
On happy homes, or where the lake in the moon
Sleeps dreaming of the mountains, fair as Ruth,
In the old Hebrew pastoral, at the feet   120
Of Boaz, even this simple lay of mine
May seem the burden of a prophecy,
Finding its late fulfillment in a change
Slow as the oak's growth lifting manhood up
Through broader culture, finer manners, love,
And reverence, to the level of the hills.

---

39 angels . . . tent, probably a reference to Genesis 18 •
110 knife-grinder . . . sings, in "The Friend of Humanity and the
Knife-Grinder," a parody written by George Canning

O Golden Age, whose light is of the dawn,
And not of sunset, forward, not behind,
Flood the new heavens and earth, and with thee bring
All the old virtues, whatsoever things   130
Are pure and honest and of good repute,
But add thereto whatever bard has sung
Or seer has told of when in trance and dream
They saw the Happy Isles of prophecy!
Let Justice hold her scale, and Truth divide
Between the right and wrong; but give the heart
The freedom of its fair inheritance;
Let the poor prisoner, cramped and starved so long,
At Nature's table feast his ear and eye
With joy and wonder; let all harmonies   140
Of sound, form, color, motion, wait upon
The princely guest, whether in soft attire
Of leisure clad, or the coarse frock of toil,
And, lending life to the dead form of faith,
Give human nature reverence for the sake
Of One who bore it, making it divine
With the ineffable tenderness of God;
Let common need, the brotherhood of prayer,
The heirship of an unknown destiny,
The unsolved mystery round about us, make   150
A man more precious than the gold of Ophir.
Sacred, inviolate, unto whom all things
Should minister, as outward types and signs
Of the eternal beauty which fulfils
The one great purpose of creation, Love,
The sole necessity of Earth and Heaven!

AMONG THE HILLS

For weeks the clouds had raked the hills
    And vexed the vales with raining,
And all the woods were sad with mist,
    And all the brooks complaining.   160

At last, a sudden night-storm tore
    The mountain veils asunder,
And swept the valleys clean before
    The besom of the thunder.

Through Sandwich notch the west-wind sang
    Good morrow to the cotter;
And once again Chocorua's horn
    Of shadow pierced the water.

Above his broad lake Ossipee,
    Once more the sunshine wearing,   170
Stooped, tracing on that silver shield
    His grim armorial bearing.

Clear drawn against the hard blue sky
    The peaks had winter's keenness;
And, close on autumn's frost, the vales
    Had more than June's fresh greenness.

Again the sodden forest floors
    With golden lights were checkered,
Once more rejoicing leaves in wind
    And sunshine danced and flickered.   180

It was as if the summer's late
    Atoning for its sadness
Had borrowed every season's charm
    To end its days in gladness.

I call to mind those banded vales
    Of shadow and of shining,
Through which, my hostess at my side,
    I drove in day's declining.

We held our sideling way above
    The river's whitening shallows,   190
By homesteads old, with wide-flung barns
    Swept through and through by swallows,—

By maple orchards, belts of pine
    And larches climbing darkly
The mountain slopes, and, over all,
    The great peaks rising starkly.

You should have seen that long hill-range
    With gaps of brightness riven,—
How through each pass and hollow streamed
    The purpling lights of heaven,—   200

Rivers of gold-mist flowing down
    From far celestial fountains,—

---

151 **Ophir,** a region mentioned in the Old Testament as a source
of gold and jewels • 165 **Sandwich notch,** an entrance to the White
Mountains • 167 **Chocorua,** one of the White Mountains • 169
lake Ossipee, in eastern New Hampshire

The great sun flaming through the rifts
  Beyond the wall of mountains!

We paused at last where home-bound cows
  Brought down the pasture's treasure,
And in the barn the rhythmic flails
  Beat out a harvest measure.

We heard the night-hawk's sullen plunge,
  The crow his tree-mates calling: 210
The shadows lengthening down the slopes
  About our feet were falling.

And through them smote the level sun
  In broken lines of splendor,
Touched the gray rocks and made the green
  Of the shorn grass more tender.

The maples bending o'er the gate,
  Their arch of leaves just tinted
With yellow warmth, the golden glow
  Of coming autumn hinted.   220

Keen white between the farm-house showed,
  And smiled on porch and trellis,
The fair democracy of flowers
  That equals cot and palace.

And weaving garlands for her dog,
  'Twixt chidings and caresses,
A human flower of childhood shook
  The sunshine from her tresses.

On either hand we saw the signs
  Of fancy and of shrewdness,   230
Where taste had wound its arms of vines
  Round thrift's uncomely rudeness.

The sun-brown farmer in his frock
  Shook hands, and called to Mary:
Bare-armed, as Juno might, she came,
  White-aproned from her dairy.

Her air, her smile, her motions, **told**
  Of womanly completeness;
A music as of household songs
  Was in her voice of sweetness.   240

Not fair alone in curve and line,
  But something more and better,
The secret charm eluding art,
  Its spirit, not its letter;—

An inborn grace that nothing lacked
  Of culture or appliance,—
The warmth of genial courtesy,
  The calm of self-reliance.

Before her queenly womanhood
  How dared our hostess utter   250
The paltry errand of her need
  To buy her fresh-churned butter?

She led the way with housewife pride,
  Her goodly store disclosing,
Full tenderly the golden balls
  With practised hands disposing.

Then, while along the western hills
  We watched the changeful glory
Of sunset, on our homeward way,
  I heard her simple story.   260

The early crickets sang; the stream
  Plashed through my friend's narration:
Her rustic patois of the hills
  Lost in my free translation.

"More wise," she said, "than those who swarm
  Our hills in middle summer,
She came, when June's first roses blow,
  To greet the early comer.

"From school and ball and rout she came,
  The city's fair, pale daughter,   270
To drink the wine of mountain air
  Beside the Bearcamp Water.

"Her step grew firmer on the hills
  That watch our homesteads over;

---

241 **Not fair . . . line.** For about a dozen years, this line read "Not
beautiful in curve or line." The present line is said to have been
suggested by (then Senator) James G. Blaine • 272 **Bearcamp Water,**
the Bear Camp River, near Ossipee, New Hampshire

On cheek and lip, from summer fields,
 She caught the bloom of clover.

"For health comes sparkling in the streams
 From cool Chocorua stealing:
There's iron in our Northern winds;
 Our pines are trees of healing.   280

"She sat beneath the broad-armed elms
 That skirt the mowing-meadow,
And watched the gentle west-wind weave
 The grass with shine and shadow.

"Beside her, from the summer heat
 To share her grateful screening,
With forehead bared, the farmer stood,
 Upon his pitchfork leaning.

"Framed in its damp, dark locks, his face
 Had nothing mean or common,—   290
Strong, manly, true, the tenderness
 And pride beloved of woman.

"She looked up, glowing with the health
 The country air had brought her,
And, laughing, said: 'You lack a wife,
 Your mother lacks a daughter.

" 'To mend your frock and bake your bread
 You do not need a lady:
Be sure among these brown old homes
 Is some one waiting ready,—   300

" 'Some fair, sweet girl with skilful hand
 And cheerful heart for treasure,
Who never played with ivory keys,
 Or danced the polka's measure.'

"He bent his black brows to a frown,
 He set his white teeth tightly.
' 'Tis well,' he said, 'for one like you
 To choose for me so lightly.

" 'You think, because my life is rude
 I take no note of sweetness: 310
I tell you love has naught to do
 With meetness or unmeetness.

" 'Itself its best excuse, it asks
 No leave of pride or fashion
When silken zone or homespun frock
 It stirs with throbs of passion.

" 'You think me deaf and blind: you bring
 Your winning graces hither
As free as if from cradle-time
 We two had played together.   320

" 'You tempt me with your laughing eyes,
 Your cheek of sundown's blushes,
A motion as of waving grain,
 A music as of thrushes.

" 'The plaything of your summer sport,
 The spells you weave around me
You cannot at your will undo,
 Nor leave me as you found me.

" 'You go as lightly as you came,
 Your life is well without me;   330
What care you that these hills will close
 Like prison-walls about me?

" 'No mood is mine to seek a wife,
 Or daughter for my mother:
Who loves you loses in that love
 All power to love another!

" 'I dare your pity or your scorn,
 With pride your own exceeding;
I fling my heart into your lap
 Without a word of pleading.'   340

"She looked up in his face of pain
 So archly, yet so tender:
'And if I lend you mine,' she said,
 'Will you forgive the lender?

" 'Nor frock nor tan can hide the man;
 And see you not, my farmer,
How weak and fond a woman waits
 Behind this silken armor?

" 'I love you: on that love alone,
 And not my worth, presuming,   350

Will you not trust for summer fruit
    The tree in May-day blooming?'

"Alone the hangbird overhead,
    His hair-swung cradle straining,
Looked down to see love's miracle,—
    The giving that is gaining.

"And so the farmer found a wife,
    His mother found a daughter:
There looks no happier home than hers
    On pleasant Bearcamp Water.   360

"Flowers spring to blossom where she walks
    The careful ways of duty;
Our hard, stiff lines of life with her
    Are flowing curves of beauty.

"Our homes are cheerier for her sake,
    Our door-yards brighter blooming,
And all about the social air
    Is sweeter for her coming.

"Unspoken homilies of peace
    Her daily life is preaching;   370
The still refreshment of the dew
    Is her unconscious teaching.

"And never tenderer hand than hers
    Unknits the brow of ailing;
Her garments to the sick man's ear
    Have music in their trailing.

"And when, in pleasant harvest moons,
    The youthful huskers gather,
Or sleighdrives on the mountain ways
    Defy the winter weather,—   380

"In sugar-camps, when south and warm
    The winds of March are blowing,
And sweetly from its thawing veins
    The maple's blood is flowing,—

"In summer, where some lilied pond
    Its virgin zone is bearing,
Or where the ruddy autumn fire
    Lights up the apple-paring,—

"The coarseness of a ruder time
    Her finer mirth displaces,   390
A subtler sense of pleasure fills
    Each rustic sport she graces.

"Her presence lends its warmth and health
    To all who come before it.
If woman lost us Eden, such
    As she alone restore it.

"For larger life and wiser aims
    The farmer is her debtor;
Who holds to his another's heart
    Must needs be worse or better.   400

"Through her his civic service shows
    A purer-toned ambition;
No double consciousness divides
    The man and politician.

"In party's doubtful ways he trusts
    Her instincts to determine;
At the loud polls, the thought of her
    Recalls Christ's Mountain Sermon.

"He owns her logic of the heart,
    And wisdom of unreason,   410
Supplying, while he doubts and weighs,
    The needed word in season.

"He sees with pride her richer thought,
    Her fancy's freer ranges;
And love thus deepened to respect
    Is proof against all changes.

"And if she walks at ease in ways
    His feet are slow to travel,
And if she reads with cultured eyes
    What his may scarce unravel,   420

"Still clearer, for her keener sight
    Of beauty and of wonder,
He learns the meaning of the hills
    He dwelt from childhood under.

"And higher, warmed with summer lights,
    Or winter-crowned and hoary,

The ridged horizon lifts for him
   Its inner veils of glory.

"He has his own free, bookless lore,
   The lessons nature taught him,
The wisdom which the woods and hills
   And toiling men have brought him:

"The steady force of will whereby
   Her flexile grace seems sweeter;
The sturdy counterpoise which makes
   Her woman's life completer:

"A latent fire of soul which lacks
   No breath of love to fan it;
And wit, that, like his native brooks,
   Plays over solid granite.

"How dwarfed against his manliness
   She sees the poor pretension,
The wants, the aims, the follies, born
   Of fashion and convention!

"How life behind its accidents
   Stands strong and self-sustaining,
The human fact transcending all
   The losing and the gaining.

"And so, in grateful interchange
   Of teacher and of hearer,
Their lives their true distinctness keep
   While daily drawing nearer.

"And if the husband or the wife
   In home's strong light discovers
Such slight defaults as failed to meet
   The blinded eyes of lovers,

"Why need we care to ask?—who dreams
   Without their thorns of roses,
Or wonders that the truest steel
   The readiest spark discloses?

"For still in mutual sufferance lies
   The secret of true living:
Love scarce is love that never knows
   The sweetness of forgiving.

"We send the Squire to General Court,
   He takes his young wife thither;
No prouder man election day
   Rides through the sweet June weather.

"He sees with eyes of manly trust
   All hearts to her inclining;
Not less for him his household light
   That others share its shining."

Thus, while my hostess spake, there grew
   Before me, warmer tinted
And outlined with a tenderer grace,
   The picture that she hinted.

The sunset smouldered as we drove
   Beneath the deep hill-shadows.
Below us wreaths of white fog walked
   Like ghosts the haunted meadows.

Sounding the summer night, the stars
   Dropped down their golden plummets;
The pale arc of the Northern lights
   Rose o'er the mountain summits,—

Until, at last, beneath its bridge,
   We heard the Bearcamp flowing,
And saw across the mapled lawn
   The welcome home-lights glowing;—

And, musing on the tale I heard,
   'T were well, thought I, if often
To rugged farm-life came the gift
   To harmonize and soften;—

If more and more we found the troth
   Of fact and fancy plighted,
And culture's charm and labor's strength
   In rural homes united,—

The simple life, the homely hearth,
   With beauty's sphere surrounding,
And blessing toil where toil abounds
   With graces more abounding.

1868

The Meeting

The first printed version of this poem appeared in the
Atlantic Monthly, February 1868. When the poem, as
it is here printed, was prepared for publication in the
book **Among the Hills** (1868), Whittier inserted a number
of lines. Says Whitman Bennett: "The man who seriously
wishes to understand Whittier's philosophic attachment to
Quakerism should read, line by line, 'The Meeting' . . .
and get the information at the source."

The elder folks shook hands at last,
Down seat by seat the signal passed.
To simple ways like ours unused,
Half solemnized and half amused,
With long-drawn breath and shrug, my guest
His sense of glad relief expressed.
Outside the hills lay warm in sun;
The cattle in the meadow-run
Stood half-leg deep; a single bird
The green repose above us stirred.   10
"What part or lot have you," he said,
"In these dull rites of drowsy-head?
Is silence worship? Seek it where
It soothes with dreams the summer air,
Not in this close and rude-benched hall,
But where soft lights and shadows fall,
And all the slow, sleep-walking hours
Glide soundless over grass and flowers!
From time and place and form apart,
Its holy ground the human heart,   20
Nor ritual-bound nor templeward
Walks the free spirit of the Lord!
Our common Master did not pen
His followers up from other men;
His service liberty indeed,
He built no church, he framed no creed;
But while the saintly Pharisee
Made broader his phylactery,
As from the synagogue was seen
The dusty-sandalled Nazarene   30
Through ripening cornfields lead the way

Upon the awful Sabbath day.
His sermons were the healthful talk
That shorter made the mountain-walk,
His wayside texts were flowers and birds,
Where mingled with His gracious words
The rustle of the tamarisk-tree
And ripple-wash of Galilee."

"Thy words are well, O friend," I said;
"Unmeasured and unlimited,   40
With noiseless slide of stone to stone,
The mystic Church of God has grown.
Invisible and silent stands
The temple never made with hands,
Unheard the voices still and small
Of its unseen confessional.
He needs no special place of prayer
Whose hearing ear is everywhere;
He brings not back the childish days
That ringed the earth with stones of praise,   50
Roofed Karnak's hall of gods, and laid
The plinths of Philae's colonnade.
Still less He owns the selfish good
And sickly growth of solitude,—
The worthless grace that, out of sight,
Flowers in the desert anchorite;
Dissevered from the suffering whole,
Love hath no power to save a soul.
Not out of Self, the origin
And native air and soil of sin,   60
The living waters spring and flow,
The trees with leaves of healing grow.

"Dream not, O friend, because I seek
This quiet shelter twice a week,
I better deem its pine-laid floor
Than breezy hill or sea-sung shore;
But nature is not solitude:
She crowds us with her thronging wood;

51 **Karnak's hall,** the great temple of Ammon on the east bank of the
Nile, some three hundred and fifty miles from Cairo • 52 **Philae's
colonnade.** Philae is a small island in the upper Egyptian Nile. The
island was sacred to the deity Isis and holds the remains of temples
• 67 **But nature.** . . . The lines from this point to l. 106 were added
after the first version appeared

Her many hands reach out to us,
Her many tongues are garrulous;   70
Perpetual riddles of surprise
She offers to our ears and eyes;
She will not leave our senses still,
But drags them captive at her will:
And, making earth too great for heaven,
She hides the Giver in the given.

"And so, I find it well to come
For deeper rest to this still room,
For here the habit of the soul
Feels less the outer world's control;   80
The strength of mutual purpose pleads
More earnestly our common needs;
And from the silence multiplied
By these still forms on either side,
The world that time and sense have known
Falls off and leaves us God alone.

"Yet rarely through the charmed repose
Unmixed the stream of motive flows,
A flavor of its many springs,
The tints of earth and sky it brings;   90
In the still waters needs must be
Some shade of human sympathy;
And here, in its accustomed place,
I look on memory's dearest face;
The blind by-sitter guesseth not
What shadow haunts that vacant spot;
No eyes save mine alone can see
The love wherewith it welcomes me!
And still, with those alone my kin,
In doubt and weakness, want and sin,   100
I bow my head, my heart I bare
As when that face was living there,
And strive (too oft, alas! in vain)
The peace of simple trust to gain,
Fold fancy's restless wings, and lay
The idols of my heart away.

"Welcome the silence all unbroken,
Nor less the words of fitness spoken,—
Such golden words as hers for whom
Our autumn flowers have just made room;   110

Whose hopeful utterance through and through
The freshness of the morning blew;
Who loved not less the earth that light
Fell on it from the heavens in sight,
But saw in all fair forms more fair
The Eternal beauty mirrored there.
Whose eighty years but added grace
And saintlier meaning to her face,—
The look of one who bore away
Glad tidings from the hills of day,   120
While all our hearts went forth to meet
The coming of her beautiful feet!
Or haply hers, whose pilgrim tread
Is in the paths where Jesus led;
Who dreams her childhood's Sabbath dream
By Jordan's willow-shaded stream,
And, of the hymns of hope and faith,
Sung by the monks of Nazareth,
Hears pious echoes, in the call
To prayer, from Moslem minarets fall,   130
Repeating where His works were wrought
The lesson that her Master taught,
Of whom an elder Sibyl gave,
The prophecies of Cumae's cave!

"I ask no organ's soulless breath
To drone the themes of life and death,
No altar candle-lit by day,
No ornate wordsman's rhetoric-play,
No cool philosophy to teach
Its bland audacities of speech   140
To double-tasked idolators
Themselves their gods and worshippers,
No pulpit hammered by the fist
Of loud-asserting dogmatist,
Who borrows from the hand of love
The smoking thunderbolts of Jove.
I know how well the fathers taught,
What work the later schoolmen wrought;
I reverence old-time faith and men,
But God is near us now as then;   150
His force of love is still unspent,

123 **Or haply hers.** . . . This line and the eleven which follow were
added to the first version • 134 **Cumae's cave.** Near Cumae, in Italy,
was a cave where Aeneas consulted a Sibyl who uttered dark prophecies

His hate of sin as imminent;
And still the measure of our needs
Outgrows the cramping bounds of creeds;
The manna gathered yesterday
Already savors of decay;
Doubts to the world's child-heart unknown
Question us now from star and stone;
Too little or too much we know,
And sight is swift and faith is slow;   160
The power is lost to self-deceive
With shallow forms of make-believe.
We walk at high noon, and the bells
Call to a thousand oracles,
But the sound deafens, and the light
Is stronger than our dazzled sight;
The letters of the sacred Book
Glimmer and swim beneath our look;
Still struggles in the Age's breast
With deepening agony of quest   170
The old entreaty: 'Art thou He,
Or look we for the Christ to be?'

"God should be most where man is least:
So, where is neither church nor priest,
And never rag of form or creed
To clothe the nakedness of need,—
Where farmer-folk in silence meet,—
I turn my bell-unsummoned feet;
I lay the critic's glass aside,
With deepening agony of quest   180
And, lowest-seated, testify
To the oneness of humanity;
Confess the universal want,
And share whatever Heaven may grant.
He findeth not who seeks his own,
The soul is lost that's saved alone.
Not on one favored forehead fell
Of old the fire-tongued miracle,
But flamed o'er all the thronging host
The baptism of the Holy Ghost;   190
Heart answers heart: in one desire
The blending lines of prayer aspire;
'Where, in my name, meet two or three,'
Our Lord hath said, 'I there will be!'
"So sometimes comes to soul and sense
The feeling which is evidence

That very near about us lies
The realm of spiritual mysteries.
The sphere of the supernal powers
Impinges on this world of ours.   200
The low and dark horizon lifts,
To light the scenic terror shifts;
The breath of a diviner air
Blows down the answer of a prayer:
That all our sorrow, pain, and doubt
A great compassion clasps about,
And law and goodness, love and force,
Are wedded fast beyond divorce.
When duty leaves to love its task,
The beggar Self forgets to ask;   210
With smile of trust and folded hands,
The passive soul in waiting stands
To feel, as flowers the sun and dew,
The One true Life its own renew.

"So, to the calmly gathered thought
The innermost of truth is taught,
The mystery dimly understood,
That love of God is love of good,
And, chiefly, its divinest trace
In Him of Nazareth's holy face;   220
That to be saved is only this,—
Salvation from our selfishness,
From more than elemental fire,
The soul's unsanctified desire,
From sin itself, and not the pain
That warns us of its chafing chain;
That worship's deeper meaning lies
In mercy, and not sacrifice,
Not proud humilities of sense
And posturing of penitence,   230
But love's unforced obedience;
That Book and Church and Day are given
For man, not God,—for earth, not heaven,—
The blessed means to holiest ends,
Not masters, but benignant friends;
That the dear Christ dwells not afar,
The king of some remoter star,

---

219 **And, chiefly.** . . . This line and the next were inserted after the
first printing • 223 **From more.** . . . The passage through l. 231 was
also inserted later

Listening, at times, with flattered ear
To homage wrung from selfish fear,
But here, amidst the poor and blind,   240

The bound and suffering of our kind,
In works we do, in prayers we pray,
Life of our life, he lives to-day."

1868

Harriet Beecher Stowe

1811 · 1896

Litchfield, Connecticut, was the birthplace of Harriet Beecher, and the first twenty-one years of her life were spent in New England. Her father was a rigid Calvinist, and six of her brothers were eventually to become ministers, one of them the famous pulpit orator, Henry Ward Beecher. At fourteen, after an education in private religious schools, Harriet became a teacher.

When she was twenty-one, she moved with her family to Cincinnati, where her father served as the first president of Lane Theological Seminary, and for a time Harriet taught in the seminary. At twenty-four, she married Calvin Stowe, a member of the faculty. In 1850 the Stowe family moved East, and there Stowe taught in Bowdoin and in Andover.

From childhood, Mrs. Stowe escaped some of the grimness of her pious surroundings by imagining interesting adventures for herself. The imaginative faculty thus developed was of service to her when, in Cincinnati, she composed stories to be read to a literary club. The sale of some of these stories launched her upon her writing career. Financial returns became very important additions to the meager income of Professor Stowe, an income insufficient to provide for a rapidly growing family. Somehow, in intervals between caring for her large family and keeping a big house, she found time to write numerous stories and sketches.

Shortly after going to Bowdoin, Mrs. Stowe wrote *Uncle Tom's Cabin* for serial publication, in 1851, in *The National Era,* an abolitionist publication. Published as a book in 1852, this novel was sensationally successful, not only as a book but also in dramatic form (see p. 64). It did so much to advance the cause of abolition that later, when its housewifely author was presented to President Lincoln, he said quizzically, "So this is the little woman who wrote the book which caused the great war!" Mrs. Stowe followed it with *Dred* (1856), another abolitionistic work.

Less sensational, but probably of more lasting value than these novels, was a series of books dealing with life in prewar New England, important contributions to the local color movement—*The Minister's Wooing* (1859), *Oldtown Folks* (1869), *Sam Lawson's Fireside Stories* (later known as *Oldtown Fireside Stories*) (1871), and *Poganuc People* (1878).

In writing these later books, said Mrs. Stowe, "I have tried to make my mind as still and passive as a looking-glass, or a mountain lake, and then to give you merely the images reflected there. I desire that you should see the characteristic persons of those times, and hear them talk." *Fireside Stories* was a collection of stories unfolded by that admirable Yankee, Sam Lawson, to entertain two childish listeners. For these narratives, Mrs. Stowe drew largely upon not only her own memories but also those of her husband, "an inimitable mimic and story-teller." A reviewer in *Scribner's* for April 1872, called Sam Lawson "the best drawn Yankee in print," and that discerning critic, William Dean Howells, saw his tales as brilliant re-creations of a whole Yankee village world.

And in addition to being authentic, the yarns are charming and comic—the mature creations of a great author.

Constance M. Rourke, **Trumpets of Jubilee**, New York, 1927 • H. R. Brown, **The Sentimental Novel in America 1789-1860**, Durham, North Carolina, 1940 • Forrest Wilson, **Crusader in Crinoline**, Philadelphia, 1941

From

Oldtown Fireside Stories

CAPTAIN KIDD'S MONEY

One of our most favorite legendary resorts was the old barn.

Sam Lawson preferred it on many accounts. It was quiet and retired, that is to say, at such a distance from his own house, that he could not hear if Hepsy called ever so loudly, and farther off than it would be convenient for that industrious and painstaking woman to follow him. Then there was the soft fragrant cushion of hay, on which his length of limb could be easily bestowed.

Our barn had an upper loft with a swinging outer door that commanded a view of the old mill, the waterfall, and the distant windings of the river, with its grassy green banks, its graceful elm draperies, and its white flocks of water-lilies; and then on this Saturday afternoon we had Sam all to ourselves. It was a drowsy, dreamy October day, when the hens were lazily "craw, crawing," in a soft, conversational undertone with each other, as they scratched and picked the hay-seed under the barn windows. Below in the barn black Caesar sat quietly hatchelling flax, sometimes gurgling and giggling to himself with an overflow of that interior jollity with which he seemed to be always full. The African in New England was a curious contrast to everybody around him in the joy and satisfaction that he seemed to feel in the mere fact of being alive. Every white person was glad or sorry for some appreciable cause in the past, present, or future, which was capable of being definitely stated; but black Caesar was in an eternal giggle and frizzle and simmer of enjoyment for which he could give no earthly reason: he was an "embodied joy," like Shelley's skylark.

"Jest hear him," said Sam Lawson, looking pensively over the haymow, and strewing hayseed down on his wool. "How that 'ere critter seems to tickel and laugh all the while 'bout nothin'. Lordy massy, he don't seem never to consider that this life's a dream, an empty show."

"Look here, Sam," we broke in, anxious to cut short a threatened stream of morality, "you promised to tell us about Captain Kidd, and how you dug for his money."

"Did I, now? Wal, boys, that 'are history o' Kidd's is a warnin' to fellers. Why, Kidd had pious parents and Bible and sanctuary privileges when he was a boy, and yet come to be hanged. It's all in this 'ere song I'm a-goin' to sing ye. Lordy massy! I wish I had my bass-viol now. Caesar," he said, calling down from his perch, "can't you strike the pitch o' 'Cap'n Kidd' on your fiddle?"

Caesar's fiddle was never far from him. It was, in fact, tucked away in a nice little nook just over the manger; and he often caught an interval from his work to scrape a dancing-tune on it, keeping time with his heels, to our great delight.

A most wailing minor-keyed tune was doled forth, which seemed quite refreshing to Sam's pathetic vein, as he sang in his most lugubrious tones:—

> " 'My name was Robert Kidd
>   As I sailed, as I sailed,
>   My name was Robert Kidd;
>   God's laws I did forbid,
>   And so wickedly I did,
>   As I sailed, as I sailed.'

"Now ye see, boys, he's a-goin' to tell how he abused his religious privileges; just hear now:—

'My father taught me well,
    As I sailed, as I sailed;
My father taught me well
To shun the gates of hell,
But yet I did rebel,
    As I sailed, as I sailed.

'He put a Bible in my hand,
    As I sailed, as I sailed;
He put a Bible in my hand,
And I sunk it in the sand
Before I left the strand,
    As I sailed, as I sailed.'

"Did ye ever hear o' such a hardened, contrary critter, boys? It's awful to think on. Wal, ye see that 'are's the way fellers allers begin the ways o' sin, by turning their backs on the Bible and the advice o' pious parents. Now hear what he come to:—

'Then I murdered William More,
    As I sailed, as I sailed;
I murdered William More,
And left him in his gore,
Not many leagues from shore,
    As I sailed, as I sailed.

'To execution dock
    I must go, I must go.
To execution dock,
While thousands round me flock,
To see me on the block,
    I must go, I must go.'

"There was a good deal more on 't," said Sam, pausing, "but I don't seem to remember it; but it's real solemn and affectin'."

"Who was Capt. Kidd, Sam?" said I.

"Wal, he was an officer in the British navy, and he got to bein' a pirate: used to take ships and sink 'em, and murder the folks; and so they say he got no end o' money,—gold and silver and precious stones as many as the wise men in the East. But ye see, what good did it all do him? He couldn't use it, and dar'sn't keep it; so he used to bury it in spots round here and there in the awfullest heathen way ye ever heard of. Why, they say he allers used to kill one or two men or women or children of his prisoners, and bury with it, so that their sperits might keep watch on it ef anybody was to dig arter it. That 'are thing has been tried and tried, but no man nor mother's son on 'em ever got a cent that dug. 'T was tried here 'n Oldtown; and they come pretty nigh gettin' on 't, but it gin 'em the slip. Ye see, boys, *it's the Devil's money,* and he holds a pretty tight grip on 't."

"Well, how was it about digging for it? Tell us, did you do it? Were you there? Did you see it? And why couldn't they get it?" we both asked eagerly and in one breath.

"Why, Lordy massy! boys, your questions tumbles over each other thick as martins out o' a martin-box. Now, you jest be moderate and let alone, and I'll tell you all about it from the beginnin' to the end. I didn't railly have no hand in 't, though I was knowin' to 't, as I be to most things that goes on round here; but my conscience wouldn't railly a let me start on no such undertakin'.

"Wal, the one that fust sot the thing a-goin' was old Mother Hokum, that used to live up in that tumble-down shed by the cranberry-pond up beyond the spring pastur'. They had a putty bad name, them Hokums. How they got a livin' nobody knew; for they didn't seem to pay no attention to raisin' nothin' but childun, but the deuce knows, there was plenty o' them. Their old hut was like a rabbit-pen: there was a tow-head to every crack and cranny. 'Member what old Caesar said once when the word come to the store that old Hokum had got twins. 'S'pose de Lord knows best,' says Caesar, 'but *I* thought dere was Hokums enough afore.' Wal, even poor workin' industrious folks like me finds it's hard gettin' along when there's so many mouths to feed. Lordy massy! there don't never seem to be no end on 't, and so it ain't wonderful, come to think on 't, ef folks like them Hokums gets tempted to help along in ways that ain't quite right. Anyhow, folks did use to think that old Hokum was too sort o' familiar with their wood-piles 'long in the night, though they couldn't never prove it on him; and when Mother Hokum come to houses round to wash, folks use sometimes to miss pieces, here and there, though they never could find 'em on her; then they was allers a gettin' in debt here and a gettin' in debt there. Why, they got to owin' two dollars to Joe Gidger for butcher's meat, 'cause Hokum he promised so fair to pay; but he couldn't never get it out o' him. 'Member once Joe walked clear up to the cranberry-pond arter that 'are two dollars; but Mother Hokum she see him a-comin' jest as he come past the juniper-bush on the corner. She says to Hokum, 'Get into bed, old man, quick, and let me tell the story,' says she. So she covered him up; and when Gidger come in she come up to him, and says she, 'Why, Mr. Gidger, I'm jest ashamed to see ye: why, Mr. Hokum was jest a-comin' down to pay ye that 'are money last week, but ye see he was took down with the small-pox'—Joe didn't hear no more: he just turned round, and streaked it out that 'are door with his coat-tails flyin' out straight ahind him; and old Mother Hokum she jest stood at the window holdin' her sides and laughin' fit to split, to see him run. That 'are's jest a sample o' the ways them Hokums cut up.

"Wal, you see, boys, there's a queer kind o' rock down on the bank o' the river, that looks sort o' like a grave-stone. The biggest part on 't is sunk down under ground, and it's pretty well growed over with black-berry-vines; but, when you scratch the bushes away, they used to make out some queer marks on that 'are rock. They was sort o' lines and crosses; and folks would have it that them was Kidd's private marks, and that there was one o' the places where he hid his money.

"Wal, there's no sayin' fairly how it come to be thought so; but fellers used to say so, and they used sometimes to talk it over to the tahvern, and kind o' wonder whether or no, if they should dig, they wouldn't come to suthin'.

"Wal, old Mother Hokum she heard on 't, and she was sort o' enterprisin' old crittur; fact was, she had to be, 'cause the young Hokums was jest like bag-worms, the more they growed the more they eat, and I expect she found it pretty hard to fill their mouths; and so she said ef there *was* anything under that 'are rock, they'd as good's have it as the Devil; and so she didn't give old Hokum no peace o' his life, but he must see what there was there.

"Wal, I was with 'em the night they was a-talkin' on 't up. Ye see, Hokum he got thirty-seven cents' worth o' lemons and sperit. I see him goin' by as I was out a splittin' kindlin's; and says he: 'Toddy Whitney and Harry Wiggin's comin' up, and we're goin' to have a little suthin' hot,' says he; and he kind o' showed me the lemons and sperit. And I told him I guessed I would go 'long. Wal, I kind o' wanted to see what they'd be up to, ye know.

"Wal, come to find out, they was a talkin' about Cap'n Kidd's treasures, and layin' out how they should get it, and a settin' one another on with gret stories about it.

Sam Lawson—illustration by Darley for the 1872 edition

"'I've heard that there was whole chists full o' gold guineas,' says one.

"'And I've heard o' gold bracelets and ear-rings and finger-rings all sparklin' with diamonds,' says another.

"'Maybe it's old silver plate from some o' them old West Indian grandees,' says another.

"'Wal, whatever it is,' says Mother Hokum, 'I want to be into it,' says she.

"'Wal, Sam, won't you jine?' says they.

"'Wal, boys,' says I, 'I kind o' don't feel jest like

i'inin'. I sort o' ain't clear about the rights on 't: seems to me it's mighty like goin' to the Devil for money.'

"'Wal,' says Mother Hokum, 'what if 'tis? Money's money, get it how ye will; and the Devil's money'll buy as much meat as any. I'd go to the Devil if he gave good money.'

"'Wal, I guess I wouldn't,' says I. 'Don't you 'member the sermon Parson Lothrop preached about hastin' to be rich, last sabba' day?'

"'Parson Lothrop be hanged!' says she. 'Wal, now,' says she, 'I like to see a parson with his silk stockin's and great gold-headed cane, a lollopin' on his carriage behind his fat, prancin' hosses, comin' to meetin' to preach to us poor folks not to want to be rich! How'd he like it to have forty-'leven children, and nothin' to put onto 'em or into 'em, I wonder? Guess if Lady Lothrop had to rub and scrub, and wear her fingers to the bone as I do, she'd want to be rich; and I guess the parson, if he couldn't get a bellyful for a week, would be for diggin' up Kidd's money, or doing 'most anything else to make the pot bile.'

"'Wal,' says I, 'I'll kind o' go with ye, boys, and sort o' see how things turn out; but I guess I won't take no shere in 't,' says I.

"Wal, they got it all planned out. They was to wait till the full moon, and then they was to get Primus King to go with 'em and help do the diggin'. Ye see, Hokum and Toddy Whitney and Wiggin are all putty softly fellers, and hate dreffully to work; and I tell you the Kidd money ain't to be got without a pretty tough piece o' diggin'. Why, it's jest like diggin' a well to get at it. Now, Primus King was the master hand for diggin' wells, and so they said they'd get him by givin' on him a shere.

"Harry Wiggin he didn't want no nigger a sherin' in it, he said; but Toddy and Hokum they said that when there was such stiff diggin' to be done, they did n't care if they did go in with a nigger.

"Wal, Wiggin he said he hadn't no objection to havin' the nigger do the diggin', it was *sherin' the profits* he objected to.

"'Wal,' said Hokum, 'you can't get him without,' says he. 'Primus knows too much,' says he: 'you can't fool him.' Finally they 'greed that they was to give Primus twenty dollars, and shere the treasure 'mong themselves.

"Come to talk to Primus, he wouldn't stick in a spade, unless they'd pay him aforehand. Ye see, Primus was up to 'em; he knowed about Gidger, and there wa'n't none on 'em that was particular good pay; and so they all jest hed to rake and scrape, and pay him down the twenty dollars among 'em; and they 'greed for the fust full moon, at twelve o'clock at night, the 9th of October.

"Wal, ye see, I had to tell Hepsy I was goin' out to watch. Wal, so I was; but not jest in the way she took it; but Lordy massy! a feller has to tell his wife suthin' to keep her quiet, ye know, 'specially Hepsy.

"Wal, wal, of all the moonlight nights that ever I did see, I never did see one equal to that. Why, you could see the color o' everything. I 'member I could see how the huckleberry-bushes on the rock was red as blood when the moonlight shone through 'em; 'cause the leaves, you see, had begun to turn.

"Goin' on our way we got to talkin' about the sperits.

"'I ain't afraid on 'em,' says Hokum. 'What harm can a sperit do me?' says he. 'I don't care ef there's a dozen on 'em,' and he took a swig at his bottle.

"'Oh! there ain't no sperits,' says Harry Wiggin. 'That 'are talk's all nonsense;' and he took a swig at *his* bottle.

"'Wal,' says Toddy, 'I don't know 'bout that 'ere. Me and Ike Sanders has seen the sperits in the Cap'n Brown house. We thought we'd jest have a peek into the window one night; and there was a whole flock o' black colts without no head on come rushin' on us and knocked us flat.'

"'I expect you'd been at the tahvern,' says Hokum.

"'Wal, yes, we had; but them was sperits; we wa'n't drunk, now; we was jest as sober as ever we was.'

"'Wal, they won't get away my money,' says Primus, 'for I put it safe away in Dinah's teapot afore I come out;' and then he showed all his ivories from ear to ear. 'I think all this 'are's sort o' foolishness,' says Primus.

"'Wal', says I, 'boys, I ain't a-goin' to have no part or lot in this 'ere matter, but I'll jest lay it off to you how it's to be done. Ef Kidd's money is under this rock, there's *sperits* that watch it, and you mustn't give 'em no advantage. There mustn't be a word spoke from the time ye get sight o' the treasure till ye get it safe up on to firm ground,' says I. 'Ef ye do, it'll vanish right out o' sight. I've talked with them that has dug down to it and seen it; but they allers lost it, 'cause they'd call out and say suthin'; and the minute they spoke, away it went.'

"Wal, so they marked off the ground; and Primus he begun to dig, and the rest kind o' sot around. It was so still it was kind o' solemn. Ye see, it was past twelve o'clock, and every critter in Oldtown was asleep; and there was two whipporwills on the great Cap'n Brown elm-trees, that kep' a answerin' each other back and forward sort o' solitary like; and then every once in a while there'd come a sort o' strange whisper up among the elm-tree leaves, jest as if there was talkin' goin' on; and every time Primus struck his spade into the ground it sounded sort o' holler, jest as if he'd been a-diggin' a grave. 'It's kind o' melancholy,' says I, 'to think o' them poor critters that had to be killed and buried jest to keep this 'ere treasure. What awful thing'll be brought to light in the judgment day! Them poor critters they loved to live and hated to die as much as any on us; but no, they hed to die jest to satisfy that critter's wicked will. I've heard them as thought they could tell the Cap'n Kidd places by layin' their ear to the ground at midnight, and they'd hear groans and wailin's.'"

"Why, Sam! were there really people who could tell where Kidd's money was?" I here interposed.

"Oh, sartin! why, yis. There was Shebna Bascom, he was one. Shebna could always tell what was under the earth. He'd cut a hazel-stock, and hold it in his hand when folks was wantin' to know where to dig wells; and that 'are stick would jest turn in his hands, and p'int down till it would fairly grind the bark off; and ef you dug in that place you was sure to find a spring. Oh, yis! Shebna he's told many where the Kidd money was, and been with 'em when they dug for it; but the pester on 't was they allers lost it, 'cause they would some on 'em speak afore they thought."

"But, Sam, what about this digging? Let's know what came of it," said we, as Sam appeared to lose his way in his story.

"Wal, ye see, they dug down about five feet, when Primus he struck his spade smack on something that chinked like iron.

"Wal, then Hokum and Toddy Whitney was into the hole in a minute; they made Primus get out, and they took the spade, 'cause they wanted to be sure to come on it themselves.

"Wal, they begun, and they dug and he scraped, and sure enough they come to a gret iron pot as big as your granny's dinner-pot, with an iron bale to it.

"Wal, then they put down a rope, and he put the rope through the handle; then Hokum and Toddy they clambered upon the bank, and all on 'em began to draw up jest as still and silent as could be. They drawed and drawed, till they jest got it even with the ground, when Toddy spoke out all in a tremble, 'There,' says he, *'we've got it!'* And the minit he spoke they was both struck by *suthin'* that knocked 'em clean over; and the rope give a crack like a pistol-shot, and broke short off; and the pot went down, down, down, and they heard it goin', jink, jink, jink; and it went way down into the earth, and the ground closed over it; and then they heard the screechin'est laugh ye ever did hear."

"I want to know, Sam, did you see that pot?" I exclaimed at this part of the story.

"Wal, no, I didn't. Ye see, I jest happened to drop asleep while they was diggin', I was so kind o' tired, and I did n't wake up till it was all over.

"I was waked up, 'cause there was consid'able of a scuffle; for Hokum was so mad at Toddy for speakin', that he was a-fistin' on him; and old Primus he jest haw-hawed and laughed. 'Wal, I got *my* money safe, anyhow,' says he.

" 'Wal, come to,' says I. ' 'Tain't no use cryin' for spilt milk: you've jest got to turn in now and fill up this 'ere hole, else the selectmen'll be down on ye.'

" 'Wal,' says Primus, 'I did n't engage to fill up no holes;' and he put his spade on his shoulder and trudged off.

"Wal, it was putty hard work, fillin' in that hole; but Hokum and Toddy and Wiggin had to do it, 'cause they did n't want to have everybody a-laughin' at 'em; and I kind o' tried to set it home to 'em, showin' on 'em that 'twas all for the best.

" 'Ef you'd 'a' been left to get that 'ere money, there'd 'a' come a cuss with it,' says I. 'It shows the vanity o' hastin' to be rich.'

" 'Oh, you shet up!' says Hokum, says he. 'You never hasted to anything,' says he. Ye see, he was riled, that's why he spoke so."

"Sam," said we, after maturely reflecting over the story, "what do you suppose was in that pot?"

"Lordy massy, boys! ye never will be done askin' questions. Why, how should I know?"

1871

Bret Harte

1836 · 1902

"The writer of the epic of the gold rush," Francis Bret Harte, lived in California only during the period from 1854 to 1871. The rest of his life he lived in the East or abroad. Yet his stay in California gave him his most important material for poetry and for fiction which won remarkable popularity for him.

Harte was born in Albany, New York, August 25, 1836. He had a rather sketchy education. After his widowed mother moved the family to San Francisco, he joined them—in 1854—on the Pacific Coast. There he taught school, worked in the mines for a short time, served as a Wells Fargo Express messenger, and eventually became a printer. Developing his skill as a writer, he in time worked into various editorial jobs on some of the California magazines.

In 1868 he published "The Luck of Roaring Camp" in the newly founded *Overland Monthly,* of which he was editor. When the issue containing the story reached the East, the story was an immediate sensational success. Other stories in the same vein augmented Harte's popularity, and a poem, "Plain Language from Truthful James," was another extraordinary hit, read and quoted by everyone. In 1871, with an impressive contract from the *Atlantic Monthly* in his pocket, Harte started East, leaving the Far West permanently. His journey across the continent was a triumphant progress, and he was hailed in the East as a new genius.

The part of his life which came after this journey was pretty much of an anticlimax. A few more stories—"The Outcasts of Poker Flat," and "Tennessee's Partner," and "How Santa Claus Came to Simpson's Bar," for in-

stance—and some of his many poems were up to the early standard, but his work became repetitious, and, in the end, not much more than the working out of a formula. In 1878 he went abroad on a consular appointment to Germany. From 1888 until his death in 1902 he lived in England.

Harte believed that his art derived from that of American humor, and much of the comedy he mingles with pathos is obviously related to the humorous writings of pre-Civil War humorists. From the same group he evidently learned much about the picturing in fiction of the teeming life of a frontier section. From Dickens, his favorite author, he also apparently learned a great deal—particularly a way of merging his background into a story and a way of making characters memorable by giving them grotesque or unexpected traits. From post-war humorists, he borrowed various tricks of phrasing. His fame derived in part from the skill with which he blended these elements in his stories, in part from the interest the public had in the picturesque life of the latest American frontier.

An element in Harte's writings which also helped their popularity was a novel twist which he used again and again in the time-worn plot of sacrifice. In earlier sentimental stories, sweet and gracious characters habitually had made touching sacrifices in behalf of weak or wicked characters. Harte reversed the rôle of the rougher characters, and showed prostitutes, gamblers, or other besmirched men and women of the mining camps bravely making sacrifices. In "The Luck of Roaring Camp" the old formula of "innocent character saves ignoble character" is reversed when the rough Kentuck sacrifices his life to rescue little Tom Luck. In "Tennessee's Partner" the person for whom the sacrifice is made is, of course, a typical rascal of the old-fashioned sort; but the partner who is the hero shows the tenderness which lurks beneath a tough exterior.

Harte's great success is important in American literary history because of the impetus it gave to local color writing, which in time was to acquaint the public with

life in most of the other sections of the country. The unconventional morality—for the time—of his fiction prepared the way for characterizations and scenes in later fiction which increasingly departed from prudish standards.

The Writings of Bret Harte, Standard Library Edition, 20 vols., Boston, 1896-1903 • Bret Harte, Representative Selections (American Writers Series), ed. J. B. Harrison, Cincinnati, 1941 • G. R. Stewart, Jr., Bret Harte, Argonaut and Exile, New York, 1931

— Local color writer!

Local color story

Kentuck — Played up

The Luck of Roaring Camp

they played all day long.

Glorification of the sinner

There was commotion in Roaring Camp. It could not have been a fight, for in 1850 that was not novel enough to have called together the entire settlement. The ditches and claims were not only deserted, but "Tuttle's grocery" had contributed its gamblers, who, it will be remembered, calmly continued their game the day that French Pete and Kanaka Joe shot each other to death over the bar in the front room. The whole camp was collected before a rude cabin on the outer edge of the clearing. Conversation was carried on in a low tone, but the name of a woman was frequently repeated. It was a name familiar enough in the camp,—"Cherokee Sal."

Perhaps the less said of her the better. She was a coarse, and it is to be feared, a very sinful woman. But at that time she was the only woman in Roaring Camp, and was just then lying in sore extremity, when she most needed the ministration of her own sex. Dissolute, abandoned, and irreclaimable, she was yet suffering a martyrdom hard enough to bear even when veiled by sympathizing womanhood, but now terrible in her loneliness. The primal curse had come to her in that

original isolation which must have made the punishment of the first transgression so dreadful. It was, perhaps, part of the expiation of her sin, that, at a moment when she most lacked her sex's intuitive tenderness and care, she met only the half-contemptuous faces of her masculine associates. Yet a few of the spectators were, I think, touched by her sufferings. Sandy Tipton thought it was "rough on Sal," and, in the contemplation of her condition, for a moment rose superior to the fact that he had an ace and two bowers in his sleeve.

It will be seen, also, that the situation was novel. Deaths were by no means uncommon in Roaring Camp, but a birth was a new thing. People had been dismissed from the camp effectively, finally, and with no possibility of return; but this was the first time that anybody had been introduced *ab initio.* Hence the excitement.

"You go in there, Stumpy," said a prominent citizen known as "Kentuck," addressing one of the loungers. "Go in there, and see what you kin do. You've had experience in them things."

Perhaps there was a fitness in the selection. Stumpy, in other climes, had been the putative head of two families; in fact, it was owing to some legal informality in these proceedings that Roaring Camp—a city of refuge—was indebted to his company. The crowd approved the choice, and Stumpy was wise enough to bow to the majority. The door closed upon the extempore surgeon and midwife, and Roaring Camp sat down outside, smoked its pipe, and awaited the issue.

The assemblage numbered about a hundred men. One or two of these were actual fugitives from justice, some were criminal, and all were reckless. Physically, they exhibited no indication of their past lives and

→ a "novel twist" bad characters made selfless sacrifices rather than good characters —

character. The greatest scamp had a Raphael face, with a profusion of blond hair; Oakhurst, a gambler, had the melancholy air and intellectual abstraction of a Hamlet; the coolest and most courageous man was scarcely over five feet in height, with a soft voice and an embarrassed, timid manner. The term "roughs" applied to them was a distinction rather than a definition. Perhaps in the minor details of fingers, toes, ears, etc., the camp may have been deficient, but these slight omissions did not detract from their aggregate force. The strongest man had but three fingers on his right hand; the best shot had but one eye.

Such was the physical aspect of the men that were dispersed around the cabin. The camp lay in a triangular valley, between two hills and a river. The only outlet was a steep trail over the summit of a hill that faced the cabin, now illuminated by the rising moon. The suffering woman might have seen it from the rude bunk whereon she lay,—seen it winding like a silver thread until it was lost in the stars above.

A fire of withered pine boughs added sociability to the gathering. By degrees the natural levity of Roaring Camp returned. Bets were freely offered and taken regarding the result. Three to five that "Sal would get through with it"; even, that the child would survive; side bets as to the sex and complexion of the coming stranger. In the midst of an excited discussion an exclamation came from those nearest the door, and the camp stopped to listen. Above the swaying and moaning of the pines, the swift rush of the river, and the crackling of the fire rose a sharp, querulous cry—a cry unlike anything heard before in the camp. The pines stopped moaning, the river ceased to rush, and the fire to crackle. It seemed as if Nature had stopped to listen too.

The camp rose to its feet as one man! It was proposed to explode a barrel of gun-powder, but, in consideration of the situation of the mother, better counsels prevailed, and only a few revolvers were discharged; for, whether owing to the rude surgery of the camp, or some other reason, Cherokee Sal was sinking fast. Within an hour she had climbed, as it were, that rugged road that led to the stars, and so passed out of Roaring Camp, its sin and shame forever. I do not think that the announcement disturbed them much, except in speculation as to the fate of the child. "Can he live now?" was asked of Stumpy. The answer was doubtful. The only other being of Cherokee Sal's sex and maternal condition in the settlement was an ass. There was some conjecture as to fitness, but the experiment was tried. It was less problematical than the ancient treatment of Romulus and Remus, and apparently as successful.

When these details were completed, which exhausted another hour, the door was opened, and the anxious crowd, who had already formed themselves into a queue, entered in single file. Beside the low bunk or shelf, on which the figure of the mother was starkly outlined below the blankets, stood a pine table. On this a candle-box was placed, and within it, swathed in staring red flannel, lay the last arrival at Roaring Camp. Beside the candle-box was placed a hat. Its use was soon indicated. "Gentlemen," said Stumpy, with a singular mixture of authority and *ex officio* complacency—"Gentlemen will please pass in at the front door, round the table, and out at the back door. Them as wishes to contribute anything toward the orphan will find a hat handy." The first man entered with his hat on; he uncovered, however, as he looked about him, and so, unconsciously, set an example to the next. In such communities good and bad actions are catching. As the procession filed in, comments were audible,—criticisms addressed, perhaps, rather to Stumpy, in the character of showman,—"Is that him?" "Mighty small specimen"; "Hasn't more'n got the color"; "Ain't bigger nor a derringer." The contributions were as characteristic: A silver tobacco box; a doubloon; a navy revolver, silver mounted; a gold specimen; a very beautifully embroidered lady's handkerchief (from Oakhurst the gambler); a diamond breastpin; a diamond ring (suggested by the pin, with the remark from the giver that he "saw that pin and went two diamonds better"); a slung shot; a Bible (contributor not detected); a golden spur; a silver teaspoon (the initials, I regret to say, were not the giver's); a pair of surgeon's shears; a lancet; a Bank of England note for £5; and about $200 in loose gold and silver coin. During these proceedings Stumpy maintained a silence as impassive as the dead on his left—a gravity as inscrutable as that of the newly-born on his right. Only one incident occurred to break the monotony of the curious procession. As Kentuck bent over the candle-box half curiously, the child turned, and, in a spasm of pain, caught at his groping finger, and held it fast for a moment. Kentuck looked foolish and embarrassed. Something like a blush tried to assert itself in his weather-beaten cheek. "The d—d little cuss!" he said, as he extricated his finger, with, perhaps, more tenderness and care than he might have been deemed capable of showing. He held that finger a little apart from its fellows as he went out, and examined it curiously. The examination provoked the same original remark in regard to the child. In fact, he seemed to enjoy repeating it. "He rastled with my finger," he remarked to Tipton, holding up the member, "the d—d little cuss!"

It was four o'clock before the camp sought repose. A light burnt in the cabin where the watchers sat, for Stumpy did not go to bed that night. Nor did Kentuck. He drank quite freely and related with great gusto his experience, invariably ending with his characteristic condemnation of the newcomer. It seemed to relieve him of any unjust implication of sentiment, and Kentuck had the weaknesses of the nobler sex. When everybody else had gone to bed, he walked down to the river, and whistled reflectingly. Then he walked up the gulch, past the cabin, still whistling with demonstrative unconcern. At a large redwood tree he paused and retraced his steps, and again passed the cabin. Halfway down to the river's bank he again paused, and then returned and knocked at the door. It was opened by Stumpy. "How goes it?" said Kentuck, looking past Stumpy toward the candle-box. "All serene," replied Stumpy. "Anything up?" "Nothing." There was a pause —an embarrassing one—Stumpy still holding the door. Then Kentuck had recourse to his finger, which he held up to Stumpy. "Rastled with it,—the d—d little cuss," he said, and retired.

The next day Cherokee Sal had such rude sepulture as Roaring Camp afforded. After her body had been committed to the hillside, there was a formal meeting of the camp to discuss what should be done with her infant. A resolution to adopt it was unanimous and enthusiastic. But an animated discussion in regard to the manner and feasibility of providing for its wants at once sprung up. It was remarkable that the argument partook of none of those fierce personalities with which discussions were usually conducted at Roaring Camp. Tipton proposed that they should send the child to Red Dog—a distance of forty miles—where female attention could be procured. But the unlucky suggestion met with fierce and unanimous opposition. It was evident that no plan which entailed parting from their new acquisition would for a moment be entertained. "Besides," said Tom Ryder, "them fellows at Red Dog would swap it, and ring in somebody else on us." A disbelief in the honesty of other camps prevailed at Roaring Camp as in other places.

The introduction of a female nurse in the camp also met with objection. It was argued that no decent woman could be prevailed to accept Roaring Camp as her home, and the speaker urged that "they didn't want any more of the other kind." This unkind allusion to the defunct mother, harsh as it may seem, was the first spasm of propriety—the first symptom of the camp's regeneration. Stumpy advanced nothing. Perhaps he felt a certain delicacy in interfering with the selection of a possible successor in office. But when questioned, he averred stoutly that he and "Jinny"—the mammal before alluded to—could manage to rear the child. There was something original, independent, and heroic about the plan that pleased the camp. Stumpy was retained. Certain articles were sent for to Sacramento. "Mind," said the treasurer, as he pressed a bag of gold-dust into the expressman's hand, "the best that can be got—lace, you know, and filigree-work and frills,—d—n the cost!"

Strange to say, the child thrived. Perhaps the invigorating climate of the mountain camp was compensation for material deficiencies. Nature took the foundling to her broader breast. In that rare atmosphere of the Sierra foothills—that air pungent with balsamic odor, that ethereal cordial, at once bracing and exhilarating, he may have found food and nourishment, or a subtle chemistry that transmuted asses' milk to lime and phosphorus. Stumpy inclined to the belief that it was the latter and good nursing. "Me and that ass," he would say, "has been father and mother to him! Don't you," he would add, apostrophizing the helpless bundle before him, "never go back on us."

By the time he was a month old, the necessity of giving him a name became apparent. He had generally been known as "the Kid," "Stumpy's boy," "the Cayote" (an allusion to his vocal powers) and even by Kentuck's endearing diminutive of "the d—d little cuss." But these were felt to be vague and unsatisfactory, and were at last dismissed under another influence. Gamblers and adventurers are generally superstitious, and Oakhurst one day declared that the baby had brought "the luck" to Roaring Camp. It was certain that of late they had been successful. "Luck" was the name agreed upon, with the prefix of Tommy for greater convenience. No allusion was made to the mother, and the father was unknown. "It's better," said the philosophical Oakhurst, "to take a fresh deal all round. Call him Luck, and start him fair." A day was accordingly set apart for the christening. What was meant by this ceremony the reader may imagine, who has already gathered some idea of the reckless irreverence of Roaring Camp. The master of ceremonies was one "Boston," a noted wag, and the occasion seemed to promise the greatest facetiousness. This ingenious satirist had spent two days in preparing a burlesque of the church service, with pointed local allusions. The choir was properly trained, and Sandy Tipton was to stand godfather. But after the procession had marched to the grove with music and banners, and the child had been deposited before a mock altar, Stumpy stepped before the expectant crowd. "It ain't my style to spoil fun, boys," said the little man, stoutly, eyeing the faces around him, "but it strikes me that this thing ain't exactly on the squar. It's playing it pretty low down on this yer baby to ring in fun on him that he ain't goin' to understand. And ef there's going to be any god-fathers round, I'd like to see who's got any better rights than me." A silence followed Stumpy's speech. To the credit of all humorists be it said that the first man to acknowledge its justice was the satirist, thus stopped of his fun. "But," said Stumpy, quickly, following up his advantage, "we're here for a christening, and we'll have it. I proclaim you Thomas Luck, according to the laws of the United States and the State of California, so help me God." It was the first time that the name of the Deity had been uttered otherwise but profanely in the camp. The form of christening was perhaps even more ludicrous than the satirist had conceived; but strangely enough, nobody saw it and nobody laughed. "Tommy" was christened as seriously as he would have been under a Christian roof, and cried and was comforted in as orthodox fashion.

And so the work of regeneration began in Roaring Camp. Almost imperceptibly a change came over the settlement. The cabin assigned to "Tommy Luck"—or "The Luck," as he was more frequently called—first showed signs of improvement. It was kept scrupulously clean and whitewashed. Then it was boarded, clothed and papered. The rosewood cradle—packed eighty miles by mule—had, in Stumpy's way of putting it, "sorter killed the rest of the furniture." So the rehabilitation of the cabin became a necessity. The men who were in the habit of lounging in at Stumpy's to see "how The Luck got on" seemed to appreciate the change, and, in self-defense, the rival establishment of "Tuttle's grocery" bestirred itself, and imported a carpet and mirrors. The reflections of the latter on the appearance of Roaring Camp tended to produce stricter habits of personal cleanliness. Again Stumpy imposed a kind of quarantine upon those who aspired to the honor and privilege of holding "The Luck." It was a cruel mortification to Kentuck—who, in the carelessness of a large nature and the habits of frontier life, had begun to regard all garments as a second cuticle, which, like a snake's, only sloughed off through decay—to be debarred this privilege from certain prudential reasons. Yet such was the subtle influence of innovation that he thereafter appeared regularly every afternoon in a clean shirt, and face still shining from his ablutions. Nor were moral and social sanitary laws neglected. "Tommy," who was supposed to spend his whole existence in a persistent attempt to repose, must not be disturbed by noise. The shouting and yelling which had gained the camp its infelicitous title were not permitted within hearing distance of Stumpy's. The men conversed in whispers, or smoked with Indian gravity. Profanity was tacitly given up in these sacred precincts, and throughout the camp a popular form of expletive, known as "D—n the luck!" and "Curse the luck!" was abandoned, as having a new personal bearing. Vocal music was not interdicted, being supposed to have a soothing, tranquilizing quality, and one song, sung by "Man-o'-War Jack," an English sailor from Her Majesty's Australian colonies, was quite popular as a lullaby. It was a lugubrious recital of the exploits of "the *Arethusa,* Seventy-four,*" in a muffled minor, ending with a prolonged dying fall at the burden of each verse, "On b-o-o-o-ard of the *Arethusa.*" It was a fine sight to see Jack holding The Luck, rocking from side to side as if with the motion of a ship, and crooning forth this naval ditty. Either through the peculiar rocking of Jack or the length of his song—it contained ninety stanzas, and was continued with conscientious deliberation to the bitter end—the lullaby generally had the desired effect. At such times the men would lie at full length under the trees, in the soft summer twilight, smoking their pipes and drinking in the melodious utterances. An indistinct idea that this was pastoral happiness pervaded the camp. "This 'ere kind o' think," said the Cockney Simmons, meditatively reclining on his elbow, "is 'evingly." It reminded him of Greenwich.

On the long summer days The Luck was usually carried to the gulch, from whence the golden store of Roaring Camp was taken. There, on a blanket spread over pine boughs, he would lie while the men were working in the ditches below. Latterly, there was a rude attempt to decorate this bower with flowers and sweet-smelling shrubs, and generally some one would bring him a cluster of wild honey-suckles, azaleas, or the painted blossoms of Las Mariposas. The men had suddenly awakened to the fact that there were beauty and significance in these trifles, which they had so long trodden carelessly beneath their feet. A flake of glittering mica, a fragment of variegated quartz, a bright pebble from the bed of the creek, became beautiful to eyes thus cleared and strengthened, and were invariably put aside for "The Luck." It was wonderful how many treasures the woods and hillsides yielded that "would do for Tommy." Surrounded by playthings such as never child out of fairyland had before, it is to be hoped that Tommy was content. He appeared to be serenely happy, albeit there was an infantine gravity about him, a contemplative light in his round gray eyes, that sometimes worried Stumpy. He was always tractable and quiet, and it is recorded that once, having crept beyond his "corral"—a hedge of tessellated pine boughs, which surrounded his bed—he dropped over the bank on his head in the soft earth, and remained with his mottled legs in the air in that position for at least five minutes with unflinching gravity. He was extricated without a murmur. I hesitate to record the many other instances of his sagacity, which rest, unfortunately, upon the statements of prejudiced friends. Some of them were not without a tinge of superstition. "I crep' up the bank just now," said Kentuck one day, in a breathless state of excitement, "and dern my skin if he wasn't a talking to a jaybird as was a-sittin' on his lap. There they was, just as free and sociable as anything you please, a-jawin at each other just like two cherrybums." Howbeit,

whether creeping over the pine boughs or lying lazily on his back, blinking at the leaves above him, to him the birds sang, the squirrels chattered, and the flowers bloomed. Nature was his nurse and playfellow. For him she would let slip between the leaves golden shafts of sunlight that fell just within his grasp; she would send wandering breezes to visit him with the balm of bay and resinous gums; to him the tall redwoods nodded familiarly and sleepily, the bumblebees buzzed, and the rooks cawed a slumbrous accompaniment.

Such was the golden summer of Roaring Camp. They were "flush times"—and the Luck was with them. The claims had yielded enormously. The camp was jealous of its privileges and looked suspiciously on strangers. No encouragement was given to immigration, and, to make their seclusion more perfect, the land on either side of the mountain wall that surrounded the camp they duly pre-empted. This, and a reputation for singular proficiency with the revolver, kept the reserve of Roaring Camp inviolate. The expressman—their only connecting link with the surrounding world—sometimes told wonderful stories of the camp. He would say, "They've a street up there in 'Roaring,' that would lay over any street up there in Red Dog. They've got vines and flowers round their houses, and they wash themselves twice a day. But they're mighty rough on strangers, and they worship an Ingin baby."

With the prosperity of the camp came a desire for further improvement. It was proposed to build a hotel in the following spring, and to invite one or two decent families to reside there for the sake of "The Luck," who might perhaps profit by female companionship. The sacrifice that this concession to the sex cost these men, who were fiercely skeptical in regard to its general virtue and usefulness, can only be accounted for by their affection for Tommy. A few still held out. But the resolve could not be carried into effect for three months, and the minority meekly yielded in the hope that something might turn up to prevent it. And it did.

The winter of '51 will long be remembered in the foothills. The snow lay deep on the sierras, and every mountain creek became a river, and every river a lake. Each gorge and gulch was transformed into a tumultuous watercourse that descended the hillsides, tearing down giant trees and scattering its drift and debris along the

6. began to enjoy beauty (especially) nature—

plain. Red Dog had been twice under water, and Roaring Camp had been forewarned. "Water put the gold into them gulches," said Stumpy; "it's been here once and will be here again!" And that night the North Fork suddenly leaped over its banks, and swept up the triangular valley of Roaring Camp.

In the confusion of rushing water, crashing trees, and crackling timber, and the darkness which seemed to flow with the water and blot out the fair valley, but little could be done to collect the scattered camp. When the morning broke, the cabin of Stumpy nearest the river-bank was gone. Higher up the gulch they found the body of its unlucky owner; but the pride—the hope—the joy—the Luck—of Roaring Camp had disappeared. They were returning with sad hearts, when a shout from the bank recalled them.

It was a relief-boat from down the river. They had picked up, they said, a man and an infant, nearly exhausted, about two miles below. Did anybody know them, and did they belong here?

It needed but a glance to show them Kentuck lying there, cruelly crushed and bruised, but still holding The Luck of Roaring Camp in his arms. As they bent over the strangely assorted pair, they saw that the child was cold and pulseless. "He is dead," said one. Kentuck opened his eyes. "Dead?" he repeated feebly. "Yes, my man, and you are dying too." A smile lit the eyes of the expiring Kentuck. "Dying!" he repeated, "he's a-taking me with him—tell the boys I've got the Luck with me now"; and the strong man, clinging to the frail babe as a drowning man is said to cling to a straw, drifted away into the shadowy river that flows forever to the unknown sea.

1868

Tennessee's Partner

came in & was going to bribe the court to get back his partner, Tenn. who was up for trial!

I do not think that we ever knew his real name. Our ignorance of it certainly never gave us any social inconvenience, for at Sandy Bar in 1854 most men were christened anew. Sometimes these appellatives were derived from some distinctiveness of dress, as in the case of "Dungaree Jack;" or from some peculiarity of habit, as shown in "Saleratus Bill," so called from an undue proportion of that chemical in his daily bread; or from some unlucky slip, as exhibited in "The Iron Pirate," a mild, inoffensive man, who earned that baleful title by his unfortunate mispronunciation of the term "iron pyrites." Perhaps this may have been the beginning of a rude heraldry; and I am constrained to think that it was because a man's real name in that day rested solely upon his own unsupported statement. "Call yourself Clifford, do you?" said Boston, addressing a timid newcomer with infinite scorn; "hell is full of such Cliffords!" He then introduced the unfortunate man, whose name happened to be really Clifford, as "Jaybird Charley,"—an unhallowed inspiration of the moment that clung to him ever after.

But to return to Tennessee's Partner, whom we never knew by any other than this relative title. That he had ever existed as a separate and distinct individuality we only learned later. It seems that in 1853 he left Poker Flat to go to San Francisco, ostensibly to procure a wife. He never got any farther than Stockton. At that place he was attracted by a young person who waited upon the table at the hotel where he took his meals. One morning he said something to her which caused her to smile not unkindly, to somewhat coquettishly break a plate of toast over his upturned, serious, simple face, and to retreat to the kitchen. He followed her, and emerged a few moments later, covered with more toast and victory. That day week they were married by a justice of the peace, and returned to Poker Flat. I am aware that something more might be made of this episode, but I prefer to tell it as it was current at Sandy Bar,—in the gulches and bar-rooms,—where all sentiment was modified by a strong sense of humor.

Of their married felicity but little is known, perhaps for the reason that Tennessee, then living with his partner, one day took occasion to say something to the bride on her own account, at which, it is said, she smiled not

[margin note, vertical:] true name

unkindly and chastely retreated,—this time as far as Marysville, where Tennessee followed her, and where they went to house-keeping without the aid of a justice of the peace. Tennessee's Partner took the loss of his wife simply and seriously, as was his fashion. But to everybody's surprise, when Tennessee one day returned from Marysville, without his partner's wife,—she having smiled and retreated with somebody else,—Tennessee's Partner was the first man to shake his hand and greet
10 him with affection. The boys who had gathered in the canon to see the shooting were naturally indignant. Their indignation might have found vent in sarcasm but for a certain look in Tennessee's Partner's eyes that indicated a lack of humorous appreciation. In fact, he was a grave man, with a steady application to practical detail which was unpleasant in a difficulty.

Meanwhile a popular feeling against Tennessee had grown up on the Bar. He was known to be a gambler; he was suspected to be a thief. In these suspicions Ten-
20 nessee's Partner was equally compromised; his continued intimacy with Tennessee after the affair above quoted could only be accounted for on the hypothesis of a co-partnership of crime. At last Tennessee's guilt became flagrant. One day he overtook a stranger on his way to Red Dog. The stranger afterward related that Tennessee beguiled the time with interesting anecdote and reminiscence, but illogically concluded the interview in the following words: "And now, young man, I'll trouble you for your knife, your pistols, and your money. You see
30 your weppings might get you into trouble at Red Dog, and your money's a temptation to the evilly disposed. I think you said your address was San Francisco. I shall endeavor to call." It may be stated here that Tennessee had a fine flow of humor, which no business preoccupation could wholly subdue.

This exploit was his last. Red Dog and Sandy Bar made common cause against the highwayman. Tennessee was hunted in very much the same fashion as his prototype, the grizzly. As the toils closed around him, he
40 made a desperate dash through the Bar, emptying his revolver at the crowd before the Arcade Saloon, and so on up Grizzly Canon; but at its farther extremity he was stopped by a small man on a gray horse. The men looked at each other a moment in silence. Both were fearless, both self-possessed and independent, and both types of a civilization that in the seventeenth century would

have been called heroic, but in the nineteenth simply "reckless."

"What have you got there?—I call," said Tennessee
quietly. 50

"Two bowers and an ace," said the stranger as quietly, showing two revolvers and a bowie-knife.

"That takes me," returned Tennessee; and, with this gambler's epigram, he threw away his useless pistol and rode back with his captor. *he is captured*

It was a warm night. The cool breeze which usually sprang up with the going down of the sun behind the chaparral-crested mountain was that evening withheld from Sandy Bar. The little canon was stifling with heated resinous odors, and the decaying driftwood on 60 the Bar sent forth faint sickening exhalations. The feverishness of day and its fierce passions still filled the camp. Lights moved restlessly along the bank of the river, striking no answering reflection from its tawny current. Against the blackness of the pines the windows of the old loft above the express-office stood out staringly bright; and through their curtainless panes the loungers below could see the forms of those who were even then deciding the fate of Tennessee. And above all this, etched on the dark firmament, rose the Sierra, remote 70 and passionless, crowned with remoter passionless stars.

The trial of Tennessee was conducted as fairly as was consistent with a judge and jury who felt themselves to some extent obliged to justify, in their verdict, the previous irregularities of arrest and indictment. The law of Sandy Bar was implacable, but not vengeful. The excitement and personal feeling of the chase were over; with Tennessee safe in their hands, they were ready to listen patiently to any defense, which they were already satisfied was insufficient. There being no doubt in their 80 own minds, they were willing to give the prisoner the benefit of any that might exist. Secure in the hypothesis that he ought to be hanged on general principles, they indulged him with more latitude of defense than his reckless hardihood seemed to ask. The Judge appeared to be more anxious than the prisoner, who, otherwise unconcerned, evidently took a grim pleasure in the responsibility he had created. "I don't take any hand in this yer game," had been his invariable but good-humored reply to all questions. The Judge—who was also 90 his captor—for a moment vaguely regretted that he had not shot him "on sight" that morning, but presently dismissed this human weakness as unworthy of the judicial mind. Nevertheless, when there was a tap at the door, and it was said that Tennessee's Partner was there on behalf of the prisoner, he was admitted at once without question. Perhaps the younger members of the jury, to whom the proceedings were becoming irksomely thoughtful, hailed him as a relief.

For he was not, certainly, an imposing figure. Short and stout, with a square face, sunburned into a preternatural redness, clad in a loose duck "jumper" and trousers streaked and splashed with red soil, his aspect under any circumstances would have been quaint, and was now even ridiculous. As he stooped to deposit at his feet a heavy carpetbag he was carrying, it became obvious, from partially developed legends and inscriptions, that the material with which his trousers had been patched had been originally intended for a less ambitious covering. Yet he advanced with great gravity, and after shaking the hand of each person in the room with labored cordiality, he wiped his serious perplexed face on a red bandana handkerchief, a shade lighter than his complexion, laid his powerful hand upon the table to steady himself, and thus addressed the Judge:—

"I was passin' by," he began, by way of apology, "and I thought I'd just step in and see how things was gettin' on with Tennessee thar,—my pardner. It's a hot night. I disremember any sich weather before on the Bar." He paused a moment, but nobody volunteering any other meteorological recollection, he again had recourse to his pocket-handkerchief, and for some moments mopped his face diligently.

"Have you anything to say on behalf of the prisoner?" said the Judge finally.

"Thet's it," said Tennessee's Partner, in a tone of relief. "I come yar as Tennessee's pardner,—knowing him nigh on four year, off and on, wet and dry, in luck and out o' luck. His ways ain't aller my ways, but thar ain't any p'ints in that young man, thar ain't any liveliness as he's been up to, as I don't know. And you sez to me, sez you,—confidential-like, and between man and man, —sez you, 'Do you know anything in his behalf?' and I sez to you, sez I,—confidential-like, as between man and man,—'What should a man know of his pardner?'"

"Is this all you have to say?" asked the Judge impatiently, feeling, perhaps, that a dangerous sympathy of humor was beginning to humanize the court.

"Thet's so," continued Tennessee's Partner. "It ain't for me to say anything agin' him. And now, what's the case? Here's Tennessee wants money, wants it bad, and does n't like to ask it of his old pardner. Well, what does Tennessee do? He lays for a stranger, and he fetches that stranger; and you lays for *him,* and you fetches *him;* and the honors is easy. And I put it to you, bein' a fa'r-minded man, and to you, gentlemen all, as fa'r-minded men, ef this is n't so."

"Prisoner," said the Judge, interrupting, "have you any questions to ask this man?"

"No! no!" continued Tennessee's Partner hastily. "I play this yer hand alone. To come down to the bedrock, its just this: Tennessee, thar, has played it pretty rough and expensive-like on a stranger, and on this yer camp. And now, what's the fair thing? Some would say more, some would say less. Here's seventeen hundred dollars in coarse gold and a watch,—it's about all my pile,—and call it square!" And before a hand could be raised to prevent him he had emptied the contents of the carpetbag upon the table.

For a moment his life was in jeopardy. One or two men sprang to their feet, several hands groped for hidden weapons, and a suggestion to "throw him from the window" was only overridden by a gesture from the Judge. Tennessee laughed. And apparently oblivious of the excitement, Tennessee's Partner improved the opportunity to mop his face again with his handkerchief.

When order was restored, and the man was made to understand, by the use of forcible figures and rhetoric, that Tennessee's offense could not be condoned by money, his face took a more serious and sanguinary hue, and those who were nearest to him noticed that his rough hand trembled slightly on the table. He hesitated a moment as he slowly returned the gold to the carpetbag, as if he had not yet entirely caught the elevated sense of justice which swayed the tribunal, and was perplexed with the belief that he had not offered enough. Then he turned to the Judge, and saying, "This yer is a lone hand, played alone, and without my pardner," he bowed to the jury and was about to withdraw, when the Judge called him back:—

"If you have anything to say to Tennessee, you had better say it now."

For the first time that evening the eyes of the prisoner and his strange advocate met. Tennessee smiled, showed his white teeth, and saying, "Euchred, old man!" held out his hand. Tennessee's Partner took it in his own, and saying, "I just dropped in as I was passin' to see how things was gettin' on," let the hand passively fall, and adding that "it was a warm night," again mopped his face with his handkerchief, and without another word withdrew.

The two men never again met each other alive. For the unparalleled insult of a bribe offered to Judge Lynch —who, whether bigoted, weak, or narrow, was at least incorruptible—firmly fixed in the mind of that mythical personage any wavering determination of Tennessee's fate; and at the break of day he was marched, closely guarded, to meet it at the top of Marley's Hill.

How he met it, how cool he was, how he refused to say anything, how perfect were the arrangements of the committee, were all duly reported, with the addition of a warning moral and example to all future evil-doers, in the "Red Dog Clarion," by its editor, who was present, and to whose vigorous English I cheerfully refer the reader. But the beauty of that midsummer morning, the blessed amity of earth and air and sky, the awakened life of the free woods and hills, the joyous renewal and promise of Nature, and above all, the infinite serenity that thrilled through each, was not reported, as not being a part of the social lesson. And yet, when the weak and foolish deed was done, and a life, with its possibilities and responsibilities, had passed out of the misshapen thing that dangled between earth and sky, the birds sang, the flowers bloomed, the sun shone, as cheerily as before; and possibly the "Red Dog Clarion" was right.

Tennessee's Partner was not in the group that surrounded the ominous tree. But as they turned to disperse, attention was drawn to the singular appearance of a motionless donkey-cart halted at the side of the road. As they approached, they at once recognized the venerable "Jenny" and the two-wheeled cart as the property of Tennessee's Partner, used by him in carrying dirt from his claim; and a few paces distant the owner of the equipage himself, sitting under the buckeye-tree, wiping the perspiration from his glowing face. In answer to an inquiry, he said he had come for the body of the "diseased," "if it was all the same to the committee." He did n't wish to "hurry anything"; he could "wait." He was not working that day; and when the gentlemen were done with the "diseased," he would take him. "Ef thar is any present," he added, in his simple, serious way, "as would care to jine in the fun'l, they kin come." Per-

haps it was from a sense of humor, which I have already intimated was a feature of Sandy Bar,—perhaps it was from something even better than that, but two thirds of the loungers accepted the invitation at once.

It was noon when the body of Tennessee was delivered into the hands of his partner. As the cart drew up to the fatal tree, we noticed that it contained a rough oblong box,—apparently made from a section of sluicing,—and half filled with bark and the tassels of pine. The cart was further decorated with slips of willow and made fragrant with buckeye-blossoms. When the body was deposited in the box, Tennessee's Partner drew over it a piece of tarred canvas, and gravely mounting the narrow seat in front, with his feet upon the shafts, urged the little donkey forward. The equipage moved slowly on, at that decorous pace which was habitual with Jenny even under less solemn circumstances. The men—half curiously, half jestingly, but all good-humoredly—strolled along beside the cart, some in advance, some a little in the rear of the homely catafalque. But whether from the narrowing of the road or some present sense of decorum, as the cart passed on, the company fell to the rear in couples, keeping step, and otherwise assuming the external show of a formal procession. Jack Folinsbee, who had at the outset played a funeral march in dumb show upon an imaginary trombone, desisted from a lack of sympathy and appreciation,—not having, perhaps, your true humorist's capacity to be content with the enjoyment of his own fun.

The way led through Grizzly Canon, by this time clothed in funereal drapery and shadows. The red-woods, burying their moccasined feet in the red soil, stood in Indian file along the track, trailing an uncouth benediction from their bending boughs upon the passing bier. A hare, surprised into helpless inactivity, sat upright and pulsating in the ferns by the roadside as the cortege went by. Squirrels hastened to gain a secure outlook from higher boughs; and the blue-jays, spreading their wings, fluttered before them like outriders, until the outskirts of Sandy Bar were reached, and the solitary cabin of Tennessee's Partner.

Viewed under more favorable circumstances, it would not have been a cheerful place. The unpicturesque site, the rude and unlovely outlines, the unsavory details, which distinguish the nest-building of the California miner were all here with the dreariness of decay superadded. A few paces from the cabin there was a rough inclosure, which, in the brief days of Tennessee's Partner's matrimonial felicity, had been used as a garden, but was now overgrown with fern. As we approached it, we were surprised to find that what we had taken for a recent attempt at cultivation was the broken soil about an open grave.

The cart was halted before the inclosure, and rejecting the offers of assistance with the same air of simple self-reliance he had displayed throughout, Tennessee's Partner lifted the rough coffin on his back, and deposited it unaided within the shallow grave. He then nailed down the board which served as a lid, and mounting the little mound of earth beside it, took off his hat and slowly mopped his face with his handkerchief. This the crowd felt was a preliminary to speech, and they disposed themselves variously on stumps and boulders, and sat expectant.

"When a man," began Tennessee's Partner slowly, "has been running free all day, what's the natural thing for him to do? Why, to come home. And if he ain't in a condition to go home, what can his best friend do? Why, bring him home. And here's Tennessee has been running free, and we brings him home from his wandering." He paused and picked up a fragment of quartz, rubbed it thoughtfully on his sleeve, and went on: "It ain't the first time that I've packed him on my back, as you see'd me now. It ain't the first time that I brought him to this yer cabin when he could n't help himself; it ain't the first time that I and Jinny have waited for him on yon hill, and picked him up and so fetched him home, when he could n't speak and did n't know me. And now that it's the last time, why"—he paused and rubbed the quartz gently on his sleeve—"you see it's sort of rough on his pardner. And now, gentlemen," he added abruptly, picking up his long-handled shovel, "the fun's over; and my thanks, and Tennessee's thanks, to you for your trouble."

Resisting any proffers of assistance, he began to fill

in the grave, turning his back upon the crowd, that after a few moments' hesitation gradually withdrew. As they crossed the little ridge that hid Sandy Bar from view, some, looking back, thought they could see Tennessee's Partner, his work done, sitting upon the grave, his shovel between his knees, and his face buried in his red bandana handkerchief. But it was argued by others that you could n't tell his face from his handkerchief at that distance, and this point remained undecided.

In the reaction that followed the feverish excitement of that day, Tennessee's Partner was not forgotten. A secret investigation had cleared him of any complicity in Tennessee's guilt, and left only a suspicion of his general sanity. Sandy Bar made a point of calling on him, and proffering various uncouth but well-meant kindnesses. But from that day his rude health and great strength seemed visibly to decline; and when the rainy season fairly set in, and the tiny grass-blades were beginning to peep from the rocky mound above Tennessee's grave, he took to his bed.

One night, when the pines beside the cabin were swaying in the storm and trailing their slender fingers over the roof, and the roar and rush of the swollen river were heard below, Tennessee's Partner lifted his head from the pillow, saying, "It is time to go for Tennessee; I must put Jinny in the cart;" and would have risen from his bed but for the restraint of his attendant. Struggling, he still pursued his singular fancy: "There, now, steady, Jinny,—steady, old girl. How dark it is! Look out for the ruts,—and look out for him, too, old gal. Sometimes, you know, when he's blind drunk, he drops down right in the trail. Keep on straight up to the pine on the top of the hill. Thar! I told you so!—thar he is,—coming this way, too,—all by himself, sober, and his face a-shining. Tennessee! Pardner!"

And so they met.

1869

Plain Language from Truthful James

Written in 1870 and published in September of the same year, this poem, known to many as "The Heathen Chinee," had a success comparable with that of "The Luck." News-

papers in every part of the country printed it; it was issued as a broadside; song versions were published; and several lithograph illustrations found ready buyers. According to George R. Stewart, "It was said that President Grant had intended to take up the Chinese problem in his message to Congress, but refrained after the poem had made the whole matter the occasion of hilarity."

Harte was rather distressed by the fame of the poem, partly because he felt that some people, failing to perceive its irony, used it to justify a prejudice against the Chinese; partly because he thought it was a bad poem. Today it seems a rather pleasant bit of nonsense, amusing because of the story it tells and because of the galloping meter. The metrics, Harte said, were influenced by Swinburne's **Atalanta in Calydon.**

Which I wish to remark,
　And my language is plain,
That for ways that are dark
　And for tricks that are vain,
The heathen Chinee is peculiar,
　Which the same I would rise to explain.

Ah Sin was his name;
　And I shall not deny,
In regard to the same,
　What the name might imply;　　　　10
But his smile it was pensive and childlike,
　As I frequent remarked to Bill Nye.

It was August the third,
　And quite soft was the skies;
Which it might be inferred
　That Ah Sin was likewise;
Yet he played it that day upon William
　And me in a way I despise.

Which we had a small game,
　And Ah Sin took a hand;　　　　20
It was Euchre. The same
　He did not understand;
But he smiled as he sat by the table,
　With the smile that was childlike and bland.

Yet the cards they were stocked
　In a way that I grieve,
And my feelings were shocked
　At the state of Nye's sleeve,
Which was stuffed full of aces and bowers,
　And the same with intent to deceive.　　30

But the hands that were played
　By that heathen Chinee,
And the points that he made,

Were quite frightful to see,—
Till at last he put down a right bower,
　Which the same Nye had dealt unto me.

Then I looked up at Nye,
　And he gazed upon me;
And he rose with a sigh,
　And said, "Can this be?　　　　40
We are ruined by Chinese cheap labor,"—
　And he went for that heathen Chinee.

In the scene that ensued
　I did not take a hand,
But the floor it was strewed
　Like the leaves on the strand
With the cards that Ah Sin had been hiding,
　In the game "he did not understand."

In his sleeves which were long,
　He had twenty-four jacks,—　　　50
Which was coming it strong,
　Yet I state but the facts;

"... his smile it was pensive and childlike ..."—illustration by Sol Eytinge, Jr. in Every Saturday, April 1871

Plain Talk from Truthful James　349

And we found on his nails, which were taper,
   What is frequent in tapers,—that's wax.

Which is why I remark,
   And my language is plain,

That for ways that are dark
   And for tricks that are vain,
The heathen Chinee is peculiar,—
   Which the same I am free to maintain.

Edward Eggleston
1837 · 1902

Edward Eggleston, "the first of the Hoosiers" in literature, wrote novels which greatly increased the number of novel-readers in America and which had an important influence in turning the American novel toward realism.

Eggleston was born in Vevay, Indiana, in 1837. He attended the public schools there but was prevented by ill health from going to college. Brought up a devout Methodist, he soon became a "circuit rider," preaching at ten widely separated stations on a four weeks' circuit in southern Indiana. His health broke under the strain of such strenuous employment, and he spent some nine years in Minnesota as Bible agent and pastor of small churches. He gave up the ministry in 1866 and turned to writing for religious papers; some of his most famous stories first appeared in such papers, and his writing always retained some of the marks of the Sunday School juvenile. He made a reputation with *The Hoosier Schoolmaster* (1871), and added to that reputation with *The Circuit Rider* (1874), *Roxy* (1878), a story of married life in Indiana, and *The Graysons* (1888), in which young Lincoln appears briefly.

After 1870 Eggleston lived in the East, in Brooklyn and New York, and at Joshua's Rock on Lake George. About 1890, or earlier, his interest shifted from fiction to history (the change was not radical, for he had always thought of his fiction as a kind of history), and he

projected too ambitiously a comprehensive account of the growth of American civilization, two volumes of which he completed. As president of the American Historical Association in 1900, he expressed the view (less generally recognized then than now) that the best history is a record, not of a people's politics and wars, but of its culture. In a very real sense, his novels were such a history of the Indiana country in the early days.

His most authentic and valuable social record is probably found in *The Circuit Rider*. He knew the subject from his own experience. There are crudities of style, but perhaps such a narrative would not greatly profit by the finished treatment of a sophisticated artist. Eggleston saw the Middlewestern frontier of the early nineteenth century as a chaos of contrasts: of corn-shuckings and camp meetings, of wild revels and wilder revivals, of highwaymen and preachers, of abandoned wickedness and austere piety. The dominating figure in this primitive society, he thought, was the Methodist circuit rider. "More than anyone else," he said, "the early circuit preachers brought order out of this chaos. In no other class was the real heroic element so finely displayed."

G. C. Eggleston, **The First of the Hoosiers**, Philadelphia, 1903 • W. P. Randel, **Edward Eggleston**, New York, 1946 • F. L. Pattee, "The Discovery of Pike County," **A History of American Literature Since 1870**, New York, 1915

From

The Circuit Rider

Spread of Metho. in South. Ohio

CHAPTER XX

The Circuit Rider tells the story of the spread of Methodism in southern Ohio in the early nineteenth century (the events of the book occur in the years from 1809 to 1812). The Methodists were opposed by the more conservative sects, particularly by the Presbyterians, who objected to the hysteria of camp meetings. They were opposed also by the lawless element in the outlying districts—the Methodist circuit rider had to fight as well as preach.

Morton Goodwin, the hero of Eggleston's story, so completely loses social caste by being converted to Methodism and becoming a circuit rider that Patty Lumsden, of a proud Virginia family (her mother, before migrating from Virginia to Ohio, had belonged to the Episcopal Church), breaks off their engagement. Toward the end of the book, Patty herself becomes a Methodist and the lovers, of course, are happily married.

Eggleston is at his best in his description of the Methodist meetings. One kind of meeting was the annual conference, where ministers assembled from all over the district and, after a season of religious devotion, received their appointments for the following year from the presiding bishop. The selection given here describes such a meeting; among those attending are Morton Goodwin, the fighting parson, and young Kike, his sick, pietistic friend. The author shows a warm admiration for these religious pioneers. Writing in 1878—to him a time of irreligion and sophistication—he speaks up for the simple virtues of the Western pioneer folk and for the religion of the early Methodists. Whatever its limitations as a novel, **The Circuit Rider** is an invaluable contribution to our religious and social history.

More than two years have passed since Morton made his great sacrifice. You may see him now riding up to the Hickory Ridge Church—a "hewed-log" country meeting-house. He is dressed in homespun clothes. At the risk of compromising him forever, I must confess that his coat is straight-breasted—shad-bellied as the profane call it—and his best hat a white one with a broad brim. The face is still fresh, despite the conflicts and hardships of one year's travel in the mountains of Eastern Kentucky, and the sickness and exposure of another year in the malarious cane-brakes of Western Tennessee. Perils of Indians, perils of floods, perils of alligators, perils of bad foods, perils of cold beds, perils of robbers, perils of rowdies, perils of fevers, and the weariness of five thousand miles of horseback riding in a year, with five or six hundred preachings in the same time, and the care of numberless scattered churches in the wilderness have conspired to give sedateness to his countenance. And yet there is a youthfulness about the sun-browned cheeks, and a lingering expression of that sort of humor which Western people call "mischief" about the eyes, that match but grotesquely with white hat and shad-bellied coat.

He has been a preacher almost ever since he became a Methodist. How did he get his theological education? It used to be said that Methodist preachers were educated by the old ones telling the young ones all they knew; but besides this oral instruction Morton carried in his saddle-bags John Wesley's simple, solid sermons, Charles Wesley's hymns, and a Bible. Having little of the theory and system of theology, he was free to take lessons in the larger school of life and practical observation. For the rest, the free criticism to which he was subject from other preachers, and the contact with a few families of refinement, had obliterated his dialect. Naturally a gentleman at heart, he had, from the few stately gentlemen that he met, quickly learned to be a gentleman in manners. He is regarded as a young man of great promise by the older brethren; his clear voice is very charming, his strong and manly speech and his tender feeling are very inspiring, and on his two circuits he has reported extraordinary revivals. Some of the old men sagely predict that "he's got bishop-timber in him," but no such ambitious dreams disturb his sleep. He has not "gone into a

---

2 great sacrifice. The reference is to Morton's conversion to Methodism and the consequent loss of Patty (see headnote) • **6 shad-bellied,** slender and sloping away in the abdomen • **28 John Wesley** (1703-1791), was the founder of Methodism in England (1738) • **28 Charles Wesley** (1707-1788), English Methodist preacher and hymn writer, was one of John Wesley's brothers

decline" on account of Patty. A healthy nature will bear heavy blows. But there is a pain, somewhere—everywhere—in his being, when he thinks of the girl who stood just above him in the spelling-class, and who looked so divine when she was spinning her two dozen cuts a day. He does not like this regretful feeling. He prays to be forgiven for it. He acknowledges in class-meeting and in love-feast that he is too much like Lot's wife—he finds his heart prone to look back toward the objects he once loved. Often in riding through the stillness of a deep forest—and the primeval forest is to him the peculiar abode of the Almighty—his noble voice rings out fervently and even pathetically with that stanza:

> "The dearest idol I have known,
> Whate'er that idol be,
> Help me to tear it from thy throne
> And worship only Thee!"

No man can enjoy a joke with more zest than he, and none can tell a story more effectively in a generation of preachers who are all good story-tellers. He loves his work; its dangers and difficulties satisfy the ambition of his boyhood; and he has had no misgivings, except when once or twice he has revisited his parents in the Hissawachee Bottom. Then the longing to see Patty has seized him and he has been fain to hurry away, praying to be delivered from every snare of the enemy.

He is not the only man in a straight-breasted coat who is approaching the country meeting-house. It is conference-time, and the greetings are hearty and familiar. Everybody is glad to see everybody, and, after a year of separation, nobody can afford to stand on ceremony with anybody else. Morton has hardly alighted before half a dozen preachers have rushed up to him and taken him by the hand. A tall brother, with a grotesque twitch in his face, cries out:

"How do you do, Brother Goodwin? Glad to see the alligators haven't finished you!"

To which Morton returns a laughing reply; but suddenly he sees, standing back of the rest and waiting his turn, a young man with a solemn, sallow face, pinched by sickness and exposure, and bordered by the straight black hair that falls on each side of it. He wears over his clothes a blanket with arm-holes cut through, and seems to be perpetually awaiting an ague-chill. Seeing him, Morton pushes the rest aside, and catches the wan hand

in both of his own with a cry: "Kike, God bless you! How are you, dear old fellow? You look sick."

Kike smiled faintly, and Morton threw his arm over his shoulder and looked in his face. "I am sick, Mort. Cast down, but not destroyed, you know. I hope I am ready to be offered up."

"Not a bit of it. You've got to get better. Offered up? Why, you aren't fit to offer to an alligator. Where are you staying?"

"Out there." Kike pointed to the tents of a camp-meeting barely visible through the trees. The people in the neighborhood of the Hickory Ridge Church, being unable to entertain the Conference in their homes, had resorted to the device of getting up a camp-meeting. It was easier to take care of the preachers out of doors than in. Morton shook his head as he walked with Kike to the thin canvas tent under which he had been assigned to sleep. The white spot on the end of Kike's nose and the blue lines under his finger-nails told plainly of the on-coming chill, and Morton hurried away to find some better shelter for him than under this thin sheet. But this was hard to do. The few brethren in the neighborhood had already filled their cabins full of guests, mostly in infirm health, and Kike, being one of the younger men, renowned only for his piety and his revivals, had not been thought of for a place elsewhere than on the camp-ground. Finding it impossible to get a more comfortable resting place for his friend, Morton turned to seek for a physician. The only doctor in the neighborhood was a Presbyterian minister, retired from the ministry on account of his impaired health. To him Morton went to ask for medicine for Kike.

"Dr. Morgan, there is a preacher sick down at the camp-ground," said Morton, "and—"

"And you want me to see him," said the doctor in an alert, anticipative fashion, seizing his "pill-bags" and donning his hat.

When the two rode up to the tent in which Kike was lodged they found a prayer-meeting of a very exciting kind going on in the tent adjoining. There were cries and groans and amens and hallelujahs commingled in a way

---

6 cuts, lengths of yarn • 7 class-meeting . . . love-feast, meetings in which the Methodists told their "experiences" • 8 Lot's wife looked back upon Sodom and Gomorrah and became a pillar of salt. See Genesis 19:26 • 50 Cast . . . destroyed, verbatim from II Corinthians 4:9

quite intelligible to the experienced ear of Morton, but quite unendurable to the orderly doctor.

"A bad place for a sick man, sir," he said to Morton, with great positiveness.

"I know it is, doctor," said Morton; "and I've done my best to get him out of it, but I cannot. See how thin this tent-cover is."

"And the malaria of these woods is awful. Camp meetings, sir, are always bad. And this *fuss* is enough to
10 drive a patient crazy."

Morton thought the doctor prejudiced, but he said nothing. They had now reached the corner of the tent where Kike lay on a straw pallet, holding his hands to his head. The noise from the prayer-meeting was more than his weary brain would bear.

"Can you sit on my horse?" said the doctor, promptly proceeding to lift Kike without even explaining to him who he was, or where he proposed to take him.

Morton helped to place Kike in the saddle, but the
20 poor fellow was shaking so that he could not sit there. Morton then brought out Dolly—she was all his own now—and took the slight form of Kike in his arms, he riding on the croup, and the sick man in the saddle.

"Where shall I ride to, doctor?"

"To my house," said the doctor, mounting his own horse and spurring off to have a bed made ready for Kike.

As Morton rode up to the doctor's gate, the shaking Kike roused a little and said, "She's the same fine old Dolly, Mort."
30 "A little more sober. The long rides in the cane-brakes, and the responsibility of the Methodist itinerancy, have given her the gravity that belongs to the ministry."

Such a bed as Kike found in Dr. Morgan's house! After the rude bear-skins upon which he had languished in the backwoods cabins, after the musty feather-beds in freezing lofts, and the pallets of leaves upon which he had shivered and scorched and fought fleas and mosquitoes, this clean white bed was like a foretaste of heaven. But Kike was almost too sick to be grateful.
40 The poor frame had been kept up by will so long, that now that he was in a good bed and had Morton he felt that he could afford to be sick. What had been ague settled into that wearisome disease called bilious fever. Morton staid by him nearly all of the time, looking into the conference now and then to see the venerable Asbury in the chair, listening to a grand speech from Mc-

Kendree, attending on the third day of the session, when, with the others who had been preaching two years on probation, he was called forward to answer the "ques-
50 tions" always propounded to "Candidates for admission to the conference." Kike only was missing from the list of those who were to have heard the bishop's exhortations, full of martial fire, and to have answered his questions in regard to their spiritual state. For above all gifts of speech or depths of learning, or acuteness of reasoning, the early Methodists esteemed devout affections; and no man was of account for the ministry who was not "groaning to be made perfect in this life." The question stands in the discipline yet, but very many young men who assent to it groan after nothing so much as a city
60 church with full galleries.

Morton Goodwin—engraving by J. Karst for the 1878 edition

The strange mystery in which appointments were involved could not but pique curiosity. Morton having had one year of mountains, and one year of cane-brakes, had come to wish for one year of a little more comfort, and a little better support. There is a romance about

45 Asbury. Born in England, Francis Asbury (1745-1816) became the first Methodist bishop in America ° 46 McKendree, William McKendree (1757-1835), first American-born bishop of the Methodist Church

The Circuit Rider 353

going threadbare and tattered in a good cause, but even the romance gets threadbare and tattered if it last too long, and one wishes for a little sober reality of warm clothes to relieve a romance, charming enough in itself, but dull when it grows monotonous.

The awful hour of appointments came on at last. The brave-hearted men sat down before the bishop, and before God, not knowing what was to be their fate. Morton could not guess where he was going. A miasmatic cane-
10 brake, or a deadly cypress swamp, might be his doom, or he might—but no, he would not hope that his lot might fall in Ohio. He was a young man, and a young man must take his chances. Morton found himself more anxious about Kike than about himself. Where would the bishop send the invalid? With Kike it might be a matter of life and death, and Kike would not hear to being left without work. He meant, he said, to cease at once to work and live.

The brethren, still in sublime ignorance of their des-
20 tiny, sang fervently that fiery hymn of Charles Wesley's:

> "Jesus, the name high over all,
>   In hell or earth or sky.
> Angels and men before him fall,
>   And devils fear and fly.

> "O that the world might taste and see,
>   The riches of his grace,
> The arms of love that compass me
>   Would all mankind embrace."

And when they reached the last stanzas there was the
30 ring of soldiers ready for battle in their martial voices. That some of them would die from exposure, malaria, or accident during the next year was probable. Tears came to their eyes, and they involuntarily began to grasp the hands of those who stood next them as they approached the climax of the hymn, which the bishop read impressively, two lines at a time, for them to sing:

> "His only righteousness I show,
>   His saving truth proclaim,
> 'Tis all my business here below
40 >   To cry, 'Behold the Lamb.'

> "Happy if with my latest breath
>   I may but gasp his name,

Preach him to all and cry in death,
  'Behold, behold the Lamb!' "

Then, with suffused eyes, they resumed their seats, and the venerable Asbury, with calmness and with a voice faltering with age, made them a brief address; tender and sympathetic at first, earnest as he proceeded, and full of ardor and courage at the close.

"When the British Admiralty," he said, "wanted some 50 man to take Quebec, they began with the oldest General first, asking him: 'General, will you go and take Quebec?' To which he made reply, 'It is a very difficult enterprise.' 'You may stand aside,' they said. One after another the Generals answered that they would, in some more or less indefinite manner, until the youngest man on the list was reached. 'General Wolfe,' they said, 'will you go and take Quebec?' 'I'll do it or die,' he replied." Here the bishop paused, looked round about upon them, and added, with a voice full of emotion, "He went, and did both. We 60 send you first to take the country allotted to you. We want only men who are determined to do it or die! Some of you, dear brethren, will do both. If you fall, let us hear that you fell like Methodist preachers at your post, face to the foe, and the shout of victory on your lips."

The effect of this speech was beyond description. There were sobs, and cries of "Amen," "God grant it," "Halleluiah!" from every part of the old log church. Every man was ready for the hardest place, if he must. Gravely, as one who trembles at his responsibility, the 70 bishop brought out his list. No man looked any more upon his fellow. Every one kept his eyes fixed upon the paper from which the bishop read the appointments, until his own name was reached. Some showed pleasure when their names were called, some could not conceal a look of pain. When the reading had proceeded half way down the list, Morton heard, with a little start, the words slowly enounced as the bishop's eyes fell on him: "Jenkinsville Circuit—Morton Goodwin."

Well, at least Jenkinsville was in Ohio. But it was in 80 the wickedest part of Ohio. Morton half suspected that he was indebted to his muscle, his courage, and his quick wit for the appointment. The rowdies of Jenkinsville

57 Wolfe . . . Quebec. The English, led by General James Wolfe (1727-1759), captured Quebec from the French in 1759. Wolfe was killed in the battle

Circuit were worse than the alligators of Mississippi. But he was young, hopeful and brave, and rather relished a difficult field than otherwise. He listened now for Kike's name. It came at the bottom of the list:

"Pottawottomie Creek—W. T. Smith, Hezekiah Lumsden."

The bishop had not dared to entrust a circuit to a man so sick as Kike was. He had, therefore, sent him as a "second man" or "junior preacher" on a circuit in the wilderness of Michigan.

The last appointment having been announced, a simple benediction closed the services, and the brethren who had foregone houses and homes and fathers and mothers and wives and children for the kingdom of heaven's sake saddled their horses, called, one by one, at Dr. Morgan's to say a brotherly "God bless you!" to the sick Kike, and rode away, each in his own direction, and all with a self-immolation to the cause rarely seen since the Middle-Age.

They rode away, all but Kike, languishing yet with fever, and Morton watching by his side.

1874

George Washington Cable

1844 · 1925

George Washington Cable's father came from an old slaveholding family in Virginia; his mother was a native of New England and a strict Puritan. There were thus conflicting strains in his inheritance, the influences of which can be traced in his life and writings.

Cable was born in New Orleans, where his father was a not too successful merchant. From the age of fourteen George helped, by miscellaneous jobs, to support the family left destitute by the death of his father. During the Civil War he served with a troop of Mississippi cavalry and was severely wounded. For more than ten years after the war, he was clerk and bookkeeper for a cotton firm in New Orleans. During the clerking and bookkeeping years, however, he read much, delved into the old French and Spanish records of New Orleans, and (because, as he said, it seemed a pity that such rich materials should go to waste) began to write. His first story, "'Sieur George," appeared in Scribner's Monthly in 1873. Other stories of romantic New Orleans followed

and were collected in Old Creole Days (1879). He worked the Creole vein further in The Grandissimes (1880) and in Madame Delphine (1881). Despite the success of these and other similar books, Cable—his Puritan inheritance asserting itself—turned reformer, and in The Silent South (1885) zealously advocated reforms in racial relations. The book made him so unpopular in the South that he moved to Northampton, Massachusetts. His later works are of interest chiefly to the social historian.

Cable deserves to be remembered as the literary discoverer of New Orleans and as the facile recorder of his discoveries there. Like many other writers of local color fiction, he was a romantic realist and was inclined to play up picturesqueness and the moral ending: the established standards of the genre seem to have required that a story be at once edifying and exotic. If Cable's edification is sometimes a little forced, his exoticism is at least based on fact. The New Orleans of the early nineteenth century was a colorful *mélange* of races, and therefore of languages and of mores. With a sensitive, skillful talent, Cable caught, and preserved in several of his early pieces, this extraordinary life and color. At his best, he has, as Professor Pattee has said, a "Gallic brilliance" unique in American literature. The question of the complete accuracy of Cable's pictures may well be left to the histor-

ical specialist, for the pictures themselves have a verisimilitude quite sufficient for the purposes of good literature.

Lucy Cable Biklé, George W. Cable, His Life and Letters, New York, 1928 • F. L. Pattee, "The New Romance," A History of American Literature Since 1870, New York, 1915 • E. L. Tinker, "Cable and the Creoles," American Literature, January 1934

"Blood runs thicker than water"

Belles Demoiselles Plantation

like — "Fall of House of Usher"

A Creole is a white person who is descended from the French or Spanish settlers of Louisiana and the Gulf States, and who preserves their characteristic speech and culture. "The title [of Creole]," to quote Cable's own definition, ". . . came early to include any native of French or Spanish descent whose non-alliance with the slave race entitled him to social rank."

"Belles Demoiselles Plantation" is discursive and almost plotless (the dénouement seems reminiscent of "The Fall of the House of Usher") and the conclusion is too sentimental for modern taste. But the story is excellent in its rendering of locale and manners. With many deft touches Cable conveys the hauteur, the grace, the French gaiety of his Creole characters.

First printed in Scribner's Monthly, April 1874, the story was reprinted in Old Creole Days, 1879.

The original grantee was Count——, assume the name to be De Charleu; the old Creoles never forgive a public mention. He was the French king's commissary. One day, called to France to explain the lucky accident of the commissariat having burned down with his account-books inside, he left his wife, a Choctaw Comptesse, behind.

Arrived at court, his excuses were accepted, and that tract granted him where afterwards stood Belles Demoiselles Plantation. A man cannot remember every thing! 10 In a fit of forgetfulness he married a French gentlewoman, rich and beautiful, and 'brought her out.' However, 'All's well that ends well'; a famine had been in the colony, and the Choctaw Comptesse had starved, leaving nought but a half-caste orphan family lurking on the edge of the settlement, bearing our French gentlewoman's own new name, and being mentioned in Monsieur's will.

And the new Comptesse—she tarried but a twelvemonth, left Monsieur a lovely son, and departed, led out 20 of this vain world by the swamp-fever. From this son sprang the proud Creole family of De Charleu. It rose straight up, up, up, generation after generation, tall, branchless, slender, palm-like; and finally, in the time of which I am to tell, flowered with all the rare beauty of a century-plant, in Artemise, Innocente, Felicité, the twins Marie and Martha, Leontine and little Septima; the seven beautiful daughters for whom their home had been fitly named Belles Demoiselles.

The Count's grant had once been a long Pointe, round 30 which the Mississippi used to whirl, and seethe, and foam, that it was horrid to behold. Big whirlpools would open and wheel about in the savage eddies under the low bank, and close up again, and others open, and spin, and disappear. Great circles of muddy surface would boil up from hundreds of feet below, and gloss over, and seem to float away,—sink, come back again under water, and with only a soft hiss surge up again, and again drift off,

---

Belles Demoiselles, beautiful young ladies • 12 brought . . . out, brought her from France to Louisiana • 14 starved, died of starvation (the etymological meaning of the word is "to die")

and vanish. Every few minutes the loamy bank would tip down a great load of earth upon its besieger, and fall back a foot,—sometimes a yard,—and the writhing river would press after, until at last the Pointe was quite swallowed up, and the great river glided by in a majestic curve, and asked no more; the bank stood fast, the 'caving' became a forgotten misfortune, and the diminished grant was a long, sweeping, willowy bend, rustling with miles of sugarcane.

10 Coming up the Mississippi in the sailing craft of those early days, about the time one first could descry the white spires of the old St. Louis Cathedral, you would be pretty sure to spy, just over to your right under the levee, Belles Demoiselles Mansion, with its broad veranda and red painted cypress roof, peering over the embankment, like a bird in the nest, half hid by the avenue of willows which one of the departed De Charleus,—he that married a Marot,—had planted on the levee's crown.

The house stood unusually near the river, facing east-20 ward, and standing foursquare, with an immense veranda about its sides, and a flight of steps in front spreading broadly downward, as we open arms to a child. From the veranda nine miles of river were seen; and in their compass, near at hand, the shady garden full of rare and beautiful flowers; farther away broad fields of cane and rice, and the distant quarters of the slaves, and on the horizon everywhere a dark belt of cypress forest.

The master was old Colonel De Charleu,—Jean Albert Henri Joseph De Charleu-Marot, and 'Colonel' by the 30 grace of the first American governor. Monsieur,—he would not speak to any one who called him 'Colonel,'—was a hoary-headed patriarch. His step was firm, his form erect, his intellect strong and clear, his countenance classic, serene, dignified, commanding, his manners courtly, his voice musical,—fascinating. He had had his vices,—all his life; but had borne them, as his race do, with a serenity of conscience and a cleanness of mouth that left no outward blemish on the surface of the gentleman. He had gambled in Royal Street, drunk hard 40 in Orleans Street, run his adversary through in the duelling-ground at Slaughter-house Point, and danced and quarrelled at the St. Philippe Street Theatre quadroon balls. Even now, with all his courtesy and bounty, and a hospitality which seemed to be entertaining angels, he was bitter-proud and penurious, and deep down in his hard-finished heart loved nothing but himself, his name,

and his motherless children. But these!—their ravishing beauty was all but excuse enough for the unbounded idolatry of their father. Against these seven goddesses he never rebelled. Had they even required him to de- 50 fraud old De Carlos—

I can hardly say.

Old De Carlos was his extremely distant relative on the Choctaw side. With this single exception, the narrow thread-like line of descent from the Indian wife, diminished to a mere strand by injudicious alliances, and deaths in the gutters of old New Orleans, was extinct. The name, by Spanish contact, had become De Carlos; but this one surviving bearer of it was known to all, and known only, as Injin Charlie. 60

One thing I never knew a Creole to do. He will not utterly go back on the ties of blood, no matter what sort of knots those ties may be. For one reason, he is never ashamed of his or his father's sins; and for another,—he will tell you—he is 'all heart!'

So the different heirs of the De Charleu estate had always strictly regarded the rights and interests of the De Carloses, especially their ownership of a block of dilapidated buildings in a part of the city, which had once been very poor property, but was beginning to be valuable. 70 This block had much more than maintained the last De Carlos through a long and lazy lifetime, and, as his household consisted only of himself, and an aged and crippled Negress, the inference was irresistible that he 'had money.' Old Charlie, though by *alias* an 'Injin,' was plainly a dark white man, about as old as Colonel De Charleu, sunk in the bliss of deep ignorance, shrewd, deaf, and, by repute at least, unmerciful.

The Colonel and he always conversed in English. This rare accomplishment, which the former had learned from 80 his Scotch wife,—the latter from up-river traders,—they found an admirable medium of communication, answering, better than French could, a similar purpose to that of the stick which we fasten to the bit of one horse and breast-gear of another, whereby each keeps his distance. Once in a while, too, by way of jest, English found its way among the ladies of Belles Demoiselles, always signifying that their sire was about to have business with old Charlie.

---

12 **St. Louis Cathedral** in New Orleans was completed in 1794 • 30 **first . . . governor.** Louisiana was acquired from France in 1803

Belles Demoiselles Plantation 357

Now a long-standing wish to buy out Charlie troubled the Colonel. He had no desire to oust him unfairly; he was proud of being always fair; yet he did long to engross the whole estate under one title. Out of his luxurious idleness he had conceived this desire, and thought little of so slight an obstacle as being already somewhat in debt to old Charlie for money borrowed, and for which Belles Demoiselles was, of course, good, ten times over. Lots, buildings, rents, all, might as well be his, he thought, to give, keep, or destroy. 'Had he but the old man's heritage. Ah! he might bring that into existence which his *belles demoiselles* had been begging for, "since many years;" a home,—and such a home,—in the gay city. Here he should tear down this row of cottages, and make his garden wall; there that long rope-walk should give place to vine-covered arbors; the bakery yonder should make way for a costly conservatory; that wine warehouse should come down, and the mansion go up. It should be the finest in the state. Men should never pass it, but they should say—"the palace of the De Charleus; a family of grand descent, a people of elegance and bounty, a line as old as France, a fine old man, and seven daughters as beautiful as happy; whoever dare attempt to marry there must leave his own name behind him!"

'The house should be of stones fitly set, brought down in ships from the land of "les Yankees," and it should have an airy belvedere, with a gilded image tip-toeing and shining on its peak, and from it you should see, far across the gleaming folds of the river, the red roof of Belles Demoiselles, the country-seat. At the big stone gate there should be a porter's lodge, and it should be a privilege even to see the ground.'

Truly they were a family fine enough, and fancy-free enough to have fine wishes, yet happy enough where they were, to have had no wish but to live there always.

To those, who, by whatever fortune, wandered into the garden of Belles Demoiselles some summer afternoon as the sky was reddening towards evening, it was lovely to see the family gathered out upon the tile pavement at the foot of the broad front steps, gayly chatting and jesting, with that ripple of laughter that comes so pleasingly from a bevy of girls. The father would be found seated in their midst, the centre of attention and compliment, witness, arbiter, umpire, critic, by his beautiful children's unanimous appointment, but the single vassal, too, of seven absolute sovereigns.

Now they would draw their chairs near together in eager discussion of some new step in the dance, or the adjustment of some rich adornment. Now they would start about him with excited comments to see the eldest fix a bunch of violets in his button-hole. Now the twins would move down a walk after some unusual flower, and be greeted on their return with the high pitched notes of delighted feminine surprise.

As evening came on they would draw more quietly about their paternal centre. Often their chairs were forsaken, and they grouped themselves on the lower steps, one above another, and surrendered themselves to the tender influences of the approaching night. At such an hour the passer on the river, already attracted by the dark figures of the broad-roofed mansion, and its woody garden standing against the glowing sunset, would hear the voices of the hidden group rise from the spot in the soft harmonies of an evening song; swelling clearer and clearer as the thrill of music warmed them into feeling, and presently joined by the deeper tones of the father's voice; then, as the daylight passed quite away, all would be still, and he would know that the beautiful home had gathered its nestlings under its wings.

And yet, for mere vagary, it pleased them not to be pleased.

'Arti!' called one sister to another in the broad hall, one morning,—mock amazement in her distended eyes,—'something is goin' to took place!'

'*Comm-e-n-t?*'—long-drawn perplexity.

'Papa is goin' to town!'

The news passed up stairs.

'Inno!'—one to another meeting in a doorway,—'something is goin' to took place!'

'*Qu'est-ce-que c'est!*'—vain attempt at gruffness.

'Papa is goin' to town!'

The unusual tidings were true. It was afternoon of the same day that the Colonel tossed his horse's bridle to his groom, and stepped up to old Charlie, who was sitting on his bench under a China-tree, his head, as was his fashion, bound in a Madras handkerchief. The 'old man'

---

26 **les Yankees,** the Yankees • 27 **belvedere,** an open, roofed gallery or loggia on the top of a house for the purpose of commanding a view • 33 **fancy-free,** free from the power of love. See A Midsummer-Night's Dream, Act II, sc. i, l. 64 • 75 **Comm-e-n-t?** Indeed? Why do you say that? • 80 **Qu'est-ce-que c'est!** What is it!

was plainly under the effect of spirits, and smiled a deferential salutation without trusting himself to his feet.

'Eh, well Charlie!'—the Colonel raised his voice to suit his kinsman's deafness,—'how is those times with my friend Charlie?'

'Eh?' said Charlie, distractedly.

'Is that goin' well with my friend Charlie?'

'In de house,—call her,'—making a pretence of rising.

'Non, non! I don't want,' the speaker paused to breathe—''ow is collection?'

'Oh!' said Charlie, 'every day he make me more poorer!'

'What do you hask for it?' asked the planter indifferently, designating the house by a wave of his whip.

'Ask for w'at?' said Injin Charlie.

'De house! What you ask for it?'

'I don't believe,' said Charlie.

'What you would take for it!' cried the planter.

'Wait for w'at?'

'What you would take for the whole block?'

'I don't want to sell him!'

'I'll give you ten thousand dollah for it.'

'Ten t'ousand dollah for dis house? Oh, no, dat is no price. He is blame good old house,—dat old house.' (Old Charlie and the Colonel never swore in presence of each other.) 'Forty years dat old house didn't had to be paint! I easy can get fifty t'ousand dollah for dat old house.'

'Fifty thousand picayunes; yes,' said the Colonel.

'She's a good house. Can make plenty money,' pursued the deaf man.

'That's what makes you so rich, eh, Charlie?'

'Non, I don't make nothing. Too blame clever, me, dat's de troub'. She's a good house,—make money fast like a steamboat,—make a barrel full in a week! Me, I lose money all de days. Too blame clever.'

'Charlie!'

'Eh?'

'Tell me what you'll take.'

'Make? I don't make nothing. Too blame clever.'

'What will you take?'

'Oh! I got enough already,—half drunk now.'

'What will you take for the 'ouse?'

'You want to buy her?'

'I don't know,'—(shrug),—'maybe,—if you sell it cheap.'

'She's a bully old house.'

There was a long silence. By and by old Charlie commenced—

'Old Injin Charlie is a low-down dog.'

'C'est vrai, oui!' retorted the Colonel in an undertone.

'He's got Injin blood in him.'

The Colonel nodded assent.

'But he's got some blame good blood, too, ain't it?'

The Colonel nodded impatiently.

'Bien! Old Charlie's Injin blood says, "sell de house, Charlie, you blame old fool!" Mais, old Charlie's good blood says, "Charlie! if you sell dat old house, Charlie, you low-down old dog, Charlie, what de Compte De Charleu make for you grace-granmuzzer, de dev' can eat you, Charlie, I don't care."'

'But you'll sell it anyhow, won't you, old man?'

'No!' And the no rumbled off in muttered oaths like thunder out on the Gulf. The incensed old Colonel wheeled and started off.

'Curl!' (Colonel) said Charlie, standing up unsteadily. The planter turned with an inquiring frown.

'I'll trade with you!' said Charlie.

The Colonel was tempted. ''Ow'l you trade?' he asked.

'My house for yours!'

The old Colonel turned pale with anger. He walked very quickly back, and came close up to his kinsman.

'Charlie!' he said.

'Injin Charlie,'—with a tipsy nod.

But by this time self-control was returning. 'Sell Belles Demoiselles to you?' he said in a high key, and then laughed 'Ho, ho, ho!' and rode away.

A cloud, but not a dark one, overshadowed the spirits of Belles Demoiselles' plantation. The old master, whose beaming presence had always made him a shining Saturn, spinning and sparkling within the bright circle of his daughters, fell into musing fits, started out of frowning reveries, walked often by himself, and heard business from his overseer fretfully.

No wonder. The daughters knew his closeness in trade, and attributed to it his failure to negotiate for

---

29 **picayune**, small coin worth five or six cents • 33 **clever**, good-natured, obliging • 51 **C'est vrai, oui!** That is indeed true! • 56 **Bien!** Well! • 57 **Mais**, but • 60 **you grace-granmuzzer**, your great-grandmother • 60 **dev'**, devil • 80 **Saturn**, a reference to the planet and its encircling rings

the Old Charlie buildings,—so to call them. They began to depreciate Belles Demoiselles. If a north wind blew, it was too cold to ride. If a shower had fallen, it was too muddy to drive. In the morning the garden was wet. In the evening the grasshopper was a burden. *Ennui* was turned into capital; every headache was interpreted a premonition of ague; and when the native exuberance of a flock of ladies without a want or a care burst out in laughter in the father's face, they spread their French eyes, rolled up their little hands, and with rigid wrists and mock vehemence vowed and vowed again that they only laughed at their misery, and should pine to death unless they could move to the sweet city. 'Oh! the theatre! Oh! Orleans Street! Oh! the masquerade! the Place d'Armes! the ball!' and they would call upon Heaven with French irreverence, and fall into each other's arms, and whirl down the hall singing a waltz, end with a grand collision and fall, and, their eyes streaming merriment, lay the blame on the slippery floor, that would some day be the death of the whole seven.

Three times more the fond father, thus goaded, managed, by accident,—business accident,—to see old Charlie and increase his offer; but in vain. He finally went to him formally.

'Eh?' said the deaf and distant relative. 'For what you want him, eh? Why you don't stay where you halways be 'appy? Dis is a blame old rat-hole,—good for old Injin Charlie,—da's all. Why you don't stay where you be halways 'appy? Why you don't buy somewheres else?'

'That's none of your business,' snapped the planter. Truth was, his reasons were unsatisfactory even to himself.

A sullen silence followed. Then Charlie spoke:

'Well, now, look here; I sell you old Charlie's house.'

'*Bien!* and the whole block,' said the Colonel.

'Hold on,' said Charlie. 'I sell you de 'ouse and de block. Den I go and git drunk, and go to sleep; de dev' comes along and says, "Charlie! old Charlie, you blame low-down old dog, wake up! What you doin' here? Where's de 'ouse what Monsieur le Compte give your grace-gran-muzzer? Don't you see dat fine gentyman, De Charleu, done gone and tore him down and make him over new, you blame old fool, Charlie, you low-down old Injin dog!"'

'I'll give you forty thousand dollars,' said the Colonel.

'For de 'ouse?'

'For all.'

The deaf man shook his head.

'Forty-five!' said the Colonel.

'What a lie? For what you tell me "What a lie?" I don't tell you no lie.'

'*Non, non!* I give you *forty-five!*' shouted the Colonel.

Charlie shook his head again.

'Fifty!'

He shook it again.

The figures rose and rose to—

'Seventy-five!'

The answer was an invitation to go away and let the owner alone, as he was, in certain specified respects, the vilest of living creatures, and no company for a fine gentyman.

The 'fine gentyman' longed to blaspheme,—but before old Charlie!—in the name of pride, how could he? He mounted and started away.

'Tell you what I'll make wid you,' said Charlie.

The other, guessing aright, turned back without dismounting, smiling.

'How much Belles Demoiselles hoes me now?' asked the deaf one.

'One hundred and eighty thousand dollars,' said the Colonel, firmly.

'Yass,' said Charlie. 'I don't want Belles Demoiselles.'

The old Colonel's quiet laugh intimated it made no difference either way.

'But me,' continued Charlie, 'me,—I'm got le Compte De Charleu's blood in me, any'ow,—a litt' bit, any'ow, ain't it?'

The Colonel nodded that it was.

'*Bien!* If I go out of dis place and don't go to Belles Demoiselles, de peoples will say,—dey will say, "Old Charlie he been all doze time tell a blame *lie!* He ain't no kin to his old grace-gran-muzzer, not a blame bit! He don't got nary drop of De Charleu blood to save his blame low-down old Injin soul!" No, sare! What I want wid money, den? No, sare! My place for yours!'

He turned to go into the house, just too soon to see the Colonel make an ugly whisk at him with his riding-whip. Then the Colonel, too, moved off.

---

5 **grasshopper . . . burden.** Compare Ecclesiastes 12:5: ". . . and the grasshopper shall be a burden, and desire shall fail"

Two or three times over, as he ambled homeward, laughter broke through his annoyance, as he recalled old Charlie's family pride and the presumption of his offer. Yet each time he could but think better of—not the offer to swap, but the preposterous ancestral loyalty. It was so much better than he could have expected from his 'low-down' relative, and not unlike his own whim withal —the proposition which went with it was forgiven.

This last defeat bore so harshly on the master of Belles Demoiselles, that the daughters, reading chagrin in his face, began to repent. They loved their father as daughters can, and when they saw their pretended dejection harassing him seriously they restrained their complaints, displayed more than ordinary tenderness, and heroically and ostentatiously concluded there was no place like Belles Demoiselles. But the new mood touched him more than the old, and only refined his discontent. Here was a man, rich without the care of riches, free from any real trouble, happiness as native to his house as perfume to his garden, deliberately, as it were with premeditated malice, taking joy by the shoulder and bidding her be gone to town, whither he might easily have followed, only that the very same ancestral nonsense that kept Injin Charlie from selling the old place for twice its value prevented him from choosing any other spot for a city home.

But by and by the charm of nature and the merry hearts around him prevailed; the fit of exalted sulks passed off, and after a while the year flared up at Christmas, flickered, and went out.

New Year came and passed; the beautiful garden of Belles Demoiselles put on its spring attire; the seven fair sisters moved from rose to rose; the cloud of discontent had warmed into invisible vapor in the rich sunlight of family affection, and on the common memory the only scar of last year's wound was old Charlie's sheer impertinence in crossing the caprice of the De Charleus. The cup of gladness seemed to fill with the filling of the river.

How high that river was! Its tremendous current rolled and tumbled and spun along, hustling the long funeral flotillas of drift,—and how near shore it came! Men were out day and night, watching the levee. On windy nights even the old Colonel took part, and grew light-hearted with occupation and excitement, as every minute the river threw a white arm over the levee's top, as though

it would vault over. But all held fast, and, as the summer drifted in, the water sunk down into its banks and looked quite incapable of harm.

On a summer afternoon of uncommon mildness, old Colonel Jean Albert Henri Joseph De Charleu-Marot, being in a mood for revery, slipped the custody of his feminine rulers and sought the crown of the levee, where it was his wont to promenade. Presently he sat upon a stone bench,—a favorite seat. Before him lay his broad-spread fields; near by, his lordly mansion; and being still, —perhaps by female contact,—somewhat sentimental, he fell to musing on his past. It was hardly worthy to be proud of. All its morning was reddened with mad frolic, and far toward the meridian it was marred with elegant rioting. Pride had kept him well-nigh useless, and despised the honors won by valor; gaming had dimmed prosperity; death had taken his heavenly wife; voluptuous ease had mortgaged his lands; and yet his house still stood, his sweet-smelling fields were still fruitful, his name was fame enough; and yonder and yonder, among the trees and flowers, like angels walking in Eden, were the seven goddesses of his only worship.

Just then a slight sound behind him brought him to his feet. He cast his eyes anxiously to the outer edge of the little strip of bank between the levee's base and the river. There was nothing visible. He paused, with his ear toward the water, his face full of frightened expectation. Ha! There came a single plashing sound, like some great beast slipping into the river, and little waves in a wide semi-circle came out from under the bank and spread over the water!

'My God!'

He plunged down the levee and bounded through the low weeds to the edge of the bank. It was sheer, and the water about four feet below. He did not stand quite on the edge, but fell upon his knees a couple of yards away, wringing his hands, moaning and weeping, and staring through his watery eyes at a fine, long crevice just discernible under the matted grass, and curving outward on either hand toward the river.

'My God!' he sobbed aloud; 'my God!' and even while he called, his God answered: the tough Bermuda grass stretched and snapped, the crevice slowly became a gape, and softly, gradually, with no sound but the closing of the water at last, a ton or more of earth settled into the boiling eddy and disappeared.

At the same instant a pulse of the breeze brought from the garden behind, the joyous, thoughtless laughter of the fair mistresses of Belles Demoiselles.

The old Colonel sprang up and clambered over the levee. Then forcing himself to a more composed movement, he hastened into the house and ordered his horse.

'Tell my children to make merry while I am gone,' he left word. 'I shall be back to-night,' and the horse's hoofs clattered down a by-road leading to the city.

'Charlie,' said the planter, riding up to a window, from which the old man's nightcap was thrust out, 'what you say, Charlie,—my house for yours, eh, Charlie—what you say?'

''Ello!' said Charlie; 'from where you come from dis time of to-night?'

'I come from the Exchange in St. Louis Street.' (A small fraction of the truth.)

'What you want?' said matter-of-fact Charlie.

'I come to trade.'

The low-down relative drew the worsted off his ears. 'Oh! yass,' he said with an uncertain air.

'Well, old man Charlie, what you say: my house for yours,—like you said,—eh, Charlie?'

'I dunno,' said Charlie; 'it's nearly mine now. Why you don't stay dare youse'f?'

'*Because I don't want!*' said the Colonel savagely. 'Is dat reason enough for you? You better take me in de notion, old man, I tell you,—yes!'

Charlie never winced; but how his answer delighted the Colonel! Quoth Charlie:

'I don't care—I take him!—*mais*, possession give right off.'

'Not the whole plantation, Charlie; only'—

'I don't care,' said Charlie; 'we easy can fix dat. *Mais*, what for you don't want to keep him? I don't want him. You better keep him.'

'Don't you try to make no fool of me, old man,' cried the planter.

'Oh, no!' said the other. 'Oh, no! but you make a fool of yourself, ain't it?'

The dumbfounded Colonel stared; Charlie went on:

'Yass! Belles Demoiselles is more wort' dan tree block like dis one. I pass by dare since two weeks. Oh, pritty Belles Demoiselles! De cane was wave in de wind, de garden smell like a bouquet, de white-cap was jump up and down on de river; seven *belles demoiselles* was ridin'

362 *Cable*

on horses. "Pritty, pritty, pritty!" says old Charlie. Ah! *Monsieur le père,* 'ow 'appy, 'appy, 'appy!

'Yass!' he continued—the Colonel still staring—'le Compte De Charleu have two familie. One was low-down Choctaw, one was high up *noblesse.* He gave the low-down Choctaw dis old rat-hole; he give Belles Demoiselles to you gran-fozzer; and now you don't be *satisfait.* What I'll do wid Belles Demoiselles? She'll break me in two years, yass. And what you'll do wid old Charlie's house, eh? You'll tear her down and make you'se'f a blame old fool. I rather wouldn't trade!'

The planter caught a big breathful of anger, but Charlie went straight on:

'I rather wouldn't, *mais* I will do it for you;—just the same, like Monsieur le Compte would say, "Charlie, you old fool, I want to shange houses wid you."'

So long as the Colonel suspected irony he was angry, but as Charlie seemed, after all, to be certainly in earnest, he began to feel conscience-stricken. He was by no means a tender man, but his lately-discovered misfortune had unhinged him, and this strange, undeserved, disinterested family fealty on the part of Charlie touched his heart. And should he still try to lead him into the pitfall he had dug? He hesitated;—no, he would show him the place by broad daylight, and if he chose to overlook the 'caving bank,' it would be his own fault;—a trade's a trade.

'Come,' said the planter, 'come at my house to-night; to-morrow we look at the place before breakfast, and finish the trade.'

'For what?' said Charlie.

'Oh, because I got to come in town in the morning.'

'I don't want,' said Charlie. 'How I'm goin' to come dere?'

'I git you a horse at the liberty stable.'

'Well—anyhow—I don't care—I'll go.' And they went.

When they had ridden a long time, and were on the road darkened by hedges of Cherokee rose, the Colonel called behind him to the 'low-down' scion:

'Keep the road, old man.'

'Eh?'

'Keep the road.'

'Oh, yes; all right; I keep my word; we don't goin' to play no tricks, eh?'

---

49 Monsieur le père, the father • 54 satisfait, satisfied • 81 liberty stable, livery stable, where horses and vehicles are kept for hire

But the Colonel seemed not to hear. His ungenerous design was beginning to be hateful to him. Not only old Charlie's unprovoked goodness was prevailing; the eulogy on Belles Demoiselles had stirred the depths of an intense love for his beautiful home. True, if he held to it, the caving of the bank, at its present fearful speed, would let the house into the river within three months; but were it not better to lose it so, than sell his birthright? Again,—coming back to the first thought,—to betray his own blood! It was only Injin Charlie; but had not the De Charleu blood just spoken out in him? Unconsciously he groaned.

After a time they struck a path approaching the plantation in the rear, and a little after, passing from behind a clump of live-oaks, they came in sight of the villa. It looked so like a gem, shining through its dark grove, so like a great glow-worm in the dense foliage, so significant of luxury and gayety, that the poor master, from an over-flowing heart, groaned again.

'What?' asked Charlie.

The Colonel only drew his rein, and, dismounting mechanically, contemplated the sight before him. The high, arched doors and windows were thrown wide to the summer air; from every opening the bright light of numerous candelabra darted out upon the sparkling foliage of magnolia and bay, and here and there in the spacious verandas a colored lantern swayed in the gentle breeze. A sound of revel fell on the ear, the music of harps; and across one window, brighter than the rest, flitted, once or twice, the shadows of dancers. But oh! the shadows flitting across the heart of the fair mansion's master!

'Old Charlie,' said he, gazing fondly at his house, 'You and me is both old, eh?'

'Yaas,' said the stolid Charlie.

'And we has both been bad enough in our time, eh, Charlie?'

Charlie, surprised at the tender tone, repeated 'Yaas.'

'And you and me is mighty close?'

'Blame close, yaas.'

'But you never know me to cheat, old man!'

'No,'—impassively.

'And do you think I would cheat you now?'

'I dunno,' said Charlie. 'I don't believe.'

'Well, old man, old man,'—his voice began to quiver,— 'I sha'n't cheat you now. My God!—old man, I tell you— you better not make the trade!'

'Because for what?' asked Charlie in plain anger; but both looked quickly toward the house! The Colonel tossed his hands wildly in the air, rushed forward a step or two, and giving one fearful scream of agony and fright, fell forward on his face in the path. Old Charlie stood transfixed with horror. Belles Demoiselles, the realm of maiden beauty, the home of merriment, the house of dancing, all in the tremor and glow of pleasure, suddenly sunk, with one short, wild wail of terror—sunk, sunk, down, down, down, into the merciless, unfathomable flood of the Mississippi.

Twelve long months were midnight to the mind of the childless father; when they were only half gone, he took his bed; and every day, and every night, old Charlie, the 'low-down,' the 'fool,' watched him tenderly, tended him lovingly, for the sake of his name, his misfortunes, and his broken heart. No woman's step crossed the floor of the sick-chamber, whose western dormer-windows overpeered the dingy architecture of old Charlie's block; Charlie and a skilled physician, the one all interest, the other all gentleness, hope, and patience—these only entered by the door; but by the window came in a sweet-scented evergreen vine, transplanted from the caving bank of Belles Demoiselles. It caught the rays of sunset in its flowery net and let them softly in upon the sick man's bed; gathered the glancing beams of the moon at midnight, and often wakened the sleeper to look, with his mindless eyes, upon their pretty silver fragments strewn upon the floor.

By and by there seemed—there was—a twinkling dawn of returning reason. Slowly, peacefully, with an increase unseen from day to day, the light of reason came into the eyes, and speech became coherent; but withal there came a failing of the wrecked body, and the doctor said that monsieur was both better and worse.

One evening, as Charlie sat by the vine-clad window with his fireless pipe in his hand, the old Colonel's eyes fell full upon his own, and rested there.

'Charl—,' he said with an effort, and his delighted nurse hastened to the bedside and bowed his best ear. There was an unsuccessful effort or two, and then he whispered, smiling with sweet sadness,—

'We didn't trade.'

The truth, in this case, was a secondary matter to Charlie; the main point was to give a pleasing answer. So he nodded his head decidedly, as who should say— 'Oh yes, we did, it was a bona-fide swap!' but when he saw the smile vanish, he tried the other expedient and shook his head with still more vigor, to signify that they had not so much as approached a bargain; and the smile returned.

Charlie wanted to see the vine recognized. He stepped backward to the window with a broad smile, shook the foliage, nodded and looked smart.

'I know,' said the Colonel, with beaming eyes, '—many weeks.'

The next day—

'Charl—'

The best ear went down.

'Send for a priest.'

The priest came, and was alone with him a whole afternoon. When he left, the patient was very haggard and exhausted, but smiled and would not suffer the crucifix to be removed from his breast.

One more morning came. Just before dawn Charlie, lying on a pallet in the room, thought he was called, and came to the bedside.

'Old man,' whispered the failing invalid, 'is it caving yet?'

Charlie nodded.

'It won't pay you out.'

'Oh, dat makes not'ing,' said Charlie. Two big tears rolled down his brown face. 'Dat makes not'in'.'

The Colonel whispered once more:

'*Mes belles demoiselles!* in paradise;—in the garden— I shall be with them at sunrise;' and so it was.

1874

Mary Noailles Murfree (Charles Egbert Craddock)

1850 · 1922

Mary Noailles Murfree, who wrote under the pseudonym of Charles Egbert Craddock, was one of the most prominent among the many local colorists who flourished during the last three decades of the nineteenth century, and whose work amounted to a literary discovery of America.

She was born in 1850 in middle Tennessee near the fine old town of Murfreesboro (named at the beginning of the century for her great-grandfather, a Revolutionary officer from North Carolina). Her father was a successful lawyer, an owner of plantations in the delta country, and an admirer of Scott and Dickens. Miss Murfree was educated in the traditional Southern manner at young ladies' finishing schools—at the Nashville Female Academy and at Chegary Institute in Philadelphia. The Murfrees spent some fifteen summers at Beersheba Springs, a fashionable resort in the Cumberland Mountains; it was the country around Beersheba which furnished the materials for Miss Murfree's early stories, though she later visited, and utilized in her fiction, the wilder, more primitive Great Smokies, which lie to the east of the Cumberland range. Her first story to attract attention, "Dancin' Party at Harrison's Cove," was published in the *Atlantic Monthly* in 1878; other mountain stories appeared in the same magazine, and the group was collected in 1884 under the title *In the Tennessee*

Mountains. In 1885 appeared *The Prophet of the Great Smoky Mountains,* a novel of considerable power. Miss Murfree's reputation rests chiefly upon these books, although she wrote many volumes of mountain stories and of historical fiction dealing with the colonial Southwest and the Civil War.

Her work, like that of most of the writers of the local color school, seems much less important now than it did at the end of the last century. The modern reader of *In the Tennessee Mountains* is likely to object to the studied search for the quaint and picturesque, the moral emphasis, the purple style of the descriptive passages, and the intrusions of the author, a cultivated lady, among her uncultivated mountain characters. It was an artistic disadvantage, though inevitable, that Miss Murfree should approach her east Tennessee mountain folk as an outsider from the middle Tennessee aristocracy. Certainly, a sharp and instructive contrast could be pointed out between her stories and those of George W. Harris, who, dealing with the life of the same region, was closer to his subjects and less inhibited by genteel tradition in his treatment of them. But despite Miss Murfree's shortcomings in art and in realism, her writings have a charm of their own. The dialect is adequately rendered. Her account of the life of the mountaineer is entirely faithful to her vision, if not entirely so to reality. Her descriptions of mountain scenery, though sometimes a burden upon the story, often have an old-fashioned beauty. Her name is associated enduringly with the Tennessee mountains.

In the Tennessee Mountains, 1884 • The Prophet of the Great Smoky Mountains, 1885 • E. W. Parks, Charles Egbert Craddock, Chapel Hill, 1941

Over on the T'other Mounting

"Over on the T'other Mounting," like most of Miss Murfree's work, contains two different kinds of writing which are somewhat at odds with each other: the passages which render the speech and manners of the mountain folk, and the literary passages in which the author describes her settings and comments upon the action. But despite this lack of integration, Miss Murfree's stories deserve a permanent place in American literature. If the reader is tempted to dismiss many passages as "fine writing," he will be arrested by the accuracy and skill with which the author records the dialect, superstitions, and idiosyncrasies of her mountain characters.

First printed in the **Atlantic Monthly,** June 1881, the story was reprinted in **In the Tennessee Mountains,** 1884.

Stretching out laterally from a long oblique line of the Southern Alleghanies are two parallel ranges, following the same course through several leagues, and separated by a narrow strip of valley hardly half a mile in width. As they fare along arm in arm, so to speak, sundry differences between the close companions are distinctly apparent. One is much the higher, and leads the way; it strikes out all the bold curves and angles of the course, meekly attended by the lesser ridge; its shadowy coves and sharp ravines are repeated in miniature as its comrade falls into the line of march; it seems to have its companion in charge, and to conduct it away from the majestic procession of mountains that traverses the State.

But, despite its more imposing appearance, all the tangible advantages are possessed by its humble neighbor. When Old Rocky-Top, as the lower range is called, is fresh and green with the tender verdure of spring, the snow still lies on the summit of the T'other Mounting, and drifts deep into treacherous rifts and chasms, and muffles the voice of the singing pines; and all the crags are hung with gigantic glittering icicles, and the woods are gloomy and bleak. When the sun shines bright on Old Rocky-Top, clouds often hover about the loftier mountain, and storms brew in that higher atmosphere; the all-pervading winter winds surge wildly among the groaning forests, and wrench the limbs from the trees, and dash huge fragments of cliffs down deep gorges, and spend their fury before they reach the sheltered lower spur. When the kindly shades of evening slip softly down on drowsy Rocky-Top, and the work is laid by in the rough little houses, and the simple homefolks draw around the hearth, day still lingers in a weird, paralytic life among the tree-tops of the T'other Mounting; and the only remnant of the world visible is that stark black line of its summit, stiff and hard against the faint green and saffron tints of the sky. Before the birds are well awake on Old Rocky-Top, and while the shadows are still thick, the T'other Mounting has been called up to a new day. Lonely dawns these: the pale gleam strikes along the October woods, bringing first into uncertain twilight the dead yellow and red of the foliage, presently heightened into royal gold and crimson by the first ray of sunshine; it rouses the timid wild-fowl; it drives home the plundering fox; it meets, perhaps, some lumbering bear or skulking mountain wolf; it flecks with light and shade the deer, all gray and antlered; it falls upon no human habitation, for the few settlers of the region have a persistent predilection for Old Rocky-Top. Somehow, the T'other Mounting is vaguely in ill repute among its neighbors,—it has a bad name.

"It 's the onluckiest place ennywhar nigh about," said Nathan White, as he sat one afternoon upon the porch of his log-cabin, on the summit of Old Rocky-Top, and gazed up at the heights of the T'other Mounting across the narrow valley. "I hev hearn tell all my days ez how, ef ye go up thar on the T'other Mounting, suthin' will happen ter ye afore ye kin git away. An' I knows myself ez how—'t war ten year ago an' better—I went up thar, one Jan'ry day, a-lookin' fur my cow, ez hed strayed off through not hevin' enny calf ter our house; an' I fund the cow, but jes' tuk an' slipped on a icy rock, an' bruk my ankle-bone. 'T war sech a job a-gittin' off 'n that thar T'other Mounting an' back over hyar, it hev l'arned me ter stay away from thar."

"Thar war a man," piped out a shrill quavering voice from within the door,—the voice of Nathan White's father, the oldest inhabitant of Rocky-Top,—"thar war a man hyar, nigh on ter fifty year ago,—he war mightily gin ter thievin' horses; an' one time, while he war a-runnin' away with Pete Dilks's dapple-gray mare,—they called her Luce, five year old she war,—Pete, he war a-ridin' a-hint him on his old sorrel mare,—her name 't war Jane, an'—the Jeemes boys, they war a-ridin' arter the horse-thief too. Thar, now! I clar forgits what horses them Jeemes boys war a-ridin' of." He paused for an instant in anxious reflection. "Waal, sir! it do beat all that I can't remember them Jeemes boys' horses! Anyways, they got ter that thar tricky ford through Wild-Duck River, thar on the side o' the T'other Mounting, an' the horse-thief war ahead, an' he hed ter take it fust. An' that thar river,—it rises yander in them pines, nigh about," pointing with a shaking fore-finger, —"an' that thar river jes' spun him out'n the saddle like a top, an' he war n't seen no more till he hed floated nigh ter Colbury, ez dead ez a door-nail, nor Pete's dapple-gray mare nuther; she bruk her knees agin them high stone banks. But he war a good swimmer, an' he war drowned. He war witched with the place, ez sure ez ye air born."

A long silence ensued. Then Nathan White raised his pondering eyes with a look of slow curiosity. "What did Tony Britt say he war a-doin' of, when ye kem on him suddint in the woods on the T'other Mounting?" he asked, addressing his son, a stalwart youth, who was sitting upon the step, his hat on the back of his head, and his hands in the pockets of his jeans trousers.

"He said he war a-huntin', but he hed n't hed no sort 'n luck. It 'pears ter me ez all the game thar is witched somehow, an' ye can't get no good shot at nuthin'. Tony tole me to-day that he got up three deer, an' hed toler'ble aim; an' he missed two, an' the t'other jes' trotted off with a rifle-ball in his flank, ez onconsarned ez ef he hed hit him with an acorn."

"I hev always hearn ez everything that belongs on that thar T'other Mounting air witched, an' ef ye brings away so much ez a leaf, or a stone, or a stick, ye fotches a curse with it," chimed in the old man, "'kase thar hev been sech a many folks killed on the T'other Mounting."

"I tole Tony Britt that thar word," said the young fellow, "an' 'lowed ter him ez how he hed tuk a mighty bad spot ter go a-huntin'."

"What did he say?" demanded Nathan White.

"He say he never knowed ez thar war murders com-

---

64 witched, bewitched • 82 fotches, fetch, bring

T'other mountain bad folks hide they you can't catch animals there when hunting "its witched"!

mit on T'other Mounting, an' ef thar war he 'spects 't war nuthin' but Injuns, long time ago. But he 'lowed the place war powerful onlucky, an' he believed the mounting war witched."

"Ef Tony Britt's arter enny harm," said the octogenarian, "he 'll never come off 'n that thar T'other Mounting. It 's a mighty place fur bad folks ter make thar eend. Thar 's that thar horse thief I war a-tellin' 'bout, an' that dapple-gray mare,—her name 't war Luce. An' folks ez is a-runnin' from the sheriff jes' takes ter the T'other Mounting ez nateral ez ef it war home; an' ef they don't git cotched, they is never hearn on no more." He paused impressively. "The rocks falls on 'em, an' kills 'em; an' I'll tell ye jes' how I knows," he resumed, oracularly. "'T war sixty year ago, nigh about, an' me an' them Jeemes boys war a-burnin' of lime tergether over on the T'other Mounting. We hed a lime-kiln over thar, jes' under Piney Notch, an' never hed no luck, but jes' stuck ter it like fools, till Hiram Jeemes got one of his eyes put out. So we quit burnin' of lime on the T'other Mounting, 'count of the place bein' witched, an' kem over hyar ter Old Rocky-Top, an' got along toler'ble well, cornsiderin'. But one day, whilst we war a-workin' on the T'other Mounting, what d' ye think I fund in the rock? The print of a bare foot in the solid stone, ez plain an' ez nateral ez ef the track hed been lef' in the clay yestiddy. Waal, I knowed it war the track o' Jeremiah Stubbs, what shot his step-brother, an' gin the sheriff the slip, an' war las' seen on the T'other Mounting, 'kase his old shoe jes' fit the track, fur we tried it. An' a good while arterward I fund on that same T'other Mounting—in the solid stone, mind ye—a fish, what he had done br'iled fur supper, jes' turned ter a stone."

"So thar's the Bible made true," said an elderly woman, who had come to the door to hear this reminiscence, and stood mechanically stirring a hoe-cake batter in a shallow wooden bowl. "Ax fur a fish, an' ye 'll git a stone."

The secret history of the hills among which they lived was indeed as a sealed book to these simple mountaineers.

"The las' time I war ter Colbury," said Nathan White, "I hearn the sheriff a-talkin' 'bout how them evil-doers an' sech runs fur the T'other Mounting fust thing; though he 'lowed ez it war powerful foxy in 'em ter try ter hide thar, kase he said, ef they wunst reaches it, he mought ez well look fur a needle in a hay-stack. He

'lowed ef he hed a posse a thousand men strong he could n't git 'em out."

"He can't find 'em, 'kase the rocks falls on 'em, or swallers 'em in," said the old man. "Ef Tony Britt is up ter mischief he'll never come back no more. He'll git into worser trouble than ever he see afore."

"He hev done seen a powerful lot of trouble, fust one way an' another, 'thout foolin' round the T'other Mounting," said Nathan White. "They tells me ez he got hisself indicted, I believes they calls it, or suthin', down yander ter the court at Colbury,—that war year afore las',—an' he hed ter pay twenty dollars fine; 'kase when he war overseer of the road he jes' war constant in lettin' his friends, an' folks ginerally, off 'thout hevin' 'em fined, when they did n't come an' work on the road, —though that air the way ez the overseers hev always done, without nobody a-tellin' on 'em an' sech. But them ez war n't Tony Britt's friends seen a mighty differ. He war dead sure ter fine Caleb Hoxie seventy-five cents, 'cordin' ter the law, fur every day that he war summonsed ter work an' never come; 'kase Tony an' Caleb hed some sort 'n grudge agin one another 'count of a spavined horse what Caleb sold ter Tony, makin' him out to be a sound critter,—though Caleb swears he never knowed the horse war spavined when he sold him ter Tony, no more 'n nuthin'. Caleb war mightily worked up 'bout this hyar finin' business, an' him an' Tony hed a tussle 'bout it every time they kem tergether. But Caleb war always sure ter git the worst of it, 'kase Tony, though he air toler'ble spindling sort o' build, he air somehow or other sorter stringy an' tough, an' makes a right smart show in a reg'lar knock-down an' drag-out fight. So Caleb he war beat every time, an' fined too. An' he tried wunst ter shoot Tony Britt, but he missed his aim. An' when he war a-layin' off how ter fix Tony, fur treatin' him that way, he war a-stoppin', one day, at Jacob Green's black-smith's shop, yander, a mile down the valley, an' he war a-talkin' 'bout it ter a passel o' folks thar. An' Lawyer Rood from Colbury war thar, an' Jacob war a-shoein' of his mare; an' he hearn the tale, an' axed Caleb why n't he report Tony ter the court, an' git him fined fur neglect of his duty, bein' overseer of

---

37 **Ax . . . stone.** Compare Matthew 7:9: "Or what man is there of you, whom if his son ask bread, will he give him a stone" • 84 **passel,** parcel, a group of indefinite number

evil people hide out t'other mountain!

the road. An' Caleb never knowed before that it war the law that everybody what war summonsed an' did n't come must be fined, or the overseer must be fined hisself; but he knowed that Tony hed been a-lettin' of his friends off, an' folks ginerally, an' he jes' 'greed fur Lawyer Rood ter stir up trouble fur Tony. An' he done it. An' the court fined Tony twenty dollars fur them ways o' his'n. An' it kept him so busy a-scufflin' ter raise the twenty dollars that he never hed a chance ter give Caleb Hoxie more'n one or two beatin's the whole time he war a-scrapin' up the money."

This story was by no means unknown to the little circle, nor did its narrator labor under the delusion that he was telling a new thing. It was merely a verbal act of recollection, and an attentive silence reigned as he related the familiar facts. To people who live in lonely regions this habit of retrospection (especially noticeable in them) and an enduring interest in the past may be something of a compensation for the scanty happenings of the present. When the recital was concluded, the hush for a time was unbroken, save by the rush of the winds, bringing upon their breath the fragrant woodland odors of balsams and pungent herbs, and a fresh and exhilarating suggestion of sweeping over a volume of falling water. They stirred the fringed shadow of a great pine that stood, like a sentinel, before Nathan White's door and threw its colorless simulacrum, a boastful lie twice its size, far down the sunset road. Now and then the faint clangor of a cow-bell came from out the tangled woods about the little hut, and the low of homeward-bound cattle sounded upon the air, mellowed and softened by the distance. The haze that rested above the long, narrow valley was hardly visible, save in the illusive beauty with which it invested the scene,—the tender azure of the far-away ranges; the exquisite tones of the gray and purple shadows that hovered about the darkening coves and along the deep lines marking the gorges; the burnished brilliance of the sunlight, which, despite its splendor, seemed lonely enough, lying motionless upon the lonely landscape and on the still figures clustered about the porch. Their eyes were turned toward the opposite steeps, gorgeous with scarlet oak and sumac, all in autumnal array, and their thoughts were busy with the hunter on the T'other Mounting and vague speculations concerning his evil intent.

"It 'pears ter me powerful strange ez Tony goes a-foolin' round that thar T'other Mounting, cornsiderin' what happened yander in its shadow," said the woman, coming again to the door, and leaning idly against the frame; the bread was baking over the coals. "That thar wife o' his'n, afore she died, war always frettin' 'kase way down thar on the backbone, whar her house war, the shadow o' the T'other Mounting laid on it fur an hour an' better every day of the worl'. She 'lowed ez it always put her in mind o' the shadow o' death. An' I thought 'bout that thar sayin' o' hern the day when I see her a-lyin' stiff an' cold on the bed, an' the shadow of the T'other Mounting drapping in at the open door, an' a-creepin' an' a-creepin' over her face. An' I war plumb glad when they got that woman under ground, whar, ef the sunshine can't git ter her, neither kin the shadow. Ef ever thar war a murdered woman, she war one. Arter all that hed come an' gone with Caleb Hoxie, fur Tony Britt ter go arter him, 'kase he war a yerb-doctor, ter git him ter physic his wife, who war nigh about dead with the lung fever, an' gin up by old Dr. Marsh!—it looks ter me like he war plumb crazy,—though him an' Caleb hed sorter made friends 'bout the spavined horse an' sech afore then. Jes' ez soon ez she drunk the stuff that Caleb fixed fur her she laid her head back an' shet her eyes, an' never opened 'em no more in this worl'. She war a murdered woman, an' Caleb Hoxie done it through the yerbs he fixed fur her."

A subtile amethystine mist had gradually overlaid the slopes of the T'other Mounting, mellowing the brilliant tints of the variegated foliage to a delicious hazy sheen of mosaics; but about the base the air seemed dun-colored, though transparent; seen through it, even the red of the crowded trees was but a sombre sort of magnificence, and the great masses of gray rocks, jutting out among them here and there, wore a darkly frowning aspect. Along the summit there was a blaze of scarlet and gold in the full glory of the sunshine; the topmost cliffs caught its rays, and gave them back in unexpected gleams of green or grayish-yellow, as of mosses, or vines, or huckleberry bushes, nourished in the heart of the deep fissures.

"Waal," said Nathan White, "I never did believe ez Caleb gin her ennythink ter hurt,—though I knows thar

66 **yerb-doctor,** herb doctor

is them ez does. Caleb is the bes' yerb-doctor I ever see. The rheumatiz would nigh on ter hev killed me, ef it war n't fur him, that spell I had las' winter. An' Dr. Marsh, what they hed up afore the gran' jury, swore that the yerbs what Caleb gin her war nuthin' ter hurt; *he* said, though, they could n't holp nor hender. An' but fur Dr. Marsh they would hev jailed Caleb ter stand his trial, like Tony wanted 'em ter do. But Dr. Marsh said she died with the consumption, jes' the same, an' Caleb's yerbs war wholesome, though they war n't no 'count at all."

"I knows I ain't a-goin' never ter tech nuthin' he fixes fur me no more," said his wife, "an' I'll be bound nobody else in these hyar mountings will, nuther."

"Waal," drawled her son, "I knows fur true ez he air tendin' now on old Gideon Croft, what lives over yander in the valley on the t'other side of the T'other Mounting, an' is down with the fever. He went over thar yestiddy evening, late; I met him when he war goin', an' he tole me."

"He hed better look out how he comes across Tony Britt," said Nathan White; "fur I hearn, the las' time I war ter the Settlemint, how Tony hev swore ter kill him the nex' time he see him, fur a-givin' of pizenous yerbs ter his wife. Tony air mightily outdone 'kase the gran' jury let him off. Caleb hed better be sorter keerful how he goes a-foolin' round these hyar dark woods."

The sun had sunk, and the night, long held in abeyance, was coming fast. The glooms gathered in the valley; a soft gray shadow hung over the landscape, making familiar things strange. The T'other Mounting was all a dusky, sad purple under the faintly pulsating stars, save that high along the horizontal line of its summit gleamed the strange red radiance of the dead and gone sunset. The outline of the foliage was clearly drawn against the pure lapis lazuli tint of the sky behind it; here and there the uncanny light streamed through the bare limbs of an early leafless tree, which looked in the distance like some bony hand beckoning, or warning, or raised in horror.

"*Anythink* mought happen thar!" said the woman, as she stood on night-wrapped Rocky-Top and gazed up at the alien light, so red in the midst of the dark landscape. When she turned back to the door of the little hut, the meagre comforts within seemed almost luxury, in their cordial contrast to the desolate, dreary mountain yonder and the thought of the forlorn, wandering hunter. A genial glow from the hearth diffused itself over the puncheon floor; the savory odor of broiling venison filled the room as a tall, slim girl knelt before the fire and placed the meat upon the gridiron, her pale cheeks flushing with the heat; there was a happy suggestion of peace and unity when the four generations trooped in to their supper, grandfather on his grandson's arm, and a sedate two-year-old bringing up the rear. Nathan White's wife paused behind the others to bar the door, and once more, as she looked up at the T'other Mounting, the thought of the lonely wanderer smote her heart. The red sunset light had died out at last, but a golden aureola heralded the moon-rise, and a gleaming thread edged the masses of foliage; there was no faint suggestion now of mist in the valley, and myriads of stars filled a cloudless sky. "He hev done gone home by this time," she said to her daughter-in-law, as she closed the door, "an' ef he ain't, he'll hev a moon ter light him."

"Air ye a-studyin' 'bout Tony Britt yit?" asked Nathan White. "He hev done gone home a good hour by sun, I'll be bound. Jes' ketch Tony Britt a-huntin' till sundown, will ye! He air a mighty pore hand ter work. 'Stonishes me ter hear he air even a-huntin' on the T'other Mounting."

"I don't believe he's up ter enny harm," said the woman; "he hev jes' tuk ter the woods with grief."

"'Pears ter me," said the daughter-in-law, rising from her kneeling posture before the fire, and glancing reproachfully at her husband,—"'pears ter me ez ye mought hev brought him hyar ter eat his supper along of we-uns, stiddier a-leavin' him a-grievin' over his dead wife in them witched woods on the T'other Mounting."

The young fellow looked a trifle abashed at this suggestion. "I never wunst thought of it," he said. "Tony never stopped ter talk more'n a minit, nohow."

The evening wore away; the octogenarian and the sedate two-year-old fell asleep in their chairs shortly after supper; Nathan White and his son smoked their cob-pipes, and talked fitfully of the few incidents of the day; the women sat in the firelight with their knitting, silent and absorbed, except that now and then the elder, breaking from her reverie, declared, "I can't git Tony Britt out'n my head nohow in the worl'."

The moon had come grandly up over the T'other

---

6 **holp,** help • 35 **lapis lazuli,** a blue stone • 47 **puncheon floor,** made of rough boards • 65 **hour by sun,** an hour before sundown • 75 **along of we-uns,** with us • 76 **stiddier,** instead

Over on the T'other Mounting 369

Mounting, casting long silver lights and deep black shadows through all the tangled recesses and yawning chasms of the woods and rocks. In the vast wilderness the bright rays met only one human creature, the belated hunter making his way homeward through the dense forest with an experienced woodman's craft. For no evil intent had brought Tony Britt to the T'other Mounting; he had spent the day in hunting, urged by that strong necessity without which the mountaineer seldom makes any exertion. Dr. Marsh's unavailing skill had cost him dear; his only cow was sold to make up the twenty dollars fine which his revenge on Caleb Hoxie had entailed upon him; without even so much as a spavined horse tillage was impossible, and the bounteous harvest left him empty-handed, for he had no crops to gather. The hardships of extreme poverty had reinforced the sorrows that came upon him in battalions, and had driven him far through long aisles of the woods, where the night fell upon him unaware. The foliage was all embossed with exquisite silver designs that seemed to stand out some little distance from the dark masses of leaves; now and then there came to his eyes that emerald gleam never seen upon verdure in the day-time,—only shown by some artificial light, or the moon's sweet uncertainty. The wind was strong and fresh, but not cold; here and there was a glimmer of dew. Once, and once only, he thought of the wild traditions which peopled the T'other Mounting with evil spirits. He paused with a sudden chill; he glanced nervously over his shoulder down the illimitable avenues of the lonely woods. The grape-vines, hanging in festoons from tree to tree, were slowly swinging back and forth, stirred by the wind. There was a dizzy dance of shadows whirling on every open space where the light lay on the ground. The roar and fret of Wild-Duck River, hidden there somewhere in the pines, came on the breeze like a strange, weird, fitful voice, crying out amid the haunted solitudes of the T'other Mounting. He turned abruptly, with his gun on his shoulder, and pursued his way through the trackless desert in the direction of his home. He had been absorbed in his quest and his gloomy thoughts, and did not realize the distance he had traversed until it lay before him to be retraced; but his superstitious terror urged him to renewed exertions. "Ef ever I gits off'n this hyar witched mounting," he said to himself, as he tore away the vines and brambles that beset his course, "I'll never come back agin while I lives." He grew

calmer when he paused on a huge projecting crag, and looked across the narrow valley at the great black mass opposite, which he knew was Old Rocky-Top; its very presence gave him a sense of companionship and blunted his fear, and he sat down to rest for a few minutes, gazing at the outline of the range he knew so well, so unfamiliar from a new stand-point. How low it seemed from the heights of the T'other Mounting! Could that faint gleam be the light in Nathan White's house? Tony Britt glanced further down the indistinct slope, where he knew his own desolate, deserted hut was crouched. "Jes' whar the shadow o' the T'other Mounting can reach it," he thought, with a new infusion of bitterness. He averted his eyes; he would look no longer; he threw himself at full length among the ragged clumps of grass and fragments of rock, and turned his face to the stars. It all came back to him then. Sometimes, in his sordid cares and struggles for his scanty existence, his past troubles were dwarfed by the present. But here on the lonely cliff, with the infinite spaces above him and the boundless forest below, he felt anew his isolation. No light on earth save the far gleam from another man's home, and in heaven only the drowning face of the moon, drifting slowly through the blue floods of the skies. He was only twenty-five; he had youth and health and strength, but he felt that he had lived his life; it seemed long, marked as it was by cares and privation and persistent failure. Little as he knew of life, he knew how hard his had been, even meted by those of the poverty-stricken wretches among whom his lot was cast. "An' sech luck!" he said, as his sad eyes followed the drifting dead face of the moon. "Along o' that thar step-mother o' mine till I war growed; an' then when I war married, an' we hed got the house put up, an' war beginnin' ter git along like other folks kin, an' Car'-line's mother gin her that thar calf what growed ter a cow, an' through pinchin' and' savin' we made out ter buy that thar horse from Caleb Hoxie, jes' ez we war a-startin' ter work a crap he lays down an' dies; an' that cussed twenty dollars ez I hed ter pay ter the court; an' Car'line jes' a-gettin' sick, an' a-wastin' an' a-wastin' away, till I, like a fool, brung Caleb thar, an' he pizens her with his yerbs—God A'mighty! ef I could jes' lay my hands wunst on that scoundrel I would n't leave a mite of him,

16 **sorrows . . . battalions.** Compare Hamlet, Act IV, sc. v, ll. 78-79: "When sorrows come, they come not single spies, But in battalions" 84 **crap**, crop

ef he war pertected by a hundred lyin', thievin' gran' juries! But he can't stay a-hidin' forevermo'. He's got ter 'count ter me, ef he ain't ter the law; an' he'll see a mighty differ atwixt us. I swear he'll never draw another breath!"

He rose with a set, stern face, and struck a huge bowlder beside him with his hard clenched hand as he spoke. He had not even an ignorant idea of an impressive dramatic pose; but if the great gaunt cliff had been the stage of a theatre his attitude and manner at that instant would have won him applause. He was all alone with his poverty and his anguished memories, as men with such burdens are apt to be.

The bowlder on which, in his rude fashion, he had registered his oath was harder than his hard hand, and the vehemence of the blow brought blood; but he had scarcely time to think of it. His absorbed reverie was broken by a rustling other than that of the eddying wind. He raised his head and looked about him, half expecting to see the antlers of a deer. Then there came to his ears the echo of the tread of man. His eyes mechanically followed the sound. Forty feet down the face of the crag a broad ledge jutted out, and upon it ran a narrow path, made by stray cattle, or the feet of their searching owners; it was visible from the summit for a distance of a hundred yards or so, and the white glamour of the moonbeams fell full upon it. Before a speculation had suggested itself, a man walked slowly into view along the path, and with starting eyes the hunter recognized his dearest foe. Britt's hand lay upon the bowlder; his oath was in his mind; his unconscious enemy had come within his power. Swifter than a flash the temptation was presented. He remembered the warnings of his lawyer at Colbury last week, when the grand jury had failed to find a true bill against Caleb Hoxie,—that he was an innocent man, and must go unscathed, that any revenge for fancied wrongs would be dearly rued; he remembered, too, the mountain traditions of the falling rocks burying evil-doers in the heart of the hills. Here was his opportunity. He would have a life for a life, and there would be one more legend of the very stones conspiring to punish malefactors escaped from men added to the terrible "sayin's" of the T'other Mounting. A strong belief in the supernatural influences of the place was rife within him; he knew nothing of Gideon Croft's fever and the errand that had brought the herb-doctor through the "witched

mounting;" had he not been transported thither by some invisible agency, that the rocks might fall upon him and crush him?

The temptation and the resolve were simultaneous. With his hand upon the bowlder, his hot heart beating fast, his distended eyes burning upon the approaching figure, he waited for the moment to come. There lay the long, low, black mountain opposite, with only the moon beams upon it, for the lights in Nathan White's house were extinguished; there was the deep, dark gulf of the valley; there, forty feet below him, was the narrow, moon-flooded path on the ledge, and the man advancing carelessly. The bowlder fell with a frightful crash, the echoes rang with a scream of terror, and the two men—one fleeing from the dreadful danger he had barely escaped, the other from the hideous deed he thought he had done—ran wildly in opposite directions through the tangled autumnal woods.

Was every leaf of the forest endowed with a woful voice, that the echo of that shriek might never die from Tony Britt's ears? Did the storied, retributive rocks still vibrate with this new victim's frenzied cry? And what was this horror in his heart! Now,—so late,—was coming a terrible conviction of his enemy's innocence, and with it a fathomless remorse.

All through the interminable night he fled frantically along the mountain's summit, scarcely knowing whither, and caring for nothing except to multiply the miles between him and the frightful object that he believed lay under the bowlder which he had dashed down the precipice. The moon sank beneath the horizon; the fantastic shadows were merged in the darkest hour of the night; the winds died, and there was no voice in all the woods, save the wail of Wild-Duck River and the forever-resounding screams in the flying wretch's ears. Sometimes he answered them in a wild, hoarse, inarticulate cry; sometimes he flung his hands above his head and wrung them in his agony; never once did he pause in his flight. Panting, breathless, exhausted, he eagerly sped through the darkness; tearing his face upon the brambles; plunging now and then into gullies and unseen quagmires; sometimes falling heavily, but recovering himself in an instant, and once more struggling on; striving to elude the pursuing voices, and to distance forever his conscience and his memory.

And then came that terrible early daylight that was

wont to dawn upon the T'other Mounting when all the world besides was lost in slumber; the wan, melancholy light showed dimly the solemn trees and dense undergrowth; the precarious pitfalls about his path; the long deep gorges; the great crags and chasms; the cascades, steely gray, and white; the huge mass, all hung about with shadows, which he knew was Old Rocky-Top, rising from the impenetrably dark valley below. It seemed wonderful to him, somehow, that a new day should 10 break at all. If, in a revulsion of nature, that utter blackness had continued forever and ever it would not have been strange, after what had happened. He could have borne it better than the sight of the familiar world gradually growing into day, all unconscious of his secret. He had begun the descent of the T'other Mounting, and he seemed to carry that pale dawn with him; day was breaking when he reached the foot of Old Rocky-Top, and as he climbed up to his own deserted, empty little shanty, it too stood plainly defined in the morning light. He dragged 20 himself to the door, and impelled by some morbid fascination he glanced over his shoulder at the T'other Mounting. There it was, unchanged, with the golden largess of a gracious season blazing upon every autumnal leaf. He shuddered, and went into the fireless, comfortless house. And then he made an appalling discovery. As he mechanically divested himself of his shot-pouch and powder-horn he was stricken by a sudden consciousness that he did not have his gun! One doubtful moment, and he remembered that he had laid it upon the crag when 30 he had thrown himself down to rest. Beyond question, it was there yet. His conscience was still now,—his remorse had fled. It was only a matter of time when his crime would be known. He recollected his meeting with young White while he was hunting, and then Britt cursed the gun which he had left on the cliff. The discovery of the weapon there would be strong evidence against him, taken in connection with all the other circumstances. True, he could even yet go back and recover it, but he was mastered by the fear of meeting some one on the un-40 frequented road, or even in the loneliness of the T'other Mounting, and strengthening the chain of evidence against him by the fact of being once more seen in the fateful neighborhood. He resolved that he would wait until night-fall, and then he would retrace his way, secure his gun, and all might yet be well with him. As to the bowlder,—were men never before buried under the falling rocks of the T'other Mounting?

Without food, without rest, without sleep, his limbs rigid with the strong tension of his nerves, his eyes bloodshot, haggard, and eager, his brain on fire, he sat through 50 the long morning hours absently gazing across the narrow valley at the solemn, majestic mountain opposite, and that sinister jutting crag with the indistinctly defined ledges of its rugged surface.

After a time, the scene began to grow dim; the sun was still shining, but through a haze becoming momently more dense. The brilliantly tinted foliage upon the T'other Mounting was fading; the cliffs showed strangely distorted faces through the semi-transparent blue vapor, and presently they seemed to recede altogether; the valley 60 disappeared, and all the country was filled with the smoke of distant burning woods. He was gasping when he first became sensible of the smoke-laden haze, for he had seen nothing of the changing aspect of the landscape. Before his vision was the changeless picture of a night of mingled moonlight and shadow, the ill-defined black mass where Old Rocky-Top rose into the air, the impenetrable gloom of the valley, the ledge of the crag, and the unconscious figure slowly coming within the power of his murderous hand. His eyes would look on no 70 other scene, no other face, so long as he should live.

He had a momentary sensation of stifling, and then a great weight was lifted. For he had begun to doubt whether the unlucky locality would account satisfactorily for the fall of that bowlder and the horrible object beneath it; a more reasonable conclusion might be deduced from the fact that he had been seen in the neighborhood, and the circumstances of the deadly feud. But what wonder would there be if the dry leaves on T'other Mounting should be ignited and the woods burned! What expla-80 nations might not such a catastrophe suggest!—a frantic flight from the flames toward the cliff and an accidental fall. And so he waited throughout the long day, that was hardly day at all, but an opaque twilight, through which could be discerned only the stony path leading down the slope from his door, only the blurred outlines of the bushes close at hand, only the great gaunt limbs of a lightning-scathed tree, seeming entirely severed from the unseen trunk, and swinging in the air sixty feet above the earth. 90

Toward night-fall the wind rose and the smoke-curtain lifted, once more revealing to the settlers upon Old Rocky-Top the sombre T'other Mounting, with the belated evening light still lurid upon the trees,—only a strange, faint resemblance of the sunset radiance, rather the ghost of a dead day. And presently this apparition was gone, and the deep purple line of the witched mountain's summit grew darker against the opaline skies, till it was merged in a dusky black, and the shades of the night fell thick on the landscape.

The scenic effects of the drama, that serve to widen the mental vision and cultivate the imagination of even the poor in cities, were denied these primitive, simple people;
10 but that magnificent pageant of the four seasons, wherein was forever presented the imposing splendor of the T'other Mounting in an ever-changing grandeur of aspect, was a gracious recompense for the spectacular privileges of civilization. And this evening the humble family party on Nathan White's porch beheld a scene of unique impressiveness.

The moon had not yet risen; the winds were awhirl; the darkness draped the earth as with a pall. Out from the impenetrable gloom of the woods on the T'other
20 Mounting there started, suddenly, a scarlet globe of fire; one long moment it was motionless, but near it the spectral outline of a hand appeared beckoning, of warning, or raised in horror,—only a leafless tree, catching in the distance a semblance of humanity. Then from the still ball of fire there streamed upward a long, slender plume of golden light, waving back and forth against the pale horizon. Across the dark slope of the mountain below, flashes of lightning were shooting in zigzag lines, and wherever they gleamed were seen those frantic skeleton
30 hands raised and wrung in anguish. It was cruel sport for the cruel winds; they maddened over gorge and cliff and along the wooded steeps, carrying far upon their wings the sparks of desolation. From the summit, myriads of jets of flame reached up to the placid stars; about the base of the mountain lurked a lake of liquid fire, with wreaths of blue smoke hovering over it; ever and anon, athwart the slope darted the sudden lightning, widening into sheets of flame as it conquered new ground.

The astonishment on the faces grouped about Nathan
40 White's door was succeeded by a startled anxiety. After the first incoherent exclamations of surprise came the pertinent inquiry from his wife, "Ef Old Rocky-Top war ter ketch too, whar would we-uns run ter?"

Nathan White's countenance had in its expression more of astounded excitement than of bodily fear. "Why, bless my soul!" he said at length, "the woods away over yander, what hev been burnin' all day, ain't nigh enough

ter the T'other Mounting ter ketch it,—nuthin' like it."

"The T'other Mounting would burn, though, ef fire war put ter it," said his son. The two men exchanged a 50 glance of deep significance.

"Do ye mean ter say," exclaimed Mrs. White, her fire-lit face agitated by a sudden superstitious terror, "that that thar T'other Mounting is fired by witches an' sech?"

"Don't talk so loud, Matildy," said her husband. "Them knows best ez done it."

"Thar's one thing sure," quavered the old man: "that thar fire will never tech a leaf on Old Rocky-Top. Thar's a church on this hyar mounting,—bless the Lord fur it!—an' we lives in the fear o' God." 60

There was a pause, all watching with distended eyes the progress of the flames.

"It looks like it mought hev been kindled in torment," said the young daughter-in-law.

"It looks down thar," said her husband, pointing to the lake of fire, "like the pit itself."

The apathetic inhabitants of Old Rocky-Top were stirred into an activity very incongruous with their habits and the hour. During the conflagration they traversed long distances to reach each other's houses and confer 70 concerning the danger and the questions of supernatural agency provoked by the mysterious firing of the woods. Nathan White had few neighbors, but above the crackling of the timber and the roar of the flames there rose the quick beat of running footsteps; the undergrowth of the forest near at hand was in strange commotion; and at last, the figure of a man burst forth, the light of the fire showing the startling pallor of his face as he staggered to the little porch and sank, exhausted, into a chair.

"Waal, Caleb Hoxie!" exclaimed Nathan White, in 80 good-natured raillery; "ye 're skeered, fur true! What ails ye, ter think Old Rocky-Top air a-goin' ter ketch too? 'Tain't nigh dry enough, I'm a-thinkin'."

"Fire kindled that thar way can't tech a leaf on Old Rocky-Top," sleepily piped out the old man, nodding in his chair, the glare of the flames which rioted over T'other Mounting gilding his long white hair and peaceful, slumberous face. "Thar's a church on Old Rocky-Top, —bless the"—The sentence drifted away with his dreams. 90

"Does ye believe—them—them"—Caleb Hoxie's

---

63 **torment,** hell. See Luke 16:28: "For I have five brethren; that he may testify unto them, lest they also come into this place of torment"

trembling white lips could not frame the word—"them—done it?"

"Like ez not," said Nathan White. "But that ain't a-troublin' of ye an' me. I ain't never hearn o' them witches a-tormentin' of honest folks what ain't done nuthin' hurtful ter nobody," he added, in cordial reassurance.

His son was half hidden behind one of the rough cedar posts, that his mirth at the guest's display of cowardice might not be observed. But the women, always quick to suspect, glanced meaningly at each other with widening eyes, as they stood together in the door-way.

"I dunno,—I dunno," Caleb Hoxie declared huskily. "I ain't never done nuthin' ter nobody, an' what do ye s'pose them witches an' sech done ter me las' night, on that T'other Mounting? I war a-goin' over yander to Gideon Croft's fur ter physic him, ez he air mortal low with the fever; an' ez I war a-comin' alongside o' that thar high bluff"—it was very distinct, with the flames wreathing fantastically about its gray, rigid features— "they throwed a bowlder ez big ez this hyar porch down on ter me. It jes' grazed me, an' knocked me down, an' kivered me with dirt. An' I run home a-hollerin'; an' it seemed ter me ter-day ez I war a-goin' ter screech an' screech all my life, like some onsettled crazy critter. It 'peared like 'twould take a bar'l o' hop tea ter git me quiet. An' now look yander!" and he pointed tremulously to the blazing mountain.

There was an expression of conviction on the women's faces. All their lives afterward it was there whenever Caleb Hoxie's name was mentioned; no more to be moved or changed than the stern, set faces of the crags among the fiery woods.

"Thar's a church on this hyar mounting," said the old man feebly, waking for a moment, and falling asleep the next.

Nathan White was perplexed and doubtful, and a superstitious awe had checked the laughing youngster behind the cedar post.

A great cloud of flame came rolling through the sky toward them, golden, pellucid, spangled through and through with fiery red stars; poising itself for one moment high above the valley, then breaking into myriads of sparks, and showering down upon the dark abysses below.

"Look-a-hyar!" said the elder woman in a frightened under-tone to her daughter-in-law; "this hyar wicked critter air too onlucky ter be a-sittin' 'longside of us; we'll all be burnt up afore he gits hisself away from hyar. An' who is that a-comin' yander?" For from the encompassing woods another dark figure had emerged, and was slowly approaching the porch. The wary eyes near Caleb Hoxie saw that he fell to trembling, and that he clutched at a post for support. But the hand pointing at him was shaken as with a palsy, and the voice hardly seemed Tony Britt's as it cried out, in an agony of terror, "What air ye a-doin' hyar, a-sittin' 'longside o' livin' folks? Yer bones air under a bowlder on the T'other Mounting, an' ye air a dead man!"

They said ever afterward that Tony Britt had lost his mind "through goin' a-huntin' jes one time on the T'other Mounting. His spirit air all broke, an' he's a mighty tame critter nowadays." Through his persistent endeavor he and Caleb Hoxie became quite friendly, and he was even reported to "'low that he war sati'fied that Caleb never gin his wife nuthin' ter hurt." "Though," said the gossips of Old Rocky-Top, "them women up ter White's will hev it no other way but that Caleb pizened her, an' they would n't take no yerbs from him no more'n he war a rattlesnake. But Caleb always 'pears sorter skittish when he an' Tony air tergether, like he did n't know when Tony war a-goin' ter fotch him a lick. But law! Tony air that changed that ye can't make him mad 'thout ye mind him o' the time he called Caleb a ghost."

A dark, gloomy, deserted place was the charred T'other Mounting through all the long winter. And when spring came, and Old Rocky-Top was green with delicate fresh verdure, and melodious with singing birds and chorusing breezes, and bedecked as for some great festival with violets and azaleas and laurel-blooms, the T'other Mounting was stark and wintry and black with its desolate, leafless trees. But after a while the spring came for it, too: the buds swelled and burst; flowering vines festooned the grim gray crags; and the dainty freshness of the vernal season reigned upon its summit, while all the world below was growing into heat and dust. The circuit-rider said it reminded him of a tardy change in a sinner's heart: though it come at the eleventh hour, the glorious summer is before it, and a full fruition; though it work but an hour in the Lord's vineyard, it receives the same reward as those who labored through all the day.

---

89 **Lord's vineyard.** See the parable of the laborers in the vineyard, Matthew 20:1-16

"An' it always did 'pear ter me ez thar war mighty little jestice in that," was Mrs. White's comment.

But at the meeting when that sermon was preached Tony Britt told his "experience." It seemed a confession, for according to the gossips he "'lowed that he hed flung that bowlder down on Caleb Hoxie,—what the witches flung, ye know,—'kase he believed then that Caleb hed killed his wife with pizenous yerbs; an' he went back the nex' night an' fired the woods, ter make folks think when they fund Caleb's bones that he war a-runnin' from the blaze an' fell off'n the bluff." And everybody on Old Rocky-Top said incredulously, "Pore Tony Britt! He hev los' his mind through goin' a-huntin' jes one time on the T'other Mounting."

1881

Joel Chandler Harris

1848 · 1908

Writing in *Life on the Mississippi* in 1883, Mark Twain called Joel Chandler Harris "the only master" of the Negro dialect. Twain himself was something of a master in this kind; but Harris' supremacy, then and even now, may well pass unquestioned.

Harris was born near Eatonton, Georgia. His mother, deserted by his father, took in sewing for a living. Between the ages of thirteen and seventeen (these were the Civil War years), Harris lived on the nearby plantation of Joseph Addison Turner and helped Turner print a weekly paper. At this time, he got an education by working on the paper and by reading in Turner's excellent library; he also became intimately acquainted with the life of the Southern plantation and especially with the speech and folklore of the Negroes. After the war he worked for brief periods on newspapers in Macon, New Orleans, and Savannah. In 1876 he joined the staff of the Atlanta *Constitution,* and for twenty-four years, through editorials, book reviews, feature articles, and the Uncle Remus stories (the last especially, of course), he helped mightily to make the *Constitution* the most influential newspaper ever published in the South. The stories of Uncle Remus were first collected in *Uncle Remus: His Songs and Sayings* in 1880.

Their popularity, both South and North, was so great that new volumes followed: *Nights with Uncle Remus* (1883), *Uncle Remus and His Friends* (1892), *Told by Uncle Remus* (1905), and still others.

Recent historical critics have stressed Harris' aim in the Uncle Remus stories of reconciling the North and the South. "With Harris," says Professor Buck, "the desire to reconcile amounted almost to a passion." Harris "must have worked consciously," Professor Wade believes, "to make those stories propagandist in nature. He must have realized that his propaganda, through Uncle Remus, had proved effective, and he could tell himself with all justice that much sectional rancour had evaporated before that old man's wit." Theodore Roosevelt praised Harris' writings in 1901, chiefly "for the blotting out of sectional antagonism." One can be glad that the Uncle Remus tales contributed to this happy result, without esteeming them the less as comic masterpieces of their kind, or enjoying them the less for their unalloyed humor.

Julia C. Harris, The Life and Letters of Joel Chandler Harris, Boston, 1918 • J. D. Wade, "Joel Chandler Harris," The American Review, April 1933 • P. H. Buck, "The South Begins to Write," The Road to Reunion, Boston, 1937.

From

Uncle Remus: His Songs and Sayings

Uncle Remus is Harris' version of the ante-bellum Negro who remained loyal to his master during the Civil War and after, and Harris' writings assure the reader of the kindly relations between the races on a Southern plantation.

The tales themselves belong to the folklore of the Negro race, though analogues can be found in the beast fables once popular in the literatures of Europe. Abundant humor is provided by the incongruity in the fact that the behavior of the animals closely approximates that of human beings. Uncle Remus' hero, Brer Rabbit (as Harris pointed out), "is the weakest and most harmless of all animals," and yet "is victorious in contests with the bear, the wolf, and the fox. It is not virtue that triumphs, but helplessness; it is not malice, but mischievousness." Historical critics have seen in Uncle Remus and his stories an embodiment of the "primitive outlook" of the ante-bellum Southern Negro.

UNCLE REMUS INITIATES THE LITTLE BOY

One evening recently, the lady whom Uncle Remus calls "Miss Sally" missed her little seven-year-old. Making search for him through the house and through the yard, she heard the sound of voices in the old man's cabin, and, looking through the window, saw the child sitting by Uncle Remus. His head rested against the old man's arm, and he was gazing with an expression of the most intense interest into the rough, weather-beaten face, that beamed so kindly upon him. This is what "Miss Sally"
10 heard:

"Bimeby, one day, arter Brer Fox bin doin' all dat he could fer ter ketch Brer Rabbit, en Brer Rabbit bin doin' all he could fer ter keep 'im fum it, Brer Fox say to hisse'f dat he'd put up a game on Brer Rabbit, en he ain't mo'n got de wuds out'n his mouf twel Brer Rabbit come a

376   J. C. Harris

lopin' up de big road, lookin' des ez plump, en ez fat, en ez sassy ez a Moggin hoss in a barley-patch.

"'Hol' on dar, Brer Rabbit,' sez Brer Fox, sezee.

"'I ain't got time, Brer Fox,' sez Brer Rabbit, sezee, sorter mendin' his licks.   20

"'I wanter have some confab wid you, Brer Rabbit,' sez Brer Fox, sezee.

"'All right, Brer Fox, but you better holler fum whar you stan'. I'm monstus full er fleas dis mawnin',' sez Brer Rabbit, sezee.

"'I seed Brer B'ar yistiddy,' sez Brer Fox, sezee, 'en he sorter rake me over de coals kaze you en me ain't make frens en live naberly, en I tole 'im dat I'd see you.'

"Den Brer Rabbit scratch one year wid his off hinefoot sorter jub'usly, en den he ups en sez, sezee: 30

"'All a settin', Brer Fox. Spose'n you drap roun' termorrer en take dinner wid me. We ain't got no great doin's at our house, but I speck de ole 'oman en de chilluns kin sorter scramble roun' en git up sump'n fer ter stay yo' stummuck.'

"'I'm 'gree'ble, Brer Rabbit,' sez Brer Fox, sezee.

"'Den I'll 'pen' on you,' sez Brer Rabbit, sezee.

"Nex' day, Mr. Rabbit an' Miss Rabbit got up soon, 'fo' day, en raided on a gyarden like Miss Sally's out dar, en got some cabbiges, en some roas'n years, en some sparrer-   40 grass, en dey fix up a smashin' dinner. Bimeby one er de little Rabbits, playin' out in de back-yard, come runnin' in hollerin', 'Oh, ma! oh, ma! I seed Mr. Fox a comin'!' En den Brer Rabbit he tuck de chilluns by der years en make um set down, en den him en Miss Rabbit sorter dally roun' waitin' for Brer Fox. En dey keep on waitin', but no Brer Fox ain't come. Atter'while Brer Rabbit goes to de do', easy like, en peep out, en dar, stickin' out fum behime de cornder, wuz de tip-een' er Brer Fox tail. Den Brer Rabbit shut de do' en sot down, en put his paws be-   50 hime his years en begin fer ter sing:

"'De place wharbouts you spill de grease,
    Right dar youer boun' ter slide,
  An' whar you fine a bunch er ha'r,
    You'll sholy fine de hide.'

---

17 **Moggin hoss,** Morgan horse, a celebrated breed which originated in Vermont • **20 mendin'** . . . licks, increasing his speed • **29 off, right** • **30 jub'usly,** dubiously • **31 All a settin',** agreed • **40 roas'n years,** green corn • **40 sparrer-grass,** asparagus

"Nex' day, Brer Fox sont word by Mr. Mink, en skuze hisse'f kaze he wuz too sick fer ter come, en he ax Brer Rabbit fer ter come en take dinner wid him, en Brer Rabbit say he wuz 'gree'ble.

"Bimeby, w'en de shadders wuz at der shortes', Brer Rabbit he sorter brush up en santer down ter Brer Fox's house, en w'en he got dar, he yer somebody groanin', en he look in de do' en dar he see Brer Fox settin' up in a rockin' cheer all wrop up wid flannil, en he look mighty 10 weak. Brer Rabbit look all 'roun', he did, but he ain't see no dinner. De dishpan wuz settin' on de table, en close by wuz a kyarvin' knife.

"'Look like you gwineter have chicken fer dinner, Brer Fox,' sez Brer Rabbit, sezee.

"'Yes, Brer Rabbit, deyer nice, en fresh, en tender,' sez Brer Fox, sezee.

"Den Brer Rabbit sorter pull his mustarsh, en say: 'You ain't got no calamus root, is you, Brer Fox? I done got so now dat I can't eat no chicken 'ceppin she's 20 seasoned up wid calamus root.' En wid dat Brer Rabbit lipt out er de do' and dodge 'mong de bushes, en sot dar watchin' fer Brer Fox; en he ain't watch long, nudder, kaze Brer Fox flung off de flannil en crope out er de house en got whar he could close in on Brer Rabbit, en bimeby Brer Rabbit holler out: 'Oh, Brer Fox! I'll des put yo' calamus root out yer on dish yer stump. Better come git it while hit's fresh,' and wid dat Brer Rabbit gallop off home. En Brer Fox ain't never kotch 'im yit, en w'at's mo', honey, he ain't gwineter."

HOW MR. RABBIT SAVED HIS MEAT

30 "One time," said Uncle Remus, whetting his knife slowly and thoughtfully on the palm of his hand, and gazing reflectively in the fire—"one time Brer Wolf—"

"Why, Uncle Remus!" the little boy broke in, "I thought you said the Rabbit scalded the Wolf to death a long time ago."

The old man was fairly caught and he knew it; but this made little difference to him. A frown gathered on his usually serene brow as he turned his gaze upon the child—a frown in which both scorn and indignation 40 were visible. Then all at once he seemed to regain control of himself. The frown was chased away by a look of Christian resignation.

"Dar now! W'at I tell you?" he exclaimed as if addressing a witness concealed under the bed. "Ain't I done tole you so? Bless grashus! ef chilluns ain't gittin' so dey knows mo'n ole fokes, en dey'll spute longer you en spute longer you, ceppin der ma call um, w'ich I speck twon't be long 'fo' she will, en den I'll set yere by de chimbly-cornder en git some peace er mine. W'en ole Miss wuz livin'," continued the old man, still addressing 50 some imaginary person, "hit 'uz mo'n enny her chilluns 'ud dast ter do ter come 'sputin' longer me, en Mars John'll tell you de same enny day you ax 'im."

"Well, Uncle Remus, you know you said the Rabbit poured hot water on the Wolf and killed him," said the little boy.

The old man pretended not to hear. He was engaged in searching among some scraps of leather under his chair, and kept on talking to the imaginary person. Finally, he found and drew forth a nicely plaited whip- 60 thong with a red snapper all waxed and knotted.

"I wuz fixin' up a w'ip fer a little chap," he continued, with a sigh, "but, bless grashus! 'fo' I kin git 'er done, de little chap done grow'd up twel he know mo'n I duz."

The child's eyes filled with tears and his lips began to quiver, but he said nothing; whereupon Uncle Remus immediately melted.

"I 'clar' to goodness," he said, reaching out and taking the little boy tenderly by the hand, "ef you ain't de ve'y spit en image er ole Miss w'en I brung 'er de las' news 70 er de war. Hit's des like skeerin' up a ghos' w'at you ain't fear'd un."

Then there was a pause, the old man patting the little child's hand caressingly.

"You ain't mad, is you, honey?" Uncle Remus asked finally, "kaze ef you is, I'm gwine out yere en butt my head 'gin de do' jam'."

But the little boy wasn't mad. Uncle Remus had conquered him and he had conquered Uncle Remus in pretty much the same way before. But it was some time 80 before Uncle Remus would go on with the story. He had to be coaxed. At last, however, he settled himself back in the chair and began:

"Co'se, honey, hit mout er bin ole Brer Wolf, er hit mout er bin er n'er Brer Wolf; it mout er bin 'fo' he got

---

46 **spute longer,** contradict • 72 **fear'd un,** afraid of • 85 **er n'er,** another

Uncle Remus—illustration by E. W. Kemble for Mark Twain's Library of Wit and Humor, *1888*

kotch up wid, er it mout er bin atterwards. Ez de tale were gun to me des dat away I gin it unter you. One time Brer Wolf wuz comin' 'long home fum a fishin' frolic. He s'anter 'long de road, he did, wid his string er fish 'cross his shoulder, wen fus news you know ole Miss Pa'tridge, she hop outer de bushes en flutter 'long right at Brer Wolf nose. Brer Wolf he say ter hisse'f dat ole Miss Pa'tridge tryin' fer ter toll 'im 'way fum her nes', en wid dat he lay his fish down en put out inter de
10 bushes whar ole Miss Pa'tridge come fum, en 'bout dat time Brer Rabbit, he happen 'long. Dar wuz de fishes, en dar wuz Brer Rabbit, en w'en dat de case w'at you speck a sorter innerpen'ent man like Brer Rabbit gwine do? I kin tell you dis, dat dem fishes ain't stay whar Brer Wolf put um at, en w'en Brer Wolf come back dey wuz gone.

"Brer Wolf, he sot down en scratch his head, he did, en study en study, en den hit sorter rush inter his mine dat Brer Rabbit bin 'long dar, en den Brer Wolf, he put
20 out fer Brer Rabbit house, en w'en he git dar he hail 'im. Brer Rabbit, he dunno nuthin' tall 'bout no fishes. Brer Wolf he up'n say he bleedzd ter b'leeve Brer Rabbit got dem fishes. Brer Rabbit 'ny it up en down, but Brer Wolf stan' to it dat Brer Rabbit got dem fishes. Brer Rabbit, he say dat if Brer Wolf b'leeve he got de fishes, den he give Brer Wolf lief fer ter kill de bes' cow he got. Brer Wolf, he tuck Brer Rabbit at his word, en go off ter de pastur' en drive up de cattle en kill Brer Rabbit bes' cow.

"Brer Rabbit, he hate mighty bad fer ter lose his cow, but he lay his plans, en he tell his chilluns dat he gwineter 30 have dat beef yit. Brer Wolf, he bin tuck up by de patter-rollers 'fo' now, en he mighty skeerd un um, en fus news you know, yer come Brer Rabbit hollerin' en tellin' Brer Wolf dat de patter-rollers comin'.

"'You run en hide, Brer Wolf,' sez Brer Rabbit, sezee, 'en I'll stay yer en take keer er de cow twel you gits back,' sezee.

"Soon's Brer Wolf hear talk er de patter-rollers, he scramble off inter de underbresh like he bin shot out'n a gun. En he want mo'n gone 'fo' Brer Rabbit, he whirl 40 in en skunt de cow en salt de hide down, en den he tuck'n cut up de kyarkiss en stow it 'way in de smoke-'house, en den he tuck'n stick de een' er de cow-tail in de groun'. Atter he gone en done all dis, den Brer Rabbit he squall out fer Brer Wolf:

"'Run yer, Brer Wolf! Run yer! Yo' cow gwine in de groun'! Run yer!'

"W'en ole Brer Wolf got dar, w'ich he come er scootin', dar wuz Brer Rabbit hol'in' on ter de cow-tail, fer ter keep it fum gwine in de groun'. Brer Wolf, he 50 kotch holt, en dey 'gin a pull er two en up come de tail. Den Brer Rabbit, he wink his off eye en say, sezee:

"'Dar! de tail done pull out en de cow gone,' sezee.

"But Brer Wolf he wer'n't de man fer ter give it up dat away, en he got 'im a spade, en a pick-axe, en a shovel, en he dig en dig fer dat cow twel diggin' wuz pas' all endu'unce, en ole Brer Rabbit he sot up dar in his front po'ch en smoke his seegyar. Eve'y time ole Brer Wolf stuck de pick-axe in de clay, Brer Rabbit, he giggle ter his chilluns: 60

"'He diggy, diggy, diggy, but no meat dar! He diggy, diggy, diggy, but no meat dar!'"

---

2 gun, given or told • **22 bleedzd,** obliged • **32 patter-rollers,** probably the night patrollers who determined whether Negro slaves were illegally at large • **40 want,** wasn't • **41 skunt,** skinned

"Kaze all de time de cow wuz layin' pile up in his smoke-'ouse, en him en his chilluns wuz eatin' fried beef en inguns eve'y time dey mouf water.

"Now den, honey, you take dis yer w'ip," continued the old man, twining the leather thong around the little boy's neck, "en scamper up ter de big 'ouse en tell Miss Sally fer ter gin you some un it de nex' time she fine yo' tracks in de sugar-bairl."

MR. RABBIT MEETS HIS MATCH AGAIN

"Dere wuz nudder man dat sorter play it sharp on Brer Rabbit," said Uncle Remus, as, by some mysterious process, he twisted a hog's bristle into the end of a piece of thread—an operation which the little boy watched with great interest. "In dem days," continued the old man, "de beastesses kyar'd on marters same ez fokes. Dey went inter fahmin', en I speck ef de troof wuz ter come out, dey kep' sto', en had der camp-meetin' times en der bobbycues w'en de wedder wuz 'greeble."

Uncle Remus evidently thought that the little boy wouldn't like to hear of any further discomfiture of Brer Rabbit, who had come to be a sort of hero, and he was not mistaken.

"I thought the Terrapin was the only one that fooled the Rabbit," said the little boy, dismally.

"Hit's des like I tell you, honey. Dey ain't no smart man, 'cep' w'at dey's a smarter. Ef ole Brer Rabbit hadn't er got kotch up wid, de nabers 'ud er tuck 'im for a h'ant, en in dem times dey bu'nt witches 'fo' you could squinch yo' eyeballs. Dey did dat."

"Who fooled the Rabbit this time?" the little boy asked.

When Uncle Remus had the bristle "sot" in the thread, he proceeded with the story:

"One time Brer Rabbit en ole Brer Buzzard 'cluded dey'd sorter go snacks, en crap tergedder. Hit wuz a mighty good year, en de truck tu'n out monstus well, but bimeby, w'en de time come fer dividjun, hit come ter light dat ole Brer Buzzard ain't got nuthin'. De crap wuz all gone, en dey want nuthin' dar fer ter show fer it. Brer Rabbit, he make like he in a wuss fix'n Brer Buzzard, en he mope 'roun', he did, like he fear'd dey gwineter sell 'im out.

"Brer Buzzard, he ain't sayin' nuthin', but he keep up a monstus thinkin', en one day he come 'long en holler en tell Brer Rabbit dat he done fine rich gole-mine des 'cross de river.

"'You come en go 'longer me, Brer Rabbit,' sez Brer Tukky Buzzard, sezee. 'I'll scratch en you kin grabble, en 'tween de two un us we'll make short wuk er dat gole-mine,' sezee.

"Brer Rabbit, he wuz high up fer de job, but he study en study, he did, how he gwineter git 'cross de water, kaze ev'y time he git his foot wet all de fambly kotch cole. Den he up'n ax Brer Buzzard how he gwine do, en Brer Buzzard he up'n say dat he kyar Brer Rabbit 'cross, en wid dat ole Brer Buzzard, he squot down, he did, en spread his wings, en Brer Rabbit, he mounted, en up dey riz." There was a pause.

"What did the Buzzard do then?" asked the little boy.

"Dey riz," continued Uncle Remus, "en w'en dey lit, dey lit in de top er de highest sorter pine, en de pine w'at dey lit in wuz growin' on er ilun, en de ilun wuz in de middle er de river, wid de deep water runnin' all 'roun'. Dey ain't mo'n lit 'fo' Brer Rabbit, he know w'ich way de win' 'uz blowin', en by de time ole Brer Buzzard got hisse'f ballunce on a lim', Brer Rabbit, he up'n say, sezee:

"'W'iles we er res'n here, Brer Buzzard, en bein's you bin so good, I got sump'n fer ter tell you,' sezee. 'I got a gole-mine er my own, one w'at I make myse'f, en I speck we better go back ter mine 'fo' we bodder 'longer yone,' sezee.

"Den ole Brer Buzzard, he laff, he did, twel he shake, en Brer Rabbit, he sing out:

"'Hole on, Brer Buzzard! Don't flop yo' wings w'en you laff, kaze den ef you duz, sump'n 'ill drap fum up yer, en my gole-mine won't do you no good, en needer will yone do me no good.'

"But 'fo' dey got down fum dar, Brer Rabbit done tole all 'bout de crap, en he hatter promus fer ter 'vide fa'r en squar. So Brer Buzzard, he kyar 'im back, en Brer Rabbit he walk weak in de knees a mont' atterwuds."

1880

---

3 inguns, onions • 14 kyar'd on marters, carried on matters • 15 fahmin', farming • 33 go snacks, share • 69 bodder . . . yone, bother with yours

From

Nights with Uncle Remus

MR. BENJAMIN RAM AND HIS WONDERFUL FIDDLE

I 'speck you done year tell er ole man Benjermun Ram," said Uncle Remus, with a great affectation of indifference, after a pause.

"Old man who?" asked the little boy.

"Old man Benjermun Ram. I 'speck you done year tell er him too long 'go ter talk 'bout."

"Why, no, I haven't, Uncle Remus!" exclaimed the little boy, protesting and laughing. "He must have been a mighty funny old man."

10 "Dat's ez may be," responded Uncle Remus, sententiously. "Fun deze days wouldn't er counted fer fun in dem days; en many's de time w'at I see folks laughin'," continued the old man, with such withering sarcasm that the little boy immediately became serious,—"many's de time w'at I sees um laughin' en laughin', w'en I lay dey ain't kin tell w'at deyer laughin' at deyse'f. En 'tain't der laughin' w'at pesters me, nudder,"—relenting a little,— "hit's dish yer ev'lastin' snickle en giggle, giggle en snickle."

20 Having thus mapped out, in a dim and uncertain way, what older people than the little boy might have been excused for accepting as a sort of moral basis, Uncle Remus proceeded:

"Dish yer Mr. Benjermun Ram, w'ich he done come up inter my min', was one er deze yer ole-timers. Dey tells me dat he 'uz a fiddler fum away back yander—one er dem ar kinder fiddlers w'at can't git de chune down fine 'less dey pats der foot. He stay all by he own-alone se'f 'way out in de middle un a big new-groun', en he sech a 30 handy man fer ter have at a frolic dat de yuther creeturs like 'im mighty well, en w'en dey tuck a notion fer ter shake der foot, w'ich de notion tuck'n' struck um eve'y once in a w'ile, nuthin' 'ud do but dey mus' sen' fer ole man Benjermun Ram en he fiddle; en dey do say," continued Uncle Remus, closing his eyes in a sort of ecstasy,

"dat w'en he squar' hisse'f back in a cheer, en git in a weavin' way, he kin des snatch dem old-time chunes fum who lay de rail. En den, w'en de frolic wuz done, dey'd all fling in, dem yuther creeturs would, en fill up a bag er peas fer ole Mr. Benjermun Ram fer ter kyar 40 home wid 'im.

"One time, des 'bout Christmas, Miss Meadows en Miss Motts en de gals, dey up 'n' say dat dey'd sorter gin a blow-out, en dey got wud ter ole man Benjermun Ram w'ich dey 'speckted 'im fer ter be on han'. W'en de time come fer Mr. Benjermun Ram fer ter start, de win' blow cole en de cloud 'gun ter spread out 'cross de elements—but no marter fer dat; ole man Benjermun Ram tuck down he walkin'-cane, he did, en tie up de fiddle in a bag, en sot out fer Miss Meadows. He thunk 50 he know de way, but hit keep on gittin' col'er, en col'er, en mo' cloudy, twel bimeby, fus' news you know, ole Mr. Benjermun Ram done lose de way. Ef he'd er kep' on down de big road fum de start, it moughter bin diffunt, but he tuck a nigh-cut, en he ain't git fur 'fo' he done los' sho' 'nuff. He go dis away, en he go dat away, en he go de yuther way, yit all de same he wus done los'. Some folks would er sot right flat down whar dey wus en study out de way, but ole man Benjermun Ram ain't got wrinkle on he hawn fer nothin', kaze he done got de 60 name er ole Billy Hardhead long 'fo' dat. Den ag'in, some folks would er stop right still in der tracks en holler en bawl fer ter see ef dey can't roust up some er de neighbors, but ole Mr. Benjermun Ram, he des stick he jowl in de win', he did, en he march right on des 'zackly like he know he ain't gwine de wrong way. He keep on, but 'twan't long 'fo' he 'gun ter feel right lonesome, mo' speshually w'en hit come up in he min' how Miss Meadows en de galls en all de comp'ny be bleedz ter do de bes' dey kin bidout any fiddlin'; en hit kinder make he marrer 70 git cole w'en he study 'bout how he gotter sleep out dar in de woods by hisse'f.

"Yit, all de same, he keep on twel de dark 'gun ter drap down, en den he keep on still, en bimeby he come ter a little rise whar dey wuz a clay-gall. W'en he git dar he stop en look 'roun', he did, en 'way off down in de holler, dar he see a light shinin', en w'en he see dis, ole

---

29 **new-groun'**, newly cleared ground • 38 **fum . . . rail**, from the foundation or beginning • 44 **wud**, word • 60 **hawn**, horn • 75 **clay-gall**, a bare patch that has resisted erosion

man Benjermun Ram tuck he foot in he han', en make he way todes it des lak it de ve'y place w'at he bin huntin'. 'Twan't long 'fo' he come ter de house whar de light is, en, bless you soul, he don't make no bones er knockin'. Den somebody holler out:

"'Who dat?'

"'I'm Mr. Benjermun Ram, en I done lose de way, en I come fer ter ax you ef you can't take me in fer de night,' sezee.

"In common," continued Uncle Remus, "ole Mr. Benjermun Ram wuz a mighty rough-en-spoken somebody, but you better b'leeve he talk monst'us perlite dis time.

"Den some un on t'er side er de do' ax Mr. Benjermun Ram fer ter walk right in, en wid dat he open de do' en walk in, en make a bow like fiddlin' folks does w'en dey goes in comp'ny; but he ain't no sooner made he bow en look 'roun' twel he 'gun ter shake en shiver lak he done bin stricken wid de swamp ager, kaze, settin' right dar 'fo' de fier wuz ole Brer Wolf, wid his toofies showin' up all w'ite en shiny like dey wuz bran new. Ef ole Mr. Benjermun Ram ain't bin so ole en stiff I boun' you he'd er broke en run, but 'mos' 'fo' he had time fer ter study 'bout gittin' 'way, ole Brer Wolf done bin jump up en shet de do' en fassen' 'er wid a great big chain. Ole Mr. Benjermun Ram he know he in fer't, en he tuck'n put on a bol' face ez he kin, but he des nat'ally hone fer ter be los' in de woods some mo'. Den he make 'n'er low bow, en he hope Brer Wolf and all his folks is well, en den he say, sezee, dat he des drap in fer ter wom hisse'f, en 'quire uv de way ter Miss Meadows', en ef Brer Wolf be so good ez ter set 'im in de road ag'in, he be off putty soon en be much 'blige in de bargains.

"'Tooby sho', Mr. Ram,' sez Brer Wolf, sezee, w'iles he lick he chops en grin; 'des put yo' walkin'-cane in de cornder over dar, en set yo' bag down on de flo', en make yo'se'f at home,' sezee. 'We ain't got much,' sezee, 'but w'at we is got is yone w'iles you stays, en I boun' we'll take good keer un you,' sezee; en wid dat Brer Wolf laugh en show his toofies so bad dat ole man Benjermun Ram come mighty nigh havin' 'n'er ager.

"Den Brer Wolf tuck'n' flung 'n'er lighter'd-knot on de fier, en den he slip inter de back room, en present'y, w'iles ole Mr. Benjermun Ram wuz settin' dar shakin' in he shoes, he year Brer Wolf whispun' ter he ole 'oman:

"'Ole 'oman! ole 'oman! Fling 'way yo' smoke meat— fresh meat fer supper! Fling 'way yo' smoke meat—fresh meat fer supper!'

"Den ole Miss Wolf, she talk out loud, so Mr. Benjermun Ram kin year:

"'Tooby sho' I'll fix 'im some supper. We er 'way off yer in de woods, so fur fum comp'ny dat goodness knows I'm mighty glad ter see Mr. Benjermun Ram.'

"Den Mr. Benjermun Ram year ole Miss Wolf whettin' 'er knife on a rock—*shirrah! shirrah! shirrah!*—en ev'y time he year de knife say *shirrah!* he know he dat much nigher de dinner-pot. He know he can't git 'way, en w'iles he settin' dar studyin', hit 'come 'cross he min' dat he des mought ez well play one mo' chune on he fiddle 'fo' de wuss come ter de wuss. Wid dat he ontie de bag en take out de fiddle, en 'gun ter chune 'er up—*plink, plank, plunk, plink! plunk, plank, plink, plunk!*"

Uncle Remus's imitation of the tuning of a fiddle was marvellous enough to produce a startling effect upon a much less enthusiastic listener than the little boy. It was given in perfect good faith, but the serious expression on the old man's face was so irresistibly comic that the child laughed until the tears ran down his face. Uncle Remus very properly accepted this as a tribute to his wonderful resources as a story-teller, and continued, in great good-humor:

"W'en ole Miss Wolf year dat kinder fuss, co'se she dunner w'at is it, en she drap 'er knife en lissen. Ole Mr. Benjermun Ram ain't know dis, en he keep on chunin' up—*plank, plink, plunk, plank!* Den ole Miss Wolf, she tuck'n' hunch Brer Wolf wid'er elbow, en she say, sez she:

"'Hey, ole man! w'at dat?'

"'Den bofe un um cock up der years en lissen, en des 'bout dat time, ole Mr. Benjermun Ram he sling de butt er de fiddle up und' he chin, en struck up one er dem ole-time chunes."

"Well, what tune was it, Uncle Remus?" the little boy asked, with some display of impatience.

"Ef I ain't done gone en fergit dat chune off'n my min'," continued Uncle Remus; "hit sorter went like dat ar song 'bout 'Sheep shell co'n wid de rattle er his ho'n;' en yit hit mout er been dat ar yuther one 'bout 'Roll de key, ladies, roll dem keys.' Brer Wolf

---

2 todes, toward • 13 t'er, the other • 18 ager, ague • 27 'n'er, another • 41 lighter'd-knot, pine knot

en ole Miss Wolf, dey lissen en lissen, en de mo' w'at dey lissen de skeerder dey git, twel bimeby dey tuck ter der heels en make a break fer de swamp at de back er de house des lak de patter-rollers wuz atter um.

"W'en ole man Benjermun Ram sorter let up wid he fiddlin', he don't see no Brer Wolf, en he don't year no ole Miss Wolf. Den he look in de back room; no Wolf dar. Den he look in de back po'ch; no Wolf dar. Den he look in de closet en de cubberd; no Wolf aint dar yit. Den ole Mr. Benjermun Ram, he tuck 'n' shot all de do's en lock um, en he s'arch 'roun' en he fine some peas en fodder in de lof', w'ich he et um fer he supper, en den he lie down front er de fier en sleep soun' ez a log.

"Nex' mawnin' he 'uz up en stirrin' monst'us soon,

en he put out fum dar, en he fine de way ter Miss Meadows' time 'nuff fer ter play at de frolic. W'en he git dar, Miss Meadows en de gals, dey run ter de gate fer ter meet 'im, en dis un tuck he hat, en dat un tuck he cane, en t'er 'n tuck he fiddle, en den dey up 'n' say:

"'Law, Mr. Ram! whar de name er goodness is you bin? We so glad you come. Stir 'roun' yer, folks, en git Mr. Ram a cup er hot coffee.'

"Dey make a mighty big ter-do 'bout Mr. Benjermun Ram, Miss Meadows en Miss Motts en de gals did, but 'twix' you en me en de bedpos', honey, dey'd er had der frolic wh'er de ole chap 'uz dar er not, kaze de gals done made 'rangements wid Brer Rabbit fer ter pat fer um, en in dem days Brer Rabbit wuz a patter, mon. He mos' sho'ly wuz."

1883

Sarah Orne Jewett

1849 · 1909

"If I were asked to name three American books," wrote Willa Cather in 1925, "which have the possibility of a long, long life, I would say at once, *The Scarlet Letter, Huckleberry Finn,* and *The Country of the Pointed Firs.* I can think of no others that confront time and change so serenely."

Sarah Orne Jewett, the author of *The Country of the Pointed Firs,* was born in the village of South Berwick, in the southwest corner of Maine, just ten miles from the seacoast. Although she became a cosmopolitan person, traveling in Europe and spending a good deal of time with friends in Boston (Annie Fields, Howells, Thomas Bailey Aldrich, and others), South Berwick was

her lifelong home and she always returned there to write. Like all good regionalists, she believed with Whittier that

> . . . he who wanders widest lifts
> No more of beauty's jealous veils
> Than he who from his doorway sees
> The miracle of flowers and trees.

Her formal schooling was irregular and fragmentary. Her real education for writing came from riding and talking with her father, a country doctor, as he visited his many patients in the fishing villages and on the upland farms, and from reading in her father's library.

Although she read widely in the modern English and Continental novel (in Jane Austen, Thackeray, Flaubert, Tolstoy), she was influenced especially by Mrs. Stowe's account of life along the Maine coast and by Howells, who had emphasized, in *A Chance Acquaintance*, the "pleasure in finding out the small graces and beauties of the poverty-stricken subjects." Her first story appeared in the *Atlantic Monthly* in 1869, when she was only twenty. In 1877 was published *Deephaven*, a collection of stories and sketches about a Maine village, nominally Deephaven but really South Berwick. Miss Jewett wrote many such sketches and stories, which appeared at frequent intervals in the *Atlantic* and were collected from time to time in book form: *Country By-Ways* (1881), *A White Heron and Other Stories* (1886), *A Native of Winby and Other Tales* (1893), *The Country of the Pointed Firs* (1896) are a partial list.

"The thing that teases the mind over and over for years," Miss Jewett once said, "and at last gets itself put down rightly on paper—whether little or great, **it** belongs to Literature." Her work shows the knowledge that comes only with long saturation, and the fine selective process of the artist. Her stories of New England are the best that have been written since Hawthorne. They are not as great as Hawthorne's (Miss Cather's praise, quoted earlier, is a little extravagant), because Miss Jewett lacks Hawthorne's grasp, his tragic power. She deals with the gentle, the amiable, the picturesque, and, at times, the trivial, and she sometimes fails to make their significance convincing. But her work is authentic literary art: she adds a delicate grace to the New England spareness. Her best writing has been justly called "a miracle in pastel shades."

The Best Stories of Sarah Orne Jewett (selected and arranged with a preface by Willa Cather), 2 vols., Boston, 1925 • F. O. Matthiessen, Sarah Orne Jewett, Boston, 1929

The Courting of Sister Wisby

Discursive and plotless, "The Courting of Sister Wisby" finds ample literary justification in its portrayal of New England life and manners. The author herself is present in the story, and the characters are seen from her point of view. Although the critical reader may detect the faintest suggestion of condescension toward "dear old Mrs. Goodsoe" and the others and an air of exhibiting them as interesting "specimens," Miss Jewett's treatment is firmly based upon an intimate knowledge and a genuine sympathy.

The story was printed in **The King of Folly Island and Other People**, 1888.

All the morning there had been an increasing temptation to take an out-door holiday, and early in the afternoon the temptation outgrew my power of resistance. A far-away pasture on the long southwestern slope of a high hill was persistently present to my mind, yet there seemed to be no particular reason why I should think of it. I was not sure that I wanted anything from the pasture, and there was no sign, except the temptation, that the pasture wanted anything of me. But I was on the farther side of as many as three fences before I stopped to think again where I was going, and why. 10

There is no use in trying to tell another person about that afternoon unless he distinctly remembers weather exactly like it. No number of details concerning an Arctic ice-blockade will give a single shiver to a child of the tropics. This was one of those perfect New England days in late summer, when the spirit of autumn takes a first stealthy flight, like a spy, through the ripening country-side, and, with feigned sympathy for those who droop with August heat, puts her cool cloak of bracing air about leaf and flower and human shoulders. Every living thing grows suddenly cheerful and strong; it is only when you catch sight of a horror-stricken little maple in swamp soil—a little maple that has second sight 20

and fore-knowledge of coming disaster to her race—
only then does a distrust of autumn's friendliness dim
your joyful satisfaction.

In midwinter there is always a day when one has the
first foretaste of spring; in late August there is a morning when the air is for the first time autumn-like. Perhaps it is a hint to the squirrels to get in their first supplies for the winter hoards, or a reminder that summer
will soon end, and everybody had better make the most
of it. We are always looking forward to the passing and
ending of winter, but when summer is here it seems as
if summer must always last. As I went across the fields
that day, I found myself half lamenting that the world
must fade again, even that the best of her budding and
bloom was only a preparation for another springtime,
for an awakening beyond the coming winter's sleep.

The sun was slightly veiled; there was a chattering
group of birds, which had gathered for a conference
about their early migration. Yet, oddly enough, I heard
the voice of a belated bobolink, and presently saw him
rise from the grass and hover leisurely, while he sang a
brief tune. He was much behind time if he were still
a housekeeper; but as for the other birds who listened,
they cared only for their own notes. An old crow went
sagging by, and gave a croak at his despised neighbor,
just as a black reviewer croaked at Keats—so hard it
is to be just to one's contemporaries. The bobolink was
indeed singing out of season, and it was impossible to
say whether he really belonged most to this summer or
to the next. He might have been delayed on his northward journey; at any rate, he had a light heart now, to
judge from his song, and I wished that I could ask him
a few questions—how he liked being the last man among
the bobolinks, and where he had taken singing lessons
in the South.

Presently I left the lower fields, and took a path that
led higher, where I could look beyond the village to the
northern country mountainward. Here the sweet fern
grew thick and fragrant, and I also found myself heed-
lessly treading on pennyroyal. Nearby, in a field corner,
I long ago made a most comfortable seat by putting a
stray piece of board and bit of rail across the angle of
the fences. I have spent many a delightful hour there,
in the shade and shelter of a young pitch-pine and a
wild-cherry tree, with a lovely outlook toward the village, just far enough away beyond the green slopes and

tall elms of the lower meadows. But that day I still had
the feeling of being outward bound, and did not turn
aside nor linger. The high pasture land grew more and
more enticing.

I stopped to pick some blackberries that twinkled at
me like beads among their dry vines, and two or three
yellow-birds fluttered up from the leaves of a thistle and
then came back again, as if they had complacently discovered that I was only an overgrown yellow-bird, in
strange disguise but perfectly harmless. They made me
feel as if I were an intruder, though they did not offer to
peck at me, and we parted company very soon. It was
good to stand at last on the great shoulder of the hill.
The wind was coming in from the sea, there was a fine
fragrance from the pines, and the air grew sweeter every
moment. I took new pleasure in the thought that in a
piece of wild pasture land like this one may get closest
to Nature, and subsist upon what she gives of her own
free will. There have been no drudging, heavy-shod
ploughmen to overturn the soil, and vex it into yielding
artificial crops. Here one has to take just what Nature
is pleased to give, whether one is a yellow-bird or a human being. It is very good entertainment for a summer
wayfarer, and I am asking my reader now to share the
winter provision which I harvested that day. Let us
hope that the small birds are also faring well after their
fashion, but I give them an anxious thought while the
snow goes hurrying in long waves across the buried fields,
this windy winter night.

I next went farther down the hill, and got a drink of
fresh cool water from the brook, and pulled a tender
sheaf of sweet flag beside it. The mossy old fence just
beyond was the last barrier between me and the pasture
which had sent an invisible messenger earlier in the day,
but I saw that somebody else had come first to the rendezvous: there was a brown gingham cape-bonnet and a
sprigged shoulder-shawl bobbing up and down, a little
way off among the junipers. I had taken such uncommon pleasure in being alone that I instantly felt a sense
of disappointment; then a warm glow of pleasant satisfaction rebuked my selfishness. This could be no one
but dear old Mrs. Goodsoe, the friend of my childhood

26 **black . . . Keats,** an allusion to the contemptuous review of Keats'
''Endymion'' by John Wilson Croker in the **Quarterly Review** for
April 1818

and fond dependence of my maturer years. I had not seen her for many weeks, but here she was, out on one of her famous campaigns for herbs, or perhaps just returning from a blueberrying expedition. I approached with care, so as not to startle the gingham bonnet; but she heard the rustle of the bushes against my dress, and looked up quickly, as she knelt, bending over the turf. In that position she was hardly taller than the luxuriant junipers themselves.

10 "I'm a-gittin' in my mulleins," she said briskly, "an' I've been thinking o' you these twenty times since I come out o' the house. I begun to believe you must ha' forgot me at last."

"I have been away from home," I explained. "Why don't you get in your pennyroyal too? There's a great plantation of it beyond the next fence but one."

"Pennyr'yal!" repeated the dear old woman, with an air of compassion for inferior knowledge; "'tain't the right time, darlin'. Pennyr'yal's too rank now. But for 20 mulleins this day is prime. I've got a dreadful graspin' fit for 'em this year; seems if I must be goin' to need 'em extry. I feel like the squirrels must when they know a hard winter's comin'." And Mrs. Goodsoe bent over her work again, while I stood by and watched her carefully cut the best fullgrown leaves with a clumsy pair of scissors, which might have served through at least half a century for herb-gathering. They were fastened to her apron-strings by a long piece of list.

"I'm going to take my jack-knife and help you," I 30 suggested, with some fear of refusal. "I just passed a flourishing family of six or seven heads that must have been growing on purpose for you."

"Now be keerful, dear heart," was the anxious response; "choose 'em well. There's odds in mulleins same's there is in angels. Take a plant that's all run up to stalk, and there ain't but little goodness in the leaves. This one I'm at now must ha' been stepped on by some creatur and blighted of its bloom, and the leaves is han'some! When I was small I used to have a notion that Adam an' 40 Eve must a took mulleins for their winter wear. Ain't they just like flannel, for all the world? I've had experience, and I know there's plenty of sickness might be saved to folks if they'd quit horse-radish and such fiery, exasperating things, and use mullein drarves in proper season. Now I shall spread these an' dry 'em nice on my spare floor in the garrit, an' come to steam 'em for use

along in the winter there'll be the vally of the whole summer's goodness in 'em, sartin." And she snipped away with the dull scissors while I listened respectfully, and took great pains to have my part of the harvest present 50 a good appearance.

"This is most too dry a head," she added presently, a little out of breath. "There! I can tell you there's win'rows o' young doctors, bilin' over with book-larnin', that is truly ignorant of what to do for the sick, or how to p'int out those paths that well people foller toward sickness. Book-fools I call 'em, them young men, an' some on 'em never'll live to know much better, if they git to be Methuselahs. In my time every middle-aged woman who had brought up a family had some proper ideas of dealin' 60 with complaints. I won't say but there was some fools amongst *them,* but I'd rather take my chances, unless they'd forsook herbs and gone to dealin' with patent stuff. Now my mother really did sense the use of herbs and roots. I never see anybody that come up to her. She was a meek-looking woman, but very understandin' mother was."

"Then that's where you learned so much yourself, Mrs. Goodsoe," I ventured to say.

"Bless your heart, I don't hold a candle to her; 'tis but 70 little I can recall of what she used to say. No, her l'arnin' died with her," said my friend, in a self-deprecating tone. "Why, there was as many as twenty kinds of roots alone that she used to keep by her, that I forgot the use of; an' I'm sure I shouldn't know where to find most of 'em, any. There was an herb"—*airb* she called it—"an herb called masterwort, that she used to get way from Pennsylvany; and she used to think everything of noble-liverwort, but I never could seem to get the right effects from it as she could. Though I don't know as she ever really 80 did use masterwort where somethin' else wouldn't a served. She had a cousin married out in Pennsylvany that used to take pains to get it to her every year or two, and so she felt 't was important to have it. Some set more by such things as come from a distance, but I

28 list, a strip of cloth • 34 odds, difference, inequality • 35 angels. There are nine ranks of angels in the generally accepted hierarchy: in descending order, Seraphim, Cherubim, Thrones, Dominions or Dominations, Virtues, Powers, Principalities, Archangels, and Angels • 44 drarves, draws, young shoots or sprouts • 47 vally, value • 53 win'rows, windrows, rows of hay raked up to dry • 59 Methuselah, according to Genesis 5:27, lived to be 969 years old

The Courting of Sister Wisby   385

rec'lect mother always used to maintain that folks was meant to be doctored with the stuff that grew right about 'em; 'twas sufficient, an' so ordered. That was before the whole population took to livin' on wheels, the way they do now. 'Twas never my idee that we was meant to know what's goin' on all over the world to once. There's goin' to be some sort of a set-back one o' these days, with these telegraphs an' things, an' letters comin' every hand's turn, and folks leavin' their proper work to answer 'em. I may not live to see it. 'Twas allowed to be difficult for folks to get about in old times, or to git word across the country, and they stood in their lot an' place, and weren't all just alike, either, same as pine-spills."

We were kneeling side by side now, as if in penitence for the march of progress, but we laughed as we turned to look at each other.

"Do you think it did much good when everybody brewed a cracked quart mug of herb-tea?" I asked, walking away on my knees to a new mullein.

"I've always lifted my voice against the practice, far's I could," declared Mrs. Goodsoe; "an' I won't deal out none o' the herbs I save for no such nonsense. There was three houses along our road—I call no names—where you couldn't go into the livin' room without findin' a mess o' herb-tea drorin' on the stove or side o' the fireplace, winter or summer, sick or well. One was thoroughwut, one would be camomile, and the other, like as not, yellow dock; but they all used to put in a little new rum to git out the goodness, or keep it from spilin'." (Mrs. Goodsoe favored me with a knowing smile.) "Land, how mother used to laugh! But poor creatures, they had to work hard, and I guess it never done 'em a mite o' harm; they was all good herbs. I wish you could hear the quawkin' there used to be when they was indulged with a real case o' sickness. Everybody would collect from far an' near; you'd see 'em coming along the road and across the pastures then; everybody clamorin' that nothin' would do no kind o' good but her choice o' teas or drarves to the feet. I wonder there was a babe lived to grow up in the whole lower part o' the town; an' if nothin' else 'peared to ail 'em, word was passed about that 'twas likely Mis' So-and-So's last young one was goin' to be foolish. Land, how they'd gather! I know one day the doctor come to Widder Peck's and the house was crammed so't he could scercely git inside the door; and he says, just as polite, 'Do send for some of the neighbors!' as if there wa'n't a soul to turn to, right or left. You'd ought to seen 'em begin to scatter."

"But don't you think the cars and telegraphs have given people more to interest them, Mrs. Goodsoe? Don't you believe people's lives were narrower then, and more taken up with little things?" I asked, unwisely, being a product of modern times.

"Not one mite, dear," said my companion stoutly. "There was as big thoughts then as there is now; these times was born o' them. The difference is in folks themselves; but now, instead o' doin' their own housekeepin' and watchin' their own neighbors—though that was carried to excess—they git word that a niece's child is ailin' the other side o' Massachusetts, and they drop everything and git on their best clothes, and off they jiggit in the cars. 'Tis a bad sign when folks wear out their best clothes faster 'n they do their everyday ones. The other side o' Massachusetts has got to look after itself by rights. An' besides that, Sunday-keepin's all gone out o' fashion. Some lays it to one thing an' some another, but some o' them old ministers that folks are all a-sighin' for did preach a lot o' stuff that wa'n't nothin' but chaff; 'twa'n't the word o' God out o' either Old Testament or New. But everybody went to meetin' and heard it, and come home, and was set to fightin' with their next door neighbor over it. Now I'm a believer, and I try to live a Christian life, but I'd as soon hear a surveyor's book read out, figgers an' all, as try to get any simple truth out o' most sermons. It's them as is most to blame."

"What was the matter that day at Widow Peck's?" I hastened to ask, for I knew by experience that the good, clear-minded soul beside me was apt to grow unduly vexed and distressed when she contemplated the state of religious teaching.

"Why, there wa'n't nothin' the matter, only a gal o' Miss Peck's had met with a dis'pintment and had gone into screechin' fits. 'Twas a rovin' creatur' that had come along hayin' time, and he'd gone off an' forsook her betwixt two days; nobody ever knew what become of him. Them Pecks was 'Good Lord, anybody!' kind o' gals, and took up with whoever they could get. One of 'em married Heron, the Irishman; they lived in that little house that was burnt this summer, over on the edge o' the plains.

13 **pine-spills**, pine needles • 25 **drorin'**, drawing

He was a good-hearted creatur', with a laughin' eye and a clever word for everybody. He was the first Irishman that ever came this way, and we was all for gettin' a look at him, when he first used to go by. Mother's folks was what they call Scotch-Irish, though; there was an old race of 'em settled about here. They could foretell events, some on 'em, and had second sight. I know folks used to say mother's grandmother had them gifts, but mother was never free to speak about it to us. She remembered her well, too."

"I suppose that you mean old Jim Heron, who was such a famous fiddler?" I asked with great interest, for I am always delighted to know more about that rustic hero, parochial Orpheus that he must have been!

"Now, dear heart, I suppose you don't remember him, do you?" replied Mrs. Goodsoe, earnestly. "Fiddle! He'd about break your heart with them tunes of his, or else set your heels flying up the floor in a jig, though you was minister o' the First Parish and all wound up for a funeral prayer. I tell ye there ain't no tunes sounds like them used to. It used to seem to me summer nights when I was comin' along the plains road, and he set by the window playin', as if there was a bewitched human creatur' in that old red fiddle o' his. He could make it sound just like a woman's voice tellin' somethin' over and over, as if folks could help her out o' her sorrows if she could only make 'em understand. I've set by the stone-wall and cried as if my heart was broke, and dear knows it wa'n't in them days. How he would twirl off them jigs and dance tunes! He used to make somethin' han'-some out of 'em in fall an' winter, playin' at huskins and dancin' parties; but he was unstiddy by spells, as he got along in years, and never knew what it was to be fore-handed. Everybody felt bad when he died; you couldn't help likin' the creatur'. He'd got the gift—that's all you could say about it.

"There was a Mis' Jerry Foss, that lived over by the brook bridge, on the plains road, that had lost her husband early, and was left with three child'n. She set the world by 'em, and was a real pleasant, ambitious little woman, and was workin' on as best she could with that little farm, when there come a rage o' scarlet fever, and her boy and two girls was swept off and laid dead within the same week. Every one o' the neighbors did what they could, but she'd had no sleep since they was taken sick, and after the funeral she set there just like a piece o' marble, and would only shake her head when you spoke to her. They all thought her reason would go; and 'twould certain, if she couldn't have shed tears. An' one o' the neighbors—'twas like mother's sense, but it might have been somebody else—spoke o' Jim Heron. Mother an' one or two o' the women that knew her best was in the house with her. 'T was right in the edge o' the woods and some of us younger ones was over by the wall on the other side of the road where there was a couple of old willows—I remember just how the brook damp felt—and we kept quiet's we could, and some other folks come along down the road, and stood waitin' on the little bridge, hopin' somebody'd come out, I suppose, and they'd git news. Everybody was wrought up, and felt a good deal for her, you know. By an' by Jim Heron come stealin' right out o' the shadows an' set down on the door-step, an' 'twas a good while before we heard a sound; then, oh, dear me! 'twas what the whole neighborhood felt for that mother all spoke in the notes, an' they told me afterwards that Mis' Foss's face changed in a minute, and she come right over an' got into my mother's lap—she was a little woman—an' laid her head down, and there she cried herself into a blessed sleep. After a while one o' the other women stole out an' told the folks, and we all went home. He only played that one tune.

"But there!" resumed Mrs. Goodsoe, after a silence, during which my eyes were filled with tears. "His wife always complained that the fiddle made her nervous. She never 'peared to think nothin' o' poor Heron after she'd once got him."

"That's often the way," said I, with harsh cynicism, though I had no guilty person in my mind at the moment; and we went straying off, not very far apart, up through the pasture. Mrs. Goodsoe cautioned me that we must not get so far off that we could not get back the same day. The sunshine began to feel very hot on our backs, and we both turned toward the shade. We had already collected a large bundle of mullein leaves, which were carefully laid into a clean, calico apron, held together by the four corners, and proudly carried by me, though my companion regarded them with anxious eyes. We sat down together at the edge of the pine woods, and Mrs.

14 **parochial Orpheus.** The lyre of Orpheus, in Greek mythology, could charm beasts and make trees and rocks move. "Parochial" means restricted to a parish, provincial

Good example
"The dried herself with the plants —
so she would keep her goodness longer"

story began

spirit bride

Goodsoe proceeded to fan herself with her limp cape-bonnet.

"I declare, how hot it is! The east wind's all gone again," she said. "It felt so cool this forenoon that I overburdened myself with as thick a petticoat as any I've got. I'm despri't afeared of having a chill, now that I ain't so young as once. I hate to be housed up."

"It's only August, after all," I assured her unnecessarily, confirming my statement by taking two peaches out of my pocket, and laying them side by side on the brown pine needles between us.

"Dear sakes alive!" exclaimed the old lady, with evident pleasure. "Where did you get them, now? Doesn't anything taste twice better out-o'-doors? I ain't had such a peach for years. Do le's keep the stones, an' I'll plant 'em; it only takes four years for a peach pit to come to bearing, an' I guess I'm good for four years, 'thout I meet with some accident."

I could not help agreeing, or taking a fond look at the thin little figure, and her wrinkled brown face and kind, twinkling eyes. She looked as if she had properly dried herself, by mistake, with some of her mullein leaves, and was likely to keep her goodness, and to last the longer in consequence. There never was a truer, simple-hearted soul made out of the old-fashioned country dust than Mrs. Goodsoe. I thought, as I looked away from her across the wide country, that nobody was left in any of the farmhouses so original, so full of rural wisdom and reminiscence, so really able and dependable, as she. And nobody had made better use of her time in a world foolish enough to sometimes under-value medicinal herbs.

When we had eaten our peaches we still sat under the pines, and I was not without pride when I had poked about in the ground with a little twig, and displayed to my crony a long fine root, bright yellow to the eye, and a wholesome bitter to the taste.

"Yis, dear, goldthread," she assented indulgently. "Seems to me there's more of it than anything except grass an' hardhack. Good for canker, but no better than two or three other things I can call to mind; but I always lay in a good wisp of it, for old times' sake. Now, I want to know why you should a bit it, and took away all the taste o' your nice peach? I was just thinkin' what a han'some entertainment we've had. I've got so I 'sociate certain things with certain folks, and goldthread was somethin' Lizy Wisby couldn't keep house without,

no ways whatever. I believe she took so much it kind o' puckered her disposition."

"Lizy Wisby?" I repeated inquiringly.

"You knew her, if ever, by the name of Mis' Deacon Brimblecom," answered my friend, as if this were only a brief preface to further information, so I waited with respectful expectation. Mrs. Goodsoe had grown tired out in the sun, and a good story would be an excuse for sufficient rest. It was a most lovely place where we sat, half-way up the long hillside; for my part, I was perfectly contented and happy. "You've often heard of Deacon Brimblecom?" she asked, as if a great deal depended upon his being properly introduced.

"I remember him," said I. "They called him Deacon Brimfull, you know, and he used to go about with a witchhazel branch to show people where to dig wells."

"That's the one," said Mrs. Goodsoe, laughing. "I didn't know's you could go so far back. I'm always divided between whether you can remember everything I can, or are only a babe in arms."

"I have a dim recollection of there being something strange about their marriage," I suggested, after a pause, which began to appear dangerous. I was so much afraid the subject would be changed.

"I can tell you all about it," I was quickly answered. "Deacon Brimblecom was very pious accordin' to his lights in his early years. He lived way back in the country then, and there come a rovin' preacher along, and set everybody up that way all by the ears. I've heard the old folks talk it over, but I forget most of his doctrine, except some of his followers was persuaded they could dwell among the angels while yet on airth, and this Deacon Brimfull, as you call him, felt sure he was called by the voice of a spirit bride. So he left a good, deservin' wife he had, an' four children, and built him a new house over to the other side of the land he'd had from his father. They didn't take much pains with the buildin', because they expected to be translated before long, and then the spirit brides and them folks was goin' to appear and divide up the airth amongst 'em, and the world's folks and onbelievers was goin' to serve 'em or be sent to torments. They had meetin's about in the school-

84 translated, removed to heaven without a natural death • 87 onbelievers, unbelievers • 88 torments, hell. See note, p. 393

houses, an' all sorts o' goin's on; some on 'em went crazy, but the deacon held on to what wits he had, an' by an' by the spirit bride didn't turn out to be much of a house-keeper an' he had always been used to good livin' so he sneaked home ag'in. One o' mother's sisters married up to Ash Hill, where it all took place; that's how I come to have the particulars."

"Then how did he come to find his Eliza Wisby?" I inquired. "Do tell me the whole story; you've got mul-
10 lein leaves enough."

"There's all yesterday's at home, if I haven't," replied Mrs. Goodsoe. "The way he come a-courtin' o' Sister Wisby was this: she went a-courtin' o' him.

"There was a spell he lived to home, and then his poor wife died, and he had a spirit bride in good earnest, an' the child'n was placed about with his folks and hers, for they was both out o' good families; and I don't know what come over him, but he had another pious fit that looked for all the world like the real thing. He hadn't
20 no family cares, and he lived with his brother's folks, and turned his land in with theirs. He used to travel to every meetin' an' conference that was within reach of his old sorrel hoss's feeble legs; he j'ined the Christian Baptists that was just in their early prime, and he was a great ex-horter, and got to be called deacon, though I guess he wa'n't deacon, 'less it was for a spare hand when deacon timber was scercer'n usual. An' one time there was a four-days' protracted meetin' to the church in the lower part of the town. 'Twas a real solemn time; somethin'
30 more'n usual was goin' forward, an' they collected from the whole country round. Women folks liked it, an' the men too; it give 'em a change, an' they was quartered round free, same as conference folks now. Some on 'em, for a joke, sent Silas Brimblecom up to Lizy Wisby's, though she'd give out she couldn't accommodate nobody, because of expectin' her cousin's folks. Everybody knew 'twas a lie; she was amazin' close considerin' she had plenty to do with. There was a streak that wa'n't just right somewheres in Lizy's wits, I always thought. She
40 was very kind in case o' sickness, I'll say that for her.

"You know where the house is, over there on what they call Windy Hill? There the deacon went, all un-suspectin', and 'stead o' Lizy's resentin' of him she put in her own hoss, and they come back together to evenin' meetin'. She was prominent among the sect herself, an' he bawled and talked, and she bawled and talked, an'

took up more'n the time allotted in the exercises, just as if they was showin' off to each other what they was able to do at expoundin'. Everybody was laughin' at 'em af-
50 ter the meetin' broke up, and that next day an' the next an' all through, they was constant, and seemed to be havin' a beautiful occasion. Lizy had always give out she scorned the men, but when she got a chance at a particu-lar one 'twas altogether different, and the deacon seemed to please her somehow or 'nother, and—There! you don't want to listen to this old stuff that's past an' gone?"

"Oh, yes, I do," said I.

"I run on like a clock that's onset her striking hand," said Mrs. Goodsoe mildly. "Sometimes my kitchen time-
60 piece goes on half the forenoon, and I says to myself the day before yesterday I would let it be a warnin', and keep it in mind for a check on my own speech. The next news that was heard was that the deacon an' Lizy—well, opinions differed which of 'em had spoke first, but them fools settled it before the protracted meetin' was over, and give away their hearts before he started for home. They considered 'twould be wise, though, considerin' their short acquaintance, to take one another on trial a spell; 'twas Lizy's notion, and she asked him why he wouldn't come over and stop with her till spring, and
70 then, if they both continued to like, they could git mar-ried any time 'twas convenient. Lizy, she come and talked it over with mother, and mother disliked to of-fend her, but she spoke pretty plain; and Lizy felt hurt, an' thought they was showin' excellent judgment, so much harm come from hasty unions and folks comin' to a realizin' sense of each other's failin's when 'twas too late.

"So one day our folks saw Deacon Brimfull a-ridin' by with a gre't coopful of hens in the back o' his wagon, and bundles o' stuff tied on top and hitched to the exes un-
80 derneath; and he riz a hymn just as he passed the house, and was speedin' the old sorrel with a willer switch. 'Twas most Thanksgivin' time, an' sooner'n she expected him. New Year's was the time she set; but he thought he'd come while the roads was fit for wheels. They was out to meetin' together Thanksgivin' Day, an' that used to be a gre't season for marryin'; so the young folks nudged each other, and some on 'em ventured to speak to the couple as they come down the aisle. Lizy carried

80 exes, axles

The Courting of Sister Wisby   389

it off real well; she wa'n't afraid o' what nobody said or thought, and so home they went. They'd got out her yaller sleigh and her hoss; she never would ride after the deacon's poor old creatur', and I believe it died long o' the winter from stiffenin' up.

"Yes," said Mrs. Goodsoe, emphatically, after we had silently considered the situation for a short space of time, "yes, there was consider'ble talk, now I tell you! The raskil boys pestered 'em just about to death for a while. They used to collect up there an' rap on the winders, and they'd turn out all the deacon's hens 'long at nine o'clock o' night, and chase 'em all over the dingle; an' one night they even lugged the pig right out o' the sty, and shoved it into the back entry, an' run for their lives. They'd stuffed its mouth full o' somethin', so it couldn't squeal till it got there. There wa'n't a sign o' nobody to be seen when Lizy hasted out with the light, and she an' the deacon had to persuade the creatur' back as best they could; 'twas a cold night, and they said it took 'em till towards mornin'. You see the deacon was just the kind of a man that a hog wouldn't budge for; it takes a masterful man to deal with a hog. Well, there was no end to the works nor the talk, but Lizy left 'em pretty much alone. She did 'pear kind of dignified about it, I must say!"

"And then, were they married in the spring?"

"I was tryin' to remember whether it was just before Fast Day or just after," responded my friend, with a careful look at the sun, which was nearer the west than either of us had noticed. "I think likely 'twas along in the last o' April, any way some of us looked out o' the window one Monday mornin' early, and says, 'For goodness' sake! Lizy's sent the deacon home again!' His old sorrel havin' passed away, he was ridin' in Ezry Welsh's hoss-cart, with his hen-coop and more bundles than he had when he come, and looked as meechin' as ever you see. Ezry was drivin', and he let a glance fly swiftly round to see if any of us was lookin' out; an' then I declare if he didn't have the malice to turn right in towards the barn, where he see my oldest brother, Joshuay, an' says he real natural, 'Joshuay, just step out with your wrench. I believe I hear my kingbolt rattlin' kind o' loose.' Brother, he went out an' took in the sitooation, an' the deacon bowed kind of stiff. Joshuay was so full o' laugh, and Ezry Welsh, that they couldn't look one another in the face. There wa'n't nothing ailed the kingbolt, you know, an' when

Josh riz up he says, 'Goin' up country for a spell, Mr. Brimblecom?'

"'I be,' says the deacon, lookin' dreadful mortified and cast down.

"'Ain't things turned out well with you an' Sister Wisby?' says Joshuay. 'You had ought to remember that the woman is the weaker vessel.'

"'Hang her, let her carry less sail, then!' the deacon bu'st out, and he stood right up an' shook his fist there by the hen-coop, he was so mad; an' Ezry's hoss was a young creatur' an' started up and set the deacon right over backwards into the chips. We didn't know but he'd broke his neck; but when he see the women folks runnin' out he jumped up quick as a cat, an' clim' into the cart, an' off they went. Ezry said he told him that he couldn't git along with Lizy, she was so fractious in thundery weather; if there was a rumble in the daytime she must go right to bed an' screech, and if 'twas night she must git right up an' go an' call him out of a sound sleep. But everybody knew he'd never a gone home unless she'd sent him.

"Somehow they made it up ag'in, him an' Lizy, and she had him back. She'd been countin' all along on not havin' to hire nobody to work about the gardin an' so on, an' she said she wa'n't goin' to let him have a whole winter's board for nothin'. So the old hens was moved back, and they was married right off fair an' square, an' I don't know but they got along well as most folks. He brought his youngest girl down to live with 'em after a while, an' she was a real treasure to Lizy; everybody spoke well o' Phœbe Brimblecom. The deacon got over his pious fit, and there was consider'ble work in him if you kept right after him. He was an amazin' cider-drinker, and he airnt the name you know him by in his latter days. Lizy never trusted him with nothin', but she kep' him well. She left everything she owned to Phœbe, when she died, 'cept somethin' to satisfy the law. There, they're all gone now; seems to me sometimes, when I get thinkin', as if I'd lived a thousand years!"

I laughed, but I found Mrs. Goodsoe's thoughts had taken a serious turn.

---

12 **dingle**, small ravine or valley • 36 **meechin'**, miching, lying hidden, skulking • 53 **woman . . . vessel**, an allusion to I Peter 3:7: "Likewise, ye husbands . . . giving honour unto the wife, as unto the weaker vessel . . . ." • 80 **airnt**, earned

"There, I come by some old graves down here in the lower edge of the pasture," she said as we rose to go. "I couldn't help thinking how I should like to be laid right out in the pasture ground, when my time comes; it looked sort o' comfortable, and I have ranged these slopes so many summers. Seems as if I could see right up through the turf and tell when the weather was pleasant, and get the goodness o' the sweet fern. Now, dear, just hand me my apernful o' mulleins out o' the shade. I hope you won't come to need none this winter, but I'll dry some special for you."

"I'm going by the road," said I, "or else by the path across the meadows, so I will walk as far as the house with you. Aren't you pleased with my company?" for she demurred at my going the least bit out of the way.

So we strolled toward the little gray house, with our plunder of mullein leaves slung on a stick which we carried between us. Of course I went in to make a call, as if I had not seen my hostess before; she is the last maker of muster-gingerbread, and before I came away I was kindly measured for a pair of mittens.

"You'll be sure to come an' see them two peach-trees after I get 'em well growin'?" Mrs. Goodsoe called after me when I had said good-by, and was almost out of hearing down the road.

1888

Mary E. Wilkins Freeman

1852 · 1930

The most realistic of the New England local colorists, Mary E. Wilkins was born in Randolph, a village in eastern Massachusetts. She attended the schools of Randolph and of Brattleboro, Vermont, where her family lived for a while and her father kept a store, and she spent one year (1870-1871) at Mount Holyoke Female Seminary. After the death of her parents in 1883, she returned to her native village to live; the Massachusetts village and the country around it furnished the materials for her early stories. The best of these are found in *A Humble Romance and Other Stories* (1887), *A New England Nun and Other Stories* (1891), and *People of Our Neighborhood* (1898). After her marriage in 1902 to Dr. Charles M. Freeman of Metuchen, New Jersey, Mrs. Freeman attempted, with indifferent success, to enlarge the scope of her writing. Despite a voluminous and varied output, her reputation and importance still rest upon the early stories of Massachusetts village and rural life.

The style of these stories is as spare and angular as the characters it is used to describe. The stories themselves are concentrated and dramatic: they move inexorably to a climax which often takes the form of open revolt. For, in the author's view, the New England nature holds within itself "the elements of revolution": this repressed nature "has a floodgate, and the power which it releases is an accumulation." Compared with Miss Jewett, she is pessimistic. "What Miss Jewett with her love of the idyllic did not see," says Parrington, "—the grim and stark ugliness that resulted from the long Puritan repression—Mary Wilkins was to make the very warp of her work." Van Wyck Brooks, however, regards the ugliness in the lives of Miss Wilkins' people as less important than the heroism: "Better than anyone else, she pictured the powers of last resistance in the Yankee soul. . . . All these villagers lived with a vengeance . . . . Thus, underneath Miss Wilkins's village something lurked that was still sublime." Such an interpretation would seem to have been at least a part of the author's intention. A case in point is Sarah Penn in "The Revolt of 'Mother' ": she performed a "feat," says the author,

which "was equal in its way to Wolfe's storming of the Heights of Abraham."

F. L. Pattee, "Recorders of the New England Decline," A History of American Literature Since 1870, New York, 1915 • V. L. Parrington, "The New England Scene," The Beginnings of Critical Realism in America, New York, 1930 • Van Wyck Brooks, "Country Pictures," New England: Indian Summer, New York, 1940

Her Pessimism dramatic stories often ended in a climatic revolt

The Revolt of 'Mother'

"The Revolt of 'Mother' " is remarkable for its penetrating insight into the New England character, for its economy, and for its dramatic power.

First printed in Harper's New Monthly Magazine, September 1890, the story was reprinted in A New England Nun and Other Stories, 1891.

"Father!"

"What is it?"

"What are them men diggin' over there in the field for?"

There was a sudden dropping and enlarging of the lower part of the old man's face, as if some heavy weight had settled therein; he shut his mouth tight, and went on harnessing the great bay mare. He hustled the collar on to her neck with a jerk.

"Father!"

The old man slapped the saddle upon the mare's back.

"Look here, father, I want to know what them men are diggin' over in the field for, an' I'm goin' to know."

"I wish you'd go into the house, mother, an' 'tend to your own affairs," the old man said then. He ran his

words together, and his speech was almost as inarticulate as a growl.

But the woman understood; it was her most native tongue. "I ain't goin' into the house till you tell me what them men are doin' over there in the field," said she. 20

Then she stood waiting. She was a small woman, short and straight-waisted like a child in her brown cotton gown. Her forehead was mild and benevolent between the smooth curves of gray hair; there were meek downward lines about her nose and mouth; but her eyes, fixed upon the old man, looked as if the meekness had been the result of her own will, never of the will of another.

They were in the barn, standing before the wide open doors. The spring air, full of the smell of growing 30 grass and unseen blossoms, came in their faces. The deep yard in front was littered with farm wagons and piles of wood; on the edges, close to the fence and the house, the grass was a vivid green, and there were some dandelions.

The old man glanced doggedly at his wife as he tightened the last buckles on the harness. She looked as immovable to him as one of the rocks in his pastureland, bound to the earth with generations of blackberry vines. He slapped the reins over the horse, and started 40 forth from the barn.

"Father!" said she.

The old man pulled up. "What is it?"

"I want to know what them men are diggin' over there in that field for."

"They're diggin' a cellar, I s'pose, if you've got to know."

"A cellar for what?"

"A barn."

"A barn? You ain't goin' to build a barn over there 50 where we was goin' to have a house, father?"

The old man said not another word. He hurried the horse into the farm wagon, and clattered out of the yard, jouncing as sturdily on his seat as a boy.

The woman stood a moment looking after him, then she went out of the barn across a corner of the yard to the house. The house, standing at right angles with the great barn and a long reach of sheds and out-buildings, was infinitesimal compared with them. It was scarcely as commodious for people as the little boxes under the barn eaves were for doves.

A pretty girl's face, pink and delicate as a flower, was looking out of one of the house windows. She was watching three men who were digging over in the field which bounded the yard near the road line. She turned quietly when the woman entered.

"What are they digging for, mother?" said she. "Did he tell you?"

"They're diggin' for—a cellar for a new barn."

"Oh, mother, he ain't going to build another barn?"

"That's what he says."

A boy stood before the kitchen glass combing his hair. He combed slowly and painstakingly, arranging his brown hair in a smooth hillock over his forehead. He did not seem to pay any attention to the conversation.

"Sammy, did you know father was going to build a new barn?" asked the girl.

The boy combed assiduously.

"Sammy!"

He turned, and showed a face like his father's under his smooth crest of hair. "Yes, I s'pose I did," he said, reluctantly.

"How long have you known it?" asked his mother.

"'Bout three months, I guess."

"Why didn't you tell of it?"

"Didn't think 'twould do no good."

"I don't see what father wants another barn for," said the girl, in her sweet, slow voice. She turned again to the window, and stared out at the digging men in the field. Her tender, sweet face was full of a gentle distress. Her forehead was as bald and innocent as a baby's with the light hair strained back from it in a row of curl-papers. She was quite large, but her soft curves did not look as if they covered muscles.

Her mother looked sternly at the boy. "Is he goin' to buy more cows?"

The boy did not reply; he was tying his shoes.

"Sammy, I want you to tell me if he's goin' to buy more cows."

"I s'pose he is."

"How many?"

"Four, I guess."

His mother said nothing more. She went into the pantry, and there was a clatter of dishes. The boy got his cap from a nail behind the door, took an old arithmetic from the shelf, and started for school. He was lightly built, but clumsy. He went out of the yard with a curious spring in the hips, that made his loose home-made jacket tilt up in the rear.

The girl went to the sink, and began to wash the dishes that were piled up there. Her mother came promptly out of the pantry, and shoved her aside. "You wipe 'em," said she, "I'll wash. There's a good many this mornin'."

The mother plunged her hands vigorously into the water, the girl wiped the plates slowly and dreamily. "Mother," said she, "don't you think it's too bad father's going to build that new barn, much as we need a decent house to live in?"

Her mother scrubbed a dish fiercely. "You ain't found out yet we're women-folks, Nanny Penn," said she. "You ain't seen enough of men-folks yet to. One of these days you'll find it out, an' then you'll know that we know only what men-folks think we do, so far as any use of it goes, an' how we'd ought to reckon men-folks in with Providence, an' not complain of what they do any more than we do of the weather."

"I don't care; I don't believe George is anything like that, anyhow," said Nanny. Her delicate face flushed pink, her lips pouted softly, as if she were going to cry.

"You wait an' see. I guess George Eastman ain't no better than other men. You hadn't ought to judge father, though. He can't help it, 'cause he don't look at things jest the way we do. An' we've been pretty comfortable here, after all. The roof don't leak—ain't never but once—that's one thing. Father's kept it shingled right up."

"I do wish we had a parlor."

"I guess it won't hurt George Eastman any to come to see you in a nice clean kitchen. I guess a good many girls don't have as good a place as this. Nobody's ever heard me complain."

"I ain't complained either, mother."

The Revolt of 'Mother' 393

"Well, I don't think you'd better, a good father an' a good home as you've got. S'pose your father made you go out an' work for your livin'? Lots of girls have to that ain't no stronger an' better able to than you be."

Sarah Penn washed the frying-pan with a conclusive air. She scrubbed the outside of it as faithfully as the inside. She was a masterly keeper of her box of a house. Her one living-room never seemed to have in it any of the dust which the friction of life with inanimate matter produces. She swept, and there seemed to be no dirt to go before the broom; she cleaned, and one could see no difference. She was like an artist so perfect that he has apparently no art. To-day she got out a mixing bowl and a board, and rolled some pies, and there was no more flour upon her than upon her daughter who was doing finer work. Nanny was to be married in the fall, and she was sewing on some white cambric and embroidery. She sewed industriously while her mother cooked; her soft milk-white hands and wrists showed whiter than her delicate work.

"We must have the stove moved out in the shed before long," said Mrs. Penn. "Talk about not havin' things, it's been a real blessin' to be able to put a stove up in that shed in hot weather. Father did one good thing when he fixed that stove-pipe out there."

Sarah Penn's face as she rolled her pies had that expression of meek vigor which might have characterized one of the New Testament saints. She was making mince-pies. Her husband, Adoniram Penn, liked them better than any other kind. She baked twice a week. Adoniram often liked a piece of pie between meals. She hurried this morning. It had been later than usual when she began, and she wanted to have a pie baked for dinner. However deep a resentment she might be forced to hold against her husband, she would never fail in sedulous attention to his wants.

Nobility of character manifests itself at loop-holes when it is not provided with large doors. Sarah Penn's showed itself to-day in flaky dishes of pastry. So she made the pies faithfully, while across the table she could see, when she glanced up from her work, the sight that rankled in her patient and steadfast soul—the digging of the cellar of the new barn in the place where Adoniram forty years ago had promised her their new house should stand.

The pies were done for dinner. Adoniram and Sammy were home a few minutes after twelve o'clock. The dinner was eaten with serious haste. There was never much conversation at the table in the Penn family. Adoniram asked a blessing, and they ate promptly, then rose up and went about their work.

Sammy went back to school, taking soft sly lopes out of the yard like a rabbit. He wanted a game of marbles before school, and feared his father would give him some chores to do. Adoniram hastened to the door and called after him, but he was out of sight.

"I don't see what you let him go for, mother," said he. "I wanted him to help me unload that wood."

Adoniram went to work out in the yard unloading wood from the wagon. Sarah put away the dinner dishes, while Nanny took down her curl papers and changed her dress. She was going down to the store to buy some more embroidery and thread.

When Nanny was gone, Mrs. Penn went to the door. "Father!" she called.

"Well, what is it!"

"I want to see you jest a minute, father."

"I can't leave this wood nohow. I've got to git it unloaded an' go for a load of gravel afore two o'clock. Sammy had ought to helped me. You hadn't ought to let him go to school so early."

"I want to see you jest a minute."

"I tell ye I can't, nohow, mother."

"Father, you come here." Sarah Penn stood in the door like a queen; she held her head as if it bore a crown; there was that patience which makes authority royal in her voice. Adoniram went.

Mrs. Penn led the way into the kitchen, and pointed to a chair. "Sit down, father," said she; "I've got somethin' I want to say to you."

He sat down heavily; his face was quite stolid, but he looked at her with restive eyes. "Well, what is it, mother?"

"I want to know what you're buildin' that new barn for, father?"

"I ain't got nothin' to say about it."

"It can't be you think you need another barn?"

"I tell ye I ain't got nothin' to say about it, mother; an' I ain't goin' to say nothin'."

"Be you goin' to buy more cows?"

Adoniram did not reply; he shut his mouth tight.

"I know you be, as well as I want to. Now, father,

look here"—Sarah Penn had not sat down; she stood before her husband in the humble fashion of a Scripture woman—"I'm goin' to talk real plain to you; I never have sence I married you, but I'm goin' to now. I ain't never complained, an' I ain't goin' to complain now, but I'm goin' to talk plain. You see this room here, father; you look at it well. You see there ain't no carpet on the floor, an' you see the paper is all dirty, an' droppin' off the wall. We ain't had no new paper on it for ten year, an' then I put it on myself, an' it didn't cost but ninepence a roll. You see this room, father; it's all the one I've had to work in an' eat in an' sit in sence we was married. There ain't another woman in the whole town whose husband ain't got half the means you have but what's got better. It's all the room Nanny's got to have her company in; an' there ain't one of her mates but what's got better, an' their fathers not so able as hers is. It's all the room she'll have to be married in. What would you have thought, father, if we had had our weddin' in a room no better than this? I was married in my mother's parlor, with a carpet on the floor, an' stuffed furniture, an' a mahogany card-table. An' this is all the room my daughter will have to be married in. Look here, father!"

Sarah Penn went across the room as though it were a tragic stage. She flung open a door and disclosed a tiny bedroom, only large enough for a bed and bureau, with a path between. "There, father," said she—"there's all the room I've had to sleep in forty year. All my children were born there—the two that died, an' the two that's livin'. I was sick with a fever there."

She stepped to another door and opened it. It led into the small, ill-lighted pantry. "Here," said she, "is all the buttery I've got—every place I've got for my dishes, to set away my victuals in, an' to keep my milk-pans in. Father, I've been takin' care of the milk of six cows in this place, an' now you're goin' to build a new barn, an' keep more cows, an' give me more to do in it."

She threw open another door. A narrow crooked flight of stairs wound upward from it. "There, father," said she, "I want you to look at the stairs that go up to them two unfinished chambers that are all the places our son an' daughter have had to sleep in all their lives. There ain't a prettier girl in town nor a more ladylike one than Nanny, an' that's the place she has to sleep in. It ain't so good as your horse's stall; it ain't so warm an' tight."

Sarah Penn went back and stood before her husband. "Now, father," said she, "I want to know if you think you're doin' right an' accordin' to what you profess. Here, when we was married, forty year ago, you promised me faithful that we should have a new house built in that lot over in the field before the year was out. You said you had money enough, an' you wouldn't ask me to live in no such place as this. It is forty year now, an' you've been makin' more money, an' I've been savin' of it for you ever since, an' you ain't built no house yet. You've built sheds an' cow-houses an' one new barn, an' now you're goin' to build another. Father, I want to know if you think it's right. You're lodgin' your dumb beasts better than you are your own flesh an' blood. I want to know if you think it's right."

"I ain't got nothin' to say."

"You can't say nothin' without ownin' it ain't right, father. An' there's another thing—I ain't complained; I've got along forty year, an' I s'pose I should forty more, if it wasn't for that—if we don't have another house. Nanny she can't live with us after she's married. She'll have to go somewhere else to live away from us, an' it don't seem as if I could have it so, noways, father. She wasn't ever strong. She's got considerable color, but there wasn't never any backbone to her. I've always took the heft of everything off her, an' she ain't fit to keep house an' do everything herself. She'll be all worn out inside of a year. Think of her doin' all the washin' an' ironin' an' bakin' with them soft white hands an' arms, an' sweepin'! I can't have it so, noways, father."

Mrs. Penn's face was burning; her mild eyes gleamed. She had pleaded her little cause like a Webster; she had ranged from severity to pathos; but her opponent employed that obstinate silence which makes eloquence futile with mocking echoes. Adoniram arose clumsily.

"Father, ain't you got nothin' to say?" said Mrs. Penn.

"I've got to go off after that load of gravel. I can't stan' here talkin' all day."

"Father, won't you think it over, an' have a house built there instead of a barn?"

"I ain't got nothin' to say."

Adoniram shuffled out. Mrs. Penn went into her bedroom. When she came out, her eyes were red. She had a roll of unbleached cotton cloth. She spread it out on the kitchen table, and began cutting out some shirts for her husband. The men over in the field had a team

makes shirts for him

to help them this afternoon; she could hear their halloos. She had a scanty pattern for the shirts; she had to plan and piece the sleeves.

Nanny came home with her embroidery, and sat down with her needlework. She had taken down her curl-papers, and there was a soft roll of fair hair like an aureole over her forehead; her face was as delicately fine and clear as porcelain. Suddenly she looked up, and the tender red flamed all over her face and neck. "Mother," said she.

"What say?"

"I've been thinking—I don't see how we're goin' to have any—wedding in this room. I'd be ashamed to have his folks come if we didn't have anybody else."

"Mebbe we can have some new paper before then; I can put it on. I guess you won't have no call to be ashamed of your belongin's."

"We might have the wedding in the new barn," said Nanny, with gentle pettishness. "Why, mother, what makes you look so?"

Mrs. Penn had started, and was staring at her with a curious expression. She turned again to her work, and spread out a pattern carefully on the cloth. "Nothin'," said she.

Presently Adoniram clattered out of the yard in his two-wheeled dump cart, standing as proudly upright as a Roman charioteer. Mrs. Penn opened the door and stood there a minute looking out; the halloos of the men sounded louder.

It seemed to her all through the spring months that she heard nothing but the halloos and the noises of saws and hammers. The new barn grew fast. It was a fine edifice for this little village. Men came on pleasant Sundays, in their meeting suits and clean shirt bosoms, and stood around it admiringly. Mrs. Penn did not speak of it, and Adoniram did not mention it to her, although sometimes, upon a return from inspecting it, he bore himself with injured dignity.

"It's a strange thing how your mother feels about the new barn," he said, confidentially, to Sammy one day.

Sammy only grunted after an odd fashion for a boy; he had learned it from his father.

The barn was all completed ready for use by the third week in July. Adoniram had planned to move his stock in on Wednesday; on Tuesday he received a letter which changed his plans. He came in with it early in the morning. "Sammy's been to the post-office," said he,

"an' I've got a letter from Hiram." Hiram was Mrs. Penn's brother, who lived in Vermont.

"Well," said Mrs. Penn, "what does he say about the folks?"

"I guess they're all right. He says he thinks if I come up country right off there's a chance to buy jest the kind of a horse I want." He stared reflectively out of the window at the new barn.

Mrs. Penn was making pies. She went on clapping the rolling-pin into the crust, although she was very pale, and her heart beat loudly.

"I dun' know but what I'd better go," said Adoniram. "I hate to go off jest now, right in the midst of hayin', but the ten-acre lot's cut, an' I guess Rufus an' the others can git along without me three or four days. I can't get a horse round here to suit me, nohow, an' I've got to have another for all that wood-haulin' in the fall. I told Hiram to watch out, an' if he got wind of a good horse to let me know. I guess I'd better go."

"I'll get out your clean shirt an' collar," said Mrs. Penn calmly.

She laid out Adoniram's Sunday suit and his clean clothes on the bed in the little bedroom. She got his shaving-water and razor ready. At last she buttoned on his collar and fastened his black cravat.

Adoniram never wore his collar and cravat except on extra occasions. He held his head high, with a rasped dignity. When he was all ready, with his coat and hat brushed, and a lunch of pie and cheese in a paper bag, he hesitated on the threshold of the door. He looked at his wife, and his manner was definitely apologetic. "If them cows come to-day, Sammy can drive 'em into the new barn," said he; "an' when they bring the hay up, they can pitch it in there."

"Well," replied Mrs. Penn.

Adoniram set his shaven face ahead and started. When he had cleared the door-step, he turned and looked back with a kind of nervous solemnity. "I shall be back by Saturday if nothin' happens," said he.

"Do be careful, father," returned his wife.

She stood in the door with Nanny at her elbow and watched him out of sight. Her eyes had a strange, doubtful expression in them; her peaceful forehead was contracted. She went in, and about her baking again. Nanny sat sewing. Her wedding-day was drawing nearer, and she was getting pale and thin with her steady sewing. Her mother kept glancing at her.

"Have you got that pain in your side this mornin'?" she asked.

"A little."

Mrs. Penn's face, as she worked, changed, her perplexed forehead smoothed, her eyes were steady, her lips firmly set. She formed a maxim for herself, although incoherently with her unlettered thoughts. "Unsolicited opportunities are the guide-posts of the Lord to the new roads of life," she repeated in effect, 10 and she made up her mind to her course of action.

"S'posin' I *had* wrote to Hiram," she muttered once, when she was in the pantry—"s'posin' I had wrote, an' asked him if he knew of any horse? But I didn't, an' father's goin' wa'n't none of my doin'. It looks like a providence." Her voice rang out quite loud at the last.

"What you talkin' about, mother?" called Nanny.

"Nothin'."

Mrs. Penn hurried her baking; at eleven o'clock it 20 was all done. The load of hay from the west field came slowly down the cart track, and drew up at the new barn. Mrs. Penn ran out. "Stop!" she screamed, "stop!"

The men stopped and looked; Sammy upreared from the top of the load, and stared at his mother.

"Stop!" she cried out again. "Don't you put the hay in that barn; put it in the old one."

"Why, he said to put it in here," returned one of the haymakers, wonderingly. He was a young man, a neighbor's son, whom Adoniram hired by the year to 30 help on the farm.

"Don't you put the hay in the new barn; there's room enough in the old one, ain't there?" said Mrs. Penn.

"Room enough," returned the hired man, in his thick, rustic tones. "Didn't need the new barn, nohow, far as room's concerned. Well, I s'pose he changed his mind." He took hold of the horses' bridles.

Mrs. Penn went back to the house. Soon the kitchen windows were darkened, and a fragrance like warm honey came into the room.

40 Nanny laid down her work. "I thought father wanted them to put the hay into the new barn?" she said, wonderingly.

"It's all right," replied her mother.

Sammy slid down from the load of hay, and came in to see if dinner was ready.

"I ain't goin' to get a regular dinner to-day, as long as father's gone," said his mother. "I've let the fire go out.

You can have some bread an' milk an' pie. I thought we could get along." She set out some bowls of milk, some bread, and a pie on the kitchen table. "You'd better 50 eat your dinner now," said she. "You might jest as well get through with it. I want you to help me afterwards."

Nanny and Sammy stared at each other. There was something strange in their mother's manner. Mrs. Penn did not eat anything herself. She went into the pantry, and they heard her moving dishes while they ate. Presently she came out with a pile of plates. She got the clothes-basket out of the shed, and packed them in it. Nanny and Sammy watched. She brought out cups and saucers, and put them in with the plates. 60

"What you goin' to do, mother?" inquired Nanny, in a timid voice. A sense of something unusual made her tremble, as if it were a ghost. Sammy rolled his eyes over his pie.

"You'll see what I'm goin' to do," replied Mrs. Penn. "If you're through, Nanny, I want you to go up-stairs an' pack up your things; an' I want you, Sammy, to help me take down the bed in the bedroom."

"Oh, mother, what for?" gasped Nanny.

"You'll see." 70

During the next few hours a feat was performed by this simple, pious New England mother which was equal in its way to Wolfe's storming of the Heights of Abraham. It took no more genius and audacity of bravery for Wolfe to cheer his wondering soldiers up those steep precipices, under the sleeping eyes of the enemy, than for Sarah Penn, at the head of her children, to move all their little household goods into the new barn while her husband was away.

Nanny and Sammy followed their mother's instruc- 80 tions without a murmur; indeed, they were overawed. There is a certain uncanny and superhuman quality about all such purely original undertakings as their mother's was to them. Nanny went back and forth with her light load, and Sammy tugged with sober energy.

At five o'clock in the afternoon the little house in which the Penns had lived for forty years had emptied itself into the new barn.

Every builder builds somewhat for unknown purposes, and is in a measure a prophet. The architect of Adoniram 90 Penn's barn, while he designed it for the comfort of four-footed animals, had planned better than he knew

---

73 Wolfe's . . . Abraham. See note, p. 354

for the comfort of humans. Sarah Penn saw at a glance its possibilities. Those great box-stalls, with quilts hung before them, would make better bedrooms than the one she had occupied for forty years, and there was a tight carriage-room. The harness-room, with its chimney and shelves, would make a kitchen of her dreams. The great middle space would make a parlor, by-and-by, fit for a palace. Up-stairs there was as much room as down. With partitions and windows, what a house would there be! Sarah looked at the row of stanchions before the allotted space for cows, and reflected that she would have her front entry there.

At six o'clock the stove was up in the harness room, the kettle was boiling, and the table set for tea. It looked almost as home-like as the abandoned house across the yard had ever done. The young hired man milked, and Sarah directed him calmly to bring the milk to the new barn. He came gaping, dropping little blots of foam from the brimming pails on the grass. Before the next morning he had spread the story of Adoniram Penn's wife moving into the new barn all over the little village. Men assembled in the store and talked it over, women with shawls over their heads scuttled into each other's houses before their work was done. Any deviation from the ordinary course of life in this quiet town was enough to stop all progress in it. Everybody paused to look at the staid, independent figure on the side track. There was a difference of opinion with regard to her. Some held her to be insane; some, of a lawless and rebellious spirit.

Friday the minister went to see her. It was in the forenoon, and she was at the barn door shelling peas for dinner. She looked up and returned his salutation with dignity, then she went on with her work. She did not invite him in. The saintly expression of her face remained fixed, but there was an angry flush over it.

The minister stood awkwardly before her, and talked. She handled the peas as if they were bullets. At last she looked up, and her eyes showed the spirit that her meek front had covered for a lifetime.

"There ain't no use talkin', Mr. Hersey," said she. "I've thought it all over an' over, an' I believe I'm doin' what's right. I've made it the subject of prayer, an' it's betwixt me an' the Lord an' Adoniram. There ain't no call for nobody else to worry about it."

"Well, of course, if you have brought it to the Lord in prayer, and feel satisfied that you are doing right, Mrs. Penn," said the minister, helplessly. His thin gray-bearded face was pathetic. He was a sickly man; his youthful confidence had cooled; he had to scourge himself up to some of his pastoral duties as relentlessly as a Catholic ascetic, and then he was prostrated by the smart.

"I think it's right jest as much as I think it was right for our forefathers to come over here from the old country 'cause they didn't have what belonged to 'em," said Mrs. Penn. She arose. The barn threshold might have been Plymouth Rock from her bearing. "I don't doubt you mean well, Mr. Hersey," said she, "but there are things people hadn't ought to interfere with. I've been a member of the church for over forty years. I've got my own mind an' my own feet, an' I'm goin' to think my own thoughts an' go my own way, an' nobody but the Lord is goin' to dictate to me unless I've a mind to have him. Won't you come in an' set down? How is Mis' Hersey?"

"She is well, I thank you," replied the minister. He added some more perplexed apologetic remarks; then he retreated.

He could expound the intricacies of every character study in the Scriptures, he was competent to grasp the Pilgrim Fathers and all historical innovators, but Sarah Penn was beyond him. He could deal with primal cases, but parallel ones worsted him. But, after all, although it was aside from his province, he wondered more how Adoniram Penn would deal with his wife than how the Lord would. Everybody shared the wonder. When Adoniram's four new cows arrived, Sarah ordered three to be put in the old barn, the other in the house shed where the cooking-stove had stood. That added to the excitement. It was whispered that all four cows were domiciled in the house.

Towards sunset on Saturday, when Adoniram was expected home, there was a knot of men in the road near the new barn. The hired man had milked, but he still hung around the premises. Sarah Penn had supper all ready. There were brown-bread and baked beans and a custard pie; it was the supper that Adoniram loved on a Saturday night. She had on a clean calico, and she bore herself imperturbably. Nanny and Sammy kept close at her heels. Their eyes were large, and Nanny was full of nervous tremors. Still there was to them more pleasant excitement than anything else. An in-born confidence in their mother over their father asserted itself.

Sammy looked out of the harness-room window. "There he is," he announced, in an awed whisper. He and Nanny peeped around the casing. Mrs. Penn kept on about her work. The children watched Adoniram leave the new horse standing in the drive while he went to the house door. It was fastened. Then he went around to the shed. That door was seldom locked, even when the family was away. The thought how her father would be confronted by the cow flashed upon Nanny. There was a hysterical sob in her throat. Adoniram emerged from the shed and stood looking about in a dazed fashion. His lips moved; he was saying something, but they could not hear what it was. The hired man was peeping around a corner of the old barn, but nobody saw him.

Adoniram took the new horse by the bridle and led him across the yard to the new barn. Nanny and Sammy slunk close to their mother. The barn doors rolled back, and there stood Adoniram, with the long mild face of the great Canadian farm horse looking over his shoulder.

Nanny kept behind her mother, but Sammy stepped suddenly forward, and stood in front of her.

Adoniram stared at the group. "What on airth you all down here for?" said he. "What's the matter over to the house?"

"We've come here to live, father," said Sammy. His shrill voice quavered out bravely.

"What"—Adoniram sniffed—"what is it smells like cookin'?" said he. He stepped forward and looked in the open door of the harness-room. Then he turned to his wife. His old bristling face was pale and frightened. "What on airth does this mean, mother?" he gasped.

"You come in here, father," said Sarah. She led the way into the harness-room and shut the door. "Now, father," said she, "you needn't be scared. I ain't crazy. There ain't nothin' to be upset over. But we've come here to live, an' we're goin' to live here. We've got jest as good a right here as new horses an' cows. The house wasn't fit for us to live in any longer, an' I made up my mind I wa'n't goin' to stay there. I've done my duty by you forty year, an' I'm goin' to do it now; but I'm goin' to live here. You've got to put in some windows and partitions; an' you'll have to buy some furniture."

"Why, mother!" the old man gasped.

"You'd better take your coat off an' get washed—there's the wash basin—an' then we'll have supper."

"Why, mother!"

Sammy went past the window, leading the new horse to the old barn. The old man saw him, and shook his head speechlessly. He tried to take off his coat, but his arms seemed to lack the power. His wife helped him. She poured some water into the tin basin, and put in a piece of soap. She got the comb and brush, and smoothed his thin gray hair after he had washed. Then she put the beans, hot bread, and tea on the table. Sammy came in, and the family drew up. Adoniram sat looking dazedly at his plate, and they waited.

"Ain't you goin' to ask a blessin', father?" said Sarah.

And the old man bent his head and mumbled.

All through the meal he stopped eating at intervals, and stared furtively at his wife; but he ate well. The home food tasted good to him, and his old frame was too sturdily healthy to be affected by his mind. But after supper he went out, and sat down on the step of the smaller door at the right of the barn, through which he had meant his Jerseys to pass in stately file, but which Sarah designed for her front house door, and he leaned his head on his hands.

After the supper dishes were cleared away and the milk-pans washed, Sarah went out to him. The twilight was deepening. There was a clear green glow in the sky. Before them stretched the smooth level of field; in the distance was a cluster of hay-stacks like the huts of a village; the air was very cool and calm and sweet. The landscape might have been an ideal one of peace.

Sarah bent over and touched her husband on one of his thin, sinewy shoulders. "Father!"

The old man's shoulders heaved: he was weeping.

"Why, don't do so, father," said Sarah.

"I'll—put up the—partitions, an'—everything you—want, mother."

Sarah put her apron up to her face; she was overcome by her own triumph.

Adoniram was like fortress whose walls had no active resistance, and went down the instant the right besieging tools were used. "Why, mother," he said, hoarsely, "I hadn't no idee you was so set on't as all this comes to."

1890

The Revolt of Mother' **399**

William Sydney Porter
(O. Henry)

1862 · 1910

William Sydney Porter—at one time somewhat extravagantly called "the American de Maupassant"—was born in Greensboro, North Carolina. After clerking in a drug store, he went to Texas, where he lived on a ranch and later was a bank teller in Austin. Accused of embezzlement, he fled to Central America only to return because of his wife's illness and (after trial and conviction) to serve a term of three years (1897-1900) in the federal penitentiary at Columbus, Ohio. While in the penitentiary, he began to write short stories for the magazines under the pen name of "O. Henry." The last ten years of his life were spent in New York producing many stories which proved to be enormously popular all over the United States.

O. Henry's stories are not great literature. They rely for their interest chiefly upon ingenuity of plot—the "surprise ending"—the achievement of which depends too much upon accident and coincidence. The style is marked by a journalistic smartness. His work, however, has a social significance. In *The Four Million*, he described aspects of life in New York which previous writers had missed. "In spite of his preposterous absurdities," says Ludwig Lewisohn, "he caught the tang of, let us say, Herald Square in 1907. A perished, amusing moment is somehow captured and held fast."

C. A. Smith, O. Henry (biography), Garden City, 1916 • E. H. Long, O. Henry, the Man and His Work, Philadelphia, 1949

From · The Four Million

The Furnished Room

"The Furnished Room" is taken from O. Henry's famous collection of stories about New York City, **The Four Million**, published in 1909.

The story is thoroughly characteristic in its use of coin-cidence and surprise, its picturesque detail, its facile, journalistic style. A larger significance may be found in its social connotation: the migration of countless young people to New York and other big cities to seek their fortunes. As Lewisohn has observed, "O. Henry discovered the hall bedroom."

Restless, shifting, fugacious as time itself is a certain vast bulk of the population of the red brick district of the lower West Side. Homeless, they have a hundred homes. They flit from furnished room to furnished room, transients forever—transients in abode, transients in heart and mind. They sing "Home, Sweet Home" in rag-time; they carry their *lares et penates* in a bandbox; their vine is entwined about a picture hat; a rubber plant is their fig tree.

Hence the houses of this district, having had a thousand dwellers, should have a thousand tales to tell, mostly dull ones no doubt; but it would be strange if there could not be found a ghost or two in the wake of all these vagrant guests.

One evening after dark a young man prowled among these crumbling red mansions, ringing their bells. At the twelfth he rested his lean hand-baggage upon the step and wiped the dust from his hat-band and forehead. The bell sounded faint and far away in some remote, hollow depths.

To the door of this, the twelfth house whose bell he had rung, came a housekeeper who made him think of an unwholesome surfeited worm that had eaten its nut to a hollow shell and now sought to fill the vacancy with edible lodgers.

He asked if there was a room to let.

"Come in," said the housekeeper. Her voice came from her throat; her throat seemed lined with fur. "I have the third floor back, vacant since a week back. Should you wish to look at it?"

The young man followed her up the stairs. A faint light from no particular source mitigated the shadows of the halls. They trod noiselessly upon a stair carpet that its own loom would have forsworn. It seemed to have become vegetable; to have degenerated in that rank, sunless air to lush lichen or spreading moss that grew in patches to the staircase and was viscid under the foot like organic matter. At each turn of the stairs were vacant niches in the wall. Perhaps plants had once been set within them. If so they had died in that foul and tainted air. It may be that statues of the saints had stood there, but it was not difficult to conceive that imps and devils had dragged them forth in the darkness and down to the unholy depths of some furnished pit below.

"This is the room," said the housekeeper, from her furry throat. "It's a nice room. It ain't often vacant. I had some most elegant people in it last summer—no trouble at all, and paid in advance to the minute. The water's at the end of the hall. Sprowls and Mooney kept it three months. They done a vaudeville sketch. Miss B'retta Sprowls—you may have heard of her—Oh, that was just the stage names—right there over the dresser is where

the marriage certificate hung, framed. The gas is here, and you see there is plenty of closet room. It's a room everybody likes. It never stays idle long."

"Do you have many theatrical people rooming here?" asked the young man.

"They comes and goes. A good proportion of my lodgers is connected with the theatres. Yes, sir, this is the theatrical district. Actor people never stays long anywhere. I get my share. Yes, they comes and they goes."

He engaged the room, paying for a week in advance. He was tired, he said, and would take possession at once. He counted out the money. The room had been made ready, she said, even to towels and water. As the housekeeper moved away he put, for the thousandth time, the question that he carried at the end of his tongue.

"A young girl—Miss Vashner—Miss Eloise Vashner—do you remember such a one among your lodgers? She would be singing on the stage, most likely. A fair girl, of medium height and slender, with reddish, gold hair and a dark mole near her left eyebrow."

"No, I don't remember the name. Them stage people has names they changes as often as their rooms. They comes and they goes. No, I don't call that one to mind."

No. Always no. Five months of ceaseless interrogation and the inevitable negative. So much time spent by day in questioning managers, agents, schools and choruses; by night among the audiences of theatres from all-star casts down to music halls so low that he dreaded to find what he most hoped for. He who had loved her best had tried to find her. He was sure that since her disappearance from home this great, water-girt city held her somewhere, but it was like a monstrous quicksand, shifting its particles constantly, with no foundation, its upper granules of to-day buried to-morrow in ooze and slime.

The furnished room received its latest guest with a first glow of pseudo-hospitality, a hectic, haggard, perfunctory welcome like the specious smile of a demirep. The sophistical comfort came in reflected gleams from the decayed furniture, the ragged brocade upholstery of a couch and two chairs, a foot-wide cheap pier glass between two windows, from one or two gilt picture frames and a brass bedstead in a corner.

The guest reclined, inert, upon a chair, while the room,

---

2 *lares et penates*, Roman household gods • 3 *vine . . . fig tree*, symbols of the householder in the Old Testament. Compare I Kings 4:25: ". . . every man under his vine and under his fig tree . . ."

confused in speech as though it were an apartment in Babel, tried to discourse to him of its diverse tenantry.

A polychromatic rug like some brilliant-flowered rectangular, tropical islet lay surrounded by a billowy sea of soiled matting. Upon the gray-papered wall were those pictures that pursue the homeless one from house to house—The Huguenot Lovers, The First Quarrel, The Wedding Breakfast, Psyche at the Fountain. The mantel's chastely severe outline was ingloriously veiled behind some pert drapery drawn rakishly askew like the sashes of the Amazonian ballet. Upon it were some desolate flotsam cast aside by the room's marooned when a lucky sail had borne them to a fresh port—a trifling vase or two, pictures of actresses, a medicine bottle, some stray cards out of a deck.

One by one, as the characters of a cryptograph become explicit, the little signs left by the furnished room's procession of guests developed a significance. The threadbare space in the rug in front of the dresser told that lovely woman had marched in the throng. Tiny finger prints on the wall spoke of little prisoners trying to feel their way to sun and air. A splattered stain, raying like the shadow of a bursting bomb, witnessed where a hurled glass or bottle had splintered with its contents against the wall. Across the pier glass had been scrawled with a diamond in staggering letters the name "Marie." It seemed that the succession of dwellers in the furnished room had turned in fury—perhaps tempted beyond forbearance by its garish coldness—and wreaked upon it their passions. The furniture was chipped and bruised; the couch, distorted by bursting springs, seemed a horrible monster that had been slain during the stress of some grotesque convulsion. Some more potent upheaval had cloven a great slice from the marble mantel. Each plank in the floor owned its particular cant and shriek as from a separate and individual agony. It seemed incredible that all this malice and injury had been wrought upon the room by those who had called it for a time their home; and yet it may have been the cheated home instinct surviving blindly, the resentful rage at false household gods that had kindled their wrath. A hut that is our own we can sweep and adorn and cherish.

The young tenant in the chair allowed these thoughts to file, softshod, through his mind, while there drifted into the room furnished sounds and furnished scents. He heard in one room a tittering and incontinent, slack laughter; in others the monologue of a scold, the rattling of dice, a lullaby, and one crying dully; above him a banjo tinkled with spirit. Doors banged somewhere; the elevated trains roared intermittently; a cat yowled miserably upon a back fence. And he breathed the breath of the house—a dank savour rather than a smell —a cold, musty effluvium as from underground vault mingled with the reeking exhalations of linoleum and mildewed and rotten woodwork.

Then suddenly, as he rested there, the room was filled with the strong, sweet odour of mignonette. It came as upon a single buffet of wind with such sureness and fragrance and emphasis that it almost seemed a living visitant. And the man cried aloud: "What, dear?" as if he had been called, and sprang up and faced about. The rich odour clung to him and wrapped him around. He reached out his arms for it, all his senses for the time confused and commingled. How could one be peremptorily called by an odour? Surely it must have been a sound. But, was it not the odour that had touched, that had caressed him?

"She has been in this room," he cried, and he sprang to wrest from it a token, for he knew he would recognize the smallest thing that had belonged to her or that she had touched. This enveloping scent of mignonette, the odour that she had loved and made her own—whence came it?

The room had been but carelessly set in order. Scattered upon the flimsy dresser scarf were half a dozen hairpins—those discreet, indistinguishable friends of womankind, feminine of gender, infinite of mood, and uncommunicative of tense. These he ignored, conscious of their triumphant lack of identity. Ransacking the drawers of the dresser he came upon a discarded, tiny, ragged handkerchief. He pressed it to his face. It was racy and insolent with heliotrope; he hurled it to the floor. In another drawer he found odd buttons, a theatre programme, a pawnbroker's card, two lost marshmallows, a book on the divination of dreams. In the last was a woman's black satin hair-bow, which halted him, poised between ice and fire. But the black satin hair-bow also is femininity's demure, impersonal, common ornament, and tells no tales.

---

2 Babel, a reference to the confusion of languages at the tower of Babel, described in Genesis 11:1-9

And then he traversed the room like a hound on the scent, skimming the walls, considering the corners of the bulging matting on his hands and knees, rummaging mantel and tables, the curtains and hangings, the drunken cabinet in the corner, for a visible sign, unable to perceive that she was there beside, around, against, within, above him, clinging to him, wooing him, calling him so poignantly through the finer senses that even his grosser ones became cognisant of the call. Once again he answered loudly: "Yes, dear!" and turned, wild-eyed, to gaze on vacancy, for he could not yet discern form and colour and love and outstretched arms in the odour of mignonette. Oh, God! whence that odour, and since when have odours had a voice to call? Thus he groped.

He burrowed in crevices and corners, and found corks and cigarettes. These he passed in passive contempt. But once he found in a fold of the matting a half-smoked cigar, and this he ground beneath his heel with a green and trenchant oath. He sifted the room from end to end. He found dreary and ignoble small records of many a peripatetic tenant; but of her whom he sought, and who may have lodged there, and whose spirit seemed to hover there, he found no trace.

And then he thought of the housekeeper.

He ran from the haunted room downstairs and to a door that showed a crack of light. She came out to his knock. He smothered his excitement as best he could.

"Will you tell me, madam," he besought her, "who occupied the room I have before I came?"

"Yes, sir. I can tell you again. 'Twas Sprowls and Mooney, as I said. Miss B'retta Sprowls it was in the theatres, but Missis Mooney she was. My house is well known for respectability. The marriage certificate hung, framed, on a nail over——"

"What kind of a lady was Miss Sprowls—in looks, I mean?"

"Why, black-haired, sir, short, and stout, with a comical face. They left a week ago Tuesday."

"And before they occupied it?"

"Why, there was a single gentleman connected with the draying business. He left owing me a week. Before him was Missis Crowder and her two children, that stayed four months; and back of them was old Mr. Doyle, whose sons paid for him. He kept the room six months. That goes back a year, sir, and further I do not remember."

He thanked her and crept back to his room. The room

was dead. The essence that had vivified it was gone. The perfume of mignonette had departed. In its place was the old, stale odour of mouldy house furniture, of atmosphere in storage.

The ebbing of his hope drained his faith. He sat staring at the yellow, singing gaslight. Soon he walked to the bed and began to tear the sheets into strips. With the blade of his knife he drove them tightly into every crevice around windows and door. When all was snug and taut he turned out the light, turned the gas full on again, and laid himself gratefully upon the bed.

. . . . . .

It was Mrs. McCool's night to go with the can for beer. So she fetched it and sat with Mrs. Purdy in one of those subterranean retreats where housekeepers foregather and the worm dieth seldom.

"I rented out my third floor, back, this evening," said Mrs. Purdy across a fine circle of foam. "A young man took it. He went up to bed two hours ago."

"Now, did ye, Mrs. Purdy, ma'am?" said Mrs. McCool, with intense admiration. "You do be a wonder for rentin' rooms of that kind. And did ye tell him, then?" she concluded in a husky whisper, laden with mystery.

"Rooms," said Mrs. Purdy, in her furriest tones, "are furnished for to rent. I did not tell him, Mrs. McCool."

"'Tis right ye are, ma'am; 'tis by renting rooms we kape alive. Ye have the rale sense for business, ma'am. There be many people will rayjict the rentin' of a room if they be tould a suicide has been after dyin' in the bed of it."

"As you say, we has our living to be making," remarked Mrs. Purdy.

"Yis, ma'am; 'tis true. 'Tis just one wake ago this day I helped ye lay out the third floor, back. A pretty slip of a colleen she was to be killin' herself wid the gas— a swate little face she had, Mrs. Purdy, ma'am."

"She'd a-been called handsome, as you say," said Mrs. Purdy, assenting but critical, "but for that mole she had a-growin' by her left eyebrow. Do fill up your glass again, Mrs. McCool."

1909

---

21 **peripatetic**, walking about, itinerant • 61 **worm dieth seldom**, a humorous adaptation of Mark 9:44: "Where their worm dieth not, and the fire is not quenched." The Biblical worm of remorse becomes a symbol of thirst which is seldom "quenched"

BROOKLYN ACADEMY OF MUSIC, FEB. 7th

*Tickets at 244 Fulton St. and
172 Montague St.*

Samuel L. Clemens
(Mark Twain)

1835 · 1910

Perhaps the happiest circumstance in Samuel Langhorne Clemens' life, as far as rich material for literature was concerned, was that he spent his boyhood years in Hannibal, Missouri. Just about in the center of the United States, this little town had the mile-wide Mississippi rolling before it, and on the other sides were countryside, prairie, and forest. The river, the farm, and the out-of-doors of his boyhood were part and parcel not only of Clemens' life but also of his great books. At sixty-two he wrote: "I can call back the solemn twilight and the mystery of the deep woods, the earthy smells, the faint odors of the wild flowers, the sheen of rain-washed foliage . . . the far-off hammering of woodpeckers . . . in the remoteness of the forest . . . I can call it all back and make it as real as it ever was, and as blessed. I can call back the prairie and its loneliness and peace, and a vast hawk hanging motionless in the sky."

He could call back such memories of his boyhood, and he could set them down with gusto and with affection in his best books. But, as he said, "if I confine myself to boy life at times, it is because that life had a peculiar charm for me, and not because I was unfamiliar with other phases of life." A life full of wide experience preceded and included his career as an author. In turn a printer's devil, journeyman printer, steamboat pilot, soldier, miner, newspaper reporter, traveling correspondent, lecturer, author, editor, and publisher, he had enough "careers" to give several authors materials for books, and each pursuit contributed to his understanding of human nature.

Illustration: advertisement of a lecture given about 1869 by Mark Twain

Clemens became a printer's apprentice during his boyhood in Hannibal. Having learned to set type, he wandered eastward as far as New York, picking up printing jobs in one city after another. Then, back in the Middle West in the fifties, he learned the pilot's trade and spent some of his happiest years steering boats up and down the Mississippi. (When, later, he adopted a pseudonym, it was an expression used by steamboatmen when testing the depth of the channel.) The job of piloting lasted through the boom days of river trade which were cut off by the Civil War. In 1861, after brief service in the Confederate army, he went out to the Far West. There, he took some fliers in mining stock, did some prospecting, and finally got into journalism of the masculine humorous sort which flourished in the Far West.

The journalistic work, in Nevada and California, launched him on his career as a humorist. Pieces he had written in the Far West were printed in the East, and one of his tales, "The Celebrated Jumping Frog of Calaveras County," first heard in a mining camp, won national acclaim in 1865. Travel letters about a trip to Europe and the Holy Land, published in newspapers in 1867 and put into book form as *The Innocents Abroad* (1869), established him as an outstandingly popular humorist. *Roughing It* (1872), *The Gilded Age* (in collaboration with Charles Dudley Warner, 1873), *The Adventures of Tom Sawyer* (1876), *A Tramp Abroad* (1880), *The Prince and the Pauper* (1882), *Life on the Mississippi* (1883), *The Adventures of Huckleberry Finn* (1884), and *A Connecticut Yankee in King Arthur's Court* (1889) were all widely purchased. The success of various books made work other than writing unnecessary, but Clemens, a son of the boomtime frontier who had a love for speculation and a childlike reverence for wealth, tried to swell a generous income by making investments. Having invested some of his royalties from his first popular book in a Buffalo newspaper, Clemens was an editor for a time. He financed many inventions and get-rich schemes, and eventually set up as a large-scale publisher of books —his own as well as those by other authors.

In Buffalo and Hartford, abroad and in New York, he lived lavishly on his excellent income. His Hartford mansion, for instance, was a massive, showy structure incorporating a number of costly features, and his monthly expenditures for living and entertaining were huge. In 1893, when the author-businessman was fifty-eight, some important financial investments proved unwise, his publishing house failed, and he faced financial ruin. Refusing to accept bankruptcy, he paid off his debts dollar for dollar, earning enough to do so by making a lecture trip around the world and by publishing *Tom Sawyer Abroad* and *Pudd'nhead Wilson* (1894), *Joan of Arc* (1896), and *Following the Equator* (1897). His last great books, published posthumously, were *The Mysterious Stranger* (1916), and his *Autobiography* (1924, 1940).

In all of Twain's writings, his personality was an important element. Those who knew the humorist best emphasize the fact that his character had extraordinarily varied facets. Olivia Langdon, whom he married in 1870, loved him not only for his chivalry and his tenderness, but also for his tendency, freely indulged, to tease her and the children unmercifully. Close associates saw him, on alternate visits, as an outrageous prankster and a gloomy pessimist. Surprisingly, his intimate friend, Howells, thought that a certain delicacy was an intrinsic trait. "Among the half-dozen . . . personalities that each of us becomes," Howells wrote, "I should say that Clemens's central and final personality was something exquisite. His casual acquaintances might know him, perhaps, from his fierce intensity, his wild pleasure in shocking people . . . as anything but exquisite, and yet that was what in the last analysis he was. . . . One could not know him well without realizing him the most serious, the most humane, the most conscientious of men."

The first works by Twain to attract national attention—"The Jumping Frog" and *Innocents Abroad*—represented two aspects of his work. The former was a tall tale much like those Sam Clemens, as a boyish printer's devil, had seen in newspapers or had heard told in yarnspinning sessions. Its affiliations with "The Big Bear" or "A Coon Hunt in a Fency Country" are obvious. A large share of *Innocents Abroad* was popular humor similar, in important ways, to the kind of humor which had been flourishing when Clemens had set up as a humorist—the humor of such professional "Funny Men" as Artemus Ward and Josh Billings. After he had hit upon his mature technique, the two methods—that of the old Southwestern humorists and that of the funny men—were intermingled in most of his writings. The travel books, for example, increasingly gained in variety and interest by alternating literary-comedian material with anecdotes.

When, in his fiction, the training Twain had had as a professional humorist caused him to mingle buffoonery and burlesque with materials inhospitable to the broadest comedy, his writings tended to suffer from unevenness of tone. His masterpiece, *Huckleberry Finn,* for instance, particularly in the chapters concerning the rescue of Jim, contained passages of broad humor and parody which frequently clashed in tone with the style of the long oral tale used throughout the volume. But this book, like others which showed him at his best, triumphed over such faults. It triumphed, for one thing, because, taking a hint from local colorists of the day, and recalling his varied past, Clemens freighted his pages with vivid regional details which were instinct with life. Moreover, although he was as contemptuous of poetry as Shakespeare's rough soldier Hotspur, like Hotspur, Clemens was an interesting combination of masculinity and poetic sensibility, and his style revealed both qualities. More than any other classic fictionist he wrote the American language, but he also manifested a knack —comparable to the skill of the best poets— for finding the best words to represent scenes, actions, and emotions. In addition, he had genius for creating memorable characters like Colonel Sellers, Tom Sawyer, Huck, and Huck's Pappy, and for breathing the breath of life into them.

Clemens thought that another thing that helped him

survive other humorists was the philosophy he expressed in his writings. "Philosophy" is too highfalutin a word, perhaps, for the notions, hunches, and prejudices which this emotional and often cantankerous individual expressed in his books. Yet the attitudes of this highly American author give his writings an element of interest over and above that supplied by their artistry and the peculiar quirks of his own personality. He reveals the nostalgia for the old America, the distrust of religion, the zeal for political and social reform, and the pessimism which were being voiced by other authors, particularly in the period from 1865 to 1900.

All these qualities have helped Twain overcome the handicap any American author must overcome if he starts writing what his countrymen are likely to call "mere humor." Although critics still now and then reach up to pat him condescendingly on the head, it now seems reasonably certain that Mark Twain will grow in stature with the passage of time. Increasingly, Clemens' countrymen appreciate the charm of his personality, the breadth and depth of his richly native experiences, the unostentatious artistry revealed by his best writings. More and more, Americans are agreeing with Howells' estimate of him as "sole and incomparable, the Lincoln of our literature."

Writings of Mark Twain, 25 vols., New York, 1904-1907 • A. B. Paine, *Mark Twain: A Biography,* 3 vols., New York, 1912 • W. D. Howells, *My Mark Twain,* New York, 1910 • Bernard De Voto, **Mark Twain's America,** Boston, 1932 • Dixon Wecter, **Sam Clemens of Hannibal,** Boston, 1952

The Celebrated Jumping Frog of Calaveras County

a tall tale —

On December 4, 1864, Clemens arrived for a visit at Jim Gillis' cabin on Jackass Hill, in the Tuolumne district. On pleasant days, Clemens worked at pocket mining. On rainy days the author, Gillis, and neighboring miners sat around the stove in the dilapidated tavern at Angel's Camp and told stories. One afternoon Ben Coon, a former Illinois river pilot, spun a yarn which had been going the

rounds of the camps and the newspapers—the one about the jumping frog.

In time the humorist told the story to his friend, Artemus Ward. Ward, liking it, asked him to write it out for use in a forthcoming book, **Artemus Ward's Travels.** Arriving too late for inclusion in the volume, it was printed, instead, in the **Saturday Press,** November 18, 1865. The piece, an immediate hit, was reprinted in newspapers throughout the country.

The teller of the tale at Angel's Camp, Clemens said later, "was entirely serious, for he was dealing with what for him were austere facts; . . . he saw no humor in the tale, neither did his listeners; neither he nor they ever smiled or laughed; in my time I have not attended a more solemn conference." In writing his own version,

1. distrust of religion
2. Zeal for reform — Polit. & social
3. Pessimism

Clemens perhaps tried to reproduce the ludicrous elements in this scene by having humorless Simon Wheeler tell his comic narrative to an equally humorless, painfully bored listener. Based on an oral narrative, the tale in many ways—especially in its "humanization" of animals—shows its relationship to the frontier humor which the humorist had enjoyed as a boy.

In compliance with the request of a friend of mine, who wrote me from the East, I called on good-natured, garrulous old Simon Wheeler, and inquired after my friend's friend, *Leonidas W. Smiley*, as requested to do, and I hereunto append the result. I have a lurking suspicion that *Leonidas W.* Smiley is a myth; that my friend never knew such a personage; and that he only conjectured that, if I asked old Wheeler about him, it would remind him of his infamous *Jim* Smiley, and
10 he would go to work and bore me nearly to death with some exasperating reminiscence of him as long and tedious as it should be useless to me. If that was the design, it succeeded.

I found Simon Wheeler dozing comfortably by the bar-room stove of the dilapidated tavern in the decayed mining camp of Angel's, and I noticed that he was fat and bald-headed, and had an expression of winning gentleness and simplicity upon his tranquil countenance. He roused up and gave me good-day. I told him a friend
20 of mine had commissioned me to make some inquiries about a cherished companion of his boyhood named *Leonidas W. Smiley—Rev. Leonidas W. Smiley—a* young minister of the Gospel, who he had heard was at one time a resident of Angel's Camp. I added that, if Mr. Wheeler could tell me anything about this Rev. Leonidas W. Smiley, I would feel under many obligations to him.

Simon Wheeler backed me into a corner and blockaded me there with his chair, and then sat me down
30 and reeled off the monotonous narrative which follows this paragraph. He never smiled, he never frowned, he never changed his voice from the gentle-flowing key to which he tuned the initial sentence, he never betrayed the slightest suspicion of enthusiasm; but all through the interminable narrative there ran a vein of impressive earnestness and sincerity, which showed me plainly that, so far from his imagining that there was anything

ridiculous or funny about his story, he regarded it as a really important matter, and admired its two heroes as men of transcendent genius in *finesse*. I let him go on 40 in his own way, and never interrupted him once:

"Rev. Leonidas W. H'm, Reverend Le—well, there was a feller here once by the name of *Jim* Smiley, in the winter of '49—or may be it was the spring of '50— I don't recollect exactly, somehow, though what makes me think it was one or the other is because I remember the big flume wasn't finished when he first came to the camp; but any way, he was the curiosest man about always betting on any thing that turned up you ever see, if he could get any body to bet on the other side; 50 and if he couldn't, he'd change sides. Any way that suited the other man would suit him—any way just so's he got a bet, *he* was satisfied. But still he was lucky, un- common lucky; he most always come out winner. He was always ready and laying for a chance; there couldn't be no solit'ry thing mentioned but that feller'd offer to bet on it, and take any side you please, as I was just tell- ing you. If there was a horse-race, you'd find him flush, or you'd find him busted at the end of it; if there was a dog-fight, he'd bet on it; if there was a cat-fight, he'd 60 bet on it; if there was a chicken-fight, he'd bet on it; why, if there was two birds setting on a fence, he would bet you which one would fly first; or if there was a camp-meeting, he would be there reg'lar, to bet on Parson Walker, which he judged to be the best exhorter about there, and so he was, too, and a good man. If he even seen a straddle-bug start to go anywheres, he would bet you how long it would take him to get wherever he was going to, and if you took him up, he would foller that straddle-bug to Mexico but what he would find out 70 where he was bound for and how long he was on the road. Lots of the boys here has seen that Smiley, and can tell you about him. Why, it never made no differ- ence to *him*—he would bet on *any* thing—the dangdest feller. Parson Walker's wife laid very sick once, for a good while, and it seemed as if they warn't going to save her; but one morning he come in, and Smiley asked how she was, and he said she was considerable better— thank the Lord for his inf'nite mercy—and coming on so smart that, with the blessing of Prov'dence, she'd 80 get well yet; and Smiley, before he thought, says, "Well, I'll resk two-and-a-half that she don't, anyway."

Thish-yer Smiley had a mare—the boys called her the fifteen-minute nag, but that was only in fun, you

The Celebrated Jumping Frog 407

know, because, of course, she was faster than that—and he used to win money on that horse, for all she was so slow and always had the asthma, or the distemper, or the consumption, or something of that kind. They used to give her two or three hundred yards start, and then pass her under way; but always at the fag-end of the race she'd get excited and desperate-like, and come cavorting and straddling up, and scattering her legs around limber, sometimes in the air, and sometimes out to one side amongst the fences, and kicking up m-o-r-e dust, and raising m-o-r-e racket with her coughing and sneezing and blowing her nose—and always fetch up at the stand just about a neck ahead, as near as you could cipher it down.

And he had a little small bull pup, that to look at him you'd think he wa'nt worth a cent, but to set around and look ornery, and lay for a chance to steal something. But as soon as money was up on him, he was a different dog; his under-jaw'd begin to stick out like the fo'castle of a steamboat, and his teeth would uncover, and shine savage like the furnaces. And a dog might tackle him, and bully-rag him, and bite him, and throw him over his shoulder two or three times, and Andrew Jackson—which was the name of the pup—Andrew Jackson would never let on but what *he* was satisfied, and hadn't expected nothing else—and the bets being doubled and doubled on the other side all the time, till the money was all up; and then all of a sudden he would grab that other dog jest by the j'int of his hind leg and freeze to it—not chaw, you understand, but only jest grip and hang on till they throwed up the sponge, if it was a year. Smiley always come out winner on that pup, till he harnessed a dog once that didn't have no hind legs, because they'd been sawed off by a circular saw, and when the thing had gone along far enough, and the money was all up, and he come to make a snatch for his pet holt, he saw in a minute how he'd been imposed on, and how the other dog had him in the door, so to speak, and he 'peared surprised, and then he looked sorter discouraged-like, and didn't try no more to win the fight, and so he got shucked out bad. He give Smiley a look, as much as to say his heart was broke, and it was *his* fault, for putting up a dog that hadn't no hind legs for him to take holt of, which was his main dependence in a fight, and then he limped off a piece and laid down and died. It was a good pup, was that Andrew Jackson, and would have made a name

for hisself if he'd lived, for the stuff was in him, and he had genius—I know it, because he hadn't had no opportunities to speak of, and it don't stand to reason that a dog could make such a fight as he could under them circumstances, if he hadn't no talent. It always makes me feel sorry when I think of that last fight of his'n, and the way it turned out.

Well, thish-yer Smiley had rat-tarriers, and chicken cocks, and tom-cats, and all them kind of things, till you couldn't rest, and you couldn't fetch nothing for him to bet on but he'd match you. He ketched a frog one day, and took him home, and said he calk'lated to edercate him; and so he never done nothing for three months but set in his back yard and learn that frog to jump. And you bet he *did* learn him, too. He'd give him a little punch behind, and the next minute you'd see that frog whirling in the air like a doughnut—see him turn one summerset, or may be a couple, if he got a good start, and come down flat-footed and all right, like a cat. He got him up so in the matter of catching flies, and kept him in practice so constant, that he'd nail a fly every time as far as he could see him. Smiley said all a frog wanted was education, and he could do most anything—and I believe him. Why, I've seen him set Dan'l Webster down here on this floor—Dan'l Webster was the name of the frog—and sing out, "Flies, Dan'l, flies!" and quicker'n you could wink, he'd spring straight up, and snake a fly off'n the counter there, and flop down on the floor again as solid as a gob of mud, and fall to scratching the side of his head with his hind foot as indifferent as if he hadn't no idea he'd been doin' any more'n any frog might do. You never see a frog so modest and straightfor'ard as he was, for all he was so gifted. And when it come to fair and square jumping on a dead level, he could get over more ground at one straddle than any animal of his breed you ever see. Jumping on a dead level was his strong suit, you understand; and when it come to that, Smiley would ante up money on him as long as he had a red. Smiley was monstrous proud of his frog, and well he might be, for fellers that had traveled and been everywheres, all said he laid over any frog that ever *they* see.

Well, Smiley kept the beast in a little lattice box, and he used to fetch him down town sometimes and lay for a bet. One day a feller—a stranger in the camp, he was—come across him with his box, and says:

"What might it be that you've got in the box?"

And Smiley says, sorter indifferent like, "It might be a parrot, or it might be a canary, may be, but it ain't—it's only just a frog."

And the feller took it, and looked at it careful, and turned it round this way and that, and says, "H'm—so 'tis. Well, what's *he* good for?"

"Well," Smiley says, easy and careless, "he's good enough for *one* thing, I should judge—he can outjump ary frog in Calaveras county."

The feller took the box again, and took another long, particular look, and give it back to Smiley, and says, very deliberate, "Well, I don't see no p'ints about that frog that's any better'n any other frog."

"May be you don't," Smiley says. "May be you understand frogs, and maybe you don't understand 'em; may be you've had experience, and may be you ain't only a amature, as it were. Anyways I've got *my* opinion, and I'll risk forty dollars he can outjump any frog in Calaveras county."

And the feller studied a minute, and then says, kinder sad like, "Well, I'm only a stranger here, and I ain't got no frog; but if I had a frog, I'd bet you."

And then Smiley says, "That's all right—that's all right—if you'll hold my box a minute, I'll go and get you a frog." And so the feller took the box, and put up his forty dollars along with Smiley's, and set down to wait.

So he set there a good while thinking and thinking to hisself, and then he got the frog out and prized his mouth open and took a teaspoon and filled him full of quail shot—filled him pretty near up to his chin—and set him on the floor. Smiley he went to the swamp and slopped around in the mud for a long time, and finally he ketched a frog, and fetched him in, and give him to this feller, and says:

"Now, if you're ready, set him alongside of Dan'l, with his fore-paws just even with Dan'l, and I'll give the word." Then he says, "One—two—three—jump!" and him and the feller touched up the frogs from behind, and the new frog hopped off, but Dan'l give a heave, and hysted up his shoulders—so—like a Frenchman, but it wan't no use—he couldn't budge; he was planted as solid as an anvil, and he couldn't no more stir than if he was anchored out. Smiley was a good deal surprised, and he was disgusted too, but he didn't have no idea what the matter was, of course.

The feller took the money and started away; and when

" '—he 'pears to look mighty baggy . . .' "—illustration by Kemble for Mark Twain's Library of Wit and Humor

he was going out at the door, he sorter jerked his thumb over his shoulders—this way—at Dan'l, and says again, very deliberate, "Well, *I* don't see no p'ints about that frog that's any better'n any other frog."

Smiley he stood scratching his head and looking down at Dan'l a long time, and at last he says, "I do wonder what in the nation that frog throw'd off for—I wonder if there ain't something the matter with him—he 'pears to look mighty baggy, somehow." And he ketched Dan'l by the nap of the neck, and lifted him up and says, "Why, blame my cats, if he don't weigh five pound!" and turned him upside down, and he belched out a double handful of shot. And then he see how it was, and he was the maddest man—he set the frog down and took out after that feller, but he never ketched him. And—

(Here Simon Wheeler heard his name called from the front yard, and got up to see what was wanted.) And turning to me as he moved away, he said: "Just set where you are, stranger, and rest easy—I ain't going to be gone a second."

But, by your leave, I did not think that a continuation of the history of the enterprising vagabond *Jim* Smiley would be likely to afford me much information concerning the *Rev. Leonidas W.* Smiley, and so I started away.

At the door I met the sociable Wheeler returning, and he buttonholed me and recommenced:

"Well, thish-yer Smiley had a yeller one-eyed cow that didn't have no tail, only jest a short stump like a bannanner, and—"

"Oh! hang Smiley and his afflicted cow!" I muttered, good-naturedly, and bidding the old gentleman good-day, I departed.

1865

The Celebrated Jumping Frog 409

The Innocents Abroad

With a band of nineteenth-century pilgrims, Clemens made a trip abroad between June 8 and November 19, 1867. During the journey he sent accounts from various stopping places to some American newspapers. These accounts, which had been well liked by readers, were revised and published in the book The Innocents Abroad in 1869. Within a year, some sixty-seven thousand copies were sold. The humorist's fame was established.

The book, as its Preface proclaimed, had as its purpose "to suggest to the reader how he would be likely to see Europe and the East if he looked at them with his own eyes instead of the eyes of those who traveled in those countries before him." Previous travelers, guidebooks in hand, had been overawed by the antiquity and the romance of the Old World; this author was determined to judge for himself. The two passages which follow were among the most admired in the book. In each the naïve tourists were satirized, but two distinctly different methods were used. In "The Old Masters," perhaps the most famous chapter in the volume, Clemens wrote as a sensible man, sickened by the ecstasies and idiocies of tourists who depend upon guidebooks to suggest how they shall react to works of art. The way Clemens built up his devastating attack on "The Last Supper," after an ingratiating start, offers an interesting study in rhetorical method. In "The Tomb of Adam," he wrote as if he himself were a sentimental, credulous traveler, believing everything he was told—no matter how preposterous—and trying to pump up appropriate emotions for the occasion. (The titles have been inserted by the editors.)

Chapter XIX

[THE OLD MASTERS]

Here, in Milan, in an ancient tumble-down ruin of a church, is the mournful wreck of the most celebrated painting in the world—"The Last Supper," by Leonardo

da Vinci. We are not infallible judges of pictures, but of course we went there to see this wonderful painting, once so beautiful, always so worshipped by masters in art, and forever to be famous in song and story. And the first thing that occurred was the infliction on us of a placard fairly reeking with wretched English. Take a morsel of it: 10

"Bartholomew (that is the first figure on the left hand side at the spectator), uncertain and doubtful about what he thinks to have heard, and upon which he wants to be assured by himself at Christ and by no others."

Good, isn't it? And then Peter is described as "argumenting in a threatening and angrily condition at Judas Iscariot."

This paragraph recalls the picture. "The Last Supper" is painted on the dilapidated wall of what was a little 20 chapel attached to the main church in ancient times, I suppose. It is battered and scarred in every direction, and stained and discolored by time, and Napoleon's horses kicked the legs off most the disciples when they (the horses, not the disciples,) were stabled there more than a half century ago.

I recognized the old picture in a moment—the Saviour with bowed head seated at the centre of a long, rough table with scattering fruits and dishes upon it, and six disciples on either side in their long robes, talking to 30 each other—the picture from which all engravings and all copies have been made for three centuries. Perhaps no living man has ever known an attempt to paint the Lord's Supper differently. The world seems to have become settled in the belief, long ago, that it is not possible for human genius to outdo this creation of Da Vinci's. I suppose painters will go on copying it as long as any of the original is left visible to the eye. There were a dozen easels in the room, and as many artists transferring the great picture to their canvases. Fifty proofs of 40 steel engravings and lithographs were scattered around, too. And as usual, I could not help noticing how superior the copies were to the original, that is, to my inexperienced eye. Wherever you find a Raphael, a Rubens, a Michael Angelo, a Caracci, or a Da Vinci (and we see them every day,) you find artists copying them, and the copies are always the handsomest. Maybe the originals were handsome when they were new, but they are not now.

This picture is about thirty feet long, and ten or twelve high, I should think, and the figures are at least life size. It is one of the largest paintings in Europe.

The colors are dimmed with age; the countenances are scaled and marred, and nearly all expression is gone from them; the hair is a dead blur upon the wall, and there is no life in the eyes. Only the attitudes are certain.

People come here from all parts of the world, and glorify this masterpiece. They stand entranced before it 10 with bated breath and parted lips, and when they speak, it is only in the catchy ejaculations of rapture:

"O, wonderful!"

"Such expression!"

"Such grace of attitude!"

"Such dignity!"

"Such faultless drawing!"

"Such matchless coloring!"

"Such feeling!"

"What delicacy of touch!"

20 "What sublimity of conception!"

"A vision! A vision!"

satire

I only envy those people; I envy them their honest admiration, if it be honest—their delight, if they feel delight. I harbor no animosity toward any of them. But at the same time the thought *will* intrude itself upon me, how can they see what is not visible? What would you think of a man who looked at some decayed, blind, toothless, pock-marked Cleopatra, and said: "What matchless beauty! What soul! What expression!" What would you 30 think of a man who gazed upon a dingy, foggy sunset, and said: "What sublimity! What feeling! What richness of coloring!" What would you think of a man who stared in ecstasy upon a desert of stumps and said: "Oh, my soul, my beating heart, what a noble forest is here!"

You would think that those men had an astonishing talent for seeing things that had already passed away. It was what I thought when I stood before the "Last Supper" and heard men apostrophizing wonders, and 40 beauties and perfections which had faded out of the picture and gone, a hundred years before they were born. We can imagine the beauty that was once in an aged face; we can imagine the forest if we see the stumps; but we can not absolutely *see* these things when they are not there. I am willing to believe that the eye of the practiced artist can rest upon the "Last Supper"

and renew a lustre where only a hint of it is left, supply a tint that has faded away, restore an expression that is gone; patch, and color, and add, to the dull canvas until at last its figures shall stand before him aglow with the 50 life, the feelings, the freshness, yea, with all the noble beauty that was theirs when first they came from the hand of the master. But *I* can not work this miracle. Can those other uninspired visitors do it, or do they only happily imagine they do?

After reading so much about it, I am satisfied that the "Last Supper" was a very miracle of art once. But it was three hundred years ago.

It vexes me to hear people talk so glibly of "feeling," "expression," "tone," and those other easily acquired and 60 inexpensive technicalities of art that make such a fine show in conversations concerning pictures. There is not one man in seventy-five hundred that can tell what a pictured face is intended to express. There is not one man in five hundred that can go into a court-room and be sure that he will not mistake some harmless innocent of a juryman for the black-hearted assassin on trial. Yet such people talk of "character" and presume to interpret "expression" in pictures. There is an old story that Matthews, the actor, was once lauding the ability of the 70 human face to express the passions and emotions hidden in the breast. He said the countenance could disclose what was passing in the heart plainer than the tongue could.

"Now," he said, "observe my face—what does it express?"

"Despair!"

"Bah, it expresses peaceful resignation! What does *this* express?"

"Rage!"

80 "Stuff! it means terror! This!"

"Imbecility!"

"Fool! It is smothered ferocity! Now *this!*"

"Joy!"

"Oh, perdition! *Any* ass can see it means insanity!"

Expression! People coolly pretend to read it who would think themselves presumptuous if they pretended to interpret the hieroglyphics on the obelisks of Luxor—yet they are fully as competent to do the one thing as the other. I have heard two very intelligent critics speak of 90 Murillo's Immaculate Conception (now in the museum at Seville) within the past few days. One said:

"Oh, the Virgin's face is full of the ecstasy of a joy that is complete—that leaves nothing more to be desired on earth!"

The other said:

"Ah, that wonderful face is so humble, so pleading—it says as plainly as words could say it: 'I fear; I tremble; I am unworthy. But Thy will be done; sustain Thou Thy servant!'"

The reader can see the picture in any drawing-room; it can be easily recognized; the Virgin (the only young and really beautiful Virgin that was ever painted by one of the old masters, some of us think,) stands in the crescent of the new moon, with a multitude of cherubs hovering about her, and more coming; her hands are crossed upon her breast, and upon her uplifted countenance falls a glory out of the heavens. The reader may amuse himself, if he chooses, in trying to determine which of these gentlemen read the Virgin's "expression" aright, or if either of them did it.

Any one who is acquainted with the old masters will comprehend how much the Last Supper is damaged when I say that the spectator can not really tell, now, whether the disciples are Hebrews or Italians. These ancient painters never succeeded in denationalizing themselves. The Italian artists painted Italian Virgins, the Dutch painted Dutch Virgins, the Virgins of the French painters were Frenchwomen—none of them ever put into the face of the Madonna that indescribable something which proclaims the Jewess, whether you find her in New York, in Constantinople, in Paris, Jerusalem, or in the Empire of Morocco. I saw in the Sandwich Islands, once, a picture, copied by a talented German artist from an engraving in one of the American illustrated papers. It was an allegory, representing Mr. Davis in the act of signing a secession act or some such document. Over him hovered the ghost of Washington in warning attitude, and in the background a troop of shadowy soldiers in Continental uniform were limping with shoeless, bandaged feet through a driving snow-storm. Valley Forge was suggested, of course. The copy seemed accurate, and yet there was a discrepancy somewhere. After a long examination I discovered what it was—the shadowy soldiers were all Germans! Jeff Davis was a German! Even the hovering ghost was a German ghost! The artist had unconsciously worked his nationality into the picture. To tell the truth, I am getting a little perplexed

about John the Baptist and his portraits. In France I finally grew reconciled to him as a Frenchman; here he is unquestionably an Italian. What next? Can it be possible that the painters make John the Baptist a Spaniard in Madrid and an Irishman in Dublin?

Chapter LIII

[THE TOMB OF ADAM]

The Greek Chapel is the most roomy, the richest and the showiest chapel in the Church of the Holy Sepulchre. Its altar, like that of all the Greek churches, is a lofty screen that extends clear across the chapel, and is gorgeous with gilding and pictures. The numerous lamps that hang before it are of gold and silver, and cost great sums.

But the feature of the place is a short column that rises from the middle of the marble pavement of the chapel, and marks the exact *centre of the earth.* The most reliable traditions tell us that this was known to be the earth's centre, ages ago, and that when Christ was upon earth he set all doubts upon the subject forever, by stating with his own lips that the tradition was correct. Remember, He said that that particular column stood upon the centre of the world. If the centre of the world changes, the column changes its position accordingly. This column has moved three different times, of its own accord. This is because, in great convulsions of nature, at three different times, masses of the earth—whole ranges of mountains, probably—have flown off into space, thus lessening the diameter of the earth, and changing the exact locality of its centre by a point or two. This is a very curious and interesting circumstance, and is a withering rebuke to those philosophers who would make us believe that it is not possible for any portion of the earth to fly off into space.

To satisfy himself that this spot was really the centre of the earth, a sceptic once paid well for the privilege of ascending to the dome of the church to see if the sun gave him a shadow at noon. He came down perfectly convinced. The day was very cloudy and the sun threw no shadows at all; but the man was satisfied that if the sun had come out and made shadows it could not have

---

34 **Mr. Davis,** Jefferson Davis (1808-1889), president of the Confederate States of America

made any for him. Proofs like these are not to be set aside by the idle tongues of cavilers. To such as are not bigoted, and are willing to be convinced, they carry a conviction that nothing can ever shake.

If even greater proofs than those I have mentioned are wanted, to satisfy the headstrong and the foolish that this is the genuine centre of the earth, they are here. The greatest of them lies in the fact that from under this very column was taken the *dust from which Adam was* 10 *made.* This can surely be regarded in the light of a settler. It is not likely that the original first man would have been made from an inferior quality of earth when it was entirely convenient to get first quality from the world's centre. This will strike any reflecting mind forcibly. That Adam was formed of dirt procured in this very spot is amply proven by the fact that in six thousand years no man has ever been able to prove that the dirt was *not* procured here whereof he was made.

It is a singular circumstance that right under the roof 20 of this same church, and not far away from that illustrious column, Adam himself, the father of the human race, lies buried. There is no question that he is actually buried in the grave which is pointed out as his—there can be none—because it has never yet been proven that that grave is not the grave in which he is buried.

The tomb of Adam! How touching it was, here in a land of strangers, far away from home, and friends, and all who cared for me, thus to discover the grave of a blood relation. The unerring instinct of nature thrilled its recognition. The fountain of my filial affection was 30 stirred to its profoundest depths, and I gave way to tumultuous emotion. I leaned upon a pillar and burst into tears. I deem it no shame to have wept over the grave of my poor dead relative. Let him who would sneer at my emotion close this volume here, for he will find little to his taste in my journeyings through Holy Land. Noble old man—he did not live to see me—he did not live to see his child. And I—I—alas, I did not live to see *him.* Weighed down by sorrow and disappointment, he died before I was born—six thousand brief summers 40 before I was born. But let us try to bear it with fortitude. Let us trust that he is better off, where he is. Let us take comfort in the thought that his loss is our eternal gain.

1869

---

33 **I deem it. . . .** Three chapters earlier, Clemens had quoted at length from a book by ''Wm. C. Grimes''—**Nomadic Life in Palestine,** ''the representative,'' he called it, ''of a class of Palestine books.'' Actually the book was W. C. Prime's **Tent Life in the Holy Land.** In one of the passages quoted, Prime had pointed out proudly how often he had wept. ''It is no shame,'' Prime had said, ''to have wept in Palestine. . . . Let him who would sneer at my emotion close this volume here, for he will find little to his taste in my journeyings through Holy Land''

From

shows how the author, by alternating exposition and description with humorous anecdotes, secured variety. The tall tales about the speed of the jackass rabbit and the appetite of the camel were vastly admired.

Roughing It

Chapter III

JACKASS RABBITS AND SAGEBRUSH

Published in 1871, **Roughing It,** for its subject matter, went back a few years in Clemens' life to the period when he had gone to the Far West. Informatively and amusingly, he recounted his journey across country and his Western adventures. Like **Innocents Abroad,** this volume was highly successful, its sales aggregating almost forty thousand copies in three months. The following chapter

About an hour and a half before daylight we were bowling along smoothly over the road—so smoothly that our cradle only rocked in a gentle, lulling way, that was gradually soothing us to sleep, and dulling our consciousness—when something gave away under us! We were dimly aware of it, but indifferent to it. The coach stopped. We heard the driver and conductor talking together outside, and rummaging for a lantern, and swearing because they could not find it—but we had no interest in whatever had happened, and it only added to our comfort to think of those people out there at work in the murky night, and we snug in our nest with the curtains drawn. But presently, by the sounds, there seemed to be an examination going on, and then the driver's voice said:

"By George, the thoroughbrace is broke!"

This startled me broad awake—as an undefined sense 10 of calamity is always apt to do. I said to myself: "Now, a thoroughbrace is probably part of a horse; and doubtless a vital part, too, from the dismay in the driver's voice. Leg, maybe—and yet how could he break his leg waltzing along such a road as this? No, it can't be his leg. That is impossible, unless he was reaching for the driver. Now, what can be the thorough-brace of a horse, I wonder? Well, whatever comes, I shall not air my ignorance in this crowd, anyway."

Just then the conductor's face appeared at a lifted 20 curtain, and his lantern glared in on us and our wall of mail matter. He said:

"Gents, you'll have to turn out a spell. Thorough-brace is broke."

We climbed out into a chill drizzle, and felt ever so homeless and dreary. When I found that the thing they called a "Thoroughbrace" was the massive combination of bolts and springs which the coach rocks itself in, I said to the driver:

"I never saw a thoroughbrace used up like that, 30 before, that I can remember. How did it happen?"

"Why, it happened by trying to make one coach carry three days' mail—that's how it happened," said he. "And right here is the very direction which is wrote on all the newspaper-bags which was to be put out for the Injuns for to keep 'em quiet. It's most uncommon lucky, becuz it's so nation dark I should 'a' gone by unbe-knowns if that air thoroughbrace hadn't broke."

I knew that he was in labor with another of those winks of his, though I could not see his face, because 40 he was bent down at work; and wishing him a safe delivery, I turned to and helped the rest get out the mail-sacks. It made a great pyramid by the roadside when it was all out. When they had mended the thoroughbrace we filled the two boots again, but put no mail on top, and only half as much inside as there was before. The conductor bent all the seats back down, and then filled the coach just half full of mail-bags from

end to end. We objected loudly to this, for it left us no seats. But the conductor was wiser than we, and said a bed was better than seats, and, moreover, this 50 plan would protect his thoroughbraces. We never wanted any seats after that. The lazy bed was in-finitely preferable. I had many an exciting day, subse-quently, lying on it reading the statutes and the diction-ary, and wondering how the characters would turn out.

The conductor said he would send back a guard from the next station to take charge of the abandoned mail-bags, and we drove on.

It was now just dawn; and as we stretched our cramped legs full length on the mail sacks, and gazed 60 out through the windows across the wide wastes of greensward clad in cool, powdery mist, to where there was an expectant look in the eastern horizon, our perfect enjoyment took the form of a tranquil and contented ecstasy. The stage whirled along at a spanking gait, the breeze flapping curtains and suspended coats in a most exhilarating way; the cradle swayed and swung luxuri-ously, the pattering of the horses' hoofs, the cracking of the driver's whip, and his "Hi-yi! g'lang!" were music; the spinning ground and the waltzing trees ap- 70 peared to give us a mute hurrah as we went by, and then slack up and look after us with interest, or envy, or something; and as we lay and smoked the pipe of peace and compared all this luxury with the years of tiresome city life that had gone before it, we felt that there was only one complete and satisfying happiness in the world, and we had found it.

After breakfast, at some station whose name I have forgotten, we three climbed up on the seat behind the driver, and let the conductor have our bed for a nap. 80 And by and by, when the sun made me drowsy, I lay down on my face on top of the coach, grasping the slender iron railing, and slept for an hour more. That will give one an appreciable idea of those matchless roads. Instinct will make a sleeping man grip a fast hold of the railing when the stage jolts, but when it only swings and sways, no grip is necessary. Overland drivers and conductors used to sit in their places and sleep thirty of forty minutes at a time, on good roads, while spinning along at the rate of eight or ten miles an hour. I saw 90 them do it, often. There was no danger about it; a sleeping man *will* seize the irons in time when the coach jolts. These men were hard worked, and it was not possible for them to stay awake all the time.

By and by we passed through Marysville, and over the Big Blue and Little Sandy thence about a mile, and entered Nebraska. About a mile further on, we came to the Big Sandy—one hundred and eighty miles from St. Joseph.

As the sun was going down, we saw the first specimen of an animal known familiarly over two thousand miles of mountain and desert—from Kansas clear to the Pacific Ocean—as the "jackass rabbit." He is well named. He is just like any other rabbit, except that he is from one-third to twice as large, has longer legs in proportion to his size, and has the most preposterous ears that ever were mounted on any creature *but* a jackass. When he is sitting quiet, thinking about his sins, or is absent-minded or unapprehensive of danger, his majestic ears project above him conspicuously; but the breaking of a twig will scare him nearly to death, and then he tilts his ears back gently and starts for home. All you can see, then, for the next minute, is his long gray form stretched out straight and "streaking it" through the low sage-brush, head erect, eyes right, and ears just canted a little to the rear, but showing you where the animal is, all the time, the same as if he carried a jib. Now and then he makes a marvelous spring with his long legs, high over the stunted sage-brush, and scores a leap that would make a horse envious. Presently, he comes down to a long, graceful "lope," and shortly he mysteriously disappears. He has crouched behind a sage-brush, and will sit there and listen and tremble until you get within six feet of him, when he will get under way again. But one must shoot at this creature once, if he wishes to see him throw his heart into his heels, and do the best he knows how. He is frightened clear through, now, and he lays his long ears down on his back, straightens himself out like a yard-stick every spring he makes, and scatters miles behind him with an easy indifference that is enchanting.

Our party made this specimen "hump himself," as the conductor said. The Secretary started him with a shot from the Colt; I commenced spitting at him with my weapon; and all in the same instant the old "Allen's" whole broadside let go with a rattling crash, and it is not putting it too strong to say that the rabbit was frantic! He dropped his ears, set up his tail, and left for San Francisco at a speed which can only be described as a flash and a vanish! Long after he was out of sight we could hear him whiz.

I do not remember where we first came across "sage-brush," but as I have been speaking of it I may as well describe it. This is easily done, for if the reader can imagine a gnarled and venerable live oak tree reduced to a little shrub two feet high, with its rough bark, its foliage, its twisted boughs, all complete, he can picture the "sage-brush" exactly. Often, on lazy afternoons in the mountains I have lain on the ground with my face under a sage-brush, and entertained myself with fancying that the gnats among its foliage were lilliputian birds, and that the ants marching and countermarching about its base were lilliputian flocks and herds, and myself some vast loafer from Brobdingnag waiting to catch a little citizen and eat him.

It is an imposing monarch of the forest in exquisite miniature, is the "sage-brush." Its foliage is a grayish green, and gives that tint to desert and mountain. It smells like our domestic sage, and "sage-tea" made from it tastes like the sage-tea which all boys are so well acquainted with. The sage-brush is a singularly hardy plant, and grows right in the midst of deep sand, and among barren rocks, where nothing else in the vegetable world would try to grow, except "bunch-grass." The sage-bushes grow from three to six or seven feet apart, all over the mountains and deserts of the Far West, clear to the borders of California. There is not a tree of any kind in the deserts, for hundreds of miles—there is no vegetation at all in a regular desert, except the sage-brush and its cousin the "greasewood," which is so much like the sage-brush that the difference amounts to little. Camp-fires and hot suppers in the deserts would be impossible but for the friendly sage-brush. Its trunk is as large as a boy's wrist (and from that up to a man's arm), and its crooked branches are half as large as its trunk—all good, sound, hard wood, very like oak.

When a party camps, the first thing to be done is to cut sage-brush; and in a few minutes there is an opulent pile of it ready for use. A hole a foot wide, two feet deep, and two feet long, is dug, and sage-brush chopped up and burned in it till it is full to the brim with glowing coals; then the cooking begins, and there is no smoke, and consequently no swearing. Such a fire will keep all night, with very little replenishing; and it makes a very sociable camp-fire, and one around which the most impossible reminiscences sound plausible, instructive, and profoundly entertaining.

Sage-brush is very fair fuel, but as a vegetable it is a

distinguished failure. Nothing can abide the taste of it but the jackass and his illegitimate child, the mule. But their testimony to its nutritiousness is worth nothing, for they will eat pine knots, or anthracite coal, or brass filings, or lead pipe, or old bottles, or anything that comes handy, and then go off looking as grateful as if they had had oysters for dinner. Mules and donkeys and camels have appetites that anything will relieve temporarily, but nothing satisfy. In Syria, once, at the headwaters of the Jordan, a camel took charge of my overcoat while the tents were being pitched, and examined it with a critical eye, all over, with as much interest as if he had an idea of getting one made like it; and then, after he was done figuring on it as an article of apparel, he began to contemplate it as an article of diet. He put his foot on it, and lifted one of the sleeves out with his teeth, and chewed and chewed at it, gradually taking it in, and all the while opening and closing his eyes in a kind of religious ecstasy, as if he had never tasted anything as good as an overcoat before in his life. Then he smacked his lips once or twice, and reached after the other sleeve. Next he tried the velvet collar, and smiled a smile of such contentment that it was plain to see that he regarded that as the daintiest thing about an overcoat. The tails went next, along with some per-

cussion caps and cough candy, and some fig-paste from Constantinople. And then my newspaper correspondence dropped out, and he took a chance in that—manuscript letters written for the home papers. But he was treading on dangerous ground, now. He began to come across solid wisdom in those documents that was rather weighty on his stomach; and occasionally he would take a joke that would shake him up till it loosened his teeth; it was getting to be perilous times with him, but he held his grip with good courage and hopefully, till at last he began to stumble on statements that not even a camel could swallow with impunity. He began to gag and gasp, and his eyes to stand out, and his forelegs to spread, and in about a quarter of a minute he fell over as stiff as a carpenter's workbench, and died a death of indescribable agony. I went and pulled the manuscript out of his mouth, and found that the sensitive creature had choked to death on one of the mildest and gentlest statements of fact that I ever laid before a trusting public.

I was about to say, when diverted from my subject, that occasionally one finds sage-bushes five or six feet high, and with a spread of branch and foliage in proportion, but two or two and a half feet is the usual height.

1872

From

The Gilded Age

During 1873 Charles Dudley Warner (1829-1900), the author of a number of books, and his family were neighbors of the Clemens family in Hartford. One February evening when the Warners were dining with the Clemenses, Warner and his host said stern things about contemporary novels. Urged by their wives to show what they could do in the field, the two men accepted the challenge and collaborated on The Gilded Age (1873). The novel is remarkably good in some ways, remarkably bad in others.

Some characterizations, the account of the speculative activity of the period, and the indictments of corruption in government are excellent; but the rest is melodramatic and needlessly complicated. In some of the best parts, such as Chapters VII and VIII, here reprinted, Clemens created one of his great characters, Colonel Sellers. As the first passage opens, Washington Hawkins, a relative of the Colonel, arrives in Hawkeye, where the Colonel lives.

Chapter VII

COLONEL SELLERS'S SCHEMES FOR MONEY-MAKING

Bearing Washington Hawkins and his fortunes, the stage-coach tore out of Swansea at a fearful gait, with horn tooting gaily and half the town admiring from doors and windows. But it did not tear any more after it got to the outskirts; it dragged along stupidly enough, then —till it came in sight of the next hamlet; and then the bugle tooted gaily again, and again the vehicle went tearing by the houses. This sort of conduct marked every entry to a station and every exit from it; and so in those days children grew up with the idea that stage-coaches always tore and always tooted; but they also grew up with the idea that pirates went into action in their Sunday clothes, carrying the black flag in one hand and pistoling people with the other, merely because they were so represented in the pictures: but these illusions vanished when later years brought their disenchanting wisdom. They learned then that the stagecoach is but a poor, plodding, vulgar thing in the solitudes of the highway; and that the pirate is only a seedy, unfantastic "rough," when he is out of the pictures.

Toward evening, the stage-coach came thundering into Hawkeye with a perfectly triumphant ostentation—which was natural and proper, for Hawkeye was a pretty large town for interior Missouri. Washington, very stiff and tired and hungry, climbed out, and wondered how he was to proceed now. But his difficulty was quickly solved. Colonel Sellers came down the street on a run and arrived panting for breath. He said:

"Lord bless you—I'm glad to see you, Washington—perfectly delighted to see you, my boy! I got your message. Been on the lookout for you. Heard the stage horn, but had a party I couldn't shake off—man that's got an enormous thing on hand—wants me to put some capital into it—and I tell you, my boy, I could do worse, I could do a deal worse. No, now, let that luggage alone; I'll fix that. Here, Jerry, got anything to do? All right—shoulder this plunder and follow me. Come along, Washington. Lord, I'm glad to see you! Wife and the children are just perishing to look at you. Bless you, they won't know you, you've grown so. Folks all well, I suppose? That's good—glad to hear that. We're always going to run down and see them, but I'm into so many operations, and they're not things a man feels like trusting to other people, and so somehow we keep putting it off. Fortunes in them! Good gracious, it's the country to pile up wealth in! Here we are—here's where the Sellers dynasty hangs out. Dump it on the doorstep, Jerry—the blackest Negro in the state, Washington, but got a good heart—mighty likely boy, is Jerry. And now

I suppose you've got to have ten cents, Jerry. That's all right—when a man works for me—when a man—in the other pocket, I reckon—when a man—why, where the mischief is that portmonnaie!—when a—well now that's odd—Oh, now I remember, must have left it at the bank; and b' George I've left my check-book, too—Polly says I ought to have a nurse—well, no matter. Let me have a dime, Washington, if you've got—ah, thanks. Now clear out, Jerry, your complexion has brought on the twilight half an hour ahead of time. Pretty fair joke—pretty fair. Here he is, Polly! Washington's come, children!—come now, don't eat him up—finish him in the house. Welcome, my boy, to a mansion that is proud to shelter the son of the best man that walks on the ground. Si Hawkins has been a good friend to me, and I believe I can say that whenever I've had a chance to put him into a good thing I've done it, and done it pretty cheerfully, too. I put him into that sugar speculation—what a grand thing that was, if we hadn't held on too long!"

True enough; but holding on too long had utterly ruined both of them; and the saddest part of it was, that they never had had so much money to lose before, for Sellers's sale of their mule crop that year in New Orleans had been a great financial success. If he had kept out of sugar and gone back home content to stick to mules it would have been a happy wisdom. As it was, he managed to kill two birds with one stone—that is to say, he killed the sugar speculation by holding for high rates till he had to sell at the bottom figure, and that calamity killed the mule that laid the golden egg—which is but a figurative expression and will be so understood. Sellers had returned home cheerful but empty-handed, and the mule business lapsed into other hands. The sale of the Hawkins property by the sheriff had followed, and the Hawkins hearts been torn to see Uncle Dan'l and his wife pass from the auction-block into the hands of a Negro trader and depart for the remote South to be seen no more by the family. It had seemed like seeing their own flesh and blood sold into banishment.

Washington was greatly pleased with the Sellers mansion. It was a two-story-and-a-half brick, and much more stylish than any of its neighbors. He was borne to the family sitting-room in triumph by the swarm of little Sellerses, the parents following with their arms about each other's waists.

The whole family were poorly and cheaply dressed; and the clothing, although neat and clean, showed many evidences of having seen long service. The Colonel's "stovepipe" hat was napless and shiny with much polishing, but nevertheless it had an almost convincing expression about it of having been just purchased new. The rest of his clothing was napless and shiny, too, but it had the air of being entirely satisfied with itself and blandly sorry for other people's clothes. It was growing rather dark in the house, and the evening air was chilly, too. Sellers said:

"Lay off your overcoat, Washington, and draw up to the stove and make yourself at home—just consider yourself under your own shingles, my boy—I'll have a fire going, in a jiffy. Light the lamp, Polly, dear, and let's have things cheerful—just as glad to see you, Washington, as if you'd been lost a century and we'd found you again!"

By this time the Colonel was conveying a lighted match into a poor little stove. Then he propped the stove-door to its place by leaning the poker against it, for the hinges had retired from business. This door framed a small square of isinglass, which now warmed up with a faint glow. Mrs. Sellers lit a cheap, showy lamp, which dissipated a good deal of the gloom, and then everybody gathered into the light and took the stove into close companionship.

The children climbed all over Sellers, fondled him, petted him, and were lavishly petted in return. Out from this tugging, laughing, chattering disguise of legs and arms and little faces, the Colonel's voice worked its way and his tireless tongue ran blithely on without interruption; and the purring little wife, diligent with her knitting, sat near at hand and looked happy and proud and grateful; and she listened as one who listens to oracles and gospels and whose grateful soul is being refreshed with the bread of life. By and by the children quieted down to listen; clustered about their father, and resting their elbows on his legs, they hung upon his words as if he were uttering the music of the spheres.

A dreary old haircloth sofa against the wall; a few damaged chairs; the small table the lamp stood on; the crippled stove—these things constituted the furniture of the room. There was no carpet on the floor; on the wall were occasional square-shaped interruptions of the general tint of the plaster which betrayed that there used to be pictures in the house—but there were none

now. There were no mantel ornaments, unless one might bring himself to regard as an ornament a clock which never came within fifteen strokes of striking the right time, and whose hands always hitched together at twenty-two minutes past anything and traveled in company the rest of the way home.

"Remarkable clock!" said Sellers, and got up and wound it. "I've been offered—well, I wouldn't expect you to believe what I've been offered for that clock. Old Governor Hager never sees me but he says, 'Come, now, Colonel, name your price—I *must* have that clock!' But my goodness I'd as soon think of selling my wife. As I was saying to—silence in the court, now, she's begun to strike! You can't talk against her—you have to just be patient and hold up till she's said her say. Ah—well, as I was saying, when—she's beginning again! Nineteen, twenty, twenty-one, twenty-two, twen—ah, that's all. Yes, as I was saying to old Judge—go it, old girl, don't mind me. Now how is that? Isn't that a good, spirited tone? She can wake the dead! Sleep? Why you might as well try to sleep in a thunder factory. Now just listen at that. She'll strike a hundred and fifty, now, without stopping—you'll see. There ain't another clock like that in Christendom."

Washington hoped that this might be true, for the din was distracting—though the family, one and all, seemed filled with joy; and the more the clock "buckled down to her work" as the Colonel expressed it, and the more insupportable the clatter became, the more enchanted they all appeared to be. When there was silence, Mrs. Sellers lifted upon Washington a face that beamed with a childlike pride, and said:

"It belonged to his grandmother."

The look and the tone were a plain call for admiring surprise, and therefore Washington said—(it was the only thing that offered itself at the moment):

"Indeed!"

"Yes, it did, didn't it, father!" exclaimed one of the twins. "She was my great-grandmother—and George's too; wasn't she, father! *You* never saw her, but Sis has seen her, when Sis was a baby—didn't you, Sis! Sis has seen her most a hundred times. She was awful deef—she's dead, now. Ain't she, father!"

All the children chimed in, now, with one general Babel of information about deceased—nobody offering to read the riot act or seeming to discountenance the insurrection or disapprove of it in any way—but the head twin drowned all the turmoil and held his own against the field:

"It's our clock, now—and it's got wheels inside of it, and a thing that flutters every time she strikes—don't it, father! Great-grandmother died before hardly any of us were born—she was an Old-School Baptist and had warts all over her—you ask father if she didn't. She had an uncle once that was baldheaded and used to have fits; he wasn't *our* uncle, I don't know what he was to us—some kin or another I reckon—father's seen him a thousand times—hain't you father! We used to have a calf that et apples and just chawed up dishrags like nothing, and if you stay here you'll see lots of funerals—won't he, Sis! Did you ever see a house afire? I have! Once me and Jim Terry—"

But Sellers began to speak now, and the storm ceased. He began to tell about an enormous speculation he was thinking of embarking some capital in—a speculation which some London bankers had been over to consult with him about—and soon he was building glittering pyramids of coin, and Washington was presently growing opulent under the magic of his eloquence. But at the same time Washington was not able to ignore the cold entirely. He was nearly as close to the stove as he could get, and yet he could not persuade himself that he felt the slightest heat, notwithstanding the isinglass door was still gently and serenely glowing. He tried to get a trifle closer to the stove, and the consequence was, he tripped the supporting poker and the stove-door tumbled to the floor. And then there was a revelation—there was nothing in the stove but a lighted tallow candle!

The poor youth blushed and felt as if he must die with shame. But the Colonel was only disconcerted for a moment—he straightway found his voice again:

"A little idea of my own, Washington—one of the greatest things in the world! You must write and tell your father about it—don't forget that, now. I have been reading up some European scientific reports—friend of mine, Count Fugier, sent them to me—sends me all sorts of things from Paris—he thinks the world of me, Fugier does. Well, I saw that the Academy of France had been testing the properties of heat, and they came to the conclusion that it was a non-conductor or something like that, and of course its influence must necessarily be deadly in nervous organizations with excitable temperaments, especially where there is any tendency toward rheumatic affections. Bless you, I saw in a moment what was the matter with us, and says I, out goes your fires!—no more slow torture and certain death for me, sir. What you want is the *appearance* of heat, not the heat itself—that's the idea. Well, how to do it was the next thing. I just put my head to work, pegged away a couple of days, and here you are! Rheumatism? Why a man can't any more start a case of rheumatism in this house than he can shake an opinion out of a mummy! Stove with a candle in it and a transparent door—that's it—it has been the salvation of this family. Don't you fail to write your father about it, Washington. And tell him the idea is mine—I'm no more conceited than most people, I reckon, but you know it is human nature for a man to want credit for a thing like that."

Washington said with his blue lips that he would, but he said in his secret heart that he would promote no such iniquity. He tried to believe in the healthfulness of the invention, and succeeded tolerably well; but after all he could not feel that good health in a frozen body was any real improvement on the rheumatism.

Chapter VIII

COLONEL SELLERS ENTERTAINS WASHINGTON HAWKINS

The supper at Colonel Sellers's was not sumptuous, in the beginning, but it improved on acquaintance. That is to say, that what Washington regarded at first sight as mere lowly potatoes, presently became awe-inspiring agricultural productions that had been reared in some ducal garden beyond the sea, under the sacred eye of the duke himself, who had sent them to Sellers; the bread was from corn which could be grown in only one favored locality in the earth and only a favored few could get it; the Rio coffee, which at first seemed execrable to the taste, took to itself an improved flavor when Washington was told to drink it slowly and not hurry what should be a lingering luxury in order to be fully appreciated—it was from the private stores of a Brazilian nobleman with an unrememberable name. The Colonel's tongue was a magician's wand that turned dried apples into figs and water into wine as easily as it could change a hovel into a palace and present poverty into imminent future riches.

Washington slept in a cold bed in a carpetless room

and woke up in a palace in the morning; at least the palace lingered during the moment that he was rubbing his eyes and getting his bearings—and then it disappeared and he recognized that the Colonel's inspiring talk had been influencing his dreams. Fatigue had made him sleep late; when he entered the sitting-room he noticed that the old haircloth sofa was absent; when he sat down to breakfast the Colonel tossed six or seven dollars in bills on the table, counted them over, said he was a little short and must call upon his banker; then returned the bills to his wallet with the indifferent air of a man who is used to money. The breakfast was not an improvement upon the supper, but the Colonel talked it up and transformed it into an oriental feast. By and by, he said:

"I intend to look out for you, Washington, my boy. I hunted up a place for you yesterday, but I am not referring to that, now—that is a mere livelihood—mere bread and butter; but when I say I mean to look out for you I mean something very different. I mean to put things in your way that will make a mere livelihood a trifling thing. I'll put you in a way to make more money than you'll ever know what to do with. You'll be right here where I can put my hand on you when anything turns up. I've got some prodigious operations on foot; but I'm keeping quiet; mum's the word; your old hand don't go around powwowing and letting everybody see his k'yards and find out his little game. But all in good time, Washington, all in good time. You'll see. Now, there's an operation in corn that looks well. Some New York men are trying to get me to go into it—buy up all the growing crops and just boss the market when they mature—ah, I tell you it's a great thing. And it only costs a trifle; two millions or two and a half will do it. I haven't exactly promised yet—there's no hurry—the more indifferent I seem, you know, the more anxious those fellows will get. And then there is the hog speculation—that's bigger still. We've got quiet men at work," (he was very impressive here,) "mousing around, to get propositions out of all the farmers in the whole West and Northwest for the hog crop, and other agents quietly getting propositions and terms out of all the manufactories—and don't you see, if we can get all the hogs and all the slaughter-houses into our hands on the dead quiet—whew! it would take three ships to carry the money. I've looked into the thing—calculated all the chances for and all the chances against, and though I

shake my head and hesitate and keep on thinking, apparently, I've got my mind made up that if the thing can be done on a capital of six millions, that's the horse to put up money on! Why, Washington—but what's the use of talking about it—any man can see that there's whole Atlantic oceans of cash in it, gulfs and bays thrown in. But there's a bigger thing than that, yet—a bigger—"

"Why, Colonel, you can't want anything bigger!" said Washington, his eyes blazing. "Oh, I wish I could go into either of those speculations—I only wish I had money—I wish I wasn't cramped and kept down and fettered with poverty, and such prodigious chances lying right here in sight! Oh, it is a fearful thing to be poor. But don't throw away those things—they are so splendid and I can see how sure they are. Don't throw them away for something still better and maybe fail in it! I wouldn't, Colonel. I would stick to these. I wish father were here and were his old self again. Oh, he never in his life had such chances as these are. Colonel, you *can't* improve on these—no man can improve on them!"

A sweet, compassionate smile played about the Colonel's features, and he leaned over the table with the air of a man who is "going to show you" and do it without the least trouble:

"Why Washington, my boy, these things are nothing. They *look* large—of course they look large to a novice, but to a man who has been all his life accustomed to large operations—pshaw! They're well enough to while away an idle hour with, or furnish a bit of enjoyment that will give a trifle of idle capital a chance to earn its bread while it is waiting for something to *do*, but—now just listen a moment—just let me give you an idea of what we old veterans of commerce call 'business.' Here's the Rothschilds' proposition—this is between you and me, you understand—"

Washington nodded three or four times impatiently, and his glowing eyes said, "Yes, yes—hurry—I understand—"

"—for I wouldn't have it get out for a fortune. They want me to go in with them on the sly—agent was here two weeks ago about it—go in on the sly" (voice down to an impressive whisper, now) "and buy up a hundred and thirteen wildcat banks in Ohio, Indiana, Kentucky, Illinois, and Missouri—notes of these banks are at all sorts of discount now—average discount of the hundred and thirteen is forty-four per cent,—buy them all up, you see, and then all of a sudden let the cat out of the bag! Whiz! the stock of every one of those wild-cats would spin up to a tremendous premium before you could turn a handspring—profit on the speculation not a dollar less than forty millions!" (An eloquent pause, while the marvelous vision settled into W.'s focus.) "Where's your hogs now! Why, my dear innocent boy, we would just sit down on the front door-steps and peddle banks like lucifer matches!"

10   Washington finally got his breath and said:

"Oh, it is perfectly wonderful! Why couldn't these things have happened in father's day? And I—it's of no use—they simply lie before my face and mock me. There is nothing for me but to stand helpless and see other people reap the astonishing harvest."

"Never mind, Washington, don't you worry. I'll fix you. There's plenty of chances. How much money have you got?"

In the presence of so many millions, Washington 20 could not keep from blushing when he had to confess that he had eighteen dollars in the world.

"Well, all right—don't despair. Other people have been obliged to begin with less. I have a small idea that may develop into something for us both, all in good time. Keep your money close and add to it. I'll make it breed. I've been experimenting (to pass away the time) on a little preparation for curing sore eyes—a kind of decoction nine-tenths water and the other tenth drugs that don't cost more than a dollar a barrel; I'm still ex-30 perimenting; there's one ingredient wanted yet to perfect the thing, and somehow I can't just manage to hit upon the thing that's necessary, and I don't dare talk with a chemist, of course. But I'm progressing, and before many weeks I wager the country will ring with the fame of Beriah Sellers's Infallible Imperial Oriental Optic Liniment and Salvation for Sore Eyes—the Medical Wonder of the Age! Small bottles fifty cents, large ones a dollar. Average cost, five and seven cents for the two sizes. The first year sell, say, ten thousand 40 bottles in Missouri, seven thousand in Iowa, three thousand in Arkansas, four thousand in Kentucky, six thousand in Illinois, and say twenty-five thousand in the rest of the country. Total, fifty-five thousand bottles; profit clear of all expenses, twenty thousand dollars at the very lowest calculation. All the capital needed is to manufacture the first two thousand bottles—say a hundred and fifty dollars—then the money would begin to flow in.

The second year, sales would reach two hundred thousand bottles—clear profit, say seventy-five thousand dollars—and in the mean time the great factory would be build-50 ing in St. Louis, to cost, say, one hundred thousand dollars. The third year we could easily sell one million bottles in the United States and—"

"O, splendid!" said Washington. "Let's commence right away—let's—"

"—one million bottles in the United States—profit at least three hundred and fifty thousand dollars—and then it would begin to be time to turn our attention toward the real idea of the business."

"The real idea of it! Ain't three hundred and fifty 60 thousand dollars a year a pretty real—"

"Stuff! Why, what an infant you are, Washington—what a guileless, short-sighted, easily contented innocent you are, my poor little country-bred know-nothing! Would I go to all that trouble and bother for the poor crumbs a body might pick up in this country? Now do I look like a man who—does my history suggest that I am a man who deals in trifles, contents himself with the narrow horizon that hems in the common herd, sees no further than the end of his nose? Now, 70 you know that that is not me—couldn't be me. You ought to know that if I throw my time and abilities into a patent medicine, it's a patent medicine whose field of operations is the solid earth! its clients the swarming nations that inhabit it! Why what is the republic of America for an eye-water country? Lord bless you, it is nothing but a barren highway that you've got to cross to get to the true eye-water market! Why, Washington, in the Oriental countries people swarm like the sands of the desert; every square mile of ground 80 upholds its thousands upon thousands of struggling human creatures—and every separate and individual devil of them's got the ophthalmia! It's as natural to them as noses are—and sin. It's born with them, it stays with them, it's all that some of them have left when they die. Three years of introductory trade in the Orient and what will be the result? Why, our headquarters would be in Constantinople and our hindquarters in Further India! Factories and warehouses in Cairo, Ispahan, Bagdad, Damascus, Jerusalem, Yedo, 90 Peking, Bangkok, Delhi, Bombay, and Calcutta! Annual income—well, God only knows how many millions and millions apiece!"

Washington was so dazed, so bewildered—his heart

and his eyes had wandered so far away among the strange lands beyond the seas, and such avalanches of coin and currency had fluttered and jingled confusedly down before him, that he was now as one who has been whirling round and round for a time, and, stopping all at once, finds his surroundings still whirling and all objects a dancing chaos. However, little by little the Sellers family cooled down and crystallized into shape, and the poor room lost its glitter and resumed its poverty. Then the youth found his voice and begged Sellers to drop everything and hurry up the eye-water; and he got his eighteen dollars and tried to force it upon the Colonel—pleaded with him to take it —implored him to do it. But the Colonel would not; said he would not need the capital (in his native magnificent way he called that eighteen dollars capital) till the eye-water was an accomplished fact. He made Washington easy in his mind, though, by promising that he would call for it just as soon as the invention was finished, and he added the glad tidings that nobody but just they two should be admitted to a share in the speculation.

When Washington left the breakfast-table he could have worshiped that man. Washington was one of that kind of people whose hopes are in the very clouds one day, and in the gutter the next. He walked on air, now. The Colonel was ready to take him around and introduce him to the employment he had found for him, but Washington begged for a few moments in which to write home; with his kind of people, to ride today's new interest to death and put off yesterday's till another time, is nature itself. He ran up-stairs and wrote glowingly, enthusiastically, to his mother about the hogs and the corn, the banks and the eye-water—and added a few inconsequential millions to each project. And he said that people little dreamed what a man Colonel Sellers was, and that the world would open its eyes when it found out. And he closed his letter thus:

So make yourself perfectly easy, mother—in a little while you shall have everything you want, and more. I am not likely to stint *you* in anything, I fancy. This money will not be for me, alone, but for all of us. I want all to share alike; and there is going to be far more for each than one person can spend. Break it to father cautiously—you understand the need of that—break it to him cautiously, for he has had such cruel hard fortune, and is so stricken by it that great good news might prostrate him more surely than even bad, for he is used to the bad but is grown sadly unaccustomed to the other. Tell Laura—tell all the children. And write to Clay about it if he is not with you yet. You may tell Clay that whatever I get he can freely share in—freely. He knows that that is true— there will be no need that I should swear to that to make him believe it. Good-by—and mind what I say: Rest perfectly easy, one and all of you, for our troubles are nearly at an end.

Poor lad, he could not know that his mother would cry some loving, compassionate tears over his letter and put off the family with a synopsis of its contents which conveyed a deal of love to them but not much idea of his prospects or projects. And he never dreamed that such a joyful letter could sadden her and fill her night with sighs, and troubled thoughts, and bodings of the future, instead of filling it with peace and blessing it with restful sleep.

When the letter was done, Washington and the Colonel sallied forth, and as they walked along Washington learned what he was to be. He was to be a clerk in a real-estate office. Instantly the fickle youth's dreams forsook the magic eye-water and flew back to the Tennessee Land. And the gorgeous possibilities of that great domain straightway began to occupy his imagination to such a degree that he could scarcely manage to keep even enough of his attention upon the Colonel's talk to retain the general run of what he was saying. He was glad it was a real-estate office—he was a made man now, sure.

The Colonel said that General Boswell was a rich man and had a good and growing business; and that Washington's work would be light and he would get forty dollars a month and be boarded and lodged in the General's family—which was as good as ten dollars more; and even better, for he could not live as well even at the "City Hotel" as he would there, and yet the hotel charged fifteen dollars a month where a man had a good room.

General Boswell was in his office; a comfortable-looking place, with plenty of outline maps hanging about the walls and in the windows, and a spectacled man was marking out another one on a long table. The office was in the principal street. The General received Washington with a kindly but reserved politeness. Washington rather liked his looks. He was about fifty years old, dignified, well preserved, and well dressed. After the Colonel took his leave, the General talked awhile with Washington—his talk consisting chiefly of instructions about the clerical duties of the place.

He seemed satisfied as to Washington's ability to take care of the books, he was evidently a pretty fair theoretical bookkeeper, and experience would soon harden theory into practice. By and by dinner-time came, and the two walked to the General's house; and now Washington noticed an instinct in himself that moved him to keep not in the General's rear, exactly, but yet not at his side—somehow the old gentleman's dignity and reserve did not inspire familiarity.

1873

From

Old Times on the Mississippi

Out for a long walk in the woods with his friend the Rev. Joseph Twichell in 1874, Clemens got to reminiscing about "old Mississippi days of steamboating glory and grandeur as I saw them . . . from the pilot-house." "What a virgin subject to hurl into a magazine!" said Twichell. When Clemens wrote about the experience to his friend William Dean Howells, editor of the **Atlantic**, Howells urged him to write a series of reminiscences. "Old Times on the Mississippi" appeared in six installments between January and July 1875. In 1883 the articles, augmented with new material, were published as **Life on the Mississippi**, in which "A Daring Deed" became Chapter VII and "Continued Perplexities" became Chapter IX.

The following passages are part of Clemens' account of his apprenticeship as a pilot. The first paragraph—a transitional paragraph—is omitted from "A Daring Deed."

A DARING DEED

The pilot-house was full of pilots, going down to "look at the river." What is called the "upper river" (the two hundred miles between St. Louis and Cairo, where the Ohio comes **in)** was low; and the Mississippi changes its channel so constantly that the pilots used to always find it necessary to run down to Cairo to take a fresh look, when their boats were to lie in port a week; that is, when the water was at a low stage. A deal of this "looking at the river" was done by poor fellows who seldom had a berth, and whose only hope of getting one lay in their being always freshly posted and therefore ready to drop into the shoes of some reputable pilot, for a single trip, on account of such pilot's sudden illness, or some other necessity. And a good many of them constantly ran up and down inspecting the river, not because they ever really hoped to get a berth, but because (they being guests of the boat) it was cheaper to "look at the river" than stay ashore and pay board. In time these fellows grew dainty in their tastes, and only infested boats that had an established reputation for setting good tables. All visiting pilots were useful, for they were always ready and willing, winter or summer, night or day, to go out in the yawl and help buoy the channel or assist the boat's pilots in any way they could. They were likewise welcomed because all pilots are tireless talkers, when gathered together, and as they talk only about the river they are always understood and are always interesting. Your true pilot cares nothing about anything on earth but the river, and his pride in his occupation surpasses the pride of kings.

We had a fine company of these river inspectors along this trip. There were eight or ten, and there was abundance of room for them in our great pilot-house. Two or three of them wore polished silk hats, elaborate shirt-fronts, diamond breastpins, kid gloves, and patent-leather boots. They were choice in their English, and bore themselves with a dignity proper to men of solid means and prodigious reputation as pilots. The others were more or less loosely clad, and wore upon their heads tall felt cones that were suggestive of the days of the Commonwealth.

I was a cipher in this august company, and felt subdued, not to say torpid. I was not even of sufficient consequence to assist at the wheel when it was necessary to put the tiller hard down in a hurry; the guest that stood nearest did that when occasion required—and this was pretty much all the time, because of the crookedness of the channel and the scant water. I stood in a corner; and the talk I listened to took the hope all out of me. One visitor said to another:

"Jim, how did you run Plum Point, coming up?"

"It was in the night, there, and I ran it the way one of the boys on the *Diana* told me; started out about fifty yards above the wood-pile on the false point, and held on the cabin under Plum Point till I raised the reef—quarter less twain—then straightened up for the middle bar till I got well abreast the old one-limbed cottonwood in the bend, then got my stern on the cottonwood, and head on the low place above the point, and came through a-booming—nine and a half."

"Pretty square crossing, an't it?"

"Yes, but the upper bar's working down fast."

Another pilot spoke up and said:

"I had better water than that, and ran it lower down; started out from the false point—mark twain—raised the second reef abreast the big snag in the bend, and had quarter less twain."

One of the gorgeous ones remarked:

"I don't want to find fault with your leadsmen, but that's a good deal of water for Plum Point, it seems to me."

There was an approving nod all around as this quiet snub dropped on the boaster and "settled" him. And so they went on talk-talk-talking. Meantime, the thing that was running in my mind was, "Now, if my ears hear aright, I have not only to get the names of all the towns and islands and bends, and so on, by heart, but I must even get up a warm personal acquaintanceship with every old snag and one-limbed cottonwood and obscure wood-pile that ornaments the banks of this river for twelve hundred miles; and more than that, I must actually know where these things are in the dark, unless these guests are gifted with eyes that can pierce through

two miles of solid blackness. I wish the piloting business was in Jericho and I had never thought of it."

At dusk Mr. Bixby tapped the big bell three times (the signal to land), and the captain emerged from his drawing-room in the forward end of the "texas," and looked up inquiringly. Mr. Bixby said:

"We will lay up here all night, captain."

"Very well, sir."

That was all. The boat came to shore and was tied up for the night. It seemed to me a fine thing that the pilot could do as he pleased, without asking so grand a captain's permission. I took my supper and went immediately to bed, discouraged by my day's observations and experiences. My late voyage's note-booking was but a confusion of meaningless names. It had tangled me all up in a knot every time I had looked at it in the daytime. I now hoped for respite in sleep; but no, it reveled all through my head till sunrise again, a frantic and tireless nightmare.

Next morning I felt pretty rusty and low-spirited. We went booming along, taking a good many chances, for we were anxious to "get out of the river" (as getting out to Cairo was called) before night should overtake us. But Mr. Bixby's partner, the other pilot, presently grounded the boat, and we lost so much time getting her off that it was plain the darkness would overtake us a good long way above the mouth. This was a great misfortune, especially to certain of our visiting pilots, whose boats would have to wait for their return, no matter how long that might be. It sobered the pilot-house talk a good deal. Coming up-stream, pilots did not mind low water or any kind of darkness; nothing stopped them but fog. But down-stream work was different; a boat was too nearly helpless, with a stiff current pushing behind her; so it was not customary to run down-stream at night in low water.

There seemed to be one small hope, however: if we could get through the intricate and dangerous Hat Island crossing before night, we could venture the rest, for we would have plainer sailing and better water. But it would be insanity to attempt Hat Island at night. So there was a deal of looking at watches all the rest of the day, and a constant ciphering upon the speed we were making; Hat Island was the eternal subject, sometimes hope was high and sometimes we were delayed in a bad crossing, and down it went again. For hours all hands lay under the burden of this suppressed excitement; it was even communicated to me, and I got to feeling so solicitous about Hat Island, and under such an awful pressure of responsibility, that I wished I might have five minutes on shore to draw a good, full, relieving breath, and start over again. We were standing no regular watches. Each of our pilots ran such portions of the river as he had run when coming upstream, because of his greater familiarity with it; but both remained in the pilot-house constantly.

An hour before sunset Mr. Bixby took the wheel, and Mr. W. stepped aside. For the next thirty minutes every man held his watch in his hand and was restless, silent, and uneasy. At last somebody said, with a doomful sigh:

"Well, yonder's Hat Island—and we can't make it."

All the watches closed with a snap, everybody sighed and muttered something about its being "too bad, too bad—ah, if we could *only* have got here half an hour sooner!" and the place was thick with the atmosphere of disappointment. Some started to go out, but loitered, hearing no bell-tap to land. The sun dipped behind the horizon, the boat went on. Inquiring looks passed from one guest to another; and one who had his hand on the door-knob and had turned it, waited, then presently took away his hand and let the knob turn back again. We bore steadily down the bend. More looks were exchanged, and nods of surprised admiration—but no words. Insensibly the men drew together behind Mr. Bixby, as the sky darkened and one or two dim stars came out. The dead silence and sense of waiting became oppressive. Mr. Bixby pulled the cord, and two deep, mellow notes from the big bell floated off on the night. Then a pause, and one more note was struck. The watchman's voice followed, from the hurricane-deck:

"Labboard lead, there! Stabboard lead!"

The cries of the leadsmen began to rise out of the distance, and were gruffly repeated by the word-passers on the hurricane-deck.

"M-a-r-k three! M-a-r-k three! Quarter-less-three! Half twain! Quarter twain! M-a-r-k twain! Quarter-less—"

Mr. Bixby pulled two bell-ropes, and was answered by faint jinglings far below in the engine-room, and our speed slackened. The steam began to whistle through the gauge-cocks. The cries of the leadsmen went on—and it is a weird sound, always, in the night. Every pilot in the lot was watching now, with fixed eyes, and talking under his breath. Nobody was calm and easy but Mr. Bixby. He would put his wheel down and stand on a spoke, and as the steamer swung into her (to me) utterly invisible marks—for we seemed to be in the midst of a wide and gloomy sea—he would meet and fasten her there. Out of the murmur of half-audible talk, one caught a coherent sentence now and then—such as:

"There; she's over the first reef all right!"

After a pause, another subdued voice:

"Her stern's coming down just *exactly* right, by George!"

"Now she's in the marks; over she goes!"

Somebody else muttered:

"Oh, it was done beautiful—*beautiful!*"

Now the engines were stopped altogether, and we drifted with the current. Not that I could see the boat drift, for I could not, the stars being all gone by this time. This drifting was the dismalest work; it held one's heart still. Presently I discovered a blacker gloom than that which surrounded us. It was the head of the island. We were closing right down upon it. We entered its deeper shadow, and so imminent seemed the peril that I was likely to suffocate; and I had the strongest impulse to do *something,* anything, to save the vessel. But still Mr. Bixby stood by his wheel, silent, intent as a cat, and all the pilots stood shoulder to shoulder at his back.

"She'll not make it!" somebody whispered.

The water grew shoaler and shoaler, by the leadsman's cries, till it was down to:

"Eight-and-a-half! E-i-g-h-t feet! E-i-g-h-t feet! Seven-and—"

Mr. Bixby said warningly through his speaking-tube to the engineer:

"Stand by, now!"

"Ay, ay, sir!"

"Seven-and-a-half! Seven feet! *Six*-and—"

We touched bottom! Instantly Mr. Bixby set a lot of bells ringing, shouted through the tube, *"Now,* let her have it—every ounce you've got!" then to his partner, "Put her hard down! snatch her! snatch her!" The boat rasped and ground her way through the sand, hung upon the apex of disaster a single tremendous instant, and then over she went! And such a shout as went up at Mr. Bixby's back never loosened the roof of a pilot-house before!

There was no more trouble after that. Mr. Bixby was a hero that night; and it was some little time, too, before his exploit ceased to be talked about by river-men.

Fully to realize the marvelous precision required in laying the great steamer in her marks in that murky waste of water, one should know that not only must she pick her intricate way through snags and blind reefs, and then shave the head of the island so closely as to brush the overhanging foliage with her stern, but at one place she must pass almost within arm's reach of a sunken and invisible wreck that would snatch the hull timbers from under her if she should strike it, and destroy a quarter of a million dollars' worth of steamboat and cargo in five minutes, and maybe a hundred and fifty human lives into the bargain.

The last remark I heard that night was a compliment to Mr. Bixby, uttered in soliloquy and with unction by one of our guests. He said:

"By the Shadow of Death, but he's a lightning pilot!"

CONTINUED PERPLEXITIES

I promptly put such a strain on my memory that by and by even the shoal water and the countless crossing-marks began to stay with me. But the result was just the same. I never could more than get one knotty thing learned before another presented itself. Now I had often seen pilots gazing at the water and pretending to read it as if it were a book; but it was a book that told me nothing. A time came at last, however, when Mr. Bixby seemed to think me far enough advanced to bear a lesson on water-reading. So he began:

"Do you see that long, slanting line on the face of the water? Now, that's a reef. Moreover, it's a bluff reef. There is a solid sand-bar under it that is nearly as straight up and down as the side of a house. There is plenty of water close up to it, but mighty little on top of it. If you were to hit it you would knock the boat's brains out. Do you see where the line fringes out at the upper end and begins to fade away?"

"Yes, sir."

"Well, that is a low place; that is the head of the reef. You can climb over there, and not hurt anything. Cross over, now, and follow along close under the reef—easy water there—not much current."

I followed the reef along till I approached the fringed end. Then Mr. Bixby said:

"Now get ready. Wait till I give the word. She won't want to mount the reef; a boat hates shoal water. Stand by—wait—*wait*—keep her well in hand. *Now* cramp her down! Snatch her! snatch her!"

He seized the other side of the wheel and helped to spin it around until it was hard down, and then we held it so. The boat resisted, and refused to answer for a while, and next she came surging to starboard, mounted the reef, and sent a long, angry ridge of water foaming away from her bows.

"Now watch her; watch her like a cat, or she'll get away from you. When she fights strong and the tiller slips a little, in a jerky, greasy sort of way, let up on her a trifle; it is the way she tells you at night that the water is too shoal; but keep edging her up, on the bar now; there is a bar under every point, because the water that comes down around it forms an eddy and allows the sediment to sink. Do you see those fine lines on the face of the water that branch out like the ribs of a fan? Well, those are little reefs; you want to just miss the ends of them, but run them pretty close. Now look out—look out! Don't you crowd that slick, greasy-looking place; there ain't nine feet there; she won't stand it. She begins to smell it; look sharp, I tell you! Oh, blazes, there you go! Stop the starboard wheel! Quick! Ship up to back! Set her back!"

The engine bells jingled and the engines answered promptly, shooting white columns of steam far aloft out of the 'scape-pipes, but it was too late. The boat had "smelt" the bar in good earnest; the foamy ridges that radiated from her bows suddenly disappeared, a great dead swell came rolling forward, and swept ahead of her, she careened far over to larboard, and went tearing away toward the shore as if she were about scared to death. We were a good mile from where we ought to have been when we finally got the upper hand of her again.

During the afternoon watch the next day, Mr. Bixby asked me if I knew how to run the next few miles. I said:

"Go inside the first snag above the point, outside the next one, start out from the lower end of Higgins's woodyard, make a square crossing, and—"

"That's all right. I'll be back before you close up on the next point."

But he wasn't. He was still below when I rounded it and entered upon a piece of the river which I had some misgivings about. I did not know that he was hiding behind a chimney to see how I would perform. I went gaily along, getting prouder and prouder, for he had never left the boat in my sole charge such a length of time before. I even got to "setting" her and letting the wheel go entirely, while I vaingloriously turned my back and inspected the stern marks and hummed a tune, a sort of easy indifference which I had prodigiously admired in Bixby and other great pilots. Once I inspected rather long, and when I faced to the front again my heart flew into my mouth so suddenly that if I hadn't clapped my teeth together I should have lost it. One of those frightful bluff reefs was stretching its deadly length right across our bows! My head was gone in a moment; I did not know which end I stood on; I gasped and could not get my breath; I spun the wheel down with such rapidity that it wove itself together like a spider's web; the boat answered and turned square away from the reef, but the reef followed her! I fled, but still it followed, still it kept—right across my bows! I never looked to see where I was going, I only fled. The awful crash was imminent. Why didn't that villain come? If I committed the crime of ringing a bell I might get thrown overboard. But better that than kill the boat. So in blind desperation, I started such a rattling "shivaree" down below as never had astounded an engineer in this world before, I fancy. Amidst the frenzy of the bells the engines began to back and fill in a curious way, and my reason forsook its throne—we were about to crash into the woods on the other side of the river. Just then Mr. Bixby stepped calmly into view on the hurricane-deck. My soul went out to him in gratitude. My distress vanished; I would have felt safe on the brink of Niagara with Mr. Bixby on the hurricane-deck. He blandly and sweetly took his toothpick out of his mouth between his fingers, as if it were a cigar— we were just in the act of climbing an overhanging big tree, and the passengers were scudding astern like rats— and lifted up these commands to me ever so gently:

"Stop the starboard! Stop the larboard! Set her back on both!"

The boat hesitated, halted, pressed her nose among the boughs a critical instant, then reluctantly began to back away.

"Stop the larboard! Come ahead on it! Stop the starboard! Come ahead on it! Point her for the bar!"

I sailed away as serenely as a summer's morning. Mr. Bixby came in and said, with mock simplicity:

"When you have a hail, my boy, you ought to tap the big bell three times before you land, so that the engineers can get ready."

I blushed under the sarcasm, and said I hadn't had any hail.

"Ah! Then it was for wood, I suppose. The officer of the watch will tell you when he wants to wood up."

I went on consuming, and said I wasn't after wood.

"Indeed? Why, what could you want over here in the bend, then? Did you ever know of a boat following a bend up-stream at this stage of the river?"

"No, sir—and I wasn't trying to follow it. I was getting away from a bluff reef."

"No, it wasn't a bluff reef; there isn't one within three miles of where you were."

"But I saw it. It was as bluff as that one yonder."

"Just about. Run over it!"

"Do you give it as an order?"

"Yes. Run over it!"

"If I don't, I wish I may die."

"All right; I am taking the responsibility."

I was just as anxious to kill the boat, now, as I had been to save it before. I impressed my orders upon my memory, to be used at the inquest, and made a straight break for the reef. As it disappeared under our bows I held my breath; but we slid over it like oil.

"Now, don't you see the difference? It wasn't anything but a *wind* reef. The wind does that."

"So I see. But it is exactly like a bluff reef. How am I ever going to tell them apart?"

"I can't tell you. It is an instinct. By and by you will just naturally *know* one from the other, but you never will be able to explain why or how you know them apart."

It turned out to be true. The face of the water, in time, became a wonderful book—a book that was a dead language to the uneducated passenger, but which told its mind to me without reserve, delivering its most cherished secrets as clearly as if it uttered them with a voice. And it was not a book to be read once and thrown

aside, for it had a new story to tell every day. Throughout the long twelve hundred miles there was never a
page that was void of interest, never one that you could
leave unread without loss, never one that you would
want to skip, thinking you could find higher enjoyment
in some other thing. There never was so wonderful a
book written by man; never one whose interest was so
absorbing, so unflagging, so sparklingly renewed with
every reperusal. The passenger who could not read it
10 was charmed with a peculiar sort of faint dimple on its
surface (on the rare occasions when he did not overlook
it altogether); but to the pilot that was an *italicized* passage; indeed, it was more than that, it was a legend of
the largest capitals, with a string of shouting exclama-
tion-points at the end of it, for it meant that a wreck
or a rock was buried there that could tear the life out of
the strongest vessel that ever floated. It is the faintest
and simplest expression the water ever makes, and the
most hideous to a pilot's eye. In truth, the passenger
20 who could not read this book saw nothing but all
manner of pretty pictures in it, painted by the sun and
shaded by the clouds, whereas to the trained eye these
were not pictures at all, but the grimmest and most
dead-earnest of reading-matter.

Now when I had mastered the language of this water,
and had come to know every trifling feature that bordered the great river as familiarly as I knew the letters
of the alphabet, I had made a valuable acquisition. But
I had lost something, too. I had lost something which
30 could never be restored to me while I lived. All the
grace, the beauty, the poetry, had gone out of the majestic river! I still kept in mind a certain wonderful
sunset which I witnessed when steamboating was new
to me. A broad expanse of the river was turned to
blood; in the middle distance the red hue brightened
into gold, through which a solitary log came floating,
black and conspicuous; in one place a long, slanting
mark lay sparkling upon the water; in another the surface was broken by boiling, tumbling rings, that were as
40 many-tinted as an opal; where the ruddy flush was faintest, was a smooth spot that was covered with graceful
circles and radiating lines, ever so delicately traced; the
shore on our left was densely wooded, and the somber
shadow that fell from this forest was broken in one
place by a long, ruffled trail that shone like silver; and
high above the forest wall a clean-stemmed dead tree

waved a single leafy bough that glowed like a flame in
the unobstructed splendor that was flowing from the
sun. There were graceful curves, reflected images, woody
heights, soft distances; and over the whole scene, far 50
and near, the dissolving lights drifted steadily, enriching
it every passing moment with new marvels of coloring.

I stood like one bewitched. I drank it in, in a speechless rapture. The world was new to me, and I had never
seen anything like this at home. But as I have said, a
day came when I began to cease from noting the glories
and the charms which the moon and the sun and the
twilight wrought upon the river's face; another day came
when I ceased altogether to note them. Then, if that
sunset scene had been repeated, I should have looked up- 60
on it without rapture, and should have commented upon
it, inwardly, after this fashion: "This sun means that we
are going to have wind to-morrow; that floating log
means that the river is rising, small thanks to it; that
slanting mark on the water refers to a bluff reef which
is going to kill somebody's steamboat one of these nights,
if it keeps on stretching out like that; those tumbling
'boils' show a dissolving bar and a changing channel
there; the lines and circles in the slick water over yonder are a warning that that troublesome place is shoal- 70
ing up dangerously; that silver streak in the shadow of
the forest is the 'break' from a new snag, and he has
located himself in the very best place he could have
found to fish for steamboats; that tall dead tree, with a
single living branch, is not going to last long, and then
how is a body ever going to get through this blind place
at night without the friendly old landmark?"

No, the romance and beauty were all gone from the
river. All the value any feature of it had for me now was
the amount of usefulness it could furnish toward com- 80
passing the safe piloting of a steamboat. Since those
days, I have pitied doctors from my heart. What does
the lovely flush in a beauty's cheek mean to a doctor
but a "break" that ripples above some deadly disease?
Are not all her visible charms sown thick with what are
to him the signs and symbols of hidden decay? Does he
ever see her beauty at all, or doesn't he simply view her
professionally, and comment upon her unwholesome
condition all to himself? And doesn't he sometimes
wonder whether he has gained most or lost most by 90
learning his trade?

1875·1883

From

A Tramp Abroad

Baker's Blue-Jay Yarn

This selection is part of Chapter II and all of Chapter III of **A Tramp Abroad** (1880). The storyteller is modeled after Jim Gillis, the old character at whose hut Clemens was a delighted visitor for a time in the sixties.

Notable in the handling is the transition from the actual world of the Neckar hills to the fantastic world where blue-jays talk. Notable, too, as Mr. De Voto remarks, are the origin and the artistry of this mock oral tale: "Its material comes from the Negro's bestiary, interstitial with the life of his [Clemens'] boyhood in Hannibal; and in this way the humor rises from fantasy, from the imaginative myth-making of the slaves and the frontier. But also, Jim Baker, the narrator, exists; he is a creation from the world of reality. He lives, and no fantasy has gone into his creation, but only the sharp perception of an individual. His patient, explanatory mind actually works before our eyes and no one can doubt him. His speech has been caught so cunningly that its rhythms produce complete conviction. Fantasy is thus an instrument of realism and the humor of Mark Twain merges into the fiction that is his highest reach."

If any particular piece of humor is typical of the American brand, this is the one. Here, in admirable proportions, are combined the satirical philosophy of the horse-sense school, the realistic portrayal of earthy characters, and the fantasy blended of poetry and vulgarity which runs through much of our humor.

One never tires of poking about in the dense woods that clothe all these lofty Neckar hills to their tops. The great deeps of a boundless forest have a beguiling and impressive charm in any country; but German legends and fairy tales have given these an added charm. They have peopled all that region with gnomes, and dwarfs, and all sorts of mysterious and uncanny creatures. At the time I am writing of, I had been reading so much of this literature that sometimes I was not sure but I was beginning to believe in the gnomes and fairies as realities.

One afternoon I got lost in the woods about a mile from the hotel, and presently fell into a train of dreamy thought about animals which talk, and kobolds, and enchanted folk, and the rest of the pleasant legendary stuff; and so, by stimulating my fancy, I finally got to imagining I glimpsed small flitting shapes here and there down the columned aisles of the forest. It was a place which was peculiarly meet for the occasion. It was a pine wood, with so thick and soft a carpet of brown needles that one's footfall made no more sound than if he were treading on wool; the tree-trunks were as round and straight and smooth as pillars, and stood close together; they were bare of branches to a point about twenty-five feet above ground, and from there upward so thick with boughs that not a ray of sunlight could pierce through. The world was bright with sunshine outside, but a deep and mellow twilight reigned in there, and also a silence so profound that I seemed to hear my own breathings.

When I had stood ten minutes, thinking and imagining, and getting my spirit in tune with the place, and in the right mood to enjoy the supernatural, a raven suddenly uttered a hoarse croak over my head. It made me start; and then I was angry because I started. I looked up, and the creature was sitting on a limb right over me, looking down at me. I felt something of the same sense of humiliation and injury which one feels when he finds that a human stranger has been clandestinely inspecting him in his privacy and mentally commenting upon him. I eyed the raven, and the raven eyed me. Nothing was said during some seconds. Then the bird stepped a little way along his limb to get a better point of observation, lifted his wings, stuck his head far down below his shoulders toward me, and croaked again —a croak with a distinctly insulting expression about it. If he had spoken in English he could not have said any more plainly than he did say in raven, "Well, what do *you* want here?" I felt as foolish as if I had been caught in some mean act by a responsible being, and reproved for it. However, I made no reply; I would not bandy words with a raven. The adversary waited a while, with his shoulders still lifted, his head thrust down between them, and his keen bright eye fixed on me; then he threw out two or three more insults, which I could not understand, further than that I knew a portion of them consisted of language not used in church.

I still made no reply. Now the adversary raised his head and called. There was an answering croak from a little distance in the wood,—evidently a croak of inquiry. The adversary explained with enthusiasm, and the other raven dropped everything and came. The two sat side by side on the limb and discussed me as freely and offensively as two great naturalists might discuss a new kind of bug. The thing became more and more embarrassing. They called in another friend. This was too much. I saw that they had the advantage of me, and so I concluded to get out of the scrape by walking out of it. They enjoyed my defeat as much as any low white people could have done. They craned their necks and laughed at me (for a raven *can* laugh, just like a man), they squalled insulting remarks after me as long as they could see me. They were nothing but ravens— I knew that,—what they thought about me could be a matter of no consequence,—and yet when even a raven shouts after you, "What a hat!" "Oh, pull down your vest!" and that sort of thing, it hurts you and humiliates you and there is no getting around it with fine reasoning and pretty arguments.

Animals talk to each other, of course. There can be no question about that; but I suppose there are very few people who can understand them. I never knew but one man who could. I knew he could, however, because he told me so himself. He was a middle-aged, simple-hearted miner who had lived in a lonely corner of California, among the woods and mountains, a good many years, and had studied the ways of his only neighbors, the beasts and the birds, until he believed he could accurately translate any remark which they made. This was Jim Baker. According to Jim Baker, some animals have only a limited education, and use only very simple words, and scarcely ever a comparison or a flowery figure; whereas, certain other animals have a large vocabulary, a fine command of language and a ready and fluent delivery; consequently these latter talk a great deal; they like it; they are conscious of their talent, and they enjoy "showing off." Baker said, that after long and careful observation, he had come to the con-

clusion that the bluejays were the best talkers he had found among birds and beasts. Said he:

"There's more *to* a bluejay than any other creature. He has got more moods, and more different kinds of feelings than other creatures; and, mind you, whatever a bluejay feels, he can put into language. And no mere commonplace language, either, but rattling, out-and-out book-talk—and bristling with metaphor, too—just bristling! And as for command of language—why *you* never see a bluejay get stuck for a word. No man ever did. They just boil out of him! And another thing: I've noticed a good deal, and there's no bird, or cow, or anything that uses as good grammar as a bluejay. You may say a cat uses good grammar. Well, a cat does— but you let a cat get excited once; you let a cat get to pulling fur with another cat on a shed, nights, and you'll hear grammar that will give you the lockjaw. Ignorant people think it's the *noise* which fighting cats make that is so aggravating, but it ain't so; it's the sickening grammar they use. Now I've never heard a jay use bad grammar but very seldom; and when they do, they are as ashamed as a human; they shut right down and leave.

"You may call a jay a bird. Well, so he is, in a measure—because he's got feathers on him, and don't belong to no church, perhaps; but otherwise he is just as much a human as you be. And I'll tell you for why. A jay's gifts, and instincts, and feelings, and interests, cover the whole ground. A jay hasn't got any more principle than a Congressman. A jay will lie, a jay will steal, a jay will deceive, a jay will betray; and four times out of five, a jay will go back on his solemnest promise. The sacredness of an obligation is a thing which you can't cram into no bluejay's head. Now, on top of all this, there's another thing; a jay can out-swear any gentleman in the mines. You think a cat can swear. Well, a cat can; but you give a bluejay a subject that calls for his reserve-powers, and where is your cat? Don't talk to *me* —I know too much about this thing. And there's yet another thing; in the one little particular of scolding— just good, clean, out-and-out scolding—a bluejay can lay over anything, human or divine. Yes, sir, a jay is everything that a man is. A jay can cry, a jay can laugh, a jay can feel shame, a jay can reason and plan and discuss, a jay likes gossip and scandal, a jay has got a sense of humor, a jay knows when he is an ass just as well as you do—maybe better. If a jay ain't human, he better take in his sign, that's all. Now I'm going to tell you a perfectly true fact about some bluejays.

"When I first begun to understand jay language correctly, there was a little incident happened here. Seven years ago, the last man in this region but me moved away. There stands his house,—been empty ever since; a log house, with a plank roof—just one big room, and no more; no ceiling—nothing between the rafters and the floor. Well, one Sunday morning I was sitting out here in front of my cabin, with my cat, taking the sun, and looking at the blue hills, and listening to the leaves rustling so lonely in the trees, and thinking of the home away yonder in the states, that I hadn't heard from in thirteen years, when a bluejay lit on that house, with an acorn in his mouth, and says, 'Hello, I reckon I've struck something.' When he spoke, the acorn dropped out of his mouth and rolled down the roof, of course, but he didn't care; his mind was all on the thing he had struck. It was a knot-hole in the roof. He cocked his head to one side, shut one eye and put the other one to the hole, like a 'possum looking down a jug; then he glanced up with his bright eyes, gave a wink or two with his wings—which signifies gratification, you understand,—and says, 'It looks like a hole, it's located like a hole,—blamed if I don't believe it *is* a hole!'

"Then he cocked his head down and took another look; he glances up perfectly joyful, this time; winks his wings and his tail both, and says, 'Oh, no, this ain't no fat thing, I reckon! If I ain't in luck!—why it's a perfectly elegant hole!' So he flew down and got that acorn, and fetched it up and dropped it in, and was just tilting his head back, with the heavenliest smile on his face, when all of a sudden he was paralyzed into a listening attitude and that smile faded gradually out of his countenance like breath off'n a razor, and the queerest look of surprise took its place. Then he says, 'Why, I didn't hear it fall!' He cocked his eye at the hole again, and took a long look; raised up and shook his head; stepped around to the other side of the hole and took another look from that side; shook his head again. He studied a while, then he just went into the *details*—walked round and round the hole and spied into it from every point of the compass. No use. Now he took a thinking attitude on the comb of the roof and scratched the back of his head with his right foot a minute, and finally says, 'Well, it's too many for *me,* that's certain; must be a mighty long hole; however, I ain't got no time to fool around here, I got to 'tend to business; I reckon it's all right—chance it, anyway.'

"So he flew off and fetched another acorn and dropped it in, and tried to flirt his eye to the hole quick enough to see what become of it, but he was too late. He held his eye there as much as a minute; then he raised up and sighed, and says, 'Confound it, I don't seem to understand this thing, no way; however, I'll tackle her again.' He fetched another acorn, and done his level best to see what become of it, but he couldn't. He says, 'Well, *I* never struck no such a hole as this before; I'm of the opinion it's a totally new kind of a hole.' Then he begun to get mad. He held in for a spell, walking up and down the comb of the roof and shaking his head and muttering to himself; but his feelings got the upper hand of him, presently, and he broke loose and cussed himself black in the face. I never see a bird take on so about a little thing. When he got through he walks to the hole and looks in again for half a minute; then he says, 'Well, you're a long hole, and a deep hole, and a mighty singular hole altogether—but I've started in to fill you, and I'm d—d if I *don't* fill you, if it takes a hundred years!'

"And with that, away he went. You never see a bird work so since you was born. He laid into his work like a nigger, and the way he hove acorns into that hole for about two hours and a half was one of the most exciting and astonishing spectacles I ever struck. He never stopped to take a look any more—he just hove 'em in and went for more. Well, at last he could hardly flop his wings, he was so tuckered out. He comes a-drooping down, once more, sweating like an ice-pitcher, drops his acorn in and says, '*Now* I guess I've got the bulge on you by this time!' So he bent down for a look. If you'll believe me, when his head come up again he was just pale with rage. He says, 'I've shoveled acorns enough in there to keep the family thirty years, and if I can see a sign of one of 'em I wish I may land in a museum with a belly full of sawdust in two minutes!'

"He just had strength enough to crawl up on to the comb and lean his back agin the chimbly, and then he collected his impressions and begun to free his mind. I see in a second that what I had mistook for profanity in the mines was only just the rudiments, as you may say.

"Another jay was going by, and heard him doing his devotions, and stops to inquire what was up. The

sufferer told him the whole circumstance, and says, 'Now yonder's the hole, and if you don't believe me, go and look for yourself.' So this fellow went and looked, and comes back and says, 'How many did you say you put in there?' 'Not any less than two tons,' says the sufferer. The other jay went and looked again. He couldn't seem to make it out, so he raised a yell, and three more jays come. They all examined the hole, they all made the sufferer tell it over again, then they
10 all discussed it, and got off as many leather-headed opinions about it as an average crowd of humans could have done.

"They called in more jays; then more and more, till pretty soon this whole region 'peared to have a blue flush about it. There must have been five thousand of them; and such another jawing and disputing and fipping and cussing, you never heard. Every jay in the whole lot put his eye to the hole and delivered a more chuckle-headed opinion about the mystery than the jay
20 that went there before him. They examined the house all over, too. The door was standing half open, and at last one old jay happened to go and light on it and look in. Of course, that knocked the mystery galley-

west in a second. There lay the acorns, scattered all over the floor. He flopped his wings and raised a whoop 'Come here!' he says, 'Come here, everybody; hang'd if this fool hasn't been trying to fill up a house with acorns!' They all came a-swooping down like a blue cloud, and as each fellow lit on the door and took a glance, the whole absurdity of the contract that that 30 first jay had tackled hit him home and he fell over backwards suffocating with laughter, and the next jay took his place and done the same.

"Well, sir, they roosted around here on the housetop and the trees for an hour, and guffawed over that thing like human beings. It ain't any use to tell me a bluejay hasn't got a sense of humor, because I know better. And memory, too. They brought jays here from all over the United States to look down that hole, every summer for three years. Other birds, too. And they 40 could all see the point, except an owl that come from Nova Scotia to visit the Yo Semite, and he took this thing in on his way back. He said he couldn't see anything funny in it. But then he was a good deal disappointed about Yo Semite, too."

1880

From

Life on the Mississippi

Chapter III

FRESCOES FROM THE PAST

A chapter written for **Huckleberry Finn**, but never included in it, is the one which follows. Clemens placed it in Chapter III of **Life on the Mississippi**, with introductory remarks which throw some light on his conception of the nature of **The Adventures of Huckleberry Finn**. The "tall talk" and the fanciful yarning in the passage are among Clemens' happiest achievements in this vein. The boasts of Bob and the Pet Child of Calamity represent a convention in the prewar humor of the frontier—the convention whereby authors pictured contestants preceding all fights with similar proclamations about their prowess. The

author evidently remembered and recorded some of the favorite phrases of the Hannibal town drunkard whom he had known when he was a boy. Just why Clemens left this passage out of **Huckleberry Finn** has puzzled his critics, since it is rich in invention and humor.

By way of illustrating keelboat talk and manners, and that now departed and hardly-remembered raft-life, I will throw in, in this place, a chapter from a book which I have been working at, by fits and starts, during the past five or six years, and may possibly finish in the course of five or six more. The book is a story which details some passages in the life of an ignorant village boy, Huck Finn, son of the town drunkard of my time out West, there. He has run away from his persecuting father, and from a persecuting good widow who wishes 10 to make a nice, truth-telling, respectable boy of him; and with him a slave of the widow's has also escaped. They have found a fragment of a lumber-raft (it is high

water and dead summer-time), and are floating down
the river by night, and hiding in the willows by day—
bound for Cairo, whence the Negro will seek freedom in
the heart of the free states. But, in a fog, they pass Cairo
without knowing it. By and by they begin to suspect
the truth, and Huck Finn is persuaded to end the dismal
suspense by swimming down to a huge raft which they
have seen in the distance ahead of them, creeping
aboard under cover of the darkness, and gathering the
needed information by eavesdropping:

But you know [writes Huck] a young person can't
wait very well when he is impatient to find a thing out.
We talked it over, and by and by Jim said it was such
a black night, now, that it wouldn't be no risk to swim
down to the big raft and crawl aboard and listen—they
would talk about Cairo, because they would be calculating to go ashore there for a spree, maybe; or anyway
they would send boats ashore to buy whisky or fresh
meat or something. Jim had a wonderful level head,
for a nigger: he could most always start a good plan
when you wanted one.

I stood up and shook my rags off and jumped into
the river, and struck out for the raft's light. By and by,
when I got down nearly to her, I eased up and went
slow and cautious. But everything was all right—nobody
at the sweeps. So I swum down along the raft till I was
most abreast the camp-fire in the middle, then I crawled
aboard and inched along and got in among some bundles
of shingles on the weather side of the fire. There was
thirteen men there—they was the watch on deck of
course. And a mighty rough-looking lot, too. They had
a jug, and tin cups, and they kept the jug moving. One
man was singing—roaring, you may say; and it wasn't
a nice song—for a parlor, anyway. He roared through
his nose, and strung out the last word of every line very
long. When he was done they all fetched a kind of Injun
warwhoop, and then another was sung. It begun:

"There was a woman in our towdn,
    In our towdn did dwed'l [dwell],
    She loved her husband dear-i-lee,
    But another man twyste as wed'l.

"Singing too, riloo, riloo, riloo,
    Ri-too, riloo, rilay - - - e,
    She loved her husband dear-i-lee,
    But another man twyste as wed'l."

And so on—fourteen verses. It was kind of poor, and
when he was going to start on the next verse one of them
said it was the tune the old cow died on; and another
one said: "Oh, give us a rest!" And another one told him
to take a walk. They made fun of him till he got mad
and jumped up and begun to cuss the crowd, and said
he could lam any thief in the lot.

They was all about to make a break for him, but the
biggest man there jumped up and says:

"Set whar you are, gentlemen. Leave him to me; he's
my meat."

Then he jumped up in the air three times, and cracked
his heels together every time. He flung off a buckskin
coat that was all hung with fringes, and says, "You lay
thar tell the chawin-up's done"; and flung his hat down,
which was all over ribbons, and says, "You lay thar tell
his sufferin's is over."

Then he jumped up in the air and cracked his heels
together again, and shouted out:

"Whoo-oop! I'm the old original iron-hawed, brass-
mounted, copper-bellied corpse-maker from the wilds
of Arkansaw! Look at me! I'm the man they call Sudden
Death and General Desolation! Sired by a hurricane,
dam'd by an earthquake, half-brother to the cholera,
nearly related to the smallpox on the mother's side!
Look at me! I take nineteen alligators and a bar'l of
whisky for breakfast when I'm in robust health, and a
bushel of rattlesnakes and a dead body when I'm ailing.
I split the everlasting rocks with my glance, and I squench
the thunder when I speak! Whoo-oop! Stand back and
give me room according to my strength! Blood's my
natural drink, and the wails of the dying is music to my
ear. Cast your eye on me, gentlemen! and lay low and
hold your breath, for I'm 'bout to turn myself loose!"

All the time he was getting this off, he was shaking
his head and looking fierce, and kind of swelling around
in a little circle, tucking up his wristbands, and now and
then straightening up and beating his breast with his
fist, saying, "Look at me, gentlemen!" When he got
through, he jumped up and cracked his heels together
three times, and let off a roaring "Whoo-oop! I'm the
bloodiest son of a wildcat that lives!"

Then the man that had started the row tilted his old
slouch hat down over his right eye; then he bent stooping
forward, with his back sagged and his south end sticking
out far, and his fists a-shoving out and drawing in in
front of him, and so went around in a little circle about

three times, swelling himself up and breathing hard. Then he straightened, and jumped up and cracked his heels together three times before he lit again (that made them cheer), and he began to shout like this:

"Whoo-oop! bow your neck and spread, for the kingdom of sorrow's a-coming! Hold me down to the earth, for I feel my powers a-working! whoo-oop! I'm a child of sin, *don't* let me get a start! Smoked glass, here, for all! Don't attempt to look at me with the naked eye, gentlemen! When I'm playful I use the meridians of longitude and parallels of latitude for a seine, and drag the Atlantic Ocean for whales! I scratch my head with the lightning and purr myself to sleep with the thunder! When I'm cold, I bile the Gulf of Mexico and bathe in it; when I'm hot I fan myself with an equinoctial storm; when I'm thirsty I reach up and suck a cloud dry like a sponge; when I range the earth hungry, famine follows in my tracks! Whoo-oop! Bow your neck and spread! I put my hand on the sun's face and make it night in the earth; I bite a piece out of the moon and hurry the seasons; I shake myself and crumble the mountains! Contemplate me through leather—*don't* use the naked eye! The massacre of isolated communities is the pastime of my idle moments, the destruction of nationalities the serious business of my life! The boundless vastness of the great American desert is my enclosed property, and I bury my dead on my own premises!" He jumped up and cracked his heels together three times before he lit (they cheered him again), and as he come down he shouted out: "Whoo-oop! bow your neck and spread, for the Pet Child of Calamity's a-coming!"

Then the other one went to swelling around and blowing again—the first one—the one they called Bob; next, the Child of Calamity chipped in again, swelling round and round each other and punching their fists most into each other's faces, and whooping and jawing like Injuns; then Bob called the Child names, and the Child called him names back again; next, Bob called him a heap rougher names; and the Child come back at him with the very worst kind of language; next, Bob knocked the Child's hat off, and the Child picked it up and kicked Bob's ribbony hat about six foot; Bob went and got it and said never mind, this warn't going to be the last of this thing, because he was a man that never forgot and never forgive, and so the Child better look out, for there was a time a-coming, just as sure as he was a living man,

that he would have to answer to him with the best blood in his body. The Child said no man was willinger than he for that time to come, and he would give Bob fair warning, *now,* never to cross his path again, for he could never rest till he had waded in his blood, for such was his nature, though he was sparing him now on account of his family, if he had one.

Both of them was edging away in different directions, growling and shaking their heads and going on about what they was going to do; but a little black-whiskered chap skipped up and says:

"Come back here, you couple of chicken-livered cowards, and I'll thrash the two of ye!"

And he done it, too. He snatched them, he jerked them this way and that, he booted them around, he knocked them sprawling faster than they could get up. Why, it warn't two minutes till they begged like dogs—and how the other lot did yell and laugh and clap their hands all the way through, and shout, "Sail in, Corpse-Maker!" "Hi! at him again, Child of Calamity!" "Bully for you, little Davy!" Well, it was a perfect pow-wow for a while, Bob and the Child had red noses and black eyes when they got through. Little Davy made them own up that they was sneaks and cowards and not fit to eat with a dog or drink with a nigger; then Bob and the Child shook hands with each other, very solemn, and said they had always respected each other and was willing to let bygones be bygones. So then they washed their faces in the river; and just then there was a loud order to stand by for a crossing, and some of them went forward to man the sweeps there, and the rest went aft to handle the after sweeps.

I lay still and waited for fifteen minutes, and had a smoke out of a pipe that one of them left in reach; then the crossing was finished, and they stumped back and had a drink around and went to talking and singing again. Next they got out an old fiddle, and one played, and another patted juba, and the rest turned themselves loose on a regular old-fashioned keelboat breakdown. They couldn't keep that up very long without getting winded, so by and by they settled around the jug again.

They sung "Jolly, Jolly Raftsman's the Life for Me," with a rousing chorus, and then they got to talking about differences betwixt hogs, and their different kind of habits; and next about women and their different kind of ways; and next about the best ways to put out houses that was afire; and next about what ought to be done with the Injuns; and next what a king had to do, and how much he got; and next about how to make cats fight; and next what to do when a man has fits; and next about the differences betwixt clear-water rivers and muddy-water ones. The man they called Ed said the muddy Mississippi water was wholesomer to drink than the clear water of the Ohio; he said if you let a pint of yaller Mississippi water settle, you would have about a half to three-quarters of an inch of mud in the bottom, according to the stage of the river, and then it warn't no better than Ohio water—what you wanted to do was to keep it stirred up—and when the river was low, keep mud on hand to put in and thicken the water up the way it ought to be.

The Child of Calamity said that was so; he said there was nutritiousness in the mud, and a man that drunk Mississippi water could grow corn in his stomach if he wanted to. He says:

"You look at the graveyards; that tells the tale. Trees won't grow worth shucks in a Cincinnati graveyard, but in a Sent Louis graveyard they grow upwards of eight hundred foot high. It's all on account of the water the people drunk before they laid up. A Cincinnati corpse don't richen a soil any."

And they talked about how Ohio water didn't like to mix with Mississippi water. Ed said if you take the Mississippi on a rise when the Ohio is low, you'll find a wide band of clear water all the way down the east side of the Mississippi for a hundred mile or more, and the minute you get out a quarter of a mile from shore and pass the line, it is all thick and yaller the rest of the way across. They talked about how to keep tobacco from getting mouldy, and from that they went to ghosts and told about a lot that other folks had seen; but Ed says:

"Why don't you tell something that you've seen yourselves? Now let me have a say. Five years ago I was on a raft as big as this, and right along here it was a bright moonshiny night, and I was on watch and boss of the stabboard oar forrard, and one of my pards was a man named Dick Allbright, and he come along to where I was sitting, forrard—gaping and stretching, he was— and stooped down on the edge of the raft and washed his face in the river, and come and set down by me and

got out his pipe, and had just got it filled, when he looks up and says:

"'Why looky-here,' he says, 'ain't that Buck Miller's place, over yander in the bend?'

"'Yes,' says I, 'it is—why?' He laid his pipe down and leaned his head on his hand, and says:

"'I thought we'd be furder down.' I says:

"'I thought it, too, when I went off watch'—we was standing six hours on and six off—'but the boys told me,' I says, 'that the raft didn't seem to hardly move, for the last hour,' says I, 'though she's a-slipping along all right now,' says I. He give a kind of a groan, and says:

"'I seed a raft act so before, along here,' he says, ''pears to me the current has most quit above the head of this bend durin' the last two years,' he says.

"Well, he raised up two or three times, and looked away off and around on the water. That started me at it, too. A body is always doing what he sees somebody else doing, though there mayn't be no sense in it. Pretty soon I see a black something floating on the water away

Huck Finn—this drawing and the four following were done by Kemble for the first edition of Huckleberry Finn

off to stabboard and quartering behind us. I see he was looking at it, too, I says:

"'What's that?' He says, sort of pettish:

"'Tain't nothing but an old empty bar'l.'

"'An empty bar'l!' says I, 'why,' says I, 'a spy-glass is a fool to *your* eyes. How can you tell it's an empty bar'l?' He says:

"'I don't know; I reckon it ain't a bar'l, but I thought it might be,' says he.

"'Yes,' I says, 'so it might be, and it might be any-thing else, too; a body can't tell nothing about it, such a distance as that,' I says:

"We hadn't nothing else to do, so we kept on watch-ing it. By and by I says,

"'Why, looky-here, Dick Allbright, that thing's a-gaining on us, I believe.'

"He never said nothing. The thing gained and gained, and I judged it must be a dog that was about tired out. Well, we swung down into the crossing, and the thing floated across the bright streak of the moonshine, and by George, it *was* a bar'l. Says I:

"'Dick Allbright, what made you think that thing was a bar'l, when it was half a mile off?' says I. Says he:

"'I don't know.' Says I:

"'You tell me, Dick Allbright.' Says he:

"'Well, I knowed it was a bar'l; I've seen it before; lots has seen it; they says it's a ha'nted bar'l.'

"I called the rest of the watch, and they come and stood there, and I told them what Dick said. It floated right along abreast, now, and didn't gain any more. It was about twenty foot off. Some was for having it aboard, but the rest didn't want to. Dick Allbright said rafts that had fooled with it had got bad luck by it. The captain of the watch said he didn't believe in it. He said he reckoned the bar'l gained on us because it was in a little better current than what we was. He said it would leave by and by.

"So then we went to talking about other things, and we had a song, and then a breakdown; and after that the captain of the watch called for another song; but it was clouding up now, and the bar'l stuck right thar in the same place, and the song didn't seem to have much warm-up to it, somehow, and so they didn't finish it, and there warn't any cheers, but it sort of dropped flat, and nobody said anything for a minute. Then every-body tried to talk at once, and one chap got off a joke,

but it warn't no use, they didn't laugh, and even the chap that made the joke didn't laugh at it, which ain't usual. We all just settled down glum, and watched the bar'l, and was oneasy and oncomfortable. Well, sir, it shut down black and still, and then the wind began to moan around, and next the lightning began to play and the thunder to grumble. And pretty soon there was a regular storm, and in the middle of it a man that was running aft stumbled and fell and sprained his ankle so that he had to lay up. This made the boys shake their heads. And every time the lightning come, there was that bar'l, with the blue lights winking around it. We was always on the lookout for it. But by and by, toward dawn, she was gone. When the day come we couldn't see her anywhere, and we warn't sorry, either.

"But next night about half past nine, when there was songs and high jinks going on, here she comes again, and took her old roost on the stabboard side. There warn't no more high jinks. Everybody got solemn; nobody talked; you couldn't get anybody to do anything but set around moody and look at the bar'l. It begun to cloud up again. When the watch changed, the off watch stayed up, 'stead of turning in. The storm ripped and roared around all night, and in the middle of it another man tripped and sprained his ankle, and had to knock off. The bar'l left toward day, and nobody see it go.

"Everybody was sober and down in the mouth all day. I don't mean the kind of sober that comes of leav-ing liquor alone—not that. They was quiet, but they all drunk more than usual—not together, but each man sidled off and took it private, by himself.

"After dark the off watch didn't turn in; nobody sung, nobody talked; the boys didn't scatter around, neither; they sort of huddled together, forrard; and for two hours they set there, perfectly still, looking steady in the one direction, and heaving a sigh once in a while. And then, here comes the bar'l again. She took up her old place. She stayed there all night; nobody turned in. The storm come on again, after midnight. It got awful dark; and the rain poured down; hail, too; the thunder boomed and roared and bellowed; the wind blowed a hurricane; and the lightning spread over everything in big sheets of glare, and showed the whole raft as plain as day; and the river lashed up white as milk as far as you could see for miles, and there was that bar'l jiggering along, same as ever. The captain ordered the watch to man the after sweeps for a crossing, and nobody would go—no more sprained ankles for them, they said. They wouldn't even *walk* aft. Well, then, just then the sky split wide open, with a crash, and the lightning killed two men of the after watch, and crippled two more. Crippled them how, say you? Why, *sprained their ankles!*

"The bar'l left in the dark betwixt lightnings, toward dawn. Well, not a body eat a bite at breakfast that morning. After that the men loafed around in twos and threes, and talked low together. But none of them herded with Dick Allbright. They all give him the cold shake. If he come around where any of the men was, they split up and sidled away. They wouldn't man the sweeps with him. The captain had all the skiffs hauled up on the raft, alongside of his wigwam, and wouldn't let the dead men be took ashore to be planted; he didn't believe a man that got ashore would come back; and he was right.

"After night come, you could see pretty plain that there was going to be trouble if that bar'l come again; there was such a muttering going on. A good many wanted to kill Dick Allbright, because he'd seen the bar'l on other trips, and that had an ugly look. Some wanted to put him ashore. Some said: 'Let's all go ashore in a pile, if the bar'l comes again.'

"This kind of whispers was still going on, the men being bunched together forrard watching for the bar'l, when lo and behold you here she comes again. Down she comes, slow and steady, and settles into her old tracks. You could 'a' heard a pin drop. Then up comes the captain, and says:

"'Boys, don't be a pack of children and fools; I don't want this bar'l to be dogging us all the way to Orleans, and *you* don't: Well, then, how's the best way to stop it? Burn it up—that's the way. I'm going to fetch it aboard,' he says. And before anybody could say a word, in he went.

"He swum to it, and as he come pushing it to the raft, the men spread to one side. But the old man got it aboard and busted in the head, and there was a baby in it! Yes, sir; a stark-naked baby. It was Dick Allbright's baby; he owned up and said so.

"'Yes,' he says, a-leaning over it, 'yes, it is my own lamented darling, my poor lost Charles William Allbright deceased,' says he—for he could curl his tongue around the bulliest words in the language when he was of a mind to, and lay them before you without a jint started anywheres. Yes, he said, he used to live up at the head of this bend, and one night he choked his child, which was crying, not intending to kill it—which was prob'ly a lie—and then he was scared, and buried it in a bar'l, before his wife got home, and off he went, and struck the northern trail and went to rafting; and this was the third year that the bar'l had chased him. He said the bad luck always begun light, and lasted till four men was killed, and then the bar'l didn't come any more after that. He said if the men would stand it one more night—and was a-going on like that—but the men had got enough. They started to get out a boat to take him ashore and lynch him, but he grabbed the little child all of a sudden and jumped overboard with it, hugged up to his breast and shedding tears, and we never see him again, poor old suffering soul, nor Charles William neither."

"*Who* was shedding tears?" says Bob; "was it Allbright or the baby?"

"Why, Allbright, of course; didn't I tell you the baby was dead? Been dead three years—how could it cry?"

"Well, never mind how it could cry—how could it *keep* all that time?" says Davy. "You answer me that."

"I don't know how it done it," says Ed. "It done it, though—that's all I know about it."

"Say—what did they do with the bar'l?" says the Child of Calamity.

"Why, they hove it overboard, and it sunk like a chunk of lead."

"Edward, did the child look like it was choked?" says one.

"Did it have its hair parted?" says another.

"What was the brand on that bar'l, Eddy?" says a fellow they called Bill.

"Have you got the papers for them statistics, Edmund?" says Jimmy.

"Say, Edwin, was you one of the men that was killed by the lightning?" says Davy.

"Him? Oh, no! he was both of 'em," says Bob. Then they all haw-hawed.

"Say, Edward, don't you reckon you'd better take a pill? You look bad—don't you feel pale?" says the Child of Calamity.

"Oh, come, now, Eddy," says Jimmy, "show up; you must 'a' kept part of that bar'l to prove the thing by. Show us the bung-hole—*do*—and we'll all believe you."

"Say, boys," says Bill, "less divide it up. Thar's thirteen of us. I can swaller a thirteenth of the yarn, if you can worry down the rest."

Ed got up mad and said they could all go to some place which he ripped out pretty savage, and then walked off aft, cussing to himself, and they yelling and jeering at him, and roaring and laughing so you could hear them a mile.

"Boys, we'll split a watermelon on that," says the Child of Calamity; and he came rummaging around in the dark amongst the shingle bundles where I was, and put his hand on me. I was warm and soft and naked; so he says "Ouch!" and jumped back.

"Fetch a lantern or a chunk of fire here, boys—there's a snake here as big as a cow!"

So they run there with a lantern, and crowded up and looked in on me.

"Come out of that, you beggar!" says one.

"Who are you?" says another.

"What are you after here? Speak up prompt, or overboard you go."

"Snake him out, boys. Snatch him out by the heels."

I began to beg, and crept out amongst them trembling. They looked me over, wondering, and the Child of Calamity says:

"A cussed thief! Lend me a hand and less heave him overboard!"

"No," says Big Bob, "less get out the paint-pot and paint him a sky-blue all over from head to heel, and *then* heave him over."

"Good! that's it. Go for the paint, Jimmy."

When the paint come, and Bob took the brush and was just going to begin, the others laughing and rubbing their hands, I begun to cry, and that sort of worked on Davy, and he says:

"'Vast there. He's nothing but a cub. I'll paint the man that teches him!"

So I looked around on them, and some of them grumbled and growled, and Bob put down the paint, and the others didn't take it up.

"Come here to the fire, and less see what you're up to here," says Davy. "Now set down there and give an account of yourself. How long have you been aboard here?"

"Not over a quarter of a minute, sir," says I.

"How did you get dry so quick?"

"I don't know, sir. I'm always that way, mostly."

"Oh, you are, are you? What's your name?"

I warn't going to tell my name. I didn't know what to say, so I just says:

"Charles William Allbright, sir."

Then they roared—the whole crowd; and I was mighty glad I said that, because, maybe, laughing would get them in a better humor.

When they got done laughing, Davy says:

"It won't hardly do, Charles William. You couldn't have growed this much in five year, and you was a baby, when you come out of the bar'l, you know, and dead at that. Come now, tell a straight story, and nobody'll hurt you, if you ain't up to anything wrong. What *is* your name?"

"Aleck Hopkins, sir. Aleck James Hopkins."

"Well, Aleck, where did you come from here?"

"From a trading-scow. She lays up the bend yonder. I was born on her. Pap has traded up and down here all his life; and he told me to swim off here, because when you went by he said he would like to get some of you to speak to a Mr. Jonas Turner, in Cairo, and tell him—"

"Oh, come!"

"Yes, sir, it's as true as the world. Pap he says—"

"Oh, your grandmother!"

They all laughed, and I tried again to talk, but they broke in on me and stopped me.

"Now, looky-here," says Davy; "you're scared, and so you talk wild. Honest, now do you live in a scow, or is it a lie?"

"Yes, sir, in a trading-scow. She lays up at the head of the bend. But I warn't born in her. It's our first trip."

"Now you're talking! What did you come aboard here for? To steal?"

"No, sir, I didn't. It was only to get a ride on the raft. All boys does that."

"Well, I know that. But what did you hide for?"

"Sometimes they drive the boys off."

"So they do. They might steal. Looky-here; if we let you off this time, will you keep out of these kind of scrapes hereafter?"

"'Deed I will, boss. You try me."

"All right, then. You ain't but little ways from shore.

Overboard with you, and don't you make a fool of yourself another time this way. Blast it, boy, some raftsmen would rawhide you till you were black and blue!"

I didn't wait to kiss good-by, but went overboard and broke for shore. When Jim come along by and by, the big raft was far away out of sight around the point. I swum out and got aboard, and was mighty glad to see home again.

The boy did not get the information he was after, but his adventure has furnished the glimpse of the departed raftsman and keelboatman which I desire to offer in this place.

1876?·1883

Chapter XXXVIII

THE HOUSE BEAUTIFUL

Because "Old Times on the Mississippi" was not lengthy enough to fill a large book of the sort sold by subscription, Clemens hit upon the idea of supplementing it with an account of a visit, made in 1882, to the river. He took the trip and wrote the story of the journey. This account was presented in Chapters XXI-LX of **Life on the Mississippi**, published in 1883. In the chapter which follows, he includes a description of the exterior and the interior of an ante-bellum Southern mansion, one so detailed and authentic that at least two social historians have quoted it at length to acquaint readers with pre-Civil War ways of living. In 1884 and the years which followed, readers were to have a chance to contrast this account with a description of the same room—or one very like it— written by naïve Huck Finn.

We took passage in a Cincinnati boat for New Orleans; or on a Cincinnati boat—either is correct; the former is the Eastern form of putting it, the latter the Western.

Mr. Dickens declined to agree that the Mississippi steamboats were "magnificent," or that they were "floating palaces"—terms which had always been applied to them; terms which did not over-express the admiration with which the people viewed them.

Mr. Dickens's position was unassailable, possibly; the people's position was certainly unassailable. If Mr. Dickens was comparing these boats with the crown jewels; or with the Taj, or with the Matterhorn; or with some other priceless or wonderful thing which he had seen, they were not magnificent—he was right. The people compared them with what *they* had seen; and, thus measured, thus judged, the boats were magnificent—the term was the correct one, it was not at all too strong. The people were as right as was Mr. Dickens. The steamboats were finer than anything on shore. Compared with superior dwelling-houses and first-class hotels in the valley, they were indubitably magnificent, they were "palaces." To a few people living in New Orleans and St. Louis they were not magnificent, perhaps; not palaces; but to the great majority of those populations, and to the entire populations spread over both banks between Baton Rouge and St. Louis, they were palaces; they tallied with the citizen's dream of what magnificence was, and satisfied it.

Every town and village along that vast stretch of double river-frontage had a best dwelling, finest dwelling, mansion—the home of its wealthiest and most conspicuous citizens. It is easy to describe it: large grassy yard, with paling fence painted white—in fair repair; brick walk from gate to door; big, square, two-story "frame" house, painted white and porticoed like a Grecian temple—with this difference, that the imposing fluted columns and Corinthian capitals were a pathetic sham, being made of white pine, and painted; iron knocker; brass door-knob—discolored, for lack of polishing. Within, an uncarpeted hall, of planed boards; opening out of it, a parlor, fifteen feet by fifteen—in some instances five or ten feet larger; ingrain carpet; mahogany center-table; lamp on it, with green-paper shade—standing on a gridiron, so to speak, made of high-colored yarns, by the young ladies of the house, and called a lamp-mat; several books, piled and disposed, with cast-iron exactness, according to an inherited and unchangeable plan; among them, Tupper, much penciled;

---

18 **Mr. Dickens.** Charles Dickens (1812-1870) in **American Notes** (1842), to which Clemens refers, gave an account of a journey through parts of the United States • 26 **Taj,** the Taj Mahal • 26 **Matterhorn,** one of the most famous mountains in the Alps • 62 **Tupper.** Martin Farquhar Tupper (1810-1889) was the author of **Proverbial Philosophy** (1838), a collection of very inferior and very popular poems

also, *Friendship's Offering,* and *Affection's Wreath,* with their sappy inanities illustrated in die-away mezzotints; also, Ossian; *Alonzo and Melissa,* maybe *Ivanhoe;* also "Album," full of original "poetry" of the Thou-hast-wounded-the-spirit-that-loved-thee breed; two or three goody-goody works—*Shepherd of Salisbury Plain,* etc.; current number of the chaste and innocuous *Godey's Lady's Book,* with painted fashion-plate of wax-figure women with mouths all alike—lips and eyelids the same 10 size—each five-foot woman with a two-inch wedge sticking from under her dress and letting on to be half of her foot. Polished air-tight stove (new and deadly invention), with pipe passing through a board which closes up the discarded good old fireplace. On each end of the wooden mantel, over the fireplace, a large basket of peaches and other fruits, natural size, all done in plaster, rudely, or in wax, and painted to resemble the originals—which they don't. Over middle of mantel, engraving—"Washington Crossing the Delaware"; on the 20 wall by the door, copy of it done in thunder-and-lightning crewels by one of the young ladies—work of art which would have made Washington hesitate about crossing, if he could have foreseen what advantage was going to be taken of it. Piano—kettle in disguise—with music, bound and unbound, piled on it, and on a stand near by: "Battle of Prague"; "Bird Waltz"; "Arkansas Traveler"; "Rosin the Bow"; "Marseillaise Hymn"; "On a Lone Barren Isle" (St. Helena); "The Last Link Is Broken"; "She Wore a Wreath of Roses the Night 30 When Last We Met"; "Go, Forget Me, Why Should Sorrow o'er That Brow a Shadow Fling"; "Hours That Were to Memory Dearer"; "Long, Long Ago"; "Days of Absence"; "A Life on the Ocean Wave, a Home on the Rolling Deep"; "Bird at Sea"; and spread open on the rack where the plaintive singer has left it, *"Ro-*holl on, silver *moo-*hoon, guide the *trav-*el-err on his *way,"* etc. Tilted pensively against the piano, a guitar—guitar capable of playing the Spanish fandango by itself, if you give it a start. Frantic work of art on the wall—pious 40 motto, done on the premises, sometimes in colored yarns, sometimes in faded grasses: progenitor of the "God Bless Our Home" of modern commerce. Framed in black moldings on the wall, other works of art, conceived and committed on the premises, by the young ladies; being grim black-and-white crayons; landscapes, mostly: lake, solitary sailboat, petrified clouds, pregeological trees on shore, anthracite precipice; name of criminal conspicuous in the corner. Lithograph, "Napoleon Crossing the Alps." Lithograph, "The Grave at St. Helena." Steel plates, Trumbull's "Battle of Bunker 50 Hill," and the "Sally from Gibraltar." Copper plates, "Moses Smiting the Rock," and "Return of the Prodigal Son." In big gilt frame, slander of the family in oil: papa holding a book ("Constitution of the United States"); guitar leaning against mamma, blue ribbons fluttering from its neck; the young ladies, as children, in slippers and scalloped pantalettes, one embracing toy horse, the other beguiling kitten with ball of yarn, and both simpering up at mamma, who simpers back. These persons all fresh, raw, and red—apparently skinned. Op- 60 posite, in gilt frame, grandpa and grandma, at thirty and twenty-two, stiff, old-fashioned, high-collared, puff-sleeved, glaring pallidly out from a background of solid Egyptian night. Under a glass French clock dome, large bouquet of stiff flowers done in corpsy-white wax. Pyramidal what-not in the corner, the shelves occupied chiefly with bric-à-brac of the period, disposed with an eye to best effect: shell, with the Lord's Prayer carved on it; another shell—of the long-oval sort, narrow, straight orifice, three inches long, running from end to end—por- 70 trait of Washington carved on it; not well done; the shell had Washington's mouth, originally—artist should have built to that. These two are memorials of the long-ago bridal trip to New Orleans and the French Market. Other bric-à-brac: Californian "specimens"—quartz, with gold wart adhering; old Guinea-gold locket, with circlet of ancestral hair in it; Indian arrow-heads, of flint; pair of bead moccasins, from uncle who crossed the Plains; three "alum" baskets of various colors—being skeleton-frame of wire, clothed on with cubes of 80 crystallized alum in the rock-candy style—works of art which were achieved by the young ladies; their doubles

---

1 Friendship's Offering . . . Affection's Wreath, elaborate "annuals" which flourished as gift books, 1835-1855 • 3 Ossian, an alleged author of a folk epic, which was actually written by James Macpherson (1736-1796), a Scottish author. It was quite popular both in England and in the United States • 3 Alonzo and Melissa, a sentimental novel, The Asylum, or, Alonzo and Melissa (1811), by Isaac Mitchell • 7 Godey's Lady's Book, the most popular women's magazine in America in the 1840's

and duplicates to be found upon all what-nots in the land; convention of desiccated bugs and butterflies pinned to a card; painted toy dog, seated upon bellows attachment—drops its under-jaw and squeaks when pressed upon; sugar-candy rabbit—limbs and features merged together, not strongly defined; pewter presidential-campaign medal; miniature cardboard wood-sawyer, to be attached to the stovepipe and operated by the heat; small Napoleon, done in wax; spread-open daguerreotypes of dim children, parents, cousins, aunts, and friends, in all attitudes but customary ones; no templed portico at back, and manufactured landscape stretching away in the distance—that came in later, with the photograph; all these vague figures lavishly chained and ringed— metal indicated and secured from doubt by stripes and splashes of vivid gold bronze; all of them too much combed, too much fixed up; and all of them uncomfortable in inflexible Sunday clothes of a pattern which the spectator cannot realize could ever have been in fashion; husband and wife generally grouped together—husband sitting, wife standing, with hand on his shoulder—and both preserving, all these fading years, some traceable effect of the daguerreotypist's brisk "Now smile, if you please!" Bracketed over what-not—place of special sacredness—an outrage in water-color, done by the young niece that came on a visit long ago, and died. Pity, too; for she might have repented of this in time. Horsehair chairs, horsehair sofa which keeps sliding from under you. Window-shades, of oil stuff, with milkmaids and ruined castles stenciled on them in fierce colors. Lambrequins dependent from gaudy boxings of beaten tin, gilded. Bedrooms with rag carpets; bedsteads of the "corded" sort, with a sag in the middle, the cords needing tightening; snuffy feather-bed—not aired often enough; cane-seat chairs, splint-bottomed rocker; looking-glass on wall, school-slate size, veneered frame; inherited bureau; wash-bowl and pitcher, possibly—but not certainly; brass candlestick, tallow candle, snuffers. Nothing else in the room. Not a bathroom in the house; and no visitor likely to come along who has ever seen one.

That was the residence of the principal citizen, all the way from the suburbs of New Orleans to the edge of St. Louis. When he stepped aboard a big fine steamboat, he entered a new and marvelous world: chimney-tops cut to counterfeit a spraying crown of plumes—and maybe painted red; pilot-house, hurricane-deck, boiler-deck guards, all garnished with white wooden filigree-work of fanciful patterns; gilt acorns topping the derricks; gilt deerhorns over the big bell; gaudy symbolical picture on the paddle-box, possibly; big roomy boiler-deck, painted blue, and furnished with Windsor armchairs; inside, a far-receding snow-white "cabin"; porcelain knob and oil-picture on every stateroom door; curving patterns of filigree-work touched up with gilding, stretching overhead all down the converging vista; big chandeliers every little way, each an April shower of glittering glass-drops; lovely rainbow-light falling everywhere from the colored glazing of the skylights; the whole a long-drawn, resplendent tunnel, a bewildering and soul-satisfying spectacle! in the ladies' cabin a pink and white Wilton carpet, as soft as mush, and glorified with a ravishing pattern of gigantic flowers. Then the Bridal Chamber—the animal that invented that idea was still alive and unhanged, at that day—Bridal Chamber whose pretentious flummery was necessarily overawing to the now tottering intellect of that hosannahing citizen. Every stateroom had its couple of cozy clean bunks, and perhaps a looking-glass and a snug closet, and sometimes there was even a wash-bowl and pitcher, and part of a towel which could be told from mosquito-netting by an expert—though generally these things were absent, and the shirt-sleeved passengers cleansed themselves at a long row of stationary bowls in the barber shop, where were also public towels, public combs, and public soap.

Take the steamboat which I have just described, and you have her in her highest and finest, and most pleasing, and comfortable, and satisfactory estate. Now cake her over with a layer of ancient and obdurate dirt, and you have the Cincinnati steamer awhile ago referred to. Not all over—only inside; for she was ably officered in all departments except the steward's.

But wash that boat and repaint her, and she would be about the counterpart of the most complimented boat of the old flush times: for the steamboat architecture of the West has undergone no change; neither has steamboat furniture and ornamentation undergone any.

1882·1883

From

Huckleberry Finn

When Twain himself published this episode as a unit in the Century for December 1884, he explained its context in the book for the magazine readers as follows: "The Negro Jim is escaping from slavery in Missouri, and Huck Finn is running away from a drunken father, who maltreats him. The two fugitives are floating down the Mississippi on a fragment of a lumber-raft, doing their voyaging by night and hiding themselves and the raft in the day-time. When this chapter opens they have already floated four hundred miles—a trip which has occupied ten or twelve adventurous nights."

The following passage (part of Chapter XVI and all of Chapters XVII and XVIII) typifies much that made the book memorable. Here, in rich detail, is a segment of life along the river in the 1840's. Here is Huck's character, revealed by what he does and says. And here is an employment of the American language for varying purposes —for humor ranging from broad, low comedy to something much higher, for description, for the portrayal of action, and for Huck's restrained account of how he felt after the death of his friend, Buck Grangerford.

THE GRANGERFORDS TAKE ME IN

Well, the night got gray and rather thick, which is the next meanest thing to fog. You can't tell the shape of the river, and you can't see no distance. It got to be very late and still, and then along comes a steamboat up the river. We lit the lantern, and judged she would see it. Up-stream boats didn't generly come close to us; they go out and follow the bars and hunt for easy water under the reefs; but nights like this they bull right up the channel against the whole river.

We could hear her pounding along, but we didn't 10 see her good till she was close. She aimed right for us. Often they do that and try to see how close they can come without touching; sometimes the wheel bites off a sweep, and then the pilot sticks his head out and laughs, and thinks he's mighty smart. Well, here she comes, and we said she was going to try and shave us; but she didn't seem to be sheering off a bit. She was a big one, and she was coming in a hurry, too, looking like a black cloud with rows of glow-worms around it; but all of a sudden she bulged out, big and scary, with a 20 long row of wide-open furnace doors shining like red-hot teeth, and her monstrous bows and guards hanging right over us. There was a yell at us, and a jingling of bells to stop the engines, a powwow of cussing, and whistling of steam—and as Jim went overboard on one side and I on the other, she come smashing straight through the raft.

I dived—and I aimed to find the bottom, too, for a thirty-foot wheel had got to go over me, and I wanted it to have plenty of room. I could always stay under 30 water a minute; this time I reckon I stayed under a minute and a half. Then I bounced for the top in a hurry, for I was nearly busting. I popped out to my armpits and blowed the water out of my nose, and puffed a bit. Of course there was a booming current; and of course that boat started her engines again ten seconds after she stopped them, for they never cared much for raftsmen; so now she was churning along up the river, out of sight in the thick weather, though I could hear her. 40

I sung out for Jim about a dozen times, but I didn't get any answer; so I grabbed a plank that touched me while I was "treading water," and struck out for shore, shoving it ahead of me. But I made out to see that the drift of the current was towards the left-hand shore, which meant that I was in a crossing; so I changed off and went that way.

It was one of these long, slanting, two-mile crossings; so I was a good long time in getting over. I made a safe landing, and clumb up the bank. I couldn't see but 50 a little ways, but I went poking along over rough ground for a quarter of a mile or more, and then I run across a big old-fashioned double log house before I noticed it. I was going to rush by and get away, but a lot of dogs jumped out and went to howling and barking at me, and I knowed better than to move another peg.

In about a minute somebody spoke out of a window without putting his head out, and says:

"Be done, boys! Who's there?"

I says:

"It's me."

"Who's me?"

"George Jackson, sir."

10 "What do you want?"

"I don't want nothing, sir. I only want to go along by, but the dogs won't let me."

"What are you prowling around here this time of night for—hey?"

"I warn't prowling around, sir; I fell overboard off of the steamboat."

"Oh, you did, did you? Strike a light there, somebody. What did you say your name was?"

"George Jackson, sir. I'm only a boy."

20 "Look here, if you're telling the truth you needn't be afraid—nobody 'll hurt you. But don't try to budge; stand right where you are. Rouse out Bob and Tom, some of you, and fetch the guns. George Jackson, is there anybody with you?"

"No, sir, nobody."

I heard the people stirring around in the house now, and see a light. The man sung out:

"Snatch that light away, Betsy, you old fool—ain't you got any sense? Put it on the floor behind the front 30 door. Bob, if you and Tom are ready, take your places."

"All ready."

"Now, George Jackson, do you know the Shepherdsons?"

"No, sir; I never heard of them."

"Well, that may be so, and it mayn't. Now, all ready. Step forward, George Jackson. And mind, don't you hurry—come mighty slow. If there's anybody with you, let him keep back—if he shows himself he'll be shot. Come along now. Come slow; push the door open your- 40 self—just enough to squeeze in, d'you hear?"

I didn't hurry; I couldn't if I'd a-wanted to. I took one slow step at a time and there warn't a sound, only I thought I could hear my heart. The dogs were as still as the humans, but they followed a little behind me. When I got to the three log doorsteps I heard them un-

Colonel Grangerford

locking and unbarring and unbolting. I put my hand on the door and pushed it a little and a little more till somebody said, "There, that's enough—put your head in." I done it, but I judged they would take it off.

The candle was on the floor, and there they all was, 50 looking at me, and me at them, for about a quarter of a minute: Three big men with guns pointed at me, which made me wince, I tell you; the oldest, gray and about sixty, the other two thirty or more—all of them fine and handsome—and the sweetest old gray-headed lady, and back of her two young women which I couldn't see right well. The old gentleman says:

"There; I reckon it's all right. Come in."

As soon as I was in the old gentleman he locked the door and barred it and bolted it, and told the young 60 men to come in with their guns, and they all went in a big parlor that had a new rag carpet on the floor, and got together in a corner that **was** out of the range of the front windows—there warn't none on the side. They held the candle, and took a good look at me, and all said, "Why, *he* ain't a Shepherdson—no, there ain't any Shepherdson about him." Then the old man said he hoped I wouldn't mind being searched for arms, because he didn't mean no harm by it—it was only to make sure. So he didn't pry into my pockets, but only felt outside with his hands, and said it was all right. He told me to make myself easy and at home, and tell all about myself; but the old lady says:

"Why, bless you, Saul, the poor thing's as wet as he can be; and don't you reckon it may be he's hungry?"

"True for you, Rachel—I forgot."

So the old lady says:

"Betsy" (this was a nigger woman), "you fly around and get him something to eat as quick as you can, poor thing; and one of you girls go and wake up Buck and tell him—oh, here he is himself. Buck, take this little stranger and get the wet clothes off from him and dress him up in some of yours that's dry."

Buck looked about as old as me—thirteen or fourteen or along there, though he was a little bigger than me. He hadn't on anything but a shirt, and he was very frowzy-headed. He came in gaping and digging one fist into his eyes, and he was dragging a gun along with the other one. He says:

"Ain't they no Shepherdsons around?"

They said, no, 'twas a false alarm.

"Well," he says, "if they'd 'a' ben some, I reckon I'd 'a' got one."

They all laughed, and Bob says:

"Why, Buck, they might have scalped us all, you've been so slow in coming."

"Well, nobody come after me, and it ain't right. I'm always kept down; I don't get no show."

"Never mind, Buck, my boy," says the old man, "you'll have show enough, all in good time, don't you fret about that. Go 'long with you now, and do as your mother told you."

When we got up-stairs to his room he got me a coarse shirt and a roundabout and pants of his, and I put them on. While I was at it he asked me what my name was, but before I could tell him he started to tell me about a bluejay and a young rabbit he had catched in the woods day before yesterday, and he asked me where Moses was when the candle went out. I said I didn't know; I hadn't heard about it before, no way.

"Well, guess," he says.

"How'm I going to guess," says I, "when I never heard tell of it before?"

"But you can guess, can't you? It's just as easy."

"*Which* candle?" I says.

"Why, any candle," he says.

"I don't know where he was," says I; "where was he?"

"Why, he was in the *dark!* That's where he was!"

"Well, if you knowed where he was, what did you ask me for?"

"Why, blame it, it's a riddle, don't you see? Say, how long are you going to stay here? You got to stay always. We can just have booming times—they don't have no school now. Do you own a dog? I've got a dog—and he'll go in the river and bring out chips that you throw in. Do you like to comb up Sundays, and all that kind of foolishness? You bet I don't, but ma she makes me. Confound these ole britches! I reckon I'd better put 'em on, but I'd ruther not, it's so warm. Are you all ready? All right. Come along, old hoss."

Cold corn-pone, cold corn-beef, butter and buttermilk—that is what they had for me down there, and there ain't nothing better that ever I've come across yet. Buck and his ma and all of them smoked cob pipes, except the nigger woman, which was gone, and the two young women. They all smoked and talked, and I eat and talked. The young women had quilts around them, and their hair down their backs. They all asked me questions, and I told them how pap and me and all the family was living on a little farm down at the bottom of Arkansaw, and my sister Mary Ann run off and got married and never was heard of no more, and Bill went to hunt them and he warn't heard of no more, and Tom and Mort died, and then there warn't nobody but just me and pap left, and he was just trimmed down to nothing, on account of his troubles; so when he died I took what there was left, because the farm didn't belong to us, and started up the river, deck passage, and fell overboard; and that was how I come to be here. So they said I could have a home there as long as I wanted it. Then it was most daylight and everybody went to bed, and I went to bed with Buck, and when I waked up in the morning, drat it all, I had forgot what my name was. So I laid there about an hour trying to think, and when Buck waked up I says:

"Can you spell, Buck?"

"Yes," he says.

"I bet you can't spell my name," says I.

"I bet you what you dare I can," says he.

"All right," says I, "go ahead."

"G-e-o-r-g-e J-a-x-o-n—there now," he says.

"Well," says I, "you done it, but I didn't think you 10 could. It ain't no slouch of a name to spell—right off without studying."

I set it down, private, because somebody might want *me* to spell it next, and so I wanted to be handy with it and rattle it off like I was used to it.

It was a mighty nice family, and a mighty nice house, too. I hadn't seen no house out in the country before that was so nice and had so much style. It didn't have an iron latch on the front door, nor a wooden one with a buckskin string, but a brass knob to turn, the same 20 as houses in town. There warn't no bed in the parlor, nor a sign of a bed; but heaps of parlors in towns has beds in them. There was a big fireplace that was bricked on the bottom, and the bricks was kept clean and red by pouring water on them and scrubbing them with another brick; sometimes they wash them over with red water-paint that they call Spanish-brown, same as they do in town. They had big brass dog-irons that could hold up a saw-log. There was a clock on the middle of the mantelpiece, with a picture of a town painted on the 30 bottom half of the glass front, and a round place in the middle of it for the sun, and you could see the pendulum swinging behind it. It was beautiful to hear that clock tick; and sometimes when one of these peddlers had been along and scoured her up and got her in good shape, she would start in and strike a hundred and fifty before she got tuckered out. They wouldn't took any money for her.

Well, there was a big outlandish parrot on each side of the clock, made out of something like chalk, and 40 painted up gaudy. By one of the parrots was a cat made of crockery, and a crockery dog by the other; and when you pressed down on them they squeaked, but didn't open their mouths nor look different nor interested. They squeaked through underneath. There was a couple of big wild-turkey-wing fans spread out behind those things. On the table in the middle of the room was a kind of a lovely crockery basket that had apples and oranges and peaches and grapes piled up in it, which was much redder and yellower and prettier than real ones is, but they warn't real because you could 50 see where pieces had got chipped off and showed the white chalk, or whatever it was, underneath.

This table had a cover made out of beautiful oil-cloth, with a red and blue spread-eagle painted on it, and a painted border all around. It come all the way from Philadelphia, they said. There was some books, too, piled up perfectly exact on each corner of the table. One was a big family Bible full of pictures. One was *Pilgrim's Progress,* about a man that left his family, it didn't say why. I read considerable in it now 60 and then. The statements was interesting, but tough. Another was *Friendship's Offering,* full of beautiful stuff and poetry; but I didn't read the poetry. Another was Henry Clay's Speeches, and another was Dr. Gunn's *Family Medicine,* which told you all about what to do if a body was sick or dead. There was a hymn-book, and a lot of other books. And there was nice split-bottom chairs, and perfectly sound, too—not bagged down in the middle and busted, like an old basket.

They had pictures hung on the walls—mainly Wash- 70 ingtons and Lafayettes, and battles, and Highland Marys, and one called "Signing the Declaration." There was some that they called crayons, which one of the daughters which was dead made her own self when she was only fifteen years old. They was different from any pictures I ever see before—blacker, mostly, than is common. One was a woman in a slim black dress, belted small under the armpits, with bulges like a cabbage in the middle of the sleeves, and a large black scoop-shovel bonnet with a black veil, and white slim ankles crossed 80 about with black tape, and very wee black slippers, like a chisel, and she was leaning pensive on a tombstone on her right elbow, under a weeping willow, and her other hand hanging down her side holding a white handkerchief and a reticule, and underneath the picture it said "Shall I Never See Thee More Alas." Another one was a young lady with her hair all combed up straight to the top of her head, and knotted there in front of a comb like a chair-back, and she was crying into a handkerchief and had a dead bird laying on its back in her other 90 hand with its heels up, and underneath the picture it said "I Shall Never Hear Thy Sweet Chirrup More Alas."

Huckleberry Finn 445

There was one where a young lady was at a window looking up at the moon, and tears running down her cheeks; and she had an open letter in one hand with black sealing-wax showing on one edge of it, and she was mashing a locket with a chain to it against her mouth, and underneath the picture it said "And Art Thou Gone Yes Thou Art Gone Alas." These was all nice pictures, I reckon, but I didn't somehow seem to take to them, because if ever I was down a little they always give me the fan-tods. Everybody was sorry she died, because she had laid out a lot more of these pictures to do, and a body could see by what she had done what they had lost. But I reckoned that with her disposition she was having a better time in the graveyard. She was at work on what they said was her greatest picture when she took sick, and every day and every night it was her prayer to be allowed to live till she got it done, but she never got the chance. It was a picture of a young woman in a long white gown, standing on the rail of a bridge all ready to jump off, with her hair all down her back, and looking up to the moon, with the tears running down her face, and she had two arms folded across her breast, and two arms stretched out in front, and two more reaching up toward the moon—and the idea was to see which pair would look best, and then scratch out all the other arms; but, as I was saying, she died before she got her mind made up, and now they kept this picture over the head of the bed in her room, and every time her birthday come they hung flowers on it. Other times it was hid with a little curtain. The young woman in the picture had a kind of a nice sweet face, but there was so many arms it made her look too spidery, seemed to me.

This young girl kept a scrap-book when she was alive, and used to paste obituaries and accidents and cases of patient suffering in it out of the *Presbyterian Observer*, and write poetry after them out of her own head. It was very good poetry. This is what she wrote about a boy by the name of Stephen Dowling Bots that fell down a well and was drowned:

ODE TO STEPHEN DOWLING BOTS, DEC'D

And did young Stephen sicken,
　And did young Stephen die?
And did the sad hearts thicken,
　And did the mourners cry?

No; such was not the fate of
　Young Stephen Dowling Bots;
Though sad hearts round him thickened,
　'Twas not from sickness' shots.

No whooping-cough did rack his frame,
　Nor measles drear with spots;
Not these impaired the sacred name
　Of Stephen Dowling Bots.

Despised love struck not with woe
　That head of curly knots,
Nor stomach troubles laid him low,
　Young Stephen Dowling Bots.

O no. Then list with tearful eye,
　Whilst I his fate do tell.
His soul did from this cold world fly
　By falling down a well.

They got him out and emptied him;
　Alas it was too late;
His spirit was gone for to sport aloft
　In the realms of the good and great.

If Emmeline Grangerford could make poetry like that before she was fourteen, there ain't no telling what she could 'a' done by and by. Buck said she could rattle off poetry like nothing. She didn't ever have to stop to think. He said she would slap down a line, and if she couldn't find anything to rhyme with it would just scratch it out and slap down another one, and go ahead. She warn't particular; she could write about anything you choose to give her to write about just so it was sadful. Every time a man died, or a woman died, or a child died, she would be on hand with her "tribute" before he was cold. She called them tributes. The neighbors said it was the doctor first, then Emmeline, then the undertaker—the undertaker never got in ahead of Emmeline but once, and then she hung fire on a rhyme for the dead person's name, which was Whistler. She warn't ever the same after that; she never complained, but she kinder pined away and did not live long. Poor thing, many's the time I made myself go up to the little room that used to be hers and get out her poor old scrap-book and read in it when her pictures had been

ladies sing "The Last Link is Broken" and play "The Battle of Prague" on it. The walls of all the rooms was plastered, and most had carpets on the floors, and the whole house was whitewashed on the outside.

It was a double house, and the big open place betwixt them was roofed and floored, and sometimes the table was set there in the middle of the day, and it was a cool, comfortable place. Nothing couldn't be better. And warn't the cooking good, and just bushels of it too!

Col. Grangerford was a gentleman, you see. He was a gentleman all over; and so was his family. He was well born, as the saying is, and that's worth as much in a man as it is in a horse, so the Widow Douglas said, and nobody ever denied that she was of the first aristocracy in our town; and pap he always said it, too, though he warn't no more quality than a mudcat himself. Col. Grangerford was very tall and very slim, and had a darkish-paly complexion, not a sign of red in it anywheres; he was clean-shaved every morning all over his thin face, and he had the thinnest kind of lips, and the thinnest kind of nostrils, and a high nose, and heavy eyebrows, and the blackest kind of eyes, sunk so deep back that they seemed like they was looking out of caverns at you, as you may say. His forehead was high, and his hair was gray and straight and hung to his shoulders. His hands was long and thin, and every day of his life he put on a clean shirt and a full suit from head to foot made out of linen so white it hurt your eyes to look at it; and on Sundays he wore a blue tail-coat with brass buttons on it. He carried a mahogany cane with a silver head to it. There warn't no frivolishness about him, not a bit, and he warn't ever loud. He was as kind as he could be—you could feel that, you know, and so you had confidence. Sometimes he smiled, and it was good to see; but when he straightened himself up like a liberty-pole, and the lightning begun to flicker out from under his eyebrows, you wanted to climb a tree first, and find out what the matter was afterwards. He didn't ever have to tell anybody to mind their manners—everybody was always good-mannered where he was. Everybody loved to have him around, too; he was sunshine most always—I mean he made it seem like good weather. When he turned into a cloud-bank it was awful dark for half a minute, and that was enough; there wouldn't nothing go wrong again for a week.

" . . . *so many arms it made her look too spidery. . . .* "

aggravating me and I had soured on her a little. I liked all that family, dead ones and all, and warn't going to let anything come between us. Poor Emmeline made poetry about all the dead people when she was alive, and it didn't seem right that there warn't nobody to make some about her now she was gone; so I tried to sweat out a verse or two myself, but I couldn't seem to make it go somehow. They kept Emmeline's room trim and nice, and all the things fixed in it just the way she liked to have them when she was alive, and nobody ever slept there. The old lady took care of the room herself, though there were plenty of niggers, and she sewed there a good deal and read her Bible there mostly.

Well, as I was saying about the parlor, there was beautiful curtains on the windows: white, with pictures painted on them of castles with vines all down the walls, and cattle coming down to drink. There was a little old piano, too, that had tin pans in it, I reckon, and nothing was ever so lovely as to hear the young

excellent Characterization

When him and the old lady come down in the morning all the family got up out of their chairs and give them good day, and didn't set down again till they had set down. Then Tom and Bob went to the sideboard where the decanter was, and mixed a glass of bitters and handed it to him, and he held it in his hand and waited till Tom's and Bob's was mixed, and then they bowed and said, "Our duty to you, sir, and madam"; and *they* bowed the least bit in the world and said thank you, and so they drank, all three, and Bob and Tom poured a spoonful of water on the sugar and the mite of whisky or apple-brandy in the bottom of their tumblers, and give it to me and Buck, and we drank to the old people too.

Bob was the oldest and Tom next—tall, beautiful men with very broad shoulders and brown faces, and long black hair and black eyes. They dressed in white linen from head to foot, like the old gentleman, and wore broad Panama hats.

Then there was Miss Charlotte; she was twenty-five, and tall and proud and grand, but as good as she could be when she warn't stirred up; but when she was she had a look that would make you wilt in your tracks, like her father. She was beautiful.

So was her sister, Miss Sophia, but it was a different kind. She was gentle and sweet like a dove, and she was only twenty.

Each person had their own nigger to wait on them—Buck too. My nigger had a monstrous easy time, because I warn't used to having anybody do anything for me, but Buck's was on the jump most of the time.

This was all there was of the family now, but there used to be more—three sons; they got killed; and Emmeline that died.

The old gentleman owned a lot of farms and over a hundred niggers. Sometimes a stack of people would come there, horseback, from ten or fifteen mile around, and stay five or six days, and have such junketings round about and on the river, and dances and picnics in the woods daytimes, and balls at the house nights. These people was mostly kinfolks of the family. The men brought their guns with them. It was a handsome lot of quality, I tell you.

There was another clan of aristocracy around there—five or six families—mostly of the name of Shepherdson.

They was as high-toned and well born and rich and grand as the tribe of Grangerfords. The Shepherdsons and Grangerfords used the same steamboat-landing, which was about two mile above our house; so sometimes when I went up there with a lot of our folks I used to see a lot of the Shepherdsons there on their fine horses.

One day Buck and me was away out in the woods hunting, and heard a horse coming. We was crossing the road. Buck says:

"Quick! Jump for the woods!"

We done it, and then peeped down the woods through the leaves. Pretty soon a splendid young man came galloping down the road, setting his horse easy and looking like a soldier. He had his gun across his pommel. I had seen him before. It was young Harney Shepherdson. I heard Buck's gun go off at my ear, and Harney's hat tumbled off from his head. He grabbed his gun and rode straight to the place where we was hid. But we didn't wait. We started through the woods on a run. The woods warn't thick, so I looked over my shoulder to dodge the bullet, and twice I seen Harney cover Buck with his gun; and then he rode away the way he come—to get his hat, I reckon, but I couldn't see. We never stopped running till we got home. The old gentleman's eyes blazed a minute—'twas pleasure, mainly, I judged—then his face sort of smoothed down, and he says, kind of gentle:

"I don't like that shooting from behind a bush. Why didn't you step into the road, my boy?"

"The Shepherdsons don't, father. They always take advantage."

Miss Charlotte she held her head up like a queen while Buck was telling his tale, and her nostrils spread and her eyes snapped. The two young men looked dark, but never said nothing. Miss Sophia she turned pale, but the color come back when she found the man warn't hurt.

Soon as I could get Buck down by the corn-cribs under the trees by ourselves, I says:

"Did you want to kill him, Buck?"

"Well, I bet I did."

"What did he do to you?"

"Him? He never done nothing to me."

"Well, then, what did you want to kill him for?"

"Why, nothing—only it's on account of the feud."

"What's a feud?"

"Why, where was you raised? Don't you know what a feud is?"

"Never heard of it before—tell me about it."

"Well," says Buck, "a feud is this way: A man has a quarrel with another man, and kills him; then that other man's brother kills *him;* then the other brothers, on both sides, goes for one another; then the *cousins* chip in—and by and by everybody's killed off, and there ain't no more feud. But it's kind of slow, and takes a long time."

"Has this one been going on long, Buck?"

"Well, I should *reckon!* It started thirty year ago, or som'ers along there. There was trouble 'bout something, and then a lawsuit to settle it; and the suit went agin one of the men, and so he up and shot the man that won the suit—which he would naturally do, of course. Anybody would."

"What was the trouble about, Buck?—land?"

"I reckon maybe—I don't know."

"Well, who done the shooting? Was it a Grangerford or a Shepherdson?"

"Laws, how do *I* know? It was so long ago."

"Don't anybody know?"

"Oh, yes, pa knows, I reckon, and some of the other old people; but they don't know now what the row was about in the first place."

"Has there been many killed, Buck?"

"Yes; right smart chance of funerals. But they don't always kill. Pa's got a few buckshot in him; but he don't mind it 'cuz he don't weigh much, anyway. Bob's been carved up some with a bowie, and Tom's been hurt once or twice."

"Has anybody been killed this year, Buck?"

"Yes; we got one and they got one. 'Bout three months ago my cousin Bud, fourteen year old, was riding through the woods on t'other side of the river, and didn't have no weapon with him, which was blame' foolishness, and in a lonesome place he hears a horse a-coming behind him, and sees old Baldy Shepherdson a-linkin' after him with his gun in his hand and his white hair a-flying in the wind; and 'stead of jumping off and taking to the brush, Bud 'lowed he could outrun him; so they had it, nip and tuck, for five mile or more, the old man a-gaining all the time; so at last Bud seen it warn't any use, so he stopped and faced around so as to have the bullet-holes in front, you know, and the old man he rode up and shot him down. But he didn't git much chance to enjoy his luck, for inside of a week our folks laid *him* out."

"I reckon that old man was a coward, Buck."

"I reckon he *warn't* a coward. Not by a blame' sight. There ain't a coward amongst them Shepherdsons—not a one. And there ain't no cowards amongst the Grangerfords either. Why, that old man kep' up his end in a fight one day for half an hour against three Grangerfords, and come out winner. They was all a-horseback; he lit off of his horse and got behind a little woodpile, and kep' his horse before him to stop the bullets; but the Grangerfords stayed on their horses and capered around the old man, and peppered away at him, and he peppered away at them. Him and his horse both went home pretty leaky and crippled, but the Grangerfords had to be *fetched* home—and one of 'em was dead, and another died the next day. No, sir; if a body's out hunting for cowards he don't want to fool away any time amongst them Shepherdsons, becuz they don't breed any of that *kind.*"

Next Sunday we all went to church, about three mile, everybody a-horseback. The men took their guns along, so did Buck, and kept them between their knees or stood them handy against the wall. The Shepherdsons done the same. It was pretty ornery preaching—all about brotherly love, and such-like tiresomeness; but everybody said it was a good sermon, and they all talked it over going home, and had such a powerful lot to say about faith and good works and free grace and pre-foreordestination, and I don't know what all, that it did seem to me to be one of the roughest Sundays I had run across yet.

About an hour after dinner everybody was dozing around, some in their chairs and some in their rooms, and it got to be pretty dull. Buck and a dog was stretched out on the grass in the sun sound asleep. I went up to our room, and judged I would take a nap myself. I found that sweet Miss Sophia standing in her door, which was next to ours, and she took me in her room and shut the door very soft, and asked me if I liked her, and I said I did; and she asked me if I would do something for her and not tell anybody, and I said I would. Then she said she'd forgot her Testament, and left it in the seat at church between two other books, and would I slip out quiet and go there and fetch it to her, and not say nothing to nobody. I said I would. So I slid out and slipped off up the road, and there warn't anybody at the church, except maybe a hog or two, for there warn't any lock on the door, and hogs likes a puncheon floor in summer-time because it's cool. If you notice, most folks don't go to church only when they've got to; but a hog is different.

Says I to myself, something's up; it ain't natural for a girl to be in such a sweat about a Testament. So I give ₁₀ it a shake, and out drops a little piece of paper with *"Half past two"* wrote on it with a pencil. I ransacked it, but couldn't find anything else. I couldn't make anything out of that, so I put the paper in the book again, and when I got home and upstairs there was Miss Sophia in her door waiting for me. She pulled me in and shut the door; then she looked in the Testament till she found the paper, and as soon as she read it she looked glad; and before a body could think she grabbed me and give me a squeeze, and said I was the best boy in the ₂₀ world, and not to tell anybody. She was mighty red in the face for a minute, and her eyes lighted up, and it made her powerful pretty. I was a good deal astonished, but when I got my breath I asked her what the paper was about, and she asked me if I had read it, and I said no, and she asked me if I could read writing, and I told her "no, only coarse-hand," and then she said the paper warn't anything but a book-mark to keep her place, and I might go and play now.

I went off down to the river, studying over this thing, ₃₀ and pretty soon I noticed that my nigger was following along behind. When we was out of sight of the house he looked back and around a second, and then comes a-running, and says:

"Mars Jawge, if you'll come down into de swamp I'll show you a whole stack o' water-moccasins."

Thinks I, that's mighty curious; he said that yesterday. He oughter know a body don't love water-moccasins enough to go around hunting for them. What is he up to, anyway? So I says:

₄₀ "All right; trot ahead."

I followed a half a mile; then he struck out over the swamp, and waded ankle-deep as much as another half-mile. We come to a little flat piece of land which was dry and very thick with trees and bushes and vines, and he says:

"You shove right in dah jist a few steps, Mars Jawge;

dah's whah dey is. I's seed 'm befo'; I don't k'yer to see 'em no mo'."

Then he slopped right along and went away, and pretty soon the trees hid him. I poked into the place a ₅₀ ways and come to a little open patch as big as a bed-room all hung around with vines, and found a man laying there asleep—and, by jings, it was my old Jim!

I waked him up, and I reckoned it was going to be a grand surprise to him to see me again, but it warn't. He nearly cried he was so glad, but he warn't surprised. Said he swum along behind me that night, and heard me yell every time, but dasn't answer, because he didn't want nobody to pick *him* up and take him into slavery again. Says he: ₆₀

"I got hurt a little, en couldn't swim fas', so I wuz a considerable ways behine you towards de las'; when you landed I reck'ned I could ketch up wid you on de lan' 'dout havin' to shout at you, but when I see dat house I begin to go slow. I 'uz off too fur to hear what dey say to you—I wuz 'fraid o' de dogs; but when it 'uz all quiet ag'in I knowed you's in de house, so I struck out for de woods to wait for day. Early in de mawnin' some er de niggers come along, gwyne to de fields, en dey tuk me ₇₀ en showed me dis place, whah de dogs can't track me on accounts o' de water, en dey brings me truck to eat every night, en tells me how you's a-gittin' along."

"Why didn't you tell my Jack to fetch me here sooner, Jim?"

"Well, 'twarn't no use to 'sturb you, Huck, tell we could do sumfn—but we's all right now. I ben a-buyin' pots en pans en vittles, as I got a chanst, en a-patchin' up de raf' nights when—"

"*What* raft, Jim?"

"Our ole raf'." ₈₀

"You mean to say our old raft warn't smashed all to flinders?"

"No, she warn't. She was tore up a good deal—one en' of her was; but dey warn't no great harm done, on'y our traps was mos' all los'. Ef we hadn' dive' so deep en swum so fur under water, en de night hadn't ben so dark, en we warn't so sk'yerd, en ben sick punkin-heads, as de sayin' is, we'd a seed de raf'. But it's jis' as well we didn't, 'kase now she's all fixed up ag'in mos' as good as new, en we's got a new lot o' stuff, in de place o' what 'uz los'." ₉₀

"Why, how did you get hold of the raft again, Jim—did you catch her?"

"How I gwyne to ketch her en I out in de woods? No; some er de niggers foun' her ketched on a snag along heah in de ben', en dey hid her in a crick 'mongst de willows, en dey wuz so much jawin' 'bout which un 'um she b'long to de mos' dat I come to heah 'bout it pooty soon, so I ups en settles de trouble by tellin' 'um she don't b'long to none uv 'um, but to you en me; en I ast 'm if dey gwyne to grab a young white genlman's propaty, en git a hid'n for it? Den I gin 'm ten cents
10 apiece, en dey 'uz mighty well satisfied, en wisht some mo' raf's 'ud come along en make 'm rich ag'in. Dey's mighty good to me, dese niggers is, en whatever I wants 'm to do fur me I doan' have to ast 'm twice, honey. Dat Jack's a good nigger, en pooty smart."

"Yes, he is. He ain't ever told me you was here; told me to come, and he'd show me a lot of water-moccasins. If anything happens *he* ain't mixed up in it. He can say he never seen us together, and it'll be the truth."

I don't want to talk much about the next day. I
20 reckon I'll cut it pretty short. I waked up about dawn, and was a-going to turn over and go to sleep again when I noticed how still it was—didn't seem to be anybody stirring. That warn't usual. Next I noticed that Buck was up and gone. Well, I gets up, a-wondering, and goes down-stairs—nobody around; everything as still as a mouse. Just the same outside. Thinks I, what does it mean? Down by the woodpile I comes across my Jack, and says:

"What's it all about?"
30   Says he:

"Don't you know, Mars Jawge?"

"No," says I, "I don't."

"Well, den, Miss Sophia's run off! 'deed she has. She run off in de night some time—nobody don't know jis' when; run off to get married to dat young Harney Shepherdson, you know—leastways, so dey 'spec. De fambly foun' it out 'bout half an hour ago—maybe a little mo'—en I *tell* you dey warn't no time los'. Sich another hurryin' up guns en hosses *you* never see! De
40 women folks has gone for to stir up de relations, en ole Mars Saul en de boys tuck dey guns en rode up de river road for to try to ketch dat young man en kill him 'fo' he kin git acrost de river wid Miss Sophia. I reck'n dey's gwyne to be mighty rough times."

"Buck went off 'thout waking me up."

"Well, I reck'n he *did!* Dey warn't gwyne to mix you

" . . . *trying to get at a couple of young chaps that was behind the wood-rank.* . . ."

up in it. Mars Buck he loaded up his gun en 'lowed he's gwyne to fetch home a Shepherdson or bust. Well, dey'll be plenty un 'm dah, I reck'n, en you bet you he'll fetch one ef he gits a chanst."
50   I took up the river road as hard as I could put. By and by I begin to hear guns a good ways off. When I came in sight of the log store and the woodpile where the steamboats lands I worked along under the trees and brush till I got to a good place, and then I clumb up into the forks of a cottonwood that was out of reach, and watched. There was a wood-rank four foot high a little ways in front of the tree, and first I was going to hide behind that; but maybe it was luckier I didn't.

There was four or five men cavorting around on their
60 horses in the open place before the log store, cussing and yelling, and trying to get at a couple of young chaps that was behind the wood-rank alongside of the steamboat-landing; but they couldn't come it. Every time one of them showed himself on the river side of the woodpile he got shot at. The two boys was squatting back to back behind the pile, so they could watch both ways.

By and by the men stopped cavorting around and yelling. They started riding towards the store; then up
70 gets one of the boys, draws a steady bead over the wood-rank, and drops one of them out of his saddle. All the men jumped off of their horses and grabbed the hurt one and started to carry him to the store; and that minute the two boys started on the run. They got half-way to the tree I was in before the men noticed. Then the men see them, and jumped on their horses and took out

after them. They gained on the boys, but it didn't do no good, the boys had too good a start; they got to the woodpile that was in front of my tree, and slipped in behind it, and so they had the bulge on the men again. One of the boys was Buck, and the other was a slim young chap about nineteen years old.

The men ripped around awhile, and then rode away. As soon as they was out of sight I sung out to Buck and told him. He didn't know what to make of my voice coming out of the tree at first. He was awful surprised. He told me to watch out sharp and let him know when the men come in sight again; said they was up to some devilment or other—wouldn't be gone long. I wished I was out of that tree, but I dasn't come down. Buck begun to cry and rip, and 'lowed that him and his cousin Joe (that was the other young chap) would make up for this day yet. He said his father and his two brothers was killed, and two or three of the enemy. Said the Shepherdsons laid for them in ambush. Buck said his father and brothers ought to waited for their relations—the Shepherdsons was too strong for them. I asked him what was become of young Harney and Miss Sophia. He said they'd got across the river and was safe. I was glad of that; but the way Buck did take on because he didn't manage to kill Harney that day he shot at him—I hain't ever heard anything like it.

All of a sudden, bang! bang! bang! goes three or four guns—the men had slipped around through the woods and come in from behind without their horses! The boys jumped for the river—both of them hurt—and as they swum down the current the men run along the bank shooting at them and singing out, "Kill them, kill them!" It made me so sick I most fell out of the tree. I ain't a-going to tell *all* that happened—it would make me sick again if I was to do that. I wished I hadn't ever come ashore that night to see such things. I ain't ever going to get shut of them—lots of times I dream about them.

I stayed in the tree till it begun to get dark, afraid to come down. Sometimes I heard guns away off in the woods; and twice I seen little gangs of men gallop past the log store with guns; so I reckoned the trouble was still a-going on. I was mighty down-hearted; so I made up my mind I wouldn't ever go anear that house again, because I reckoned I was to blame, somehow. I judged that that piece of paper meant that Miss Sophia was to meet Harney somewheres at half past two and run off; and I judged I ought to told her father about that paper and the curious way she acted, and then maybe he would 'a' locked her up, and this awful mess wouldn't ever have happened.

When I got down out of the tree I crept along down the river-bank a piece, and found the two bodies laying in the edge of the water, and tugged at them till I got them ashore; then I covered up their faces, and got away as quick as I could. I cried a little when I was covering up Buck's face, for he was mighty good to me.

It was just dark now. I never went near the house, but struck through the woods and made for the swamp. Jim warn't on his island, so I tramped off in a hurry for the crick, and crowded through the willows, red-hot to jump aboard and get out of that awful country. The raft was gone! My souls, but I was scared! I couldn't get my breath for most a minute. Then I raised a yell. A voice not twenty-five foot from me says:

"Good lan'! is dat you, honey? Doan' make no noise."

It was Jim's voice—nothing ever sounded so good before. I run along the bank a piece and got aboard, and Jim he grabbed me and hugged me, he was so glad to see me. He says:

"Laws bless you, chile, I 'uz right down sho' you's dead ag'in. Jack's been heah; he say he rek'n you's ben shot, kase you didn' come home no mo'; so I's jes' dis minute a-startin' de raf' down towards de mouf er de crick, so's to be all ready for to shove out en leave soon as Jack comes ag'in en tells me for certain you *is* dead. Lawsy, I's mighty glad to git you back ag'in, honey."

I says:

"All right—that's mighty good; they won't find me, and they'll think I've been killed, and floated down the river—there's something up there that'll help them think so—so don't you lose no time, Jim, but just shove off for the big water as fast as ever you can."

I never felt easy till the raft was two mile below there and out in the middle of the Mississippi. Then we hung up our signal lantern, and judged that we was free and safe once more. I hadn't had a bite to eat since yesterday, so Jim he got out some corn-dodgers and buttermilk, and pork and cabbage and greens—there ain't nothing in the world so good when it's cooked right—and whilst I eat my supper we talked and had a good time. I was powerful glad to get away from the feuds, and so was

Jim to get away from the swamp. We said there warn't no home like a raft, after all. Other places do seem so cramped up and smothery, but a raft don't. You feel mighty free and easy and comfortable on a raft.

1883·1884

AN ARKANSAW DIFFICULTY

Down the river below the Grangerford plantation, Huck and Jim, against their will, were joined by two rascals who called themselves the king and the duke. These two, who were glad to collect any dishonest pennies available, brought the raft ashore in Bricksville, Arkansas, to give a performance of a Shakespearean play, and Huck saw the incidents here described. The passage, part of Chapter XXI, starts just after the duke has hired the courthouse and has posted bills advertising the play.

When Clemens printed a long selection about Huck, Jim, the king, and the duke in the February 1885 issue of the Century, most of this passage was omitted for fear that it might offend the sensibilities of subscribers. (See Bernard DeVoto, Mark Twain's America, pp. 212-216, for a detailed study of the excisions.) Sherburn's speech to the mob, with its commentaries on what Clemens called "The damned human race," is an articulation of some of the pessimistic attitudes which were to become more and more important to Clemens as the years passed. In What Is Man? and The Mysterious Stranger, he was to give them their most detailed expression.

Then we went loafing around town. The stores and houses was most all old, shackly, dried-up frame concerns that hadn't ever been painted; they was set up three or four foot above ground on stilts, so as to be out of reach of the water when the river was overflowed. The houses had little gardens around them, but they didn't seem to raise hardly anything in them but jimpson-weeds, and sunflowers, and ashpiles, and old curled-up boots and shoes, and pieces of bottles, and rags, and played-out tinware. The fences was made of different kinds of boards, nailed on at different times; and they leaned every which way, and had gates that didn't generly have but one hinge—a leather one. Some of the fences had been whitewashed some time or another, but the duke said it was in Columbus's time, like enough. There was generly hogs in the garden, and people driving them out.

All the stores was along one street. They had white domestic awnings in front, and the country-people hitched their horses to the awning-posts. There was empty dry-goods boxes under the awnings, and loafers roosting on them all day long, whittling them with their Barlow knives; and chawing tobacco, and gaping and yawning and stretching—a mighty ornery lot. They generly had on yellow straw hats most as wide as an umbrella, but didn't wear no coats nor waistcoats; they called one another Bill, and Buck, and Hank, and Joe, and Andy, and talked lazy and drawly, and used considerable many cuss-words. There was as many as one loafer leaning up against every awning-post, and he most always had his hands in his britches pockets, except when he fetched them out to lend a chaw of tobacco or scratch. What a body was hearing amongst them all the time was:

"Gimme a chaw 'v tobacker, Hank."

"Cain't; I hain't got but one chaw left. Ask Bill."

Maybe Bill he gives him a chaw; maybe he lies and says he ain't got none. Some of them kinds of loafers never has a cent in the world, nor a chaw of tobacco of their own. They get all their chawing by borrowing; they say to a fellow, "I wisht you'd len' me a chaw, Jack, I jist this minute give Ben Thompson the last chaw I had"—which is a lie pretty much every time; it don't fool nobody but a stranger; but Jack ain't no stranger, so he says:

"You give him a chaw, did you? So did your sister's cat's grandmother. You pay me back the chaws you've awready borry'd off'n me, Lafe Buckner, then I'll loan you one or two ton of it, and won't charge you no back intrust, nuther."

"Well, I did pay you back some of it wunst."

"Yes, you did—'bout six chaws. You borry'd store tobacker and paid back nigger-head."

Store tobacco is flat black plug, but these fellows mostly chaws the natural leaf twisted. When they borrow a chaw they don't generly cut it off with a knife, but set the plug in between their teeth, and gnaw with their teeth and tug at the plug with their hands till they get it in two; then sometimes the one that owns the tobacco looks mournful at it when it's handed back, and says, sarcastic:

"I'm on the waw-path, and the price uv coffins is a-gwyne to raise."

"Here, gimme the *chaw*, and you take the *plug.*"

All the streets and lanes was just mud; they warn't nothing else *but* mud—mud as black as tar and nigh about a foot deep in some places, and two or three inches deep in *all* the places. The hogs loafed and grunted around everywheres. You'd see a muddy sow and a litter of pigs come lazying along the street and whollop herself right down in the way, where folks had to walk around her, and she'd stretch out and shut her eyes and wave her ears whilst the pigs was milking her, and look as happy as if she was on salary. And pretty soon you'd hear a loafer sing out, "Hi! *so* boy! sick him, Tige!" and away the sow would go, squealing most horrible, with a dog or two swinging to each ear, and three or four dozen more a-coming; and then you would see all the loafers get up and watch the thing out of sight, and laugh at the fun and look grateful for the noise. Then they'd settle back again till there was a dog-fight. There couldn't anything wake them up all over, and make them happy all over, like a dog-fight—unless it might be putting turpentine on a stray dog and setting fire to him, or tying a tin pan to his tail and see him run himself to death.

On the river-front some of the houses was sticking out over the bank, and they was bowed and bent, and about ready to tumble in. The people had moved out of them. The bank was caved away under one corner of some others, and that corner was hanging over. People lived in them yet, but it was dangersome, because sometimes a strip of land as wide as a house caves in at a time. Sometimes a belt of land a quarter of a mile

deep will start in and cave along and cave along till it all caves into the river in one summer. Such a town as that has to be always moving back, and back, and back, because the river's always gnawing at it.

The nearer it got to noon that day the thicker and thicker was the wagons and horses in the streets, and more coming all the time. Families fetched their dinners with them from the country, and eat them in the wagons. There was considerable whisky-drinking going on, and I seen three fights. By and by somebody sings out:

"Here comes old Boggs!—in from the country for his little old monthly drunk; here he comes, boys!"

All the loafers looked glad; I reckoned they was used to having fun out of Boggs. One of them says:

"Wonder who he's a-gwyne to chaw up this time. If he'd a-chawed up all the men he's ben a-gwyne to chaw up in the last twenty year he'd have considerable ruputation now."

Another one says, "I wisht old Boggs 'd threaten me, 'cuz then I'd know I warn't gwyne to die for a thousan' year."

Boggs comes a-tearing along on his horse, whooping and yelling like an Injun, and singing out:

"Cler the track, thar. I'm on the waw-path, and the price uv coffins is a-gwyne to raise."

He was drunk, and weaving about in his saddle; he was over fifty year old, and had a very red face. Everybody yelled at him and laughed at him and sassed him, and he sassed back, and said he'd attend to them and lay them out in their regular turns, but he couldn't wait now because he'd come to town to kill old Colonel Sherburn, and his motto was, "Meat first, and spoon vittles to top off on."

He see me, and rode up and says:

"Whar'd you come f'm, boy? You prepared to die?"

Then he rode on. I was scared, but a man says:

"He don't mean nothing; he's always a-carryin' on like that when he's drunk. He's the best-naturedest old fool in Arkansaw—never hurt nobody, drunk nor sober."

Boggs rode up before the biggest store in town, and bent his head down so he could see under the curtain of the awning and yells:

"Come out here, Sherburn! Come out and meet the man you've swindled. You're the houn' I'm after, and I'm a-gwyne to have you, too!"

And so he went on, calling Sherburn everything he

could lay his tongue to, and the whole street packed with people listening and laughing and going on. By and by a proud-looking man about fifty-five—and he was a heap the best-dressed man in that town, too—steps out of the store, and the crowd drops back on each side to let him come. He says to Boggs, mighty ca'm and slow—he says:

"I'm tired of this, but I'll endure it till one o'clock. Till one o'clock, mind—no longer. If you open your mouth against me only once after that time you can't travel so far but I will find you."

Then he turns and goes in. The crowd looked mighty sober; nobody stirred, and there warn't no more laughing. Boggs rode off blackguarding Sherburn as loud as he could yell, all down the street; and pretty soon back he comes and stops before the store, still keeping it up. Some men crowded around him and tried to get him to shut up, but he wouldn't; they told him it would be one o'clock in about fifteen minutes, and so he *must* go home —he must go right away. But it didn't do no good. He cussed away with all his might, and throwed his hat down in the mud and rode over it, and pretty soon away he went a-raging down the street again, with his gray hair a-flying. Everybody that could get a chance at him tried their best to coax him off of his horse so they could lock him up and get him sober; but it warn't no use—up the street he would tear again, and give Sherburn another cussing. By and by somebody says:

"Go for his daughter!—quick, go for his daughter; sometimes he'll listen to her. If anybody can persuade him, she can."

So somebody started on a run. I walked down street a ways and stopped. In about five or ten minutes here comes Boggs again, but not on his horse. He was a-reeling across the street towards me, bareheaded, with a friend on both sides of him a-holt of his arms and hurrying him along. He was quiet, and looked uneasy; and he warn't hanging back any, but was doing some of the hurrying himself. Somebody sings out:

"Boggs!"

I looked over there to see who said it, and it was that Colonel Sherburn. He was standing perfectly still in the street, and had a pistol raised in his right hand—not aiming it, but holding it out with the barrel tilted up towards the sky. The same second I see a young girl coming on the run, and two men with her. Boggs and the men turned round to see who called him, and when they see the pistol the men jumped to one side, and the pistol-barrel come down slow and steady to a level—both barrels cocked. Boggs throws up both of his hands and says, "O Lord, don't shoot!" Bang! goes the first shot, and he staggers back, clawing at the air—bang! goes the second one, and he tumbles backwards onto the ground, heavy and solid, with his arms spread out. That young girl screamed out and comes rushing, and down she throws herself on her father, crying, and saying, "Oh, he's killed him, he's killed him!" The crowd closed up around them, and shouldered and jammed one another, with their necks stretched, trying to see, and people on the inside trying to shove them back and shouting, "Back, back! give him air, give him air!"

Colonel Sherburn he tossed his pistol onto the ground, and turned around on his heels and walked off.

They took Boggs to a little drug store, the crowd pressing around just the same, and the whole town following, and I rushed and got a good place at the window, where I was close to him and could see in. They laid him on the floor and put one large Bible under his head, and opened another one and spread it on his breast; but they tore open his shirt first, and I seen where one of the bullets went in. He made about a dozen long gasps, his breast lifting the Bible up when he drawed in his breath, and letting it down again when he breathed it out—and after that he laid still; he was dead. Then they pulled his daughter away from him, screaming and crying, and took her off. She was about sixteen, and very sweet and gentle looking, but awful pale and scared.

Well, pretty soon the whole town was there, squirming and scrouging and pushing and shoving to get at the window and have a look, but people that had the places wouldn't give them up, and folks behind them was saying all the time, "Say, now, you've looked enough, you fellows; 'tain't right and 'tain't fair for you to stay thar all the time, and never give nobody a chance; other folks has their rights as well as you."

There was considerable jawing back, so I slid out, thinking maybe there was going to be trouble. The streets was full, and everybody was excited. Everybody that seen the shooting was telling how it happened, and there was a big crowd packed around each one of these fellows, stretching their necks and listening. One long, lanky man, with long hair and a big white fur stovepipe

hat on the back of his head, and a crooked-handled cane, marked out the places on the ground where Boggs stood and where Sherburn stood, and the people following him around from one place to t'other and watching everything he done, and bobbing their heads to show they understood, and stooping a little and resting their hands on their thighs to watch him mark the places on the ground with his cane; and then he stood up straight and stiff where Sherburn had stood, frowning and
10 having his hat-brim down over his eyes, and sung out, "Boggs!" and then fetched his cane down slow to a level, and says "Bang!" staggered backwards, says "Bang!" again, and fell down flat on his back. The people that had seen the thing said he done it perfect; said it was just exactly the way it all happened. Then as much as a dozen people got out their bottles and treated him.

Well, by and by somebody said Sherburn ought to be lynched. In about a minute everybody was saying it; so
20 away they went, mad and yelling, and snatching down every clothes-line they come to to do the hanging with.

They swarmed up towards Sherburn's house, a-whooping and raging like Injuns, and everything had to clear the way or get run over and tromped to mush, and it was awful to see. Children was heeling it ahead of the mob, screaming and trying to get out of the way; and every window along the road was full of women's heads, and there was nigger boys in every tree, and bucks and wenches looking over every fence; and as soon as the
30 mob would get nearly to them they would break and skaddle back out of reach. Lots of the women and girls was crying and taking on, scared most to death.

They swarmed up in front of Sherburn's palings as thick as they could jam together, and you couldn't hear yourself think for the noise. It was a little twenty-foot yard. Some sung out "Tear down the fence! tear down the fence!" Then there was a racket of ripping and tearing and smashing, and down she goes, and the front wall of the crowd begins to roll in like a wave.
40 Just then Sherburn steps out onto the roof of his little front porch, with a double-barrel gun in his hand, and takes his stand, perfectly ca'm and deliberate, not saying a word. The racket stopped, and the wave sucked back.

Sherburn never said a word—just stood there, looking down. The stillness was awful creepy and uncomfortable.

456 *Clemens*

Sherburn run his eye slow along the crowd; and wherever it struck the people tried a little to outgaze him, but they couldn't; they dropped their eyes and looked sneaky. Then pretty soon Sherburn sort of laughed; not 50 the pleasant kind, but the kind that makes you feel like when you are eating bread that's got sand in it.

Then he says, slow and scornful:

"The idea of *you* lynching anybody! It's amusing. The idea of you thinking you had pluck enough to lynch a *man!* Because you're brave enough to tar and feather poor friendless cast-out women that come along here, did that make you think you had grit enough to lay your hands on a *man?* Why, a *man's* safe in the hands of ten thousand of your kind—as long as it's daytime and 60 you're not behind him.

"Do I know you? I know you clear through. I was born and raised in the South, and I've lived in the North; so I know the average all around. The average man's a coward. In the North he lets anybody walk over him that wants to, and goes home and prays for a humble spirit to bear it. In the South one man, all by himself, has stopped a stage full of men in the daytime, and robbed the lot. Your newspapers call you a brave people so much that you think you *are* braver than any other 70 people—whereas you're just *as* brave, and no braver. Why don't your juries hang murderers? Because they're afraid the man's friends will shoot them in the back, in the dark—and it's just what they *would* do.

"So they always acquit; and then a *man* goes in the night, with a hundred masked cowards at his back, and lynches the rascal. Your mistake is, that you didn't bring a man with you; that's one mistake, and the other is that you didn't come in the dark and fetch your masks. You brought *part* of a man—Buck Harkness, there— 80 and if you hadn't had him to start you, you'd 'a' taken it out in blowing.

"You didn't want to come. The average man don't like trouble and danger. *You* don't like trouble and danger. But if only *half* a man—like Buck Harkness, there—shouts 'Lynch him! lynch him!' you're afraid to back down—afraid you'll be found out to be what you are—*cowards*—and so you raise a yell, and hang yourselves onto that half-a-man's coat-tail, and come raging up here, swearing what big things you're going to do. 90 The pitifulest thing out is a mob; that's what an army is —a mob; they don't fight with courage that's born in them, but with courage that's borrowed from their mass,

Satire

and from their officers. But a mob without any _man_ at the head of it is _beneath_ pitifulness. Now the thing for _you_ to do is to droop your tails and go home and crawl in a hole. If any real lynching's going to be done it will be done in the dark, Southern fashion; and when they come they'll bring their masks, and fetch a _man_ along. Now _leave_—and take your half-a-man with you"—

tossing his gun up across his left arm and cocking it when he says this.

The crowd washed back sudden, and then broke all apart, and went tearing off every which way, and Buck Harkness he heeled it after them, looking tolerable cheap. I could 'a' stayed if I wanted to, but I didn't want to. 1884

From

Mark Twain's Autobiography

THE CHARACTER OF MAN

In this brief passage, dictated in 1906, Clemens sums up some of the attitudes which were part of the pessimism which became increasingly important in his thinking during his later years. He explains why he feels man is the most detestable of all creatures and why certain claims about man's superiority are unjustifiable. Some of the concepts had been set forth in Colonel Sherburn's speech in Huckleberry Finn (p. 456), others in such pessimistic works as What Is Man? and The Mysterious Stranger, his most extreme voicings of this attitude. Logicians have noted inconsistencies between Twain's position that man is not responsible for his actions and his position that man is to be condemned for his misdeeds.

Concerning man—he is too large a subject to be treated as a whole; so I will merely discuss a detail or two of him at this time. I desire to contemplate him from this point of view—this premise: that he was not made for any useful purpose, for the reason that he hasn't served any; that he was most likely not even made _intentionally_; and that his working himself up out of the oyster bed to his present position was probably matter of surprise and regret to the Creator. . . . For his history, in all climes, all ages and all circumstances, furnishes oceans and continents of proof that of all the creatures that were made he is the most detestable. Of the entire brood he is the only one—the solitary one—that possesses malice.

That is the basest of all instincts, passions, vices—the most hateful. That one thing puts him below the rats, the grubs, the trichinæ. He is the only creature that inflicts pain for sport, knowing it to _be_ pain. But if the cat knows she is inflicting pain when she plays with the frightened mouse, then we must make an exception here; we must grant that in one detail man is the moral peer of the cat. _All_ creatures kill—there seems to be no exception; but of the whole list, man is the only one that kills for fun; he is the only one that kills in malice, the only one that kills for revenge. Also—in all the list he is the only creature that has a nasty mind.

Shall he be extolled for his noble qualities, for his gentleness, his sweetness, his amiability, his lovingness, his courage, his devotion, his patience, his fortitude, his prudence, the various charms and graces of his spirit? The other animals share _all_ these with him, yet are free from the blacknesses and rottennesses of his character.

. . . There are certain sweet-smelling sugar-coated lies current in the world which all politic men have apparently tacitly conspired together to support and perpetuate. One of these is, that there is such a thing in the world as independence: independence of thought, independence of opinion, independence of action. Another is, that the world loves _to see_ independence—admires it, applauds it. Another is, that there is such a thing in the world as toleration—in religion, in politics, and such matters; and with it trains that already mentioned auxiliary lie that toleration is admired and applauded. Out of these trunk-lies spring many branch ones: to wit, the lie that not all men are slaves; the lie that men are glad when other men succeed; glad when they prosper;

glad to see them reach lofty heights; sorry to see them fall again. And yet other branch lies: to wit, that there is heroism in man, that he is not mainly made up of malice and treachery; that he is sometimes not a coward; that there is something about him that ought to be perpetuated—in heaven, or hell, or somewhere. And these other branch lies, to wit: that conscience, man's moral medicine chest, is not only created by the Creator, but is put into man ready charged with the right and only true and authentic correctives of conduct—and the duplicate chest, with the self-same correctives, unchanged, unmodified, distributed to all nations and all epochs. And yet one other branch lie: to wit, that I am I, and you are you; that we are units, individuals, and have natures of our own, instead of being the tail end of a tapeworm eternity of ancestors extending in linked procession back and back and back—to our source in the monkeys, with this so-called individuality of ours a decayed and rancid mush of inherited instincts and teachings derived, atom by atom, stench by stench, from the entire line of that sorry column, and not so much new and original matter in it as you could balance on a needle point and examine under a microscope. This makes wellnigh fantastic the suggestion that there can be such a thing as a personal, original, and responsible nature in a man, separable from that in him which is not original, and findable in such quantity as to enable the observer to say, This is a man, not a procession.

. . . Consider the first-mentioned lie: that there is such a thing in the world as independence; that it exists in individuals; that it exists in bodies of men. Surely if anything *is* proven, by whole oceans and continents of evidence, it is that the quality of independence was almost wholly left out of the human race. The scattering exceptions to the rule only emphasize it, light it up, make it glare. The whole population of New England meekly took their turns, for years, in standing up in the railway trains, without so much as a complaint above their breath, till at last these uncounted millions were able to produce exactly one single independent man, who stood to his rights and made the railroad give him a seat. Statistics and the law of probabilities warrant the assumption that it will take New England forty years to breed his fellow. There is a law, with a penalty attached, forbidding trains to occupy the Asylum Street crossing more than five minutes at a time. For years people and carriages used to wait there nightly as much as twenty minutes on a stretch while New England trains monopolized that crossing. I used to hear men use vigorous language about that insolent wrong—But they waited, just the same.

We are discreet sheep; we wait to see how the drove is going, and then go with the drove. We have two opinions: one private, which we are afraid to express; and another one—the one we use—which we force ourselves to wear to please Mrs. Grundy, until habit makes us comfortable in it, and the custom of defending it presently makes us love it, adore it, and forget how pitifully we came by it. Look at it in politics. Look at the candidates whom we loathe, one year, and are afraid to vote against, the next; whom we cover with unimaginable filth, one year, and fall down on the public platform to worship, the next—and keep on doing it until the habitual shutting of our eyes to last year's evidences brings us presently to a sincere and stupid belief in this year's. Look at the tyranny of party—at what is called party allegiance, party loyalty—a snare invented by designing men for selfish purposes—and which turns voters into chattels, slaves, rabbits, and all the while their masters, and they themselves are shouting rubbish about liberty, independence, freedom of opinion, freedom of speech, honestly unconscious of the fantastic contradiction; and forgetting or ignoring that their fathers and the churches shouted the same blasphemies a generation earlier when they were closing their doors against the hunted slave, beating his handful of humane defenders with Bible texts and billies, and pocketing the insults and licking the shoes of his Southern master.

If we would learn what the human race really *is* at bottom, we need only observe it in election times. A Hartford clergyman met me in the street and spoke of a new nominee—denounced the nomination, in strong, earnest words—words that were refreshing for their independence, their manliness. He said, "I ought to be proud, perhaps, for this nominee is a relative of mine; on the contrary, I am humiliated and disgusted, for I know him intimately—familiarly—and I know that he is an unscrupulous scoundrel, and always has been." You should have seen this clergyman preside at a political meeting forty days later, and urge, and plead, and gush

---

80 **Hartford Clergyman.** "Jan. 11, '06.—I can't remember his name. It began with K, I think. He was one of the American revisers of the New Testament, and was nearly as great a scholar as Hammond Trumbull."—Clemens

—and you should have heard him paint the character of this same nominee. You would have supposed he was describing the Cid, and Greatheart, and Sir Galahad, and Bayard the Spotless all rolled into one. Was he sincere? Yes—by that time; and therein lies the pathos of it all, the hopelessness of it all. It shows at what trivial cost of effort a man can teach himself to lie, and learn to believe it, when he perceives, by the general drift, that that is the popular thing to do. Does he believe his lie yet? Oh, probably not; he has no further use for it. It was but a passing incident; he spared to it the moment that was its due, then hastened back to the serious business of his life.

And what a paltry poor lie is that one which teaches that independence of action and opinion is prized in men, admired, honored, rewarded. When a man leaves a political party, he is treated as if the party owned him—as if he were its bond slave, as most party men plainly are—and had stolen himself, gone off with what was not his own. And he is traduced, derided, despised, held up to public obloquy and loathing. His character is remorselessly assassinated; no means, however vile, are spared to injure his property and his business.

The preacher who casts a vote for conscience' sake runs the risk of starving. And is rightly served, for he has been teaching a falsity—that men respect and honor independence of thought and action.

Mr. Beecher may be charged with a _crime_, and his whole following will rise as one man, and stand by him to the bitter end; but who so poor to be his friend when he is charged with casting a vote for conscience' sake? Take the editor so charged—take—take anybody.

All the talk about tolerance, in anything or anywhere, is plainly a gentle lie. It does not exist. It is in no man's heart; but it unconsciously and by moss-grown inherited habit, drivels and slobbers from all men's lips. Intolerance is everything for oneself, and nothing for the other person. The mainspring of man's nature is just that—selfishness.

Let us skip the other lies, for brevity's sake. To consider them would prove nothing, except that man is what he is—loving toward his own, lovable to his own—his family, his friends—and otherwise the buzzing, busy, trivial enemy of his race—who tarries his little day, does his little dirt, commends himself to God, and then goes out into the darkness, to return no more, and send no messages back—selfish even in death.

1906 • 1924

HOWELLS

William Dean Howells

1837 • 1920

"Ah! poor Real Life, which I love, can I make others share the delight I find in thy foolish and insipid face?" William Dean Howells exclaimed in _Their Wedding Journey_ (1872), his first novel. He loved "Real Life," particularly American life, and he communicated his delight in it to many readers in many books.

Howells was born at Martin's Ferry, Ohio, in 1837. His father was a printer and journalist in several Ohio towns, and the boy learned early to help. He received little formal education, but he had a passion for languages, especially German, and for literature, especially the poems of Heine. From 1856 to 1861 Howells was

Howells 459

reporter and editorial writer on the *Ohio State Journal* of Columbus. He wrote in 1860 a campaign biography of Lincoln and was rewarded by an appointment in 1861 as consul at Venice. In the meantime, he had been trying his hand at poetry. "Ah! if I only could write something worthy of the *Atlantic!*" he said to a friend; the ambition was realized in 1860 when three of his poems appeared in that magazine. In the same year occurred his first visit to New England, which is charmingly remembered in *Literary Friends and Acquaintance* (1900). To the young Howells the journey was a pilgrimage to the Holy Land of American literature. James T. Fields, editor of the *Atlantic,* Lowell, and Holmes received him most cordially. Hawthorne, after talking with Howells on the hilltop back of "The Wayside," wrote on his card as an introduction to Emerson, "I find this young man worthy."

Howells was in Venice from 1861 to 1865. In 1862 he married Eleanor Mead, of Brattleboro, Vermont. (She had visited in Columbus in 1860, and upon expressing surprise at seeing a copy of the *Atlantic,* had been informed, "There are several *contributors* to the *Atlantic* in Columbus!") The literary fruits of Howells' Italian experience were to appear later in *Venetian Life* (1866), *Modern Italian Poets* (1887), and elsewhere. In 1866 he returned to America, was made assistant editor of the *Atlantic* (blessed consummation), and settled in Cambridge. In 1872 he became editor-in-chief and continued in that high office until 1881. His acceptance by the literary celebrities is sufficiently attested by the fact that he was among the select group invited to Craigie House for the "Dante evenings," when Longfellow read installments of his translation of the *Divine Comedy* and the company sat down to a nine o'clock supper. During these years, Howells seems to have been especially under the somewhat awe-inspiring mentorship of Lowell, of whom he wrote to Charles Eliot Norton, "His strength is felt throughout the whole puny body of our literature."

Howells moved in 1888 to New York, where he lived —allowing for excursions back to New England and to Europe—the rest of his life. After two months there, he wrote: "I have been trying to catch on to the bigger life of the place. It's immensely interesting . . . and the place is lordly free, with foreign touches of all kinds all through its abounding Americanism: Boston seems of another planet." And a little later (to Henry James):

"At the bottom of our wicked hearts, we all like New York, and I hope to use some of its vast, gay, shapeless life in my fiction." In 1889 he attended a Socialist meeting: "It was as quiet and orderly as a Sunday School, and people whom the reporters represent as violent conspirators were poorly-dressed, well-behaved listeners to a lecture which dealt patiently with hard facts." It is clear that Howells' residence in New York extended his social horizon. As early as 1886 he had established a connection with Harper and Brothers. From 1900 on he wrote the "Easy Chair" department of *Harper's Monthly,* which brought him increasing influence and prestige. He received honorary degrees from Harvard, Yale, Columbia, and Oxford, and for many years was president of the American Academy of Arts and Letters.

In addition to many volumes of travel, autobiography, literary criticism, and plays, Howells wrote thirty-eight novels. Three of these have generally been regarded as decidedly better than the rest: *A Modern Instance* (1882), *The Rise of Silas Lapham* (1885), and *A Hazard of New Fortunes* (1890). The setting of the first and second is New England, chiefly Boston; of the third, New York. *A Modern Instance* is an intense story —intense, that is, for the mild Howells—of the failure of the marriage of a young journalist of weak moral principle and an inexperienced, temperamental girl from a Maine village. The characters and scenes are drawn with knowledge and skill. *The Rise of Silas Lapham* is the story of the career of a "self-made" Boston businessman who is awkward in society but honorable in business; the author is especially expert in depicting contrasts between the Brahmins and the parvenus of the Boston social world. In *A Hazard of New Fortunes* Howells essayed a larger canvas. A half-dozen or more individuals living in New York, each representing a different social background and attitude, are brought together, somewhat artificially, by means of their connection with a magazine: a Boston dilettante, a professional Southerner, a promoter, a millionaire from the Middle West, an immigrant Socialist, a social worker from fashionable society, and a social visionary. The climactic event is a streetcar strike, which is treated sympathetically. "No other American novel of the nineteenth century, except possibly *The Gilded Age,*" says Granville Hicks, "can be compared in its scope with *A Hazard of New Fortunes.*" A fourth book of considerable interest—*A Traveler from Altruria* (1894)—may be added, though it is more nearly a tract than a novel. Altruria is Howells' Utopia, and his "traveler," after having been sufficiently pained by what he has seen at a summer hotel in the White Mountains, describes the ideal society in a lecture which shows, still further, Howells' increasing interest in social problems and the influence of his reading of Edward Bellamy and Tolstoy.

Howells has been sharply criticized since his death. The naturalists have objected to his reticence and decency, his suppression of sex and crime. The Freudians (see Ludwig Lewisohn, *Expression in America*) have discovered in his prudishness the "violent sex-consciousness" of the Victorian mind. The Socialist critics (see Granville Hicks, *The Great Tradition*) have condemned him for his failure to come to grips with the problems of capital and labor; Hicks cannot forgive him, particularly, for presenting in Silas Lapham an honorable capitalist. In defense, it may be urged that Howells dealt with the life he knew, and that he should be judged by what he wrote, rather than by what he didn't write. He thought, a little naïvely perhaps, that "the more smiling aspects of life are the more American." The new realism in fiction, he maintained, should portray the typical, the representative, rather than the exceptional; and he persisted in his belief that the typical, the representative phenomena of American life were comparatively decent. From this point of view, his books give a valuable picture. He had a facile pen; he had skill in dialogue and dramatic situation; he was marvelously adept in depicting the domestic commonplaces and the foibles of "society." During the last two decades of the nineteenth century, he was our chief recorder in prose fiction of the domestic life of middle-class America.

O. W. Firkins, **William Dean Howells: A Study**, Cambridge, 1924 • **Life in Letters of William Dean Howells**, ed. Mildred Howells, 2 vols., New York, 1928 • **William Dean Howells: Representative Selections**, ed. C. M. Kirk and R. Kirk, New York, 1950 • W. M. Gibson and George Arms, **A Bibliography of William Dean Howells**, New York, 1948

From

[handwritten: Artists are imitators ~~of~~ of men rather than of nature]

Criticism and Fiction

[handwritten: Critics seek art in standards put up by previous great artists & an original is not accepted at first]

Criticism and Fiction is not only the best statement of Howells' aims but also a significant document in the history of the "new realism" in American prose fiction.

As for those called critics," the author says, "they have generally sought the rule of the arts in the wrong place; they have sought among poems, pictures, engravings, statues, and buildings; but art can never give the rules that make an art. This is, I believe, the reason why artists in general, and poets principally, have been confined in so narrow a circle; they have been rather imitators of one another than of nature. Critics follow them, and therefore can do little as guides. I can judge but poorly of anything while I measure it by no other standard than itself. The true standard of the arts is in every man's power; and an easy observation of the most common, sometimes of the meanest things, in nature will give the truest lights, where the greatest sagacity and industry that slights such observation must leave us in the dark, or, what is worse, amuse and mislead us by false lights."

If this should happen to be true—and it certainly commends itself to acceptance—it might portend an immediate danger to the vested interests of criticism, only that it was written a hundred years ago; and we shall probably have the "sagacity and industry that slights the observation" of nature long enough yet to allow most critics the time to learn some more useful trade than criticism as they pursue it. Nevertheless, I am in hopes that the communistic era in taste foreshadowed by Burke is approaching, and that it will occur within the lives of men now overawed by the foolish old super-

---

1 author. Howells is quoting from Edmund Burke's **Philosophical Inquiry into the Origin of Our Ideas on the Sublime and Beautiful** (1756)

stition that literature and art are anything but the expression of life, and are to be judged by any other test than that of their fidelity to it. The time is coming, I hope, when each new author, each new artist, will be considered, not in his proportion to any other author or artist, but in his relation to the human nature, known to us all, which it is his privilege, his high duty, to interpret. "The true standard of the artist is in every man's power" already, as Burke says; Michelangelo's "light of the piazza," the glance of the common eye, is and always was the best light on a statue; Goethe's "boys and blackbirds" have in all ages been the real connoisseurs of berries; but hitherto the mass of common men have been afraid to apply their own simplicity, naturalness, and honesty to the appreciation of the beautiful. They have always cast about for the instruction of some one who professed to know better, and who browbeat wholesome commonsense into the self-distrust that ends in sophistication. They have fallen generally to the worst of this bad species, and have been "amused and misled" (how pretty that quaint old use of amuse is!) "by the false lights" of critical vanity and self-righteousness. They have been taught to compare what they see and what they read, not with the things that they have observed and known, but with the things that some other artist or writer has done. Especially if they have themselves the artistic impulse in any direction they are taught to form themselves, not upon life, but upon the masters who became masters only by forming themselves upon life. The seeds of death are planted in them, and they can produce only the still-born, the academic. They are not told to take their work into the public square and see if it seems true to the chance passer, but to test it by the work of the very men who refused and decried any other test of their own work. The young writer who attempts to report the phrase and carriage of every-day life, who tries to tell just how he has heard men talk and seen them look, is made to feel guilty of something low and unworthy by the stupid people who would like to have him show how Shakespeare's men talked and looked, or Scott's, or Thackeray's, or Balzac's, or Hawthorne's, or Dickens's; he is instructed to idealize his personages, that is, to take the life-likeness out of them, and put the book-likeness into them. He is approached in the spirit of the wretched pedantry into which learning, much or little, always decays when it withdraws itself and stands apart from experience in an attitude of imagined superiority, and which would say

with the same confidence to the scientists: "I see that you are looking at a grasshopper there which you have found in the grass, and I suppose you intend to describe it. Now don't waste your time and sin against culture in that way. I've got a grasshopper here, which has been evolved at considerable pains and expense out of the grasshopper in general; in fact, it's a type. It's made up of wire and card-board, very prettily painted in a conventional tint, and it's perfectly indestructible. It isn't very much like a real grasshopper, but it's a great deal nicer, and it's served to represent the notion of a grasshopper ever since man emerged from barbarism. You may say that it's artificial. Well, it is artificial; but then it's ideal too; and what you want to do is to cultivate the ideal. You'll find the books full of my kind of grasshopper, and scarcely a trace of yours in any of them. The thing that you are proposing to do is commonplace; but if you say that it isn't commonplace, for the very reason that it hasn't been done before, you'll have to admit that it's photographic."

As I said, I hope the time is coming when not only the artist, but the common, average man, who always "has the standard of the arts in his power," will have also the courage to apply it, and will reject the ideal grasshopper wherever he finds it, in science, in literature, in art, because it is not "simple, natural, and honest," because it is not like a real grasshopper. But I will own that I think the time is yet far off, and that the people who have been brought up on the ideal grasshopper, the heroic grasshopper, the impassioned grasshopper, the self-devoted, adventureful, good old romantic card-board grasshopper, must die out before the simple, honest, and natural grasshopper can have a fair field. I am in no haste to compass the end of these good people, whom I find in the mean time very amusing. It is delightful to meet one of them, either in print or out of it—some sweet elderly lady or excellent gentleman whose youth was pastured on the literature of thirty or forty years ago —and to witness the confidence with which they preach their favorite authors as all the law and the prophets. They have commonly read little or nothing since, or, if they have, they have judged it by a standard taken from these authors, and never dreamed of judging it by nature;

---

11 **Goethe,** Johann Wolfgang von Goethe (1749-1832), German author • 20 **amused,** distracted, bewildered • 41 **Balzac,** Honoré de Balzac (1799-1850), French novelist

they are destitute of the documents in the case of the later writers; they suppose that Balzac was the beginning of realism, and that Zola is its wicked end; they are quite ignorant, but they are ready to talk you down, if you differ from them, with an assumption of knowledge sufficient for any occasion. The horror, the resentment, with which they receive any question of their literary saints is genuine; you descend at once very far in the moral and social scale, and anything short of offensive personality is too good for you; it is expressed to you that you are one to be avoided, and put down even a little lower than you have naturally fallen.

These worthy persons are not to blame; it is part of their intellectual mission to represent the petrifaction of taste, and to preserve an image of a smaller and cruder and emptier world than we now live in, a world which was feeling its way towards the simple, the natural, the honest, but was a good deal "amused and misled" by lights now no longer mistakable for heavenly luminaries. They belong to a time, just passing away, when certain authors were considered authorities in certain kinds, when they must be accepted entire and not questioned in any particular. Now we are beginning to see and to say that no author is an authority except in those moments when he held his ear close to Nature's lips and caught her very accent. These moments are not continuous with any authors in the past, and they are rare with all. Therefore I am not afraid to say now that the greatest classics are sometimes not at all great, and that we can profit by them only when we hold them, like our meanest contemporaries, to a strict accounting, and verify their work by the standard of the arts which we all have in our power, the simple, the natural, and the honest.

Those good people, those curious and interesting if somewhat musty back-numbers, must always have a hero, an idol of some sort, and it is droll to find Balzac, who suffered from their sort such bitter scorn and hate for his realism while he was alive, now become a fetich in his turn, to be shaken in the faces of those who will not blindly worship him. But it is no new thing in the history of literature; whatever is established is sacred with those who do not think. At the beginning of the century, when romance was making the same fight against effete classicism which realism is making to-day against effete romanticism, the Italian poet Monti declared that "the romantic was the cold grave of the Beautiful," just as the realistic is now supposed to be. The romantic of that day and the real of this are in certain degree the same. Romanticism then sought, as realism seeks now, to widen the bounds of sympathy, to level every barrier against æsthetic freedom, to escape from the paralysis of tradition. It exhausted itself in this impulse; and it remained for realism to assert that fidelity to experience and probability of motive are essential conditions of a great imaginative literature. It is not a new theory, but it has never before universally characterized literary endeavor. When realism becomes false to itself, when it heaps up facts merely, and maps life instead of picturing it, realism will perish too. Every true realist instinctively knows this, and it is perhaps the reason why he is careful of every fact, and feels himself bound to express or to indicate its meaning at the risk of over-moralizing. In life he finds nothing insignificant; all tells for destiny and character; nothing that God has made is contemptible. He cannot look upon human life and declare this thing or that thing unworthy of notice, any more than the scientist can declare a fact of the material world beneath the dignity of his inquiry. He feels in every nerve the equality of things and the unity of men; his soul is exalted, not by vain shows and shadows and ideals, but by realities, in which alone the truth lives. In criticism it is his business to break the images of false gods and misshapen heroes, to take away the poor silly toys that many grown people would still like to play with. He cannot keep terms with Jack the Giant-killer or Puss in Boots, under any name or in any place, even when they reappear as the convict Vautrec, or the Marquis de Montrivaut, or the Sworn Thirteen Noblemen. He must say to himself that Balzac, when he imagined these monsters, was not Balzac, he was Dumas; he was not realistic, he was romantic . . . .

Which brings us again, after this long way about, to the divine Jane and her novels . . . . She was great and they were beautiful, because she and they were honest, and dealt with nature nearly a hundred years ago as realism deals with it to-day. Realism is nothing more and nothing less than the truthful treatment of material, and

3 Zola, Émile Zola (1840-1902), French naturalistic novelist • 45 Monti, Vincenzo Monti (1754-1828), Italian poet • 77 Vautrec . . . Noblemen, characters in Balzac's Comédie humaine • 80 Dumas, Alexandre Dumas (1803-1870), French romantic novelist, author of The Three Musketeers • 83 divine Jane, Jane Austen (1775-1817), English novelist

Jane Austen was the first and the last of the English novelists to treat material with entire truthfulness. Because she did this, she remains the most artistic of the English novelists, and alone worthy to be matched with the great Scandinavian and Slavic and Latin artists. It is not a question of intellect, or not wholly that. The English have mind enough; but they have not taste enough; or, rather, their taste has been perverted by their false criticism, which is based upon personal preference, and not upon principle; which instructs a man to think that what he likes is good, instead of teaching him first to distinguish what is good before he likes it. The art of fiction, as Jane Austen knew it, declined from her through Scott, and Bulwer, and Dickens, and Charlotte Brontë, and Thackeray, and even George Eliot, because the mania of romanticism had seized upon all Europe, and these great writers could not escape the taint of their time; but it has shown few signs of recovery in England, because English criticism, in the presence of the Continental masterpieces, has continued provincial and special and personal, and has expressed a love and a hate which had to do with the quality of the artist rather than the character of his work. It was inevitable that in their time the English romanticists should treat, as Señor Valdés says, "the barbarous customs of the Middle Ages, softening and disfiguring them, as Walter Scott and his kind did"; that they should "devote themselves to falsifying nature, refining and subtilizing sentiment, and modifying psychology after their own fancy," like Bulwer and Dickens, as well as like Rousseau and Madame de Staël, not to mention Balzac, the worst of all that sort at his worst. This was the natural course of the disease; but it really seems as if it were their criticism that was to blame for the rest: not, indeed, for the performance of this writer or that, for criticism can never affect the actual doing of a thing; but for the esteem in which this writer or that is held through the perpetuation of false ideals. The only observer of English middle-class life since Jane Austen worthy to be named with her was not George Eliot, who was first ethical and then artistic, who transcended her in everything but the form and method most essential to art, and there fell hopelessly below her. It was Anthony Trollope who was most like her in simple honesty and instinctive truth, as unphilosophized as the light of common day; but he was so warped from a wholesome ideal as to wish at times to be like the caricaturist Thackeray, and to stand

about in his scene, talking it over with his hands in his pockets, interrupting the action, and spoiling the illusion in which alone the truth of art resides. Mainly, his instinct was too much for his ideal, and with a low view of life in its civic relations and a thoroughly bourgeois soul, he yet produced works whose beauty is surpassed only by the effect of a more poetic writer in the novels of Thomas Hardy. Yet if a vote of English criticism even at this late day, when all continental Europe has the light of æsthetic truth, could be taken, the majority against these artists would be overwhelmingly in favor of a writer who had so little artistic sensibility, that he never hesitated on any occasion, great or small, to make a foray among his characters, and catch them up to show them to the reader and tell him how beautiful or ugly they were; and cry out over their amazing properties.

Doubtless the ideal of those poor islanders will be finally changed. If the truth could become a fad it would be accepted by all their "smart people," but truth is something rather too large for that; and we must await the gradual advance of civilization among them. Then they will see that their criticism has misled them; and that it is to this false guide they owe, not precisely the decline of fiction among them, but its continued debasement as an art . . . .

One of the great newspapers the other day invited the prominent American authors to speak their minds upon a point in the theory and practice of fiction which had already vexed some of them. It was the question of how much or how little the American novel ought to deal with certain facts of life which are not usually talked of before young people, and especially young ladies. Of course the question was not decided, and I forget just how far the balance inclined in favor of a larger freedom in the matter. But it certainly inclined that way; one or two writers of the sex which is somehow supposed to have purity in its keeping (as if purity were a thing that did not practically concern the other sex, preoccupied with serious affairs) gave it a rather vigorous tilt to that side. In view of this fact it would not be the part of prudence to make an effort to dress the balance;

---

14 **Scott . . . Eliot**, English novelists of the nineteenth century • 25 **Valdés**, Armando Palacio Valdés (1853-1938), Spanish novelist • 30 **Rousseau**, Jean Jacques Rousseau (1712-1778), French romantic philosopher and author • 30 **Madame de Staël** (1766-1817), French novelist • 58 **a writer.** Thackeray is meant

and indeed I do not know that I was going to make any such effort. But there are some things to say, around and about the subject, which I should like to have some one else say, and which I may myself possibly be safe in suggesting.

One of the first of these is the fact, generally lost sight of by those who censure the Anglo-Saxon novel for its prudishness, that it is really not such a prude after all; and that if it is sometimes apparently anxious to avoid those experiences of life not spoken of before young people, this may be an appearance only. Sometimes a novel which has this shuffling air, this effect of truckling to propriety, might defend itself, if it could speak for itself, by saying that such experiences happened not to come within its scheme, and that, so far from maiming or mutilating itself in ignoring them, it was all the more faithfully representative of the tone of modern life in dealing with love that was chaste, and with passion so honest that it could be openly spoken of before the tenderest society bud at dinner. It might say that the guilty intrigue, the betrayal, the extreme flirtation even, was the exceptional thing in life, and unless the scheme of the story necessarily involved it, that it would be bad art to lug it in, and as bad taste as to introduce such topics in a mixed company. It could say very justly that the novel in our civilization now always addresses a mixed company, and that the vast majority of the company are ladies, and that very many, if not most, of these ladies are young girls. If the novel were written for men and for married women alone, as in continental Europe, it might be altogether different. But the simple fact is that it is not written for them alone among us, and it is a question of writing, under cover of our universal acceptance, things for young girls to read which you would be put out-of-doors for saying to them, or frankly giving notice of your intention, and so cutting yourself off from the pleasure—and it is a very high and sweet one—of appealing to these vivid, responsive intelligences, which are none the less brilliant and admirable because they are innocent.

One day a novelist who liked, after the manner of other men, to repine at his hard fate, complained to his friend, a critic, that he was tired of the restriction he had put upon himself in this regard; for it is a mistake, as can be readily shown, to suppose that others impose it. "See how free those French fellows are!" he rebelled. "Shall we always be shut up to our tradition of decency?"

"Do you think it's much worse than being shut up to their tradition of indecency?" said his friend.

Then that novelist began to reflect, and he remembered how sick the invariable motive of the French novel made him. He perceived finally that, convention for convention, ours was not only more tolerable, but on the whole was truer to life, not only to its complexion, but also to its texture. No one will pretend that there is not vicious love beneath the surface of our society; if he did, the fetid explosions of the divorce trials would refute him; but if he pretended that it was in any just sense characteristic of our society, he could be still more easily refuted. Yet it exists, and it is unquestionably the material of tragedy, the stuff from which intense effects are wrought. The question, after owning this fact, is whether these intense effects are not rather cheap effects. I incline to think they are, and I will try to say why I think so, if I may do so without offence. The material itself, the mere mention of it, has an instant fascination; it arrests, it detains, till the last word is said, and while there is anything to be hinted. This is what makes a love intrigue of some sort all but essential to the popularity of any fiction. Without such an intrigue the intellectual equipment of the author must be of the highest, and then he will succeed only with the highest class of readers. But any author who will deal with a guilty love intrigue holds all readers in his hand, the highest with the lowest, as long as he hints the slightest hope of the smallest potential naughtiness. He need not at all be a great author; he may be a very shabby wretch, if he has but the courage or the trick of that sort of thing. The critics will call him "virile" and "passionate"; decent people will be ashamed to have been limed by him; but the low average will only ask another chance of flocking into his net. If he happens to be an able writer, his really fine and costly work will be unheeded, and the lure to the appetite will be chiefly remembered. There may be other qualities which make reputations for other men, but in his case they will count for nothing. He pays this penalty for his success in that kind; and every one pays some such penalty who deals with some such material. It attaches in like manner to the triumphs of the writers who now almost form a school among us, and who may be said to have established themselves in an

80 limed, entangled, ensnared

easy popularity simply by the study of erotic shivers and fervors. They may find their account in the popularity, or they may not; there is no question of the popularity.

But I do not mean to imply that their case covers the whole ground. So far as it goes, though, it ought to stop the mouths of those who complain that fiction is enslaved to propriety among us. It appears that of a certain kind of impropriety it is free to give us all it will, and more. But this is not what serious men and women writing fiction mean when they rebel against the limitations of their art in our civilization. They have no desire to deal with nakedness, as painters and sculptors freely do in the worship of beauty; or with certain facts of life, as the stage does, in the service of sensation. But they ask why, when the conventions of the plastic and histrionic arts liberate their followers to the portrayal of almost any phase of the physical or of the emotional nature, an American novelist may not write a story on the lines of *Anna Karenina* or *Madame Bovary*. *Sapho* they put aside, and from Zola's work they avert their eyes. They do not condemn him or Daudet, necessarily, or accuse their motives; they leave them out of the question; they do not want to do that kind of thing. But they do sometimes wish to do another kind, to touch one of the most serious and sorrowful problems of life in the spirit of Tolstoï and Flaubert, and they ask why they may not. At one time, they remind us, the Anglo-Saxon novelist did deal with such problems—De Foe in his spirit, Richardson in his, Goldsmith in his. At what moment did our fiction lose this privilege? In what fatal hour did the Young Girl arise and seal the lips of Fiction, with a touch of her finger, to some of the most vital interests of life?

Whether I wished to oppose them in their aspiration for greater freedom, or whether I wished to encourage them, I should begin to answer them by saying that the Young Girl had never done anything of the kind. The manners of the novel have been improving with those of its readers; that is all. Gentlemen no longer swear or fall drunk under the table, or abduct young ladies and shut them up in lonely country-houses, or so habitually set about the ruin of their neighbors' wives, as they once did. Generally, people now call a spade an agricultural implement; they have not grown decent without having also grown a little squeamish, but they have grown comparatively decent; there is no doubt

about that. They require of a novelist whom they respect unquestionable proof of his seriousness, if he proposes to deal with certain phases of life; they require a sort of scientific decorum. He can no longer expect to be received on the ground of entertainment only; he assumes a higher function, something like that of a physician or a priest, and they expect him to be bound by laws as sacred as those of such professions; they hold him solemnly pledged not to betray them or abuse their confidence. If he will accept the conditions, they give him their confidence, and he may then treat to his greater honor, and not at all to his disadvantage, of such experiences, such relations of men and women as George Eliot treats in *Adam Bede,* in *Daniel Deronda,* in *Romola,* in almost all her books; such as Hawthorne treats in the *Scarlet Letter;* such as Dickens treats in *David Copperfield;* such as Thackeray treats in *Pendennis,* and glances at in every one of his fictions; such as most of the masters of English fiction have at some time treated more or less openly. It is quite false or quite mistaken to suppose that our novels have left untouched these most important realities of life. They have not only made them their stock in trade; they have kept a true perspective in regard to them; they have relegated them in their pictures of life to the space and place they occupy in life itself, as we know it in England and America. They have kept a correct proportion, knowing perfectly well that unless the novel is to be a map, with everything scrupulously laid down in it, a faithful record of life in far the greater extent could be made to the exclusion of guilty love and all its circumstances and consequences.

I justify them in this view not only because I hate what is cheap and meretricious, and hold in peculiar loathing the cant of the critics who require "passion" as something in itself admirable and desirable in a novel, but because I prize fidelity in the historian of feeling and character. Most of these critics who demand "passion" would seem to have no conception of any passion but one. Yet there are several other passions: the passion of grief, the passion of avarice, the passion

---

19 **Anna Karenina,** famous novel by the Russian novelist Tolstoy (1828-1910) • 19 **Madame Bovary,** famous novel by the French novelist Gustave Flaubert (1821-1880) • 19 **Sapho,** a novel by Daudet, published in 1884 • 21 **Daudet** (1840-1897), French author • 28 **De Foe . . . Goldsmith,** English novelists of the eighteenth century

of pity, the passion of ambition, the passion of hate, the passion of envy, the passion of devotion, the passion of friendship; and all these have a greater part in the drama of life than the passion of love, and infinitely greater than the passion of guilty love. Wittingly or unwittingly, English fiction and American fiction have recognized this truth, not fully, not in the measure it merits, but in greater degree than most other fictions.

1891

Fulkerson desires an Editor for a newspaper new magazine & he a westerner living in east desires march, another westerner living in east & in unsatisfactory Insurance business, to be his Editor?

A Hazard of New Fortunes

A Hazard of New Fortunes begins with the difficult decision of the Marches (especially difficult for Mrs. March, who is a native Bostonian) to move from Boston to New York, where Mr. March, who in many ways resembles Howells himself, is to edit the magazine **Every Other Week.** Howells' delicate realism is exhibited at its best in the scene in which Mr. and Mrs. March face this turning point in their lives. The later scenes, in which the Marches look for living quarters in New York, show both the niceties of Howells' realism and his expanding social consciousness.

A discussion on labor unions and capitalism in end

PART FIRST

Chapter I

Now, you think this thing over, March, and let me know the last of next week," said Fulkerson. He got up from the chair which he had been sitting astride, with his face to its back, and tilting toward March on its hind-legs, and came and rapped upon his table with his thin bamboo stick. "What you want to do is to get out of the insurance business, anyway. You acknowledge that yourself. You never liked it, and now it makes you sick; in other words, it's killing you. You ain't an insurance man by nature. You're a natural-born literary man; and you've been going against the grain. Now, I offer you a chance to go *with* the grain. I don't say you're going to make your everlasting fortune, but I'll give you a living salary, and if the thing succeeds you'll share in its success. We'll all share in its success. That's the beauty of it. I tell you, March, this is the greatest idea that has been struck since——" Fulkerson stopped and searched his mind for a fit image—"since the creation of man."

He put his leg up over the corner of March's table and gave himself a sharp cut on the thigh, and leaned forward to get the full effect of his words upon his listener.

March had his hands clasped together behind his head, and he took one of them down long enough to put his inkstand and mucilage-bottle out of Fulkerson's way. After many years' experiment of a moustache and whiskers, he now wore his grizzled beard full, but cropped close; it gave him a certain grimness, corrected by the gentleness of his eyes.

"Some people don't think much of the creation of man, nowadays. Why stop at that? Why not say since the morning stars sang together?"

"No, sir; no, sir! I don't want to claim too much, and I draw the line at the creation of man. I'm satisfied with that. But if you want to ring the morning stars into the prospectus, all right; I won't go back on you."

"But I don't understand why you've set your mind on *me,*" March said. "I haven't had any magazine experience, you know that; and I haven't seriously attempted to do anything in literature since I was married. I gave up smoking and the Muse together. I suppose I could still manage a cigar, but I don't believe I could——"

"Muse worth a cent." Fulkerson took the thought out of his mouth and put it into his own words. "I know. Well, I don't want you to. I don't care if you never

33 **morning . . . together.** See Job 38:7: "When the morning stars sang together, and all the sons of God shouted for joy"

write a line for the thing, though you needn't reject anything of yours, if it happens to be good, on that account. And I don't want much experience in my editor; rather not have it. You told me, didn't you, that you used to do some newspaper work before you settled down?"

"Yes; I thought my lines were permanently cast in those places once. It was more an accident than anything else that I got into the insurance business. I sup-
10 pose I secretly hoped that if I made my living by something utterly different, I could come more freshly to literature proper in my leisure."

"I see; and you found the insurance business too many for you. Well, anyway, you've always had a hankering for the inkpots; and the fact that you first gave me the idea of this thing shows that you've done more or less thinking about magazines."

"Yes—less."

"Well, all right. Now don't you be troubled. I know
20 what I want, generally speaking, and in this particular instance I want *you*. I might get a man of more experience, but I should probably get a man of more prejudice and self-conceit along with him, and a man with a following of the literary hangers-on that are sure to get round an editor sooner or later. I want to start fair; and I've found out in the syndicate business all the men that are worth having. But they know me, and they don't know you, and that's where we shall have the pull on them. They won't be able to work the thing.
30 Don't you be anxious about the experience. I've got experience enough of my own to run a dozen editors. What I want is an editor who has taste, and you've got it; and conscience, and you've got it; and horse-sense, and you've got that. And I like you because you're a Western man, and I'm another. I do cotton to a Western man when I find him off East here, holding his own with the best of 'em, and showing 'em that he's just as much civilised as they are. We both know what it is to have our bright home in the setting sun; heigh?"
40 "I think we Western men who've come East are apt to take ourselves a little too objectively, and to feel ourselves rather more representative than we need," March remarked.

Fulkerson was delighted. "You've hit it! We do! We are!"

"And as for holding my own, I'm not very proud

of what I've done in that way; it's been very little to hold. But I know what you mean, Fulkerson, and I've felt the same thing myself; it warmed me toward you when we first met. I can't help suffusing a little to any 50 man when I hear that he was born on the other side of the Alleghanies. It's perfectly stupid. I despise the same thing when I see it in Boston people."

Fulkerson pulled first one of his blond whiskers and then the other, and twisted the end of each into a point, which he left to untwine itself. He fixed March with his little eyes, which had a curious innocence in their cunning, and tapped the desk immediately in front of him. "What I like about you is that you're broad in your sympathies. The first time I saw you, that night 60 on the Quebec boat, I said to myself, 'There's a man I want to know. There's a human being.' I was a little afraid of Mrs. March and the children, but I felt at home with you—thoroughly domesticated—before I passed a word with you; and when you spoke first, and opened up with a joke over that fellow's tableful of light literature and Indian moccasins and birch-bark toy canoes and stereoscopic views, I knew that we were brothers—spiritual twins. I recognised the Western style of fun, and I thought, when you said you were from 70 Boston, that it was some of the same. But I see now that it's being a cold fact, as far as the last fifteen or twenty years count, is just so much gain. You know both sections, and you can make this thing go, from ocean to ocean."

"We might ring that into the prospectus, too," March suggested, with a smile. "You might call the thing *From Sea to Sea*. By the way, what are you going to call it?"

"I haven't decided yet; that's one of the things I wanted to talk with you about. I *had* thought of *The* 80 *Syndicate;* but it sounds kind of dry, and it don't seem to cover the ground exactly. I should like something that would express the co-operative character of the thing; but I don't know as I can get it."

"Might call it *The Mutual*."

"They'd think it was an insurance paper. No, that won't do. But Mutual comes pretty near the idea. If we could get something like that, it would pique curiosity;

---

7 lines . . . places. Compare Psalms 16:6: "The lines are fallen unto me in pleasant places; yea, I have a goodly heritage" • 35 cotton to, readily make friends with

and then if we could get paragraphs afloat explaining that the contributors were to be paid according to the sales, it would be a first rate ad."

He bent a wide, anxious, inquiring smile upon March, who suggested lazily, "You might call it *The Round-Robin.* That would express the central idea of irresponsibility. As I understand, everybody is to share the profits and be exempt from the losses. Or, if I'm wrong, and the reverse is true, you might call it *The Army of Martyrs.* Come, that sounds attractive, Fulkerson! Or what do you think of *The Fifth Wheel?* That would forestall the criticism that there are too many literary periodicals already. Or, if you want to put forward the idea of complete independence, you could call it *The Free Lance;* or——"

"Or *The Hog on Ice*—either stand up or fall down, you know," Fulkerson broke in coarsely. "But we'll leave the name of the magazine till we get the editor. I see the poison's beginning to work in you, March; and if I had time, I'd leave the result to time. But I haven't. I've got to know inside of the next week. To come down to business with you, March, I shan't start this thing unless I can get you to take hold of it."

He seemed to expect some acknowledgment, and March said, "Well, that's very nice of you, Fulkerson."

"No, sir; no, sir! I've always liked you, and wanted you, ever since we met that first night. I had this thing inchoately in my mind then, when I was telling you about the newspaper syndicate business—beautiful vision of a lot of literary fellows breaking loose from the bondage of publishers, and playing it alone——"

"You might call it *The Lone Hand;* that would be attractive," March interrupted. "The whole West would know what you meant."

Fulkerson was talking seriously, and March was listening seriously; but they both broke off and laughed. Fulkerson got down off the table, and made some turns about the room. It was growing late; the October sun had left the top of the tall windows; it was still clear day, but it would soon be twilight; they had been talking a long time. Fulkerson came and stood with his little feet wide apart, and bent his little lean, square face on March: "See here! How much do you get out of this thing here, anyway?"

"The insurance business?" March hesitated a moment, and then said, with a certain effort of reserve, "At present

about three thousand." He looked up at Fulkerson with a glance, as if he had a mind to enlarge upon the fact, and then dropped his eyes without saying more.

Whether Fulkerson had not thought it so much or not, he said, "Well, I'll give you thirty-five hundred. Come! And your chances in the success."

"We won't count the chances in the success. And I don't believe thirty-five hundred would go any further in New York than three thousand in Boston."

"But you don't live on three thousand here?"

"No; my wife has a little property."

"Well, she won't lose the income if you go to New York. I suppose you pay six or seven hundred a year for your house here. You can get plenty of flats in New York for the same money; and I understand you can get all sorts of provisions for less than you pay now—three or four cents on the pound. Come!"

This was by no means the first talk they had had about the matter; every three or four months during the past two years the syndicate man had dropped in upon March to air the scheme and to get his impressions of it. This had happened so often that it had come to be a sort of joke between them. But now Fulkerson clearly meant business, and March had a struggle to maintain himself in a firm poise of refusal.

"I dare say it wouldn't—or it needn't—cost so very much more, but I don't want to go to New York; or my wife doesn't. It's the same thing."

"A good deal samer," Fulkerson admitted.

March did not quite like his candour, and he went on with dignity. "It's very natural she shouldn't. She has always lived in Boston; she's attached to the place. Now, if you were going to start *The Fifth Wheel* in Boston—"

Fulkerson slowly and sadly shook his head, but decidedly. "Wouldn't do. You might as well say St. Louis or Cincinnati. There's only one city that belongs to the whole country, and that's New York."

"Yes, I know," sighed March; "and Boston belongs to the Bostonians; but they like you to make yourself at home while you're visiting."

"If you'll agree to make phrases like that, right along, and get them into *The Round-Robin* somehow, I'll say four thousand," said Fulkerson. "You think it over now, March. You *talk* it over with Mrs. March; I know you will, anyway; and I might as well make a virtue of advising you to do it. Tell her I advised you to do it, and you let me know before next Saturday what you've decided."

March shut down the rolling top of his desk in the corner of the room, and walked Fulkerson out before him. It was so late that the last of the chore-women who washed down the marble halls and stairs of the great building had wrung out her floor-cloth and departed, leaving spotless stone and a clean damp smell in the darkening corridors behind her.

"Couldn't offer you such swell quarters in New York, March," Fulkerson said as he went tack-tacking down the steps with his small boot-heels. "But I've got my eye on a little house round in West Eleventh Street, that I'm going to fit up for my bachelor's hall in the third story, and adapt for *The Lone Hand* in the first and second, if this thing goes through; and I guess we'll be pretty comfortable. It's right on the Sand Strip—no malaria of *any* kind."

"I don't know that I'm going to share its salubrity with you yet," March sighed in an obvious travail which gave Fulkerson hopes.

"Oh yes, you are," he coaxed. "Now, you talk it over with your wife. You give her a fair, unprejudiced chance at the thing on its merits, and I'm very much mistaken in Mrs. March if she doesn't tell you to go in and win. We're bound to win!"

They stood on the outside steps of the vast edifice beetling like a granite crag above them, with the stone groups of an allegory of life-insurance fore-shortened in the bas-relief overhead. March absently lifted his eyes to it. It was suddenly strange after so many years' familiarity, and so was the well-known street in its Saturday-evening solitude. He asked himself, with prophetic homesickness, if it were an omen of what was to be. But he only said musingly, "A fortnightly. You know that didn't work in England. *The Fortnightly* is published once a month now."

"It works in France," Fulkerson retorted. "The *Revue des Deux Mondes* is still published twice a month. I guess we can make it work in America—with illustrations."

"Going to have illustrations?"

"My dear boy! What are you giving me? Do I look like the sort of lunatic who would start a thing in the twilight of the nineteenth century *without* illustrations? *Come* off!"

"Ah, that complicates it! I don't know anything about art." March's look of discouragement confessed the hold the scheme had taken upon him.

"I don't want you to!" Fulkerson retorted. "Don't you suppose I shall have an art man?"

"And will they—the artists—work at a reduced rate too, like the writers, with the hopes of a share in the success?"

"Of course they will! And if I want any particular man, for a card, I'll pay him big money besides. But I can get plenty of first-rate sketches on my own terms. You'll see! They'll *pour* in!"

"Look here, Fulkerson," said March, "you'd better call this fortnightly of yours *The Madness of the Half-Moon;* or *Bedlam Broke Loose* wouldn't be bad! Why do you throw away all your hard earnings on such a crazy venture? Don't do it!" The kindness which March had always felt, in spite of his wife's first misgivings and reservations, for the merry, hopeful, slangy, energetic little creature trembled in his voice. They had both formed a friendship for Fulkerson during the week they were together in Quebec. When he was not working the newspapers there, he went about with them over the familiar ground they were showing their children, and was simply grateful for the chance, as well as very entertaining about it all. The children liked him, too; when they got the clew to his intention, and found that he was not quite serious in many of the things he said, they thought he was great fun. They were always glad when their father brought him home on the occasion of Fulkerson's visits to Boston; and Mrs. March, though of a charier hospitality, welcomed Fulkerson with a grateful sense of his admiration for her husband. He had a way of treating March with deference, as an older and abler man, and of qualifying the freedom he used toward every one with an implication that March tolerated it voluntarily, which she thought very sweet, and even refined.

"Ah, *now* you're talking like a man and a brother," said Fulkerson. "Why, March, old man, do you suppose I'd come on here and try to talk you into this thing if I wasn't morally, if I wasn't perfectly, *sure* of success? There isn't any if or and about it. I know my ground, every inch; and I don't stand alone on it," he added,

57 **for a card,** that is, to play a winning card

over confident?
??

with a significance which did not escape March. "When you've made up your mind, I can give you the proof; but I'm not at liberty now to say anything more. I tell you it's going to be a triumphal march from the word go, with coffee and lemonade for the procession along the whole line. All you've got to do is to fall in." He stretched out his hand to March. "You let me know as soon as you can."

March deferred taking his hand till he could ask, "Where are you going?"

"Parker House. Take the half-past ten for New York to-night."

"I thought I might walk your way." March looked at his watch. "But I shouldn't have time. Good-bye!"

He now let Fulkerson have his hand, and they exchanged a cordial pressure. Fulkerson started off at a quick, light pace. Half a block away he stopped, turned round, and seeing March still standing where he had left him, he called back joyously, "I've got the name!"

"What?"

"Every Other Week."

"It isn't bad."

"Ta-ta!"

Chapter II

All the way up to the South End March prolonged his talk with Fulkerson, and at his door in Nankeen Square he closed the parley with a plump refusal to go to New York on any terms. His daughter Bella was lying in wait for him in the hall, and she threw her arms round his neck with the exuberance of her fourteen years, and with something of the histrionic intention of her sex. He pressed on, with her clinging about him, to the library, and, in the glow of his decision against Fulkerson, kissed his wife, where she sat by the study lamp reading the *Transcript* through her first pair of eyeglasses: it was agreed in the family that she looked distinguished in them, or at any rate cultivated. She took them off to give him a glance of question, and their son Tom looked up from his book for a moment; he was in his last year at the high-school, and was preparing for Harvard.

"I didn't get away from the office till half-past five," March explained to his wife's glance, "and then I walked. I suppose dinner's waiting. I'm sorry, but I won't do it any more."

At table he tried to be gay with Bella, who babbled at him with a voluble pertness, which her brother had often advised her parents to check in her, unless they wanted her to be universally despised.

"Papa," she shouted, at last, "you're not listening!"

As soon as possible his wife told the children they might be excused. Then she asked, "What *is* it, Basil?"

"What is what?" he retorted, with a specious brightness that did not avail.

"What is on your mind?"

"How do you know there's anything?"

"Your kissing me so when you came in, for one thing."

"Don't I always kiss you when I come in?"

"Not now. I suppose it isn't necessary any more. *Cela va sans baiser.*"

"Yes, I guess it's so; we get along without the symbolism now." He stopped, but she knew that he had not finished.

"Is it about your business? Have they done anything more?"

"No; I'm still in the dark. I don't know whether they mean to supplant me, or whether they ever did. But I wasn't thinking about that. Fulkerson has been to see me again."

"Fulkerson?" She brightened at the name, and March smiled too. "Why didn't you bring him to dinner?"

"I wanted to talk with you. Then you *do* like him?"

"What has that got to do with it, Basil?"

"Nothing! nothing! That is, he was boring away about that scheme of his again. He's got it into definite shape at last."

"What shape?"

March outlined it for her, and his wife seized its main features with the intuitive sense of affairs which makes women such good business-men, when they will let it.

"It *sounds* perfectly crazy," she said finally. "But it mayn't be. The only thing I didn't like about Mr. Fulkerson was his always wanting to chance things. But what have you got to do with it?"

"What have I got to do with it?" March toyed with the delay the question gave him; then he said, with a

34 Transcript. The Boston Evening Transcript, discontinued in 1941, was for many years the favorite newspaper of the more cultivated in Boston • 59 Cela . . . baiser, it goes without kissing (on the analogy of "cela va sans dire," it goes without saying)

sort of deprecatory laugh, "It seems that Fulkerson has had his eye on me ever since we met that night on the Quebec boat. I opened up pretty freely to him, as you do to a man you never expect to see again, and when I found he was in that newspaper syndicate business, I told him about my early literary ambitions——"

"You can't say that *I* ever discouraged them, Basil," his wife put in. "I should have been willing, any time, to give up everything for them."

10 "Well, he says that I first suggested this brilliant idea to him. Perhaps I did; I don't remember. When he told me about his supplying literature to newspapers for simultaneous publication, he says I asked, 'Why not apply the principle of co-operation to a magazine, and run it in the interest of the contributors?' and that set him to thinking, and he thought out his plan of a periodical, which should pay authors and artists a low price outright for their work, and give them a chance of the profits in the way of a percentage. After all, it isn't 20 so very different from the chances an author takes when he publishes a book. And Fulkerson thinks that the novelty of the thing would pique public curiosity, if it didn't arouse public sympathy. And the long and short of it is, Isabel, that he wants me to help edit it."

"To edit it?" His wife caught her breath, and she took a little time to realise the fact, while she stared hard at her husband to make sure he was not joking.

"Yes. He says he owes it all to me; that I invented the idea—the germ—the microbe."

30 His wife had now realised the fact, at least in a degree that excluded trifling with it. "That is very honourable of Mr. Fulkerson; and if he owes it to you, it was the least he could do." Having recognised her husband's claim to the honour done him, she began to kindle with a sense of the honour itself, and the value of the opportunity. "It's a very high compliment to *you,* Basil; a *very* high compliment. And you could give up this wretched insurance business that you've always hated so, and that's making you so unhappy now that 40 you think they're going to take it from you. Give it up, and take Mr. Fulkerson's offer! It's a perfect interposition, coming just at this time! Why, do it! Mercy!" she suddenly arrested herself, "he wouldn't expect *you* to get along on the possible profits?" Her face expressed the awfulness of the notion.

March smiled reassuringly, and waited to give him-

self the pleasure of the sensation he meant to give her. "If I'll make striking phrases for it and edit it too, he'll give me four thousand dollars."

50 He leaned back in his chair, and stuck his hands deep into his pockets, and watched his wife's face, luminous with the emotions that flashed through her mind—doubt, joy, anxiety.

"Basil! You don't mean it! Why, *take* it! Take it *instantly! Oh,* what a thing to happen! *Oh,* what luck! But you deserve it, if you first suggested it. What an escape, what a triumph over all those hateful insurance people! O Basil, I'm afraid he'll change his mind! You ought to have accepted on the spot. You might have 60 *known* I would approve, and you could *so* easily have taken it back if I didn't. Telegraph him now! Run right out with the despatch! Or we can send Tom!"

In these imperatives of Mrs. March's there was always much of the conditional. She meant that he should do what she said, if it were entirely right; and she never meant to be considered as having urged him.

"And suppose his enterprise went wrong?" her husband suggested.

"It won't *go* wrong. Hasn't he made a success of his syndicate?" 70

"He says so—yes."

"Very well, then, it stands to reason that he'll succeed in this, too. He wouldn't undertake it if he didn't know it would succeed; he must have capital."

"It will take a great deal to get such a thing going; and even if he's got an Angel behind him——"

She caught at the word: "An Angel?"

"It's what the theatrical people call a financial backer. He dropped a hint of something of that kind."

"Of course, he's got an Angel," said his wife, promptly 80 adopting the word. "And even if he hadn't, still, Basil, I should be willing to have you risk it. The risk isn't so great, is it? We shouldn't be ruined if it failed altogether. With our stocks we have two thousand a year, anyway, and we could pinch through on that till you got into some other business afterward, especially if we'd saved something out of your salary while it lasted. Basil, I want you to try it! I know it will give you a new lease of life to have a congenial occupation." March laughed, but his wife persisted. "I'm all for your trying it, Basil; 90 indeed I am. If it's an experiment, you can give it up."

"It can give me up, too."

"Oh, nonsense! I guess there's not much fear of that. Now, I want you to telegraph Mr. Fulkerson, so that he'll find the despatch waiting for him when he gets to New York. I'll take the whole responsibility, Basil, and I'll risk all the consequences."

Chapter III

March's face had sobered more and more as she followed one hopeful burst with another, and now it expressed a positive pain. But he forced a smile, and said: "There's a little condition attached. Where did
10 you suppose it was to be published?"

"Why, in Boston, of course. Where else should it be published?"

She looked at him for the intention of his question so searchingly that he quite gave up the attempt to be gay about it. "No," he said gravely, "it's to be published in New York."

She fell back in her chair. "In New York?" She leaned forward over the table toward him, as if to make sure that she heard aright, and said, with all the keen
20 reproach that he could have expected, *In New York, Basil!* Oh, how *could* you have let me go on?"

He had a sufficiently rueful face in owning, "I oughtn't to have done it, but I got started wrong. I couldn't help putting the best foot forward at first— or as long as the whole thing was in the air. I didn't know that you would take so much to the general enterprise, or else I should have mentioned the New York condition at once; but of course that puts an end to it."

30 "Oh, of course," she assented sadly. "We *couldn't* go to New York."

"No, I know that," he said; and with this a perverse desire to tempt her to the impossibility awoke in him, though he was really quite cold about the affair himself now. "Fulkerson thought we could get a nice flat in New York for about what the interest and taxes came to here, and provisions are cheaper. But I should rather not experiment at my time of life. If I could have been caught younger, I might have been inured to New York,
40 but I don't believe I could stand it now."

"How I hate to have you talk that way, Basil! You are young enough to try anything—anywhere; but you know I don't like New York. I don't approve of it. It's

so *big,* and *so* hideous! Of course I shouldn't mind that; but I've always lived in Boston, and the children were born and have all their friendships and associations here." She added, with helplessness that discredited her good-sense and did her injustice, "I have just got them both into the Friday afternoon class at Papanti's, and you know how difficult that is."
50
March could not fail to take advantage of an occasion like this. "Well, that alone ought to settle it. Under the circumstances it would be flying in the face of Providence to leave Boston. The mere fact of a brilliant opening like that offered me on *The Microbe,* and the halcyon future which Fulkerson promises if we'll come to New York, is as dust in the balance against the advantages of the Friday afternoon class."

"Basil," she appealed solemnly, "have I ever interfered with your career?"
60
"I never had any for you to interfere with, my dear."

"Basil! Haven't I always had faith in you? And don't you suppose that if I thought it would really be for your advancement, I would go to New York or anywhere with you?"

"No, my dear, I don't," he teased. "If it would be for my salvation, yes, perhaps; but not short of that; and I should have to prove by a cloud of witnesses that it would. I don't blame you. I wasn't born in Boston, but I understand how you feel. And really, my dear," he
70 added, without irony, "I never seriously thought of asking you to go to New York. I *was* dazzled by Fulkerson's offer, I'll own that; but his choice of me as editor sapped my confidence in him."

"I don't like to hear you say that, Basil," she entreated.

"Well, of course there were mitigating circumstances. I could see that Fulkerson meant to keep the whip-hand himself, and that was reassuring. And besides, if the Reciprocity Life should happen not to want my services any longer, it wouldn't be quite like giving up a
80 certainty; though, as a matter of business, I let Fulkerson get that impression; I felt rather sneaking to do it. But, if the worst comes to the worst, I can look about for something to do in Boston; and, anyhow, people don't starve on two thousand a year, though it's convenient to

---

49 **class at Papanti's,** dancing class of select young people • 68 **cloud of witnesses.** See Hebrews 12:1: "Wherefore seeing we also are compassed about with so great a cloud of witnesses . . ."

have five. The fact is, I'm too old to change so radically. If you don't like my saying that, then *you* are, Isabel, and so are the children. I've no right to take them from the home we've made, and to change the whole course of their lives, unless I can assure them of something, and I can't assure them of anything. Boston is big enough for us, and it's certainly prettier than New York. I always feel a little proud of hailing from Boston; my pleasure in the place mounts the further I get away from it. But I do appreciate it, my dear, I've no more desire to leave it than you have. You may be sure that if you don't want to take the children out of the Friday afternoon class, I don't want to leave my library here, and all the ways I've got set in. We'll keep on. Very likely the company won't supplant me, and if it does, and Watkins gets the place, he'll give me a subordinate position of some sort. Cheer up, Isabel! I have put Satan and his angel, Fulkerson, behind me, and it's all right. Let's go in to the children."

He came round the table to Isabel, where she sat in a growing distraction, and lifted her by the waist from her chair.

She sighed deeply. "Shall we tell the children about it?"

"No. What's the use, now?"

"There wouldn't be any," she assented. When they entered the family room, where the boy and girl sat on either side of the lamp working out the lessons for Monday which they had left over from the day before, she asked, "Children, how would you like to live in New York?"

Bella made haste to get in her word first. "And give up the Friday afternoon class?" she wailed.

Tom growled from his book, without lifting his eyes, "I shouldn't want to go to Columbia. They haven't got any dormitories, and you have to board round anywhere. Are you going to New York?" He now deigned to look up at his father.

"No, Tom. You and Bella have decided me against it. Your perspective shows the affair in its true proportions. I had an offer to go to New York, but I've refused it...."

[After a prolonged consideration, the Marches decide to accept Fulkerson's offer and move to New York. Renouncing her initial objection, Mrs. March insists that she has always wanted her husband to try his hand at literature. The final decision is hastened by the almost certain

prospect of March's being transferred to a less desirable position in the insurance company. When the following chapter opens, the Marches have for some time been looking for a house or apartment in New York without much success.]

Chapter IX

Their house-hunting no longer had novelty, but it still had interest; and they varied their day by taking a coupé, by renouncing advertisements, and by reverting to agents. Some of these induced them to consider the idea of furnished houses; and Mrs. March learned tolerance for Fulkerson by accepting permits to visit flats and houses which had none of the qualifications she desired in either, and were as far beyond her means as they were out of the region to which she had geographically restricted herself. They looked at three-thousand and four-thousand dollar apartments, and rejected them for one reason or another which had nothing to do with the rent; the higher the rent was, the more critical they were of the slippery inlaid floors and the arrangement of the richly decorated rooms. They never knew whether they had deceived the janitor or not; as they came in a coupé, they hoped they had.

They drove accidentally through one street that seemed gayer in the perspective than an L road. The fire-escapes, with their light iron balconies and ladders of iron, decorated the lofty house fronts; the roadway and sidewalks and door-steps swarmed with children; women's heads seemed to show at every window. In the basements, over which flights of high stone steps led to the tenements, were green-grocers' shops abounding in cabbages, and provision stores running chiefly to bacon and sausages, and cobblers' and tinners' shops, and the like, in proportion to the small needs of a poor neighbourhood. Ash barrels lined the sidewalks, and garbage heaps filled the gutters; teams of all trades stood idly about; a peddler of cheap fruit urged his cart through the street, and mixed his cry with the joyous screams and shouts of the children and the scolding and gossiping voices of the

---

1 **radically** suggests the idea of uprooting • 17 **put . . . me.** Compare Luke 4:8 from the account of the temptation of Jesus: "And Jesus answered and said unto him, Get thee behind me, Satan . . ." • 43 **coupé**, a four-wheeled closed carriage for two persons inside, with an outside seat for the driver • 60 **L road**, the elevated railroad, then new in New York and only recently (1941) dismantled

women; the burly blue bulk of a policeman defined it-self at the corner; a drunkard zigzagged down the side-walk toward him. It was not the abode of the extremest poverty, but of a poverty as hopeless as any in the world, transmitting itself from generation to generation, and establishing conditions of permanency to which human life adjusts itself as it does to those of some incurable disease, like leprosy.

10 The time had been when the Marches would have taken a purely æsthetic view of the facts as they glimpsed them in this street of tenement-houses; when they would have contented themselves with saying that it was as picturesque as a street in Naples or Florence, and with wondering why nobody came to paint it; they would have thought they were sufficiently serious about it in blaming the artists for their failure to appreciate it, and going abroad for the picturesque when they had it here under their noses. It was to the nose that the street made one of its strongest appeals, and Mrs. March pulled up 20 her window of the coupé. "Why does he take us through such a disgusting street?" she demanded, with an exas-peration of which her husband divined the origin.

"This driver may be a philanthropist in disguise," he answered, with dreamy irony, "and may want us to think about the people who are not merely carried through this street in a coupé, but have to spend their whole lives in it, winter and summer, with no hopes of driving out of it, except in a hearse. I must say they don't seem to mind it. I haven't seen a jollier crowd anywhere in New 30 York. They seem to have forgotten death a little more completely than any of their fellow-citizens, Isabel. And I wonder what they think of us, making this gorgeous progress through their midst. I suppose they think we're rich, and hate us—if they hate rich people; they don't look as if they hated anybody. Should we be as patient as they are with their discomfort? I don't believe there's steam-heat or an elevator in the whole block. Seven rooms and a bath would be more than the largest and genteelest family would know what to do with. They 40 wouldn't know what to do with the bath anyway."

His monologue seemed to interest his wife apart from the satirical point it had for themselves. "You ought to get Mr. Fulkerson to let you work some of these New York sights up for *Every Other Week,* Basil; you could do them very nicely."

"Yes; I've thought of that. But don't let's leave the personal ground. Doesn't it make you feel rather small

and otherwise unworthy when you see the kind of street these fellow-beings of yours live in, and then think how particular you are about locality and the number of bell- 50 pulls? I don't see even ratchets and speaking-tubes at these doors." He craned his neck out of the window for a better look, and the children of discomfort cheered him, out of sheer good feeling and high spirits. "I didn't know I was so popular. Perhaps it's a recognition of my humane sentiments."

"Oh, it's very easy to have humane sentiments, and to satirise ourselves for wanting eight rooms and a bath in a good neighbourhood, when we see how these wretched creatures live," said his wife. "But if we shared all we 60 have with them, and then settled down among them, what good would it do?"

"Not the least in the world. It might help us for the moment, but it wouldn't keep the wolf from their doors for a week; and then they would go on just as before, only they wouldn't be on such good terms with the wolf. The only way for them is to keep up an unbroken inti-macy with the wolf; then they can manage him some-how. I don't know how, and I'm afraid I don't want to. Wouldn't you like to have this fellow drive us round 70 among the halls of pride somewhere for a little while? Fifth Avenue or Madison, up-town?"

"No; we've no time to waste. I've got a place near Third Avenue, on a nice cross street, and I want him to take us there." It proved that she had several addresses near together, and it seemed best to dismiss their coupé and do the rest of their afternoon's work on foot. It came to nothing; she was not humbled in the least by what she had seen in the tenement-house street; she yielded no point in her ideal of a flat, and the flats per- 80 sistently refused to lend themselves to it. She lost all patience with them.

"Oh, I don't say the flats are in the right of it," said her husband, when she denounced their stupid inade-quacy to the purposes of a Christian home. "But I'm not so sure that we are either. I've been thinking about that home business ever since my sensibilities were dragged —in a coupé—through that tenement-house street. Of course no child born and brought up in such a place as that could have any conception of home. But that's be- 90 cause those poor people can't give character to their habi-

---

50 **number of bell-pulls,** one for each flight up

tations. They have to take what they can get. But people like us—that is, of our means—do give character to the average flat. It's made to meet their tastes, or their supposed tastes; and so it's made for social show, not for family life at all. Think of a baby in a flat! It's a contradiction in terms; the flat is the negation of motherhood. The flat means society life; that is, the pretence of social life. It's made to give artificial people a society basis on a little money—too much money, of course, for what they get. So the cost of the building is put into marble halls and idiotic decoration of all kinds. I don't object to the conveniences, but none of these flats have a living-room. They have drawing-rooms to foster social pretence, and they have dining-rooms and bedrooms; but they have no room where the family can all come together and feel the sweetness of being a family. The bedrooms are black-holes mostly, with a sinful waste of space in each. If it were not for the marble halls, and the decorations, and the foolishly expensive finish, the houses could be built round a court, and the flats could be shaped something like a Pompeiian house, with small sleeping closets—only lit from the outside—and the rest of the floor thrown into two or three large cheerful halls, where all the family life could go on, and society could be transacted unpretentiously. Why, those tenements are better and humaner than those flats! There the whole family lives in the kitchen, and has its consciousness of being; but the flat abolishes the family consciousness. It's confinement without coziness; it's cluttered without being snug. You couldn't keep a self-respecting cat in a flat; you couldn't go down cellar to get cider. No: the Anglo-Saxon home, as we know it in the Anglo-Saxon house, is simply impossible in the Franco-American flat, not because it's humble, but because it's false."

"Well, then," said Mrs. March, "let's look at houses."

He had been denouncing the flat in the abstract, and he had not expected this concrete result. But he said, "We will look at houses, then."

Chapter X

Nothing mystifies a man more than a woman's aberrations from some point at which he supposes her fixed as a star. In these unfurnished houses, without steam or elevator, March followed his wife about with patient wonder. She rather liked the worst of them best; but

she made him go down into the cellars and look at the furnaces; she exacted from him a rigid inquest of the plumbing. She followed him into one of the cellars by the fitful glare of successively lighted matches, and they enjoyed a moment in which the anomaly of their presence there on that errand, so remote from all the facts of their long-established life in Boston, realised itself for them.

"Think how easily we might have been murdered and nobody been any the wiser!" she said when they were comfortably out-doors again.

"Yes, or made way with ourselves in an access of emotional insanity, supposed to have been induced by unavailing flat-hunting," he suggested.

She fell in with the notion. "I'm beginning to *feel* crazy. But I don't want *you* to lose your head, Basil. And I don't want you to sentimentalise any of the things you see in New York. I think you were disposed to do it in that street we drove through. I don't believe there's any *real* suffering—not real *suffering*—among those people; that is, it would be suffering from our point of view, but they've been used to it all their lives, and they don't feel their discomfort so much."

"Of course I understand that, and I don't propose to sentimentalise them. I think when people get used to a bad state of things they had better stick to it; in fact they don't usually like a better state so well, and I shall keep that firmly in mind."

She laughed with him, and they walked along the L-bestridden avenue, exhilarated by their escape from murder and suicide in that cellar, toward the nearest crosstown track, which they meant to take home to their hotel. "Now to-night we will go to the theatre," she said, "and get this whole house business out of our minds, and be perfectly fresh for a new start in the morning." Suddenly she clutched his arm. "Why, did you *see* that man?" and she signed with her head toward a decently dressed person who walked beside them, next to the gutter, stooping over as if to examine it, and half halting at times.

"No. What?"

"Why, I saw him pick up a dirty bit of cracker from the pavement and cram it into his mouth and eat it down as if he were famished. And look! he's actually hunting for more in those garbage heaps!"

This was what the decent-looking man with the hard hands and broken nails of a workman was doing—like a hungry dog. They kept up with him, in the fascination of the sight, to the next corner, where he turned down the side street still searching the gutter.

They walked on a few paces. Then March said, "I must go after him," and he left his wife standing.

"Are you in want—hungry?" he asked the man.

The man said he could not speak English, monsieur. March asked his question in French.

The man shrugged a pitiful, desperate shrug, "Mais, monsieur——"

March put a coin in his hand, and then suddenly the man's face twisted up; he caught the hand of this almsgiver in both of his, and clung to it. "Monsieur! monsieur!" he gasped, and the tears rained down his face.

His benefactor pulled himself away, shocked and ashamed, as one is by such a chance, and got back to his wife, and the man lapsed back into the mystery of misery out of which he had emerged.

March felt it laid upon him to console his wife for what had happened. "Of course we might live here for years and not see another case like that; and of course there are twenty places where he could have gone for help if he had known where to find them."

"Ah, but it's the possibility of his needing the help so badly as that!" she answered. "That's what I can't bear, and I shall not come to a place where such things are possible, and we may as well stop our house-hunting here at once."

"Yes? And what part of Christendom will you live in? Such things are possible everywhere in our conditions."

"Then we must change the conditions——"

"Oh no; we must go to the theatre and forget them. We can stop at Brentano's for our tickets as we pass through Union Square."

"I am not going to the theatre, Basil. I am going home to Boston to-night. You can stay and find a flat."

He convinced her of the absurdity of her position and even of its selfishness; but she said that her mind was quite made up irrespective of what had happened; that she had been away from the children long enough; that she ought to be at home to finish up the work of leaving it. The word brought a sigh. "Ah, I don't know why we should see nothing but sad and ugly things now. When we were young——"

"Younger," he put in. "We're still young."

"That's what we pretend, but we know better. But I was thinking how pretty and pleasant things used to be turning up all the time on our travels in the old days. Why, when we were in New York here on our wedding journey the place didn't seem half so dirty as it does now, and none of these dismal things happened."

"It was a good deal dirtier," he answered; "and I fancy worse in every way—hungrier, raggeder, more wretchedly housed. But that wasn't the period of life for us to notice it. Don't you remember, when we started to Niagara the last time, how everybody seemed middle-aged and commonplace; and when we got there there were no evident brides; nothing but elderly married people?"

"At least they weren't starving," she rebelled.

"No, you don't starve in parlour cars and first-class hotels; but if you step out of them you run your chance of seeing those who do, if you're getting on pretty well in the forties. If it's the unhappy who see unhappiness, think what misery must be revealed to people who pass their lives in the really squalid tenement-house streets—I don't mean picturesque avenues like that we passed through."

"But we are *not* unhappy," she protested, bringing the talk back to the personal base again, as women must to get any good out of talk. "We're really no unhappier than we were when we were young."

"We're more serious."

"Well, I hate it; and I wish you *wouldn't* be so serious, if that's what it brings us to."

"I will be trivial from this on," said March. "Shall we go to the *Hole in the Ground* to-night?"

"I am going to Boston."

"It's much the same thing. How do you like that for triviality? It's a little blasphemous, I'll allow."

"It's very silly," she said.

At the hotel they found a letter from the agent who had sent them the permit to see Mrs. Grosvenor Green's apartment. He wrote that she had heard they were pleased with her apartment, and that she thought she could make the terms to suit. She had taken her passage to Europe, and was very anxious to let the flat before she sailed. She would call that evening at seven.

"Mrs. Grosvenor Green!" said Mrs. March. "Which of the ten thousand flats is it, Basil?"

8 Mais, monsieur, Why, sir • 34 Brentano's, a bookstore and ticket agency • 50 our wedding journey. Howells began the story of the Marches in Their Wedding Journey

A Hazard of New Fortunes 477

"The gimcrackery," he answered. "In the Xenophon, you know."

"Well, she may save herself the trouble. I shall not see her. Or yes—I must. I *couldn't* go away without seeing what sort of creature could have planned that fly-away flat. She must be a perfect—"

"Parachute," March suggested.

"No: anybody so light as that couldn't come **down.**"

"Well, toy balloon."

"Toy balloon will do for the present," Mrs. March admitted. "But I feel that naught but herself can be her parallel for volatility."

When Mrs. Grosvenor Green's card came up they both descended to the hotel parlour, which March said looked like the saloon of a Moorish day-boat; not that he knew of any such craft, but the decorations were so Saracenic and the architecture so Hudson Riverish. They found there on the grand central divan a large lady whose vast smoothness, placidity, and plumpness set at defiance all their preconceptions of Mrs. Grosvenor Green, so that Mrs. March distinctly paused with her card in her hand before venturing even tentatively to address her. Then she was astonished at the low calm voice in which Mrs. Green acknowledged herself, and slowly proceeded to apologise for calling. It was not quite true that she had taken her passage for Europe, but she hoped soon to do so, and she confessed that in the meantime she was anxious to let her flat. She was a little worn out with the care of house-keeping—Mrs. March breathed, "Oh yes!" in the sigh with which ladies recognise one another's martyrdom—and Mr. Green had business abroad, and she was going to pursue her art studies in Paris; she drew in Mr. Ilcomb's class now, but the instruction was so much better in Paris; and as the Superintendent seemed to think the price was the only objection, she had ventured to call.

"Then we didn't deceive him in the least," thought Mrs. March, while she answered sweetly: "No; we were only afraid that it would be too small for our family. We require a good many rooms." She could not forego the opportunity of saying, "My husband is coming to New York to take charge of a literary periodical, and he will have to have a room to write in," which made Mrs. Green bow to March, and made March look sheepish. "But we did think the apartment very charming (It *was* architecturally charming," she protested to her conscience), "and we should have been so glad if we could have got

into it." She followed this with some account of their house-hunting, amid soft murmurs of sympathy from Mrs. Green, who said that she had been through all that, and that if she could have shown her apartment to them she felt sure that she could have explained it so that they would have seen its capabilities better. Mrs. March assented to this, and Mrs. Green added that if they found nothing exactly suitable she would be glad to have them look at it again; and then Mrs. March said that she was going back to Boston herself, but she was leaving Mr. March to continue the search, and she had no doubt he would be only *too* glad to see the apartment by daylight. "But if you take it, Basil," she warned him, when they were alone, "I shall simply renounce you. I wouldn't live in that junk shop if you gave it to me. But who would have thought she was that kind of looking person? Though of course I might have known if I had stopped to think once. It's because the place doesn't express her at all that it's so unlike her. It couldn't be like anybody, or anything that flies in the air, or creeps upon the earth, or swims in the waters under the earth. I wonder where in the world she's from; she's no New-Yorker; even we can see that; and she's not quite a country person either; she seems like a person from some large town, where she's been an æsthetic authority. And she can't find good enough art instruction in New York, and has to go to Paris for it! Well, it's pathetic, after all, Basil. I can't help feeling sorry for a person who mistakes herself to that extent."

"I can't help feeling sorry for the husband of a person who mistakes herself to that extent. What is Mr. Grosvenor Green going to do in Paris while she's working her way into the Salon?"

"Well, you keep away from her apartment, Basil; that's all I've got to say to *you*. And yet I do like some things about her."

"I like everything about her but her apartment," said March.

"I like her going to be out of the country," said his wife. "We shouldn't be overlooked. And the place was

---

6 **fly-away,** flighty, eccentric • 16 **Saracenic,** pertaining to the Moslems • 67 **flies . . . earth.** Mrs. March's language is reminiscent of Genesis 1:26: "And God said, Let us make man in our image . . . and let them have dominion over the fish of the sea, and over the fowl of the air, and over the cattle, and over all the earth, and over every creeping thing . . ."

prettily shaped, you can't deny it. And there was an elevator and steam-heat. And the location *is* very convenient. And there was a hall-boy to bring up cards. The halls and stairs were kept very clean and nice. But it wouldn't do. I could put you a folding bed in the room where you wrote, and we could even have one in the parlour—"

"Behind a portière? I couldn't stand any more portières!"

10 "And we could squeeze the two girls into one room, or perhaps only bring Margaret, and put out the whole of the wash. Basil!" she almost shrieked, "it isn't to be thought of!"

He retorted, "I'm not thinking of it, my dear."

Fulkerson came in just before they started for Mrs. March's train, to find out what had become of them, he said, and to see whether they had got anything to live in yet.

"Not a thing," she said. "And I'm just going back 20 to Boston, and leaving Mr. March here to do anything he pleases about it. He has *carte blanche.*"

"But freedom brings responsibility, you know, Fulkerson, and it's the same as if I'd no choice. I'm staying behind because I'm left, not because I expect to do anything."

"Is that so?" asked Fulkerson. "Well, we must see what can be done. I supposed you would be all settled by this time, or I should have humped myself to find you something. None of those places I gave you amount 30 to anything?"

"As much as forty thousand others we've looked at," said Mrs. March. "Yes, one of them, *does* amount to something. It comes so near being what we want that I've given Mr. March particular instructions not to go near it."

She told him about Mrs. Grosvenor Green and her flat, and at the end he said—

"Well, well, we must look out for that. I'll keep an eye on him, Mrs. March, and see that he doesn't do 40 anything rash, and I won't leave him till he's found just the right thing. It exists, of course; it must in a city of eighteen hundred thousand people, and the only question is where to find it. You leave him to me, Mrs. March; I'll watch out for him."

Fulkerson showed some signs of going to the station when he found they were not driving, but she bade him a peremptory good-bye at the hotel door.

"He's very nice, Basil, and his way with you is perfectly charming. It's very sweet to see how really fond of you he is. But I didn't want him stringing along up 50 to Forty-second Street with us, and spoiling our last moments together."

At Third Avenue they took the Elevated, for which she confessed an infatuation. She declared it the most ideal way of getting about in the world, and was not ashamed when he reminded her of how she used to say that nothing under the sun could induce her to travel on it. She now said that the night transit was even more interesting than the day, and that the fleeting intimacy you formed with people in second and third floor in- 60 teriors, while all the usual street life went on underneath, had a domestic intensity mixed with a perfect repose that was the last effect of good society with all its security and exclusiveness. He said it was better than the theatre, of which it reminded him, to see those people through their windows: a family party of work-folk at a late tea, some of the men in their shirt sleeves; a woman sewing by a lamp; a mother laying her child in its cradle; a man with his head fallen on his hands upon a table; a girl and her lover leaning over the window- 70 sill together. What suggestion! what drama! what infinite interest! At the Forty-second Street station they stopped a minute on the bridge that crosses the track to the branch road for the Central Depôt, and looked up and down the long stretch of the elevated to north and south. The track that found and lost itself a thousand times in the flare and tremor of the innumerable lights; the moony sheen of the electrics mixing with the reddish points and blots of gas far and near; the architectural shapes of houses and churches and towers, rescued 80 by the obscurity from all that was ignoble in them, and the coming and going of the trains marking the stations with vivider or fainter plumes of flame-shot steam— formed an incomparable perspective. They often talked afterward of the superb spectacle, which in a city full of painters nightly works its unrecorded miracles; and they were just to the Arachne roof spun in iron over the cross street on which they ran to the depôt; but for the present they were mostly inarticulate before it. They had another moment of rich silence when they paused 90

---

10 **two girls**, servants • 87 **Arachne**, according to Ovid's **Metamorphoses**, a maiden turned into a spider by Minerva for competing with her in the arts of weaving and embroidery

A Hazard of New Fortunes 479

in the gallery that leads from the elevated station to the waiting-rooms in the Central Depôt and looked down upon the great night trains lying on the tracks dim under the rain of gas-lights that starred without dispersing the vast darkness of the place. What forces, what fates, slept in these bulks which would soon be hurling themselves north and east and west through the night! Now they waited there like fabled monsters of Arab story ready for the magician's touch, tractable, reckless, will-less—

10 organised lifelessness full of a strange semblance of life.

The Marches admired the impressive sight with a thrill of patriotic pride in the fact that the whole world perhaps could not afford just the like. Then they hurried down to the ticket offices, and he got her a lower berth in the Boston sleeper, and went with her to the car. They made the most of the fact that her berth was in the very middle of the car; and she promised to write as soon as she reached home. She promised also that having seen the limitations of New York in respect to flats, she

20 would not be hard on him if he took something not quite ideal. Only he must remember that it was not to be above Twentieth Street nor below Washington Square; it must not be higher than the third floor; it must have an elevator, steam-heat, hall-boys, and a pleasant janitor. These were essentials; if he could not get them, then they must do without. But he must get them. . . .

[The Marches soon find themselves, strangely enough, established in Mrs. Grosvenor Green's apartment, which Mrs. March takes a real pleasure in adapting to the needs of her family; and March embarks upon his new career as editor of **Every Other Week.** The magazine is the device by which Howells brings together in New York an interesting assortment of people. Fulkerson, a "go-getter" from the West, is the promoter and business manager of the magazine. Dryfoos, recently made rich by the discovery of natural gas on his Indiana farm, is the "angel" or financial backer; he is presented as a crude and unscrupulous capitalist. The Dryfoos household includes the infirm and ineffectual Mrs. Dryfoos, who has been unhappy ever since she left the old homestead in the West; a son, Conrad, who is bookkeeper for the magazine but who is more interested (much to his father's disgust) in religious and social work; two daughters, Mela and Christine; and a chaperone, Mrs. Mandel, who has been employed to educate the young ladies in the social graces. Others connected more or less directly with the magazine are:

Lindau, an immigrant Socialist from Germany, who lost an arm in the American Civil War; Colonel Woodburn, a "professional" Southerner, and his daughter; Kendricks, a dilettante writer; Beaton, a dilettante painter who has shown Christine Dryfoos an equivocal attention; and Margaret Vance, of aristocratic family, who shares Conrad Dryfoos' interest in social reform.

The selection which follows is an account of a stag dinner at the Dryfoos house, the affair having been engineered by the genial Fulkerson to bring together in friendly fashion the people connected with the magazine. The intrusion of the question of capital and labor, however, mars the harmony of the occasion.]

PART FOURTH

Chapter VI

So far as the Dryfoos family was concerned, the dinner might as well have been given at Frescobaldi's rooms. None of the ladies appeared. Mrs. Dryfoos was glad to escape to her own chamber, where she sat before an 30 autumnal fire, shaking her head and talking to herself at times, with the foreboding of evil which old women like her make part of their religion. The girls stood just out of sight at the head of the stairs, and disputed which guest it was at each arrival; Mrs. Mandel had gone to her room to write letters, after beseeching them not to stand there. When Kendricks came, Christine gave Mela a little pinch, equivalent to a little mocking shriek; for, on the ground of his long talk with Mela at Mrs. Horn's, in the absence of any other admirer, they based 40 a superstition of his interest in her; when Beaton came, Mela returned the pinch, but awkwardly, so that it hurt, and then Christine involuntarily struck her.

Frescobaldi's men were in possession everywhere: they had turned the cook out of her kitchen and the waitress out of her pantry; the reluctant Irishman at the door was supplemented by a vivid Italian, who spoke French with the guests, and said, "*Bien, Monsieur,*" and "*Toute suite,*" and "*Merci!*" to all, as he took their hats and coats, and effused a hospitality that needed no lan- 50 guage but the gleam of his eyes and teeth and the play of his eloquent hands. From his professional dress-coat,

---

23 **Frescobaldi,** a caterer employed for the occasion

lustrous with the grease spotted on it at former dinners and parties, they passed to the frocks of the elder and younger Dryfoos in the drawing-room, which assumed informality for the affair, but did not put their wearers wholly at their ease. The father's coat was of black broadcloth, and he wore it unbuttoned; the skirts were long, and the sleeves came down to his knuckles; he shook hands with his guests, and the same dryness seemed to be in his palm and throat, as he huskily asked each to take a chair. Conrad's coat was of modern texture and cut, and was buttoned about him as if it concealed a bad conscience within its lapels; he met March with his entreating smile, and he seemed no more capable of coping with the situation than his father. They both waited for Fulkerson, who went about and did his best to keep life in the party during the half-hour that passed before they sat down at dinner. Beaton stood gloomily aloof, as if waiting to be approached on the right basis before yielding an inch of his ground; Colonel Woodburn, awaiting the moment when he could sally out on his hobby, kept himself intrenched within the dignity of a gentleman, and examined askance the figure of old Lindau as he stared about the room, with his fine head up, and his empty sleeve dangling over his wrist. March felt obliged to him for wearing a new coat in the midst of that hostile luxury, and he was glad to see Dryfoos make up to him and begin to talk with him, as if he wished to show him particular respect, though it might have been because he was less afraid of him than of the others. He heard Lindau saying, "Boat, the name is Choarman?" and Dryfoos beginning to explain his Pennsylvania Dutch origin, and he suffered himself, with a sigh of relief, to fall into talk with Kendricks, who was always pleasant; he was willing to talk about something besides himself, and had no opinions that he was not ready to hold in abeyance for the time being out of kindness to others. In that group of impassioned individualities, March felt him a refuge and comfort—with his harmless dilettante intention of some day writing a novel, and his belief that he was meantime collecting material for it.

Fulkerson, while breaking the ice for the whole company, was mainly engaged in keeping Colonel Woodburn thawed out. He took Kendricks away from March and presented him to the Colonel as a person who, like himself, was looking into social conditions; he put one hand on Kendricks' shoulder, and one on the colonel's, and

made some flattering joke, apparently at the expense of the young fellow, and then left them. March heard Kendricks protest in vain, and the colonel say gravely: "I do not wonder, sir, that these things interest you. They constitute a problem which society must solve or which will dissolve society," and he knew from that formula, which the colonel had once used with him, that he was laying out a road for the exhibition of the hobby's paces later.

Fulkerson came back to March, who had turned toward Conrad Dryfoos, and said, "If we don't get this thing going pretty soon, it'll be the death of me," and just then Frescobaldi's butler came in and announced to Dryfoos that dinner was served. The old man looked toward Fulkerson with a troubled glance, as if he did not know what to do; he made a gesture to touch Lindau's elbow. Fulkerson called out, "*Here's* Colonel Woodburn, Mr. Dryfoos," as if Dryfoos were looking for him; and he set the example of what he was to do by taking Lindau's arm himself. "Mr. Lindau is going to sit at my end of the table, alongside of March. Stand not upon the order of your going, gentlemen, but fall in at once." He contrived to get Dryfoos and the colonel before him, and he let March follow with Kendricks. Conrad came last with Beaton, who had been turning over the music at the piano, and chafing inwardly at the whole affair. At the table Colonel Woodburn was placed on Dryfoos's right, and March on his left. March sat on Fulkerson's right, with Lindau next him; and the young men occupied the other seats.

"Put you next to March, Mr. Lindau," said Fulkerson, "so you can begin to put Apollinaris in his champagne-glass at the right moment; you know his little weakness of old; sorry to say it's grown on him."

March laughed with kindly acquiescence in Fulkerson's wish to start the gaiety, and Lindau patted him on the shoulder. "I know hiss veakness. If he liges a class of vine, it iss begause his loaf ingludes efen hiss enemy, as Shakespeare galled it."

"Ah, but Shakespeare couldn't have been thinking of champagne," said Kendricks.

---

30 Boat . . . Choarman, but . . . German • 68 Stand . . . once. Compare Macbeth, Act III, sc. iv, ll. 118-119 • 79 Apollinaris, an effervescing alkaline mineral water • 85 loaf . . . it, a double allusion to the Bible ("Love your enemies," Matthew 5:44) and to Shakespeare ("Oh God, that men should put an enemy in their mouths to steal away their brains!" Othello, Act II, sc. iii, l. 291)

"I suppose, sir," Colonel Woodburn interposed with lofty courtesy, "champagne could hardly have been known in his day."

"I suppose not, colonel," returned the younger man deferentially. "He seemed to think that sack and sugar might be a fault; but he didn't mention champagne."

"Perhaps he felt there was no question about that," suggested Beaton, who then felt that he had not done himself justice in the sally.

"I wonder just when champagne did come in," said March.

"I know when it ought to come in," said Fulkerson. "Before the soup!"

They all laughed, and gave themselves the air of drinking champagne out of tumblers every day, as men like to do. Dryfoos listened uneasily; he did not quite understand the allusions, though he knew what Shakespeare was, well enough; Conrad's face expressed a gentle deprecation of joking on such a subject, but he said nothing.

The talk ran on briskly through the dinner. The young men tossed the ball back and forth; they made some wild shots, but they kept it going, and they laughed when they were hit. The wine loosed Colonel Woodburn's tongue; he became very companionable with the young fellows; with the feeling that a literary dinner ought to have a didactic scope, he praised Scott and Addison as the only authors fit to form the minds of gentlemen.

Kendricks agreed with him, but wished to add the name of Flaubert as a master of style. "Style, you know," he added, "is the man."

"Very true, sir; you are quite right, sir," the colonel assented; he wondered who Flaubert was.

Beaton praised Baudelaire and Maupassant; he said these were the masters. He recited some lurid verses from Baudelaire; Lindau pronounced them a disgrace to human nature, and gave a passage from Victor Hugo on Louis Napoleon, with his heavy German accent, and then he quoted Schiller. "Ach, boat that iss peaudifool! Not zo?" he demanded of March.

"Yes, beautiful; but, of course, you know I think there's nobody like Heine!"

Lindau threw back his great old head and laughed, showing a want of teeth under his moustache. He put his hand on March's back. "This poy—he wass a poy den—wass so gracy to pekin reading Heine that he gommence with the tictionary bevore he knows any crammar, and ve bick it out vort by vort togeder."

"He was a pretty cay poy in those days, heigh, Lindau?" asked Fulkerson, burlesquing the old man's accent, with an impudent wink that made Lindau himself laugh. "Back in the dark ages, I mean, there in Indianapolis. Just how long ago did you old codgers meet there, anyway?" Fulkerson saw the restiveness in Dryfoos's eye at the purely literary course the talk had taken; he had intended it to lead up that way to business, to *Every Other Week;* but he saw that it was leaving Dryfoos too far out, and he wished to get it on the personal ground, where everybody is at home.

"Ledt me zee," mused Lindau. "Wass it in fifty-nine or zixty, Passil? Idt wass a year or dwo pefore the war proke oudt, anyway."

"Those were exciting times," said Dryfoos, making his first entry into the general talk. "I went down to Indianapolis with the first company from our place, and I saw the red-shirts pouring in everywhere. They had a song—

> "Oh, never mind the weather, but git over
>   double trouble,
> For we're bound for the land of Canaan."

The fellows locked arms and went singin' it up and down four or five abreast in the moonlight; crowded everybody else off the sidewalk."

"I rememper, I rememper," said Lindau, nodding his head slowly up and down. "A coodt many off them nefer gome pack from that landt of Ganaan, Mr. Dryfoos?"

"You're right, Mr. Lindau. But I reckon it was worth it—the country we've got now. Here, young man!" He caught the arm of the waiter who was going round with the champagne bottle. "Fill up Mr. Lindau's glass, there. I want to drink the health of those old times with him. Here's to your empty sleeve, Mr. Lindau. God bless it! No offence to *you,* Colonel Woodburn," said Dryfoos, turning to him before he drank.

---

5 sack . . . fault, from Falstaff's speech to Hal, I Henry IV, Act II, sc. iv, l. 517: "If sack and sugar be a fault, God help the wicked" • 31 Style . . . man. "The style is the man himself" ("Le style est l'homme même") occurs in a Discourse by the Comte de Buffon written in 1750 • 43 nobody like Heine. Howells gives to March one of his own early preferences

"Not at all, sir, not at all," said the colonel. "I will drink with you, if you will permit me."

"We'll all drink—standing," cried Fulkerson. "Help March to get up, somebody! Fill high the bowl with Samian Apollinaris for Coonrod! Now, then, hurrah for Lindau!"

They cheered, and hammered on the table with the butts of their knife-handles. Lindau remained seated. The tears came into his eyes; he said, "I thank you, chendlemen," and hiccoughed.

"I'd 'a' went into the war myself," said Dryfoos, "but I was raisin' a family of young children, and I didn't see how I could leave my farm. But I helped to fill up the quota at every call, and when the volunteering stopped I went round with the subscription paper myself; and we offered as good bounties as any in the State. My substitute was killed in one of the last skirmishes—in fact, after Lee's surrender—and I've took care of his family, more or less, ever since."

"By the way, March," said Fulkerson, "what sort of an idea would it be to have a good war-story—might be a serial—in the magazine? The war has never fully panned out in fiction yet. It was used a good deal just after it was over, and then it was dropped. I think it's time to take it up again. I believe it would be a card."

It was running in March's mind that Dryfoos had an old rankling shame in his heart for not having gone into the war, and that he had often made that explanation of his course without having ever been satisfied with it. He felt sorry for him; the fact seemed pathetic; it suggested a dormant nobleness in the man.

Beaton was saying to Fulkerson, "You might get a series of sketches by substitutes; the substitutes haven't been much heard from in the war literature. How would 'The Autobiography of a Substitute' do? You might follow him up to the moment he was killed in the other man's place, and inquire whether he had any right to the feelings of a hero when he was only hired in the place of one. Might call it 'The Career of a Deputy Hero.'"

"I fancy," said March, "that there was a great deal of mixed motive in the men who went into the war as well as in those who kept out of it. We canonised all that died or suffered in it, but some of them must have been self-seeking and low-minded, like men in other vocations." He found himself saying this in Dryfoos's

behalf; the old man looked at him gratefully at first, he thought, and then suspiciously.

Lindau turned his head toward him and said: "You are righdt, Passil; you are righdt. I haf zeen on the fieldt of pattle the voarst eggsipitions of human paseness —chelousy, fanity, ecodistic bridte. I haf zeen men in the face off death itself gofferened by motifes as low as— as pusiness motifes."

"Well," said Fulkerson, "it would be a grand thing for *Every Other Week* if we could get some of those ideas worked up into a series. It would make a lot of talk."

Colonel Woodburn ignored him in saying, "I think, Major Lindau——"

"High brifate; prefet gorporal," the old man interrupted, in rejection of the title.

Kendricks laughed and said, with a glance of appreciation at Lindau, "Brevet corporal is good."

Colonel Woodburn frowned a little, and passed over the joke. "I think Mr. Lindau is right. Such exhibitions were common to both sides, though if you gentlemen will pardon me for saying so, I think they were less frequent on ours. We were fighting more immediately for existence; we were fewer than you were, and we knew it; we felt more intensely that if each were not for all, then none was for any."

The colonel's words made their impression. Dryfoos said with authority, "That is so."

"Colonel Woodburn," Fulkerson called out, "if you'll work up those ideas into a short paper—say three thousand words—I'll engage to make March take it."

The colonel went on without replying: "But Mr. Lindau is right in characterising some of the motives that led men to the cannon's mouth as no higher than business motives, and his comparison is the most forcible that he could have used. I was very much struck by it."

The hobby was out, the colonel was in the saddle with so firm a seat that no effort sufficed to dislodge him. The dinner went on from course to course with barbaric profusion, and from time to time Fulkerson tried to bring the talk back to *Every Other Week*. But perhaps because that was only the ostensible and not the real object of

<hr>

4 Fill . . . Samian. Compare "The Isles of Greece" in Byron's **Don Juan**, Canto III, l. 61: "Fill high the bowl with Samian wine" • 64 **Brevet**, by honorary promotion

the dinner, which was to bring a number of men together under Dryfoos's roof, and make them the witnesses of his splendour, make them feel the power of his wealth, Fulkerson's attempts failed. The colonel showed how commercialism was the poison at the heart of our national life; how we began as a simple, agricultural people, who had fled to these shores with the instinct, divinely implanted, of building a State such as the sun never shone upon before; how we had conquered the wilderness and the savage; how we had flung off, in our struggle with the mother-country, the trammels of tradition and precedent, and had settled down, a free nation, to the practice of the arts of peace; how the spirit of commercialism had stolen insidiously upon us, and the infernal impulse of competition had embroiled us in a perpetual warfare of interests, developing the worst passions of our nature, and teaching us to trick and betray and destroy one another in the strife for money, till now that impulse had exhausted itself, and we found competition gone and the whole economic problem in the hands of monopolies—the Standard Oil Company, the Sugar Trust, the Rubber Trust, and what not. And now what was the next thing? Affairs could not remain as they were; it was impossible; and what was the next thing?

The company listened for the main part silently. Dryfoos tried to grasp the idea of commercialism as the colonel seemed to hold it; he conceived of it as something like the dry-goods business on a vast scale, and he knew he had never been in that. He did not like to hear competition called infernal; he had always supposed it was something sacred; but he approved of what Colonel Woodburn said of the Standard Oil Company; it was all true; the Standard Oil Company had squeezed Dryfoos once, and made him sell it a lot of oil-wells by putting down the price of oil so low in that region that he lost money on every barrel he pumped.

All the rest listened silently, except Lindau; at every point the colonel made against the present condition of things he said more and more fiercely, "You are righdt, you are righdt." His eyes glowed, his hand played with his knife-hilt. When the colonel demanded, "And what is the next thing?" he threw himself forward, and repeated, "Yes, sir! What is the next thing?"

"Natural gas, by thunder!" shouted Fulkerson.

One of the waiters had profited by Lindau's posture to lean over him and put down in the middle of the table a structure in white sugar. It expressed Frescobaldi's conception of a derrick, and a touch of nature had been added in the flame of brandy, which burned luridly up from a small pit in the centre of the base, and represented the gas in combustion as it issued from the ground. Fulkerson burst into a roar of laughter with the words that recognised Frescobaldi's personal tribute to Dryfoos. Everybody rose and peered over at the thing, while he explained the work of sinking a gas-well, as he had already explained it to Frescobaldi. In the midst of his lecture he caught sight of the caterer himself, where he stood in the pantry doorway, smiling with an artist's anxiety for the effect of his masterpiece.

"Come in, come in, Frescobaldi! We want to congratulate you," Fulkerson called to him. "Here, gentlemen! Here's Frescobaldi's health."

They all drank; and Frescobaldi, smiling brilliantly and rubbing his hands as he bowed right and left, permitted himself to say to Dryfoos, "You are please; no? You like?"

"First-rate, first-rate!" said the old man; but when the Italian had bowed himself out and his guests had sunk into their seats again, he said dryly to Fulkerson, "I reckon they didn't have to torpedo that well, or the derrick wouldn't look quite so nice and clean."

"Yes," Fulkerson answered, "and that ain't quite the style—that little wiggly-waggly blue flame—that the gas acts when you touch off a good vein of it. This might do for weak-gas;" and he went on to explain: "They call it weak-gas when they tap it two or three hundred feet down; and anybody can sink a well in his backyard and get enough gas to light and heat his house. I remember one fellow that had it blazing up from a pipe through a flower-bed, just like a jet of water from a fountain. My, my, my! You fel—you gentlemen—ought to go out and see that country, all of you. Wish we *could* torpedo this well, Mr. Dryfoos, and let 'em see how it works! Mind that one you torpedoed for me? You know, when they sink a well," he went on to the company, "they can't always most generally sometimes tell whether they're goin' to get gas or oil or salt-water. Why, when they first began to bore for salt-water out on the Kanawha, back about the beginning of the century, they used to get gas now and then, and then they considered it a

---

89 Kanawha, a river which flows through West Virginia into the Ohio River

failure; they called a gas-well a blower, and give it up in disgust; the time wasn't ripe for gas yet. Now they bore away sometimes till they get half-way to China, and don't seem to strike anything worth speaking of. Then they put a dynamite torpedo down in the well and explode it. They have a little bar of iron that they call a Go-devil, and they just drop it down on the business end of the torpedo, and then stand from under, if *you* please! You hear a noise, and in about a half a minute you begin to *see* one, and it begins to rain oil and mud and salt-water and rocks and pitchforks and adoptive citizens; and when it clears up the derrick's painted—got a coat on that'll wear in any climate. That's what our honoured host meant. Generally get some visiting lady, when there's one round, to drop the Go-devil. But that day we had to put up with Conrad here. They offered to let me drop it, but I declined. I told 'em I hadn't much practice with Go-devils in the newspaper syndicate business, and I wasn't very well myself, anyway. Astonishing," Fulkerson continued, with the air of relieving his explanation by an anecdote, "how reckless they get using dynamite when they're torpedoing wells. We stopped at one place where a fellow was handling the cartridges pretty freely, and Mr. Dryfoos happened to caution him a little, and that ass came up with one of 'em in his hand, and began to pound it on the buggy-wheel to show us how safe it was. I turned green, I was so scared; but Mr. Dryfoos kept his colour, and kind of coaxed the fellow till he quit. You could see he was the fool kind, that if you tried to stop him he'd keep on hammering that cartridge, just to show that it wouldn't explode, till he blew you into Kingdom Come. When we got him to go away, Mr. Dryfoos drove up to his foreman. 'Pay Sheney off, and discharge him on the spot,' says he. 'He's too safe a man to have round; he knows too much about dynamite.' I never saw anybody so cool."

Dryfoos modestly dropped his head under Fulkerson's flattery and, without lifting it, turned his eyes toward Colonel Woodburn. "I had all sorts of men to deal with in developing my property out there, but I had very little trouble with them, generally speaking."

"Ah, ah! you foundt the labouring-man reasonable—dractable—tocile?" Lindau put in.

"Yes, generally speaking," Dryfoos answered. "They mostly knew which side of their bread was buttered. I did have one little difficulty at one time. It happened to

be when Mr. Fulkerson was out there. Some of the men tried to form a union——"

"No, no!" cried Fulkerson. "Let *me* tell that! I know you wouldn't do yourself justice, Mr. Dryfoos, and I want 'em to know how a strike can be managed, if you take it in time. You see, some of those fellows got a notion that there ought to be a union among the working-men to keep up wages, and dictate to the employers, and Mr. Dryfoos's foreman was the ringleader in the business. They understood pretty well that as soon as he found it out that foreman would walk the plank, and so they watched out till they thought they had Mr. Dryfoos just where they wanted him—everything on the keen jump, and every man worth his weight in diamonds—and then they come to him, and told him to sign a promise to keep that foreman to the end of the season, or till he was through with the work on the Dryfoos and Hendry Addition, under penalty of having them all knock off. Mr. Dryfoos smelt a mice, but he couldn't tell where the mice was; he saw that they did have him, and he signed, of course. There wasn't anything really against the fellow, anyway; he was a first-rate man, and he did his duty every time; only he'd got some of those ideas into his head, and they turned it. Mr. Dryfoos signed, and then he laid low."

March saw Lindau listening with a mounting intensity, and heard him murmur in German, "Shameful! shameful!"

Fulkerson went on: "Well, it wasn't long before they began to show their hand, but Mr. Dryfoos kept dark. He agreed to everything; there never was such an obliging capitalist before; there wasn't a thing they asked of him that he didn't do, with the greatest of pleasure, and all went merry as a marriage-bell till one morning a whole gang of fresh men marched into the Dryfoos and Hendry Addition, under the escort of a dozen Pinkertons with repeating rifles at half-cock, and about fifty fellows found themselves out of a job. You never saw such a mad set."

"Pretty neat," said Kendricks, who looked at the affair purely from an æsthetic point of view. "Such a *coup* as that would tell tremendously in a play."

"That was vile treason," said Lindau in German to

81 merry . . . marriage-bell, from Byron's **Childe Harold**, Canto III, I. 188: ''And all went merry as a marriage bell'' • 83 Pinker-tons, detectives employed by an agency founded by Allan Pinkerton in Chicago in 1850

March. "He's an infamous traitor! I cannot stay here. I must go."

He struggled to rise, while March held him by the coat, and implored him under his voice, "For Heaven's sake, don't, Lindau! You owe it to yourself not to make a scene, if you come here." Something in it all affected him comically; he could not help laughing.

The others were discussing the matter, and seemed not to have noticed Lindau, who controlled himself and
10 sighed: "You are right. I must have patience."

Beaton was saying to Dryfoos, "Pity your Pinkertons couldn't have given them a few shots before they left."

"No, that wasn't necessary," said Dryfoos. "I succeeded in breaking up the union. I entered into an agreement with other parties not to employ any man who would not swear that he was non-union. If they had attempted violence, of course they could have been shot. But there was no fear of that. Those fellows can always be depended upon to cut each other's throats in
20 the long-run."

"But sometimes," said Colonel Woodburn, who had been watching throughout for a chance to mount his hobby again, "they make a good deal of trouble first. How was it in the great railroad strike of '77?"

"Well, I guess there was a little trouble that time, colonel," said Fulkerson. "But the men that undertake to override the laws and paralyse the industries of a country like this generally get left in the end."

"Yes, sir, generally; and up to a certain point, always.
30 But it's the exceptional that is apt to happen, as well as the unexpected. And a little reflection will convince any gentleman here that there is always a danger of the exceptional in your system. The fact is, those fellows have the game in their own hands already. A strike of the whole body of the Brotherhood of Engineers alone would starve out the entire Atlantic seaboard in a week; labour insurrection could make head at a dozen given points, and your government couldn't move a man over the roads without the help of the engineers."

40 "That is so," said Kendricks, struck by the dramatic character of the conjecture. He imagined a fiction dealing with the situation as something already accomplished.

"Why don't some fellow do the *Battle of Dorking* act with that thing?" said Fulkerson. "It would be a card."

"Exactly what I was thinking, Mr. Fulkerson," said Kendricks.

Fulkerson laughed. "Telepathy—clear case of mind-transference. Better see March, here, about it. *I'd* like to have it in *Every Other Week*. It would make talk."

"Perhaps it might set your people to thinking as well 50 as talking," said the colonel.

"Well, sir," said Dryfoos, setting his lips so tightly together that his imperial stuck straight outward, "if I had my way, there wouldn't *be* any Brotherhood of Engineers, nor any other kind of labour union in the whole country."

"What!" shouted Lindau. "You would sobbress the unionss of the voarking-men?"

"Yes, I would."

"And what would you do with the unionss of the 60 gabidalists—the drosts—and gompines, and boolss? Would you dake the righdt from one and gif it to the odder?"

"Yes, sir, I would," said Dryfoos, with a wicked look at him.

Lindau was about to roar back at him with some furious protest, but March put his hand on his shoulder imploringly, and Lindau turned to him to say in German, "But it is infamous—infamous! What kind of man is this? Who is he? He has the heart of a tyrant."   70

Colonel Woodburn cut in. "You couldn't do that, Mr. Dryfoos, under your system. And if you attempted it, with your conspiracy laws, and that kind of thing, it might bring the climax sooner than you expected. Your commercialised society has built its house on the sands. It will have to go. But I should be sorry if it went before its time."

"You are righdt, sir," said Lindau. "It would be a bity. I hobe it will last till it feelss its rottenness, like Herodt. Boat, when its hour gomes, when it trops to bieces with 80 the veight off its own gorrubtion—what then?"

"It's not to be supposed that a system of things like this can drop to pieces of its own accord, like the old Republic of Venice," said the colonel. "But when the last vestige of commercial society is gone, then we can

---

24 **strike of '77.** Railroad riots in 1877 throughout the East, and especially in Pennsylvania, resulted from the reduction of wages • 43 **Battle of Dorking,** by Sir G. T. Chesney (1833-1895), appeared in **Blackwood's Magazine** in 1871. Designed to point up a lack of military preparation, the book gave an imaginary account of the invasion and ultimate conquest of England by a foreign power • 53 **imperial,** a pointed beard on a man's chin and lower lip

Conrad – a
dreamy
visionary

begin to build anew; and we shall build upon the
central idea, not of the false liberty you now worship,
but of responsibility—responsibility. The enlightened,
the moneyed, the cultivated class shall be responsible to
the central authority—emperor, duke, president; the
name does not matter—for the national expense and
the national defence, and it shall be responsible to the
working-classes of all kinds for homes and lands and
implements, and the opportunity to labour at all times.
10 The working-classes shall be responsible to the leisure
class for the support of its dignity in peace, and shall be
subject to its command in war. The rich shall warrant
the poor against planless production and the ruin that
now follows, against danger from without and famine
from within, and the poor——"

"No, no, no!" shouted Lindau. "The *State* shall do
that—the whole beople. The men who voark shall have
and shall eat; and the men that will not voark, they shall
sdarfe. But no man need sdarfe. He will go to the
20 State, and the State will see that he haf voark, and that
he haf foodt. All the roadts and mills and mines and
landts shall be the beople's and be ron *by* the beople
for the beople. There shall be no rich and no boor; and
there shall not be war any more, for what bower wouldt
dare to addack a beople bound togeder in a broderhood
like that?"

"Lion and lamb act," said Fulkerson, not well knowing, after so much champagne, what words he was using.

No one noticed him, and Colonel Woodburn said
30 coldly to Lindau, "You are talking paternalism, sir."

"And *you* are dalking *feutalism!*" retorted the old man.

The Colonel did not reply. A silence ensued, which
no one broke till Fulkerson said: "Well, now, look here.
If either one of these millenniums was brought about,
by force of arms, or otherwise, what would become of
Every Other Week? Who would want March for an
editor? How would Beaton sell his pictures? Who
would print Mr. Kendricks' little society verses and
short stories? What would become of Conrad and his
40 good works?" Those named grinned in support of Fulkerson's diversion, but Lindau and the colonel did not
speak; Dryfoos looked down at his plate, frowning.
A waiter came round with cigars, and Fulkerson took
one. "Ah," he said, as he bit off the end, and leaned
over to the emblematic masterpiece, where the brandy
was still feebly flickering, "I wonder if there's enough

natural gas left to light my cigar." His effort put the *very*
flame out and knocked the derrick over; it broke in *wages*
fragments on the table. Fulkerson cackled over the ruin:
"I wonder if all Moffitt will look that way after labour 50
and capital have fought it out together. I hope this ain't
ominous of anything personal, Dryfoos?"

"I'll take the risk of it," said the old man harshly.

He rose mechanically, and Fulkerson said to Frescobaldi's man, "You can bring us the coffee in the
library."

The talk did not recover itself there. Lindau would
not sit down; he refused coffee, and dismissed himself
with a haughty bow to the company; Colonel Woodburn shook hands elaborately all round, when he had 60
smoked his cigar; the others followed him. It seemed
to March that his own good-night from Dryfoos was
dry and cold. . . .

[A streetcar strike furnishes the dramatic climax of
Howells' story; such a strike had occurred in New York a
few months before the publication of the book. In the
chapters that follow, the strike is presented in such a way
as to show the reactions of various characters to it: the
hostility of the elder Dryfoos; the sympathy of Lindau,
young Dryfoos, and Margaret Vance; the indifference of
Fulkerson; the detachment of March. Whatever Howells'
own attitude may have been, the emphasis given to the
subject shows the author's growing awareness of the
problem.]

PART FIFTH

Chapter III

indifference

The strike made a good deal of talk in the office of
Every Other Week—that is, it made Fulkerson talk
a good deal. He congratulated himself that he was not
personally incommoded by it, like some of the fellows
who lived up-town, and had not everything under one
roof, as it were. He enjoyed the excitement of it, and
he kept the office-boy running out to buy the extras 70
which the newsmen came crying through the street
almost every hour with a lamentable, unintelligible noise.
He read not only the latest intelligence of the strike, but
the editorial comments on it, which praised the firm at-

titude of both parties, and the admirable measures taken by the police to preserve order. Fulkerson enjoyed the interviews with the police captains and the leaders of the strike; he equally enjoyed the attempts of the reporters to interview the road managers, which were so graphically detailed, and with such a fine feeling for the right use of scareheads as to have almost the value of direct expressions from them, though it seemed that they had resolutely refused to speak. He said, at second-hand from the papers, that if the men behaved themselves and respected the rights of property, they would have public sympathy with them every time; but just as soon as they began to interfere with the roads' right to manage their own affairs in their own way, they must be put down with an iron hand; the phrase "iron hand" did Fulkerson almost as much good as if it had never been used before. News began to come of fighting between the police and the strikers when the roads tried to move their cars with men imported from Philadelphia, and then Fulkerson rejoiced at the splendid courage of the police. At the same time he believed what the strikers said, and that the trouble was not made by them, but by gangs of roughs acting without their approval. In this juncture he was relieved by the arrival of the State Board of Arbitration, which took up its quarters, with a great many scareheads, at one of the principal hotels, and invited the roads and the strikers to lay the matter in dispute before them; he said that now we should see the working of the greatest piece of social machinery in modern times. But it appeared to work only in the alacrity of the strikers to submit their grievance. The roads were as one road in declaring that there was nothing to arbitrate, and that they were merely asserting their right to manage their own affairs in their own way. One of the presidents was reported to have told a member of the Board, who personally summoned him, to get out and to go about his business. Then, to Fulkerson's extreme disappointment, the august tribunal, acting on behalf of the sovereign people in the interest of peace, declared itself powerless and got out, and would, no doubt, have gone about its business if it had had any. Fulkerson did not know what to say, perhaps because the extras did not; but March laughed at this result.

"It's a good deal like the military manœuvre of the King of France and his forty thousand men. I suppose

somebody told him at the top of the hill that there was nothing to arbitrate, and to get out and go about his business, and that was the reason he marched down after he had marched up with all that ceremony. What amuses me is to find that in an affair of this kind the roads have rights and the strikers have rights, but the public has no rights at all. The roads and the strikers are allowed to fight out a private war in our midst—as thoroughly and precisely a private war as any we despise the Middle Ages for having tolerated—as any street war in Florence or Verona—and to fight it out at our pains and expense, and we stand by like sheep, and wait till we get tired. It's a funny attitude for a city of fifteen hundred thousand inhabitants."

"What would you do?" asked Fulkerson, a good deal daunted by this view of the case.

"Do? Nothing. Hasn't the State Board of Arbitration declared itself powerless? We have no hold upon the strikers; and we're so used to being snubbed and disobliged by common carriers that we have forgotten our hold on the roads, and always allow them to manage their own affairs in their own way, quite as if we had nothing to do with them, and they owed us no services in return for their privileges."

"That's a good deal so," said Fulkerson, disordering his hair. "Well, it's nuts for the colonel nowadays. He says if he was boss of this town he would seize the roads on behalf of the people, and man 'em with policemen, and run 'em till the managers had come to terms with the strikers; and he'd do that every time there was a strike."

"Doesn't that rather savour of the paternalism he condemned in Lindau?" asked March.

"I don't know. It savours of horse-sense."

"You are pretty far gone, Fulkerson. I thought you were the most engaged man I ever saw; but I guess you're more father-in-lawed. And before you're married too."

"Well, the colonel's a glorious old fellow, March. I wish he had the power to do that thing, just for the fun of looking on while he waltzed in. He's on the

7 scareheads, sensational headlines • 45 military . . . men, an allusion to the nursery rhyme: "The King of France with forty thousand men/ Marched up the hill and then marched down again" • 82 engaged man. Fulkerson has become engaged to marry Colonel Woodburn's daughter

keen jump from morning till night, and he's up late and early to see the row. I'm afraid he'll get shot at some of the fights; he sees them all; *I* can't get any show at them: haven't seen a brickbat shied or a club swung yet. Have you?"

"No, I find I can philosophise the situation about as well from the papers, and that's what I really want to do, I suppose. Besides I'm solemnly pledged by Mrs. March not to go near any sort of crowd, under penalty of having her bring the children and go with me. Her theory is that we must all die together; the children haven't been at school since the strike began. There's no precaution that Mrs. March hasn't used. She watches me whenever I go out, and sees that I start straight for this office."

Fulkerson laughed and said: "Well, it's probably the only thing that's saved your life. Have you seen anything of Beaton lately?"

"No. You don't mean to say *he's* killed!"

"Not if he knows it. But I don't know——. What do you say, March? What's the reason you couldn't get us up a paper on the strike?"

"I knew it would fetch round to *Every Other Week,* somehow."

"No, but seriously. There'll be plenty of newspaper accounts. But you could treat it in the historical spirit —like something that happened several centuries ago; De Foe's Plague of London style. Heigh? What made me think of it was Beaton. If I could get hold of him, you two could go round together and take down its æsthetic aspects. It's a big thing, March, this strike is. I tell you it's imposing to have a private war, as you say, fought out this way, in the heart of New York, and New York not minding it a bit. See? Might take that view of it. With your descriptions and Beaton's sketches—well, it would just be the greatest card! Come! What do you say?"

"Will you undertake to make it right with Mrs. March if I'm killed and she and the children are not killed with me?"

"Well, it would be difficult. I wonder how it would do to get Kendricks to do the literary part?"

"I've no doubt he'd jump at the chance. I've yet to see the form of literature that Kendricks wouldn't lay down his life for."

"Say!" March perceived that Fulkerson was about to

vent another inspiration, and smiled patiently. "Look here! What's the reason we couldn't get one of the strikers to write it up for us?"

"Might have a symposium of strikers and presidents," March suggested.

"No; I'm in earnest. They say some of those fellows —especially the foreigners—are educated men. I know one fellow—a Bohemian—that used to edit a Bohemian newspaper here. He could write it out in his kind of Dutch, and we could get Lindau to translate it."

"I guess not," said March dryly.

"Why not? He'd do it for the cause, wouldn't he? Suppose you put it up on him, the next time you see him."

"I don't see Lindau any more," said March. He added, "I guess he's renounced me along with Mr. Dryfoos's money."

"Pshaw! You don't mean he hasn't been round since?"

"He came for a while, but he's left off coming now. I don't feel particularly gay about it," March said, with some resentment of Fulkerson's grin. "He's left me in debt to him for lessons to the children."

Fulkerson laughed out. "Well, he *is* the greatest old fool! Who'd 'a' thought he'd 'a' been in earnest with those 'brincibles' of his? But I suppose there have to be just such cranks; it takes all kinds to make a world."

"There has to be *one* such crank, it seems," March partially assented. "One's enough for me."

"I reckon this thing is nuts for Lindau, too," said Fulkerson. "Why, it must act like a schooner of beer on him all the while, to see 'gabidal' embarrassed like it is by this strike. It must make old Lindau feel like he was back behind those barricades at Berlin. Well, he's a splendid old fellow; pity he drinks, as I remarked once before."

When March left the office he did not go home so directly as he came, perhaps because Mrs. March's eye was not on him. He was very curious about some aspects of the strike, whose importance, as a great social convulsion, he felt people did not recognise; and with his temperance in everything, he found its negative ex-

---

28 **De Foe's . . . London.** Defoe's **Journal of the Plague Year** (1722) was a fictitious narrative which seemed so authentic that it was later quoted as authoritative • 79 **barricades at Berlin,** a reference to the Revolution of 1848 in Prussia

pressions as significant as its more violent phases. He had promised his wife solemnly that he would keep away from these, and he had a natural inclination to keep his promise; he had no wish to be that peaceful spectator who always gets shot when there is any firing on a mob. He interested himself in the apparent indifference of the mighty city, which kept on about its business as tranquilly as if the private war being fought out in its midst were a vague rumour of Indian troubles
10 on the frontier; and he realised how there might once have been a street feud of forty years in Florence without interfering materially with the industry and prosperity of the city. On Broadway there was a silence where a jangle and clatter of horse-car bells and hoofs had been, but it was not very noticeable; and on the avenues, roofed by the elevated roads, this silence of the surface tracks was not noticeable at all in the roar of the trains overhead. Some of the cross-town cars were beginning to run again; with a policeman on
20 the rear of each; on the Third Avenue line, operated by non-union men, who had not struck, there were two policemen beside the driver of every car, and two beside the conductor, to protect them from the strikers. But there were no strikers in sight, and on Second Avenue they stood quietly about in groups on the corners. While March watched them at a safe distance, a car laden with policemen came down the track, but none of the strikers offered to molest it. In their simple Sunday best, March thought them very quiet, decent-
30 looking people, and he could well believe that they had nothing to do with the riotous outbreaks in other parts of the city. He could hardly believe that there were any such outbreaks; he began more and more to think them mere newspaper exaggerations in the absence of any disturbance, or the disposition to it, that he could see. He walked on to the East River: Avenues A, B, and C presented the same quiet aspect as Second Avenue; groups of men stood on the corners, and now and then a police-laden car was brought unmolested down
40 the tracks before them; they looked at it and talked together, and some laughed, but there was no trouble.

March got a cross-town car, and came back to the West side. A policeman, looking very sleepy and tired, lounged on the platform.

"I suppose you'll be glad when this cruel war is over," March suggested, as he got in.

The officer gave him a surly glance and made him no answer.

His behaviour, from a man born to the joking give and take of our life, impressed March. It gave him a 50 fine sense of the ferocity which he had read of the French troops putting on toward the populace just before the *coup d'état;* he began to feel like populace; but he struggled with himself and regained his character of philosophical observer. In this character he remained in the car and let it carry him by the corner where he ought to have got out and gone home, and let it keep on with him to one of the furthermost tracks westward, where so much of the fighting was reported to have taken place. But everything on the 60 way was as quiet as on the East side.

Suddenly the car stopped with so quick a turn of the brake that he was half thrown from his seat, and the policeman jumped down from the platform and ran forward.

Chapter IV

Dryfoos sat at breakfast that morning with Mrs. Mandel as usual to pour out his coffee. Conrad had already gone down-town; the two girls lay abed much later than their father breakfasted, and their mother had gradually grown too feeble to come down till lunch. Suddenly 70 Christine appeared at the door. Her face was white to the edges of her lips, and her eyes were blazing.

"Look here, father! Have you been saying anything to Mr. Beaton?"

The old man looked up at her across his coffee-cup through his frowning brows. "No."

Mrs. Mandel dropped her eyes, and the spoon shook in her hand.

"Then what's the reason he don't come here any more?" demanded the girl; and her glance darted 80 from her father to Mrs. Mandel. "Oh, it's *you,* is it? I'd like to know who told *you* to meddle in other people's business?"

"*I* did," said Dryfoos savagely. "*I* told her to ask him what he wanted here, and he said he didn't want

---

53 coup d'état, the sudden stroke of policy by which Louis Napoleon became emperor of France (1851-1852)

anything, and he stopped coming. That's all. I did it myself."

"Oh, you *did,* did you?" said the girl, scarcely less insolently than she had spoken to Mrs. Mandel. "I should like to know what you did it for? I'd like to know what made you think I wasn't able to take care of myself. I just knew somebody had been meddling, but I didn't suppose it was *you.* I can manage my own affairs in my own way, if you please, and I'll thank you after this to leave me to myself in what don't concern you."

"Don't concern me? You impudent jade!" her father began.

Christine advanced from the doorway toward the table; she had her hands closed upon what seemed trinkets, some of which glittered and dangled from them. She said, "Will you go to him and tell him that this meddlesome minx here had no business to say anything about me to him, and you take it all back?"

"No!" shouted the old man. "And if——"

"That's all I want of *you!*" the girl shouted in her turn. "Here are your presents." With both hands she flung the jewels—pins and rings and earrings and bracelets—among the breakfast dishes, from which some of them sprang to the floor. She stood a moment to pull the intaglio ring from the finger where Beaton put it a year ago, and dashed that at her father's plate. Then she whirled out of the room, and they heard her running upstairs.

The old man made a start toward her, but he fell back in his chair before she was gone, and with a fierce, grinding movement of his jaws, controlled himself. "Take—take those things up," he gasped to Mrs. Mandel. He seemed unable to rise again from his chair, but when she asked him if he were unwell, he said no, with an air of offence, and got quickly to his feet. He mechanically picked up the intaglio ring from the table while he stood there, and put it on his little finger; his hand was not much bigger than Christine's. "How do you suppose she found it out?" he asked, after a moment.

"She seems to have merely suspected it," said Mrs. Mandel, in a tremor, and with the fright in her eyes which Christine's violence had brought there.

"Well, it don't make any difference. She had to know, somehow, and now she knows." He started toward the door of the library, as if to go into the hall, where his hat and coat always hung.

"Mr. Dryfoos," palpitated Mrs. Mandel, "I can't remain here, after the language your daughter has used to me— I can't let you leave me—I—I'm afraid of her——"

"Lock yourself up, then," said the old man rudely. He added, from the hall before he went out, "I reckon she'll quiet down now."

He took the elevated road. The strike seemed a very far-off thing, though the paper he bought to look up the stock market was full of noisy typography about yesterday's troubles on the surface lines. Among the millions in Wall Street there was some joking and some swearing, but not much thinking about the six thousand men who had taken such chances in their attempt to better their condition. Dryfoos heard nothing of the strike in the lobby of the Stock Exchange, where he spent two or three hours watching a favourite stock of his go up and go down under the betting. By the time the Exchange closed it had risen eight points, and on this and some other investments he was five thousand dollars richer than he had been in the morning. But he had expected to be richer still, and he was by no means satisfied with his luck. All through the excitement of his winning and losing had played the dull, murderous rage he felt toward the child who had defied him, and when the game was over and he started home, his rage mounted into a sort of frenzy; he would teach her, he would break her. He walked a long way without thinking, and then waited for a car. None came, and he hailed a passing coupé.

"What has got all the cars?" he demanded of the driver, who jumped down from his box to open the door for him and get his direction.

"Been away?" asked the driver. "Hasn't been any car along for a week. Strike."

"Oh yes," said Dryfoos. He felt suddenly giddy, and he remained staring at the driver after he had taken his seat.

The man asked, "Where to?"

Dryfoos could not think of his street or number, and he said with uncontrollable fury, "I told you once! Go up to West Eleventh, and drive along slow on the south side; I'll show you the place."

He could not remember the number of *Every Other Week* office, where he suddenly decided to stop before he went home. He wished to see Fulkerson, and ask him something about Beaton: whether he had been about lately, and whether he had dropped any hint of what had happened concerning Christine; Dryfoos believed that Fulkerson was in the fellow's confidence.

There was nobody but Conrad in the counting-room, whither Dryfoos returned after glancing into Fulkerson's empty office. "Where's Fulkerson?" he asked, sitting down with his hat on.

"He went out a few moments ago," said Conrad, glancing at the clock. "I'm afraid he isn't coming back again to-day, if you wanted to see him."

Dryfoos twisted his head sidewise and upward to indicate March's room. "That other fellow out, too?"

"He went just before Mr. Fulkerson," answered Conrad.

"Do you generally knock off here in the middle of the afternoon?" asked the old man.

"No," said Conrad, as patiently as if his father had not been there a score of times, and found the whole staff of *Every Other Week* at work between four and five. "Mr. March, you know, always takes a good deal of his work home with him, and I suppose Mr. Fulkerson went out so early because there isn't much doing to-day. Perhaps it's the strike that makes it dull."

"The strike—yes! It's a pretty piece of business to have everything thrown out because a parcel of lazy hounds want a chance to lay off and get drunk." Dryfoos seemed to think Conrad would make some answer to this, but the young man's mild face merely saddened, and he said nothing. "I've got a coupé out there now that I had to take because I couldn't get a car. If I had my way I'd have a lot of those vagabonds hung. They're waiting to get the city into a snarl, and then rob the houses—pack of dirty, worthless whelps. They ought to call out the militia, and fire into 'em. Clubbing is too good for them." Conrad was still silent, and his father sneered, "But I reckon *you* don't think so."

"I think the strike is useless," said Conrad.

"Oh, you *do*, do you? Comin' to your senses a little. Gettin' tired walkin' so much. I should like to know what your gentlemen over there on the East side think about the strike, anyway."

The young fellow dropped his eyes. "I am not authorised to speak for them."

"Oh, indeed! And perhaps you're not authorised to speak for yourself?"

"Father, you know we don't agree about these things. I'd rather not talk——"

"But I'm goin' to *make* you talk this time!" cried Dryfoos, striking the arm of the chair he sat in with the side of his fist. A maddening thought of Christine came over him. "As long as you eat my bread, you have got to do as I say. I won't have my children telling me what I shall do and sha'n't do, or take on airs of being holier than me. Now, you just speak up! Do you think those loafers are right, or don't you? Come!"

Conrad apparently judged it best to speak. "I think they were very foolish to strike—at this time, when the elevated roads can do the work."

"Oh, at this time, heigh! And I suppose they think over there on the East side that it'd been wise to strike before we got the elevated." Conrad again refused to answer, and his father roared, "What do you think?"

"I think a strike is always bad business. It's war; but sometimes there don't seem any other way for the working men to get justice. They say that sometimes strikes do raise the wages, after a while."

"Those lazy devils were paid enough already," shrieked the old man. "They got two dollars a day. How much do you think they ought to 'a' got? Twenty?"

Conrad hesitated with a beseeching look at his father. But he decided to answer. "The men say that with partial work, and fines, and other things they get sometimes a dollar, and sometimes ninety cents a day."

"They lie, and you *know* they lie," said his father, rising and coming toward him. "And what do you think the upshot of it all will be, after they've ruined business for another week, and made people hire hacks, and stolen the money of honest men? How is it going to end?"

"They will have to give in."

"Oh, give in, heigh! And what will you say *then*, I should like to know? How will you feel about it then? Speak!"

"I shall feel as I do now. I know you don't think that way, and I don't blame you—or anybody. But if I have got to say how I shall feel, why, I shall feel sorry they didn't succeed, for I believe they have a righteous cause, though they go the wrong way to help themselves."

His father came close to him, his eyes blazing, his teeth set. "Do you *dare* to say that to me?"

"Yes. I can't help it. I pity them; my whole heart is with those poor men."

"You impudent puppy!" shouted the old man. He lifted his hand and struck his son in the face. Conrad caught his hand with his own left, and while the blood began to trickle from a wound that Christine's intaglio ring had made in his temple, he looked at him with a kind of grieving wonder, and said, "Father!"

The old man wrenched his fist away, and ran out of the house. He remembered his address now, and he gave it as he plunged into the coupé. He trembled with his evil passion, and glared out of the windows at the passers as he drove home; he only saw Conrad's mild grieving, wondering eyes, and the blood slowly trickling from the wound in his temple.

Conrad went to the neat set-bowl in Fulkerson's comfortable room, and washed the blood away, and kept bathing the wound with the cold water till it stopped bleeding. The cut was not deep, and he thought he would not put anything on it. After a while he locked up the office, and started out, he hardly knew where. But he walked on, in the direction he had taken, till he found himself in Union Square, on the pavement in front of Brentano's. It seemed to him that he heard some one calling gently to him, "Mr. Dryfoos!"

Chapter V

Conrad looked confusedly around, and the same voice said again, "Mr. Dryfoos!" and he saw that it was a lady speaking to him from a coupé beside the curbing, and then he saw that it was Miss Vance.

She smiled when he gave signs of having discovered her, and came up to the door of her carriage. "I am so glad to meet you. I have been longing to talk to somebody; nobody seems to feel about it as I do. Oh, isn't it horrible? *Must* they fail? I saw cars running on all the lines as I came across; it made me sick at heart. *Must* those brave fellows give in? And everybody seems to hate them so—I can't bear it." Her face was estranged with excitement, and there were traces of tears on it. "You must think me almost crazy to stop you in the street this way; but when I caught sight of you I had to

speak. I knew you would sympathise—I knew you would feel as I do. Oh, how can anybody help honouring those poor men for standing by one another as they do? They are risking all they have in the world for the sake of justice! Oh, they are true heroes! They are staking the bread of their wives and children on the dreadful chance they've taken! But no one seems to understand it. No one seems to see that they are willing to suffer more now that other poor men may suffer less hereafter. And those wretched creatures that are coming in to take their places—those traitors——"

"We can't blame them for wanting to earn a living, Miss Vance," said Conrad.

"No, no! I don't blame them. Who am I, to do such a thing? It's *we*—people like me, of my class—who make the poor betray one another. But this dreadful fighting—this hideous paper is full of it." She held up an extra, crumpled with her nervous reading. "Can't something be done to stop it? Don't you think that if some one went among them, and tried to make them see how perfectly hopeless it was to resist the companies, and drive off the new men, he might do some good? I have wanted to go and try; but I am a woman, and I mustn't! I shouldn't be afraid of the strikers, but I'm afraid of what people would say!" Conrad kept pressing his handkerchief to the cut in his temple, which he thought might be bleeding, and now she noticed this. "Are you hurt, Mr. Dryfoos? You look so pale."

"No, it's nothing—a little scratch I've got."

"Indeed you look pale. Have you a carriage? How will you get home? Will you get in here with me, and let me drive you?"

"No, no," said Conrad, smiling at her excitement. "I'm perfectly well——"

"And you don't think I'm foolish and wicked for stopping you here, and talking in this way? But I know you feel as I do!"

"Yes, I feel as you do. You are right—right in every way—I mustn't keep you—Good-bye." He stepped back to bow, but she put her beautiful hand out of the window, and when he took it she wrung his hand hard.

"Thank you, thank you! You are good and you are just! But no one can do anything. It's useless!"

The type of irreproachable coachman on the box whose respectability had suffered through the strange behaviour of his mistress in this interview, drove quickly off at her signal, and Conrad stood a moment looking after the carriage. His heart was full of joy; it leaped; he thought it would burst. As he turned to walk away it seemed to him as if he mounted upon the air. The trust she had shown him, the praise she had given him; that crush of the hand: he hoped nothing, he formed no idea from it, but it all filled him with love that cast out the pain and shame he had been suffering. He believed that he could never be unhappy any more; the hardness that was in his mind toward his father went out of it; he saw how sorely he had tried him; he grieved that he had done it, but the means, the difference of his feelings about the cause of their quarrel, he was solemnly glad of that since she shared it. He was only sorry for his father. "Poor father!" he said under his breath as he went along. He explained to her about his father in his reverie, and she pitied his father too.

He was walking over toward the West side, aimlessly at first, and then at times with the longing to do something to save those mistaken men from themselves forming itself into a purpose. Was not that what she meant, when she bewailed her woman's helplessness? She must have wished him to try, if he, being a man, could not do something; or if she did not, still he would try, and if she heard of it, she would recall what she had said, and would be glad he had understood her so. Thinking of her pleasure in what he was going to do, he forgot almost what it was; but when he came to a street-car track he remembered it, and looked up and down to see if there were any turbulent gathering of men, whom he might mingle with and help to keep from violence. He saw none anywhere; and then suddenly, as if at the same moment, for in his exalted mood all events had a dreamlike simultaneity, he stood at the corner of an avenue, and in the middle of it, a little way off, was a street-car, and around the car a tumult of shouting, cursing, struggling men. The driver was lashing his horses forward, and a policeman was at their heads, with the conductor, pulling them; stones, clubs, brick-bats hailed upon the car, the horses, the men trying to move them. The mob closed upon them in a body, and then a patrol-wagon whirled up from the other side, and a squad of policemen leaped out, and began to club the rioters. Conrad could see how they struck them under the rims of their hats; the blows on their skulls sounded as if they had fallen on stone; the rioters ran in all directions.

One of the officers rushed up toward the corner where Conrad stood, and then he saw at his side a tall old man with a long white beard. He was calling out at the policeman: "Ah yes! Glup the strikerss—gif it to them! Why don't you co and glup the bresidents that insoalt your lawss, and gick your Boart of Arpidration out-of-toors? Glup the strikerss—they cot no friendts! They cot no money to pribe you, to dreat you!"

The officer lifted his club, and the old man threw his left arm up to shield his head. Conrad recognised Lindau, and now he saw the empty sleeve dangle in the air, over the stump of his wrist. He heard a shot in that turmoil beside the car, and something seemed to strike him in the breast. He was going to say to the policeman, "Don't strike him! He's an old soldier! You see he has no hand!" but he could not speak, he could not move his tongue. The policeman stood there; he saw his face: it was not bad, not cruel; it was like the face of a statue, fixed, perdurable; a mere image of irresponsible and involuntary authority. Then Conrad fell forward, pierced through the heart by that shot fired from the car.

March heard the shot as he scrambled out of his car, and at the same moment he saw Lindau drop under the club of the policeman, who left him where he fell, and joined the rest of the squad in pursuing the rioters. The fighting round the car in the avenue ceased; the driver whipped his horses into a gallop, and the place was left empty.

March would have liked to run; he thought how his wife had implored him to keep away from the rioting; but he could not have left Lindau lying there if he would. Something stronger than his will drew him to the spot, and there he saw Conrad dead beside the old man. . . .

[The concluding chapters tell briefly of the death of Lindau, the remorse of Dryfoos for his treatment of his son, the transfer of the ownership of Every Other Week from Dryfoos to Fulkerson and March, the Dryfooses' departure for Europe, the marriage of Fulkerson and Miss Woodburn, and the entrance of Margaret Vance into an order of nuns. Thus Howells concludes his rich and varied study of the New York of the 1880's.]

1890

doing, for it constrained the artist to a lifelong pursuit of intangible realities that existed only in his imagination. ... Even in his subtle psychological inquiries he remained shut up within his own skull-pan. His characters are only projections of his brooding fancy, externalizations of hypothetical subtleties." It is true that James was alienated from America and that he became increasingly obsessed with psychological subtleties which he described in an increasingly difficult style. Quite possibly, however, Parrington, and those who agree with the judgments just quoted, do James less than justice. It may be urged that there is more of America in James' books than appears at first glance. His books contain scores of Americans; his most admirable characters are, repeatedly, Americans; and, paradoxically enough in view of his high regard for the "culture" of Europe, his Europeans and his Europeanized Americans are likely to betray a moral decadence—a moral decadence which the author unmistakably condemns. America does not come off nearly so badly in James' books as some suppose, nor Europe nearly so well. It is arguable, moreover, that the psychological subtleties of the later works have a valid basis in fact. Civilized human relations are almost infinitely complex and subtle. Most novelists greatly simplify, or pass superficially over, these relations; James was a specialist in them. He was perhaps the first novelist to recognize fully the complexities which may grow out of the relationship of one sensitive personality to another, and to record them with fine discrimination and microscopic detail. The reading of his best work requires attention and patience, but it may be, "under the right persuasion," an immensely rewarding experience.

The Novels and Tales of Henry James, New York edition, 26 vols., New York, 1907-1917 • The Letters of Henry James, ed. Percy Lubbock, 2 vols., New York, 1920 • The Notebooks of Henry James, ed. F. O. Matthiessen and K. B. Murdock, New York, 1947 • J. W. Beach, The Method of Henry James, New Haven, 1918 • Pelham Edgar, Henry James: Man and Author, London, 1927 • The Art of the Novel: Critical Prefaces by Henry James, ed. R. P. Blackmur, New York, 1934 • F. O. Matthiessen, Henry James: The Major Phase, New York, 1944 • The Question of Henry James, ed. F. W. Dupee, New York, 1945 • F. O. Matthiessen, The James Family, New York, 1947 • Leon Edel, Henry James: The Untried Years, 1843-1870, Philadelphia, 1953

From

Hawthorne

THE HOUSE OF THE SEVEN GABLES

Hawthorne belonged to the older, romantic period of the novel, while James represented the new era of realism. In writing about Hawthorne, therefore, James quite naturally was thinking of, among other things, the differences between the two styles or modes. "It cannot be too often repeated," he said, "that Hawthorne was not a realist. ... He never attempted to render exactly or closely the actual facts of the society that surrounded him." Hawthorne's story is of interest, James pointed out, not so much for its own sake as for its "symbolic" value. The characters of The House of the Seven Gables "are all figures rather than characters—they are all pictures rather than persons"; they are "light and vague"; "they are all types . . . of something general." James felt, however, that Hawthorne's method was well adapted to his characters, with a single exception: the portrait of Holgrave, who represents the modern American, would have profited, he thought, by the realistic method.

James recognized Hawthorne's greatness despite "the absence of the realistic mode of treatment." He admired Hawthorne's art. He was willing to admit that Hawthorne's method was nearly always suited to his subject matter and purpose. And he found in The House of the Seven Gables the characteristic which all great fiction, whether romantic or realistic, must possess—the "hum . . . of the whole multitudinous life of man."

The House of the Seven Gables was written at Lenox, among the mountains of Massachusetts, a village nestling, rather loosely, in one of the loveliest corners of New England, to which Hawthorne had betaken himself after the success of The Scarlet Letter became conspicuous, in the summer of 1850, and where he occupied for two years an uncomfortable little red house, which is now pointed out to the inquiring stranger. The inquiring stranger is now a frequent figure at Lenox, for the place has suffered the process of lionisation. It has become a prosperous watering-place, or at least (as there are no waters), as they say in America, a summer-resort. It is a brilliant and generous landscape, and thirty years ago a man of fancy, desiring to apply himself, might have found both inspiration and tranquillity there. Hawthorne found so much of both that he wrote more during his two years of residence at Lenox than at any period of his career. He began with *The House of the Seven Gables,* which was finished in the early part of 1851. This is the longest of his three American novels; it is the most elaborate, and in the judgment of some persons it is the finest. It is a rich, delightful, imaginative work, larger and more various than its companions, and full of all sorts of deep intentions, of interwoven threads of suggestion. But it is not so rounded and complete as *The Scarlet Letter;* it has always seemed to me more like a prologue to a great novel than a great novel itself. I think this is partly owing to the fact that the subject, the *donnée,* as the French say, of the story, does not quite fill it out, and that we get at the same time an impression of certain complicated purposes on the author's part, which seem to reach beyond it. I call it larger and more various than its companions, and it has, indeed, a greater richness of tone and density of detail. The colour, so to speak, of *The House of the Seven Gables* is admirable. But the story has a sort of expansive quality which never wholly fructifies, and as I lately laid it down, after reading it for the third time, I had a sense of having interested myself in a magnificent fragment. Yet the book has a great fascination; and of all of those of its author's productions which I have read over while writing this sketch, it is perhaps the one that has gained most by re-perusal. If it be true of the others that the pure, natural quality of the imaginative strain is their great merit, this is at least as true of *The House of the Seven Gables,* the charm of which is in a peculiar degree of the kind that we fail to reduce to its grounds—like that of the sweetness of a piece of music, or the softness of fine September weather. It is vague, indefinable, ineffable; but it is the sort of thing we must always point to in justification of the high claim that we make for Hawthorne. In this case, of course, its vagueness is a drawback, for it is difficult to point to ethereal beauties; and if the reader whom

we have wished to inoculate with our admiration inform us, after looking awhile, that he perceives nothing in particular, we can only reply that, in effect, the object is a delicate one.

The House of the Seven Gables comes nearer being a picture of contemporary American life than either of its companions; but on this ground it would be a mistake to make a large claim for it. It cannot be too often repeated that Hawthorne was not a realist. He had a high sense of reality—his Note-Books superabundantly testify to it; and fond as he was of jotting down the items that make it up, he never attempted to render exactly or closely the actual facts of the society that surrounded him. I have said—I began by saying—that his pages were full of its spirit, and of a certain reflected light that springs from it; but I was careful to add that the reader must look for his local and national qualities between the lines of his writing and in the *indirect* testimony of his tone, his accent, his temper, of his very omissions and suppressions. *The House of the Seven Gables* has, however, more literal actuality than the others, and if it were not too fanciful an account of it, I should say that it renders, to an initiated reader, the impression of a summer afternoon in an elm-shadowed New England town. It leaves upon the mind a vague correspondence to some such reminiscence, and in stirring up the association it renders it delightful. The comparison is to the honour of the New England town, which gains in it more than it bestows. The shadows of the elms, in *The House of the Seven Gables,* are exceptionally dense and cool; the summer afternoon is peculiarly still and beautiful; the atmosphere has a delicious warmth, and the long daylight seems to pause and rest. But the mild provincial quality is there, the mixture of shabbiness and freshness, the paucity of ingredients. The end of an old race—this is the situation that Hawthorne has depicted, and he has been admirably inspired in the choice of the figures in

1 two years. Hawthorne resided at Lenox from May 1850 until November 1851 • **2 now pointed out.** The "little red house" was destroyed by fire in 1890. It is soon to be rebuilt by the National Federation of Music Clubs and will be used in connection with the Berkshire Music Festivals • **14 three . . . novels.** The Blithedale Romance (1852) is the third • **71 New England town.** Interestingly enough, James had attempted in the opening chapters of **Roderick Hudson** (1876) the "evocation" (to quote from his later Preface to the novel) of a "small New England town." He thought that the attempt "failed of intensity," owing partly to his "scant experience" with the subject whom he seeks to interest us. They are all figures rather than characters—they are all pictures rather than persons. But if their reality is light and vague, it is sufficient, and it is in harmony with the low relief and dimness of outline of the objects that surrounded them. They are all types, to the author's mind, of something general, of something that is bound up with the history, at large, of families and individuals, and each of them is the centre of a cluster of those ingenious and meditative musings, rather melancholy, as a general thing, than joyous, which melt into the current and texture of the story and give it a kind of moral richness. A grotesque old spinster, simple, childish, penniless, very humble at heart, but rigidly conscious of her pedigree; an amiable bachelor, of an epicurean temperament and an enfeebled intellect, who has passed twenty years of his life in penal confinement for a crime of which he was unjustly pronounced guilty; a sweet-natured and bright-faced young girl from the country, a poor relation of these two ancient decrepitudes, with whose moral mustiness her modern freshness and soundness are contrasted; a young man still more modern, holding the latest opinions, who has sought his fortune up and down the world, and, though he has not found it, takes a genial and enthusiastic view of the future: these, with two or three remarkable accessory figures, are the persons concerned in the little drama. The drama is a small one, but as Hawthorne does not put it before us for its own superficial sake, for the dry facts of the case, but for something in it which he holds to be symbolic and of large application, something that points a moral and that it behooves us to remember, the scenes in the rusty wooden house whose gables give its name to the story, have something of the dignity both of history and of tragedy. Miss Hepzibah Pyncheon, dragging out a disappointed life in her paternal dwelling, finds herself obliged in her old age to open a little shop for the sale of penny toys and gingerbread. This is the central incident of the tale, and, as Hawthorne relates it, it is an incident of the most impressive magnitude and most touching interest. Her dishonoured and vague-minded brother is released from prison at the same moment, and returns to the ancestral roof to deepen her perplexities. But, on the other hand, to alleviate them, and to introduce a breath of the air of the outer world into this long unventilated interior, the little country cousin also arrives, and proves the good angel of the feebly distracted household. All this episode is exquisite—admirably conceived

and executed, with a kind of humorous tenderness, an equal sense of everything in it that is picturesque, touching, ridiculous, worthy of the highest praise. Hepzibah Pyncheon, with her near-sighted scowl, her rusty joints, her antique turban, her map of a great territory to the eastward which ought to have belonged to her family, her vain terrors, and scruples, and resentments, the inaptitude and repugnance of an ancient gentlewoman to the vulgar little commerce which a cruel fate has compelled her to engage in—Hepzibah Pyncheon is a masterly picture. I repeat that she is a picture, as her companions are pictures; she is a charming piece of descriptive writing, rather than a dramatic exhibition. But she is described like her companions, too, so subtly and lovingly that we enter into her virginal old heart and stand with her behind her abominable little counter. Clifford Pyncheon is a still more remarkable conception, though he is, perhaps, not so vividly depicted. It was a figure needing a much more subtle touch, however, and it was of the essence of his character to be vague and unemphasised. Nothing can be more charming than the manner in which the soft, bright, active presence of Phoebe Pyncheon is indicated, or than the account of her relations with the poor, dimly sentient kinsman for whom her light-handed sisterly offices, in the evening of a melancholy life, are a revelation of lost possibilities of happiness. "In her aspect," Hawthorne says of the young girl, "there was a familiar gladness, and a holiness that you could play with, and yet reverence it as much as ever. She was like a prayer offered up in the homeliest beauty of one's mother-tongue. Fresh was Phoebe, moreover, and airy, and sweet in her apparel; as if nothing that she wore—neither her gown, nor her small straw bonnet, nor her little kerchief, any more than her snowy stockings—had ever been put on before; or, if worn, were all the fresher for it, and with a fragrance as if they had lain among the rose-buds." Of the influence of her maidenly salubrity upon poor Clifford, Hawthorne gives the prettiest description, and then, breaking off suddenly, renounces the attempt in language which, while pleading its inadequacy, conveys an exquisite satisfaction to the reader. I quote the passage for the sake of its extreme felicity, and of the charming image with which it concludes.

"But we strive in vain to put the idea into words. No adequate expression of the beauty and profound pathos with which it impresses us is attainable. This being, made only for happiness, and heretofore so miserably failing to be happy—his tendencies so hideously thwarted that, some unknown time ago, the delicate springs of his character, never morally or intellectually strong, had given way, and he was now imbecile—this poor forlorn voyager from the Islands of the Blest, in a frail bark, on a tempestuous sea, had been flung by the last mountain-wave of his shipwreck into a quiet harbour. There, as he lay more than half lifeless on the strand, the fragrance of an earthly rose-bud had come to his nostrils, and, as odours will, had summoned up reminiscences or visions of all the living and breathing beauty amid which he should have had his home. With his native susceptibility of happy influences, he inhales the slight ethereal rapture into his soul, and expires!"

I have not mentioned the personage in *The House of the Seven Gables* upon whom Hawthorne evidently bestowed most pains, and whose portrait is the most elaborate in the book; partly because he is, in spite of the space he occupies, an accessory figure, and partly because, even more than the others, he is what I have called a picture rather than a character. Judge Pyncheon is an ironical portrait, very richly and broadly executed, very sagaciously composed and rendered—the portrait of a superb, full-blown hypocrite, a large-based, full-nurtured Pharisee, bland, urbane, impressive, diffusing about him a "sultry" warmth of benevolence, as the author calls it again and again, and basking in the noontide of prosperity and the consideration of society; but in reality hard, gross, and ignoble. Judge Pyncheon is an elaborate piece of description, made up of a hundred admirable touches, in which satire is always winged with fancy, and fancy is linked with a deep sense of reality. It is difficult to say whether Hawthorne followed a model in describing Judge Pyncheon; but it is tolerably obvious that the picture is an impression—a copious impression—of an individual. It has evidently a definite starting-point in fact, and the author is able to draw, freely and confidently, after the image established in his mind. Holgrave, the modern young man, who has been a Jack-of-all-trades, and is at the period of the story a daguerreotypist, is an attempt to render a kind of national type—that of the young citizen of the United States whose fortune is simply in his lively intelligence, and who

stands naked, as it were, unbiased and unencumbered alike, in the centre of the far-stretching level of American life. Holgrave is intended as a contrast; his lack of traditions, his democratic stamp, his condensed experience, are opposed to the desiccated prejudices and exhausted vitality of the race of which poor feebly-scowling, rusty-jointed Hepzibah is the most heroic representative. It is, perhaps, a pity that Hawthorne should not have proposed to himself to give the old Pyncheon qualities some embodiment which would help them to balance more fairly with the elastic properties of the young daguerreotypist—should not have painted a lusty conservative to match his strenuous radical. As it is, the mustiness and mouldiness of the tenants of the House of the Seven Gables crumble away rather too easily. Evidently, however, what Hawthorne designed to represent was not the struggle between an old society and a new, for in this case he would have given the old one a better chance; but simply, as I have said, the shrinkage and extinction of a family. This appealed to his imagination; and the idea of long perpetuation and survival always appears to have filled him with a kind of horror and disapproval. Conservative, in a certain degree, as he was himself, and fond of retrospect and quietude and the mellowing influences of time, it is singular how often one encounters in his writings some expression of mistrust of old houses, old institutions, long lines of descent. He was disposed, apparently, to allow a very moderate measure in these respects, and he condemns the dwelling of the Pyncheons to disappear from the face of the earth because it has been standing a couple of hundred years. In this he was an American of Americans; or, rather, he was more American than many of his countrymen, who, though they are accustomed to work for the short run rather than the long, have often a lurking esteem for things that show the marks of having lasted. I will add that Holgrave is one of the few figures, among those which Hawthorne created, with regard to which the absence of the realistic mode of treatment is felt as a loss. Holgrave is not sharply enough characterised; he lacks features; he is not an individual, but a type. But my last word about this admirable novel must not be a restrictive one. It is a large and generous production, pervaded with that vague hum, that indefinable echo, of the whole multitudinous life of man, which is the real sign of a great work of fiction. . . .

1879

The Art of Fiction

James at odds with both
1. Romanticists +
2 Naturalists

James was at odds with two schools of fiction popular in this period: the school of romantic adventure, best represented by Robert Louis Stevenson, and the school of detailed social documentation—the naturalistic school—best represented by Émile Zola. James' own work was neither "adventurous" nor "sociological." With a minimum of plot, in the usual sense of the term, and of external details, James' stories tended more and more to concentrate upon the fascinating problem of the expanding consciousness of a character. The result was much less popular than the work of the other schools, and James felt the challenge.

To those of the naturalistic school, who insisted that the novelist should write from a large and varied experience of life, James replied that experience is properly "an immense sensibility" and that insight is more important than "experience" as ordinarily construed. The English woman novelist (in James' illustration) who succeeded so admirably in giving a convincing picture of French Protestant youth had had, as a matter of "experience," only a momentary glimpse of such a group; but she had had the all-important faculty of "insight." To those who insisted upon exciting incident, James answered that excitement does not necessarily consist of physical action, does not absolutely require moving accidents by flood and field. "It is an incident," he remarked characteristically, "for a woman to stand up with her hand resting on a table and look out at you in a certain way"—an exciting incident, too, he meant to imply, particularly if the young woman happened to be Miss Isabel Archer in **The Portrait of a Lady.** The "psychological" subjects, he argued, have an interest and validity of their own. For example, the "moral consciousness of a child," which Edmond de Goncourt and George Eliot had employed with varying success, and which James himself was to employ, rather abstrusely, in **What Maisie Knew,** may be more exciting to a subtle intelligence than Stevenson's adventures on the Spanish

Main. From James' standpoint, the first is the more valid subject because it comes within the range of every reader's experience, while the second subject is known to most readers "only in supposition."

Both in motivation, therefore, and in its essential argument, James' essay was a criticism of popular current schools of fiction and a spirited defense of his own fictional practice.

"The Art of Fiction" was first published in **Longman's Magazine** in 1884; it was collected with other essays in **Partial Portraits** in 1888.

James Concentrates on consciousness of character

I should not have affixed so comprehensive a title to these few remarks, necessarily wanting in any completeness upon a subject the full consideration of which would carry us far, did I not seem to discover a pretext for my temerity in the interesting pamphlet lately published under this name by Mr. Walter Besant. Mr. Besant's lecture at the Royal Institution—the original form of his pamphlet—appears to indicate that many persons are interested in the art of fiction, and are not indifferent to such remarks, as those who practise it may attempt to make about it. I am therefore anxious not to lose the benefit of this favourable association, and to edge in a few words under cover of the attention which Mr. Besant is sure to have excited. There is something very encouraging in his having put into form certain of his ideas on the mystery of story-telling.

It is a proof of life and curiosity—curiosity on the part of the brotherhood of novelists as well as on the part of their readers. Only a short time ago it might have been supposed that the English novel was not what the French call *discutable.* It had no air of having a theory, a conviction, a consciousness of itself behind it— of being the expression of an artistic faith, the result of choice and comparison. I do not say it was necessarily the worse for that; it would take much more courage than I possess to intimate that the form of the novel as Dickens and Thackeray (for instance) saw it had any taint of incompleteness. It was, however, *naïf* (if I may help myself out with another French word); and evi-

---

6 Besant, Sir Walter Besant (1836-1901), English novelist and critic •
21 discutable, debatable

dently if it be destined to suffer in any way for having lost its *naïveté* it has now an idea of making sure of the corresponding advantages. During the period I have alluded to there was a comfortable good-humoured feeling abroad that a novel is a novel, as a pudding is a pudding, and that our only business with it could be to swallow it. But within a year or two, for some reason or other, there have been signs of returning animation— the era of discussion would appear to have been to a certain extent opened. Art lives upon discussion, upon experiment, upon curiosity, upon variety of attempt, upon the exchange of views and the comparison of standpoints; and there is a presumption that those times when no one has anything particular to say about it, and has no reason to give for practice or preference, though they may be times of honour, are not times of development— are times, possibly, even a little of dulness. The successful application of any art is a delightful spectacle, but the theory too is interesting; and though there is a great deal of the latter without the former I suspect there has never been a genuine success that has not had a latent core of conviction. Discussion, suggestion, formulation, these things are fertilizing when they are frank and sincere. Mr. Besant has set an excellent example in saying what he thinks, for his part, about the way in which fiction should be written, as well as about the way in which it should be published; for his view of the "art," carried on into an appendix, covers that too. Other labourers in the same field will doubtless take up the argument, they will give it the light of their experience, and the effect will surely be to make our interest in the novel a little more what it had for some time threatened to fail to be —a serious, active, inquiring interest, under protection of which this delightful study may, in moments of confidence, venture to say a little more what it thinks of itself.

It must take itself seriously for the public to take it so. The old superstition about fiction being "wicked" has doubtless died out in England; but the spirit of it lingers in a certain oblique regard directed toward any story which does not more or less admit that it is only a joke. Even the most jocular novel feels in some degree the weight of the proscription that was formerly directed against literary levity: the jocularity does not always succeed in passing for orthodoxy. It is still expected, though perhaps people are ashamed to say it, that a pro-duction which is after all only a "make-believe" (for what else is a "story"?) shall be in some degree apologetic—shall renounce the pretension of attempting really to represent life. This, of course, any sensible, wide-awake story declines to do, for it quickly perceives that the tolerance granted to it on such a condition is only an attempt to stifle it disguised in the form of generosity. The old evangelical hostility to the novel, which was as explicit as it was narrow, and which regarded it as little less favourable to our immortal part than a stage-play, was in reality far less insulting. The only reason for the existence of a novel is that it does attempt to represent life. When it relinquishes this attempt, the same attempt that we see on the canvas of the painter, it will have arrived at a very strange pass. It is not expected of the picture that it will make itself humble in order to be forgiven; and the analogy between the art of the painter and the art of the novelist is, so far as I am able to see, complete. Their inspiration is the same, their process (allowing for the different quality of the vehicle) is the same, their success is the same. They may learn from each other, they may explain and sustain each other. Their cause is the same, and the honour of one is the honour of another. The Mahometans think a picture an unholy thing, but it is a long time since any Christian did, and it is therefore the more odd that in the Christian mind the traces (dissimulated though they may be) of a suspicion of the sister art should linger to this day. The only effectual way to lay it to rest is to emphasize the analogy to which I just alluded—to insist on the fact that as the picture is reality, so the novel is history. That is the only general description (which does it justice) that we may give of the novel. But history also is allowed to represent life; it is not, any more than painting, expected to apologize. The subject-matter of fiction is stored up likewise in documents and records, and if it will not give itself away, as they say in California, it must speak with assurance, with the tone of the historian. Certain accomplished novelists have a habit of giving themselves away which must often bring tears to the eyes of people who take their fiction seriously. I was lately struck, in reading over many pages of Anthony Trollope, with his want of discretion in this particular. In a digression, a parenthesis or an aside, he concedes to the reader that he and this trusting friend are only "making believe." He admits that the events he narrates have not really happened, and that he can give his narrative any turn the reader may like best. Such a betrayal of a sacred office seems to me, I confess, a terrible crime; it is what I mean by the attitude of apology, and it shocks me every whit as much in Trollope as it would have shocked me in Gibbon or Macaulay. It implies that the novelist is less occupied in looking for the truth (the truth, of course I mean, that he assumes, the premises that we must grant him, whatever they may be) than the historian, and in doing so it deprives him at a stroke of all his standing-room. To represent and illustrate the past, the actions of men, is the task of either writer, and the only difference that I can see is, in proportion as he succeeds, to the honour of the novelist, consisting as it does in his having more difficulty in collecting his evidence, which is so far from being purely literary. It seems to me to give him a great character, the fact that he has at once so much in common with the philosopher and the painter; this double analogy is a magnificent heritage.

It is of all this evidently that Mr. Besant is full when he insists upon the fact that fiction is one of the *fine* arts, deserving in its turn of all the honours and emoluments that have hitherto been reserved for the successful profession of music, poetry, painting, architecture. It is impossible to insist too much on so important a truth, and the place that Mr. Besant demands for the work of the novelist may be represented, a trifle less abstractly, by saying that he demands not only that it shall be reputed artistic, but that it shall be reputed very artistic indeed. It is excellent that he should have struck this note, for his doing so indicates that there was need of it, that his proposition may be to many people a novelty. One rubs one's eyes at the thought; but the rest of Mr. Besant's essay confirms the revelation. I suspect in truth that it would be possible to confirm it still further, and that one would not be far wrong in saying that in addition to the people to whom it has never occurred that a novel ought to be artistic, there are a great many others who, if this principle were urged upon them, would be filled with an indefinable mistrust. They would find it difficult to explain their repugnance, but it would operate strongly to put them on their guard. "Art," in our Protestant communities, where so many things have got so strangely twisted about, is supposed in certain circles to have some vague injurious effect upon those who make it an important consideration, who let it

weigh in the balance. It is assumed to be opposed in some mysterious manner to morality, to amusement, to instruction. When it is embodied in the work of the painter (the sculptor is another affair!) you know what it is: it stands there before you, in the honesty of pink and green and a gilt frame; you can see the worst of it at a glance, and you can be on your guard. But when it is introduced into literature it becomes more insidious—there is danger of its hurting you before you know it. Literature should be either instructive or amusing, and there is in many minds an impression that these artistic preoccupations, the search for form, contribute to neither end, interfere indeed with both. They are too frivolous to be edifying, and too serious to be diverting; and they are moreover priggish and paradoxical and superfluous. That, I think, represents the manner in which the latent thought of many people who read novels as an exercise in skipping would explain itself if it were to become articulate. They would argue, of course, that a novel ought to be "good," but they would interpret this term in a fashion of their own, which indeed would vary considerably from one critic to another. One would say that being good means representing virtuous and aspiring characters placed in prominent positions; another would say that it depends on a "happy ending," on a distribution at the last of prizes, pensions, husbands, wives, babies, millions, appended paragraphs, and cheerful remarks. Another still would say that it means being full of incident and movement, so that we shall wish to jump ahead, to see who was the mysterious stranger, and if the stolen will was ever found, and shall not be distracted from this pleasure by any tiresome analysis or "description." But they would all agree that the "artistic" idea would spoil some of their fun. One would hold it accountable for all the description, another would see it revealed in the absence of sympathy. Its hostility to a happy ending would be evident, and it might even in some cases render any ending at all impossible. The "ending" of a novel is, for many persons, like that of a good dinner, a course of dessert and ices, and the artist in fiction is regarded as a sort of meddlesome doctor who forbids agreeable aftertastes. It is therefore true that this conception of Mr. Besant's of the novel as a superior form encounters not only a negative but a positive indifference. It matters little that as a work of art it should really be as little or as much of its essence to supply happy endings, sympathetic characters, and an objective tone, as if it were a work of mechanics: the association of ideas, however incongruous, might easily be too much for it if an eloquent voice were not sometimes raised to call attention to the fact that it is at once as free and as serious a branch of literature as any other.

Certainly this might sometimes be doubted in presence of the enormous number of works of fiction that appeal to the credulity of our generation, for it might easily seem that there could be no great character in a commodity so quickly and easily produced. It must be admitted that good novels are much compromised by bad ones, and that the field at large suffers discredit from overcrowding. I think, however, that this injury is only superficial, and that the superabundance of written fiction proves nothing against the principle itself. It has been vulgarised, like all other kinds of literature, like everything else to-day, and it has proved more than some kinds accessible to vulgarisation. But there is as much difference as there ever was between a good novel and a bad one: the bad is swept with all the daubed canvases and spoiled marble into some unvisited limbo, or infinite rubbish-yard beneath the back-windows of the world, and the good subsists and emits its light and stimulates our desire for perfection. As I shall take the liberty of making but a single criticism of Mr. Besant, whose tone is so full of love of his art, I may as well have done with it at once. He seems to me to mistake, in attempting to say so definitely beforehand, what sort of an affair the good novel will be. To indicate the danger of such an error as that has been the purpose of these few pages; to suggest that certain traditions on the subject, applied *a priori*, have already had much to answer for, and that the good health of an art which undertakes so immediately to reproduce life must demand that it be perfectly free. It lives upon exercise, and the very meaning of exercise is freedom. The only obligation to which in advance we may hold a novel, without incurring the accusation of being arbitrary, is that it be interesting. That general responsibility rests upon it, but it is the only one I can think of. The ways in which it is at liberty to accomplish this result (of interesting us) strike me as innumerable, and such as can only suffer from being marked out or fenced in by prescription. They are as various as the temperament of man, and they are successful in proportion as they reveal a particular mind, different from others. A novel is in its broadest definition a personal, a direct impression of life: that, to begin with, constitutes its value, which is greater or less according to the intensity of the impression. But there will be no intensity at all, and therefore no value, unless there is freedom to feel and say. The tracing of a line to be followed, of a tone to be taken, of a form to be filled out, is a limitation of that freedom and a suppression of the very thing that we are most curious about. The form, it seems to me, is to be appreciated after the fact: then the author's choice has been made, his standard has been indicated; then we can follow lines and directions and compare tones and resemblances. Then in a word we can enjoy one of the most charming of pleasures, we can estimate quality, we can apply the test of execution. The execution belongs to the author alone; it is what is most personal to him, and we measure him by that. The advantage, the luxury, as well as the torment and responsibility of the novelist, is that there is no limit to what he may attempt as an executant—no limit to his possible experiments, efforts, discoveries, successes. Here it is especially that he works, step by step, like his brother of the brush, of whom we may always say that he has painted his picture in a manner best known to himself. His manner is his secret, not necessarily a jealous one. He cannot disclose it as a general thing if he would; he would be at a loss to teach it to others. I say this with a due recollection of having insisted on the community of method of the artist who paints a picture and the artist who writes a novel. The painter *is* able to teach the rudiments of his practice, and it is possible, from the study of good work (granted the aptitude), both to learn how to paint and to learn how to write. Yet it remains true, without injury to the *rapprochement,* that the literary artist would be obliged to say to his pupil much more than the other, "Ah, well, you must do it as you can!" It is a question of degree, a matter of delicacy. If there are exact sciences, there are also exact arts, and the grammar of painting is so much more definite that it makes the difference.

I ought to add, however, that if Mr. Besant says at the beginning of his essay that the "laws of fiction may be laid down and taught with as much precision and exact-

---

79 **rapprochement,** comparison or analogy (between the art of painting and the art of fiction)

ness as the laws of harmony, perspective, and proportion," he mitigates what might appear to be an extravagance by applying his remark to "general" laws, and by expressing most of these rules in a manner with which it would certainly be unaccommodating to disagree. That the novelist must write from his experience, that his "characters must be real and such as might be met with in actual life;" that "a young lady brought up in a quiet country village should avoid descriptions of garrison life," and "a writer whose friends and personal experiences belong to the lower middle-class should carefully avoid introducing his characters into society;" that one should enter one's notes in a common-place book; that one's figures should be clear in outline; that making them clear by some trick of speech or of carriage is a bad method, and "describing them at length" is a worse one; that English Fiction should have a "conscious moral purpose;" that "it is almost impossible to estimate too highly the value of careful workmanship—that is, of style;" that "the most important point of all is the story," that "the story is everything:" these are principles with most of which it is surely impossible not to sympathise. That remark about the lower middle-class writer and his knowing his place is perhaps rather chilling; but for the rest I should find it difficult to dissent from any one of these recommendations. At the same time, I should find it difficult positively to assent to them, with the exception, perhaps, of the injunction as to entering one's notes in a common-place book. They scarcely seem to me to have the quality that Mr. Besant attributes to the rules of the novelist—the "precision and exactness" of "the laws of harmony, perspective, and proportion." They are suggestive, they are even inspiring, but they are not exact, though they are doubtless as much so as the case admits of: which is a proof of that liberty of interpretation for which I just contended. For the value of these different injunctions—so beautiful and so vague—is wholly in the meaning one attaches to them. The characters, the situation, which strike one as real will be those that touch and interest one most, but the measure of reality is very difficult to fix. The reality of Don Quixote or of Mr. Micawber is a very delicate shade; it is a reality so coloured by the author's vision that, vivid as it may be, one would hesitate to propose it as a model: one would expose one's self to some very embarrassing questions on the part of a pupil. It goes without saying that you will

not write a good novel unless you possess the sense of reality; but it will be difficult to give you a recipe for calling that sense into being. Humanity is immense, and reality has a myriad forms; the most one can affirm is that some of the flowers of fiction have the odour of it, and others have not; as for telling you in advance how your nosegay should be composed, that is another affair. It is equally excellent and inconclusive to say that one must write from experience; to our supposititious aspirant such a declaration might savour of mockery. What kind of experience is intended, and where does it begin and end? Experience is never limited, and it is never complete; it is an immense sensibility, a kind of huge spiderweb of the finest silken threads suspended in the chamber of consciousness, and catching every air-borne particle in its tissue. It is the very atmosphere of the mind; and when the mind is imaginative—much more when it happens to be that of a man of genius—it takes to itself the faintest hints of life, it converts the very pulses of the air into revelations. The young lady living in a village has only to be a damsel upon whom nothing is lost to make it quite unfair (as it seems to me) to declare to her that she shall have nothing to say about the military. Greater miracles have been seen than that, imagination assisting, she should speak the truth about some of these gentlemen. I remember an English novelist, a woman of genius, telling me that she was much commended for the impression she had managed to give in one of her tales of the nature and way of life of the French Protestant youth. She had been asked where she learned so much about this recondite being, she had been congratulated on her peculiar opportunities. These opportunities consisted in her having once, in Paris, as she ascended a staircase, passed an open door where, in the household of a *pasteur,* some of the young Protestants were seated at table round a finished meal. The glimpse made a picture; it lasted only a moment, but that moment was experience. She had got her direct personal impression, and she turned out her type. She knew what youth was, and what Protestantism; she also had the advantage of having seen what it was to be French, so that she converted these ideas into a concrete image and produced a reality. Above all, however, she was blessed with

42 Micawber, in Dickens' David Copperfield • 81 pasteur, pastor
72 English novelist . . . youth. The reference is to **The Story of Elizabeth** (1863) by Anne Isabella Thackeray, later Lady Ritchie

the faculty which when you give it an inch takes an ell, and which for the artist is a much greater source of strength than any accident of residence or of place in the social scale. The power to guess the unseen from the seen, to trace the implication of things, to judge the whole piece by the pattern, the condition of feeling life in general so completely that you are well on your way to knowing any particular corner of it—this cluster of gifts may almost be said to constitute experience, and they occur in country and in town, and in the most differing stages of education. If experience consists of impressions, it may be said that impressions *are* experience, just as (have we not seen it?) they are the very air we breathe. Therefore, if I should certainly say to a novice, "Write from experience and experience only," I should feel that this was rather a tantalising monition if I were not careful immediately to add, "Try to be one of the people on whom nothing is lost!"

I am far from intending by this to minimise the importance of exactness—of truth of detail. One can speak best from one's own taste, and I may therefore venture to say that the air of reality (solidity of specification) seems to me to be the supreme virtue of a novel—the merit on which all its other merits (including that conscious moral purpose of which Mr. Besant speaks) helplessly and submissively depend. If it be not there they are all as nothing, and if these be there, they owe their effect to the success with which the author has produced the illusion of life. The cultivation of this success, the study of this exquisite process, form, to my taste, the beginning and the end of the art of the novelist. They are his inspiration, his despair, his reward, his torment, his delight. It is here in very truth that he competes with life; it is here that he competes with his brother the painter in *his* attempt to render the look of things, the look that conveys their meaning, to catch the colour, the relief, the expression, the surface, the substance of the human spectacle. It is in regard to this that Mr. Besant is well inspired when he bids him take notes. He cannot possibly take too many, he cannot possibly take enough. All life solicits him, and to "render" the simplest surface, to produce the most momentary illusion, is a very complicated business. His case would be easier, and the rule would be more exact, if Mr. Besant had been able to tell him what notes to take. But this, I fear, he can never learn in any manual; it is the business of his life. He has to take a great many in order to select a few, he has to work them up as he can, and even the guides and philosophers who might have most to say to him must leave him alone when it comes to the application of precepts, as we leave the painter in communion with his palette. That his characters "must be clear in outline," as Mr. Besant says—he feels that down to his boots; but how he shall make them so is a secret between his good angel and himself. It would be absurdly simple if he could be taught that a great deal of "description" would make them so, or that on the contrary the absence of description and the cultivation of dialogue, or the absence of dialogue and the multiplication of "incident," would rescue him from his difficulties. Nothing, for instance, is more possible than that he be of a turn of mind for which this odd, literal opposition of description and dialogue, incident and description, has little meaning and light. People often talk of these things as if they had a kind of internecine distinctness, instead of melting into each other at every breath, and being intimately associated parts of one general effort of expression. I cannot imagine composition existing in a series of blocks, nor conceive, in any novel worth discussing at all, of a passage of description that is not in its intention narrative, a passage of dialogue that is not in its intention descriptive, a touch of truth of any sort that does not partake of the nature of incident, or an incident that derives its interest from any other source than the general and only source of the success of a work of art—that of being illustrative. A novel is a living thing, all one and continuous, like any other organism, and in proportion as it lives will it be found, I think, that in each of the parts there is something of each of the other parts. The critic who over the close texture of a finished work shall pretend to trace a geography of items will mark some frontiers as artificial, I fear, as any that have been known to history. There is an old-fashioned distinction between the novel of character and the novel of incident which must have cost many a smile to the intending fabulist who was keen about his work. It appears to me as little to the point as the equally celebrated distinction between the novel and the romance—to answer as little to any

---

1 **ell.** A measure whose length varies in different countries; the English ell is 45 inches

reality. There are bad novels and good novels, as there are bad pictures and good pictures; but that is the only distinction in which I see any meaning, and I can as little imagine speaking of a novel of character as I can imagine speaking of a picture of character. When one says picture one says of character, when one says novel one says of incident, and the terms may be transposed at will. What is character but the determination of incident? What is incident but the illustration of character? What is either a picture or a novel that is *not* of character? What else do we seek in it and find in it? It is an incident for a woman to stand up with her hand resting on a table and look at you in a certain way; or if it be not an incident I think it will be hard to say what it is. At the same time it is an expression of character. If you say you don't see it (character in *that*—*allons donc!*), this is exactly what the artist who has reasons of his own for thinking he *does* see it undertakes to show you. When a young man makes up his mind that he has not faith enough after all to enter the church as he intended, that is an incident, though you may not hurry to the end of the chapter to see whether perhaps he doesn't change once more. I do not say that these are extraordinary or startling incidents. I do not pretend to estimate the degree of interest proceeding from them, for this will depend upon the skill of the painter. It sounds almost puerile to say that some incidents are intrinsically much more important than others, and I need not take this precaution after having professed my sympathy for the major ones in remarking that the only classification of the novel that I can understand is into that which has life and that which has it not.

The novel and the romance, the novel of incident and that of character—these clumsy separations appear to me to have been made by critics and readers for their own convenience, and to help them out of some of their occasional predicaments, but to have little reality or interest for the producer, from whose point of view it is of course that we are attempting to consider the art of fiction. The case is the same with another shadowy category which Mr. Besant apparently is disposed to set up—that of the "modern English novel;" unless indeed it be that in this matter he has fallen into an accidental confusion of standpoints. It is not quite clear whether he intends the remarks in which he alludes to it to be didactic or historical. It is as difficult to suppose a person intending to write a modern English as to suppose him writing an ancient English novel: that is a label which begs the question. One writes the novel, one paints the picture, of one's language and of one's time, and calling it modern English will not, alas! make the difficult task any easier. No more, unfortunately, will calling this or that work of one's fellow-artist a romance —unless it be, of course, simply for the pleasantness of the thing, as for instance when Hawthorne gave this heading to his story of *Blithedale*. The French, who have brought the theory of fiction to remarkable completeness, have but one name for the novel, and have not attempted smaller things in it, that I can see, for that. I can think of no obligation to which the "romancer" would not be held equally with the novelist; the standard of execution is equally high for each. Of course it is of execution that we are talking—that being the only point of a novel that is open to contention. This is perhaps too often lost sight of, only to produce interminable confusions and cross-purposes. We must grant the artist his subject, his idea, his *donnée*: our criticism is applied only to what he makes of it. Naturally I do not mean that we are bound to like it or find it interesting: in case we do not our course is perfectly simple—to let it alone. We may believe that of a certain idea even the most sincere novelist can make nothing at all, and the event may perfectly justify our belief; but the failure will have been a failure to execute, and it is in the execution that the fatal weakness is recorded. If we pretend to respect the artist at all, we must allow him his freedom of choice, in the face, in particular cases, of innumerable presumptions that the choice will not fructify. Art derives a considerable part of its beneficial exercise from flying in the face of presumptions, and some of the most interesting experiments of which it is capable are hidden in the bosom of common things. Gustave Flaubert has written a story about the devotion of a servant-girl to a parrot, and the production, highly finished as it is, cannot on the whole be called a success. We are perfectly free to find it flat, but I think it might have been interesting; and I, for my part, am extremely glad he should have written it; it is a contribution to our knowledge of what

16 *allons donc!* come now! nonsense! • 32 *novel . . . romance.* Hawthorne distinguished between the two in the Preface to **The House of the Seven Gables** • 55 **Blithedale**, Hawthorne's **Blithedale Romance** • 66 *donnée*, theme, subject

The Art of Fiction 507

can be done—or what cannot. Ivan Turgénieff has written a tale about a deaf and dumb serf and a lap-dog, and the thing is touching, loving, a little masterpiece. He struck the note of life where Gustave Flaubert missed it—he flew in the face of a presumption and achieved a victory.

Nothing, of course, will ever take the place of the good old fashion of "liking" a work of art or not liking it: the most improved criticism will not abolish that primitive, that ultimate test. I mention this to guard myself from the accusation of intimating that the idea, the subject, of a novel or a picture, does not matter. It matters, to my sense, in the highest degree, and if I might put up a prayer it would be that artists should select none but the richest. Some, as I have already hastened to admit, are much more remunerative than others, and it would be a world happily arranged in which persons intending to treat them should be exempt from confusions and mistakes. This fortunate condition will arrive only, I fear, on the same day that critics become purged from error. Meanwhile, I repeat, we do not judge the artist with fairness unless we say to him, "Oh, I grant you your starting-point, because if I did not I should seem to prescribe to you, and heaven forbid I should take that responsibility. If I pretend to tell you what you must not take, you will call upon me to tell you then what you must take; in which case I shall be prettily caught. Moreover, it isn't till I have accepted your data that I can begin to measure you. I have the standard, the pitch; I have no right to tamper with your flute and then criticise your music. Of course I may not care for your idea at all; I may think it silly, or stale, or unclean; in which case I wash my hands of you altogether. I may content myself with believing that you will not have succeeded in being interesting, but I shall, of course, not attempt to demonstrate it, and you will be as indifferent to me as I am to you. I needn't remind you that there are all sorts of tastes: who can know it better? Some people, for excellent reasons, don't like to read about carpenters; others, for reasons even better, don't like to read about courtesans. Many object to Americans. Others (I believe they are mainly editors and publishers) won't look at Italians. Some readers don't like quiet subjects; others don't like bustling ones. Some enjoy a complete illusion, others the consciousness of large concessions. They choose their novels accord-

ingly, and if they don't care about your idea they won't, *a fortiori*, care about your treatment."

So that it comes back very quickly, as I have said, to the liking: in spite of M. Zola, who reasons less powerfully than he represents, and who will not reconcile himself to this absoluteness of taste, thinking that there are certain things that people ought to like, and that they can be made to like. I am quite at a loss to imagine anything (at any rate in this matter of fiction) that people *ought* to like or to dislike. Selection will be sure to take care of itself, for it has a constant motive behind it. That motive is simply experience. As people feel life, so they will feel the art that is most closely related to it. This closeness of relation is what we should never forget in talking of the effort of the novel. Many people speak of it as a factitious, artificial form, a product of ingenuity, the business of which it is to alter and arrange the things that surround us, to translate them into conventional, traditional moulds. This, however, is a view of the matter which carries us but a very short way, condemns the art to an eternal repetition of a few familiar *clichés,* cuts short its development, and leads us straight up to a dead wall. Catching the very note and trick, the strange irregular rhythm of life, that is the attempt whose strenuous force keeps Fiction upon her feet. In proportion as in what she offers us we see life *without* rearrangement do we feel that we are touching the truth; in proportion as we see it *with* rearrangement do we feel that we are being put off with a substitute, a compromise and convention. It is not uncommon to hear an extraordinary assurance of remark in regard to this matter of rearranging, which is often spoken of as if it were the last word of art. Mr. Besant seems to me in danger of falling into the great error with his rather unguarded talk about "selection." Art is essentially selection, but it is a selection whose main care is to be typical, to be inclusive. For many people art means rose-coloured window-panes, and selection means picking a bouquet for Mrs. Grundy. They will tell you glibly that artistic considerations have nothing to do with the disagreeable, with the ugly; they will rattle off shallow commonplaces about the province of art and the limits of art till you are

48 *a fortiori,* by the stronger reason • 51 **represents,** portrays in his fiction • 85 **Mrs. Grundy,** a person referred to in Thomas Morton's comedy **Speed the Plough** (1798), has become the stock symbol of narrow conventionalism and prudery.

moved to some wonder in return as to the province and the limits of ignorance. It appears to me that no one can ever have made a seriously artistic attempt without becoming conscious of an immense increase—a kind of revelation—of freedom. One perceives in that case—by the light of a heavenly ray—that the province of art is all life, all feeling, all observation, all vision. As Mr. Besant so justly intimates, it is all experience. That is a sufficient answer to those who maintain that it must not touch the sad things of life, who stick into its divine unconscious bosom little prohibitory inscriptions on the end of sticks, such as we see in public gardens—"It is forbidden to walk on the grass; it is forbidden to touch the flowers; it is not allowed to introduce dogs or to remain after dark; it is requested to keep to the right." The young aspirant in the line of fiction whom we continue to imagine will do nothing without taste, for in that case his freedom would be of little use to him; but the first advantage of his taste will be to reveal to him the absurdity of the little sticks and tickets. If he have taste, I must add, of course, he will have ingenuity, and my disrespectful reference to that quality just now was not meant to imply that it is useless in fiction. But it is only a secondary aid; the first is a capacity for receiving straight impressions.

Mr. Besant has some remarks on the question of "the story" which I shall not attempt to criticise, though they seem to me to contain a singular ambiguity, because I do not think I understand them. I cannot see what is meant by talking as if there were a part of a novel which is the story and part of it which for mystical reasons is not—unless indeed the distinction be made in a sense in which it is difficult to suppose that any one should attempt to convey anything. "The story," if it represents anything, represents the subject, the idea, the *donnée* of the novel; and there is surely no "school"—Mr. Besant speaks of a school—which urges that a novel should be all treatment and no subject. There must assuredly be something to treat; every school is intimately conscious of that. This sense of the story being the idea, the starting-point, of the novel, is the only one that I see in which it can be spoken of as something different from its organic whole; and since in proportion as the work is successful the idea permeates and penetrates it, informs and animates it, so that every word and every punctuation-point contribute directly to the expression,

in that proportion do we lose our sense of the story being a blade which may be drawn more or less out of its sheath. The story and the novel, the idea and the form, are the needle and thread, and I never heard of a guild of tailors who recommended the use of the thread without the needle, or the needle without the thread. Mr. Besant is not the only critic who may be observed to have spoken as if there were certain things in life which constitute stories, and certain others which do not. I find the same odd implication in an entertaining article in the *Pall Mall Gazette*, devoted, as it happens, to Mr. Besant's lecture. "The story is the thing!" says this graceful writer, as if with a tone of opposition to some other idea. I should think it was, as every painter who, as the time for "sending in" his picture looms in the distance, finds himself still in quest of a subject—as every belated artist not fixed about his theme will heartily agree. There are some subjects which speak to us and others which do not, but he would be a clever man who should undertake to give a rule—an index expurgatorius—by which the story and the no-story should be known apart. It is impossible (to me at least) to imagine any such rule which shall not be altogether arbitrary. The writer in the *Pall Mall* opposes the delightful (as I suppose) novel of *Margot la Balafrée* to certain tales in which "Bostonian nymphs" appear to have "rejected English dukes for psychological reasons." I am not acquainted with the romance just designated, and can scarcely forgive the *Pall Mall* critic for not mentioning the name of the author, but the title appears to refer to a lady who may have received a scar in some heroic adventure. I am inconsolable at not being acquainted with this episode, but am utterly at a loss to see why it is a story when the rejection (or acceptance) of a duke is not, and why a reason, psychological or other, is not a subject when a cicatrix is. They are all particles of the multitudinous life with which the novel deals, and surely no dogma which pretends to make it lawful to touch the one and unlawful to touch the other will stand for a moment on its feet. It is the special picture that must stand or fall, according as it seems to possess truth or to lack it. Mr.

---

71 **Bostonian . . . reasons,** presumably a reference to James' **Portrait of a Lady,** in which Isabel Archer, an American girl, rejects a proposal of marriage from an English lord • 82 **cicatrix,** scar; **la Balafrée** means "the scarred woman"

Besant does not, to my sense, light up the subject by intimating that a story must, under penalty of not being a story, consist of "adventures." Why of adventures more than of green spectacles? He mentions a category of impossible things, and among them he places "fiction without adventure." Why without adventure, more than without matrimony, or celibacy, or parturition, or cholera, or hydropathy, or Jansenism? This seems to me to bring the novel back to the hapless little *rôle* of being an artificial, ingenious thing—bring it down from its large, free character of an immense and exquisite correspondence with life. And what *is* adventure when it comes to that, and by what sign is the listening pupil to recognize it? It is an adventure—an immense one—for me to write this little article; and for a Bostonian nymph to reject an English duke is an adventure only less stirring, I should say, than for an English duke to be rejected by a Bostonian nymph. I see dramas within dramas in that, and innumerable points of view. A psychological reason is, to my imagination, an object adorably pictorial; to catch the tint of its complexion—I feel as if that idea might inspire one to Titianesque efforts. There are few things more exciting to me, in short, than a psychological reason, and yet, I protest, the novel seems to me the most magnificent form of art. I have just been reading, at the same time, the delightful story of *Treasure Island,* by Mr. Robert Louis Stevenson and, in a manner less consecutive, the last tale from M. Edmond de Goncourt, which is entitled *Chérie.* One of these works treats of murders, mysteries, islands of dreadful renown, hairbreadth escapes, miraculous coincidences, and buried doubloons. The other treats of a little French girl who lived in a fine house in Paris, and died of wounded sensibility because no one would marry her. I call *Treasure Island* delightful, because it appears to me to have succeeded wonderfully in what it attempts; and I venture to bestow no epithet upon *Chérie*, which strikes me as having failed deplorably in what it attempts—that is, in tracing the development of the moral consciousness of a child. But one of these productions strikes me as exactly as much of a novel as the other, and as having a "story" quite as much. The moral consciousness of a child is as much a part of life as the islands of the Spanish Main, and the one sort of geography seems to me to have those "surprises" of which Mr. Besant speaks quite as much as the other. For myself (since it comes back in the last

resort, as I say, to the preference of the individual), the picture of the child's experience has the advantage that I can at successive steps (an immense luxury, near to the "sensual pleasure" of which Mr. Besant's critic in the *Pall Mall* speaks) say Yes or No, as it may be, to what the artist puts before me. I have been a child in fact, but I have been on a quest for a buried treasure only in supposition, and it is a simple accident that with M. de Goncourt I should have for the most part to say No. With George Eliot, when she painted that country with a far other intelligence, I always said Yes.

The most interesting part of Mr. Besant's lecture is unfortunately the briefest passage—his very cursory allusion to the "conscious moral purpose" of the novel. Here again it is not very clear whether he be recording a fact or laying down a principle; it is a great pity that in the latter case he should not have developed his idea. This branch of the subject is of immense importance, and Mr. Besant's few words point to considerations of the widest reach, not to be lightly disposed of. He will have treated the art of fiction but superficially who is not prepared to go every inch of the way that these considerations will carry him. It is for this reason that at the beginning of these remarks I was careful to notify the reader that my reflections on so large a theme have no pretension to be exhaustive. Like Mr. Besant, I have left the question of the morality of the novel till the last, and at the last I find I have used up my space. It is a question surrounded with difficulties, as witness the very first that meets us, in the form of a definite question, on the threshold. Vagueness, in such a discussion, is fatal, and what is the meaning of your morality and your conscious moral purpose? Will you not define your terms and explain how (a novel being a picture) a picture can be either moral or immoral? You wish to paint a moral picture or carve a moral statue: will you not tell us how you would set about it? We are discussing the Art of Fiction; questions of art are questions (in the widest sense) of execution; questions of morality are quite another affair, and will you not let us see how it is that you

8 **Jansenism.** The doctrines propounded by Cornelis Jansen (1585-1638), bishop of Ypres, and pronounced heretical by the Catholic Church • 22 **Titianesque,** referring to Titian (1477-1576), Venetian painter • 39 **tracing . . . child.** James himself was to do just this, superbly, in his novel **What Maisie Knew** (1897) • 56 **George Eliot.** The reference is to George Eliot's **Silas Marner**

find it so easy to mix them up? These things are so clear to Mr. Besant that he has deduced from them a law which he sees embodied in English Fiction, and which is "a truly admirable thing and a great cause for congratulation." It is a great cause for congratulation indeed when such thorny problems become as smooth as silk. I may add that in so far as Mr. Besant perceives that in point of fact English Fiction has addressed itself preponderantly to these delicate questions he will appear to many people to have made a vain discovery. They will have been positively struck, on the contrary, with the moral timidity of the usual English novelist; with his (or with her) aversion to face the difficulties with which on every side the treatment of reality bristles. He is apt to be extremely shy (whereas the picture that Mr. Besant draws is a picture of boldness), and the sign of his work, for the most part, is a cautious silence on certain subjects. In the English novel (by which of course I mean the American as well), more than in any other, there is a traditional difference between that which people know and that which they agree to admit that they know, that which they see and that which they speak of, that which they feel to be a part of life and that which they allow to enter into literature. There is the great difference, in short, between what they talk of in conversation and what they talk of in print. The essence of moral energy is to survey the whole field, and I should directly reverse Mr. Besant's remark and say not that the English novel has a purpose, but that it has a diffidence. To what degree a purpose in a work of art is a source of corruption I shall not attempt to inquire; the one that seems to me least dangerous is the purpose of making a perfect work. As for our novel, I may say lastly on this score that as we find it in England to-day it strikes me as addressed in a large degree to "young people," and that this in itself constitutes a presumption that it will be rather shy. There are certain things which it is generally agreed not to discuss, not even to mention, before young people. That is very well, but the absence of discussion is not a symptom of the moral passion. The purpose of the English novel—"a truly admirable thing, and a great cause for congratulation"—strikes me therefore as rather negative.

There is one point at which the moral sense and the artistic sense lie very near together; that is in the light of the very obvious truth that the deepest quality of a work of art will always be the quality of the mind of the producer. In the proportion as that intelligence is fine will the novel, the picture, the statue partake of the substance of beauty and truth. To be constituted of such elements is, to my vision, to have purpose enough. No good novel will ever proceed from a superficial mind; that seems to me an axiom which, for the artist in fiction, will cover all needful moral ground: if the youthful aspirant take it to heart it will illuminate for him many of the mysteries of "purpose." There are many other useful things that might be said to him, but I have come to the end of my article, and can only touch them as I pass. The critic in the *Pall Mall Gazette,* whom I have already quoted, draws attention to the danger, in speaking of the art of fiction, of generalising. The danger that he has in mind is rather, I imagine, that of particularising, for there are some comprehensive remarks which, in addition to those embodied in Mr. Besant's suggestive lecture, might without fear of misleading him be addressed to the ingenuous student. I should remind him first of the magnificence of the form that is open to him, which offers to sight so few restrictions and such innumerable opportunities. The other arts, in comparison, appear confined and hampered; the various conditions under which they are exercised are so rigid and definite. But the only condition that I can think of attaching to the composition of the novel is, as I have already said, that it be sincere. This freedom is a splendid privilege, and the first lesson of the young novelist is to learn to be worthy of it. "Enjoy it as it deserves," I should say to him; "take possession of it, explore it to its utmost extent, publish it, rejoice in it. All life belongs to you, and do not listen either to those who would shut you up into corners of it and tell you that it is only here and there that art inhabits, or to those who would persuade you that this heavenly messenger wings her way outside of life altogether, breathing a superfine air, and turning away her head from the truth of things. There is no impression of life, no manner of seeing it and feeling it, to which the plan of the novelist may not offer a place; you have only to remember that talents so dissimilar as those of Alexandre Dumas and Jane Austen, Charles Dickens and Gustave Flaubert have worked in this field with equal glory. Do not think too much about optimism and pessimism; try and catch the colour of life itself. In France to-day we see a prodigious effort (that of

Emile Zola, to whose solid and serious work no explorer of the capacity of the novel can allude without respect), we see an extraordinary effort, vitiated by a spirit of pessimism on a narrow basis. M. Zola is magnificent, but he strikes an English reader as ignorant; he has an air of working in the dark; if he had as much light as energy, his results would be of the highest value. As for the aberrations of a shallow optimism, the ground (of English fiction especially) is strewn with their brittle particles as with broken glass. If you must indulge in conclusions, let them have the taste of a wide knowledge. Remember that your first duty is to be as complete as possible—to make as perfect a work. Be generous and delicate and pursue the prize."

1884

Daisy Miller

Satirical Portrait of an American girl!

The story of Daisy Miller owed its genesis to a hint from a friend in Rome during the autumn of 1877. The friend told the author of a young American girl—"a child of nature and of freedom"—who had innocently violated the strict decorums of Roman society. James' imagination did the rest. The result was a **nouvelle**, or short novel, in which the author saw a certain "flatness" and at the same time "a shy incongruous charm." (See James' Preface in the New York edition of **The Novels and Tales of Henry James**, Vol. XVIII, pp. v-viii, or **The Art of the Novel**, ed. R. P. Blackmur, pp. 267-270.)

Unlike any other work by James, **Daisy Miller** created a small furor and thus became, as he later said, "the most prosperous child of my invention." Its popularity was partly a success of scandal, for many readers in this country resented what they supposed to be a satirical portrait of the American girl. Writing in James' defense (**Century Magazine**, November 1882), W. D. Howells declared truly that "so far as the average American girl was studied at all in Daisy Miller, her indestructible innocence, her invulnerable new-worldliness, had never been so delicately appreciated."

Technically, the story is remarkable for the consistent use of the restricted point of view. Told in the third person, the narrative presents the characters and situations as seen through the eyes of one actor; if in the course of the story there is uncertainty about Miss Miller, it is because the evidence is often confusing to Winterbourne. Though an American, he has lived too long in Europe to understand American ways. His expanding consciousness affords the pattern of the story. James was to develop and refine this method in his later works, but rarely, if ever, with a more delightful result.

Daisy Miller is here given in the original version; around 1905-1906, James made the style of this work, and of other early works, conform more nearly to that of his "later manner." (The revised version of **Daisy Miller** can be consulted in the New York edition, Vol. XVIII.) A comparison between **Daisy Miller**, as here given, and later pieces like "The Middle Years" and "The Beast in the Jungle," which follow, will afford the student an opportunity of measuring James' stylistic development. For the nature of James' later revisions, the student should read "The Painter's Sponge and Varnish Bottle" in F. O. Matthiessen's **Henry James: The Major Phase**.

PART I

At the little town of Vevey, in Switzerland, there is a particularly comfortable hotel. There are, indeed, many hotels; for the entertainment of tourists is the business of the place, which, as many travellers will remember, is seated upon the edge of a remarkably blue lake—a lake that it behooves every tourist to visit. The shore of the lake presents an unbroken array of establishments of this order, of every category, from the "grand hotel" of the newest fashion, with a chalk-white front, a hundred

---

5 lake, Lake Geneva

balconies, and a dozen flags flying from its roof, to the little Swiss *pension* of an elder day, with its name inscribed in German-looking lettering upon a pink or yellow wall, and an awkward summer-house in the angle of the garden. One of the hotels in Vevey, however, is famous, even classical, being distinguished from many of its upstart neighbors by an air both of luxury and of maturity. In this region, in the month of June, American travellers are extremely numerous; it may be said, indeed, that Vevey assumes at this period some of the characteristics of an American watering-place. There are sights and sounds which evoke a vision, an echo, of Newport and Saratoga. There is a flitting hither and thither of "stylish" young girls, a rustling of muslin flounces, a rattle of dance-music in the morning hours, a sound of high-pitched voices at all times. You receive an impression of these things at the excellent inn of the "Trois Couronnes," and are transported in fancy to the Ocean House or to Congress Hall. But at the "Trois Couronnes," it must be added, there are other features that are much at variance with these suggestions: neat German waiters, who look like secretaries of legation; Russian princesses sitting in the garden; little Polish boys walking about, held by the hand, with their governors; a view of the sunny crest of the Dent du Midi and the picturesque towers of the Castle of Chillon.

I hardly know whether it was the analogies or the differences that were uppermost in the mind of a young American, who, two or three years ago, sat in the garden of the "Trois Couronnes," looking about him, rather idly, at some of the graceful objects I have mentioned. It was a beautiful summer morning, and in whatever fashion the young American looked at things, they must have seemed to him charming. He had come from Geneva the day before, by the little steamer, to see his aunt, who was staying at the hotel—Geneva having been for a long time his place of residence. But his aunt had a headache—his aunt had almost always a headache—and now she was shut up in her room, smelling camphor, so that he was at liberty to wander about. He was some seven-and-twenty years of age; when his friends spoke of him, they usually said that he was at Geneva, "studying." When his enemies spoke of him, they said—but, after all, he had no enemies; he was an extremely amiable fellow, and universally liked. What I should say is, simply, that when certain persons spoke of him they affirmed that the reason of his spending so much time at Geneva was that he was extremely devoted to a lady who lived there—a foreign lady—a person older than himself. Very few Americans—indeed I think none— had ever seen this lady, about whom there were some singular stories. But Winterbourne had an old attachment for the little metropolis of Calvinism; he had been put to school there as a boy, and he had afterwards gone to college there—circumstances which had led to his forming a great many youthful friendships. Many of these he had kept, and they were a source of great satisfaction to him.

After knocking at his aunt's door and learning that she was indisposed, he had taken a walk about the town, and then he had come in to his breakfast. He had now finished his breakfast; but he was drinking a small cup of coffee, which had been served to him on a little table in the garden by one of the waiters who looked like an *attaché*. At last he finished his coffee and lit a cigarette. Presently a small boy came walking along the path—an urchin of nine or ten. The child, who was diminutive for his years, had an aged expression of countenance, a pale complexion, and sharp little features. He was dressed in knickerbockers, with red stockings, which displayed his poor little spindleshanks; he also wore a brilliant red cravat. He carried in his hand a long alpenstock, the sharp point of which he thrust into everything that he approached—the flower-beds, the garden-benches, the trains of the ladies' dresses. In front of Winterbourne he paused, looking at him with a pair of bright, penetrating little eyes.

"Will you give me a lump of sugar?" he asked, in a sharp, hard little voice—a voice immature, and yet, somehow, not young.

Winterbourne glanced at the small table near him, on which his coffee-service rested, and saw that several morsels of sugar remained. "Yes, you may take one," he answered; "but I don't think sugar is good for little boys."

This little boy stepped forward and carefully selected three of the coveted fragments, two of which he buried in the pocket of his knickerbockers, depositing the other as promptly in another place. He poked his alpenstock, lance-fashion, into Winterbourne's bench, and tried to crack the lump of sugar with his teeth.

---

2 **pension,** boarding house • 25 **Dent du Midi,** a high peak of the Swiss Alps • 53 **metropolis of Calvinism.** John Calvin (1509-1564), the Protestant theologian, lived at Geneva

"Oh, blazes; it's har-r-d!" he exclaimed, pronouncing the adjective in a peculiar manner.

Winterbourne had immediately perceived that he might have the honour of claiming him as a fellow-countryman. "Take care you don't hurt your teeth," he said, paternally.

"I haven't got any teeth to hurt. They have all come out. I have only got seven teeth. My mother counted them last night, and one came out right afterwards. She said she'd slap me if any more came out. I can't help it. It's this old Europe. It's the climate that makes them come out. In America they didn't come out. It's these hotels."

Winterbourne was much amused, "If you eat three lumps of sugar, your mother will certainly slap you," he said.

"She's got to give me some candy, then," rejoined his young interlocutor. "I can't get any candy here—any American candy. American candy's the best candy."

"And are American little boys the best little boys?" asked Winterbourne.

"I don't know. I'm an American boy," said the child.

"I see you are one of the best!" laughed Winterbourne.

"Are you an American man?" pursued this vivacious infant. And then, on Winterbourne's affirmative reply —"American men are the best," he declared.

His companion thanked him for the compliment; and the child, who had now got astride of his alpenstock, stood looking about him, while he attacked a second lump of sugar. Winterbourne wondered if he himself had been like this in his infancy, for he had been brought to Europe at about this age.

"Here comes my sister!" cried the child, in a moment. "She's an American girl."

Winterbourne looked along the path and saw a beautiful young lady advancing. "American girls are the best girls," he said, cheerfully, to his young companion.

"My sister ain't the best!" the child declared. "She's always blowing at me."

"I imagine that is your fault, not hers," said Winterbourne. The young lady meanwhile had drawn near. She was dressed in white muslin, with a hundred frills and flounces, and knots of pale-colored ribbon. She was bare-headed; but she balanced in her hand a large parasol, with a deep border of embroidery; and she was strikingly, admirably pretty. "How pretty they are!" thought Winterbourne, straightening himself in his seat, as if he were prepared to rise.

The young lady paused in front of his bench, near the parapet of the garden, which overlooked the lake. The little boy had now converted his alpenstock into a vaulting-pole, by the aid of which he was springing about in the gravel, and kicking it up not a little.

"Randolph," said the young lady, "what *are* you doing?"

"I'm going up the Alps," replied Randolph. "This is the way!" And he gave another little jump, scattering the pebbles about Winterbourne's ears.

"That's the way they come down," said Winterbourne.

"He's an American man!" cried Randolph, in his little hard voice.

The young lady gave no heed to this announcement, but looked straight at her brother. "Well, I guess you had better be quiet," she simply observed.

It seemed to Winterbourne that he had been in a manner presented. He got up and stepped slowly towards the young girl, throwing away his cigarette. "This little boy and I have made acquaintance," he said, with great civility. In Geneva, as he had been perfectly aware, a young man was not at liberty to speak to a young unmarried lady except under certain rarely-occurring conditions; but here at Vevey, what conditions could be better than these?—a pretty American girl coming and standing in front of you in a garden. This pretty American girl, however, on hearing Winterbourne's observation, simply glanced at him; she then turned her head and looked over the parapet, at the lake and the opposite mountains. He wondered whether he had gone too far; but he decided that he must advance farther, rather than retreat. While he was thinking of something else to say, the young lady turned to the little boy again.

"I should like to know where you got that pole," she said.

"I bought it!" responded Randolph.

"You don't mean to say you're going to take it to Italy."

"Yes, I am going to take it to Italy!" the child declared.

The young girl glanced over the front of her dress, and smoothed out a knot or two of ribbon. Then she rested her eyes upon the prospect again. "Well, I guess

---

39 blowing at, scolding

you had better leave it somewhere," she said, after a moment.

"Are you going to Italy?" Winterbourne inquired, in a tone of great respect.

The young lady glanced at him again. "Yes, sir," she replied. And she said nothing more.

"Are you—a—going over the Simplon?" Winterbourne pursued, a little embarrassed.

"I don't know," she said. "I suppose it's some mountain. Randolph, what mountain are we going over?"

"Going where?" the child demanded.

"To Italy," Winterbourne explained.

"I don't know," said Randolph. "I don't want to go to Italy. I want to go to America."

"Oh, Italy is a beautiful place!" rejoined the young man.

"Can you get candy there?" Randolph loudly inquired.

"I hope not," said his sister. "I guess you have had enough candy, and mother thinks so too."

"I haven't had any for ever so long—for a hundred weeks!" cried the boy, still jumping about.

The young lady inspected her flounces and smoothed her ribbons again; and Winterbourne presently risked an observation upon the beauty of the view. He was ceasing to be embarrassed, for he had begun to perceive that she was not in the least embarrassed herself. There had not been the slightest alteration in her charming complexion; she was evidently neither offended nor fluttered. If she looked another way when he spoke to her, and seemed not particularly to hear him, this was simply her habit, her manner. Yet, as he talked a little more, and pointed out some of the objects of interest in the view, with which she appeared quite unacquainted, she gradually gave him more of the benefit of her glance; and then he saw that this glance was perfectly direct and unshrinking. It was not, however, what would have been called an immodest glance, for the young girl's eyes were singularly honest and fresh. They were wonderfully pretty eyes; and, indeed, Winterbourne had not seen for a long time anything prettier than his fair countrywoman's various features—her complexion, her nose, her ears, her teeth. He had a great relish for feminine beauty; he was addicted to observing and analyzing it; and as regards this young lady's face he made several observations. It was not at all insipid, but it was not exactly expressive; and though it was eminently delicate Winterbourne mentally accused it—very forgivingly—

of a want of finish. He thought it very possible that Master Randolph's sister was a coquette; he was sure she had a spirit of her own; but in her bright, sweet, superficial little visage there was no mockery, no irony. Before long it became obvious that she was much disposed towards conversation. She told him that they were going to Rome for the winter—she and her mother and Randolph. She asked him if he was a "real American"; she shouldn't have taken him for one; he seemed more like a German—this was said after a little hesitation, especially when he spoke. Winterbourne, laughing, answered that he had met Germans who spoke like Americans; but that he had not, so far as he remembered, met an American who spoke like a German. Then he asked her if she should not be more comfortable in sitting upon the bench which he had just quitted. She answered that she liked standing up and walking about; but she presently sat down. She told him she was from New York State—"if you know where that is." Winterbourne learned more about her by catching hold of her small, slippery brother and making him stand a few minutes by his side.

"Tell me your name, my boy," he said.

"Randolph C. Miller," said the boy, sharply. "And I'll tell you her name;" and he levelled his alpenstock at his sister.

"You had better wait till you are asked!" said this young lady, calmly.

"I should like very much to know your name," said Winterbourne.

"Her name is Daisy Miller!" cried the child. "But that isn't her real name; that isn't her name on her cards."

"It's a pity you haven't got one of my cards!" said Miss Miller.

"Her real name is Annie P. Miller," the boy went on.

"Ask him his name," said his sister, indicating Winterbourne.

But on this point Randolph seemed perfectly indifferent; he continued to supply information in regard to his own family. "My father's name is Ezra B. Miller," he announced. "My father ain't in Europe; my father's in a better place than Europe."

Winterbourne imagined for a moment that this was the manner in which the child had been taught to inti-

7 **Simplon**, a pass through the Alps

mate that Mr. Miller had been removed to the sphere of celestial rewards. But Randolph immediately added, "My father's in Schenectady. He's got a big business. My father's rich, you bet."

"Well!" ejaculated Miss Miller, lowering her parasol and looking at the embroidered border. Winterbourne presently released the child, who departed, dragging his alpenstock along the path. "He doesn't like Europe," said the young girl. "He wants to go back."

"To Schenectady, you mean?"

"Yes; he wants to go right home. He hasn't got any boys here. There is one boy here, but he always goes round with a teacher; they won't let him play."

"And your brother hasn't any teacher?" Winterbourne inquired.

"Mother thought of getting him one to travel round with us. There was a lady told her of a very good teacher; an American lady—perhaps you know her—Mrs. Sanders. I think she came from Boston. She told her of this teacher, and we thought of getting him to travel round with us. But Randolph said he didn't want a teacher travelling round with us. He said he wouldn't have lessons when he was in the cars. And we *are* in the cars about half the time. There was an English lady we met in the cars—I think her name was Miss Featherstone; perhaps you know her. She wanted to know why I didn't give Randolph lessons—give him 'instructions,' she called it. I guess he could give me more instructions than I could give him. He's very smart."

"Yes," said Winterbourne; "he seems very smart."

"Mother's going to get a teacher for him as soon as we get to Italy. Can you get good teachers in Italy?"

"Very good, I should think," said Winterbourne.

"Or else she's going to find some school. He ought to learn some more. He's only nine. He's going to college." And in this way Miss Miller continued to converse upon the affairs of her family, and upon other topics. She sat there with her extremely pretty hands, ornamented with very brilliant rings, folded in her lap, and with her pretty eyes now resting upon those of Winterbourne, now wandering over the garden, the people who passed by, and the beautiful view. She talked to Winterbourne as if she had known him a long time. He found it very pleasant. It was many years since he had heard a young girl talk so much. It might have been said of this unknown young lady, who had come and sat down beside him upon a

bench, that she chattered. She was very quiet; she sat in a charming tranquil attitude, but her lips and her eyes were constantly moving. She had a soft, slender, agreeable voice, and her tone was decidedly sociable. She gave Winterbourne a history of her movements and intentions, and those of her mother and brother, in Europe, and enumerated, in particular, the various hotels at which they had stopped. "That English lady, in the cars," she said—"Miss Featherstone—asked me if we didn't all live in hotels in America. I told her I had never been in so many hotels in my life as since I came to Europe. I have never seen so many—it's nothing but hotels." But Miss Miller did not make this remark with a querulous accent; she appeared to be in the best humor with everything. She declared that the hotels were very good, when once you got used to their ways, and that Europe was perfectly sweet. She was not disappointed—not a bit. Perhaps it was because she had heard so much about it before. She had ever so many intimate friends that had been there ever so many times. And then she had had ever so many dresses and things from Paris. Whenever she put on a Paris dress she felt as if she were in Europe.

"It was a kind of a wishing-cap," said Winterbourne.

"Yes," said Miss Miller, without examining this analogy; "it always made me wish I was here. But I needn't have done that for dresses. I am sure they send all the pretty ones to America; you see the most frightful things here. The only thing I don't like," she proceeded, "is the society. There isn't any society; or, if there is, I don't know where it keeps itself. Do you? I suppose there is some society somewhere, but I haven't seen anything of it. I'm very fond of society, and I have always had a great deal of it. I don't mean only in Schenectady, but in New York. I used to go to New York every winter. In New York I had lots of society. Last winter I had seventeen dinners given me; and three of them were by gentlemen," added Daisy Miller. "I have more friends in New York than in Schenectady—more gentlemen friends; and more young lady friends too," she resumed in a moment. She paused again for an instant; she was looking at Winterbourne with all her prettiness in her lively eyes and in her light, slightly monotonous smile. "I have always had," she said, "a great deal of gentlemen's society."

Poor Winterbourne was amused, perplexed, and de-

perplexed by her because he has lost his idea of what a typical American girl is like!

cidedly charmed. He had never yet heard a young girl
express herself in just this fashion; never, at least, save
in cases where to say such things seemed a kind of demonstrative evidence of a certain laxity of deportment.
And yet was he to accuse Miss Daisy Miller of actual or
potential *inconduite,* as they said at Geneva? He felt
that he had lived at Geneva so long that he had lost a
good deal; he had become dishabituated to the American
tone. Never, indeed, since he had grown old enough to
10 appreciate things, had he encountered a young American
girl of so pronounced a type as this. Certainly she was
very charming, but how deucedly sociable! Was she
simply a pretty girl from New York State—were they
all like that, the pretty girls who had a good deal of
gentlemen's society? Or was she also a designing, an
audacious, an unscrupulous young person? Winterbourne
had lost his instinct in this matter, and his reason could
not help him. Miss Daisy Miller looked extremely innocent. Some people had told him that, after all, Ameri-
20 can girls were exceedingly innocent; and others had told
him that, after all, they were not. He was inclined to
think Miss Daisy Miller was a flirt—a pretty American
flirt. He had never, as yet, had any relations with young
ladies of this category. He had known, here in Europe,
two or three women—persons older than Miss Daisy
Miller, and provided, for respectability's sake, with
husbands—who were great coquettes—dangerous, terrible women, with whom one's relations were liable to
take a serious turn. But this young girl was not a
30 coquette in that sense; she was very unsophisticated;
she was only a pretty American flirt. Winterbourne was
almost grateful for having found the formula that applied to Miss Daisy Miller. He leaned back in his seat;
he remarked to himself that she had the most charming nose he had ever seen; he wondered what were the
regular conditions and limitations of one's intercourse
with a pretty American flirt. It presently became apparent that he was on the way to learn.

"Have you been to that old castle?" asked the young
40 girl, pointing with her parasol to the far-gleaming walls
of the Château de Chillon.

"Yes, formerly, more than once," said Winterbourne.
"You too, I suppose, have seen it?"

"No; we haven't been there. I want to go there dreadfully. Of course I mean to go there. I wouldn't go away
from here without having seen that old castle."

"It's a very pretty excursion," said Winterbourne, "and
very easy to make. You can drive, you know, or you
can go by the little steamer."

"You can go in the cars," said Miss Miller. 50

"Yes; you can go in the cars," Winterbourne assented.

"Our courier says they take you right up to the castle,"
the young girl continued. "We were going last week;
but my mother gave out. She suffers dreadfully from
dyspepsia. She said she couldn't go. Randolph wouldn't
go either; he says he doesn't think much of old castles.
But I guess we'll go this week, if we can get Randolph."

"Your brother is not interested in ancient monuments?" Winterbourne inquired, smiling.

"He says he don't care much about old castles. He's 60
only nine. He wants to stay at the hotel. Mother's
afraid to leave him alone, and the courier won't stay with
him; so we haven't been to many places. But it will be
too bad if we don't go up there." And Miss Miller
pointed again at the Château de Chillon.

"I should think it might be arranged," said Winterbourne. "Couldn't you get some one to stay—for the
afternoon—with Randolph?"

Miss Miller looked at him a moment; and then, very
placidly, "I wish *you* would stay with him!" she said. 70

Winterbourne hesitated a moment. "I should much
rather go to Chillon with you."

"With me?" asked the young girl, with the same
placidity.

She didn't rise, blushing, as a young girl at Geneva
would have done; and yet Winterbourne, conscious
that he had been very bold, thought it possible she
was offended. "With your mother," he answered, very
respectfully.

But it seemed that both his audacity and his respect 80
were lost upon Miss Daisy Miller. "I guess my mother
won't go after all," she said. "She don't like to ride round
in the afternoon. But did you really mean what you said
just now; that you would like to go up there?"

"Most earnestly," Winterbourne declared.

"Then we may arrange it. If mother will stay with
Randolph, I guess Eugenio will."

"Eugenio?" the young man inquired.

---

6 inconduite, misconduct • 41 Château de Chillon, made famous by
Byron's poem, "The Prisoner of Chillon"

"Eugenio's our courier. He doesn't like to stay with Randolph; he's the most fastidious man I ever saw. But he's a splendid courier. I guess he'll stay at home with Randolph if mother does, and then we can go to the castle."

Winterbourne reflected for an instant as lucidly as possible—"we" could only mean Miss Daisy Miller and himself. This programme seemed almost too agreeable for credence; he felt as if he ought to kiss the young lady's hand. Possibly he would have done so—and quite spoiled the project; but at this moment another person —presumably Eugenio—appeared. A tall, handsome man, with superb whiskers, wearing a velvet morning-coat and a brilliant watch-chain, approached Miss Miller, looking sharply at her companion. "Oh, Eugenio!" said Miss Miller, with the friendliest accent.

Eugenio had looked at Winterbourne from head to foot; he now bowed gravely to the young lady. "I have the honour to inform mademoiselle that luncheon is upon the table."

Miss Miller slowly rose. "See here, Eugenio," she said. "I'm going to that old castle, anyway."

"To the Château de Chillon, mademoiselle?" the courier inquired. "Mademoiselle has made arrangements?" he added, in a tone which struck Winterbourne as very impertinent.

Eugenio's tone apparently threw, even to Miss Miller's own apprehension, a slightly ironical light upon the young girl's situation. She turned to Winterbourne, blushing a little—a very little. "You won't back out?" she said.

"I shall not be happy till we go!" he protested.

"And you are staying in this hotel?" she went on. "And you are really an American?"

The courier stood looking at Winterbourne, offensively. The young man, at least, thought his manner of looking an offence to Miss Miller; it conveyed an imputation that she "picked up" acquaintances. "I shall have the honour of presenting to you a person who will tell you all about me," he said, smiling, and referring to his aunt.

"Oh, well, we'll go some day," said Miss Miller. And she gave him a smile and turned away. She put up her parasol and walked back to the inn beside Eugenio. Winterbourne stood looking after her; and as she moved away, drawing her muslin furbelows over the gravel,

said to himself that she had the *tournure* of a princess.

He had, however, engaged to do more than proved feasible, in promising to present his aunt, Mrs. Costello, to Miss Daisy Miller. As soon as the former lady had got better of her headache he waited upon her in her apartment; and, after the proper inquiries in regard to her health, he asked her if she had observed, in the hotel, an American family—a mamma, a daughter, and a little boy.

"And a courier?" said Mrs. Costello. "Oh, yes, I have observed them. Seen them—heard them—and kept out of their way." Mrs. Costello was a widow with a fortune; a person of much distinction, who frequently intimated that, if she were not so dreadfully liable to sick-headaches, she would probably have left a deeper impress upon her time. She had a long pale face, a high nose, and a great deal of very striking white hair, which she wore in large puffs and *rouleaux* over the top of her head. She had two sons married in New York, and another who was now in Europe. This young man was amusing himself at Hombourg, and, though he was on his travels, was rarely perceived to visit any particular city at the moment selected by his mother for her own appearance there. Her nephew, who had come up to Vevey expressly to see her, was therefore more attentive than those who, as she said, were nearer to her. He had imbibed at Geneva the idea that one must always be attentive to one's aunt. Mrs. Costello had not seen him for many years, and she was greatly pleased with him, manifesting her approbation by initiating him into many of the secrets of that social sway which, as she gave him to understand, she exerted in the American capital. She admitted that she was very exclusive; but, if he were acquainted with New York, he would see that one had to be. And her picture of the minutely hierarchical constitution of the society of that city, which she presented to him in many different lights, was, to Winterbourne's imagination, almost oppressively striking.

He immediately perceived, from her tone, that Miss Daisy Miller's place in the social scale was low. "I am afraid you don't approve of them," he said.

"They are very common," Mrs. Costello declared. "They

---

47 tournure, figure and style • 64 rouleaux, coils • 67 Hombourg, a watering place in Prussia, famous for its mineral springs

are the sort of Americans that one does one's duty by not—not accepting."

"Ah, you don't accept them?" said the young man.

"I can't, my dear Frederick. I would if I could, but I can't."

"The young girl is very pretty," said Winterbourne, in a moment.

"Of course she's pretty. But she is very common."

"I see what you mean, of course," said Winterbourne, after another pause.

"She has that charming look that they all have," his aunt resumed. "I can't think where they pick it up; and she dresses in perfection—no, you don't know how well she dresses. I can't think where they get their taste."

"But, my dear aunt, she is not, after all, a Comanche savage."

"She is a young lady," said Mrs. Costello, "who has an intimacy with her mamma's courier."

"An intimacy with the courier?" the young man demanded.

"Oh, the mother is just as bad! They treat the courier like a familiar friend—like a gentleman. I shouldn't wonder if he dines with them. Very likely they have never seen a man with such good manners, such fine clothes, so like a gentleman. He probably corresponds to the young lady's idea of a count. He sits with them in the garden, in the evening. I think he smokes."

Winterbourne listened with interest to these disclosures; they helped him to make up his mind about Miss Daisy. Evidently she was rather wild.

"Well," he said, "I am not a courier, and yet she was very charming to me."

"You had better have said at first," said Mrs. Costello with dignity, "that you had made her acquaintance."

"We simply met in the garden, and we talked a bit."

"*Tout bonnement!* And pray what did you say?"

"I said I should take the liberty of introducing her to my admirable aunt."

"I am much obliged to you."

"It was to guarantee my respectability," said Winterbourne.

"And pray who is to guarantee hers?"

"Ah, you are cruel!" said the young man. "She's a very nice young girl."

"You don't say that as if you believed it," Mrs. Costello observed.

"She is completely uncultivated," Winterbourne went on. "But she is wonderfully pretty, and, in short, she is very nice. To prove that I believe it, I am going to take her to the Château de Chillon."

"You two are going off there together? I should say it proved just the contrary. How long had you known her, may I ask, when this interesting project was formed? You haven't been twenty-four hours in the house."

"I had known her half an hour!" said Winterbourne, smiling.

"Dear me!" cried Mrs. Costello. "What a dreadful girl!"

Her nephew was silent for some moments. "You really think, then," he began, earnestly, and with a desire for trustworthy information—"you really think that—" But he paused again.

"Think what, sir?" said his aunt.

"That she is the sort of young lady who expects a man —sooner or later—to carry her off?"

"I haven't the least idea what such young ladies expect a man to do. But I really think that you had better not meddle with little American girls that are uncultivated, as you call them. You have lived too long out of the country. You will be sure to make some great mistake. You are too innocent."

"My dear aunt, I am not so innocent," said Winterbourne, smiling and curling his moustache.

"You are too guilty, then!"

Winterbourne continued to curl his moustache, meditatively. "You won't let the poor girl know you, then?" he asked at last.

"Is it literally true that she is going to the Château de Chillon with you?"

"I think that she fully intends it."

"Then, my dear Frederick," said Mrs. Costello, "I must decline the honour of her acquaintance. I am an old woman, but I am not too old—thank Heaven—to be shocked!"

"But don't they all do these things—the young girls in America?" Winterbourne inquired.

Mrs. Costello stared a moment. "I should like to see my granddaughters do them!" she declared, grimly.

This seemed to throw some light upon the matter,

36 *Tout bonnement!* very well!

for Winterbourne remembered to have heard that his pretty cousins in New York were "tremendous flirts." If, therefore, Miss Daisy Miller exceeded the liberal margin allowed to these young ladies, it was probable that anything might be expected of her. Winterbourne was impatient to see her again, and he was vexed with himself that, by instinct, he should not appreciate her justly.

Though he was impatient to see her, he hardly knew what he should say to her about his aunt's refusal to become acquainted with her; but he discovered, promptly enough, that with Miss Daisy Miller there was no great need of walking on tiptoe. He found her that evening in the garden, wandering about in the warm starlight, like an indolent sylph, and swinging to and fro the largest fan he had ever beheld. It was ten o'clock. He had dined with his aunt, had been sitting with her since dinner, and had just taken leave of her till the morrow. Miss Daisy Miller seemed very glad to see him; she declared it was the longest evening she had ever passed.

"Have you been all alone?" he asked.

"I have been walking round with mother. But mother gets tired walking round," she answered.

"Has she gone to bed?"

"No; she doesn't like to go to bed," said the young girl. "She doesn't sleep—not three hours. She says she doesn't know how she lives. She's dreadfully nervous. I guess she sleeps more than she thinks. She's gone somewhere after Randolph; she wants to try to get him to go to bed. He doesn't like to go to bed."

"Let us hope she will persuade him," observed Winterbourne.

"She will talk to him all she can; but he doesn't like her to talk to him," said Miss Daisy, opening her fan. "She's going to try to get Eugenio to talk to him. But he isn't afraid of Eugenio. Eugenio's a splendid courier, but he can't make much impression on Randolph! I don't believe he'll go to bed before eleven." It appeared that Randolph's vigil was in fact triumphantly prolonged, for Winterbourne strolled about with the young girl for some time without meeting her mother. "I have been looking round for that lady you want to introduce me to," his companion resumed. "She's your aunt." Then, on Winterbourne's admitting the fact, and expressing some curiosity as to how she had learned it, she said she had heard all about Mrs. Costello from the chambermaid. She was very quiet, and very *comme il faut;* she wore white puffs; she spoke to no one, and she never dined at the *table d'hôte.* Every two days she had a headache. "I think that's a lovely description, headache and all!" said Miss Daisy, chattering along in her thin, gay voice. "I want to know her ever so much. I know just what *your* aunt would be; I know I should like her. She would be very exclusive. I like a lady to be exclusive; I'm dying to be exclusive myself. Well, we *are* exclusive, mother and I. We don't speak to every one—or they don't speak to us. I suppose it's about the same thing. Anyway, I shall be ever so glad to know your aunt."

Winterbourne was embarrassed. "She would be most happy," he said; "but I am afraid those headaches will interfere."

The young girl looked at him through the dusk. "But I suppose she doesn't have a headache every day," she said, sympathetically.

Winterbourne was silent a moment. "She tells me she does," he answered at last—not knowing what to say.

Miss Daisy Miller stopped, and stood looking at him. Her prettiness was still visible in the darkness; she was opening and closing her enormous fan. "She doesn't want to know me!" she said, suddenly. "Why don't you say so? You needn't be afraid. I'm not afraid!" And she gave a little laugh.

Winterbourne fancied there was a tremor in her voice; he was touched, shocked, mortified by it. "My dear young lady," he protested, "she knows no one. It's her wretched health."

The young girl walked on a few steps, laughing still. "You needn't be afraid," she repeated. "Why should she want to know me?" Then she paused again; she was close to the parapet of the garden, and in front of her was the starlit lake. There was a vague sheen upon its surface, and in the distance were dimly-seen mountain forms. Daisy Miller looked out upon the mysterious prospect, and then she gave another little laugh. "Gracious! she *is* exclusive!" she said. Winterbourne wondered whether she was seriously wounded, and for a moment almost wished that her sense of injury might be such as to make it becoming in him to attempt to reassure and comfort her. He had a pleasant sense that she would be

---

47 comme il faut, proper

very approachable for consolatory purposes. He felt then, for the instant, quite ready to sacrifice his aunt, conversationally; to admit that she was a proud, rude woman, and to declare that they needn't mind her. But before he had time to commit himself to this perilous mixture of gallantry and impiety, the young lady, resuming her walk, gave an exclamation in quite another tone. "Well; here's mother! I guess she hasn't got Randolph to go to bed." The figure of a lady appeared, at a distance, very indistinct in the darkness, and advancing with a slow and wavering movement. Suddenly it seemed to pause.

"Are you sure it is your mother? Can you distinguish her in this thick dusk?" Winterbourne asked.

"Well!" cried Miss Daisy Miller, with a laugh, "I guess I know my own mother. And when she has got on my shawl, too! She is always wearing my things."

The lady in question, ceasing to advance, hovered vaguely about the spot at which she had checked her steps. "I am afraid your mother doesn't see you," said Winterbourne. "Or perhaps," he added—thinking, with Miss Miller, the joke permissible—"perhaps she feels guilty about your shawl."

"Oh, it's a fearful old thing!" the young girl replied, serenely. "I told her she could wear it. She won't come here, because she sees you."

"Ah, then," said Winterbourne, "I had better leave you."

"Oh, no; come on!" urged Miss Daisy Miller.

"I'm afraid your mother doesn't approve of my walking with you."

Miss Miller gave him a serious glance. "It isn't for me; it's for you—that is, it's for her. Well, I don't know who it's for! But mother doesn't like any of my gentlemen friends. She's right down timid. She always makes a fuss if I introduce a gentleman. But I do introduce them—almost always. If I didn't introduce my gentlemen friends to mother," the young girl added, in her little soft, flat monotone, "I shouldn't think I was natural."

"To introduce me," said Winterbourne, "you must know my name." And he proceeded to pronounce it.

"Oh, dear, I can't say all that!" said his companion, with a laugh. But by this time they had come up to Mrs. Miller, who, as they drew near, walked to the parapet of the garden and leaned upon it, looking intently at the lake, and turning her back to them.

"Mother!" said the young girl, in a tone of decision. Upon this the elder lady turned round. "Mr. Winterbourne," said Miss Daisy Miller, introducing the young man very frankly and prettily. "Common" she was, as Mrs. Costello had pronounced her; yet it was a wonder to Winterbourne that, with her commonness, she had a singularly delicate grace.

Her mother was a small, spare, light person, with a wandering eye, a very exiguous nose, and a large forehead, decorated with a certain amount of thin, much-frizzled hair. Like her daughter, Mrs. Miller was dressed with extreme elegance; she had enormous diamonds in her ears. So far as Winterbourne could observe, she gave him no greeting—she certainly was not looking at him. Daisy was near her, pulling her shawl straight. "What are you doing, poking round here?" this young lady inquired; but by no means with that harshness of accent which her choice of words may imply.

"I don't know," said her mother, turning towards the lake again.

"I shouldn't think you'd want that shawl!" Daisy exclaimed.

"Well—I do!" her mother answered, with a little laugh.

"Did you get Randolph to go to bed?" asked the young girl.

"No; I couldn't induce him," said Mrs. Miller, very gently. "He wants to talk to the waiter. He likes to talk to that waiter."

"I was telling Mr. Winterbourne," the young girl went on; and to the young man's ear her tone might have indicated that she had been uttering his name all her life.

"Oh, yes!" said Winterbourne; "I have the pleasure of knowing your son."

Randolph's mamma was silent; she turned her attention to the lake. But at last she spoke. "Well, I don't see how he lives!"

"Anyhow, it isn't so bad as it was at Dover," said Daisy Miller.

"And what occurred at Dover?" Winterbourne asked.

"He wouldn't go to bed at all. I guess he sat up all night—in the public parlour. He wasn't in bed at twelve o'clock; I know that."

"It was half-past twelve," declared Mrs. Miller, with mild emphasis.

"Does he sleep much during the day?" Winterbourne demanded.

"I guess he doesn't sleep much," Daisy rejoined.

"I wish he would!" said her mother. "It seems as if he couldn't."

"I think he's real tiresome," Daisy pursued.

Then, for some moments, there was silence. "Well, Daisy Miller," said the elder lady, presently, "I shouldn't think you'd want to talk against your own brother!"

"Well, he *is* tiresome, mother," said Daisy, quite without the asperity of a retort.

"He's only nine," urged Mrs. Miller.

"Well, he wouldn't go to that castle," said the young girl. "I'm going there with Mr. Winterbourne."

To this announcement, very placidly made, Daisy's mamma offered no response. Winterbourne took for granted that she deeply disapproved of the projected excursion; but he said to himself that she was a simple, easily-managed person, and that a few deferential protestations would take the edge from her displeasure.

"Yes," he began; "your daughter has kindly allowed me the honour of being her guide."

Mrs. Miller's wandering eyes attached themselves, with a sort of appealing air, to Daisy, who, however, strolled a few steps farther, gently humming to herself. "I presume you will go in the cars," said her mother.

"Yes; or in the boat," said Winterbourne.

"Well, of course, I don't know," Mrs. Miller rejoined. "I have never been to that castle."

"It is a pity you shouldn't go," said Winterbourne, beginning to feel reassured as to her opposition. And yet he was quite prepared to find that, as a matter of course, she meant to accompany her daughter.

"We've been thinking ever so much about going," she pursued; "but it seems as if we couldn't. Of course Daisy—she wants to go round. But there's a lady here—I don't know her name—she says she shouldn't think we'd want to go to see castles *here;* she should think we'd want to wait till we got to Italy. It seems as if there would be so many there," continued Mrs. Miller, with an air of increasing confidence. "Of course, we only want to see the principal ones. We visited several in England," she presently added.

"Ah, yes! in England there are beautiful castles," said Winterbourne. "But Chillon, here, is very well worth seeing."

"Well, if Daisy feels up to it—," said Mrs. Miller, in a tone impregnated with a sense of the magnitude of the enterprise. "It seems as if there was nothing she wouldn't undertake."

"Oh, I think she'll enjoy it!" Winterbourne declared. And he desired more and more to make it a certainty that he was to have the privilege of a *tête-à-tête* with the young lady, who was still strolling along in front of them, softly vocalizing. "You are not disposed, madam," he inquired, "to undertake it yourself?"

Daisy's mother looked at him, an instant, askance, and then walked forward in silence. Then—"I guess she had better go alone," she said, simply. Winterbourne observed to himself that this was a very different type of maternity from that of the vigilant matrons who massed themselves in the forefront of social intercourse in the dark old city at the other end of the lake. But his meditations were interrupted by hearing his name very distinctly pronounced by Mrs. Miller's unprotected daughter.

"Mr. Winterbourne!" murmured Daisy.

"Mademoiselle!" said the young man.

"Don't you want to take me out in a boat?"

"At present?" he asked.

"Of course!" said Daisy.

"Well, Annie Miller!" exclaimed her mother.

"I beg you, madam, to let her go," said Winterbourne, ardently; for he had never yet enjoyed the sensation of guiding through the summer starlight a skiff freighted with a fresh and beautiful young girl.

"I shouldn't think she'd want to," said her mother. "I should think she'd rather go indoors."

"I'm sure Mr. Winterbourne wants to take me," Daisy declared. "He's so awfully devoted!"

"I will row you over to Chillon, in the starlight."

"I don't believe it!" said Daisy.

"Well!" ejaculated the elder lady again.

"You haven't spoken to me for half an hour," her daughter went on.

"I have been having some very pleasant conversation with your mother," said Winterbourne.

"Well, I want you to take me out in a boat!" Daisy repeated. They had all stopped, and she had turned round and was looking at Winterbourne. Her face wore a charming smile, her pretty eyes were gleaming, she was swinging her great fan about. No; it's impossible to be prettier than that, thought Winterbourne.

"There are half a dozen boats moored at that landing-place," he said, pointing to certain steps which descended from the garden to the lake. "If you will do me the honour to accept my arm, we will go and select one of them."

Daisy stood there smiling; she threw back her head and gave a little, light laugh. "I like a gentleman to be formal!" she declared.

10 "I assure you it's a formal offer."

"I was bound I would make you say something," Daisy went on.

"You see it's not very difficult," said Winterbourne. "But I am afraid you are chaffing me."

"I think not, sir," remarked Mrs. Miller, very gently.

"Do, then, let me give you a row," he said to the young girl.

"It's quite lovely, the way you say that!" cried Daisy.

"It will be still more lovely to do it."

20 "Yes, it would be lovely!" said Daisy. But she made no movement to accompany him; she only stood there laughing.

"I should think you had better find out what time it is," interposed her mother.

"It is eleven o'clock, madam," said a voice, with a foreign accent, out of the neighbouring darkness; and Winterbourne, turning, perceived the florid personage who was in attendance upon the two ladies. He had apparently just approached.

30 "Oh, Eugenio," said Daisy, "I am going out in a boat!"

Eugenio bowed. "At eleven o'clock, mademoiselle?"

"I am going with Mr. Winterbourne. This very minute."

"Do tell her she can't," said Mrs. Miller to the courier.

"I think you had better not go out in a boat, mademoiselle," Eugenio declared.

Winterbourne wished to Heaven this pretty girl were not so familiar with her courier; but he said nothing.

"I suppose you don't think it's proper!" Daisy ex-
40 claimed. "Eugenio doesn't think anything's proper."

"I am at your service," said Winterbourne.

"Does mademoiselle propose to go alone?" asked Eugenio of Mrs. Miller.

"Oh, no; with this gentleman!" answered Daisy's mamma.

The courier looked for a moment at Winterbourne—the latter thought he was smiling—and then, solemnly, with a bow, "As mademoiselle pleases!" he said.

"Oh, I hoped you would make a fuss!" said Daisy. "I don't care to go now." 50

"I myself shall make a fuss if you don't go," said Winterbourne.

"That's all I want—a little fuss!" And the young girl began to laugh again.

"Mr. Randolph has gone to bed!" the courier announced, frigidly.

"Oh, Daisy; now we can go!" said Mrs. Miller.

Daisy turned away from Winterbourne, looking at him, smiling, and fanning herself. "Good-night," she said; "I hope you are disappointed, or disgusted, or 60 something!"

He looked at her, taking the hand she offered him. "I am puzzled," he answered.

"Well, I hope it won't keep you awake!" she said, very smartly; and, under the escort of the privileged Eugenio, the two ladies passed towards the house.

Winterbourne stood looking after them; he was indeed puzzled. He lingered beside the lake for a quarter of an hour, turning over the mystery of the young girl's sudden familiarities and caprices. But the 70 only very definite conclusion he came to was that he should enjoy deucedly "going off" with her somewhere.

Two days afterwards he went off with her to the Castle of Chillon. He waited for her in the large hall of the hotel, where the couriers, the servants, the foreign tourists were lounging about and staring. It was not the place he should have chosen, but she had appointed it. She came tripping downstairs, buttoning her long gloves, squeezing her folded parasol against her pretty figure, dressed in the perfection of a soberly elegant 80 travelling-costume. Winterbourne was a man of imagination and, as our ancestors used to say, sensibility; as he looked at her dress and, on the great staircase, her little rapid, confiding step, he felt as if there were something romantic going forward. He could have believed he was going to elope with her. He passed out with her among all the idle people that were assembled there; they were all looking at her very hard; she had begun to chatter as soon as she joined him. Winterbourne's

---

82 sensibility, delicacy of feeling, as in Jane Austen's Sense and Sensibility

preference had been that they should be conveyed to Chillon in a carriage; but she expressed a lively wish to go in the little steamer; she declared that she had a passion for steamboats. There was always such a lovely breeze upon the water, and you saw such lots of people. The sail was not long, but Winterbourne's companion found time to say a great many things. To the young man himself their little excursion was so much of an escapade—an adventure—that, even allowing for her habitual sense of freedom, he had some expectation of seeing her regard it in the same way. But it must be confessed that, in this particular, he was disappointed. Daisy Miller was extremely animated, she was in charming spirits; but she was apparently not at all excited; she was not fluttered; she avoided neither his eyes nor those of any one else; she blushed neither when she looked at him nor when she felt that people were looking at her. People continued to look at her a great deal, and Winterbourne took much satisfaction in his pretty companion's distinguished air. He had been a little afraid that she would talk loud, laugh overmuch, and even, perhaps, desire to move about the boat a good deal. But he quite forgot his fears; he sat smiling, with his eyes upon her face, while, without moving from her place, she delivered herself of a great number of original reflections. It was the most charming garrulity he had ever heard. He had assented to the idea that she was "common"; but was she so, after all, or was he simply getting used to her commonness? Her conversation was chiefly of what metaphysicians term the objective cast; but every now and then it took a subjective turn.

"What on *earth* are you so grave about?" she suddenly demanded, fixing her agreeable eyes upon Winterbourne's.

"Am I grave?" he asked. "I had an idea I was grinning from ear to ear."

"You look as if you were taking me to a funeral. If that's a grin, your ears are very near together."

"Should you like me to dance a hornpipe on the deck?"

"Pray do, and I'll carry round your hat. It will pay the expenses of our journey."

"I never was better pleased in my life," murmured Winterbourne.

She looked at him a moment, and then burst into a little laugh. "I like to make you say those things! You're a queer mixture!"

In the castle, after they had landed, the subjective element decidedly prevailed. Daisy tripped about the vaulted chambers, rustled her skirts in the corkscrew staircases, flirted back with a pretty little cry and a shudder from the edge of the *oubliettes,* and turned a singularly well-shaped ear to everything that Winterbourne told her about the place. But he saw that she cared very little for feudal antiquities, and that the dusky traditions of Chillon made but a slight impression upon her. They had the good fortune to have been able to walk without other companionship than that of the custodian; and Winterbourne arranged with this functionary that they should not be hurried—that they should linger and pause wherever they chose. The custodian interpreted the bargain generously—Winterbourne, on his side, had been generous—and ended by leaving them quite to themselves. Miss Miller's observations were not remarkable for logical consistency; for anything she wanted to say she was sure to find a pretext. She found a great many pretexts in the rugged embrasures of Chillon for asking Winterbourne sudden questions about himself—his family, his previous history, his tastes, his habits, his intentions—and for supplying information upon corresponding points in her own personality. Of her own tastes, habits, and intentions Miss Miller was prepared to give the most definite, and, indeed, the most favourable, account.

"Well, I hope you know enough!" she said to her companion, after he had told her the history of the unhappy Bonnivard. "I never saw a man that knew so much!" The history of Bonnivard had evidently, as they say, gone into one ear and out of the other. But Daisy went on to say that she wished Winterbourne would travel with them, and "go round" with them; they might know something in that case. "Don't you want to come and teach Randolph?" she asked. Winterbourne said that nothing could possibly please him so much; but that he had unfortunately other occupations. "Other occupations? I don't believe it!" said Miss Daisy. "What do you mean? You are not in business." The young man admitted that he was not in business; but he had

---

51 oubliettes, dungeons with trap doors • 76 **Bonnivard,** François de Bonnivard (1496-1570), Swiss patriot who was imprisoned in the Castle of Chillon from 1530 to 1536. His story is the subject of Byron's "Prisoner of Chillon"

engagements which, even within a day or two, would force him to go back to Geneva. "Oh, bother!" she said; "I don't believe it!" and she began to talk about something else. But a few moments later, when he was pointing out to her the pretty design of an antique fireplace, she broke out irrelevantly, "You don't mean to say you are going back to Geneva?"

"It is a melancholy fact that I shall have to return to-morrow."

10 "Well, Mr. Winterbourne," said Daisy, "I think you're horrid!"

"Oh, don't say such dreadful things!" said Winterbourne—"just at the last!"

"The last!" cried the young girl; "I call it the first. I have half a mind to leave you here and go straight back to the hotel alone." And for the next ten minutes she did nothing but call him horrid. Poor Winterbourne was fairly bewildered; no young lady had as yet done him the honour to be so agitated by the announcement of his 20 movements. His companion, after this, ceased to pay any attention to the curiosities of Chillon or the beauties of the lake; she opened fire upon the mysterious charmer in Geneva, whom she appeared to have instantly taken for granted that he was hurrying back to see. How did Miss Daisy Miller know that there was a charmer in Geneva? Winterbourne, who denied the existence of such a person, was quite unable to discover; and he was divided between amazement at the rapidity of her induction and amusement at the frankness of her *persiflage.* 30 She seemed to him, in all this, an extraordinary mixture of innocence and crudity. "Does she never allow you more than three days at a time?" asked Daisy, ironically. "Doesn't she give you a vacation in summer? There is no one so hard worked but they can get leave to go off somewhere at this season. I suppose, if you stay another day, she'll come after you in the boat. Do wait over till Friday, and I will go down to the landing to see her arrive!" Winterbourne began to think he had been wrong to feel disappointed in the temper in which the 40 young lady had embarked. If he had missed the personal accent, the personal accent was now making its appearance. It sounded very distinctly, at last, in her telling him she would stop "teasing" him if he would promise her solemnly to come down to Rome in the winter.

"That's not a difficult promise to make," said Winterbourne. "My aunt has taken an apartment in Rome for the winter, and has already asked me to come and see her."

"I don't want you to come for your aunt," said Daisy; "I want you to come for me." And this was the only 50 allusion that the young man was ever to hear her make to his invidious kinswoman. He declared that, at any rate, he would certainly come. After this Daisy stopped teasing. Winterbourne took a carriage, and they drove back to Vevey in the dusk; the young girl was very quiet.

In the evening Winterbourne mentioned to Mrs. Costello that he had spent the afternoon at Chillon with Miss Daisy Miller.

"The Americans—of the courier?" asked this lady.

"Ah, happily," said Winterbourne, "the courier stayed 60 at home."

"She went with you all alone?"

"All alone."

Mrs. Costello sniffed a little at her smelling-bottle. "And that," she exclaimed, "is the young person whom you wanted me to know!"

PART II

Winterbourne, who had returned to Geneva the day after his excursion to Chillon, went to Rome towards the end of January. His aunt had been established there for several weeks, and he had received a couple of letters 70 from her. "Those people you were so devoted to last summer at Vevey have turned up here, courier and all," she wrote. "They seem to have made several acquaintances, but the courier continues to be the most *intime.* The young lady, however, is also very intimate with some third-rate Italians, with whom she rackets about in a way that makes much talk. Bring me that pretty novel of Cherbuliez's—*Paule Méré*—and don't come later than the 23rd."

In the natural course of events, Winterbourne, on 80 arriving in Rome, would presently have ascertained Mrs. Miller's address at the American banker's, and have gone to pay his compliments to Miss Daisy. "After what happened at Vevey I think I may certainly call upon them," he said to Mrs. Costello.

"If, after what happens—at Vevey and everywhere—

---

78 **Cherbuliez,** Victor Cherbuliez (1829-1899), French novelist

you desire to keep up the acquaintance, you are very welcome. Of course a man may know every one. Men are welcome to the privilege!"

"Pray what is it that happens—here, for instance?" Winterbourne demanded.

"The girl goes about alone with her foreigners. As to what happens further, you must apply elsewhere for information. She has picked up half-a-dozen of the regular Roman fortune-hunters, and she takes them
10 about to people's houses. When she comes to a party she brings with her a gentleman with a good deal of manner and a wonderful moustache."

"And where is the mother?"

"I haven't the least idea. They are very dreadful people."

Winterbourne meditated a moment. "They are very ignorant—very innocent only. Depend upon it they are not bad."

"They are hopelessly vulgar," said Mrs. Costello.
20 "Whether or no being hopelessly vulgar is being 'bad' is a question for the metaphysicians. They are bad enough to dislike, at any rate; and for this short life that is quite enough."

The news that Daisy Miller was surrounded by half-a-dozen wonderful moustaches checked Winterbourne's impulse to go straightway to see her. He had perhaps not definitely flattered himself that he had made an ineffaceable impression upon her heart, but he was annoyed at hearing of a state of affairs so little in harmony
30 with an image that had lately flitted in and out of his own meditations; the image of a very pretty girl looking out of an old Roman window and asking herself urgently when Mr. Winterbourne would arrive. If, however, he determined to wait a little before reminding Miss Miller of his claims to her consideration, he went very soon to call upon two or three other friends. One of these friends was an American lady who had spent several winters at Geneva, where she had placed her children at school. She was a very accomplished woman,
40 and she lived in the Via Gregoriana. Winterbourne found her in a little crimson drawing-room, on a third floor; the room was filled with southern sunshine. He had not been there ten minutes when the servant came in, announcing "Madame Mila!" This announcement was presently followed by the entrance of little Randolph Miller, who stopped in the middle of the room and

stood staring at Winterbourne. An instant later his pretty sister crossed the threshold; and then, after a considerable interval, Mrs. Miller slowly advanced.

"I know you!" said Randolph.   50

"I'm sure you know a great many things," exclaimed Winterbourne, taking him by the hand. "How is your education coming on?"

Daisy was exchanging greetings very prettily with her hostess; but when she heard Winterbourne's voice she quickly turned her head. "Well, I declare!" she said.

"I told you I should come, you know," Winterbourne rejoined, smiling.

"Well—I didn't believe it," said Miss Daisy.

"I am much obliged to you," laughed the young man. 60

"You might have come to see me!" said Daisy.

"I arrived only yesterday."

"I don't believe that!" the young girl declared.

Winterbourne turned with a protesting smile to her mother; but this lady evaded his glance, and, seating herself, fixed her eyes upon her son. "We've got a bigger place than this," said Randolph. "It's all gold on the walls."

Mrs. Miller turned uneasily in her chair. "I told you if I were going to bring you, you would say something!" 70
she murmured.

"I told *you!*" Randolph exclaimed. "I tell *you,* sir!" he added, jocosely, giving Winterbourne a thump on the knee. "It *is* bigger, too!"

Daisy had entered upon a lively conversation with her hostess; and Winterbourne judged it becoming to address a few words to her mother. "I hope you have been well since we parted at Vevey," he said.

Mrs. Miller now certainly looked at him—at his chin. "Not very well, sir," she answered.   80

"She's got the dyspepsia," said Randolph. "I've got it, too. Father's got it. I've got it most!"

This announcement, instead of embarrassing Mrs. Miller, seemed to relieve her. "I suffer from the liver," she said. "I think it's this climate; it's less bracing than Schenectady, especially in the winter season. I don't know whether you know we reside at Schenectady. I was saying to Daisy that I certainly hadn't found any one like Dr. Davis, and I didn't believe I should. Oh, at Schenectady he stands first; they think everything of 90
him. He has so much to do, and yet there was nothing he wouldn't do for me. He said he never saw anything

like my dyspepsia, but he was bound to cure it. I'm sure there was nothing he wouldn't try. He was just going to try something new when we came off. Mr. Miller wanted Daisy to see Europe for herself. But I wrote to Mr. Miller that it seems as if I couldn't get on without Dr. Davis. At Schenectady he stands at the very top; and there's a great deal of sickness there, too. It affects my sleep."

Winterbourne had a good deal of pathological gossip with Dr. Davis's patient, during which Daisy chattered unremittingly to her own companion. The young man asked Mrs. Miller how she was pleased with Rome. "Well, I must say I am disappointed," she answered. "We had heard so much about it; I suppose we had heard too much. But we couldn't help that. We had been led to expect something different."

"Ah, wait a little, and you will become very fond of it," said Winterbourne.

"I hate it worse and worse every day!" cried Randolph.

"You are like the infant Hannibal," said Winterbourne.

"No, I ain't!" Randolph declared, at a venture.

"You are not much like an infant," said his mother. "But we have seen places," she resumed, "that I should put a long way before Rome." And in reply to Winterbourne's interrogation, "There's Zürich," she concluded; "I think Zürich is lovely; and we hadn't heard half so much about it."

"The best place we've seen is the City of Richmond!" said Randolph.

"He means the ship," his mother explained. "We crossed in that ship. Randolph had a good time on the *City of Richmond.*"

"It's the best place I've seen," the child repeated. "Only it was turned the wrong way."

"Well, we've got to turn the right way some time," said Mrs. Miller, with a little laugh. Winterbourne expressed the hope that her daughter at least found some gratification in Rome, and she declared that Daisy was quite carried away. "It's on account of the society—the society's splendid. She goes round everywhere; she has made a great number of acquaintances. Of course she goes round more than I do. I must say they have been very sociable; they have taken her right in. And then she knows a great many gentlemen. Oh, she thinks there's nothing like Rome. Of course, it's a great deal pleasanter for a young lady if she knows plenty of gentlemen."

By this time Daisy had turned her attention again to Winterbourne. "I've been telling Mrs. Walker how mean you were!" the young girl announced.

"And what is the evidence you have offered?" asked Winterbourne, rather annoyed at Miss Miller's want of appreciation of the zeal of an admirer who on his way down to Rome had stopped neither at Bologna nor at Florence, simply because of a certain sentimental impatience. He remembered that a cynical compatriot had once told him that American women—the pretty ones, and this gave a largeness to the axiom—were at once the most exacting in the world and the least endowed with a sense of indebtedness.

"Why, you were awfully mean at Vevey," said Daisy. "You wouldn't do anything. You wouldn't stay there when I asked you."

"My dearest young lady," cried Winterbourne, with eloquence, "have I come all the way to Rome to encounter your reproaches?"

"Just hear him say that!" said Daisy to her hostess, giving a twist to a bow on this lady's dress. "Did you ever hear anything so quaint?"

"So quaint, my dear?" murmured Mrs. Walker, in a tone of a partisan of Winterbourne.

"Well, I don't know," said Daisy, fingering Mrs. Walker's ribbons. "Mrs. Walker, I want to tell you something."

"Mother-r," interposed Randolph, with his rough ends to his words, "I tell you you've got to go. Eugenio'll raise —something!"

"I'm not afraid of Eugenio," said Daisy, with a toss of her head. "Look here, Mrs. Walker," she went on, "you know I'm coming to your party."

"I am delighted to hear it."

"I've got a lovely dress!"

"I am very sure of that."

"But I want to ask a favour—permission to bring a friend."

"I shall be happy to see any of your friends," said Mrs. Walker, turning with a smile to Mrs. Miller.

"Oh, they are not my friends," answered Daisy's

---

20 like . . . Hannibal, in his intense hatred of Rome

mamma, smiling shyly, in her own fashion. "I never spoke to them."

"It's an intimate friend of mine—Mr. Giovanelli," said Daisy, without a tremor in her clear little voice, or a shadow on her brilliant little face.

Mrs. Walker was silent a moment; she gave a rapid glance at Winterbourne. "I shall be glad to see Mr. Giovanelli," she then said.

"He's an Italian," Daisy pursued, with the prettiest
10 serenity. "He's a great friend of mine—he's the handsomest man in the world—except Mr. Winterbourne! He knows plenty of Italians, but he wants to know some Americans. He thinks ever so much of Americans. He's tremendously clever. He's perfectly lovely!"

It was settled that this brilliant personage should be brought to Mrs. Walker's party, and then Mrs. Miller prepared to take her leave. "I guess we'll go back to the hotel," she said.

"You may go back to the hotel, mother, but I'm going
20 to take a walk," said Daisy.

"She's going to walk with Mr. Giovanelli," Randolph proclaimed.

"I am going to the Pincio," said Daisy, smiling.

"Alone, my dear—at this hour?" Mrs. Walker asked. The afternoon was drawing to a close—it was the hour for the throng of carriages and of contemplative pedestrians. "I don't think it's safe, my dear," said Mrs. Walker.

"Neither do I," subjoined Mrs. Miller. "You'll get
30 the fever, as sure as you live. Remember what Dr. Davis told you!"

"Give her some medicine before she goes," said Randolph.

The company had risen to its feet; Daisy, still showing her pretty teeth, bent over and kissed her hostess. "Mrs. Walker, you are too perfect," she said. "I'm not going alone; I am going to meet a friend."

"Your friend won't keep you from getting the fever," Mrs. Miller observed.

40 "Is it Mr. Giovanelli?" asked the hostess.

Winterbourne was watching the young girl; at this question his attention quickened. She stood there smiling and smoothing her bonnet ribbons; she glanced at Winterbourne. Then, while she glanced and smiled, she answered, without a shade of hesitation, "Mr. Giovanelli—the beautiful Giovanelli."

"My dear young friend," said Mrs. Walker, taking her hand, pleadingly, "don't walk off to the Pincio at this hour to meet a beautiful Italian."

"Well, he speaks English," said Mrs. Miller. 50

"Gracious me!" Daisy exclaimed, "I don't want to do anything improper. There's an easy way to settle it." She continued to glance at Winterbourne. "The Pincio is only a hundred yards distant, and if Mr. Winterbourne were as polite as he pretends, he would offer to walk with me!"

Winterbourne's politeness hastened to affirm itself, and the young girl gave him gracious leave to accompany her. They passed down stairs before her mother, and at the door Winterbourne perceived Mrs. Miller's 60 carriage drawn up, with the ornamental courier whose acquaintance he had made at Vevey seated within. "Good-bye, Eugenio!" cried Daisy, "I'm going to take a walk." The distance from the Via Gregoriana to the beautiful garden at the other end of the Pincian Hill is, in fact, rapidly traversed. As the day was splendid, however, and the concourse of vehicles, walkers, and loungers numerous, the young Americans found their progress much delayed. This fact was highly agreeable to Winterbourne, in spite of his consciousness of his 70 singular situation. The slow-moving, idly-gazing Roman crowd bestowed much attention upon the extremely pretty young foreign lady who was passing through it upon his arm; and he wondered what on earth had been in Daisy's mind when she proposed to expose herself, unattended, to its appreciation. His own mission, to her sense, apparently, was to consign her to the hands of Mr. Giovanelli; but Winterbourne, at once annoyed and gratified, resolved that he would do no such thing.

"Why haven't you been to see me?" asked Daisy. 80 "You can't get out of that."

"I have had the honour of telling you that I have only just stepped out of the train."

"You must have stayed in the train a good while after it stopped!" cried the young girl, with her little laugh. "I suppose you were asleep. You have had time to go to see Mrs. Walker."

"I knew Mrs. Walker—" Winterbourne began to explain.

---

23 Pincio, Monte Pincio, a small hill just within the walls of Rome

"I know where you knew her. You knew her at Geneva. She told me so. Well, you knew me at Vevey. That's just as good. So you ought to have come." She asked him no other question than this; she began to prattle about her own affairs. "We've got splendid rooms at the hotel; Eugenio says they're the best rooms in Rome. We are going to stay all winter, if we don't die of the fever; and I guess we'll stay then. It's a great deal nicer than I thought; I thought it would be fear-
10 fully quiet; I was sure it would be awfully poky. I was sure we should be going round all the time with one of those dreadful old men that explain about the pictures and things. But we only had about a week of that, and now I'm enjoying myself. I know ever so many people, and they are all so charming. The society's extremely select. There are all kinds—English, and Germans, and Italians. I think I like the English best. I like their style of conversation. But there are some lovely Americans. I never saw anything so hospitable. There's something or
20 other every day. There's not much dancing; but I must say I never thought dancing was everything. I was al-ways fond of conversation. I guess I shall have plenty at Mrs. Walker's—her rooms are so small." When they had passed the gate of the Pincian Gardens, Miss Miller began to wonder where Mr. Giovanelli might be. "We had better go straight to that place in front," she said, "where you look at the view."

"I certainly shall not help you to find him," Winter-bourne declared.

30 "Then I shall find him without you," said Miss Daisy.

"You certainly won't leave me!" cried Winterbourne.

She burst into her little laugh. "Are you afraid you'll get lost—or run over? But there's Giovanelli, leaning against that tree. He's staring at the women in the carriages; did you ever see anything so cool?"

Winterbourne perceived at some distance a little man standing with folded arms, nursing his cane. He had a handsome face, an artfully poised hat, a glass in one eye, and a nosegay in his buttonhole. Winterbourne looked
40 at him a moment, and then said, "Do you mean to speak to that man?"

"Do I mean to speak to him? Why, you don't suppose I mean to communicate by signs?"

"Pray understand, then," said Winterbourne, "that I intend to remain with you."

Daisy stopped and looked at him, without a sign of troubled consciousness in her face; with nothing but the presence of her charming eyes and her happy dimples. "Well, she's a cool one!" thought the young man.

"I don't like the way you say that," said Daisy. "It's 50 too imperious."

"I beg your pardon if I say it wrong. The main point is to give you an idea of my meaning."

The young girl looked at him more gravely, but with eyes that were prettier than ever. "I have never allowed a gentleman to dictate to me, or to interfere with any-thing I do."

"I think you have made a mistake," said Winter-bourne. "You should sometimes listen to a gentleman— the right one." 60

Daisy began to laugh again. "I do nothing but listen to gentlemen!" she exclaimed. "Tell me if Mr. Giovanelli is the right one."

The gentleman with the nosegay in his bosom had now perceived our two friends, and was approaching the young girl with obsequious rapidity. He bowed to Winterbourne as well as to the latter's companion; he had a brilliant smile, an intelligent eye; Winterbourne thought him not a bad-looking fellow. But he never-theless said to Daisy, "No, he's not the right one." 70

Daisy evidently had a natural talent for performing introductions; she mentioned the name of each of her companions to the other. She strolled along with one of them on each side of her; Mr. Giovanelli, who spoke English very cleverly—Winterbourne afterwards learned that he had practised the idiom upon a great many American heiresses—addressed to her a great deal of very polite nonsense; he was extremely urbane, and the young American, who said nothing, reflected upon that profundity of Italian cleverness which enables people to 80 appear more gracious in proportion as they are more acutely disappointed. Giovanelli, of course, had counted upon something more intimate; he had not bargained for a party of three. But he kept his temper in a manner which suggested far-stretching intentions. Winterbourne flattered himself that he had taken his measure. "He is not a gentleman," said the young American; "he is only a clever imitation of one. He is a music-master, or a penny-a-liner, or a third-rate artist. Damn his good

---

89 penny-a-liner, hack writer

looks!" Mr. Giovanelli had certainly a very pretty face; but Winterbourne felt a superior indignation at his own lovely fellow-country woman's not knowing the difference between a spurious gentleman and a real one. Giovanelli chattered and jested, and made himself wonderfully agreeable. It was true that, if he was an imitation, the imitation was brilliant. "Nevertheless," Winterbourne said to himself, "a nice girl ought to know!" And then he came back to the question whether this was, in fact, a nice girl. Would a nice girl—even allowing for her being a little American flirt—make a rendezvous with a presumably low-lived foreigner? The rendezvous in this case, indeed, had been in broad daylight, and in the most crowded corner of Rome; but was it not possible to regard the choice of these circumstances as a proof of extreme cynicism? Singular though it may seem, Winterbourne was vexed that the young girl, in joining her *amoroso,* should not appear more impatient of his own company, and he was vexed because of his inclination. It was impossible to regard her as a perfectly well-conducted young lady; she was wanting in a certain indispensable delicacy. It would therefore simplify matters greatly to be able to treat her as the object of one of those sentiments which are called by romancers "lawless passions." That she should seem to wish to get rid of him would help him to think more lightly of her, and to be able to think more lightly of her would make her much less perplexing. But Daisy, on this occasion, continued to present herself as an inscrutable combination of audacity and innocence.

She had been walking some quarter of an hour, attended by her two cavaliers, and responding in a tone of very childish gaiety, as it seemed to Winterbourne. to the pretty speeches of Mr. Giovanelli, when a carriage that had detached itself from the revolving train drew up beside the path. At the same moment Winterbourne perceived that his friend Mrs. Walker—the lady whose house he had lately left—was seated in the vehicle, and was beckoning to him. Leaving Miss Miller's side, he hastened to obey her summons. Mrs. Walker was flushed; she wore an excited air. "It is really too dreadful," she said. "That girl must not do this sort of thing. She must not walk here with you two men. Fifty people have noticed her."

Winterbourne raised his eyebrows. "I think it's a pity to make too much fuss about it."

"It's a pity to let the girl ruin herself!"

"She is very innocent," said Winterbourne.

"She's very crazy!" cried Mrs. Walker. "Did you ever see anything so imbecile as her mother? After you had all left me, just now, I could not sit still for thinking of it. It seemed too pitiful not even to attempt to save her. I ordered the carriage and put on my bonnet, and came here as quickly as possible. Thank Heaven I have found you!"

"What do you propose to do with us?" asked Winterbourne, smiling.

"To ask her to get in, to drive her about here for half-an-hour, so that the world may see that she is not running absolutely wild, and then to take her safely home."

"I don't think it's a very happy thought," said Winterbourne; "but you can try."

Mrs. Walker tried. The young man went in pursuit of Miss Miller, who had simply nodded and smiled at his interlocutor in the carriage, and had gone her way with her companion. Daisy, on learning that Mrs. Walker wished to speak to her, retraced her steps with a perfect good grace and with Mr. Giovanelli at her side. She declared that she was delighted to have a chance to present this gentleman to Mrs. Walker. She immediately achieved the introduction, and declared that she had never in her life seen anything so lovely as Mrs. Walker's carriage-rug.

"I am glad you admire it," said this lady, smiling sweetly. "Will you get in and let me put it over you?"

"Oh no, thank you," said Daisy. "I shall admire it much more as I see you driving round with it."

"Do get in and drive with me!" said Mrs. Walker.

"That would be charming, but it's so enchanting just as I am!" and Daisy gave a brilliant glance at the gentlemen on either side of her.

"It may be enchanting, dear child, but it is not the custom here," urged Mrs. Walker, leaning forward in her victoria, with her hands devoutly clasped.

"Well, it ought to be, then!" said Daisy. "If I didn't walk I should expire."

"You should walk with your mother, dear," cried the lady from Geneva, losing patience.

"With my mother, dear!" exclaimed the young girl. Winterbourne saw that she scented interference. "My mother never walked ten steps in her life. And then, you know," she added, with a laugh, "I am more than five years old."

"You are old enough to be more reasonable. **You** are old enough, dear Miss Miller, to be talked about."

Daisy looked at Mrs. Walker, smiling intensely. "Talked about? What do you mean?"

"Come into my carriage, and I will tell you."

Daisy turned her quickened glance again from one of the gentlemen beside her to the other. Mr. Giovanelli was bowing to and fro, rubbing down his gloves and laughing very agreeably; Winterbourne thought it a most unpleasant scene. "I don't think I want to know what you mean," said Daisy, presently. "I don't think I should like it."

Winterbourne wished that Mrs. Walker would tuck in her carriage-rug and drive away; but this lady did not enjoy being defied, as she afterwards told him. "Should you prefer being thought a very reckless girl?" she demanded.

"Gracious!" exclaimed Daisy. She looked again at Mr. Giovanelli, then she turned to Winterbourne. There was a little pink flush in her cheek; she was tremendously pretty. "Does Mr. Winterbourne think," she asked slowly, smiling, throwing back her head and glancing at him from head to foot, "that—to save my reputation—I ought to get into the carriage?"

Winterbourne coloured; for an instant he hesitated greatly. It seemed so strange to hear her speak that way of her "reputation." But he himself, in fact, must speak in accordance with gallantry. The finest gallantry here was simply to tell her the truth; and the truth for Winterbourne—as the few indications I have been able to give have made him known to the reader—was that Daisy Miller should take Mrs. Walker's advice. He looked at her exquisite prettiness; and then said, very gently, "I think you should get into the carriage."

Daisy gave a violent laugh. "I never heard anything so stiff! If this is improper, Mrs. Walker," she pursued, "then I am all improper, and you must give me up. Good-bye; I hope you'll have a lovely ride!" and, with Mr. Giovanelli, who made a triumphantly obsequious salute, she turned away.

Mrs. Walker sat looking after her, and there were tears in Mrs. Walker's eyes. "Get in here, sir," she said to Winterbourne, indicating the place beside her. The young man answered that he felt bound to accompany Miss Miller; whereupon Mrs. Walker declared that if he refused her this favour she would never speak to him again. She was evidently in earnest. Winterbourne overtook Daisy and her companion, and, offering the young girl his hand, told her that Mrs. Walker had made an imperious claim upon his society. He expected that in answer she would say something rather free, something to commit herself still further to that "recklessness" from which Mrs. Walker had so charitably endeavoured to dissuade her. But she only shook his hand, hardly looking at him; while Mr. Giovanelli bade him farewell with a too emphatic flourish of the hat.

Winterbourne was not in the best possible humour as he took his seat in Mrs. Walker's victoria. "That was not clever of you," he said, candidly, while the vehicle mingled again with the throng of carriages.

"In such a case," his companion answered, "I don't wish to be clever; I wish to be *earnest!*"

"Well, your earnestness has only offended her and put her off."

"It has happened very well," said Mrs. Walker. "If she is perfectly determined to compromise herself, the sooner one knows it the better; one can act accordingly."

"I suspect she meant no harm," Winterbourne rejoined.

"So I thought a month ago. But she has been going too far."

"What has she been doing?"

"Everything that is not done here. Flirting with any man she could pick up; sitting in corners with mysterious Italians; dancing all the evening with the same partners; receiving visits at eleven o'clock at night. Her mother goes away when visitors come."

"But her brother," said Winterbourne, laughing, "sits up till midnight."

"He must be edified by what he sees. I'm told that at their hotel every one is talking about her, and that a smile goes round among all the servants when a gentleman comes and asks for Miss Miller."

"The servants be hanged!" said Winterbourne, angrily. "The poor girl's only fault," he presently added, "is that she is very uncultivated."

"She is naturally indelicate," Mrs. Walker declared. "Take that example this morning. How long had you known her at Vevey?"

"A couple of days."

"Fancy, then, her making it a personal matter that you should have left the place!"

Winterbourne was silent for some moments; then he said, "I suspect, Mrs. Walker, that you and I have lived too long at Geneva!" And he added a request that she should inform him with what particular design she had made him enter her carriage.

"I wished to beg you to cease your relations with Miss Miller—not to flirt with her—to give her no further opportunity to expose herself—to let her alone, in short."

"I'm afraid I can't do that," said Winterbourne. "I like her extremely."

"All the more reason that you shouldn't help her to make a scandal."

"There shall be nothing scandalous in my attentions to her."

"There certainly will be in the way she takes them. But I have said what I had on my conscience," Mrs. Walker pursued. "If you wish to rejoin the young lady I will put you down. Here, by-the-way, you have a chance."

The carriage was traversing that part of the Pincian Garden that overhangs the wall of Rome and overlooks the beautiful Villa Borghese. It is bordered by a large parapet, near which there are several seats. One of the seats, at a distance, was occupied by a gentleman and a lady, towards whom Mrs. Walker gave a toss of her head. At the same moment these persons rose and walked towards the parapet. Winterbourne had asked the coachman to stop; he now descended from the carriage. His companion looked at him a moment in silence; then, while he raised his hat, she drove majestically away. Winterbourne stood there: he had turned his eyes towards Daisy and her cavalier. They evidently saw no one; they were too deeply occupied with each other. When they reached the low garden-wall they stood a moment looking off at the great flat-topped pine-clusters of the Villa Borghese; then Giovanelli seated himself familiarly upon the broad ledge of the wall. The western sun in the opposite sky sent out a brilliant shaft through a couple of cloud-bars, whereupon Daisy's companion took her parasol out of her hands and opened it. She came a little nearer, and he held the parasol over her; then, still holding it, he let it rest upon her shoulder, so that both of their heads were hidden from Winterbourne. This young man lingered a moment, then he began to walk. But he walked—not towards the couple with the parasol—towards the residence of his aunt, Mrs. Costello.

He flattered himself on the following day that there was no smiling among the servants when he, at least, asked for Mrs. Miller at her hotel. This lady and her daughter, however, were not at home; and on the next day after, repeating his visit, Winterbourne again had the misfortune not to find them. Mrs. Walker's party took place on the evening of the third day, and, in spite of the frigidity of his last interview with the hostess, Winterbourne was among the guests. Mrs. Walker was one of those American ladies who, while residing abroad, make a point, in their own phrase, of studying European society; and she had on this occasion collected several specimens of her diversely-born fellow-mortals to serve, as it were, as text-books. When Winterbourne arrived, Daisy Miller was not there, but in a few moments he saw her mother come in alone, very shyly and ruefully. Mrs. Miller's hair above her exposed-looking temples was more frizzled than ever. As she approached Mrs. Walker, Winterbourne also drew near.

"You see I've come all alone," said poor Mrs. Miller. "I'm so frightened I don't know what to do. It's the first time I've ever been to a party alone, especially in this country. I wanted to bring Randolph, or Eugenio, or some one, but Daisy just pushed me off by myself. I ain't used to going round alone."

"And does not your daughter intend to favour us with her society?" demanded Mrs. Walker, impressively.

"Well, Daisy's all dressed," said Mrs. Miller, with that accent of the dispassionate, if not of the philosophic historian with which she always recorded the current incidents of her daughter's career. "She got dressed on purpose before dinner. But she's got a friend of hers there; that gentleman—the Italian—that she wanted to bring. They've got going at the piano; it seems as if they couldn't leave off. Mr. Giovanelli sings splendidly. But I guess they'll come before very long," concluded Mrs. Miller, hopefully.

"I'm sorry she should come—in that way," said Mrs. Walker.

"Well, I told her that there was no use in her getting dressed before dinner if she was going to wait three hours," responded Daisy's mamma. "I didn't see the use of her putting on such a dress as that to sit round with Mr. Giovanelli."

"This is most horrible!" said Mrs. Walker, turning away and addressing herself to Winterbourne. *"Elle s'affiche.* It's her revenge for my having ventured to remonstrate with her. When she comes I shall not speak to her."

Daisy came after eleven o'clock; but she was not, on such an occasion, a young lady to wait to be spoken to. She rustled forward in radiant loveliness, smiling and chattering, carrying a large bouquet, and attended by Mr. Giovanelli. Every one stopped talking, and turned and looked at her. She came straight to Mrs. Walker. "I'm afraid you thought I never was coming, so I sent mother off to tell you. I wanted to make Mr. Giovanelli practise some things before he came; you know he sings beautifully, and I want you to ask him to sing. This is Mr. Giovanelli; you know I introduced him to you; he's got the most lovely voice, and he knows the most charming set of songs. I made him go over them this evening on purpose; we had the greatest time at the hotel." Of all this Daisy delivered herself with the sweetest, brightest audibleness, looking now at her hostess and now round the room, while she gave a series of little pats round her shoulders to the edges of her dress. "Is there any one I know?" she asked.

"I think every one knows you!" said Mrs. Walker, pregnantly, and she gave a very cursory greeting to Mr. Giovanelli. This gentleman bore himself gallantly. He smiled and bowed, and showed his white teeth; he curled his moustaches and rolled his eyes, and performed all the proper functions of a handsome Italian at an evening party. He sang very prettily half-a-dozen songs, though Mrs. Walker afterwards declared that she had been quite unable to find out who asked him. It was apparently not Daisy who had given him his orders. Daisy sat at a distance from the piano; and though she had publicly, as it were, professed a high admiration for his singing, talked, not inaudibly, while it was going on.

"It's a pity these rooms are so small; we can't dance," she said to Winterbourne, as if she had seen him five minutes before.

"I am not sorry we can't dance," Winterbourne answered; "I don't dance."

"Of course you don't dance; you're too stiff," said Miss Daisy. "I hope you enjoyed your drive with Mrs. Walker!"

"No, I didn't enjoy it; I preferred walking with you."

"We paired off; that was much better," said Daisy.

"But did you ever hear anything so cool as Mrs. Walker's wanting me to get into her carriage and drop poor Mr. Giovanelli, and under the pretext that it was proper? People have different ideas! It would have been most unkind; he had been talking about that walk for ten days."

"He should not have talked about it at all," said Winterbourne; "he would never have proposed to a young lady of this country to walk about the streets with him."

"About the streets?" cried Daisy, with her pretty stare. "Where, then, would he have proposed to her to walk? The Pincio is not the streets, either; and I, thank goodness, am not a young lady of this country. The young ladies of this country have a dreadfully poky time of it, so far as I can learn; I don't see why I should change my habits for *them.*"

"I am afraid your habits are those of a flirt," said Winterbourne, gravely.

"Of course they are," she cried, giving him her little smiling stare again. "I'm a fearful, frightful flirt! Did you ever hear of a nice girl that was not? But I suppose you will tell me now that I am not a nice girl."

"You're a very nice girl; but I wish you would flirt with me, and me only," said Winterbourne.

"Ah! thank you—thank you very much; you are the last man I should think of flirting with. As I have had the pleasure of informing you, you are too stiff."

"You say that too often," said Winterbourne.

Daisy gave a delighted laugh. "If I could have the sweet hope of making you angry, I should say it again."

"Don't do that; when I am angry I'm stiffer than ever. But if you won't flirt with me, do cease, at least, to flirt with your friend at the piano; they don't understand that sort of thing here."

"I thought they understood nothing else!" exclaimed Daisy.

"Not in young unmarried women."

"It seems to me much more proper in young unmarried women than in old married ones," Daisy declared.

"Well," said Winterbourne, "when you deal with natives you must go by the custom of the place. Flirting is a purely American custom; it doesn't exist here. So when you show yourself in public with Mr. Giovanelli, and without your mother—"

---

2 *Elle s'affiche.* She is seeking notoriety

"Gracious! poor mother!" interposed Daisy.

"Though you may be flirting, Mr. Giovanelli is not; he means something else."

"He isn't preaching, at any rate," said Daisy with vivacity. "And if you want very much to know, we are neither of us flirting; we are too good friends for that; we are very intimate friends."

"Ah!" rejoined Winterbourne, "if you are in love with each other it is another affair."

She had allowed him up to this point to talk so frankly that he had no expectation of shocking her by this ejaculation; but she immediately got up, blushing visibly, and leaving him to exclaim mentally that little American flirts were the queerest creatures in the world. "Mr. Giovanelli, at least," she said, giving her interlocutor a single glance, "never says such very disagreeable things to me."

Winterbourne was bewildered; he stood staring. Mr. Giovanelli had finished singing; he left the piano and came over to Daisy. "Won't you come into the other room and have some tea?" he asked, bending before her with his ornamental smile.

Daisy turned to Winterbourne, beginning to smile again. He was still more perplexed, for this inconsequent smile made nothing clear, though it seemed to prove, indeed, that she had a sweetness and softness that reverted instinctively to the pardon of offences. "It has never occurred to Mr. Winterbourne to offer me any tea," she said, with her little tormenting manner.

"I have offered you advice," Winterbourne rejoined.

"I prefer weak tea!" cried Daisy, and she went off with the brilliant Giovanelli. She sat with him in the adjoining room, in the embrasure of the window, for the rest of the evening. There was an interesting performance at the piano, but neither of these young people gave heed to it. When Daisy came to take leave of Mrs. Walker, this lady conscientiously repaired the weakness of which she had been guilty at the moment of the young girl's arrival. She turned her back straight upon Miss Miller and left her to depart with what grace she might. Winterbourne was standing near the door; he saw it all. Daisy turned very pale and looked at her mother, but Mrs. Miller was humbly unconscious of any violation of the usual social forms. She appeared, indeed, to have felt an incongruous impulse to draw attention to her own striking observance of them. "Good-night, Mrs.

Walker," she said; "we've had a beautiful evening. You see, if I let Daisy come to parties without me, I don't want her to go away without me." Daisy turned away, looking with a pale, grave face at the circle near the door; Winterbourne saw that, for the first moment, she was too much shocked and puzzled even for indignation. He on his side was greatly touched.

"That was very cruel," he said to Mrs. Walker.

"She never enters my drawing room again!" replied his hostess.

Since Winterbourne was not to meet her in Mrs. Walker's drawing-room, he went as often as possible to Mrs. Miller's hotel. The ladies were rarely at home; but when he found them the devoted Giovanelli was always present. Very often the brilliant little Roman was in the drawing-room with Daisy alone, Mrs. Miller being apparently constantly of the opinion that discretion is the better part of surveillance. Winterbourne noted, at first with surprise, that Daisy on these occasions was never embarrassed or annoyed by his own entrance; but he very presently began to feel that she had no more surprises for him; the unexpected in her behaviour was the only thing to expect. She showed no displeasure at her *tête-à-tête* with Giovanelli being interrupted; she could chatter as freshly and freely with two gentlemen as with one; there was always, in her conversation, the same odd mixture of audacity and puerility. Winterbourne remarked to himself that if she was seriously interested in Giovanelli, it was very singular that she should not take more trouble to preserve the sanctity of their interviews; and he liked her the more for her innocent-looking indifference and her apparently inexhaustible good humour. He could hardly have said why, but she seemed to him a girl who would never be jealous. At the risk of exciting a somewhat derisive smile on the reader's part, I may affirm that with regard to the women who had hitherto interested him, it very often seemed to Winterbourne among the possibilities that, given certain contingencies, he should be afraid—literally afraid—of these ladies; he had a pleasant sense that he should never be afraid of Daisy Miller. It must be added that this sentiment was not altogether flattering to Daisy; it was part of his conviction, or rather of his apprehension, that she would prove a very light young person.

But she was evidently very much interested in Giovanelli. She looked at him whenever he spoke; she was

perpetually telling him to do this and to do that; she was constantly "chaffing" and abusing him. She appeared completely to have forgotten that Winterbourne had said anything to displease her at Mrs. Walker's little party. One Sunday afternoon, having gone to St. Peter's with his aunt, Winterbourne perceived Daisy strolling about the great church in company with the inevitable Giovanelli. Presently he pointed out the young girl and her cavalier to Mrs. Costello. This lady looked at them
10 a moment through her eyeglass, and then she said,

"That's what makes you so pensive in these days, eh?"

"I had not the least idea I was pensive," said the young man.

"You are very much pre-occupied; you are thinking of something."

"And what is it," he asked, "that you accuse me of thinking of?"

"Of that young lady's—Miss Baker's, Miss Chandler's —what's her name?—Miss Miller's intrigue with that
20 little barber's block."

"Do you call it an intrigue," Winterbourne asked— "an affair that goes on with such peculiar publicity?"

"That's their folly," said Mrs. Costello, "it's not their merit."

"No," rejoined Winterbourne, with something of that pensiveness to which his aunt had alluded. "I don't believe that there is anything to be called an intrigue."

"I have heard a dozen people speak of it; they say she is quite carried away by him."

30 "They are certainly very intimate," said Winterbourne.

Mrs. Costello inspected the young couple again with her optical instrument. "He is very handsome. One easily sees how it is. She thinks him the most elegant man in the world, the finest gentleman. She has never seen anything like him; he is better even than the courier. It was the courier, probably, who introduced him; and if he succeeds in marrying the young lady, the courier will come in for a magnificent commission."

"I don't believe she thinks of marrying him," said Win-
40 terbourne, "and I don't believe he hopes to marry her."

"You may be very sure she thinks of nothing. She goes on from day to day, from hour to hour, as they did in the Golden Age. I can imagine nothing more vulgar. And at the same time," added Mrs. Costello, "depend upon it that she may tell you any moment that she is 'engaged.'"

"I think that is more than Giovanelli expects," said Winterbourne.

"Who is Giovanelli?"

"The little Italian. I have asked questions about him 50 and learned something. He is apparently a perfectly respectable little man. I believe he is, in a small way, a *cavaliere avvocato*. But he doesn't move in what are called the first circles. I think it is really not absolutely impossible that the courier introduced him. He is evidently immensely charmed with Miss Miller. If she thinks him the finest gentleman in the world, he, on his side, has never found himself in personal contact with such splendor, such opulence, such expensiveness, as this young lady's. And then she must seem to him wonder- 60 fully pretty and interesting. I rather doubt that he dreams of marrying her. That must appear to him too impossible a piece of luck. He has nothing but his handsome face to offer, and there is a substantial Mr. Miller in that mysterious land of dollars. Giovanelli knows that he hasn't a title to offer. If he were only a count or a *marchese!* He must wonder at his luck, at the way they have taken him up."

"He accounts for it by his handsome face, and thinks Miss Miller a young lady *qui se passe ses fantaisies!*" 70 said Mrs. Costello.

"It is very true," Winterbourne pursued, "that Daisy and her mamma have not yet risen to that stage of— what shall I call it?—of culture, at which the idea of catching a count or a *marchese* begins. I believe that they are intellectually incapable of that conception."

"Ah! but the *avvocato* can't believe it," said Mrs. Costello.

Of the observation excited by Daisy's "intrigue," Winterbourne gathered that day at St. Peter's sufficient evi- 80 dence. A dozen of the American colonists in Rome came to talk with Mrs. Costello, who sat on a little portable stool at the base of one of the great pilasters. The vesper service was going forward in splendid chants and organ-tones in the adjacent choir, and meanwhile, between Mrs. Costello and her friends, there was a great deal said about poor little Miss Miller's going really "too far." Winterbourne was not pleased with what he heard;

---

53 **cavaliere avvocato,** a lawyer • 67 **marchese,** an Italian noble; a rank above a count and below a prince • 70 **qui . . . fantaisies,** who indulges her whims

but when, coming out upon the great steps of the church, he saw Daisy, who had emerged before him, get into an open cab with her accomplice and roll away through the cynical streets of Rome, he could not deny to himself that she was going very far indeed. He felt very sorry for her—not exactly that he believed that she had completely lost her head, but because it was painful to hear so much that was pretty, and undefended, and natural, assigned to a vulgar place among the categories of dis-
10 order. He made an attempt after this to give a hint to Mrs. Miller. He met one day in the Corso a friend—a tourist like himself, who had just come out of the Doria Palace, where he had been walking through the beautiful gallery. His friend talked for a moment about the superb portrait of Innocent X., by Velasquez, which hangs in one of the cabinets of the palace, and then said, "And in the same cabinet, by-the-way, I had the pleasure of contemplating a picture of a different kind—that pretty American girl whom you pointed out to me last
20 week." In answer to Winterbourne's inquiries, his friend narrated that the pretty American girl—prettier than ever—was seated with a companion in the secluded nook in which the great papal portrait was enshrined.

"Who was her companion?" asked Winterbourne.

"A little Italian with a bouquet in his button-hole. The girl is delightfully pretty; but I thought I understood from you the other day that she was a young lady *du meilleur monde.*"

30 "So she is!" answered Winterbourne; and having assured himself that his informant had seen Daisy and her companion but five minutes before, he jumped into a cab and went to call on Mrs. Miller. She was at home; but she apologized to him for receiving him in Daisy's absence.

"She's gone out somewhere with Mr. Giovanelli," said Mrs. Miller. "She's always going round with Giovanelli."

"I have noticed that they are very intimate," Winterbourne observed.

40 "Oh, it seems as if they couldn't live without each other!" said Mrs. Miller. "Well, he's a real gentleman, anyhow. I keep telling Daisy she's engaged!"

"And what does Daisy say?"

"Oh, she says she isn't engaged. But she might as well be!" this impartial parent resumed. "She goes on as if she was. But I've made Mr. Giovanelli promise to tell

me, if *she* doesn't. I should want to write to Mr. Miller about it—shouldn't you?"

Winterbourne replied that he certainly should; and the state of mind of Daisy's mamma struck him as so un- 50 precedented in the annals of parental vigilance that he gave up as utterly irrelevant the attempt to place her upon her guard.

After this Daisy was never at home, and Winterbourne ceased to meet her at the houses of their common acquaintants because, as he perceived, these shrewd people had quite made up their minds that she was going too far. They ceased to invite her, and they intimated that they desired to express to observant Europeans the great truth that, though Miss Daisy Miller was a young 60 American lady, her behaviour was not representative—was regarded by her compatriots as abnormal. Winterbourne wondered how she felt about all the cold shoulders that were turned towards her, and sometimes it annoyed him to suspect that she did not feel at all. He said to himself that she was too light and childish, too uncultivated and unreasoning, too provincial, to have reflected upon her ostracism, or even to have perceived it. Then at other moments he believed that she carried about in her elegant and irresponsible little organism a 70 defiant, passionate, perfectly observant consciousness of the impression she produced. He asked himself whether Daisy's defiance came from the consciousness of innocence, or from her being, essentially, a young person of the reckless class. It must be admitted that holding one's self to a belief in Daisy's "innocence" came to seem to Winterbourne more and more a matter of fine-spun gallantry. As I have already had occasion to relate, he was angry at finding himself reduced to chopping logic about this young lady; he was vexed at his want of instinctive 80 certitude as to how far her eccentricities were generic, national, and how far they were personal. From either view of them he had somehow missed her, and now it was too late. She was "carried away" by Mr. Giovanelli.

A few days after his brief interview with her mother, he encountered her in that beautiful abode of flowering desolation known as the Palace of the Caesars. The early

---

15 Velasquez, Diego Rodriguez de Silva y Velásquez (1599-1660), Spanish painter • 29 **du meilleur monde,** of the best **society**

Roman spring had filled the air with bloom and perfume, and the rugged surface of the Palatine was muffled with tender verdure. Daisy was strolling along the top of one of those great mounds of ruin that are embanked with mossy marble and paved with monumental inscriptions. It seemed to him that Rome had never been so lovely as just then. He stood looking off at the enchanting harmony of line and colour that remotely encircles the city, inhaling the softly humid odours, and feeling the freshness of the year and the antiquity of the place reaffirm themselves in mysterious interfusion. It seemed to him, also, that Daisy had never looked so pretty; but this had been an observation of his whenever he met her. Giovanelli was at her side, and Giovanelli, too, wore an aspect of even unwonted brilliancy.

"Well," said Daisy, "I should think you would be lonesome!"

"Lonesome?" asked Winterbourne.

"You are always going round by yourself. Can't you get any one to walk with you?"

"I am not so fortunate," said Winterbourne, "as your companion."

Giovanelli, from the first, had treated Winterbourne with distinguished politeness; he listened with a deferential air to his remarks; he laughed, punctiliously, at his pleasantries; he seemed disposed to testify to his belief that Winterbourne was a superior young man. He carried himself in no degree like a jealous wooer; he had obviously a great deal of tact; he had no objection to your expecting a little humility of him. It even seemed to Winterbourne at times that Giovanelli would find a certain mental relief in being able to have a private understanding with him—to say to him, as an intelligent man, that, bless you, *he* knew how extraordinary was this young lady, and didn't flatter himself with delusive—or, at least, *too* delusive—hopes of matrimony and dollars. On this occasion he strolled away from his companion to pluck a sprig of almond-blossom, which he carefully arranged in his button-hole.

"I know why you say that," said Daisy, watching Giovanelli. "Because you think I go round too much with *him*." And she nodded at her attendant.

"Every one thinks so—if you care to know," said Winterbourne.

"Of course I care to know!" Daisy exclaimed, seriously. "But I don't believe it. They are only pretending to be shocked. They don't really care a straw what I do. Besides, I don't go round so much."

"I think you will find they do care. They will show it—disagreeably."

Daisy looked at him a moment. "How—disagreeably?"

"Haven't you noticed anything?" Winterbourne asked.

"I have noticed you. But I noticed you were as stiff as an umbrella the first time I saw you."

"You will find I am not so stiff as several others," said Winterbourne, smiling.

"How shall I find it?"

"By going to see the others."

"What will they do to me?"

"They will give you the cold shoulder. Do you know what that means?"

Daisy was looking at him intently; she began to colour. "Do you mean as Mrs. Walker did the other night?"

"Exactly!" said Winterbourne.

She looked away at Giovanelli, who was decorating himself with his almond-blossom. Then, looking back at Winterbourne, "I shouldn't think you would let people be so unkind!" she said.

"How can I help it?" he asked.

"I should think you would say something."

"I did say something;" and he paused a moment. "I say that your mother tells me that she believes you are engaged."

"Well, she does," said Daisy very simply.

Winterbourne began to laugh. "And does Randolph believe it?" he asked.

"I guess Randolph doesn't believe anything," said Daisy. Randolph's scepticism excited Winterbourne to further hilarity, and he observed that Giovanelli was coming back to them. Daisy, observing it too, addressed herself again to her countryman. "Since you have mentioned it," she said, "I *am* engaged." . . . Winterbourne looked at her; he had stopped laughing. "You don't believe it!" she added.

He was silent a moment; and then, "Yes, I believe it," he said.

"Oh, no, you don't!" she answered. "Well, then—I am not!"

The young girl and her cicerone were on their way

2 Palatine, one of Rome's Seven Hills

to the gate of the enclosure, so that Winterbourne, who had but lately entered, presently took leave of them. A week afterwards he went to dine at a beautiful villa on the Caelian Hill, and, on arriving, dismissed his hired vehicle. The evening was charming, and he promised himself the satisfaction of walking home beneath the Arch of Constantine and past the vaguely-lighted monuments of the Forum. There was a waning moon in the sky, and her radiance was not brilliant, but she was veiled in a thin cloud-curtain which seemed to diffuse and equalize it. When, on his return from the villa (it was eleven o'clock), Winterbourne approached the dusky circle of the Colosseum, it occurred to him, as a lover of the picturesque, that the interior, in the pale moonshine, would be well worth a glance. He turned aside and walked to one of the empty arches, near which, as he observed, an open carriage—one of the little Roman streetcabs—was stationed. Then he passed in, among the cavernous shadows of the great structure, and emerged upon the clear and silent arena. The place had never seemed to him more impressive. One-half of the gigantic circus was in deep shade; the other was sleeping in the luminous dusk. As he stood there he began to murmur Byron's famous lines, out of "Manfred"; but before he had finished his quotation he remembered that if nocturnal meditations in the Colosseum are recommended by the poets, they are deprecated by the doctors. The historic atmosphere was there certainly; but the historic atmosphere, scientifically considered, was no better than a villainous miasma. Winterbourne walked to the middle of the arena, to take a more general glance, intending thereafter to make a hasty retreat. The great cross in the centre was covered with shadow; it was only as he drew near it that he made it out distinctly. Then he saw that two persons were stationed upon the low steps which formed its base. One of these was a woman, seated; her companion was standing in front of her.

Presently the sound of the woman's voice came to him distinctly in the warm night-air. "Well, he looks at us as one of the old lions or tigers may have looked at the Christian martyrs!" These were the words he heard, in the familiar accent of Miss Daisy Miller.

"Let us hope he is not very hungry," responded the ingenious Giovanelli. "He will have to take me first; you will serve for dessert!"

Winterbourne stopped, with a sort of horror; and, it must be added, with a sort of relief. It was as if a sudden illumination had been flashed upon the ambiguity of Daisy's behaviour, and the riddle had become easy to read. She was a young lady whom a gentleman need no longer be at pains to respect. He stood there looking at her—looking at her companion, and not reflecting that though he saw them vaguely, he himself must have been more brightly visible. He felt angry with himself that he had bothered so much about the right way of regarding Miss Daisy Miller. Then, as he was going to advance again, he checked himself; not from the fear that he was doing her injustice, but from the sense of the danger of appearing unbecomingly exhilarated by this sudden revulsion from cautious criticism. He turned away towards the entrance of the place; but, as he did so, he heard Daisy speak again.

"Why, it was Mr. Winterbourne! He saw me—and he cuts me!"

What a clever little reprobate she was, and how smartly she played at injured innocence! But he wouldn't cut her. Winterbourne came forward again, and went towards the great cross. Daisy had got up; Giovanelli lifted his hat. Winterbourne had now begun to think simply of the craziness, from a sanitary point of view, of a delicate young girl lounging away the evening in this nest of malaria. What if she *were* a clever little reprobate? that was no reason for her dying of the *perniciosa*. "How long have you been here?" he asked, almost brutally.

Daisy, lovely in the flattering moonlight, looked at him a moment. Then—"All the evening," she answered, gently. . . . "I never saw anything so pretty."

"I am afraid," said Winterbourne, "that you will not think Roman fever very pretty. This is the way people catch it. I wonder," he added, turning to Giovanelli, "that you, a native Roman, should countenance such a terrible indiscretion."

"Ah," said the handsome native, "for myself I am not afraid."

"Neither am I—for you! I am speaking for this young lady."

Giovanelli lifted his well-shaped eyebrows and showed

---

24 Byron's . . . "Manfred." See the passage in Act III, sc. iv • 73
perniciosa, malaria

his brilliant teeth. But he took Winterbourne's rebuke with docility. "I told the signorina it was a grave indiscretion; but when was the signorina ever prudent?"

"I never was sick, and I don't mean to be!" the signorina declared. "I don't look like much, but I'm healthy! I was bound to see the Colosseum by moonlight; I shouldn't have wanted to go home without that; and we have had the most beautiful time, haven't we, Mr. Giovanelli? If there has been any danger, Eugenio can give me some pills. He has got some splendid pills."

"I should advise you," said Winterbourne, "to drive home as fast as possible and take one!"

"What you say is very wise," Giovanelli rejoined. "I will go and make sure the carriage is at hand." And he went forward rapidly.

Daisy followed with Winterbourne. He kept looking at her; she seemed not in the least embarrassed. Winterbourne said nothing; Daisy chattered about the beauty of the place. "Well, I *have* seen the Colosseum by moonlight!" she exclaimed. "That's one good thing." Then, noticing Winterbourne's silence, she asked him why he didn't speak. He made no answer; he only began to laugh. They passed under one of the dark archways; Giovanelli was in front with the carriage. Here Daisy stopped a moment, looking at the young American. *"Did* you believe I was engaged the other day?" she asked.

"It doesn't matter what I believed the other day," said Winterbourne, still laughing.

"Well, what do you believe now?"

"I believe that it makes very little difference whether you are engaged or not!"

He felt the young girl's pretty eyes fixed upon him through the thick gloom of the archway; she was apparently going to answer. But Giovanelli hurried her forward. "Quick! quick!" he said; "if we get in by midnight we are quite safe."

Daisy took her seat in the carriage, and the fortunate Italian placed himself beside her. "Don't forget Eugenio's pills!" said Winterbourne, as he lifted his hat.

"I don't care," said Daisy, in a little strange tone, "whether I have Roman fever or not!" Upon this the cab-driver cracked his whip, and they rolled away over the desultory patches of the antique pavement.

Winterbourne—to do him justice, as it were—mentioned to no one that he had encountered Miss Miller, at midnight, in the Colosseum with a gentleman; but,

nevertheless, a couple of days later, the fact of her having been there under these circumstances was known to every member of the little American circle, and commented accordingly. Winterbourne reflected that they had of course known it at the hotel, and that, after Daisy's return, there had been an exchange of remarks between the porter and the cab-driver. But the young man was conscious, at the same moment, that it had ceased to be a matter of serious regret to him that the little American flirt should be "talked about" by low-minded menials. These people, a day or two later, had serious information to give: the little American flirt was alarmingly ill. Winterbourne, when the rumour came to him, immediately went to the hotel for more news. He found that two or three charitable friends had preceded him, and that they were being entertained in Mrs. Miller's salon by Randolph.

"It's going round at night," said Randolph—"that's what made her sick. She's always going round at night. I shouldn't think she'd want to—it's so plaguy dark. You can't see anything here at night, except when there's a moon! In America there's always a moon!" Mrs. Miller was invisible; she was now, at least, giving her daughter the advantage of her society. It was evident that Daisy was dangerously ill.

Winterbourne went often to ask for news of her, and once he saw Mrs. Miller, who, though deeply alarmed, was—rather to his surprise—perfectly composed, and, as it appeared, a most efficient and judicious nurse. She talked a good deal about Dr. Davis, but Winterbourne paid her the compliment of saying to himself that she was not, after all, such a monstrous goose. "Daisy spoke of you the other day," she said to him. "Half the time she doesn't know what she's saying, but that time I think she did. She gave me a message; she told me to tell you—she told me to tell you that she never was engaged to that handsome Italian. I am sure I am very glad; Mr. Giovanelli hasn't been near us since she was taken ill. I thought he was so much of a gentleman; but I don't call that very polite! A lady told me that he was afraid I was angry with him for taking Daisy round at night. Well, so I am; but I suppose he knows I'm a lady. I would scorn to scold him. Anyway, she says she's not engaged. I don't know why she wanted you to know; but she said to me three times, 'Mind you tell Mr. Winterbourne.' And then she told me to ask if you remembered the time you went to that castle in Switzerland. But I said I wouldn't give any such messages as that. Only, if she is not engaged, I'm sure I'm glad to know it."

But, as Winterbourne had said, it mattered very little. A week after this the poor girl died; it had been a terrible case of the fever. Daisy's grave was in the little Protestant cemetery, in an angle of the wall of the imperial Rome, beneath the cypresses and the thick spring-flowers. Winterbourne stood there beside it, with

10 a number of other mourners—a number larger than the scandal excited by the young lady's career would have led you to expect. Near him stood Giovanelli, who came nearer still before Winterbourne turned away. Giovanelli was very pale; on this occasion he had no flower in his button-hole; he seemed to wish to say something. At last he said, "She was the most beautiful young lady I ever saw, and the most amiable." And then he added in a moment, "and she was the most innocent."

Winterbourne looked at him, and presently repeated

20 his words, "And the most innocent?"

"The most innocent!"

Winterbourne felt sore and angry. "Why the devil," he asked, "did you take her to that fatal place?"

Mr. Giovanelli's urbanity was apparently imperturbable. He looked on the ground a moment, and then he said, "For myself, I had no fear; and she wanted to go."

"That was no reason!" Winterbourne declared.

The subtle Roman again dropped his eyes. "If she had lived, I should have got nothing. She would never have

30 married me, I am sure."

"She would never have married you?"

"For a moment I hoped so. But no, I am sure."

Winterbourne listened to him; he stood staring at the raw protuberance among the April daisies. When he turned away again, Mr. Giovanelli with his light, slow step, had retired.

Winterbourne almost immediately left Rome; but the following summer he again met his aunt, Mrs. Costello, at Vevey. Mrs. Costello was fond of Vevey. In the interval Winterbourne had often thought of Daisy 40 Miller and her mystifying manners. One day he spoke of her to his aunt—said it was on his conscience that he had done her injustice.

"I am sure I don't know," said Mrs. Costello. "How did your injustice affect her?"

"She sent me a message before her death which I didn't understand at the time. But I have understood it since. She would have appreciated one's esteem."

"Is that a modest way," asked Mrs. Costello, "of saying that she would have reciprocated one's affection?" 50

Winterbourne offered no answer to this question; but he presently said, "You were right in that remark that you made last summer. I was booked to make a mistake. I have lived too long in foreign parts."

Nevertheless, he went back to live at Geneva, whence there continue to come the most contradictory accounts of his motives of sojourn: a report that he is "studying" hard—an intimation that he is much interested in a very clever foreign lady.

1878

The Middle Years

"The Middle Years" first appeared in Scribner's Magazine in 1893; it was collected with other stories in Terminations in 1895.

Technically, the story is an interesting example of James' mature mastery of "point of view." Although told in the third person, the narrative is managed, carefully and consistently, from the point of view of a single character. Placing himself at the center of Dencombe's consciousness, the author surveys the scene through Dencombe's—never another's—eyes. The conversation is reported as Dencombe hears it. At no point in the story does the reader know for certain more than Dencombe himself knows. The management is especially ingenious in the opening paragraphs, where Dencombe, upon the basis of the evidence at hand, makes conjectures, tentative and sometimes incorrect, concerning the "group of three persons." The rich potentialities of the restricted point of view were to be more fully realized in the late novels, notably in **The Wings of** the Dove, The Ambassadors, and **The Golden Bowl.**

Like several of James' best stories, "The Middle Years" has for its subject the life of the creative artist in literature. Two points are stressed in the following story: the artist's desire for perfection and the artist's desire for intelligent appreciation.

Dencombe's life has been one of complete devotion to his art. The mastery of his art has been achieved slowly and with great difficulty. He is a perfectionist. Although he reads his latest book with a good deal of pride, it does not completely satisfy him. He makes numerous small revisions of style: "Dencombe was a passionate corrector, a fingerer of style; the last thing he ever arrived at was a form final for himself." Moreover, he looks forward to even better work in the future: "a certain splendid 'last manner,' the very citadel, as it would prove, of his reputation." This characterization of Dencombe is applicable to James himself.

A second point of emphasis is Dencombe's feeling that his work is not rightly understood or appreciated by the reading public. Even Dr. Hugh, the only enthusiastic admirer whom he has chanced to meet, "fails to guess" Dencombe's "intention" in his latest novel. Possibly we are to infer that "poor Dencombe" dies of the sheer lack of appreciation. The autobiographical parallel here, of course, is much less close. Although the story probably reflects the author's disappointment at the failure of his works to win a large audience, James has never been without discerning readers. Moreover, James did not die of frustration; he lived actually to accomplish what Dencombe could only grandly envisage: "the jewels rare, strings of pearls, he would hang between the columns of his temple."

Henry James—caricature by Sir Max Beerbohm from The Academy, *November 26, 1898*

T he April day was soft and bright, and poor Dencombe, happy in the conceit of reasserted strength, stood in the garden of the hotel, comparing, with a deliberation in which, however, there was still something of languor, the attractions of easy strolls. He liked the feeling of the south, so far as you could have it in the north, he liked the sandy cliffs and the clustered pines, he liked even the colorless sea. "Bournemouth as a health resort" had sounded like a mere advertisement, but now he was
10 reconciled to the prosaic. The sociable country postman, passing through the garden, had just given him a small parcel, which he took out with him, leaving the hotel to the right and creeping to a convenient bench that he knew of, a safe recess in the cliff. It looked to the south, to the tinted walls of the Island, and was protected behind by the sloping shoulder of the down. He was tired enough when he reached it, and for a moment he was disappointed; he was better, of course, but better, after all, than what? He should never again, as at one or two great moments of the past be better than himself. The 20 infinite of life had gone, and what was left of the dose was a small glass engraved like a thermometer by the apothecary. He sat and stared at the sea, which appeared

8 **Bournemouth,** on the southern coast of England

The Middle Years 541

all surface and twinkle, far shallower than the spirit of man. It was the abyss of human illusion that was the real, the tideless deep. He held his packet, which had come by book post, unopened on his knee, liking, in the lapse of so many joys (his illness had made him feel his age), to know that it was there, but taking for granted there could be no complete renewal of the pleasure, dear to young experience, of seeing oneself "just out." Dencombe, who had a reputation, had come out too often and knew too well in advance how he should look.

His postponement associated itself vaguely, after a little, with a group of three persons, two ladies and a young man, whom, beneath him, straggling and seemingly silent, he could see move slowly together along the sands. The gentleman had his head bent over a book, and was occasionally brought to a stop by the charm of this volume, which, as Dencombe could perceive even at a distance, had a cover alluringly red. Then his companions, going a little further, waited for him to come up, poking their parasols into the beach, looking around them at the sea and sky, and clearly sensible of the beauty of the day. To these things the young man with the book was still more clearly indifferent; lingering, credulous, absorbed, he was an object of envy to an observer from whose connection with literature all such artlessness had faded. One of the ladies was large and mature; the other had the spareness of comparative youth and of a social situation possibly inferior. The large lady carried back Dencombe's imagination to the age of crinoline; she wore a hat of the shape of a mushroom, decorated with a blue veil, and had the air, in her aggressive amplitude, of clinging to a vanished fashion or even a lost cause. Presently her companion produced from under the folds of a mantle a limp, portable chair which she stiffened out and of which the large lady took possession. This act, and something in the movement of either party, instantly characterized the performers—they performed for Dencombe's recreation—as opulent matron and humble dependent. What, moreover, was the use of being an approved novelist if one couldn't establish a relation between such figures; the clever theory, for instance, that the young man was the son of the opulent matron, and that the humble dependent, the daughter of a clergyman or an officer, nourished a secret passion for him? Was that not visible from the way she stole

behind her protectress to look back at him? back to where he had let himself come to a full stop when his mother sat down to rest. His book was a novel; it had the catch-penny cover, and while the romance of life stood neglected at his side he lost himself in that of the circulating library. He moved mechanically to where the sand was softer, and ended by plumping down in it to finish his chapter at his ease. The humble dependent, discouraged by his remoteness, wandered, with a martyred droop of the head, in another direction, and the exorbitant lady, watching the waves, offered a confused resemblance to a flying machine that had broken down.

When his drama began to fail Dencombe remembered that he had, after all, another pastime. Though such promptitude on the part of the publisher was rare, he was already able to draw from its wrapper his "latest," perhaps his last. The cover of *The Middle Years* was duly meretricious, the smell of the fresh pages the very odor of sanctity; but for the moment he went no further —he had become conscious of a strange alienation. He had forgotten what his book was about. Had the assault of his old ailment, which he had so fallaciously come to Bournemouth to ward off, interposed utter blankness as to what had preceded it? He had finished the revision of proof before quitting London, but his subsequent fortnight in bed had passed the sponge over color. He couldn't have chanted to himself a single sentence, couldn't have turned with curiosity or confidence to any particular page. His subject had already gone from him, leaving scarcely a superstition behind. He uttered a low moan as he breathed the chill of this dark void, so desperately it seemed to represent the completion of a sinister process. The tears filled his mild eyes; something precious had passed away. This was the pang that had been sharpest during the last few years—the sense of ebbing time, of shrinking opportunity; and now he felt not so much that his last chance was going as that it was gone indeed. He had done all that he should ever do, and yet he had not done what he wanted. This was the laceration—that practically his career was over; it was as violent as a rough hand at his throat. He rose from his seat nervously, like a creature hunted by a

---

8 oneself "just out," that is, one's book just published

dread; then he fell back in his weakness and nervously opened his book. It was a single volume; he preferred single volumes and aimed at a rare compression. He began to read, and little by little, in this occupation, he was pacified and reassured. Everything came back to him, but came back with a wonder, came back, above all, with a high and magnificent beauty. He read his own prose, he turned his own leaves, and had, as he sat there with the spring sunshine on the page, an emotion peculiar and intense. His career was over, no doubt, but it was over, after all, with *that*.

He had forgotten during his illness the work of the previous year; but what he had chiefly forgotten was that it was extraordinarily good. He lived once more into his story and was drawn down, as by a siren's hand, to where, in the dim underworld of fiction, the great glazed tank of art, strange, silent subjects float. He recognized his motive and surrendered to his talent. Never, probably, had that talent, such as it was, been so fine. His difficulties were still there, but what was also there, to his perception, though probably, alas! to nobody's else, was the art that in most cases had surmounted them. In his surprised enjoyment of this ability he had a glimpse of a possible reprieve. Surely its force was not spent—there were life and service in it yet. It had not come to him easily, it had been backward and round-about. It was the child of time, the nursling of delay; he had struggled and suffered for it, making sacrifices not to be counted, and now that it was really mature was it to cease to yield, to confess itself brutally beaten? There was an infinite charm for Dencombe in feeling as he had never felt before that diligence *vincit omnia*. The result produced in his little book was somehow a result beyond his conscious intention: it was as if he had planted his genius, had trusted his method, and they had grown up and flowered with this sweetness. If the achievement had been real, however, the process had been manful enough. What he saw so intensely today, what he felt as a nail driven in, was that only now, at the very last, had he come into possession. His development had been abnormally slow, almost grotesquely gradual. He had been hindered and retarded by experience, and for long periods had only groped his way. It had taken too much of his life to produce too little of his art. The art had come, but it had come after everything else. At such a rate a first existence was too

short—long enough only to collect material; so that to fructify, to use the material, one must have a second age, an extension. This extension was what poor Dencombe sighed for. As he turned the last leaves of his volume he murmured: "Ah, for another go! ah, for a better chance!"

The three persons he had observed on the sands had vanished and then reappeared; they had now wandered up a path, an artificial and easy ascent, which led to the top of the cliff. Dencombe's bench was halfway down, on a sheltered ledge, and the large lady, a massive, heterogeneous person, with bold black eyes and kind red cheeks, now took a few moments to rest. She wore dirty gauntlets and immense diamond earrings; at first she looked vulgar, but she contradicted this announcement in an agreeable offhand tone. While her companions stood waiting for her she spread her skirts on the end of Dencombe's seat. The young man had gold spectacles, through which, with his finger still in his red-covered book, he glanced at the volume, bound in the same shade of the same color, lying on the lap of the original occupant of the bench. After an instant Dencombe understood that he was struck with a resemblance, had recognized the gilt stamp on the crimson cloth, was reading *The Middle Years,* and now perceived that somebody else had kept pace with him. The stranger was startled, possibly even a little ruffled, to find that he was not the only person who had been favored with an early copy. The eyes of the two proprietors met for a moment, and Dencombe borrowed amusement from the expression of those of his competitor, those, it might even be inferred, of his admirer. They confessed to some resentment—they seemed to say: "Hang it, has he got it *already?* Of course he's a brute of a reviewer!" Dencombe shuffled his copy out of sight while the opulent matron, rising from her repose, broke out: "I feel already the good of this air!"

"I can't say I do," said the angular lady. "I find myself quite let down."

"I find myself horribly hungry. At what time did you order lunch?" her protectress pursued.

The young person put the question by. "Dr. Hugh always orders it."

---

32 *vincit omnia,* conquers all things

"I ordered nothing today—I'm going to make you diet," said their comrade.

"Then I shall go home and sleep. *Qui dort, dîne!*"

"Can I trust you to Miss Vernham?" asked Dr. Hugh of his elder companion.

"Don't I trust *you?*" she archly inquired.

"Not too much!" Miss Vernham, with her eyes on the ground, permitted herself to declare. "You must come with us at least to the house," she went on, while the personage on whom they appeared to be in attendance began to mount higher. She had got a little out of earshot; nevertheless Miss Vernham became, as far as Dencombe was concerned, less distinctly audible to murmur to the young man: "I don't think you realize all you owe the countess!"

Absently, a moment, Dr. Hugh caused his gold-rimmed spectacles to shine at her.

"Is that the way I strike you? I see—I see!"

"She's awfully good to us," continued Miss Vernham, compelled by her interlocutor's immovability to stand there in spite of his discussion of private matters. Of what use would it have been that Dencombe should be sensitive to shades had he not detected in that immovability a strange influence from the quiet old convalescent in the great tweed cape? Miss Vernham appeared suddenly to become aware of some such connection, for she added in a moment: "If you want to sun yourself here you can come back after you've seen us home."

Dr. Hugh, at this, hesitated, and Dencombe, in spite of a desire to pass for unconscious, risked a covert glance at him. What his eyes met this time, as it happened, was on the part of the young lady a queer stare, naturally vitreous, which made her aspect remind him of some figure (he couldn't name it) in a play or a novel, some sinister governess or tragic old maid. She seemed to scrutinize him, to challenge him, to say, from general spite: "What have you got to do with us?" At the same instant the rich humor of the countess reached them from above: "Come, come, my little lambs, you should follow your old *bergère!*" Miss Vernham turned away at this, pursuing the ascent, and Dr. Hugh, after another mute appeal to Dencombe and a moment's evident demur, deposited his book on the bench, as if to keep his place or even as a sign that he would return, and bounded without difficulty up the rougher part of the cliff.

Equally innocent and infinite are the pleasures of observation and the resources engendered by the habit of analyzing life. It amused poor Dencombe, as he dawdled in his tepid air bath, to think that he was waiting for a revelation of something at the back of a fine young mind. He looked hard at the book on the end of the bench, but he wouldn't have touched it for the world. It served his purpose to have a theory which should not be exposed to refutation. He already felt better of his melancholy; he had, according to his old formula, put his head at the window. A passing countess could draw off the fancy when, like the elder of the ladies who had just retreated, she was as obvious as the giantess of a caravan. It was indeed general views that were terrible; short ones, contrary to an opinion sometimes expressed, were the refuge, were the remedy. Dr. Hugh couldn't possibly be anything but a reviewer who had understandings for early copies with publishers or with newspapers. He reappeared in a quarter of an hour, with visible relief at finding Dencombe on the spot, and the gleam of white teeth in an embarrassed but generous smile. He was perceptibly disappointed at the eclipse of the other copy of the book; it was a pretext the less for speaking to the stranger. But he spoke notwithstanding; he held up his own copy and broke out pleadingly:

"*Do* say, if you have occasion to speak of it, that it's the best thing he has done yet!"

Dencombe responded with a laugh: "Done yet" was so amusing to him, made such a grand avenue of the future. Better still, the young man took *him* for a reviewer. He pulled out *The Middle Years* from under his cape, but instinctively concealed any telltale look of fatherhood. This was partly because a person was always a fool for calling attention to his work. "Is that what you're going to say yourself?" he inquired of his visitor.

"I'm not quite sure I shall write anything. I don't as a regular thing—I enjoy in peace. But it's awfully fine."

Dencombe debated a moment. If his interlocutor had begun to abuse him he would have confessed on the spot to his identity, but there was no harm in drawing him on a little to praise. He drew him on with such success that in a few moments his new acquaintance, seated by

3 *Qui dort, dîne!* Sleeping is as good as eating • 41 **bergère,** shepherdess

his side, was confessing candidly that Dencombe's novels were the only ones he could read a second time. He had come the day before from London, where a friend of his, a journalist, had lent him his copy of the last—the copy sent to the office of the journal and already the subject of a "notice" which, as was pretended there (but one had to allow for "swagger"), it had taken a full quarter of an hour to prepare. He intimated that he was ashamed for his friend, and in the case of a work demanding and repaying study, of such inferior manners; and, with his fresh appreciation and inexplicable wish to express it, he speedily became for poor Dencombe a remarkable, a delightful apparition. Chance had brought the weary man of letters face to face with the greatest admirer in the new generation whom it was supposable he possessed. The admirer, in truth, was mystifying, so rare a case was it to find a bristling young doctor—he looked like a German physiologist—enamored of literary form. It was an accident, but happier than most accidents, so that Dencombe, exhilarated as well as confounded, spent half an hour in making his visitor talk while he kept himself quiet. He explained his premature possession of *The Middle Years* by an allusion to the friendship of the publisher, who, knowing he was at Bournemouth for his health, had paid him this graceful attention. He admitted that he had been ill, for Dr. Hugh would infallibly have guessed it; he even went so far as to wonder whether he mightn't look for some hygienic "tip" from a personage combining so bright an enthusiasm with a presumable knowledge of the remedies now in vogue. It would shake his faith a little perhaps to have to take a doctor seriously who could take *him* so seriously, but he enjoyed this gushing modern youth, and he felt with an acute pang that there would still be work to do in a world in which such odd combinations were presented. It was not true, what he had tried for renunciation's sake to believe, that all the combinations were exhausted. They were not, they were not—they were infinite; the exhaustion was in the miserable artist.

Dr. Hugh was an ardent physiologist, saturated with the spirit of the age—in other words he had just taken his degree; but he was independent and various, he talked like a man who would have preferred to love literature best. He would fain have made fine phrases, but nature had denied him the trick. Some of the finest in *The Middle Years* had struck him inordinately, and he took the liberty of reading them to Dencombe in support of his plea. He grew vivid, in the balmy air, to his companion, for whose deep refreshment he seemed to have been sent; and was particularly ingenuous in describing how recently he had become acquainted, and how instantly infatuated, with the only man who had put flesh between the ribs of an art that was starving on superstitions. He had not yet written to him—he was deterred by a sentiment of respect. Dencombe at this moment felicitated himself more than ever on having never answered the photographers. His visitor's attitude promised him a luxury of intercourse, but he surmised that a certain security in it, for Dr. Hugh, would depend not a little on the countess. He learned without delay with what variety of countess they were concerned, as well as the nature of the tie that united the curious trio. The large lady, an Englishwoman by birth and the daughter of a celebrated baritone, whose taste, without his talent, she had inherited, was the widow of a French nobleman and mistress of all that remained of the handsome fortune, the fruit of her father's earnings, that had constituted her dower. Miss Vernham, an odd creature but an accomplished pianist, was attached to her person at a salary. The countess was generous, independent, eccentric; she traveled with her minstrel and her medical man. Ignorant and passionate, she had nevertheless moments in which she was almost irresistible. Dencombe saw her sit for her portait in Dr. Hugh's free sketch, and felt the picture of his young friend's relation to her frame itself in his mind. This young friend, for a representative of the new psychology, was himself easily hypnotized, and if he became abnormally communicative it was only a sign of his real subjection. Dencombe did accordingly what he wanted with him, even without being known as Dencombe.

Taken ill on a journey in Switzerland the countess had picked him up at an hotel, and the accident of his happening to please her had made her offer him, with her imperious liberality, terms that couldn't fail to dazzle a practitioner without patients and whose resources had been drained dry by his studies. It was not the way he would have elected to spend his time, but it was time that would pass quickly, and meanwhile she was wonderfully kind. She exacted perpetual attention, but it was impossible not to like her. He gave details about his queer patient, a "type" if there ever was one, who had in connection with her flushed obesity and in addition to the morbid strain of a violent and aimless will a grave organic disorder; but he came back to his loved novelist, whom he was so good as to pronounce more essentially a poet than many of those who went in for verse, with a zeal excited, as all his indiscretion had been excited, by the happy chance of Dencombe's sympathy and the coincidence of their occupation. Dencombe had confessed to a slight personal acquaintance with the author of *The Middle Years,* but had not felt himself as ready as he could have wished when his companion, who had never yet encountered a being so privileged, began to be eager for particulars. He even thought that Dr. Hugh's eye at that moment emitted a glimmer of suspicion. But the young man was too inflamed to be shrewd, and repeatedly caught up the book to exclaim: "Did you notice this?" or "Weren't you immensely struck with that?" "There's a beautiful passage toward the end," he broke out; and again he laid his hand upon the volume. As he turned the pages he came upon something else, while Dencombe saw him suddenly change color. He had taken up, as it lay on the bench, Dencombe's copy instead of his own, and his neighbor immediately guessed the reason of his start. Dr. Hugh looked grave an instant; then he said: "I see you've been altering the text!" Dencombe was a passionate corrector, a fingerer of style; the last thing he ever arrived at was a form final for himself. His ideal would have been to publish secretly, and then, on the published text, treat himself to the terrified revise, sacrificing always a first edition and beginning for posterity and even for the collectors, poor dears, with a second. This morning, in *The Middle Years,* his pencil had pricked a dozen lights. He was amused at the effect of the young man's reproach; for an instant it made him change color. He stammered, at any rate, ambiguously; then, through a blur of ebbing consciousness, saw Dr. Hugh's mystified eyes. He only had time to feel he was about to be ill again—that emotion, excitement, fatigue, the heat of the sun, the solicitation of the air, had combined to play him a trick, before, stretching out a hand to his visitor with a plaintive cry, he lost his senses altogether.

Later he knew that he had fainted and that Dr. Hugh had got him home in a bath chair, the conductor of which, prowling within hail for custom, had happened to remember seeing him in the garden of the hotel. He had recovered his perception in the transit, and had, in bed, that afternoon, a vague recollection of Dr. Hugh's young face, as they went together, bent over him in a comforting laugh and expressive of something more than a suspicion of his identity. That identity was ineffaceable now, and all the more that he was disappointed, disgusted. He had been rash, been stupid, had gone out too soon, stayed out too long. He oughtn't to have exposed himself to strangers, he ought to have taken his servant. He felt as if he had fallen into a hole too deep to descry any little patch of heaven. He was confused about the time that had elapsed—he pieced the fragments together. He had seen his doctor, the real one, the one who had treated him from the first and who had again been very kind. His servant was in and out on tiptoe, looking very wise after the fact. He said more than once something about the sharp young gentleman. The rest was vagueness, in so far as it wasn't despair. The vagueness, however, justified itself by dreams, dozing anxieties from which he finally emerged to the consciousness of a dark room and a shaded candle.

"You'll be all right again—I know all about you now," said a voice near him that he knew to be young. Then his meeting with Dr. Hugh came back. He was too discouraged to joke about it yet, but he was able to perceive, after a little, that the interest of it was intense for his visitor. "Of course I can't attend you professionally—you've got your own man, with whom I've talked and who's excellent," Dr. Hugh went on. "But you must let me come to see you as a good friend. I've just looked in before going to bed. You're doing beautifully, but it's a good job I was with you on the cliff. I shall come in early tomorrow. I want to do something for you. I want to do everything. You've done a tremendous lot for me." The young man held his hand, hanging over him, and poor Dencombe, weakly aware of this living pressure, simply lay there and accepted his devotion. He couldn't do anything less—he needed help too much.

The idea of the help he needed was very present to him that night, which he spent in a lucid stillness, an intensity of thought that constituted a reaction from his hours of stupor. He was lost, he was lost—he was lost if he couldn't be saved. He was not afraid of suffering,

of death; he was not even in love with life; but he had
had a deep demonstration of desire. It came over him
in the long, quiet hours that only with *The Middle Years*
had he taken his flight; only on that day, visited by
soundless processions, had he recognized his kingdom.
He had had a revelation of his range. What he dreaded
was the idea that his reputation should stand on the
unfinished. It was not with his past but with his future
that it should properly be concerned. Illness and age
rose before him like specters with pitiless eyes: how was
he to bribe such fates to give him the second chance?
He had had the one chance that all men have—he had
had the chance of life. He went to sleep again very late,
and when he awoke Dr. Hugh was sitting by his head.
There was already, by this time, something beautifully
familiar in him.

"Don't think I've turned out your physician," he said;
"I'm acting with his consent. He has been here and seen
you. Somehow he seems to trust me. I told him how
we happened to come together yesterday, and he recognizes that I've a peculiar right."

Dencombe looked at him with a calculating earnestness. "How have you squared the countess?"

The young man blushed a little, but he laughed.
"Oh, never mind the countess!"

"You told me she was very exacting."

Dr. Hugh was silent a moment. "So she is."

"And Miss Vernham's an *intrigante*."

"How do you know that?"

"I know everything. One *has* to, to write decently!"

"I think she's mad," said limpid Dr. Hugh.

"Well, don't quarrel with the countess—she's a present
help to you."

"I don't quarrel," Dr. Hugh replied. "But I don't get
on with silly women." Presently he added: "You seem
very much alone."

"That often happens at my age. I've outlived, I've lost
by the way."

Dr. Hugh hesitated; then surmounting a soft scruple:
"Whom have you lost?"

"Everyone."

"Ah, no!" the young man murmured, laying a hand
on his arm.

"I once had a wife—I once had a son. My wife died
when my child was born, and my boy, at school, was
carried off by typhoid."

"I wish I'd been there!" said Dr. Hugh simply.

"Well—if you're here!" Dencombe answered, with a
smile that, in spite of dimness, showed how much he
liked to be sure of his companion's whereabouts.

"You talk strangely of your age. You're not old."

"Hypocrite—so early!"

"I speak physiologically."

"That's the way I've been speaking for the last five
years, and it's exactly what I've been saying to myself.
It isn't till we *are* old that we begin to tell ourselves
we're not!"

"Yet I know I myself am young," Dr. Hugh declared.

"Not so well as I!" laughed his patient, whose visitor
indeed would have established the truth in question
by the honesty with which he changed the point of view,
remarking that it must be one of the charms of age—at
any rate in the case of high distinction—to feel that one
has labored and achieved. Dr. Hugh employed the common phrase about earning one's rest, and it made poor
Dencombe, for an instant, almost angry. He recovered
himself, however, to explain, lucidly enough, that if he,
ungraciously, knew nothing of such a balm, it was doubtless because he had wasted inestimable years. He had
followed Literature from the first, but he had taken a
lifetime to get alongside of her. Only today, at last, had
he begun to *see,* so that what he had hitherto done was
a movement without a direction. He had ripened too
late, and was so clumsily constituted that he had had
to teach himself by mistakes.

"I prefer your flowers, then, to other people's fruit,
and your mistakes to other people's successes," said gallant Dr. Hugh. "It's for your mistakes I admire you."

"You're happy—you don't know," Dencombe answered.

Looking at his watch the young man had got up; he
named the hour of the afternoon at which he would
return. Dencombe warned him against committing himself too deeply, and expressed again all his dread of
making him neglect the countess—perhaps incur her
displeasure.

"I want to be like you—I want to learn by mistakes!"
Dr. Hugh laughed.

"Take care you don't make too grave a one! But do
come back," Dencombe added, with the glimmer of a
new idea.

"You should have had more vanity!" Dr. Hugh spoke

as if he knew the exact amount required to make a man of letters normal.

"No, no—I only should have had more time. I want another go."

"Another go?"

"I want an extension."

"An extension?" Again Dr. Hugh repeated Dencombe's words, with which he seemed to have been struck.

"Don't you know?—I want to what they call 'live.'"

The young man, for good-by, had taken his hand, which closed with a certain force. They looked at each other hard a moment. "You *will* live," said Dr. Hugh.

"Don't be superficial. It's too serious!"

"You *shall* live!" Dencombe's visitor declared, turning pale.

"Ah, that's better!" And as he retired the invalid, with a troubled laugh, sank gratefully back.

All that day and all the following night he wondered if it mightn't be arranged. His doctor came again, his servant was attentive, but it was to his confident young friend that he found himself mentally appealing. His collapse on the cliff was plausibly explained, and his liberation, on a better basis, promised for the morrow; meanwhile, however, the intensity of his meditations kept him tranquil and made him indifferent. The idea that occupied him was none the less absorbing because it was a morbid fancy. Here was a clever son of the age, ingenious and ardent, who happened to have set him up for connoisseurs to worship. This servant of his altar had all the new learning in science and all the old reverence in faith; wouldn't he therefore put his knowledge at the disposal of his sympathy, his craft at the disposal of his love? Couldn't he be trusted to invent a remedy for a poor artist to whose art he had paid a tribute? If he couldn't, the alternative was hard: Dencombe would have to surrender to silence, unvindicated and undivined. The rest of the day and all the next he toyed in secret with this sweet futility. Who would work the miracle for him but the young man who could combine such lucidity with such passion? He thought of the fairy tales of science, and charmed himself into forgetting that he looked for a magic that was not of this world. Dr. Hugh was an apparition, and that placed him above the law. He came and went while his patient, who sat up, followed him with supplicating eyes. The interest

of knowing the great author had made the young man begin *The Middle Years* afresh, and would help him to find a deeper meaning in its pages. Dencombe had told him what he "tried for"; with all his intelligence, on a first perusal, Dr. Hugh had failed to guess it. The baffled celebrity wondered then who in the world *would* guess it; he was amused once more at the fine, full way with which an intention could be missed. Yet he wouldn't rail at the general mind today—consoling as that ever had been: the revelation of his own slowness had seemed to make all stupidity sacred.

Dr. Hugh, after a little, was visibly worried, confessing, on inquiry, to a source of embarrassment at home. "Stick to the countess—don't mind me," Dencombe said repeatedly; for his companion was frank enough about the large lady's attitude. She was so jealous that she had fallen ill—she resented such a breach of allegiance. She paid so much for his fidelity that she must have it all; she refused him the right to other sympathies, charged him with scheming to make her die alone, for it was needless to point out how little Miss Vernham was a resource in trouble. When Dr. Hugh mentioned that the countess would already have left Bournemouth if he hadn't kept her in bed, poor Dencombe held his arm tighter and said with decision: "Take her straight away." They had gone out together, walking back to the sheltered nook in which, the other day, they had met. The young man, who had given his companion a personal support, declared with emphasis that his conscience was clear—he could ride two horses at once. Didn't he dream, for his future, of a time when he should have to ride five hundred? Longing equally for virtue, Dencombe replied that in that golden age no patient would pretend to have contracted with him for his whole attention. On the part of the countess was not such an avidity lawful? Dr. Hugh denied it, said there was no contract, but only a free understanding, and that a sordid servitude was impossible to a generous spirit; he liked moreover to talk about art, and that was the subject on which, this time, as they sat together on the sunny bench, he tried most to engage the author of *The Middle Years*. Dencombe, soaring again a little on the weak wings of convalescence and still haunted by that happy notion of an organized rescue, found another strain of eloquence to plead the cause of a certain splendid "last manner," the very citadel, as it would prove, of his reputation, the stronghold into which his real treasure would be gathered. While his listener gave up the morning and the great, still sea appeared to wait, he had a wonderful explanatory hour. Even for himself he was inspired as he told of what his treasure would consist—the precious metals he would dig from the mine, the jewels rare, strings of pearls, he would hang between the columns of his temple. He was wonderful for himself, so thick his convictions crowded; but he was still more wonderful for Dr. Hugh, who assured him, none the less, that the very pages he had just published were already encrusted with gems. The young man, however, panted for the combinations to come, and, before the face of the beautiful day renewed to Dencombe his guarantee that his profession would hold itself responsible for such a life. Then he suddenly clapped his hand upon his watch pocket and asked leave to absent himself for half an hour. Dencombe waited there for his return, but was at last recalled to the actual by the fall of a shadow across the ground. The shadow darkened into that of Miss Vernham, the young lady in attendance on the countess; whom Dencombe, recognizing her, perceived so clearly to have come to speak to him that he rose from his bench to acknowledge the civility. Miss Vernham indeed proved not particularly civil; she looked strangely agitated, and her type was now unmistakable.

"Excuse me if I inquire," she said, "whether it's too much to hope that you may be induced to leave Dr. Hugh alone." Then, before Dencombe, greatly disconcerted, could protest: "You ought to be informed that you stand in his light; that you may do him a terrible injury."

"Do you mean by causing the countess to dispense with his services?"

"By causing her to disinherit him." Dencombe stared at this, and Miss Vernham pursued, in the gratification of seeing she could produce an impression: "It has depended on himself to come into something very handsome. He has had a magnificent prospect, but I think you've succeeded in spoiling it."

"Not intentionally, I assure you. Is there no hope that the accident may be repaired?" Dencombe asked.

"She was ready to do anything for him. She takes great fancies, she lets herself go—it's her way. She has no relations, she's free to dispose of her money, and she's very ill."

"I'm very sorry to hear it," Dencombe stammered.

"Wouldn't it be possible for you to leave Bournemouth? That's what I've come to ask of you."

Poor Dencombe sank down on his bench. "I'm very ill myself, but I'll try!"

Miss Vernham still stood there with her colorless eyes and the brutality of her good conscience. "Before it's too late, please!" she said; and with this she turned her back, in order, quickly, as if it had been a business to which she could spare but a precious moment, to pass out of his sight.

Oh, yes! after this Dencombe was certainly very ill. Miss Vernham had upset him with her rough, fierce news; it was the sharpest shock to him to discover what was at stake for a penniless young man of fine parts. He sat trembling on his bench, staring at the waste of waters, feeling sick with the directness of the blow. He was indeed too weak, too unsteady, too alarmed; but he would make the effort to get away, for he couldn't accept the guilt of interference, and his honor was really involved. He would hobble home, at any rate, and then he would think what was to be done. He made his way back to the hotel and, as he went, had a characteristic vision of Miss Vernham's great motive. The countess hated women, of course; Dencombe was lucid about that; so the hungry pianist had no personal hopes and could only console herself with the bold conception of helping Dr. Hugh in order either to marry him after he should get his money or to induce him to recognize her title to compensation and buy her off. If she had befriended him at a fruitful crisis he would really, as a man of delicacy, and she knew what to think of that point, have to reckon with her.

At the hotel Dencombe's servant insisted on his going back to bed. The invalid had talked about catching a train and had begun with orders to pack; after which his humming nerves had yielded to a sense of sickness. He consented to see his physician, who immediately was sent for, but he wished it to be understood that his door was irrevocably closed to Dr. Hugh. He had his plan, which was so fine that he rejoiced in it after getting back to bed. Dr. Hugh, suddenly finding himself snubbed without mercy, would, in natural disgust and to the joy of Miss Vernham, renew his allegiance to the countess. When his physician arrived Dencombe learned that he was feverish and that this was very wrong; he was to cultivate calmness and try, if possible, not to think. For the rest of the day he wooed stupidity; but there was an ache that kept him sentient, the probable sacrifice of his "extension," the limit of his course. His medical adviser was anything but pleased; his successive relapses were ominous. He charged this personage to put out a strong hand and take Dr. Hugh off his mind—it would contribute so much to his being quiet. The agitating name, in his room, was not mentioned again, but his security was a smothered fear, and it was not confirmed by the receipt, at ten o'clock that evening, of a telegram which his servant opened and read for him and to which, with an address in London, the signature of Miss Vernham was attached. "Beseech you to use all influence to make our friend join us here in the morning. Countess much the worse for dreadful journey, but everything may still be saved." The two ladies had gathered themselves up and had been capable in the afternoon of a spiteful revolution. They had started for the capital, and if the elder one, as Miss Vernham had announced, was very ill, she had wished to make it clear that she was proportionately reckless. Poor Dencombe, who was not reckless, and who only desired that everything should indeed be "saved," sent this missive straight off to the young man's lodging and had on the morrow the pleasure of knowing that he had quitted Bournemouth by an early train.

Two days later he pressed in with a copy of a literary journal in his hand. He had returned because he was anxious and for the pleasure of flourishing the great review of *The Middle Years*. Here at least was something adequate—it rose to the occasion; it was an acclamation, a reparation, a critical attempt to place the author in the niche he had fairly won. Dencombe accepted and submitted; he made neither objection nor inquiry, for old complications had returned and he had had two atrocious days. He was convinced not only that he should never again leave his bed, so that his young friend might pardonably remain, but that the demand he should make on the patience of beholders would be very moderate indeed. Dr. Hugh had been to town, and he tried to find in his eyes some confession that the countess was pacified and his legacy clinched; but all he could see there was the light of his juvenile joy in two or three of the phrases of the newspaper. Dencombe couldn't read them, but when his visitor had insisted on repeating them more than once he was able to shake an unintoxi-

cated head. "Ah, no! but they would have been true of what I *could* have done!"

"What people 'could have done' is mainly what they've in fact done," Dr. Hugh contended.

"Mainly, yes; but I've been an idiot!" said Dencombe.

Dr. Hugh did remain; the end was coming fast. Two days later Dencombe observed to him, by way of the feeblest of jokes, that there would now be no question whatever of a second chance. At this the young man stared; then he exclaimed: "Why, it has come to pass—it has come to pass! The second chance has been the public's—the chance to find the point of view, to pick up the pearl!"

"Oh, the pearl!" poor Dencombe uneasily sighed. A smile as cold as a winter sunset flickered on his drawn lips as he added: "The pearl is the unwritten—the pearl is the unalloyed, the *rest,* the lost!"

From that moment he was less and less present, heedless to all appearance of what went on around him. His disease was definitely mortal, of an action as relentless, after the short arrest that had enabled him to fall in with Dr. Hugh, as a leak in a great ship. Sinking steadily, though this visitor, a man of rare resources, now cordially approved by his physician, showed endless art in guarding him from pain, poor Dencombe kept no reckoning of favor or neglect, betrayed no symptom of regret or speculation. Yet toward the last he gave a sign of having noticed that for two days Dr. Hugh had not been in his room, a sign that consisted of his suddenly opening his eyes to ask of him if he had spent the interval with the countess.

"The countess is dead," said Dr. Hugh. "I knew that in a particular contingency she wouldn't resist. I went to her grave."

Dencombe's eyes opened wider. "She left you 'something handsome'?"

The young man gave a laugh almost too light for a chamber of woe. "Never a penny! She roundly cursed me."

"Cursed you?" Dencombe murmured.

"For giving her up. I gave her up for *you.* I had to choose," his companion explained.

"You chose to let a fortune go?"

"I chose to accept, whatever they might be, the consequences of my infatuation," smiled Dr. Hugh. Then, as a larger pleasantry: "A fortune be hanged! It's your own fault if I can't get your things out of my head."

The immediate tribute to his humor was a long, bewildered moan; after which, for many hours, many days, Dencombe lay motionless and absent. A response so absolute, such a glimpse of a definite result, and such a sense of credit worked together in his mind and producing a strange commotion, slowly altered and transfigured his despair. The sense of cold submersion left him—he seemed to float without an effort. The incident was extraordinary as evidence, and it shed an intenser light. At the last he signed to Dr. Hugh to listen, and, when he was down on his knees by the pillow, brought him very near.

"You've made me think it all a delusion."

"Not your glory, my dear friend," stammered the young man.

"Not my glory—what there is of it! It *is* glory—to have been tested, to have had our little quality, and cast our little spell. The thing is to have made somebody care. You happen to be crazy, of course, but that doesn't affect the law."

"You're a great success!" said Dr. Hugh, putting into his young voice the ring of a marriage bell.

Dencombe lay taking this in; then he gathered strength to speak once more. "A second chance—*that's* the delusion. There never was to be but one. We work in the dark—we do what we can—we give what we have. Our doubt is our passion, and our passion is our task. The rest is the madness of art."

"If you've doubted, if you've despaired, you've always 'done' it," his visitor subtly argued.

"We've done something or other," Dencombe conceded.

"Something or other is everything. It's the feasible. It's *you!*"

"Comforter!" poor Dencombe ironically sighed.

"But it's true," insisted his friend.

"It's true. It's frustration that doesn't count."

"Frustration's only life," said Dr. Hugh.

"Yes, it's what passes." Poor Dencombe was barely audible, but he had marked with the words the virtual end of his first and only chance.

1895

The Beast in the Jungle

"The Beast in the Jungle" has been justly celebrated as not only one of James' best works but one of the most distinguished short novels in English.

John Marcher had had from early youth—he told his friend and confidante, May Bartram—"the sense of being kept for something rare and strange, possibly prodigious and terrible, that was sooner or later to happen" to him. His life became one of self-centered expectation; he was constantly on the watch for this rare happening, and May Bartram watched with him. The lady, quite naturally, had her own idea of what Marcher's fate would be: namely, his falling in love with her. But she was disappointed, for the only love of which Marcher proved to be capable was self-love.

The story is concerned with a quiet, insidious selfishness which is fatal to the life of the soul. Marcher cultivated an "inner detachment," he watched his own "state of mind." He is symbolical of what Allen Tate (in another connection—see his "Narcissus as Narcissus," p. 873) has called, variously and accurately, "the remarkable self-consciousness of our age," "the modern squirrel cage of our sensibility," "the locked-in ego," "the cut-offness of the modern 'intellectual' man from the world." James' story is indeed an anticipation in subject and theme of Eliot's "Prufrock," Tate's "Ode to the Confederate Dead," and other classics of our time.

James' method moves between narrative and drama. Much of the story is narrative, touched lightly or not at all by the dramatic. The author reserves his greatest intensity for two scenes, where the action is powerfully dramatized: the scene in May Bartram's parlor on an April afternoon when May, aging and ill but still lovely, offered herself to Marcher as she stood before him "all draped and all soft, in her fairness and slimness," and Marcher remained unresponsive, unaware; and the scene in the cemetery where the chance encounter with the ravaged countenance of a stranger showed him "what passion meant," what sorrow over the death of a woman meant when the woman "had been loved for herself." Marcher recognized too late his tragic error, stated explicitly by the author as follows: "The escape would have been to love her; then, **then** he would have lived. **She** had lived—who could say now with what passion?—since she had loved him for himself; whereas he had never thought of her (ah how it hugely glared at him!) but in the chill of his egotism and the light of her use."

The story is told from the restricted point of view—the point of view of Marcher. This method is much employed by James, especially in his later work, but its use here involves a special difficulty, for whereas James' center of revelation is ordinarily a person of large insight, Marcher's insight is very limited. The perception of a Dencombe (in "The Middle Years") or a Strether (in **The Ambassadors**) is large enough to meet the requirements of truth. But it is necessary for the author to go beyond the perception of Marcher, who—until the very end—saw so little of the truth of his situation. The way in which James manages to use his central intelligence and at the same time convey impressions of which this intelligence is unaware is a triumph of technical skill.

The use of the stranger for the purpose of catastrophe (the climax is the scene in section IV where Marcher misses his last chance) may be objected to as fortuitous and unprepared-for. The author might plead, however, classical precedent, for the stranger is truly a **deus ex machina:** an agent from a world outside Marcher's own is necessary to shock him into awareness.

What is the meaning of the central symbol? "Something or other lay in wait for him," we are told, "amid the twists and the turns of the months and the years, like a crouching beast in the jungle." The beast had sprung on that April afternoon (Marcher eventually comes to realize) as May "hopelessly turned from him." At the very end, he sees, in a kind of hallucination, the beast "rise, huge and hideous, for the leap that was to settle him." The beast, then, may be symbolical of the insidious, monstrous egotism which ironically robs Marcher's life of meaning and makes of him "the man, to whom nothing on earth was to have happened."

W hat determined the speech that startled him in the course of their encounter scarcely matters, being probably but some words spoken by himself quite without intention—spoken as they lingered and slowly moved together after their renewal of acquaintance. He had been conveyed by friends an hour or two before to the house at which she was staying; the party of visitors at the other house, of whom he was one, and thanks to whom it was his theory, as always, that he was lost in the crowd, had been invited over to luncheon. There had 10 been after luncheon much dispersal, all in the interest of the original motive, a view of Weatherend itself and the fine things, intrinsic features, pictures, heirlooms, treasures of all the arts, that made the place almost famous; and the great rooms were so numerous that guests could wander at their will, hang back from the principal group and in cases where they took such matters with the last seriousness give themselves up to mysterious appreciations and measurements. There were persons to be observed, singly or in couples, bending 20 toward objects in out-of-the-way corners with their hands on their knees and their heads nodding quite as with the emphasis of an excited sense of smell. When they were two they either mingled their sounds of ecstasy or melted into silences of even deeper import, so that there were aspects of the occasion that gave it for Marcher much the air of the "look round," previous to a sale highly advertised, that excites or quenches, as may be, the dream of acquisition. The dream of acquisition at Weatherend would have had to be wild indeed, 30 and John Marcher found himself, among such suggestions, disconcerted almost equally by the presence of those who knew too much and by that of those who knew nothing. The great rooms caused so much poetry and history to press upon him that he needed some straying apart to feel in a proper relation with them, though this impulse was not, as happened, like the gloating of some of his companions, to be compared to the movements of a dog sniffing a cupboard. It had an issue promptly enough in a direction that was not to 40 have been calculated.

It led, briefly, in the course of the October afternoon,

to his closer meeting with May Bartram, whose face, a reminder, yet not quite a remembrance, as they sat much separated at a very long table, had begun merely by troubling him rather pleasantly. It affected him as the sequel of something of which he had lost the beginning. He knew it, and for the time quite welcomed it, as a continuation, but didn't know what it continued, which was an interest or an amusement the greater as he was also somehow aware—yet without a direct sign from her —that the young woman herself hadn't lost the thread. She hadn't lost it, but she wouldn't give it back to him, he saw, without some putting forth of his hand for it; and he not only saw that, but saw several things more, things odd enough in the light of the fact that at the moment some accident of grouping brought them face to face he was still merely fumbling with the idea that any contact between them in the past would have had no importance. If it had had no importance he scarcely knew why his actual impression of her should so seem to have so much; the answer to which, however, was that in such a life as they all appeared to be leading for the moment one could but take things as they came. He was satisfied, without in the least being able to say why, that this young lady might roughly have ranked in the house as a poor relation; satisfied also that she was not there on a brief visit, but was more or less a part of the establishment—almost a working, a remunerated part. Didn't she enjoy at periods a protection that she paid for by helping, among other services, to show the place and explain it, deal with the tiresome people, answer questions about the dates of the building, the styles of the furniture, the authorship of the pictures, the favourite haunts of the ghost? It wasn't that she looked as if you could have given her shillings—it was impossible to look less so. Yet when she finally drifted toward him, distinctly handsome, though ever so much older—older than when he had seen her before—it might have been as an effect of her guessing that he had, within the couple of hours, devoted more imagination to her than to all the others put together, and had thereby penetrated to a kind of truth that the others were too stupid for. She *was* there on harder terms than any one; she was there as a consequence of things suffered, one way and another, in the interval of years; and she remembered him very much as she was remembered—only a good deal better.

By the time they at last thus came to speech they were alone in one of the rooms—remarkable for a fine portrait over the chimney-place—out of which their friends had passed, and the charm of it was that even before they had spoken they had practically arranged with each other to stay behind for talk. The charm, happily, was in other things too—partly in there being scarce a spot at Weatherend without something to stay behind for. It was in the way the autumn day looked into the high windows as it waned; the way the red light, breaking at the close from under a low sombre sky, reached out in a long shaft and played over old wainscots, old tapestry, old gold, old colour. It was most of all perhaps in the way she came to him as if, since she had been turned on to deal with the simpler sort, he might, should he choose to keep the whole thing down, just take her mild attention for a part of her general business. As soon as he heard her voice, however, the gap was filled up and the missing link supplied; the slight irony he divined in her attitude lost its advantage. He almost jumped at it to get there before her. "I met you years and years ago in Rome. I remember all about it." She confessed to disappointment —she had been so sure he didn't; and to prove how well he did he began to pour forth the particular recollections that popped up as he called for them. Her face and her voice, all at his service now, worked the miracle—the impression operating like the torch of a lamplighter who touches into flame, one by one, a long row of gas-jets. Marcher flattered himself the illumination was brilliant, yet he was really still more pleased on her showing him, with amusement, that in his haste to make everything right he had got most things rather wrong. It hadn't been at Rome—it had been at Naples; and it hadn't been eight years before—it had been more nearly ten. She hadn't been, either, with her uncle and aunt, but with her mother and her brother; in addition to which it was not with the Pembles *he* had been, but with the Boyers, coming down in their company from Rome—a point on which she insisted, a little to his confusion, and as to which she had her evidence in hand. The Boyers she had known, but didn't know the Pembles, though she had heard of them, and it was the people he was with who had made them acquainted. The incident of the thunderstorm that had raged round them with such violence as to drive them for refuge into an excavation—this incident had not occurred at the Palace of the Cæsars, but at Pompeii, on an occasion when they had been present there at an important find.

The Beast in the Jungle   **553**

He accepted her amendments, he enjoyed her corrections, though the moral of them was, she pointed out, that he *really* didn't remember the least thing about her; and he only felt it as a drawback that when all was made strictly historic there didn't appear much of anything left. They lingered together still, she neglecting her office —for from the moment he was so clever she had no proper right to him—and both neglecting the house, just waiting as to see if a memory or two more wouldn't again breathe on them. It hadn't taken them many minutes, after all, to put down on the table, like the cards of a pack, those that constituted their respective hands; only what came out was that the pack was unfortunately not perfect—that the past, invoked, invited, encouraged, could give them, naturally, no more than it had. It had made them anciently meet—her at twenty, him at twenty-five; but nothing was so strange, they seemed to say to each other, as that, while so occupied, it hadn't done a little more for them. They looked at each other as with the feeling of an occasion missed; the present would have been so much better if the other, in the far distance, in the foreign land, hadn't been so stupidly meagre. There weren't apparently, all counted, more than a dozen little old things that had succeeded in coming to pass between them; trivialities of youth, simplicities of freshness, stupidities of ignorance, small possible germs, but too deeply buried—too deeply (didn't it seem?) to sprout after so many years. Marcher could only feel he ought to have rendered her some service—saved her from a capsized boat in the Bay or at least recovered her dressing-bag, filched from her cab in the streets of Naples by a lazzarone with a stiletto. Or it would have been nice if he could have been taken with fever all alone at his hotel, and she could have come to look after him, to write to his people, to drive him out in convalescence. *Then* they would be in possession of the something or other that their actual show seemed to lack. It yet somehow presented itself, this show, as too good to be spoiled; so that they were reduced for a few minutes more to wondering a little helplessly why—since they seemed to know a certain number of the same people—their reunion had been so long averted. They didn't use that name for it, but their delay from minute to minute to join the others was a kind of confession that they didn't quite want it to be a failure. Their attempted supposition of reasons for their not having met but showed how little they knew of each other. There came in fact a moment when Marcher felt a positive pang. It was vain to pretend she was an old friend, for all the communities were wanting, in spite of which it was as an old friend that he saw she would have suited him. He had new ones enough—was surrounded with them for instance on the stage of the other house—as a new one he probably wouldn't have so much as noticed her. He would have liked to invent something, get her to make-believe with him that some passage of a romantic or critical kind *had* originally occurred. He was really almost reaching out in imagination—as against time—for something that would do, and saying to himself that if it didn't come this sketch of a fresh start would show for quite awkwardly bungled. They would separate, and now for no second or no third chance. They would have tried and not succeeded. Then it was, just at the turn, as he afterwards made it out to himself, that, everything else failing, she herself decided to take up the case and, as it were, save the situation. He felt as soon as she spoke that she had been consciously keeping back what she said and hoping to get on without it; a scruple in her that immensely touched him when, by the end of three or four minutes more, he was able to measure it. What she brought out, at any rate, quite cleared the air and supplied the link—the link it was so odd he should frivolously have managed to lose.

"You know you told me something I've never forgotten and that again and again has made me think of you since; it was that tremendously hot day when we went to Sorrento, across the bay, for the breeze. What I allude to was what you said to me, on the way back, as we sat under the awning of the boat enjoying the cool. Have you forgotten?"

He had forgotten and was even more surprised than ashamed. But the great thing was that he saw in this no vulgar reminder of any "sweet" speech. The vanity of women had long memories, but she was making no claim on him of a compliment or a mistake. With another woman, a totally different one, he might have feared the recall possibly even of some imbecile "offer." So, in having to say that he had indeed forgotten, he was conscious rather of a loss than of a gain; he already saw an interest in the matter of her mention. "I try to think— but I give it up. Yet I remember the Sorrento day."

"I'm not very sure you do," May Bartram after a moment said; "and I'm not very sure I ought to want you to. It's dreadful to bring a person back at any time to what he was ten years before. If you've lived away from it," she smiled, "so much the better."

"Ah if *you* haven't why should I?" he asked.

"Lived away, you mean, from what I myself was?"

"From what *I* was. I was of course an ass," Marcher went on; "but I would rather know from you just the sort of ass I was than—from the moment you have something in your mind—not know anything."

Still, however, she hesitated. "But if you've completely ceased to be that sort—?"

"Why I can then all the more bear to know. Besides, perhaps I haven't."

"Perhaps. Yet if you haven't," she added, "I should suppose you'd remember. Not indeed that *I* in the least connect with my impression the invidious name you use. If I had only thought you foolish," she explained, "the thing I speak of wouldn't so have remained with me. It was about yourself." She waited as if it might come to him; but as, only meeting her eyes in wonder, he gave no sign, she burnt her ships. "Has it ever happened?"

Then it was that, while he continued to stare, a light broke for him and the blood slowly came to his face, which began to burn with recognition. "Do you mean I told you—?" But he faltered, lest what came to him shouldn't be right, lest he should only give himself away.

"It was something about yourself that it was natural one shouldn't forget—that is if one remembered you at all. That's why I ask you," she smiled, "if the thing you then spoke of has ever come to pass?"

Oh then he saw, but he was lost in wonder and found himself embarrassed. This, he also saw, made her sorry for him, as if her allusion had been a mistake. It took him but a moment, however, to feel it hadn't been, much as it had been a surprise. After the first little shock of it her knowledge on the contrary began, even if rather strangely, to taste sweet to him. She was the only other person in the world then who would have it, and she had had it all these years, while the fact of his having so breathed his secret had unaccountably faded from him. No wonder they couldn't have met as if nothing had happened. "I judge," he finally said, "that I know what you mean. Only I had strangely enough lost any sense of having taken you so far into my confidence."

"Is it because you've taken so many others as well?"

"I've taken nobody. Not a creature since then."

"So that I'm the only person who knows?"

"The only person in the world."

"Well," she quickly replied, "I myself have never spoken. I've never, never repeated of you what you told me." She looked at him so that he perfectly believed her. Their eyes met over it in such a way that he was without a doubt. "And I never will."

She spoke with an earnestness that, as if almost excessive, put him at ease about her possible derision. Somehow the whole question was a new luxury to him—that is from the moment she was in possession. If she didn't take the sarcastic view she clearly took the sympathetic, and that was what he had had, in all the long time, from no one whomsoever. What he felt was that he couldn't at present have begun to tell her, and yet could profit perhaps exquisitely by the accident of having done so of old. "Please don't then. We're just right as it is."

"Oh I am," she laughed, "if you are!" To which she added: "Then you do still feel in the same way?"

It was impossible he shouldn't take to himself that she was really interested, though it all kept coming as perfect surprise. He had thought of himself so long as abominably alone, and lo he wasn't alone a bit. He hadn't been, it appeared, for an hour—since those moments on the Sorrento boat. It was *she* who had been, he seemed to see as he looked at her—she who had been made so by the graceless fact of his lapse of fidelity. To tell her what he had told her—what had it been but to ask something of her? something that she had given, in her charity, without his having, by a remembrance, by a return of the spirit, failing another encounter, so much as thanked her. What he had asked of her had been simply at first not to laugh at him. She had beautifully not done so for ten years, and she was not doing so now. So he had endless gratitude to make up. Only for that he must see just how he had figured to her. "What, exactly, was the account I gave—?"

"Of the way you did feel? Well, it was very simple. You said you had had from your earliest time, as the deepest thing within you, the sense of being kept for something rare and strange, possibly prodigious and terrible, that was sooner or later to happen to you, that you had in your bones the foreboding and the conviction of, and that would perhaps overwhelm you."

The Beast in the Jungle 555

"Do you call that very simple?" John Marcher asked.

She thought a moment. "It was perhaps because I seemed, as you spoke, to understand it."

"You do understand it?" he eagerly asked.

Again she kept her kind eyes on him. "You still have the belief?"

"Oh!" he exclaimed helplessly. There was too much to say.

"Whatever it's to be," she clearly made out, "it hasn't yet come."

He shook his head in complete surrender now. "It hasn't yet come. Only, you know, it isn't anything I'm to *do,* to achieve in the world, to be distinguished or admired for. I'm not such an ass as *that.* It would be much better, no doubt, if I were."

"It's to be something you're merely to suffer?"

"Well, say to wait for—to have to meet, to face, to see suddenly break out in my life; possibly destroying all further consciousness, possibly annihilating me; possibly, on the other hand, only altering everything, striking at the root of all my world and leaving me to the consequences, however they shape themselves."

She took this in, but the light in her eyes continued for him not to be that of mockery. "Isn't what you describe perhaps but the expectation—or at any rate the sense of danger, familiar to so many people—of falling in love?"

John Marcher wondered. "Did you ask me that before?"

"No—I wasn't so free-and-easy then. But it's what strikes me now."

"Of course," he said after a moment, "it strikes you. Of course it strikes *me.* Of course what's in store for me may be no more than that. The only thing is," he went on, "that I think if it had been that I should by this time know."

"Do you mean because you've *been* in love?" And then as he but looked at her in silence: "You've been in love, and it hasn't meant such a cataclysm, hasn't proved the great affair?"

"Here I am, you see. It hasn't been overwhelming."

"Then it hasn't been love," said May Bartram.

"Well, I at least thought it was. I took it for that—I've taken it till now. It was agreeable, it was delightful, it was miserable," he explained. "But it wasn't strange. It wasn't what *my* affair's to be."

"You want something all to yourself—something that nobody else knows or *has* known?"

"It isn't a question of what I 'want'—God knows I don't want anything. It's only a question of the apprehension that haunts me—that I live with day by day."

He said this so lucidly and consistently that he could see it further impose itself. If she hadn't been interested before she'd have been interested now. "Is it a sense of coming violence?"

Evidently now too again he liked to talk of it. "I don't think of it as—when it does come—necessarily violent. I only think of it as natural and as of course above all unmistakeable. I think of it simply as *the* thing. *The* thing will of itself appear natural."

"Then how will it appear strange?"

Marcher bethought himself. "It won't—to *me.*"

"To whom then?"

"Well," he replied, smiling at last, "say to you."

"Oh then I'm to be present?"

"Why you *are* present—since you know."

"I see." She turned it over. "But I mean at the catastrophe."

At this, for a minute, their lightness gave way to their gravity; it was as if the long look they exchanged held them together. "It will only depend on yourself—if you'll watch with me."

"Are you afraid?" she asked.

"Don't leave me *now,*" he went on.

"Are you afraid?" she repeated.

"Do you think me simply out of my mind?" he pursued instead of answering. "Do I merely strike you as a harmless lunatic?"

"No," said May Bartram. "I understand you. I believe you."

"You mean you feel how my obsession—poor old thing!—may correspond to some possible reality?"

"To some possible reality."

"Then you *will* watch with me?"

She hesitated, then for the third time put her question. "Are you afraid?"

"Did I tell you I was—at Naples?"

"No, you said nothing about it."

"Then I don't know. And I should *like* to know," said John Marcher. "You'll tell me yourself whether you think so. If you'll watch with me you'll see."

"Very good then." They had been moving by this time

across the room, and at the door, before passing out, they paused as for the full wind-up of their understanding. "I'll watch with you," said May Bartram.

II

The fact that she "knew"—knew and yet neither chaffed him nor betrayed him—had in a short time begun to constitute between them a goodly bond, which became more marked when, within the year that followed their afternoon at Weatherend, the opportunities for meeting multiplied. The event that thus promoted these occasions was the death of the ancient lady her great-aunt, under whose wing since losing her mother, she had to such an extent found shelter, and who, though but the widowed mother of the new successor to the property, had succeeded—thanks to a high tone and a high temper—in not forfeiting the supreme position at the great house. The deposition of this personage arrived but with her death, which, followed by many changes, made in particular a difference for the young woman in whom Marcher's expert attention had recognised from the first a dependent with a pride that might ache though it didn't bristle. Nothing for a long time had made him easier than the thought that the aching must have been much soothed by Miss Bartram's now finding herself able to set up a small home in London. She had acquired property, to an amount that made that luxury just possible, under her aunt's extremely complicated will, and when the whole matter began to be straightened out, which indeed took time, she let him know that the happy issue was at last in view. He had seen her again before that day, both because she had more than once accompanied the ancient lady to town and because he had paid another visit to the friends who so conveniently made of Weatherend one of the charms of their own hospitality. These friends had taken him back there; he had achieved there again with Miss Bartram some quiet detachment; and he had in London succeeded in persuading her to more than one brief absence from her aunt. They went together, on these latter occasions, to the National Gallery and the South Kensington Museum, where, among vivid reminders, they talked of Italy at large—not now attempting to recover, as at first, the taste of their youth and their ignorance. That recovery, the first day at Weatherend, had served its purpose well, had given them quite enough; so that they were, to Marcher's sense, no longer hovering

about the headwaters of their stream, but had felt their boat pushed sharply off and down the current.

They were literally afloat together; for our gentleman this was marked, quite as marked as that the fortunate cause of it was just the buried treasure of her knowledge. He had with his own hands dug up this little hoard, brought to light—that is to within reach of the dim day constituted by their discretions and privacies—the object of value the hiding-place of which he had, after putting it into the ground himself, so strangely, so long forgotten. The rare luck of his having again just stumbled on the spot made him indifferent to any other question; he would doubtless have devoted more time to the odd accident of his lapse of memory if he hadn't been moved to devote so much to the sweetness, the comfort, as he felt, for the future, that this accident itself had helped to keep fresh. It had never entered into his plan that any one should "know," and mainly for the reason that it wasn't in him to tell any one. That would have been impossible, for nothing but the amusement of a cold world would have waited on it. Since, however, a mysterious fate had opened his mouth betimes, in spite of him, he would count that a compensation and profit by it to the utmost. That the right person *should* know tempered the asperity of his secret more than his shyness had permitted him to imagine; and May Bartram was clearly right, because— well, because there she was. Her knowledge simply settled it; he would have been sure enough by this time had she been wrong. There was that in his situation, no doubt, that disposed him too much to see her as a mere confidant, taking all her light for him from the fact—the fact only—of her interest in his predicament; from her mercy, sympathy, seriousness, her consent not to regard him as the funniest of the funny. Aware, in fine, that her price for him was just in her giving him this constant sense of his being admirably spared, he was careful to remember that she had also a life of her own, with things that might happen to *her*, things that in friendship one should likewise take account of. Something fairly remarkable came to pass with him, for that matter, in this connexion —something represented by a certain passage of his consciousness, in the suddenest way, from one extreme to the other.

He had thought himself, so long as nobody knew, the most disinterested person in the world, carrying his concentrated burden, his perpetual suspense, ever so quietly,

The Beast in the Jungle **557**

holding his tongue about it, giving others no glimpse of it nor of its effect upon his life, asking of them no allowance and only making on his side all those that were asked. He hadn't disturbed people with the queerness of their having to know a haunted man, though he had had moments of rather special temptation on hearing them say they were forsooth "unsettled." If they were as unsettled as he was—he who had never been settled for an hour in his life—they would know what it meant. Yet it wasn't, all the same, for him to make them, and he listened to them civilly enough. This was why he had such good—though possibly such rather colourless—manners; this was why, above all, he could regard himself, in a greedy world, as decently—as in fact perhaps even a little sublimely—unselfish. Our point is accordingly that he valued this character quite sufficiently to measure his present danger of letting it lapse, against which he promised himself to be much on his guard. He was quite ready, none the less, to be selfish just a little, since surely no more charming occasion for it had come to him. "Just a little," in a word, was just as much as Miss Bartram, taking one day with another, would let him. He never would be in the least coercive, and would keep well before him the lines on which consideration for her— the very highest—ought to proceed. He would thoroughly establish the heads under which her affairs, her requirements, her peculiarities—he went so far as to give them the latitude of that name—would come into their intercourse. All this naturally was a sign of how much he took the intercourse itself for granted. There was nothing more to be done about *that*. It simply existed; had sprung into being with her first penetrating question to him in the autumn light there at Weatherend. The real form it should have taken on the basis that stood out large was the form of their marrying. But the devil in this was that the very basis itself put marrying out of the question. His conviction, his apprehension, his obsession, in short, wasn't a privilege he could invite a woman to share; and that consequence of it was precisely what was the matter with him. Something or other lay in wait for him, amid the twists and the turns of the months and the years, like a crouching beast in the jungle. It signified little whether the crouching beast were destined to slay him or to be slain. The definite point was the inevitable spring of the creature; and the definite lesson from that was that a man of feeling didn't cause himself to be accompanied by a lady on a tiger-hunt. Such was the image under which he had ended by figuring his life.

They had at first, none the less, in the scattered hours spent together, made no allusion to that view of it; which was a sign he was handsomely alert to give that he didn't expect, that he in fact didn't care, always to be talking about it. Such a feature in one's outlook was really like a hump on one's back. The difference it made every minute of the day existed quite independently of discussion. One discussed of course *like* a hunchback, for there was always, if nothing else, the hunchback face. That remained, and she was watching him; but people watched best, as a general thing, in silence, so that such would be predominantly the manner of their vigil. Yet he didn't want, at the same time, to be tense and solemn; tense and solemn was what he imagined he too much showed for with other people. The thing to be, with the one person who knew, was easy and natural—to make the reference rather than be seeming to avoid it, to avoid it rather than be seeming to make it, and to keep it, in any case, familiar, facetious even, rather than pedantic and portentous. Some such consideration as the latter was doubtless in his mind for instance when he wrote pleasantly to Miss Bartram that perhaps the great thing he had so long felt as in the lap of the gods was no more than this circumstance, which touched him so nearly, of her acquiring a house in London. It was the first allusion they had yet again made, needing any other hitherto so little; but when she replied, after having given him the news, that she was by no means satisfied with such a trifle as the climax to so special a suspense, she almost set him wondering if she hadn't even a larger conception of singularity for him than he had for himself. He was at all events destined to become aware little by little, as time went by, that she was all the while looking at his life, judging it, measuring it, in the light of the thing she knew, which grew to be at last, with the consecration of the years, never mentioned between them save as "the real truth" about him. That had always been his own form of reference to it, but she adopted the form so quietly that, looking back at the end of a period, he knew there was no moment at which it was traceable that she had, as he might say, got inside his idea, or exchanged the attitude of beautifully indulging for that of still more beautifully believing him.

It was always open to him to accuse her of seeing him but as the most harmless of maniacs, and this, in the long run—since it covered so much ground—was his easiest description of their friendship. He had a screw loose for her, but she liked him in spite of it and was practically, against the rest of the world, his kind wise keeper, unremunerated but fairly amused and, in the absence of other near ties, not disreputably occupied. The rest of the world of course thought him queer, but she, she only, knew how, and above all why, queer; which was precisely what enabled her to dispose the concealing veil in the right folds. She took his gaiety from him—since it had to pass with them for gaiety—as she took everything else; but she certainly so far justified by her unerring touch his finer sense of the degree to which he had ended by convincing her. *She* at least never spoke of the secret of his life except as "the real truth about you," and she had in fact a wonderful way of making it seem, as such, the secret of her own life too. That was in fine how he so constantly felt her as allowing for him; he couldn't on the whole call it anything else. He allowed for himself, but she, exactly, allowed still more; partly because, better placed for a sight of the matter, she traced his unhappy perversion through reaches of its course into which he could scarce follow it. He knew how he felt, but, besides knowing that, she knew how he *looked* as well; he knew each of the things of importance he was insidiously kept from doing, but she could add up the amount they made, understand how much, with a lighter weight on his spirit, he might have done, and thereby establish how, clever as he was, he fell short. Above all she was in the secret of the difference between the forms he went through—those of his little office under Government, those of caring for his modest patrimony, for his library, for his garden in the country, for the people in London whose invitations he accepted and repaid—and the detachment that reigned beneath them and that made of all behaviour, all that could in the least be called behaviour, a long act of dissimulation. What it had come to was that he wore a mask painted with the social simper, out of the eye-holes of which there looked eyes of an expression not in the least matching the other features. This the stupid world, even after years, had never more than half-discovered. It was only May Bartram who had, and she achieved, by an art indescribable, the feat of at once—or perhaps it was only alternately—meeting the eyes from in front and mingling her own vision, as from over his shoulder, with their peep through the apertures.

So while they grew older together she did watch with

him, and so she let this association give shape and colour to her own existence. Beneath *her* forms as well detachment had learned to sit, and behaviour had become for her, in the social sense, a false account of herself. There was but one account of her that would have been true all the while and that she could give straight to nobody, least of all to John Marcher. Her whole attitude was a virtual statement, but the perception of that only seemed called to take its place for him as one of the many things necessarily crowded out of his consciousness. If she had moreover, like himself, to make sacrifices to their real truth, it was to be granted that her compensation might have affected her as more prompt and more natural. They had long periods, in this London time, during which, when they were together, a stranger might have listened to them without in the least pricking up his ears; on the other hand the real truth was equally liable at any moment to rise to the surface, and the auditor would then have wondered indeed what they were talking about. They had from an early hour made up their mind that society was, luckily, unintelligent, and the margin allowed them by this had fairly become one of their commonplaces. Yet there were still moments when the situation turned almost fresh—usually under the effect of some expression drawn from herself. Her expressions doubtless repeated themselves, but her intervals were generous. "What saves us, you know, is that we answer so completely to so usual an appearance: that of the man and woman whose friendship has become such a daily habit—or almost—as to be at last indispensable." That for instance was a remark she had frequently enough had occasion to make, though she had given it at different times different developments. What we are especially concerned with is the turn it happened to take from her one afternoon when he had come to see her in honour of her birthday. This anniversary had fallen on a Sunday, at a season of thick fog and general outward gloom; but he had brought her his customary offering, having known her now long enough to have established a hundred small traditions. It was one of his proofs to himself, the present he made her on her birthday, that he hadn't sunk into real selfishness. It was mostly nothing more than a small trinket, but it was always fine of its kind, and he was regularly careful to pay for it more than he thought he could afford. "Our habit saves you at least, don't you see? because it makes you, after all, for the vulgar, indistinguishable from other men. What's the most inveterate

The Beast in the Jungle 559

mark of men in general? Why the capacity to spend end-less time with dull women—to spend it I won't say with-out being bored, but without minding that they are, without being driven off at a tangent by it; which comes to the same thing. I'm your dull woman, a part of the daily bread for which you pray at church. That covers your tracks more than anything."

"And what covers yours?" asked Marcher, whom his dull woman could mostly to this extent amuse. "I see of course what you mean by your saving me, in this way and that, so far as other people are concerned—I've seen it all along. Only what is it that saves *you?* I often think, you know, of that."

She looked as if she sometimes thought of that too, but rather in a different way. "Where other people, you mean, are concerned?"

"Well, you're really so in with me, you know—as a sort of result of my being so in with yourself. I mean of my having such an immense regard for you, being so tremendously mindful of all you've done for me. I some-times ask myself if it's quite fair. Fair I mean to have so involved and—since one may say it—interested you. I almost feel as if you hadn't really had time to do anything else."

"Anything else but be interested?" she asked. "Ah what else does one ever want to be? If I've been 'watching' with you, as we long ago agreed I was to do, watching's always in itself an absorption."

"Oh certainly," John Marcher said, "if you hadn't had your curiosity—! Only doesn't it sometimes come to you as time goes on that your curiosity isn't being particu-larly repaid?"

May Bartram had a pause. "Do you ask that, by any chance, because you feel at all that yours isn't? I mean because you have to wait so long."

Oh he understood what she meant! "For the thing to happen that never does happen? For the beast to jump out? No, I'm just where I was about it. It isn't a matter as to which I can *choose,* I can decide for a change. It isn't one as to which there *can* be a change. It's in the lap of the gods. One's in the hands of one's law—there one is. As to the form the law will take, the way it will op-erate, that's its own affair."

"Yes," Miss Bartram replied; "of course one's fate's coming, of course it *has* come in its own form and its own way, all the while. Only, you know, the form and the way in your case were to have been—well, something so exceptional and, as one may say, so particularly *your* own."

Something in this made him look at her with suspi-cion. "You say 'were to *have* been,' as if in your heart you had begun to doubt."

"Oh!" she vaguely protested.

"As if you believe," he went on, "that nothing will now take place."

She shook her head slowly but rather inscrutably. "You're far from my thought."

He continued to look at her. "What then is the matter with you?"

"Well," she said after another wait, "the matter with me is simply that I'm more sure than ever my curiosity, as you call it, will be but too well repaid."

They were frankly grave now; he had got up from his seat, had turned once more about the little drawing-room to which, year after year, he brought his inevitable topic; in which he had, as he might have said, tasted their in-timate community with every sauce, where every object was as familiar to him as the things of his own house and the very carpets were worn with his fitful walk very much as the desks in old counting-houses are worn by the elbows of generations of clerks. The generations of his nervous moods had been at work there, and the place was the written history of his whole middle life. Under the impression of what his friend had just said he knew himself, for some reason, more aware of these things; which made him, after a moment, stop again before her. "Is it possibly that you've grown afraid?"

"Afraid?" He thought, as she repeated the word, that his question had made her, a little, change colour; so that, lest he should have touched on a truth, he explained very kindly: "You remember that that was what you asked *me* long ago—the first day at Weatherend."

"Oh yes, and you told me you didn't know—that I was to see for myself. We've said little about it since, even in so long a time."

"Precisely," Marcher interposed—"quite as if it were too delicate a matter for us to make free with. Quite as if we might find, on pressure, that I *am* afraid. For then," he said, "we shouldn't, should we? quite know what to do."

She had for the time no answer to his question. "There have been days when I thought you were. Only, of course," she added, "there have been days when we have thought almost anything."

"Everything. Oh!" Marcher softly groaned as with a gasp, half-spent, at the face, more uncovered just then than it had been for a long while, of the imagination always with them. It had always had its incalculable moments of glaring out, quite as with the very eyes of the very Beast, and, used as he was to them, they could still draw from him the tribute of a sigh that rose from the depths of his being. All they had thought, first and last, rolled over him; the past seemed to have been reduced to mere barren speculation. This in fact was what the place had just struck him as so full of—the simplification of everything but the state of suspense. That remained only by seeming to hang in the void surrounding it. Even his original fear, if fear it had been, had lost itself in the desert. "I judge, however," he continued, "that you see I'm not afraid now."

"What I see, as I make it out, is that you've achieved something almost unprecedented in the way of getting used to danger. Living with it so long and so closely you've lost your sense of it; you know it's there, but you're indifferent, and you cease even, as of old, to have to whistle in the dark. Considering what the danger is," May Bartram wound up, "I'm bound to say I don't think your attitude could well be surpassed."

John Marcher faintly smiled. "It's heroic?"

"Certainly—call it that."

It was what he would have liked indeed to call it. "I *am* then a man of courage?"

"That's what you were to show me."

He still, however, wondered. "But doesn't the man of courage know what he's afraid of—or *not* afraid of? I don't know *that,* you see. I don't focus it. I can't name it. I only know I'm exposed."

"Yes, but exposed—how shall I say?—so directly. So intimately. That's surely enough."

"Enough to make you feel then—as what we may call the end and the upshot of our watch—that I'm not afraid?"

"You're not afraid. But it isn't," she said, "the end of our watch. That is it isn't the end of yours. You've everything still to see."

"Then why haven't *you?*" he asked. He had had, all along, today, the sense of her keeping something back, and he still had it. As this was his first impression of that it quite made a date. The case was the more marked as she didn't at first answer; which in turn made him go on. "You know something I don't." Then his voice, for that

of a man of courage, trembled a little. "You know what's to happen." Her silence, with the face she showed, was almost a confession—it made him sure. "You know, and you're afraid to tell me. It's so bad that you're afraid I'll find out."

All this might be true, for she did look as if, unexpectedly to her, he had crossed some mystic line that she had secretly drawn round her. Yet she might, after all, not have worried; and the real climax was that he himself, at all events, needn't. "You'll never find out."

III

It was all to have made, none the less, as I have said, a date; which came out in the fact that again and again, even after long intervals, other things that passed between them wore in relation to this hour but the character of recalls and results. Its immediate effect had been indeed rather to lighten insistence—almost to provoke a reaction; as if their topic had dropped by its own weight and as if moreover, for that matter, Marcher had been visited by one of his occasional warnings against egotism. He had kept up, he felt, and very decently on the whole, his consciousness of the importance of not being selfish, and it was true that he had never sinned in that direction without promptly enough trying to press the scales the other way. He often repaired his fault, the season permitting, by inviting his friend to accompany him to the opera; and it not infrequently thus happened that, to show he didn't wish her to have but one sort of food for her mind, he was the cause of her appearing there with him a dozen nights in the month. It even happened that, seeing her home at such times, he occasionally went in with her to finish, as he called it, the evening, and, the better to make his point, sat down to the frugal but always careful little supper that awaited his pleasure. His point was made, he thought, by his not eternally insisting with her on himself; made for instance, at such hours, when it befell that, her piano at hand and each of them familiar with it, they went over passages of the opera together. It chanced to be on one of these occasions, however, that he reminded her of her not having answered a certain question he had put to her during the talk that had taken place between them on her last birthday. "What is it that saves *you?*"—saved her, he meant, from that appearance of variation from the usual human type. If he had practically escaped remark, as she pretended, by doing, in the most important particular, what most men do—find the answer to life in patching up an alliance of a sort with a woman no better than himself—how had she escaped it, and how could the alliance, such as it was, since they must suppose it had been more or less noticed, have failed to make her rather positively talked about?

"I never said," May Bartram replied, "that it hadn't made me a good deal talked about."

"Ah well then you're not 'saved.'"

"It hasn't been a question for me. If you've had your woman I've had," she said, "my man."

"And you mean that makes you all right?"

Oh it was always as if there were so much to say! "I don't know why it shouldn't make me—humanly, which is what we're speaking of—as right as it makes you."

"I see," Marcher returned. "'Humanly,' no doubt, as showing that you're living for something. Not, that is, just for me and my secret."

May Bartram smiled. "I don't pretend it exactly shows that I'm not living for you. It's my intimacy with you that's in question."

He laughed as he saw what she meant. "Yes, but since, as you say, I'm only, so far as people make out, ordinary, you're—aren't you?—no more than ordinary either. You help me to pass for a man like another. So if I *am*, as I understand you, you're not compromised. Is that it?"

She had another of her waits, but she spoke clearly enough. "That's it. It's all that concerns me—to help you to pass for a man like another."

He was careful to acknowledge the remark handsomely. "How kind, how beautiful, you are to me! How shall I ever repay you?"

She had her last grave pause, as if there might be a choice of ways. But she chose. "By going on as you are."

It was into this going on as he was that they relapsed, and really for so long a time that the day inevitably came for a further sounding of their depths. These depths, constantly bridged over by a structure firm enough in spite of its lightness and of its occasional oscillation in the somewhat vertiginous air, invited on occasion, in the interest of their nerves, a dropping of the plummet and a measurement of the abyss. A difference had been made moreover, once for all, by the fact that she had all the while not appeared to feel the need of rebutting his charge of an idea within her that she didn't dare to express—a charge uttered just before one of the fullest of their later discussions ended. It had come up for him

then that she "knew" something and that what she knew was bad—too bad to tell him. When he had spoken of it as visibly so bad that she was afraid he might find it out, her reply had left the matter too equivocal to be let alone and yet, for Marcher's special sensibility, almost too formidable again to touch. He circled about it at a distance that alternately narrowed and widened and that still wasn't much affected by the consciousness in him that there was nothing she could "know," after all, any better than he did. She had no source of knowledge he hadn't equally—except of course that she might have finer nerves. That was what women had where they were interested; they made out things, where people were concerned, that the people often couldn't have made out for themselves. Their nerves, their sensibility, their imagination, were conductors and revealers, and the beauty of May Bartram was in particular that she had given herself so to his case. He felt in these days what, oddly enough, he had never felt before, the growth of a dread of losing her by some catastrophe—some catastrophe that yet wouldn't at all be *the* catastrophe: partly because she had almost of a sudden begun to strike him as more useful to him than ever yet, and partly by reason of an appearance of uncertainty in her health, coincident and equally new. It was characteristic of the inner detachment he had hitherto so successfully cultivated and to which our whole account of him is a reference, it was characteristic that his complications, such as they were, had never yet seemed so as at this crisis to thicken about him, even to the point of making him ask himself if he were, by any chance, of a truth, within sight or sound, within touch or reach, within the immediate jurisdiction, of the thing that waited.

When the day came, as come it had to, that his friend confessed to him her fear of a deep disorder in her blood, he felt somehow the shadow of a change and the chill of a shock. He immediately began to imagine aggravations and disasters, and above all to think of her peril as the direct menace for himself of personal privation. This indeed gave him one of those partial recoveries of equanimity that were agreeable to him—it showed him that what was still first in his mind was the loss she herself might suffer. "What if she should have to die before knowing, before seeing—?" It would have been brutal, in the early stages of her trouble, to put that question to her; but it had immediately sounded for him to his own concern, and the possibility was what most made him sorry for her. If she did "know," moreover, in the sense of her having had some—what should he think?—mystical irresistible light, this would make the matter not better, but worse, inasmuch as her original adoption of his own curiosity had quite become the basis of her life. She had been living to see what would *be* to be seen, and it would quite lacerate her to have to give up before the accomplishment of the vision. These reflexions, as I say, quickened his generosity; yet, make them as he might, he saw himself, with the lapse of the period, more and more disconcerted. It lapsed for him with a strange steady sweep, and the oddest oddity was that it gave him, independently of the threat of much inconvenience, almost the only positive surprise his career, if career it could be called, had yet offered him. She kept the house as she had never done; he had to go to her to see her—she could meet him nowhere now, though there was scarce a corner of their loved old London in which she hadn't in the past, at one time or another, done so; and he found her always seated by her fire in the deep old-fashioned chair she was less and less able to leave. He had been struck one day, after an absence exceeding his usual measure, with her suddenly looking much older to him than he had ever thought of her being; then he recognised that the suddenness was all on his side—he had just simply and suddenly noticed. She looked older because inevitably, after so many years, she *was* old, or almost; which was of course true in still greater measure of her companion. If she was old, or almost, John Marcher assuredly was, and yet it was her showing of the lesson, not his own, that brought the truth home to him. His surprises began here; when once they had begun they multiplied; they came rather with a rush: it was as if, in the oddest way in the world, they had all been kept back, sown in a thick cluster, for the late afternoon of life, the time at which for people in general the unexpected has died out.

One of them was that he should have caught himself —for he *had* so done—*really* wondering if the great accident would take form now as nothing more than his being condemned to see this charming woman, this admirable friend, pass away from him. He had never so unreservedly qualified her as while confronted in thought with such a possibility; in spite of which there was small doubt for him that as an answer to his long riddle the mere effacement of even so fine a feature of his situation would be an abject anti-climax. It would represent,

as connected with his past attitude, a drop of dignity under the shadow of which his existence could only become the most grotesque of failures. He had been far from holding it a failure—long as he had waited for the appearance that was to make it a success. He had waited for quite another thing, not for such a thing as that. The breath of his good faith came short, however, as he recognised how long he had waited, or how long at least his companion had. That she, at all events, might be recorded as having waited in vain—this affected him sharply, and all the more because of his at first having done little more than amuse himself with the idea. It grew more grave as the gravity of her condition grew, and the state of mind it produced in him, which he himself ended by watching as if it had been some definite disfigurement of his outer person, may pass for another of his surprises. This conjoined itself still with another, the really stupefying consciousness of a question that he would have allowed to shape itself had he dared. What did everything mean—what, that is, did *she* mean, she and her vain waiting and her probable death and the soundless admonition of it all—unless that, at this time of day, it was simply, it was overwhelmingly too late? He had never at any stage of his queer consciousness admitted the whisper of such a correction; he had never till within these last few months been so false to his conviction as not to hold that what was to come to him had time, whether *he* struck himself as having it or not. That at last, at last, he certainly hadn't it, to speak of, or had it but in the scantiest measure—such, soon enough, as things went with him, became the inference with which his old obsession had to reckon: and this it was not helped to do by the more and more confirmed appearance that the great vagueness casting the long shadow in which he had lived had, to attest itself, almost no margin left. Since it was in Time that he was to have met his fate, so it was in Time that his fate was to have acted; and as he waked up to the sense of no longer being young, which was exactly the sense of being stale, just as that, in turn, was the sense of being weak, he waked up to another matter beside. It all hung together; they were subject, he and the great vagueness, to an equal and indivisible law. When the possibilities themselves had accordingly turned stale, when the secret of the gods had grown faint, had perhaps even quite evaporated, that, and that only, was failure. It wouldn't have been failure to be bankrupt, dishonoured, pilloried, hanged; it was

The Beast in the Jungle 563

failure not to be anything. And so, in the dark valley into which his path had taken its unlooked-for twist, he wondered not a little as he groped. He didn't care what awful crash might overtake him, with what ignominy or what monstrosity he might yet be associated—since he wasn't after all too utterly old to suffer—if it would only be decently proportionate to the posture he had kept, all his life, in the threatened presence of it. He had but one desire left—that he shouldn't have been "sold."

IV

Then it was that, one afternoon, while the spring of the year was young and new she met all in her own way his frankest betrayal of these alarms. He had gone in late to see her, but evening hadn't settled and she was presented to him in that long fresh light of waning April days which affects us often with a sadness sharper than the greyest hours of autumn. The week had been warm, the spring was supposed to have begun early, and May Bartram sat, for the first time in the year, without a fire; a fact that, to Marcher's sense, gave the scene of which she formed part a smooth and ultimate look, an air of knowing in its immaculate order and cold meaningless cheer, that it would never see a fire again. Her own aspect—he could scarce have said why—intensified this note. Almost as white as wax, with the marks and signs in her face as numerous and as fine as if they had been etched by a needle, with soft white draperies relieved by a faded green scarf on the delicate tone of which the years had further refined, she was the picture of a serene and exquisite but impenetrable sphinx, whose head, or indeed all whose person, might have been powdered with silver. She was a sphinx, yet with her white petals and green fronds she might have been a lily too—only an artificial lily, wonderfully imitated and constantly kept, without dust or stain, though not exempt from a slight droop and a complexity of faint creases, under some clear glass bell. The perfection of household care, of high polish and finish, always reigned in her rooms, but they now looked most as if everything had been wound up, tucked in, put away, so that she might sit with folded hands and with nothing more to do. She was "out of it," to Marcher's vision; her work was over; she communicated with him as across some gulf or from some island of rest that she had already reached, and it made him feel strangely abandoned. Was it—or rather wasn't it—that if for so long she had been watching with him the answer to their

question must have swum into her ken and taken on its name, so that her occupation was verily gone? He had as much as charged her with this in saying to her, many months before, that she even then knew something she was keeping from him. It was a point he had never since ventured to press, vaguely fearing as he did that it might become a difference, perhaps a disagreement, between them. He had in this later time turned nervous, which was what he in all the other years had never been; and the oddity was that his nervousness should have waited till he had begun to doubt, should have held off so long as he was sure. There was something, it seemed to him, that the wrong word would bring down on his head, something that would so at least ease off his tension. But he wanted not to speak the wrong word; that would make everything ugly. He wanted the knowledge he lacked to drop on him, if drop it could, by its own august weight. If she was to forsake him it was surely for her to take leave. This was why he didn't directly ask her again what she knew; but it was also why, approaching the matter from another side, he said to her in the course of his visit: "What do you regard as the very worst that at this time of day *can* happen to me?"

He had asked her that in the past often enough; they had, with the odd irregular rhythm of their intensities and avoidances, exchanged ideas about it and then had seen the ideas washed away by cool intervals, washed like figures traced in sea-sand. It had ever been the mark of their talk that the oldest allusions in it required but a little dismissal and reaction to come out again, sounding for the hour as new. She could thus at present meet his enquiry quite freshly and patiently. "Oh yes, I've repeatedly thought, only it always seemed to me of old that I couldn't quite make up my mind. I thought of dreadful things, between which it was difficult to choose; and so must you have done."

"Rather! I feel now as if I had scarce done anything else. I appear to myself to have spent my life in thinking of nothing *but* dreadful things. A great many of them I've at different times named to you, but there were others I couldn't name."

"They were too, too dreadful?"

"Too, too dreadful—some of them."

She looked at him a minute, and there came to him as he met it an inconsequent sense that her eyes, when one got their full clearness, were still as beautiful as they had been in youth, only beautiful with a strange cold light—a light that somehow was a part of the effect, if it wasn't rather a part of the cause, of the pale hard sweetness of the season and the hour. "And yet," she said at last, "there are horrors we've mentioned."

It deepened the strangeness to see her, as such a figure in such a picture, talk of "horrors," but she was to do in a few minutes something stranger yet—though even of this he was to take the full measure but afterwards—and the note of it already trembled. It was, for the matter of that, one of the signs that her eyes were having again the high flicker of their prime. He had to admit, however, what she said. "Oh yes, there were times when we did go far." He caught himself in the act of speaking as if it all were over. Well, he wished it were; and the consummation depended for him clearly more and more on his friend.

But she had now a soft smile. "Oh far—!"

It was oddly ironic. "Do you mean you're prepared to go further?"

She was frail and ancient and charming as she continued to look at him, yet it was rather as if she had lost the thread. "Do you consider that we went far?"

"Why I thought it the point you were just making— that we *had* looked most things in the face."

"Including each other?" She still smiled. "But you're quite right. We've had together great imaginations, often great fears; but some of them have been unspoken."

"Then the worst—we haven't faced that. I *could* face it, I believe, if I knew what you think it. I feel," he explained, "as if I had lost my power to conceive such things." And he wondered if he looked as blank as he sounded. "It's spent."

"Then why do you assume," she asked, "that mine isn't?"

"Because you've given me signs to the contrary. It isn't a question for you of conceiving, imagining, comparing. It isn't a question now of choosing." At last he came out with it. "You know something I don't. You've shown me that before."

These last words had affected her, he made out in a moment, exceedingly, and she spoke with firmness. "I've shown you, my dear, nothing."

He shook his head. "You can't hide it."

"Oh, oh!" May Bartram sounded over what she couldn't hide. It was almost a smothered groan.

"You admitted it months ago, when I spoke of it to you as of something you were afraid I should find out.

Your answer was that I couldn't, that I wouldn't, and I don't pretend I have. But you had something therefore in mind, and I now see how it must have been, how it still is, the possibility that, of all possibilities, has settled itself for you as the worst. This," he went on, "is why I appeal to you. I'm only afraid of ignorance to-day—I'm not afraid of knowledge." And then as for a while she said nothing: "What makes me sure is that I see in your face and feel here, in this air and amid these appearances, that you're out of it. You've done. You've had your experience. You leave me to my fate."

Well, she listened, motionless and white in her chair, as on a decision to be made, so that her manner was fairly an avowal, though still, with a small fine inner stiffness, an imperfect surrender. "It *would* be the worst," she finally let herself say. "I mean the thing I've never said."

It hushed him a moment. "More monstrous than all the monstrosities we've named?"

"More monstrous. Isn't that what you sufficiently express," she asked, "in calling it the worst?"

Marcher thought. "Assuredly—if you mean, as I do, something that includes all the loss and all the shame that are thinkable."

"It would if it *should* happen," said May Bartram. "What we're speaking of, remember, is only my idea."

"It's your belief," Marcher returned. "That's enough for me. I feel your beliefs are right. Therefore if, having this one, you give me no more light on it, you abandon me."

"No, no!" she repeated. "I'm with you—don't you see? —still." And as to make it more vivid to him she rose from her chair—a movement she seldom risked in these days—and showed herself, all draped and all soft, in her fairness and slimness. "I haven't forsaken you."

It was really, in its effort against weakness, a generous assurance, and had the success of the impulse not, happily, been great, it would have touched him to pain more than to pleasure. But the cold charm in her eyes had spread, as she hovered before him, to all the rest of her person, so that it was for the minute almost a recovery of youth. He couldn't pity her for that; he could only take her as she showed—as capable even yet of helping him. It was as if, at the same time, her light might at any instant go out; wherefore he must make the most of it. There passed before him with intensity the three or four things he wanted most to know; but the question

The Beast in the Jungle

that came of itself to his lips really covered the others. "Then tell me if I shall consciously suffer."

She promptly shook her head. "Never!"

It confirmed the authority he imputed to her, and it produced on him an extraordinary effect. "Well, what's better than that? Do you call that the worst?"

"You think nothing is better?" she asked.

She seemed to mean something so special that he again sharply wondered, though still with the dawn of a prospect of relief. "Why not, if one doesn't *know?*" After which, as their eyes, over his question, met in silence, the dawn deepened and something to his purpose came prodigiously out of her very face. His own, as he took it in, suddenly flushed to the forehead, and he gasped with the force of a perception to which, on the instant, everything fitted. The sound of his gasp filled the air; then he became articulate. "I see—if I don't suffer!"

In her own look, however, was doubt. "You see what?"

"Why what you mean—what you've always meant."

She again shook her head. "What I mean isn't what I've always meant. It's different."

"It's something new?"

She hung back from it a little. "Something new. It's not what you think. I see what you think."

His divination drew breath then; only her correction might be wrong. "It isn't that I *am* a blockhead?" he asked between faintness and grimness. "It isn't that it's all a mistake?"

"A mistake?" she pityingly echoed. *That* possibility, for her, he saw, would be monstrous; and if she guaranteed him the immunity from pain it would accordingly not be what she had in mind. "Oh no," she declared; "It's nothing of that sort. You've been right."

Yet he couldn't help asking himself if she weren't, thus pressed, speaking but to save him. It seemed to him he should be most in a hole if his history should prove all a platitude. "Are you telling me the truth, so that I shan't have been a bigger idiot than I can bear to know? I *haven't* lived with a vain imagination, in the most besotted illusion? I haven't waited but to see the door shut in my face?"

She shook her head again. "However the case stands *that* isn't the truth. Whatever the reality, it *is* a reality. The door isn't shut. The door's open," said May Bartram.

"Then something's to come?"

She waited once again, always with her cold sweet eyes on him. "It's never too late." She had, with her gliding step, diminished the distance between them, and she stood nearer to him, close to him, a minute, as if still charged with the unspoken. Her movement might have been for some finer emphasis of what she was at once hesitating and deciding to say. He had been standing by the chimney-piece, fireless and sparely adorned, a small perfect old French clock and two morsels of rosy Dresden constituting all its furniture; and her hand grasped the shelf while she kept him waiting, grasped it a little as for support and encouragement. She only kept him waiting, however; that is he only waited. It had become suddenly, from her movement and attitude, beautiful and vivid to him that she had something more to give him; her wasted face delicately shone with it—it glittered almost as with the white lustre of silver in her expression. She was right, incontestably, for what he saw in her face was the truth, and strangely, without consequence, while their talk of it as dreadful was still in the air, she appeared to present it as inordinately soft. This, prompting bewilderment, made him but gape the more gratefully for her revelation, so that they continued for some minutes silent, her face shining at him, her contact imponderably pressing, and his stare all kind but all expectant. The end, none the less, was that what he had expected failed to come to him. Something else took place instead, which seemed to consist at first in the mere closing of her eyes. She gave way at the same instant to a slow fine shudder, and though he remained staring—though he stared in fact but the harder—turned off and regained her chair. It was the end of what she had been intending, but it left him thinking only of that.

"Well, you don't say—?"

She had touched in her passage a bell near a chimney and had sunk back strangely pale. "I'm afraid I'm too ill."

"Too ill to tell me?" It sprang up sharp to him, and almost to his lips, the fear she might die without giving him light. He checked himself in time from so expressing his question, but she answered as if she had heard the words.

"Don't you know—now?"

" 'Now'—?" She had spoken as if some difference had been made within the moment. But her maid, quickly obedient to her bell, was already with them. "I know nothing." And he was afterwards to say to himself that he must have spoken with odious impatience, such an impatience as to show that, supremely disconcerted, he washed his hands of the whole question.

"Oh!" said May Bartram.

"Are you in pain?" he asked as the woman went to her.

"No," said May Bartram.

Her maid, who had put an arm round her as if to take her to her room, fixed on him eyes that appealingly contradicted her; in spite of which, however, he showed once more his mystification. "What then has happened?"

She was once more, with her companion's help, on her feet, and, feeling withdrawal imposed on him, he had blankly found his hat and gloves and had reached the door. Yet he waited for her answer. "What *was* to," she said.

V

He came back the next day, but she was then unable to see him, and as it was literally the first time this had occurred in the long stretch of their acquaintance he turned away, defeated and sore, almost angry—or feeling at least that such a break in their custom was really the beginning of the end—and wandered alone with his thoughts, especially with the one he was least able to keep down. She was dying and he would lose her; she was dying and his life would end. He stopped in the Park, into which he had passed, and stared before him at his recurrent doubt. Away from her the doubt pressed again; in her presence he had believed her, but as he felt his forlornness he threw himself into the explanation that, nearest at hand, had most of a miserable warmth for him and least of a cold torment. She had deceived him to save him—to put him off with something in which he should be able to rest. What could the thing that was to happen to him be, after all, but just this thing that had begun to happen? Her dying, her death, his consequent solitude—*that* was what he had figured as the Beast in the Jungle, that was what had been in the lap of the gods. He had had her word for it as he left her—what else on earth could she have meant? It wasn't a thing of a monstrous order; not a fate rare and distinguished; not a stroke of fortune that overwhelmed and immortalised; it had only the stamp of the common doom. But poor Marcher at this hour judged the common doom sufficient. It would serve his turn, and even as the consum-

mation of infinite waiting he would bend his pride to accept it. He sat down on a bench in the twilight. He hadn't been a fool. Something had *been,* as she had said, to come. Before he rose indeed it had quite struck him that the final fact really matched with the long avenue through which he had had to reach it. As sharing his suspense and as giving herself all, giving her life, to bring it to an end, she had come with him every step of the way. He had lived by her aid, and to leave her behind would be cruelly, damnably to miss her. What could be more overwhelming than that?

Well, he was to know within the week, for though she kept him a while at bay, left him restless and wretched during a series of days on each of which he asked about her only again to have to turn away, she ended his trial by receiving him where she had always received him. Yet she had been brought out at some hazard into the presence of so many of the things that were, consciously, vainly, half their past, and there was scant service left in the gentleness of her mere desire, all too visible, to check his obsession and wind up his long trouble. That was clearly what she wanted, the one thing more for her own peace while she could still put out her hand. He was so affected by her state that, once seated by her chair, he was moved to let everything go; it was she herself therefore who brought him back, took up again, before she dismissed him, her last word of the other time. She showed how she wished to leave their business in order. "I'm not sure you understood. You've nothing to wait for more. It *has* come."

Oh how he looked at her! "Really?"

"Really."

"The thing that, as you said, *was* to?"

"The thing that we began in our youth to watch for."

Face to face with her once more he believed her; it was a claim to which he had so abjectly little to oppose. "You mean that it has come as a positive definite occurrence, with a name and a date?"

"Positive. Definite. I don't know about the 'name,' but oh with a date!"

He found himself again too helplessly at sea. "But come in the night—come and passed me by?"

May Bartram had her strange faint smile. "Oh no, it hasn't passed you by!"

"But if I haven't been aware of it and it hasn't touched me—?"

"Ah your not being aware of it"—and she seemed to hesitate an instant to deal with this—"your not being aware of it is the strangeness *in* the strangeness. It's the wonder *of* the wonder." She spoke as with the softness almost of a sick child, yet now at last, at the end of all, with the perfect straightness of a sibyl. She visibly knew that she knew, and the effect on him was of something co-ordinate, in its high character, with the law that had ruled him. It was the true voice of the law; so on her lips would the law itself have sounded. "It *has* touched you," she went on. "It has done its office. It has made you all its own."

"So utterly without my knowing it?"

"So utterly without your knowing it." His hand, as he leaned to her, was on the arm of her chair, and, dimly smiling always now, she placed her own on it. "It's enough if *I* know it."

"Oh!" he confusedly breathed, as she herself of late so often had done.

"What I long ago said is true. You'll never know now, and I think you ought to be content. You've *had* it," said May Bartram.

"But had what?"

"Why what was to have marked you out. The proof of your law. It has acted. I'm too glad," she then bravely added, "to have been able to see what it's *not*."

He continued to attach his eyes to her, and with the sense that it was all beyond him, and that *she* was too, he would still have sharply challenged her hadn't he so felt it an abuse of her weakness to do more than take devoutly what she gave him, take it hushed as to a revelation. If he did speak, it was out of the fore-knowledge of his loneliness to come. "If you're glad of what it's 'not' it might then have been worse?"

She turned her eyes away, she looked straight before her; with which after a moment: "Well, you know our fears."

He wondered. "It's something then we never feared?"

On this slowly she turned to him. "Did we ever dream, with all our dreams, that we should sit and talk of it thus?"

He tried for a little to make out that they had; but it was as if their dreams, numberless enough, were in solution in some thick cold mist through which thought lost itself. "It might have been that we couldn't talk?"

"Well"—she did her best for him—"not from this side. This, you see," she said, "is the *other* side."

"I think," poor Marcher returned, "that all sides are the same to me." Then, however, as she gently shook her head in correction: "We mightn't, as it were, have got across—?"

"To where we are—no. We're *here*"—she made her weak emphasis.

"And much good does it do us!" was her friend's frank comment.

"It does us the good it can. It does us the good that *it* isn't here. It's past. It's behind," said May Bartram. "Before—" but her voice dropped.

He had got up, not to tire her, but it was hard to combat his yearning. She after all told him nothing but that his light had failed—which he knew well enough without her. "Before—?" he blankly echoed.

"Before, you see, it was always to *come*. That kept it present."

"Oh I don't care what comes now! Besides," Marcher added, "it seems to me I liked it better present, as you say, than I can like it absent with *your* absence."

"Oh mine!"—and her pale hands made light of it.

"With the absence of everything." He had a dreadful sense of standing there before her for—so far as anything but this proved, this bottomless drop was concerned—the last time of their life. It rested on him with a weight he felt he could scarce bear, and this weight it apparently was that still pressed out what remained in him of speakable protest. "I believe you; but I can't begin to pretend I understand. *Nothing,* for me, is past; nothing *will* pass till I pass myself, which I pray my stars may be as soon as possible. Say, however," he added, "that I've eaten my cake, as you contend, to the last crumb—how can the thing I've never felt at all be the thing I was marked out to feel?"

She met him perhaps less directly, but she met him unperturbed. "You take your 'feelings' for granted. You were to suffer your fate. That was not necessarily to know it."

"How in the world—when what is such knowledge but suffering?"

She looked up at him a while in silence. "No—you don't understand."

"I suffer," said John Marcher.

"Don't, don't!"

"How can I help at least *that?*"

"*Don't!*" May Bartram repeated.

She spoke it in a tone so special, in spite of her weakness, that he stared an instant—stared as if some light, hitherto hidden, had shimmered across his vision. Darkness again closed over it, but the gleam had already become for him an idea. "Because I haven't the right—?"

"Don't *know*—when you needn't," she mercifully urged. "You needn't—for we shouldn't."

"Shouldn't?" If he could but know what she meant!

"No—it's too much."

"Too much?" he still asked but, with a mystification that was the next moment of a sudden to give way. Her words, if they meant something, affected him in this light—the light also of her wasted face—as meaning *all,* and the sense of what knowledge had been for herself came over him with a rush which broke through into a question. "Is it of that then you're dying?"

But she watched him, gravely at first, as to see, with this, where he was, and she might have seen something or feared something that moved her sympathy. "I would live for you still—if I could." Her eyes closed for a little, as if, withdrawn into herself, she were for a last time trying. "But I can't!" she said as she raised them again to take leave of him.

She couldn't indeed, as but too promptly and sharply appeared, and he had no vision of her after this that was anything but darkness and doom. They had parted for ever in that strange talk; access to her chamber of pain, rigidly guarded, was almost wholly forbidden him; he was feeling now moreover, in the face of doctors, nurses, the two or three relatives attracted doubtless by the presumption of what she had to "leave," how few were the rights, as they were called in such cases, that he had to put forward, and how odd it might even seem that their intimacy shouldn't have given him more of them. The stupidest fourth cousin had more, even though she had been nothing in such a person's life. She had been a feature of features in *his,* for what else was it to have been so indispensable? Strange beyond saying were the ways of existence, baffling for him the anomaly of his lack, as he felt it to be, of producible claim. A woman might have been, as it were, everything to him, and it might yet present him in no connexion that any one seemed held to recognise. If this was the case in these closing weeks it was the case more sharply on the occasion of the last offices rendered, in the great grey London cemetery, to what had been mortal, to what had been precious, in his friend. The concourse at her grave was not numerous, but he saw himself treated as scarce

more nearly concerned with it than if there had been a thousand others. He was in short from this moment face to face with the fact that he was to profit extraordinarily little by the interest May Bartram had taken in him. He couldn't quite have said what he expected, but he hadn't surely expected this approach to a double privation. Not only had her interest failed him, but he seemed to feel himself unattended—and for a reason he couldn't seize—by the distinction, the dignity, the propriety, if nothing else, of the man markedly bereaved. It was as if in the view of society he had not *been* markedly bereaved, as if there still failed some sign or proof of it, and as if none the less his character could never be affirmed nor the deficiency ever made up. There were moments as the weeks went by when he would have liked, by some almost aggressive act, to take his stand on the intimacy of his loss, in order that it *might* be questioned and his retort, to the relief of his spirit, so recorded; but the moments of an irritation more helpless followed fast on these, the moments during which, turning things over with a good conscience but with a bare horizon, he found himself wondering if he oughn't to have begun, so to speak, further back.

He found himself wondering indeed at many things, and this last speculation had others to keep it company. What could he have done, after all, in her lifetime, without giving them both, as it were, away? He couldn't have made known she was watching him, for that would have published the superstition of the Beast. This was what closed his mouth now—now that the Jungle had been threshed to vacancy and that the Beast had stolen away. It sounded too foolish and too flat; the difference for him in this particular, the extinction in his life of the element of suspense, was such as in fact to surprise him. He could scarce have said what the effect resembled; the abrupt cessation, the positive prohibition, of music perhaps, more than anything else, in some place all adjusted and all accustomed to sonority and to attention. If he could at any rate have conceived lifting the veil from his image at some moment of the past (what had he done, after all, if not lift it to *her?*) so to do this to-day, to talk to people at large of the Jungle cleared and confide to them that he now felt it as safe, would have been not only to see them listen as to a goodwife's tale, but really to hear himself tell one. What it presently came to in truth was that poor Marcher waded through his beaten grass, where no life stirred, where no breath sounded, where no evil eye seemed to gleam from a possible lair, very much as if vaguely looking for the Beast, and still more as if acutely missing it. He walked about in an existence that had grown strangely more spacious, and, stopping fitfully in places where the undergrowth of life struck him as closer, asked himself yearningly, wondered secretly and sorely, if it would have lurked here or there. It would have at all events *sprung;* what was at least complete was his belief in the truth itself of the assurance given him. The change from his old sense to his new was absolute and final: what was to happen *had* so absolutely and finally happened that he was as little able to know a fear for his future as to know a hope; so absent in short was any question of anything still to come. He was to live entirely with the other question, that of his unidentified past, that of his having to see his fortune impenetrably muffled and masked.

The torment of this vision became then his occupation; he couldn't perhaps have consented to live but for the possibility of guessing. She had told him, his friend, not to guess; she had forbidden him, so far as he might, to know, and she had even in a sort denied the power in him to learn: which were so many things, precisely, to deprive him of rest. It wasn't that he wanted, he argued for fairness, that anything past and done should repeat itself; it was only that he shouldn't, as an anticlimax, have been taken sleeping so sound as not to be able to win back by an effort of thought the lost stuff of consciousness. He declared to himself at moments that he would either win it back or have done with consciousness for ever; he made this idea his one motive in fine, made it so much his passion that none other, to compare with it, seemed ever to have touched him. The lost stuff of consciousness became thus for him as a strayed or stolen child to an unappeasable father; he hunted it up and down very much as if he were knocking at doors and enquiring of the police. This was the spirit in which, inevitably, he set himself to travel; he started on a journey that was to be as long as he could make it; it danced before him that, as the other side of the globe couldn't possibly have less to say to him, it might, by a possibility of suggestion, have more. Before he quitted London, however, he made a pilgrimage to May Bartram's grave, took his way to it through the endless avenues of the grim suburban metropolis, sought it out in the wilderness of tombs, and, though he had come but for the renewal of the act of farewell, found himself, when he had at last

stood by it, beguiled into long intensities. He stood for an hour, powerless to turn away and yet powerless to penetrate the darkness of death; fixing with his eyes her inscribed name and date, beating his forehead against the fact of the secret they kept, drawing his breath, while he waited, as if some sense would in pity of him rise from the stones. He kneeled on the stones, however, in vain; they kept what they concealed; and if the face of the tomb did become a face for him it was because her two names became a pair of eyes that didn't know him. He gave them a last long look, but no palest light broke.

VI

He stayed away, after this, for a year; he visited the depths of Asia, spending himself on scenes of romantic interest, of superlative sanctity; but what was present to him everywhere was that for a man who had known what *he* had known the world was vulgar and vain. The state of mind in which he had lived for so many years shone out to him, in reflexion, as a light that coloured and refined, a light beside which the glow of the East was garish cheap and thin. The terrible truth was that he had lost—with everything else—a distinction as well; the things he saw couldn't help being common when he had become common to look at them. He was simply now one of them himself—he was in the dust, without a peg for the sense of difference; and there were hours when, before the temples of gods and the sepulchres of kings, his spirit turned for nobleness of association to the barely discriminated slab in the London suburb. That had become for him, and more intensely with time and distance, his one witness of a past glory. It was all that was left to him for proof or pride, yet the past glories of Pharaohs were nothing to him as he thought of it. Small wonder then that he came back to it on the morrow of his return. He was drawn there this time as irresistibly as the other, yet with a confidence, almost, that was doubtless the effect of the many months that had elapsed. He had lived, in spite of himself, into his change of feeling, and in wandering over the earth had wandered, as might be said, from the circumference to the centre of his desert. He had settled to his safety and accepted perforce his extinction; figuring to himself, with some colour, in the likeness of certain little old men he remembered to have seen, of whom, all meagre and wizened as they might look, it was related that they had in their time fought twenty duels or been loved by ten princesses. They indeed had been wondrous for others while he was but wondrous for himself; which, however, was exactly the cause of his haste to renew the wonder by getting back, as he might put it, into his own presence. That had quickened his steps and checked his delay. If his visit was prompt it was because he had been separated so long from the part of himself that alone he now valued.

It's accordingly not false to say that he reached his goal with a certain elation and stood there again with a certain assurance. The creature beneath the sod *knew* of his rare experience, so that, strangely now, the place had lost for him its mere blankness of expression. It met him in mildness—not, as before, in mockery; it wore for him the air of conscious greeting that we find, after absence, in things that have closely belonged to us and which seem to confess of themselves to the connexion. The plot of ground, the graven tablet, the tended flowers affected him so as belonging to him that he resembled for the hour a contented landlord reviewing a piece of property. Whatever had happened—well, had happened. He had not come back this time with the vanity of that question, his former worrying "what, *what?*" now practically so spent. Yet he would none the less never again so cut himself off from the spot; he would come back to it every month, for if he did nothing else by its aid he at least held up his head. It thus grew for him, in the oddest way, a positive resource; he carried out his idea of periodical returns, which took their place at last among the most inveterate of his habits. What it all amounted to, oddly enough, was that in his finally so simplified world this garden of death gave him the few square feet of earth on which he could still most live. It was as if, being nothing anywhere else for any one, nothing even for himself, he were just everything here, and if not for a crowd of witnesses or indeed for any witness but John Marcher, then by clear right of the register that he could scan like an open page. The open page was the tomb of his friend, and *there* were the facts of the past, there the truth of his life, there the backward reaches in which he could lose himself. He did this from time to time with such effect that he seemed to wander through the old years with his hand in the arm of a companion who was, in the most extraordinary manner, his other, his younger self; and to wander, which was more extraordinary yet, round and round a third presence—not wandering she, but stationary, still, whose eyes, turn-

ing with his revolution, never ceased to follow him, and whose seat was his point, so to speak, of orientation. Thus in short he settled to live—feeding all on the sense that he once *had* lived, and dependent on it not alone for a support but for an identity.

It sufficed him in its way for months and the year elapsed; it would doubtless even have carried him further but for an accident, superficially slight, which moved him, quite in another direction, with a force beyond any of his impressions of Egypt or of India. It was a thing of the merest chance—the turn, as he afterwards felt, of a hair, though he was indeed to live to believe that if light hadn't come to him in this particular fashion it would still have come in another. He was to live to believe this, I say, though he was not to live, I may not less definitely mention, to do much else. We allow him at any rate the benefit of the conviction, struggling up for him at the end, that, whatever might have happened or not happened, he would have come round of himself to the light. The incident of an autumn day had put the match to the train laid from of old by his misery. With the light before him he knew that even of late his ache had only been smothered. It was strangely drugged, but it throbbed; at the touch it began to bleed. And the touch, in the event, was the face of a fellow mortal. This face, one grey afternoon when the leaves were thick in the alleys, looked into Marcher's own, at the cemetery, with an expression like the cut of a blade. He felt it, that is, so deep down that he winced at the steady thrust. The person who so mutely assaulted him was a figure he had noticed, on reaching his own goal, absorbed by a grave a short distance away, a grave apparently fresh, so that the emotion of the visitor would probably match it for frankness. This fact alone forbade further attention, though during the time he stayed he remained vaguely conscious of his neighbour, a middle-aged man apparently, in mourning, whose bowed back, among the clustered monuments and mortuary yews, was constantly presented. Marcher's theory that these were elements in contact with which he himself revived, had suffered, on this occasion, it may be granted, a marked, an excessive check. The autumn day was dire for him as none had recently been, and he rested with a heaviness he had not yet known on the low stone table that bore May Bartram's name. He rested without power to move, as if some spring in him, some spell vouchsafed, had suddenly been broken for ever. If he could have done that mo-

The Beast in the Jungle 571

ment as he wanted he would simply have stretched himself on the slab that was ready to take him, treating it as a place prepared to receive his last sleep. What in all the wide world had he now to keep awake for? He stared before him with the question, and it was then that, as one of the cemetery walks passed near him, he caught the shock of the face.

His neighbour at the other grave had withdrawn, as he himself, with force enough in him, would have done by now, and was advancing along the path on his way to one of the gates. This brought him close, and his pace was slow, so that—and all the more as there was a kind of hunger in his look—the two men were for a minute directly confronted. Marcher knew him at once for one of the deeply stricken—a perception so sharp that nothing else in the picture comparatively lived, neither his dress, his age, nor his presumable character and class; nothing lived but the deep ravage of the features he showed. He *showed* them—that was the point; he was moved, as he passed, by some impulse that was either a signal for sympathy or, more possibly, a challenge to an opposed sorrow. He might already have been aware of our friend, might at some previous hour have noticed in him the smooth habit of the scene, with which the state of his own senses so scantly consorted, and might thereby have been stirred as by an overt discord. What Marcher was at all events conscious of was in the first place that the image of scarred passion presented to him was conscious too—of something that profaned the air; and in the second that, roused, startled, shocked, he was yet the next moment looking after it, as it went, with envy. The most extraordinary thing that had happened to him— though he had given that name to other matters as well —took place, after his immediate vague stare, as a consequence of this impression. The stranger passed, but the raw glare of his grief remained, making our friend wonder in pity what wrong, what wound it expressed, what injury not to be healed. What had the man *had,* to make him by the loss of it so bleed and yet live?

Something—and this reached him with a pang—that *he,* John Marcher, hadn't; the proof of which was precisely John Marcher's arid end. No passion had ever touched him, for this was what passion meant; he had survived and maundered and pined, but where had been *his* deep ravage? The extraordinary thing we speak of was the sudden rush of the result of this question. The sight that had just met his eyes named to him, as in letters of quick flame, something he had utterly, insanely missed, and what he had missed made these things a train of fire, made them mark themselves in an anguish of inward throbs. He had seen *outside* of his life, not learned it within, the way a woman was mourned when she had been loved for herself: such was the force of his conviction of the meaning of the stranger's face, which still flared for him as a smoky torch. It hadn't come to him, the knowledge, on the wings of experience; it had brushed him, jostled him, upset him, with the disrespect of chance, the insolence of accident. Now that the illumination had begun, however, it blazed to the zenith, and what he presently stood there gazing at was the sounded void of his life. He gazed, he drew breath, in pain; he turned in his dismay, and, turning, he had before him in sharper incision than ever the open page of his story. The name on the table smote him as the passage of his neighbour had done, and what it said to him, full in the face, was that *she* was what he had missed. This was the awful thought, the answer to all the past, the vision at the dread clearness of which he grew as cold as the stone beneath him. Everything fell together, confessed, explained, overwhelmed; leaving him most of all stupefied at the blindness he had cherished. The fate he had been marked for he had met with a vengeance—he had emptied the cup to the lees; he had been the man of his time, *the* man, to whom nothing on earth was to have happened. That was the rare stroke—that was his visitation. So he saw it, as we say, in pale horror, while the pieces fitted and fitted. So *she* had seen it while he didn't, and so she served at this hour to drive the truth home. It was the truth, vivid and monstrous, that all the while he had waited the wait was itself his portion. This the companion of his vigil had at a given moment made out, and she had then offered him the chance to baffle his doom. One's doom, however, was never baffled, and on the day she told him his own had come down she had seen him but stupidly stare at the escape she offered him.

The escape would have been to love her; then, *then* he would have lived. *She* had lived—who could say now with what passion?—since she had loved him for himself; whereas he had never thought of her (ah how it hugely glared at him!) but in the chill of his egotism and the light of her use. Her spoken words came back to him—the chain stretched and stretched. The Beast had lurked indeed, and the Beast, at its hour, had sprung; it had sprung in that twilight of the cold April when, pale, ill, wasted, but all beautiful, and perhaps even then recoverable, she had risen from her chair to stand before him and let him imaginably guess. It had sprung as he didn't guess; it had sprung as she hopelessly turned from him, and the mark, by the time he left her, had fallen where it *was* to fall. He had justified his fear and achieved his fate; he had failed, with the last exactitude, of all he was to fail of; and a moan now rose to his lips as he remembered she had prayed he mightn't know. This horror of waking—*this* was knowledge, knowledge under the breath of which the very tears in his eyes seemed to

freeze. Through them, none the less, he tried to fix it and hold it; he kept it there before him so that he might feel the pain. That at least, belated and bitter, had something of the taste of life. But the bitterness suddenly sickened him, and it was as if, horribly, he saw, in the truth, in the cruelty of his image, what had been appointed and done. He saw the Jungle of his life and saw the lurking Beast; then, while he looked, perceived it, as by a stir of the air, rise, huge and hideous, for the leap that was to settle him. His eyes darkened—it was close; and, instinctively turning, in his hallucination, to avoid it, he flung himself, face down, on the tomb.   1903

REALISTS AND NATURALISTS:

Howe   Kirkland   Garland   Frederic

Crane   Norris   Dreiser

Edgar Watson Howe

1853 · 1937

The printer's case, where so many American writers in the latter half of the nineteenth century were schooled in writing, was the Harvard and Yale of Edgar Watson Howe. Born in Indiana, Howe, as a child, moved to Fairview, Missouri. His brief common-school education was broken off at the age of eleven when, having to fend for himself, he learned the printer's trade. He set up type for newspapers in Missouri, Nebraska, Colorado, Iowa, and Kansas and eventually became a journalist.

Howe was editor of the *Atchison* (Kansas) *Daily Globe* when he wrote *The Story of a Country Town,* his

first novel, in evenings after work. Unable to find a publishing house willing to accept the realistic manuscript, he printed the book in his own printshop in 1883. So successful was the book—if a claim which he made later is to be credited—that several publishers' readers were dismissed for having rejected it. A number of other books, none so noteworthy, followed. Howe continued his association with the *Globe* until 1927, building up a national reputation for the newspaper. He died in 1937.

By the time Howe began to write his novel, realistic

"The grave by the path"—frontispiece from E. W. Howe, The Story of a Country Town, *1883*

methods had evidently become so widespread that he could employ them without any great amount of self-consciousness. His brand of realism was, for the time, particularly frank and grim in its portrayal of the harshness of life in a pioneer Western community. In the days of Edgar Lee Masters' *Spoon River Anthology* (1914), a book of poetry which won sensational fame for its stern pictures of rural life, Howe was rediscovered as a pioneer in the movement Carl Van Doren has called "revolt from the Village." He was thus an initiator of a development which culminated in writings by Zona Gale and Sinclair Lewis and a number of other authors.

E. W. Howe, **Plain People** (an autobiography), New York, 1929 • Carl Van Doren, "Introduction" to **The Story of a Country Town**, New York, 1927

From

The Story of a Country Town

"The sternest, the grimmest of American novels," Carl Van Doren said in 1921, was **The Story of a Country Town.**

"I became early impressed," says the narrator, Ned Westlock, "with the fact that our people seemed to be miserable and discontented, and frequently wondered that they did not . . . move away from a place which made all the men surly and rough, and the women pale and fretful." The chief characters in the novel, John Westlock and Jo Erring, were tragic figures. John, Ned's father, for instance, often sat for hours grimly thinking—"tempted and beckoned by the invisible and mysteriously potent forces he pretended to despise"; and eventually he yielded to temptation and eloped with a vulgar woman whom he did not love. Jo ended his unhappy life by committing suicide.

A quiet, rather colorless style and an easy-going narrative method gave the novel much of its impact. The following portion of one chapter is not a high point in the book but a typical passage which shows the shallow religion, the poverty, the unhappiness, and the aimlessness of Twin Mounds and which gives a revealing glimpse of the discontented John Westlock.

Chapter XVI

MORE OF THE VILLAGE OF TWIN MOUNDS

In Twin Mounds the citizens spent their idle time in religious discussions, and although I lived there a great many years I do not remember that any of the questions in dispute were ever settled. They never discussed politics with any animation, and read but little, except in the Bible to find points to dispute; but of religion they never tired, and many of them could quote the sacred word by the page. No two of them ever exactly agreed in their ideas, for men who thought alike
10 on baptism violently quarrelled when the resurrection was mentioned, and two of them who engaged a hell-redemptionist one night would in all probability fail to agree themselves the next, on the atonement. The merchants neglected their customers, when they had them, to discuss points in the Bible which I used to think were not of the slightest consequence, and in many instances the men who argued the most were those who chased deer with hounds on Sunday, and ran horse races, for they did not seem to discuss the
20 subject so much on account of its importance as because of its fitness as a topic to quarrel about.

There was always a number of famous discussions going on, as between the lawyer and the storekeeper, or the blacksmith and the druggist, or the doctor and the carpenter, and whenever I saw a crowd gathering hurriedly in the evening I knew that two of the disputants had got together again to renew their old difficulty, which they kept up until a late hour, in the presence of half the town.

30 There was a certain man who kept a drug store, who was always in nervous excitement from something a fat blacksmith had said to him in their discussions, and who had a habit of coming in on him suddenly in the middle of the day; and whenever I went into the place of business of either one of them I heard them telling those present how they had triumphed the night before, or intended to triumph on a future occasion. Some of the greatest oaths I have ever heard were uttered by these men while discussing religion, and frequently the little and nervous drug-store keeper had to be forcibly 40 prevented from jumping at his burly opponent and striking him. The drug store was not far away from the office where I worked, and whenever loud and boisterous talking was heard in that direction a smile went round, for we knew the blacksmith had suddenly come upon his enemy, and attacked him with something he had thought up while at his work. I never knew exactly what the trouble between them was, though I heard enough of it; but I remember that it had some reference to a literal resurrection, and a new 50 body; and I often thought it queer that each one was able to take the Bible and establish his position so clearly. Whenever I heard the blacksmith talk I was sure that the druggist was wrong, but when the druggist called upon the blacksmith to stop right there, and began his argument, I became convinced that, after all, there were two sides to the question.

These two men, as well as most of the others, were members of a church known then as the Campbellite, for I do not remember that there was an infidel or 60 unbeliever in the place. There were a great many backsliders, but none of them ever questioned religion itself, though they could never agree on doctrine. It has occurred to me since that if one of them had thought to dispute the inspiration of the Bible, and argued about that, the people would have been entirely happy, for the old discussions in time became very tiresome.

The people regarded religion as a struggle between the Campbellite church and the Devil, and a sensation 70 was developed one evening when my father remarked to the druggist, in the presence of the usual crowd— he happened to be in the place on an errand, as he never engaged in the amusement of the town—that sprinkling answered every purpose of baptism. The druggist became very much excited immediately and prepared for a discussion, but my father only laughed at him and walked away. The next Sunday, however, he preached a sermon on the subject in the court-house, and attacked the town's religion with so much vigor that the excitement was very intense.

Most of the citizens of Twin Mounds came from the surrounding country, and a favorite way of increasing the population was to elect the county officers from the country, but after their terms expired a new set moved in, for it was thought they became so corrupt by a two years' residence that they could not be trusted to a re-election. The town increased in size a little in this manner, for none of these men ever went back to their farms again, though they speedily lost standing after they retired from their positions. Many others who left their farms to move to the town said in excuse that the school advantages were better, and seemed very anxious for a time that their children should be educated, but once they were established in Twin Mounds they abused the school a great deal, and said it was not satisfactory, and allowed their children to remain away if they were so inclined.

There was the usual number of merchants, professional men, mechanics, etc., who got along well enough, but I never knew how at least one half the inhabitants lived. Some of them owned teams, and farmed in the immediate vicinity; others "hauled," and others did whatever offered, but they were all poor, and were constantly changing from one house to another. These men usually had great families of boys, who grew up in the same indifferent fashion, and drifted off in time nobody knew where, coming back occasionally, after a long absence, well-dressed, and with money to rattle in their pockets. But none of them ever came back who had business of sufficient importance elsewhere to call them away again, for they usually remained until their good clothes wore out, the delusion of their respectability was broken, and they became town loafers again, or engaged in the hard pursuits of their fathers. The only resident of Twin Mounds who ever distinguished himself ran away with a circus and never came back, for although he was never heard of it was generally believed that he must have become famous in some way to induce him to forego the pleasure of returning home in good

clothes, and swaggering up and down the street to allow the people to shake his hand.

This class of men never paid their debts, and to get credit for an amount was equal to earning it, to their way of thinking, and a new merchant who came in did a great business until he found them out. I have said they never paid; they did sometimes, but if they paid a dollar on account they bought three or four times that amount to go on the books.

They always seemed to me to be boys yet, surprised at being their own masters, and only worked when they had to, as boys do. They engaged in boys' amusements, too, for most of them owned packs of dogs, and short-distance racehorses, and it was one of their greatest accomplishments to drive a quarter-horse to a wood-wagon to some out-of-the-way neighborhood, match it against a farmer's horse threatened with speed, and come back with all the money owned in that direction. I suppose they came West to grow up with the country, like the rest of us, but they were idle where they came from, and did not improve in the West, because work was necessary, whereupon the thought no doubt occurred to them that they could have grown rich in that way anywhere.

A few of them were away most of the time—I never knew where, but so far away that they seldom came home—and their families supported themselves as best they could, but were always expecting the husbands and fathers to return and take them away to homes of luxury. Occasionally news came that they were killed by Indians, and occasionally this was contradicted by the certainty that they were locked up for disreputable transactions, or hanged. Whenever a Twin Mounds man died away from home otherwise than honorably, it was always said that he had been killed by the Indians.

All of this, and much more, I learned during the first three years of my residence there . . . .

During this time I had mastered the mystery of the boxes [of the printer's case] so well that I wondered how it was possible I had puzzled my brain over them, they seemed so simple and easy, and if I improved the time well, I am sure it was due to the kindly encouragement and help of Martin, who was not only a very clever printer, but an intelligent man besides. It had always been a part of his work, I believe, to write the few local items of the town, and he taught me to help him; making me do it my way first, and then, after he had explained the errors, I wrote them all over again. If I employed a bad sentence, or an inappropriate word, he explained his objections at length, and I am certain that had I been less dull I should have become a much better writer than I am, for he was very competent to teach me.

My father, as an editor, was earnest and vigorous, and the subjects of which he wrote required columns for expression, so that his page of the paper was always full. I spent a quite recent rainy holiday in a dusty attic looking over an old file of the "Union of States" when he was its editor, and was surprised at the ability he displayed. The simple and honest manner in which he discussed the questions of the day became very popular, for he always advocated that which was right, and there was always more presswork to do every week, which he seemed to regard as an imposition on Martin, who had formerly had that hard part of the work to perform, and on the plea of needing exercise he early began to run the press himself, and in the history of the business at that time no man was known who could equal him in the rapid and steady manner in which he went about it.

Soon after my introduction into the office I had learned to ink the forms so acceptably with a hand roller that I was forced to keep at it, for a suitable successor could not be found, but at last we found a young man who had a passion for art (it was none other than my old enemy, Shorty Wilkinson; I fought him regularly every week during the first year of my residence in town, but we finally agreed to become friends), and after that Martin and I spent a portion of the two press days of the week in adorning our page with paragraphs of local happenings; or rather in rambling through the town hunting for them. Sometimes we invented startling things at night, and spent the time given us in wandering through the woods like idle boys, bathing and fishing in the streams in summer, and visiting the sugar-camps in early spring, where we heard many tales of adventure which afterwards appeared in print under great headings.

By reason of the fact that it was conducted by a careful and industrious man, and the great number of law advertisements which came in from that and two of the adjoining counties, the "Union of States" made a good deal of money, and certainly it was improved under my father's proprietorship. Before it came into his possession it was conducted by a man who had ideas, but not talents, beyond a country newspaper, who regarded it as a poor field in which to expect either reputation or money; but my father made it as readable as he could, and worked every day and night at something designed to improve it. The result was that its circulation rapidly extended, and the business was very profitable.

His disposition had not changed with his residence, except that he turned me over entirely to Martin, and a room had been fitted up in the building where the paper was printed for our joint occupancy, where we spent our evenings as we saw fit, but always to some purpose, for the confidence reposed in Martin was deserved.

From my mother, who was more lonely than ever in the stone house in which we lived, I learned occasionally that the Rev. John Westlock still read and thought far into every night. Into the room in which he slept was brought every evening the dining-table, and sitting before this, spread out to its full size, he read, wrote, or thought until he went to bed, which was always at a late hour.

It occurred to me once or twice, in an indifferent sort of way, that a man who had no greater affairs than a country printing office, and a large amount of wild land constantly increasing in value, had no reason to think so much as he did, but I never suspected what his trouble was until it was revealed to me, as I shall presently relate.

When I rambled through the town at night, and passed that way, if I looked in at his window, which was on the ground floor, he was oftener thinking than reading or writing, leaning back in his chair, with a scowl on his face which frightened me. Whether the procession of forbidden pictures was still passing before him, and the figures accompanying them were still beckoning, will never be known until the Great Book of Men's Actions, said to be kept in Heaven, is opened, and I hope that those who are permitted to look at the writing under the head of John Westlock will be able to read, through the mercy of God: "Tempted and tried; but forgiven."

Almost every Saturday afternoon he drove away into the country without explanation, and did not return until Sunday night or early Monday morning. Where he went we never knew, but we supposed he had gone to preach in some of the country churches or schoolhouses, for persons who came into the office through the week spoke in a way which led us to believe that such was the case, although he was not often at Fairview, Jo told me, but he heard of him frequently in the adjoining neighborhoods.

During the latter part of the second year of our residence in Twin Mounds, my father came home one Monday morning in an unusually bad humor, and though he went away occasionally after that, it was usually late in the evening, and I came to understand somehow that he did not preach any more, the result of some sort of a misunderstanding. Even had I been anxious to know the particulars, there was no one to inform me, as no one seemed to know, and in a little while I ceased to think about it entirely, for he at once gave me more to do by teaching me the details of the business. The men who came to the office to see him after that annoyed him, and made him more irritable, therefore he taught me the routine of his affairs, that I might relieve him of them. We all usually worked together, but after this he took whatever he had to do into the room where Martin had his bed, and when the people came in I was expected to attend to them. From my going into the bedroom to ask him questions about his land business, which I did not so well understand, it came to be believed that he was failing in health, and his old friends frequently expressed the hope that he would soon be better. If I had trouble in settling with any one, he came out impatiently, and acted as if he would like to pitch the man into the street, for his affairs were always straight and honest, and there was no occasion for trouble. Frequently he would propose to work in my place if I would go out in town, and solicit business, and when there were bills to collect, I was put about it, so that for weeks at a time he did not see any one, and trusted almost everything to me.

When my father was away, I was expected to stay at home, and I could not help noticing that my mother was growing paler and weaker, and that the old trouble of which she had spoken to Jo was no better. The house in which we lived was built of square blocks of stone, and the walls were so thick, and the windows so small, that I used to think of her as a prisoner shut up in it. The upper part was not used, except when I went there to sleep, and it was such a dismal and lonely place that I was often awakened in the night with bad dreams, but I always had company, for I found her sleeping on a pallet by the side of my bed, as though she was glad to be near me. I never heard her come, or go away, but if I awoke in the night I was sure to find her by my side.

"There is a great change in you, Ned," she said to me one evening when I had gone to stay with her, "since coming to town."

I replied that I was glad to hear her say so, as I was very ignorant when I went into the office to work.

"The rest of us are unchanged," she said. "We are no happier here than in Fairview; just the same, I think."

It was the only reference she had ever made to the subject to me, and I did not press it, for I feared she would break down and confess the sorrow which filled her life. A great many times afterwards I could have led her up to talk about it, fully and freely, I think, but I dreaded to hear from her own lips how unhappy she really was. Had I those days to live over—how often are those words said and written, as though there is a consciousness with every man of having been unwise as well as unhappy in his youth—I would pursue a different course, but it never occurred to me then that I could be of more use to her than I was, or that I could in any way lessen her sorrow. She never regretted that I no longer slept in the house, nor that I was growing as cold toward her as my father, which must have been the case, so I never knew that she cared much about it. Indeed, I interpreted her unhappiness as indifference toward me, and it had been that way since I could remember. Had she put her arms around me, and asked me to love her because no one else did, I am sure I should have been devoted to her, but her quietness convinced me that she was so troubled in other ways that there was no time to think of me, and while I believe I was always kind and thoughtful of her, I fear I was never affectionate.

1883

Joseph Kirkland

1830 · 1894

Details in the biography of Joseph Kirkland in the years before he became an author hardly suggest that he was preparing for a literary career. He was born in Geneva, New York, January 7, 1830. In his early boyhood, he moved westward to Michigan with his family. His formal education was confined to a few years. In 1843 he returned east with his family—to New York City; in 1847 he took a trip to England. Shortly after that he began a career in business, interrupted by a few years of service in the United States army during the Civil War. He was a clerk in New York, an auditor, a coal-mine operator, a worker in an Internal Revenue office in Illinois. At fifty, after study in night school, he was admitted to the bar, and he practiced law until his death in 1894.

The outline does not indicate any preparation for authorship, but there had been preparation, nevertheless. His parents had both been schoolteachers, and they had given him a good deal of informal education at home. His mother, furthermore, was the author Caroline Kirkland who, in the 1840's, had written several books about life on the Michigan frontier. During the trip to England, at seventeen, Kirkland had carefully kept a journal in which he had attempted to write vividly of his experiences. He had long been interested in literature, and had come to believe that the best fiction was the sort which drew most directly upon life and which "told the truth." His belief was that earlier fictionists dealing with the Middle West had great faults: Eggleston

had been too humorous to be accurate; Howe, too "melodramatic."

He thought that by writing more nearly in the fashion of Thomas Hardy and by drawing upon his own rich experience, he could improve upon their work. So he wrote the novel *Zury: The Meanest Man in Spring County*, published in 1887, when he was in his late fifties. Hamlin Garland, pleased with the book, visited its author in Chicago. He found that Kirkland was "a small man, alert and humorous, with keen, black eyes." "His," said Garland, "was the keenest mind I had ever met in the West." When Garland asked him how he happened to write his book, Kirkland explained that he had lived almost all his life in Illinois, part of the time in a small town. "I am the son of a pioneer woman writer, Caroline Kirkland," he said, "and I know farm life. All the characters in *Zury* have their prototypes in my down-state acquaintances. The book is as true as I could make it. Many of its incidents are literally exact." Howells, in his review of the novel, indicated that it conformed to his own theories about fiction which was a "transcript from life": "Those gaunt, sallow, weary, work-worn women, those tireless, rude, independent, and mutually helpful men, belong to a period now driven to the furthest frontier; their look and speech are caught here with a certainty that can come only of personal knowledge. But personal knowledge alone does not suffice in such a case, and we are to be glad of an artist with clear eyes and an honest hand in the author of *Zury*—one incapable of painting life other than he has found it."

The general approval that *Zury* received from critics encouraged Kirkland to devote an increasing amount of his time to literature. He wrote plays, historical books about Chicago, magazine articles, and numerous book reviews. More notable achievements, however, were two novels. The first was *The McVeys* (1888), a sequel to *Zury* which pictured life in rural Illinois. The second was *The Captain of Company K* (1891). This book was based upon Kirkland's experiences during the Civil War, which he had entered as a private, following the first call for volunteers, and from which he had emerged, in 1863, as a major. The book was dedicated "to the surviving men of the firing line, the men who could see the enemy in front of them with the naked eye while they would have needed a field-glass to see the history-makers behind them." The dedication shows

something of the spirit of the book: written mainly from the point of view of the common soldier, it was a pioneer work in its realistic account of some of the less glamorous aspects of the war.

Kirkland is probably more important historically than he is when judged by positive standards. He was not untouched by romanticism; he was not particularly skilled as a storyteller, and he did not have a great deal of power. Yet he could write better than average dialogue, he had a flair for setting down details, and he could attract attention as a writer whose creed was that fiction should tell the truth. Undoubtedly he was very important as a trail blazer for the American realistic movement.

Hamlin Garland, **Roadside Meetings**, New York, 1930, 106-112 • W. D. Howells, "The Editor's Study," **Harper's Magazine**, New York, June 1888, LXXVII, 152-153 • Lloyd Lewis, "Letters of a Pioneer Realist," **Newberry Library Bulletin**, Chicago, December 1945

From

Zury: The Meanest Man in Spring County

Chapter V

HOW THE MEANEST MAN GOT SO MEAN, AND HOW MEAN HE GOT

Ephraim wanted Zury to marry, but it was with "a sharp eye to the main chance." Property and personal service at no wages might both be secured by a judicious choice. Girls were not plenty, but at the Peddicombs' there were three of marriageable age. Their place was only three miles from Prouder's, and they were still the nearest neighbors. Mrs. Peddicomb had not long survived the birth of her three daughters. She died (as was and is common among farmers' wives) at not much over

thirty years of age, just when her life ought to have been in its prime. 10

She was called a "Come-gals kind of woman" by neighbors; partly in ridicule of her enthusiasm, and partly in admiration of her energy. It was told of her that she would get up before light on Monday, "fly 'raound," uncover the fire, hang on the kettle, and call up the ladder to the loft,—

"Come gals! *Dew* git up 'n' start in! To-day's Monday, to-morrow's Tuesday, 'n' next day's Wednesday; 'n' then comes Thursday, Friday, 'n' Saturday,—the hull week 20 gone 'n' nothin' done."

The two younger girls had been cared for by the oldest, and so had retained some girlish freshness and delicacy, but as for Mary (the caretaker after her mother's death), she was "good-looking" only because she looked good.

On this marriage subject Ephraim took occasion to speak to Zury.

"Mary Peddicomb, she's a likely gal."

"Mary? Why not S'manthy 'n' Flory?" 30

"Oh, yes; they're all right tew. Th' ol' man he's got th' best part of a section. Some stawk, tew; 'n' th' haouse 'n' barn's fust rate."

"Ya-as. Ef th' haouse 'n' barn worn't so good he'd have more stawk th't 'd pay him right smart better'n th' haouse 'n' barn dooz."

"Peddicomb ain't like t' marry ag'in. Mary she'll have her sheer."

"Any more'n th' others?"

"Oh, no. All same. But I reck'n Mary she'd be more of a manager. *She* kin work. I've watched her ever sence she wuz knee-high to a hoppy-toad, 'n' *I* tell ye she kin work!"

"Ef ye mean more manageable ye mought's well say so."

"Wal, I dew 'llaow she'd be full 's little likely t' be uppish 's th' others."

"Ye 'llaow 't humbly and humble goes t'gether?"

"Wal, yes; 'mongst the wimmin folks, substantially. Nothin' sets 'em so bad up 's bein' ha'ans'm. Spiles 'em fer use abaout the place. Th' humbly ones take t' milkin' more willin' like; 'n' I don't see but what the caows give daown tew 'em full 's well 's tew the ha'ans'm ones. 'N' then when ther' looks goes the' 're apt t' kick."

"What, the caows?"

"No, the wimmin."

("Humbly" in country parlance is a corruption of "homely," the opposite of handsome; plain, ungainly. "Humbly as a hedge fence.")

Zury pondered on this shrewd counsel from time to time, but took no step toward marrying.

"Right smart o' things t' think on afore th' 'll be any hurry 'baout a-gittin' marr'd. Th' feller th't 's in an orfle sweat t' marry, he 's li'ble t' be the very feller th't 's behind-hand with everythin' else. Takes Time by the forelock 'baout gittin' a wife; 'n' by the fetlock 'baout gittin' suthin' fer her t' eat."

The boy was wedded to his idols quite as faithfully, if not quite so sordidly, as was his father. Their dispositions were much alike. No draft on their powers of endurance and self-denial could be too great.

As to niggardliness, there was a confessed rivalry between them. Each would tell of the money-making and money-saving exploits of the other, and of his efforts to surpass them.

"Dad's a screamer t' save money! D' ye ever see him withe a plaow-pint ontew a plaow? Give him a hickory grub, 'n' he kin dew it so it'll run a good half a day; 'n' then withe it on agin in noon-spell whilst th' team

's a eatin', 'n' then withe it on agin come night so 's t' be ready fer nex' morn'n', 'n' keep it up fer a week that-a-way, sooner 'n pay th' smith a cent t' rivit it fast."

"Thasso, thasso, Zury. Hickory twigs is cheaper ner iron any day."

"Ya-as, dad; but then I kin make a shillin' while ye 're a savin' a cent. Look at it wunst. I upped 'n' sold the smith a half an acre, 'n' took a mortgage on it, 'n' made him dew all aour repairin' b' way of interest on the mortgage, 'n' then foreclosed th' mortgage when it come dew, 'n' got th' land back, shop 'n' all. Business is business!"

Ephraim always wanted to buy at the shop where they wrapped up the purchases with the largest and strongest paper and twine, and the harnesses on the farm gradually grew to be largely composed of twine. Zury could buy everything at wholesale, half price, including merchandise, paper, twine, harnesses, and all.

One day Zury came across a poor little boy carrying a poorer little puppy and crying bitterly.

"What 's the matter, sonny?"

"Our folks gimme a dime t' draownd this h'yer purp, 'n' I—I—I—hate t' dew it."

"Wal, ne' mind, bub; gimme the dime 'n' I'll draownd him fer ye."

Whereupon he took the cash and the pup and walked to the mill-pond, while the boy ran home. Zury threw the little trembling creature as far as he could into the pond. A few seconds of wildly waving small ears, legs, and tail, and then a splash, and then nothing but widening ripples. But out of one of the ripples is poked a little round object, which directs itself bravely toward the shore. Nearer and nearer struggles the small black nozzle, sometimes under water, and sometimes on top, but always nearer.

"Ye mis'able, ornery little fyce, ye! Lemme ketch ye swimmin' ashore! I'll throw ye furder nex' time."

At last poor little roly-poly drags itself to the land and squats down at the very water's edge, evidently near to the end of its powers. Zury picks it up and swings it for a mighty cast, but stops and studies it a moment.

"Looks fer all the world like a sheep-dawg-purp."

Whereupon he slipped it into his pocket and carried it home, where it grew up to be a fit mate to old Shep, and the ancestress of a line of sheep dogs which ornament Spring County to this day.

Later, when the same boy, grown older, applied to Zury for one of the pups, he charged him the full price, fifty cents, took all he had, thirty-six cents, and his note on interest for the balance, the dog being pledged as security. The note being unpaid when due, Zury took back the dog. "Business is business!"

Years passed and it came time for the old man to be gathered to his fathers and the son to reign in his stead. When Ephraim lay on his deathbed, he whispered to
10 Zury:—

"What day 's to-day?"

"Tuesday, father."

"I hope I'll live ontel Thursday, 'n' then ye kin hev the fun'r'l Sunday, 'n' not lose a day's work with the teams."

He did not die till Saturday night, but Zury had the funeral on Sunday all the same, like a dutiful son as he was, bent on carrying out his father's last request.

After Zury had grown to be a prosperous farmer, Chi-
20 cago became the great market for the sale of grain. Teams by the score would start out from far down the State, and, driving during the day and camping at night, make the long journey. They would go in pairs or squads so as to be able to double teams over the bad places. Forty or fifty bushels could thus be carried in one load, when the chief parts of the roads were good, and "the ready john" (hard cash), could be got for the grain, at twenty or thirty cents a bushel for corn or wheat. This sum would provide a barrel or two of salt,
30 and perhaps a plow and a bundle of dry goods and knick-knacks for the women folks, the arrival of which was a great event in the lonely farm-houses.

Zury had now working for him (beside Jule, who kept house and attended to the live stock), a young fellow who became a score of years afterward private, corporal, sergeant, lieutenant, and captain in the —th Illinois Volunteer Infantry in the great war. From his stories, told in bivouacs and beside camp fires, to toiling, struggling, suffering "boys in blue," these tales are taken
40 almost verbatim. (Some of them have already found their way into print.)

"Zury always wanted to get onto the road with farmers whose housekeeping was good, because his own was—well, wuss th'n what we git down here in Dixie, an' there's no need of *that*. Well, when they'd halt for noon-

spell, Zury he'd happen along promiscuous-like, an' most generally some of 'em would make him stop an' take a bite. He was good company if he *was* so near. 'N' then a man's feed warn't counted fer much, unless it was some store-truck or boughten stuff. 50

"But one day they jest passed the wink and sot it up on him, and come noon-spell nobody asked Zury an' me to eat. Zury left me to take care of both teams while he walked up and down the line of wagins. Everybody who hadn't 'jest eat,' warn't 'quite ready' yet, an' by the next time he came to those who hadn't been 'quite ready,' they'd 'jest eat.'

"Wal, Zury swallered his disappointment and I swallered all the chawed wheat I could git away with, and the first settlement we passed Zury went and bought a mon- 60 strous big bag of sody-crackers, and we eat them for supper and breakfast. And still we were not happy.

"Next noon-spell Zury said, 'Boys, s'posin' we kinder whack up 'n' mess together.' Wal, the others 'd had enough of their joke, and so they all agreed, and chipped in. Ham, pickles, pies, cakes, honey, eggs, apples, and one thing another. Ye see every man's o' woman knew that when they got together, her housekeep would be compared with everybody else's; so these long drives were like donation parties, or weddings, or funerals,—well fed. 70

"Of course, Zury's sody-crackers went in with the rest, an' me an' Zury always ate *some* anyhow for appearance sake. I could see the fellers were all makin' fun of Zury's cute dodge of gettin' a dozen good meals for him an' me at the price of a few pounds of sody-crackers. But *then*, they did n't know Zury so well as they thought they did. By an' by the trip was done an' settlin'-up-time came, when each man was called on for his share of pasturage, ferriage, an' one thing another. Zury paid his, but he deducted out twenty-five cents paid for sody- 80 crackers. Said it was one of the cash outlays for the common good, an' if any of the rest of 'em spent money an' did n't put it in, more fools they. Business is business."

So Zury in the soda-cracker episode came out "top of the heap" as usual. The top of the heap was his accustomed place, but still he perceived that he was living under one useless disability, and, with his quick adaptation of means to ends and remedies to deficiencies, he simply—married. In doing this, he was guided by his father's shrewd words; counsel which had lain fallow 90 in his memory for years.

Zury's marriageability had, of course, not been un-observed in the household of the three daughters. Peddi-comb had remarked what a good "outin'" the Prouders had made in their purchase of swine from him, and cherished the same kind of feeling toward them that most of us experience when some other person has done better in a joint transaction than we did.

"Them Praouders, the' 'll skin outer the land all the' kin skin, 'n' then sell offen the place all 't anybody 'll buy, 'n' then feed t' the hawgs all a hawg 'll eat, 'n' then give th' rest t' th' dawg, 'n' then what th' dawg won't tech the' 'll live on theirselves."

"Yew bet," tittered Samantha, the second. "That thar ornery Zury Praouder he'd let a woman starve t' death ef he could. 'N' o' man Praouder wuz th' same way, tew. Th' o' woman she wuz near abaout skin 'n' bone when the' buried her. I seen her in her coffin, 'n' I know."

"Oh, don't *yew* be scaret, S'manthy. I hain't saw Zury a-lookin' over t' your side o' the meetin'-haouse, no gre't," kindly rejoined Flora, the youngest daughter.

"Who, me? He knows better! Not ef husbands wuz scarcer ner hen's teeth."

"Six hundred 'n' forty acres o' good land, all fenced 'n' paid fer; 'n' a big orchard; 'n' all well stocked, tew." (He added this with a pang, remembering once more the pig-purchase, which by this time had grown to a mighty drove, in spite of many sales.)

"Don't care ef he owned all ou' doors. Th' more the' 've got, th' more it shows haow stingy the' be."

Then the meek Mary ventured a remark.

"Mebbe ef Zury wuz t' marry a good gal it 'd be the makin' on him."

"Oh, Mary, *yew* hain't no call t' stan' up fer Zury! Th' o' man he 'd a ben more in yewr line."

"No, Zury would n't want *me,* ner no other man, I don't expect," she answered with a laugh—and a sigh.

One Sunday afternoon Zury rode over to Peddicomb's to get a wife. He tried to decide which girl to ask, but his mind would wander off to other subjects,—crops, live stock, bargains, investments. He did n't much think that either girl he asked would say no, but if she did, he could ask the others. When he came near the house he caught sight of one of the girls, in her Sunday clothes, picking a "posy" in the "front garding." It was Mary.

"Good day, Mary. Haow 's all the folks?"

"Good day, Zury—Mr. Praouder, I s'pose I should say. Won't ye 'light?"

"Wal, I guess not. I jes' wanted t' speak abaout a little matter."

"Wal, father he 's raoun' some 'ers. Haow 's the folks t' your 'us?"

"All peart; that is t' say th' ain't no one naow ye know, but me 'n' Jule 'n' Mac. That makes a kind of a bob-tail team, ye know, Mary. Nobody but Jule t' look out fer things. Not b't what he 's a pretty fair of a nigger as niggers go. He c'd stay raoun' 'n' help some aoutside."

"Whatever is he a-drivin' at?" thought Mary, but she said nothing.

"The's three of you gals to hum. Ye don't none of ye seem t' go off yit, tho' I sh'd a-thought Flory she 'd a-ben picked up afore this, 'n' S'manthy tew fer that matter."

Neither of them saw the unintended slur this rough speech cast upon poor Mary.

"Don't ye think we'd better git married, Mary?"

"What, *me?*"

"Wal, yes." He answered this in a tone where she might have detected the suggestion, "Or one of your sisters," if she had been keen and critical. But she was neither. She simply rested her work-worn hand upon the gate post and her chin upon her hand, and looked dreamily off over the prairie. She pondered the novel proposition for some time, but fortunately not quite long enough to cause Zury to ask if either of her sisters was at home, as he was quite capable of doing.

She looked up at him, the blood slowly mounting to her face, and considered how to say yes. He saw that she meant yes, so he helped her out a little. He wanted to have it settled and go.

"Wal, Mary, silence gives consent, they say. When shall it be?"

"Oh, yew ain't in no hurry, Zury, I don't expect."

He was about to urge prompt action, but the thought occurred to him that she must want to get her "things" ready, and the longer she waited the more "things" she would bring with her. So he said:—

"Suit yerself, Mary. I'll drop over 'n' see ye nex' Sun-day, 'n' we 'll fix it all up."

Mary had no objection to urge, though possibly in her secret heart she wished there had been a little more sentiment and romance about it. No woman likes "to be cheated out of her wooing," but then this might come

Joseph Kirkland—frontispiece from Joseph Kirkland,
The Captain of Company K, *1891*

later. He called for her with the wagon on the appointed day, and they drove to the house of a justice of the peace who lived a good distance away. This was not for the sake of making a wedding trip, but because this particular justice owed Zury money, as Zury carefully explained.

And so Mary went to work for Zury very much as Jule did, only it was for less wages, as Jule got a dollar a month besides his board and clothes, while Mary did not.

For a year or two or three after marriage (during which two boys were born to them) Zury found that he had gained, by this investment, something more than mere profit and economy—that affection and sympathy were realities in life. But gradually the old dominant mania resumed its course, and involved in its current the weak wife as well as the strong husband. The general verdict was that both Zury and Mary were "jest 's near 's they could stick 'n' live." "They 'd skin a flea fer its hide 'n' taller."

"He gin an acre o' graound fer the church 'n' scule-house, 'n' it raised the value of his hull farm more 'n' a dollar an acre. 'N' when he got onto the scule-board *she* 'lloawed she had n't released her daower right, 'n' put him up t' tax the deestrick fer the price of that same acre o' ground."

So Zury, claiming the proud position of "the meanest ma-an in Spring Caounty," would like to hear his claim disputed. If he had a rival he would like to have him pointed out, and would "try pootty hard but what he 'd match him."

Strange as it may seem, these grasping characteristics did not make Zury despised or even disliked among his associates. His "meanness" was not underhanded.

"Th' ain't nothin' *mean* abaout Zury, *mean* 's he is. Gimme a man as sez right aout 'look aout fer yerself,' 'n' I kin git along with him. It 's these h'yer sneakin' fellers th't 's one thing afore yer face 'n' another behind yer back th't I can't abide. Take ye by th' beard with one hand 'n' smite ye under th' fifth rib with t' other! He pays his way 'n' dooz 's he 'grees every time. When he buys 'taters o' me, I 'd jest 's live 's hev him measure 'em 's measure 'em myself with him a-lookin' on. He knows hoaw t' trade, 'n' ef yew don't, he don't want ye t' trade with him, that 's all; ner t' grumble if ye git holt o' the hot eend o' th' poker arter he 's give ye fair notice. Better be shaved with a sharp razor than a dull one."

On an occasion when the honesty of a more pretentious citizen was compared with Zury's to the advantage of the latter, he said:—

"Honest? Me? Wal, I guess so. Fustly, I would n't be noth'n' else, nohaow; seck'ndly, I kin 'fford t' be, seein' 's hoaw it takes a full bag t' stand alone; thirdly, I can't 'fford t' be noth'n' else, coz honesty 's th' best policy."

He was evidently quoting, unconsciously but by direct inheritance, the aphorisms of his fellow Pennsylvanian, Dr. Franklin.

In peace as in war strong men love "foemen worthy of their steel." Men liked to be with Zury and hear his gay, shrewd talk; to trade with him, and meet his frankly brutal greed. He enjoyed his popularity, and liked to do good turns to others when it cost him nothing. When elected to local posts of trust and confidence he served the public in the same efficient fashion in which he served himself, and he was therefore continually elected to school directorships and other like "thank 'ee jobs."

1887

Hamlin Garland

1860 · 1940

In the battle of the realists against "effete romanticism" in the 1890's, William Dean Howells had perhaps his most militant ally in Hamlin Garland, a large-framed and indefatigable Middlewesterner. For Garland, indeed, "realism" was too tame a term; he preferred to call himself a "veritist" or truth stater and his first important book, *Main-Travelled Roads* (1891), came close to being the most completely honest volume of its decade. Garland lacked the deep-rooted convictions and infinite patience that Howells had; he fought with pitchforks and was easily discouraged. To most critics, therefore, Garland's is a story of failure, of giving way to economic and social pressure; he has been called an "author of wax."

The details of Garland's life are to be found in numerous autobiographical books, of which the most notable is *A Son of the Middle Border* (1917). Born in 1860 on a farm in western Wisconsin, he moved with his family first to northeastern Iowa, where he attended Cedar Valley Seminary at Osage, and then to northeastern South Dakota. As a boy he learned the endless routine of the dirt farmer—caring for stock, plowing, dragging, sowing, cultivating, harvesting. He found farmwork drudgery, although he liked the prairies and the clear blue Western skies. The world of books was more attractive, and at an early age, encouraged by his mother, he determined to make himself a teacher. Yet he was twenty-four before, mortgaging the homestead he had staked out, he really broke with farming.

He chose to study in Boston and there, between 1884 and 1887, he quickly educated himself in the theaters, in the homes of friendly writers, actors, and artists, most of all in the Boston Public Library. He discovered Herbert Spencer and Henrik Ibsen and impressionism and the new novelists of Europe, realists most of them. Gradually he made friends and found modest employment as a lecturer, teacher, and reviewer. Unsophisticated and far from intellectually radical, he was nevertheless deeply influenced by the restlessness of the age, perhaps because he fell among the young men who were sensing literary and artistic revolution in the air. Although he had practically no money and failed to make much impression by the poems, essays, and sketches which he sent around to the magazines, he was stirred by many enthusiasms, awakened almost overnight to the excitement of ideas.

Then, in 1887, he returned to South Dakota to visit his parents. Very probably he would have been shocked at the meanness of the life in which he had grown up had he seen it at its best, but his visit was to a West suffering the ills which were soon to call forth the People's Party and the oratory of William Jennings Bryan. Garland had acquired enough perspective to see that farm life was far from idyllic and that the frontier had not fulfilled its promise. When he returned to Boston he wrote the tales collected in *Main-Travelled Roads*.

Garland's tragedy was that he never surpassed this initial effort. For a time, encouraged by the friendship of B. O. Flower, editor of *The Arena*, he thought of himself as a reformer; his anger at the plight of his native section and his reading of Henry George found expression in several political novels in 1892. None was really well written, perhaps because Garland was more fascinated by the rôle of prophet. With the World's Columbian Exposition being advertised, he envisioned a great literary renaissance centering in Chicago and described the shape of things to come in the essays collected as *Crumbling Idols* (1894). For nearly twenty years he devoted himself to exemplifying the virtues of Western literature, only to find that Western themes and Western scenes were of themselves no guarantee of greatness. He wrote sixteen novels between 1895 and 1916. They show an increasing command of structure and are perhaps as good as the better magazine fiction of the period. Not one of them, however, is truly memorable and some are almost gushingly sentimental. The best that can be said for them is that Garland treated the American Indian with objective fairness and provided many colorful pictures of the high plains and mountains. In his search for fresh local color he failed to correct his greatest weakness as a novelist—his thin characterization. It is obvious that Garland's fondness for family and club life, for travel, for literary friendships, however satisfying to him personally, cost him much as an artist. The power which he had briefly in the years between 1887 and 1891 was largely gone. He himself admitted in 1924 (see "Limitations of Authorship in America," *The Bookman*, May) that he had compromised to keep his market. All through his later life he showed a tendency to deplore the constantly lowering standards of public taste and the commercialization of literature.

After 1916, when he moved to New York, Garland attained a new popularity by turning to autobiography. The writer who had insisted that "the present is the vital theme" ransacked his journals and notebooks and memory for five volumes dealing with the "Middle Border" and four volumes of literary gossip. In 1922 *A Daughter of the Middle Border* won the Pulitzer Prize for biography. Social and literary historians will doubtless find these books invaluable. They make it clear, however, that Garland was never really a rebel. What seemed like revolt was an intensely personal emotional reaction to a particular situation; the true Garland was respectful of tradition and of success, wherever he found them. He was interested, moreover, in many things, perhaps too many for his artistic salvation. Veritism was only one cause among many, and although he tried to present life truthfully he never had an irrepressible passion to say something important supremely well.

A Son of the Middle Border, New York, 1917 • Roadside Meetings, New York, 1930 • F. B. Millett, Contemporary American Authors: A Critical Survey and 219 Bio-Bibliographies, New York, 1940 • V. L. Parrington, The Beginnings of Critical Realism in America, 1860-1920, New York, 1930, 288-300 • W. F. Taylor, The Economic Novel in America, Chapel Hill, 1942, 148-183

Mrs. Ripley's Trip

In a Foreword to **Main-Travelled Roads** written in 1922 Garland told of his trip to South Dakota in 1887, after three years in Boston. On his way he stopped in Chicago to visit Joseph Kirkland (see p. 579), who suggested that Garland ought to write fiction (see **A Son of the Middle Border**). The farther he got beyond Chicago the more depressing he found the landscape, and when he got to Ordway, South Dakota, he found his mother "imprisoned in a small cabin on the enormous sunburnt, treeless plain, with no expectation of ever living anywhere else." "In that hot little house," he added in **Roadside Meetings**, "I wrote my first story, a sketch descriptive of the life I had known as a boy. It was in truth only the amplification of a tale which my mother retold of an old neighbor in Iowa who, after many years of border life, went 'back to York State' on a visit. 'Mrs. Ripley' was not unlike a character in Mary Wilkins' stories [he was probably thinking of "The Revolt of 'Mother' "] and I wrote nearly two thousand words of her story one Sunday forenoon." Completed after Garland's return to Boston, "Mrs. Ripley's Trip" was accepted by **Harper's Weekly** and printed in the issue for November 24, 1888. Garland was paid seventy dollars for it, half of which he sent his mother as coauthor. Although not so bitter as some of the stories written a few months later, "Mrs. Ripley's Trip" is an excellent example of the regard for truthful depiction of farm life which made Garland's early work outstanding.

The night was in windy November, and the blast, threatening rain, roared around the poor little shanty of Uncle Ripley, set like a chicken-trap on the vast Iowa prairie. Uncle Ethan was mending his old violin, with many York State "dums!" and "I gol darns!" totally oblivious of his tireless old wife, who, having "finished the supper-dishes," sat knitting a stocking, evidently for the little grandson who lay before the stove like a cat.

Neither of the old people wore glasses, and their light
10 was a tallow candle; they couldn't afford "none o' them new-fangled lamps." The room was small, the chairs were wooden, and the walls bare—a home where poverty was a never-absent guest. The old lady looked pathetically little, weazened, and hopeless in her ill-fitting garments (whose original color had long since vanished), intent as she was on the stocking in her knotted, stiffened fingers, and there was a peculiar sparkle in her little black eyes, and an unusual resolution in the straight line of her withered and shapeless lips.
20 Suddenly she paused, stuck a needle in the spare knob of her hair at the back of her head, and looking at Ripley, said decisively: "Ethan Ripley, you'll haff to do your own cooking from now on to New Year's. I'm goin' back to Yaark State."

The old man's leather-brown face stiffened into a look of quizzical surprise for a moment; then he cackled, incredulously: "Ho! Ho! har! Sho! be y', now? I want to know if y' be."

"Well, you'll find out."

30 "Goin' to start to-morrow, mother?"

"No, sir, I ain't; but I am on Thursday. I want to get to Sally's by Sunday, sure, an' to Silas's on Thanksgivin'."

There was a note in the old woman's voice that brought genuine stupefaction into the face of Uncle Ripley. Of course in this case, as in all others, the money consideration was uppermost.

"Howgy 'xpect to get the money, mother? Anybody died an' left yeh a pile?"

"Never you mind where I get the money, so 's 't you don't haff to bear it. The land knows if I'd 'a' waited for 40 you to pay my way—"

"You needn't twit me of bein' poor, old woman," said Ripley, flaming up after the manner of many old people. "I've done my part t' get along. I've worked day in and day out—"

"Oh! I ain't done no work, have I?" snapped she, laying down the stocking and levelling a needle at him, and putting a frightful emphasis on "I."

"I didn't say you hadn't done no work."

"Yes, you did!" 50

"I didn't neither. I said—"

"I know what you said."

"I said I'd done my part!" roared the husband, dominating her as usual by superior lung power. "I didn't say you hadn't done your part," he added with an unfortunate touch of emphasis.

"I know y' didn't say it, but y' meant it. I don't know what y' call doin' my part, Ethan Ripley; but if cookin' for a drove of harvest hands and thrashin' hands, takin' care o' the eggs and butter, 'n' diggin' 'taters an' milkin' 60 ain't my part, I don't never expect to do my part, 'n' you might as well know it fust 's last.

"I'm sixty years old," she went on, with a little break in her harsh voice, dominating him now by woman's logic, "an' I've never had a day to myself, not even Fourth o' July. If I've went a-visitin' 'r to a picnic, I've had to come home an' milk 'n' get supper for you men-folks. I ain't been away t' stay overnight for thirteen years in this house, 'n' it was just so in Davis County for ten more. For twenty-three years, Ethan Ripley, I've 70 stuck right to the stove an' churn without a day or a night off."

Her voice choked again, but she rallied, and continued impressively, "And now I'm a-goin' back to Yaark State."

Ethan was vanquished. He stared at her in speechless surprise, his jaw hanging. It was incredible.

"For twenty-three years," she went on, musingly, "I've just about promised myself every year I'd go back an' see my folks." She was distinctly talking to herself now, and her voice had a touching, wistful cadence. "I've 80 wanted to go back an' see the old folks, an' the hills where we played, an' eat apples off the old tree down by the well. I've had them trees an' hills in my mind days and days—nights, too—an' the girls I used to know, an' my own folks—"

She fell into a silent muse, which lasted so long that the ticking of the clock grew loud as a gong in the man's ears, and the wind outside seemed to sound drearier than usual. He returned to the money problem; kindly, though.

"But how y' goin' t' raise the money? I ain't got no extra cash this time. Agin Roach is paid, an' the interest paid, we ain't got no hundred dollars to spare, Jane, not by a jugful."

"Wal, don't you lay awake nights studyin' on where I'm a-goin' to get the money," said the old woman, taking delight in mystifying him. She had him now, and he couldn't escape. He strove to show his indifference, however, by playing a tune or two on the violin.

"Come, Tukey, you better climb the wooden hill," Mrs. Ripley said, a half-hour later, to the little chap on the floor, who was beginning to get drowsy under the influence of his grandpa's fiddling. "Pa, you had orta 'a' put that string in the clock to-day—on the 'larm side the string is broke," she said, upon returning from the boy's bedroom. "I orta git up early to-morrow, to git some sewin' done. Land knows, I can't fix up much, but they is a little I c'n do. I want to look decent."

They were alone now, and they both sat expectantly.

"You 'pear to think, mother, that I'm agin yer goin'."

"Wal, it would kinder seem as if y' hadn't hustled yerself any t' help me git off."

He was smarting under the sense of being wronged. "Wal, I'm just as willin' you should go as I am for myself, but if I ain't got no money I don't see how I'm goin' to send—"

"I don't want ye to send; nobody ast ye to, Ethan Ripley. I guess if I had what I've earnt since we came on this farm I'd have enough to go to Jericho with."

"You've got as much out of it as I have," he replied gently. "You talk about your goin' back. Ain't I been wantin' to go back myself? And ain't I kep' still 'cause I see it wa'n't no use? I guess I've worked jest as long and as hard as you, an' in storms an' in mud an' heat, ef it comes t' that."

The woman was staggered, but she wouldn't give up; she must get in one more thrust.

"Wal, if you'd 'a' managed as well as I have, you'd have some money to go with." And she rose and went to mix her bread and set it "raisin'."

He sat by the fire twanging his fiddle softly. He was plainly thrown into gloomy retrospection, something quite unusual for him. But his fingers picking out the bars of a familiar tune set him to smiling, and whipping his bow across the strings, he forgot all about his wife's resolutions and his own hardships. "Trouble always slid off his back like punkins off a haystack, anyway," his wife said.

The old man still sat fiddling softly after his wife disappeared in the hot and stuffy little bedroom off the kitchen. His shaggy head bent lower over his violin. He heard her shoes drop—*one, two.* Pretty soon she called:

"Come, put up that squeakin' old fiddle, and go to bed. Seems as if you orta have sense enough not to set there keepin' everybody in the house awake."

"You hush up," retorted he. "I'll come when I git ready, and not till. I'll be glad when you're gone—"

"Yes, I warrant *that.*"

With which amiable good-night they went off to sleep, or at least she did, while he lay awake pondering on "where under the sun she was goin' t' raise that money."

The next day she was up bright and early, working away on her own affairs, ignoring Ripley entirely, the fixed look of resolution still on her little old wrinkled face. She killed a hen and dressed and baked it. She fried up a pan of doughnuts and made a cake. She was engaged in the doughnuts when a neighbor came in, one of these women who take it as a personal affront when any one in the neighborhood does anything without asking their advice. She was fat, and could talk a man blind in three minutes by the watch. Her neighbor said:

"What's this I hear, Mis' Ripley?"

"I dun know. I expect you hear about all they is goin' on in this neighborhood," replied Mrs. Ripley, with crushing bluntness; but the gossip did not flinch.

"Well, Sett Turner told *me* that her husband told *her* that Ripley told *him* this mornin' that you was goin' back East on a visit."

"Wal, what of it?"

"Well, air yeh?"

"The Lord willin' an' the weather permittin', I expect I be."

"Good land, I want to know! Well, well! I never was

so astonished in my whole life. I said, says I, 'It can't be.' 'Well,' ses 'e, 'tha's what *she* told me,' ses 'e. 'But,' says I, 'she is the last woman in the world to go gallavantin' off East,' ses I. 'An',' ses he, 'but it comes from good authority,' ses he. 'Well, then, it must be so,' ses I. But, land sakes! do tell me all about it. How come you to make up y'r mind? All these years you've been kind a' talkin' it over, an' now y'r actshelly goin'—well, I *never!* 'I s'pose Ripley furnishes the money,' ses I to him. 'Well, no,' ses 'e. 'Ripley says he'll be blowed if he sees where the money's coming from,' ses 'e; and ses I, 'But maybe she's jest jokin',' ses I. 'Not much,' he says. S' 'e: 'Ripley believes she's goin' fast enough. He's jest as anxious to find out as we be—'"

Here Mrs. Doudney paused for breath; she had walked so fast and rested so little that her interminable flow of "ses I's" and "ses he's" ceased necessarily. She had reached, moreover, the point of most vital interest—the money.

"An' you'll find out jest 'bout as soon as he does," was the dry response from the figure hovering over the stove; and with all her manoeuvring that was all she got.

All day Ripley went about his work exceedingly thoughtful for him. It was cold blustering weather. The wind rustled among the cornstalks with a wild and mournful sound, the geese and ducks went sprawling down the wind, and the horses' coats were ruffled and backs raised.

The old man was husking all alone in the field, his spare form rigged out in two or three ragged coats, his hands inserted in a pair of gloves minus nearly all the fingers, his thumbs done up in "stalls," and his feet thrust into huge coarse boots. The "down ears" wet and chapped his hands, already worn to the quick. Toward night it grew colder and threatened snow. In spite of all these attacks he kept his cheerfulness, and though he was very tired, he was softened in temper.

Having plenty of time to think matters over, he had come to the conclusion that the old woman needed a play-spell. "I ain't likely to be no richer next year than I am this one; if I wait till I'm able to send her she won't never go. I calc'late I c'n git enough out o' them shoats to send her. I'd kind a' lotted on eat'n' them pigs done up in sassengers, but if the ol' woman goes East, Tukey an' me'll kind a' haff to pull through without 'em. We'll have a turkey f'r Thanksgivin', an' a chicken once 'n a

while. Lord! but we'll miss the gravy on the flapjacks." (He smacked his lips over the thought of the lost dainty.) "But let 'er rip! We can stand it. Then there is my buffalo overcoat. I'd kind a' calc'lated on havin' a buffalo—but that's gone up the spout along with them sassengers."

These heroic sacrifices having been determined upon, he put them into effect at once.

This he was able to do, for his corn-rows ran alongside the road leading to Cedarville, and his neighbors were passing almost all hours of the day.

It would have softened Jane Ripley's heart could she have seen his bent and stiffened form among the corn-rows, the cold wind piercing to the bone through his threadbare and insufficient clothing. The rising wind sent the snow rattling among the moaning stalks at intervals. The cold made his poor dim eyes water, and he had to stop now and then to swing his arms about his chest to warm them. His voice was hoarse with shouting at the shivering team.

That night as Mrs. Ripley was clearing the dishes away she got to thinking about the departure of the next day, and she began to soften. She gave way to a few tears when little Tewksbury Gilchrist, her grandson, came up and stood beside her.

"Gran'ma, you ain't goin' to stay away always, are yeh?"

"Why, course not, Tukey. What made y' think that?"

"Well, y' ain't told us nawthin' 't all about it. An' yeh kind o' look 's if yeh was mad."

"Well, I ain't mad; I'm jest a-thinkin', Tukey. Y' see, I come away from them hills when I was a little girl a'most; before I married y'r grandad. And I ain't never been back. 'Most all my folks is there, sonny, an' we've been s' poor all these years I couldn't seem t' never git started. Now, when I'm 'most ready t' go, I feel kind a queer—'s if I'd cry."

And cry she did, while little Tewksbury stood patting her trembling hands. Hearing Ripley's step on the porch, she rose hastily and, drying her eyes, plunged at the work again.

Ripley came in with a big armful of wood, which he rolled into the wood-box with a thundering crash. Then he pulled off his mittens, slapped them together to knock off the ice and snow, and laid them side by side under the stove. He then removed cap, coat, blouse, and finally his boots, which he laid upon the wood-box, the soles turned toward the stove-pipe.

As he sat down without speaking, he opened the front doors of the stove, and held the palms of his stiffened hands to the blaze. The light brought out a thoughtful look on his large, uncouth, yet kindly, visage. Life had laid hard lines on his brown skin, but it had not entirely soured a naturally kind and simple nature. It had made him penurious and dull and iron-muscled; had stifled all the slender flowers of his nature; yet there was warm soil somewhere hid in his heart.

"It's snowin' like all p'ssessed," he remarked finally. "I guess we'll have a sleigh-ride to-morrow. I calc'late t' drive y' daown in scrumptious style. If you must leave, why, we'll give yeh a whoopin' old send-off—won't we, Tukey?"

Nobody replying, he waited a moment. "I've ben a-thinkin' things over kind o' t'-day, mother, an' I've come t' the conclusion that we *have* been kind o' hard on yeh, without knowin' it, y' see. Y' see I'm kind o' easy-goin', an' little Tuke he's only a child, an' we ain't c'nsidered how you felt."

She didn't appear to be listening, but she was, and he didn't appear, on his part, to be talking to her, and he kept his voice as hard and dry as he could.

"An' I was tellin' Tukey t'-day that it was a dum shame our crops hadn't turned out better. An' when I saw ol' Hatfield go by I hailed him, an' asked him what he'd gimme for two o' m' shoats. Wal, the upshot is, I sent t' town for some things I calc'late you'd need. An' here's a ticket to Georgetown, and ten dollars. Why, ma, what's up?"

Mrs. Ripley broke down, and with her hands all wet with dishwater, as they were, covered her face, and sobbed. She felt like kissing him, but she didn't. Tewksbury began to whimper too; but the old man was astonished. His wife had not wept for years (before him). He rose and walking clumsily up to her timidly touched her hair—

"Why, mother! What's the matter? What've I done now? I was calc'latin' to sell them pigs anyway. Hatfield jest advanced the money on 'em."

She hopped up and dashed into the bedroom, and in a few minutes returned with a yarn mitten, tied around the wrist, which she laid on the table with a thump, saying: "I don't want yer money. There's money enough to take me where I want to go."

"Whee—ew! Thunder and gimpsum root! Where 'd ye get that? Didn't dig it out of a hole?"

"No, I jest saved it—a dime at a time—see!"

Here she turned it out on the table—some bills, but mostly silver dimes and quarters.

"Thunder and scissors! Must be two er three hundred dollars there," he exclaimed.

"They's jest seventy-five dollars and thirty cents; jest about enough to go back on. Tickets is fifty-five dollars, goin' and comin'. That leaves twenty dollars for other expenses, not countin' what I've already spent, which is six-fifty," said she, recovering her self-possession. "It's plenty."

"But y' ain't calc'lated on no sleepers nor hotel bills."

"I ain't goin' on no sleeper. Mis' Doudney says it's jest scandalous the way things is managed on them cars. I'm goin' on the old-fashioned cars, where they ain't no half-dressed men runnin' around."

"But *you* needn't be afraid of them, mother; at your age—"

"There! you needn't throw my age an' homeliness into my face, Ethan Ripley. If I hadn't waited an' tended on you so long, I'd look a little more's I did when I married yeh."

Ripley gave it up in despair. He didn't realize fully enough how the proposed trip had unsettled his wife's nerves. She didn't realize it herself.

"As for the hotel bills, they won't be none. I ain't agoin' to pay them pirates as much for a day's board as we'd charge for a week's, and have nawthin' to eat but dishes. I'm goin' to take a chicken an' some hard-boiled eggs, an' I'm goin' right through to Georgetown."

"Wal, all right, mother; but here's the ticket I got."

"I don't want yer ticket."

"But you've got to take it."

"Well, I haint."

"Why, yes, ye have. It's bought, an' they won't take it back."

"Won't they?" She was perplexed again.

"Not much they won't. I ast 'em. A ticket sold is sold."

"Wal, if they won't—"

"You bet they won't."

"I s'pose I'll haff to use it." And that ended it.

They were a familiar sight as they rode down the road toward town next day. As usual, Mrs. Ripley sat up straight and stiff as "a half-drove wedge in a white-oak log." The day was cold and raw. There was some snow on the ground, but not enough to warrant the use of sleighs. It was "neither sleddin' nor wheelin'." The old people sat on a board laid across the box, and had an old quilt or two drawn up over their knees. Tewksbury lay in the back part of the box (which was filled with hay), where he jounced up and down, in company with a queer old trunk and a brand-new imitation-leather hand-bag.

There is no ride quite so desolate and uncomfortable as a ride in a lumber-wagon on a cold day in autumn, when the ground is frozen, and the wind is strong and raw with threatening snow. The wagon-wheels grind along in the snow, the cold gets in under the seat at the calves of one's legs, and the ceaseless bumping of the bottom of the box on the feet is almost intolerable.

There was not much talk on the way down, and what little there was related mainly to certain domestic regulations, to be strictly followed, regarding churning, pickles, pancakes, etc. Mrs. Ripley wore a shawl over her head, and carried her queer little black bonnet in her hand. Tewksbury was also wrapped in a shawl. The boy's teeth were pounding together like castanets by the time they reached Cedarville, and every muscle ached with the fatigue of shaking.

After a few purchases they drove down to the station, a frightful little den (common in the West), which was always too hot or too cold. It happened to be hot just now—a fact which rejoiced little Tewksbury.

"Now git my trunk *stamped,* 'r *fixed,* 'r whatever they call it," she said to Ripley, in a commanding tone, which gave great delight to the inevitable crowd of loafers beginning to assemble. "Now remember, Tukey, have grandad kill that biggest turkey night before Thanksgiving, an' then you run right over to Mis' Doudney's— she's got a nawful tongue, but she can bake a turkey first-rate—an' she'll fix up some squash-pies for yeh. You can warm up one o' them mince-pies. I wish ye could be with me, but ye can't; so do the best ye can."

Ripley returning now, she said: "Wal, now, I've fixed things up the best I could. I've baked bread enough to last a week, an' Mis' Doudney has promised to bake for yeh—"

"I don't like her bakin'."

"Wal, you'll haff to stand it till I get back, 'n' you'll find a jar o' sweet pickles an' some crab-apple sauce down suller, 'n' you'd better melt up brown sugar for 'lasses, 'n' for goodness' sake don't eat all them mince-pies up the fust week, 'n' see that Tukey ain't froze goin'

to school. An' now you'd better get out for home. Good-by! an' remember them pies."

As they were riding home, Ripley roused up after a long silence.

"Did she—a—kiss you good-by, Tukey?"

"No, sir," piped Tewksbury.

"Thunder! didn't she?" After a silence: "She didn't me, neither. I guess she kind a' sort a' forgot it, bein' so flustrated, y' know."

One cold, windy, intensely bright day, Mrs. Stacey, who lives about two miles from Cedarville, looking out of the window, saw a queer little figure struggling along the road, which was blocked here and there with drifts. It was an old woman laden with a good half-dozen parcels, which the wind seemed determined to wrench from her.

She was dressed in black, with a full skirt, and her cloak being short, the wind had excellent opportunity to inflate her garments and sail her off occasionally into the deep snow outside the track, but she held out bravely till she reached the gate. As she turned in, Mrs. Stacey cried:

"Why! it's Gran'ma Ripley, just getting back from her trip. Why! how do you do? Come in. Why! you must be nearly frozen. Let me take off your hat and veil."

"No, thank ye kindly, but I can't stop," was the given reply. "I must be gittin' back to Ripley. I expec' that man has jest let ev'rything go six ways f'r Sunday."

"Oh, you *must* sit down just a minute and warm."

"Wal, I will; but I've got to git home by sundown sure. I don't s'pose they's a thing in the house to eat," she said solemnly.

"Oh, dear! I wish Stacey was here, so he could take you home. An' the boys at school—"

"Don't need any help, if 't wa'nt for these bundles an' things. I guess I'll jest leave some of 'em here, an'— Here! take one of these apples. I brought 'em from Lizy Jane's suller, back to Yaark State."

"Oh! they're delicious! You must have had a lovely time."

"Pretty good. But I kep' thinkin' of Ripley an' Tukey all the time. I s'pose they have had a gay time of it" (she meant the opposite of gay). "Wal, as I told Lizy Jane, I've had my spree, an' now I've got to git back to work. They ain't no rest for such as we are. As I told Lizy Jane, them folks in the big houses have Thanksgiv-in' dinners every day of their lives, and men an' women

unrealistic talk! of farmers people!

in splendid clo's to wait on 'em, so 't Thanksgivin' don't mean anything to 'em; but we poor critters, we make a great to-do if we have a good dinner onct a year. I've saw a pile o' this world, Mrs. Stacey—a pile of it! I didn't think they was so many big houses in the world as I saw b'tween here an' Chicago. Wal, I can't set here gabbin'." She rose resolutely. "I must get home to Ripley. Jest kind o' stow them bags away. I'll take two an' leave them three others. Good-by! I must be gittin'
10 home to Ripley. He'll want his supper on time."

And off up the road the indomitable little figure trudged, head held down to the cutting blast—little snow-fly, a speck on a measureless expanse, crawling along with painful breathing, and slipping, sliding steps —"Gittin' home to Ripley an' the boy."

Ripley was out to the barn when she entered, but Tewksbury was building a fire in the old cook-stove. He sprang up with a cry of joy, and ran to her. She seized him and kissed him, and it did her so much good she
20 hugged him close, and kissed him again and again, crying hysterically.

"Oh, gran'ma, I'm so glad to see you! We've had an awful time since you've been gone."

She released him, and looked around. A lot of dirty dishes were on the table, the table-cloth was a "sight to behold" (as she afterward said), and so was the stove— kettle-marks all over the table-cloth, splotches of pan-cake batter all over the stove.

"Wal, I sh'd say as much," she dryly assented, untying her bonnet-strings. 30

When Ripley came in she had her regimentals on, the stove was brushed, the room swept, and she was elbow-deep in the dish-pan. "Hullo, mother! Got back, hev yeh?"

"I sh'd say it was about *time*," she replied curtly, without looking up or ceasing work. "Has ol' 'Crumpy' dried up yit?" This was her greeting.

Her trip was a fact now; no chance could rob her of it. She had looked forward twenty-three years toward it, and now she could look back at it accomplished. She 40 took up her burden again, never more thinking to lay it down.

1887·1888

---

42 down. The only extensive revision of the *Harper's Weekly* text was Garland's fortunate omission of the following ending: ". . . till her poor work-weary, bony hands should be folded finally on her lean, pathetic old bosom. Her next trip will be so far away she will never return—far past the gates of space and time"

From

Crumbling Idols

Crumbling Idols: Twelve Essays on Art Dealing Chiefly with Literature, Painting and the Drama, published by the newly founded firm of Stone and Kimball in 1894, was an expansion, revision, and rearrangement of various critical articles and (presumably) lectures which Garland had written in the preceding several years. Although he was inclined in his later life to be a little scornful of his violence and youthfulness, Crumbling Idols is historically important. It reflects Garland's acceptance of Howells' faith in realism, his conviction (which he later recanted) that the literary center of the future was to be Chicago, his awareness of the interrelation of the arts, and the characteristic enthusiasms of the 1890's for Ibsen, impressionism, and local color. If there was any "manifesto" defending the general position of the local colorists, this book contained it. Of the two chapters here reprinted, "Local Color in Art" seems not to have been printed previously, but "The Local Novel" was apparently part of a lecture delivered as early as 1891 (see Roadside Meetings, p. 189) and is substantially the same as "The Future of Fiction," which had appeared in The Arena for April 1893. Other portions of the book had appeared in The Arena and The Forum.

V

LOCAL COLOR IN ART

Local color in fiction is demonstrably the life of fiction. It is the native element, the differentiating element. It corresponds to the endless and vital charm of individual peculiarity. It is the differences which interest us; the similarities do not please, do not forever stimulate and feed as do the differences. Literature would die of dry rot if it chronicled the similarities only, or even largely.

Historically, the local color of a poet or dramatist is of the greatest value. The charm of Horace is the side light he throws on the manners and customs of his time. The vital in Homer lies, after all, in his local color, not in his abstractions. Because the sagas of the North delineate more exactly how men and women lived and wrought in those days, therefore they have always appealed to me with infinitely greater power than Homer.

Similarly, it is the local color of Chaucer that interests us to-day. We yawn over his tales of chivalry which were in the manner of his contemporaries, but the Miller and the Priest interest us. Wherever the man of the past in literature showed us what he really lived and loved, he moves us. We understand him, and we really feel an interest in him.

Historically, local color has gained in beauty and suggestiveness and humanity from Chaucer down to the present day. Each age has embodied more and more of its actual life and social conformation until the differentiating qualities of modern art make the best paintings of Norway as distinct in local color as its fiction is vital and indigenous.

Every great moving literature to-day is full of local color. It is this element which puts the Norwegian and Russian almost at the very summit of modern novel writing, and it is the comparative lack of this distinctive flavor which makes the English and French take a lower place in truth and sincerity.

Everywhere all over the modern European world, men are writing novels and dramas as naturally as the grass or corn or flax grows. The Provençal, the Hun, the Catalonian, the Norwegian, is getting a hearing. This literature is not the literature of scholars; it is the literature of lovers and doers; of men who love the modern and who have not been educated to despise common things.

These men are speaking a new word. They are not hunting themes, they are struggling to express.

Conventional criticism does not hamper or confine them. They are rooted in the soil. They stand among the corn-fields and they dig in the peat-bogs. They concern themselves with modern and very present words and themes, and they have brought a new word which is to divide in half the domain of beauty.

They have made art the re-creation of the beautiful *and the significant*. Mere beauty no longer suffices. Beauty is the world-old aristocrat who has taken for mate this mighty young plebeian Significance. Their child is to be the most human and humane literature ever seen.

It has taken the United States longer to achieve independence of English critics than it took to free itself from old-world political and economic rule. Its political freedom was won, not by its gentlemen and scholars, but by its yeomanry; and in the same way our national literature will come in its fulness when the common American rises spontaneously to the expression of his concept of life.

The fatal blight upon most American art has been, and is to-day, its imitative quality, which has kept it characterless and factitious,—a forced rose-culture rather than the free flowering of native plants.

Our writers despised or feared the home market. They rested their immortality upon the "universal theme," which was a theme of no interest to the public and of small interest to themselves.

During the first century and a half, our literature had very little national color. It was quite like the utterance of corresponding classes in England. But at length Bryant and Cooper felt the influence of our mighty forests and prairies. Whittier uttered something of New England boy-life, and Thoreau prodded about among newly discovered wonders, and the American literature got its first start.

Under the influence of Cooper came the stories of wild life from Texas, from Ohio, and from Illinois. The wild, rough settlements could not produce smooth and cultured poems or stories; they only furnished forth rough-and-ready anecdotes, but in these stories there were hints of something fine and strong and native.

As the settlements increased in size, as the pressure of the forest and the wild beast grew less, expression

28 **Norwegian and Russian.** Garland refers to the work of Björnstjerne Björnson (1832-1910) and Ivan Turgenev (1818-1883), two of the most famous novelists of the latter nineteenth century • 35 **Provençal . . . Catalonian,** a reference to the regional and national literatures of southern France, Hungary, and northeastern Spain, best represented perhaps by the poetry of the Provençal Frédéric Mistral (1830-1914) and the Hungarians Sándor Petöfi (1823-1849) and János Arany (1817-1882), and by the plays of the Catalonian Ángel Guimerá (1847-1924). The local color movement of the United States was preceded and paralleled by widespread regionalism in Europe

rose to a higher plane; men softened in speech and manner. All preparations were being made for a local literature raised to the level of art.

The Pacific slope was first in the line. By the exceptional interest which the world took in the life of the gold fields, and by the forward urge which seems always to surprise the pessimist and the scholiast, two young men were plunged into that wild life, led across the plains set in the shadow of Mount Shasta, and local literature received its first great marked, decided impetus.

To-day we have in America, at last, a group of writers who have no suspicion of imitation laid upon them. Whatever faults they may be supposed to have, they are at any rate, themselves. American critics can depend upon a characteristic American literature of fiction and the drama from these people.

The corn has flowered, and the cotton-boll has broken into speech.

Local color—what is it? It means that the writer spontaneously reflects the life which goes on around him. It is natural and unstrained art.

It is, in a sense, unnatural and artificial to find an American writing novels of Russia or Spain or the Holy Land. He cannot hope to do it so well as the native. The best he can look for is that poor word of praise, "He does it very well, considering he is an alien."

If a young writer complain that there are no themes at home, that he is forced to go abroad for perspective and romance, I answer there is something wrong in his education or his perceptive faculty. Often he is more anxious to win a money success than to be patiently one of art's unhurried devotees.

I can sympathize with him, however, for criticism has not helped him to be true. Criticism of the formal kind and spontaneous expression are always at war, like the old man and the youth. They may politely conceal it, but they are mutually destructive.

Old men naturally love the past; the books they read are the master-pieces; the great men are all dying off, they say; the young man should treat lofty and universal themes, as they used to do. These localisms are petty. These truths are disturbing. Youth annoys them. Spontaneousness is formlessness, and the criticism that does not call for the abstract and the ideal and the beautiful is leading to destruction, these critics say.

And yet there is a criticism which helps, which tends to keep a writer at his best; but such criticism recognizes

the dynamic force of a literature, and tries to spy out tendencies. This criticism to-day sees that local color means national character, and is aiding the young writer to treat his themes in the best art.

I assert it is the most natural thing in the world for a man to love his native land and his native, intimate surroundings. Born into a web of circumstances, enmeshed in common life, the youthful artist begins to think. All the associations of that childhood and the love-life of youth combine to make that web of common affairs, threads of silver and beads of gold; the near-at-hand things are the dearest and sweetest after all.

As the reader will see, I am using local color to mean something more than a forced study of the picturesque scenery of a State.

Local color in a novel means that it has such quality of texture and back-ground that it could not have been written in any other place or by any one else than a native.

It means a statement of life as indigenous as the plant-growth. It means that the picturesque shall not be seen by the author,—that every tree and bird and mountain shall be dear and companionable and necessary, not picturesque; the tourist cannot write the local novel.

From this it follows that local color must not be put in for the sake of local color. It must go in, it *will* go in, because the writer naturally carries it with him half unconsciously, or conscious only of its significance, its interest to him.

He must not stop to think whether it will interest the reader or not. He must be loyal to himself, and put it in because he loves it. If he is an artist, he will make his reader feel it through his own emotion.

What we should stand for is not universality of theme, but beauty and strength of treatment, leaving the writer to choose his theme because he loves it.

Here is the work of the critic. Recognizing that the theme is beyond his control, let him aid the young writer to delineate simply and with unwavering strokes. Even here the critic can do little, if he is possessed of the idea that the young writer of to-day should model upon Addison or Macaulay or Swift.

There are new criterions to-day in writing as in paint-

---

7 **two young men,** presumably Bret Harte (see p. 338) and Joaquin Miller (1841?-1913) • 9 **Mount Shasta,** in northern California

ing, and individual expression is the aim. The critic can do much to aid a young writer to *not* copy an old master or any other master. Good criticism can aid him to be vivid and simple and unhackneyed in his technique, the subject is his own affair.

I agree with him who says, Local art must be raised to the highest levels in its expression; but in aiding this perfection of technique we must be careful not to cut into the artist's spontaneity. To apply ancient dogmas of criticism to our life and literature would be benumbing to artist and fatal to his art.

VI

THE LOCAL NOVEL

The local novel seems to be the heir-apparent to the kingdom of poesy. It is already the most promising of all literary attempts to-day; certainly it is the most sincere. It seems but beginning its work. It is "hopelessly contemporaneous"; that is its strength. It is (at its best) unaffected, natural, emotional. It is sure to become all-powerful. It will redeem American literature, as it has already redeemed the South from its conventional and highly wrought romanticism.

By reason of growing truth and sincerity the fiction of the South has risen from the dead. It is now in the spring season of shooting wilding plants and timorous blades of sown grains. Its future is assured. Its soil is fertilized with the blood of true men. Its women are the repositories of great, vital, sincere, emotional experiences which will inevitably appear in their children, and at last in art, and especially in fiction. The Southern people are in the midst of a battle more momentous than the Rebellion, because it is the result of the Rebellion; that is, the battle of intrenched privilege against the swiftly-spreading democratic idea of equality before the law and in the face of nature.

They have a terribly, mightily dramatic race-problem on their hands. The South is the meeting-place of winds. It is the seat of swift and almost incalculable change; and this change, this battle, this strife of invisible powers, is about to enter their fiction.

The Negro has already entered it. He has brought a musical speech to his masters, and to the new fiction. He has brought a strange and pleading song into music. The finest writers of the New South already find him a never-failing source of interest. He is not, of course, the only subject of Southern fiction, nor even the principal figure; but he is a necessary part, and a most absorbingly interesting part.

The future of fiction in the South will also depict the unreconstructed rebel unreservedly, and the race-problem without hate or contempt or anger; for the highest art will be the most catholic in its sympathy. It will delineate vast contending forces, and it will be a great literature.

The Negro will enter the fiction of the South, first, as subject; second, as artist in his own right. His first attempts will be imitative, but he will yet utter himself, as surely as he lives. He will contribute a poetry and a novel as peculiarly his own as the songs he sings. He may appear, also, in a strange half-song, half-chant, and possibly in a drama peculiar to himself; but in some form of fiction he will surely utter the sombre and darkly-florid genius for emotional utterance which characterizes him.

In the North the novel will continue local for some time to come. It will delineate the intimate life and speech of every section of our enormous and widely scattered republic. It will catch and fix in charcoal the changing, assimilating races, delineating the pathos and humor and the infinite drama of their swift adjustment to new conditions. California, New Mexico, Idaho, Utah, Oregon, each wonderful locality in our Nation of Nations will yet find its native utterance. The superficial work of the tourist and outsider will not do. The real novelist of these sections is walking behind the plow or trudging to school in these splendid potential environments.

This local movement will include the cities as well, and St. Louis, Chicago, San Francisco, will be delineated by artists born of each city, whose work will be so true that it could not have been written by any one from the outside. The real utterance of a city or a locality can only come when a writer is born out of its intimate heart. To such an one, nothing will be "strange" or "picturesque;" all will be familiar, and full of significance or beauty. The novel of the slums must be written by one who has played there as a child, and taken part in all its amusements; not out of curiosity, but out of pleasure seeking. It cannot be done from above nor from the outside. It must be done out of a full heart and without seeking for effect.

The artist should not look abroad to see how others

are succeeding. Success does not always measure merit. It took nearly a third of a century for Whitman and Monet to be recognized. The great artist never conforms. He does not trail after some other man's success. He works out his individual perception of things.

The contrast of city and country, everywhere growing sharper, will find its reflection in this local novel of the immediate future,—the same tragedies and comedies, with the essential difference called local color, and taking place all over the land, wherever cities arise like fungi, unhealthy, yet absorbing as subjects of fictional art.

As I have elsewhere pointed out, the drama will join the novel in this study of local conditions. It will be derived from fiction, and in many cases the dramatist and novelist will be the same person. In all cases the sincerity of the author's love for his scenes and characters will find expression in tender care for truth, and there will be made to pass before our eyes wonderfully suggestive pictures of other lives and landscapes. The drama will grow in dignity and importance along these lines.

Both drama and novel will be colloquial. This does not mean that they will be exclusively in the dialects, but the actual speech of the people of each locality will unquestionably be studied more closely than ever before. Dialect is the life of a language, precisely as the common people of the nation form the sustaining power of its social life and art.

And so in the novel, in the short story, and in the drama—by the work of a multitude of loving artists, not by the work of an over-topping personality—will the intimate social, individual life of the nation be depicted. Before this localism shall pass away, such a study will have been made of this land and people as has never been made by any other age or social group,—a literature from the plain people, reflecting their unrestrained outlook on life, subtle in speech and color, humane beyond precedent, humorous, varied, simple in means, lucid as water, searching as sunlight.

To one who believes each age to be its own best interpreter, the idea of "decay of fiction" never comes. That which the absolutist takes for decay is merely change. The conservative fears change; the radical welcomes it. The conservative tries to argue that fundamentals cannot change; that they are the same yesterday, to-day, and to-morrow. If that were true, then a sorrowful outlook on the future would be natural. Such permanency would be death. Life means change.

As a matter of fact, the minute differentiations of literature which the conservative calls its non-essentials, are really its essentials. Vitality and growth are in these "non-essentials." It is the difference in characters, not their similarity, which is forever interesting. It is the subtle coloring individuality gives which vitalizes landscape art, and so it is the subtle differences in the interpretation of life which each age gives that vitalizes its literature and makes it its own.

The individuality of the artist is the saving grace of art; and landscape painting will not be fantastic so long as men study nature. It will never be mere reproduction so long as the artist represents it as he sees it. The fact will correct the fantasy. The artist will color the fact.

The business of the present is not to express fundamentals, but to sincerely present its own minute and characteristic interpretation of life. This point cannot be too often insisted upon. Unless a writer add something to the literature of his race, has he justification? Is there glory in imitation? Is the painter greatest who copies old masters, or is it more praiseworthy to embody an original conception? These are very important questions for the young artist.

To perceive the hopelessness of absolutism in literature, you have but to stop a moment to think. Admit that there are perfect models to which must be referred all subsequent writing, and we are committed to a barren round of hopeless imitations. The young writer is disheartened or drawn off into imitations, and ruined for any real expression. This way of looking at literature produced our Barlows and Coltons and Hillhouses, with their "colossi of cotton-batting," and it produces blank-verse dramas to-day.

But the relativists in art are full of hope. They see that life is the model,—or, rather, that each man stands accountable to himself first, and to the perceived fact of life second. Life is always changing, and literature

3 Monet, Claude Monet (1840-1926), French painter, who applied to his art the scientific principles of light and is regarded as the leader of the impressionists • 78 Barlows . . . Hillhouses. Garland is probably echoing some contemporary judgment of early American literature, but the editors have been unable to place the phrase "colossi of cotton-batting." All the writers named were overambitious—Joel Barlow (1754-1812) in his epic, The Columbiad; James A. Hillhouse (1789-1841) in his blank-verse drama, Hadad (1825); and George Hooker Colton (1818-1847) in Tecumseh, or, The West Thirty Years Since (1842), a romantic poem of nine cantos in the manner of Sir Walter Scott

changes with it. It never decays; it changes. Poetry— that is to say *impassioned personal outlook on life*—is in no more danger of extinction to-day than in the days of Edmund Spenser. The American novel will continue to grow in truth to American life without regard to the form and spirit of the novel or drama of the past. Consciously or unconsciously, the point of view of the modern writer is that of the veritist, or truth stater.

Once out of the period of tutelage, it is natural for youth to overleap barriers. He naturally discards the wig and cloak of his grandfathers. He comes at last to reject, perhaps a little too brusquely, the models which conservatism regards with awe. He respects them as history, but he has life, abounding, fresh, contiguous life; life that stings and smothers and overwhelms and exalts, like the salt, green, snow-tipped ocean surf; life, with its terrors and triumphs, right here and now; its infinite drama, its allurement, its battle, and its victories. Life is the model, truth is the master, the heart of the man himself his motive power. The pleasure of re-creating in the image of nature is the artist's unfailing reward.

To him who sees that difference, not similarity, is the vitalizing quality, there is no sorrow at change. The future will take care of itself. In the space of that word "difference" lies all the infinite range of future art. Some elements are comparatively unchanging. The snow will fall, spring will come, men and women love, the stars will rise and set, and grass return again and again in vast rhythms of green, but society will not be the same.

The physical conformation of our nation will change. It will lose its wildness, its austerity. Its unpeopled plains will pass away, and gardens will bloom where the hot sand now drifts. Cities will rise where now the elk and the mountain lions are. Swifter means of transportation will bring the lives of different sections into closer relationship. It will tend to equalize intellectual opportunities. The physical and mental life of men and women will be changed, the relation of man to man, and man to woman, will change in detail, and the fiction of the future will express these changes.

To the veritist, therefore, the present is the vital theme. The past is dead, and the future can be trusted to look after itself. The young men and maidens of that time will find the stars of their present brighter than the stars of '92, the people around them more absorbing than books, and their own outlook on life more reasonable than that of dead men. Their writing and painting, in proportion to its vitality and importance, will reflect this, their natural attitude, toward life and history.

1891-1893·1894

Harold Frederic

1856 · 1898

Dutch, French, and New England blood flowed in the veins of Harold Frederic, though his birthplace was Utica, New York. The boy was eighteen months old when his father died, and his mother thereafter supported the family by operating a dairy. During his school days, Frederic helped her. "I spent my boyhood," he recalled later, "in getting out of bed at five in the morning to look after the cattle, and until I was fourteen, I drove a milk wagon as a 'side issue' in my agricultural duties." Later, he was successively an office boy, a retoucher of photographs, and a farm hand. At twenty he became a reporter, at twenty-four an editor, on a Utica newspaper. From 1884 to the year of his death, he served as a London correspondent for the New York *Times*.

It was while Frederic was abroad that he wrote his best-known fictional works, alternating days on which he toiled over his novels with days devoted to journalism. Vivid memories of the life he had seen during his varied career in upstate New York entered into his writings. His novels include *Seth's Brother's Wife* (1887), which exposes the seamy side of farm life and rural politics; *The Lawton Girl* (1890), based on the conflict between capital and labor in a manufacturing town; and *The Copperhead* (1893), which indicts political intolerance. More notable than any of these, and more notable, too, than several novels concerned with American history or with British backgrounds, is *The Damnation of Theron Ware* (1896), published two years before Frederic's early death.

The careful method of writing typical of Frederic was exemplified by his work on this novel. Believing that it was his duty to know everything each of his characters did, he spent five years making detailed studies of their fields of special interest. Since one was a biologist, for instance, he learned everything he could about appropriate aspects of science. And since the main character was a Methodist preacher, Frederic taught himself, as he said, "all the details of a Methodist minister's work, obligations, and daily routine, and all the machinery of his church." In addition he drew freely upon his recollections of the folk whom he had known during his boyhood. The result was that he wrote a novel which went beyond others of the period in its authenticity. Because the book which was thus carefully written treated religion critically, it caused something of a furor in its day and was much discussed. It was reprinted as recently as 1924, and even today historians of American fiction consider it an outstanding achievement.

E. S. Bates, "Harold Frederic," **Dictionary of American Biography,** New York, 1931 • A. H. Quinn, **American Fiction,** New York, 1936

From

The Damnation of Theron Ware

The protagonist in Frederic's best novel is a young Methodist minister, Theron Ware, sincere, ambitious, but half-educated, impressionable, and unstable. Assigned by the bishop to serve in the raw little town of Octavius, in central New York, Ware undergoes a moral transformation. Acquaintanceship with a group of characters of a very different background from his makes him poignantly aware of his own limitations, and at the same time his growing insight into the pettiness and emotionalism of small-town Methodism causes his faith to waver. In the end, thanks to the common-sense advice of a revivalist, he makes a halfway recovery from his "damnation." Chapter III of the novel offers a sample of the author's satirical realism. (The title has been supplied by the editors.)

[THE TRUSTEES AND THE REV. MR. WARE]

When the three trustees had been shown in by the Rev. Mr. Ware, and had taken seats, an awkward little pause ensued. The young minister looked doubtingly from one face to another, the while they glanced with inquiring interest about the room, noting the pictures and appraising the furniture in their minds.

The obvious leader of the party, Loren Pierce, a rich quarryman, was an old man of medium size and mean attire, with a square, beardless face as hard and impassive in expression as one of his blocks of limestone. The irregular, thin-lipped mouth, slightly sunken, 10 and shut with vice-like firmness, the short snub nose, and the little eyes squinting from half-closed lids beneath slightly marked brows, seemed scarcely to attain to the dignity of features, but evaded attention instead, as if feeling that they were only there at all from plain necessity, and ought not to be taken into account. Mr. Pierce's face did not know how to smile,— what was the use of smiles?—but its whole surface radiated secretiveness. Portrayed on canvas by a master 10 brush, with a ruff or a red robe for masquerade, generations of imaginative amateurs would have seen in it vast-reaching plots, the skeletons of a dozen dynastic cupboards, the guarded mysteries of half a century's international diplomacy. The amateurs would have been wrong again. There was nothing behind Mr. Pierce's juiceless countenance more weighty than a general determination to exact seven per cent for his money, and some specific notions about capturing certain brick-yards which were interfering with his quarry-sales. But 20 Octavius watched him shamble along its sidewalks quite as the Vienna of dead and forgotten yesterday might have watched Metternich.

Erastus Winch was of a breezier sort,—a florid, stout, and sandy man, who spent most of his life driving over evil country roads in a buggy, securing orders for dairy furniture and certain allied lines of farm utensils. This practice had given him a loud voice and a deceptively hearty manner, to which the other avocation of cheese-buyer, which he pursued at the Board of Trade meet-30 ings every Monday afternoon, had added a considerable command of persuasive yet non-committal language. To look at him, still more to hear him, one would have sworn he was a good fellow, a trifle rough and noisy, perhaps, but all right at bottom. But the County Clerk of Dearborn County could have told you of agriculturists who knew Erastus from long and unhappy experience, and who held him to be even a tighter man than Loren Pierce in the matter of a mortgage.

The third trustee, Levi Gorringe, set one wondering at 40 the very first glance what on earth he was doing in that company. Those who had known him longest had the least notion; but it may be added that no one knew him well. He was a lawyer, and had lived in Octavius for upwards of ten years; that is to say, since early manhood. He had an office on the main street, just under the principal photograph gallery. Doubtless he was some-times in this office; but his fellow-townsmen saw him more often in the street doorway, with the stairs behind him, and the flaring show-cases of the photographer on either side, standing with his hands in his pockets and 50 an unlighted cigar in his mouth, looking at nothing in particular. About every other day he went off after breakfast into the country roundabout, sometimes with a rod, sometimes with a gun, but always alone. He was a bachelor, and slept in a room at the back of his office, cooking some of his meals himself, getting others at a restaurant close by. Though he had little visible practice, he was understood to be well-to-do and even more, and people tacitly inferred that he "shaved notes." The Methodists of Octavius looked upon him as a queer 60 fish, and through nearly a dozen years had never quite outgrown their hebdomadal tendency to surprise at seeing him enter church. He had never, it is true, pro-fessed religion, but they had elected him as a trustee now for a number of terms, all the same,—partly be-cause he was their only lawyer, partly because he, like both his colleagues, held a mortgage on the church edi-fice and lot. In person, Mr. Gorringe was a slender man, with a skin of a clear, uniform citron tint, black waving hair, and dark gray eyes, and a thin, high-featured face. 70 He wore a mustache and pointed chin-tuft; and, though he was of New England parentage and had never been further south than Ocean Grove, he presented a general effect of old Mississippian traditions and tastes star-tlingly at variance with the standards of Dearborn County Methodism. Nothing could convince some of the elder sisters that he was not a drinking man.

The three visitors had completed their survey of the room now; and Loren Pierce emitted a dry, harsh little cough, as a signal that business was about to begin. At 80 this sound, Winch drew up his feet, and Gorringe untied a parcel of account-books and papers that he held on his knee. Theron felt that his countenance must be ex-hibiting to the assembled brethren an unfortunate sense of helplessness in their hands. He tried to look more resolute, and forced his lips into a smile.

"Brother Gorringe allus acts as Seckertary," said Erastus Winch, beaming broadly upon the minister, as if the mere mention of the fact promoted jollity. "That's it, Brother Gorringe,—take your seat at Brother Ware's 90 desk. Mind the Dominie's pen don't play tricks on you, an' start off writin' out sermons instid of figgers." The humorist turned to Theron as the lawyer walked over to the desk at the window. "I allus have to caution him about that," he remarked with great joviality. "An' do *you* look out afterwards, Brother Ware, or else you'll catch that pen o' yours scribblin' lawyer's lingo in place o' the Word."

Theron felt bound to exhibit a grin in acknowledgment of this pleasantry. The lawyer's change of position had involved some shifting of the others' chairs, and the young minister found himself directly confronted by Brother Pierce's hard and colorless old visage. Its little eyes were watching him, as through a mask, and under their influence the smile of politeness fled from his lips. The lawyer on his right, the cheese-buyer to the left, seemed to recede into distance as he for the moment returned the gaze of the quarryman. He waited now for him to speak, as if the others were of no importance.

"We are a plain sort o' folks up in these parts," said Brother Pierce, after a slight further pause. His voice was as dry and rasping as his cough, and its intonations were those of authority. "We walk here," he went on, eying the minister with a sour regard, "in a meek an' humble spirit, in the straight an' narrow way which leadeth unto life. We ain't gone traipsin' after strange gods, like some people that call themselves Methodists in other places. We stick by the Discipline an' the ways of our fathers in Israel. No new-fangled notions can go down here. Your wife'd better take them flowers out of her bunnit afore next Sunday."

Silence possessed the room for a few moments, the while Theron, pale-faced and with brows knit, studied the pattern of the ingrain carpet. Then he lifted his head, and nodded it in assent. "Yes," he said; "we will do nothing by which our 'brother stumbleth, or is offended, or is made weak.'"

Brother Pierce's parchment face showed no sign of surprise or pleasure at this easy submission. "Another thing: We don't want no book-learnin' or dictionary words in our pulpit," he went on coldly. "Some folks may stomach 'em; we won't. Them two sermons o' yours, p'r'aps they'd do down in some city place; but they're like your wife's bunnit here, they're too flowery to suit us. What we want to hear is the plain, old-fashioned Word of God, without any palaver or 'hems and ha's. They tell me there's some parts where hell's treated as played-out,—where our ministers don't like

to talk much about it because people don't want to hear about it. Such preachers ought to be put out. They ain't Methodists at all. What we want here, sir, is straight-out, flat-footed hell,—the burnin' lake o' fire an' brimstone. Pour it into 'em, hot an' strong. We can't have too much of it. Work in them awful deathbeds of Voltaire an' Tom Paine, with the Devil right there in the room, reachin' for 'em, an' they yellin' for fright; that's what fills the anxious seat an' brings in souls hand over fist."

Theron's tongue dallied for an instant with the temptation to comment upon these old-wife fables, which were so dear to the rural religious heart when he and I were boys. But it seemed wiser to only nod again, and let his mentor go on.

"We ain't had no trouble with the Free Methodists here," continued Brother Pierce, "jest because we kept to the old paths, an' seek for salvation in the good old way. Everybody can shout 'Amen!' as loud and as long as the Spirit moves him, with us. Some one was sayin' you thought we ought to have a choir and an organ. No, sirree! No such tom-foolery for us! You'll only stir up feelin' agin yourself by hintin' at such things. And then, too, our folks don't take no stock in all that pack o' nonsense about science, such as tellin' the age of the earth by crackin' up stones. I've b'en in the quarry line all my life, an' I know it's all humbug! Why, they say some folks are goin' round now preachin' that our grandfathers were all monkeys. That comes from departin' from the ways of our forefathers, an' puttin' in organs an' choirs, an' deckin' our women-folks out with gewgaws, an' apin' the fashions of the worldly. I should n't wonder if them kind did have some monkey blood in 'em. You'll find we're a different sort here."

The young minister preserved silence for a little, until it became apparent that the old trustee had had his say out. Even then he raised his head slowly, and at last made answer in a hesitating and irresolute way.

"You have been very frank," he said. "I am obliged to you. A clergyman coming to a new charge cannot be better served than by having laid before him a clear statement of the views and—and spiritual tendencies— of his new flock, quite at the outset. I feel it to be of especial value in this case, because I am young in years and in my ministry, and am conscious of a great weakness of the flesh. I can see how daily contact with a people so attached to the old, simple, primitive Methodism of Wesley and Asbury may be a source of much strength to me. I may take it," he added upon second thought, with an inquiring glance at Mr. Winch, "that Brother Pierce's description of our charge, and its tastes and needs, meets with your approval?"

Erastus Winch nodded his head and smiled expansively. "Whatever Brother Pierce says, goes!" he declared. The lawyer, sitting behind at the desk by the window, said nothing.

"The place is jest overrun with Irish," Brother Pierce began again. "They've got two Catholic churches here now to our one, and they do jest as they blamed please at the charter elections. It'd be a good idea to pitch into Catholics in general whenever you can. You could make a hit that way. I say the State ought to make 'em pay taxes on their church property. They've no right to be exempted, because they ain't Christians at all. They're idolaters, that's what they are! I know 'em! I've had 'em in my quarries for years, an' they ain't got no idee of decency or fair dealin'. Every time the price of stone went up, every man of 'em would jine to screw more wages out o' me. Why, they used to keep account o' the amount o' business I done, an' figger up my profits, an' have the face to come an' talk to me about 'em, as if that had anything to do with wages. It's my belief their priests put 'em up to it. People don't begin to reelize,—that church of idolatry'll be the ruin o' this country, if it ain't checked in time. Jest you go at 'em hammer'n' tongs! I've got Eyetalians in the quarries now. They're sensible fellows: they know when they're well off; a dollar a day, an' they're satisfied, an' everything goes smooth."

"But they're Catholics, the same as the Irish," suddenly interjected the lawyer, from his place by the window. Theron pricked up his ears at the sound of his voice. There was an anti-Pierce note in it, so to speak, which it did him good to hear. The consciousness of sympathy began on the instant to inspire him with courage.

"I know some people *say* they are," Brother Pierce guardedly retorted; "but I've summered an' wintered both kinds, an' I hold to it they're different. I grant ye, the Eyetalians *are* some given to jabbin' knives into each other, but they never git up strikes, an' they don't grumble about wages. Why, look at the way they live,—

jest some weeds an' yarbs dug up on the roadside, an' stewed in a kettle with a piece o' fat the size o' your finger, an' a loaf o' bread, an' they're happy as a king. There's some sense in *that;* but the Irish, they've got to have meat an' potatoes an' butter jest as if—as if—"

"As if they'd b'en used to 'em at home," put in Mr. Winch, to help his colleague out.

The lawyer ostentatiously drew up his chair to the desk, and began turning over the leaves of his biggest book. "It's getting on toward noon, gentlemen," he said, in an impatient voice.

The business meeting which followed was for a considerable time confined to hearing extracts from the books and papers read in a swift and formal fashion by Mr. Gorringe. If this was intended to inform the new pastor of the exact financial situation in Octavius, it lamentably failed of its purpose. Theron had little knowledge of figures; and though he tried hard to listen, and to assume an air of comprehension, he did not understand much of what he heard. In a general way he gathered that the church property was put down at $12,000, on which there was a debt of $4,800. The annual expenses were $2,250, of which the principal items were $800 for his salary, $170 for the rent of the parsonage, and $319 for interest on the debt. It seemed that last year the receipts had fallen just under $2,000, and they now confronted the necessity of making good this deficit during the coming year, as well as increasing the regular revenues. Without much discussion, it was agreed that they should endeavor to secure the services of a celebrated "debt-raiser," early in the autumn, and utilize him in the closing days of a revival.

Theron knew this "debt-raiser," and had seen him at work,—a burly, bustling, vulgar man who took possession of the pulpit as if it were an auctioneer's block, and pursued the task of exciting liberality in the bosoms of the congregation by alternating prayer, anecdote, song, and cheap buffoonery in a manner truly sickening. Would it not be preferable, he feebly suggested, to raise the money by a festival, or fair, or some other form of entertainment which the ladies could manage?

Brother Pierce shook his head with contemptuous emphasis. "Our women-folks ain't that kind," he said. "They did try to hold a sociable once, but nobody came, and we didn't raise more'n three or four dollars. It ain't their line. They lack the worldly arts. As the

Discipline commands, they avoid the evil of putting on gold and costly apparel, and taking such diversions as cannot be used in the name of the Lord Jesus."

"Well—of course—it you prefer the 'debt-raiser'—" Theron began, and took the itemized account from Gorringe's knee as an excuse for not finishing the hateful sentence.

He looked down the foolscap sheet, line by line, with no special sense of what it signified, until his eye caught
10 upon this little section of the report, bracketed by itself in the Secretary's neat hand:

INTEREST CHARGE.

First mortgage (1873) $1,000 (E. Winch) @ 7. $ 70
Second mortgage (1876) 1,700 (L. Gorringe) @ 6. 102
Third mortgage (1878) 2,100 (L. Pierce) @ 7. 147
$4,800 $319

It was no news to him that the three mortgages on the church property were held by the three trustees. But as he looked once more, another feature of the thing struck him as curious.

"I notice that the rates of interest vary," he remarked without thinking, and then wished the words unsaid, for the two trustees in view moved uneasily on their seats.

"Oh, that's nothing," exclaimed Erastus Winch, with
20 a boisterous display of jollity. "It's only Brother Gorringe's pleasant little way of making a contribution to our funds. You will notice that, at the date of all these mortgages, the State rate of interest was seven per cent. Since then it's b'en lowered to six. Well, when that happened, you see, Brother Gorringe, not being a professin' member, and so not bound by our rules, he could just as well as not let his interest down a cent. But Brother Pierce an' me, we talked it over, an' we made up our minds we were tied hand an' foot by our contract. You
30 know how strong the Discipline lays it down that we must be bound to the letter of our agreements. That bein' so, we seen it in the light of duty not to change what we'd set our hands to. That's how it is, Brother Ware."

"I understand," said Theron, with an effort at polite calmness of tone. "And—is there anything else?"

"There's this," broke in Brother Pierce: "we're commanded to be law-abiding people, an' seven per cent *was* the law—an' would be now if them ragamuffins in
40 the Legislation—"

"Surely we need n't go further into that," interrupted

the minister, conscious of a growing stiffness in his moral spine. "Have we any other business before us?"

Brother Pierce's little eyes snapped, and the wrinkles in his forehead deepened angrily. "Business?" he demanded. "Yes, plenty of it. We've got to reduce expenses. We're nigh onto $300 behind-hand this minute. Besides your house-rent, you get $800 free an' clear, —that is $15.38 every week, an' only you an' your wife to keep out of it. Why, when I was your age, young 50 man, and after that too, I was glad to get $6 a week."

"I don't think my salary is under discussion, Mr. Pierce—"

"*Brother* Pierce!" suggested Winch, in a half-chuckling undertone.

"Brother Pierce, then!" echoed Theron, impatiently. "The Quarterly Conference and the Estimating Committee deal with that. The trustees have no more to do with it than the man in the moon."

"Come, come, Brother Ware," put in Erastus Winch, 60 "we must n't have no hard feelin's. Brotherly love is what we're all lookin' after. Brother Pierce's meanin' was n't agin your drawin' your full salary, every cent of it, only—only there are certain little things connected with the parsonage here that we feel you ought to bear. F'r instance, there's the new sidewalk we had to lay in front of the house here only a month ago. Of course, if the treasury was flush we would n't say a word about it. An' then there's the gas bill here. Seein' as you get your rent for nothin', it don't seem much to ask that you 70 should see to lightin' the place yourself."

"No, I don't think that either is a proper charge upon me," interposed Theron. "I decline to pay them."

"We can have the gas shut off," remarked Brother Pierce, coldly.

"As soon as you like," responded the minister, sitting erect and tapping the carpet nervously with his foot. "Only you must understand that I will take the whole matter to the Quarterly Conference in July. I already see a good many other interesting questions about the 80 financial management of this church which might be appropriately discussed there."

"Oh, come, Brother Ware!" broke in Trustee Winch, with a somewhat agitated assumption of good-feeling. "Surely these are matters we ought to settle amongst ourselves. We never yet asked outsiders to meddle with our business here. It's our motto, Brother Ware. I say, if you've got a motto, stand by it."

"Well, my motto," said Theron, "is to be behaved decently to by those with whom I have to deal; and I also propose to stand by it."

Brother Pierce rose gingerly to his feet, with the hesitation of an old man not sure about his knees. When he had straightened himself, he put on his hat, and eyed the minister sternly from beneath its brim.

"The Lord gives us crosses grievous to our natur'," he said, "an' we're told to bear 'em cheerfully as long as they're on our backs; but there ain't nothin' said agin our unloadin' 'em in the ditch the minute we git the chance. I guess you won't last here more 'n a twelve-month."

He pulled his soft and discolored old hat down over his brows with a significantly hostile nod, and, turning, stumped toward the hall-door without offering to shake hands.

The other trustees had risen likewise, in tacit recognition that the meeting was over. Winch clasped the minister's hand in his own broad, hard palm, and squeezed it in an exuberant grip. "Don't mind his little ways, Brother Ware," he urged in a loud, unctuous whisper, with a grinning backward nod: "he's a trifle skittish sometimes when you don't give him free rein; but he's all wool an' a yard wide when it comes to right-down hard-pan religion. My love to Sister Ware;" and he followed the senior trustee into the hall.

Mr. Gorringe had been tying up his books and papers. He came now with the bulky parcel under his arm, and his hat and stick in the other hand. He could give little but his thumb to Theron to shake. His face wore a grave expression, and not a line relaxed as, catching the minister's look, he slowly covered his left eye in a deliberate wink.

* * * * *

"Well?—and how did it go off?" asked Alice, from where she knelt by the oven door, a few minutes later.

For answer, Theron threw himself wearily into the big old farm rocking-chair on the other side of the stove, and shook his head with a lengthened sigh.

"If it was n't for that man Gorringe of yours," he said dejectedly, "I think I should feel like going off— and learning a trade."

1896

Stephen Crane

1871 · 1900

Stephen Crane has been called "the Chatterton of American literature"—a comparison which implies that, like the young English poet, he was (in Wordsworth's phrase) a "marvelous boy" who "perished in his pride." Although Crane himself would not have liked such a romantic tag, it contains an element of truth; a writer of indisputable genius, Crane died prematurely, leaving a body of work which, while excellent in itself, gave promise of still better work to come.

Crane was born in Newark, New Jersey, the son of a Methodist preacher. He spent one year at Lafayette College, where he shocked his English professor by declaring that Tennyson's poetry was "swill"; and another year at Syracuse University, where he played shortstop on the varsity nine. Believing earnestly that he must devote his life to "the business of writing," he began with journalism. His brief career as a newspaper writer gave him rich and varied opportunities for observation: in the New York Bowery, in Texas and Mexico, and—under war conditions—in Greece and in Cuba. After his marriage in 1896 he lived in England; one of his close friends there was Joseph Conrad. Crane died in the Black Forest, in Germany, where he had gone with the hope of improving his health.

His fame rests upon a few poems, several short stories, and two short novels—*Maggie: A Girl of the Streets* (1893) and *The Red Badge of Courage* (1895). As a poet, Crane is an interesting link between Emily Dickinson and the Imagists of the 1910's. As a writer of fiction, he is important both as an early naturalist and as an expert craftsman. *Maggie* has been called the first naturalistic American novel. An honest picture of the brutal and sordid life of the New York slums, the book was such a novelty in 1893 that the author had to publish it at his own expense. *The Red Badge* is remarkable in both substance and technique. It is nominally the story of a battle in the Civil War; but any war and any battle would have served, because there is no attempt at localization. At the time of writing, Crane knew nothing of war at first hand. After his experiences in Greece and Cuba, he could say to a friend, *"The Red Badge* is all right!"* Later experience had confirmed the truth first apprehended chiefly by the imagination. Henry Fleming, the soldier, ran panic-stricken when the enemy charged; but with experience, he gained courage. Before the end of the story, "he had been to touch the great death, and found that, after all, it was but the great death." *The Red Badge* is an acute psychological study of the raw recruit in action. Technically, the book is comparable with James' mature work in that the story, though written in the third person, is managed consistently from the point of view of the distraught soldier.

Crane was above all else (and in a sense applicable to comparatively few American writers) the disinterested artist. He aimed at complete honesty of treatment. He wrote with economy, restraint, and a respect for point of view. He chose words precisely and created images which are colorful and impressionistic. He was a master of irony. It was ironical that a nice girl like Maggie should have "blossomed in a mud puddle." It was ironical that the soldier, Henry Fleming, should have gained courage through an accidental knock on the head. Man's self-importance, to Crane, and his self-pity were ironical in a universe indifferent to man.

The Works of Stephen Crane, ed. Wilson Follett, 12 vols., New York, 1926 • Thomas Beer, Stephen Crane, New York, 1923 • John Berryman, Stephen Crane, New York, 1951

The Open Boat

A Tale intended to be after the Fact. Being the Experience of Four Men from the Sunk Steamer 'Commodore'

In December 1896, the steamer **Commodore**, carrying ammunition and a party of Cuban insurrectionists, sailed from Jacksonville, Florida, for Cuba, where a revolution was in progress. Crane was on board as war correspondent for a newspaper syndicate. The ship went down off the Florida coast, and Crane got into the last of the boats to leave the sinking vessel; the other men in the open boat were the ship's cook, the oiler, and the injured captain. Crane's story is based upon his actual experiences; it is indeed "after the fact."

The story is told from the point of view of the men in the boat; more especially from the point of view of the correspondent, who was Crane himself. If there are a few violations of this rule (as when the author intrudes to say that "there was not a life-saving station within twenty miles") the violations are designed to heighten the desired effect (in the instance cited, the effect of irony). "The Open Boat" is Crane at his best. Sustained point of view, restraint, ironical wit, poetic images and cadences, and Poe's virtue of totality—these are some of the characteristic qualities of Crane which make "The Open Boat" one of the short masterpieces of modern American prose.

I

None of them knew the colour of the sky. Their eyes glanced level, and were fastened upon the waves that swept toward them. These waves were of the hue of slate, save for the tops, which were of foaming white, and all of the men knew the colours of the sea. The horizon narrowed and widened, and dipped and rose, and at all times its edge was jagged with waves that seemed thrust up in points like rocks.

Many a man ought to have a bath-tub larger than the boat which here rode upon the sea. These waves were most wrongfully and barbarously abrupt and tall, and each froth-top was a problem in small boat navigation.

The cook squatted in the bottom and looked with both eyes at the six inches of gunwale which separated him from the ocean. His sleeves were rolled over his fat forearms, and the two flaps of his unbuttoned vest dangled as he bent to bail out the boat. Often he said: 'Gawd! That was a narrow clip.' As he remarked it he invariably gazed eastward over the broken sea.

The oiler, steering with one of the two oars in the boat, sometimes raised himself suddenly to keep clear of water that swirled in over the stern. It was a thin little oar and it seemed often ready to snap.

The correspondent, pulling at the other oar, watched the waves and wondered why he was there.

The injured captain, lying in the bow, was at this time buried in that profound dejection and indifference which comes, temporarily at least, to even the bravest and most enduring when, willy nilly, the firm fails, the army loses, the ship goes down. The mind of the master of a vessel is rooted deep in the timbers of her, though he command for a day or a decade, and this captain had on him the stern impression of a scene in the greys of dawn of seven turned faces, and later a stump of a top-mast with a white ball on it that slashed to and fro at the waves, went low and lower, and down. Thereafter there was something strange in his voice. Although steady, it was deep with mourning, and of a quality beyond oration or tears.

'Keep 'er a little more south, Billie,' said he.

'A little more south, sir,' said the oiler in the stern.

A seat in this boat was not unlike a seat upon a bucking broncho, and, by the same token, a broncho is not much smaller. The craft pranced and reared, and plunged like an animal. As each wave came, and she rose for it, she seemed like a horse making at a fence outrageously high. The manner of her scramble over these walls of water is a mystic thing, and, moreover, at the top of them were ordinarily these problems in white water, the foam racing down from the summit of each wave, requiring a new leap, and a leap from the air. Then, after scornfully bumping a crest, she would slide, and race, and splash down a long incline, and arrive bobbing and nodding in front of the next menace.

A singular disadvantage of the sea lies in the fact that after successfully surmounting one wave you discover that there is another behind it just as important and just as nervously anxious to do something effective in the way of swamping boats. In a ten-foot dingey one can get an idea of the resources of the sea in the line of waves that is not probable to the average experience which is never at sea in a dingey. As each slaty wall of water approached, it shut all else from the view of the men in the boat, and it was not difficult to imagine that this particular wave was the final outburst of the ocean, the last effort of the grim water. There was a terrible grace in the move of the waves, and they came in silence, save for the snarling of the crests.

In the wan light, the faces of the men must have been grey. Their eyes must have glinted in strange ways as they gazed steadily astern. Viewed from a balcony, the whole thing would doubtless have been weirdly picturesque. But the men in the boat had no time to see it, and if they had had leisure there were other things to occupy their minds. The sun swung steadily up the sky, and they knew it was broad day because the colour of the sea changed from slate to emerald-green, streaked with amber lights, and the foam was like tumbling snow. The process of the breaking day was unknown to them. They were aware only of this effect upon the colour of the waves that rolled toward them.

In disjointed sentences the cook and the correspondent argued as to the difference between a life-saving station and a house of refuge. The cook had said: 'There's a house of refuge just north of the Mosquito Inlet Light, and as soon as they see us, they'll come off in their boat and pick us up.'

'As soon as who see us?' said the correspondent.

'The crew,' said the cook.

'Houses of refuge don't have crews,' said the correspondent. 'As I understand them, they are only places where clothes and grub are stored for the benefit of shipwrecked people. They don't carry crews.'

'Oh, yes, they do,' said the cook.

'No, they don't,' said the correspondent.

---

16 **oiler,** an engine-room greaser

'Well, we're not there yet, anyhow,' said the oiler, in the stern.

'Well,' said the cook, 'perhaps it's not a house of refuge that I'm thinking of as being near Mosquito Inlet Light. Perhaps it's a life-saving station.'

'We're not there yet,' said the oiler, in the stern.

II

As the boat bounced from the top of each wave, the wind tore through the hair of the hatless men, and as the craft plopped her stern down again the spray slashed
10 past them. The crest of each of these waves was a hill, from the top of which the men surveyed, for a moment, a broad tumultuous expanse, shining and wind-riven. It was probably splendid. It was probably glorious, this play of the free sea, wild with lights of emerald and white and amber.

'Bully good thing it's an on-shore wind,' said the cook. 'If not, where would we be? Wouldn't have a show.'

'That's right,' said the correspondent.

The busy oiler nodded his assent.

20 Then the captain, in the bow, chuckled in a way that expressed humour, contempt, tragedy, all in one. 'Do you think we've got much of a show now, boys?' said he.

Whereupon the three were silent, save for a trifle of hemming and hawing. To express any particular optimism at this time they felt to be childish and stupid, but they all doubtless possessed this sense of the situation in their mind. A young man thinks doggedly at such times. On the other hand, the ethics of their condition was decidedly against any open suggestion of
30 hopelessness. So they were silent.

'Oh, well,' said the captain, soothing his children, 'we'll get ashore all right.'

But there was that in his tone which made them think, so the oiler quoth: 'Yes! If this wind holds!'

The cook was bailing: 'Yes! If we don't catch hell in the surf.'

Canton flannel gulls flew near and far. Sometimes they sat down on the sea, near patches of brown seaweed that rolled over the waves with a movement like carpets on a
40 line in a gale. The birds sat comfortably in groups, and they were envied by some in the dingey, for the wrath of the sea was no more to them than it was to a covey of prairie chickens a thousand miles inland. Often they came very close and stared at the men with black bead-like eyes. At these times they were uncanny and sinister in their unblinking scrutiny, and the men hooted angrily at them, telling them to be gone. One came, and evidently decided to alight on the top of the captain's head. The bird flew parallel to the boat and did not circle, but made short sidelong jumps in the air in chicken-fashion. His 50 black eyes were wistfully fixed upon the captain's head. 'Ugly brute,' said the oiler to the bird. 'You look as if you were made with a jack-knife.' The cook and the correspondent swore darkly at the creature. The captain naturally wished to knock it away with the end of the heavy painter; but he did not dare do it, because anything resembling an emphatic gesture would have capsized this freighted boat, and so with his open hand, the captain gently and carefully waved the gull away. After it had been discouraged from the pursuit the captain breathed 60 easier on account of his hair, and others breathed easier because the bird struck their minds at this time as being somehow gruesome and ominous.

In the meantime the oiler and the correspondent rowed. And also they rowed.

They sat together in the same seat, and each rowed an oar. Then the oiler took both oars; then the correspondent took both oars; then the oiler; then the correspondent. They rowed and they rowed. The very ticklish part of the business was when the time came for the reclining 70 one in the stern to take his turn at the oars. By the very last star of truth, it is easier to steal eggs from under a hen than it was to change seats in the dingey. First the man in the stern slid his hand along the thwart and moved with care, as if he were of Sèvres. Then the man in the rowing seat slid his hand along the other thwart. It was all done with the most extraordinary care. As the two sidled past each other, the whole party kept watchful eyes on the coming wave, and the captain cried: 'Look out now! Steady there!' 80

The brown mats of seaweed that appeared from time to time were like islands, bits of earth. They were travelling, apparently, neither one way nor the other. They were, to all intents, stationary. They informed the men in the boat that it was making progress slowly toward the land.

The captain, rearing cautiously in the bow, after the

---

37 **Canton flannel,** cotton fabric with a long, fleecy nap • 56 **painter,** a rope, usually at the bow, for fastening a boat • 74 **thwart,** a rower's seat • 75 **Sèvres,** costly porcelain manufactured at Sèvres, France

dingey soared on a great swell, said that he had seen the lighthouse at Mosquito Inlet. Presently the cook remarked that he had seen it. The correspondent was at the oars then, and for some reason he too wished to look at the lighthouse, but his back was toward the far shore and the waves were important, and for some time he could not seize an opportunity to turn his head. But at last there came a wave more gentle than the others, and when at the crest of it he swiftly scoured the western

10 horizon.

'See it?' said the captain.

'No,' said the correspondent slowly, 'I didn't see anything.'

'Look again,' said the captain. He pointed. 'It's exactly in that direction.'

At the top of another wave. the correspondent did as he was bid, and this time his eyes chanced on a small still thing on the edge of the swaying horizon. It was precisely like the point of a pin. It took an anxious eye

20 to find a lighthouse so tiny.

'Think we'll make it, captain?'

'If this wind holds and the boat don't swamp, we can't do much else,' said the captain.

The little boat, lifted by each towering sea, and splashed viciously by the crests, made progress that in the absence of seaweed was not apparent to those in her. She seemed just a wee thing wallowing, miraculously top up, at the mercy of five oceans. Occasionally, a great spread of water, like white flames, swarmed into her.

30 'Bail her, cook,' said the captain serenely.

'All right, captain,' said the cheerful cook.

III

It would be difficult to describe the subtle brotherhood of men that was here established on the seas. No one said that it was so. No one mentioned it. But it dwelt in the boat, and each man felt it warm him. They were a captain, an oiler, a cook, and a correspondent, and they were friends, friends in a more curiously iron-bound degree than may be common. The hurt captain, lying against the water-jar in the bow, spoke always in a low

40 voice and calmly, but he could never command a more ready and swiftly obedient crew than the motley three of the dingey. It was more than a mere recognition of what was best for the common safety. There was surely in it a quality that was personal and heartfelt. And after this devotion to the commander of the boat there was

this comradeship that the correspondent, for instance, who had been taught to be cynical of men, knew even at the time was the best experience of his life. But no one said that it was so. No one mentioned it.

'I wish we had a sail,' remarked the captain. 'We might 50 try my overcoat on the end of an oar and give you two boys a chance to rest.' So the cook and the correspondent held the mast and spread wide the overcoat. The oiler steered, and the little boat made good way with her new rig. Sometimes the oiler had to scull sharply to keep a sea from breaking into the boat, but otherwise sailing was a success.

Meanwhile the lighthouse had been growing slowly larger. It had now almost assumed colour, and appeared like a little grey shadow on the sky. The man 60 at the oars could not be prevented from turning his head rather often to try for a glimpse of this little grey shadow.

At last, from the top of each wave the men in the tossing boat could see land. Even as the lighthouse was an upright shadow on the sky, this land seemed but a long black shadow on the sea. It certainly was thinner than paper. 'We must be about opposite New Smyrna,' said the cook, who had coasted this shore often in schooners. 'Captain, by the way, I believe they abandoned that life-saving station there about a year ago.' 70

'Did they?' said the captain.

The wind slowly died away. The cook and the correspondent were not now obliged to slave in order to hold high the oar. But the waves continued their old impetuous swooping at the dingey, and the little craft, no longer under way, struggled woundily over them. The oiler or the correspondent took the oars again.

Shipwrecks are apropos of nothing. If men could only train for them and have them occur when the men had reached pink condition, there would be less drowning at 80 sea. Of the four in the dingey none had slept any time worth mentioning for two days and two nights previous to embarking in the dingey, and in the excitement of clambering about the deck of a foundering ship they had also forgotten to eat heartily.

For these reasons, and for others, neither the oiler nor the correspondent was fond of rowing at this time. The correspondent wondered ingenuously how in the name of all that was sane could there be people who thought

---

67 **New Smyrna,** a town on the east coast of Florida • 76 **woundily,** excessively

it amusing to row a boat. It was not an amusement; it was a diabolical punishment, and even a genius of mental aberrations could never conclude that it was anything but a horror to the muscles and a crime against the back. He mentioned to the boat in general how the amusement of rowing struck him, and the weary-faced oiler smiled in full sympathy. Previously to the foundering, by the way, the oiler had worked double-watch in the engine-room of the ship.

10 'Take her easy, now, boys,' said the captain. 'Don't spend yourselves. If we have to run a surf you'll need all your strength, because we'll sure have to swim for it. Take your time.'

Slowly the land arose from the sea. From a black line it became a line of black and a line of white, trees and sand. Finally, the captain said that he could make out a house on the shore. 'That's the house of refuge, sure,' said the cook. 'They'll see us before long, and come out after us.'

20 The distant-lighthouse reared high. 'The keeper ought to be able to make us out now, if he's looking through a glass,' said the captain. 'He'll notify the life-saving people.'

'None of those other boats could have got ashore to give word of the wreck,' said the oiler, in a low voice. 'Else the lifeboat would be out hunting us.'

Slowly and beautifully the land loomed out of the sea. The wind came again. It had veered from the north-east to the south-east. Finally, a new sound struck 30 the ears of the men in the boat. It was the low thunder of the surf on the shore. 'We'll never be able to make the lighthouse now,' said the captain. 'Swing her head a little more north, Billie.'

'A little more north, sir,' said the oiler.

Whereupon the little boat turned her nose once more down the wind, and all but the oarsmen watched the shore grow. Under the influence of this expansion doubt and direful apprehension was leaving the minds of the men. The management of the boat was still most ab- 40 sorbing, but it could not prevent a quiet cheerfulness. In an hour, perhaps, they would be ashore.

Their backbones had become thoroughly used to balancing in the boat, and they now rode this wild colt of a dingey like circus men. The correspondent thought that he had been drenched to the skin, but happening to feel in the top pocket of his coat, he found therein eight cigars. Four of them were soaked with sea-water;

four were perfectly scatheless. After a search, somebody produced three dry matches, and thereupon the four waifs rode impudently in their little boat, and with an 50 assurance of an impending rescue shining in their eyes, puffed at the big cigars and judged well and ill of all men. Everybody took a drink of water.

IV

'Cook,' remarked the captain, 'there don't seem to be any signs of life about your house of refuge.'

'No,' replied the cook. 'Funny they don't see us!'

A broad stretch of lowly coast lay before the eyes of the men. It was of low dunes topped with dark vegetation. The roar of the surf was plain, and sometimes they could see the white lip of a wave as it spun up the 60 beach. A tiny house was blocked out black upon the sky. Southward, the slim lighthouse lifted its little grey length.

Tide, wind, and waves were swinging the dingey northward. 'Funny they don't see us,' said the men.

The surf's roar was here dulled, but its tone was, nevertheless, thunderous and mighty. As the boat swam over the great rollers, the men sat listening to this roar. 'We'll swamp sure,' said everybody.

It is fair to say here that there was not a life-saving station within twenty miles in either direction, but the men 70 did not know this fact, and in consequence they made dark and opprobrious remarks concerning the eyesight of the nation's life-savers. Four scowling men sat in the dingey and surpassed records in the invention of epithets.

'Funny they don't see us.'

The light-heartedness of a former time had completely faded. To their sharpened minds it was easy to conjure pictures of all kinds of incompetency and blindness and, indeed, cowardice. There was the shore of the populous land, and it was bitter and bitter to them that from it 80 came no sign.

'Well,' said the captain, ultimately, 'I suppose we'll have to make a try for ourselves. If we stay out here too long, we'll none of us have strength left to swim after the boat swamps.'

And so the oiler, who was at the oars, turned the boat straight for the shore. There was a sudden tightening of muscles. There was some thinking.

'If we don't all get ashore—' said the captain. 'If we don't all get ashore, I suppose you fellows know where 90 to send news of my finish?'

They then briefly exchanged some addresses and admonitions. As for the reflections of the men, there was a great deal of rage in them. Perchance they might be formulated thus: 'If I am going to be drowned—if I am going to be drowned—if I am going to be drowned, why, in the name of the seven mad gods who rule the sea, was I allowed to come thus far and contemplate sand and trees? Was I brought here merely to have my nose dragged away as I was about to nibble the sacred cheese of life? It is preposterous. If this old ninny-woman, Fate, cannot do better than this, she should be deprived of the management of men's fortunes. She is an old hen who knows not her intention. If she has decided to drown me, why did she not do it in the beginning and save me all this trouble? The whole affair is absurd. . . . But no, she cannot mean to drown me. She dare not drown me. She cannot drown me. Not after all this work.' Afterward the man might have had an impulse to shake his fist at the clouds: 'Just you drown me, now, and then hear what I call you!'

The billows that came at this time were more formidable. They seemed always just about to break and roll over the little boat in a turmoil of foam. There was a preparatory and long growl in the speech of them. No mind unused to the sea would have concluded that the dingey could ascend these sheer heights in time. The shore was still afar. The oiler was a wily surfman. 'Boys,' he said swiftly, 'she won't live three minutes more, and we're too far out to swim. Shall I take her to sea again, captain?'

'Yes! Go ahead!' said the captain.

This oiler, by a series of quick miracles, and fast and steady oarsmanship, turned the boat in the middle of the surf and took her safely to sea again.

There was a considerable silence as the boat bumped over the furrowed sea to deeper water. Then somebody in gloom spoke. 'Well, anyhow, they must have seen us from the shore by now.'

The gulls went in slanting flight up the wind toward the grey desolate east. A squall, marked by dingy clouds, and clouds brick-red, like smoke from a burning building, appeared from the south-east.

'What do you think of those life-saving people? Ain't they peaches?'

'Funny they haven't seen us.'

'Maybe they think we're out here for sport! Maybe they think we're fishin'. Maybe they think we're damned fools.'

It was a long afternoon. A changed tide tried to force them southward, but wind and wave said northward. Far ahead, where coastline, sea, and sky formed their mighty angle, there were little dots which seemed to indicate a city on the shore.

'St. Augustine?'

The captain shook his head. 'Too near Mosquito Inlet.'

And the oiler rowed, and then the correspondent rowed. Then the oiler rowed. It was a weary business. The human back can become the seat of more aches and pains than are registered in books for the composite anatomy of a regiment. It is a limited area, but it can become the theatre of innumerable muscular conflicts, tangles, wrenches, knots, and other comforts.

'Did you ever like to row, Billie?' asked the correspondent.

'No,' said the oiler. 'Hang it.'

When one exchanged the rowing-seat for a place in the bottom of the boat, he suffered a bodily depression that caused him to be careless of everything save an obligation to wiggle one finger. There was cold sea-water swashing to and fro in the boat, and he lay in it. His head, pillowed on a thwart, was within an inch of the swirl of a wave crest, and sometimes a particularly obstreperous sea came in-board and drenched him once more. But these matters did not annoy him. It is almost certain that if the boat had capsized he would have tumbled comfortably out upon the ocean as if he felt sure that it was a great soft mattress.

'Look! There's a man on the shore!'

'Where?'

'There! See 'im? See 'im?'

'Yes, sure! He's walking along.'

'Now he's stopped. Look! He's facing us!'

'He's waving at us!'

'So he is! By thunder!'

'Ah, now we're all right! Now we're all right! There'll be a boat out here for us in half an hour.'

'He's going on. He's running. He's going up to that house there.'

The remote beach seemed lower than the sea, and it required a searching glance to discern the little black figure. The captain saw a floating stick and they rowed to it. A bath-towel was by some weird chance in the boat, and, tying this on the stick, the captain waved it. The oarsman did not dare turn his head, so he was obliged to ask questions.

'What's he doing now?'

'He's standing still again. He's looking, I think. . . . There he goes again. Toward the house. . . . Now he stopped again.'

'Is he waving at us?'

'No, not now! he was, though.'

'Look! There comes another man!'

'He's running.'

'Look at him go, would you.'

'Why, he's on a bicycle. Now he's met the other man. They're both waving at us. Look!'

'There comes something up the beach.'

'What the devil is that thing?'

'Why, it looks like a boat.'

'Why, certainly it's a boat.'

'No, it's on wheels.'

'Yes, so it is. Well, that must be the life-boat. They drag them along shore on a wagon.'

'That's the life-boat, sure.'

'No, by—, it's—it's an omnibus.'

'I tell you it's a life-boat.'

'It is not! It's an omnibus. I can see it plain. See? One of these big hotel omnibuses.'

'By thunder, you're right. It's an omnibus, sure as fate. What do you suppose they are doing with an omnibus? Maybe they are going around collecting the life-crew, hey?'

'That's it, likely. Look! There's a fellow waving a little black flag. He's standing on the steps of the omnibus. There come those other two fellows. Now they're all talking together. Look at the fellow with the flag. Maybe he ain't waving it.'

'That ain't a flag, is it? That's his coat. Why, certainly, that's his coat.'

'So it is. It's his coat. He's taken it off and is waving it around his head. But would you look at him swing it.'

'Oh, say, there isn't any life-saving station there. That's just a winter resort hotel omnibus that has brought over some of the boarders to see us drown.'

'What's that idiot with the coat mean? What's he signaling, anyhow?'

'It looks as if he were trying to tell us to go north. There must be a life-saving station up there.'

'No! He thinks we're fishing. Just giving us a merry hand. See? Ah, there, Willie.'

'Well, I wish I could make something out of those signals. What do you suppose he means?'

'He don't mean anything. He's just playing.'

'Well, if he'd just signal us to try the surf again, or to go to sea and wait, or go north, or go south, or go to hell —there would be some reason in it. But look at him. He just stands there and keeps his coat revolving like a wheel. The ass!'

'There come more people.'

'Now there's quite a mob. Look! Isn't that a boat?'

'Where? Oh, I see where you mean. No, that's no boat.'

'That fellow is still waving his coat.'

'He must think we like to see him do that. Why don't he quit it? It don't mean anything.'

'I don't know. I think he is trying to make us go north. It must be that there's a life-saving station there somewhere.'

'Say, he ain't tired yet. Look at 'im wave.'

'Wonder how long he can keep that up. He's been revolving his coat ever since he caught sight of us. He's an idiot. Why aren't they getting men to bring a boat out? A fishing boat—one of those big yawls—could come out here all right. Why don't he do something?'

'Oh, it's all right, now.'

'They'll have a boat out here for us in less than no time, now that they've seen us.'

A faint yellow tone came into the sky over the low land. The shadows on the sea slowly deepened. The wind bore coldness with it, and the men began to shiver.

'Holy smoke!' said one, allowing his voice to express his impious mood, 'if we keep on monkeying out here! If we've got to flounder out here all night!'

'Oh, we'll never have to stay here all night! Don't you worry. They've seen us now, and it won't be long before they'll come chasing out after us.'

The shore grew dusky. The man waving a coat blended gradually into this gloom, and it swallowed in the same manner the omnibus and the group of people. The spray, when it dashed uproariously over the side, made the voyagers shrink and swear like men who were being branded.

'I'd like to catch the chump who waved that coat. I feel like soaking him one, just for luck.'

'Why? What did he do?'

'Oh, nothing, but then he seemed so damned cheerful.'

In the meantime the oiler rowed, and then the correspondent rowed, and then the oiler rowed. Grey-faced and bowed forward, they mechanically, turn by turn, plied the leaden oars. The form of the lighthouse had vanished from the southern horizon, but finally a pale star appeared, just lifting from the sea. The streaked saffron in the west passed before the all-merging darkness, and the sea to the east was black. The land had vanished, and was expressed only by the low and drear thunder of the surf.

'If I am going to be drowned—if I am going to be drowned—if I am going to be drowned, why, in the name of the seven mad gods who rule the sea, was I allowed to come thus far and contemplate sand and trees?
10 Was I brought here merely to have my nose dragged away as I was about to nibble the sacred cheese of life?'

The patient captain, drooped over the water-jar, was sometimes obliged to speak to the oarsman.

'Keep her head up! Keep her head up!'

'"Keep her head up," sir.' The voices were weary and low.

This was surely a quiet evening. All save the oarsman lay heavily and listlessly in the boat's bottom. As for him, his eyes were just capable of noting the tall
20 black waves that swept forward in a most sinister silence, save for an occasional subdued growl of a crest.

The cook's head was on a thwart, and he looked without interest at the water under his nose. He was deep in other scenes. Finally he spoke. 'Billie,' he murmured, dreamfully, 'what kind of pie do you like best?'

V

'Pie,' said the oiler and the correspondent, agitatedly. 'Don't talk about those things, blast you!'

'Well,' said the cook, 'I was just thinking about ham sandwiches, and—'
30 A night on the sea in an open boat is a long night. As darkness settled finally, the shine of the light, lifting from the sea in the south, changed to full gold. On the northern horizon a new light appeared, a small bluish gleam on the edge of the waters. These two lights were the furniture of the world. Otherwise there was nothing but waves.

Two men huddled in the stern, and distances were so magnificent in the dingey that the rower was enabled to keep his feet partly warmed by thrusting them under
40 his companions. Their legs indeed extended far under the rowing-seat until they touched the feet of the captain forward. Sometimes, despite the efforts of the tired oarsman, a wave came piling into the boat, an icy wave of the night, and the chilling water soaked them anew. They would twist their bodies for a moment and groan,

and sleep the dead sleep once more, while the water in the boat gurgled about them as the craft rocked.

The plan of the oiler and the correspondent was for one to row until he lost the ability, and then arouse the other from his sea-water couch in the bottom of the boat. 50

The oiler plied the oars until his head drooped forward, and the overpowering sleep blinded him. And he rowed yet afterward. Then he touched a man in the bottom of the boat, and called his name. 'Will you spell me for a little while?' he said, meekly.

'Sure, Billie,' said the correspondent, awakening and dragging himself to a sitting position. They exchanged places carefully, and the oiler, cuddling down in the sea-water at the cook's side, seemed to go to sleep instantly.

The particular violence of the sea had ceased. The 60 waves came without snarling. The obligation of the man at the oars was to keep the boat headed so that the tilt of the rollers would not capsize her, and to preserve her from filling when the crests rushed past. The black waves were silent and hard to be seen in the darkness. Often one was almost upon the boat before the oarsman was aware.

In a low voice the correspondent addressed the captain. He was not sure that the captain was awake, although this iron man seemed to be always awake. 70 'Captain, shall I keep her making for that light north, sir?'

The same steady voice answered him. 'Yes. Keep it about two points off the port bow.'

The cook had tied a life-belt around himself in order to get even the warmth which this clumsy cork contrivance could donate, and he seemed almost stove-like when a rower, whose teeth invariably chattered wildly as soon as he ceased his labour, dropped down to sleep.

The correspondent, as he rowed, looked down at the 80 two men sleeping underfoot. The cook's arm was around the oiler's shoulders, and, with their fragmentary clothing and haggard faces, they were the babes of the sea, a grotesque rendering of the old babes in the wood.

Later he must have grown stupid at his work, for suddenly there was a growling of water, and a crest came with a roar and a swash into the boat, and it was a wonder that it did not set the cook afloat in his lifebelt. The cook continued to sleep, but the oiler sat up, blinking his eyes and shaking with the new cold. 90

'Oh, I'm awful sorry, Billie,' said the correspondent, contritely.

'That's all right, old boy,' said the oiler, and lay down again and was asleep.

Presently it seemed that even the captain dozed, and the correspondent thought that he was the one man afloat on all the oceans. The wind had a voice as it came over the waves, and it was sadder than the end.

There was a long, loud swishing astern of the boat, and a gleaming trail of phosphorescence, like blue flame, was furrowed on the black waters. It might have been 10 made by a monstrous knife.

Then there came a stillness, while the correspondent breathed with the open mouth and looked at the sea.

Suddenly there was another swish and another long flash of bluish light, and this time it was alongside the boat, and might almost have been reached with an oar. The correspondent saw an enormous fin speed like a shadow through the water, hurling the crystalline spray and leaving the long glowing trail.

The correspondent looked over his shoulder at the 20 captain. His face was hidden, and he seemed to be asleep. He looked at the babes of the sea. They certainly were asleep. So, being bereft of sympathy, he leaned a little way to one side and swore softly into the sea.

But the thing did not then leave the vicinity of the boat. Ahead or astern, on one side or the other, at intervals long or short, fled the long sparkling streak, and there was to be heard the whiroo of the dark fin. The speed and power of the thing was greatly to be admired. It cut the water like a gigantic and keen projectile.

30 The presence of this biding thing did not affect the man with the same horror that it would if he had been a picknicker. He simply looked at the sea dully and swore in an undertone.

Nevertheless, it is true that he did not wish to be alone with the thing. He wished one of his companions to awaken by chance and keep him company with it. But the captain hung motionless over the water-jar, and the oiler and the cook in the bottom of the boat were plunged in slumber.

VI

40 'If I am going to be drowned—if I am going to be drowned—if I am going to be drowned, why, in the name of the seven mad gods who rule the sea, was I allowed to come thus far and contemplate sand and trees?'

During this dismal night, it may be remarked that a man would conclude that it was really the intention of the seven mad gods to drown him, despite the abominable injustice of it. For it was certainly an abominable injustice to drown a man who had worked so hard, so hard. The man felt it would be a crime most unnatural. 50 Other people had drowned at sea since galleys swarmed with painted sails, but still—

When it occurs to a man that nature does not regard him as important, and that she feels she would not maim the universe by disposing of him, he at first wishes to throw bricks at the temple, and he hates deeply the fact that there are no bricks and no temples. Any visible expression of nature would surely be pelleted with his jeers.

Then, if there be no tangible thing to hoot he feels, 60 perhaps, the desire to confront a personification and indulge in pleas, bowed to one knee, and with hands supplicant, saying: 'Yes, but I love myself.'

A high cold star on a winter's night is the word he feels that she says to him. Thereafter he knows the pathos of his situation.

The men in the dingey had not discussed these matters, but each had, no doubt, reflected upon them in silence and according to his mind. There was seldom any expression upon their faces save the general one of com- 70 plete weariness. Speech was devoted to the business of the boat.

To chime the notes of his emotion, a verse mysteriously entered the correspondent's head. He had even forgotten that he had forgotten this verse, but it suddenly was in his mind.

'A soldier of the Legion lay dying in Algiers,
There was lack of woman's nursing, there was
    dearth of woman's tears;
But a comrade stood beside him, and he took
    that comrade's hand,
And he said: "I shall never see my own,
    my native land."'
80

In his childhood, the correspondent had been made acquainted with the fact that a soldier of the Legion lay dying in Algiers, but he had never regarded the fact as

---

77 A soldier . . . land, from "Bingen on the Rhine," by Caroline E. S. Norton (1808-1877)

important. Myriads of his school-fellows had informed him of the soldier's plight, but the dinning had naturally ended by making him perfectly indifferent. He had never considered it his affair that a soldier of the Legion lay dying in Algiers, nor had it appeared to him as a matter for sorrow. It was less to him than the breaking of a pencil's point.

Now, however, it quaintly came to him as a human, living thing. It was no longer merely a picture of a few throes in the breast of a poet, meanwhile drinking tea and warming his feet at the grate; it was an actuality— stern, mournful, and fine.

The correspondent plainly saw the soldier. He lay on the sand with his feet out straight and still. While his pale left hand was upon his chest in an attempt to thwart the going of his life, the blood came between his fingers. In the far Algerian distance, a city of low square forms was set against a sky that was faint with the last sunset hues. The correspondent, plying the oars and dreaming of the slow and slower movements of the lips of the soldier, was moved by a profound and perfectly impersonal comprehension. He was sorry for the soldier of the Legion who lay dying in Algiers.

The thing which had followed the boat and waited had evidently grown bored at the delay. There was no longer to be heard the slash of the cut-water, and there was no longer the flame of the long trail. The light in the north still glimmered, but it was apparently no nearer to the boat. Sometimes the boom of the surf rang in the correspondent's ears, and he turned the craft seaward then and rowed harder. Southward, someone had evidently built a watch-fire on the beach. It was too low and too far to be seen, but it made a shimmering, roseate reflection upon the bluff back of it, and this could be discerned from the boat. The wind came stronger, and sometimes a wave suddenly raged out like a mountain-cat, and there was to be seen the sheen and sparkle of a broken crest.

The captain, in the bow, moved on his water-jar and sat erect. 'Pretty long night,' he observed to the correspondent. He looked at the shore. 'Those life-saving people take their time.'

'Did you see that shark playing around?'

'Yes, I saw him. He was a big fellow, all right.'

'Wish I had known you were awake.'

Later the correspondent spoke into the bottom of the boat.

'Billie!' There was a slow and gradual disentanglement. 'Billie, will you spell me?'

'Sure,' said the oiler.

As soon as the correspondent touched the cold comfortable sea-water in the bottom of the boat, and had huddled close to the cook's life-belt he was deep in sleep, despite the fact that his teeth played all the popular airs. This sleep was so good to him that it was but a moment before he heard a voice call his name in a tone that demonstrated the last stages of exhaustion. 'Will you spell me?'

'Sure, Billie.'

The light in the north had mysteriously vanished, but the correspondent took his course from the wide-awake captain.

Later in the night they took the boat farther out to sea, and the captain directed the cook to take one oar at the stern and keep the boat facing the seas. He was to call out if he should hear the thunder of the surf. This plan enabled the oiler and the correspondent to get respite together. 'We'll give those boys a chance to get into shape again,' said the captain. They curled down and, after a few preliminary chatterings and trembles, slept once more the dead sleep. Neither knew they had bequeathed to the cook the company of another shark, or perhaps the same shark.

As the boat caroused on the waves, spray occasionally bumped over the side and gave them a fresh soaking, but this had no power to break their repose. The ominous slash of the wind and the water affected them as it would have affected mummies.

'Boys,' said the cook, with the notes of every reluctance in his voice, 'she's drifted in pretty close. I guess one of you had better take her to sea again.' The correspondent, aroused, heard the crash of the toppled crests.

As he was rowing, the captain gave him some whisky-and-water, and this steadied the chills out of him. 'If I ever get ashore and anybody shows me even a photograph of an oar—'

At last there was a short conversation.

'Billie. . . . Billie, will you spell me?'

'Sure,' said the oiler.

VII

When the correspondent again opened his eyes, the sea and the sky were each of the grey hue of the dawning. Later, carmine and gold was painted upon the waters. The morning appeared finally, in its splendour, with a sky of pure blue, and the sunlight flamed on the tips of the waves.

On the distant dunes were set many little black cottages, and a tall white windmill reared above them. No man, nor dog, nor bicycle appeared on the beach. The cottages might have formed a deserted village.

The voyagers scanned the shore. A conference was held in the boat. 'Well,' said the captain, 'if no help is coming, we might better try a run through the surf right away. If we stay out here much longer we will be too weak to do anything for ourselves at all.' The others silently acquiesced in this reasoning. The boat was headed for the beach. The correspondent wondered if none ever ascended the tall wind-tower, and if then they never looked seaward. This tower was a giant, standing with its back to the plight of the ants. It represented in a degree, to the correspondent, the serenity of nature amid the struggles of the individual—nature in the wind, and nature in the vision of men. She did not seem cruel to him then, nor beneficent, nor treacherous, nor wise. But she was indifferent, flatly indifferent. It is, perhaps, plausible that a man in this situation, impressed with the unconcern of the universe, should see the innumerable flaws of his life, and have them taste wickedly in his mind and wish for another chance. A distinction between right and wrong seems absurdly clear to him, then, in this new ignorance of the grave-edge, and he understands that if he were given another opportunity he would mend his conduct and his words, and be better and brighter during an introduction or at a tea.

'Now, boys,' said the captain, 'she is going to swamp sure. All we can do is to work her in as far as possible, and then when she swamps, pile out and scramble for the beach. Keep cool now, and don't jump until she swamps sure.'

The oiler took the oars. Over his shoulders he scanned the surf. 'Captain,' he said, 'I think I'd better bring her about, and keep her head-on to the seas and back her in.'

'All right, Billie,' said the captain. 'Back her in.' The oiler swung the boat then and, seated in the stern, the cook and the correspondent were obliged to look over their shoulders to contemplate the lonely and indifferent shore.

The monstrous in-shore rollers heaved the boat high until the men were again enabled to see the white sheets of water scudding up the slanted beach. 'We won't get in very close,' said the captain. Each time a man could wrest his attention from the rollers, he turned his glance toward the shore, and in the expression of the eyes during this contemplation there was a singular quality. The correspondent, observing the others, knew that they were not afraid, but the full meaning of their glances was shrouded.

As for himself, he was too tired to grapple fundamentally with the fact. He tried to coerce his mind into thinking of it, but the mind was dominated at this time by the muscles, and the muscles said they did not care. It merely occurred to him that if he should drown it would be a shame.

There were no hurried words, no pallor, no plain agitation. The men simply looked at the shore. 'Now, remember to get well clear of the boat when you jump,' said the captain.

Seaward the crest of a roller suddenly fell with a thunderous crash, and the long white comber came roaring down upon the boat.

'Steady now,' said the captain. The men were silent. They turned their eyes from the shore to the comber and waited. The boat slid up the incline, leaped at the furious top, bounced over it, and swung down the long back of the waves. Some water had been shipped and the cook bailed it out.

But the next crest crashed also. The tumbling boiling flood of white water caught the boat and whirled it almost perpendicular. Water swarmed in from all sides. The correspondent had his hands on the gunwale at this time, and when the water entered at that place he swiftly withdrew his fingers, as if he objected to wetting them.

The little boat, drunken with this weight of water, reeled and snuggled deeper into the sea.

'Bail her out, cook! Bail her out,' said the captain.

'All right, captain,' said the cook.

'Now, boys, the next one will do for us, sure,' said the oiler. 'Mind to jump clear of the boat.'

The third wave moved forward, huge, furious, implacable. It fairly swallowed the dingey, and almost simultaneously the men tumbled into the sea. A piece of life-belt had lain in the bottom of the boat, and as the correspondent went overboard he held this to his chest with his left hand.

The January water was icy, and he reflected immediately that it was colder than he had expected to find it off the coast of Florida. This appeared to his dazed mind as a fact important enough to be noted at the time. The coldness of the water was sad; it was tragic. This fact was somehow so mixed and confused with his opinion of his own situation that it seemed almost a proper reason for tears. The water was cold.

When he came to the surface he was conscious of little but the noisy water. Afterward he saw his companions in the sea. The oiler was ahead in the race. He was swimming strongly and rapidly. Off to the correspondent's left, the cook's great white and corked back bulged out of the water, and in the rear the captain was hanging with his one good hand to the keel of the overturned dingey.

There is a certain immovable quality to a shore, and the correspondent wondered at it amid the confusion of the sea.

It seemed also very attractive, but the correspondent knew that it was a long journey, and he paddled leisurely. The piece of life-preserver lay under him, and sometimes he whirled down the incline of a wave as if he were on a hand-sled.

But finally he arrived at a place in the sea where travel was beset with difficulty. He did not pause swimming to inquire what manner of current had caught him, but there his progress ceased. The shore was set before him like a bit of scenery on a stage, and he looked at it and understood with his eyes each detail of it.

As the cook passed, much farther to the left, the captain was calling to him, 'Turn over on your back, cook! Turn over on your back and use the oar.'

'All right, sir.' The cook turned on his back, and, paddling with an oar, went ahead as if he were a canoe.

Presently the boat also passed to the left of the correspondent with the captain clinging with one hand to the keel. He would have appeared like a man raising himself to look over a board fence, if it were not for the extraordinary gymnastics of the boat. The correspondent marvelled that the captain could still hold to it.

They passed on, nearer to shore—the oiler, the cook, the captain—and following them went the water-jar, bouncing gaily over the seas.

The correspondent remained in the grip of this strange new enemy—a current. The shore, with its white slope of sand and its green bluff, topped with little silent cottages, was spread like a picture before him. It was very near to him then, but he was impressed as one who in a gallery looks at a scene from Brittany or Algiers.

He thought: 'I am going to drown? Can it be possible? Can it be possible? Can it be possible?' Perhaps an individual must consider his own death to be the final phenomenon of nature.

But later a wave perhaps whirled him out of this small deadly current, for he found suddenly that he could again make progress toward the shore. Later still, he was aware that the captain, clinging with one hand to the keel of the dingey, had his face turned away from the shore and toward him, and was calling his name. 'Come to the boat! Come to the boat!'

In his struggle to reach the captain and the boat, he reflected that when one gets properly wearied, drowning must really be a comfortable arrangement, a cessation of hostilities accompanied by a large degree of relief, and he was glad of it, for the main thing in his mind for some moments had been horror of the temporary agony. He did not wish to be hurt.

Presently he saw a man running along the shore. He was undressing with most remarkable speed. Coat, trousers, shirt, everything flew magically off him.

'Come to the boat,' called the captain.

'All right, captain.' As the correspondent paddled, he saw the captain let himself down to bottom and leave the boat. Then the correspondent performed his one little marvel of the voyage. A large wave caught him and flung him with ease and supreme speed completely over the boat and far beyond it. It struck him even then as an event in gymnastics, and a true miracle of the sea. An overturned boat in the surf is not a plaything to a swimming man.

The correspondent arrived in water that reached only to his waist, but his condition did not enable him to stand for more than a moment. Each wave knocked him into a heap, and the under-tow pulled at him.

Then he saw the man who had been running and undressing, and undressing and running, come bounding into the water. He dragged ashore the cook, and then waded toward the captain, but the captain waved him away, and sent him to the correspondent. He was naked, naked as a tree in winter, but a halo was about his head, and he shone like a saint. He gave a strong pull, and a long drag, and a bully heave at the correspondent's hand.

The correspondent, schooled in the minor formulæ, said: 'Thanks, old man.' But suddenly the man cried: 'What's that?' He pointed a swift finger. The correspondent said: 'Go.'

In the shallows, face downward, lay the oiler. His forehead touched sand that was periodically, between each wave, clear of the sea.

The correspondent did not know all that transpired afterward. When he achieved safe ground he fell, strik-
10 ing the sand with each particular part of his body. It was as if he had dropped from a roof, but the thud was grateful to him.

It seems that instantly the beach was populated with men with blankets, clothes, and flasks, and women with coffee-pots and all the remedies sacred to their minds. The welcome of the land to the men from the sea was warm and generous, but a still and dripping shape was carried slowly up the beach, and the land's welcome for it could only be the different and sinister hospitality of the grave.
20

When it came night, the white waves paced to and fro in the moonlight, and the wind brought the sound of the great sea's voice to the men on shore, and they felt that they could then be interpreters.

1898

Frank Norris

1870 · 1902

"Give us stories now," was Norris' plea; "give us men, strong, brutal men, with red-hot blood in 'em, blood and bones and viscera in 'em, and women, too, that move and have their being." As well as any utterance of Norris this entreaty shows his alliance not with reticent realism of the sort Howells wrote but with the naturalistic school which flourished in France in the later years of the nineteenth century.

Frank Norris adopted this creed after he had experimented with other methods of artistic expression. Born in Chicago to well-to-do parents in 1870, he moved with his family to San Francisco in 1884. Somehow, at the age of seventeen, he persuaded his family to allow him to study art in Paris. During his stay abroad, however, he changed his allegiance from the Atelier Julien to literature—literature, furthermore, of a romantic sort influenced by the French romantic writer

Froissart and the English romantic writer Stevenson. Some of Norris' earlier writings were clearly of the cloak-and-dagger school.

Back in California as a student at the University of California (1890-1894), he discovered the appeal of the French naturalistic school led by Zola, and of Rudyard Kipling. As a student at Harvard (1894-1895), he wrote two novels showing this newer influence: *Vandover and the Brute,* not published until 1914, and *McTeague,* published in 1899. Later, he wrote the two novels for which he is best remembered, *The Octopus* (1901) and *The Pit* (1903).

In part, Norris' enthusiasm for "living" characters derived from his feeling that life was superior to art. "Of all the difficult things," he said, "that enter into the learning of a difficult profession, the most difficult of all for the intended novelist . . . is that life is better

Frank Norris—from W. T. Witham, Living American Literature, *Bk. I, 1947, published by Stephen Daye Press*

than literature. The amateur will say this with conviction, will preach it in public and practise the exact reverse in private. But it still remains true that all the temperament, all the sensitiveness to impressions, all the education in the world will not help one little, little bit in the writing of the novel if life itself, the crude, the vulgar, if you will, is not studied. An hour's experience is worth ten years of study."

Gifted with a talent for friendship, Norris took great delight in becoming one of the Bohemian group in Paris and equal delight in becoming a friend of athletes, men-about-the-campus, and scholars in his college fraternity. At the same time he was very much of a conscious literary artist, and his critical writings attest that he had thoroughly developed theories about technique. Each chapter of a novel, he felt, should be "distinct, separate, having a definite beginning, rise, height and end, the action continuous, containing no break in time, the locality unchanged throughout. . . ."

Norris liked to think of himself as a naturalist, and he believed naturalist to be an author who attended to elemental forces in such a way as to give his narratives the sweep of epics. In *The Octopus* Norris pictured a poet eager to do what he approved—to strive, as he put it, "for the diapason, the great song which should embrace in itself a whole epoch, a complete era, the voice of the entire people." The scientific doctrine of the survival of the fittest and the sociological doctrine of economic determinism, also championed by naturalists, found expression in his books. *The Octopus* and *The Pit* were parts of a projected trilogy which was to show in epic terms the importance of wheat to all men's lives.

The career which came to an untimely end when Norris died in 1902 had, indeed, been a promising one. Norris' novels, it is true, for all his concern with the art of storytelling, were rather chaotic, but it seems very likely that, in time, he might have learned more about giving them unity. He is to be credited with introducing naturalism and what it stood for to a country in which naturalism was to be increasingly important. He foreshadows some of the aspects of the writings of notable modern authors—the unflinching depiction of sordid detail of Faulkner, the brutality of Hemingway, the poetic fervor of Wolfe.

The Complete Works of Frank Norris, 10 vols., Garden City, 1928 • Franklin Walker, Frank Norris, Garden City, 1943 • Ernest Marchand, Frank Norris: A Study, Stanford University, 1942

handwritten margin notes: "symbolizing the railroad getting 'a stranglehold on the wheat fields + farms'"

The Octopus

Norris was employed for several years by **McClure's Magazine** as a reader and author. The association was important, since he worked at an office with such socially conscious authors as Ray Stannard Baker, Ida Tarbell, and Lincoln Steffens. All these authors helped drive home a lesson that he felt he had learned from the great Zola—that the best novel was "the novel of purpose." He planned The Octopus as such a work.

"I am leaving for California Monday next," wrote Norris to a friend, April 5, 1899, "to be gone, very likely, until fall. It . . . is the result of a talk I had with the firm here. They believe with me that the big American novel is going to come out of the West—California. . . . I've got an idea that is as big as all outdoors and McClure is going to back me up while I put it through. . . . It involves a very long, a very serious, and perhaps a very terrible novel. It will be about the San Joaquin wheat raisers and the Southern Pacific, and I guess we'll call it The Octopus—catch on? . . . There's the chance for the big, epic, dramatic thing in this, and I mean to do it thoroughly—get at it from every point of view, the social, agricultural, and political. . . ."

Norris spent four months in California, collecting materials. Then he returned to New York and started work on the book. Says his biographer, Franklin Walker: "He wrote plot summaries, he wrote out an 'index sheet' for each character, he tabulated and arranged his notes, he made a map of the country where his action was to take place." In a sense he considered himself a research worker, unfolding a more or less objective "case study" which would reveal sociological truths. Such a study, inevitably, in his opinion, would be admirable as art. The writing itself, after the preliminaries had been completed, took a full year, and the novel was published in the spring of 1901.

Norris announced that this work was the first of "A Trilogy of the Epic of the Wheat"—three novels which were to tell, respectively, of "1) the production, 2) the distribution, 3) the consumption of American wheat." The first dealt, as he said, with "the war between the wheat grower and the Railroad Trust." Follower of Zola that he was, Norris naturally saw these two as particular symbols of more universal elements. For him, the wheat was a primitive force, nourished by the earth and a perennial, irresistible nourisher of life. The Trust—the Octopus—was the artificial exploiter and enemy of this life force.

To develop his thesis, Norris told his story very largely as it was seen by Presley, a poet who had a great longing to write an epic of the West in stirring hexameters. Presley was admirable for the author's purposes because of his ability to see with a poet's eye the life of south-central California and the symbolism of various events and happenings. Portions of the novel tell of mystic and romantic adventures of the characters which are related poetically to the main theme. The excerpts presented hereafter, however, tell only of the central conflict—that between the ranchers and the Railroad.

The time at the start is late September, with the harvest in the San Joaquin Valley just completed. Presley, who lives with the Derrick family at Los Muertos Rancho, pays a visit to some of the neighbors. Returning from a visit to Vanamee, a sheepherder and range rider, he is horrified by a scene which foreshadows the course of the narrative.

from Book I, Chapter I

THE SLAUGHTER OF THE SHEEP

Presley had climbed the fence at the limit of the Quien Sabe ranch. Beyond was Los Muertos, but between the two ran the railroad. He had only time to jump back upon the embankment when, with a quivering of all the earth, a locomotive, single, unattached, shot by him with a roar, filling the air with the reek of hot oil, vomiting smoke and sparks; its enormous eye, cyclopean, red, throwing a glare far in advance, shooting by in a sudden crash of confused thunder; filling the night with the terrific clamor of its iron hoofs.

Abruptly Presley remembered. This must be the crack passenger engine of which Dyke had told him, the one delayed by the accident on the Bakersfield division, and for whose passage the track had been opened all the way to Fresno.

10

Before Presley could recover the shock of the irruption, while the earth was still vibrating, the rails still humming, the engine was far away, flinging the echo of its frantic gallop over all the valley. For a brief instant it roared with a hollow diapason on the Long Trestle over Broderson Creek, then plunged into a cutting further on, the quivering glare of its fires losing itself in the night, its thunder abruptly diminishing to a subdued and distant humming. All at once this ceased. The engine was gone.

But the moment the noise of the engine lapsed, Presley —about to start forward again—was conscious of a confusion of lamentable sounds that rose into the night from out the engine's wake. Prolonged cries of agony, sobbing wails of infinite pain, heartrending, pitiful.

The noises came from a little distance. He ran down the track, crossing the culvert, over the irrigating ditch, and at the head of the long reach of track—between the culvert and the Long Trestle—paused abruptly, held immovable at the sight of the ground and rails all about him.

In some way, the herd of sheep—Vanamee's herd— had found a breach in the wire fence by the right of way and had wandered out upon the tracks. A band had been crossing just at the moment of the engine's passage. The pathos of it was beyond expression. It was a slaughter, a massacre of innocents. The iron monster had charged full into the midst, merciless, inexorable. To the right and left, all the width of the right of way, the little bodies had been flung; backs were snapped against the fence posts; brains knocked out. Caught in the barbs of the wire, wedged in, the bodies hung suspended. Under foot it was terrible. The black blood, winking in the starlight, seeped down into the clinkers between the ties with a prolonged sucking murmur.

Presley turned away, horror-struck, sick at heart, overwhelmed with a quick burst of irresistible compassion for this brute agony he could not relieve. The sweetness was gone from the evening, the sense of peace, of security, and placid contentment was stricken from the landscape. The hideous ruin in the engine's path drove all thought of his poem from his mind. The inspiration vanished like a mist. The *de Profundis* had ceased to ring.

He hurried on across the Los Muertos ranch, almost running, even putting his hands over his ears till he was out of hearing distance of that all but human distress. Not until he was beyond earshot did he pause,

looking back, listening. The night had shut down again. For a moment the silence was profound, unbroken.

Then, faint and prolonged, across the levels of the ranch, he heard the engine whistling for Bonneville. Again and again, at rapid intervals in its flying course, it whistled for road crossings, for sharp curves, for trestles; ominous notes, hoarse, bellowing, ringing with the accents of menace and defiance; and abruptly Presley saw again, in his imagination, the galloping monster, the terror of steel and steam, with its single eye, cyclopean, red, shooting from horizon to horizon; but saw it now as the symbol of a vast power, huge, terrible, flinging the echo of its thunder over all the reaches of the valley, leaving blood and destruction in its path; the leviathan, with tentacles of steel clutching into the soil, the soulless Force, the iron-hearted Power, the monster, the Colossus, the Octopus.

[The book moves on to represent the growers of wheat who are the intended victims of the Octopus. The following chapter describes the plowing at the Quien Sabe Rancho, the proprietor of which is Annixter, a leading character in the book.]

from Book I, Chapter IV

THE PLOWING

The day was fine. Since the first rain of the season there had been no other. Now the sky was without a cloud, pale blue, delicate, luminous, scintillating with morning. The great brown earth turned a huge flank to it, exhaling the moisture of the early dew. The atmosphere, washed clean of dust and mist, was translucent as crystal. Far off to the east, the hills on the other side of Broderson Creek stood out against the pallid saffron of the horizon as flat and as sharply outlined as if pasted on the sky. The campanile of the ancient Mission of San Juan seemed as fine as frost work. All about between the horizons, the carpet of the land unrolled itself to infinity. But now it was no longer parched with heat, cracked and warped by a merciless sun, powdered with

---

43 **de Profundis,** from the depths, the first words of the Latin version of Psalm 130. Before the opening of this selection Presley had heard the nearby mission bells sounding this part of the nightfall service

dust. The rain had done its work; not a clod that was not swollen with fertility, not a fissure that did not exhale the sense of fecundity. One could not take a dozen steps upon the ranches without the brusque sensation that underfoot the land was alive; roused at last from its sleep, palpitating with the desire of reproduction. Deep down there in the recesses of the soil, the great heart throbbed once more, thrilling with passion, vibrating with desire, offering itself to the caress of the plow, in-sistent, eager, imperious. Dimly one felt the deep-seated trouble of the earth, the uneasy agitation of its members, the hidden tumult of its womb, demanding to be made fruitful, to reproduce, to disengage the eternal renascent germ of Life that stirred and struggled in its loins.

The plows, thirty-five in number, each drawn by its team of ten, stretched in an interminable line, nearly a quarter of a mile in length, behind and ahead of Vanamee. They were arranged, as it were, *en echelon*, not in file—not one directly behind the other, but each succeeding plow its own width further in the field than the one in front of it. Each of these plows held five shears, so that when the entire company was in motion, one hundred and seventy-five furrows were made at the same instant. At a distance, the plows resembled a great column of field artillery. Each driver was in his place, his glance alternating between his horses and the foreman nearest at hand. Other foremen, in their bug-gies or buckboards, were at intervals along the line, like battery lieutenants. Annixter himself, on horseback, in boots and campaign hat, a cigar in his teeth, over-looked the scene.

The division superintendent, on the opposite side of the line, galloped past to a position at the head. For a long moment there was a silence. A sense of prepared-ness ran from end to end of the column. All things were ready, each man in his place. The day's work was about to begin.

Suddenly, from a distance at the head of the line came the shrill trilling of a whistle. At once the fore-man nearest Vanamee repeated it, at the same time turn-ing down the line and waving one arm. The signal was repeated, whistle answering whistle, till the sounds lost themselves in the distance. At once the line of plows lost its immobility, moving forward, getting slowly under way, the horses straining in the traces. A prolonged movement rippled from team to team, disengaging in its passage a multitude of sounds—the click of buckles,

the creak of straining leather, the subdued clash of ma-chinery, the cracking of whips, the deep breathing of nearly four hundred horses, the abrupt commands and cries of the drivers, and, last of all, the prolonged, sooth-ing murmur of the thick brown earth turning steadily from the multitude of advancing shears.

The plowing, thus commenced, continued. The sun rose higher. Steadily, the hundred iron hands kneaded and furrowed and stroked the brown, humid earth, the hundred iron teeth bit deep into the Titan's flesh. Perched on his seat, the moist, living reins slipping and tugging in his hands, Vanamee, in the midst of this steady confusion of constantly varying sensation, sight interrupted by sound, sound mingling with sight, on this swaying, vibrating seat, quivering with the prolonged thrill of the earth, lapsed to a sort of pleasing numbness, in a sense, hypnotized by the weaving maze of things in which he found himself involved. To keep his team at an even, regular gait, maintaining the precise interval, to run his furrows as closely as possible to those already made by the plow in front—this for the moment was the entire sum of his duties. But while one part of his brain, alert and watchful, took cognizance of these mat-ters, all the greater part was lulled and stupefied with the long monotony of the affair.

The plowing, now in full swing, enveloped him in a vague, slow-moving whirl of things. Underneath him was the jarring, jolting, trembling machine; not a clod was turned, not an obstacle encountered, that he did not receive the swift impression of it through all his body, the very friction of the damp soil, sliding incessantly from the shiny surface of the shears, seemed to repro-duce itself in his finger tips and along the back of his head. He heard the horse-hoofs by the myriads crushing down easily, deeply, into the loam, the prolonged clink-ing of trace-chains, the working of the smooth, brown flanks in the harness, the clatter of wooden hames, the champing of bits, the click of iron shoes against pebbles, the brittle stubble of the surface ground crackling and snapping as the furrows turned, the sonorous, steady breaths wrenched from the deep, laboring chests, strap-bound, shining with sweat, and all along the line the voices of the men talking to the horses. Everywhere there were visions of glossy brown backs, straining, heaving, swollen with muscle; harness streaked with specks of froth, broad, cup-shaped hoofs, heavy with brown loam, men's faces red with tan, blue overalls spotted with axle-grease; muscled hands, the knuckles whitened in their grip on the reins, and through it all the ammoniacal smell of the horses, the bitter reek of perspiration of beasts and men, the aroma of warm leather, the scent of dead stubble—and stronger and more penetrating than everything else, the heavy, enervating odor of the up-turned, living earth.

At intervals, from the top of one of the rare, low swells of the land, Vanamee overlooked a wider horizon. On the other divisions of Quien Sabe the same work was in progress. Occasionally he could see another column of plows in the adjoining division—sometimes so close at hand that the subdued murmur of its movements reached his ear; sometimes so distant that it resolved itself into a long, brown streak upon the gray of the ground. Further off to the west on the Osterman ranch other columns came and went, and, once, from the crest of the highest swell on his division, Vanamee caught a distant glimpse of the Broderson ranch. There, too, moving specks indicated that the plowing was under way. And further away still, far off there beyond the fine line of the horizons, over the curve of the globe, the shoulder of the earth, he knew were other ranches, and beyond these others, and beyond these still others, the immensi-ties multiplying to infinity.

Everywhere throughout the great San Joaquin, unseen and unheard, a thousand plows up-stirred the land, tens of thousands of shares clutched deep into the warm, moist soil.

It was the long stroking caress, vigorous, male, power-ful, for which the Earth seemed panting. The heroic embrace of a multitude of iron hands, gripping deep into the brown, warm flesh of the land that quivered responsive and passionate under this rude advance, so robust as to be almost an assault, so violent as to be veritably brutal. There, under the sun and under the speckless sheen of the sky, the wooing of the Titan began, the vast primal passion, the two world-forces, the ele-mental Male and Female, locked in a colossal embrace, at grapples in the throes of an infinite desire, at once terrible and divine, knowing no law, untamed, savage, natural, sublime.

From time to time the gang in which Vanamee worked halted on the signal from foreman or overseer. The horses came to a standstill, the vague clamor of the work lapsed away. Then the minutes passed. The whole work hung suspended. All up and down the line one demanded what had happened. The division superintendent gal-loped past, perplexed and anxious. For the moment, one of the plows was out of order, a bolt had slipped, a lever refused to work, or a machine had become immobilized in heavy ground, or a horse had lamed himself. Once, even, toward noon, an entire plow was taken out of the line, so out of gear that a messenger had to be sent to the division forge to summon the machinist.

Annixter had disappeared. He had ridden further on to the other divisions of his ranch, to watch the work in progress there. At twelve o'clock, according to his orders, all the division superintendents put themselves in communication with him by means of the telephone wires that connected each of the division houses, report-ing the condition of the work, the number of acres covered, the prospects of each plow traversing its daily average of twenty miles.

At half-past twelve, Vanamee and the rest of the drivers ate their lunch in the field, the tin buckets having been distributed to them that morning after breakfast. But in the evening, the routine of the previous day was repeated, and Vanamee, unharnessing his team, riding one horse and leading the others, returned to the division barns and bunk-house.

It was between six and seven o'clock. The half hun-dred men of the gang threw themselves upon the supper the Chinese cooks had set out in the shed of the eating-house, long as a bowling alley, unpainted, crude, the seats benches, the table covered with oilcloth. Overhead a half-dozen kerosene lamps flared and smoked.

The table was taken as if by assault; the clatter of iron knives upon the tin plates was as the reverberation of hail upon a metal roof. The plowmen rinsed their throats with great draughts of wine, and, their elbows wide, their foreheads flushed, resumed the attack upon the beef and bread, eating as though they would never have enough. All up and down the long table, where the kerosene lamps reflected themselves deep in the oilcloth cover, one heard the incessant sounds of mastication, and saw the uninterrupted movement of great jaws. At every moment one or another of the men demanded a fresh portion of beef, another pint of wine, another half-loaf of bread. For upward of an hour the gang ate. It was no longer a supper. It was a veritable barbecue, a crude and primitive feasting, barbaric, homeric.

But in all this scene Vanamee saw nothing repulsive. Presley would have abhorred it—this feeding of the People, this gorging of the human animal, eager for its meat. Vanamee, simple, uncomplicated, living so close to nature and the rudimentary life, understood its significance. He knew very well that within a short half-hour after this meal the men would throw themselves down in their bunks to sleep without moving, inert and stupefied with fatigue, till the morning. Work, food, and sleep, all life reduced to its bare essentials, uncomplex, honest, healthy. They were strong, these men, with the strength of the soil they worked, in touch with the essential things, back again to the starting point of civilization, coarse, vital, real, and sane.

[Agent for the railroad in the district of the story is S. Behrman, grossly fat, avaricious, cruel. For the men of the valley, S. Behrman is the Pacific and Southwestern Railroad. His peremptory handling of freight rates riles the farmers, and they are further distressed by rumors that the railroad may shortly revalue the land which they have been leasing. At the celebration of the completion of a big barn on Annixter's ranch, their fears are confirmed and they take action.]

from Book I, Chapter VI

THE ORGANIZATION OF THE LEAGUE

It was almost midnight. The dance drew toward its close in a storm of jubilation. The perspiring musicians toiled like galley slaves; the guests singing as they danced.

The group of men reassembled in the harness room. Even Magnus Derrick condescended to enter and drink a toast. Presley and Vanamee, still holding themselves aloof, looked on, Vanamee more and more disgusted. Dabney, standing to one side, overlooked and forgotten, continued to sip steadily at his glass, solemn, reserved. Garnett of the Ruby rancho, Keast from the ranch of the same name, Gethings of the San Pablo, and Chattern of the Bonanza, leaned back in their chairs, their waistcoats unbuttoned, their legs spread wide, laughing— they could not tell why. Other ranchers, men whom Annixter had never seen, appeared in the room, wheat growers from places as far distant as Goshen and Pixley; young men and old, proprietors of veritable principalities, hundreds of thousands of acres of wheat lands, a dozen of them, a score of them; men who were strangers to each other, but who made it a point to shake hands

with Magnus Derrick, the "prominent man" of the valley. Old Broderson, whom every one had believed had gone home, returned, though much sobered, and took his place, refusing, however, to drink another spoonful.

Soon the entire number of Annixter's guests found themselves in two companies, the dancers on the floor of the barn, frolicking through the last figures of the Virginia reel, and the boisterous gathering of men in the harness room, downing the last quarts of fertilizer. Both assemblies had been increased. Even the older people had joined in the dance, while nearly every one of the men who did not dance had found his way into the harness room. The two groups rivaled each other in their noise. Out on the floor of the barn was a very whirlwind of gayety, a tempest of laughter, hand-clapping, and cries of amusement. In the harness room the confused shouting and singing, the stamping of heavy feet, set a quivering reverberation in the oil of the kerosene lamps, the flame of the candles in the Japanese lanterns flaring and swaying in the gusts of hilarity. At intervals, between the two, one heard the music, the wailing of the violins, the vigorous snarling of the cornet, and the harsh, incessant rasping of the snare drum.

And at times all these various sounds mingled in a single vague note, huge, clamorous, that rose up into the night from the colossal, reverberating compass of the barn and sent its echoes far off across the unbroken levels of the surrounding ranches, stretching out to infinity under the clouded sky, calm, mysterious, still.

Annixter, the punch bowl clasped in his arms, was pouring out the last spoonful of liquor into Caraher's glass when he was aware that some one was pulling at the sleeve of his coat. He set down the punch bowl.

"Well, where did *you* come from?" he demanded.

It was a messenger from Bonneville, the uniformed boy that the telephone company employed to carry messages. He had just arrived from town on his bicycle, out of breath and panting.

"Message for you, sir. Will you sign?"

He held the book to Annixter, who signed the receipt, wondering.

The boy departed, leaving a thick envelope of yellow paper in Annixter's hands, the address typewritten, the word "Urgent" written in blue pencil in one corner.

Annixter tore it open. The envelope contained other sealed envelopes, some eight or ten of them, addressed to Magnus Derrick, Osterman, Broderson, Garnett, Keast,

Gethings, Chattern, Dabney, and to Annixter himself.

Still puzzled, Annixter distributed the envelopes, muttering to himself:

"What's up now?"

The incident had attracted attention. A comparative quiet followed, the guests following the letters with their eyes as they were passed around the table. They fancied that Annixter had arranged a surprise.

Magnus Derrick, who sat next to Annixter, was the first to receive his letter. With a word of excuse he opened it.

"Read it, read it, Governor," shouted a half-dozen voices. "No secrets, you know. Everything above-board here to-night."

Magnus cast a glance at the contents of the letter, then rose to his feet and read:

Magnus Derrick,
   Bonneville, Tulare Co., Cal.
Dear Sir:
   By regrade of October 1st, the value of the Railroad land you occupy, included in your ranch of Los Muertos, has been fixed at $27.00 per acre. The land is now for sale at that price to any one.
          Yours, etc.,
             Cyrus Blakelee Ruggles,
             Land Agent, P. and S. W. R. R.
             S. Behrman,
             Local Agent, P. and S. W. R. R.

In the midst of the profound silence that followed, Osterman was heard to exclaim grimly:

"*That's* a pretty good one. Tell us another."

But for a long moment this was the only remark.

The silence widened, broken only by the sound of torn paper as Annixter, Osterman, old Broderson, Garnett, Keast, Gethings, Chattern, and Dabney opened and read their letters. They were all to the same effect, almost word for word like the Governor's. Only the figures and the proper names varied. In some cases the price per acre was twenty-two dollars. In Annixter's case it was thirty.

"And—and the Company promised to sell to me, to—to all of us," gasped old Broderson, "at *two dollars and a half* an acre."

It was not alone the ranchers immediately around Bonneville who would be plundered by this move on the part of the Railroad. The "alternate section" system applied throughout all the San Joaquin. By striking at the Bonneville ranchers a terrible precedent was established. Of the crowd of guests in the harness room alone, nearly every man was affected, every man menaced with ruin. All of a million acres was suddenly involved.

Then suddenly the tempest burst. A dozen men were on their feet in an instant, their teeth set, their fists clinched, their faces purple with rage. Oaths, curses, maledictions exploded like the firing of successive mines. Voices quivered with wrath, hands flung upward, the fingers hooked, prehensile, trembled with anger. The sense of wrongs, the injustices, the oppression, extortion, and pillage of twenty years suddenly culminated and found voice in a raucous howl of execration. For a second there was nothing articulate in that cry of savage exasperation, nothing even intelligent. It was the human animal hounded to its corner, exploited, harried to its last stand, at bay, ferocious, terrible, turning at last with bared teeth and upraised claws to meet the death grapple. It was the hideous squealing of the tormented brute, its back to the wall, defending its lair, its mate and its whelps, ready to bite, to rend, to trample, to batter out the life of The Enemy in a primeval, bestial welter of blood and fury.

The roar subsided to intermittent clamor, in the pauses of which the sounds of music and dancing made themselves audible once more.

"S. Behrman again," vociferated Harran Derrick.

"Chose his moment well," muttered Annixter. "Hits his hardest when we're all rounded up having a good time."

"Gentlemen, this is ruin."

"What's to be done now?"

"*Fight!* My God! do you think we are going to stand this? Do you think we *can?*"

The uproar swelled again. The clearer the assembly of ranchers understood the significance of this move on the part of the Railroad, the more terrible it appeared, the more flagrant, the more intolerable. Was it possible, was it within the bounds of imagination, that this tyranny should be contemplated? But they knew—past years had driven home the lesson—the implacable, iron monster with whom they had to deal, and again and again the sense of outrage and oppression lashed them to their feet, their mouths wide with curses, their fists clinched tight, their throats hoarse with shouting.

"Fight! How fight? What *are* you going to do?"

"If there's a law in this land—"

"If there is, it is in Shelgrim's pocket. Who owns the courts in California? Ain't it Shelgrim?"

"God damn him."

"Well, how long are you going to stand it? How long before you'll settle up accounts with six inches of plugged gas-pipe?"

"And our contracts, the solemn pledges of the corporation to sell to us first of all—"

"And now the land is for sale to anybody."

"Why, it is a question of my home. Am I to be turned out? Why, I have put eight thousand dollars into improving this land."

"And I six thousand, and now that I have, the Railroad grabs it."

"And the system of irrigating ditches that Derrick and I have been laying out. There's thousands of dollars in that!"

"I'll fight this out till I've spent every cent of my money."

"Where? In the courts that the Company owns?"

"Think I am going to give in to this? Think I am to get off my land? By God, gentlemen, law or no law, railroad or no railroad, I—will—not."

"Nor I."

"Nor I."

"Nor I."

"This is the last. Legal means first; if those fail—the shotgun."

"They can kill me. They can shoot me down, but I'll die—die fighting for my home—before I'll give in to this."

At length Annixter made himself heard:

"All out of the room but the ranch owners," he shouted. "Hooven, Caraher, Dyke, you'll have to clear out. This is a family affair. Presley, you and your friend can remain."

Reluctantly the others filed through the door. There remained in the harness room—besides Vanamee and Presley—Magnus Derrick, Annixter, old Broderson, Harran, Garnett from the Ruby rancho, Keast from the ranch of the same name, Gethings of the San Pablo, Chattern of the Bonanza, about a score of others, ranchers from various parts of the county, and, last of all, Dabney, ignored, silent, to whom nobody spoke and who, as yet, had not uttered a word.

But the men who had been asked to leave the harness room spread the news throughout the barn. It was repeated from lip to lip. One by one the guests dropped out of the dance. Groups were formed. By swift degrees the gayety lapsed away. The Virginia reel broke up. The musicians ceased playing, and in the place of the noisy, effervescent revelry of the previous half hour, a subdued murmur filled all the barn, a mingling of whispers, lowered voices, the coming and going of light footsteps, the uneasy shifting of positions, while from behind the closed doors of the harness room came a prolonged, sullen hum of anger and strenuous debate. The dance came to an abrupt end. The guests, unwilling to go as yet, stunned, distressed, stood clumsily about, their eyes vague, their hands swinging at their sides, looking stupidly into each other's faces. A sense of impending calamity, oppressive, foreboding, gloomy, passed through the air overhead in the night, a long shiver of anguish and of terror, mysterious, despairing.

In the harness room, however, the excitement continued unchecked. One rancher after another delivered himself of a torrent of furious words. There was no order, merely the frenzied outcry of blind fury. One spirit alone was common to all—resistance at whatever cost and to whatever lengths.

Suddenly Osterman leaped to his feet, his bald head gleaming in the lamp-light, his red ears distended, a flood of words filling his great, horizontal slit of a mouth, his comic actor's face flaming. Like the hero of a melodrama, he took the stage with a great sweeping gesture.

"Organization," he shouted, "that must be our watchword. The curse of the ranchers is that they fritter away their strength. Now, we must stand together, now, *now*. Here's the crisis, here's the moment. Shall we meet it? *I call for the League.* Not next week, not to-morrow, not in the morning, but now, now, now, this very moment, before we go out of that door. Every one of us here to join it, to form the beginnings of a vast organization, banded together to death, if needs be, for the protection of our rights and homes. Are you ready? Is it now or never? I call for the League."

Instantly there was a shout. With an actor's instinct, Osterman had spoken at the precise psychological moment. He carried the others off their feet, glib, dexterous, voluble. Just what was meant by the League the others did not know, but it was something, a vague engine, a machine with which to fight. Osterman had not done speaking before the room rang with outcries, the crowd of men shouting, for what they did not know:

"The League! The League!"

"Now, to-night, this moment; sign our names before we leave."

"He's right. Organization! The League!"

"We have a committee at work already," Osterman vociferated. "I am a member, and also Mr. Broderson, Mr. Annixter, and Mr. Harran Derrick. What our aims are we will explain to you later. Let this committee be the nucleus of the League—temporarily, at least. Trust us. We are working for you and with you. Let this committee be merged into the larger committee of the League, and for President of the League"—he paused the fraction of a second—"for President there can be but one name mentioned, one man to whom we all must look as leader—Magnus Derrick."

The Governor's name was received with a storm of cheers. The harness room re-echoed with the shouts of:

"Derrick! Derrick!"

"Magnus for President!"

"Derrick, our natural leader."

"Derrick, Derrick, Derrick for President."

Magnus rose to his feet. He made no gesture. Erect as a cavalry officer, tall, thin, commanding, he dominated the crowd in an instant. There was a moment's hush.

"Gentlemen," he said, "if organization is a good word, moderation is a better one. The matter is too grave for haste. I would suggest that we each and severally return to our respective homes for the night, sleep over what has happened, and convene again to-morrow, when we are calmer and can approach this affair in a more judicious mood. As for the honor with which you would inform me, I must affirm that that, too, is a matter for grave deliberation. This League is but a name as yet. To accept control of an organization whose principles are not yet fixed is a heavy responsibility. I shrink from it—"

But he was allowed to proceed no further. A storm of protest developed. There were shouts of:

"No, no. The League to-night and Derrick for President."

"We have been moderate too long."

"The League first, principles afterward."

"We can't wait," declared Osterman. "Many of us can not attend a meeting to-morrow. Our business af-

fairs would prevent it. Now we are all together. I propose a temporary chairman and secretary be named and a ballot be taken. But first the League. Let us draw up a set of resolutions to stand together, for the defence of our homes, to death, if needs be, and each man present affix his signature thereto."

He subsided amid vigorous applause. The next quarter of an hour was a vague confusion, every one talking at once, conversations going on in low tones in various corners of the room. Ink, pens, and a sheaf of foolscap were brought from the ranch house. A set of resolutions was drafted, having the force of a pledge, organizing the League of Defence. Annixter was the first to sign. Others followed, only a few holding back, refusing to join till they had thought the matter over. The roll grew; the paper circulated about the table; each signature was welcomed by a salvo of cheers. At length, it reached Harran Derrick, who signed amid tremendous uproar. He released the pen only to shake a score of hands.

"Now, Magnus Derrick."

"Gentlemen," began the Governor, once more rising, "I beg of you to allow me further consideration. Gentlemen—"

He was interrupted by renewed shouting.

"No, no, now or never. Sign, join the League."

"Don't leave us. We look to you to help."

But presently the excited throng that turned their faces toward the Governor were aware of a new face at his elbow. The door of the harness room had been left unbolted and Mrs. Derrick, unable to endure the heartbreaking suspense of waiting outside, had gathered up all her courage and had come into the room. Trembling, she clung to Magnus's arm, her pretty light-brown hair in disarray, her large young girl's eyes wide with terror and distrust. What was about to happen she did not understand, but these men were clamoring for Magnus to pledge himself to something, to some terrible course of action, some ruthless, unscrupulous battle to the death with the iron-hearted monster of steel and steam. Nerved with a coward's intrepidity, she, who so easily obliterated herself, had found her way into the midst of this frantic crowd, into this hot, close room, reeking of alcohol and tobacco smoke, into this atmosphere surcharged with hatred and curses. She seized her husband's arm imploring, distraught with terror.

"No, no," she murmured, "no, don't sign."

She was the feather caught in the whirlwind. *En masse,* the crowd surged toward the erect figure of the Governor, the pen in one hand, his wife's fingers in the other, the roll of signatures before him. The clamor was deafening; the excitement culminated brusquely. Half a hundred hands stretched toward him; thirty voices, at top pitch, implored, expostulated, urged, almost commanded. The reverberation of the shouting was as the plunge of a cataract.

It was the uprising of The People; the thunder of the outbreak of revolt; the mob demanding to be led, aroused at last, imperious, resistless, overwhelming. It was the blind fury of insurrection, the brute, many-tongued, red-eyed, bellowing for guidance, baring its teeth, unsheathing its claws, imposing its will with the abrupt, resistless pressure of the relaxed piston, inexorable, knowing no pity.

"No, no," implored Annie Derrick. "No, Magnus, don't sign."

"He *must,*" declared Harran, shouting in her ear to make himself heard, "he must. Don't you understand?"

Again the crowd surged forward, roaring. Mrs. Derrick was swept back, pushed to one side. Her husband no longer belonged to her. She paid the penalty for being the wife of a great man. The world, like a colossal iron wedge, crushed itself between. She was thrust to the wall. The throng of men, stamping, surrounded Magnus; she could no longer see him, but, terror-struck, she listened. There was a moment's lull, then a vast thunder of savage jubilation. Magnus had signed.

Harran found his mother leaning against the wall, her hands shut over her ears; her eyes, dilated with fear, brimming with tears. He led her from the harness room to the outer room, where Mrs. Tree and Hilma took charge of her, and then, impatient, refusing to answer the hundreds of anxious questions that assailed him, hurried back to the harness room.

Already the balloting was in progress, Osterman acting as temporary chairman. On the very first ballot he was made secretary of the League *pro tem.,* and Magnus unanimously chosen for its President. An executive committee was formed, which was to meet the next day at the Los Muertos ranch house.

It was half-past one o'clock. In the barn outside the greater number of the guests had departed. Long since the musicians had disappeared. There only remained the families of the ranch owners involved in the meeting in the harness room. These huddled in isolated groups in corners of the garish, echoing barn, the women in their wraps, the young men with their coat collars turned up against the draughts that once more made themselves felt.

For a long half hour the loud hum of eager conversation continued to issue from behind the door of the harness room. Then, at length, there was a prolonged scraping of chairs. The session was over. The men came out in groups, searching for their families.

At once the homeward movement began. Every one was worn out. Some of the ranchers' daughters had gone to sleep against their mothers' shoulders.

Billy, the stableman, and his assistant were awakened, and the teams were hitched up. The stable yard was full of a maze of swinging lanterns and buggy lamps. The horses fretted, champing the bits; the carry-alls creaked with the straining of leather and springs as they received their loads. At every instant one heard the rattle of wheels, as vehicle after vehicle disappeared in the night. A fine drizzling rain was falling, and the lamps began to show dim in a vague haze of orange light.

Magnus Derrick was the last to go. At the doorway of the barn he found Annixter, the roll of names—which it had been decided he was to keep in his safe for the moment—under his arm. Silently the two shook hands. Magnus departed. The grind of the wheels of his carry-all grated sharply on the gravel of the driveway in front of the ranch house, then, with a hollow roll across a little plank bridge, gained the roadway. For a moment the beat of the horses' hoofs made itself heard on the roadway. It ceased. Suddenly there was a great silence.

Annixter, in the doorway of the great barn, stood looking about him for a moment, alone, thoughtful. The barn was empty. That astonishing evening had come to an end. The whirl of things and people, the crowd of dancers, Delaney, the gun fight, Hilma Tree, her eyes fixed on him in mute confession, the rabble in the harness room, the news of the regrade, the fierce outburst of wrath, the hasty organizing of the League, all went spinning confusedly through his recollection. But he was exhausted. Time enough in the morning to think it all over. By now it was raining sharply. He put the roll of names into his inside pocket, threw a sack over his head and shoulders, and went down to the ranch house.

But in the harness room, lighted by the glittering lanterns and flaring lamps, in the midst of overturned chairs, spilled liquor, cigar stumps, and broken glasses, Vanamee and Presley still remained talking, talking. At length, they rose, and came out upon the floor of the barn and stood for a moment looking about them.

Billy, the stableman, was going the rounds of the walls, putting out light after light. By degrees, the vast interior was growing dim. Upon the roof overhead the rain drummed incessantly, the eaves dripping. The floor was littered with pine needles, bits of orange peel, ends and fragments of torn organdies and muslins and bits of tissue paper from the "Phrygian Bonnets" and "Liberty Caps." The buckskin mare in the stall, dozing on three legs, changed position with a long sigh. The sweat stiffening the hair upon her back and loins, as it dried, gave off a penetrating, ammoniacal odor that mingled with the stale perfume of sachet and wilted flowers.

Presley and Vanamee stood looking at the deserted barn. There was a long silence. Then Presley said:

"Well . . . what do you think of it all?"

"I think," answered Vanamee slowly, "I think that there was a dance in Brussels the night before Waterloo."

[Despite the opposition of Magnus, the League decides to use money to bring about the election of two of the three members of the State Railway Commission, which is to fix the valuation of their property and the rates for the transportation of their wheat. One of the members backed by the League is Lyman Derrick, the "Governor's" eldest son, a corporation lawyer. At a meeting of the Executive Committee of the League which is held at the Los Muertos ranch, Lyman appears to tell about the new rates which the commissioners have fixed.]

from Book II, Chapter IV

LYMAN'S REPORT TO THE COMMITTEE

At the time appointed, the men composing the Committee gathered about the table in the dining-room of the Los Muertos ranch house. It was almost a reproduction of the scene of the famous evening when Osterman had proposed the plan of the Ranchers' Railroad Commission. Magnus Derrick sat at the head of the table, in his buttoned frock coat. Whiskey bottles and siphons of soda-water were within easy reach. Presley, who by now was considered the confidential friend of every member of the Committee, lounged as before on the sofa, smoking cigarettes, the cat Nathalie on his knee. Besides Magnus and Annixter, Osterman was present, and old Broderson and Harran; Garnett from the Ruby Rancho and Gethings of the San Pablo, who were also members of the Executive Committee, were on hand, preoccupied, bearded men, smoking black cigars, and, last of all, Dabney, the silent old man, of whom little was known but his name, and who had been made a member of the Committee, nobody could tell why.

"My son Lyman should be here, gentlemen, within at least ten minutes. I have sent my team to meet him at Bonneville," explained Magnus, as he called the meeting to order. "The secretary will call the roll."

Osterman called the roll, and, to fill in the time, read over the minutes of the previous meeting. The treasurer was making his report as to the funds at the disposal of the League when Lyman arrived.

Magnus and Harran went forward to meet him, and the Committee rather awkwardly rose and remained standing while the three exchanged greetings, the members, some of whom had never seen their commissioner, eying him out of the corners of their eyes.

Lyman was dressed with his usual correctness. His cravat was of the latest fashion, his clothes of careful design and unimpeachable fit. His shoes, of patent leather, reflected the lamplight, and he carried a drab overcoat over his arm. Before being introduced to the Committee, he excused himself a moment and ran to see his mother, who waited for him in the adjoining sitting-room. But in a few moments he returned, asking pardon for the delay.

He was all affability; his protruding eyes, that gave such an unusual, foreign appearance to his very dark face, radiated geniality. He was evidently anxious to please, to produce a good impression upon the grave, clumsy farmers before whom he stood. But at the same time, Presley, watching him from his place on the sofa, could imagine that he was rather nervous. He was too nimble in his cordiality, and the little gestures he made in bringing his cuffs into view and in touching the ends of his tight, black mustache with the ball of his thumb were repeated with unnecessary frequency.

"Mr. Broderson, my son, Lyman, my eldest son. Mr. Annixter, my son, Lyman."

The Governor introduced him to the ranchers, proud of Lyman's good looks, his correct dress, his ease of manner. Lyman shook hands all around, keeping up a flow of small talk, finding a new phrase for each member, complimenting Osterman, whom he already knew, upon
10 his talent for organization, recalling a mutual acquaintance to the mind of old Broderson. At length, however, he sat down at the end of the table, opposite his brother. There was a silence.

Magnus rose to recapitulate the reasons for the extra session of the Committee, stating again that the Board of Railway Commissioners which they—the ranchers—had succeeded in seating had at length issued the new schedule of reduced rates, and that Mr. Derrick had been obliging enough to offer to come down to Los Muertos
20 in person to acquaint the wheat-growers of the San Joaquin with the new rates for the carriage of their grain.

But Lyman very politely protested, addressing his father punctiliously as "Mr. Chairman," and the other ranchers as "Gentlemen of the Executive Committee of the League." He had no wish, he said, to disarrange the regular proceedings of the Committee. Would it not be preferable to defer the reading of his report till "new business" was called for? In the meanwhile, let the Committee proceed with its usual work. He understood
30 the necessarily delicate nature of this work, and would be pleased to withdraw till the proper time arrived for him to speak.

"Good deal of backing and filling about the reading of a column of figures," muttered Annixter to the man at his elbow.

Lyman "awaited the Committee's decision." He sat down, touching the ends of his mustache.

"Oh, play ball," growled Annixter.

Gethings rose to say that as the meeting had been
40 called solely for the purpose of hearing and considering the new grain tariff, he was of the opinion that routine business could be dispensed with and the schedule read at once. It was so ordered.

Lyman rose and made a long speech. Voluble as Osterman himself, he, nevertheless, had at his command a vast number of readymade phrases, the staples

of a political speaker, the stock in trade of the commercial lawyer, which rolled off his tongue with the most persuasive fluency. By degrees, in the course of his speech, he began to insinuate the idea that the wheat-
50 growers had never expected to settle their difficulties with the Railroad by the work of a single commission; that they had counted upon a long, continued campaign of many years, railway commission succeeding railway commission, before the desired low rates should be secured; that the present Board of Commissioners was only the beginning and that too great results were not expected from them. All this he contrived to mention casually, in the talk, as if it were a foregone conclusion, a matter understood by all. 60

As the speech continued, the eyes of the ranchers around the table were fixed with growing attention upon this well-dressed, city-bred young man, who spoke so fluently and who told them of their own intentions. A feeling of perplexity began to spread, and the first taint of distrust invaded their minds.

"But the good work has been most auspiciously inaugurated," continued Lyman. "Reforms so sweeping as the one contemplated can not be accomplished in a single night. Great things grow slowly, benefits to be 70 permanent must accrue gradually. Yet, in spite of all this, your commissioners have done much. Already the phalanx of the enemy is pierced, already his armor is dinted. Pledged as were your commissioners to an average ten per cent reduction in rates for the carriage of grain by the Pacific and Southwestern Railroad, we have rigidly adhered to the demands of our constituency, we have obeyed the People. The main problem has not yet been completely solved; that is for later, when we shall have gathered sufficient strength to attack the 80 enemy in his very stronghold; *but an average ten per cent cut has been made all over the State.* We have made a great advance, have taken a great step forward, and if the work is carried ahead, upon the lines laid down by the present commissioners and their constituents, there is every reason to believe that within a very few years equitable and stable rates for the shipment of grain from the San Joaquin Valley to Stockton, Port Costa, and tidewater will be permanently imposed."

"Well, hold on," exclaimed Annixter, out of order 90 and ignoring the Governor's reproof, "hasn't your commission reduced grain rates in the San Joaquin?"

"We have reduced grain rates by ten per cent all over the State," rejoined Lyman. "Here are copies of the new schedule."

He drew them from his valise and passed them around the table.

"You see," he observed, "the rate between Mayfield and Oakland, for instance, has been reduced by twenty-five cents a ton."

"Yes—but—but—" said old Broderson, "it is rather unusual, isn't it, for wheat in that district to be sent to Oakland?"

"Why, look here," exclaimed Annixter, looking up from the schedule, "where is there any reduction in rates in the San Joaquin—from Bonneville and Guadalajara, for instance? I don't see as you've made any reduction at all. Is this right? Did you give me the right schedule?"

"Of course, all the points in the State could not be covered at once," returned Lyman. "We never expected, you know, that we could cut rates in the San Joaquin the very first move; that is for later. But you will see we made very material reductions on shipments from the upper Sacramento Valley; also the rate from Ione to Marysville has been reduced eighty cents a ton."

"Why, rot," cried Annixter, "no one ever ships wheat that way."

"The Salinas rate," continued Lyman, "has been lowered seventy-five cents; the St. Helena rate fifty cents, and please notice the very drastic cut from Red Bluff, north, along the Oregon route, to the Oregon State Line."

"Where not a carload of wheat is shipped in a year," commented Gethings of the San Pablo.

"Oh, you will find yourself mistaken there, Mr. Gethings," returned Lyman courteously. "And for the matter of that, a low rate would stimulate wheat-production in that district."

The order of the meeting was broken up, neglected; Magnus did not even pretend to preside. In the growing excitement over the inexplicable schedule, routine was not thought of. Every one spoke at will.

"Why, Lyman," demanded Magnus, looking across the table to his son, "is this schedule correct? You have not cut rates in the San Joaquin at all. We—these gentlemen here and myself—we are no better off than we were before we secured your election as commissioner."

"We were pledged to make an average ten per cent cut, sir—"

"It is an average ten per cent cut," cried Osterman. "Oh, yes, that's plain. It's an average ten per cent cut all right, but you've made it by cutting grain rates between points where practically no grain is shipped. We, the wheat-growers in the San Joaquin, where all the wheat is grown, are right where we were before. The Railroad won't lose a nickel. By Jingo, boys," he glanced around the table, "I'd like to know what this means."

"The Railroad, if you come to that," returned Lyman, "has already lodged a protest against the new rate."

Annixter uttered a derisive shout.

"A protest! That's good, that is. When the P. and S. W. objects to rates it don't 'protest,' m' son. The first you hear from Mr. Shelgrim is an injunction from the courts preventing the order for new rates from taking effect. By the Lord," he cried angrily, leaping to his feet, "I would like to know what all this means, too. Why didn't you reduce our grain rates? What did we elect you for?"

"Yes, what did we elect you for?" demanded Osterman and Gethings, also getting to their feet.

"Order, order, gentlemen," cried Magnus, remembering the duties of his office and rapping his knuckles on the table. "This meeting has been allowed to degenerate too far already."

"You elected us," declared Lyman doggedly, "to make an average ten per cent cut on grain rates. We have done it. Only because you don't benefit at once, you object. It makes a difference whose ox is gored, it seems."

"Lyman!"

It was Magnus who spoke. He had drawn himself to his full six feet. His eyes were flashing direct into his son's. His voice rang with severity.

"Lyman, what does this mean?"

The other spread out his hands.

"As you see, sir. We have done our best. I warned you not to expect too much. I told you that this question of transportation was difficult. You would not wish to put rates so low that the action would amount to confiscation of property."

"Why did you not lower rates in the valley of the San Joaquin?"

"That was not a *prominent* issue in the affair,"

responded Lyman, carefully emphasizing his words. "I understand, of course, it was to be approached *in time*. The main point was *an average ten per cent reduction*. Rates *will* be lowered in the San Joaquin. The ranchers around Bonneville will be able to ship to Port Costa at equitable rates, but so radical a measure as that can not be put through in a turn of the hand. We must study—"

"You *knew* the San Joaquin rate *was* an issue," shouted Annixter, shaking his finger across the table. "What do we men who backed you care about rates up in Del Norte and Siskiyou Counties? Not a whoop in hell. It was the San Joaquin rate we were fighting for, and we elected you to reduce that. You didn't do it and you don't intend to, and, by the Lord Harry, I want to know why."

"You'll know, sir—" began Lyman.

"Well, I'll tell you why," vociferated Osterman. "I'll tell you why. It's because we have been sold out. It's because the P. and S. W. have had their spoon in this boiling. It's because our commissioners have betrayed us. It's because we're a set of damn fool farmers and have been cinched again."

Lyman paled under his dark skin at the direct attack. He evidently had not expected this so soon. For the fraction of one instant he lost his poise. He strove to speak, but caught his breath, stammering.

"What have you to say, then?" cried Harran, who, until now, had not spoken.

"I have this to say," answered Lyman, making head as best he might, "that this is no proper spirit in which to discuss business. The Commission has fulfilled its obligations. It has adjusted rates to the best of its ability. We have been at work for two months on the preparation of this schedule—"

"That's a lie," shouted Annixter, his face scarlet; "that's a lie. That schedule was drawn in the offices of the Pacific and Southwestern and you know it. It's a scheme of rates made for the Railroad and by the Railroad and you were bought over to put your name to it."

There was a concerted outburst at the words. All the men in the room were on their feet, gesticulating and vociferating.

"Gentlemen, gentlemen," cried Magnus, "are we schoolboys, are we ruffians of the street?"

"We're a set of fool farmers and we've been betrayed," cried Osterman.

"Well, what have you to say? What have you to say?" persisted Harran, leaning across the table toward his brother. "For God's sake, Lyman, you've got *some* explanation."

"You've misunderstood," protested Lyman, white and trembling. "You've misunderstood. You've expected too much. Next year—next year—soon now, the Commission will take up the—the Commission will consider the San Joaquin rate. We've done our best, that is all."

"Have you, sir?" demanded Magnus.

The Governor's head was in a whirl; a sensation, almost of faintness, had seized upon him. Was it possible? Was it possible?

"Have you done your best?" For a second he compelled Lyman's eye. The glances of father and son met, and, in spite of his best efforts, Lyman's eyes wavered. He began to protest once more, explaining the matter over again from the beginning. But Magnus did not listen. In that brief lapse of time he was convinced that the terrible thing had happened, that the unbelievable had come to pass. It was in the air. Between father and son, in some subtle fashion, the truth that was a lie stood suddenly revealed. But even then Magnus would not receive it. Lyman do this! His son, his eldest son, descend to this! Once more and for the last time he turned to him and in his voice there was that ring that compelled silence.

"Lyman," he said, "I adjure you—I—I demand of you as you are my son and an honorable man, explain yourself. What is there behind all this? It is no longer as Chairman of the Committee I speak to you, you a member of the Railroad Commission. It is your father who speaks, and I address you as my son. Do you understand the gravity of this crisis; do you realize the responsibility of your position; do you not see the importance of this moment? Explain yourself."

"There is nothing to explain."

"You have not reduced rates in the San Joaquin? You have not reduced rates between Bonneville and tidewater?"

"I repeat, sir, what I said before. An average ten per cent cut—"

"Lyman, answer me, yes or no. Have you reduced the Bonneville rate?"

"It could not be done so soon. Give us time. We—"

"Yes or no! By God, sir, do you dare equivocate with me? Yes or no; have you reduced the Bonneville rate?"

"No."

"And answer *me,*" shouted Harran, leaning far across the table, "answer *me.* Were you paid by the Railroad to leave the San Joaquin rate untouched?"

Lyman, whiter than ever, turned furiously upon his brother.

"Don't you dare put that question to me again."

"No, I won't," cried Harran, "because I'll *tell* you to your villain's face that you *were* paid to do it."

On the instant the clamor burst forth afresh. Still on their feet, the ranchers had, little by little, worked around the table, Magnus alone keeping his place. The others were in a group before Lyman, crowding him, as it were, to the wall, shouting into his face with menacing gestures. The truth that was a lie, the certainty of a trust betrayed, a pledge ruthlessly broken, was plain to every one of them.

"By the Lord! men have been shot for less than this," cried Osterman. "You've sold us out, you, and if you ever bring that dago face of yours on a level with mine again, I'll slap it."

"Keep your hands off," exclaimed Lyman quickly, the aggressiveness of the cornered rat flaming up within him. "No violence. Don't you go too far."

"How much were you paid? How much were you paid?" vociferated Harran.

"Yes, yes, what was your price?" cried the others. They were beside themselves with anger; their words came harsh from between their set teeth; their gestures were made with their fists clinched.

"You know the Commission acted in good faith," retorted Lyman. "You know that all was fair and above-board."

"Liar," shouted Annixter; "liar, bribe-eater. You were bought and paid for," and with the words his arm seemed almost of itself to leap out from his shoulder. Lyman received the blow squarely in the face and the force of it sent him staggering backward toward the wall. He tripped over his valise and fell half-way, his back supported against the closed door of the room. Magnus sprang forward. His son had been struck, and the instincts of a father rose up in instant protest; rose for a moment, then forever died away in his heart. He checked the words that flashed to his mind. He lowered

his upraised arm. No, he had but one son. The poor, staggering creature with the fine clothes, white face, and blood-streaked lips was no longer his. A blow could not dishonor him more than he had dishonored himself.

But Gethings, the older man, intervened, pulling Annixter back, crying:

"Stop, this won't do. Not before his father."

"I am no father to this man, gentlemen," exclaimed Magnus. "From now on I have but one son. You, sir," he turned to Lyman, "you, sir, leave my house."

Lyman, his handkerchief to his lips, his smart cravat in disarray, caught up his hat and coat. He was shaking with fury, his protruding eyes were bloodshot. He swung open the door.

"Ruffians," he shouted from the threshold, "ruffians, bullies. Do your own dirty business yourselves after this. I'm done with you. How is it, all of a sudden, you talk about honor? How is it that all at once you're so clean and straight? You weren't so particular at Sacramento just before the nominations. How was the Board elected? I'm a bribe-eater, am I? Is it any worse than *giving* a bribe? Ask Magnus Derrick what he thinks about that. Ask him how much he paid the Democratic bosses at Sacramento to swing the convention."

He went out, slamming the door.

Presley followed. The whole affair made him sick at heart, filled him with infinite disgust, infinite weariness. He wished to get away from it all. He left the dining-room and the excited, clamoring men behind him and stepped out on the porch of the ranch house, closing the door behind him. Lyman was nowhere in sight. Presley was alone. It was late, and after the lamp-heated air of the dining-room the coolness of the night was delicious, and its vast silence, after the noise and fury of the committee meeting, descended from the stars like a benediction. Presley stepped to the edge of the porch, looking off to southward.

And there before him, mile after mile, illimitable, covering the earth from horizon to horizon, lay the Wheat. The growth, now many days old, was already high from the ground. There it lay, a vast, silent ocean, shimmering a pallid green under the moon and under the stars; a mighty force, the strength of nations, the life of the world. There in the night, under the dome of the sky, it was growing steadily. To Presley's mind, the scene in the room he had just left dwindled to paltry insignificance before this sight. Ah, yes, the Wheat—it was over this that the Railroad, the ranchers, the traitor false to his trust, all the members of an obscure conspiracy, were wrangling. As if human agency could affect this colossal power! What were these heated, tiny squabbles, this feverish, small bustle of mankind, this minute swarming of the human insect, to the great, majestic, silent ocean of the Wheat itself! Indifferent, gigantic, resistless, it moved in its appointed grooves. Men, Liliputians, gnats in the sunshine, buzzed impudently in their tiny battles, were born, lived through their little day, died, and were forgotten; while the Wheat, wrapped in Nirvanic calm, grew steadily under the night, alone with the stars and with God.

[Thus betrayed by the agent whom they had expected to protect them, baffled in every other attempt they make to battle the forces against them, the ranchers are desperate. When, at a barbecue, some of the ranchers receive word that they have been dispossessed, open warfare ensues.]

from Book II, Chapter VI

OPEN WARFARE

Annixter, Harran, and Presley climbed to the level plateau where the games were to be held, to lay out the courses, and mark the distances. It was the very place where once Presley had loved to lounge entire afternoons, reading his books of poems, smoking and dozing. From this high point one dominated the entire valley to the south and west. The view was superb. The three men paused for a moment on the crest of the hill to consider it.

Young Vacca came running and panting up the hill after them, calling for Annixter.

"Well, well, what is it?"

"Mr. Osterman's looking for you, sir, you and Mr. Harran. Vanamee, that cowboy over at Derrick's, has just come from the Governor with a message. I guess it's important."

"Hello, what's up now?" muttered Annixter, as they turned back.

They found Osterman saddling his horse in furious haste. Near by him was Vanamee holding by the bridle an animal that was one lather of sweat. A few of the picnickers were turning their heads curiously in that direction. Evidently something of moment was in the wind.

"What's all up?" demanded Annixter, as he and Harran, followed by Presley, drew near.

"There's hell to pay," exclaimed Osterman under his breath. "Read that. Vanamee just brought it."

He handed Annixter a sheet of note paper, and turned again to the cinching of his saddle.

"We've got to be quick," he cried. "They've stolen a march on us."

Annixter read the note, Harran and Presley looking over his shoulder.

"Ah, it's them, is it?" exclaimed Annixter.

Harran set his teeth. "Now for it," he exclaimed.

"They've been to your place already, Mr. Annixter," said Vanamee. "I passed by it on my way up. They have put Delaney in possession, and have set all your furniture out in the road."

Annixter turned about, his lips white. Already Presley and Harran had run to their horses.

"Vacca," cried Annixter, "where's Vacca? Put the saddle on the buckskin, *quick*. Osterman, get as many of the League as are here together at *this* spot, understand. I'll be back in a minute. I must tell Hilma this."

Hooven ran up as Annixter disappeared. His little eyes were blazing, he was dragging his horse with him.

"Say, dose fellers come, hey? Me, I'm alretty, see I hev der guhn."

"They've jumped the ranch, little girl," said Annixter, putting one arm around Hilma. "They're in our house now. I'm off. Go to Derrick's and wait for me there."

She put her arms around his neck.

"You're going?" she demanded.

"I must. Don't be frightened. It will be all right. Go to Derrick's and—good-by."

She said never a word. She looked once long into his eyes, then kissed him on the mouth.

Meanwhile, the news had spread. The multitude rose to its feet. Women and men, with pale faces, looked at each other speechless, or broke forth into inarticulate exclamations. A strange, unfamiliar murmur took the place of the tumultuous gayety of the previous moments. A sense of dread, of confusion, of impending terror weighed heavily in the air. What was now to happen?

When Annixter got back to Osterman, he found a number of the Leaguers already assembled. They were all mounted. Hooven was there and Harran, and besides these, Garnett of the Ruby rancho and Gethings of the San Pablo, Phelps, the foreman of Los Muertos, and, last of all, Dabney, silent as ever, speaking to no one. Presley came riding up.

"Best keep out of this, Pres," cried Annixter.

"Are we ready?" exclaimed Gethings.

"Ready, ready, we're all here."

"*All*. Is this all of us?" cried Annixter. "Where are the six hundred men who were going to rise when this happened?"

They had wavered, these other Leaguers. Now, when the actual crisis impended, they were smitten with confusion. Ah, no, they were not going to stand up and be shot at just to save Derrick's land. They were not armed. What did Annixter and Osterman take them for? No, sir; the Railroad had stolen a march on them. After all his big talk Derrick had allowed them to be taken by surprise. The only thing to do was to call a meeting of the Executive Committee. That was the only thing. As for going down there with no weapons in their hands, *no*, sir. That was asking a little *too* much.

"Come on, then, boys," shouted Osterman, turning his back on the others. "The Governor says to meet him at Hooven's. We'll make for the Long Trestle and strike the trail to Hooven's there."

They set off. It was a terrible ride. Twice during the scrambling descent from the hills, Presley's pony fell beneath him. Annixter, on his buckskin, and Osterman, on his thoroughbred, good horsemen both, led the others, setting a terrific pace. The hills were left behind. Broderson Creek was crossed and on the levels of Quien Sabe, straight through the standing wheat, the nine horses, flogged and spurred, stretched out to their utmost. Their passage through the wheat sounded like the rip and tear of a gigantic web of cloth. The landscape on either hand resolved itself into a long blur. Tears came to the eyes, flying pebbles, clods of earth, grains of wheat flung up in the flight, stung the face like shot. Osterman's thoroughbred took the second crossing of Broderson Creek in a single leap. Down under the Long Trestle tore the cavalcade in a shower of mud and gravel; up again on the further bank, the horses blowing like steam engines; on into the trail to Hooven's, single file now, Presley's pony lagging, Hooven's horse bleeding at the eyes, the buckskin, game as a fighting cock, catching her second

wind, far in the lead now, distancing even the English thoroughbred that Osterman rode.

At last Hooven's unpainted house, beneath the enormous live-oak tree, came in sight. Across the Lower Road, breaking through fences and into the yard around the house, thundered the Leaguers. Magnus was waiting for them.

The riders dismounted, hardly less exhausted than their horses.

"Why, where's all the men?" Annixter demanded of Magnus.

"Broderson is here and Cutter," replied the Governor, "no one else. I thought *you* would bring more men with you."

"There are only nine of us."

"And the six hundred Leaguers who were going to rise when this happened!" exclaimed Garnett, bitterly.

"Rot the League," cried Annixter. "It's gone to pot— went to pieces at the first touch."

"We have been taken by surprise, gentlemen, after all," said Magnus. "Totally off our guard. But there are eleven of us. It is enough."

"Well, what's the game? Has the marshal come? How many men are with him?"

"The United States marshal from San Francisco," explained Magnus, "came down early this morning and stopped at Guadalajara. We learned it all through our friends in Bonneville about an hour ago. They telephoned me and Mr. Broderson. S. Behrman met him and provided about a dozen deputies. Delaney, Ruggles, and Christian joined them at Guadalajara. They left Guadalajara, going toward Mr. Annixter's ranch house on Quien Sabe. They are serving the writs in ejectment and putting the dummy buyers in possession. They are armed. S. Behrman is with them."

"Where are they now?"

"Cutter is watching them from the Long Trestle. They returned to Guadalajara. They are there now."

"Well," observed Gethings, "from Guadalajara they can only go to two places. Either they will take the Upper Road and go on to Osterman's next, or they will take the Lower Road to Mr. Derrick's."

"That is as I supposed," said Magnus. "That is why I wanted you to come here. From Hooven's here, we can watch both roads simultaneously."

"Is anybody on the lookout on the Upper Road?"

"Cutter. He is on the Long Trestle."

"Say," observed Hooven, the instincts of the old-time soldier stirring him, "say, dose feller pretty demn schmart, I tink. We got to put some picket way oudt bei der Lower Roadt alzoh, und he tek dose glassus Mist'r Ennixt'r got bei um. Say, look at dose irregation ditsch. Dot ditsch he run righd across *both* dose road, hey? Dat's some fine entrenchment, you bedt. We fighd um from dose ditsch."

In fact, the dry irrigating ditch was a natural trench, admirably suited to the purpose, crossing both roads as Hooven pointed out and barring approach from Guadalajara to all the ranches save Annixter's—which had already been seized.

Gethings departed to join Cutter on the Long Trestle, while Phelps and Harran, taking Annixter's field glasses with them, and mounting their horses, went out toward Guadalajara on the Lower Road to watch for the marshal's approach from that direction.

After the outposts had left them, the party in Hooven's cottage looked to their weapons. Long since, every member of the League had been in the habit of carrying his revolver with him. They were all armed and, in addition, Hooven had his rifle. Presley alone carried no weapon.

The main room of Hooven's house, in which the Leaguers were now assembled, was barren, poverty-stricken, but tolerably clean. An old clock ticked vociferously on a shelf. In one corner was a bed, with a patched, faded quilt. In the centre of the room, straddling over the bare floor, stood a pine table. Around this the men gathered, two or three occupying chairs, Annixter sitting sidewise on the table, the rest standing.

"I believe, gentlemen," said Magnus, "that we can go through this day without bloodshed. I believe not one shot need be fired. The Railroad will not force the issue, will not bring about actual fighting. When the marshal realizes that we are thoroughly in earnest, thoroughly determined, I am convinced that he will withdraw."

There were murmurs of assent.

"Look here," said Annixter, "if this thing can by any means be settled peaceably, I say let's do it, so long as we don't give in."

The others stared. Was this Annixter who spoke—the Hotspur of the League, the quarrelsome, irascible fellow who loved and sought a quarrel? Was it Annixter, who now had been the first and only one of them

all to suffer, whose ranch had been seized, whose household possessions had been flung out into the road?

"When you come right down to it," he continued, "killing a man, no matter what he's done to you, is a serious business. I propose we make one more attempt to stave this thing off. Let's see if we can't get to talk with the marshal himself; at any rate, warn him of the danger of going any further. Boys, let's not fire the first shot. What do you say?"

The others agreed unanimously and promptly; and old Broderson, tugging uneasily at his long beard, added:

"No—no—no violence, no *unnecessary* violence, that is. I should hate to have innocent blood on my hands—that is, if it *is* innocent. I don't know, that S. Behrman—ah, he is a—a—surely he had innocent blood on *his* head. That Dyke affair, terrible, terrible; but then Dyke *was* in the wrong—driven to it, though; the Railroad did drive him to it. I want to be fair and just to everybody—"

"There's a team coming up the road from Los Muertos," announced Presley from the door.

"Fair and just to everybody," murmured old Broderson, wagging his head, frowning perplexedly. "I don't want to—to—to harm anybody unless they harm me."

"Is the team going toward Guadalajara?" inquired Garnett, getting up and coming to the door.

"Yes, it's a Portuguese, one of the garden truck men."

"We must turn him back," declared Osterman. "He can't go through here. We don't want him to take any news on to the marshal and S. Behrman."

"I'll turn him back," said Presley.

He rode out toward the market cart, and the others, watching from the road in front of Hooven's, saw him halt it. An excited interview followed. They could hear the Portuguese expostulating volubly, but in the end he turned back.

"Martial law on Los Muertos, isn't it?" observed Osterman. "Steady all," he exclaimed as he turned about, "here comes Harran."

Harran rode up at a gallop. The others surrounded him.

"I saw them," he cried. "They are coming this way. S. Behrman and Ruggles are in a two-horse buggy. All the others are on horseback. There are eleven of them.

44 Hotspur, a proud, quarrelsome character in I Henry IV

Christian and Delaney are with them. Those two have rifles. I left Hooven watching them."

"Better call in Gethings and Cutter right away," said Annixter. "We'll need all our men."

"I'll call them in," Presley volunteered at once. "Can I have the buckskin? My pony is about done up."

He departed at a brisk gallop, but on the way met Gethings and Cutter returning. They, too, from their elevated position, had observed the marshal's party leav-10 ing Guadalajara by the Lower Road. Presley told them of the decision of the Leaguers not to fire until fired upon.

"All right," said Gethings. "But if it comes to a gun-fight, that means it's all up with at least one of us. Delaney never misses his man."

When they reached Hooven's again, they found that the Leaguers had already taken their position in the ditch. The plank bridge across it had been torn up. Magnus, two long revolvers lying on the embankment in front of him, was in the middle, Harran at his side. On either 20 side, some five feet intervening between each man, stood the other Leaguers, their revolvers ready. Dabney, the silent old man, had taken off his coat.

"Take your places between Mr. Osterman and Mr. Bro-derson," said Magnus, as the three men rode up. "Presley," he added, "I forbid you to take any part in this affair."

"Yes, keep him out of it," cried Annixter from his position at the extreme end of the line. "Go back to Hooven's house, Pres, and look after the horses," he added. "This is no business of yours. And keep the road 30 behind us clear. Don't let *any one* come near, not *any one,* understand?"

Presley withdrew, leading the buckskin and the horses that Gethings and Cutter had ridden. He fastened them under the great live-oak and then came out and stood in the road in front of the house to watch what was going on.

In the ditch, shoulder deep, the Leaguers, ready, watchful, waited in silence, their eyes fixed on the white shimmer of the road leading to Guadalajara.

"Where's Hooven?" inquired Cutter.

40 "I don't know," Osterman replied. "He was out watch-ing the Lower Road with Harran Derrick. Oh, Harran," he called, "isn't Hooven coming in?"

"I don't know what he is waiting for," answered Har-ran. "He was to have come in just after me. He thought maybe the marshal's party might make a feint in this direction, then go around by the Upper Road, after all.

He wanted to watch them a little longer. But he ought to be here now."

"Think he'll take a shot at them on his own account?"

"Oh, no, he wouldn't do that."   50

"Maybe they took him prisoner."

"Well, that's to be thought of, too."

Suddenly there was a cry. Around the bend of the road in front of them came a cloud of dust. From it emerged a horse's head.

"Hello, hello, there's something."

"Remember, we are not to fire first."

"Perhaps that's Hooven; I can't see. Is it? There only seems to be one horse."

"Too much dust for one horse."   60

Annixter, who had taken his field glasses from Har-ran, adjusted them to his eyes.

"That's not them," he announced presently, "nor Hooven either. That's a cart." Then, after another mo-ment, he added, "The butcher's cart from Guadalajara."

The tension was relaxed. The men drew long breaths, settling back in their places.

"Do we let him go on, Governor?"

"The bridge is down. He can't go by and we must not let him go back. We shall have to detain him and ques-   70 tion him. I wonder the marshal let him pass."

The cart approached at a lively trot.

"Anybody else in that cart, Mr. Annixter?" asked Magnus. "Look carefully. It may be a ruse. It is strange the marshal should have let him pass."

The Leaguers roused themselves again. Osterman laid his hand on his revolver.

"No," called Annixter, in another instant, "no, there's only one man in it."

The cart came up, and Cutter and Phelps, clambering 80 from the ditch, stopped it as it arrived in front of the party.

"Hey—what—what?" exclaimed the young butcher, pulling up. "Is that bridge broke?"

But at the idea of being held, the boy protested at top voice, badly frightened, bewildered, not knowing what was to happen.

"No, no, I got my meat to deliver. Say, you let me go. Say, I ain't got nothing to do with you."

He tugged at the reins, trying to turn the cart about. 90 Cutter, with his jack-knife, parted the reins just back of the bit.

"You'll stay where you are, m' son, for a while. We're not going to hurt you. But you are not going back to town till we say so. Did you pass anybody on the road out of town?"

In reply to the Leaguers' questions, the young butcher at last told them he had passed a two-horse buggy and a lot of men on horseback just beyond the railroad tracks. They were headed for Los Muertos.

"That's them, all right," muttered Annixter. "They're coming by this road, sure."

The butcher's horse and cart were led to one side of the road, and the horse tied to the fence with one of the severed lines. The butcher himself was passed over to Presley, who locked him in Hooven's barn.

"Well, what the devil," demanded Osterman, "has become of Bismarck?"

In fact, the butcher had seen nothing of Hooven. The minutes were passing, and still he failed to appear.

"What's he up to, anyways?"

"Bet you what you like, they caught him. Just like that crazy Dutchman to get excited and go too near. You can always depend on Hooven to lose his head."

Five minutes passed, then ten. The road toward Guadalajara lay empty, baking and white under the sun.

"Well, the marshal and S. Behrman don't seem to be in any hurry, either."

"Shall I go forward and reconnoitre, Governor?" asked Harran.

But Dabney, who stood next to Annixter, touched him on the shoulder and, without speaking, pointed down the road. Annixter looked, then suddenly cried out:

"Here comes Hooven."

The German galloped into sight, around the turn of the road, his rifle laid across his saddle. He came on rapidly, pulled up, and dismounted at the ditch.

"Dey're commen," he cried, trembling with excitement. "I watch um long dime bei der side oaf der roadt in der busches. Dey shtop bei der gate oder side der relroadt trecks and talk long dime mit one n'udder. Den dey gome on. Dey're gowun sure do zum monkey-doodle pizeness. Me, I see Gritschum put der kertridges in his guhn. I tink they gowun to gome *my* place first. Dey gowun to try to put me off, tek my home, bei Gott."

"All right, get down in here and keep quiet, Hooven. Don't fire unless—"

"Here they are."

A half-dozen voices uttered the cry at once.

There could be no mistake this time. A buggy, drawn by two horses, came into view around the curve of the road. Three riders accompanied it, and behind these, seen at intervals in a cloud of dust, were two—three—five—six others.

This, then, was S. Behrman with the United States marshal and his posse. The event that had been so long in preparation, the event which it had been said would never come to pass, the last trial of strength, the last fight between the Trust and the People, the direct, brutal grapple of armed men, the law defied, the Government ignored, behold, here it was close at hand.

Osterman cocked his revolver, and in the profound silence that had fallen upon the scene, the click was plainly audible from end to end of the line.

"Remember our agreement, gentlemen," cried Magnus, in a warning voice. "Mr. Osterman, I must ask you to let down the hammer of your weapon."

No one answered. In absolute quiet, standing motionless in their places, the Leaguers watched the approach of the marshal.

Five minutes passed. The riders came on steadily. They drew nearer. The grind of the buggy wheels in the grit and dust of the road, and the prolonged clatter of the horses' feet began to make itself heard. The Leaguers could distinguish the faces of their enemies.

In the buggy were S. Behrman and Cyrus Ruggles, the latter driving. A tall man in a frock coat and slouched hat—the marshal, beyond question—rode at the left of the buggy; Delaney, carrying a Winchester, at the right. Christian, the real estate broker, S. Behrman's cousin, also with a rifle, could be made out just behind the marshal. Back of these, riding well up, was a group of horsemen, indistinguishable in the dust raised by the buggy's wheels.

Steadily the distance between the Leaguers and the posse diminished.

"Don't let them get too close, Governor," whispered Harran.

When S. Behrman's buggy was about one hundred yards distant from the irrigating ditch, Magnus sprang out upon the road, leaving his revolvers behind him. He beckoned Garnett and Gethings to follow, and the three ranchers, who, with the exception of Broderson, were the oldest men present, advanced, without arms, to meet the marshal.

Magnus cried aloud:

"Halt where you are."

From their places in the ditch, Annixter, Osterman, Dabney, Harran, Hooven, Broderson, Cutter, and Phelps, their hands laid upon their revolvers, watched silently, alert, keen, ready for anything.

At the Governor's words, they saw Ruggles pull sharply on the reins. The buggy came to a standstill, the riders doing likewise. Magnus approached the marshal, still followed by Garnett and Gethings, and began to speak. His voice was audible to the men in the ditch, but his words could not be made out. They heard the marshal reply quietly enough and the two shook hands. Delaney came around from the side of the buggy, his horse standing before the team across the road. He leaned from the saddle, listening to what was being said, but made no remark. From time to time, S. Behrman and Ruggles, from their seats in the buggy, interposed a sentence or two into the conversation, but at first, so far as the Leaguers could discern, neither Magnus nor the marshal paid them any attention. They saw, however, that the latter repeatedly shook his head and once they heard him exclaim in a loud voice:

"I only know my duty, Mr. Derrick."

Then Gethings turned about, and seeing Delaney close at hand, addressed an unheard remark to him. The cowpuncher replied curtly and the words seemed to anger Gethings. He made a gesture, pointing back to the ditch, showing the intrenched Leaguers to the posse. Delaney appeared to communicate the news that the Leaguers were on hand and prepared to resist, to the other members of the party. They all looked toward the ditch and plainly saw the ranchers there, standing to their arms.

But meanwhile Ruggles had addressed himself more directly to Magnus, and between the two an angry discussion was going forward. Once even Harran heard his father exclaim:

"The statement is a lie and no one knows it better than yourself."

"Here," growled Annixter to Dabney, who stood next him in the ditch, "those fellows are getting too close. Look at them edging up. Don't Magnus see that?"

The other members of the marshal's force had come forward from their places behind the buggy and were spread out across the road. Some of them were gathered about Magnus, Garnett, and Gethings; and some were talking together, looking and pointing toward the ditch. Whether acting upon signal or not, the Leaguers in the ditch could not tell, but it was certain that one or two of the posse had moved considerably forward. Besides this, Delaney had now placed his horse between Magnus and the ditch, and two others riding up from the rear had followed his example. The posse surrounded the three ranchers, and by now everybody was talking at once.

"Look here," Harran called to Annixter, "this won't do. I don't like the looks of this thing. They all seem to be edging up, and before we know it they may take the Governor and the other men prisoners."

"They ought to come back," declared Annixter.

"Somebody ought to tell them that those fellows are creeping up."

By now the angry argument between the Governor and Ruggles had become more heated than ever. Their voices were raised; now and then they made furious gestures.

"They ought to come back," cried Osterman. "We couldn't shoot now if anything should happen, for fear of hitting them."

"Well, it sounds as though something were going to happen pretty soon."

They could hear Gethings and Delaney wrangling furiously; another deputy joined in.

"I'm going to call the Governor back," exclaimed Annixter, suddenly clambering out of the ditch.

"No, no," cried Osterman, "keep in the ditch. They can't drive us out if we keep here."

Hooven and Harran, who had instinctively followed Annixter, hesitated at Osterman's words and the three halted irresolutely on the road before the ditch, their weapons in their hands.

"Governor," shouted Harran, "come on back. You can't do anything."

Still the wrangle continued, and one of the deputies, advancing a little from out the group, cried out:

"Keep back there! Keep back there, you!"

"Go to hell, will you?" shouted Harran on the instant. "You're on my land."

"Oh, come back here, Harran," called Osterman. "That ain't going to do any good."

"There—listen," suddenly exclaimed Harran. "The Governor is calling us. Come on; I'm going."

Osterman got out of the ditch and came forward, catching Harran by the arm and pulling him back.

"He didn't call. Don't get excited. You'll ruin everything. Get back into the ditch again."

But Cutter, Phelps, and the old man Dabney, misunderstanding what was happening, and seeing Osterman leave the ditch, had followed his example. All the
10 Leaguers were now out of the ditch, and a little way down the road, Hooven, Osterman, Annixter, and Harran in front, Dabney, Phelps, and Cutter coming up from behind.

"Keep back, you," cried the deputy again.

In the group around S. Behrman's buggy, Gethings and Delaney were yet quarreling, and the angry debate between Magnus, Garnett, and the marshal still continued.

Till this moment, the real estate broker, Christian, had
20 taken no part in the argument, but had kept himself in the rear of the buggy. Now, however, he pushed forward. There was but little room for him to pass, and, as he rode by the buggy, his horse scraped his flank against the hub of the wheel. The animal recoiled sharply, and, striking against Garnett, threw him to the ground. Delaney's horse stood between the buggy and the Leaguers gathered on the road in front of the ditch; the incident, indistinctly seen by them, was misinterpreted.

30 Garnett had not yet risen when Hooven raised a great shout:

"*Hoch, der Kaiser! Hoch, der Vaterland!*"

With the words he dropped to one knee, and, sighting his rifle carefully, fired into the group of men around the buggy.

Instantly the revolvers and rifles seemed to go off of themselves. Both sides, deputies and Leaguers, opened fire simultaneously. At first, it was nothing but a confused roar of explosions; then the roar lapsed to an
40 irregular, quick succession of reports, shot leaping after shot; then a moment's silence, and, last of all, regular as clock-ticks, three shots at exact intervals. Then stillness.

Delaney, shot through the stomach, slid down from his horse, and, on his hands and knees, crawled from the road into the standing wheat. Christian fell backward from the saddle toward the buggy, and hung suspended

in that position, his head and shoulders on the wheel, one stiff leg still across his saddle. Hooven, in attempting to rise from his kneeling position, received a rifle ball 50 squarely in the throat, and rolled forward upon his face. Old Broderson crying out, "Oh, they've shot me, boys," staggered sideways, his head bent, his hands rigid at his sides, and fell into the ditch. Osterman, blood running from his mouth and nose, turned about and walked back. Presley helped him across the irrigating ditch and Osterman laid himself down, his head on his folded arms. Harran Derrick dropped where he stood, turning over on his face, and lay motionless, groaning terribly, a pool of blood forming under his stomach. 60 The old man Dabney, silent as ever, received his death speechless. He fell to his knees, got up again, fell once more, and died without a word. Annixter, instantly killed, fell his length to the ground, and lay without movement, just as he had fallen, one arm across his face.

[This bloody conflict marks the end of the struggle of the ranchers. The Railroad has been victorious—has rapaciously taken from the tillers of the soil their land. Presley writes in his journal his impressions of the unequal contest and its conclusion.]

from Book II, Chapter VII

PRESLEY'S JOURNAL

Presley did not close his eyes once during the night; he did not even remove his clothes. Long after the doctor had departed and that house of tragedy had quieted down, he still remained in his place by the open win- 70 dow of his little room, looking off across the leagues of growing wheat, watching the slow kindling of the dawn. Horror weighed intolerably upon him. Monstrous things, huge, terrible, whose names he knew only too well, whirled at a gallop through his imagination, or rose spectral and grisly before the eyes of his mind. Harran dead, Annixter dead, Broderson dead, Osterman, perhaps, even at that moment dying. Why, these men had made up his world. Annixter had been his best friend, Harran, his almost daily companion; Broderson and Oster- 80 man were familiar to him as brothers. They were all his

32 *Hoch . . . Vaterland!* Hail the Emperor! Hail the Fatherland!

associates, his good friends, the group was his environment, belonging to his daily life. And he, standing there in the dust of the road by the irrigating ditch, had seen them shot. He found himself suddenly at his table, the candle burning at his elbow, his journal before him, writing swiftly, the desire for expression, the craving for outlet to the thoughts that clamored tumultuous at his brain, never more insistent, more imperious. Thus he wrote:

"Dabney dead, Hooven dead, Harran dead, Annixter dead, Broderson dead, Osterman dying, S. Behrman alive, successful; the Railroad in possession of Quien Sabe. I saw them shot. Not twelve hours since I stood there at the irrigating ditch. Ah, that terrible moment of horror and confusion! powder smoke—flashing pistol barrels—blood stains—rearing horses—men staggering to their death—Christian in a horrible posture, one rigid leg high in the air across his saddle—Broderson falling sidewise into the ditch—Osterman laying himself down, his head on his arms, as if tired, tired out. These things, I have seen them. The picture of this day's work is from henceforth part of my mind, part of *me*. They have done it, S. Behrman and the owners of the railroad have done it, while all the world looked on, while the people of these United States looked on. Oh, come now and try your theories upon us, us of the ranchos, us, who have suffered, us, who *know*. Oh, talk to *us* now of the 'rights of Capital,' talk to *us* of the Trust, talk to *us* of the 'equilibrium between the classes.' Try your ingenious ideas upon us. *We know.* I can not tell whether or not your theories are excellent. I do not know if your ideas are plausible. I do not know how practical is your scheme of society. I do not know if the Railroad has a right to our lands, but I *do* know that Harran is dead, that Annixter is dead, that Broderson is dead, that Hooven is dead, that Osterman is dying, and that S. Behrman is alive, successful, triumphant; that he has ridden into possession of a principality over the dead bodies of five men shot down by his hired associates.

"I can see the outcome. The Railroad will prevail. The Trust will overpower us. Here in this corner of a great nation, here, on the edge of the continent, here, in this valley of the West, far from the great centres, isolated, remote, lost, the great iron hand crushes life from us, crushes liberty and the pursuit of happiness from us, and our little struggles, our moment's convulsion of death agony causes not one jar in the vast, clashing machinery of the nation's life; a fleck of grit in the wheels, perhaps, a grain of sand in the cogs—the momentary creak of the axle is the mother's wail of bereavement, the wife's cry of anguish—and the great wheel turns, spinning smooth again, even again, and the tiny impediment of a second, scarce noticed, is forgotten. Make the people believe that the faint tremor in their great engine is a menace to its function? What a folly to think of it. Tell them of the danger and they will laugh at you. Tell them, five years from now, the story of the fight between the League of the San Joaquin and the Railroad and it will not be believed. What! a pitched battle between Farmer and Railroad, a battle that cost the lives of seven men? Impossible, it could not have happened. Your story is fiction—is exaggerated.

"Yet it is Lexington—God help us, God enlighten us, God rouse us from our lethargy—it is Lexington; farmers with guns in their hands fighting for Liberty. Is our State of California the only one that has its ancient and hereditary foe? Are there no other Trusts between the oceans than this of the Pacific and Southwestern Railroad? Ask yourselves, you of the Middle West, ask yourselves, you of the North, ask yourselves, you of the East, ask yourselves, you of the South—ask yourselves, every citizen of every State from Maine to Mexico, from the Dakotas to the Carolinas, have you not the monster in your boundaries? If it is not a Trust of transportation, it is only another head of the same Hydra. Is not our death struggle typical? Is it not one of many, is it not symbolical of the great and terrible conflict that is going on everywhere in these United States? Ah, you people, blind, bound, tricked, betrayed, can you not see it? Can you not see how the monsters have plundered your treasures and holding them in the grip of their iron claws, dole them out to you only at the price of your blood, at the price of the lives of your wives and your little children? You give your babies to Moloch for the loaf of bread you have kneaded yourselves. You offer your starved wives to Juggernaut for the iron nail you have yourselves compounded."

1899-1900·1901

---

84 **Moloch,** a Semitic god who was worshiped with human sacrifices • 86 **Juggernaut,** a Hindu god (a form of Vishnu). Legend had it that frenzied devotees allowed themselves to be crushed by the wheels of the car in which the idol of this deity was drawn during the festival of the god's car

A Neglected Epic

In this plea for a proper literary treatment of an American subject, Norris indicates some of the ideas which impelled him to attempt his epic trilogy, of which **The Octopus** was a part. The essay was first published in **World's Work**, December 1902.

Suddenly we have found that there is no longer any Frontier. The westward-moving course of empire has at last crossed the Pacific Ocean. Civilization has circled the globe and has come back to its starting point, the vague and mysterious East.

The thing has not been accomplished peacefully. From the very first it has been an affair of wars—of invasions. Invasions of the East by the West, and of raids North and South—raids accomplished by flying columns that dashed out from both sides of the main army. Sometimes even the invaders have fought among themselves, as, for instance, the Trojan War, or the civil wars of Italy, England, and America; sometimes they have turned back on their tracks and, upon one pretext or another, reconquered the races behind them, as for instance Alexander's wars to the eastward, the Crusades, and Napoleon's Egyptian campaigns.

Retarded by all these obstacles, the march has been painfully slow. To move from Egypt to Greece took centuries of time. More centuries were consumed in the campaign that brought empire from Greece to Rome, and still more centuries passed before it crossed the Alps and invaded northern and western Europe.

But observe. Once across the Mississippi, the West—our Far West—was conquered in about forty years. In all the vast campaign from east to west here is the most signal victory, the swiftest, the completest, the most brilliant achievement—the wilderness subdued at a single stroke.

Now all these various fightings to the westward, these mysterious race-movements, migrations, wars and wan-derings have produced their literature, distinctive, peculiar, excellent. And this literature we call epic. The Trojan War gave us the "Iliad," the "Odyssey," and the "Aeneid;" the campaign of the Greeks in Asia Minor produced the "Anabasis;" a whole cycle of literature grew from the conquest of Europe after the fall of Rome— "The Song of Roland," "The Nibelungenlied," "The Romance of the Rose," "Beowulf," "Magnusson," "The Scotch Border Ballads," "The Poem of the Cid," "The Hemskringla," "Orlando Furioso," "Jerusalem Delivered," and the like.

On this side of the Atlantic, in his clumsy, artificial way, but yet recognized as a producer of literature, Cooper has tried to chronicle the conquest of the eastern part of our country. Absurd he may be in his ideas of life and character, the art in him veneered over with charlatanism; yet the man was solemn enough and took his work seriously, and his work is literature.

Also a cycle of romance has grown up around the Civil War. The theme has had its poets to whom the public have been glad to listen. The subject is vast, noble; is, in a word, epic, just as the Trojan War and the Retreat of the Ten Thousand were epic.

But when at last one comes to look for the literature that sprang from and has grown up about the last great epic event in the history of civilization, the event which in spite of stupendous difficulties was consummated more swiftly, more completely, more satisfactorily than any like event since the westward migration began— I mean the conquering of the West, the subduing of the wilderness beyond the Mississippi—what has this produced in the way of literature? The dime novel! The dime novel and nothing else. The dime novel and nothing better.

The Trojan War left to posterity the character of Hector; the wars with the Saracens gave us Roland; the folklore of Iceland produced Grettir; the Scotch

---

1 **no . . . Frontier.** The disappearance of the frontier was announced by the federal government in 1890; and in 1893 Frederick Jackson Turner published the first significant study of the frontier in our history • 34 **Iliad . . . Odyssey . . . Aeneid.** These, like others listed, were, as Norris says, epic works—with one exception: there was no Magnusson epic. Probably Norris' error arose from the fact that Eirikr Magnusson aided William Norris in translating some sagas into English • 54 **Retreat . . . Thousand,** the defeat of the army of Cyrus at Cunaxa (401 B.C.), reported by Xenophon in his **Anabasis** • 63 **dime novel,** a type of cheap thriller written and sold in this country between 1860 and about 1895

border poetry brought forth Douglas; the Spanish epic the Cid. But the American epic, just as heroic, just as elemental, just as important and as picturesque, will fade into history, leaving behind no finer type, no nobler hero than Buffalo Bill.

The young Greeks sat on marble terraces overlooking the Aegean Sea and listened to the thunderous roll of Homer's hexameter. In the feudal castles the minstrel sang to the young boys, of Roland. The farm folk of Iceland to this very day treasure up and read to their little ones hand-written copies of the Gretla Saga chronicling the deeds and death of Grettir the Strong. But the youth of the United States learn of their epic by paying a dollar to see the "Wild West Show."

The plain truth of the matter is that we have neglected our epic—the black shame of it be on us—and no contemporaneous poet or chronicler thought it worth his while to sing the song or tell the tale of the West because literature in the day when the West was being won was a cult indulged in by certain well-bred gentlemen in New England who looked eastward to the Old World, to the legends of England and Norway and Germany and Italy for their inspiration, and left the great, strong, honest, fearless, resolute deeds of their own countrymen to be defamed and defaced by the nameless hacks of the "yellow back" libraries.

One man—who wrote "How Santa Claus Came to Simpson's Bar"—one poet, one chronicler did, in fact, arise for the moment, who understood that wild, brave life and who for a time gave promise of bearing record of things seen.

One of the requirements of an epic—a true epic—is that its action must devolve upon some great national event. There was no lack of such in those fierce years after '49. Just that long and terrible journey from the Mississippi to the ocean is an epic in itself. Yet no serious attempt has ever been made by an American author to render into prose or verse this event in our history as "national" in scope, in origin and in results as the Revolution itself. The prairie schooner is as large a figure in the legends as the black ship that bore Ulysses homeward from Troy. The sea meant as much to the Argonauts of the fifties as it did to the ten thousand.

And the Alamo! There is a trumpet-call in the word; and only the look of it on the printed page is a flash of fire. But the very histories slight the deed, and to many an American, born under the same flag that the Mexican rifles shot to ribbons on that splendid day, the word is meaningless. Yet Thermopylae was less glorious, and in comparison with that siege the investment of Troy was mere wanton riot. At the very least the Texans in that battered adobe church fought for the honour of their flag and the greater glory of their country, not for loot or the possession of the person of an adultress. Young men are taught to consider the "Iliad," with its butcheries, its glorification of inordinate selfishness and vanity, as a classic. Achilles, murderer, egotist, ruffian, and liar, is a hero. But the name of Bowie, the name of the man who gave his life to his flag at the Alamo, is perpetuated only in the designation of a knife. Crockett is the hero of a "funny story" about a sagacious 'coon; while Travis, the boy commander who did what Gordon with an empire back of him failed to do, is quietly and definitely ignored.

Because we have done nothing to get at the truth about the West; because our best writers have turned to the old-country folklore and legends for their inspiration; because "melancholy harlequins" strut in fringed leggings upon the street-corners, one hand held out for pennies, we have come to believe that our West, our epic, was an affair of Indians, road-agents, and desperadoes, and have taken no account of the brave men who stood for law and justice and liberty, and for those great ideas died by the hundreds, unknown and unsung—died that the West might be subdued, that the last stage of the march should be accomplished, that the Anglo-Saxon should fulfil his destiny and complete the cycle of the world.

The great figure of our neglected epic, the Hector of our ignoble Iliad, is not, as the dime novels would have us believe, a lawbreaker, but a lawmaker; a fighter, it is true, as is always the case with epic figures, but a fighter for peace, a calm, grave, strong man who hated the lawbreaker as the hound hates the wolf.

He did not lounge in barrooms; he did not cheat at

---

5 **Buffalo Bill,** William F. Cody (1846-1917), the hero of many dime novels, notably those of Ned Buntline and Prentiss Ingraham • 14 **Wild West Show,** a traveling tent show in which feats of marksmanship and Indian raids were reënacted • 27 **One man.** Bret Harte was the author of the story mentioned • 43 **Argonauts,** American goldseekers. The name came from the Greek legend concerning those who sailed with Jason on the ship **Argo** to find the golden fleece • 44 **Alamo.** See note, p. 167 • 58 **Bowie.** James Bowie was one of the heroes • 61 **Travis.** William Travis died in the Alamo • 62 **Gordon,** Charles George Gordon (1833-1885), British general who died defending Khartoum against the Sudanese

cards; he did not drink himself to maudlin fury; he did not "shoot at the drop of the hat." But he loved his horse, he loved his friend, he was kind to little children; he was always ready to side with the weak against the strong, with the poor against the rich. For hypocrisy, and pretense, for shams and subterfuges, he had no mercy, no tolerance. He was too brave to lie and too strong to steal. The odds in that lawless day were ever against him; his enemies were many and his friends were few; but his face was always set bravely against evil, and fear was not in him even at the end. For such a man as this could die no quiet death in a land where law went no further than the statute books and life lay in the crook of his neighbour's forefinger.

He died in defense of an ideal, an epic hero, a legendary figure, formidable, sad. He died facing down injustice, dishonesty, and crime; died "in his boots;" and the same world which has glorified Achilles and forgotten Travis finds none too poor to do him reverence. No literature has sprung up around him—this great character native to America. He is of all the world-types the one distinctive to us—peculiar, particular and unique. He is dead and even his work is misinterpreted and misunderstood. His very memory will soon be gone, and the American epic, which, on the shelves of posterity, should have stood shoulder to shoulder with the "Hemskringla" and the "Tales of the Nibelungen" and the "Song of Roland," will never be written.

1902

A Plea for Romantic Fiction

Readers who believe that such terms as "realism" and "romanticism" have had unchanging definitions throughout their history will be puzzled by this plea. The fact of the matter, of course, is that both terms have been used by critics and authors with a variety of denotations. Here, as Norris urges "romantic" writing, defining the term in his own individual way, he offers insight not only into the nature of critical controversies of the day but also into his own objectives and methods as an author.

Let us at the start make a distinction. Observe that one speaks of romanticism and not of sentimentalism. One claims that the latter is as distinct from the former as is that other form of art which is called Realism. Romance has been often put upon and overburdened by being forced to bear the onus of abuse that by right should fall to sentiment; but the two should be kept very distinct; for a very high and illustrious place will be claimed for romance, while sentiment will be handed down the scullery stairs.

Many people to-day are composing mere sentimentalism, and calling it and causing it to be called romance; so with those who are too busy to think much upon these subjects, but who none the less love honest literature, Romance, too, has fallen into disrepute. Consider now the cut-and-thrust stories. They are all labeled Romances, and it is very easy to get the impression that Romance must be an affair of cloaks and daggers, or moonlight and golden hair. But this is not so at all. The true Romance is a more serious business than this. It is not merely a conjurer's trick-box full of flimsy quackeries, tinsel and claptraps, meant only to amuse, and relying upon deception to do even that. Is it not something better than this? Can we not see in it an instrument, keen, finely tempered, flawless—an instrument with which we may go straight through the clothes and tissues and wrappings of flesh down deep into the red, living heart of things?

Is all this too subtle, too merely speculative and intrinsic, too *precieuse* and nice and "literary"? Devoutly one hopes the contrary. So much is made of so-called Romanticism in present-day fiction that the subject seems worthy of discussion, and a protest against the misuse of a really noble and honest formula of literature appears to be timely—misuse, that is, in the sense of a limited use. Let us suppose for the moment that a romance can be made out of a cut-and-thrust business. Good

---

30 precieuse, affected

Heavens, are there no other things that are romantic, even in this—falsely, falsely called—humdrum world of today? Why should it be that so soon as the novelist addresses himself—seriously—to the consideration of contemporary life he must abandon Romance and take up the harsh, loveless, colourless, blunt tool called Realism?

Now, let us understand at once what is meant by Romance and what by Realism. Romance, I take it, is the kind of fiction that takes cognizance of variations
10 from the type of normal life. Realism is the kind of fiction that confines itself to the type of normal life. According to this definition, then, Romance may even treat of the sordid, the unlovely—as for instance, the novels of M. Zola. (Zola has been dubbed a Realist, but he is, on the contrary, the very head of the Romanticists.) Also, Realism, used as it sometimes is as a term of reproach, need not be in the remotest sense or degree offensive, but on the other hand respectable as a church and proper as a deacon—as, for instance, the
20 novels of Mr. Howells.

The reason why one claims so much for Romance, and quarrels so pointedly with Realism, is that Realism stultifies itself. It notes only the surface of things. For it, Beauty is not even skin deep, but only a geometrical plane, without dimensions and depth, a mere outside. Realism is very excellent so far as it goes, but it goes no further than the Realist himself can actually see, or actually hear. Realism is minute; it is the drama of a broken teacup, the tragedy of a walk down the block,
30 the excitement of an afternoon call, the adventure of an invitation to dinner. It is the visit to my neighbour's house, a formal visit, from which I may draw no conclusions. I see my neighbour and his friends—very, oh, such very! probable people—and that is all. Realism bows upon the doormat and goes away and says to me, as we link arms on the sidewalk: "That is life." And I say it is not. It is not, as you would very well see if you took Romance with you to call upon your neighbour.

Lately you have been taking Romance a weary journey
40 across the water—ages and the flood of years—and haling her into the fuzzy, musty, worm-eaten, moth-riddled, rust-corroded "Grandes Salles" of the Middle Ages and the Renaissance, and she has found the drama of a bygone age for you there. But would you take her across the street to your neighbour's front parlour (with the bisque fisher-boy on the mantel and the photograph of Niagara Falls on glass hanging in the front window);

would you introduce her there? Not you. Would you take a walk with her on Fifth Avenue, or Beacon Street, or Michigan Avenue? No, indeed. Would you choose 50 her for a companion of a morning spent in Wall Street, or an afternoon in the Waldorf-Astoria? You just guess you would not.

She would be out of place, you say—inappropriate. She might be awkward in my neighbour's front parlour, and knock over the little bisque fisher-boy. Well, she might. If she did, you might find underneath the base of the statuette, hidden away, tucked away—what? God knows. But something that would be a complete revelation of my neighbour's secretest life. 60

So you think Romance would stop in the front parlour and discuss medicated flannels and mineral waters with the ladies? Not for more than five minutes. She would be off upstairs with you, prying, peeping, peering into the closets of the bedroom, into the nursery, into the sitting-room; yes, and into that little iron box screwed to the lower shelf of the closet in the library; and into those compartments and pigeon-holes of the *secretaire* in the study. She would find a heartache (maybe) between the pillows of the mistress's bed, and a memory carefully 70 secreted in the master's deed-box. She would come upon a great hope amid the books and papers of the study-table of the young man's room, and—perhaps—who knows—an affair, or, great Heavens, an intrigue, in the scented ribbons and gloves and hairpins of the young lady's bureau. And she would pick here a little and there a little, making up a bag of hopes and fears and a package of joys and sorrows—great ones, mind you—and then come down to the front door, and, stepping out into the street, hand you the bags and 80 package and say to you—"That is Life!"

Romance does very well in the castles of the Middle Ages and the Renaissance chateaux, and she has the *entree* there and is very well received. That is all well and good. But let us protest against limiting her to such places and such times. You will find her, I grant you, in the chatelaine's chamber and the dungeon of the man-at-arms; but, if you choose to look for her, you will find her equally at home in the brownstone house on the corner and in the office-building downtown. And 90

---

14 **M. Zola**, Émile Zola. See note, p. 463 • 42 **Grandes Salles**, great rooms • 49 **Fifth . . . Avenue**, fashionable streets in New York, Boston, and Chicago, respectively

this very day, in this very hour, she is sitting among the rags and wretchedness, the dirt and despair of the tenements of the East Side of New York.

"What?" I hear you say, "look for Romance—the lady of the silken robes and golden crown, our beautiful, chaste maiden of soft voice and gentle eyes—look for her among the vicious ruffians, male and female, of Allen Street and Mulberry Bend?" I tell you she is there, and to your shame be it said you will not know her in those surroundings. You, the aristocrats, who demand the fine linen and the purple in your fiction; you, the sensitive, the delicate, who will associate with your Romance only so long as she wears a silken gown. You will not follow her to the slums, for you believe that Romance should only amuse and entertain you, singing you sweet songs and touching the harp of silver strings with rosy-tipped fingers. If haply she should call to you from the squalour of a dive, or the awful degradation of a disorderly house, crying: "Look! listen! This, too, is life. These, too, are my children! Look at them, know them and, knowing, help!" Should she call thus you would stop your ears; you would avert your eyes and you would answer, "Come from there, Romance. Your place is not there!" And you would make of her a harlequin, a tumbler, a sword-dancer, when, as a matter of fact, she should be by right divine a teacher sent from God.

She will not often wear the robe of silk, the gold crown, the jeweled shoon; will not always sweep the silver harp. An iron note is hers if so she choose, and coarse garments, and stained hands; and, meeting her thus, it is for you to know her as she passes—know her for the same young queen of the blue mantle and lilies. She can teach you if you will be humble to learn—teach you by showing. God help you if at last you take from Romance her mission of teaching; if you do not believe that she has a purpose—a nobler purpose and a mightier than mere amusement, mere entertainment. Let Realism do the entertaining with its meticulous presentation of teacups, rag carpets, wall-paper and haircloth sofas, stopping with these, going no deeper than it sees, choosing the ordinary, the untroubled, the commonplace.

But to Romance belongs the wide world for range, and the unplumbed depths of the human heart, and the mystery of sex, and the problems of life, and the black, unsearched penetralia of the soul of man. You, the indolent, must not always be amused. What matter the silken clothes, what matter the prince's houses? Romance, too, is a teacher, and if—throwing aside the purple— she wears the camel's-hair and feeds upon the locusts, it is to cry aloud unto the people, "Prepare ye the way of the Lord; make straight his path."

1902

---

3 **the East Side,** tenement district • 7 **Allen . . . Bend,** parts of New York's tenement district • 50 **Prepare . . . path,** Matthew 3:3

Theodore Dreiser

1871 · 1945

Theodore Dreiser was our first full-fledged naturalist in fiction. Although Frederic, Crane, and Norris had pioneered in the naturalistic direction, a fully developed naturalism did not appear in the American novel until Theodore Dreiser's *Sister Carrie:* for the first time in American fiction, the actions of the characters were determined entirely by "natural" causes.

The twelfth in a family of thirteen children, Dreiser was born in 1871, in Terre Haute, Indiana, where his father, a German emigrant, was proprietor of a woolen mill. The burning of the mill, which was not insured, left the family in extreme poverty. Dreiser's formal schooling was received in an Indiana high school and at Indiana University, where he stayed only one year because he felt that the curriculum "did not concern ordinary life at all." More useful than college to Dreiser were various odd jobs in Chicago—washing dishes in a restaurant, shoveling coal in a railroad yard, working in a hardware factory, collecting bills for a furniture store. Valuable also to the future novelist were his experiences as a reporter on the Chicago *Globe* and on other newspapers in St. Louis, Cleveland, Pittsburgh, and New York. His newspaper career extended until about 1905. For a while he was connected with certain "pulp" magazines, and from 1907 to 1910 he was editor of *The Delineator.* Jobs like these were necessary to pay expenses; his novels brought him little money for many years. In the meantime, he had married but did not find marriage to his liking. "It was a binding state," he said, "and I was not to be bound. I begged her to set me free, and she did." Perhaps he depicts in the story "Free" the tragedy which he felt he had escaped.

For more than twenty years, Dreiser was the center of a great controversy. His books were condemned as "immoral." *Sister Carrie,* though printed in 1900, was not released for sale in America until 1906. His second novel, *Jennie Gerhardt* (1911), like *Sister Carrie,* was objected to because it told a story of unconventional sex relationships. Dreiser did not hold up Carrie or Jennie as examples for other girls to follow, nor did he treat sex salaciously; but conventional moralists found objectionable his sympathetic attitude toward his characters and his failure to mete out the usual rewards and punishments. *The Financier* (1912) and *The Titan* (1914), which describe the unscrupulous career of Frank Cowperwood, were attacked with especial violence by Stuart P. Sherman ("The Barbaric Naturalism of Theodore Dreiser," *On Contemporary Literature,* 1918), who declared, "Dreiser has just two things to tell us about Cowperwood: that he has a rapacious appetite for money; and that he has a rapacious appetite for women." *The "Genius"* (1915), an inferior and innocuous work, was suppressed for eight years. Dreiser's champions, chief among whom was H. L. Mencken, editor of *The Smart Set,* defended him ably; but the attack continued until 1925, the year of *An American*

Theodore Dreiser, 1943—Wide World Photo

Tragedy. Although *An American Tragedy* was not radically different from its predecessors, it was an instantaneous success. No more striking evidence can be cited of the change in the intellectual and moral atmosphere of postwar America. Mencken could put up his bright sword.

It is easy to point out weaknesses in Dreiser's novels: he lacks a sense of humor; his prose is pedestrian; the piling up of detail often makes for dull reading. But his work is important, both historically and intrinsically. No other American novelist has documented his stories quite so carefully or has written a social record of American life so convincingly authentic. No other American novelist has treated his subjects so sympathetically. Human actions, to Dreiser, are largely the result of social forces from without, and of chemical forces from within. Men and women, therefore, are not too much to blame for what they are and do. There is no satire or cynicism or smartness in Dreiser, no prurient exploitation of sex, no manipulation of plot or trick of style. He recorded life as he saw it—with naturalness, candor, and compassion. Sherwood Anderson wrote in

1921: "Theodore Dreiser is a man who, with the passage of time, is bound to loom larger and larger in the awakening aesthetic consciousness of America." The prophecy is in process of fulfillment. Now that Dreiser is no longer a subject of controversy, as he was in the 1910's and 1920's, his work can be studied dispassionately. Two important books (sympathetic but dispassionate) have already shown Dreiser beginning to loom in the modern intellectual and aesthetic consciousness: R. H. Elias' *Theodore Dreiser: Apostle of* *Nature* (1949) traces the growth of Dreiser's mind; and F. O. Matthiessen's *Theodore Dreiser* (1951) gives to the major fictions, and makes them seem worthy of it, the kind of acute analysis which this critic gave in his *American Renaissance* (1941) to the fictions of Hawthorne and Melville.

Theodore Dreiser, **Dawn** (an autobiography), New York, 1931 • H. L. Mencken, **A Book of Prefaces**, New York, 1917 • Dorothy Dudley, **Forgotten Frontiers: Dreiser and the Land of the Free**, New York, 1932

The Second Choice

Although Dreiser can be best appreciated in the mass, a short story like "The Second Choice" illustrates well enough the essential characteristics of his work: prosaic, commonplace detail; a plodding style; a compassion which may easily be mistaken for sentimentality but which at its best has a genuine poignance; a natural narrative method free from trick or artifice. The last named characteristic is of special importance, for it marks Dreiser's break with the traditional short story in America. The traditional short story, as written by Poe, Bret Harte, and O. Henry, seemed meretricious to Dreiser and his followers because it sacrificed realism to artifice of plot and the surprise ending. "The Second Choice" does not properly end at all: Shirley simply "proceeded to set the table."

"The Second Choice" is taken from **Free and Other Stories**, published in 1918. But it is similar to the work which had made Dreiser an important force in American fiction since the beginning of the century.

*S*hirley Dear:

You don't want the letters. There are only six of them, anyhow, and think, they're all I have of you to cheer me on my travels. What good would they be to you—

little bits of notes telling me you're sure to meet me—but me—think of me! If I send them to you, you'll tear them up, whereas if you leave them with me I can dab them with musk and ambergris and keep them in a little silver box, always beside me.

Ah, Shirley dear, you really don't know how sweet I think you are, how dear! There isn't a thing we have ever done together that isn't as clear in my mind as this great big skyscraper over the way here in Pittsburgh, and far more pleasing. In fact, my thoughts of you are the most precious and delicious things I have, Shirley.

But I'm too young to marry now. You know that, Shirley, don't you? I haven't placed myself in any way yet, and I'm so restless that I don't know whether I ever will, really. Only yesterday, old Roxbaum—that's my new employer here—came to me and wanted to know if I would like an assistant overseership on one of his coffee plantations in Java, said there would not be much money in it for a year or two, a bare living, but later there would be more—and I jumped at it. Just the thought of Java and going there did that, although I knew I could make more staying right here. Can't you see how it is with me, Shirl? I'm too restless and too young. I couldn't take care of you right, and you wouldn't like me after a while if I didn't.

But ah, Shirley sweet, I think the dearest things of you! There isn't an hour, it seems, but some little bit of you comes back—a dear, sweet bit—the night we sat on the grass in Tregore Park and counted the stars through the trees; that first evening at Sparrows Point when we missed the last train and had to walk to Langley. Remember the tree-toads, Shirl? And then that warm April Sunday in Atholby woods! Ah, Shirl, you don't want the six notes! Let me keep them. But think of me, will you, sweet, wherever you go and whatever you do? I'll always think of you, and wish that you had met a better, saner man than me, and that I really could have married you and been all you wanted me to be. By-by, sweet. I may start for Java within the month. If so, and you would want them, I'll send you some cards from there—if they have any.

Your worthless

ARTHUR.

She sat and turned the letter in her hand, dumb with despair. It was the very last letter she would ever get from him. Of that she was certain. He was gone now, once and for all. She had written him only once, not making an open plea but asking him to return her letters, and then there had come this tender but evasive reply, saying nothing of a possible return but desiring to keep her letters for old times' sake—the happy hours they had spent together.

The happy hours! Oh, yes, yes, yes—the happy hours!

In her memory now, as she sat here in her home after the day's work, meditating on all that had been in the few short months since he had come and gone, was a world of color and light—a color and light so transfiguring as to seem celestial, but now, alas, wholly dissipated. It had contained so much of all she had desired—love, romance, amusement, laughter. He had been so gay and thoughtless, or headstrong, so youthfully romantic, and with such a love of play and change and to be saying and doing anything and everything. Arthur could dance in a gay way, whistle, sing after a fashion, play. He could play cards and do tricks, and he had such a superior air, so genial and brisk, with a kind of innate courtesy in it and yet an intolerance for slowness and stodginess or anything dull or dingy, such as characterized—But here her thoughts fled from him. She refused to think of any one but Arthur.

Sitting in her little bedroom now, off the parlor on the ground floor in her home in Bethune Street, and looking out over the Kessels' yard, and beyond that—there being no fences in Bethune Street—over the "yards" or lawns of the Pollards, Bakers, Cryders, and others, she thought of how dull it must all have seemed to him, with his fine imaginative mind and experiences, his love of change and gaiety, his atmosphere of some-thing better than she had ever known. How little she had been fitted, perhaps, by beauty or temperament to overcome this—the something—dullness in her work or her home, which possibly had driven him away. For, although many had admired her to date, and she was young and pretty in her simple way and constantly receiving suggestions that her beauty was disturbing to some, still, he had not cared for her—he had gone.

And now, as she meditated, it seemed that this scene, and all that it stood for—her parents, her work, her daily shuttling to and fro between the drug company for which she worked and this street and house—was typical of her life and what she was destined to endure always. Some girls were so much more fortunate. They had fine clothes, fine homes, a world of pleasure and op-portunity in which to move. They did not have to scrimp and save and work to pay their own way. And yet she had always been compelled to do it, but had never complained until now—or until he came, and after. Bethune Street, with its commonplace front yards and houses nearly all alike, and this house, so like the others, room for room and porch for porch, and her parents, too, really like all the others, had seemed good enough, quite satisfactory, indeed, until then. But now, now!

Here, in their kitchen, was her mother, a thin, pale, but kindly woman, peeling potatoes and washing lettuce, and putting a bit of steak or a chop or a piece of liver in a frying pan day after day, morning and evening, month after month, year after year. And next door was Mrs. Kessel doing the same thing. And next door Mrs. Cryder. And next door Mrs. Pollard. But, until now, she had not thought it so bad. But now—now—oh! And on all the porches or lawns all along this street were the husbands and fathers, mostly middle-aged or old men like her father, reading their papers or cutting the grass before dinner, or smoking and meditating afterward. Her father was out in front now, a stooped, forbearing, meditative soul, who had rarely anything to say—leaving it all to his wife, her mother, but who was fond of her in his dull, quiet way. He was a pattern-maker by trade, and had come into possession of this small, ordinary home via years of toil and saving, her mother helping him. They had no particular religion, as he often said, thinking reasonably human conduct a sufficient passport to heaven, but they had gone occasionally to the Methodist Church over in Nicholas Street, and she had once joined it. But of late she had not gone, weaned away by the other commonplace pleasures of her world.

And then in the midst of it, the dull drift of things, as she now saw them to be, he had come—Arthur Bristow—young, energetic, good-looking, ambitious, dreamful, and instanter, and with her never knowing quite how, the whole thing had been changed. He had appeared so swiftly—out of nothing, as it were.

Previous to him had been Barton Williams, stout, phlegmatic, good-natured, well-meaning, who was, or had been before Arthur came, asking her to marry him, and whom she allowed to half assume that she would. She had liked him in a feeble, albeit, as she thought, tender way, thinking him the kind, according to the logic of her neighborhood, who would make her a good husband, and, until Arthur appeared on the scene, had really intended to marry him. It was not really a love-match, as she saw now, but she thought it was, which was much the same thing, perhaps. But, as she now recalled, when Arthur came, how the scales fell from her eyes! In a trice, as it were, nearly, there was a new heaven and a new earth. Arthur had arrived, and with him a sense of something different.

Mabel Gove had asked her to come over to her house in Westleigh, the adjoining suburb, for Thanksgiving eve and day, and without a thought of anything, and because Barton was busy handling a part of the work in the despatcher's office of the Great Eastern and could not see her, she had gone. And then, to her surprise and strange, almost ineffable delight, the moment she had seen him, he was there—Arthur, with his slim, straight figure and dark hair and eyes and clean-cut features, as clean and attractive as those of a coin. And as he had looked at her and smiled and narrated humorous bits of things that had happened to him, something had come over her—a spell—and after dinner they had all gone round to Edith Barringer's to dance, and there as she had danced with him, somehow, without any seeming boldness on his part, he had taken possession of her, as it were, drawn her close, and told her she had beautiful eyes and hair and such a delicately rounded chin, and that he thought she danced gracefully and was sweet. She had nearly fainted with delight.

"Do you like me?" he had asked in one place in the dance, and, and, in spite of herself, she had looked up into his eyes, and from that moment she was almost mad over him, could think of nothing else but his hair and eyes and his smile and his graceful figure.

Mabel Gove had seen it all, in spite of her determination that no one should, and on their going to bed later, back at Mabel's home, she had whispered:

"Ah, Shirley, I saw. You like Arthur, don't you?"

"I think he's very nice," Shirley recalled replying, for Mabel knew of her affair with Barton and liked him, "but I'm not crazy over him." And for this bit of treason she had sighed in her dreams nearly all night.

And the next day, true to a request and a promise made by him, Arthur had called again at Mabel's to take her and Mabel to a "movie" which was not so far away, and from there they had gone to an ice-cream parlor, and during it all, when Mabel was not looking, he had squeezed her arm and hand and kissed her neck, and she had held her breath, and her heart had seemed to stop.

"And now you're going to let me come out to your place to see you, aren't you?" he had whispered.

And she had replied, "Wednesday evening," and then written the address on a little piece of paper and given it to him.

But now it was all gone, gone!

This house, which now looked so dreary—how romantic it had seemed that first night *he* called—the front room with its commonplace furniture, and later in the spring, the veranda, with its vines just sprouting, and the moon in May. Oh, the moon in May, and June and July, when he was here! How she had lied to Barton to make evenings for Arthur, and occasionally to Arthur to keep him from contact with Barton. She had not even mentioned Barton to Arthur because—because— well, because Arthur was so much better, and somehow (she admitted it to herself now) she had not been sure that Arthur would care for her long, if at all, and then —well, and then, to be quite frank, Barton might be good enough. She did not exactly hate him because she had found Arthur—not at all. She still liked him in a way—he was so kind and faithful, so very dull and straightforward and thoughtful of her, which Arthur was certainly not. Before Arthur had appeared, as she well remembered, Barton had seemed to be plenty good enough—in fact, all that she desired in a pleasant, companionable way, calling for her, taking her places, bringing her flowers and candy, which Arthur rarely did, and for that, if nothing more, she could not help continuing to like him and to feel sorry for him, and, besides, as she had admitted to herself before, if Arthur left her—. . . Weren't his parents better off than hers—and hadn't he a good position for such a man as he—one hundred and fifty dollars a month and the certainty of more later on? A little while before meeting Arthur, she had thought this very good, enough for two to live on at least, and 10 she had thought some of trying it at some time or other— but now—now—

And that first night he had called—how well she remembered it—how it had transfigured the parlor next this in which she was now, filling it with something it had never had before, and the porch outside, too, for that matter, with its gaunt, leafless vine, and this street, too, even—dull, commonplace Bethune Street. There had been a flurry of snow during the afternoon while she was working at the store, and the ground was white 20 with it. All the neighboring homes seemed to look sweeter and happier and more inviting than ever they had as she came past them, with their lights peeping from under curtains and drawn shades. She had hurried into hers and lighted the big red-shaded parlor lamp, her one artistic treasure, as she thought, and put it near the piano, between it and the window, and arranged the chairs, and then bustled to the task of making herself as pleasing as she might. For him she had gotten out her one best filmy house dress and done up her hair in 30 the fashion she thought most becoming—and that he had not seen before—and powdered her cheeks and nose and darkened her eyelashes, as some of the girls at the store did, and put on her new gray satin slippers, and then, being so arrayed, waited nervously, unable to eat anything or to think of anything but him.

And at last, just when she had begun to think he might not be coming, he had appeared with that arch smile and a "Hello! It's here you live, is it? I was wondering. George, but you're twice as sweet as I thought you 40 were, aren't you?" And then, in the little entryway, behind the closed door, he had held her and kissed her on the mouth a dozen times while she pretended to push against his coat and struggle and say that her parents might hear.

And, oh, the room afterward, with him in it in the red glow of the lamp, and with his pale handsome face made handsomer thereby, as she thought! He had made her sit near him and had held her hands and told her about his work and his dreams—all that he expected to do in the future—and then she had found herself wish- 50 ing intensely to share just such a life—his life—anything that he might wish to do; only, she kept wondering, with a slight pain, whether he would want her to—he was so young, dreamful, ambitious, much younger and more dreamful than herself, although, in reality, he was several years older.

And then followed that glorious period from December to this late September, in which everything which was worth happening in love had happened. Oh, those wondrous days the following spring, when, with the 60 first burst of buds and leaves, he had taken her one Sunday to Atholby, where all the great woods were, and they had hunted spring beauties in the grass, and sat on a slope and looked at the river below and watched some boys fixing up a sailboat and setting forth in it quite as she wished she and Arthur might be doing— going somewhere together—far, far away from all commonplace things and life! And then he had slipped his arm about her and kissed her cheek and neck, and tweaked her ear and smoothed her hair—and oh, there 70 on the grass, with the spring flowers about her and a canopy of small green leaves above, the perfection of love had come—love so wonderful that the mere thought of it made her eyes brim now! And then had been days, Saturday afternoons and Sundays, at Atholby and Sparrows Point, where the great beach was, and in lovely Tregore Park, a mile or two from her home, where they could go of an evening and sit in or near the pavilion and have ice-cream and dance or watch the dancers. Oh, the stars, the winds, the summer breath of those days! 80 Ah, me! Ah, me!

Naturally, her parents had wondered from the first about her and Arthur, and her and Barton, since Barton had already assumed a proprietary interest in her and she had seemed to like him. But then she was an only child and a pet, and used to presuming on that, and they could not think of saying anything to her. After all, she was young and pretty and was entitled to change her

---

4 her— . . . The dots throughout the selection are Dreiser's and do not indicate an omission

mind; only, only—she had had to indulge in a career of lying and subterfuge in connection with Barton, since Arthur was headstrong and wanted every evening that he chose—to call for her at the store and keep her downtown to dinner and a show.

Arthur had never been like Barton, shy, phlegmatic, obedient, waiting long and patiently for each little favor, but, instead, masterful and eager, rifling her of kisses and caresses and every delight of love, and teasing and playing with her as a cat would a mouse. She could never resist him. He demanded of her her time and her affection without let or hindrance. He was not exactly selfish or cruel, as some might have been, but gay and unthinking at times, unconsciously so, and yet loving and tender at others—nearly always so. But always he would talk of things in the future as if they really did not include her—and this troubled her greatly—of places he might go, things he might do, which, somehow, he seemed to think or assume that she could not or would not do with him. He was always going to Australia sometime, he thought, in a business way, or to South Africa, or possibly to India. He never seemed to have any fixed clear future for himself in mind.

A dreadful sense of helplessness and of impending disaster came over her at these times, of being involved in some predicament over which she had no control, and which would lead her on to some sad end. Arthur, although plainly in love, as she thought, and apparently delighted with her, might not always love her. She began, timidly at first (and always, for that matter), to ask him pretty, seeking questions about himself and her, whether their future was certain to be together, whether he really wanted her—loved her—whether he might not want to marry some one else or just her, and whether she wouldn't look nice in a pearl satin wedding-dress with a long creamy veil and satin slippers and a bouquet of bridalwreath. She had been so slowly but surely saving to that end, even before he came, in connection with Barton; only, after *he* came, all thought of the import of it had been transferred to him. But now, also, she was beginning to ask herself sadly, "Would it ever be?" He was so airy, so inconsequential, so ready to say: "Yes, yes," and "Sure, sure! That's right! Yes, indeedy; you bet! Say, kiddie, but you'll look sweet!" but, somehow, it had always seemed as if this whole thing were a glorious interlude and that it could not

last. Arthur was too gay and ethereal and too little settled in his own mind. His ideas of travel and living in different cities, finally winding up in New York or San Francisco, but never with her exactly until she asked him, were too ominous, although he always reassured her gaily: "Of course! Of course!" But somehow she could never believe it really, and it made her intensely sad at times, horribly gloomy. So often she wanted to cry, and she could scarcely tell why.

And then, because of her affection for him, she had finally quarreled with Barton, or nearly that, if one could say that one ever really quarreled with him. It had been because of a certain Thursday evening a few weeks before about which she had disappointed him. In a fit of generosity, knowing that Arthur was coming Wednesday, and because Barton had stopped in at the store to see her, she had told him that he might come, having regretted it afterward, so enamored was she of Arthur. And then when Wednesday came, Arthur had changed his mind, telling her he would come Friday instead, but on Thursday evening he had stopped in at the store and asked her to go to Sparrows Point, with the result that she had no time to notify Barton. He had gone to the house and sat with her parents until ten-thirty, and then, a few days later, although she had written him offering an excuse, had called at the store to complain slightly.

"Do you think you did just right, Shirley? You might have sent word, mightn't you? Who was it—the new fellow you won't tell me about?"

Shirley flared on the instant.

"Supposing it was? What's it to you? I don't belong to you yet, do I? I told you there wasn't any one, and I wish you'd let me alone about that. I couldn't help it last Thursday—that's all—and I don't want you to be fussing with me—that's all. If you don't want to, you needn't come any more, anyhow."

"Don't say that, Shirley," pleaded Barton. "You don't mean that. I won't bother you, though, if you don't want me any more."

And because Shirley sulked, not knowing what else to do, he had gone and she had not seen him since.

And then sometime later when she had thus broken with Barton, avoiding the railway station where he worked, Arthur had failed to come at his appointed time, sending no word until the next day, when a note came to the store saying that he had been out of town for his firm over Sunday and had not been able to notify her, but that he would call Tuesday. It was an awful blow. At the time, Shirley had a vision of what was to follow. It seemed for the moment as if the whole world had suddenly been reduced to ashes, that there was nothing but black charred cinders anywhere—she felt that about all life. Yet it all came to her clearly then that this was but the beginning of just such days and just such excuses, and that soon, soon, he would come no more. He was beginning to be tired of her and soon he would not even make excuses. She felt it, and it froze and terrified her.

And then, soon after, the indifference which she feared did follow—almost created by her own thoughts, as it were. First, it was a meeting he had to attend somewhere one Wednesday night when he was to have come for her. Then he was going out of town again, over Sunday. Then he was going away for a whole week —it was absolutely unavoidable, he said, his commercial duties were increasing—and once he had casually remarked that nothing could stand in the way where she was concerned—never! She did not think of reproaching him with this; she was too proud. If he was going, he must go. She would not be willing to say to herself that she had ever attempted to hold any man. But, just the same, she was agonized by the thought. When he was with her, he seemed tender enough; only, at times, his eyes wandered and he seemed slightly bored. Other girls, particularly pretty ones, seemed to interest him as much as she did.

And the agony of the long days when he did not come any more for a week or two at a time! The waiting, the brooding, the wondering, at the store and here in her home—in the former place making mistakes at times because she could not get her mind off him and being reminded of them, and here at her own home at nights, being so absent-minded that her parents remarked on it. She felt sure that her parents must be noticing that Arthur was not coming any more, or as much as he had— for she pretended to be going out with him, going to Mabel Gove's instead—and that Barton had deserted her too, he having been driven off by her indifference, never to come any more, perhaps, unless she sought him out.

And then it was that the thought of saving her own face by taking up with Barton once more occurred to her, of using him and his affections and faithfulness and dullness, if you will, to cover up her own dilemma. Only, this ruse was not to be tried until she had written Arthur this one letter—a pretext merely to see if there was a single ray of hope, a letter to be written in a gentle-enough way and asking for the return of the few notes she had written him. She had not seen him now in nearly a month, and the last time she had, he had said he might soon be compelled to leave her awhile—to go to Pittsburgh to work. And it was his reply to this that she now held in her hand—from Pittsburgh! It was frightful! The future without him!

But Barton would never know really what had transpired, if she went back to him. In spite of all her delicious hours with Arthur, she could call him back, she felt sure. She had never really entirely dropped him, and he knew it. He had bored her dreadfully on occasion, arriving on off days when Arthur was not about, with flowers or candy, or both, and sitting on the porch steps and talking of the railroad business and of the whereabouts and doings of some of their old friends. It was shameful, she had thought at times, to see a man so patient, so hopeful, so good-natured as Barton, deceived in this way, and by her, who was so miserable over another. Her parents must see and know, she had thought at these times, but still, what else was she to do?

"I'm a bad girl," she kept telling herself. "I'm all wrong. What right have I to offer Barton what is left?" But still, somehow, she realized that Barton, if she chose to favor him, would only be too grateful for even the leavings of others where she was concerned, and that even yet, if she but deigned to crook a finger, she could have him. He was so simple, so good-natured, so stolid and matter of fact, so different to Arthur whom (she could not help smiling at the thought of it) she was loving now about as Barton loved her—slavishly, hopelessly.

And then, as the days passed and Arthur did not write any more—just this one brief note—she at first grieved horribly, and then in a fit of numb despair attempted, bravely enough from one point of view, to adjust herself to the new situation. Why should she despair? Why die of agony where there were plenty who would still sigh for her—Barton among others? She was young, pretty, very—many told her so. She could, if she chose, achieve a vivacity which she did not feel. Why should she brook this unkindness without a thought of retaliation? Why shouldn't she enter upon a gay and heartless career, indulging in a dozen flirtations at once—dancing and killing all thoughts of Arthur in a round of frivolities? There were many who beckoned to her. She stood at her counter in the drug store on many a day and brooded over this, but at the thought of which one to begin with, she faltered. After her late love, all were so tame, for the present anyhow.

And then—and then—always there was Barton, the humble or faithful, to whom she had been so unkind and whom she had used and whom she still really liked. So often self-reproaching thoughts in connection with him crept over her. He must have known, must have seen how badly she was using him all this while, and yet he had not failed to come and come, until she had actually quarreled with him, and any one would have seen that it was literally hopeless. She could not help remembering, especially now in her pain, that he adored her. He was not calling on her now at all—by her indifference she had finally driven him away—but a word, a word—she waited for days, weeks, hoping against hope, and then—

The office of Barton's superior in the Great Eastern terminal had always made him an easy object for her blandishments, coming and going, as she frequently did, via this very station. He was in the office of the assistant train-despatcher on the ground floor, where passing to and from the local, which, at times, was quicker than a street-car, she could easily see him by peering in; only, she had carefully avoided him for nearly a year. If she chose now, and would call for a message blank at the adjacent telegraph-window which was a part of his room, and raised her voice as she often had in the past, he could scarcely fail to hear, if he did not see her. And if he did, he would rise and come over—of that she was sure, for he never could resist her. It had been a wile of hers in the old days to do this or to make her presence felt by idling outside. After a month of brooding, she felt that she must act—her position as a deserted girl was too much. She could not stand it any longer really—the eyes of her mother, for one.

It was six-fifteen one evening when, coming out of the store in which she worked, she turned her step disconsolately homeward. Her heart was heavy, her face rather pale and drawn. She had stopped in the store's retiring-room before coming out to add to her charms as much as possible by a little powder and rouge and to smooth her hair. It would not take much to reallure her former sweetheart, she felt sure—and yet it might not be so easy after all. Suppose he had found another? But she could not believe that. It had scarcely been long enough since he had last attempted to see her, and he was really so very, very fond of her and so faithful. He was too slow and certain in his choosing—he had been so with her. Still, who knows? With this thought, she went forward in the evening, feeling for the first time the shame and pain that comes of deception, the agony of having to relinquish an ideal and the feeling of despair that comes to those who find themselves in the position of suppliants, stooping to something which in better days and better fortune they would not know. Arthur was the cause of this.

When she reached the station, the crowd that usually filled it at this hour was swarming. There were so many pairs like Arthur and herself laughing and hurrying away or so she felt. First glancing in the small mirror of a weighing scale to see if she were still of her former charm, she stopped thoughtfully at a little flower stand which stood outside, and for a few pennies purchased a tiny bunch of violets. She then went inside and stood near the window, peering first furtively to see if he were present. He was. Bent over his work, a green shade over his eyes, she could see his solid genial figure at a table. Stepping back a moment to ponder, she finally went forward and, in a clear voice asked,

"May I have a blank, please?"

The infatuation of the discarded Barton was such that it brought him instantly to his feet. In his stodgy, stocky way he rose, his eyes glowing with a friendly hope, his mouth wreathed in smiles, and came over. At the sight of her, pale, but pretty—paler and prettier, really, than he had ever seen her—he thrilled dumbly.

"How are you, Shirley?" he asked sweetly, as he drew near, his eyes searching her face hopefully. He had not seen her for so long that he was intensely hungry, and her paler beauty appealed to him more than ever. Why wouldn't she have him? he was asking himself. Why wouldn't his persistent love yet win her? Perhaps it might. "I haven't seen you in a month of Sundays, it seems. How are the folks?"

"They're all right, Bart," she smiled archly, "and so am I. How have you been? It has been a long time since I've seen you. I've been wondering how you were. Have you been all right? I was just going to send a message."

As he had approached, Shirley had pretended at first not to see him, a moment later to affect surprise, although she was really suppressing a heavy sigh. The sight of him, after Arthur, was not reassuring. Could she really interest herself in him any more? Could she?

"Sure, sure," he replied genially; "I'm always all right. You couldn't kill me, you know. Not going away, are you, Shirl?" he queried interestedly.

"No; I'm just telegraphing to Mabel. She promised to meet me to-morrow, and I want to be sure she will."

"You don't come past here as often as you did, Shirley," he complained tenderly. "At least, I don't seem to see you so often," he added with a smile. "It isn't anything I have done, is it?" he queried, and then, when she protested quickly, added: "What's the trouble, Shirl? Haven't been sick, have you?"

She affected all her old gaiety and ease, feeling as though she would like to cry.

"Oh, no," she returned; "I've been all right. I've been going through the other door, I suppose, or coming in and going out on the Langdon Avenue car." (This was true, because she had been wanting to avoid him.) "I've been in such a hurry, most nights, that I haven't had time to stop, Bart. You know how late the store keeps us at times."

He remembered, too, that in the old days she had made time to stop or meet him occasionally.

"Yes, I know," he said tactfully. "But you haven't been to any of our old card-parties either of late, have you? At least, I haven't seen you. I've gone to two or three, thinking you might be there."

That was another thing Arthur had done—broken up her interest in these old store and neighborhood parties and a banjo-and-mandolin club to which she had once belonged. They had all seemed so pleasing and amusing in the old days—but now. . . In those days Bart had been her usual companion when his work permitted.

"No," she replied evasively, but with a forced air of pleasant remembrance; "I have often thought of how

much fun we had at those, though. It was a shame to drop them. You haven't seen Harry Stull or Trina Trask recently, have you?" she inquired, more to be saying something than for any interest she felt.

He shook his head negatively, then added:

"Yes, I did, too; here in the waiting-room a few nights ago. They were coming down-town to a theater, I suppose."

His face fell slightly as he recalled how it had been their custom to do this, and what their one quarrel had been about. Shirley noticed it. She felt the least bit sorry for him, but much more for herself, coming back so disconsolately to all this.

"Well, you're looking as pretty as ever, Shirley," he continued, noting that she had not written the telegram and that there was something wistful in her glance. "Prettier, I think," and she smiled sadly. Every word that she tolerated from him was as so much gold to him, so much of dead ashes to her. "You wouldn't like to come down some evening this week and see 'The Mouse-Trap,' would you? We haven't been to a theater together in I don't know when." His eyes sought hers in a hopeful, doglike way.

So—she could have him again—that was the pity of it! To have what she really did not want, did not care for! At the least nod now he would come, and this very devotion made it all but worthless, and so sad. She ought to marry him now for certain, if she began in this way, and could in a month's time if she chose, but oh, oh—could she? For the moment she decided that she could not, would not. If he had only repulsed her—told her to go—ignored her—but no; it was her fate to be loved by him in this moving, pleading way, and hers not to love him as she wished to love—to be loved. Plainly, he needed some one like her, whereas she, she—She turned a little sick, a sense of the sacrilege of gaiety at this time creeping into her voice, and exclaimed:

"No, no!" Then seeing his face change, a heavy sadness come over it, "Not this week, anyhow, I mean" ("Not so soon," she had almost said). "I have several engagements this week and I'm not feeling well. But"—seeing his face change, and the thought of her own state returning—"you might come out to the house some evening instead, and then we can go some other time." His face brightened intensely. It was wonderful how he longed to be with her, how the least favor from her comforted and lifted him up. She could see also now, however, how little it meant to her, how little it could ever mean, even if to him it was heaven. The old relationship would have to be resumed in toto, once and for all, but did she want it that way now that she was feeling so miserable about this other affair? As she meditated, these various moods racing to and fro in her mind, Barton seemed to notice, and now it occurred to him that perhaps he had not pursued her enough—was too easily put off. She probably did like him yet. This evening, her present visit, seemed to prove it.

"Sure, sure!" he agreed. "I'd like that. I'll come out Sunday, if you say. We can go any time to the play. I'm sorry, Shirley, if you're not feeling well. I've thought of you a lot these days. I'll come out Wednesday, if you don't mind."

She smiled a wan smile. It was all so much easier than she had expected—her triumph—and so ashenlike in consequence, a flavor of dead-sea fruit and defeat about it all, that it was pathetic. How could she, after Arthur? How could he, really?

"Make it Sunday," she pleaded, naming the farthest day off, and then hurried out.

Her faithful lover gazed after her, while she suffered an intense nausea. To think—to think—it should all be coming to this! She had not used her telegraph-blank, and now had forgotten all about it. It was not the simple trickery that discouraged her, but her own future which could find no better outlet than this, could not rise above it apparently, or that she had no heart to make it rise above it. Why couldn't she interest herself in some one different to Barton? Why did she have to return to him? Why not wait and meet some other— ignore him as before? But no, no; nothing mattered now —no one—it might as well be Barton as any one, and she would at least make him happy and at the same time solve her own problem. She went out into the train-shed and climbed into her train. Slowly, after the usual pushing and jostling of a crowd, it drew out toward Latonia, that suburban region in which her home lay. As she rode, she thought.

"What have I just done? What am I doing?" she kept asking herself as the clacking wheels on the rails fell into a rhythmic dance and the houses of the brown, dry, endless city fled past in a maze. "Severing myself decisively from the past—the happy past—for suppos-

ing, once I am married, Arthur should return and want me again—suppose! Suppose!"

Below at one place, under a shed, were some market-gardeners disposing of the last remnants of their day's wares—a sickly, dull life, she thought. Here was Rutgers Avenue, with its line of red street-cars, many wagons and tracks and counter-streams of automobiles—how often had she passed it morning and evening in a shuttle-like way, and how often would, unless she got married! And here, now, was the river flowing smoothly between its banks lined with coal-pockets and wharves— away, away to the huge deep sea which she and Arthur had enjoyed so much. Oh, to be in a small boat and drift out, out into the endless, restless, pathless deep! Somehow the sight of this water, to-night and every night, brought back those evenings in the open with Arthur at Sparrows Point, the long line of dancers in Eckert's Pavilion, the woods at Atholby, the park, with the dancers in the pavilion—she choked back a sob. Once Arthur had come this way with her on just such an evening as this, pressing her hand and saying how wonderful she was. Oh, Arthur! Arthur! And now Barton was to take his old place again—forever, no doubt. She could not trifle with her life longer in this foolish way, or his. What was the use? But think of it!

Yes, it must be—forever now, she told herself. She must marry. Time would be slipping by and she would become too old. It was her only future—marriage. It was the only future she had ever contemplated really, a home, children, the love of some man whom she could love as she loved Arthur. Ah, what a happy home that would have been for her! But now, now—

But there must be no turning back now, either. There was no other way. If Arthur ever came back—but fear not, he wouldn't! She had risked so much and lost—lost him. Her little venture into true love had been such a failure. Before Arthur had come all had been well enough. Barton, stout and simple and frank and direct, had in some way—how, she could scarcely realize now— offered sufficient of a future. But now, now! He had enough money, she knew, to build a cottage for the two of them. He had told her so. He would do his best always to make her happy, she was sure of that. They could live in about the state her parents were living in— or a little better, not much—and would never want. No doubt there would be children, because he craved them

—several of them—and that would take up her time, long years of it—the sad, gray years! But then Arthur, whose children she would have thrilled to bear, would be no more, a mere memory—think of that!—and Barton, the dull, the commonplace, would have achieved his finest dream—and why?

Because love was a failure for her—that was why—and in her life there could be no more true love. She would never love any one again as she had Arthur. It could not be, she was sure of it. He was too fascinating, too wonderful. Always, always, wherever she might be, whoever she might marry, he would be coming back, intruding between her and any possible love, receiving any possible kiss. It would be Arthur she would be loving or kissing. She dabbed at her eyes with a tiny handkerchief, turned her face close to the window and stared out, and then as the environs of Latonia came into view, wondered (so deep is romance): What if Arthur should come back at some time—or now! Supposing he should be here at the station now, accidentally or on purpose, to welcome her, to soothe her weary heart. He had met her here before. How she would fly to him, lay her head on his shoulder, forget forever that Barton ever was, that they had ever separated for an hour. Oh, Arthur! Arthur!

But no, no; here was Latonia—here the viaduct over her train, the long business street and the cars marked "Center" and "Langdon Avenue" running back into the great city. A few blocks away in tree-shaded Bethune Street, duller and plainer than ever, was her parents' cottage and the routine of that old life which was now, she felt, more fully fastened upon her than ever before—the lawn-mowers, the lawns, the front porches all alike. Now would come the going to and fro of Barton to business as her father and she now went to business, her keeping house, cooking, washing, ironing, sewing for Barton as her mother now did these things for her father and herself. And she would not be in love really, as she wanted to be. Oh, dreadful! She could never escape it really, now that she could endure it less, scarcely for another hour. And yet she must, must, for the sake of—for the sake of—she closed her eyes and dreamed.

She walked up the street under the trees, past the houses and lawns all alike to her own, and found her father on their veranda reading the evening paper. She sighed at the sight.

"Back, daughter?" he called pleasantly.

"Yes."

"Your mother is wondering if you would like steak or liver for dinner. Better tell her."

"Oh, it doesn't matter."

She hurried into her bedroom, threw down her hat and gloves, and herself on the bed to rest silently, and groaned in her soul. To think that it had all come to this!—Never to see him any more!—To see only Barton, and marry him and live in such a street, have four or five children, forget all her youthful companionships—and all to save her face before her parents, and her future. Why must it be? Should it be, really? She choked and stifled. After a little time her mother, hearing her come in, came to the door—thin, practical, affectionate, conventional.

"What's wrong, honey? Aren't you feeling well to-night? Have you a headache? Let me feel."

Her thin cool fingers crept over her temples and hair. She suggested something to eat or a headache powder right away.

"I'm all right, mother. I'm just not feeling well now. Don't bother. I'll get up soon. Please don't."

"Would you rather have liver or steak to-night, dear?"

"Oh, anything—nothing—please don't bother—steak will do—anything"—if only she could get rid of her and be at rest.

Her mother looked at her and shook her head sympathetically, then retreated quietly, saying no more. Lying so, she thought and thought—grinding, destroying thoughts about the beauty of the past, the darkness of the future—until able to endure them no longer she got up and, looking distractedly out of the window into the yard and the house next door, stared at her future fixedly. What should she do? What should she really do? There was Mrs. Kessel in her kitchen getting her dinner as usual, just as her own mother was now, and Mr. Kessel out on the front porch in his shirt-sleeves reading the evening paper. Beyond was Mr. Pollard in his yard, cutting the grass. All along Bethune Street were such houses and such people—simple, commonplace souls all—clerks, managers, fairly successful craftsmen, like her father and Barton, excellent in their way but not like Arthur the beloved, the lost—and here was she, perforce, or by decision of necessity, soon to be one of them, in some such street as this no doubt, forever and—. For the moment it choked and stifled her.

The Second Choice 655

She decided that she would not. No, no, no! There must be some other way—many ways. She did not have to do this unless she really wished to—would not—only—. Then going to the mirror she looked at her face and smoothed her hair.

"But what's the use?" she asked of herself wearily and resignedly after a time. "Why should I cry? Why shouldn't I marry Barton? I don't amount to anything, anyhow. Arthur wouldn't have me. I wanted him, and I am compelled to take some one else—or no one—what difference does it really make who? My dreams are too high, that's all. I wanted Arthur, and he wouldn't have me. I don't want Barton, and he crawls at my feet. I'm a failure, that's what's the matter with me."

And then, turning up her sleeves and removing a fichu which stood out too prominently from her breast, she went into the kitchen and, looking about for an apron, observed:

"Can't I help? Where's the tablecloth?" and finding it among napkins and silverware in a drawer in the adjoining room, proceeded to set the table.

1918

POETS "IN TIME OF HESITATION":

Hayne   Lanier

Sill   Dickinson   Crane   Moody

Paul Hamilton Hayne

1830 · 1886

A native of Charleston, and the nephew of Robert Y. Hayne, to whom Webster made his famous reply in the year of the poet's birth, Paul Hamilton Hayne was educated at the Coates School, where his lifelong friendship with Henry Timrod began, and at the College of Charleston. He was a member of the Charleston literary group, presided over by William Gilmore Simms, which founded *Russell's Magazine* in 1857, and during its short life of four years Hayne was the editor of that notable literary journal. His house and library were destroyed when Sherman took Charleston in 1865. After the war, he lived at "Copse Hill" in the pine barrens near Augusta, Georgia, where he managed to support himself and his wife by his writing.

Hayne's best poems describe emotionally and pictorially the aspects of nature which he knew most intimately—the mocking bird, for example, and the pine forest. His effects are vivid and delicate, though even his happiest work is marred by trite phrasing ("sylvan scene," "stately queen") and there is no great power of thought. While his poems of protest to the North, written during reconstruction, show that he was capable of impassioned feeling and utterance, he lacked Timrod's iron strength as well as Timrod's control, metrical skill, and classical purity. Hayne is worthy of study, never-theless, as a minor poet whose work is representative of much of the romantic verse of the Old South.

The Complete Poems of Hayne, Boston, 1882 • Edwin Mims, "Paul Hamilton Hayne," Library of Southern Literature, New Orleans, 1909, V • A Collection of Hayne Letters, ed. D. M. McKeithan, Austin, Texas, 1944

Aspects of the Pines

Tall, sombre, grim, against the morning sky
   They rise, scarce touched by melancholy airs,
Which stir the fadeless foliage dreamfully,
   As if from realms of mystical despairs.

Tall, sombre, grim, they stand with dusky gleams
   Brightening to gold within the woodland's core,
Beneath the gracious noontide's tranquil beams—
   But the weird winds of morning sigh no more.

A stillness, strange, divine, ineffable,
   Broods round and o'er them in the wind's surcease, 10
And on each tinted copse and shimmering dell
   Rests the mute rapture of deep-hearted peace.

Last, sunset comes—the solemn joy and might
   Borne from the West when cloudless day declines—
Low, flutelike breezes sweep the waves of light,
   And lifting dark green tresses of the pines,

Till every lock is luminous—gently float,
   Fraught with hale odors up the heavens afar
To faint when twilight on her virginal throat
   Wears for a gem the tremulous vesper star. 20

1875

"Copse Hill," home of Paul Hamilton Hayne — from Poems of Paul Hamilton Hayne, 1882

The Mocking-Bird

A golden pallor of voluptuous light
Filled the warm southern night:
The moon, clear orbed, above the sylvan scene
Moved like a stately queen,
So rife with conscious beauty all the while,
What could she do but smile
At her own perfect loveliness below,
Glassed in the tranquil flow
Of crystal fountains and unruffled streams?
Half lost in waking dreams, 10
As down the loneliest forest dell I strayed,
Lo! from a neighboring glade,
Flashed through the drifts of moonshine, swiftly came

A fairy shape of flame.
It rose in dazzling spirals overhead,
Whence to wild sweetness wed,
Poured marvellous melodies, silvery trill on trill;
The very leaves grew still
On the charmed trees to hearken; while for me,
Heart-trilled to ecstasy,   20
I followed—followed the bright shape that flew,
Still circling up the blue,
Till as a fountain that has reached its height,
Falls back in sprays of light
Slowly dissolved, so that enrapturing lay,
Divinely melts away
Through tremulous spaces to a music-mist,
Soon by the fitful breeze
　　How gently kissed
Into remote and tender silences.   30

1882

Poverty

Once I beheld thee, a lithe mountain maid,
Embrowned by wholesome toils in lusty air;
Whose clear blood, nurtured by strong, primitive cheer,
Through Amazonian veins, flowed unafraid.
Broad-breasted, pearly-teethed, thy pure breath strayed,
Sweet as deep-uddered kine's curled in the rare
Bright spaces of thy lofty atmosphere,
O'er some rude cottage in a fir-grown glade.
Now, of each brave ideal virtue stripped,
O Poverty! I behold thee as thou art,   10
A ruthless hag, the image of woeful dearth
Or brute despair, gnawing its own starved heart.
Thou ravening wretch! fierce-eyed and monster-lipped,
Why scourge forevermore God's beauteous earth?

1882

Sidney Lanier

1842 · 1881

Sidney Lanier was a Southerner, but he did not belong to the planter aristocracy, nor was he in sympathy with their feudal ideals. His background was urban and professional: his father was a lawyer, and the boy grew up in the little city of Macon, Georgia. When the Civil War broke out shortly after his graduation from Oglethorpe College, he enlisted as a Confederate soldier, and he served faithfully for the war's duration, spending the last five months in a federal prison. But in the novel based upon his war experiences (*Tiger Lilies,* 1867), there is no glorification of war as such, nor idealization of the "lost cause," nor nostalgia for the Southern order destroyed by the war. According to one of the characters in the story, the war was "a rich man's war and a poor man's fight."

Lanier wanted ardently to be a musician and a poet. And since there was little opportunity for the cultivation of music and poetry in the South during the reconstruction years, he sought a more favorable environment, and found it in Baltimore. In that half-Northern, half-Southern city, in the 1870's, he played the flute with professional skill in the Peabody Symphony Orchestra. His studies at this time of Old and Middle English and of the Elizabethan period resulted in a series of lectures at Peabody Institute and in an appointment, in 1879, as lecturer on English literature at Johns Hopkins University. Before he was quite forty, death of tuberculosis cut short a career of promise.

In addition to *Tiger Lilies,* his prose works include *The English Novel, Shakspere and His Forerunners,* and *The Science of English Verse.* In *The English Novel* he prudishly condemns the eighteenth-century English novel as "unsavory muck," and finds the perfect flower of the novel's development in the work of George Eliot. In *Shakspere and His Forerunners* he shows a surprising range of reading (in view of his limited opportunities) in English poetry, including Anglo-Saxon poetry, and is especially attracted to the Elizabethan sonnets. His most significant prose work is *The Science of English Verse,* which is an original and ingenious, though unconvincing, treatment of verse in terms of music. Verse he regards as "in all respects a phenomenon of sound"; "the main distinction between music and verse is . . . the difference between the scale of tones used in music and the scale of tones used by the human speaking-voice." His method of scansion, which employs the musical system of notation, makes a metronome an almost indispensable part of one's equipment.

Ardent and excitable, Lanier wrote poetry which suffers from the lack of emotional and intellectual control. His eagerness to embrace all that seemed to him beautiful and noble and his attempt to deal with the problems of modern life resulted in poetry that is frequently confused and febrile, despite the sincerity of its moral idealism. Moreover, his metaphors are often unsuccessful. In "My Springs" his wife's eyes are "two dove-cotes of gray doves"—which is too unnatural. In "Sunrise" the sun is "the great Sun-Bee," that flashes from its "hive-hole"—which is belittling. In "Corn" the abandoned Georgia hill is "gashed and hairy Lear" —which is too tragic. Perhaps Lanier read too indiscriminately and too susceptibly in the conceitful English sonnets of the 1590's.

That he was capable of writing with clearly focused objectivity, however, is shown in his narrative poems (notably, "The Revenge of Hamish") and in brief passages in the philosophical poems. One is grateful for many true objective renderings of Southern landscape, even though the objectivity may be only briefly sustained: "the zigzag-cornered fence" and the intrenched sassafras of "Corn"; the marsh-grass, "waist-high, broad in the blade" of "The Marshes of Glynn." Lanier is worthy of praise also for his experiments with musical effects in verse. "The Symphony" contains some extraordinary descriptions of the sounds of individual instruments: the flute, the violin, "the melting clarinet," "the bold straightforward horn." Equally remarkable is his attempt at "symphonic" structure. The problem must be referred to the musical experts; it has never been dealt with adequately by Lanier's critics, who, unfortunately, have not been musicologists. But it may be said here, simply, that "The Marshes of Glynn," for example, appears to be constructed after the manner of a symphony, and should be read as a sequence of symphonic movements, the first of which is the magnificently sustained opening of twenty lines.

Lanier's reputation as a poet does not stand nearly so high today as it did at the turn of the century. Hard-boiled critics have resented his prudishness and sentimentality. Logical critics have objected to both the unsoundness of his metaphors and the vagueness and confusion in his thought (a vagueness and confusion, it may be added, which can be found in generous measure in the Victorian poets of England). An influential school of Southern regionalists (see John Crowe Ransom, "Hearts and Heads," *The American Review,* March 1934) has condemned Lanier for the very qualities which had recommended him to progressive Southerners in 1900, namely, in Professor Edwin Mims' phrase, "the cosmopolitanism and modernness of his mind." But after whatever deductions, one may still find much in Lanier to admire. His high devotion to music and poetry was admirable. He has many lines which are felicitous and true. And the musical aspects of his verse are yet to be properly appreciated.

Poems of Sidney Lanier, ed. Mary Day Lanier, New York, 1884 • **Centennial Edition of the Writings of Sidney Lanier,** 10 vols., ed. C. R. Anderson and others, Baltimore, 1946 • Edwin Mims, **Sidney Lanier,** Boston, 1905 • A. H. Starke, **Sidney Lanier,** Chapel Hill, 1933 • S. T. Williams, "Lanier," **American Writers on American Literature,** ed. John Macy, New York, 1931

Corn

In sending the manuscript of "Corn" to a friend for criticism, Lanier wrote as follows: "I inclose the manuscript of a poem in which I have endeavored to carry some very prosaic matters up to a loftier plane. I have been struck with alarm in seeing the number of old, deserted home-steads and gullied hills in the older counties of Georgia; and though they are dreadfully commonplace, I have thought they are surely mournful enough to be poetic." For further evidence of Lanier's constructive interest in Southern agricultural problems, the student should read his essay "The New South," published in 1880.

After having been rejected by William Dean Howells, editor of the Atlantic Monthly, "Corn" was accepted by Lippincott's Magazine, in Philadelphia, and appeared in the February 1875 number. It was Lanier's first poem to win wide recognition.

Today the woods are trembling through and through
With shimmering forms, that flash before my view,
Then melt in green as dawn-stars melt in blue.
   The leaves that wave against my cheek caress
   Like women's hands; the embracing boughs express
   A subtlety of mighty tenderness;
   The copse-depths into little noises start,
   That sound anon like beatings of a heart,
   Anon like talk 'twixt lips not far apart.
   The beech dreams balm, as a dreamer hums a song; 10
   Through that vague wafture, expirations strong
   Throb from young hickories breathing deep and long
With stress and urgence bold of prisoned spring
     And ecstasy of burgeoning.
   Now, since the dew-plashed road of morn is dry,
   Forth venture odors of more quality
   And heavenlier giving. Like Jove's locks awry,
     Long muscadines
Rich-wreathe the spacious foreheads of great pines,
And breathe ambrosial passion from their vines. 20
   I pray with mosses, ferns and flowers shy
   That hide like gentle nuns from human eye
   To lift adoring perfumes to the sky.

I hear faint bridal-sighs of brown and green
Dying to silent hints of kisses keen
As far lights fringe into a pleasant sheen.
   I start at fragmentary whispers, blown
   From undertalks of leafy souls unknown,
   Vague purports sweet, of inarticulate tone.

Dreaming of gods, men, nuns, and brides, between 30
Old companies of oaks that inward lean
To join their radiant amplitudes of green
   I slowly move, with ranging looks that pass
   Up from the matted miracles of grass
Into yon veined complex of space,
Where sky and leafage interlace
   So close, the heaven of blue is seen
   Inwoven with a heaven of green.

I wander to the zigzag-cornered fence
Where sassafras, intrenched in brambles dense, 40
Contests with solid vehemence
   The march of culture, setting limb and thorn
   As pikes against the army of the corn.

There, while I pause, my fieldward-faring eyes
Take harvests, where the stately corn-ranks rise,
   Of inward dignities
And large benignities and insights wise,
   Graces and modest majesties.
Thus, without theft, I reap another's field;
Thus, without tilth, I house a wondrous yield, 50
And heap my heart with quintuple crops concealed.

Look, out of line one tall corn-captain stands
Advanced beyond the foremost of his bands,
   And waves his blades upon the very edge
   And hottest thicket of the battling hedge.
Thou lustrous stalk, that ne'er mayst walk nor talk,
   Still shalt thou type the poet-soul sublime
   That leads the vanward of his timid time
   And sings up cowards with commanding rhyme—
Soul calm, like thee, yet fain, like thee, to grow 60
By double increment, above, below;
   Soul homely, as thou art, yet rich in grace like thee,

---

50 tilth, act of tilling or cultivating the soil

Teaching the yeomen selfless chivalry
That moves in gentle curves of courtesy;
Soul filled like thy long veins with sweetness tense,
    By every godlike sense
Transmuted from the four wild elements.
    Drawn to high plans,
Thou lift'st more stature than a mortal man's,
Yet ever piercest downward in the mold   70
    And keepest hold
Upon the reverend and steadfast earth
    That gave thee birth;
Yea, standest smiling in thy future grave,
    Serene and brave,
With unremitting breath
Inhaling life from death,
Thine epitaph writ fair in fruitage eloquent,
    Thyself thy monument.

    As poets should   80
Thou hast built up thy hardihood
With universal food,
    Drawn in select proportion fair
    From honest mold and vagabond air;
From darkness of the dreadful night,
    And joyful light;
From antique ashes, whose departed flame
    In thee has finer life and longer fame;
From wounds and balms,
From storms and calms,   90
    From potsherds and dry bones
    And ruin-stones.
Into thy vigorous substance thou hast wrought
Whate'er the hand of Circumstance hath brought;
    Yea, into cool solacing green hast spun
    White radiance hot from out the sun.
So thou dost mutually leaven
Strength of earth with grace of heaven;
    So thou dost marry new and old
    Into a one of higher mold;   100
    So thou dost reconcile the hot and cold,
    The dark and bright,
And many a heart-perplexing opposite:
    And so,
    Akin by blood to high and low,
Fitly thou playest out thy poet's part,
Richly expending thy much-bruisèd heart
In equal care to nourish lord in hall

Or beast in stall:
    Thou took'st from all that thou might'st give to all. 110

O steadfast dweller on the selfsame spot
Where thou wast born, that still repinest not—
Type of the home-fond heart, the happy lot!—
    Deeply thy mild content rebukes the land
    Whose flimsy homes, built on the shifting sand
Of trade, forever rise and fall
With alternation whimsical,
    Enduring scarce a day,
    Then swept away
By swift engulfments of incalculable tides   120
Whereon capricious Commerce rides.
Look, thou substantial spirit of content!
Across this little vale, thy continent,
    To where, beyond the moldering mill,
    Yon old deserted Georgian hill
Bares to the sun his piteous aged crest
    And seamy breast,
    By restless-hearted children left to lie
    Untended there beneath the heedless sky,
    As barbarous folk expose their old to die.   130
Upon that generous-rounding side,
    With gullies scarified
    Where keen Neglect his lash hath plied,
Dwelt one I knew of old, who played at toil,
And gave to coquette Cotton soul and soil.
    Scorning the slow reward of patient grain,
    He sowed his heart with hopes of swifter gain,
    Then sat him down and waited for the rain.
He sailed in borrowed ships of usury—
A foolish Jason on a treacherous sea,   140
Seeking the Fleece and finding misery.
    Lulled by smooth-rippling loans, in idle trance
    He lay, content that unthrift Circumstance
    Should plow for him the stony field of Chance.
Yea, gathering crops whose worth no man might tell,
He staked his life on games of Buy-and-Sell,
And turned each field into a gambler's hell.
    Aye, as each year began,
    My farmer to the neighboring city ran;

91 **potsherds,** fragments of broken earthen pots, as in Job 2:8: "And he took a potsherd to scrape himself withal . . ." • 132 **scarified,** cut • 135 **coquette Cotton.** Contrast Timrod's attitude toward cotton in "Ethnogenesis" and "The Cotton Boll" • 140 **Jason,** in Greek mythology, went in quest of the Golden Fleece

Passed with a mournful anxious face   150
Into the banker's inner place;
Parleyed, excused, pleaded for longer grace;
  Railed at the drought, the worm, the rust, the grass;
  Protested ne'er again 'twould come to pass;
  With many an *oh* and *if* and *but alas*
Parried or swallowed searching questions rude,
And kissed the dust to soften Dives's mood.
At last, small loans by pledges great renewed,
  He issues smiling from the fatal door,
  And buys with lavish hand his yearly store   160
  Till his small borrowings will yield no more.
Aye, as each year declined,
With bitter heart and ever-brooding mind
He mourned his fate unkind.
  In dust, in rain, with might and main,
  He nursed his cotton, cursed his grain,
  Fretted for news that made him fret again,
Snatched at each telegram of Future Sale,
And thrilled with Bulls' or Bears' alternate wail—
In hope or fear alike forever pale.   170
  And thus from year to year, through hope and fear,
  With many a curse and many a secret tear,
  Striving in vain his cloud of debt to clear,
    At last
He woke to find his foolish dreaming past,
  And all his best-of-life the easy prey
Of squandering scamps and quacks that lined his way
    With vile array,
From rascal statesman down to petty knave;
Himself, at best, for all his bragging brave,   180
A gamester's catspaw and a banker's slave.
  Then, worn and gray, and sick with deep unrest,
  He fled away into the oblivious West,
  Unmourned, unblest.

Old hill! old hill! thou gashed and hairy Lear
Whom the divine Cordelia of the year,
E'en pitying Spring, will vainly strive to cheer—
  King, that no subject man nor beast may own,
  Discrowned, undaughtered and alone—
Yet shall the great God turn thy fate,   190
And bring thee back into thy monarch state
    And majesty immaculate.
  Lo, through hot waverings of the August morn,
  Thou givest from thy vasty sides forlorn
  Visions of golden treasuries of corn—

Ripe largesse lingering for some bolder heart
That manfully shall take thy part,
    And tend thee,
    And defend thee,
With antique sinew and with modern art.   200

1874·1875

The Symphony

Lanier wrote to a friend on March 24, 1875, concerning the composition of "The Symphony": "About four days ago, a certain poem which I had vaguely ruminated a week before took hold of me like a real James River ague, and I have been in a mortal shake with the same, day and night, ever since. I call it 'The Symphony': I personify each instrument in the orchestra, and make them discuss various deep social questions of the times, in the progress of the music." The "deep social questions" have to do with the evils of "Trade": the poem is an indictment of "Trade," by which Lanier means not only industrialism or the factory system, but all competitive business.

Does business mean, **Die, you—live, I?**
Then 'Trade is trade' but sings a lie:
'Tis only war grown miserly.

Humanitarian sympathy, moral idealism, an artist's temperament, devotion to the chivalric code ("Trade killed Chivalry," he said), and the aristocratic Southern tradition—all unite, no doubt, to explain his contempt for the commercial spirit of the modern age.

---

153 **worm**, bollworm, which devours the bolls of the cotton plant. The boll weevil did not invade the South until the 1890's • 157 **Dives**, the rich man in "the parable of the rich man and Lazarus." The proper name does not appear in the Biblical account (Luke 16:19-31), but owes its origin to the Latin adjective "dives" (meaning "rich") in the Vulgate. The name is here applied to the banker of l. 151 • 168 **Future Sale**, speculative selling for delivery at a future time; dealing in "futures" • 169 **Bulls**, those who buy, expecting a rise in price • 169 **Bears**, those who sell, expecting a fall in price • 181 **gamester's catspaw**, gambler's tool • 185 **Lear . . . Cordelia**, a reference to King Lear, of Shakespeare's play, who was cruelly abused by his older daughters, and devotedly cared for by his youngest daughter, Cordelia • 194 **vasty**, vast. This word occurs in Shakespeare • 196 **largesse**, bounty or reward. The word is Chaucerian

The poem's argument is less interesting than its style. Many lines are marvelously suggestive of the tones of the individual instruments and of orchestral effects.

The poem first appeared in **Lippincott's Magazine** for June 1875.

"O Trade! O Trade! would thou wert dead!
The Time needs heart—'tis tired of head:
We're all for love," the violins said.
"Of what avail the rigorous tale
Of bill for coin and box for bale?
Grant thee, O Trade! thine uttermost hope:
Level red gold with blue sky-slope,
And base it deep as devils grope:
When all's done, what hast thou won
Of the only sweet that's under the sun?   10
Ay, canst thou buy a single sigh
Of true love's least, least ecstasy?"
Then, with a bridegroom's heart-beats trembling,
All the mightier strings assembling
Ranged them on the violins' side
As when the bridegroom leads the bride,
And, heart in voice, together cried:
"Yea, what avail the endless tale
Of gain by cunning and plus by sale?
Look up the land, look down the land,   20
The poor, the poor, the poor, they stand
Wedged by the pressing of Trade's hand
Against an inward-opening door
That pressure tightens evermore:
They sigh a monstrous foul-air sigh
For the outside leagues of liberty,
Where Art, sweet lark, translates the sky
Into a heavenly melody.
'Each day, all day' (these poor folks say),
'In the same old year-long, drear-long way,   30
We weave in the mills and heave in the kilns,
We sieve mine-meshes under the hills,
And thieve much gold from the Devil's bank tills,
To relieve, O God, what manner of ills?—
The beasts, they hunger, and eat, and die;
And so do we, and the world's a sty;
Hush, fellow-swine: why nuzzle and cry?
Swinehood hath no remedy

Say many men, and hasten by,
Clamping the nose and blinking the eye.   40
But who said once, in the lordly tone,
Man shall not live by bread alone
But all that cometh from the Throne?
　Hath God said so?
　But Trade saith *No:*
And the kilns and the curt-tongued mills say *Go!*
There's plenty that can, if you can't: we know.
Move out, if you think you're underpaid.
The poor are prolific; we're not afraid;
'Trade is trade.'"   50
Thereat this passionate protesting
Meekly changed, and softened till
It sank to sad requesting
And suggesting sadder still:
"And oh, if men might some time see
How piteous-false the poor decree
That trade no more than trade must be!
Does business mean, *Die, you—live, I?*
Then 'Trade is trade' but sings a lie:
'Tis only war grown miserly.   60
If business is battle, name it so:
War-crimes less will shame it so,
And widows less will blame it so.
Alas, for the poor to have some part
In yon sweet living lands of Art,
Makes problem not for head, but heart.
Vainly might Plato's brain revolve it:
Plainly the heart of a child could solve it."

And then, as when from words that seem but rude
We pass to silent pain that sits abroad   70
Back in our heart's great dark and solitude,
So sank the strings to gentle throbbing
Of long chords change-marked with sobbing—
Motherly sobbing, not distinctlier heard
Than half wing-openings of the sleeping bird,
Some dream of danger to her young hath stirred.
Then stirring and demurring ceased, and lo!
Every least ripple of the strings' song-flow
Died to a level with each level bow
And made a great chord tranquil-surfaced so,   80

---

4 tale, a reckoning by numbers • 42 Man . . . Throne. Compare Luke 4:4

As a brook beneath his curving bank doth go
To linger in the sacred dark and green
Where many boughs the still pool overlean
And many leaves make shadow with their sheen.
  But presently
A velvet flute-note fell down pleasantly
Upon the bosom of that harmony,
And sailed and sailed incessantly,
As if a petal from a wild-rose blown
Had fluttered down upon that pool of tone   90
And boatwise dropped o' the convex side
And floated down the glassy tide
And clarified and glorified
The solemn spaces where the shadows bide.
From the warm concave of that fluted note
Somewhat, half song, half odor, forth did float,
As if a rose might somehow be a throat:
"When Nature from her far-off glen
Flutes her soft messages to men,
  The flute can say them o'er again;   100
  Yea, Nature, singing sweet and lone,
Breathes through life's strident polyphone
The flute-voice in the world of tone.
  Sweet friends,
  Man's love ascends
To finer and diviner ends
Than man's mere thought e'er comprehends,
For I, e'en I,
As here I lie,
A petal on a harmony,   110
Demand of Science whence and why
Man's tender pain, man's inward cry,
When he doth gaze on earth and sky?
I am not overbold:
  I hold
Full powers from Nature manifold.
I speak for each no-tonguèd tree
That, spring by spring, doth nobler be,
And dumbly and most wistfully
His mighty prayerful arms outspreads   120
Above men's oft-unheeding heads,
And his big blessing downward sheds.
I speak for all-shaped blooms and leaves,
Lichens on stones and moss on eaves,
Grasses and grains in ranks and sheaves;
Broad-fronded ferns and keen-leaved canes,

And briery mazes bounding lanes,
And marsh-plants, thirsty-cupped for rains,
And milky stems and sugary veins;
For every long-armed woman-vine   130
That round a piteous tree doth twine;
For passionate odors, and divine
Pistils, and petals crystalline;
All purities of shady springs,
All shynesses of film-winged things
That fly from tree-trunks and bark-rings;
All modesties of mountain-fawns
That leap to covert from wild lawns,
And tremble if the day but dawns;
All sparklings of small beady eyes   140
Of birds, and sidelong glances wise
Wherewith the jay hints tragedies;
All piquancies of prickly burs,
And smoothnesses of downs and furs,
Of eiders and of minivers;
All limpid honeys that do lie
At stamen-bases, nor deny
The humming-birds' fine roguery,
Bee-thighs, nor any butterfly;
All gracious curves of slender wings,   150
Bark-mottlings, fibre-spiralings,
Fern-wavings and leaf-flickerings;
Each dial-marked leaf and flower-bell
Wherewith in every lonesome dell
Time to himself his hours doth tell;
All tree-sounds, rustlings of pine-cones,
Wind-sighings, doves' melodious moans,
And night's unearthly under-tones;
All placid lakes and waveless deeps,
All cool reposing mountain-steeps,   160
Vale-calms and tranquil lotos-sleeps;—
Yea, all fair forms, and sounds, and lights,
And warmths, and mysteries, and mights,
Of Nature's utmost depths and heights.
—These doth my timid tongue present,
Their mouthpiece and leal instrument

---

126 Broad-fronded, broad-leafed • 145 minivers, ermines or
weasels in white winter coats • 157 doves' . . . moans echoes
Tennyson's "moan of doves in immemorial elms" in The Princess,
Song VII, l. 207 • 161 lotos-sleeps. The lotus fruit, when eaten, produced a dreamy contentment and complete forgetfulness of home and
friends; see Tennyson's "Lotus-Eaters"

And servant, all love-eloquent.
I heard, when *'All for love'* the violins cried:
So, Nature calls through all her system wide,
Give me thy love, O man, so long denied.   170
Much time is run, and man hath changed his ways,
Since Nature, in the antique fable-days,
Was hid from man's true love by proxy fays,
False fauns and rascal gods that stole her praise.
The nymphs, cold creatures of man's colder brain,
Chilled Nature's streams till man's warm heart was fain
Never to lave its love in them again.
Later, a sweet Voice *Love thy neighbor* said,
Then first the bounds of neighborhood outspread
Beyond all confines of old ethnic dread,   180
Vainly the Jew might wag his covenant head:
'All men are neighbors,' so the sweet Voice said.
So, when man's arms had circled all man's race,
The liberal compass of his warm embrace
Stretched bigger yet in the dark bounds of space;
With hands a-grope he felt smooth Nature's grace,
Drew her to breast and kissed her sweetheart face:
Yea, man found neighbors in great hills and trees
And streams and clouds and suns and birds and bees,
And throbbed with neighbor-loves in loving these.   190
But oh, the poor! the poor! the poor!
That stand by the inward-opening door
Trade's hand doth tighten ever more,
And sigh their monstrous foul-air sigh
For the outside hills of liberty,
Where Nature spreads her wild blue sky
For Art to make into melody!
Thou Trade! thou king of the modern days!
      Change thy ways,
      Change thy ways;   200
Let the sweaty laborers file
      A little while,
      A little while,
Where Art and Nature sing and smile.
Trade! is thy heart all dead, all dead?
And hast thou nothing but a head?
I'm all for heart," the flute-voice said,
And into sudden silence fled,
Like as a blush that while 'tis red
Dies to a still, still white instead.   210

   Thereto a thrilling calm succeeds,
Till presently the silence breeds

A little breeze among the reeds
That seems to blow by sea-marsh weeds:
Then from the gentle stir and fret
Sings out the melting clarionet,
Like as a lady sings while yet
Her eyes with salty tears are wet.
"O Trade! O Trade!" the Lady said,
"I too will wish thee utterly dead   220
If all thy heart is in thy head.
For O my God! and O my God!
What shameful ways have women trod
At beckoning of Trade's golden rod!
Alas when sighs are traders' lies,
And heart's-ease eyes and violet eyes
      Are merchandise!
O purchased lips that kiss with pain!
O cheeks coin-spotted with smirch and stain!
O trafficked hearts that break in twain!   230
—And yet what wonder at my sister's crime?
So hath Trade withered up Love's sinewy prime,
Men love not women as in olden time.
Ah, not in these cold merchantable days
Deem men their life an opal gray, where plays
The one red Sweet of gracious ladies'-praise.
Now, comes a suitor with sharp prying eye—
Says, *Here, you Lady, if you'll sell, I'll buy:*
Come, heart for heart—a trade? What! weeping? why?
Shame on such wooers' dapper mercery!   240
I would my lover kneeling at my feet
In humble manliness should cry, *O sweet!*
I know not if thy heart my heart will greet:
I ask not if thy love my love can meet:
Whate'er thy worshipful soft tongue shall say,
I'll kiss thine answer, be it yea or nay:
I do but know I love thee, and I pray
To be thy knight until my dying day.
Woe him that cunning trades in hearts contrives!
Base love good women to base loving drives.   250
If men loved larger, larger were our lives;
And wooed they nobler, won they nobler wives."

There thrust the bold straightforward horn
To battle for that lady lorn,

---

178 Love . . . neighbor. See Matthew 22:39 • 181 **covenant** refers to the legalism of the Old Testament • 240 **dapper mercery,** slick bargaining

With heartsome voice of mellow scorn,
Like any knight in knighthood's morn.
   "Now comfort thee," said he,
     "Fair Lady.
For God shall right thy grievous wrong,
And man shall sing thee a true-love song,   260
Voiced in act his whole life long,
   Yea, all thy sweet life long,
     Fair Lady.
Where's he that craftily hath said,
The day of chivalry is dead?
I'll prove that lie upon his head,
   Or I will die instead,
     Fair Lady.
Is Honor gone into his grave?
Hath Faith become a caitiff knave,   270
And Selfhood turned into a slave
   To work in Mammon's cave,
     Fair Lady?
Will Truth's long blade ne'er gleam again?
Hath Giant Trade in dungeons slain
All great contempts of mean-got gain
   And hates of inward stain,
     Fair Lady?
For aye shall name and fame be sold,
And place be hugged for the sake of gold,   280
And smirch-robed Justice feebly scold
   At Crime all money-bold,
     Fair Lady?
Shall self-wrapt husbands aye forget
Kiss-pardons for the daily fret
Wherewith sweet wifely eyes are wet—
   Blind to lips kiss-wise set—
     Fair Lady?
Shall lovers higgle, heart for heart,
Till wooing grows a trading mart   290
Where much for little, and all for part,
   Make love a cheapening art,
     Fair Lady?
Shall woman scorch for a single sin
That her betrayer may revel in,
And she be burnt, and he but grin
   When that the flames begin,
     Fair Lady?
Shall ne'er prevail the woman's plea,
We maids would far, far whiter be   300
If that our eyes might sometimes see

Men maids in purity,
   Fair Lady?
Shall Trade aye salve his conscience-aches
With jibes at Chivalry's old mistakes—
The wars that o'erhot knighthood makes
   For Christ's and ladies' sakes,
     Fair Lady?
Now by each knight that e'er hath prayed
To fight like a man and love like a maid,   310
Since Pembroke's life, as Pembroke's blade,
   I' the scabbard, death, was laid,
     Fair Lady,
I dare avouch my faith is bright
That God doth right and God hath might.
Nor time hath changed His hair to white,
   Nor His dear love to spite,
     Fair Lady.
I doubt no doubts: I strive, and shrive my clay,
And fight my fight in the patient modern way   320
For true love and for thee—ah me! and pray
   To be thy knight until my dying day,
     Fair Lady."
Made end that knightly horn, and spurred away
Into the thick of the melodious fray.

And then the hautboy played and smiled,
And sang like any large-eyed child,
Cool-hearted and all undefiled.
   "Huge Trade!" he said,
"Would thou wouldst lift me on thy head   330
And run where'er my finger led!
Once said a Man—and wise was He—
Never shalt thou the heavens see,
Save as a little child thou be."
Then o'er sea-lashings of commingling tunes
The ancient wise bassoons,
   Like weird,

---

264 **Where's . . . dead,** an allusion to a famous passage in Edmund Burke's **Reflections on the Revolution in France** ("But the age of chivalry is gone. . . ."), though "craftly" is meant to apply not at all to Burke, but perhaps to some anonymous cynic • 272 **Mammon's cave,** described in Spenser's **Faerie Queene,** Bk. II, Canto vii, is filled with "great heapes of gold" • 292 **cheapening,** bargaining • 311 **Pembroke,** probably William Herbert, third Earl of Pembroke (1580-1630). Lanier may have had in mind Pembroke's participation in 1606 in a tournament, in which he spoke a challenge to all "knights adventurers of hereditary note" • 333 **Never . . . be.** See Matthew 18:3

Gray-beard
Old harpers sitting on the high sea-dunes,
    Chanted runes: 340
"Bright-waved gain, gray-waved loss,
The sea of all doth lash and toss,
One wave forward and one across:
But now 'twas trough, now 'tis crest,
And worst doth foam and flash to best,
    And curst to blest.

"Life! Life! thou sea-fugue, writ from east to west,
    Love, Love alone can pore
    On thy dissolving score
    Of harsh half-phrasings,   350
      Blotted ere writ,
    And double erasings
      Of chords most fit.
Yea, Love, sole music-master blest,
May read thy weltering palimpsest.
To follow Time's dying melodies through,
And never to lose the old in the new,
And ever to solve the discords true—
    Love alone can do.
And ever Love hears the poor-folks' crying,   360
And ever Love hears the women's sighing,
And ever sweet knighthood's death-defying,
And ever wise childhood's deep implying,
But never a trader's glozing and lying.

"And yet shall Love himself be heard,
Though long deferred, though long deferred:
O'er the modern waste a dove hath whirred:
Music is Love in search of a word."

                                  1875

The Revenge of Hamish

The story of "The Revenge of Hamish" was based upon
an incident in William Black's **Macleod of Dare**, a novel
appearing serially in **Harper's Magazine** in 1878 (see
A. H. Starke, **Sidney Lanier**, p. 310). Lanier achieves in
this poem something of the economy, naturalness, and
directness of the old ballads. Different in both style and
subject matter from his usual work, "The Revenge of
Hamish" is interesting not only in itself but as evidence
of the craftsman's virtuosity and the catholic literary interests of its author.

It was three slim does and a ten-tined buck in the
    bracken lay;
    And all of a sudden the sinister smell of a man,
    Awaft on a wind-shift, wavered and ran,
Down the hill-side and sifted along through the bracken
    and passed that way.

Then Nan got a-tremble at nostril; she was the dainti-
    est doe;
    In the print of her velvet flank on the velvet fern
    She reared, and rounded her ears in turn.
Then the buck leapt up, and his head as a king's to a
    crown did go

Full high in the breeze, and he stood as if Death had the
    form of a deer;
    And the two slim does long lazily stretching arose,   10
    For their day-dream slowlier came to a close,
Till they woke and were still, breath-bound with waiting
    and wonder and fear.

Then Alan the huntsman sprang over the hillock, the
    hounds shot by,
    The does and the ten-tined buck made a marvellous
      bound,
    The hounds swept after with never a sound,
But Alan loud winded his horn in sign that the quarry
    was nigh.

For at dawn of that day proud Maclean of Lochbuy to
    the hunt had waxed wild,
    And he cursed at old Alan till Alan fared off with the
      hounds
    For to drive him the deer to the lower glen-grounds:
"I will kill a red deer," quoth Maclean, "in the sight of
    the wife and the child."   20

The Symphony • 367 O'er . . . whirred recalls the dove sent from
Noah's ark; see Genesis 8:8-12
The Revenge of Hamish • 1 ten-tined, ten branches of the antler

So gayly he paced with the wife and the child to his
    chosen stand;
    But he hurried tall Hamish the henchman ahead:
      "Go turn,"—
Cried Maclean,—"if the deer seek to cross to the burn,
Do thou turn them to me: nor fail, lest thy back be red
    as thy hand."

Now hard-fortuned Hamish, half blown of his breath
    with the height of the hill,
    Was white in the face when the ten-tined buck and
    the does
    Drew leaping to burn-ward; huskily rose
His shouts, and his nether lip twitched, and his legs were
    o'er-weak for his will.

So the deer darted lightly by Hamish and bounded away
    to the burn.
    But Maclean never bating his watch tarried wait-
    ing below;   30
    Still Hamish hung heavy with fear for to go
All the space of an hour; then he went, and his face was
    greenish and stern,

And his eye sat back in the socket, and shrunken the
    eye-balls shone,
    As withdrawn from a vision of deeds it were shame
    to see.
    "Now, now, grim henchman, what is 't with thee?"
Brake Maclean, and his wrath rose red as a beacon the
    wind path upblown.

"Three does and a ten-tined buck made out," spoke
    Hamish, full mild,
    "And I ran for to turn, but my breath it was blown;
    and they passed;
    I was weak, for ye called ere I broke me my fast."
Cried Maclean: "Now a ten-tined buck in the sight of
    the wife and the child   40

I had killed if the gluttonous kern had not wrought me
    a snail's own wrong!"
    Then he sounded, and down came kinsmen and clans-
    men all:
    "Ten blows, for ten tine, on his back let fall,

And reckon no stroke if the blood follow not at the bite
    of thong!"

So Hamish made bare, and took him his strokes; at the
    last he smiled.
    "Now I'll to the burn," quoth Maclean, "for it still
    may be,
    If a slimmer-paunched henchman will hurry with
    me,
I shall kill me the ten-tined buck for a gift to the wife
    and the child!"

Then the clansmen departed, by this path and that; and
    over the hill
    Sped Maclean with an outward wrath for an inward
    shame;   50
    And that place of the lashing full quiet became;
And the wife and the child stood sad; and bloody-backed
    Hamish sat still.

But look! red Hamish has risen; quick about and about
    turns he.
    "There is none betwixt me and the crag-top!" he
    screams under breath.
    Then, livid as Lazarus lately from death,
He snatches the child from the mother, and clambers the
    crag toward the sea.

Now the mother drops breath; she is dumb, and her
    heart goes dead for a space,
    Till the motherhood, mistress of death, shrieks, shrieks
    through the glen,
    And that place of the lashing is live with men,
And Maclean, and the gillie that told him, dash up in a
    desperate race.   60

Not a breath's time for asking; an eye-glance reveals all
    the tale untold.
    They follow mad Hamish afar up the crag toward
    the sea,
    And the lady cries: "Clansmen, run for a fee!
Yon castle and lands to the two first hands that shall
    hook him and hold

---

23 **burn**, brook • 41 **kern**, peasant, boor • 55 **Lazarus.** The account
of the raising of Lazarus from the dead is given in John 11

"Fast Hamish back from the brink!"—and ever she flies
   up the steep,
   And the clansmen pant, and they sweat, and they
      jostle and strain.
   But, mother, 'tis vain; but, father, 'tis vain;
Stern Hamish stands bold on the brink, and dangles the
   child o'er the deep.

Now a faintness falls on the men that run, and they all
   stand still.
   And the wife prays Hamish as if he were God, on
      her knees,   70
   Crying: "Hamish! O Hamish! but please, but please
For to spare him!" and Hamish still dangles the child,
   with a wavering will.

On a sudden he turns; with a sea-hawk scream, and a
   gibe, and a song,
   Cries: "So; I will spare ye the child if, in sight of ye all,
   Ten blows on Maclean's bare back shall fall,
And ye reckon no stroke if the blood follow not at the
   bite of the thong!"

Then Maclean he set hardly his tooth to his lip that his
   tooth was red,
   Breathed short for a space, said: "Nay, but it never
      shall be!
   Let me hurl off the damnable hound in the sea!"
But the wife: "Can Hamish go fish us the child from
   the sea, if dead?   80

"Say yea!—Let them lash *me*, Hamish?"—"Nay!"—
   "Husband, the lashing will heal;
   But, oh, who will heal me the bonny sweet bairn in
      his grave?
   Could ye cure me my heart with the death of a knave?
Quick! Love! I will bare thee—so—kneel!" Then
   Maclean 'gan slowly to kneel

With never a word, till presently downward he jerked
   to the earth.
   Then the henchman—he that smote Hamish—would
      tremble and lag;
   "Strike, hard!" quoth Hamish, full stern, from the crag;
Then he struck him, and "One!" sang Hamish, and
   danced with the child in his mirth.

And no man spake beside Hamish; he counted each
   stroke with a song.
   When the last stroke fell, then he moved him a pace
      down the height,   90
   And he held forth the child in the heartaching sight
Of the mother, and looked all pitiful grave, as repenting
   a wrong.

And there as the motherly arms stretched out with the
   thanksgiving prayer—
   And there as the mother crept up with a fearful
      swift pace,
   Till her finger nigh felt of the bairnie's face—
In a flash fierce Hamish turned round and lifted the
   child in the air,

And sprang with the child in his arms from the horrible
   height in the sea,
   Shrill screeching, "Revenge!" in the wind-rush; and
      pallid Maclean,
   Age-feeble with anger and impotent pain,
Crawled up on the crag, and lay flat, and locked hold
   of dead roots of a tree—   100

And gazed hungrily o'er, and the blood from his back
   drip-dripped in the brine,
   And a sea-hawk flung down a skeleton fish as he flew,
   And the mother stared white on the waste of blue,
And the wind drove a cloud to seaward, and the sun
   began to shine.

                                                      1878

The Marshes of Glynn

"The Marshes of Glynn" first appeared in **A Masque of Poets**, a collection of anonymous verse by various authors published in Boston in 1878. The marshes described are located near Brunswick, Georgia. The poem shows "Lanier's spiritual maturity," says Starke, "to which he has worked through all his other poems." It is the best known and perhaps the best loved of his compositions.

Glooms of the live-oaks, beautiful-braided and woven
With intricate shades of the vines that myriad-cloven
   Clamber the forks of the multiform boughs,—

Emerald twilights,—
  Virginal shy lights,
Wrought of the leaves to allure to the whisper of vows,
When lovers pace timidly down through the green
    colonnades
Of the dim sweet woods, of the dear dark woods,
  Of the heavenly woods and glades,
That run to the radiant marginal sand-beach within   10
  The wide sea-marshes of Glynn;—

Beautiful glooms, soft dusks in the noon-day fire,—
Wildwood privacies, closets of lone desire,
Chamber from chamber parted with wavering arras of
    leaves,—
Cells for the passionate pleasure of prayer to the soul
    that grieves,
Pure with a sense of the passing of saints through the
    wood,
Cool for the dutiful weighing of ill with good;—

O braided dusks of the oak and woven shades of the vine,
While the riotous noon-day sun of the June-day long
    did shine
Ye held me fast in your heart and I held you fast in
    mine;   20
But now when the noon is no more, and riot is rest,
And the sun is a-wait at the ponderous gate of the West,
And the slant yellow beam down the wood-aisle doth
    seem
Like a lane into heaven that leads from a dream,—
Ay, now, when my soul all day hath drunken the soul of
    the oak,
And my heart is at ease from men, and the wearisome
    sound of the stroke
  Of the scythe of time and the trowel of trade is low,
  And belief overmasters doubt, and I know that I know,
  And my spirit is grown to a lordly great compass
      within,
That the length and the breadth and the sweep of the
    marshes of Glynn   30
Will work me no fear like the fear they have wrought
    me of yore
When length was fatigue, and when breadth was but
    bitterness sore,
And when terror and shrinking and dreary unnam-
    able pain
Drew over me out of the merciless miles of the plain,—

Oh, now, unafraid, I am fain to face
  The vast sweet visage of space.
To the edge of the wood I am drawn, I am drawn,
Where the gray beach glimmering runs, as a belt of
    the dawn,
  For a mete and a mark
    To the forest-dark:—   40
      So:
Affable live-oak, leaning low,—
Thus—with your favor—soft, with a reverent hand
(Not lightly touching your person, Lord of the land!),
Bending your beauty aside, with a step I stand
On the firm-packed sand,
      Free
By a world of marsh that borders a world of sea.
  Sinuous southward and sinuous northward the shim-
      mering band
  Of the sand-beach fastens the fringe of the marsh to
      the folds of the land.   50
Inward and outward to northward and southward the
    beach-lines linger and curl
As a silver-wrought garment that clings to and follows
    the firm sweet limbs of a girl.
Vanishing, swerving, evermore curving again into sight,
Softly the sand-beach wavers away to a dim gray looping
    of light.
And what if behind me to westward the wall of the
    woods stands high?
The world lies east: how ample, the marsh and the sea
    and the sky!
A league and a league of marsh-grass, waist-high, broad
    in the blade,
Green, and all of a height, and unflecked with a light
    or a shade,
Stretch leisurely off, in a pleasant plain,
To the terminal blue of the main.   60

Oh, what is abroad in the marsh and the terminal sea?
  Somehow my soul seems suddenly free
From the weighing of fate and the sad discussion of sin,
By the length and the breadth and the sweep of the
    marshes of Glynn.

Ye marshes, how candid and simple and nothing-with-
    holding and free
Ye publish yourselves to the sky and offer yourselves
    to the sea!

Tolerant plains, that suffer the sea and the rains and
　　the sun,
Ye spread and span like the catholic man who hath
　　mightily won
God out of knowledge and good out of infinite pain
And sight out of blindness and purity out of a stain.　70

As the marsh-hen secretly builds on the watery sod,
Behold I will build me a nest on the greatness of God:
I will fly in the greatness of God as the marsh-hen flies
In the freedom that fills all the space 'twixt the marsh
　　and the skies:
By so many roots as the marsh-grass sends in the sod
I will heartily lay me a-hold on the greatness of God:
Oh, like to the greatness of God is the greatness within
The range of the marshes, the liberal marshes of Glynn.

And the sea lends large, as the marsh: lo, out of his
　　plenty the sea
Pours fast: full soon the time of the flood-tide must
　　be:　　　　　　　　　　　　　　　　　　　　　80
Look how the grace of the sea doth go
About and about through the intricate channels that flow
　　　　Here and there,
　　　　　　Everywhere,
Till his waters have flooded the uttermost creeks and
　　the low-lying lanes,

And the marsh is meshed with a million veins,
That like as with rosy and silvery essences flow
　In the rose-and-silver evening glow.
　　　　Farewell, my lord Sun!
The creeks overflow: a thousand rivulets run　　　　90
'Twixt the roots of the sod; the blades of the marsh-
　　grass stir;
Passeth a hurrying sound of wings that westward whirr;
Passeth, and all is still; and the currents cease to run;
And the sea and the marsh are one.

How still the plains of the waters be!
The tide is in his ecstasy.
The tide is at his highest height:
　　　　And it is night.

And now from the Vast of the Lord will the waters of
　　sleep
Roll in on the souls of men,　　　　　　　　　　　100
But who will reveal to our waking ken
The forms that swim and the shapes that creep
　　　　Under the waters of sleep?
And I would I could know what swimmeth below when
　　the tide comes in
On the length and the breadth of the marvellous marshes
　　of Glynn.

internal rhyme.

　　　　　　　　　　　　　　　　　　　　　　1878

Edward Rowland Sill

1841 · 1887

Edward Rowland Sill, born in Windsor, Connecticut,
in 1841, was the descendant of a distinguished line of
New England ancestors which included several ministers. He prepared for college at Phillips Exeter and
attended Yale. Then followed a period of indecision
which ended with his becoming a teacher and author at
the University of California. In 1882 he retired from
teaching and returned to the East, where he died in 1887.

With some differences in time and place, the pattern
of Sill's living was reminiscent of the lives of earlier
Brahmin poets. Sill thought of poetry much as they had.
It should express "a pure and rich nature." It should

be "full of lovely images" and "in every way musical." It should be concerned with "both thought and feeling," should "bring about us troops of high and pure associations," and "leave us purer and richer than it found us." Putting such beliefs into practice in creative writing, Sill produced a number of poems which were very much in the vein of Longfellow—"The Arch," for instance, and "Spring Twilight," and two very popular poems, "The Fool's Prayer" and "Opportunity."

In cherishing such concepts and in producing such poetry, Sill showed his relationship with a sizable group of poets contemporaneous with him—Thomas Bailey Aldrich, Edmund Clarence Stedman, Richard Watson Gilder, and others. These writers carried over into the last decades of the nineteenth century the so-called "genteel tradition" of the prewar period. As a rule, they were reminiscent, derivative, echoing songs of British or American Victorians. They prolonged a way of thinking about literature and a way of writing it which had flourished in different days. Hence Sill, though a minor poet, merits attention as a representative poet.

But Sill, in some of his poems, contrasted with these anachronistic authors in reflecting more of the puzzlement and the doubt of his period than they did. The certainties which had given the Brahmins both their stodginess and their appeal were crumbling, and, as Professor Newton Arvin has noted, "unlike any American poet before him, or among his contemporaries, Sill had the hardihood to express in verse a metaphysical anxiety." Professor Arvin points out the significance of this fact when he says: "It is an old story to us now, this poetry of negation; but it was not an old story sixty years ago. It took an uncommon moral refinement then to have even the glimpses which Sill had into the Waste Land . . . . Sill was no Robinson, no Eliot, no Jeffers. But what is striking is that he gave so much play to negation as he did."

Alfred Kreymborg also sees Sill as an author worthy of study: "Sill fell between the New England decline and the national renascence, of which he was an obscure forerunner . . . . Next to the jocund Longfellow, he looms a courageous, truth-seeking individual; and he was Poe's equal in the esthetic realm. And since his esthetic power bent his melancholia to an objective resolution, his poems have a more decided reality than Poe's . . . . Within the limits he set himself, he was the purest artist in Nineteenth Century American Poetry."

The Poetical Works of Edward Rowland Sill, Boston, 1906 • William Belmont Parker, Edward Rowland Sill, His Life and Work, Boston, 1915

Morning

One of Sill's Yale classmates, as quoted by W. B. Parker, observed that while he and Sill were in college, the faculty was so strong for discipline that it often deliberately erected obstacles for students to overcome: "When [for instance], President Woolsey offered to cushion the bare seats in the chapel at his own expense, the proposition was turned down as tending to make the students effeminate. To this hated chapel, we were driven twice a day and four times on Sunday, one of the daily herdings being before daylight in winter. Some compensation for these monastic rigors lies in the fact that during one of them, Sill got the idea for 'Morning,' and it symbolized his feeling regarding the lights our teachers read by."

A fellow editor of the **Yale Literary Magazine**, in which the poem first appeared, said that the original composition contained a final line, "Was there not meaning in my dream?" "I struck out the last line," he said, "because, as I told Sill afterwards, 'a finger-post wasn't needed.' Instead of being vexed, he was grateful." Undoubtedly, Sill's symbolism was adequate without the line. The composition, although an early one, is indicative of the author's discontent with older solutions, his eagerness to find better new ones.

I entered once, at break of day,
A chapel, lichen-stained and gray,
Where a congregation dozed and heard
An old monk read from a written Word.
No light through the window-panes could pass,
For shutters were closed on the rich stained-glass;
And in a gloom like the nether night
The monk read on by a taper's light.

Ghostly with shadows, that shrank and grew
As the dim light flared, were aisle and pew;   10
And the congregation that dozed around
Listened without a stir or sound—
Save one, who rose with wistful face,
And shifted a shutter from its place.
Then light flashed in like a flashing gem—
For dawn had come unknown to them—
And a slender beam, like a lance of gold,
Shot to the crimson curtain-fold,
Over the bended head of him
Who pored and pored by the taper dim;   20
And it kindled over his wrinkled brow
Such words: "The law which was till now;"
And I wondered that, under that morning ray,
When night and shadow were scattered away,
The monk should bow his locks of white
By a taper's feebly flickering light—
Should pore, and pore, and never seem
To notice the golden morning-beam.

    1860

The Fool's Prayer

W. C. Bartlett, a contemporary of Sill, at a memorial meeting in 1887, read a paper which told of the contemporary estimate of this poem: "The grandest sermon that has been uttered in rhythmic lines in the last half-century, is in . . . 'The Fool's Prayer.' Not many fugitive poems have been more widely read. It has in it the voice of the prophet and the priest. It turns the footstool of the king into a confessional. It abases and lifts up the fool into the holier atmosphere of humiliation, penitence and prayer. It convicts the scoffing king and sends him away murmuring, 'Be merciful to me, a fool.' It is a ritual fit not only for fools and kings, but for that large class who, being neither fools nor kings, prefer the ignoble and scoffing jest to any reverent expression for a faith that can save the world." A modern critic, probably, would be less enthusiastic.

The royal feast was done; the King
    Sought some new sport to banish care,

And to his jester cried: "Sir Fool,
    Kneel now, and make for us a prayer!"

The jester doffed his cap and bells,
    And stood the mocking court before;
They could not see the bitter smile
    Behind the painted grin he wore.

He bowed his head, and bent his knee
    Upon the monarch's silken stool;   10
His pleading voice arose: "O Lord,
    Be merciful to me, a fool!

"No pity, Lord, could change the heart
    From red with wrong to white as wool;
The rod must heal the sin: but, Lord,
    Be merciful to me, a fool!

" 'T is not by guilt the onward sweep
    Of truth and right, O Lord, we stay;
'T is by our follies that so long
    We hold the earth from heaven away.   20

"These clumsy feet, still in the mire,
    Go crushing blossoms without end;
These hard, well-meaning hands we thrust
    Among the heart-strings of a friend.

"The ill-timed truth we might have kept—
    Who knows how sharp it pierced and stung?
The word we had not sense to say—
    Who knows how grandly it had rung?

"Our faults no tenderness should ask,
    The chastening stripes must cleanse them all;   30
But for our blunders—oh, in shame
    Before the eyes of heaven we fall.

"Earth bears no balsam for mistakes;
    Men crown the knave, and scourge the tool
That did his will; but Thou, O Lord,
    Be merciful to me, a fool!"

The room was hushed, in silence rose
    The King, and sought his gardens cool,
And walked apart, and murmured low,
    "Be merciful to me, a fool!"   40

    1879

Opportunity

Like "The Fool's Prayer," this poem was very popular among the readers of the day; frequently it was reprinted in newspapers and grade-school readers. In setting and verse form, it resembles the work of one of the author's idols, Tennyson. It also continues the genteel tradition of Lowell and Longfellow.

This I beheld, or dreamed it in a dream:—
There spread a cloud of dust along a plain;
And underneath the cloud, or in it, raged
A furious battle, and men yelled, and swords
Shocked upon swords and shields. A prince's banner
Wavered, then staggered backward, hemmed by foes.
A craven hung along the battle's edge,
And thought, "Had I a sword of keener steel—
That blue blade that the king's son bears,—but this
Blunt thing—!" he snapt and flung it from his hand,   10
And lowering crept away and left the field.
Then came the king's son, wounded, sore bestead,
And weaponless, and saw the broken sword,
Hilt-buried in the dry and trodden sand,
And ran and snatched it, and with battle-shout
Lifted afresh he hewed his enemy down,
And saved a great cause that heroic day.

                                                1880

The Book of Hours

"Certainly," says Professor Arvin, "Sill was tormented more than most men by his incapacity to see into the heart of things; more painfully haunted by doubtfulness and perplexity. There is a sonnet called 'The Book of Hours,' in which he figures himself as a man vainly attempting to read a tale in a language he imperfectly understands, and failing to be touched by its grace. . . ."

As one who reads a tale writ in a tongue
    He only partly knows,—runs over it

And follows but the story, losing wit
And charm, and half the subtle links among
The haps and harms that the book's folk beset,—
    So do we with our life. Night comes, and morn:
    I know that one has died and one is born;
That this by love and that by hate is met.
But all the grace and glory of it fail
    To touch me, and the meanings they enfold.   10
The Spirit of the World hath told the tale,
    And tells it: and 't is very wise and old.
But o'er the page there is a mist and veil:
    I do not know the tongue in which 't is told.

                                                1885

Roland

Alfred Kreymborg sees in this poem a foretaste of "the cryptic Robinson and the later and still more cryptic Eliot"; the style, indeed, is terse and suggestive rather than discursive. Thinking rather more of content than of style, perhaps, Professor Arvin sees it as foreshadowing both "Miniver Cheevy" (p. 890) and "J. Alfred Prufrock" (p. 942). It should be noted, however, that the resolution of the poem shows the ironically named hero—far from being a romantically valiant man—finding a solution of his problem. It is interesting and significant to note that it was a solution of a sort the author himself had sought throughout life.

A foolish creature full of fears,
    He trembled for his fate,
And stood aghast to feel the earth
    Swing round her dizzy freight.

With timid foot he touched each plan,
    Sure that each plan would fail;
Behemoth's tread was his, it seemed,
    And every bridge too frail.

No glory of the night or day
    Lit any crown for him,   10
The tranquil past but breathed a mist
    To make the future dim.

The world, his birthright, seemed a cell,
  An iron heritage;
Man, a trapped creature, left to die
  Forgotten in his cage.

In every dark he held his breath
  And warded off a blow;
While at his shoulder still he sought
  Some tagging ghost of woe.   20

Spying the thorns but not the flowers,
  Through all the blossoming land
He hugged his careful heart and shunned
  The path on either hand.

The buds that broke their hearts to give
  New odors to the air
He saw not; but he caught the scent
  Of dead leaves everywhere.

Till on a day he came to know
  He had not made the world;   30

That if he slept, as when he ran,
  Each onward planet whirled.

He knew not where the vision fell,
  Only all things grew plain—
As if some thatch broke through and let
  A sunbeam cross his brain.

In beauty flushed the morning light,
  With blessing dropped the rain,
All creatures were to him most fair,
  Nor anything in vain.   40

He breathed the space that links the stars,
  He rested on God's arm—
A man unmoved by accident,
  Untouched by any harm.

The weary doubt if all is good,
  They doubt if all is ill,
He left to Him who leaves to us
  To know that all is well.

                                              1900

Emily Dickinson

1830 · 1886

On April 16, 1862, Thomas Wentworth Higginson, a clergyman in Worcester, Mass., found in his mailbox a strange little note. "Mr. Higginson,—" it began, "Are you too deeply occupied to say if my verse is alive?" Enclosed were four extraordinary little poems and, tucked away in a separate envelope, as if the writer had wished to hide it, the poet's name—Emily Dickinson.

Higginson, intrigued by the quaint way his corre-

spondent had written him and impressed by the unusual talent shown in the poetry, wrote of his admiration for Miss Dickinson's songs, asked to see more, and made some inquiries about his reticent correspondent's life. Her reply contained vague answers to his questions, as if she were eager to keep details about her life secret. To his query about her age, for instance, she replied somewhat irrelevantly that she had written little

Emily Dickinson—from Letters of Emily Dickinson, *ed. Mabel Loomis Todd, Harper & Brothers, 1931*

poetry "until this winter, sir." "You ask of my companions," she said a few lines later. "Hills, sir, and the sundown, and a dog large as myself, that my father bought me. They are better than beings because they know, but do not tell; and the noise in the pool at noon excels my piano." At the end she expressed fear that her "story" was growing fatiguing and asked innocently whether her letter told what he had asked her to tell.

The incident might typify the way knowledge of this shy, playful, odd poet has eluded biographers. Some facts about her are clear enough: that she was the daughter of Lawyer Edward Dickinson of Amherst, Massachusetts, a rather stern Calvinist; that despite her repressive surroundings she was a vivacious, fun-loving girl; that she was well educated in the Amherst Academy and Mount Holyoke; that in time, something happened to her which caused her to become a recluse in her house in Amherst, writing much verse but refusing to publish it.

Exactly what led to Miss Dickinson's reclusiveness

has been explained in various ways by various biographers, most of whom have found evidence of an unhappy love affair, though agreement has not been reached about even the identity of the man she supposedly loved. Probably the most believable version of her story is that written by Professor George F. Whicher. His thesis is that most of Miss Dickinson's few relationships with men were completely intellectual, her only "love" was all on her side and the object of it was never aware of it, and she did not become a recluse suddenly and dramatically but drifted by degrees into her habit of living apart from the world.

What is even more puzzling than the details of her life is the paradox of her personality. Here is a child of New England Puritanism sternly reared in a strict household, shut off from much of life, increasingly retiring. But here also is a playful humorist, a passionate rebel, daring in her feeling, thinking, and expression. Here, too, as more and more readers recognize, is a fine poet. For, though details about Miss Dickinson's biography have led, in studies of her, to somewhat more emphasis on her personal history, somewhat less on her work, than may be desirable, she has been given growing recognition as a poet of significance. The first selection of her poetry, published posthumously in 1890, was frequently reprinted, and other selections appeared in 1892, 1896, 1914, 1924, 1929, 1936, and 1945. Beginning in the 1920's many critics have praised her, along with Whitman, for pioneering in modern poetry.

The uses Miss Dickinson made of imperfect rhyme or eye-rhyme, the liberties she took with grammar and rhythm, and, in particular, her habit of packing her lines with cryptic meanings have endeared her to present-day readers. Too, her vivid imagination and her playful spirit made her as fond of poetic conceits as John Donne, idol of the moderns, had been in the seventeenth century. The resemblance to Donne was almost certainly not the result of imitation: like the best modern poets, Miss Dickinson evolved a way of her own with words. Higginson, on reading her verse, thought perhaps Whitman's style had influenced her; but she said she had never read him—that she had been told "that he was disgraceful." Emerson, however, she knew in person and as an author, and Professor Boynton has noted important stylistic resemblances between the verse of the Transcendentalist leader and that of Miss Dickinson. "How many fairly discriminating readers," asks

Mr. Boynton, "might be puzzled if asked to tell which of the poets wrote the following quatrains?

> He who has no hands
> Perforce must use his tongue;
> Foxes are so cunning
> Because they are not strong.

> Ever the Rock of Ages melts
>   Into the mineral air,
> To be the quarry whence to build
>   Thought and its mansions fair.

They are, in fact, both Emerson's; but it is doubtful if any but Emersoniacs and Emilists could be certain in their ascriptions, and even then the answer would depend more on recognition than on judgment." Mr. Boynton correctly adds that despite this similarity it would be wrong to see in the younger poet either an imitator or an unconscious reflection of the older—that Emerson's influence at most, simply was "effective in reinforcing what 'the candidate preliminary was.'" Yet the kinship of her technique with that of two of the most radical prosodic innovators of her time is significant.

Significant also is the kinship of Miss Dickinson's way of thinking with that of her day. As Professor Whicher says, "What she actually represents is the last surprising bloom—the November witch-hazel blossom—of New England's flowering time . . . . She was a child of the Golden Day and never lost the impress of the period. Three of its strongest currents came to a confluence in her poetry: The Puritan tradition in which she was nurtured; the Yankee or, more broadly, American humor that was just coming out of the ground; and the spiritual unrest, typified by Emerson, which everywhere was melting the frost of custom . . . . Each was implicit in her surroundings and was absorbed from the atmosphere of her time. Blended, they gave her a style that was both original and native."

The Collected Poems of Emily Dickinson, ed. Martha Dickinson Bianchi and A. L. Hampson, Boston, 1937 • Bolts of Melody, ed. Millicent Todd Bingham, New York, 1945 • Letters of Emily Dickinson, New and Enlarged Edition, ed. Mabel Loomis Todd, New York, 1931 • G. F. Whicher, This Was a Poet, New York, 1939 • Millicent Todd Bingham, Ancestors' Brocades, New York, 1945

My Sabbath

This poem was one of the few published by Miss Dickinson herself during her lifetime: it appeared in **The Round Table**, edited by the author's cousins, Henry E. and Charles H. Sweetser, on March 12, 1864. Millicent Todd Bingham, in **Ancestors' Brocades**, suggests that it might have been the reception given to this poem which convinced the poet that "it was useless to attempt to gain a hearing."

Some keep the Sabbath going to church,
    I keep it staying at home,
With a bobolink for a chorister,
    And an orchard for a dome.

Some keep the Sabbath in surplice,
    I just wear my wings,
And instead of tolling the bell for church,
    Our little sexton sings.

God preaches—a noted clergyman,
    And the sermon is never long;

So instead of going to heaven at last,
    I'm going all along.

1864

The Snake

Miss Dickinson had not consented to its publication when this poem appeared in the **Springfield Republican**, February 14, 1866. She was annoyed with some liberties taken by the editor in the division of lines and in the punctuation. But she later made only a few changes in the wording: l. 4, "sudden" was substituted for "instant"; l. 11, "child" for "boy"; l. 12, "morn" for "noon." Here, as in other poems, the author uses figurative expressions which not only portray accurately but also connote the emotion of the poet. Increasingly, it suggests the effects of the snake which are summarized in the last line—"zero at the bone."

A narrow fellow in the grass
Occasionally rides;
You may have met him,—did you not?
His notice instant is.

The grass divides as with a comb,
A spotted shaft is seen;
And then it closes at your feet
And opens further on.

He likes a boggy acre,
A floor too cool for corn,   10
Yet when a boy, and barefoot,
I more than once, at noon,

Have passed, I thought, a whip-lash
Unbraiding in the sun,—
When, stooping to secure it,
It wrinkled, and was gone.

Several of nature's people
I know, and they know me;
I feel for them a transport
Of cordiality;   20

But never met this fellow,
Attended or alone,
Without a tighter breathing,
And zero at the bone.

                                                              1866

This Is My Letter

Poems of Emily Dickinson (1890), as the title-page announced, was "edited by two of her friends, Mabel Loomis Todd and T. W. Higginson." The editors chose "This Is My Letter" as a fitting prelude. Despite its simplicity of form and language, the poem indicates the author's feeling about the nature of her work and typifies her compact yet rich way of expressing her ideas. The selections from Miss Dickinson's writings printed hereafter, unlike our selections from other authors, do not have the dates of publication affixed. These writings were all published posthumously, and the dates of their appearance have no relevance to the dates of their composition.

This is my letter to the world,
   That never wrote to me,—

The simple news that Nature told,
   With tender majesty.

Her message is committed
   To hands I cannot see;
For love of her, sweet countrymen,
   Judge tenderly of me!

The Preacher

Brought up by a strict Puritan father, Miss Dickinson, despite her rebellion against some of the excesses of Calvinism, probably resented the highly intellectualized and at times snobbish liberal religion which was replacing it. The pretentious "modern" preacher, talking at length about virtues which perhaps could better be practiced than defined, gets his "come-uppance" in this ironic poem. The final lines gibe at the figure conjured up at the start of the poem, first by comparing mock gold (pyrites) with gold (here, as elsewhere in Miss Dickinson's poetry, a symbol of integrity) and then by imagining how Christ would feel upon confronting him.

He preached upon "breadth" till it argued him narrow.—
The broad are too broad to define;
And of "truth" until it proclaimed him a liar,—
The truth never flaunted a sign.

Simplicity fled from this counterfeit presence
As gold the pyrites would shun.
What confusion would cover the innocent Jesus
To meet so enabled a man!

I Like to See It Lap the Miles

"Your true poet," a character in Santayana's writings is made to say, "catches the charm of something or anything, dropping the thing itself." Here Miss Dickinson depicts a locomotive as if it were a mythical and mighty horse. The metaphor makes possible suggestions of the superhuman power and the paradoxical servitude of this lapper of miles and parer of quarries.

I like to see it lap the miles,
And lick the valleys up,
And stop to feed itself at tanks;
And then, prodigious, step

Around a pile of mountains,
And, supercilious, peer
In shanties by the sides of roads;
And then a quarry pare

To fit its sides, and crawl between,
Complaining all the while   10
In horrid, hooting stanza;
Then chase itself down hill

And neigh like Boanerges;
Then, punctual as a star,
Stop—docile and omnipotent—
At its own stable door.

The Humming Bird

"The Humming Bird" is a revision of an earlier version, and Professor Whicher (This Was a Poet, pp. 261-262) gives an interesting analysis of the changes made. "Here," he says of the final version, "is the whole sensation of hummingbird: first, a dazzle of sudden sense impressions, movement, motion of wings, color, and whir (in the re-iterated r's), all at once; then (the bird's departure taken for granted) the emptiness emphasized by the clear picture of nodding blossoms; and finally the startled mind of the (assumed) spectator regaining its poise with a whimsical comment. Nothing could be spared and no more is needed. Emily Dickinson was never to write a better nature poem than this, but the stepping-stones that led up to her finest achievement are, many of them, monuments of an artistry only slightly less perfect." As this analysis indicates, the poem is a striking example of the author's skill in giving concrete expression to abstract ideas—one of her most notable abilities.

A route of evanescence
With a revolving wheel;
A resonance of emerald,
A rush of cochineal;
And every blossom on the bush
Adjusts its tumbled head,—
The mail from Tunis, probably,
An easy morning's ride.

The Chariot

This poem illustrates how, in Professor Whicher's words, Miss Dickinson's line of thinking at times "rises to a . . . level where abstract ideas are personified and dramatized, filled with vital breath, and placed in exciting relation with each other." By telling vividly of the start of a journey by carriage to eternity, with Death as the coachman, the poem thus fancifully gives concrete expression to the hope for immortality. The details of the poem are arranged so as to disassociate the travelers more and more from earthly life. In the opening lines, "I could not stop" ambiguously suggests a laborer who could not put off toil. The second stanza shows that the poet has "put away" not only toil but also leisure. Now the slow carriage passes children at play, oblivious of the nearby travelers; next it passes fields which emphasize the lifelessness of the poet and the driver by "gazing" at them. After the darkness has come with the passing by of the setting sun, the travelers pause before a grave whose tenant has crumbled to dust: even that semblance of being has disappeared. Such is the preparation for the final stanza, in which immortality has replaced completely the mortality of earth.

Because I could not stop for Death,
He kindly stopped for me;
The carriage held but just ourselves
And Immortality.

We slowly drove, he knew no haste,
And I had put away
My labor and my leisure too,
For his civility.

We passed the school where children played
At wrestling in a ring;   10
We passed the fields of gazing grain,
We passed the setting sun.

We paused before a house that seemed
A swelling of the ground;
The roof was scarcely visible,
The cornice but a mound.

Since then 't is centuries; but each
Feels shorter than the day
I first surmised the horses' heads
Were toward eternity.   20

---

irreverant

Papa Above

This is a mockery of anthropomorphism, the tendency of
man to create God in his own image. "Suppose," Miss
Dickinson seems to have thought, "suppose a mouse conjured up a vision of God and eternity—what would this
vision be like?" Playfully, then, she pictured the animal
considering a Cat as the angel of death and conceiving of
heaven as a snug cupboard where, for all eternity, the
angel-mouse might nibble at his cheese. The irreverent
way she played with religious concepts was much in
the spirit of many contemporaneous nineteenth-century
American humorists. Robert Burdette's "The Brakeman at
Church" (1879), for instance, was a translation of the
tenets of various religious sects into the jargon of the
railroad man.

Papa above!
                    Regard a Mouse
O'erpowered by the Cat;

Reserve within thy Kingdom
A "mansion" for the Rat!

Snug in seraphic cupboards
To nibble all the day,
While unsuspecting cycles
Wheel pompously away.

As Imperceptibly as Grief

Although it ostensibly tells of the imperceptible passing of
summer, this composition also may be read as a comment upon change and death. The meaning is subtly
suggested by figures such as "as imperceptibly as grief"
and "without a wing," and by symbols. The symbols are
figures perhaps only vaguely suggestive of their implications unless Miss Dickinson's peculiarly personal ways of
using them in a number of her poems are taken into
account. As Mr. Thomas Dillon Howells has noticed in
an unpublished Master's dissertation, morning, for her,
signifies "hope, purity, innocence"; afternoon, customarily,
is associated with death, funerals; twilight or dusk, "a
solemn time of day, completion, peace."

change + death

As imperceptibly as grief
The summer lapsed away,—   *death came*
Too imperceptible, at last,
To seem like perfidy.

A quietness distilled,
As twilight long begun,
Or Nature, spending with herself
Sequestered afternoon.

The dusk drew earlier in,
The morning foreign shone,—   10

Papa Above • 5 **Rat.** Evidently the mouse thinks of rathood as a
heavenly glorification of the mouse

A courteous, yet harrowing grace,
As guest who would be gone.

And thus, without a wing,
Or service of a keel,
Our summer made her light escape
Into the beautiful.

Farther in Summer than the Birds

Mr. Yvor Winters, who considers this poem one of the five or six of the greatest by Miss Dickinson, says that in it "we are shown the essential cleavage between man, as represented by the author-reader, and nature, as represented by the insects in the late summer grass; the subject is the plight of man, the willing and freely-moving entity, in a universe in which he is by virtue of his essential qualities a foreigner. . . . The change described in the last two lines is the change in the appearance of nature and in the feeling of the observer which results from a recognition of the cleavage. . . . The first two lines of the last stanza are written in the author's personal grammatical shorthand; they are no doubt defective in this respect, but the defect is minor. They mean: There is as yet no diminution of beauty, no mark of change on the brightness. The twelfth line contains a meaningless inversion. On the other hand, the false rhymes are employed with unusually fine modulation; the first rhyme is perfect, the second and third represent successive stages of departure, and the last a return to what is roughly the stage of the second. These effects are complicated by the rhyming, both perfect and imperfect, from stanza to stanza. The intense strangeness of the poem could not have been achieved with standard rhyming."

Farther in summer than the birds,
Pathetic from the grass,
A minor nation celebrates
Its unobtrusive mass.

No ordinance is seen,
So gradual the grace,

A pensive custom it becomes,
Enlarging loneliness

Antiquest felt at noon
When August, burning low,
Calls forth this spectral canticle,
Repose to typify.

Remit as yet no grace,
No furrow on the glow,
Yet a druidic difference
Enhances nature now.

I Taste a Liquor Never Brewed

Thomas Bailey Aldrich thought that this composition needed "only a slight revision of the initial stanza to entitle it to rank with some of the swallow flights in Heine's lyrical intermezzos." He "tucked a rhyme into that opening stanza" to make it read:

> I taste a liquor never brewed
> In vats along the Rhine;
> No tankard ever held a draught
> Of alcohol like mine.

Miss Genevieve Taggard, in **The Life and Mind of Emily Dickinson**, defends the original version thus: " 'From tankards scooped in pearl' enjoins our attention, after being so vandalized. Quite apart from the sounds received and carried on by it, it runs the voice from the a's in 'tankards' to the o's in 'scooped' and then produces the word 'pearl,' on which to let them culminate; the nk and the r in 'tankard' catching all the other consonants as the ripple of tone-colour runs down the line. If anyone needs the pale device of rhyme after such interplay of sound, culminating in 'Yield such an alcohol,' he is tone-deaf and deserves to be so. But he should be told that, while he was hearing nothing, the stanza as a whole has been giving off the variations on the sound of I, firmly placed in the middle of the first line, at the end of the second, near the beginning of the third to culminate in 'yield' and the I's of 'alcohol.' "

I taste a liquor never brewed,
From tankards scooped in pearl;
Not all the vats upon the Rhine
Yield such an alcohol!

Inebriate of air am I,
And debauchee of dew,
Reeling, through endless summer days,
From inns of molten blue.

When landlords turn the drunken bee
Out of the foxglove's door,
When butterflies renounce their drams,
I shall but drink the more!

Till seraphs swing their snowy hats,
And saints to windows run,
To see the little tippler
Leaning against the sun!

[Handwritten annotations: general Theme — the taste a wine of summer & spring that cannot be brewed on earth — wine glasses — tankards scooped of pearl — The containers would be nature itself — priceless — beautiful surroundings — an intoxication of spring + summer — intoxicated — Spring — air — dew — the bee — the grape — foxglove flower — beauty of summer days — makes her intoxicated]

I'll Tell You How the Sun Rose

I'll tell you how the sun rose,—
A ribbon at a time.
The steeples swam in amethyst,
The news like squirrels ran.

The hills untied their bonnets,
The bobolinks begun.
Then I said softly to myself,
"That must have been the sun!"

*   *   *

But how he set, I know not.
There seemed a purple stile   10
Which little yellow boys and girls
Were climbing all the while

Till when they reached the other side,
A dominie in gray
Put gently up the evening bars,
And led the flock away.

If You Were Coming in the Fall

If you were coming in the fall,
I'd brush the summer by
With half a smile and half a spurn,
As housewives do a fly.

If I could see you in a year,
I'd wind the months in balls,
And put them each in separate drawers,
Until their time befalls.

If only centuries delayed,
I'd count them on my hand,   10
Subtracting till my fingers dropped
Into Van Dieman's land.

If certain, when this life was out,
That yours and mine should be,
I'd toss it yonder like a rind,
And taste eternity.

But now, all ignorant of the length
Of time's uncertain wing,
It goads me, like the goblin bee,
That will not state its sting.   20

If You Were Coming in the Fall • 12 Van Dieman's land, Tasmania; here used as a symbol for a remote and far-distant place

The Wife

She rose to his requirement, dropped
The playthings of her life
To take the honorable work
Of woman and of wife.

If aught she missed in her new day
Of amplitude, or awe,

Or first prospective, or the gold
In using wore away,

It lay unmentioned, as the sea
Develops pearl and weed,
But only to himself is known   10
The fathoms they abide.

Real

I like a look of agony,   *sincerity*
Because I know it's true;
Men do not sham convulsion,
Nor simulate a throe.

The eyes glaze once, and that is death.
Impossible to feign
The beads upon the forehead
By homely anguish strung.

The Bustle in a House

The bustle in a house
The morning after death
Is solemnest of industries
Enacted upon earth,—

The sweeping up the heart,
And putting love away
We shall not want to use again
Until eternity.

I Died for Beauty

I died for beauty, but was scarce
Adjusted in the tomb,
When one who died for truth was lain
In an adjoining room.

He questioned softly why I failed?
"For beauty," I replied.
"And I for truth—the two are one;
We brethren are," he said.

And so, as kinsmen met a night,
We talked between the rooms,   10
Until the moss had reached our lips,
And covered up our names.

'Twas Warm at First like Us

'Twas warm at first like us,
Until there crept thereon
A chill, like frost upon a glass
Till all the scene be gone.

The forehead copied stone,   *what is it?*
The fingers grew too cold
To ache, and like a skater's brook
The busy eyes congealed.

It straightened—that was all.
It crowded cold to cold—
It multiplied indifference   10
As Pride were all it could.

And even when with cords
'T was lowered like a freight,
It made no signal, nor demurred,
But dropped like adamant.

Contrast of warmth & life to chill & death

There's a Certain Slant of Light

There's a certain slant of light,
On winter afternoons,
That oppresses like the weight
Of cathedral tunes.

Heavenly hurt it gives us;
We can find no scar,

But internal difference
Where the meanings are.

None may teach it anything,
'T is the seal, despair,—
An imperial affliction
Sent us of the air.

When it comes, the landscape listens,
Shadows hold their breath;
When it goes, 't is like the distance
On the look of death.

I've Seen a Dying Eye

I've seen a dying eye
Run round and round a room
In search of something, as it seemed,
Then cloudier become;
And then, obscure with fog,
And then be soldered down, —*casket put down*
Without disclosing what it be,
'T were blessed to have seen.

The Robin's My Criterion of Tune

The Robin's my criterion of tune
Because I grow where robins do—
But were I Cuckoo born
I'd swear by him—
The ode familiar rules the morn.
The Buttercup's my whim
For bloom—
Because we're orchard-sprung—
But were I Britain-born
I'd daisies spurn—
None but the Nut October fits
Because through dropping it
The seasons flit, I'm taught.
Without the snow's tableau

Winter were lie to me—
Because I see New Englandly.
The Queen discerns like me
Provincially.

S.

Death Is a Dialogue

Death is a dialogue between
The spirit and the dust.
"Dissolve," says Death. The Spirit, "Sir, *very good!*
I have another trust."

Death doubts it, argues from the ground.
The Spirit turns away,
Just laying off, for evidence,
An overcoat of clay.

A Wounded Deer Leaps Highest

A wounded deer leaps highest,
I've heard the hunter tell;
'Tis but the ecstasy of death,
And then the brake is still.

The smitten rock that gushes,
The trampled steel that springs:
A cheek is always redder
Just where the hectic stings!

Mirth is the mail of anguish, ✳
In which it cautious arm,
Lest anybody spy the blood
And "You're hurt" exclaim!

Exclusion

The soul selects her own society,
Then shuts the door;

On her divine majority
Obtrude no more.

Unmoved, she notes the chariot's pausing
At her low gate;
Unmoved, an emperor is kneeling
Upon her mat.

I've known her from an ample nation
Choose one;   10
Then close the valves of her attention
Like stone.

We Learned the Whole of Love

We learned the whole of love,
The alphabet, the words,
A chapter, then the mighty book—
Then revelation closed.

But in each other's eyes
An ignorance beheld
Diviner than the childhood's,
And each to each a child

Attempted to expound
What neither understood.   10
Alas, that wisdom is so large
And truth so manifold!

My Life Had Stood a Loaded Gun

My life had stood a loaded gun
In corners, till a day
The owner passed—identified,
And carried me away.

And now we roam the sov'reign woods,
And now we hunt the doe—
And every time I speak for him
The mountains straight reply.

And do I smile, such cordial light
Upon the valley glow—
It is as a Vesuvian face
Had let its pleasure through.

And when at night, our good day done,
I guard my master's head,
'Tis better than the eider duck's
Deep pillow to have shared.

To foe of his I'm deadly foe,
None stir the second time
On whom I lay a yellow eye
Or an emphatic thumb.   20

Though I than he may longer live,
He longer must than I,
For I have but the art to kill—
Without the power to die.

Summer Has Two Beginnings

Summer has two beginnings,
Beginning once in June,
Beginning in October
Affectingly again,

Without perhaps the riot,
But graphicker for grace—
As finer is a going
Than a remaining face—

Departing then forever,
Forever until May.   10
Forever is deciduous
Except to those who die.

1871 · 1900

For a biographical account of Stephen Crane and a consideration of his novels and short stories, **see** pages 603-604.

Poems

Poems numbered 1-2 appeared in **The Black Riders and Other Lines** in 1895; poems numbered 3-6 appeared in **War Is Kind and Other Lines** in 1899.

Critics have often pointed out Crane's indebtedness to Emily Dickinson and his anticipation of the Imagist poets. Reacting against the popular tradition of Tennyson and Longfellow, Crane achieved something of the concentration, the impressionistic pictorial effect, and the irony of modern American poetry.

1

God fashioned the ship of the world carefully.
With the infinite skill of an All-Master
Made He the hull and the sails,
Held He the rudder
Ready for adjustment.
Erect stood He, scanning His work proudly.
Then—at fateful time—a wrong called,
And God turned, heeding.
Lo, the ship, at this opportunity, slipped slyly,

Making cunning noiseless travel down the ways.   10
So that, for ever rudderless, it went upon the seas
Going ridiculous voyages,
Making quaint progress,
Turning as with serious purpose
Before stupid winds.
And there were many in the sky
Who laughed at this thing.

2

Should the wide world roll away,
Leaving black terror,
Limitless night,
Nor God, nor man, nor place to stand
Would be to me essential,
If thou and thy white arms were there,
And the fall to doom a long way.

3

Do not weep, maiden, for war is kind.
Because your lover threw wild hands toward the sky

And the affrighted steed ran on alone,
Do not weep.
War is kind.

   Hoarse, booming drums of the regiment,
   Little souls who thirst for fight,
   These men were born to drill and die.
   The unexplained glory flies above them,
   Great is the battle-god, great, and his kingdom—   10
   A field where a thousand corpses lie.

Do not weep, babe, for war is kind.
Because your father tumbled in the yellow trenches,
Raged at his breast, gulped and died,
Do not weep.
War is kind.

   Swift blazing flag of the regiment,
   Eagle with crest of red and gold,
   These men were born to drill and die.
   Point for them the virtue of slaughter,   20
   Make plain to them the excellence of killing
   And a field where a thousand corpses lie.

Mother whose heart hung humble as a button
On the bright splendid shroud of your son,
Do not weep.
War is kind.

4

The wayfarer,
Perceiving the pathway to truth,
Was struck with astonishment.
It was thickly grown with weeds.
"Ha," he said,
"I see that none has passed here
"In a long time."
Later he saw that each weed
Was a singular knife.
"Well," he mumbled at last,   10
"Doubtless there are other roads."

5

A man said to the universe:
"Sir, I exist!"
"However," replied the universe,

"The fact has not created in me
"A sense of obligation."

6

The trees in the garden rained flowers.
Children ran there joyously.
They gathered the flowers
Each to himself.
Now there were some
Who gathered great heaps—
Having opportunity and skill—
Until, behold, only chance blossoms
Remained for the feeble.
Then a little spindling tutor   10
Ran importantly to the father, crying:
'Pray, come hither!
See this unjust thing in your garden!'
But when the father had surveyed,
He admonished the tutor:
'Not so, small sage!
This thing is just.
For, look you,
Are not they who possess the flowers
Stronger, bolder, shrewder   20
Than they who have none?
Why should the strong—
The beautiful strong—
Why should they not have the flowers?'
Upon reflection, the tutor bowed to the ground,
'My lord,' he said,
'The stars are displaced
By this towering wisdom.'

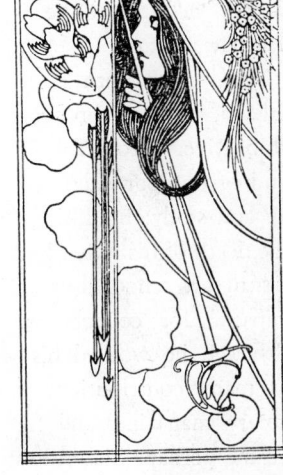

*Illustration by Will Brad-
ley for the poem "War Is
Kind" from Stephen Crane,*
War Is Kind, *1899*

William Vaughn Moody

1869 · 1910

The one American poet who stood out from among his fellows in the first decade of the twentieth century was William Vaughn Moody. Like his friend Edwin Arlington Robinson (see p. 888), whose fame was to come later, Moody was on the whole traditional in his forms, although not slavishly so. Frequently reminiscent of the later English Victorians, his verses nevertheless have the distinction of revealing a sensitive and observant individual whose bookishness did not obscure his fresh perceptions of a uniquely puzzling world. Moody saw the United States in the "progressive" era and he did not like its lack of direction, its materialism, its apparent desertion of ideals. But he was not bitter, as Crane was, nor a crusader, as were some of the novelists of his generation. His very detachment was to a degree a virtue, for it enabled him to describe with admirable balance the state of the American mind at the opening of a new century.

Moody was born in a small town in south-central Indiana, but was brought up in New Albany, on the Ohio River across from Louisville. As a boy he was fond of outdoor exercise, but also of music and painting and study; his liking for all these stayed with him. The death of his father broke up the family while Moody was in art school, but with the help of an uncle he prepared for college and in 1889 entered Harvard. Although he worked his way through, he found time for many contributions to the *Harvard Monthly,* the literary magazine, and for the rich friendships which became perhaps his greatest glory.

Having satisfied the requirements for graduation in three years, Moody spent his senior year in Europe, tutoring a young man getting ready for Harvard. They walked through the English lake country and the Black Forest, saw the sights of Paris, Florence, and Athens. Before he died, he returned to Europe five more times, sometimes for months on end; like Howells and Henry James and many other Americans he found the other side of the Atlantic a second home. In 1893, however, he went back to Cambridge for his own commencement to read the Class Day poem, staying on at Harvard for two years of graduate study. He then accepted an instructorship in English at the University of Chicago, which was rising dramatically to eminence. In Chicago he spent the larger part of seven years, teaching, editing school textbooks to supplement his income, enjoying the companionship of a lively literary and artistic set, leaving at intervals for vacations in Europe, northern Michigan, and Colorado. Always, moreover, there was writing, which he was coming to regard as his real profession. In 1902 he was enabled to give it his full time through the success of a textbook, *A History of English Literature,* written in collaboration with his friend Robert Morss Lovett. Its royalties supported a farewell to the classroom.

His true work had already begun with a poetic drama, *The Masque of Judgment* (1898), and a thin volume of *Poems* (1901), containing twenty-five pieces, some of them previously published in magazines. His production in the eight remaining years of his life was not large, primarily because he was fighting a losing battle with the tumorous condition which caused his death in 1910. Of the quality of what he did, however, there has never been any question. A dozen additional short poems, *The Fire-Bringer* (1904, a second poetic drama which with *The Masque of Judgment* and the uncompleted "Death of Eve" forms his most ambitious work), and two prose plays, *The Great Divide* (produced in 1906, it ran for two years and gave him his first genuine financial security) and *The Faith Healer* (1909)—these and his letters are all that we have.

There is nothing quite like Moody's writings in American literature for the combination of fresh experience and scholarship. The two poles of Moody's life and thought were Chicago and Europe—crude, throbbing, undisciplined force on the one hand, the shaping and ever-present awareness of past excellence on the other. Respect for power and a sense of the merits of tradition are combined in almost everything that Moody wrote, from his short lyrics to the trilogy in which he hoped to display the unity of God and man by reinterpreting the stories of Prometheus, the Day of Judgment, and Eve. Curiously enough, the combination is a fairly happy one. Like Whitman before him, Moody accepted the world and humanity, whatever their manifestations, as ultimately good and meaningful, refusing to separate the spiritual from the physical. He was no doubter, although he was often discouraged. Like Robert Browning, whom he much resembles, Moody had the intellectuality and fastidiousness that come with systematic study of literary art. He lived in an age of doubt and uncertainty which he quite fully shared, but his humanism carried him through and he was able to comment with quiet penetration upon the world he saw.

The Poems and Plays of William Vaughn Moody, ed. J. M. Manly, 2 vols., Boston, 1912 • Selected Poems of William Vaughn Moody, ed. R. M. Lovett, Boston, 1931 • Some Letters of William Vaughn Moody, ed. D. G. Mason, Boston, 1913 • Letters to Harriet, ed. Percy Mackaye, Boston, 1935 • D. D. Henry, William Vaughn Moody: A Study, Boston, 1934

An Ode in Time of Hesitation

[After seeing at Boston the statue of Robert Gould Shaw, killed while storming Fort Wagner, July 18, 1863, at the head of the first enlisted Negro regiment, the 54th Massachusetts.]

On one of his walking tours in Europe in July 1897 Moody read the account of the dedication of Saint Gaudens' monument to Col. Robert Gould Shaw, on Boston Common across from the State House. Professor Lovett, his companion, was able to tell of the stories of jeering at Shaw and his Negro regiment before their departure for the South. After his return to the United States, Moody saw the monument and in 1900, deeply distressed that American troops were being used to put down the insurrection of the Filipinos led by Emilio Aguinaldo, he wrote the following poem, based upon the contrast between Shaw's idealism and the imperialistic policy which he believed was being followed in the Philippines. It was published in the Atlantic Monthly for May 1900. A few words were changed when Moody collected his poems for the 1901 volume.

The "Ode" was much admired from the first. Its relatively free form is typical of Moody, who in many ways anticipated the "new poetry" which became popular after 1915. Typical also are its allusions and literary echoes, its occasionally archaic diction and venturesome metaphor. Bookish but not exotic, it is a courageous political poem on a subject of which Americans have not yet heard the last word.

I

Before the solemn bronze Saint Gaudens made
To thrill the heedless passer's heart with awe,
And set here in the city's talk and trade
To the good memory of Robert Shaw,

1 Saint Gaudens, Augustus Saint Gaudens (1848-1907), Irish-born American sculptor, best known perhaps for his mantled figure over the grave of Mrs. Henry Adams in Rock Creek Cemetery, Washington, D. C. He dominated sculpture in the United States after 1880, and the Shaw monument is only one of many commissions commemorating Civil War heroes

This bright March morn I stand,
And hear the distant spring come up the land;
Knowing that what I hear is not unheard
Of this boy soldier and his Negro band,
For all their gaze is fixed so stern ahead,
For all the fatal rhythm of their tread.   10
The land they died to save from death and shame
Trembles and waits, hearing the spring's great name,
And by her pangs these resolute ghosts are stirred.

II

Through street and mall the tides of people go
Heedless; the trees upon the Common show
No hint of green; but to my listening heart
The still earth doth impart
Assurance of her jubilant emprise,
And it is clear to my long-searching eyes
That love at last has might upon the skies.   20
The ice is runneled in the little pond;
A telltale patter drips from off the trees;
The air is touched with southland spiceries,
As if but yesterday it tossed the frond
Of pendent mosses where the live-oaks grow
Beyond Virginia and the Carolines,
Or had its will among the fruits and vines
Of aromatic isles asleep beyond
Florida and the Gulf of Mexico.

III

Soon shall the Cape Ann children shout in glee,   30
Spying the arbutus, spring's dear recluse;
Hill lads at dawn shall hearken the wild goose
Go honking northward over Tennessee;
West from Oswego to Sault Sainte-Marie,
And on to where the Pictured Rocks are hung,
And yonder where, gigantic, willful, young,
Chicago sitteth at the northwest gates,
With restless violent hands and casual tongue
Moulding her mighty fates,
The Lakes shall robe them in ethereal sheen;   40
And like a larger sea, the vital green
Of springing wheat shall vastly be outflung
Over Dakota and the prairie states.
By desert people immemorial
On Arizonan mesas shall be done
Dim rites unto the thunder and the sun;

Nor shall the primal gods lack sacrifice
More splendid, when the white Sierras call
Unto the Rockies straightway to arise
And dance before the unveiled ark of the year,   50
Sounding their windy cedars as for shawms,
Unrolling rivers clear
For flutter of broad phylacteries;
While Shasta signals to Alaskan seas
That watch old sluggish glaciers downward creep
To fling their icebergs thundering from the steep,
And Mariposa through the purple calms
Gazes at far Hawaii crowned with palms
Where East and West are met,—
A rich seal on the ocean's bosom set   60
To say that East and West are twain,
With different loss and gain:
The Lord hath sundered them; let them be sundered yet.

IV

Alas! what sounds are these that come
Sullenly over the Pacific seas,—
Sounds of ignoble battle, striking dumb
The season's half-awakened ecstasies?
Must I be humble, then,
Now when my heart hath need of pride?
Wild love falls on me from these sculptured men;   70
By loving much the land for which they died
I would be justified.
My spirit was away on pinions wide
To soothe in praise of her its passionate mood
And ease it of its ache of gratitude,
Too sorely heavy is the debt they lay
On me and the companions of my day.
I would remember now
My country's goodliness, make sweet her name.
Alas! what shade art thou   80
Of sorrow or of blame
Liftest the lyric leafage from her brow,
And pointest a slow finger at her shame?

---

30 Cape Ann. See note, p. 57 • 35 Pictured Rocks, on the south
shore of Lake Superior, east of Marquette, Michigan • 50 unveiled
ark, an allusion to the ark of the covenant, symbol of the favor of
God to the Jews, and referred to frequently in the Bible • 57 Mariposa, a town and county of the high Sierras, in California

V

Lies! lies! It cannot be! The wars we wage
Are noble, and our battles still are won
By justice for us, ere we lift the gage.
We have not sold our loftiest heritage.
The proud republic hath not stooped to cheat
And scramble in the market-place of war;
Her forehead weareth yet its solemn star.   90
Here is her witness: this, her perfect son,
This delicate and proud New England soul
Who leads despisèd men, with just-unshackled feet,
Up the large ways where death and glory meet,
To show all peoples that our shame is done,
That once more we are clean and spirit-whole

VI

Crouched in the sea fog on the moaning sand
All night he lay, speaking some simple word
From hour to hour to the slow minds that heard,
Holding each poor life gently in his hand   100
And breathing on the base rejected clay
Till each dark face shone mystical and grand
Against the breaking day;
And lo, the shard the potter cast away
Was grown a fiery chalice crystal-fine
Fulfilled of the divine
Great wine of battle wrath by God's ring-finger stirred.
Then upward, where the shadowy bastion loomed
Huge on the mountain in the wet sea light,
Whence now, and now, infernal flowerage bloomed, 110
Bloomed, burst, and scattered down its deadly seed,—
They swept, and died like freemen on the height,
Like freemen, and like men of noble breed;
And when the battle fell away at night
By hasty and contemptuous hands were thrust
Obscurely in a common grave with him
The fair-haired keeper of their love and trust.
Now limb doth mingle with dissolvèd limb
In nature's busy old democracy
To flush the mountain laurel when she blows   120
Sweet by the southern sea,
And heart with crumbled heart climbs in the rose:—
The untaught hearts with the high heart that knew
This mountain fortress for no earthly hold
Of temporal quarrel, but the bastion old

Of spiritual wrong,
Built by an unjust nation sheer and strong,
Expugnable but by a nation's rue
And bowing down before that equal shrine
By all men held divine,   130
Whereof his band and he were the most holy sign.

VII

O bitter, bitter shade!
Wilt thou not put the scorn
And instant tragic question from thine eyes?
Do thy dark brows yet crave
That swift and angry stave—
Unmeet for this desirous morn—
That I have striven, striven to evade?
Gazing on him, must I not deem they err
Whose careless lips in street and shop aver   140
As common tidings, deeds to make his cheek
Flush from the bronze, and his dead throat to speak?
Surely some elder singer would arise,
Whose harp hath leave to threaten and to mourn
Above this people when they go astray.
Is Whitman, the strong spirit, overworn?
Has Whittier put his yearning wrath away?
I will not and I dare not yet believe!
Though furtively the sunlight seems to grieve,
And the spring-laden breeze   150
Out of the gladdening west is sinister
With sounds of nameless battle overseas;
Though when we turn and question in suspense
If these things be indeed after these ways,
And what things are to follow after these,
Our fluent men of place and consequence
Fumble and fill their mouths with hollow phrase,
Or for the end-all of deep arguments
Intone their dull commercial liturgies—
I dare not yet believe! My ears are shut!   160
I will not hear the thin satiric praise
And muffled laughter of our enemies,
Bidding us never sheathe our valiant sword
Till we have changed our birthright for a gourd
Of wild pulse stolen from a barbarian's hut;
Showing how wise it is to cast away
The symbols of our spiritual sway,
That so our hands with better ease
May wield the driver's whip and grasp the jailer's keys.

An Ode in Time of Hesitation   691

VIII

Was it for this our fathers kept the law? 170
This crown shall crown their struggle and their ruth?
Are we the eagle nation Milton saw
Mewing its mighty youth,
Soon to possess the mountain winds of truth,
And be a swift familiar of the sun
Where aye before God's face his trumpets run?
Or have we but the talons and the maw,
And for the abject likeness of our heart
Shall some less lordly bird be set apart?—
Some gross-billed wader where the swamps are fat? 180
Some gorger in the sun? Some prowler with the bat?

IX

Ah no!
We have not fallen so.
We are our fathers' sons: let those who lead us know!
'T was only yesterday sick Cuba's cry
Came up the tropic wind, "Now help us, for we die!"
Then Alabama heard,
And rising, pale, to Maine and Idaho
Shouted a burning word.
Proud state with proud impassioned state conferred, 190
And at the lifting of a hand sprang forth,
East, west, and south, and north,
Beautiful armies. Oh, by the sweet blood and young
Shed on the awful hill slope at San Juan,
By the unforgotten names of eager boys
Who might have tasted girls' love and been stung
With the old mystic joys
And starry griefs, now the spring nights come on,
But that the heart of youth is generous,—
We charge you, ye who lead us, 200
Breathe on their chivalry no hint of stain!
Turn not their new-world victories to gain!
One least leaf plucked for chaffer from the bays
Of their dear praise,
One jot of their pure conquest put to hire,
The implacable republic will require;
With clamor, in the glare and gaze of noon,
Or subtly, coming as a thief at night,
But surely, very surely, slow or soon
That insult deep we deeply will requite. 210
Tempt not our weakness, our cupidity!
For save we let the island men go free,
Those baffled and dislaureled ghosts

Will curse us from the lamentable coasts
Where walk the frustrate dead.
The cup of trembling shall be drainèd quite,
Eaten the sour bread of astonishment,
With ashes of the hearth shall be made white
Our hair, and wailing shall be in the tent;
Then on your guiltier head 220
Shall our intolerable self-disdain
Wreak suddenly its anger and its pain;
For manifest in that disastrous light
We shall discern the right
And do it, tardily.—O ye who lead,
Take heed!
Blindness we may forgive, but baseness we will smite.

1900

On a Soldier Fallen in the Philippines

Moody's opposition to imperialism was perhaps pre sented even more effectively in this poem, first published in the **Atlantic Monthly** in February 1901, than in "Ar Ode in Time of Hesitation." In March of the same year, with the capture of Aguinaldo, the Filipino independence movement was crushed.

Streets of the roaring town,
Hush for him, hush, be still!
He comes, who was stricken down
Doing the word of our will.
Hush! Let him have his state,
Give him his soldier's crown.
The grists of trade can wait
Their grinding at the mill,
But he cannot wait for his honor, now the trumpet has
been blown.
Wreathe pride now for his granite brow, lay love on his
breast of stone. 10

An Ode . . . 172 Milton. John Milton (1608-1674) wrote of England as "an eagle mewing her mighty youth" • 194 San Juan. San Juan Hill, near Santiago de Cuba, was taken by American forces on July 1, 1898, with casualties amounting to 10 per cent of the attacking force. It was in this action that Theodore Roosevelt won distinction as a military leader

Toll! Let the great bells toll
Till the clashing air is dim.
Did we wrong this parted soul?
We will make it up to him.
Toll! Let him never guess
What work we set him to.
Laurel, laurel, yes;
He did what we bade him do.
Praise, and never a whispered hint but the fight he
    fought was good;
Never a word that the blood on his sword was his coun-
    try's own heart's-blood.   20

A flag for the soldier's bier
Who dies that his land may live;
O, banners, banners here,
That he doubt not nor misgive!
That he heed not from the tomb
The evil days draw near
When the nation, robed in gloom,
  With its faithless past shall strive.
Let him never dream that his bullet's scream went wide
    of its island mark,
Home to the heart of his darling land where she stumbled
    and sinned in the dark.   30
                 1901

The Menagerie

First published in the 1901 collection, "The Menagerie" is
a dramatic monologue. The "little man in trousers, slightly
jagged," reflects, with a penetration which somewhat
belies his condition, upon his place in the evolutionary
scheme of things. More simply and attractively than
anywhere else, perhaps, Moody here presents his faith
in the unity of the universe, the inseparableness of soul and
body, and the potential capacity of human beings for improvement. The humor is not without its sting.

Thank God my brain is not inclined to cut
Such capers every day! I'm just about
Mellow, but then—There goes the tent-flap shut.
Rain's in the wind. I thought so: every snout
Was twitching when the keeper turned me out.

That screaming parrot makes my blood run cold.
Gabriel's trump! the big bull elephant
Squeals "Rain!" to the parched herd. The monkeys scold,
And jabber that it's rain water they want.
(It makes me sick to see a monkey pant.)   10

I'll foot it home, to try and make believe
I'm sober. After this I stick to beer,
And drop the circus when the sane folks leave.
A man's a fool to look at things too near:
They look back, and begin to cut up queer.

Beasts do, at any rate; especially
Wild devils caged. They have the coolest way
Of being something else than what you see:
You pass a sleek young zebra nosing hay,
A nylghau looking bored and distingué,—   20

And think you've seen a donkey and a bird.
Not on your life! Just glance back, if you dare
The zebra chews, the nylghau hasn't stirred;
But something's happened, Heaven knows what or
    where,
To freeze your scalp and pompadour your hair.

I'm not precisely an æolian lute
Hung in the wandering winds of sentiment,
But drown me if the ugliest, meanest brute
Grunting and fretting in that sultry tent
Didn't just floor me with embarrassment!   30

'Twas like a thunder-clap from out the clear,—
One minute they were circus beasts, some grand,
Some ugly, some amusing, and some queer:
Rival attractions to the hobo band,
The flying jenny, and the peanut stand.

Next minute they were old hearth-mates of mine!
Lost people, eyeing me with such a stare!
Patient, satiric, devilish, divine;
A gaze of hopeless envy, squalid care,
Hatred, and thwarted love, and dim despair.   40

Within my blood my ancient kindred spoke,—
Grotesque and monstrous voices, heard afar
Down ocean caves when behemoth awoke,
Or through fern forests roared the plesiosaur
Locked with the giant-bat in ghastly war.

And suddenly, as in a flash of light,
I saw great Nature working out her plan;
Through all her shapes from mastodon to mite
Forever groping, testing, passing on
To find at last the shape and soul of Man.   50

Till in the fullness of accomplished time,
Comes brother Forepaugh, upon business bent,
Tracks her through frozen and through torrid clime,
And shows us, neatly labeled in a tent,
The stages of her huge experiment;

Blabbing aloud her shy and reticent hours;
Dragging to light her blinking, slothful moods;
Publishing fretful seasons when her powers
Worked wild and sullen in her solitudes,
Or when her mordant laughter shook the woods.   60

Here, round about me, were her vagrant births;
Sick dreams she had, fierce projects she essayed;
Her qualms, her fiery prides, her crazy mirths;
The troublings of her spirit as she strayed,
Cringed, gloated, mocked, was lordly, was afraid,

On that long road she went to seek mankind;
Here were the darkling coverts that she beat
To find the Hider she was sent to find;
Here the distracted footprints of her feet
Whereby her soul's Desire she came to greet.   70

But why should they, her botch-work, turn about
And stare disdain at me, her finished job?
Why was the place one vast suspended shout
Of laughter? Why did all the daylight throb
With soundless guffaw and dumb-stricken sob?

Helpless I stood among those awful cages;
The beasts were walking loose, and I was bagged!
I, I, last product of the toiling ages,
Goal of heroic feet that never lagged,—
A little man in trousers, slightly jagged.   80

Deliver me from such another jury!
The Judgment-day will be a picnic to 't.
Their satire was more dreadful than their fury,
And worst of all was just a kind of brute
Disgust, and giving up, and sinking mute.

Survival of the fittest, adaptation,
And all their other evolution terms,
Seem to omit one small consideration,
To wit, that tumblebugs and angleworms
Have souls: there's soul in everything that squirms.   90

And souls are restless, plagued, impatient things,
All dream and unaccountable desire;
Crawling, but pestered with the thought of wings;
Spreading through every inch of earth's old mire
Mystical hanker after something higher.

Wishes *are* horses, as I understand.
I guess a wistful polyp that has strokes
Of feeling faint to gallivant on land
Will come to be a scandal to his folks;
Legs he will sprout, in spite of threats and jokes.   100

And at the core of every life that crawls
Or runs or flies or swims or vegetates—
Churning the mammoth's heart-blood, in the galls
Of shark and tiger planting gorgeous hates,
Lighting the love of eagles for their mates;

Yes, in the dim brain of the jellied fish
That is and is not living—moved and stirred
From the beginning a mysterious wish,
A vision, a command, a fatal Word:
The name of Man was uttered, and they heard.   110

Upward along the æons of old war
They sought him: wing and shank-bone, claw and bill
Were fashioned and rejected; wide and far
They roamed the twilight jungles of their will;
But still they sought him, and desired him still.

Man they desired, but mind you, Perfect Man,
The radiant and the loving, yet to be!
I hardly wonder, when they came to scan
The upshot of their strenuosity,
They gazed with mixed emotions upon *me*.   120

Well, my advice to you is, Face the creatures,
Or spot them sideways with your weather eye,

---

52 Forepaugh, Adam Forepaugh (1831-1890), American circus proprietor, after 1867, Barnum's chief rival

Just to keep tab on their expansive features;
It isn't pleasant when you're stepping high
To catch a giraffe smiling on the sly.

If nature made you graceful, don't get gay
Back-to before the hippopotamus;
If meek and godly, find some place to play
Besides right where three mad hyenas fuss:

You may hear language that we won't discuss.

If you're a sweet thing in a flower-bed hat,
Or her best fellow with your tie tucked in,
Don't squander love's bright springtime girding at
An old chimpanzee with an Irish chin:
There may be hidden meaning in his grin.

1901

CRITICS OF AMERICAN SOCIETY:

George   Bellamy   Steffens   Dunne   Sinclair   Adams

Henry George

1839 · 1897

"Depression" is still a painful word to most Americans, who more than a decade later cannot erase the memories of personal misery which the history books will never quite catch in their accounts of the stock-market crash of 1929, the closing of the banks in 1933, and the measures of the "alphabet" agencies—NRA, RFC, AAA, CCC, PWA, and WPA. Yet depressions have come so regularly to the United States—one about every twenty years—that many persons regard them as the in-

evitable end and fresh beginning of the "business cycle" of capitalist economy.

Others have always insisted that an industrialized society of enormous productive capacity ought somehow to be able to find a way of avoiding periodic breakdowns in its system of distribution. Wholesale bankruptcies,

Illustration: "And he asks for more"—an anti-trust cartoon by Dalrymple for **Puck**, March 7, 1890. King Monopoly, sitting in state upon American industry, receives tribute from the entire nation.

the unemployment of able-bodied men and women, and starvation not for lack of food but for lack of buying power—these have seemed too high a price to pay for free enterprise. In the distress of deflationary eras the critics have always commanded attention. Brook Farm and the Socialism of Fourier were not lightly dismissed while the memories of the Panic of 1837 lingered. Technocracy and the Townsend Plan had their vogue in the nineteen-thirties, and the strength of the New Deal lay in the conviction of a majority of Americans that economic stability must be a concern of government. But when times are good, "experimentation" is unpopular.

In the aftermath of the Civil War there was a long stretch of hard times; between the Panic of 1873 and that of 1893 there was no genuine recovery. Social planners had time to perfect their schemes of amelioration through years when almost everyone demanded change. The result was a vast literature of social criticism, of which Henry George's *Progress and Poverty* (1879) and Edward Bellamy's *Looking Backward* (1888) are the best examples. Neither is perhaps a literary masterpiece, but few American books have been so directly influential. They and other works like them helped direct the political thought and action of two generations.

Henry George was a Philadelphian by birth. He did not do well in school and at thirteen was working as an errand boy. He clerked a bit, attended lectures at the Franklin Institute, went to sea for a year's voyage to Australia and India, learned the trade of typesetter, shipped again as a steward on a vessel bound for California. In San Francisco he left his ship, and there he lived for most of the time between 1858 and 1880. He did not find life easy, particularly after his marriage at twenty-one in 1860, and the arrival of four children in quick succession. He worked at what he could find, but chiefly at printing, reporting, and editing. For a year, in 1867-1868, he was managing editor of the San Francisco *Times,* at fifty dollars a week.

Early in 1869 he was in New York City, organizing a wire news service for the San Francisco *Herald.* There he had two revealing experiences. He had a first-hand demonstration of the power of monopoly when he saw his news service killed by the opposition of the Associated Press and its influence with, so he believed, the Western Union Telegraph Company. And in the streets of the city he had what he later called a "vision, a call."

"I saw," he said, "and recognized for the first time the shocking contrast between monstrous wealth and debasing want. And here I made a vow from which I have never faltered, to seek out, and remedy, if I could, the cause that condemned little children to lead such a life as you know them to lead in the squalid districts."

Later in the same year, back in California, he found what he believed to be the cause, the reason for the shocking contrast he had noted. Riding in the hills around Oakland, a city just then in the grip of a fever of land speculation, he asked a passing teamster what land thereabouts was worth. He was told that its worth was uncertain, but that a man "over there" would sell for a thousand dollars an acre. "Like a flash it came upon me that there was the reason of advancing poverty with advancing wealth. With the growth of population, land grows in value, and the men who work it must pay more for the privilege."

Land monopoly, he decided, had to be destroyed. God gave the land for the use of men—of all men, not merely a fortunate few. He sat down to work out some means of halting the trend which he observed all around him, and which he was now convinced was the chief cause of poverty. In 1871 he published a forty-eight-page pamphlet, *Our Land and Land Policy, National and State,* in which he argued that land should be taxed for its unearned value, that is to say in accordance with the difference between what it is worth when used and what it is worth by reason of its location. Improvements would not be considered; the owner of a vacant lot would have to pay just as much as the owner who had a store building on his lot. By this method of taxation, he argued, land speculation would be brought to an end, and the whole cost of government would be borne by land alone.

George's pamphlet found few readers, and perhaps did not deserve to win more, for his knowledge of previous writers on political economy at this stage was relatively slight. But he had his idea, and he went on studying it. The Panic of 1873 and the long period of distress which followed accentuated his desire to make himself clear. In 1879 he printed, at his own expense, *Progress and Poverty: An Inquiry into the Cause of Industrial Depressions and of Increase of Want with Increase of Wealth.* Early in 1880 Appleton's of New York undertook a commercial edition, and within a few months Henry George's program for social and economic reform was everywhere under discussion. He took it on the lecture platform; he moved to New York and found generous support there; he visited Ireland and England. In *Social Problems* (1883) he wrote on the relation of his scheme to such subjects as "Over-Production," "The Effects of Machinery," and "The Functions of Government." He founded and edited *The Standard* (1886-1892), a weekly magazine. After 1888 his plan was known as the Single Tax, and was frequently an issue in municipal, state, and even national elections. Twice he ran for mayor of New York City, dying in the last days of his second campaign. By that time he had become one of the best-known public figures in the nation, a powerful force in tax reform and in various other movements designed to limit special privilege.

The majority of economists and tax experts have dismissed George's solution as oversimplified or unworkable, and the left wing of the present day is likely to be scornful of his rejection of Karl Marx' interpretation of history as class struggle. Yet George remains admired, for his clear criticism of certain positions of the English economists of the classical school (Thomas Robert Malthus, David Ricardo, and John Stuart Mill), for his powerful reaffirmation and extension to the economic sphere of the "natural rights" theories of the American Revolution, and for his basic moral strength, a quality none too common in the acquisitive era known as the Gilded Age.

The Writings of Henry George, Memorial Edition, 10 vols., New York, 1898-1900 • R. A. Sawyer, Henry George and the Single Tax: A Catalogue of the Collection in the New York Public Library, New York, 1926 • G. R. Geiger, The Philosophy of Henry George, New York, 1933 • V. L. Parrington, The Beginnings of Critical Realism in America, 1860-1920, New York, 1930, 125-136 • R. H. Gabriel, The Course of American Democratic Thought, New York, 1940, 198-204

From

Progress and Poverty

The forty-five chapters of **Progress and Poverty** are divided into ten books, preceded by the introduction which is here reprinted, and followed by a conclusion which is in actuality a brief sermon on Truth. The full argument cannot be summarized, but, after stating his problem, George devotes about half his space to an examination of what is true and what false in economic science as developed before his time, the remainder of the book to a description of his remedy for the condition which he regards as the basic cause of poverty. All but the last paragraph of Chapter II, Book VIII, is here reprinted—the author's statement of the principle of the Single Tax. Thereafter, as he himself said in a Preface written for the fourth edition (1880), George's inquiry passes into the realms of ethics and practical statesmanship. The student interested in economic theory will need to read the whole to understand George's position. He himself remarked of it, in summary: "What I have done in this book, if I have correctly solved the great problem I have sought to investigate, is, to unite the truth perceived by the schools of Smith and Ricardo to the truth perceived by the schools of Proudhon and LaSalle; to show that laissez faire (in its full true meaning) opens the way to a realization of the noble dreams of socialism; to identify social law with moral law, and to disprove ideas which in the minds of many cloud grand and elevating perceptions." The selections which follow are enough, however, to suggest the literary excellence of George's presentation. The clarity of his language, the richness of his allusions (surprisingly frequent for a man so largely self-taught), and the sweeping grandeur of his moral earnestness—these account for the vast audience which he has found. **Progress and Poverty** has been translated into many foreign languages and several millions of copies have been printed.

Introductory

THE PROBLEM

The present century has been marked by a prodigious increase in wealth-producing power. The utilization of steam and electricity, the introduction of improved processes and labor-saving machinery, the greater subdivision

and grander scale of production, the wonderful facilita-
tion of exchanges, have multiplied enormously the effectiveness of labor.

At the beginning of this marvelous era it was natural
to expect, and it was expected, that labor-saving inventions would lighten the toil and improve the condition
of the laborer; that the enormous increase in the power of producing wealth would make real poverty a thing
of the past. Could a man of the last century—a Franklin or a Priestley—have seen, in a vision of the future,
the steamship taking the place of the sailing vessel, the
railroad train of the wagon, the reaping machine of the
scythe, the threshing machine of the flail; could he have
heard the throb of the engines that in obedience to human will, and for the satisfaction of human desire, exert
a power greater than that of all the men and all the beasts
of burden of the earth combined; could he have seen the
forest tree transformed into finished lumber—into doors,
sashes, blinds, boxes or barrels, with hardly the touch of
a human hand; the great workshops where boots and
shoes are turned out by the case with less labor than the
old-fashioned cobbler could have put on a sole; the factories where, under the eye of a girl, cotton becomes
cloth faster than hundreds of stalwart weavers could
have turned it out with their hand-looms; could he have
seen steam hammers shaping mammoth shafts and
mighty anchors, and delicate machinery making tiny
watches; the diamond drill cutting through the heart of
the rocks, and coal oil sparing the whale; could he have
realized the enormous saving of labor resulting from
improved facilities of exchange and communication—
sheep killed in Australia eaten fresh in England, and the
order given by the London banker in the afternoon
executed in San Francisco in the morning of the same
day; could he have conceived of the hundred thousand
improvements which these only suggest, what would he
have inferred as to the social condition of mankind?

It would not have seemed like an inference; further
than the vision went it would have seemed as though he
saw; and his heart would have leaped and his nerves
would have thrilled, as one who from a height beholds
just ahead of the thirst-stricken caravan the living gleam
of rustling woods and the glint of laughing waters.
Plainly, in the sight of the imagination, he would have
beheld these new forces elevating society from its very
foundations, lifting the very poorest above the possibility

of want, exempting the very lowest from anxiety for
the material needs of life; he would have seen these
slaves of the lamp of knowledge taking on themselves
the traditional curse, these muscles of iron and sinews
of steel making the poorest laborer's life a holiday, in
which every high quality and noble impulse could have
scope to grow.

And out of these bounteous material conditions he
would have seen arising, as necessary sequences, moral
conditions realizing the golden age of which mankind
have always dreamed. Youth no longer stunted and
starved; age no longer harried by avarice; the child at
play with the tiger; the man with the muck-rake drinking in the glory of the stars. Foul things fled, fierce
things tame; discord turned to harmony! For how could
there be greed where all had enough? How could the
vice, the crime, the ignorance, the brutality, that spring
from poverty and the fear of poverty, exist where poverty had vanished? Who should crouch where all were
freemen; who oppress where all were peers?

More or less vague or clear, these have been the
hopes, these the dreams born of the improvements which
give this wonderful century its preëminence. They have
sunk so deeply into the popular mind as radically to
change the currents of thought, to recast creeds and dis-
place the most fundamental conceptions. The haunting
visions of higher possibilities have not merely gathered
splendor and vividness, but their direction has changed
—instead of seeing behind the faint tinges of an expiring sunset, all the glory of the daybreak has decked the
skies before.

It is true that disappointment has followed disappointment, and that discovery upon discovery, and invention
after invention, have neither lessened the toil of those
who most need respite, nor brought plenty to the poor.
But there have been so many things to which it seemed
this failure could be laid, that up to our time the new
faith has hardly weakened. We have better appreciated
the difficulties to be overcome; but not the less trusted
that the tendency of the times was to overcome them.

Now, however, we are coming into collision with

Text: the Fiftieth Anniversary Edition, New York, 1933 • 10 Priestley,
Joseph Priestley (1733-1804), English scientist and Unitarian clergyman
who settled in Pennsylvania in 1794. Like Franklin, he was an enthusiastic believer in scientific progress

facts which there can be no mistaking. From all parts of the civilized world come complaints of industrial depression; of labor condemned to involuntary idleness; of capital massed and wasting; of pecuniary distress among business men; of want and suffering and anxiety among the working classes. All the dull, deadening pain, all the keen, maddening anguish, that to great masses of men are involved in the words "hard times," afflict the world to-day. This state of things, common to communities differing so widely in situation, in political institutions, in fiscal and financial systems, in density of population and in social organization, can hardly be accounted for by local causes. There is distress where large standing armies are maintained, but there is also distress where the standing armies are nominal; there is distress where protective tariffs stupidly and wastefully hamper trade, but there is also distress where trade is nearly free; there is distress where autocratic government yet prevails, but there is also distress where political power is wholly in the hands of the people; in countries where paper is money, and in countries where gold and silver are the only currency. Evidently, beneath all such things as these, we must infer a common cause.

That there is a common cause, and that it is either what we call material progress or something closely connected with material progress, becomes more than an inference when it is noted that the phenomena we class together and speak of as industrial depressions are but intensifications of phenomena which always accompany material progress, and which show themselves more clearly and strongly as material progress goes on. Where the conditions to which material progress everywhere tends are most fully realized—that is to say, where population is densest, wealth greatest, and the machinery of production and exchange most highly developed—we find the deepest poverty, the sharpest struggle for existence, and the most of enforced idleness.

It is to the newer countries—that is, to the countries where material progress is yet in its earlier stages—that laborers emigrate in search of higher wages, and capital flows in search of higher interest. It is in the older countries—that is to say, the countries where material progress has reached later stages—that widespread destitution is found in the midst of the greatest abundance. Go into one of the new communities where Anglo-Saxon vigor is just beginning the race of progress; where the machinery of production and exchange is yet rude and inefficient; where the increment of wealth is not yet great enough to enable any class to live in ease and luxury; where the best house is but a cabin of logs or a cloth and paper shanty, and the richest man is forced to daily work—and though you will find an absence of wealth and all its concomitants, you will find no beggars. There is no luxury, but there is no destitution. No one makes an easy living, nor a very good living; but every one *can* make a living, and no one able and willing to work is oppressed by the fear of want.

But just as such a community realizes the conditions which all civilized communities are striving for, and advances in the scale of material progress—just as closer settlement and a more intimate connection with the rest of the world, and greater utilization of labor-saving machinery, make possible greater economies in production and exchange, and wealth in consequence increases, not merely in the aggregate, but in proportion to population—so does poverty take a darker aspect. Some get an infinitely better and easier living, but others find it hard to get a living at all. The "tramp" comes with the locomotive, and almshouses and prisons are as surely the marks of "material progress" as are costly dwellings, rich warehouses, and magnificent churches. Upon streets lighted with gas and patrolled by uniformed policemen, beggars wait for the passer-by, and in the shadow of college, and library, and museum, are gathering the more hideous Huns and fiercer Vandals of whom Macaulay prophesied.

This fact—the great fact that poverty and all its concomitants show themselves in communities just as they develop into the conditions toward which material progress tends—proves that the social difficulties existing wherever a certain stage of progress has been reached, do not arise from local circumstances, but are, in some way or another, engendered by progress itself.

And, unpleasant as it may be to admit it, it is at last becoming evident that the enormous increase in productive power which has marked the present century and is still going on with accelerating ratio, has no tendency

---

76 **Macaulay,** Thomas Babington Macaulay (1800-1859), English author and statesman. His prophecy of "more hideous Huns and fiercer Vandals" was made in a letter to an American friend

to extirpate poverty or to lighten the burdens of those compelled to toil. It simply widens the gulf between Dives and Lazarus, and makes the struggle for existence more intense. The march of invention has clothed mankind with powers of which a century ago the boldest imagination could not have dreamed. But in factories where labor-saving machinery has reached its most wonderful development, little children are at work; wherever the new forces are anything like fully utilized, large classes are maintained by charity or live on the verge of recourse to it; amid the greatest accumulations of wealth, men die of starvation, and puny infants suckle dry breasts; while everywhere the greed of gain, the worship of wealth, shows the force of the fear of want. The promised land flies before us like the mirage. The fruits of the tree of knowledge turn as we grasp them to apples of Sodom that crumble at the touch.

It is true that wealth has been greatly increased, and that the average of comfort, leisure, and refinement has been raised; but these gains are not general. In them the lowest class do not share. I do not mean that the condition of the lowest class has nowhere nor in anything been improved; but that there is nowhere any improvement which can be credited to increased productive power. I mean that the tendency of what we call material progress is in nowise to improve the condition of the lowest class in the essentials of healthy, happy human life. Nay, more, that it is still further to depress the condition of the lowest class. The new forces, elevating in their nature though they be, do not act upon the social fabric from underneath, as was for a long time hoped and believed, but strike it at a point intermediate between top and bottom. It is as though an immense wedge were being forced, not underneath society, but through society. Those who are above the point of separation are elevated, but those who are below are crushed down.

This depressing effect is not generally realized, for it is not apparent where there has long existed a class just able to live. Where the lowest class barely lives, as has been the case for a long time in many parts of Europe, it is impossible for it to get any lower, for the next lowest step is out of existence, and no tendency to further depression can readily show itself. But in the progress of new settlements to the conditions of older communities it may clearly be seen that material progress does not merely fail to relieve poverty—it actually produces it. In the United States it is clear that squalor and misery, and the vices and crimes that spring from them, everywhere increase as the village grows to the city, and the march of development brings the advantages of the improved methods of production and exchange. It is in the older and richer sections of the Union that pauperism and distress among the working classes are becoming most painfully apparent. If there is less deep poverty in San Francisco than in New York, is it not because San Francisco is yet behind New York in all that both cities are striving for? When San Francisco reaches the point where New York now is, who can doubt that there will also be ragged and barefooted children on her streets?

This association of poverty with progress is the great enigma of our times. It is the central fact from which spring industrial, social, and political difficulties that perplex the world, and with which statesmanship and philanthropy and education grapple in vain. From it come the clouds that overhang the future of the most progressive and self-reliant nations. It is the riddle which the Sphinx of Fate puts to our civilization, and which not to answer is to be destroyed. So long as all the increased wealth which modern progress brings goes but to build up great fortunes, to increase luxury and make sharper the contrast between the House of Have and the House of Want, progress is not real and cannot be permanent. The reaction must come. The tower leans from its foundations, and every new story but hastens the final catastrophe. To educate men who must be condemned to poverty, is but to make them restive; to base

3 **Dives and Lazarus.** See note, p. 662 • 16 **apples of Sodom,** attractive fruit which when picked turned to ashes, according to ancient writers; it is believed to have been a variety of nightshade • 21 **share.** "It is true that the poorest may now in certain ways enjoy what the richest a century ago could not have commanded, but this does not show improvement of condition so long as the ability to obtain the necessaries of life is not increased. The beggar in a great city may enjoy many things from which the backwoods farmer is debarred, but that does not prove the condition of the city beggar better than that of the independent farmer."—George • 69 **Sphinx,** an allusion to the monster of Thebes which killed travelers who could not answer the riddle, "What animal is it that walks on four legs in the morning, two at noon, and three in the evening?"

on a state of most glaring social inequality political institutions under which men are theoretically equal, is to stand a pyramid on its apex.

All-important as this question is, pressing itself from every quarter painfully upon attention, it has not yet received a solution which accounts for all the facts and points to any clear and simple remedy. This is shown by the widely varying attempts to account for the prevailing depression. They exhibit not merely a divergence between vulgar notions and scientific theories, but also show that the concurrence which should exist between those who avow the same general theories breaks up upon practical questions into an anarchy of opinion. Upon high economic authority we have been told that the prevailing depression is due to over-consumption; upon equally high authority, that it is due to over-production; while the wastes of war, the extension of railroads, the attempts of workmen to keep up wages, the demonetization of silver, the issues of paper money, the increase of labor-saving machinery, the opening of shorter avenues to trade, etc., are separately pointed out as the cause, by writers of reputation.

And while professors thus disagree, the ideas that there is a necessary conflict between capital and labor, that machinery is an evil, that competition must be restrained and interest abolished, that wealth may be created by the issue of money, that it is the duty of government to furnish capital or to furnish work, are rapidly making way among the great body of the people, who keenly feel a hurt and are sharply conscious of a wrong. Such ideas, which bring great masses of men, the repositories of ultimate political power, under the leadership of charlatans and demagogues, are fraught with danger; but they cannot be successfully combated until political economy shall give some answer to the great question which shall be consistent with all her teachings, and which shall commend itself to the perceptions of the great masses of men.

It must be within the province of political economy to give such an answer. For political economy is not a set of dogmas. It is the explanation of a certain set of facts. It is the science which, in the sequence of certain phenomena, seeks to trace mutual relations and to identify cause and effect, just as the physical sciences seek to do in other sets of phenomena. It lays its foundations upon firm ground. The premises from which it makes its deductions are truths which have the highest sanction; axioms which we all recognize; upon which we safely base the reasoning and actions of everyday life, and which may be reduced to the metaphysical expression of the physical law that motion seeks the line of least resistance —viz., that men seek to gratify their desires with the least exertion. Proceeding from a basis thus assured, its processes, which consist simply in identification and separation, have the same certainty. In this sense it is as exact a science as geometry, which, from similar truths relative to space, obtains its conclusions by similar means, and its conclusions when valid should be as self-apparent. And although in the domain of political economy we cannot test our theories by artificially produced combinations or conditions, as may be done in some of the other sciences, yet we can apply tests no less conclusive, by comparing societies in which different conditions exist, or by, in imagination, separating, combining, adding or eliminating forces or factors of known direction.

I propose in the following pages to attempt to solve by the methods of political economy the great problem I have outlined. I propose to seek the law which associates poverty with progress, and increases want with advancing wealth; and I believe that in the explanation of this paradox we shall find the explanation of those recurring seasons of industrial and commercial paralysis which, viewed independently of their relations to more general phenomena, seem so inexplicable. Properly commenced and carefully pursued, such an investigation must yield a conclusion that will stand every test, and as truth, will correlate with all other truth. For in the sequence of phenomena there is no accident. Every effect has a cause, and every fact implies a preceding fact.

That political economy, as at present taught, does not explain the persistence of poverty amid advancing wealth in a manner which accords with the deep-seated perceptions of men; that the unquestionable truths which it does teach are unrelated and disjointed; that it has failed to make the progress in popular thought that truth, even when unpleasant, must make; that, on the contrary, after a century of cultivation, during which it has engrossed the attention of some of the most subtle and powerful intellects, it should be spurned by the statesman, scouted by the masses, and relegated in the opinion of many educated and thinking men to the rank of a pseudo-science in which nothing is fixed or can be fixed—must, it seems to me, be due not to any inability of the science when properly pursued, but to some false step in its premises, or overlooked factor in its estimates. And as such mistakes are generally concealed by the respect paid to authority, I propose in this inquiry to take nothing for granted, but to bring even accepted theories to the test of first principles, and should they not stand the test, freshly to interrogate facts in the endeavor to discover their law.

I propose to beg no question, to shrink from no conclusion, but to follow truth wherever it may lead. Upon us is the responsibility of seeking the law, for in the very heart of our civilization to-day women faint and little children moan. But what that law may prove to be is not our affair. If the conclusions that we reach run counter to our prejudices, let us not flinch; if they challenge institutions that have long been deemed wise and natural, let us not turn back.

Book VIII, Chapter II

HOW EQUAL RIGHTS TO THE LAND MAY BE ASSERTED AND SECURED

We have traded the want and suffering that everywhere prevail among the working classes, the recurring paroxysms of industrial depression, the scarcity of employment, the stagnation of capital, the tendency of wages to the starvation point, that exhibit themselves more and more strongly as material progress goes on, to the fact that the land on which and from which all must live is made the exclusive property of some.

We have seen that there is no possible remedy for these evils but the abolition of their cause; we have seen that private property in land has no warrant in justice, but stands condemned as the denial of natural right—a subversion of the law of nature that as social development goes on must condemn the masses of men to a slavery the hardest and most degrading.

We have weighed every objection, and seen that neither on the ground of equity or expediency is there anything to deter us from making land common property by confiscating rent.

But a question of method remains. How shall we do it?

We should satisfy the law of justice, we should meet all economic requirements, by at one stroke abolishing all private titles, declaring all land public property, and letting it out to the highest bidders in lots to suit, under such conditions as would sacredly guard the private right to improvements.

Thus we should secure, in a more complex state of society, the same equality of rights that in a ruder state were secured by equal partitions of the soil, and by giving the use of the land to whoever could procure the most from it, we should secure the greatest production.

Such a plan, instead of being a wild, impracticable vagary, has (with the exception that he suggests compensation to the present holders of land—undoubtedly a careless concession which he upon reflection would reconsider) been indorsed by no less eminent a thinker than Herbert Spencer, who ("Social Statics," Chap. IX, Sec. 8) says of it:

"Such a doctrine is consistent with the highest state of civilization; may be carried out without involving a community of goods, and need cause no very serious revolution in existing arrangements. The change required would simply be a change of landlords. Separate ownership would merge into the joint-stock ownership of the public. Instead of being in the possession of individuals, the country would be held by the great corporate body—society. Instead of leasing his acres from an isolated proprietor, the farmer would lease them from the nation. Instead of paying his rent to the agent of Sir John or his Grace, he would pay it to an agent or deputy agent of the community. Stewards would be public officials instead of private ones, and tenancy the only land tenure. A state of things so ordered would be in perfect harmony with the moral law. Under it all men would be equally landlords, all men would be alike free to become tenants. * * * Clearly, therefore, on such a system, the earth might be enclosed, occupied and

---

60 **Herbert Spencer** (1820-1903), English philosopher, who published Social Statics in 1851

cultivated, in entire subordination to the law of equal freedom."

But such a plan, though perfectly feasible, does not seem to me the best. Or rather I propose to accomplish the same thing in a simpler, easier, and quieter way, than that of formally confiscating all the land and formally letting it out to the highest bidders.

To do that would involve a needless shock to present customs and habits of thought—which is to be avoided.

To do that would involve a needless extension of governmental machinery—which is to be avoided.

It is an axiom of statesmanship, which the successful founders of tyranny have understood and acted upon— that great changes can best be brought about under old forms. We, who would free men, should heed the same truth. It is the natural method. When nature would make a higher type, she takes a lower one and develops it. This, also, is the law of social growth. Let us work by it. With the current we may glide fast and far. Against it, it is hard pulling and slow progress.

I do not propose either to purchase or to confiscate private property in land. The first would be unjust; the second, needless. Let the individuals who now hold it still retain, if they want to, possession of what they are pleased to call *their* land. Let them continue to call it *their* land. Let them buy and sell, and bequeath and devise it. We may safely leave them the shell, if we take the kernel. *It is not necessary to confiscate land; it is only necessary to confiscate rent.*

Nor to take rent for public uses is it necessary that the State should bother with the letting of lands, and assume the chances of the favoritism, collusion, and corruption this might involve. It is not necessary that any new machinery should be created. The machinery already exists. Instead of extending it, all we have to do is to simplify and reduce it. By leaving to land owners a percentage of rent which would probably be much less than the cost and loss involved in attempting to rent lands through State agency, and by making use of this existing machinery, we may, without jar or shock, assert the common right to land by taking rent for public uses.

We already take some rent in taxation. We have only to make some changes in our modes of taxation to take it all.

What I, therefore, propose, as the simple yet sovereign remedy, which will raise wages, increase the earnings of capital, extirpate pauperism, abolish poverty, give remunerative employment to whoever wishes it, afford free scope to human powers, lessen crime, elevate morals, and taste, and intelligence, purify government and carry civilization to yet nobler heights, is—*to appropriate rent by taxation.*

In this way the State may become the universal landlord without calling herself so, and without assuming a single new function. In form, the ownership of land would remain just as now. No owner of land need be dispossessed, and no restriction need be placed upon the amount of land any one could hold. For, rent being taken by the State in taxes, land, no matter in whose name it stood, or in what parcels it was held, would be really common property, and every member of the community would participate in the advantages of its ownership.

Now, insomuch as the taxation of rent, or land values, must necessarily be increased just as we abolish other taxes, we may put the proposition into practical form by proposing—

To abolish all taxation save that upon land values.

As we have seen, the value of land is at the beginning of society nothing, but as society develops by the increase of population and the advance of the arts, it becomes greater and greater. In every civilized country, even the newest, the value of the land taken as a whole is sufficient to bear the entire expenses of government. In the better developed countries it is much more than sufficient. Hence it will not be enough merely to place all taxes upon the value of land. It will be necessary, where rent exceeds the present governmental revenues, commensurately to increase the amount demanded in taxation, and to continue this increase as society progresses and rent advances. But this is so natural and easy a matter, that it may be considered as involved, or at least understood, in the proposition to put all taxes on the value of land. That is the first step, upon which the practical struggle must be made. When the hare is once caught and killed, cooking him will follow as a matter of course. When the common right to land is so far appreciated that all taxes are abolished save those which fall upon rent, there is no danger of much more than is necessary to induce them to collect the public revenues being left to individual land holders.

Experience has taught me (for I have been for some

years endeavoring to popularize this proposition) that wherever the idea of concentrating all taxation upon land values finds lodgment sufficient to induce consideration, it invariably makes way, but there are few of the classes most to be benefited by it, who at first, or even for a long time afterward, see its full significance and power. It is difficult for workingmen to get over the idea that there is a real antagonism between capital and labor. It is difficult for small farmers and homestead owners to get over the idea that to put all taxes on the value of land would be unduly to tax them. It is difficult for both classes to get over the idea that to exempt capital from taxation would be to make the rich richer, and the poor poorer. These ideas spring from confused thought. But behind ignorance and prejudice there is a powerful interest, which has hitherto dominated literature, education, and opinion. A great wrong always dies hard, and the great wrong which in every civilized country condemns the masses of men to poverty and want, will not die without a bitter struggle. . . .

1877-1879·1879

Edward Bellamy

1850 · 1898

Like Henry George, Edward Bellamy was both a moralist and a product of long-continued hard times. He too had a "call" to reaffirm the philosophy of the rights of man and a "vision" of a society in which there would no longer be poverty for the many and riches for the few but abundance for all. The similarity between George and Bellamy does not, however, go much further. Bellamy, a preacher's son with a highly developed social conscience, was interested in many things, not in a single-minded study of economic science. His better world was to be achieved by a new nationalism, best described as a religion of democracy, closely akin to Christian socialism. Bellamy belongs with the long line of New England reformers rather than with the philosophers, although no one would minimize his moral force. Very probably he reached more readers more quickly than did the author of *Progress and Poverty*. His vivid and concrete description of a technology organized for production rather than for profit is the most famous of American Utopias, and among the best visualizations of an ideal society in all literature. As Ida M. Tarbell remarked not long ago, "there has never been one which gained the lasting hold on popular imagination or which carried with it such a sense of something reasoned, workable, and fool-proof as that of Edward Bellamy."

Bellamy was born in Chicopee Falls, Massachusetts, in 1850. Failing to achieve his ambition of an appointment to West Point, he entered Union College, but stayed only one year. At eighteen he spent the better part of a year in Europe, where, as he wrote later, "my eyes were first fully opened to the extent and consequences of man's inhumanity to man." After 1869 there is almost continuous evidence of his anxiety to do something to better the condition of the oppressed and the unfortunate. After two years of study he was admitted to the bar, but he gave up law almost at once in favor of journalism. Seven of the next nine years he spent as editorial writer and reviewer, on the New York *Evening Post* (seven months in 1871-1872), the Springfield *Union* (1872-1877), and the Springfield *Penny News* (1880), in the last of which he was a partner with his brother. In 1875 Bellamy began to contribute short stories to the national magazines and by 1880 had published nine times in *Scribner's Monthly* (later *Century*), *Lippincott's,* and *Appleton's.* Two novelettes came out in book form and a portion of a serial appeared in a Great Barrington, Massachusetts, newspaper. The serial, *The Duke of Stockbridge: A Romance of Shays' Rebellion,* reflects Bellamy's concern with Populism and the debtor classes. Although most of it was written before 1880, the book was not completed and published until 1900, two years after Bellamy's death. *Six to One: A Nantucket Idyl* (1878), a somewhat callow study of feminine psychology, is an early example of his persistent romanticism about women. *Dr. Heidenhoff's Progress* (1880) was a Hawthornesque treatment of the psychological effects of evil upon the evildoer. In the early eighties, after Bellamy had decided to give all of his time to his writing, another handful of short stories appeared and a third novelette, *Miss Ludington's Sister: A Romance of Immortality* (1884).

Then, late in 1886, the year of the Haymarket affair in Chicago, that most appalling testimony of the decade to the social and economic insecurity of the nation, Bellamy sat down at his desk "with the definite purpose of trying to reason out a method of economic organization by which the republic might guarantee the livelihood and material welfare of its citizens on a basis of equality corresponding to and supplementing their political equality." *Looking Backward: 2000-1887,* the novel which resulted, was completed in August 1887 and published in the following January. It changed its author from a somewhat casual liberal to a leader of a Socialistic movement.

Looking Backward convinced thousands of Americans that the society it described was just what they wanted. By the middle of June 1888 there was talk of a "Nationalist" movement and by the end of the year Nationalist clubs were being organized. A monthly magazine, *The Nationalist,* began publication in Boston, May 1889. As the sales of his novel skyrocketed into the hundreds of thousands Bellamy elaborated his program in lectures and articles. In January 1891 he founded his own weekly, *The New Nation,* and it is probable that his followers lent their influence to the formation of the People's Party, founded in May 1891 on a platform which included, among other items, "national ownership of all means of public communication and transportation." Nationalism faded, however, even more quickly than Populism, partly because of lack of leadership but largely because of the same forces of conservatism which defeated William Jennings Bryan in the election of 1896.

The opposition to Nationalism is well summarized in the review of *Looking Backward* by W. T. Harris, one of the foremost philosophers and educators of his time, which appeared in *The Forum* for October 1889. Harris asserted that two assumptions of Bellamy's were unsupported by fact. The first is that under the principle of competition the rich grow richer and fewer while the poor grow poorer and more numerous. This idea Harris attributed to Karl Marx, "evolved from the depths of his consciousness, but not supported by any reliable or pertinent statistics." The second is that the few rich people are rich at the expense of the poor. Harris also objected to the regimentation of Bellamy's system, concluding that "private property and free competition constitute the simple device by which civilization has been able to isolate individuals from one another and develop a sense of the sacredness of personality."

Bellamy, never robust, was a sick man after 1896, but he managed a sequel to *Looking Backward. Equality* (1897), though much more a tract than a novel, is well worth reading for its revelation of the breadth of his interests and his prophetic views of developments which have come in the last half century. Of especial interest are his comments on "How the Profit System Nullified the Benefit of Inventions" and "What Became of the Great Cities." There is scarcely an aspect of present-day social planning with which he did not deal in some detail.

Edward Bellamy Speaks Again, Kansas City, 1937 • A. E. Morgan, Edward Bellamy, New York, 1944 • Lewis Mumford, The Story of Utopias, New York, 1922, 159-169 • A. B. Forbes, "The Literary Quest for Utopia, 1880-1900," Social Forces, December 1927, VI, 179-189

Looking Backward

Julian West, the narrator, is a wealthy Bostonian who in 1887 is engaged to be married to Edith Bartlett. He is subject to insomnia and sleeps in a tomblike chamber beneath the foundation of his house, sometimes hiring a hypnotist to put him to sleep. No one knows of these arrangements except his servant and the hypnotist, and on May 30 the hypnotist leaves town and the servant dies in a fire which destroys West's house and, presumably, West himself. In September of the year 2000 a Boston physician, Dr. Leete, uncovers a mass of masonry in his garden, finds West, and resuscitates him. **Looking Backward** is West's account of what he finds at the end of the twentieth century. Among the wonders are airplanes, the radio, television, paper fabrics for clothing and draperies, electrical heat—all of them unknown in 1887. More important, however, is the peaceful Socialistic society, so much in contrast with that of 1887, which West describes as like a coach to which the masses of humanity are harnessed, while a few ride on top. The climax of the story is a nightmare in which West finds himself back in 1887, tries to tell of what he has seen, and is denounced as an anarchist. Running through the story is the romance of West and Edith Leete, who turns out to be the great-granddaughter of Edith Bartlett.

In the chapters reprinted here will be found Dr. Leete's account of how the change to the new society was accomplished and of how the "dirty work" gets done by the "industrial army," together with the description of the means by which regimentation is avoided. These are the crucial matters if we may believe the critics who attacked Bellamy. It should be added that many pages are devoted to displaying the extensive recreational facilities and the material comforts provided by the nationalized state.

When, in the course of the evening the ladies retired, leaving Dr. Leete and myself alone, he sounded me as to my disposition for sleep, saying that if I felt like it my bed was ready for me; but if I was inclined to wakefulness nothing would please him better than to bear me company. "I am a late bird, myself," he said, "and, without suspicion of flattery, I may say that a companion more interesting than yourself could scarcely be imagined. It is decidedly not often that one has a chance to converse with a man of the nineteenth century." 10

Now I had been looking forward all the evening with some dread to the time when I should be alone, on retiring for the night. Surrounded by these most friendly strangers, stimulated and supported by their sympathetic interest, I had been able to keep my mental balance. Even then, however, in pauses of the conversation I had had glimpses, vivid as lightning flashes, of the horror of strangeness that was waiting to be faced when I could no longer command diversion. I knew I could not sleep 20 that night, and as for lying awake and thinking, it argues no cowardice, I am sure, to confess that I was afraid [of] it. When, in reply to my host's question, I frankly told him this, he replied, that it would be strange if I did not feel just so, but that I need have no anxiety about sleeping; whenever I wanted to go to bed, he would give me a dose which would insure me a sound night's sleep without fail. Next morning, no doubt, I would awake with the feeling of an old citizen.

"Before I acquire that," I replied, "I must know a little 30 more about the sort of Boston I have come back to. You told me when we were upon the housetop that though a century only had elapsed since I fell asleep, it had been marked by greater changes in the conditions of humanity than many a previous millennium. With the city before me I could well believe that, but I am very curious to know what some of the changes have been. To make a beginning somewhere, for the subject is doubtless a large one, what solution, if any, have you found for the labor question? It was the Sphinx's riddle of the nine- 40 teenth century, and when I dropped out the Sphinx was threatening to devour society, because the answer was not forthcoming. It is well worth sleeping a hundred years to learn what the right answer was, if, indeed, you have found it yet."

"As no such thing as the labor question is known nowadays," replied Dr. Leete, "and there is no way in which it could arise, I suppose we may claim to have solved it. Society would indeed have fully deserved being devoured if it had failed to answer a riddle so entirely simple. In fact, to speak by the book, it was not necessary for society to solve the riddle at all. It may be said to have solved itself. The solution came as the result of a process of industrial evolution which could not have terminated otherwise. All that society had to do was to recognize and co-operate with that evolution, when its tendency had become unmistakable."

"I can only say," I answered, "that at the time I fell asleep no such evolution had been recognized."

"It was in 1887 that you fell into this sleep, I think you said."

"Yes, May 30th, 1887."

My companion regarded me musingly for some moments. Then he observed, "And you tell me that even then there was no general recognition of the nature of the crisis which society was nearing? Of course, I fully credit your statement. The singular blindness of your contemporaries to the signs of the times is a phenomenon commented on by many of our historians, but few facts of history are more difficult for us to realize, so obvious and unmistakable as we look back seem the indications, which must also have come under your eyes, of the transformation about to come to pass. I should be interested, Mr. West, if you would give me a little more definite idea of the view which you and men of your grade of intellect took of the state and prospects of society in 1887. You must, at least, have realized that the widespread industrial and social troubles, and the underlying dissatisfaction of all classes with the inequalities of society, and the general misery of mankind, were portents of great changes of some sort."

"We did, indeed, fully realize that," I replied. "We felt that society was dragging anchor and in danger of going adrift. Whither it would drift nobody could say, but all feared the rocks."

"Nevertheless," said Dr. Leete, "the set of the current was perfectly perceptible if you had but taken pains to observe it, and it was not toward the rocks, but toward a deeper channel."

"We had a popular proverb," I replied, "that 'hindsight is better than foresight,' the force of which I shall now, no doubt, appreciate more fully than ever. All I can say is, that the prospect was such when I went into that long sleep that I should not have been surprised had I looked down from your housetop to-day on a heap of charred and moss-grown ruins instead of this glorious city."

Dr. Leete had listened to me with close attention and nodded thoughtfully as I finished speaking. "What you have said," he observed, "will be regarded as a most valuable vindication of Storiot, whose account of your era has been generally thought exaggerated in its picture of the gloom and confusion of men's minds. That a period of transition like that should be full of excitement and agitation was indeed to be looked for, but seeing how plain was the tendency of the forces in operation, it was natural to believe that hope rather than fear would have been the prevailing temper of the popular mind."

"You have not yet told me what was the answer to the riddle which you found," I said. "I am impatient to know by what contradiction of natural sequence the peace and prosperity which you now seem to enjoy could have been the outcome of an era like my own."

"Excuse me," replied my host, "but do you smoke?" It was not till our cigars were lighted and drawing well that he resumed. "Since you are in the humor to talk rather than to sleep, as I certainly am, perhaps I cannot do better than to try to give you enough idea of our modern industrial system to dissipate at least the impression that there is any mystery about the process of its evolution. The Bostonians of your day had the reputation of being great askers of questions, and I am going to show my descent by asking you one to begin with. What should you name as the most prominent feature of the labor troubles of your day?"

"Why, the strikes, of course," I replied.

"Exactly; but what made the strikes so formidable?"

"The great labor organizations."

"And what was the motive of these great organizations?"

Text: the first edition (1888). Bellamy later made some changes and revisions in the details of his scheme, good evidence of the seriousness of his social purpose • 58 Storiot, evidently a historian of Dr. Leete's time

"The workmen claimed they had to organize to get their rights from the big corporations," I replied.

"That is just it," said Dr. Leete; "the organization of labor and the strikes were an effect, merely, of the concentration of capital in greater masses than had ever been known before. Before this concentration began, while as yet commerce and industry were conducted by innumerable petty concerns with small capital, instead of a small number of great concerns with vast capital, the individual workman was relatively important and independent in his relations to the employer. Moreover, when a little capital or a new idea was enough to start a man in business for himself, workingmen were constantly becoming employers and there was no hard and fast line between the two classes. Labor unions were needless then, and general strikes out of the question. But when the era of small concerns with small capital was succeeded by that of the great aggregations of capital, all this was changed. The individual laborer who had been relatively important to the small employer was reduced to insignificance and powerlessness over against the great corporation, while, at the same time, the way upward to the grade of employer was closed to him. Self-defence drove him to union with his fellows.

"The records of the period show that the outcry against the concentration of capital was furious. Men believed that it threatened society with a form of tyranny more abhorrent than it had ever endured. They believed that the great corporations were preparing for them the yoke of a baser servitude than had ever been imposed on the race, servitude not to men but to soulless machines incapable of any motive but insatiable greed. Looking back, we cannot wonder at their desperation, for certainly humanity was never confronted with a fate more sordid and hideous than would have been the era of corporate tyranny which they anticipated.

"Meanwhile, without being in the smallest degree checked by the clamor against it, the absorption of business by ever larger monopolies continued. In the United States, where this tendency was later in developing than in Europe, there was not, after the beginning of the last quarter of the century, any opportunity whatever for individual enterprise in any important field of industry, unless backed by a great capital. During the last decade of the century, such small businesses as still remained were fast failing survivals of a past epoch, or mere parasites on the great corporations, or else existed in fields too small to attract the great capitalists. Small businesses, as far as they still remained, were reduced to the condition of rats and mice, living in holes and corners, and counting on evading notice for the enjoyment of existence. The railroads had gone on combining till a few great syndicates controlled every rail in the land. In manufactories, every important staple was controlled by a syndicate. These syndicates, pools, trusts, or whatever their name, fixed prices and crushed all competition except when combinations as vast as themselves arose. Then a struggle, resulting in a still greater consolidation, ensued. The great city bazar crushed its country rivals with branch stores, and in the city itself absorbed its smaller rivals till the business of a whole quarter was concentrated under one roof, with a hundred former proprietors of shops serving as clerks. Having no business of his own to put his money in, the small capitalist, at the same time that he took service under the corporation, found no other investment for his money but its stocks and bonds, thus becoming doubly dependent upon it.

"The fact that the desperate popular opposition to the consolidation of business in a few powerful hands had no effect to check it, proves that there must have been a strong economical reason for it. The small capitalists, with their innumerable petty concerns, had, in fact, yielded the field to the great aggregations of capital, because they belonged to a day of small things and were totally incompetent to the demands of an age of steam and telegraphs and the gigantic scale of its enterprises. To restore the former order of things, even if possible, would have involved returning to the day of stage-coaches. Oppressive and intolerable as was the regime of the great consolidations of capital, even its victims, while they cursed it, were forced to admit the prodigious increase of efficiency which had been imparted to the national industries, the vast economies effected by concentration of management and unity of organization, and to confess that since the new system had taken the place of the old, the wealth of the world had increased at a rate before undreamed of. To be sure this vast increase had gone chiefly to make the rich richer, increasing the gap between them and the poor; but the fact remained that, as a means merely of producing wealth, capital had been proved efficient in proportion to its consolidation. The restoration of the old system with the subdivision of capital, if it were possible, might indeed bring back a greater equality of conditions with more individual dignity and freedom, but it would be at the price of general poverty and the arrest of material progress.

"Was there, then, no way of commanding the services of the mighty wealth-producing principle of consolidated capital, without bowing down to a plutocracy like that of Carthage? As soon as men began to ask themselves these questions, they found the answer ready for them. The movement toward the conduct of business by larger and larger aggregations of capital, the tendency toward monopolies, which had been so desperately and vainly resisted, was recognized at last, in its true significance, as a process which only needed to complete its logical evolution to open a golden future to humanity.

"Early in the last century the evolution was completed by the final consolidation of the entire capital of the nation. The industry and commerce of the country, ceasing to be conducted by a set of irresponsible corporations and syndicates of private persons at their caprice and for their profit, were intrusted to a single syndicate representing the people, to be conducted in the common interest for the common profit. The nation, that is to say, organized as the one great business corporation in which all other corporations were absorbed; it became the one capitalist in the place of all other capitalists, the sole employer, the final monopoly in which all previous and lesser monopolies were swallowed up, a monopoly in the profits and economies of which all citizens shared. In a word, the people of the United States concluded to assume the conduct of their own business, just as one hundred odd years before they had assumed the conduct of their own government, organizing now for industrial purposes on precisely the same grounds that they had then organized for political purposes. At last, strangely late in the world's history, the obvious fact was perceived that no business is so essentially the public business as the industry and commerce on which the people's livelihood depends, and that to entrust it to private persons to be managed for private profit, is a folly similar in kind, though vastly greater in magnitude, to that of surrendering the functions of political government to kings and nobles to be conducted for their personal glorification."

"Such a stupendous change as you describe," said I, "did not, of course, take place without great bloodshed and terrible convulsions."

"On the contrary," replied Dr. Leete, "there was absolutely no violence. The change had been long foreseen. Public opinion had become fully ripe for it, and the whole mass of the people was behind it. There was no more possibility of opposing it by force than by argument. On the other hand the popular sentiment toward the great corporations and those identified with them had ceased to be one of bitterness, as they came to realize their necessity as a link, a transition phase, in the evolution of the true industrial system. The most violent foes of the great private monopolies were now forced to recognize how invaluable and indispensable had been their office in educating the people up to the point of assuming control of their own business. Fifty years before, the consolidation of the industries of the country under national control would have seemed a very daring experiment to the most sanguine. But by a series of object lessons, seen and studied by all men, the great corporations had taught the people an entirely new set of ideas on this subject. They had seen for many years syndicates handling revenues greater than those of states, and directing the labors of hundreds of thousands of men with an efficiency and economy unattainable in smaller operations. It had come to be recognized as an axiom that the larger the business the simpler the principles that can be applied to it; that, as the machine is truer than the hand, so the system, which in a great concern does the work of the master's eye in a small business, turns out more accurate results. Thus it came about that, thanks to the corporations themselves, when it was proposed that the nation should assume their functions, the suggestion implied nothing which seemed impracticable even to the timid. To be sure it was a step beyond any yet taken, a broader generalization, but the very fact that the nation would be the sole corporation in the field would, it was seen, relieve the undertaking of many difficulties with which the partial monopolies had contended."

CHAPTER VI

Dr. Leete ceased speaking, and I remained silent, endeavoring to form some general conception of the changes in the arrangements of society implied in the tremendous revolution which he had described.

---

7 **Carthage,** which was an oligarchy dominated by commercial interests • 28 **shared.** In later editions Bellamy inserted the sentence: "The epoch of trusts had ended in The Great Trust"

Finally I said, "The idea of such an extension of the functions of government is, to say the least, rather overwhelming."

"Extension!" he repeated, "where is the extension?"

"In my day," I replied, "it was considered that the proper functions of government, strictly speaking, were limited to keeping the peace and defending the people against the public enemy, that is, to the military and police powers."

"And, in heaven's name, who are the public enemies?" exclaimed Dr. Leete. "Are they France, England, Germany, or hunger, cold and nakedness? In your day governments were accustomed, on the slightest international misunderstanding, to seize upon the bodies of citizens and deliver them over by hundreds of thousands to death and mutilation, wasting their treasures the while like water; and all this oftenest for no imaginable profit to the victims. We have no wars now, and our governments no war powers, but in order to protect every citizen against hunger, cold and nakedness, and provide for all his physical and mental needs, the function is assumed of directing his industry for a term of years. No, Mr. West, I am sure on reflection you will perceive that it was in your age, not in ours, that the extension of the functions of governments was extraordinary. Not even for the best ends would men now allow their governments such powers as were then used for the most maleficent."

"Leaving comparisons aside," I said, "the demagoguery and corruption of our public men would have been considered, in my day, insuperable objections to any assumption by government of the charge of the national industries. We should have thought that no arrangement could be worse than to entrust the politicians with control of the wealth-producing machinery of the country. Its material interests were quite too much the football of parties as it was."

"No doubt you were right," rejoined Dr. Leete, "but all that is changed now. We have no parties or politicians, and as for demagoguery, and corruption, they are words having only an historical significance."

"Human nature itself must have changed very much," I said.

"Not at all," was Dr. Leete's reply, "but the conditions of human life have changed, and with them the motives of human action. The organization of society no longer offers a premium on baseness. But these are matters which you can only understand as you come, with time, to know us better."

"But you have not yet told me how you have settled the labor problem. It is the problem of capital which we have been discussing," I said. "After the nation had assumed conduct of the mills, machinery, railroads, farms, mines and capital in general of the country, the labor question still remained. In assuming the responsibilities of capital the nation had assumed the difficulties of the capitalist's position."

"The moment the nation assumed the responsibilities of capital, those difficulties vanished," replied Dr. Leete. "The national organization of labor under one direction was the complete solution of what was, in your day and under your system, justly regarded as the insoluble labor problem. When the nation became the sole employer, all the citizens, by virtue of their citizenship, became employees, to be distributed according to the needs of industry."

"That is," I suggested, "you have simply applied the principle of universal military service, as it was understood in our day, to the labor question."

"Yes," said Dr. Leete, "that was something which followed as a matter of course as soon as the nation had become the sole capitalist. The people were already accustomed to the idea that the obligation of every citizen, not physically disabled, to contribute his military services to the defence of the nation, was equal and absolute. That it was equally the duty of every citizen to contribute his quota of industrial or intellectual services to the maintenance of the nation, was equally evident, though it was not until the nation became the employer of labor that citizens were able to render this sort of service with any pretence either of universality or equity. No organization of labor was possible when the employing power was divided among hundreds or thousands of individuals and corporations, between which concert of any kind was neither desired, nor indeed feasible. It constantly happened then that vast numbers who desired to labor could find no opportunity, and on the other hand, those who desired to evade a part or all of their debt could easily do so."

---

47 baseness. The point here was expanded by several sentences in later editions

"Service, now, I suppose, is compulsory upon all," I suggested.

"It is rather a matter of course than of compulsion," replied Dr. Leete. "It is regarded as so absolutely natural and reasonable that the idea of its being compulsory has ceased to be thought of. He would be thought to be an incredibly contemptible person who should need compulsion in such a case. Nevertheless, to speak of service being compulsory would be a weak way to state its absolute inevitableness. Our entire social order is so wholly based upon and deduced from it that if it were conceivable that a man could escape it, he would be left with no possible way to provide for his existence. He would have excluded himself from the world, cut himself off from his kind, in a word, committed suicide."

"Is the term of service in this industrial army for life?"

"Oh, no; it both begins later and ends earlier than the average working period in your day. Your workshops were filled with children and old men, but we hold the period of youth sacred to education, and the period of maturity, when the physical forces begin to flag, equally sacred to ease and agreeable relaxation. The period of industrial service is twenty-four years, beginning at the close of the course of education at twenty-one and terminating at forty-five. After forty-five, while discharged from labor, the citizen still remains liable to special calls, in case of emergencies causing a sudden great increase in the demand for labor, till he reaches the age of fifty-five, but such calls are rarely, in fact almost never, made. The fifteenth day of October of every year is what we call Muster Day, because those who have reached the age of twenty-one are then mustered into the industrial service, and at the same time those who, after twenty-four years service, have reached the age of forty-five are honorably mustered out. It is the great day of the year with us, whence we reckon all other events, our Olympiad, save that it is annual."

CHAPTER VII

"It is after you have mustered your industrial army into service," I said, "that I should expect the chief difficulty to arise, for there its analogy with a military army must cease. Soldiers have all the same thing, and a very simple thing, to do, namely, to practice the manual of arms, to march and stand guard. But the industrial army must learn and follow two or three hundred diverse trades and avocations. What administrative talent can be equal to determining wisely what trade or business every individual in a great nation shall pursue?"

"The administration has nothing to do with determining that point."

"Who does determine it, then?" I asked.

"Every man for himself in accordance with his natural aptitude, the utmost pains being taken to enable him to find out what his natural aptitude really is. The principle on which our industrial army is organized is that a man's natural endowments, mental and physical, determine what he can work at most profitably to the nation and most satisfactorily to himself. While the obligation of service in some form is not to be evaded, voluntary election, subject only to necessary regulation, is depended on to determine the particular sort of service every man is to render. As an individual's satisfaction during his term of service depends on his having an occupation to his taste, parents and teachers watch from early years for indications of special aptitudes in children. Manual industrial training is no part of our educational system, which is directed to general culture and the humanities, but a theoretical knowledge of the processes of the various industries is given, and our youth are constantly encouraged to visit the workshops, and are frequently taken on long excursions to acquire familiarity with special industries. Usually, long before he is mustered into service, a young man, if he has a taste for any special pursuit, has found it out and probably acquired a great deal of information about it. If, however, he has no special taste, and makes no election when opportunity is offered, he is assigned to any avocation among those of an unskilled character which may be in need of men."

"Surely," I said, "it can hardly be that the number of volunteers for any trade is exactly the number needed in that trade. It must be generally either under or over the demand."

"The supply of volunteers is always expected to fully equal the demand," replied Dr. Leete. "It is the business of the administration to see that this is the case. The rate of volunteering for each trade is closely watched.

---

65 children. The remainder of this paragraph was later much revised

If there be a noticeably greater excess of volunteers over men needed in any trade, it is inferred that the trade offers greater attractions than others. On the other hand, if the number of volunteers for a trade tends to drop below the demand, it is inferred that it is thought more arduous. It is the business of the administration to seek constantly to equalize the attractions of the trades, so far as the conditions of labor in them are concerned, so that all trades shall be equally attractive to persons having natural tastes for them. This is done by making the hours of labor in different trades to differ according to their arduousness. The lighter trades, prosecuted under the most agreeable circumstances, have in this way the longest hours, while an arduous trade, such as mining, has very short hours. There is no theory, no *a priori* rule, by which the respective attractiveness of industries is determined. The administration, in taking burdens off one class of workers and adding them to other classes, simply follows the fluctuations of opinion among the workers themselves as indicated by the rate of volunteering. The principle is that no man's work ought to be, on the whole, harder for him than any other man's for him, the workers themselves to be the judges. There are no limits to the application of this rule. If any particular occupation is in itself so arduous or so oppressive that, in order to induce volunteers, the day's work in it had to be reduced to ten minutes, it would be done. If, even then, no man was willing to do it, it would remain undone. But of course, in point of fact, a moderate reduction in the hours of labor, or addition of other privileges, suffices to secure all needed volunteers for any occupation necessary to men. If, indeed, the unavoidable difficulties and dangers of such a necessary pursuit were so great that no inducement of compensating advantages would overcome men's repugnance to it, the administration would only need to take it out of the common order of occupations by declaring it 'extra hazardous,' and those who pursued it especially worthy of the national gratitude, to be overrun with volunteers. Our young men are very greedy of honor, and do not let slip such opportunities. Of course you will see that dependence on the purely voluntary choice of avocations involves the abolition in all of anything like unhygienic conditions or special peril to life and limb. Health and safety are conditions common to all industries. The nation does not maim and slaughter its workmen by thousands, as did the private capitalists and corporations of your day."

"When there are more who want to enter a particular trade than there is room for, how do you decide between the applicants?" I inquired.

"Preference is given to those with the best general records in their preliminary service as unskilled laborers, and as youths in their educational course. No man, however, who through successive years remains persistent in his desire to show what he can do at any particular trade, is in the end denied an opportunity. I should add, in reference to the counter-possibility of some sudden failure of volunteers in a particular trade, or some sudden necessity of an increased force, that the administration, while depending on the voluntary system for filling up the trades as a rule, holds always in reserve the power to call for special volunteers, or draft any force needed from any quarter. Generally, however, all needs of this sort can be met by details from the class of unskilled or common laborers."

"How is this class of common laborers recruited?" I asked. "Surely nobody voluntarily enters that."

"It is the grade to which all new recruits belong for the first three years of their service. It is not till after this period, during which he is assignable to any work at the discretion of his superiors, that the young man is allowed to elect a special avocation. These three years of stringent discipline none are exempt from."

"As an industrial system, I should think this might be extremely efficient," I said, "but I don't see that it makes any provision for the professional classes, the men who serve the nation with brains instead of hands. Of course you can't get along without the brain-workers. How, then, are they selected from those who are to serve as farmers and mechanics? That must require a very delicate sort of sifting process, I should say."

"So it does," replied Dr. Leete; "the most delicate possible test is needed here, and so we leave the question whether a man shall be a brain or hand worker entirely to him to settle. At the end of the term of three years as a common laborer, which every man must serve, it is for him to choose in accordance to his natural tastes whether he will fit himself for an art or profession, or be a farmer or mechanic. If he feels that he can do better work with his brains than his muscles he finds every facility provided for testing the reality of his sup-

51 **Preference.** In later editions this point was more fully dealt with

posed bent, of cultivating it, and if fit, of pursuing it as his avocation. The schools of technology, of medicine, or art, of music, of histrionics and of higher liberal learning, are always open to aspirants without condition."

"Are not the schools flooded with young men whose only motive is to avoid work?"

Dr. Leete smiled a little grimly.

"No one is at all likely to enter the professional schools for the purpose of avoiding work, I assure you,"
10 he said. "They are intended for those with special aptitude for the branches they teach, and any one without it would find it easier to do double hours at his trade than try to keep up with the classes. Of course many honestly mistake their vocation, and, finding themselves unequal to the requirements of the schools, drop out and return to the industrial service; no discredit attaches to such persons, for the public policy is to encourage all to develop suspected talents which only actual tests can prove the reality of. The professional and
20 scientific schools of your day depended on the patronage of their pupils for support, and the practice appears to have been common of giving diplomas to unfit persons, who afterwards found their way into the professions. Our schools are national institutions, and to have passed their tests is a proof of special abilities not to be questioned.

"This opportunity for a professional training," the doctor continued, "remains open to every man till the age of thirty-five is reached, after which students are
30 not received, as there would remain too brief a period before the age of discharge in which to serve the nation in their professions. In your day young men had to choose their professions very young, and therefore, in a large proportion of instances, wholly mistook their vocations. It is recognized nowadays that the natural aptitudes of some are later than those of others in developing, and therefore, while the choice of profession may be made as early as twenty-four, it remains open for eleven years longer. I should add that the right
40 of transfer, under proper restrictions, from a trade first chosen to one preferred later in life, also remains open to a man till thirty-five."

A question which had a dozen times before been on my lips, now found utterance, a question which touched upon what, in my time, had been regarded the most vital difficulty in the way of any final settlement of the industrial problem. "It is an extraordinary thing," I said,

"that you should not yet have said a word about the method of adjusting wages. Since the nation is the sole employer the government must fix the rate of wages and 50 determine just how much everybody shall earn, from the doctors to the diggers. All I can say is, that this plan would never have worked with us, and I don't see how it can now unless human nature has changed. In my day, nobody was satisfied with his wages or salary. Even if he felt he received enough, he was sure his neighbor had too much, which was as bad. If the universal discontent on this subject, instead of being dissipated in curses and strikes directed against innumerable employers, could have been concentrated upon one, and that 60 the government, the strongest ever devised would not have seen two pay days."

Dr. Leete laughed heartily.

"Very true, very true," he said, "a general strike would most probably have followed the first pay day, and a strike directed against a government is a revolution."

"How, then, do you avoid a revolution every pay day?" I demanded. "Has some prodigious philosopher devised a new system of calculus satisfactory to all for determining the exact and comparative value of all sorts of serv- 70 ice, whether by brawn or brain, by hand or voice, by ear or eye? Or has human nature itself changed, so that no man looks upon his own things but 'every man on the things of his neighbor?' One or the other of these events must be the explanation."

"Neither one nor the other, however, is," was my host's laughing response. "And now, Mr. West," he continued, "you must remember that you are my patient as well as my guest, and permit me to prescribe sleep for you before we have any more conversation. It is after 80 three o'clock."

"The prescription is, no doubt, a wise one," I said; "I only hope it can be filled."

"I will see to that," the doctor replied, and he did, for he gave me a wine glass of something or other which sent me to sleep as soon as my head touched the pillow.

1886-1887·1888

---

29 **thirty-five.** Bellamy later reduced the age to thirty • 75 **explanation.** In the next chapter, not here reprinted, Dr. Leete explains how wages and money have been eliminated, each citizen being given at the beginning of each year a credit corresponding to his share of the annual product of the nation, on which he can obtain what he needs from the public storehouses

Lincoln Steffens

1866 · 1936

In the second part of Bunyan's *Pilgrim's Progress* Christian and his wife, visiting the Interpreter's House, are shown into a room "where was a man that could look no way but downwards, with a muck-rake in his hand," although one who stood over him was proffering in exchange a celestial crown. The scene revealed, so the Interpreter says, "that heaven is but as a fable to some, and that things here are counted the only things substantial." In 1906, when President Theodore Roosevelt wearied of the sensational disclosures of political and business corruption in *McClure's, Collier's,* and other popular magazines, he remembered his Bunyan and labeled the magazine writers "muckrakers." Because the reformers of the age of Roosevelt I devoted themselves largely to uncovering the unpalatable facts of graft and boss rule, without envisioning such futures as had guided Henry George and Edward Bellamy, muckraking is an apt description of an era.

The chief of the muckrakers (although Roosevelt, his personal friend, specifically excepted him from the charge) was Lincoln Steffens. A Californian whose father was, up to a point, indulgent, Steffens graduated from the university of his native state in 1889, and then spent nearly three years in study in Berlin, Heidelberg, Leipzig, Paris, and London. He married a fellow American in Europe, but neglected to inform his family of the fact. When he landed in New York City in 1892, vaguely expecting to go West "to teach or lecture on the theories of ethics while making a study of morals: the professional ethics and the actual conduct of men in business, politics, and the professions," he found a letter

from his father. It informed him that he was now to support himself and contained a hundred dollars to carry him until he could find a job.

Steffens found a place, not too easily, on the New York *Evening Post,* and was soon extraordinarily successful as a reporter. He had the knack of asking questions with such intelligence and penetration that important men took him into their confidence. Within six years he knew a great deal about Wall Street and the police department, and had become city editor of the *Commercial Advertiser,* a paper which contributed largely to the early political career of Theodore Roosevelt. By the investment of a small legacy from one of his Leipzig classmates he obtained financial freedom, which enabled him to pursue with few restrictions the task he set himself—an understanding of the ethical implications of social and political processes.

His first real fame came in 1903, after he had joined the editorial staff of *McClure's.* Visiting the great cities of the Middle West to investigate boss rule and reform movements, he was struck by the similarity between conditions in New York and those elsewhere, and gradually came to the conviction that corruption in politics and business was no local phenomenon, that democracy was on trial everywhere. Unlike most reformers he could not lay all the blame upon "evil" individuals; he saw bribery and bossism and crime and organized vice as connected parts of a vast "System," for which the citizens themselves, however moral and upright might be their individual beliefs, were responsible.

Steffens explored the System in a series of magazine

articles, later collected as *The Shame of the Cities* (1904); in *The Struggle for Self-Government* (1906), which was the most extensive interpretation of his collection of facts; and in various other books and articles, including some attempts at fiction. Steffens also wrote extensively for *The American Magazine* and *Everybody's*. His *Autobiography* (1931) seems likely to survive as one of the best first-hand reports on the years between 1900 and 1913 (the age of "Teddy" the trust-buster and of progressivism) and as an intelligent man's effort to understand the forces of the twentieth-century world. Steffens came in the end to prophesy the end of the middle class and a contest, not between capital and labor, but between ownership and management, with the fundamental issue being whether economic life (and hence political life as well) should be regulated to protect those who live on dividends and interest or those who live on wages. His final conclusion was that "reform" was futile.

Whatever one may think of that, Steffens will never be found a dull writer. His intellectual curiosity, his liking for human beings whatever their state, condition, or morals, his lively style—all are suggested in the last sentences of his autobiography. "My life was worth my living. And as for the world in general, all that was or is or ever will be wrong with that is my—our thinking about it."

The Autobiography of Lincoln Steffens, New York, 1931 • The Letters of Lincoln Steffens, New York, 1938 • C. C. Regier, The Era of the Muckrakers, Chapel Hill, 1932 • John Chamberlain, Farewell to Reform: The Rise, Life and Decay of the Progressive Mind in America, second edition, New York, 1933 • Louis Filler, Crusaders for American Liberalism, Yellow Springs, 1950

From • The Shame of the Cities

Philadelphia: Corrupt and Contented

"Tweed Days in St. Louis," the first of Steffens' famous series, was written in collaboration with a St. Louis reporter and appeared in **McClure's** for October 1902. The other articles quickly followed: "The Shame of Minneapolis" (January 1903), "The Shamelessness of St. Louis" (March), "Pittsburg: A City Ashamed" (May), "Philadelphia: Corrupt and Contented" (July), "Chicago: Half Free and Fighting On" (October), and "New York: Good Government to the Test" (November). When their author collected them in book form he added an introduction with "some conclusions," asserting that for misgovernment no one class, no one breed, no one group of interests was at fault. He refused to blame the conditions he observed upon foreigners, upon politicians, or upon the absence of businessmen in government. "We Americans," he concluded, "may have failed. We may be mercenary and selfish. Democracy with us may be impossible and corruption inevitable, but these articles . . . have demonstrated that we can stand the truth; that there is pride in the character of American citizenship; and that this pride may be a power in the land. So this little volume, a record of shame and yet of self-respect, a disgraceful confession, yet a declaration of honor, is dedicated, in all good faith, to the accused—to all the citizens of all the cities in the United States."

Noteworthy in Steffens' style is the constant alternation between his generalizations and the facts which he accumulated from his informants with the great care which was necessary to avoid libel suits. "Philadelphia: Corrupt and Contented" is an excellent example of the journalistic exposé, a type of writing by no means dead. The reader should remember that the entire state of Pennsylvania was dominated by Matthew S. Quay, from 1885 until his death in 1904 one of the most powerful political "bosses" in American history.

Other American cities, no matter how bad their own condition may be, all point with scorn to Philadelphia as worse—"the worst-governed city in the country." St. Louis, Minneapolis, Pittsburg submit with some patience to the jibes of any other community; the most friendly suggestion from Philadelphia is rejected with contempt. The Philadelphians are "supine," "asleep"; hopelessly ring-ruled, they are "complacent." "Politically benighted," Philadelphia is supposed to have no light to throw upon a state of things that is almost universal.

This is not fair. Philadelphia is, indeed, corrupt; but it is not without significance. Every city and town in the country can learn something from the typical political experience of this great representative city. New York is excused for many of its ills because it is the metropolis, Chicago because of its forced development; Philadelphia is our "third largest" city and its growth has been gradual and natural. Immigration has been blamed for our municipal conditions; Philadelphia, with 47 per cent of the population native-born of native-born parents, is the most American of our greater cities. It is "good," too, and intelligent. I don't know just how to measure the intelligence of a community, but a Pennsylvania college professor who declared to me his belief in education for the masses as a way out of political corruption, himself justified the "rake-off" of preferred contractors on public works on the ground of a "fair business profit." Another plea we have made is that we are too busy to attend to public business, and we have promised, when we come to wealth and leisure, to do better. Philadelphia has long enjoyed great and widely distributed prosperity; it is the city of homes; there is a dwelling house for every five persons,—men, women, and children,—of the population; and the people give one a sense of more leisure and repose than any community I ever dwelt in. Some Philadelphians account for their political state on the ground of their ease and comfort. There is another class of optimists whose hope is in an "aristocracy" that is to come by and by; Philadelphia is surer that it has a "real aristocracy" than any other place in the world, but its aristocrats, with few exceptions, are in the ring, with it, or of no political use. Then we hear that we are a young people and that when we are older and "have traditions," like some of the old countries, we also will be honest. Philadelphia is one of the oldest of our cities and treasures for us scenes and relics of some of the noblest traditions of "our fair land." Yet I was told how once "for a joke" a party of boodlers counted out the "divvy" of their graft in unison with the ancient chime of Independence Hall.

Philadelphia is representative. This very "joke," told, as it was, with a laugh, is typical. All our municipal governments are more or less bad, and all our people are optimists. Philadelphia is simply the most corrupt and the most contented. Minneapolis has cleaned up, Pittsburg has tried to, New York fights every other election, Chicago fights all the time. Even St. Louis has begun to stir (since the elections are over), and at the worst was only shameless. Philadelphia is proud; good people there defend corruption and boast of their machine. My college professor, with his philosophic view of "rake-offs," is one Philadelphia type. Another is the man, who, driven to bay with his local pride, says: "At least you must admit that our machine is the best you have ever seen."

Disgraceful? Other cities say so. But I say that if Philadelphia is a disgrace, it is a disgrace not to itself alone, nor to Pennsylvania, but to the United States and to American character. For this great city, so highly representative in other respects, is not behind in political experience, but ahead, with New York. Philadelphia is a city that has had its reforms. Having passed through all the typical stages of corruption, Philadelphia reached the period of miscellaneous loot with a boss for chief thief, under James McManes and the Gas Ring 'way back in the late sixties and seventies. This is the Tweed stage of corruption from which St. Louis, for example, is just emerging. Philadelphia, in two inspiring popular revolts, attacked the Gas Ring, broke it, and in 1885 achieved that dream of American cities—a good charter. The present condition of Philadelphia, therefore, is not that which precedes, but that which follows reform, and in this distinction lies its startling general significance. What has happened since the Bullitt Law or charter went into effect in Philadelphia may happen in any American city "after reform is over."

For reform with us is usually revolt, not government, and is soon over. Our people do not seek, they avoid self-rule, and "reforms" are spasmodic efforts to punish bad rulers and get somebody that will give us good

---

70 **James McManes** (1822-1899), trustee of the municipal gasworks for most of his life after 1865 and dominant in Philadelphia city politics until 1881 • 71 **Tweed**, William Marcy Tweed (1823-1878), Democratic boss of New York City from about 1861 until 1873, when he was convicted of grand larceny • 79 **Bullitt Law** (1885), which permitted the reorganization of the Philadelphia city government, so called from its author, John C. Bullitt (1824-1902)

government or something that will make it. A self-acting form of government is an ancient superstition. We are an inventive people and we all think that we shall devise some day a legal machine that will turn out good government automatically. The Philadelphians have treasured this belief longer than the rest of us and have tried it more often. Throughout their history they have sought this wonderful charter and they thought they had it when they got the Bullitt Law, which con-
10 centrates in the Mayor ample power, executive and political, and complete responsibility. Moreover, it calls for very little thought and action on the part of the people. All they expected to have to do when the Bullitt Law went into effect was to elect as mayor a good business man, who with his probity and common sense would give them that good business administration which is the ideal of many reformers.

The Bullitt Law went into effect in 1887. A committee of twelve—four men from the Union League,
20 four from business organizations, and four from the bosses—picked out the first man to run under it on the Republican ticket, Edwin H. Fitler, an able, upright business man, and he was elected. Strange to say, his administration was satisfactory to the citizens, who speak well of it to this day, and to the politicians also; Boss McManes (the ring was broken, not the boss) took to the next national convention from Philadelphia a delegation solid for Fitler for President of the United States. It was a farce, but it pleased Mr. Fitler, so Matthew S.
30 Quay, the State boss, let him have a complimentary vote on the first ballot. The politicians "fooled" Mr. Fitler, and they "fooled" also the next business mayor, Edwin S. Stuart, likewise a most estimable gentleman. Under these two administrations the foundation was laid for the present government of Philadelphia, the corruption to which Philadelphians seem so reconciled, and the machine which is "at least the best you have ever seen."

The Philadelphia machine isn't the best. It isn't sound,
40 and I doubt if it would stand in New York or Chicago. The enduring strength of the typical American political machine is that it is a natural growth—a sucker, but deep-rooted in the people. The New Yorkers vote for Tammany Hall. The Philadelphians do not vote; they are disfranchised, and their disfranchisement is one anchor of the foundation of the Philadelphia organization.

This is no figure of speech. The honest citizens of Philadelphia have no more rights at the polls than the Negroes down South. Nor do they fight very hard for this basic privilege. You can arouse their Republican 50 ire by talking about the black Republican votes lost in the Southern States by white Democratic intimidation, but if you remind the average Philadelphian that he is in the same position, he will look startled, then say, "That's so, that's literally true, only I never thought of it in just that way." And it is literally true.

The machine controls the whole process of voting, and practices fraud at every stage. The assessor's list is the voting list, and the assessor is the machine's man. "The assessor of a division kept a disorderly house; he padded 60 his lists with fraudulent names registered from his house; two of these names were used by election officers. . . . The constable of the division kept a disreputable house; a policeman was assessed as living there. . . . The election was held in the disorderly house maintained by the assessor. . . . The man named as judge had a criminal charge for a life offense pending against him. . . . Two hundred and fifty-two votes were returned in a division that had less than one hundred legal votes within its boundaries." These extracts from a report of the 70 Municipal League suggest the election methods. The assessor pads the list with the names of dead dogs, children, and non-existent persons. One newspaper printed the picture of a dog, another that of a little four-year-old Negro boy, down on such a list. A ring orator in a speech resenting sneers at his ward as "low down" reminded his hearers that that was the ward of Independence Hall, and, naming over signers of the Declaration of Independence, he closed his highest flight of eloquence with the statement that "these men, the 80 fathers of American liberty, voted down here once. And," he added, with a catching grin, "they vote here yet." Rudolph Blankenburg, a persistent fighter for the right and the use of the right to vote (and, by the way, an immigrant), sent out just before one election a regis-

22 **Edwin H. Fitler** (1825-1896), cordage manufacturer and Republican mayor, 1887-1891 • 29 **Matthew S. Quay** (1833-1904), Republican state leader from 1885 until his death, and United States senator, 1887-1899, 1901-1904 • 33 **Edwin S. Stuart** (1853-1937), Republican mayor, 1891-1895, later (1907-1911) governor • 83 **Rudolph Blankenburg** (1843-1918), wealthy businessman, later (1912-1916) mayor

Philadelphia: Corrupt and Contented 717

tered letter to each voter on the rolls of a certain selected division. Sixty-three per cent. were returned marked "not at," "removed," "deceased," etc. From one four-story house where forty-four voters were addressed, eighteen letters came back undelivered; from another of forty-eight voters, came back forty-one letters; from another sixty-one out of sixty-two; from another forty-four out of forty-seven. Six houses in one division were assessed at one hundred and seventy-two voters, more than the votes cast in the previous election in any one of two hundred entire divisions.

The repeating is done boldly, for the machine controls the election officers, often choosing them from among the fraudulent names; and when no one appears to serve, assigning the heeler ready for the expected vacancy. The police are forbidden by law to stand within thirty feet of the polls, but they are at the box and they are there to see that the machine's orders are obeyed and that repeaters whom they help to furnish are permitted to vote without "intimidation" on the names they, the police, have supplied. The editor of an anti-machine paper who was looking about for himself once told me that a ward leader who knew him well asked him into a polling place. "I'll show you how it's done," he said, and he had the repeaters go round and round voting again and again on the names handed them on slips. "But," as the editor said, "that isn't the way it's done." The repeaters go from one polling place to another, voting on slips, and on their return rounds change coats, hats, etc. The business proceeds with very few hitches; there is more jesting than fighting. Violence in the past has had its effect; and is not often necessary nowadays, but if it is needed the police are there to apply it. Several citizens told me that they had seen the police help to beat citizens or election officers who were trying to do their duty, then arrest the victim; and Mr. Clinton Rogers Woodruff, the executive counsel of the Municipal League, has published a booklet of such cases. But an official statement of the case is at hand in an announcement by John Weaver, the new machine mayor of Philadelphia, that he is going to keep the police out of politics and away from the polls. "I shall see," he added, "that every voter enjoys the full right of suffrage and that ballots may be placed in the ballot box without fear of intimidation."

But many Philadelphians do not try to vote. They leave everything to the machine, and the machine casts their ballots for them. It is estimated that 150,000 voters did not go to the polls at the last election. Yet the machine rolled up a majority of 130,000 for Weaver, with a fraudulent vote estimated all the way from forty to eighty thousand, and this in a campaign so machine-made that it was called "no contest." Francis Fisher Kane, the Democrat, got 32,000 votes out of some 204,000. "What is the use of voting?" these stay-at-homes ask. A friend of mine told me he was on the lists in the three wards in which he had successively dwelt. He votes personally in none, but the leader of his present ward tells him how he has been voted. Mr. J. C. Reynolds, the proprietor of the St. James Hotel, went to the polls at eleven o'clock last election day, only to be told that he had been voted. He asked how many others from his house had voted. An election officer took up a list, checked off twelve names, two down twice, and handed it to him. When Mr. Reynolds got home he learned that one of these had voted, the others had been voted. Another man said he rarely attempted to vote, but when he did, the officers let him, even though his name had already been voted on; and then the Negro repeaters would ask if his "brother was coming 'round to-day." They were going to vote him, as they vote all good-natured citizens who stay away. "When this kind of man turns out," said a leader to me, "we simply have two repeaters extra—one to balance him and one more to the good." If necessary, after all this, the machine counts the vote "right," and there is little use appealing to the courts, since they have held, except in one case, that the ballot box is secret and cannot be opened. The only legal remedy lies in the purging of the assessors' lists, and when the Municipal League had this done in 1899, they reported that there was "wholesale voting on the very names stricken off."

Deprived of self-government, the Philadelphians haven't even self-governing machine government. They have their own boss, but he and his machine are subject to the State ring and take their orders from the

37 Clinton Rogers Woodruff (1868-   ), counsel for the Municipal League from 1891 until 1904, long nationally famous for his work for better municipal government • 40 John Weaver (1861-1928), independent Republican mayor, 1903-1907 • 53 Francis Fisher Kane (1866-   ), lawyer, Democratic nominee for mayor in 1903

State boss, Matthew S. Quay, who is the proprietor of Pennsylvania and the real ruler of Philadelphia, just as William Penn, the Great Proprietor, was. Philadelphians, especially the local bosses, dislike this description of their government, and they point for refutation to their charter. But this very Bullitt Law was passed by Quay, and he put it through the Legislature, not for reform reasons, but at the instance of David H. Lane, his Philadelphia lieutenant, as a check upon the power of Boss McManes. Later, when McManes proved hopelessly insubordinate, Quay decided to have done with him forever. He chose David Martin for boss, and from his seat in the United States Senate, Penn's successor raised up his man and set him over the people. Croker, who rose by his own strength to the head of Tammany Hall, has tried twice to appoint a successor; no one else could, and he failed. The boss of Tammany Hall is a growth. So Croker has attempted to appoint district leaders and failed; a Tammany district leader is a growth. Boss Martin, picked up and set down from above, was accepted by Philadelphia and the Philadelphia machine, and he removed old ward leaders and appointed new ones. Some leaders in Philadelphia own their wards, of course, but Martin and, after him, Durham have sent men into a ward to lead it, and they have led it.

The Philadelphia organization is upside down. It has its root in the air, or, rather, like the banyan tree, it sends its roots from the center out both up and down and all around, and there lies its peculiar strength. For when I said it was dependent and not sound, I did not mean that it was weak. It is dependent as a municipal machine, but the organization that rules Philadelphia is, as we have seen, not a mere municipal machine, but a city, State, and national organization. The people of Philadelphia are Republicans in a Republican city in a Republican State in a Republican nation, and they are bound ring on ring on ring. The President of the United States and his patronage; the National Cabinet and their patronage; the Congress and the patronage of the Senators and the Congressmen from Pennsylvania; the Governor of the State and the State Legislature with their powers and patronage; and all that the mayor and city councils have of power and patronage—all these bear down upon Philadelphia to keep it in the control of Quay's boss and his little ring. This is the ideal of party organization, and, possibly, is the end toward which our democratic republic is tending. If it is, the end is absolutism. Nothing but a revolution could overthrow this oligarchy, and there is its danger. With no outlet at the polls for public feeling, the machine cannot be taught anything it does not know excepting at the cost of annihilation.

But the Philadelphia machine-leaders know their business. As I said in "Tweed Days in St. Louis," the politicians will learn, if the people won't, from exposure and reform. The Pennsylvania bosses learned the "uses of reform"; we have seen Quay applying it to discipline McManes, and he since has turned reformer himself, to punish local bosses. The bosses have learned also the danger of combination between citizens and the Democrats. To prevent this, Quay and his friends have spread sedulously the doctrine of "reform within the party," and, from the Committee of One Hundred on, the reformers have stuck pretty faithfully to this principle. But lest the citizens should commit such a sin against their party, Martin formed a permanent combination of the Democratic with the Republican organization, using to that end a goodly share of the Federal and county patronage. Thus the people of Philadelphia were "fixed" so that they couldn't vote if they wanted to, and if they should want to, they couldn't vote for a Democrat, except of Republican or independent choosing. In other words, having taken away their ballot, the bosses took away also the choice of parties.

But the greatest lesson learned and applied was that of conciliation and "good government." The people must not want to vote or rebel against the ring. This ring, like any other, was formed for the exploitation of the city for private profit, and the cementing force is the "cohesive power of public plunder." But McManes and Tweed had proved that miscellaneous larceny was dangerous, and why should a lot of cheap politicians get

---

8 **David H. Lane,** Republican associate of Quay; in his autobiography Samuel W. Pennypacker says: "he is very much of a philosopher and has often been called the brains of the party in Philadelphia" • 12 **David Martin,** later state insurance commissioner • 14 **Croker,** Richard Croker (1841-1922), leader of Tammany Hall from 1886 until 1903; he was one of Steffens' early "contacts" in New York City and is described at some length in the **Autobiography** • 24 **Durham,** Israel W. Durham, the Philadelphia boss to whom Steffens devotes a whole chapter in the **Autobiography,** and the subject of one of his later works of fiction, "The Dying Boss"

so much and the people nothing at all? The people had been taught to expect but little from their rulers: good water, good light, clean streets well paved, fair transportation, the decent repression of vice, public order and public safety, and no scandalous or open corruption, would more than satisfy them. It would be good business and good politics to give them these things. Like Chris Magee, who studied out the problem with him, Martin took away from the rank and file of the party and from the ward leaders and office holders the privilege of theft, and he formed companies and groups to handle the legitimate public business of the city. It was all graft, but it was to be all lawful, and, in the main, it was. Public franchises, public works, and public contracts were the principal branches of the business, and Martin adopted the dual boss idea which we have seen worked out by Magee and Flinn in Pittsburg. In Philadelphia it was Martin and Porter, and just as Flinn had a firm, Booth & Flinn, Ltd., so Porter was Filbert and Porter.

Filbert and Porter got all the public contracts they could handle, and the rest went to other contractors friendly to them and to the ring. Sometimes the preferred contractor was the lowest bidder, but he did not have to be. The law allowed awards to the "lowest and best," and the courts held that this gave the officials discretion. But since public criticism was to be considered, the ring, to keep up appearances, resorted to many tricks. One was to have fake bids made above the favorite. Another was to have the favorite bid high, but set an impossible time limit; the department of the city councils could extend the time afterwards. Still another was to arrange for specifications which would make outsiders bid high, then either openly alter the plans or let the ring firm perform work not up to requirements.

Many of Martin's deals and jobs were scandals, but they were safe; they were in the direction of public service; and the great mass of the business was done quietly. Moreover, the public was getting something for its money,—not full value, but a good percentage. In other words, there was a limit to the "rake-off," and some insiders have told me that it had been laid down as a principle with the ring that the people should have in value (that is in work or benefit, including a fair profit) ninety-five cents out of every dollar. In some of the deals I investigated, the "rake-off" over and above profit was as high as twenty-five per cent. Still, even at this, there was "a limit," and the public was getting, as one of the leaders told me, "a run for its money." Cynical as it all sounds, this view is taken by many Philadelphians almost if not quite as intelligent as my college professor.

But there was another element in the policy of conciliation which is a potent factor in the contentment of Philadelphia, and I regard it as the key to that "apathy" which has made the community notorious. We have seen how Quay had with him the Federal resources and those of the State, and the State ring, and we have seen how Martin, having the city, mayor and councils, won over the Democratic city leaders. Here they had under pay in office at least 15,000 men and women. But each of these 15,000 persons was selected for office because he could deliver votes, either by organizations, by parties, or by families. These must represent pretty near a majority of the city's voters. But this is by no means the end of the ring's reach. In the State ring are the great corporations, the Standard Oil Company, Cramp's Ship Yard, and the steel companies, with the Pennsylvania Railroad at their head, and all the local transportation and other public utility companies following after. They get franchises, privileges, exemptions, etc.; they have helped finance Quay through deals: the Pennsylvania paid Martin, Quay said once, a large yearly salary; the Cramps get contracts to build United States ships, and for years have been begging for a subsidy on homemade ships. The officers, directors, and stockholders of these companies, with their friends, their bankers, and their employees, are of the organization. Better still, one of the local bosses of Philadelphia told me he could always give a worker a job with these companies, just as he could in a city department, or in the mint, or postoffice. Then there are the bankers who enjoy, or may some day enjoy, public deposits; those that profit on loans to finance political financial deals; the promoting capitalists who share with the bosses on franchises; and

---

8 **Chris Magee,** Christopher L. Magee (1848-1901), Republican boss of Pittsburgh from about 1877; in "Pittsburg: A City Ashamed" Steffens remarked that "in the management of a city Croker was a child beside Chris Magee" • 17 **Flinn,** William Flinn, a Pittsburgh contractor; see "Pittsburg: A City Ashamed," for the process of graft Steffens is describing • 18 **Porter,** Charles A. Porter (1836-?), contractor and Republican state senator, 1890-1896 • 66 **Cramp's Ship Yard.** William Cramp and Sons, under Charles Henry Cramp (1828-1913) was the largest shipbuilding company in the United States

the brokers who deal in ring securities and speculate upon ring tips. Through the exchange the ring financiers reach the investing public, which is a large and influential body. The traction companies, which bought their way from beginning to end by corruption, which have always been in the ring, and whose financiers have usually shared in other big ring deals, adopted early the policy of bribing the people with "small blocks of stock."
Dr. Frederick Speirs, in his "The Street Railway System of Philadelphia," came upon transactions which "indicate clearly that it is the policy of the Union Company to get the securities into the hands of a large number of small holders, the plain inference being that a wide distribution of securities will fortify the company against possible attacks by the public." In 1895 he found a director saying: "Our critics have engaged the Academy of Music, and are to call an assemblage of people opposed to the street railways as now managed. It would take eight Academies of Music to hold the stock-holders of the Union Traction Company."

But we are not yet through. Quay has made a specialty all his life of reformers, and he and his local bosses have won over so many that the list of former reformers is very, very long. Martin drove down his roots through race and religion, too. Philadelphia was one of the hot-beds of "know-nothingism." Martin recognized the Catholic, and the Irish-Irish, and so drew off into the Republican party the great natural supply of the Democrats; and his successors have given high places to representative Jews. "Surely this isn't corruption!" No, and neither is that corruption which makes the heads of great educational and charity institutions "go along," as they say in Pennsylvania, in order to get appropriations for their institutions from the State and land from the city. They know what is going on, but they do not join reform movements. The provost of the University of Pennsylvania declined to join in a revolt because, he said, it might impair his usefulness to the University. And so it is with others, and with clergymen who have favorite charities; with Sabbath associations and City Beautiful clubs; with lawyers who want briefs; with real estate dealers who like to know in advance about public improvements, and real estate owners who appreciate light assessments; with shopkeepers who don't want to be bothered with strict inspections.

If there is no other hold for the ring on a man there always is the protective tariff. "I don't care," said a manufacturer. "What if they do plunder and rob us, it can't hurt me unless they raise the tax rates, and even that won't ruin me. Our party keeps up the tariff. If they should reduce that, my business would be ruined."

Such, then, are the ramifications of this machine, such is its strength. No wonder Martin could break his own rules, as he did, and commit excesses. Philadelphia is not merely corrupt, it is corrupted. Martin's doom was proclaimed not in Philadelphia, but in the United States Senate, and his offense was none of this business of his, but his failure to nominate as successor to Mayor Stuart the man, Boise Penrose, whom Matt Quay chose for that place. Martin had consented, but at the last moment he ordered the nomination of Charles F. War-wick instead. The day that happened Mr. Quay arose on the floor of the Senate and, in a speech so irrelevant to the measure under consideration that nobody out of Pennsylvania understood it, said that there was in his town a man who had given as his reason for not doing what he had promised to do, the excuse that he was "under a heavy salary from a great corporation (the Pennsylvania Railroad) and was compelled to do what the corporation wished him to do. And," added Senator Quay, "men in such a position with high power for good or evil ought . . . to go about . . . with the dol-lar mark of the corporation on their foreheads." Quay named as the new boss Israel W. Durham, a ward leader under Martin.

Martin having the city through Mayor Warwick fought Quay in the State, with Chris Magee for an ally, but Quay beat them both there and then prepared to beat them in their own cities. His cry was Reform, and he soon had the people shouting for it.

Quay responded with a Legislative committee to investigate abuses in the cities, but this so-called "Lexow" was called off before it amounted to much more than a momentary embarrassment to Martin. Martin's friends, on the other hand, caught Quay and nearly sent him

---

26 **know-nothingism**, a "native American" political movement of the 1850's, taking its name from the oath of its members to answer all questions about their purposes with "I don't know" • 59 **Boise Penrose**, Boies Penrose (1860-1921), United States senator from 1897 until 1921 • 61 **Charles F. Warwick** (1852-1913), Republican mayor, 1895-1899 • 82 **Lexow**, from the investigation of the New York City police in 1898, instigated by Clarence Lexow (1852-1910), then state senator

to prison. The People's Bank, James McManes, president, failed. The cashier, John S. Hopkins, had been speculating and letting Quay and other politicians have bank funds without collateral for stock gambling. In return Quay and the State Treasurer left heavy State deposits with the bank. Hopkins lost his nerve and shot himself. McManes happened to call in friends of Martin and advise him, and these suggested a Martin man for receiver. They found among the items money
10 lent to Quay without security, except the State funds, and telegrams asking Hopkins to buy "1000 Met" (Metropolitan) and promising in return to "shake the plum tree." Quay, his son, Richard R., and Benjamin J. Haywood, the State Treasurer, were indicted for conspiracy, and every effort was made to have the trial precede the next election for the Legislature which was to elect a successor to Quay in the United States Senate; but Quay got stays and postponements in the hopes that a more friendly District Attorney could be put in that office.
20 Martin secured the election of Peter F. Rothermel, who was eager to try the case, and Quay had to depend on other resources. The trial came in due course, and failed; Judge Biddle ruled out the essential evidence on the ground that it was excluded by the statute of limitation. Rothermel went on with the trial, but it was hopeless; Quay was acquitted and the other cases were abandoned.

Popular feeling was excited by this exposure of Quay, but there was no action till the factional fighting sug-
30 gested a use for it. Quay had refused the second United States Senatorship to John Wanamaker, and Wanamaker led through the State and in Philadelphia a fight against the boss, which has never ceased. It took the form of a reform campaign, and Quay's methods were made plain, but the boss beat Wanamaker at every point, had Penrose made Senator, and through Penrose and Durham was gradually getting possession of Philadelphia. The final triumph came with the election of Samuel H. Ashbridge as mayor.

40 "Stars-and-Stripes Sam," as Ashbridge is sometimes called, was a speech-maker and a "joiner." That is to say, he made a practice of going to lodges, associations, brotherhoods, Sunday-schools, and all sorts of public and private meetings, joining some, but making at all speeches patriotic and sentimental. He was very popular. Under the Bullitt Law, as I have said, all that is

necessary to a good administration and complete, though temporary reform, is a good mayor. The politicians feel that they must nominate a man in whom the people as well as themselves have faith. They had had faith in 50 Warwick, both the ring and the people, and Warwick had found it impossible to satisfy two such masters. Now they put their faith in Ashbridge, and so did Durham, and so did Martin. All interests accepted him, therefore, and all watched him with hope and more or less assurance; none more than the good people. And, indeed, no man could have promised more or better public service than Ashbridge. The result, however, was distracting.

Mr. Ashbridge "threw down" Martin, and he recog- 60 nized Quay's man, "Is" Durham, as the political boss. Durham is a high type of boss, candid, but of few words; generous, but businesslike; complete master of himself, and a genius at organization. For Pennsylvania politics he is a conservative leader, and there would have been no excesses under him, as there have been few "rows." But Mr. Durham has not been the master of the Philadelphia situation. He bowed to Quay, and he could not hold Ashbridge. Philadelphians say that if it should come to a fight, Durham could beat Quay in 70 Philadelphia, but it doesn't come to a fight. Another thing Philadelphians say is that he "keeps his word," yet he broke it (with notice) when Quay asked him to stand for Pennypacker for Governor. As I said before, however, Philadelphia is so constituted that it apparently cannot have self-government, not even its own boss, so that the allegiance paid to Quay is comprehensible. But the submission of the boss to the mayor was extraordinary, and it seemed to some sagacious politicians dangerous.
80
For Mr. Ashbridge broke through all the principles of moderate grafting developed by Martin. Durham formed his ring—taking in James P. McNichol as co-ruler and preferred contractor; John M. Mack as promoter and financier, and he widened the inside circle to include more individuals. But while he was more liberal

20 **Peter F. Rothermel** (1850-1929), district attorney of Philadelphia County, 1899-1902 • 31 **John Wanamaker** (1838-1922), foremost merchant of the city, and active all his life in reform movements • 38 **Samuel H. Ashbridge** (1849-1906), Republican mayor, 1899-1903 • 83 **James P. McNichol**, later a state senator • 84 **John M. Mack** (1852-1915), a contractor and street-railway promoter

toward his leaders, and not inclined "to grab off everything for himself," as one leader told me, he maintained the principle of concentration and strict control as good politics and good business. So, too, he adopted Martin's program of public improvements, the filtration, boulevards, etc., and added to it. When Ashbridge was well settled in office, these schemes were all started, and the mayor pushed them with a will. According to the "Philadelphia Plan," the mayor should not be in the ring. He should be an ambitious man, and his reward promotion, not riches. If he is "out for the stuff," he is likely to be hurried by the fretful thought that his term is limited to four years, and since he cannot succeed himself as mayor, his interest in the future of the machine is less than that of a boss, who goes on forever.

When he was nominated, Ashbridge had debts of record amounting to some $40,000. Before he was elected these were satisfied. Soon after he took office he declared himself to former Postmaster Thomas L. Hicks. Here is Mr. Hicks's account of the incident:

"At one of the early interviews I had with the mayor in his office, he said to me: 'Tom, I have been elected mayor of Philadelphia. I have four years to serve. I have no further ambitions. I want no other office when I am out of this one, and I shall get out of this office all there is in it for Samuel H. Ashbridge.'

"I remarked that this was a very foolish thing to say. 'Think how that could be construed,' I said.

"'I don't care anything about that,' he declared. 'I mean to get out of this office everything there is in it for Samuel H. Ashbridge.'"

When he retired from office last April, he became the president of a bank, and was reputed to be rich. Here is the summary published by the Municipal League at the close of his labors:

"The four years of the Ashbridge administration have passed into history, leaving behind them a scar on the fame and reputation of our city which will be a long time healing. Never before, and let us hope never again, will there be such brazen defiance of public opinion, such flagrant disregard of public interest, such abuse of powers and responsibilities for private ends. These are not generalizations, but each statement can be abundantly proved by numerous instances."

These "numerous instances" are notorious in Philadelphia; some of them were reported all over the country.

One of them was the attempted intimidation of John Wanamaker. Thomas B. Wanamaker, John Wanamaker's son, bought the *North American,* a newspaper which had been, and still is, exposing the abuses and corruption of the political ring. Abraham L. English, Mr. Ashbridge's Director of the Department of Public Safety, called on Mr. John Wanamaker, said he had been having him watched, and was finally in a position to demand that the newspaper stop the attacks. The merchant exposed the whole thing, and a committee appointed to investigate reported that: "Mr. English has practically admitted that he attempted to intimidate a reputable citizen and unlawfully threatened him in an effort to silence criticism of a public newspaper; that from the mayor's refusal to order an investigation of the conduct of Mr. English on the request of a town meeting of representative citizens, the community is justified in regarding him as aiding and abetting Mr. English in the corrupt act committed, and that the mayor is therefore to be equally censured by the community."

The other "instances of brazen abuse of power" were the increase of protected vice—the importation from New York of the "white slavery system of prostitution," the growth of "speak-easies," and the spread of gambling and of policy-playing until it took in the school children. This last the *North American* exposed, but in vain till it named police officers who had refused when asked to interfere. Then a judge summoned the editors and reporters of the paper, the mayor, Director English, school children, and police officers to appear before him. The mayor's personal attorney spoke for the police during the inquiry, and it looked black for the newspaper till the children began to tell their stories. When the hearing was over the judge said:

"The evidence shows conclusively that our public school system in this city is in danger of being corrupted at its fountain; that in one of the schools over one hundred and fifty children were buyers of policy, as were also a large number of scholars in other schools. It was first discovered about eighteen months ago, and for about one year has been in full operation." The police officers were not punished, however.

That corruption had reached the public schools and was spreading rapidly through the system, was discovered by the exposure and conviction of three school directors of the twenty-eighth ward. It was known before that teachers and principals, like any other office holders, had to have a "pull" and pay assessments for election expenses. "Voluntary contributions" was the term used, but over the notices in blue pencil was written "2 per cent.," and teachers who asked directors and ward bosses what to do, were advised that they would "better pay." Those that sent less than the amount suggested, got receipts: "check received; shall we hold for balance or enter on account?" But the exposure in the twenty-eighth ward brought it home to the parents of the children that the teachers were not chosen for fitness, but for political reasons, and that the political reasons had become cash.

Miss Rena A. Haydock testified as follows: "I went to see Mr. Travis, who was a friend of mine, in reference to getting a teacher's certificate. He advised me to see all of the directors, especially Mr. Brown. They told me that it would be necessary for me to pay $120 to get the place. They told me of one girl who had offered $250, and her application had been rejected. That was before they broached the subject of money to me. I said that I didn't have $120 to pay, and they replied that it was customary for teachers to pay $40 a month out of their first three months' salary. The salary was $47. They told me they didn't want the money for themselves, but that it was necessary to buy the other faction. Finally I agreed to the proposition, and they told me that I must be careful not to mention it to anybody or it would injure my reputation. I went with my brother to pay the money to Mr. Johnson. He held out a hat, and when my brother handed the money to him he took it behind the hat."

The regular business of the ring was like that of Pittsburg, but more extensive. I have space only for one incident of one phase of it: Widener and Elkins, the national franchise buyers, are Philadelphians, and they were in the old Martin ring. They had combined all the street railways of the city before 1900, and they were withdrawing from politics, with their traction system. But the Pennsylvania rings will not let corporations that have risen in corruption reform and retire, and, besides, it was charged that in the Martin-Quay fight, the street railways had put up money to beat Quay for the United States Senate. At any rate, plans were laid to "mace" the street railways.

"Macing" is a form of high blackmail. When they have sold out all they have, the politicians form a competing company and compel the old concern to buy out or sell out. While Widener and Elkins were at sea, bound for Europe, in 1901, the Philadelphia ring went to the Legislature and had introduced there two bills, granting a charter to practically all the streets and alleys not covered by tracks in Philadelphia, and to run short stretches of the old companies' tracks to make connections. Clinton Rogers Woodruff, who was an Assemblyman, has told the story. Without notice the bills were introduced at 3 P.M. on Monday, May 29; they were reported from committee in five minutes; by 8:50 P.M. they were printed and on the members' desk, and by 9 P.M. were passed on first reading. The bills passed second reading the next day, Memorial Day, and on the third day were passed from the Senate to the House, where they were "jammed through" with similar haste and worse trickery. In six legislative days the measures were before Governor Stone, who signed them June 7, at midnight, in the presence of Quay, Penrose, Congressman Foerderer, Mayor Ashbridge's Banker, James P. McNichol, John M. Mack, and other capitalists and politicians. Under the law, one hundred charters were applied for the next morning—thirteen for Philadelphia. The charters were granted on June 5, and that same day a special meeting of the Philadelphia Select Council was called for Monday. There the citizens of Philadelphia met the oncoming charters, but their hearing was brief. The charters went through without a hitch, and were sent to Mayor Ashbridge on June 13.

The mayor's secretary stated authoritatively in the morning that the mayor would not sign that day. But he did. An unexpected incident forced his hand. John Wanamaker sent him an offer of $2,500,000 for the franchises about to be given away. Ashbridge threw the letter into the street unread. Mr. Wanamaker had deposited $250,000 as a guarantee of good faith and his action was becoming known. The ordinances were signed by midnight, and the city lost at least two and

35 **Widener and Elkins,** Peter A. Brown Widener (1834-1915) and William L. Elkins (1852-1903), active in street-railway manipulations in several large cities and in extensive real estate operations; their fortunes were among the largest of their day • 65 **Governor Stone,** William Alexis Stone (1846-1920), Republican governor, 1899-1903 • 67 **Congressman Foerderer,** Robert Herman Foerderer (1860-1903), leather manufacturer who was congressman-at-large in 1900-1903

one-half millions of dollars; but the ring made it and much more. When Mr. Wanamaker's letter was published, Congressman Foerderer, an incorporator of the company, answered for the machine. He said the offer was an advertisement; that it was late, and that they were sorry they hadn't had a chance to "call the bluff." Mr. Wanamaker responded with a renewal of the offer of $2,500,000 to the city, and, he said, "I will add $500,000 as a bonus to yourself and your associates personally for the conveyance of the grants and corporate privileges you now possess." That ended the controversy.

But the deal went on. Two more bills, called "Trolley Chasers," were put through, to finish off the legislation, too hurriedly done to be perfect. One was to give the company the right to build either elevated or underground, or both; the second to forbid all further such grants without a hearing before a board consisting of the Governor, the Secretary of the Commonwealth, and the Attorney-General. With all these franchises and exclusive privileges, the new company made the old one lease their plant in operation to the company which had nothing but "rights," or, in Pennsylvania slang, a "good, husky mace."

Ashbridgeism put Philadelphia and the Philadelphia machine to a test which candid ring leaders did not think it would stand. What did the Philadelphians do? Nothing. They have their reformers: they have men like Francis B. Reeves, who fought with every straight reform movement from the days of the Committee of One Hundred; they have men like Rudolph Blankenburg, who have fought with every reform that promised any kind of relief; there are the Municipal League, with an organization by wards, the Citizens' Municipal League, the Allied Reform League, and the Law and Order Society; there are young men and veterans; there are disappointed politicians and ambitious men who are not advanced fast enough by the machine. There is discontent in a good many hearts, and some men are ashamed. But "the people" won't follow. One would think the Philadelphians would follow any leader; what should they care whether he is pure white or only gray? But they do care. "The people" seem to prefer to be ruled by a known thief than an ambitious reformer. They will make you convict their Tweeds, McManeses, Butlers, and Shepherds, and even then they may forgive them and talk of monuments to their precious memory, but they

take delight in the defeat of John Wanamaker because they suspect that he is a hypocrite and wants to go to the United States Senate.

All the stout-hearted reformers had made a campaign to re-elect Rothermel, the District Attorney who had dared to try Quay. Surely there was an official to support! But no, Quay was against him. The reformers used money, some $250,000, I believe,—fighting the devil with fire,—but the machine used more money, $700,000, from the teachers, "speak-easies," office holders, bankers, and corporations. The machine handled the ballot. Rothermel was beaten by John Weaver. There have been other campaigns, before and since, led by the Municipal League, which is managed with political sense, but each successive defeat was by a larger majority for the machine.

There is no check upon this machine excepting the chance of a mistake, the imminent fear of treachery, and the remote danger of revolt. To meet this last, the machine, as a State organization, has set about throttling public criticism. Ashbridge found that blackmail was ineffective. Durham, Quay, and Governor Pennypacker have passed a libel law which meant to muzzle the press. The Governor was actuated apparently only by his sufferings from cartoons and comments during his campaign; the Philadelphia ring has boodling plans ahead which exposure might make exasperating to the people. The Philadelphia *Press,* the leading Republican organ in the State, puts it right: "The Governor wanted it [the law] in the hope of escaping from the unescapable cartoon. The gang wanted it in the hope of muzzling the opposition to jobs. . . . The act is distinctly designed to gag the press in the interest of the plunderers and against the interest of the people."

Disfranchised, without a choice of parties; denied, so the Municipal League declares, the ancient right of petition; and now to lose "free speech,"—is there no

---

28 **Francis B. Reeves** (1836-?), chairman of the executive committee of the Municipal Reform Committee of 100 • 44 **Butlers, and Shepherds,** city bosses. Edward Butler was Democratic boss of St. Louis (see "The Shamelessness of St. Louis"); A. R. Shepherd (1835-1902) controlled the District of Columbia between 1871 and 1874, when Washington businessmen wished to have the District organized as a territory • 68 **Governor Pennypacker.** Samuel Whitaker Pennypacker (1843-1916), Republican governor, 1903-1907, was author of **The Autobiography of a Pennsylvanian** (1918), an interesting view of the politics of Pennsylvania by an admirer of Quay

hope for Philadelphia? Yes, the Philadelphians have a very present hope. It is in their new mayor, John Weaver. There is nothing in his record to inspire faith in an outsider. He speaks himself of two notorious "miscarriages of justice" during his term as District Attorney; he was the nominee of the ring; and the ring men have confidence in him. But so have the people, and Mr. Weaver makes fair promises. So did Ashbridge. There is this difference, however: Mr. Weaver has made
10 a good start. He compromised with the machine on his appointments, but he declared against the protection of vice, for free voting, and he stopped some "wholesale grabs" or "maces" that appeared in the Legislature, just before he took office.

One was a bill to enable (ring) companies to "appropriate, take, and use all water within this commonwealth and belonging either to public or to private persons as it may require for its private purposes." This was a scheme to sell out the water works of Philadelphia, and
20 all other such plants in the State. Another bill was to open the way to a seizure of the light and power of the city and of the State. Martin and Warwick "leased" the city gas works. Durham and his crowd wanted a whack at it. "It shall be lawful," the bill read, "for any

city, town or borough owning any gas works or electric light plant for supplying light, heat, and power, to sell, lease or otherwise dispose of the same to individuals or corporations, and in order to obtain the best possible returns therefor, such municipal body may . . . vest in the lessees or purchasers the exclusive right, both as 30 against such municipal corporations and against any and all other persons and corporations, to supply gas or electricity. . . ." As in St. Louis, the public property of Philadelphia is to be sold off. These schemes are to go through later, I am told, but on Mr. Weaver's declarations that he would not "stand for them," they were laid over.

It looks as if the Philadelphians were right about Mr. Weaver, but what if they are? Think of a city putting its whole faith in one man, in the *hope* that John 40 Weaver, an Englishman by birth, will *give* them good government! And why should he do that? Why should he serve the people and not the ring? The ring can make or break him; the people of Philadelphia can neither reward nor punish him. For even if he restores to them their ballots and proves himself a good mayor, he cannot succeed himself; the good charter forbids more than one term.

1902•1903

Finley Peter Dunne

1867 • 1936

What Jack Downing was for the opening decades of the nineteenth century, Mr. Dooley, the character created by Finley Peter Dunne, was for its closing years. In Chicago, which had been Dunne's birthplace, he attended high school and worked his way up from office boy on a newspaper to a job as a reporter. When in 1892 he chanced to put a piece commenting on current affairs into the dialect of an Irish saloonkeeper, he hit upon a way of writing destined to make him famous.

After some experiments and changes, the saloonkeeper became Martin Dooley, who, in his place on Archey Road, talked at length on all sorts of subjects. At first it was chiefly a Chicago audience which enjoyed his remarks; but when Mr. Dooley got to talking about the Spanish-American War in 1898, he became a national favorite. His monologues appeared in many newspapers, and when they were collected in books they found many purchasers. Dunne's books included *Mr. Dooley in Peace and in War* (1898), *Mr. Dooley in the Hearts of His Countrymen* (1899), *Mr. Dooley's Philosophy* (1900), *Mr. Dooley's Opinions* (1901), *Observations of Mr. Dooley* (1902), *Dissertations by Mr. Dooley* (1906), *Mr. Dooley Says* (1910), *New Dooley Book* (1911), and *Mr. Dooley on Making a Will* (1919). After a long career as a satirical writer, Dunne died in 1936.

Mr. Dooley's relationship with the long line of horse-sense humorists admired by Americans is clear. His unlearned but vivid diction and his common-sensical philosophy show his alliance with such commentators. It is noteworthy, however, that this well-realized character was more closely related to the earlier figures, such as Downing and Biglow, than to the literary comedians almost contemporaneous with him. For his im-

mediate readers, as Mr. Mark Sullivan says, "Mr. Dooley supplied the softening solvent of humor to the American atmosphere in times of acute controversy. Just when we were getting worked up into factional passion, with everybody searching the cellar of his vocabulary for verbal lumps of coal, Mr. Dooley would come out in the Sunday papers with a picture of the situation that made every reader laugh at it, and at himself." For later readers, Dunne furnished saltily phrased essays which amusingly illuminate the times which produced them. They do more: because they are rich in their commentary upon human foibles of all periods, they have enduring merit. Much of Mr. Dooley's talk, without change or, at most, with changes in only a few names, has the sting of satire on affairs of the present day. And Mr. Dooley and a good many of those whom he talks about continue to be vividly human characterizations.

Mr. Dooley at His Best, ed. Elmer Ellis, New York, 1938 • Elmer Ellis, Mr. Dooley's America: A Life of Finley Peter Dunne, New York, 1941

From

Mr. Dooley in Peace and in War

ON WAR PREPARATIONS

Says Professor Ellis, introducing this piece: "The opera bouffe character of certain aspects of the Spanish-American War in 1898 furnished Mr. Dooley with subjects for comment that increased his circle of admirers enormously. The confusion of organizing an army was more than evident in the newspapers of the day. The two chief concentration camps were at Chickamauga Park and Tampa. The fondness of the commanding general, Nelson A. Miles, for public statements and gold braids was often noted. When he left Washington to 'take the field' at Tampa, he was accompanied by Mrs. Miles, a daughter, and a son."

Mr. Dooley, one of the few of our crackerbox sages to be blessed, himself, with a sense of humor, has a delightful time ironically jesting about Gin'ral Miles' strange preparations for warfare.

"Well," Mr. Hennessy asked, "how goes th' war?"

"Splendid, thank ye," said Mr. Dooley. "Fine, fine. It makes me hear-rt throb with pride that I'm a citizen iv th' Sixth Wa-ard."

"Has th' ar-rmy started f'r Cuba yet?"

"Wan ar-rmy, says ye? Twinty! Las' Choosdah an advance ar-rmy iv wan hundherd an' twinty thousand men landed fr'm th' Gussie, with tin thousand cannons hurlin' projick-tyles weighin' eight hundherd pounds sivinteen miles. Winsdah night a second ar-rmy iv injineers, miners, plumbers, an' lawn tinnis experts, numberin' in all four hundherd an' eighty thousand men, ar-rmed with death-dealin' canned goods, was hurried to Havana to storm th' city.

"Thursdah mornin' three thousand full rigimints iv r-rough r-riders swum their hor-rses acrost to Matoonzas, an' afther a spirited battle captured th' Rainy Christiny golf links, two up an' hell to play, an' will hold thim again all comers. Th' same afthernoon th' reg'lar cavalry, con-sistin' iv four hundherd an' eight thousan' well-mounted men, was loaded aboard th' tug Lucy J., and departed on their earned iv death amidst th' cheers iv eight millyon sojers left behind at Chickamaha. These cav'lry'll cooperate with Commodore Schlow; an' whin he desthroys th' Spanish fleet, as he does ivry Sundah an' holy day except in Lent, an' finds out where they ar-re an' desthroys thim, but thinks they ar-re on their way f'r to fight Cousin George Dooley, th' cav'lry will make a dash back to Tampa, where Gin'ral Miles is preparin' to desthroy th' Spanish at wan blow, —an' he's th' boy to blow.

"The gin'ral arrived th' other day, fully prepared f'r
10 th' bloody wurruk iv war. He had his intire fam'ly with him. He r-rode recklessly into camp, mounted on a superb specyal ca-ar. As himsilf an' Uncle Mike Miles, an' Cousin Hennery Miles, an' Master Miles, aged eight years, dismounted fr'm th' specyal train, they were received with wild cheers be eight millyon iv th' bravest sojers that iver give up their lives f'r their country. Th' press cinchorship is so pow'rful that no news is allowed to go out; but I have it fr'm th' specyal corryspondint iv Mesilf, Clancy th' Butcher, Mike Casey,
20 an' th' City Direchtry that Gin'ral Miles instantly repaired himsilf to th' hotel, where he made his plans f'r cr-rushin' th' Spanyards at wan blow. He will equip th' ar-rmy with blow-guns at wanst. His uniforms ar-re comin' down in specyal steel protected buhyon trains fr'm th' mint, where they've been kept f'r a year. He has ordhered out th' gold resarve f'r to equip his staff, numberin' eight thousan' men, manny iv whom ar-re clubmen; an', as soon as he can have his pitchers took, he will cr-rush th' Spanish with wan blow. Th' pur-pose
30 iv th' gin'ral is to permit no delay. Decisive action is demanded be th' people. An', whin th' hot air masheens has been sint to th' front, Gin'ral Miles will strike wan blow that'll be th' damdest blow since th' year iv th' big wind in Ireland.

"Iv coorse, they'se dissinsions in th' cabinet; but they don't amount to nawthin'. Th' Sicrety iv War is in favor iv sawin' th' Spanish ar-rmy into two-be-four joists. Th' Sicrety iv th' Threeasury has a scheme f'r roonin' thim be lindin' thim money. Th' Sicrety iv th' Navy
40 wants to sue thim befure th' Mattsachusetts Supreme Coort. I've heerd that th' Prisident is arrangin' a knee dhrill, with th' idee iv prayin' th' villyans to th' divvil. But these diff'rences don't count. We're all wan people, an' we look to Gin'ral Miles to desthroy th' Spanish with wan blow. Whin it comes, trees will be lifted out be th' roots. Morro Caste'll cave in, an' th' air'll

be full iv Spanish whiskers. A long blow, a sthrong blow, an' a blow all together."

"We're a gr-reat people," said Mr. Hennessy, earnestly.

"We ar-re," said Mr. Dooley. "We ar-re that. An' th' 50
best iv it is, we know we ar-re."

ON REFORM CANDIDATES

A product of the dissatisfaction of some with local government in this period was the "reform candidate," here satirized by Mr. Dooley. Too often, as the sage Irishman points out, the silk-stocking office seeker was completely unaware of the mass of voters who lived out beyond the best business and residential districts—a mass so numerous that it could decide many elections. Willie Boye, amusingly sketched by Mr. Dooley, is an example. Flannigan, on the other hand, is the practical ward politician who gets acquainted intimately with the people of the slums. Mr. Dooley's story is a vivid little parable about impractical versus practical politics.

"That frind iv ye'ers, Dugan, is an intilligent man," said Mr. Dooley. "All he needs is an index an' a few illusthrations to make him a bicyclopedja iv useless information."

"Well," said Mr. Hennessy, judiciously, "he ain't no Socrates an' he ain't no answers-to-questions colum; but he's a good man that goes to his jooty, an' as handy with a pick as some people are with a cocktail spoon. What's he been doin' again ye?" 60

"Nawthin'," said Mr. Dooley, "but he was in here Choosday. 'Did ye vote?' says I. 'I did,' says he. 'Which wan iv th' distinguished bunko steerers got ye'er invalu'ble suffrage?' says I. 'I didn't have none with me,' says he, 'but I voted f'r Charter Haitch,' says he. 'I've been with him in six ilictions,' says he, 'an' he's a good man,' he says. 'D'ye think ye're votin' f'r th' best?' says I. 'Why, man alive,' I says, 'Charter Haitch was assassinated three years ago,' I says. 'Was he?' says Dugan. 'Ah, well, he's lived that down be this time. He was a good man,' 70
he says.

"Ye see, that's what thim rayform lads wint up again. If I liked rayformers, Hinnissy, an' wanted f'r to see thim win out wanst in their lifetime, I'd buy thim each a suit iv chilled steel, ar-rm thim with raypeatin' rifles, an' take thim east iv State Sthreet an' south iv Jackson Bullyvard. At prisint th' opinion that pre-vails in th' ranks iv th' gloryous ar-rmy iv ray-form is that there ain't annything worth seein' in this lar-rge an' commodyous desert but th' pest-house an' the bridewell. Me frind Willum J. O'Brien is no rayformer. But Willum J. undhershstands that there's a few hundherds iv thousands iv people livin' in a part iv th' town that 10 looks like nawthin' but smoke fr'm th' roof iv th' Onion League Club that have on'y two pleasures in life, to wur-ruk an' to vote, both iv which they do at th' uniform rate iv wan dollar an' a half a day. That's why Willum J. O'Brien is now a sinitor an' will be an aldherman afther next Thursdah, an' it's why other people are sinding him flowers.

"This is th' way a rayform candydate is ilicted. Th' boys down town has heerd that things ain't goin' r-right somehow. Franchises is bein' handed out to none iv 20 thim; an' wanst in a while a mimber iv th' club, comin' home a little late an' thryin' to riconcile a pair iv r-round feet with an embroidered sidewalk, meets a sthrong ar-rm boy that pushes in his face an' takes away all his marbles. It begins to be talked that th' time has come f'r good citizens f'r to brace up an' do somethin', an' they agree to nomynate a candydate f'r aldherman. 'Who'll we put up?' says they. 'How's Clarence Doolittle?' says wan. 'He's laid up with a coupon thumb, an' can't r-run.' 'An' how about Arthur Doheny?' 'I 30 swore an oath whin I came out iv colledge I'd niver vote f'r a man that wore a made tie.' 'Well, thin, let's thry Willie Boye.' 'Good,' says th' comity. 'He's jus' th' man f'r our money.' An' Willie Boye, after thinkin' it over, goes to his tailor an' ordhers three dozen pairs iv pants, an' decides f'r to be th' sthandard-bearer iv th' people. Musin' over his fried eyesthers an' asparagus an' his champagne, he bets a polo pony again a box of golfballs he'll be ilicted unanimous; an' all th' good citizens make a vow f'r to set th' alar-rm clock f'r half-past three 40 on th' afthernoon iv iliction day, so's to be up in time to vote f'r th' riprisintitive iv pure gover'mint.

"'Tis some time befure they comprehind that there ar-re other candydates in th' field. But th' other candydates know it. Th' sthrongest iv thim—his name is Flannigan, an' he's a re-tail dealer in wines an' liquors, an' he lives over his establishment. Flannigan was nomy-

Mr. Dooley and Mr. Hennessey—illustration by Kemble for Mr. Dooley's Philosophy, *1900*

nated enthusyastically at a prim'ry held in his bar-rn; an' befure Willie Boye had picked out pants that wud match th' color iv th' Austhreelyan ballot this here Flannigan had put a man on th' day watch, tol' him to speak gently 50 to anny raygistered voter that wint to sleep behind th' sthove, an' was out that night visitin' his frinds. Who was it judged th' cake walk? Flannigan. Who was it carrid th' pall? Flannigan. Who was it sthud up at th' christening? Flannigan. Whose ca-ards did th' grievin' widow, and th' blushin' bridegroom, or th' happy father find in th' hack? Flannigan's. Ye bet ye'er life. Ye see Flannigan wasn't out f'r th' good iv th' community. Flannigan was out f'r Flannigan an' th' stuff.

"Well, iliction day come around; an' all th' imminent 60 frinds iv good gover'mint had special wires sthrung into th' club, an' waited f'r th' returns. Th' first precin't showed 28 votes f'r Willie Boye to 14 f'r Flannigan. 'That's my precin't,' says Willie. 'I wondher who voted thim fourteen?' 'Coachmen,' says Clarence Doolittle. 'There are thirty-five precin'ts in this ward,' says th' leader iv th' rayform ilimint. 'At this rate, I'm sure iv 440 meejority. Gossoon,' he says, 'put a keg iv sherry

---

28 **coupon thumb,** a thumb made sore by clipping many coupons to collect interest on bonds

wine on th' ice,' he says. 'Well,' he says, 'at last th' community is relieved fr'm misrule,' he says. 'To-mor-rah I will start in arrangin' amindmints to th' tariff schedool an' th' ar-bitration threety,' he says. 'We must be up an' doin',' he says. 'Hol' on there,' says wan iv th' comity. 'There must be some mistake in this fr'm th' sixth precin't,' he says. 'Where's the sixth precin't?' says Clarence. 'Over be th' dumps,' says Willie. 'I told me futman to see to that. He lives at th' corner iv Des-plaines an Bloo Island Av'noo on Goose's Island,' he says. 'What does it show?' 'Flannigan, three hundherd an' eighty-five; Hansen, forty-eight; Schwartz, twinty; O'Malley, sivinteen; Casey, ten; O'Day, eight; Larsen, five; O'Rourke, three; Mulcahy, two; Schmitt, two; Mo-loney, two; Riordon, two; O'Malley, two; Willie Boye, wan.' 'Gintlemin,' says Willie Boye, arisin' with a stern look in his eyes, 'Th' rascal has bethrayed me. Waither, take th' sherry wine off th' ice. They'se no hope f'r sound financial legislation this year. I'm goin' home.'

"An', as he goes down th' sthreet, he hears a band play an' sees a procission headed be a calceem light; an', in a carredge, with his plug hat in his hand an' his di'mond makin' th' calceem look like a piece iv punk in a smoke-house, is Flannigan, payin' his first visit this side iv th' thracks."

ON CHARITY

The preceding accounts of Mr. Dooley show his practical mind, his sense of humor, his witty way of making a point. "On Charity" not only sets forth his ideas but also catches some of the tenderer qualities of the man. His charity, inconsistent as it is with his preachments, makes him not only an amusing character but also a lovable one.

"Br-r-r!" cried Mr. McKenna, entering stiffly and spread-ing his hands over the potbellied stove. "It's cold."

"Where?" asked Mr. Dooley. "Not here."

"It's cold outside," said Mr. McKenna. "It was ten be-low at Shannahan's grocery when I went by, and the wind blowing like all possessed. Lord love us, but I pity them that's got to be out to-night."

"Save ye'er pity," said Mr. Dooley, comfortably. "It ain't cowld in here. There's frost on th' window, 'tis thrue for ye; an' th' wheels has been singin' th' live-long day. But what's that to us? Here I am, an' there ye are, th' stove between us an' th' kettle hummin'. In a minyit it'll bile, an' thin I'll give ye a taste iv what'll make a king iv ye.

"Well, tubby sure, 'tis thryin' to be dhrivin' a coal wagon or a sthreet-car; but 'tis all in a lifetime. Th' dif-f'rence between me an' th' man that sets up in th' seat thumpin' his chest with his hands is no more thin th' diff'rence between him an' th' poor divvle that walks along behind th' wagon with his shovel on his shoulder, an' 'll thank th' saints f'r th' first chanst to put tin ton iv ha-ard coal into a cellar f'r a quarther iv a dollar. Th' lad afoot invies th' dhriver, an' th' dhriver invies me; an' might invy big Cleveland if it wasn't f'r th' hivinly smell iv this here noggin. An' who does Cleveland invy? Sure, it'd be sacreliege f'r me to say.

"Me ol' father, who was as full iv sayin's as an al-manac, used to sink his spoon into th' stirabout, an' say, 'Well, lads, this ain't bacon an' greens an' porther; but it'll be annything ye like if ye'll on'y think iv th' Cassidys.' Th' Cassidys was th' poorest fam'ly in th' parish. They waked th' oldest son in small beer, an' was little thought of. Did me father iver ask thim in to share th' stir-about? Not him. An' he was the kindest man in th' wurruld. He had a heart in him as big as a lump iv turf, but he'd say, 'Whin ye grow up, take no wan's sor-rows to ye'ersilf,' he says. ''Tis th' wise man that goes through life thinkin' iv himsilf, fills his own stomach, an' takes away what he can't ate in his pocket.' An' he was r-right, Jawn. We have throubles enough iv our own. Th' wurruld goes on just th' same, an' ye can find fifty men to say th' lit'ny f'r ye to wan that'll give ye what'll relieve a fastin' spit. Th' dead ar-re always pop'lar. I knowed a society wanst to vote a monymint to a man an' refuse to help his fam'ly, all in wan night. 'Tis cowld outside th' dure, ye say, but 'tis war-rum in here; an' I'm gettin' in me ol' age to think that the dif-f'rence between hivin an' hell is no broader"—

Mr. Dooley's remarks were cut short by a cry from the back room. It was unmistakably a baby's cry. Mr. McKenna turned suddenly in amazement as Mr. Dooley bolted.

"Well, in the name of the saints, what's all this?" he cried, following his friend into the back room. He found the philosopher, with an expression of the utmost sternness, sitting on the side of his bed, with a little girl of two or three in his arms. The philosopher was singing:—

> Ar-rah rock-a-bye, babby, on th' three top:
> Whin th' wind blo-ows, th' cradle ull r-rock;
> An', a-whin th' bough breaks, th' cradle ull fa-a-a-ll,
> An' a-down ull come babby, cradle, an' all.

Then he sang:—

> In th' town iv Kilkinny there du-wilt a fair ma-aid,
> In th' town iv Kilkinny there du-wilt a fair ma-aid.
> She had cheeks like th' roses, an' hair iv th' same,
> An' a mouth like ripe sthrawburries burrid in crame.

He rocked the child to and fro, and its crying ceased while he sang:—

> Chip, chip, a little horse;
> Chip, chip, again, sir.
> How manny miles to Dublin?
> Threescure an' tin, sir.

The little girl went to sleep on Mr. Dooley's white apron. He lifted her tenderly, and carried her over to his bed. Then he tiptoed out with an apprehensive face, and whispered: "It's Jawn Donahue's kid that wandherd away fr'm home, an' wint to sleep on me dure-step. I sint th' Dorsey boy to tell th' mother, but he's a long time gone. Do ye run over, Jawn, an' lave thim know."

1898

Upton Sinclair

1878 ·

"Readers of my novels," Upton Sinclair has said in his autobiography, *American Outpost,* "know that I have one favorite theme, the contrast of the social classes; there are characters from both worlds, the rich and the poor, and the plot is contrived to carry you from one to the other." He might have added that his rich folk are useless, extravagant, and, with a few exceptions, unprincipled, while his poor and essentially noble characters are almost invariably pushed around by an industrial and capitalistic society. Sinclair is, in short, the foremost of our "proletarian" writers, a Socialist who has long been certain that in practically every American institution there is a canker of plutocracy. Author of nearly one hundred books and pamphlets on nearly every conceivable aspect of modern life, he is master of the literary method of "exposure," and is best known for

The Jungle (1906) and *Dragon's Teeth* (1942). The former, a revelation of the conditions in Chicago's meatpacking industry, helped to strengthen the first Pure Food and Drug Act; the latter, third of the "Lanny Budd" series, won the Pulitzer Prize for fiction by portraying conditions in Nazi-dominated Europe.

Sinclair was born in Baltimore but brought up in New York, where he was graduated from the College of the City of New York in 1898. By that time he was already earning his own living by selling stories and jokes. He estimates that for a stretch of some months he turned out fifty-six thousand words a week for the pulp-paper magazines, an almost incredible task. His first serious novel was published in 1901, shortly before he became active as a Socialist. "Muckraking" made him famous, as it did his friend Lincoln Steffens, but Sinclair did not grow discouraged with the failure of progressivism. Despite much ridicule and some actual persecution, he has remained a wholehearted believer in the perfectibility of man and the ultimate triumph of social justice.

Nor have his energies gone entirely into his books. The League for Industrial Democracy (formerly the Intercollegiate Socialist Society) and the American Civil Liberties Union are largely of his creation. Three times he has run for Congress, and three times for the governorship of California, where he has lived since 1915. Usually he has been a Socialist, but he supported Woodrow Wilson, and his last campaign for the governorship was waged as a Democrat. In *I, Governor of California and How I Ended Poverty* (1933) and other pamphlets he set forth his platform, EPIC (End Poverty in California), explaining the depression as a result of private ownership of complex tools and of the "economic insanity" of limiting production. His program found wide public support in the early days of the New Deal and he was very nearly elected.

In addition to the books already mentioned, the best examples of Sinclair's fiction are *King Coal* (1917), *Oil!* (1927), *Boston* (1928), and *The Wet Parade* (1931), which deal with coal strikes in Colorado, the exploitation of the California oil fields, the Sacco-Vanzetti case, and prohibition, respectively. Like the Lanny Budd novels, which have been more widely read, these books are essentially current history, interpreted less as class warfare than as a lesson to the middle-class liberal, to whom Sinclair has hoped to bring home his conviction of brotherhood with the workers. His best-known direct attacks on the *status quo* are probably *The Brass Check* (1919), a blast at the capitalist press, and *The Goose-Step* (1923), which charges American schools with subservience to upper-class ideals.

Sinclair has always written with amazing fluency and a consequent unevenness. He is a propagandist, akin in spirit to Thomas Paine but writing in the idiom of an industrialized nation well aware of the theories of Karl Marx. A chronic protester and iconoclast, he has enough good nature and humor to lighten the tedium of innumerable and often repetitive details. Much of his work has been translated from the English and he is doubtless one of the chief interpreters of the United States to other nations. Conservative critics have found him radical and unsound; extreme left-wing thinkers have condemned him for not adhering strictly enough to the Marxist line. Of his earnestness and honesty there is no longer much question.

American Outpost: A Book of Reminiscences, Pasadena, 1932 • Floyd Dell, **Upton Sinclair: A Study in Social Protest**, New York, 1927 • Louis Filler, **Crusaders for American Liberalism**, Yellow Springs, 1950 • Granville Hicks, **The Great Tradition: An Interpretation of American Literature since the Civil War**, Revised Edition, New York, 1935 • Robert Cantwell, "Upton Sinclair," **New Republic**, February 24, 1937 • Malcolm Cowley, "Man of Good Will," **New Republic,** January 11, 1943

From

The Jungle

The circumstances of composition, publication, and reception of **The Jungle** are explained by Sinclair in **American Outpost** (pp. 153-171). The story was commissioned by a Socialist magazine, **The Appeal to Reason,** which advanced $500 for a novel of wage-slavery. Sinclair selected the Chicago stockyards for his scene, spent seven weeks there in the fall of 1904, and after a month of collecting data found his characters by observing a wedding party in the rear room of a saloon. Returning to a farm near Princeton, New Jersey, he began writing on Christmas Day, completing the novel in the summer of 1905. It was by that time appearing as a serial. Five publishers refused to print the novel in book form, although one of them had advanced another $500 after reading the first chapters. Before Doubleday, Page and Company took it over, having made a careful investigation to avoid possible libel suits, Sinclair had made arrangements to print it himself. The trade edition appeared in February 1906. Unperturbed by the condition of the workers, the public was horrified by the evidence of criminal negligence in meat inspection. The packers aided the success of the book by efforts to answer its charges and President Theodore Roosevelt, prodded by a flood of letters from convinced readers, arranged an investigation. The Pure Food and Drug Act was at that time being perfected: Roosevelt signed it on June 30. For six months **The Jungle** was a best seller and it was soon translated into seventeen languages. Sinclair was famous although, as he said, he aimed at the public's heart and hit its stomach.

The Jungle retains its power even though not all readers will agree with Jack London's conviction that it is the **Uncle Tom's Cabin** of wage-slavery, "written of sweat and blood, and groans and tears." The chapter which follows is not the most spectacular in the novel, but it shows its author's Socialism and contains numerous implications that Brown's and Durham's were not over-careful of public health. It is also notable as a description of industrial processes, a type of exposition at which Sinclair excels.

CHAPTER III

I n his capacity as delicatessen vender, Jokubas Szedvilas had many acquaintances. Among these was one of the special policemen employed by Durham, whose duty it frequently was to pick out men for employment. Jokubas had never tried it, but he expressed a certainty that he could get some of his friends a job through this man. It was agreed, after consultation, that he should make the effort with old Antanas and with Jonas. Jurgis was confident of his ability to get work for himself, unassisted
10 by any one.

As we have said before, he was not mistaken in this. He had gone to Brown's and stood there not more than half an hour before one of the bosses noticed his form towering above the rest, and signalled to him. The colloquy which followed was brief and to the point:—

"Speak English?"

"No; Lít-uanian." (Jurgis had studied this word carefully.)

"Job?"

20 "Je." (A nod.)

"Worked here before?"

"No 'stand."

(Signals and gesticulations on the part of the boss. Vigorous shakes of the head by Jurgis.)

"Shovel guts?"

"No 'stand." (More shakes of the head.)

"Zarnos. Pagaiksztis. Szluota!" (Imitative motions.)

"Je."

"See door. Durys?" (Pointing.)

"Je."

"To-morrow, seven o'clock. Understand? Rytoj!
Prieszpietys! Septyni!"

"Dekui, tamistai!" (Thank you, sir.) And that was all. Jurgis turned away, and then in a sudden rush the full realization of his triumph swept over him, and he gave a yell and a jump, and started off on a run. He had a job! He had a job! And he went all the way home as if upon wings, and burst into the house like a cyclone, to the rage of the numerous lodgers who had just turned in for their daily sleep.

Meantime Jokubas had been to see his friend the policeman, and received encouragement, so it was a happy party. There being no more to be done that day, the shop was left under the care of Lucija, and her husband sallied forth to show his friends the sights of Packingtown. Jokubas did this with the air of a country gentleman escorting a party of visitors over his estate; he was an old-time resident, and all these wonders had grown up under his eyes, and he had a personal pride in them. The packers might own the land, but he claimed the landscape, and there was no one to say nay to this.

They passed down the busy street that led to the yards. It was still early morning, and everything was at its high tide of activity. A steady stream of employees was pouring through the gate—employees of the higher sort, at this hour, clerks and stenographers and such. For the women there were waiting big two-horse wagons, which set off at a gallop as fast as they were filled. In the distance there was heard again the lowing of the cattle, a sound as of a far-off ocean calling. They followed it, this time, as eager as children in sight of a circus menagerie—which, indeed, the scene a good deal resembled. They crossed the railroad tracks, and then on each side of the street were the pens full of cattle; they would have stopped to look, but Jokubas hurried them on, to where there was a stairway and a raised gallery, from which everything could be seen. Here they stood, staring, breathless with wonder.

There is over a square mile of space in the yards, and more than half of it is occupied by cattle-pens; north and south as far as the eye can reach there stretches a sea of pens. And they were all filled—so many cattle no one had ever dreamed existed in the world. Red cattle, black, white, and yellow cattle; old cattle and young cattle; great
10 bellowing bulls and little calves not an hour born; meek-eyed milch cows and fierce, long-horned Texas steers. The sound of them here was as of all the barnyards of the universe; and as for counting them—it would have taken all day simply to count the pens. Here and there ran long alleys, blocked at intervals by gates; and Jokubas told them that the number of these gates was twenty-five thousand. Jokubas had recently been reading a newspaper article which was full of statistics such as that, and he was very proud as he repeated them and made his
20 guests cry out with wonder. Jurgis too had a little of this sense of pride. Had he not just gotten a job, and become a sharer in all this activity, a cog in this marvellous machine?

Here and there about the alleys galloped men upon horseback, booted, and carrying long whips; they were very busy, calling to each other, and to those who were driving the cattle. They were drovers and stock-raisers, who had come from far states, and brokers and commission-merchants, and buyers for all the big packing-houses.
30 Here and there they would stop to inspect a bunch of cattle, and there would be a parley, brief and businesslike. The buyer would nod or drop his whip, and that would mean a bargain; and he would note it in his little book, along with hundreds of others he had made that morning. Then Jokubas pointed out the place where the cattle were driven to be weighed, upon a great scale that would weigh a hundred thousand pounds at once and record it automatically. It was near to the east entrance that they stood, and all along this east side of the yards ran the
40 railroad tracks, into which the cars were run, loaded with cattle. All night long this had been going on, and now the pens were full; by to-night they would all be empty, and the same thing would be done again.

"And what will become of all these creatures?" cried Teta Elzbieta.

"By to-night," Jokubas answered, "they will all be killed and cut up; and over there on the other side of the packing-houses are more railroad tracks, where the cars come to take them away."

There were two hundred and fifty miles of track within 50 the yards, their guide went on to tell them. They brought about ten thousand head of cattle every day, and as many hogs, and half as many sheep—which meant some eight or ten million live creatures turned into food every year. One stood and watched, and little by little caught the drift of the tide, as it set in the direction of the packing-houses. There were groups of cattle being driven to the chutes, which were roadways about fifteen feet wide, raised high above the pens. In these chutes the stream of animals was continuous; it was quite uncanny to 60 watch them, pressing on to their fate, all unsuspicious— a very river of death. Our friends were not poetical, and the sight suggested to them no metaphors of human destiny; they thought only of the wonderful efficiency of it all. The chutes into which the hogs went climbed high up—to the very top of the distant buildings; and Jokubas explained that the hogs went up by the power of their own legs, and then their weight carried them back through all the processes necessary to make them into pork. 70

"They don't waste anything here," said the guide, and then he laughed and added a witticism, which he was pleased that his unsophisticated friends should take to be his own: "They use everything about the hog except the squeal." In front of Brown's General Office building there grows a tiny plot of grass, and this, you may learn, is the only bit of green thing in Packingtown; likewise this jest about the hog and his squeal, the stock in trade of all the guides, is the one gleam of humor that you will find there. 80

After they had seen enough of the pens, the party went up the street, to the mass of buildings which occupy the centre of the yards. These buildings, made of brick and stained with innumerable layers of Packingtown smoke, were painted all over with advertising signs, from which the visitor realized suddenly that he had come to the home of many of the torments of his life. It was here that they made those products with the wonders of which they pestered him so—by placards that defaced the landscape when he travelled, and by staring advertisements in 90 the newspapers and magazines—by silly little jingles that he could not get out of his mind, and gaudy pictures that lurked for him around every street corner. Here was where they made Brown's Imperial Hams and Bacon, Brown's Dressed Beef, Brown's Excelsior Sausages! Here was the headquarters of Durham's Pure Leaf Lard, of Durham's Breakfast Bacon, Durham's Canned Beef, Potted Ham, Devilled Chicken, Peerless Fertilizer!

Entering one of the Durham buildings, they found a
10 number of other visitors waiting; and before long there came a guide, to escort them through the place. They make a great feature of showing strangers through the packing-plants, for it is a good advertisement. But *ponas* Jokubas whispered maliciously that the visitors did not see any more than the packers wanted them to.

They climbed a long series of stairways outside of the building, to the top of its five or six stories. Here were the chute, with its river of hogs, all patiently toiling upward; there was a place for them to rest to cool off, and
20 then through another passageway they went into a room from which there is no returning for hogs.

It was a long, narrow room, with a gallery along it for visitors. At the head there was a great iron wheel, about twenty feet in circumference, with rings here and there along its edge. Upon both sides of this wheel there was a narrow space, into which came the hogs at the end of their journey; in the midst of them stood a great burly Negro, bare-armed and bare-chested. He was resting for the moment, for the wheel had stopped while men were
30 cleaning up. In a minute or two, however, it began slowly to revolve, and then the men upon each side of it sprang to work. They had chains which they fastened about the leg of the nearest hog, and the other end of the chain they hooked into one of the rings upon the wheel. So, as the wheel turned, a hog was suddenly jerked off his feet and borne aloft.

At the same instant the ear was assailed by a most terrifying shriek; the visitors started in alarm, the women turned pale and shrank back. The shriek was followed
40 by another, louder and yet more agonizing—for once started upon that journey, the hog never came back; at the top of the wheel he was shunted off upon a trolley, and went sailing down the room. And meantime another was swung up, and then another, and another, until there was a double line of them, each dangling by a foot and

kicking in frenzy—and squealing. The uproar was appalling, perilous to the ear-drums; one feared there was too much sound for the room to hold—that the walls must give way or the ceiling crack. There were high squeals and low squeals, grunts, and wails of agony; there 50 would come a momentary lull, and then a fresh outburst, louder than ever, surging up to a deafening climax. It was too much for some of the visitors—the men would look at each other, laughing nervously, and the women would stand with hands clenched, and the blood rushing to their faces, and the tears starting in their eyes.

Meanwhile, heedless of all these things, the men upon the floor were going about their work. Neither squeals of hogs nor tears of visitors made any difference to them; one by one they hooked up the hogs, and one by one 60 with a swift stroke they slit their throats. There was a long line of hogs, with squeals and life-blood ebbing away together; until at last each started again, and vanished with a splash into a huge vat of boiling water.

It was all so very businesslike that one watched it fascinated. It was pork-making by machinery, pork-making by applied mathematics. And yet somehow the most matter-of-fact person could not help thinking of the hogs; they were so innocent, they came so very trustingly; and they were so very human in their protests—and so 70 perfectly within their rights! They had done nothing to deserve it; and it was adding insult to injury, as the thing was done here, swinging them up in this cold-blooded, impersonal way, without a pretence at apology, without the homage of a tear. Now and then a visitor wept, to be sure; but this slaughtering-machine ran on, visitors or no visitors. It was like some horrible crime committed in a dungeon, all unseen and unheeded, buried out of sight and of memory.

One could not stand and watch very long without 80 becoming philosophical, without beginning to deal in symbols and similes, and to hear the hog-squeal of the universe. Was it permitted to believe that there was nowhere upon the earth, or above the earth, a heaven for hogs, where they were requited for all this suffering?

---

13 ponas, master or lord • 84 heaven for hogs. "For twenty-six years," writes Sinclair (American Outpost, p. 229), "I have been ridiculed for a passage . . . discussing the moral claims of dying hogs—which passage was intended as hilarious farce"

Each one of these hogs was a separate creature. Some were white hogs, some were black; some were brown, some were spotted; some were old, some were young; some were long and lean, some were monstrous. And each of them had an individuality of his own, a will of his own, a hope and a heart's desire; each was full of self-confidence, of self-importance, and a sense of dignity. And trusting and strong in faith he had gone about his business, the while a black shadow hung over him and a horrid Fate waited in his pathway. Now suddenly it had swooped upon him, and had seized him by the leg. Relentless, remorseless, it was; all his protests, his screams, were nothing to it—it did its cruel will with him, as if his wishes, his feelings, had simply no existence at all; it cut his throat and watched him gasp out his life. And now was one to believe that there was nowhere a god of hogs, to whom this hog-personality was precious, to whom these hog-squeals and agonies had a meaning? Who would take this hog into his arms and comfort him, reward him for his work well done, and show him the meaning of his sacrifice? Perhaps some glimpse of all this was in the thoughts of our humble-minded Jurgis, as he turned to go on with the rest of the party, and muttered: "Dieve—but I'm glad I'm not a hog!"

The carcass hog was scooped out of the vat by machinery, and then it fell to the second floor, passing on the way through a wonderful machine with numerous scrapers, which adjusted themselves to the size and shape of the animal, and sent it out at the other end with nearly all of its bristles removed. It was then again strung up by machinery, and sent upon another trolley ride; this time passing between two lines of men, who sat upon a raised platform, each doing a certain single thing to the carcass as it came to him. One scraped the outside of a leg; another scraped the inside of the same leg. One with a swift stroke cut the throat; another with two swift strokes severed the head, which fell to the floor and vanished through a hole. Another made a slit down the body; a second opened the body wider; a third with a saw cut the breast-bone; a fourth loosened the entrails; a fifth pulled them out—and they also slid through a hole in the floor. There were men to scrape each side and men to scrape the back; there were men to clean the carcass inside, to trim it and wash it. Looking down this room, one saw, creeping slowly, a line of dangling hogs a hundred yards in length; and for every yard there was a man, working as if a demon were after him. At the end of this hog's progress every inch of the carcass had been gone over several times; and then it was rolled into the chilling-room, where it stayed for twenty-four hours, and where a stranger might lose himself in a forest of freezing hogs.

Before the carcass was admitted here, however, it had to pass a government inspector, who sat in the doorway and felt of the glands in the neck for tuberculosis. This government inspector did not have the manner of a man who was worked to death; he was apparently not haunted by a fear that the hog might get by him before he had finished his testing. If you were a sociable person, he was quite willing to enter into conversation with you, and to explain to you the deadly nature of the ptomaines which are found in tubercular pork; and while he was talking with you you could hardly be so ungrateful as to notice that a dozen carcasses were passing him untouched. This inspector wore an imposing silver badge, and he gave an atmosphere of authority to the scene, and, as it were, put the stamp of official approval upon the things which were done in Durham's.

Jurgis went down the line with the rest of the visitors, staring open-mouthed, lost in wonder. He had dressed hogs himself in the forest of Lithuania; but he had never expected to live to see one hog dressed by several hundred men. It was like a wonderful poem to him, and he took it all in guilelessly—even to the conspicuous signs demanding immaculate cleanliness of the employees. Jurgis was vexed when the cynical Jokubas translated these signs with sarcastic comments, offering to take them to the secret rooms where the spoiled meats went to be doctored.

The party descended to the next floor, where the various waste materials were treated. Here came the entrails, to be scraped and washed clean for sausage-casings; men and women worked here in the midst of a sickening stench, which caused the visitors to hasten by, gasping. To another room came all the scraps to be "tanked," which meant boiling and pumping off the grease to make soap and lard; below they took out the refuse, and this, too, was a region in which the visitors did not linger. In still other places men were engaged in cutting up the carcasses that had been through the chilling-rooms. First there were the "splitters," the most expert workmen in the plant, who earned as high as fifty cents an hour, and did not a thing all day except chop hogs down the middle. Then there were "cleaver men," great giants with muscles of iron; each had two men to attend him—to slide the half carcass in front of him on the table, and hold it while he chopped it, and then turn each piece so that he might chop it once more. His cleaver had a blade about two feet long, and he never made but one cut; he made it so neatly, too, that his implement did not smite through and dull itself—there was just enough force for a perfect cut, and no more. So through various yawning holes there slipped to the floor below—to one room hams, to another forequarters, to another sides of pork. One might go down to this floor and see the pickling-rooms, where the hams were put into vats, and the great smoke-rooms, with their airtight iron doors. In other rooms they prepared saltpork—there were whole cellars full of it, built up in great towers to the ceiling. In yet other rooms they were putting up meat in boxes and barrels, and wrapping hams and bacon in oiled paper, sealing and labelling and sewing them. From the doors of these rooms went men with loaded trucks, to the platform where freight-cars were waiting to be filled; and one went out there and realized with a start that he had come at last to the ground floor of this enormous building.

Then the party went across the street to where they did the killing of beef—where every hour they turned four or five hundred cattle into meat. Unlike the place they had left, all this work was done on one floor; and instead of there being one line of carcasses which moved to the workmen, there were fifteen or twenty lines, and the men moved from one to another of these. This made a scene of intense activity, a picture of human power wonderful to watch. It was all in one great room, like a circus amphitheatre, with a gallery for visitors running over the centre.

Along one side of the room ran a narrow gallery, a few feet from the floor; into which gallery the cattle were driven by men with goads which gave them electric shocks. Once crowded in here, the creatures were prisoned, each in a separate pen, by gates that shut, leaving them no room to turn around; and while they stood bellowing and plunging, over the top of the pen there leaned one of the "knockers," armed with a sledge-hammer, and watching for a chance to deal a blow. The room echoed with the thuds in quick succession, and the stamping and kicking of the steers. The instant the animal had fallen, the "knocker" passed on to another; while a second man raised a lever, and the side of the pen was raised, and the animal, still kicking and struggling, slid out to the "killing-bed." Here a man put shackles about one leg, and pressed another lever, and the body was jerked up into the air. There were fifteen or twenty such pens, and it was a matter of only a couple of minutes to knock fifteen or twenty cattle and roll them out. Then once more the gates were opened, and another lot rushed in; and so out of each pen there flowed a steady stream of carcasses, which the men upon the killing-beds had to get out of the way.

The manner in which they did this was something to be seen and never forgotten. They worked with furious intensity, literally upon the run—at a pace with which there is nothing to be compared except a football game. It was all highly specialized labor, each man having his task to do; generally this would consist of only two or three specific cuts, and he would pass down the line of fifteen or twenty carcasses, making these cuts upon each. First there came the "butcher," to bleed them; this meant one swift stroke, so swift that you could not see it—only the flash of the knife; and before you could realize it, the man had darted on to the next line, and a stream of bright red was pouring out upon the floor. This floor was half an inch deep with blood, in spite of the best efforts of men who kept shovelling it through holes; it must have made the floor slippery, but no one could have guessed this by watching the men at work.

The carcass hung for a few minutes to bleed; there was no time lost, however, for there were several hanging in each line, and one was always ready. It was let down to the ground, and there came the "headsman," whose task it was to sever the head, with two or three swift strokes. Then came the "floorsman," to make the first cut in the skin; and then another to finish ripping the skin down the centre; and then half a dozen more in swift succession, to finish the skinning. After they were through, the carcass was again swung up; and while a man with a stick examined the skin, to make sure that it had not been cut, and another rolled it up and tumbled it through one of the inevitable holes in the floor, the beef proceeded on its journey. There were men to cut it, and men to split it, and men to gut it and scrape it clean inside. There were some with hose which threw jets of boiling water upon it, and others who removed the feet and added the final touches. In the end, as with the hogs, the finished beef was run into the chilling-room, to hang its appointed time.

10 The visitors were taken there and shown them, all neatly hung in rows, labeled conspicuously with the tags of the government inspectors—and some, which had been killed by a special process, marked with the sign of the "kosher" rabbi, certifying that it was fit for sale to the orthodox. And then the visitors were taken to the other parts of the building, to see what became of each particle of the waste material that had vanished through the floor; and to the pickling-rooms, and the salting-rooms, the canning-rooms, and the packing-rooms, where 20 choice meat was prepared for shipping in refrigerator-cars, destined to be eaten in all the four corners of civilization. Afterward they went outside, wandering about among the mazes of buildings in which was done the work auxiliary to this great industry. There was scarcely a thing needed in the business that Durham and Company did not make for themselves. There was a great steam-power plant and an electricity plant. There was a barrel factory, and a boiler-repair shop. There was a building to which the grease was piped, and made into 30 soap and lard; and then there was a factory for making lard cans, and another for making soap boxes. There was a building in which the bristles were cleaned and dried, for the making of hair cushions and such things; there was a building where the skins were dried and tanned, there was another where heads and feet were made into glue, and another where bones were made into fertilizer. No tiniest particle of organic matter was wasted in Durham's. Out of the horns of the cattle they made combs, buttons, hair-pins, and imitation ivory; out of the 40 shin bones and other big bones they cut knife and tooth-brush handles, and mouthpieces for pipes; out of the hoofs they cut hair-pins and buttons, before they made the rest into glue. From such things as feet, knuckles, hide clippings, and sinews came such strange and un-likely products as gelatin, isinglass, and phosphorus, bone-black, shoe-blacking, and bone-oil. They had curled-hair works for the cattle tails, and a "wool-pullery" for the sheep skins; they made pepsin from the stomachs of the pigs, and albumen from the blood, and violin strings from the ill-smelling entrails. When there was nothing 50 else to be done with a thing, they first put it into a tank and got out of it all the tallow and grease, and then they made it into fertilizer. All these industries were gathered into buildings near by, connected by galleries and railroads with the main establishment; and it was esti-mated that they had handled nearly a quarter of a billion of animals since the founding of the plant by the elder Durham a generation and more ago. If you counted with it the other big plants—and they were now really all one —it was, so Jokubas informed them, the greatest aggre- 60 gation of labor and capital ever gathered in one place. It employed thirty thousand men; it supported directly two hundred and fifty thousand people in its neighborhood, and indirectly it supported half a million. It sent its products to every country in the civilized world, and it furnished the food for no less than thirty million people!

To all of these things our friends would listen open-mouthed—it seemed to them impossible of belief that anything so stupendous could have been devised by mor-tal man. That was why to Jurgis it seemed almost pro- 70 fanity to speak about the place as did Jokubas, sceptically; it was a thing as tremendous as the universe—the laws and ways of its working no more than the universe to be questioned or understood. All that a mere man could do, it seemed to Jurgis, was to take a thing like this as he found it, and do as he was told; to be given a place in it and a share in its wonderful activities was a blessing to be grateful for, as one was grateful for the sunshine and the rain. Jurgis was even glad that he had not seen the place before meeting with his triumph, for he felt 80 that the size of it would have overwhelmed him. But now he had been admitted—he was a part of it all! He had the feeling that this whole huge establishment had taken him under its protection, and had become respon-sible for his welfare. So guileless was he, and ignorant of the nature of business, that he did not even realize that he had become an employee of Brown's, and that Brown and Durham were supposed by all the world to be deadly rivals—were even required to be deadly rivals by the law of the land, and ordered to try to ruin each 90 other under penalty of fine and imprisonment!

1905·1906

Henry Adams

1838 · 1918

"Probably no child, born in the same year, held better cards than he." In these words Henry Adams, in mature life, assessed the circumstances of his own birth, which had occurred in Boston in 1838. His remark was less a snobbish boast than an objective statement of fact. The cards had been good indeed: no financial problem faced him; his mother was the daughter of the wealthiest man in his native city. Part of the infant's heritage was a brilliant mind, and his family cherished fine old traditions of culture and useful service. His forebears, including two Presidents of the United States and three ministers to England as well as several notable scholars, had been most distinguished. The Adamses were one of the honored families of Massachusetts, and many people in New England took for granted that any member of the tribe was destined to have an outstanding career.

It was not surprising that, after Henry Adams had been trained in a Boston private school, then in Harvard, and finally—for some years—in centers of European culture, he showed real talents for several different kinds of endeavor. During the Civil War period, he efficiently acted as secretary to his father, who served for a time as United States congressman and later as minister to England. Between 1868 and 1870, he was a journalistic commentator, of much promise, upon domestic and foreign affairs. Between 1870 and 1876, he was the competent editor of a long-established and distinguished magazine, the *North American Review*. Simultaneously he was a highly successful teacher of medieval history at Harvard, where, among other important innovations, he introduced the graduate seminar.

Henry Adams—crayon drawing by J. B. Potter

In Washington, D. C., to which he moved from Boston, Adams composed two noteworthy novels, *Democracy* (1880) and *Esther* (1884), as well as several studies in American history. These included, in addition to shorter works, a pair of excellent biographies, *Life of Albert Gallatin* (1879) and *John Randolph* (1882), and a much admired nine-volume *History of the United States During the Administrations of Jefferson and Madison* (1889-1891). His interpretation of medieval life, *Mont-Saint-Michel and Chartres* (1904, revised in 1913), was praised by literary critics as well as by historians. (Professor John Spencer Bassett, in the *Cambridge History of American Literature*, calls the book "probably the best expression of the Middle Ages yet published in the English language.") His crowning achievement, in the opinion of most, was a philosophical autobiography cryptically titled *The Education of Henry Adams*, privately printed in 1907 but not made available to the general public until 1918, the year of the author's death.

The aptitudes thus displayed, considering Adams' nature and nurture, were not surprising. But the varied nature of his efforts was an outward sign of an inward discontent. The "education" which he achieved, one which did not end with college but extended throughout a long lifetime, was, in Adams' opinion, an indecisive one. Despite the fine cards dealt to him by fate, he said, characteristically writing of himself in the third person, "he never got to the point of playing the game at all; he lost himself in the study of it, watching the errors of the players . . . ." His aim, in large part, as he watched and thoughtfully pondered what he saw, was to find some secret of orderliness, some meaningful scheme, in the complex world of his time. Widely traveled though he was not only in Europe but in America, Mexico, the South Seas, Egypt, and Russia as well; closely acquainted though he was with a host of the leading figures of the day in several fields; well read though he was in books on many subjects, he found that the answer consistently proved elusive.

Adams' first novel, *Democracy*, shows what discouraging conclusions he reached when he studied and weighed the values of one important phase of American life— our governmental system. Sternly, in the spirit of doubt which was moving many of our authors in the 1880's, Adams tells a story underlining faults which he had seen in our government while living in Washington. As Ludwig Lewisohn observes, in *Expression in America*, "He rejects the life of the American collectivity at its densest and most representative place and point; he despairs of the Republic; he leaves the reader with not a shred of illusion concerning the national government and its method." And Adams' skepticism about ways of living in his era became much more inclusive by the time he reached his sixties and wrote his two most famous books.

These books, *Mont-Saint-Michel and Chartres* and *The Education*, dramatically indicate the great problem which this author attempted to solve, and record his search for a solution. The former examines the point in the long history of the human race at which, he believes, "man had held the highest idea of himself as a unit in a unified universe." The art and the architecture of the medieval period during which were erected the two great cathedrals of his title, Adams contends, are symbols of an age of unity, an age during which man had found answers satisfactory to himself to questions about the nature of the universe and man's place in it. Such an age of peaceful adjustment was made possible, Adams holds, by man's transference of the vital power of the Virgin—Mary, the central figure of medieval faith— into both belief and action.

Adams thus looks back with wistful nostalgia at the distant age which had solved the problem of living. But when he turns to his own time he sees a contrast which creates a different mood. He sees the age in which he has lived as one not of unity but of chaotic multiplicity. His *Education* gives an account of its author's continuously baffled search—in many parts of the earth during a long period—for some up-to-date, unified meaning or faith comparable to that which had motivated medieval worshipers. In politics, in religion, in philosophy, in physics, in biology, in psychology, he finds evidence which leads him to draw a distressing conclusion: "Chaos was the law of nature; Order was the dream of man." Adams' autobiography, therefore, marks the attainment of a high point in the skepticism characteristic of its author's period. But it has more than a negative value: for one thing, it sets forth Adams' "dynamic theory of history," which interestingly attempts to interpret cause-effect relationships in our past in terms of certain laws of the physical world. For another, it positively insists upon our need for "a new social mind" to grapple with complex modern life, and thus it foreshadows a growing concern of the present day.

The form employed by Adams in his life story makes both the account and the message memorable. No hysteria of the sort far too frequent in American pessimistic writing enters into it; rather the whole thoughtful narrative is set down with detachment and quiet irony. Adams was equipped, by training and temperament, not only for an objective, amused consideration of the world in which he lived but also for something even more noteworthy—a smiling contemplation of himself, scion of the great Adams family, scurrying over the face of the earth to carry on a lifelong quest which, although it is always frustrated, is eternally hopeful. His very use of the third person (instead of the first person typical of autobiography) emphasizes his playful objectivity. His refusal to consider in any detail several deeply tragic events in his life—such as the death of his wife in 1885—helps him maintain the tone of high comedy. His style is quiet, reserved, cynical—implicit in its nuances rather than explicit and direct. *The Education,* descriptive of chaos though it is, is anything but chaotic: subtlety and sureness make the book an outstanding masterpiece among American works of its genre.

J. T. Adams, **Henry Adams,** New York, 1933 • Ernest Samuels, **Young Henry Adams,** Cambridge, 1948 • R. A. Hume, ''The Style and Literary Background of Henry Adams, with Attention to The Education,'' **American Literature,** January 1945 • R. F. Nichols, ''The Dynamic Interpretation of History,'' **New England Quarterly,** June 1935 • T. K. Whipple, ''Henry Adams,'' **Spokesmen: Modern Writers and American Life,** New York, 1928

From

The Education of Henry Adams

Chapter XXV

THE DYNAMO AND THE VIRGIN (1900)

Chapter XXV of Adams' autobiography tells how, at the Paris Exposition of 1900, instructed by the scientist Langley, Adams became aware of the power and the mystery of the dynamo. "As he grew accustomed to the great gallery of machines," he writes of himself, "he began to feel the forty-foot dynamos as a moral force, much as the early Christians felt the Cross." Was it possible, he wondered, for a historian to chart man's development in terms of this twentieth-century embodiment of force? "Symbol or energy," he writes, "the Virgin had acted as the greatest force the Western world ever felt and had drawn man's activities to herself more strongly than any other power, natural or supernatural, had ever done; the historian's business was to follow the track of the energy; to find where it came from and where it went to; its complex source and shifting channels; its values, equivalents, conversions." The chapter tells how the dynamo and the thoughts it stimulated brought additional puzzlement to Adams and started him on a new search for understanding.

Until the Great Exposition of 1900 closed its doors in November, Adams haunted it, aching to absorb knowledge, and helpless to find it. He would have liked to know how much of it could have been grasped by the best-informed man in the world. While he was thus meditating chaos, Langley came by, and showed it to him. At Langley's behest, the Exhibition dropped its superfluous rags and stripped itself to the skin, for Langley knew what to study, and why, and how; while Adams might as well have stood outside in the night, 10 staring at the Milky Way. Yet Langley said nothing new, and taught nothing that one might not have learned from Lord Bacon, three hundred years before; but though one should have known the "Advancement of Science" as well as one knew the "Comedy of Errors," the literary knowledge counted for nothing until some teacher should show how to apply it. Bacon took a vast deal of trouble in teaching King James I and his subjects, American or other, towards the year 1620, that true science was the development or economy of forces; 20 yet an elderly American in 1900 knew neither the formula nor the forces; or even so much as to say to himself that his historical business in the Exposition

13 **Lord Bacon,** Francis Bacon (1561-1626), English philosopher, whose work on ''Advancement of Science'' was **The Advancement of Learning** (1605) • 15 **Comedy of Errors,** Shakespeare's play • 18 **King James I** (1566-1625) was king of Great Britain from 1603 until his death

concerned only the economies or developments of force since 1893, when he began the study at Chicago.

Nothing in education is so astonishing as the amount of ignorance it accumulates in the form of inert facts. Adams had looked at most of the accumulations of art in the storehouses called Art Museums; yet he did not know how to look at the art exhibits of 1900. He had studied Karl Marx and his doctrines of history with profound attention, yet he could not apply them at Paris. Langley, with the ease of a great master of experiment, threw out of the field every exhibit that did not reveal a new application of force, and naturally threw out, to begin with, almost the whole art exhibit. Equally, he ignored almost the whole industrial exhibit. He led his pupil directly to the forces. His chief interest was in new motors to make his airship feasible, and he taught Adams the astonishing complexities of the new Daimler motor, and of the automobile, which, since 1893, had become a nightmare at a hundred kilometres an hour, almost as destructive as the electric tram which was only ten years older; and threatening to become as terrible as the locomotive steam-engine itself, which was almost exactly Adams's own age.

Then he showed his scholar the great hall of dynamos, and explained how little he knew about electricity or force of any kind, even of his own special sun, which spouted heat in inconceivable volume, but which, as far as he knew, might spout less or more, at any time, for all the certainty he felt in it. To him, the dynamo itself was but an ingenious channel for conveying somewhere the heat latent in a few tons of poor coal hidden in a dirty engine-house carefully kept out of sight; but to Adams the dynamo became a symbol of infinity. As he grew accustomed to the great gallery of machines, he began to feel the forty-foot dynamos as a moral force, much as the early Christians felt the Cross. The planet itself seemed less impressive, in its old-fashioned, deliberate, annual or daily revolution, than this huge wheel, revolving within arm's-length at some vertiginous speed, and barely murmuring—scarcely humming an audible warning to stand a hair's-breadth further for respect of power—while it would not wake the baby lying close against its frame. Before the end, one began to pray to it; inherited instinct taught the natural expression of man before silent and infinite force. Among the thousand symbols of ultimate energy, the dynamo was not so human as some, but it was the most expressive.

Yet the dynamo, next to the steam-engine, was the most familiar of exhibits. For Adams's objects its value lay chiefly in its occult mechanism. Between the dynamo in the gallery of machines and the engine-house outside, the break of continuity amounted to abysmal fracture for a historian's objects. No more relation could he discover between the steam and the electric current than between the Cross and the cathedral. The forces were interchangeable if not reversible, but he could see only an absolute *fiat* in electricity as in faith. Langley could not help him. Indeed, Langley seemed to be worried by the same trouble, for he constantly repeated that the new forces were anarchical, and specially that he was not responsible for the new rays, that were little short of parricidal in their wicked spirit towards science. His own rays, with which he had doubled the solar spectrum, were altogether harmless and beneficent; but Radium denied its God—or, what was to Langley the same thing, denied the truths of his Science. The force was wholly new.

A historian who asked only to learn enough to be as futile as Langley or Kelvin, made rapid progress under this teaching, and mixed himself up in the tangle of ideas until he achieved a sort of Paradise of ignorance vastly consoling to his fatigued senses. He wrapped himself in vibrations and rays which were new, and he would have hugged Marconi and Branly had he met them, as he hugged the dynamo; while he lost his arithmetic in trying to figure out the equation between the discoveries and the economies of force. The economies, like the discoveries, were absolute, supersensual, occult; incapable of expression in horse-power. What mathematical equivalent could he suggest as the value of a Branly coherer? Frozen air, or the electric furnace, had some scale of measurement, no doubt, if somebody could invent a thermometer adequate to the purpose; but X-rays had played no part whatever in man's con-

---

2 1893, the year of the World's Columbian Exposition at Chicago, which Adams had visited. In Chapter XXII, he told of the questions raised by the scientific and industrial exhibits • 18 **Daimler**, Gottlieb Daimler (1834-1900), the discoverer of important improvements in the gasoline engine • 65 **Radium . . . God.** Scientists were still puzzled by the activity of this recently discovered element • 69 **Kelvin**, William Thomson Kelvin, Baron (1824-1907), British mathematician and physicist, an authority on molecular dynamics • 74 **Branly**, Édouard Branly (1846-1940), French physicist. Branly's coherer was useful in detecting electric waves

sciousness, and the atom itself had figured only as a fiction of thought. In these seven years man had translated himself into a new universe which had no common scale of measurement with the old. He had entered a supersensual world, in which he could measure nothing except by chance collisions of movements imperceptible to his senses, perhaps even imperceptible to his instruments, but perceptible to each other, and so to some known ray at the end of the scale. Langley seemed 10 prepared for anything, even for an indeterminable number of universes interfused—physics stark mad in metaphysics.

Historians undertake to arrange sequences,—called stories, or histories—assuming in silence a relation of cause and effect. These assumptions, hidden in the depths of dusty libraries, have been astounding, but commonly unconscious and childlike; so much so, that if any captious critic were to drag them to light, historians would probably reply, with one voice, that they had never 20 supposed themselves required to know what they were talking about. Adams, for one, had toiled in vain to find out what he meant. He had even published a dozen volumes of American history for no other purpose than to satisfy himself whether, by the severest process of stating, with the least possible comment, such facts as seemed sure, in such order as seemed rigorously consequent, he could fix for a familiar moment a necessary sequence of human movement. The result had satisfied him as little as at Harvard College. Where he saw 30 sequence, other men saw something quite different, and no one saw the same unit of measure. He cared little about his experiments and less about his statesmen, who seemed to him quite as ignorant as himself and, as a rule, no more honest; but he insisted on a relation of sequence, and if he could not reach it by one method, he would try as many methods as science knew. Satisfied that the sequence of men led to nothing and that the sequence of their society could lead no further, while the mere sequence of time was artificial, and the sequence of 40 thought was chaos, he turned at last to the sequence of force; and thus it happened that, after ten years' pursuit, he found himself lying in the Gallery of Machines at the Great Exposition of 1900, his historical neck broken by the sudden irruption of forces totally new.

Since no one else showed much concern, an elderly person without other cares had no need to betray alarm. The year 1900 was not the first to upset schoolmasters.

Copernicus and Galileo had broken many professorial necks about 1600; Columbus had stood the world on its head towards 1500; but the nearest approach to the 50 revolution of 1900 was that of 310, when Constantine set up the Cross. The rays that Langley disowned, as well as those which he fathered, were occult, supersensual, irrational; they were what, in terms of medieval science, were called immediate modes of the divine substance.

The historian was thus reduced to his last resources. Clearly if he was bound to reduce all these forces to a common value, this common value could have no measure but that of their attraction on his own mind. He must treat them as they had been felt; as convertible, 60 reversible, interchangeable attractions on thought. He made up his mind to venture it; he would risk translating rays into faith. Such a reversible process would vastly amuse a chemist, but the chemist could not deny that he, or some of his fellow physicists, could feel the force of both. When Adams was a boy in Boston, the best chemist in the place had probably never heard of Venus except by way of scandal, or of the Virgin except as idolatry; neither had he heard of dynamos or automobiles or radium; yet his mind was ready to feel the 70 force of all, though the rays were unborn and the women were dead.

Here opened another totally new education, which promised to be by far the most hazardous of all. The knife-edge along which he must crawl, like Sir Lancelot in the twelfth century, divided two kingdoms of force which had nothing in common but attraction. They were as different as a magnet is from gravitation, supposing one knew what a magnet was, or gravitation, or love. The force of the Virgin was still felt at Lourdes, 80 and seemed to be as potent as X-rays but in America neither Venus nor Virgin ever had value as a force— at most as sentiment. No American had ever truly been afraid of either.

This problem in dynamics gravely perplexed an American historian. The Woman had once been su-

---

48 **Copernicus**, Nikolaus Copernicus (1473-1543), Polish astronomer who had revolutionized thought concerning the mechanics of the universe • 48 **Galileo**, Galileo Galilei (1564-1642), Italian astronomer • 51 **Constantine** (272?-337), Roman emperor who was converted to Christianity about 310 • 75 **Sir Lancelot**, according to one medieval story, had to crawl along a knife-edge to enter a castle from which he rescued Guinevere • 80 **Lourdes**, town in southwestern France, famous for its miraculous grotto • 86 **The Woman**, the feminine force

preme; in France she still seemed potent, not merely as a sentiment, but as a force. Why was she unknown in America? For evidently America was ashamed of her, and she was ashamed of herself, otherwise they would not have strewn fig-leaves so profusely all over her. When she was a true force, she was ignorant of fig-leaves, but the monthly-magazine-made American female had not a feature that would have been recognized by Adam. The trait was notorious, and often
10 humorous, but any one brought up among Puritans knew that sex was a sin. In any previous age, sex was strength. Neither art nor beauty was needed. Every one, even among Puritans, knew that neither Diana of the Ephesians nor any of the Oriental goddesses was worshipped for her beauty. She was goddess because of her force; she was the animated dynamo; she was reproduction—the greatest and most mysterious of all energies; all she needed was to be fecund. Singularly enough, not one of Adams's many schools of education had ever
20 drawn his attention to the opening lines of Lucretius, though they were perhaps the finest in all Latin literature, where the poet invoked Venus exactly as Dante invoked the Virgin:—

"Quae quoniam rerum naturam *sola* gubernas."

The Venus of Epicurean philosophy survived in the Virgin of the Schools:—

"Donna, sei tanto grande, e tanto vali,
Che qual vuol grazia, e a te non ricorre,
Sua disianza vuol volar senz' ali."

30 All this was to American thought as though it had never existed. The true American knew something of the facts, but nothing of the feelings; he read the letter, but he never felt the law. Before this historical chasm, a mind like that of Adams felt itself helpless; he turned from the Virgin to the Dynamo as though he were a Branly coherer. On one side, at the Louvre and at Chartres, as he knew by the record of work actually done and still before his eyes, was the highest energy ever known to man, the creator of four-fifths of his noblest
40 art, exercising vastly more attraction over the human mind than all the steam-engines and dynamos ever dreamed of; and yet this energy was unknown to the American mind. An American Virgin would never dare command; an American Venus would never dare exist.

The question, which to any plain American of the nineteenth century seemed as remote as it did to Adams, drew him almost violently to study, once it was posed; and on this point Langleys were as useless as though they were Herbert Spencers or dynamos. The idea survived only as art. There one turned as naturally as
50 though the artist were himself a woman. Adams began to ponder, asking himself whether he knew of any American artist who had ever insisted on the power of sex, as every classic had always done; but he could think only of Walt Whitman; Bret Harte, as far as the magazines would let him venture; and one or two painters, for the flesh-tones. All the rest had used sex for sentiment, never for force; to them, Eve was a tender flower, and Herodias an unfeminine horror. American art, like the American language and American
60 education, was as far as possible sexless. Society regarded this victory over sex as its greatest triumph, and the historian readily admitted it, since the moral issue, for the moment, did not concern one who was studying the relations of unmoral force. He cared nothing for the sex of the dynamo until he could measure its energy.

Vaguely seeking a clue, he wandered through the art exhibit, and, in his stroll, stopped almost every day before St. Gaudens's General Sherman, which had been given the central post of honor. St. Gaudens himself
70 was in Paris, putting on the work his usual interminable last touches, and listening to the usual contradictory suggestions of brother sculptors. Of all the American artists who gave to American art whatever life it breathed in the seventies, St. Gaudens was perhaps the most sympathetic, but certainly the most inarticulate. General Grant or Don Cameron had scarcely less in-

---

13 **Diana,** fertility goddess of Ephesus • 20 **Lucretius,** Titus Lucretius Carus (96-55 B.C.), Roman poet • 24 **Quae quoniam** . . . . "Since thou art, then, sole mistress of the nature of things."—Lucretius, **On the Nature of Things,** I. 21 • 27 **Donna, sei tanto** . . . .

Lady, thou are so great, and so prevailing,
That he who wishes grace, nor runs to thee,
His aspirations without wings would fly.

—Dante, "Paradiso," XXXIII, II. 13-15 (Longfellow's translation) • 49 **Herbert Spencer.** See note, p. 702 • 59 **Herodias,** the wife of Herod Antipas; by feminine guile, she brought about the death of John the Baptist • 69 **St. Gaudens's . . . Sherman.** Augustus Saint Gaudens (see note, p. 689) was a friend of Adams. His statue of General Sherman, then on display in Paris, now stands in Central Park, New York • 77 **Don Cameron,** J. D. Cameron (1833-1918), a senator from Pennsylvania and another friend of Adams

stinct of rhetoric than he. All the others—the Hunts, Richardson, John La Farge, Stanford White—were exuberant; only St. Gaudens could never discuss or dilate on an emotion, or suggest artistic arguments for giving to his work the forms that he felt. He never laid down the law, or affected the despot, or became brutalized like Whistler by the brutalities of his world. He required no incense; he was no egoist; his simplicity of thought was excessive; he could not imitate, or give any form but his own to the creations of his hand. No one felt more strongly than he the strength of other men, but the idea that they could affect him never stirred an image in his mind.

This summer his health was poor and his spirits were low. For such a temper, Adams was not the best companion, since his own gaiety was not *folle;* but he risked going now and then to the studio on Mont Parnasse to draw him out for a stroll in the Bois de Boulogne, or dinner as pleased his moods, and in return St. Gaudens sometimes let Adams go about in his company.

Once St. Gaudens took him down to Amiens, with a party of Frenchmen, to see the cathedral. Not until they found themselves actually studying the sculpture of the western portal, did it dawn on Adams's mind that, for his purposes, St. Gaudens on that spot had more interest to him than the cathedral itself. Great men before great monuments express great truths, provided they are not taken too solemnly. Adams never tired of quoting the supreme phrase of his idol Gibbon, before the Gothic cathedrals: "I darted a contemptuous look on the stately monuments of superstition." Even in the footnotes of his history, Gibbon had never inserted a bit of humor more human than this, and one would have paid largely for a photograph of the fat little historian, on the background of Notre Dame of Amiens, trying to persuade his readers—perhaps himself—that he was darting a contemptuous look on the stately monument, for which he felt in fact the respect which every man of his vast study and active mind always feels before objects worthy of it; but besides the humor, one felt also the relation. Gibbon ignored the Virgin, because in 1789 religious monuments were out of fashion. In 1900 his remark sounded fresh and simple as the green fields to ears that had heard a hundred years of other remarks, mostly no more fresh and certainly less simple. Without malice, one might find it more instructive than a whole lecture of Ruskin. One sees what one brings, and at that moment Gibbon brought the French Revolution. Ruskin brought reaction against the Revolution. St. Gaudens had passed beyond all. He liked the stately monuments much more than he liked Gibbon or Ruskin; he loved their dignity; their unity; their scale; their lines; their lights and shadows; their decorative sculpture; but he was even less conscious than they of the force that created it all—the Virgin, the Woman—by whose genius "the stately monuments of superstition" were built, through which she was expressed. He would have seen more meaning in Isis with the cow's horns, at Edfoo, who expressed the same thought. The art remained, but the energy was lost even upon the artist.

Yet in mind and person St. Gaudens was a survival of the 1500; he bore the stamp of the Renaissance, and should have carried an image of the Virgin round his neck, or stuck in his hat, like Louis XI. In mere time he was a lost soul that had strayed by chance into the twentieth century, and forgotten where it came from. He writhed and cursed at his ignorance, much as Adams did at his own, but in the opposite sense. St. Gaudens was a child of Benvenuto Cellini, smothered in an American cradle. Adams was a quintessence of Boston, devoured by curiosity to think like Benvenuto. St. Gaudens's art was starved from birth, and Adams's instinct was blighted from babyhood. Each had but half of a nature, and when they came together before the Virgin of Amiens they ought both to have felt in her the force that made them one; but it was not so. To Adams she became more than ever a channel of force; to St. Gaudens she remained as before a channel of taste.

For a symbol of power, St. Gaudens instinctively preferred the horse, as was plain in his horse and Victory of the Sherman monument. Doubtless Sherman also

1 the Hunts, Richard Morris Hunt (1827-1895), an architect; William Morris Hunt (1824-1879), a painter • 2 Richardson, Henry H. Richardson (1838-1886), an architect • 2 John La Farge (1835-1910), painter and sculptor • 2 Stanford White (1853-1906), an architect • 7 Whistler, James M. Whistler (1834-1903), sharp-tongued American artist who lived in Europe • 16 folle, mad or extravagant • 29 Gibbon, Edward Gibbon (1737-1794), English historian and skeptic • 47 Ruskin, John Ruskin (1819-1900), English art critic whose philosophizing about cathedrals differed greatly from Adams' • 58 Isis. Adams had seen a statue of this Egyptian goddess of fertility in Edfu, Egypt • 64 Louis XI (1423-1483), king of France • 69 Benvenuto Cellini (1500-1571), a great Italian craftsman in metals, here used to represent the artistry of the Renaissance

The Education of Henry Adams

felt it so. The attitude was so American that, for at least forty years, Adams had never realized that any other could be in sound taste. How many years had he taken to admit a notion of what Michael Angelo and Rubens were driving at? He could not say; but he knew that only since 1895 had he begun to feel the Virgin or Venus as force, and not everywhere even so. At Chartres—perhaps at Lourdes—possibly at Cnidos if one could still find there the divinely naked Aphrodite of Praxiteles—but otherwise one must look for force to the goddesses of Indian mythology. The idea died out long ago in the German and English stock. St. Gaudens at Amiens was hardly less sensitive to the force of the female energy than Matthew Arnold at the Grande Chartreuse. Neither of them felt goddesses as power— only as reflected emotion, human expression, beauty, purity, taste, scarcely even as sympathy. They felt a railway train as power; yet they, and all other artists, constantly complained that the power embodied in a railway train could never be embodied in art. All the steam in the world could not, like the Virgin, build Chartres.

Yet in mechanics, whatever the mechanicians might think, both energies acted as interchangeable forces on man, and by action on man all known force may be measured. Indeed, few men of science measured force in any other way. After once admitting that a straight line was the shortest distance between two points, no serious mathematician cared to deny anything that suited his convenience, and rejected no symbol, un-proved or unproveable, that helped him to accomplish work. The symbol was force, as a compass-needle or a triangle was force, as the mechanist might prove by losing it, and nothing could be gained by ignoring their value. Symbol or energy, the Virgin had acted as the greatest force the Western world ever felt, and had drawn man's activities to herself more strongly than any other power, natural or supernatural, had ever done; the historian's business was to follow the track of the en-ergy; to find where it came from and where it went to; its complex source and shifting channels; its values, equivalents, conversions. It could scarcely be more com-plex than radium; it could hardly be deflected, diverted, polarized, absorbed more perplexingly than other radiant matter. Adams knew nothing about any of them, but as a mathematical problem of influence on human prog-ress, though all were occult, all reacted on his mind,

and he rather inclined to think the Virgin easiest to handle.

The pursuit turned out to be long and tortuous, lead-ing at last into the vast forests of scholastic science. From Zeno to Descartes, hand in hand with Thomas Aquinas, Montaigne, and Pascal, one stumbled as stupidly as though one were still a German student of 1860. Only with the instinct of despair could one force one's self into this old thicket of ignorance after having been repulsed at a score of entrances more promising and more popular. Thus far, no path had led anywhere, un-less perhaps to an exceedingly modest living. Forty-five years of study had proved to be quite futile for the pursuit of power; one controlled no more force in 1900 than in 1850, although the amount of force controlled by society had enormously increased. The secret of education still hid itself somewhere behind ignorance, and one fumbled over it as feebly as ever. In such laby-rinths, the staff is a force almost more necessary than the legs; the pen becomes a sort of blind-man's dog, to keep him from falling into the gutters. The pen works for itself, and acts like a hand, modelling the plastic material over and over again to the form that suits it best. The form is never arbitrary, but is a sort of growth like crystallization, as any artist knows too well; for often the pencil or pen runs into side-paths and shape-lessness, loses its relations, stops or is bogged. Then it has to return on its trail, and recover, if it can, its line of force. The result of a year's work depends more on what is struck out than on what is left in; on the sequence of the main lines of thought, than on their play or variety. Compelled once more to lean heavily on this support, Adams covered more thousands of pages with figures as formal as though they were algebra, laboriously striking out, altering, burning, experimenting, until the year had expired, the Exposition had long been closed, and winter drawing to its end before he sailed from Cherbourg, on January 19, 1901 for home.

---

8 **Cnidos,** site of the temple in which was placed the statue of Aphro-dite which was the masterpiece of the great Greek sculptor, Praxiteles • 14 **Matthew Arnold** (1822-1888), English poet and critic, told, in his poem "Stanzas from the Grande Chartreuse," of his religious expe-riences • 52 **Zeno,** Greek philosopher of the fourth century B.C.; founder of stoicism • 52 **Descartes,** René Descartes (1596-1650), French philosopher—a rationalist • 52 **Aquinas,** Saint Thomas Aquinas (1225?-1274), Catholic philosopher • 53 **Montaigne,** Michel Eyquem de Montaigne (1533-1592), French essayist and philosopher • 53 **Pascal,** Blaise Pascal (1623-1662), French mathematician and philosopher

Chapter XXXIII

A DYNAMIC THEORY OF HISTORY (1904)

In 1910, Adams sent out to a number of his fellow historians **A Letter to American Teachers of History.** In his letter, he (1) held that the hypothesis of evolution had been overthrown by a discovery in physics—the second law of thermodynamics, which suggested that the unrestorable mechanical energy of the earth was being dissipated; (2) urged his colleagues to work out a formula for the course of history in terms of this law. Though historians in general worked on no such scheme, Adams had tentatively formulated his use of the principle in an essay, "The Rule of Phase Applied to History" (later published in **The Degradation of the Democratic Dogma** in 1918), and in two chapters (XXXIII and XXXIV) of **The Education.** In "Henry Adams on History" (**New England Quarterly,** June 1935), Roy F. Nichols summarizes the theory thus: "Adams's studies of force led him to believe that thought followed its developments. The order of the appearance of the great forces conveniently corresponded to the order of their intensity. First, there was human reproductive energy as represented by women; second, faith, culminating in Christianity; third, mechanical power; fourth, electricity; and finally, radium."

Chapter XXXIII applies the formula to the course of man's experiences down to 1900. The concluding lines are transitional to Chapter XXXIV, "A Law of Acceleration," which suggests that as the forces involved in successive phases became increasingly powerful, the phases became of briefer and briefer duration.

Mr. Nichols notes "the veritable revolution in science" which has taken place since Adams' day because "the theory of relativity, the phenomena of radioactivity, and quantum mechanics have come to the fore." As a result, he concludes, "Henry Adams's challenge to teachers of history to seek a dynamic interpretation still stands, even though his own attempt to formulate it must be discarded. Historian and scientist may well work together—but they will work in a different direction from that pointed out by Adams." Even after historian and scientist succeed in this endeavor, however—if they ever do—Adams' account will continue to be of interest as an interpretation of the past of mankind based upon the suggestions of the science of the day and also upon the pessimistic conclusions of its author.

A dynamic theory, like most theories, begins by begging the question: it defines Progress as the development and economy of Forces. Further, it defines force as anything that does, or helps to do work. Man is a force; so is the sun; so is a mathematical point, though without dimensions or known existence.

Man commonly begs the question again by taking for granted that he captures the forces. A dynamic theory, assigning attractive force to opposing bodies in proportion to the law of mass, takes for granted that the forces of nature capture man. The sum of force attracts; the feeble atom or molecule called man is attracted; he suffers education or growth; he is the sum of the forces that attract him; his body and his thought are alike their product; the movement of the forces controls the progress of his mind, since he can know nothing but the motions which impinge on his senses, whose sum makes education.

For convenience as an image, the theory may liken man to a spider in its web, watching for chance prey. Forces of nature dance like flies before the net, and the spider pounces on them when it can; but it makes many fatal mistakes, though its theory of force is sound. The spider-mind acquires a faculty of memory, and, with it, a singular skill of analysis and synthesis, taking apart and putting together in different relations the meshes of its trap. Man had in the beginning no power of analysis or synthesis approaching that of the spider, or even of the honey-bee; but he had acute sensibility to the higher forces. Fire taught him secrets that no other animal could learn; running water probably taught him even more, especially in his first lessons of mechanics; the animals helped to educate him, trusting themselves into his hands merely for the sake of their food, and carrying his burdens or supplying his clothing; the grasses and grains were academies of study. With little or no effort on his part, all these forces formed his thought, induced his action, and even shaped his figure.

Long before history began, his education was complete, for the record could not have been started until he had been taught to record. The universe that had formed him took shape in his mind as a reflection of his own unity, containing all forces except himself. Either separately, or in groups, or as a whole, these forces never ceased to act on him, enlarging his mind as they enlarged the surface foliage of a vegetable, and the mind needed only to respond, as the forests did, to these attractions. Susceptibility to the highest forces is the highest genius; selection between them is the highest science; their mass is the highest educator. Man always made, and still makes, grotesque blunders in selecting and measuring forces, taken at random from the heap, but he never made a mistake in the value he set on the whole, which he symbolized as unity and worshipped as God. To this day, his attitude towards it has never changed, though science can no longer give to force a name.

10 Man's function as a force of nature was to assimilate other forces as he assimilated food. He called it the love of power. He felt his own feebleness, and he sought for an ass or a camel, a bow or a sling, to widen his range of power, as he sought a fetish or a planet in the world beyond. He cared little to know its immediate use, he could afford to throw nothing away which he could conceive to have possible value in this or any other existence. He waited for the object to teach him its use, or want of use, and the process was slow. He may 20 have gone on for hundreds of thousands of years, waiting for Nature to tell him her secrets; and, to his rivals among the monkeys, Nature has taught no more than at their start; but certain lines of force were capable of acting on individual apes, and mechanically selecting types of race or sources of variation. The individual that responded or reacted to lines of new force then was possibly the same individual that reacts on it now, and his conception of the unity seems never to have changed in spite of the increasing diversity of forces; but 30 the theory of variation is an affair of other science than history, and matters nothing to dynamics. The individual or the race would be educated on the same lines of illusion, which, according to Arthur Balfour, had not essentially varied down to the year 1900.

To the highest attractive energy, man gave the name of divine, and for its control he invented the science called Religion, a word which meant, and still means, cultivation of occult force whether in detail or mass. Unable to define Force as a unity, man symbolized it 40 and pursued it, both in himself, and in the infinite, as philosophy and theology; the mind is itself the subtlest of all known forces, and its self-introspection necessarily created a science which had the singular value of lifting his education, at the start, to the finest, subtlest, and broadest training both in analysis and synthesis, so that, if language is a test, he must have reached his highest powers early in his history; while the mere motive re-

mained as simple an appetite for power as the tribal greed which led him to trap an elephant. Hunger, whether for food or for the infinite, sets in motion 50 multiplicity and infinity of thought, and the sure hope of gaining a share of infinite power in eternal life would lift most minds to effort.

He had reached this completeness five thousand years ago, and added nothing to his stock of known forces for a very long time. The mass of nature exercised on him so feeble an attraction that one can scarcely account for his apparent motion. Only a historian of very exceptional knowledge would venture to say at what date between 3000 B.C. and 1000 A.D., the momentum of 60 Europe was greatest; but such progress as the world made consisted in economies of energy rather than in its development; it was proved in mathematics, measured by names like Archimedes, Aristarchus, Ptolemy, and Euclid; or in Civil Law, measured by a number of names which Adams had begun life by failing to learn; or in coinage, which was most beautiful near its beginning, and most barbarous at its close; or it was shown in roads, or the size of ships, or harbors; or by the use of metals, instruments, and writing; all of them economies 70 of force, sometimes more forceful than the forces they helped; but the roads were still travelled by the horse, the ass, the camel, or the slave; the ships were still propelled by sails or oars; the lever, the spring, and the screw bounded the region of applied mechanics. Even the metals were old.

Much of the same thing could be said of religious or supernatural forces. Down to the year 300 of the Christian era they were little changed, and in spite of Plato and the sceptics were more apparently chaotic than ever. 80 The experience of three thousand years had educated society to feel the vastness of Nature, and the infinity of her resources of power, but even this increase of attraction had not yet caused economies in its methods of pursuit.

There the Western world stood till the year A.D. 305, when the Emperor Diocletian abdicated; and there it

---

33 Arthur Balfour, the Earl of Balfour (1848-1930), British philosopher and statesman • 64 Archimedes (287?-212 B.C.), Greek mathematician • 64 Aristarchus, a third-century B.C. philosopher and a native of Samos, was the chief exponent of the heliocentric theory of the universe • 64 Ptolemy, a second-century Greco-Egyptian astronomer • 65 Euclid, Greek geometer who lived about 300 B.C. • 86 Diocletian (245-313), Roman emperor

was that Adams broke down on the steps of Ara Cœli, his path blocked by the scandalous failure of civilization at the moment it had achieved complete success. In the year 305 the empire had solved the problems of Europe more completely than they have ever been solved since. The Pax Romana, the Civil Law, and Free Trade should, in four hundred years, have put Europe far in advance of the point reached by modern society in the four hundred years since 1500, when conditions were less simple.

The efforts to explain, or explain away, this scandal had been incessant, but none suited Adams unless it were the economic theory of adverse exchanges and exhaustion of minerals; but nations are not ruined beyond a certain point by adverse exchanges, and Rome had by no means exhausted her resources. On the contrary, the empire developed resources and energies quite astounding. No other four hundred years of history before A.D. 1800 knew anything like it; and although some of these developments, like the Civil Law, the roads, aqueducts, and harbors, were rather economies than force, yet in northwestern Europe alone the empire had developed three energies—France, England, and Germany—competent to master the world. The trouble seemed rather to be that the empire developed too much energy, and too fast.

A dynamic law requires that two masses—nature and man—must go on, reacting upon each other, without stop, as the sun and a comet react on each other, and that any appearance of stoppage is illusive. The theory seems to exact excess, rather than deficiency, of action and reaction to account for the dissolution of the Roman Empire, which should, as a problem of mechanics, have been torn to pieces by acceleration. If the student means to try the experiment of framing a dynamic law, he must assign values to the forces of attraction that caused the trouble; and in this case he has them in plain evidence. With the relentless logic that stamped Roman thought, the empire, which had established unity on earth, could not help establishing unity in heaven. It was induced by its dynamic necessities to economize the gods.

The Church has never ceased to protest against the charge that Christianity ruined the empire, and, with its usual force, has pointed out that its reforms alone saved the State. Any dynamic theory gladly admits it. All it asks is to find and follow the force that attracts. The Church points out this force in the Cross, and history needs only to follow it. The empire loudly asserted its motive. Good taste forbids saying that Constantine the Great speculated as audaciously as a modern stock-broker on values of which he knew at the utmost only the volume; or that he merged all uncertain forces into a single trust, which he enormously overcapitalized, and forced on the market; but this is the substance of what Constantine himself said in his Edict of Milan in the year 313, which admitted Christianity into the Trust of State Religions. Regarded as an Act of Congress, it runs: "We have resolved to grant to Christians as well as all others the liberty to practise the religion they prefer, in order that whatever exists of divinity or celestial power may help and favor us and all who are under our government." The empire pursued power—not merely spiritual but physical—in the sense in which Constantine issued his army order the year before, at the battle of the Milvian Bridge: *In hoc signo vinces!* using the Cross as a train of artillery, which, to his mind, it was. Society accepted it in the same character. Eighty years afterwards, Theodosius marched against his rival Eugene with the Cross for physical champion; and Eugene raised the image of Hercules to fight for the pagans; while society on both sides looked on, as though it were a boxing-match, to decide a final test of force between the divine powers. The Church was powerless to raise the ideal. What is now known as religion affected the mind of old society but little. The laity, the people, the million, almost to a man, bet on the gods as they bet on a horse.

No doubt the Church did all it could to purify the process, but society was almost wholly pagan in its point of view, and was drawn to the Cross because, in its system of physics, the Cross had absorbed all the old occult or fetish-power. The symbol represented the sum of nature—the Energy of modern science—and society believed it to be as real as X-rays; perhaps it was! The emperors used it like rays in medicine; the dying clung to it as the quintessence of force, to protect them from the forces of evil on their road to the next life.

Throughout these four centuries the empire knew

---

6 Pax Romana, Roman peace • 49 Constantine. See note, p. 743 • 65 Milvian Bridge, ancient bridge over the Tiber, where Maxentius was drowned after his defeat (312 A.D.) by Constantine • 65 In hoc . . . vinces! "In this sign you will conquer!" • 68 Theodosius (346?-395), Roman emperor • 69 Eugene, or Eugenius, a Roman emperor who was defeated and slain by Theodosius in 394

that religion disturbed economy, for even the cost of heathen incense affected the exchanges; but no one could afford to buy or construct a costly and complicated machine when he could hire an occult force at trifling expense. Fetish-power was cheap and satisfactory, down to a certain point. Turgot and Auguste Comte long ago fixed this stage of economy as a necessary phase of social education, and historians seem now to accept it as the only gain yet made towards scientific history. Great numbers of educated people—perhaps a majority—cling to the method still, and practise it more or less strictly; but, until quite recently, no other was known. The only occult power at man's disposal was fetish. Against it, no mechanical force could compete except within narrow limits.

Outside of occult or fetish-power, the Roman world was incredibly poor. It knew but one productive energy resembling a modern machine—the slave. No artificial force of serious value was applied to production or transportation, and when society developed itself so rapidly in political and social lines, it had no other means of keeping its economy on the same level than to extend its slave-system and its fetish-system to the utmost.

The result might have been stated in a mathematical formula as early as the time of Archimedes, six hundred years before Rome fell. The economic needs of a violently centralizing society forced the empire to enlarge its slave-system until the slave-system consumed itself and the empire too, leaving society no resource but further enlargement of its religious system in order to compensate for the losses and horrors of the failure. For a vicious circle, its mathematical completeness approached perfection. The dynamic law of attraction and reaction needed only a Newton to fix it in algebraic form.

At last, in 410, Alaric sacked Rome, and the slave-ridden, agricultural, uncommercial Western Empire—the poorer and less Christianized half—went to pieces. Society, though terribly shocked by the horrors of Alaric's storm, felt still more deeply the disappointment in its new power, the Cross, which had failed to protect its Church. The outcry against the Cross became so loud among Christians that its literary champion, Bishop Augustine of Hippo—a town between Algiers and Tunis—was led to write a famous treatise in defence of the Cross, familiar still to every scholar, in which he defended feebly the mechanical value of the symbol—arguing only that pagan symbols equally failed—but insisted on its spiritual value in the *Civitas Dei* which had taken the place of the *Civitas Romae* in human interest. "Granted that we have lost all we had! Have we lost faith? Have we lost piety? Have we lost the wealth of the inner man who is rich before God? These are the wealth of Christians!" The *Civitas Dei,* in its turn, became the sum of attraction for the Western world, though it also showed the same weakness in mechanics that had wrecked the *Civitas Romae.* St. Augustine and his people perished at Hippo towards 430, leaving society in appearance dull to new attraction.

Yet the attraction remained constant. The delight of experimenting on occult force of every kind is such as to absorb all the free thought of the human race. The gods did their work; history has no quarrel with them; they led, educated, enlarged the mind; taught knowledge; betrayed ignorance, stimulated effort. So little is known about the mind—whether social, racial, sexual or heritable; whether material or spiritual; whether animal, vegetable or mineral—that history is inclined to avoid it altogether; but nothing forbids one to admit, for convenience, that it may assimilate food like the body, storing up new force and growing, like a forest, with the storage. The brain has not yet revealed its mysterious mechanism of gray matter. Never has Nature offered it so violent a stimulant as when she opened to it the possibility of sharing infinite power in eternal life, and it might well need a thousand years of prolonged and intense experiment to prove the value of the motive. During these so-called Middle Ages, the Western mind reacted in many forms, on many sides, expressing its motives in modes, such as Romanesque and Gothic architecture, glass windows and mosaic walls, sculpture and poetry, war and love, which still affect some people as the noblest work of man, so that, even today, great masses of idle and ignorant tourists travel from far countries to look at Ravenna and San Marco, Palermo and Pisa, Assisi, Cordova, Chartres, with vague notions about the force that created them, but with a certain surprise that a social mind of such singular energy and unity should still lurk in their shadows.

6 **Turgot,** Anne Robert Jacques Turgot (1727-1781), French economist • 6 **Auguste Comte** (1798-1857), French philosopher • 33 **Newton,** Sir Isaac Newton (1642-1727), English mathematician • 34 **Alaric** (370?-410), king of the Visigoths who conquered Rome • 41 **Bishop Augustine,** Augustinus (354-430), early Christian philosopher, author of **City of God** • 47 **Civitas Dei,** "City of God" • 83 **Ravenna . . . Chartres,** Old World cities the architecture of which embodies the Christian culture of the medieval period

The tourist more rarely visits Constantinople or studies the architecture of Sancta Sofia, but when he does, he is distinctly conscious of forces not quite the same. Justinian has not the simplicity of Charlemagne. The Eastern Empire showed an activity and variety of forces that classical Europe had never possessed. The navy of Nicephoras Phocas in the tenth century would have annihilated in half an hour any navy that Carthage or Athens or Rome ever set afloat. The dynamic scheme
10 began by asserting rather recklessly that between the Pyramids (B.C. 3000), and the Cross (A.D. 300), no new force affected Western progress, and antiquarians may easily dispute the fact; but in any case the motive influence, old or new, which raised both Pyramids and Cross was the same attraction of power in a future life that raised the dome of Sancta Sofia and the Cathedral at Amiens, however much it was altered, enlarged, or removed to distance in space. Therefore, no single event has more puzzled historians than the sudden, unexplained
20 appearance of at least two new natural forces of the highest educational value in mechanics, for the first time within record of history. Literally, these two forces seemed to drop from the sky at the precise moment when the Cross on one side and the Crescent on the other, proclaimed the complete triumph of the *Civitas Dei*. Had the Manichean doctrine of Good and Evil as rival deities been orthodox, it would alone have accounted for this simultaneous victory of hostile powers.

Of the compass, as a step towards demonstration of
30 the dynamic law, one may confidently say it proved, better than any other force, the widening scope of the mind, since it widened immensely the range of contact between nature and thought. The compass educated. This must prove itself as needing no proof.

Of Greek fire and gunpowder, the same thing cannot certainly be said, for they have the air of accidents due to the attraction of religious motives. They belong to the spiritual world; or to the doubtful ground of Magic which lay between Good and Evil. They were
40 chemical forces, mostly explosive, which acted and still act as the most violent educators ever known to man, but they were justly feared as diabolic, and whatever insolence man may have risked towards the milder teachers of his infancy, he was an abject pupil towards explosives. The Sieur de Joinville left a record of the energy with which the relatively harmless Greek fire educated and enlarged the French mind in a single night

in the year 1249, when the crusaders were trying to advance on Cairo. The good king St. Louis and all his staff dropped on their knees at every fiery flame that 50 flew by, praying—"God have pity on us!" and never man had more reason to call on his gods than they, for the battle of religion between Christian and Saracen was trifling compared with that of education between gunpowder and the Cross.

The fiction that society educated itself, or aimed at a conscious purpose, was upset by the compass and gunpowder which dragged and drove Europe at will through frightful bogs of learning. At first, the apparent lag for want of volume in the new energies lasted one or two 60 centuries, which closed the great epochs of emotion by the Gothic cathedrals and scholastic theology. The moment had Greek beauty and more than Greek unity, but it was brief; and for another century or two, Western society seemed to float in space without apparent motion. Yet the attractive mass of nature's energy continued to attract, and education became more rapid than ever before. Society began to resist, but the individual showed greater and greater insistence, without realizing what he was doing. When the Crescent drove 70 the Cross in ignominy from Constantinople in 1453, Gutenberg and Fust were printing their first Bible at Mainz under the impression that they were helping the Cross. When Columbus discovered the West Indies in 1492, the Church looked on it as a victory for the Cross. When Luther and Calvin upset Europe half a century later, they were trying, like St. Augustine, to substitute the *Civitas Dei* for the *Civitas Romae*. When the Puritans set out for New England in 1620, they too were looking to found a *Civitas Dei* in State Street; 80

---

4 Justinian, Flavius Anicius Justinianus (483-565), Byzantine emperor • 4 Charlemagne, Charles I (742-814), emperor of the West, 800-814 • 7 Nicephoras Phocas (913?-969), emperor of the Eastern Roman Empire, 963-969 • 24 the Crescent, the emblem of the Turkish empire • 26 Manichean doctrine, the doctrine of the third century Persian, Mani, who taught the dualistic belief that although man's body is the product of the Kingdom of Darkness (Evil), his soul is the product of the Kingdom of Light (Good) • 45 Sieur de Joinville, Sire Jean de Joinville (1224?-1317), French chronicler • 49 St. Louis, King Louis IX (1214-1270) of France • 72 Gutenberg, Johann Gutenberg (1397?-1468), alleged inventor of printing from movable types • 72 Fust, Johann Fust (1400?-1466), German pioneer printer associated with Gutenberg • 76 Luther, Martin Luther (1483-1546), leader of the German Reformation • 76 Calvin, John Calvin. See note, p. 513 • 80 State Street, a figurative term for the location of New England government

and when Bunyan made his Pilgrimage in 1678, he repeated St. Jerome. Even when, after centuries of license, the Church reformed its discipline, and, to prove it, burned Giordano Bruno in 1600, besides condemning Galileo in 1630—as science goes on repeating to us every day—it condemned anarchists, not atheists. None of the astronomers were irreligious men; all of them made a point of magnifying God through his works; a form of science which did their religion no credit. Neither Galileo nor Kepler, neither Spinoza nor Descartes, neither Leibnitz nor Newton, any more than Constantine the Great—if so much—doubted Unity. The utmost range of their heresies reached only its personality.

This persistence of thought-inertia is the leading idea of modern history. Except as reflected in himself, man has no reason for assuming unity in the universe, or an ultimate substance, or a prime-motor. The *a priori* insistence on this unity ended by fatiguing the more active—or reactive—minds; and Lord Bacon tried to stop it. He urged society to lay aside the idea of evolving the universe from a thought, and to try evolving thought from the universe. The mind should observe and register forces—take them apart and put them together—without assuming unity at all. "Nature, to be commanded, must be obeyed." "The imagination must be given not wings but weights." As Galileo reversed the action of earth and sun, Bacon reversed the relation of thought to force. The mind was thenceforth to follow the movement of matter, and unity must be left to shift for itself.

The revolution in attitude seemed voluntary, but in fact was as mechanical as the fall of a feather. Man created nothing. After 1500, the speed of progress so rapidly surpassed man's gait as to alarm every one, as though it were the acceleration of a falling body which the dynamic theory takes it to be. Lord Bacon was as much astonished by it as the Church was, and with reason. Suddenly society felt itself dragged into situations altogether new and anarchic—situations which it could not affect, but which painfully affected it. Instinct taught it that the universe in its thought must be in danger when its reflection lost itself in space. The danger was all the greater because men of science covered it with "larger synthesis," and poets called the undevout astronomer mad. Society knew better. Yet the telescope held it rigidly standing on its head; the microscope revealed a universe that defied the senses; gunpowder killed whole races that lagged behind; the compass coerced the most imbruted mariner to act on the impossible idea that the earth was round; the press drenched Europe with anarchism. Europe saw itself, violently resisting, wrenched into false positions, drawn along new lines as a fish that is caught on a hook; but unable to understand by what force it was controlled. The resistance was often bloody, sometimes humorous, always constant. Its contortions in the eighteenth century are best studied in the wit of Voltaire, but all history and all philosophy from Montaigne and Pascal to Schopenhauer and Nietzsche deal with nothing else; and still, throughout it all, the Baconian law held good; thought did not evolve nature, but nature evolved thought. Not one considerable man of science dared face the stream of thought; and the whole number of those who acted, like Franklin, as electric conductors of the new forces from nature to man, down to the year 1800, did not exceed a few score, confined to a few towns in Western Europe. Asia refused to be touched by the stream, and America, except for Franklin, stood outside.

Very slowly the accretion of these new forces, chemical and mechanical, grew in volume until they acquired sufficient mass to take the place of the old religious science, substituting their attraction for the attractions of the *Civitas Dei,* but the process remained the same. Nature, not mind, did the work that the sun does on the planets. Man depended more and more absolutely on forces other than his own, and on instruments which superseded his senses. Bacon foretold it: "Neither the naked hand nor the understanding, left to itself, can effect much. It is by instruments and helps that work is done." Once done, the mind resumed its illusion, and society forgot its impotence; but no one better than Bacon knew its tricks and for his true followers science always meant

1 **Bunyan,** John Bunyan (1628-1688), author of **Pilgrim's Progress** • 2 **St. Jerome** (340?-420), Latin church father • 4 **Giordano Bruno** (1548?-1600), Italian philosopher who was burned at the stake • 10 **Kepler,** Johannes Kepler (1571-1630), German astronomer • 10 **Spinoza,** Baruch Spinoza (1632-1677), Dutch philosopher • 11 **Leibnitz,** Gottfried Wilhelm von Leibnitz (1646-1716), German philosopher • 58 **Voltaire,** François Marie Arouet de Voltaire (1694-1778), French philosopher and author • 60 **Schopenhauer and Nietzsche,** Arthur Schopenhauer (1778-1860) and Friedrich W. Nietzsche (1844-1900), German philosophers

self-restraint, obedience, sensitiveness to impulse from without. "Non fingendum aut excogitandum sed inveniendum quid Natura faciat aut ferat."

The success of this method staggers belief, and even to-day can be treated by history only as a miracle of growth, like the sports of nature. Evidently a new variety of mind had appeared. Certain men merely held out their hands—like Newton, watched an apple; like Franklin, flew a kite; like Watt, played with a tea-kettle—and great forces of nature stuck to them as though she were playing ball. Governments did almost nothing but resist. Even gunpowder and ordnance, the great weapon of government, showed little development between 1400 and 1800. Society was hostile or indifferent, as Priestly and Jenner, and even Fulton, with reason complained in the most advanced societies in the world, while its resistance became acute wherever the Church held control; until all mankind seemed to draw itself out in a long series of groups, dragged on by an attractive power in advance, which even the leaders obeyed without understanding, as the planets obeyed gravity, or the trees obeyed heat and light.

The influx of new force was nearly spontaneous. The reaction of mind on the mass of nature seemed not greater than that of a comet on the sun; and had the spontaneous influx of force stopped in Europe, society must have stood still, or gone backward, as in Asia or Africa. Then only economies of process would have counted as new force, and society would have been better pleased; for the idea that new force must be in itself a good is only an animal or vegetable instinct. As Nature developed her hidden energies, they tended to become destructive. Thought itself became tortured, suffering reluctantly, impatiently, painfully, the coercion of new method. Easy thought had always been movement of inertia, and mostly mere sentiment; but even the processes of mathematics measured feebly the needs of force.

The stupendous acceleration after 1800 ended in 1900 with the appearance of the new class of supersensual forces, before which the man of science stood at first as bewildered and helpless, as in the fourth century, a priest of Isis before the Cross of Christ.

This, then, or something like this, would be a dynamic formula of history. Any schoolboy knows enough to object at once that it is the oldest and most universal of all theories. Church and State, theology and philosophy, have always preached it, differing only in the allotment

of energy between nature and man. Whether the attractive energy has been called God or Nature, the mechanism has been always the same, and history is not obliged to decide whether the Ultimate tends to a purpose or not, or whether ultimate energy is one or many. Every one admits that the will is a free force, habitually decided by motives. No one denies that motives exist adequate to decide the will; even though it may not always be conscious of them. Science has proved that forces, sensible and occult, physical and metaphysical, simple and complex, surround, traverse, vibrate, rotate, repel, attract, without stop; that man's senses are conscious of few, and only in a partial degree; but that, from the beginning of organic existence his consciousness has been induced, expanded, trained in the lines of his sensitiveness; and that the rise of his faculties from a lower power to a higher, or from a narrower to a wider field, may be due to the function of assimilating and storing outside force or forces. There is nothing unscientific in the idea that, beyond the lines of force felt by the senses, the universe may be—as it has always been—either a supersensuous chaos or a divine unity, which irresistibly attracts, and is either life or death to penetrate. Thus far, religion, philosophy, and science seem to go hand in hand. The schools begin their vital battle only there. In the earlier stages of progress, the forces to be assimilated were simple and easy to absorb, but, as the mind of man enlarged its range, it enlarged the field of complexity, and must continue to do so, even into chaos, until the reservoirs of sensuous or supersensuous energies are exhausted, or cease to affect him, or until he succumbs to their excess.

For past history, this way of grouping its sequences may answer for a chart of relations although any serious student would need to invent another, to compare or correct its errors; but past history is only a value of relation to the future, and this value is wholly one of convenience, which can be tested only by experiment. Any law of movement must include, to make it a convenience, some mechanical formula of acceleration.

1907

---

2 **Non fingendum.** . . . "One must not invent or excogitate what nature does or produces, but one must find out" • 9 Watt, James Watt (1736-1819), Scottish inventor of the steam engine • 14 **Priestly,** Joseph Priestly. See note, p. 698 • 15 **Jenner,** Edward Jenner (1749-1823), famous English physician • 15 **Fulton,** Robert Fulton (1765-1815), American engineer and inventor

Chapter **6**

U. S. A.   1914 to the present

"U.S.A. is the slice of a continent. . . .
U.S.A. is the world's greatest rivervalley
fringed with mountains and hills. . . .
But mostly U.S.A. is the speech of the people."

Dos Passos

I. Intellectual Currents

The Modern Pessimism

Thinking of the Civil War, Hawthorne spoke of the tragedy in the lives of the women whose husbands and sweethearts were killed in battle: "The girls that would have loved them," he said, "and made happy firesides for them, will pine and wither, and tread along many sour and discontented years, and at last go out of life without knowing what life is. Every shot that takes effect kills one and worse than kills the other." This aspect of war's aftermath found expression in many literary works during and after World War I. Two illustrations will suffice: Amy Lowell's "Patterns" (1915) and Eugene O'Neill's *Strange Interlude* (1928). The poem is a powerful expression of sexual frustration:

> For the man who should loose me is dead,
> Fighting with the Duke of Flanders,
> In a pattern called a war.
> Christ! What are patterns for?

In the "strangled explosion" of the last line, "half-oath, half-prayer" (as Foster Damon, Miss Lowell's biographer, aptly describes it) is compressed much of war's misery. Instead of the rigid self-control described in Miss Lowell's poem, O'Neill, in a similar situation, shows breakdown. After the death of her fiancé in the war, Nina Leeds went to pieces, giving herself promiscuously to the men in an army hospital. One of the characters in the play attributed her behavior to "a desire to be kind" and "a morbid longing for martyrdom." In both instances the psychological effects of war on women are poignantly portrayed.

Other literary works deal with actual participants in World War I. John Dos Passos' *Three Soldiers* (1921) is concerned chiefly with the irksomeness of army life to a man of aesthetic temperament. John Andrews, graduate of Harvard, wanted to write great music. When he was arrested for desertion at the end of the story, the wind scattered about the room the leaves of the musical score on which he had been working. War is hateful to the artist, Dos Passos said, and destructive of his art. In the minds of many men—whether artists or persons of average sensitivity—the war left memories of experiences which they tried in vain to forget. The case of the war veteran, Stetson, in T. S. Eliot's *The Waste Land* (1922) is a classic instance. Stetson's tragic experience is likened to a corpse "planted" in a garden, which will either be dug up by "the Dog" of memory or "sprout" and "bloom" in the subconscious mind.

The tragic effects of World War I are best epitomized, perhaps, in Ernest Hemingway's *The Sun Also Rises* (1926) and *A Farewell to Arms* (1929). In *The Sun Also Rises* we are shown the "lost generation" of expatriates who, with shattered nerves and illusions, sought amusement and forgetfulness at bullfights in Spain and in the cafés of Paris. The chief character, Jake Barnes, had been made sexually impotent by a physical injury received in the war. His condition is symbolic of the spiritual impotence of the "lost generation." In *A Farewell to Arms* the war again deprived its victims of high aims and ideals. After the "Retreat from Caporetto" (which has been justly called the finest account in all literature of the collapse of an army) Frederic Henry, the American ambulance driver, could see nothing worth living for except physical satisfactions. In the wreckage of the world about him, thought became a torment and a futile occupation. Hence his famous conclusion: "I was not made to think. I was made to eat. My God, yes. Eat and drink and sleep with Catherine."

A New Criticism of America

We had entered World War I, as Woodrow Wilson (p. 793) expressed it, "to make the world safe for democracy," and the failure of that high mission produced a cynical reaction in many minds. Possibly the United States was hardly qualified to play such an exalted rôle. It was natural that many writers should turn a critical—sometimes a jaundiced—eye upon the American scene and that they should see much more to condemn than to admire. "Debunking" became a favorite literary approach; after Pearl Harbor it was called "selling America short."

Biographers of the 1920's attempted to show that our national idols had feet of clay. Historians insisted that

"The Survivor"—pen and ink drawing by George Grosz, 1936. Courtesy of the Art Institute of Chicago. The reaction of the artist to war and its horrors is dramatically illustrated in this drawing.

materialistic rather than idealistic motives had determined the entire course of our history since Jamestown and Plymouth Rock. The most popular magazine of the period among the literate was H. L. Mencken's *American Mercury,* which exposed in a monthly department called "Americana" a wealth of current stupidities—at once laughable and deplorable—culled from the newspapers of the forty-eight states.

The most effective and the most popular criticism of the American scene of the twenties was written by Sinclair Lewis (p. 1036). His *Main Street* (p. 1037) satirized the small town of the Middle West, where Lewis found "dullness made God." *Babbitt* (1922) ridiculed the American businessman so successfully that "Babbitt" and "Babbittry" were added to the dictionary. The hard-hitting satire got under the skins of many Rotarians and boosters. Among the items in Lewis' indictment were questionable business ethics, an undeveloped literary taste, commercial criteria of success, and ultraconservatism in social and political thinking. *Babbitt* epitomized the unlovely aspects of the Harding era. *Arrowsmith* (1925) showed an America inimical to scholarship and pure research. Heroically devoted to medical experimentation, Dr. Martin Arrowsmith found many stupid obstacles in his path. *Dodsworth* (1929) satirized the American woman. Fran Dodsworth was unmercifully exposed as a pampered, selfish, superficial, pretentious snob;

she is the most damning portrait in Lewis' entire gallery. Reading between the lines today, one can see that Lewis really enjoyed many of the people whom he ridiculed and relished much in the life which he professed to view with contempt, and that he would not exchange his Gopher Prairie or his Zenith for Utopia. But readers in the 1920's saw only the devastating satire; they hailed him as the greatest of all debunkers, being unaware that he transcended the narrow boundaries of the debunking age. His greatness may very well lie in the subtle quality which escaped his current readers.

Though Lewis was the chief of the satirists in the 1920's, many other writers presented indictments of America. Theodore Dreiser's *An American Tragedy* (1925) showed a society vitiated by perverted notions of the good life. Though the reader might wonder if Clyde Griffiths would have amounted to much under ideal conditions, the mores of his materialistic and class-conscious world were bad enough to corrupt a stronger character. Carl Sandburg (p. 904) exposed the increasing evils of capitalism: "people living in shanties," "$6 a week department store girls," "steel trust wops, dead without having lived, gray and shrunken at forty years of age." Allied with Big Business, the Church, Sandburg charged, travestied the teachings of Jesus. Following Sandburg's lead, other writers directed attention to conditions among the workers, and the word "proletariat" came for the first time into general American use. O'Neill's *The Hairy Ape* (p. 976) presented the worker's growing dissociation from his work, his growing feeling of not "belonging." Carlyle had pointed out nearly a hundred years earlier the inadequacy, from the human standpoint, of the "cash-payment nexus": a feeling of loyalty, of belonging, is necessary to a man's satisfaction in his work. It is still perhaps the central problem of modern industrialism. While O'Neill expressed the problem in stirring modern terms, he offered nothing constructive: the conclusion of *The Hairy Ape* is futile and defeatist. In another remarkable play of the twenties (*The Adding Machine,* 1923), Elmer Rice argued that the modern machine had a degrading effect upon the worker, that machine-tending is the lowest of all serfdoms in human history, and that man deteriorates as the machine improves. It seemed bitterly ironical to the author that "the finest triumph of the evolutionary process" should be a machine-tender, "operating a super-hyper-adding

machine with the great toe of his right foot." A distinguished anthropologist expressed a similar view of the problem when he said: "There is real danger that the engineers will make apes of all of us. By the invention of tools, engineers brought man up from the level of an ape, but the human curve starts downward when tools can be used without cerebral exertion, when the individual is allowed not only to stop sweating but also to stop thinking."

Despite these and other searching criticisms, the general public of the 1920's was relatively complacent. For the three consecutive administrations of Harding, Coolidge, and Hoover, political conservatism was predominant. Successful investors enjoyed a rapidly mounting "prosperity." Yale undergraduates (see Lewis' *Dodsworth*) aspired to become Wall Street brokers and owners of yachts. Poor boys with ability and nerve, like Fitzgerald's Gatsby, (*The Great Gatsby*, 1925), amassed wealth quickly and spent it gaudily in the attempt to realize the dreams of their youth; Fitzgerald's novel, indeed, is a brilliant representation of the tinsel and corruption of this whole fabulous era. A few economists foresaw the crash of 1929, but their warnings were overridden by the mania for money. Irving Fisher and President Hoover assured us to the bitter end that the economic structure of the country was "fundamentally sound." After the crash came the Great Depression.

During the years of the Great Depression, criticism of America in literature became more serious, more bitter, and more brutal. Whether the accounts presented were of contemporary life or of life in an earlier period, many writers joined in a strident, damning chorus. With lurid, Gothic power, William Faulkner's novels told of violence and moral perversion in "Jefferson," Mississippi. These works were to acquire for later readers rich symbolic meanings: in the words of his best interpreter, George Marion O'Donnell, Faulkner "projected in fiction the conflict between his inherent traditional values and the modern world." Nearer the naturalistic level was James T. Farrell's *Studs Lonigan* (1932-1935), which showed the collapse of middle-class morality in southside Chicago. The traditional character-building institutions—the home, the school, and the church—were powerless to prevent the moral ruin of Studs. Again starkly, but with human warmth, John Steinbeck's *The Grapes of Wrath* (p. 1150)—perhaps the best single ex-

"*Years of Dust*"—*poster by Ben Shahn for the Resettlement Administration, 1936. Courtesy of the Downtown Gallery*

pression in our literature of the difficulties peculiar to the Depression—told of the Joads of Oklahoma, who were tractored off the land, of their Westward migration in a jalopy, and of their sufferings in California, where the family of seven workers, including women and children, were able to earn the sum total of $3.50 a day. The book gives an impression of a powerful mass movement: the Okies are less arresting as individuals than as representatives of the mass. The proletarian novel "arrived" in *The Grapes of Wrath*.

The Dominance of Science and Quasi-Science

Not only the wreckage of war and the mounting criticism of American economic and social life, but science too contributed to the dominant mood of pessimism be-

tween the wars. Perhaps it would be more correct to say "popular science," for the reference is not to science as such, but to its embodiment in literature, where it is easily susceptible of misconstruction and falsification. In any case, the scientist is hardly to blame. It is regrettable that some of his discoveries had unfortunate results.

The new physics gave the impression to the lay mind that the universe is somehow doomed. Historians and interpreters of science had much to say in the twenties and thirties about the second law of thermodynamics or the law of entropy, which seemed to mean that energy is deteriorating or becoming less available, that the universe is cooling off and running down, and that the earth will someday be unfit for human habitation. The ultimate destination of man on this planet appeared to be the "heat-death." This view of things colored the thinking of many moderns, writers and readers alike; it found its most forceful literary expression in the poetry of Robinson Jeffers (p. 932), who wrote in "To the Stone-Cutters":

. . . man will be blotted out, the blithe earth die,
the brave sun Die blind, his heart blackening.

It was better so, the poet reasoned, for he saw in man's deepest nature a subconscious desire to return to the pre-natal darkness and silence of the womb. In "Night" he declared,

The sun-lovers have a blond favorite,
A father of lights and noises, wars, weeping, and laughter,
Hot labor, lust and delight and the other blemishes. Quietness
Flows from her deeper fountain; and he [the sun] will die; and she [the night] is immortal.

Inspired by the new physics, Jeffers regarded life as a "blemish," and extinction as the greatest good.

Freudian psychology, too, left its mark everywhere in the literature between the wars. Possibly the first fictional work in America to exemplify the conscious and deliberate use of Freudian principles was Sherwood Anderson's *Winesburg, Ohio* (1919, see p. 1015), where almost everyone is abnormal and the abnormalities are explained in terms of sexual repression. O'Neill's *Strange Interlude* and *Mourning Becomes Electra* (1931) appear to have been constructed from Freudian blue-prints. The new psychological principles were employed also in biography and literary history. Psychoanalyzing Poe (*Edgar Allan Poe,* 1926), Joseph Wood Krutch believed that Poe's sexual impotence accounted for much that is distinctive in his poems and tales. Applying Freud to American literary history (*Expression in America,* 1932), Ludwig Lewisohn was able to reveal an amazing number and variety of psychological maladies among men of letters: Hawthorne's sense of guilt, for example, was "precipitated by the incest wish of infancy." By the middle thirties many sophisticated moderns, through a kind of "scientific" mania for sex-analysis and sex-experimentation, had succeeded in making themselves almost as morbid on the subject as the prudish, hypocritical Victorians, whom they regarded with unmitigated horror (note Lewisohn's remarks on Howells in *Expression in America*).

Closely associated in the popular mind with Freudian psychology was the biology of glandular secretions, which, to many, seemed a new source of tyranny. Oversexed persons, like Lady Brett in Hemingway's *The Sun Also Rises,* could blame the endocrine or some other glands for their immoral behavior. Stupid, brutal persons, like Lennie in Steinbeck's *Of Mice and Men* (1937), could point to hypothyroidism as the sign of their fate. Little by little, the modern sciences, which had begun as a great liberating force, seemed to be imprisoning man as tightly as he had ever been imprisoned by the pseudo-sciences of the Middle Ages.

The new sciences of economics and sociology also tended to overplay their legitimate rôles. Charles A. Beard (*An Economic Interpretation of the Constitution,* 1913) and his successors exaggerated the importance of economic factors in American history. V. L. Parrington (*Main Currents in American Thought,* 1927-1930) and his disciples likewise exaggerated the importance of economic elements in American literature. It is not surprising that in much of the fiction of the period economic pressure appeared decisive or that before the end of the period man's life appeared to consist, contrary to Holy Writ, in the amount of commodities which he possessed. Meanwhile, social pressures vied strenuously with the economic ones for the honor of being the chief determinant in human destiny. William Graham Sumner had declared that folkways were decisive, and his successors elaborated and illustrated the proposition. Clyde Griffiths

in Dreiser's *An American Tragedy* and Studs Lonigan in Farrell's trilogy demonstrated brilliantly enough the apparent impossibility of escape from the mores.

The Helplessness of the Individual

Many signs, in short, seemed to point to the growing helplessness of the individual. There appeared no longer to be any such thing as an autonomous and morally responsible person. In actual life, of course, there continued to be many such persons, but the species well-nigh disappeared from books written in the spirit of the age. This spirit found its best philosophical statement in Joseph Wood Krutch's *The Modern Temper* (1929). Modern civilization, to Krutch, was decadent, for thought itself is a mark of decadence. The future belongs, as always, to the barbarians, "absorbed in the processes of life for their own sake, eating without asking if it is worth while to eat, begetting children without asking why they should beget them, and conquering without asking for what purpose they conquer."

The poets brilliantly expressed the mood of failure and despair. Robinson's "man against the sky" was by no means sure that he was not pursuing a

> blind atomic pilgrimage
> Whereon by crass chance billeted we go. . . .

Eliot gave the classic picture of futility in "Prufrock" (p. 942):

"I have measured out my life with coffee spoons. . . ."

The Hamlet of A. MacLeish (1928) echoed, with modern mutations and overtones, the despair of Shakespeare's Hamlet:

> Thou wouldst not think
> How ill all's here about my heart!

These three poems may be taken as sufficiently characteristic of the period. The Hamlet mood was congenial to all of them, but they exemplified Hamlet's confusion and indecision rather than his capacity for heroic action. Hart Crane's suicide in 1932 was a shocking and symbolic dramatization of the poet's despair in an age of doubt and anxiety.

While Krutch and the intellectual poets were displaying the helplessness of the thinking man, entangled in the toils of thought, the novelists were discovering an-

other kind of helplessness in the masses of men—a helplessness obviously not explicable by intellectualism, but by biological and social determinism. Several novels already mentioned—*An American Tragedy, Studs Lonigan, The Grapes of Wrath*—abundantly illustrate the tyranny of social and economic pressure and the impotence of the individual in the face of overwhelming circumstance. But the most complete illustration in American fiction of the modern determinism is Dos Passos' *U.S.A.* (1930-1936), which is at once—in the apt description of Alfred Kazin—"the dominant social novel of the thirties" and "the coldest and most mechanical of tragic novels." It is indeed our largest and most comprehensive fictional gallery of human automatons. The reader finds it difficult, if not impossible, to take an interest in its people as persons: it has been justly said that Dos Passos did not create character. The twenty-odd people in *U.S.A.* (p. 1098) exhibit the mechanical behavior, the unawareness, the moral irresponsibility, of robots, as they are pushed about over the continents by irrational force. A contradiction in the novel, of which the author may not have been aware, affords the only ground for hope: unlike the fictional characters, the subjects of the "biographies," which were taken from contemporary history, are by no means helpless. The discrepancy suggests how far the pattern of the social novel in the middle thirties had deviated from life.

Counter Attitudes

American literature between the wars was thus predominantly pessimistic. It would be a mistake, however, to suppose that all American literature in this period was negative and despairing. The old positive forces were not dead; they were rooted too deep in man's nature to die. It goes without saying that certain names appearing among those supporting the prevalent pessimism will reappear among those expressing more positive views, for few writers were entirely negative or completely pessimistic.

First among the positive forces was what Browning called "our manhood's prime vigor": "How good is man's life, the mere living!" exclaimed that now unfashionable Victorian poet. However outmoded his message, one would not expect to find an entire generation of Ameri-

can writers silent on this theme. In fact, it appears frequently in the literature of the period between the wars. The most notable examples of *élan vital* are found in the writings of those incorrigible romanticists, Ernest Hemingway (p. 1124) and Thomas Wolfe (p. 1133). Whatever the state of the world at large might be, these writers were still able to enjoy living. No author has ever shown a greater avidity for life than Wolfe. In this respect he stands at the opposite pole from Jeffers. No author has ever celebrated friendship and love with greater ardor and tenderness than Hemingway. At the end of *For Whom the Bell Tolls* (1940), Robert Jordan "told himself," "You had a lot of luck to have had such a good life."

Other instinctive forces which would not down, no matter how mechanical or scientific the age, were the love of the earth, the love of humanity, the love of country—they appeared separately and combined in a variety of patterns. The good earth was never better than in the poems of Robert Frost (p. 893), and was never exhibited with greater tang or economic urgency than in the essays of the Southern Agrarians (*I'll Take My Stand,* 1930), who brilliantly argued for the way of life of Thomas Jefferson and John Taylor of Caroline. Love of humanity still manifested itself, ranging from individuals to the mass, from personal kindness to faith in the common man. Sandburg was devoted to "the people" with an ardor as warm as Whitman's and more militant. People were "beautiful" to William Saroyan. Steinbeck's characters had a friendly warmth: human kindness could hardly go further than in the concluding scene of *The Grapes of Wrath.* Love of country still flourished, ranging between a lively sense of the past and its historic glories and a passionate, instinctive attachment to the place of one's birth. Stephen Vincent Benét (p. 1005) was inspired by the history of the Civil War to write our best historical narrative in verse in *John Brown's Body* (1928). Wolfe's devotion to America was more instinctive. To him, it was the "fabulous country —the place where miracles not only happen, but where they happen all the time" (*Of Time and the River,* 1935). Like Whitman, he tried to take in all of America equally, though neither quite succeeded; for just as Whitman's affection was intensely localized in Manhattan and the Brooklyn Ferry, so Wolfe's was rooted deepest in "old Catawba, there in the hills of home."

The positive forces thus far considered were largely instinctive, but there were also positive intellectual and moral forces at work in the literature of the twenties and thirties. In the midst of a world which appeared given over to naturalism and lawlessness, the "neo-humanists"—Paul Elmer More, Irving Babbitt, and Norman Foerster—argued for the necessity of discipline, of standards of excellence, and of traditional values. Control must come from within, they reasoned; the "inner check" is the only saving virtue, and the most available sources of that virtue are the classic disciplines (*Humanism and America,* 1930, by Foerster and others). Less "humanistic" but more human and genuinely fortifying was the note sounded with charm and firmness by two of the finest novelists of the period—Ellen Glasgow and Willa Cather. While most of the male novelists were advertising failure, Miss Glasgow and Miss Cather preferred to show the possibility of success. In *Barren Ground* (1925), Miss Glasgow reversed two stock pictures of failure: failure on the farm and failure through disappointment in love. It had been generally supposed that success of any sort on a farm was no longer possible, but Dorinda Oakley actually reclaimed the barren ground, thereby fulfilling Lanier's prophecy in "Corn" fifty years earlier. It had been generally supposed, too—especially in the South—that a girl could scarcely survive disappointment in love, but Dorinda survived. "Dorinda exists," Miss Glasgow declared, "wherever the spirit of fortitude has triumphed over the sense of futility." Miss Cather also showed the triumph of fortitude. *My Antonia* (1918) portrayed a pioneer immigrant woman, passionately devoted to her family and to her life on the Nebraska prairie, triumphant over difficulties which would have defeated a less robust soul. It is a beautiful and heart-warming picture. *Death Comes for the Archbishop* (1927) is likewise a story of heroism—the heroism of two Catholic missionaries in the Spanish Southwest. They made a great team: Latour curbing Vaillant's rashness, Vaillant stimulating and inspiring Latour. The building of the cathedral in Santa Fé was a splendid culmination of their efforts. Even in the pessimistic gloom of the years between the wars, Miss Cather and Miss Glasgow—brave women—were able to say: Success is the reward of the stronghearted. This is the meaning of America, and of life.

One other force on the positive side must be men-

tioned, religious faith. In the literature of no other period in our history had the note of religious faith been so nearly absent. Its rare occurrence seemed anachronistic to many readers, though later generations may judge otherwise of—to mention two commanding examples—*Death Comes for the Archbishop* and *Ash-Wednesday* (1930). "Where there is great love," Father Latour said, "there are always miracles. The miracles of the Church seem to me to rest not so much upon faces or voices or healing power coming suddenly near to us from afar off, but upon our perceptions being made finer, so that for a moment our eyes can see and our ears can hear what there is about us always." If Miss Cather's case for religion was chiefly emotional and aesthetic, T. S. Eliot's was chiefly intellectual. After the futility of "The Love Song of J. Alfred Prufrock" (1917) and the despair of *The Waste Land*—the most powerful single statement of the aridity of the world between the wars and the most influential poem of the century —Eliot moved firmly on to the religious position of *Ash-Wednesday* (p. 956). The poem does not record an easy victory. There is no disposition to nurse the illusion that the modern man can recover the spontaneous, unquestioning faith of an earlier age: the poet does not "hope to know again the infirm glory of the positive hour." The road to belief is a tortuous one, and is symbolized in the poem by a staircase which one climbs with difficulty, and down which one can see the "twisted shapes" left below. Final attainment is possible only through realizing the necessity of surrendering the individual will to the divine will. *Ash-Wednesday* concludes with Dante's words, "Our peace in His will," which are themselves a rephrasing of the words of Jesus, "Not my will but thine be done."

The usual contemporary comment on the religious attitudes of Miss Cather and Eliot was that they were impossible because they were essentially medieval attitudes inapplicable to modern times. The objection loses its weight if the values of religion are timeless.

The Political Struggle

The years between 1914 and the present seem to fall into a series of periods each of which profoundly affected the lives of all Americans: World War I, reluctantly entered by the United States in 1917; the period of peacemaking, which ended with general disillusionment about the value of the war; the boom-time era, which, after several portents had been unnoted, ended with the stock-market crash of 1929; the period of depression, followed by slow recovery; then the period during which the world drifted toward another great war; and finally World War II and its aftermath.

Each of these eras was marked by political disputes, some of them unusually bitter. Looking back, we may see that the domestic conflict centered upon the rôle of the state versus the rôle of the individual, while the conflict concerning our foreign relations set isolationism against participation in world affairs.

The domestic policies of the Democrats under Woodrow Wilson (p. 793) were thus summarized by the party in 1916: "We found our country hampered by

"The Campaign"—cartoon by Hugh Hutton from **The** Philadelphia Inquirer, *October 1936. See page 762 for a cartoon favorable to the New Deal.*

special privilege, a vicious tariff, obsolete banking laws and an inelastic currency. . . . Under our administration, under a leadership that has never faltered, these abuses have been corrected and our people freed therefrom." Such was the work of Wilson's "New Freedom," as seen by his followers. The Republican presidents who came into office after the war, by contrast, tended to give business a freer hand and to increase tariffs. Harding, Coolidge, and Hoover (p. 807) tended to emphasize free enterprise and minimize governmental control. Hoover wrote in 1922: "Salvation will not come to us out of the wreckage of individualism. What we need today is steady devotion to a better, brighter, broader individualism—an individualism that carries increasing responsibilty and service to our fellows." Those who took an opposing point of view, championed by Franklin D. Roosevelt (p. 820), came into power after Hoover's policies failed to end the depression which had begun in 1929. Their position was that the federal government had to assume a greater responsibility in curbing a ruthless economic individualism and in assisting

its victims. The "New Deal," as a result, comprised many measures which limited the scope of free enterprise. On into the 1940's and 1950's the battle of free enterprise versus a modified form of collectivism continued.

The attitude of the general public moved more in harmony in the discussion of international affairs. At the end of World War I, the public was in favor of the League of Nations and the participation of the United States in world affairs. After the disillusionment of the peace, however, the country tended toward pacifism and isolationism. As Fascism and Nazism developed in the 1930's, and as the inevitability of war became increasingly apparent, a growing and soon dominant group became convinced that the United States could no longer separate itself, either in war or in peace, from the rest of the world.

The Impact of World War II

The outbreak of war in Europe in 1939, our lend-lease to Britain and to Russia, our own entrance into the War following Japan's attack on Pearl Harbor in December 1941, all had the effect, primarily, of stepping up the tempo of American production and, secondarily, of throwing into partial eclipse the social objectives of the New Deal. Once more, American initiative, resourcefulness, and know-how were lauded to the skies; once more the American entrepreneur became the man of the hour. Certain aspects of American life which had been objects of scorn or disdain by writers like Lewis and Dos Passos suddenly became things to be cherished. During the war years, 1941-1945, and for a good while thereafter, one heard no slurs at Babbittry, or American industrialism, or the Middle West, that favorite butt of the 1920's; the Middle West, indeed, was now "the bread basket of the free world," "the arsenal of democracy." We were engaged in a war of survival, and the chief factors which were to contribute to our victory were the superior technology and productive power of American industry and American agriculture.

After World War II, the demand for top production continued with little if any abatement. For several years America was called upon to feed the ravaged portions of Europe. And not long after the War's end, despite

THE WAILING WALL!

"The Wailing Wall!"—cartoon by H. M. Talburt in Scripps-Howard Newspapers, May 1935

the hopeful auspices under which the United Nations organization had been launched in San Francisco in 1945, a new tension and rivalry came into being between the United States and Russia and assumed, before a great while, alarming proportions. One result of this new international rivalry was an intense and tremendously expensive competition in armaments, especially in the development and production of atomic bombs and other new weapons. American industry was again called upon for all-out production. In short, since 1941 and earlier, American material productivity has been, and continues to be, essential to our national survival. It is small wonder, therefore, that some of the older satire of the American scene has seemed less forceful and that some of the older subjects of satire have become less available, despite the fact that American materialism and its concomitants are scarcely more lovely now than they were in the 1920's. It is one of the greater contemporary misfortunes that American materialism must be more emphasized than ever before as the price of existence itself.

Postwar Attitudes

At the midcentury and after, it became increasingly clear that a changed attitude toward America on the part of our writers and artists, and on the part of intellectuals generally, was gradually taking shape. The editors of one of our more advanced literary quarterlies, for example, implied their belief, in 1952, that "a re-affirmation and rediscovery of America is under way" ("Our Country and Our Culture: A Symposium," *Partisan Review,* May-June 1952). The editors went on to quote Edmund Wilson, distinguished critic and for many years literary editor of *The New Yorker:*

> My optimistic opinion is that the United States at the present time is politically more advanced than any other part of the world. . . . We have seen in the last fifty years a revival of the democratic creativeness which presided at the birth of the Republic and flourished through the Civil War. This began to assert itself strongly during the first two decades of this century, was stimulated by the depression that followed the blowing-up of the Stock Market, and culminated in the New Deal.

It was accompanied by a remarkable renascence of American arts and letters.*

One may well inquire, what is the nature of this changed attitude? What are some of the reasons for the change, and how valid are these reasons? And what has been the effect upon the course of American letters?

The altered international situation has been, to be sure, a basic factor in producing a changed intellectual climate. Reduced to a state of collapse by World War II, Western Europe found itself dependent upon the United States both economically and politically. The United States, almost overnight, became the chief bulwark of Western culture. The alternative offered by Soviet Russia in 1950 was intolerable even to those who had liked (or thought they liked) Soviet Russia in 1930. The threatened destruction by Russia of all that we hold dear has stimulated on all sides, and especially among those who felt themselves estranged at an earlier time or were most vocal in their censure, the fresh realization that America is the last best hope of earth.

An equally important reason, no doubt, for a changed attitude toward America on the part of our writers is the simple fact that far-reaching social and economic reform at home during the first half of the twentieth century has removed many of the grievances which prompted our earlier fiction of protest. At the midcentury, the condition of the laborer had been improved to the point where books like Mary Wilkins Freeman's *Portion of Labor* and Upton Sinclair's *Jungle* had no contemporary relevance. Supported by government subsidies, the long-underpaid farmers had achieved such prosperity, by and large, that there was no further need for pleas and angry protests in their behalf, like Hamlin Garland's *Main-Travelled Roads* or John Steinbeck's *The Grapes of Wrath*. Government regulation of business had put an end to the predatory practices which "Big Business" had often indulged in during an earlier age, as well as to such shenanigans as those exposed in books like Dreiser's *The Financier* and *The Titan*.

This, of course, is not to say that evils deserving exposure and satire no longer exist. The position of minority groups, for example, is still just cause for grief, and books like Lillian Smith's *Strange Fruit* (1944) and

---

*From **Europe Without Baedeker** by Edmund Wilson, Doubleday & Co., Inc.

Laura Hobson's *Gentleman's Agreement* (1947) are sufficient indication that our novelists are still alive to the need for social reform. But the social progress achieved by the "trust-busting" of Theodore Roosevelt, the New Freedom of Woodrow Wilson, and the New Deal of Franklin Roosevelt has had the effect of making American society comparatively enlightened and has minimized for the novelist of today an area which was of major importance in an earlier era.

Still another factor in the altered climate of the mid-century years has been the rediscovery and reappraisal of some of the traditional items and values in the American experience. Thrown back upon our own country, as it were, and finding ourselves in a position of world leadership, we were not long in discovering some good things previously scorned or underrated, but now seen as worthy to be admired and cherished. One thing found good, and worthy of appreciative study, was the evolution of American democratic thought from Jefferson through subsequent leaders like Jackson, Lincoln, Wilson, and Franklin Roosevelt. Another discovery exciting to many readers, was the older literature of America; it was suddenly seen that writers like Thoreau, Hawthorne, Melville, Whitman, Mark Twain, Dickinson, and James required no apology in any court of literary opinion, that they were among the great writers of modern times. And still another good thing of the American past—now poignantly recognized as good and essential, though difficult to regain if once lost—was religious faith. World War II and its aftermath seemed to inculcate anew man's sinfulness, and man's need for God. Neo-Thomism and Neo-Orthodoxy were names given to movements of thought which looked for solutions, respectively, to Catholic and to Protestant fountains of truth and inspiration. The popular influence of a Catholic writer like Fulton John Sheen and the more intellectual influence of a Protestant theologian like Reinhold Niebuhr are indications of midcentury trends toward religion. The midcentury literary critics also began to strike the religious note. Though apparently concerned primarily with questions of technique, they began to find in the literature they admired—whether Donne or Shakespeare or Hawthorne or Melville or James—moral and religious values. Writers lacking moral profundity and religious insight, writers who were not serious, and had no helpful realistic light to throw upon the human condition, were more and more ignored by the reigning critics of the period.

These and other causes, then, have contributed to an altered attitude toward America. It must not be supposed, however, that there are just grounds for complacency, for new dangers confront us. Fear of Russia already tends to establish a rigid patriotic conformity as the order of the day, threatening that spirit of nonconformity which has been one of the chief glories of the American tradition—whether in Roger Williams or Thoreau or Whitman or Thomas Wolfe. The emphasis upon accelerated material production in the continuing national emergency, the diversion of scientific research into military channels, the growing reliance upon technology—these and other foes arise, threatening to bind our souls with secular chains. Our writers have been aware of these dangers.

If John Dos Passos in his later trilogy, *District of Columbia,* published in 1952, takes a more favorable view of the American way of life than in his famous earlier trilogy, *U.S.A.,* published in 1937; if Van Wyck Brooks in his widely read literary histories—beginning with *The Flowering of New England* (1936) and continuing through *The Confident Years* (1952)—shows an America hospitable to the writer and his art, instead of hostile, as Brooks had argued in earlier works like *Letters and Leadership* (1918) and *The Ordeal of Mark Twain* (1920); still it must not be inferred that Dos Passos and Brooks and other older writers whom we have seen change their view of America have ended in fatuous complacency. It is rather that the years which bring the philosophic mind have brought to these older writers a realistic adjustment to the world in which we live.

Such an adjustment is difficult for the very young, and perhaps even undesirable. John W. Aldridge's sober and objective report (in *After the Lost Generation,* 1951) on the young novelists who have emerged since World War II* shows that these young men have been much less successful in finding their métier than were their distinguished predecessors—Hemingway, Fitzgerald, and Dos Passos—in the years just after World War

---

* The young novelists treated in Aldridge's survey are: Norman Mailer, Irwin Shaw, John Horne Burns, Truman Capote, Gore Vidal, Alfred Hayes, Paul Bowles, Merle Miller, Frederick Buechner, and Vance Bourjaily

I. Aldridge sums up the plight of beginning writers today as follows:

> They are finding that modern life is still basically purposeless, that the typical condition of modern man is still doubt, confusion, and fear. But because they have never known life otherwise and were not exposed, as their predecessors were, to the process by which it became as it now is, they can write of it from neither the perspective of protest nor that of disillusionment and loss . . . . Loss is no longer the spiritual climate of the age, but the chaos of loss is still its typical material.

There is no denying the difficulties which confront the young writer today. But, by the same token, there is no denying the difficulties which confront the young writer in any period. A certain robustness and toughness are always requisite. Aldridge well states the omnipresent need as follows:

> What we need today to give us a literature of vitality and significance . . . is a few writers of genius, men who would be able to go on day in and day out, year in and year out, patiently creating out of their own spiritual resources master works of art . . . . They would have to be big enough and dedicated enough to withstand all our efforts to kill them, frighten them, buy them off, or send them to prison.

It is perhaps too early to say if the young novelists discussed by Aldridge (and other young novelists not discussed by him) are writers of true genius, "able to go on day in and day out." It is perhaps too early also to make confident predictions about the young poets presented with admirable commentary (by the editor and by the poets themselves) in John Ciardi's anthology, *Mid-Century American Poets* (1950) * Ciardi's description of the temper of these poets and their work is doubtless applicable to the most recent trends in American verse generally:

> These poets will listen to the authority of sense and talent, as it is, for instance, obvious that all of them have paid homage to Mr. Eliot's poetry and criticism, but once they have listened, they all in-

sist on their own freedom to accept or reject according to their own view. It is never, then, a poetry of movements and manifestoes. It is more nearly a blend of the classical and the metaphysical, a poetry of individual appraisal, tentative, self-questioning, introspective, socially involved, and always reserving for itself the right to meet experience in its humanistic environment—the uncoerced awareness of the individual man, which in art must be subjected always to principles of craftsmanship. It is therefore a poetry of great variety, and of some difficulty, but a poetry capable of offering great rewards.

This is doubtless a valuable statement. And yet, despite the emphasis here on independence, freshness, and variety, it seems clear enough that at the midcentury the modes established by Eliot and Pound more than thirty years earlier were still regnant in American verse.

The New Criticism

Possibly the outstanding new trend in literature during the 1940's and 1950's was the prominence given to the so-called "New Criticism." For the first time in our literary history, there seemed to be more practicing critics than poets, or novelists, or dramatists. Literary quarterlies like *The Kenyon Review, The Sewanee Review, The Partisan Review, The Hopkins Review,* and *The Hudson Review*—and many others of a similar kind—were so largely devoted to criticism that some midcentury observers said that our age had become more critical than creative.

The New Criticism was, in its inception, primarily a protest against the historical approach emphasized by professors and graduate schools. The new critics rightly insisted that a literary work—whether poem, play, story, or novel—is a work of art, that it has a uniqueness, an independent life of its own, that it is its own excuse for

---

* The young poets included in Ciardi's anthology are: Richard Wilbur, Peter Viereck, Muriel Rukeyser, Theodore Roethke, Karl Shapiro, Winfield Townley Scott, John Frederick Nims, E. L. Mayo, Robert Lowell, Randall Jarrell, John Holmes, Richard Eberhart, John Ciardi, Elizabeth Bishop, and Delmore Schwartz

being. They deplored the historical emphasis, which substituted for the close analysis of a literary work a biographical and historical commentary on the author's life and his age, the circumstances of composition, textual variants, and other matters which the new critics maintained were irrelevant to the aesthetic question. Allen Tate threw down the gauntlet in his "Miss Emily and the Bibliographers" (1940). For a good many years there were lively skirmishes between "historians" and "critics."

The most valuable product of the movement was a considerable body of important critical writing, writing which subjected literature—particularly individual works of literature—to a new kind of scrutiny. Critics had not often before examined literary texts so closely and so perceptively. T. S. Eliot and I. A. Richards were early leaders. They were soon followed by such expert practitioners as Yvor Winters, R. P. Blackmur, Allen Tate, John Crowe Ransom, Kenneth Burke, Cleanth Brooks, Robert Penn Warren, Philip Rahv, and Lionel Trilling, to name only a few. These critics differ a good deal among themselves: Brooks, for example, has been concerned largely with the tensions and paradoxes of the individual poem; Burke, with semantic suggestiveness; Trilling, with symbolic overtones; and so on. But they all agree in placing the individual work at the center and in focusing our attention upon that. Meanwhile, *Understanding Poetry* (1938) by Brooks and Warren, and many subsequent volumes modeled after it, brought about important changes in the reading and teaching of literature in America.

The new critical movement for a time seemed in danger of carrying its principles too far when it tended to divorce the literary work from its milieu. A more recent trend seems to recognize the fact that history as well as analysis has its place in literary study, and many signs now point to a rapprochement between the warring schools. But the contribution of the New Criticism—despite the inevitable vagaries—remains a solid one. Thanks to the efforts of its practitioners, the literary work itself has regained its rightful primacy.

Southern Revival

Regionally speaking, the most dramatic aspect of American literary history in the 1940's and 1950's has been the renaissance in the Southern states. The award of the Nobel Prize to William Faulkner in 1950 brought to the world's attention a literary state of affairs which students had been aware of for some time. In recent Southern literature, surely, we find none of the decline, the negation, the impotence which Aldridge laments in his group of jaded, world-weary young novelists—the writers who are denied even the stimulus of disillusion, because they have never had any illusions to lose. When one recalls the poetry and criticism of John Crowe Ransom, Allen Tate, and Randall Jarrell, and the prose fiction of Katherine Anne Porter, William Faulkner, and Robert Penn Warren (to mention a few of the chief practitioners), one realizes the vitality and strength, as well as artistry, of the Southern movement.

It may well be that the Southern writers have drawn upon a reservoir of power long since denied to writers elsewhere. Southern writers as a class are more indigenous, and more deeply rooted in, and more loyal to, their nativity than most modern writers of other regions. The South, moreover, has been less affected than other regions by certain modern movements and attitudes; by industry, by science, by progressive thought, by amorality, by ennui—by a number of modern influences, in short, which have perhaps made the writer's task more difficult. The South, instead, has preserved tenaciously its traditional beliefs, its religion, its superstitions and folklore, its speech, its feudal arrangements, its code of manners. These things make up a rich fund of materials for the writer, and if a radical social change is taking place (as is the case in the contemporary South), then the writer's awareness of the old order and its passing becomes acute, and a condition favorable to literary creation (or so goes a theory which seems plausible enough) is thereby brought about.

But in whatever way one explains the extraordinary literary activity of the modern South, this much at least can be said: that a good many Southern writers today appear "big enough and dedicated enough" to withstand any efforts from whatever source that might be made "to kill them, frighten them, buy them off, or send them to prison." At this late date, the Southern experience is finding for the first time a full, free expression in literature. Enriched and matured by defeat, conflict, and tragedy, this experience seems peculiarly usable today in the dramatic presentation (as in books like Faulkner's *Light in August* and Warren's *All the King's Men*) of the paradoxes of life and the contradictions at the heart of all human truth.

It remains to be seen if the modern Southern flowering can furnish to the country at large a literary leadership comparable to that furnished by the New England flowering of a century ago. Faulkner's Nobel Prize Speech, which struck a humanistic note too rare in our century, seemed to evoke, encouragingly enough, a sympathetic response everywhere. In this memorable little speech, which recalled in a surprising manner one of the chief writers of the New England flowering, Nathaniel Hawthorne, Faulkner said that "the problems of the human heart in conflict with itself . . . alone can make good writing because only that is worth writing about, worth the agony and the sweat." "A writer," he said, "should have no room in his workshop for anything but the old verities and truths of the heart, the old universal truths, lacking which any story is ephemeral and doomed —love and honor and pity and pride and compassion and sacrifice." He refused "to accept the end of man." Man, he declared, is "immortal . . . because he has a soul, a spirit capable of compassion and sacrifice and endurance." The writer's great function is to "help man endure by lifting up his heart." The writer's works should be "not merely the record of man" but "one of the props, the pillars, to help him endure and prevail."

These words of William Faulkner at Stockholm—the most impressive words that were spoken in the mid-century years by a creative writer anywhere in the Western world—suggest to us the direction which humane letters must always take.   R.S.

II. Literary Trends

If names meant anything, the literary movement which began about 1914 was, at first, a "little" movement. In cities and towns all over the nation and, after World War I, in Paris and London, "little groups" devoted themselves to the modest project of revolutionizing literature. They produced plays in "little theaters" and pub-

First Expatriate American: "Garçon, what was that piece the orchestra just played?" "That, M'sieu, was 'The Star Spangled Banner'!"—cartoon by Gardner Rea from Life, *April 5, 1929*

lished poems and stories in "little magazines." The oft-repeated word "little" proclaimed hostility to "big" theatrical producers and "big" national magazines and publishing houses which catered to masses of people.

The word also implied rebellion against the alleged conservatism and shallowness of writers for large audiences. Such writers, the rebels contended, prolonged the thoughtless optimism, the prudishness, the simple and unlifelike depictions, of "The Victorians." Like literary rebels who had started movements in previous ages, modern writers looked to other times and other lands for models which met their peculiar needs. Dramatists turned for inspiration to the experimental playwrights of Europe. Poets turned to radical American poets of the past (such as Emily Dickinson, Walt Whitman, and Stephen Crane) and to the poets of France and Great Britain. Novelists looked back to American realists and naturalists or looked abroad for contemporary models. Adapting the methods of a host of un-Victorian authors, American writers between World Wars I and II produced highly experimental works which they believed represented life more truly than older writings had.

And though the movement, at the start, was "little," in the end it tended to dominate our national literature. Group theaters developed leading playwrights; and several poets and fiction writers who had started as contributors to *Poetry, The Little Review, transition, Story,* or other little magazines eventually won national or even international recognition. Other authors of importance who came late in the period clearly showed the influence of the "little group" pioneers. In the end, drama, poetry, and fiction, the outstanding literary forms of the period, were greatly changed as a result of the movement.

Experiments in Drama

After 1910, many intelligent Americans felt that the commercial theater in this country was unsatisfactory because, having capitulated to the movies, it no longer provided "road shows" carrying drama to remote parts of the country, and because it was too much concerned with box-office success to give art much of a chance. Many young Americans traveling abroad between 1900 and 1916 found European theaters very stimulating. The Théâtre-Libre of Paris, which had been founded in 1887, the Abbey Theater of Dublin (1894), the Moscow Art Theater (1897), the Kleines Theater of Berlin (1902) all were carrying on interesting experiments in the drama which seemed to point the way to healthy changes.

Returning home, these travelers preached their new gospel and won converts. During the first two decades of the twentieth century, numerous community playhouses or workshops—little theaters—were established all over the country, from Boston, where the Toy Theater produced plays, to Palo Alto, California, where the Stanford University Theater was active. A number of colleges, simultaneously, offered work in playwriting and production under such teachers as George Pierce Baker of Harvard, Thomas Wood Stevens of Carnegie Institute of Technology, A. M. Drummond of Cornell, E. C. Mabie of Iowa, and Frederick Henry Koch of North Carolina.

In little theaters and campus workshops, amateur authors, actors, and producers carried on experiments more radical than any which commercial theatrical folk were likely to attempt.

In time, this movement had impacts upon the commercial theater. It cultivated audiences receptive to novelty in dramatic writing and staging. It supplied producers, actors, and playwrights who had learned their trade in community playhouses and college classrooms. And in three important instances, little theater groups became leading commercial producers: The Washington Square Players, founded in Greenwich Village in 1915, became the Theatre Guild in 1918; the Provincetown Players, also founded in 1915, left their fishing smack playhouse on Cape Cod to go to New York City and to become active in production there; and the Group Theatre, founded by some insurgent Theatre Guild members, became professionally active in 1931. These organizations, which were successful both commercially and artistically, were responsible for initial productions of plays by outstanding authors such as Edna St. Vincent Millay, Paul Green, Eugene O'Neill, and Clifford Odets.

Imagination and Realism

Authors writing for the new theater not only tried to avoid the clichés of plot, characterization, dialogue, acting, and staging which had caused the older theater to become dull; in addition, they experimented in a very imaginative fashion with modes and methods. Even when they were highly successful with one type of play, a number of authors gladly tried their hands at completely different types.

Two men trained by Professor Baker of Harvard, for instance, alternated between the writing of highly successful social comedies in the tradition of Royall Tyler's *The Contrast* and the writing of fantasies: Philip Barry won success with his sparkling *You and I* (1922), then wrote a poetic play about street cleaners—*White Wings* (1926); and S. N. Behrman, after making a hit with *The Second Man* (1927), offered a comic version of a classic legend in *Amphitryon 38* (1937). Later, both wrote additional social comedies. Marc Connelly, who began his career as a collaborator with George S. Kaufman in writing satirical comedies such as *To the Ladies* (1922), turned, with Kaufman, to the writing of the expressionistic play, *Beggar on Horseback* (1924), and

A scene from the original production of The Adding Machine, *1923—photograph by Vandamn*

later wrote, solo, the prize-winning folk Biblical play, *The Green Pastures* (1930), based upon Roark Bradford's Negro Sunday School stories. Elmer Rice, trained by the Morningside Players, a little theater group, succeeded equally well in writing his expressionistic *The Adding Machine* and his realistic *Street Scene* (1929); Maxwell Anderson, a graduate of Stanford, collaborated with Laurence Stallings in the realistic war play *What Price Glory?* (1924), and later authored verse dramas such as *Elizabeth the Queen* (1930) and *Winterset* (1935); the prose satire, *Both Your Houses;* and a musical comedy satire, *Knickerbocker Holiday* (1938). Paul Green, trained in the playwrighting courses of the University of North Carolina, became widely known for his realistic Negro play, *In Abraham's Bosom* (1926) but followed it with *Roll, Sweet Chariot* (1934), "a symphonic play of the Negro people," then with *Johnny Johnson* (1937), a musical comedy fantasy.

Clearly, the writers and the public of this period saw values in both realistic modes of writing and the more imaginative modes. Such hospitality led to one development, evident in some dramas, which was more or less peculiar to the period—the mingling of the realistic with the romantic or the fanciful. The "folk plays" of Paul Green, staged by little theater groups and by experimental New York producers, are an example, since they show life close to the soil but employ songs and poetic dialogue.

Expressionism and "The Hairy Ape"

An extreme of this sort of mingling is found in various expressionistic plays popular during the period—*Beggar on Horseback,* for instance. This play starts with a scene in the apartment of the hero, Neil, a penniless composer. The settings are realistic. The characters are introduced as true-to-life figures—the workingwoman with whom the hero is in love, the rich Gladys Cady, whom he is tempted to marry, and Gladys' money-grubbing family. Then the hero takes a sedative and has a dream forecasting the life he is to have if he marries the rich girl. The dream, thereafter, is presented objectively on the stage, with the distortion, the stylization, the symbolism of some dreams, set forth in dialogue which often has the repetitious quality, the rhythmic cadences, and the vocabulary of poetry. The costumes and settings are not realistic but are like those in dreams. A few lines of the stage directions at the time the dream starts suggest the technique:

> . . . it begins to grow light again—but it is no longer Neil's room. It is a railway station, with the arch of Track 37 prominently visible, and other arches flanking it at the side. A muddled train schedule is printed on the station walls, with strange towns that never existed. Neil's piano, however, has remained where it was, and so has his easy chair. Then, down the aisles of the lighted theatre, there comes suddenly a double wedding procession. One section is headed by Mr. Cady and Gladys—Mr. Cady in golf knickers and sox, knitted vest, and frock coat, with a silk hat prominently on his arm. Gladys is the gorgeously attired bride, bearing proudly a bouquet that consists entirely of banknotes. Behind them stream four ushers—spats, frock coats, and high hats, to say nothing of huge bridal veils, draped over their heads.

When the dream has concluded, the scene again becomes the composer's apartment, and the action returns to the realm of the everyday world.

Similar experiments mark this whole period. In addition, the drama, rather more than in previous periods, spoke out in behalf of political, social, and economic beliefs, many of them decidedly leftist in tendency. In the 1920's, *Beggar on Horseback* satirized wealth and big business. Later, as the populace in general tended leftward, authors such as Lillian Hellman and Clifford Odets wrote plays supporting labor or attacking Fascistic tendencies. The Group Theatre, quite active in this movement, attracted attention when, in 1935, it produced Odets' *Waiting for Lefty*. This depiction of a strike of taxicab drivers used a number of the devices of little theater productions—the presentation of action in the auditorium as well as on the stage, the unfolding of the story in episodic blackouts, and the employment of rhetorical language. And its purpose was to vivify the difficulties of laborers and to plead their cause.

Eugene O'Neill (p. 976), who was, by general agreement, the outstanding dramatist of the interwar period, represents several of the main tendencies of the time. He studied playwrighting in Professor Baker's class at Harvard, and he had his first plays produced by the Provincetown Players and his later ones by the Theatre Guild. A highly experimental author, he shifted from realistic writing in plays such as *Beyond the Horizon* (1920) and *Anna Christie* (1922) to expressionistic writing in plays such as *The Emperor Jones* (1921) and *The Hairy Ape* (1922), then to naturalistic dramas, and then to still other types.

The Hairy Ape (p. 978) is an expressionistic drama which forcefully voices the discontentment of the proletariat. Some of the scenery and much of the dialogue and action are realistic. In some scenes, however, the masked characters, the marionette-like processions, the monologues, and the choric effects lift the action into the realm of fantasy. The primitive Yank, despite his tough vocabulary, has an articulateness which is more in character for O'Neill than for the battered stoker. The rhythms of much of the dialogue are much more poetic than those of ordinary speech. Reading this play one easily sees why O'Neill, as he once wrote Professor Quinn, "sets most store by himself as a bit of a poet, who has labored with the spoken word to evolve original rhythms of beauty where beauty apparently isn't—*Jones, Ape, God's Chillun, Desire*, etc.—and to see the transfiguring nobility of tragedy, in as near the Greek sense as one can grasp it, in seemingly the most ignoble, debased lives." The formula is one which applies to many dramatists of the period. O'Neill stands out from the rest, not because he has attempted something entirely unique, but because he brings to his task a unique talent.

The Poetic Renaissance

Although various dates have been mentioned as marking the beginning of the poetic renaissance, the date most widely accepted is 1912, the year of the founding of *Poetry, A Magazine of Verse* by Harriet Monroe (1860-1936) and a group of subscribers. The motive of this publication, as the first issue stated it, was "to give to poetry her own place, her own voice." "The popular magazines," explained the editors, "can afford her but scant courtesy—a Cinderella corner in the ashes—because they seek a large public which is not hers, **a public** which buys them not for their verse but for their stories, pictures, journalism, rarely for their literature even in prose. . . . We believe that there is a public for poetry, that it will grow, and that as it becomes more numerous and more appreciative the work produced in this art will grow in power, in beauty, in significance."

The magazine, from its founding down to the present, has admirably fulfilled its function, and in time its prophecy was justified. *Poetry* introduced many new poets to the public. The books of some poets, notably Masters' *Spoon River Anthology* (1915), which was extraordinarily popular for poetry, attracted additional readers. Poets who lectured—Frost, Sandburg, and Lindsay, in particular—won a wider audience. Then there were various little magazines which, following the lead of *Poetry,* devoted much space to poems and to critical discussion: *Contemporary Verse* (1916-1929), *The Double Dealer* (1921-1926), *The Fugitive* (1922-1925), *Palms* (1923-1940), and others. Books on the new poetry by persuasive critics (Amy Lowell, Louis Untermeyer, John Crowe Ransom, Cleanth Brooks, and Allen Tate, to name but a few) helped cultivate understanding and appreciation. The result was the creation of a sizable cultured public which bought books of contemporary poetry and read it with enthusiasm.

Critics of modern poetry, many of whom urged the detailed analysis of poems (illustrated by Tate's "Narcissus as Narcissus," p. 873), found that a common attitude among the new poets was one of rebellion against Victorian poetry. Sometimes, as in the works of E. A. Robinson (p. 888), this rebellion was visible chiefly in *what* the poet said—the voicing of un-Victorian philosophical attitudes. More often, however, the poets rebelled not only against conventional beliefs but also against conventional poetic techniques—a rebellion indicated by *how* the poet expressed himself.

In poetry, as in the drama, there were innumerable experiments. As Frost observed humorously, "Poetry . . . was tried without punctuation. It was tried without capital letters. It was tried without any image but those to the eye. . . . It was tried without content under the name of poesie pure. It was tried without phrase, epigram, coherence, logic, and consistency. It was tried without ability. . . . It was tried without feeling or sentiment. . . ." The sources of these experimental techniques were also numerous—the English metaphys-

ical poets of the seventeenth century, the symbolists of France, the "radical" American poets of the nineteenth century, and others. A complete consideration of the period, therefore, would deal with innovations and influences by the score. Our more limited consideration will deal with three of the chief rebellions against older techniques: (1) against the older ideas about the "seriousness" proper to poetry, (2) against conventional versification, and (3) against conventional "poetic" diction.

"Serious Humor"

During the last decades of the nineteenth century and the early years of the twentieth century, poets in general lagged behind radical realistic and naturalistic fiction writers in adapting their methods to changing views of life in the United States. The more advanced novelists, dissatisfied with what they had thought were romantic simplifications, had turned to realism and naturalism partly because they believed that these modes made possible more inclusive—and truer—representations of life. But most poets had continued to write romantic poetry. Love or hate or sorrow had continued to be an "all out" business with them, completely disconnected from workaday concerns such as digging ditches, say, or sipping coffee, or selecting neckties. The attitude of the best poetry, in literal accordance with the urgings of Matthew Arnold and other leading critics, was one of "high seriousness." Poets had values about which they cherished no doubts, and though their poems sometimes showed vacillations, they moved forward steadily to firm conclusions.

There had been some exceptions: Whitman (p. 134) had fused "fleshly" and "spiritual" viewpoints; Emily Dickinson (p. 675) had been simultaneously playful and serious while writing of love, religion, or even death; William Vaughn Moody (p. 688) had assumed the comic rôle of "a little man in trousers, slightly jagged," to discuss the serious problem of evolution; Stephen Crane (p. 686) had told with irony of the indifference of the universe to man's suffering. These poets, it now developed, foreshadowed the conception of "seriousness" combined with humor which was to shape interwar poetry. Cleanth Brooks, in *Modern Poetry and the Tradition,* interestingly contrasts the new conception with the older one:

The two conceptions are almost diametrically opposed. Arnold's sincerity expresses itself as a vigilance which keeps out of the poem all those extraneous and distracting elements which might seem to contradict what the poet wishes to communicate to his audience. It is the sincerity of the conscientious expositor who makes his point, even at the expense of suppressions and exclusions. . . . The second conception of poetry, on the other hand, reveals itself as an unwillingness to ignore the complexity of experience. The poet attempts to fuse the conflicting elements in a harmonious whole.

Modern poets, in other words, feeling that life is more complicated than most romantic poets have admitted, reveal its conflicting aspects, its colliding values. Inevitably, therefore, their poems—excepting those of Jeffers and others who view life as completely tragic—deal with incongruities; and humor, wit, or irony of varied shades become important even in very serious poems. The poet is not necessarily vacillating indecisively; in making up his mind, he is trying to take into account manifold aspects of life.

Incongruity in many of Lindsay's best poems, for instance, is akin to that in American folklore. In such poems, one may hear echoes of the fireside talk of frontier yarnspinners. Lindsay is a mythmaker, and though his myths stop short of the most inventive tall tales, they achieve comparable fusings of the real and the imagined. His Andrew Jackson "was eight feet tall. . . . His sword was so long he dragged it on the ground." His General Booth (p. 922) enters a Heaven which is part supernatural, part Illinois country town. His Simon Legree is the legendary creation of a Negro poet, and his Congo blacks (p. 924) are a white man's fabulous interpretation of savagery. Even his Lincoln, stalking through Springfield at night (p. 928), assumes the guise of a folk creation.

Sandburg, likewise, embodies playful myths and imaginative tall tales in serious poems. His "Chicago" (p. 905) is a giant personification comparable to the frontier braggarts; he re-creates a half-mythical Lincoln by giving folk pictures of him (p. 916); he praises the people by telling of their folklore. In addition to frontier or rural humor, however, he makes use of the wry humor of the dispossessed as it is voiced in hobo ballads which he has reproduced in his *American Songbag:* it mingles hate, bitter contempt, and tenderness in "To a Contemporary Bunkshooter" (p. 906) and "A.E.F." (p. 912).

The humor of two New England poets, Robinson and Frost, as Constance Rourke has remarked in *American Humor,* also prolongs an older tradition:

> For companions in the legendary village of Tilbury Town Robinson has chosen types recurrent throughout early American comedy, ne'er-do-wells, liars, the quirky, the large-hearted and lost, spendthrifts of time and money and love. Robinson is master of that unobtrusive irony that has belonged to the Yankee; like the older Yankee he turns constantly to a dry metaphor—"an old vanity that is half as rich in salvage as old ashes.". . . A reticent humor runs through much of Robinson's poetry, so quietly as to pass unnoticed by many readers, yet producing a constant lightning and relief and change, with a balance of forces against the impending tragedy. . . . Frost [too] has kept the native humor, often deepened to a bitter irony, but delicately infused; most of his humor, like that of the early Yankee tradition, is so deeply inwoven with his further speech as to be almost inseparable from it.

These poets of New England, then, show relationships to the Yankee humor of the *Farmer's Almanacs* and of Seba Smith.

Four modern poets, to summarize, re-create in serious poetry the extravagant humor of the old West or the dry humor of Down East. Another group—which is represented in this text by T. S. Eliot, Wallace Stevens, Hart Crane, Karl Shapiro, and Gwendolyn Brooks—embodies more subtle (albeit ironic) incongruities in its poetry. Cleanth Brooks sees "wit" as the instrument used by these poets in fusing disparates; and his definition of wit shows how it may be used for serious purposes:

> Wit is not only an acute perception of analogies; it is a lively awareness of the fact that the obvious attitude toward a given situation is not the only possible attitude. Because wit, for us, is still associ-

ated with levity, it may be well to state it in its most serious terms. The witty poet's glancing at other attitudes is not merely "play"—an attempt to puzzle or show off his acuteness of perception; it is possible to describe it as merely his refusal to blind himself to a multiplicity which exists.

The perception of such multiplicity has frequently caused poets in this group to discard or greatly modify older ways of organizing poems in favor of "witty" organizations which emphasize ironic incongruities. Contrasting aspects or values are placed side by side and their disparate qualities are emphasized by the omission of most transitions. What Eliot calls " 'links in the chain,' of explanatory and connecting matter" are left out. Though such arrangements may, for a time, puzzle readers used to Victorian poetry, they are, considering the poets' assumptions about reality, inevitable. As Eliot has pointed out, "Such selection of sequences of images and ideas has nothing chaotic about it. There is a logic of imagination as well as a logic of concepts." Eliot and others of his group, in their poems, seek to arrange details in accordance with what he calls "the logic of the imagination."

A poem held together by what Eliot calls "the logic of concepts" might begin with a poetic statement of the idea that modern man is less romantic than man was in the past. "Look upon modern man," it might continue, and thereupon it might describe modern man in unromantic terms. The description might be followed by a transition—"It was not so with man in other days"—and the transition might introduce a description of a romantic character of the past. Possibly the poet might thereafter summarize the whole idea of the poem, and then lament the departure of romance. In such a structure no "links in the chain" would be missing and the meaning would be explicitly formulated. Contrast Eliot's "logic of imagination" in a terse passage in *The Waste Land* (p. 946). Note that there are no transitions, generalizations, or statements of attitudes—simply juxtaposed images, with those of the opening two lines providing a meaningful ironic contrast with those of the last four:

At the violet hour, the evening hour that strives
Homeward, and brings the sailor home from sea,
The typist home at teatime, clears her breakfast, lights

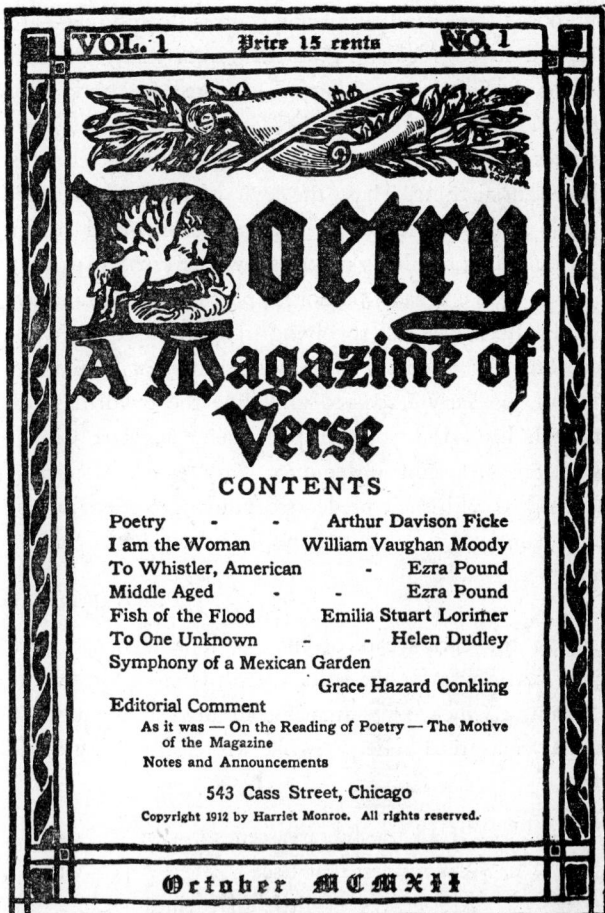

Cover of first issue of Poetry, A Magazine of Verse, October 1912. In the editorial comment it was stated that "poetry alone, of all the fine arts, has been left to shift for herself in a world unaware of its immediate and desperate need of her. . . . The present venture is a modest effort to give to poetry her own place, her own voice. . . ."

Her stove, and lays out food in tins.
Out of the window perilously spread
Her drying combinations touched by the sun's last rays. . . .

The opening two lines here connote the romance of purple twilight for adventurous sailors turning homeward; the remaining lines show the drab office worker clearing up dirty breakfast dishes, dining on canned food, and then washing and hanging out her underwear.

Comparable ironic contrasts or ironic parallelisms—

The Poetic Renaissance 773

or, more often, parallelisms and contrasts combined—are implied in the order of the images in many modern poems. In "The Love Song of J. Alfred Prufrock" (p. 942), "The Hippopotamus," or "Gerontion" (p. 945) the images are much more complex, but the juxtaposition is the essential thing. Thus "the logic of the imagination" which shapes these poems expresses irony, and in its "serious humor" Eliot's poetry shows its kinship to that of even such a broadly humorous poet as Vachel Lindsay. Similar juxtapositions involving irony are used by Wallace Stevens, often for a purpose somewhat similar to that of the early Eliot—to underline the tawdriness of modern life. And younger poets such as Hart Crane, Karl Shapiro, and Gwendolyn Brooks, all doubtless acquainted with their predecessors among modern poets, have employed the device in ways of their own.

New Rhythms

During the early years of the poetic renaissance, one great battle was for the recognition of free verse. Keith Preston, a Chicago newspaper columnist, implied what was a widespread belief when he wrote, in a witty quatrain:

> Of all the literary scenes,
> The saddest that I see
> Are graves of little magazines
> That died to make verse free.

Casual readers, for a long time, thought that "the new poetry" and "free verse" were synonymous. Many leaders in the movement did for a time write much free verse— Amy Lowell, Edgar Lee Masters, John Gould Fletcher, Hilda Doolittle, and others. Writers of such verse, obviously in the tradition of Whitman, are represented in this text by Carl Sandburg and Wallace Stevens.

By degrees, poets won this battle. They were aided by the growth of Whitman's reputation which took place during this period, by the popular success of the *Spoon River Anthology,* by critics, poets, and teachers who championed vers libre. By 1940, radio plays written in free verse appealed to wide audiences, and many an amateur poet who mailed his early efforts to the home-town newspaper wrote, without any sense of being daring, in free verse.

Free verse won its spurs, but after a period during which it was used by more and more poets, there came

a period during which it was used by fewer and fewer, and by 1941 many leading poets considered it rather old-fashioned. Having won all the freedom they wanted, many poets eventually decided that they could do with less freedom than vers libre allowed. Nevertheless, free verse had important effects, for it offered clues about possible variations in verse forms. Robinson, for instance, in some ways highly conventional in his prosody, diverged from regularity rather more than he probably would have done in an earlier period—and was less criticized for his divergences. And other poets, when they departed from established prosodic methods, did so without a twinge and without disastrous consequences.

Even so "classical" a poet as Robert Frost has not been untouched by the new tendency toward freedom. His theory of prosody, as Lawrance Thompson explains in *Fire and Ice,* attempts to reconcile "three separate planes of sound" which affect rhythms:

> The first of these is the basic and theoretically rigid meter, which Frost is willing to reduce "virtually" to "strict iambic" and "loose iambic." These basic accents, fitted to the variable structure of the line and of the stanza, offer an underlying foundation of words and phrases. The second plane of sound is derived from the words and phrases as they might be pronounced without regard to meaning, without regard to context. The third plane of sound is derived from the tones of voice which give particularly intended shades of meaning to the words when they are spoken as units in their contexts of phrases and sentences.

For example, in the opening lines of "Mending Wall" (p. 896) the "basic pattern" is iambic pentameter. However, normal accentuation, regardless of contexts, in such words as "something," "ground-swell," and "makes gaps" causes deviations from the regular iambic pattern. A proper reading of the poem, also, will suggest the character of the speaker and the quizzical, teasing tone of his remarks: such a character, probably, would maliciously emphasize and caress with his tongue the word "spills"— a word which embodies the whole playful destruction of walls by nature which so distresses the orderly neighbor. And later, in line 15, the word "between," important as it is in the concept being developed, may properly be given a stress—may properly be set off by significant pause—suggestive of its contextual importance. The sense Frost manifests, here and in other poems, of these three different planes of sound doubtless does much to account for a quality which many critics have seen in his poems: for poetry, they are often extraordinarily close in their rhythms to the everyday talk of New England farmers.

Vachel Lindsay, as his remarks here and there about metrics indicate, learned a great deal about versification from three poets: John Dryden (1631-1700), Edgar Allan Poe (1809-1849), and Algernon Charles Swinburne (1837-1909). Each of these achieved noteworthy effects by varying established rhythms and by exploiting, to the full, possibilities of tone-color—vowel and consonant arrangements. Dryden's "A Song for St. Cecilia's Day" brilliantly utilizes variations possible in an irregular ode to contrast the sounds of musical instruments, and it is not difficult to imagine Lindsay writing a gloss for Dryden comparable to that on "The Congo" offering instructions like those below for the reading of the lines:

The trumpet's loud clangor	Shrilly and with
Excites us to arms	increasing speed.
With shrill notes of anger	
And mortal alarms.	
·The double, double, double beat	To be chanted in
Of the thundering drum	deep bass, all the
Cries hark! the foes come;	heavy accents
	very heavy.
Charge, charge, 'tis too late to retreat!	
The soft complaining flute	To be read slowly and
In dying notes discovers	softly in the manner of
	insinuating music, all the o
The woes of hopeless lovers,	sounds very golden.
Whose dirge is whispered by the warbling lute.	

So glossed, Dryden's lines show clearly the source of some of Lindsay's practices.

But Lindsay's rhythms also had more immediate sources. During his boyhood in Springfield, Lindsay came to know well the rhythms of church oratory, both white and Negro, and also those of open-air political oratory. While at Hiram College, he was well trained in the florid public speaking fashionable during his young manhood. The rhythms of the Gregorian Chant were also, he acknowledged, influential. "From Boston to Los Angeles," he wrote, "we American versifiers, democratic poets, face the problem of our potential audiences of one million or one hundred million that we have never conquered, but which the Chatauqua orator like Bryan . . . may reach any day. From this standpoint, Bryan is the one living American poet till we make a few songs sturdy enough to endure the confusion of the Chatauqua tent. . . ." To capture such audiences, Lindsay wrote such poems as "General William Booth Enters into Heaven" and "The Congo"—experiments in what he called "The Higher Vaudeville"—designed to attract popular attention. Recited as this poet recited such poems,* these and other songs proved attractive to unsophisticated high-school students and even to tired businessmen.

Although T. S. Eliot, Wallace Stevens, Hart Crane, Allen Tate, and others of their "school" probably are not overfond of Lindsay, they adapt rhythms to materials in a comparable fashion. Eliot, who wrote a few poems close to free verse in form during his early career, eventually came to use rhyme and fairly conventional meters. Like Lindsay, however, he found contrasts in rhythms useful to enforce contrasting moods, attitudes, or materials. That Tate conceives of rhythm similarly is indicated by his discussion of his own prosody in "Narcissus as Narcissus."

Jeffers started his career as a conventional versifier, but his later poetry—that most admired by his critics—follows a metrical scheme which, as he says, is a "compromise" avoiding both "arbitrary form and capricious lack or disruption of form." Jeffers says of his meter:

> I want it rhythmic and not rhymed—moulded more closely to the subject than in older English poetry—but as formed as alcaics if that were possible too. The event is of course a compromise. . . . My feeling is for the number of beats to the line. There is a quantitative element too in which the unstressed syllables have part.

Taking this statement as a clue, Herbert Klein made a study reported in *The Prosody of Robinson Jeffers* (1930). His finding was that, considered carefully, the rhythms of this poet are much less chaotic than, at first

---

*Some of his readings are available on records issued by Columbia University. Listening to such records, or to those of Frost, Sandburg, or Eliot, is of great value to the student

glance, they appear to be. The reason is that Jeffers has been aware not only of the patterns of English verse but also of the quantitative patterns common to classical poetry. Says Klein:

> Briefly, my conclusion is that Jeffers uses stress to define and limit the line; quantity to regulate it. That is to say, the sheer possible syllabic length of the line is set (within exceptionally broad limits) by the number of stresses which the beat pattern of the poem permits. But the tempo of the lines, the contrast of breathless haste in one line (or joyful skipping) with sonorous deliberation (or hard wrenching plodding) in another is due to quantity.

Because of a knowledge of ancient poetry rather uncommon for modern American poets (with the exception of Frost), Jeffers has achieved metrical effects which are new, individual, and arresting.

The effect, in the end, of all the experimentation with rhythms was to give modern poets a very wide range indeed in their handling of rhythms. Patterns of emphasis could be adjusted in many ways to the thoughts and emotions expressed in poems, and readers accustomed to the new poetry readily accepted any metrical patterns, no matter how bizarre, which justified themselves by their achievements. And the flexible rhythms became highly appropriate to the expression of the contrasts and the incongruities so important in many modern poems.

The Language of Modern Poetry

After 1914 there was about as much variety in the kinds of language used as there was in the kinds of rhythms. Robinson, in general, used the same sort of diction as had been used in the Victorian period, though shorn of clichés and many of its ornaments, and so did some other poets. However, at the start of the period, some poets—like Dryden, Wordsworth, and Whitman before them—consciously rebelled against what they believed to be "unnatural" or ineffective ways of saying things, characteristic of older poetry. The rebellion was justified, so writers said, by several convictions: that a new language was needed to cope in a real way with the modern world, that expressions not worn threadbare had particular im-

pact, that concrete rather than abstract words were best for stating truth, and that poets did well to draw upon the common speech which still was a great source of poetry.

The ways of rebelling, however, differed. They differed, quite often, in accordance with the poets' ideas about the ways "common speech" should be translated into poetry. For in this period when the talk of various classes differed greatly, naturally it was possible to disagree about the class of men whose talk should be imitated. Should it be the class of the factory worker, say, of the farmer, or of the learned scholar? And naturally, even after deciding upon the kind of speech to be used in poetry, poets differed about the selection, the intensification necessary if ordinary talk was to be transmuted.

Robert Frost conceives of himself as a user of the talk of New Hampshire farmers. He has approvingly quoted Emerson's lines about Down East talk in "Monadnock," lines which point out that country folk, with their paltry vocabularies of a hundred words or so, are "the masters who can teach" the poet our "ancient speech," and he has admired dialogues in Shakespeare, made up as they are of "lean sharp sentences, with the give and take, the thread of thought and action quick, nor lost in a maze of metaphor and adjective." Frost usually lives up to his implied ideal. He uses an extraordinarily large proportion of monosyllables (forty in a row, for instance, at one point in "The Death of the Hired Man," p. 897), and very few long words; he often employs provincialisms. His lines, whether they serve as dialogue or as first-person voicings of the poet's thought, often have a sparse epigrammatic quality like that of folk speech. (Note, for instance, ll. 1, 27, 32-33 in "Mending Wall," p. 896.) Since Frost deliberately uses such simple, undecorated diction, very close to ordinary speech, he perforce suggests poetic meanings in subtle and delicate ways; and the unwary reader is likely to miss complexities firmly embodied in his laconic poems.

Lindsay and Sandburg employ words in a fashion in some ways comparable to Frost: some of their poems are couched in the Middlewestern counterpart of New England farm language. Each of these poets, however, following the example of Whitman (whom both admire), mingles poetic words with more vernacular expressions. And each experiments with somewhat different elements in our national speech. The language which Lindsay calls "really American" is the pure and simple English of the Elizabethan period, still spoken in unspoiled rural districts: he cites as an example of it Mark Twain's *Roughing It* (see p. 413). But he conceives of this language as potentially "eloquent" since its speakers "are all orators and preserve in eloquent periods the United States language." Such are the elements in our speech which Lindsay tries to utilize in his poetry—"the Grand Style," but employed with earthiness and native humor. Sandburg draws upon the talk of common men for the epigrams and sayings in some of his poems. He draws, in addition, upon the language of the factory or of the city sidewalk for such expressions as "where do you get that stuff"; "the . . . bunch backing you"; "a good four flusher"; and "he starts people puking" (all in "To a Contemporary Bunkshooter")—language highly appropriate to express the proletarian sentiments of the speaker.

Jeffers, over the years, has varied his diction. His earlier poems are, on the whole, pretty conventional: they embody expressions typical of older poetry and contain frequent inversions. Later poems are couched in a larger vocabulary which draws upon science—physics, biochemistry, geology, botany—for many words. But mingled with these learned expressions are colloquial phrases and contractions. And the style also is richly figurative.

Jeffers, at times, writes moderately obscure lines—one may cite these in "Roan Stallion" (p. 934):

> The atom bounds-breaking,
> Nucleus to sun, electrons to planets, with recognition
> Not praying, self-equaling, the whole to the whole,
>   the microcosm
> Not entering nor accepting entrance, more equally,
>   more utterly, more incredibly conjugate
> With the other extreme and greatness; passionately
>   perceptive of identity. . . .

But he is not alone in being obscure. Even such an old-fashioned poet as Robinson is obscure now and then, and so are such ordinarily forthright poets as Lindsay and Sandburg. Modern poetry, as a matter of fact, has been much criticized for the obscurity of its language.

Such obscurity is not, as some claim, the result of a deliberate attempt to blur meaning: actually it attempts to express meaning which is hard to decipher chiefly because it is complicated. Many difficult passages are at least as justifiable as those explained by Tate in his convincing apologia for their use in a specific poem (p. 873). Tate—like Stevens, Crane, Shapiro, and Brooks—works in a fashion similar to that of Eliot, and though Eliot writes poetry not immediately clear even to sophisticated readers, he amply justifies his diction, and that of other modern poets, in notably intelligent critical writings.

Difficult though some of his poetry is, Eliot indicates in his writings that he shares the belief that poets do well to write verse after the manner of the actual talk of men. He praises Donne, the seventeenth-century British metaphysical poet, for "managing to maintain a tone of direct and informal address"; he commends Dryden for having a talent which is "exactly the same" as Donne's; he holds that "no serious critic" will disapprove of Wordsworth's avowed attempt "to imitate, and as far as possible, to adopt, the very language of men." In general, carrying out his own theories, Eliot does achieve a conversational tone in his poems.

But Eliot sees clearly that at times certain demands of poetry may make conversational language unsatisfactory. "There is," he says, "no conversational or other form which can be applied indiscriminately": some ideas and feelings may be best expressed in other styles. Moreover, he feels that the poet cannot "talk like *any* class of society," since he has to talk "like himself—rather better, we hope, than any actual class; though when any class of society happens to have the best word, phrase, or expletive for anything, then the poet is entitled to it."

And indeed the poet who achieves all that Eliot sees him doing must be an artist in manipulating language. The language important to the poet, Eliot feels, "is that which is struggling to digest and express new objects, new groups of objects, new feelings, new aspects. . . ." Such living language, this poet holds, combines traditional with novel meanings: "whatever words a writer employs, he benefits by knowing as much as possible of the history of those words, of the uses to which they have already been applied. . . . The essential of tradition is this: in getting as much as possible the whole weight of the history of the language behind his word." Hence a sense of the traditional is valuable. The essential of novelty, by contrast, is the expression of that which is characteristic not only of the age but also of the individual poet. The modern poet, aware of the complexity of his period and of his reactions to it, must "become more and more comprehensive, more allusive, more indirect, in order to force, to dislocate if necessary, language into his meaning." In addition to thus expressing what is traditional and what is unique, the language of today's poetry, Eliot thinks, fuses two other elements—feeling and thought. Poets of today will be condemned if, like Tennyson and Browning, "they do not feel their thought as immediately as the odour of the rose." Instead each should reveal in his words "a direct sensuous apprehension of thought, or re-creation of thought into feeling, which is exactly what we find in Donne," greatly admired by Eliot as well as other modern authors.

The title and one of the lines of a poem by Eliot offer examples of these fusings in diction. The words "love song" in the title, "The Love Song of J. Alfred Prufrock," have *traditional* signification: in past periods, they stood for an expression of affection which was direct and passionate. This *individual* love song, by contrast, represents our peculiar era by not expressing affection and by being indirect and unimpassioned. Similarly, the word "song," which in the past stood for simple singing, in this poem stands for complex thinking. Again, in "J. Alfred Prufrock" (one of those names "parted on the side," today typical of some pretentious people), "Alfred" has been *traditionally* associated with the man of action, Alfred the Great; but in this *individual* poem, it applies to a "hero" who is exactly the opposite of a man of action. Fusion of *thought* and *feeling* is illustrated by line 51, in which Prufrock thinks "I have measured out my life with coffee spoons." Prufrock's thought is that he has wasted his life in meaningless social rituals; but this is expressed in sensory terms—terms of feeling—in the image of annoyed frustration: the delicate handling of ineffectual little spoons from which coffee cannot be savored but must be sipped.

Some modern poets, then, for all their approval of the use of conversational language, often depart from the simplicities of social talk in order to express complex meanings. Therefore the language aids the "serious humor" and the varied rhythms in appropriately voicing the ideas and feelings poets have about the modern world.

The New Fiction

During the period between 1912 and 1920, as we have seen, "the new drama" and "the new poetry" reached notable heights. "The new fiction," by contrast—at least that which people bought and talked about a great deal—lagged behind. Consistent authors of best sellers included Gene Stratton Porter, Harold Bell Wright, Zane Grey, and Eleanor H. Porter. The most popular novels left out the less savory aspects of American life, and their optimistic plots showed virtuous characters triumphant, after a struggle, over vicious villains. Obviously this fiction, although written in the twentieth century, prolonged the tradition of nineteenth-century sentimentalism.

Early in the 1920's, though, the beginnings of a change became apparent. On the best-seller list appeared F. Scott Fitzgerald's *This Side of Paradise,* Edith Wharton's *The Age of Innocence,* and Sinclair Lewis' *Main Street,* books in sharp contrast with previous best sellers. The last of these shortly became sensationally successful. In an article in *Bookman,* September 1921, a British novelist, Archibald Marshall, considered "half a dozen novels said to represent a new development in American fiction, all of which are now being widely read." There was, indeed, "a new development." During the years that followed, pre-1920 novelists tended slowly to recede in importance while very different writers such as Lewis, Hemingway, Faulkner, Dos Passos, Steinbeck, and Wolfe replaced them not only in critical esteem but also—at least at times—in general popularity.

Probably the huge audience which fictionists had was in large measure responsible for the late burgeoning of the new fiction. A larger audience than either poetry or drama reached, fiction readers were, for a long time, content with old-fashioned narratives. They preferred "pure" and "sweet" stories to the more rugged works of the Stephen Cranes and the Theodore Dreisers. But after many readers had been disillusioned by the outcome of World War I or had been converted by preachers of disillusionment such as Henry Adams and H. L. Mencken, a part of the older audience seceded and began to demand fictional works of a different sort. These were joined by a large share of the younger readers. Increasing numbers approved of the tendency which Archibald Marshall saw in best sellers "to portray the meanness of life in a particular [American] community." Attacks made by older neglected novelists, voiced anew, were considered with respect. Interest in Howe, Kirkland, and Crane was reawakened and redoubled. Dreiser's reputation prospered, and in 1925, when Dreiser published *An American Tragedy*, he found to his pleased surprise that the new audience was large enough to make that book for a time a best seller. By the 1930's, many books as stern as Dreiser's managed to win wide and appreciative audiences—not such wide ones, to be sure, as escapist novels like *Anthony Adverse* and *Gone with the Wind*, but very respectable audiences nevertheless.

Readers, then, who turned to fiction writers of the newer sort did so less because of their manner than because of their matter. But the authors of the new fiction, like the interwar poets, rebelled against older techniques, and they naturally needed new techniques appropriate to their preachments. Looking back to their most sympathetic predecessors, the realists and naturalists of the period 1880-1920, they found useful hints. And considering their new views of life, they hit upon methods of unfolding narratives which served their purposes.

Regardless of the sources of their procedures, fiction writers tended to drop the old argument concerning the relative merits of romanticism, realism, naturalism, expressionism, and other "isms," and to agree with Percy Lubbock, an admired critic of fiction, when he wrote: "The best form is that which makes the most of its subject—there is no other definition of the meaning of form in fiction." Authors and critics admired equally the novels of Dreiser and Farrell, cast in the form of naturalism; those of James Branch Cabell, written after the pattern of romances; and those of Robert Nathan, in the form of fantasy. What mattered most was that the fiction, as the phrase constantly had it, should "tell the real truth about life as it was." Detail, plot, and characterization were manipulated chiefly to achieve the end Mencken had in mind when he spoke of the "fundamental purpose" as being "to make the novel true."

Detail in Modern Fiction

Two ways of handling detail, perhaps, are outstanding in modern fiction—the "documentary" way and the "poetic" way. The documentary method, discoverable in Fitzgerald's *This Side of Paradise* and in the writings of Sinclair Lewis, John Dos Passos, and many other modern novelists, is notable for its mass of detail. Probably Dreiser, as much as any previous author, is its parent,

and its ideal is something like scientific accuracy and completeness. An example of this method in an extreme form is the chapter in *Main Street* wherein Lewis tells of Carol Kennicott's stroll down the street after which the novel is named. A grocery is thus described:

> Howland & Gould's Grocery. In the display window, black, overripe bananas and lettuce on which a cat was sleeping. Shelves lined with red crêpe paper which was now faded and torn and concentrically spotted. Flat against the wall of the second story the signs of lodges—the Knights of Pythias, the Maccabees, the Woodmen, the Masons.

In similar detail, for several pages, Lewis tells about building after building along the street—a total of twenty-five of them. The method is almost photographic in the multiplicity of descriptive touches used. The intention behind it, apparently, is to give such overwhelming documentation that the reader feels that the picture must be accurate.

Similarly, when Lewis records conversations, he sets down something close to a complete transcript: the repetitions of phrase and the peculiarities of expression seem to be mimicked to perfection. Consider this snatch of conversation between Babbitt and Littlefield, after Babbitt has brought up the subject of politics:

> "In my opinion, what the country needs, first and foremost, is a good, sound, business-like conduct of its affairs. What we need is—a business administration!" said Littlefield.
>
> "I'm glad to hear you say that! [said Babbitt] I certainly am glad to hear you say that! I didn't know how you'd feel about it with all your associations with colleges and so on, and I'm glad you feel that way. What the country needs—just at this present juncture—is neither a college president nor a lot of monkeying with foreign affairs, but a good—sound—economical—business—administration, that will give us a chance to have something like a decent turnover."

The details in this speech and others monotonously repeating phrases and "thoughts" seem almost stenographic in their accuracy and their completeness.

Of course, there is selection even in such passages as

Mr. and Mrs. Sinclair Lewis in a Model T Ford touring car on Main Street—photo Brown Brothers

these, and other authors who use this method are likely to be somewhat more selective than Lewis. The basis of the selection is the author's view of the scene or speech he is presenting. Lewis, for instance, gives an impression of the tawdriness, the dullness of Main Street in the first passage, and an impression of the unintellectual, standardized attitudes of Americans in the second. The abundant details are so chosen as to document amply each interpretation.

The "poetic" handling of detail, by contrast, is very highly selective, and although the details are likely to be literally accurate, they are also likely to be symbolically, i.e., poetically, significant—reminiscent not so much of Dreiser as of Stephen Crane and Frank Norris.

Willa Cather discusses the problem of detail in "The Novel Démeublé" (the unfurnished novel). She quotes approvingly Mérimée's dictum to the effect that the art of choosing from innumerable details is more important than attentive observation or exact rendition, and scoffs at the "popular superstition that 'realism' asserts itself in the cataloguing of a great number of material objects . . . and in minutely and unsparingly describing physical sensations." Balzac, she holds, failed as an artist in so far as he "tried out the value of literalness . . . to the uttermost." Tolstoy, by contrast, succeeded because he made the physical details "so much a part of the emotions of the people that they are perfectly synthesized." Hawthorne, too, used details sparsely but made all he used unobtrusively valuable to the mood of the story. Miss Cather concludes:

> Whatever is felt upon the page without being specifically named there—that, one might say, is created. It is the inexplicable presence of the thing

not named, of the overtone divined by the ear but not heard by it, the verbal mood, the emotional aura of the fact or the thing or the deed, that gives high quality to the novel or the drama, as well as to poetry itself.

The implication, of course, is that the details in a novel by Miss Cather should have an "emotional aura," an implicit value, comparable to that of the images in poetry.

Ernest Hemingway, although unlike Miss Cather in many respects, has similar theories about the handling of details. In all save one of his books (*To Have and Have Not,* 1937, wherein he briefly tries, with dubious success, to write like Dos Passos), Hemingway reduces descriptive detail to the minimum. His problem—the problem of all writers—as he sees it, consists of "knowing what you truly felt, rather than what you were supposed to feel," and then setting down "the real thing, the sequence of motion and fact which made the emotion." Details, in other words, primarily are valuable to suggest the experiencing of feelings, and Hemingway believes that if these are stated "purely enough," they will be "valid . . . always." "All good books are alike," he has said, "in that they are truer than if they had really happened and after you are finished reading one you will feel that all that happened to you and afterwards it all belongs to you: the good and the bad, the ecstasy, the remorse and the sorrow, the people and the places and how the weather was. If you can get so you can give that to people, then you are a writer." The details, selected with the lyric skill necessary for such an achievement, ideally get what this author calls "a fourth and a fifth dimension"—perhaps the prototype of Miss Cather's "whatever is felt upon the page without being specifically named." The fact or the detail becomes a symbol, and Hemingway, like his master, the Mark Twain of *Huckleberry Finn,* achieves poetry in what appears to be matter-of-fact prose.

This may be seen in the opening paragraph of "In Another Country" (p. 1130):

> In the fall the war was always there, but we did not go to it any more. It was cold in the fall in Milan and the dark came very early. Then the electric lights came on, and it was pleasant along the streets looking in the windows. There was much game hanging outside the shops, and the snow

powdered in the fur of the foxes and wind blew their tails. The deer hung stiff and heavy and empty, and small birds blew in the wind and the wind turned their feathers. It was a cold fall and the wind came down from the mountains.

The paragraph is factual, but it contrasts with Lewis' description of *Main Street* because of the nature of its details. Hemingway's details are sparse, and they are more than literal: they are symbolic as well as accurate. Poetically they stand for the "other countries" which the lonely characters portrayed in the story sense but do not enter—the country of battle from which their wounds have removed them, that of peace which they glimpse through lighted windows from darkened streets, the country of nature symbolized by the game, and the country, finally, of death—connoted by the cold, the dark, and by the wind which blows from the mountains.

Poetic details comparable to those in the passage by Hemingway just quoted are to be found, as one would expect, in the writings of Willa Cather. They are to be found in Steinbeck and Wolfe (although both of these writers often employ the literal method characteristic of Lewis) and in the packed long stories of Katherine Anne Porter. In fact, if a trend in the handling of detail is to be discovered in the modern period, it is a trend toward selectivity and poetic suggestion rather than exhaustive documentation. F. Scott Fitzgerald interestingly represents this trend: one may see it very clearly by contrasting his handling of detail in *This Side of Paradise* (1920) and *The Great Gatsby* (1925). Between the two novels, he revised his method in the direction to be followed by many major writers of the period.

Plot Patterns

When, in December 1930, Sinclair Lewis accepted the Nobel Prize, he made an address, "The American Fear of Literature," in which he catalogued conservative criticisms of contemporaneous writers. Eugene O'Neill, for instance, who had transformed American drama "from a false world of neat and complete trickery to a world of splendor and fear and greatness," was criticized because "he has seen life as not to be neatly arranged in the study of a scholar but as a terrifying, magnificent, and often quite horrible thing akin to the tornado, the earthquake, the devastating fire." The description applies not only to this dramatist but also to a number of fiction writers. They, too, refused to arrange happenings in neat and complete patterns comparable to those in older fiction. It was this fact, probably, that Archibald Marshall had in mind when he accused the new fictionists of failing to tell a story. "There is no progress," he complained.

Like Marshall, readers fond of Victorian plots believe that many modern novels, especially those of the twenties, bewilderingly depart from established narrative forms. Often, novelists like Dreiser, whom many of them admire, are satisfied to write simply the biographies of characters—sometimes from birth to death, sometimes from day to day over a shorter but not particularly exciting period. Such biographies often tell of characters who do not change: like picaresque figures they merely do various things and meet a series of people. Marshall instanced Carol Kennicott in *Main Street,* who, he said, "remains at the end much as she was at the beginning." "And her successive revolts," he added, "have little dramatic quality in them." Similarly, in *Babbitt, Arrowsmith, Elmer Gantry, Dodsworth,* and other novels, as Carl Van Doren notices, Lewis "employs an easy arrangement nearer chronicle than drama." James T. Farrell and Thomas Wolfe, in their novels, also use such arrangements as are supplied by apparently unmanipulated biography, although they continue their biographies through several volumes. In *All the King's Men* by Robert Penn Warren, the narrative thread is the biography of the demagogue chief character, Willie Stark.

John Dos Passos uses a similar technique in *Three Soldiers,* but he tends to complicate his story element by unfolding, simultaneously, several biographical chronicles—moving briskly and without transitions from one to the other. *"Manhattan Transfer,"* as Professor J. W. Beach remarks in *American Fiction, 1920-1940,* "is a picture of chaos moral and social; and the narrative technique corresponds to the theme. Each chapter is a loose bundle of incidents from the lives of many different persons or groups, anywhere from four or sixteen in number, completely unrelated save in time and their common involvement in the chaos of Manhattan" *U.S.A.* does much the same thing with a broader picture screen, the entire nation, as a background. The biographies of twelve people, scattered from the East to the West coast, are presented in fragmentary parts.

These people encounter many characters who move into and out of their lives. In addition, at intervals, "Newsreels," "The Camera Eye," and biographies of leading public figures are interspersed. The newsreels present impressionistic pictures of the nation of the day. The "Camera Eye" passages offer stream-of-consciousness interpretations. The brief biographies show, with selected details, the lives of leaders in ways which emphasize the trends of the times. These thumb-nail biographical accounts are comparable, as a result, to the biographies of major characters, although their parts are drawn together—are not separated by stretches of narrative.

But there are many modern narratives, nevertheless, which do show developments, developments which occur when the characters learn something—discover something. Faulkner's narratives often show a discovery of the terrible in human existence. "A Rose for Emily" (p. 1110), although it is comparatively uncomplicated, shows the method in miniature, for it tells how the villagers learn, detail by detail, of the horror of Miss Emily Grierson's life. Sometimes it is not the characters so much as the readers who make the discovery. *The Sound and the Fury* (1929), for example, one of Faulkner's best works, follows a jumbled plan, even as to time, which is justifiable largely because it makes such an unfolding possible. The order and relationships of happenings are further obscured because the story is told as it is seen not by one character but by three characters, in turn, and then the author. But the result of the whole procedure is a parading of various fragments which finally cease to be disconnected and become, instead, interrelated parts of a terrible picture. The discovery, therefore, takes place in the mind of the reader rather than in that of anyone in the story. Faulkner uses similar schemes—in eventual effect, at any rate—in other narratives.

The plot of discovery may be useful, of course, for affirmative as well as negative fictional works. Willa Cather often shows characters seeking and finding satisfactory self-fulfillment—the artist in *Song of the Lark,* the pioneer in *My Ántonia,* the soldier in *One of Ours,* the intellectual in *The Professor's House,* religious men in *Death Comes for the Archbishop.* When, in the latter part of the 1930's, fiction writers (like writers in other fields) began to forsake critical attacks in favor of positive preachments, this pattern tended to be prevalent.

Hemingway marks this transition. His "The Killers" (p. 1125) shows the youthful Nick apprehending some of the terror of the world—apprehending ruthlessness and violence, not through books and motion pictures but through first-hand experiences. Hemingway's early novels (*The Sun Also Rises* and *A Farewell to Arms*) and various short stories show characters making discoveries, usually of such a primitive sort that they indicate not the rehabilitation of human values so much as their disintegration. The chief character in *To Have and Have Not* and even more notably the chief character in *For Whom the Bell Tolls* find a faith beyond individual creature comfort, a social faith. Increasingly, as the United States moved toward World War II, and affirmations became more important for some novelists than attacks, fictional narratives tended to show similar discoveries—in Lewis' *Work of Art* and *It Can't Happen Here,* in Steinbeck's *The Grapes of Wrath* (p. 1150), and in Wolfe's *You Can't Go Home Again* (p. 1137). In the later part of the period, nevertheless, as in the earlier, the plots of discovery served admirably for the development of the authors' ideas.

Characterization and Psychology

From the beginning, authors of fiction have had certain limited ways of characterizing—showing the characteristics of the people about whose lives they wrote: they could comment upon them, describe their physical backgrounds and their outward appearance, tell of their actions or of their thoughts, set forth their conversations or the conversations of others about them. During the interwar period, fictionists did not manage to hit upon any new devices, but in various ways they manipulated and modified the older ones. One older device tended to disappear altogether: the comment of the author upon the characters. Fearful of appearing to moralize, and dubious, as a matter of fact, about their ability to state positive values, the authors in these years tended to drop out of their stories and to become relatively dramatic—objective—in their characterization. Description, too, was used less frequently as a characterizing device, although some authors (as has been suggested) continued to rely upon detailed description of background and physical appearance. For the most part, however, modern fiction writers depended for characterization upon the presentation of the words, deeds, and thoughts of their characters.

The handling of these characters was shaped largely by the science of psychology, which, as has been stated (p. 758), was of great importance in modern fiction. Seemingly, like Henry James before them (see p. 495), modern authors found central to their writing problem the selection of a fictional point of view—the kind of insight or insights they as authors were to have into the minds of their characters. And, of course, the statement of the insights was determined by the authors' concepts of psychology. Sherwood Anderson, for instance, was strongly influenced by the Freudian concept of human behavior, and stories in *Winesburg, Ohio* (p. 1015), his most famous collection, almost all dealt with complexes or phobias.

Hemingway, in some of his writings, seems to follow one lead suggested by behavioristic psychologists* when they scoffed at the scientific value of a study of "consciousness" and urged, instead, the observation of human activity—behavior. Often, Hemingway objectively sets down remarks and actions of the characters, or, as he puts it, "what really happens in action"—but he leaves to be inferred what the characters feel or think. "The Killers" is a perfect example, set forth as it is without a single glimpse into its characters' thoughts: it has the dramatic objectivity of a play. "In Another Country," though a first-person narrative, holds to a minimum the unfolding of the narrator's thoughts. When such a technique is used, whether Hemingway's characters are sophisticates or prizefighters, the subtle nuances of their thoughts and feelings—exactly the things with which Henry James was chiefly concerned—are not and cannot be presented. Hemingway's belief, apparently, is that such subtleties are relatively unimportant—that the primitive and universal emotions related to physical pleasure or pain are those most significant both in life and in art. Hence Hemingway, at times, has been classified as a "primitivist."

Steinbeck, too, is often a primitivist in his psychology.

---

* The chief scholarly consideration is J. B. Watson's **Behavior: An Introduction to Comparative Psychology,** New York, 1914; the chief popular study is a best-selling book by G. A. Dorsey, **Why We Behave Like Human Beings,** New York, 1925. In the 1920's, behaviorism was quite influential in psychological study

His tendency, as Edmund Wilson notices in *The Boys in the Back Room* (1941), is "to present life in animal terms," to deal "either with the lower animals or with human beings so rudimentary that they are almost on the animal level." In consequence, as Wilson says, "The chief subject of Mr. Steinbeck's fiction has been . . . not those aspects of humanity in which it is most thoughtful, imaginative, constructive, nor even those aspects of animals that seem most attractive to humans, but rather the processes of life itself. . . . And it is only, as a rule, on this primitive level that Mr. Steinbeck deals with moral questions: the virtues like the crimes for Mr. Steinbeck are still a part of . . . planless and almost aimless, of . . . almost unconscious, processes of life." Even the psychology of labor movements, as this author sees it, is animal-like. Striking fruit-pickers become "groupmen," and a character thus describes them: "It was like all of them disappeared, and it was just one big animal, going down the road. Just all one animal. . . ."

The somewhat similar psychological technique employed by Dos Passos also might well have stemmed from the "animal psychology" of the behaviorists—a psychology which tends to reduce action to two elements, stimuli and responses. His vast collection of human beings, though varied, seem (as Professor Beach suggests) to be capable of only a few responses to basic stimuli. "The presence of a given organism within the field of vision provokes the response of 'love'; discomfort drives one to a more comfortable attitude; a feeling of emptiness provokes boredom and sets one on the track of entertainment and novelty; a business opportunity releases effort and ambition." Dos Passos' human beings are comparable to laboratory mice which react one way when a bell rings, another way when a light flashes.

This type of psychology tends to make characterization simpler in modern fiction than it was in the older fiction. In some instances, by contrast, modern psychological concepts tend to make characterization rather more complex. Freud and his various followers have made authors aware of the complexity of some human motives and of the strangely illogical processes of the subconscious. Therefore, when some writers peer into the minds of characters, they see thoughts following devious pathways. These complicated mental processes the writers may reproduce by the "stream-of-consciousness" tech-

nique, the strange digressions, the random associations, which take place in the mind. In *The Sound and the Fury,* Faulkner, using the "floating point of view" described earlier, records different happenings as they are held or considered in the thoughts—both conscious and unconscious—of a series of characters. (The device, incidentally, is very helpful to the gradual unfolding of horror which his narrative achieves.) Katherine Anne Porter, in a number of outstanding stories—for example, "Flowering Judas" (p. 1071)—has focused upon the happenings by showing the thoughts a leading character has about them. Hemingway, in some of the most important passages of *A Farewell to Arms, To Have and Have Not,* and *For Whom the Bell Tolls,* momentarily departs from his characteristic dramatic method. Peering into the excited minds of his characters, he uses the stream-of-consciousness technique to tell what thoughts and fragments of thoughts are running through their minds. And Wolfe, when he tells what a leading character is thinking, may resort to poetic prose suggestive of both thought and emotion.

Modern Humor

Through the difficult years from 1914 down into the 1950's, Americans managed to retain their love for laughter, and humor flourished in many guises. The older forms did not disappear. Innumerable comics in movies, on radio, and on television continued to make use of materials and techniques passed along to them by the Literary Comedians. Will Rogers (1879-1935) and others followed the patterns of horse-sense commentary which dated back a century or more. Chic Sale, Bob Burns, and Herb Shriner amused modern audiences by telling tales not unlike those of oldtime yarnspinners. Writers on occasion found to their taste the substance and manner typical of the mock oral anecdote: Faulkner's "Spotted Horses" (p. 1115) is a splendid example. The tall tale, too, had its twentieth-century practitioners, some of whom, like Sandburg (p. 904), retold whoppers about Paul Bunyan, and some of whom celebrated such traditional comic demigods as Davy Crockett, John Henry, Pecos Bill, and Joe Magarac. Stephen Vincent Benét combined the outrageously impossible with the commonplace, after the manner of the Southwestern yarnspinners, in a series of fantasies of his own invention, of which "Daniel Webster and the Sea Serpent" (p. 1006) is typical.

Although the older forms of humor continued to be used, much modern humor underwent important changes. In Sinclair Lewis' novels, caricature and exaggeration were used in new ways for social satire. In poetry, as has been seen, humor often became bitterly ironic.

The humor published in humorous magazines, particularly in the outstanding one for the period, *The New Yorker,* often differed from that of earlier periods in the direction of its satire. "Father," for instance, in Clarence Day's *Life with Father* (p. 999), was in some essentials like the traditional horse-sense character: he was a man of intelligence and experience who used both to solve problems. But whereas in the past humorists had used such characters as oracular *raisonneurs* and had shown them wisely solving problems of all kinds, Day pictured Father as lovable but quaint and told how he was baffled again and again. Mother, his foil, featherbrained and innocent of experience—in some ways comparable to the genial idiot of the Literary Comedians—was, by contrast, portrayed more sympathetically and was shown succeeding where her spouse failed. The veer in satirical direction, typical of much humor of the time, embodied in comic terms modern man's doubts concerning the the validity of any system for solving problems and discovering truths.

James Thurber, like Day, has had doubts about man's ability not only to master the universe but also to solve his own minor problems. "Man," he once wrote, "is surely farther away from the Answer than any other animal this side of the ladybug." Much of Thurber's comedy, as in "The Night the Bed Fell" (p. 1003), hilariously depicts ineptitudes and chaotic confusions. Like many modern fictionists, Thurber often uses present-day psychology in characterizing; but unlike the fictionists he makes the phobias, complexes, and maladjustments which burgeon in life as he represents it not abnormal and tragic, but commonplace and tremendously funny. In contrast to earlier humorists who equipped their heroes with superhuman muscles or prodigious quantities of gumption, Thurber equips his with magnificent psy-

"Never say die!"—self-portrait by Clarence Day from Thoughts Without Words, © *1923*

choses. With other modern humorists, he has (as Bernard DeVoto has put it) transformed Genial Idiots into Perfect Neurotics; and thus his narratives direct their satire against modern man's worriments about his maladjustments.

The forms and techniques of humor, then, (like those of drama, poetry, and fiction) have been shaped by the intellectual concepts of the period. Anyone who has followed the devious pathways of our literature from colonial times to the midyears of the twentieth century will realize that such a shaping was typical. As we have traced the multiple changes in writing methods which have taken place as the nation grew from a tiny group of colonies to one of the great nations of the world, we have seen how, in era after era, the thought of the period, the historical developments, and the personalities of authors have profoundly influenced the methods whereby writers have told—seriously or comically—of our struggles, of our failures and successes, and of our vista of the future.   W.B.

Chronological Table
of Literature and History

1914 Theodore Dreiser's **The Titan** • Robert Frost's **North of Boston** • Vachel Lindsay's **The Congo and Other Poems** • Amy Lowell's **Sword Blades and Poppy Seed** • Eugene O'Neill's **Thirst and Other One Act Plays**
World War I began in Europe, 1 August

1915 Willa Cather's **The Song of the Lark** • Dreiser's **The "Genius"** • Edgar Lee Masters' **Spoon River Anthology**
The Provincetown Players, Washington Square Players, The Playhouse established • **Lusitania** sunk, 7 May, with loss of American lives

1916 Sherwood Anderson's **Windy McPherson's Son** • Frost's **Mountain Interval** • Robinson Jeffers' **Californians** • Lindsay's **A Handy Guide for Beggars** • O'Neill's **Bound East for Cardiff** • Edwin Arlington Robinson's **The Man Against the Sky** • Carl Sandburg's **Chicago Poems** • Mark Twain's **The Mysterious Stranger**
Woodrow Wilson reëlected President

1917 Anderson's **Marching Men** • T. S. Eliot's **Prufrock and Other Observations** • Hamlin Garland's **A Son of the Middle Border** • Lindsay's **The Chinese Nightingale and Other Poems** • Robinson's **Merlin**
Germany began unrestricted submarine warfare, 1 February • United States severed diplomatic relations with Germany, 2 February; declared war, 6 April • Czar Nicholas of Russia abdicated, 15 March • First troops of American Expeditionary Force landed in France, 26 June • Bolshevists under Lenin assumed power in Russia, 7 November

1918 Stephen Vincent Benét's **Young Adventure** • Cather's **My Antonia** • Sandburg's **Cornhuskers**

• **The Education of Henry Adams** first made available to the general public, became a best seller
Wilson outlined Fourteen Points for peace, 8 January • Russia, with treaty of Brest-Litovsk, made separate peace with Central Powers, 3 March • Revolution in Germany, 7 November; Kaiser Wilhelm abdicated, a German Republic proclaimed, 9 November • Armistice signed, 11 November

1919 Anderson's **Winesburg, Ohio** • Irving Babbitt's **Rousseau and Romanticism** • H. L. Mencken's **Prejudices** (first series) and **The American Language** • O'Neill's **The Moon of the Caribbees, and Six Other Plays**
The Theatre Guild established • Communist International (Comintern) organized in Russia • Benito Mussolini organized Italian Fascist movement, 23 March • Treaty of Versailles signed, 28 June; rejected by United States Senate, 19 November

1920 Anderson's **Poor White** • Benét's **Heavens and Earth** • Clarence Day's **This Simian World** • John Dos Passos' **One Man's Initiation—1917** • Eliot's **The Sacred Wood** • F. Scott Fitzgerald's **This Side of Paradise** • Sinclair Lewis' **Main Street** • O'Neill's **Beyond the Horizon** • Robinson's **Lancelot** • Sandburg's **Smoke and Steel**
League of Nations established at Geneva, Switzerland, 10 January • Warren Gamaliel Harding elected twenty-ninth President • Transcontinental air-mail service and commercial radio broadcasting initiated • United States census: population 105,710,620

1921 Anderson's **The Triumph of the Egg** • Dos Passos' **Three Soldiers** • O'Neill's **The Emperor Jones**

Washington Conference opened, 11 November; concluded 6 February 1922, after which President Harding submitted to the Senate seven treaties designed to ease tensions with Japan in the Pacific

1922 Benét's **Young People's Pride** • Eliot's **The Waste Land** • Fitzgerald's **The Beautiful and Damned** • Lewis' **Babbitt** • O'Neill's **Anna Christie** and **The Hairy Ape**
Mussolini and the Fascists took over the government of Italy, 28 October • Russian government organized as the Union of Socialist Soviet Republics, December

1923 Anderson's **Many Marriages** and **Horses and Men** • Cather's **A Lost Lady** • Frost's **New Hampshire** • Robinson's **Roman Bartholow** • Wallace Stevens' **Harmonium**
President Harding died, 2 August; Calvin Coolidge became thirtieth President • Munich "Beer-Hall Putsch" by German National Socialists failed, 9 November; Adolf Hitler captured and imprisoned, 12 November

1924 Kenneth Burke's **The White Oxen** • Eliot's **Homage to John Dryden** • Ernest Hemingway's **In Our Time: Stories** • Jeffers' **Tamar and Other Poems** • Herman Melville's **Billy Budd, Foretopman** first published
Lenin died, 21 January; after some years Joseph Stalin emerged as virtual dictator of Soviet Russia • Coolidge elected to full term as President

1925 Anderson's **Dark Laughter** • Cather's **The Professor's House** • Dos Passos' **Manhattan Transfer** • Dreiser's **An American Tragedy** • Fitzgerald's **The Great Gatsby** • Jeffers' **Roan Stallion** • Lewis' **Arrowsmith**

1926 Cather's **My Mortal Enemy** • Hart Crane's **White Buildings** • William Faulkner's **Soldiers' Pay** • Hemingway's **The Sun Also Rises** and **The Torrents of Spring** • O'Neill's **The Great God Brown** • Sandburg's **Abraham Lincoln: The Prairie Years**
Germany admitted to League of Nations

1927 Cather's **Death Comes for the Archbishop** • Faulkner's **Mosquitoes** • Hemingway's **Men Without Women** • Jeffers' **The Women at Point Sur** • Lewis' **Elmer Gantry** • O'Neill's **Marco Millions** and **Lazarus Laughed** • Robinson's **Tristram** • Sandburg's **The American Songbag**
Chiang Kai-shek, leader of the Kuomintang government, established capitol at Nanking and became virtual ruler of China until 1949

1928 Benét's **John Brown's Body** • Eliot's **For Lancelot Andrewes** • Frost's **West-Running Brook** • Jeffers' **Cawdor and Other Poems** • O'Neill's **Strange Interlude** • Sandburg's **Good Morning, America** • Allen Tate's **Mr. Pope and Other Poems**
First Russian Five-Year Plan for industrialization organized by Stalin • Herbert Hoover elected thirty-first President

1929 Faulkner's **Sartoris** and **The Sound and the Fury** • Hemingway's **A Farewell to Arms** • Jeffers' **Dear Judas and Other Poems** • Lewis' **Dodsworth** • Robinson's **Cavender's House** • James Thurber and E. B. White's **Is Sex Necessary?** • Thomas Wolfe's **Look Homeward, Angel: A Story of the Buried Life**
Postwar prosperity ended with stock market crash, 29 October, the beginning of the Great Depression

1930 Crane's **The Bridge** • Dos Passos' **The 42nd Parallel** • Eliot's **Ash-Wednesday** • Faulkner's **As I Lay Dying** • Twelve Authors (the Southern Agrarians), **I'll Take My Stand: The South and the Agrarian Tradition**
Sinclair Lewis became the first American to win the Nobel Prize in Literature • United States census: population 122,775,046

1931 Anderson's **Perhaps Women** • Burke's **Counter-Statement** • Cather's **Shadows on the Rock** • Faulkner's **Sanctuary** • O'Neill's **Mourning Becomes Electra** • Lincoln Steffens' **Autobiography** • Thurber's **The Owl in the Attic** • Edmund Wilson's **Axel's Castle**
King Alfonso XIII forced to leave Spain, 14 April, and a republic proclaimed • Japanese troops invaded Manchuria, 18 September; a puppet state, Manchukuo, was created 18 February 1932

1932 Anderson's **Beyond Desire** • Day's **God and My Father** • Dos Passos' **1919** • Faulkner's **Light in August** • Hemingway's **Death in the Afternoon** • Jeffers' **Thurso's Landing and Other Poems** • Tate's **Robert E. Lee**

Secretary of State Henry L. Stimson protested Japanese occupation of Manchuria • Congress authorized, 2 February, establishment of Reconstruction Finance Corporation (RFC) to aid railroads and financial institutions affected by the depression • Franklin Delano Roosevelt elected thirty-second President

1933 Hemingway's **Winner Take Nothing** • Jeffers' **Give Your Heart to the Hawks and Other Poems** • Lewis' **Ann Vickers** • O'Neill's **Ah, Wilderness!** • Robinson's **Talifer**

Hitler became Chancellor of Germany, January, was granted dictatorial power in March and began persecution of Jews and proscription of anti-Nazi parties • Roosevelt inaugurated numerous measures to relieve severe economic distress: National Industrial Recovery Act (NRA), Agricultural Adjustment Act (AAA), Civilian Conservation Corps (CCC), Tennessee Valley Authority (TVA) • Japan signified intent to withdraw from the League of Nations

1934 Lewis' **Work of Art** • O'Neill's **Days Without End**

Securities Exchange Act (establishing SEC), Home Owners' Loan Act (HOLC) enacted for recovery from depression • After death of President von Hindenburg, Hitler combined presidency and chancellorship of Germany and assumed title of "Der Fuehrer," 16 August

1935 Burke's **Permanence and Change: Anatomy of Purpose** • Cather's **Lucy Gayheart** • Day's **Life with Father** • Eliot's **Murder in the Cathedral** • Jeffers' **Solstice and Other Poems** • Lewis' **It Can't Happen Here** • Robinson's **King Jasper** • John Steinbeck's **Tortilla Flat** • Stevens' **Ideas of Order** • Wolfe's **Of Time and the River**

Works Projects Administration (WPA), National Youth Administration (NYA) set up to provide "work relief" • NRA declared unconstitutional • Social Security Act passed • Committee for Indus-

trial Organization (CIO) founded • Italian forces invaded Ethiopia, 3 October, having been massed on Somaliland border since December 1934; economic sanctions against Italy applied by fifty-three nations after Ethiopian appeal to League • German rearmament begun

1936 Faulkner's **Absalom, Absalom!** • Frost's **A Further Range** • Sandburg's **The People, Yes** • Steinbeck's **In Dubious Battle** • Stevens' **Owl's Clover** • Robert Penn Warren's **Thirty-six Poems**

AAA declared unconstitutional • King George V of England died, 20 January; his eldest son, Edward VIII, succeeded, but abdicated, 11 December, and was in turn succeeded by George VI • German troops began to occupy the Rhineland, 7 March, defying treaty agreement • Revolt against Spanish Republican Government began in Morocco, 17 July; Gen. Francisco Franco invested with title of Chief of the Spanish Nationalist Government, 1 October • Roosevelt reëlected President

1937 Benét's **The Devil and Daniel Webster** • Dos Passos' **The Big Money** • Hemingway's **To Have and Have Not** • Jeffers' **Such Counsels You Gave to Me and Other Poems** • Steinbeck's **Of Mice and Men** • Stevens' **The Man with the Blue Guitar and Other Poems** • Thurber's **Let Your Mind Alone**

Japan invaded China, 7 July, occupying both Peiping and Shanghai before the end of the year • Roosevelt called for "quarantine" of aggressors in Chicago address, 5 October

1938 Benét's **Johnny Pye and the Fool-Killer** • Faulkner's **The Unvanquished** • Hemingway's **The Fifth Column and the First Forty-nine Stories** • Lewis' **The Prodigal Parents** • Steinbeck's **The Long Valley** • Wilson's **The Triple Thinkers**

Hitler invaded Austria, 11 March; German-Austrian union (Anschluss) proclaimed two days later • Prime Minister Neville Chamberlain of Britain signed a "Peace Declaration" with Hitler at Munich, 30 September, yielding to Nazi demands that Czechoslovakia cede the Sudetenland to Germany; Czechoslovakia subsequently partitioned among Germany, Hungary, and Poland

1939 Dos Passos' **Adventures of a Young Man** • Eliot's **The Idea of a Christian Society** • Faulkner's **The Wild Palms** • Katherine Anne Porter's **Pale Horse, Pale Rider** • Sandburg's **Abraham Lincoln: The War Years** • Steinbeck's **The Grapes of Wrath** • Warren's **Night Rider** • Wolfe's **The Web and the Rock**

Franco completed conquest of Spain, 29 March • Italian troops invaded Albania, 7 April • Germany and Italy announced military and political alliance, 7 May • Germany and Soviet Russia signed ten-year nonaggression pact, 24 August • Germany attacked Poland, 1 September • Britain and France declared war on Germany, 3 September • Roosevelt proclaimed a national emergency, 8 September • Poland occupied by Germany and Russia, September • Russia invaded Finland, 30 November; Finland made peace and ceded territory, March 1940

1940 Cather's **Sapphira and the Slave Girl** • Faulkner's **The Hamlet** • Hemingway's **For Whom the Bell Tolls** • Lewis' **Bethel Merriday** • Carson McCullers' **The Heart Is a Lonely Hunter** • Mencken's **Happy Days, 1880-1892** • Thurber's **The Male Animal** (with Elliott Nugent) • Wolfe's **You Can't Go Home Again**

German armies swept across Europe, conquering Holland, 13 May; Belgium, 28 May; France, 22 June • Winston Churchill replaced Chamberlain as Prime Minister of Britain • Italy and Germany invaded Greece • First peacetime conscription inaugurated in the United States, 29 October • Roosevelt elected President for third term • United States pledged aid to Britain "short of war" • United States census: population 131,669,275

1941 Burke's **The Philosophy of Literary Form** • Dos Passos' **The Ground We Stand On** • Fitzgerald's **The Last Tycoon** • McCullers' **Reflections in a Golden Eye** • Mencken's **Newspaper Days, 1899-1906** • Steinbeck's **Sea of Cortez** (with E. F. Ricketts) • Wilson's **The Boys in the Back Room** and **The Wound and the Bow**

Roosevelt proclaimed the Four Freedoms, 6 January • Congress passed the Lend-Lease Act,

March • Russia and Japan signed five-year neutrality treaty, 13 April • German troops invaded Russia, 22 June • Atlantic Charter announced, 14 August • Pearl Harbor attacked by Japan, 7 December; Japanese troops simultaneously occupied Guam and Wake Island and landed in the Philippines • United States declared war on Japan, 8 December • Germany and Italy declared war on the United States, 11 December • United States declared war on Germany and Italy, 13 December

1942 Frost's **A Witness Tree** • Marion Hargrove's **See Here, Private Hargrove** • Randall Jarrell's **Blood for a Stranger** • Karl Shapiro's **Person, Place, and Thing** • Steinbeck's **The Moon Is Down** and **Bombs Away** • Stevens' **Parts of a World** • Thurber's **My World—and Welcome to It** • Eudora Welty's **The Robber Bridegroom**

Declaration of the United Nations issued, 1 January • Japanese occupied Singapore, 15 February • Threat of invasion of Australia lessened by naval air engagement, Battle of the Coral Sea, 4-8 May • Last American troops in the Philippines surrendered Corregidor Island, 6 May • Japanese invasion fleet turned back at Midway Island, 4-7 June • American and Australian troops began offensive, establishing bases in New Guinea and on Guadalcanal in the Solomon Islands • Allied troops occupied French North Africa, 7-8 November • German armies pushed to the Caucasus and threatened both Leningrad and Moscow, being held there and at Stalingrad

1943 Dos Passos' **Number One** • Eliot's **Four Quartets** • Lewis' **Gideon Planish** • Mencken's **Heathen Days, 1890-1936** • Frederick Prokosch's **The Conspirators** • Ernie Pyle's **Here Is Your War** • Thurber's **Men, Women, and Dogs** • Wendell Willkie's **One World**

Roosevelt and Churchill conferred at Casablanca, Morocco, 14-24 January, choosing Dwight D. Eisenhower as supreme commander for attack on Italy • Russia announced, 3 February, destruction of German army of 300,000, encircled at Stalingrad since November • Allies occupied Tunis and

Bizerte, last Axis positions in North Africa, 8-12 May; conquered Sicily, 10 July-17 August • Mussolini resigned, 23 July • Pietro Badoglio, Mussolini's successor, signed armistice, 3 September; Allies landed on Italian mainland • Roosevelt, Churchill, and Chiang Kai-shek conferred at Cairo, Egypt, 21-26 November, agreeing that postwar Korea should be independent • Roosevelt, Churchill, and Stalin conferred at Teheran, Iran, 22 November-2 December, guaranteeing independence of postwar Iran

1944   Dos Passos' **State of the Nation** • John Hersey's **A Bell for Adano** • Robert Lowell's **Land of Unlikeness** • Katherine Anne Porter's **The Leaning Tower** • Shapiro's **V-Letter and Other Poems** • Jean Stafford's **Boston Adventure**
American troops invaded Marshall Islands, 2 February • Rome liberated, 5 June • Allied invasion of Western Europe began, 6 June (D-Day), with landings in Normandy, Eisenhower, supreme commander • American troops returned to Guam, 20 July • Paris liberated, 29 August • Germany invaded from the west, 12 September • American troops returned to the Philippines, landing on Leyte, 19 October • Roosevelt elected for fourth term as President

1945   Benét's **Western Star** • Gwendolyn Brooks' **A Street in Bronzeville** • Burke's **A Grammar of Motives** • Frost's **A Masque of Reason** • Jarrell's **Little Friend, Little Friend** • Mencken's **The American Language, Supplement One** • Shapiro's **Essay on Rime** • Steinbeck's **Cannery Row**
Russian troops invaded Germany from the east, 19 January • Yugoslavia became a federated republic, after the soviet model, with Marshal Tito as head of state • Roosevelt, Churchill, and Stalin conferred at Yalta, in the Crimea, discussing postwar policies, 4-11 February • Manila liberated, 3 February • American troops landed on Iwo Jima, 18 February • American troops crossed the Rhine, 8 March • American troops invaded Okinawa, 325 miles from Japan, 1 April • Roosevelt died, 12 April; Harry S. Truman became thirty-third President • Russians occupied

Vienna and entered Berlin, April • Death of Hitler announced, 1 May; Admiral Doenitz proclaimed himself successor • Germany surrendered unconditionally, 7 May (V-E Day) • Labor Party won British general election, 26 July; Clement R. Atlee became Prime Minister • Truman, Churchill, and Stalin, with their foreign ministers, conferred at Potsdam, 17 July-2 August, providing for occupation of Germany, reparations, and procedure for peace treaties • Charter of the United Nations issued by the San Francisco conference, 26 June; ratification completed by the United States, 8 August, and by Russia, 24 October • Atomic bomb dropped on Hiroshima, Japan, 6 August • Russia declared war on Japan, 8 August • Unconditional surrender of Japan announced by President Truman, 14 August (V-J Day)

1946   Dos Passos' **Tour of Duty** • Dreiser's **The Bulwark** • Hersey's **Hiroshima** • Jeffers' **Medea** • Lowell's **Lord Weary's Castle** • McCullers' **The Member of the Wedding** • O'Neill's **The Iceman Cometh** • Warren's **All the King's Men** and **Blackberry Winter**
First Assembly of the United Nations met at London, 10 January • League of Nations dissolved itself, 18 April, turning over its assets to the United Nations • Philippines became independent, 4 July • First convictions of high-ranking Nazis for war crimes announced by International Military Tribunal, at Nuremberg, 30 September

1947   Dreiser's **The Stoic** • Frost's **A Steeple Bush** and **A Masque of Mercy** • A. B. Guthrie's **The Big Sky** • Lewis' **Kingsblood Royal** • James Michener's **Tales of the South Pacific** • Shapiro's **Trial of a Poet and Other Poems** • Steinbeck's **The Pearl** and **The Wayward Bus** • Stevens' **Transport to Summer** • Warren's **The Circus in the Attic and Other Stories**
Foreign ministers of Britain, France, the United States, and Russia ended a six-week conference in Moscow, 24 April, without reaching agreement on peace terms for Germany and Austria • "Truman Doctrine" inaugurated by Congressional appropriations for economic and military aid to Greece and Turkey, where Communist

coups were feared • "Marshall Plan" of aid to free nations announced by Secretary of State George C. Marshall, 5 June • Taft-Hartley Labor Act passed by Congress over Truman's veto, 23 June • Gen. Andrei A. Zhdanov called upon all Communists to oppose Marshall Plan, 22 October • King Michael of Rumania abdicated and a People's Republic (Communist) proclaimed

1948 Cather's **The Old Beauty and Others** • Faulkner's **Intruder in the Dust** • Jeffers' **The Double Axe and Other Poems** • **Literary History of the United States**, ed. R. E. Spiller and others • Norman Mailer's **The Naked and the Dead** • William Van O'Connor's **Sense and Sensibility in Modern Poetry** • Sandburg's **Remembrance Rock** • Irwin Shaw's **The Young Lions** • Stevens' **A Primitive Like an Orb** • Thurber's **The Beast in Me and Other Animals** • Peter Viereck's **Terror and Decorum**

Communists seized power in Czechoslovakia, 25 February • Britain, France, Belgium, the Netherlands, and Luxemburg signed a fifty-year mutual defense treaty, 17 March • Western Berlin blockaded by refusal of Russians to permit train or truck traffic through the Soviet occupation zone, 1 April; supplies delivered by airlift for seventeen months • Congress approved organization of Economic Coöperation Administration (ECA) to supervise aid to free nations, 2 April • Following failure by the United States and Russia and by the United Nations to arrange for free elections and a united Korea, that country was in effect partitioned by organization of the northern People's Democratic Republic (Communist), 1 May, and the southern Republic of Korea, 10 May • Yugoslavia expelled from the Cominform and denounced by Soviet Russia, June • Peacetime Selective Service Act became law, 24 June • Truman elected to full term as President

1949 Nelson Algren's **The Man with the Golden Arm** • Brooks' **Annie Allen** • Dos Passos' **The Grand Design** • Faulkner's **Knight's Gambit** • Lewis' **The God-seeker** • René Wellek and Austin Warren's **Theory of Literature** • Welty's **The Golden Apples**

Chiang Kai-shek resigned as President of China, 21 January, in the face of growing power of Chinese Communists • North Atlantic Defense Treaty, basis of North Atlantic Defense Organization (NATO), signed 4 April by United States, Canada, Britain, France, Belgium, the Netherlands, Luxemburg, Norway, Denmark, Iceland, Italy, and Portugal; ratified by Senate, 21 July • Britain, France, and the United States agreed to establish a West German republic, 8 April; Federal Republic of Western Germany proclaimed, 23 May • German Democratic Republic (Communist) proclaimed in Eastern Germany, 7 October • People's Republic of China (Communist) proclaimed in Peiping, 21 September • Congress appropriated funds for military aid to NATO members, 27 September • Chinese Nationalist government of Chiang Kai-shek labelled "reactionary" by Secretary of State Dean Acheson, 6 August • Chinese Nationalist government fled to Formosa, 7 December

1950 Burke's **A Rhetoric of Motives** • Dos Passos' **The Prospect Before Us** • Hemingway's **Across the River and into the Trees** • Hersey's **The Wall** • Steinbeck's **Burning Bright** • Stevens' **The Auroras of Autumn** • Viereck's **Strike Through the Mask!** • Warren's **World Enough and Time**

Britain recognized the Peiping Communist regime as the **de facto** government of China, 6 January • United Nations Security Council rejected Russia's resolution to unseat the representative of Nationalist China, 10 January, after which the Russian member walked out and did not return for six months • Mao Tse-tung, leader of the Chinese Communists, signed a mutual defense treaty with Stalin, in Moscow, 15 February • North Korean troops invaded South Korea, 25 June; U. N. Security Council declared this action a breach of peace and called upon all U. N. members to aid in enforcing its order for withdrawal of North Koreans to the 38th parallel of latitude; Truman ordered Gen. Douglas MacArthur, commander of American forces in Japan, to assist the South Koreans, and sent the Seventh Fleet to Formosan waters to prevent conflict between

Nationalist and Communist China • United States census: population 150,697,261

1951 Truman Capote's **The Grass Harp** • Faulkner's **Requiem for a Nun** • James Jones' **From Here to Eternity** • Lewis' **World So Wide** • Mailer's **Barbary Shore** • J. D. Salinger's **The Catcher in the Rye** • Shaw's **The Troubled Air** • Richard Wilbur's **Ceremony and Other Poems** • Herman Wouk's **The Caine Mutiny**

U. N. General Assembly named Communist China the aggressor in Korea, 1 February • Arms embargo against Communist China voted, 19 May • Chinese Communists "liberated" Tibet, 27 May • Japanese Peace Treaty signed by United States and forty-eight other nations, San Francisco, 8 September • Greece and Turkey admitted to NATO, September • Mutual Security Agency (MSA) replaced ECA, 10 October • Conservative Party won general election in Britain, 25 October, Churchill returning as Prime Minister

1952 Hemingway's **The Old Man and the Sea** • O'Connor's **An Age of Criticism** • O'Neill's **A Moon for the Misbegotten** • Sandburg's **Always the Young Strangers** • Steinbeck's **East of Eden** • Wilson's **The Shores of Light**

King George VI of Britain died, 6 February; Elizabeth II proclaimed Queen • NATO Council, meeting at Lisbon, February, approved a European army, with use of German troops • Proposals for German and Austrian peace treaties failed, March • Communist Party in Russia reorganized, 5-15 October • Dwight D. Eisenhower elected thirty-fourth President

1953 Stalin died, 5 March; succeeded by Georgi M. Malenkov • Korean armistice signed, 27 July

Woodrow Wilson

1856 · 1924

The ideals of the American people in World War I were most fully expressed by Woodrow Wilson, twenty-eighth President of the United States. Within a few months after the Armistice of 1918, however, Wilson's scheme to fulfill his promise to "make the world safe for democracy" had been rejected and his leadership had ended in failure as complete as that of any political figure in American history. Whose fault it was—his own, that of his enemies in the Senate, or that of the people themselves—is still acrimoniously debated. Now, after a second and far more destructive World War, it seems likely that the final measure of Wilson's greatness will be the degree to which the world succeeds in its continuing effort to substitute law for force as the ultimate settlement of international disputes. If strong armies and navies and air forces are to be the only assurance of peace, Wilson was and will remain an impractical dreamer. If an international organization capable of ending war and of dealing justly with the wrongs which cause war can be perfected, Wilson was an inspired prophet and may yet regain the vast prestige which he had in 1918 and 1919.

The most remarkable thing about Wilson as a man

is that he should have become a political leader. The son of a Presbyterian clergyman, he was born at Staunton, Virginia, in 1856, and brought up in Georgia

Woodrow Wilson—photo Brown Brothers

and the Carolinas. His biographers have made much of both the Presbyterian and the Southern background in explaining Wilson's moralistic political philosophy. After a year at Davidson College in North Carolina he went to Princeton, where he was graduated in 1879. He then studied law at the University of Virginia, practicing briefly in Atlanta before deciding to prepare himself for teaching and writing on the science of politics, the subject which had attracted him strongly during his undergraduate days. From 1883 until 1885 he worked at Johns Hopkins University, where he took his Ph.D. degree in 1886. By that time his first book, *Congressional Government* (1885), had brought him the attention of scholars, and he had begun his teaching career in a post at Bryn Mawr. A long series of contributions to history and political science followed—the accompaniment of a brilliant teaching record at Bryn Mawr (1885-1888), Wesleyan (1888-1890), and Princeton (1890-1910). *The State* (1889), *Division and Reunion, 1829-1889* (1893), *George Washington* (1896), *A History of the American People* (1902), and *Constitutional Government in the United States* (1908) did not exhaust his energies; he was also interested in educational reorganization and from 1902 until 1910 was the president of Princeton. At fifty-four, indeed, he was the pattern of a modern college administrator. Few persons would have guessed that three years later he would be President of the United States, and that within eight years he would symbolize the hopes of peoples the world over that they would have the chance to determine for themselves under what government they wished to live.

Wilson's spectacular rise in politics was the result of several circumstances: the need of the Democratic party for a reform candidate to challenge the Republican leadership of Theodore Roosevelt; the widespread feeling that the Republicans, for all their "trust-busting," had not gone far enough toward economic justice; and, most important of all, the internal strife in the Republican party which resulted in the Progressive or "Bull Moose" ticket of 1912. As governor of New Jersey in 1910-1912 Wilson showed himself willing to fight "bossism" to the bitter end; his earnestness and honesty commended him to the rank and file throughout the nation. Unpalatable as he was to many Democratic leaders, he won enough support to win, with the assistance of William Jennings Bryan, the Presidential nomination in 1912—on the forty-sixth ballot in one of the stormiest conventions in American history. Campaigning for what he called the "New Freedom," a domestic program comprising conservation of natural resources, fair access to raw materials and financial credits, and the elimination of all forms of monopoly, he was elected by a vast majority in the electoral college, although Theodore Roosevelt and William Howard Taft (Progressive and Republican opponents) between them polled over a million more votes than the 6,300,000 cast for Wilson. With large Democratic majorities in both houses of Congress, Wilson was offered an opportunity for practical achievement such as very seldom comes to a political scientist.

Remarkable domestic legislation was soon pushed through—a sharp downward revision of the protective tariff, the Federal Reserve Act, various measures for improving the condition of farmers and workingmen. Almost at once, however, Wilson was plagued by the necessity of dealing with all but insoluble problems in foreign affairs. Revolution in Mexico was followed by such disorder that many Americans demanded intervention; before that matter was settled, war had broken out in Europe. The familiar difficulties of neutrality followed, with a new variation provided by German submarine warfare. It is not necessary here to retell the story of the steps which led to the declaration of war against the German Empire, the sending of the American Expeditionary Force under General Pershing, and, after the Armistice, Wilson's personal participation in the framing of the Treaty of Versailles, with the League of Nations as its basic feature. Most of this tale is related in Wilson's own words. For Wilson and for the United States, however, the climax was tragic—a retirement into isolationism. Less than a generation was required to prove that the principle of national self-determination, unsupported by an effective international organization, cannot be sustained.

As a writer Wilson had the virtues and the weaknesses of a good college lecturer. He is clear; he leaves no doubt of the organization of his material; he makes effective use of allusion and the well-rounded phrase. On the other hand, he tends to overwork repetition for emphasis, intensification by superlatives, adjectives, and nouns in couplets and series, and his tone is sometimes almost arrogantly dogmatic. His rhetoric is that of the public speaker, the master of persuasion, self-confident and earnest, a little impatient, perhaps, of interruption. The style, however, is the man himself, hard to fit into precise categories and capable of widely divergent interpretation.

The Public Papers of Woodrow Wilson, ed. R. S. Baker and W. E. Dodd, Authorized Edition (Bibliographies, II, 475-506; IV, 437-483, VI, 543-636), 6 vols., New York, 1925-1927 • W. B. Hale, The Story of a Style, New York, 1920 • R. S. Baker, Woodrow Wilson: Life and Letters, 8 vols., New York, 1927-1939 • G. W. Johnson, with the collaboration of the editors of Look, Woodrow Wilson: The Unforgettable Figure Who Has Returned to Haunt Us, New York, 1944

War Message

Address... Delivered at a Joint Session of the Two Houses of Congress, April 2, 1917

The circumstances of the composition and delivery of Wilson's "War Message" have been described by a number of his close associates, most notably by Colonel House (Intimate Papers), David F. Houston, his secretary of agriculture (Eight Years in Wilson's Cabinet), and Frank I. Cobb, editor of the New York World. Excellent summaries may be found in the fifth volume of Mark Sullivan's Our Times (1933) and in Walter Millis' Road to War: America, 1914-1917 (1935). The crisis developed immediately after Wilson's second inauguration. On March 9 the President called for a special session of Congress to meet on April 16; on March 21 the date was advanced by two weeks to April 2. On Saturday night, March 31, unable to sleep, Wilson carried his small typewriter to the south portico of the White House and there, in bathrobe and slippers, with a bowl of crackers and milk beside him, he wrote what is probably his greatest speech. It is well to remember that he had labored to maintain American neutrality long after great blocs of his countrymen and the majority of his cabinet and advisers were more than ready to fight. He knew that his call to arms would have great popular appeal, and he had, as more than one observer has noted, an almost unparalleled skill in the choice of emotion-laden words. His purpose, however, was not merely to create national unity, but also to turn the war frenzy to the moral level which to him was the sole justification for sending American forces to Europe. His careful distinction between the German government and the German people was an ingenious way of waging war with ideas; but his moralistic line of thought shows most clearly in the eloquent summary of American war aims, with its promise of "a universal dominion of right by such a concert of free peoples as shall bring peace and safety to all nations and make the world itself at last free."

I have called the Congress into extraordinary session because there are serious, very serious, choices of policy to be made, and made immediately, which it was neither right nor constitutionally permissible that I should assume the responsibility of making.

On the third of February last I officially laid before you the extraordinary announcement of the Imperial German Government that on and after the first day of February it was its purpose to put aside all restraints of law or of humanity and use its submarines to sink every vessel that sought to approach either the ports of Great Britain and Ireland or the western coasts of Europe or any of the ports controlled by the enemies of Germany within the Mediterranean. That had seemed to be the object of the German submarine warfare earlier in the war, but since April of last year the Imperial Government has somewhat restrained the commanders of its undersea craft in conformity with its promise then given to us that passenger boats should not be sunk and that

10

4 **constitutionally permissible.** Under Article I, Section 8, Paragraph 11 of the Constitution, the power to declare war is given to Congress • 6 **third of February,** the date on which Wilson had announced to a joint session the severing of all diplomatic relations with the German government • 16 **April of last year.** A note to the German government dated April 18, 1916, had threatened to sever diplomatic relations unless submarine warfare against American ships was abandoned

due warning would be given to all other vessels which its submarines might seek to destroy, when no resistance was offered or escape attempted, and care taken that their crews were given at least a fair chance to save their lives in their open boats. The precautions taken were meager and haphazard enough, as was proved in distressing instance after instance in the progress of the cruel and unmanly business, but a certain degree of restraint was observed. The new policy has swept every restriction aside. Vessels of every kind, whatever their flag, their character, their cargo, their destination, their errand, have been ruthlessly sent to the bottom without warning and without thought of help or mercy for those on board, the vessels of friendly neutrals along with those of belligerents. Even hospital ships and ships carrying relief to the sorely bereaved and stricken people of Belgium, though the latter were provided with safe conduct through the proscribed areas by the German Government itself and were distinguished by unmistakable marks of identity, have been sunk with the same reckless lack of compassion or of principle.

I was for a little while unable to believe that such things would in fact be done by any government that had hitherto subscribed to the humane practices of civilized nations. International law had its origin in the attempt to set up some law which would be respected and observed upon the seas, where no nation had right of dominion and where lay the free highways of the world. By painful stage after stage has that law been built up, with meager enough results, indeed, after all was accomplished that could be accomplished, but always with a clear view, at least, of what the heart and conscience of mankind demanded. This minimum of right the German Government has swept aside under the plea of retaliation and necessity and because it had no weapons which it could use at sea except those which it is impossible to employ as it is employing them without throwing to the winds all scruples of humanity or of respect for the understandings that were supposed to underlie the intercourse of the world. I am not now thinking of the loss of property involved, immense and serious as that is, but only of the wanton and wholesale destruction of the lives of non-combatants, men, women, and children, engaged in pursuits which have always, even in the darkest periods of modern history, been

deemed innocent and legitimate. Property can be paid for; the lives of peaceful and innocent people cannot be. The present German submarine warfare against commerce is a warfare against mankind.

It is a war against all nations. American ships have been sunk, American lives taken, in ways which it has stirred us very deeply to learn of, but the ships and people of other neutral and friendly nations have been sunk and overwhelmed in the waters in the same way. There has been no discrimination. The challenge is to all mankind. Each nation must decide for itself how it will meet it. The choice we make for ourselves must be made with a moderation of counsel and a temperateness of judgment befitting our character and our motives as a nation. We must put excited feeling away. Our motive will not be revenge, or the victorious assertion of the physical might of the nation, but only the vindication of right, of human right, of which we are only a single champion.

When I addressed the Congress on the twenty-sixth of February last I thought that it would suffice to assert our neutral rights with arms; our right to use the seas against unlawful interference; our right to keep our people safe against unlawful violence. But armed neutrality, it now appears, is impracticable. Because submarines are in effect outlaws when used as the German submarines have been used against merchant shipping, it is impossible to defend ships against their attacks as the law of nations has assumed that merchantmen would defend themselves against privateers or cruisers, visible craft giving chase upon the open sea. It is common prudence in such circumstances, grim necessity indeed, to endeavour to destroy them before they have shown their own intention. They must be dealt with upon sight, if dealt with at all. The German Government denies the right of neutrals to use arms at all within the areas of the sea which it has proscribed, even in the defense of rights which no modern publicist has ever before questioned their right to defend. The intimation is conveyed that the armed guards which we have placed on our merchant ships will be treated as beyond the pale of law and subject to be dealt with as pirates would be. Armed neutrality is ineffectual enough

---

66 **twenty-sixth of February,** the date on which Wilson had asked Congress for authority to arm American merchant ships

at best; in such circumstances and in the face of such pretensions it is worse than ineffectual: it is likely only to produce what it was meant to prevent; it is practically certain to draw us into the war without either the rights or the effectiveness of belligerents. There is one choice we cannot make, we are incapable of making:—we will not choose the path of submission and suffer the most sacred rights of our nation and our people to be ignored or violated. The wrongs against which we now array ourselves are no common wrongs; they cut to the very roots of human life.

With a profound sense of the solemn and even tragic character of the step I am taking and of the grave responsibilities which it involves, but in unhesitating obedience to what I deem my constitutional duty, I advise that Congress declare the recent course of the Imperial German Government to be in fact nothing less than war against the government and people of the United States; that it formally accept the status of belligerent which has thus been thrust upon it, and that it take immediate steps not only to put the country in a more thorough state of defense but also to exert all its power and employ all its resources to bring the Government of the German Empire to terms and end the war.

What this will involve is clear. It will involve the utmost practicable coöperation in counsel and action with the governments now at war with Germany; and, as incident to that, the extension to those Governments of the most liberal financial credits, in order that our resources may so far as possible be added to theirs. It will involve the organization and mobilization of all the material resources of the country to supply the materials of war and serve the incidental needs of the nation in the most abundant and yet the most economical and efficient way possible. It will involve the immediate full equipment of the navy in all respects but particularly in supplying it with the best means of dealing with the enemy's submarines. It will involve the immediate addition to the armed forces of the United States already provided for by law in case of war at least five hundred thousand men, who should, in my opinion, be chosen upon the principle of universal liability to service, and also the authorization of subsequent additional increments of equal force so soon as they may be needed and can be handled in training.

It will involve also, of course, the granting of adequate credits to the Government, sustained, I hope, so far as they can equitably be sustained by the present generation, by well-conceived taxation.

I say sustained so far as may be equitable by taxation because it seems to me that it would be most unwise to base the credits which will now be necessary entirely on money borrowed. It is our duty, I most respectfully urge, to protect our people so far as we may against the very serious hardships and evils which would be likely to arise out of the inflation which would be produced by vast loans.

In carrying out the measures by which these things are to be accomplished we should keep constantly in mind the wisdom of interfering as little as possible in our own preparation and in the equipment of our own military forces with the duty,—for it will be a very practical duty,—of supplying the nations already at war with Germany with the materials which they can obtain only from us or by our assistance. They are in the field and we should help them in every way to be effective there.

I shall take the liberty of suggesting, through the several executive departments of the Government, for the consideration of your committees, measures for the accomplishment of the several objects I have mentioned. I hope that it will be your pleasure to deal with them as having been framed after very careful thought by the branch of the Government upon which the responsibility of conducting the war and safeguarding the nation will most directly fall.

While we do these things, these deeply momentous things, let us be very clear, and make very clear to all the world what our motives and our objects are. My own thought has not been driven from its habitual and normal course by the unhappy events of the last two months, and I do not believe that the thought of the nation has been altered or clouded by them. I have exactly the same things in mind now that I had in mind

7 **path of submission.** At this point Wilson was interrupted by a roar of applause led by Chief Justice White. Cheering was almost continuous throughout the remainder of his address • 29 **Governments,** Great Britain, France, and Italy • 41 **already provided for,** by the National Defence Act, signed by the President on June 3, 1916 • 43 **universal liability,** Wilson's acceptance of the principle of conscription as opposed to dependence upon volunteers

when I addressed the Senate on the twenty-second of January last; the same that I had in mind when I addressed the Congress on the third of February and on the twenty-sixth of February. Our object now, as then, is to vindicate the principles of peace and justice in the life of the world as against selfish and autocratic power and to set up amongst the really free and self-governed peoples of the world such a concert of purpose and of action as will henceforth insure the observance of those principles. Neutrality is no longer feasible or desirable where the peace of the world is involved and the freedom of its peoples, and the menace to that peace and freedom lies in the existence of the autocratic governments backed by organized force which is controlled wholly by their will, not by the will of their people. We have seen the last of neutrality in such circumstances. We are at the beginning of an age in which it will be insisted that the same standards of conduct and of responsibility for wrong done shall be observed among nations and their governments that are observed among the individual citizens of civilized states.

We have no quarrel with the German people. We have no feeling towards them but one of sympathy and friendship. It was not upon their impulse that their government acted in entering this war. It was not with their previous knowledge or approval. It was a war determined upon as wars used to be determined upon in the old, unhappy days when peoples were nowhere consulted by their rulers and wars were provoked and waged in the interests of dynasties or of little groups of ambitious men who were accustomed to use their fellow-men as pawns or tools. Self-governed nations do not fill their neighbour states with spies or set the course of intrigue to bring about some critical posture of affairs which will give them an opportunity to strike and make conquest. Such designs can be successfully worked out only under cover and where no one has the right to ask questions. Cunningly contrived plans of deception or aggression, carried, it may be, from generation to generation, can be worked out and kept from the light only within the privacy of courts or behind the carefully guarded confidences of a narrow and privileged class. They are happily impossible where public opinion commands and insists upon full information concerning all the nation's affairs.

A steadfast concert for peace can never be maintained except by a partnership of democratic nations. No autocratic government could be trusted to keep faith within it or observe its covenants. It must be a league of honour, a partnership of opinion. Intrigue would eat its vitals away; the plottings of inner circles who could plan what they would and render account to no one would be a corruption seated at its very heart. Only free peoples can hold their purpose and their honour steady to a common end and prefer the interests of mankind to any narrow interest of their own.

Does not every American feel that assurance has been added to our hope for the future peace of the world by the wonderful and heartening things that have been happening within the last few weeks in Russia? Russia was known by those who knew it best to have been always in fact democratic at heart, in all the vital habits of her thought, in all the intimate relationships of her people that spoke their natural instinct, their habitual attitude toward life. The autocracy that crowned the summit of her political structure, long as it had stood and terrible as was the reality of its power, was not in fact Russian in origin, character or purpose; and it has been shaken off and the great, generous Russian people have been added in all their native majesty and might to the forces that are fighting for freedom in the world, for justice, and for peace. Here is a fit partner for a League of Honour.

One of the things that has served to convince us that the Prussian autocracy was not and could never be our

1 **twenty-second of January**, the date of an address in which Wilson had discussed the war aims of the belligerents, pleading for a "peace without victory." Both sides claimed, he said, to be fighting for a just and secure peace, not for the humiliation of the enemy. Such a peace, he believed, was possible on four conditions: the acceptance of "the principle that governments derive their just powers from the consent of the governed"; the acceptance of the principle that all great powers "be assured a direct outlet to the great highways of the sea"; the acceptance of genuine freedom of the seas; and world-wide limitation of armaments. Because it foreshadowed most of Wilson's argument for the kind of peace he wanted, this address ranks among the most important of his state papers • 23 **German people.** The device of separating a people from their corrupt or autocratic government had been used previously by Wilson in his dealings with the Huerta regime in Mexico • 61 **happening . . . Russia.** The abdication of Czar Nicholas II had come on March 15, after little more than two weeks of revolution. The coup d'état of the Bolshevists led by Lenin was still seven months in the future when Wilson spoke, since it came on November 7

friend is that from the very outset of the present war it has filled our unsuspecting communities and even our offices of government with spies and set criminal intrigues everywhere afoot against our national unity of counsel, our peace within and without, our industries and our commerce. Indeed it is now evident that its spies were here even before the war began; and it is unhappily not a matter of conjecture but a fact proved in our courts of justice that the intrigues which have

10 more than once come perilously near to disturbing the peace and dislocating the industries of the country have been carried on at the instigation, with the support, and even under the personal direction of official agents of the Imperial Government accredited to the Government of the United States. Even in checking these things and trying to extirpate them we have sought to put the most generous interpretation possible upon them because we knew that their source lay, not in any hostile feeling or purpose of the German people to-

20 wards us (who were, no doubt, as ignorant of them as we ourselves were), but only in the selfish designs of a Government that did what it pleased and told its people nothing. But they have played their part in serving to convince us at last that that Government entertains no real friendship for us and means to act against our peace and security at its convenience. That it means to stir up enemies against us at our very doors the intercepted note to the German Minister at Mexico City is eloquent evidence.

30 We are accepting this challenge of hostile purpose because we know that in such a government, following such methods, we can never have a friend; and that in the presence of its organized power, always lying in wait to accomplish we know not what purpose, there can be no assured security for the democratic governments of the world. We are now about to accept gauge of battle with this natural foe to liberty and shall, if necessary, spend the whole force of the nation to check and nullify its pretensions and its power. We are glad, now that we

40 see the facts with no veil of false pretence about them, to fight thus for the ultimate peace of the world and for the liberation of its peoples, the German peoples included: for the rights of nations great and small and the privilege of men everywhere to choose their way of life and of obedience. The world must be made safe for democracy. Its peace must be planted upon the tested

foundations of political liberty. We have no selfish ends to serve. We desire no conquest, no dominion. We seek no indemnities for ourselves, no material compensation for the sacrifices we shall freely make. We are but one of 50 the champions of the rights of mankind. We shall be satisfied when those rights have been made as secure as the faith and the freedom of nations can make them.

Just because we fight without rancour and without selfish object, seeking nothing for ourselves but what we shall wish to share with all free peoples, we shall, I feel confident, conduct our operations as belligerents without passion and ourselves observe with proud punctilio the principles of right and of fair play we profess to be fighting for. 60

I have said nothing of the Governments allied with the Imperial Government of Germany because they have not made war upon us or challenged us to defend our right and our honour. The Austro-Hungarian Government has, indeed, avowed its unqualified indorsement and acceptance of the reckless and lawless submarine warfare adopted now without disguise by the Imperial German Government, and it has therefore not been possible for this Government to receive Count Tarnowski, the Ambassador recently accredited to this 70 Government by the Imperial and Royal Government of Austria-Hungary; but that Government has not actually engaged in warfare against citizens of the United States on the seas, and I take the liberty, for the present at least, of postponing a discussion of our relations with the authorities at Vienna. We enter this war only where we are clearly forced into it because there are no other means of defending our rights.

It will be all the easier for us to conduct ourselves as belligerents in a high spirit of right and fairness because we act without animus, not in enmity towards a people or with the desire to bring any injury or disadvantage upon them, but only in armed opposition to an irresponsible government which has thrown aside all considerations of humanity and of right and is running amuck.
10 We are, let me say again, the sincere friends of the German people, and shall desire nothing so much as the early re-establishment of intimate relations of mutual advantage between us,—however hard it may be for them, for the time being, to believe that this is spoken from our hearts. We have borne with their present government through all these bitter months because of that friendship,—exercising a patience and forbearance which would otherwise have been impossible. We shall, happily, still have an opportunity to prove that friendship in
20 our daily attitude and actions towards the millions of men and women of German birth and native sympathy who live among us and share our life, and we shall be proud to prove it toward all who are in fact loyal to their neighbours and to the Government in the hour of test. They are, most of them, as true and loyal Americans as if they had never known any other fealty or allegiance. They will be prompt to stand with us in rebuking and restraining the few who may be of a different mind and purpose. If there should be disloyalty, it will be dealt
30 with with a firm hand of stern repression; but, if it lifts

its head at all, it will lift it only here and there and without countenance except from a lawless and malignant few.

It is a distressing and oppressive duty, Gentlemen of the Congress, which I have performed in thus addressing you. There are, it may be, many months of fiery trial and sacrifice ahead of us. It is a fearful thing to lead this great peaceful people into war, into the most terrible and disastrous of all wars, civilization itself seeming to be in the balance. But the right is more precious than peace, and we shall fight for the things which we have 40 always carried nearest our hearts,—for democracy, for the right of those who submit to authority to have a voice in their own governments, for the rights and liberties of small nations, for a universal dominion of right by such a concert of free peoples as shall bring peace and safety to all nations and make the world itself at last free. To such a task we can dedicate our lives and our fortunes, everything that we are and everything that we have, with the pride of those who know that the day has come when America is privileged to spend her blood 50 and her might for the principles that gave her birth and happiness and the peace which she has treasured. God helping her, she can do no other.

1917

---

53 she . . . other. "Probably not one of a hundred of his American hearers," says Mark Sullivan, "recognized that paraphrase of Martin Luther's declaration, immortal to every German Lutheran, 'ich kann nicht anders' (I can do no other). And Germans, in America as well as in Germany, who felt the sentimental pull of it, did not recognize the Wilsonian art of it"

League of Nations

Address at Columbus, Ohio,
September 4, 1919

Wilson's failure to make his vision of a League of Nations to end war prevail may be explained in part by the natural reaction of the American people to peace. That he made

innumerable mistakes which a more astute politician might have avoided cannot, however, be denied. His decision to go himself to the peace conference forced him to make compromises which from a distance he might have avoided; his egotistic by-passing of Senate leadership and prerogatives and his appeal to the people for a Democratic Congress counted heavily against him. When it appeared that the Senate was likely to emasculate by reservations the treaty which he had done his best to achieve, he decided to take his case to the public. He left Washington on September 3, 1919, on a nation-wide speaking tour, with a schedule of approximately forty speeches. Although often received with great enthusiasm, he was tired and seriously ill, not always at his best. The emotional strain was so great that at Pueblo, Colorado, on September 25, he broke into tears while he was speaking, and that night on the train suffered a paralytic stroke from which he never fully recovered. A year later his party and his League were rejected by the voters.

The speech which follows was the first and perhaps the most characteristic of his series in explanation of the treaty. Largely extemporaneous, as is revealed by the numerous repetitions of phrases, it is nevertheless well-organized and often eloquent. It is not the speech of a tactful man, but few will deny its honesty and its essential truth. Without a strong League of Nations the Treaty of Versailles was not destined to be what Wilson thought it was; a league of some nations turned out not to be enough.

Mr. Chairman, Gov. Campbell, my fellow citizens, it is with very profound pleasure that I find myself face to face with you. I have for a long time chafed at the confinement of Washington. I have for a long time wished to fulfill the purpose with which my heart was full when I returned to our beloved country, namely, to go out and report to my fellow countrymen concerning those affairs of the world which now need to be settled. The only people I owe any report to are you and the
10 other citizens of the United States.

And it has become increasingly necessary, apparently, that I should report to you. After all the various angles at which you have heard the treaty held up, perhaps you would like to know what is in the treaty. I find it very difficult in reading some of the speeches that I have read to form any conception of that great document. It is a document unique in the history of the world for many reasons, and I think I can not do you a better service, or the peace of this world a better service, than by pointing
20 out to you just what this treaty contains and what it seeks to do.

In the first place, my fellow countrymen, it seeks to punish one of the greatest wrongs ever done in history, the wrong which Germany sought to do to the world and to civilization; and there ought to be no weak purpose with regard to the application of the punishment. She attempted an intolerable thing, and she must be made to

pay for the attempt. The terms of the treaty are severe, but they are not unjust. I can testify that the men associated with me at the peace conference in Paris had it in 30 their hearts to do justice and not wrong. But they knew, perhaps, with a more vivid sense of what had happened than we could possibly know on this side of the water, the many solemn covenants which Germany had disregarded, the long preparation she had made to overwhelm her neighbors, and the utter disregard which she had shown for human rights, for the rights of women, of children, of those who were helpless. They had seen their lands devast[at]ed by an enemy that devoted himself not only to the effort at victory, but to the effort at 40 terror—seeking to terrify the people whom he fought. And I wish to testify that they exercised restraint in the terms of this treaty. They did not wish to overwhelm any great nation. They acknowledged that Germany was a great nation, and they had no purpose of overwhelming the German people, but they did think that it ought to be burned into the consciousness of men forever that no people ought to permit its government to do what the German Government did.

In the last analysis, my fellow countrymen, as we in 50 America would be the first to claim, a people are responsible for the acts of their government. If their government purposes things that are wrong, they ought to take measures to see to it that that purpose is not executed. Germany was self-governed; her rulers had not concealed the purposes that they had in mind, but they had deceived their people as to the character of the methods they were going to use, and I believe from what I can learn that there is an awakened consciousness in Germany itself of the deep iniquity of the thing that was at- 60 tempted. When the Austrian delegates came before the peace conference, they in so many words spoke of the origination of the war as a crime and admitted in our presence that it was a thing intolerable to contemplate. They knew in their hearts that it had done them the deepest conceivable wrong, that it had put their people and the people of Germany at the judgment seat of mankind, and throughout this treaty every term that was applied to Germany was meant, not to humiliate Germany, but to rectify the wrong that she had done. 70

1 Gov. Campbell, James Edwin Campbell (1843-1924), Democratic governor of Ohio in 1890-1892

Look even into the severe terms of reparation—for there was no indemnity. No indemnity of any sort was claimed, merely reparation, merely paying for the destruction done, merely making good the losses so far as such losses could be made good which she had unjustly inflicted, not upon the governments, for the reparation is not to go to the governments, but upon the people whose rights she had trodden upon with absolute absence of everything that even resembled pity. There was no indemnity in this treaty, but there is reparation, and even in the terms of reparation a method is devised by which the reparation shall be adjusted to Germany's ability to pay it.

I am astonished at some of the statements I hear made about this treaty. The truth is that they are made by persons who have not read the treaty or who, if they have read it, have not comprehended its meaning. There is a method of adjustment in that treaty by which the reparation shall not be pressed beyond the point which Germany can pay, but which will be pressed to the utmost point that Germany can pay—which is just, which is righteous. It would have been intolerable if there had been anything else. For, my fellow citizens, this treaty is not meant merely to end this single war. It is meant as a notice to every government which in the future will attempt this thing that mankind will unite to inflict the same punishment. There is no national triumph sought to be recorded in this treaty. There is no glory sought for any particular nation. The thought of the statesmen collected around that table was of their people, of the sufferings that they had gone through, of the losses they had incurred—that great throbbing heart which was so depressed, so forlorn, so sad in every memory that it had had of the five tragical years that have gone. Let us never forget those years, my fellow countrymen. Let us never forget the purpose—the high purpose, the disinterested purpose—with which America lent its strength not for its own glory but for the defense of mankind.

As I said, this treaty was not intended merely to end this war. It was intended to prevent any similar war. I wonder if some of the opponents of the league of nations have forgotten the promises we made our people before we went to that peace table. We had taken by processes of law the flower of our youth from every household, and we told those mothers and fathers and sisters and wives and sweethearts that we were taking those men to fight a war which would end business of that sort; and if we do not end it, if we do not do the best that human concert of action can do to end it, we are of all men the most unfaithful, the most unfaithful to the loving hearts who suffered in this war, the most unfaithful to those households bowed in grief and yet lifted with the feeling that the lad laid down his life for a great thing and, among other things, in order that other lads might never have to do the same thing. That is what the league of nations is for, to end this war justly, and then not merely to service notice on governments which would contemplate the same things that Germany contemplated, but also concerning the combination of power which will prove to them that they will do it at their peril. It is idle to say the world *will* combine against you, because it may not, but it is persuasive to say the world *is* combined against you, and will remain combined against the things that Germany attempted. The league of nations is the only thing that can prevent the recurrence of this dreadful catastrophe and redeem our promises.

The character of the league is based upon the experience of this very war. I did not meet a single public man who did not admit these things, that Germany would not have gone into this war if she had thought Great Britain was going into it, and that she most certainly would never have gone into this war if she dreamed America was going into it. And they all admitted that a notice beforehand that the greatest powers of the world would combine to prevent this sort of thing would prevent it absolutely. When gentlemen tell you, therefore, that the league of nations is intended for some other purpose than this, merely reply this to them: If we do not do this thing, we have neglected the central covenant that we made to our people, and there will then be no statesman of any country who can thereafter promise his people alleviation from the perils of war. The passions of this world are not dead. The rivalries of this world have not cooled. They have been rendered hotter than ever. The harness that is to unite nations is more neces-

44 flower . . . youth. Mark Sullivan's description of the formula of Wilson's speeches is well illustrated by this sentence. The sense of his speech completed, Sullivan says, "he then picks up a salt-cellar containing the word 'heart,' and sprinkles the manuscript, and another salt-cellar containing a store of 'rights,' and sprinkles again, and others containing 'hold dear's,' and similar emotion-provoking, atmosphere-creating words"

sary now than it ever was before, and unless there is this assurance of combined action before wrong is attempted, wrong will be attempted just as soon as the most ambitious nations can recover from the financial stress of this war.

Now, look what else is in the treaty. This treaty is unique in the history of mankind, because the center of it is the redemption of weak nations. There never was a congress of nations before that considered the rights of those who could not enforce their rights. There never was a congress of nations before that did not seek to effect some balance of power brought about by means of serving the strength and interest of the strongest powers concerned; whereas this treaty builds up nations that never could have won their freedom in any other way; builds them up by gift, by largess, not by obligations; builds them up because of the conviction of the men who wrote the treaty that the rights of people transcend the rights of governments, because of the conviction of the men who wrote that treaty that the fertile source of war is wrong. The Austro-Hungarian Empire, for example, was held together by military force and consisted of peoples who did not want to live together, who did not have the spirit of nationality as toward each other, who were constantly chafing at the bands that held them. Hungary, though a willing partner of Austria, was willing to be a partner because she could share Austria's strength to accomplish her own ambitions, and her own ambitions were to hold under her the Jugo-Slavic peoples that lay to the south of her; Bohemia, an unhappy partner, a partner by duress, beating in all her veins the strongest national impulse that was to be found anywhere in Europe; and north of that, pitiful Poland, a great nation divided up among the great powers of Europe, torn asunder, kinship disregarded, natural ties treated with contempt, and an obligatory division among sovereigns imposed upon her—a part of her given to Russia, a part of her given to Austria, a part of her given to Germany —great bodies of Polish people never permitted to have the normal intercourse with their kinsmen for fear that that fine instinct of the heart should assert itself which binds families together. Poland could never have won her independence. Bohemia never could have broken away from Austro-Hungarian combination. The Slavic peoples to the south, running down into the great Balkan Peninsula, had again and again tried to assert their na-

tionality and independence, and had as often been crushed, not by the immediate power they were fighting, but by the combined power of Europe. The old alliances, the old balances of power, were meant to see to it that no little nation asserted its right to the disturbance of the peace of Europe, and every time an assertion of rights was attempted they were suppressed by combined influence and force.

This treaty tears away all that: says these people have a right to live their own lives under the governments which they themselves choose to set up. That is the American principle, and I was glad to fight for it. When strategic claims were urged, it was matter of common counsel that such considerations were not in our thought. We were not now arranging for future wars. We were giving people what belonged to them. My fellow citizens, I do not think there is any man alive who has a more tender sympathy for the great people of Italy than I have, and a very stern duty was presented to us when we had to consider some of the claims of Italy on the Adriatic, because strategically, from the point of view of future wars, Italy needed a military foothold on the other side of the Adriatic, but her people did not live there except in little spots. It was a Slavic people, and I had to say to my Italian friends, "Everywhere else in this treaty we have given territory to the people who lived on it, and I do not think that it is for the advantage of Italy, and I am sure it is not for the advantage of the world, to give Italy territory where other people live." I felt the force of the argument for what they wanted, and it was the old argument that had always prevailed, namely, that they needed it from a military point of view, and I have no doubt that if there is no league of nations, they will need it from a military point of view; but if there is a league of nations, they will not need it from a military point of view.

If there is no league of nations, the military point of view will prevail in every instance, and peace will be brought into contempt, but if there is a league of nations, Italy need not fear the fact that the shores on the other side of the Adriatic tower above the lower and sandy shores on her side of the sea, because there will be no threatening guns there, and the nations of the world will have concerted, not merely to see that the Slavic peoples have their rights, but that the Italian people have their rights as well. I had rather have everybody on my side than to be armed to the teeth. Every settlement that is right, every settlement that is based on the principles I have alluded to, is a safe settlement, because the sympathy of mankind will be behind it.

Some gentlemen have feared with regard to the league of nations that we will be obliged to do things we do not want to do. If the treaty were wrong, that might be so, but if the treaty is right, we will wish to preserve right. I think I know the heart of this great people whom I, for the time being, have the high honor to represent, better than some other men that I hear talk. I have been bred, and am proud to have been bred, in the old revolutionary school which set this Government up, when it was set up as the friend of mankind, and I know if they do not that America has never lost that vision or that purpose. But I have not the slightest fear that arms will be necessary if the purpose is there. If I know that my adversary is armed and I am not, I do not press the controversy, and if any nation entertains selfish purposes set against the principles established in this treaty, and is told by the rest of the world that it must withdraw its claims, it will not press them.

The heart of this treaty then, my fellow citizens, is not even that it punishes Germany. That is a temporary thing. It is that it rectifies the age-long wrongs which characterized the history of Europe. There were some of us who wished that the scope of the treaty would reach some other age-long wrongs. It was a big job, and I do not say that we wished that it were bigger, but there were other wrongs elsewhere than in Europe and of the same kind which no doubt ought to be righted, and some day will be righted, but which we could not draw into the treaty because we could deal only with the countries whom the war had engulfed and affected. But so far as the scope of our authority went, we rectified the wrongs which have been the fertile source of war in Europe.

Have you ever reflected, my fellow countrymen, on the real source of revolution? Men do not start revolutions in a sudden passion. Do you remember what Thomas Carlyle said about the French Revolution? He was speaking of the so-called Hundred Days Terror which reigned not only in Paris, but throughout France, in the days of the French Revolution, and he reminded his readers that back of that hundred days lay several hundred years of agony and of wrong. The French people had been deeply and consistently wronged by their Government, robbed, their human rights disregarded, and the slow agony of those hundreds of years had after awhile gathered into a hot anger that could not be suppressed. Revolutions do not spring up overnight. Revolutions come from the long suppression of the human spirit. Revolutions come because men know that they have rights and that they are disregarded; and when we think of the future of the world in connection with this treaty we must remember that one of the chief efforts of those who made this treaty was to remove that anger from the heart of great peoples, great peoples who had always been suppressed, who had always been used, and who had always been the tools in the hands of governments, generally alien governments, not their own. The makers of the treaty knew that if these wrongs were not removed, there could be no peace in the world, because, after all, my fellow citizens, war comes from the seed of wrong and not from the seed of right. This treaty is an attempt to right the history of Europe, and, in my humble judgment, it is a measurable success. I say "measurable," my fellow citizens, because you will realize the difficulty of this:

Here are two neighboring peoples. The one people have not stopped at a sharp line, and the settlements of the other people or their migrations have not begun at a sharp line. They have intermingled. There are regions where you can not draw a national line and say there are Slavs on this side [illustrating] and Italians on that [illustrating]. It can not be done. You have to approximate the line. You have to come as near to it as you can, and then trust to the processes of history to redistribute, it may be, the people that are on the wrong side of the line. There are many such lines drawn in this treaty and to be drawn in the Austrian treaty, where there are perhaps more lines of that sort than in the German treaty. When we came to draw the line between the Polish people and the German people—not the line between Germany and Poland; there was no Poland, strictly speaking, but the line between the German and the Polish people —we were confronted by such problems as the disposition of districts like the eastern part of Silesia, which is called Upper Silesia because it is mountainous and the

40 **Thomas Carlyle** (1795-1881), Scotch essayist and historian. The passage alluded to is Chap. I of Bk. V of the third volume of **The French Revolution** (1837)

other part is not. Upper Silesia is chiefly Polish, and when we came to draw the line of what should be Poland it was necessary to include Upper Silesia if we were really going to play fair and make Poland up of the Polish peoples wherever we found them in sufficiently close neighborhood to one another, but it was not perfectly clear that Upper Silesia wanted to be part of Poland. At any rate, there were Germans in Upper Silesia who said that it did not, and therefore we did there what we did in many other places. We said, "Very well, then, we will let the people that live there decide. We will have a referendum. Within a certain length of time after the war, under the supervision of an international commission which will have a sufficient armed force behind it to preserve order and see that nobody interferes with the elections, we will have an absolutely free vote and Upper Silesia shall go either to Germany or to Poland, as the people in Upper Silesia prefer." That illustrates many other cases where we provided for a referendum, or a plebiscite, as they chose to call it. We are going to leave it to the people themselves, as we should have done, what Government they shall live under. It is none of my prerogative to allot peoples to this Government or the other. It is nobody's right to do that allotting except the people themselves, and I want to testify that this treaty is shot through with the American principle of the choice of the governed.

Of course, at times it went further than we could make a practical policy of, because various peoples were keen upon getting back portions of their population which were separated from them by many miles of territory, and we could not spot the map over with little pieces of separated States. I even reminded my Italian colleagues that if they were going to claim every place where there was a large Italian population, we would have to cede New York to them, because there are more Italians in New York than in any Italian city. But I hope, I believe, that the Italians in New York City are as glad to stay there as we are to have them. But I would not have you suppose that I am intimating that my Italian colleagues entered any claim for New York City.

We of all peoples in the world, my fellow citizens, ought to be able to understand the questions of this treaty without anybody explaining them to us, for we are made up out of all the peoples of the world. I dare say that in this audience there are representatives of practically all the people dealt with in this treaty. You do not have to have me explain national aspirations to you. You have been brought up on them. You have learned of them since you were children, and it is those national aspirations which we sought to release and give an outlet to in this great treaty.

But we did much more than that. This treaty contains among other things a Magna Charta of labor—a thing unheard of until this interesting year of grace. There is a whole section of the treaty devoted to arrangements by which the interests of those who labor with their hands all over the world, whether they be men or women or children, are sought to be safeguarded; and next month there is to meet the first assembly under this section of the league. Let me tell you, it will meet whether the treaty is ratified by that time or not. There is to meet an assembly which represents the interests of laboring men throughout the world. Not their political interests; there is nothing political about it. It is the interests of men concerning the conditions of their labor, concerning the character of labor which women shall engage in, the character of labor which children shall be permitted to engage in; the hours of labor; and, incidentally, of course, the remuneration of labor; that labor shall be remunerated in proportion, of course, to the maintenance of the standard of living, which is proper, for the man who is expected to give his whole brain and intelligence and energy to a particular task. I hear very little said about the Magna Charta of labor which is embodied in this treaty. It forecasts the day, which ought to have come long ago, when statesmen will realize that no nation is fortunate which is not happy and that no nation can be happy whose people are not contented; contented in their lives and fortunate in the circumstances of their lives.

If I were to state what seems to me the central idea of this treaty, it would be this: It is almost a discovery in international conventions that nations do not consist of their governments but consist of their people. That is a rudimentary idea. It seems to us in America to go with-

---

20 **plebiscite.** The plebiscite referred to was held in 1920, resulting in 717,122 votes for Germany, 483,514 for Poland. A commission of the Council of the League of Nations awarded the southeastern districts of Upper Silesia to Poland on October 20, 1921. The partition of Silesia was one of the reasons for Hitler's denouncing of the Treaty of Versailles and its results

out saying, but, my fellow citizens, it was never the leading idea in any other international congress that I ever heard of; that is to say, any international congress made up of the representatives of governments. They were always thinking of national policy, of national advantage, of the rivalries of trade, of the advantages of territorial conquest. There is nothing of that in this treaty. You will notice that even the territories which are taken away from Germany, like her colonies, are not given to anybody. There is not a single act of annexation in this treaty. Territories inhabited by people not yet to govern themselves, either because of economical or other circumstances, are put under the care of powers, who are to act as trustees—trustees responsible in the forum of the world at the bar of the league of nations, and the terms upon which they are to exercise their trusteeship are outlined. They are not to use those people by way of draft to fight their wars for them. They are not to permit any form of slavery among them, or of enforced labor. They are to see to it that there are humane conditions of labor with regard not only to the women and children but to the men also. They are to establish no fortifications. They are to regulate the liquor and the opium traffic. They are to see to it, in other words, that the lives of the people whose care they assume—not sovereignty over whom they assume—are kept clean and safe and wholesome. There again the principle of the treaty comes out, that the object of the arrangement is the welfare of the people who live there, and not the advantage of the trustee.

It goes beyond that. It seeks to gather under the common supervision of the league of nations the various instrumentalities by which the world has been trying to check the evils that were in some places debasing men, like the opium traffic, like the traffic—for it was a traffic —in women and children, like the traffic in other dangerous drugs, like the traffic in arms among uncivilized people who could use arms only for their own detriment. It provides for sanitation, for the work of the Red Cross. Why, those clauses, my fellow citizens, draw the hearts of the world into league, draw the noble impulses of the world together and make a team of them.

I used to be told that this was an age in which mind was monarch, and my comment was that if that was true, the mind was one of those modern monarchs that reigns and does not govern; that, as a matter of fact, we were governed by a great representative assembly made up of the human passions, and that the best we could manage was that the high and fine passions should be in a majority so that they could control the baser passions, so that they could check the things that were wrong. This treaty seeks something like that. In drawing the humane endeavors of the world together it makes a league of the fine passions of the world, of its philanthropic passions, of its passion of pity, of its passion of human sympathy, of its passion of human friendliness and helpfulness, for there is such a passion. It is the passion which has lifted us along the slow road of civilization. It is the passion which has made organized government possible. It is the passion which has made justice and established it in the world.

That is the treaty. Did you ever hear of it before? Did you ever know before what was in this treaty? Did anybody before ever tell you what the treaty was intended to do? I beg, my fellow citizens, that you and the rest of those Americans with whom we are happy to be associated all over this broad land will read the treaty yourselves, or, if you will not take the time to do that—for it is a technical document—that you will accept the interpretation of those who made it and know what the intentions were in the making of it. I hear a great deal, my fellow citizens, about the selfishness and the selfish ambitions of other governments, and I would not be doing justice to the gifted men with whom I was associated on the other side of the water if I did not testify that the purposes that I have outlined were their purposes. We differed as to the method very often. We had discussions as to the details, but we never had any serious discussion as to the principle. While we all acknowledged that the principles might perhaps in detail have been better realized, we are all back of those principles. There is a concert of mind and of purpose and of policy in the world that was never in existence before. I am not saying that by way of credit to myself or to those colleagues to whom I have alluded, because what happened to us was that we got messages from our people. We were under instructions, whether they were written down or not, and we did not dare come home without fulfilling those instruc-

---

62 **Did you ever hear. . . .** The tone of this paragraph, although intended to be ironic, is an excellent illustration of Wilson's tendency to introduce an unfortunate professorial effect

tions. If I could not have brought back the kind of treaty that I did bring back, I never would have come back, because I would have been an unfaithful servant, and you would have had the right to condemn me in any way that you chose to use. So that I testify that this is an American treaty not only, but it is a treaty that expresses the heart of the great peoples who were associated together in the war against Germany.

I said at the opening of this informal address, my fellow citizens, that I had come to make a report to you. I want to add to that a little bit. I have not come to debate the treaty. It speaks for itself, if you will let it. The arguments directed against it are directed against it with a radical misunderstanding of the instrument itself. Therefore, I am not going anywhere to debate the treaty. I am going to expound it, and I am going, as I do here, now, to-day, to urge you in every vocal method that you can use to assert the spirit of the American people in support of it. Do not let men pull it down. Do not let them misrepresent it. Do not let them lead this Nation away from the high purposes with which this war was inaugurated and fought. As I came through that line of youngsters in khaki a few minutes ago I felt that I could

salute them because I had done the job in the way I promised them I would do it, and when this treaty is accepted, men in khaki will not have to cross the seas again. That is the reason I believe in it.

I say "when it is accepted," for it will be accepted. I have never entertained a moment's doubt of that, and the only thing I have been impatient of has been the delay. It is not dangerous delay, except for the temper of the peoples scattered throughout the world who are waiting. Do you realize, my fellow citizens, that the whole world is waiting on America? The only country in the world that is trusted at this moment is the United States, and the peoples of the world are waiting to see whether their trust is justified or not. That has been the ground of my impatience. I knew their trust was justified, but I begrudged the time that certain gentlemen wish to take in telling them so. We shall tell them so in a voice as authentic as any voice in history, and in the years to come men will be glad to remember that they had some part in the great struggle which brought this incomparable consummation of the hopes of mankind.

1919

Herbert Clark Hoover

1874 ·

Ray Lyman Wilbur and Arthur Mastick Hyde preface their *The Hoover Policies* with a contrast between "two clashing philosophies of government" of modern times: "The first proposes to find solutions through a vast turn toward centralization of government, 'economic planning' with its strong measures of coercion of individuals. The second proposes to accomplish the same ends within the framework of a strong local as well as Federal Government and the development of understanding and

voluntary co-operative action among free men. The one drives toward personal government where the state is the master of men. The other drives toward a government of laws where men are masters of the state. The one drives toward Collectivism. The other drives toward American Individualism." The former, these authors who were sympathetic to Hoover claimed, was the concept of Franklin Delano Roosevelt; the latter, the concept of Hoover. Many of Hoover's supporters—

and at least some of his opponents—probably would have agreed that this was a proper statement of what Hoover has stood for.

Herbert Clark Hoover's life up until the time when he ran for the Presidency cultivated his firm faith in what he called "rugged individualism." His birthplace was West Branch, Iowa, and his ancestors were pioneer Quaker stock. Orphaned before he had reached his teens, he went, at twelve, to live with an uncle on the extreme frontier in Oregon. There he worked on a farm and absorbed much of the Far Western faith in thrift and industry. Later he worked his way through Stanford University, as a clerk, a distributor of newspapers, and a campus entrepreneur. In 1895, after he had acquired a degree in engineering, he went to Nevada City to work as a laborer in the mines. He left this district to become associated with a prominent California mining engineer, Louis Janin. Though he started as a personal secretary, he soon made such an impression that Janin began to assign him to work in mines in every part of the West. In 1897, at twenty-three, he was sent to Western Australia, where he successfully directed mining operations in the desert country. When, two years later, he went to China to carry out a new assignment, it was at a salary of ten thousand dollars a year. By 1902, he was ready for an executive position, first as a junior partner in a London mining firm, then later in 1908 as an independent consulting engineer with offices scattered over the face of the earth. By 1914, the man who had started his career with only a few dollars had become a rich man —one who, understandably enough, believed devoutly in private industry and enterprise.

His public career, which began in 1913 when he was sent abroad to arrange for exhibits at the San Francisco Exposition, established his reputation as a man who could use efficient business methods in government. In Europe when World War I began, he accepted the chairmanship of the Commission for the Relief of Belgium. After the United States became a belligerent, he became National Food Administrator. During the Presidencies of Harding and Coolidge (1921-1928), he served as secretary of commerce. His aggressive administration, combined with his habit of introducing engineering methods to solve economic problems, won widespread admiration.

When Coolidge "did not choose to run" for reëlection in 1928, Republicans thought of Hoover as his logical successor. In the election, Hoover received 444 electoral votes to the 87 of his opponent, Al Smith. Hoover, as President, continued to voice his lifelong belief in individualism, yet his administration marked the beginnings of socialized economy, and several of his measures were carried forward by the Roosevelt administration. The reason was that, though he thought highly of individualistic enterprise, he was, after all, an engineer who had great faith in planning. Furthermore, in 1929 and the years which followed, the United States was gripped by a devastating depression. Although Hoover firmly believed that the bad state of affairs was temporary, eventually he came to believe that action was necessary. Characteristically, he attempted a fusion, both in theory and in practice, of the laissez-faire philosophy and planning. He conceived of government operating to help rather than to restrain business and individual enterprise which, with slight regulation, acted for social good. The creation of the Reconstruction Finance Corporation and the passage of an Emergency Relief Act and the Federal Home Loan Bank Act embodied his policy. Fearing that private and local initiative would be damaged by national measures, Hoover did not develop many federal relief measures until late in his administration. The effects of the legislation adopted had not appeared sufficient, in the opinion of the voters in 1932, and he was defeated by Franklin D. Roosevelt by a large majority.

After his defeat, Hoover retired to his home in Palo Alto, California. He did not, however, retire from the political arena. He has continued to be a power in the Republican party; he has frequently issued statements about the world food supply, and has consistently attacked both national and international Democratic policies, in books such as *The Challenge to Liberty* (1934), *American Ideals and the New Deal* (1936), and *America's Way Forward* (1939) as well as in numerous speeches. All of these utterances set forth Hoover's political philosophy very clearly.

W. S. Myers and W. H. Newton, **The Hoover Administration,** New York, 1936 • R. L. Wilbur and A. M. Hyde, **The Hoover Policies,** New York, 1937

The Choice for Youth

Address before the
Young Republican League of Colorado
Colorado Springs
March 7, 1936

Hoover, as a rule has been an adequate but hardly an exciting speaker. Showing little feeling for effective sentence rhythms, he has tended to use abstract or latinate words rather than homespun or common phrases. At times, however, he uses figures of speech with some effect. (Instances in this speech are the claim that youthful opportunities were being "mortgaged" and the "spilt milk-jug" figure). And consistently, as in this address, he has given an impression of earnest belief in his principles and of abhorrence of those of his opponents.

PART I

This assembly marks the anxiety which stirs the nation. Never before have our young men and women so interested themselves in public questions.

It was not long since we fought a great war to "make the world safe for democracy." Hardly four years ago we accepted freedom as we accepted the air we breathed. No man thought our ideals were endangered in his lifetime. Yet now men freely propose how much of liberty we shall sacrifice. Certainly your freedom and your opportunities in life are being mortgaged.

Naturally I have been interested in the New Deal replies since I began discussion of these critical issues. The President said on January 3, 1936: "We have been specific in our affirmative action. Let them be specific in their negative attack." I have tried to be obliging.

But they have made no answer to facts or chapters or verses given in proofs. They, however, are not taciturn as to personal remarks. I did note that one of the New Deal spokesmen in this debate seeks to justify the violation of their platform promises by claiming that I did not hold to our platform promises. There were thirty-nine promises in the Republican platform of 1928. Of these, thirty-seven were carried out even in depression by my administration. And those fulfilled promises included upholding the Constitution and the preservation of national honor. Two secondary promises broke against the obstinacy of a Democratic Congress.

I leave research into their platform promises to well-known Democratic leaders. The examination of spilt milk is of importance. It shows that certain people cannot be safely entrusted with the jug.

The New Deal was not included in the Democratic platform of 1932. But the interpretation of political forces does not rest alone upon platforms. It rests also upon a knowledge of the motives and aims of men and the forces they represent. Eight days before that election I stated that the real intention of these men was to tinker with the currency. I said their program would raise government expenditures to nine billion a year. I said it was their intention to put the government into business. I said it was their intention to undermine state and local government by centralization in Washington. I said it was their intention to regiment our people and undermine the American System with imported European philosophies. That was all vociferously denied. All those interpretations have come true except as to that nine billion—it was only 95 per cent correct.

During the past few months I have made some further interpretations of where we are now headed. I hear again from the New Deal spokesmen the old cat-calls of 1932 —"creating fear," "creating fear."

The Formulas of Revolution

For many years I have studied the tactics and techniques in European countries by which Liberty has been dethroned and dictatorship erected by men greedy for power.

First they ascribed the tragic miseries of the times not to the Great War, where it belongs, but to some party or class. The great phrases born from the finest emotions of mankind were used to camouflage the greed for power. They made great promises. They demanded violent action against human ills that are only slowly curable. They claimed that sporadic wickedness in high places had permeated the whole system of liberty. They shouted new destructive slogans and phrases day by day to inflame the people. They implanted unreasoning hates in the souls of men. They first grasped at power through elections which Liberty provided. Then began the "must emergency instruments of power," "to save the nation." The first demands were powers of dictation over industry and agriculture and finance and labor. Legislatures were reduced to rubber stamps. Honest debate was shut off in the halls of deliberation. A powerful government propaganda was put on the taxpayers' bill, that hates and suspicions could be further inflamed. And all of these men insisted that civilization had begun all over again when they came into power.

In the final stages of European degeneration Liberty died from the waters of her own well. That was when the waters of free speech were poisoned by untruth. Then have followed the last steps to dictatorship, with suppression of freedom of speech, freedom of worship, of the courts, and all other freedoms. Men were goose-stepped in a march back to the Middle Ages.

Whether they know it or not, the New Deal has imitated the intellectual and vocal technique of typical European revolution. In the talking and legislative stages they made some progress. You will recollect also the claim that even civilization came to a dead stop on March 4, 1933.

But America has not reached these final stages. Thanks to a people of a great heritage, to the press and the radio, free speech still lives in America. I intend to use a little more of it tonight.

PART II

The American System of Liberty

My remarks tonight are addressed in large measure to the younger generation. It is you who will have to bear these increased burdens. It is you and your children whose opportunities are being limited.

But far beyond that, our immense objectives upon which depend the welfare of mankind require the faith, the idealism, the courage of youth that they shall not fail. This is more than an acceptance or a rejection of the collectivist ideas and blunders of the New Deal. You must carry forward. The problems of today are different from those of 3 years ago or 10 years ago.

But what sort of an America do we want? What should be our foundations? What should be our ideals?

Perhaps without immodesty I can claim to have had some experience in American life. I have lived all kinds of it. I have seen it in contrast with many countries.

I lived my early boyhood on an Iowa farm. I lived it later as the ward of a country doctor in Oregon. I lived among those to whom hard work was the price of existence. The opportunities of America opened out to me the public schools. They carried me to professional training of an American university. I began by working with my own hands for my daily bread. I have tasted the despair of fruitless search for a job. I know now there was an economic depression either coming or going at that time. Nobody told me of it. So I did not have the additional worry of what the government would do about it.

But I have lived the problems of labor both as a workman and with the men who had to find the payroll. I have lived in the administration of industry with its problems of production and the well-being of men.

My profession took me into many foreign lands under many kinds of government, both of free men and of tyrannies. I saw the squalor of Asia, the frozen class barriers of Europe. I was not a tourist. I was associated in their working lives and problems. I had to deal with their social systems and their governments. And everywhere to the common people America was the hope of the world.

Every yearly homecoming was again to me a proof of the glory of America. I was each time refreshed by the sight of its less grinding poverty, of its greater kindliness and its greater spread of opportunity to the common man. It was more than that. It was a land of self-respect that comes alone from freedom of the spirit.

I participated on behalf of America in a great war. I saw untold misery and revolution. I have seen liberty die and tyranny rise. I learned of its unending calamities.

I have been repeatedly placed by my countrymen where I had need to deal with the hurricanes of social and economic destruction which swept the world. I have had every honor that any man could want, and I have seen the worst misery that men can produce.

These experiences with all these mighty forces which influence the destiny of humanity make for humility of conclusions. And I recount all this to give emphasis to one great conviction.

I believe in the American System of Liberty. I believe in it from thousands of experiences. I believe that upon its foundation is the one hope of the common man. It has faults. But it contains the only real ferment of progress.

There are other systems of Liberty. But at the heart

of our American System is embedded a great ideal unique in the world. That is the ideal that there shall be an opportunity in life, and equal opportunity, for every boy and girl, every man and woman. It holds that they have the chance to rise to any position to which their character and ability may entitle them. That ideal is limited or ended if this nation is to be goose-stepped from Washington.

About every outstanding advance which has promoted the welfare of mankind in the last century has been born in countries of free men and women. The steam engine, electricity, automobiles, telephones, airplanes, radio, free schooling, the great advances in biology, are but part of them. I might include the adding machine but its present use by the New Deal raises doubts as to its contribution to the welfare of mankind.

On the other hand almost every one of the world's mistakes has its origin in personal government. Violation of treaties, great wars, persecution of the Jews and other religionists, and so on down to the fantastic laws by a Must Congress, and the slaughter of pigs.

Youth and American Liberty

American young men and women should have the right to plan, to live their own lives with just one limitation —that they shall not injure their neighbors. What they want of government is to keep the channels of opportunity open and equal, not to block them and then charge them for doing it. They want rewards to the winners in the race. They do not want to be planed down to a pattern. To red-blooded men and women there is joy of work and joy in the battle of competition. There is the daily joy of doing something worth while, of proving one's own worth, of telling every evil person where he can go. There is the joy of championing justice to the weak and downtrodden. These are the battles which create the national fiber of self-reliance and self-respect. That is what made America. If you concentrate all adventure in the government it does not leave much constructive joy for the governed.

In economic life there is but one hope of increased security and comfort for the common man, of opportunity for all. That is to adopt every labor-saving device, every discovery, every idea to reduce waste and the cost of producing goods. We must work our machines heartlessly but not our men. Thereby goods can be sold cheaper and more people can buy. That is the only sure road to a job for every man. It is the only road to restored employment. That production of a plenty can spring alone from the initiative and enterprise of free men. That is no system of robbery. It is action for the common service. That is destroyed at once by the grotesque notion that government shall limit production.

We cannot operate this world of machines and men without leadership. Competent leadership can come only by the rise of men and women in a free society by the impulse of their own ambition, character, and abilities. That leadership cannot come by birth, or by wealth, or be nursed like queen bees. That leadership cannot be chosen by bureaucrats. It comes from the ambition of free men and women against the polishing-wheels of competition. It comes in a system of rewards. America should not be divided into the "haves" and "have nots," but into the "doers" and the "do nots."

There are those who scoff at individual liberty as of no consequence to the poor or unemployed. Yet it is alone through the creative impulses of free and confident spirits that redemption of their suffering must come. It is through them alone that social security can be attained. Our job is not to pull down the great majority but to pull up those who lag behind.

PART III
Business and American Liberty

And at once we come to the relation of government to economic life. I have discussed many of its phases elsewhere. On this occasion time permits me to refer only to the relations of government to business. For in this field lies a large part of the choice that youth must make.

We have three alternatives.

First: Unregulated business.

Second: Government-regulated business, which I believe is the American System.

Third: Government-dictated business, whether by dictation to business or by government in business. This is the New Deal choice. These ideas are dipped from cauldrons of European Fascism or Socialism.

Unregulated Business

While some gentlemen may not agree, we may dismiss any system of unregulated business. We know from experience that the vast tools of technology and mechanical power can be seized for purposes of oppression. They have been used to limit production and to strangle competition and opportunity. We can no more have economic power without checks and balances than we can have political power without checks and balances. Either one leads to tyranny.

And there must be regulation of the traffic even when it is honest. We have too many people and too many devices to allow them to riot all over the streets of commerce. But a traffic policeman must only enforce the rules. He will block the traffic if he stands on the corner demanding to know their business and telling them how to run it.

The American System of Regulation

I am one who believes that the only system which will preserve liberty and hold open the doors of opportunity is government-regulated business. And this is as far from government-dictated business as the two poles. Democracy can regulate its citizens through law and judicial bodies. No democracy can dictate and survive as a democracy. The only way to preserve individual initiative and enterprise is for the government to make the same rules for everybody and act as umpire.

But if we are to preserve freedom we must face the fact that ours is a regulatory system.

And let us be definite once and for all as to what we mean by a system of regulation. It looms up more clearly against the past three years.

1. A great area of business will regulate its own prices and profits through competition. Competition is also the restless pillow of progress. But we must compel honest competition through prevention of monopolies and unfair practices. That is indirect regulation.

2. The semi-yet natural monopolies, such as railways and utilities, must be directly regulated as to rates to prevent the misuse of their privilege.

3. Banking, finance, public markets, and other functions of trust must be regulated to prevent abuse and misuse of trust.

The failure of the states, particularly New York, to do their part during the boom years has necessitated an extension of Federal action. The New Deal regulations of stock and security promotion in various aspects have the right objectives. They were hastily and poorly formed without proper consideration by Congress. But they point right.

4. Certain groups must be appropriately regulated to prevent waste of natural resources.

5. Labor must have the right to free collective bargaining. But it must have responsibilities as well as rights.

6. At one time we relied upon the theory of "shirt sleeves to shirt sleeves in three generations" to regulate over-accumulations of wealth. This is now guaranteed by our income and inheritance taxes. Some people feel these taxes take the shirt also.

But there are certain principles that must run through these methods.

1. The first principle of regulation is the least regulation that will preserve equality of opportunity and liberty itself. We cannot afford to stifle a thousand honest men in order to smother one evil person.

2. To preserve Liberty the major burden of regulation must fall upon the States and local government. But where the States hopelessly fail or when the problem grows beyond their powers we should call upon the Federal government. Or we should invoke the machinery of interstate compacts.

3. Regulation should be by specific law, that all who run may read. That alone holds open the doors of the courts to the citizen. This must be "a government of laws and not of men."

4. And the American System of Liberty will not function solely through traffic policemen. The fundamental regulation of the nation is the Ten Commandments and the Sermon on the Mount.

Incidentally, the government might regulate its own business by some of the standards it imposes on others.

There are certain humanities which run through all business. As we become more experienced, more humane, as conditions change, we recognize things as abuses which we once passed over. There are the abuses of slums, child-labor, sweated hours, and sweated wages. They have been diminishing for decades before the New Deal. They have not been solved yet. They must be solved. We must not be afraid to use the powers of government to eliminate them.

There will be periodic unemployment in any system. It is even so in the self-declared economic heavens of Socialism and Fascism. With common sense we could provide insurance programs against it. We could go further and prevent many causes of depressions.

Out of medical and public health discoveries we have in eighty years increased the number of people over sixty years of age from four per cent to eight per cent. That imposes another problem upon us.

This American System has sprung from the spirit of our people. It has been developing progressively over many generations. However grave its faults may be they are but marginal to a great area of human well-being. The test of a system is its comparative results with others and whether it has the impulses within to cure its faults. This system based on ordered liberty alone answers these tests.

The doors of opportunity cannot be held open by inaction. That is an ideal that must be incessantly fought for.

These doors are partly closed by every gentleman who hatches some special privilege. They are closed to somebody by every betrayal of trust. But because brickbats can be used for murder we do not need stop building houses. These doors are partly shut by every needless bureaucrat. And there is the tax collector. He stands today right in the door.

Every new invention, every new idea, every new war shifts and changes our economic life. That greatest instrument of American joy, the automobile, has in twenty years shifted regulation in a hundred directions.

Many obstructions and abuses have been added by the New Deal. Many of them are older but no worse. While the inspiration to reform comes from the human heart, it is achieved only by the intellect. Enthusiastic hearts have flooded us with illusions. Ideals without illusions are good. Ideals with illusions are no good. You may remember that youth with a banner of strange device. Was it "Excelsior" or was it "Planned economy"? He froze to death.

PART IV
Government-Dictated Economic Life

Young men and women have grave need to look into this New Deal alternative to our American System.

If anyone does not believe there is a bite in that innocent term "Planned Economy," he might re-read this paragraph from one of the leading New Deal spokesmen:

"It is . . . a logical impossibility to have a *planned economy* and to *have business operating its industries,* just as it is also impossible to have one within our present *constitutional* and *statutory structure.* Modifications in both, so serious as to mean *destruction* and *re-beginning,* are required."

That is involved language but if it means anything it means that both private business and the Constitution must be modified so seriously as to mean destruction and re-beginning.

The President, far from repudiating these ideas, has continuously supported "Planned Economy." On one occasion he said, ". . . All of the proposals and all of the legislation since the fourth of March have not been just a collection of haphazard schemes but rather the orderly component parts of a connected and logical whole."

The Supreme Court has removed some ten of these component parts. And rather than have the score raised to thirteen before an election we have seen three more quietly removed. However, if the New Deal is reelected they will be found to have a lot of spare parts.

Do not mistake. The choice is still yours. But the New Deal has no choice. The New Deal is committed to drive ahead for government dictation of our economic life. It is committed by a thousand statements, by a thousand actions. It is committed by the supporters upon whom it is dependent.

The President assures them "we will not retreat." They did mention a breathing spell. A spell is a very limited period.

I have spoken at length upon these subjects elsewhere, but I may remind you of a few examples of the choice that the New Deal offers to youth. Under that "connected and logical whole" a man could be fined and sent to jail for starting a new business of his own; for refusing to sell his own products as directed; for not reducing his production; for increasing his production if his energies found a market; for selling at prices below his competitors; or for having 101 gold dollars.

Also you might note that when you ask the man with a profit and loss motive for a job, he asks just one thing, "Can you do the job?" When you ask the government for a job, your ability is second to your politics, your delivery of votes, and your affiliations generally. That is not equality of opportunity.

And what of this managed currency and this managed credit, which threaten Liberty and opportunity with the poison of inflation? What of this governmentally raised cost of living? What of all this continued waste and folly wrought in the name of relief? What of the folly of these purchases of foreign silver? What of the debauchery of the Civil Service and the politics in relief?

What of the taxes that will ooze from this spending and debt all your lives?

Do not mistake. The new taxes of today are but part of them. More of them are as inevitable as the first of the month. The only alternatives are repudiation or inflation. No matter what nonsense you are told about corporations and the rich paying the bill, there will be two-thirds of it for the common man to pay after the corporations and the rich are sucked dry.

Taxation enslaves as well as dictatorship. Every increased dollar in taxes is a limitation upon your opportunities. It means you have to work that many days more for the government instead of for your own advancement. Your fireside talks in the future will be with the tax collector.

And where do we get to after all this attempt to supplant the American System? At the time of the election day in 1932 the American Federation of Labor reported 11,600,000 unemployed. Today, after three years of the New Deal, they report 11,000,000 unemployed. To get these people back to their jobs was the outstanding job of our government. It was the excuse given for all these doings. But the grim fact remains that it has failed in its primary purpose. And fifteen billion dollars will be added to the national debt before the New Deal is over.

PART V

What Is Real Liberalism?

We hear much as to who is a Tory, a Reactionary, a Conservative, a Liberal, or a Radical. These terms when used honestly reflect an attitude of mind. The political use of them was imported from England. They do not fit well in America. However, they have certain advantages. You can elect yourself to any one of these groups if you say it often enough. If you do not like anybody you can consign him to the one which is most hated by your listener.

Taking a compound of definitions coming out of Washington, the impression would be that the Tories do the money-changing. The Reactionaries are members of well-warmed and well-stocked clubs. The Conservatives are greedily trying to keep their jobs and their savings. The Liberals have the exclusive right to define the opinions of others. The Radicals do not know what to do but do it in every direction.

As a matter of serious fact, these terms have been used mostly for camouflage and for political assassination.

The natural choice of youth is toward true liberalism. True liberalism seeks all legitimate freedom first, in the confident belief that without such freedom the pursuit of other blessings is in vain. Liberalism is a force true of the spirit, proceeding from the deep realization that economic freedom cannot be sacrificed if political freedom is to be preserved.

It is a false liberalism that interprets itself into dictation by government. Every step in that direction crushes the very roots of liberalism. It is the road not to liberty but to less liberty. The spirit of liberalism is to create free men. It is not the regimentation of men. It is not the extension of bureaucracy. You cannot extend the mastery of government over the daily life of a people without somewhere making it master of people's souls and thoughts.

Today, however, the term Liberal is claimed by every sect that would limit human freedom and stagnate the human soul—whether they be Fascists, Socialists, Communists, Epics, or New Dealers.

This misuse of English political terms is used to cover the confusion of thought that pumps from the New Deal. Yet our American problems cut squarely across such muddy classification.

If an open mind, free to search for the truth and apply it in government, is liberal, then you should be liberal.

If belief in open opportunity and equal opportunity has become conservative, then you should be conservative.

If belief that this can be held only in a society of orderly individual initiative and enterprise is conservative, then you should be conservative.

If opposition to those things which abuse and limit equal opportunity, such as privilege, monopolies, exploitation, or oppression whether in business or in government, is liberal, then you should be liberal.

If opposition to managed economy whether of the Socialist, Fascist, or New Deal pattern is Tory, then you should be Tory.

If the humane action to eliminate such abominations as slum squalor, child labor, and sweated labor, to give greater protection from unemployment and old age is radical, then you should be radical.

If the use of all the powers of the government to relieve our people from hunger and cold in calamity is radical, then you should be radical.

If belief in the old-fashioned virtues of self-reliance, thrift, government economy, of a balanced budget, of a stable currency, of fidelity of government to its obligations is reactionary, then you should be reactionary.

If holding to the Bill of Rights with its safeguards of the balance of powers and local government is Tory, then you should be Tory.

If demand that change in the Constitution be by open submission to the people and not by subterfuge constitutes reaction, then again you should be reactionary.

If demand that we have a government of laws and not of bureaucrats is conservative, then you should be conservative.

If you agree with all this, then you have shed yourselves of many "isms" or you have melted them into plain Americanism.

If you add to that a belief in decency of Americans, a conception of spiritual prosperity, and a faith in the greatness of America, you will have lifted these realities to the realms of idealism.

But it all sums up to this—whether the choice of youth will be to carry on that liberty for which Americans have died upon a thousand battlefields.

PART VI

Expanding Opportunities of Youth

I hear much that new opportunity for youth is gone. It occurs to me that for 150 years God-fearing people under the blessings of freedom built up quite a plant and equipment on this continent. It teems with millions of farms and homes and cattle and pigs, despite the AAA. There are railroads, highways, power plants and factories, stores and banks, and money-changers. There are towns and magnificent cities. There are newspapers, colleges, libraries, orchestras, bands, radios, and other noises. It is very sad, but did it ever occur to you that all the people who live in these houses, and all those who run this complicated machine are going to die? Just as sure as death the job is yours. And there are opportunities in every inch of it.

The New Deal would dim your dreams of new adventure by telling you that there is nothing to do any more but run the old plant. The President on one occasion stated: "Our industrial plant is built. . . . Our last frontier has been reached. . . . Our task now . . . is the sober, less dramatic business of administering the resources and plants already in hand, etc." That no doubt excepts the new government plants.

As a matter of fact, science and invention during even these troubled years since the war have given us further mighty powers of progress. These inventions will create a thousand new frontiers. You have the blood and the urge of your American forebears. You are as good stuff as they. You are better trained and equipped than they were. I have no doubt of your character and your resolution. I know American youth is champing at the bit to take advantage of an opening world. From that, if we preserve the American System of liberty, we could have a century of glorious opportunity to every young man and woman. We could have a century of unparalleled progress to the nation.

1936

President Roosevelt's New Foreign Policies

The Great Debate over American foreign policy was reaching its height when Hoover addressed the Council on Foreign Relations in Chicago, February 1, 1939. Hoover spoke for more than Republicans; he spoke for millions of Americans who, quite aside from party lines, sincerely felt that the country could best save itself and serve the world by avoiding involvement in a war against Germany, Japan, and Italy. The debate came to a dramatic end with the bombing of Pearl Harbor.

I wish to talk on peace. We are deluged with talk of war. Our minds are being prepared to accept war as inevitable. We need to keep our heads.

And I say this as one who in positions of responsibility saw every stage in the development of the last war. And I have seen the bitterness of its failure to bring blessings to mankind.

I have no need to recite the malevolent forces rampant in the world. In twenty nations desperate peoples have surrendered personal liberty for some form of authoritarian government. They are placing their trust in dictatorship clothed in new ideologies of Utopia. Some of them are making war or are aggressively threatening other nations. The world is taut with fear. Five times more men are under arms than before the Great War.

We in America are indignant at the brutalities of these systems and their cruel wrongs to minorities. We are fearful of the penetration of their ideologies. We are alarmed at their military preparations and their aggressiveness.

Their neighboring democracies are consciously or unconsciously flooding us with propaganda that we, too, are in danger, that we will inevitably be drawn in.

We have need to strip emotion from these questions as much as we can. They are questions of life or death not only to men but also to nations.

We have need to appraise coolly these dangers. We have need of sober, analytical debate upon the policies of government toward them. We must do so without partisanship.

Our Foreign Policies

Amid these agitations, President Roosevelt has now announced a new departure in foreign policies.

Beginning with his suggestion of fourteen months ago of quarantining dictatorships, he now states: "We have learned that God-fearing democracies . . . cannot forever let pass without effective protest acts of aggression against sister nations. . . . There are many methods short of war, but stronger and more effective than mere words, of bringing home to aggressor governments the aggregate sentiments of our own people."

Mr. Roosevelt has also proposed to the country a huge increase in our already large armament. Under his plans we are on the way to become possibly the largest naval power and certainly the largest air power in the world.

Let me say at once that if our defense requires it every American will willingly bear that burden though it contributes to lower the standard of living of every American and though it plunges us further into debt.

It does mean an increase in our military expenditure from 650 millions of only six years ago to 1400 or 1500 millions next year.

But the proper degree of our military preparedness depends first upon what our foreign policies are to be, and second, upon where and from what our dangers come. When these are determined then the size of our armament is for our Army and Navy experts to say. Without these determinations they can give no competent advice.

Our foreign policies in these major dimensions must be determined by the American people and the Congress, not by the President alone. The citizens can also in some degree appraise our dangers. After all it is the people who are made poor and who sacrifice their lives and the lives of their sons.

Our Traditional Policies

For a hundred and thirty years before the Great War and since we rejected the League of Nations our foreign policies have been simple and emphatic.

First, to keep out of foreign entanglements and other peoples' wars; not to interfere in the affairs of other nations.

Second, our armament is for defense, not aggression.

Third, that defense to include the Western Hemisphere by enforcement of the Monroe Doctrine.

Fourth, to protect by force if necessary, the lives of Americans who are of necessity abroad, but to depend upon the peaceful processes of negotiation to protect their rights and property.

Fifth, to cooperate in peaceful movements to promote peace and in economic movements to promote world prosperity. And to insist that neither by spirit nor action do we imply either military or economic force for these purposes.

Sixth. Under the recent Neutrality Law we presumably prohibit the purchase of arms in the United States by other nations while actually at war, together with some restrictions upon credit and travel. Such purchases are without restrictions until we declare that a war exists. And let me say parenthetically that this arms provision needs immediate revision. In effect it compels us to take sides rather than be neutral.

---

31 quarantining dictatorships, a reference to Roosevelt's speech of October 5, 1937 (see p. 829)

I believe these are the full dimensions of American policies that have been approved by the American people up to now.

Mr. Roosevelt's New Expansion of Foreign Policies

Mr. Roosevelt now proposes to expand these policies. The sum of his proposal is that we make effective protest at acts of aggression against sister nations. He says we must use methods stronger than words and short of war. He asks for armament to back his extensions. As Daniel Webster said in his reply to Hayne, "Let me run the honorable gentleman's doctrine a little into its practical application."

First. The only known effective methods short of war and more than words are that we either support one side with supplies of food, raw materials, finance and munitions, or that we deny these to the other side by embargoes, boycotts or other economic sanctions.

Second. The aggressions against sister nations that Mr. Roosevelt is discussing are not alone in the Western Hemisphere. They are in reality aggressions across the Atlantic and the Pacific, in Europe and Asia.

Third. This new policy means that we are to determine who are the aggressors in the world.

The determination of the who and when of aggression sounds easy. It sometimes is easy. But if one examines the history of the world the distinction between legitimate expansion and wicked aggression becomes confused. The League of Nations after some years of effort failed to find even a definition of aggressor. We are to set ourselves up as the oracle of righteousness in age-old quarrels that began before our nation was born. A large part of the United States was the result of aggression under any definition; likewise parts of the British Empire and France. The world will not remain static, for the pressures of populations, economic life, and defense are not static forces. In any event, it does not seem to be a job that America should undertake. More especially as each case must needs be debated in Congress and divided by the emotions of our racial origins.

Fourth. These proposals to use some sort of coercion against nations are of course a complete departure from neutrality in other peoples' wars. It is the method of coercion, not persuasion. It is in direct violation of Secretary Hull's reaffirmation, on which the ink is but sixty days dry, of an old American policy that "the

intervention of any state in the internal and external affairs of another is inadmissible."

Fifth. Such measures are obviously futile unless undertaken in cooperation with other nations. Without joint action supplies of food or oil or cotton or munitions can be obtained elsewhere. And joint action means at least temporary alliances with countries in Europe or Asia.

Sixth. Such policies are provocative of reprisals and must be backed by armament far beyond that required for defense of the Western Hemisphere. If we are to provoke we must be prepared to enforce.

Seventh. Economic pressures inevitably run into pressures upon civil populations. Civil populations are mostly women and children. The morals of starvation by force rank no higher than killing from the air.

Eighth. Any nation which sets up such policies and builds an armament of dimensions to back them is sure to arouse fear. This idea of America sitting alone determining who and what in the world shall stop and go would make us suspect of the whole world. It is certain that combinations of power will arise against a nation which does that, no matter how good-neighborly its words may be.

Let me say at once that any form of direct or indirect coercion of nations is force and is the straight path to war itself. No husky nation will stand such pressures without bloody resistance.

Those who think in terms of economic sanctions should also think in terms of war.

It will be said that these measures will preserve peace; that if nations know we will throw our weight into the balance they will not transgress on others. That is worldwide power politics. That is the exact theory of joining in the balance of power throughout the world. That setting has in the long and tragic history of Europe inevitably exploded in war.

All this becomes the most momentous change in American policies of peace and war since we entered the Great War.

Moreover the European democracies have accepted it as a complete change of national policy by the United States. If it is not a proposal to change radically our policies then they are under a misapprehension.

But to determine the issue, let me propose some questions that the American people deserve to have answered.

1. Shall we reverse our traditional policies at this time?

2. Shall we set ourselves up to determine who the aggressor is in the world?

3. Shall we engage in embargoes, boycotts, economic sanctions against aggressor nations?

4. Shall we do this where the Western Hemisphere is not attacked?

5. Shall we provide an armament greater than that necessary to protect the Western Hemisphere from military invasion?

6. Shall we take collective action with other nations to make these more than words and short of war policies effective?

7. Are we to be the policemen of the world?

Certainly it is due to Mr. Roosevelt, to the Congress, and to the American people that we know exactly what all this means. The Congress should have this adventure clarified before we go blindly into great increases in armament.

The Dangers of the Western Hemisphere

Before we answer these questions and before we venture into these paths of force and conflict, even short of war, we should realistically examine how serious the so-called imminent dangers are from aggressive nations.

Our dangers are obviously in two forms—the penetration of their ideologies, which would destroy democracies, and their military aggressiveness.

And their military aggressiveness has to be appraised in two aspects. First, the direct dangers to the Western Hemisphere, and second, our further concern in the dangers to our sister democracies in Europe and Asia.

Penetration of Ideologies

The first segment of this danger is the ideologies. The penetration of these ideologies, whether it be the Communism of Russia, the National Socialism of Germany, or the Fascism of Italy, is an internal problem for each country where they penetrate. Ideas cannot be cured with battleships or aeroplanes. I say this as I do not assume that we intend to attack dictators or extirpate ideologies in their home sources. That would lead the world to worse destruction than the religious wars of the Middle Ages.

Our job of defense against these un-American ideologies is to eliminate Communist, Socialist and Fascist ideas and persons from our own institutions. It is to maintain the ideals of free men, which make this unprofitable soil for such alien seed.

I am confident that if the lamp of liberty can be kept alight these ideologies will yet die of their own falsity. They spring not from moral and spiritual inspirations but from the cupidity of men. In any event no additional appropriations for arms will settle those problems.

The Military Dangers

The second segment of danger is that of military attack of the dictatorships upon democracies.

And we may first explore the imminent dangers of military attack upon the Western Democracies. And again we should consider it in the light of realism rather than the irritating words that emanate from world capitals.

Our people must realize that even if there were no dictators present, the blunders in the peace treaties, the pressures of population, the impoverishment of peoples will create periodic European crises. That has been the history of Europe since long before America was born.

As terrifying as these crises look in the morning paper, there are more realistic pressures for peaceful adjustments than for war.

Since the Great War land fortifications for defense have increased in power faster than offensive land weapons. The dictatorships know that if they were to attack the Western Democracies they would probably find their land and sea defenses impregnable. Attack from the air offers hideous destruction, but it also brings sobering reprisals. It stiffens resolution and it does not capture capital cities. It is my belief that the Western Democracies of Europe can amply defend themselves against military attack.

And in this connection we must not close our eyes to one condition under which the American people, disregarding all other questions, might join in European war. We are a humane people, and our humanity can be overstrained by brutality. That was one of the causes of our entry into the last war. For instance, if wholesale attack were made upon women and children by the deliberate destruction of cities from the air, then the indignation of the American people could not be restrained from action.

I do not believe officials of any nation have become so foolish or dare the depth of barbarism of such an undertaking. The indignation in the United States today at such killings in Spain and China, where it is excused as the accident of attempts to demoralize munitions supply, should be a warning of the temper which would be raised.

There are other realistic forces which weigh against military attack by the Dictatorships on the Democracies. Despite various so-called "demands" the Dictatorships are in reality mainly interested elsewhere. The face of Germany is turned more East than toward Western Europe. The face of Japan is turned West into Asia. The Russians are amply engaged at home. The Italians claim grievances with England and France arising out of the treaties under which they came into the Great War, but these are not impossible of solution.

Beyond all this, every one of the totalitarian states has its own grave internal weaknesses.

Above all, the common people in no country in Europe want war. They are terrified of it.

Do not think I believe the situation is not dangerous in Europe. Far from it. But it is not so imminent as the speeches abroad might make it appear. And what is not imminent is often preventable.

Obviously our dangers are much less than those of the overseas democracies. The Western Hemisphere is still protected by a moat of 3000 miles of ocean on the East and 6000 miles on the West. No aeroplane has yet been built that can come one-third the way across the Atlantic and one-fifth of the way across the Pacific with destructive bombs and fly home again. In any event, these dictatorships have nothing to gain by coming 3000 miles or 6000 miles to attack the Western Hemisphere. So long as our defenses are maintained they have everything to lose.

That any of these dictatorships, whether Japan, Germany, Italy, or Russia, or all of them together, have the remotest idea of military attack upon the Western Hemisphere is sheer hysteria.

It will be said that we must be prepared to go across the seas and enforce lawful rights for American trade by military action. I do not agree with that thesis. There always comes a time, with patience, when such ends can be accomplished by the processes of peace.

Some Ultimate Possible Consequences

There are other factors that we need to consider also before we decide to use force beyond protection of the Western Hemisphere. We must not refuse to look at the possible ultimates before we start down these paths.

If we join with force in Europe or Asia, even though it be short of war, we must consider its consequences should it lead to war. For that is the most probable result. The call to join is based upon the preservation of human liberty in the world. Our first purpose is to maintain liberty in America. If civilization based on liberty fails in the United States it is gone from the earth. We must safeguard that, not only in our own interest but in the interest of the world.

Personal liberty and free economic life are not built for modern war. A great war today is a mobilization of the whole people. That means democracy must temporarily surrender to dictatorship, no matter what one may call it, in order that we may bend our full energies to war.

It means that our country must be mobilized into practically a Fascist state. It would be so organized. It went some distance in the last Great War, although we did not use that term at the time. It would have gone much farther if the war had extended longer.

I speak of this not from hearsay but as one who participated in the economic organization of the Great War. I saw the rise of opposition to demobilization of the interests which benefited. But we secured the immediate and courageous demobilization of this economic power over the daily lives of our people because of the backing of a real lover of human liberty—Woodrow Wilson.

Today the lowered vitality of free enterprise, the necessity to subordinate or repudiate our enormous peace-time national debt to make way for finance of a new war, together with the ideas of economic power which impregnate our government, all drive to the improbability of after-war demobilization of centralized power.

If it were that or the loss of our national independence it would not be too great a price. But let us at least recognize that a war to save liberty would probably destroy liberty. In my view another great war will make dictatorship universal.

Even if we escaped this result, yet the sacrifice of our sons and the moral and economic destruction are a bitter prospect to contemplate. Surely we learned this from the last war. As we look back over our participation in that war there is still another cup of bitterness. America can make war but we cannot make permanent peace in Europe or Asia. The peace after the Great War sowed the dragon's teeth whose growth confronts us today.

Conclusion

And now a word in conclusion. As a nation we must

weigh all these experiences, these forces and factors as best we can. We may not agree upon the importance to lay upon any one of them. But from the total of them it is my belief that at this time the country should say an emphatic No to the questions of clarification which I have proposed above.

This world can never reach peace by threats and force. If this is to be the blind leadership of men, nothing can save the world from a catastrophe to civilization.

No nation has alone built this civilization. We all live by heritages which have been enriched by every nation and every century. And to save this civilization there must be a changed attitude of men. Our country standing apart can make a contribution of transcendent service in holding aloft the banner of moral relationships.

If we are to hold that banner of morals aloft the people of America should express unhesitatingly their indignation against wrong and persecution. They should extend aid to the suffering.

We should not be isolationists in promoting peace by the methods of peace. We should not be isolationists in proposals to join in the most healing of all processes of peace—economic cooperation to restore prosperity.

But surely all reason, all history, all our own experience show that wrongs cannot be righted and durable peace cannot be imposed on nations by force, threats, economic pressures, or war. I want America to stand against that principle if it is the last nation under that banner. I want it to stand there because it is the only hope of preserving liberty on this continent.

That is America's greatest service to mankind.

1939

Franklin Delano Roosevelt

1882 · 1945

Constantly, between 1932 and 1945, Franklin Delano Roosevelt was bitterly attacked by his opponents and enthusiastically praised by his adherents. His opponents called him a dictator, a destroyer of our capitalistic society, a warmonger. His adherents claimed that he was a great democratic leader, a preserver of free enterprise and protector of the weak. Even Roosevelt's death in 1945 did not end the fierce dispute, and it was clear that many years would have to pass before history could render an impartial verdict. Yet none denied that Roosevelt, for better or worse, had wielded tremendous influence upon the history of the world in his time.

The background of Franklin Delano Roosevelt was a rather unusual one for a political leader in recent times.

His birthplace was a family estate in Hyde Park, New York, and his family was patrician and well-to-do. He was educated in Europe, in an exclusive private school— Groton, at Harvard, and in the Columbia law school. In 1905, while still in law school, he married Eleanor Roosevelt, his distant cousin, a niece of Theodore Roosevelt. The marriage was described in detail in the newspapers because it was a match between members of old families, the headmaster of Groton officiated, and President Theodore Roosevelt himself gave away the bride.

After admission to the bar, Franklin Roosevelt practiced in New York for a time. His political career began in 1910 when he was persuaded to run for state senator in the "silk stocking" Dutchess County District, which included Hyde Park. He campaigned energetically and was elected. As a legislator, he won state-wide attention by taking a stand against the New York political machine, and won reëlection. When Woodrow Wilson became a Presidential candidate, he was one of the few New York delegates who staunchly supported him in the convention. He was rewarded by an appointment to an assistant secretaryship in the navy (1913-1921) and became a nationally known political figure. His association in Washington with such liberal leaders as Wilson, Bryan, and Daniels developed his political philosophy. In 1920, he was a vice-presidential candidate, but he and his running-mate, James M. Cox, were defeated.

At this point, Roosevelt's career in politics might well have ended, since a defeated vice-presidential candidate might easily have been forgotten. The likelihood appeared to be increased when, in 1921, he was stricken with infantile paralysis, a disease which threatened him with death or with inaction throughout the rest of his life. His conquest over his illness was a remarkable achievement. "Once," he said later, "I spent two years lying in bed, trying to move my big toe. That was the hardest job I ever had to do. After that, anything else seems easy."

As if to establish the point, despite the lameness resulting from his sickness he became increasingly active in law, in business, and in politics. The battle with disease had given him time to study books and documents on political problems and to write many letters to fellow Democrats, and as a result he had become both well-informed and widely known when, in 1924, he made the convention speech nominating Al Smith as candidate for the Presidency. In 1928 he was elected governor of New York, a state in the national limelight and a state, furthermore, which decides 45 electoral votes; when, therefore, he was reëlected, in 1930, he became a logical contender for the Presidential nomination. From the beginning Roosevelt excited controversy. Many competent observers considered him unpromising material. Walter Lippmann, a much respected newspaper commentator, called him "an amiable man with many philanthropic impulses who, without any important qualification for the office, would very much like to be President." Others maintained that as governor of New York he had been a much-needed progressive force toward social legislation. He was elected partly, of course, because of

President Roosevelt in Quebec in 1944 for a conference with Winston Churchill—International News Photos

the ardent desire of the electorate to replace Hoover, whom they held responsible for the ills of the country. Partly responsible for his election was a vigorous nation-wide campaign during which many voters were won over by his extraordinary personal magnetism.

His first term showed that he was capable of proposing extreme measures in an attempt to end the greatest depression in history and capable, too, of bringing about their enactment. He seemed to thrive upon controversy; he had a genius for practical politics; and when he chose to appeal for popular support in one of his radio "fireside chats" his eloquent voice was often extraordinarily effective. The New Deal was eventually implemented, therefore, by a series of measures designed to stabilize commercial institutions, to encourage agriculture, to administer relief, and to modify the political and economic structure of the country. The nation showed its approval of Roosevelt's domestic policies by reëlecting him in 1936.

During Roosevelt's second term, additional measures similar to those of the first term were passed. During this term, too, he, among others, began to discern distressing signs of international trouble, and as early as

1937, his so-called "Quarantine Address" in Chicago (p. 829) emphasized the danger. By 1940 Europe was embroiled in war, and international as well as domestic issues were stressed in the campaign that year. When he was victorious over Wendell Willkie, Roosevelt became the first man ever elected to a third term. Domestic issues yielded the place of primary importance to international issues. Roosevelt hastened the strengthening of our armed forces, and urged increasing aid to Britain and then to Russia. The attack on Pearl Harbor, followed by declarations of war, put an end to all national hesitation. Roosevelt became an international as well as a national leader as the United States joined her allies in a concerted assault. Supplies, aircraft, arms, and men poured across the Atlantic and the Pacific. In 1944 the nation indicated its approval of Roosevelt's wartime administration by electing him to his fourth term. He died in the spring of 1945, a few months before Germany and Japan capitulated.

A descendant of an old and wealthy family, Roosevelt often proclaimed his enmity to privileged groups and his friendship to the "Forgotten Man," and urged measures in accord with these attitudes. Roosevelt therefore was disliked by many who considered him a traitor to his class. A canny politician, gifted with personal charm, he was also opposed by those who considered him a slick finagler bent upon gaining power. A proponent of a planned economy, he was attacked by many for his "socialistic tendencies." His supporters, many of them as fanatical as his most bitter enemies, held that he was leading a crusade for the many against the few who had disproportionate powers and privileges. Thus the nation argued about his domestic policies. In the argument about foreign affairs, some saw him as a catspaw—a dupe—of other countries, needlessly involving his nation in foreign controversies with which it should have no concern. Others, by contrast, saw him as a far-sighted leader who wisely perceived that the United States was destined to take its full part in the affairs of the world. Thus, in times of bitter controversy, Roosevelt became a symbol for certain domestic and certain international attitudes. No other President, including even Jackson and Lincoln, was the object of so much dislike and so much affection during his lifetime.

The Public Papers and Addresses of Franklin D. Roosevelt, 9 vols., New York, 1938-1940 • D. P. Geddes, ed., Franklin Delano Roosevelt, A Memorial, New York, 1945 • Robert Sherwood, Roosevelt and Hopkins, New York, 1948 • Donald Day, Franklin D. Roosevelt's Own Story, Boston, 1951

Progressive Government

In September 1932, when Franklin Roosevelt gave the following address in San Francisco, the United States was suffering from the most severe economic depression the country had ever known. Factories by the hundred were closed or closing, millions of workers were unemployed and uncertain of food and shelter, farmers in frightening numbers were losing their lands in foreclosures as their markets faded—or were openly resisting officers of the law attempting to evict them. Pessimism mounting to despair was the American mood, and the nation was indeed in crisis.

Against this backdrop the Presidential contest between Herbert Hoover and Franklin Roosevelt became a conflict which voters followed with passionate interest. Mr. Hoover earnestly sought recovery in what he considered the traditional "American Way" of relatively unrestricted private enterprise, which was certainly under challenge by the developments of the day and which his personal manner, not particularly well suited to radio or newsreel, did not help to make more appealing. Mr. Roosevelt espoused a "New Deal" for the "Forgotten Man," stressing redefinitions of basic American concepts, a greater rôle for government in economic affairs. He added an optimism, a warm smile, and a remarkable personal magnetism to the attraction of a philosophy toward which many in his audiences, victims of the times, were already predisposed. With such speeches as the following, Mr. Roosevelt won the election by an overwhelming majority. Seldom if ever did President Roosevelt, even in later years, set forth his philosophy more clearly or completely than in "Progressive Government."

M*y friends:*

I count it a privilege to be invited to address the Commonwealth Club. It has stood in the life of this city and State, and it is perhaps accurate to add, the Nation, as a group of citizen leaders interested in fundamental problems of Government, and chiefly concerned with achievement of progress in Government through non-partisan means. The privilege of addressing you, therefore, in the heat of a political campaign, is great. I want to re-
10 spond to your courtesy in terms consistent with your policy.

I want to speak not of politics but of Government. I want to speak not of parties, but of universal principles. They are not political, except in that larger sense in which a great American once expressed a definition of politics, that nothing in all of human life is foreign to the science of politics.

I do want to give you, however, a recollection of a long life spent for a large part in public office. Some of
20 my conclusions and observations have been deeply accentuated in these past few weeks. I have traveled far— from Albany to the Golden Gate. I have seen many people, and heard many things, and today, when in a sense my journey has reached the half-way mark, I am glad of the opportunity to discuss with you what it all means to me.

Sometimes, my friends, particularly in years such as these, the hand of discouragement falls upon us. It seems that things are in a rut, fixed, settled, that the world has
30 grown old and tired and very much out of joint. This is the mood of depression, of dire and weary depression.

But then we look around us in America, and everything tells us that we are wrong. America is new. It is in the process of change and development. It has the great potentialities of youth, and particularly is this true of the great West, and of this coast, and of California.

I would not have you feel that I regard this as in any sense a new community. I have traveled in many parts of the world, but never have I felt the arresting thought
40 of the change and development more than here, where the old, mystic East would seem to be near to us, where the currents of life and thought and commerce of the whole world meet us. This factor alone is sufficient to cause man to stop and think of the deeper meaning of things, when he stands in this community.

But more than that, I appreciate that the membership of this club consists of men who are thinking in terms beyond the immediate present, beyond their own immediate tasks, beyond their own individual interests. I
50 want to invite you, therefore, to consider with me in the large, some of the relationships of Government and economic life that go deeply into our daily lives, our happiness, our future and our security.

The issue of Government has always been whether individual men and women will have to serve some system of Government or economics, or whether a system of Government and economics exists to serve individual men and women. This question has persistently dominated the discussion of Government for many gen-
60 erations. On questions relating to these things men have differed, and for time immemorial it is probable that honest men will continue to differ.

The final word belongs to no man; yet we can still believe in change and in progress. Democracy, as a dear old friend of mine in Indiana, Meredith Nicholson, has called it, is a quest, a never-ending seeking for better things, and in the seeking for these things and the striving for them, there are many roads to follow. But, if we map the course of these roads, we find that there
70 are only two general directions.

When we look about us, we are likely to forget how hard people have worked to win the privilege of Government. The growth of the national Governments of Europe was the struggle for the development of a centralized force in the Nation, strong enough to impose peace upon ruling barons. In many instances the victory of the central Government, the creation of a strong central Government, was a haven of refuge to the individual. The people preferred the master far away to the ex-
80 ploitation and cruelty of the smaller master near at hand.

But the creators of national Government were perforce ruthless men. They were often cruel in their methods, but they did strive steadily toward something that society needed and very much wanted, a strong central State able to keep the peace, to stamp out civil war, to put the unruly nobleman in his place, and to permit the bulk of individuals to live safely. The man of ruthless force had his place in developing a pioneer country, just as he did in fixing the power of the cen-

---

65 **Meredith Nicholson** (1866-1947), an Indiana novelist, was to serve as minister to Paraguay, to Venezuela, and to Nicaragua during Roosevelt's Presidency

tral Government in the development of Nations. Society paid him well for his services and its development. When the development among the Nations of Europe, however, had been completed, ambition and ruthlessness, having served their term, tended to overstep their mark.

There came a growing feeling that Government was conducted for the benefit of a few who thrived unduly at the expense of all. The people sought a balancing—a limiting force. There came gradually, through town councils, trade guilds, national parliaments, by constitution and by popular participation and control, limitations on arbitrary power.

Another factor that tended to limit the power of those who ruled, was the rise of the ethical conception that a ruler bore a responsibility for the welfare of his subjects.

The American colonies were born in this struggle. The American Revolution was a turning point in it. After the Revolution the struggle continued and shaped itself in the public life of the country. There were those who because they had seen the confusion which attended the years of war for American independence surrendered to the belief that popular Government was essentially dangerous and essentially unworkable. They were honest people, my friends, and we cannot deny that their experience had warranted some measure of fear. The most brilliant, honest and able exponent of this point of view was Hamilton. He was too impatient of slow-moving methods. Fundamentally he believed that the safety of the republic lay in the autocratic strength of its Government, that the destiny of individuals was to serve that Government, and that fundamentally a great and strong group of central institutions, guided by a small group of able and public spirited citizens, could best direct all Government.

But Mr. Jefferson, in the summer of 1776, after drafting the Declaration of Independence turned his mind to the same problem and took a different view. He did not deceive himself with outward forms. Government to him was a means to an end, not an end in itself; it might be either a refuge and a help or a threat and a danger, depending on the circumstances. We find him carefully analyzing the society for which he was to organize a Government. "We have no paupers. The great mass of our population is of laborers, our rich who cannot live without labor, either manual or professional, being few and of moderate wealth. Most of the labor-ing class possess property, cultivate their own lands, have families and from the demand for their labor, are enabled to exact from the rich and the competent such prices as enable them to feed abundantly, clothe above mere decency, to labor moderately and raise their families."

These people, he considered, had two sets of rights, those of "personal competency" and those involved in acquiring and possessing property. By "personal competency" he meant the right of free thinking, freedom of forming and expressing opinions, and freedom of personal living, each man according to his own lights. To insure the first set of rights, a Government must so order its functions as not to interfere with the individual. But even Jefferson realized that the exercise of the property rights might so interfere with the rights of the individual that the Government, without whose assistance the property rights could not exist, must intervene, not to destroy individualism, but to protect it.

You are familiar with the great political duel which followed; and how Hamilton, and his friends, building toward a dominant centralized power were at length defeated in the great election of 1800, by Mr. Jefferson's party. Out of that duel came the two parties, Republican and Democratic, as we know them today.

So began, in American political life, the new day, the day of the individual against the system, the day in which individualism was made the great watchword of American life. The happiest of economic conditions made that day long and splendid. On the Western frontier, land was substantially free. No one, who did not shirk the task of earning a living, was entirely without opportunity to do so. Depressions could, and did, come and go; but they could not alter the fundamental fact that most of the people lived partly by selling their labor and partly by extracting their livelihood from the soil, so that starvation and dislocation were practically impossible. At the very worst there was always the possibility of climbing into a covered wagon and moving west where the untilled prairies afforded a haven for men to whom the East did not provide a place. So great were our natural resources that we could offer this relief not only to our own people, but to the distressed of all the world; we could invite immigration from Europe, and welcome it with open arms. Traditionally, when a depression came a new section of land was opened in the West; and even our temporary misfortune served our manifest destiny.

It was in the middle of the nineteenth century that a new force was released and a new dream created. The force was what is called the industrial revolution, the advance of steam and machinery and the rise of the forerunners of the modern industrial plant. The dream was the dream of an economic machine, able to raise the standard of living for everyone; to bring luxury within the reach of the humblest; to annihilate distance by steam power and later by electricity, and to release everyone from the drudgery of the heaviest manual toil. It was to be expected that this would necessarily affect Government. Heretofore, Government had merely been called upon to produce conditions within which people could live happily, labor peacefully, and rest secure. Now it was called upon to aid in the consummation of this new dream. There was, however, a shadow over the dream. To be made real, it required use of the talents of men of tremendous will and tremendous ambition, since by no other force could the problems of financing and engineering and new developments be brought to a consummation.

So manifest were the advantages of the machine age, however, that the United States fearlessly, cheerfully, and, I think, rightly, accepted the bitter with the sweet. It was thought that no price was too high to pay for the advantages which we could draw from a finished industrial system. The history of the last half century is accordingly in large measure a history of a group of financial Titans whose methods were not scrutinized with too much care, and who were honored in proportion as they produced the results, irrespective of the means they used. The financiers who pushed the railroads to the Pacific were always ruthless, often wasteful, and frequently corrupt; but they did build railroads, and we have them today. It has been estimated that the American investor paid for the American railroad system more than three times over in the process; but despite this fact the net advantage was to the United States. As long as we had free land; as long as population was growing by leaps and bounds; as long as our industrial plants were insufficient to supply our own needs, society chose to give the ambitious man free play and unlimited reward provided only that he produced the economic plant so much desired.

During this period of expansion, there was equal opportunity for all, and the business of Government was not to interfere but to assist in the development of industry. This was done at the request of business men themselves. The tariff was originally imposed for the purpose of "fostering our infant industry," a phrase I think the older among you will remember as a political issue not so long ago. The railroads were subsidized, sometimes by grants of money, oftener by grants of land; some of the most valuable oil lands in the United States were granted to assist the financing of the railroad which pushed through the Southwest. A nascent merchant marine was assisted by grants of money, or by mail subsidies, so that our steam shipping might ply the seven seas. Some of my friends tell me that they do not want the Government in business. With this I agree; but I wonder whether they realize the implications of the past. For while it has been American doctrine that the Government must not go into business in competition with private enterprises, still it has been traditional, particularly in Republican administrations, for business urgently to ask the Government to put at private disposal all kinds of Government assistance. The same man who tells you that he does not want to see the Government interfere in business—and he means it, and has plenty of good reasons for saying so—is the first to go to Washington and ask the Government for a prohibitory tariff on his product. When things get just bad enough, as they did two years ago, he will go with equal speed to the United States Government and ask for a loan; and the Reconstruction Finance Corporation is the outcome of it. Each group has sought protection from the Government for its own special interests, without realizing that the function of Government must be to favor no small group at the expense of its duty to protect the rights of personal freedom and of private property of all its citizens.

In retrospect we can now see that the turn of the tide came with the turn of the century. We were reaching our last frontier; there was no more free land and our industrial combinations had become great uncontrolled and irresponsible units of power within the State. Clear-sighted men saw with fear the danger that opportunity would no longer be equal; that the growing corporation, like the feudal baron of old, might threaten the economic freedom of individuals to earn a living. In that hour, our anti-trust laws were born. The cry was raised against the great corporations, Theodore Roosevelt, the first great Republican Progressive, fought a Presidential campaign on the issue of "trust busting" and talked freely about malefactors of great wealth. If the Government had a policy it was rather to turn the clock back, to destroy the large combinations and to return to the time when every man owned his individual small business.

This was impossible; Theodore Roosevelt, abandoning the idea of "trust busting," was forced to work out a difference between "good" trusts and "bad" trusts. The Supreme Court set forth the famous "rule of reason" by which it seems to have meant that a concentration of industrial power was permissible if the method by which it got its power, and the use it made of that power, were reasonable.

Woodrow Wilson, elected in 1912, saw the situation more clearly. Where Jefferson had feared the encroachment of political power on the lives of individuals, Wilson knew that the new power was financial. He saw, in the highly centralized economic system, the despot of the twentieth century, on whom great masses of individuals relied for their safety and their livelihood, and whose irresponsibility and greed (if they were not controlled) would reduce them to starvation and penury. The concentration of financial power had not proceeded so far in 1912 as it has today; but it had grown far enough for Mr. Wilson to realize fully its implications. It is interesting, now, to read his speeches. What is called "radical" today (and I have reason to know whereof I speak) is mild compared to the campaign of Mr. Wilson. "No man can deny," he said, "that the lines of endeavor have more and more narrowed and stiffened; no man who knows anything about the development of industry in this country can have failed to observe that the larger kinds of credit are more and more difficult to obtain unless you obtain them upon terms of uniting your efforts with those who already control the industry of the country, and nobody can fail to observe that every man who tries to set himself up in competition with any process of manufacture which has taken place under the control of large combinations of capital will presently find himself either squeezed out or obliged to sell and allow himself to be absorbed." Had there been no World War—had Mr. Wilson been able to devote eight years to domestic instead of to international affairs—we might have had a wholly different situation at the present time. However, the then distant roar of European cannon, growing ever louder, forced him to abandon the study of this issue. The problem he saw so clearly is left with

us as a legacy; and no one of us on either side of the political controversy can deny that it is a matter of grave concern to the Government.

A glance at the situation today only too clearly indicates that equality of opportunity as we have known it no longer exists. Our industrial plant is built; the problem just now is whether under existing conditions it is not overbuilt. Our last frontier has long since been reached, and there is practically no more free land. More than half of our people do not live on the farms or on lands and cannot derive a living by cultivating their own property. There is no safety valve in the form of a Western prairie to which those thrown out of work by Eastern economic machines can go for a new start. We are not able to invite the immigration from Europe to share our endless plenty. We are now providing a drab living for our own people.

Our system of constantly rising tariffs has at last reacted against us to the point of closing our Canadian frontier on the north, our European markets on the east, many of our Latin-American markets to the south, and a goodly proportion of our Pacific markets on the west, through the retaliatory tariffs of those countries. It has forced many of our great industrial institutions which exported their surplus production to such countries, to establish plants in such countries, within the tariff walls. This has resulted in the reduction of the operation of their American plants, and opportunity for employment.

Just as freedom to farm has ceased, so also the opportunity in business has narrowed. It still is true that men can start small enterprises, trusting to native shrewdness and ability to keep abreast of competitors; but area after area has been preempted altogether by the great corporations, and even in the fields which still have no great concerns, the small man starts under a handicap. The unfeeling statistics of the past three decades show that the independent business man is running a losing race. Perhaps he is forced to the wall; perhaps he cannot command credit; perhaps he is "squeezed out," in Mr. Wilson's words, by highly organized corporate competitors, as your corner grocery man can tell you. Recently a careful study was made of the concentration of business in the United States. It showed that our economic life was dominated by some six hundred odd corporations who controlled two-thirds of American industry. Ten million small business men divided the other third. More striking still, it appeared that if the process of concentration goes on at the same rate, at the end of another century we shall have all American industry controlled by a dozen corporations, and run by perhaps a hundred men. Put plainly, we are steering a steady course toward economic oligarchy, if we are not there already.

Clearly, all this calls for a re-appraisal of values. A mere builder of more industrial plants, a creator of more railroad systems, an organizer of more corporations, is as likely to be a danger as a help. The day of the great promoter or the financial Titan, to whom we granted anything if only he would build, or develop, is over. Our task now is not discovery or exploitation of natural resources, or necessarily producing more goods. It is the soberer, less dramatic business of administering resources and plants already in hand, of seeking to re-establish foreign markets for our surplus production, of meeting the problem of underconsumption, of adjusting production to consumption, of distributing wealth and products more equitably, of adapting existing economic organizations to the service of the people. The day of enlightened administration has come.

Just as in older times the central Government was first a haven of refuge, and then a threat, so now in a closer economic system the central and ambitious financial unit is no longer a servant of national desire, but a danger. I would draw the parallel one step farther. We did not think because national Government had become a threat in the 18th century that therefore we should abandon the principle of national Government. Nor today should we abandon the principle of strong economic units called corporations, merely because their power is susceptible of easy abuse. In other times we dealt with the problem of an unduly ambitious central Government by modifying it gradually into a constitutional democratic Government. So today we are modifying and controlling our economic units.

As I see it, the task of Government in its relation to business is to assist the development of an economic declaration of rights, an economic constitutional order. This is the common task of statesman and business man. It is the minimum requirement of a more permanently safe order of things.

Happily, the times indicate that to create such an order not only is the proper policy of Government, but

it is the only line of safety for our economic structures as well. We know, now, that these economic units cannot exist unless prosperity is uniform, that is, unless purchasing power is well distributed throughout every group in the Nation. That is why even the most selfish of corporations for its own interest would be glad to see wages restored and unemployment ended and to bring the Western farmer back to his accustomed level of prosperity and to assure a permanent safety to both groups. That is why some enlightened industries themselves endeavor to limit the freedom of action of each man and business group within the industry in the common interest of all; why business men everywhere are asking a form of organization which will bring the scheme of things into balance, even though it may in some measure qualify the freedom of action of individual units within the business.

The exposition need not further be elaborated. It is brief and incomplete, but you will be able to expand it in terms of your own business or occupation without difficulty. I think everyone who has actually entered the economic struggle—which means everyone who was not born to safe wealth—knows in his own experience and his own life that we have now to apply the earlier concepts of American Government to the conditions of today.

The Declaration of Independence discusses the problem of Government in terms of a contract. Government is a relation of give and take, a contract, perforce, if we would follow the thinking out of which it grew. Under such a contract rulers were accorded power, and the people assented to that power on consideration that they be accorded certain rights. The task of statesmanship has always been the re-definition of these rights in terms of a changing and growing social order. New conditions impose new requirements upon Government and those who conduct Government.

I held, for example, in proceedings before me as Governor, the purpose of which was the removal of the Sheriff of New York, that under modern conditions it was not enough for a public official merely to evade the legal terms of official wrong-doing. He owed a positive duty as well. I said in substance that if he had acquired large sums of money, he was when accused required to explain the sources of such wealth. To that extent this wealth was colored with a public interest. I said that in financial matters, public servants should, even beyond private citizens, be held to a stern and uncompromising rectitude.

I feel that we are coming to a view through the drift of our legislation and our public thinking in the past quarter century that private economic power is, to enlarge an old phrase, a public trust as well. I hold that continued enjoyment of that power by any individual or group must depend upon the fulfillment of that trust. The men who have reached the summit of American business life know this best; happily, many of these urge the binding quality of this greater social contract.

The terms of that contract are as old as the Republic, and as new as the new economic order.

Every man has a right to life; and this means that he has also a right to make a comfortable living. He may by sloth or crime decline to exercise that right; but it may not be denied him. We have no actual famine or dearth; our industrial and agricultural mechanism can produce enough and to spare. Our Government formal and informal, political and economic, owes to everyone an avenue to possess himself of a portion of that plenty sufficient for his needs, through his own work.

Every man has a right to his own property; which means a right to be assured, to the fullest extent attainable, in the safety of his savings. By no other means can men carry the burdens of those parts of life which, in the nature of things, afford no chance of labor; childhood, sickness, old age. In all thought of property, this right is paramount; all other property rights must yield to it. If, in accord with this principle, we must restrict the operations of the speculator, the manipulator, even the financier, I believe we must accept the restriction as needful, not to hamper individualism but to protect it.

These two requirements must be satisfied, in the main, by the individuals who claim and hold control of the great industrial and financial combinations which dominate so large a part of our industrial life. They have undertaken to be, not business men, but princes of property. I am not prepared to say that the system which produces them is wrong. I am very clear that they must fearlessly and competently assume the responsibility which goes with the power. So many enlightened business men know this that the statement would be little more than a platitude, were it not for an added implication.

This implication is, briefly, that the responsible heads of finance and industry instead of acting each for himself, must work together to achieve the common end. They must, where necessary, sacrifice this or that private advantage; and in reciprocal self-denial must seek a general advantage. It is here that formal Government—political Government, if you choose—comes in. Whenever in the pursuit of this objective the lone wolf, the unethical competitor, the reckless promoter, the Ishmael or Insull whose hand is against every man's, declines to join in achieving an end recognized as being for the public welfare, and threatens to drag the industry back to a state of anarchy, the Government may properly be asked to apply restraint. Likewise, should the group ever use its collective power contrary to the public welfare, the Government must be swift to enter and protect the public interest.

The Government should assume the function of economic regulation only as a last resort, to be tried only when private initiative, inspired by high responsibility, with such assistance and balance as Government can give, has finally failed. As yet there has been no final failure, because there has been no attempt; and I decline to assume that this Nation is unable to meet the situation.

The final term of the high contract was for liberty and the pursuit of happiness. We have learned a great deal of both in the past century. We know that individual liberty and individual happiness mean nothing unless both are ordered in the sense that one man's meat is not another man's poison. We know that the old "rights of personal competency," the right to read, to think, to speak, to choose and live a mode of life, must be respected at all hazards. We know that liberty to do anything which deprives others of those elemental rights is outside the protection of any compact; and that Government in this regard is the maintenance of a balance, within which every individual may have a place if he will take it; in which every individual may find safety if he wishes it; in which every individual may attain such power as his ability permits, consistent with his assuming the accompanying responsibility.

All this is a long, slow talk. Nothing is more striking than the simple innocence of the men who insist, whenever an objective is present, on the prompt production of a patent scheme guaranteed to produce a result. Human endeavor is not so simple as that. Government includes the art of formulating a policy, and using the political technique to attain so much of that policy as will receive general support; persuading, leading, sacrificing, teaching always, because the greatest duty of a statesman is to educate. But in the matters of which I have spoken, we are learning rapidly, in a severe school. The lessons so learned must not be forgotten, even in the mental lethargy of a speculative upturn. We must build toward the time when a major depression cannot occur again; and if this means sacrificing the easy profits of inflationist booms, then let them go; and good riddance.

Faith in America, faith in our tradition of personal responsibility, faith in our institutions, faith in ourselves demand that we recognize the new terms of the old social contract. We shall fulfill them, as we fulfilled the obligation of the apparent Utopia which Jefferson imagined for us in 1776, and which Jefferson, Roosevelt and Wilson sought to bring to realization. We must do so, lest a rising tide of misery, engendered by our common failure, engulf us all. But failure is not an American habit; and in the strength of great hope we must all shoulder our common load.

1932

Address at Chicago

October 5, 1937

The so-called "Quarantine Speech" was delivered at the dedication of a new bridge over the Chicago River, constructed with Public Works Administration funds. The President was completing an eight-thousand-mile trip which had carried him into the Far West. The crowd gathered was estimated at a hundred thousand. Said a contemporary—rather unfriendly—account (**Newsweek**, October 18, 1937): "About as soon as he started to speak he made it plain that this would be no jovial chat peppered with complimentary local allusions. Those close enough saw that he had dropped his usual 'personality' smile: he looked over the crowd with a mien almost as set as those of the feather-crowned braves . . . who had come up the river in canoes to greet him with a war dance. . . . Beneath the speaker's rostrum, telegraph keys rattled. Wires flashed to every continent of the world the words of this man who looms to millions abroad as virtual dictator of the richest and most enterprising—and potentially the most formidable—of all powers. . . . In Japan, Italy, and Germany, the censor worked fast—newspapers carried little more than brief paraphrases. . . ." At the time the

address was delivered, a large majority, according to a national public opinion poll, favored stricter neutrality laws for keeping the United States out of war.

I am glad to come once again to Chicago and especially to have the opportunity of taking part in the dedication of this important project of civic betterment.

On my trip across the continent and back I have been shown many evidences of the result of commonsense co-operation between municipalities and the Federal Government, and I have been greeted by tens of thousands of Americans who have told me in every look and word that their material and spiritual well-being has made great strides forward in the past few years.

And yet, as I have seen with my own eyes the prosperous farms, the thriving factories and the busy railroads—as I have seen the happiness and security and peace which covers our wide land—almost inevitably I have been compelled to contrast our peace with very different scenes being enacted in other parts of the world.

It is because the people of the United States under modern conditions must, for the sake of their own future, give thought to the rest of the world, that I, as the responsible executive head of the nation, have chosen this great inland city and this gala occasion to speak to you on a subject of definite national importance.

The political situation in the world, which of late has been growing progressively worse, is such as to cause grave concern and anxiety to all the peoples and nations who wish to live in peace and amity with their neighbors.

Some nine years ago the hopes of mankind for a continuing era of international peace were raised to great heights when more than sixty nations solemnly pledged themselves not to resort to arms in furtherance of their national aims and policies. The high aspirations expressed in the Briand-Kellogg Peace Pact and the hopes for peace thus raised have of late given way to a haunting fear of calamity.

The present reign of terror and international lawlessness began a few years ago. It began through unjustified interference in the internal affairs of other nations or the invasion of alien territory in violation of treaties, and has now reached a stage where the very foundations of civilization are seriously threatened.

The landmarks and traditions which have marked the progress of civilization toward a condition of law, order and justice are being wiped away.

Without a declaration of war and without warning or justification of any kind, civilians, including women and children, are being ruthlessly murdered with bombs from the air.

In times of so-called peace, ships are being attacked and sunk by submarines without cause or notice. Nations are fomenting and taking sides in civil warfare in nations that have never done them any harm. Nations claiming freedom for themselves deny it to others.

Innocent peoples and nations are being cruelly sacrificed to a greed for power and supremacy which is devoid of all sense of justice and humane consideration.

To paraphrase a recent author: "Perhaps we foresee a time when men, exultant in the technique of homicide, will rage so hotly over the world that every precious thing will be in danger, every book and picture and harmony, every treasure garnered through two millenniums, the small, the delicate, the defenseless—all will be lost or wrecked or utterly destroyed."

If those things come to pass in other parts of the world, let no one imagine that America will escape, that it may expect mercy, that this Western Hemisphere will not be attacked and that it will continue tranquilly and peacefully to carry on the ethics and the arts of civilization.

If those days come, "there will be no safety by arms, no help from authority, no answer in science. The storm will rage till every flower of culture is trampled and all human beings are leveled in a vast chaos."

If those days are not to come to pass—if we are to have a world in which we can breathe freely and live in amity without fear—the peace-loving nations must make a concerted effort to uphold laws and principles on which alone peace can rest secure.

The peace-loving nations must make a concerted effort in opposition to those violations of treaties and those ignorings of humane instincts which today are creating a state of international anarchy and instability from which there is no escape through mere isolation or neutrality.

Those who cherish their freedom and recognize and respect the equal right of their neighbors to be free and live in peace must work together for the triumph of law and moral principles in order that peace, justice and confidence may prevail in the world.

There must be a return to a belief in the pledged word, in the value of a signed treaty. There must be recognition of the fact that national morality is as vital as private morality.

A Bishop wrote me the other day:

"It seems to me that something greatly needs to be said in behalf of ordinary humanity against the present practice of carrying the horrors of war to helpless civilians, especially women and children.

"It may be that such a protest might be regarded by many, who claim to be realists, as futile, but may it not be that the heart of mankind is so filled with horror at the present needless suffering that that force could be mobilized in sufficient volume to lessen such cruelty in the days ahead?

"Even though it may take twenty years, which God forbid, for civilization to make effective its corporate protest against this barbarism, surely strong voices may hasten the day."

There is a solidarity and interdependence about the modern world, both technically and morally, which

5 **Briand-Kellogg Peace Pact.** The Pact of Paris, formulated chiefly by Aristide Briand, French premier, and Frank B. Kellogg, secretary of state of the United States, was a multilateral treaty between sixty-two nations signed August 27, 1928, in Paris. It "condemned recourse to war for the solution of international controversies and renounced it as an instrument of national policy." It was completely lacking in sanctions and was not, even at the time, the source of much hope for lasting peace • 8 **present reign of terror.** See Chronological Table, p. 788 • 22 **Nations . . . sides.** Shortly before this address England and France, jointly, had sent a note to Mussolini urging that Italian forces be withdrawn from Spain

makes it impossible for any nation completely to isolate itself from economic and political upheavals in the rest of the world, especially when such upheavals appear to be spreading and not declining.

There can be no stability or peace either within nations or between nations except under laws and moral standards adhered to by all. International anarchy destroys every foundation for peace. It jeopardizes either the immediate or the future security of every nation, large or small.

It is, therefore, a matter of vital interest and concern to the people of the United States that the sanctity of international treaties and the maintenance of international morality be restored.

The overwhelming majority of the peoples and nations of the world today want to live in peace.

They seek the removal of barriers against trade.

They want to exert themselves in industry, in agriculture and in business, that they may increase their wealth through the production of wealth-producing goods, rather than striving to produce military planes and bombs and machine guns and cannon for the destruction of human lives and useful property.

In those nations of the world which seem to be piling armament on armament for purposes of aggression, and those other nations which fear acts of aggression against them and their security, a very high proportion of the national income is being spent directly for armaments. It runs from 30 to as high as 50 per cent.

The proportion that we in the United States spend is far less—11 or 12 per cent.

How happy we are that the circumstances of the moment permit us to put our money into bridges and boulevards, dams and reforestation, the conservation of our soil and many other kinds of useful works, rather than into huge standing armies and vast supplies of implements of war.

I am compelled and you are compelled, nevertheless, to look ahead. The peace, the freedom and the security of 90 per cent of the population of the world is being jeopardized by the remaining 10 per cent who are threatening a break-down of all international order and law.

Surely the 90 per cent who want to live in peace under law and in accordance with moral standards that have received almost universal acceptance through the centuries can and must find some way to make their will prevail.

The situation is definitely of universal concern. The questions involved relate not merely to violations of specific provisions of particular treaties; they are questions of war and of peace, of international law, and especially of principles of humanity. It is true that they involve definite violations of agreements, and especially of the Covenant of the League of Nations, the Briand-Kellogg Pact and the Nine-Power Treaty. But they also involve problems of world economy, world security and world humanity.

It is true that the moral consciousness of the world must recognize the importance of removing injustices and well-founded grievances; but at the same time it must be aroused to the cardinal necessity of honoring sanctity of treaties, of respecting the rights and liberties of others and of putting an end to acts of international aggression.

It seems to be unfortunately true that the epidemic of world lawlessness is spreading.

When an epidemic of physical disease starts to spread, the community approves and joins in a quarantine of the patients in order to protect the health of the community against the spread of the disease.

It is my determination to pursue a policy of peace and to adopt every practicable measure to avoid involvement in war.

It ought to be inconceivable that in this modern era, and in the face of experience, any nation could be so foolish and ruthless as to run the risk of plunging the whole world into war by invading and violating, in contravention of solemn treaties, the territory of other nations that have done them no real harm and which are too weak to protect themselves adequately. Yet the peace of the world and the welfare and security of every nation is today being threatened by that very thing.

No nation which refuses to exercise forbearance and to respect the freedom and rights of others can long

41 remaining 10 per cent. The total population of Germany, Italy, and Japan was exactly 10 per cent of the estimated population of the world • 56 Nine-Power Treaty, signed February 6, 1922, by the United States, Great Britain, France, Japan, Italy, Belgium, the Netherlands, Portugal, and China, had as its purpose "safeguarding the rights and the interest of China" by guaranteeing its sovereignty, independence, and territorial administrative integrity

remain strong and retain the confidence and respect of other nations. No nation ever loses its dignity or good standing by conciliating its differences, and by exercising great patience with, and consideration for, the rights of other nations.

War is a contagion, whether it be declared or undeclared. It can engulf states and peoples remote from the original scene of hostilities. We are determined to keep out of war, yet we cannot insure ourselves against 10 the disastrous effects of war and the dangers of involvement. We are adopting such measures as will minimize our risk of involvement, but we cannot have complete protection in a world of disorder in which confidence and security have broken down.

If civilization is to survive, the principles of the Prince of Peace must be restored. Shattered trust between nations must be revived.

Most important of all, the will for peace on the part of peace-loving nations must express itself to the end that nations that may be tempted to violate their agreements 20 and the rights of others will desist from such a cause. There must be positive endeavors to preserve peace.

America hates war. America hopes for peace. Therefore, America actively engages in the search for peace.

1937

Dwight D. Eisenhower

1890 ·

The thirty-fourth President of the United States, Dwight David Eisenhower, was born in Denison, Texas, October 14, 1890, and grew up in Abilene, Kansas. He was graduated from the United States Military Academy (West Point) in 1915, and on July 1, 1916, he was married to Mamie Geneva Doud. Having advanced steadily through the military grades, he held the rank of Lieutenant General at the outbreak of World War II, and was elevated to the rank of General of the Army in December 1944. He was Allied Commander-in-Chief in North Africa in 1942-1943, and later in the War was made Commanding General of the Allied Forces in the European Theater of Operations. After victory in Europe in 1945, General Eisenhower was made Chief of Staff—a post which he held from 1945 to 1948, when he became president of Columbia University. His career as the president of Columbia was interrupted in 1951, when President Truman appointed him to take charge of the military organiza-

tion of Western Europe under the North Atlantic Pact.

In the presidential election in November 1952, Eisenhower was the Republican candidate; his Democratic opponent was the brilliant Adlai Stevenson, Governor of Illinois. Eisenhower's supporters could point to a record which had been consistently impressive both militarily and diplomatically, a career in which their candidate had evidenced efficiency, alertness, insight, generalship, and tact. His tact, especially, and his obvious sincerity, and other personable qualities recommended him to the American voters as they had recommended him to the Europeans and to his own soldiers, and it was his personal popularity, very largely, which enabled the Republicans to win their first presidential election in twenty-four years. Their slogan, quite appropriately, was "We like Ike."

Dwight Eisenhower, **Crusade in Europe**, New York, 1948 • John Gunther, **Eisenhower, the Man and the Symbol**, New York, 1952

Inaugural Address

The following address, President Eisenhower's Inaugural, was delivered in the nation's capital, before the capitol building, on January 20, 1953, at noon. It was the first presidential inaugural to be televised from coast to coast.

The address should be read against the background of contemporary events. It was indeed a complex and parlous background, comprising in part: the military stalemate in Korea, where the United Nations forces had halted Communist aggression without being able to bring the campaign to a successful conclusion; the growing tension between the United States and Russia; the mounting strain of atomic armaments; the mounting governmental expenditures (chiefly for armaments), and the still unchecked inflation; the fear, which threatened to get out of hand, of subversive Communist agents and activities within our own borders. Hence the emphasis in the address upon firmness, courage, and confidence in our future.

My fellow citizens:

The world and we have passed the midway point of a century of continuing challenge. We sense with all our faculties that forces of good and evil are massed and armed and opposed as rarely before in history.

This fact defines the meaning of this day. We are summoned, by this honored and historic ceremony, to witness more than the act of one citizen swearing his oath of service, in the presence of his God. We are called as a people, to give testimony, in the sight of the world, to our faith that the future shall belong to the free.

Since this century's beginning, a time of tempest has seemed to come upon the continents of the earth. Masses of Asia have wakened to strike off shackles of the past. Great nations of Europe have waged their bloodiest wars. Thrones have toppled and their vast empires have disappeared. New nations have been born.

For our own country, it has been a time of recurring trial. We have grown in power and in responsibility. We have passed through the anxieties of depression and of war to a summit unmatched in man's history. Seeking to secure peace in the world, we have had to fight our way through the forests of the Argonne to the shores of Iwo Jima, and to the cold mountains of Korea.

In the swift rush of great events, we find ourselves groping to know the full sense and meaning of the times in which we live. In our quest of understanding, we beseech God's guidance. We summon all our knowledge of the past and we scan all signs of the future. We bring all our wit and will to meet the question: How far have we come in man's long pilgrimage from darkness toward light? Are we nearing the light— a day of freedom and of peace for all mankind? Or are the shadows of another night closing in upon us?

Great as are the preoccupations absorbing us at home, concerned as we are with the matters that deeply affect our livelihood today and our vision of the future, each of these domestic problems is dwarfed by, and often even created by, this question that involves all human kind.

This trial comes at a moment when man's power to achieve good or to inflict evil surpasses the brightest hopes and the sharpest fears of all ages. We can turn rivers in their courses, level mountains to the plains. Ocean and land and sky are avenues for our colossal commerce. Disease diminishes and life lengthens.

Yet the promise of this life is imperiled by the very genius that has made it possible. Nations amass wealth. Labor sweats to create—and turn out devices to level not only mountains but also cities. Science seems ready to confer upon us, as its final gift, the power to erase human life from this planet.

At such a time in history, we who are free must proclaim anew our faith.

This faith is the abiding creed of our fathers. It is our faith in the deathless dignity of man, governed by eternal moral and natural laws.

This faith defines our full view of life. It establishes, beyond debate, those gifts of the Creator that are man's inalienable rights, and that make all men equal in His sight.

In the light of this equality, we know that the virtues most cherished by free people—love of truth, pride of work, devotion to country—all are treasures equally precious in the lives of the most humble and of the most exalted. The men who mine coal and fire furnaces and balance ledgers and turn lathes and pick cotton and heal the sick and plant corn—all serve as proudly, and as profitably, for America as the statesmen who draft treaties or the legislators who enact laws.

This faith rules our whole way of life. It decrees that we, the people, elect leaders not to rule but to serve. It asserts that we have the right to choice of our own work and to the reward of our own toil. It inspires the initiative that makes our productivity the wonder of the world. And it warns that any man who seeks to deny equality in all his brothers betrays the spirit of the free and invites the mockery of the tyrant.

It is because we, all of us, hold to these principles that the political changes accomplished this day do not imply turbulence, upheaval, or disorder. Rather this change expresses a purpose of strengthening our dedication and devotion to the precepts of our founding documents, a conscious renewal of faith in our country and in the watchfulness of a divine Providence.

The enemies of this faith know no God but force, no devotion but its use. They tutor men in treason. They feed upon the hunger of others. Whatever defies them, they torture, especially the truth.

Here, then, is joined no pallid argument between slightly differing philosophies. This conflict strikes directly at the faith of our fathers and the lives of our sons. No principle or treasure that we hold, from the spiritual knowledge of our free schools and churches to the creative magic of free labor and capital, nothing lies safely beyond the reach of the struggle.

Freedom is pitted against slavery; light against dark.

The faith we hold belongs not to us alone but to the free of all the world. This common bond binds the grower of rice in Burma and the planter of wheat in Iowa, the shepherd in Southern Italy and the mountaineer in the Andes. It confers a common dignity upon the French soldier who dies in Indochina, the British soldier killed in Malaya, the American life given in Korea.

We know, beyond this, that we are linked to all free peoples not merely by a noble idea but by a simple need. No free people can for long cling to any privilege or enjoy any safety in economic solitude. For all our own material might, even we need markets in the world for the surpluses of our farms and of our factories. Equally, we need for these same farms and factories vital materials and products of distant lands. This basic law of interdependence, so manifest in the commerce of peace, applies with thousand-fold intensity in the event of war.

So are we persuaded by necessity and by belief that the strength of all free peoples lies in unity, their danger in discord.

To produce this unity, to meet the challenge of our time, destiny has laid upon our country the responsibility of the free world's leadership. So it is proper that we assure our friends once again that, in the discharge of this responsibility, we Americans know and observe the difference between world leadership and imperialism; between firmness and truculence; between a thoughtfully calculated goal and spasmodic reaction to the stimulus of emergencies.

We wish our friends the world over to know this above all: We face the threat—not with dread and confusion—but with confidence and conviction.

We feel this moral strength because we know that we are not helpless prisoners of history. We are free men. We shall remain free, never to be proven guilty of the one capital offense against freedom, a lack of staunch faith.

In pleading our just cause before the bar of history and in pressing our labor for world peace, we shall be guided by certain fixed principles.

These principles are:

(1) Abhorring war as a chosen way to balk the purposes of those who threaten us, we hold it to be the first task of statesmanship to develop the strength that will deter the forces of aggression and promote the conditions of peace. For, as it must be the supreme purpose of all free men, so it must be the dedication of their leaders, to save humanity from preying upon itself.

In the light of this principle, we stand ready to engage with any and all others in joint effort to remove the causes of mutual fear and distrust among nations, and so to make possible drastic reduction of armaments. The sole requisites for undertaking such effort are that—in their purpose—they be aimed logically and honestly toward secure peace for all; and that—in their result—they provide methods by which every participating nation will prove good faith in carrying out its pledge.

(2) Realizing that common sense and common decency alike dictate the futility of appeasement, we shall never try to placate an aggressor by the false and wicked bargain of trading honor for security. For in the final choice a soldier's pack is not so heavy a burden as a prisoner's chains.

(3) Knowing that only a United States that is strong and immensely productive can help defend freedom in

our world, we view our nation's strength and security as a trust upon which rests the hope of free men everywhere. It is the firm duty of each of our free citizens and of every free citizen everywhere to place the cause of his country before the comfort and convenience of himself.

(4) Honoring the identity and heritage of each nation of the world, we shall never use our strength to try to impress upon another people our own cherished political and economic institutions.

(5) Assessing realistically the needs and capacities of proven friends of freedom, we shall strive to help them to achieve their own security and well-being. Likewise, we shall count upon them to assume, within the limits of their resources, their full and just burden, in the common defense of freedom.

(6) Recognizing economic health as an indispensable basis of military strength and the free world's peace, we shall strive to foster everywhere, and to practice ourselves, policies that encourage productivity and profitable trade. For the impoverishment of any single people in the world means danger to the well-being of all other peoples.

(7) Appreciating that economic need, military security and political wisdom combine to suggest regional groupings of free peoples, we hope, within the framework of the United Nations, to help strengthen such special bonds the world over. The nature of these ties must vary with the different problems of different areas.

In the Western Hemisphere, we enthusiastically join with all our neighbors in the work of perfecting a community of fraternal trust and common purpose.

In Europe, we ask that enlightened and inspired leaders of the Western nations strive with renewed vigor to make the unity of their peoples a reality. Only as free Europe unitedly marshals its strength can it effectively safeguard, even with our help, its spiritual and cultural heritages.

(8) Conceiving the defense of freedom, like freedom itself, to be one and indivisible, we hold all continents and peoples in equal regard and honor. We reject any insinuation that one race or another, one people or another, is in any sense inferior or expendable.

(9) Respecting the United Nations as the living sign of all peoples' hope for peace, we shall strive to make it not merely an eloquent symbol but an effective force. And in our quest of honorable peace, we shall neither compromise, nor tire, nor ever cease.

By these rules of conduct, we hope to be known to all peoples.

By their observance, an earth of peace may become not a vision but a fact.

This hope—this supreme aspiration—must rule the way we live.

We must be ready to dare all for our country. For history does not long entrust the care of freedom to the weak or the timid. We must acquire proficiency in defense and display stamina in purpose.

We must be willing, individually and as a nation, to accept whatever sacrifices may be required of us. A people that values its privileges above its principles soon loses both.

These basic precepts are not lofty abstractions, far removed from matters of daily living. They are laws of spiritual strength that generate and define our material strength. Patriotism means equipped forces and a prepared citizenry. Moral stamina means more energy and more productivity, on the farm and in the factory. Love of liberty means the guarding of every resource that makes freedom possible—from the sanctity of our families and the wealth of our soil to the genius of our scientists.

So each citizen plays an indispensable role. The productivity of our heads, our hands and our hearts is the source of all the strength we can command, for both the enrichment of our lives and the winning of peace.

No person, no home, no community can be beyond the reach of this call. We are summoned to act in wisdom and in conscience; to work with industry, to teach with persuasion, to preach with conviction, to weigh our every deed with care and with compassion. For this truth must be clear before us: Whatever America hopes to bring to pass in the world must first come to pass in the heart of America.

The peace we seek, then, is nothing less than the practice and the fulfillment of our whole faith, among ourselves and in our dealings with others. It signifies more than stilling the guns, easing the sorrow of war.

More than an escape from death, it is a way of life.

More than a haven for the weary, it is a hope for the brave.

This is the hope that beckons us onward in this century of trial. This is the work that awaits us all, to be done with bravery, with charity—and with prayer to Almighty God.   1953

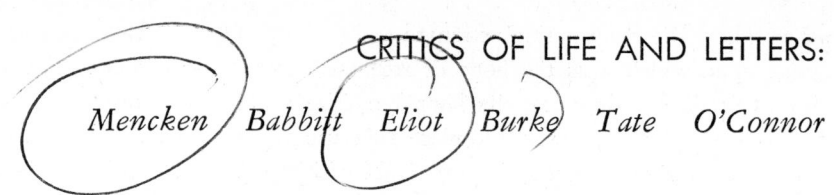

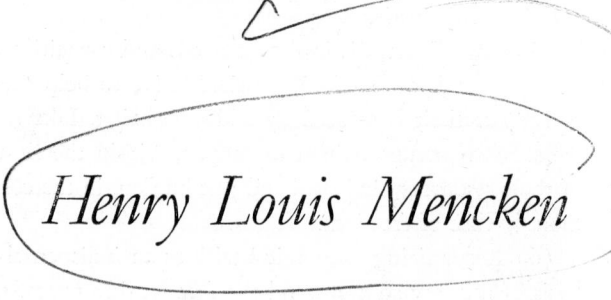

Henry Louis Mencken

1880 · 1956

The impact of Henry Louis Mencken upon the United States of the 1920's and 1930's was truly remarkable. Because, as an announcer of the cynicism of the times, he ferociously attacked many cherished beliefs and established institutions, intellectuals idolized him. His enemies, however, were as vituperative as he was. The *New Haven Union,* for instance, called him "a treacherous alien sapping at the vitals of America's proudest and most essential institutions, an indecent buffoon wallowing in obscenity as he howls with glee." During 1926 he was castigated in more than four hundred editorials, usually in very strong language.

Mencken was born in Baltimore in 1880, of German ancestry. His education at Baltimore Polytechnic was augmented by some correspondence-school work, but he never attended college. After becoming a reporter at nineteen, he plied his trade so successfully that within a couple of years he became an editor. In those two years he had launched into creative work to produce some short stories and a book of mediocre poetry, *Ventures in Verse,* which was to appear in 1903. He worked as a journalist on the Baltimore *Herald* (1903-1906), and intermittently on the Baltimore *Sun* papers (1906-1941).

When a book by Mencken on George Bernard Shaw (1905) and another on the philosophy of Nietzsche (1908) attracted attention beyond Baltimore, he became editor of a national magazine, *Smart Set* (1908-1914). His writings for this periodical and his syndicated weekly column for the *Evening Sun* won him a national following. In 1924, when the *American Mercury* was established, he became its editor, to serve until 1933.

It was while Mencken, assisted by George Jean Nathan, was directing this magazine that he was most influential. He championed authors such as Dreiser, Cather, and Lewis, but his attacks were more heeded than his defenses. In article after article, he lambasted Rotarians, fundamentalists, reformers, professors, and leading politicians. He sneered and snorted at the masses, at government by the masses, at Victorian morality, at sentimental literature, at prohibition, at poetry.

His style had much to do with his appeal. The love for words which led him to compile the scholarly study *The American Language* (1919, revised in 1921, 1923, 1936, and supplemented in 1945) helped him find and employ words which gave his writing gusto and power. His mastery of invective led to his introducing telling phrases such as "Bible Belt," "Yahoo," and "booboisie." His sentences mingled elegant words with such nicknames, with slang, with metaphors, and with words borrowed from foreign tongues, all placed in the right order

H. L. Mencken—photo by A. Aubrey Bodine

wanted. As Oscar Cargill recounts in *Intellectual America,* "Over the verdant countryside poured a green flood of *Mercuries,* sweeping away palings, fences, and battlements, erasing marshes and boundaries, wetting priest and parishman, destroying every convention, moral and taboo. The liberated masses and the ebullient bourgeoisie read together from the same page, forgetting all class distinctions. Stenographers went to work with the *Mercury* under their arms; millionaries laid it aside on their blotters. . . . It became a badge of freedom, a visible symbol of intelligence, the sure sign of sophistication." Mencken's followers regarded him as a great emancipator, their leader in attacks upon old-fashioned conventions and values.

In 1933, however, when Mencken retired from the *Mercury* editorship, many of the battles he had fought had been won, and others had begun to seem less significant. His political tenets, to many, appeared to be as old-fashioned as those of Thomas Jefferson, from which they had been derived, though with many changes. His influence was definitely on the wane, and no one was much surprised when he began to write his reminiscences. Nor was anyone surprised when the reminiscences, upon publication, proved to be gusty, vivid, and highly amusing.

Selected Prejudices, New York, 1927 • Treatise on the Gods, New York, 1930 • Days of H. L. Mencken, New York, 1947 • Edgar Kemler, The Irreverent Mr. Mencken, Boston, 1950 • W. R. Manchester, Disturber of the Peace, New York, 1951

for climactic emphasis. And his articles and essays, like his sentences, were full of fire and force.

This was just what many people, at the time,

From • Prejudices: Third Series

On Being an American

Characteristic of the rough and derisive criticism leveled at the United States by Mencken in the 1920's is "On Being an American." Here, as he offers his reasons for not joining the migrants of the day in their self-exile to Europe, he jeers with characteristic gusto at a whole series of faults and foibles in American life.

Apparently there are those who begin to find it disagreeable—nay, impossible. Their anguish fills the Liberal weeklies, and every ship that puts out from New York carries a groaning cargo of them, bound for Paris, London, Munich, Rome and way points—anywhere to escape the great curses and atrocities that make life intolerable for them at home. Let me say at once that I find little to cavil at in their basic complaints. In more than one direction, indeed, I probably go a great deal further than even the Young Intellectuals. It is, for example, 10 one of my firmest and most sacred beliefs, reached after

Reprinted from **Prejudices; Third Series**, by H. L. Mencken, by permission of Alfred A. Knopf, Inc. Copyright 1922 by Alfred A. Knopf, Inc.
10 Young Intellectuals, the intellectual members of the "lost generation," many of whom, in the 1920's, left this country for Europe

On Being an American **837**

an inquiry extending over a score of years and supported by incessant prayer and meditation, that the government of the United States, in both its legislative arm and its executive arm, is ignorant, incompetent, corrupt, and disgusting—and from this judgment I except no more than twenty living lawmakers and no more than twenty executioners of their laws. It is a belief no less piously cherished that the administration of justice in the Republic is stupid, dishonest, and against all reason and equity—and from this judgment I except no more than thirty judges, including two upon the bench of the Supreme Court of the United States. It is another that the foreign policy of the United States—its habitual manner of dealing with other nations, whether friend or foe—is hypocritical, disingenuous, knavish, and dishonorable—and from this judgment I consent to no exceptions whatever, either recent or long past. And it is my fourth (and, to avoid too depressing a bill, final) conviction that the American people taking one with another, constitute the most timorous, sniveling, poltroonish, ignominious mob of serfs and goose-steppers ever gathered under one flag in Christendom since the end of the Middle Ages, and that they grow more timorous, more sniveling, more poltroonish, more ignominious every day.

So far I go with the fugitive Young Intellectuals—and into the Bad Lands beyond. Such, in brief, are the cardinal articles of my political faith, held passionately since my admission to citizenship and now growing stronger and stronger as I gradually disintegrate into my component carbon, oxygen, hydrogen, phosphorus, calcium, sodium, nitrogen and iron. This is what I believe and preach, *in nomine Domini*, Amen. Yet I remain on the dock, wrapped in the flag, when the Young Intellectuals set sail. Yet here I stand, unshaken and undespairing, a loyal and devoted Americano, even a chauvinist, paying taxes without complaint, obeying all laws that are physiologically obeyable, accepting all the searching duties and responsibilities of citizenship unprotestingly, investing the sparse usufructs of my miserable toil in the obligations of the nation, avoiding all commerce with men sworn to overthrow the government, contributing my mite toward the glory of the national arts and sciences, enriching and embellishing the native language, spurning all lures (and even all invitations) to get out and stay out—here am I, a bachelor of easy means,

forty-two years old, unhampered by debts or issue, able to go wherever I please and to stay as long as I please—here am I, contentedly and even smugly basking beneath the Stars and Stripes, a better citizen, I daresay, and certainly a less murmurous and exigent one, than thousands who put the Hon. Warren Gamaliel Harding beside Friedrich Barbarossa and Charlemagne, and hold the Supreme Court to be directly inspired by the Holy Spirit, and belong ardently to every Rotary Club, Ku Klux Klan, and Anti-Saloon League, and choke with emotion when the band plays "The Star-Spangled Banner," and believe with the faith of little children that one of Our Boys, taken at random, could dispose in a fair fight of ten Englishmen, twenty Germans, thirty Frogs, forty Wops, fifty Japs, or a hundred Bolsheviki.

Well, then, why am I still here? Why am I so complacent (perhaps even to the point of offensiveness), so free from bile, so little fretting and indignant, so curiously happy? Why did I answer only with a few academic "Hear, Hears" when Henry James, Ezra Pound, Harold Stearns and the *emigrés* of Greenwich Village issued their successive calls to the corn-fed *intelligentsia* to flee the shambles, escape to fairer lands, throw off the curse forever? The answer, of course, is to be sought in the nature of happiness, which tempts to metaphysics. But let me keep upon the ground. To me, at least (and I can only follow my own nose) happiness presents itself in an aspect that is tripartite. To be happy (reducing the thing to its elementals) I must be:

a. Well-fed, unhounded by sordid cares, at ease in Zion.

---

33 **in nomine Domini,** in the name of the Lord • 52 **Warren Gamaliel Harding** (1865-1923), twenty-ninth President of the United States • 53 **Friedrich Barbarossa** (1123?-1190), emperor of Germany, 1152-1190 • 55 **Rotary Club,** the well-known business and professional men's club founded in 1905; a target of many jeers from the intelligentsia in the 1920's • 55 **Ku Klux Klan,** a nation-wide secret organization founded in Georgia in 1915 under the name used by a reconstruction society. It preached white supremacy, anti-Semitism, and anti-Catholicism and was influential in the politics of the 1920's • 60 **Frogs . . . Wops,** insulting nicknames used by intolerant Americans —the former, for Frenchmen; the latter, for Italians • 61 **Bolsheviki,** the Russian Socialists who were feared by many in the 1920's—the equivalent, in that period, of today's Russian Communists • 66 **Ezra Pound** (1885-   ), Idaho-born poet who, in 1908, went abroad to live • 67 **Harold Stearns** (1891-1943), an expatriate American writer who, in **America and the Young Intellectual** (1923), sternly criticized civilization in the United States

b. Full of a comfortable feeling of superiority to the masses of my fellow-men.

c. Delicately and unceasingly amused according to my taste.

It is my contention that, if this definition be accepted, there is no country on the face of the earth wherein a man roughly constituted as I am—a man of my general weaknesses, vanities, appetites, prejudices, and aversions—can be so happy, or even one-half so happy, as he can be in these free and independent states. Going further, I lay down the proposition that it is a sheer physical impossibility for such a man to live in These States and *not* be happy—that it is as impossible to him as it would be to a schoolboy to weep over the burning down of his school-house. If he says that he isn't happy here, then he either lies or is insane. Here the business of getting a living, particularly since the war brought the loot of all Europe to the national strong-box, is enormously easier than it is in any other Christian land —so easy, in fact, that an educated and forehanded man who fails at it must actually make deliberate efforts to that end. Here the general average of intelligence, of knowledge, of competence, of integrity, of self-respect, of honor is so low that any man who knows his trade, does not fear ghosts, has ready fifty good books, and practices the common decencies stands out as brilliantly as a wart on a bald head, and is thrown willy-nilly into a meager and exclusive aristocracy. And here, more than anywhere else that I know of or have heard of, the daily panorama of human existence, of private and communal folly—the unending procession of governmental extortions and chicaneries, of commercial brigandages and throat-slittings, of theological buffooneries, of aesthetic ribaldries, of legal swindles and harlotries, of miscellaneous rogueries, villainies, imbecilities, grotesqueries, and extravagances—is so inordinately gross and preposterous, so perfectly brought up to the highest conceivable amperage, so steadily enriched with an almost fabulous daring and originality, that only the man who was born with a petrified diaphragm can fail to laugh himself to sleep every night, and to awake every morning with all the eager, unflagging expectation of a Sunday-school superintendent touring the Paris peep-shows.

A certain sough of rhetoric may be here. Perhaps I yield to words as a chautauqua lecturer yields to them, be-

laboring and fermenting the hinds with his Message from the New Jerusalem. But fundamentally I am quite as sincere as he is. For example, in the matter of attaining to ease in Zion, of getting a fair share of the national swag, now piled so mountainously high. It seems to me, sunk in my Egyptian night, that the man who fails to do this in the United States to-day is a man who is somehow stupid—maybe not on the surface, but certainly deep down. Either he is one who cripples himself unduly, say by setting up a family before he can care for it, or by making a bad bargain for the sale of his wares, or by concerning himself too much about the affairs of other men; or he is one who endeavors fatuously to sell something that no normal American wants. Whenever I hear a professor of philosophy complain that his wife has eloped with some moving-picture actor or bootlegger who can at least feed and clothe her, my natural sympathy for the man is greatly corrupted by contempt for his lack of sense. Would it be regarded as sane and laudable for a man to travel the Soudan trying to sell fountain-pens, or Greenland offering to teach double-entry bookkeeping or counterpoint? Coming closer, would the judicious pity or laugh at a man who opened a shop for the sale of incunabula in Little Rock, Ark., or who demanded a living in McKeesport, Pa., on the ground that he could read Sumerian? In precisely the same way it seems to me to be nonsensical for a man to offer generally some commodity that only a few rare and dubious Americans want, and then weep and beat his breast because he is not patronized. One seeking to make a living in a country must pay due regard to the needs and tastes of that country. Here in the United States we have no jobs for grand dukes, and none for *Wirkliche Geheimräte,* and none for palace eunuchs, and none for masters of the buckhounds, and none (any more) for brewery *Todsaufer* —and very few for oboe-players, metaphysicians, astrophysicists, assyriologists, water-colorists, stylites and epic poets. There was a time when the *Todsaufer* served a public need and got an adequate reward, but it is no more. There may come a time when the composer of string quartettes is paid as much as a railway conductor, but it is not yet. Then why practice such trades—that is,

---

78 Wirkliche Geheimräte, real privy councilor • 80 **Todsaufer,** a taster of brews whose function was to insure against poison

as trades? The man of independent means may venture into them prudently; when he does so, he is seldom molested; it may even be argued that he performs a public service by adopting them. But the man who has a living to make is simply silly if he goes into them; he is like a soldier going over the top with a coffin strapped to his back. Let him abandon such puerile vanities, and take to the uplift instead, as, indeed, thousands of other victims of the industrial system have already done. Let him bear in mind that, whatever its neglect of the humanities and their monks, the Republic has never got half enough bond salesmen, quack doctors, ward leaders, phrenologists, Methodist evangelists, circus clowns, magicians, soldiers, farmers, popular song writers, moonshine distillers, forgers of gin labels, mine guards, detectives, spies, snoopers, and *agents provocateurs*. The rules are set by Omnipotence; the discreet man observes them. Observing them, he is safe beneath the starry bed-tick, in fair weather or foul. The *boobus Americanus* is a bird that knows no closed season—and if he won't come down to Texas oil stock, or one-night cancer cures, or building lots in Swampshurst, he will always come down to Inspiration and Optimism, whether political, theological, pedagogical, literary, or economic.

The doctrine that it is *infra dignitatem* for an educated man to take a hand in the snaring of this goose is one in which I see nothing convincing. It is a doctrine chiefly voiced, I believe, by those who have tried the business and failed. They take refuge behind the childish notion that there is something honorable about poverty *per se*—the Greenwich Village complex. This is nonsense. Poverty may be an unescapable misfortune, but that no more makes it honorable than a cocked eye is made honorable by the same cause. Do I advocate, then, the ceaseless, senseless hogging of money? I do not. All I advocate—and praise as virtuous—is the hogging of enough to provide security and ease. Despite all the romantic superstitions to the contrary, the artist cannot do his best work when he is oppressed by unsatisfied wants. Nor can the philosopher. Nor can the man of science. The best and clearest thinking of the world is done and the finest art is produced, not by men who are hungry, ragged and harassed, but by men who are well-fed, warm and easy in mind. It is the artist's first duty to his art to achieve that tranquility for himself. Shakespeare tried to achieve it; so did Beethoven, Wagner, Brahms,

Ibsen and Balzac. Goethe, Schopenhauer, Schumann and Mendelssohn were born to it. Joseph Conrad, Richard Strauss and Anatole France have got it for themselves in our own day. In the older countries, where competence is far more general and competition is thus more sharp, the thing is often cruelly difficult, and sometimes almost impossible. But in the United States it is absurdly easy, given ordinary luck. Any man with a superior air, the intelligence of a stockbroker, and the resolution of a hatcheck girl—in brief, any man who believes in himself enough, and with sufficient cause, to be called a **journeyman**—can cadge enough money, in this glorious commonwealth of morons, to make life soft for him.

And if a lining for the purse is thus facilely obtainable, given a reasonable prudence and resourcefulness, then balm for the ego is just as unlaboriously got, given ordinary dignity and decency. Simply to exist, indeed, on the plane of a civilized man is to attain, in the Republic, to a distinction that should be enough for all save the most vain; it is even likely to be too much, as the frequent challenges of the Ku Klux Klan, the American Legion, the Anti-Saloon League, and other such vigilance committees of the majority testify. Here is a country in which all political thought and activity are concentrated upon the scramble for jobs—in which the normal politician, whether he be a President or a village road supervisor, is willing to renounce any principle, however precious to him, and to adopt any lunacy, however offensive to him, in order to keep his place at the trough. Go into politics, then, without seeking or wanting office, and at once you are as conspicuous as a red-haired blackamoor—in fact, a great deal more conspicuous, for red-haired blackamoors have been seen, but who has ever seen or heard of an American politician, Democrat or Republican, Socialist or Liberal, Whig or Tory, who did not itch for a job? Again, here is a country in which it is an axiom that a business man shall be a member of a Chamber of Commerce, an admirer of Charles M. Schwab, a reader of the *Saturday Evening Post*, a golfer—in brief, a vegetable. Spend your hours

---

19 **boobus Americanus,** American boob or dumbbell—a phrase coined and frequently used by Mencken • 25 **infra dignitatem,** undignified • 31 **Greenwich . . . complex.** In the 1920's, Greenwich Village was famous as the proud dwelling place of indigent artists • 85 **Charles M. Schwab** (1862-1939), a steel tycoon

of escape from *Geschäft* reading Remy de Gourmont or practicing the violoncello, and the local Sunday newspaper will infallibly find you out and hymn the marvel —nay, your banker will summon you to discuss your notes, and your rivals will spread the report (probably truthful) that you were pro-German during the war. Yet again, here is a land in which women rule and men are slaves. Train your women to get your slippers for you, and your ill fame will match Galileo's or Darwin's. Once more, here is the Paradise of back-slappers, of democrats, of mixers, of go-getters. Maintain ordinary reserve, and you will arrest instant attention—and have your hand kissed by multitudes who, despite democracy, have all the inferior man's unquenchable desire to grovel and admire.

Nowhere else in the world is superiority more easily attained or more eagerly admitted. The chief business of the nation, as a nation, is the setting up of heroes, mainly bogus. It admired the literary style of the late Woodrow; it respects the theological passion of Bryan; it venerates J. Pierpont Morgan; it takes Congress seriously; it would be unutterably shocked by the proposition (with proof) that a majority of its judges are ignoramuses, and that a respectable minority of them are scoundrels. The manufacture of artificial *Durchlauchten, k. k. Hoheiten* and even gods goes on feverishly and incessantly; the will to worship never flags. Ten iron-molders meet in the back-room of a near-beer saloon, organize a lodge of the Noble and Mystic Order of American Rosicrucians, and elect a wheelwright Supreme Worthy Whimwham; a month later they send a notice to the local newspaper that they have been greatly honored by an official visit from that Whimwham, and that they plan to give him a jeweled fob for his watch-chain. The chief national heroes—Lincoln, Lee, and so on—cannot remain mere men. The mysticism of the mediæval peasantry gets into the communal view of them, and they begin to sprout haloes and wings. As I say, no intrinsic merit—at least, none commensurate with the mob estimate—is needed to come to such august dignities. Everything American is a bit amateurish and childish, even the national gods. The most conspicuous and respected American in nearly every field of endeavor, saving only the purely commercial (I exclude even the financial) is a man who would attract little attention in any other country. The leading American critic of literature, after twenty years of diligent exposition of his

ideas, has yet to make it clear what he is in favor of, and why. The queen of the *haut monde,* in almost every American city, is a woman who regards Lord Reading as an aristocrat and her superior, and whose grandfather slept in his underclothes. The leading American musical director, if he went to Leipzig, would be put to polishing trombones and copying drum parts. The chief living American military-man—the national heir to Frederick, Marlborough, Wellington, Washington and Prince Eugene—is a member of the Elks, and proud of it. The leading American philosopher (now dead, with no successor known to the average pedagogue) spent a lifetime erecting an epistemological defense for the national aesthetic maxim: "I don't know nothing about music, but I know what I like." The most eminent statesman the United States has produced since Lincoln was fooled by Arthur James Balfour, and miscalculated his public support by more than 5,000,000 votes. And the current Chief Magistrate of the nation—its defiant substitute for czar and kaiser—is a small-town printer who, when he wishes to enjoy himself in the Executive Mansion, invites in a homeopathic doctor, a Seventh Day Adventist evangelist, and a couple of moving-picture actresses . . . .

IV

All the while I have been forgetting the third of my reasons for remaining so faithful a citizen of the Federation, despite all the lascivious inducements from expatriates to follow them beyond the seas, and all the surly suggestions from patriots that I succumb. It is the reason which grows out of my mediæval but unashamed taste for the bizarre and indelicate, my congenital weakness for comedy of the grosser varieties. The United States, to my eye, is incomparably the greatest show on earth. It is a show which avoids diligently all the kinds of clowning which tire me most quickly—for example,

---

1 **Geschäft,** employment • 1 **Remy de Gourmont** (1858-1915), a French dramatist and novelist • 19 **Woodrow,** Woodrow Wilson (1856-1924), twenty-eighth President of the United States • 19 **Bryan,** William Jennings Bryan (1860-1925), an enthusiastic fundamentalist who fought against teaching evolution in the schools • 20 **J. Pierpont Morgan** (1837-1913), American financier • 24 **Durchlauchten,** Highnesses • 25 **k. k. Hoheiten,** royal imperial Highnesses • 29 **Rosicrucians,** a mystic religious order • 48 **haut monde,** world of fashion • 63 **Balfour.** See note, p. 748. Mencken here assumes that Balfour misled the "eminent statesman," Woodrow Wilson • 65 **Chief Magistrate,** Warren G. Harding

royal ceremonials, the tedious hocus-pocus of *haut poli-tique,* the taking of politics seriously—and lays chief stress upon the kinds which delight me unceasingly—for example, the ribald combats of demagogues, the exquisitely ingenious operations of master rogues, the pursuit of witches and heretics, the desperate struggles of inferior men to claw their way into Heaven. We have clowns in constant practice among us who are as far above the clowns of any other great state as a Jack Demp-
10 sey is above a paralytic—and not a few dozen or score of them, but whole droves and herds. Human enterprises which, in all other Christian countries, are resigned despairingly to an incurable dullness—things that seem devoid of exhilarating amusement by their very nature—are here lifted to such vast heights of buffoonery that contemplating them strains the midriff almost to breaking. I cite an example: the worship of God. Everywhere else on earth it is carried on in a solemn and dispiriting manner; in England, of course, the bishops are obscene,
20 but the average man seldom gets a fair chance to laugh at them and enjoy them. Now come home. Here we not only have bishops who are enormously more obscene than even the most gifted of the English bishops; we have also a huge force of lesser specialists in ecclesiastical mountebankery—tin-horn Loyolas, Savonarolas and Xaviers of a hundred fantastic rites, each performing untiringly and each full of a grotesque and illimitable whimsicality. Every American town, however small, has one of its own: a holy clerk with so fine a talent for in-
30 troducing the arts of jazz into the salvation of the damned that his performance takes on all the gaudiness of a four-ring circus, and the bald announcement that he will raid Hell on such and such a night is enough to empty all the town blind-pigs and bordellos and pack his sanctuary to the doors. And to aid him and inspire him there are traveling experts to whom he stands in the relation of a wart to the Matterhorn—stupendous masters of theological imbecility, contrivers of doctrines utterly preposterous, heirs to the Joseph Smith, Mother Eddy
40 and John Alexander Dowie tradition—Bryan, Sunday, and their like. These are the eminences of the American Sacred College. I delight in them. Their proceedings make me a happier American.

Turn, now, to politics. Consider, for example, a campaign for the Presidency. Would it be possible to imagine anything more uproariously idiotic—a deafening, nerve-wracking battle to the death between Tweedledum and Tweedledee, Harlequin and Sganarelle, Gobbo and Dr. Cook—the unspeakable, with fearful snorts, gradually swallowing the inconceivable? I defy any one to 50 match it elsewhere on this earth. In other lands, at worst, there are at least intelligible issues, coherent ideas, salient personalities. Somebody says something, and somebody replies. But what did Harding say in 1920, and what did Cox reply? Who was Harding, anyhow, and who was Cox? Here, having perfected democracy, we lift the whole combat to symbolism, to transcendentalism, to metaphysics. Here we load a pair of palpably tin cannon with blank cartridges charged with talcum powder, and so let fly. Here one may howl over the show without any 60 uneasy reminder that it is serious, and that some one may be hurt. I hold that this elevation of politics to the plane of undiluted comedy is peculiarly American, that nowhere else on this disreputable ball has the art of the sham-battle been developed to such fineness. Two experiences are in point. During the Harding-Cox combat of bladders an article of mine, dealing with some of its more melodramatic phases, was translated into German and reprinted by a Berlin paper. At the head of it the editor was careful to insert a preface explaining to his 70 readers, but recently delivered to democracy, that such contests were not taken seriously by intelligent Americans, and warning them solemnly against getting into sweats over politics. At about the same time I had dinner with an Englishman. From cocktails to bromo seltzer he bewailed the political lassitude of the English populace—its growing indifference to the whole partisan harlequinade. Here were two typical foreign attitudes: the Germans were in danger of making politics too harsh and implacable, and the English were in danger 80 of forgetting politics altogether. Both attitudes, it must be plain, make for bad shows. Observing a German

---

1 **haut politique,** political ceremony • 25 **Loyolas . . . Xaviers,** religious leaders • 39 **Joseph Smith** (1805-1844), American founder of Mormonism • 39 **Mother Eddy,** Mary Baker Eddy (1821-1910), founder of Christian Science • 40 **John Alexander Dowie,** a famed evangelist • 40 **Sunday,** Billy Sunday, an evangelist • 47 **Tweedledum . . . Dr. Cook,** disputes between nonentities, clowns, and prevaricators • 55 **Cox.** James Cox was Harding's rival candidate for the Presidency in 1920

campaign, one is uncomfortably harassed and stirred up; observing an English campaign (at least in times of peace), one falls asleep. In the United States the thing is done better. Here politics is purged of all menace, all sinister quality, all genuine significance, and stuffed with such gorgeous humors, such inordinate farce that one comes to the end of a campaign with one's ribs loose, and ready for "King Lear," or a hanging, or a course of medical journals.

But feeling better for the laugh. *Ridi si sapis,* said Martial. Mirth is necessary to wisdom, to comfort, above all, to happiness. Well, here is the land of mirth, as Germany is the land of metaphysics and France is the land of fornication. Here the buffoonery never stops. What could be more delightful than the endless struggle of the Puritan to make the joy of the minority unlawful and impossible? The effort is itself a greater joy to one standing on the side-lines than any or all of the carnal joys that it combats. Always, when I contemplate an uplifter at his hopeless business, I recall a scene in an old-time burlesque show, witnessed for hire in my days as a dramatic critic. A chorus girl executed a fall upon the stage, and Rudolph Krausemeyer, the Swiss comedian, rushed to her aid. As he stooped painfully to succor her, Irving Rabinovitz, the Zionist comedian, fetched him a fearful clout across the cofferdam with a slap-stick. So the uplifter, the soul-saver, the Americanizer, striving to make the Republic fit for Y. M. C. A. secretaries. He is the eternal American, ever moved by the best intentions, ever running *à la* Krausemeyer to the rescue of virtue, and ever getting his pantaloons fanned by the Devil. I am naturally sinful, and such spectacles caress me. If the slap-stick were a sash-weight the show would be cruel, and I'd probably complain to the *Polizei.* As it is, I know that the uplifter is not really hurt, but simply shocked. The blow, in fact, does him good, for it helps to get him into Heaven, as exegetes prove from Matthew V, ii: *Heureux serez-vous, lorsqu'on vous outragera, qu'on vous persécutera,* and so on. As for me, it makes me a more contented man, and hence a better citizen. One man prefers the Republic because it pays better wages than Bulgaria. Another because it has laws to keep him sober and his daughter chaste. Another because the Woolworth Building is higher than the cathedral at Chartres. Another because,

living here, he can read the New York *Evening Journal.* Another because there is a warrant out for him somewhere else. Me, I like it because it amuses me to my taste. I never get tired of the show. It is worth every cent it costs.

That cost, it seems to me is very moderate. Taxes in the United States are not actually high. I figure, for example, that my private share of the expense of maintaining the Hon. Mr. Harding in the White House this year will work out to less than 80 cents. Try to think of better sport for the money: in New York it has been estimated that it costs $8 to get comfortably tight, and $17.50, on an average, to pinch a girl's arm. The United States Senate will cost me perhaps $11 for the year, but against that expense set the subscription price of the *Congressional Record,* about $15, which as a journalist, I receive for nothing. For $4 less than nothing I am thus entertained as Solomon never was by his hooch dancers. Col. George Brinton McClellan Harvey costs me but 25 cents a year; I get Nicholas Murray Butler free. Finally, there is young Teddy Roosevelt, the naval expert. Teddy costs me, as I work it out, about 11 cents a year, or less than a cent a month. More, he entertains me doubly for the money, first as a naval expert, and secondly as a walking *attentat* upon democracy, a devastating proof that there is nothing, after all, in that superstition. We Americans subscribe to the doctrine of human equality—and the Rooseveltii reduce it to an absurdity as brilliantly as the sons of Veit Bach. Where is your equal opportunity now? Here in this Eden of clowns, with the highest rewards of clowning theoretically open to every poor boy—here in the very citadel of democracy we found and cherish a clown *dynasty!*

1922

---

11 **Martial,** Marcus Valerius Martialis (40?-102?), Latin author of epigrams • 35 **Polizei,** police • 38 **Heureux serez-vous** . . . . The beginning of a French translation of Matthew 5:2, which, in the King James version, reads: "Blessed are ye, when men shall revile you, and persecute you, and say all manner of evil against you, for my sake" • 64 **George Brinton McClellan Harvey** (1864-1928), American journalist who was influential in politics • 65 **Nicholas Murray Butler,** long-time president of Columbia University and a pundit on national and international affairs • 66 **Teddy Roosevelt,** son of Theodore Roosevelt • 70 **attentat,** outrage • 74 **Veit Bach** (born about 1555), believed to be the founder of the famous Bach family; great-great-grandfather of Johann Sebastian Bach

From · Prejudices: Fourth Series

The American Novel

In "The American Novel," Mencken preaches a doctrine which is highly characteristic not only of his own thinking, but also of the thinking of the period. In a period of revolt against established standards, he and others, naturally enough, tended to rate fiction according to its success in attacking traditions. American novelists, Mencken alleges, have learned to be free and frank; therefore they are bound to be great. The piece comes from a volume called **Prejudices**, and true to his title, Mencken reveals along the way a number of his personal distastes—for Anglicized American writers, the Victorians, professional critics, literary censors, commercialized authors, Greenwich Village modern poets, and others. The prediction about the future course of American literature contained in the final paragraphs has not, in the long run, proved to be very accurate.

It is an ancient platitude of historical criticism that great wars and their sequelæ are inimical to the fine arts, and particularly to the art of letters. The kernel of truth in it lies in the obvious fact that a people engaged in a bitter struggle for existence have no time for such concerns, which demand not only leisure but also a certain assured feeling of security, well-being and self-sufficiency—in brief, the thing often called aristocratic (or sometimes intellectual) detachment. No man ever wrote good poetry with his wife in parturition in the next room, or the police preparing to raid his house, or his shirt-tail afire. He needs to be comfortable to do it, and if not actually comfortable, then at all events safe. Wars tend to make life uncomfortable and unsafe —but not, it must be observed, inevitably and necessarily, not always and invariably. A bitter and demoralizing struggle goes with wars that are lost, and the same struggle goes with wars that are won only by dint of

stupendous and ruinous effort, but it certainly does not go with wars that are won easily. These last do not palsy and asphyxiate the artist, as he is palsied and asphyxiated by cholera morbus, suits for damages or marriage. On the contrary, they pump him full of ozone, and he is never more alive and lively than following them. I point to a few familiar examples. The Civil War, as everyone knows, bankrupted the South and made life a harsh and bitter struggle for its people, and especially for the gentler and more civilized minority of its people. In consequence, the South became as sterile artistically, after Lee's surrender, as Mexico or Portugal, and even today it lags far behind the North in beautiful letters, and even further behind in music, painting and architecture. But the war, though it went on for four years, strained the resources of the North very little, either in men or in money, and so its conclusion found the Northerners very rich and cocky, and full of a yearning to astonish the world, and that yearning, in a few decades set up a new and extremely vigorous American literature, created an American architecture of a revolutionary character, and even laid the first courses of American schools of music and painting. Mark Twain, Walt Whitman, Henry James and William Dean Howells, all of them draft dodgers in the war itself, were in a very real sense products of the war, for they emerged as phenomena of the great outburst of creative energy that followed it, and all of them, including even James, were as thoroughly American as Jay Gould, P. T. Barnum or Jim Fisk. The stars of the national letters in the years before the war had been Americans only by geographical accident. About Emerson there hung a smell of Königsberg and Weimar; Irving was simply a New York Englishman; Poe was a citizen of No Man's Land; even Hawthorne and Cooper, despite their concern with American themes, showed not the slightest evidence of an American point of view. But Mark Twain, Howells and Whitman belonged to the Republic as palpably as Niagara Falls or Tammany Hall belonged to it, and so

Reprinted from **Prejudices, Fourth Series**, by H. L. Mencken, by permission of Alfred A. Knopf, Inc. • Copyright 1924 by Alfred A. Knopf, Inc.
48 **Jay Gould** (1836-1892), American financier • 48 **P. T. Barnum** (1810-1891), American showman • 48 **Jim Fisk** (1834-1872), American financier • 51 **Königsberg and Weimar**, cities in Germany, famous in philosophical history

did James, though the thought horrified him and we must look at him through his brother William to get the proof. Turn now to Europe. France, harshly used in the war of 1870-71, was sterile for a decade, but the wounds were not deep, and recovery was in full swing by 1880. Germany, injured scarcely at all, produced Nietzsche almost before the troops got home, and was presently offering an asylum and an inspiration to Ibsen, preparing the way for the reform and moderni-
10 zation of the theatre, and making contributions of the utmost value to practically all of the arts and sciences. Spain, after the Armada, gave the world Cervantes and then expired; England produced Shakespeare and founded a literature that is not surpassed in history.

What has thus happened over and over again in the past—and I might pile up examples for pages—may be in process of repetition today, and under our very noses. All Europe, plainly enough, is in a state of exhaustion and depression, and in no department of human activity
20 is the fact more visible than in that of the arts. Not only are the defeated nations, Russia, Germany and Austria, producing nothing save a few extravagant ec-centricities; there is also a great lowness of spirit in the so-called victorious nations, for their victory was almost as ruinous as defeat. France, as after 1870, is running to a pretentious and artificial morbidity in letters, and marking time in music and painting; Italy is producing little save psychopathological absurdities by such mounte-banks as D'Annunzio and Papini; even England shows
30 all the signs of profound fatigue. The great English writers of the age before the war are passing. Meredith is gone; Hardy has put up his shutters; Kipling went to wreck in the war itself; Conrad is dead; Shaw, once so agile and diverting, becomes a seer and prophet. Nor is there any sign of sound progress among the younger men. Arnold Bennett, a star of brilliant promise in 1913, is today a smoking smudge. Wells has ceased to be an artist and become a prophet in the Sunday sup-plements. Masefield has got no further than he was on
40 August 2, 1914. The rest of the novelists are simply chasing their own tails. The Georgian poets, having emerged gloriously during the war, now disappear be-hind their manners. Only a few women, led by May Sinclair, and a few iconoclastic young men, led by Aldous Huxley, are still indubitably alive.

It seems to me that, in the face of this dark depression

across the water, the literary spectacle on this side takes on an aspect that is extremely reassuring, and even a bit exhilarating. For the first time in history, there begins to show itself the faint shadow of a hope that, 50 if all goes well, leadership in the arts, and especially in all the art of letters, may eventually transfer itself from the eastern shore of the Atlantic to the western shore. Our literature, as I have more than once pointed out in the past, is still oppressed by various heavy handi-caps, chiefly resident in the failure of the new aristocracy of money to function as an aristocracy of taste. The artist among us is still a sort of pariah, beset by public contempt on the one hand and by academic enmity on the other; he still lacks the public position that his 60 brothers enjoy in older and more civilized countries. Nevertheless, it must be obvious to everyone that his condition tends to improve materially—that, in our own time, it *has* improved materially—that though his rewards remain meagre, save in mere money, his free-dom grows steadily greater. And it must be obvious, too, that he begins to show that that increasing free-dom is not wholly wasted upon him—that he knows how to use it, and is disposed to do so with some gusto. What all the younger American writers have in com- 70 mon is a sort of new-found elasticity or goatishness, a somewhat exaggerated sense of aliveness, a glowing delight in the spectacle before them, a vigorous and naïve self-consciousness. The schoolmaster critics be-labor them for it, and call it a disrespect for tradition, and try to put it down by denouncing it as due to cor-rupt foreign influences. But it is really a proof of the rise of nationalism—perhaps of the first dawn of a genuine sense of nationality. No longer imitative and timorous, as most of their predecessors were, these 80 youngsters are attempting a first-hand examination of the national scene, and making an effort to represent it in terms that are wholly American. They are the pioneers of a literature that, whatever its defects in the abstract, will at least be a faithful reflection of the national life, that will be more faithful, indeed, in its defects than in its merits. In England the novel sub-

7 **Nietzsche**, Friedrich Wilhelm Nietzsche. See note, p. 752 • 12 **Cer-vantes**, Miguel de Cervantes (1547-1616), Spanish author who wrote **Don Quixote** • 29 **D'Annunzio**, Gabriele D'Annunzio (1863-1938), Italian author • 29 **Papini**, Giovanni Papini (1881-   ), Italian philosopher and author

sides into formulæ, the drama is submerged in artificialities, and even poetry, despite occasional revolts, moves toward scholarliness and emptiness. But in America, since the war, all three show the artless and superabundant energy of little children. They lack, only too often, manner and urbanity; it is no wonder that they are often shocking to pedants. But there is the breath of life in them, and that life is far nearer its beginning than its end.

The causes of all this are not far to seek. The American Legion is right: we won the war. It cost us nothing in men; it brought us a huge profit in money; as Europe has gone down, we have gone up. Moreover, it produced a vast discharge of spiritual electricity, otherwise and more injuriously dissipated in the countries more harshly beset. The war was fought ignobly; its first and most obvious effect was to raise up a horde of cads, and set them in authority as spokesmen of the nation. But out of that swinishness there was bound to come reaction, and out of the reaction there was bound to flow a desire to re-examine the whole national pretension—to turn on the light, to reject old formulæ, to think things out anew and in terms of reality. Suddenly the old houses of cards came tumbling down, and the professors inhabiting them ran about in their nightshirts, bawling for the police. The war, first and last, produced a great deal more than John Dos Passos' "Three Soldiers." It also produced Lewis' "Babbitt," and Cabell's "Jurgen," and Fergusson's "Capitol Hill," and O'Neill's "The Emperor Jones." And, producing them, it ended an epoch of sweetness and light.

II

The young American literatus of today, with publishers ready and eager to give him a hearing, can scarcely imagine the difficulties which beset his predecessor of twenty years ago; he is, indeed, far too little appreciative of the freedom he has, and far too prone to flee from hard work to the solace of the martyr's shroud. When I first began practise as a critic, in 1908, there was yet plenty of excuse for putting it on. It was a time of almost inconceivable complacency and conformity. Hamilton Wright Mabie was still alive and still taken seriously, and all the young pedagogues who aspired to the critical gown imitated him in his watchful stupidity. This camorra had delivered a violent wallop to Theodore Dreiser eight years before, and he was yet

suffering from his bruises; it was not until 1911 that he printed "Jennie Gerhardt." Miss Harriet Monroe and her gang of new poets were still dispersed and inarticulate; Miss Amy Lowell, as yet unaware of Imagism, was writing polite doggerel in the manner of a New England schoolmarm; the reigning dramatists of the nation were Augustus Thomas, David Belasco and Clyde Fitch; Miss Cather was imitating Mrs. Wharton; Hergesheimer had six years to go before he'd come to "The Lay Anthony"; Cabell was known only as one who provided the text for illustrated gift-books; the American novelists most admired by most publishers, by most readers and by all practising critics were Richard Harding Davis, Robert W. Chambers and James Lane Allen. It is hard indeed, in retrospect, to picture those remote days just as they were. They seem almost fabulous. The chief critical organ of the Republic was actually the Literary Supplement of the New York *Times.* The *Dial* was down with diabetes in Chicago; the *Nation* was made dreadful by the gloomy humors of Paul Elmer More; the *Bookman* was even more saccharine and sophomoric than it is today. When the mild and *pianissimo* revolt of the middle 90's—a feeble echo of the English revolt—had spent itself, the Presbyterians marched in and took possession of the works. Most of the erstwhile revoltés boldly took the veil— notably Hamlin Garland. No novel that told the truth about life as Americans were living it, no poem that departed from the old patterns, no play that had the merest ghost of an idea in it had a chance. When, in

28 **Jurgen,** a sexy novel by James Branch Cabell (1879-   ) which, following its appearance in 1919, was the object of much discussion by critics • 28 **Capitol Hill,** a realistic portrayal of life in Washington, D. C., by Harvey Fergusson (1890-   ) • 40 **Hamilton Wright Mabie** (1846-1916), American critic and editor • 48 **Amy Lowell** (1874-1925) was a leader in the poetry of the day • 48 **Imagism,** a movement in poetry (1909-1917) which emphasized terseness, clarity, and sharpness of imagery. Miss Lowell was one of the most famous of the imagists • 52 **Mrs. Wharton,** Edith Wharton (1862-1937), a novelist in the tradition of Henry James • 53 **Hergesheimer,** Joseph Hergesheimer (1880-   ), author of novels, some of which exploited picturesque details in American history, others of which limned the society of the day • 57 **Richard Harding Davis** (1864-1916), newspaper correspondent as well as a facile novelist and playwright. In his fiction he wrote romantically of New York dandies and of soldiers of fortune • 58 **Robert W. Chambers** (1865-1933) wrote popular fictional works about the past and his own day • 58 **James Lane Allen** (1849-1925), a Kentuckian, was the author of romantic novels about his region

an author should present America or his nation — and not be afraid to be realistic

1908, Mrs. Mary Roberts Rinehart printed a conventional mystery story which yet managed to have a trace of sense in it, it caused a sensation. And when, two years later, Dr. William Lyon Phelps printed a book of criticism in which he actually ranked Mark Twain alongside Emerson and Hawthorne, there was as great a stirring beneath the college elms as if a naked fancy woman had run across the campus. If Hergesheimer had come into New York in 1908 with "Cytherea" under his arm, he would have worn out his pantaloons on publishers' benches without getting so much as a polite kick. If Eugene O'Neill had come to Broadway with "The Hairy Ape," he would have been sent to Edward E. Rose to learn the elements of his trade. The devilish and advanced thing, in those days, was for the fat lady star to give a couple of matinees of Ibsen's "A Doll's House."

A great many men and a few women addressed themselves to the dispersal of this fog. Some of them were imaginative writers who found it simply impossible to bring themselves within the prevailing rules; some were critics; others were young publishers. As I look back, I can't find any sign of concerted effort; it was, in the main, a case of each on his own. The more contumacious of the younger critics, true enough, tended to rally 'round Huneker, who, as a matter of fact, was very little interested in American letters, and the young novelists had a leader in Dreiser, who, I suspect, was quite unaware of most of them. However, it was probably Dreiser who chiefly gave form to the movement, despite the fact that for eleven long years he was silent. Not only was there a useful rallying-point in the idiotic suppression of "Sister Carrie"; there was also the encouraging fact of the man's massive immovability. Physically and mentally he loomed up like a sort of headland—a great crag of basalt that no conceivable assault seemed able to touch. His predecessor, Frank Norris, was of much softer stuff. Norris, had he lived longer, would have been wooed and ruined, I fear, by the Mabies, Boyntons and other such Christian critics, as Garland had been wooed and ruined before him. Dreiser, fortunately for American letters, never had to face any such seduction. The critical schoolmarms, young and old, fell upon him with violence the moment he appeared above the horizon of his native steppe, and soon he was the storm center of a battle-royal that lasted nearly twenty years. The man himself was solid, granitic, without nerves. Very little cunning was in him and not much bellicose enterprise, but he showed a truly appalling tenacity. The pedagogues tried to scare him to death, they tried to stampede his partisans and they tried to put him into Coventry and get him forgotten, but they failed every time. The more he was reviled, sneered at, neglected, the more resolutely he stuck to his formula. That formula is now every serious American novelist's formula. They all try to write better than Dreiser, and not a few of them succeed, but they all follow him in his fundamental purpose—to make the novel true. Dreiser added something, and here following him is harder: he tried to make the novel poignant—to add sympathy, feeling, imagination to understanding. It will be a long while before that enterprise is better managed than he managed it in "Jennie Gerhardt."

Today, it seems to me, the American imaginative writer, whether he be novelist, poet or dramatist, is quite as free as he deserves to be. He is free to depict the life about him precisely as he sees it, and to interpret it in any manner he pleases. The publishers of the land, once so fearful of novelty, are now so hospitable to it that they constantly fail to distinguish the novelty that has hard thought behind it from that which has only some Village mountebank's desire to stagger the wives of Rotarians. Our stage is perhaps the freest in the world—not only to sensations, but also to ideas. Our poets get into print regularly with stuff so bizarre and unearthly that only Christian Scientists can understand it. The extent of this new freedom, indeed, is so great that large numbers of persons appear to be unable to believe in it; they are constantly getting into sweats about the taboos and inhibitions that remain, for example, those nourished by comstockery. But the im-

---

1 **Mary Roberts Rinehart** (1876-   ), prolific author of mystery novels • 4 **William Lyon Phelps** (1865-1943), popular Yale professor who was one of the first academic men to give serious attention to contemporary literature • 10 **Cytherea** (1922) was a somewhat dramatic psychological novel about the search of a middle-aged businessman for ideal love • 26 **Huneker**, James Gibbons Huneker (1860-1921), a distinguished critic of music, art, and literature • 40 **Boynton**, Percy H. Boynton (1875-1946), a professor at the University of Chicago and author of several books about contemporary literature • 81 **comstockery**, a noun honoring Anthony Comstock (1844-1915), famous in a battle against what he considered obscenity in literature

to make the novel true! to American life!

portance and puissance of comstockery, I believe, is quite as much overestimated as the importance and puissance of the objurgations still hurled at sense and honesty by the provincial professors of American Idealism, the Genius of America, and other such phantasms. The Comstocks, true enough, still raid an occasional book, particularly when their funds are running low and there is need to inflame Christian men, but that their monkeyshines ever actually *suppress* a book of any consequence I very much doubt. The flood is too vast for them. Chasing a minnow with desperate passion, they let a whole school of whales go by. In any case, they confine their operations to the single field of sex, and it must be plain that it is not in the field of sex that the hottest battles against the old American manner have been fought and won. "Three Soldiers" was far more subversive of that manner than all the stories of sex ever written in America—and yet "Three Soldiers" came out with the imprint of one of the most respectable of American publishers, and was scarcely challenged. "Babbitt" scored a victory that was still easier, and yet more significant, for its target was the double one of American business and American Christianity; it set the whole world to laughing at two things that are far more venerated in the United States than the bodily chastity of women. Nevertheless, "Babbitt" went down so easily that even the alfalfa *Gelehrten* joined in whooping for it, apparently on the theory that praising Lewis would make the young of the national species forget Dreiser. Victimized by their own craft, the *Gelehrten* thus made a foul attack upon their own principles, for if their principles did not stand against just such anarchistic and sacrilegious books, then they were without any sense whatever, as was and is, indeed, the case.

I shall not rehearse the steps in the advance from "Sister Carrie," suppressed and proscribed, to "Babbitt," swallowed and hailed. The important thing is that, despite the caterwauling of the Comstocks and the pedagogues, a reasonable freedom for the serious artist now prevails—that publishers stand ready to print him, that critics exist who are competent to recognize him and willing to do battle for him, and that there is a large public eager to read him. What use is he making of his opportunity? Certainly not the worst use possible, but also certainly not the best. He is free, but he is not yet, perhaps, worthy of freedom. He lets the popular magazine, the movie and the cheap-John publisher pull him too hard in one direction; he lets the vagaries of his politics pull him too hard in another. Back in 1908 I predicted the destruction of Upton Sinclair the artist by Upton Sinclair the visionary and reformer. Sinclair's bones now bleach upon the beach. Beside them repose those of many another man and woman of great promise—for example, Winston Churchill. Floyd Dell is on his way—one novel and two doses of Greenwich Village psychology. Hergesheimer writes novelettes for the *Saturday Evening Post*. Willa Cather has won the Pulitzer Prize—a transaction comparable to the election of Charles W. Eliot to the Elks. Masters turns to prose that somehow fails to come off. Dreiser, forgetting his trilogy, experiments rather futilely with the drama, the essay, free verse. Fuller renounces the novel for book reviewing. Tarkington is another Pulitzer prizeman, always on the verge of first-rate work but always falling short by an inch. Many of the White Hopes of ten or fifteen years ago perished in the war, as surely victims of its slaughter as Rupert Brooke or Otto Braun; it is, indeed, curious to note that practically every American author who moaned and sobbed for democracy between the years 1914 and 1919 is now extinct. The rest have gone down the chute of the movies.

But all this, after all, may signify little. The shock troops have been piled up in great masses, but the ground is cleared for those that follow. Well, then, what of the youngsters? Do they show any sign of seizing their chance? The answer is yes and no. On the one hand there is a group which, revolving 'round the *Bookman*, talks a great deal and accomplishes nothing. On the other hand there is a group which, revolving 'round

27 **Gelehrten,** learned folk • 55 **Winston Churchill** (1871-1947), American author who wrote a number of historical novels of distinction • 55 **Floyd Dell** (1887-   ) was noted in the twenties as a psychological novelist. Some of his writings concerned the revolt against convention sponsored in Greenwich Village • 60 **Charles W. Eliot** (1834-1926), president of Harvard (1869-1909), sponsored the elective system of undergraduate courses • 60 **Masters,** Edgar Lee Masters (1869-1950), author of **Spoon River Anthology** (1915) • 63 **Fuller,** Henry Blake Fuller (1857-1929), Chicago novelist whose promising career began in 1890, had not written a novel since **Bertram Cope's Year** (1919). His next novel did not appear until 1929 • 64 **Tarkington,** Booth Tarkington (1869-1946), creator of Penrod among others. His career as a novelist began in 1899 and continued into the 1940's • 67 **White Hopes.** When Jack Johnson, Negro, was heavyweight champion, rising white prizefighters were called "White Hopes"

the *Dial* and the *Little Review,* talks even more and does
even less. But on the third hand, as it were, there is a
group which says little and saws wood. There seems to
be little in common between its members, no sign of a
formal movement, with its *blague* and its bombast, but
all of them have this in common: that they owe both
their opportunity and their method to the revolution
that followed "Sister Carrie." Most of them are from
the Middle West, but they are distinct from the Chicago
crowd, now degenerated to posturing and worse. They
are sophisticated, disillusioned, free from cant, and
yet they have imagination. The raucous protests of the
evangelists of American Idealism seem to have no more
effect upon them than the advances of the Expres-
sionists, Dadaists and other such cafe-table prophets.
Out of this dispersed and ill-defined group, I believe,

something will come. Its members are those who are
free from the two great delusions which, from the beginning, have always cursed American letters: the delusion
that a work of art is primarily a moral document, that its
purpose is to make men better Christians and more
docile cannon-fodder, and the delusion that it is an exercise in logic, that its purpose is to prove something
These delusions, lingering beyond their time, are
responsible for most of the disasters visible in the national literature today—the disasters of the radicals as
well as those of the 100 per cent dunderheads. The
writers of the future, I hope and believe, will carefully
avoid both of them.

1924

5 blague, humbug • 15 Dadaists, a radical French literary group

[handwritten notes: for all lit., many critics have set up 2 standards 1. It must be a moral piece with purpose to make better Christians 2. + it must be an exercise in logic — to prove something this leaves out all realism]

Irving Babbitt

1865 · 1933

During the late 1920's and early 1930's, rebellion against
what was called "Victorianism"—that is, against any
kind of established standards—was pretty general. Opposed to this rebellion was a group called "the New
Humanists," a group which sturdily reaffirmed certain
older faiths. The members of this learned critical school
(most of them were professors) asserted kinship with
the sixteenth-century European Humanists. Like their
predecessors (John Colet, Thomas More, Desiderius
Erasmus, and others), the modern group tried to revi-
talize interest in the classics. Like their predecessors,
too, the modern group urged that life should be lived
for its opportunities of individual development through
discipline.

Outstanding were Paul Elmer More, Robert Shafer,
Norman Foerster, Frank Mather, Stuart Sherman, Sher-
lock Bronson Gass, Harry Hayden Clark, and others;
but their acknowledged leader was Professor Irving Babbitt. Babbitt was the most militant and the most formidable member of the group, and it was he who leveled
and received the most ferocious blows in the battle which
raged concerning the proper nature of criticism and the
merits of contemporary literature.

Paradoxically, the undisciplined childhood of Irving
Babbitt in his native Dayton, Ohio, stimulated instead
of discouraged a faith in self-discipline which he was to
preach throughout most of his life. His reading of the
classics in high school enlarged that faith. Study at Harvard and abroad—more of it out of classes than in
classes—gave him great learning which he felt bolstered
his initial belief in self-discipline. His wide study, too,
evidently only confirmed his early tendency toward

dualism—a belief that two forces, one good, one evil, ruled the universe. Such, at least, was the impression of Paul Elmer More when, in 1934, he recalled the big man as a fellow student at Harvard in the 1890's, pacing back and forth in a dormitory room and vehemently arguing in behalf of his beliefs. "Not only had Babbitt at an early age—how early I do not know—reached . . . settled convictions," said More, "but at least from the beginning of our acquaintance they were knit together into a system of logical bonds which were perfectly clear to his mind. . . ."

Babbitt taught a year at Williams College (1892-1893), then returned to Harvard, to teach there in the romance languages department the rest of his life (1894-1933). Hoffman Nickerson, in 1934, tried to suggest how, as a teacher, Babbitt appeared to the enthusiastic students in his classes: "After a quarter of a century, one still vividly recalls the absorbing interest, almost the excitement, of his lectures. Into the austere and bare Harvard lecture room there would walk powerfully a strongly-built, slightly awkward, six-foot man, his hair brown turning to grey, his eyes a light grey-blue—always brilliant, usually tranquil, but capable of blazing. . . . Hardly had his clear, carefully-controlled, but vibrant voice made itself heard than one sat bolt upright in the realization that here was a master-anatomist of the whole modernist menagerie. . . . To hear him was to understand the modern world."

Babbitt's first book, *Literature and the American College* (1908), had as its motto a quotation from Emerson which summarized the basis of Babbitt's particular brand of Humanistic philosophy:

> There are two laws discrete
> Not reconciled,
> Law for man, and law for thing;
> The last builds town and fleet,
> But it runs wild,
> And doth the man unking.

"The first article of Babbitt's humanist creed," writes Nickerson, "was the dual nature of man. He saw clearly that all men are born with a desire for beauty, truth, and goodness, which if perfectly combined would result in perfect order; and at the same time with a tendency to evil, which tendency, if not grasped by the intellect and opposed by the will, results in intolerable disorder. He taught that this basic fact of man's dual nature has been obscured by the naturalistic school of thought. . . ." In later books as well as his first, Babbitt preached this doctrine—*The New Laokoön* (1910), *The Masters of French Criticism* (1912), *Rousseau and Romanticism* (1919), *Democracy and Leadership* (1924), and *On Being Creative* (1932).

He not only supported his thesis; he also vigorously opposed forces in literature which he saw working against it. The subtitle of *The New Laokoön*, for instance, was "An Essay on the Confusion of the Arts," and after arguing that there was confusion, Babbitt ascribed the lack of "dignity, centrality, repose" to the fact that "the men of the present have no centre, no sense of anything fixed or permanent either within or without themselves." In *Rousseau and Romanticism*, Babbitt traced the blame for much modern confusion to the romantic, undisciplined trend which had been initiated by the French philosopher, Jean Jacques Rousseau. Following that trend, he claimed, "those who call themselves modern have come to adopt a purely exploratory attitude towards life. 'On desperate seas long wont to roam,' they have lost more and more the sense of what is normal and central in human experience. But to get away from what is normal and central is to get away from wisdom." With such views of the faults of modern society and of the necessary remedies for those faults, Babbitt necessarily condemned much of the writing of the day. Creative writing, he held, lacked philosophical depth of the sort needed for greatness; critical writing was impressionistic and superficial. Although they differed from him about some matters, most of Babbitt's fellow Humanists agreed with his diagnosis and offered similar antidotes for the modern "disease." For a time, Babbitt and his associates were in the spotlight; but a few years after Babbitt's death, the general impression was that Humanism, as a movement, had pretty well ended. Nevertheless the Humanists had a real impact upon modern thought. And in the late 1930's and the 1940's, when social changes and World War II stimulated affirmative thinking, an increasing number of American writers were echoing Babbitt's plea for firmly held critical and ethical standards.

F. E. McMahon, **The Humanism of Irving Babbitt**, Washington, D. C., 1931 • P. E. More, "Irving Babbitt," **University of Toronto Quarterly**, January 1934 • Hoffman Nickerson, "Irving Babbitt," **American Review**, February 1934

The Critic and American Life

"The Critic and American Life," an essay by Professor Babbitt published in Forum, February 1928, came as close as any document to constituting a "manifesto" of Babbitt's group. It provoked much general discussion, and was answered and interpreted by a number of critics in both parties. Not only does it summarize the Humanist's dissatisfaction with contemporary writers in general and in particular, in addition it admirably states the philosophy of the leader of the group.

A frequent remark of the French about Americans is: "They're children"; which, interpreted, means that from the French point of view Americans are childishly uncritical. The remark is relevant only in so far as it refers to general critical intelligence. In dealing with the special problems of a commercial and industrial society Americans have shown that they can be abundantly critical. Certain Americans, for example, have developed a critical keenness in estimating the value of stocks and
10 bonds that is nothing short of uncanny. The very persons, however, who are thus keen in some particular field are when confronted with questions that call for general critical intelligence, often puerile. Yet in an age like the present, which is being subjected to a constant stream of propaganda in everything from the choice of its religion to its cigarettes, general critical intelligence would seem desirable.

As a matter of fact, most persons nowadays aspire to be not critical but creative. We have not merely creative
20 poets and novelists, but creative readers and listeners and dancers. Lately a form of creativeness has appeared that may in time swallow up all the others—creative salesmanship. The critic himself has caught the contagion and also aspires to be creative. He is supposed to become so when he receives from the creation of another, con-

ceived as pure temperamental overflow, so vivid an impression that, when passed through his temperament, it issues forth as a fresh creation. What is eliminated in both critic and creator is any standard that is set above temperament and that therefore might interfere with 30 their eagerness to get themselves expressed.

This notion of criticism as self-expression is important for our present subject, for it has been adopted by the writer who is, according to the last edition of the *Encyclopaedia Britannica,* "the greatest critical force in America"—Mr. H. L. Mencken. "The critic is first and last," says Mr. Mencken, "simply trying to express himself; he is trying to achieve thereby for his own inner ego the grateful feeling of a function performed, a tension relieved, a katharsis attained which Wagner achieved when 40 he wrote *Die Walküre,* and a hen achieves every time she lays an egg." This creative self-expression, as practiced by himself and others, has, according to Mr. Mencken, led to a salutary stirring up of the stagnant pool of American letters: "To-day for the first time in years there is strife in American criticism. . . . Heretics lay on boldly and the professors are forced to make some defence. Often going further they attempt counter-attacks. Ears are bitten off, noses are bloodied. There are wallops both above and below the belt." 50

But it may be that criticism is something more than Mr. Mencken would have us believe, more in short than a squabble between Bohemians, each eager to capture the attention of the public for his brand of self-expression. To reduce criticism indeed to the satisfaction of a temperamental urge, to the uttering of one's gustos and disgustos (in Mr. Mencken's case chiefly the latter) is to run counter to the very etymology of the word which implies discrimination and judgment. The best one would anticipate from a writer like Mr. Mencken, pos- 60 sessing an unusual verbal virtuosity and at the same time temperamentally irresponsible, is superior intellectual vaudeville. One must grant him, however, certain genuine critical virtues—for example, a power of shrewd observation within rather narrow limits. Yet the total effect of his writing is nearer to intellectual vaudeville than to serious criticism.

The serious critic is more concerned with achieving a correct scale of values and so seeing things proportion-

34 **last edition,** the thirteenth edition • 40 **Wagner,** Richard Wagner (1813-1883), German composer of the opera **Die Walküre**

ately than with self-expression. His essential virtue is poise. The specific benefit he confers is to act as a moderating influence on the opposite insanities between which mankind in the lump is constantly tending to oscillate—oscillations that Luther compares to the reelings of a drunken peasant on horseback. The critic's survey of any particular situation may very well seem satirical. The complaint that Mr. Mencken is too uniformly disgruntled in his survey of the American situation rather misses the point. Behind the pleas for more constructiveness it is usually easy to detect the voice of the booster. A critic who did not get beyond a correct diagnosis of existing evils might be very helpful. If Mr. Mencken has fallen short of being such a diagnostician, the failure is due not to his excess of severity but to his lack of discrimination.

The standards with reference to which men have discriminated in the past have been largely traditional. The outstanding fact of the present period, on the other hand, has been the weakening of traditional standards. An emergency has arisen not unlike that with which Socrates sought to cope in ancient Athens. Anyone who is untraditional and seeks at the same time to be discriminating must almost necessarily own Socrates as his master. As is well known, Socrates sought above all to be discriminating in his use of general terms. The importance of the art of inductive defining that he devised may perhaps best be made clear by bringing together two sayings, one of Napoleon—"Imagination governs mankind"—and one of John Selden—"Syllables govern mankind." Before allowing one's imagination and finally one's conduct to be controlled by a general term, it would seem wise to submit it to a Socratic scrutiny.

It is, therefore, unfortunate that at a time like the present, which plainly calls for a Socrates, we should instead have got a Mencken. One may take as an example of Mr. Mencken's failure to discriminate adequately, his attitude toward the term that for several generations past has been governing the imagination of multitudes—democracy. His view of democracy is simply that of Rousseau turned upside down, and nothing, as has been remarked, resembles a hollow so much as a swelling. A distinction of which he has failed to recognize the importance is that between a direct or unlimited and a constitutional democracy. In the latter we probably have the best thing in the world. The former, on the other hand, as all thinkers of any penetration from Plato and

Aristotle down have perceived, leads to the loss of liberty and finally to the rise of some form of despotism. The two conceptions of democracy involve not merely incompatible views of government but ultimately of human nature. The desire of the constitutional democrat for institutions that act as checks on the immediate will of the people implies a similar dualism in the individual —a higher self that acts restrictively on his ordinary and impulsive self. The partisan of unlimited democracy on the other hand is an idealist in the sense of that the term assumed in connection with the so-called romantic movement. His faith in the people is closely related to the doctrine of natural goodness proclaimed by the sentimentalists of the eighteenth century and itself marking an extreme recoil from the dogma of total depravity. The doctrine of natural goodness favors the free temperamental expansion that I have already noticed in speaking of the creative critic.

It is of the utmost importance, however, if one is to understand Mr. Mencken, to discriminate between two types of temperamentalist—the soft and sentimental type, who cherishes various "ideals," and the hard, or Nietzschean type, who piques himself on being realistic. As a matter of fact, if one sees in the escape from traditional controls merely an opportunity to live temperamentally, it would seem advantageous to pass promptly from the idealistic to the Nietzschean phase, sparing oneself as many as possible of the intermediary disillusions. It is at all events undeniable that the rise of Menckenism has been marked by a certain collapse of romantic idealism in the political field and elsewhere. The numerous disillusions that have supervened upon the War have provided a favoring atmosphere.

The symptoms of Menckenism are familiar: a certain hardness and smartness and disposition to rail at everything that, rightly or wrongly, is established and respected; a tendency to identify the real with what Mr. Mencken terms "the cold and clammy facts" and to assume that the only alternative to facing these facts is to fade away into sheer romantic unreality. These and similar traits are becoming so widely diffused that, whatever one's opinion of Mr. Mencken as a writer and thinker, one must grant him representativeness. He is a chief

5 Luther, Martin Luther. See note, p. 751 • 30 John Selden (1584-1654), British jurist, scholar, and author • 70 Nietzschean, based upon the philosophy of Friedrich Wilhelm Nietzsche. See note, p. 752

prophet at present of those who deem themselves emancipated but who are, according to Mr. Brownell,[2] merely unbuttoned.

The crucial point in any case is one's attitude toward the principle of control. Those who stand for this principle in any form or degree are dismissed by the emancipated as reactionaries or, still graver reproach, as Puritans. Mr. Mencken would have us believe that the historical Puritan was not even sincere in his moral rigorism, but was given to "lamentable transactions with loose women and fiery jugs." This may serve as a sample of the assertions, picturesquely indiscriminate, by which a writer wins immediate notoriety at the expense of his permanent reputation. The facts about the Puritan happen to be complex and need to be dealt with very Socratically. It has been affirmed that the point of view of the Puritan was Stoical rather than truly Christian, and the affirmation is not wholly false. The present discussion of the relationship between Puritanism and the rise of capitalism with its glorification of the acquisitive life also has its justification. It is likewise a fact that the Puritan was from the outset unduly concerned with reforming others as well as himself, and this trait relates him to the humanitarian meddler or "wowser" of the present day, who is Mr. Mencken's pet aversion.

Yet it remains true that awe and reverence and humility are Christian virtues and that there was some survival of these virtues in the Puritan. For a representative Puritan like Jonathan Edwards they were inseparable from the illumination of grace, from what he terms "a divine and supernatural light." In the passage from the love and fear of God of an Edwards to the love and service of man professed by the humanitarian, something has plainly dropped out, something that is very near the centre. What has tended to disappear is the inner life with the special type of control it imposes. With the decline of this inner control there has been an increasing resort to outer control. Instead of the genuine Puritan we then have the humanitarian legalist who passes innumerable laws for the control of people who refuse to control themselves. The activity of our uplifters is scarcely suggestive of any "divine and supernatural light." Here is a discrimination of the first importance that has been obscured by the muddy thinking of our half-baked intelligentsia. One is thus kept from perceiving the real problem, which is to retain the inner life, even though one refuse to accept the theological nightmare with which the Puritan associated it. More is involved in the failure to solve this problem than the Puritan tradition. It is the failure of our contemporary life in general. Yet, unless some solution is reached by a full and free exercise of the critical spirit, one remains a mere modernist and not a thoroughgoing and complete modern; for the modern spirit and the critical spirit are in their essence one.

What happens, when one sets out to deal with questions of this order without sufficient depth of reflection and critical maturity, may be seen in Mr. Sinclair Lewis's last novel. He has been lured from art into the writing of a wild diatribe which, considered even as such, is largely beside the mark. If the Protestant Church is at present threatened with bankruptcy, it is not because it has produced an occasional Elmer Gantry. The true reproach it has incurred is that, in its drift toward modernism, it has lost its grip not merely on certain dogmas but, simultaneously, on the facts of human nature. It has failed above all to carry over in some modern and critical form the truth of a dogma that unfortunately receives much support from these facts—the dogma of original sin. At first sight Mr. Mencken would appear to have a conviction of evil—when, for example, he reduces democracy in its essential aspect to a "combat between jackals and jackasses"—that establishes at least one bond between him and the austere Christian.

The appearance, however, is deceptive. The Christian is conscious above all of the "old Adam" in himself: hence his humility. The effect of Mr. Mencken's writing, on the other hand, is to produce pride rather than humility, a pride ultimately based on flattery. The reader, especially the young and callow reader, identifies himself imaginatively with Mr. Mencken and conceives of himself as a sort of morose and sardonic divinity surveying from some superior altitude an immeasurable expanse of "boobs." This attitude will not seem especially novel to anyone who has traced the modern movement. One is reminded in particular of Flaubert, who showed a diligence in collecting bourgeois imbecilities comparable to that displayed by Mr. Mencken in his *Americana*. Flau-

2 Brownell, William Crary Brownell (1851-1928), American literary critic associated with the New Humanists • 57 Lewis's last novel. Babbitt refers to Elmer Gantry (1927), which satirized religious shams and the ministers who allegedly perpetrated them • 87 Americana, a department in the American Mercury wherein Mencken and a fellow editor, George Jean Nathan, offered excerpts from newspapers and magazines purportedly typical of the asinine features of American life

bert's discovery that one does not add to one's happiness in this way would no doubt be dismissed by Mr. Mencken as irrelevant, for he has told us that he does not believe in happiness. Another discovery of Flaubert's may seem to him more worthy of consideration. "By dint of railing at idiots," Flaubert reports, "one runs the risk of becoming idiotic oneself."

It may be that the only way to escape from the unduly complacent cynicism of Mr. Mencken and his school is to reaffirm once more the truths of the inner life. In that case it would seem desirable to disengage, so far as possible, the principle of control on which the inner life finally depends from mere creeds and traditions and assert it as a psychological fact; a fact, moreover, that is neither "cold" nor "clammy." The coldness and clamminess of much so called realism arises from its failure to give this fact due recognition. A chief task, indeed, of the Socratic critic would be to rescue the noble term "realist" from its present degradation. A view of reality that overlooks the element in man that moves in an opposite direction from mere temperament, the specifically human factor in short, may prove to be singularly one-sided. Is the Puritan, John Milton, when he declares that "he who reigns within himself and rules passions, desires, and fears is more than a king," less real than Mr. Theodore Dreiser when he discourses in his peculiar dialect of "those rearranging chemisms upon which all the morality or immorality of the world is based?"

As a matter of fact, according to the degree and nature of the exercise of the principle of control, one may distinguish two main types of realism which may be denominated respectively religious and humanistic: as the principle of control falls into abeyance, a third type tends to emerge, which may be termed naturalistic realism. That the decline of the traditional controls has been followed by a lapse to the naturalistic level is indubitable. The characteristic evils of the present age arise from unrestraint and violation of the law of measure and not, as our modernists would have us believe, from the tyranny of taboos and traditional inhibitions. The facts cry to heaven. The delicate adjustment that is required between the craving for emancipation and the need of control has been pointed out once for all by Goethe, speaking not as a Puritan but as a clear-eyed man of the world. Everything, he says, that liberates the spirit without a corresponding growth in self-mastery is pernicious.

This one sentence would seem to cover the case of our "flaming youth" rather completely.

The movement in the midst of which we are still living was from its inception unsound in its dealing with the principle of control. It is vain to expect from the dregs of this movement what its "first sprightly running failed to give." Mr. Carl Sandburg speaks of the "marvelous rebellion of man at all signs reading 'Keep off.'" An objection to this purely insurrectional attitude is that, as a result of its endless iteration during the past century and more, it has come to savor too strongly of what has been called "the humdrum of revolt." A more serious objection to the attitude is that it encourages an unrestricted and merely temperamental liberty which, paradoxically enough at first sight, affords the modern man no avenue of escape from the web that is being woven about him by the scientific determinist.

Realists of the current type are in point of fact intimately allied with the psychologists,—glandular, behavioristic, and psychoanalytical,—who, whatever their divergences among themselves, unite in their deterministic trend and therefore clash fundamentally with both religious and humanistic realists. The proper method of procedure in defending the freedom of the will would seem to be to insist upon it as a fact of experience, a fact so primary that the position of the determinist involves an evasion of one of the immediate data of consciousness in favor of a metaphysical dream. What is genuinely experimental in naturalistic psychology should of course be received with respect; but the facts of which it takes account in its experiments are unimportant compared with the facts it either neglects or denies. Practically it is running into grotesque extremes of pseudo-science that make of it a shining mark for the Socratic critic.

Here at all events is the issue on which all other issues finally hinge; for until the question of moral freedom—the question whether man is a responsible agent or only the plaything of his impulses and impressions—is decided, nothing is decided; and to decide the question under existing circumstances calls for the keenest critical discrimination. Creation that is not sufficiently supported by such discrimination is likely to prove premature.

One may illustrate from Mr. Dreiser's *American Trage-*

---

48 flaming youth, a term used in the 1920's to designate the thrill-seeking younger generation

dy, hailed in certain quarters as the "Mt. Everest" of recent fiction. He has succeeded in producing in this work something genuinely harrowing; but one is harrowed to no purpose. One has in more than full measure the tragic qualm but without the final relief and enlargement of spirit that true tragedy succeeds somehow in giving, and that without resort to explicit moralizing. It is hardly worth while to struggle through eight hundred and more very pedestrian pages to be left at the end with a feeling of sheer oppression. The explanation of this oppression is that Mr. Dreiser does not rise sufficiently above the level of "rearranging chemisms," in other words, of animal behavior. Tragedy may admit fate— Greek tragedy admits it—but not of the naturalistic variety. Confusion on this point may compromise in the long run the reputation of writers more eminent than Mr. Dreiser—for example, of Thomas Hardy. Fatalism of the naturalistic type is responsible in large measure for the atmosphere of futility and frustration that hangs heavily over so much contemporary writing. One finally comes to feel with a recent poet that "dust" is the common source from which

> stream
> The cricket's cry and Dante's dream.

Anyone who admits reality only in what derives from the dust, whether in a cricket or a Dante, must, from the point of view of the religious or the humanistic realist, be prepared to make substantial sacrifices. In the first place, he must sacrifice the depth and subtlety that arise from the recognition in some form of the duality of man's nature. For the interest that may arise from the portrayal of the conflict between a law of the spirit and a law of the members, the inordinate interest in sex for its own sake promoted by most of the so-called realists is a rather shabby substitute. A merely naturalistic realism also involves the sacrifice of beauty in almost any sense of that elusive term. Closely related to this sacrifice is the sacrifice of delicacy, elevation, and distinction. The very word realism has come to connote the opposite of these qualities. When we learn, for example, that someone has written a realistic study of a great man, we are sure in advance that he has devoted his main effort to proving that "Plutarch lied." The more the great man is reduced to the level of commonplace or worse, the more we feel he has been "humanized."

Mr. Sherwood Anderson has argued ingeniously that, in as much as we ourselves are crude, our literature, if it is not to be unreal and factitious, should be crude likewise. But the writer who hopes to achieve work of importance cannot afford to be too deeply immersed in the atmosphere of the special place and passing moment. Still less can he afford to make us feel, as writers like Mr. Anderson and Mr. Dreiser and Mr. Sinclair Lewis do, that, if there were any lack of vulgarity in what they are depicting they would be capable of supplying the defect from their own abundance. More is involved here than mere loss of distinction. We have come, indeed, to the supreme sacrifice that every writer must make who does not transcend a naturalistic realism. He must forego the hope of the enduring appeal—the hope that every writer worthy of his salt cherishes in some degree. In the absence of humanistic or religious standards, he is prone to confound the real with the welter of the actual, and so to miss what Dr. Johnson terms the "grandeur of generality."

Certain books in the current mode are so taken up with the evanescent surfaces of life that they will survive, if at all, not as literature but as sociological documents. The very language in which they are written will, in a generation or two, require a glossary. So far from imposing an orderly pattern on the raw material of experience, they rather emphasize the lack of pattern. The resulting effect, to borrow a phrase from the late Stephen Crane, who has had a marked influence on the recent movement, is that of a "cluttered incoherency." As an extreme example of the tendency one may cite *Manhattan Transfer* by John Dos Passos. In the name of reality, Mr. Dos Passos has perpetrated a literary nightmare. Such a work would seem to have slight value even as a sociological document; unless, indeed, one is prepared to admit that contemporary Manhattan is inhabited chiefly by epileptic Bohemians.

"It is as much a trade," says La Bruyère, "to make a book as it is to make a clock"; in short, literature is largely a matter of technique. The technique of *Manhattan Transfer* is as dubious as its underlying philoso-

---

43 **Plutarch** (46?-120?), Greek biographer who wrote early studies of the great men of antiquity • 64 **Dr. Johnson,** Samuel Johnson (1709-1784), British author • 83 **La Bruyère,** Jean de La Bruyère (1645-1696), French novelist and essayist

phy. Neither can be justified save on the assumption that the aim of art is to exaggerate the clutter and incoherency of the mundane spectacle instead of eliciting its deeper meaning. Technique counts for even more in poetry than in prose. It would be possible to base on technical grounds alone a valid protest against the present preposterous overestimate of Walt Whitman. Fundamental questions need, in these very untraditional days, to be critically elucidated with a view to right definition if the poet is not to lack technique or still worse, if he is not, like certain recent practitioners of free verse, to be hagridden by a false technique. It evidently concerns both the form and substance of poetry, whether one define it with Aristotle as the portrayal of representative human action, or whether one define it with Mr. Carl Sandburg as a "mystic, sensuous mathematics of fire, smokestacks, waffles, pansies, people, and purple sunsets."

There is no doubt much in the America of to-day that suggests a jazzy impressionism. Still our naturalistic deliquescence has probably not gone so far as one might infer from poetry like that of Mr. Sandburg or fiction like that of Mr. Dos Passos. The public response to some of the realistic novels has been considerable: allowance must be made however for the *succès de scandale,* also for the skill attained by the modern publisher in the art of merchandising. The reputation of certain books one might mention may be regarded as a triumph of "creative" advertising. What has been created is a mirage of masterpieces where no masterpieces are. It is well also to remember in regard to some of the works that have been most discussed that, so far from being an authentic reflection of the American scene, they are rather a belated echo of certain European movements. For it is as certain that in our literary and artistic modes we follow Europe —usually at an interval of from five to forty years—as it is that we lead Europe in our bathtubs and sanitary plumbing. Any one who resided in Paris in the nineties and later in America, will, as I can testify from personal experience, have the sense of having lived through the same literary fads twice. Mr. Dreiser reminds one of Zola and his school. The technique of Mr. Dos Passos recalls that of the Goncourts. Our experimenters in free verse have followed in the wake not merely of Walt Whitman but of the French symbolists, and so on.

We shall presently begin to hear of certain new developments in French literature and critical thought that point, though indecisively as yet, to a radical departure from what has been the main current since the eighteenth century and in some respects since the Renaissance. It is well that we should become familiar with the writers who reveal in different ways this latest trend,—notably with Maritain, Maurras, Lasserre, Seillière, and Benda; for they give evidence of a quality of cerebration that is rare in our own literati. At the same time we should not adopt with our usual docility the total outlook of any of these writers: for no one of them has worked out a point of view exactly adapted to our requirements. In general, it is not fitting that a great nation at the very height of its power should go on indefinitely trailing after Europe. It is time for us to initiate something of our own. This does not mean that we should proceed forthwith to inbreed our own "originality." It means almost the exact opposite. The most original thing one could do nowadays would be to question the whole theory of originality as mere temperamental overflow and self-expression that has prevailed from the "geniuses" of the eighteenth century down to one of our youthful and very minor bards who aspires to "spill his bright illimitable soul."

A genuinely critical survey would make manifest that the unsatisfactoriness of our creative effort is due to a lack of the standards that culture alone can supply. Our cultural crudity and insignificance can be traced in turn to the inadequacy of our education, especially our higher education. Mr. Mencken's attack on the "professors" is therefore largely justified; for if the professors were performing their function properly Mr. Mencken himself would not be possible. One must add in common justice that the professors themselves, or at least some of them, are becoming aware that all is not well with existing conditions. One could not ask anything more perspicacious than the following paragraph from a recent report of Committee G to the American Association of University Professors:

---

24 *succès de scandale,* a work which is popular because it includes racy material • 42 the Goncourts. Edmond de Goncourt (1822-1896) and Jules de Goncourt (1830-1870), brothers, were French fiction writers • 52 Maritain . . . Benda, French critics of recent times who championed attitudes similar to those of Babbitt. Jacques Maritain, for instance, urged Thomism as a basis for modern criticism; Maurras attacked romanticism and urged a return to classical standards; Benda attacked the prevalent "social sensibility" of the twentieth century and indicated a preference for the ways and the works of the Old Regime

American education has suffered from the domination, conscious or unconscious, direct or indirect, of political and sentimental, as well as educational, theories that are demonstrably false. If the views of some men are to prevail the intellectual life of the country is doomed; everybody except the sheer idiot is to go to college and pursue chiefly sociology, nature study, child study, and community service —and we shall have a society unique only in its mediocrity, ignorance and vulgarity. It will not do to dismiss lightly even so extreme a view as this; it is too indicative. Such influences are very strong, their pressure is constant; and if education has largely failed in America it has been due primarily to them.

In short, as a result of the encroachments of an equalitarian democracy, the standards of our higher education have suffered in two distinct particulars: first, as regards the quality of students; second, as regards the quality of the studies these students pursue. The first of these evils is generally recognized. There is even some prospect of remedial measures. Certain institutions, Harvard, for example, without being as yet severely selective, are becoming more critical of the incompetent student. On the other hand, there seems to be less hope than ever of any righting of the second and more serious evil—the failure to distinguish qualitatively between studies. The main drift is still toward what one may term the blanket degree. (Dartmouth, for example, has just merged its bachelor of arts and bachelor of science.) Yet rather than blur certain distinctions it would have been better, one might suppose, to use up all the letters of the alphabet devising new degrees to meet the real or supposed educational needs of the modern man. To bestow the A.B. degree indiscriminately on a student for whom education has meant primarily a specialization in chemistry and on one for whom it has meant primarily an assimilation of the masterpieces of Greek literature is to empty it of any effective meaning. At the present rate, indeed, the time may come when the A.B. will not throw much more light on the cultural quality of its recipient than it would, if, as has been suggested, it were bestowed on every American child at birth.

It goes without saying that those who have been lowering and confusing educational standards have been profuse in their professions of "service." A critical examination, not merely of American education but of American life at the present time will almost necessarily hinge on this term. The attitude of the Socratic critic toward it is not to be confounded with that of Mr. Mencken and the "hard-boiled" contingent. "When a gang of real estate agents," says Mr. Mencken, "bond salesmen, and automobile dealers gets together to sob for Service, it takes no Freudian to surmise that someone is about to be swindled." But if one entertain doubts about this current American gospel, why waste one's ammunition on any such small fry? Other and more exalted personages than the members of the Rotary Club at Zenith have, in Mr. Sinclair Lewis's elegant phrase, been "yipping for Service." If one is to deal with this idea of service Socratically, one needs to consider it in its relation to the two figures who have rightly been taken to be the most representative in our cultural background—Benjamin Franklin and Jonathan Edwards. Franklin's idea of service is already humanitarian. Edwards' idea is still traditionally Christian service not of man but of God. What Franklin stood for is flourishing prodigiously at the present moment, so much so that he may perhaps be defined in his chief line of influence as the great superrotarian. What Edwards stood for is, on the other hand, largely obsolete or survives only in the form of habits, which, lacking doctrinal support, are steadily declining along with the whole Puritan culture.

Intermediary types are possible. One may in one's character reflect the Puritan background and at the same time in one's idea of service derive rather from Franklin. Precisely that combination is found in the most influential of our recent educational leaders—the late President Eliot. A legitimate admiration for his personal qualities should not interfere with the keenest critical scrutiny of his views about education, for the two things stand in no necessary connection. Practically this means to scrutinize the humanitarian idealism that he probably did more than any other man of his generation to promote. In this respect most of the heads of our institutions of learning have been and still are understudies of President Eliot.

In an address on the occasion of his ninetieth birthday

---

58 **Rotary . . . Zenith,** portrayed in Sinclair Lewis' *Babbitt* (1922) •
78 **President Eliot.** See note, p. 848

President Eliot warned his hearers against introspection, lest it divert them from a whole-hearted devotion to service. Between this attitude and a religious or humanistic attitude there is a clash of first principles. Both humanism and religion require introspection as a prerequisite of the inner life and its appropriate activity. With the disappearance of this activity what is left is the outer activity of the utilitarian, and this leads straight to the one-sided cult of material efficiency and finally to the standardization that is, according to nearly all foreign critics and many of our own, a chief American danger. We cannot return to the introspection of the Puritan. We shudder at the theology an Edwards would impose as the condition of his "divine and supernatural light." Yet it does not follow, as I have already suggested, that we should reject the inner life itself along with this theology. One may recognize innumerable incidental advantages in the gospel of service and yet harbor an uneasy suspicion withal that in the passage from the older religion to the modern humanitarian dispensation something vital has disappeared, something of which neither the outer working of the utilitarian nor again the expansive sympathy of the sentimentalist can offer an equivalent.

The problem of the inner life is very much bound up with two other problems that are now pressing for solution in our higher education and have as yet found none: the problem of the specialist and the problem of leisure. The man of leisure is engaged in an inner and specifically human form of activity, a form that is, according to Aristotle, needful if he is to compass the end of ends—his own happiness. The question is whether one should consent like the specialist to forego this activity and to live partially and as a mere instrument for the attainment of some outer end—even though this end be the progress of humanity. We are beginning to hear a great deal nowadays about the "menace" of leisure. It has been estimated that with the perfecting of mechanical devices the man of the future will be able to satisfy his material wants by working not more than four hours a day. It is vain to anticipate that the rank and file will use this release from outer activity intelligently unless the leaders, notably those in high academic station, show the way. The notion of true leisure is the ultimate source of the standards of any education that deserves to be called liberal. When even a few of our college and university presidents show that they are thinking to some purpose on the nature of leisure it will be time enough to talk of "America's coming of age."

As it is, our institutions of learning seem to be becoming more and more hotbeds of "idealism." Their failure, on the whole, to achieve standards as something quite distinct from ideals on the one hand, and standardization on the other, may prove a fact of sinister import for the future of American civilization. The warfare that is being waged at the present time by Mr. Sinclair Lewis and others against a standardized Philistinism continues in the main the protest that has been made for several generations past by the temperamentalists, hard or soft, against the mechanizing of life by the utilitarian. This protest has been, and is likely to continue to be, ineffectual. The fruitful opposite of the standardized Philistine is not the Bohemian, nor again the hard temperamentalist or superman, as Mr. Mencken conceives him, but the man of leisure. Leisure involves an inner effort with reference to standards that is opposed to the sheer expansion of temperament, as it is to every other form of sheer expansion.

Perhaps a reason why the standards of the humanist are less popular in this country than the ideals of the humanitarian is that these standards set bounds to the acquisitive life; whereas it seems possible to combine a perfect idealism with an orgy of unrestricted commercialism. It is well for us to try to realize how we appear to others in this matter. Our growing unpopularity abroad is due no doubt in part to envy of our material success, but it also arises from the proneness of the rest of the world to judge us, not by the way we feel about ourselves, but by our actual performance. If we are in our own eyes a nation of idealists, we are, according to our most recent French critic, M. André Siegfried, a "nation of Pharisees." The European, M. Siegfried would have us believe, still has a concern for the higher values of civilization, whereas the American is prepared to sacrifice these values ruthlessly to mass production and material efficiency.

It is easy to detect under this assumption the latest form of a "certain condescension in foreigners." The breakdown of cultural standards is European as well as American. It is not clear that M. Siegfried himself has

81 André Siegfried (1875-   ), French interpreter of American life. "See his volume Les États-Unis d'aujourd'hui (1927) translated under the title America Comes of Age."—Babbitt

an adequate notion of the form of effort that can alone serve as a counterpoise to the one-sided activity of the utilitarian. His assertion that Europe, appalled at the American excess of standardization, is inclined to turn from Henry Ford to Gandhi is more picturesque than convincing. At the same time his anatomy of our favorite ideal of service is not without interest. This ideal opposes no effective barrier to our expansiveness. An unchecked expansiveness on the national scale is always imperialistic. Among the ingredients of a possible American imperialism M. Siegfried enumerates the American's "great self-satisfaction, his rather brutal sense of his own interests, and *the consciousness, still more dangerous, of his 'duties' towards humanity.*" M. Siegfried admits however that our imperialism is likely to be of a new and subtle essence, not concerned primarily with territorial aggrandizement.

A proper discussion of Mr. Siegfried's position as well as of other issues I have been raising would transcend the limits of an article. My end has been accomplished if I have justified in some measure the statement with which I started as to the importance of cultivating a general critical intelligence. James Russell Lowell's dictum that before having an American literature we must have an American criticism was never truer than it is to-day. The obvious reply to those who call for more creation and less criticism is that one needs to be critical above all in examining what now passes for creation. A scrutiny of this kind would, I have tried to show, extend beyond the bounds of literature to various aspects of our national life and would converge finally on our higher education.

We cannot afford to accept as a substitute for this true criticism the self-expression of Mr. Mencken and his school, unless indeed we are to merit the comment that is, I am told, made on us by South Americans: "They are not a very serious people!" To be sure, the reader may reflect that I am myself a critic, or would-be critic. I can only express the hope that, in my magnifying of the critical function, I do not offer too close a parallel to the dancing-master in Molière who averred, it will be remembered, that "all the mistakes of men, the fatal reverses that fill the world's annals, the shortcomings of statesmen, and the blunders of great captains arise from not knowing how to dance."

1928

---

40 **Molière,** pseudonym of Jean Baptiste Poquelin (1622-1673), French dramatist

---

Thomas Stearns Eliot

1888 ·

Born in St. Louis, where his grandfather had founded Washington University, and educated at Harvard, where he was influenced by George Santayana and Irving Babbitt, Thomas Stearns Eliot has resided in England since 1914 and since 1927 has been a British subject. The award to him of the Nobel Prize in 1948 was an appropriate recognition of his great fame.

During the nineteen twenties and early nineteen thirties, Eliot was more influential than any other poet or critic writing in English. His *The Waste Land* (1922) set the style for a whole generation of younger poets. His essays—especially "The Metaphysical Poets" (1921), "Andrew Marvell" (1921), and "John Dryden" (1922)—altered the current of literary criticism. At a time when the influence of the nineteenth century was still dominant, Eliot brushed that century aside, a little contemptuously, and sought standards in an earlier tradition, particularly that of the seventeenth century. He

T. S. Eliot—photo by Kay Bell

and English and American poets were reappraised in the light of this new standard. Many idols were shattered: Tennyson and even Keats suffered. John Donne became the pattern of the perfect poet; almost everyone could quote Marvell's "To His Coy Mistress"; Gerard Manley Hopkins and Emily Dickinson—nineteenth-century poets who wrote "metaphysical" poetry—were raised to a new eminence. In the essays of Eliot and others (notably John Crowe Ransom, Allen Tate, Cleanth Brooks, R. P. Blackmur, and Yvor Winters), the metaphysical revolution produced a body of criticism which is remarkable for its close analysis of the relation of structure and style to content.

Eliot's influence waned somewhat after 1930. His famous announcement that he had become "an Anglo-Catholic in religion, a classicist in literature, and a royalist in politics" presented difficulties to many of his admirers in two of the three categories named: in politics and in religion. The religious, if not the political, development, however, seemed natural enough in Eliot's case. The return to the seventeenth century (and to Dante) implied a deep religious interest. The world described in the early poems ("Prufrock," 1917, "Gerontion," 1920, and *The Waste Land,* 1922, for example) was obviously a world paralyzed by the loss of religious faith. The decay of Protestantism, Eliot believed, was the most significant and the most tragic fact in modern history. The religious argument of *Ash-Wednesday* (1930), therefore, was a logical step in his development. The "Word" of St. John was "lost": the poem attempted to answer the question, "Where shall the Word be found?" The argument was continued in *Four Quartets* (1943): in the chaos of the modern world, we have only "hints and guesses"—"the rest is prayer, observance, discipline, thought and action."

But Eliot ultimately transcends political and religious questions and literary theories, for he is preëminently a poet. In poetry, he has striven for, and achieved, the utmost condensation. His aim, he has said, is "to write poetry which should be essentially poetry, with nothing 'poetic' about it, poetry standing naked in its bare bones."

H. R. Williamson, The Poetry of T. S. Eliot, New York, 1933 • F. O. Matthiessen, The Achievement of T. S. Eliot, Boston, 1935 • Cleanth Brooks, Modern Poetry and the Tradition, Chapel Hill, 1939 • J. C. Ransom, The New Criticism, Norfolk, Connecticut, 1941 • Leonard Unger, T. S. Eliot: A Selected Critique, New York, 1948

raised the question in 1921 whether the virtue of the seventeenth-century English poets "was not something permanently valuable, which subsequently disappeared, but ought not to have disappeared." His affirmative answer, elaborated in his essays and demonstrated in his poetry, wrought a revolution in critical taste. Eliot contrasted, for example, the "mistiness" and "vagueness" of William Morris (1834-1896) with the "bright, hard precision" of Marvell (1621-1678). Good poetry must have "wit"—"a tough reasonableness beneath the slight lyric grace." "When a poet's mind is perfectly equipped for its work," he declared, "it is constantly amalgamating disparate experience"—a description which gave a favorable turn to Dr. Johnson's famous objection that the metaphysical poets yoked together by violence the most heterogeneous ideas. If the metaphysical method failed, the failure, Eliot insisted, was not in the heterogeneousness of the ideas but in the imperfect yoking or amalgamation. Owing largely to Eliot's original influence, the "metaphysical" became a mark of excellence,

Literature and the Modern World

"Literature and the Modern World" is a good example of Eliot's later philosophical essays. Here he points out the dangers of an all-absorbing social consciousness. Religion and poetry, Eliot believes, languish in the completely socialized state; they are of great importance in the modern world both as expressions of, and as aids to, a proper balance between the individual person and society.

People may be conscious of their age without knowing very much about it. I believe that most of us are influenced, more than we realize, by a kind of deterministic conception of history. That may be all right for the Marxian, who has a reasoned theory about it; but it has no advantage as an unconscious assumption. The assumption of the inevitability of progress has, we all know, been discarded in its nineteenth century form: it is the butt of popular philosophers like Dean Inge. But
10 actually, what we have discarded is a particular variety of the theory of progress: that which is associated with Darwin, Tennyson, free-trade, and the industrial development of the latter part of the last century: in short, with Liberalism. Our beliefs have been shaken in detail: for instance, no one now is convinced of the automatic beneficence of scientific invention. Invention may be applied to destructive, rather than to creative activity; and it throws people out of work and it stimulates production while it diminishes consumption: these are commonplaces. Nevertheless, we retain the essential of the
20 doctrine of progress: we have no faith in the present.

In popularizing the belief in the future in a crude form we have, I think, a good deal for which to thank Mr. H. G. Wells. His superficial philosophy has had an extensive influence. Whatever Mr. Wells may explicitly disclaim, I think that the effect of his writing has been something like this: to propagate a belief that the value of the present resides in its service to the future, and nowhere else. Morality consists in working to

forward the happiness of future generations, "happiness" of a not remarkably spiritualized kind. We
30 are to find our happiness in scientific work which will benefit future humanity, and for the rest get anything out of life that we can. I do not want to let my words be twisted to suggest that we should take no concern with the lives of future generations. It is very much our business. What I object to is the complete dislocation of values. It is important not only that we should try to want the right things for the future. It is important also that we should have just as much respect for
40 ourselves; and remember that we, as human beings, are individually just as valuable as the men of the future. Mr. Wells seems to propagate a strange false humility of evolutionism: as the higher apes are to us, he says in effect, so are we to the men of the future; and as we regard our animal ancestors, whether apes, lemurs or opossums, so will they of the future regard us. This is, of course, the quite natural corollary of a naïf faith in perpetual evolution, combined with a denial of any sharp dividing line between the human and the animal: that
50 is, a denial of the human soul.

Now, one effect of this is to justify a contempt for humanity as we find it today, and the admission of any means, at whatever cost to human dignity, which will bring about the kind of future which Mr. Wells contemplates with such rapture. I confess that I cannot see why we should take such pains to produce a race of men, millennia hence, who will only look down upon *us* as apes, lemurs, or opossums. It seems a thankless labor. We
60 must affirm that there is no more value in the future than there is in the present. That is to say, we must affirm the eternal against the transient; the eternal which has been realized in the past, can be realized in the present; and it is our business to try to bring about a future in which the obstacles to this realization will be less, for the mass of humanity, than they are today. And these obstacles are not all of a material kind; they are in ourselves too. Our attitude may seem less ambitious than that of Mr. Wells; but it is more definite. It is simply that of the humble parent who wants his child to have a better
70

9 Dean Inge, William R. Inge (1860-   ), for many years dean of St. Paul's in London and popularly known as the "gloomy dean" • 24 H. G. Wells (1866-1946), English novelist, historian, and popular scientist, famous for such works as Tono-Bungay, The Outline of History, and The War of the Worlds

some writers feel
they must only
write tit what
is useful to
society.

chance in life than he had, and to lead a better life than he has led.

I said at the beginning that this modern eschatology begins in optimism and easily ends in despair. But I do not draw the moral of the proprietor whose granary was full. We are obviously at the end of an age, oppressed by the sense of corruption and decay, and fearful of the kinds of change which may come, since some change must. And since our minds must needs be filled with thought about the future, thought affecting our own action tomorrow perhaps, and our consciences disturbed by what we find about us and within us, it is all the more important to keep our heads, our sense of values; all the more important that we should hold fast to the things which were, and are, and shall be, world without end.

My immediate occupation, however, is with the effect upon modern literature of this dislocation of values and this moral subservience of the present to the future. As a kind of consultant, as well as a potential impresario, I have to see a good deal of what is being written, in some forms, by those much younger than myself. In the better writers there is strongly developed a kind of social conscience, a notion that literature ought to be useful to society. In the inferior writers this conscience may, of course, take the form merely of a determination not to miss the boat; but I confidently assure you of the existence of a fair proportion of sincerity. Now this devotion to society may involve precisely the same dislocation of values as the devotion to the future; and I propose to try to come to a conclusion about the proper relation of the poet today to himself and to society. The preoccupation of which I speak is inevitable, it is right; but how is it to be adjusted to the permanent values which literature is supposed to realize?

Here we get to the point. Should a literary artist have this acute sense of a social duty obliging him to convey a message; and if so, when is the "message" beneficial and when detrimental to the "art"?

I believe that the man of letters at the present day ought to have this sense. But the great danger for the artist is always that of conscientiously trying to feel what he does not feel. I will venture the following formulation. What is desirable is a harmony between the individual and sub-individual passions of the artist, and the social ideas and feelings which he wishes to propagate.

In this harmony, he neither exploits a conscious doctrine as a vehicle for his personality, nor cramps or distorts his personality to adapt it to a social doctrine. This requires some little amplification.

A man is both an individual and a member. Instead of "individual" I shall use the word "person." His *personality* is unique and not to be violated; but he is equally created to be a *member* of society. When society is conceived as merely a sum of individuals, you get the chaos of liberal democracy. When the person is wholly subordinated to society, you get the dehumanization of fascism or communism. The extremes, however, may meet. For what liberal democracy really recognizes is a sum, not of persons, but of individuals: that is to say, not the variety and uniqueness of persons, but the purely material individuation of the old-fashioned or Democritean atom. And this is a disrespect to the person. For the person is no longer a person if wholly isolated from the community; and the community is no longer a community if it does not consist of persons. A man is not himself unless he is a member; and he cannot be a member unless he is also something alone. Man's membership and his solitude must be taken together. There are moments, perhaps not known to everyone, when a man may be nearly crushed by the terrible awareness of his isolation from every other human being; and I pity him if he finds himself only alone with himself and his meanness and futility, alone without God. It is after these moments, alone *with* God and aware of our worthiness, but for Grace, of nothing but damnation, that we turn with most thankfulness and appreciation to the awareness of our *membership:* for we appreciate and are thankful for nothing fully until we see where it begins and where it ends. All that I have been saying is recognized by the Church, and the balance is maintained only by the Church: it is not recognized, but is made manifest by, the endless seesaw of political tendency between anarchy and tyranny: a seesaw which, in the secular world, I believe has no end.

---

5 moral . . . full, possibly an allusion to the story of Joseph, whose storehouses had been well stocked with grain against the famine years (see Genesis 41). The "moral" may be that, unlike Joseph, the modern "liberal" is ill-prepared for reversals • 61 Democritean atom. The atoms of Democritus, Greek philosopher of the fourth century B.C., were identical in chemical quality but differed in size and form

Menchen believes
Artist? It must have sense of usefulness to society
but not to place that he writes what he doesnt

Now all this may sound perfectly irrelevant to my subject; but it is not so. This same balance ought to exist, on its plane, in the activity of the artist. For the artist cannot devote himself truly to any cause unless by that devotion he is also most truly being, and becoming, himself. The artist may, as Remy de Gourmont profoundly says, "in writing himself, write his age"; but I think that we should add that he may sometimes in writing his age, write himself: which will come to the same thing. But it is from himself that he must start. It is sometimes helpful to put things in an extreme, and therefore dangerous way. So I may say that in one aspect the true artist may be said to be simply *exploiting* the things he believes in for the purpose of making art:—only if he does this *consciously* is he a false artist.

Whereas a man like D. H. Lawrence is in danger of manipulating his philosophy to fit his private needs and to justify his private weaknesses, the adherent of an objective creed is in danger of denying, or distorting himself to fit his beliefs; and the opposite insincerity becomes possible. This is equally a danger for the Christian and for the communist, and especially at those moments when personal inspiration fails. How far can one go in identifying a creed with oneself, or oneself with a creed? The development of the person may be twisted, or the purity of the creed may be polluted. I believe, naturally, that the Christian, if he understands his Christianity, has safeguards which the mere social revolutionist cannot have: safeguards of the personal emotion. For instance: social enthusiasm alone, however intense, does not seem to have the substance needed to make poetry. What is the difference between Dante's denunciation of the vices of his time, and Shelley's denunciation of kings, tyrants, and priests? Shelley's excitement is in his head, and therefore emits rather shrill and inapplicable head noises; whereas Dante's is involved with all his own sufferings—definite grievances and definite humiliations at the hands of particular people, of all of which he is conscious: self-interested grudges and deprivations, earthly if you like, but primarily *real*, and that is the first thing. Only the greatest, the Hebrew Prophets, seem to be utterly caught up and possessed by God as mouthpieces; in ordinary human poets the human personal loss, the private grievance and bitterness and loneliness, must be present. Even when the poet is aware of nothing, interested in nothing,

beyond his personal feelings, these may have, by their intensity, a representative value, so that we envisage him, like Villon, not as wrapped up in his private griefs, but reliving them, holding nothing back, in a passionate cry to God—and there is, in the end, no one else to cry to. But in the greatest poets these private passions are completed in a passionate belief in objective moral values, in a striving towards justice and the life of the spirit among men.

Now the tendency of secular revolution today seems to me to be to diminish the value of the person. Of what importance, we may say currently, is all this expression of personal feeling and private suffering, in a world of so much general injustice and oppression? and this is the secular point of view: of what importance one man, when the life of society is at stake! We are back with the modern eschatology of which Mr. Wells is the popular preacher. The present order is damned, let us snatch what satisfaction we can, say some; and, the present order is damned, let us sacrifice—not our pleasure, but our *selves*—to the future, say others; and one may perhaps maintain both conclusions at once. And behind is the master idea which has been working unobtrusively throughout our time, an idea which in the forms of heresy has always been waiting for us: the idea of the *"group consciousness"*—modest, and scientific and certain it sounds under that name.

In a recent article called "The Real Issue," which I have read with interest and approval, Mr. Christopher Dawson makes some pertinent remarks about the position of the individual in the classless society:

> . . . the orthodox Communist will deny that this total subordination and sacrifice of humanity to the State machine is of the essence of Communism, for did not Marx and Lenin expressly teach that the dictatorship of the proletariat is only a temporary phase, and that the State itself will eventually wither away and give place to a classless and Stateless society? But how will this end

---

6 **Remy de Gourmont.** See note, p. 841 • 16 **D. H. Lawrence** (1885-1930), English writer famous for such novels as **Sons and Lovers** and **Lady Chatterley's Lover** and for such critical works as **Studies in Classic American Literature** • 48 **Villon,** François Villon, French lyric poet of the fifteenth century

be attained? Only when the individual is so completely socialized that he will instinctively devote all his energies to working for society and will be unable to conceive of any other end than that of the economic organism of which he forms part. In such an order there will be no need for a State any more than it is necessary for ants or bees to have a State. But is it a human order, and is it possible for humanity to rise or sink to such a level?

10 I do not, any more than Mr. Dawson, think such a consummation likely; but if I did not think it possible I should not take the trouble of attacking the idea of it. It would be brought about, not by the diabolic cleverness of scheming philosophers and politicians, but by the natural aversion of human beings to the responsibility and strain of being *human*. For we must remember that it *is* a great strain for the erect animal to persist in being erect, a physical and still more a moral strain. With or without mechanical aids of movement and 20 noise, most people spend a good deal of their time avoiding the human responsibility; and we only remain human because of the continual vicarious sacrifice of a few dedicated lives. And the "group consciousness," the heresy bred within the antithetical heresy of liberalism, has a great seductive charm; for it helps to release us from the burden of responsibility. It would more likely, I think, be a reversion to a lower kind of consciousness, than an ascent to a higher one; it is largely, in fact, to the speculations, which profess to be 30 based on the study of primitive races, of such writers as Durkheim and Lévy-Bruhl, that we owe the conceptions. That such a state of humanity would be unfavorable to poetry follows from what I have said earlier. That is not perhaps of the utmost importance in itself; there are matters more important than the perpetual production of new poetry, though we must remember that a people which ceases to create the new will also lose the power to appreciate the *old*. What is important is that the creation of poetry depends upon the maintenance of 40 the person, of the person in relation to other individuals, to God, and to society.

There is much, however, in the aspirations of poetry today with which I am in full sympathy. When we compare the state of poetry now with that of forty years ago, towards the end of the last century, I think we may see, without drawing any comparison between the merits of individual poets (and even if that comparison were to result to our disadvantage), that the social earnestness and dissatisfaction which have been lately expressing themselves have been all to the good; and poetry has 50 taken on a new seriousness and a new social importance. It is perhaps not insignificant that the one great poet we have who belongs to both periods, Mr. William Butler Yeats, has been writing his finest poetry within recent years. With all we owe him, I find it difficult to regard Mr. Yeats as anything but a *contemporary;* and if anyone said that of me, when I arrive at his present age, I should consider it the highest of compliments. What I think we have missed, and have been struggling for, is the recognition of poetry as something other than ex- 60 quisite pleasure for a small number of people who have the taste for it—as something having a function of social value. The poet must assume his rôle of moralist, and thus manifest his relation to society.

I think however that the passion for social righteousness will prove in the end not enough in itself. The danger of what I have called the modern eschatology, the danger of neglecting the permanent for the transitory, the personal for the social, is one to which the poet is exposed in common with everyone else: but 70 he has a peculiar responsibility not to be deluded. Yet I would ask you to have some sympathy with his difficulties. An age of change, and a period of incessant apprehension of war, do not form a favorable environment. There is a temptation to welcome change for its own sake, to sink our minds in some desperate philosophy of *action;* and several such philosophies are being urged upon us. Contempt for the past, and even ignorance of it, is on the increase, and many are ready for the unlimited experiment. We cannot effect intelli- 80 gent change, unless we hold fast to the permanent essentials; and a clear understanding of what we should hold fast to, and what abandon, should make us all the better prepared to carry out the changes that are needed. Thus we can look back upon the past without regret, and to the future without fear.

1935

---

31 **Durkheim**, Émile Durkheim (1858-1917), French sociologist and philosopher • 31 **Lévy-Bruhl**, Lucian Lévy-Bruhl (1857-1939), French philosopher and ethnologist

[handwritten annotation at top:] Marxism is not successful as a method alone "" in literature "" " " indirect alone
If an artist is only objective, not introducing his own views he isn't as realistic as he would be by being both objective & subjective

Kenneth Burke

1897 ·

[handwritten annotation:] he must however — not just give pleasure — but function of social value —

The best of the New Critics have been men of extraordinary breadth. Kenneth Burke, for example, knows music, psychology, and political philosophy as well as many specialists. His most recent books, *A Grammar of Motives* (1945) and *A Rhetoric of Motives* (1950), venture into the common ground of psychological, ethical, economic, and political behavior, where most "authorities" are timidly apologetic.

Burke was born in Pittsburgh, Pennsylvania, on May 5, 1897. He studied at Ohio State and Columbia universities, but in his twenties plunged into the New York world of letters, as reviewer, translator, and roving critic. His first book, *The White Oxen* (1924), was fiction, but he made his real reputation as a music critic, first on the avant garde magazine of the Twenties, *The Dial*, in 1927-1929, and then, 1934-1936, on *The Nation*.

He gradually emerged, however, as a notable theorist on aesthetics in general and on literary criticism in particular. His best-known books are *Counter-Statement* (1931), *Permanence and Change—Anatomy of Purpose* (1935), and *Philosophy of Literary Form—Studies in Symbolic Action* (1941). They show a preoccupation with the purposes of art and with its place in modern culture. In the process of making up his mind about these matters Burke has lectured at the New School for Social Research, at the University of Chicago, and at Bennington College. In 1948-1949 he was a Fellow of the Institute of Advanced Study.

F. B. Millett, Contemporary American Authors, New York, 1940 • M. D. Zabel, Literary Opinion in America, Revised Edition, New York, 1951

Psychology and Form

This essay appeared originally in **The Dial** for July 1925; it was later reprinted in **Counter-Statement**. Typically Burkean in its delicate combination of learning and reflection, it explores one of the standard questions of the New Criticism: What makes a given piece of literary art "work"? The emphasis upon "internal structure" is typical, but the exploration has unusual subtlety and clarity.

It is not until the fourth scene of the first act that Hamlet confronts the ghost of his father. As soon as the situation has been made clear, the audience has been, consciously or unconsciously, waiting for this ghost to appear, while in the fourth scene this moment has been definitely promised. For earlier in the play Hamlet had arranged to come to the platform at night with Horatio to meet the ghost, and it is now night, he is with Horatio and Marcellus, and they are standing on the platform. Hamlet asks Horatio the hour.

Hor. I think it lacks of twelve.
Mar. No, it is struck.
Hor. Indeed? I heard it not: then it draws near the season
Wherein the spirit held his wont to walk.

Promptly hereafter there is a sound off-stage. "A flourish of trumpets, and ordnance shot off within." Hamlet's friends have established the hour as twelve. It is time for the ghost. Sounds off-stage, and of course it is not the ghost. It is, rather, the sound of the king's carousal, for the king "keeps wassail." A tricky and useful detail. We have been waiting for a ghost, and get, startlingly, a blare of trumpets. And, once the trumpets are silent, we feel how desolate are these three men waiting for a ghost, on a bare "platform," feel it by this sudden juxtaposition of an imagined scene of lights and merriment. But the trumpets announcing a carousal have suggested a subject of conversation. In the darkness Hamlet discusses the excessive drinking of his countrymen. He points out that it tends to harm their reputation abroad, since, he argues, this one showy vice makes their virtues "in the general censure take corruption." And for this reason, although he himself is a native of this place, he does not approve of the custom. Indeed, there in the gloom he is talking very intelligently on these matters, and Horatio answers, "Look, my Lord, it comes." All this time we had been waiting for a ghost, and it comes at the one moment which was not pointing towards it. This ghost, so assiduously prepared for, is yet a surprise. And now that the ghost has come, we are waiting for something further. Program: a speech from Hamlet. Hamlet must confront the ghost. Here again Shakespeare can feed well upon the use of contrast for his effects. Hamlet has just been talking in a sober, rather argumentative manner—but now the flood-gates are unloosed:

Angels and ministers of grace defend us!
Be thou a spirit of health or goblin damn'd,

Bring with thee airs from heaven or blasts from hell . . .

and the transition from the matter-of-fact to the grandiose, the full-throated and full-voweled, is a second burst of trumpets, perhaps more effective than the first, since it is the rich fulfillment of a promise. Yet this satisfaction in turn becomes an allurement, an itch for further developments. At first desiring solely to see Hamlet confront the ghost, we now want Hamlet to learn from the ghost the details of the murder—which are, however, with shrewdness and husbandry, reserved for "Scene V— Another part of the Platform."

I have gone into this scene at some length, since it illustrates so perfectly the relationship between psychology and form, and so aptly indicates how the one is to be defined in terms of the other. That is, the psychology here is not the psychology of the *hero,* but the psychology of the *audience.* And by that distinction, form would be the psychology of the audience. Or, seen from another angle, form is the creation of an appetite in the mind of the auditor, and the adequate satisfying of that appetite. This satisfaction—so complicated is the human mechanism—at times involves a temporary set of frustrations, but in the end these frustrations prove to be simply a more involved kind of satisfaction, and furthermore serve to make the satisfaction of fulfillment more intense. If, in a work of art, the poet says something, let us say, about a meeting, writes in such a way that we desire to observe that meeting, and then, if he places that meeting before us—that is form. While obviously, that is also the psychology of the audience, since it involves desires and their appeasements.

The seeming breach between form and subject-matter, between technique and psychology, which has taken place in the last century is the result, it seems to me, of scientific criteria being unconsciously introduced into matters of purely esthetic judgment. The flourishing of science has been so vigorous that we have not yet had time to make a spiritual readjustment adequate to the changes in our resources of material and knowledge. There are disorders of the social system which are caused solely by our undigested wealth (the basic disorder being, perhaps, the phenomenon of overproduction: to remedy this, instead of having all workers employed on half time, we have half working full time and the other half idle, so that whereas overproduction could be the greatest reward of applied science, it has been, up to now, the most menacing condition our modern civilization has had to face). It would be absurd to suppose that such social disorders would not be paralleled by disorders of culture and taste, especially since science is so pronouncedly a spiritual factor. So that we are, owing to the sudden wealth science has thrown upon us, all *nouveaux-riches* in matters of culture, and most poignantly in that field where lack of native firmness is most readily exposed, in matters of esthetic judgment.

One of the most striking derangements of taste which science has temporarily thrown upon us involves the understanding of psychology in art. Psychology has become a body of information (which is precisely what psychology in science should be, or must be). And similarly, in art, we tend to look for psychology as the purveying of information. Thus, a contemporary writer has objected to Joyce's *Ulysses* on the ground that there are more psychoanalytic data available in Freud. (How much more drastically he might, by the same system, have destroyed Homer's *Odysseus!*) To his objection it was answered that one might, similarly. denounce Cézanne's trees in favor of state forestry bulletins. Yet are not Cézanne's landscapes themselves tainted with the psychology of information? Has he not, by perception, *pointed out* how one object lies against another, *indicated* what takes place between two colors (which is the psychology of science, and is less successful in the medium of art than in that of science, since in art such processes are at best implicit, whereas in science they are so readily made explicit)? Is Cézanne not, to that extent, a state forestry bulletin, except that he tells what goes on in the eye instead of on the tree? And do not the true values of his work lie elsewhere—and precisely in what I distinguish as the psychology of form?

Thus, the great influx of information has led the artist also to lay his emphasis on the giving of information— with the result that art tends more and more to substitute the psychology of the hero (the subject) for the psychology of the audience. Under such an attitude, when form is preserved it is preserved as an annex, a luxury, or, as some feel, a downright affectation. It remains, though sluggish, like the human appendix, for occasional demands are still made upon it; but its true vigor is gone, since it is no longer organically required. Proposition: The hypertrophy of the psychology of information is accompanied by the corresponding atrophy of the psychology of form.

In information, the matter is intrinsically interesting. And by intrinsically interesting I do not necessarily mean intrinsically valuable, as witness the intrinsic interest of backyard gossip or the most casual newspaper items. In art, at least the art of the great ages (Aeschylus, Shakespeare, Racine), the matter is interesting by means of an extrinsic use, a function. Consider, for instance, the speech of Mark Antony, the "Brutus is an honourable man." Imagine in the same place a very competently developed thesis on human conduct, with statistics, intelligence tests, definitions; imagine it as the finest thing of the sort ever written, and as really being at the roots of an understanding of Brutus. Obviously, the play would simply stop until Antony had finished. For in the case of Antony's speech, the value lies in the fact that his words are shaping the future of the audience's desires, not the desires of the Roman populace, but the desires of the pit. This is the psychology of form as distinguished from the psychology of information.

The distinction is, of course, absolutely true only in its nonexistent extremes. Hamlet's advice to the players, for instance, has little of the quality which distinguishes Antony's speech. It is, rather, intrinsically interesting, although one could very easily prove how the play would benefit by some such delay at this point, and that anything which made this delay possible without violating the consistency of the subject would have, in this, its formal justification. It would, furthermore, be absurd to rule intrinsic interest out of literature. I wish simply to

10 **nouveaux-riches**, the recently wealthy • 20 **Ulysses** (1922), a famous stream-of-consciousness novel by the Irish author, James Joyce (1882-1941) • 21 **Freud**, Sigmund Freud (1856-1939), Austrian neurologist and psychologist, whose epochal writings on psychoanalysis appeared between 1895 and 1900 • 25 **Cézanne's trees**. Paul Cézanne (1839-1906), French painter, is noted for his composition, in which color relationships are examined by means of the interplay of sharply defined planes • 55 **Aeschylus, Shakespeare, Racine**, the foremost tragic dramatists of their respective nations and periods. Aeschylus (525-456 B.C.) is best known for **Seven against Thebes** and a Prometheus trilogy, Jean Racine (1639-1699) for his **Phèdre** (1677) • 58 **speech of Mark Antony**, Julius Caesar, Act II, sc. ii

have it restored to its properly minor position, seen as merely one out of many possible elements of style. Goethe's prose, often poorly imagined or neutral in its line-for-line texture, especially in the treatment of romantic episode—perhaps he felt that the romantic episode in itself was enough?—is strengthened into a style possessing affirmative virtues by his rich use of aphorism. But this is, after all, but one of many possible facets of appeal. In some places, notably in *Wilhelm Meisters Lehrjahre* when Wilhelm's friends disclose the documents they have been collecting about his life unbeknown to him, the aphorisms are almost rousing in their efficacy, since they involve the story. But as a rule the appeal of aphorism is intrinsic: that is, it satisfies without being functionally related to the context. Also, to return to the matter of Hamlet, it must be observed that the style in this passage is no mere "information-giving" style; in its alacrity, its development, it really makes this one fragment into a kind of miniature plot.

One reason why music can stand repetition so much more sturdily than correspondingly good prose is because music, of all the arts, is by its nature least suited to the psychology of information, and has remained closer to the psychology of form. Here form cannot atrophy. Every dissonant chord cries for its solution, and whether the musician resolves or refuses to resolve this dissonance into the chord which the body cries for, he is dealing in human appetites. Correspondingly good prose, however, more prone to the temptations of pure information, cannot so much bear repetition since the esthetic value of information is lost once that information is imparted. If one returns to such a work again it is purely because, in the chaos of modern life, he has been able to forget it. With a desire, on the other hand, its recovery is as agreeable as its discovery. One can memorize the dialogue between Hamlet and Guildenstern, where Hamlet gives Guildenstern the pipe to play on. For, once the speech is known, its repetition adds a new element to compensate for the loss of novelty. We cannot take a recurrent pleasure in the new (in information) but we can in the natural (in form). Already, at the moment when Hamlet is holding out the pipe to Guildenstern and asking him to play upon it, we "gloat over" Hamlet's triumphal descent upon Guildenstern, when, after Guildenstern has, under increasing embarrassment, pro-

tested three times that he cannot play the instrument, Hamlet launches the retort for which all this was preparation:

> Why, look you now, how unworthy a thing you make of me. You would play upon me, you would seem to know my stops; you would pluck out the heart of my mystery; you would sound me from my lowest note to the top of my compass; and there is much music, excellent voice, in this little organ, yet cannot you make it speak. 'Sblood, do you think I am easier to be played on than a pipe? Call me what instrument you will, though you can fret me, you cannot play upon me.

In the opening lines we hear the promise of the close, and thus feel the emotional curve even more keenly than at first reading. Whereas in most modern art this element is underemphasized. It gives us the gossip of a plot, a plot which too often has for its value the mere fact that we do not know its outcome.

Music, then, fitted less than any other art for imparting information, deals minutely in frustrations and ful-

---

3 **Goethe's.** Johann Wolfgang von Goethe (1749-1832), the foremost German author, wrote two novels, **The Sorrows of Werther** (1774) and **Wilhelm Meister** (in parts, 1795-1829), as well as much other prose • 15 **related to the context.** "Similarly, the epigram of Racine is 'pure art,' because it usually serves to formulate or clarify some situation within the play itself. In Goethe the epigram is most often of independent validity, as in **Die Wahlverwandtschaften**, where the ideas of Ottilie's diary are obviously carried over boldly from the author's notebook. In Shakespeare we have the union of extrinsic and intrinsic epigram, the epigram growing out of its context and yet valuable independent of its context."—Burke • 36 **dialogue,** Hamlet, Act III, sc. ii • 58 **play upon me.** "One might indicate still further appropriateness here. As Hamlet finishes his speech, Polonius enters, and Hamlet turns to him, 'God bless you, sir!' Thus, the plot is continued (for Polonius is always the promise of action) and a full stop is avoided: the embarrassment laid upon Rosencrantz and Guildenstern is not laid upon the audience." —Burke • 64 **do not know its outcome.** "Yet modern music has gone far in the attempt to renounce this aspect of itself. Its dissonances become static, demanding no particular resolution. And whereas an unfinished modulation by a classic musician occasions positive dissatisfaction, the refusal to resolve a dissonance in modern music does not dissatisfy us, but irritates or stimulates. Thus, 'energy' takes the place of style."—Burke • 66 **fulfillments of desire.** "Suspense is the least complex kind of anticipation, as surprise is the least complex kind of fulfillment."—Burke

fillments of desire, and for that reason more often gives us those curves of emotion which, because they are natural, can bear repetition without loss. It is for this reason that music, like folk tales, is most capable of lulling us to sleep. A lullaby is a melody which comes quickly to rest, where the obstacles are easily overcome—and this is precisely the parallel to those waking dreams of struggle and conquest which (especially during childhood) we permit ourselves when falling asleep or when trying to induce sleep. Folk tales are just such waking dreams. Thus it is right that art should be called a "waking dream." The only difficulty with this definition (indicated by Charles Baudouin in his *Psychoanalysis and Aesthetics,* a very valuable study of Verhaeren) is that today we understand it to mean art as a waking dream for the artist. Modern criticism, and psychoanalysis in particular, is too prone to define the essence of art in terms of the artist's weaknesses. It is, rather, the audience which dreams, while the artist oversees the conditions which determine this dream. He is the manipulator of blood, brains, heart, and bowels which, while we sleep, dictate the mold of our desires. This is, of course, the real meaning of artistic felicity—an exaltation at the correctness of the procedure, so that we enjoy the steady march of doom in a Racinian tragedy with exactly the same equipment as that which produces our delight with Benedick's "Peace! I'll stop your mouth. *(Kisses her)"* which terminates the imbroglio of *Much Ado About Nothing.*

The methods of maintaining interest which are most natural to the psychology of information (as it is applied to works of pure art) are surprise and suspense. The method most natural to the psychology of form is eloquence. For this reason the great ages of Aeschylus, Shakespeare, and Racine, dealing as they did with material which was more or less a matter of common knowledge so that the broad outlines of the plot were known in advance (while it is the broad outlines which are usually exploited to secure surprise and suspense) developed formal excellence, or eloquence, as the basis of appeal in their work.

Not that there is any difference in kind between the classic method and the method of the cheapest contemporary melodrama. The drama, more than any other form, must never lose sight of its audience: here the failure to satisfy the proper requirements is most disastrous. And since certain contemporary work is successful, it follows that rudimentary laws of composition are being complied with. The distinction is one of intensity rather than of kind. The contemporary audience hears the lines of a play or novel with the same equipment as it brings to reading the lines of its daily paper. It is content to have facts placed before it in some more or less adequate sequence. Eloquence is the minimizing of this interest in fact, *per se,* so that the "more or less adequate sequence" of their presentation must be relied on to a much greater extent. Thus, those elements of surprise and suspense are subtilized, carried down into the writing of a line or a sentence, until in all its smallest details the work bristles with disclosures, contrasts, restatements with a difference, ellipses, images, aphorism, volume, sound-values, in short all that complex wealth of minutiae which in their line-for-line aspect we call style and in their broader outlines we call form.

As a striking instance of a modern play with potentialities in which the intensity of eloquence is missing, I might cite a recent success, Capek's *R. U. R.* Here, in a melodrama which was often astonishing in the rightness of its technical procedure, when the author was finished he had written nothing but the scenario for a play by Shakespeare. It was a play in which the author produced time and again the opportunity, the demand, for eloquence, only to move on. (At other times, the most successful moments, he utilized the modern discovery of silence, writing moments wherein words could not possibly serve but to detract from the effect: this we might call the "flowering" of information.) The Adam and Eve scene of the last act, a "commission" which the Shakespeare of the comedies would have loved to fill, was in the verbal barrenness of Capek's play something shameless to the point of blushing. The Robot, turned human, prompted by the dawn of love to see his first sunrise, or hear the bird-call, and forced merely to say, "Oh, see the sunrise," or, "Hear the pretty birds"—here one could do

13 **Baudouin,** L. Charles-Baudouin, author of *Le Symbole chez Verhaeren* (fourth edition, 1924) • 14 **Verhaeren,** Émile Verhaeren (1855-1916), Belgian poet and critic, known as a defender of the French Impressionist painters • 67 **R.U.R.** (1923), by Karl Capek (1850-1938), a Czechoslovakian author, deals with robots or mechanical workmen

nothing but wring his hands at the absence of that esthetic mold which produced the overslung "speeches" of
Romeo and Juliet.

Suspense is the concern over the possible outcome of
some specific detail of plot rather than for general qualities. Thus, "Will A marry B or C?" is suspense. In
Macbeth, the turn from the murder scene to the porter
scene is a much less literal channel of development.
Here the presence of one quality calls forth the demand
for another, rather than one tangible incident of plot
awaking an interest in some other possible tangible incident of plot. To illustrate more fully, if an author managed over a certain number of his pages to produce a
feeling of sultriness, or oppression, in the reader, this
would unconsciously awaken in the reader the desire for
a cold, fresh north wind—and thus some aspect of a
north wind would be effective if called forth by some
aspect of stuffiness. A good example of this is to be found
in a contemporary poem, T. S. Eliot's *The Waste Land,*
where the vulgar, oppressively trivial conversation in the
public house calls forth in the poet a memory of a line
from Shakespeare. These slobs in a public house, after
a desolately low-visioned conversation, are now forced by
closing time to leave the saloon. They say good-night.
And suddenly the poet, feeling his release, drops into
another good-night, a good-night with *désinvolture,* a
good-night out of what was, within the conditions of the
poem at least, a graceful and irrecoverable past.

"Well that Sunday Albert was home, they had a
    hot gammon,
And they asked me in to dinner, to get the beauty
    of it hot"—

    [at this point the bartender interrupts: it is
    closing time]

"Goonight Bill. Goonight Lou. Goonight May.
    Goonight. Ta ta. Goonight. Goonight.
Good-night, ladies, good-night, sweet ladies,
    good-night, good-night."

There is much more to be said on these lines, which I
have shortened somewhat in quotation to make my issue
clearer. But I simply wish to point out here that this
transition is a bold juxtaposition of one quality created
by another, an association in ideas which, if not logical,
is nevertheless emotionally natural. In the case of *Mac-*
beth, similarly, it would be absurd to say that the audience,
after the murder scene, wants a porter scene. But the
audience does want the quality which this porter par-
ticularizes. The dramatist might, conceivably, have introduced some entirely different character or event in
this place, provided only that the event produced the
same quality of relationship and contrast (grotesque
seriousness followed by grotesque buffoonery). One of
the most beautiful and satisfactory "forms" of this sort
is to be found in Baudelaire's "Femmes Damnées," where
the poet, after describing the business of a Lesbian seduction, turns to the full oratory of his apostrophe:

Descendez, descendez, lamentables victimes,
Descendez le chemin de l'enfer éternel . . .

while the stylistic efficacy of this transition contains a
richness which transcends all moral (or unmoral) sophistication: the efficacy of appropriateness, of exactly
the natural curve in treatment. Here is morality even for
the godless, since it is a morality of art, being justified,
if for no other reason, by its paralleling of that staleness,
that disquieting loss of purpose, which must have followed the procedure of the two characters, the *femmes*
damnées themselves, a remorse which, perhaps only physical in its origin, nevertheless becomes psychic.

But to return, we have made three terms synonymous:
form, psychology, and eloquence. And eloquence thereby
becomes the essence of art, while pity, tragedy, sweetness, humor, in short all the emotions which we experience in life proper, as non-artists, are simply the material on which eloquence may feed. The arousing of pity,
for instance, is not the central purpose of art, although

---

19 **The Waste Land.** See p. 946 • 50 **"Femmes Damnées,"** by the
French poet, Charles Pierre Baudelaire (1821-1867) • 53 **Descendez,**
. . . éternel. Go down, go down, miserable victims, go down the road
to eternal hell • 64 **nevertheless becomes psychic.** "As another
aspect of the same subject, I could cite many examples from the fairy
tale. Consider, for instance, when the hero is to spend the night in a
bewitched castle. Obviously, as darkness descends, weird adventures
must befall him. His bed rides him through the castle; two halves
of a man challenge him to a game of nine-pins played with thigh
bones and skulls. Or entirely different incidents may serve instead of
these. The quality comes first, the particularization follows."—Burke

it may be an adjunct of artistic effectiveness. One can feel pity much more keenly at the sight of some actual misfortune—and it would be a great mistake to see art merely as a weak representation of some actual experience. That artists today are content to write under such an esthetic accounts in part for the inferior position which art holds in the community. Art, at least in the great periods when it has flowered, was the conversion, or transcendence, of emotion into eloquence, and was thus a factor added to life. I am reminded of St. Augustine's caricature of the theatre: that whereas we do not dare to wish people unhappy, we do want to feel sorry for them, and therefore turn to plays so that we can feel sorry although no real misery is involved. One might apply the parallel interpretation to the modern delight in happy endings, and say that we turn to art to indulge our humanitarianism in a well-wishing which we do not permit ourselves towards our actual neighbors. Surely the catharsis of art is more complicated than this, and more reputable.

Eloquence itself, as I hope to have established in the instance from *Hamlet* which I have analyzed, is no mere plaster added to a framework of more stable qualities. Eloquence is simply the end of art, and is thus its essence. Even the poorest is eloquent, but in a poor way, with less intensity, until this aspect is obscured by others fattening upon its leanness. Eloquence is not showiness; it is, rather, the result of that desire in the artist to make a work perfect by adapting it in every minute detail to the racial appetites.

The distinction between the psychology of information and the psychology of form involves a definition of esthetic truth. It is here precisely, to combat the deflection which the strength of science has caused to our tastes, that we must examine the essential breach between scientific and artistic truth. Truth in art is not the discovery of facts, not an addition to human knowledge in the scientific sense of the word. It is, rather, the exercise of human propriety, the formulation of symbols which rigidify our sense of poise and rhythm. Artistic truth is the externalization of taste. I sometimes wonder, for instance, whether the "artificial" speech of John Lyly might perhaps be "truer" than the revelations of Dostoevsky. Certainly at its best, in its feeling for a statement which returns upon itself, which attempts the systole to

a diastole, it *could* be much truer than Dostoevsky. And if it is not, it fails not through a mistake of Lyly's esthetic, but because Lyly was a man poor in character whereas Dostoevsky was rich and complex. When Swift, making the women of Brobdingnag enormous, deduces from this discrepancy between their size and Gulliver's that Gulliver could sit astride their nipples, he has written

4 **some actual experience.** "Could not the Greek public's resistance to Euripides be accounted for in the fact that he, of the three great writers of Greek tragedy, betrayed his art, was guilty of esthetic impiety, in that he paid more attention to the arousing of emotion *per se* than to the sublimation of emotion into eloquence?"—Burke. Euripides, a Greek tragic dramatist of the fifth century B.C., is best known for his *Medea* • 10 **St. Augustine's caricature of the theatre.** Like most of the early Church Fathers, Augustine (354-430) was opposed to the theater • 38 **scientific sense of the word.** "One of the most striking examples of the encroachment of scientific truth into art is the doctrine of 'truth by distortion,' whereby one aspect of an object is suppressed the better to emphasize some other aspect; this is, obviously, an attempt to indicate by art some fact of knowledge, to make some implicit aspect of an object as explicit as one can by means of the comparatively dumb method of art (dumb, that is, as compared to the perfect ease with which science can indicate its discoveries). Yet science has already made discoveries in the realm of this 'factual truth,' this 'truth by distortion' which must put to shame any artist who relies on such matter for his effects. Consider, for instance, the motion-picture of a man vaulting. By photographing this process very rapidly, and running the reel very slowly, one has upon the screen the most striking set of factual truths to aid in our understanding of an athlete vaulting. Here, at our leisure, we can observe the contortions of four legs, a head, and a butt. This squirming thing we saw upon the screen showed us an infinity of factual truths anent the balances of an athlete vaulting. We can, from this, observe the marvelous system of balancing which the body provides for itself in the adjustments of moving. Yet, so far as the esthetic truth is concerned, this on the screen was not an athlete, but a squirming thing, a horror, displaying every fact of vaulting except the exhilaration of the act itself."—Burke • 41 **externalization of taste.** "The procedure of science involves the elimination of taste, employing as a substitute the corrective norm of the pragmatic test, the empirical experiment, which is entirely intellectual. Those who oppose the 'intellectualism' of critics like Matthew Arnold are involved in an hilarious blunder, for Arnold's entire approach to the appreciation of art is through delicacies of taste intensified to the extent almost of squeamishness."—Burke. Matthew Arnold (1822-1888), English critic and poet, is famous for his "touchstone" method of evaluation and for the strongly moral flavor of his literary judgments • 42 **John Lyly** (1554?-1606), English dramatist (*Endymion*, 1579) and novelist (*Euphues*, 1580) • 43 **Dostoevsky,** Fyodor Mikhailovich Dostoevsky (1821-1881), Russian author of *Crime and Punishment* (1866), *The Brothers Karamazov* (1879-1880), and other famous novels • 46 **truer than Dostoevsky.** "As for instance, the 'conceit' of Endymion's awakening, when he forgets his own name, yet recalls that of his beloved."—Burke • 49 **Swift,** Jonathan Swift (1667-1745), English satirist, author of *Gulliver's Travels* (1726)

something which is esthetically true, which is, if I may be pardoned, profoundly "proper," as correct in its Euclidean deduction as any corollary in geometry. Given the companions of Ulysses in the cave of Polyphemus, it is true that they would escape clinging to the bellies of the herd let out to pasture. St. Ambrose, detailing the habits of God's creatures, and drawing from them moral maxims for the good of mankind, St. Ambrose in his limping natural history rich in scientific inaccuracies that are at the very heart of emotional rightness, St. Ambrose writes "Of night-birds, especially the nightingale which hatches her eggs by song; of the owl, the bat, and the cock at cockcrow; in what these may apply to the guidance of our habits," and in the sheer rightness of that program there is the truth of art. In introducing this talk of night-birds, after many pages devoted to other of God's creatures, he says:

What now! While we have been talking, you will notice how the birds of night have already started fluttering about you, and, in this same fact of warning us to leave off with our discussion, suggest thereby a further topic—

and this seems to me to contain the best wisdom of which the human frame is capable, an address, a discourse, which can make our material life seem blatant almost to the point of despair. And when the cock crows, and the thief abandons his traps, and the sun lights up, and we are in every way called back to God by the well-meaning admonition of this bird, here the very blindnesses of religion become the deepest truths of art.

1925

3 the companions . . . Polyphemus. See Homer's Odyssey, Bk. IX •
6 St. Ambrose (339?-397), bishop of Milan

Allen Tate

1899 •

In the 1920's, Vanderbilt University in Nashville, Tennessee, was the center of a fruitful and significant literary movement. Headed by John Crowe Ransom, a graduate of Vanderbilt in the class of 1909 and a member of the English department there after 1914, the Nashville group consisted for the most part of men who, as Ransom's students, had caught the sharp contagion of his influence. It is doubtful if, in our entire history, another college (except Harvard in the 1820's and 1830's) has graduated in one generation a "school" of writers who have had such a strong impact upon American literature. The chief writers, besides Ransom himself, were Donald Davidson, Allen Tate, Andrew Nelson Lytle, Cleanth Brooks, and Robert Penn Warren. The bibliography appended to this sketch will suggest the range of their achievements.

There appear to have been three stages of development. The group began as poets: "The Fugitives"—as they styled themselves—wrote intellectual poetry which may be regarded as a part of the general reaction of the twenties against the nineteenth century. Though continuing to write poetry, the group turned, in 1930, to Southern economic and social questions: *I'll Take My Stand* argued for a return to agrarianism and vigorously combated the "progressive" assumption that the true welfare of the South could be best served by an accelerated program of industrialization. The book provoked for its authors the somewhat misleading label of "neo-Confederates." After 1930 the group became less unified in literary output, if not in spirit. The fugitives and agrarians of former years turned to the novel, and, to an even greater extent, to literary criticism. Many critical essays by members of the group appeared in *The Southern Review* (1935-1944), edited by Warren and Brooks, *The Kenyon Review* (1938—), edited by Ransom, and *The Sewanee Review,* edited by Tate in 1944-1945, as well as *The Virginia Quarterly Review* and other journals. Although this criticism owed something to T. S. Eliot and I. A. Richards, the work of each man bore the stamp of his own originality.

If the poetry of the Nashville writers seems hardly different in kind from the main body of modern intellectual poetry, and if the social-economic thesis of *I'll Take My Stand* seems a beautiful but ineffectual dream, the literary criticism exerted a wide influence. Through a new, close examination of the text of the individual poem, *Understanding Poetry,* by Brooks and Warren worked a major revolution in reading and teaching. The great virtue of the movement was that it redirected attention to the literature itself, which was about to be submerged by historical matter; its dangers were a tendency to regard literature *in vacuo,* to carry analysis to a point of overrefinement, and to employ a terminology too abstruse for the general reader.

Allen Tate, a distinguished member of the Nashville group, was born in Kentucky. He attended Vanderbilt, where he was graduated in 1922. Although engaged almost continuously in writing, he has found time for other employments: in the 1930's he was a member at different times of the English departments of Southwestern University at Memphis, the North Carolina Woman's College at Greensboro, and Princeton; in 1942-1944, he held the chair of poetry in the Library of Congress. Later, he taught at New York University. In 1951, he joined the English faculty of the University of Minnesota. Like most intellectual writers of our time, Tate and his Nashville associates are "reactionary" in the better sense of the word. They have sought to recover certain values of the past: the Southern cultural tradition, the religious point of view, and an intellectual fiber best exemplified in the poets of seventeenth-century England. Tate's "Ode to the Confederate Dead" (p. 966) and "Narcissus as Narcissus" afford a unique opportunity to study the work of a modern poet in the closest possible relation to the critical ideas which it embodies.

Mr. Pope and Other Poems, New York, 1928 • **Stonewall Jackson** (biography), New York, 1928 • **Jefferson Davis** (biography), New York, 1929 • **The Fathers** (novel), New York, 1938 • **Reason in Madness** (essays), New York, 1941 • **Forlorn Demon** (essays), Chicago, 1953

The following is a partial bibliography of other members of the Nashville group: Cleanth Brooks, **Understanding Poetry** (with Robert Penn Warren), New York, 1938; **The Well-Wrought Urn,** New York, 1947 • Donald Davidson, **The Tall Men** (poems), Boston, 1927; **Lee in the Mountains and Other Poems,** Boston, 1938; **The Attack on Leviathan** (essays), Chapel Hill, 1938 • A. N. Lytle, **The Long Night** (novel), Indianapolis, 1936 • J. C. Ransom, **Poems about God,** New York, 1919; **Chills and Fever** (poems), New York, 1924; **The World's Body** (essays), New York, 1938; **New Criticism,** Norfolk, Connecticut, 1941 • R. P. Warren, see p. 1171 • All except Brooks contributed essays to **I'll Take My Stand,** New York, 1930. See further for the entire group, **A Vanderbilt Miscellany,** ed. R. C. Beatty, Nashville, 1944

Narcissus as Narcissus

"Narcissus as Narcissus" first appeared in **The Virginia Quarterly Review,** Winter 1938, and was reprinted in **Reason in Madness** (1941). The close attention to the nature of poetry and poetic structure—well exemplified in Tate's essay—is typical of much modern criticism.

On this first occasion, which will probably be the last of my talking about my own verse, I could plead the example of Edgar Allan Poe, who wrote an essay entitled "The Philosophy of Composition." But in our age the appeal to authority is weak, and I am of my age. I prefer to leave the propriety of self-discussion to the reader. You will remember the Englishman who refuted an

American's criticism of Drinkwater, who had, on the opening night of his "Robert E. Lee," permitted Grant to appear in gray and Lee in blue: "Oh, I should think that Drinkwater would know about that." I am willing to let Drinkwater know about that, with the reminder to the reader that what I happen to know about the poem I shall discuss is limited. I remember merely my intention in writing it; I do not know whether the poem is good; and I do not know its obscure origins.

How does one come to write a poem: where does it come from? That is the question asked by the psychologists or the geneticists of poetry. Of late I have not been able to read any of their theories through: years ago I read one by Mr. Conrad Aiken; another, I think, by Mr. Robert Graves; but I have forgotten them. I am not throwing off on verbal mechanisms, dreams, or repressions as origins of poetry; all three of them and more besides may have a great deal to do with it. Nor should I ignore Mr. I. A. Richards, whose theories I have read a great deal: to him a poem seems to be a kind of ideal harmony among the greatest number of our appetites, which ordinarily jangle, and the reader gets the same harmony or "ordering of the mind" second-hand—only it is really as good as first-hand since the poet differs from the mere reader by the hair of a talent for constructing appetitive harmonies in words. While this theory may be false, I can only say that given a few premises which I shall not discuss, it is logical: I do not care whether it is false or true.

Other psychological theories today—I speak from rusty acquaintance—say a good deal about compensation. A poem is an indirect effort of a shaky man to justify himself to happier men, or to present a superior account of his relation to a world that allows him but little certainty, and would allow as little to the happier men if they did not wear blinders—according to the poet. For example, a poet might be a fellow who could not get enough self-justification out of being an automobile salesman (whose certainty is a fixed quota of cars every month) to rest comfortably upon it. So the poet, who wants to be something that he cannot be, and is a failure in plain life, makes up fictitious versions of his predicament that are interesting even to other persons because nobody is a perfect automobile salesman. Everybody, alas, suffers a little. . . . I constantly read this kind of criticism of my own verse. According to its doctors, my one intransigent desire is to have been a Confederate general, and because I could not or would not become anything else, I set up for poet and began to invent fictions about the personal ambitions that my society has no use for.

Although a theory may not be "true," it may make certain insights available for a while; and I have deemed it proper to notice theories of the genetic variety because a poet talking about himself is often expected, as the best authority, to explain the origins of his poems. But persons interested in origins are seldom quick to use them. Poets, in their way, are practical men; they are interested in results. What is the poem, after it is written? That is the question. Not where it came from, or why. The Why and Where can never get beyond the guessing stage because, in the language of those who think it can, poetry cannot be brought to "laboratory conditions." The only real evidence that any critic may bring before his gaze is the finished poem. For some reason most critics have a hard time fixing their minds directly under their noses, and before they see what is there they use a telescope upon the horizon to see where it came from. They are woodcutters who do their job by finding out where the ore came from in the iron of the steel of the blade of the axe that Jack built. I do not say that this procedure is without its own contributory insights; but the insights are merely contributory and should not replace the object that gives rise to them. A poem may be an instance of morality, of social conditions, of psychological history; it may instance all its qualities, but never one of them alone, nor any two or three; nor ever less than all. In making women "instances" of sex we make them whores.

Genetic theories, I gather, have been cherished academically with detachment. Among "critics" they have been useless and not quite disinterested: I have myself found them applicable to the work of poets whom I did not like. That is the easiest way.

I say all this because it seems to me that my verse or anybody else's is merely a way of knowing something: if the poem is a real creation, it is a kind of knowledge that we did not possess before. It is not knowledge

---

1 Drinkwater, John Drinkwater (1882-1937), English dramatist • 15 Robert Graves, contemporary English poet and novelist • 19 I. A. Richards, an English critic, author of **Principles of Literary Criticism**, **Practical Criticism**, and other critical works. For an extended consideration of Richards, see Ransom's **The New Criticism**

"about" something else; the poem is the fulness of that knowledge. We know the particular poem, not what it says that we can restate. In a manner of speaking, the poem is its own knower, neither poet nor reader knowing anything that the poem says apart from the words of the poem. I have expressed this view elsewhere in other terms, and it has been accused of æstheticism or art for art's sake. But let the reader recall the historic position of Catholicism: *nulla salus extra ecclesiam*. That must be religion*ism*. There is probably nothing wrong with art for art's sake if we take the phrase seriously, and not take it to mean the kind of poetry written in England forty years ago. Religion always ought to transcend any of its particular uses; the true art for art's sake view can be held only by religious persons who are always looking for something that they can respect apart from use (though it may be useful), like poems, fly-rods, and formal gardens. . . . These are negative postulates, and I am going to illustrate them with some commentary on a poem called "Ode to the Confederate Dead."

II

That poem is "about" solipsism or Narcissism, or any other *ism* that denotes the failure of the human personality to function properly in nature and society. Society (and "nature" as modern society constructs it) appears to offer limited fields for the exercise of the whole man, who wastes his energy piecemeal over separate functions that ought to come under a unity of being. (Until the last generation, only certain women were whores, having been set aside as special instances of sex amid a social scheme that held the general belief that sex must be part of a whole; now the general belief is that sex must be special.) Without unity we get the remarkable self-consciousness of our age. Everybody is talking about this evil, and a great many persons know what ought to be done to correct it. As a citizen I have my own prescription, but as a poet I am concerned with the experience of solipsism. And an experience *of* it is very different from a theory *about* it.

I should have trouble connecting solipsism and the Confederate dead, as a rational thesis; I should make a fool of myself in the discussion, because I know no more of the Confederate dead or of solipsism than hundreds of other people. (Possibly less: the dead Confederates may be presumed to have a certain privacy; and as for solip-

sism, I blush to the philosophers who know all about Bishop Berkeley; I use the term here in its strict etymology.) And if I call this interest in one's ego Narcissism, I make myself a logical ignoramus, as well as a loose-mouth with mythology. I use Narcissism to mean only preoccupation with self; it may be love or hate. But a good psychiatrist knows that it means self-love only, and otherwise he can talk about it more coherently, knows more about it than I ever hope or desire to know. He would look at me professionally if I piped up with the remark that the modern squirrel cage of our sensibility, the extreme introspection of our time, has anything whatever to do with the Confederate dead.

But when the doctor looks at literature it is a question whether he sees it: the sea boils and pigs have wings because in poetry all things are possible—if, as the drug-store cowboys would put it, you are man enough. They are possible because in poetry the disparate elements are not combined in logic, which can combine only under certain categories and under the law of contradiction; they are combined rather as experience, and experience has decided to ignore logic, except perhaps as another field of experience. Experience means conflict, our natures being what they are, and conflict means drama. Dramatic experience is not logical; it may be subdued to the kind of coherence that we indicate when we speak, in criticism, of form. Indeed, as experience, this conflict is always a logical contradiction, or philosophically an antinomy. Serious poetry deals with the fundamental conflicts that cannot be logically resolved: we can state the conflicts rationally, but reason does not relieve us of them. Their only final coherence is the formal re-creation of art, which "freezes" the experience as permanently as a logical formula, but without, like the formula, leaving all but the logic out.

Narcissism and the Confederate dead cannot be connected logically, or even historically; even were the connection an historical fact, they would not stand connected as art, for no one experiences raw history. The

9 nulla . . . ecclesiam, no salvation outside the church • 21 solipsism, the assumption that the self knows and can know nothing but its own modification and states • 21 Narcissism. Narcissus, in Greek mythology, fell in love with his own reflection in a fountain. Narcissism, as used here, means simply (to quote the author) "preoccupation with self" • 46 Bishop Berkeley, George Berkeley (1685-1753), Irish idealistic philosopher

proof of the connection must lie, if anywhere, in the experienced conflict which is the poem itself. Since one set of references for the conflict is the historic Confederates, the poem, if it is successful, is a certain section of history made into experience, but only on this occasion, and on these terms: even the author of the poem has no experience of its history apart from the occasion and the terms.

It will be understood that I do not claim even a partial success in the junction of the two "ideas" in the poem I am about to discuss. I am describing an intention, and the labor of revising the poem—a labor spread over ten years—fairly exposes the lack of confidence that I have felt and still feel in it. All the tests of its success in style and versification would come in the end to a single test, an answer, yes or no, to the question: Assuming that the Confederates and Narcissus are not yoked together by mere violence, has the poet convinced the reader that, on the specific occasion of this poem, there is a necessary yet hitherto undetected relation between them? By necessary I mean dramatically relevant, a relation "discovered" in terms of the particular occasion, not historically argued or philosophically deduced. Should the question that I have just asked be answered yes, then this poem or any other with its specific problem could be said to have form: what was previously a merely felt quality of life has been raised to the level of experience—it has become specific, local, dramatic, "formal"—that is to say, *in*-formed.

III

The structure of the Ode is simple. Figure to yourself a man stopping at the gate of a Confederate graveyard on a late autumn afternoon. The leaves are falling; his first impressions bring him the "rumor of mortality"; and the desolation barely allows him, at the beginning of the second stanza, the heroically conventional surmise that the dead will enrich the earth, "where these memories grow." From those quoted words to the end of that passage he pauses for a baroque meditation on the ravages of time, concluding with the figure of the "blind crab." This creature has mobility but no direction, energy but no purposeful world to use it in: in the entire poem there are only two explicit symbols for the locked-in ego; the crab is the first and less explicit sym-

bol, a mere hint, a planting of the idea that will become overt in its second instance—the jaguar towards the end. The crab is the first intimation of the nature of the moral conflict upon which the drama of the poem develops: the cut-off-ness of the modern "intellectual man" from the world.

The next long passage or "strophe," beginning "You know who have waited by the wall," states the other term of the conflict. It is the theme of heroism, not merely moral heroism, but heroism in the grand style, elevating even death from mere physical dissolution into a formal ritual: this heroism is a formal ebullience of the human spirit in an entire society, not private, romantic illusion—something better than moral heroism, great as that may be, for moral heroism, being personal and individual, may be achieved by certain men in all ages, even ages of decadence. But the late Hart Crane's commentary is better than any I can make: "The theme of chivalry, a tradition of excess (not literally excess, rather active faith) which cannot be perpetuated in the fragmentary cosmos of today—'those desires which should be yours tomorrow,' but which, you know, will not persist nor find any way into action."

The structure then is a tension between the two themes, "active faith" which has decayed, and the "fragmentary cosmos" which surrounds us. (I must repeat here that this is not a philosophical thesis; it is an impressionistic rendering of a conflict that is concrete within the poem.) In contemplating the heroic theme the man at the gate never quite commits himself to the illusion of its availability to him. The most that he can allow himself is the fancy that the blowing leaves are charging soldiers, but he rigorously returns to the refrain: "Only the wind"—or the "leaves flying." I suppose it is a commentary on our age that the man at the gate never quite achieves the illusion that the leaves are heroic men, so that he may identify himself with them, as Keats and Shelley easily and beautifully did with nightingales and west winds. More than this, he cautions himself, reminds himself repeatedly of his subjective prison, his solipsism, by breaking off the half-illusion

---

18 **yoked . . . violence.** Dr. Johnson, who, in his **Life of Cowley,** first applied the term "metaphysical" to certain English poets of the seventeenth century, said that in their poetry "the most heterogeneous ideas are yoked by violence together" • 60 **Hart Crane** (1899-1932, p. 961), an American poet, author of **The Bridge**

and coming back to the refrain of wind and leaves—a refrain that, as Hart Crane said, is necessary to the "subjective continuity."

These two themes struggle for mastery up to the passage,

> We shall say only the leaves whispering
> In the improbable mist of nightfall

which is near the end. It will be observed that the passage begins with a phrase taken from the wind-leaves refrain—the signal that it has won. The refrain has been fused with the main stream of the man's reflections, dominating them; and he cannot return even to an ironic vision of the heroes. There is nothing but death, the mere naturalism of death at that. Autumn and the leaves are death; the men who exemplified in a grand style an "active faith" are dead; there are only the leaves.

Shall we then worship death?

> . . . set up the grave
> In the house? The ravenous grave . . .

that will take us before our time? The question is not answered, although as a kind of romanticism it might, if answered affirmatively, provide an illusory solution to the solipsism of the man; but he cannot accept it. Nor has he been able to live in his immediate world, the fragmentary cosmos. There is no practical solution, no solution offered for the edification of moralists. (To those who may identify the man at the gate with the author of the poem I would say: He differs from the author in not accepting a "practical solution," for the author's dilemma is perhaps not quite so exclusive as that of the meditating man.) The main intention of the poem has been to state the conflict, to concentrate it, to present it, in Mr. R. P. Blackmur's phrase, as experienced form—not as a logical dilemma.

The closing image, that of the serpent, is the ancient symbol of time, and I tried to give it the credibility of the commonplace by placing it in a mulberry bush—with the faint hope that the silkworm would somehow be implicit. But time is also death. If that is so, then space, or the Becoming, is life; and I believe there is not a single spatial symbol in the poem. "Sea-space" is allowed the "blind crab"; but the sea, as appears plainly in the passage beginning, "Now that the salt

of their blood . . ." is life only in so far as it is the source of the lowest forms of life, the source perhaps of all life, but life undifferentiated, halfway between life and death. This passage is a contrasting inversion of the conventional

> . . . inexhaustible bodies that are not
> Dead, but feed the grass . . .

the reduction of the earlier, literary conceit to a more naturalistic figure derived from modern biological speculation. These "buried Cæsars" will not bloom in the hyacinth but will only make saltier the sea.

The wind-leaves refrain was added to the poem in 1930, nearly five years after the first draft was written. I felt that the danger of adding it was small because, implicit in the long strophes of meditation, the ironic commentary on the vanished heroes was already there, giving the poem such dramatic tension as it had in the earlier version. The refrain makes the commentary more explicit, more visibly dramatic, and renders quite plain, as Hart Crane intimated, the subjective character of the imagery throughout. But there was another reason for it, besides the increased visualization that it imparts to the dramatic conflict. It "times" the poem better, offers the reader frequent pauses in the development of the two themes, allows him occasions of assimilation; and on the whole—this was my hope and intention—the refrain makes the poem seem longer than it is and thus eases the concentration of imagery—without, I hope, sacrificing a possible effect of concentration.

IV

I have been asked why I called the poem an ode. I first called it an elegy. It is an ode only in the sense in which Cowley in the seventeenth century misunderstood the real structure of the Pindaric ode. Not only are the metre and rhyme without fixed pattern, but in another feature the poem is even further removed from Pindar than Abraham Cowley was: a purely subjective medita-

---

34 **R. P. Blackmur**, a contemporary American critic • 54 **buried . . . hyacinth.** See The Rubaiyat:

> I sometimes think that never blows so red
> The Rose as where some buried Caesar bled;
> That every Hyacinth the Garden wears
> Dropt in her Lap from some once lovely Head

tion would not in Cowley's age have been called an ode. I suppose in so calling it I intended an irony: the scene of the poem is not a public celebration, it is a lone man by a gate.

The dominant rhythm is "falling," the dominant metre iambic pentameter varied with six-, four-, and three-stressed lines; but this was not planned in advance for variety. I adapted the metre to the effect desired at the moment. The model for the irregular rhyming was "Lycidas," but for that other models could have served. The rhymes in a given strophe I tried to adjust to the rhythm and the texture of feeling and image. For example, take this passage in the second strophe:

> Autumn is desolation in the plot
> Of a thousand acres where these memories grow
> From the inexhaustible bodies that are not
> Dead, but feed the grass row after rich row.
> Think of the autumns that have come and gone!—
> Ambitious November with the humors of the year,
> With a particular zeal for every slab,
> Staining the uncomfortable angels that rot
> On the slabs, a wing chipped here, an arm there:
> The brute curiosity of an angel's stare
> Turns you, like them, to stone,
> Transforms the heaving air
> Till plunged to a heavier world below
> You shift your sea-space blindly
> Heaving, turning like the blind crab.

There is rhymed with *year* (to many persons, perhaps, only a half-rhyme), and I hoped the reader would unconsciously assume that he need not expect further use of that sound for some time. So when the line, "The brute curiosity of an angel's stare," comes a moment later, rhyming with *year-there,* I hoped that the violence of image would be further reinforced by the repetition of a sound that was no longer expected. I wanted the shock to be heavy; so I felt that I could not afford to hurry the reader away from it until he had received it in full. The next two lines carry on the image at a lower intensity: the rhyme, "Transforms the heaving *air,"* prolongs the moment of attention upon that passage, while at the same time it ought to begin dissipating the shock, both by the introduction of a new image and by reduction of the "meaning" to a pattern of sound,

the *ere*-rhymes. I calculated that the third use of that sound *(stare)* would be a surprise, the fourth a monotony. I purposely made the end words of the third from last and last lines—*below* and *crab*—delayed rhymes for *row* and *slab,* the last being an internal and half-dissonant rhyme for the sake of bewilderment and incompleteness, qualities by which the man at the gate is at the moment possessed.

This is elementary but I cannot vouch for its success. As the dramatic situation of the poem is the tension that I have already described, so the rhythm is an attempt at a series of "modulations" back and forth between a formal regularity, for the heroic emotion, and a broken rhythm, with scattering imagery, for the failure of that emotion. I have pointed out that the passage, "You know who have waited by the wall," presents the heroic theme of "active faith"; it will be observed that the rhythm, increasingly after "You who have waited for the angry resolution," is almost perfectly regular iambic, with only a few initial inversions and weak endings. The passage is meant to convey a plenary vision, the actual presence, of the exemplars of active faith: the man at the gate at that moment is nearer to realizing them than at any other in the poem; hence the formal rhythm. But the vision breaks down; the wind-leaves refrain intervenes; and the next passage, "Turn your eyes to the immoderate past," is the irony of the preceding realization. With the self-conscious historical sense he turns his eyes into the past. The next passage after this, beginning "You hear the shout . . ." is the failure of the vision in both phases, the pure realization and the merely historical. He cannot "see" the heroic virtues; there is wind, rain, leaves. But there is sound; for a moment he deceives himself with it. It is the noise of the battles that he has evoked. Then comes the figure of the rising sun of those battles; he is "lost in that orient of the thick and fast," and he curses his own moment, "the setting sun." The "setting sun" I tried to use as a triple image, for the decline of the heroic age and for the actual scene of late afternoon, the latter being not only natural desolation but spiritual desolation as well. . . . Again for a moment he thinks he hears the battle shout, but only for a moment; then the silence reaches him.

Corresponding to the disintegration of the vision just described, there has been a breaking down of the formal rhythm. The complete breakdown comes with the images of the "mummy" and the "hound bitch." (*Hound* bitch because the hound is a hunter, participant of a formal ritual.) The failure of the vision throws the man back upon himself, but upon himself he cannot bring to bear the force of a sustained imagination. He sees himself in random images (random to him, deliberate with the author) of something lower than he ought to be: the human image is only that of preserved death; but if he is alive he is an old hunter, dying. The passages about the mummy and the bitch are deliberately brief—slight rhythmic stretches. (These are the only verses I have written for which I thought of the movement first, then cast about for the symbols.)

I believe the term modulation denotes in music the uninterrupted shift from one key to another: I do not know the term for change of rhythm without change of measure. I wish to describe a similar change in verse rhythm; it may be convenient to think of it as also modulation of a kind. At the end of the passage that I have been discussing the final words are "Hears the wind only." The phrase closes the first main division of the poem. I have loosely called the longer passages strophes, but if I were hardy enough to impose the classical organization of the lyric ode upon a baroque poem, I should say that these words bring to an end the Strophe, after which must come the next main division, or Antistrophe, which was often employed to answer the matter set forth in the Strophe or to present it from another point of view. And that is precisely the significance of the next main division. But I wanted this second division of the poem to arise out of the collapse of the first. It is plain that it would not have suited my purpose to round off the first section with some sort of formal rhythm; I ended it with an unfinished line. The next division must therefore begin by finishing that line, not merely in metre but with an integral rhythm. I will quote the passage:

> The hound bitch
> Toothless and dying, in a musty cellar
> Hears the wind only.

> Now that the salt of their blood
> Stiffens the saltier oblivion of the sea,
> Seals the malignant purity of the flood, . . .

The cæsura, after *only,* is thus at the middle of the third foot. (These are the familiar terms; I should use others in an extended discussion of prosody.) The reader expects the foot to be completed by the stress on the next word, *Now,* as in a sense it is; but the phrase, "Now that the salt of their blood," is also the beginning of a new movement; it is two "dactyls" creating momentarily a mounting rhythm counter to the falling rhythm that has prevailed. But with the finishing off of the line with *blood,* the falling rhythm is restored; the whole line from *Hears* to *blood* is actually an iambic pentameter with liberal inversions and substitutions that were expected to create a counter-rhythm within the line. From the cæsura on the rhythm is new; it has—or was expected to have—an organic relation to the preceding rhythm; and it signals the rise of a new statement of the theme.

I have gone into this passage in detail—I might have chosen another—not because I think it is successful, but because I labored with it; if it is a failure, or even an uninteresting success, it ought to offer as much technical instruction to other persons as it would were it both successful and interesting. But a word more: the broader movement introduced by the new rhythm was meant to correspond, as a sort of Antistrophe, to the earlier formal movement beginning, "You know who have waited by the wall." It is a new formal movement with new feeling and new imagery. The precarious illusion of the earlier movement has broken down into the personal symbols of the mummy and the hound; the pathetic fallacy of the leaves as charging soldiers and the conventional "buried Cæsar" theme have become rotten leaves and dead bodies wasting in the earth, to return after long erosion to the sea. In the midst of this naturalism, what shall the man say?—What shall all humanity say in the presence of decay? The two themes, then, have been struggling for mastery; the structure of the poem thus exhibits the development of two formal passages that contrast the two themes. The two formal passages break down, the first shading off into the second ("Now that the salt of their blood . . ."), the second one concluding with the figure of the

75 **pathetic fallacy,** *a phrase first used by Ruskin to mean the attribution of human traits or feelings to inanimate nature*

jaguar, which is presented in a distracted rhythm left hanging in the air from a weak ending—the word *victim*. This figure of the jaguar is the only explicit rendering of the Narcissus motif in the poem, but instead of a youth gazing into a pool, a predatory beast stares at a jungle stream, and leaps to devour himself.

The next passage begins:

What shall we say who have knowledge
Carried to the heart?

Should the reader care to think of this as the gathering up of the two themes, now fused, into a final statement, I should see no objection to calling it the Epode. But upon the meaning of the lines from here to the end I see no need for further commentary. I have talked about the structure of the poem, not its quality. One can no more find the quality of one's own verse than one can find its value, and to try to find either is like looking into a glass for the effect that one's face has upon other persons.

If anybody ever wished to know anything about this poem that he could not interpret for himself, he is still in the dark. I cannot believe that I have illuminated the difficulties that some readers have found in the style. But then I cannot, have never been able to, see any difficulties of that order. The poem has been much revised. I still think there is much to be said for the original *barter* instead of *yield* in the second line, and for *Novembers* instead of *November* in line fifteen. The revisions were not undertaken for the convenience of the reader but for the poem's own clarity, so that, word, phrase, line, passage, the poem might at worst come near its best expression.

I know that this long commentary has been a long presumption. But perhaps I have not been talking chiefly of the ostensible subject. At any rate, the presumption cannot be so egregious as the shorter presumption of the poem itself. There is nothing so presumptuous as poetry.

1938

William Van O'Connor

1915 ·

As the first managing editor of *American Quarterly,* the general editor (with Frederick J. Hoffman) of *Twentieth-Century Literature in America,* a series of mid-century evaluations, a frequent contributor to the critical journals, and the author of five books, William Van O'Connor has shown himself to be one of the most tireless men of letters of the present day. He brings to the judgment of contemporary literature a discrimination which is the product of professional concern with literary tradition but is not narrowly "academic."

O'Connor was born in Syracuse, New York, on Jan-

uary 10, 1915. He was graduated from Syracuse University in 1936 and took his M.A. degree there in the following year. World War II interrupted his study for the Ph.D. degree at Columbia University and his teaching apprenticeship. Before entering the army he had been instructor in English at St. Francis College, Brooklyn (1937-1940), Ohio State University (1940-1941), and Louisiana State University (1941-1942).

The war carried O'Connor to the South Pacific but did not cut off his literary activity completely. He not only sent back critical articles and poems to the United

States, but he also published in Australian and Filipino magazines and newspapers. At Milne Bay, in New Guinea, he met Karl Shapiro (p. 967), whose *Essay on Rime* reflects an extraordinary wartime debate on contemporary poetry and poets.

O'Connor's chief publications are *The New Woman of the Renaissance* (1942), *Climates of Tragedy* (1943), *Sense and Sensibility in Modern Poetry* (1948), *The Shaping Spirit: A Study of Wallace Stevens* (1950), and *An Age of Criticism* (1952). He was also the editor and a contributor to *Forms of Modern Fiction* (1948). Since 1946 he has been a member of the staff of the University of Minnesota, teaching courses in literary criticism and contemporary literature.

O'Connor's work has two distinctive features. Like that of many war generation writers it displays a hatred of sham and affectation, an allergy for what is "phony." With this is combined unusual breadth, the result of a refusal to embrace the doctrine of any narrow school of critical thought. The important question, O'Connor says at one point in *An Age of Criticism,* is this: "why in all its complexities modern literature is what it is." This is not merely an important question; it is also a demanding one, to be answered only by the exertion of the best talents of many types of minds.

Directory of American Scholars, Second Edition, Lancaster, Pa., 1951

A Short View of the New Criticism

This essay first appeared in **College English** for November 1949 (XI, 63-71). A revised and expanded version constitutes "Analytical Criticism," the ninth and final chapter of O'Connor's **An Age of Criticism, 1900-1950.** All footnotes to this essay are the author's; the editors have made no attempt to annotate an unusually allusive discussion which makes its own suggestions of additional reading.

I

No relatively brief discussion of the new criticism can take into account the many and divergent lines of inquiry which one or another of its practitioners has investigated. The bibliography appended to Robert Stallman's *Critiques,* an anthology of the new criticism, lists hundreds of articles and books. Cleanth Brooks, for one, has said that the term "the new criticism" has hardly proved a happy designation because it seems to imply a "literary guild" and to stress novelty.

Many critics now find themselves, however, with interests and, in general, even a method in common. Most of them would probably agree that the critic should (1) center his attention on the literary work itself, (2) study the various problems arising from examining relationships between a subject matter and the final form of a work, and (3) consider ways in which the moral and philosophical elements get into or are related to the literary work.

Their emphases are suggested by this statement from T. S. Eliot:

> You can never draw the line between aesthetic criticism and moral and social criticism; you cannot draw a line between criticism and metaphysics; you start with literary criticism, and however rigorous an aesthete you may be, you are over the frontier into something else sooner or later. The best you can do is to accept these conditions and know what you are doing when you do it. And, on the other hand, you must know how and when to retrace your steps.

The chief differences between the new criticism and scholarship are that the former attempts to hold more closely to the literary work itself than it does to the

4 The . . . books. "William Elton's **A Glossary of the New Criticism,** published by **Poetry** is a convenient manual for those interested in a more selective bibliography or in a brief discussion of many of the issues and questions raised in this criticism."—O'Connor

social or biographical origins of the work and, second, to evolve criteria that make possible judgments about literary worth.

That the new criticism is a continuation of older English criticism might be demonstrated in various ways, most readily perhaps by reference to Samuel Taylor Coleridge. His study of "Venus and Adonis," in *Biographia Literaria,* furnishes a kind of epitome of many of the considerations that recur over and over again in the new criticism: imagination as it relates to versification and the ability to reduce a multitude of feelings to their proper proportion in relation to the total unity of the work; dissociating the literary work from its origins in the writer's own life—so that the work, as Eliot has demanded, lives impersonally and with its own kind of wholeness; dramatizing, or, as James would say, "rendering, not reporting"; union of "creative power and intellectual energy," or, as we say more commonly now, "the union of thought and feeling"; complexity in the sense that one perceives the "flux and reflux of the mind in all its subtlest thoughts" and in the sense that imagery, versification, tone, and so forth, contribute in the most minute ways to the dominant feeling and thematic lines unifying the work. I. A. Richards and T. E. Hulme, two of the seminal figures in the new criticism, are greatly indebted to Coleridge. So also are later critics like Herbert Read and Kenneth Burke. In fact, Coleridge is so much a part of the preconceptions of contemporary criticism that there is probably no critic who is not greatly in his debt. In this sense, then, the new criticism is not *new*—it is a continuation of nineteenth-century English criticism. It is undoubtedly more intensive than Coleridge's. And it is new in that it borrows from contemporary anthropology, philosophy, and psychology—just as Coleridge borrowed from German philosophy.

But the new critics cannot be considered members of a "literary guild." One might think of T. S. Eliot (at least in his earlier work), William Empson, R. P. Blackmur, Robert Penn Warren, Cleanth Brooks, and John Crowe Ransom as being in agreement about most of their critical standards. There is considerable agreement among them, but anyone reading through Mr. Ransom's *The New Criticism* will also be struck by the extent of their disagreements. Ransom's theory, for instance, that much of the concrete detail of the poem is to be looked upon as interesting and pleasant in its own right but

irrelevant to the logical or "prose" meaning of the poem is not evident in the work of these other critics; some of them are explicitly in disagreement with it. And *The Anatomy of Nonsense* offers abundant evidence that Yvor Winters is in very considerable disagreement, not merely with Mr. Ransom's theory, but with the theories of most of their contemporaries.

These disagreements might be documented at length, but to emphasize the disagreements might lead us to overlook the fact that each critic is attempting to establish a body of definable criteria. A concern with such terms as "tension" and "ambiguity" or "expressive form" and "pseudo-reference" or "paradox" and "irony" implies an attempt to establish a body of criteria. Each critic is concerned to develop techniques that will enable the reader to explore the complex parts of the literary work and to make some attempt to evaluate its worth.

Almost all the contemporary critics would probably agree with Robert Penn Warren's statement, in his essay on *The Ancient Mariner,* that the primary problem in examining the meanings of a work of literature is to get at its "internal consistency." The stated intention of the author, if available, may or may not be relevant. Nor will it suffice to say that *the* meaning is the meaning a work had for its contemporary audience. "Every work,"

---

4 That . . . ways. "See, for example, the Johns Hopkins University Lectures in Criticism ('Bollingen Series,' No. XVI, 1949)."—O'Connor • 7 His . . . reporting. "In praising 'Venus and Adonis' Coleridge said, 'You seem to be told nothing but to see and hear everything.' "—O'Connor • 68 internal consistency. "The problem of internal consistency is often raised in conjunction with the problem of multiple interpretations. For instance, in his analysis of The Tempest Mark Van Doren makes these comments: 'The Tempest does bind up in final form a host of themes with which the author has been concerned. . . . One interpretation of The Tempest does not agree with another. And there is a deeper trouble in the truth that any interpretation, even the wildest, is more or less plausible. . . . Any set of symbols, moved close to the play, lights up as in an electric field. Its meaning, in other words, is precisely as rich as the human mind, and it says that the world is what it is. But what the world is cannot be said in a sentence. . . .' Obviously, not every play or poem is as rich in multiple meanings as The Tempest. Although it seems likely that a play or poem rich in meanings is likely to last a longer time, it does not seem necessary to add that the presence of multiple meanings, which could be fatuous and confused, is an indisputable test of literary value. In other words, multiple meaning, of itself, is no test of greatness. The reader interested in an example of a contemporary poem that has been interpreted in two different ways, each plausible, may read the Brooks and Warren analysis of 'The Love Song of J. Alfred Prufrock' in Understanding Poetry and compare it with Roy Basler's analysis in Sex, Symbolism and Psychology in Literature."—O'Connor

as C. S. Lewis says in *The Personal Heresy,* "that lasts long in the world is continually taking on . . . colors which the artist neither foresaw nor intended." Lionel Trilling, in "Freud and Literature," emphasizes the fact that a twentieth-century audience sees the Oedipus factor —which is not the *sole* factor—in *Hamlet* in a way the Elizabethans were not prepared to see it. Elizabethan psychology, as scholars like Lily Bess Campbell and Hardin Craig have made evident, led Shakespeare's audiences to stress other factors, even to see the play in terms that are no longer meaningful or significant to us. If we grant, as we should, the value in attempting to approximate a vision of *Hamlet* as seen by Elizabethan eyes, we do not have to grant that such a vision has exhausted the values of *Hamlet.*

The problem of meaning is phrased somewhat differently by René Wellek and Austin Warren in *Theory of Literature.* "A poem, we have to conclude," they say, "is not an individual experience or a sum of experiences, but only a potential cause of experiences. . . . Thus the real poem must be conceived as a structure of norms, realized only partially in the actual experience of its readers." It is true, they admit, that each work of art has unique aspects, but to overstress uniqueness invites complete critical relativism and an indifference to the similarities and common elements that would make it possible to discuss not merely genre but literature in general. They discuss the division of the literary work into such factors as sound, meaning, character, setting, and point of view, each factor having its subordinate considerations and each interrelated with the other factors. "The work of art, then, appears as an object of knowledge *sui generis. . . .*" Wellek and Warren admit that the *Iliad* as understood by the Greeks is not identical with the *Iliad* we are capable of understanding. Nonetheless, there must be a "substantial identity of 'structure' which has remained the same throughout the ages."

The obvious danger in the effort of the new criticism to set up criteria is that such criteria could become frozen or rigid. Criticism demands acuteness, imagination, and sensibility. Epigones could vulgarize criticism by applying formulas mechanically. The willingness of sensitive critics to realize that each original work may be at variance in some respects with certain of their preconceptions should minimize the danger of employing criteria in a vulgar or mechanical way. To deny the possibility of standards is, on the other hand, to deny the validity of all literary criticism.

II

If one is to discuss the work of literature as literature, it is not enough to attempt to reduce it to its social or biographical origins. Nor is it enough to restate it in terms of its "content." When it has been organized or transmuted into a literary work, the original idea or original lump of experience is a part of the "structure" or "form" of the work. It is no longer, in any complete sense, "content." In other words, the new criticism objects to the old dichotomy of content and form. The principle, simply enough, is that we know in part what a writer says by the way he says it. If he alters the way he says it, he has probably affected not only the appropriateness of his manner or style but the actual meaning of what he has said.

The dichotomy of content and form is apparently a Cartesian and Kantian inheritance. Meaning was commonly held to have a mind-body relationship; rhetorical figures were a dress put upon meaning, like the glove put on the hand. (The attempted divorce of meaning from matter, which was a part of the effort to achieve "mathematical unfeeling" or objectivity, is discussed in the new criticism usually as a part of the phenomenon labeled by T. S. Eliot the "dissociation of sensibility.") The concern with structure in the new criticism implies some degree of recognition that abstraction emerges from matter. Walter J. Ong, in "The Meaning of the 'New Criticism,'" writes:

> The understanding is defective if it does not observe that, however they may be handled in

3 Lionel . . . it. "W. K. Wimsatt and M. C. Beardsley, in 'The Intentional Fallacy' and 'The Affective Fallacy,' discuss those methods of criticism and scholarship that do not concentrate on 'internal consistency.' " —O'Connor • 35 Nonetheless . . . ages. "Not all the viewpoints in terms of which the structure is seen will be equally capable of grasping it most meaningfully. Therefore, some 'hierarchy of viewpoints, a criticism of the grasp of norms, is implied in the concept of the adequacy of interpretation.' This dependence on a 'system of norms' more or less completely realized by various generations of readers (as well as individuals) would avoid the extremes of absolutism and relativism. It would seem to follow also that one might, after all, by knowing the full potentialities of poetic language, be able to say that particular generations of poets held viewpoints that enabled them to make excellent or poor use of the potentialities of their medium, poetry."—O'Connor

mathematics and minor logic, the most abstract abstractions always come to us in ways which reflect their origins out of material existents. . . . Abstractions cannot be preserved and packaged, but are known and used only as they are being drawn in some way or another out of matter.

The "total meaning" has been one of the chief concerns of I. A. Richards. Meter, diction, metaphor, methods of organizing the poem, and so forth, are to him not ornamental but parts of the total meaning. The poet's attitude toward his subject matter is, or should be, implicit in his meter (the use of the spondee, for example, to slow the metrical movement) and in his diction (the "Mister Death" phrase in Cummings' poem on Buffalo Bill suggests the poet's attitude toward death in this particular context). The meter and the diction are among the factors that generate the tone. And the method of organizing the elements in the poem—the incidental ironies, the juxtaposing of unlike elements, the bringing together of homogeneous elements, the use of alliteration, of internal rhyme, and so forth—also contributes to its meaning. The employment of assonance, for example, can enable a poet to echo and stress a word he does not want to repeat explicitly. The interest in total meaning is related to the belief that there is in literature no true separation of form and content. Meter, diction, and alliteration are not only a part of the form; they are a part of the meaning. Form in this sense is not an envelope; it is a vehicle for the emergence of the total meaning or total abstraction the writer has made available.

The reader of *The Well Wrought Urn* will be able to observe that Cleanth Brooks thinks of the poem as a structure or form in the sense indicated above. He justifies his use of "paradox" and "irony" as the most available terms to suggest the kinds of indirection and the kinds of qualification he has observed to be characteristic of the total statement (or structure) that composes the poem. To substitute a paraphrase, a simplified meaning, is to destroy a part of the structure and therefore a part of the meaning. (In a somewhat similar way, Allen Tate's analyses of verses by Edna Millay, James Thomson, and John Donne in his "Tension in Poetry" are examinations into patterns of coherent relationships between denotative and connotative meanings in poetry.)

Structure or form is also a key concept in the criticism of the novel. A novelist succeeds or fails in terms of his structure. Mark Schorer says: "What we need in fiction is a devoted fidelity to every technique which will help us discover and evaluate our subject matter, and more than that, to discover the amplifications of meaning of which our subject matter is capable." To take a specific instance, Robert Penn Warren's essay on Hemingway has as its center the concept of an appropriate structure. He explains, first, what he calls the "characteristic Hemingway 'point.'" This includes comments on the initiates in Hemingway's God-abandoned world, the hard-bitten, disciplined men and women who not only savor drinking and sex but have a sharp awareness of the physical world and of light and darkness. Drinking and sex are dramatized as forces that dull the sense of *nada* (death and the meaninglessness of the physical world), except that with love a margin of human significance or meaning is achieved, and so forth. The successful Hemingway stories occur, Warren says, when "the essential limitations of his premises" have been accepted. The "failures occur when we feel that Hemingway has not respected the limitations of his premises." In the failures, not merely the moral significance or judgment, which we expect to be implied in the action, becomes blurred, but the characteristic irony and the simplified style sound empty and pretentious. Warren's focus, in other words, is on the structure of the stories. Critics like R. P. Blackmur, M. D. Zabel, and F. R. Leavis, we may assume, look to James and to Conrad, in particular, because in them they find artists who have learned how to inform a given subject matter with maximum resonance, meaning, and significance.

Kenneth Burke in "Psychology and Form" is concerned with the contemporary desire for "content," a result, he thinks, of "scientific criteria being unconsciously introduced into matters of purely esthetic judgment." Early in the same essay he shows that the success of *Hamlet,* Act I, is the result of its *form.* Eloquence, he continues, demands a minimizing of interest in fact per se, which is not, of course, a minimizing of interest in fact as it is made available through form or structure. Through an interest in structure

those elements of surprise and suspense are subtilized, carried down into the writing of a line or a sentence, until in all its smallest detail the work bristles with disclosures, contrasts, restatements with a difference, ellipses, images, aphorism, volume, sound-values, in short all that complex wealth of minutiae which in their line-for-line aspect we call style and in their broader outlines we call form.

An aspect of what I have called the aesthetic emphasis can be stated in the terms Wallace Stevens used in disagreeing with the Marxists about his function as a poet. He wrote that "one's objective as a poet is to achieve poetry, precisely as one's objective in music is to achieve music." Stevens is saying not that poetry is nonsense but that whatever literary significance it has is not as philosophy or politics but as poetry. Eliot is in partial disagreement on this matter: "The 'greatness' of literature cannot be determined solely by literary standards; though we must remember that whether it is literature or not can be determined only by literary standards."

One of the arguments directed against the new criticism is that by emphasizing form it fails to emphasize moral values and other extra-aesthetic values (content). This argument again is dependent upon the assumption that form and content can be separated. One answer would be in the emphasis in the new criticism on synthesis, tension, irony, complexity, and inclusiveness as opposed to the sentimental, the arbitrary, the merely asserted, and so forth. The maturity with which a moral or political view emerges from the aesthetic form is dependent in part on how well, how impressively, and how vividly the view has been investigated and refracted through the aesthetic medium. The very nature of literary form, demanding, as it does, stylization, that is, selection of detail, understatement, parody, or the manipulation of characters within a given, concrete situation, precludes the possibility of its offering easy rules of thumb for moral, political, or social action. Henry James was given to commenting on the relation between morality and the novel as an art form. Two passages suggest that James saw, first, the need for considering a subject in its complexity (as the new critics do) in order to arrive at a mature view of the experience being transmuted into art and, second, the necessity to see the moral situation not as a universally valid rule but as an abstraction emerging from a given, concrete instance. The first of these is from *The Art of the Novel:*

There is one point at which the moral sense and the artistic sense lie very close together; that is in the light of the very obvious truth that the deepest

quality of a work of art will always be the quality of the mind of the producer. In proportion as that intelligence is fine will the novel, the picture, the statue partake of the substance of beauty and truth. To be constituted of such elements is, to my vision, to have purpose enough. No good novel will ever proceed from a superficial mind; that seems to me an axiom which, for the artist in fiction, will cover all needful moral ground.

The second is from the Preface to *The Portrait of a Lady.* On the novelist's ability to project any vision of life depends his ability to project a moral view:

Here we get exactly the high price of the novel as a literary form—its power not only, while preserving that form with closeness, to range through all the differences of the individual relation to its general subject-matter, all the varieties of outlook on life, of disposition to reflect and project, created by conditions that are never the same from man to man (or, as far as that goes, from woman to woman), but positively to appear more true to its character in proportion as it strains, or tends to burst, with a latent extravagance, its mould.

The very character of the morality implicit in the situation is dependent upon how fully the novelist has been able to dramatize and evoke the thematic lines quickening and informing his structure. In formalist terms, as Wellek and Warren suggest, Eliot's statement about non-literary standards of greatness is a loose statement. In the final analysis, statements about the moral or philosophical elements in a literary work are made inside an aesthetic framework, in terms of the structure that makes these elements available for discussion.

Anyone reading through the new critics will be struck by the frequency with which a number of them give up their close readings, analyses, and evaluations in order to theorize about poetry as knowledge, the cognitive aspects of poetry, the ontology of poetry, and so forth. Richards, in his *Science and Poetry,* discussed as "pseudo-statements" those statements which are not verifiable in scientific terms but which satisfy our emotional needs. But he was unable to recover poetry as a form of knowledge from those (Mr. Tate in his "Literature as Knowledge" and elsewhere lumps them all under the term "Positivist") who assume that only what is verifiable in terms of scientific proofs is knowledge, the rest, irresponsible emotion. Poetic statements were "useful" but not "true." But the later Richards, of the *Philosophy of Rhetoric* and *Coleridge on the Imagination,* got away from the notion that poetry, although valuable in ordering our minds, is irrelevant to the "real" world. In the volume on Coleridge he says: *"Poetry is the completest mode of utterance."* And in this volume he places poetic language in the realm of myth (with no such pejorative connotations as "pseudo" or "false"). Myths "are those hard realities in projection, their symbolic recognition, coordination and acceptance. . . . Without his mythologies man is only a cruel animal without a soul . . . a congeries of possibilities without order or aim." Philip Wheelwright in "Poetry, Myth, and Religion," Mark Schorer in *William Blake,* and Richard Chase in *Quest for Myth* also provide valuable studies of myth in relation to poetry. And there are discussions of myth throughout the various works of the southern critics.

Empson, in his much discussed *Seven Types of Ambiguity,* is, although not explicitly, concerned with poetic statements as cognitive. The older preconception is that cognitive language, simple idea, is abstract, is language with fixed meanings. Ong quotes Hugh Blair, a late neoclassical rhetorician whose *Lectures on Rhetoric* was widely used in the nineteenth century: "Simple expression just makes our ideas known to others; but figurative language, over and above, bestows a particular dress upon that idea; a dress which both makes it to be remarked and adorns it." Empson, by showing that the new meaning (tenor) and metaphor (vehicle) *interact,* thereby suggesting a considerable number of meanings (abstractions), is showing that meanings have their origin in matter, in the concrete.

Critics now stress particularity or the concrete and want to insist on its value as a contribution to our knowledge. In myth and archetypal images (studied, for example, by Maud Bodkin), in our affective responses to color and image, and in the way our sensibilities are aroused by what Mr. Ransom has called "the world's body" they want to find evidence of the ways in which literature gives us a kind of knowledge with which science and philosophy are not concerned. Aristotle had said that literature gives us a superior form of knowledge; but Aristotle did not live under the aegis of modern science, which says that only what is verifiable is true. This would seem to put literature, which lives out of the intuition, insights, and imagination of its creators, in a realm of, at best, the delightful or the useful. Almost all the contemporary critics have been concerned with the status of literature in a scientific-minded world.

Certain of the most zealous proponents of criticism have already given notice that they are more concerned with functioning as critics than with serving literature. The critic as critic is neither philosopher, moralist, nor theoretician. The job of the critic is to help us perceive the nature and worth of the literary work. It is not the function of the critic to offer us coherent systems of philosophy, coherent theories of the nature of language, or even ideological systems that include accounts of poetry as a substitute for religion and the relation of the poet to the economic order. He can use all the information he can get; but, strictly speaking, he can employ his theory or knowledge as a critic only in so far as it is relevant to the particular work or works he is discussing and attempting to make more available for the reader. Once in a while some educationist magnanimously offers to subsume the study of literature under sociology— which would mean the end of the study of literature as an art. It would be ironic, indeed, if a few zealots in criticism managed to raise a complex edifice composed of interrelated lines of knowledge in philosophy, anthropology, and linguistics that was so massive that the literary work beneath it became merely an excuse for the superstructure. Almost everyone in the twentieth century is looking for a kind of knowledge that will be as a Second Coming. It is too much to hope that such knowledge is resting like a genie in the bottle labeled "the new criticism." In "The Function of Criticism" Eliot refers to a criticism that is self-serving as "autotelic." Tate, in a more homely phrase, has discussed it as "the picture apologizing to the frame."

V

In 1858, Sainte-Beuve, in a lecture entitled "A Literary Tradition," distinguished between the duty of the professor of literature and the critic. It is the duty of the professor, he said, to maintain a tradition of good taste and of the critic to discover new talent. He also pointed out that one of the dangers of historical scholarship was to allow, by failing to revivify the past through reinterpretation and reanalysis, a tradition to become moribund.

A tradition of good taste can be kept alive only by re-examining it in terms of the sensibility of the contemporary world. Certainly this implies a knowledge of the modern sensibility as it has been expressed and in part formed by modern literature. But literary scholarship until the advent of the critical movement in the universities tended to ignore aesthetic principles as a means of studying literature and attempted to live off the sensibility or taste that had been formed by earlier societies. An increasingly larger number of students and scholars have perceived that they were in the anomalous position of having, in effect, to deny the existence of modern literature and of their own sensibilities, formed, willy-nilly, by the inescapable fact of their living in the twentieth century. They were being asked to perform the feat of admiring the more remote past through, at the latest, the eyes of Matthew Arnold, a man who never forgot that he was writing about his own world. They were not to ask what it is that Wallace Stevens or T. S. Eliot have in common with Crashaw or Pope. A literary tradition, as Sainte-Beuve suggested, is deeply significant only when it is re-examined by each generation. By ignoring basic aesthetic considerations, scholars were allowing our literary tradition to petrify, to become antiquarian facts. As a consequence, there is now a growing feeling that the scholar should be a critic before he can be trusted as a keeper of the tradition.

In "Miss Emily and the Bibliographer" Tate attacks the notion of a "fixed hierarchy," the illusion, as he calls it, that history has ordered the place to be held by writers in a hierarchy of worth. The assumption that their places are fixed implies that the standards for evaluating them are also rigidly fixed. It implies that a new generation attempting to understand and use the literature of the past has no business altering or modifying any of these fixed judgments. To give concrete instances, it implies that the generation which has written our literature had no business raising Skelton, the Jacobean poets, Dryden, Pope, and Swift to a new eminence while allowing Browning, Swinburne, and many others in the nineteenth century to take lower places. If scholars encouraged, rather than discouraged, acts of critical judgment, if they looked upon our literary tradition as living, then these changes would not seem heretical. Nor would they lead to a chaos of new judgments or even, by and large, harm the reputations of established figures. The willingness to look upon a literary tradition as alive rather than as dead and fixed was discussed by Eliot in "Tradition and the Individual Talent," in these sentences (which he repeated in "The Function of Criticism"):

> The existing monuments form an ideal order among themselves, which is modified by the introduction of the new (the really new) work of art among them. The existing order is complete before the new work arrives; for order to persist after the supervention of novelty, the *whole* existing order must be, if ever so slightly, altered; and so the relations, proportions, values of each work of art toward the whole are readjusted; and this is conformity between the old and the new. Whoever has approved this idea of order, of the form of European, of English literature will not find it preposterous that the past should be altered by the present as much as the present is directed by the past. And the poet who is aware of this will be aware of great difficulties and responsibilities.

One of the functions of the critic, as Eliot has observed obliquely in his essay on Johnson's "Vanity of Human Wishes" and as Leavis has stated explicitly, is "to define, help form, and organize the contemporary sensibility, and to make conscious the 'standards' in it." Perhaps T. E. Hulme's *Speculations,* a tremendous formative influence on Eliot, Pound, Tate, and, to a lesser extent, Herbert Read, did more than any other book, not merely to help "make conscious the 'standards'" in contemporary literature and criticism, but to define the contemporary sensibility. It also defined the break with Victorianism. (In Hulme there are dicta, sometimes worked out, sometimes not, about scientism, romanticism, the need for a system of religious values, and the structure of poetry.) Hulme discussed the breakup of religious belief and the awful burden thereby thrown on the individual poet to establish, not only his own scale of values, but the vehicles for giving them literary expression. One of the persistent themes running through the new criticism is the consequences of the decay of a religious order. In other words, the new critics, like the cultural historians, are concerned with the rise of science and the decline of religion in the post-Renaissance world. As literary critics, they are concerned with the ways these developments are manifest in language and in literary forms.   1949

Edwin Arlington Robinson

1869 · 1935

In the second decade of the twentieth century, a poetic renaissance burst upon America. Poetry fairly boomed, as never before or since in our history. The following names and titles were some of the highlights of the period: Amy Lowell, *Sword Blades and Poppy Seed* (1914); Robert Frost, *North of Boston* (1914); Vachel Lindsay, *The Congo and Other Poems* (1914); Edgar Lee Masters, *Spoon River Anthology* (1915); Carl Sandburg, *Chicago Poems* (1916); and Edna St. Vincent Millay, *Renascence* (1917). An important organ of the movement was *Poetry: A Magazine of Verse,* edited in Chicago by Harriet Monroe. The poetic renaissance flourished for about ten years; by the early twenties, these writers had said about all that they had to say. World War I, moreover, interrupted the movement and produced a spiritual climate which required a different kind of poetry. The appearance of Eliot's *The Waste Land* in 1922 marked the beginning of a new phase.

Edwin Arlington Robinson is associated in popular memory with the renaissance. His *Man Against the Sky* (1916) was hailed along with the works of the new poets. Yet Robinson was not really one of the new poets; he had been publishing poetry for twenty years before he achieved recognition, which was a by-product of the renaissance proper. But if Robinson preceded the new poets, his belated fame, which they

helped him to achieve, more than kept pace with theirs. In the twenties, he was generally regarded as America's greatest living poet, and was awarded the Pulitzer

Edwin Arlington Robinson—caricature by William Gropper from The Literary Spotlight, *ed. John Farrar, 1924*

Prize three times—in 1922 for *Collected Poems,* in 1925 for *The Man Who Died Twice,* and in 1928 for *Tristram.*

Robinson was born in the village of Head Tide, Maine, and spent his youth in nearby Gardiner, the "Tilbury Town" of his poems. After finishing the high-school course in Gardiner, he entered Harvard, but left after two years, returning to Gardiner to devote himself to the writing of poetry. In 1897 he moved to New York, where he lived for the rest of his life, except for summers spent, after 1911, at the MacDowell Colony near Peterborough, New Hampshire. He went to Europe once, but never traveled in the United States beyond New England and New York City. Unmarried and shy, he lived quietly and inexpensively; he had little money, but, like another New Englander, Henry Thoreau, he could be rich by making his wants few. He published over twenty volumes of poetry, some of the more notable of which are: *The Children of the Night* (1897), *Captain Craig* (1902), *The Town Down the River* (1910), *The Man Against the Sky* (1916), *Merlin* (1917), *Lancelot* (1920), *Dionysus in Doubt* (1925), *Tristram* (1927), and *Matthias at the Door* (1931). Though written in conventional nineteenth-century forms, Robinson's poetry is "modern" in diction and temper. He may have been influenced by Robert Browning's dramatic monologue and analysis of men and women, but his view of life is nearer Thomas Hardy's than any other earlier poet's. His poetry is sober, reflective, pessimistic, and now and then obscure.

Robinson's development was, roughly, in two phases. Before 1916 he excelled in "Tilbury" portraits which were sharply etched and indigenous to New England. In the second phase Robinson became medieval and philosophical. He retold the Arthurian stories in *Merlin, Lancelot,* and *Tristram,* and gave free rein, in these poems and in others, to philosophical disquisition. At their best, the philosophical parts have dignity and strength; at their worst, they are wordy and vague. Although his fame dates from the second phase, critical opinion today, ironically enough, seems to prefer the early portraits of Tilbury Town.

The Man Against the Sky suggests Robinson's qualities as a philosophical poet. The Man Against the Sky, Robinson's Everyman, is a figure of doubtful heroism. His course is ambiguous. But his road—whatever it may have been—was a dark one and led only to apparent failure or, at best, to an equivocal success. This being so, "Why live?" the poet asks. The answer is a little uncertain: there is, he says, "an orient Word that will not be erased." This "orient Word" makes life significant even though its meaning is but dimly understood. The poet seems to counsel a kind of despairing courage to seek out the meaning.

Other poems suggest similar moods and attitudes. In "Flammonde," "we've each a darkening hill to climb." Miniver Cheevy "scratched his head and kept on thinking." In "Credo," the poet could not find his way, though he felt "the coming glory of the Light."

Despite his large use of Arthurian materials, Robinson is in the native New England tradition. He reflects that tradition, though, in the process of decay. The accent is still Puritan, but no longer vigorous and triumphant.

Collected Poems, New York, 1937 • Amy Lowell, **Tendencies in Modern American Poetry,** Boston, 1917 • Mark Van Doren, **Edwin Arlington Robinson,** New York, 1927

Cliff Klingenhagen

Cliff Klingenhagen had me in to dine
With him one day; and after soup and meat,
And all the other things there were to eat,
Cliff took two glasses and filled one with wine
And one with wormwood. Then, without a sign
For me to choose at all, he took the draught
Of bitterness himself, and lightly quaffed
It off, and said the other one was mine.

And when I asked him what the deuce he meant
By doing that, he only looked at me   10
And smiled, and said it was a way of his.
And though I know the fellow, I have spent
Long time a-wondering when I shall be
As happy as Cliff Klingenhagen is.

1897

Cliff Klingenhagen   **889**

handwritten: "Added lines" Post script →

Richard Cory

handwritten: Cory wasn't strong enough to take a hard life.

Whenever Richard Cory went down town,
We people on the pavement looked at him:
He was a gentleman from sole to crown,
Clean favored, and imperially slim.

And he was always quietly arrayed,
And he was always human when he talked;
But still he fluttered pulses when he said,
'Good-morning,' and he glittered when he walked.

handwritten: essential superficiality

And he was rich—yes, richer than a king—
And admirably schooled in every grace:
In fine, we thought that he was everything
To make us wish that we were in his place.

10

So on we worked, and waited for the light,
And went without the meat, and cursed the bread;
And Richard Cory, one calm summer night,
Went home and put a bullet through his head.

1897

handwritten: no courage — to wait for light

handwritten: he appeared fine - but he couldn't take life

handwritten: dazzling personality but not depth -

L'Envoi

handwritten: elaborates on his Credo

Now in a thought, now in a shadowed word,
Now in a voice that thrills eternity,
Ever there comes an onward phrase to me
Of some transcendent music I have heard;
No piteous thing by soft hands dulcimered,
No trumpet crash of blood-sick victory,
But a glad strain of some vast harmony
That no brief mortal touch has ever stirred.
There is no music in the world like this,
No character wherewith to set it down,
No kind of instrument to make it sing.
No kind of instrument? Ah, yes, there is;
And after time and place are overthrown,
God's touch will keep its one chord quivering.

10

1897

handwritten: there's harmony, true, coaxed just heard.

handwritten: a logical plan in the universe that man is not always aware of — ordered universe — music of man sees the caos!

Credo

handwritten: belief — Robinson's beliefs

I cannot find my way: there is no star
In all the shrouded heavens anywhere;
And there is not a whisper in the air
Of any living voice but one so far
That I can hear it only as a bar
Of lost, imperial music, played when fair
And angel fingers wove, and unaware,
Dead leaves to garlands where no roses are.
No, there is not a glimmer, nor a call,
For one that welcomes, welcomes when he fears, 10
The black and awful chaos of the night;
For through it all—above, beyond it all—
I know the far-sent message of the years,
I feel the coming glory of the Light.

1897

Miniver Cheevy

Although it reads like a satire on nineteenth-century medievalism—shades of Mark Twain's **Connecticut Yankee!**—this poem actually foreshadows the poet's deep interest in the Arthurian stories. If Miniver Cheevy could have written **Merlin** and **Tristram**, perhaps he would not have required the solace of alcohol.

handwritten: Combination alcoholist Romantic

Miniver Cheevy, child of scorn, *handwritten:* — alcoholic
Grew lean while he assailed the seasons;
He wept that he was ever born,
And he had reasons.

Miniver loved the days of old
When swords were bright and steeds were prancing;
The vision of a warrior bold
Would set him dancing.

"Miniver Cheevy" from **The Town Down the River** by Edwin Arlington Robinson; published by Charles Scribner's Sons; copyright, 1910, by Charles Scribner's Sons and 1938 by Ruth Niveson; used by permission of the publishers

Miniver sighed for what was not,
    And dreamed, and rested from his labors; 10
He dreamed of Thebes and Camelot,
    And Priam's neighbors.

Miniver mourned the ripe renown
    That made so many a name so fragrant;
He mourned Romance, now on the town,
    And Art, a vagrant.

Miniver loved the Medici,
    Albeit he had never seen one;
He would have sinned incessantly
    Could he have been one. 20

Miniver cursed the commonplace
    And eyed a khaki suit with loathing;
He missed the mediaeval grace
    Of iron clothing.

Miniver scorned the gold he sought,
    But sore annoyed was he without it;
Miniver thought, and thought, and thought,
    And thought about it.

Miniver Cheevy, born too late,
    Scratched his head and kept on thinking; 30
Miniver coughed, and called it fate,
    And kept on drinking.

                          1907

Flammonde

"Flammonde" illustrates Robinson's fascinated interest in psychological enigmas: what "satanic kink" in the mind of Flammonde prevented him from being the grand success that he might otherwise have been?

The man Flammonde, from God knows where,
With firm address and foreign air,
With news of nations in his talk
And something royal in his walk,
With glint of iron in his eyes,
But never doubt, nor yet surprise,

Appeared, and stayed, and held his head
As one by kings accredited.

Erect, with his alert repose
About him, and about his clothes, 10
He pictured all tradition hears
Of what we owe to fifty years.
His cleansing heritage of taste
Paraded neither want nor waste;
And what he needed for his fee
To live, he borrowed graciously.

He never told us what he was,
Or what mischance, or other cause,
Had banished him from better days
To play the Prince of Castaways. 20
Meanwhile he played surpassing well
A part, for most, unplayable;
In fine, one pauses, half afraid
To say for certain that he played.

For that, one may as well forego
Conviction as to yes or no;
Nor can I say just how intense
Would then have been the difference
To several, who, having striven
In vain to get what he was given,
Would see the stranger taken on 30
By friends not easy to be won.

Moreover, many a malcontent
He soothed and found munificent;
His courtesy beguiled and foiled
Suspicion that his years were soiled;
His mien distinguished any crowd,
His credit strengthened when he bowed;
And women, young and old, were fond
Of looking at the man Flammonde.

There was a woman in our town 40
On whom the fashion was to frown;
But while our talk renewed the tinge
Of a long-faded scarlet fringe,
The man Flammonde saw none of that,
And what he saw we wondered at—
That none of us, in her distress,
Could hide or find our littleness.

[handwritten: Flammonde got group together to raise money to send talented boy to school.]

There was a boy that all agreed
Had shut within him the rare seed
Of learning. We could understand,
But none of us could lift a hand.
The man Flammonde appraised the youth,
And told a few of us the truth;
And thereby, for a little gold,
A flowered future was unrolled.

There were two citizens who fought
For years and years, and over nought;
They made life awkward for their friends,
And shortened their own dividends.
The man Flammonde said what was wrong
Should be made right; nor was it long
Before they were again in line,
And had each other in to dine.

[in margin: 50]
[in margin: 60]

[handwritten: (3) Flammond becomes a preach between 2 enemies]

And these I mention are but four
Of many out of many more.
So much for them. But what of him—
So firm in every look and limb?
What small satanic sort of kink
Was in his brain? What broken link
Withheld him from the destinies
That came so near to being his?

[in margin: 70]

What was he, when we came to sift
His meaning, and to note the drift
Of incommunicable ways
That make us ponder while we praise?
Why was it that his charm revealed
Somehow the surface of a shield?
What was it that we never caught?
What was he, and what was he not?

[handwritten: he hid behind Something!]
[in margin: 80]

How much it was of him we met
We cannot ever know; nor yet
Shall all he gave us quite atone
For what was his, and his alone;
Nor need we now, since he knew best,
Nourish an ethical unrest:
Rarely at once will nature give
The power to be Flammonde and live.

[handwritten: Key of poem]

We cannot know how much we learn
From those who never will return,

[in margin: 90]

Until a flash of unforseen
Remembrance falls on what has been.
We've each a darkening hill to climb;
And this is why, from time to time
In Tilbury Town, we looked beyond
Horizons for the man Flammonde.

1915

[handwritten: satanic kink - love of drink.]

Mr. Flood's Party

[handwritten: Portrait of social failure]

"Mr. Flood's Party" is another of Robinson's masterful Tilbury Town portraits, clearly conceived and sharply etched. The "party" consists of only one person, since Mr. Flood's contemporaries have long been dead, and the younger generation of Tilbury are unfriendly to him. Mr. Flood is thus reduced to the misfortune of drinking alone. In a special sense, the poem suggests the loneliness of rural New England, but in a larger sense, the loneliness of old age anywhere.

The reference to Roland seems quaintly incongruous in a New England setting. There is little resemblance between Mr. Flood and the famous knight of medieval romance except that each fought a losing battle alone and went down in defeat at last.

[handwritten: lonely alcoholic.]

Old Eben Flood, climbing alone one night
Over the hill between the town below
And the forsaken upland hermitage
That held as much as he should ever know
On earth again of home, paused warily.
The road was his with not a native near;
And Eben, having leisure, said aloud,
For no man else in Tilbury Town to hear:

'Well, Mr. Flood, we have the harvest moon
Again, and we may not have many more;
The bird is on the wing, the poet says,
And you and I have said it here before.
Drink to the bird.' He raised up to the light
The jug that he had gone so far to fill,
And answered huskily: 'Well, Mr. Flood,
Since you propose it, I believe I will.'

[in margin: 10]

[handwritten at bottom: Citizens of this town won't quite forgive him because he would reveal his private affairs or past or confide with truth in spite of the things he'd done for them.]

Alone, as if enduring to the end
A valiant armor of scarred hopes outworn,
He stood there in the middle of the road
Like Roland's ghost winding a silent horn.
Below him, in the town among the trees,
Where friends of other days had honored him,
A phantom salutation of the dead
Rang thinly till old Eben's eyes were dim.

Then, as a mother lays her sleeping child
Down tenderly, fearing it may awake,
He set the jug down slowly at his feet
With trembling care, knowing that most things break;
And only when assured that on firm earth
It stood, as the uncertain lives of men
Assuredly did not, he paced away,
And with his hand extended paused again:

'Well, Mr. Flood, we have not met like this
In a long time; and many a change has come
To both of us, I fear, since last it was
We had a drop together. Welcome home!'
Convivially returning with himself,
Again he raised the jug up to the light;

And with an acquiescent quaver said:
'Well, Mr. Flood, if you insist, I might.   40

'Only a very little, Mr. Flood—
For auld lang syne. No more, sir; that will do.'
So, for the time, apparently it did,
And Eben evidently thought so too;
For soon amid the silver loneliness
Of night he lifted up his voice and sang,
Secure, with only two moons listening,
Until the whole harmonious landscape rang—

'For auld lang syne.' The weary throat gave out,
The last word wavered, and the song was done.   50
He raised again the jug regretfully
And shook his head, and was again alone.
There was not much that was ahead of him,
And there was nothing in the town below—
Where strangers would have shut the many doors
That many friends had opened long ago.

1921

20 **Roland's ghost,** an allusion to the hero of the famous French romance of the eleventh century, the **Chanson de Roland.** The reference obliquely reflects Robinson's absorbing interest in the European Middle Ages

[handwritten annotations:]
his calling out for help but it's too late—too late, gone too far
Song of Roland — Roland blew his horn too late in battle
Robinson's economy of words
in life — most joys, friendships, marriages etc in life break!

Robert Frost

1875 ·

[handwritten annotations:]
Flammonde is isolated from the people of silvery town. He's isolated not because people don't find him nice or friendly, but because he has so much more humanity + love for humanity that people could not understand him. He was lonely. People don't usually have this much love for others; therefore can't understand ones who do.
his "satanic tint" made him "misunderstood"

Despite the fact that his natal place was San Francisco, California, Robert Frost's forebears for nine generations had been New Englanders, and most of his life, from 1885 to the present, has been lived in New England. Frost's father died in San Francisco when the boy was ten, and the widow went East to Lawrence, Massachusetts, with her children, to live with their grandfather. Frost attended school in Lawrence, and did such good work that, at graduation, he was high-school valedictorian. In the autumn of 1892 Frost entered Dartmouth, but, finding college life unattractive, he shortly withdrew. During the next few years, he worked in a mill for a time, took a tramping trip through the South, did some teaching, some newspaper work, and married Elinor White, who in high school had been his only rival for class valedictorian. In 1897, he tried college again, this time Harvard, where he enjoyed the study of Latin, Greek, and philosophy. At the end of two years, however, he again left college, and moved to a farm near Derry, New Hampshire, which had been given to him by his grandfather. Because farming, during a period of eleven years, proved pretty unprofitable, Frost turned to teaching at nearby Pinkerton Academy (1905-1911) and then at New Hampshire State Normal (1911-1912).

Meanwhile, he had made a rather discouraging start as a poet. He had from early boyhood been an enthusiastic reader and writer of poetry. In his teens he had begun to publish a few of his poems in magazines. His poetry, however, did not seem very attractive to most buyers: in twenty years, he earned about two hundred dollars, in all, from his verses. In 1911, at thirty-six, he decided to sell his farm and to spend a few years in concentrated poetic work, to determine once and for all whether he could succeed in literature. Attracted by the relatively low cost of living in England, he went there, with his family, in 1912. By 1913 he managed to find a British publisher for his first book of verse, *A Boy's Will.* This, as well as his second book, *North of Boston* (1914), was very favorably received by English readers and critics.

When, in 1915, Frost returned to America, he learned that his two books, upon re-publication in this country, had won appreciation of a sort to make him rub his eyes. Regardless, he resumed his old vocations of farming—in New Hampshire and Vermont—and of teaching; but now he gave more time to composition. Since 1915, he has taught at Amherst College, the University of Michigan, the University of Vermont, and Bread Loaf School of English at Middlebury College. He has published several books of verse, notably *Mountain Interval* (1916), *New Hampshire* (1924), *West-Running Brook* (1928), *A Further Range* (1936), *A Witness Tree* (1942), *Come In* (1943), *A Masque of Reason* (1945), *Steeple Bush* (1947), *A Masque of Mercy* (1948), and three issues of *Selected Poems* (1923, 1931, 1934). Frost has received the Pulitzer Award for American poetry four times: 1924, 1931, 1937, and 1943.

The poetry of Frost has been influenced, of course, by various authors whom he admires. Vergil, the Latin poet of the *Georgics* and the *Eclogues,* has left his imprint. Frost's work is in the tradition, too, of New England predecessors such as Emerson, Thoreau, and Emily Dickinson. Yet, for the most part, bookish influences seem less important than those of the poet's inheritance and environment. The scenery, the characters, the habits of life in his section north of Boston are the stuff of much of the verse. The rocky farms, the lush woodlands, the old houses, and the stone fences of Yankeeland are in his poems. So are the rugged folk of the section—their hard lives devoted to tilling thin soil, their quirks, their ironic humor, their emotional crises. Writing of such people, often in monologues and dialogues, the poet subtly translates into rhythms the intonations, as well as expressions, which are pure New England. And much of the verse is read best when the reader uses the tight-lipped way of talking characteristic of farm folk in New Hampshire and Vermont. Frost himself, a stalwart, rough-hewn figure of a man with the weathered face of a farmer, so reads them to perfection.

Although, at first reading or hearing, the poems may seem to be lucidly simple, after better acquaintance they turn out to be, in many instances, rich in hidden meanings. Some words which Emily Dickinson applied to herself apply to Frost; like her, he "thinks New Englandly." There is a certain reticence, a teasing indirectness, in his way of telling his thought. Generally he avoids personal involvement by dramatizing: "Everything written," he has said, "is as good as it is dramatic." Often he merely presents an incident or scene, and leaves to the reader the search for any implied significance; and even when he states a moral (as in "Mending Wall") frequently a more general meaning is implied. "If I must be classified as a poet," he once said, half jestingly, half earnestly, "I might be called a Synecdochist; for I prefer the synecdoche in poetry—that figure of speech in which we use a part for the whole." Furthermore, it appears that he avoids explicit formulations partly, at least, because he does not want to commit himself to any solution which runs the danger of being simple-minded. Life, he sees, is full of apparent paradoxes. It is tragic and hilariously comic, beautiful and ugly, chaotic and unified, and he refuses to take an extreme "either-or" position. Therefore, as Mark Van Doren has said (*American Scholar,* 1936), "Mr. Frost's place is and always has been singularly central. He has nothing to do with the extremes where most of our shouting has been heard. . . . There is an ignoble way of avoiding extremes. It is the way of being nobody and saying nothing; or never, at any rate, being or saying enough to count. But there is another way which, difficult though it may be to define, is the only way worth considering. It consists in occupying or touching both extremes at once, and inhabiting all the space between. It consists in being capable of excess while actually achieving more than excess achieves. It consists in finding the golden mean which, far from signifying that the extremes have been avoided, signifies that they have been enclosed and contained." A careful study of the poetry of Robert Frost will show that, for all his appearance of rustic simplicity, he has more of significance to say than many of the contemporaneous poets among whom he holds a high position.

Collected Poems, New York, 1930 • R. P. Coffin, New Poetry of New England, Baltimore, 1938 • Recognition of Robert Frost, ed. Richard Thornton, New York, 1937 • Lawrance Thompson, Fire and Ice: The Art and Thought of Robert Frost, New York, 1942

Mowing

A one-sentence interpretation of this poem by its author is, "The youth takes up life simply with the small tasks." Wrote T. K. Whipple, in Spokesmen: "Robert Frost's is preëminently a farmer's poetry. His familiarity with nature and with objects is not, for all his deservedly famous observation, that of the observer or spectator, but that of the man who has worked with them and used them. His acquaintance with them is more intimate and more intuitive than that of the onlooker. A grindstone to him is not a quaint object with rustic associations, but something which has made him groan and sweat; a scythe does not remind him of Theocritus but of the feel of the instrument as he swung it." In "Mowing," the poet is concerned with suggesting to the reader his "intimate and intuitive acquaintance" with a swinging scythe—his sensing of significance in an ordinary task. The verse form, since it is a sonnet with its own individual rhyme-scheme, and since its iambic rhythms are adjusted to those of a conversational tone, represents the modified modernism of the author's versification.

There was never a sound beside the wood but one,
And that was my long scythe whispering to the ground.
What was it it whispered? I knew not well myself;
Perhaps it was something about the heat of the sun,
Something, perhaps, about the lack of sound—
And that was why it whispered and did not speak.
It was no dream of the gift of idle hours,
Or easy gold at the hand of fay or elf:

Anything more than the truth would have seemed too weak
To the earnest love that laid the swale in rows,   10
Not without feeble-pointed spikes of flowers
(Pale orchises), and scared a bright green snake.
The fact is the sweetest dream that labor knows.
My long scythe whispered and left the hay to make.
1913

The Demiurge's Laugh

A "demiurge," according to Greek mythology, was a subordinate god who created or fashioned the world. Frost has said that "The Demiurge's Laugh" is "about science." Hence "the Demon" whom the poet pursued may have been some false god worshiped by science as a creator, perhaps creative evolution as a final explanation of all history and progress. Thinking he was on the trail of this scientific fable, the poet heard a sound "behind him instead of before"—a mocking sound which made him realize that his belief that he was progressing toward understanding was fallacious. Abashed by this realization, he abandoned the search. Such an interpretation of the poem (others are possible) at least is consistent with the author's lifelong habit of rejecting over-simplified solutions and faiths.

It was far in the sameness of the wood;
    I was running with joy on the Demon's trail,

Though I knew what I hunted was no true god.

    It was just as the light was beginning to fail
That I suddenly heard—all I needed to hear.
It has lasted me many and many a year.

The sound was behind me instead of before,
    A sleepy sound, but mocking half,
As of one who utterly couldn't care.

    The Demon arose from his wallow to laugh,   10
Brushing the dirt from his eye as he went;
And well I knew what the Demon meant.

I shall not forget how his laugh rang out.
    I felt as a fool to have been so caught,
And checked my steps to make pretence
    It was something among the leaves I sought
(Though doubtful whether he stayed to see).
Thereafter I sat me against a tree.

                           1913

Mending Wall

Characteristic details often repeated in the New England landscape are stone fences, laboriously kept in neat repair by their owners. In this poem, which tells of the springtime ritual of mending such a wall, two kinds of Yankees—or of men—are dramatically contrasted. The "I" of the poem is unconventional in his thinking and impish in his discourse; his neighbor is a person who doggedly takes for granted that anything which his father has thought and said must be a final fact. The narrator opens with some of his reflections about the way nature seems to battle, in its mysterious way, against a wall. He then tells of an annual arrangement he has with his neighbor to repair winter damages—"to set the wall between us once again." There is irony, of course, in the fact that those who live near to one another thus coöperate to set themselves apart, an irony which is heightened by the fact that this particular wall has no real purpose. In the brief argument which follows, the narrator teases his neighbor about this situation; but the neighbor repeats, with unction, an old adage which he has thoughtlessly accepted. Some will take this poem to be a little character etching; others, perhaps, will take it to be a parable about the way tradition works against nature to keep men or even nations apart. Frost merely tells the story. Writes G. R. Elliott, in *The Nation*, 1919, " 'Good fences make good neighbors'; but also, on the other hand, 'Something there is that doesn't love a wall.' This two-sided text . . . is the underlying theme of the poet's whole work. Does it not also represent, in miniature, the great paradox which now confronts human society? 'Walls' are indispensable, we find, and yet our progress toward human brotherhood seems sadly cramped by 'walls.' That this paradox is soluble in the spirit of true neighborliness, but that the solution of it is laborious and exciting, is what one is made to feel keenly in reading Mr. Frost's poetry."

Something there is that doesn't love a wall,
That sends the frozen-ground-swell under it,
And spills the upper boulders in the sun;
And makes gaps even two can pass abreast.
The work of hunters is another thing:
I have come after them and made repair
Where they have left not one stone on a stone,
But they would have the rabbit out of hiding,
To please the yelping dogs. The gaps I mean,
No one has seen them made or heard them made,
But at spring mending-time we find them there.
I let my neighbour know beyond the hill;
And on a day we meet to walk the line
And set the wall between us once again.
We keep the wall between us as we go.
To each the boulders that have fallen to each.
And some are loaves and some so nearly balls
We have to use a spell to make them balance:
'Stay where you are until our backs are turned!'
We wear our fingers rough with handling them.   20
Oh, just another kind of out-door game,
One on a side. It comes to little more:
There where it is we do not need the wall:
He is all pine and I am apple orchard.
My apple trees will never get across
And eat the cones under his pines, I tell him.
He only says, 'Good fences make good neighbours.'
Spring is the mischief in me, and I wonder
If I could put a notion in his head:

'Why do they make good neighbours? Isn't it   30
Where there are cows? But here there are no cows.
Before I built a wall I'd ask to know
What I was walling in or walling out,
And to whom I was like to give offence.
Something there is that doesn't love a wall,
That wants it down.' I could say 'Elves' to him,
But it's not elves exactly, and I'd rather
He said it for himself. I see him there
Bringing a stone grasped firmly by the top
In each hand, like an old-stone savage armed.   40
He moves in darkness as it seems to me,
Not of woods only and the shade of trees.
He will not go behind his father's saying,
And he likes having thought of it so well
He says again, 'Good fences make good neighbours.'
                                                1914

The Death of the Hired Man

"The Death of the Hired Man," like "Mending Wall,"
dramatically presents a group of contrasting characters,
but here there are three instead of two. Aside from some
brief descriptive and narrative passages, it is a dialogue,
and the conversation typifies Robert Frost's skill in making
verse sound like talk and in delineating the folk of his
region. The temperament and history of the hired man,
Silas, are shown indirectly by the discussion about him,
and his return and death are important incidents. Silas
is a lazy, sponging rogue who, on many occasions, has
wandered away only to return and take advantage of the
kindness of his employers, Mary and Warren. These employers reveal their characters as they converse about
the latest return of this pathetic but rather ingratiating
creature. In the discussion which follows, the wife deftly
wins the farmer over to her point of view. When Warren
goes to speak with Silas, he makes an ironic discovery.

Mary sat musing on the lamp-flame at the table
Waiting for Warren. When she heard his step,
She ran on tip-toe down the darkened passage
To meet him in the doorway with the news

And put him on his guard. 'Silas is back.'
She pushed him outward with her through the door
And shut it after her. 'Be kind,' she said.
She took the market things from Warren's arms
And set them on the porch, then drew him down
To sit beside her on the wooden steps.   10

'When was I ever anything but kind to him?
But I'll not have the fellow back,' he said.
'I told him so last haying, didn't I?
"If he left then," I said, "that ended it."
What good is he? Who else will harbour him
At his age for the little he can do?
What help he is there's no depending on.
Off he goes always when I need him most.
"He thinks he ought to earn a little pay,
Enough at least to buy tobacco with,   20
So he won't have to beg and be beholden."
"All right," I say, "I can't afford to pay
Any fixed wages, though I wish I could."
"Someone else can." "Then someone else will have to."
I shouldn't mind his bettering himself
If that was what it was. You can be certain,
When he begins like that, there's someone at him
Trying to coax him off with pocket-money,—
In haying time, when any help is scarce.
In winter he comes back to us. I'm done.'   30

'Sh! not so loud: he'll hear you,' Mary said.

'I want him to: he'll have to soon or late.'

'He's worn out. He's asleep beside the stove.
When I came up from Rowe's I found him here,
Huddled against the barn-door fast asleep,
A miserable sight, and frightening, too—
You needn't smile—I didn't recognise him—
I wasn't looking for him—and he's changed.
Wait till you see.'

                   'Where did you say he'd been?' 40

'He didn't say. I dragged him to the house,
And gave him tea and tried to make him smoke.
I tried to make him talk about his travels.
Nothing would do: he just kept nodding off.'

'What did he say? Did he say anything?'

'But little.'

                        'Anything? Mary, confess
He said he'd come to ditch the meadow for me.'

'Warren!'

                'But did he? I just want to know.' 50

'Of course he did. What would you have him say?
Surely you wouldn't grudge the poor old man
Some humble way to save his self-respect.
He added, if you really care to know,
He meant to clear the upper pasture, too.
That sounds like something you have heard before?
Warren, I wish you could have heard the way
He jumbled everything. I stopped to look
Two or three times—he made me feel so queer—
To see if he was talking in his sleep.   60
He ran on Harold Wilson—you remember—
The boy you had in haying four years since.
He's finished school, and teaching in his college.
Silas declares you'll have to get him back.
He says they two will make a team for work:
Between them they will lay this farm as smooth!
The way he mixed that in with other things.
He thinks young Wilson a likely lad, though daft
On education—you know how they fought
All through July under the blazing sun,   70
Silas up on the cart to build the load,
Harold along beside to pitch it on.'

'Yes, I took care to keep well out of earshot.'

'Well, those days trouble Silas like a dream.
You wouldn't think they would. How some things linger!
Harold's young college boy's assurance piqued him.
After so many years he still keeps finding
Good arguments he sees he might have used.
I sympathise. I know just how it feels
To think of the right thing to say too late.   80
Harold's associated in his mind with Latin.
He asked me what I thought of Harold's saying
He studied Latin like the violin

Because he liked it—that an argument!
He said he couldn't make the boy believe
He could find water with a hazel prong—
Which showed how much good school had ever done him.
He wanted to go over that. But most of all
He thinks if he could have another chance
To teach him how to build a load of hay—'   90

'I know, that's Silas' one accomplishment.
He bundles every forkful in its place,
And tags and numbers it for future reference,
So he can find and easily dislodge it
In the unloading. Silas does that well.
He takes it out in bunches like big birds' nests.
You never see him standing on the hay
He's trying to lift, straining to lift himself.'

'He thinks if he could teach him that, he'd be
Some good perhaps to someone in the world.   100
He hates to see a boy the fool of books.
Poor Silas, so concerned for other folk,
And nothing to look backward to with pride,
And nothing to look forward to with hope,
So now and never any different.'

Part of a moon was falling down the west,
Dragging the whole sky with it to the hills.
Its light poured softly in her lap. She saw it
And spread her apron to it. She put out her hand
Among the harp-like morning-glory strings,   110
Taut with the dew from garden bed to eaves,
As if she played unheard some tenderness
That wrought on him beside her in the night.
'Warren,' she said, 'he has come home to die:
You needn't be afraid he'll leave you this time.'

'Home,' he mocked gently.

                        'Yes, what else but home?
It all depends on what you mean by home.
Of course he's nothing to us, any more
Than was the hound that came a stranger to us   120
Out of the woods, worn out upon the trail.'

'Home is the place where, when you have to go there,
They have to take you in.'

'I should have called it
Something you somehow haven't to deserve.'

Warren leaned out and took a step or two,
Picked up a little stick, and brought it back
And broke it in his hand and tossed it by.
'Silas has better claim on us you think
Than on his brother? Thirteen little miles   130
As the road winds would bring him to his door.
Silas has walked that far no doubt to-day.
Why didn't he go there? His brother's rich,
A somebody—director in the bank.'

'He never told us that.'

'We know it though.'

'I think his brother ought to help, of course.
I'll see to that if there is need. He ought of right
To take him in, and might be willing to—
He may be better than appearances.   140
But have some pity on Silas. Do you think
If he had any pride in claiming kin
Or anything he looked for from his brother,
He'd keep so still about him all this time?'

'I wonder what's between them.'

'I can tell you.
Silas is what he is—we wouldn't mind him—
But just the kind that kinsfolk can't abide.
He never did a thing so very bad.
He don't know why he isn't quite as good   150
As anybody. Worthless though he is,
He won't be made ashamed to please his brother.'

'I can't think Si ever hurt anyone.'

'No, but he hurt my heart the way he lay
And rolled his old head on that sharp-edged chair-
    back.
He wouldn't let me put him on the lounge.
You must go in and see what you can do.
I made the bed up for him there to-night.
You'll be surprised at him—how much he's broken.
His working days are done; I'm sure of it.'   160

'I'd not be in a hurry to say that.'

'I haven't been. Go, look, see for yourself.
But, Warren, please remember how it is:
He's come to help you ditch the meadow.
He has a plan. You mustn't laugh at him.
He may not speak of it, and then he may.
I'll sit and see if that small sailing cloud
Will hit or miss the moon.'

It hit the moon.
Then there were three there, making a dim row,   170
The moon, the little silver cloud, and she.

Warren returned—too soon, it seemed to her,
Slipped to her side, caught up her hand and waited.

'Warren?' she questioned.

'Dead,' was all he answered.
                                                    1914

The Hill Wife

In Fire and Ice, an illuminating study of Robert Frost,
Professor Thompson writes these helpful comments: "An
implied dramatic narrative is fashioned from five very
short lyrics in 'The Hill Wife'. . . . It stands out by implication as a miniature lyric drama in five scenes. The first
scene, of twelve lines only, sets the stage for tragedy, and
establishes the theme of fear-in-loneliness. The Hill Wife
tries to tell her husband that something must be wrong
with them to be so sad and lonely. . . . The second scene is
even shorter than the first. In it a chorus voice describes
the fear of the empty house when the Hill Wife returns
with her husband at night. . . . In the third scene, the Hill
Wife describes her fear caused by the way a passing
tramp smiled strangely and unfathomably at her before
he walked into the woods with the bread she had given
him. Fear of yet another kind shows itself in the fourth
scene. Briefly the chorus voice tells how the Hill Wife
is troubled by the persistent scrape of a pine branch which

her bedroom window with 'tireless but
~~~~~.' The fifth scene, entitled 'The Impulse,'
contains climax and denouement. The chorus voice tells
how the Hill Wife followed her silent husband in field
and wood, hoping that his nearness might relieve her
fear of loneliness. Once, when she strayed off so far that
she scarcely heard when he shouted to her, she hid herself instead of answering him. The conclusion [comprising
the last two stanzas] is terse enough. In 'The Hill Wife'
the psychological analysis is developed entirely through
implication, and hinges on the growing failure of the
man to sympathize with the woman's accumulated psy-
chosis."

LONELINESS

Her Word

One ought not to have to care
    So much as you and I
Care when the birds come round the house
    To seem to say good-bye;

Or care so much when they come back
    With whatever it is they sing;
The truth being we are as much
    Too glad for the one thing

As we are too sad for the other here—
    With birds that fill their breasts   10
But with each other and themselves
    And their built or driven nests.

HOUSE FEAR

Always—I tell you this they learned—
Always at night when they returned
To the lonely house from far away
To lamps unlighted and fire gone gray,
They learned to rattle the lock and key
To give whatever might chance to be
Warning and time to be off in flight:
And preferring the out- to the in-door night,   20
They learned to leave the house-door wide
Until they had lit the lamp inside.

900   *Frost*

THE SMILE

Her Word

I didn't like the way he went away.
That smile! It never came of being gay.
Still he smiled—did you see him?—I was sure!
Perhaps because we gave him only bread
And the wretch knew from that that we were poor.
Perhaps because he let us give instead
Of seizing from us as he might have seized.
Perhaps he mocked at us for being wed,   30
Or being very young (and he was pleased
To have a vision of us old and dead).
I wonder how far down the road he's got.
He's watching from the woods as like as not.

THE OFT-REPEATED DREAM

She had no saying dark enough
    For the dark pine that kept
Forever trying the window-latch
    Of the room where they slept.

The tireless but ineffectual hands
    That with every futile pass   40
Made the great tree seem as a little bird
    Before the mystery of glass!

It never had been inside the room,
    And only one of the two
Was afraid in an oft-repeated dream
    Of what the tree might do.

THE IMPULSE

It was too lonely for her there,
    And too wild,
And since there were but two of them,
    And no child,   50

And work was little in the house,
    She was free,
And followed where he furrowed field,
    Or felled tree.

She rested on a log and tossed
    The fresh chips,

Frontispiece from Robert Frost, New Hampshire, *1923.*
Woodcut by J. J. Lankes

With a song only to herself
    On her lips.

And once she went to break a bough
    Of black alder.   60
She strayed so far she scarcely heard
    When he called her—

And didn't answer—didn't speak—
    Or return.
She stood, and then she ran and hid
    In the fern.

He never found her, though he looked
    Everywhere,
And he asked at her mother's house
    Was she there.   70

Sudden and swift and light as that
    The ties gave,
And he learned of finalities
    Besides the grave.

1916

Birches

A man, upon seeing bent birches, recalls how, as a boy, he had swung upon such trees. Then, by means of an analogy, he contrasts the swinging of a boy, toward Heaven and back to earth, with death.

When I see birches bend to left and right
Across the lines of straighter darker trees,
I like to think some boy's been swinging them.
But swinging doesn't bend them down to stay.
Ice-storms do that. Often you must have seen them
Loaded with ice a sunny winter morning
After a rain. They click upon themselves
As the breeze rises, and turn many-colored
As the stir cracks and crazes their enamel.
Soon the sun's warmth makes them shed crystal shells   10
Shattering and avalanching on the snow-crust—
Such heaps of broken glass to sweep away
You'd think the inner dome of heaven had fallen.
They are dragged to the withered bracken by the load,
And they seem not to break; though once they are bowed
So low for long, they never right themselves:
You may see their trunks arching in the woods
Years afterwards, trailing their leaves on the ground
Like girls on hands and knees that throw their hair
Before them over their heads to dry in the sun.   20
But I was going to say when Truth broke in
With all her matter-of-fact about the ice-storm
I should prefer to have some boy bend them
As he went out and in to fetch the cows—
Some boy too far from town to learn baseball,
Whose only play was what he found himself,
Summer or winter, and could play alone.
One by one he subdued his father's trees

By riding them down over and over again
Until he took the stiffness out of them,
And not one but hung limp, not one was left
For him to conquer. He learned all there was
To learn about not launching out too soon
And so not carrying the tree away
Clear to the ground. He always kept his poise
To the top branches, climbing carefully
With the same pains you use to fill a cup
Up to the brim, and even above the brim.
Then he flung outward, feet first, with a swish,
Kicking his way down through the air to the ground. 40
So was I once myself a swinger of birches.
And so I dream of going back to be.
It's when I'm weary of considerations,
And life is too much like a pathless wood
Where your face burns and tickles with the cobwebs
Broken across it, and one eye is weeping
From a twig's having lashed across it open.
I'd like to get away from earth awhile
And then come back to it and begin over.
May no fate willfully misunderstand me   50
And half grant what I wish and snatch me away
Not to return. Earth's the right place for love:
I don't know where it's likely to go better.
I'd like to go by climbing a birch tree,
And climb black branches up a snow-white trunk
Toward heaven, till the tree could bear no more,
But dipped its top and set me down again.
That would be good both going and coming back.
One could do worse than be a swinger of birches.

1916

Stopping by Woods on a Snowy Evening

The speaker in this brief monologue is a farmer who has
stopped his sleigh for a time to admire the snow falling
over the night-darkened woods. His horse, puzzled by
the pause, takes the same attitude toward it which would
be taken by anyone with a worldly scheme of values:

the stop serves no material purpose, so why make it? In
time, the traveler himself recalls worldly demands—remembers that he has "promises to keep" and a schedule
to follow. It is, perhaps, a simple story of a momentary
halt to admire beauty, in the business of living. Or perhaps—if one wants to follow some of the unobtrusive
suggestions—it is a picture of a man who, in the midst
of life, has a brief and dim comprehension of the inevitable sleep which is death.

Whose woods these are I think I know.
His house is in the village though;
He will not see me stopping here
To watch his woods fill up with snow.

My little horse must think it queer
To stop without a farmhouse near
Between the woods and frozen lake
The darkest evening of the year.

He gives his harness bells a shake
To ask if there is some mistake.   10
The only other sound's the sweep
Of easy wind and downy flake.

The woods are lovely, dark and deep.
But I have promises to keep,
And miles to go before I sleep,
And miles to go before I sleep.

1923

Two Tramps in Mud-Time

In splitting wood, a man may find a physical and
emotional pleasure similar to the one Frost describes
in this poem and in "Mowing." Suppose, though, that
someone who has a financial need for work asks for the
ax or the scythe? This question is posed by "Two Tramps
in Mud-Time." Cleanth Brooks notices that the opening
stanzas "establish the character of the speaker so that the

generalization . . . is dramatically justified." He criticizes Frost, however, because here the generalization "is made finally in the mode of prose rather than in terms of symbol." The criticism might not be valid if, as some may hold, the solution is not Frost's own, or if the solution—like the moral of "Mending Wall"—has emotional and logical implications above and beyond those explicitly stated.

Out of the mud two strangers came
And caught me splitting wood in the yard.
And one of them put me off my aim
By hailing cheerily "Hit them hard!"
I knew pretty well why he dropped behind
And let the other go on a way.
I knew pretty well what he had in mind:
He wanted to take my job for pay.

Good blocks of beech it was I split,
As large around as the chopping-block;   10
And every piece I squarely hit
Fell splinterless as a cloven rock.
The blows that a life of self-control
Spares to strike for the common good
That day, giving a loose to my soul,
I spent on the unimportant wood.

The sun was warm but the wind was chill.
You know how it is with an April day:
When the sun is out and the wind is still,
You're one month on in the middle of May.   20
But if you so much as dare to speak,
A cloud comes over the sunlit arch,
A wind comes off a frozen peak,
And you're two months back in the middle of March.

A bluebird comes tenderly up to alight
And fronts the wind to unruffle a plume,
His song so pitched as not to excite
A single flower as yet to bloom.
It is snowing a flake: and he half knew
Winter was only playing possum.   30
Except in color he isn't blue,
But he wouldn't advise a thing to blossom.

The water for which we may have to look
In summertime with a witching-wand,
In every wheelrut's now a brook,
In every print of a hoof a pond.
Be glad of water, but don't forget
The lurking frost in the earth beneath
That will steal forth after the sun is set
And show on the water its crystal teeth.   40

The time when most I loved my task
These two must make me love it more
By coming with what they came to ask.
You'd think I never had felt before
The weight of an ax head poised aloft,
The grip on earth of outspread feet,
The life of muscles rocking soft
And smooth and moist in vernal heat.

Out of the woods two hulking tramps
(From sleeping God knows where last night   50
But not long since in the lumber camps).
They thought all chopping was theirs of right.
Men of the woods and lumber-jacks,
They judged me by their appropriate tool.
Except as a fellow handled an ax,
They had no way of knowing a fool.

Nothing on either side was said.
They knew they had but to stay their stay
And all their logic would fill my head:
As that I had no right to play   60
With what was another man's work for gain.
My right might be love but theirs was need.
And where the two exist in twain
Theirs was the better right—agreed.

But yield who will to their separation,
My object in life is to unite
My avocation and my vocation
As my two eyes make one in sight.
Only where love and need are one,
And the work is play for mortal stakes,   70
Is the deed ever really done
For Heaven and the future's sakes.

1936

Two Tramps in Mud-Time   903

Carl Sandburg

1878 ·

Back in the later years of the nineteenth century, a large number of recently arrived Swedish immigrants were working in Galesburg, Illinois, and several of them had the common Swedish name, Johnson. To avoid confusion, August Johnson, a blacksmith with a railway construction gang, changed his name to Sandburg. Thus when August's son, born in Galesburg in 1878, became well-known, he was famous not as Carl Johnson but as Carl Sandburg. Probably Sandburg would have been pleased to have a more ordinary name than he has. For as a writer, he conceived of his work as the articulation of the experiences, the thoughts, and the dreams of ordinary men and women.

When he was thirteen, Carl Sandburg left school to drive a milkwagon. Later he was a porter in a Galesburg barber shop, and then a worker in a brickyard. In the years before the Spanish-American War began, he traveled a good deal (mostly on the underside of boxcars), stopping off in Kansas, say, to work in the wheatfields, or in Denver or Omaha to wash dishes in a hotel. It was during his eight-month enlistment for the Spanish-American War that he was persuaded by an alumnus of Lombard College at Galesburg that he ought to go to college.

After working his way through Lombard, he became a traveling salesman of stereopticon slides, and he was engaged in this work when, in 1904, a former professor arranged for the publication of his first book, a little pamphlet called *In Reckless Ecstasy*. Sandburg later was to be glad that this collection of rather imitative poems had not had a wide sale, but he never renounced the passages in it which foreshadowed all his future work. "I glory," one such passage went, "in this world of men and women, torn with troubles and lost in sorrow, yet living on to love and laugh and play through it all. My eyes range with pleasure over flowers, prairies, woods, grass, and running water, and the sea, and the sky and the clouds."

A few years after his first book appeared, Sandburg became a journalist in Milwaukee, working as labor reporter on Socialist Victor Berger's *Milwaukee Leader*. For a time, he was secretary to Milwaukee's Socialist mayor, Emil Seidel. In Milwaukee in 1908, he married Lillian Steichen, who, like him, was interested in the fortunes of laborers. In 1912 he and his wife drifted to Chicago, where he worked for several publications, notably the *Daily News*.

When *Poetry* was started in Chicago, Sandburg was one of its early contributors; and in 1916 his first book of poems to be put out by a nationally known publisher appeared. *Chicago Poems* was followed by *Cornhuskers* (1918), *Smoke and Steel* (1920), *Slabs of the Sunburnt West* (1922), *Good Morning, America* (1928), *The People, Yes* (1936), and *Collected Poems* (1951).

Meanwhile, Sandburg had become well known as a singer of ballads. In various parts of the country, he had appeared on platforms to sing the folk songs collected on his travels—songs of cowboys, hobos, and workmen, and spirituals learned from their Negro makers. In time, some of the songs he sang, accompanying himself on a guitar, were recorded. In time, too, the folk songs he had collected were published in *The American Songbag* (1927), a book admired by the scholar and the general reader alike.

When Sandburg eventually turned to the writing of history, he produced a biography of Lincoln. *The Prairie Years* (1926) carried Lincoln's story down to the time Lincoln left for the White House and *The War Years* (1940) told of Lincoln as President.

The poetry, the ballad collecting, the biography, and a rather chaotic historical novel, *Remembrance Rock* (1948), are all of a piece. Frequently Sandburg has quoted with admiration the saying of one of Kipling's characters—"I will be the word of the people. Mine will be the bleeding mouth from which the gag is snatched. I will say everything." As Sandburg has conceived of his task, it has been to voice the thoughts and feelings of the common folk; and he believes that he expresses them in his poems, in his folk songs, and in the biography of the American people's greatest hero.

His poetry is expressive of his times in both its form and its subject matter. It is free verse of the sort becoming fashionable when he started to write. His diction is the American language, the richness of which was being discovered in Sandburg's young manhood. He, like others, was bewildered by the shift of America from the agrarian way of living to the industrial way. He, like others, was resentful of the injustices and the hypocrisies of a transitional period. Finally he, like others, found a hope and a belief which he could affirm. For him, these

Carl Sandburg, 1941—Wide World Photo

grew, naturally enough, from what he had seen and learned of the people—*The People, Yes*.

Harry Hansen, **Midwest Portraits**, New York, 1923 • Bruce Weirick, **From Whitman to Sandburg in American Poetry**, New York, 1928 • T. K. Whipple, **Spokesmen: Modern Writers and American Life**, New York, 1928 • Vernon Loggins, **I Hear America . . . : Literature in the United States Since 1900**, New York, 1937

Chicago

"What Sandburg likes in Chicago," note Carl and Mark Van Doren, "is its newness and hopefulness, which a different poet might call its rawness and callowness. . . .

Above all he admires the superb insolence of the untamed capital. . . . Sandburg is equally insolent. He too discards the past and its patterns; he too reaches out and grasps whatever seems to him full of life and molds it to his own uses; he too speaks his own language, though it comes to him from the streets rather than from the dictionaries. To the extent that Chicago is the metropolis of the present and the future, Sandburg is the poet of these eras."

When "Chicago" appeared in **Poetry** in 1914, it was the subject of a great deal of controversy. Its unconventional rhythms, diction, and imagery seemed to some to depart deliberately from those of conventional poetry. Nevertheless, the poem has something more than a casual structure. The opening lines offer a series of descriptions summarized in the fifth line, "City of the Big Shoulders"—a suggestion of the city's power. Lines 6-8 show the grim aspects, but line 9 marks a turn, and the defense of the city begins with other details about strength. In lines 19-23, climactically, this strength is shown overcoming the sorrow and sordidness earlier described, and in the final line the words of the opening lines are repeated, this time linked with the pride and the laughter of Chicago.

Hog Butcher for the World
Tool Maker, Stacker of Wheat,
Player with Railroads and the Nation's Freight
    Handler;
Stormy, husky, brawling,
City of the Big Shoulders:

They tell me you are wicked and I believe them, for I
    have seen your painted women under the gas lamps
    luring the farm boys.
And they tell me you are crooked and I answer: Yes, it
    is true I have seen the gunman kill and go free to
    kill again.
And they tell me you are brutal and my reply is: On the
    faces of women and children I have seen the marks
    of wanton hunger.
And having answered so I turn once more to those who
    sneer at this my city, and I give them back the sneer
    and say to them:
Come and show me another city with lifted head singing
    so proud to be alive and coarse and strong and
    cunning.   10
Flinging magnetic curses amid the toil of piling job on
    job, here is a tall bold slugger set vivid against the
    little soft cities;
Fierce as a dog with tongue lapping for action, cunning
    as a savage pitted against the wilderness,
        Bareheaded,
        Shoveling,

        Wrecking,
        Planning,
        Building, breaking, rebuilding,
Under the smoke, dust all over his mouth, laughing with
    white teeth,
Under the terrible burden of destiny laughing as a young
    man laughs,
Laughing even as an ignorant fighter laughs who has
    never lost a battle,   20
Bragging and laughing that under his wrist is the pulse,
    and under his ribs the heart of the people,
        Laughing!
Laughing the stormy, husky, brawling laughter of Youth,
    half-naked, sweating, proud to be Hog Butcher,
    Tool Maker, Stacker of Wheat, Player with Railroads and Freight Handler to the Nation.

                1914

To a Contemporary Bunkshooter
Billy Sunday

In this fierce poem, Sandburg angrily contrasts the preachments of the theatrical revivalist of the day with the teachings of Christ. The author's sympathy with the underprivileged makes him contemptuous of sermonizing under the guise of religion which serves the purpose of their exploiters by urging people to suffer wrongs with a humble spirit. His conception of Jesus is of a quiet man who gave his life as a sacrifice for humble sufferers—a very different sort from the encourager of exploitation pictured by the athletic preacher here apostrophized.

You come along . . . tearing your shirt . . . yelling about
    Jesus.
    Where do you get that stuff?
    What do you know about Jesus?
Jesus had a way of talking soft and outside of a few
    bankers and higher-ups among the con men of Jeru-
    salem everybody liked to have this Jesus around
    because he never made any fake passes and every-
    thing he said went and he helped the sick and **gave**
    the people hope.

You come along squirting words at us, shaking your fist and call us all dam fools so fierce the froth slobbers over your lips . . . always blabbing we're all going to hell straight off and you know all about it.

I've read Jesus' words. I know what he said. You don't throw any scare into me. I've got your number. I know how much you know about Jesus.

He never came near clean people or dirty people but they felt cleaner because he came along. It was your crowd of bankers and business men and lawyers hired the sluggers and murderers who put Jesus out of the running.

I say the same bunch backing you nailed the nails into the hands of this Jesus of Nazareth. He had lined up against him the same crooks and strong-arm men now lined up with you paying your way.

This Jesus was good to look at, smelled good, listened good. He threw out something fresh and beautiful from the skin of his body and the touch of his hands wherever he passed along.

You slimy bunkshooter, you put a smut on every human blossom in reach of your rotten breath belching about hell-fire and hiccupping about this Man who lived a clean life in Galilee.   10

When are you going to quit making the carpenters build emergency hospitals for women and girls driven crazy with wrecked nerves from your gibberish about Jesus?— I put it to you again: Where do you get that stuff? What do you know about Jesus?

Go ahead and bust all the chairs you want to. Smash a whole wagon-load of furniture at every performance. Turn sixty somersaults and stand on your nutty head. If it wasn't for the way you scare the women and kids I'd feel sorry for you and pass the hat.

I like to watch a good four-flusher work, but not when he starts people puking and calling for the doctors.

I like a man that's got nerve and can pull off a great original performance, but you — you're only a bughouse pedlar of second-hand gospel — you're only shoving out a phoney imitation of the goods this Jesus wanted free as air and sunlight.

You tell people living in shanties Jesus is going to fix it up all right with them by giving them mansions in the skies after they're dead and the worms have eaten 'em.

You tell $6 a week department store girls all they need is Jesus; you take a steel trust wop, dead without having lived, grey and shrunken at forty years of age, and you tell him to look at Jesus on the cross and he'll be all right.

You tell poor people they don't need any more money on pay day and even if it's fierce to be out of a job, Jesus'll fix that up all right, all right — all they gotta do is take Jesus the way you say.

I'm telling you Jesus wouldn't stand for the stuff you're handing out. Jesus played it different. The bankers and lawyers of Jerusalem got their sluggers and murderers to go after Jesus just because Jesus wouldn't play their game. He didn't sit in with the big thieves.

I don't want a lot of gab from a bunkshooter in my religion.

I won't take my religion from any man who never works except with his mouth and never cherishes any memory except the face of the woman on the American silver dollar.   20

I ask you to come through and show me where you're pouring out the blood of your life.

I've been to this suburb of Jerusalem they call Golgotha, where they nailed Him, and I know if the story is straight it was real blood ran from His hands and the nail-holes, and it was real blood spurted in red drops where the spear of the Roman soldier rammed in between the ribs of this Jesus of Nazareth.

1914

The Harbor

"Poems," Sandburg has said, "are the results of moods. I don't approach a subject in the same mood every day." A comparison between the picture of Chicago given here and that presented in "Chicago" shows how the poet's mood determines what details he will present. Here, instead of being lusty and gay, the city is cramped and tragic. The confinement of its walls and the bafflement of its inhabitants are set off against the lack of restraint and the freedom of the open sky. In one mood, at any rate, Sandburg saw the city as something evil and frustrating—something opposed to the goodness of unspoiled nature.

Passing through huddled and ugly walls
By doorways where women
Looked from their hunger-deep eyes,
Haunted with shadows of hunger-hands,
Out from the huddled and ugly walls,
I came sudden, at the city's edge,
On a blue burst of lake,
Long lake waves breaking under the sun
On a spray-flung curve of shore;
And a fluttering storm of gulls,   10
Masses of great gray wings
And flying white bellies
Veering and wheeling free in the open.

1916

I Am the People, the Mob

This poem comes as near as anything Sandburg has written to expressing one of the poet's most important beliefs. Here is a positive statement of his remedy for the evils he sees in the world of his day—a realization, on the part of the people, of their needs and their own power to supply them.

I am the people — the mob — the crowd — the mass.
Do you know that all the great work of the world is done through me?
I am the workingman, the inventor, the maker of the world's food and clothes.
I am the audience that witnesses history. The Napoleons come from me and the Lincolns.
They die. And then I send forth more Napoleons and Lincolns.
I am the seed ground. I am a prairie that will stand for much plowing. Terrible storms pass over me. I

forget. The best of me is sucked out and wasted. I forget. Everything but Death comes to me and makes me work and give up what I have. And I forget.
Sometimes I growl, shake myself and spatter a few red drops for history to remember. Then — I forget.
When I, the People, learn to remember, when I, the People, use the lessons of yesterday and no longer forget who robbed me last year, who played me for a fool,— then there will be no speaker in all the world say the name: "The People," with any fleck of a sneer in his voice or any far-off smile of derision.
The mob — the crowd — the mass — will arrive then.

1916

Prairie

"Ostensibly," writes Harry Hansen, "he [Sandburg] was of the city, but the great wide prairie was close at hand; he was to grow up with the music of the wind through its corn fields in his ears; like the young Lincoln he was to tread the furrows of rich, black loam and feel the soft grass of the meadow lands under his bare feet." This song expresses his kinship, his affection.

More than the preceding poems in this text, this poem shows Sandburg's considerable indebtedness to Whitman. Not only are the phrasings and rhythms similar, but the mood is Whitmanesque. Perhaps this is because Sandburg here is praising the vast American landscape, the joy of work, and the brotherhood of man. There is a difference, however, which is rather hard to define. Perhaps the most important fact is that Sandburg worked a great deal in the fields before he wrote about them, and his experience gave his poem somewhat more particularity than a typical poem by Whitman about farming.

I was born on the prairie and the milk of its wheat, the red of its clover, the eyes of its women, gave me a song and a slogan.

Here the water went down, the icebergs slid with gravel, the gaps and the valleys hissed, and the black loam came, and the yellow sandy loam.

Here between the sheds of the Rocky Mountains and the Appalachians, here now a morning star fixes a fire sign over the timber claims and cow pastures, the corn belt, the cotton belt, the cattle ranches.

Here the gray geese go five hundred miles and back with a wind under their wings honking the cry for a new home.

Here I know I will hanker after nothing so much as one more sunrise or a sky moon of fire doubled to a river moon of water.

The prairie sings to me in the forenoon and I know in the night I rest easy in the prairie arms, on the prairie heart.

•   •   •

After the sunburn of the day
handling a pitchfork at a hayrack,
after the eggs and biscuit and coffee,
the pearl-gray haystacks   10
in the gloaming
are cool prayers
to the harvest hands.

In the city among the walls the overland passenger train is choked and the pistons hiss and the wheels curse.
On the Prairie the overland flits on phantom wheels and the sky and the soil between them muffle the pistons and cheer the wheels.

•   •   •

I am here when the cities are gone.
I am here before the cities come.
I nourished the lonely men on horses.
I will keep the laughing men who ride iron.
I am dust of men.   20

The running water babbled to the deer, the cottontail, the gopher.
You came in wagons, making streets and schools,
Kin of the ax and rifle, kin of the plow and horse,
Singing *Yankee Doodle, Old Dan Tucker, Turkey in the Straw,*

You in the coonskin cap at a log house door hearing a lone wolf howl,
You at a sod house door reading the blizzards and chinooks let loose from Medicine Hat,
I am dust of your dust, as I am brother and mother
To the copper faces, the worker in flint and clay,
The singing women and their sons a thousand years ago
Marching single file the timber and the plain.   30

I hold the dust of these amid changing stars.
I last while old wars are fought, while peace broods mother-like,
While new wars arise and the fresh killings of young men.
I fed the boys who went to France in great dark days.
Appomattox is a beautiful word to me and so is Valley Forge and the Marne and Verdun,
I who have seen the red births and the red deaths
Of sons and daughters, I take peace or war, I say nothing and wait.

Have you seen a red sunset drip over one of my cornfields, the shore of night stars, the wave lines of dawn up a wheat valley?
Have you heard my threshing crews yelling in the chaff of a strawpile and the running wheat of the wagonboards, my cornhuskers, my harvest hands hauling crops, singing dreams of women, worlds, horizons?

•   •   •

Rivers cut a path on flat lands.   40
The mountains stand up.
The salt oceans press in
And push on the coast lines.
The sun, the wind, bring rain
And I know what the rainbow writes across
the east or west in a half-circle:
A love-letter pledge to come again.

•   •   •

Towns on the Soo Line,
Towns on the Big Muddy,
Laugh at each other for cubs
And tease as children.   50

Omaha and Kansas City, Minneapolis and St. Paul, sisters
    in a house together, throwing slang, growing up.
Towns in the Ozarks, Dakota wheat towns, Wichita,
    Peoria, Buffalo, sisters throwing slang, growing up.

        • • •

Out of prairie-brown grass crossed with a streamer of
    wigwam smoke — out of a smoke pillar, a blue
    promise — out of wild ducks woven in greens and
    purples —
Here I saw a city rise and say to the peoples round
    world: Listen, I am strong, I know what I want.
Out of log houses and stumps — canoes stripped from
    tree-sides — flatboats coaxed with an ax from the
    timber claims — in the years when the red and the
    white men met — the houses and streets rose.

A thousand red men cried and went away to new places
    for corn and women: a million white men came and
    put up skyscrapers, threw out rails and wires, feelers
    to the salt sea: now the smokestacks bite the skyline
    with stub teeth.

In an early year the call of a wild duck woven in greens
    and purples: now the riveter's chatter, the police
    patrol, the song-whistle of the steamboat.

To a man across a thousand years I offer a handshake.
I say to him: Brother, make the story short, for the stretch
    of a thousand years is short.

        • • •

What brothers these in the dark?   60
What eaves of skyscrapers against a smoke moon?
These chimneys shaking on the lumber shanties
When the coal boats plow by on the river —
The hunched shoulders of the grain elevators —
The flame sprockets of the sheet steel mills
And the men in the rolling mills with their shirts off
Playing their flesh arms against the twisting wrists of
    steel:
            what brothers these
            in the dark
            of a thousand years?   70

        • • •

A headlight searches a snowstorm.
A funnel of white light shoots from over the pilot of the
    Pioneer Limited crossing Wisconsin.

In the morning hours, in the dawn,
The sun puts out the stars of the sky
And the headlight of the Limited train.

The fireman waves his hand to a country school teacher
    on a bobsled.
A boy, yellow hair, red scarf and mittens, on the bobsled,
    in his lunch box a pork chop sandwich and a V of
    gooseberry pie.

The horses fathom a snow to their knees.
Snow hats are on the rolling prairie hills.
The Mississippi bluffs wear snow hats.   80

        • • •

Keep your hogs on changing corn and mashes of grain,
    O farmerman.
    Cram their insides till they waddle on short legs
    Under the drums of bellies, hams of fat.
    Kill your hogs with a knife slit under the ear.
    Hack them with cleavers.
    Hang them with hooks in the hind legs.

        • • •

A wagonload of radishes on a summer morning.
Sprinkles of dew on the crimson-purple balls.
The farmer on the seat dangles the reins on the rumps of
    dapple-gray horses.   90
The farmer's daughter with a basket of eggs dreams of a
    new hat to wear to the county fair.

        • • •

On the left- and right-hand side of the road,
         Marching corn —
I saw it knee high weeks ago — now it is head high —
    tassels of red silk creep at the ends of the ears.

        • • •

I am the prairie, mother of men, waiting.
They are mine, the threshing crews eating beefsteak,
    the farmboys driving steers to the railroad cattle
    pens.

They are mine, the crowds of people at a Fourth of July basket picnic, listening to a lawyer read the Declaration of Independence, watching the pinwheels and Roman candles at night, the young men and women two by two hunting the bypaths and kissing bridges.

They are mine, the horses looking over a fence in the frost of late October saying good-morning to the horses hauling wagons of rutabaga to market.

They are mine, the old zigzag rail fences, the new barb wire.

. . .

The cornhuskers wear leather on their hands.   100
There is no let-up to the wind.
Blue bandannas are knotted at the ruddy chins.

Falltime and winter apples take on the smolder of the five-o'clock November sunset: falltime, leaves, bonfires, stubble, the old things go, and the earth is grizzled.

The land and the people hold memories, even among the anthills and the angleworms, among the toads and woodroaches — among gravestone writings rubbed out by the rain — they keep old things that never grow old.

The frost loosens corn husks.
The sun, the rain, the wind
          loosen corn husks.
The men and women are helpers.
They are all cornhuskers together.
I see them late in the western evening   110
          in a smoke-red dust.

. . .

The phantom of a yellow rooster flaunting a scarlet comb, on top of a dung pile crying hallelujah to the streaks of daylight,
The phantom of an old hunting dog nosing in the underbrush for muskrats, barking at a coon in a treetop at midnight, chewing a bone, chasing his tail round a corncrib,
The phantom of an old workhorse taking the steel point of a plow across a forty-acre field in spring, hitched to a harrow in summer, hitched to a wagon among cornshocks in fall,

These phantoms come into the talk and wonder of people on the front porch of a farmhouse late summer nights.
"The shapes that are gone are here," said an old man with a cob pipe in his teeth one night in Kansas with a hot wind on the alfalfa.

. . .

Look at six eggs
In a mockingbird's nest.

Listen to six mockingbirds
Flinging follies of O-be-joyful   120
Over the marshes and uplands.

Look at songs
Hidden in eggs.

. . .

When the morning sun is on the trumpet-vine blossoms, sing at the kitchen pans: Shout All Over God's Heaven.
When the rain slants on the potato hills and the sun plays a silver shaft on the last shower, sing to the bush at the backyard fence: Mighty Lak a Rose.
When the icy sleet pounds on the storm windows and the house lifts to a great breath, sing for the outside hills: The Ole Sheep Done Know the Road, the Young Lambs Must Find the Way.

. . .

Spring slips back with a girl face calling always: "Any new songs for me? Any new songs?"

O prairie girl, be lonely, singing, dreaming, waiting — your lover comes — your child comes — the years creep with toes of April rain on new-turned sod.
O prairie girl, whoever leaves you only crimson poppies to talk with, whoever puts a good-by kiss on your lips and never comes back —
There is a song deep as the falltime redhaws, long as the layer of black loam we go to, the shine of the morning star over the corn belt, the wave line of dawn up a wheat valley.   130

O prairie mother, I am one of your boys.
I have loved the prairie as a man with a heart shot full
    of pain over love.   130
Here I know I will hanker after nothing so much as one
    more sunrise or a sky moon of fire doubled to a
    river moon of water.

• • •

I speak of new cities and new people.
I tell you the past is a bucket of ashes.
I tell you yesterday is a wind gone down, a sun dropped
    in the west.
I tell you there is nothing in the world only an ocean of
    to-morrows, a sky of to-morrows.

I am a brother of the cornhuskers who say at sun-
    down:
        To-morrow is a day.

                              1918

Cool Tombs

When Abraham Lincoln was shoveled into the tombs,
    he forgot the copperheads and the assassin . . . in
    the dust, in the cool tombs.

And Ulysses Grant lost all thought of con men and Wall
    Street, cash and collateral turned ashes . . . in the
    dust, in the cool tombs.

Pocahontas' body, lovely as a poplar, sweet as a red haw
    in November or a pawpaw in May, did she wonder?
    does she remember? . . . in the dust, in the cool
    tombs?

Take any streetful of people buying clothes and groceries,
    cheering a hero or throwing confetti and blowing
    tin horns . . . tell me if the lovers are losers . . .
    tell me if any get more than the lovers . . . in the
    dust . . . in the cool tombs.

                              1918

A. E. F.

In 1920, when this poem was written, many authors were expressing, as Sandburg does here, their belief that World War I had been futile. The reverie-like quietness of this poem makes it rather more impressive than some of the more strident announcements of the same idea. So, too, does the contrast of the final slangy clause with the different kind of language in the earlier lines. The slangy advice to the spider, coming in a climactic phrase at the conclusion, forcefully summarizes the poet's ironic feeling about the war.

There will be a rusty gun on the wall, sweetheart,
The rifle grooves curling with flakes of rust.
A spider will make a silver string nest in the darkest,
    warmest corner of it.
The trigger and the range-finder, they too will be rusty.
And no hands will polish the gun, and it will hang on
    the wall.
Forefingers and thumbs will point absently and casually
    toward it.
It will be spoken among half-forgotten, wished-to-be-
    forgotten things.
They will tell the spider: Go on, you're doing good work.
                            1920

From

The People, Yes

In his fifty-ninth year, Sandburg published a book-long poem made up pretty largely of the sayings and tales of the people—"stories and psalms nobody would laugh at," but which represent the unending quest of the masses for happiness and truth. Sandburg thus developed in detail a theme which he had stated in a brief poem, "I Am the People, the Mob," in 1916.

The following are two excerpts from **The People, Yes.** The first collects some of the yarns produced by the folk of America, many of them exaggerations of a sort long popular in American comic humor. The second tells of one of the great American folk heroes, Paul Bunyan, the creation of the loggers, whose biography has been presented notably by Esther Shephard in **Paul Bunyan**. Both represent the modern tendency to embody folklore in literature.

THEY HAVE YARNS

They have yarns
Of a skyscraper so tall they had to put hinges
On the two top stories so to let the moon go by,
Of one corn crop in Missouri when the roots
Went so deep and drew off so much water
The Mississippi riverbed that year was dry,
Of pancakes so thin they only had one side,
Of "a fog so thick we shingled the barn and six feet out
    on the fog,"
Of Pecos Pete straddling a cyclone in Texas and riding
    it to the west coast where "it rained out under him,"
Of the man who drove a swarm of bees across the Rocky
    Mountains and the Desert "and didn't lose a
    bee,"   10
Of a mountain railroad curve where the engineer in his
    cab can touch the caboose and spit in the con-
    ductor's eye,
Of the boy who climbed a cornstalk growing so fast he
    would have starved to death if they hadn't shot bis-
    cuits up to him,
Of the old man's whiskers: "When the wind was with
    him his whiskers arrived a day before he did,"
Of the hen laying a square egg and cackling "Ouch!" and
    of hens laying eggs with the dates printed on them,
Of the ship captain's shadow: it froze to the deck one
    cold winter night,
Of mutineers on that same ship put to chipping rust
    with rubber hammers,
Of the sheep counter who was fast and accurate: "I just
    count their feet and divide by four,"
Of the man so tall he must climb a ladder to shave him-
    self,
Of the runt so teeny-weeny it takes two men and a boy
    to see him,
Of mosquitoes: one can kill a dog, two of them a man,   20

Of a cyclone that sucked cookstoves out of the kitchen,
    up the chimney flue, and on to the next town,
Of the same cyclone picking up wagon-tracks in Ne-
    braska and dropping them over in the Dakotas,
Of the hook-and-eye snake unlocking itself into forty
    pieces, each piece two inches long, then in nine
    seconds flat snapping itself together again,
Of the watch swallowed by the cow — when they butch-
    ered her a year later the watch was running and
    had the correct time,
Of horned snakes, hoop snakes that roll themselves where
    they want to go, and rattlesnakes carrying bells
    instead of rattles on their tails,
Of the herd of cattle in California getting lost in a giant
    redwood tree that had hollowed out,
Of the man who killed a snake by putting its tail in its
    mouth so it swallowed itself,
Of railroad trains whizzing along so fast they reach the
    station before the whistle,

---

2 **skyscraper so tall.** The structure so tall that hinges are needed to protect the moon and the sun turns up frequently in American folklore. Captain Stormalong, hero of New England tall tales, built a mast with such an arrangement, according to Charles Edward Brown's **Old Stormalong Yarns.** Paul Bunyan built an oil rig with a similar arrangement, according to John Lee Brooks' "Paul Bunyan, Oil Man" in **Follow de Drinkin' Gou'd** • 9 **Pecos Pete,** or Pecos Bill (the name usually given him in Texas windies), thus busted a cyclone. See Edward O'Reilly, "The Saga of Pecos Bill," **Century,** October 1923 • 10 **swarm of bees.** The boast about herding the swarm of bees occurs in the play **Lightnin'** (1918) by Winchell Smith and Frank Bacon • 12 **the boy . . . cornstalk.** This story is told of Paul Bunyan's handy man, Swede Charlie, in Ida Turney's "The Scissorbills" in **Paul Bunyan Marches On** • 15 **ship captain's shadow.** In Mark Twain's **Following the Equator,** Chap. 26, the ship's mate had this difficulty with his shadow on an arctic voyage • 20 **mosquitoes.** Sandburg may be recalling the mosquitoes described by a steamboat mate, Mr. H., in Chap. 34 of Mark Twain's **Life on the Mississippi.** If so, he errs in his statistics. Says Twain of Mr. H.: "He said that two of them could whip a dog, and that four of them could hold a man down . . . 'butcher' him." Mr. Sandburg appears to be exaggerating somewhat • 25 **horned snakes.** Sandburg may have confused these with "horn-snakes," which are described in H. E. Taliaferro's **Fisher's River Scenes and Characters.** This snake, as described by Uncle Davy, an eyewitness, was ten feet long, had a head as big as a saucer, and had a stinger in his tail which was "six inches long and sharp as a needle." "This snake," said Uncle Davy, "he cotched the eend uv his tail in his mouth, he did, and come rollin' down the mounting . . . jist like a hoop." The snake landed, by chance, so that his stinger caught in a tree, and soon the tree was "dead as a herrin'; all the leaves was wilted like a fire had gone through its branches." This happened in North Carolina

Of pigs so thin the farmer had to tie knots in their tails
    to keep them from crawling through the cracks in
    their pens,
Of Paul Bunyan's big blue ox, Babe, measuring between
    the eyes forty-two ax-handles and a plug of Star
    tobacco exactly,   30
Of John Henry's hammer and the curve of its swing
    and his singing of it as "a rainbow round my
    shoulder."

    "Do tell!"
    "I want to know!"
    "You don't say so!" ·
    "For the land's sake!"
    "Gosh all fish-hooks!"
    "Tell me some more.
    I don't believe a word you say
    but I love to listen
    to your sweet harmonica   40
    to your chin-music.
    Your fish stories hang together
    when they're just a pack of lies:
    you ought to have a leather medal:
    you ought to have a statue
    carved of butter: you deserve
    a large bouquet of turnips."

"Yessir," the traveler drawled,
"Away out there in the petrified forest
everything goes on the same as usual.   50
The petrified birds sit in their petrified nests
and hatch their petrified young from petrified eggs."

A high pressure salesman jumped off the Brooklyn Bridge
    and was saved by a policeman. But it didn't take
    him long to sell the idea to the policeman. So to-
    gether they jumped off the bridge.

One of the oil men in heaven started a rumor of a gusher
    down in hell. All the other oil men left in a hurry
    for hell. As he gets to thinking about the rumor he
    had started he says to himself there might be some-
    thing in it after all. So he leaves for hell in a hurry.

"The number 42 will win this raffle, that's my number."
    And when he won they asked him whether he

guessed the number or had a system. He said he had
a system, "I took up the old family album and there
on page 7 was my grandfather and grandmother
both on page 7. I said to myself this is easy for 7
times 7 is the number that will win and 7 times 7
is 42."

Once a shipwrecked sailor caught hold of a stateroom
door and floated for hours till friendly hands from
out of the darkness threw him a rope. And he called
across the night, "What country is this?" and hearing voices answer, "New Jersey," he took a fresh
hold on the floating stateroom door and called back
half-wearily, "I guess I'll float a little farther."

An Ohio man bundled up the tin roof of a summer
    kitchen and sent it to a motor car maker with a com-
    plaint of his car not giving service. In three weeks
    a new car arrived for him and a letter: "We regret
    delay in shipment but your car was received in a very
    bad order."
A Dakota cousin of this Ohio man sent six years of tin
    can accumulations to the same works, asking them
    to overhaul his car. Two weeks later came a rebuilt
    car, five old tin cans, and a letter: "We are also
    forwarding you five parts not necessary in our new
    model."
Thus fantasies heard at filling stations in the midwest.
    Another relates to a Missouri mule who took aim
    with his heels at an automobile rattling by. The car
    turned a somersault, lit next a fence, ran right along
    through a cornfield till it came to a gate, moved
    onto the road and went on its way as though nothing
    had happened. The mule heehawed with desolation,
    "What's the use?"
Another tells of a farmer and his family stalled on a rail-
    road crossing, how they jumped out in time to see

---

30 **blue ox, Babe,** a wonderful animal, very helpful on logging
operations. Babe could pull great sleds of logs, could pile lumber
with his tail, and make himself useful in many other ways • 31
John Henry, folk hero of the Negroes, was a great steel-driver. He
died in a steel-driving contest with a machine. See p. 262 and also
"John Henry of the Cape Fear," in **Bundles of Troubles and Other
Tarheel Tales** • 49 **the petrified forest,** a forest in Yellowstone
Park apparently discovered by Jim Bridger. See J. Cecil Alter, **James
Bridger.** One of the most remarkable facts about this forest was
that there the law of gravity was petrified

a limited express knock it into flinders, the farmer calling, "Well, I always did say that car was no shucks in a real pinch." 60

When the Masonic Temple in Chicago was the tallest building in the United States west of New York, two men who would cheat the eyes out of you if you gave 'em a chance, took an Iowa farmer to the top of the building and asked him, "How is this for high?" They told him that for $25 they would go down in the basement and turn the building around on its turn-table for him while he stood on the roof and saw how this seventh wonder of the world worked. He handed them $25. They went. He waited. They never came back.

This is told in Chicago as a folk tale, the same as the legend of Mrs. O'Leary's cow kicking over the barn lamp that started the Chicago fire, when the Georgia visitor, Robert Toombs, telegraphed an Atlanta crony, "Chicago is on fire, the whole city burning down, God be praised!"

Nor is the prize sleeper Rip Van Winkle and his scolding wife forgotten, nor the headless horseman scooting through Sleepy Hollow

Nor the sunken treasure-ships in coves and harbors, the hideouts of gold and silver sought by Coronado, nor the Flying Dutchman rounding the Cape doomed to nevermore pound his ear nor ever again take a snooze for himself

Nor the sailor's caretaker Mother Carey seeing to it that every seafaring man in the afterworld has a seabird to bring him news of ships and women, an albatross for the admiral, a gull for the deckhand

Nor the sailor with a sweetheart in every port of the world, nor the ships that set out with flying colors and all the promises you could ask, the ships never heard of again,

Nor Jim Liverpool, the riverman who could jump across any river and back without touching land he was that quick on his feet,

Nor Mike Fink along the Ohio and the Mississippi, half wild horse and half cock-eyed alligator, the rest of him snags and snapping turtle. "I can out-run, out-jump, out-shoot, out-brag, out-drink, and out-fight, rough and tumble, no holts barred, any man on both

sides of the river from Pittsburgh to New Orleans and back again to St. Louis. My trigger finger itches and I want to go redhot. War, famine and bloodshed puts flesh on my bones, and hardship's my daily bread."

Nor the man so lean he threw no shadow: six rattlesnakes struck at him at one time and every one missed him.

WHO MADE PAUL BUNYAN?

Who made Paul Bunyan, who gave him birth as a myth, who joked him into life as the Master Lumberjack, who fashioned him forth as an apparition easing the hours of men amid axes and trees, saws and lumber? The people, the bookless people, they made Paul and had him alive long before he got into the books for those who read. He grew up in shanties, around the hot stoves of winter, among socks and mittens drying, in the smell of tobacco smoke and the roar of laughter mocking the outside weather. And some of Paul came overseas in wooden bunks below decks in sailing vessels. And some of Paul is old as the hills, young as the alphabet. 70

The Pacific Ocean froze over in the winter of the Blue Snow and Paul Bunyan had long teams of oxen hauling regular white snow over from China. This was the winter Paul gave a party to the Seven Axmen. Paul fixed a granite floor sunk two hundred feet deep for them to dance on. Still, it tipped and tilted as the dance went on. And because the Seven Axmen refused to take off their hob-nailed boots, the sparks from the nails of their dancing feet lit up the place so that Paul didn't light the kerosene lamps. No women being on the Big Onion river at that time the Seven Axmen had to dance with each other, the one left over in each set taking Paul as a partner. The commotion of the dancing that night brought on an earthquake and the Big Onion river moved over three counties to the east.

---

64 hideouts . . . silver. See J. Frank Dobie, Coronado's Children, for some of these legends • 68 Mike Fink (1770?-1823) was a boastful and brash ranger, keelboatman, and trapper. The remarks quoted are one of his boasts. See Walter Blair and F. J. Meine, Mike Fink

One year when it rained from St. Patrick's Day till the Fourth of July, Paul Bunyan got disgusted because his celebration of the Fourth was spoiled. He dived into Lake Superior and swam to where a solid pillar of water was coming down. He dived under this pillar, swam up into it and climbed with powerful swimming strokes, was gone about an hour, came splashing down, and as the rain stopped, he explained, "I turned the dam thing off." This is told in the Big North Woods and on the Great Lakes, with many particulars.

Two mosquitoes lighted on one of Paul Bunyan's oxen, killed it, ate it, cleaned the bones, and sat on a grub shanty picking their teeth as Paul came along. Paul sent to Australia for two special bumble bees to kill these mosquitoes. But the bees and the mosquitoes intermarried; their children had stingers on both ends. And things kept getting worse till Paul brought a big boatload of sorghum up from Louisiana and while all the bee-mosquitoes were eating at the sweet sorghum he floated them down to the Gulf of Mexico. They got so fat that it was easy to drown them all between New Orleans and Galveston.

Paul logged on the Little Gimlet in Oregon one winter. The cook stove at that camp covered an acre of ground. They fastened the side of a hog on each snowshoe and four men used to skate on the griddle while the cook flipped the pancakes. The eating table was three miles long; elevators carried the cakes to the ends of the table where boys on bicycles rode back and forth on a path down the center of the table dropping the cakes where called for.

Benny, the Little Blue Ox of Paul Bunyan, grew two feet every time Paul looked at him, when a youngster. The barn was gone one morning and they found it on Benny's back; he grew out of it in a night. One night he kept pawing and bellowing for more pancakes, till there were two hundred men at the cook shanty stove trying to keep him fed. About breakfast time Benny broke loose, tore down the cook shanty, ate all the pancakes piled up for the loggers' breakfast. And after that Benny made his mistake; he ate the red hot stove; and that finished him. This is only one of the hot stove stories told in the North Woods.

1935·1936

From

Abraham Lincoln: The Prairie Years

When Abraham Lincoln: The Prairie Years, Sandburg's first biographical work, appeared in 1926, some critics mentioned that they were surprised to find that a poet could write history so well. But there was no need for surprise, for the biography was very much of a piece with Sandburg's earlier writings. The background of the book was that of the author who had sung, "O prairie mother, I am one of your boys"; and much of it was a re-creation of a way of living that was common to Lincoln and his biographer. Of course, a great deal of research had been necessary, but it had been a sort of study particularly likely to appeal to Sandburg. Much of it had been concerned with the prairie folk of Lincoln's day—their ways of working, their religious beliefs, their songs, their superstitions, their yarns and jests, their proverbs. Other research had uncovered details about the man who, more than any other, seemed to Sandburg representative of the finest qualities of common Americans.

The book, therefore, was in a sense a poem about Lincoln and the America in which he had his roots. And as in other poems, Sandburg selected, marshaled, and voiced his facts to give them emotional impact. The following passage, though it says relatively little about Lincoln's prairie background, shows how the author turned mundane facts into rather stirring prose poetry.

LINCOLN AT THIRTY-SEVEN

The thirty-seven-year-old son of Thomas Lincoln and Nancy Hanks Lincoln had changed with a changing western world. His feet had worn deerskin moccasins as a boy; they were put into rawhide boots when he was full-grown; now he had them in dressed calf leather. His head-cover was a coonskin cap when he was a boy, and all men and boys wore the raccoon tail as a high head-piece; floating down the Mississippi to New Orleans he wore a black felt hat from an eastern factory and it held the post-office mail of New Salem; now he was a prominent politician and lawyer wearing a tall, stiff, silk hat known as a "stovepipe," also called a "plug hat."

In this "stovepipe" hat he carried letters, newspaper clippings, deeds, mortgages, checks, receipts. Once he apologized to a client for not replying to a letter; he had bought a new hat and in cleaning out the old hat he missed this particular letter. The silk stovepipe hat was nearly a foot high, with a brim only an inch or so in width; it was a high, lean, longish hat and it made Lincoln look higher, leaner, more longish.

As he had gone along farther in law practice and politics, he had taken more care of his looks. His first partner, John T. Stuart, was one of the handsomest figures and best-dressed men in Springfield; and Lincoln had to take Stuart's place once in a courthouse near Springfield, handling a case for a client; when Lincoln introduced himself as the man sent by Stuart to take Stuart's place, the client, an Englishman accustomed to wigs and gowns in a courtroom, refused to take Lincoln as his lawyer, snorted with disgust, and hired another lawyer.

And though Lincoln had begun wearing broadcloth and white shirts with a white collar and black silk cravat, and a suggestion of sideburns coming down three-fourths the length of his ears, he was still known as one of the carelessly dressed men of Springfield, along with Stephen Logan, who wore unbleached cotton shirts and had sat two years as a circuit-court judge wearing an unbleached cotton shirt with no cravat or stock.

The loose bones of Lincoln were hard to keep neat; trousers go baggy at the knees of a story-teller who has the habit, at the end of a story, where the main laugh comes in, of putting his arms around his knees, raising his knees to his chin, and rocking to and fro. Those who spoke of his looks often mentioned his trousers creeping to the ankles and higher; his rumpled hair, his wrinkled vest. When he wasn't away making speeches, electioneering or practicing law on the circuit, he cut kindling wood, tended to the cordwood for the stoves in the house,

milked the cow, gave her a few forks of hay and changed her straw bedding every day.

He analyzed the tariff, the national banks, the public lands, and the annexation of Texas, while pailing a cow. One evening he went to where his cow was pastured with other cows, and as he told it: "I found the calves all together and away from the cows, and I didn't know my calf well enough to distinguish her from the others. Still, I picked out one that I thought was mine. Presently that identical calf went and sucked my cow, and then I knew it was mine."

He looked like a farmer, it was often said; he seemed to have come from prairies and barns rather than city streets and barber shops; and in his own way he admitted and acknowledged it; he told voters from the stump that it was only a few years since he had worn buckskin breeches and they shrank in the rain and crept to his knees leaving the skin blue and bare. The very words that came off his lips in tangled important discussions among lawyers had a wilderness air and a log-cabin smack. The way he pronounced the word "idea" was more like "idee," the word "really" more like a drawled Kentucky "ra-a-ly."

As he strode or shambled into a gathering of men, he stood out as a special figure for men to look at; it was a little as though he had come farther on harder roads and therefore had longer legs for the traveling; and a little as though he had been where life is stripped to its naked facts and it would be useless for him to try to put on certain pretenses of civilization. He may have figured out for himself about how far he could go and find it easy and healthy and comfortable for him to be in speech and looks the Indiana cornhusker and the Mississippi River flatboatman. The manners of a gentleman and a scholar dropped off him sometimes like a cloak, and his speech was that of a farmer who works his own farm, or a lawyer who pails a cow morning and evening and might refer to it incidentally in polite company or in a public address. He was not embarrassed, and nobody else was embarrassed, when at the Bowling Green funeral he had stood up and, instead of delivering a formal funeral address on the character of the deceased, had shaken with grief and put a handkerchief to his face and wept tears, and motioned to the body-bearers to take his dead friend away. There was a natural grace to it; funerals should be so conducted; a man who loves a dead man should stand up and try to speak and find himself overwhelmed with grief so that instead of speaking he smothers his face in a handkerchief and weeps. This was the eloquence of naked fact beyond which there is no eloquence.

At the death of a great friend he could weep without shame, lone and inevitable; at a petty campaign lie alluding to his aristocratic relatives visiting him, he could laugh and say that only one had made a visit and he was arrested for stealing a jew's-harp. He could be immensely solemn, tenderly grave, quizzically humorous, and flatly comic. As he strode or shambled into a gathering of men, he stood out as a special figure to look at; some of the range of his feeling, the gamut of the solemn and comic, was registered in the angles of his body, in the sweeping lengths of extra long arms and legs, in the panther slouch of running and throwing muscles, in the wiry, rawbone frame that seemed to have been at home once handling an ax in tall timber, with the silent silhouette of an eagle watching.

Standing, Lincoln loomed tall with his six feet, four inches of height; sitting in a chair he looked no taller than other men, except that his knees rose higher than the level of the seat of the chair. Seated on a low chair or bench he seemed to be crouching. The shoulders were stooped and rounded, the head bent forward and turned downward; shirt-collars were a loose fit; an Adam's apple stood out on a scrawny neck; his voice was a tenor that carried song-tunes poorly but had clear and appealing modulations in his speeches; in rare moments of excitement it rose to a startling and unforgettable falsetto tone that carried every syllable with unmistakable meaning. In the stoop of his shoulders and the forward bend of his head there was a grace and familiarity so that it was easy for shorter people to look up into his face and talk with him.

The mouth and eyes, and the facial muscles running back from the mouth and eyes, masked a thousand shades of meaning. In hours of melancholy, when poisons of dejection dragged him, the underlip and its muscles drooped; his friends felt either that he then was a sick man with a disorder of bile and secretions or else that his thoughts roamed in farther and darker caverns than ordinary men ventured into. Ordinarily there was a fresh, gracious calm; it was a grave, sad calm, perhaps gloomy, but strong with foundations resting on substrata of granite; a mouth shaped with depths of hope that its fixed resolves would be kept and held. And between this solemn mouth of Lincoln and at the other end of the gamut, his comic mouth, there was the play of a thousand shades of meaning. Besides being tragedian, he was comedian. Across the mask of his dark gravity could come a light-ray of the quizzical, the puzzled. This could spread into the beginning of a smile and then spread farther into wrinkles and wreaths of laughter that lit the whole face into a glow; and it was of the quality of his highest laughter that it traveled through his whole frame, currents of it vitalizing his toes.

A fine chiseling of lines on the upper lip seemed to be some continuation of the bridge of the nose, forming a feature that ended in a dimple at the point of the chin. The nose was large; if it had been a trifle larger he would have been called big-nosed; it was a nose for breathing deep sustained breaths of air, a strong shapely nose, granitic with resolve and patience. Two deepening wrinkles started from the sides of the right and left nostrils and ran down the outer rims of the upper lip; farther out on the two cheeks were deepening wrinkles that had been long crude dimples when he was a boy; hours of toil, pain, and laughter were deepening these wrinkles. From the sides of the nose, angular cheek-bones branched right and left toward the large ears, forming a base for magnificently constructed eye-sockets. Bushy black eyebrows shaded the sockets where the eyeballs rested with gray transformers of action, thought, laughter. Shaded into the gray of his eyes was a tinting of hazel. In his eyes as nowhere else was registered the shifting light of his moods; their language ran from rapid twinkles of darting hazel that won the hearts of children on to a fixed baffling gray that the shrewdest lawyers and politicians could not read, to find there an intention he wanted to hide.

The thatch of coarse hair on the head was black when seen from a distance, but close up it had a brownish, rough, sandy tint. He had been known to comb it, parting it far on the right side, and slicking it down so that it looked groomed by a somewhat particular man; but most of the time it was loose and rumpled. The comb might have parted it either on the far right or on the far left side; he wasn't particular.

Throughout his life as a grown man he was holding to the hacked-out slants of body that his father had in mind in the younger days when his frame stretched upward in a rapid, uneven growth, and his father said he looked like he needed a carpenter's plane put to him. In those days they had called him "Long Shanks"; and as a

grown man his long shanks were a dominant feature of his physical presence. Yet it was true that men and women as varied as Stephen T. Logan and Hannah Armstrong felt about him something elusive, glancing, elfin, off and beyond all that was told by the gaunt, rambling lines of his physical structure. The eyes, the laughter, the play of words, a scrutinizing, drawling poise, curves that came and went with the tricks of sun-showers and rainbows — he gave out echoes and values. A cherishing of
10 true testimonies ran out from his face and form. All he could do for Bowling Green was to weep; the words had not been made that could tell what he wanted to say in that hour. As the day came near for his marriage to the brilliant, fashionable daughter of a Kentucky bank president, he held odds even by writing an old friend — also of hacked-out and slanted structure — the plain, old dependable, silent, truth-telling John Hanks who could not write his own name: "I hope you will come over; be sure to be on deck by early candlelight." The lizard story
20 might be a rehearsal of a comic pantomime with two players having a line each to speak; and still further it might be a portentous allegory in democratic and religious behavior and words.

When he had bought his house at Eighth and Jackson streets from Rev. Charles Dresser there was a mortgage of $900 on it. And in the deed of title from Dresser to Lincoln this $900 mortgage wasn't mentioned. He trusted Dresser, took a chance on losing $900, just the personal assurance of the preacher who had married him. And the money was later paid in full.

30 It was natural that Abraham Lincoln was many things to many people; some believed him a cunning, designing lawyer and politician who coldly figured all his moves in advance; some believed him a sad, odd, awkward man trying to find a niche in life where his hacked-out frame could have peace and comfort; some believed him a superb human struggler with solemn and comic echoes and values far off and beyond the leashes and bones that held him to earth and law and politics.

40 In his own mind he did not divide people into good people and bad people. As he walked from his own home close to the cornfields near the city limits of Springfield and met people on his way to the courthouse and the post office, and as he watched the two-legged figures on their many errands or, forgetting their errands, moving around the public square, he saw good mixed in the bad and bad mixed in the good.

In his own mind he made the note: "The true rule in determining to embrace or reject anything, is not whether it have any evil in it, but whether it have more of evil
50 than of good. There are few things wholly evil or wholly good. Almost everything is an inseparable compound of the two; so that our best judgment of the preponderance between them is continually demanded."

1926

Vachel Lindsay

1879 · 1931

Better, perhaps, than any recent poet, Vachel Lindsay represented some of the important attitudes of the great Middle West — its agrarianism, its democracy, and its evangelism. Born and reared in Springfield, Illinois, he spent his youth in a city which is the capital of the largely rural state of Illinois. Andrew Jackson, Walt Whitman, and Lincoln were his political idols. From childhood, he was a member of the intensely evangelical Disciples of Christ church. And each of these influences, as well as his work in art, did much to determine the nature of Lindsay's poetry.

Both of Lindsay's parents were Kentuckians whose

thinking had been molded by that of the agrarian South. Each summer, the boy visited his grandparents' farm in Indiana, where he heard the talk of pioneers and farmers. The ideal oratory of his childhood was that of the pulpit, the political stump, and the Fourth of July platform.

Study in the Springfield public schools was followed by work in Hiram College in Ohio. Later he lived in Chicago, studying in the Art Institute (1900-1903) and eking out his meager allowance by working at various part-time jobs. He also studied in the New York School of Art (1904-1905), "drawing architecture, drawing sculpture, trying to draw the Venus of Milo, and imitating the Japanese Prints and Beardsley, and trying to draw like Blake and all such masters."

Lindsay's art work and his thinking next led him into some ventures which seem strange but were definitely in character. Impelled by his faith in art and literature as regenerating forces in American life, he went on tramping trips (1906, 1908, 1912) to various parts of the country, and he made still other tours as a lecturer for the Y.M.C.A. and the Anti-Saloon League. In his travels, he was a sort of lay evangelist, attempting to convert his countrymen to a way of living in which art was important. Some of his experiences were recounted in a volume called *Adventures While Preaching the Gospel of Beauty* (1914).

Vachel Lindsay—self-portrait from The Village Magazine, *1925*

It was during a walking trip from Illinois to New Mexico in 1912 that he composed the poem "General William Booth Enters into Heaven," which, because of the novelty of its material and its form, was to win Lindsay's first national acclaim when it was published in *Poetry,*

the newly founded magazine. *General William Booth Enters into Heaven and Other Poems* was published in 1913; *The Congo and Other Poems,* in 1914; *The Chinese Nightingale and Other Poems,* in 1917; *The Golden Whales of California and Other Rhymes,* in 1920.

Shortly after his first success, Lindsay became a favorite of the lecture platform, one who traveled to every corner of the country. His success, to some extent, was the result of his invention of what he called "the higher vaudeville," devised to convert indifferent audiences to the beauties of poetry. This consisted, as he said, of "elaborate reading . . . reading that comes to the edge of a chant without having the literary meaning crowded by the chant." Some idea of his reading is suggested by marginal notations on a number of his poems, but the best way to learn how he sounded is to listen to records of some of his recitations. His flexible voice and his handling of rhythms gave his poetry unique appeal.

The poems thus presented were typical of the man in several ways. They showed the student of art in their techniques, their images. In the rhythms of country oratory, they set forth myths and folklore. They were frequently the product of the robust imaginative humor of the common man. They preached Lindsay's deeply held convictions—his ethical and religious ideals and the tenets of his political faith. Finally, they mirrored emotions which ranged from bounding exuberance to sadness—emotions which he experienced in alternating moods.

In the end Lindsay wearied of his platform appearances, since he felt that the theatrical quality of his reading obscured not only his message but also his lyrical artistry. His later books of poetry—*Going-to-the-Sun* (1923), *Going-to-the-Stars* and *The Candle in the Cabin* (1926), and *Every Soul Is a Circus* (1929)—which were more lyrical in nature, did not succeed as his earlier works had. Supporting his wife and their two children was almost impossible on his small income. Always subject to occasional fits of melancholia, in his last years he gave way more and more frequently to a feeling of depression. He died by his own hand in 1931.

Collected Poems, Revised and Illustrated Edition (contains poems before 1923; later poems have not been collected), New York, 1925 • A. E. Trombley, Lindsay, Adventurer, Columbia, Missouri, 1929 • E. L. Masters, Vachel Lindsay: A Poet in America, New York, 1935

Proclamations

At the conclusion of his tramping trip of 1912, Lindsay issued a series of proclamations, which were published first in a national magazine, **Farm and Fireside,** and later at the conclusion of **Adventures While Preaching the Gospel of Beauty.** The following two selections touch upon tenets which were to be developed in his prose and poetry during the rest of his career. The first offers rural ways of living and thinking as a substitute for the woeful existence offered by cities. The second urges a reconciliation of "Religion, Equality, and Beauty."

A PROCLAMATION OF BALM IN GILEAD

Go to the fields, O city laborers, till your wounds are healed. Forget the streetcars, the skyscrapers, the slums, the Marseillaise song.

We proclaim to the broken-hearted, still able to labor, the glories of the ploughed land. The harvests are wonderful. And there is a spiritual harvest appearing. A great agricultural flowering of art and song is destined soon to appear. Where corn and wheat are growing, men are singing the psalms of David, not the Marseillaise.

10 You to whom the universe has become a blast-furnace, a coke-oven, a cinder-strewn freight-yard, to whom the history of all ages is a tragedy with the climax now, to whom our democracy and our flag are but playthings of the hypocrite,— turn to the soil, turn to the earth, your mother, and she will comfort you. Rest, be it ever so little, from your black broodings. Think with the farmer once more, as your fathers did. Revere with the farmer our centuries-old civilization, however little it meets the city's trouble. Revere the rural customs that have their
20 roots in the immemorial benefits of nature.

With the farmer look again upon the Constitution as something brought by Providence, prepared for by the ages. Go to church, the cross-roads church, and say the Lord's Prayer again. Help them with their temperance crusade. It is a deeper matter than you think. Listen to the laughter of the farmer's children. Know that not all

the earth is a-weeping. Know that so long as there is black soil deep on the prairie, so long as grass will grow on it, we have a vast green haven.

The roots of some of our trees are still in the earth. 30 Our mountains need not to be moved from their places. Wherever there is tillable land, there is a budding and blooming of old-fashioned Americanism, which the farmer is making splendid for us against the better day.

There is perpetual balm in Gilead, and many city workmen shall turn to it and be healed. This by faith, and a study of the signs, we proclaim!

PROCLAMATION

Of the Coming of Religion, Equality and Beauty

In our new day, so soon upon us, for the first time in the history of Democracy, art and the church shall be hand in hand and equally at our service. Neither craftsman- 40 ship nor prayer shall be purely aristocratic any more, nor at war with each other, nor at war with the State. The priest, the statesman and the singer shall discern one another's work more perfectly and give thanks to God.

Even now our best churches are blossoming in beauty. Our best political life, whatever the howlers may say, is tending toward equality, beauty and holiness.

Political speech will cease to turn only upon the price of grain, but begin considering the price of cross-roads fountains and people's palaces. Our religious life will no 50 longer trouble itself with the squabbles of orthodoxy. It will give us the outdoor choral procession, the ceremony of dedicating the wheat-field or the new-built private house to God. That politician who would benefit the people will not consider all the world wrapped up in the defence or destruction of a tariff schedule. He will serve the public as did Pericles, with the world's greatest dramas. He will rebuild the local Acropolis. He will make his particular Athens rule by wisdom and philosophy, not trade alone. Our crowds shall be audiences, 60 not hurrying mobs; dancers, not brawlers; observers, not restless curiosity-seekers. Our mobs shall become assemblies and our assemblies religious; devout in a subtle sense, equal in privilege and courtesy, delicate of spirit, a perfectly rounded democracy.

All this shall come through the services of three kinds of men in wise coöperation: the priests, the statesmen and the artists. Our priests shall be religious men like

St. Francis, or John Wesley, or General Booth, or Cardinal Newman. They shall be many types, but supreme of their type.

Our statesmen shall find their exemplars and their inspiration in Washington, Jefferson and Lincoln, as all good Americans devoutly desire.

But even these cannot ripen the land without the work of men as versatile as William Morris or Leonardo. Our artists shall fuse the work of these other workers, and
10 give expression to the whole cry and the whole weeping and rejoicing of the land. We shall have Shelleys with a heart for religion, Ruskins with a comprehension of equality.

Religion, equality and *beauty!* By these America shall come into a glory that shall justify the yearning of the sages for her perfection, and the prophecies of the poets, when she was born in the throes of Valley Forge.

This by faith and a study of the signs, we proclaim!
1913

---

8 **William Morris** (1834-1896) was not only an English author but also an artisan and a designer • 8 **Leonardo**, Leonardo da Vinci (1452-1510), in addition to being an artist, was also an architect and an engineer • 11 **Shelley**, Percy Bysshe Shelley (1792-1822), British poet, was an atheist and hence, in Lindsay's opinion, irreligious • 12 **Ruskin**. See note, p. 745. Ruskin had views of democracy with which Lindsay did not agree

---

General William Booth Enters into Heaven

This poem is a fanciful memorial of General William Booth (1829-1912), the English founder of the Salvation Army. Like many of Lindsay's poems, it is notable for its rhythm. Here the beat is determined by the music of the Salvation Army band: the first line, and other lines in the poem, echo the "boom-boom-Boom-Boom-Boom" of a drum, and the refrain, "Are you washed in the blood of the Lamb?" is a line from a favorite song of the evangelists whom Booth led. Notable, too, is the imagery: Lindsay here shows why he urged that his poems be judged "for lifetime and even hereditary thoughts and memories of painting." Like the old medieval plays which localized Biblical scenes in terms of the experiences of the audience, this poem shows Heaven in the guise of a county seat in a little Midwestern town. Around the courthouse square, Booth leads the band of bedraggled sinners whom his army has saved, and like a local mayor welcoming a visiting celebrity, Jesus comes from the courthouse to welcome Booth. The English evangelist doubtless appealed to the poet because of the democratic faith which both championed. The author's evangelism is displayed in the picturing of the regeneration of the motley marchers and in the repeated refrain which, at the end, is addressed directly to the reader.

(To be sung to the tune of "The Blood of the Lamb" with indicated instruments.)

I

(Bass drum beaten loudly.)
Booth led boldly with his big bass drum,
(Are you washed in the blood of the Lamb?)
The saints smiled gravely, and they said,
"He's come."
(Are you washed in the blood of the Lamb?)
Walking lepers followed, rank on rank,
Lurching bravos from the ditches dank,
Drabs from the alleyways and drug-fiends pale—
Minds still passion-ridden, soul-powers frail!
Vermin-eaten saints with moldy breath   10
Unwashed legions with the ways of death—
(Are you washed in the blood of the Lamb?)

(Banjos.)
Every slum had sent its half-a-score
The round world over.— (Booth had groaned for more.)
Every banner that the wide world flies
Bloomed with glory and transcendent dyes.
Big-voiced lasses made their banjos bang;
Tranced, fanatical, they shrieked and sang;—
"Are you washed in the blood of the Lamb?"
Hallelujah! It was queer to see   20
Bull-necked convicts with that land make free!
Loons with trumpets blowed a blare, blare, blare—
On, on, upward thro' the golden air!
(Are you washed in the blood of the Lamb?)

II

(Bass drum slower and softer.)
Booth died blind, and still by faith he trod,
Eyes still dazzled by the ways of God.
Booth led boldly, and he looked the chief:
Eagle countenance in sharp relief,
Beard a-flying, air of high command
Unabated in that holy land.   30

(Sweet flute music.)
Jesus came from out the Courthouse door,
Stretched His hands above the passing poor.
Booth saw not, but led his queer ones there
'Round and 'round the mighty Courthouse square.
Yet in an instant all that blear review
Marched on spotless, clad in raiment new.
The lame were straightened, withered limbs uncurled,
And blind eyes opened on a new sweet world.

(Bass drum louder.)
Drabs and vixens in a flash made whole!
Gone was the weasel-head, the snout, the jowl!   40
Sages and sibyls now, and athletes clean,
Rulers of empires, and of forests green!

*(Grand chorus of all instruments. Tambourines to the
foreground.)*
The hosts were sandaled and their wings were fire!
    (Are you washed in the blood of the Lamb?)
But their noise played havoc with the angel-choir.
    (Are you washed in the blood of the Lamb?)
Oh, shout Salvation! it was good to see
Kings and Princes by the Lamb set free.
The banjos rattled and the tambourines
Jing-jing-jingled in the hands of Queens!   50

(Reverently sung, no instruments.)
And when Booth halted by the curb for prayer
He saw his Master thro' the flag-filled air.
Christ came gently with a robe and crown
For Booth the soldier, while the throng knelt down.
He saw King Jesus. They were face to face,
And he knelt a-weeping in that holy place.
    Are you washed in the blood of the Lamb?

                                            1912·1913

The Eagle That Is Forgotten

John Altgeld, governor of Illinois during Lindsay's youth,
won the poet's respect by championing the liberal cause.
Altgeld's ideas on the penal system and taxation, his par-
doning of anarchists, and his protest against the breaking
of strikes by federal troops caused him to be abused as a
"radical" by many newspapers. Lindsay was sympathetic
to the liberal agrarian movement symbolized by Altgeld.

Sleep softly . . . eagle forgotten . . . under the stone.
Time has its way with you there, and the clay has its own.

"We have buried him now," thought your foes, and in
    secret rejoiced.
They made a brave show of their mourning, their hatred
    unvoiced.
They had snarled at you, barked at you, foamed at you,
    day after day.
Now you were ended. They praised you . . . and laid
    you away.

The others, that mourned you in silence and terror and
    truth,
The widow bereft of her crust, and the boy without
    youth,
The mocked and the scorned and the wounded, the lame
    and the poor,
That should have remembered forever, . . . Remember
    no more.   10

Where are those lovers of yours, on what name do they
    call,
The lost, that in armies wept over your funeral pall?
They call on the names of a hundred high-valiant ones,
A hundred white eagles have risen, the sons of your sons,
The zeal in their wings is a zeal that your dreaming began,
The valor that wore out your soul in the service of man.

Sleep softly . . . eagle forgotten . . . under the stone.
Time has its way with you there, and the clay has its own.
Sleep on, O brave-hearted, O wise man that kindled the
    flame —
To live in mankind is far more than to live in a name,   20
To live in mankind, far, far more than . . . to live in a
    name.

                                            1912?·1913

From

The Congo

A Study of the Negro Race

(Being a memorial to Ray Eldred,
a Disciple missionary of the Congo River)

Perhaps the most famous of Lindsay's poems, "The Congo" fully exploits rhythm and tone-coloring for its purpose. The marginal suggestions make clear how the reading of the poem may not only give it variety but also emphasize shifts in mood comparable to those in Dryden's odes, which Lindsay greatly admired.

The three sections of the poem, since they treat three aspects of Negro character—savagery, high spirits, religiousness—justify the subtitle. But the parts of the poem are complexly related and integrated. For one thing, each section begins with a modern scene, and then, following a refrain (ll. 12-13, 37-38), shifts to the Congo of the African jungles, where similar but more primitive or fantastic scenes are enacted. Thus the shift is from the drunken bellicosity of Negroes in a saloon to the savage deeds of Negroes in Africa, then from the juba dance in a gambling hall to a gaudy and fantastic cakewalk performed in "a Negro fairyland" by "a minstrel river." The third section, "The Hope of Their Religion," shifts from a Negro revival meeting to a regenerated "Congo Paradise." The Mumbo-Jumbo refrain, recurrent throughout, is made to represent the savagery of the race, at first triumphant, then laughed to scorn by the high-spirited dancers, and finally (in Section III) utterly defeated by the hope of religion.

I. THEIR BASIC SAVAGERY

Fat black bucks in a wine-barrel room,
Barrel-house kings, with feet unstable,
Sagged and reeled and pounded on the table,

A deep rolling bass.

Pounded on the table,
Beat an empty barrel with the handle of a broom
Hard as they were able,
Boom, boom, BOOM,
With a silk umbrella and the handle of a broom,
Boomlay, boomlay, boomlay, BOOM.

THEN I had religion, THEN I had a vision   10
I could not turn from their revel in derision.

THEN I SAW THE CONGO, CREEPING THROUGH THE BLACK,
CUTTING THROUGH THE FOREST WITH A GOLDEN TRACK.

More deliberate. Solemnly chanted.

Then along the riverbank
A thousand miles
Tattooed cannibals danced in files;
Then I heard the boom of the blood-lust song
And a thigh-bone beating on a tin-pan gong.

A rapidly piling climax of speed and racket.

And "BLOOD" screamed the whistles and the fifes of the warriors,
"BLOOD" screamed the skull-faced, lean witch-doctors,   20
"Whirl ye the deadly voo-doo rattle,
Harry the uplands,
Steal all the cattle,

Rattle-rattle, rattle-rattle,
Bing.
Boomlay, boomlay, boomlay, BOOM,"

A roaring, epic, rag-time tune
From the mouth of the Congo
To the Mountains of the Moon
Death is an Elephant,   30
Torch-eyed and horrible,

Foam-flanked and terrible.
BOOM, steal the pygmies,
BOOM, kill the Arabs,
BOOM, kill the white men,
HOO, HOO, HOO.
Listen to the yell of Leopold's ghost
Burning in Hell for his hand-maimed host.

Hear how the demons chuckle and yell
Cutting his hands off, down in Hell.   40
Listen to the creepy proclamation,
Blown through the lairs of the forest-nation,
Blown past the white-ant's hill of clay.
Blown past the marsh where the butterflies play:—
"Be careful what you do,
Or Mumbo-Jumbo, God of the Congo,
And all of the other

Gods of the Congo,
Mumbo-Jumbo will hoo-doo you,
Mumbo-Jumbo will hoo-doo you,   50
Mumbo-Jumbo will hoo-doo you."

II. THEIR IRREPRESSIBLE HIGH SPIRITS

Wild crap-shooters with a whoop and a call
Danced the juba in their gambling hall

And laughed fit to kill, and shook the town,
And guyed the policemen and laughed them down
With a boomlay, boomlay, boomlay, BOOM.
THEN I SAW THE CONGO, CREEPING THROUGH THE BLACK,
CUTTING THROUGH THE FOREST WITH A GOLDEN TRACK.

A Negro fairyland swung into view,
A minstrel river   60
Where dreams come true.

The ebony palace soared on high
Through the blossoming trees to the evening sky.
The inlaid porches and casements shone

With gold and ivory and elephant-bone.
And the black crowd laughed till their sides were sore.
At the baboon butler in the agate door,
And the well-known tunes of the parrot band
That trilled on the bushes of that magic land.

A troupe of skull-faced witch-men came

70

With pomposity.

Through the agate doorway in suits of flame,
Yea, long-tailed coats with a gold-leaf crust
And hats that were covered with diamond-dust.
And the crowd in the court gave a whoop and a call
And danced the juba from wall to wall.
But the witch-men suddenly stilled the throng

With a great de-
liberation and
ghostliness.

With a stern cold glare, and a stern old song:—
"Mumbo-Jumbo will hoo-doo you." . . .
Just then from the doorway, as fat as shotes,
Came the cake-walk princes in their long red coats,

80

With overwhelm-
ing assurance,
good cheer, and
pomp.

Canes with a brilliant lacquer shine,
And tall silk hats that were red as wine.
And they pranced with their butterfly partners there,
Coal-black maidens with pearls in their hair,

With growing speed
and sharply
marked dance-
rhythm.

Knee-skirts trimmed with the jassamine sweet,
And bells on their ankles and little black-feet.
And the couples railed at the chant and the frown
Of the witch-men lean, and laughed them down.
(Oh rare was the revel, and well worth while
That made those glowering witch-men smile.)

90

The cake-walk royalty then began
To walk for a cake that was tall as a man
To the tune of "Boomlay, boomlay, BOOM,"
While the witch-men laughed, with a sinister air,
And sang with the scalawags prancing there:—

With a touch of
Negro dialect,
and as rapidly
as possible
toward the end.

"Walk with care, walk with care,
Or Mumbo-Jumbo, God of the Congo,
And all of the other
Gods of the Congo,
Mumbo-Jumbo will hoo-doo you.

100

Beware, beware, walk with care,
Boomlay, boomlay, boomlay, boom.
Boomlay, boomlay, boomlay, boom,
Boomlay, boomlay, boomlay, boom,
Boomlay, boomlay, boomlay,
BOOM."
Oh rare was the revel, and well worth while
That made those glowering witch-men smile.

Slow philosophic
calm.

A good old negro in the slums of the town
Preached at a sister for her velvet gown.
Howled at a brother for his low-down ways,
His prowling, guzzling, sneak-thief days.
Beat on the Bible till he wore it out
Starting the jubilee revival shout.
And some had visions, as they stood on chairs,
And sang of Jacob, and the golden stairs,
And they all repented, a thousand strong
From their stupor and savagery and sin and wrong
And slammed with their hymn books till they shook the room
With "glory, glory, glory,"
And "Boom, boom, BOOM."
THEN I SAW THE CONGO, CREEPING THROUGH THE BLACK,
CUTTING THROUGH THE JUNGLE WITH A GOLDEN TRACK.
And the gray sky opened like a new-rent veil
And showed the Apostles with their coats of mail.
In bright white steele they were seated round
And their fire-eyes watched where the Congo wound.
And the twelve Apostles, from their thrones on high
Thrilled all the forest with their heavenly cry:—
"Mumbo-Jumbo will die in the jungle;
Never again will he hoo-doo you,
Never again will he hoo-doo you."

Then along that river, a thousand miles
The vine-snared trees fell down in files.
Pioneer angels cleared the way
For a Congo paradise, for babes at play,
For sacred capitals, for temples clean.
Gone were the skull-faced witch-men lean.
There, where the wild ghost-gods had wailed
A million boats of the angels sailed
With oars of silver, and prows of blue
And silken pennants that the sun shone through.
'Twas a land transfigured, 'twas a new creation.
Oh, a singing wind swept the negro nation
And on through the backwoods clearing flew:—
"Mumbo-Jumbo is dead in the jungle.
Never again will he hoo-doo you,
Never again will he hoo-doo you."

Redeemed were the forests, the beasts and the men,
And only the vulture dared again

Marginal notes:

110 — Heavy bass. With a literal imitation of camp-meeting racket, and trance.

120 — Exactly as in the first section. Begin with terror and power, end with joy.

130 — Sung to the tune of "Hark ten thousand harps and voices."

With growing deliberation and joy.

140 — In a rather high key—as delicately as possible.

To the tune of "Hark, ten thousand harps and voices."

150

By the far, lone mountains of the moon
To cry, in the silence, the Congo tune:—
"Mumbo-Jumbo will hoo-doo you,
Mumbo-Jumbo will hoo-doo you.
Mumbo . . . Jumbo . . . will . . . hoo-doo . . . you."

Dying down
into a pene-
trating,
terrified
whisper.

1914

Abraham Lincoln Walks at Midnight

(In Springfield, Illinois)

Professor T. K. Whipple sees in this poem an example of what he calls Lindsay's "myth-making faculty." The myths in the poet's works, he notes, "partake of the nature of visions" such as "the figure of Lincoln walking through the streets of Springfield in the darkness. . . . Such phantasms have an epic scope, legendary, fabulous, racial. All Lindsay's best work has this folk-quality. No one equals him in ability to discern symbols of national significance underlying the national life. . . . Always at his best he has this intimate relationship with the American scene; like other American writers, he profits by staying close to the soil. . . ."

It is portentous, and a thing of state
That here at midnight, in our little town
A mourning figure walks, and will not rest,
Near the old courthouse pacing up and down,

Or by his homestead, or in shadowed yards
He lingers where his children used to play,
Or through the market, on the well-worn stones
He stalks until the dawn-stars burn away.

A bronzed, lank man! His suit of ancient black,
A famous high top-hat and plain worn shawl   10
Make him the quaint great figure that men love,
The prairie-lawyer, master of us all.

He cannot sleep upon his hillside now.
He is among us:—as in times before!

928   *Lindsay*

And we who toss and lie awake for long
Breathe deep, and start, to see him pass the door.

His head is bowed. He thinks on men and kings.
Yea, when the sick world cries, how can he sleep?
Too many peasants fight, they know not why,
Too many homesteads in black terror weep.   20

The sins of all the war-lords burn his heart.
He sees the dreadnaughts scouring every main.
He carries on his shawl-wrapped shoulders now
The bitterness, the folly and the pain.

He cannot rest until a spirit-dawn
Shall come;—the shining hope of Europe free:
The league of sober folk, the Workers' Earth,
Bringing long peace to Cornland, Alp and Sea.

It breaks his heart that kings must murder still,
That all his hours of travail here for men   30
Seem yet in vain. And who will bring white peace
That he may sleep upon his hill again?

1914

The Flower-Fed Buffaloes

The flower-fed buffaloes of the spring
In the days of long ago,
Ranged where the locomotives sing
And the prairie flowers lie low:—
The tossing, blooming, perfumed grass
Is swept away by the wheat,

Wheels and wheels and wheels spin by
In the spring that still is sweet.
But the flower-fed buffaloes of the spring
Left us, long ago. 10
They gore no more, they bellow no more,

They trundle around the hills no more:—
With the Blackfeet, lying low.
With the Pawnees, lying low,
Lying low.

1924

Wallace Stevens

1879 · 1955

Wallace Stevens was born in Reading, Pennsylvania, on October 2, 1879—the same year as Vachel Lindsay. His mother was of Pennsylvania descent and his father, a lawyer, of Dutch ancestry. After attending Harvard and New York Law School, Stevens entered law practice in New York City, and it was during his years as a lawyer that he began to publish poems in the newly founded *Poetry* and the more *avant-garde* New York magazine, *Others*. In 1916 he moved to Hartford to work for an insurance company, continuing his writing of poetry but not publishing his first volume, *Harmonium,* until 1923. In 1931 he published a revised version of this first book, adding a few new poems. Stevens' period of greatest productivity, however, did not begin until after 1934, when he became vice-president of the insurance company by which he was employed. *Ideas of Order* appeared in 1935 and *Owl's Clover* in 1936, both volumes in limited editions. These were followed by *The Man with a Blue Guitar and Other Poems* (1937), *Parts of a World* (1942), *Notes Toward a Supreme Fiction* (1942), *Transport to Summer* (1947), and *Three Academic Pieces* (1948).

Stevens was a rare phenomenon in the contemporary American scene—a highly successful businessman who was also an outstanding poet. His poetry, however, particu-

larly at the start, seemed to be disassociated from the prosaic, the everyday. It made use of luxurious backgrounds, exotic place names, foreign words and phrases. The color and texture of Stevens' settings were compared by critics with impressionistic paintings which may, in fact, have had some influence upon them. His literary alliances, apparently, were also exotic—with the French Symbolists and Parnassians of the late nineteenth century. The strange titles of his poems not infrequently showed resemblances to those used by the French composer, Claude Debussy, or by surrealistic painters and abstractionists, e.g., "Hymn from a Watermelon Pavilion," "The Paltry Nude Starts on a Spring Voyage," "The Worms at Heaven's Gate," and "Dominance of Black." Stevens had a taste, too, for extraordinary sound combinations: he often wrote sonorous nonsense lines or lines whose meanings tended to be obscured by alliterative or rhyming sounds, e.g., "Chieftan Iffucan of Azcan in caftan / Often with henna hackles, halt!"

Stevens' matter and manner, divorced as they frequently were from the mundane, had relevance to one of his major concerns—concern about the loss from man's life of belief and direction. Stevens' first poems dealt chiefly with a nostalgic longing for beauty and perfection (represented often by strange and exotic cenes) which are not to be found in the commonplaces of the workaday world. With increasing frequency in his later poems, though, he was interested in finding solutions to this tragic problem. The reconciliation between man and his environment, he claimed repeatedly, may be achieved by a sensuous unity with nature or—more important—by the achievement of a poet's insight. For the power of the poet, Stevens explained, derives from the fact that "he creates the world to which we turn incessantly and without knowing it and that he gives to life the supreme fiction without which we are unable to conceive of it." In some later poems, Stevens conceived of this insight, too, as revealing the way man's lot may be improved by heroic actions or by social changes.

Stevens' career was a long one. He did not go unappreciated during his early years as a poet: Harriet Monroe of *Poetry* honored him with an award, critics spoke of him with respect, and he had a devoted (though small) group of admirers. But it was not until he entered his second period of productivity in the 1930's and 1940's that his originality, his sense of form and drama, his control of words, and his mature insights won for him wide appreciation among readers of poetry as well as a secure place among the leading American poets of the twentieth century.

William Van O'Connor, **The Shaping Spirit: A Study of Wallace Stevens**, Chicago, 1950 • James V. Cunningham, "The Poetry of Wallace Stevens," **Poetry**, December 1950, LXXV, 149-165

The Emperor of Ice-Cream

Stevens once wrote of this poem: "This wears a deliberately commonplace costume, and yet it seems to me to contain something of the essential gaudiness of poetry." The commonplace elements are the muscular cigar roller (a symbol of materialism), the wenches in their everyday dresses, the boys who bring flowers in old newspapers (stanza one), the battered dresser, the sheet, the corpse with unlovely calloused feet (stanza two). The "gaudiness" is supplied, perhaps, by the sound of the lines, particularly the alliterative third line, and the stanzaic refrains with their ritualistic praise of the emperor—a figure whose rulership is of the inconsequential. By using such details in his depiction of preparations for a funeral, the poet ironically comments upon the meaninglessness of a great reality, death, in the modern world. Louise Bogan has said of Stevens: "His sense of form and his gifts of language were extraordinary; these, added to his dramatic power, which produced many moments of tension—'The Emperor of Ice-Cream' is an example of such a moment—lifted his work from the realm of the arabesque and the rococo."

Call the roller of big cigars,
The muscular one, and bid him whip

In kitchen cups concupiscent curds.
Let the wenches dawdle in such dress
As they are used to wear, and let the boys
Bring flowers in last month's newspapers.
Let be be finale of seem.
The only emperor is the emperor of ice-cream.

Take from the dresser of deal,
Lacking the three glass knobs, that sheet   10
On which she embroidered fantails once
And spread it so as to cover her face.
If her horny feet protrude, they come
To show how cold she is, and dumb.
Let the lamp affix its beam.
The only emperor is the emperor of ice-cream.

1923

Sunday Morning

The details of the first, sixth, and seventh stanzas exemplify Stevens' fondness for brilliantly colored backgrounds, particularly evident in his early poems. "Sunday Morning," as James V. Cunningham has described it, "has as its subject a deep emotional attachment to traditional Christianity and a rejection of Christianity in favor of the clear and felt apprehension of sensory detail in life, together with an attempt to preserve in the new setting the emotional aspects of the old values." The poem shows a woman musing while at a late Sunday morning breakfast. It tells what she sees, feels, and thinks, and also sets forth comments of the poet upon her experience. The wish of the poet, typically, is, as Cunningham puts it, "to be at peace with his surroundings, with this world, and with himself. He requires for this an experience of the togetherness of himself and nature, an interpenetration of himself and his environment, along with some intuition of permanence in the experience of absoluteness."

I

Complacencies of the peignoir, and late
Coffee and oranges in a sunny chair,
And the green freedom of a cockatoo
Upon a rug mingle to dissipate
The holy hush of ancient sacrifice.
She dreams a little, and she feels the dark
Encroachment of that old catastrophe,
As a calm darkens among water-lights.
The pungent oranges and bright, green wings
Seem things in some procession of the dead,   10
Winding across wide water, without sound.
The day is like wide water, without sound,
Stilled for the passing of her dreaming feet
Over the seas, to silent Palestine,
Dominion of the blood and sepulchre.

II

Why should she give her bounty to the dead?
What is divinity if it can come
Only in silent shadows and in dreams?
Shall she not find in comforts of the sun,
In pungent fruit and bright, green wings, or else   20
In any balm or beauty of the earth,
Things to be cherished like the thought of heaven?
Divinity must live within herself:
Passions of rain, or moods in falling snow;
Grievings in loneliness, or unsubdued
Elations when the forest blooms; gusty
Emotions on wet roads on autumn nights;
All pleasures and all pains, remembering
The bough of summer and the winter branch.
These are the measures destined for her soul.   30

III

Jove in the clouds had his inhuman birth.
No mother suckled him, no sweet land gave
Large-mannered motions to his mythy mind.
He moved among us, as a muttering king,
Magnificent, would move among his hinds,
Until our blood, commingling, virginal,
With heaven, brought such requital to desire
The very hinds discerned it, in a star.
Shall our blood fail? Or shall it come to be
The blood of paradise? And shall the earth   40
Seem all of paradise that we shall know?
The sky will be much friendlier then than now,
A part of labor and a part of pain,
And next in glory to enduring love,
Not this dividing and indifferent blue.

IV

She says, "I am content when wakened birds,
Before they fly, test the reality
Of misty fields, by their sweet questionings;
But when the birds are gone, and their warm fields
Return no more, where, then, is paradise?"   50
There is not any haunt of prophesy,
Nor any old chimera of the grave,
Neither the golden underground, nor isle
Melodious, where spirits gat them home,
Nor visionary south, nor cloudy palm
Remote on heaven's hill, that has endured
As April's green endures; or will endure
Like her remembrance of awakened birds,
Or her desire for June and evening, tipped
By the consummation of the swallow's wings.   60

V

She says, "But in contentment I still feel
The need of some imperishable bliss."
Death is the mother of beauty; hence from her,
Alone, shall come fulfilment to our dreams
And our desires. Although she strews the leaves
Of sure obliteration on our paths,
The path sick sorrow took, the many paths
Where triumph rang its brassy phrase, or love
Whispered a little out of tenderness,
She makes the willow shiver in the sun   70
For maidens who were wont to sit and gaze
Upon the grass, relinquished to their feet.

She causes boys to pile new plums and pears
On disregarded plate. The maidens taste
And stray impassioned in the littering leaves.

VI

Is there no change of death in paradise?
Does ripe fruit never fall? Or do the boughs
Hang always heavy in that perfect sky,
Unchanging, yet so like our perishing earth,
With rivers like our own that seek for seas   80
They never find, the same receding shores
That never touch with inarticulate pang?
Why set the pear upon those river-banks
Or spice the shores with odors of the plum?
Alas, that they should wear our colors there,
The silken weavings of our afternoons,
And pick the strings of our insipid lutes!
Death is the mother of beauty, mystical,
Within whose burning bosom we devise
Our earthly mothers waiting, sleeplessly.   90

VII

Supple and turbulent, a ring of men
Shall chant in orgy on a summer morn
Their boisterous devotion to the sun,
Not as a god, but as a god might be,
Naked among them, like a savage source.

Their chant shall be a chant of paradise,
Out of their blood, returning to the sky;
And in their chant shall enter, voice by voice,
The windy lake wherein their lord delights,
The trees, like serafin, and echoing hills,   100
That choir among themselves long afterward.
They shall know well the heavenly fellowship
Of men that perish and of summer morn.
And whence they came and whither they shall go
The dew upon their feet shall manifest.

VIII

She hears, upon that water without sound,
A voice that cries, "The tomb in Palestine
Is not the porch of spirits lingering
It is the grave of Jesus, where he lay."
We live in an old chaos of the sun,   110
Or old dependency of day and night,
Or island solitude, unsponsored, free,
Of that wide water, inescapable.
Deer walk upon our mountains, and the quail
Whistle about us their spontaneous cries;
Sweet berries ripen in the wilderness;
And, in the isolation of the sky,
At evening, casual flocks of pigeons make
Ambiguous undulations as they sink,
Downward to darkness, on extended wings.   120

1915 • 1923

Robinson Jeffers

1887 •

Why write about men and women if they are ignoble
and inadequate creatures is a question which more than
one reader has asked of Robinson Jeffers, the most blackly

pessimistic of contemporary American poets. One answer
might be that we might as well solace ourselves with
conversation; another is that which might have been

given by Swift or Voltaire: mean and contemptible as humanity is, there are some individuals whose strength and dignity may be admired even in failure and whose tragic transcience even a misanthrope can pity. Yet it is useless to deny the nihilism of Jeffers, who obviously believes that human beings are so bad that their destruction, which he regards as inevitable, can hardly be deplored. His God is power, impersonal and inhuman, and His finest attribute is that He is utterly unlike man.

This conclusion did not come to Jeffers all at once. He arrived at it only in his thirties, after an unusually thorough exploration of literature and of science and the shattering disillusion of World War I. He was born in Pittsburgh in 1887, to an elderly father who was a classical scholar and a theologian. At the age of five he was reading Greek; at fifteen, after two years in European boarding schools, he had some mastery of Italian, French, and German, together with a love of mountains and of poetry. After a year at the University of Western Pennsylvania (now Pittsburgh), he entered Occidental College as a junior (his family having moved to California) and in 1905, aged eighteen, he took his B.A. degree. Precocious, shy, but blessed with a rugged physique and a love for the outdoor life, he would probably have found any of the workaday vocations difficult. He added a further complication to his life by falling in love with a woman who was already married, Mrs. Una Call Kester, a fellow graduate student at the University of Southern California. He married her eventually, after she had won a divorce, but that was not until 1913, and in the interval there were many tribulations. Graduate work in English gave way to preparation for medicine, medical school to a determination to write, although it was accompanied by enrollment in courses in forestry, zoology, and law in the University of Washington. Finally, in 1912, he attained the independence of a small income from the legacy of a distant relative, and late in the following year he was married. A plan to live abroad was spoiled by the outbreak of war in Europe, and late in 1914 Jeffers and his wife settled at Carmel-by-the-Sea, on the Monterey peninsula. There they have lived ever since, and there Jeffers built a house with his own hands and found the materials for most of his distinctive poetry. He has made the "feel" of the Carmel coast familiar to many readers who have never seen the Pacific Ocean.

Reputation came belatedly, after remarkable changes in style and in philosophy. There is foreshadowing of unorthodoxy and metrical experimentation in *Flagons and Apples* (1912) and *Californians* (1916), but the former is the record of disappointment in love and the latter, written in the first serenity of his marriage, a well-nigh cheerful book. He has not cared to reprint any of the poems which appeared in either of them. The war made personalities insignificant; maturity and the temper of the twenties played their part; *Tamar and Other Poems* (1924) was at once recognized as the work of a poet who had something to say and who had found a fresh way of saying it. Republished in 1925, with additions, this book, with its free rhythms and striking metaphors, its brutal and unforgettable narratives, its subtle symbolism and its gloomy world-view, gave Jeffers the audience which he has held ever since. It was followed by *The Women at Point Sur* (1927), *Cawdor* (1928), *Dear Judas* (1929), *Thurso's Landing* (1932), *Give Your Heart to the Hawks* (1933), *Solstice* (1935), *Such Counsels You Gave to Me* (1937), *Be Angry at the Sun* (1941), and a free adaptation of Euripides' play, *Medea* (1946), to name only the most important volumes.

Jeffers has often been compared with Eugene O'Neill, and it is true that they share a temperamental melancholy which critics like to call Celtic, as well as a great debt to the themes and methods of Greek tragedy. Jeffers, however, is more clearly the product of an age which by Freudian psychology, biochemistry, and nuclear physics has destroyed most of the basic assumptions of the past. He cannot be explained in a few sentences or paragraphs, for no American poet has faced more squarely the insoluble problems: Where does modern man stand now, nearing the middle of the twentieth century? and What has man to look forward to? Jeffers has not, most of us hope, given the final answers, but few of us find it easy to refute him. He is not precisely a materialist, for matter, too, is but a symbol for his remote and mysterious moving power, but landscapes and seascapes mean more to him than human beings, and the background of existence has little discernible meaning. He has now entered his sixth decade of living, but it would seem doubtful that the spectacle of the atomic era, which has shocked many less intellectual persons these last years, will mellow his opinions. The appalling prospect of man's destiny is no news to Robinson Jeffers.

The Selected Poetry of Robinson Jeffers, New York, 1937 • S. S. Alberts, A Bibliography of the Works of Robinson Jeffers, New York, 1933 • Delmore Schwartz and Frajam Taylor, "The Enigma of Robinson Jeffers," Poetry, October 1939, LV, 30-46 • L. C. Powell, Robinson Jeffers; the Man and His Work, Revised Edition, Pasadena, 1940

Roan Stallion

In the Foreword to **Selected Poetry** Jeffers has said that he remembers clearly the moment of conception of this poem, alone of all his poems. Having finished "The Tower of Tragedy," he was seeking a contemporary subject, "because I repented of using a Greek story when there were so many new ones at hand." While Jeffers was sitting on a rock to look at the sunset after quarrying granite, there came into his mind the memory of an abandoned cabin in the hills, of which it was said that the owner had been killed by a stallion. "Immediately, for persons of the drama, came the Indian woman and her white husband, real persons whom I had often seen driving through our village in a ramshackle buggy. The episode of the woman swimming her horse through a storm-swollen ford at night came also; it was part of her actual history. . . . So that when I stood up and began to handle stones again, the poem had already made itself in my mind." Jeffers has also indicated that the poem owes something to a statue of a horse in Turin, of which the legend went that it was the tribute of a woman; it owes something also to the myth of Leda, the woman whom Jove, in the form of a swan, wooed and won.

Whatever its origins, the story is typical of its author in its violence, in its contrast of the tawdriness of the human characters and the grandeur of mountain and storm setting, in the boldness of its figures of speech (Jeffers is more "poetic" in his metaphors than in his rhythms), in the Freud-like fusion of sexual and religious emotion, and, not least of all, in the interpolated denial of man's oneness with God (ll. 164-174). Oscar Cargill has suggested, in **Intellectual America,** that the poem is sensational rather than truly tragic, because it is psychologically impossible to pity the stallion. One may also question whether such a primitive type of woman would see angels with hawks' heads or even subconsciously intermingle the Christ story with paganism. Jeffers, as always, is concerned with ideas rather than with human beings.

The dog barked; then the woman stood in the doorway,
    and hearing iron strike stone down the steep road
Covered her head with a black shawl and entered the light
    rain; she stood at the turn of the road.
A nobly formed woman; erect and strong as a new tower;
    the features stolid and dark
But sculptured into a strong grace; straight nose with a
    high bridge, firm and wide eyes, full chin,
Red lips; she was only a fourth part Indian; a Scottish
    sailor had planted her in young native earth,
Spanish and Indian, twenty-one years before. He had
    named her California when she was born;
That was her name; and had gone north.

                She heard the hooves and
    wheels come nearer, up the steep road.
The buckskin mare, leaning against the breastpiece,
    plodded into sight round the wet bank.
The pale face of the driver followed; the burnt-out eyes;
    they had fortune in them. He sat twisted   10
On the seat of the old buggy, leading a second horse by a
    long halter, a roan, a big one,
That stepped daintily; by the swell of the neck, a stallion.
    "What have you got, Johnny?" "Maskerel's stallion.
Mine now. I won him last night, I had very good luck."
    He was quite drunk. "They bring their mares up
    here now.

I keep this fellow. I got money besides, but I'll not show
you." "Did you buy something, Johnny,
For our Christine? Christmas comes in two days, Johnny."
"By God, forgot," he answered laughing.
"Don't tell Christine it's Christmas; after while I get her
something, maybe." But California:
"I shared your luck when you lost: you lost *me* once,
Johnny, remember? Tom Dell had me two nights
Here in the house: other times we've gone hungry: now
that you've won, Christine will have her Christmas.
We share your luck, Johnny. You give me money, I go
down to Monterey to-morrow,
Buy presents for Christine, come back in the evening. 20
Next day Christmas." "You have wet ride," he
answered
Giggling. "Here money. Five dollar; ten; twelve dollar.
You buy two bottles of rye whiskey for Johnny."
"All right. I go to-morrow."
                    He was an outcast Hollander; not old, but
shriveled with bad living.
The child Christine inherited from his race blue eyes,
from his life a wizened forehead; she watched
From the house-door her father lurch out of the buggy
and lead with due respect the stallion
To the new corral, the strong one; leaving the wearily
breathing buckskin mare to his wife to unharness.

Storm in the night; the rain on the thin shakes of the roof
like the ocean on rock streamed battering; once
thunder
Walked down the narrow canyon into Carmel valley and
wore away westward; Christine was wakeful
With fears and wonders; her father lay too deep for
storm to touch him.
                    Dawn comes late in the year's dark, 30
Later into the crack of a canyon under redwoods; and
California slipped from bed
An hour before it; the buckskin would be tired; there was
a little barley, and why should Johnny
Feed all the barley to his stallion? That is what he would
do. She tiptoed out of the room.
Leaving her clothes, he'd waken if she waited to put them
on, and passed from the door of the house
Into the dark of the rain; the big black drops were cold
through the thin shift, but the wet earth

Pleasant under her naked feet. There was a pleasant smell
in the stable; and moving softly,
Touching things gently with the supple bend of the un-
clothed body, was pleasant. She found a box,
Filled it with sweet dry barley and took it down to the
old corral. The little mare sighed deeply
At the rail in the wet darkness; and California returning
between two redwoods up to the house
Heard the happy jaws grinding the grain. Johnny could
mind the pigs and chickens. Christine called to
her   40
When she entered the house, but slept again under her
hand. She laid the wet night-dress on a chair-back
And stole into the bedroom to get her clothes. A plank
creaked, and he wakened. She stood motionless
Hearing him stir in the bed. When he was quiet she
stooped after her shoes, and he said softly,
"What are you doing? Come back to bed." "It's late, I'm
going to Monterey, I must hitch up."
"You come to bed first. I been away three days. I give you
money, I take back the money
And what you do in town then?" She sighed sharply and
came to the bed.
                    He reaching his hands from it
Felt the cool curve and firmness of her flank, and half
rising caught her by the long wet hair.
She endured, and to hasten the act she feigned desire; she
had not for long, except in dream, felt it.
Yesterday's drunkenness made him sluggish and exacting; she saw, turning her head sadly,   50
The windows were bright gray with dawn; he embraced
her still, stopping to talk about the stallion.
At length she was permitted to put on her clothes. Clear
daylight over the steep hills;
Gray-shining cloud over the tops of the redwoods; the
winter stream sang loud; the wheels of the buggy
Slipped in deep slime, ground on washed stones at the
road-edge. Down the hill the wrinkled river smothered the ford.
You must keep to the bed of stones: she knew the way by
willow and alder: the buckskin halted mid-stream,
Shuddering, the water her own color washing up to the
traces; but California, drawing up
Her feet out of the whirl onto the seat of the buggy
swung the whip over the yellow water
And drove to the road.

All morning the clouds were racing northward like a river. At noon they thickened.
When California faced the southwind home from Monterey it was heavy with level rainfall.   60
She looked seaward from the foot of the valley; red rays cried sunset from a trumpet of streaming
Cloud over Lobos, the southwest occident of the solstice. Twilight came soon, but the tired mare
Feared the road more than the whip. Mile after mile of slow gray twilight.
          Then, quite suddenly, darkness.
"Christine will be asleep. It is Christmas Eve. The ford. That hour of daylight wasted this morning!"
She could see nothing; she let the reins lie on the dashboard and knew at length by the cramp of the wheels
And the pitch down, they had reached it. Noise of wheels on stones, plashing of hooves in water; a world
Of sounds; no sight; the gentle thunder of water; the mare snorting, dipping her head, one knew,
To look for footing, in the blackness, under the stream. The hushing and creaking of the sea-wind
In the passion of invisible willows.   70
          The mare stood still; the woman shouted to her; spared whip,
For a false leap would lose the track of the ford. She stood. "The baby's things," thought California,
"Under the seat: the water will come over the floor"; and rising in the midst of the water
She tilted the seat; fetched up the doll, the painted wooden chickens, the woolly bear, the book
Of many pictures, the box of sweets: she brought them all from under the seat and stored them, trembling,
Under her clothes, about the breasts, under the arms; the corners of the cardboard boxes
Cut into the soft flesh; but with a piece of rope for a girdle and wound about the shoulders
All was made fast. The mare stood still as if asleep in the midst of the water. Then California
Reached out a hand over the stream and fingered her rump; the solid wet convexity of it
Shook like the beat of a great heart. "What are you waiting for?" But the feel of the animal surface   80
Had wakened a dream, obscured real danger with a dream of danger. "What for? for the water-stallion
To break out of the stream, that is what the rump strains for, him to come up flinging foam sidewise,

Fore-hooves in air, crush me and the rig and curl over his woman." She flung out with the whip then;
The mare plunged forward. The buggy drifted sidelong: was she off ground? Swimming? No: by the splashes.
The driver, a mere prehensile instinct, clung to the side-irons of the seat and felt the force
But not the coldness of the water, curling over her knees, breaking up to the waist
Over her body. They'd turned. The mare had turned up stream and was wallowing back into shoal water.
Then California dropped her forehead to her knees, having seen nothing, feeling a danger,
And felt the brute weight of a branch of alder, the pendulous light leaves brush her bent neck
Like a child's fingers. The mare burst out of water and stopped on the slope to the ford. The woman climbed down   90
Between the wheels and went to her head. "Poor Dora," she called her by her name, "there, Dora. Quietly,"
And led her around, there was room to turn on the margin, the head to the gentle thunder of the water.
She crawled on hands and knees, felt for the ruts, and shifted the wheels into them. "You can see, Dora.
I can't. But this time you'll go through it." She climbed into the seat and shouted angrily. The mare
Stopped, her two forefeet in the water. She touched with the whip. The mare plodded ahead and halted.
Then California thought of prayer: "Dear little Jesus,
Dear baby Jesus born to-night, your head was shining
Like silver candles. I've got a baby too, only a girl. You had light wherever you walked.
Dear baby Jesus give me light." Light streamed: rose, gold, rich purple, hiding the ford like a curtain.
The gentle thunder of water was a noise of wing-feathers, the fans of paradise lifting softly.   100
The child afloat on radiance had a baby face, but the angels had birds' heads, hawks' heads,
Bending over the baby, weaving a web of wings about him. He held in the small fat hand
A little snake with golden eyes, and California could see clearly on the under radiance
The mare's pricked ears, a sharp black fork against the shining light-fall. But it dropped; the light of heaven
Frightened poor Dora. She backed; swung up the water,
And nearly oversetting the buggy turned and scrambled backward; the iron wheel-tires rang on boulders.

Then California weeping climbed between the wheels.
Her wet clothes and the toys packed under

Dragged her down with their weight; she stripped off
cloak and dress and laid the baby's things in the
buggy;

Brought Johnny's whiskey out from under the seat;
wrapped all in the dress, bottles and toys, and tied
them

Into a bundle that would sling over her back. She
unharnessed the mare, hurting her fingers   110

Against the swollen straps and the wet buckles. She tied
the pack over her shoulders, the cords

Crossing her breasts, and mounted. She drew up her shift
about her waist and knotted it, naked thighs

Clutching the sides of the mare, bare flesh to the wet
withers, and caught the mane with her right hand,

The looped-up bridle-reins in the other. "Dora, the baby
gives you light." The blinding radiance

Hovered the ford. "Sweet baby Jesus give us light." Cataracts of light and Latin singing

Fell through the willows; the mare snorted and reared:
the roar and thunder of the invisible water;

The night shaking open like a flag, shot with the flashes;
the baby face hovering; the water

Beating over her shoes and stockings up to the bare
thighs; and over them, like a beast

Lapping her belly; the wriggle and pitch of the mare
swimming; the drift, the sucking water; the blinding

Light above and behind with not a gleam before,
in the throat of darkness; the shock of the fore-
hooves   120

Striking bottom, the struggle and surging lift of the
haunches. She felt the water streaming off her

From the shoulders down; heard the great strain and sob
of the mare's breathing, heard the horseshoes grind
on gravel.

When California came home the dog at the door snuffed
at her without barking; Christine and Johnny

Both were asleep; she did not sleep for hours, but kindled fire and knelt patiently over it,

Shaping and drying the dear-bought gifts for Christmas
morning.

She hated (she thought) the proud-necked stallion.
He'd lean the big twin masses of his breast on the rail, his
red-brown eyes flash the white crescents,

She admired him then, she hated him for his uselessness,
serving nothing

But Johnny's vanity. Horses were too cheap to breed. She
thought, if he could range in freedom,

Shaking the red-roan mane for a flag on the bare
hills.   130

                A man
brought up a mare in April;

Then California, though she wanted to watch, stayed
with Christine indoors. When the child fretted

The mother told her once more about the miracle of the
ford; her prayers to the little Jesus

The Christmas Eve when she was bringing the gifts
home; the appearance, the lights, the Latin singing,

The thunder of wing-feathers and water, the shining
child, the cataracts of splendor down the darkness.

"A little baby," Christine asked, "the God is a baby?"
"The child of God. That was his birthday.

His mother was named Mary: we pray to her too: God
came to her. He was not the child of a man

Like you or me. God was his father: she was the stallion's
wife—what did I say—God's wife,"

She said with a cry, lifting Christine aside, pacing the
planks of the floor. "She is called more blessed

Than any woman. She was so good, she was more loved."
"Did God live near her house?" "He lives   140

Up high, over the stars; he ranges on the bare blue hill of
the sky." In her mind a picture

Flashed, of the red-roan mane shaken out for a flag on
the bare hills, and she said quickly, "He's more

Like a great man holding the sun in his hand." Her mind
giving her words the lie, "But no one

Knows, only the shining and the power. The power, the
terror, the burning fire covered her over . . ."

"Was she burnt up, mother?" "She was so good and
lovely, she was the mother of the little Jesus.

If you are good nothing will hurt you." "What did she
think?" "She loved, she was not afraid of the
hooves—

Hands that had made the hills and sun and moon,
and the sea and the great redwoods, the terrible
strength,

She gave herself without thinking." "You only saw the
baby, mother?" "Yes, and the angels about him,

The great wild shining over the black river." Three times
she had walked to the door, three times returned,

And now the hand that had thrice hung on the knob,
    full of prevented action, twisted the cloth   150
Of the child's dress that she had been mending. "Oh, oh,
    I've torn it." She struck at the child and then em-
    braced her
Fiercely, the small blond sickly body.
                         Johnny came in, his face
    reddened as if he had stood
Near fire, his eyes triumphing. "Finished," he said, and
    looked with malice at Christine. "I go
Down valley with Jim Carrier; owes me five dollar,
    fifteen I charge him, he brought ten in his pocket.
Has grapes on the ranch, maybe I take a barrel red wine
    instead of money. Be back to-morrow.
To-morrow night I tell you—Eh, Jim," he laughed over
    his shoulder, "I say to-morrow evening
I show her how the red fellow act, the big fellow. When
    I come home." She answered nothing, but stood
In front of the door, holding the little hand of her daugh-
    ter, in the path of sun between the redwoods,
While Johnny tied the buckskin mare behind Carrier's
    buggy, and bringing saddle and bridle tossed
    them   160
Under the seat. Jim Carrier's mare, the bay, stood with
    drooped head and started slowly, the men
Laughing and shouting at her; their voices could be heard
    down the steep road, after the noise
Of the iron-hooped wheels died from the stone. Then one
    might hear the hush of the wind in the tall red-
    woods,
The tinkle of the April brook, deep in its hollow.
                        Humanity is the
    start of the race; I say
Humanity is the mould to break away from, the crust to
    break through, the coal to break into fire,
The atom to be split.
                Tragedy that breaks man's face and a white
    fire flies out of it; vision that fools him
Out of his limits, desire that fools him out of his limits,
    unnatural crime, inhuman science,
Slit eyes in the mask; wild loves that leap over the walls
    of nature, the wild fence-vaulter science,   170
Useless intelligence of far stars, dim knowledge of the
    spinning demons that make an atom,
These break, these pierce, these deify, praising their

God shrilly with fierce voices: not in man's shape
He approves the praise, he that walks lightning-naked on
    the Pacific, that laces the suns with planets,
The heart of the atom with electrons: what is humanity
    in this cosmos? For him, the last
Least taint of a trace in the dregs of the solution; for
    itself, the mould to break away from, the coal
To break into fire, the atom to be split.

                     After the child slept, after
    the leopard-footed evening
Had glided oceanward, California turned the lamp to its
    least flame and glided from the house.
She moved sighing, like a loose fire, backward and for-
    ward on the smooth ground by the door.
She heard the night-wind that draws down the valley like
    the draught in a flue under clear weather   180
Whisper and toss in the tall redwoods; she heard the
    tinkle of the April brook deep in its hollow.
Cooled by the night the odors that the horses had left
    behind were in her nostrils; the night
Whitened up the bare hill; a drift of coyotes by the river
    cried bitterly against moonrise;
Then California ran to the old corral, the empty one
    where they kept the buckskin mare,
And leaned, and bruised her breasts on the rail, feeling
    the sky whiten. When the moon stood over the hill
She stole to the house. The child breathed quietly. Her-
    self: to sleep? She had seen Christ in the night at
    Christmas.
The hills were shining open to the enormous night of the
    April moon: empty and empty,
The vast round backs of the bare hills? If one should ride
    up high might not the Father himself
Be seen brooding His night, cross-legged, chin in hand,
    squatting on the last dome? More likely
Leaping the hills, shaking the red-roan mane for a flag
    on the bare hills. She blew out the lamp.   190
Every fiber of flesh trembled with faintness when she
    came to the door; strength lacked, to wander
Afoot into the shining of the hill, high enough, high
    enough . . . the hateful face of a man had taken
The strength that might have served her, the corral was
    empty. The dog followed her, she caught him by the
    collar,

Dragged him in fierce silence back to the door of the
house, latched him inside.

It was like daylight

Out-doors and she hastened without faltering down the
footpath, through the dark fringe of twisted oak-
brush,

To the open place in a bay of the hill. The dark strength
of the stallion had heard her coming; she heard him

Blow the shining air out of his nostrils, she saw him in
the white lake of moonlight

Move like a lion along the timbers of the fence, shaking
the nightfall

Of the great mane; his fragrance came to her; she leaned
on the fence;   200

He drew away from it, the hooves making soft thunder
in the trodden soil.

Wild love had trodden it, his wrestling with the stranger,
the shame of the day

Had stamped it into mire and powder when the heavy
fetlocks

Strained the soft flanks. "Oh, if I could bear you!

If I had the strength. O great God that came down to
Mary, gently you came. But I will ride him

Up into the hill, if he throws me, if he tramples me, is it
not my desire

To endure death?" She climbed the fence, pressing her
body against the rail, shaking like fever,

And dropped inside to the soft ground. He neither threatened her with his teeth nor fled from her coming,

And lifting her hand gently to the upflung head she
caught the strap of the headstall,

That hung under the quivering chin. She unlooped the
halter from the high strength of the neck   210

And the arch the storm-cloud mane hung with live
darkness. He stood; she crushed her breasts

On the hard shoulder, an arm over the withers, the other
under the mass of his throat, and murmuring

Like a mountain dove, "If I could bear you." No way, no
help, a gulf in nature. She murmured, "Come,

We will run on the hill. O beautiful, O beautiful," and
led him

To the gate and flung the bars on the ground. He threw
his head downward

To snuff at the bars; and while he stood, she catching
mane and withers with all sudden contracture

And strength of her lithe body, leaped, clung hard, and
was mounted. He had been ridden before; he did not

Fight the weight but ran like a stone falling;

Broke down the slope into the moon-glass of the stream,
and flattened to his neck

She felt the branches of a buck-eye tree fly over her, saw
the wall of the oak-scrub   220

End her world: but he turned there, the matted branches

Scraped her right knee, the great slant shoulders

Laboring the hill-slope, up, up, the clear hill. Desire had
died in her

At the first rush, the falling like death, but now it revived,

She feeling between her thighs the labor of the great engine, the running muscles, the hard swiftness,

She riding the savage and exultant strength of the world.
Having topped the thicket he turned eastward,

Running less wildly; and now at length he felt the halter
when she drew on it; she guided him upward;

He stopped and grazed on the great arch and pride of the
hill, the silent calvary. A dwarfish oakwood

Climbed the other slope out of the dark of the unknown
canyon beyond; the last wind-beaten bush of it

Crawled up to the height, and California slipping from
her mount tethered him to it. She stood then,   230

Shaking. Enormous films of moonlight

Trailed down from the height. Space, anxious whiteness,
vastness. Distant beyond conception the shining
ocean

Lay light like a haze along the ledge and doubtful world's
end. Little vapors gleaming, and little

Darknesses on the far chart underfoot symbolized wood
and valley; but the air was the element, the moon-

Saturate arcs and spires of the air.

Here is solitude, here on the
calvary, nothing conscious

But the possible God and the cropped grass, no witness,
no eye but that misformed one, the moon's past
fullness.

Two figures on the shining hill, woman and stallion, she
kneeling to him, brokenly adoring.

He cropping the grass, shifting his hooves, or lifting the
long head to gaze over the world,

Tranquil and powerful. She prayed aloud, "O God, I
am not good enough, O fear, O strength, I am
draggled.   240

Johnny and other men have had me, and O clean power!
    Here am I," she said, falling before him,
And crawled to his hooves. She lay a long while, as if
    asleep, in reach of the fore-hooves, weeping. He
    avoided
Her head and the prone body. He backed at first; but
    later plucked the grass that grew by her shoulder.
The small dark head under his nostrils: a small round
    stone, that smelt human, black hair growing
    from it:
The skull shut the light in it: it was not possible for
    any eyes
To know what throbbed and shone under the sutures of
    the skull, or a shell full of lightning
Had scared the roan strength, and he'd have broken
    tether, screaming, and run for the valley.
                      The atom bounds-breaking,
Nucleus to sun, electrons to planets, with recognition
Not praying, self-equaling, the whole to the whole, the
    microcosm   250
Not entering nor accepting entrance, more equally, more
    utterly, more incredibly conjugate
With the other extreme and greatness; passionately per-
    ceptive of identity. . . .
              The fire threw up figures
And symbols meanwhile, racial myths formed and dis-
    solved in it, the phantom rulers of humanity
That without being are yet more real than what they are
    born of, and without shape, shape that which makes
    them:
The nerves and the flesh go by shadowlike, the limbs and
    the lives shadowlike, these shadows remain, these
    shadows
To whom temples, to whom churches, to whom labors
    and wars, visions and dreams are dedicate:
Out of the fire in the small round stone that black moss
    covered, a crucified man writhed up in anguish;
A woman covered by a huge beast in whose mane the
    stars were netted, sun and moon were his eye-
    balls,
Smiled under the unendurable violation, her throat swol-
    len with the storm and blood-flecks gleaming   260
On the stretched lips; a woman—no, a dark water, split
    by jets of lightning, and after a season
What floated up out of the furrowed water, a boat, a fish,
    a fire-globe?

              It had wings, the creature,
And flew against the fountain of lightning, fell burnt out
    of the cloud back to the bottomless water . . .
Figures and symbols, castlings of the fire, played in her
    brain; but the white fire was the essence,
The burning in the small round shell of bone that black
    hair covered, that lay by the hooves on the hilltop.

She rose at length, she unknotted the halter; she walked
    and led the stallion; two figures, woman and stallion,
Came down the silent emptiness of the dome of the hill,
    under the cataract of the moonlight.

The next night there was moon through cloud. Johnny
    had returned half drunk toward evening, and
    California
Who had known him for years with neither love nor
    loathing to-night hating him had let the child
    Christine   270
Play in the light of the lamp for hours after her bedtime;
    who fell asleep at length on the floor
Beside the dog; then Johnny: "Put her to bed." She
    gathered the child against her breasts, she laid her
In the next room, and covered her with a blanket. The
    window was white, the moon had risen. The mother
Lay down by the child, but after a moment Johnny stood
    in the doorway. "Come drink." He had brought
    home
Two jugs of wine slung from the saddle, part payment
    for the stallion's service; a pitcher of it
Was on the table, and California sadly came and emptied
    her glass. Whiskey, she thought,
Would have erased him till to-morrow; the thin red
    wine . . .
    "We have a good evening," he laughed, pouring it.
"One glass yet then I show you what the red fellow did."
    She moving toward the house-door his eyes
Followed her, the glass filled and the red juice ran over
    the table. When it struck the floor-planks   280
He heard and looked. "Who stuck the pig?" he muttered
    stupidly, "here's blood, here's blood," and trailed
    his fingers
In the red lake under the lamplight. While he was look-
    ing down the door creaked, she had slipped out-
    doors,

And he, his mouth curving like a faun's imagined the
chase under the solemn redwoods, the panting

And unresistant victim caught in a dark corner. He
emptied the glass and went outdoors

Into the dappled lanes of moonlight. No sound but the
April brook's. "Hey Bruno," he called, "find her.

Bruno, go find her." The dog after a little understood
and quested, the man following.

When California crouching by an oak-bush above the
house heard them come near she darted

To the open slope and ran down hill. The dog barked at
her heels, pleased with the game, and Johnny

Followed in silence. She ran down to the new corral, she
saw the stallion

Move like a lion along the timbers of the fence, the dark
arched neck shaking the nightfall   290

Of the great mane; she threw herself prone and writhed
under the bars, his hooves backing away from her

Made muffled thunder in the soft soil. She stood in the
midst of the corral, panting, but Johnny

Paused at the fence. The dog ran under it, and seeing the
stallion move, the woman standing quiet,

Danced after the beast, with white-toothed feints and
dashes. When Johnny saw the formidable dark
strength

Recoil from the dog, he climbed up over the fence.

The child Christine waked when her mother left her

And lay half dreaming, in the half-waking dream she
saw the ocean come up out of the west

And cover the world, she looked up through clear
water at the tops of the redwoods. She heard the
door creak

And the house empty; her heart shook her body, sitting
up on the bed, and she heard the dog

And crept toward light, where it gleamed under the
crack of the door. She opened the door, the room
was empty,   300

The table-top was a red lake under the lamplight. The
color of it was terrible to her;

She had seen the red juice drip from a coyote's muzzle
her father had shot one day in the hills

And carried him home over the saddle: she looked at the
rifle on the wall-rack: it was not moved:

She ran to the door, the dog was barking and the moon
was shining: she knew wine by the odor

But the color frightened her, the empty house frightened
her, she followed down hill in the white lane of
moonlight

The friendly noise of the dog. She saw in the big horse's
corral, on the level shoulder of the hill,

Black on white, the dark strength of the beast, the dancing fury of the dog, and the two others.

One fled, one followed; the big one charged, rearing; one
fell under his fore-hooves. She heard her mother

Scream: without thought she ran to the house, she dragged
a chair past the red pool and climbed to the rifle,

Got it down from the wall and lugged it somehow
through the door and down the hillside, under the
hard weight   310

Sobbing. Her mother stood by the rails of the corral,
she gave it to her. On the far side

The dog flashed at the plunging stallion; in the midst of
the space the man, slow-moving, like a hurt worm

Crawling, dragged his body by inches toward the fence-
line. Then California, resting the rifle

On the top rail, without doubting, without hesitance,

Aimed for the leaping body of the dog, and when it
stood, fired. It snapped, rolled over, lay quiet.

"O mother, you've hit Bruno!" "I couldn't see the sights
in the moonlight," she answered quietly. She stood

And watched, resting the rifle-butt on the ground. The
stallion wheeled, freed from his torment, the man

Lurched up to his knees, wailing a thin and bitter bird's
cry, and the roan thunder

Struck; hooves left nothing alive but teeth tore up the
remnant. "O mother, shoot, shoot!" Yet California

Stood carefully watching, till the beast having fed all his
fury stretched neck to utmost, head high,   320

And wrinkled back the upper lip from the teeth, yawning
obscene disgust over—not a man—

A smear on the moon-lake earth: then California moved
by some obscure human fidelity

Lifted the rifle. Each separate nerve-cell of her brain
flaming the stars fell from their places

Crying in her mind: she fired three times before the
haunches crumpled sidewise, the forelegs stiffening,

And the beautiful strength settled to earth: she turned
then on her little daughter the mask of a woman

Who has killed God. The night-wind veering, the smell
of the spilt wine drifted down hill from the house.

1925

Thomas Stearns Eliot

1888 ·

See page 859 for a biographical account of Eliot.

The Love Song of J. Alfred Prufrock

Written while Eliot was still an undergraduate at Harvard, "The Love Song of J. Alfred Prufrock" has attained the rank of an American classic. Prufrock is a modern Hamlet, that is, a Hamlet without the capacity for heroic action. The poem is a consummate portrait of the modern intellectual who is inhibited and bewildered by his intellectualism. (For an extraordinarily acute analysis, see Brooks and Warren, **Understanding Poetry.**)

S'io credesse che mia risposta fosse
A persona che mai tornasse al mondo,
Questa fiamma staria senza piu scosse.
Ma perciocche giammai di questo fondo
Non torno vivo alcun, s'i'odo il vero,
Senza tema d'infamia ti rispondo.

Let us go then, you and I,
When the evening is spread out against the sky
Like a patient etherized upon a table;
Let us go, through certain half-deserted streets,

The muttering retreats
Of restless nights in one-night cheap hotels
And sawdust restaurants with oyster-shells:
Streets that follow like a tedious argument
Of insidious intent
To lead you to an overwhelming question. . .   10
Oh, do not ask, 'What is it?'
Let us go and make our visit.

In the room the women come and go
Talking of Michelangelo.

The yellow fog that rubs its back upon the window-panes,
The yellow smoke that rubs its muzzle on the window-
            panes
Licked its tongue into the corners of the evening,
Lingered upon the pools that stand in drains,
Let fall upon its back the soot that falls from chimneys,
Slipped by the terrace, made a sudden leap,   20
And seeing that it was a soft October night,
Curled once about the house, and fell asleep.

S'io . . . rispondo. If I could believe that my answer might be to a person who should ever return into the world, this flame would stand without more quiverings; but inasmuch as, if I hear the truth, never from this depth did any living man return, without fear of infamy I answer thee (from Dante's "Inferno," Canto XXVII, ll. 61-66)

And indeed there will be time
For the yellow smoke that slides along the street,
Rubbing its back upon the window-panes;
There will be time, there will be time
To prepare a face to meet the faces that you meet;
There will be time to murder and create,
And time for all the works and days of hands
That lift and drop a question on your plate; 30
Time for you and time for me,
And time yet for a hundred indecisions,
And for a hundred visions and revisions,
Before the taking of a toast and tea.

In the room the women come and go
Talking of Michelangelo.

And indeed there will be time
To wonder, 'Do I dare?' and, 'Do I dare?'
Time to turn back and descend the stair,
With a bald spot in the middle of my hair— 40
(They will say: 'How his hair is growing thin!')
My morning coat, my collar mounting firmly to the chin,
My necktie rich and modest, but asserted by a simple
　　　pin—
(They will say: 'But how his arms and legs are thin!')
Do I dare
Disturb the universe?
In a minute there is time
For decisions and revisions which a minute will reverse.

For I have known them all already, known them all:—
Have known the evenings, mornings, afternoons, 50
I have measured out my life with coffee spoons;
I know the voices dying with a dying fall
Beneath the music from a farther room.
　　So how should I presume?

And I have known the eyes already, known them all—
The eyes that fix you in a formulated phrase,
And when I am formulated, sprawling on a pin,
When I am pinned and wriggling on the wall,
Then how should I begin
To spit out all the butt-ends of my days and ways? 60
　　And how should I presume?

And I have known the arms already, known them all—

Arms that are braceleted and white and bare
(But in the lamplight, downed with light brown hair!)
Is it perfume from a dress
That makes me so digress?
Arms that lie along a table, or wrap about a shawl.
　　And should I then presume?
　　And how should I begin?

　　　　　·　·　·　·　·　·

Shall I say, I have gone at dusk through narrow streets 70
And watched the smoke that rises from the pipes
Of lonely men in shirt-sleeves, leaning out of windows? ...
I should have been a pair of ragged claws
Scuttling across the floors of silent seas.

　　　　　·　·　·　·　·　·

And the afternoon, the evening, sleeps so peacefully!
Smoothed by long fingers,
Asleep ... tired ... or it malingers,
Stretched on the floor, here beside you and me.
Should I, after tea and cakes and ices,
Have the strength to force the moment to its crisis? 80
But though I have wept and fasted, wept and prayed,
Though I have seen my head (grown slightly bald)
　　　brought in upon a platter,
I am no prophet—and here's no great matter;
I have seen the moment of my greatness flicker,
And I have seen the eternal Footman hold my coat,
　　and snicker,
And in short, I was afraid.

And would it have been worth it, after all,
After the cups, the marmalade, the tea,
Among the porcelain, among some talk of you and me,
Would it have been worth while, 90
To have bitten off the matter with a smile,
To have squeezed the universe into a ball
To roll it toward some overwhelming question,
To say: 'I am Lazarus, come from the dead,
Come back to tell you all, I shall tell you all'—
If one, settling a pillow by her head,
　　Should say: 'That is not what I
　　　meant at all,

---

82 **head . . . platter,** an allusion to the beheading of John the
Baptist, whose head was brought to Herod "in a charger." See
Matthew 14:1-11 • 94 **Lazarus.** See John 11

The Love Song of J. Alfred Prufrock　943

That is not it, at all.'

＊　　＊　　＊　　＊　　＊

And would it have been worth it, after all,
Would it have been worth while,   100
After the sunsets and the dooryards and the sprinkled
    streets,
After the novels, after the teacups, after the skirts that
    trail along the floor—
And this, and so much more?—
It is impossible to say just what I mean!
But as if a magic lantern threw the nerves in patterns
    on a screen:
Would it have been worth while
If one, settling a pillow or throwing off a shawl,
And turning toward the window, should say:
   'That is not it at all,
   That is not what I meant, at all.'   110

＊　　＊　　＊　　＊　　＊

No! I am not Prince Hamlet, nor was meant to be;
Am an attendant lord, one that will do
To swell a progress, start a scene or two,
Advise the prince; no doubt, an easy tool,
Deferential, glad to be of use,
Politic, cautious, and meticulous;
Full of high sentence, but a bit obtuse;
At times, indeed, almost ridiculous—
Almost, at times, the Fool.

I grow old . . . I grow old . . .   120
I shall wear the bottoms of my trousers rolled.

Shall I part my hair behind? Do I dare to eat a peach?
I shall wear white flannel trousers, and walk upon the
    beach.
I have heard the mermaids singing, each to each.

I do not think that they will sing to me.

I have seen them riding seaward on the waves
Combing the white hair of the waves blown back
When the wind blows the water white and black.

We have lingered in the chambers of the sea
By sea-girls wreathed with seaweed red and brown   130
Till human voices wake us, and we drown.

           1917

944 *Eliot*

Sweeney among the Nightingales

Matthiessen's comment is helpful: "Eliot once remarked that all he consciously set out to create in 'Sweeney among the Nightingales' was a sense of foreboding. Yet the very exactitude with which he has built up his impression by means of the close details of his night-town scene, as well as by the way he underlines his effect through a reference both in the epigraph and in the final stanza to another scene of foreboding that ended in the murder of Agamemnon, inevitably causes his delineation to take on wider implications. The sharp contrast that seems at first simply to be mocking a debased present as it juxtaposes Sweeney with the hero of antiquity, ends in establishing also an undercurrent of moving drama: for a sympathetic feeling for Sweeney is set up by the realization that he is a man as well as Agamemnon, and that his plotted death is therefore likewise a human tragedy."

ὤμοι πέπληγμαι καιρίαν πληγὴν ἔσω.

Apeneck Sweeney spreads his knees
Letting his arms hang down to laugh,
The zebra stripes along his jaw
Swelling to maculate giraffe.

The circles of the stormy moon
Slide westward toward the River Plate,
Death and the Raven drift above
And Sweeney guards the hornèd gate.

Gloomy Orion and the Dog
Are veiled; and hushed the shrunken seas;   10

The Love Song of J. Alfred Prufrock • 117 **Full . . . sentence,** full of wisdom, said of the speech of Chaucer's "clerk of Oxenford." See the "Prologue" to the **Canterbury Tales,** l. 306
Sweeney among the Nightingales • ὤμοι . . . ἔσω. Alas! I am stricken by a timely blow within (from the **Agamemnon** of Aeschylus) • 6 **River Plate,** Río de la Plata, an estuary in South America • 8 **hornèd gate.** In classical mythology, the gate of horn is the gate of the abode of Sleep through which true dreams come forth • 9 **Orion . . . Dog,** constellations

The person in the Spanish cape
Tries to sit on Sweeney's knees

Slips and pulls the table cloth
Overturns a coffee-cup,
Reorganized upon the floor
She yawns and draws a stocking up;

The silent man in mocha brown
Sprawls at the window-sill and gapes;
The waiter brings in oranges
Bananas figs and hothouse grapes;   20

The silent vertebrate in brown
Contracts and concentrates, withdraws;
Rachel *née* Rabinovitch
Tears at the grapes with murderous paws;

She and the lady in the cape
Are suspect, thought to be in league;
Therefore the man with heavy eyes
Declines the gambit, shows fatigue,

Leaves the room and reappears
Outside the window, leaning in,   30
Branches of wistaria
Circumscribe a golden grin;

The host with someone indistinct
Converses at the door apart,
The nightingales are singing near
The Convent of the Sacred Heart,

And sang within the bloody wood
When Agamemnon cried aloud,
And let their liquid siftings fall
To stain the stiff dishonoured shroud.   40
                                                     1920

[handwritten annotations: withdraws with / when poisonous fruits brought in / Rachel – offers grapes to Sweeney – She's animal in that she's murderous – to murder him / grapes !! (poisoned) / out played the murderers / suggestion of his death! / alliteration / dead man]

Gerontion

Broadly speaking, "Gerontion" repeats the general situation of "Prufrock," but Gerontion is a more tragic figure:

he had more brilliant capacities than Prufrock and his disintegration is more complete. The poem is a masterly
embodiment of the metaphysical method described by
Eliot in his essay on "The Metaphysical Poets" as "a development by rapid association of thought which requires
considerable agility on the part of the reader." Matthiessen comments as follows on the method: "The transitions are sudden, but, in terms of the context, unmistakable. There could hardly be a more effective way
of stressing the intimate connection between the mysteries
of religion and sex than by linking together the Christian
story with the upsurging energies of spring. Yet it is also
'depraved' May, and suddenly we are aware that it is not
simply the Holy Communion that is being eaten and
drunk 'among whispers': that last phrase also relates to
the empty, slightly sinister cosmopolitan world in which
Gerontion's life has been betrayed, his passion and
ardour have been divided and lost."

Thou hast nor youth nor age
But as it were an after dinner sleep
Dreaming of both.

Here I am, an old man in a dry month,
Being read to by a boy, waiting for rain.
I was neither at the hot gates
Nor fought in the warm rain
Nor knee deep in the salt marsh, heaving a cutlass,
Bitten by flies, fought.
My house is a decayed house,
And the jew squats on the window sill, the owner,
Spawned in some estaminet of Antwerp,
Blistered in Brussels, patched and peeled in London. 10
The goat coughs at night in the field overhead;
Rocks, moss, stonecrop, iron, merds.
The woman keeps the kitchen, makes tea,
Sneezes at evening, poking the peevish gutter.
                                    I an old man,
A dull head among windy spaces.

Sweeney among the Nightingales • 28 gambit, strategy in chess by
which a player gives up a piece to gain an advantage • 38 **Agamemnon.**
His murder by his wife and her lover is the basis of the play by Aeschylus
Gerontion • **Thou . . . both.** See Measure for Measure, Act III, sc. i,
ll. 32-34 • 2 **waiting for rain.** Drought reappears as a recurrent theme
in **The Waste Land** • 12 **merds,** dung

Signs are taken for wonders. 'We would see a sign!'
The word within a word, unable to speak a word,
Swaddled with darkness. In the juvescence of the year
Came Christ the tiger   20

In depraved May, dogwood and chestnut, flowering judas,
To be eaten, to be divided, to be drunk
Among whispers; by Mr. Silvero
With caressing hands, at Limoges
Who walked all night in the next room;
By Hakagawa, bowing among the Titians;
By Madame de Tornquist, in the dark room
Shifting the candles; Fräulein von Kulp
Who turned in the hall, one hand on the door. Vacant
     shuttles
Weave the wind. I have no ghosts,   30
An old man in a draughty house
Under a windy knob.

After such knowledge, what forgiveness? Think now
History has many cunning passages, contrived corridors
And issues, deceives with whispering ambitions,
Guides us by vanities. Think now
She gives when our attention is distracted
And what she gives, gives with such supple confusions
That the giving famishes the craving. Gives too late
What's not believed in, or if still believed,   40
In memory only, reconsidered passion. Gives too soon
Into weak hands, what's thought can be dispensed with
Till the refusal propagates a fear. Think
Neither fear nor courage saves us. Unnatural vices
Are fathered by our heroism. Virtues
Are forced upon us by our impudent crimes.
These tears are shaken from the wrath-bearing tree.

The tiger springs in the new year. Us he devours. Think
     at last
We have not reached conclusion, when I
Stiffen in a rented house. Think at last   50
I have not made this show purposelessly
And it is not by any concitation
Of the backward devils
I would meet you upon this honestly.
I that was near your heart was removed therefrom
To lose beauty in terror, terror in inquisition.
I have lost my passion: why should I need to keep it
Since what is kept must be adulterated?

I have lost my sight, smell, hearing, taste and touch:
How should I use them for your closer contact?   60

These with a thousand small deliberations
Protract the profit of their chilled delirium,
Excite the membrane, when the sense has cooled,
With pungent sauces, multiply variety
In a wilderness of mirrors. What will the spider do,
Suspend its operations, will the weevil
Delay? De Bailhache, Fresca, Mrs. Cammel, whirled
Beyond the circuit of the shuddering Bear
In fractured atoms. Gull against the wind, in the windy
     straits
Of Belle Isle, or running on the Horn,   70
White feathers in the snow, the Gulf claims,
And an old man driven by the Trades
To a sleepy corner.

                              Tenants of the house,
Thoughts of a dry brain in a dry season.
                                                    1920

The Waste Land

"When a poet's mind is perfectly equipped for its work,"
Eliot has said, "it is constantly amalgamating disparate

17 We . . . sign! Compare Matthew 12:38-39: "Then certain of the
scribes and of the Pharisees answered, saying, Master, we would see a
sign from thee. But he answered and said unto them, An evil and
adulterous generation seeketh after a sign, and there shall no sign
be given to it . . ." • 18 word . . . word. Compare John 1:1: "In the
beginning was the Word, and the Word was with God, and the Word
was God." The lost "Word" reappears as a theme in Ash-Wednesday
• 19 Swaddled . . . darkness. Compare Job 38:9: "When I made
. . . thick darkness a swaddling-band for it [the sea]." Mary wrapped
the infant Jesus "in swaddling clothes" (Luke 2:7) • 19 juvescence
. . . year, when the year was growing young • 21 In depraved . . .
judas. Yvor Winters has pointed out the interesting fact that this line
is based upon the first paragraph of Chap. 18 in The Education of
Henry Adams • 23 Mr. Silvero. This name and other names of persons
in the poem are those of former acquaintances of Gerontion • 33
Think. The repetition of "think" recalls the similar use of "thinketh"
in the monologue of Browning's "Caliban upon Setebos" • 52 concitation, concerted agitation • 70 Belle Isle, between Labrador and Newfoundland • 72 Trades, the trade winds

experience." If the juxtapositions and transitions of this method present an unusual difficulty, Eliot's defense is that modern poetry must be difficult because, he argues, "our civilization comprehends great variety and complexity, and this variety and complexity, playing upon a refined sensibility, must produce various and complex results."

The Waste Land is, in part, a collection of characters and scenes drawn from the modern world: Madame Sosostris, the fortune teller; the crowd crossing London Bridge in the early morning fog; the woman sitting at her dressing table, and talking or trying to talk with her husband, or lover; the woman in an English pub discussing Lil with another woman; Mr. Eugenides, the Smyrna merchant; the typist and the clerk; the girl from Highbury and her experience in a canoe on the Thames; and others. These characters and scenes are symbols of the degradation and despair of the modern world.

But "realistic" scenes like these are only a part of the representation. The poem's intention is to show these things in relation to other things, to show them both in time and in eternity, and thereby achieve a rich dimensional development. The modern scene is shown, first, in relation to the historical past, and it would seem that there has been a decline. The bored woman is compared unfavorably with Cleopatra, whom age could not wither nor custom stale, the comparison being suggested by the verbal reminiscence of Shakespeare's description of Cleopatra's barge. The Thames, now littered with "cardboard boxes, cigarette ends / Or other testimony of summer nights," has deteriorated since Elizabethan times, when it was the scene of stately bridals, suggested by a line from Spenser's "Prothalamion." Apparent deterioration is everywhere: the typist is a degradation of Goldsmith's "lovely woman"; Sweeney and Mrs. Porter lack the dignity of Marvell's lovers, suggested by the verbal echo of "To His Coy Mistress"; and so on.

Further development in dimension (or depth of perspective) is achieved by showing the contemporary scene in a frame of reference which is essentially timeless, and which is drawn from ancient myths. Old Tiresias, who has suffered all, knowing "both sides of love," and "foresuffered all," having the power to foresee the future, is a dispassionate spectator and chorus. If the suggested comparisons between the present and the past seem to point to present deterioration, the commentary of Tire-

sias suggests the view that the decline is more apparent than real. The Fisher King, from the Grail legend, and the desert country, repeatedly described, are other symbols of timelessness: the evil of the world, the poem intends to say, is as old as the world itself. The present evil, however, is not nullified, or mitigated even, by the larger frames of reference; it is, rather, given added weight and significance when seen in the perspective of man's long and ageless experience.

The ironic futility of "Prufrock" is continued in The Waste Land, but the despair is greater and the religious implications (it is important to note) are correspondingly more emphatic. It is as if the poem meant to say that man must be reduced to utter despair before there can be a conscious striving toward religious faith. Many passages in The Waste Land suggest a religious "solution" (Eliot's solution was to be developed in "Ash-Wednesday" and Four Quartets). The desert passages recall the Old Testament in both tone and language. Compare, for example, Eliot's "Son of man, / You cannot say, or guess, for you know only / A heap of broken images" with Ezekiel's "Son of man, can these bones live? And I answered, O Lord God, thou knowest." Ecclesiastes 12 describes a waste land similar to that of the poem: ". . . and the grasshopper shall be a burden, and desire shall fail. . . ." The allusion to Christ's agony and death ("After the torchlight red on sweaty faces / After the frosty silence in the garden / After the agony ————") connotes Christian belief. The poem, however, reaches out to include all religions. Christ is associated with the Fisher King and other "hanged gods," and becomes one of many examples of the basic doctrine of life through death. Among the illustrations of the doctrine in the poem are the corpse buried in the garden, (emblem of fertility rites), which the Dog threatens to exhume and thereby prevent the rebirth of life, and the drowned Phoenician Sailor, whose eyes undergo a supernatural change. The Sanskrit words at the end (meaning "give, sympathize, control," and "the peace which passeth understanding") point up the antiquity and unity of religious belief.

Two of the best of the now numerous discussions of The Waste Land are that by Cleanth Brooks in Modern Poetry and the Tradition and that by George Williamson in Reader's Guide to T. S. Eliot. Other examples and references can be found in Leonard Unger's T. S. Eliot: A Selected Critique.

I

THE BURIAL OF THE DEAD

April is the cruellest month, breeding
Lilacs out of the dead land, mixing
Memory and desire, stirring
Dull roots with spring rain.
Winter kept us warm, covering
Earth in forgetful snow, feeding
A little life with dried tubers.
Summer surprised us, coming over the Starnbergersee
With a shower of rain; we stopped in the colonnade,
And went on in sunlight, into the Hofgarten,   10
And drank coffee, and talked for an hour.
Bin gar keine Russin, stamm' aus Litauen, echt deutsch.
And when we were children, staying at the archduke's,
My cousin's, he took me out on a sled,
And I was frightened. He said, Marie,
Marie, hold on tight. And down we went.
In the mountains, there you feel free.
I read, much of the night, and go south in the winter.

What are the roots that clutch, what branches grow
Out of this stony rubbish? Son of man,   20
You cannot say, or guess, for you know only
A heap of broken images, where the sun beats,
And the dead tree gives no shelter, the cricket no relief,
And the dry stone no sound of water. Only
There is shadow under this red rock,
(Come in under the shadow of this red rock),
And I will show you something different from either
Your shadow at morning striding behind you
Or your shadow at evening rising to meet you;
I will show you fear in a handful of dust.   30

> *Frisch weht der Wind*
> *Der Heimat zu*
> *Mein Irisch Kind,*
> *Wo weilest du?*

"You gave me hyacinths first a year ago;
"They called me the hyacinth girl."
—Yet when we came back, late, from the Hyacinth
    garden,
Your arms full, and your hair wet, I could not
Speak, and my eyes failed, I was neither
Living nor dead, and I knew nothing,   40
Looking into the heart of light, the silence.
Oed' und leer das Meer.

Madame Sosostris, famous clairvoyante,
Had a bad cold, nevertheless
Is known to be the wisest woman in Europe,
With a wicked pack of cards. Here, said she,
Is your card, the drowned Phoenician Sailor,
(Those are pearls that were his eyes. Look!)
Here is Belladonna, the Lady of the Rocks,
The lady of situations.   50
Here is the man with three staves, and here the Wheel,

In the following annotations on **The Waste Land**, Eliot's own notes (from his **Collected Poems**, 1936) are identified by quotation marks and by (Eliot) after each note. Supplementary notes have been supplied by the editors

"Not only the title, but the plan and a good deal of the incidental symbolism of the poem were suggested by Miss Jessie L. Weston's book on the Grail legend: **From Ritual to Romance** (Cambridge). Indeed, so deeply am I indebted, Miss Weston's book will elucidate the difficulties of the poem much better than my notes can do; and I recommend it (apart from the great interest of the book itself) to any who think such elucidation of the poem worth the trouble. To another work of anthropology I am indebted in general, one which has influenced our generation profoundly; I mean **The Golden Bough**; I have used especially the two volumes **Adonis, Attis, Osiris.** Anyone who is acquainted with these works will immediately recognise in the poem certain references to vegetation ceremonies." (Eliot) "NAM . . . θέλω," "Yes, and I myself saw with my own eyes the Sibyl of Cumae hanging in a cage; and when the children cried at her, 'Sibyl, what do you want?' she used to reply, 'I want to die.' " Petronius, **Satyricon**, XLVIII • 12 **Bin . . . deutsch,** I am no Russian, I come from Lithuania, true German • 20 **Son of man,** "Cf. Ezekiel 2:1." (Eliot) • 23 **cricket no relief,** "Cf. Ecclesiastes 12:5." (Eliot) • 31 **Frisch . . . du?** "V. Tristan und Isolde, I, verses 5-8." (Eliot) "The wind blows fresh homeward, my Irish child, where do you tarry?" From the opera by Wagner • 42 **Oed'** . . . **Meer,** "Id. III, verse 24." (Eliot) "Desolate and empty the sea" • 46 **pack of cards.** "I am not familiar with the exact constitution of the Tarot pack of cards, from which I have obviously departed to suit my own convenience. The Hanged Man, a member of the traditional pack, fits my purpose in two ways: because he is associated in my mind with the Hanged God of Frazer, and because I associate him with the hooded figure in the passage of the disciples to Emmaus in Part V. The Phoenician Sailor and the Merchant appear later; also the 'crowds of people,' and Death by Water is executed in Part IV. The Man with Three Staves (an authentic member of the Tarot pack) I associate, quite arbitrarily, with the Fisher King himself." (Eliot) Frazer is the author of **The Golden Bough**; the Fisher King is the impotent ruler of the waste land described in **From Ritual to Romance** • 48 **Those . . . eyes,** from Ariel's song in Shakespeare's **The Tempest**, Act I, sc. ii, l. 398

And here is the one-eyed merchant, and this card,
Which is blank, is something he carries on his back,
Which I am forbidden to see. I do not find
The Hanged Man. Fear death by water.
I see crowds of people, walking round in a ring.
Thank you. If you see dear Mrs. Equitone,
Tell her I bring the horoscope myself:
One must be so careful these days.

Unreal City,   60
Under the brown fog of a winter dawn,
A crowd flowed over London Bridge, so many,
I had not thought death had undone so many.
Sighs, short and infrequent, were exhaled,
And each man fixed his eyes before his feet.
Flowed up the hill and down King William Street,
To where Saint Mary Woolnoth kept the hours
With a dead sound on the final stroke of nine.
There I saw one I knew, and stopped him, crying:
      "Stetson!
"You who were with me in the ships at Mylae!   70
"That corpse you planted last year in your garden,
"Has it begun to sprout? Will it bloom this year?
"Or has the sudden frost disturbed its bed?
"Oh keep the Dog far hence, that's friend to men,
"Or with his nails he'll dig it up again!
"You! hypocrite lecteur!—mon semblable,—mon frère!"

                                                        II

                                    A GAME OF CHESS

The chair she sat in, like a burnished throne,
Glowed on the marble, where the glass
Held up by standards wrought with fruited vines
From which a golden Cupidon peeped out   80
(Another hid his eyes behind his wing)
Doubled the flames of sevenbranched candelabra
Reflecting light upon the table as
The glitter of her jewels rose to meet it,
From satin cases poured in rich profusion;
In vials of ivory and coloured glass
Unstoppered, lurked her strange synthetic perfumes,
Unguent, powdered, or liquid—troubled, confused
And drowned the sense in odours; stirred by the air
That freshened from the window, these ascended   90
In fattening the prolonged candle-flames,
Flung their smoke into the laquearia,

Stirring the pattern on the coffered ceiling.
Huge sea-wood fed with copper
Burned green and orange, framed by the coloured stone,
In which sad light a carvèd dolphin swam.
Above the antique mantel was displayed
As though a window gave upon the sylvan scene
The change of Philomel, by the barbarous king
So rudely forced; yet there the nightingale   100
Filled all the desert with inviolable voice
And still she cried, and still the world pursues,
"Jug Jug" to dirty ears.
And other withered stumps of time

---

60 **Unreal City,** "Cf. Baudelaire:
   'Fourmillante cité, cité pleine de rêves,
   'Où le spectre en plein jour raccroche le passant.' " (Eliot)
"Swarming city, city full of dreams, where a ghost in broad daylight
accosts the passerby." From "Les Sept Vieillards" • 63 **I had . . .
so many,** "Cf. Inferno III, 55-57:
                        'si lunga tratta
   di gente, ch'io non avrei mai creduto
   che morte tanta n'avesse disfatta.' " (Eliot)
"So long a train of people, I never should have believed death had
undone so many" • 64 **Sighs . . . exhaled,** "Cf. Inferno IV, 25-27:
   'Quivi, secondo che per ascoltare,
   'non avea pianto, ma' che di sospiri,
   'che l'aura eterna facevan tremare.' " (Eliot)
"Here, as one listened, there was no complaining, but only sighs, which
made the eternal air tremble" • 68 **With . . . nine,** "A phenomenon
which I have often noticed." (Eliot) • 70 **Mylae,** Roman naval victory
over Carthage in 260 B.C. • 74 **Dog,** "Cf. the Dirge in Webster's
White Devil." (Eliot) The lines referred to occur in Act V, sc. iv of
John Webster's play: "But keep the wolf far thence, that's foe to
men,/For with his nails he'll dig them up again." The "corpse" has
been taken to refer to the fertility god, and the "sprouting" to the
god's resurrection. An analogous concept occurs in Romans 6:5: "For if
we have been planted together in the likeness of His death, we shall
be also in the likeness of His resurrection" • 76 **hypocrite . . . frère,**
"V. Baudelaire, Preface to **Fleurs du Mal.**" (Eliot) "Hypocritical reader,
my likeness, my brother" • 77 **The chair . . . throne,** "Cf. **Antony
and Cleopatra,** II, ii, l. 190." (Eliot) The famous passage in Shakespeare describing Cleopatra's barge begins "The barge she sat in,
like a burnished throne . . ." • 92 **laquearia,** "V. Aeneid, I. 726:
   'dependent lychni laquearibus aureis incensi, et noctem flammis
   funalia vincunt.' " (Eliot)
"Lighted lamps hang from the fretted ceiling of gold, and flaming
torches overcome the night" • 98 **sylvan scene,** "V. Milton, **Paradise
Lost,** IV, 140." (Eliot) Here Milton describes the Garden of Eden as
first viewed by Satan • 99 **Philomel,** "V. Ovid, **Metamorphoses,** VI,
Philomela." (Eliot) Here Ovid tells the story of the rape of Philomela
by Tereus, the cutting out of her tongue, and her subsequent change
into a nightingale. The words "jug, jug" (l. 103) were used by English
poets to represent the nightingale's song. See, for example, John Lyly's
"Alexander and Campaspe": "What bird so sings, yet does so wail?/
Oh, 'tis the ravished nightingale,/Jug, jug, jug, jug, tereu, she cries,/
And still her woes at midnight rise" • 100 **nightingale,** "Cf. Part III,
l. 204." (Eliot)

Were told upon the walls; staring forms
Leaned out, leaning, hushing the room enclosed.
Footsteps shuffled on the stair.
Under the firelight, under the brush, her hair
Spread out in fiery points
Glowed into words, then would be savagely still.   110

"My nerves are bad to-night. Yes, bad. Stay with me.
"Speak to me. Why do you never speak. Speak.
"What are you thinking of? What thinking? What?
      What?
"I never know what you are thinking. Think."

I think we are in rats' alley
Where the dead men lost their bones.

"What is that noise?"
                              The wind under the door.
"What is that noise now? What is the wind doing?"
                              Nothing again nothing.   120
                                                    "Do
"You know nothing? Do you see nothing? Do you
      remember
"Nothing?"

              I remember
Those are pearls that were his eyes.
"Are you alive, or not? Is there nothing in your head?"
                                                    But
O O O O that Shakespeherian Rag—
It's so elegant
So intelligent   130
"What shall I do now? What shall I do?"
"I shall rush out as I am, and walk the street
"With my hair down, so. What shall we do to-morrow?
"What shall we ever do?"
                              The hot water at ten.
And if it rains, a closed car at four.
And we shall play a game of chess,
Pressing lidless eyes and waiting for a knock upon the
      door.

When Lil's husband got demobbed, I said—
I didn't mince my words, I said to her myself,   140
HURRY UP PLEASE ITS TIME

Now Albert's coming back, make yourself a bit smart.
He'll want to know what you done with that money he
      gave you
To get yourself some teeth. He did, I was there.
You have them all out, Lil, and get a nice set,
He said, I swear, I can't bear to look at you.
And no more can't I, I said, and think of poor Albert,
He's been in the army four years, he wants a good time,
And if you don't give it him, there's others will, I said.
Oh is there, she said. Something o' that, I said.   150
Then I'll know who to thank, she said, and give me a
      straight look.
HURRY UP PLEASE ITS TIME
If you don't like it you can get on with it, I said.
Others can pick and choose if you can't.
But if Albert makes off, it won't be for lack of telling.
You ought to be ashamed, I said, to look so antique.
(And her only thirty-one.)
I can't help it, she said, pulling a long face,
It's them pills I took, to bring it off, she said.
(She's had five already and nearly died of young George.)
The chemist said it would be all right, but I've never
      been the same.   161
You *are* a proper fool, I said.
Well, if Albert won't leave you alone, there it is, I said,
What you get married for if you don't want children?
HURRY UP PLEASE ITS TIME
Well, that Sunday Albert was home, they had a hot
      gammon,
And they asked me in to dinner, to get the beauty of it
      hot—
HURRY UP PLEASE ITS TIME
HURRY UP PLEASE ITS TIME
Goonight Bill. Goonight Lou. Goonight May. Goonight.
Ta ta. Goonight. Goonight.   171
Good night ladies, good night, sweet ladies, good night,
      good night.

---

115 rats' alley, "Cf. Part III, I. 195." (Eliot) • 118 The wind,
"Cf. Webster: 'Is the wind in that door still?'" (Eliot) The quotation
is from John Webster's The Devil's Law Case, Act III, sc. ii, I. 162 •
125 Those . . . eyes, "Cf. Part I, I. 37, 48." (Eliot) • 137 game
of chess, "Cf. the game of chess in Middleton's Women Beware
Women." (Eliot) In Act II, sc. ii, of Thomas Middleton's play, a chess
game is used to distract the attention of a mother-in-law while her
daughter-in-law is being seduced by a highborn lover, the husband
being absent • 141 HURRY . . . TIME, the call denoting closing time
in an English pub • 172 Good . . . night. The line is taken from
Ophelia's mad speech in Hamlet, Act IV, sc. v, I. 74

III

THE FIRE SERMON

The river's tent is broken: the last fingers of leaf
Clutch and sink into the wet bank. The wind
Crosses the brown land, unheard. The nymphs are
    departed.
Sweet Thames, run softly, till I end my song.
The river bears no empty bottles, sandwich papers,
Silk handkerchiefs, cardboard boxes, cigarette ends
Or other testimony of summer nights. The nymphs are
    departed.
And their friends, the loitering heirs of city directors;
Departed, have left no addresses.   181
By the waters of Leman I sat down and wept . . .
Sweet Thames, run softly till I end my song,
Sweet Thames, run softly, for I speak not loud or long.
But at my back in a cold blast I hear
The rattle of the bones, and chuckle spread from ear to
    ear.
A rat crept softly through the vegetation
Dragging its slimy belly on the bank
While I was fishing in the dull canal
On a winter evening round behind the gashouse   190
Musing upon the king my brother's wreck
And on the king my father's death before him.
White bodies naked on the low damp ground
And bones cast in a little low dry garret,
Rattled by the rat's foot only, year to year.
But at my back from time to time I hear
The sound of horns and motors, which shall bring
Sweeney to Mrs. Porter in the spring.
O the moon shone bright on Mrs. Porter
And on her daughter   200
They wash their feet in soda water
Et O ces voix d'enfants, chantant dans la coupole!

Twit twit twit
Jug jug jug jug jug jug
So rudely forc'd.
Tereu

Unreal City
Under the brown fog of a winter noon
Mr. Eugenides, the Smyrna merchant
Unshaven, with a pocket full of currants
C.i.f. London: documents at sight,   210

Asked me in demotic French
To luncheon at the Cannon Street Hotel
Followed by a weekend at the Metropole.
At the violet hour, when the eyes and back
Turn upward from the desk, when the human engine
    waits
Like a taxi throbbing waiting,
I Tiresias, though blind, throbbing between two lives,

---

176 **Sweet . . . song,** "V. Spenser, *Prothalamion.*" (Eliot) The line
is the refrain of Edmund Spenser's poem • 182 **By . . . wept,**
Cf. Psalms 137: "By the rivers of Babylon, there we sat down, yea,
we wept, when we remembered Zion." "Leman" is the Swiss name
for Lake Geneva. The three dots, here and elsewhere in the poem, are
the author's, and do not denote omissions • 192 **the king . . .
father's death,** "Cf. **The Tempest,** I, ii." (Eliot) Compare especially
lines 389-391: "Sitting on a bank, / Weeping again the King my
father's wrack, / This music crept by me upon the waters. . . ."
Eliot's passage alludes obliquely to the Fisher King of the Grail
Legend • 196 **But . . . hear,** "Cf. Marvell, **To His Coy Mistress.**"
(Eliot) The especially relevant lines are: "But ever at my back I hear /
Time's winged chariot, hurrying near . . ." • 197 **The sound . . .
bring,** "Cf. Day, **Parliament of Bees:**
    'When of the sudden, listening, you shall hear,
    'A noise of horns and hunting, which shall bring
    'Actaeon to Diana in the spring,
    'Where all shall see her naked skin . . .' " (Eliot)
• 199 **O the moon,** "I do not know the origin of the ballad from
which these lines are taken: it was reported to me from Sydney,
Australia." (Eliot) Eliot may possibly have known also the popular
American song whose chorus begins with the line, "O the moon
shines tonight on pretty Redwing" • 202 **Et . . . coupole,** "V. Verlaine,
Parsifal." (Eliot) "And O the voices of the children chanting in the
choir" • 210 **currants.** "The currants were quoted at a price 'carriage
and insurance free to London'; and the Bill of Lading etc. were to be
handed to the buyer upon payment of the sight draft." (Eliot) • 218
Tiresias. "Tiresias, although a mere spectator and not indeed a
'character,' is yet the most important personage in the poem, uniting
all the rest. Just as the one-eyed merchant, seller of currants, melts
into the Phoenician Sailor, and the latter is not wholly distinct from
Ferdinand Prince of Naples, so all the women are one woman, and
the two sexes meet in Tiresias. What Tiresias sees, in fact, is the
substance of the poem. The whole passage from Ovid is of great
anthropological interest:
    '. . . .Cum Iunone iocos et maior vestra profecto est
    Quam, quae contingit maribus,' dixisse, 'voluptas.'
    Illa negat; placuit quae sit sententia docti
    Quaerere Tiresiae: venus huic erat utraque nota.
    Nam duo magnorum viridi coeuntia silva
    Corpora serpentum baculi violaverat ictu
    Deque viro factus, mirabile, femina septem
    Egerat autumnos; octavo rursus eosdem
    Vidit et 'est vestrae si tanta potentia plagae,'
    Dixit 'ut auctoris sortem in contraria mutet,
    Nunc quoque vos feriam!' percussis anguibus isdem
    Forma prior rediit genetivaque venit imago.
    Arbiter hic igitur sumptus de lite iocosa
    Dicta Iovis firmat; gravius Saturnia iusto
218 continued on following page

Old man with wrinkled female breasts, can see
At the violet hour, the evening hour that strives   220
Homeward, and brings the sailor home from sea,
The typist home at teatime, clears her breakfast, lights
Her stove, and lays out food in tins.
Out of the window perilously spread
Her drying combinations touched by the sun's last rays,
On the divan are piled (at night her bed)
Stockings, slippers, camisoles, and stays.
I Tiresias, old man with wrinkled dugs
Perceived the scene, and foretold the rest—
I too awaited the expected guest.   230
He, the young man carbuncular, arrives,
A small house agent's clerk, with one bold stare,
One of the low on whom assurance sits
As a silk hat on a Bradford millionaire.
The time is now propitious, as he guesses,
The meal is ended, she is bored and tired,
Endeavours to engage her in caresses
Which still are unreproved, if undesired.
Flushed and decided, he assaults at once;
Exploring hands encounter no defence;   2:0
His vanity requires no response,
And makes a welcome of indifference.
(And I Tiresias have foresuffered all
Enacted on this same divan or bed;
I who have sat by Thebes below the wall
And walked among the lowest of the dead.)
Bestows one final patronising kiss,
And gropes his way, finding the stairs unlit . . .

She turns and looks a moment in the glass,
Hardly aware of her departed lover;   )
Her brain allows one half-formed thought to pass
"Well now that's done; and I'm glad it's over."
When lovely woman stoops to folly and
Paces about her room again, alone,
She smoothes her hair with automatic hand,
And puts a record on the gramaphone.

"This music crept by me upon the waters"
And along the Strand, up Queen Victoria Street.
O City city, I can sometimes hear
Beside a public bar in Lower Thames Street,   260
The pleasant whining of a mandoline
And a clatter and a chatter from within
Where fishmen lounge at noon: where the walls

Of Magnus Martyr hold
Inexplicable splendour of Ionian white and gold.

> The river sweats
> Oil and tar
> The barges drift
> With the turning tide
> Red sails   270
> Wide

218 continued from preceding page
> Nec pro materia fertur doluisse suique
> Iudicis aeterna damnavit lumina nocte,
> At pater omnipotens (neque enim licet irrita cuiquam
> Facta dei fecisse deo) pro lumine adempto
> Scire futura dedit poenamque levavit honore.'' (Eliot)
"Jupiter, by chance, well drenched with nectar, laid aside all weighty cares, and engaged in some free jokes with Juno, in her idle moments, and said: 'Decidedly the pleasure of you females, is greater than that which falls to the lot of us males.' She denied it. It was agreed between them, to ask what was the opinion of the experienced Tiresias. To him both pleasures were well known. For he had separated with a blow of his staff two bodies of large serpents as they were coupling in a green wood; and (passing strange) become a woman from a man, he had spent seven autumns. In the eighth, he again saw the same serpents, and said, 'If the power of a stroke given you is so great as to change the condition of the giver into the opposite one, I will now strike you again.' Having struck the same snakes, his former sex returned, and his original shape came again. He, therefore, being chosen as umpire in this sportive contest, confirmed the words of Jove. The daughter of Saturn is said to have grieved more than was fit, and not in proportion to the subject; and she condemned the eyes of the umpire to eternal darkness. But the omnipotent father (for it is not allowed any God to cancel the acts of another Deity) gave him the knowledge of things to come, in recompense for his loss of sight, and alleviated his punishment by this honour.'' Ovid's **Metamorphoses**, III, 320-338. Translation of Henry T. Riley • **221 brings . . . sea**, "This may not appear as exact as Sappho's lines, but I had in mind the 'longshore' or 'dory' fisherman, who returns at nightfall.'' (Eliot) Eliot refers to Sappho's apostrophe to the Evening Star: "Hesperus, you bring home all things the bright morning dispersed—the sheep, the goat, the child to its mother,'' Byron paraphrased Sappho in the famous stanza in **Don Juan** (III, 107) beginning: "Oh, Hesperus! thou bringest all good things—/Home to the weary, to the hungry cheer . . . .'' Cf. also the well-known line from Robert Louis Stevenson's "Requiem": "Home is the sailor, home from sea'' • **253 When . . . folly**, "V. Goldsmith, the song in **The Vicar of Wakefield**." (Eliot) The lines, in Chap. XXIV, are as follows: "When lovely woman stoops to folly,/And finds too late that men betray,/What charm can soothe her melancholy?/What art can wash her guilt away?/The only art her guilt to cover,/To hide her shame from every eye,/To give repentance to her lover,/And wring his bosom—is to die'' • **257 "This . . . waters**," "V. **The Tempest**, as above." (Eliot) See the note on l. 192 • **264 Magnus Martyr**. "The interior of St. Magnus Martyr is to my mind one of the finest among Wren's interiors. See **The Proposed Demolition of Nineteen City Churches** (P. S. King & Son, Ltd.)." (Eliot) • **266 The river sweats**. "The Song of the (three) Thames-daughters begins here. From line 292 to 306 inclusive they speak in turn. V. **Götterdämmerung**, III, i: the Rhine-daughters." (Eliot) In the passage referred to in Wagner's work, the three Rhine-daughters lament the loss of the gold entrusted to their custody

To leeward, swing on the heavy spar.
The barges wash
Drifting logs
Down Greenwich reach
Past the Isle of Dogs.
    Weialala leia
    Wallala leialala

Elizabeth and Leicester
Beating oars 280
The stern was formed
A gilded shell
Red and gold
The brisk swell
Rippled both shores
Southwest wind
Carried down stream
The peal of bells
White towers
    Weialala leia
    Wallala leialala 290

"Trams and dusty trees.
Highbury bore me. Richmond and Kew
Undid me. By Richmond I raised my knees
Supine on the floor of a narrow canoe."

"My feet are at Moorgate, and my heart
Under my feet. After the event
He wept. He promised 'a new start.'
I made no comment. What should I resent?"

"On Margate Sands. 300
I can connect
Nothing with nothing.
The broken fingernails of dirty hands.
My people humble people who expect
Nothing."
    la la

To Carthage then I came

Burning burning burning burning
O Lord Thou pluckest me out
O Lord Thou pluckest 310

burning

DEATH BY WATER

Phlebas the Phoenician, a fortnight dead,
Forgot the cry of gulls, and the deep sea swell
And the profit and loss.
       A current under sea
Picked his bones in whispers. As he rose and fell
He passed the stages of his age and youth
Entering the whirlpool.
       Gentile or Jew
O you who turn the wheel and look to windward, 320
Consider Phlebas, who was once handsome and tall as you.

V

WHAT THE THUNDER SAID

After the torchlight red on sweaty faces
After the frosty silence in the gardens
After the agony in stony places
The shouting and the crying
Prison and palace and reverberation

---

279 **Elizabeth and Leicester,** "V. Froude, **Elizabeth,** Vol. I, ch. iv, letter of De Quadra to Philip of Spain: 'In the afternoon we were in a barge, watching the games on the river. (The queen) was alone with Lord Robert and myself on the poop, when they began to talk nonsense, and went so far that Lord Robert at last said, as I was on the spot there was no reason why they should not be married if the queen pleased.' " (Eliot) De Quadra, a Catholic bishop, was Spanish Ambassador at Elizabeth's court • 293 **Highbury . . . Undid me,** "Cf. Purgatorio, V, 133:

    'Ricorditi di me, che son la Pia;
    'Siena mi fe', disfecemi Maremma,' " (Eliot)

"Remember me, who am La Pia; Siena made me, Maremma unmade me" • 307 **To Carthage . . . came,** "V. St. Augustine's **Confessions:** 'to Carthage then I came, where a cauldron of unholy loves sang all about mine ears.' " (Eliot) • 308 **Burning . . . burning.** "The complete text of the Buddha's Fire Sermon (which corresponds in importance to the Sermon on the Mount) from which these words are taken, will be found translated in the late Henry Clarke Warren's **Buddhism in Translation** (Harvard Oriental Series). Mr. Warren was one of the great pioneers of Buddhist studies in the Occident." (Eliot) • 309 **O Lord . . . out,** "From St. Augustine's **Confessions** again. The collocation of these two representatives of eastern and western asceticism, as the culmination of this part of the poem, is not an accident." (Eliot) **V. What the Thunder Said:** "In the first part of Part V three themes are employed: the journey to Emmaus, the approach to the Chapel Perilous (see Miss Weston's book) and the present decay of eastern Europe." (Eliot) For the journey to Emmaus, see Luke 24 • 322 **torch-light.** The opening lines refer to events preceding the crucifixion of Christ. Cf. particularly Luke 22:23

Of thunder of spring over distant mountains
He who was living is now dead
We who were living are now dying
With a little patience   330

Here is no water but only rock
Rock and no water and the sandy road
The road winding above among the mountains
Which are mountains of rock without water
If there were water we should stop and drink
Amongst the rock one cannot stop or think
Sweat is dry and feet are in the sand
If there were only water amongst the rock
Dead mountain mouth of carious teeth that cannot spit
Here one can neither stand nor lie nor sit   340
There is not even silence in the mountains
But dry sterile thunder without rain
There is not even solitude in the mountains
But red sullen faces sneer and snarl
From doors of mudcracked houses
                        If there were water
        And no rock
        If there were rock
        And also water
        And water   350
        A spring
        A pool among the rock
        If there were the sound of water only
        Not the cicada
        And dry grass singing
        But sound of water over a rock
        Where the hermit-thrush sings in the pine trees
        Drip drop drip drop drop drop drop
        But there is no water

Who is the third who walks always beside you?   360
When I count, there are only you and I together
But when I look ahead up the white road
There is always another one walking beside you
Gliding wrapt in a brown mantle, hooded
I do not know whether a man or a woman
—But who is that on the other side of you?

What is that sound high in the air
Murmur of maternal lamentation

Who are those hooded hordes swarming
Over endless plains, stumbling in cracked earth   370
Ringed by the flat horizon only
What is the city over the mountains
Cracks and reforms and bursts in the violet air
Falling towers
Jerusalem Athens Alexandria
Vienna London
Unreal

A woman drew her long black hair out tight
And fiddled whisper music on those strings
And bats with baby faces in the violet light   380
Whistled, and beat their wings
And crawled head downward down a blackened wall
And upside down in air were towers
Tolling reminiscent bells, that kept the hours
And voices singing out of empty cisterns and exhausted
        wells.

In this decayed hole among the mountains
In the faint moonlight, the grass is singing
Over the tumbled graves, about the chapel

357 hermit-thrush. "This is Turdus aonalaschkae pallasii, the hermit-
thrush which I have heard in Quebec County. Chapman says (Handbook of Birds of Eastern North America) 'it is most at home in
secluded woodland and thickety retreats. . . . Its notes are not
remarkable for variety or volume, but in purity and sweetness of tone
and exquisite modulation they are unequalled.' Its 'water-dripping
song' is justly celebrated." (Eliot) • 360 the third. "The following
lines were stimulated by the account of one of the Antarctic expeditions (I forget which, but I think one of Shackleton's): it was related
that the party of explorers, at the extremity of their strength, had the
constant delusion that there was one more member than could actually
be counted." (Eliot) Cf. also the journey to Emmaus, Luke 24. Eliot's
account is symbolical of the resurrection of the fertility god, and the
lack of faith and consequent blindness in the Waste Land • 367-377
What . . . Unreal, "Cf. Hermann Hesse, Blick ins Chaos: 'Schon ist
halb Europa, schon ist zumindest der halbe Osten Europas auf dem
Wege zum Chaos, fährt betrunken im heiligem Wahn am Abgrund
entlang und singt dazu, singt betrunken und hymnisch wie Dmitri
Karamasoff sang. Ueber diese Lieder lacht der Bürger beleidigt, der
Heilige und Seher hört sie mit Tränen.' " (Eliot) "Already half of Europe,
already at least half of Eastern Europe, is on the way to chaos, going
drunk in holy folly along the edge of the abyss and singing drunken
hymns as Dmitri Karamasoff did. The burgher laughs scornfully at these
songs while the saint and seer hear them with tears." The allusion is
to Dostoievski's The Brothers Karamazov • 388 chapel, the Chapel
Perilous (cf. Jessie L. Weston's From Ritual to Romance, already
referred to) where, according to the legends of the Holy Grail, the
knight must endure supernatural terrors as a preparation for his quest

There is the empty chapel, only the wind's home.
It has no windows, and the door swings,   390
Dry bones can harm no one.
Only a cock stood on the rooftree
Co co rico co co rico
In a flash of lightning. Then a damp gust
Bringing rain

Ganga was sunken, and the limp leaves
Waited for rain, while the black clouds
Gathered far distant, over Himavant.
The jungle crouched, humped in silence.
Then spoke the thunder   400
DA
Datta: what have we given?
My friend, blood shaking my heart
The awful daring of a moment's surrender
Which an age of prudence can never retract
By this, and this only, we have existed
Which is not to be found in our obituaries
Or in memories draped by the beneficent spider
Or under seals broken by the lean solicitor
In our empty rooms   410
DA
Dayadhvam: I have heard the key
Turn in the door once and turn once only
We think of the key, each in his prison
Thinking of the key, each confirms a prison
Only at nightfall, aethereal rumours
Revive for a moment a broken Coriolanus
DA
Damyata: The boat responded
Gaily, to the hand expert with sail and oar   420
The sea was calm, your heart would have responded
Gaily, when invited, beating obedient
To controlling hands

       I sat upon the shore
Fishing, with the arid plain behind me
Shall I at least set my lands in order?
London Bridge is falling down falling down falling down
Poi s'ascose nel foco che gli affina
Quando fiam uti chelidon—O swallow swallow
Le Prince d'Aquitaine à la tour abolie   430
These fragments I have shored against my ruins

Why then Ile fit you. Hieronymo's mad againe.
Datta. Dayadhvam. Damyata.
    Shantih shantih shantih

1922

---

393 **Co . . . rico.** The crowing of the cock has at least a double association: the dispersal of ghosts and evil spirits (cf. **Hamlet,** Act I, sc. ii, I. 160), and Peter's denial of Christ (see Matthew 26:74) • 402 **Datta,** " 'Datta, dayadhvam, damyata' (Give, sympathise, control). The fable of the meaning of the Thunder is found in the **Brihadaranyaka-Upanishad,** 5, 1. A translation is found in Deussen's **Sechzig Upanishads des Veda,** p. 489." (Eliot) • 408 **draped . . . spider,** "Cf. Webster, **The White Devil,** V, vi:

      '. . . they'll remarry
  Ere the worm pierce your winding-sheet, ere the spider
  Make a thin curtain for your epitaphs.' " (Eliot)

• 412 **the key,** "Cf. **Inferno,** XXXIII, 46:
  'ed io sentii chiavar l'uscio di sotto
  all 'orribile torre.'
[" . . . and below I heard the door of the horrible tower being closed up," said by Ugolino to Dante] Also F. H. Bradley, **Appearance and Reality,** p. 346: 'My external sensations are no less private to myself than are my thoughts or my feelings. In either case my experience falls within my own circle, a circle closed on the outside; and, with all its elements alike, every sphere is opaque to the others which surround it . . . . In brief, regarded as an existence which appears in a soul, the whole world for each is peculiar and private to that soul.' " (Eliot) • 417 **broken Coriolanus,** the hero of Shakespeare's play of that name, a Roman general and aristocrat, who fell the victim of his own pride and the people's ingratitude • 425 **Fishing,** "V. Weston: **From Ritual to Romance:** chapter on the Fisher King." (Eliot) "The title of Fisher," says Miss Weston. "has, from the earliest ages, been associated with Deities who were held to be specially connected with the origin and preservation of life." In Eliot's treatment, the Fisher King, like Christ and the Fertility gods, is symbolical of life through death • 428 **Poi . . . affina,** "V. **Purgatorio,** XXVI, 148:
  ' "Ara vos prec per aquella valor
  "que vos guida al som de l'escalina,
  "sovegna vos a temps de ma dolor."
  Poi s'ascose nel foco che gli affina.' " (Eliot)
" 'Now I pray you by that power which guides you to the top of this stairway, be mindful of my pain in proper season.' He hid himself then in the fire which refines them." In this passage, the purgatorial fires consume the lusts of the flesh • 429 **Quando . . . swallow,** "V. **Pervigilium Veneris.** Cf. Philomela in Parts II and III." (Eliot) "When shall I be like the swallow," from **Pervigilium Veneris,** a mediaeval poem describing the joy of nature on the night of Venus • 430 **Le Prince . . . abolie,** "V. Gerard de Nerval, Sonnet **El Desdichado.**" (Eliot) "The Prince of Aquitaine in the ruined tower" • 432 **Why . . . againe,** "V. Kyd's **Spanish Tragedy,**" (Eliot) The first sentence occurs in Act IV, sc. i, of Thomas Kyd's **Spanish Tragedy,** where Hieronymo agrees to present at court a play by which he secretly plans to take revenge on the murderers of his son; the second sentence is the subtitle of the play • 434 **Shantih.** "Shantih. Repeated as here, a formal ending to an Upanishad. 'The Peace which passeth understanding' is our equivalent to this word." (Eliot) Cf. Philippians 4:7: "And the peace of God, which passeth all understanding . . . ."

Ash-Wednesday

a Ceremonial day of catholic Church

Ash-Wednesday is one of the most important religious poems which have been written in English during the present century. Although Eliot's religious position is specifically Anglo-Catholic, the poem has a broad validity for all religious experience.

The poem describes the progress of the soul from despair to hope, from unbelief to belief. The hopelessness in the early stanzas seems as profound as that expressed in **The Waste Land,** and more apathetic: "Because I do not hope," the poet says—and "I no longer strive to strive." But by means and in ways which defy scientific description, the upward movement of the soul begins in Section 3, where the poet employs the symbol of an ascending stair. At the second and at the third turning of the stair, the soul pauses to look back upon the "twisted shapes" below —its former unhappy states. At length, the soul attains the goal happily epitomized in the phrase from Dante, "Our peace in His will." The poem concludes with a prayer to the "Blessed sister, holy mother." In developing and expressing his thought, Eliot has drawn upon the Bible, Dante, and the liturgies of the Roman and English Churches.

Like much modern poetry of the intellectual school, **Ash-Wednesday** is a difficult poem, even to the sympathetic reader, and gives up its meaning slowly. The student may derive some aid from F. O. Matthiessen's **The Achievement of T. S. Eliot** and Theodore Morrison's "Ash Wednesday: A Religious History," **New England Quarterly,** XI, June 1938.

I

Because I do not hope to turn again
Because I do not hope
Because I do not hope to turn
Desiring this man's gift and that man's scope
I no longer strive to strive towards such things
(Why should the agèd eagle stretch its wings?)
Why should I mourn
The vanished power of the usual reign?

Because I do not hope to know again
The infirm glory of the positive hour   10

Because I do not think
Because I know I shall not know
The one veritable transitory power
Because I cannot drink
There, where trees flower, and springs flow, for there is
    nothing again

Because I know that time is always time
And place is always and only place
And what is actual is actual only for one time
And only for one place
I rejoice that things are as they are and   20
I renounce the blessèd face
And renounce the voice
Because I cannot hope to turn again
Consequently I rejoice, having to construct something
Upon which to rejoice

And pray to God to have mercy upon us
And I pray that I may forget
These matters that with myself I too much discuss
Too much explain
Because I do not hope to turn again   30
Let these words answer
For what is done, not to be done again
May the judgment not be too heavy upon us

Because these wings are no longer wings to fly
But merely vans to beat the air
The air which is now thoroughly small and dry
Smaller and dryer than the will
Teach us to care and not to care
Teach us to sit still   *

Prayer to Vir. Mary—

Pray for us sinners now and at the hour of our death   40
Pray for us now and at the hour of our death.

II

Lady, three white leopards sat under a juniper-tree

Ash-Wednesday, the first day of Lent; so called from a custom, observed on that day, in the Roman Catholic Church, of putting ashes upon the head as a symbol of contrition, while the priest says, "Remember, man, that thou art dust, and unto dust thou shalt return" • 4 **Desiring . . . scope.** Compare "Desiring this man's art, and that man's scope," from Shakespeare's **Sonnets,** number 29 • 42 **Lady.** The Lady seems a personification of religious faith • 42 **leopards.** The three leopards may represent "the world, the flesh, and the devil," but it is not necessary to be so specific

In the cool of the day, having fed to satiety
On my legs my heart my liver and that which had been
    contained
In the hollow round of my skull. And God said
Shall these bones live? shall these
Bones live? And that which had been contained
In the bones (which were already dry) said chirping:
Because of the goodness of this Lady
And because of her loveliness, and because   50
She honours the Virgin in meditation,
We shine with brightness. And I who am here dissembled
Proffer my deeds to oblivion, and my love
To the posterity of the desert and the fruit of the gourd.
It is this which recovers
My guts the strings of my eyes and the indigestible
    portions
Which the leopards reject. The Lady is withdrawn
In a white gown, to contemplation, in a white gown.
Let the whiteness of bones atone to forgetfulness.
There is no life in them. As I am forgotten   60
And would be forgotten, so I would forget
Thus devoted, concentrated in purpose. And God said
Prophesy to the wind, to the wind only for only
The wind will listen. And the bones sang chirping
With the burden of the grasshopper, saying

Lady of silences
Calm and distressed
Torn and most whole
Rose of memory
Rose of forgetfulness   70
Exhausted and life-giving
Worried reposeful
The single Rose
Is now in the Garden
Where all loves end
Terminate torment
Of love unsatisfied
The greater torment
Of love satisfied
End of the endless
Journey to no end
Conclusion of all that
Is inconclusible
Speech without word and
Word of no speech
Grace to the Mother

For the Garden
Where all love ends.

Under a juniper-tree the bones sang, scattered and
    shining
We are glad to be scattered, we did little good to each
    other,   90
Under a tree in the cool of the day, with the blessing of
    sand,
Forgetting themselves and each other, united
In the quiet of the desert. This is the land which ye
Shall divide by lot. And neither division nor unity
Matters. This is the land. We have our inheritance.

At the first turning of the second stair
I turned and saw below
The same shape twisted on the banister
Under the vapour in the fetid air
Struggling with the devil of the stairs who wears   100
The deceitful face of hope and of despair.

At the second turning of the second stair
I left them twisting, turning below;
There were no more faces and the stair was dark,
Damp, jagged, like an old man's mouth drivelling, beyond
    repair,
Or the toothed gullet of an agèd shark.

At the first turning of the third stair
Was a slotted window bellied like the fig's fruit
And beyond the hawthorn blossom and a pasture scene
The broadbacked figure drest in blue and green   110
Enchanted the maytime with an antique flute.
Blown hair is sweet, brown hair over the mouth blown,
Lilac and brown hair;
Distraction, music of the flute, stops and steps of the
    mind over the third stair,
Fading, fading; strength beyond hope and despair
Climbing the third stair.

Lord, I am not worthy

[handwritten annotations: "change begins from exact land & despair to rise to place & faith   III"]

45 And God . . . live. Compare Ezekiel 37:3: "And he said unto me,
Son of man, can these bones live" • 62 God . . . wind. Compare
Ezekiel 37:9: "Then said he unto me, Prophesy unto the wind, prophesy,
son of man, and say to the wind . . ." • 93 This . . . lot. Compare
Ezekiel 48:29: "This is the land which ye shall divide by lot unto the
tribes of Israel for inheritance . . ."

Lord, I am not worthy

but speak the word only.

IV

Who walked between the violet and the violet   120
Who walked between
The various ranks of varied green
Going in white and blue, in Mary's colour,
Talking of trivial things
In ignorance and in knowledge of eternal dolour
Who moved among the others as they walked,
Who then made strong the fountains and made fresh
    the springs

Made cool the dry rock and made firm the sand
In blue of larkspur, blue of Mary's colour,
Sovegna vos   130

Here are the years that walk between, bearing
Away the fiddles and the flutes, restoring
One who moves in the time between sleep and waking,
    wearing

White light folded, sheathed about her, folded.
The new years walk, restoring
Through a bright cloud of tears, the years, restoring
With a new verse the ancient rhyme. Redeem
The time. Redeem
The unread vision in the higher dream
While jewelled unicorns draw by the gilded hearse.   140

The silent sister veiled in white and blue
Between the yews, behind the garden god,
Whose flute is breathless, bent her head and signed but
    spoke no word

But the fountain sprang up and the bird sang down
Redeem the time, redeem the dream
The token of the word unheard, unspoken

Till the wind shake a thousand whispers from the yew

And after this our exile

V

If the lost word is lost, if the spent word is spent

If the unheard, unspoken   150
Word is unspoken, unheard;
Still is the unspoken word, the Word unheard,
The Word without a Word, the Word within
The world and for the world;
And the light shone in darkness and
Against the Word the unstilled world still whirled
About the centre of the silent Word.

O my people, what have I done unto thee.

Where shall the word be found, where will the word
Resound? Not here, there is not enough silence   160
Not on the sea or on the islands, not
On the mainland, in the desert or the rain land,
For those who walk in darkness
Both in the day time and in the night time
The right time and the right place are not here
No place of grace for those who avoid the face
No time to rejoice for those who walk among noise and
    deny the voice

Will the veiled sister pray for
Those who walk in darkness, who chose thee and oppose
    thee,
Those who are torn on the horn between season and
    season, time and time, between   170
Hour and hour, word and word, power and power, those
    who wait
In darkness? Will the veiled sister pray
For children at the gate
Who will not go away and cannot pray:
Pray for those who chose and oppose

O my people, what have I done unto thee.

Will the veiled sister between the slender
Yew trees pray for those who offend her
And are terrified and cannot surrender

---

130 **Sovegna vos,** remember • 137 **Redeem The time.** Compare
Ephesians 5:16: "Redeeming the time, because the days are evil"
• 148 **after . . . exile,** a phrase from the prayer "Salve Regina,"
which follows the Catholic Mass. Eliot has said, "The consummation
of the drama, the perfect and ideal drama, is to be found in the
ceremony of the Mass" • 149 **word,** the revelation of God to man,
as in John 1:1. See note, p. 946 • 158 **O my people . . . thee,**
taken verbatim from Micah 6:3

And affirm before the world and deny between the
    rocks   180
In the last desert between the last blue rocks
The desert in the garden the garden in the desert
Of drouth, spitting from the mouth the withered apple-
    seed.

    O my people.

                          VI
Although I do not hope to turn again
Although I do not hope
Although I do not hope to turn

Wavering between the profit and the loss
In this brief transit where the dreams cross
The dreamcrossed twilight between birth and dying   190
(Bless me father) though I do not wish to wish these
    things
From the wide window towards the granite shore
The white sails still fly seaward, seaward flying
Unbroken wings

And the lost heart stiffens and rejoices
In the lost lilac and the lost sea voices
And the weak spirit quickens to rebel
For the bent golden-rod and the lost sea smell

Quickens to recover
The cry of quail and the whirling plover   200
And the blind eye creates
The empty forms between the ivory gates
And smell renews the salt savour of the sandy earth

This is the time of tension between dying and birth
The place of solitude where three dreams cross
Between blue rocks
But when the voices shaken from the yew tree drift away
Let the other yew be shaken and reply.

7 : mary!

Blessèd sister, holy mother, spirit of the fountain, spirit
    of the garden,
Suffer us not to mock ourselves with falsehood   210
Teach us to care and not to care
Teach us to sit still
Even among these rocks,
Our peace in His will
And even among these rocks
Sister, mother
And spirit of the river, spirit of the sea,
Suffer me not to be separated

And let my cry come unto Thee.

                                      1930

214 Our peace . . . will. See Dante's **Divine Comedy**, Bk. III, l. 85

Hart Crane

1899 · 1932

Hart Crane was born in Garrettsville, Ohio, and later lived in Cleveland, where he attended a public high school for three years. He did not go to college, but while still in his teens dedicated himself to a poetic career. Writing to a friend in 1921, he expressed his literary

likes and aversions as follows: "I do not care greatly for Mme. Browning. And on the top of my dislike for this lady, Tennyson, Thompson, Chatterton, Byron, Moore, Milton and several more. . . . But you will notice that I *do* run joyfully towards Messrs. Poe, Whitman, Shake-

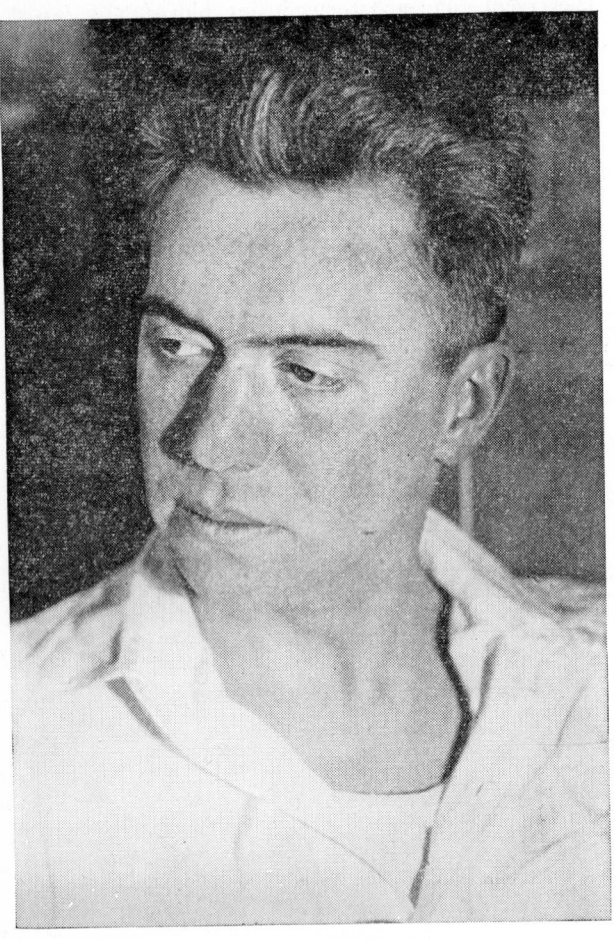

Hart Crane—photo courtesy of Walker Evans

speare, Keats, Shelley, Coleridge, John Donne, John Webster, Marlowe, Baudelaire, Laforgue, Dante. . . ." Crane might have added to this list of favorites the contemporary names of T. S. Eliot and Ezra Pound, who influenced Crane's own poetry more than did any of the others.

For a livelihood, Crane did various jobs in his father's candy business, working as clerk in a candy store, traveling salesman, warehouse manager, and the like, but later found less uncongenial employment as a writer for advertising agencies, first in Cleveland and then in New York. Like Sherwood Anderson, whom he admired, he gravitated to New York and its literary coteries. Here Crane profited by his associations with Gorham Munson, Waldo Frank, Allen Tate, Malcolm Cowley, and others. Otto Kahn, the philanthropist, gave him a thousand dollars

(and offered more) so that he might have leisure for his poetry. His magnum opus, *The Bridge,* was published in 1930 and met with a mixed reception. Neurotically unhappy for a long while, Crane sought peace of mind, without success, in the Adirondacks, Europe, Cuba, Mexico. En route to the United States from Mexico, April 27, 1932, he committed suicide by jumping from the deck of a steamship into the waters of the Caribbean Sea. Many factors had doubtless contributed to his acute neurotic state: among them, the separation of his parents since his early boyhood; their failure to sympathize with his literary ambitions; a sexual maladjustment; his loss of faith in the grand theme of *The Bridge*—the future of America—precipitated possibly by the Great Depression and his reading of Spengler.

Crane's fame, it now appears, rests securely upon *The Bridge,* perhaps the most ambitious poem in English since *The Waste Land,* to which it is in some ways similar, though it is neither as well unified nor as firmly sustained as Eliot's masterpiece. In *The Bridge,* Crane was attempting a modern synthesis of the American experience. In the early stages of composition, he described his aim as follows: "Very roughly, the poem concerns a mystical synthesis of America. History and fact, location, etc., all have to be transfigured into abstract form. . . . The initial impulses of our people will have to be gathered up toward the climax of the bridge, symbol of our constructive future, our unique identity, in which is also included our scientific hopes and achievements of the future." "What I am after," he explained to Kahn in 1927, "is an assimilation of this [the American] experience, a more organic panorama, showing the continuous and living evidence of the past in the inmost vital substance of the present. . . . What I am really handling, you see, is the Myth of America. . . . I am really writing an epic of the modern consciousness." Crane's aim was a noble one. If the poem does not entirely succeed, the chief reason may be found in the almost insuperable difficulties imposed by the conflicts and scepticisms of the "modern consciousness."

Allen Tate, "Hart Crane," **Reactionary Essays on Poetry and Ideas,** New York, 1936 • Philip Horton, **Hart Crane: The Life of an American Poet,** New York, 1937 • Brom Weber, **Hart Crane: A Biographical and Critical Study,** New York, 1948

From

The Bridge

The Bridge consists of fifteen parts. These parts, however, are rather loosely held together, and can be read separately as well as in conjunction. Crane, in fact, succeeds better in the individual poems which compose **The Bridge** than he does in their amalgamation into an integrated whole.

The three poems which follow—"Proem: To Brooklyn Bridge," "The River," and "The Tunnel"—are representative of Crane's best poetry and show the kind of "mystical synthesis" which he was attempting in **The Bridge**. Here indeed we see, as Crane put it, "the continuous and living evidence of the past in the inmost vital substance of the present."

The "Proem" is a beautiful and moving apostrophe to Brooklyn Bridge as "harp and altar."

"The River," says Allen Tate, "has some blemishes towards the end, but by and large it is a masterpiece of order and style; it alone is enough to place Crane in the first rank of American poets, living or dead." Of this poem, Crane gave to Otto Kahn the following illuminating explication:

> The subway is simply a figurative, psychological 'vehicle' for transporting the reader to the Middle West. He lands on the railroad tracks in the company of several tramps in the twilight. The extravagance of the first twenty-three lines of this section is an intentional burlesque on the cultural confusion of the present—a great conglomeration of noises analogous to the strident impression of a fast express rushing by. The rhythm is jazz. Thenceforward the rhythm settles down to a steady pedestrian gait, like that of wanderers plodding along. My tramps are psychological vehicles, also. Their wanderings, as you will notice, carry the reader into interior after interior, all of it funneled by the Mississippi. They are the leftovers of the pioneers in at least this respect—that abstractly their wanderings carry the reader through certain experiences roughly parallel to that of the traders, adventurers, Boone and others. I think I have caught some of the essential spirit of the Great Valley here. . . . (Quoted in Weber, p. 353)

Of "The Tunnel," Weber says: "It is as a description of an urban experience that the poem attains its greatest distinction, and it is unquestionably one of Crane's most successfully integrated pieces. The horrors of subway transportation—the noise, the broken conversations, the staring eyes, the lights, the spasmodic stops and starts at stations, the rounding of curves—are masterfully presented." In an early synopsis, Crane spoke of this section as "a kind of purgatory," its subject being "the encroachment of machinery on humanity." Although the effect of the subway picture is undoubtedly depressing, the poem ends with buoyant, essentially religious, references: to Lazarus, who rose from the dead, to the "Word that will not die," to the purifying, sacramental "Hand of Fire."

PROEM: TO BROOKLYN BRIDGE

How many dawns, chill from his rippling rest
The seagull's wings shall dip and pivot him,
Shedding white rings of tumult, building high
Over the chained bay waters Liberty—

Then, with inviolate curve, forsake our eyes
As apparitional as sails that cross
Some page of figures to be filed away;
—Till elevators drop us from our day . . .

I think of cinemas, panoramic sleights
With multitudes bent toward some flashing scene   10
Never disclosed, but hastened to again,
Foretold to other eyes on the same screen;

And Thee, across the harbor, silver-paced
As though the sun took step of thee, yet left
Some motion ever unspent in thy stride,—
Implicitly thy freedom staying thee!

Proem • 8 The three dots here and elsewhere in the selections from Crane are the author's, and do not indicate omissions

Out of some subway scuttle, cell or loft
A bedlamite speeds to thy parapets,
Tilting there momently, shrill shirt ballooning,
A jest falls from the speechless caravan.   20

Down Wall, from girder into street noon leaks,
A rip-tooth of the sky's acetylene;
All afternoon the cloud-flown derricks turn . . .
Thy cables breathe the North Atlantic still.

And obscure as that heaven of the Jews,
Thy guerdon . . . Accolade thou dost bestow
Of anonymity time cannot raise:
Vibrant reprieve and pardon thou dost show.

O harp and altar, of the fury fused,
(How could mere toil align thy choiring strings!)   30
Terrific threshold of the prophet's pledge,
Prayer of pariah, and the lover's cry,—

Again the traffic lights that skim thy swift
Unfractioned idiom, immaculate sigh of stars,
Beading thy path—condense eternity:
And we have seen night lifted in thine arms.

Under thy shadow by the piers I waited;
Only in darkness is thy shadow clear.
The City's fiery parcels all undone,
Already snow submerges an iron year . . .   40

O Sleepless as the river under thee,
Vaulting the sea, the prairies' dreaming sod,
Unto us lowliest sometimes sweep, descend
And of the curveship lend a myth to God.

THE RIVER

Stick your patent name on a signboard
brother—all over—going west—young man
Tintex—Japalac—Certain-teed Overalls ads
and lands sakes! under the new playbill ripped
in the guaranteed corner—see Bert Williams what?
Minstrels when you steal a chicken just
save me the wing, for if it isn't
Erie it ain't for miles around a
Mazda—and the telegraphic night coming on Thomas

a Ediford—and whistling down the tracks   10
a headlight rushing with the sound—can you
imagine—while an EXPRESS makes time like
SCIENCE—COMMERCE and the HOLYGHOST
RADIO ROARS IN EVERY HOME WE HAVE THE NORTHPOLE
WALLSTREET AND VIRGINBIRTH WITHOUT STONES OR
WIRES OR EVEN RUNNing brooks connecting ears
and no more sermons windows flashing roar
Breathtaking—as you like it . . . eh?

So the 20th Century—so
whizzed the Limited—roared by and left   20
three men, still hungry on the tracks, ploddingly
watching the tail lights wizen and converge, slipping gimleted and neatly out of sight.

The last bear, shot drinking in the Dakotas,
Loped under wires that span the mountain stream.
Keen instruments, strung to a vast precision
Bind town to town and dream to ticking dream.
But some men take their liquor slow—and count
—Though they'll confess no rosary nor clue—
The river's minute by the far brook's year.   30
Under a world of whistles, wires and steam
Caboose-like they go ruminating through
Ohio, Indiana—blind baggage—
To Cheyenne tagging . . . Maybe Kalamazoo.

Time's rendings, time's blendings they construe
As final reckonings of fire and snow;
Strange bird-wit, like the elemental gist
Of unwalled winds they offer, singing low
My Old Kentucky Home and Casey Jones,
Some Sunny Day. I heard a road-gang chanting so.   40
And afterwards, who had a colt's eyes—one said,
"Jesus! Oh I remember watermelon days!" And sped
High in a cloud of merriment, recalled
"—And when my Aunt Sally Simpson smiled," he
            drawled—
"It was almost Louisiana, long ago."

"There's no place like Booneville though, Buddy,"
One said, excising a last burr from his vest,
"—For early trouting." Then peering in the can,
"—But I kept on the tracks." Possessed, resigned,
He trod the fire down pensively and grinned,
Spreading dry shingles of a beard. . . .   50

Behind
My father's cannery works I used to see
Rail-squatters ranged in nomad raillery,
The ancient men—wifeless or runaway
Hobo-trekkers that forever search
An empire wilderness of freight and rails.
Each seemed a child, like me, on a loose perch,
Holding to childhood like some termless play.
John, Jake, or Charley, hopping the slow freight   60
—Memphis to Tallahassee—riding the rods,
Blind fists of nothing, humpty-dumpty clods.

Yet they touch something like a key perhaps.
From pole to pole across the hills, the states
—They know a body under the wide rain;
Youngsters with eyes like fjords, old reprobates
With racetrack jargon,—dotting immensity
They lurk across her, knowing her yonder breast
Snow-silvered, sumac-stained or smoky blue,
Is past the valley-sleepers, south or west.   70
—As I have trod the rumorous midnights, too.

And past the circuit of the lamp's thin flame
(O Nights that brought me to her body bare!)
Have dreamed beyond the print that bound her name.
Trains sounding the long blizzards out—I heard
Wail into distances I knew were hers.
Papooses crying on the wind's long mane
Screamed redskin dynasties that fled the brain,
—Dead echoes! But I knew her body there,
Time like a serpent down her shoulder, dark,   80
And space, an eaglet's wing, laid on her hair.

Under the Ozarks, domed by Iron Mountain,
The old gods of the rain lie wrapped in pools
Where eyeless fish curvet a sunken fountain
And re-descend with corn from querulous crows.
Such pilferings make up their timeless eatage,
Propitiate them for their timber torn
By iron, iron—always the iron dealt cleavage!
They doze now, below axe and powder horn.

And Pullman breakfasters glide glistening steel   90
From tunnel into field—iron strides the dew—
Straddles the hill, a dance of wheel on wheel.
You have a half-hour's wait at Siskiyou,

Or stay the night and take the next train through.
Southward, near Cairo passing, you can see
The Ohio merging,—borne down Tennessee;
And if it's summer and the sun's in dusk
Maybe the breeze will lift the River's musk
—As though the waters breathed that you might know
Memphis Johnny, Steamboat Bill, Missouri Joe.   100
Oh, lean from the window, if the train slows down,
As though you touched hands with some ancient clown,
—A little while gaze absently below
And hum *Deep River* with them while they go.

Yes, turn again and sniff once more—look see,
O Sheriff, Brakeman and Authority—
Hitch up your pants and crunch another quid,
For you, too, feed the River timelessly.
And few evade full measure of their fate;
Always they smile out eerily what they seem.   110
I could believe he joked at heaven's gate—
Dan Midland—jolted from the cold brake-beam.

Down, down—born pioneers in time's despite,
Grimed tributaries to an ancient flow—
They win no frontier by their wayward plight,
But drift in stillness, as from Jordan's brow.

You will not hear it as the sea; even stone
Is not more hushed by gravity . . . But slow,
As loth to take more tribute—sliding prone
Like one whose eyes were buried long ago   120

The River, spreading, flows—and spends your dream.
What are you, lost within this tideless spell?
You are your father's father, and the stream—
A liquid theme that floating niggers swell.

Damp tonnage and alluvial march of days—
Nights turbid, vascular with silted shale
And roots surrendered down of moraine clays:
The Mississippi drinks the farthest dale.

O quarrying passion, undertowed sunlight!
The basalt surface drags a jungle grace   130
Ochreous and lynx-barred in lengthening might;
Patience! and you shall reach the biding place!

Over De Soto's bones the freighted floors
Throb past the City storied of three thrones.
Down two more turns the Mississippi pours
(Anon tall ironsides up from salt lagoons)

And flows within itself, heaps itself free.
All fades but one thin skyline 'round . . . Ahead
No embrace opens but the stinging sea;
The River lifts itself from its long bed,   140

Poised wholly on its dream, a mustard glow,
Tortured with history, its one will—flow!
—The Passion spreads in wide tongues, choked and slow,
Meeting the Gulf, hosannas silently below.

THE TUNNEL

To find the Western path
Right thro' the Gates of Wrath—BLAKE

Performances, assortments, résumés—
Up Times Square to Columbus Circle lights
Channel the congresses, nightly sessions,
Refractions of the thousand theaters, faces—
Mysterious kitchens . . . You shall search them all.
Some day by heart you'll learn each famous sight
And watch the curtain lift in hell's despite;
You'll find the garden in the third act dead,
Finger your knees—and wish yourself in bed
With tabloid crime-sheets perched in easy sight.

    Then let you reach your hat
    and go.
    As usual, let you—also
    walking down—exclaim
    to twelve upward leaving
    a subscription praise
    for what time slays . . .

Or can't you quite make up your mind to ride;
A walk is better underneath the L a brisk
Ten blocks or so before? But you find yourself   20
Preparing penguin flexions of the arms—
As usual you will meet the scuttle yawn:
The subway yawns the quickest promise home.

Be minimum, then, to swim the hiving swarms

Out of the Square, the Circle burning bright—
Avoid the glass doors gyring at your right,
Where boxed alone a second, eyes take fright
—Quite unprepared rush naked back to light:
And down beside the turnstile press the coin
Into the slot. The gongs already rattle.   30

    And so
    of cities you bespeak
    subways, rivered under streets
    and rivers . . . In the car
    the overtone of motion
    underground, the monotone
    of motion is the sound
    of other faces, also underground—

"Let's have a pencil Jimmy—living now
at Floral Park   40
Flatbush—on the fourth of July—
like a pigeon's muddy dream—potatoes
to dig in the field—travlin the town too—
night after night—the Culver line—the
girls all shaping up—it used to be—"

Our tongues recant like beaten weather vanes.
This answer lives like verdigris, like hair
Beyond extinction, surcease of the bone;
And repetition freezes—"What
what do you want? getting weak on the links?   50
fandaddle daddy don't ask for change—IS THIS
FOURTEENTH? it's half-past six she said—if
you don't like my gate why did you
swing on it, why *didja*
swing on it
anyhow—"

    And somehow anyhow swing—

The phonographs of hades in the brain
Are tunnels that re-wind themselves, and love
A burnt match skating in a urinal—   60
Somewhere above Fourteenth TAKE THE EXPRESS

The Tunnel • To find . . . Wrath, Blake's "Morning," ll. 1-2 • 1
résumés, one of the special usages of Walt Whitman (whom Crane particularly admired—"Cape Hatteras," in **The Bridge**, is an explicit tribute
to Whitman); for an example of Whitman's use of the word, see "Thou
Mother with Thy Equal Brood," section 4, p. 209

To brush some new presentiment of pain—

"But I want service in this office SERVICE
I said—after
the show she cried a little afterwards but—"

Whose head is swinging from the swollen strap?
Whose body smokes along the bitten rails,
Bursts from a smoldering bundle far behind
In back forks of the chasms of the brain—
Puffs from a riven stump far out behind   70
In interborough fissures of the mind . . . ?
And why do I often meet your visage here,
Your eyes like agate lanterns—on and on
Below the toothpaste and the dandruff ads?
—And did their riding eyes right through your side,
And did their eyes like unwashed platters ride?
And Death, aloft—gigantically down
Probing through you toward me, O Evermore!
And when they dragged your retching flesh,
Your trembling hands that night through Baltimore—
That last night on the ballot rounds, did you,   81
Shaking—did you deny the ticket, Poe?

For Gravesend Manor change at Chambers Street.
The platform hurries along to a dead stop.

The intent escalator lifts a serenade
Stilly
Of shoes, umbrellas, each eye attending its shoe, then
Bolting outright somewhere above where streets
Burst suddenly in rain . . . The gongs recur:
Elbows and levers, guard and hissing door.   90
Thunder is galvothermic here below . . . The car
Wheels off. The train rounds, bending to a scream,
Taking the final level for the dive
Under the river—
And somewhat emptier than before,
Demented, for a hitching second, humps; then
Lets go . . . Toward corners of the floor
Newspapers wing, revolve and wing.
Blank windows gargle signals through the roar.
And does the Daemon take you home, also,   100
Wop washerwoman, with the bandaged hair?
After the corridors are swept, the cuspidors—
The gaunt sky-barracks cleanly now, and bare,

O Genoese, do you bring mother-eyes and hands
Back home to children and to golden hair?

Daemon, demurring and eventful yawn!
Whose hideous laughter is a bellows mirth.
—Or the muffled slaughter of a day in birth—
O cruelly to inoculate the brinking dawn
With antennae toward worlds that glow and sink—   110
To spoon us out more liquid than the dim
Locution of the eldest star, and pack
The conscience naveled in the plunging wind,
Umbilical to call—and straightway die!
O caught like pennies beneath soot and steam,
Kiss of our agony thou gatherest;
Condensed, thou takest all—shrill ganglia
Impassioned with some song we fail to keep.

And yet, like Lazarus, to feel the slope,
The sod and billow breaking—lifting ground,   120
—A sound of waters bending astride the sky
Unceasing with some Word that will not die!

• • •

A tugboat, wheezing wreaths of steam,
Lunged past, with one galvanic blare stove up the River.
I counted the echoes assembling, one after one,
Searching, thumbing the midnight on the piers.
Lights, coasting, left the oily tympanum of waters;
The blackness somewhere gouged glass on a sky.

And this thy harbor, O my City, I have driven under,
Tossed from the coil of ticking towers . . . Tomorrow,
And to be . . . Here by the River that is East—   131
Here at the waters' edge the hands drop memory;
Shadowless in that abyss they unaccounting lie.
How far away the star has pooled the sea—
Or shall the hands be drawn away, to die?
Kiss of our agony Thou gatherest,
               O Hand of Fire
                   gatherest—

                                    1930

---

77 **gigantically down.** Compare Poe's "The City in the Sea," ll. 28-29:
"While from a proud tower in the town / Death looks gigantically down"
• 104 **O Genoese.** Compare "Ah Genoese" in l. 65 of Whitman's
"Passage to India" (p. 203), a poem which undoubtedly influenced
some of the fundamental concepts of **The Bridge**

Allen Tate

1899 ·

See page 872 for a biographical account of Tate.

Ode to the Confederate Dead

Row after row with strict impunity
The headstones yield their names to the element,
The wind whirrs without recollection;
In the riven troughs the splayed leaves
Pile up, of nature the casual sacrament
To the seasonal eternity of death;
Then driven by the fierce scrutiny
Of heaven to their election in the vast breath,
They sough the rumor of mortality.

Autumn is desolation in the plot   10
Of a thousand acres where these memories grow
From the inexhaustible bodies that are not
Dead, but feed the grass row after rich row.
Think of the autumns that have come and gone!—
Ambitious November with the humors of the year,
With particular zeal for every slab,
Staining the uncomfortable angels that rot
On the slabs, a wing chipped here, an arm there:
The brute curiosity of an angel's stare
Turns you, like them, to stone,   20
Transforms the heaving air
Till plunged to a heavier world below
You shift your sea-space blindly
Heaving, turning like the blind crab.

    Dazed by the wind, only the wind
    The leaves flying, plunge

You know who have waited by the wall
The twilight certainty of an animal,
Those midnight restitutions of the blood
You know—the immitigable pines, the smoky
    frieze   30
Of the sky, the sudden call: you know the rage,
The cold pool left by the mounting flood,
Of muted Zeno and Parmenides.
You who have waited for the angry resolution
Of those desires that should be yours tomorrow,
You know the unimportant shrift of death
And praise the vision
And praise the arrogant circumstance
Of those who fall
Rank upon rank, hurried beyond decision—   40
Here by the sagging gate, stopped by the wall.

    Seeing, seeing only the leaves
    Flying, plunge and expire

Turn your eyes to the immoderate past,
Turn to the inscrutable infantry rising
Demons out of the earth—they will not last.
Stonewall, Stonewall, and the sunken fields of hemp,
Shiloh, Antietam, Malvern Hill, Bull Run.

From **Selected Poems** by Allen Tate; published by Charles Scribner's Sons; copyright, 1937, by Charles Scribner's Sons • Used by permission of the publishers

Lost in that orient of the thick and fast
You will curse the setting sun.   50

    Cursing only the leaves crying
    Like an old man in a storm

You hear the shout, the crazy hemlocks point
With troubled fingers to the silence which
Smothers you, a mummy, in time.

                  The hound bitch
Toothless and dying, in a musty cellar
Hears the wind only.

             Now that the salt of their blood
Stiffens the saltier oblivion of the sea,   60
Seals the malignant purity of the flood,
What shall we who count our days and bow
Our heads with a commemorial woe
In the ribboned coats of grim felicity,
What shall we say of the bones, unclean,
Whose verdurous anonymity will grow?
The ragged arms, the ragged heads and eyes
Lost in these acres of the insane green?
The gray lean spiders come, they come and go;
In a tangle of willows without light   70

The singular screech-owl's tight
Invisible lyric seeds the mind
With the furious murmur of their chivalry.

    We shall say only the leaves
    Flying, plunge and expire

We shall say only the leaves whispering
In the improbable mist of nightfall
That flies on multiple wing:
Night is the beginning and the end
And in between the ends of distraction   80
Waits mute speculation, the patient curse
That stones the eyes, or like the jaguar leaps
For his own image in a jungle pool, his victim.

What shall we say who have knowledge
Carried to the heart? Shall we take the act
To the grave? Shall we, more hopeful, set up the grave
In the house? The ravenous grave?

                Leave now
The shut gate and the decomposing wall:
The gentle serpent, green in the mulberry bush,   90
Riots with his tongue through the hush—
Sentinel of the grave who counts us all!

                     1928

Karl Jay Shapiro

1913 •

The general recognition that a serious writer is doing outstanding work comes usually when he is between thirty and forty years old. Of course, the time of such recognition varies greatly, but among the authors encountered in this chapter only two, Wolfe and Dos Passos, could possibly be considered "established" in their late twenties, and only four, Robinson, Frost, Willa Cather, and Babbitt, achieved that eminence after forty.

This means that the new writers of 1945 or later were likely to have been born no earlier than 1910, to have lived through World War I as children, to have been college students or job hunters in the Great Depression, and to have been or military age in December 1941, when the Japanese attack on Pearl Harbor plunged the United States into World War II and into the subsequent awareness of world-wide responsibilities and genuine danger of still another and even more terrible struggle for survival. It is not at all surprising, then, that almost every one of the authors of this generation, which has seen the failure of internationalism, economic collapse, the rise of dictatorships, and, not seldom, the actuality of total war, shows the effect of a psychic shock beyond that of any earlier group of Americans. They have lived with violence and death on a larger scale than their predecessors ever dreamed would be possible by the middle of the twentieth century.

Their varied reactions to this grim fact constitute the chief pattern of contemporary literature. Some have continued to explore the mazes of politics, economics, and sociology, in the faint hope of at least fixing the responsibility for what they have endured. Others have accepted sin and guilt as man's inevitable burden and, like their remote forebears, turned in one way or another to God as the only refuge or solace. Still others have decided, as did so many soldiers, that there is nothing to do but "sweat it out," to do, that is, the best one can to adjust to an unintelligible and unintelligent situation, maintaining meanwhile what personal integrity is possible in a military-minded world.

It is to this last group that Karl Shapiro most clearly belongs. His *V-Letter and Other Poems,* published in 1944 while he was with the United States Army in the South Pacific, won the Pulitzer Prize for him at thirty-one. It, with his other work, is among the best records thus far available of what the war has done to his generation.

Shapiro was born in Baltimore, Maryland, in 1913, the son of a Jewish father and a Catholic mother. "Recapitulations," a sequence in *Trial of a Poet* (1947), tells us something of his youth, and many of his shorter pieces build up a picture of a sensitive but self-reliant person, early aware of snobbery and sham, of cruelty and conflict. A year at the University of Virginia, perhaps a shade more committed than most American colleges to the ancient cult of the "gentleman," was obviously painful. Shapiro was publishing poetry at twenty-one, and a slim collection, *Poems,* appeared in 1935. Between 1936 and 1940 he was a student at Johns Hopkins University. There he evidently read to good purpose, for his later verses reveal an acquaintance with a wide range of subjects and poetic devices. Selective Service caught him in 1941, and at the time Evelyn Katz, his fiancée, saw *Person, Place and Thing* through the press in 1942, he was on active duty "somewhere in the Pacific." His postwar work has included a year as poetry consultant at the Library of Congress, several years of teaching at Hopkins, and, since 1950, the editorship of *Poetry, A Magazine of Verse.* Important books, in addition to those already mentioned, are *Essay on Rime* (1945) and *Bibliography of Modern Prosody* (1948).

Some critics have complained of a certain superficial cleverness in Shapiro's work, and it must be admitted that some of his earlier poems overwork sensational juxtapositions (for instance, the first line of "The Fly": "O hideous little bat, the size of snot"), but his range is wide and thoroughly characteristic of his time. Department store, restaurant, cathedral, hospital, theater, honky-tonk, railroad station, drug store, barber shop, graveyard —all these he has named as Emerson would have put it, "sometimes after their appearance, sometimes after their essence," and the lasting impression is not of technical skill alone but of an honest and intelligent man probing and expressing the meanings of life and love, suffering and beauty, peace and war. There is not much, perhaps, to believe in passionately, but there remain courage and sensitivity and, above all, honesty.

David Daiches, "The Poetry of Karl Shapiro," **Poetry, A Magazine of Verse,** August 1945

V-Letter

The V-Letter was devised to facilitate correspondence between World War II soldiers and their wives and sweethearts and families. Letters written on special stationery were microfilmed and sent by air; in the United States the film was "blown up" and printed before delivery. This poem, originally printed in **The New Yorker,** January 12, 1943, has a smooth but intricate rhythm which helps to give sophistication to a subject as old as soldiering.

I love you first because your face is fair,
  Because your eyes Jewish and blue,
Set sweetly with the touch of foreignness
Above the cheekbones, stare rather than dream.
Often your countenance recalls a boy
  Blue-eyed and small, whose silent mischief
Tortured his parents and compelled my hate
    To wish his ugly death.
Because of this reminder, my soul's trouble,
And for your face, so often beautiful,   10
    I love you, wish you life.

I love you first because you wait, because
  For your own sake I cannot write
Beyond these words. I love you for these words
That sting and creep like insects and leave filth.
I love you for the poverty you cry
  And I bend down with tears of steel
That melt your hand like wax, not for this war
    The droplets shattering
Those candle-glowing fingers of my joy,   20
But for your name of agony, my love,
    That cakes my mouth with salt.

And all your imperfections and perfections
  And all your magnitude of grace
And all this love explained and unexplained
Is just a breadth. I see you woman-size
And this looms larger and more goddess-like
  Than silver goddesses on screens.
I see you in the ugliness of light
    Yet you are beautiful,   30
And in the dark of absence your full length
Is such as meets my body to the full
    Though I am starved and huge.

You turn me from these days as from a scene
  Out of an open window far
Where lies the foreign city and the war.
You are my home and in your spacious love
I dream to march as under flaring flags
  Until the door is gently shut.
Give me the tearless lesson of your pride,   40
  Teach me to live and die
As one deserving anonymity,
The mere devotion of a house to keep
    A woman and a man.

Give me the free and poor inheritance
  Of our own kind, not furniture
Of education, nor the prophet's pose,
The general cause of words, the hero's stance,
The ambitions incommensurable with flesh,
  But the drab makings of a room   50
Where sometimes in the afternoon of thought
    The brief and blinding flash
May light the enormous chambers of your will
And show the gracious Parthenon that time
    Is ever measured by.

As groceries in a pantry gleam and smile
  Because they are important weights
Bought with the metal minutes of your pay,
So do these hours stand in solid rows,
The dowry for a use in common life.   60
  I love you first because your years
Lead to my matter-of-fact and simple death
  Or to our open marriage,
And I pray nothing for my safety back,
Not even luck, because our love is whole
    Whether I live or fail.

1943

Troop Train

In this poem Shapiro has caught not only the universal isolation and foreboding of soldiers but also the peculiar character of global war, which carries men and matériel in wearying journeys halfway around the world.

It stops the town we come through. Workers raise
Their oily arms in good salute and grin.
Kids scream as at a circus. Business men
Glance hopefully and go their measured way.
And women standing at their dumbstruck door
More slowly wave and seem to warn us back,
As if a tear blinding the course of war
Might once dissolve our iron in their sweet wish.

Fruit of the world, O clustered on ourselves
We hang as from a cornucopia   10
In total friendliness, with faces bunched
To spray the streets with catcalls and with leers.
A bottle smashes on the moving ties
And eyes fixed on a lady smiling pink
Stretch like a rubber-band and snap and sting
The mouth that wants the drink-of-water kiss.

And on through crummy continents and days,
Deliberate, grimy, slightly drunk we crawl,
The good-bad boys of circumstance and chance,
Whose bucket-helmets bang the empty wall   20
Where twist the murdered bodies of our packs
Next to the guns that only seem themselves.
And distance like a strap adjusted shrinks,
Tightens across the shoulder and holds firm.

Here is a deck of cards; out of this hand
Dealer, deal me my luck, a pair of bulls,
The right draw to a flush, the one-eyed jack.
Diamonds and hearts are red but spades are black,
And spades are spades and clubs are clovers—black.
But deal me winners, souvenirs of peace.   30
This stands to reason and arithmetic,
Luck also travels and not all come back.

Trains lead to ships and ships to death or trains,
And trains to death or trucks, and trucks to death,
Or trucks lead to the march, the march to death,
Or that survival which is all our hope;
And death leads back to trucks and trains and ships,
But life leads to the march, O flag! at last
The place of life found after trains and death
—Nightfall of nations brilliant after war.

                                                  1943

The Intellectual

The perennial impatience of the artist with those who only talk about art is increased here by the conviction of the war generation that its miseries are at least partially the result of indecision.

What should the wars do with these figging fools?

The man behind the book may not be man,
His own man or the book's or yet the time's,
But still be whole, deciding what he can
In praise of politics or German rimes.

But the intellectual lights a cigarette
And offers it lit to the lady, whose odd smile
Is the merest hyphen—lest he should forget
What he has been resuming all the while.

He talks to overhear, she to withdraw
To some interior feminine fireside   10
Where the back arches, beauty puts forth a paw
Like a black puma stretching in velvet pride,

Making him think of cats, a stray of which
Some days sets up a howling in his brain,
Pure interference such as this neat bitch
Seems to create from listening disdain.

But talk is all the value, the release,
Talk is the very fillip of an act,
The frame and subject of the masterpiece
Under whose film of age the face is cracked.   20

His own forehead glows like expensive wood,
But back of it the mind is disengaged,
Self-sealing clock recording bad and good
At constant temperature, intact, unaged.

But strange, his body is an open house
Inviting every passerby to stay;
The city to and fro beneath his brows
Wanders and drinks and chats from night to day.

Think of a private thought, indecent room
Where one might kiss his daughter before bed!   30
Life is embarrassed; shut the family tomb,
Console your neighbor for his recent dead;

Troop Train • **26 pair of bulls**, aces. Draw poker, in which the dealer sometimes chooses to call the jack of hearts a "wild" card, is the game which supplies the images in these lines
The Intellectual • Reprinted by permission of Random House, Inc. • Copyright, 1944, by Karl Shapiro

Do something! die in Spain or paint a green
Gouache, go into business (Rimbaud did),
Or start another Little Magazine,
Or move in with a woman, have a kid.

Invulnerable, impossible, immune,
Do what you will, your will will not be done
But dissipate the light of afternoon
Till evening flickers like the midnight sun,   40

And midnight shouts and dies: I'd rather be
A milkman walking in his sleep at dawn
Bearing fat quarts of cream, and so be free,
Crossing alone and cold from lawn to lawn.

I'd rather be a barber and cut hair
Than walk with you in gilt museum halls,
You and the puma-lady, she so rare
Exhaling her silk soul upon the walls.

Go take yourself apart, but let me be
The fault you find with everyman. I spit,   50
I laugh, I fight; and you, *l'homme qui rit,*
Swallow your stale saliva, and still sit.

                                                        1944

Homecoming

This poem was first printed in **The New Yorker** for June
23, 1945.

Lost in the vastness of the void Pacific
My thousand days of exile, pain,
Bid me farewell. Gone is the Southern Cross
To her own sky, fallen a continent
Under the wave, dissolved the bitterest isles
In their salt element,
And here upon the deck the mist encloses
My smile that would light up all darkness
And ask forgiveness of the things that thrust
Shame and all death on millions and on me.   10

We bring no raw materials from the East
But green-skinned men in blue-lit holds

And lunatics impounded between-decks;
The mighty ghoul-ship that we ride exhales
The sickly-sweet stench of humiliation,
And even the majority, untouched by steel
Or psychoneurosis, stare with eyes in rut,
Their hands a rabble to snatch the riches
Of glittering shops and girls.

Because I am angry at this kindness which   20
Is both habitual and contradictory
To the life of armies, now I stand alone
And hate the swarms of khaki men that crawl
Like lice upon the wrinkled hide of earth,
Infesting ships as well. Not otherwise
Could I lean outward piercing fog to find
Our sacred bridge of exile and return.
My tears are psychological, not poems
To the United States; my smile is prayer.

Gnawing the thin slops of anxiety,   30
Escorted by the ground swell and by gulls,
In silence and with mystery we enter
The territorial waters. Not till then
Does that convulsive terrible joy, more sudden
And brilliant than the explosion of a ship,
Shatter the tensions of the heaven and sea
To crush a hundred thousand skulls
And liberate in that high burst of love
The imprisoned souls of soldiers and of me.

                                                        1945

From

Recapitulations

"Recapitulations" is a series of sixteen short poems, at the
beginning of **Trial of a Poet**.   Five of these are reprinted

The Intellectual • 33 **die in Spain,** an allusion to the Spanish Civil
War, in which numerous American opponents of Fascism took a part
• 34 **Rimbaud,** Arthur Rimbaud (1854-1891), French poet, who gave up
poetry for trading in Africa • 35 **Little Magazine,** a magazine designed usually to print the work of young and unknown writers. See
p. 767 • 41 **I'd rather be,** an echo of Wordsworth's sonnet, "The
World Is Too Much with Us," which, although written in another time
and place, is almost an epitome of Shapiro's view of the present era
Homecoming • Reprinted by permission of Random House, Inc. •
Copyright, 1945, by Karl Shapiro

here. All except XIII appeared first in **Poetry** for December 1946.

II

At one the Apocalypse had spoken,
Von Moltke fell, I was housebroken.

At two how could I understand
The murder of Archduke Ferdinand?

France was involved with history,
I with my thumbs when I was three.

A sister came, we neared a war,
Paris was shelled when I was four.

I joined in our peach-kernel drive
For poison gas when I was five.

At six I cheered the big parade,
Burned sparklers and drank lemonade.

At seven I passed at school though I
Was far too young to say *Versailles*.

At eight the boom began to tire,
I tried to set our house on fire.

The Bolshevists had drawn the line,
Lenin was stricken, I was nine.

What evils do not retrograde
To my first odious decade?   20

IV

I lived in a house of panels,
    Victorian, darkly made;
A virgin in bronze and marble
    Leered from the balustrade.

The street was a tomb of virtues,
    Autumnal for dreams and haunts;
I gazed from the polished windows
    Toward a neighborhood of aunts.

Mornings I practiced piano,
    Wrote elegies and sighed;
The evenings were conversations
    Of poetry and suicide.

Weltschmerz and mysticism,
    What tortures we undergo!

I loved with the love of Heinrich
    And the poison of Edgar Poe.

VIII

For four years stupefied by martial law
The poet in khaki held his tongue. Coward
Or patriot or both, he learned the raw
Truth of the life where only rifles flowered.

His primum mobile was inertia, Fate
As the poor devils called it when they tried
To justify the distance of their state
From that of free men on the civilian side.

The chief hell was stupidity, the vast
And national ignorance of the dividing line
Between the many and the few. He classed
The majority of his fellowmen as swine.

Unlike the others, he revered the bar
And eagle of authority. He loathed
The naked officer and his choice cigar
Yet loved him dutifully when fully clothed.

He seldom doubted that the Cause was just
And did his service with a soldier's sloth.
In his commanders he imposed his trust
—God, he presumed, was on the side of both.   20

XII

I plucked the bougainvillea
    In Queensland in time of war;
The train stopped at the station
    And I reached it from my door.

I have never kept a flower
    And this one I never shall

II • 2 **Von Moltke** (1848-1916), chief of the German general staff, was relieved of his post in 1914, following the French victory in the first Battle of the Marne • 4 **Archduke Ferdinand** (1863-1914), of Austria, whose assassination at Sarajevo was the inflammatory incident of World War I • 8 **Paris was shelled,** in the latter part of World War I, by specially built German artillery, capable of shooting over seventy-five miles • 14 **Versailles,** where the peace treaty was signed on June 28, 1919 • 18 **Lenin was stricken,** by a paralytic stroke months before his death in 1924 • **IV** • 15 **Heinrich,** Heinrich Heine (1797-1850), German poet famous for love lyrics

From **Recapitulations** • Reprinted by permission of Random House, Inc. • Copyright, 1946, by Karl Shapiro

I thought as I laid the blossom
  In the leaves of *Les Fleurs du Mal.*

I read my book in the desert
  In the time of death and fear,
The flower slipped from the pages
  And fell to my lap, my dear.

I sent it inside my letter,
  The purplest kiss I knew,
And thus you abused my passion
  With "A most Victorian Jew."

When nuns were spitted and poets fell
And Spain the medieval hell
Became our modern one as well
  And I, a Hamlet, held my tongue,
  Tell me, conscience, was I wrong?

When matters on the Ebro failed
And Cornford died and Campbell railed
And I to my Tahiti sailed
  To ape Loti and Rupert's throng,
  Tell me, conscience, was I wrong?

When Russia smote the sledded Finn
And generals of the French let in
Germans to practice mutual sin,

And I read Horace all night long,
  Tell me, conscience, was I wrong?

When London like the phoenix burned
And flew in fire and fire returned
And peace beneath the umbrella spurned,
  Did I to either side belong?
  Tell me, conscience, was I wrong?   20

When dolls in armor from their toys
Scuttled our fleet with frightful noise
And I obeyed the White House voice,
  My best friend was in a prison flung.
  Tell me, conscience, was I wrong?

                                                        1946

XII • 8 Les Fleurs du Mal (1857), a volume by the French poet,
Charles Pierre Baudelaire (1821-1887) • XIII • 6 Ebro, a river in
northeastern Spain, forming the last defense line of the Republicans
and their friends for nearly four months in 1938 • 7 Cornford . . .
Campbell, presumably personal acquaintances of Shapiro • 9 Loti . . .
Rupert's throng. Pierre Loti (1850-1923), in his best-known novel,
Pecheur d'Islande (The Iceland Fisherman), glorified the life of
simple folk. The other allusion is perhaps to Rupert Brooke (1887-
1915), English poet, who in 1913 went on a trip to the South Seas. He
died in the First World War • 11 Russia smote. Russia invaded
Finland in 1939, and again in June 1941. Cf. Hamlet, Act I, sc. i, l.
63, "He smote the sledded Polacks on the ice" • 18 peace beneath
the umbrella. Prime Minister Neville Chamberlain carried his umbrella
on his two trips to confer with Hitler at Munich in September 1938, which
he thought achieved "peace in our time." Political cartoonists made the
umbrella famous • 22 Scuttled our fleet, at Pearl Harbor, December 7,
1941

Gwendolyn Brooks

1917 •

Chicago's South Side, a vast sprawling exhibit of the most crucial social problems of the nation, has provided the materials for two distinguished contemporary Negro writers: Richard Wright and Gwendolyn Brooks. The South Side was the home of Bigger Thomas, tragic hero of *Native Son,* Wright's novel of 1940, which has gained an international reputation. And it was the home of Annie Allen, the sensitive and highly articulate heroine of the book by Miss Brooks which won the Pulitzer Prize for poetry published in 1949. Both books are sharp reminders that the dreams and ideals of American Negroes are the dreams and ideals of all Americans, but that American democracy still denies to some of its citizens a full spiritual partnership. Of the two, *Annie Allen* probably makes its point more subtly and with more force.

Miss Brooks (since 1939 Mrs. Henry Lowington Blakely) was born in Kansas but taken only a month later to Chicago. There she grew up, went to college, worked, married, lived through World War II. She never lost an early pleasure in poetry, and in 1944 some of her writing was printed in *Poetry, A Magazine of Verse*. A year later *A Street in Bronzeville* was published, bringing her a number of fellowships and grants-in-aid which were amply rewarded by *Annie Allen*.

Annie Allen is essentially a novel, the story of a Negro girl's life from childhood to maturity. Part I, "Notes from the Childhood and the Girlhood," contains eleven poems. Part II, "The Anniad," is a long poem of forty-three seven-line stanzas, with an appendix of three short pieces; its portrayal of a marriage interrupted by the husband's going off to war is extraordinarily moving. Part III, "The Womanhood," is in fifteen sections, some of them made up of several poems. Much of the material is probably autobiographical, but Annie Allen exists apart from her creator, an unforgettable and appealing character.

Technically Miss Brooks' poetry is impressive for range and variety of form. She delicately combines direct and vivid sense impressions with the somewhat elliptical style characteristic of T. S. Eliot and his admirers. She is not always successful, for sometimes a phrase or line does not quite sustain the level of the rest, but she is invariably interesting. She evidently has a social conscience, but she also has a delight in life and in the music of words. One feels that she has something important to say, that she possesses a healthy and highly original mind and that she never poses. These are rare qualities in a contemporary poet, and it seems very probable that with her the best is yet to come. The war, for her, was a maturing force, merely enlarging her compassion for humanity.

Stanley Kunitz, "Bronze by Gold," **Poetry, A Magazine of Verse**, April 1950

The Birth in a Narrow Room

This poem is the first of the "Notes from the Childhood and the Girlhood."

Weeps out of western country something new.
Blurred and stupendous. Wanted and unplanned.
  Winks. Twines, and weakly winks
Upon the milk-glass fruit bowl, iron pot,
The bashful china child tipping forever
Yellow apron and spilling pretty cherries.

Now, weeks and years will go before she thinks
"How pinchy is my room! how can I breathe!
I am not anything and I have got
Not anything, or anything to do!"—   10

But prances nevertheless with gods and fairies
Blithely about the pump and then beneath
The elms and grapevines, then in darling endeavor
By privy foyer, where the screenings stand
And where the bugs buzz by in private cars
Across old peach cans and old jelly beans.

1949

Pygmies are Pygmies Still, Though Percht on Alps
—EDWARD YOUNG

This poem is the tenth of the "Notes." Young (1683-1765), an English poet, rephrased a classical source in line 309 of "Night, VI," in **The Complaint: or Night Thoughts on Life, Death, and Immortality** (1742-1745).

But can see better there, and laughing there
Pity the giants wallowing on the plain.
Giants who bleat and chafe in their small grass,
Seldom to spread the palm; to spit; come clean.

Pygmies expand in cold impossible air,
Cry fie on giantshine, poor glory which
Pounds breast-bone punily, screeches, and has
Reached no Alps: or, knows no Alps to reach.

1949

What Shall I Give My Children? Who Are Poor

Part I of "The Womanhood" consists of five sonnets entitled "the children of the poor," of which this is the second. The group first appeared in **Poetry** for March 1949. The suggestion that the isolation of the Negro is more spiritual than economic is an important aspect of Miss Brooks' thought. The imagery, too, is characteristically mixed, with the dominant image (that of the engraver and his stone) embedded in others, more feminine and naïve.

What shall I give my children? who are poor,
Who are adjudged the leastwise of the land,
Who are my sweetest lepers, who demand
No velvet and no velvety velour;
But who have begged me for a brisk contour,
Crying that they are quasi, contraband
Because unfinished, graven by a hand
Less than angelic, admirable or sure.
My hand is stuffed with mode, design, device.
But I lack access to my proper stone.   10
And plenitude of plan shall not suffice
Nor grief nor love shall be enough alone
To ratify my little halves who bear
Across an autumn freezing everywhere.

1949

Manicure

This poem, a short story in verse, is from "Beauty Shoppe," Part XII of "The Womanhood."

He's betting on it this yellow mellow bit
Is buyable. Regal or Met, he'd say,
A Gordon's Dry at the Tavern. And she's got.
Her signals call. The undernourished brows.
The red fat smudge that won't make up its mind
Whether to nip nose, chin, or both together.
The face snowed under. The irresolute modesty.
Those eyes—Mayhap this chick is on the House!
To the approach. Outrageous? guy-gallant?
Paternal? frosty-with-the-heart-of-fire?   10
Already, this hors-d'oeuvre is in the teeth,
And all a brother has to do is bite.
Ready! . . . Aim! . . . Fire! The glass eyes break. The red
Fat moves and melts. Brows rise in lean surprise.
Bosom awakes. Maybe, she says. She might.
Well, possibly. . .Well, call at nine tonight.

1949

Men of Careful Turns

Part XV of "The Womanhood" would seem to be Miss Brooks' personal comment on inter-racial tensions. Few statements make clearer the emotional context of prejudice as it affects its objects.

Men of careful turns, haters of forks in the road,
The strain at the eye, that puzzlement, that awe—
Grant me that I am human, that I hurt,
That I can cry.

Not that I now ask alms, in shame gone hollow,
Nor cringe outside the loud and sumptuous gate.
Admit me to our mutual estate.

Open my rooms, let in the light and air.
Reserve me service at the human feast.
And let the joy continue. Do not hoard silence   10
For the moment when I enter, tardily,
To enjoy my height among you. And to love you
No more as a woman loves a drunken mate,
Restraining full caress and good My Dear,
Even pity for the heaviness and the need—
Fearing sudden fire out of the uncaring mouth,
Boiling in the slack eyes, and the traditional blow.
Next, the indifference formal, deep and slow.

Comes in your graceful glider and benign,
To smile upon me bigly; now desires   20
Me easy, easy; claims the days are softer
Than they were; murmurs reflectively "Remember
When cruelty, metal, public, uncomplex,
Trampled you obviously and every hour. . . ."
(Now cruelty flaunts diplomas, is elite,
Delicate, has polish, knows how to be discreet):
   Requests my patience, wills me to be calm,
Brings me a chair, but the one with broken straw,
Whispers "My friend, no thing is without flaw.

If prejudice is native—and it is—you   30
Will find it ineradicable—not to
Be juggled, not to be altered at all,
But left unvexed at its place in the properness
Of things, even to be given (with grudging) honor.
   What
We are to hope is that intelligence
Can sugar up our prejudice with politeness.
Politeness will take care of what needs caring.
For the line is there.
And has a meaning. So our fathers said—   40
And they were wise—we think—At any rate,
They were older than ourselves. And the report is
What's old is wise. At any rate, the line is
Long and electric. Lean beyond and nod.
Be sprightly. Wave. Extend your hand and teeth.
   But never forget it stretches there beneath."
The toys are all grotesque
And not for lovely hands; are dangerous,
Serrate in open and artful places. Rise.
Let us combine. There are no magics or elves   50
Or timely godmothers to guide us. We are lost, must
Wizard a track through our own screaming weed.

                                                      1949

---

39 line, the color line

Eugene O'Neill, Dramatist

Eugene O'Neill

1888 · 1953

The 1920's and early 1930's were the greatest period
in the history of the American drama; during those
years, a dramatic revival was in full swing. In comedy
there were—to select only a few of the more brilliant
examples—Philip Barry's *Paris Bound* (1927) and *Holiday* (1929), S. N. Behrman's *The Second Man* (1927)
and *Biography* (1932), George Kelly's *The Show-Off*
(1924) and *Craig's Wife* (1925), George S. Kauf-

man's *Beggar on Horseback* (with Marc Connelly, 1924) and *The Royal Family* (with Edna Ferber, 1927), and Robert Sherwood's *Road to Rome* (1927) and *Reunion in Vienna* (1931). And in tragedy, there were the plays of Eugene O'Neill—by common consent the greatest dramatist whom America has yet produced. Among O'Neill's more important works were: *Beyond the Horizon* (1920), *The Emperor Jones* (1921), *Anna Christie* and *The Hairy Ape* (1922), *Desire under the Elms* (1924), *The Great God Brown* (1926), *Strange Interlude* (1928); and *Mourning Becomes Electra* (1931). O'Neill's creativity has declined in later years (owing perhaps to ill-health). His *The Iceman Cometh* (1946) and *Moon for the Misbegotten* (1952) met with an equivocal reception. Interesting drama was not lacking in the 1930's and 1940's, as is evidenced by such distinguished plays as Maxwell Anderson's *Winterset*, Clifford Odets' *Waiting for Lefty*, Lillian Hellman's *The Little Foxes*, and Tennessee Williams' *A Street-Car Named Desire*. But despite successes like these, the great work of O'Neill in the 1920's stands out, still, as the high point in American dramatic literature.

Son of the famous actor James O'Neill, Eugene O'Neill was born in New York City. After a varied experience which included not only academic study (at Princeton, 1906-1907, and at Harvard, 1914-1915) but also two years at sea, a tour in vaudeville, and a turn at newspaper reporting, he began his career as dramatist in 1916.

His plays are interesting, first of all, for their bold experimentation. Restive under the restraints imposed by the theater, and never satisfied with an achieved form, O'Neill constantly experimented with new techniques. *The Emperor Jones* and *The Hairy Ape* were experiments in monodrama—a type of play whose purpose is the exhibition of a single character. *Desire under the Elms* employed a novel stage set, showing by means of the cross-section of a house simultaneous actions in the different rooms. *The Great God Brown* used masks to distinguish between the assumed and the real attitudes of the characters, and *Strange Interlude* used the aside for the same purpose. Many plays (*The Hairy Ape* among them) employed "expressionism"—a technique which sought to convey the meaning symbolically rather than by a literal realism. Even though the auditor sometimes questioned the success of these experiments, he always applauded their brilliance and originality. O'Neill's plays are interesting, in the second place, for their psycho-

Eugene O'Neill—drawing by Karl Woerner from The Forum, *October 1932*

logical insight. The author achieved his most powerful effects in studies of the disintegration of personality. In *The Emperor Jones*, the theme was the breakdown of a Negro's mentality under the stress of fear; in *The Hairy Ape*, a worker's loss of motivation when he could no longer feel that he "belonged"; in *Strange Interlude*, the mental and moral disintegration of a woman whose fiancé had been killed in war. Although the Freudian psychology was too prominently displayed—a fact which may prove injurious to O'Neill's future reputation—there is no denying the originality and power of his best work.

A. H. Quinn, **A History of the American Drama from the Civil War to the Present Day**, 2 vols., New York, 1927 • S. K. Winther, **Eugene O'Neill**, New York, 1934 • R. D. Skinner, **Eugene O'Neill; A Poet's Quest**, New York, 1935 • B. H. Clark, **Eugene O'Neill**, New York, 1936

The Hairy Ape

A Comedy of Ancient and Modern Life in Eight Scenes

The Hairy Ape was first produced by the Provincetown Players at their theater, the Provincetown Playhouse, 183 Macdougal Street, New York City, March 9, 1922. Louis Wolheim took the part of "Yank."

The play is significant technically because of its strong emphasis upon a single character and its use of "expressionism." Although it is employed throughout, the expressionistic method—which at intervals substitutes a fantastic kind of symbolism for external realism—is prominent in Scene V, for example, where Yank lunges against the pedestrians on Fifth Avenue without producing any visible effect upon them. The play is important also for its content. Although O'Neill, here as elsewhere, is concerned primarily with psychological processes, he presents in The Hairy Ape a psychological problem which is broadly social in its implications—the divorce, in the modern industrial world, of the worker from his work. It is a problem which came into being with the industrial revolution, which goes much deeper than hours and wages, and for which no solution has yet been found.

Characters

Robert Smith, "Yank"
Paddy
Long
Mildred Douglas
Her Aunt
Second Engineer
A Guard
A Secretary of an Organization
Stokers, Ladies, Gentlemen, etc.

Scenes

Scene I: The firemen's forecastle of an ocean liner—an hour after sailing from New York.
Scene II: Section of promenade deck, two days out—morning.
Scene III: The stokehole. A few minutes later.
Scene IV: Same as Scene I. Half an hour later.
Scene V: Fifth Avenue, New York. Three weeks later.
Scene VI: An island near the city. The next night.
Scene VII: In the city. About a month later.
Scene VIII: In the city. Twilight of the next day.

SCENE I

SCENE. The firemen's forecastle of a transatlantic liner an hour after sailing from New York for the voyage across. Tiers of narrow, steel bunks, three deep, on all sides. An entrance in rear. Benches on the floor before the bunks. The room is crowded with men, shouting, cursing, laughing, singing—a confused, inchoate uproar swelling into a sort of unity, a meaning—the bewildered, furious, baffled defiance of a beast in a cage. Nearly all the men are drunk. Many bottles are passed from hand to hand. All are dressed in dungaree pants, heavy ugly shoes. Some wear singlets, but the majority are stripped to the waist.

The treatment of this scene, or of any other scene in the play, should by no means be naturalistic. The effect sought after is a cramped space in the bowels of a ship, imprisoned by white steel. The lines of bunks, the uprights supporting them, cross each other like the steel framework of a cage. The ceiling crushes down upon the men's heads. They cannot stand upright. This accentuates the natural stooping posture which shoveling coal and the resultant over-development of back and shoulder muscles have given them. The men themselves should resemble those pictures in which the appearance of Neanderthal Man is guessed at. All are hairy-chested, with long arms of tremendous power, and low, receding brows above their small, fierce, resentful eyes. All the civilized white races are represented, but except for the slight differentiation in color of hair, skin, eyes, all these men are alike.

The curtain rises on a tumult of sound. Yank is seated in the foreground. He seems broader, fiercer, more truculent, more powerful, more sure of himself than the rest. They respect his superior strength—the grudging respect of fear.

Then, too, he represents to them a self-expression, the very last word in what they are, their most highly developed individual.

VOICES. Gif me trink dere, you!
'Ave a wet!
Salute!
Gesundheit!
Skoal!
Drunk as a lord, God stiffen you!
Here's how!
Luck!
Pass back that bottle, damn you!
Pourin' it down his neck!
Ho, Froggy! Where the devil have you been?
La Touraine.
I hit him smash in yaw, py Gott!
Jenkins—the First—he's a rotten swine——
And the coppers nabbed him—and I run——
I like peer better. It don't pig head gif you.
A slut, I'm sayin'! She robbed me aslape——
To hell with 'em all!
You're a bloody liar!
Say dot again!
[*Commotion. Two men about to fight are pulled apart.*]
No scrappin' now!
To-night——
See who's the best man!
Bloody Dutchman!
To-night on the for'ard square.
I'll bet on Dutchy.
He packa da wallop, I tella you!
Shut up, Wop!
No fightin', maties. We're all chums, ain't we?
[*A voice starts bawling a song.*]
        "Beer, beer, glorious beer!
        Fill yourselves right up to here."
YANK. [*For the first time seeming to take notice of the uproar about him, turns around threateningly—in a tone of contemptuous authority.*] Choke off dat noise! Where d'yuh get dat beer stuff? Beer, hell! Beer's for goils—and Dutchmen. Me for somep'n wit a kick to it! Gimme a drink, one of youse guys. [*Several bottles are eagerly offered. He takes a tremendous gulp at one of them; then, keeping the bottle in his hand, glares bel-*

ligerently at the owner, who hastens to acquiesce in this robbery by saying.] All righto, Yank. Keep it and have another. [YANK *contemptuously turns his back on the crowd again. For a second there is an embarrassed silence. Then——*]
VOICES. We must be passing the Hook.
She's beginning to roll to it.
Six days in hell—and then Southampton.
Py Yesus, I vish somepody take my first vatch for me!
Gittin' seasick, Square-head?
Drink up and forget it!
What's in your bottle?
Gin.
Dot's nigger trink.
Absinthe? It's doped. You'll go off your chump, Froggy!
Cochon!
Whisky, that's the ticket!
Where's Paddy?
Going asleep.
Sing us that whisky song, Paddy.
[*They all turn to an old, wizened Irishman who is dozing, very drunk, on the benches forward. His face is extremely monkey-like with all the sad, patient pathos of that animal in his small eyes.*]
Singa da song, Caruso Pat!
He's gettin' old. The drink is too much for him.
He's too drunk.
PADDY. [*Blinking about him, starts to his feet resentfully, swaying, holding on to the edge of a bunk.*] I'm never too drunk to sing. 'Tis only when I'm dead to the world I'd be wishful to sing at all. [*With a sort of sad contempt.*] "Whisky Johnny," ye want? A chanty, ye want? Now that's a queer wish from the ugly like of you, God help you. But no matther. [*He starts to sing in a thin, nasal, doleful tone.*]
Oh, whisky is the life of man!
    Whisky! O Johnny! [*They all join in on this.*]
Oh, whisky is the life of man!
    Whisky for my Johnny! [*Again chorus.*]
Oh, whisky drove my old man mad!
    Whisky! O Johnny!
Oh, whisky drove my old man mad!
    Whisky for my Johnny!
YANK. [*Again turning around scornfully.*] Aw hell!

The Hairy Ape 979

Nix on dat old sailing ship stuff! All dat bull's dead, see? And you're dead, too, yuh damned old Harp, on'y yuh don't know it. Take it easy, see. Give us a rest. Nix on de loud noise. [*With a cynical grin.*] Can't youse see I'm tryin' to t'ink?

ALL. [*Repeating the word after him as one with the same cynical amused mockery.*] Think! [*The chorused word has a brazen metallic quality as if their throats were phonograph horns. It is followed by a general uproar of hard, barking laughter.*]

VOICES. Don't be cracking your head wit ut, Yank.

You gat headache, py yingo!

One thing about it—it rhymes with drink!

Ha, ha, ha!

Drink, don't think!

Drink, don't think!

Drink, don't think!

[*A whole chorus of voices has taken up this refrain, stamping on the floor, pounding on the benches with fists.*]

YANK. [*Taking a gulp from his bottle—goodnaturedly.*] Aw right. Can de noise. I got yuh de foist time.

[*The uproar subsides. A very drunken sentimental tenor begins to sing.*]

"Far away in Canada,
Far across the sea,
There's a lass who fondly waits
Making a home for me——"

YANK. [*Fiercely contemptuous.*] Shut up, yuh lousy boob! Where d'yuh yet dat tripe? Home? Home, hell! I'll make a home for yuh! I'll knock yuh dead. Home! T'hell wit home! Where d'yuh get dat tripe? Dis is home, see? What d'yuh want wit home? [*Proudly.*] I runned away from mine when I was a kid. On'y too glad to beat it, dat was me. Home was lickings for me, dat's all. But yuh can bet your shoit no one ain't never licked me since! Wanter try it, any of youse? Huh! I guess not. [*In a more placated but still contemptuous tone.*] Goils waitin' for yuh, huh? Aw, hell! Dat's all tripe. Dey don't wait for no one. Dey'd double-cross yuh for a nickel. Dey're all tarts, get me? Treat 'em rough, dat's me. To hell wit 'em. Tarts, dat's what, de whole bunch of 'em.

LONG. [*Very drunk, jumps on a bench excitedly, gesticulating with a bottle in his hand.*] Listen 'ere, Comrades! Yank 'ere is right. 'E says this 'ere stinkin' ship is our 'ome. And 'e says as 'ome is 'ell. And 'e's right! This is 'ell. We lives in 'ell, Comrades—and right enough we'll die in it. [*Raging.*] And who's ter blame, I arsks yer? We ain't. We wasn't born this rotten way. All men is born free and ekal. That's in the bleedin' Bible, maties. But what d'they care for the Bible—them lazy, bloated swine what travels first cabin? Them's the ones. They dragged us down 'til we're on'y wage slaves in the bowels of a bloody ship, sweatin', burnin' up, eatin' coal dust! Hit's them's ter blame—the damned Capitalist clarss!

[*There had been a gradual murmur of contemptuous resentment rising among the men until now he is interrupted by a storm of catcalls, hisses, boos, hard laughter.*]

VOICES. Turn it off!

Shut up!

Sit down!

Closa da face!

Tamn fool! [*Etc.*]

YANK. [*Standing up and glaring at* LONG.] Sit down before I knock yuh down! [LONG *makes haste to efface himself.* YANK *goes on contemptuously.*] De Bible, huh? De Cap'tlist class, huh? Aw nix on dat Salvation Army-Socialist bull. Git a soapbox! Hire a hall! Come and be saved, huh? Jerk us to Jesus, huh? Aw g'wan! I've listened to lots of guys like you, see. Yuh're all wrong. Wanter know what I t'ink? Yuh ain't no good for no one. Yuh're de bunk. Yuh ain't got no noive, get me? Yuh're yellow, dat's what. Yellow, dat's you. Say! What's dem slobs in de foist cabin got to do wit us? We're better men dan dey are, ain't we? Sure! One of us guys could clean up de whole mob wit one mit. Put one of 'em down here for one watch in de stokehole, what'd happen? Dey'd carry him off on a stretcher. Dem boids don't amount to nothin'. Dey're just baggage. Who makes dis old tub run? Ain't it us guys? Well den, we belong, don't we? We belong and dey don't. Dat's all. [*A loud chorus of approval.* YANK *goes on.*] As for dis bein' hell—aw, nuts! Yuh lost your noive, dat's what. Dis is a man's job, get me? It belongs. It runs dis tub. No stiffs need apply. But yuh're a stiff, see? Yuh're yellow, dat's you.

VOICES. [*With a great hard pride in them.*]

Righto!

A man's job!

Talk is cheap, Long.

He never could hold up his end.

Divil take him!

Yank's right. We make it go.

Py Gott, Yank say right ting!

We don't need no one cryin' over us.

Makin' speeches.

Throw him out!

Yellow!

Chuck him overboard!

I'll break his jaw for him!

[*They crowd around* LONG *threateningly.*]

YANK. [*Half good-natured again—contemptuously.*] Aw, take it easy. Leave him alone. He ain't woith a punch. Drink up. Here's how, whoever owns dis. [*He takes a long swallow from his bottle. All drink with him. In a flash all is hilarious amiability again, back-slapping, loud talk, etc.*]

PADDY. [*Who has been sitting in a blinking, melancholy daze—suddenly cries out in a voice full of old sorrow.*] We belong to this, you're saying? We make the ship to go, you're saying? Yerra then, that Almighty God have pity on us! [*His voice runs into the wail of a keen, he rocks back and forth on his bench. The men stare at him, startled and impressed in spite of themselves.*] Oh, to be back in the fine days of my youth, ochone! Oh, there was fine beautiful ships them days—clippers wid tall masts touching the sky—fine strong men in them—men that was sons of the sea as if 'twas the mother that bore them. Oh, the clean skins of them, and the clear eyes, the straight backs and full chests of them! Brave men they was, and bold men surely! We'd be sailing out, bound down round the Horn maybe. We'd be making sail in the dawn, with a fair breeze, singing a chanty song wid no care to it. And astern the land would be sinking low and dying out, but we'd give it no heed but a laugh, and never a look behind. For the day that was, was enough, for we was free men—and I'm thinking 'tis only slaves do be giving heed to the day that's gone or the day to come—until they're old like me. [*With a sort of religious exaltation.*] Oh, to be scudding south again wid the power of the Trade Wind driving her on steady through the nights and the days! Full sail on her! Nights and days! Nights when the foam of the wake would be flaming wid fire, when the sky'd be blazing and winking wid stars. Or the full of the moon maybe. Then you'd see her driving through the gray night, her sails stretching aloft all silver and white, not a sound on the deck, the lot of us dreaming dreams, till you'd believe 'twas no real ship at all you was on but a ghost ship like the *Flying Dutchman* they say does be roaming the seas forevermore without touching a port. And there was the days, too. A warm sun on the clean decks. Sun warming the blood of you, and wind over the miles of shiny green ocean like strong drink to your lungs. Work—aye, hard work—but who'd mind that at all? Sure, you worked under the sky and 'twas work wid skill and daring to it. And wid the day done, in the dog watch, smoking me pipe at ease, the lookout would be raising land maybe, and we'd see the mountains of South Americy wid the red fire of the setting sun painting their white tops and the clouds floating by them! [*His tone of exaltation ceases. He goes on mournfully.*] Yerra, what's the use of talking? 'Tis a dead man's whisper. [*To* YANK *resentfully.*] 'Twas them days men belonged to ships, not now. 'Twas them days a ship was part of the sea, and a man was part of a ship, and the sea joined all together and made it one. [*Scornfully.*] Is it one wid this you'd be, Yank—black smoke from the funnels smudging the sea, smudging the decks—the bloody engines pounding and throbbing and shaking—wid divil a sight of sun or a breath of clean air—choking our lungs wid coal dust—breaking our backs and hearts in the hell of the stokehole—feeding the bloody furnace—feeding our lives along wid the coal, I'm thinking—caged in by steel from a sight of the sky like bloody apes in the Zoo! [*With a harsh laugh.*] Ho-ho, divil mend you! Is it to belong to that you're wishing? Is it a flesh and blood wheel of the engines you'd be?

YANK. [*Who has been listening with a contemptuous sneer, barks out the answer.*] Sure ting! Dat's me. What about it?

PADDY. [*As if to himself—with great sorrow.*] Me time is past due. That a great wave wid sun in the heart of it may sweep me over the side sometime I'd be dreaming of the days that's gone!

YANK. Aw, yuh crazy Mick! [*He springs to his feet and advances on* PADDY *threateningly—then stops, fighting some queer struggle within himself—lets his hands*

22 keen, a lamentation or dirge • 25 ochone, alas

The Hairy Ape   981

fall to his sides—contemptuously.] Aw, take it easy. Yuh're aw right at dat. Yuh're bugs, dat's all—nutty as a cuckoo. All dat tripe yuh been pullin'——Aw, dat's all right. On'y it's dead, get me? Yuh don't belong no more, see. Yuh don't get de stuff. Yuh're too old. [*Disgustedly.*] But aw say, come up for air onct in a while, can't yuh? See what's happened since yuh croaked. [*He suddenly bursts forth vehemently, growing more and more excited.*] Say! Sure! Sure I meant
10 it! What de hell—— Say, lemme talk! Hey! Hey, you old Harp! Hey, youse guys! Say, listen to me—wait a moment—I gotter talk, see. I belong and he don't. He's dead but I'm livin'. Listen to me! Sure I'm part of de engines! Why de hell not! Dey move, don't dey? Dey're speed, ain't dey! Dey smash trou, don't dey? Twenty-five knots a hour! Dat's goin' some! Dat's new stuff! Dat belongs! But him, he's too old. He gets dizzy. Say, listen. All dat crazy tripe about nights and days; all dat crazy tripe about stars and moons; all dat crazy tripe about
20 suns and winds, fresh air and de rest of it—— Aw hell, dat's all a dope dream! Hittin' de pipe of de past, dat's what he's doin'. He's old and don't belong no more. But me, I'm young! I'm in de pink! I move wit it! It, get me! I mean de ting dat's de guts of all dis. It ploughs trou all de tripe he's been sayin'. It blows dat up! It knocks dat dead! It slams dat offen de face of de oith! It, get me! De engines and de coal and de smoke and all de rest of it! He can't breathe and swallow coal dust, but I kin, see? Dat's fresh air for me! Dat's food
30 for me! I'm new, get me? Hell in de stokehole? Sure! It takes a man to work in hell. Hell, sure, dat's my fav'rite climate. I eat it up! I git fat on it! It's me makes it hot! It's me makes it roar! It's me makes it move! Sure, on'y for me everyting stops. It all goes dead, get me? De noise and smoke and all de engines movin' de woild, dey stop. Dere ain't nothin' no more! Dat's what I'm sayin'. Everyting else dat makes de woild move, somep'n makes it move. It can't move witout somep'n else, see? Den yuh get down to me. I'm at de bottom, get me!
40 Dere ain't nothin' foither. I'm de end! I'm de start! I start somep'n and de woild moves! It—dat's me!—de new dat's moiderin' de old! I'm de ting in coal dat makes it boin; I'm steam and oil for de engines; I'm de ting in noise dat makes yuh hear it; I'm smoke and express trains and steamers and factory whistles; I'm de ting in gold dat makes it money! And I'm what

makes iron into steel! Steel, dat stands for de whole ting! And I'm steel—steel—steel! I'm de muscles in steel, de punch behind it! [*As he says this he pounds with his fist against the steel bunks. All the men,* 50 *roused to a pitch of frenzied self-glorification by his speech, do likewise. There is a deafening metallic roar, through which* YANK'S *voice can be heard bellowing.*] Slaves, hell! We run de whole woiks. All de rich guys dat tink dey're somep'n, dey ain't nothin'! Dey don't belong. But us guys, we're in de move, we're at de bottom, de whole ting is us! [PADDY *from the start of* YANK'S *speech has been taking one gulp after another from his bottle, at first frightenedly, as if he were afraid to listen, then desperately, as if to drown his senses,* 60 *but finally has achieved complete indifferent, even amused, drunkenness.* YANK *sees his lips moving. He quells the uproar with a shout.*] Hey, youse guys, take it easy! Wait a moment! De nutty Harp is sayin' somep'n.

PADDY. [*Is heard now—throws his head back with a mocking burst of laughter.*] Ho-ho-ho-ho-ho——

YANK. [*Drawing back his fist, with a snarl.*] Aw! Look out who yuh're givin' the bark!

PADDY. [*Begins to sing the "Miller of Dee" with enormous good nature.*] 70

"I care for nobody, no, not I,
    And nobody cares for me."

YANK. [*Good-natured himself in a flash, interrupts* PADDY *with a slap on the bare back like a report.*] Dat's de stuff! Now yuh're gettin' wise to somep'n. Care for nobody, dat's de dope! To hell wit 'em all! And nix on nobody else carin'. I kin care for myself, get me! [*Eight bells sound, muffled, vibrating through the steel walls as if some enormous brazen gong were imbedded in the heart of the ship. All the men jump up mechanically,* 80 *file through the door silently close upon each other's heels in what is very like a prisoners' lockstep.* YANK *slaps* PADDY *on the back.*] Our watch, yuh old Harp! [*Mockingly.*] Come on down in hell. Eat up de coal dust. Drink in de heat. It's it, see! Act like yuh liked it, yuh better—or croak yuhself.

PADDY. [*With jovial defiance.*] To the divil wid it! I'll not report this watch. Let them log me and be damned. I'm no slave the like of you. I'll be sittin' here at me ease, and drinking, and thinking, and dreaming dreams. 90

YANK. [*Contemptuously.*] Tinkin' and dreamin', what'll that get yuh? What's tinkin' got to do wit it?

We move, don't we? Speed, ain't it? Fog, dat's all you stand for. But we drive trou dat, don't we? We split dat up and smash trou—twenty-five knots a hour! [*Turns his back on* PADDY *scornfully.*] Aw, yuh make me sick! Yuh don't belong! [*He strides out the door in rear.* PADDY *hums to himself, blinking drowsily.*]

[*Curtain*]

SCENE II

SCENE. Two days out. A section of the promenade deck. **Mildred Douglas** and her aunt are discovered reclining in deck chairs. The former is a girl of twenty, slender, delicate, with a pale, pretty face marred by a self-conscious expression of disdainful superiority. She looks fretful, nervous, and discontented, bored by her own anemia. Her aunt is a pompous and proud—and fat—old lady. She is a type even to the point of a double chin and lorgnettes. She is dressed pretentiously, as if afraid her face alone would never indicate her position in life. **Mildred** is dressed all in white.

The impression to be conveyed by this scene is one of the beautiful, vivid life of the sea all about—sunshine on the deck in a great flood, the fresh sea wind blowing across it. In the midst of this, these two incongruous, artificial figures, inert and disharmonious, the elder like a gray lump of dough touched up with rouge, the younger looking as if the vitality of her stock had been sapped before she was conceived, so that she is the expression not of its life energy but merely of the artificialities that energy had won for itself in the spending.

MILDRED. [*Looking up with affected dreaminess.*] How the black smoke swirls back against the sky! Is it not beautiful?

10 AUNT. [*Without looking up.*] I dislike smoke of any kind.

MILDRED. My great-grandmother smoked a pipe—a clay pipe.

AUNT. [*Ruffling.*] Vulgar.

MILDRED. She was too distant a relative to be vulgar. Time mellows pipes.

AUNT. [*Pretending boredom but irritated.*] Did the sociology you took up at college teach you that—to play the ghoul on every possible occasion, excavating old bones?

20 Why not let your great-grandmother rest in her grave?

MILDRED. [*Dreamily.*] With her pipe beside her—puffing in Paradise.

AUNT. [*With spite.*] Yes, you are a natural born ghoul. You are even getting to look like one, my dear.

MILDRED. [*In a passionless tone.*] I detest you, Aunt. [*Looking at her critically.*] Do you know what you remind me of? Of a cold pork pudding against a background of linoleum tablecloth in the kitchen of a—but the possibilities are wearisome. [*She closes her eyes.*]

AUNT. [*With a bitter laugh.*] Merci for your candor. 30 But since I am and must be your chaperon—in appearance, at least—let us patch up some sort of armed truce. For my part you are quite free to indulge any pose of eccentricity that beguiles you—as long as you observe the amenities——

MILDRED. [*Drawling.*] The inanities?

AUNT. [*Going on as if she hadn't heard.*] After exhausting the morbid thrills of social service work on New York's East Side—how they must have hated you, by the way, the poor that you made so much poorer in 40 their own eyes!—you are now bent on making your slumming international. Well, I hope Whitechapel will provide the needed nerve tonic. Do not ask me to chaperon you there, however. I told your father I would not. I loathe deformity. We will hire an army of detectives and you may investigate everything—they allow you to see.

MILDRED. [*Protesting with a trace of genuine earnestness.*] Please do not mock at my attempts to discover how the other half lives. Give me credit for some sort 50 of groping sincerity in that at least. I would like to help them. I would like to be some use in the world. Is it my fault I don't know how? I would like to be sincere, to touch life somewhere. [*With weary bitterness.*] But I'm afraid I have neither the vitality nor integrity. All that was burnt out in our stock before I was born. Grandfather's blast furnaces, flaming to the sky, melting steel, making millions—then father keeping those home fires burning, making more millions— and little me at the tail-end of it all. I'm a waste product 60 in the Bessemer process—like the millions. Or rather, I inherit the acquired trait of the by-product, wealth, but none of the energy, none of the strength of the steel

---

42 **Whitechapel,** a quarter of London just east of the city

that made it. I am sired by gold and damned by it, as they say at the race track—damned in more ways than one. [*She laughs mirthlessly.*]

AUNT. [*Unimpressed—superciliously.*] You seem to be going in for sincerity to-day. It isn't becoming to you, really—except as an obvious pose. Be as artificial as you are, I advise. There's a sort of sincerity in that, you know. And, after all, you must confess you like that better.

MILDRED. [*Again affected and bored.*] Yes, I suppose 10 I do. Pardon me for my outburst. When a leopard complains of its spots, it must sound rather grotesque. [*In a mocking tone.*] Purr, little leopard. Purr, scratch, tear, kill, gorge yourself and be happy—only stay in the jungle where your spots are camouflage. In a cage they make you conspicuous.

AUNT. I don't know what you are talking about.

MILDRED. It would be rude to talk about anything to you. Let's just talk. [*She looks at her wrist watch.*] Well, thank goodness, it's about time for them to come 20 for me. That ought to give me a new thrill, Aunt.

AUNT. [*Affectedly troubled.*] You don't mean to say you're really going? The dirt—the heat must be frightful——

MILDRED. Grandfather started as a puddler. I should have inherited an immunity to heat that would make a salamander shiver. It will be fun to put it to the test.

AUNT. But don't you have to have the captain's—or someone's—permission to visit the stokehole?

MILDRED. [*With a triumphant smile.*] I have it—both 30 his and the chief engineer's. Oh, they didn't want to at first, in spite of my social service credentials. They didn't seem a bit anxious that I should investigate how the other half lives and works on a ship. So I had to tell them that my father, the president of Nazareth Steel, chairman of the board of directors of this line, had told me it would be all right.

AUNT. He didn't.

MILDRED. How naïve age makes one! But I said he did, Aunt. I even said he had given me a letter to them— 40 which I had lost. And they were afraid to take the chance that I might be lying. [*Excitedly.*] So it's ho! for the stokehole. The second engineer is to escort me. [*Looking at her watch again.*] It's time. And here he comes, I think.

[*The* SECOND ENGINEER *enters. He is a husky, fine-looking man of thirty-five or so. He stops before the*

two and tips his cap, visibly embarrassed and ill-at-ease.]

SECOND ENGINEER. Miss Douglas?

MILDRED. Yes. [*Throwing off her rugs and getting to her feet.*] Are we all ready to start?

SECOND ENGINEER. In just a second, ma'am. I'm waiting for the Fourth. He's coming along.

MILDRED. [*With a scornful smile.*] You don't care to 50 shoulder this responsibility alone, is that it?

SECOND ENGINEER. [*Forcing a smile.*] Two are better than one. [*Disturbed by her eyes, glances out to sea—blurts out.*] A fine day we're having.

MILDRED. Is it?

SECOND ENGINEER. A nice warm breeze——

MILDRED. It feels cold to me.

SECOND ENGINEER. But it's hot enough in the sun——

MILDRED. Not hot enough for me. I don't like Nature. I was never athletic. 60

SECOND ENGINEER. [*Forcing a smile.*] Well, you'll find it hot enough where you're going.

MILDRED. Do you mean hell?

SECOND ENGINEER. [*Flabbergasted, decides to laugh.*] Ho-ho! No, I mean the stokehole.

MILDRED. My grandfather was a puddler. He played with boiling steel.

SECOND ENGINEER. [*All at sea—uneasily.*] Is that so? Hum, you'll excuse me, ma'am, but are you intending to wear that dress? 70

MILDRED. Why not?

SECOND ENGINEER. You'll likely rub against oil and dirt. It can't be helped.

MILDRED. It doesn't matter. I have lots of white dresses.

SECOND ENGINEER. I have an old coat you might throw over——

MILDRED. I have fifty dresses like this. I will throw this one into the sea when I come back. That ought to wash it clean, don't you think?

SECOND ENGINEER. [*Doggedly.*] There's ladders to 80 climb down that are none too clean—and dark alleyways——

MILDRED. I will wear this very dress and none other.

SECOND ENGINEER. No offense meant. It's none of my business. I was only warning you——

MILDRED. Warning? That sounds thrilling.

SECOND ENGINEER. [*Looking down the deck—with a sigh of relief.*] There's the Fourth now. He's waiting for us. If you'll come——

MILDRED. Go on. I'll follow you. [*He goes.* MILDRED *turns a mocking smile on her aunt.*] An oaf—but a handsome, virile oaf.

AUNT. [*Scornfully.*] Poser!

MILDRED. Take care. He said there were dark alley-ways——

AUNT. [*In the same tone.*] Poser!

MILDRED. [*Biting her lips angrily.*] You are right. But would that my millions were not so anemically chaste!

AUNT. Yes, for a fresh pose I have no doubt you would drag the name of Douglas in the gutter!

MILDRED. From which it sprang. Goodby, Aunt. Don't pray too hard that I may fall into the fiery furnace.

AUNT. Poser!

MILDRED. [*Viciously.*] Old hag! [*She slaps her aunt insultingly across the face and walks off, laughing gayly.*]

AUNT. [*Screams after her.*] I said poser!

[*Curtain*]

SCENE III

SCENE. The stokehole. In the rear, the dimly-outlined bulks of the furnaces and boilers. High overhead one hanging electric bulb sheds just enough light through the murky air laden with coal dust to pile up masses of shadows everywhere. A line of men, stripped to the waist, is before the furnace doors. They bend over, looking neither to right nor left, handling their shovels as if they were part of their bodies, with a strange, awkward, swinging rhythm. They use the shovels to throw open the furnace doors. Then from these fiery round holes in the black a flood of terrific light and heat pours full upon the men who are outlined in silhouette in the crouching, inhuman attitudes of chained gorillas. The men shovel with a rhythmic motion, swinging as on a pivot from the coal which lies in heaps on the floor behind to hurl it into the flaming mouths before them. There is a tumult of noise— the brazen clang of the furnace doors as they are flung open or slammed shut, the grating, teeth-gritting grind of steel against steel, of crunching coal. This clash of sounds stuns one's ears with its rending dissonance. But there is order in it, rhythm, a mechanical regulated recurrence, a tempo. And rising above all, making the air hum with the quiver of liberated energy, the roar of leaping flames in the furnaces, the monotonous throbbing beat of the engines.

As the curtain rises, the furnace doors are shut. The men are taking a breathing spell. One or two are arranging the coal behind them, pulling it into more accessible heaps. The others can be dimly made out leaning on their shovels in relaxed attitudes of exhaustion.

PADDY. [*From somewhere in the line—plaintively.*] Yerra, will this divil's own watch nivir end? Me back is broke. I'm destroyed entirely.

YANK. [*From the center of the line—with exuberant scorn.*] Aw, yuh make me sick! Lie down and croak, why don't yuh? Always beefin', dat's you! Say, dis is a cinch! Dis was made for me! It's my meat, get me! [*A whistle is blown—a thin, shrill note from somewhere overhead in the darkness.* YANK *curses without resentment.*] Dere's de damn engineer crackin' de whip. He tinks we're loafin'.

PADDY. [*Vindictively.*] God stiffen him!

YANK. [*In an exultant tone of command.*] Come on, youse guys! Git into de game! She's gittin hungry! Pile some grub in her. Trow it into her belly! Come on now, all of youse! Open her up!

[*At this last all the men, who have followed his movements of getting into position, throw open their furnace doors with a deafening clang. The fiery light floods over their shoulders as they bend round for the coal. Rivulets of sooty sweat have traced maps on their backs. The enlarged muscles form bunches of high light and shadow.*]

YANK. [*Chanting a count as he shovels without seeming effort.*] One—two—tree—— [*His voice rising exultantly in the joy of battle.*] Dat's de stuff! Let her have it! All togedder now! Sling it into her! Let her ride! Shoot de piece now! Call de toin on her! Drive her into it! Feel her move! Watch her smoke! Speed, dat's her middle name! Give her coal, youse guys! Coal, dat's her booze! Drink it up, baby! Let's see yuh sprint! Dig in and gain a lap! Dere she go-o-es. [*This last in the chanting formula of the gallery gods at the six-day bike race. He slams his furnace door shut. The others do likewise with as much unison as their wearied bodies will permit. The effect is of one fiery eye after another being blotted out with a series of accompanying bangs.*]

PADDY. [*Groaning.*] Me back is broke. I'm bate out— bate——

[*There is a pause. Then the inexorable whistle sounds*

again from the dim regions above the electric light.
There is a growl of cursing rage from all sides.]

YANK. [*Shaking his fist upward—contemptuously.*]
Take it easy dere, you! Who d'yuh tinks runnin' dis
game, me or you? When I git ready, we move. Not
before! When I git ready, get me!

VOICES. [*Approvingly.*] That's the stuff!
      Yank tal him, py golly!
      Yank ain't afeerd.
      Goot poy, Yank!
      Give him hell!
10   Tell 'im 'e's a bloody swine!
      Bloody slave-driver!

YANK. [*Contemptuously.*] He ain't got no noive. He's
yellow, get me? All de engineers is yellow. Dey got
streaks a mile wide. Aw, to hell wit him! Let's move,
youse guys. We had a rest. Come on, she needs it! Give
her pep! It ain't for him. Him and his whistle, dey don't
belong. But we belong, see! We gotter feed de baby!
Come on! [*He turns and flings his furnace door open.*
They all follow his lead. At this instant the SECOND
20 *and* FOURTH ENGINEERS *enter from the darkness on the*
left with MILDRED *between them. She starts, turns paler,*
her pose is crumbling, she shivers with fright in spite
of the blazing heat, but forces herself to leave the
ENGINEERS *and take a few steps nearer the men. She*
is right behind YANK. *All this happens quickly while*
the men have their backs turned.]

YANK. Come on, youse guys! [*He is turning to get*
coal when the whistle sounds again in a peremptory, ir-
ritating note. This drives YANK *into a sudden fury.*
30 *While the other men have turned full around and*
stopped dumfounded by the spectacle of MILDRED *stand-*
ing there in her white dress, YANK *does not turn far*
enough to see her. Besides, his head is thrown back, he
blinks upward through the murk trying to find the owner
of the whistle, he brandishes his shovel murderously over
his head in one hand, pounding on his chest, gorilla-like,
with the other, shouting.] Toin off dat whistle! Come
down outa dere, yuh yellow, brass-buttoned, Belfast
bum, yuh! Come down and I'll knock yer brains out!
40 Yuh lousy, stinkin', yellow mut of a Catholic-moiderin'
bastard! Come down and I'll moider yuh! Pullin' dat
whistle on me, huh? I'll show yuh! I'll crash yer skull in!
I'll drive yer teet' down yer troat! I'll slam yer nose
trou de back of yer head! I'll cut yer guts out for a

nickel, yuh lousy boob, yuh dirty, crummy, muck-eatin'
son of a——[*Suddenly he becomes conscious of all the*
other men staring at something directly behind his back.
He whirls defensively with a snarling, murderous growl,
crouching to spring, his lips drawn back over his teeth,
his small eyes gleaming ferociously. He sees MILDRED, 50
like a white apparition in the full light from the open
furnace doors. He glares into her eyes, turned to stone.
As for her, during his speech she has listened, paralyzed
with horror, terror, her whole personality crushed, beaten
in, collapsed, by the terrific impact of this unknown,
abysmal brutality, naked and shameless. As she looks
at his gorilla face, as his eyes bore into hers, she utters a
low, choking cry and shrinks away from him, putting
both hands up before her eyes to shut out the sight of
his face, to protect her own. This startles YANK *to a re-* 60
action. His mouth falls open, his eyes grow bewildered.]

MILDRED. [*About to faint—to the* ENGINEERS, *who*
now have her one by each arm—whimperingly.] Take
me away! Oh, the filthy beast! [*She faints. They carry*
her quickly back, disappearing in the darkness at the left,
rear. An iron door clangs shut. Rage and bewildered
fury rush back on YANK. *He feels himself insulted in*
some unknown fashion in the very heart of his pride.
He roars.] God damn yuh! [*And hurls his shovel after*
them at the door which has just closed. It hits the steel 70
bulkhead with a clang and falls clattering on the steel
floor. From overhead the whistle sounds again in a long,
angry, insistent command.]

[*Curtain.*]

SCENE IV

SCENE. The firemen's forecastle. **Yank's** watch has just
come off duty and had dinner. Their faces and bodies
shine from a soap and water scrubbing but around their
eyes, where a hasty dousing does not touch, the coal dust
sticks like black make-up, giving them a queer, sinister
expression. **Yank** has not washed either face or body.
He stands out in contrast to them, a blackened, brooding
figure. He is seated forward on a bench in the exact
attitude of Rodin's "The Thinker." The others, most of
them smoking pipes, are staring at **Yank** half-apprehen-
sively, as if fearing an outburst; half-amusedly, as if they
saw a joke somewhere that tickled them.

VOICES. He ain't ate nothin'.

Py golly, a fallar gat to gat grub in him.

Divil a lie.

Yank feeda da fire, no feeda da face.

Ha-ha.

He ain't even washed hisself.

He's forgot.

Hey, Yank, you forgot to wash.

YANK. [*Sullenly.*] Forgot nothin'! To hell wit washin'.

VOICES. It'll stick to you.

It'll get under your skin.

Give yer the bleedin' itch, that's wot.

It makes spots on you—like a leopard.

Like a piebald nigger, you mean.

Better wash up, Yank.

You sleep better.

Wash up, Yank.

Wash up! Wash up!

YANK. [*Resentfully.*] Aw say, youse guys. Lemme alone. Can't youse see I'm tryin' to tink?

ALL. [*Repeating the word after him as one with cynical mockery.*] Think! [*The word has a brazen, metallic quality as if their throats were phonograph horns. It is followed by a chorus of hard, barking laughter.*]

YANK. [*Springing to his feet and glaring at them belligerently.*] Yes, tink! Tink, dat's what I said. What about it? [*They are silent, puzzled by his sudden resentment at what used to be one of his jokes. YANK sits down again in the same attitude of "The Thinker."*]

VOICES. Leave him alone.

He's got a grouch on.

Why wouldn't he?

PADDY. [*With a wink at the others.*] Sure I know what's the matther. 'Tis aisy to see. He's fallen in love, I'm telling you.

ALL. [*Repeating the word after him as one with cynical mockery.*] Love! [*The word has a brazen, metallic quality as if their throats were phonograph horns. It is followed by a chorus of hard, barking laughter.*]

YANK. [*With a contemptuous snort.*] Love, hell! Hate, dat's what. I've fallen in hate, get me?

PADDY. [*Philosophically.*] 'Twould take a wise man to tell one from the other. [*With a bitter, ironical scorn, increasing as he goes on.*] But I'm telling you it's love that's in it. Sure what else but love for us poor bastes in the stokehole would be bringing a fine lady, dressed like a white quane, down a mile of ladders and steps to be havin' a look at us?

[*A growl of anger goes up from all sides.*]

LONG. [*Jumping on a bench—hecticly.*] Hinsultin' us! Hinsultin' us, the bloody cow! And them bloody engineers! What right 'as they got to be exhibitin' us 's if we was bleedin' monkeys in a menagerie? Did we sign for hinsults to our dignity as 'onest workers? Is that in the ship's articles? You kin bloody well bet it ain't! But I knows why they done it. I arsked a deck steward 'o she was and 'e told me. 'Er old man's a bleedin' millionaire, a bloody Capitalist! 'E's got enuf bloody gold to sink this bleedin' ship! 'E makes arf the bloody steel in the world! 'E owns this bloody boat! And you and me, Comrades, we're 'is slaves! And the skipper and mates and engineers, they're 'is slaves! And she's 'is bloody daughter and we're all 'er slaves, too! And she gives 'er orders as 'ow she wants to see the bloody animals below decks and down they takes 'er!

[*There is a roar of rage from all sides.*]

YANK. [*Blinking at him bewilderedly.*] Say! Wait a moment! Is all dat straight goods?

LONG. Straight as string! The bleedin' steward as waits on 'em, 'e told me about 'er. And what're we goin' ter do, I asks yer? 'Ave we got ter swaller 'er hinsults like dogs? It ain't in the ship's articles. I tell yer we got a case. We kin go to law——

YANK. [*With abysmal contempt.*] Hell! Law!

ALL. [*Repeating the word after him as one with cynical mockery.*] Law! [*The word has a brazen metallic quality as if their throats were phonograph horns. It is followed by a chorus of hard, barking laughter.*]

LONG. [*Feeling the ground slipping from under his feet—desperately.*] As voters and citizens we kin force the bloody governments——

YANK. [*With abysmal contempt.*] Hell! Governments!

ALL. [*Repeating the word after him as one with cynical mockery.*] Governments! [*The word has a brazen metallic quality as if their throats were phonograph horns. It is followed by a chorus of hard, barking laughter.*]

LONG. [*Hysterically.*] We're free and equal in the sight of God——

YANK. [*With abysmal contempt.*] Hell! God!

---

28 **The Thinker,** the famous statue by Auguste Rodin (1840-1917), a French sculptor

ALL. [*Repeating the word after him as one with cynical mockery.*] God! [*The word has a brazen metallic quality as if their throats were phonograph horns. It is followed by a chorus of hard, barking laughter.*]

YANK. [*Witheringly.*] Aw, join de Salvation Army!

ALL. Sit down! Shut up! Damn fool! Sea-lawyer! [LONG *slinks back out of sight.*]

PADDY. [*Continuing the trend of his thoughts as if he had never been interrupted—bitterly.*] And there she was standing behind us, and the Second pointing at us like a man you'd hear in a circus would be saying: In this cage is a queerer kind of baboon than ever you'd find in darkest Africy. We roast them in their own sweat —and be damned if you won't hear some of thim saying they like it! [*He glances scornfully at* YANK.]

YANK. [*With a bewildered uncertain growl.*] Aw!

PADDY. And there was Yank roarin' curses and turning round wid his shovel to brain her—and she looked at him, and him at her——

YANK. [*Slowly.*] She was all white. I tought I was a ghost. Sure.

PADDY. [*With heavy, biting sarcasm.*] 'Twas love at first sight, divil a doubt of it! If you'd seen the endearin' look on her pale mug when she shriveled away with her hands over her eyes to shut out the sight of him! Sure, 'twas as if she'd seen a great hairy ape escaped from the Zoo!

YANK. [*Stung—with a growl of rage.*] Aw!

PADDY. And the loving way Yank heaved his shovel at the skull of her, only she was out the door! [*A grin breaking over his face.*] 'Twas touching, I'm telling you! It put the touch of home, swate home in the stokehole.

[*There is a roar of laughter from all.*]

YANK. [*Glaring at* PADDY *menacingly.*] Aw, choke dat off, see!

PADDY. [*Not heeding him—to the others.*] And her grabbin' at the Second's arm for protection. [*With a grotesque imitation of a woman's voice.*] Kiss me, Engineer dear, for it's dark down here and me old man's in Wall Street making money! Hug me tight, darlin', for I'm afeerd in the dark and me mother's on deck makin' eyes at the skipper!

[*Another roar of laughter.*]

YANK. [*Threateningly.*] Say! What yuh tryin' to do, kid me, yuh old Harp?

PADDY. Divil a bit! Ain't I wishin' myself you'd brained her?

YANK. [*Fiercely.*] I'll brain her! I'll brain her yet, wait 'n' see! [*Coming over to* PADDY—*slowly.*] Say, is dat what she called me—a hairy ape?

PADDY. She looked it at you if she didn't say the word itself.

YANK. [*Grinning horribly.*] Hairy ape, huh? Sure! Dat's de way she looked at me, aw right. Hairy ape! So dat's me, huh? [*Bursting into rage—as if she were still in front of him.*] Yuh skinny tart! Yuh whitefaced bum, yuh! I'll show yuh who's a ape! [*Turning to the others, bewilderment seizing him again.*] Say, youse guys. I was bawlin' him out for pullin' de whistle on us. You heard me. And den I seen youse lookin' at somep'n and I tought he'd sneaked down to come up in back of me, and I hopped round to knock him dead wit de shovel. And dere she was wit de light on her! Christ, yuh coulda pushed me over with a finger! I was scared, get me? Sure! I tought she was a ghost, see? She was all in white like dey wrap around stiffs. You seen her. Kin yuh blame me? She didn't belong, dat's what. And den when I come to and seen it was a real skoit and seen de way she was lookin' at me—like Paddy said—Christ, I was sore, get me? I don't stand for dat stuff from nobody. And I flung de shovel—on'y she'd beat it. [*Furiously.*] I wished it'd banged her! I wished it'd knocked her block off!

LONG. And be 'anged for murder or 'lectrocuted? She ain't bleedin' well worth it.

YANK. I don't give a damn what! I'd be square wit her, wouldn't I? Tink I wanter let her put somep'n over on me? Tink I'm goin' to let her git away wit dat stuff? Yuh don't know me! No one ain't never put nothin' over on me and got away wit it, see!—not dat kind of stuff—no guy and no skoit neither! I'll fix her! Maybe she'll come down again——

VOICE. No chance, Yank. You scared her out of a year's growth.

YANK. I scared her? Why de hell should I scare her? Who de hell is she? Ain't she de same as me? Hairy ape, huh? [*With his old confident bravado.*] I'll show her I'm better'n her, if she on'y knew it. I belong and she don't, see! I move and she's dead! Twenty-five knots a hour, dat's me! Dat carries her but I make dat. She's on'y baggage. Sure! [*Again bewilderedly.*] But, Christ, she was funny lookin'! Did yuh pipe her hands? White and skinny. Yuh could see de bones trough 'em. And her

mush, dat was dead white, too. And her eyes, dey was like dey'd seen a ghost. Me, dat was! Sure! Hairy ape! Ghost, huh? Look at dat arm! [*He extends his right arm, swelling out the great muscles.*] I coulda took her wit dat, wit just my little finger even, and broke her in two. [*Again bewilderedly.*] Say, who is dat skoit, huh? What is she? What's she come from? Who made her? Who give her de noive to look at me like dat? Dis ting's got my goat right. I don't get her. She's new
10 to me. What does a skoit like her mean, huh? She don't belong, get me! I can't see her. [*With growing anger.*] But one ting I'm wise to, aw right, aw right! Youse all kin bet your shoits I'll get even wit her. I'll show her if she tinks she—— She grinds de organ and I'm on de string, huh? I'll fix her! Let her come down again and I'll fling her in de furnace! She'll move den! She won't shiver at nothin', den! Speed, dat'll be her! She'll belong den! [*He grins horribly.*]

PADDY. She'll never come. She's had her belly-full,
20 I'm telling you. She'll be in bed now, I'm thinking, wid ten doctors and nurses feedin' her salts to clean the fear out of her.

YANK. [*Enraged.*] Yuh tink I made her sick, too, do yuh? Just lookin' at me, huh? Hairy ape, huh? [*In a frenzy of rage.*] I'll fix her! I'll tell her where to git off! She'll git down on her knees and take it back or I'll bust de face offen her! [*Shaking one fist upward and beating on his chest with the other.*] I'll find yuh! I'm comin', d'yuh hear? I'll fix yuh, God damn yuh! [*He makes a
30 rush for the door.*]

VOICES. Stop him!
He'll get shot!
He'll murder her!
Trip him up!
Hold him!
He's gone crazy!
Gott, he's strong!
Hold him down!
Look out for a kick!
40 Pin his arms!

[*They have all piled on him and, after a fierce struggle, by sheer weight of numbers have borne him to the floor just inside the door.*]

PADDY. [*Who has remained detached.*] Kape him down till he's cooled off. [*Scornfully.*] Yerra, Yank, you're a great fool. Is it payin' attention at all you

are to the like of that skinny sow widout one drop of rale blood in her?

YANK. [*Frenziedly, from the bottom of the heap.*] She done me doit! She done me doit, didn't she? I'll git square wit her! I'll get her some way! Git offen me, youse guys! Lemme up! I'll show her who's a ape!

[*Curtain.*]

SCENE V

SCENE. Three weeks later. A corner of Fifth Avenue in the Fifties on a fine Sunday morning. A general atmosphere of clean, well-tidied, wide street; a flood of mellow, tempered sunshine; gentle, genteel breezes. In the rear, the show windows of two shops, a jewelry establishment on the corner, a furrier's next to it. Here the adornments of extreme wealth are tantalizingly displayed. The jeweler's window is gaudy with glittering diamonds, emeralds, rubies, pearls, etc., fashioned in ornate tiaras, crowns, necklaces, collars, etc. From each piece hangs an enormous tag from which a dollar sign and numerals in intermittent electric lights wink out the incredible prices. The same in the furrier's. Rich furs of all varieties hang there bathed in a downpour of artificial light. The general effect is of a background of magnificence cheapened and made grotesque by commercialism, a background in tawdry disharmony with the clear light and sunshine on the street itself.

Up the side street Yank and Long come swaggering. Long is dressed in shore clothes, wears a black Windsor tie, cloth cap. Yank is in his dirty dungarees. A fireman's cap with black peak is cocked defiantly on the side of his head. He has not shaved for days and around his fierce, resentful eyes—as around those of Long to a lesser degree —the black smudge of coal dust still sticks like make-up. They hesitate and stand together at the corner, swaggering, looking about them with a forced, defiant contempt.

LONG. [*Indicating it all with an oratorical gesture.*] 50 Well, 'ere we are. Fif' Avenoo. This 'ere's their bleedin' private lane, as yer might say. [*Bitterly.*] We're trespassers 'ere. Proletarians keep orf the grass!

YANK. [*Dully.*] I don't see no grass, yuh boob. [*Staring at the sidewalk.*] Clean, ain't it? Yuh could eat a fried egg offen it. The white wings got some job sweepin' dis up. [*Looking up and down the avenue—*

surlily.] Where's all de white-collar stiffs yuh said was here—and de skoits—*her* kind?

LONG. In church, blarst 'em! Arskin' Jesus to give 'em more money.

YANK. Choich, huh? I useter go to choich onct—sure—when I was a kid. Me old man and woman, dey made me. Dey never went demselves, dough. Always got too big a head on Sunday mornin', dat was dem. [*With a grin.*] Dey was scrappers for fair, bot' of dem. On Satiday nights when dey bot' got a skinful dey could put up a bout oughter been staged at de Garden. When dey got trough dere wasn't a chair or table wit a leg under it. Or else dey bot' jumped on me for somep'n. Dat was where I loined to take punishment. [*With a grin and a swagger.*] I'm a chip offen de old block, get me?

LONG. Did yer old man follow the sea?

YANK. Naw. Worked along shore. I runned away when me old lady croaked wit de tremens. I helped at truckin' and in de market. Den I shipped in de stokehole. Sure. Dat belongs. De rest was nothin'. [*Looking around him.*] I ain't never seen dis before. De Brooklyn waterfront, dat was where I was dragged up. [*Taking a deep breath.*] Dis ain't so bad at dat, huh?

LONG. Not bad? Well, we pays for it wiv our bloody sweat, if yer wants to know!

YANK. [*With sudden angry disgust.*] Aw, hell! I don't see no one, see—like her. All dis gives me a pain. It don't belong. Say, ain't dere a back room around dis dump? Let's go shoot a ball. All dis is too clean and quiet and dolled-up, get me! It gives me a pain.

LONG. Wait and yer'll bloody well see——

YANK. I don't wait for no one. I keep on de move. Say, what yuh drag me up here for, anyway? Tryin' to kid me, yuh simp, yuh?

LONG. Yer wants to get back at 'er, don't yer? That's what yer been sayin' every bloomin' hour since she hinsulted yer.

YANK. [*Vehemently.*] Sure ting I do! Didn't I try to get even with her in Southampton? Didn't I sneak on de dock and wait for her by de gangplank? I was goin' to spit in her pale mug, see! Sure, right in her pop-eyes! Dat woulda made me even, see? But no chanct. Dere was a whole army of plain-clothes bulls around. Dey spotted me and gimme de bum's rush. I never seen her. But I'll git square wit her yet, you

watch! [*Furiously.*] De lousy tart! She tinks she kin get away wit moider—but not wit me! I'll fix her! I'll tink of a way!

LONG. [*As disgusted as he dares to be.*] Ain't that why I brought yer up 'ere—to show yer? Yer been lookin' at this 'ere 'ole affair wrong. Yer been actin' an' talkin' 's if it was all a bleedin' personal matter between yer and that bloody cow. I wants to convince yer she was on'y a representative of 'er clarss. I wants to awaken yer bloody clarss consciousness. Then yer'll see it's 'er clarss yer've got to fight, not 'er alone. There's a 'ole mob of 'em like 'er, Gawd blind 'em!

YANK. [*Spitting on his hands—belligerently.*] De more de merrier when I gits started. Bring on de gang!

LONG. Yer'll see 'em in arf a mo', when that church lets out. [*He turns and sees the window display in the two stores for the first time.*] Blimey! Look at that, will yer? [*They both walk back and stand looking in the jeweler's.* LONG *flies into a fury.*] Just look at this 'ere bloomin' mess! Just look at it! Look at the bleedin' prices on 'em—more'n our 'ole bloody stokehole makes in ten voyages sweatin' in 'ell! And they—'er and 'er bloody clarss—buys 'em for toys to dangle on 'em! One of these 'ere would buy scoff for a starvin' family for a year!

YANK. Aw, cut de sob stuff! T' hell wit de starvin' family! Yuh'll be passin' de hat to me next. [*With naïve admiration.*] Say, dem tings is pretty, huh? Bet yuh dey'd hock for a piece of change aw right. [*Then turning away, bored.*] But, aw hell, what good are dey? Let her have 'em. Dey don't belong no more'n she does. [*With a gesture of sweeping the jewelers into oblivion.*] All dat don't count, get me?

LONG. [*Who has moved to the furrier's—indignantly.*] And I s'pose this 'ere don't count neither—skins of poor, 'armless animals slaughtered so as 'er and 'ers can keep their bleedin' noses warm!

YANK. [*Who has been staring at something inside—with queer excitement.*] Take a slant at dat! Give it de once-over! Monkey fur—two t'ousand bucks! [*Bewilderedly.*] Is dat straight goods—monkey fur? What de hell——?

LONG. [*Bitterly.*] It's straight enuf. [*With grim humor.*] They wouldn't bloody well pay that for a 'airy ape's skin—no, nor for the 'ole livin' ape with all 'is 'ead, and body, and soul thrown in!

YANK. [*Clenching his fists, his face growing pale with rage as if the skin in the window were a personal insult.*] Trowin' it up in my face! Christ! I'll fix her!

LONG. [*Excitedly.*] Church is out. 'Ere they come, the bleedin' swine. [*After a glance at YANK's lowering face—uneasily.*] Easy goes, Comrade. Keep yer bloomin' temper. Remember force defeats itself. It ain't our weapon. We must impress our demands through peaceful means—the votes of the on-marching proletarians of the bloody world!

YANK. [*With abysmal contempt.*] Votes, hell! Votes is a joke, see. Votes for women! Let dem do it!

LONG. [*Still more uneasily.*] Calm, now. Treat 'em wiv the proper contempt. Observe the bleedin' parasites but 'old yer 'orses.

YANK. [*Angrily.*] Git away from me! Yuh're yellow, dat's what. Force, dat's me! De punch, dat's me every time, see!

[*The crowd from church enter from the right, sauntering slowly and affectedly, their heads held stiffly up, looking neither to right nor left, talking in toneless, simpering voices. The women are rouged, calcimined, dyed, over-dressed to the nth degree. The men are in Prince Alberts, high hats, spats, canes, etc. A procession of gaudy marionettes, yet with something of the relentless horror of Frankensteins in their detached, mechanical unawareness.*]

VOICES. Dear Doctor Caiaphas! He is so sincere!
What was the sermon? I dozed off.
About the radicals, my dear—and the false doctrines that are being preached.
We must organize a hundred per cent American bazaar.
And let everyone contribute one one-hundredth per cent of their income tax.
What an original idea!
We can devote the proceeds to rehabilitating the veil of the temple.
But that has been done so many times.

YANK. [*Glaring from one to the other of them—with an insulting snort of scorn.*] Huh! Huh!

[*Without seeming to see him, they make wide detours to avoid the spot where he stands in the middle of the sidewalk.*]

LONG. [*Frightenedly.*] Keep yer bloomin' mouth shut, I tells yer.

YANK. [*Viciously.*] G'wan! Tell it to Sweeney! [*He swaggers away and deliberately lurches into a top-hatted gentleman, then glares at him pugnaciously.*] Say, who d'yuh tink yuh're bumpin'? Tink yuh own de oith?

GENTLEMAN. [*Coldly and affectedly.*] I beg your pardon. [*He has not looked at YANK and passes on without a glance, leaving him bewildered.*]

LONG. [*Rushing up and grabbing YANK's arm.*] 'Ere! Come away! This wasn't what I meant. Yer'll 'ave the bloody coppers down on us.

YANK. [*Savagely—giving him a push that sends him sprawling.*] G'wan!

LONG. [*Picks himself up—hysterically.*] I'll pop orf then. This ain't what I meant. And whatever 'appens, yer can't blame me. [*He slinks off left.*]

YANK. T' hell wit youse! [*He approaches a lady —with a vicious grin and a smirking wink.*] Hello, Kiddo. How's every little ting? Got anyting on for to-night? I know an old boiler down to de docks we kin crawl into. [*The lady stalks by without a look, without a change of pace. YANK turns to others—insultingly.*] Holy smokes, what a mug! Go hide yuhself before de horses shy at yuh. Gee, pipe de heine on dat one! Say, youse, yuh look like de stoin of a ferryboat. Paint and powder! All dolled up to kill! Yuh look like stiffs laid out for de boneyard! Aw, g'wan, de lot of youse! Yuh give me de eye-ache. Yuh don't belong, get me! Look at me, why don't youse dare? I belong, dat's me! [*Pointing to a skyscraper across the street which is in process of construction—with bravado.*] See dat building goin' up dere? See de steel work? Steel, dat's me! Youse guys live on it and tink yuh're somep'n. But I'm *in* it, see! I'm de hoistin' engine dat makes it go up! I'm it—de inside and bottom of it! Sure! I'm steel and steam and smoke and de rest of it! It moves —speed—twenty-five stories up—and me at de top and bottom—movin'! Youse simps don't move. Yuh're on'y dolls I winds up to see 'm spin. Yuh're de garbage, get me—de leavins—de ashes we dump over de side! Now, what 'a' yuh gotta say? [*But as they seem neither to see nor hear him, he flies into a fury.*] Bums! Pigs! Tarts!

Frankensteins. The author means "Frankenstein's monsters," from the monster created by Frankenstein in Mrs. Shelley's novel of that name. "The blunder," says H. W. Fowler in **Modern English Usage,** "is very common indeed, almost, but surely not quite, sanctioned by custom"

Bitches! [*He turns in a rage on the men, bumping viciously into them but not jarring them the least bit. Rather it is he who recoils after each collision. He keeps growling.*] Git off de oith! G'wan, yuh bum! Look where yuh're goin', can't yuh? Git outa here! Fight, why don't yuh? Put up yer mits! Don't be a dog! Fight or I'll knock yuh dead! [*But, without seeming to see him, they all answer with mechanical affected politeness.*] I beg your pardon. [*Then at a cry from one of the women, they all scurry to the furrier's window.*]

THE WOMAN. [*Ecstatically, with a gasp of delight.*] Monkey fur! [*The whole crowd of men and women chorus after her in the same tone of affected delight.*] Monkey fur!

YANK. [*With a jerk of his head back on his shoulders, as if he had received a punch full in the face—raging.*] I see yuh, all in white! I see yuh, yuh white-faced tart, yuh! Hairy ape, huh? I'll hairy ape yuh! [*He bends down and grips at the street curbing as if to pluck it out and hurl it. Foiled in this, snarling with passion, he leaps to the lamp-post on the corner and tries to pull it up for a club. Just at that moment a bus is heard rumbling up. A fat, high-hatted, spatted gentleman runs out from the side street. He calls out plaintively.*] Bus! Bus! Stop there! [*And runs full tilt into the bending, straining* YANK, *who is bowled off his balance.*]

YANK. [*Seeing a fight—with a roar of joy as he springs to his feet.*] At last! Bus, huh? I'll bust yuh! [*He lets drive a terrific swing, his fist landing full on the fat gentleman's face. But the gentleman stands unmoved as if nothing had happened.*]

GENTLEMAN. I beg your pardon. [*Then irritably.*] You have made me lose my bus. [*He claps his hands and begins to scream:*] Officer! Officer!

[*Many police whistles shrill out on the instant and a whole platoon of policemen rush in on* YANK *from all sides. He tries to fight but is clubbed to the pavement and fallen upon. The crowd at the window have not moved or noticed this disturbance. The clanging gong of the patrol wagon approaches with a clamoring din.*]

[*Curtain.*]

SCENE VI

SCENE. Night of the following day. A row of cells in the prison on Blackwell's Island. The cells extend back diagonally from right front to left rear. They do not stop, but disappear in the dark background as if they ran on, numberless, into infinity. One electric bulb from the low ceiling of the narrow corridor sheds its light through the heavy steel bars of the cell at the extreme front and reveals part of the interior. Yank can be seen within, crouched on the edge of his cot in the attitude of Rodin's "The Thinker." His face is spotted with black and blue bruises. A blood-stained bandage is wrapped around his head.

YANK. [*Suddenly starting as if awakening from a dream, reaches out and shakes the bars—aloud to himself, wonderingly.*] Steel. Dis is de Zoo, huh? [*A burst of hard, barking laughter comes from the unseen occupants of the cells, runs back down the tier, and abruptly ceases.*]

VOICES. [*Mockingly.*] The Zoo? That's a new name for this coop—a damn good name!

Steel, eh? You said a mouthful. This is the old iron house.

Who is that boob talkin'?

He's the bloke they brung in out of his head. The bulls had beat him up fierce.

YANK. [*Dully.*] I musta been dreamin'. I tought I was in a cage at de Zoo—but de apes don't talk, do dey?

VOICES. [*With mocking laughter.*] You're in a cage aw right.

A coop!

A pen!

A sty!

A kennel! [*Hard laughter—a pause.*]

Say, guy! Who are you? No, never mind lying. What are you?

Yes, tell us your sad story. What's your game?

What did they jug yuh for?

YANK. [*Dully.*] I was a fireman—stokin' on de liners. [*Then with sudden rage, rattling his cell bars.*] I'm a hairy ape, get me? And I'll bust youse all in de jaw if yuh don't lay off kiddin' me.

VOICES. Huh! You're a hard boiled duck, ain't you!

When you spit, it bounces! [*Laughter.*]

Aw, can it. He's a regular guy. Ain't you?

What did he say he was—a ape?

YANK. [*Defiantly.*] Sure ting! Ain't dat what youse all are—apes? [*A silence. Then a furious rattling of bars from down the corridor.*]

A VOICE. [*Thick with rage.*] I'll show yuh who's a ape, yuh bum!

VOICES. Ssshh! Nix!

Can de noise!

Piano!

You'll have the guard down on us!

YANK. [*Scornfully.*] De guard? Yuh mean de keeper, don't yuh? [*Angry exclamations from all the cells.*]

VOICE. [*Placatingly.*] Aw, don't pay no attention to him. He's off his nut from the beatin'-up he got. Say, you guy! We're waitin' to hear what they landed you for—or ain't yuh tellin'?

YANK. Sure, I'll tell youse. Sure! Why de hell not? On'y—youse won't get me. Nobody gets me but me, see? I started to tell de Judge and all he says was: "Toity days to tink it over." Tink it over! Christ, dat's all I been doin' for weeks! [*After a pause.*] I was tryin' to git even wit someone, see?—someone dat done me doit.

VOICES. [*Cynically.*] De old stuff, I bet. Your goil, huh?

Give yuh the double-cross, huh?

That's them every time!

Did yuh beat up de odder guy?

YANK. [*Disgustedly.*] Aw, yuh're all wrong! Sure dere was a skoit in it—but not what youse mean, not dat old tripe. Dis was a new kind of skoit. She was dolled up all in white—in de stokehole. I tought she was a ghost. Sure. [*A pause.*]

VOICES. [*Whispering.*] Gee, he's still nutty.

Let him rave. It's fun listenin'.

YANK. [*Unheeding—groping in his thoughts.*] Her hands—dey was skinny and white like dey wasn't real but painted on somep'n. Dere was a million miles from me to her—twenty-five knots a hour. She was like some dead ting de cat brung in. Sure, dat's what. She didn't belong. She belonged in de window of a toy store, or on de top of a garbage can, see! Sure! [*He breaks out angrily.*] But would yuh believe it, she had de noive to do me doit. She lamped me like she was seein' somep'n broke loose from de menagerie. Christ, yuh'd oughter seen her eyes! [*He rattles the bars of his cell furiously.*] But I'll get back at her yet, you watch! And if I can't find her I'll take it out on de gang she runs wit. I'm wise to where dey hangs out now. I'll show her who belongs! I'll show her who's in de move and who ain't. You watch my smoke!

VOICES. [*Serious and joking.*] Dat's de talkin'!

Take her for all she's got!

What was this dame, anyway? Who was she, eh?

YANK. I dunno. First cabin stiff. Her old man's a millionaire, dey says—name of Douglas.

VOICES. Douglas? That's the president of the Steel Trust, I bet.

Sure. I seen his mug in de papers.

He's filthy with dough.

VOICE. Hey, feller, take a tip from me. If you want to get back at that dame, you better join the Wobblies. You'll get some action then.

YANK. Wobblies? What de hell's dat?

VOICE. Ain't you ever heard of the I. W. W.?

YANK. Naw. What is it?

VOICE. A gang of blokes—a tough gang. I been readin' about 'em to-day in the paper. The guard give me the *Sunday Times*. There's a long spiel about 'em. It's from a speech made in the Senate by a guy named Senator Queen. [*He is in the cell next to* YANK'S. *There is a rustling of paper.*] Wait'll I see if I got light enough and I'll read you. Listen. [*He reads:*] "There is a menace existing in this country to-day which threatens the vitals of our fair Republic—as foul a menace against the very life-blood of the American Eagle as was the foul conspiracy of Catiline against the eagles of ancient Rome!"

VOICE. [*Disgustedly.*] Aw, hell! Tell him to salt de tail of dat eagle!

VOICE. [*Reading.*] "I refer to that devil's brew of rascals, jailbirds, murderers and cut-throats who libel all honest workingmen by calling themselves the Industrial Workers of the World; but in the light of their nefarious plots, I call them the Industrious *Wreckers* of the World!"

YANK. [*With vengeful satisfaction.*] Wreckers, dat's de right dope! Dat belongs! Me for dem!

VOICE. Ssshh! [*Reading.*] "This fiendish organization is a foul ulcer on the fair body of our Democracy——"

VOICE. Democracy, hell! Give him the boid, fellers —the raspberry! [*They do.*]

VOICE. Ssshh! [*Reading:*] "Like Cato I say to this Senate, the I. W. W. must be destroyed! For they repre-

---

72 **Catiline**, Lucius Sergius Catilina (108?-62 B.C.), a Roman conspirator against whom Cicero delivered his famous orations • 87 **Cato**, Marcus Porcius Cato, the Elder (234-149 B.C.), whose famous saying, "Carthage must be destroyed," is referred to

sent an ever-present dagger pointed at the heart of the greatest nation the world has ever known, where all men are born free and equal, with equal opportunities to all, where the Founding Fathers have guaranteed to each one happiness, where Truth, Honor, Liberty, Justice, and the Brotherhood of Man are a religion absorbed with one's mother's milk, taught at our father's knee, sealed, signed, and stamped upon in the glorious Constitution of these United States!" [*A perfect storm of hisses, catcalls, boos, and hard laughter.*]

VOICES. [*Scornfully.*] Hurrah for de Fort' of July!

Pass de hat!

Liberty!

Justice!

Honor!

Opportunity!

Brotherhood!

ALL. [*With abysmal scorn.*] Aw, hell!

VOICE. Give that Queen Senator guy the bark! All togedder now—one—two—tree—— [*A terrific chorus of barking and yapping.*]

GUARD. [*From a distance.*] Quiet there, youse—or I'll git the hose. [*The noise subsides.*]

YANK. [*With growling rage.*] I'd like to catch dat Senator guy alone for a second. I'd loin him some trute!

VOICE. Ssshh! Here's where he gits down to cases on the Wobblies. [*Reads:*] "They plot with fire in one hand and dynamite in the other. They stop not before murder to gain their ends, nor at the outraging of defenseless womanhood. They would tear down society, put the lowest scum in the seats of the mighty, turn Almighty God's revealed plan for the world topsy-turvy, and make of our sweet and lovely civilization a shambles, a desolation where man, God's masterpiece, would soon degenerate back to the ape!"

VOICE. [*To* YANK.] Hey, you guy. There's your ape stuff again.

YANK. [*With a growl of fury.*] I got him. So dey blow up tings, do dey? Dey turn tings round, do dey? Hey, lend me dat paper, will yuh?

VOICE. Sure. Give it to him. On'y keep it to yourself, see. We don't wanter listen to no more of that slop.

VOICE. Here you are. Hide it under your mattress.

YANK. [*Reaching out.*] Tanks. I can't read much but I kin manage. [*He sits, the paper in the hand at his side, in the attitude of Rodin's "The Thinker." A pause. Several snores from down the corridor. Sud-* denly YANK *jumps to his feet with a furious groan as if some appalling thought had crashed on him—bewilderedly.*] Sure—her old man—president of de Steel Trust—makes half de steel in de world—steel—where I tought I belonged—drivin' trou—movin'—in dat—to make *her*—and cage me in for her to spit on! Christ! [*He shakes the bars of his cell door till the whole tier trembles. Irritated, protesting exclamations from those awakened or trying to get to sleep.*] He made dis—dis cage! Steel! *It* don't belong, dat's what! Cages, cells, locks, bolts, bars—dat's what it means!—holdin' me down wit him at de top! But I'll drive trou! Fire, dat melts it! I'll be fire—under de heap—fire dat never goes out—hot as hell—breakin' out in de night—— [*While he has been saying this last he has shaken his cell door to a clanging accompaniment. As he comes to the "breakin' out" he seizes one bar with both hands and, putting his two feet up against the others so that his position is parallel to the floor like a monkey's, he gives a great wrench backwards. The bar bends like a licorice stick under his tremendous strength. Just at this moment the* PRISON GUARD *rushes in, dragging a hose behind him.*]

GUARD. [*Angrily.*] I'll loin youse bums to wake me up! [*Sees* YANK.] Hello, it's you, huh? Got the D. Ts., hey? Well, I'll cure 'em. I'll drown your snakes for yuh! [*Noticing the bar.*] Hell, look at dat bar bended! On'y a bug is strong enough for dat!

YANK. [*Glaring at him.*] Or a hairy ape, yuh big yellow bum! Look out! Here I come! [*He grabs another bar.*]

GUARD. [*Scared now—yelling off left.*] Toin de hose on, Ben!—full pressure! And call de others—and a straitjacket! [*The curtain is falling. As it hides* YANK *from view, there is a splattering smash as the stream of water hits the steel of* YANK'S *cell.*]

[*Curtain.*]

SCENE VII

SCENE. Nearly a month later. An I. W. W. local near the waterfront, showing the interior of a front room on the ground floor, and the street outside. Moonlight on the narrow street, buildings massed in black shadow. The interior of the room, which is general assembly room, office, and reading-room, resembles some dingy settlement boys' club. A desk and high stool are in one corner. A table with papers, stacks of pamphlets, chairs about it, is at center. The whole is decidedly cheap, banal, commonplace, and unmysterious as a room could well be. The secretary is perched on the stool making entries in a large ledger. An eye shade casts his face into shadows. Eight or ten men, longshoremen, iron workers, and the like, are grouped about the table. Two are playing checkers. One is writing a letter. Most of them are smoking pipes. A big signboard is on the wall at the rear, "Industrial Workers of the World—Local No. 57."

[YANK *comes down the street outside. He is dressed as in Scene Five. He moves cautiously, mysteriously. He comes to a point opposite the door; tiptoes softly up to it, listens, is impressed by the silence within, knocks carefully, as if he were guessing at the password to some secret rite. Listens. No answer. Knocks again a bit louder. No answer. Knocks impatiently, much louder.*]

SECRETARY. [*Turning around on his stool.*] What the hell is that—someone knocking? [*Shouts.*] Come in, why don't you? [*All the men in the room look up.* YANK *opens the door slowly, gingerly, as if afraid of an ambush. He looks around for secret doors, mystery, is taken aback by the commonplaceness of the room and the men in it, thinks he may have gotten in the wrong place, then sees the signboard on the wall and is reassured.*]

YANK. [*Blurts out.*] Hello.

10 MEN. [*Reservedly.*] Hello.

YANK. [*More easily.*] I tought I'd bumped into de wrong dump.

SECRETARY. [*Scrutinizing him carefully.*] Maybe you have. Are you a member?

YANK. Naw, not yet. Dat's what I come for—to join.

SECRETARY. That's easy. What's your job—longshore?

YANK. Naw. Fireman—stoker on de liners.

SECRETARY. [*With satisfaction.*] Welcome to our city. Glad to know you people are waking up at last. We

20 haven't got many members in your line.

YANK. Naw. Dey're all dead to de woild.

SECRETARY. Well, you can help to wake 'em. What's your name? I'll make out your card.

YANK. [*Confused.*] Name? Lemme tink.

SECRETARY. [*Sharply.*] Don't you know your own name?

YANK. Sure; but I been just Yank for so long—Bob, dat's it—Bob Smith.

SECRETARY. [*Writing.*] Robert Smith. [*Fills out the

30 rest of card.*] Here you are. Cost you half a dollar.

YANK. Is dat all—four bits? Dat's easy. [*Gives the Secretary the money.*]

SECRETARY. [*Throwing it in drawer.*] Thanks. Well, make yourself at home. No introductions needed. There's literature on the table. Take some of those pamphlets with you to distribute aboard ship. They may bring results. Sow the seed, only go about it right. Don't get caught and fired. We got plenty out of work. What we need is men who can hold their jobs—and work for us at the same time. 40

YANK. Sure. [*But he still stands, embarrassed and uneasy.*]

SECRETARY. [*Looking at him—curiously.*] What did you knock for? Think we had a coon in uniform to open doors?

YANK. Naw. I tought it was locked—and dat yuh'd wanter give me the once-over trou a peep-hole or somep'n to see if I was right.

SECRETARY. [*Alert and suspicious but with an easy laugh.*] Think we were running a crap game? That door 50 is never locked. What put that in your nut?

YANK. [*With a knowing grin, convinced that this is all camouflage, a part of the secrecy.*] Dis burg is full of bulls, ain't it?

SECRETARY. [*Sharply.*] What have the cops got to do with us? We're breaking no laws.

YANK. [*With a knowing wink.*] Sure. Youse wouldn't for woilds. Sure. I'm wise to dat.

SECRETARY. You seem to be wise to a lot of stuff none of us knows about. 60

YANK. [*With another wink.*] Aw, dat's aw right, see. [*Then made a bit resentful by the suspicious glances from all sides.*] Aw, can it! Youse needn't put me trou de toid degree. Can't youse see I belong? Sure! I'm reg'lar. I'll stick, get me? I'll shoot de woiks for youse. Dat's why I wanted to join in.

SECRETARY. [*Breezily, feeling him out.*] That's the right spirit. Only are you sure you understand what you've joined? It's all plain and above board; still, some guys get a wrong slant on us. [*Sharply.*] What's your 70 notion of the purpose of the I. W. W.?

YANK. Aw, I know all about it.

SECRETARY. [*Sarcastically.*] Well, give us some of your valuable information.

YANK. [*Cunningly.*] I know enough not to speak outa my toin. [*Then, resentfully again.*] Aw, say! I'm reg'lar. I'm wise to de game. I know yuh got to watch your step wit a stranger. For all youse know, I might be a plain-clothes dick, or somep'n, dat's what yuh're tinkin', huh? Aw, forget it! I belong, see? Ask any guy down to de docks if I don't.

SECRETARY. Who said you didn't?

YANK. After I'm 'nitiated, I'll show yuh.

SECRETARY. [*Astounded.*] Initiated? There's no initiation.

YANK. [*Disappointed.*] Ain't there no password—no
10 grip nor nothin'?

SECRETARY. What'd you think this is—the Elks—or the Black Hand?

YANK. De Elks, hell! De Black Hand, dey're a lot of yellow backstickin' Ginees. Naw. Dis is a man's gang, ain't it?

SECRETARY. You said it! That's why we stand on our two feet in the open. We got no secrets.

YANK. [*Surprised but admiringly.*] Yuh mean to say yuh always run wide open—like dis?

20 SECRETARY. Exactly.

YANK. Den yuh sure got your noive wit youse!

SECRETARY. [*Sharply.*] Just what was it made you want to join us? Come out with that straight.

YANK. Yuh call me? Well, I got noive, too! Here's my hand. Yuh wanter blow tings up, don't yuh? Well, dat's me! I belong!

SECRETARY. [*With pretended carelessness.*] You mean change the unequal conditions of society by legitimate direct action—or with dynamite?

30 YANK. Dynamite! Blow it offen de oith—steel—all de cages—all de factories, steamers, buildings, jails—de Steel Trust and all dat makes it go.

SECRETARY. So—that's your idea, eh? And did you have any special job in that line you wanted to propose to us? [*He makes a sign to the men, who get up cautiously one by one and group behind YANK.*]

YANK. [*Boldly.*] Sure, I'll come out wit it. I'll show youse I'm one of de gang. Dere's dat millionaire guy, Douglas——

40 SECRETARY. President of the Steel Trust, you mean? Do you want to assassinate him?

YANK. Naw, dat don't get you nothin'. I mean blow up de factory, de woiks, where he makes de steel. Dat's what I'm after—to blow up de steel, knock all de steel in de woild up to de moon. Dat'll fix tings! [*Eagerly, with a touch of bravado.*] I'll do it by me lonesome! I'll

show yuh! Tell me where his woiks is, how to git there, all de dope. Gimme de stuff, de old butter—and watch me do de rest! Watch de smoke and see it move! I don't give a damn if dey nab me—long as it's done! I'll soive 50 life for it—and give 'em de laugh! [*Half to himself.*] And I'll write her a letter and tell her de hairy ape done it. Dat'll square tings.

SECRETARY. [*Stepping away from YANK.*] Very interesting. [*He gives a signal. The men, huskies all, throw themselves on YANK and before he knows it they have his legs and arms pinioned. But he is too flabbergasted to make a struggle, anyway. They feel him over for weapons.*]

MAN. No gat, no knife. Shall we give him what's 60 what and put the boots to him?

SECRETARY. No. He isn't worth the trouble we'd get into. He's too stupid. [*He comes closer and laughs mockingly in YANK's face.*] Ho-ho! By God, this is the biggest joke they've put up on us yet. Hey, you Joke! Who sent you—Burns or Pinkerton? No, by God, you're such a bonehead I'll bet you're in the Secret Service! Well, you dirty spy, you rotten agent provocator, you can go back and tell whatever skunk is paying you blood-money for betraying your brothers that he's wasting his 70 coin. You couldn't catch a cold. And tell him that all he'll ever get on us, or ever has got, is just his own sneaking plots that he's framed up to put us in jail. We are what our manifesto says we are, neither more nor less— and we'll give him a copy of that any time he calls. And as for you—— [*He glares scornfully at YANK, who is sunk in an oblivious stupor.*] Oh, hell, what's the use of talking? You're a brainless ape.

YANK. [*Aroused by the word to fierce but futile struggles.*] What's dat, yuh Sheeny bum, yuh! 80

SECRETARY. Throw him out, boys. [*In spite of his struggles, this is done with gusto and éclat. Propelled by several parting kicks, YANK lands sprawling in the middle of the narrow cobbled street. With a growl he starts to get up and storm the closed door, but stops bewildered by the confusion in his brain, pathetically impotent. He sits there, brooding, in as near to the attitude of Rodin's "Thinker" as he can get in his position.*]

---

12 **Black Hand,** an Italian criminal society, originating about 1868, members of which formed the nucleus of a blackmailing society in the United States • 14 **Ginees,** derisive slang for Italians • 66 **Burns or Pinkerton,** detective agencies

YANK. [*Bitterly.*] So dem boids don't tink I belong, neider. Aw, to hell wit 'em! Dey're in de wrong pew— de same old bull—soapboxes and Salvation Army—no guts! Cut out an hour offen de job a day and make me happy! Gimme a dollar more a day and make me happy! Tree square a day, and cauliflowers in de front yard— ekal rights—a woman and kids—a lousy vote—and I'm all fixed for Jesus, huh? Aw, hell! What does dat get yuh? Dis ting's in your inside, but it ain't your belly. Feedin' your face—sinkers and coffee—dat don't touch it. It's way down—at de bottom. Yuh can't grab it, and yuh can't stop it. It moves, and everything moves. It stops and de whole woild stops. Dat's me now—I don't tick, see?—I'm a busted Ingersoll, dat's what. Steel was me, and I owned de woild. Now I ain't steel, and de woild owns me. Aw, hell! I can't see—it's all dark, get me? It's all wrong! [*He turns a bitter mocking face up like an ape gibbering at the moon.*] Say, youse up dere, Man in de Moon, yuh look so wise, gimme de answer, huh? Slip me de inside dope, de information right from de stable— where do I get off at, huh?

A POLICEMAN. [*Who has come up the street in time to hear this last—with grim humor.*] You'll get off at the station, you boob, if you don't get up out of that and keep movin'.

YANK. [*Looking up at him—with a hard, bitter laugh.*] Sure! Lock me up! Put me in a cage! Dat's de on'y answer yuh know. G'wan, lock me up!

POLICEMAN. What you been doin'?

YANK. Enuf to gimme life for! I was born, see? Sure, dat's de charge. Write it in de blotter. I was born, get me!

POLICEMAN. [*Jocosely.*] God pity your old woman! [*Then matter-of-fact.*] But I've no time for kidding. You're soused. I'd run you in but it's too long a walk to the station. Come on now, get up, or I'll fan your ears with this club. Beat it now! [*He hauls YANK to his feet.*]

YANK. [*In a vague mocking tone.*] Say, where do I go from here?

POLICEMAN. [*Giving him a push—with a grin, indifferently.*] Go to hell.

[*Curtain.*]

SCENE VIII

SCENE. Twilight of the next day. The monkey house at the Zoo. One spot of clear gray light falls on the front of one cage so that the interior can be seen. The other cages are vague, shrouded in shadow from which chatterings pitched in a conversational tone can be heard. On the one cage a sign from which the word "Gorilla" stands out. The gigantic animal himself is seen squatting on his haunches on a bench in much the same attitude as Rodin's "Thinker." Yank enters from the left. Immediately a chorus of angry chattering and screeching breaks out. The gorilla turns his eyes but makes no sound or move.

YANK. [*With a hard, bitter laugh.*] Welcome to your city, huh? Hail, hail, de gang's all here! [*At the sound of his voice the chattering dies away into an attentive silence.* YANK *walks up to the gorilla's cage and, leaning over the railing, stares in at its occupant, who stares back at him, silent and motionless. There is a pause of dead stillness. Then* YANK *begins to talk in a friendly confidential tone, half-mockingly, but with a deep undercurrent of sympathy.*] Say, yuh're some hard-lookin' guy, ain't yuh? I seen lots of tough nuts dat de gang called gorillas, but yuh're de foist real one I ever seen. Some chest yuh got, and shoulders, and dem arms and mits! I bet yuh got a punch in eider fist dat'd knock 'em all silly! [*This with genuine admiration. The gorilla, as if he understood, stands upright, swelling out his chest and pounding on it with his fist.* YANK *grins sympathetically.*] Sure, I get yuh. Yuh challenge de whole woild, huh? Yuh got what I was sayin' even if yuh muffed de woids. [*Then bitterness creeping in.*] And why wouldn't yuh get me? Ain't we both members of de same club—de Hairy Apes? [*They stare at each other—a pause— then* YANK *goes on slowly and bitterly.*] So yuh're what she seen when she looked at me, de white-faced tart! I was you to her, get me? On'y outa de cage—broke out—free to moider her, see? Sure! Dat's what she tought. She wasn't wise dat I was in a cage, too—worser'n yours— sure—a damn sight—'cause you got some chanct to bust loose—but me—— [*He grows confused.*] Aw, hell! It's all wrong, ain't it? [*A pause.*] I s'pose yuh wanter know what I'm doin' here, huh? I been warmin' a bench down to de Battery—ever since last night. Sure. I seen de sun come up. Dat was pretty, too—all red and pink and green. I was lookin' at de skyscrapers—steel—and all de ships comin' in, sailin' out, all over de oith—and dey was steel, too. De sun was warm, dey wasn't no clouds, and dere was a breeze blowin'. Sure, it was great

The Hairy Ape   997

stuff. I got it aw right—what Paddy said about dat bein' de right dope—on'y I couldn't get *in* it, see? I couldn't belong in dat. It was over my head. And I kept tinkin'—and den I beat it up here to see what youse was like. And I waited till dey was all gone to git yuh alone. Say, how d'yuh feel sittin' in dat pen all de time, havin' to stand for 'em comin' and starin' at yuh—de white-faced, skinny tarts and de boobs what marry 'em —makin' fun of yuh, laughin' at yuh, gittin' scared of yuh—damn 'em! [*He pounds on the rail with his fist.* 10 *The gorilla rattles the bars of his cage and snarls. All the other monkeys set up an angry chattering in the darkness.* YANK *goes on excitedly.*] Sure! Dat's de way it hits me, too. On'y yuh're lucky, see? Yuh don't belong wit 'em and yuh know it. But me, I belong wit 'em —but I don't, see? Dey don't belong wit me, dat's what. Get me? Tinkin' is hard—[*He passes one hand across his forehead with a painful gesture. The gorilla growls impatiently.* YANK *goes on gropingly.*] It's dis way, what I'm drivin' at. Youse can sit and dope dream in de 20 past, green woods, de jungle and de rest of it. Den yuh belong and dey don't. Den yuh kin laugh at 'em, see? Yuh're de champ of de woild. But me—I ain't got no past to tink in, nor nothin' dat's comin', on'y what's now—and dat don't belong. Sure, you're de best off! Yuh can't tink, can yuh? Yuh can't talk neider. But I kin make a bluff at talkin' and tinkin'—a'most git away wit it—a'most!—and dat's where de joker comes in. [*He laughs.*] I ain't on oith and I ain't in heaven, get me? I'm in de middle tryin' to separate 'em, takin' all de 30 woist punches from bot' of 'em. Maybe dat's what dey call hell, huh? But you, yuh're at de bottom. You belong! Sure! Yuh're de on'y one in de woild dat does, yuh lucky stiff! [*The gorilla growls proudly.*] And dat's why dey gotter put yuh in a cage, see? [*The gorilla roars angrily.*] Sure! Yuh get me. It beats it when you try to tink it or talk it—it's way down—deep—behind— you 'n' me we feel it. Sure! Bot' members of dis club! [*He laughs—then in a savage tone.*] What de hell! T' hell wit it! A little action, dat's our meat! Dat 40 belongs! Knock 'em down and keep bustin' 'em till dey croaks yuh wit a gat—wit steel! Sure! Are yuh game? Dey've looked at youse, ain't dey—in a cage? Wanter git even? Wanter wind up like a sport 'stead of croakin' slow in dere? [*The gorilla roars an emphatic affirmative.* YANK *goes on with a sort of furious exaltation.*] Sure!

Yuh're reg'lar! Yuh'll stick to de finish! Me 'n' you, huh?—bot' members of this club! We'll put up one last star bout dat'll knock 'em offen deir seats! Dey'll have to make de cages stronger after we're trou! [*The* 50 *gorilla is straining at his bars, growling, hopping from one foot to the other.* YANK *takes a jimmy from under his coat and forces the lock on the cage door. He throws this open.*] Pardon from de governor! Step out and shake hands! I'll take yuh for a walk down Fif' Avenoo. We'll knock 'em offen de oith and croak wit de band playin'. Come on, Brother. [*The gorilla scrambles gingerly out of his cage. Goes to* YANK *and stands looking at him.* YANK *keeps his mocking tone—holds out his hand.*] Shake—de secret grip of our order. [*Some-* 60 *thing, the tone of mockery, perhaps, suddenly enrages the animal. With a spring he wraps his huge arms around* YANK *in a murderous hug. There is a crackling snap of crushed ribs—a gasping cry, still mocking, from* YANK.] Hey, I didn't say kiss me! [*The gorilla lets the crushed body slip to the floor; stands over it uncertainly, considering; then picks it up, throws it in the cage, shuts the door, and shuffles off menacingly into the darkness at left. A great uproar of frightened chattering and whimpering comes from the other cages. Then* 70 YANK *moves, groaning, opening his eyes, and there is silence. He mutters painfully.*] Say—dey oughter match him—wit Zybszko. He got me, aw right. I'm trou. Even him didn't tink I belonged. [*Then, with sudden passionate despair.*] Christ, where do I get off at? Where do I fit in? [*Checking himself as suddenly.*] Aw, what de hell! No squawkin', see! No quittin', get me! Croak wit your boots on! [*He grabs hold of the bars of the cage and hauls himself painfully to his feet—looks around him bewilderedly—forces a mocking laugh.*] 80 In de cage, huh? [*In the strident tones of a circus barker.*] Ladies and gents, step forward and take a slant at de one and only—[*His voice weakening.*]—one and original—Hairy Ape from de wilds of—— [*He slips in a heap on the floor and dies. The monkeys set up a chattering, whimpering wail. And, perhaps, the Hairy Ape at last belongs.*]

[*Curtain.*]

1922

---

73 Zybszko, Stanislaus Zbyszko, a famous wrestler of the twenties

Clarence Shepard Day, Jr.

1874 · 1935

In the trying period of the Depression which began in 1929, and in the tense days before, during, and after World War II, a large share of the American reading public was particularly fond of autobiographical reminiscences, in sketches and books, of family life. Many readers, possibly, found it pleasant to visit vicariously periods during which problems—in retrospect at least—seemed less serious and pressing than those of the twentieth century. Several authors, furthermore, wrote in an extremely appealing fashion about their families, depicting memorable characters with infectious tenderness and amusement. One of the most successful of such authors was Clarence Shepard Day, Jr.

Day was born in New York City in 1874, the grandson of the founder of a great metropolitan newspaper and the son of a Wall Street broker. He attended Yale, graduating in 1896, then began to work in the Stock Exchange. Having found that he had little enthusiasm for finance, Day joined the navy during the Spanish-American War. A severe attack of arthritis ended his period of service and left him partially crippled throughout the rest of his life. Despite his crippled hands, Day became a cartoonist of some repute: his deft impressionistic line drawings in some ways foreshadowed those of such imaginative moderns as William Steig and James Thurber. Day also became a journalist and a writer of essays, sketches, and books.

Day's first book, *This Simian World* (1920), was a somewhat Swiftean satire in which man was compared, usually to his disadvantage, to other animals, and his faults were ascribed to his simian ancestry. His second book, *The Crow's Nest* (1921), was a collection of ironic essays. *Thoughts Without Words* (1928) was made up of comic drawings, most of them accompanied by brief bits of light verse. Day found and worked his best vein—that of comic family reminiscence—in *God and My Father* (1932). This was followed by *In the Green Mountain Country* (1934), *Life with Father* (1935), and *Life with Mother* (1937), published posthumously. Day died in 1935.

From

Life with Father

FATHER AND HIS HARD-ROCKING SHIP

Life with Father was a Book-of-the-Month Club choice and a best-seller. A dramatic version was one of America's most durable plays; a motion picture version was well received; and translations of both book and dramatic versions were very popular in Europe after World War II. The sketch which follows is quite typical of those in Day's most popular book. It shows Father Day, an opinionated, systematic, would-be tyrant, trying in vain to rule his far less systematic wife and family. This particular adventure is one of many which Father had with household finances and Mrs. Day's haphazard methods of keeping books. The unlabored style, the characterization, the incongruities between the characters, and the author's unobtrusive amusement are elements here that are typical of Day's writing.

Father said that one great mystery about the monthly household expenses was what made them jump up and down so. "Anyone would suppose that there would be some regularity after a while which would let a man try to make plans, but I never know from one month to another what to expect."

Mother said she didn't, either. Things just seemed to go that way.

"But they have no business to go that way, Vinnie," Father declared. "And what's more I won't allow it."

Mother said she didn't see what she could do about it. All she knew was that when the bills mounted up, it didn't mean that she had been extravagant.

"Well, it certainly means that you've spent a devil of a lot of money," said Father.

Mother looked at him obstinately. She couldn't exactly deny this, but she said that it wasn't fair.

Appearances were often hopelessly against Mother but that never daunted her. She wasn't afraid of Father or anybody. She was a woman of great spirit who would have flown at and pecked any tyrant. It was only when she had a bad conscience that she had no heart to fight. Father had the best of her there because he never had a bad conscience. And he didn't know that he was a tyrant. He regarded himself as a long-suffering man who asked little of anybody, and who showed only the greatest moderation in his encounters with unreasonable beings like Mother. Mother's one advantage over him was that she was quicker. She was particularly elusive when Father was trying to hammer her into shape.

When the household expenses shot up very high, Father got frightened. He would then, as Mother put it, yell his head off. He always did some yelling anyhow, merely on general principles, but when his alarm was genuine he roared in real anguish.

Usually this brought the total down again, at least for a while. But there were times when no amount of noise seemed to do any good, and when every month for one reason or another the total went on up and up. And then, just as Father had almost resigned himself to this awful outgo, and just as he had eased up on his yelling and had begun to feel grim, the expenses, to his utter amazement, would take a sharp drop.

Mother didn't keep track of these totals. She was too busy watching small details, and Father never knew whether to tell her the good news or not. He always did

tell her, because he couldn't keep things to himself. But he always had cause to regret it.

When he told her, he did it in as disciplinary a manner as possible. He didn't congratulate her on the expenses having come down. He appeared at her door, waving the bills at her with a threatening scowl, and said, "I've told you again and again that you could keep the expenses down if you tried, and this shows I was right."

Mother was always startled at such attacks, but she didn't lose her presence of mind. She asked how much less the amount was and said it was all due to her good management, of course, and Father ought to give her the difference.

At this point Father suddenly found himself on the defensive and the entire moral lecture that he had intended to deliver was wrecked. The more they talked, the clearer it seemed to Mother that he owed her that money. Only when he was lucky could he get out of her room without paying it.

He said that this was one of the things about her that was enough to drive a man mad.

The other thing was her lack of system, which was always cropping up in new ways. He sometimes looked at Mother as though he had never seen her before. "Upon my soul," he said, "I almost believe you don't know what system is. You don't even want to know, either."

He had at last invented what seemed a perfect method of recording expenses. Whenever he gave any money to Mother, he asked her what it was for and made a note of it in his pocket notebook. His idea was that these items, added to those in the itemized bills, would show him exactly where every dollar had gone.

But they didn't.

He consulted his notebook. "I gave you six dollars in cash on the twenty-fifth of last month," he said, "to buy a new coffeepot."

"Yes," Mother said, "because you broke your old one. You threw it right on the floor."

Father frowned. "I'm not talking about that," he answered. "I am simply endeavoring to find out from you, if I can—"

"But it's so silly to break a nice coffeepot, Clare, and

that was the last of those French ones, and there was nothing the matter with the coffee that morning; it was made just the same as it always is."

"It wasn't," said Father. "It was made in a damned barbaric manner."

"And I couldn't get another French one," Mother continued, "because that little shop the Auufmordts told us about has stopped selling them. They said the tariff wouldn't let them any more, and I told Monsieur Duval he ought to be ashamed of himself to stand there and say so. I said that if I had a shop, I'd like to see the tariff keep me from selling things."

"But I gave you six dollars to buy a new pot," Father firmly repeated, "and now I find that you apparently got one at Lewis & Conger's and charged it. Here's their bill: 'one brown earthenware drip coffeepot, five dollars.'"

"So I saved you a dollar," Mother triumphantly said, "and you can hand it right over to me."

"Bah! What nonsense you talk!" Father cried. "Is there no way to get this thing straightened out? What did you do with the six dollars?"

"Why, Clare! I can't tell you now, dear. Why didn't you ask me at the time?"

"Oh, my God!" Father groaned.

"Wait a moment," said Mother. "I spent four dollars and a half for that new umbrella I told you I wanted, and you said I didn't need a new one, but I did, very much."

Father got out his pencil and wrote "New Umbrella for V." in his notebook.

"And that must have been the week," Mother went on, "that I paid Mrs. Tobin for two extra days' washing, so that was two dollars more out of it, which makes it six-fifty. There's another fifty cents that you owe me."

"I don't owe you anything," Father said. "You have managed to turn a coffeepot for me into a new umbrella for you. No matter what I give you money for, you buy something else with it, and if this is to keep on, I might as well not keep account books at all."

"I'd like to see you run this house without having any money on hand for things," Mother said.

"I am not made of money," Father replied. "You seem to think I only have to put my hand in my pocket to get some."

Mother not only thought this, she knew it. His wallet always was full. That was the provoking part of it—she knew he had the money right there, but he tried to keep from giving it to her. She had to argue it out of him.

"Well, you can put your hand in your pocket and give me that dollar-fifty this minute," she said. "You owe me that, anyhow."

Father said he didn't have a dollar-fifty to spare and tried to get back to his desk, but Mother wouldn't let him go till he paid her. She said she wouldn't put up with injustice.

Mother said it hampered her dreadfully never to have any cash. She was always having to pay out small amounts for demands that she had forgot to provide for, and in such emergencies the only way to do was to juggle things around. One result, however, of all these more or less innocent shifts was that in this way she usually took care of all her follies herself. All the small ones, at any rate. They never got entered on Father's books, except when they were monstrous.

She came home one late afternoon in a terrible state. "Has it come yet?" she asked the waitress.

The waitress said nothing had come that she knew of.

Mother ran upstairs with a hunted expression and flung herself down on her bed. When we looked in, she was sobbing.

It turned out that she had gone to an auction, and she had become so excited that she had bought but not paid for a grandfather's clock.

Mother knew in her heart that she had no business going to auctions. She was too suggestible, and if an hypnotic auctioneer once got her eye, she was lost. Besides, an auction aroused all her worst instincts—her combativeness, her recklessness, and her avaricious love of a bargain. And the worst of it was that this time it wasn't a bargain at all. At least she didn't think it was now. The awful old thing was about eight feet tall, and it wasn't the one she had wanted. It wasn't half as nice as the clock that old Miss Van Derwent had bought. And inside the hood over the dial, she said, there was a little ship which at first she hadn't noticed, a horrid ship that rocked up and down every time the clock ticked. It made her ill just to look at it. And she didn't have the money, and the man said he'd have to send it this evening, and what would Father say?

She came down to dinner, and left half-way through. Couldn't stand it. But an hour or two later, when the doorbell rang, she bravely went to tell Father.

She could hardly believe it, but she found that luck was with her, for once. If the clock had come earlier, there might have been a major catastrophe, but Father was in a good mood and he had had a good dinner. And though he never admitted it or spoke of it, he had a weakness for clocks. There were clocks all over the house, which he would allow no one to wind but himself. Every Sunday between breakfast and church he made the rounds, setting them at the right time by his infallible watch, regulating their speed, and telling us about every clock's little idiosyncrasies. When he happened to be coming downstairs on the hour, he cocked his ear, watch in hand, to listen to as many of them as

he could, in the hope that they would all strike at once. He would reprove the impulsive pink clock in the spare room for striking too soon, and the big solemn clock in the dining-room for being a minute too late.

So when Mother led him out in the hall to confess to him and show him what she had bought, and he saw it was a clock, he fell in love with it, and made almost no fuss at all.

The let-down was too much for Mother. She tottered off to her room without another word and went straight to bed, leaving Father and the auctioneer's man setting up the new clock alongside the hatrack. Father was especially fascinated by the hard-rocking ship.

1935

James Grover Thurber

1894 ·

A number of Clarence Day's best sketches were written for *The New Yorker,* the leading humorous magazine in the United States from the time of its founding in 1924 to the present. James Grover Thurber was even more closely associated with this periodical than Day was; for a time he was one of its editors, a large share of his drawings and sketches have appeared there, and he has been generally thought of as the best humorist of many discovered by the magazine.

Despite his identification with this Eastern metropolitan publication, Thurber was born and reared in the Middle West, and the best of his writing has been of his life and that of his family in this section. He was born in Columbus, Ohio, December 8, 1894. He attended grade school, then high school, and finally Ohio State University in Columbus. When World War I began, Thurber quit the university without completing his work for the B.A. degree. Unable to enlist because an accident

in boyhood had blinded him in one eye and because the sight of his other eye had deteriorated, Thurber became a code clerk in the State Department in Paris and served until 1920.

He next became a journalist, first on the *Columbus Dispatch,* then on the *Chicago Tribune* in Paris, then on the *New York Evening Post.* In 1926, he began selling to *The New Yorker,* and in 1927, he became a member of the staff. He served briefly as managing editor but resigned to devote a larger share of his time to writing. Since 1926 Thurber's drawings and writings have been featured by the magazine.

Thurber's books, several of them collections of magazine sketches, include: *Is Sex Necessary?* written in collaboration with E. B. White (1929), *The Owl in the Attic* (1931), *The Seal in the Bedroom* (1932), *My Life and Hard Times* (1933), *The Middle-Aged Man on the Flying Trapeze* (1935), *Let Your Mind Alone*

(1937), *Fables for Our Time* (1940), *The Male Animal,* a play written in collaboration with Elliott Nugent (1940), *The White Deer* (1945), *The Beast in Me and Other Animals* (1948), *The Thirteen Clocks* (1950), and *The Thurber Album* (1952). These show great versatility, including as they do parodies and burlesques,

fiction, fables, fairy tales, a drama, and books of humorous reminiscence.

Leonard Bacon, "Humors and Careers," **Saturday Review of Literature,** April 20, 1939 • Robert M. Coates, "Thurber, Inc.," **Saturday Review of Literature,** December 2, 1939

From

My Life and Hard Times

THE NIGHT THE BED FELL

Generally regarded as Thurber's most amusing book is **My Life and Hard Times,** a collection of remembrances of hilarious happenings in the Thurber home in Columbus and in Ohio State University. The sketches show Thurber's typical preoccupation with what he considers a "genius for getting into minor difficulties" which swell to major proportions. They show, too, the author's tendency to deal with psychological maladjustments of a grimly amusing sort—genial exaggerations of the troublesome times and of man's resulting bewilderment.

I suppose that the high-water mark of my youth in Columbus, Ohio, was the night the bed fell on my father. It makes a better recitation (unless, as some friends of mine have said, one has heard it five or six times) than it does a piece of writing, for it is almost necessary to throw furniture around, shake doors, and bark like a dog, to lend the proper atmosphere and verisimilitude to what is admittedly a somewhat incredible tale. Still, it did take place.

10   It happened, then, that my father had decided to sleep in the attic one night, to be away where he could think. My mother opposed the notion strongly because, she said, the old wooden bed up there was unsafe: it was wobbly and the heavy headboard would crash down on father's head in case the bed fell, and kill him. There was no dissuading him, however, and at a quarter past

ten he closed the attic door behind him and went up the narrow twisting stairs. We later heard ominous creakings as he crawled into bed. Grandfather, who usually slept in the attic bed when he was with us, had dis- 20 appeared some days before. (On these occasions he was usually gone six or eight days and returned growling and out of temper, with the news that the federal Union was run by a passel of blockheads and that the Army of the Potomac didn't have any more chance than a fiddler's bitch.)

We had visiting us at this time a nervous first cousin of mine named Briggs Beall, who believed that he was likely to cease breathing when he was asleep. It was his feeling that if he were not awakened every hour during 30 the night, he might die of suffocation. He had been accustomed to setting an alarm clock to ring at intervals until morning, but I persuaded him to abandon this. He slept in my room and I told him that I was such a light sleeper that if anybody quit breathing in the same room with me, I would wake instantly. He tested me the first night—which I had suspected he would—by holding his breath after my regular breathing had convinced him I was asleep. I was not asleep, however, and called to him. This seemed to allay his fears a little, but he took the 40 precaution of putting a glass of spirits of camphor on a little table at the head of his bed. In case I didn't arouse him until he was almost gone, he said, he would sniff the camphor, a powerful reviver. Briggs was not the only member of his family who had his crotchets. Old Aunt Melissa Beall (who could whistle like a man, with two fingers in her mouth) suffered under the premonition that she was destined to die on South High Street, because she had been born on South High Street and married on South High Street. Then there was Aunt 50 Sarah Shoaf, who never went to bed at night without

"Some nights she threw them all"—drawing by James Thurber. By permission. Copyright 1933 James Thurber. In The Thurber Carnival, *Harper & Brothers*

the fear that a burglar was going to get in and blow chloroform under her door through a tube. To avert this calamity—for she was in greater dread of anesthetics than of losing her household goods—she always piled her money, silverware, and other valuables in a neat stack just outside her bedroom, with a note reading: "This is all I have. Please take it and do not use your chloroform, as this is all I have." Aunt Gracie Shoaf also had a burglar phobia, but she met it with more fortitude. She was confident that burglars had been getting into her house every night for forty years. The fact that she never missed anything was to her no proof to the contrary. She always claimed that she scared them off before they could take anything, by throwing shoes down the hallway. When she went to bed she piled, where she could get at them handily, all the shoes there were about her house. Five minutes after she had turned off the light, she would sit up in bed and say "Hark!" Her husband, who had learned to ignore the whole situation as long ago as 1903, would either be sound asleep or pretend to be

sound asleep. In either case he would not respond to her tugging and pulling, so that presently she would arise, tiptoe to the door, open it slightly and heave a shoe down the hall in one direction and its mate down the hall in the other direction. Some nights she threw them all, some nights only a couple of pairs.

But I am straying from the remarkable incidents that took place during the night that the bed fell on father. By midnight we were all in bed. The layout of the rooms and this disposition of their occupants is important to an understanding of what later occurred. In the front room upstairs (just under father's attic bedroom) were my mother and my brother Herman, who sometimes sang in his sleep, usually "Marching Through Georgia" or "Onward, Christian Soldiers." Briggs Beall and myself were in a room adjoining this one. My brother Roy was in a room across the hall from ours. Our bull terrier, Rex, slept in the hall.

My bed was an army cot, one of those affairs which are made wide enough to sleep on comfortably only by putting up, flat with the middle section, the two sides which ordinarily hang down like the sideboards of a dropleaf table. When these sides are up, it is perilous to roll too far toward the edge, for then the cot is likely to tip completely over, bringing the whole bed down on top of one with a tremendous banging crash. This, in fact, is precisely what happened, about two o'clock in the morning. (It was my mother who, in recalling the scene later, first referred to it as "the night the bed fell on your father.")

Always a deep sleeper, slow to arouse (I had lied to Briggs), I was at first unconscious of what had happened when the iron cot rolled me onto the floor and toppled over on me. It left me still warmly bundled up and unhurt, for the bed rested above me like a canopy. Hence I did not wake up, only reached the edge of consciousness and went back. The racket, however, instantly awakened my mother, in the next room, who came to the immediate conclusion that her worst dread was realized: the big wooden bed upstairs had fallen on father. She therefore screamed, "Let's go to your poor father!" It was this shout, rather than the noise of my cot falling, that awakened Herman, in the same room with her. He thought that mother had become, for no apparent reason, hysterical. "You're all right, Mamma!" he shouted, trying to calm her. They exchanged shout for shout for perhaps ten seconds: "Let's go to your poor father!" and "You're all right!" That woke up Briggs. By this time I was conscious of what was going on, in a vague way, but did not yet realize that I was under my bed instead of on it. Briggs, awakening in the midst of loud shouts of fear and apprehension, came to the quick conclusion that he was suffocating and that we were all trying to "bring him out." With a low moan, he grasped the glass of camphor at the head of his bed and instead of sniffing it poured it over himself. The room reeked of camphor. "Ugf, ahfg," choked Briggs, like a drowning man, for he had almost succeeded in stopping his breath under the deluge of pungent spirits. He leaped out of bed and groped toward the open window, but he came up against one that was closed. With his hand, he beat out the glass, and I could hear it crash and tinkle in the alleyway below. It was at this juncture that I, in trying to get up, had the uncanny sensation of feeling my bed above me! Foggy with sleep, I now suspected, in my turn, that the whole uproar was being made in a frantic endeavor to extricate me from what must be an unheard-of and perilous situation. "Get me out of this!" I bawled. "Get me out!" I think I had the nightmarish belief that I was entombed in a mine. "Gugh," gasped Briggs, floundering in his camphor.

By this time my mother, still shouting, pursued by Herman, still shouting, was trying to open the door to the attic, in order to go up and get my father's body out of the wreckage. The door was stuck, however, and wouldn't yield. Her frantic pulls on it only added to the general banging and confusion. Roy and the dog were now up, the one shouting questions, the other barking.

Father, farthest away and soundest sleeper of all, had by this time been awakened by the battering on the attic door. He decided that the house was on fire. "I'm coming, I'm coming!" he wailed in a slow, sleepy voice —it took him many minutes to regain full consciousness. My mother, still believing he was caught under the bed, detected in his "I'm coming!" the mournful, resigned note of one who is preparing to meet his Maker. "He's dying!" she shouted.

"I'm all right!" Briggs yelled to reassure her. "I'm all right!" He still believed that it was his closeness to death that was worrying mother. I found at last the light switch in my room, unlocked the door, and Briggs and I joined the others at the attic door. The dog, who never did like Briggs, jumped for him—assuming that he was the culprit in whatever was going on—and Roy had to throw Rex and hold him. We could hear father crawling out of bed upstairs. Roy pulled the attic door open, with a mighty jerk, and father came down the stairs, sleepy and irritable but safe and sound. My mother began to weep when she saw him. Rex began to howl. "What in the name of heaven is going on here?" asked father.

The situation was finally put together like a gigantic jigsaw puzzle. Father caught a cold from prowling around in his bare feet but there were no other bad results. "I'm glad," said mother, who always looked on the bright side of things, "that your grandfather wasn't here."

1933

Stephen Vincent Benét

1898 · 1943

A versatile and prolific author, Stephen Vincent Benét wrote poems of varied sorts, novels, book reviews, short stories, a history, movie and radio scripts, and an opera.

Humor figured importantly in works of many genres— even in his youthful poems and in his epic, *John Brown's Body*. Probably more admired and possibly more durable than any of his other popular writings was a series of stories in which he made use of materials and methods of writing typical of old-time tall tales.

Benét was born in Bethlehem, Pennsylvania, in July 1898, the descendant of three generations of professional soldiers. Both his grandfather and his father had tastes for literature: the former had ably translated a military history into English; the latter was a student and collector of poetry who habitually read aloud to his family. A frail youngster, Benét early became an avid reader and a writer of stories and poems, some of which were published while he was still a schoolboy. He left Yale in his junior year to enlist for World War I. Rejected because of defective eyesight, he became a code clerk in the State Department, serving for a time in the same office as James Thurber. After the war, he returned to college for his B.A. and M.A.

As an undergraduate, Benét had published his first book of poems, *Five Men and Pompey,* in 1915. In 1918 had appeared *Young Adventure; a Book of Poems.* Another collection of poems, *Heaven and Earth,* was accepted as his master's thesis and was published in 1920. His first novel, *The Beginning of Wisdom* (1921), he wrote the summer after leaving Yale; his second, *Young People's Pride* (1922), after a period in Paris. After 1923, he resumed the writing of poetry and became a successful writer of magazine stories. A Guggenheim fellowship enabled him to go to France and to concentrate upon *John Brown's Body* (1928), an epic which not only became a best-seller but also won a Pulitzer Prize.

Benét was enabled by this successful venture to write at a rather more leisurely pace and to develop a talent which had been shown in some parts of his long poem —a talent for mingling legend and history with humor. This ability was evidenced in a number of playful ballad-like poems which he wrote—some in collaboration with his wife—celebrating historical and legendary American heroes and heroines. He also wrote a number of short stories after the manner of the Southwest Yarnspinners (p. 270) and the Mark Twain of "Baker's Bluejay Yarn" (p. 429), mingling folklore, wild fantasy, and poetic imaginings with homely detail, and written in the American language. Examples included "The Devil and Daniel Webster," "A Tooth for Paul Revere," "The Sobbin' Women," "Johnny Pye and the Fool Killer," and the story here reprinted.

Quite a few of these stories developed patriotic themes, underlining traditional American beliefs and virtues. When in the 1930's and 1940's, Benét felt that the attitudes and the safety of the United States were endangered, he devoted much of his energy to the writing of poems, stories, and radio dramas dealing with social and political ameliorations and with American participation in World War II. He died in March 1943, leaving uncompleted an epic account of the settlement of the Eastern Seaboard, *Western Star,* published in incomplete form in 1943.

William Rose Benét, "My Brother Steve," **Saturday Review of Literature,** November 15, 1941

From · Thirteen O'Clock

Daniel Webster and the Sea Serpent

It happened, one summer's day, that Dan'l Webster and some of his friends were out fishing. That was in the high days of his power and his fame, when the question wasn't if he was going to be President but when he was going to be President, and everybody at Kingston depot stood up when Dan'l Webster arrived to take the cars. But in spite of being Secretary of State and the biggest man in New England, he was just the same Dan'l

From **Thirteen O'Clock** published by Rinehart & Company, Inc. • Copyright, 1936, by Stephen Vincent Benét

Webster. He bought his Jamaica personal and in the jug at Colonel Sever's store in Kingston, right under a sign saying ENGLISH AND WEST INDIA GOODS, and he never was too busy to do a hand's turn for a friend. And, as for his big farm at Marshfield, that was just the apple of his eye. He buried his favorite horses with their shoes on, standing up, in a private graveyard, and wrote Latin epitaphs for them, and he often was heard to say that his big Hungarian bull, Saint Stephen, had more sense in his rear off hoof than most politicians. But, if there was one thing he loved better than Marshfield itself, it was the sea and the waters around it, for he was a fisherman born.

This time, he was salt-water fishing in the Comet, well out of sight of land. It was a good day for fishing, not too hazy, but not too clear, and Dan'l Webster enjoyed it, as he enjoyed everything in life, except maybe listening to the speeches of Henry Clay. He'd stolen a half-dozen days to come up to Marshfield, and well he needed the rest, for we'd nearly gone to war with England the year before, and now he was trying to fix up a real copper-riveted treaty that would iron out all the old differences that still kept the two countries unfriendly. And that was a job, even for Dan'l Webster. But as soon as he stepped aboard the Comet, he was carefree and heartwhole. He had his real friends around him and he wouldn't allow a word of politics talked on the boat—though that rule got broken this time, and for a good reason, as you'll see. And when he struck his first cod, and felt the fish take the hook, a kind of big slow smile went over his features, and he said, "Gentlemen, this is solid comfort." That was the kind of man he was.

I don't know how many there were of them aboard—half a dozen or so—just enough for good company. We'll say there were George Blake and Rufus Choate and young Peter Harvey and a boy named Jim Billings. And, of course, there was Seth Peterson, Dan'l's boat captain, in his red flannel shirt, New England as cod and beach plums, and Dan'l Webster's fast friend. Dan'l happened to be Secretary of State, and Seth Peterson happened to be a boat captain, but that didn't make any difference between them. And, once the Comet left the dock, Seth Peterson ran the show, as it's right that a captain should.

Well, they'd fished all morning and knocked off for a bite of lunch, and some had had segars and snoozes afterward, and some hadn't, but in any case, it was around midafternoon, and everybody was kind of comfortable and contented. They still fished, and they fished well, but they knew in an hour or so they'd be heading back for home with a fine catch on board. So maybe there was more conversation than Seth Peterson would have approved of earlier, and maybe some jokes were passed and some stories told. I don't know, but you know how it is when men get together at the end of a good day. All the same, they were still paying attention to their business—and I guess it was George Blake that noticed it first.

"Dan'l," he said, breathing hard, "I've got something on my line that pulls like a Morgan horse."

"Well, yank him in!" sang out Dan'l, and then his face changed as his own line began to stiffen and twang. "George," he said, "I beat you! I got something on my line that pulls like a pair of steers!"

"Give 'em more line, Mr. Webster!" yells Seth Peterson, and Dan'l did. But at that, the line ran out so fast that it smoked when it hit the water, and any hands but Dan'l Webster's would have been cut to the bone. Nor you couldn't see where it went to, except Something deep in the waters must be pulling it out as a cat pulls yarn from a ball. The veins in Dan'l Webster's arm stood out like cords. He played the fish and played the fish; he fought it with every trick he knew. And still the little waves danced and the other men gaped at the fight —and still he couldn't bring the Something to time.

"By the big elm at Marshfield!" he said at last, with his dark face glowing and a fisherman's pride in his eyes. "Have I hooked on to a frigate with all sails set? I've payed out a mile of my own particular line, and she still pulls like ten wild horses. Gentlemen, what's this?"

And even as he said it, the tough line broke in two with a crack like a musket-shot, and out of the deep of ocean, a mile away, the creature rose, majestic. Neighbors, that was a sight! Shaking the hook from its jaw, it rose, the sea serpent of the Scriptures, exact and to specifications as laid down in the Good Book, with its hairy face and its furlong on furlong of body, wallowing and thrashing in the troubled sea. As it rose, it gave a long low melancholy hoot, like a kind of forsaken steamboat; and when it gave out that hoot, young Jim Billings,

Daniel Webster and the Sea Serpent 1007

the boy, fainted dead away on the deck. But nobody even noticed him—they were all staring at the sea serpent with bulging eyes.

Even Dan'l Webster was shaken. He passed his hand for a moment across his brow and gave a sort of inquiring look at the jug of Jamaica by the hatch.

"Gentlemen," he said in a low voice, "the evidence—the ocular evidence would seem to be conclusive. And yet, speaking as a lawyer—"

"Thar she blows! I never thought to see her again!" yells Seth Peterson, half driven out of his mind by the sight, as the sea serpent roiled the waters. "Thar she blows, by the Book of Genesis! Oh, why ain't I got a harpoon?"

"Quiet, Seth," said Dan'l Webster. "Let us rather give thanks for being permitted to witness this glorious and unbelievable sight." And then you could see the real majesty of the man, for no sooner were the words out of his mouth than the sea serpent started swimming straight toward the Comet. She came like a railway train and her wake boiled out behind her for an acre. And yet, there was something kind of skittish about her, too—you might say that she came kind of shaking her skirts and bridling. I don't know what there was about her that made you sure she was a female, but they were all sure.

She came, direct as a bullet, till you could count the white teeth shining in her jaws. I don't know what the rest of them did—though doubtless some prayers were put up in a hasty way—but Dan'l Webster stood there and faced her, with his brow dark and his eyes like a sleepy lion's giving her glance for glance. Yes, there was a minute, there, when she lifted her head high out of water and they looked at each other eye to eye. They say hers were reddish but handsome. And then, just as it seemed she'd crash plumb through the Comet, she made a wide wheel and turned. Three times she circled the boat, hooting lonesomely, while the Comet danced up and down like a cork on the waves. But Dan'l Webster kept his footing, one hand gripping the mast, and whenever he got a chance, he fixed her with his eye. Till finally, on the third circuit, she gave one last long hoot—like twenty foghorns at once, it was, and nearly deafened them all—and plunged back whence she'd come, to the bottomless depths of the sea.

But even after the waters were calm again, they didn't say anything for quite a while. Till, finally, Seth Peterson spoke.

"Well, Mr. Webster," he said, "that one got away" —and he grinned a dry grin.

"Leviathan of the Scriptures! Give me paper and pen," said Dan'l Webster. "We must write this down and attest it." And then they all began to talk.

Well, he wrote an account of just what they'd seen, very plain and honest. And everybody there signed his name to it. Then he read it over to them again aloud. And then there was another silence, while they looked at one another.

Finally, Seth Peterson shook his head, slow and thoughtful.

"It won't do, Dan'l," he said, in a deep voice.

"Won't do?" said Dan'l Webster, with his eyes blazing. "What do you mean, Seth?"

"I mean it just won't do, Dan'l," said Seth Peterson, perfectly respectful, but perfectly firm. "I put it up to you, gentlemen," he said, turning to the others. "I can go home and say I've seen the sea serpent. And everybody'll say, 'Oh, that's just that old liar, Seth Peterson.' But if it's Dan'l Webster says so—can't you see the difference?"

He paused for a minute, but nobody said a word.

"Well, I can," he said. He drawled out the words very slow. "Dan'l Webster—Secretary of State—sees and talks to a sea serpent—off Plymouth Bay. Why, it would plumb ruin him! And I don't mind being ruint, but it's different with Dan'l Webster. Would you vote for a man for President who claimed he'd saw the sea serpent? Well, would you? Would anybody?"

There was another little silence, and then George Blake spoke.

"He's right, Dan'l," he said, while the others nodded. "Give me that paper." He took it from Dan'l Webster's hand and threw it in the sea.

"And now," he said in a firm voice, "I saw cod. Nothing but cod. Except maybe a couple of halibut. Did any gentlemen here see anything else?"

Well, at that, it turned out, of course, that nobody aboard had seen anything but cod all day. And with that, they put back for shore. All the same, they all looked over their shoulders a good deal till they got back to harbor.

And yet Dan'l Webster wasn't too contented that evening, in spite of his fine catch. For, after all, he had seen the sea serpent, and not only seen her but played her on the line for twenty-seven minutes by his gold repeater, and, being a fisherman, he'd like to have said so. And yet, if he did—Seth was right—folks would think him crazy or worse. It took his mind off Lord Ashburton and the treaty with England—till, finally, he pushed aside the papers on his desk.

"Oh, a plague on the beast!" he said, kind of crossly. "I'll leave it alone and hope it leaves me alone." So he took his candle and went up to bed. But just as he was dropping off to sleep, he thought he heard a long low hoot from the mouth of Green Harbor River, two miles away.

The next night the hooting continued, and the third day there was a piece in the Kingston paper about the new Government foghorn at Rocky Ledge. Well, the thing began to get on Dan'l Webster's nerves, and when his temper was roused, he wasn't a patient man. Moreover, the noises seemed to disturb the stock—at least his overseer said so—and the third night his favorite gray kicked half the door out of her stall. "That sea serpent's getting to be an infernal nuisance," thought Dan'l Webster. "I've got to protect my property." So, the fourth night he put on his old duck-shooting clothes and took his favorite shotgun, Learned Selden, and went down to a blind at the mouth of Green Harbor River, to see what he could see. He didn't tell anybody else about his intentions, because he still felt kind of sensitive about the whole affair.

Well, there was a fine moon that night, and sure enough, about eleven o'clock, the sea serpent showed up, steaming in from ocean, all one continuous wave length, like a giant garden hose. She was quite a handsome sight, all speckled with the moonlight, but Dan'l Webster couldn't rightly appreciate it. And just as she came to the blind, she lifted her head and looked sorrowfully in the direction of Marshfield and let out a long low soulful hoot like a homesick train.

Dan'l Webster hated to do it. But he couldn't have a sea serpent living in Green Harbor River and scaring the stock—not to speak of the universal consternation and panic there'd be in the countryside when such a thing was known. So he lifted Learned Selden and gave her both barrels for a starter, just a trifle over her head. And as soon as the gun exploded, the sea serpent let out a screech you could hear a mile and headed back for open sea. If she'd traveled fast before, she traveled like lightning now, and it wasn't any time before she was just a black streak on the waters.

Dan'l Webster stepped out of the blind and wiped his brow. He felt sorry, but he felt relieved. He didn't think she'd be back, after that sort of scare, and he wanted to leave everything shipshape before he went down to Washington, next morning. But next day, when he told Seth Peterson what he'd done, he didn't feel so chipper. For, "You shouldn't have done that, Mr. Webster," said Seth Peterson, shaking his head, and that was all he would say except a kind of mutter that sounded like "Samanthy was always particular set in her likes." But Dan'l didn't pay any attention to that, though he remembered it later, and he was quite short with Seth for the first time in their long relationship. So Seth shut up like a quahog, and Dan'l took the cars for Washington.

When he got there he was busy enough, for the British treaty was on the boil, and within twenty-four hours he'd forgot all about the sea serpent. Or thought he had. But three days later, as he was walking home to his house on Lafayette Square, with a senator friend of his, in the cool of the evening, they heard a curious noise. It seemed to come from the direction of the Potomac River.

"Must have got a new whistle for the Baltimore night boat," said the senator. "Noisy too."

"Oh, that's just the bullfrogs on the banks," said Dan'l Webster steadily. But he knew what it was, just the same, and his heart sank within him. But nobody ever called Dan'l Webster a coward. So, as soon as he'd got rid of the senator, he went down to the banks of the Potomac. Well, it was the sea serpent, all right.

She looked a little tired, as well she might, having swum from Plymouth Bay. But as soon as she saw Dan'l Webster, she stretched out her neck and gave a long low loving hoot. Then Dan'l knew what the trouble was and for once in his life, he didn't know what to do. But he'd brought along a couple of roe herring, in a paper, just in case; so he fed them to her and she hooted, affectionate and grateful. Then he walked back to his house with his

Daniel Webster and the Sea Serpent 1009

head bowed. And that very night he sent a special express letter to Seth Peterson at Marshfield, for, it seemed to him, Seth must know more about the business than he let on.

Well, Seth got to Washington as fast as the cars would bring him, and the very evening he arrived Dan'l sent him over to interview the serpent. But when Seth came back, Dan'l could see by his face that he hadn't made much progress.

"Could you talk to her, Seth?" he said, and his voice was eager. "Can she understand United States?"

"Oh, she can understand it all right," said Seth. "She's even picking up a few words. They was always a smart family, those Rock Ledge serpents, and she's the old maid of the lot, and the best educated. The only trouble with 'em is, they're so terrible sot in their ways."

"You might have warned me, Seth," said Dan'l Webster, kind of reproachful, and Seth looked uncomfortable.

"Well, to tell you the truth," he said, "I thought all of 'em was dead. Nor I never thought she'd act up like this—her father was as respectable a serpent as you'd see in a long summer's day. Her father—"

"Bother her father!" said Dan'l Webster and set his jaw. "Tell me what she says."

"Well, Mr. Webster," said Seth, and stared at his boots, "she says you're quite a handsome man. She says she never did see anybody quite like you," he went on. "I hate to tell you this, Mr. Webster, and I feel kind of responsible, but I think you ought to know. And I told you that you oughtn't to have shot at her—she's pretty proud of that. She says she knows just how you meant it. Well, I'm no great hand at being embarrassed, Mr. Webster, but, I tell you, she embarrassed me. You see, she's been an old maid for about a hundred and fifty years, I guess, and that's the worst of it. And being the last of her folks in those particular waters, there's just no way to restrain her—her father and mother was as sensible, hard-working serpents as ever gave a fellow a tow through a fog, but you know how it is with those old families. Well, she says wherever you go, she'll follow you, and she claims she wants to hear you speak before the Supreme Court—"

"Did you tell her I'm a married man?" said Dan'l. "Did you tell her that?"

"Yes, I told her," said Seth, and you could see the perspiration on his forehead. "But she says tnat doesn't signify—her being a serpent and different—and she's fixing to move right in. She says Washington's got a lovely climate and she's heard all about the balls and the diplomatic receptions. I don't know how she's heard about them, but she has." He swallowed. "I got her to promise she'd kind of lie low for two weeks and not come up the Potomac by daylight—she was fixing to do that because she wants to meet the President. Well, I got her to promise that much. But she says, even so, if you don't come to see her once an evening, she'll hoot till you do, and she told me to tell you that you haven't heard hooting yet. And as soon as the fish market's open, I better run down and buy a barrel of flaked cod, Mr. Webster—she's partial to flaked cod and she usually takes it in the barrel. Well, I don't want to worry you, Mr. Webster, but I'm afraid that we're in a fix."

"A fix!" said Dan'l Webster. "It's the biggest fix I ever was in in my life!"

"Well, it's kind of complimentary, in a way, I guess," said Seth Peterson, "but—"

"Does she say anything else?" said Dan'l Webster, drawing a long breath.

"Yes, Mr. Webster," said Seth Peterson, his eyes on his boots. "She says you're a little shy. But she says she likes that in a man."

Dan'l Webster went to bed that night, but he didn't sleep. He worked and worked those great brains of his till he nearly wore out the wheels, but he still couldn't think of a way to get rid of the sea serpent. And just about the time dawn broke, he heard one long low hoot, faithful and reminiscent, from the direction of the Potomac.

Well, the next two weeks were certainly bad ones for him. For, as the days wore on, the sea serpent got more and more restive. She wanted him to call her Samanthy, which he wouldn't, and she kept asking him when he was going to introduce her into society, till he had to feed her Italian sardines in olive oil to keep her quiet. And that ran up a bill at the fish market that he hated to think of—besides, her continually threatening to come up the Potomac by day. Moreover, and to put the cap on things, the great Webster-Ashburton treaty that was to make his name as Secretary of State had struck a snag and England didn't seem at all partial to admitting the American claims. Oh, it was a weary fortnight and a troublesome one!

The last afternoon of the fortnight, he sat in his office and he didn't know where to turn. For Lord Ashburton was coming to see him for a secret conference that night at nine, and he had to see the sea serpent at ten, and how to satisfy either of them he didn't know. His eyes stared wearily at the papers on his desk. He rang the bell for his secretary.

"The corvette Benjamin Franklin reports—" he said. "This should have gone to the Navy Department, Mr. Jones." Then he glanced at the naval report again and his eyes began to glow like furnaces. "By the bones of Leviathan! I've got it!" he said, with a shout. "Where's my hat, Mr. Jones. I must see the President at once!"

There was a different feeling about the house on Lafayette Square that evening, for Dan'l Webster was himself again. He cracked a joke with Seth Peterson and took a glass of Madeira and turned it to the light. And when Lord Ashburton was announced—a nice, white-haired old gentleman, though a little stiff in his joints—he received him with all the courtesy of a king.

"I am glad to see you so much restored, Mr. Webster," said Lord Ashburton, when the greetings had been exchanged. "And yet I fear I bring you bad news. Concerning clauses six and seven of the proposed treaty between Her Majesty's Government and the United States of America, it is my duty to state—"

"My lord, let us drop the clauses for a moment and take the wider view," said Dan'l Webster, smiling. "This is a matter concerning the future welfare and peace of two great nations. Your government claims the right to search our ships; that right we deny. And our attitude seems to you preposterous. Is that not so?"

"I would hesitate to use the word 'preposterous,' " said Lord Ashburton cautiously. "Yet—"

"And yet," said Dan'l Webster, leaning forward, "there are things which may seem preposterous, and yet are not. Let me put a case. Let us say that Great Britain has the strongest navy afloat."

"Britannia rules the waves," said Lord Ashburton, with a noble smile.

"There were a couple she didn't rule in 1812," said Dan'l Webster, "but let that pass. Let me ask you, Lord Ashburton, and let me ask you solemnly, what could even the power and might of Britain's navy avail against Leviathan?"

"Leviathan?" said Lord Ashburton, rather coldly. "Naturally, I understand the Biblical illusion. Yet—"

"The sea serpent," said Dan'l Webster, kind of impatient. "What could all Britain's navy do against the sea serpent out of the Scriptures?"

Lord Ashburton stared at him as if he had gone mad. "God bless my soul, Mr. Secretary!" he said. "But I fail to see the point of your question. The sea serpent doesn't exist!"

"Doesn't he—I mean she?" said Dan'l Webster, calmly. "And suppose I should prove to you that it does exist?"

"Well, 'pon my word! God bless my soul!" said Lord Ashburton, kind of taken aback. "Naturally—in that case—however—but even so—"

Dan'l Webster touched a bell on his desk. "Lord Ashburton," he said, kind of solemn, "I am putting my life, and what is dearer to me, my honor and reputation, in your hands. Nevertheless, I feel it necessary, for a better understanding between our two countries."

Seth Peterson came into the room and Dan'l nodded at him.

"Seth," he said, "Lord Ashburton is coming with us to see Samanthy."

"It's all right if you say so, Mr. Webster," said Seth Peterson, "but he'll have to help carry the sardines."

"Well, 'pon my word! Bless my soul! A very strange proceeding!" said Lord Ashburton, but he followed along.

Well, they got to the banks of the Potomac, the three of them, and when they were there, Seth whistled. Samanthy was lying mostly under water, behind a little brushy island, but when she heard the whistle, she began to heave up and uncoil, all shining in the moonlight. It was what you might call a kind of impressive sight. Dan'l Webster looked at Lord Ashburton, but Lord Ashburton's words seemed sort of stuck in his throat.

Finally he got them out. "Bless my soul!" he said. "You Americans are very extraordinary! Is it alive?"

But then all he could do was goggle, for Samanthy had lifted her head, and giving a low friendly hoot, she commenced to swim around the island.

"Now, is that a sea serpent or isn't it?" said Dan'l Webster, with a kind of quiet pride.

"Indubitably," said Lord Ashburton, staring through his eyeglass. "Indubitably," and he kind of cleared his throat. "It is, indeed and in fact, a serpent of the sea. And I am asleep and in bed, in my room at the British Embassy." He pinched himself. "Ouch!" he said. "No, I am not."

"Would you call it sizable, for a sea serpent?" persisted Dan'l Webster.

Lord Ashburton stared again through his eyeglass. "Quite," he said. "Oh, yes, quite, quite!"

"And powerful?" asked Dan'l.

"I should judge so," said Lord Ashburton, faintly, as the sea serpent swam around and around the island and the waves of its wake broke crashing on the bank. "Yes, indeed, a very powerful engine of destruction. May I ask what it feeds upon?"

"Italian sardines for preference," said Dan'l. "But that's beside the point." He drew a long breath. "Well, my lord," he said, "we're intending to commission that sea serpent as a regular and acknowledged war vessel in the United States Navy. And then, where's your wooden walls?"

Lord Ashburton, he was a diplomat, and his face didn't change expression as he stared first at the sea serpent and then at the face of Dan'l Webster. But after a while, he nodded. "You need not labor the point, Mr. Secretary," he said. "My Government, I am sure, will be glad to reconsider its position on the last two clauses and the right of search."

"Then I'm sure we can reach an agreement," said Dan'l Webster, and wiped the sweat from his brow. "And now, let's feed Samanthy."

He whistled to her himself, a long musical whistle, and she came bounding and looping in toward shore. It took all three of them to heave her the barrel of sardines, and she swallowed it down in one gulp. After that, she gave a hoot of thanks and gratitude, and Lord Ashburton sat down on the bank for a minute and took snuff. He said that he needed something to clear his mind.

"Naturally," he said, after a while. "Her Majesty's Government must have adequate assurances as to the good conduct of this—this lady." He'd meant to say "creature" at first, but Samanthy rolled her eye at him just then, and he changed the word.

"You shall have them," said Dan'l Webster, and whistled Samanthy even closer. She came in kind of skittish, flirting her coils, and Lord Ashburton closed his eyes for a minute. But when Dan'l Webster spoke, it was in the voice that hushed the Senate whenever he rose.

"Samanthy," he said, "I speak to you now as Secretary of State of the United States of America." It was the great voice that had rung in the Supreme Court and replied to Hayne, and even a sea serpent had to listen respectful. For the voice was mellow and deep, and he pictured Samanthy's early years as a carefree young serpent, playing with her fellows, and then her hard life of toil and struggle when she was left lone and lorn, till even Seth Peterson and Lord Ashburton realized the sorrow and tragedy of her lonely lot. And then, in the gentlest and kindest way you could ask, he showed her where her duty lay.

"For, if you keep on hooting in the Potomac, Samanthy," he said, "you'll become a public menace to navigation and get sat upon by the Senate Committee for Rivers and Harbors. They'll drag you up on land, Samanthy, and put you in the Smithsonian Institution; they'll stick you in a stagnant little pool and children will come to throw you peanuts on Sundays, and their nurses will poke you with umbrellas if you don't act lively enough. The U.S. Navy will shoot at you for target practice, Samanthy, and the scientists will examine you, and the ladies of the Pure Conduct League will knit you a bathing suit, and you'll be bothered every minute by congressmen and professors and visitors and foreign celebrities till you won't be able to call your scales your own. Oh, yes, it'll be fame, Samanthy, but it won't be good enough. Believe me, I know something about fame and it's begging letters from strangers and calls from people you don't know and don't want to know, and the burden and wear and tear of being a public character till it's enough to break your heart. It isn't good enough, Samanthy; it won't give you back your free waters and your sporting in the deep. Yes, Samanthy, it's a remarkable thing to have you here in Washington, but it isn't the life you were meant for and I can't take advantage of your trust. And now," he said to Seth Peterson, "just what does she say?"

Seth Peterson listened, attentive, to the hootings.

"She says the Washington climate isn't what she thought it was," he said. "And the Potomac River's too warm; it's bad for her sciatica. And she's plumb tired of sardines."

"Does she say anything about me?" asked Dan'l Webster anxiously.

"Well," said Seth Peterson, listening, "she says—if you'll excuse me, Mr. Webster—that you may be a great man, but you wouldn't make much of a sea serpent. She says you haven't got enough coils. She says—well, she says no hard feelings, but she guesses it was a mistake on both sides."

He listened again. "But she says one thing," he said. "She says she's got to have recognition and a husband, if she has to take this Lord Ashburton. She says he doesn't look like much, but he might get her introduced at Court."

A great light broke over Dan'l's face and his voice rang out like thunder. "She shall have them both," he said. "Come here, Samanthy. By virtue of the authority vested in me as Secretary of State, and by special order of the President of the United States and the Secretary of the Navy, as witness the attached commission in blank which I now fill in with your name, I hereby attach you to the United States Navy, to rank as a forty-four-gun frigate on special duty, rating a rear admiral's flag and a salute of the appropriate number of guns, wherever encountered in American waters. And, by virtue of the following special order, I hereby order you to the South Seas, there to cruise until further orders for the purpose of seeking a suitable and proper husband, with all the rights, privileges, duties and appurtenances pertaining to said search and said American citizenship, as aforesaid and Hail Columbia. Signed John Tyler, President. With which is subjoined a passport signed by Daniel Webster, Secretary of State, bidding all foreign nations let pass without hindrance the American citizen, Samanthy Doe, on her lawful journeys and errands." He dropped his voice for a moment and added reflectively, "The American corvette, Benjamin Franklin, reports sighting a handsome young male sea serpent on February third of the present year, just off the coast of the Sandwich Islands. Said serpent had forty-two coils by

actual count, and when last sighted was swimming SSW at full speed."

But hardly had he spoken when Samanthy, for the last time, lifted her head and gave out a last long hoot. She looked upon Dan'l Webster as she did so, and there was regret in her eye. But the regret was tinctured with eagerness and hope.

Then she beat the water to a froth, and, before they really saw her go, she was gone, leaving only her wake on the moonlit Potomac.

"Well," said Dan'l Webster, yawning a little, "there we are. And now, Lord Ashburton, if you'll come home with me, we can draw up that treaty."

"Gladly," said Lord Ashburton, brushing his coat with his handkerchief. "Is it really gone? 'Pon my soul! You know, for a moment, I imagined that I actually saw a sea serpent. You have a very vivid way of putting things, Mr. Webster. But I think I understand the American attitude now, from the—er—analogy you were pleased to draw between such a—er—fabulous animal and the young strength of your growing country."

"I was confident that you would appreciate it, once it was brought to your attention," said Dan'l Webster. But he winked one eye at Seth Peterson, and Seth Peterson winked back.

And I'll say this for Dan'l Webster, too—he kept his promises. All through the time he was Secretary of State, he saw to it that the forty-four-gun frigate, Samanthy Doe, was carried on a special account on the books of the Navy. In fact, there's some people say that she's still so carried, and that it was her give Ericsson the idea for building the Monitor in the Civil War—if she wasn't the Monitor herself. And when the White Fleet went around the world in Teddy Roosevelt's time—well, there was a lookout in the crow's-nest of the flagship, one still calm night, as they passed by the palmy isles of the South Seas. And all of a sudden, the water boiled, tremendous and phosphorescent, and there was a pair of sea serpents and seven young ones, circling, calm and majestic, three times around the fleet. He rubbed his eyes and he stared, but there they were. Well, he was the only one that saw it, and they put him in the brig for it next morning. But he swore, till the day he died, they were flying the Stars and Stripes.

1937

Daniel Webster and the Sea Serpent   1013

Sherwood Anderson

1876 · 1941

Sherwood Anderson was born in Camden, Ohio, and much of his boyhood was spent in Clyde, another small Ohio town. The poverty of his family was perhaps the chief reason why he quit school at the age of fourteen and got a job. Thereafter, for a good many years, he worked at a great variety of jobs (all requiring manual labor), first in Clyde and then in Chicago. In 1898, he joined the National Guard, and his company was sent to Cuba for patrol duty after the defeat of the Spanish forces. Upon his return from Cuba in 1899, he enrolled (somewhat belatedly—he was twenty-three) in Wittenberg Academy, a preparatory school in Springfield, Ohio, and was graduated the following year. Soon thereafter, he became a writer of advertising copy. He was so successful in this line that he organized, in 1907, in Elyria, Ohio, the Anderson Manufacturing Company, which specialized in roof-paint. In 1912, Anderson—though married and the father of three children, and eminently successful in the manufacture and sale of roof-paint—left his factory and did not return. "My feet are cold and wet. I have been walking too long on the bed of a river," he said to his secretary.

It was a dramatic and memorable moment; nothing quite like it had happened before in our literary history: a successful businessman abandoning his business at the age of thirty-six in order to devote his life to writing. Anderson went at once to Chicago, where he soon became a member (though he perforce continued for a good many years to write advertising copy for a living) of the circle of writers who were making the "Chicago Renaissance" the most important and exciting literary movement in contemporary America: Floyd Dell, Ben

Sherwood Anderson—caricature by William Gropper from The Literary Spotlight, *ed. John Farrar, 1924*

Hecht, Carl Sandburg, Theodore Dreiser, Edgar Lee Masters, and others. Seven years later, Anderson published—in 1919—*Winesburg, Ohio,* his masterpiece. This was followed by two other collections of short narratives similar to *Winesburg* and almost as good: *The Triumph of the Egg* in 1921, and *Horses and Men* in 1923. The intense and unconventional stories in these books are Anderson's special contribution to American literature.

His long list of publications includes other kinds of writing. Among his novels are *Poor White* (1921), *Many Marriages* (1923), and *Dark Laughter* (1925). He wrote several ostensibly autobiographical works, such as *A Story Teller's Story* (1924) and *Tar: A Midwest Childhood* (1926). *Perhaps Women* (1931) and *Puzzled America* (1935) are social reports which deal sympathetically with the mill workers of the new industrial South.

Though the Midwest was his rightful milieu, and Chicago his proper cosmopolitan center, Anderson moved restlessly to this place and that, always seeking a fulfillment which he could never achieve: to New York, which he mistakenly regarded as a better place for him to be than Chicago, and where he sought the guidance of Waldo Frank and Van Wyck Brooks; to Paris, where he met Ernest Hemingway and Gertrude Stein; to New Orleans, where his association with William Faulkner

probably contributed little to his literary career. After 1927, he lived (with his fourth wife) on a farm near Marion, Virginia, and, having bought the two newspapers in the town, gave much of his time to journalism. Even here, though, in a handsome house of native stone built into the Virginia hillside, he was unhappy, presumably because of the failure of his creative powers, and the decline of his literary reputation. During his later years, he espoused with noble (if sometimes ingenuous and misguided) fervor the cause of the Southern textile workers.

"To say that cultivated readers of the early 1920's," Irving Howe accurately remarked in 1951, "admired Anderson's work as highly as such readers today admire Faulkner's is to exaggerate only a little." Anderson's subsequent fame has fallen somewhat below the high mark first inspired by *Winesburg,* but his best work remains important, and its importance continues to be rediscovered by new generations of readers.

Letters of Sherwood Anderson, eds. H. M. Jones and W. B. Rideout, Boston, 1953 • Irving Howe, Sherwood Anderson, New York, 1951 • James Schevill, Sherwood Anderson, His Life and Work, Denver, 1951 • Norman Holmes Pearson, "Anderson and the New Puritanism," The Newberry Library Bulletin, December 1948 • William L. Phillips, "How Sherwood Anderson Wrote Winesburg, Ohio," American Literature, March 1951, XXIII, 7-30

From · Winesburg, Ohio

Adventure

Winesburg, Ohio, from which the following selection is taken, is a collection of sketches held together by a unity of theme and mood. Pieces like the following were something new in American literature in 1919. Hawthorne (and other American writers to a lesser degree) had dealt perceptively with neurotic states, but several new elements gave to Winesburg a uniqueness and special power: the pervasive tenderness; the simplicity, directness, and understatement of the writing; the Freudian view of sex-repres-

sion, were for the first time frankly embodied in American fiction.

Terms like "realism" and "naturalism" seem inappropriate here. Nor is it satisfactory to take the book, in any special sense, as a picture of the Midwest, or as an allied part of the "revolt from the village," the chief manifesto of which was Sinclair Lewis' Main Street. Winesburg is rather a parable of the human condition, with reference to the world in general, and more particularly perhaps to modern industrial America. Anderson called his characters "grotesques." He was dissatisfied with the surface realism popularized by Howells. He had "a hunger," he said, "to see beneath the surface of lives."

Winesburg, Ohio, in the words of Anderson's best critic, Irving Howe, "may be read as a fable of American estrangement, its theme the loss of love. The book's major characters are alienated from the basic sources of emotional sustenance . . . . They are distraught communicants in search of a ceremony, a social value, a manner of living, a lost ritual that may, by some means, re-establish a flow and exchange of emotion."

Alice Hindman, a woman of twenty-seven when George Willard was a mere boy, had lived in Winesburg all her life. She clerked in Winney's Dry Goods Store and lived with her mother who had married a second husband.

Alice's step-father was a carriage painter, and given to drink. His story is an odd one. It will be worth telling some day.

At twenty-seven Alice was tall and somewhat slight. Her head was large and overshadowed her body. Her shoulders were a little stooped and her hair and eyes brown. She was very quiet but beneath a placid exterior a continual ferment went on.

When she was a girl of sixteen and before she began to work in the store, Alice had an affair with a young man. The young man, named Ned Currie, was older than Alice. He, like George Willard, was employed on the *Winesburg Eagle* and for a long time he went to see Alice almost every evening. Together the two walked under the trees through the streets of the town and talked of what they would do with their lives. Alice was then a very pretty girl and Ned Currie took her into his arms and kissed her. He became excited and said things he did not intend to say and Alice, betrayed by her desire to have something beautiful come into her rather narrow life, also grew excited. She also talked. The outer crust of her life, all of her natural diffidence and reserve, was torn away and she gave herself over to the emotions of love. When, late in the fall of her sixteenth year, Ned Currie went away to Cleveland where he hoped to get a place on a city newspaper and rise in the world, she wanted to go with him. With a trembling voice she told him what was in her mind. "I will work and you can work," she said. "I do not want to harness you to a needless expense that will prevent your making progress. Don't marry me now. We will get along without that and we can be together. Even though we live in the same house no one will say anything. In the city we will be unknown and people will pay no attention to us."

Ned Currie was puzzled by the determination and abandon of his sweetheart and was also deeply touched. He had wanted the girl to become his mistress but changed his mind. He wanted to protect and care for her. "You don't know what you're talking about," he said sharply; "you may be sure I'll let you do no such thing. As soon as I get a good job I'll come back. For the present you'll have to stay here. It's the only thing we can do."

On the evening before he left Winesburg to take up his new life in the city, Ned Currie went to call on Alice. They walked about through the streets for an hour and then got a rig from Wesley Moyer's livery and went for a drive in the country. The moon came up and they found themselves unable to talk. In his sadness the young man forgot the resolutions he had made regarding his conduct with the girl.

They got out of the buggy at a place where a long meadow ran down to the bank of Wine Creek and there in the dim light became lovers. When at midnight they returned to town they were both glad. It did not seem to them that anything that could happen in the future could blot out the wonder and beauty of the thing that had happened. "Now we will have to stick to each other, whatever happens we will have to do that," Ned Currie said as he left the girl at her father's door.

The young newspaper man did not succeed in getting a place on a Cleveland paper and went west to Chicago. For a time he was lonely and wrote to Alice almost every day. Then he was caught up by the life of the city; he began to make friends and found new interests in life. In Chicago he boarded at a house where there were several women. One of them attracted his attention and he forgot Alice in Winesburg. At the end of a year he had stopped writing letters, and only once in a long time, when he was lonely or when he went into one of the city parks and saw the moon shining on the grass as it had shone that night on the meadow by Wine Creek, did he think of her at all.

In Winesburg the girl who had been loved grew to be a woman. When she was twenty-two years old her father, who owned a harness repair shop, died suddenly. The harness maker was an old soldier, and after a few months his wife received a widow's pension. She used

From **Winesburg, Ohio** by Sherwood Anderson • Copyright 1919 by B. W. Huebsch, Inc., 1947 by Eleanor Copenhaver Anderson • Reprinted by permission of The Viking Press, Inc., New York

the first money she got to buy a loom and became a weaver of carpets, and Alice got a place in Winney's store. For a number of years nothing could have induced her to believe that Ned Currie would not in the end return to her.

She was glad to be employed because the daily round of toil in the store made the time of waiting seem less long and uninteresting. She began to save money, thinking that when she had saved two or three hundred dollars she would follow her lover to the city and try if her presence would not win back his affections.

Alice did not blame Ned Currie for what had happened in the moonlight in the field, but felt that she could never marry another man. To her the thought of giving to another what she still felt could belong only to Ned seemed monstrous. When other young men tried to attract her attention she would have nothing to do with them. "I am his wife and shall remain his wife whether he comes back or not," she whispered to herself, and for all of her willingness to support herself could not have understood the growing modern idea of a woman's owning herself and giving and taking for her own ends in life.

Alice worked in the dry goods store from eight in the morning until six at night and on three evenings a week went back to the store to stay from seven until nine. As time passed and she became more and more lonely she began to practice the devices common to lonely people. When at night she went upstairs into her room she knelt on the floor to pray and in her prayers whispered things she wanted to say to her lover. She became attached to inanimate objects, and because it was her own, could not bear to have anyone touch the furniture of her room. The trick of saving money, begun for a purpose, was carried on after the scheme of going to the city to find Ned Currie had been given up. It became a fixed habit, and when she needed new clothes she did not get them. Sometimes on rainy afternoons in the store she got out her bank book and, letting it lie open before her, spent hours dreaming impossible dreams of saving money enough so that the interest would support both herself and her future husband.

"Ned always liked to travel about," she thought. "I'll give him the chance. Some day when we are married and I can save both his money and my own, we will be rich. Then we can travel together all over the world."

In the dry goods store weeks ran into months and months into years as Alice waited and dreamed of her lover's return. Her employer, a grey old man with false teeth and a thin grey mustache that drooped down over his mouth, was not given to conversation, and sometimes, on rainy days and in the winter when a storm raged in Main Street, long hours passed when no customers came in. Alice arranged and rearranged the stock. She stood near the front window where she could look down the deserted street and thought of the evenings when she had walked with Ned Currie and of what he had said. "We will have to stick to each other now." The words echoed and re-echoed through the mind of the maturing woman. Tears came into her eyes. Sometimes when her employer had gone out and she was alone in the store she put her head on the counter and wept. "Oh, Ned, I am waiting," she whispered over and over, and all the time the creeping fear that he would never come back grew stronger within her.

In the spring when the rains have passed and before the long hot days of summer have come, the country about Winesburg is delightful. The town lies in the midst of open fields, but beyond the fields are pleasant patches of woodlands. In the wooded places are many little cloistered nooks, quiet places where lovers go to sit on Sunday afternoons. Through the trees they look out across the fields and see farmers at work about the barns or people driving up and down on the roads. In the town bells ring and occasionally a train passes, looking like a toy thing in the distance.

For several years after Ned Currie went away Alice did not go into the wood with other young people on Sunday, but one day after he had been gone for two or three years and when her loneliness seemed unbearable, she put on her best dress and set out. Finding a little sheltered place from which she could see the town and a long stretch of the fields, she sat down. Fear of age and ineffectuality took possession of her. She could not sit still, and arose. As she stood looking out over the land something, perhaps the thought of never ceasing life as it expresses itself in the flow of the seasons, fixed her mind on the passing years. With a shiver of dread, she realized that for her the beauty and freshness of youth had passed. For the first time she felt that she had been cheated. She did not blame Ned Currie and did not know what to blame. Sadness swept over her. Dropping to her knees, she tried to pray, but instead of prayers words of protest came to her lips. "It is not going to come to me. I will never find happiness. Why do I tell myself lies?" she cried, and an odd sense of relief came with this, her first bold attempt to face the fear that had become a part of her everyday life.

In the year when Alice Hindman became twenty-five two things happened to disturb the dull uneventfulness of her days. Her mother married Bush Milton, the carriage painter of Winesburg, and she herself became a member of the Winesburg Methodist Church. Alice joined the church because she had become frightened by the loneliness of her position in life. Her mother's second marriage had emphasized her isolation. "I am becoming old and queer. If Ned comes he will not want me. In the city where he is living men are perpetually young. There is so much going on that they do not have time to grow old," she told herself with a grim little smile, and went resolutely about the business of becoming acquainted with people. Every Thursday evening when the store had closed she went to a prayer meeting in the basement of the church and on Sunday evening attended a meeting of an organization called The Epworth League.

When Will Hurley, a middle-aged man who clerked in a drug store and who also belonged to the church, offered to walk home with her she did not protest. "Of course I will not let him make a practice of being with me, but if he comes to see me once in a long time there can be no harm in that," she told herself, still determined in her loyalty to Ned Currie.

Without realizing what was happening, Alice was trying feebly at first, but with growing determination, to get a new hold upon life. Beside the drug clerk she walked in silence, but sometimes in the darkness as they went stolidly along she put out her hand and touched softly the folds of his coat. When he left her at the gate before her mother's house she did not go indoors, but stood for a moment by the door. She wanted to call to the drug clerk, to ask him to sit with her in the darkness on the porch before the house, but was afraid he would not understand. "It is not him that I want," she told herself; "I want to avoid being so much alone. If I am not careful I will grow unaccustomed to being with people."

. . .

During the early fall of her twenty-seventh year a passionate restlessness took possession of Alice. She could not bear to be in the company of the drug clerk, and when, in the evening, he came to walk with her she sent him away. Her mind became intensely active and when, weary from the long hours of standing behind the counter in the store, she went home and crawled into bed, she could not sleep. With staring eyes she looked into the darkness. Her imagination, like a child awakened from long sleep, played about the room. Deep within her there was something that would not be cheated by phantasies and that demanded some definite answer from life.

Alice took a pillow into her arms and held it tightly against her breasts. Getting out of bed, she arranged a blanket so that in the darkness it looked like a form lying between the sheets and, kneeling beside the bed, she caressed it, whispering words over and over, like a refrain. "Why doesn't something happen? Why am I left here alone?" she muttered. Although she sometimes thought of Ned Currie, she no longer depended on him. Her desire had grown vague. She did not want Ned Currie or any other man. She wanted to be loved, to have something answer the call that was growing louder and louder within her.

And then one night when it rained Alice had an adventure. It frightened and confused her. She had come home from the store at nine and found the house empty. Bush Milton had gone off to town and her mother to the house of a neighbor. Alice went upstairs to her room and undressed in the darkness. For a moment she stood by the window hearing the rain beat against the glass and then a strange desire took possession of her. Without stopping to think of what she intended to do, she ran downstairs through the dark house and out into the rain. As she stood on the little grass plot before the house and felt the cold rain on her body a mad desire to run naked through the streets took possession of her.

She thought that the rain would have some creative and wonderful effect on her body. Not for years had she felt so full of youth and courage. She wanted to leap and run, to cry out, to find some other lonely human and embrace him. On the brick sidewalk before the house a man stumbled homeward. Alice started to run. A wild, desperate mood took possession of her. "What do I care who it is. He is alone, and I will go to him," she thought; and then without stopping to consider the possible result of her madness, called softly. "Wait!"

she cried. "Don't go away. Whoever you are, you must wait."

The man on the sidewalk stopped and stood listening. He was an old man and somewhat deaf. Putting his hand to his mouth, he shouted: "What? What say?" he called.

Alice dropped to the ground and lay trembling. She was so frightened at the thought of what she had done that when the man had gone on his way she did not dare get to her feet, but crawled on hands and knees through the grass to the house. When she got to her own room she bolted the door and drew her dressing table across the doorway. Her body shook as with a chill and her hands trembled so that she had difficulty getting into her nightdress. When she got into bed she buried her face in the pillow and wept brokenheartedly. "What is the matter with me? I will do something dreadful if I am not careful," she thought, and turning her face to the wall, began trying to force herself to face bravely the fact that many people must live and die alone, even in Winesburg.

1919

Willa Sibert Cather

1876 · 1947

The secure position of Willa Cather among present-day American writers is the result of her allegiance to the belief that fiction is a form of art worth practicing with the utmost seriousness. To her it was not merely a business, the providing of entertainment to a magazine-reading public, or a means to the improvement of society. Like Henry James and Sarah Orne Jewett, to whom she acknowledged her indebtedness, she always thought of storytelling in qualitative terms and her work was a constant striving for perfection. In "The Novel Démeublé," first published in *The New Republic* for April 12, 1922, she expounded her doctrine that literary art is primarily a matter of selection and simplification, the learning of when to subordinate detail to the desired effect. The effects which she chiefly sought were in the realm of subtleties of character and situation. She was akin to James in her aims, but was perhaps more aware than he was of the importance of setting and of physical action; she was, in short, somewhat closer to tradition and on the whole more popular. Seldom if ever, however, did she compromise with her artistic conscience. It is easy to complain of her limited range and to question the ethical and social bases of her thinking, but no one is likely to deny her integrity.

Miss Cather was born in 1876 near Winchester, in the northern tip of Virginia. From her ninth to her nineteenth year, she was a Nebraskan, growing up in what was then a pioneer rural community, settled largely by Norwegian and Bohemian immigrants. After some tutoring at home she went to high school at Red Cloud, and then to the University of Nebraska, where she was graduated in 1895. By that time she had acquired a deep interest in good music, an enthusiasm for the work of Henry James, and a desire to write, heightened by some experience with newspaper work and a few appearances in the college magazine. Only gradually did she find her power as a writer. Her first published stories and poems appeared in 1900. She had then worked for five years on the Pittsburgh *Daily Leader.* Her first book, *April Twilights* (1903), a volume of poems, came out while she was teaching English in Allegheny High School. Her mood in these years was chiefly the familiar one of rebellion against the cultural bleakness of the small town and the small-town mind, later so fully exploited by Sinclair Lewis in *Main Street* and *Babbitt.* Her best-known short stories, "The Sculptor's Funeral," "A Wagner Matinée," and "Paul's Case," all collected in *The Troll Garden* (1905), utilize this mood. In 1906 she moved to New York City to work on *McClure's Magazine,* of which she was managing editor from 1908 until 1911.

It seems likely that the most important event of Miss Cather's years as editor was her connection with Sarah Orne Jewett, who advised her late in 1908 to find time and quiet to perfect her work if she wished her gifts to mature. Following this advice, Miss Cather resigned her editorship to write a novel. *Alexander's Bridge* (1912; previously serialized in *McClure's* as "Alexander's Masquerade") was imitative of Henry James in its London setting and mild ethical theme, but it was followed a year later by *O Pioneers!* in which Miss Cather returned to the immigrant folk she had known as a child. It and *My Ántonia* (1918) must be ranked with the finest of Middlewestern novels for their unforgettable central characters and their rich detail of pioneer life in Nebraska. With them and *The Song of the Lark* (1915), the story of a girl whose voice carried her from Colorado to the Metropolitan Opera Company, Miss Cather's reputation was firmly established. It has never since been in danger.

The remainder of Miss Cather's work consists of three collections of short stories (*Youth and the Bright Medusa,* 1920; *Obscure Destinies,* 1932; and *The Old Beauty and Others,* 1948), one volume of critical and reminiscent essays (*Not under Forty,* 1936), and eight relatively short novels (*One of Ours,* 1922, which won the Pulitzer Prize; *A Lost Lady,* 1923; *The Professor's House,* 1925; *My Mortal Enemy,* 1926; *Death Comes for the Archbishop,* 1927; *Shadows on the Rock,* 1931; *Lucy Gayheart,* 1935; and *Sapphira and the Slave Girl,* 1940). Each of the novels has its partisans; a number of them have been best sellers. As a whole they show admirable mastery of the novel form for the purposes which Miss Cather avowed, together with an increasing preoccupation with the lack of meaningful orderliness in the contemporary world. The ethical and social values which Miss Cather cherished appear to grow harder and harder to hang on to. She stood essentially for tradition and refinement, for art in life as well as in fiction, and it is not surprising that she turned more and more to the past and found Roman Catholicism the best of possible faiths. Sometimes, in troublous times, Miss Cather was more than a trifle sad that the simplicity of the old days is past.

The Novels and Stories of Willa Cather, Library Edition, 11 vols., Boston, 1937-1941 • E. K. Brown, Willa Cather: A Critical Biography, New York, 1953 • T. K. Whipple, Spokesmen: Modern Writers and American Life, New York, 1928 • Carl Van Doren, The American Novel, 1789-1939, Revised and Enlarged Edition, New York, 1940 • Maxwell Giesmar, The Last of the Provincials, Boston, 1947, 153-226 • Granville Hicks, "The Case Against Willa Cather," English Journal, November 1933, XXII, 703-710 • Lionel Trilling, "Willa Cather," The New Republic, February 10, 1937, XC, 10-13 • Letters of Sarah Orne Jewett, ed. Annie Fields, Boston, 1911

From • Obscure Destinies

Neighbour Rosicky

In "Neighbour Rosicky," the longest of the three stories in **Obscure Destinies** (1932), Miss Cather returned to the immigrant folk who had been her neighbors in her girlhood in Nebraska, of whom she has also written in **My Ántonia** and **O Pioneers!** Her respect for the basic values of rural life—security and humaneness and family solidarity—will be evident to any reader. The story is in her mature style, marked by restraint and a careful subordination of detail to the achievement of a mood. Like most of her later work this story makes clear her belief that the good life is well worth the living and that it can be achieved most readily by simplification. "Neighbour Rosicky" was written in New York in 1928.

When Doctor Burleigh told neighbour Rosicky he had a bad heart, Rosicky protested.

"So? No, I guess my heart was always pretty good. I got a little asthma, maybe. Just a awful short breath when I was pitchin' hay last summer, dat's all."

"Well now, Rosicky, if you know more about it than I do, what did you come to me for? It's your heart that makes you short of breath, I tell you. You're sixty-five years old, and you've always worked hard, and your heart's tired. You've got to be careful from now on, and you can't do heavy work any more. You've got five boys at home to do it for you."

The old farmer looked up at the Doctor with a gleam of amusement in his queer, triangular-shaped eyes. His eyes were large and lively, but the lids were caught up in the middle in a curious way, so that they formed a triangle. He did not look like a sick man. His brown face was creased but not wrinkled, he had a ruddy colour in his smooth-shaven cheeks and in his lips, under his long brown moustache. His hair was thin and ragged around his ears, but very little grey. His forehead, naturally high and crossed by deep parallel lines, now ran all the way up to his pointed crown. Rosicky's face had the habit of looking interested,—suggested a contented disposition and a reflective quality that was gay rather than grave. This gave him a certain detachment, the easy manner of an on-looker and observer.

"Well, I guess you ain't got no pills for a bad heart, Doctor Ed. I guess the only thing is fur me to git me a new one."

Doctor Burleigh swung round in his desk-chair and frowned at the old farmer. "I think if I were you I'd take a little care of the old one, Rosicky."

Rosicky shrugged. "Maybe I don't know how. I expect you mean fur me not to drink my coffee no more."

"I wouldn't, in your place. But you'll do as you choose about that. I've never yet been able to separate a Bohemian from his coffee or his pipe. I've quit trying. But the sure thing is you've got to cut out farm work. You can feed the stock and do chores about the barn, but you can't do anything in the fields that makes you short of breath."

"How about shelling corn?"

"Of course not!"

Rosicky considered with puckered brows.

"I can't make my heart go no longer'n it wants to, can I, Doctor Ed?"

"I think it's good for five or six years yet, maybe more, if you'll take the strain off it. Sit around the house and help Mary. If I had a good wife like yours, I'd want to stay around the house."

His patient chuckled. "It ain't no place fur a man. I don't like no old man hanging round the kitchen too much. An' my wife, she's a awful hard worker her own self."

"That's it; you can help her a little. My Lord, Rosicky, you are one of the few men I know who has a family he can get some comfort out of; happy dispositions, never quarrel among themselves, and they treat you right. I want to see you live a few years and enjoy them."

"Oh, they're good kids, all right," Rosicky assented.

The Doctor wrote him a prescription and asked him how his oldest son, Rudolph, who had married in the spring, was getting on. Rudolph had struck out for himself, on rented land. "And how's Polly? I was afraid Mary mightn't like an American daughter-in-law, but it seems to be working out all right."

"Yes, she's a fine girl. Dat widder woman bring her daughters up very nice. Polly got lots of spunk, an' she got some style, too. Da's nice, for young folks to have some style." Rosicky inclined his head gallantly. His voice and his twinkly smile were an affectionate compliment to his daughter-in-law.

"It looks like a storm, and you'd better be getting home before it comes. In town in the car?" Doctor Burleigh rose.

"No, I'm in de wagon. When you got five boys, you ain't got much chance to ride round in de Ford. I ain't much for cars, noway."

"Well, it's a good road out to your place; but I don't want you bumping around in a wagon much. And never again on a hay-rake, remember!"

Rosicky placed the Doctor's fee delicately behind the desk-telephone, looking the other way, as if this were an absent-minded gesture. He put on his plush

Reprinted from **Obscure Destinies** by Willa Cather, by permission of Alfred A. Knopf, Inc. • Copyright, 1932, by Willa Cather

cap and his corduroy jacket with a sheepskin collar, and went out.

The Doctor picked up his stethoscope and frowned at it as if he were seriously annoyed with the instrument. He wished it had been telling tales about some other man's heart, some old man who didn't look the Doctor in the eye so knowingly, or hold out such a warm brown hand when he said good-bye. Doctor Burleigh had been a poor boy in the country before he
10 went away to medical school; he had known Rosicky almost ever since he could remember, and he had a deep affection for Mrs. Rosicky.

Only last winter he had had such a good breakfast at Rosicky's, and that when he needed it. He had been out all night on a long, hard confinement case at Tom Marshall's,—a big rich farm where there was plenty of stock and plenty of feed and a great deal of expensive farm machinery of the newest model, and no comfort whatever. The woman had too many children and too
20 much work, and she was no manager. When the baby was born at last, and handed over to the assisting neighbour woman, and the mother was properly attended to, Burleigh refused any breakfast in that slovenly house, and drove his buggy—the snow was too deep for a car—eight miles to Anton Rosicky's place. He didn't know another farm-house where a man could get such a warm welcome, and such good strong coffee with rich cream. No wonder the old chap didn't want to give up his coffee!
30 He had driven in just when the boys had come back from the barn and were washing up for breakfast. The long table, covered with a bright oilcloth, was set out with dishes waiting for them, and the warm kitchen was full of the smell of coffee and hot biscuit and sausage. Five big handsome boys, running from twenty to twelve, all with what Burleigh called natural good manners,—they hadn't a bit of the painful self-consciousness he himself had to struggle with when he was a lad. One ran to put his horse away, another helped
40 him off with his fur coat and hung it up, and Josephine, the youngest child and the only daughter, quickly set another place under her mother's direction.

With Mary, to feed creatures was the natural expression of affection,—her chickens, the calves, her big hungry boys. It was a rare pleasure to feed a young man

whom she seldom saw and of whom she was as proud as if he belonged to her. Some country housekeepers would have stopped to spread a white cloth over the oilcloth, to change the thick cups and plates for their best china, and the wooden-handled knives for plated 50 ones. But not Mary.

"You must take us as you find us, Doctor Ed. I'd be glad to put out my good things for you if you was expected, but I'm glad to get you any way at all."

He knew she was glad,—she threw back her head and spoke out as if she were announcing him to the whole prairie. Rosicky hadn't said anything at all; he merely smiled his twinkling smile, put some more coal on the fire, and went into his own room to pour the Doctor a little drink in a medicine glass. When they 60 were all seated, he watched his wife's face from his end of the table and spoke to her in Czech. Then, with the instinct of politeness which seldom failed him, he turned to the Doctor and said slyly, "I was just tellin' her not to ask you no questions about Mrs. Marshall till you eat some breakfast. My wife, she's terrible fur to ask questions."

The boys laughed, and so did Mary. She watched the Doctor devour her biscuit and sausage, too much excited to eat anything herself. She drank her coffee and 70 sat taking in everything about her visitor. She had known him when he was a poor country boy, and was boastfully proud of his success, always saying: "What do people go to Omaha for, to see a doctor, when we got the best one in the State right here?" If Mary liked people at all, she felt physical pleasure in the sight of them, personal exultation in any good fortune that came to them. Burleigh didn't know many women like that, but he knew she was like that.

When his hunger was satisfied, he did, of course, have 80 to tell them about Mrs. Marshall, and he noticed what a friendly interest the boys took in the matter.

Rudolph, the oldest one (he was still living at home then), said: "The last time I was over there, she was lifting them big heavy milk-cans, and I knew she ought not to be doing it."

"Yes, Rudolph told me about that when he come home, and I said it wasn't right," Mary put in warmly. "It was all right for me to do them things up to the last, for I was terrible strong, but that woman's weakly." 90

And do you think she'll be able to nurse it, Ed?" She sometimes forgot to give him the title she was so proud of. "And to think of your being up all night and then not able to get a decent breakfast! I don't know what's the matter with such people."

"Why, mother," said one of the boys, "if Doctor Ed had got breakfast there, we wouldn't have him here. So you ought to be glad."

10 "He knows I'm glad to have him, John, any time. But I'm sorry for that poor woman, how bad she'll feel the Doctor had to go away in the cold without his breakfast."

"I wish I'd been in practice when these were getting born." The doctor looked down the row of close-clipped heads. "I missed some good breakfasts by not being."

The boys began to laugh at their mother because she flushed so red, but she stood her ground and threw up her head. "I don't care, you wouldn't have got away from this house without breakfast. No doctor ever did. 20 I'd have had something ready fixed that Anton could warm up for you."

The boys laughed harder than ever, and exclaimed at her: "I'll bet you would!" "She would, that!"

"Father, did you get breakfast for the doctor when we were born?"

"Yes, and he used to bring me my breakfast, too, mighty nice. I was always awful hungry!" Mary admitted with a guilty laugh.

While the boys were getting the Doctor's horse, he 30 went to the window to examine the house plants. "What do you do to your geraniums to keep them blooming all winter, Mary? I never pass this house that from the road I don't see your windows full of flowers."

She snapped off a dark red one, and a ruffled new green leaf, and put them in his buttonhole. "There, that looks better. You look too solemn for a young man, Ed. Why don't you git married? I'm worried about you. Settin' at breakfast, I looked at you real hard, and I 40 seen you've got some grey hairs already."

"Oh, yes! They're coming. Maybe they'd come faster if I married."

"Don't talk so. You'll ruin your health eating at the hotel. I could send your wife a nice loaf of nut bread, if you only had one. I don't like to see a young

man getting grey. I'll tell you something, Ed; you make some strong black tea and keep it handy in a bowl, and every morning just brush it into your hair, an' it'll keep the grey from showin' much. That's the way I do!"

50 Sometimes the Doctor heard the gossipers in the drugstore wondering why Rosicky didn't get on faster. He was industrious, and so were his boys, but they were rather free and easy, weren't pushers, and they didn't always show good judgment. They were comfortable, they were out of debt, but they didn't get much ahead. Maybe, Doctor Burleigh reflected, people as generous and warmhearted and affectionate as the Rosickys never got ahead much; maybe you could not enjoy your life and put it into the bank, too.

II

60 When Rosicky left Doctor Burleigh's office, he went into the farm-implement store to light his pipe and put on his glasses and read over the list Mary had given him. Then he went into the general merchandise place next door and stood about until the pretty girl with the plucked eyebrows, who always waited on him, was free. Those eyebrows, two thin India-ink strokes, amused him, because he remembered how they used to be. Rosicky always prolonged his shopping by a little joking; the girl knew the old fellow admired her, and she liked to chaff with him. 70

"Seems to me about every other week you buy ticking, Mr. Rosicky, and always the best quality," she remarked as she measured off the heavy bolt with red stripes.

"You see, my wife is always makin' goose-fedder pillows, an de' thin stuff don't hold in dem little downfedders."

"You must have lots of pillows at your house."

"Sure. She makes quilts of dem, too. We sleeps easy. Now she's makin' a fedder quilt for my son's wife. 80 You know Polly, that married my Rudolph. How much my bill, Miss Pearl?"

"Eight eighty-five."

"Chust make it nine, and put in some candy fur de women."

"As usual. I never did see a man buy so much candy for his wife. First thing you know, she'll be getting too fat."

"I'd like dat. I ain't much fur all dem slim women like what de style is now."

"That's one for me, I suppose, Mr. Bohunk!" Pearl sniffed and elevated her India-ink strokes.

When Rosicky went out to his wagon, it was beginning to snow,—the first snow of the season, and he was glad to see it. He rattled out of town and along the highway through a wonderfully rich stretch of country, the finest farms in the county. He admired this High Prairie, as it was called, and always liked to drive through it. His own place lay in a rougher territory, where there was some clay in the soil and it was not so productive. When he bought his land, he hadn't the money to buy on High Prairie; so he told his boys, when they grumbled, that if their land hadn't some clay in it, they wouldn't own it at all. All the same, he enjoyed looking at these fine farms, as he enjoyed looking at a prize bull.

After he had gone eight miles, he came to the graveyard, which lay just at the edge of his own hay-land. There he stopped his horses and sat still on his wagon seat, looking about at the snowfall. Over yonder on the hill he could see his own house, crouching low, with the clump of orchard behind and the windmill before, and all down the gentle hill-slope the rows of pale gold cornstalks stood out against the white field. The snow was falling over the cornfield and the pasture and the hay-land, steadily, with very little wind,—a nice dry snow. The graveyard had only a light wire fence about it and was all overgrown with long red grass. The fine snow, settling into this red grass and upon the few little evergreens and the headstones, looked very pretty.

It was a nice graveyard, Rosicky reflected, sort of snug and homelike, not cramped or mournful,—a big sweep all around it. A man could lie down in the long grass and see the complete arch of the sky over him, hear the wagons go by; in summer the mowing-machine rattled right up to the wire fence. And it was so near home. Over there across the cornstalks his own roof and windmill looked so good to him that he promised himself to mind the Doctor and take care of himself. He was awful fond of his place, he admitted. He wasn't anxious to leave it. And it was a comfort to think that he would never have to go farther than the edge of his own hayfield. The snow, falling over his barnyard and the graveyard, seemed to draw things together like. And

they were all old neighbours in the graveyard, most of them friends; there was nothing to feel awkward or embarrassed about. Embarrassment was the most disagreeable feeling Rosicky knew. He didn't often have it,—only with certain people whom he didn't understand at all.

Well, it was a nice snowstorm; a fine sight to see the snow falling so quietly and graciously over so much open country. On his cap and shoulders, on the horses' backs and manes, light, delicate, mysterious it fell; and with it a dry cool fragrance was released into the air. It meant rest for vegetation and men and beasts, for the ground itself; a season of long nights for sleep, leisurely breakfasts, peace by the fire. This and much more went through Rosicky's mind, but he merely told himself that winter was coming, clucked to his horses, and drove on.

When he reached home, John, the youngest boy, ran out to put away his team for him, and he met Mary coming up from the outside cellar with her apron full of carrots. They went into the house together. On the table, covered with oilcloth figured with clusters of blue grapes, a place was set, and he smelled hot coffee-cake of some kind. Anton never lunched in town; he thought that extravagant, and anyhow he didn't like the food. So Mary always had something ready for him when he got home.

After he was settled in his chair, stirring his coffee in a big cup, Mary took out of the oven a pan of *kolache* stuffed with apricots, examined them anxiously to see whether they had got too dry, put them beside his plate, and then sat down opposite him.

Rosicky asked her in Czech if she wasn't going to have any coffee.

She replied in English, as being somehow the right language for transacting business: "Now what did Doctor Ed say, Anton? You tell me just what."

"He said I was to tell you some compliments, but I forgot 'em." Rosicky's eyes twinkled.

"About you, I mean. What did he say about your asthma?"

"He says I ain't got no asthma." Rosicky took one of the little rolls in his broad brown fingers. The thickened nail of his right thumb told the story of his past.

"Well, what is the matter? And don't try to put me off."

"He don't say nothing much, only I'm a little older, and my heart ain't so good like it used to be."

Mary started and brushed her hair back from her temples with both hands as if she were a little out of her mind. From the way she glared, she might have been in a rage with him.

"He says there's something the matter with your heart? Doctor Ed says so?"

"Now don't yell at me like I was a hog in de garden, Mary. You know I always did like to hear a woman talk soft. He didn't say anything de matter wid my heart, only it ain't so young like it used to be, an' he tell me not to pitch hay or run de corn-sheller."

Mary wanted to jump up, but she sat still. She admired the way he never under any circumstances raised his voice or spoke roughly. He was city-bred, and she was country-bred; she often said she wanted her boys to have their papa's nice ways.

"You never have no pain there, do you? It's your breathing and your stomach that's been wrong. I wouldn't believe nobody but Doctor Ed about it. I guess I'll go see him myself. Didn't he give you no advice?"

"Chust to take it easy like, an' stay round de house dis winter. I guess you got some carpenter work for me to do. I kin make some new shelves for you, and I want dis long time to build a closet in de boys' room and make dem two little fellers keep dere clo'es hung up."

Rosicky drank his coffee from time to time, while he considered. His moustache was of the soft long variety and came down over his mouth like the teeth of a buggy-rake over a bundle of hay. Each time he put down his cup, he ran his blue handkerchief over his lips. When he took a drink of water, he managed very neatly with the back of his hand.

Mary sat watching him intently, trying to find any change in his face. It is hard to see anyone who has become like your own body to you. Yes, his hair had got thin, and his high forehead had deep lines running from left to right. But his neck, always clean-shaved except in the busiest seasons, was not loose or baggy. It was burned a dark reddish brown, and there were deep creases in it, but it looked firm and full of blood. His cheeks had a good colour. On either side of his mouth there was a half-moon down the length of his cheek, not wrinkles, but two lines that had come there from his habitual expression. He was shorter and broader than when she married him; his back had grown broad and curved, a good deal like the shell of an old turtle, and his arms and legs were short.

He was fifteen years older than Mary, but she had hardly ever thought about it before. He was her man, and the kind of man she liked. She was rough, and he was gentle,—city-bred, as she always said. They had been shipmates on a rough voyage and had stood by each other in trying times. Life had gone well with them because, at bottom, they had the same ideas about life. They agreed, without discussion, as to what was most important and what was secondary. They didn't often exchange opinions, even in Czech,—it was as if they had thought the same thought together. A good deal had to be sacrificed and thrown overboard in a hard life like theirs, and they had never disagreed as to the things that could go. It had been a hard life, and a soft life, too. There wasn't anything brutal in the short, broad-backed man with the three-cornered eyes and the forehead that went on to the top of his skull. He was a city man, a gentle man, and though he had married a rough farm girl, he had never touched her without gentleness.

They had been at one accord not to hurry through life, not to be always skimping and saving. They saw their neighbours buy more land and feed more stock than they did, without discontent. Once when the creamery agent came to the Rosickys to persuade them to sell him their cream, he told them how much money the Fasslers, their nearest neighbours, had made on their cream last year.

"Yes," said Mary, "and look at them Fassler children! Pale, pinched little things, they look like skimmed milk. I had rather put some colour into my children's faces than put money into the bank."

The agent shrugged and turned to Anton.

"I guess we'll do like she says," said Rosicky.

III

Mary very soon got into town to see Doctor Ed, and then she had a talk with her boys and set a guard over Rosicky. Even John, the youngest, had his father on his mind. If Rosicky went to throw hay down from the loft, one of the boys ran up the ladder and took the fork from him. He sometimes complained that though he was getting to be an old man, he wasn't an old woman yet.

That winter he stayed in the house in the afternoons and carpentered, or sat in the chair between the window full of plants and the wooden bench where the two pails of drinking-water stood. This spot was called "Father's corner," though it was not a corner at all. He had a shelf there, where he kept his Bohemian papers and his pipes and tobacco, and his shears and needles and thread and tailor's thimble. Having been a tailor in his youth, he couldn't bear to see a woman patching at his clothes, or at the boys'. He liked tailoring, and always patched all the overalls and jackets and work shirts. Occasionally he made over a pair of pants one of the older boys had outgrown, for the little fellow.

While he sewed, he let his mind run back over his life. He had a good deal to remember, really; life in three countries. The only part of his youth he didn't like to remember was the two years he had spent in London, in Cheapside, working for a German tailor who was wretchedly poor. Those days, when he was nearly always hungry, when his clothes were dropping off him for dirt, and the sound of a strange language kept him in continual bewilderment, had left a sore spot in his mind that wouldn't bear touching.

He was twenty when he landed at Castle Garden in New York, and he had a protector who got him work in a tailor shop in Vesey Street, down near the Washington Market. He looked upon that part of his life as very happy. He became a good workman, he was industrious, and his wages were increased from time to time. He minded his own business and envied nobody's good fortune. He went to night school and learned to read English. He often did overtime work and was well paid for it, but somehow he never saved anything. He couldn't refuse a loan to a friend, and he was self-indulgent. He liked a good dinner, and a little went for beer, a little for tobacco; a good deal went to the girls. He often stood through an opera on Saturday nights; he could get standing-room for a dollar. Those were the great days of opera in New York, and it gave a fellow something to think about for the rest of the week. Rosicky had a quick ear, and a childish love of all the stage splendour; the scenery, the costumes, the ballet. He usually went with a chum, and after the performance they had beer and maybe some oysters somewhere. It was a fine life; for the first five years or so it satisfied him completely. He was never hungry or cold or dirty, and everything amused him: a fire, a dog fight, a parade, a storm, a ferry ride. He thought New York the finest, richest, friendliest city in the world.

Moreover, he had what he called a happy home life. Very near the tailor shop was a small furniture-factory, where an old Austrian, Loeffler, employed a few skilled men and made unusual furniture, most of it to order, for the rich German housewives uptown. The top floor of Loeffler's five-story factory was a loft, where he kept his choice lumber and stored the odd pieces of furniture left on his hands. One of the young workmen he employed was a Czech, and he and Rosicky became fast friends. They persuaded Loeffler to let them have a sleeping-room in one corner of the loft. They bought good beds and bedding and had their pick of the furniture kept up there. The loft was low-pitched, but light and airy, full of windows, and good-smelling by reason of the fine lumber put up there to season. Old Loeffler used to go down to the docks and buy wood from South America and the East from the sea captains. The young men were as foolish about their house as a bridal pair. Zichec, the young cabinet-maker, devised every sort of convenience, and Rosicky kept their clothes in order. At night and on Sundays, when the quiver of machinery underneath was still, it was the quietest place in the world, and on summer nights all the sea winds blew in. Zichec often practiced on his flute in the evening. They were both fond of music and went to the opera together. Rosicky thought he wanted to live like that forever.

But as the years passed, all alike, he began to get a little restless. When spring came round, he would begin to feel fretted, and he got to drinking. He was likely to drink too much of a Saturday night. On Sunday he was languid and heavy, getting over his spree. On Monday he plunged into work again. So he never had time to figure out what ailed him, though he knew something did. When the grass turned green in Park Place, and the lilac hedge at the back of Trinity churchyard put out its blossoms, he was tormented by a longing to run away. That was why he drank too much; to get a temporary illusion of freedom and wide horizons.

Rosicky, the old Rosicky, could remember as if it were yesterday the day when the young Rosicky found out what was the matter with him. It was on a Fourth of July afternoon, and he was sitting in Park Place in the sun. The lower part of New York was empty. Wall Street, Liberty Street, Broadway, all empty. So much stone and asphalt with nothing going on, so many empty windows. The emptiness was intense, like the stillness in a great factory when the machinery stops and the belts and bands cease running. It was too great a change, it took all the strength out of one. Those blank buildings, without the stream of life pouring through them, were like empty jails. It struck young Rosicky that this was the trouble with big cities; they built you in from the earth itself, cemented you away from any contact with the ground. You lived in an unnatural world, like the fish in an aquarium, who were probably much more comfortable than they ever were in the sea.

On that very day he began to think seriously about the articles he had read in the Bohemian papers, describing prosperous Czech farming communities in the West. He believed he would like to go out there as a farmhand; it was hardly possible that he could ever have land of his own. His people had always been workmen; his father and grandfather had worked in shops. His mother's parents had lived in the country, but they rented their farm and had a hard time to get along. Nobody in his family had ever owned any land,—that belonged to a different station of life altogether. Anton's mother died when he was little, and he was sent into the country to her parents. He stayed with them until he was twelve, and formed those ties with the earth and the farm animals and growing things which are never made at all unless they are made early. After his grandfather died, he went back to live with his father and stepmother, but she was very hard on him, and his father helped him to get passage to London.

After that Fourth of July day in Park Place, the desire to return to the country never left him. To work on another man's farm would be all he asked; to see the sun rise and set and to plant things and watch them grow. He was a very simple man. He was like a tree that has not many roots, but one tap-root that goes down deep. He subscribed for a Bohemian paper printed in Chicago, then for one printed in Omaha. His mind got farther and farther west. He began to save a little money to buy his liberty. When he was thirty-five, there was a great meeting in New York of Bohemian athletic societies, and Rosicky left the tailor shop and

went home with the Omaha delegates to try his fortune in another part of the world.

IV

Perhaps the fact that his own youth was well over before he began to have a family was one reason why Rosicky was so fond of his boys. He had almost a grandfather's indulgence for them. He had never had to worry about any of them—except, just now, a little about Rudolph.

On Saturday night the boys always piled into the Ford, took little Josephine, and went to town to the moving-picture show. One Saturday morning they were talking at the breakfast table about starting early that evening, so that they would have an hour or so to see the Christmas things in the stores before the show began. Rosicky looked down the table.

"I hope you boys ain't disappointed, but I want you to let me have de car tonight. Maybe some of you can go in with de neighbours."

Their faces fell. They worked hard all week, and they were still like children. A new jack-knife or a box of candy pleased the older ones as much as the little fellow.

"If you and Mother are going to town," Frank said, "maybe you could take a couple of us along with you, anyway."

"No, I want to take de car down to Rudolph's, and let him an' Polly go in to de show. She don't git into town enough, an' I'm afraid she's gittin' lonesome, an' he can't afford no car yet."

That settled it. The boys were a good deal dashed. Their father took another piece of apple-cake and went on: "Maybe next Saturday night de two little fellers can go along wid dem."

"Oh, is Rudolph going to have the car every Saturday night?"

Rosicky did not reply at once; then he began to speak seriously: "Listen, boys; Polly ain't lookin' so good. I don't like to see nobody lookin' sad. It comes hard fur a town girl to be a farmer's wife. I don't want no trouble to start in Rudolph's family. When it starts, it ain't so easy to stop. An American girl don't git used to our ways all at once. I like to tell Polly she and Rudolph can have the car every Saturday night till after New Year's, if it's all right with you boys."

Neighbour Rosicky 1027

"Sure it's all right, Papa," Mary cut in. "And it's good you thought about that. Town girls is used to more than country girls. I lay awake nights, scared she'll make Rudolph discontented with the farm."

The boys put as good a face on it as they could. They surely looked forward to their Saturday nights in town. That evening Rosicky drove the car the half-mile down the road to Rudolph's new, bare little house.

Polly was in a short-sleeved gingham dress, clearing
10 away the supper dishes. She was a trim, slim little thing, with blue eyes and shingled yellow hair, and her eyebrows were reduced to a mere brush-stroke, like Miss Pearl's.

"Good-evening, Mr. Rosicky. Rudolph's at the barn, I guess." She never called him father, or Mary mother. She was sensitive about having married a foreigner. She never in the world would have done it if Rudolph hadn't been such a handsome, persuasive fellow and such a gallant lover. He had graduated in her class in the
20 high school in town, and their friendship began in the ninth grade.

Rosicky went in, though he wasn't exactly asked. "My boys ain't goin' to town to-night, an' I brought de car over fur you two to go in to de picture show."

Polly, carrying dishes to the sink, looked over her shoulder at him. "Thank you. But I'm late with my work tonight, and pretty tired. Maybe Rudolph would like to go in with you."

"Oh, I don't go to de shows! I'm too old-fashioned.
30 You won't feel so tired after you ride in de air a ways. It's a nice clear night, an' it ain't cold. You go an' fix yourself up, Polly, an' I'll wash de dishes an' leave everything nice fur you."

Polly blushed and tossed her bob. "I couldn't let you do that, Mr. Rosicky. I wouldn't think of it."

Rosicky said nothing. He found a bib apron on a nail behind the kitchen door. He slipped it over his head and then took Polly by her two elbows and pushed her gently toward the door of her own room. "I washed
40 up de kitchen many times for my wife, when de babies was sick or somethin'. You go an' make yourself look nice. I like you to look prettier'n any of dem town girls when you go in. De young folks must have some fun, an' I'm goin' to look out fur you, Polly."

That kind, reassuring grip on her elbows, the old man's funny bright eyes, made Polly want to drop her head on his shoulder for a second. She restrained her-self, but she lingered in his grasp at the door of her room, murmuring tearfully: "You always lived in the city when you were young, didn't you? Don't you ever
50 get lonesome out here?"

As she turned round to him, her hand fell naturally into his, and he stood holding it and smiling into her face with his peculiar, knowing, indulgent smile without a shadow of reproach in it. "Dem big cities is all right fur de rich, but dey is terrible hard fur de poor."

"I don't know. Sometimes I think I'd like to take a chance. You lived in New York, didn't you?"

"An' London. Da's bigger still. I learned my trade dere. Here's Rudolph comin', you better hurry."
60

"Will you tell me about London sometime?"

"Maybe. Only I ain't no talker, Polly. Run an' dress yourself up."

The bedroom door closed behind her, and Rudolph came in from the outside, looking anxious. He had seen the car and was sorry any of his family should come just then. Supper hadn't been a very pleasant occasion. Halting in the doorway, he saw his father in a kitchen apron, carrying dishes to the sink. He flushed crimson and something flashed in his eye.
70 Rosicky held up a warning finger.

"I brought de car over fur you an' Polly to go to de picture show, an' I made her let me finish here so you won't be late. You go put on a clean shirt, quick!"

"But don't the boys want the car, father?"

"Not tonight dey don't." Rosicky fumbled under his apron and found his pants pocket. He took out a silver dollar and said in a hurried whisper: "You go an' buy dat girl some ice cream an' candy tonight, like you was courtin'. She's awful good friends wid me."
80

Rudolph was very short of cash, but he took the money as if it hurt him. There had been a crop failure all over the country. He had more than once been sorry he'd married this year.

In a few minutes the young people came out, looking clean and a little stiff. Rosicky hurried them off, and then he took his own time with the dishes. He scoured the pots and pans and put away the milk and swept the kitchen. He put some coal in the stove and shut off the draughts, so the place would be warm for them
90 when they got home late at night. Then he sat down and had a pipe and listened to the clock tick.

Generally speaking, marrying an American girl was certainly a risk. A Czech should marry a Czech. It was lucky that Polly was the daughter of a poor widow woman; Rudolph was proud, and if she had a prosperous family to throw up at him, they could never make it go. Polly was one of four sisters, and they all worked; one was book-keeper in the bank, one taught music, and Polly and her younger sister had been clerks, like Miss Pearl. All four of them were musical, had pretty voices, and sang in the Methodist choir, which the eldest sister directed.

Polly missed the sociability of a store position. She missed the choir, and the company of her sisters. She didn't dislike housework, but she disliked so much of it. Rosicky was a little anxious about this pair. He was afraid Polly would grow so discontented that Rudy would quit the farm and take a factory job in Omaha. He had worked for a winter up there, two years ago, to get money to marry on. He had done very well, and they would always take him back at the stockyards. But to Rosicky that meant the end of everything for his son. To be a landless man was to be a wage-earner, a slave, all your life; to have nothing, to be nothing.

Rosicky thought he would come over and do a little carpentering for Polly after the New Year. He guessed she needed jollying. Rudolph was a serious sort of chap, serious in love and serious about his work.

Rosicky shook out his pipe and walked home across the fields. Ahead of him the lamplight shone from his kitchen windows. Suppose he were still in a tailor shop on Vesey Street, with a bunch of pale, narrow-chested sons working on machines, all coming home tired and sullen to eat supper in a kitchen that was a parlour also; with another crowded, angry family quarrelling just across the dumb-waiter shaft, and squeaking pulleys at the windows where dirty washings hung on dirty lines above a court full of old brooms and mops and ash-cans. . . .

He stopped by the windmill to look up at the frosty winter stars and draw a long breath before he went inside. That kitchen with the shining windows was dear to him; but the sleeping fields and bright stars and the noble darkness were dearer still.

V

On the day before Christmas the weather set in very cold; no snow, but a bitter, biting wind that whistled and sang over the flat land and lashed one's face like fine wires. There was baking going on in the Rosicky kitchen all day, and Rosicky sat inside, making over a coat that Albert had outgrown into an overcoat for John. Mary had a big red geranium in bloom for Christmas, and a row of Jerusalem cherry trees, full of berries. It was the first year she had ever grown these; Doctor Ed brought her the seeds from Omaha when he went to some medical convention. They reminded Rosicky of plants he had seen in England; and all afternoon, as he stitched, he sat thinking about those two years in London, which his mind usually shrank from even after all this while.

He was a lad of eighteen when he dropped down into London, with no money and no connexions except the address of a cousin who was supposed to be working at a confectioner's. When he went to the pastry shop, however, he found that the cousin had gone to America. Anton tramped the streets for several days, sleeping in doorways and on the Embankment, until he was in utter despair. He knew no English, and the sound of the strange language all about him confused him. By chance he met a poor German tailor who had learned his trade in Vienna, and could speak a little Czech. This tailor, Lifschnitz, kept a repair shop in a Cheapside basement, underneath a cobbler. He didn't much need an apprentice, but he was sorry for the boy and took him in for no wages but his keep and what he could pick up. The pickings were supposed to be coppers given you when you took work home to a customer. But most of the customers called for their clothes themselves, and the coppers that came Anton's way were very few. He had, however, a place to sleep. The tailor's family lived upstairs in three rooms; a kitchen, a bedroom, where Lifschnitz and his wife and five children slept, and a living-room. Two corners of this living-room were curtained off for lodgers; in one Rosicky slept on an old horsehair sofa, with a feather quilt to wrap himself in. The other corner was rented to a wretched, dirty boy, who was studying the violin. He actually practised there. Rosicky was dirty, too. There was no way to be anything else. Mrs. Lifschnitz got the water she cooked and washed with from a pump in a brick court, four flights down. There were bugs in the place, and multitudes of fleas, though the poor woman did the best she could. Rosicky knew she often went empty to give another potato or a spoonful of dripping to the two hungry, sad-eyed boys who lodged with her. He used to think he would never get out of there, never get a clean shirt to his back again. What would he do, he wondered, when his clothes actually dropped to pieces and the worn cloth wouldn't hold patches any longer?

It was still early when the old farmer put aside his sewing and his recollections. The sky had been a dark grey all day, with not a gleam of sun, and the light failed at four o'clock. He went to shave and change his shirt while the turkey was roasting. Rudolph and Polly were coming over for supper.

After supper they sat round in the kitchen, and the younger boys were saying how sorry they were it hadn't snowed. Everybody was sorry. They wanted a deep snow that would lie long and keep the wheat warm, and leave the ground soaked when it melted.

"Yes, sir!" Rudolph broke out fiercely; "if we have another dry year like last year, there's going to be hard times in this country."

Rosicky filled his pipe. "You boys don't know what hard times is. You don't owe nobody, you got plenty to eat an' keep warm, an' plenty water to keep clean. When you got them, you can't have it very hard."

Rudolph frowned, opened and shut his big right hand, and dropped it clenched upon his knee. "I've got to have a good deal more than that, Father, or I'll quit this farming gamble. I can always make good wages railroading or at the packing house, and be sure of my money."

"Maybe so," his father answered dryly.

Mary, who had just come in from the pantry and was wiping her hands on the roller towel, thought Rudy and his father were getting too serious. She brought her darning-basket and sat down in the middle of the group.

"I ain't much afraid of hard times, Rudy," she said heartily. "We've had a plenty, but we've always come through. Your father wouldn't never take nothing very hard, not even hard times. I got a mind to tell you a story on him. Maybe you boys can't hardly remember the year we had that terrible hot wind, that burned everything up on the Fourth of July? All the corn an' the gardens. An' that was in the days when we didn't have alfalfa yet,—I guess it wasn't invented.

"Well, that very day your father was out cultivatin' corn, and I was here in the kitchen makin' plum pre-
serves. We had bushels of plums that year. I noticed it was terrible hot, but it's always hot in the kitchen when you're preservin', an' I was too busy with my plums to mind. Anton come in from the field about three o'clock, an' I asked him what was the matter.

"'Nothin',' he says, 'but it's pretty hot, an' I think I won't work no more today.' He stood round for a few minutes, an' then he says: 'Ain't you near through? I want you should git up a nice supper for us tonight. It's Fourth of July.'

"I told him to git along, that I was right in the middle of preservin', but the plums would taste good on hot biscuit. 'I'm goin' to have fried chicken, too,' he says, and he went off an' killed a couple. You three oldest boys was little fellers, playin' round outside, real hot an' sweaty, an' your father took you to the horse tank down by the windmill an' took off your clothes an' put you in. Them two box-elder trees was little then, but they made shade over the tank. Then he took off all his own clothes, an' got in with you. While he was playin' in the water with you, the Methodist preacher drove into our place to say how all the neighbours was goin' to meet at the schoolhouse that night, to pray for rain. He drove right to the windmill, of course, and there was your father and you three with no clothes on. I was in the kitchen door, an' I had to laugh, for the preacher acted like he ain't never seen a naked man before. He surely was embarrassed, an' your father couldn't git to his clothes; they was all hangin' up on the windmill to let the sweat dry out of 'em. So he laid in the tank where he was, an' put one of you boys on top of him to cover him up a little, an' talked to the preacher.

"When you got through playin' in the water, he put clean clothes on you and a clean shirt on himself, and by that time I'd begun to get supper. He says: 'It's too hot in here to eat comfortable. Let's have a picnic in the orchard. We'll eat our supper behind the mulberry hedge, under them linden trees.'

"So he carried our supper down, an' a bottle of my wild-grape wine, an' everything tasted good, I can tell you. The wind got cooler as the sun was goin' down, and it turned out pleasant, only I noticed how the leaves was curled up on the linden trees. That made me think, an' I asked your father if that hot wind all day hadn't been terrible hard on the gardens an' the corn.

"'Corn,' he says, 'there ain't no corn.'

"'What you talkin' about?' I said. 'Ain't we got forty acres?'

"'We ain't got an ear,' he says, 'nor nobody else ain't got none. All the corn in this country was cooked by three o'clock today, like you'd roasted it in an oven.'

"'You mean you won't get no crop at all?' I asked him. I couldn't believe it, after he'd worked so hard.

"'No crop this year,' he says. 'That's why we're havin' a picnic. We might as well enjoy what we got.'

"An' that's how your father behaved, when all the neighbours was so discouraged they couldn't look you in the face. An' we enjoyed ourselves that year, poor as we was, an' our neighbours wasn't a bit better off for bein' miserable. Some of 'em grieved till they got poor digestions and couldn't relish what they did have."

The younger boys said they thought their father had the best of it. But Rudolph was thinking that, all the same, the neighbours had managed to get ahead more, in the fifteen years since that time. There must be something wrong about his father's way of doing things. He wished he knew what was going on in the back of Polly's mind. He knew she liked his father, but he knew, too, that she was afraid of something. When his mother sent over coffee-cake or prune tarts or a loaf of fresh bread, Polly seemed to regard them with a certain suspicion. When she observed to him that his brothers had nice manners, her tone implied that it was remarkable they should have. With his mother she was stiff and on her guard. Mary's hearty frankness and gusts of good humour irritated her. Polly was afraid of being unusual or conspicuous in any way, of being "ordinary," as she said!

When Mary had finished her story, Rosicky laid aside his pipe.

"You boys like me to tell you about some of dem hard times I been through in London?" Warmly encouraged, he sat rubbing his forehead along the deep creases. It was bothersome to tell a long story in English (he nearly always talked to the boys in Czech), but he wanted Polly to hear this one.

"Well, you know about dat tailor shop I worked in in London? I had one Christmas dere I ain't never forgot. Times was awful bad before Christmas; de boss ain't got much work, an' have it awful hard to pay his rent. It ain't so much fun, bein' poor in a big city like London, I'll say! All de windows is full of good t'ings to eat, an' all de pushcarts in de streets is full, an' you smell 'em all de time, an' you ain't got no money,—not a damn bit. I didn't mind de cold so much, though I didn't have no overcoat, chust a short jacket I'd outgrowed so it wouldn't meet on me, an' my hands was chapped raw. But I always had a good appetite, like you all know, an' de sight of dem pork pies in de windows was awful fur me!

"Day before Christmas was terrible foggy dat year, an' dat fog gits into your bones and makes you all damp like. Mrs. Lifschnitz didn't give us nothin' but a little bread an' drippin' for supper, because she was savin' to try for to give us a good dinner on Christmas Day. After supper de boss say I can go an' enjoy myself, so I went into de streets to listen to de Christmas singers. Dey sing old songs an' make very nice music, an' I run round after dem a good ways, till I got awful hungry. I t'ink maybe if I go home, I can sleep till morning an' forgit my belly.

"I went into my corner real quiet, and roll up in my fedder quilt. But I ain't got my head down, till I smell somet'ing good. Seem like it git stronger an' stronger, an' I can't git to sleep noway. I can't understand dat smell. Dere was a gas light in a hall across de court, dat always shine in at my window a little. I got up an' look round. I got a little wooden box in my corner fur a stool, 'cause I ain't got no chair. I picks up dat box, and under it dere is a roast goose on a platter! I can't believe my eyes. I carry it to de window where de light comes in, an' touch it and smell it to find out, an' den I taste it to be sure. I say, I will eat chust one little bite of dat goose, so I can go to sleep, and tomorrow I won't eat none at all. But I tell you, boys, when I stop, one half of dat goose was gone!"

The narrator bowed his head, and the boys shouted. But little Josephine slipped behind his chair and kissed him on the neck beneath his ear.

"Poor little Papa, I don't want him to be hungry!"

"Da's long ago, child. I ain't never been hungry since I had your mudder to cook fur me."

"Go on and tell us the rest, please," said Polly.

"Well, when I come to realize what I done, of course, I felt terrible. I felt better in de stomach, but very bad in de heart. I set on my bed wid dat platter on my knees, an' it all come to me; how hard dat poor woman save to buy dat goose, and how she get some neighbour to cook it dat got more fire, an' how she put it in my corner to keep it away from dem hungry children. Dey was an old carpet hung up to shut my corner off, an' de children wasn't allowed to go in dere. An' I know she put it in my corner because she trust me more'n she did de violin boy. I can't stand it to face her after I spoil de Christmas. So I put on my shoes and go out into de city. I tell myself I better throw myself in de river; but I guess I ain't dat kind of a boy.

"It was after twelve o'clock, an' terrible cold, an' I start out to walk about London all night. I walk along de river awhile, but dey was lots of drunks all along; men, and women too. I chust move along to keep away from the police. I git onto de Strand, an' den over to New Oxford Street, where dere was a big German restaurant on de ground floor, wid big windows all fixed up fine, an' I could see de people havin' parties inside. While I was lookin' in, two men and two ladies come out, laughin' and talkin' and feelin' happy about all dey been eatin' an' drinkin', and dey was speakin' Czech,—not like de Austrians, but like de home folks talk it.

"I guess I went crazy, an' I done what I ain't never done before nor since. I went right up to dem gay people an' begun to beg dem: 'Fellow countrymen, for God's sake give me money enough to buy a goose!'

"Dey laugh, of course, but de ladies speak awful kind to me, an' dey take me back into de restaurant and give me hot coffee and cakes, an' make me tell all about how I happened to come to London, an' what I was doin' dere. Dey take my name and where I work down on paper, an' both of dem ladies give me ten shillings.

"De big market at Covent Garden ain't very far away, an' by dat time it was open. I go dere an' buy a big goose an' some pork pies, an' potatoes and onions, an' cakes an' oranges fur de children,—all I could carry! When I git home, everybody is still asleep. I pile all I bought on de kitchen table, an' go in an' lay down on my bed, an' I ain't waken up till I hear dat woman scream when she come out into her kitchen. My goodness, but she was surprise! She laugh an' cry at de same time, an' hug me and waken all de children. She ain't stop fur no breakfast; she git de Christmas dinner ready dat morning; and we all sit down an' eat all we can hold. I ain't never seen dat violin boy have all he can hold before."

"Two three days after dat, de two men come to hunt me up, an' dey ask my boss, and he give me a good report an' tell dem I was a steady boy all right. One of dem Bohemians was very smart an' run a Bohemian newspaper in New York, an' de odder was a rich man, in de importing business, an' dey been travelling togedder. Dey told me how t'ings was easier in New York, an' offered to pay my passage when dey was goin' home soon on a boat. My boss say to me: 'You go. You ain't got no chance here, an' I like to see you git ahead, fur you always been a good boy to my woman, and fur dat fine Christmas dinner you give us all.' An' da's how I got to New York."

That night when Rudolph and Polly, arm in arm, were running home across the fields with the bitter wind at their backs, his heart leaped for joy when she said she thought they might have his family come over for supper on New Year's Eve. "Let's get up a nice supper, and not let your mother help at all; make her be company for once."

"That would be lovely of you, Polly," he said humbly. He was a very simple, modest boy, and he, too, felt vaguely that Polly and her sisters were more experienced and worldly than his people.

VI

The winter turned out badly for farmers. It was bitterly cold, and after the first light snows before Christmas there was no snow at all,—and no rain. March was as bitter as February. On those days when the wind fairly punished the country, Rosicky sat by his window. In the fall he and the boys had put in a big wheat planting, and now the seed had frozen in the ground. All that land would have to be ploughed up and planted over again, planted in corn. It had happened before, but he was younger then, and he never worried about what had to be. He was sure of himself and of Mary; he knew they could bear what they had to bear, that they would always pull through somehow. But he was not so sure about the young ones, and he felt troubled because Rudolph and Polly were having such a hard start.

Sitting beside his flowering window while the panes rattled and the wind blew in under the door, Rosicky gave himself to reflection as he had not done since those Sundays in the loft of the furniture-factory in

New York, long ago. Then he was trying to find what he wanted in life for himself; now he was trying to find what he wanted for his boys, and why it was he so hungered to feel sure they would be here, working this very land, after he was gone.

They would have to work hard on the farm, and probably they would never do much more than make a living. But if he could think of them as staying here on the land, he wouldn't have to fear any great un-kindness for them. Hardships, certainly; it was a hard-ship to have the wheat freeze in the ground when seed was so high; and to have to sell your stock because you had no feed. But there would be other years when everything came along right, and you caught up. And what you had was your own. You didn't have to choose between bosses and strikers, and go wrong either way. You didn't have to do with dishonest and cruel people. They were the only things in his experience he had found terrifying and horrible; the look in the eyes of a dishonest and crafty man, of a scheming and rapacious woman.

In the country, if you had a mean neighbour, you could keep off his land and make him keep off yours. But in the city, all the foulness and misery and brutal-ity of your neighbours was part of your life. The worst things he had come upon in his journey through the world were human,—depraved and poisonous speci-mens of man. To this day he could recall certain terrible faces in the London streets. There were mean people everywhere, to be sure, even in their own country town here. But they weren't tempered, hardened, sharp-ened, like the treacherous people in cities who live by grinding or cheating or poisoning their fellow-men. He had helped to bury two of his fellow-workmen in the tailoring trade, and he was distrustful of the or-ganized industries that see one out of the world in big cities. Here, if you were sick, you had Doctor Ed to look after you; and if you died, fat Mr. Haycock, the kindest man in the world, buried you.

It seemed to Rosicky that for good, honest boys like his, the worst they could do on the farm was better than the best they would be likely to do in the city. If he'd had a mean boy, now, one who was crooked and sharp and tried to put anything over on his brothers, then town would be the place for him. But he had no such boy. As for Rudolph, the discontented one,

he would give the shirt off his back to anyone who touched his heart. What Rosicky really hoped for his boys was that they could get through the world without ever knowing much about the cruelty of human beings. "Their mother an' me ain't prepared them for that," he sometimes said to himself.

These thoughts brought him back to a grateful con-sideration of his own case. What an escape he had had, to be sure! He, too, in his time, had had to take money for repair work from the hand of a hungry child who let it go so wistfully; because it was money due his boss. And now, in all these years, he had never had to take a cent from anyone in bitter need,—never had to look at the face of a woman become like a wolf's from struggle and famine. When he thought of these things, Rosicky would put on his cap and jacket and slip down to the barn and give his work-horses a little extra oats, letting them eat it out of his hand in their slobbery fashion. It was his way of expressing what he felt, and made him chuckle with pleasure.

The spring came warm, with blue skies,—but dry, dry as a bone. The boys began ploughing up the wheat-fields to plant them over in corn. Rosicky would stand at the fence corner and watch them, and the earth was so dry it blew up in clouds of brown dust that hid the horses and the sulky plough and the driver. It was a bad outlook.

The big alfalfa-field that lay between the home place and Rudolph's came up green, but Rosicky was wor-ried because during that open windy winter a great many Russian thistle plants had blown in there and lodged. He kept asking the boys to rake them out; he was afraid that their seed would root and "take the alfalfa." Rudolph said that was nonsense. The boys were working so hard planting corn, their father felt he couldn't insist about the thistles, but he set great store by that big alfalfa field. It was a feed you could depend on,—and there was some deeper reason, vague, but strong. The peculiar green of that clover woke early memories in old Rosicky, went back to some-thing in his childhood in the old world. When he was a little boy, he had played in fields of that strong blue-green colour.

One morning, when Rudolph had gone to town in the car, leaving a work-team idle in his barn, Rosicky went over to his son's place, put the horses to the buggy rake, and set about quietly raking up those thistles. He behaved with guilty caution, and rather enjoyed stealing a march on Doctor Ed, who was just then taking his first vacation in seven years of practice and was attending a clinic in Chicago. Rosicky got the thistles raked up, but did not stop to burn them. That would take some time, and his breath was pretty short, so he thought he had better get the horses back to the barn.

He got them into the barn and to their stalls, but the pain had come on so sharp in his chest that he didn't try to take the harness off. He started for the house, bending lower with every step. The cramp in his chest was shutting him up like a jack-knife. When he reached the windmill, he swayed and caught at the ladder. He saw Polly coming down the hill, running with the swiftness of a slim greyhound. In a flash she had her shoulder under his armpit.

"Lean on me, Father, hard! Don't be afraid. We can get to the house all right."

Somehow they did, though Rosicky became blind with pain; he could keep on his legs, but he couldn't steer his course. The next thing he was conscious of was lying on Polly's bed, and Polly bending over him wringing out bath towels in hot water and putting them on his chest. She stopped only to throw coal into the stove, and she kept the tea-kettle and the black pot going. She put these hot applications on him for nearly an hour, she told him afterwards, and all that time he was drawn up stiff and blue, with the sweat pouring off him.

As the pain gradually loosed its grip, the stiffness went out of his jaws, the black circles round his eyes disappeared, and a little of his natural colour came back. When his daughter-in-law buttoned his shirt over his chest at last, he sighed.

"Da's fine, de way I feel now, Polly. It was a awful bad spell, an' I was so sorry it all come on you like it did."

Polly was flushed and excited. "Is the pain really gone? Can I leave you long enough to telephone over to your place?"

Rosicky's eyelids fluttered. "Don't telephone, Polly. It ain't no use to scare my wife. It's nice and quiet here, an' if I ain't too much trouble to you, just let me lay still till I feel like myself. I ain't got no pain now. It's nice here."

Polly bent over him and wiped the moisture from his face. "Oh, I'm so glad it's over!" she broke out impulsively. "It just broke my heart to see you suffer so, Father."

Rosicky motioned her to sit down on the chair where the tea-kettle had been, and looked up at her with that lively affectionate gleam in his eyes. "You was awful good to me, I won't ever forgit dat. I hate it to be sick on you like dis. Down at de barn I say to myself, dat young girl ain't had much experience in sickness, I don't want to scare her, an' maybe she's got a baby comin' or somet'ing."

Polly took his hand. He was looking at her so intently and affectionately and confidingly; his eyes seemed to caress her face, to regard it with pleasure. She frowned with her funny streaks of eyebrows, and then smiled back at him.

"I guess maybe there is something of that kind going to happen. But I haven't told anyone yet, not my mother or Rudolph. You'll be the first to know."

His hand pressed hers. She noticed that it was warm again. The twinkle in his yellow-brown eyes seemed to come nearer.

"I like mighty well to see dat little child, Polly," was all he said. Then he closed his eyes and lay half-smiling. But Polly sat still, thinking hard. She had a sudden feeling that nobody in the world, not her mother, not Rudolph, or anyone, really loved her as much as old Rosicky did. It perplexed her. She sat frowning and trying to puzzle it out. It was as if Rosicky had a special gift for loving people, something that was like an ear for music or an eye for colour. It was quiet, unobtrusive; it was merely there. You saw it in his eyes,—perhaps that was why they were merry. You felt it in his hands, too. After he dropped off to sleep, she sat holding his warm, broad, flexible brown hand. She had never seen another in the least like it. She wondered if it wasn't a kind of gypsy hand, it was so alive and quick and light in its communications,—very strange in a farmer. Nearly all the farmers she knew had huge lumps of fists, like mauls, or they were knotty and bony and uncomfortable-looking, with stiff fingers. But Rosicky's hand was like quicksilver, flexible, muscular, about the colour of a pale cigar, with deep, deep creases across the palm. It wasn't nervous, it wasn't a stupid lump; it was a warm brown human hand, with some cleverness in it, a great deal of generosity, and something else which Polly could only call "gypsy-like,"—something nimble and lively and sure, in the way that animals are.

Polly remembered that hour long afterward; it had been like an awakening to her. It seemed to her that she had never learned so much about life from anything as from old Rosicky's hand. It brought her to herself; it communicated some direct and untranslatable message.

When she heard Rudolph coming in the car, she ran out to meet him.

"Oh, Rudy, your father's been awful sick! He raked up those thistles he's been worrying about, and afterwards he could hardly get to the house. He suffered so I was afraid he was going to die."

Rudolph jumped to the ground. "Where is he now?"

"On the bed. He's asleep. I was terribly scared, because, you know, I'm so fond of your father." She slipped her arm through his and they went into the house. That afternoon they took Rosicky home and put him to bed, though he protested that he was quite well again.

The next morning he got up and dressed and sat down to breakfast with his family. He told Mary that his coffee tasted better than usual to him, and he warned the boys not to bear any tales to Doctor Ed when he got home. After breakfast he sat down by his window to do some patching and asked Mary to thread several needles for him before she went to feed her chickens, —her eyes were better than his, and her hands steadier. He lit his pipe and took up John's overalls. Mary had been watching him anxiously all morning, and as she went out of the door with her bucket of scraps, she saw that he was smiling. He was thinking, indeed, about Polly, and how he might never have known what a tender heart she had if he hadn't got sick over there. Girls nowadays didn't wear their heart on their sleeve. But now he knew Polly would make a fine woman after the foolishness wore off. Either a woman had that sweetness at her heart or she hadn't. You couldn't always tell by the look of them; but if they had that, everything came out right in the end.

After he had taken a few stitches, the cramp began in his chest, like yesterday. He put his pipe cautiously down on the window-sill and bent over to ease the pull. No use,—he had better try to get to his bed if

he could. He rose and groped his way across the familiar floor, which was rising and falling like the deck of a ship. At the door he fell. When Mary came in, she found him lying there, and the moment she touched him she knew that he was gone.

Doctor Ed was away when Rosicky died, and for the first few weeks after he got home he was hard driven. Every day he said to himself that he must get out to see the family that had lost their father. One soft, warm moonlight night in early summer he started for the farm. His mind was on other things, and not until his road ran by the graveyard did he realize that Rosicky wasn't over there on the hill where the red lamplight shone, but here, in the moonlight. He stopped his car, shut off the engine, and sat there for a while.

A sudden hush had fallen on his soul. Everything here seemed strangely moving and significant, though signifying what, he did not know. Close by the wire fence stood Rosicky's mowing-machine, where one of the boys had been cutting hay that afternoon; his own work-horses had been going up and down there. The new-cut hay perfumed all the night air. The moonlight silvered the long, billowy grass that grew over the graves and hid the fence; the few little evergreens stood out black in it, like shadows in a pool. The sky was very blue and soft, the stars rather faint because the moon was full.

For the first time it struck Doctor Ed that this was really a beautiful graveyard. He thought of city cemeteries; acres of shrubbery and heavy stone, so arranged and lonely and unlike anything in the living world. Cities of the dead, indeed; cities of the forgotten, of the "put away." But this was open and free, this little square of long grass which the wind for ever stirred. Nothing but the sky overhead, and the many-coloured fields running on until they met that sky. The horses worked here in summer; the neighbours passed on their way to town; and over yonder, in the cornfield, Rosicky's own cattle would be eating fodder as winter came on. Nothing could be more undeathlike than this place; nothing could be more right for a man who had helped to do the work of great cities and had always longed for the open country and had got to it at last. Rosicky's life seemed to him complete and beautiful.

1928-1932

1st American to receive Nobel Prize

Satirist of conventionality, false fronts, vain society

Sinclair Lewis

1885 · 1951

Sinclair Lewis is an instance of a satirist and caricaturist whose victims generously supported their lampooner. Gibing at the supposedly sacred mores of his countrymen, he saw his books almost perennially best sellers for a quarter of a century. The fact suggests both that there was widespread agreement with his discontent about certain patterns of life in the United States and that his portrayal was far from merciless. Like a shrewdly observant and gossipy neighbor, he used his gift of gab for caustic running comment on the false fronts and pompous vanities and stupid conventions which are readily found in every level of society, and was so entertaining on the foibles of others that most of us forgave his obvious exaggeration of our own little faults. Lewis was in fact an incurable romanticist in his disappointment that life was not more like the storybooks where boy meets girl and they live happily ever after.

Lewis was born at Sauk Centre, in central Minnesota, in 1885. His father was a physician; his mother died when he was only five. Small-town life was uncongenial to him. Yearning for the romance of the East, he spent six months at Oberlin to prepare himself for college entrance examinations and entered Yale with the class of 1907. There he earned much of his way by newspaper work, spent two summer vacations on the then traditional cattle-boat tour to Europe, and gained some reputation as a writer for the college literary magazines. Dropping out of college at the beginning of his senior year, he joined the group at Helicon Hall, the Socialist community established by Upton Sinclair at

Englewood, New Jersey, with the profits from *The Jungle.* A brief stretch as janitor ended in illness. When he recovered he spent some months as a free-lance writer and editor in New York City and then returned to Yale to graduate in 1908. Seven years of odd literary jobs followed—reporting, editing, reading for publishers, writing advertising. Meanwhile he was writing fiction in his spare time. A juvenile under the pseudonym of Tom Graham, *Hike and the Aeroplane,* appeared in 1912; it was followed by *Our Mr. Wrenn* (1914), the story of a clerk who goes to Europe on a cattle boat, and *The Trail of the Hawk* (1915), which relates the rise of a typical American boy. At about the time that his third book was published Lewis at length found himself selling his short stories; he promptly gave up his job as advertising manager for the firm of George H. Doran to begin the untrammeled wandering of a free lance.

His success was almost immediate, although it was five years before he startled the literary world into heated debate on the merits of *Main Street* (1920). During the war years he sold numerous short stories and published three novels: *The Innocents* (1917), *The Job* (1917), and *Free Air* (1919), all of them essentially love stories but distinguished by a tentative use of slangy lingo and characters on the prowl for "better things" in life.

In *Main Street* Lewis' great talent as a satirist became evident to all. From the rather heavy irony of its Foreword through the sharp details of its description and the cutting edges with which the various village types are presented, Lewis hammered and slashed at smug provincialism. With few exceptions the rest of his stories have been on essentially the same theme. He devoted himself to laying bare whatever has seemed to him fraudulent in American life. *Babbitt* (1922) gave a new word to the language by its exposure of the emptiness of a businessman's world; *Arrowsmith* (1925) suggested that even a scientist cannot easily be honest; *Elmer Gantry* (1927) was a broad hint that charlatanism is not wholly absent in clerical circles; *Dodsworth* (1929) brought down the tycoon nearly, if not quite, to the humility of George F. Babbitt. These, by common consent, are Lewis' best novels. For *Arrowsmith* he was offered the Pulitzer Prize, which he dramatically refused; in 1930 he received the Nobel Prize, being the first American writer so honored. He died in Italy in 1951, and his body was returned for burial at Sauk Centre.

Among his less successful stories must be counted *Mantrap* (1926), *The Man Who Knew Coolidge* (1928), *Ann Vickers* (1933), *Work of Art* (1934), *It Can't Happen Here* (1935), *The Prodigal Parents* (1938), *Bethel Merriday* (1940), *Gideon Planish* (1943), *Cass Timberlane* (1945), *Kingsblood Royal* (1947), and *The God-seeker* (1949). However, nearly every one of them has some points of interest. Lewis'

chief handicaps were his difficulty in achieving memorable characterization and his too great fluency. His novels are peopled with allegorical figures with names carefully chosen to reveal their typical implications and his style is frequently slapstick rather than subtle.

It is now clear, however, that the novels of Sinclair Lewis are the historical record of the crassness of an epoch. The United States between World Wars I and II had need of reformers and in Lewis it had one of its most persistent, although by no means most virulent, gadflies. Lewis was a debunker, but no misanthrope. He liked the absurdities which he found everywhere in American life; he shared the aspirations of his countrymen for getting ahead in the world and their delight in mechanical gadgets and material comforts, their yearning for warm personal relationships, their basic optimism. Life seemed so interesting to him that he seldom was discouraged about it and he never plumbed the depths of pessimism as did Mark Twain.

T. K. Whipple, **Spokesmen: Modern Writers and American Life**, New York, 1928 • Harry Hartwick, **The Foreground of American Fiction**, Cincinnati, 1934 • P. H. Boynton, **America in Contemporary Fiction**, Chicago, 1940 • Alfred Kazin, **On Native Grounds: An Interpretation of Modern American Prose Literature**, New York, 1942 • Maxwell Geismar, **The Last of the Provincials**, Boston, 1947, 69-150

Main Street

In 1904-1905, when he was a sophomore at Yale, Lewis planned a novel tentatively entitled "The Village Virus," which would destroy the myth that the small town was the abiding place of virtue. He returned to it in the summer of 1919 while living in Minnesota and completed it in the following spring at Washington. Published in October, **Main Street** soon led the best-seller lists and was translated into several European languages. In some ways it is more a sociological study than a novel and it was so received by the public, which divided into those who agreed that Main Street everywhere was like Lewis'

description and those who insisted that it was not. Twenty years later it was still possible to debate whether or not small-town life was less provincial than it had been when Lewis wrote.

The distinction of **Main Street** among Lewis' novels is that Carol Kennicott, its heroine, is one of his few full-length portraits, a woman who is at once typical and to most readers real. The selections which follow are a series of vignettes from the life of Carol, a life which was a struggle with Gopher Prairie and what Gopher Prairie stood for.

FOREWORD

This is America—a town of a few thousand, in a region of wheat and corn and dairies and little groves.

The town is, in our tale, called "Gopher Prairie, Minnesota." But its Main Street is the continuation of

Main Streets everywhere. The story would be the same in Ohio or Montana, in Kansas or Kentucky or Illinois, and not very differently would it be told Up York State or in the Carolina hills.

Main Street is the climax of civilization. That this Ford car might stand in front of the Bon Ton Store, Hannibal invaded Rome and Erasmus wrote in Oxford cloisters. What Ole Jenson the grocer says to Ezra Stowbody the banker is the new law for London, Prague, and the unprofitable isles of the sea; whatsoever Ezra does not know and sanction, that thing is heresy, worthless for knowing and wicked to consider.

Our railway station is the final aspiration of architecture. Sam Clark's annual hardware turnover is the envy of the four counties which constitute God's Country. In the sensitive art of the Rosebud Movie Palace there is a Message, and humor strictly moral.

Such is our comfortable tradition and sure faith. Would he not betray himself an alien cynic who should otherwise portray Main Street, or distress the citizens by speculating whether there may not be other faiths?

[Carol Milford, when she meets Dr. Will Kennicott of Gopher Prairie, is twenty-four; the year is 1911. She is a Middlewestern girl, brought up at Mankato, where her Massachusetts-born father was a judge. Her mother has been dead since she was nine, her father since she was thirteen. She has graduated from Blodgett College, a "bulwark of sound religion" on the edge of Minneapolis, has spent a year in library school in Chicago, and for the past three years has worked in the public library of St. Paul. She is bookish, plays the violin, and is given to dramatizing herself through intense but seldom long-lived enthusiasms. Of all her "notions" the most persistent is to get her hands upon a prairie village and make it beautiful—an idea which is traceable to a sociology course in college. It is not surprising, therefore, that she tells Will at their first meeting that a doctor can, if he will, transform a whole community.]

CHAPTER II

II

Of the love-making of Carol and Will Kennicott there is nothing to be told which may not be heard on every summer evening, on every shadowy block.

They were biology and mystery; their speech was slang phrases and flares of poetry; their silences were contentment, or shaky crises when his arm took her shoulder. All the beauty of youth, first discovered when it is passing—and all the commonplaceness of a well-to-do unmarried man encountering a pretty girl at the time when she is slightly weary of her employment and sees no glory ahead nor any man she is glad to serve.

They liked each other honestly—they were both honest. She was disappointed by his devotion to making money, but she was sure that he did not lie to patients, and that he did keep up with the medical magazines. What aroused her to something more than liking was his boyishness when they went tramping.

They walked from St. Paul down the river to Mendota, Kennicott more elastic-seeming in a cap and a soft crêpe shirt, Carol youthful in a tam-o'-shanter of mole velvet, a blue serge suit with an absurdly and agreeably broad turn-down linen collar, and frivolous ankles above athletic shoes. The High Bridge crosses the Mississippi, mounting from low banks to a palisade of cliffs. Far down beneath it on the St. Paul side, upon mud flats, is a wild settlement of chicken-infested gardens and shanties patched together from discarded sign-boards, sheets of corrugated iron, and planks fished out of the river. Carol leaned over the rail of the bridge to look down at this Yang-tse village; in delicious imaginary fear she shrieked that she was dizzy with the height; and it was an extremely human satisfaction to have a strong male snatch her back to safety, instead of having a logical woman teacher or librarian sniff, "Well, if you're scared, why don't you get away from the rail, then?"

From the cliffs across the river Carol and Kennicott looked back at St. Paul on its hills; an imperial sweep from the dome of the cathedral to the dome of the state capitol.

The river road led past rocky field slopes, deep glens, woods flamboyant now with September, to Mendota, white walls and a spire among trees beneath a hill, old-world in its placid ease. And for this fresh land, the place is ancient. Here is the bold stone house which General Sibley, the king of fur-traders, built in 1835, with plaster of river mud, and ropes of twisted grass for laths. It has an air of centuries. In its solid rooms Carol and Kennicott found prints from other days which the house had seen—tail-coats of robin's-egg blue, clumsy Red River carts laden with luxurious furs, whiskered

Union soldiers in slant forage caps and rattling sabers.

It suggested to them a common American past, and it was memorable because they had discovered it together. They talked more trustingly, more personally, as they trudged on. They crossed the Minnesota River in a rowboat ferry. They climbed the hill to the round stone tower of Fort Snelling. They saw the junction of the Mississippi and the Minnesota, and recalled the men who had come here eighty years ago—Maine lumbermen, York traders, soldiers from the Maryland hills.

"It's a good country, and I'm proud of it. Let's make it all that those old boys dreamed about," the unsentimental Kennicott was moved to vow.

"Let's!"

"Come on. Come to Gopher Prairie. Show us. Make the town—well—make it artistic. It's mighty pretty, but I'll admit we aren't any too darn artistic. Probably the lumberyard isn't as scrumptious as all these Greek temples. But go to it! Make us change!"

"I would like to. Some day!"

"Now! You'd love Gopher Prairie. We've been doing a lot with lawns and gardening the past few years, and it's so homey—the big trees and—— And the best people on earth. And keen. I bet Luke Dawson——"

Carol but half listened to the names. She could not fancy their ever becoming important to her.

"I bet Luke Dawson has got more money than most of the swells on Summit Avenue; and Miss Sherwin in the high school is a regular wonder—reads Latin like I do English; and Sam Clark, the hardware man, he's a corker —not a better man in the state to go hunting with; and if you want culture, besides Vida Sherwin there's Reverend Warren, the Congregational preacher, and Professor Mott, the superintendent of schools, and Guy Pollock, the lawyer—they say he writes regular poetry and—and Raymie Wutherspoon, he's not such an awful boob when you get to *know* him, and he sings swell. And—— And there's plenty of others. Lym Cass. Only of course none of them have your finesse, you might call it. But they don't make 'em any more appreciative and so on. Come on! We're ready for you to boss us!"

They sat on the bank below the parapet of the old fort, hidden from observation. He circled her shoulder with his arm. Relaxed after the walk, a chill nipping her throat, conscious of his warmth and power, she leaned gratefully against him.

"You know I'm in love with you, Carol!"

She did not answer, but she touched the back of his hand with an exploring finger.

"You say I'm so darn materialistic. How can I help it, unless I have you to stir me up?"

She did not answer. She could not think.

"You say a doctor could cure a town the way he does a person. Well, you cure the town of whatever ails it, if anything does, and I'll be your surgical kit."

She did not follow his words, only the burning resoluteness of them.

She was shocked, thrilled, as he kissed her cheek and cried, "There's no use saying things and saying things and saying things. Don't my arms talk to you—now?"

"Oh, please, please!" She wondered if she ought to be angry, but it was a drifting thought, and she discovered that she was crying.

Then they were sitting six inches apart, pretending that they had never been nearer, while she tried to be impersonal:

"I would like to—would like to see Gopher Prairie."

"Trust me! Here she is! Brought some snapshots down to show you."

Her cheek near his sleeve, she studied a dozen village pictures. They were streaky; she saw only trees, shrubbery, a porch indistinct in leafy shadows. But she exclaimed over the lakes: dark water reflecting wooded bluffs, a flight of ducks, a fisherman in shirt sleeves and a wide straw hat, holding up a string of croppies. One winter picture of the edge of Plover Lake had the air of an etching: lustrous slide of ice, snow in the crevices of a boggy bank, the mound of a muskrat house, reeds in thin black lines, arches of frosty grasses. It was an impression of cool clear vigor.

"How'd it be to skate there for a couple of hours, or go zinging along on a fast ice-boat, and skip back home for coffee and some hot wienies?" he demanded.

"It might be—fun."

"But here's the picture. Here's where you come in."

A photograph of a forest clearing: pathetic new furrows straggling among stumps, a clumsy log cabin chinked with mud and roofed with hay. In front of it a sagging woman with tight-drawn hair, and a baby bedraggled, smeary, glorious-eyed.

"Those are the kind of folks I practise among, good share of the time. Nels Erdstrom, fine clean young

Svenska. He'll have a corking farm in ten years, but now—— I operated his wife on a kitchen table, with my driver giving the anesthetic. Look at that scared baby! Needs some woman with hands like yours. Waiting for you! Just look at that baby's eyes, look how he's begging——"

"Don't! They hurt me. Oh, it would be sweet to help him—so sweet."

As his arms moved toward her she answered all her
10 doubts with "Sweet, so sweet."

[Carol and Will marry after a year of "conversational" courtship and go to Colorado for their honeymoon. The reader meets them next upon the train going to Gopher Prairie, Carol thinking of the provinciality of the farmers who crowd the train and of the contrast between the beauty of the countryside and the bleak ugliness of the small towns. As she wonders what Gopher Prairie will be like, the train pulls in, and she knows that it is just like all the others—a "junk-heap," she decides to herself. They are met by a group of the Doctor's friends.]

CHAPTER IV

"The Clarks have invited some folks to their house to meet us, tonight," said Kennicott, as he unpacked his suit-case.

"Oh, that is nice of them!"

"You bet. I told you you'd like 'em. Squarest people on earth. Uh, Carrie—— Would you mind if I sneaked down to the office for an hour, just to see how things are?"

"Why, no. Of course not. I know you're keen to
20 get back to work."

"Sure you don't mind?"

"Not a bit. Out of my way. Let me unpack."

But the advocate of freedom in marriage was as much disappointed as a drooping bride at the alacrity with which he took that freedom and escaped to the world of men's affairs. She gazed about their bedroom, and its full dismalness crawled over her: the awkward knuckly L-shape of it; the black walnut bed with apples and spotty pears carved on the headboard; the
30 imitation maple bureau, with pink-daubed scent-bottles and a petticoated pin-cushion on a marble slab uncom-

fortably like a gravestone; the plain pine washstand and the garlanded water-pitcher and bowl. The scent was of horsehair and plush and Florida Water.

"How could people ever live with things like this?" she shuddered. She saw the furniture as a circle of elderly judges, condemning her to death by smothering. The tottering brocade chair squeaked, "Choke her—choke her—smother her." The old linen smelled of the tomb. She was alone in this house, this strange
40 still house, among the shadows of dead thoughts and haunting repressions. " I hate it! I hate it!" she panted. "Why did I ever——"

She remembered that Kennicott's mother had brought these family relics from the old home in Lac-qui-Meurt. "Stop it! They're perfectly comfortable things. They're —comfortable. Besides—— Oh, they're horrible! We'll change them, right away."

Then, "But of course he *has* to see how things are at the office——"
50

She made a pretense of busying herself with unpacking. The chintz-lined, silver-fitted bag which had seemed so desirable a luxury in St. Paul was an extravagant vanity here. The daring black chemise of frail chiffon and lace was a hussy at which the deep-bosomed bed stiffened in disgust, and she hurled it into a bureau drawer, hid it beneath a sensible linen blouse.

She gave up unpacking. She went to the window, with a purely literary thought of village charm—holly-hocks and lanes and apple-cheeked cottagers. What she 60 saw was the side of the Seventh-Day Adventist Church —a plain clapboard wall of a sour liver color; the ash-pile back of the church; an unpainted stable; and an alley in which a Ford delivery-wagon had been stranded. This was the terraced garden below her boudoir; this was to be her scenery for——

"I mustn't! I mustn't! I'm nervous this afternoon. Am I sick? . . . Good Lord, I hope it isn't that! Not now! How people lie! How these stories lie! They say the bride is always so blushing and proud and 70 happy when she finds that out, but—I'd hate it! I'd be scared to death! Some day but—— Please, dear nebulous Lord, not now! Bearded sniffy old men sitting and demanding that we bear children. If *they* had to bear them——! I wish they did have to! Not now! Not till I've got hold of this job of liking the ash-pile out there! . . . I must shut up. I'm mildly insane.

I'm going out for a walk. I'll see the town by myself. My first view of the empire I'm going to conquer!"

She fled from the house.

She stared with seriousness at every concrete crossing, every hitching-post, every rake for leaves; and to each house she devoted all her speculation. What would they come to mean? How would they look six months from now? In which of them would she be dining? Which of these people whom she passed, now mere arrangements of hair and clothes, would turn into intimates, loved or dreaded, different from all the other people in the world?

As she came into the small business-section she inspected a broad-beamed grocer in an alpaca coat who was bending over the apples and celery on a slanted platform in front of his store. Would she ever talk to him? What would he say if she stopped and stated, "I am Mrs. Kennicott. Some day I hope to confide that a heap of extremely dubious pumpkins as a window-display doesn't exhilarate me much."

(The grocer was Mr. Frederick F. Ludelmeyer, whose market is at the corner of Main Street and Lincoln Avenue. In supposing that only she was observant Carol was ignorant, misled by the indifference of cities. She fancied that she was slipping through the streets invisible; but when she had passed, Mr. Ludelmeyer puffed into the store and coughed at his clerk, "I seen a young woman, she come along the side street. I bet she iss Doc Kennicott's new bride, good-looker, nice legs, but she wore a hell of a plain suit, no style, I wonder will she pay cash, I bet she goes to Howland & Gould's more as she does here, what you done with the poster for Fluffed Oats?")

II

When Carol had walked for thirty-two minutes she had completely covered the town, east and west, north and south; and she stood at the corner of Main Street and Washington Avenue and despaired.

Main Street with its two-story brick shops, its story-and-a-half wooden residences, its muddy expanse from concrete walk to walk, its huddle of Fords and lumber-wagons, was too small to absorb her. The broad, straight, unenticing gashes of the streets let in the grasping prairie on every side. She realized the vastness and the emptiness of the land. The skeleton iron windmill on the farm a few blocks away, at the north end of Main Street, was like the ribs of a dead cow. She thought of the coming of the Northern winter, when the unprotected houses would crouch together in terror of storms galloping out of that wild waste. They were so small and weak, the little brown houses. They were shelters for sparrows, not homes for warm laughing people.

She told herself that down the street the leaves were a splendor. The maples were orange; the oaks a solid tint of raspberry. And the lawns had been nursed with love. But the thought would not hold. At best the trees resembled a thinned woodlot. There was no park to rest the eyes. And since not Gopher Prairie but Wakamin was the county-seat, there was no court-house with its grounds.

She glanced through the fly-specked windows of the most pretentious building in sight, the one place which welcomed strangers and determined their opinion of the charm and luxury of Gopher Prairie—the Minniemashie House. It was a tall lean shabby structure, three stories of yellow-streaked wood, the corners covered with sanded pine slabs purporting to symbolize stone. In the hotel office she could see a stretch of bare unclean floor, a line of rickety chairs with brass cuspidors between, a writing-desk with advertisements in mother-of-pearl letters upon the glass-covered back. The dining-room beyond was a jungle of stained table-cloths and catsup bottles.

She looked no more at the Minniemashie House.

A man in cuffless shirt-sleeves with pink arm-garters, wearing a linen collar but no tie, yawned his way from Dyer's Drug Store across to the hotel. He leaned against the wall, scratched a while, sighed, and in a bored way gossiped with a man tilted back in a chair. A lumber-wagon, its long green box filled with large spools of barbed-wire fencing, creaked down the block. A Ford, in reverse, sounded as though it were shaking to pieces, then recovered and rattled away. In the Greek candy-store was the whine of a peanut-roaster, and the oily smell of nuts.

There was no other sound nor sign of life.

She wanted to run, fleeing from the encroaching prairie demanding the security of a great city. Her dreams of creating a beautiful town were ludicrous.

Oozing out from every drab wall, she felt a forbidding spirit which she could never conquer.

She trailed down the street on one side, back on the other, glancing into the cross streets. It was a private Seeing Main Street tour. She was within ten minutes beholding not only the heart of a place called Gopher Prairie, but ten thousand towns from Albany to San Diego:

Dyer's Drug Store, a corner building of regular
10 and unreal blocks of artificial stone. Inside the store, a greasy marble soda-fountain with an electric lamp of red and green and curdled-yellow mosaic shade. Pawed-over heaps of toothbrushes and combs and packages of shaving-soap. Shelves of soap-cartons, teething-rings, garden-seeds, and patent medicines in yellow packages—nostrums for consumption, for "women's diseases"—notorious mixtures of opium and alcohol, in the very shop to which her husband sent patients for the filling of prescriptions.

20 From a second-story window the sign "W. P. Kennicott, Phys. & Surgeon," gilt on black sand.

A small wooden motion-picture theater called "The Rosebud Movie Palace." Lithographs announcing a film called "Fatty in Love."

Howland & Gould's Grocery. In the display window, black, overripe bananas and lettuce on which a cat was sleeping. Shelves lined with red crêpe paper which was now faded and torn and concentrically spotted. Flat against the wall of the second story the signs of
30 lodges—the Knights of Pythias, the Maccabees, the Woodmen, the Masons.

Dahl & Oleson's Meat Market—a reek of blood.

A jewelry shop with tinny-looking wrist-watches for women. In front of it, at the curb, a huge wooden clock which did not go.

A fly-buzzing saloon with a brilliant gold and enamel whisky sign across the front. Other saloons down the block. From them a stink of stale beer, and thick voices bellowing pidgin German or trolling out dirty songs—
40 vice gone feeble and unenterprising and dull—the delicacy of a mining-camp minus its vigor. In front of the saloons, farmwives sitting on the seats of wagons, waiting for their husbands to become drunk and ready to start home.

A tobacco shop called "The Smoke House," filled with young men shaking dice for cigarettes. Racks of magazines, and pictures of coy fat prostitutes in striped bathing-suits.

A clothing store with a display of "ox-blood-shade Oxfords with bull-dog toes." Suits which looked worn 50
and glossless while they were still new, flabbily draped on dummies like corpses with painted cheeks.

The Bon Ton Store—Haydock & Simons'—the largest shop in town. The first-story front of clear glass, the plates cleverly bound at the edges with brass. The second story of pleasant tapestry brick. One window of excellent clothes for men, interspersed with collars of floral piqué which showed mauve daisies on a saffron ground. Newness and an obvious notion of neatness and service. Haydock & Simons. Haydock. She 60
had met a Haydock at the station; Harry Haydock; an active person of thirty-five. He seemed great to her, now, and very like a saint. His shop was clean!

Axel Egge's General Store, frequented by Scandinavian farmers. In the shallow dark window-space heaps of sleazy sateens, badly woven galateas, canvas shoes designed for women with bulging ankles, steel and red glass buttons upon cards with broken edges, a cottony blanket, a granite-ware frying-pan reposing on a sun-faded crêpe blouse. 70

Sam Clark's Hardware Store. An air of frankly metallic enterprise. Guns and churns and barrels of nails and beautiful shiny butcher knives.

Chester Dashaway's House Furnishing Emporium. A vista of heavy oak rockers with leather seats, asleep in a dismal row.

Billy's Lunch. Thick handleless cups on the wet oilcloth-covered counter. An odor of onions and the smoke of hot lard. In the doorway a young man audibly sucking a toothpick. 80

The warehouse of the buyer of cream and potatoes. The sour smell of a dairy.

The Ford Garage and the Buick Garage, competent one-story brick and cement buildings opposite each other. Old and new cars on grease-blackened concrete floors. Tire advertisements. The roaring of a tested motor; a racket which beat at the nerves. Surly young men in khaki union-overalls. The most energetic and vital places in town.

A large warehouse for agricultural implements. An 90
impressive barricade of green and gold wheels, of shafts and sulky seats, belonging to machinery of which Carol

knew nothing—potato-planters, manure-spreaders, silage-cutters, disk-harrows, breaking-plows.

A feed store, its windows opaque with the dust of bran, a patent medicine advertisement painted on its roof.

Ye Art Shoppe, Prop. Mrs Mary Ellen Wilks, Christian Science Library open daily free. A touching fumble at beauty. A one-room shanty of boards recently covered with rough stucco. A show-window delicately rich in error: vases starting out to imitate tree-trunks but running off into blobs of gilt—an aluminum ash-tray labeled "Greetings from Gopher Prairie"—a Christian Science magazine—a stamped sofa-cushion portraying a large ribbon tied to a small poppy, the correct skeins of embroidery-silk lying on the pillow. Inside the shop, a glimpse of bad carbon prints of bad and famous pictures, shelves of phonograph records and camera films, wooden toys, and in the midst an anxious small woman sitting in a padded rocking chair.

A barber shop and pool room. A man in shirt sleeves, presumably Del Snafflin the proprietor, shaving a man who had a large Adam's apple.

Nat Hicks's Tailor Shop, on a side street off Main. A one-story building. A fashion-plate showing human pitchforks in garments which looked as hard as steel plate.

On another side street a raw red-brick Catholic Church with a varnished yellow door.

The post-office—merely a partition of glass and brass shutting off the rear of a mildewed room which must once have been a shop. A tilted writing-shelf against a wall rubbed black and scattered with official notices and army recruiting-posters.

The damp, yellow-brick schoolbuilding in its cindery grounds.

The State Bank, stucco masking wood.

The Farmers' National Bank. An Ionic temple of marble. Pure, exquisite, solitary. A brass plate with "Ezra Stowbody, Pres't."

A score of similar shops and establishments.

Behind them and mixed with them, the houses, meek cottages or large, comfortable, soundly uninteresting symbols of prosperity.

In all the town not one building save the Ionic bank which gave pleasure to Carol's eyes; not a dozen buildings which suggested that, in the fifty years of Gopher Prairie's existence, the citizens had realized that it was either desirable or possible to make this, their common home, amusing or attractive.

It was not only the unsparing unapologetic ugliness and the rigid straightness which overwhelmed her. It was the planlessness, the flimsy temporariness of the buildings, their faded unpleasant colors. The street was cluttered with electric light poles, telephone poles, gasoline pumps for motor cars, boxes of goods. Each man had built with the most valiant disregard of all the others. Between a large new "block" of two-story brick shops on one side, and the fire-brick Overland garage on the other side, was a one-story cottage turned into a millinery shop. The white temple of the Farmers' Bank was elbowed back by a grocery of glaring yellow brick. One store-building had a patchy galvanized iron cornice; the building beside it was crowned with battlements and pyramids of brick capped with blocks of red sandstone.

She escaped from Main Street, fled home.

She wouldn't have cared, she insisted, if the people had been comely. She had noted a young man loafing before a shop, one unwashed hand holding the cord of an awning; a middle-aged man who had a way of staring at women as though he had been married too long and too prosaically; an old farmer, solid, wholesome, but not clean—his face like a potato fresh from the earth. None of them had shaved for three days.

"If they can't build shrines, out here on the prairie, surely there's nothing to prevent their buying safety-razors!" she raged.

She fought herself: "I must be wrong. People do live here. It *can't* be as ugly as—as I know it is! I must be wrong. But I can't do it. I can't go through with it."

She came home too seriously worried for hysteria; and when she found Kennicott waiting for her, and exulting, "Have a walk? Well, like the town? Great lawns and trees, eh?" she was able to say, with a self-protective maturity new to her, "It's very interesting."

IV

The recently built house of Sam Clark, in which was given the party to welcome Carol, was one of the largest in Gopher Prairie. It had a clean sweep of clapboards, a solid squareness, a small tower, and a large screened porch. Inside, it was as shiny, as hard, and as cheerful as a new oak upright piano.

Carol looked imploringly at Sam Clark as he rolled to the door and shouted, "Welcome, little lady! The keys of the city are yourn!"

Beyond him, in the hallway and the living-room, sitting in a vast prim circle as though they were attend-ing a funeral, she saw the guests. They were *waiting* so! They were waiting for her! The determination to be all one pretty flowerlet of appreciation leaked away. She begged of Sam, "I don't dare face them! They expect so much. They'll swallow me in one mouthful—glump!—like that!"

"Why, sister, they're going to love you—same as I would if I didn't think the doc here would beat me up!"

"B-but—— I don't dare! Faces to the right of me, faces in front of me, volley and wonder!"

She sounded hysterical to herself; she fancied that to Sam Clark she sounded insane. But he chuckled, "Now you just cuddle under Sam's wing, and if anybody rubbers at you too long, I'll shoo 'em off. Here we go! Watch my smoke—Sam'l, the ladies' delight and the bridegrooms' terror!"

His arm about her, he led her in and bawled, "Ladies and worser halves, the bride! We won't introduce her round yet, because she'll never get your bum names straight anyway. Now bust up this star-chamber!"

They tittered politely, but they did not move from the social security of their circle, and they did not cease staring.

Carol had given creative energy to dressing for the event. Her hair was demure, low on her forehead with a parting and a coiled braid. Now she wished that she had piled it high. Her frock was an ingénue slip of lawn, with a wide gold sash and a low square neck, which gave a suggestion of throat and molded shoulders. But as they looked her over she was certain that it was all wrong. She wished alternately that she had worn a spinsterish high-necked dress, and that she had dared to shock them with a violent brick-red scarf which she had bought in Chicago.

She was led about the circle. Her voice mechanically produced safe remarks:

"Oh, I'm sure I'm going to like it here ever so much,"

and "Yes, we did have the best time in Colorado—moun-tains," and "Yes, I lived in St. Paul several years. Euclid P. Tinker? No, I don't *remember* meeting him, but I'm pretty sure I've heard of him."

Kennicott took her aside and whispered, "Now I'll introduce you to them, one at a time."

"Tell me about them first."

"Well, the nice-looking couple over there are Harry Haydock and his wife, Juanita. Harry's dad owns most of the Bon Ton, but it's Harry who runs it and gives it the pep. He's a hustler. Next to him is Dave Dyer the druggist—you met him this afternoon—mighty good duck-shot. The tall husk beyond him is Jack Elder—Jackson Elder—owns the planing-mill, and the Minnie-mashie House, and quite a share in the Farmers' National Bank. Him and his wife are good sports—him and Sam and I go hunting together a lot. The old cheese there is Luke Dawson, the richest man in town. Next to him is Nat Hicks, the tailor."

"Really? A tailor?"

"Sure. Why not? Maybe we're slow, but we are democratic. I go hunting with Nat same as I do with Jack Elder."

"I'm glad. I've never met a tailor socially. It must be charming to meet one and not have to think about what you owe him. And do you—— Would you go hunting with your barber, too?"

"No but—— No use running this democracy thing into the ground. Besides, I've known Nat for years, and besides, he's a mighty good shot and—— That's the way it is, see? Next to Nat is Chet Dashaway. Great fellow for chinning. He'll talk your arm off, about religion or politics or books or anything."

Carol gazed with a polite approximation to interest at Mr. Dashaway, a tan person with a wide mouth. "Oh, I know! He's the furniture-store man!" She was much pleased with herself.

"Yump, and he's the undertaker. You'll like him. Come shake hands with him."

"Oh no, no! He doesn't—he doesn't do the embalm-ing and all that—himself? I couldn't shake hands with an undertaker!"

"Why not? You'd be proud to shake hands with a great surgeon, just after he'd been carving up people's bellies."

She sought to regain her afternoon's calm of maturity.

"Yes. You're right. I want—oh, my dear, do you know how much I want to like the people you like? I want to see people as they are."

"Well, don't forget to see people as other folks see them as they are! They have the stuff. Did you know that Percy Bresnahan came from here? Born and brought up here!"

"Bresnahan?"

"Yes—you know—president of the Velvet Motor Company of Boston, Mass.—make the Velvet Twelve—biggest automobile factory in New England."

"I think I've heard of him."

"Sure you have. Why, he's a millionaire several times over! Well, Perce comes back here for the black-bass fishing almost every summer, and he says if he could get away from business, he'd rather live here than in Boston or New York or any of those places. *He* doesn't mind Chet's undertaking."

"Please! I'll—I'll like everybody. I'll be the community sunbeam!"

He led her to the Dawsons.

Luke Dawson, lender of money on mortgages, owner of Northern cut-over land, was a hesitant man in unpressed soft gray clothes, with bulging eyes in a milky face. His wife had bleached cheeks, bleached hair, bleached voice, and a bleached manner. She wore her expensive green frock, with its passementeried bosom, bead tassels, and gaps between the buttons down the back, as though she had bought it second-hand and was afraid of meeting the former owner. They were shy. It was "Professor" George Edwin Mott, superintendent of schools, a Chinese mandarin turned brown, who held Carol's hand and made her welcome.

When the Dawsons and Mr. Mott had stated that they were "pleased to meet her," there seemed to be nothing else to say, but the conversation went on automatically.

"Do you like Gopher Prairie?" whimpered Mrs. Dawson.

"Oh, I'm sure I'm going to be ever so happy."

"There's so many nice people." Mrs. Dawson looked to Mr. Mott for social and intellectual aid. He lectured:

"There's a fine class of people. I don't like some of these retired farmers who come here to spend their last days—especially the Germans. They hate to pay school-taxes. They hate to spend a cent. But the rest are a fine class of people. Did you know that Percy Bresnahan came from here? Used to go to school right at the old building!"

"I heard he did."

"Yes. He's a prince. He and I went fishing together, last time he was here."

The Dawsons and Mr. Mott teetered upon weary feet, and smiled at Carol with crystallized expressions. She went on:

"Tell me, Mr. Mott: Have you ever tried any experiments with any of the new educational systems? The modern kindergarten methods or the Gary system?"

"Oh. Those. Most of these would-be reformers are simply notoriety-seekers. I believe in manual training, but Latin and mathematics always will be the backbone of sound Americanism, no matter what these faddists advocate—heaven knows what they do want—knitting, I suppose, and classes in wiggling the ears!"

The Dawsons smiled their appreciation of listening to a savant. Carol waited till Kennicott should rescue her. The rest of the party waited for the miracle of being amused.

Harry and Juanita Haydock, Rita Simons and Dr. Terry Gould—the young smart set of Gopher Prairie. She was led to them. Juanita Haydock flung at her in a high, cackling, friendly voice:

"Well, this is *so* nice to have you here. We'll have some good parties—dances and everything. You'll have to join the Jolly Seventeen. We play bridge and we have a supper once a month. You play, of course?"

"N-no, I don't."

"Really? In St. Paul?"

"I've always been such a book-worm."

"We'll have to teach you. Bridge is half the fun of life." Juanita had become patronizing, and she glanced disrespectfully at Carol's golden sash, which she had previously admired.

Harry Haydock said politely, "How do you think you're going to like the old burg?"

"I'm sure I shall like it tremendously."

"Best people on earth here. Great hustlers, too. Course I've had lots of chances to go live in Minneapolis, but we like it here. Real he-town. Did you know that Percy Bresnahan came from here?"

Carol perceived that she had been weakened in the biological struggle by disclosing her lack of bridge. Roused to nervous desire to regain her position she turned on Dr. Terry Gould, the young and pool-playing competitor of her husband. Her eyes coquetted with him while she gushed:

"I'll learn bridge. But what I really love most is the outdoors. Can't we all get up a boating party, and fish, or whatever you do, and have a picnic supper afterwards?"

"Now you're talking!" Dr. Gould affirmed. He looked rather too obviously at the cream-smooth slope of her shoulder. "Like fishing? Fishing is my middle name. I'll teach you bridge. Like cards at all?"

"I used to be rather good at bezique."

She knew that bezique was a game of cards—or a game of something else. Roulette, possibly. But her lie was a triumph. Juanita's handsome, high-colored, horsey face showed doubt. Harry stroked his nose and said humbly, "Bezique? Used to be great gambling game, wasn't it?"

While others drifted to her group, Carol snatched up the conversation. She laughed and was frivolous and rather brittle. She could not distinguish their eyes. They were a blurry theater-audience before which she self-consciously enacted the comedy of being the Clever Little Bride of Doc Kennicott:

"These-here celebrated Open Spaces, that's what I'm going out for. I'll never read anything but the sporting-page again. Will converted me on our Colorado trip. There were so many mousey tourists who were afraid to get out of the motor 'bus that I decided to be Annie Oakley, the Wild Western Wampire, and I bought oh! a vociferous skirt which revealed my perfectly nice ankles to the Presbyterian glare of all the Ioway schoolma'ams, and I leaped from peak to peak like the nimble chamoys, and—— You may think that Herr Doctor Kennicott is a Nimrod, but you ought to have seen me daring him to strip to his B. V. D.'s and go swimming in an icy mountain brook."

She knew that they were thinking of becoming shocked, but Juanita Haydock was admiring, at least. She swaggered on:

"I'm sure I'm going to ruin Will as a respectable practitioner—— Is he a good doctor, Dr. Gould?"

Kennicott's rival gasped at this insult to professional ethics, and he took an appreciable second before he recovered his social manner. "I'll tell you, Mrs. Kennicott." He smiled at Kennicott, to imply that whatever he might say in the stress of being witty was not to count against him in the commercio-medical warfare. "There's some people in town that say the doc is a fair to middlin' diagnostician and prescription-writer, but let me whisper this to you—but for heaven's sake don't tell him I said so—don't you ever go to him for anything more serious than a pendectomy of the left ear or a strabismus of the cardiograph."

No one save Kennicott knew exactly what this meant, but they laughed, and Sam Clark's party assumed a glittering lemon-yellow color of brocade panels and champagne and tulle and crystal chandeliers and sporting duchesses. Carol saw that George Edwin Mott and the blanched Mr. and Mrs. Dawson were not yet hypnotized. They looked as though they wondered whether they ought to look as though they disapproved. She concentrated on them:

"But I know whom I wouldn't have dared to go to Colorado with! Mr. Dawson there! I'm sure he's a regular heartbreaker. When we were introduced he held my hand and squeezed it frightfully."

"Haw! Haw! Haw!" The entire company applauded. Mr. Dawson was beatified. He had been called many things—loan-shark, skinflint, tightwad, pussyfoot—but he had never before been called a flirt.

"He is wicked, isn't he, Mrs. Dawson? Don't you have to lock him up?"

"Oh no, but maybe I better," attempted Mrs. Dawson, a tint on her pallid face.

For fifteen minutes Carol kept it up. She asserted that she was going to stage a musical comedy, that she preferred café parfait to beefsteak, that she hoped Dr. Kennicott would never lose his ability to make love to charming women, and that she had a pair of gold stockings. They gaped for more. But she could not keep it up. She retired to a chair behind Sam Clark's bulk. The smile-wrinkles solemnly flattened out in the faces of all the other collaborators in having a party, and again they stood about hoping but not expecting to be amused.

Carol listened. She discovered that conversation did not exist in Gopher Prairie. Even at this affair, which brought out the young smart set, the hunting squire set, the respectable intellectual set, and the solid financial set, they sat up with gaiety as with a corpse.

Juanita Haydock talked a good deal in her rattling voice but it was invariably of personalities: the rumor that Raymie Wutherspoon was going to send for a pair of patent leather shoes with gray buttoned tops; the rheumatism of Champ Perry; the state of Guy Pollock's grippe; and the dementia of Jim Howland in painting his fence salmon-pink.

Sam Clark had been talking to Carol about motor cars, but he felt his duties as host. While he droned, his brows popped up and down. He interrupted himself, "Must stir 'em up." He worried at his wife, "Don't you think I better stir 'em up?" He shouldered into the center of the room, and cried:

"Let's have some stunts, folks."

"Yes, let's!" shrieked Juanita Haydock.

"Say, Dave, give us that stunt about the Norwegian catching a hen."

"You bet; that's a slick stunt; do that, Dave!" cheered Chet Dashaway.

Mr. Dave Dyer obliged.

All the guests moved their lips in anticipation of being called on for their own stunts.

"Ella, come on and recite 'Old Sweetheart of Mine,' for us," demanded Sam.

Miss Ella Stowbody, the spinster daughter of the Ionic bank, scratched her dry palms and blushed. "Oh, you don't want to hear that old thing again."

"Sure we do! You bet!" asserted Sam.

"My voice is in terrible shape tonight."

"Tut! Come on!"

Sam loudly explained to Carol, "Ella is our shark at elocuting. She's had professional training. She studied singing and oratory and dramatic art and shorthand for a year, in Milwaukee."

Miss Stowbody was reciting. As encore to "An Old Sweetheart of Mine," she gave a peculiarly optimistic poem regarding the value of smiles.

There were four other stunts: one Jewish, one Irish, one juvenile, and Nat Hicks's parody of Mark Antony's funeral oration.

During the winter Carol was to hear Dave Dyer's hen-catching impersonation seven times, "An Old Sweetheart of Mine" nine times, the Jewish story and the funeral oration twice; but now she was ardent and, because she did so want to be happy and simple-hearted, she was as disappointed as the others when the stunts were finished, and the party instantly sank back into coma.

They gave up trying to be festive; they began to talk naturally, as they did at their shops and homes.

The men and women divided, as they had been tending to do all evening. Carol was deserted by the men, left to a group of matrons who steadily pattered of children, sickness, and cooks—their own shop-talk. She was piqued. She remembered visions of herself as a smart married woman in a drawing-room, fencing with clever men. Her dejection was relieved by speculation as to what the men were discussing, in the corner between the piano and the phonograph. Did they rise from these housewifely personalities to a larger world of abstractions and affairs?

She made her best curtsy to Mrs. Dawson; she twittered, "I won't have my husband leaving me so soon! I'm going over and pull the wretch's ears." She rose with a *jeune fille* bow. She was self-absorbed and self-approving because she had attained that quality of sentimentality. She proudly dipped across the room and, to the interest and commendation of all beholders, sat on the arm of Kennicott's chair.

He was gossiping with Sam Clark, Luke Dawson, Jackson Elder of the planing-mill, Chet Dashaway, Dave Dyer, Harry Haydock, and Ezra Stowbody, president of the Ionic bank.

Ezra Stowbody was a troglodyte. He had come to Gopher Prairie in 1865. He was a distinguished bird of prey—swooping thin nose, turtle mouth, thick brows, port-wine cheeks, floss of white hair, contemptuous eyes. He was not happy in the social changes of thirty years. Three decades ago, Dr. Westlake, Julius Flickerbaugh the lawyer, Merriman Peedy the Congregational pastor and himself had been the arbiters. That was as it should be; the fine arts—medicine, law, religion, and finance—recognized as aristocratic; four Yankees democratically chatting with but ruling the Ohioans and Illini and Swedes and Germans who had ventured to follow them. But Westlake was old, almost retired; Julius Flickerbaugh had lost much of his practice to livelier attorneys; Reverend (not The Reverend) Peedy was dead; and nobody was impressed in this rotten age of automobiles by the "spanking grays" which Ezra still drove. The town was as heterogeneous as Chicago. Norwegians and Germans owned stores. The social leaders were common merchants. Selling nails was considered as sacred as banking. These upstarts—the Clarks, the Haydocks—had no dignity. They were sound and conservative in politics, but they talked about motor cars and pump-guns and heaven only knew what new-fangled fads. Mr. Stowbody felt out of place with them. But his brick house with the mansard roof was still the largest residence in town, and he held his position as squire by occasionally appearing among the younger men and reminding them by a wintry eye that without the banker none of them could carry on their vulgar business.

As Carol defied decency by sitting down with the men, Mr. Stowbody was piping to Mr. Dawson, "Say, Luke, when was't Biggins first settled in Winnebago Township? Wa'n't it in 1879?"

"Why no 'twa'n't!" Mr. Dawson was indignant. "He come out from Vermont in 1867—no, wait, in 1868, it must have been—and took a claim on the Rum River, quite a ways above Anoka."

"He did not!" roared Mr. Stowbody. "He settled first in Blue Earth County, him and his father!"

("What's the point at issue?") Carol whispered to Kennicott.

("Whether this old duck Biggins had an English setter or a Llewellyn. They've been arguing it all evening!")

Dave Dyer interrupted to give tidings, "D' tell you that Clara Biggins was in town couple days ago? She bought a hot-water bottle—expensive one, too—two dollars and thirty cents!"

"Yaaaaaah!" snarled Mr. Stowbody. "Course. She's just like her grandad was. Never save a cent. Two dollars and twenty—thirty, was it?—two dollars and thirty cents for a hot-water bottle! Brick wrapped up in a flannel petticoat just as good, anyway!"

"How's Ella's tonsils, Mr. Stowbody?" yawned Chet Dashaway.

While Mr. Stowbody gave a somatic and psychic study of them, Carol reflected, "Are they really so terribly interested in Ella's tonsils, or even in Ella's esophagus? I wonder if I could get them away from personalities? Let's risk damnation and try."

"There hasn't been much labor trouble around here, has there, Mr. Stowbody?" she asked innocently.

"No, ma'am, thank God, we've been free from that, except maybe with hired girls and farm-hands. Trouble enough with these foreign farmers; if you don't watch these Swedes they turn socialist or populist

or some fool thing on you in a minute. Of course, if they have loans you can make 'em listen to reason. I just have 'em come into the bank for a talk, and tell 'em a few things. I don't mind their being democrats, so much, but I won't stand having socialists around. But thank God, we ain't got the labor trouble they have in these cities. Even Jack Elder here gets along pretty well, in the planing-mill, don't you, Jack?"

"Yep. Sure. Don't need so many skilled workmen in my place, and it's a lot of these cranky, wage-hogging, half-baked skilled mechanics that start trouble —reading a lot of this anarchist literature and union papers and all."

"Do you approve of union labor?" Carol inquired of Mr. Elder.

"Me? I should say not! It's like this: I don't mind dealing with my men if they think they've got any grievances—though Lord knows what's come over workmen, nowadays—don't appreciate a good job. But still, if they come to me honestly, as man to man, I'll talk things over with them. But I'm not going to have any outsider, any of these walking delegates, or whatever fancy names they call themselves now—bunch of rich grafters, living on the ignorant workmen! Not going to have any of those fellows butting in and telling *me* how to run *my* business!"

Mr. Elder was growing more excited, more belligerent and patriotic. "I stand for freedom and constitutional rights. If any man don't like my shop, he can get up and git. Same way, if I don't like him, he gits. And that's all there is to it. I simply can't understand all these complications and hoop-te-doodles and government reports and wage-scales and God knows what all that these fellows are balling up the labor situation with, when it's all perfectly simple. They like what I pay 'em, or they get out. That's all there is to it!"

"What do you think of profit-sharing?" Carol ventured.

Mr. Elder thundered his answer, while the others nodded, solemnly and in tune, like a shop-window of flexible toys, comic mandarins and judges and ducks and clowns, set quivering by a breeze from the open door:

"All this profit-sharing and welfare work and insurance and old-age pension is simply poppycock. Enfeebles a workman's independence—and wastes a lot of honest profit. The half-baked thinker that isn't dry behind the ears yet, and these suffragettes and God knows what all buttinskis there are that are trying to tell a business man how to run his business, and some of these college professors are just about as bad, the whole kit and bilin' of 'em are nothing in God's world but socialism in disguise! And it's my bounden duty as a producer to resist every attack on the integrity of American industry to the last ditch. Yes—SIR!"

Mr. Elder wiped his brow.

Dave Dyer added, "Sure! You bet! What they ought to do is simply to hang every one of these agitators, and that would settle the whole thing right off. Don't you think so, doc?"

"You bet," agreed Kennicott.

The conversation was at last relieved of the plague of Carol's intrusions and they settled down to the question of whether the justice of the peace had sent that hobo drunk to jail for ten days or twelve. It was a matter not readily determined. Then Dave Dyer communicated his carefree adventures on the gipsy trail:

"Yep. I get good time out of the flivver. 'Bout a week ago I motored down to New Wurttemberg. That's forty-three—— No, let's see: It's seventeen miles to Belldale, and 'bout six and three-quarters, call it seven, to Torgenquist, and it's a good nineteen miles from there to New Wurttemberg—seventeen and seven and nineteen, that makes, uh, let me see: seventeen and seven 's twenty-four, plus nineteen, well say plus twenty, that makes forty-four, well anyway, say about forty-three or -four miles from here to New Wurttemberg. We got started about seven-fifteen, prob'ly seven-twenty, because I had to stop and fill the radiator, and we ran along, just keeping up a good steady gait——"

Mr. Dyer did finally, for reasons and purposes admitted and justified, attain to New Wurttemberg.

Once—only once—the presence of the alien Carol was recognized. Chet Dashaway leaned over and said asthmatically, "Say, uh, have you been reading this serial 'Two Out' in *Tingling Tales?* Corking yarn! Gosh, the fellow that wrote it certainly can sling base-ball slang!"

The others tried to look literary. Harry Haydock offered, "Juanita is a great hand for reading high-class stuff, like 'Mid the Magnolias' by this Sara Hetwiggin Butts, and 'Riders of Ranch Reckless.' Books. But me,"

he glanced about importantly, as one convinced that no other hero had ever been in so strange a plight, "I'm so darn busy I don't have much time to read."

"I never read anything I can't check against," said Sam Clark.

Thus ended the literary portion of the conversation, and for seven minutes Jackson Elder outlined reasons for believing that the pike-fishing was better on the west shore of Lake Minniemashie than on the east— though it was indeed quite true that on the east shore Nat Hicks had caught a pike altogether admirable.

The talk went on. It did go on! Their voices were monotonous, thick, emphatic. They were harshly pompous, like men in the smoking-compartments of Pullman cars. They did not bore Carol. They frightened her. She panted, "They will be cordial to me, because my man belongs to their tribe. God help me if I were an outsider!"

Smiling as changelessly as an ivory figurine she sat quiescent, avoiding thought, glancing about the living-room and hall, noting their betrayal of unimaginative commercial prosperity. Kennicott said, "Dandy interior, eh? My idea of how a place ought to be furnished. Modern." She looked polite, and observed the oiled floors, hard-wood staircase, unused fireplace with tiles which resembled brown linoleum, cut-glass vases standing upon doilies, and the barred, shut, forbidding unit bookcases that were half filled with swashbuckler novels and unread-looking sets of Dickens, Kipling, O. Henry, and Elbert Hubbard.

She perceived that even personalities were failing to hold the party. The room filled with hesitancy as with a fog. People cleared their throats, tried to choke down yawns. The men shot their cuffs and the women stuck their combs more firmly into their back hair.

Then a rattle, a daring hope in every eye, the swinging of a door, the smell of strong coffee, Dave Dyer's mewing voice in a triumphant, "The eats!" They began to chatter. They had something to do. They could escape from themselves. They fell upon the food—chicken sandwiches, maple cake, drug-store ice cream. Even when the food was gone they remained cheerful. They could go home, any time now, and go to bed!

They went, with a flutter of coats, chiffon scarfs, and good-bys.

Carol and Kennicott walked home.

"Did you like them?" he asked.

"They were terribly sweet to me."

"Uh, Carrie—— You ought to be more careful about shocking folks. Talking about gold stockings, and about showing your ankles to schoolteachers and all!" More mildly: "You gave 'em a good time, but I'd watch out for that, 'f I were you. Juanita Haydock is such a damn cat. I wouldn't give her a chance to criticize me."

"My poor effort to lift up the party! Was I wrong to try to amuse them?"

"No! No! Honey, I didn't mean—— You were the only up-and-coming person in the bunch. I just mean—— Don't get onto legs and all that immoral stuff. Pretty conservative crowd."

She was silent, raw with the shameful thought that the attentive circle might have been criticizing her, laughing at her.

"Don't, please don't worry!" he pleaded.

Silence.

"Gosh, I'm sorry I spoke about it. I just meant—— But they were crazy about you. Sam said to me, 'That little lady of yours is the slickest thing that ever came to this town,' he said; and Ma Dawson—I didn't hardly know whether she'd like you or not, she's such a dried-up old bird, but she said, 'Your bride is so quick and bright, I declare, she just wakes me up.'"

Carol liked praise, the flavor and fatness of it, but she was so energetically being sorry for herself that she could not taste this commendation.

"Please! Come on! Cheer up!" His lips said it, his anxious shoulder said it, his arm about her said it, as they halted on the obscure porch of their house.

"Do you care if they think I'm flighty, Will?"

"Me? Why, I wouldn't care if the whole world thought you were this or that or anything else. You're my—well, you're my soul!"

He was an undefined mass, as solid-seeming as rock. She found his sleeve, pinched it, cried, "I'm glad! It's sweet to be wanted! You must tolerate my frivolousness. You're all I have!"

He lifted her, carried her into the house, and with her arms about his neck she forgot Main Street.

[The persons whom Carol finds most "interesting" as she settles into her new home are the eccentrics of Gopher Prairie: Vida Sherwin, a high-school teacher who (the reader discovers later) had hoped to marry Will herself; Raymie Wutherspoon, the slightly effeminate manager of the Bon Ton Store; and the young lawyer, Guy Pollock, like Wutherspoon a bachelor. All share to some degree her rebelliousness. Gradually she learns of the narrowness of small-town life: the prying curiosity of neighbors, the humiliation of wives who have to ask their husbands for money for household expenses, the unvarying pattern of social affairs. In an attempt to break the monotony, Carol gives a housewarming with a number of "ice-breaking" games; but the next week the Dashaways give a party without such "novelties."]

CHAPTER VII

II

She had, she meditated, passed through the novelty of seeing the town and meeting people, of skating and sliding and hunting. Bea was competent; there was no household labor except sewing and darning and gossipy assistance to Bea in bed-making. She couldn't satisfy her ingenuity in planning meals. At Dahl & Oleson's Meat Market you didn't give orders—you wofully inquired whether there was anything today besides steak and pork and ham. The cuts of beef were not cuts. They were hacks. Lamb chops were as exotic as sharks' fins. The meat-dealers shipped their best to the city, with its higher prices.

In all the shops there was the same lack of choice. She could not find a glass-headed picture-nail in town; she did not hunt for the sort of veiling she wanted —she took what she could get; and only at Howland & Gould's was there such a luxury as canned asparagus. Routine care was all she could devote to the house. Only by such fussing as the Widow Bogart's could she make it fill her time.

She could not have outside employment. To the village doctor's wife it was taboo.

She was a woman with a working brain and no work.

There were only three things which she could do: Have children; start her career of reforming; or become so definitely a part of the town that she would be fulfilled by the activities of church and study-club and bridge-parties.

Children, yes, she wanted them, but—— She was

not quite ready. She had been embarrassed by Kennicott's frankness, but she agreed with him that in the insane condition of civilization, which made the rearing of citizens more costly and perilous than any other crime, it was inadvisable to have children till he had made more money. She was sorry—— Perhaps he had made all the mystery of love a mechanical cautiousness but—— She fled from the thought with a dubious, "Some day."

Her "reforms," her impulses toward beauty in raw Main Street, they had become indistinct. But she would set them going now. She would! She swore it with soft fist beating the edges of the radiator. And at the end of all her vows she had no notion as to when and where the crusade was to begin.

Become an authentic part of the town? She began to think with unpleasant lucidity. She reflected that she did not know whether the people liked her. She had gone to the women at afternoon-coffees, to the merchants in their stores, with so many outpouring comments and whimsies that she hadn't given them a chance to betray their opinions of her. The men smiled—but did they like her? She was lively among the women—but was she one of them? She could not recall many times when she had been admitted to the whispering of scandal which is the secret chamber of Gopher Prairie conversation.

She was poisoned with doubt, as she drooped up to bed.

Next day, through her shopping, her mind sat back and observed. Dave Dyer and Sam Clark were as cordial as she had been fancying; but wasn't there an impersonal abruptness in the "H' are yuh?" of Chet Dashaway? Howland the grocer was curt. Was that merely his usual manner?

"It's infuriating to have to pay attention to what people think. In St. Paul I didn't care. But here I'm spied on. They're watching me. I mustn't let it make me self-conscious," she coaxed herself—overstimulated by the drug of thought, and offensively on the defensive.

III

A thaw which stripped the snow from the sidewalks; a ringing iron night when the lakes could be heard booming; a clear roistering morning. In tam o'shanter and tweed skirt Carol felt herself a college junior going out to play hockey. She wanted to whoop, her legs ached to run. On the way home from shopping she yielded, as a pup would have yielded. She galloped down a block and as she jumped from a curb across a welter of slush, she gave a student "Yippee!"

She saw that in a window three old women were gasping. Their triple glare was paralyzing. Across the street, at another window, the curtain had secretively moved. She stopped, walked on sedately, changed from the girl Carol into Mrs. Dr. Kennicott.

She never again felt quite young enough and defiant enough and free enough to run and halloo in the public streets; and it was as a Nice Married Woman that she attended the next weekly bridge of the Jolly Seventeen.

IV

The Jolly Seventeen (the membership of which ranged from fourteen to twenty-six) was the social cornice of Gopher Prairie. It was the country club, the diplomatic set, the St. Cecilia, the Ritz oval room, the Club de Vingt. To belong to it was to be "in." Though its membership partly coincided with that of the Thanatopsis study club, the Jolly Seventeen as a separate entity guffawed at the Thanatopsis, and considered it middle-class and even "highbrow."

Most of the Jolly Seventeen were young married women, with their husbands as associate members. Once a week they had a women's afternoon-bridge; once a month the husbands joined them for supper and evening-bridge; twice a year they had dances at I.O.O.F. Hall. Then the town exploded. Only at the annual balls of the Firemen and of the Eastern Star was there such prodigality of chiffon scarfs and tangoing and heart-burnings, and these rival institutions were not select—hired girls attended the Firemen's Ball, with section-hands and laborers. Ella Stowbody had once gone to a Jolly Seventeen Soirée in the village hack, hitherto confined to chief mourners at funerals; and Harry Haydock and Dr. Terry Gould always appeared in the town's only specimen of evening clothes.

The afternoon-bridge of the Jolly Seventeen which followed Carol's lonely doubting was held at Juanita Haydock's new concrete bungalow, with its door of polished oak and beveled plate-glass, jar of ferns in the plastered hall, and in the living-room, a fumed oak Morris chair, sixteen color-prints, and a square varnished table with a mat made of cigar-ribbons on which was one Illustrated Gift Edition and one pack of cards in a burnt-leather case.

Carol stepped into a sirocco of furnace heat. They were already playing. Despite her flabby resolves she had not yet learned bridge. She was winningly apologetic about it to Juanita, and ashamed that she should have to go on being apologetic.

Mrs. Dave Dyer, a sallow woman with a thin prettiness, devoted to experiments in religious cults, illnesses, and scandal-bearing, shook her finger at Carol and trilled, "You're a naughty one! I don't believe you appreciate the honor, when you got into the Jolly Seventeen so easy!"

Mrs. Chet Dashaway nudged her neighbor at the second table. But Carol kept up the appealing bridal manner so far as possible. She twittered, "You're perfectly right. I'm a lazy thing. I'll make Will start teaching me this very evening." Her supplication had all the sound of birdies in the nest, and Easter church-bells, and frosted Christmas cards. Internally she snarled, "That ought to be saccharine enough." She sat in the smallest rocking-chair, a model of Victorian modesty. But she saw or she imagined that the women who had gurgled at her so welcomingly when she had first come to Gopher Prairie were nodding at her brusquely.

During the pause after the first game she petitioned Mrs. Jackson Elder, "Don't you think we ought to get up another bob-sled party soon?"

"It's so cold when you get dumped in the snow," said Mrs. Elder, indifferently.

"I hate snow down my neck," volunteered Mrs. Dave Dyer, with an unpleasant look at Carol and, turning her back, she bubbled at Rita Simons, "Dearie, won't you run in this evening? I've got the loveliest new Butterick pattern I want to show you."

Carol crept back to her chair. In the fervor of discussing the game they ignored her. She was not used to being a wallflower. She struggled to keep from over-sensitiveness, from becoming unpopular by the sure method of believing that she was unpopular; but she hadn't much reserve of patience, and at the end of the second game, when Ella Stowbody sniffily asked her,

"Are you going to send to Minneapolis for your dress for the next soirée—heard you were," Carol said "Don't know yet" with unnecessary sharpness.

She was relieved by the admiration with which the jeune fille Rita Simons looked at the steel buckles on her pumps; but she resented Mrs. Howland's tart demand, "Don't you find that new couch of yours is too broad to be practical?" She nodded, then shook her head, and touchily left Mrs. Howland to get out of it any meaning she desired. Immediately she wanted to make peace. She was close to simpering in the sweetness with which she addressed Mrs. Howland: "I think that is the prettiest display of beef-tea your husband has in his store."

"Oh yes, Gopher Prairie isn't so much behind the times," gibed Mrs. Howland. Some one giggled.

Their rebuffs made her haughty; her haughtiness irritated them to franker rebuffs; they were working up to a state of painfully righteous war when they were saved by the coming of food.

Though Juanita Haydock was highly advanced in the matters of finger-bowls, doilies, and bath-mats, her "refreshments" were typical of all the afternoon-coffees. Juanita's best friends, Mrs. Dyer and Mrs. Dashaway, passed large dinner plates, each with a spoon, a fork, and a coffee cup without saucer. They apologized and discussed the afternoon's game as they passed through the thicket of women's feet. Then they distributed hot buttered rolls, coffee poured from an enamel-ware pot, stuffed olives, potato salad, and angel's-food cake. There was, even in the most strictly conforming Gopher Prairie circles, a certain option as to collations. The olives need not be stuffed. Doughnuts were in some houses well thought of as a substitute for the hot buttered rolls. But there was in all the town no heretic save Carol who omitted angel's-food.

They ate enormously. Carol had a suspicion that the thriftier housewives made the afternoon treat do for evening supper.

She tried to get back into the current. She edged over to Mrs. McGanum. Chunky, amiable, young Mrs. McGanum, with her breast and arms of a milkmaid, and her loud delayed laugh which burst startlingly from a sober face, was the daughter of old Dr. Westlake, and the wife of Westlake's partner, Dr. McGanum. Kennicott asserted that Westlake and McGanum and their contaminated families were tricky, but Carol had found them gracious. She asked for friendliness by crying to Mrs. McGanum, "How is the baby's throat now?" and she was attentive while Mrs. McGanum rocked and knitted and placidly described symptoms.

Vida Sherwin came in after school, with Miss Ethel Villets, the town librarian. Miss Sherwin's optimistic presence gave Carol more confidence. She talked. She informed the circle, "I drove almost down to Wahkeenyan with Will, a few days ago. Isn't the country lovely! And I do admire the Scandinavian farmers down there so: their big red barns and silos and milking-machines and everything. Do you all know that lonely Lutheran church, with the tin-covered spire, that stands out alone on a hill? It's so bleak; somehow it seems so brave. I do think the Scandinavians are the hardiest and best people——"

"Oh, do you *think* so?" protested Mrs. Jackson Elder. "My husband says the Svenskas that work in the planing-mill are perfectly terrible—so silent and cranky, and so selfish, the way they keep demanding raises. If they had their way they'd simply ruin the business."

"Yes, and they're simply *ghastly* hired girls!" wailed Mrs. Dave Dyer. "I swear, I work myself to skin and bone trying to please my hired girls—when I can get them! I do everything in the world for them. They can have their gentleman friends call on them in the kitchen any time, and they get just the same to eat as we do, if there's any left over, and I practically never jump on them."

Juanita Haydock rattled, "They're ungrateful, all that class of people. I do think the domestic problem is simply becoming awful. I don't know what the country's coming to, with these Scandahoofian clodhoppers demanding every cent you can save, and so ignorant and impertinent, and on my word, demanding bath-tubs and everything—as if they weren't mighty good and lucky at home if they got a bath in the wash-tub."

They were off, riding hard. Carol thought of Bea and waylaid them:

"But isn't it possibly the fault of the mistresses if the maids are ungrateful? For generations we've given them the leavings of food, and holes to live in. I don't want to boast, but I must say I don't have much trouble with Bea. She's so friendly. The Scandinavians are sturdy and honest——"

Mrs. Dave Dyer snapped, "Honest? Do you call it honest to hold us up for every cent of pay they can get? I can't say that I've had any of them steal anything (though you might call it stealing to eat so much that a roast of beef hardly lasts three days), but just the same I don't intend to let them think they can put anything over on *me!* I always make them pack and unpack their trunks down-stairs, right under my eyes, and then I know they aren't being tempted to dishonesty by any slackness on *my* part!"

"How much do the maids get here?" Carol ventured.

Mrs. B. J Gougerling, wife of the banker, stated in a shocked manner, "Any place from three-fifty to five-fifty a week! I know positively that Mrs. Clark, after swearing that she wouldn't weaken and encourage them in their outrageous demands, went and paid five-fifty—think of it! practically a dollar a day for unskilled work and, of course, her food and room and a chance to do her own washing right in with the rest of the wash. *How much do you pay, Mrs. Kennicott?*"

"Yes! How much do you pay?" insisted half a dozen.

"W-why, I pay six a week," she feebly confessed.

They gasped. Juanita protested, "Don't you think it's hard on the rest of us when you pay so much?" Juanita's demand was re-inforced by the universal glower.

Carol was angry. "I don't care! A maid has one of the hardest jobs on earth. She works from ten to eighteen hours a day. She has to wash slimy dishes and dirty clothes. She tends the children and runs to the door with wet chapped hands and——"

Mrs. Dave Dyer broke into Carol's peroration with a furious, "That's all very well, but believe me, I do those things myself when I'm without a maid—and that's a good share of the time for a person that isn't willing to yield and pay exorbitant wages!"

Carol was retorting, "But a maid does it for strangers, and all she gets out of it is the pay——"

Their eyes were hostile. Four of them were talking at once. Vida Sherwin's dictatorial voice cut through, took control of the revolution:

"Tut, tut, tut, tut! What angry passions—and what an idiotic discussion! All of you getting too serious. Stop it! Carol Kennicott, you're probably right, but you're too much ahead of the times. Juanita, quit looking so belligerent. What is this, a card party or a hen fight? Carol, you stop admiring yourself as the Joan of Arc of the hired girls, or I'll spank you. You come over here and talk libraries with Ethel Villets. Boooooo! If there's any more pecking, I'll take charge of the hen roost myself!"

They all laughed artificially, and Carol obediently "talked libraries."

A small-town bungalow, the wives of a village doctor and a village dry-goods merchant, a provincial teacher, a colloquial brawl over paying a servant a dollar more a week. Yet this insignificance echoed cellar-plots and cabinet meetings and labor conferences in Persia and Prussia, Rome and Boston, and the orators who deemed themselves international leaders were but the raised voices of a billion Juanitas denouncing a million Carols, with a hundred thousand Vida Sherwins trying to shoo away the storm.

Carol felt guilty. She devoted herself to admiring the spinsterish Miss Villets—and immediately committed another offense against the laws of decency.

"We haven't seen you at the library yet," Miss Villets reproved.

"I've wanted to run in so much but I've been getting settled and—— I'll probably come in so often you'll get tired of me! I hear you have such a nice library."

"There are many who like it. We have two thousand more books than Wakamin."

"Isn't that fine. I'm sure you are largely responsible. I've had some experience, in St. Paul."

"So I have been informed. Not that I entirely approve of library methods in these large cities. So careless, letting tramps and all sorts of dirty persons practically sleep in the reading-rooms."

"I know, but the poor souls—— Well, I'm sure you will agree with me in one thing: The chief task of a librarian is to get people to read."

"You feel so? My feeling, Mrs. Kennicott, and I am merely quoting the librarian of a very large college, is that the first duty of the *conscientious* librarian is to preserve the books."

"Oh!" Carol repented her "Oh." Miss Villets stiffened, and attacked:

"It may be all very well in cities, where they have unlimited funds, to let nasty children ruin books and just deliberately tear them up, and fresh young men take more books out than they are entitled to by the regulations, but I'm never going to permit it in this library!"

"What if some children are destructive? They learn to read. Books are cheaper than minds."

"Nothing is cheaper than the minds of some of these children that come in and bother me simply because their mothers don't keep them home where they belong. Some librarians may choose to be so wishy-washy and turn their libraries into nursing-homes and kindergartens, but as long as I'm in charge, the Gopher Prairie library is going to be quiet and decent, and the books well kept!"

Carol saw that the others were listening, waiting for her to be objectionable. She flinched before their dislike. She hastened to smile in agreement with Miss Villets, to glance publicly at her wrist-watch, to warble that it was "so late—have to hurry home—husband—such nice party—maybe you were right about maids, prejudiced because Bea so nice—such perfectly divine angel's-food, Mrs. Haydock must give me the recipe—good-by, such happy party——"

She walked home. She reflected, "It was my fault. I was touchy. And I opposed them so much. Only—— I can't! I can't be one of them if I must damn all the maids toiling in filthy kitchens, all the ragged hungry children. And these women are to be my arbiters, the rest of my life!"

She ignored Bea's call from the kitchen; she ran up-stairs to the unfrequented guest-room; she wept in terror, her body a pale arc as she knelt beside a cumbrous black-walnut bed, beside a puffy mattress covered with a red quilt, in a shuttered and airless room.

CHAPTER VIII

II

Four days after the Jolly Seventeen débâcle Vida Sherwin called and casually blew Carol's world to pieces.

"May I come in and gossip a while?" she said, with such excess of bright innocence that Carol was uneasy. Vida took off her furs with a bounce, she sat down as though it were a gymnasium exercise, she flung out:

"Feel disgracefully good, this weather! Raymond Wutherspoon says if he had my energy he'd be a grand opera singer. I always think this climate is the finest in the world, and my friends are the dearest people in the world, and my work is the most essential thing in the world. Probably I fool myself. But I know one thing for certain: You're the pluckiest little idiot in the world."

"And so you are about to flay me alive." Carol was cheerful about it.

"Am I? Perhaps. I've been wondering—I know that the third party to a squabble is often the most to blame: the one who runs between A and B having a beautiful time telling each of them what the other has said. But I want you to take a big part in vitalizing Gopher Prairie and so—— Such a very unique opportunity and—— Am I silly?"

"I know what you mean. I was too abrupt at the Jolly Seventeen."

"It isn't that. Matter of fact, I'm glad you told them some wholesome truths about servants. (Though perhaps you were just a bit tactless.) It's bigger than that. I wonder if you understand that in a secluded community like this every newcomer is on test? People cordial to her but watching her all the time. I remember when a Latin teacher came here from Wellesley, they resented her broad A. Were sure it was affected. Of course they have discussed you——"

"Have they talked about me much?"

"My dear!"

"I always feel as though I walked around in a cloud, looking out at others but not being seen. I feel so inconspicuous and so normal—so normal that there's nothing about me to discuss. I can't realize that Mr. and Mrs. Haydock must gossip about me." Carol was working up a small passion of distaste. "And I don't like it. It makes me crawly to think of their daring to talk over all I do and say. Pawing me over! I resent it. I hate——"

"Wait, child! Perhaps they resent some things in you. I want you to try and be impersonal. They'd paw over anybody who came in new. Didn't you, with newcomers in College?"

"Yes."

"Well then! Will you be impersonal? I'm paying you the compliment of supposing that you can be. I want you to be big enough to help me make this town worth while."

"I'll be as impersonal as cold boiled potatoes. (Not that I shall ever be able to help you 'make the town worth while.') What do they say about me? Really. I want to know."

"Of course the illiterate ones resent your references to anything farther away than Minneapolis. They're so suspicious—that's it, suspicious. And some think you dress too well."

"Oh, they do, do they! Shall I dress in gunny-sacking to suit them?"

"Please! Are you going to be a baby?"

"I'll be good," sulkily.

"You certainly will, or I won't tell you one single thing. You must understand this: I'm not asking you to change yourself. Just want you to know what they think. You must do that, no matter how absurd their prejudices are, if you're going to handle them. Is it your ambition to make this a better town, or isn't it?"

"I don't know whether it is or not!"

"Why—why—— Tut, tut, now, of course it is! Why, I depend on you. You're a born reformer."

"I am not—not any more!"

"Of course you are."

"Oh, if I really could help—— So they think I'm affected?"

"My lamb, they do! Now don't say they're nervy. After all, Gopher Prairie standards are as reasonable to Gopher Prairie as Lake Shore Drive standards are to Chicago. And there's more Gopher Prairies than there are Chicagos. Or Londons. And—— I'll tell you the whole story: They think you're showing off when you say 'American' instead of 'Ammurrican.' They think you're too frivolous. Life's so serious to them that they can't imagine any kind of laughter except Juanita's snortling. Ethel Villets was sure you were patronizing her when——"

"Oh, I was not!"

"——you talked about encouraging reading; and Mrs. Elder thought you were patronizing when you said she had 'such a pretty little car.' She thinks it's an enormous car! And some of the merchants say you're too flip when you talk to them in the store and——"

"Poor me, when I was trying to be friendly!"

"——every housewife in town is doubtful about your being so chummy with your Bea. All right to be kind, but they say you act as though she were your cousin. (Wait now! There's plenty more.) And they think you were eccentric in furnishing this room—they think the broad couch and that Japanese dingus are absurd. (Wait! I know they're silly.) And I guess I've heard a dozen criticize you because you don't go to church oftener and——"

"I can't stand it—I can't bear to realize that they've been saying all these things while I've been going about so happily and liking them. I wonder if you ought to have told me? It will make me self-conscious."

"I wonder the same thing. Only answer I can get is the old saw about knowledge being power. And some day you'll see how absorbing it is to have power, even here; to control the town—— Oh, I'm a crank. But I do like to see things moving."

"It hurts. It makes these people seem so beastly and treacherous, when I've been perfectly natural with them. But let's have it all. What did they say about my Chinese housewarming party?"

"Why, uh——"

"Go on. Or I'll make up worse things than anything you can tell me."

"They did enjoy it. But I guess some of them felt you were showing off—pretending that your husband is richer than he is."

"I can't—— Their meanness of mind is beyond any horrors I could imagine. They really thought that I—— And you want to 'reform' people like that when dynamite is so cheap? Who dared to say that? The rich or the poor?"

"Fairly well assorted."

"Can't they at least understand me well enough to see that though I might be affected and culturine, at least I simply couldn't commit that other kind of vulgarity? If they must know, you may tell them, with my compliments, that Will makes about four thousand a year, and the party cost half of what they probably thought it did. Chinese things are not very expensive, and I made my own costume——"

"Stop it! Stop beating me! I know all that. What they meant was: they felt you were starting dangerous competition by giving a party such as most people here can't afford. Four thousand is a pretty big income for this town."

"I never thought of starting competition. Will you

believe that it was in all love and friendliness that I tried to give them the gayest party I could? It was foolish; it was childish and noisy. But I did mean it so well."

"I know, of course. And it certainly is unfair of them to make fun of your having that Chinese food —chow men, was it?—and to laugh about your wearing those pretty trousers——"

Carol sprang up, whimpering, "Oh, they didn't do that! They didn't poke fun at my feast, that I ordered so carefully for them! And my little Chinese costume that I was so happy making—I made it secretly, to surprise them. And they've been ridiculing it, all this while!"

She was huddled on the couch.

Vida was stroking her hair, muttering, "I shouldn't——"

Shrouded in shame, Carol did not know when Vida slipped away. The clock's bell, at half past five, aroused her. "I must get hold of myself before Will comes. I hope he never knows what a fool his wife is. . . . Frozen, sneering, horrible hearts."

Like a very small, very lonely girl she trudged upstairs, slow step by step, her feet dragging, her hand on the rail. It was not her husband to whom she wanted to run for protection—it was her father, her smiling understanding father, dead these twelve years.

[Carol is now aware of her precarious position in Gopher Prairie. Wanting to be tolerated, to be liked, she nevertheless cannot give up hope that in some way the town can be made more lovely. She dreams for a time that the Thanatopsis, to which the wives of all the substantial men belong, can be turned to the problem of civic improvement. But the women are quite satisfied with things as they are; their husbands are even more so. A venture into amateur dramatics is almost equally disappointing, as are later efforts to enliven the town library and the Chautauqua. Frustration and boredom drive Carol to a flirtation with Guy Pollock, but when he criticizes the "commercial hatred" of physicians she turns back to Will, and for a time dramatizes herself as the country doctor's wife. For two years after the birth of her son, Hugh, she is content; then the reform spirit stirs her once more. Meanwhile Vida Sherwin has married Raymie Wutherspoon.]

CHAPTER XXII

I

The greatest mystery about a human being is not his reaction to sex or praise, but the manner in which he contrives to put in twenty-four hours a day. It is this which puzzles the longshoreman about the clerk, the Londoner about the bushman. It was this which puzzled Carol in regard to the married Vida. Carol herself had the baby, a larger house to care for, all the telephone calls for Kennicott when he was away; and she read everything, while Vida was satisfied with newspaper headlines.

But after detached brown years in boarding-houses, Vida was hungry for housework, for the most pottering detail of it. She had no maid, nor wanted one. She cooked, baked, swept, washed supper-cloths, with the triumph of a chemist in a new laboratory. To her the hearth was veritably the altar. When she went shopping she hugged the cans of soup, and she bought a mop or a side of bacon as though she were preparing for a reception. She knelt beside a bean sprout and crooned, "I raised this with my own hands—I brought this new life into the world."

"I love her for being so happy," Carol brooded. "I ought to be that way. I worship the baby, but the housework—— Oh, I suppose I'm fortunate; so much better off than farm-women on a new clearing, or people in a slum."

It has not yet been recorded that any human being has gained a very large or permanent contentment from meditation upon the fact that he is better off than others.

In Carol's own twenty-four hours a day she got up, dressed the baby, had breakfast, talked to Oscarina about the day's shopping, put the baby on the porch to play, went to the butcher's to choose between steak and pork chops, bathed the baby, nailed up a shelf, had dinner, put the baby to bed for a nap, paid the iceman, read for an hour, took the baby out for a walk, called on Vida, had supper, put the baby to bed, darned socks, listened to Kennicott's yawning comment on what a fool Dr. McGanum was to try to use that cheap X-ray outfit of his on an epithelioma, repaired a frock, drowsily heard Kennicott stoke the furnace, tried to read a page of Thorstein Veblen—and the day was gone.

Except when Hugh was vigorously naughty, or whiney, or laughing, or saying "I like my chair" with thrilling maturity, she was always enfeebled by loneliness. She no longer felt superior about that misfortune. She would gladly have been converted to Vida's satisfaction in Gopher Prairie and mopping the floor.

II

Carol drove through an astonishing number of books from the public library and from city shops. Kennicott was at first uncomfortable over her disconcerting habit of buying them. A book was a book, and if you had several thousand of them right here in the library, free, why the dickens should you spend your good money? After worrying about it for two or three years, he decided that this was one of the Funny Ideas which she had caught as a librarian and from which she would never entirely recover.

The authors whom she read were most of them frightfully annoyed by the Vida Sherwins. They were young American sociologists, young English realists, Russian horrorists; Anatole France, Rolland, Nexo, Wells, Shaw, Key, Edgar Lee Masters, Theodore Dreiser, Sherwood Anderson, Henry Mencken, and all the other subversive philosophers and artists whom women were consulting everywhere, in batik-curtained studios in New York, in Kansas farmhouses, San Francisco drawing-rooms, Alabama schools for Negroes. From them she got the same confused desire which the million other women felt; the same determination to be class-conscious without discovering the class of which she was to be conscious.

Certainly her reading precipitated her observations of Main Street, of Gopher Prairie and of the several adjacent Gopher Prairies which she had seen on drives with Kennicott. In her fluid thought certain convictions appeared, jaggedly, a fragment of an impression at a time, while she was going to sleep, or manicuring her nails, or waiting for Kennicott.

These convictions she presented to Vida Sherwin— Vida Wutherspoon—beside a radiator, over a bowl of not very good walnuts and pecans from Uncle Whittier's grocery, on an evening when both Kennicott and Raymie had gone out of town with the other officers of the Ancient and Affiliated Order of Spartans, to inaugurate a new chapter at Wakamin. Vida had come to the house for the night. She helped in putting Hugh to bed, sputtering the while about his soft skin. Then they talked till midnight.

What Carol said that evening, what she was passionately thinking, was also emerging in the minds of women in ten thousand Gopher Prairies. Her formulations were not pat solutions but visions of a tragic futility. She did not utter them so compactly that they can be given in her words; they were roughened with "Well, you see" and "if you get what I mean" and "I don't know that I'm making myself clear." But they were definite enough, and indignant enough.

III

In reading popular stories and seeing plays, asserted Carol, she had found only two traditions of the American small town. The first tradition, repeated in scores of magazines every month, is that the American village remains the one sure abode of friendship, honesty, and clean sweet marriageable girls. Therefore all men who succeed in painting in Paris or in finance in New York at last become weary of smart women, return to their native towns, assert that cities are vicious, marry their childhood sweethearts and, presumably, joyously abide in those towns until death.

The other tradition is that the significant features of all villages are whiskers, iron dogs upon lawns, gold bricks, checkers, jars of gilded cat-tails, and shrewd comic old men who are known as "hicks" and who ejaculate "Waal I swan." This altogether admirable tradition rules the vaudeville stage, facetious illustrators, and syndicated newspaper humor, but out of actual life it passed forty years ago. Carol's small town thinks not in hoss-swapping but in cheap motor cars, telephones, ready-made clothes, silos, alfalfa, kodaks, phonographs, leather-upholstered Morris chairs, bridge-prizes, oil-stocks, motion-pictures, land-deals, unread sets of Mark Twain, and a chaste version of national politics.

With such a small-town life a Kennicott or a Champ Perry is content, but there are also hundreds of thousands, particularly women and young men, who are not at all content. The more intelligent young people (and the fortunate widows!) flee to the cities with agility and, despite the fictional tradition, resolutely stay there, seldom returning even for holidays. The most protesting patriots of the towns leave them in old age, if they can afford it, and go to live in California or in the cities.

The reason, Carol insisted, is not a whiskered rusticity. It is nothing so amusing!

It is an unimaginatively standardized background, a sluggishness of speech and manners, a rigid ruling of the spirit by the desire to appear respectable. It is contentment . . . the contentment of the quiet dead, who are scornful of the living for their restless walking. It is negation canonized as the one positive virtue. It is the prohibition of happiness. It is slavery self-sought and self-defended. It is dullness made God.

A savorless people, gulping tasteless food, and sitting afterward, coatless and thoughtless, in rocking-chairs prickly with inane decorations, listening to mechanical music, saying mechanical things about the excellence of Ford automobiles, and viewing themselves as the greatest race in the world.

IV

She had inquired as to the effect of this dominating dullness upon foreigners. She remembered the feeble exotic quality to be found in the first-generation Scandinavians; she recalled the Norwegian Fair at the Lutheran Church, to which Bea had taken her. There, in the *bondestue,* the replica of a Norse farm kitchen, pale women in scarlet jackets embroidered with gold thread and colored beads, in black skirts with a line of blue, green-striped aprons, and ridged caps very pretty to set off a fresh face, had served *rommegrod og lefse*—sweet cakes and sour milk pudding spiced with cinnamon. For the first time in Gopher Prairie Carol had found novelty. She had reveled in the mild foreignness of it.

But she saw these Scandinavian women zealously exchanging their spiced puddings and red jackets for fried pork chops and congealed white blouses, trading the ancient Christmas hymns of the fjords for "She's My Jazzland Cutie," being Americanized into uniformity, and in less than a generation losing in the grayness whatever pleasant new customs they might have added to the life of the town. Their sons finished the process. In ready-made clothes and ready-made high-school phrases they sank into propriety, and the sound American customs had absorbed without one trace of pollution another alien invasion.

And along with these foreigners, she felt herself being ironed into glossy mediocrity, and she rebelled, in fear.

The respectability of the Gopher Prairies, said Carol, is reinforced by vows of poverty and chastity in the matter of knowledge. Except for half a dozen in each town the citizens are proud of that achievement of ignorance which it is so easy to come by. To be "intellectual" or "artistic" or, in their own word, to be "highbrow," is to be priggish and of dubious virtue.

Large experiments in politics and in co-operative distribution, ventures requiring knowledge, courage, and imagination, do originate in the West and Middlewest, but they are not of the towns, they are of the farmers. If these heresies are supported by the townsmen it is only by occasional teachers, doctors, lawyers, the labor unions, and workmen like Miles Bjornstam, who are punished by being mocked as "cranks," as "half-baked parlor socialists." The editor and the rector preach at them. The cloud of serene ignorance submerges them in unhappiness and futility.

V

Here Vida observed, "Yes—well—— Do you know, I've always thought that Ray would have made a wonderful rector. He has what I call an essentially religious soul. My! He'd have read the service beautifully! I suppose it's too late now, but as I tell him, he can also serve the world by selling shoes and—— I wonder if we oughtn't to have family-prayers?"

VI

Doubtless all small towns, in all countries, in all ages, Carol admitted, have a tendency to be not only dull but mean, bitter, infested with curiosity. In France or Tibet quite as much as in Wyoming or Indiana these timidities are inherent in isolation.

But a village in a country which is taking pains to become altogether standardized and pure, which aspires to succeed Victorian England as the chief mediocrity of the world, is no longer merely provincial, no longer downy and restful in its leaf-shadowed ignorance. It is a force seeking to dominate the earth, to drain the hills and sea of color, to set Dante at boosting Gopher Prairie, and to dress the high gods in Klassy Kollege Klothes. Sure of itself, it bullies other civilizations, as a traveling salesman in a brown derby conquers the wisdom of China and tacks advertisements of cigarettes over arches for centuries dedicate to the sayings of Confucius.

Such a society functions admirably in the large production of cheap automobiles, dollar watches, and safety razors. But it is not satisfied until the entire world also admits that the end and joyous purpose of living is to ride in flivvers, to make advertising-pictures of dollar watches, and in the twilight to sit talking not of love and courage but of the convenience of safety razors.

And such a society, such a nation, is determined by the Gopher Prairies. The greatest manufacturer is but a busier Sam Clark, and all the rotund senators and presidents are village lawyers and bankers grown nine feet tall.

Though a Gopher Prairie regards itself as a part of the Great World, compares itself to Rome and Vienna, it will not acquire the scientific spirit, the international mind, which would make it great. It picks at information which will visibly procure money or social distinction. Its conception of a community ideal is not the grand manner, the noble aspiration, the fine aristocratic pride, but cheap labor for the kitchen and rapid increase in the price of land. It plays at cards on greasy oil-cloth in a shanty, and does not know that prophets are walking and talking on the terrace.

If all the provincials were as kindly as Champ Perry and Sam Clark there would be no reason for desiring the town to seek great traditions. It is the Harry Haydocks, the Dave Dyers, the Jackson Elders, small busy men crushingly powerful in their common purpose, viewing themselves as men of the world but keeping themselves men of the cash-register and the comic film, who make the town a sterile oligarchy.

VII

She had sought to be definite in analyzing the surface ugliness of the Gopher Prairies. She asserted that it is a matter of universal similarity; of flimsiness of construction, so that the towns resemble frontier camps; of neglect of natural advantages, so that the hills are covered with brush, the lakes shut off by railroads, and the creeks lined with dumping-grounds; of depressing sobriety of color; rectangularity of buildings; and excessive breadth and straightness of the gashed streets, so that there is no escape from gales and from sight of the grim sweep of land, nor any windings to coax the loiterer along, while the breadth which would be majestic in an avenue of palaces makes the low shabby shops creeping down the typical Main Street the more mean by comparison.

The universal similarity—that is the physical expression of the philosophy of dull safety. Nine-tenths of the American towns are so alike that it is the completest boredom to wander from one to another. Always, west of Pittsburg, and often, east of it, there is the same lumber yard, the same railroad station, the same Ford garage, the same creamery, the same box-like houses and two-story shops. The new, more conscious houses are alike in their very attempts at diversity: the same bungalows, the same square houses of stucco or tapestry brick. The shops show the same standardized, nationally advertised wares; the newspapers of sections three thousand miles apart have the same "syndicated features"; the boy in Arkansas displays just such a flamboyant ready-made suit as is found on just such a boy in Delaware, both of them iterate the same slang phrases from the same sporting-pages, and if one of them is in college and the other is a barber, no one may surmise which is which.

If Kennicott were snatched from Gopher Prairie and instantly conveyed to a town leagues away, he would not realize it. He would go down apparently the same Main Street (almost certainly it would be called Main Street); in the same drug store he would see the same young man serving the same ice-cream soda to the same young woman with the same magazines and phonograph records under her arm. Not till he had climbed to his office and found another sign on the door, another Dr. Kennicott inside, would he understand that something curious had presumably happened.

Finally, behind all her comments, Carol saw the fact that the prairie towns no more exist to serve the farmers who are their reason of existence than do the great capitals; they exist to fatten on the farmers, to provide for the townsmen large motors and social preferment; and, unlike the capitals, they do not give to the district in return for usury a stately and permanent center, but only this ragged camp. It is a "parasitic Greek civilization"—minus the civilization.

"There we are then," said Carol. "The remedy? Is there any? Criticism, perhaps, for the beginning of the beginning. Oh, there's nothing that attacks the Tribal God Mediocrity that doesn't help a little . . . and probably there's nothing that helps very much. Perhaps some day the farmers will build and own their market-towns. (Think of the club they could have!) But I'm afraid I haven't any 'reform program.' Not any more! The trouble is spiritual, and no League or Party can enact a preference for gardens rather than dumping-grounds. . . . There's my confession. *Well?*"

"In other words, all you want is perfection?" said Vida.

"Yes! Why not?"

"How you hate this place! How can you expect to do anything with it if you haven't any sympathy?"

"But I have! And affection. Or else I wouldn't fume so. I've learned that Gopher Prairie isn't just an eruption on the prairie, as I thought first, but as large as New York. In New York I wouldn't know more than forty or fifty people, and I know that many here. Go on! Say what you're thinking."

"Well, my dear, if I *did* take all your notions seriously, it would be pretty discouraging. Imagine how a person would feel, after working hard for years and helping to build up a nice town, to have you airily flit in and simply say 'Rotten!' Think that's fair?"

"Why not? It must be just as discouraging for the Gopher Prairieite to see Venice and make comparisons."

"It would not! I imagine gondolas are kind of nice to ride in, but we've got better bath-rooms! But—— My dear, you're not the only person in this town who has done some thinking for herself, although (pardon my rudeness) I'm afraid you think so. I'll admit we lack some things. Maybe our theater isn't as good as shows in Paris. All right! I don't want to see any foreign culture suddenly forced on us—whether it's street-planning or table-manners or crazy communistic ideas."

Vida sketched what she termed "practical things that will make a happier and prettier town, but that do belong to our life, that actually are being done." Of the Thanatopsis Club she spoke; of the rest-room, the fight against mosquitos, the campaign for more gardens and shade-trees and sewers—matters not fantastic and nebulous and distant, but immediate and sure.

Carol's answer was fantastic and nebulous enough:

"Yes. . . . Yes. . . . I know. They're good. But if I could put through all those reforms at once, I'd still want startling, exotic things. Life is comfortable and clean enough here already. And so secure. What it needs is to be less secure, more eager. The civic improvements which I'd like the Thanatopsis to advocate are Strindberg plays, and classic dancers—exquisite legs beneath tulle—and (I can see him so clearly!) a thick, black-bearded, cynical Frenchman who would sit about and drink and sing opera and tell bawdy stories and laugh at our proprieties and quote Rabelais and not be ashamed to kiss my hand!"

"Huh! Not sure about the rest of it but I guess that's what you and all the other discontented young women really want: some stranger kissing your hand!" At Carol's gasp, the old squirrel-like Vida darted out and cried, "Oh, my dear, don't take that too seriously. I just meant——"

"I know. You just meant it. Go on. Be good for my soul. Isn't it funny: here we all are—me trying to be good for Gopher Prairie's soul, and Gopher Prairie trying to be good for my soul. What are my other sins?"

"Oh, there's plenty of them. Possibly some day we shall have your fat cynical Frenchman (horrible, sneering, tobacco-stained object, ruining his brains and his digestion with vile liquor!) but, thank heaven, for a while we'll manage to keep busy with our lawns and pavements! You see, these things really are coming! The Thanatopsis is getting somewhere. And you——" Her tone italicized the words—"to my great disappointment, are doing less, not more, than the people you laugh at! Sam Clark, on the school-board, is working for better school ventilation. Ella Stowbody (whose elocuting you always think is so absurd) has persuaded the railroad to share the expense of a parked space at the station, to do away with that vacant lot."

"You sneer so easily. I'm sorry, but I do think there's something essentially cheap in your attitude. Especially about religion.

"If you must know, you're not a sound reformer at all. You're an impossibilist. And you give up too easily. You gave up on the new city hall, the anti-fly campaign, club papers, the library-board, the dramatic association—just because we didn't graduate into Ibsen the very first thing. You want perfection all at once. Do you know what the finest thing you've done is— aside from bringing Hugh into the world? It was the help you gave Dr. Will during baby-welfare week. You didn't demand that each baby be a philosopher and artist before you weighed him, as you do with the rest of us.

"And now I'm afraid perhaps I'll hurt you. We're going to have a new schoolbuilding in this town—in just a few years—and we'll have it without one bit of help or interest from you!

"Professor Mott and I and some others have been dinging away at the moneyed men for years. We didn't call on you because you would never stand the pound-pound-pounding year after year without one bit of encouragement. And we've won! I've got the promise of everybody who counts that just as soon as war-conditions permit, they'll vote the bonds for the schoolhouse. And we'll have a wonderful building— lovely brown brick, with big windows, and agricultural and manual-training departments. When we get it, that'll be my answer to all your theories!"

"I'm glad. And I'm ashamed I haven't had any part in getting it. But—— Please don't think I'm unsympathetic if I ask one question: Will the teachers in the hygienic new building go on informing the children that Persia is a yellow spot on the map, and 'Cæsar' the title of a book of grammatical puzzles?"

VIII

Vida was indignant; Carol was apologetic; they talked for another hour, the eternal Mary and Martha—an immoralist Mary and a reformist Martha. It was Vida who conquered.

The fact that she had been left out of the campaign for the new schoolbuilding disconcerted Carol. She laid her dreams of perfection aside. When Vida asked her to take charge of a group of Camp Fire Girls, she obeyed, and had definite pleasure out of the Indian dances and ritual and costumes. She went more regularly to the Thanatopsis. With Vida as lieutenant and unofficial commander she campaigned for a village nurse to attend poor families, raised the fund herself, saw to it that the nurse was young and strong and amiable and intelligent.

Yet all the while she beheld the burly cynical Frenchman and the diaphanous dancers as clearly as the child sees its air-born playmates; she relished the Camp Fire Girls not because, in Vida's words, "this Scout training 10 will help so much to make them Good Wives," but because she hoped that the Sioux dances would bring subversive color into their dinginess.

She helped Ella Stowbody to set out plants in the tiny triangular park at the railroad station; she squatted in the dirt, with a small curved trowel and the most decorous of gardening gauntlets; she talked to Ella about the public-spiritedness of fuchsias and cannas; and she felt that she was scrubbing a temple deserted by the gods and empty even of incense and the sound 20 of chanting. Passengers looking from trains saw her as a village woman of fading prettiness, incorruptible virtue, and no abnormalities; the baggageman heard her say, "Oh yes, I do think it will be a good example for the children"; and all the while she saw herself running garlanded through the streets of Babylon.

Planting led her to botanizing. She never got much farther than recognizing the tiger lily and the wild rose, but she rediscovered Hugh. "What does the buttercup say, mummy?" he cried, his hand full of 30 straggly grasses, his cheek gilded with pollen. She knelt to embrace him; she affirmed that he made life more than full; she was altogether reconciled . . . for an hour.

But she awoke at night to hovering death. She crept away from the hump of bedding that was Kennicott; tiptoed into the bathroom and, by the mirror in the door of the medicine-cabinet, examined her pallid face.

Wasn't she growing visibly older in ratio as Vida grew plumper and younger? Wasn't her nose sharper? 40 Wasn't her neck granulated? She stared and choked. She was only thirty. But the five years since her marriage—had they not gone by as hastily and stupidly as though she had been under ether; would time not slink past till death? She pounded her fist on the cool enameled rim of the bathtub and raged mutely against the indifferent gods:

"I don't care! I won't endure it! They lie so—Vida and Will and Aunt Bessie—they tell me I ought to be satisfied with Hugh and a good home and planting seven nasturtiums in a station garden! I am I! When 50 I die the world will be annihilated, as far as I'm concerned. I am I! I'm not content to leave the sea and the ivory towers to others. I want them for me! Damn Vida! Damn all of them! Do they think they can make me believe that a display of potatoes at Howland & Gould's is enough beauty and strangeness?"

[It is now 1917 and the United States is at war. Carol grows more and more away from Will, who cannot understand her concern about "highbrow stuff." When Gopher Prairie unites to persecute a youthful tailor, Erik Valborg, Carol defends him, gives him her friendship, comes perilously close to an affair with him. Will, so the reader understands, succumbs to the wiles of the neurotic Maud Dyer. In an attempt to save herself and her marriage, although she does not know about Maud, Carol asks Will to take her to California. When she returns she finds that she is still at odds with Gopher Prairie.]

CHAPTER XXXVI

I

Kennicott was not so inhumanly patient that he could continue to forgive Carol's heresies, to woo her as he had on the venture to California. She tried to be inconspicuous, but she was betrayed by her failure to 60 glow over the boosting. Kennicott believed in it; demanded that she say patriotic things about the White Way and the new factory. He snorted, "By golly, I've done all I could, and now I expect you to play the game. Here you been complaining for years about us being so poky, and now when Blausser comes along and does stir up excitement and beautify the town like you've always wanted somebody to, why, you say he's a roughneck, and you won't jump on the band-wagon."

Once, when Kennicott announced at noon-dinner, "What do you know about this! They say there's a chance we may get another factory—cream-separator works!" he added, "You might try to look interested, even if you ain't!" The baby was frightened by the Jovian roar; ran wailing to hide his face in Carol's lap; and Kennicott had to make himself humble and court both mother and child. The dim injustice of not being understood even by his son left him irritable. He felt injured.

An event which did not directly touch them brought down his wrath.

In the early autumn, news came from Wakamin that the sheriff had forbidden an organizer for the National Nonpartisan League to speak anywhere in the county. The organizer had defied the sheriff, and announced that in a few days he would address a farmers' political meeting. That night, the news ran, a mob of a hundred business men led by the sheriff—the tame village street and the smug village faces ruddled by the light of bobbing lanterns, the mob flowing between the squatty rows of shops—had taken the organizer from his hotel, ridden him on a fence-rail, put him on a freight train, and warned him not to return.

The story was threshed out in Dave Dyer's drug store, with Sam Clark, Kennicott, and Carol present.

"That's the way to treat those fellows—only they ought to have lynched him!" declared Sam, and Kennicott and Dave Dyer joined in a proud "You bet!"

Carol walked out hastily, Kennicott observing her.

Through supper-time she knew that he was bubbling and would soon boil over. When the baby was abed, and they sat composedly in canvas chairs on the porch, he experimented, "I had a hunch you thought Sam was kind of hard on that fellow they kicked out of Wakamin."

"Wasn't Sam rather needlessly heroic?"

"All these organizers, yes, and a whole lot of the German and Squarehead farmers themselves, they're seditious as the devil—disloyal, non-patriotic, pro-German pacifists, that's what they are!"

"Did this organizer say anything pro-German?"

"Not on your life! They didn't give him a chance!" His laugh was stagey.

"So the whole thing was illegal—and led by the sheriff! Precisely how do you expect these aliens to obey your law if the officer of the law teaches them to break it? Is it a new kind of logic?"

"Maybe it wasn't exactly regular, but what's the odds? They knew this fellow would try to stir up trouble. Whenever it comes right down to a question of defending Americanism and our constitutional rights, it's justifiable to set aside ordinary procedure."

"What editorial did he get that from?" she wondered, as she protested, "See here, my beloved, why can't you Tories declare war honestly? You don't oppose this organizer because you think he's seditious but because you're afraid that the farmers he is organizing will deprive you townsmen of the money you make out of mortgages and wheat and shops. Of course, since we're at war with Germany, anything that any one of us doesn't like is 'pro-German,' whether it's business competition or bad music. If we were fighting England, you'd call the radicals 'pro-English.' When this war is over, I suppose you'll be calling them 'red anarchists.' What an eternal art it is—such a glittery delightful art —finding hard names for our opponents! How we do sanctify our efforts to keep them from getting the holy dollars we want for ourselves! The churches have always done it, and the political orators—and I suppose I do it when I call Mrs. Bogart a 'Puritan' and Mr. Stowbody a 'capitalist.' But you business men are going to beat all the rest of us at it, with your simple-hearted, energetic, pompous——"

She got so far only because Kennicott was slow in shaking off respect for her. Now he bayed:

"That'll be about all from you! I've stood for your sneering at this town, and saying how ugly and dull it is. I've stood for your refusing to appreciate good fellows like Sam. I've even stood for your ridiculing our Watch Gopher Prairie Grow campaign. But one thing I'm not going to stand: I'm not going to stand my own wife being seditious. You can camouflage all you want to, but you know darn well that these radicals, as you call 'em, are opposed to the war, and let me tell you right here and now, and you and all these long-haired men and short-haired women can beef all you want to, but we're going to take these fellows, and if they ain't patriotic, we're going to make them be patriotic. And—Lord knows I never thought I'd have to say this to my own wife—but if you go defending these fellows, then the same thing applies to you! Next thing, I suppose you'll be yapping about free speech. Free speech! There's too much free speech and free gas and free beer and free love and all the rest of your damned mouthy freedom, and if I had my way I'd make you folks live up to the established rules of decency even if I had to take you——"

"Will!" She was not timorous now. "Am I pro-

German if I fail to throb to Honest Jim Blausser, too? Let's have my whole duty as a wife!"

He was grumbling, "The whole thing's right in line with the criticism you've always been making. Might have known you'd oppose any decent constructive work for the town or for——"

"You're right. All I've done has been in line. I don't belong to Gopher Prairie. That isn't meant as a condemnation of Gopher Prairie, and it may be a condemnation of me. All right! I don't care! I don't belong here, and I'm going. I'm not asking permission any more. I'm simply going."

He grunted. "Do you mind telling me, if it isn't too much trouble, how long you're going for?"

"I don't know. Perhaps for a year. Perhaps for a life-time."

"I see. Well, of course, I'll be tickled to death to sell out my practise and go anywhere you say. Would you like to have me go with you to Paris and study art, maybe, and wear velveteen pants and a woman's bonnet, and live on spaghetti?"

"No, I think we can save you that trouble. You don't quite understand. I am going—I really am— and alone! I've got to find out what my work is——"

"Work? Work? Sure! That's the whole trouble with you! You haven't got enough work to do. If you had five kids and no hired girl, and had to help with the chores and separate the cream, like these farmers' wives, then you wouldn't be so discontented."

"I know. That's what most men—and women— like you *would* say. That's how they would explain all I am and all I want. And I shouldn't argue with them. These business men, from their crushing labors of sitting in an office seven hours a day, would calmly recommend that I have a dozen children. As it happens, I've done that sort of thing. There've been a good many times when we hadn't a maid, and I did all the housework, and cared for Hugh, and went to Red Cross, and did it all very efficiently. I'm a good cook and a good sweeper, and you don't dare say I'm not!"

"N-no, you're——"

"But was I more happy when I was drudging? I was not. I was just bedraggled and unhappy. It's work —but not my work. I could run an office or a library, or nurse and teach children. But solitary dish-washing isn't enough to satisfy me—or many other women. We're going to chuck it. We're going to wash 'em by machinery, and come out and play with you men in the offices and clubs and politics you've cleverly kept for yourselves! Oh, we're hopeless, we dissatisfied women! Then why do you want to have us about the place, to fret you? So it's for your sake that I'm going!"

"Of course a little thing like Hugh makes no difference!"

"Yes, all the difference. That's why I'm going to take him with me."

"Suppose I refuse?"

"You won't!"

Forlornly, "Uh—— Carrie, what the devil is it you want, anyway?"

"Oh, conversation! No, it's much more than that. I think it's a greatness of life—a refusal to be content with even the healthiest mud."

"Don't you know that nobody ever solved a problem by running away from it?"

"Perhaps. Only I choose to make my own definition of 'running away.' I don't call—— Do you realize how big a world there is beyond this Gopher Prairie where you'd keep me all my life? It may be that some day I'll come back, but not till I can bring something more than I have now. And even if I am cowardly and run away—all right, call it cowardly, call me anything you want to! I've been ruled too long by fear of being called things. I'm going away to be quiet and think. I'm—I'm going! I have a right to my own life."

"So have I to mine!"

"Well?"

"I have a right to my life—and you're it, you're my life! You've made yourself so. I'm damned if I'll agree to all your freak notions, but I will say I've got to depend on you. Never thought of that complication, did you, in this 'off to Bohemia, and express yourself, and free love, and live your own life' stuff!"

"You have a right to me if you can keep me. Can you?"

He moved uneasily.

II

For a month they discussed it. They hurt each other very much, and sometimes they were close to weeping, and invariably he used banal phrases about her duties and she used phrases quite as banal about freedom, and through it all, her discovery that she really could get away from Main Street was as sweet as the discovery of love. Kennicott never consented definitely. At most he agreed to a public theory that she was "going to take a short trip and see what the East was like in wartime."

She set out for Washington in October—just before the war ended.

She had determined on Washington because it was less intimidating than the obvious New York, because she hoped to find streets in which Hugh could play, and because in the stress of war-work, with its demand for thousands of temporary clerks, she could be initiated into the world of offices.

Hugh was to go with her, despite the wails and rather extensive comments of Aunt Bessie.

She wondered if she might not encounter Erik in the East, but it was a chance thought, soon forgotten.

III

The last thing she saw on the station platform was Kennicott, faithfully waving his hand, his face so full of uncomprehending loneliness that he could not smile but only twitch up his lips. She waved to him as long as she could, and when he was lost she wanted to leap from the vestibule and run back to him. She thought of a hundred tendernesses she had neglected.

She had her freedom, and it was empty. The moment was not the highest of her life, but the lowest and most desolate, which was altogether excellent, for instead of slipping downward she began to climb.

She sighed, "I couldn't do this if it weren't for Will's kindness, his giving me money." But a second after: "I wonder how many women would always stay home if they had the money?"

Hugh complained, "Notice me, mummy!" He was beside her on the red plush seat of the day-coach; a boy of three and a half. "I'm tired of playing train. Let's play something else. Let's go see Auntie Bogart."

"Oh, no! Do you really like Mrs. Bogart?"

"Yes. She gives me cookies and she tells me about the Dear Lord. You never tell me about the Dear Lord. Why don't you tell me about the Dear Lord?

Auntie Bogart says I'm going to be a preacher. Can I be a preacher? Can I preach about the Dear Lord?"

"Oh, please wait till my generation has stopped rebelling before yours starts in!"

"What's a generation?"

"It's a ray in the illumination of the spirit."

"That's foolish." He was a serious and literal person, and rather humorless. She kissed his frown, and marveled:

"I am running away from my husband, after liking a Swedish ne'er-do-well and expressing immoral opinions, just as in a romantic story. And my own son reproves me because I haven't given him religious instruction. But the story doesn't go right. I'm neither groaning nor being dramatically saved. I keep on running away, and I enjoy it. I'm mad with joy over it. Gopher Prairie is lost back there in the dust and stubble, and I look forward——"

She continued it to Hugh: "Darling, do you know what mother and you are going to find beyond the blue horizon rim?"

"What?" flatly.

"We're going to find elephants with golden howdahs from which peep young maharanees with necklaces of rubies, and a dawn sea colored like the breast of a dove, and a white and green house filled with books and silver tea-sets."

"And cookies?"

"Cookies? Oh, most decidedly cookies. We've had enough of bread and porridge. We'd get sick on too many cookies, but ever so much sicker on no cookies at all."

"That's foolish."

"It is, O male Kennicott!"

"Huh!" said Kennicott II, and went to sleep on her shoulder.

IV

The theory of the *Dauntless* regarding Carol's absence:

Mrs. Will Kennicott and son Hugh left on No. 24 on Saturday last for a stay of some months in Minneapolis, Chicago, New York, and Washington. Mrs. Kennicott confided to Ye Scribe that she will be connected with one of the multifarious war activities now centering in the Nation's Capital for a brief period before returning. Her countless friends who appreciate her splendid labors with the local Red Cross realize how valuable she will be to any war board with which she chooses to become connected. Gopher Prairie thus adds another shining star to its service flag, and without wishing to knock any neighboring communities, we would like to know any town of anywheres near our size in the state that has such a sterling war record. Another reason why you'd better Watch Gopher Prairie Grow.

• • •

Mr. and Mrs. David Dyer, Mrs. Dyer's sister, Mrs. Jennie Dayborn of Jackrabbit, and Dr. Will Kennicott drove to Minniemashie on Tuesday for a delightful picnic.

[Carol lives for nearly two years in Washington, working in the Bureau of War Risk Insurance. Will comes to see her and Hugh after thirteen months, takes her on a trip through the South, and asks her to return to Gopher Prairie. At length, pregnant with her second child, she goes back.]

CHAPTER XXXIX

I

She wondered all the way home what her sensations would be. She wondered about it so much that she had every sensation she had imagined. She was excited by each familiar porch, each hearty "Well, well!" and flattered to be, for a day, the most important news of the community. She bustled about, making calls. Juanita Haydock bubbled over their Washington encounter, and took Carol to her social bosom. This ancient opponent seemed likely to be her most intimate friend, for Vida Sherwin, though she was cordial, stood back and watched for imported heresies.

In the evening Carol went to the mill. The mystical Om-Om-Om of the dynamos in the electric-light plant behind the mill was louder in the darkness. Outside sat the night watchman, Champ Perry. He held up

his stringy hands and squeaked, "We've all missed you terrible."

Who in Washington would miss her?

Who in Washington could be depended upon like Guy Pollock? When she saw him on the street, smiling as always, he seemed an eternal thing, a part of her own self.

After a week she decided that she was neither glad nor sorry to be back. She entered each day with the matter-of-fact attitude with which she had gone to her office in Washington. It was her task; there would be mechanical details and meaningless talk; what of it?

The only problem which she had approached with emotion proved insignificant. She had, on the train, worked herself up to such devotion that she was willing to give up her own room, to try to share all of her life with Kennicott.

He mumbled, ten minutes after she had entered the house, "Say, I've kept your room for you like it was. I've kind of come round to your way of thinking. Don't see why folks need to get on each other's nerves just because they're friendly. Darned if I haven't got so I like a little privacy and mulling things over by myself."

II

She had left a city which sat up nights to talk of universal transition; of European revolution, guild socialism, free verse. She had fancied that all the world was changing.

She found that it was not.

In Gopher Prairie the only ardent new topics were prohibition, the place in Minneapolis where you could get whisky at thirteen dollars a quart, recipes for homemade beer, the "high cost of living," the presidential election, Clark's new car, and not very novel foibles of Cy Bogart. Their problems were exactly what they had been two years ago, what they had been twenty years ago, and what they would be for twenty years to come. With the world a possible volcano, the husbandmen were plowing at the base of the mountain. A volcano does occasionally drop a river of lava on even the best of agriculturists, to their astonishment and considerable injury, but their cousins inherit the farms and a year or two later go back to the plowing.

She was unable to rhapsodize much over the seven new bungalows and the two garages which Kennicott had made to seem so important. Her intensest thought about them was, "Oh yes, they're all right I suppose." The change which she did heed was the erection of the schoolbuilding, with its cheerful brick walls, broad windows, gymnasium, classrooms for agriculture and cooking. It indicated Vida's triumph, and it stirred her to activity—any activity. She went to Vida with a jaunty, "I think I shall work for you. And I'll begin at the bottom."

She did. She relieved the attendant at the rest-room for an hour a day. Her only innovation was painting the pine table a black and orange rather shocking to the Thanatopsis. She talked to the farmwives and soothed their babies and was happy.

Thinking of them she did not think of the ugliness of Main Street as she hurried along it to the chatter of the Jolly Seventeen.

She wore her eye-glasses on the street now. She was beginning to ask Kennicott and Juanita if she didn't look young, much younger than thirty-three. The eye-glasses pinched her nose. She considered spectacles. They would make her seem older, and hopelessly settled. No! She would not wear spectacles yet. But she tried on a pair at Kennicott's office. They really were much more comfortable.

III

Dr. Westlake, Sam Clark, Nat Hicks, and Del Snafflin were talking in Del's barber shop.

"Well, I see Kennicott's wife is taking a whirl at the rest-room, now," said Dr. Westlake. He emphasized the "now."

Del interrupted the shaving of Sam and, with his brush dripping lather, he observed jocularly:

"What'll she be up to next? They say she used to claim this burg wasn't swell enough for a city girl like her, and would we please tax ourselves about thirty-seven point nine and fix it all up pretty, with tidies on the hydrants and statoos on the lawns——"

Sam irritably blew the lather from his lips, with milky small bubbles, and snorted, "Be a good thing for most of us roughnecks if we did have a smart woman to tell us how to fix up the town. Just as much to her kicking as there was to Jim Blausser's gassing about factories. And you can bet Mrs. Kennicott is smart, even if she is skittish. Glad to see her back."

Dr. Westlake hastened to play safe. "So was I! So was I! She's got a nice way about her, and she knows a good deal about books—or fiction anyway. Of course she's like all the rest of these women—not solidly founded—not scholarly—doesn't know anything about political economy—falls for every new idea that some windjamming crank puts out. But she's a nice woman. She'll probably fix up the rest-room, and the rest-room is a fine thing, brings a lot of business to town. And now that Mrs. Kennicott's been away, maybe she's got over some of her fool ideas. Maybe she realizes that folks simply laugh at her when she tries to tell us how to run everything."

"Sure. She'll take a tumble to herself," said Nat Hicks, sucking in his lips judicially. "As far as I'm concerned, I'll say she's as nice a looking skirt as there is in town. But yow!" His tone electrified them. "Guess she'll miss that Swede Valborg that used to work for me! They was a pair! Talking poetry and moonshine! If they could of got away with it, they'd of been so darn lovey-dovey——"

Sam Clark interrupted, "Rats, they never even thought about making love. Just talking books and all that junk. I tell you, Carrie Kennicott's a smart woman, and these smart educated women all get funny ideas, but they get over 'em after they've had three or four kids. You'll see her settled down one of these days, and teaching Sunday School and helping at sociables and behaving herself, and not trying to butt into business and politics. Sure!"

After only fifteen minutes of conference on her stockings, her son, her separate bedroom, her music, her ancient interest in Guy Pollock, her probable salary in Washington, and every remark which she was known to have made since her return, the supreme council decided that they would permit Carol Kennicott to live, and they passed on to a consideration of Nat Hicks's New One about the traveling salesman and the old maid.

IV

For some reason which was totally mysterious to Carol, Maud Dyer seemed to resent her return. At the Jolly Seventeen Maud giggled nervously, "Well, I suppose you found war-work a good excuse to stay away and have a swell time. Juanita! Don't you think we ought to make Carrie tell us about the officers she met in Washington?"

They rustled and stared. Carol looked at them. Their curiosity seemed natural and unimportant.

"Oh yes, yes indeed, have to do that some day," she yawned.

She no longer took Aunt Bessie Smail seriously enough to struggle for independence. She saw that Aunt Bessie did not mean to intrude; that she wanted to do things for all the Kennicotts. Thus Carol hit upon the tragedy of old age, which is not that it is less vigorous than youth, but that it is not needed by youth; that its love and prosy sageness, so important a few years ago, so gladly offered now, are rejected with laughter. She divined that when Aunt Bessie came in with a jar of wild-grape jelly she was waiting in hope of being asked for the recipe. After that she could be irritated but she could not be depressed by Aunt Bessie's simoom of questioning.

She wasn't depressed even when she heard Mrs. Bogart observe, "Now we've got prohibition it seems to me that the next problem of the country ain't so much abolishing cigarettes as it is to make folks observe the Sabbath and arrest these law-breakers that play baseball and go to the movies and all on the Lord's Day."

Only one thing bruised Carol's vanity. Few people asked her about Washington. They who had most admiringly begged Percy Bresnahan for his opinions were least interested in her facts. She laughed at herself when she saw that she had expected to be at once a heretic and a returned hero; she was very reasonable and merry about it; and it hurt just as much as ever.

V

Her baby, born in August, was a girl. Carol could not decide whether she was to become a feminist leader or marry a scientist or both, but did settle on Vassar and a tricolette suit with a small black hat for her Freshman year.

VI

Hugh was loquacious at breakfast. He desired to give his impressions of owls and F Street.

"Don't make so much noise. You talk too much," growled Kennicott.

Carol flared. "Don't speak to him that way! Why don't you listen to him? He has some very interesting things to tell."

"What's the idea? Mean to say you expect me to spend all my time listening to his chatter?"

"Why not?"

"For one thing, he's got to learn a little discipline. Time for him to start getting educated."

"I've learned much more discipline, I've had much more education, from him than he has from me."

"What's this? Some new-fangled idea of raising kids you got in Washington?"

"Perhaps. Did you ever realize that children are people."

"That's all right. I'm not going to have him monopolizing the conversation."

"No, of course. We have our rights, too. But I'm going to bring him up as a human being. He has just as many thoughts as we have, and I want him to develop them, not take Gopher Prairie's version of them. That's my biggest work now—keeping myself, keeping you, from 'educating' him."

"Well, let's not scrap about it. But I'm not going to have him spoiled."

Kennicott had forgotten it in ten minutes; and she forgot it—this time.

VII

The Kennicotts and the Sam Clarks had driven north to a duck-pass between two lakes, on an autumn day of blue and copper.

Kennicott had given her a light twenty-gauge shotgun. She had a first lesson in shooting, in keeping her eyes open, not wincing, understanding that the bead at the end of the barrel really had something to do with pointing the gun. She was radiant; she almost believed

Sam when he insisted that it was she who had shot the mallard at which they had fired together.

She sat on the bank of the reedy lake and found rest in Mrs. Clark's drawling comments on nothing. The brown dusk was still. Behind them were dark marshes. The plowed acres smelled fresh. The lake was garnet and silver. The voices of the men, waiting for the last flight, were clear in the cool air.

"Mark left!" sang Kennicott, in a long-drawn call.

Three ducks were swooping down in a swift line. The guns banged, and a duck fluttered. The men pushed their light boat out on the burnished lake, disappeared beyond the reeds. Their cheerful voices and the slow splash and clank of oars came back to Carol from the dimness. In the sky a fiery plain sloped down to a serene harbor. It dissolved; the lake was white marble; and Kennicott was crying, "Well, old lady, how about hiking out for home? Supper taste pretty good, eh?"

"I'll sit back with Ethel," she said, at the car.

It was the first time she had called Mrs. Clark by her given name; the first time she had willingly sat back, a woman of Main Street.

"I'm hungry. It's good to be hungry," she reflected, as they drove away.

She looked across the silent fields to the west. She was conscious of an unbroken sweep of land to the Rockies, to Alaska; a dominion which will rise to unexampled greatness when other empires have grown senile. Before that time, she knew, a hundred generations of Carols will aspire and go down in tragedy devoid of palls and solemn chanting, the humdrum inevitable tragedy of struggle against inertia.

"Let's all go to the movies tomorrow night. Awfully exciting film," said Ethel Clark.

"Well, I was going to read a new book but—— All right, let's go," said Carol.

VIII

"They're too much for me," Carol sighed to Kennicott. "I've been thinking about getting up an annual Community Day, when the whole town would forget feuds and go out and have sports and a picnic and a dance. But Bert Tybee (why did you ever elect him mayor?)— he's kidnapped my idea. He wants the Community Day, but he wants to have some politician 'give an address.' That's just the stilted sort of thing I've tried to avoid. He asked Vida, and of course she agreed with him."

Kennicott considered the matter while he wound the clock and they tramped up-stairs.

"Yes, it would jar you to have Bert butting in," he said amiably. "Are you going to do much fussing over this Community stunt? Don't you ever get tired of fretting and stewing and experimenting?"

"I haven't even started. Look!" She led him to the nursery door, pointed at the fuzzy brown head of her daughter. "Do you see that object on the pillow? Do you know what it is? It's a bomb to blow up smugness. If you Tories were wise, you wouldn't arrest anarchists; you'd arrest all these children while they're asleep in their cribs. Think what that baby will see and meddle with before she dies in the year 2000! She may see an industrial union of the whole world, she may see aeroplanes going to Mars."

"Yump, probably be changes all right," yawned Kennicott.

She sat on the edge of his bed while he hunted through his bureau for a collar which ought to be there and persistently wasn't.

"I'll go on, always. And I am happy. But this Community Day makes me see how thoroughly I'm beaten."

"That darn collar certainly is gone for keeps," muttered Kennicott and, louder, "Yes, I guess you—— I didn't quite catch what you said, dear."

She patted his pillows, turned down his sheets, as she reflected:

"But I have won in this: I've never excused my failures by sneering at my aspirations, by pretending to have gone beyond them. I do not admit that Main Street is as beautiful as it should be! I do not admit that Gopher Prairie is greater or more generous than Europe! I do not admit that dish-washing is enough to satisfy all women! I may not have fought the good fight, but I have kept the faith."

"Sure. You bet you have," said Kennicott. "Well, good night. Sort of feels to me like it might snow tomorrow. Have to be thinking about putting up the storm-windows pretty soon. Say, did you notice whether the girl put that screwdriver back?"

1920

Katherine Anne Porter

1894 ·

Katherine Anne Porter was born in Indian Creek, Texas, the great-great-great-granddaughter of Daniel Boone, and spent her early life in Texas and Louisiana. She was educated in various convent schools of the South. She married in 1933, was divorced; in 1938, she married Albert Russel Erskine, Jr.; they were divorced in 1942. Miss Porter has lived in various parts of the world: in the South, in New York City, in Europe, in Mexico. Using details from her experiences, she has therefore employed a variety of backgrounds in her fiction. She was awarded a Guggenheim Fellowship for creative writing in 1931, and again in 1938. In 1944, she was Fellow of Regional American Literature in the Library of Congress. In 1949, she held the chair of Writer-in-Residence and Lecturer in Leland Stanford University. She has worked on a novel over a number of years but so far has published only short stories and novelettes. Her most important collections of stories are *Flowering Judas and Other Stories* (1930, 1935), *Pale Horse, Pale Rider* (1939), and *The Leaning Tower and Other Stories* (1944).

"As soon as I learned to form letters on paper, at about three years," says Miss Porter, "I began to write stories, and this has been the basic and absorbing occupation, the intact line of my life which directs my actions, deter-

mines my point of view, and profoundly affects my character and personality, my social beliefs and economic status, and the kind of friendships I form." She did not attempt publication, though, until she was thirty, and throughout her career she has worked scrupulously and painstakingly, refusing to print anything until completely satisfied with it. Miss Porter's devotion to her craft has been richly rewarded, for, although she has published comparatively little, she has achieved high distinction in the art of short fiction. Robert Penn Warren finds in all of her stories "the same underlying structure of contrast and tension, the same paradoxical problems of definition, the same delicate balancing of rival considerations, the same scrupulous development of competing claims to attention and action, the same interplay of the humorous and the serious, the same refusal to take the straight line, the formula, through the matter at hand."

Robert Penn Warren, "Katherine Anne Porter: Irony with a Center," Kenyon Review, Winter 1942 • Ray B. West, Jr., "Katherine Anne Porter: Symbol and Theme in 'Flowering Judas,'" Accent, Spring 1947 (reprinted in Critiques and Essays on Modern Fiction, ed. John W. Aldridge, New York, 1952)

Flowering Judas

"Flowering Judas" is Miss Porter's best-known story, and in the opinion of some who have studied her work closely, her most successful piece of fiction. In his illuminating analysis, "Symbol and Theme in 'Flowering Judas,'" Ray B. West, Jr., has pointed out the relation of the story to the following lines in T. S. Eliot's "Gerontion" (see p. 945):

In depraved May, dogwood and chestnut, flowering judas
To be eaten, to be divided, to be drunk
Among whispers.

"If the Judas tree," West observes, "is a symbol for the betrayer of Christ, then the sacrament in which Laura participated—the eating of the buds of the Flowering Judas—is a sacrament, not of remembrance, but of betrayal. . . . She is, like Judas, the betrayer; and her betrayal, like his, consisted in an inability to believe."

Laura's tragedy grows out of her failure to achieve an adequate emotional response: either to the Catholic religion of her girlhood (it is "no good" when she secretly enters "some crumbling little church" and tries to pray); or to the revolution, which she professes to serve; or to the young man who serenades her, singing in her patio. Nobody, and no thing, quite touches her. The retributive frustration of such apartness, such indecision, is symbolically depicted at the end in her dream of Eugenio.

The story can doubtless be read as a parable of the plight of many vague young liberals of the 1920's and 1930's who, having severed themselves from their traditional ways of life, were yet unable to embrace the revolution, and still less, the revolutionaries. But the meaning should not be restricted to, or impoverished by, the merely topical. "Flowering Judas," in a broad sense, is a beautiful illustration of what Robert Penn Warren calls the "delicate balancing of rival considerations." The total effect of the work is greatly aided by the richness, precision, and subtlety of Miss Porter's carefully modulated prose.

Braggioni sits heaped upon the edge of a straight-backed chair much too small for him, and sings to Laura in a furry, mournful voice. Laura has begun to find reasons for avoiding her own house until the latest possible moment, for Braggioni is there almost every night. No matter how late she is, he will be sitting there with a surly, waiting expression, pulling at his kinky yellow hair, thumbing the strings of his guitar, snarling a tune under his breath. Lupe the Indian maid meets Laura at the door, and says with a flicker of a glance towards the upper room, "He waits." 10

Laura wishes to lie down, she is tired of her hairpins and the feel of her long tight sleeves, but she says to him, "Have you a new song for me this evening?" If he says yes, she asks him to sing it. If he says no, she remembers his favorite one, and asks him to sing it again. Lupe brings her a cup of chocolate and a plate of rice, and Laura eats at the small table under the lamp, first inviting Braggioni, whose answer is always the same: "I have eaten, and besides, chocolate thickens the voice." 20

Laura says, "Sing, then," and Braggioni heaves himself into song. He scratches the guitar familiarly as though it were a pet animal, and sings passionately off key, taking the high notes in a prolonged painful squeal. Laura, who haunts the markets listening to the ballad singers, and stops every day to hear the blind boy playing his reed-flute in Sixteenth of September Street, listens to Braggioni with pitiless courtesy, because she dares not smile at his miserable performance. Nobody dares to smile at him. Braggioni is cruel to everyone, 30 with a kind of specialized insolence, but he is so vain of his talents, and so sensitive to slights, it would require a cruelty and vanity greater than his own to lay a finger on the vast cureless wound of his self-esteem. It would require courage, too, for it is dangerous to offend him, and nobody has this courage.

Braggioni loves himself with such tenderness and amplitude and eternal charity that his followers—for he is a leader of men, a skilled revolutionist, and his skin has been punctured in honorable warfare—warm themselves 40 in the reflected glow, and say to each other: "He has a real nobility, a love of humanity raised above mere personal affections." The excess of this self-love has flowed out, inconveniently for her, over Laura, who, with so many others, owes her comfortable situation and her salary to him. When he is in a very good humor, he tells her, "I am tempted to forgive you for being a *gringa. Gringita!*" and Laura, burning, imagines herself leaning forward suddenly, and with a sound back-handed slap wiping the suety smile from his face. If he notices her eyes at these moments he gives no sign.

She knows what Braggioni would offer her, and she must resist tenaciously without appearing to resist, and if she could avoid it she would not admit even to herself the slow drift of his intention. During these long evenings which have spoiled a long month for her, she sits in her deep chair with an open book on her knees, resting her eyes on the consoling rigidity of the printed page when the sight and sound of Braggioni singing threaten to identify themselves with all her remembered afflictions and to add their weight to her uneasy premonitions of the future. The gluttonous bulk of Braggioni has become a symbol of her many disillusions, for a revolutionist should be lean, animated by heroic faith, a vessel of abstract virtues. This is nonsense, she knows it now and is ashamed of it. Revolution must have leaders, and leadership is a career for energetic men. She is, her comrades tell her, full of romantic error, for what she defines as cynicism in them is merely "a developed sense of reality." She is almost too willing to say, "I am wrong, I suppose I don't really understand the principles," and afterward she makes a secret truce with herself, determined not to surrender her will to such expedient logic. But she cannot help feeling that she has been betrayed irreparably by the disunion between her way of living and her feeling of what life should be, and at times she is almost contented to rest in this sense of grievance as a private store of consolation. Sometimes she wishes to run away, but she stays. Now she longs to fly out of this room, down the narrow stairs, and into the street where the houses lean together like conspirators under a single mottled lamp, and leave Braggioni singing to himself.

Instead she looks at Braggioni, frankly and clearly, like a good child who understands the rules of behavior. Her knees cling together under sound blue serge, and her round white collar is not purposely nun-like. She wears the uniform of an idea, and has renounced vanities. She was born Roman Catholic, and in spite of her fear of being seen by someone who might make a scandal

of it, she slips now and again into some crumbling little church, kneels on the chilly stone, and says a Hail Mary on the gold rosary she bought in Tehuantepec. It is no good and she ends by examining the altar with its tinsel flowers and ragged brocades, and feels tender about the battered doll-shape of some male saint whose white, lace-trimmed drawers hang limply around his ankles below the hieratic dignity of his velvet robe. She has encased herself in a set of principles derived from her early training, leaving no detail of gesture or of personal taste untouched, and for this reason she will not wear lace made on machines. This is her private heresy, for in her special group the machine is sacred, and will be the salvation of the workers. She loves fine lace, and there is a tiny edge of fluted cobweb on this collar, which is one of twenty precisely alike, folded in blue tissue paper in the upper drawer of her clothes chest.

Braggioni catches her glance solidly as if he had been waiting for it, leans forward, balancing his paunch between his spread knees, and sings with tremendous emphasis, weighing his words. He has, the song relates, no father and no mother, nor even a friend to console him; lonely as a wave of the sea he comes and goes, lonely as a wave. His mouth opens round and yearns sideways, his balloon cheeks grow oily with the labor of song. He bulges marvelously in his expensive garments. Over his lavender collar, crushed upon a purple necktie, held by a diamond hoop: over his ammunition belt of tooled leather worked in silver, buckled cruelly around his gasping middle: over the tops of his glossy yellow shoes Braggioni swells with ominous ripeness, his mauve silk hose stretched taut, his ankles bound with the stout leather thongs of his shoes.

When he stretches his eyelids at Laura she notes again that his eyes are the true tawny yellow cat's eyes. He is rich, not in money, he tells her, but in power, and this power brings with it the blameless ownership of things, and the right to indulge his love of small luxuries. "I have a taste for the elegant refinements," he said once, flourishing a yellow silk handkerchief before her nose. "Smell that? It is Jockey Club, imported from New York." Nonetheless he is wounded by life. He will say

---

4 gringa. Gringita, the feminine, and the diminutive feminine, respectively, of gringo, a term of ridicule and obloquy (according to the **Dictionary of American English**) applied to Americans throughout all Mexico

so presently. "It is true everything turns to dust in the hand, to gall on the tongue." He sighs and his leather belt creaks like a saddle girth. "I am disappointed in everything as it comes. Everything." He shakes his head. "You, poor thing, you will be disappointed too. You are born for it. We are more alike than you realize in some things. Wait and see. Some day you will remember what I have told you, you will know that Braggioni was your friend."

Laura feels a slow chill, a purely physical sense of danger, a warning in her blood that violence, mutilation, a shocking death, wait for her with lessening patience. She has translated this fear into something homely, immediate, and sometimes hesitates before crossing the street. "My personal fate is nothing, except as the testimony of a mental attitude," she reminds herself, quoting from some forgotten philosophic primer, and is sensible enough to add, "Anyhow, I shall not be killed by an automobile if I can help it."

"It may be true I am as corrupt, in another way, as Braggioni," she thinks in spite of herself, "as callous, as incomplete," and if this is so, any kind of death seems preferable. Still she sits quietly, she does not run. Where could she go? Uninvited she has promised herself to this place; she can no longer imagine herself as living in another country, and there is no pleasure in remembering her life before she came here.

Precisely what is the nature of this devotion, its true motives, and what are its obligations? Laura cannot say. She spends part of her days in Xochimilco, near by, teaching the Indian children to say in English, "The cat is on the mat." When she appears in the classroom they crowd about her with smiles on their wise, innocent, clay-colored faces, crying, "Good morning, my titcher!" in immaculate voices, and they make of her desk a fresh garden of flowers every day.

During her leisure she goes to union meetings and listens to busy important voices quarreling over tactics, methods, internal politics. She visits the prisoners of her own political faith in their cells, where they entertain themselves with counting cockroaches, repenting of their indiscretions, composing their memoirs, writing out manifestoes and plans for their comrades who are still walking about free, hands in pockets, sniffing fresh air. Laura brings them food and cigarettes and a little money, and she brings messages disguised in equivocal phrases from the men outside who dare not set foot in the prison for fear of disappearing into the cells kept empty for them. If the prisoners confuse night and day, and complain, "Dear little Laura, time doesn't pass in this infernal hole, and I won't know when it is time to sleep unless I have a reminder," she brings them their favorite narcotics, and says in a tone that does not wound them with pity, "Tonight will really be night for you," and though her Spanish amuses them, they find her comforting, useful. If they lose patience and all faith, and curse the slowness of their friends in coming to their rescue with money and influence, they trust her not to repeat everything, and if she inquires, "Where do you think we can find money, or influence?" they are certain to answer, "Well, there is Braggioni, why doesn't he do something?"

She smuggles letters from headquarters to men hiding from firing squads in back streets in mildewed houses, where they sit in tumbled beds and talk bitterly as if all Mexico were at their heels, when Laura knows positively they might appear at the band concert in the Alameda on Sunday morning, and no one would notice them. But Braggioni says, "Let them sweat a little. The next time they may be careful. It is very restful to have them out of the way for a while." She is not afraid to knock on any door in any street after midnight, and enter in the darkness, and say to one of these men who is really in danger: "They will be looking for you—seriously—tomorrow morning after six. Here is some money from Vicente. Go to Vera Cruz and wait."

She borrows money from the Roumanian agitator to give to his bitter enemy the Polish agitator. The favor of Braggioni is their disputed territory, and Braggioni holds the balance nicely, for he can use them both. The Polish agitator talks love to her over café tables, hoping to exploit what he believes is her secret sentimental preference for him, and he gives her misinformation which he begs her to repeat as the solemn truth to certain persons. The Roumanian is more adroit. He is generous with his money in all good causes, and lies to her with an air of ingenuous candor, as if he were her good friend and confidant. She never repeats anything they may say. Braggioni never asks questions. He has other ways to discover all that he wishes to know about them.

Nobody touches her, but all praise her gray eyes, and the soft, round under lip which promises gayety, yet is always grave, nearly always firmly closed: and they cannot understand why she is in Mexico. She walks back and forth on her errands, with puzzled eyebrows, carrying her little folder of drawings and music and school papers. No dancer dances more beautifully than Laura walks, and she inspires some amusing, unexpected ardors, which cause little gossip, because nothing comes of them. A young captain who had been a soldier in Zapata's army attempted, during a horseback ride near Cuernavaca, to express his desire for her with the noble simplicity befitting a rude folk-hero: but gently, because he was gentle. This gentleness was his defeat, for when he alighted, and removed her foot from the stirrup, and essayed to draw her down into his arms, her horse, ordinarily a tame one, shied fiercely, reared and plunged away. The young hero's horse careered blindly after his stable-mate, and the hero did not return to the hotel until rather late that evening. At breakfast he came to her table in full charro dress, gray buckskin jacket and trousers with strings of silver buttons down the leg, and he was in a humorous, careless mood. "May I sit with you?" and "You are a wonderful rider. I was terrified that you might be thrown and dragged. I should never have forgiven myself. But I cannot admire you enough for your riding!"

"I learned to ride in Arizona," said Laura.

"If you ride with me again this morning, I promise you a horse that will not shy with you," he said. But Laura remembered that she must return to Mexico City at noon.

Next morning the children made a celebration and spent their playtime writing on the blackboard, "We lov ar ticher," and with tinted chalks they drew wreaths of flowers around the words. The young hero wrote her a letter: "I am a very foolish, wasteful, impulsive man. I should have first said I love you, and then you would not have run away. But you shall see me again." Laura thought, "I must send him a box of colored crayons," but she was trying to forgive herself for having spurred her horse at the wrong moment.

A brown, shock-haired youth came and stood in her patio one night and sang like a lost soul for two hours, but Laura could think of nothing to do about it. The moonlight spread a wash of gauzy silver over the clear spaces of the garden, and the shadows were cobalt blue. The scarlet blossoms of the Judas tree were dull purple,

and the names of the colors repeated themselves automatically in her mind, while she watched not the boy, but his shadow, fallen like a dark garment across the fountain rim, trailing in the water. Lupe came silently and whispered expert counsel in her ear: "If you will throw him one little flower, he will sing another song or two and go away." Laura threw the flower, and he sang a last song and went away with the flower tucked in the band of his hat. Lupe said, "He is one of the organizers of the Typographers Union, and before that he sold corridos in the Merced market, and before that, he came from Guanajuato, where I was born. I would not trust any man, but I trust least those from Guanajuato."

She did not tell Laura that he would be back again the next night, and the next, nor that he would follow her at a certain fixed distance around the Merced market, through the Zócolo, up Francisco I. Madero Avenue, and so along the Paseo de la Reforma to Chapultepec Park, and into the Philosopher's Footpath, still with that flower withering in his hat, and an indivisible attention in his eyes.

Now Laura is accustomed to him, it means nothing except that he is nineteen years old and is observing a convention with all propriety, as though it were founded on a law of nature, which in the end it might well prove to be. He is beginning to write poems which he prints on a wooden press, and he leaves them stuck like handbills in her door. She is pleasantly disturbed by the abstract, unhurried watchfulness of his black eyes which will in time turn easily towards another object. She tells herself that throwing the flower was a mistake, for she is twenty-two years old and knows better; but she refuses to regret it, and persuades herself that her negation of all external events as they occur is a sign that she is gradually perfecting herself in the stoicism she strives to cultivate against that disaster she fears, though she cannot name it.

She is not at home in the world. Every day she teaches children who remain strangers to her, though she loves their tender round hands and their charming opportunist savagery. She knocks at unfamiliar doors not knowing whether a friend or a stranger shall answer, and even if a known face emerges from the sour gloom of that unknown interior, still it is the face of a stranger. No matter what this stranger says to her, nor what her message to him, the very cells of her flesh reject knowledge and kinship in one monotonous word. No. No. No. She draws her strength from this one holy talismanic word which does not suffer her to be led into evil. Denying everything, she may walk anywhere in safety, she looks at everything without amazement.

No, repeats this firm unchanging voice of her blood; and she looks at Braggioni without amazement. He is a great man, he wishes to impress this simple girl who covers her great round breasts with thick dark cloth, and who hides long, invaluably beautiful legs under a heavy skirt. She is almost thin except for the incomprehensible fullness of her breasts, like a nursing mother's, and Braggioni, who considers himself a judge of women, speculates again on the puzzle of her notorious virginity, and takes the liberty of speech which she permits without a sign of modesty, indeed, without any sort of sign, which is disconcerting.

"You think you are so cold, *gringita!* Wait and see. You will surprise yourself some day! May I be there to advise you!" He stretches his eyelids at her, and his ill-humored cat's eyes waver in a separate glance for the two points of light marking the opposite ends of a smoothly drawn path between the swollen curve of her breasts. He is not put off by that blue serge, nor by her resolutely fixed gaze. There is all the time in the world. His cheeks are bellying with the wind of song. "O girl with the dark eyes," he sings, and reconsiders. "But yours are not dark. I can change all that. O girl with the green eyes, you have stolen my heart away!" then his mind wanders to the song, and Laura feels the weight of his attention being shifted elsewhere. Singing thus, he seems harmless, he is quite harmless, there is nothing to do but sit patiently and say "No," when the moment comes. She draws a full breath, and her mind wanders also, but not far. She dares not wander too far.

Not for nothing has Braggioni taken pains to be a good revolutionist and a professional lover of humanity. He will never die of it. He has the malice, the cleverness, the wickedness, the sharpness of wit, the hardness of heart, stipulated for loving the world profitably. *He will never die of it.* He will live to see himself kicked out from his feeding trough by other hungry world-saviors. Traditionally he must sing in spite of his life which drives him to bloodshed, he tells Laura, for his father was a Tuscany peasant who drifted to Yucatan and married a Maya woman: a woman of race, an aristocrat. They gave him the love and knowledge of music, thus: and under the rip of his thumbnail, the strings of the instrument complain like exposed nerves.

Once he was called Delgadito by all the girls and married women who ran after him; he was so scrawny all his bones showed under his thin cotton clothing, and he could squeeze his emptiness to the very backbone with his two hands. He was a poet and the revolution was only a dream then; too many women loved him and sapped away his youth, and he could never find enough to eat anywhere, anywhere! Now he is a leader of men, crafty men who whisper in his ear, hungry men who wait for hours outside his office for a word with him, emaciated men with wild faces who waylay him at the street gate with a timid, "Comrade, let me tell you . . ." and they blow the foul breath from their empty stomachs in his face.

He is always sympathetic. He gives them handfuls of small coins from his own pocket, he promises them work, there will be demonstrations, they must join the unions and attend the meetings, above all they must be on the watch for spies. They are closer to him than his own brothers, without them he can do nothing—until tomorrow, comrade!

Until tomorrow. "They are stupid, they are lazy, they are treacherous, they would cut my throat for nothing," he says to Laura. He has good food and abundant drink, he hires an automobile and drives in the Paseo on Sunday morning, and enjoys plenty of sleep in a soft bed beside a wife who dares not disturb him; and he sits pampering his bones in easy billows of fat, singing to Laura, who knows and thinks these things about him. When he was fifteen, he tried to drown himself because he loved a girl, his first love, and she laughed at him. "A thousand women have paid for that," and his tight little mouth turns down at the corners. Now he perfumes his hair with Jockey Club, and confides to Laura: "One woman is really as good as another for me, in the dark. I prefer them all."

His wife organizes unions among the girls in the cigarette factories, and walks in picket lines, and even speaks at meetings in the evening. But she cannot be brought to acknowledge the benefits of true liberty. "I tell her I must have my freedom, net. She does not understand my point of view." Laura has heard this many times. Braggioni scratches the guitar and meditates. "She is an instinctively virtuous woman, pure gold, no doubt of that. If she were not, I should lock her up, and she knows it."

His wife, who works so hard for the good of the factory girls, employs part of her leisure lying on the floor weeping because there are so many women in the world, and only one husband for her, and she never knows where nor when to look for him. He told her: "Unless you can learn to cry when I am not here, I must go away for good." That day he went away and took a room at the Hotel Madrid.

It is this month of separation for the sake of higher principles that has been spoiled not only for Mrs. Braggioni, whose sense of reality is beyond criticism, but for Laura, who feels herself bogged in a nightmare. Tonight Laura envies Mrs. Braggioni, who is alone, and free to weep as much as she pleases about a concrete wrong. Laura has just come from a visit to the prison, and she is waiting for tomorrow with a bitter anxiety as if tomorrow may not come, but time may be caught immovably in this hour, with herself transfixed, Braggioni singing on forever, and Eugenio's body not yet discovered by the guard.

Braggioni says: "Are you going to sleep?" Almost before she can shake her head, he begins telling her about the May-day disturbances coming on in Morelia, for the Catholics hold a festival in honor of the Blessed Virgin, and the Socialists celebrate their martyrs on that day. "There will be two independent processions, starting from either end of town, and they will march until they meet, and the rest depends . . ." He asks her to oil and load his pistols. Standing up, he unbuckles his ammunition belt, and spreads it laden across her knees. Laura sits with the shells slipping through the cleaning cloth dipped in oil, and he says again he cannot understand why she works so hard for the revolutionary idea unless she loves some man who is in it. "Are you not in love with someone?" "No," says Laura. "And no one is in love with you?" "No." "Then it is your own fault. No woman need go begging. Why, what is the matter with you? The legless beggar woman in the Alameda has a perfectly faithful lover. Did you know that?"

Laura peers down the pistol barrel and says nothing, but a long, slow faintness rises and subsides in her; Braggioni curves his swollen fingers around the throat of the guitar and softly smothers the music out of it, and when she hears him again he seems to have forgotten her, and is speaking in the hypnotic voice he uses when talking in small rooms to a listening, close-gathered crowd. Some day this world, now seemingly so composed and eternal, to the edges of every sea shall be merely a tangle of gaping trenches, of crashing walls and broken bodies. Everything must be torn from its accustomed place where it has rotted for centuries, hurled skyward and distributed, cast down again clean as rain, without separate identity. Nothing shall survive that the stiffened hands of poverty have created for the rich and no one shall be left alive except the elect spirits destined to procreate a new world cleansed of cruelty and injustice, ruled by benevolent anarchy: "Pistols are good, I love them, cannons are even better, but in the end I pin my faith to good dynamite," he concludes, and strokes the pistol lying in her hands. "Once I dreamed of destroying the city, in case it offered resistance to General Ortíz, but it fell into his hands like an overripe pear."

He is made restless by his own words, rises and stands waiting. Laura holds up the belt to him: "Put that on, and go kill somebody in Morelia, and you will be happier," she says softly. The presence of death in the room makes her bold. "Today, I found Eugenio going into a stupor. He refused to allow me to call the prison doctor. He had taken all the tablets I brought him yesterday. He said he took them because he was bored."

"He is a fool, and his death is his own business," says Braggioni, fastening his belt carefully.

"I told him if he had waited only a little while longer, you would have got him set free," says Laura. "He said he did not want to wait."

"He is a fool and we are well rid of him," says Braggioni, reaching for his hat.

He goes away. Laura knows his mood has changed, she will not see him any more for a while. He will send word when he needs her to go on errands into strange streets, to speak to the strange faces that will appear, like clay masks with the power of human speech, to mutter their thanks to Braggioni for his help. Now she is free, and she thinks, I must run while there is time. But she does not go.

Braggioni enters his own house where for a month his wife has spent many hours every night weeping and tangling her hair upon her pillow. She is weeping now, and she weeps more at the sight of him, the cause of all her sorrows. He looks about the room. Nothing is changed, the smells are good and familiar, he is well acquainted with the woman who comes toward him with no reproach except grief on her face. He says to her tenderly: "You are so good, please don't cry any more, you dear good creature." She says, "Are you tired, my angel? Sit here and I will wash your feet." She brings a bowl of water, and kneeling, unlaces his shoes, and when from her knees she raises her sad eyes under her blackened lids, he is sorry for everything, and bursts into tears. "Ah, yes, I am hungry, I am tired, let us eat something together," he says, between sobs. His wife leans her head on his arm and says, "Forgive me!" and this time he is refreshed by the solemn, endless rain of her tears.

Laura takes off her serge dress and puts on a white linen nightgown and goes to bed. She turns her head a little to one side, and lying still, reminds herself that it is time to sleep. Numbers tick in her brain like little clocks, soundless doors close of themselves around her. If you would sleep, you must not remember anything, the children will say tomorrow, good morning, my teacher, the poor prisoners who come every day bringing flowers to their jailor. 1-2-3-4-5—it is monstrous to confuse love with revolution, night with day, life with death—ah, Eugenio!

The tolling of the midnight bell is a signal, but what does it mean? Get up, Laura, and follow me: come out of your sleep, out of your bed, out of this strange house. What are you doing in this house? Without a word, without fear she rose and reached for Eugenio's hand, but he eluded her with a sharp, sly smile and drifted away. This is not all, you shall see—Murderer, he said, follow me, I will show you a new country, but it is far away and we must hurry. No, said Laura, not unless you take my hand, no; and she clung first to the stair rail, and then to the topmost branch of the Judas tree that bent down slowly and set her upon the earth, and then to the rocky ledge of a cliff, then to the jagged wave of a sea that was not water but a desert of crumbling stone. Where are you taking me, she asked in wonder but without fear. To death, and it is a long way off, and we must hurry, said Eugenio. No, said Laura, not unless you take my hand. Then eat these flowers, poor prisoner, said Eugenio in a voice of pity, take and eat: and from the Judas tree he stripped the warm bleeding flowers, and held them to her lips. She saw that his hand was fleshless, a cluster of small white petrified branches, and his eye sockets were without light, but she ate the flowers greedily for they satisfied both hunger and thirst. Murderer! said Eugenio, and Cannibal! This is my body and my blood. Laura cried No! and at the sound of her own voice, she awoke trembling, and was afraid to sleep again.

1930

F. Scott Fitzgerald

1896 · 1940

F. Scott Fitzgerald was born in St. Paul, Minnesota, and educated in the public schools of St. Paul, in the Newman School of Hackensack, New Jersey, and at Princeton University, where he formed a friendship with Edmund Wilson and contributed poems and stories to *The Nassau Literary Magazine*. He left Princeton in 1917 to join the army, soon after the United States entered World War I. He was commissioned a lieutenant in the infantry but was not sent overseas. In 1920 he married Zelda Sayre of Montgomery, Alabama. In the same year he published *This Side of Paradise,* a novel of the postwar jazz era, which made him famous. Thereafter, Fitzgerald devoted himself to the writing of prose fiction.

His literary output included three other novels—*The Beautiful and Damned* (1922), *The Great Gatsby* (1925), and *Tender Is the Night* (1934)—and, in addition, an unfinished novel, *The Last Tycoon,* which was published posthumously in 1941. He also contributed many short stories to *The Saturday Evening Post, The Red Book,* and other popular magazines. Most of these stories were collected under the following titles: *Flappers and Philosophers* (1920), *Tales of the Jazz Age* (1922), *All the Sad Young Men* (1926), and *Taps at Reveille* (1935).

Fitzgerald was a very popular writer during the 1920's, and the income from his writings during the years 1920-1924 totaled $113,000, or more than $22,500 a year. But being a conscientious artist, he found it difficult if not impossible to maintain such a financial pace. He lived a good deal abroad—in Paris, in Italy, and on the French Riviera, where he wrote *The Great Gatsby.* His last years were spent in Hollywood, where he died of a heart attack, December 21, 1940.

During the late 1940's and early 1950's, there was a notable Fitzgerald revival, to which Edmund Wilson, Budd Schulberg (who treated Fitzgerald's life fictionally in his novel, *The Disenchanted*), John O'Hara, Dorothy Parker, Malcolm Cowley, Arthur Mizener, and other distinguished writers and critics contributed. Fitzgerald achieved, suddenly, a critical importance. Most students are now inclined to agree with Mizener's

F. Scott Fitzgerald—photo by E. Hazebroucq

considered judgment, expressed in 1951, that "Fitzgerald's reputation as a serious novelist is secure."

The Crack-Up, ed. Edmund Wilson, New York, 1945 • The Stories of F. Scott Fitzgerald, ed. Malcolm Cowley, New York, 1951 • F. Scott Fitzgerald: The Man and His Work, ed. Alfred Kazin, Cleveland, 1951 • Arthur Mizener, The Far Side of Paradise: A Biography of F. Scott Fitzgerald, Boston, 1951

The Rich Boy

"The Rich Boy" was Fitzgerald's first serious work after **The Great Gatsby.** It was written between April and August 1925; it appeared in **The Red Book** in 1926, and was included in his most famous collection of stories, **All the Sad Young Men,** published in the same year.

Like **The Great Gatsby,** to which it is closely akin in several respects, "The Rich Boy" shows us Fitzgerald at the top of his powers, and at the same time in his most characteristic and historically important rôle—as a critic of the American worship of wealth. Here, as in **Gatsby,** the author probes with remarkable sympathy and insight into the psychology of the very rich.

Fitzgerald made the story, says Mizener perceptively, "primarily one of how Anson's queer, rich-boy's pride deprived him of what he wanted most, a home and an ordered life. . . . He cannot commit himself to the human

muddle as he must, if he is to have the life he wants."
Mizener rightly admires the restraint—"He gets all his
climaxes with quiet moments . . . every paragraph implies
much more than it says"—and Cowley observes, likewise,
that this story admirably shows Fitzgerald's skill in "irony
and understatement."

I

Begin with an individual, and before you know it
you find that you have created a type; begin with a type,
and you find that you have created—nothing. That is because we are all queer fish, queerer behind our faces and
voices than we want any one to know or than we know
ourselves. When I hear a man proclaiming himself an
"average, honest, open fellow," I feel pretty sure that he
has some definite and perhaps terrible abnormality which
he has agreed to conceal—and his protestation of being
average and honest and open is his way of reminding
himself of his misprision.

There are no types, no plurals. There is a rich boy,
and this is his and not his brothers' story. All my life I
have lived among his brothers but this one has been my
friend. Besides, if I wrote about his brothers I should
have to begin by attacking all the lies that the poor have
told about the rich and the rich have told about themselves—such a wild structure they have erected that when
we pick up a book about the rich, some instinct prepares
us for unreality. Even the intelligent and impassioned reporters of life have made the country of the rich as unreal
as fairy-land.

Let me tell you about the very rich. They are different
from you and me. They possess and enjoy early, and it
does something to them, makes them soft where we
are hard, and cynical where we are trustful, in a way that,
unless you were born rich, it is very difficult to understand. They think, deep in their hearts, that they are
better than we are because we had to discover the com-
pensations and refuges of life for ourselves. Even when
they enter deep into our world or sink below us, they
still think that they are better than we are. They are
different. The only way I can describe young Anson
Hunter is to approach him as if he were a foreigner
and cling stubbornly to my point of view. If I accept
his for a moment I am lost—I have nothing to show but
a preposterous movie.

Anson was the eldest of six children who would some
day divide a fortune of fifteen million dollars, and he
reached the age of reason—is it seven?—at the beginning of the century when daring young women were already gliding along Fifth Avenue in electric "mobiles."
In those days he and his brother had an English governess who spoke the language very clearly and crisply and
well, so that the two boys grew to speak as she did—
their words and sentences were all crisp and clear and
not run together as ours are. They didn't talk exactly like
English children but acquired an accent that is peculiar to
fashionable people in the city of New York.

In the summer the six children were moved from the
house on 71st Street to a big estate in northern Connecticut. It was not a fashionable locality—Anson's
father wanted to delay as long as possible his children's
knowledge of that side of life. He was a man somewhat
superior to his class, which composed New York society,
and to his period, which was the snobbish and formalized
vulgarity of the Gilded Age, and he wanted his sons
to learn habits of concentration and have sound constitutions and grow up into right-living and successful men.
He and his wife kept an eye on them as well as they were
able until the two older boys went away to school, but in
huge establishments this is difficult—it was much simpler
in the series of small and medium-sized houses in which
my own youth was spent—I was never far out of the
reach of my mother's voice, of the sense of her presence,
her approval or disapproval.

Anson's first sense of his superiority came to him when
he realized the half-grudging American deference that
was paid to him in the Connecticut village. The parents
of the boys he played with always inquired after his father
and mother, and were vaguely excited when their own
children were asked to the Hunters' house. He accepted
this as the natural state of things, and a sort of impatience
with all groups of which he was not the centre—in
money, in position, in authority—remained with him
for the rest of his life. He disdained to struggle with
other boys for precedence—he expected it to be given
him freely, and when it wasn't he withdrew into his
family. His family was sufficient, for in the East money

is still a somewhat feudal thing, a clan-forming thing. In the snobbish West, money separates families to form "sets."

At eighteen, when he went to New Haven, Anson was tall and thick-set, with a clear complexion and a healthy color from the ordered life he had led in school. His hair was yellow and grew in a funny way on his head, his nose was beaked—these two things kept him from being handsome—but he had a confident charm and a certain brusque style, and the upper-class men who passed him on the street knew without being told that he was a rich boy and had gone to one of the best schools. Nevertheless, his very superiority kept him from being a success in college—the independence was mistaken for egotism, and the refusal to accept Yale standards with the proper awe seemed to belittle all those who had. So, long before he graduated, he began to shift the centre of his life to New York.

He was at home in New York—there was his own house with "the kind of servants you can't get any more" —and his own family, of which, because of his good humor and a certain ability to make things go, he was rapidly becoming the centre, and the débutante parties, and the correct manly world of the men's clubs, and the occasional wild spree with the gallant girls whom New Haven only knew from the fifth row. His aspirations were conventional enough—they included even the irreproachable shadow he would some day marry, but they differed from the aspirations of the majority of young men in that there was no mist over them, none of that quality which is variously known as "idealism" or "illusion." Anson accepted without reservation the world of high finance and high extravagance, of divorce and dissipation, of snobbery and of privilege. Most of our lives end as a compromise—it was as a compromise that his life began.

He and I first met in the late summer of 1917 when he was just out of Yale, and, like the rest of us, was swept up into the systematized hysteria of the war. In the blue-green uniform of the naval aviation he came down to Pensacola, where the hotel orchestras played "I'm sorry, dear," and we young officers danced with the girls. Every one liked him, and though he ran with the drinkers and wasn't an especially good pilot, even the instructors treated him with a certain respect. He was always having long talks with them in his confident, logical voice—

talks which ended by his getting himself, or, more frequently, another officer, out of some impending trouble. He was convivial, bawdy, robustly avid for pleasure, and we were all surprised when he fell in love with a conservative and rather proper girl.

Her name was Paula Legendre, a dark, serious beauty from somewhere in California. Her family kept a winter residence just outside of town, and in spite of her primness she was enormously popular; there is a large class of men whose egotism can't endure humor in a woman. But Anson wasn't that sort, and I couldn't understand the attraction of her "sincerity"—that was the thing to say about her—for his keen and somewhat sardonic mind.

Nevertheless, they fell in love—and on her terms. He no longer joined the twilight gathering at the De Soto bar, and whenever they were seen together they were engaged in a long, serious dialogue, which must have gone on several weeks. Long afterward he told me that it was not about anything in particular but was composed on both sides of immature and even meaningless statements—the emotional content that gradually came to fill it grew up not out of the words but out of its enormous seriousness. It was a sort of hypnosis. Often it was interrupted, giving way to that emasculated humor we call fun; when they were alone it was resumed again, solemn, low-keyed, and pitched so as to give each other a sense of unity in feeling and thought. They came to resent any interruptions of it, to be unresponsive to facetiousness about life, even to the mild cynicism of their contemporaries. They were only happy when the dialogue was going on, and its seriousness bathed them like the amber glow of an open fire. Toward the end there came an interruption they did not resent—it began to be interrupted by passion.

Oddly enough, Anson was as engrossed in the dialogue as she was and as profoundly affected by it, yet at the same time aware that on his side much was insincere, and on hers much was merely simple. At first, too, he despised her emotional simplicity as well, but with his love her nature deepened and blossomed, and he could despise it no longer. He felt that if he could enter into Paula's warm safe life he would be happy. The long preparation of the dialogue removed any constraint—he taught her some of what he had learned from more adventurous women, and she responded with a rapt holy intensity. One evening after a dance they agreed to marry, and he wrote a long letter about her to his mother. The next day Paula told him that she was rich, that she had a personal fortune of nearly a million dollars.

III

It was exactly as if they could say "Neither of us has anything: we shall be poor together"—just as delightful that they should be rich instead. It gave them the same communion of adventure. Yet when Anson got leave in April, and Paula and her mother accompanied him North, she was impressed with the standing of his family in New York and with the scale on which they lived. Alone with Anson for the first time in the rooms where he had played as a boy, she was filled with a comfortable emotion, as though she were pre-eminently safe and taken care of. The pictures of Anson in a skull cap at his first school, of Anson on horseback with the sweetheart of a mysterious forgotten summer, of Anson in a gay group of ushers and bridesmaids at a wedding, made her jealous of his life apart from her in the past, and so completely did his authoritative person seem to sum up and typify these possessions of his that she was inspired with the idea of being married immediately and returning to Pensacola as his wife.

But an immediate marriage wasn't discussed—even the engagement was to be secret until after the war. When she realized that only two days of his leave remained, her dissatisfaction crystallized in the intention of making him as unwilling to wait as she was. They were driving to the country for dinner and she determined to force the issue that night.

Now a cousin of Paula's was staying with them at the Ritz, a severe, bitter girl who loved Paula but was somewhat jealous of her impressive engagement, and as Paula was late in dressing, the cousin, who wasn't going to the party, received Anson in the parlor of the suite.

Anson had met friends at five o'clock and drunk freely and indiscreetly with them for an hour. He left the Yale Club at a proper time, and his mother's chauffeur drove him to the Ritz, but his usual capacity was not in evidence, and the impact of the steam-heated sitting-room made him suddenly dizzy. He knew it, and he was both amused and sorry.

Paula's cousin was twenty-five, but she was exceptionally naïve, and at first failed to realize what was up. She had never met Anson before, and she was surprised when he mumbled strange information and nearly fell off his chair, but until Paula appeared it didn't occur to her that what she had taken for the odor of a dry-cleaned uniform was really whiskey. But Paula understood as soon as she appeared; her only thought was to get Anson away before her mother saw him, and at the look in her eyes the cousin understood too.

When Paula and Anson descended to the limousine they found two men inside, both asleep; they were the men with whom he had been drinking at the Yale Club, and they were also going to the party. He had entirely forgotten their presence in the car. On the way to Hempstead they awoke and sang. Some of the songs were rough, and though Paula tried to reconcile herself to the fact that Anson had few verbal inhibitions, her lips tightened with shame and distaste.

Back at the hotel the cousin, confused and agitated, considered the incident, and then walked into Mrs. Legendre's bedroom, saying: "Isn't he funny?"

"Who is funny?"

"Why—Mr. Hunter. He seemed so funny."

Mrs. Legendre looked at her sharply.

"How is he funny?"

"Why, he said he was French. I didn't know he was French."

"That's absurd. You must have misunderstood." She smiled: "It was a joke."

The cousin shook her head stubbornly.

"No. He said he was brought up in France. He said he couldn't speak any English, and that's why he couldn't talk to me. And he couldn't!"

Mrs. Legendre looked away with impatience just as the cousin added thoughtfully, "Perhaps it was because he was so drunk," and walked out of the room.

This curious report was true. Anson, finding his voice thick and uncontrollable, had taken the unusual refuge of announcing that he spoke no English. Years afterwards he used to tell that part of the story, and he invariably communicated the uproarious laughter which the memory aroused in him.

Five times in the next hour Mrs. Legendre tried to get Hempstead on the phone. When she succeeded, there was a ten-minute delay before she heard Paula's voice on the wire.

"Cousin Jo told me Anson was intoxicated."

"Oh, no. . . ."

"Oh, yes. Cousin Jo says he was intoxicated. He told her he was French, and fell off his chair and behaved as if he was very intoxicated. I don't want you to come home with him."

"Mother, he's all right! Please don't worry about——"

"But I do worry. I think it's dreadful. I want you to promise me not to come home with him."

"I'll take care of it, mother. . . ."

"I don't want you to come home with him."

"All right, mother. Good-by."

"Be sure now, Paula. Ask some one to bring you."

Deliberately Paula took the receiver from her ear and hung it up. Her face was flushed with helpless annoyance. Anson was stretched out asleep in a bedroom upstairs, while the dinner-party below was proceeding lamely toward conclusion.

The hour's drive had sobered him somewhat—his arrival was merely hilarious—and Paula hoped that the evening was not spoiled, after all, but two imprudent cocktails before dinner completed the disaster. He talked boisterously and somewhat offensively to the party at large for fifteen minutes, and then slid silently under the table; like a man in an old print—but, unlike an old print, it was rather horrible without being at all quaint. None of the young girls present remarked upon the incident—it seemed to merit only silence. His uncle and two other men carried him up-stairs, and it was just after this that Paula was called to the phone.

An hour later Anson awoke in a fog of nervous agony, through which he perceived after a moment the figure of his uncle Robert standing by the door.

". . . I said are you better?"

"What?"

"Do you feel better, old man?"

"Terrible," said Anson.

"I'm going to try you on another bromo-seltzer. If you can hold it down, it'll do you good to sleep."

With an effort Anson slid his legs from the bed and stood up.

"I'm all right," he said dully.

"Take it easy."

"I thin' if you gave me a glassbrandy I could go downstairs."

"Oh, no——"

"Yes, that's the only thin'. I'm all right now. . . . I suppose I'm in Dutch dow' there."

"They know you're a little under the weather," said his uncle deprecatingly. "But don't worry about it. Schuyler didn't even get here. He passed away in the locker-room over at the Links."

Indifferent to any opinion, except Paula's, Anson was nevertheless determined to save the débris of the evening, but when after a cold bath he made his appearance most of the party had already left. Paula got up immediately to go home.

In the limousine the old serious dialogue began. She had known that he drank, she admitted, but she had never expected anything like this—it seemed to her that perhaps they were not suited to each other, after all. Their ideas about life were too different, and so forth. When she finished speaking, Anson spoke in turn, very soberly. Then Paula said she'd have to think it over; she wouldn't decide to-night; she was not angry but she was terribly sorry. Nor would she let him come into the hotel with her, but just before she got out of the car she leaned and kissed him unhappily on the cheek.

The next afternoon Anson had a long talk with Mrs. Legendre while Paula sat listening in silence. It was agreed that Paula was to brood over the incident for a proper period and then, if mother and daughter thought it best, they would follow Anson to Pensacola. On his part he apologized with sincerity and dignity—that was all; with every card in her hand Mrs. Legendre was unable to establish any advantage over him. He made no promises, showed no humility, only delivered a few serious comments on life which brought him off with rather a moral superiority at the end. When they came South three weeks later, neither Anson in his satisfaction nor Paula in her relief at the reunion realized that the psychological moment had passed forever.

IV

He dominated and attracted her, and at the same time filled her with anxiety. Confused by his mixture of solidity and self-indulgence, of sentiment and cynicism—incongruities which her gentle mind was unable to resolve—Paula grew to think of him as two alternating personalities. When she saw him alone, or at a formal party, or with his casual inferiors, she felt a tremendous pride in his strong, attractive presence, the paternal, understanding stature of his mind. In other company she became uneasy when what had been a fine imperviousness to mere gentility showed its other face. The other face was gross, humorous, reckless of everything but pleasure. It startled her mind temporarily away from him, even led her into a short covert experiment with an old beau, but it was no use—after four months of Anson's enveloping vitality there was an anæmic pallor in all other men.

In July he was ordered abroad, and their tenderness and desire reached a crescendo. Paula considered a last-minute marriage—decided against it only because there were always cocktails on his breath now, but the parting itself made her physically ill with grief. After his departure she wrote him long letters of regret for the days of love they had missed by waiting. In August Anson's plane slipped down into the North Sea. He was pulled onto a destroyer after a night in the water and sent to a hospital with pneumonia; the armistice was signed before he was finally sent home.

Then, with every opportunity given back to them, with no material obstacle to overcome, the secret weavings of their temperaments came between them, drying up their kisses and their tears, making their voices less loud to one another, muffling the intimate chatter of their hearts until the old communication was only possible by letters, from far away. One afternoon a society reporter waited for two hours in the Hunters' house for a confirmation of their engagement. Anson denied it; nevertheless an early issue carried the report as a leading paragraph—they were "constantly seen together at Southampton, Hot Springs, and Tuxedo Park." But the serious dialogue had turned a corner into a long-sustained quarrel, and the affair was almost played out. Anson got drunk flagrantly and missed an engagement with her, whereupon Paula made certain behavioristic demands. His despair was helpless before his pride and his knowledge of himself: the engagement was definitely broken.

"Dearest," said their letters now, "Dearest, Dearest, when I wake up in the middle of the night and realize that after all it was not to be, I feel that I want to die. I can't go on living any more. Perhaps when we meet this summer we may talk things over and decide differently—we were so excited and sad that day, and I don't feel that I can live all my life without you. You speak of other people. Don't you know there are no other people for me, but only you. . . ."

But as Paula drifted here and there around the East she would sometimes mention her gaieties to make him wonder. Anson was too acute to wonder. When he saw a man's name in her letters he felt more sure of her and a little disdainful—he was always superior to such things. But he still hoped that they would some day marry.

Meanwhile he plunged vigorously into all the movement and glitter of post-bellum New York, entering a brokerage house, joining half a dozen clubs, dancing late, and moving in three worlds—his own world, the world of young Yale graduates, and that section of the half-world which rests one end on Broadway. But there was always a thorough and infractible eight hours devoted to his work in Wall Street, where the combination of his influential family connection, his sharp intelligence, and his abundance of sheer physical energy brought him almost immediately forward. He had one of those invaluable minds with partitions in it; sometimes he appeared at his office refreshed by less than an hour's sleep, but such occurrences were rare. So early as 1920 his income in salary and commissions exceeded twelve thousand dollars.

As the Yale tradition slipped into the past he became more and more of a popular figure among his classmates in New York, more popular than he had ever been in college. He lived in a great house, and had the means of introducing young men into other great houses. Moreover, his life already seemed secure, while theirs, for the most part, had arrived again at precarious beginnings. They commenced to turn to him for amusement and escape, and Anson responded readily, taking pleasure in helping people and arranging their affairs.

There were no men in Paula's letters now, but a note of tenderness ran through them that had not been there before. From several sources he heard that she had "a heavy beau," Lowell Thayer, a Bostonian of wealth and position, and though he was sure she still loved him, it made him uneasy to think that he might lose her, after all. Save for one unsatisfactory day she had not been in New York for almost five months, and as the rumors multiplied he became increasingly anxious to see her. In February he took his vacation and went down to Florida.

Palm Beach sprawled plump and opulent between the sparkling sapphire of Lake Worth, flawed here and there by house-boats at anchor, and the great turquoise bar of the Atlantic Ocean. The huge bulks of the Breakers and the Royal Poinciana rose as twin paunches from the bright level of the sand, and around them clustered the Dancing Glade, Bradley's House of Chance, and a dozen modistes and milliners with goods at triple prices from New York. Upon the trellised veranda of the Breakers two hundred women stepped right, stepped left, wheeled, and slid in that then celebrated calisthenic known as the double-shuffle, while in half-time to the music two thousand bracelets clicked up and down on two hundred arms.

At the Everglades Club after dark Paula and Lowell Thayer and Anson and a casual fourth played bridge with hot cards. It seemed to Anson that her kind, serious face was wan and tired—she had been around now for four, five, years. He had known her for three.

"Two spades."

"Cigarette? . . . Oh, I beg your pardon. By me."

"By."

"I'll double three spades."

There were a dozen tables of bridge in the room, which was filling up with smoke. Anson's eyes met Paula's, held them persistently even when Thayer's glance fell between them. . . .

"What was bid?" he asked abstractedly.

"Rose of Washington Square"

sang the young people in the corners:

> *"I'm withering there*
> *In basement air——"*

The smoke banked like fog, and the opening of a door filled the room with blown swirls of ectoplasm. Little Bright Eyes streaked past the tables seeking Mr. Conan Doyle among the Englishmen who were posing as Englishmen about the lobby.

"You could cut it with a knife."

". . . cut it with a knife."

". . . a knife."

At the end of the rubber Paula suddenly got up and spoke to Anson in a tense, low voice. With scarcely a glance at Lowell Thayer, they walked out the door and descended a long flight of stone steps—in a moment they were walking hand in hand along the moonlit beach.

"Darling, darling. . . ." They embraced recklessly, passionately, in a shadow. . . . Then Paula drew back

her face to let his lips say what she wanted to hear—she could feel the words forming as they kissed again. . . . Again she broke away, listening, but as he pulled her close once more she realized that he had said nothing— only *"Darling! Darling!"* in that deep, sad whisper that always made her cry. Humbly, obediently, her emotions yielded to him and the tears streamed down her face, but her heart kept on crying: "Ask me—oh, Anson, dearest, ask me!"

"Paula. . . . *Paula!*"

The words wrung her heart like hands, and Anson, feeling her tremble, knew that emotion was enough. He need say no more, commit their destinies to no practical enigma. Why should he, when he might hold her so, biding his own time, for another year—forever? He was considering them both, her more than himself. For a moment, when she said suddenly that she must go back to her hotel, he hesitated, thinking, first, "This is the moment, after all," and then: "No, let it wait—she is mine. . . ."

He had forgotten that Paula too was worn away inside with the strain of three years. Her mood passed forever in the night.

He went back to New York next morning filled with a certain restless dissatisfaction. Late in April, without warning, he received a telegram from Bar Harbor in which Paula told him that she was engaged to Lowell Thayer, and that they would be married immediately in Boston. What he never really believed could happen had happened at last.

Anson filled himself with whiskey that morning, and going to the office, carried on his work without a break— rather with a fear of what would happen if he stopped. In the evening he went out as usual, saying nothing of what had occurred; he was cordial, humorous, unabstracted. But one thing he could not help—for three days, in any place, in any company, he would suddenly bend his head into his hands and cry like a child.

V

In 1922 when Anson went abroad with the junior partner to investigate some London loans, the journey intimated that he was to be taken into the firm. He was twenty-seven now, a little heavy without being definitely stout, and with a manner older than his years. Old people and young people liked him and trusted him, and mothers felt safe when their daughters were in his charge, for he had a way, when he came into a room, of putting himself on a footing with the oldest and most conservative people there. "You and I," he seemed to say, "we're solid. We understand."

He had an instinctive and rather charitable knowledge of the weaknesses of men and women, and, like a priest, it made him the more concerned for the maintenance of outward forms. It was typical of him that every Sunday morning he taught in a fashionable Episcopal Sunday-school—even though a cold shower and a quick change into a cutaway coat were all that separated him from the wild night before.

After his father's death he was the practical head of his family, and, in effect, guided the destinies of the younger children. Through a complication his authority did not extend to his father's estate, which was administrated by his Uncle Robert, who was the horsey member of the family, a good-natured, hard-drinking member of that set which centres about Wheatley Hills.

Uncle Robert and his wife, Edna, had been great friends of Anson's youth, and the former was disappointed when his nephew's superiority failed to take a horsey form. He backed him for a city club which was the most difficult in America to enter—one could only join if one's family had "helped to build up New York" (or, in other words, were rich before 1880)—and when Anson, after his election, neglected it for the Yale Club, Uncle Robert gave him a little talk on the subject. But when on top of that Anson declined to enter Robert Hunter's own conservative and somewhat neglected brokerage house, his manner grew cooler. Like a primary teacher who has taught all he knew, he slipped out of Anson's life.

There were so many friends in Anson's life—scarcely one for whom he had not done some unusual kindness and scarcely one whom he did not occasionally embarrass by his bursts of rough conversation or his habit of getting drunk whenever and however he liked. It annoyed him when any one else blundered in that regard—about his own lapses he was always humorous. Odd things happened to him and he told them with infectious laughter.

I was working in New York that spring, and I used to lunch with him at the Yale Club, which my university was sharing until the completion of our own. I had read of Paula's marriage, and one afternoon, when I asked him about her, something moved him to tell me the story. After that he frequently invited me to family dinners at his house and behaved as though there was a special relation between us, as though with his confidence a little of that consuming memory had passed into me.

I found that despite the trusting mothers, his attitude toward girls was not indiscriminately protective. It was up to the girl—if she showed an inclination toward looseness, she must take care of herself, even with him.

"Life," he would explain sometimes, "has made a cynic of me."

By life he meant Paula. Sometimes, especially when he was drinking, it became a little twisted in his mind, and he thought that she had callously thrown him over.

This "cynicism," or rather his realization that naturally fast girls were not worth sparing, led to his affair with Dolly Karger. It wasn't his only affair in those years, but it came nearest to touching him deeply, and it had a profound effect upon his attitude toward life.

Dolly was the daughter of a notorious "publicist" who had married into society. She herself grew up into the Junior League, came out at the Plaza, and went to the Assembly; and only a few old families like the Hunters could question whether or not she "belonged," for her picture was often in the papers, and she had more enviable attention than many girls who undoubtedly did. She was dark-haired, with carmine lips and a high, lovely color, which she concealed under pinkish-gray powder all through the first year out, because high color was unfashionable—Victorian-pale was the thing to be. She wore black, severe suits and stood with her hands in her pockets leaning a little forward, with a humorous restraint on her face. She danced exquisitely—better than anything she liked to dance—better than anything except making love. Since she was ten she had always been in love, and, usually, with some boy who didn't respond to her. Those who did—and there were many—bored her after a brief encounter, but for her failures she reserved the warmest spot in her heart. When she met them she would always try once more—sometimes she succeeded, more often she failed.

It never occurred to this gypsy of the unattainable that there was a certain resemblance in those who refused to love her—they shared a hard intuition that saw through to her weakness, not a weakness of emotion but a weakness of rudder. Anson perceived this when he first met her, less than a month after Paula's marriage. He was drinking rather heavily, and he pretended for a week that he was falling in love with her. Then he dropped her abruptly and forgot—immediately he took up the commanding position in her heart.

Like so many girls of that day Dolly was slackly and indiscreetly wild. The unconventionality of a slightly older generation had been simply one facet of a postwar movement to discredit obsolete manners—Dolly's was both older and shabbier, and she saw in Anson the two extremes which the emotionally shiftless woman seeks, an abandon to indulgence alternating with a protective strength. In his character she felt both the sybarite and the solid rock, and these two satisfied every need of her nature.

She felt that it was going to be difficult, but she mistook the reason—she thought that Anson and his family expected a more spectacular marriage, but she guessed immediately that her advantage lay in his tendency to drink.

They met at the large débutante dances, but as her infatuation increased they managed to be more and more together. Like most mothers, Mrs. Karger believed that Anson was exceptionally reliable, so she allowed Dolly to go with him to distant country clubs and suburban houses without inquiring closely into their activities or questioning her explanations when they came in late. At first these explanations might have been accurate, but Dolly's worldly ideas of capturing Anson were soon engulfed in the rising sweep of her emotion. Kisses in the back of taxis and motor-cars were no longer enough; they did a curious thing:

They dropped out of their world for a while and made another world just beneath it where Anson's tippling and Dolly's irregular hours would be less noticed and commented on. It was composed, this world, of varying elements—several of Anson's Yale friends and their wives, two or three young brokers and bond salesmen and a handful of unattached men, fresh from college, with money and a propensity to dissipation. What this world lacked in spaciousness and scale it made up for by allowing them a liberty that it scarcely permitted itself. Moreover, it centered around them and permitted Dolly the pleasure of a faint condescension—a pleasure which

Anson, whose whole life was a condescension from the certitudes of his childhood, was unable to share.

He was not in love with her, and in the long feverish winter of their affair he frequently told her so. In the spring he was weary—he wanted to renew his life at some other source—moreover, he saw that either he must break with her now or accept the responsibility of a definite seduction. Her family's encouraging attitude precipitated his decision—one evening when Mr. Karger knocked discreetly at the library door to announce that he had left a bottle of old brandy in the dining-room, Anson felt that life was hemming him in. That night he wrote her a short letter in which he told her that he was going on his vacation, and that in view of all the circumstances they had better meet no more.

It was June. His family had closed up the house and gone to the country, so he was living temporarily at the Yale Club. I had heard about his affair with Dolly as it developed—accounts salted with humor, for he despised unstable women, and granted them no place in the social edifice in which he believed—and when he told me that night that he was definitely breaking with her I was glad. I had seen Dolly here and there, and each time with a feeling of pity at the hopelessness of her struggle, and of shame at knowing so much about her that I had no right to know. She was what is known as "a pretty little thing," but there was a certain recklessness which rather fascinated me. Her dedication to the goddess of waste would have been less obvious had she been less spirited —she would most certainly throw herself away, but I was glad when I heard that the sacrifice would not be consummated in my sight.

Anson was going to leave the letter of farewell at her house next morning. It was one of the few houses left open in the Fifth Avenue district, and he knew that the Kargers, acting upon erroneous information from Dolly, had foregone a trip abroad to give their daughter her chance. As he stepped out the door of the Yale Club into Madison Avenue the postman passed him, and he followed back inside. The first letter that caught his eye was in Dolly's hand.

He knew what it would be—a lonely and tragic monologue, full of the reproaches he knew, the invoked memories, the "I wonder if's"—all the immemorial intimacies that he had communicated to Paula Legendre in what seemed another age. Thumbing over some bills, he brought it on top again and opened it. To his surprise it was a short, somewhat formal note, which said that Dolly would be unable to go to the country with him for the week-end, because Perry Hull from Chicago had unexpectedly come to town. It added that Anson had brought this on himself: "—if I felt that you loved me as I love you I would go with you at any time, any place, but Perry is *so* nice, and he so much wants me to marry him——"

Anson smiled contemptuously—he had had experience with such decoy epistles. Moreover, he knew how Dolly had labored over this plan, probably sent for the faithful Perry and calculated the time of his arrival—even labored over the note so that it would make him jealous without driving him away. Like most compromises, it had neither force nor vitality but only a timorous despair.

Suddenly he was angry. He sat down in the lobby and read it again. Then he went to the phone, called Dolly and told her in his clear, compelling voice that he had received her note and would call for her at five o'clock as they had previously planned. Scarcely waiting for the pretended uncertainty of her "Perhaps I can see you for an hour," he hung up the receiver and went down to his office. On the way he tore his own letter into bits and dropped it in the street.

He was not jealous—she meant nothing to him—but at her pathetic ruse everything stubborn and self-indulgent in him came to the surface. It was a presumption from a mental inferior and it could not be overlooked. If she wanted to know to whom she belonged she would see.

He was on the door-step at quarter past five. Dolly was dressed for the street, and he listened in silence to the paragraph of "I can only see you for an hour," which she had begun on the phone.

"Put on your hat, Dolly," he said, "we'll take a walk."

They strolled up Madison Avenue and over to Fifth while Anson's shirt dampened upon his portly body in the deep heat. He talked little, scolding her, making no love to her, but before they had walked six blocks she was his again, apologizing for the note, offering not to see Perry at all as an atonement, offering anything. She thought that he had come because he was beginning to love her.

"I'm hot," he said when they reached 71st Street. "This is a winter suit. If I stop by the house and change, would you mind waiting for me down-stairs? I'll only be a minute."

She was happy; the intimacy of his being hot, of any physical fact about him, thrilled her. When they came to the iron-grated door and Anson took out his key she experienced a sort of delight.

Down-stairs it was dark, and after he ascended in the lift Dolly raised a curtain and looked out through opaque lace at the houses over the way. She heard the lift machinery stop, and with the notion of teasing him pressed the button that brought it down. Then on what was more than an impulse she got into it and sent it up to what she guessed was his floor.

"Anson," she called, laughing a little.

"Just a minute," he answered from his bedroom . . . then after a brief delay: "Now you can come in."

He had changed and was buttoning his vest.

"This is my room," he said lightly. "How do you like it?"

She caught sight of Paula's picture on the wall and stared at it in fascination, just as Paula had stared at the pictures of Anson's childish sweethearts five years before. She knew something about Paula—sometimes she tortured herself with fragments of the story.

Suddenly she came close to Anson, raising her arms. They embraced. Outside the area window a soft artificial twilight already hovered, though the sun was still bright on a back roof across the way. In half an hour the room would be quite dark. The uncalculated opportunity overwhelmed them, made them both breathless, and they clung more closely. It was imminent, inevitable. Still holding one another, they raised their heads—their eyes fell together upon Paula's picture, staring down at them from the wall.

Suddenly Anson dropped his arms, and sitting down at his desk tried the drawer with a bunch of keys.

"Like a drink?" he asked in a gruff voice.

"No, Anson."

He poured himself half a tumbler of whiskey, swallowed it, and then opened the door into the hall.

"Come on," he said.

Dolly hesitated.

"Anson—I'm going to the country with you tonight, after all. You understand that, don't you?"

"Of course," he answered brusquely.

In Dolly's car they rode on to Long Island, closer in their emotions than they had ever been before. They knew what would happen—not with Paula's face to remind them that something was lacking, but when they were alone in the still, hot Long Island night they did not care.

The estate in Port Washington where they were to spend the week-end belonged to a cousin of Anson's who had married a Montana copper operator. An interminable drive began at the lodge and twisted under imported poplar saplings toward a huge, pink Spanish house. Anson had often visited there before.

After dinner they danced at the Linx Club. About midnight Anson assured himself that his cousins would not leave before two—then he explained that Dolly was tired; he would take her home and return to the dance later. Trembling a little with excitement, they got into a borrowed car together and drove to Port Washington. As they reached the lodge he stopped and spoke to the night-watchman.

"When are you making a round, Carl?"

"Right away."

"Then you'll be here till everybody's in?"

"Yes, sir."

"All right. Listen: if any automobile, no matter whose it is, turns in at this gate, I want you to phone the house immediately." He put a five-dollar bill into Carl's hand. "Is that clear?"

"Yes, Mr. Anson." Being of the Old World, he neither winked nor smiled. Yet Dolly sat with her face turned slightly away.

Anson had a key. Once inside he poured a drink for both of them—Dolly left hers untouched—then he ascertained definitely the location of the phone, and found that it was within easy hearing distance of their rooms, both of which were on the first floor.

Five minutes later he knocked at the door of Dolly's room.

"Anson?" He went in, closing the door behind him. She was in bed, leaning up anxiously with elbows on the pillow; sitting beside her he took her in his arms.

"Anson, darling."

He didn't answer.

"Anson. . . . Anson! I love you. . . . Say you love me. Say it now—can't you say it now? Even if you don't mean it?"

He did not listen. Over her head he perceived that the picture of Paula was hanging here upon this wall.

He got up and went close to it. The frame gleamed faintly with thrice-reflected moonlight—within was a blurred shadow of a face that he saw he did not know. Almost sobbing, he turned around and stared with abomination at the little figure on the bed.

"This is all foolishness," he said thickly. "I don't know what I was thinking about. I don't love you and you'd better wait for somebody that loves you. I don't love you a bit, can't you understand?"

His voice broke, and he went hurriedly out. Back in the salon he was pouring himself a drink with uneasy fingers, when the front door opened suddenly, and his cousin came in.

"Why, Anson, I hear Dolly's sick," she began solicitously. "I hear she's sick. . . ."

"It was nothing," he interrupted, raising his voice so that it would carry into Dolly's room. "She was a little tired. She went to bed."

For a long time afterward Anson believed that a protective God sometimes interfered in human affairs. But Dolly Karger, lying awake and staring at the ceiling, never again believed in anything at all.

VI

When Dolly married during the following autumn, Anson was in London on business. Like Paula's marriage, it was sudden, but it affected him in a different way. At first he felt that it was funny, and had an inclination to laugh when he thought of it. Later it depressed him—it made him feel old.

There was something repetitive about it—why, Paula and Dolly had belonged to different generations. He had a foretaste of the sensation of a man of forty who hears that the daughter of an old flame has married. He wired congratulations and, as was not the case with Paula, they were sincere—he had never really hoped that Paula would be happy.

When he returned to New York, he was made a partner in the firm, and, as his responsibilities increased, he had less time on his hands. The refusal of a life-insurance company to issue him a policy made such an impression on him that he stopped drinking for a year, and claimed that he felt better physically, though I think he missed the convivial recounting of those Celliniesque adventures which, in his early twenties, had played such a part in his life. But he never abandoned the Yale Club. He was a figure there, a personality, and the tendency of his class, who were now seven years out of college, to drift away to more sober haunts was checked by his presence.

His day was never too full nor his mind too weary to give any sort of aid to any one who asked it. What had been done at first through pride and superiority had become a habit and a passion. And there was always something—a younger brother in trouble at New Haven, a quarrel to be patched up between a friend and his wife, a position to be found for this man, an investment for that. But his specialty was the solving of problems for young married people. Young married people fascinated him and their apartments were almost sacred to him—he knew the story of their love-affair, advised them where to live and how, and remembered their babies' names. Toward young wives his attitude was circumspect: he never abused the trust which their husbands—strangely enough in view of his unconcealed irregularities—invariably reposed in him.

He came to take a vicarious pleasure in happy marriages, and to be inspired to an almost equally pleasant melancholy by those that went astray. Not a season passed that he did not witness the collapse of an affair that perhaps he himself had fathered. When Paula was divorced and almost immediately remarried to another Bostonian, he talked about her to me all one afternoon. He would never love any one as he loved Paula, but he insisted that he no longer cared.

"I'll never marry," he came to say; "I've seen too much of it, and I know a happy marriage is a very rare thing. Besides, I'm too old."

But he did believe in marriage. Like all men who spring from a happy and successful marriage, he believed in it passionately—nothing he had seen would change his belief, his cynicism dissolved upon it like air. But he did really believe he was too old. At twenty-eight he began to accept with equanimity the prospect of marrying without romantic love; he resolutely chose a New York girl of his own class, pretty, intelligent, congenial, above reproach—and set about falling in love with her. The things he had said to Paula with sincerity, to other girls with grace, he could no longer say at all without smiling, or with the force necessary to convince.

"When I'm forty," he told his friends, "I'll be **ripe**. I'll fall for some chorus girl like the rest."

Nevertheless, he persisted in his attempt. His mother wanted to see him married, and he could now well afford it—he had a seat on the Stock Exchange, and his earned income came to twenty-five thousand a year. The idea was agreeable: when his friends—he spent most of his time with the set he and Dolly had evolved—closed themselves in behind domestic doors at night, he no longer rejoiced in his freedom. He even wondered if he should have married Dolly. Not even Paula had loved him more, and he was learning the rarity, in a single life, of encountering true emotion.

Just as this mood began to creep over him a disquieting story reached his ear. His Aunt Edna, a woman just this side of forty, was carrying on an open intrigue with a dissolute, hard-drinking young man named Cary Sloane. Every one knew of it except Anson's Uncle Robert, who for fifteen years had talked long in clubs and taken his wife for granted.

Anson heard the story again and again with increasing annoyance. Something of his old feeling for his uncle came back to him, a feeling that was more than personal, a reversion toward that family solidarity on which he had based his pride. His intuition singled out the essential point of the affair, which was that his uncle shouldn't be hurt. It was his first experience in unsolicited meddling, but with his knowledge of Edna's character he felt that he could handle the matter better than a district judge or his uncle.

His uncle was in Hot Springs. Anson traced down the sources of the scandal so that there should be no possibility of mistake and then he called Edna and asked her to lunch with him at the Plaza next day. Something in his tone must have frightened her, for she was reluctant, but he insisted, putting off the date until she had no excuse for refusing.

She met him at the appointed time in the Plaza lobby, a lovely, faded, gray-eyed blonde in a coat of Russian sable. Five great rings, cold with diamonds and emeralds, sparkled on her slender hands. It occurred to Anson that it was his father's intelligence and not his uncle's that had earned the fur and the stones, the rich brilliance that buoyed up her passing beauty.

Though Edna scented his hostility, she was unprepared for the directness of his approach.

The Rich Boy 1089

"Edna, I'm astonished at the way you've been acting," he said in a strong, frank voice. "At first I couldn't believe it."

"Believe what?" she demanded sharply.

"You needn't pretend with me, Edna. I'm talking about Cary Sloane. Aside from any other consideration, I didn't think you could treat Uncle Robert——"

"Now look here, Anson——" she began angrily, but his peremptory voice broke through hers:

"——and your children in such a way. You've been married eighteen years, and you're old enough to know better."

"You can't talk to me like that! You——"

"Yes, I can. Uncle Robert has always been my best friend." He was tremendously moved. He felt a real distress about his uncle, about his three young cousins.

Edna stood up, leaving her crab-flake cocktail untasted.

"This is the silliest thing——"

"Very well, if you won't listen to me I'll go to Uncle Robert and tell him the whole story—he's bound to hear it sooner or later. And afterward I'll go to old Moses Sloane."

Edna faltered back into her chair.

"Don't talk so loud," she begged him. Her eyes blurred with tears. "You have no idea how your voice carries. You might have chosen a less public place to make all these crazy accusations."

He didn't answer.

"Oh, you never liked me, I know," she went on. "You're just taking advantage of some silly gossip to try and break up the only interesting friendship I've ever had. What did I ever do to make you hate me so?"

Still Anson waited. There would be the appeal to his chivalry, then to his pity, finally to his superior sophistication—when he had shouldered his way through all these there would be admissions, and he could come to grips with her. By being silent, by being impervious, by returning constantly to his main weapon, which was his own true emotion, he bullied her into frantic despair as the luncheon hour slipped away. At two o'clock she took out a mirror and a handkerchief, shined away the marks of her tears and powdered the slight hollows where they had lain. She had agreed to meet him at her own house at five.

When he arrived she was stretched on a *chaise-longue* which was covered with cretonne for the summer, and the tears he had called up at luncheon seemed still to be standing in her eyes. Then he was aware of Cary Sloane's dark anxious presence upon the cold hearth.

"What's this idea of yours?" broke out Sloane immediately. "I understand you invited Edna to lunch and then threatened her on the basis of some cheap scandal."

Anson sat down.

"I have no reason to think it's only scandal."

"I hear you're going to take it to Robert Hunter, and to my father."

Anson nodded.

"Either you break it off—or I will," he said.

"What God damned business is it of yours, Hunter?"

"Don't lose your temper, Cary," said Edna nervously. "It's only a question of showing him how absurd——"

"For one thing, it's my name that's being handed around," interrupted Anson. "That's all that concerns you, Cary."

"Edna isn't a member of your family."

"She most certainly is!" His anger mounted. "Why—she owes this house and the rings on her fingers to my father's brains. When Uncle Robert married her she didn't have a penny."

They all looked at the rings as if they had a significant bearing on the situation. Edna made a gesture to take them from her hand.

"I guess they're not the only rings in the world," said Sloane.

"Oh, this is absurd," cried Edna. "Anson, will you listen to me? I've found out how the silly story started. It was a maid I discharged who went right to Chilicheffs—all these Russians pump things out of their servants and then put a false meaning on them." She brought down her fist angrily on the table: "And after Robert lent them the limousine for a whole month when we were South last winter——"

"Do you see?" demanded Sloane eagerly. "This maid got hold of the wrong end of the thing. She knew that Edna and I were friends, and she carried it to the Chilicheffs. In Russia they assume that if a man and a woman ——"

He enlarged the theme to a disquisition upon social relations in the Caucasus.

"If that's the case it had better be explained to Uncle Robert," said Anson dryly, "so that when the rumors do reach him he'll know they're not true."

Adopting the method he had followed with Edna at luncheon he let them explain it all away. He knew that they were guilty and that presently they would cross the line from explanation into justification and convict themselves more definitely than he could ever do. By seven they had taken the desperate step of telling him the truth—Robert Hunter's neglect, Edna's empty life, the casual dalliance that had flamed up into passion—but like so many true stories it had the misfortune of being old, and its enfeebled body beat helplessly against the armor of Anson's will. The threat to go to Sloane's father sealed their helplessness, for the latter, a retired cotton broker out of Alabama, was a notorious fundamentalist who controlled his son by a rigid allowance and the promise that at his next vagary the allowance would stop forever.

They dined at a small French restaurant, and the discussion continued—at one time Sloane resorted to physical threats, a little later they were both imploring him to give them time. But Anson was obdurate. He saw that Edna was breaking up, and that her spirit must not be refreshed by any renewal of their passion.

At two o'clock in a small night-club on 53d Street, Edna's nerves suddenly collapsed, and she cried to go home. Sloane had been drinking heavily all evening, and he was faintly maudlin, leaning on the table and weeping a little with his face in his hands. Quickly Anson gave them his terms. Sloane was to leave town for six months, and he must be gone within forty-eight hours. When he returned there was to be no resumption of the affair, but at the end of a year Edna might, if she wished, tell Robert Hunter that she wanted a divorce and go about it in the usual way.

He paused, gaining confidence from their faces for his final word.

"Or there's another thing you can do," he said slowly, "if Edna wants to leave her children, there's nothing I can do to prevent your running off together."

"I want to go home!" cried Edna again. "Oh, haven't you done enough to us for one day?"

Outside it was dark, save for a blurred glow from Sixth Avenue down the street. In that light those two who had been lovers looked for the last time into each other's tragic faces, realizing that between them there was not enough youth and strength to avert their eternal parting. Sloane walked suddenly off down the street and Anson tapped a dozing taxi-driver on the arm.

It was almost four; there was a patient flow of cleaning water along the ghostly pavement of Fifth Avenue, and the shadows of two night women flitted over the dark façade of St. Thomas's church. Then the desolate shrubbery of Central Park where Anson had often played as a child, and the mounting numbers, significant as names, of the marching streets. This was his city, he thought, where his name had flourished through five generations. No change could alter the permanence of its place here, for change itself was the essential substratum by which he and those of his name identified themselves with the spirit of New York. Resourcefulness and a powerful will—for his threats in weaker hands would have been less than nothing—had beaten the gathering dust from his uncle's name, from the name of his family, from even this shivering figure that sat beside him in the cab.

Cary Sloane's body was found next morning on the lower shelf of a pillar of Queensboro Bridge. In the darkness and in his excitement he had thought that it was the water flowing black beneath him, but in less than a second it made no possible difference—unless he had planned to think one last thought of Edna, and call out her name as he struggled feebly in the water.

VII

Anson never blamed himself for his part in this affair—the situation which brought it about had not been of his making. But the just suffer with the unjust, and he found that his oldest and somehow his most precious friendship was over. He never knew what distorted story Edna told, but he was welcome in his uncle's house no longer.

Just before Christmas Mrs. Hunter retired to a select Episcopal heaven, and Anson became the responsible head of his family. An unmarried aunt who had lived with them for years ran the house, and attempted with helpless inefficiency to chaperone the younger girls. All the children were less self-reliant than Anson, more conventional both in their virtues and in their shortcomings. Mrs. Hunter's death had postponed the début of one daughter and the wedding of another. Also it had taken something deeply material from all of them, for with her passing the quiet, expensive superiority of the Hunters came to an end.

For one thing, the estate, considerably diminished by two inheritance taxes and soon to be divided among six children, was not a notable fortune any more. Anson saw a tendency in his youngest sisters to speak rather respectfully of families that hadn't "existed" twenty years ago. His own feeling of precedence was not echoed in them—sometimes they were conventionally snobbish, that was all. For another thing, this was the last summer they would spend on the Connecticut estate; the clamor against it was too loud: "Who wants to waste the best months of the year shut up in that dead old town?" Reluctantly he yielded—the house would go into the market in the fall, and next summer they would rent a smaller place in Westchester County. It was a step down from the expensive simplicity of his father's idea, and, while he sympathized with the revolt, it also annoyed him; during his mother's lifetime he had gone up there at least every other week-end—even in the gayest summers.

Yet he himself was part of this change, and his strong instinct for life had turned him in his twenties from the hollow obsequies of that abortive leisure class. He did not see this clearly—he still felt that there was a norm, a standard of society. But there was no norm, it was doubtful if there ever had been a true norm in New York. The few who still paid and fought to enter a particular set succeeded only to find that as a society it scarcely functioned—or, what was more alarming, that the Bohemia from which they fled sat above them at table.

At twenty-nine Anson's chief concern was his own growing loneliness. He was sure now that he would never marry. The number of weddings at which he had officiated as best man or usher was past all counting—there was a drawer at home that bulged with the official neckties of this or that wedding-party, neckties standing for romances that had not endured a year, for couples who had passed completely from his life. Scarf-pins, gold pencils, cuff-buttons, presents from a generation of grooms had passed through his jewel-box and been lost—and with every ceremony he was less and less able to imagine himself in the groom's place. Under his hearty good-will toward all those marriages there was despair about his own.

And as he neared thirty he became not a little depressed at the inroads that marriage, especially lately, had made upon his friendships. Groups of people had a disconcerting tendency to dissolve and disappear. The men from his own college—and it was upon them he had expended the most time and affection—were the most elusive of all. Most of them were drawn deep into domesticity, two were dead, one lived abroad, one was in Hollywood writing continuities for pictures that Anson went faithfully to see.

Most of them, however, were permanent commuters with an intricate family life centring around some suburban country club, and it was from these that he felt his estrangement most keenly.

In the early days of their married life they had all needed him; he gave them advice about their slim finances, he exercised their doubts about the advisability of bringing a baby into two rooms and a bath, especially he stood for the great world outside. But now their financial troubles were in the past and the fearfully expected child had evolved into an absorbing family. They were always glad to see old Anson, but they dressed up for him and tried to impress him with their present importance, and kept their troubles to themselves. They needed him no longer.

A few weeks before his thirtieth birthday the last of his early and intimate friends was married. Anson acted in his usual rôle of best man, gave his usual silver tea-service, and went down to the usual *Homeric* to say good-by. It was a hot Friday afternoon in May, and as he walked from the pier he realized that Saturday closing had begun and he was free until Monday morning.

"Go where?" he asked himself.

The Yale Club, of course; bridge until dinner, then four or five raw cocktails in somebody's room and a pleasant confused evening. He regretted that this afternoon's groom wouldn't be along—they had always been able to cram so much into such nights: they knew how to attach women and how to get rid of them, how much consideration any girl deserved from their intelligent hedonism. A party was an adjusted thing—you took certain girls to certain places and spent just so much on their amusement; you drank a little, not much more than you ought to drink, and at a certain time in the morning you stood up and said you were going home. You avoided college boys, sponges, future engagements, fights, sentiment, and indiscretions. That was the way it was done. All the rest was dissipation.

In the morning you were never violently sorry—you made no resolutions, but if you had overdone it and your head was slightly out of order, you went on the wagon for a few days without saying anything about it, and waited until an accumulation of nervous boredom projected you into another party.

The lobby of the Yale Club was unpopulated. In the bar three very young alumni looked up at him, momentarily and without curiosity.

"Hello, there, Oscar," he said to the bartender. "Mr. Cahill been around this afternoon?"

"Mr. Cahill's gone to New Haven."

"Oh . . . that so?"

"Gone to the ball game. Lot of men gone up."

Anson looked once again into the lobby, considered for a moment, and then walked out and over to Fifth Avenue. From the broad window of one of his clubs—one that he had scarcely visited in five years—a gray man with watery eyes stared down at him. Anson looked quickly away—that figure sitting in vacant resignation, in supercilious solitude, depressed him. He stopped and, retracing his steps, started over 47th Street toward Teak Warden's apartment. Teak and his wife had once been his most familiar friends—it was a household where he and Dolly Karger had been used to go in the days of their affair. But Teak had taken to drink, and his wife had remarked publicly that Anson was a bad influence on him. The remark reached Anson in an exaggerated form—when it was finally cleared up, the delicate spell of intimacy was broken, never to be renewed.

"Is Mr. Warden at home?" he inquired.

"They've gone to the country."

The fact unexpectedly cut at him. They were gone to the country and he hadn't known. Two years before he would have known the date, the hour, come up at the last moment for a final drink, and planned his first visit to them. Now they had gone without a word.

Anson looked at his watch and considered a week-end with his family, but the only train was a local that would jolt through the aggressive heat for three hours. And tomorrow in the country, and Sunday—he was in no mood for porch-bridge with polite undergraduates, and dancing after dinner at a rural roadhouse, a diminutive of gaiety which his father had estimated too well.

"Oh, no," he said to himself. . . . "No."

He was a dignified, impressive young man, rather stout now, but otherwise unmarked by dissipation. He could have been cast for a pillar of something—at times you were sure it was not society, at others nothing else—

for the law, for the church. He stood for a few minutes motionless on the sidewalk in front of a 47th Street apartment-house; for almost the first time in his life he had nothing whatever to do.

Then he began to walk briskly up Fifth Avenue, as if he had just been reminded of an important engagement there. The necessity of dissimulation is one of the few characteristics that we share with dogs, and I think of Anson on that day as some well-bred specimen who had been disappointed at a familiar back door. He was going to see Nick, once a fashionable bartender in demand at all private dances, and now employed in cooling non-alcoholic champagne among the labyrinthine cellars of the Plaza Hotel.

"Nick," he said, "what's happened to everything?"

"Dead," Nick said.

"Make me a whiskey sour." Anson handed a pint bottle over the counter. "Nick, the girls are different; I had a little girl in Brooklyn and she got married last week without letting me know."

"That a fact? Ha-ha-ha," responded Nick diplomatically. "Slipped it over on you."

"Absolutely," said Anson. "And I was out with her the night before."

"Ha-ha-ha," said Nick, "ha-ha-ha!"

"Do you remember the wedding, Nick, in Hot Springs where I had the waiters and the musicians singing 'God save the King'?"

"Now where was that, Mr. Hunter?" Nick concentrated doubtfully. "Seems to me that was——"

"Next time they were back for more, and I began to wonder how much I'd paid them," continued Anson.

"—seems to me that was at Mr. Trenholm's wedding."

"Don't know him," said Anson decisively. He was offended that a strange name should intrude upon his reminiscences; Nick perceived this.

"Na—aw—" he admitted, "I ought to know that. It was one of *your* crowd—Brakins . . . Baker——"

"Bicker Baker," said Anson responsively. "They put me in a hearse after it was over and covered me up with flowers and drove me away."

"Ha-ha-ha," said Nick. "Ha-ha-ha."

Nick's simulation of the old family servant paled presently and Anson went up-stairs to the lobby. He looked around—his eyes met the glance of an unfamiliar clerk at the desk, then fell upon a flower from the morning's marriage hesitating in the mouth of a brass cuspidor. He went out and walked slowly toward the blood-red sun over Columbus Circle. Suddenly he turned around and, retracing his steps to the Plaza, immured himself in a telephone-booth.

Later he said that he tried to get me three times that afternoon, that he tried every one who might be in New York—men and girls he had not seen for years, an artist's model of his college days whose faded number was still in his address book—Central told him that even the exchange existed no longer. At length his quest roved into the country, and he held brief disappointing conversations with emphatic butlers and maids. So-and-so was out, riding, swimming, playing golf, sailed to Europe last week. Who shall I say phoned?

It was intolerable that he should pass the evening alone —the private reckonings which one plans for a moment of leisure lose every charm when the solitude is enforced. There were always women of a sort, but the ones he knew had temporarily vanished, and to pass a New York evening in the hired company of a stranger never occurred to him—he would have considered that that was something shameful and secret, the diversion of a travelling salesman in a strange town.

Anson paid the telephone bill—the girl tried unsuccessfully to joke with him about its size—and for the second time that afternoon started to leave the Plaza and go he knew not where. Near the revolving door the figure of a woman, obviously with child, stood sideways to the light—a sheer beige cape fluttered at her shoulders when the door turned and, each time, she looked impatiently toward it as if she were weary of waiting. At the first sight of her a strong nervous thrill of familiarity went over him, but not until he was within five feet of her did he realize that it was Paula.

"Why, Anson Hunter!"

His heart turned over.

"Why, Paula——"

"Why, this is wonderful. I can't believe it, *Anson!*"

She took both his hands, and he saw in the freedom of the gesture that the memory of him had lost poignancy to her. But not to him—he felt that old mood that she evoked in him stealing over his brain, that gentleness with which he had always met her optimism as if afraid to mar its surface.

"We're at Rye for the summer. Pete had to come East on business—you know of course I'm Mrs. Peter Hagerty now—so we brought the children and took a house. You've got to come out and see us."

"Can I?" he asked directly. "When?"

"When you like. Here's Pete." The revolving door functioned, giving up a fine tall man of thirty with a tanned face and a trim mustache. His immaculate fitness made a sharp contrast with Anson's increasing bulk, which was obvious under the faintly tight cut-away coat.

"You oughtn't to be standing," said Hagerty to his wife. "Let's sit down here." He indicated lobby chairs, but Paula hesitated.

"I've got to go right home," she said. "Anson, why don't you—why don't you come out and have dinner with us to-night? We're just getting settled, but if you can stand that——"

Hagerty confirmed the invitation cordially.

"Come out for the night."

Their car waited in front of the hotel, and Paula with a tired gesture sank back against silk cushions in the corner.

"There's so much I want to talk to you about," she said, "it seems hopeless."

"I want to hear about you."

"Well"—she smiled at Hagerty—"that would take a long time too. I have three children—by my first marriage. The oldest is five then four, then three." She smiled again. "I didn't waste much time having them, did I?"

"Boys?"

"A boy and two girls. Then—oh, a lot of things happened, and I got a divorce in Paris a year ago and married Pete. That's all—except that I'm awfully happy."

In Rye they drove up to a large house near the Beach Club, from which there issued presently three dark, slim children who broke from an English governess and approached them with an esoteric cry. Abstractedly and with difficulty Paula took each into her arms, a caress which they accepted stiffly, as they had evidently been told not to bump into Mummy. Even against their fresh faces Paula's skin showed scarcely any weariness—for all her physical languor she seemed younger than when he had last seen her at Palm Beach seven years ago.

At dinner she was preoccupied, and afterward, during the homage to the radio, she lay with closed eyes on the sofa, until Anson wondered if his presence at this time were not an intrusion. But at nine o'clock, when Hagerty rose and said pleasantly that he was going to leave them by themselves for a while, she began to talk slowly about herself and the past.

"My first baby," she said—"the one we call Darling, the biggest little girl—I wanted to die when I knew I was going to have her, because Lowell was like a stranger to me. It didn't seem as though she could be my own. I wrote you a letter and tore it up. Oh, you were *so* bad to me, Anson."

It was the dialogue again, rising and falling. Anson felt a sudden quickening of memory.

"Weren't you engaged once?" she asked—"a girl named Dolly something?"

"I wasn't ever engaged. I tried to be engaged, but I never loved anybody but you, Paula."

"Oh," she said. Then after a moment: "This baby is the first one I ever really wanted. You see, I'm in love now—at last."

He didn't answer, shocked at the treachery of her remembrance. She must have seen that the "at last" bruised him, for she continued:

"I was infatuated with you, Anson—you could make me do anything you liked. But we wouldn't have been happy. I'm not smart enough for you. I don't like things to be complicated like you do." She paused. "You'll never settle down," she said.

The phrase struck at him from behind—it was an accusation that of all accusations he had never merited.

"I could settle down if women were different," he said. "If I didn't understand so much about them, if women didn't spoil you for other women, if they had only a little pride. If I could go to sleep for a while and wake up into a home that was really mine—why, that's what I'm made for, Paula, that's what women have seen in me and liked in me. It's only that I can't get through the preliminaries any more."

Hagerty came in a little before eleven; after a whiskey Paula stood up and announced that she was going to bed. She went over and stood by her husband.

"Where did you go, dearest?" she demanded.

"I had a drink with Ed Saunders."

"I was worried. I thought maybe you'd run away."

She rested her head against his coat.

"He's sweet, isn't he, Anson?" she demanded.

"Absolutely," said Anson, laughing.

She raised her face to her husband.

"Well, I'm ready," she said. She turned to Anson: "Do you want to see our family gymnastic stunt?"

"Yes," he said in an interested voice.

"All right. Here we go!"

Hagerty picked her up easily in his arms.

"This is called the family acrobatic stunt," said Paula. "He carries me up-stairs. Isn't it sweet of him?"

"Yes," said Anson.

Hagerty bent his head slightly until his face touched Paula's.

"And I love him," she said. "I've just been telling you, haven't I, Anson?"

"Yes," he said.

"He's the dearest thing that ever lived in this world; aren't you, darling? . . . Well, good night. Here we go. Isn't he strong?"

"Yes," Anson said.

"You'll find a pair of Pete's pajamas laid out for you. Sweet dreams—see you at breakfast."

"Yes," Anson said.

VIII

The older members of the firm insisted that Anson should go abroad for the summer. He had scarcely had a vacation in seven years, they said. He was stale and needed a change. Anson resisted.

"If I go," he declared, "I won't come back any more."

"That's absurd, old man. You'll be back in three months with all this depression gone. Fit as ever."

"No," He shook his head stubbornly. "If I stop, I won't go back to work. If I stop, that means I've given up—I'm through."

"We'll take a chance on that. Stay six months if you like—we're not afraid you'll leave us. Why, you'd be miserable if you didn't work."

They arranged his passage for him. They liked Anson—every one liked Anson—and the change that had been coming over him cast a sort of pall over the office. The enthusiasm that had invariably signalled up business, the considerations toward his equals and his inferiors, the lift of his vital presence—within the past four months his intense nervousness had melted down these qualities into the fussy pessimism of a man of forty. On every transaction in which he was involved he acted as a drag and a strain.

"If I go I'll never come back," he said.

Three days before he sailed Paula Legendre Hagerty died in childbirth. I was with him a great deal then, for we were crossing together, but for the first time in our friendship he told me not a word of how he felt, nor did I see the slightest sign of emotion. His chief preoccupation was with the fact that he was thirty years old—he would turn the conversation to the point where he could remind you of it and then fall silent, as if he assumed that the statement would start a chain of thought sufficient to itself. Like his partners, I was amazed at the change in him, and I was glad when the *Paris* moved off into the wet space between the worlds, leaving his principality behind.

"How about a drink?" he suggested.

We walked into the bar with that defiant feeling that characterizes the day of departure and ordered four Martinis. After one cocktail a change came over him—he suddenly reached across and slapped my knee with the first joviality I had seen him exhibit for months.

"Did you see that girl in the red tam?" he demanded, "the one with the high color who had the two police dogs down to bid her good-by."

"She's pretty," I agreed.

"I looked her up in the purser's office and found out that she's alone. I'm going down to see the steward in a few minutes. We'll have dinner with her to-night."

After a while he left me, and within an hour he was walking up and down the deck with her, talking to her in his strong, clear voice. Her red tam was a bright spot of color against the steel-green sea, and from time to time she looked up with a flashing bob of her head, and smiled with amusement and interest, and anticipation. At dinner we had champagne, and were very joyous— afterward Anson ran the pool with infectious gusto, and several people who had seen me with him asked me his name. He and the girl were talking and laughing together on a lounge in the bar when I went to bed.

I saw less of him on the trip than I had hoped. He wanted to arrange a foursome, but there was no one available, so I saw him only at meals. Sometimes, though, he would have a cocktail in the bar, and he told me about the girl in the red tam, and his adventures with her, making them all bizarre and amusing, as he had a way of doing, and I was glad that he was himself again, or at least the self that I knew, and with which I felt at home. I don't think he was ever happy unless some one was in love with him, responding to him like filings to a magnet, helping him to explain himself, promising him something. What it was I do not know. Perhaps they promised that there would always be women in the world who would spend their brightest, freshest, rarest hours to nurse and protect that superiority he cherished in his heart.

1926

John Dos Passos

1896 ·

John Dos Passos' father was a New York lawyer, the son of a Portuguese immigrant; his mother's family lived in Maryland and Virginia. Born in Chicago, Dos Passos (as he has put it) was "carted around a good deal as a child"—to Mexico, England, Europe, Washington City, tidewater Virginia. He prepared for college at Choate School in Wallingford, Connecticut, and was graduated from Harvard, *cum laude,* in 1916. During World War I he served first with a French ambulance unit and later in the United States Medical Corps as a private. After the war, he went to various parts of Europe and America as a newspaper correspondent.

Dos Passos' literary reputation dates from the publication of *Three Soldiers* in 1921. His importance in modern American literature has steadily grown with the appearance of his subsequent works, the most important of which have been *Manhattan Transfer* (1925), *The 42nd Parallel* (1930), *1919* (1932), and *The Big Money* (1937). The last three works were published as one volume in 1937 with the title *U. S. A.*

Dos Passos began as an aesthete but soon developed an all-embracing social consciousness. *Three Soldiers,* one of the best of American novels dealing with World War I, presented the case of an artist to whom army life was intolerably repugnant. In this work, the author was largely concerned with the sympathetic portrayal of the emotional states and problems of an individual. In the later works, however, he became concerned primarily with the social pattern. *Manhattan Transfer* was an attempt to give a cross section of New York City, in the portrayal of which he employed a bewilderingly large number of characters and scenes. The technique was so kaleidoscopic that the attention of the reader could not rest for an appreciable length of time upon a single character or situation. The author's aim was a total picture of the social organism in which many individuals were obscurely merged.

In the novels which make up *U.S.A.,* Dos Passos retained the social point of view of *Manhattan Transfer,* but made two significant changes: he enlarged his canvas to include the whole of the United States and those parts of Europe where Americans went during the first World War, and he reduced the number of characters so as to give fuller and more intelligible accounts of their lives. Despite the altered treatment, however, his characters still have little individuality and awaken in the reader only a slight interest in them as persons. Their life-stories sometimes read like sociological case histories. In addition to the stories of a dozen or more fictional characters, *U.S.A.* contains three original features interpolated throughout the work: "The Newsreel," which consists of headlines from the contemporary press; "The Camera Eye," which is a kind of stream of consciousness or interior monologue giving the narrator's relationship to passing events; and the biographical sketch, which portrays prominent contemporary Americans, sometimes in the spirit of eulogy and sometimes, of bitter irony.

U.S.A. is the most impressive "social" novel which has been written thus far in America. The author's aim was to expose folly, corruption, and injustice wherever he found them. *U.S.A.* presents an unflattering picture of twentieth-century Americans. One recalls Emerson's judgment, a century ago, on the populations of large cities: "These are not men, but hungers, thirsts, fevers, and appetites walking." Above all, *U.S.A.* conveys the impression of the domination of individual lives by social and economic forces. The style, which Kazin well calls "a hard, lean, mocking prose," is an efficient instrument for the portrayal of the modern machine age.

The books which have followed *U.S.A.* indicate that Dos Passos, like many other authors of his generation, has been moving steadily, in more recent years, away from his earlier position at the extreme left. *Adventures of a Young Man* (1939) shows a character seeking in radical groups, and failing to find there, a satisfactory social philosophy. *The Ground We Stand On* (1941) is a collection of historical studies of American leaders and their contributions to American thought: of Roger Williams and freedom of conscience; Jefferson and civil rights; Franklin and economic opportunity. *The Grand Design* (1949), a novel, is a criticism of the New Deal. Though well-intentioned in its inception, the New Deal—as seen in Dos Passos' story—soon bogged down in impractical theories, bureaucratic red tape, personal rivalries, cocktail parties, and sexual distractions. The author was accused of having turned conservative. While retaining something of the scope and technique of *U.S.A., The Grand Design* has a new depth of characterization. Another novel, *Chosen Country* (1951), shows, still more, a recognition of the importance of individual problems. The later Dos Passos is obviously less doctrinaire and mechanical, and more human and humanistic.

J. W. Beach, American Fiction, 1920-1940, New York, 1941 • Alfred Kazin, On Native Grounds: An Interpretation of Modern American Prose Literature, New York, 1942

From

U. S. A.

The following selections from **U. S. A.** illustrate the various kinds of elements which make up the work. "Newsreel I" is an impressionistic blending of headlines taken from the newspapers at the beginning of the present century, with special emphasis upon the American conquest of the Philippines. The method of "The Camera Eye" is that known in modern literature as the stream of consciousness—an attempt to reproduce realistically a sequence of private thoughts. In this case, it is the consciousness of a small child—possibly the author himself. The place is Holland at the time of the war between England and the Boers of South Africa, who were of Dutch extraction. The child's mother, who is really an American but is mistaken for an Englishwoman, is threatened with violence on a street in Holland. "Lover of Mankind" and "Tin Lizzie" illustrate the biographical sketches which are scattered through **U. S. A.**: the former is an eloquent tribute to Eugene V. Debs, the latter an unsympathetic portrait of Henry Ford done with sharp-edged irony.

"Mac" begins the fictional story of Mac McCreary, son of a Connecticut factory worker. Mac later joins the Industrial Workers of the World in the Northwest and winds up in Mexico running a radical bookstore. Interwoven with Mac's story in **U. S. A.** are the stories of J. Ward Moorehouse, who attains prosperity and prominence as a New York public relations expert and as publicity director for the Red Cross during World War I; Janey Williams, Moorehouse's secretary; Eleanor Stoddard, who cultivates art at the Chicago Art Institute and in Europe; Charley Anderson, who begins life as an automobile mechanic, makes "big money" in the airplane industry, and dies in an automobile accident; Richard Ellsworth Savage, who serves on important military staffs in Europe during the war and afterwards becomes a Washington lobbyist; and several others. These fictional life-histories aim to present the experiences of representative Americans during the first quarter of the twentieth century.

The young man walks fast by himself through the crowd that thins into the night streets; feet are tired from hours of walking; eyes greedy for warm curve of faces, answering flicker of eyes, the set of a head, the lift of a shoulder, the way hands spread and clench; blood tingles with wants; mind is a beehive of hopes buzzing and stinging; muscles ache for the knowledge of jobs, for the roadmender's pick and shovel work, the fisherman's knack with a hook when he hauls on the slithery net from the rail of the lurching trawler, the swing of the bridgeman's arm as he slings down the whitehot rivet, the engineer's slow grip wise on the throttle, the dirtfarmer's use of his whole body when, whoaing the mules, he yanks the plow from the furrow. The young man walks by himself searching through the crowd with greedy eyes, greedy ears taut to hear, by himself, alone.

The streets are empty. People have packed into subways, climbed into streetcars and buses; in the stations they've scampered for suburban trains; they've filtered into lodgings and tenements, gone up in elevators into apartmenthouses. In a showwindow two sallow windowdressers in their shirtsleeves are bringing out a dummy girl in a red evening dress, at a corner welders in masks lean into sheets of blue flame repairing a cartrack, a few drunk bums shamble along, a sad streetwalker fidgets under an arclight. From the river comes the deep rumbling whistle of a steamboat leaving dock. A tug hoots far away.

The young man walks by himself, fast but not fast enough, far but not far enough (faces slide out of sight, talk trails into tattered scraps, footsteps tap fainter in alleys); he must catch the last subway, the streetcar, the bus, run up the gangplanks of all the steamboats, register at all the hotels, work in the cities, answer the want ads, learn the trades, take up the jobs, live in all the boardinghouses, sleep in all the beds. One bed is not enough, one job is not enough, one life is not enough. At night, head swimming with wants, he walks by himself alone.

No job, no woman, no house, no city.

Only the ears busy to catch the speech are not alone; the ears are caught tight, linked tight by the tendrils

of phrased words, the turn of a joke, the singsong
fade of a story, the gruff fall of a sentence; linking
tendrils of speech twine through the city blocks, spread
over pavements, grow out along broad parked avenues,
speed with the trucks leaving on their long night runs
over roaring highways, whisper down sandy byroads
past wornout farms, joining up cities and fillingstations,
roundhouses, steamboats, planes groping along airways;
words call out on mountain pastures, drift slow down
rivers widening to the sea and the hushed beaches.

It was not in the long walks through jostling crowds
at night that he was less alone, or in the training camp
at Allentown, or in the day on the docks at Seattle, or
in the empty reek of Washington City hot boyhood
summer nights, or in the meal on Market Street, or in
the swim off the red rocks at San Diego, or in the
bed full of fleas in New Orleans, or in the cold razor-
wind off the lake, or in the gray faces trembling in the
grind of gears in the street under Michigan Avenue,
or in the smokers of limited expresstrains, or walking
across country, or riding up the dry mountain canyons,
or the night without a sleepingbag among frozen bear-
tracks in the Yellowstone, or canoeing Sundays on
the Quinnipiac;

but in his mother's words telling about longago,
in his father's telling about when I was a boy, in the
kidding stories of uncles, in the lies the kids told at
school, the hired man's yarns, the tall tales the dough-
boys told after taps;

it was the speech that clung to the ears, the link
that tingled in the blood; U. S. A.

U. S. A. is the slice of a continent. U. S. A. is a
group of holding companies, some aggregations of trade
unions, a set of laws bound in calf, a radio network,
a chain of moving picture theatres, a column of stock-
quotations rubbed out and written in by a Western
Union boy on a blackboard, a publiclibrary full of old
newspapers and dogeared historybooks with protests
scrawled on the margins in pencil. U. S. A. is the world's
greatest rivervalley fringed with mountains and hills,
U. S. A. is a set of bigmouthed officials with too many
bankaccounts. U. S. A. is a lot of men buried in their
uniforms in Arlington Cemetery. U. S. A. is the letters
at the end of an address when you are away from home.
But mostly U. S. A. is the speech of the people.

1937

From

U.S.A.: The 42nd Parallel

NEWSREEL I

It was that emancipated race
That was chargin up the hill
Up to where them insurrectos
Was afightin fit to kill

CAPITAL CITY'S CENTURY CLOSED

General Miles with his gaudy uniform and spirited
charger was the center for all eyes especially as his
steed was extremely restless. Just as the band passed
the Commanding General his horse stood upon his
hind legs and was almost erect. General Miles instantly
reined in the frightened animal and dug in his spurs
in an endeavor to control the horse which to the horror
of the spectators, fell over backwards and landed squarely
on the Commanding General. Much to the gratification
of the people General Miles was not injured but considerable skin was scraped off the flank of the horse.
Almost every inch of General Miles's overcoat was covered with the dust of the street and between the shoulders a hole about an inch in diameter was punctured.
Without waiting for anyone to brush the dust from his
garments General Miles remounted his horse and re-
viewed the parade as if it were an everyday occurrence.

The incident naturally attracted the attention of the
crowd, and this brought to notice the fact that the Commanding General never permits a flag to be carried past
him without uncovering and remaining so until the
colors have past

And the Captain bold of Company B
Was afightin in the lead
Just like a trueborn soldier he
Of them bullets took no heed

6 **General Miles.** General Nelson A. Miles (1839-1925) was in command of the American forces which took possession of the Philippines
in 1900

OFFICIALS KNOW NOTHING OF VICE

Sanitary trustees turn water of Chicago River into drainage canal LAKE MICHIGAN SHAKES HANDS WITH THE FATHER OF THE WATERS German zuchter-verein singing contest for canary-birds opens the fight for bimetallism at the ratio of 16 to 1 has not been lost says Bryan

BRITISH BEATEN AT MAFEKING

For there's many a man been murdered in Luzon

CLAIMS ISLANDS FOR ALL TIME

Hamilton Club Listens to Oratory by Ex-Congressman Posey of Indiana

NOISE GREETS NEW CENTURY

LABOR GREETS NEW CENTURY

CHURCHES GREET NEW CENTURY

Mr. McKinley is hard at work in his office when the new year begins.

NATION GREETS CENTURY'S DAWN

Responding to a toast, Hail Columbia! at the Columbia Club banquet in Indianapolis, Ind., ex-President Benjamin Harrison said in part: I have no argument to make here or anywhere against territorial expansion; but I do not, as some do, look upon territorial expansion as the safest and most attractive avenue of national development. By the advantages of abundant and cheap coal and iron, of an enormous overproduction of food products and of invention and economy in production, we are now leading by the nose the original and the greatest of the colonizing nations.

Society Girls Shocked: Danced with Detectives

For there's many a man been murdered in Luzon
and Mindanao

GAIETY GIRLS MOBBED IN NEW JERSEY

One of the lithographs of the leading lady represented her in less than Atlantic City bathing costume, sitting on a red-hot stove; in one hand she held a brimming glass of wine, in the other ribbons drawn over a pair of rampant lobsters.

For there's many a man been murdered in Luzon
and Mindanao
and in Samar

In responding to the toast, "The Twentieth Century," Senator Albert J. Beveridge said in part: *The twentieth century will be American. American thought will dominate it. American progress will give it color and direction. American deeds will make it illustrious.*

Civilization will never lose its hold on Shanghai. Civilization will never depart from Hongkong. The gates of Peking will never again be closed to the methods of modern man. The regeneration of the world, physical as well as moral, has begun, and revolutions never move backwards.

There's been many a good man murdered in the Philippines
Lies sleeping in some lonesome grave.

THE CAMERA EYE (I)

when you walk along the street you have to step carefully always on the cobbles so as not to step on the bright anxious grassblades   easier if you hold Mother's hand and hang on it that way you can kick up your toes but walking fast you have to tread on too many grassblades the poor hurt green tongues shrink under your feet   maybe thats why those people are so angry and follow us shaking their fists   they're throwing stones grownup people throwing stones She's walking fast and we're running her pointed toes sticking out sharp among the poor trodden grassblades under the shaking folds of the brown cloth dress Englander   a pebble tinkles along the cobbles

Quick darling quick in the postcard shop its quiet the angry people are outside and cant come in   non nein nicht englander amerikanisch americain   Hoch Amerika Vive l'Amerique She laughs My dear they had me right frightened

---

5 **zuchter-verein,** breeders' association • 7 **Bryan.** William Jennings Bryan as Democratic candidate for the Presidency in 1896 led the fight for the coinage of silver in the ratio of 16 to 1 to that of gold • 8 **Mafeking,** in South Africa, where the Boer War was in progress at the turn of the century • 16 **McKinley,** William McKinley (1843-1901), President of the United States, 1897-1901

war on the veldt Kruger Bloemfontein Ladysmith and Queen Victoria an old lady in a pointed lace cap sent chocolate to the soldiers at Christmas.

under the counter it's dark and the lady the nice Dutch lady who loves Americans and has relations in Trenton shows you postcards that shine in the dark pretty hotels and palaces   O que c'est beau schon prittie prittie   and the moonlight ripple ripple under a bridge and the little reverbères are alight in the dark under the counter and the little windows of hotels around the harbor   O que c'est beau la lune

and the big moon

MAC

When the wind set from the silver factories across the river the air of the gray fourfamily frame house where Fainy McCreary was born was choking all day with the smell of whaleoil soap. Other days it smelt of cabbage and babies and Mrs. McCreary's washboilers. Fainy could never play at home because Pop, a lame cavechested man with a whispy blondegray mustache, was nightwatchman at the Chadwick Mills and slept all day. It was only round five o'clock that a curling whiff of tobacco smoke would seep through from the front room into the kitchen. That was a sign that Pop was up and in good spirits, and would soon be wanting his supper.

Then Fainy would be sent running out to one of two corners of the short muddy street of identical frame houses where they lived.

To the right it was half a block to Finley's where he would have to wait at the bar in a forest of mudsplattered trouserlegs until all the rank brawling mouths of grownups had been stopped with beers and whiskeys. Then he would walk home, making each step very carefully, with the handle of the pail of suds cutting into his hand.

To the left it was half a block to Maginnis's Fancy Groceries, Home and Imported Products. Fainy liked the cardboard Cream of Wheat darkey in the window, the glass case with different kinds of salami in it, the barrels of potatoes and cabbages, the brown smell of sugar, sawdust, ginger, kippered herring, ham, vinegar, bread, pepper, lard.

"A loaf of bread, please, mister, a half pound of butter and a box of ginger snaps."

Some evenings when Mom felt poorly, Fainy had to go further; round the corner past Maginnis's, down River-side Avenue where the trolley ran, and across the red bridge over the little river that flowed black between icy undercut snowbanks in winter, yellow and spuming in the spring thaws, brown and oily in summer. Across the river all the way to the corner of Riverside and Main, where the drugstore was, lived Bohunks and Polaks. Their kids were always fighting with the kids of the Murphys and O'Haras and O'Flanagans who lived on Orchard Street.

Fainy would walk along with his knees quaking, the medicine bottle in its white paper tight in one mittened hand. At the corner of Quince was a group of boys he'd have to pass. Passing wasn't so bad; it was when he was about twenty yards from them that the first snowball would hum by his ear. There was no comeback. If he broke into a run, they'd chase him. If he dropped the medicine bottle he'd be beaten up when he got home. A soft one would plunk on the back of his head and the snow began to trickle down his neck. When he was a half a block from the bridge he'd take a chance and run for it.

"Scared cat . . . Shanty Irish . . . Bowlegged Murphy . . . Running home to tell the cop" . . . would yell the Polak and Bohunk kids between snowballs. They made their snowballs hard by pouring water on them and leaving them to freeze overnight; if one of those hit him it drew blood.

The backyard was the only place you could really feel safe to play in. There were brokendown fences, dented garbage cans, old pots and pans too nearly sieves to mend, a vacant chickencoop that still had feathers and droppings on the floor, hogweed in summer, mud in winter; but the glory of the McCreary's backyard was Tony Harriman's rabbit hutch, where he kept Belgian hares. Tony Harriman was a consumptive and lived with his mother on the ground floor left. He wanted to raise all sorts of other small animals too, raccoons, otter, even silver fox, he'd get rich that way. The day he died nobody could find the key to the big padlock on the door of the rabbit hutch. Fainy fed the hares for several days by pushing in cabbage and lettuce leaves through the double thickness of chickenwire. Then came a week of sleet and rain when he didn't go out in the yard. The first fine day, when he went to look, one of the hares was dead. Fainy turned

1 veldt, the plains of South Africa • 1 Kruger. S. J. P. Kruger (1825-1904) was president of the South African Republic • 1 Bloemfontein, in South Africa, where the British defeated the Boers • 1 Ladysmith, in South Africa, where the British were besieged by the Boers

white; he tried to tell himself the hare was asleep, but it lay gawkily stiff, not asleep. The other hares were huddled in a corner looking about with twitching noses, their big ears flopping helpless over their backs. Poor hares; Fainy wanted to cry. He ran upstairs to his mother's kitchen, ducked under the ironing board and got the hammer out of the drawer in the kitchen table. The first time he tried he mashed his finger, but the second time he managed to jump the padlock. Inside the cage there was a funny, sour smell. Fainy picked the dead hare up by its ears. Its soft white belly was beginning to puff up, one dead eye was scaringly open. Something suddenly got hold of Fainy and made him drop the hare in the nearest garbage can and run upstairs. Still cold and trembling, he tiptoed out onto the back porch and looked down. Breathlessly he watched the other hares. By cautious hops they were getting near the door of the hutch into the yard. One of them was out. It sat up on its hind legs, limp ears suddenly stiff. Mom called him to bring her a flatiron from the stove. When he got back to the porch the hares were all gone.

That winter there was a strike in the Chadwick Mills and Pop lost his job. He would sit all day in the front room smoking and cursing:

"Ablebodied man by Jesus, if I couldn't lick any one of those damn Polaks with my crutch tied behind my back . . . I says so to Mr. Barry; I ain't goin' to join no strike. Mr. Barry, a sensible quiet man, a bit of an invalid, with a wife an' kiddies to think for. Eight years I've been watchman, an' now you give me the sack to take on a bunch of thugs from a detective agency. The dirty pugnosed son of a bitch."

"If those damn lousy furreners hadn't a walked out," somebody would answer soothingly.

The strike was not popular on Orchard Street. It meant that Mom had to work harder and harder, doing bigger and bigger boilersful of wash, and that Fainy and his older sister Milly had to help when they came home from school. And then one day Mom got sick and had to go back to bed instead of starting in on the ironing, and lay with her round white creased face whiter than the pillow and her watercreased hands in a knot under her chin. The doctor came and the district nurse, and all three rooms of the flat smelt of doctors and nurses and drugs, and the only place Fainy and Milly could find to sit was on the stairs. There they sat and cried quietly together. Then Mom's face on the pillow shrank into a little

creased white thing like a rumpled up handkerchief and they said that she was dead and took her away.

The funeral was from the undertaking parlors on Riverside Avenue on the next block. Fainy felt very proud and important because everybody kissed him and patted his head and said he was behaving like a little man. He had a new black suit on, too, like a grownup suit with pockets and everything, except that it had short pants. There were all sorts of people at the undertaking parlors he had never been close to before, Mr. Russell, the butcher and Father O'Donnell and Uncle Tim O'Hara who'd come on from Chicago, and it smelt of whisky and beer like at Finley's. Uncle Tim was a skinny man with a knobbed red face and blurry blue eyes. He wore a loose black silk tie that worried Fainy, and kept leaning down suddenly, bending from the waist as if he was going to close up like a jackknife, and whispering in a thick voice in Fainy's ear.

"Don't you mind 'em, old sport, they're a bunch o' bums and hypocrytes, stewed to the ears most of 'em already. Look at Father O'Donnell the fat swine already figurin' up the burial fees. But don't you mind 'em, remember you're an O'Hara on your mother's side. I don't mind 'em, old sport, and she was my own sister by birth and blood."

When they got home he was terribly sleepy and his feet were cold and wet. Nobody paid any attention to him. He sat whimpering on the edge of the bed in the dark. In the front room there were voices and a sound of knives and forks, but he didn't dare go in there. He curled up against the wall and went to sleep. Light in his eyes woke him up. Uncle Tim and Pop were standing over him talking loud. They looked funny and didn't seem to be standing very steady. Uncle Tim held the lamp.

"Well, Fainy, old sport," said Uncle Tim giving the lamp a perilous wave over Fainy's head. "Fenian O'Hara McCreary, sit up and take notice and tell us what you think of our proposed removal to the great and growing city of Chicago. Middletown's a terrible bitch of a dump if you ask me . . . Meanin' no offense, John . . . But Chicago . . . Jesus God, man, when you get there you'll think you've been dead and nailed up in a coffin all these years."

Fainy was scared. He drew his knees up to his chin and looked tremblingly at the two big swaying figures of men lit by the swaying lamp. He tried to speak but the words dried up on his lips.

"The kid's asleep, Tim, for all your speechifyin' . . . Take your clothes off, Fainy, and get into bed and get a good night's sleep. We're leavin' in the mornin'."

And late on a rainy morning, without any breakfast, with a big old swelltop trunk tied up with rope joggling perilously on the roof of the cab that Fainy had been sent to order from Hodgeson's Livery Stable, they set out. Milly was crying. Pop didn't say a word but sucked on an unlit pipe. Uncle Tim handled everything, making little jokes all the time that nobody laughed at, pulling a roll of bills out of his pocket at every juncture, or taking great gurgling sips out of the flask he had in his pocket. Milly cried and cried. Fainy looked out with big dry eyes at the familiar streets, all suddenly odd and lopsided, that rolled past the cab; the red bridge, the scabshingled houses where the Polaks lived, Smith's and Smith's corner drug store . . . there was Billy Hogan just coming out with a package of chewing gum in his hand. Playing hookey again. Fainy had an impulse to yell at him, but something froze it . . . Main with its elms and street cars, blocks of stores round the corner of Church, and then the fire department. Fainy looked for the last time into the dark cave where shone entrancingly the brass and copper curves of the engine, then past the cardboard fronts of the First Congregational Church, the Carmel Baptist Church, St. Andrew's Episcopal Church built of brick and set catercornered on its lot instead of straight with a stern face to the street like the other churches, then the three castiron stags on the lawn in front of the Commercial House, and the residences, each with its lawn, each with its scrollsaw porch, each with its hydrangea bush. Then the houses got smaller, and the lawns disappeared; the cab trundled round past Simpson's Grain and Feed Warehouse, along a row of barbershops, saloons and lunchrooms, and they were all getting out at the station.

At the station lunchcounter Uncle Tim set everybody up to breakfast. He dried Milly's tears and blew Fainy's nose in a big new pockethandkerchief that still had the tag on the corner and set them to work on bacon and eggs and coffee. Fainy hadn't had coffee before, so the idea of sitting up like a man and drinking coffee made him feel pretty good. Milly didn't like hers, said it was bitter. They were left all alone in the lunchroom for sometime with the empty plates and empty coffee cups under the beady eyes of a woman with the long neck and pointed face of a hen who looked at them disapprovingly from behind the counter. Then with an enormous, shattering

rumble, sludgepuff sludge . . . puff, the train came into the station. They were scooped up and dragged across the platform and through a pipesmoky car and before they knew it the train was moving and the wintry russet Connecticut landscape was clattering by.

LOVER OF MANKIND

Debs was a railroad man, born in a weather-boarded shack at Terre Haute.

He was one of ten children.

His father had come to America in a sailingship in '49, an Alsatian from Colmar; not much of a moneymaker, fond of music and reading,

he gave his children a chance to finish public school and that was about all he could do.

At fifteen Gene Debs was already working as a machinist on the Indianapolis and Terre Haute Railway.

He worked as locomotive fireman,
clerked in a store
joined the local of the Brotherhood of Locomotive Firemen, was elected secretary, traveled all over the country as organizer.

He was a tall shamblefooted man, had a sort of gusty rhetoric that set on fire the railroad workers in their pineboarded halls
made them want the world he wanted,
a world brothers might own
where everybody would split even:

I am not a labor leader. I don't want you to follow me or anyone else. If you are looking for a Moses to lead you out of the capitalist wilderness you will stay right where you are. I would not lead you into this promised land if I could, because if I could lead you in, someone else would lead you out.

That was how he talked to freighthandlers and gandywalkers, to firemen and switchmen and engineers, telling them it wasn't enough to organize the railroadmen, that all workers must be organized, that all workers must be organized in the workers' cooperative commonwealth.

Locomotive fireman on many a long night's run,
under the smoke a fire burned him up, burned in

---

53 **Debs.** Eugene V. Debs (1855-1926) was the chief leader of the Socialist movement in the United States during the last thirty years of his life • 81 **gandywalkers,** more correctly, gandy dancers; workers who repair the roadbeds of railroads

gusty words that beat in pineboarded halls; he wanted his brothers to be free men.

That was what he saw in the crowd that met him at the Old Wells Street Depot when he came out of jail after the Pullman strike,

those were the men that chalked up nine hundred thousand votes for him in nineteen twelve and scared the frockcoats and the tophats and diamonded hostesses at Saratoga Springs, Bar Harbor, Lake Geneva with the bogy of a socialist president.

But where were Gene Debs' brothers in nineteen eighteen when Woodrow Wilson had him locked up in Atlanta for speaking against war,

where were the big men fond of whisky and fond of each other, gentle rambling tellers of stories over bars in small towns in the Middle West,

quiet men who wanted a house with a porch to putter around and a fat wife to cook for them, a few drinks and cigars, a garden to dig in, cronies to chew the rag with

and wanted to work for it

and others to work for it;

where were the locomotive firemen and engineers when they hustled him off to Atlanta Penitentiary?

And they brought him back to die in Terre Haute to sit on his porch in a rocker with a cigar in his mouth,

beside him American Beauty roses his wife fixed in a bowl;

and the people of Terre Haute and the people in Indiana and the people of the Middle West were fond of him and afraid of him and thought of him as an old kindly uncle who loved them, and wanted to be with him and to have him give them candy,

but they were afraid of him as if he had contracted a social disease, syphilis or leprosy, and thought it was too bad,

but on account of the flag

and prosperity

and making the world safe for democracy,

they were afraid to be with him,

or to think much about him for fear they might believe him;

for he said:

While there is a lower class I am of it, while there is a criminal class I am of it, while there is a soul in prison I am not free.   1930

---

5 **Pullman strike.** The Pullman strike paralyzed transportation throughout the Northern states in the summer of 1894. The strike was put down by President Cleveland; and Debs, who was president of the American Railway Union, was sentenced to six months' imprisonment for contempt of court when he refused to obey an injunction • 7 **nineteen twelve.** Debs was four times Socialist candidate for the Presidency • 24 **Atlanta Penitentiary.** In 1918, Debs was sentenced to ten years' imprisonment under the Espionage Act, but was released in 1921 by President Harding

---

From

U.S.A.: The Big Money

TIN LIZZIE

Mr. Ford *the automobileer,"* the featurewriter wrote in 1900,

"Mr. Ford the automobileer began by giving his steed three or four sharp jerks with the lever at the righthand side of the seat; that is, he pulled the lever up and down sharply in order, as he said, to mix air with gasoline and drive the charge into the exploding cylinder. . . . Mr.

Ford slipped a small electric switch handle and there followed a puff, puff, puff. . . . The puffing of the machine assumed a higher key. She was flying along about eight miles an hour. The ruts in the road were deep, but the machine certainly went with a dreamlike smoothness. There was none of the bumping common even to a streetcar. . . . By this time the boulevard had been reached, and the automobileer, letting a lever fall a little, let her out. Whiz! She picked up speed with infinite rapidity. As she ran on there was a clattering behind, the new noise of the automobile.

For twenty years or more,

ever since he'd left his father's farm when he was sixteen to get a job in a Detroit machineshop, Henry Ford had been nuts about machinery. First it was watches, then he designed a steamtractor, then he built a horseless carriage with an engine adapted from the Otto gasengine he'd read about in *The World of Science,* then a mechanical buggy with a onecylinder fourcycle motor, that would run forward but not back;

at last, in ninetyeight, he felt he was far enough along to risk throwing up his job with the Detroit Edison Company, where he'd worked his way up from night fireman to chief engineer, to put all his time into working on a new gasoline engine,

(in the late eighties he'd met Edison at a meeting of electriclight employees in Atlantic City. He'd gone up to Edison after Edison had delivered an address and asked him if he thought gasoline was practical as a motor fuel. Edison had said yes. If Edison said it, it was true. Edison was the great admiration of Henry Ford's life);

and in driving his mechanical buggy, sitting there at the lever jauntily dressed in a tightbuttoned jacket and a high collar and a derby hat, back and forth over the level illpaved streets of Detroit,

scaring the big brewery horses and the skinny trotting horses and the sleekrumped pacers with the motor's loud explosions,

looking for men scatterbrained enough to invest money in a factory for building automobiles.

He was the the eldest son of an Irish immigrant who during the Civil War had married the daughter of a prosperous Pennsylvania Dutch farmer and settled down to farming near Dearborn in Wayne County, Michigan;

like plenty of other Americans, young Henry grew up hating the endless sogging through the mud about the chores, the hauling and pitching manure, the kerosene lamps to clean, the irk and sweat and solitude of the farm.

He was a slender, active youngster, a good skater, clever with his hands; what he liked was to tend the machinery and let the others do the heavy work. His mother had told him not to drink, smoke, gamble or go into debt, and he never did.

When he was in his early twenties his father tried to get him back from Detroit, where he was working as mechanic and repairman for the Drydock Engine Company that built the engines for steamboats, by giving him forty acres of land.

Young Henry built himself an uptodate square white dwellinghouse with a false mansard roof and married and settled down on the farm,

but he let the hired men do the farming;

he bought himself a buzzsaw and rented a stationary engine and cut the timber off the woodlots.

He was a thrifty young man who never drank or smoked or gambled or coveted his neighbor's wife, but he couldn't stand living on the farm.

He moved to Detroit, and in the brick barn behind his house tinkered for years in his spare time with a mechanical buggy that would be light enough to run over the clayey wagonroads of Wayne County, Michigan.

By 1900 he had a practicable car to promote.

He was forty years old before the Ford Motor Company was started and production began to move.

Speed was the first thing the early automobile manufacturers went after. Races advertised the makes of cars.

Henry Ford himself hung up several records at the track at Grosse Pointe and on the ice on Lake St. Clair. In his 999 he did the mile in thirtynine and fourfifths seconds.

But it had always been his custom to hire others to do the heavy work. The speed he was busy with was speed in production, the records records in efficient output. He hired Barney Oldfield, a stunt bicyclerider from Salt Lake City, to do the racing for him.

Henry Ford had ideas about other things than the designing of motors, carburetors, magnetos, jigs and fixtures, punches and dies; he had ideas about sales,

that the big money was in economical quantity production, quick turnover, cheap interchangeable easilyreplaced standardized parts;

it wasn't until 1909, after years of arguing with his partners, that Ford put out the first Model T.

Henry Ford was right.

That season he sold more than ten thousand tin lizzies, ten years later he was selling almost a million a year.

In these years the Taylor Plan was stirring up plant-

10 **Edison,** Thomas A. Edison (1847-1931), the electrical wizard •
85 **Taylor Plan,** the science of industrial management founded by Frederick W. Taylor (1856-1915)

U.S.A. 1105

managers and manufacturers all over the country. Efficiency was the word. The same ingenuity that went into improving the performance of a machine could go into improving the performance of the workmen producing the machine.

In 1913 they established the assemblyline at Ford's. That season the profits were something like twentyfive million dollars, but they had trouble keeping the men on the job, machinists didn't seem to like it at Ford's.

10 Henry Ford had ideas about other things than production.

He was the largest automobile manufacturer in the world; he paid high wages; maybe if the steady workers thought they were getting a cut (a very small cut) in the profits, it would give trained men an inducement to stick to their jobs,

wellpaid workers might save enough money to buy a tin lizzie; the first day Ford's announced that cleancut properlymarried American workers who wanted jobs 20 had a chance to make five bucks a day (of course it turned out that there were strings to it; always there were strings to it)

such an enormous crowd waited outside the Highland Park plant

all through the zero January night

that there was a riot when the gates were opened; cops broke heads, jobhunters threw bricks; property, Henry Ford's own property, was destroyed. The company dicks had to turn on the firehose to beat back 30 the crowd.

The American Plan; automotive prosperity seeping down from above; it turned out there were strings to it.

But that five dollars a day
paid to good, clean American workmen
who didn't drink or smoke cigarettes or read or think,
and who didn't commit adultery
and whose wives didn't take in boarders,
made America once more the Yukon of the sweated workers of the world;
40 made all the tin lizzies and the automotive age, and incidentally,
made Henry Ford the automobileer, the admirer of Edison, the birdlover,
the great American of his time.

But Henry Ford had ideas about other things besides assemblylines and the livinghabits of his employees. He was full of ideas. Instead of going to the city to make his fortune, here was a country boy who'd made his fortune by bringing the city out to the farm. The precepts he'd learned out of McGuffey's Reader, his 50 mother's prejudices and preconceptions, he had preserved clean and unworn as freshprinted bills in the safe in a bank.

He wanted people to know about his ideas, so he bought the *Dearborn Independent* and started a campaign against cigarettesmoking.

When war broke out in Europe, he had ideas about that too. (Suspicion of armymen and soldiering were part of the midwest farm tradition, like thrift, sticktoativeness, temperance and sharp practice in money 60 matters.) Any intelligent American mechanic could see that if the Europeans hadn't been a lot of ignorant underpaid foreigners who drank, smoked, were loose about women and wasteful in their methods of production, the war could never have happened.

When Rosika Schwimmer broke through the stockade of secretaries and servicemen who surrounded Henry Ford and suggested to him that he could stop the war,

he said sure they'd hire a ship and go over and get the boys out of the trenches by Christmas. 70

He hired a steamboat, the *Oscar II,* and filled it up with pacifists and socialworkers,

to go over to explain to the princelings of Europe that what they were doing was vicious and silly.

It wasn't his fault that Poor Richard's commonsense no longer rules the world and that most of the pacifists were nuts,

goofy with headlines.

When William Jennings Bryan went over to Hoboken to see him off, somebody handed William Jennings 80 Bryan a squirrel in a cage; William Jennings Bryan made a speech with the squirrel under his arm. Henry Ford threw American Beauty roses to the crowd. The band played *I Didn't Raise My Boy to Be a Soldier.* Practical jokers let loose more squirrels. An eloping couple

50 **McGuffey's Reader,** the most popular of all schoolbooks in the United States during the nineteenth century • 66 **Rosika Schwimmer,** a Hungarian feminist and pacifist, largely responsible for the idea of the "peace ship" • 69 **ship.** Ford's "peace ship" sailed from Hoboken, December 4, 1915

was married by a platoon of ministers in the saloon, and Mr. Zero, the flophouse humanitarian, who reached the dock too late to sail,

dove into the North River and swam after the boat.

The *Oscar II* was described as a floating Chautauqua; Henry Ford said it felt like a middlewestern village, but by the time they reached Christiansand in Norway, the reporters had kidded him so that he had gotten cold feet and gone to bed. The world was too crazy outside of Wayne County, Michigan. Mrs. Ford and the management sent an Episcopal dean after him who brought him home under wraps,

and the pacifists had to speechify without him.

Two years later Ford's was manufacturing munitions, Eagle boats; Henry Ford was planning oneman tanks, and oneman submarines like the one tried out in the Revolutionary War. He announced to the press that he'd turn over his war profits to the government,

but there's no record that he ever did.

One thing he brought back from his trip
was the Protocols of the Elders of Zion.

He started a campaign to enlighten the world in the *Dearborn Independent;* the Jews were why the world wasn't like Wayne County, Michigan, in the old horse and buggy days;

the Jews had started the war, Bolshevism, Darwinism, Marxism, Nietzsche, short skirts and lipstick. They were behind Wall Street and the international bankers, and the whiteslave traffic and the movies and the Supreme Court and ragtime and the illegal liquor business.

Henry Ford denounced the Jews and ran for senator and sued the *Chicago Tribune* for libel,

and was the laughing stock of the kept metropolitan press;

but when the metropolitan bankers tried to horn in on his business

he thoroughly outsmarted them.

In 1918 he had borrowed on notes to buy out his minority stockholders for the picayune sum of seventyfive million dollars.

In February, 1920, he needed cash to pay off some of these notes that were coming due. A banker is supposed to have called on him and offered him every facility if the bankers' representative could be made a member of the board of directors. Henry Ford handed the banker his hat,

and went about raising the money in his own way:

he shipped every car and part he had in his plant to his dealers and demanded immediate cash payment. Let the other fellow do the borrowing had always been a cardinal principle. He shut down production and cancelled all orders from the supplyfirms. Many dealers were ruined, many supplyfirms failed, but when he reopened his plant,

he owned it absolutely,

the way a man owns an unmortgaged farm with the taxes paid up.

In 1922 there started the Ford boom for President (high wages, waterpower, industry scattered to the small towns) that was skillfully pricked behind the scenes by another crackerbarrel philosopher,

Calvin Coolidge;

but in 1922 Henry Ford sold one million three hundred and thirtytwo thousand two hundred and nine tin lizzies; he was the richest man in the world.

Good roads had followed the narrow ruts made in the mud by the Model T. The great automotive boom was on. At Ford's production was improving all the time; less waste, more spotters, strawbosses, stool pigeons (fifteen minutes for lunch, three minutes to go to the toilet, the Taylorized speedup everywhere, reach under, adjust washer, screw down bolt, shove in cotterpin, reachunder adjustwasher, screwdown bolt, reachunderadjustscrewdownreachunderadjust until every ounce of life was sucked off into production and at night the workmen went home grey shaking husks).

Ford owned every detail of the process from the ore in the hills until the car rolled off the end of the assemblyline under its own power, the plants were rationalized to the last tenthousandth of an inch as measured by the Johansen scale;

in 1926 the production cycle was reduced to eightyone hours from the ore in the mine to the finished salable car proceeding under its own power,

but the Model T was obsolete.

New Era prosperity and the American Plan

27 Nietzsche. See note, p. 752 • 69 strawbosses, assistant foremen • 81 Johansen scale, a technique for the minute measurement of parts devised for the Ford Company by C. E. Johansson (see H. W. Barclay, **Ford Production Methods**)

(there were strings to it, always there were strings
to it)
     had killed Tin Lizzie.
     Ford's was just one of many automobile plants.
     When the stockmarket bubble burst,
     Mr. Ford the crackerbarrel philosopher said jubi-
lantly,
     "I told you so.
     Serves you right for gambling and getting in debt.
10   The country is sound."
     But when the country on cracked shoes, in frayed
trousers, belts tightened over hollow bellies,
     idle hands cracked and chapped with the cold of that
coldest March day of 1932,
     started marching from Detroit to Dearborn, asking
for work and the American Plan, all they could think
of at Ford's was machineguns.
     The country was sound, but they mowed the marchers
down.
20   They shot four of them dead.
     Henry Ford as an old man
     is a passionate antiquarian,
     (lives besieged on his father's farm embedded in
an estate of thousands of millionaire acres, protected by
an army of servicemen, secretaries, secret agents, dicks
under orders of an English exprizefighter,
     always afraid of the feet in broken shoes on the roads,
afraid the gangs will kidnap his grandchildren,
     that a crank will shoot him,

that Change and the idle hands out of work will 30
break through the gates and the high fences;
     protected by a private army against
     the new America of starved children and hollow
bellies and cracked shoes stamping on souplines,
     that has swallowed up the old thrifty farmlands
     of Wayne County, Michigan,
     as if they had never been).
     Henry Ford as an old man
     is a passionate antiquarian.
     He rebuilt his father's farmhouse and put it back 40
exactly in the state he remembered it in as a boy. He
built a village of museums for buggies, sleighs, coaches,
old plows, waterwheels, obsolete models of motorcars.
He scoured the country for fiddlers to play old-fashioned
squaredances.
     Even old taverns he bought and put back into
their original shape, as well as Thomas Edison's early
laboratories.
     When he bought the Wayside Inn near Sudbury,
Massachusetts, he had the new highway where the 50
newmodel cars roared and slithered and hissed oilily
past (the new noise of the automobile),
     moved away from the door,
     put back the old bad road,
     so that everything might be
     the way it used to be,
     in the days of horses and buggies.

                                                    1937

William Faulkner

1897 ·

The fiction of William Faulkner has as many different
planes of interest as that of any contemporary American
writer. On one level much of it is sheer horror, a twentieth-century throwback to the Gothic romance. On

another it is Hawthornesque for its exploration of the
methods and effects of symbolism and allegory. On still
another it is a vast and intricate legend of the disintegration of the Old South, epiclike in conception and not

unworthy of comparison with James Joyce's portrayal of Dublin in *Ulysses*. To the student of technique it is notable for its bold experimentation with narrative point of view, while the reader with an eye for style finds it full of some of the lushest rhetoric of our time. All in all, Faulkner's stories are almost incredibly subtle. They make such great demands of their readers that the surprising thing is that they have been as popular as they have.

Faulkner's work is almost all localized in the northern part of Mississippi. There he was born, in 1897, at New Albany, and there he has lived for most of his life in the neighboring county seat, Oxford, where the University of Mississippi is situated. The Faulkner (or Falkner) family has long been prominent in politics, railroad building, and planting; one great-grandfather of William's was the author of a popular ante-bellum romance, *The White Rose of Memphis*. The Sartoris family, prominent in a number of Faulkner's novels, appears to be in part a projection of his own clan.

Early in World War I, Faulkner, just out of high school, ran off to Canada to join the British air force. He was sent to England for training and saw about a year of service in France before he was wounded in a crash. Back in Mississippi, he was for a time a student in the university; he then worked at such odd jobs as clerking in the college postal station and house-painting. Encouragement for his writing apparently came from various friends, among them Phil Stone, an Oxford lawyer; Stark Young, then teaching at Amherst; and Sherwood Anderson, with whom he lived in New Orleans in 1922. All shared with Faulkner the fascination of the South, with its biracial pattern of life and its extremes of illiteracy and cultivation.

Faulkner's first published work was a poem in *The New Republic* for August 6, 1919. In the middle twenties a number of poems and critical articles appeared in *The Double Dealer,* a New Orleans magazine, and in 1924 a thin sheaf of poems was collected as *The Marble Faun*. Faulkner's reputation among those interested in new writers was built, however, upon a series of five novels and some of his short stories. The novels were: *Soldier's Pay* (1926), a story of the return of an aviator who had been presumed dead; *Mosquitoes* (1927), which contains some discussion of writers and their aims; *Sartoris* (1929), a key volume in the saga of the town of Jefferson in Yocknapatawpha County, the

William Faulkner—photo by Lilyan Lowmans-Chauvin

fictional counterpart of Oxford and its surrounding countryside; *The Sound and the Fury* (1929), a stream of consciousness novel in which one of the central characters is an idiot; and *As I Lay Dying* (1930), a tour de force in the use of a multiple point of view. All are technically original, and it is not surprising that Faulkner's merits were quickly recognized.

He was not really well known, however, until the appearance of *Sanctuary* in 1931. A story of sexual perversion constructed like a detective story and denying anything approaching poetic justice, it established Faulkner as one of the leaders of the "cult of violence," and, thanks to its reprinting in an inexpensive edition, it remains his most widely read novel. Although Faulkner avowedly designed it as a "shocker," it is not uncharacteristic in method or matter, for it embeds in a carefully worked-out pattern of objective indirectness some most stomach-turning crimes and abnormalities. Since its appearance Faulkner has commanded a ready market for his short stories and has made his mark even in Hollywood, where his peculiar techniques have been adapted to certain motion pictures. Some of his work has been potboiling, but no other writer, with the possible exception of Erskine Caldwell, has provided such penetrating analyses of pathological specimens of degeneracy. Much of his work has been published in England as well as in the United States, and translated (one wonders how successfully) into French, Spanish, German, Norwegian, Czech, Italian, and Portuguese. The important later books include seven novels (*Light in August,* 1932; *Pylon,* 1935; *Absalom, Absalom!* 1936; *The Wild Palms,* 1939; *The Hamlet,* 1940; *Intruder in the Dust,* 1948; and *Requiem for a Nun,* 1951) and five volumes of short stories (*These 13,* 1931; *Doctor Martino and Other Stories,* 1934; *The Unvanquished,* 1938; *Go Down, Moses,* 1942; and *Knight's Gambit,* 1949). This production was given the recognition of the Nobel Prize for Literature in 1950.

Readers vary widely in what they find in Faulkner's fiction—and, by the way, in what they look for—but few who are willing to give it patient attention will miss the ingenuity and freshness of its construction and the sin-

cerity of its attempt to catch the essence of experience in a region at once desperately proud and desperately impoverished. The undercurrents of life in Jefferson, county seat and market town of a sharecropping region overwhelmingly Negro, are seldom pleasant to contemplate. In the best of the Yocknapatawpha County series the Sartorises, representative of the old order in the South, are set off against the Snopeses, poor-white opportunists without the vestiges of moral responsibility which the Sartorises retain, despite the inbred decay of the society which produced them. It is hard in such a milieu to see what is honest and what is decent, and it is not Faulkner's intent to expound his personal position. Yet there is a sense in which, for all his worrying of sexual relationships and inexplicable cruelty, he is a moralist. Life, he seems to imply, ought to be better than it is.

The Portable Faulkner, ed. Malcolm Cowley, New York, 1946 • William Faulkner, Two Decades of Criticism, ed. F. J. Hoffman and O. W. Vickery, East Lansing, Mich., 1951

From · These 13

A Rose for Emily

This story first appeared in **The Forum** for July 1930, with illustrations by Weldon Bailey. It was collected in **These 13** (1931). It belongs, as will appear, to the Sartoris cycle, and in a minor way reflects the conflict between the old and the new order which is central to so much of Faulkner's fiction. Told more directly than most of his stories, it shows his characteristic mastery of structure in the manner in which all details fit together, once the conclusion is reached. A careless reader is likely to miss the importance of the time sequence described at the beginning of the second section.

I

When Miss Emily Grierson died, our whole town went to her funeral: the men through a sort of respectful

affection for a fallen monument, the women mostly out of curiosity to see the inside of her house, which no one save an old manservant—a combined gardener and cook—had seen in at least ten years.

It was a big, squarish frame house that had once been white, decorated with cupolas and spires and scrolled balconies in the heavily lightsome style of the seventies, set on what had once been our most select street. But garages and cotton gins had encroached and obliterated even the august names of that neighborhood; only Miss Emily's house was left, lifting its stubborn and coquettish decay above the cotton wagons and the gasoline pumps—an eyesore among eyesores. And now Miss Emily had gone to join the representatives of those august names where they lay in the cedar-bemused cemetery among the ranked and anonymous graves of Union and Confederate soldiers who fell at the battle of Jefferson.

Alive, Miss Emily had been a tradition, a duty, and a care; a sort of hereditary obligation upon the town, dating from that day in 1894 when Colonel Sartoris, the mayor—he who fathered the edict that no Negro woman should appear on the streets without an apron—remitted her taxes, the dispensation dating from the death of her father on into perpetuity. Not that Miss Emily would have accepted charity. Colonel Sartoris invented an involved tale to the effect that Miss Emily's father had loaned money to the town, which the town, as a matter of business, preferred this way of repaying. Only a man of Colonel Sartoris' generation and thought could have invented it, and only a woman could have believed it.

When the next generation, with its more modern ideas, became mayors and aldermen, this arrangement created some little dissatisfaction. On the first of the year they mailed her a tax notice. February came, and there was no reply. They wrote her a formal letter, asking her to call at the sheriff's office at her convenience. A week later the mayor wrote her himself, offering to call or to send his car for her, and received in reply a note on paper of an archaic shape, in a thin flowing calligraphy in faded ink, to the effect that she no longer went out at all. The tax notice was also enclosed, without comment.

They called a special meeting of the Board of Aldermen. A deputation waited upon her, knocked at the door through which no visitor had passed since she ceased giving china-painting lessons eight or ten years earlier. They were admitted by the old Negro into a dim hall from which a stairway mounted into still more shadow. It smelled of dust and disuse—a close, dank smell. The Negro led them into the parlor. It was furnished in heavy, leather-covered furniture. When the Negro opened the blinds of one window, they could see that the leather was cracked; and when they sat down, a faint dust rose sluggishly about their thighs, spinning with slow motes in the single sun-ray. On a tarnished gilt easel before the fireplace stood a crayon portrait of Miss Emily's father.

They rose when she entered—a small, fat woman in black, with a thin gold chain descending to her waist and vanishing into her belt, leaning on an ebony cane with a tarnished gold head. Her skeleton was small and spare; perhaps that was why what would have been merely plumpness in another was obesity in her. She looked bloated, like a body long submerged in motionless water, and of that pallid hue. Her eyes, lost in the fatty ridges of her face, looked like two small pieces of coal pressed into a lump of dough as they moved from one face to another while the visitors stated their errand.

She did not ask them to sit. She just stood in the door and listened quietly until the spokesman came to a stumbling halt. Then they could hear the invisible watch ticking at the end of the gold chain.

Her voice was dry and cold. "I have no taxes in Jefferson. Colonel Sartoris explained it to me. Perhaps one of you can gain access to the city records and satisfy yourselves."

"But we have. We are the city authorities, Miss Emily. Didn't you get a notice from the sheriff, signed by him?"

"I received a paper, yes," Miss Emily said. "Perhaps he considers himself the sheriff . . . I have no taxes in Jefferson."

"But there is nothing on the books to show that, you see. We must go by the—"

"See Colonel Sartoris. I have no taxes in Jefferson."

"But, Miss Emily—"

"See Colonel Sartoris." (Colonel Sartoris had been dead almost ten years.) "I have no taxes in Jefferson. Tobe!" The Negro appeared. "Show these gentlemen out."

II

So she vanquished them, horse and foot, just as she had vanquished their fathers thirty years before about the smell. That was two years after her father's death and a short time after her sweetheart—the one we believed would marry her—had deserted her. After her father's death she went out very little; after her sweetheart went away, people hardly saw her at all. A few of the ladies had the temerity to call, but were not received, and the only sign of life about the place was the Negro man—a young man then—going in and out with a market basket.

"Just as if a man—any man—could keep a kitchen properly," the ladies said; so they were not surprised when the smell developed. It was another link between the gross, teeming world and the high and mighty Griersons.

A neighbor, a woman, complained to the mayor, Judge Stevens, eighty years old.

"But what will you have me do about it, madam?" he said.

"Why, send her word to stop it," the woman said. "Isn't there a law?"

"I'm sure that won't be necessary," Judge Stevens said. "It's probably just a snake or a rat that nigger of hers killed in the yard. I'll speak to him about it."

The next day he received two more complaints, one from a man who came in diffident deprecation. "We really must do something about it, Judge. I'd be the last one in the world to bother Miss Emily, but we've got to do something." That night the Board of Aldermen met —three graybeards and one younger man, a member of the rising generation.

"It's simple enough," he said. "Send her word to have her place cleaned up. Give her a certain time to do it in, and if she don't . . ."

"Dammit, sir," Judge Stevens said, "will you accuse a lady to her face of smelling bad?"

So the next night, after midnight, four men crossed Miss Emily's lawn and slunk about the house like burglars, sniffing along the base of the brickwork and at the cellar openings while one of them performed a regular sowing motion with his hand out of a sack slung from his shoulder. They broke open the cellar door and sprinkled lime there, and in all the outbuildings. As they recrossed the lawn, a window that had been dark was lighted and Miss Emily sat in it, the light behind her, and her upright torso motionless as that of an idol. They crept quietly across the lawn and into the shadow of the locusts that lined the street. After a week or two the smell went away.

That was when people had begun to feel really sorry for her. People in our town, remembering how old lady Wyatt, her great-aunt, had gone completely crazy at last, believed that the Griersons held themselves a little too high for what they really were. None of the young men were quite good enough to Miss Emily and such. We had long thought of them as a tableau; Miss Emily a slender figure in white in the background, her father a spraddled silhouette in the foreground, his back to her and clutching a horse-whip, the two of them framed by the back-flung front door. So when she got to be thirty and was still single, we were not pleased exactly, but vindicated; even with insanity in the family she wouldn't have turned down all of her chances if they had really materialized.

When her father died, it got about that the house was all that was left to her; and in a way, people were glad. At last they could pity Miss Emily. Being left alone, and a pauper, she had become humanized. Now she too would know the old thrill and the old despair of a penny more or less.

The day after his death all the ladies prepared to call at the house and offer condolence and aid, as is our custom. Miss Emily met them at the door, dressed as usual

and with no trace of grief on her face. She told them that her father was not dead. She did that for three days, with the ministers calling on her, and the doctors, trying to persuade her to let them dispose of the body. Just as they were about to resort to law and force, she broke down, and they buried her father quickly.

We did not say she was crazy then. We believed she had to do that. We remembered all the young men her father had driven away, and we knew that with nothing left, she would have to cling to that which had robbed her, as people will.

III

She was sick for a long time. When we saw her again, her hair was cut short, making her look like a girl, with a vague resemblance to those angels in colored church windows—sort of tragic and serene.

The town had just let the contracts for paving the sidewalks, and in the summer after her father's death they began the work. The construction company came with niggers and mules and machinery, and a foreman named Homer Barron, a Yankee—a big, dark, ready man, with a big voice and eyes lighter than his face. The little boys would follow in groups to hear him cuss the niggers, and the niggers singing in time to the rise and fall of picks. Pretty soon he knew everybody in town. Whenever you heard a lot of laughing anywhere about the square, Homer Barron would be in the center of the group. Presently we began to see him and Miss Emily on Sunday afternoons driving in the yellow-wheeled buggy and the matched team of bays from the livery stable.

At first we were glad that Miss Emily would have an interest, because the ladies all said, "Of course a Grierson would not think seriously of a Northerner, a day laborer." But there were still others, older people, who said that even grief could not cause a real lady to forget noblesse oblige—without calling it noblesse oblige. They just said, "Poor Emily. Her kinsfolk should come to her." She had some kin in Alabama; but years ago her father had fallen out with them over the estate of old lady Wyatt, the crazy woman, and there was no communication between the two families. They had not even been represented at the funeral.

And as soon as the old people said, "Poor Emily," the whispering began. "Do you suppose it's really so?" they said to one another. "Of course it is. What else could

. . ." This behind their hands; rustling of craned silk and satin behind jalousies closed upon the sun of Sunday afternoon as the thin, swift clop-clop-clop of the matched team passed: "Poor Emily."

She carried her head high enough—even when we believed that she was fallen. It was as if she demanded more than ever the recognition of her dignity as the last Grierson; as if it had wanted that touch of earthiness to reaffirm her imperviousness. Like when she bought the rat poison, the arsenic. That was over a year after they had begun to say "Poor Emily," and while the two female cousins were visiting her.

"I want some poison," she said to the druggist. She was over thirty then, still a slight woman, though thinner than usual, with cold, haughty black eyes in a face the flesh of which was strained across the temples and about the eye-sockets as you imagine a lighthouse-keeper's face ought to look. "I want some poison," she said.

"Yes, Miss Emily. What kind? For rats and such? I'd recom—"

"I want the best you have. I don't care what kind."

The druggist named several. "They'll kill anything up to an elephant. But what you want is—"

"Arsenic," Miss Emily said. "Is that a good one?"

"Is . . . arsenic? Yes, ma'am. But what you want—"

"I want arsenic."

The druggist looked down at her. She looked back at him, erect, her face like a strained flag. "Why, of course," the druggist said. "If that's what you want. But the law requires you to tell what you are going to use it for."

Miss Emily just stared at him, her head tilted back in order to look him eye for eye, until he looked away and went and got the arsenic and wrapped it up. The Negro delivery boy brought her the package; the druggist didn't come back. When she opened the package at home there was written on the box, under the skull and bones: "For rats."

IV

So the next day we all said, "She will kill herself"; and we said it would be the best thing. When she had first begun to be seen with Homer Barron, we had said, "She will marry him." Then we said, "She will persuade him yet," because Homer himself had remarked

—he liked men, and it was known that he drank with the younger men in the Elks' Club—that he was not a marrying man. Later we said, "Poor Emily" behind the jalousies as they passed on Sunday afternoon in the glittering buggy, Miss Emily with her head high and Homer Barron with his hat cocked and a cigar in his teeth, reins and whip in a yellow glove.

Then some of the ladies began to say that it was a disgrace to the town and a bad example to the young people. The men did not want to interfere, but at last the ladies forced the Baptist minister—Miss Emily's people were Episcopal—to call upon her. He would never divulge what happened during that interview, but he refused to go back again. The next Sunday they again drove about the streets, and the following day the minister's wife wrote to Miss Emily's relations in Alabama.

So she had blood-kin under her roof again and we sat back to watch developments. At first nothing happened. Then we were sure that they were to be married. We learned that Miss Emily had been to the jeweler's and ordered a man's toilet set in silver, with the letters H. B. on each piece. Two days later we learned that she had bought a complete outfit of men's clothing, including a nightshirt, and we said, "They are married." We were really glad. We were glad because the two female cousins were even more Grierson than Miss Emily had ever been.

So we were not surprised when Homer Barron—the streets had been finished some time since—was gone. We were a little disappointed that there was not a public blowing-off, but we believed that he had gone on to prepare for Miss Emily's coming, or to give her a chance to get rid of the cousins. (By that time it was a cabal, and we were all Miss Emily's allies to help circumvent the cousins.) Sure enough, after another week they departed. And, as we had expected all along, within three days Homer Barron was back in town. A neighbor saw the Negro man admit him at the kitchen door at dusk one evening.

And that was the last we saw of Homer Barron. And of Miss Emily for some time. The Negro man went in and out with the market basket, but the front door remained closed. Now and then we would see her at a window for a moment, as the men did that night when they sprinkled the lime, but for almost six months she did not appear on the streets. Then we knew that this was to be expected too; as if that quality of her father which had thwarted her woman's life so many times had been too virulent and too furious to die.

When we next saw Miss Emily, she had grown fat and her hair was turning gray. During the next few years it grew grayer and grayer until it attained an even pepper-and-salt iron-gray, when it ceased turning. Up to the day of her death at seventy-four it was still that vigorous iron-gray, like the hair of an active man.

From that time on her front door remained closed, save for a period of six or seven years, when she was about forty, during which she gave lessons in china-painting. She fitted up a studio in one of the downstairs rooms, where the daughters and granddaughters of Colonel Sartoris' contemporaries were sent to her with the same regularity and in the same spirit that they were sent to church on Sundays with a twenty-five cent piece for the collection plate. Meanwhile her taxes had been remitted.

Then the newer generation became the backbone and the spirit of the town, and the painting pupils grew up and fell away and did not send their children to her with boxes of color and tedious brushes and pictures cut from the ladies' magazines. The front door closed upon the last one and remained closed for good. When the town got free postal delivery, Miss Emily alone refused to let them fasten the metal numbers above her door and attach a mailbox to it. She would not listen to them.

Daily, monthly, yearly we watched the Negro grow grayer and more stooped, going in and out with the market basket. Each December we sent her a tax notice, which would be returned by the post office a week later, unclaimed. Now and then we would see her in one of the downstairs windows—she had evidently shut up the top floor of the house—like the carven torso of an idol in a niche, looking or not looking at us, we could never tell which. Thus she passed from generation to generation—dear, inescapable, impervious, tranquil, and perverse.

And so she died. Fell ill in the house filled with dust and shadows, with only a doddering Negro man to wait on her. We did not even know she was sick; we had long since given up trying to get any information from the Negro. He talked to no one, probably not even to her, for his voice had grown harsh and rusty, as if from disuse.

She died in one of the downstairs rooms, in a heavy walnut bed with a curtain, her gray head propped on a pillow yellow and moldy with age and lack of sunlight.

V

The Negro met the first of the ladies at the front door and let them in, with their hushed, sibilant voices and their quick, curious glances, and then he disappeared. He walked right through the house and out the back and was not seen again.

The two female cousins came at once. They held the funeral on the second day, with the town coming to look at Miss Emily beneath a mass of bought flowers, with the crayon face of her father musing profoundly above the bier and the ladies sibilant and macabre; and the very old men—some in their brushed Confederate uniforms—on the porch and the lawn, talking of Miss Emily as if she had been a contemporary of theirs, believing that they had danced with her and courted her perhaps, confusing time with its mathematical progression, as the old do, to whom all the past is not a diminishing road but, instead, a huge meadow which no winter ever quite touches, divided from them now by the narrow bottle-neck of the most recent decade of years.

Already we knew that there was one room in that region above stairs which no one had seen in forty years, and which would have to be forced. They waited until Miss Emily was decently in the ground before they opened it.

The violence of breaking down the door seemed to fill this room with pervading dust. A thin, acrid pall as of the tomb seemed to lie everywhere upon this room decked and furnished as for a bridal: upon the valence curtains of faded rose color, upon the rose-shaded lights, upon the dressing table, upon the delicate array of crystal and the man's toilet things backed with tarnished silver, silver so tarnished that the monogram was obscured. Among them lay a collar and tie, as if they had just been removed, which, lifted, left upon the surface a pale crescent in the dust. Upon a chair hung the suit, carefully folded; beneath it the two mute shoes and the discarded socks.

The man himself lay in the bed.

For a long while we just stood there, looking down at the profound and fleshless grin. The body had apparently once lain in the attitude of an embrace, but now the long sleep that outlasts love, that conquers even the grimace of love, had cuckolded him. What was left of him, rotted beneath what was left of the nightshirt, had become inextricable from the bed in which he lay; and upon him and upon the pillow beside him lay that even coating of the patient and biding dust.

Then we noticed that in the second pillow was the indentation of a head. One of us lifted something from it, and leaning forward, that faint and invisible dust dry and acrid in the nostrils, we saw a long strand of iron-gray hair.

1930? · 1930 10

Spotted Horses

Like Henry James (see p. 495), Faulkner is something of a novelist's novelist, which is to say that his experiments in technique make him unusually interesting to other writers and to students of fiction. "Spotted Horses," for example, provides a convenient way to study differing narrative points of view. In the version which is reprinted below (from **Scribner's Magazine**, June 1931), the story is told in the first person, by an unnamed participant in its events. In **The Hamlet** (1940) Faulkner expanded the episode enormously and chose to tell it in the third person. Not all readers will agree which was the better way to tell this particular story, but a comparison of the two methods suggests that Faulkner, in the later version, wished to present the setting of his incident more subtly and more pictorially than he could through the vernacular of a sewing-machine salesman. Mrs. Littlejohn's boarder obviously would be incapable of describing a scene, as the full moon rose, in such a sentence as this: "It was merely a translation from the lapidary-dimensional of day to the treacherous and silver receptivity in which the horses huddled in mazy camouflage, or singly or in pairs rushed, fluid, phantom, and unceasing, to huddle again in mirage-like clumps from which came high, abrupt squeals and the vicious thudding of hooves." It is noteworthy that both James and Faulkner (if we may judge by this instance) developed greater intricacy of style through technical experiment. James, however, came to rely more and more upon the first-person point of view, a tendency which Faulkner here reversed.

Read for itself, "Spotted Horses" is delightful in its humor—in several ways reminiscent of the humor of the Southern yarnspinners—and its portrayal of Flem Snopes, a type of Southerner for whom Faulkner clearly has no love.

I

Yes sir. Flem Snopes has filled that whole country full of spotted horses. You can hear folks running them all day and all night, whooping and hollering, and the horses running back and forth across them little wooden bridges ever now and then kind of like thunder. Here I was this morning pretty near half way to town, with the team ambling along and me setting in the buckboard about half asleep, when all of a sudden something come swurging up outen the bushes and jumped the road clean, without touching hoof to it. It flew right over my team big as a billboard and flying through the air like a hawk. It taken me thirty minutes to stop my team and untangle the harness and the buckboard and hitch them up again.

That Flem Snopes. I be dog if he ain't a case, now. One morning about ten years ago the boys was just getting settled down on Varner's porch for a little talk and tobacco, when here come Flem out from behind the counter, with his coat off and his hair all parted, like he might have been clerking for Varner for ten years already. Folks all knowed him; it was a big family of them about five miles down the bottom. That year, at least. Share-cropping. They never stayed on any place over a year. Then they would move on to another place, with the chap or maybe the twins of that year's litter. It was a regular nest of them. But Flem. The rest of them stayed tenant farmers, moving ever year, but here come Flem one day, walking out from behind Jody Varner's counter like he owned it. And he wasn't there but a year or two before folks knowed that if him and Jody was both still in that store in ten years more it would be Jody clerking for Flem Snopes. Why, that fellow could make a nickel where it wasn't but four cents to begin with. He skun me in two trades, myself and the fellow that can do that, I just hope he'll get rich before I do; that's all.

All right. So here Flem was, clerking at Varner's, making a nickel here and there and not telling nobody about it. No, sir. Folks never knowed when Flem got the better of somebody lessen the fellow he beat told it. He'd just set there in the store-chair, chewing his tobacco and keeping his own business to hisself, until about a week later we'd find out it was somebody else's business he was keeping to hisself—provided the fellow he trimmed was mad enough to tell it. That's Flem.

We give him ten years to own ever thing Jody Varner had. But he never waited no ten years. I reckon you-all know that gal of Uncle Billy Varner's, the youngest one; Eula. Jody's sister. Ever Sunday ever yellow-wheeled buggy and curried riding horse in that country would be hitched to Bill Varner's fence, and the young bucks setting on the porch, swarming around Eula like bees around a honey pot. One of these here kind of big, soft-looking gals that could giggle richer than plowed new-ground. Wouldn't none of them leave before the others, and so they would set there on the porch until time to go home, with some of them with nine and ten miles to ride and then get up tomorrow and go back to the field. So they would all leave together and they would ride in a clump down to the creek ford and hitch them curried horses and yellow-wheeled buggies and get out and fight one another. Then they would get in the buggies again and go on home.

Well, one day about a year ago, one of them yellow-wheeled buggies and one of them curried saddle-horses quit this country. We heard they was heading for Texas. The next day Uncle Billy and Eula and Flem come in to town in Uncle Bill's surrey, and when they come back, Flem and Eula was married. And on the next day we heard that two more of them yellow-wheeled buggies had left the country. They mought have gone to Texas, too. It's a big place.

Anyway, about a month after the wedding, Flem and Eula went to Texas, too. They was gone pretty near a year. Then one day last month, Eula come back, with a baby. We figgered up, and we decided that it was as well-growed a three-months-old baby as we ever see. It can already pull up on a chair. I reckon Texas makes big men quick, being a big

place. Anyway, if it keeps on like it started, it'll be chewing tobacco and voting time it's eight years old.

And so last Friday here come Flem himself. He was on a wagon with another fellow. The other fellow had one of these two-gallon hats and a ivory-handled pistol and a box of ginger snaps sticking out of his hind pocket, and tied to the tail-gate of the wagon was about two dozen of them Texas ponies, hitched to one another with barbed wire. They was colored like parrots and they was quiet as doves, and ere a one of them would kill you quick as a rattlesnake. Nere a one of them had two eyes the same color, and nere a one of them had ever see a bridle, I reckon; and when that Texas man got down offen the wagon and walked up to them to show how gentle they was, one of them cut his vest clean offen him, same as with a razor.

Flem had done already disappeared; he had went on to see his wife, I reckon, and to see if that ere baby had done gone on to the field to help Uncle Billy plow, maybe. It was the Texas man that taken the horses on to Mrs. Littlejohn's lot. He had a little trouble at first, when they come to the gate, because they hadn't never see a fence before, and when he finally got them in and taken a pair of wire cutters and unhitched them and got them into the barn and poured some shell corn into the trough, they durn nigh tore down the barn. I reckon they thought that shell corn was bugs, maybe. So he left them in the lot and he announced that the auction would begin at sunup tomorrow.

That night we was setting on Mrs. Littlejohn's porch. You-all mind the moon was nigh full that night, and we could watch them spotted varmints swirling along the fence and back and forth across the lot same as minnows in a pond. And then now and then they would all kind of huddle up against the barn and rest themselves by biting and kicking one another. We would hear a squeal, and then a set of hoofs would go Bam! against the barn, like a pistol. It sounded just like a fellow with a pistol, in a nest of cattymounts, taking his time.

II

It wasn't ere a man knowed yet if Flem owned them things or not. They just knowed one thing: that they wasn't never going to know for sho if

Flem did or not, or if maybe he didn't just get on that wagon at the edge of town, for the ride or not. Even Eck Snopes didn't know, Flem's own cousin. But wasn't nobody surprised at that. We knowed that Flem would skin Eck quick as he would ere a one of us.

They was there by sunup next morning, some of them come twelve and sixteen miles, with seed-money tied up in tobacco sacks in their overalls, standing along the fence, when the Texas man come out of Mrs. Littlejohn's after breakfast and clumb onto the gate post with that ere white pistol butt sticking outen his hind pocket. He taken a new box of ginger-snaps outen his pocket and bit the end offen it like a cigar and spit out the paper, and said the auction was open. And still they was coming up in wagons and a horse- and mule-back and hitching the teams across the road and coming to the fence. Flem wasn't nowhere in sight.

But he couldn't get them started. He begun to work on Eck, because Eck holp him last night to get them into the barn and feed them that shell corn. Eck got out just in time. He come outen that barn like a chip on the crest of a busted dam of water, and clumb into the wagon just in time.

He was working on Eck when Henry Armstid come up in his wagon. Eck was saying he was skeered to bid on one of them, because he might get it, and the Texas man says, "Them ponies? Them little horses?" He clumb down offen the gate post and went toward the horses. They broke and run, and him following them, kind of chirping to them, with his hand out like he was fixing to catch a fly, until he got three or four of them cornered. Then he jumped into them, and then we couldn't see nothing for a while because of the dust. It was a big cloud of it, and them blare-eyed, spotted things swoaring outen it twenty foot to a jump, in forty directions without counting up. Then the dust settled and there they was, that Texas man and the horse. He had its head twisted clean around like a owl's head. Its legs was braced and it was trembling like a new bride and groaning like a saw mill, and him holding its head wrung clean around on its neck so it was snuffing sky. "Look it over," he says, with his heels dug too and that white pistol sticking outen his pocket and his neck swole up like a spreading adder's until you could just tell what he was saying, cussing the horse and talking to us all

at once: "Look him over, the fiddle headed son of fourteen fathers. Try him, buy him; you will get the best—" Then it was all dust again, and we couldn't see nothing but spotted hide and mane, and that ere Texas man's boot-heels like a couple of walnuts on two strings, and after a while that two-gallon hat come sailing out like a fat old hen crossing a fence.

When the dust settled again, he was just getting outen the far fence corner, brushing himself off. He come and got his hat and brushed it off and come and clumb onto the gate post again. He was breathing hard. The hammer-head horse was still running round and round the lot like a merry-go-round at a fair. That was when Henry Armstid come shoving up to the gate in them patched overalls and one of them dangle-armed shirts of hisn. Hadn't nobody noticed him until then. We was all watching the Texas man and the horses. Even Mrs. Littlejohn; she had done come out and built a fire under the wash-pot in her back yard, and she would stand at the fence a while and then go back into the house and come out again with a arm full of wash and stand at the fence again. Well, here come Henry shoving up, and then we see Mrs. Armstid right behind him, in that ere faded wrapper and sunbonnet and them tennis shoes. "Git on back to that wagon," Henry says.

"Henry," she says.

"Here, boys," the Texas man says; "make room for missus to git up and see. Come on Henry," he says; "here's your chance to buy that saddle-horse missus has been wanting. What about ten dollars, Henry?"

"Henry," Mrs. Armstid says. She put her hand on Henry's arm. Henry knocked her hand down.

"Git on back to that wagon, like I told you," he says.

Mrs. Armstid never moved. She stood behind Henry, with her hands rolled into her dress, not looking at nothing. "He hain't no more despair than to buy one of them things," she says. "And us not five dollars ahead of the pore house, he hain't no more despair." It was the truth, too. They ain't never made more than a bare living offen that place of theirs, and them with four chaps and the very clothes they wears she earns by weaving by the fire-light at night while Henry's asleep.

"Shut your mouth and git on back to that wagon," Henry says. "Do you want I taken a wagon stake to you here in the big road?"

Well, that Texas man taken one look at her. Then he begun on Eck again; like Henry wasn't even there.

Spotted Horses 1117

But Eck was skeered. "I can git me a snapping turtle or a water moccasin for nothing. I ain't going to buy none."

So the Texas man said he would give Eck a horse. "To start the auction, and because you holp me last night. If you'll start the bidding on the next horse," he says, "I'll give you that fiddle-head horse."

I wish you could have seen them, standing there with their seed-money in their pockets, watching that Texas man give Eck Snopes a live horse, all fixed to call him a fool if he taken it or not. Finally Eck says he'll take it. "Only I just starts the bidding," he says. "I don't have to buy the next one lessen I ain't overtopped." The Texas man said all right, and Eck bid a dollar on the next one, with Henry Armstid standing there with his mouth already open, watching Eck and the Texas man like a mad-dog or something. "A dollar," Eck says.

The Texas man looked at Eck. His mouth was already open too, like he had started to say something and what he was going to say had up and died on him. "A dollar? You mean, *one* dollar, Eck?"

"Durn it," Eck says; "two dollars, then."

Well, sir, I wish you could a seen that Texas man. He taken out that gingersnap box and held it up and looked into it, careful, like it might have been a diamond ring in it, or a spider. Then he throwed it away and wiped his face with a bandanna. "Well," he says. "Well. Two dollars. Two dollars. Is your pulse all right, Eck?" he says. "Do you have ager-sweats at night, maybe?" he says. "Well," he says, "I got to take it. But are you boys going to stand there and see Eck get two horses at a dollar a head?"

That done it. I be dog if he wasn't nigh as smart as Flem Snopes. He hadn't no more than got the words outen his mouth before here was Henry Armstid, waving his hand. "Three dollars," Henry says. Mrs. Armstid tried to hold him again. He knocked her hand off, shoving up to the gate post.

"Mister," Mrs. Armstid says, "we got chaps in the house and not corn to feed the stock. We got five dollars I earned my chaps a-weaving after dark, and him snoring in the bed. And he hain't no more despair."

"Henry bids three dollars," the Texas man says. "Raise him a dollar, Eck, and the horse is yours."

"Henry," Mrs. Armstid says.

"Raise him, Eck," the Texas man says.

"Four dollars," Eck says.

"Five dollars," Henry says, shaking his fist. He shoved up right under the gate post. Mrs. Armstid was looking at the Texas man too.

"Mister," she says, "if you take that five dollars I earned my chaps a-weaving for one of them things, it'll be a curse onto you and yourn during all the time of man."

But is wasn't no stopping Henry. He had shoved up, waving his fist at the Texas man. He opened it; the money was in nickels and quarters, and one dollar bill that looked like a cow's cud. "Five dollars," he says. "And the man that raises it'll have to beat my head off, or I'll beat hisn."

"All right," the Texas man says. "Five dollars is bid. But don't you shake your hand at me."

III

It taken till nigh sundown before the last one was sold. He got them hotted up once and the bidding got up to seven dollars and a quarter, but most of them went around three or four dollars, him setting on the gate post and picking the horses out one at a time by mouthword, and Mrs. Littlejohn pumping up and down at the tub and stopping and coming to the fence for a while and going back to the tub again. She had done got done too, and the wash was hung on the line in the back yard, and we could smell supper cooking. Finally they was all sold; he swapped the last two and the wagon for a buckboard.

We was all kind of tired, but Henry Armstid looked more like a mad-dog than ever. When he bought, Mrs. Armstid had went back to the wagon, setting in it behind them two rabbit-sized, bone-pore mules, and the wagon itself looking like it would fall all to pieces soon as the mules moved. Henry hadn't even waited to pull it outen the road; it was still in the middle of the road and her setting in it, not looking at nothing, ever since this morning.

Henry was right up against the gate. He went up to the Texas man. "I bought a horse and I paid cash," Henry says. "And yet you expect me to stand around here until they are all sold before I can get my horse. I'm going to take my horse outen that lot."

The Texas man looked at Henry. He talked like he might have been asking for a cup of coffee at the table. "Take your horse," he says.

Then Henry quit looking at the Texas man. He begun to swallow, holding onto the gate. "Ain't you going to help me?" he says.

"It ain't my horse," the Texas man says.

Henry never looked at the Texas man again, he never looked at nobody. "Who'll help me catch my horse?" he says. Never nobody said nothing. "Bring the plowline," Henry says. Mrs. Armstid got outen the wagon and brought the plowline. The Texas man got down offen the post. The woman made to pass him, carrying the rope.

"Don't you go in there, missus," the Texas man says.

Henry opened the gate. He didn't look back. "Come on here," he says.

"Don't you go in there, missus," the Texas man says.

Mrs. Armstid wasn't looking at nobody, neither, with her hands across her middle, holding the rope. "I reckon I better," she says. Her and Henry went into the lot. The horses broke and run. Henry and Mrs. Armstid followed.

"Get him into the corner," Henry says. They got Henry's horse cornered finally, and Henry taken the rope, but Mrs. Armstid let the horse get out. They hemmed it up again, but Mrs. Armstid let it get out again, and Henry turned and hit her with the rope. "Why didn't you head him back?" Henry says. He hit her again. "Why didn't you?" It was about that time I looked around and see Flem Snopes standing there.

It was the Texas man that done something. He moved fast for a big man. He caught the rope before Henry could hit the third time, and Henry whirled and made like he would jump at the Texas man. But he never jumped. The Texas man went and taken Henry's arm and led him outen the lot. Mrs. Armstid come behind them and the Texas man taken some money outen his pocket and he give it into Mrs. Armstid's hand. "Get him into the wagon and take him on home," the Texas man says, like he might have been telling them he enjoyed his supper.

Then here come Flem. "What's that for Buck?" Flem says.

"Thinks he bought one of them ponies," the Texas man says. "Get him on away, missus."

But Henry wouldn't go. "Give him back that money," he says. "I bought that horse and I aim to have him if I have to shoot him."

And there was Flem, standing there with his hands in his pockets, chewing, like he had just happened to be passing.

"You take your money and I take my horse," Henry

says. "Give it back to him," he says to Mrs. Armstid.

"You don't own no horse of mine," the Texas man says. "Get him on home, missus."

Then Henry seen Flem. "You got something to do with these horses," he says. "I bought one. Here's the money for it." He taken the bill outen Mrs. Armstid's hand. He offered it to Flem. "I bought one. Ask him. Here. Here's the money," he says, giving the bill to Flem.

When Flem taken the money, the Texas man dropped the rope he had snatched outen Henry's hand. He had done sent Eck Snopes's boy up to the store for another box of gingersnaps, and he taken the box outen his pocket and looked into it. It was empty and he dropped it on the ground. "Mr. Snopes will have your money for you tomorrow," he says to Mrs. Armstid. "You can get it from him tomorrow. He don't own no horse. You get him into the wagon and get him on home." Mrs. Armstid went back to the wagon and got in. "Where's that ere buckboard I bought?" the Texas man says. It was after sundown then. And then Mrs. Littlejohn come out on the porch and rung the supper bell.

IV

I come on in and et supper. Mrs. Littlejohn would bring in a pan of bread or something, then she would go out to the porch a minute and come back and tell us. The Texas man had hitched his team to the buckboard he had swapped them last two horses for, and him and Flem had gone, and then she told that the rest of them that never had ropes had went back to the store with I. O. Snopes to get some ropes, and wasn't nobody at the gate but Henry Armstid, and Mrs. Armstid setting in the wagon in the road, and Eck Snopes and that boy of hisn. "I don't care how many of them fool men gets killed by them things," Mrs. Littlejohn says, "but I ain't going to let Eck Snopes take that boy into that lot again." So she went down to the gate, but she come back without the boy or Eck neither.

"It ain't no need to worry about that boy," I says. "He's charmed." He was right behind Eck last night when Eck went to help feed them. The whole drove of them jumped clean over that boy's head and never touched him. It was Eck that touched him. Eck snatched him into the wagon and taken a rope and frailed the tar outen him.

So I had done et and went to my room and was undressing, long as I had a long trip to make next day; I was trying to sell a machine to Mrs. Bundren up past Whiteleaf; when Henry Armstid opened that gate and went in by hisself. They couldn't make him wait for the balance of them to get back with their ropes. Eck Snopes said he tried to make Henry wait, but Henry wouldn't do it. Eck said Henry walked right up to them and that when they broke, they run clean over Henry like a hay-mow breaking down. Eck said he snatched that boy of hisn out of the way just in time and that them things went through that gate like a creek flood and into the wagons and teams hitched side the road, busting wagon tongues and snapping harness like it was fishing-line, with Mrs. Armstid still setting in their wagon in the middle of it like something carved outen wood. Then they scattered, wild horses and tame mules with pieces of harness and single trees dangling offen them, both ways up and down the road.

"There goes ourn, paw!" Eck says his boy said. "There it goes, into Mrs. Littlejohn's house." Eck says it run right up the steps and into the house like a boarder late for supper. I reckon so. Anyway, I was in my room, in my underclothes, with one sock on and one sock in my hand, leaning out the window when the commotion busted out, when I heard something run into the melodeon in the hall; it sounded like a railroad engine. Then the door to my room come sailing in like when you throw a tin bucket top into the wind and I looked over my shoulder and see something that looked like a fourteen-foot pinwheel a-blaring its eyes at me. It had to blare them fast, because I was already done jumped out the window.

I reckon it was anxious, too. I reckon it hadn't never seen barbed wire or shell corn before, but I know it hadn't never seen underclothes before, or maybe it was a sewing-machine agent it hadn't never seen. Anyway, it whirled and turned to run back up the hall and outen the house, when it met Eck Snopes and that boy just coming in, carrying a rope. It swirled again and run down the hall and out the back door just in time to meet Mrs. Littlejohn. She had just gathered up the clothes she had washed, and she was coming onto the back porch with a armful of washing in one hand and a scrubbing-board in the other, when the horse skidded up to her, trying to stop and swirl again. It never taken Mrs. Littlejohn no time a-tall.

"Git outen here, you son," she says. She hit it across the face with the scrubbing-board; that ere scrubbing-board split as neat as ere a axe could have done it, and when the horse swirled to run back up the hall, she hit it again with what was left of the scrubbing-board, not on the head this time. "And stay out," she says.

Eck and that boy was half-way down the hall by this time. I reckon that horse looked like a pinwheel to Eck too. "Get to hell outen here, Ad!" Eck says. Only there wasn't time. Eck dropped flat on his face, but the boy never moved. The boy was about a yard tall maybe, in overalls just like Eck's; that horse swoared over his head without touching a hair. I saw that, because I was just coming back up the front steps, still carrying that ere sock and still in my underclothes, when the horse come onto the porch again. It taken one look at me and swirled again and run to the end of the porch and jumped the banisters and the lot fence like a hen-hawk and lit in the lot running and went out the gate again and jumped eight or ten upside-down wagons and went on down the road. It was a full moon then. Mrs. Armstid was still setting in the wagon like she had done been carved outen wood and left there and forgot.

That horse. It ain't never missed a lick. It was going about forty miles a hour when it come to the bridge over the creek. It would have had a clear road, but it so happened that Vernon Tull was already using the bridge when it got there. He was coming back from town; he hadn't heard about the auction; him and his wife and three daughters and Mrs. Tull's aunt, all setting in chairs in the wagon bed, and all asleep, including the mules. They waked up when the horse hit the bridge one time, but Tull said the first he knew was when the mules tried to turn the wagon around in the middle of the bridge and he seen that spotted varmint run right twixt the mules and run up the wagon tongue like a squirrel. He said he just had time to hit it across the face with his ship-stock, because about that time the mules turned the wagon around on that ere one-way bridge and that horse clumb across onto the bridge again and went on, with Vernon standing up in the wagon and kicking at it.

Tull said the mules turned in the harness and clumb back into the wagon too, with Tull trying to beat them out again, with the reins wrapped around his wrist. After that he says all he seen was overturned chairs and womenfolks' legs and white drawers shining in the moonlight, and his mules and that spotted horse going on up the road like a ghost.

The mules jerked Tull outen the wagon and drug him a spell on the bridge before the reins broke. They thought at first that he was dead, and while they was kneeling around him, picking the bridge splinters outen him, here come Eck and that boy, still carrying the rope. They was running and breathing a little hard. "Where'd he go?" Eck says.

V

I went back and got my pants and shirt and shoes on just in time to go and help get Henry Armstid outen the trash in the lot. I be dog if he didn't look like he was dead, with his head hanging back and his teeth showing in the moonlight, and a little rim of white under his eye-lids. We could still hear them horses, here and there; hadn't none of them got more than four—five miles away yet, not knowing the country, I reckon. So we could hear them and folks yelling now and then: "Whooey. Head him!"

We toted Henry into Mrs. Littlejohn's. She was in the hall; she hadn't put down the armful of clothes. She taken one look at us, and she laid down the busted scrubbing-board and taken up the lamp and opened a empty door. "Bring him in here," she says.

We toted him in and laid him on the bed. Mrs. Littlejohn set the lamp on the dresser, still carrying the clothes. "I'll declare, you men," she says. Our shadows was way up the wall, tiptoeing too; we could hear ourselves breathing. "Better get his wife," Mrs. Littlejohn says. She went out, carrying the clothes.

"I reckon we had," Quick says. "Go get her, somebody."

"Whyn't you go?" Winterbottom says.

"Let Ernest git her," Durley says. "He lives neighbors with them."

Ernest went to fetch her. I be dog if Henry didn't look like he was dead. Mrs. Littlejohn come back, with a kettle and some towels. She went to work on Henry, and then Mrs. Armstid and Ernest come in. Mrs. Armstid come to the foot of the bed and stood there, with her hands rolled into her apron, watching what Mrs. Littlejohn was doing, I reckon.

"You men get outen the way," Mrs. Littlejohn says.

"Git outside," she says. "See if you can't find something else to play with that will kill some more of you."

"Is he dead?" Winterbottom says.

"It ain't your fault if he ain't," Mrs. Littlejohn says. "Go tell Will Varner to come up here. I reckon a man ain't so different from a mule, come long come short. Except maybe a mule's got more sense."

We went to get Uncle Billy. It was a full moon. We could hear them, now and then, four miles away: "Whooey. Head him." The country was full of them, one on ever wooden bridge in the land, running across it like thunder: "Whooey. There he goes. Head him."

We hadn't got far before Henry begun to scream. I reckon Mrs. Littlejohn's water had brung him to; anyway, he wasn't dead. We went on to Uncle Billy's. The house was dark. We called to him, and after a while the window opened and Uncle Billy put his head out, peart as a peckerwood, listening. "Are they still trying to catch them durn rabbits?" he says.

He come down, with his britches on over his night-shirt and his suspenders dangling, carrying his horse-doctoring grip. "Yes, sir," he says, cocking his head like a woodpecker; "they're still a-trying."

We could hear Henry before we reached Mrs. Littlejohn's. He was going Ah-Ah-Ah. We stopped in the yard. Uncle Billy went on in. We could hear Henry. We stood in the yard, hearing them on the bridges, this-a-way and that: "Whooey. Whooey."

"Eck Snopes ought to caught hisn," Ernest says.

"Looks like he ought," Winterbottom said.

Henry was going Ah-Ah-Ah steady in the house; then he begun to scream. "Uncle Billy's started," Quick says. We looked into the hall. We could see the light where the door was. Then Mrs. Littlejohn come out.

"Will needs some help," she says. "You, Ernest. You'll do." Ernest went into the house.

"Hear them?" Quick said. "That one was on Four Mile bridge." We could hear them; it sounded like thunder a long way off; it didn't last long:

"Whooey."

We could hear Henry: "Ah-Ah-Ah-Ah-Ah."

"They are both started now," Winterbottom says. "Ernest too."

That was early in the night. Which was a good thing, because it taken a long night for folks to chase them things right and for Henry to lay there and holler, being as Uncle Billy never had none of this here chloryfoam to set Henry's leg with. So it was considerate in Flem to get them started early. And what do you reckon Flem's comment was?

That's right. Nothing. Because he wasn't there. Hadn't nobody see him since that Texas man left.

VI

That was Saturday night. I reckon Mrs. Armstid got home about daylight, to see about the chaps. I don't know where they thought her and Henry was. But lucky the oldest one was a gal, about twelve, big enough to take care of the little ones. Which she did for the next two days. Mrs. Armstid would nurse Henry all night and work in the kitchen for hern and Henry's keep, and in the afternoon she would drive home (it was about four miles) to see to the chaps. She would cook up a pot of victuals and leave it on the stove, and the gal would bar the house and keep the little ones quiet. I would hear Mrs. Littlejohn and Mrs. Armstid talking in the kitchen. "How are the chaps making out?" Mrs. Littlejohn says.

"All right," Mrs. Armstid says.

"Don't they git skeered at night?" Mrs. Littlejohn says.

"Ina May bars the door when I leave," Mrs. Armstid says. "She's got the axe in bed with her. I reckon she can make out."

I reckon they did. And I reckon Mrs. Armstid was waiting for Flem to come back to town; hadn't nobody seen him until this morning; to get her money the Texas man said Flem was keeping for her. Sho. I reckon she was.

Anyway, I heard Mrs. Armstid and Mrs. Littlejohn talking in the kitchen this morning while I was eating breakfast. Mrs. Littlejohn had just told Mrs. Armstid that Flem was in town. "You can ask him for that five dollars," Mrs. Littlejohn says.

"You reckon he'll give it to me?" Mrs. Armstid says.

Mrs. Littlejohn was washing dishes, washing them like a man, like they was made out of iron. "No," she says. "But asking him won't do no hurt. It might shame him. I don't reckon it will, but it might."

"If he wouldn't give it back, it ain't no use to ask," Mrs. Armstid says.

"Suit yourself," Mrs. Littlejohn says. "It's your money."

I could hear the dishes.

"Do you reckon he might give it back to me?" Mrs.

Armstid says. "That Texas man said he would. He said I could get it from Mr. Snopes later."

"Then go and ask him for it," Mrs. Littlejohn says. I could hear the dishes.

"He won't give it back to me," Mrs. Armstid says.

"All right," Mrs. Littlejohn says. "Don't ask him for it, then."

I could hear the dishes; Mrs. Armstid was helping. "You don't reckon he would, do you?" she says. Mrs. Littlejohn never said nothing. It sounded like she was throwing the dishes at one another. "Maybe I better go and talk to Henry about it," Mrs. Armstid says.

"I would," Mrs. Littlejohn says. I be dog if it didn't sound like she had two plates in her hands, beating them together. "Then Henry can buy another five-dollar horse with it. Maybe he'll buy one next time that will out and out kill him. If I thought that, I'd give you back the money, myself."

"I reckon I better talk to him first," Mrs. Armstid said. Then it sounded like Mrs. Littlejohn taken up all the dishes and throwed them at the cook-stove, and I come away.

That was this morning. I had been up to Bundren's and back, and I thought that things would have kind of settled down. So after breakfast, I went up to the store. And there was Flem, setting in the store chair and whittling, like he might not have ever moved since he come to clerk for Jody Varner. I. O. was leaning in the door, in his shirt sleeves and with his hair parted too, same as Flem was before he turned the clerking job over to I. O. It's a funny thing about them Snopes: they all looks alike, yet there ain't ere a two of them that claims brothers. They're always just cousins, like Flem and Eck and Flem and I. O. Eck was there too, squatting against the wall, him and that boy, eating cheese and crackers outen a sack; they told me that Eck hadn't been home a-tall. And that Lon Quick hadn't got back to town, even. He followed his horse clean down to Samson's Bridge, with a wagon and a camp outfit. Eck finally caught one of hisn. It run into a blind lane at Freeman's and Eck and the boy taken and tied their rope across the end of the lane, about three foot high. The horse come to the end of the lane and whirled and run back without ever stopping. Eck says it never seen the rope a-tall. He says it looked just like one of these here Christmas pinwheels.

"Didn't it try to run again?" I says.

"No," Eck says, eating a bite of cheese offen his knife blade. "Just kicked some."

"Kicked some?" I says.

"It broke its neck," Eck says.

Well, they was squatting there, about six of them, talking, talking at Flem; never nobody knowed yet if Flem had ere a interest in them horses or not. So finally I come right out and asked him. "Flem's done skun all of us so much," I says, "that we're proud of him. Come on, Flem," I says, "how much did you and that Texas man make offen them horses? You can tell us. Ain't nobody here but Eck that bought one of them; the others ain't got back to town yet, and Eck's your own cousin; he'll be proud to hear, too. How much did you-all make?"

They was all whittling, not looking at Flem, making like they was studying. But you could a heard a pin drop. And I. O. He had been rubbing his back up and down on the door, but he stopped now, watching Flem like a pointing dog. Flem finished cutting the sliver offen his stick. He spit across the porch, into the road. "Twarn't none of my horses," he says.

I. O. cackled, like a hen, slapping his legs with both hands. "You boys might just as well quit trying to get ahead of Flem," he said.

Well, about that time I see Mrs. Armstid come outen Mrs. Littlejohn's gate, coming up the road. I never said nothing. I says, "Well, if a man can't take care of himself in a trade, he can't blame the man that trims him."

Flem never said nothing, trimming at the stick. He hadn't seen Mrs. Armstid. "Yes, sir," I says. "A fellow like Henry Armstid ain't got nobody but hisself to blame."

"Course he ain't," I. O. says. He ain't seen her, either. "Henry Armstid's a born fool. Always is been. If Flem hadn't a got his money, somebody else would."

We looked at Flem. He never moved. Mrs. Armstid come on up the road.

"That's right," I says. "But come to think of it, Henry never bought no horse." We looked at Flem; you could a heard a match drop. "That Texas man told her to get that five dollars back from Flem next day. I reckon Flem's done already taken that money to Mrs. Littlejohn's and give it to Mrs. Armstid."

We watched Flem. I. O. quit rubbing his back against the door again. After a while Flem raised his head and spit across the porch, into the dust. I. O. cackled, just like a hen. "Ain't he a beating fellow, now?" I. O. says.

Mrs. Armstid was getting closer, so I kept on talking, watching to see if Flem would look up and see her. But he never looked up. I went on talking about Tull, about how he was going to sue Flem, and Flem setting there, whittling his stick, not saying nothing else after he said they wasn't none of his horses.

Then I. O. happened to look around. He seen Mrs. Armstid. "Pssssst!" he says. Flem looked up. "Here she comes!" I. O. says. "Go out the back. I'll tell her you done went in to town today."

But Flem never moved. He just set there, whittling, and we watched Mrs. Armstid come up onto the porch, in that ere faded sunbonnet and wrapper and them tennis shoes that made a kind of hissing noise on the porch. She come onto the porch and stopped, her hands rolled into her dress in front, not looking at nothing.

"He said Saturday," she says, "that he wouldn't sell Henry no horse. He said I could get the money from you."

Flem looked up. The knife never stopped. It went on trimming off a sliver same as if he was watching it. "He taken that money off with him when he left," Flem says.

Mrs. Armstid never looked at nothing. We never looked at her, neither, except that boy of Eck's. He had a half-et cracker in his hand, watching her, chewing.

"He said Henry hadn't bought no horse," Mrs. Armstid says. "He said for me to get the money from you today."

"I reckon he forgot about it," Flem said. "He taken that money off with him Saturday." He whittled again. I. O. kept on rubbing his back, slow. He licked his lips. After a while the woman looked up the road, where it went on up the hill, toward the graveyard. She looked up that way for a while, with that boy of Eck's watching her and I. O. rubbing his back slow against the door. Then she turned back toward the steps.

Spotted Horses 1123

"I reckon it's time to get dinner started," she says.

"How's Henry this morning, Mrs. Armstid?" Winterbottom says.

She looked at Winterbottom; she almost stopped. "He's resting, I thank you kindly," she says.

Flem got up, outen the chair, putting his knife away. He spit across the porch. "Wait a minute, Mrs. Armstid," he says. She stopped again. She didn't look at him. Flem went on into the store, with I. O. done quit rubbing his back now, with his head craned after Flem, and Mrs. Armstid standing there with her hands rolled into her dress, not looking at nothing. A wagon come up the road and passed; it was Freeman, on the way to town. Then Flem come out again, with I. O. still watching him. Flem had one of these little striped sacks of Jody Varner's candy; I bet he still owes Jody that nickel, too. He put the sack into Mrs. Armstid's hand like he would have put it into a hollow stump. He spit again across the porch. "A little sweetening for the chaps," he says.

"You're right kind," Mrs. Armstid says. She held the sack of candy in her hand, not looking at nothing. Eck's boy was watching the sack, the half-et cracker in his hand; he wasn't chewing now. He watched Mrs. Armstid roll the sack into her apron. "I reckon I better get on back and help with dinner," she says. She turned and went back across the porch. Flem set down in the chair again and opened his knife. He spit across the porch again, past Mrs. Armstid where she hadn't went down the steps yet. Then she went on, in that ere sunbonnet and wrapper all the same color, back down the road toward Mrs. Littlejohn's. You couldn't see her dress move, like a natural woman walking. She looked like a old snag still standing up and moving along on a high water. We watched her turn in at Mrs. Littlejohn's and go outen sight. Flem was whittling. I. O. begun to rub his back on the door. Then he begun to cackle, just like a durn hen.

"You boys might just as well quit trying," I. O. says. "You can't git ahead of Flem. You can't touch him. Ain't he a sight, now?"

I be dog if he ain't. If I had brung a herd of wild cattymounts into town and sold them to my neighbors and kinfolks, they would have lynched me. Yes, sir.

1930

---

21 **You're right kind.** In **The Hamlet** the three concluding paragraphs here become two paragraphs, reading as follows: " 'You're right kind,' she said. She rolled the sack into the apron, the little boy's unwinking gaze fixed upon the lump her hands made beneath the cloth. She moved again. 'I reckon I better get on and help with dinner,' she said. She descended the steps, though as soon as she reached the level earth and began to retreat, the gray folds of the garment once more lost all inference and intimation of locomotion, so that she seemed to progress without motion like a figure on a retreating and diminishing flood; a gray and blasted tree-trunk moving, somehow intact and upright, upon an unhurried flood. The clerk in the doorway cackled suddenly, explosively, chortling. He slapped his thigh.

" 'By God,' he said, 'You can't beat him.' "

Ernest Hemingway

1898 ·

Ernest Hemingway was born in Oak Park, Illinois, in 1898. He went through high school, winning some fame in boxing and football, and then became a reporter on the *Kansas City Star*. During World War I, he served on the Italian front. In postwar days, as a newspaper correspondent, he was one of the expatriates who inhabited the Left Bank in Paris. He began to write fiction, and was "discovered" by the critics in the United States. He returned to his homeland to write, going abroad now and then for travel in Europe or for big game hunting in Africa. During the Spanish Revolution and World War II he was a correspondent.

Hemingway transmutes his own experiences in his writings. Those in his first impressive book, *In Our Time* (1924), are based upon his boyhood vacations in Michigan. Those in *Men Without Women* (1927), including the two printed here, treat prewar, war, and postwar experiences at home and abroad.

His first novel, *The Sun Also Rises* (1926), depicts the war-disillusioned young people of the Left Bank. His second, *A Farewell to Arms* (1929), has for its scene the Italy of World War I, for its plot the story of the disillusionment of a young American in an ambulance unit.

These early works and others established Hemingway as the fictional laureate of "the lost generation." His experiences had been typical of this generation—his youth in America, his service in World War I, his disillusionment, and his stay in Paris. The pattern was completed when, during the Spanish Civil War, while writing of the conflict for the North American Newspaper Alliance, he discovered a more affirmative faith in democratic society and the duty and destiny of the individual.

This faith was announced in a novel, *To Have and Have Not* (1937), and a play, *The Fifth Column* (1938), both of which were far below the standard set by his earlier works. Evidently, the problem of asserting his new beliefs in artistic form was a difficult one for him to solve. In the novel *For Whom the Bell Tolls* (1940), however, he successfully coped with the problem. The novel won the admiration not only of critics but also of a huge reading public. Like Hemingway, it appeared, the people of the United States in this period had regained faith in an organized society—the sort of faith that the

book attributed to its hero, Robert Jordan, in the hours before his death. Hemingway's first postwar novel, *Across the River and into the Trees* (1950), marked no perceivable progress in his development, but a novelette, *The Old Man and the Sea* (1952), was praised by critics as an incisive artistic embodiment of some favorite themes and won for him a Pulitzer Prize.

During both his earlier and his later periods, Hemingway as a writer is indebted to Mark Twain as well as to Sherwood Anderson, Gertrude Stein, and Stephen Crane. He has been influenced by Twain's style, which, though like oral speech, was notable for its poetic overtones. Anderson and Miss Stein, whom he knew in Paris, probably encouraged him to cultivate this apparently naïve colloquial style. From them, too, he may have received instruction in emphasizing basic emotions which led Oscar Cargill to classify him, as well as these two teachers of his, as "Primitivists." At any rate, whether his narratives depict Midwestern adolescents or Left Bank sophisticates, the relatively uncomplicated drives of passion, hate, hunger, fear, and courage are consistently central in them. From Crane, by contrast, Hemingway perhaps learned something about handling symbolic or connotative details to give prose what he calls "a fourth or fifth dimension." A result is that, in this author's best narratives, there is a unique combination of strength—even at times brutality—with poetic subtlety and depth of sympathy which appeals greatly to modern readers.

Alfred Kazin, **On Native Grounds: An Interpretation of Modern American Prose Literature**, New York, 1942 • Maxwell Geismar, **Writers in Crisis: The American Novel Between Two Wars**, Boston, 1942 • Malcolm Cowley, "Introduction" to **The Portable Hemingway**, New York, 1944 • Robert Penn Warren, "Hemingway," **Kenyon Review** Winter 1947 • Philip Young, **Ernest Hemingway**, New York, 1952

The Killers

T he door of Henry's lunch-room opened and two men came in. They sat down at the counter.

"What's yours?" George asked them.

"I don't know," one of the men said. "What do you want to eat, Al?"

"I don't know," said Al. "I don't know what I want to eat."

Outside it was getting dark. The street-light came on

From **Men Without Women** by Ernest Hemingway; published by Charles Scribner's Sons; copyright, 1927, by Charles Scribner's Sons; used by permission of the publishers

outside the window. The two men at the counter read the menu. From the other end of the counter Nick Adams watched them. He had been talking to George when they came in.

"I'll have a roast pork tenderloin with apple sauce and mashed potatoes," the first man said.

"It isn't ready yet."

"What the hell do you put it on the card for?"

"That's the dinner," George explained. "You can get 10 that at six o'clock."

George looked at the clock on the wall behind the counter.

"It's five o'clock."

"The clock says twenty minutes past five," the second man said.

"It's twenty minutes fast."

"Oh, to hell with the clock," the first man said. "What have you got to eat?"

"I can give you any kind of sandwiches," George said. 20 "You can have ham and eggs, bacon and eggs, liver and bacon, or a steak."

"Give me chicken croquettes with green peas and cream sauce and mashed potatoes."

"That's the dinner."

"Everything we want's the dinner, eh? That's the way you work it."

"I can give you ham and eggs, bacon and eggs, liver—"

"I'll take ham and eggs," the man called Al said. He 30 wore a derby hat and a black overcoat buttoned across the chest. His face was small and white and he had tight lips. He wore a silk muffler and gloves.

"Give me bacon and eggs," said the other man. He was about the same size as Al. Their faces were different, but they were dressed like twins. Both wore overcoats too tight for them. They sat leaning forward, their elbows on the counter.

"Got anything to drink?" Al asked.

"Silver beer, bevo, ginger-ale," George said.

40 "I mean you got anything to *drink?*"

"Just those I said."

"This is a hot town," said the other. "What do they call it?"

"Summit."

"Ever hear of it?" Al asked his friend.

"No," said the friend.

"What do you do here nights?" Al asked.

"They eat the dinner," his friend said. "They all come here and eat the big dinner."

"That's right," George said. 50

"So you think that's right?" Al asked George.

"Sure."

"You're a pretty bright boy, aren't you?"

"Sure," said George.

"Well, you're not," said the other little man. "Is he, Al?"

"He's dumb," said Al. He turned to Nick. "What's your name?"

"Adams."

"Another bright boy," Al said. "Ain't he a bright boy, Max?" 60

"The town's full of bright boys," Max said.

George put the two platters, one of ham and eggs, the other of bacon and eggs, on the counter. He set down two side-dishes of fried potatoes and closed the wicket into the kitchen.

"Which is yours?" he asked Al.

"Don't you remember?"

"Ham and eggs."

"Just a bright boy," Max said. He leaned forward and took the ham and eggs. Both men ate with their gloves 70 on. George watched them eat.

"What are *you* looking at?" Max looked at George.

"Nothing."

"The hell you were. You were looking at me."

"Maybe the boy meant it for a joke, Max," Al said. George laughed.

"*You* don't have to laugh," Max said to him. "*You* don't have to laugh at all, see?"

"All right," said George.

"So he thinks it's all right." Max turned to Al. "He 80 thinks it's all right. That's a good one."

"Oh, he's a thinker," Al said. They went on eating.

"What's the bright boy's name down the counter?" Al asked Max.

"Hey, bright boy," Max said to Nick. "You go around on the other side of the counter with your boy friend."

"What's the idea?" Nick asked.

"There isn't any idea."

"You better go around, bright boy," Al said. Nick went around behind the counter. 90

"What's the idea?" George asked.

"None of your damn business," Al said. "Who's out in the kitchen?"

"The nigger."

"What do you mean the nigger?"

"The nigger that cooks."

"Tell him to come in."

"What's the idea?"

"Tell him to come in."

"Where do you think you are?"

"We know damn well where we are," the man called Max said. "Do we look silly?"

"You talk silly," Al said to him. "What the hell do you argue with this kid for? Listen," he said to George, "tell the nigger to come out here."

"What are you going to do to him?"

"Nothing. Use your head, bright boy. What would we do to a nigger?"

George opened the slit that opened back into the kitchen. "Sam," he called. "Come in here a minute."

The door to the kitchen opened and the nigger came in. "What was it?" he asked. The two men at the counter took a look at him.

"All right, nigger. You stand right there," Al said.

Sam, the nigger, standing in his apron, looked at the two men sitting at the counter. "Yes, sir," he said. Al got down from his stool.

"I'm going back to the kitchen with the nigger and bright boy," he said. "Go on back to the kitchen, nigger. You go with him, bright boy." The little man walked after Nick and Sam, the cook, back into the kitchen. The door shut after them. The man called Max sat at the counter opposite George. He didn't look at George but looked in the mirror that ran along back of the counter. Henry's had been made over from a saloon into a lunch-counter.

"Well, bright boy," Max said, looking into the mirror, "why don't you say something?"

"What's it all about?"

"Hey, Al," Max called, "bright boy wants to know what it's all about."

"Why don't you tell him?" Al's voice came from the kitchen.

"What do you think it's all about?"

"I don't know."

"What do you think?"

Max looked into the mirror all the time he was talking.

"I wouldn't say."

"Hey, Al, bright boy says he wouldn't say what he thinks it's all about."

"I can hear you, all right," Al said from the kitchen. He had propped open the slit that dishes passed through into the kitchen with a catsup bottle. "Listen, bright boy," he said from the kitchen to George. "Stand a little further along the bar. You move a little to the left, Max." He was like a photographer arranging for a group picture.

"Talk to me, bright boy," Max said. "What do you think's going to happen?"

George did not say anything.

"I'll tell you," Max said. "We're going to kill a Swede. Do you know a big Swede named Ole Andreson?"

"Yes."

"He comes here to eat every night, don't he?"

"Sometimes he comes here."

"He comes here at six o'clock, don't he?"

"If he comes."

"We know all that, bright boy," Max said. "Talk about something else. Ever go to the movies?"

"Once in a while."

"You ought to go to the movies more. The movies are fine for a bright boy like you."

"What are you going to kill Ole Andreson for? What did he ever do to you?"

"He never had a chance to do anything to us. He never even seen us."

"And he's only going to see us once," Al said from the kitchen.

"What are you going to kill him for, then?" George asked.

"We're killing him for a friend. Just to oblige a friend, bright boy."

"Shut up," said Al from the kitchen. "You talk too goddam much."

"Well, I got to keep bright boy amused. Don't I, bright boy?"

"You talk too damn much," Al said. "The nigger and my bright boy are amused by themselves. I got them tied up like a couple of girl friends in the convent."

"I suppose you were in a convent?"

"You never know."

"You were in a kosher convent. That's where you were."

George looked up at the clock.

"If anybody comes in you tell them the cook is off, and if they keep after it, you tell them you'll go back and cook yourself. Do you get that, bright boy?"

"All right," George said. "What you going to do with us afterward?"

"That'll depend," Max said. "That's one of those things you never know at the time."

George looked up at the clock. It was a quarter past six. The door from the street opened. A street-car motorman came in.

"Hello, George," he said. "Can I get supper?"

"Sam's gone out," George said. "He'll be back in about half an hour."

"I'd better go up the street," the motorman said. George looked at the clock. It was twenty minutes past six.

"That was nice, bright boy," Max said. "You're a regular little gentleman."

"He knew I'd blow his head off," Al said from the kitchen.

"No," said Max. "It ain't that. Bright boy is nice. He's a nice boy. I like him."

At six-fifty-five George said: "He's not coming."

Two other people had been in the lunch-room. Once George had gone out to the kitchen and made a ham-and-egg sandwich "to go" that a man wanted to take with him. Inside the kitchen he saw Al, his derby hat tipped back, sitting on a stool beside the wicket with the muzzle of a sawed off shotgun resting on the ledge. Nick and the cook were back to back in the corner, a towel tied in each of their mouths. George had cooked the sandwich, wrapped it up in oiled paper, put it in a bag, brought it in, and the man had paid for it and gone out.

"Bright boy can do everything," Max said. "He can cook and everything. You'd make some girl a nice wife, bright boy."

"Yes?" George said. "Your friend, Ole Andreson, isn't going to come."

"We'll give him ten minutes," Max said.

Max watched the mirror and the clock. The hands of the clock marked seven o'clock, and then five minutes past seven.

"Come on, Al," said Max. "We better go. He's not coming."

"Better give him five minutes," Al said from the kitchen.

In the five minutes a man came in, and George explained that the cook was sick.

"Why the hell don't you get another cook?" the man asked. "Aren't you running a lunch-counter?" He went out.

"Come on, Al," Max said.

"What about the two bright boys and the nigger?"

"They're all right."

"You think so?"

"Sure. We're through with it."

"I don't like it," said Al. "It's sloppy. You talk too much."

"Oh, what the hell," said Max. "We got to keep amused, haven't we?"

"You talk too much, all the same," Al said. He came out from the kitchen. The cut-off barrels of the shotgun made a slight bulge under the waist of his too tight-fitting overcoat. He straightened his coat with his gloved hands.

"So long, bright boy," he said to George. "You got a lot of luck."

"That's the truth," Max said. "You ought to play the races, bright boy."

The two of them went out the door. George watched them, through the window, pass under the arc-light and cross the street. In their tight overcoats and derby hats they looked like a vaudeville team. George went back through the swinging-door into the kitchen and untied Nick and the cook.

"I don't want any more of that," said Sam, the cook. "I don't want any more of that."

Nick stood up. He had never had a towel in his mouth before.

"Say," he said. "What the hell?" He was trying to swagger it off.

"They were going to kill Ole Andreson," George said. "They were going to shoot him when he came in to eat."

"Ole Andreson?"

"Sure."

The cook felt the corners of his mouth with his thumbs.

"They all gone?" he asked.

"Yeah," said George. "They're gone now."

"I don't like it," said the cook. "I don't like any of it at all."

"Listen," George said to Nick. "You better go see Ole Andreson."

"All right."

"You better not have anything to do with it at all," Sam, the cook, said. "You better stay way out of it."

"Don't go if you don't want to," George said.

"Mixing up in this ain't going to get you anywhere," the cook said. "You stay out of it."

"I'll go see him," Nick said to George. "Where does he live?"

The cook turned away.

"Little boys always know what they want to do," he said.

"He lives up at Hirsch's rooming-house," George said to Nick.

"I'll go up there."

Outside the arc-light shone through the bare branches of a tree. Nick walked up the street beside the car-tracks and turned at the next arc-light down a side-street. Three houses up the street was Hirsch's rooming-house. Nick walked up the two steps and pushed the bell. A woman came to the door.

"Is Ole Andreson here?"

"Do you want to see him?"

"Yes, if he's in."

Nick followed the woman up a flight of stairs and back to the end of a corridor. She knocked on the door.

"Who is it?"

"It's somebody to see you, Mr. Andreson," the woman said.

"It's Nick Adams."

"Come in."

Nick opened the door and went into the room. Ole Andreson was lying on the bed with all his clothes on. He had been a heavyweight prizefighter and he was too long for the bed. He lay with his head on two pillows. He did not look at Nick.

"What was it?" he asked.

"I was up at Henry's," Nick said, "and two fellows came in and tied up me and the cook, and they said they were going to kill you."

It sounded silly when he said it. Ole Andreson said nothing.

"They put us out in the kitchen," Nick went on. "They were going to shoot you when you came to supper."

Ole Andreson looked at the wall and did not say anything.

"George thought I better come and tell you about it."

"There isn't anything I can do about it," Ole Andreson said.

"I'll tell you what they were like."

"I don't want to know what they were like," Ole Andreson said. He looked at the wall. "Thanks for coming to tell me about it."

"That's all right."

Nick looked at the big man lying on the bed.

"Don't you want me to go and see the police?"

"No," Ole Andreson said. "That wouldn't do any good."

"Isn't there something I could do?"

"No. There isn't anything to do."

"Maybe it was just a bluff."

"No. It ain't just a bluff."

Ole Andreson rolled over toward the wall.

"The only thing is," he said, talking toward the wall, "I just can't make up my mind to go out. I been in here all day."

"Couldn't you get out of town?"

"No," Ole Andreson said. "I'm through with all that running around."

He looked at the wall.

"There ain't anything to do now."

"Couldn't you fix it up some way?"

"No. I got in wrong." He talked in the same flat voice. "There ain't anything to do. After a while I'll make up my mind to go out."

"I better go back and see George," Nick said.

"So long," said Ole Andreson. He did not look toward Nick. "Thanks for coming around."

Nick went out. As he shut the door he saw Ole Andreson with all his clothes on, lying on the bed looking at the wall.

"He's been in his room all day," the landlady said down-stairs. "I guess he don't feel well. I said to him: 'Mr. Andreson, you ought to go out and take a walk on a nice fall day like this,' but he didn't feel like it."

"He doesn't want to go out."

"I'm sorry he don't feel well," the woman said. "He's an awfully nice man. He was in the ring, you know."

"I know it."

"You'd never know it except from the way his face is," the woman said. They stood talking just inside the street door. "He's just as gentle."

"Well, good-night, Mrs. Hirsch," Nick said.

"I'm not Mrs. Hirsch," the woman said. "She owns the place. I just look after it for her. I'm Mrs. Bell."

"Well, good-night, Mrs. Bell," Nick said.

"Good-night," the woman said.

Nick walked up the dark street to the corner under the arc-light, and then along the car-tracks to Henry's eating-house. George was inside, back of the counter.

"Did you see Ole?"

"Yes," said Nick. "He's in his room and he won't go out."

The cook opened the door from the kitchen when he heard Nick's voice.

"I don't even listen to it," he said and shut the door.

"Did you tell him about it?" George asked.

"Sure. I told him but he knows what it's all about."

"What's he going to do?"

"Nothing."

"They'll kill him."

"I guess they will."

"He must have got mixed up in something in Chicago." 20

"I guess so," said Nick.

"It's a hell of a thing."

"It's an awful thing," Nick said.

They did not say anything. George reached down for a towel and wiped the counter.

"I wonder what he did?" Nick said.

"Double-crossed somebody. That's what they kill them for."

"I'm going to get out of this town," Nick said.

"Yes," said George. "That's a good thing to do." 30

"I can't stand to think about him waiting in the room and knowing he's going to get it. It's too damned awful."

"Well," said George, "you better not think about it."

1927

In Another Country

(handwritten annotations: "Machines are used — to help putting up wound / from service" "Medals for being in service" "Milan")

In the fall the war was always there, but we did not go to it any more. It was cold in the fall in Milan and the dark came very early. Then the electric lights came on, and it was pleasant along the streets looking in the windows. There was much game hanging outside the shops, and the snow powdered in the fur of the foxes and the wind blew their tails. The deer hung stiff and heavy and empty, and small birds blew in the wind and the wind turned their feathers. It was a cold fall and the wind came down from the mountains.

We were all at the hospital every afternoon, and there were different ways of walking across the town through the dusk to the hospital. Two of the ways were alongside canals, but they were long. Always, though, you crossed a bridge across a canal to enter the hospital. There was a choice of three bridges. On one of them a woman sold roasted chestnuts. It was warm, standing in front of her charcoal fire, and the chestnuts were warm afterward in your pocket. The hospital was very old and very beautiful, and you entered through a gate and 20 walked across a courtyard and out a gate on the other side. There were usually funerals starting from the courtyard. Beyond the old hospital were the new brick pavilions, and there we met every afternoon and were all very polite and interested in what was the matter, and sat in the machines that were to make so much difference.

The doctor came up to the machine where I was sitting and said: "What did you like best to do before the war? Did you practice a sport?"

I said: "Yes, football." 30

"Good," he said. "You will be able to play football again better than ever."

My knee did not bend and the leg dropped straight from the knee to the ankle without a calf, and the machine was to bend the knee and make it move as in riding a tricycle. But it did not bend yet, and instead the machine lurched when it came to the bending part. The doctor said: "That will all pass. You are a fortunate young man. You will play football again like a champion."

In the next machine was a major who had a little hand 40

(handwritten annotation: "Soldiers — hunting hawks —")

withered

like a baby's. He winked at me when the doctor examined his hand, which was between two leather straps that bounced up and down and flapped the stiff fingers, and said: "And will I too play football, captain-doctor?" He had been a very great fencer, and before the war the greatest fencer in Italy.

The doctor went to his office in the back room and brought a photograph which showed a hand that had been withered almost as small as the major's, before it had taken a machine course, and after was a little larger. The major held the photograph with his good hand and looked at it very carefully. "A wound?" he asked.

"An industrial accident," the doctor said.

"Very interesting, very interesting," the major said, and handed it back to the doctor.

"You have confidence?"

"No," said the major.

There were three boys who came each day who were about the same age I was. They were all three from Milan, and one of them was to be a lawyer, and one was to be a painter, and one had intended to be a soldier, and after we were finished with the machines, sometimes we walked back together to the Café Cova, which was next door to the Scala. We walked the short way through the communist quarter because we were four together. The people hated us because we were officers, and from a wine-shop some one called out, "A basso gli ufficiali!" as we passed. Another boy who walked with us sometimes and made us five wore a black silk handkerchief across his face because he had no nose then and his face was to be rebuilt. He had gone out to the front from the military academy and been wounded within an hour after he had gone into the front line for the first time. They rebuilt his face, but he came from a very old family and they could never get the nose exactly right. He went to South America and worked in a bank. But this was a long time ago, and then we did not any of us know how it was going to be afterward. We only knew then that there was always the war, but that we were not going to it any more.

We all had the same medals, except the boy with the black silk bandage across his face, and he had not been at the front long enough to get any medals. The tall boy with a very pale face who was to be a lawyer had been a lieutenant of Arditi and had three medals of the sort we each had only one of. He had lived a very long time with death and was a little detached. We were all a little detached, and there was nothing that held us together except that we met every afternoon at the hospital. Although, as we walked to the Cova through the tough part of town, walking in the dark, with light and singing coming out of the wine-shops, and sometimes having to walk into the street when the men and women would crowd together on the sidewalk so that we would have had to jostle them to get by, we felt held together by there being something that had happened that they, the people who disliked us, did not understand.

We ourselves all understood the Cova, where it was rich and warm and not too brightly lighted, and noisy and smoky at certain hours, and there were always girls at the tables and the illustrated papers on a rack on the wall. The girls at the Cova were very patriotic, and I found that the most patriotic people in Italy were the café girls—and I believe they are still patriotic.

The boys at first were very polite about my medals and asked me what I had done to get them. I showed them the papers, which were written in a very beautiful language and full of *fratellanza* and *abnegazione,* but which really said, with the adjectives removed, that I had been given the medals because I was an American. After that their manner changed a little toward me, although I was their friend against outsiders. I was a friend, but I was never really one of them after they had read the citations, because it had been different with them and they had done very different things to get their medals. I had been wounded, it was true; but we all knew that being wounded, after all, was really an accident. I was never ashamed of the ribbons, though, and sometimes, after the cocktail hour, I would imagine myself having done all the things they had done to get their medals; but walking home at night through the empty streets with the cold wind and all the shops closed, trying to keep near the street lights, I knew that I would never have done such things, and I was very much afraid to die, and often lay in bed at night by myself, afraid to die and wondering how I would be when I went back to the front again.

The three with the medals were like hunting-hawks;

---

27 A basso . . . ufficiali! Down with the officers! • 68 fratellanza, brotherhood • 68 abnegazione, sacrifice

and I was not a hawk, although I might seem a hawk to those who have never hunted; they, the three, knew better and so we drifted apart. But I stayed good friends with the boy who had been wounded his first day at the front, because he would never know how he would have turned out; so he could never be accepted either, and I liked him because I thought perhaps he would not have turned out to be a hawk either.

10 The major, who had been the great fencer, did not believe in bravery, and spent much time while we sat in the machines correcting my grammar. He had complimented me on how I spoke Italian, and we talked together very easily. One day I had said that Italian seemed such an easy language to me that I could not take a great interest in it; everything was so easy to say. "Ah, yes," the major said. "Why, then, do you not take up the use of grammar?" So we took up the use of grammar, and soon Italian was such a different language that I was afraid to talk to him until I had the grammar straight in my mind.

20 The major came very regularly to the hospital. I do not think he ever missed a day, although I am sure he did not believe in the machines. There was a time when none of us believed in the machines, and one day the major said it was all nonsense. The machines were new then and it was we who were to prove them. It was an idiotic idea, he said, "a theory, like another." I had not learned my grammar, and he said I was a stupid impossible disgrace, and he was a fool to have bothered with me. He was a small man and he sat straight up in his chair 30 with his right hand thrust into the machine and looked straight ahead at the wall while the straps thumped up and down with his fingers in them.

"What will you do when the war is over if it is over?" he asked me. "Speak grammatically!"

"I will go to the States."

"Are you married?"

"No, but I hope to be."

"The more of a fool you are," he said. He seemed very angry. "A man must not marry."

40 "Why, Signor Maggiore?"

"Don't call me 'Signor Maggiore.'"

"Why must not a man marry?"

"He cannot marry. He cannot marry," he said angrily. "If he is to lose everything, he should not place himself in a position to lose that. He should not place himself in a position to lose. He should find things he cannot lose."

He spoke very angrily and bitterly, and looked straight ahead while he talked.

"But why should he necessarily lose it?"

"He'll lose it," the major said. He was looking at the 50 wall. Then he looked down at the machine and jerked his little hand out from between the straps and slapped it hard against his thigh. "He'll lose it," he almost shouted. "Don't argue with me!" Then he called to the attendant who ran the machines. "Come and turn this damned thing off."

He went back into the other room for the light treatment and the massage. Then I heard him ask the doctor if he might use his telephone and he shut the door. When he came back into the room, I was sitting in another ma- 60 chine. He was wearing his cape and had his cap on, and he came directly toward my machine and put his arm on my shoulder.

"I am so sorry," he said, and patted me on the shoulder with his good hand. "I would not be rude. My wife has just died. You must forgive me."

"Oh—" I said, feeling sick for him. "I am so sorry."

He stood there biting his lower lip. "It is very difficult," he said. "I cannot resign myself."

He looked straight past me and out through the win- 70 dow. Then he began to cry. "I am utterly unable to resign myself," he said and choked. And then crying, his head up looking at nothing, carrying himself straight and soldierly, with tears on both his cheeks and biting his lips, he walked past the machines and out the door.

The doctor told me that the major's wife, who was very young and whom he had not married until he was definitely invalided out of the war, had died of pneumonia. She had been sick only a few days. No one expected her to die. The major did not come to the hospital 80 for three days. Then he came at the usual hour, wearing a black band on the sleeve of his uniform. When he came back, there were large framed photographs around the wall, of all sorts of wounds before and after they had been cured by the machines. In front of the machine the major used were three photographs of hands like his that were completely restored. I do not know where the doctor got them. I always understood we were the first to use the machines. The photographs did not make much difference to the major because he only looked out of 90 the window.

1927

Thomas Wolfe

1900 · 1938

Thomas Wolfe was born and grew up in Asheville, North Carolina, which is situated high in the Smokies and is described with remarkable completeness in his *Look Homeward, Angel.* After graduating from the University of North Carolina, Wolfe studied at Harvard, taught at New York University, and traveled in England and France. His *Of Time and the River* is the best account in literature of a Southerner's discovery of the world outside the South and his loneliness, his feeling of strangeness, in alien places.

Wolfe's reputation rests securely upon four powerful books. *Look Homeward, Angel* (1929) and *Of Time and the River* (1935) tell the story of Eugene Gant; *The Web and the Rock* (1939) and *You Can't Go Home Again* (1940) tell the story of George Webber. Both Gant and Webber are obviously the author himself. If the third and fourth volumes show a growing maturity of thought and style, they have less of the poetic fire, the romantic abandon, which made the first and second volumes such remarkable works. It is doubtful if a romantic genius is ever improved by sobriety. For Wolfe was a great romantic genius with all of the vitality, the exuberance, the undisciplined ardor which the name implies. He was Wordsworth's "creature moving about in worlds not realized." His closest affinities were with Coleridge, whom he often quoted, and with Whitman, whom he obviously emulated. His prose at its best has a lyrical exaltation; at its worst, it is so unpruned as to verge on the bombastic. His books have the vices as well as the virtues of great romantic writing.

Wolfe attempted a synthesis of America. His aim, like Whitman's, was to absorb America into himself and to express America subjectively and emotionally through his own life-experience. He possessed enormous capacities for feeling and passionate living. "It was not his quality as a romantic," he declared of Eugene Gant, "to escape out of life, but into it. Men do not escape from life because life is dull, but life escapes from men because men are little." Wolfe was not concerned with political and social reform. Of Gant, he said, "He had no greater need for rebellion than have most Americans, which is none at all." Except toward the end of his last book (where he spoke, somewhat vaguely, of the need for "the complete revision of the structure of society as we know it"), Wolfe's great concern was to crowd into every moment the maximum of vital experience. He was convinced that the world—and preëminently America, which, unlike the expatriates of his generation, he was never tempted to renounce—"was full of pleasant places, enchanted places." More eloquently than any other writer since Whitman, Wolfe restated the American dream: the right of every man "to live, to work, to be himself, to become whatever thing his manhood and his vision can combine to make him."

Thomas Wolfe's Letters to His Mother, ed. J. S. Terry, New York, 1943 • J. P. Bishop, "The Sorrows of Thomas Wolfe," The Kenyon Review, Gambier, Ohio, Winter 1939

From

Of Time and the River

The following selection recalls, with certain differences, Whitman's "Song of Myself" (see p. 148). Notable, among other things, are the rich sense impressions, the passionate attachment to the South ("the hills of home"), and the great fondness for trains, which were important to Wolfe as a means of exploration and adventure and as a symbol not only of these but of American achievement and of American unity.

YOUNG FAUSTUS

We are so lost, so naked and so lonely in America. Immense and cruel skies bend over us, and all of us are driven on forever and we have no home. Therefore, it is not the slow, the punctual sanded dip of the unnumbered days that we remember best, the ash of time; nor is it the huge monotone of the lost years, the unswerving schedules of the lost life and the well-known faces, that we remember best. It is a face seen once and lost forever in a crowd, an eye that looked, a face that smiled and
10 vanished on a passing train, it is a prescience of snow upon a certain night, the laughter of a woman in a summer street long years ago, it is the memory of a single moon seen at the pine's dark edge in old October—and all of our lives is written in the twisting of a leaf upon a bough, a door that opened, and a stone.

For America has a thousand lights and weathers and we walk the streets, we walk the streets forever, we walk the streets of life alone.

It is the place of the howling winds, the hurrying of
20 the leaves in old October, the hard clean falling to the earth of acorns. The place of the storm-tossed moaning of the wintry mountainside, where the young men cry out in their throats and feel the savage vigor, the rude strong energies; the place also where the trains cross rivers.

It is a fabulous country, the only fabulous country; it is the one place where miracles not only happen, but where they happen all the time.

It is the place of exultancy and strong joy, the place
30 of the darkened brooding air, the smell of snow; it is the place of all the fierce, the bitten colors in October, when all of the wild, sweet woods flame up; it is also the place of the cider press and the last brown oozings of the York Imperials. It is the place of the lovely girls with good jobs and the husky voices, who will buy a round of drinks; it is the place where the women with fine legs and silken underwear lie in the pullman berth below you, it is the place of the dark-green snore of the pullman cars, and the voices in the night-time in Virginia.

It is the place where great boats are baying at the
40 harbor's mouth, where great ships are putting out to sea; it is the place where great boats are blowing in the gulf of night, and where the river, the dark and secret river, full of strange time, is forever flowing by us to the sea.

The tugs keep baying in the river; at twelve o'clock the Berengaria *moans, her lights slide gently past the piers beyond Eleventh Street; and in the night a tall tree falls in Old Catawba, there in the hills of home.*

It is the place of autumnal moons hung low and orange at the frosty edges of the pines; it is the place of frost
50 and silence, of the clean dry shocks and the opulence of enormous pumpkins that yellow on hard clotted earth; it is the place of the stir and feathery stumble of the hens upon their roost, the frosty, broken barking of the dogs, the great barnshapes and solid shadows in the running sweep of the moon-whited countryside, the wailing whistle of the fast express. It is the place of flares and steamings on the tracks, and the swing and bob and tottering dance of lanterns in the yards; it is the place of dings and knellings and the sudden glare
60 of mighty engines over sleeping faces in the night; it is the place of the terrific web and spread and smouldering, the distant glare of Philadelphia and the solid rumble of the sleepers; it is also the place where the Transcontinental Limited is stroking eighty miles an hour across the continent and the small dark towns whip by like bullets, and there is only the fanlike stroke of the secret, immense and lonely earth again.

I have foreseen this picture many times: I will buy passage on the Fast Express.
70

From **Of Time and the River** by Thomas Wolfe; published by Charles Scribner's Sons; copyright 1935 by Charles Scribner's Sons • Used by permission of the publishers
48 **Catawba,** a county in western North Carolina

It is the place of the wild and exultant winter's morning and the wind, with the powdery snow, that has been howling all night long; it is the place of solitude and the branches of the spruce and hemlock piled with snow; it is the place where the Fall River boats are tethered to the wharf, and the wild gray snow of furious, secret, and storm-whited morning whips across them. It is the place of the lodge by the frozen lake and the sweet breath and amorous flesh of sinful woman; it is the place of the tragic and lonely beauty of New England; it is the place of the red barn and the sound of the stabled hooves and of bright tatters of old circus posters; it is the place of the immense and pungent smell of breakfast, the country sausages and the ham and eggs, the smoking wheat cakes and the fragrant coffee, and of lone hunters in the frosty thickets who whistle to their lop-eared hounds.

Where is old Doctor Ballard now with all his dogs? He held that they were sacred, that the souls of all the dear lost dead went into them. His youngest sister's soul sat on the seat beside him; she had long ears and her eyes were sad. Two dozen of his other cherished dead trotted around the buggy as he went up the hill past home. And that was eleven years ago, and I was nine years old; and I stared gravely out the window of my father's house at old Doctor Ballard.

It is the place of the straight stare, the cold white bellies and the buried lust of the lovely Boston girls; it is the place of ripe brainless blondes with tender lips and a flowery smell, and of the girls with shapely arms who stand on ladders picking oranges; it is also the place where large slow-bodied girls from Kansas City, with big legs and milky flesh, are sent East to school by their rich fathers, and there are also immense and lovely girls, with the grip of a passionate bear, who have such names as Neilson, Lundquist, Jorgenson and Brandt.

I will go up and down the country, and back and forth across the country on the great trains that thunder over America. I will go out West where States are square; Oh, I will go to Boise, and Helena and Albuquerque. I will go to Montana and the two Dakotas and the unknown places.

It is the place of violence and sudden death; of the fast shots in the night, the club of the Irish cop, and the smell of brains and blood upon the pavement; it is the place of the small-town killings, and the men who shoot the lovers of their wives; it is the place where the Negroes slash with razors and the hillmen kill in the mountain meadows; it is the place of the ugly drunks and the snarling voices and of foul-mouthed men who want to fight; it is the place of the loud word and the foolish boast and the violent threat; it is also the place of the deadly little men with white faces and the eyes of reptiles, who kill quickly and casually in the dark; it is the lawless land that feeds on murder.

"Did you know the two Lipe girls?" he asked. "Yes," I said. "They lived in Biltburn by the river, and one of them was drowned in the flood. She was a cripple, and she wheeled herself along in a chair. She was strong as a bull." "That's the girl," he said.

It is the place of the crack athletes and of the runners who limber up in March; it is the place of the ten-second men and the great jumpers and vaulters; it is the place where Spring comes, and the young birch trees have white and tender barks, of the thaw of the earth, and the feathery smoke of the trees; it is the place of the burst of grass and bud, the wild and sudden tenderness of the wilderness, and of the crews out on the river and the coaches coming down behind them in the motorboats, the surges rolling out behind when they are gone with heavy sudden wash. It is the place of the baseball players, and the easy lob, the soft spring smackings of the glove and mit, the crack of the bat; it is the place of the great batters, fielders, and pitchers, of the nigger boys and the white, drawling, shirt-sleeved men, the bleachers and the resinous smell of old worn wood; it is the place of Rube Waddell, the mighty untamed and ill-fated pitcher when his left arm is swinging like a lash. It is the place of the fighters, the crafty Jewish lightweights and the mauling Italians, Leonard, Tendler, Rocky Kansas, and Dundee; it is the place where the champion looks over his rival's shoulder with a bored expression.

I shall wake at morning in a foreign land thinking I heard a horse in one of the streets of home.

It is the place where they like to win always, and boast about their victories; it is the place of quick money and sudden loss; it is the place of the mile-long freights with their strong, solid, clanking, heavy loneliness at night, and of the silent freight of cars that

---

78 **Rube Waddell,** a great, though eccentric, southpaw **for Connie** Mack's Philadelphia Athletics

Of Time and the River 1135

curve away among raw piney desolations with their promise of new lands and unknown distances—the huge attentive gape of emptiness. It is the place where the bums come singly from the woods at sunset, the huge stillness of the watertower, the fading light, the rails, secret and alive, and trembling with the oncoming train; it is the place of the great tramps, Oklahoma Red, Fargo Pete, and the Jersey Dutchman, who grab fast rattlers for the Western shore; it is the place of old blown bums who come up in October skirls of dust and wind and crumpled newspapers and beg, with canned heat on their breaths: "Help Old McGuire: McGuire's a good guy, kid. You're not so tough, kid: McGuire's your pal, kid: How about McGuire, McGuire——?"

It is the place of the poolroom players and the drug-store boys; of the town whore and her paramour, the tough town driver; it is the place where they go to the woods on Sunday and get up among the laurel and dogwood bushes and the rhododendron blossoms; it is the place of the cheap hotels and the kids who wait with chattering lips while the nigger goes to get them their first woman; it is the place of the drunken college boys who spend the old man's money and wear fur coats to the football games; it is the place of the lovely girls up North who have rich fathers, of the beautiful wives of business men.

The train broke down somewhere beyond Manassas, and I went forward along the tracks with all the other passengers. "What's the matter?" I said to the engineer. "The eccentric strap is broken, son," he said. It was a very cold day, windy and full of sparkling sun. This was the farthest north I'd ever been, and I was twelve years old and on my way to Washington to see Woodrow Wilson inaugurated. Later I could not forget the face of the engineer and the words "eccentric strap."

It is the place of the immense and lonely earth, the place of fat ears and abundance where they grow cotton, corn, and wheat, the wine-red apples of October, and the good tobacco.

It is the place that is savage and cruel, but it is also the innocent place; it is the wild lawless place, the vital earth that is soaked with the blood of the murdered men, with the blood of the countless murdered men, with the blood of the unavenged and unremembered murdered men; but it is also the place of the child and laughter, where the young men are torn apart with ecstasy, and cry out in their throats with joy, where they hear the howl of the wind and the rain and smell the thunder and the soft numb spitting of the snow, where they are drunk with the bite and sparkle of the air and mad with the solar energy, where they believe in love and victory and think that they can never die.

It is the place where you come up through Virginia on the great trains in the night-time, and rumble slowly across the wide Potomac and see the morning sunlight on the nation's dome at Washington, and where the fat man shaving in the pullman washroom grunts, "What's this? What's this we're coming to—Washington?"— And the thin man glancing out the window says, "Yep, this is Washington. That's what it is, all right. You gettin' off here?"—And where the fat man grunts, "Who —me? Naw—I'm goin' on to Baltimore." It is the place where you get off at Baltimore and find your brother waiting.

Where is my father sleeping on the land? Buried? Dead these seven years? Forgotten, rotten in the ground? Held by his own great stone? No, no! Will I say, "Father" when I come to him? And will he call me, "Son"? Oh, no, he'll never see my face: we'll never speak except to say——

It is the place of the fast approach, the hot blind smoky passage, the tragic lonely beauty of New England, and the web of Boston; the place of the mighty station there, and engines passive as great cats, the straight dense plumes of engine smoke, the acrid and exciting smell of trains and stations, and of the man-swarm passing ever in its million-footed weft, the smell of the sea in harbors and the thought of voyages—and the place of the goat cry, the strong joy of our youth, the magic city, when we knew the most fortunate life on earth would certainly be ours, that we were twenty and could never die.

And always America is the place of the deathless and enraptured moments, the eye that looked, the mouth that smiled and vanished, and the word; the stone, the leaf, the door we never found and never have forgotten. And these are the things that we remember of America, for we have known all her thousand lights and weathers, and we walk the streets, we walk the streets forever, we walk the streets of life alone.

1935

From

You Can't Go Home Again

In an age which was becoming more and more collec-
tivistic in its political and social thinking, Wolfe argued
for the prerogatives of the individual. He feared that
collectivism would reduce the individual to anonymity.
To him as to Milton, "Fame is the spur that the clear
spirit doth raise." Deprived of "that last infirmity," he
thought, man would no longer be capable of the highest
aspirations and achievements.

THE PROMISE OF AMERICA

For four years George Webber lived and wrote in
Brooklyn, and during all this time his life was about as
solitary as any that a modern man can know. Loneliness,
far from being a rare and curious circumstance, is and
always has been the central and inevitable experience of
every man. Not only has this been true of the greatest
poets, as evidenced by the huge unhappiness of their
published grief, but now it seemed to George to apply
with equal force to all the nameless ciphers who swarmed
10 about him in the streets. As he saw them in their strident
encounters with each other, and overheard their never-
varying exchanges of abuse, contempt, distrust, and
hatred, it became increasingly clear to him that one of
the contributing causes of their complaint was loneliness.

To live alone as George was living, a man should
have the confidence of God, the tranquil faith of a monastic saint, the stern impregnability of Gibraltar. Lacking
these, he finds that there are times when anything, everything, all and nothing, the most trivial incidents, the
20 most casual words, can in an instant strip him of his
armor, palsy his hand, constrict his heart with frozen
horror, and fill his bowels with the grey substance of
shuddering impotence and desolation. Sometimes it
would be a sly remark dropped by some all-knowing
literary soothsayer in the columns of one of the more
leftish reviews, such as:

"Whatever has become of our autobiographical and
volcanic friend, George Webber? Remember him? Remember the splash he made with that so-called 'novel'
of his a few years back? Some of our esteemed col- 30
leagues thought they detected signs of promise there. We
ourselves should have welcomed another book from him,
just to prove that the first was not an accident. But
tempus fugit, and where is Webber? Calling Mr. Webber! No answer? Well, a pity, perhaps; but then, who
can count the number of one-book authors? They shoot
their bolt, and after that they go into the silence and no
more is heard from them. Some of us who were more
than a little doubtful about that book of Webber's, but
whose voices were drowned out by the Oh's and Ah's 40
of those who rushed headlong to proclaim a new star
rising in the literary firmament, could now come forward, if we weren't too kindly disposed toward our more
emotional brethren of the critical fraternity, and modestly say, 'We told you so!' "

Sometimes it would be nothing but a shadow passing
on the sun, sometimes nothing but the gelid light of
March falling on the limitless, naked, sprawling ugliness
and squalid decencies of Brooklyn streets. Whatever it
was, at such a time all joy and singing would go instantly 50
out of day, Webber's heart would drop out of him like a
leaden plummet, hope, confidence, and conviction would
seem lost forever to him, and all the high and shining
truth that he had ever found and lived and known
would now turn false to mock him. Then he would feel
like one who walked among the dead, and it would be
as if the only things that were not false on earth were
the creatures of the death-in-life who moved forever in
the changeless lights and weathers of red, waning, weary
March and Sunday afternoon. 60

These hideous doubts, despairs, and dark confusions
of the soul would come and go, and George knew them
as every lonely man must know them. For he was united
to no image save that image which he himself created.
He was bolstered by no knowledge save that which he
gathered for himself out of his own life. He saw life
with no other vision save the vision of his own eyes
and brain and senses. He was sustained and cheered and
aided by no party, was given comfort by no creed, and had
no faith in him except his own. 70

---

29 **so-called 'novel.'** The reference is to **Look Homeward, Angel**

That faith, though it was made up of many articles, was at bottom a faith in himself, a faith that if he could only succeed in capturing a fragment of the truth about the life he knew, and make it known and felt by others, it would be a more glorious accomplishment than anything else he could imagine. And through it all, animating this faith and sustaining it with a promise of rewards to come, was a belief—be it now confessed—that if he could only do this, the world would thank him for it, and would crown him with the laurel of its fame.

The desire for fame is rooted in the hearts of men. It is one of the most powerful of all human desires, and perhaps for that very reason, and because it is so deep and secret, it is the desire that men are most unwilling to admit, particularly those who feel most sharply its keen and piercing spur.

The politician, for example, would never have us think that it is love of office, the desire for the notorious elevation of public place, that drives him on. No, the thing that governs him is his pure devotion to the common weal, his selfless and high-minded statesmanship, his love of his fellow man, and his burning idealism to turn out the rascal who usurps the office and betrays the public trust which he himself, as he assures us, would so gloriously and devotedly maintain.

So, too, the soldier. It is never love of glory that inspires him to his profession. It is never love of battle, love of war, love of all the resounding titles and the proud emoluments of the heroic conqueror. Oh, no. It is devotion to duty that makes him a soldier. There is no personal motive in it. He is inspired simply by the selfless ardor of his patriotic abnegation. He regrets that he has but one life to give for his country.

So it goes through every walk of life. The lawyer assures us that he is the defender of the weak, the guardian of the oppressed, the champion of the rights of defrauded widows and beleaguered orphans, the upholder of justice, the unrelenting enemy, at no matter what cost to himself, of all forms of chicanery, fraud, theft, violence, and crime. Even the business man will not admit a selfish motive in his money-getting. On the contrary, he is the developer of the nation's resources. He is the benevolent employer of thousands of working men who would be lost and on the dole without the organizing genius of his great intelligence. He is the defender of the American ideal of rugged individualism, the shining exemplar to youth of what a poor country boy may achieve in this nation through a devotion to the national virtues of thrift, industry, obedience to duty, and business integrity. He is, he assures us, the backbone of the country, the man who makes the wheels go round, the leading citizen, Public Friend No. 1.

All these people lie, of course. They know they lie, and everyone who hears them also knows they lie. The lie, however, has become a part of the convention of American life. People listen to it patiently, and if they smile at it, the smile is weary, touched with resignation and the indifferent dismissals of fatigue.

Curiously enough, the lie has also invaded the world of creation—the one place where it has no right at all to exist. There was a time when the poet, the painter, the musician, the artist of whatever sort, was not ashamed to confess that the desire for fame was one of the driving forces of his life and labor. But what a transformation from that time to this! Nowadays one will travel far and come back fruitless if he hopes to find an artist who will admit that he is devoted to anything except the service of some ideal—political, social, economic, religious, or æsthetic—which is outside himself, and to which his own humble fameforsaking person is reverently and selflessly consigned.

Striplings of twenty assure us that the desire for fame is naïvely childish, the fruit of an outworn cult of "romantic individualism." From all the falseness and self-deception of this cult these young gentlemen tell us they are free—without troubling to explain, however, by what process of miraculous purgation they achieved their freedom. It took Goethe, the strongest soul of modern times, some three and eighty years to free his mighty spirit of this last infirmity. Milton, old and blind, forsaken, and past fifty, is said to have won free of it by the end of Cromwell's revolution, in whose employment he destroyed his sight. And yet, can we be sure that even he was ever wholly clear, for what is the tremendous edifice of *Paradise Lost* except a man's final and triumphant suit against eternity?

Poor, blind Milton!

Fame is the spur that the clear spirit doth raise
(That last infirmity of Noble mind)

---

88 Fame . . . meed, from Milton's "Lycidas," ll. 70-84. The title Look Homeward, Angel is from the same poem, l. 163

To scorn delights, and live laborious dayes;
But the fair Guerdon when we hope to find,
And think to burst out into sudden blaze,
Comes the blind Fury with th'abhorred shears,
And slits the thin-spun life. But not the praise,
Phœbus repli'd, and touch'd my trembling ears;
Fame is no plant that grows on mortal soil,
Nor in the glistering foil
Set off to th'world, nor in broad rumour lies,
10 But lives and spreds aloft by those pure eyes,
And perfet witnes of all judging Jove;
As he pronounces lastly on each deed,
Of so much fame in Heav'n expect thy meed.

Deluded man! Poor vassal of corrupted time! How fair a thing for us to know that we are not such men as he and Goethe were! We live in more stirring times, and our very striplings are secure in their collective self-lessness. We have freed ourselves of all degrading vanities, choked off the ravening desire for individual 20 immortality, and now, having risen out of the ashes of our father's earth into the untainted ethers of collective consecration, we are clear at last of all that vexed, corrupted earth—clear of the sweat and blood and sorrow, clear of the grief and joy, clear of the hope and fear and human agony of which our father's flesh and that of every other man alive before us was ever wrought.

And yet, having achieved this glorious emancipation; having laid all petty dreams aside; having learned to think of life, not in terms of ourselves, but in terms of 30 the whole mass; having learned to think of life, not as it is today, but as it is going to be five hundred years from now, when all the revolutions have been made, and all the blood has been shed, and all the hundreds of millions of vain and selfish little lives, each concerned with its own individual and romantic breath, have been ruthlessly wiped out in order to usher in the collective glory that will be—having become marvelously and, as it were, overnight such paragons of collective selflessness and such scorners of the vanity of personal fame, is it 40 not strange that though we have new phrases, yet their meaning is still the same? Is it not strange that, feeling only an amused and pitying contempt for those who are still naïve enough to long for glory, we should yet lacerate our souls, poison our minds and hearts, and crucify our spirits with bitter and rancorous hatred against those who are fortunate enough to achieve fame?

Or do we err? Are we mistaken in assuming that these words we read so often are really words of hatred, malice, envy, ridicule, and jeering mockery? Are we mis-taken in assuming that the whole vocabulary of abuse 50 which is exhausted every week in the journals of our red and pink-complexioned comrades—the sneers against a man's talent, the bitter denials that his work has any substance, sincerity, truth, or reality whatever—is really what it seems to be? No doubt we *are* mistaken. It would be more charitable to believe that these pure spirits of the present day are what they say they are—collective, selfless, consecrated—and that the words they use do not mean what they seem to mean, and do not betray the romantic and deluded passions that seem to animate 60 them, but are really words used coldly, without passion, for the purposes of collective propaganda—in operations completely surgical, whereby the language of the present day, with all its overtones of superstition, prejudice, and false knowledge, is employed clinically, scientifically, simply to further the Idea of the Future State!

No more, no more! Of what avail to crush these vermin beneath our heavy boot? The locusts have no king, and lice will multiply forever. The poet must be born, and live, and sweat, and suffer, and change, and 70 grow, yet somehow maintain the changeless selfhood of his soul's integrity among all the crawling fashions of this world of lice. The poet lives, and dies, and is im-mortal; but the eternal trifler of all complexions never dies. The eternal trifler comes and goes, sucks blood of living men, is filled and emptied with the surfeit of each changing fashion. He gorges and disgorges, and is never fed. There is no nurture in him, and he draws no nurture from the food he feeds on. There is no heart, no soul, no blood, no living faith in him: the eternal trifler 80 simply swallows and remains.

And we? Made of our father's earth, blood of his blood, bone of his bone, flesh of his flesh—born like our father here to live and strive, here to win through or be defeated—here, like all the other men who went before us, not too nice or dainty for the uses of this earth —here to live, to suffer, and to die—O brothers, like our fathers in their time, we are burning, burning, burning in the night.

Go, seeker, if you will, throughout the land and you 90 will find us burning in the night.

There where the hackles of the Rocky Mountains

blaze in the blank and naked radiance of the moon, go make your resting stool upon the highest peak. Can you not see us now? The continental wall juts sheer and flat, its huge black shadow on the plain, and the plain sweeps out against the East, two thousand miles away. The great snake that you see there is the Mississippi River.

Behold the gem-strung towns and cities of the good, green East, flung like star-dust through the field of night. That spreading constellation to the north is called Chicago, and that giant wink that blazes in the moon is the pendant lake that it is built upon. Beyond, close-set and dense as a clenched fist, are all the jeweled cities of the eastern seaboard. There's Boston, ringed with the bracelet of its shining little towns, and all the lights that sparkle on the rocky indentations of New England. Here, southward and a little to the west, and yet still coasted to the sea, is our intensest ray, the splintered firmament of the towered island of Manhattan. Round about her, sown thick as grain, is the glitter of a hundred towns and cities. The long chain of lights there is the necklace of Long Island and the Jersey shore. Southward and inland, by a foot or two, behold the duller glare of Philadelphia. Southward further still, the twin constellations—Baltimore and Washington. Westward, but still within the borders of the good, green East, that nighttime glow and smolder of hell-fire is Pittsburgh. Here, St. Louis, hot and humid in the cornfield belly of the land, and bedded on the mid-length coil and fringes of the snake. There at the snake's mouth, southward six hundred miles or so, you see the jeweled crescent of old New Orleans. Here, west and south again, you see the gemmy glitter of the cities on the Texas border.

Turn now, seeker, on your resting stool atop the Rocky Mountains, and look another thousand miles or so across moon-blazing fiend-worlds of the Painted Desert and beyond Sierras' ridge. That magic congeries of lights there to the west, ringed like a studded belt around the magic setting of its lovely harbor, is the fabled town of San Francisco. Below it, Los Angeles and all the cities of the California shore. A thousand miles to north and west, the sparkling towns of Oregon and Washington.

Observe the whole of it, survey it as you might survey a field. Make it your garden, seeker, or your backyard patch. Be at ease in it. It's your oyster—yours to open if you will. Don't be frightened, it's not so big now, when your footstool is the Rocky Mountains. Reach out and dip a hatful of cold water from Lake Michigan.

Drink it—we've tried it—you'll not find it bad. Take your shoes off and work your toes down in the river oozes of the Mississippi bottom—it's very refreshing on a hot night in the summertime. Help yourself to a bunch of Concord grapes up there in northern New York State—they're getting good now. Or raid that watermelon patch down there in Georgia. Or, if you like, you can try the Rockyfords here at your elbow, in Colorado. Just make yourself at home, refresh yourself, get the feel of things, adjust your sights, and get the scale. It's your pasture now, and it's not so big—only three thousand miles from east to west, only two thousand miles from north to south—but all between, where ten thousand points of light prick out the cities, towns, and villages, there, seeker, you will find us burning in the night.

Here, as you pass through the brutal sprawl, the twenty miles of rails and rickets, of the South Chicago slums—here, in an unpainted shack, is a Negro boy, and, seeker, he is burning in the night. Behind him is a memory of the cotton fields, the flat and mournful pineland barrens of the lost and buried South, and at the fringes of the pine another nigger shack, with mammy and eleven little niggers. Farther still behind, the slave-driver's whip, the slave ship, and, far off, the jungle dirge of Africa. And before him, what? A roped-in ring, a blaze of lights, across from him a white champion; the bell, the opening, and all around the vast sea-roaring of the crowd. Then the lightning feint and stroke, the black panther's paw—the hot, rotating presses, and the rivers of sheeted print! O seeker, where is the slave ship now?

Or there, in the clay-baked piedmont of the South, that lean and tan-faced boy who sprawls there in the creaking chair among admiring cronies before the open doorways of the fire department, and tells them how he pitched the team to shut-out victory today. What visions burn, what dreams possess him, seeker of the night? The packed stands of the stadium, the bleachers sweltering with their unshaded hordes, the faultless velvet of the diamond, unlike the clay-baked outfields down in Georgia. The mounting roar of eighty thousand voices and Gehrig coming up to bat, the boy himself upon the pitching mound, the lean face steady as a hound's; then the nod, the signal, and the wind-up, the rawhide arm

55 **Rockyfords**, a cantaloupe grown in Colorado • 88 **Gehrig**, Lou Gehrig, famous home-run hitter for the New York Yankees

that snaps and crackles like a whip, the small white bullet of the blazing ball, its loud report in the oiled pocket of the catcher's mitt, the umpire's thumb jerked upward, the clean strike.

Or there again, in the East-Side Ghetto of Manhattan, two blocks away from the East River, a block away from the gas-house district and its thuggery, there in the swarming tenement, shut in his sweltering cell, breathing the sun-baked air through opened window at the
10 fire escape, celled there away into a little semblance of privacy and solitude from all the brawling and vociferous life and argument of his family and the seething hive around him, the Jew boy sits and pores upon his book. In shirt-sleeves, bent above his table to meet the hard glare of a naked bulb, he sits with gaunt, starved face converging to his huge beaked nose, the weak eyes squinting painfully through his thick-lens glasses, his

greasy hair roached back in oily scrolls above the slanting cage of his painful and constricted brow. And for what? For what this agony of concentration? For what this hell 20 of effort? For what this intense withdrawal from the poverty and squalor of dirty brick and rusty fire escapes, from the raucous cries and violence and never-ending noise? For what? Because, brother, he is burning in the night. He sees the class, the lecture room, the shining apparatus of gigantic laboratories, the open field of scholarship and pure research, certain knowledge, and the world distinction of an Einstein name.

So, then, to every man his chance—to every man, regardless of his birth, his shining, golden opportunity— 30 to every man the right to live, to work, to be himself, and to become whatever thing his manhood and his vision can combine to make him—this, seeker, is the promise of America.

1940

John Steinbeck

1902 ·

[handwritten notes:]
— wrote during great depression
— glorified the Common man / yet he generally he always gave his characters a hope for something better he felt man could survive
— his characters are victims
tk was

The foremost young American novelist of the Great Depression, which is to say of the decade between 1930 and 1940, was a Californian, John Steinbeck. What he had to say, basically, was that life goes on, is indestructible, although its forms may change and vast numbers of individual lives may be snuffed out by the catastrophic and inscrutable forces of nature. The world of Steinbeck, like that of Robinson Jeffers, is cruelly impersonal, but the conclusions of the two writers are almost diametrically opposed. Jeffers finds the human race little short of contemptible; Steinbeck, fully aware of the meanness and impotence of humanity, is temperamentally hopeful, an admirer of the infinite mani-

festations of adaptability in living organisms. It is not surprising that Steinbeck found an eager audience in an era everywhere darkened by bankruptcy, unemployment, and a sense of possible failure in the struggle for survival. He was called "Communist" and "left-wing visionary" by men angered by his tenderness for the victims of change and his broad hint of social revolution, but time has made it clear that Steinbeck is something more than a "proletarian" novelist. He is as close to being a philosopher as any popular living writer.

Steinbeck was born at Salinas, California, in 1902. He grew up in a rich but strike-tormented valley where

[handwritten notes at bottom:]
characters have a dream to become better to survive midst many Problems

he learned at first hand of the life of the agricultural and factory workers. From 1919 through 1925 he attended Stanford University, taking the courses that attracted him without worrying about degree requirements and dropping out now and then to work as a common laborer. Already determined to be a writer, he contributed to the university magazines and, after leaving Stanford, worked briefly as a reporter in New York City. Illness helped send him back to California and a job as caretaker on a mountain estate. His first published book, *Cup of Gold,* is said to be the fourth that he wrote. It appeared in August 1929, the month before the collapse of the stock market.

Cup of Gold is a fictionized biography of Sir Henry Morgan, a seventeenth-century buccaneer; it is chiefly noteworthy for its foreshadowing of Steinbeck's fondness for symbolic and poetic techniques. It was followed by *The Pastures of Heaven* (1932), a series of short stories about the folk of a California valley, and by *To a God Unknown* (1933), a mystical novel about a man's passion for the land which he was determined to make his permanent home. None of these books attracted much attention.

Steinbeck's popularity began with *Tortilla Flat* (1935), although we are told that nine publishers rejected it before it was accepted by Covici. A series of stories about the *paisano* of the Monterey peninsula, it remains a favorite with many of his readers. *In Dubious Battle,* a strike novel which is Steinbeck's most clearly "proletarian" story, appeared in 1936; *Of Mice and Men,* a novelette, in 1937; *The Long Valley,* a collection of short stories, in 1938. *Of Mice and Men* was selected by the Book-of-the-Month Club for distribution in February 1937 and was soon a best-seller; by the end of the year a dramatic version was packing in the customers in a New York theater. Steinbeck's most widely known work, however, is *The Grapes of Wrath* (1939), a novel on the migration of agricultural workers from the Oklahoma dust bowl to the green but preëmpted fields and groves of California. It roused the wrath of Oklahomans and owning-class Californians, awakened the rest of the country to the economic plight of dispossessed farmers, and was in due course awarded the Pulitzer Prize for fiction.

In some ways the best introduction to the mature Steinbeck are two books which appeared in 1941. *The*

Forgotten Village is a book of photographs with brief accompanying captions. Based upon a documentary film on the clash between magic and medical science in a small Mexican village, it is a vivid exemplification of Steinbeck's abiding confidence that man can be improved by patience and genuine affection. *Sea of Cortez,* written in collaboration with Edward T. Ricketts, a marine biologist, is an account of an expedition to the Gulf of California and perhaps the fullest revelation of Steinbeck's preoccupation with the philosophy of science.

Whether or not Steinbeck can produce another major work of fiction comparable to *The Grapes of Wrath* remains to be seen. He should be free of the economic pressure which produces potboilers and thus able to write what he wishes with the assurance that he will be read with respect. Not one book in the last dozen years has quite "come off," however. *The Moon Is Down* (1942), a short novel on the Nazi occupation of Norway, was made into a successful play and moving picture, but contained no memorable characters. *Bombs Away* (1942) is an account of the life of a British-based air squadron, *Russian Journal* (1948), a report on a trip to the Soviet Union; both are informative but scarcely indicative of growing literary power. *Cannery Row* (1945) was a return to the Monterey *paisanos,* without improving on *Tortilla Flat; The Wayward Bus* (1947), a somewhat sensational story condemning middle-class conventions. In *The Pearl* (1947), also a successful film, Steinbeck turned to parable, without achieving such success as Hemingway's in *The Old Man and the Sea. East of Eden* (1952), his most ambitious work in fourteen years, was a best-seller, but justly damned by most critics as rambling and uneven, its main argument, that the individual can to some degree control his conduct, lost in the mass of irrelevant and sometimes incredible detail.

Because he deals often in symbols and abstract ideas, he is sometimes a puzzle to the critics. Most often, perhaps, Steinbeck has been called a primitivist, and it is true that he tends to glorify rudimentary folk, people who, as he said in 1937 in a foreword to *Tortilla Flat,* "merge successfully with their habitat." Yet Steinbeck combines, as Frederick Ives Carpenter has pointed out, several of the great skeins of American thought: the mystical monism which gave

Emerson his trust in the essential goodness of the common man; the sense of the mass or the social democracy with which Whitman tempered Emersonian individualism; and that recognition of the necessity of effective action which is the core of pragmatism, sometimes called the most characteristic of American philosophical positions. A sensitive and intelligent man, fully aware of the enormity of human failure, Steinbeck still finds a core of goodness in men and women, a zest in living which is perhaps more essential for survival than an understanding of life.

H. T. Moore, The Novels of John Steinbeck: A First Critical Study, Chicago, 1939 • Edmund Wilson, The Boys in the Back Room: Notes on California Novelists, San Francisco, 1941 • F. I. Carpenter, "The Philosophical Joads," College English, January 1941 • J. W. Beach, American Fiction, 1920-1940, New York, 1941 • Maxwell Geismar, Writers in Crisis: The American Novel Between Two Wars, Boston, 1942

From · Tortilla Flat

The Pirate

How Danny's Friends Became a Force for Good. How They Succored the Poor Pirate

In 1937, writing a Foreword to The Modern Library edition of **Tortilla Flat**, Steinbeck remarked that had he known that his stories of the **paisanos** would be considered quaint he might not have written them. He liked Danny and his Monterey friends, and his original Preface compared them to the knights of the Round Table—a group of men "from which came sweetness and joy, philanthropy and, in the end, a mystic sorrow." The book consists of seventeen chapters, of which the following is the seventh. Danny, "a mixture of Spanish, Indian, Mexican, and assorted Caucasian bloods," has returned from the war (he broke mules in Texas) to find that he is a property owner, having inherited two small houses from his grandfather. His friends join him—first Pilon, then Pablo, then Jesus Maria Corcoran. When the house that they have rented from Danny burns down, they move in with him [...] ful moment, swear that th[...] house for Dann[...]

affectionate characteri[...] book.

A great many people saw the Pirate every day, and some laughed at him, and some pitied him; but no one knew him very well, and no one interfered with him. He was a huge, broad man, with tremendous black and bushy beard. He wore jeans and a blue shirt, and he had no hat. In town he wore shoes. There was a shrinking in the Pirate's eyes when he confronted any grown person, the secret look of an animal that would like to run away if it dared turn its back long enough. Because of this expression, the paisanos of Monterey knew that his head had not grown up with the rest of his body. They called him The Pirate because of his beard. Every day people saw him wheeling his barrow of pitchwood about the streets until he sold the load. And always in a cluster at his heels walked his five dogs.

Enrique was rather houndish in appearance, although his tail was bushy. Pajarito was brown and curly, and these were the only two things you could see about him. Rudolph was a dog of whom passers-by said, "H[...] American dog." Fluff was a Pug and Señor Ale[...] son seemed to be a kind of an Airedale. [...] in a squad behind the Pirate, very [...] him, and very solicitous for his ha[...] down to rest from wheeling b[...] to sit in his lap and b[...]

liked this, for his dogs kept him warm on the coldest nights. If his feet were cold, he had only to put them against the warm belly of Señor Alec Thompson. The chicken house was so low that the Pirate had to crawl in on his hands and knees.

Early every morning, well before daylight, the Pirate crawled out of his chicken house, and the dogs followed him, roughing their coats and sneezing in the cold air. Then the party went down to Monterey and worked
10 along an alley. Four or five restaurants had their back doors on this alley. The Pirate entered each one, into a restaurant kitchen, warm and smelling of food. Grumbling cooks put packages of scraps in his hands at each place. They didn't know why they did it.

When the Pirate had visited each back door and had his arms full of parcels, he walked back up the hill to Munroe Street and entered a vacant lot, and the dogs excitedly swarmed about him. Then he opened the parcels and fed the dogs. For himself he took bread or a
20 piece of meat out of each package, but he did not pick the best for himself. The dogs sat down about him, licking their lips nervously, and shifting their feet while they waited for food. They never fought over it, and that was a surprising thing. The Pirate's dogs never fought each other, but they fought everything else that wandered the streets of Monterey on four legs. It was a fine thing to see the pack of five, hunting fox-terriers and Pomeranians like rabbits.

Daylight had come by the time the meal was over.
30 The Pirate sat on the ground and watched the sky turn blue with the morning. Below him he saw the schooners put out to sea with deckloads of lumber. He heard the bell buoy ringing sweetly off China Point. The dogs sat about him and gnawed at the bones. The Pirate seemed to be listening to the day rather than seeing it, for while his eyes did not move about, there was an air of attentiveness in him. His big hands strayed to the dogs and his fingers worked soothingly in the coarse hair. After about half an hour, the Pirate went to the corner
40 of the vacant lot, threw the covering of sacks from his wheelbarrow and dug up his ax out of the ground where he buried it every evening. Then up the hill he pushed the barrow, and into the woods, until he found a dead tree, full of pitch. By noon he had a load of fine kindling; and then, still followed by his dogs, he walked the streets until he had sold the load for twenty-five cents.

It was possible to observe all this, but what he did with the quarter, no one could tell. He never spent it. In the night, guarded from danger by his dogs, he went into the woods and hid the day's quarter with hundreds of 50 others. Somewhere he had a great hoard of money.

Pilon, that acute man, from whom no details of the life of his fellows escaped, and who was doubly delighted to come upon those secrets that nestled deep in the brains of his acquaintances, discovered that Pirate's hoard by a logical process. Pilon reasoned thus: "Every day that Pirate has a quarter. If it is two dimes and a nickel, he takes it to a store and gets a twenty-five cent piece. He never spends any money at all. Therefore, he must be hiding it." 60

Pilon tried to compute the amount of the treasure. For years the Pirate had been living in this way. Six days a week he cut pitchwood, and on Sundays he went to church. His clothes he got from the back doors of houses, his food at the back doors of restaurants. Pilon puzzled with the great numbers for a while, and then gave it up. "The Pirate must have at least a hundred dollars," he thought.

For a long time Pilon had considered these things. But it was only after the foolish and enthusiastic promise 70 to feed Danny that the thought of the Pirate's hoard gained any personal significance to Pilon.

Before he approached the subject at all, Pilon put his mind through a long and stunning preparation. He felt very sorry for the Pirate. "Poor little half-formed one," he said to himself. "God did not give him all the brain he should have. That poor little Pirate cannot look after himself. For see, he lives in filth in an old chicken house. He feeds upon scraps fit only for his dogs. His clothes are thin and ragged. And because his brain is 80 not a good one, he hides his money."

Now, with his groundwork of pity laid, Pilon moved on to his solution. "Would it not be a thing of merit," he thought, "to do those things for him which he cannot do for himself? To buy him warm clothes, to feed him food fit for a human? But," he reminded himself, "I have no money to do these things, although they lie squirming in my heart. How can these charitable things be accomplished?"

Now he was getting somewhere. Like the cat, which 90 during a long hour closes in on a sparrow, Pilon was ready for his pounce. "I have it!" his brain cried. "It is like this: The Pirate has money, but he has not the brain to use it. I have the brain! I will offer my brain to his use. I will give freely of my mind. That shall be my charity toward this poor little half-made man."

It was one of the finest structures Pilon had ever built. The urge of the artist to show his work to an audience came upon him. "I will tell it to Pablo," he thought. But he wondered whether he would dare do such a thing. Was Pablo strictly honest? Would he not want to divert some of this money to his own ends? Pilon decided not to take the chance, right then, anyway.

It is astounding to find that the belly of every black and evil thing is as white as snow. And it is saddening to discover how the concealed parts of angels are leprous. Honor and peace to Pilon, for he had discovered how to uncover and to disclose to the world the good that lay in every evil thing. Nor was he blind, as so many saints are, to the evil of good things. It must be admitted with sadness that Pilon had neither the stupidity, the self-righteousness nor the greediness for reward ever to become a saint. Enough for Pilon to do good and to be rewarded by the glow of human brotherhood accomplished.

That very night he paid a visit to the chicken house where the Pirate lived with his dogs. Danny, Pablo and Jesus Maria, sitting by the stove, saw him go and said nothing. For, they thought delicately, either a vapor of love had been wafted to Pilon or else he knew where he could get a little wine. In either case it was none of their business until he told them about it.

It was well after dark, but Pilon had a candle in his pocket, for it might be a good thing to watch the expression on the Pirate's face while he talked. And Pilon had a big round sugar cookie in a bag that Susie Francisco, who worked in a bakery, had given him in return for a formula for getting the love of Charlie Guzman. Charlie was a Postal Telegraph messenger and rode a motorcycle; and Susie had a man's cap to put on backward in case Charlie should ever ask her to ride with him. Pilon thought the Pirate might like the sugar cookie.

The night was very dark. Pilon picked his way along a narrow street bordered with vacant lots and with weed-grown, neglected gardens.

Galvez' bad bulldog came snarling out of Galvez' yard, and Pilon spoke soothing compliments to him.

"Nice dog," he said gently, and "Pretty dog," both of them palpable lies. They impressed the bulldog, however, for he retired into Galvez' yard.

Pilon came at last to the vacant property where the Pirate lived. And now he knew he must be careful, for the Pirate's dogs, if they suspected ill of anyone toward their master, were known to become defending furies. As Pilon stepped into the yard, he heard deep and threatening growls from the chicken house.

"Pirate," he called. "It is thy good friend Pilon, come to talk with thee."

There was silence. The dogs stopped growling.

"Pirate, it is only Pilon."

A deep surly voice answered him, "Go away. I am sleeping now. The dogs are sleeping. It is dark, Pilon. Go to bed."

"I have a candle in my pocket," Pilon called. "It will make a light as bright as day in thy dark house. I have a big sugar cookie for thee, too."

A faint scuffling sounded in the chicken house. "Come then," the Pirate said. "I will tell the dogs it is all right."

As he advanced through the weeds, Pilon could hear the Pirate talking softly to his dogs, explaining to them that it was only Pilon, who would do no harm. Pilon bent over in front of the dark doorway and scratched a match and lighted his candle.

The Pirate was seated on the dirt floor, and his dogs were all about him. Enrique growled, and had to be reassured again. "That one is not so wise as the others," the Pirate said pleasantly. His eyes were the pleased eyes of an amused child. When he smiled his big white teeth glistened in the candlelight.

Pilon held out the bag. "It is a fine cake for you," he said.

The Pirate took the bag and looked into it; then he smiled delightedly, and brought out the cookie. The dogs all grinned and faced him, and moved their feet and licked their lips. The Pirate broke his cookie into seven pieces. The first he gave to Pilon, who was his guest. "Now, Enrique," he said. "Now Fluff. Now Señor Alec Thompson." Each dog received his piece and gulped it and looked for more. Last, the Pirate ate his and held up his hands to the dogs. "No more, you see," he told them. Immediately the dogs lay down about him.

Pilon sat on the floor and stood the candle on the ground in front of him. The Pirate questioned him self-consciously with his eyes. Pilon sat silently, to let many questions pass through the Pirate's head. At length he said, "Thou art a worry to thy friends."

The Pirate's eyes filled with astonishment. "I? To my friends? What friends?"

Pilon softened his voice. "Thou hast many friends who think of thee. They do not come to see thee because thou art proud. They think it might hurt thy pride to have them see thee living in this chicken house, clothed in rags, eating garbage with thy dogs. But these friends of thine worry for fear the bad life may make thee ill."

The Pirate was following his words with breathless astonishment, and his brain tried to realize these new things he was hearing. It did not occur to him to doubt them, since Pilon was saying them. "I have all these friends?" he said in wonder. "And I did not know it. And I am a worry to those friends. I did not know, Pilon. I would not have worried them if I had known." He swallowed to clear his throat of emotion. "You see, Pilon, the dogs like it here. And I like it because of them. I did not think I was a worry to my friends." Tears came into the Pirate's eyes.

"Nevertheless," Pilon said, "thy mode of living keeps all thy friends uneasy."

The Pirate looked down at the ground and tried to think clearly, but as always, when he attempted to cope with a problem, his brain grew gray and no help came from it, but only a feeling of helplessness. He looked to his dogs for protection, but they had gone back to sleep, for it was none of their business. And then he looked earnestly into Pilon's eyes. "You must tell me what to do, Pilon. I did not know these things."

It was too easy. Pilon was a little ashamed that it should be so easy. He hesitated; nearly gave it up; but then he knew he would be angry with himself if he did. "Thy friends are poor," he said. "They would like to help thee, but they have no money. If thou hast money hidden, bring it out into the open. Buy thyself some clothes. Eat food that is not cast out by other people. Bring thy money out of its hiding place, Pirate."

Pilon had been looking closely at the Pirate's face while he spoke. He saw the eyes droop with suspicion and then with sullenness. In a moment Pilon knew two

things certainly; first, that the Pirate had money hidden; and second, that it was not going to be easy to get at it. He was pleased at the latter fact. The Pirate had become a problem in tactics such as Pilon enjoyed.

Now the Pirate was looking at him again, and in his eyes was cunning, and on top of that, a studied ingenuousness. "I have no money anywhere," he said.

"But every day, my friend, I have seen thee get a quarter for thy wood, and never have I seen thee spend it."

This time the Pirate's brain came to his rescue. "I give it to a poor old woman," he said. "I have no money anywhere." And with his tone he closed a door tightly on the subject.

"So it must be guile," Pilon thought. So those gifts, that in him were so sharpened, must be called into play. He stood up and lifted his candle. "I only thought to tell thee how thy friends worry," he said critically. "If thou wilt not try to help, I can do nothing for thee."

The sweetness came back into the Pirate's eyes. "Tell them I am healthy," he begged. "Tell my friends to come and see me. I will not be too proud. I will be glad to see them any time. Wilt thou tell them for me, Pilon?"

"I will tell them," Pilon said ungraciously. "But thy friends will not be pleased when they see thou dost nothing to relieve their minds." Pilon blew out his candle and went away into the darkness. He knew that the Pirate would never tell where his hoard was. It must be found by stealth, taken by force and then all the good things given to the Pirate. It was the only way.

And so Pilon set himself to watch the Pirate. He followed him into the forest when he went to cut kindlings. He lay in wait outside the chicken house at night. He talked to him long and earnestly, and nothing came of it. The treasure was as far from discovery as ever. Either it lay buried in the chicken house or it was hidden deep in the forest, and was only visited at night.

The long and fruitless vigils wore out the patience of Pilon. He knew he must have help and advice. And who could better give it than those comrades, Danny, Pablo and Jesus Maria? Who could be so stealthy, so guileful? Who could melt to kindness with more ease?

Pilon took them into his confidence; but first he prepared them, as he had prepared himself: The Pirate's poverty, his helplessness, and finally—the solution. When he came to the solution, his friends were in a philanthropic frenzy. They applauded him. Their faces shone with kindness. Pablo thought there might be well over a hundred dollars in the hoard.

When their joy had settled to a working enthusiasm, they came to plans.

"We must watch him," Pablo said.

"But I have watched him," Pilon argued. "It must be that he creeps off in the night, and then one cannot follow too close, for his dogs guard him like devils. It is not going to be so easy."

"You've used every argument?" Danny asked.

"Yes. Every one."

In the end it was Jesus Maria, that humane man, who found the way out. "It is difficult while he lives in that chicken house," he said. "But suppose he lived here, with us? Either his silence would break under our kindness, or else it would be easier to know when he goes out at night."

The friends gave a good deal of thought to this suggestion. "Sometimes the things he gets out of restaurants are nearly new," mused Pablo. "I have seen him with a steak out of which only a little was missing."

"It might be as much as two hundred dollars," said Pilon.

Danny offered an objection. "But those dogs—he would bring his dogs with him."

"They are good dogs," said Pilon. "They obey him exactly. You may draw a line around a corner and say, 'Keep thy dogs within this line.' He will tell them, and those dogs will stay."

"I saw the Pirate one morning, and he had nearly half a cake, just a little bit damp with coffee," said Pablo.

The question settled itself. The house resolved itself into a committee, and the committee visited the Pirate.

It was a crowded place, that chicken house, when they all got inside. The Pirate tried to disguise his happiness with a gruff tone.

"The weather has been bad," he said socially. And, "You wouldn't believe, maybe, that I found a tick as big as a pigeon's egg on Rudolph's neck." And he spoke disparagingly of his home, as a host should. "It is too small," he said. "It is not a fit place for one's friends to come. But it is warm and snug, especially for the dogs."

Then Pilon spoke. He told the Pirate that worry was killing his friends; but if he would go to live with them, then they could sleep again, with their minds at ease.

It was a very great shock to the Pirate. He looked at his hands. And he looked to his dogs for comfort, but they would not meet his glance. At last he wiped the happiness from his eyes with the back of his hand, and he wiped his hand on his big black beard.

"And the dogs?" he asked softly. "You want the dogs, too? Are you friends of the dogs?"

Pilon nodded. "Yes, the dogs, too. There will be a whole corner set aside for the dogs."

The Pirate had a great deal of pride. He was afraid he might not conduct himself well. "Go away now," he said pleadingly. "Go home now. Tomorrow I will come."

His friends knew how he felt. They crawled out of the door and left him alone.

"He will be happy with us, that one," said Jesus Maria.

"Poor little lonely man," Danny added. "If I had known, I would have asked him long ago, even if he had no treasure."

A flame of joy burned in all of them.

They settled soon into the new relationship. Danny, with a piece of blue chalk, drew a segment of a circle, enclosing a corner of the living room, and that was where the dogs must stay when they were in the house. The Pirate slept in that corner too, with the dogs.

The house was beginning to be a little crowded, with five men and five dogs; but from the first, Danny and his friends realized that their invitation to the Pirate had been inspired by that weary and anxious angel who guarded their destinies and protected them from evil.

Every morning, long before his friends were awake, the Pirate arose from his corner and, followed by his dogs, he made the rounds of the restaurants and the wharves. He was one of those for whom every one feels a kindliness. His packages grew larger. The paisanos received his bounty and made use of it; fresh fish, half pies, untouched loaves of stale bread, meat that required only a little soda to take the green out. They began really to live.

And their acceptance of his gifts touched the Pirate more deeply than anything they could have done for him. There was a light of worship in his eyes as he watched them eat the food he brought.

In the evening, when they sat about the stove and discussed the doings of Tortilla Flat with the lazy voices of fed gods, the Pirate's eyes darted from mouth to mouth, and his own lips moved, whispering again the words his friends said. The dogs pressed in about him jealously.

These were his friends, he told himself in the night, when the house was dark, when the dogs snuggled close to him so that all might be warm. These men loved him 10 so much that it worried them to have him live alone. The Pirate had often to repeat this to himself, for it was an astounding thing, an unbelievable thing. His wheelbarrow stood in Danny's yard now, and every day he cut his pitchwood and sold it. But so afraid was the Pirate that he might miss some word his friends said in the evening, might not be there to absorb some stream of the warm companionship, that he had not visited his hoard for several days to put the new coins there.

20 His friends were kind to him. They treated him with a sweet courtesy; but always there was some eye open and upon him. When he wheeled his barrow into the woods, one of the friends walked with him, and sat on a log while he worked. When he went into the gulch, the last thing at night, Danny or Pablo or Pilon or Jesus Maria kept him company. And in the night he must have been very quiet to have crept out without a shadow behind him.

For a week, the friends merely watched the Pirate. But 30 at last the inactivity tired them. Direct action was out of the question, they knew. And so one evening the subject of the desirability of hiding one's money came up for discussion.

Pilon began it. "I had an uncle, a regular miser, and he hid his gold in the woods. And one time he went to look at it, and it was gone. Some one had found it and stolen it. He was an old man, then, and all his money was gone, and he hanged himself." Pilon noticed with some satisfaction, the look of apprehension that came upon 40 the Pirate's face.

Danny noticed it, too; and he continued, "The viejo, my grandfather, who owned this house, also buried money. I do not know how much, but he was reputed a rich man, so there must have been three or four hundred dollars. The viejo dug a deep hole and put his money in it, and then he covered it up, and then he

strewed pine needles over the ground until he thought no one could see that anything had been done there. But when he went back, the hole was open, and the money was gone." 50

The Pirate's lips followed the words. A look of terror had come into his face. His fingers picked among the neck hairs of Señor Alec Thompson. The friends exchanged a glance and dropped the subject for the time being. They turned to the love life of Cornelia Ruiz.

In the night the Pirate crept out of the house, and the dogs crept after him; and Pilon crept after all of them. The Pirate went swiftly into the forest, leaping with sure feet over logs and brush. Pilon floundered behind him. But when they had gone at least two miles, Pilon was 60 winded, and torn by vines. He paused to rest a moment; and then he realized that all sounds ahead of him had ceased. He waited and listened and crept about, but the Pirate had disappeared.

After two hours, Pilon went back again, slowly and tiredly. There was the Pirate in the house, fast asleep among his dogs. The dogs lifted their heads when Pilon entered, and Pilon thought they smiled satirically at him for a moment.

A conference took place in the gulch the next 70 morning.

"It is not possible to follow him," Pilon reported. "He vanished. He sees in the dark. He knows every tree in the forest. We must find some other way."

"Perhaps one is not enough," Pablo suggested. "If all of us should follow him, then one might not lose track of him."

"We will talk again tonight," said Jesus Maria, "only worse. A lady I know is going to give me a little wine," he added modestly. "Maybe if the Pirate has a 80 little wine in him, he will not disappear so easily." So it was left.

Jesus Maria's lady gave him a whole gallon of wine. What could compare with the Pirate's delight that evening when a fruit jar of wine was put into his hand, when he sat with his friends and sipped his wine and listened to the talk? Such joy had come rarely into the Pirate's life. He wished he might clasp these dear people to his breast and tell them how much he loved them. But that was not a thing he could do, for they might 90 think he was drunk. He wished he could do some tremendous thing to show them his love.

"We spoke last night of burying money," said Pilon. "Today I remembered a cousin of mine, a clever man. If any one in the world could hide money where it would never be found, he could do it. So he took his money and hid it. Perhaps you have seen him, that poor little one who crawls about the wharf and begs fish heads to make soup of. That is my cousin. Some one stole his buried money."

The worry came back into the Pirate's face.

Story topped story, and in each one all manner of evil dogged the footsteps of those who hid their money.

"It is better to keep one's money close, to spend some now and then, to give a little to one's friends," Danny finished.

They had been watching the Pirate narrowly, and in the middle of the worst story they had seen the worry go from his face, and a smile of relief take its place. Now he sipped his wine and his eyes glittered with joy.

The friends were in despair. All their plans had failed. They were sick at heart. After all their goodness and their charity, this had happened. The Pirate had in some way escaped the good they had intended to confer upon him. They finished their wine and went moodily to bed.

Few things could happen in the night without Pilon's knowledge. His ears remained open while the rest of him slept. He heard the stealthy exit of the Pirate and his dogs from the house. He leaped to awaken his friends; and in a moment the four were following the Pirate in the direction of the forest. It was very dark when they entered the pine forest. The four friends ran into trees, tripped on berry vines; but for a long time they could hear the Pirate marching on ahead of them. They followed as far as Pilon had followed the night before, and then, suddenly, silence, and the whispering forest and the vague night wind. They combed the woods and the brush patches, but the Pirate had disappeared again.

At last, cold and disconsolate, they came together and trudged wearily back toward Monterey. The dawn came before they got back. The sun was already shining on the bay. The smoke of the morning fires arose to them out of Monterey.

The Pirate walked out on the porch to greet them, and his face was happy. They passed him sullenly, and filed into the living room. There on the table lay a large canvas bag.

The Pirate followed them in. "I lied to thee, Pilon," he said. "I told thee I had no money, for I was afraid. I did not know about my friends, then. You have told how hidden money is so often stolen, and I am afraid again. Only last night did a way out come to me. My money will be safe with my friends. No one can steal it if my friends guard it for me."

The four men stared at him in horror. "Take thy money back to the woods and hide it," Danny said savagely. "We do not want to watch it."

"No," said the Pirate. "I would not feel safe to hide it. But I will be happy knowing my friends guard it for me. You would not believe it, but the last two nights some one followed me into the forest to steal my money."

Terrible as the blow was, Pilon, that clever man, tried to escape it. "Before this money is put into our hands, maybe you would like to take some out," he suggested smoothly.

The Pirate shook his head. "No. I cannot do that. It is promised. I have nearly a thousand two-bitses. When I have a thousand I will buy a gold candle-stick for San Francisco de Assisi.

"Once I had a nice dog, and that dog was sick; and I promised a gold candle-stick of one thousand days if that dog would get well. And," he spread his great hands, "that dog got well."

"Is it one of these dogs?" Pilon demanded.

"No," said the Pirate. "A truck ran over him a little later."

So it was over, all hope of diverting the money. Danny and Pablo morosely lifted the heavy bag of silver quarters, took it in the other room and put it under the pillow of Danny's bed. In time they would take a certain pleasure in the knowledge that this money lay under the pillow, but now their defeat was bitter. There was nothing in the world they could do about it. Their chance had come, and it had gone.

The Pirate stood before them, and there were tears of happiness in his eyes, for he had proved his love for his friends.

"To think," he said, "all those years I lay in that chicken house, and I did not know any pleasure. But now," he added, "oh, now I am very happy."

1935

From

The Grapes of Wrath

The Grapes of Wrath is both a tract and a story. As a tract, it studies the still unsettled problem of the migrant agricultural workers—the men, women, and children who may be seen crowded into trucks and rattletrap cars in all sections of the country, on their way to pick fruit or cotton or vegetables or to weed onions or sugar beets. Often desperately needed for farm production, they are nearly everywhere feared. The landowners and managers worry lest they organize and demand high wages; local officials regard them as possible public charges or vagrants; settled and prosperous citizens thoughtlessly dismiss them as mere riffraff. Steinbeck's position is that they have a right to work without being exploited, a right to self-respect and a just share of the means of subsistence. Land, he says, must not be allowed to be accumulated in the hands of the few and kept out of production while the many starve. He attacks, in short, the "economy of scarcity" in a land where scientific agriculture has made possible the production of ample food for all. In Chapter Twenty-five he presents the picture of the destruction of grapes and cotton and coffee and pigs because overproduction has depressed the price below the margin of profit, although there are hungry, despairing people to be fed and clothed. This is, he says, the path to revolution. "In the souls of the people the grapes of wrath are filling and growing heavy, growing heavy for the vintage." His title is an echo of Julia Ward Howe's Civil War poem, "The Battle Hymn of the Republic": "Mine eyes have seen the glory of the coming of the Lord: / He is trampling out the vintage where the grapes of wrath are stored . . . ."

The Grapes of Wrath differs from late nineteenth-century novels on the same theme (Bellamy's **Looking Backward**, p. 706, and Howells' **A Traveler from Altruria**) in that it emphasizes the class struggle. Its story is typical of the 1930's, when the effects of the depression were aggravated by the years of drought and dust storms which impoverished large areas in Oklahoma and neighboring states. Specifically, it is the story of the Joads, native Americans who have lived for years near Sallisaw, in east central Oklahoma. Although they are poor people, concerned with little more than their animal wants, they are a family, a unit, with the pride and the generosity and the humanity, the pleasures and the courage, that make life meaningful. Ma is their balance wheel, although she ordinarily leaves the dignity of making decisions to her husband. Her charges include Grampa and Granma; Uncle John, who is given to melancholia; Tom, on parole after a stretch in state prison for killing a man in the anger of a fight; Noah, gentle but feeble-minded; Al, a cocksure adolescent; Rose of Sharon, who is married to a weak youth named Connie; and two half-grown children, Ruthie and Winfield.

The novel begins with a dust storm. The reader then meets Tom Joad, on his way home from prison. Tom encounters Jim Casy, a former preacher with a penchant for philosophizing, and they go together to the Joad farm. They find the house deserted, but learn from Muley Bates that the family is at Uncle John's. Going there next day they find Ma and the rest preparing to go to California where they have been told that there is plenty of work and the chance for a fresh start. They have been dispossessed of their marginal land by the drought and the foreclosure of mortgages; only by large-scale mechanization can such land now be farmed profitably.

Three chapters of the novel are reprinted in the following pages. Chapter Thirteen describes the first stages of the trip, with the succession of sudden tragedies which foreshadow the later disillusion and disintegration of the family. Chapter Fourteen, with its use of biological terminology, typifies the generalizations inserted by Steinbeck at intervals throughout the novel to alternate with the Joad story. Chapter Fifteen, frequently reprinted as a separate unit, exemplifies Steinbeck's keen observation of the surface details of contemporary life and his sure grasp of the idiom of the common people. The entire section is representative of the peculiar juxtaposition of realism and sentiment which is Steinbeck's talent.

Throughout the remainder of the novel the Joads are beset by one catastrophe after another, with infrequent interludes of hope that somehow something can be worked out. Before they reach the farmlands of California, Noah wanders off and Granma dies. The promised work does not often materialize and when it does the rate of pay is determined by the number of workers available. Only in a government camp are the Joads momentarily free from the brutality and suspicion of sheriffs and deputies, and they cannot afford to stay there and starve. Connie runs away from his pregnant wife. Casy is killed when he tries, none too expertly, to lead a strike, and Tom kills the man who struck down Casy. Since Tom has broken his parole by leaving Oklahoma, he becomes a fugitive, although it is suggested that he will carry on the work of organizing the wandering workers. In the final scene Rose of Sharon is delivered of a stillborn baby in a flooded boxcar but, since life must go on, gives her milk to a starving man.

Some readers will be offended by Steinbeck's social philosophy; others are likely to object to the animality of the life of the Joads and their friends and feel that Steinbeck has given a distorted picture of migrant workers' conditions in California at that time; still others will dislike the somewhat melodramatic incidents by which the story advances. Few, however, will deny that life is too often like this, that the improvement of the social and economic system should be the constant concern of those who live in a democracy. The Joads are not to be lightly dismissed as foreigners or poor whites; they are Americans, and their condition may readily determine the quality of life in these United States.

CHAPTER THIRTEEN

The ancient overloaded Hudson creaked and grunted to the highway at Sallisaw and turned west, and the sun was blinding. But on the concrete road Al built up his speed because the flattened springs were not in danger any more. From Sallisaw to Gore is twenty-one miles and the Hudson was doing thirty-five miles an hour. From Gore to Warner thirteen miles; Warner to Checotah fourteen miles; Checotah a long jump to Henrietta—thirty-four miles, but a real town at the
10 end of it. Henrietta to Castle nineteen miles, and the sun was overhead, and the red fields, heated by the high sun, vibrated the air.

Al, at the wheel, his face purposeful, his whole body listening to the car, his restless eyes jumping from the road to the instrument panel. Al was one with his engine, every nerve listening for weaknesses, for the thumps or squeals, hums and chattering that indicate a change that may cause a breakdown. He had become the soul of the car.

Granma, beside him on the seat, half slept, and whim- 20 pered in her sleep, opened her eyes to peer ahead, and then dozed again. And Ma sat beside Granma, one elbow out the window, and the skin reddening under the fierce sun. Ma looked ahead too, but her eyes were flat and did not see the road or the fields, the gas stations, the little eating sheds. She did not glance at them as the Hudson went by.

Al shifted himself on the broken seat and changed his grip on the steering wheel. And he sighed, "Makes a racket, but I think she's awright. God knows what 30 she'll do if we got to climb a hill with the load we got. Got any hills 'tween here an' California, Ma?"

Ma turned her head slowly and her eyes came to life. "Seems to me they's hills," she said. " 'Course I dunno. But seems to me I heard they's hills an' even mountains. Big ones."

Granma drew a long whining sigh in her sleep.

Al said, "We'll burn right up if we got climbin' to do. Have to throw out some a' this stuff. Maybe we shouldn' a brang that preacher." 40

"You'll be glad a that preacher 'fore we're through," said Ma. "That preacher'll help us." She looked ahead at the gleaming road again.

Al steered with one hand and put the other on the vibrating gear-shift lever. He had difficulty in speaking. His mouth formed the words silently before he said them aloud. "Ma—" She looked slowly around at him, her head swaying a little with the car's motion. "Ma, you scared a goin'? You scared a goin' to a new place?" 50

Her eyes grew thoughtful and soft. "A little," she said. "Only it ain't like scared so much. I'm jus' a settin' here waitin'. When somepin happens that I got to do somepin—I'll do it."

"Ain't you thinkin' what's it gonna be like when we get there? Ain't you scared it wont be nice like we thought?"

"No," she said quickly. "No, I ain't. You can't do that. I can't do that. It's too much—livin' too many lives. Up ahead they's a thousan' lives we might live, 60 but when it comes, it'll on'y be one. If I go ahead on all of 'em, it's too much. You got to live ahead 'cause you're so young, but—it's jus' the road goin' by for me. An' it's jus' how soon they gonna wanta eat some more pork bones." Her face tightened. "That's all I can do. I can't do no more. All the rest'd get upset if I done any more'n that. They all depen' on me jus' thinkin' about that."

Granma yawned shrilly and opened her eyes. She looked wildly about. "I got to get out, praise Gawd," she said.

"First clump a brush," said Al. "They's one up ahead."

"Brush or no brush, I got to git out, I tell ya." And she began to whine, "I got to git out. I got to git out."

Al speeded up, and when he came to the low brush he pulled up short. Ma threw the door open and half pulled the struggling old lady out beside the road and into the bushes. And Ma held her so Granma would not fall when she squatted.

On top of the truck the others stirred to life. Their faces were shining with sunburn they could not escape. Tom and Casy and Noah and Uncle John let themselves wearily down. Ruthie and Winfield swarmed down the side-boards and went off into the bushes. Connie helped Rose of Sharon gently down. Under the canvas, Grampa was awake, his head sticking out, but his eyes were drugged and watery and still senseless. He watched the others, but there was little recognition in his watching.

Tom called to him, "Want to come down, Grampa?"

The old eyes turned listlessly to him. "No," said Grampa. For a moment the fierceness came into his eyes. "I ain't a-goin', I tell you. Gonna stay like Muley." And then he lost interest again. Ma came back, helping Granma up the bank to the highway.

"Tom," she said. "Get that pan a bones, under the canvas in back. We got to eat somepin." Tom got the pan and passed it around, and the family stood by the roadside, gnawing the crisp particles from the pork bones.

"Sure lucky we brang these along," said Pa. "Git so stiff up there can't hardly move. Where's the water?"

"Ain't it up with you?" Ma asked. "I set out that gallon jug."

Pa climbed the sides and looked under the canvas. "It ain't here. We must a forgot it."

Thirst set in instantly. Winfield moaned, "I wanta drink. I wanta drink." The men licked their lips, sud-

denly conscious of their thirst. And a little panic started.

Al felt the fear growing. "We'll get water first service station we come to. We need some gas too." The family swarmed up the truck sides; Ma helped Granma in and got in beside her. Al started the motor and they moved on.

Castle to Paden twenty-five miles and the sun passed the zenith and started down. And the radiator cap began to jiggle up and down and steam started to whish out. Near Paden there was a shack beside the road and two gas pumps in front of it; and beside a fence, a water faucet and a hose. Al drove in and nosed the Hudson up to the hose. As they pulled in, a stout man, red of face and arms, got up from a chair behind the gas pumps and moved toward them. He wore brown corduroys, and suspenders and a polo shirt; and he had a cardboard sun helmet, painted silver, on his head. The sweat beaded on his nose and under his eyes and formed streams in the wrinkles of his neck. He strolled toward the truck, looking truculent and stern.

"You folks aim to buy anything? Gasoline or stuff?" he asked.

Al was out already, unscrewing the steaming radiator cap with the tips of his fingers, jerking his hand away to escape the spurt when the cap should come loose. "Need some gas, mister."

"Got any money?"

"Sure. Think we're beggin'?"

The truculence left the fat man's face. "Well, that's all right, folks. He'p yourself to water." And he hastened to explain. "Road is full a people, come in, use water, dirty up the toilet, an' then, by God, they'll steal stuff an' don't buy nothin'. Got no money to buy with. Come beggin' a gallon gas to move on."

Tom dropped angrily to the ground and moved toward the fat man. "We're payin' our way," he said fiercely. "You got no call to give us a goin'-over. We ain't asked you for nothin'."

"I ain't," the fat man said quickly. The sweat began to soak through his short-sleeved polo shirt. "Jus' he'p yourself to water, and go use the toilet if you want."

Winfield had got the hose. He drank from the end and then turned the stream over his head and face and emerged dripping. "It ain't cool," he said.

"I don't know what the country's comin' to," the fat man continued. His complaint had shifted now and he was no longer talking to or about the Joads. "Fifty-sixty cars a folks go by ever' day, folks all movin' west with kids an' househol' stuff. Where they goin'? What they gonna do?"

"Doin' the same as us," said Tom. "Goin' someplace to live. Tryin' to get along. That's all."

"Well, I don't know what the country's comin' to. I jus' don' know. Here's me tryin' to get along, too. Think any them big new cars stops here? No, sir! They go on to them yella-painted company stations in town. They don't stop no place like this. Most folks stops here ain't got nothin'."

Al flipped the radiator cap and it jumped into the air with a head of steam behind it, and a hollow bubbling sound came out of the radiator. On top of the truck, the suffering hound dog crawled timidly to the edge of the load and looked over, whimpering, toward the water. Uncle John climbed up and lifted him down by the scruff of the neck. For a moment the dog staggered on stiff legs, and then he went to lap the mud under the faucet. In the highway the cars whizzed by, glistening in the heat, and the hot wind of their going fanned into the service-station yard. Al filled the radiator with the hose.

"It ain't that I'm tryin' to git trade outa rich folks," the fat man went on. "I'm jus' tryin' to git trade. Why, the folks that stops here begs gasoline an' they trades for gasoline. I could show you in my back room the stuff they'll trade for gas an' oil: beds an' baby buggies an' pots an' pans. One family traded a doll their kid had for a gallon. An' what'm I gonna do with the stuff, open a junk shop? Why, one fella wanted to gimme his shoes for a gallon. An' if I was that kinda fella I bet I could git—" He glanced at Ma and stopped.

Jim Casy had wet his head, and the drops still coursed down his high forehead, and his muscled neck was wet, and his shirt was wet. He moved over beside Tom. "It ain't the people's fault," he said. "How'd you like to sell the bed you sleep on for a tankful a gas?"

"I know it ain't their fault. Ever' person I talked to is on the move for a damn good reason. But what's the country comin' to? That's what I wanta know. What's it comin to? Fella can't make a livin' no more. Folks can't make a livin' farmin'. I ask you, what's it comin' to? I can't figure her out. Ever'body I ask, they can't figure her out. Fella wants to trade his shoes

so he can git a hunderd miles on. I can't figure her out." He took off his silver hat and wiped his forehead with his palm. And Tom took off his cap and wiped his forehead with it. He went to the hose and wet the cap through and squeezed it and put it on again. Ma worked a tin cup out through the side bars of the truck, and she took water to Granma and to Grampa on top of the load. She stood on the bars and handed the cup to Grampa, and he wet his lips, and then shook his head and refused more. The old eyes looked up at Ma in pain and bewilderment for a moment before the awareness receded again.

Al started the motor and backed the truck to the gas pump. "Fill her up. She'll take about seven," said Al. "We'll give her six so she don't spill none."

The fat man put the hose in the tank. "No, sir," he said. "I jus' don't know what the country's comin' to. Relief an' all."

Casy said, "I been walkin' aroun' in the country. Ever'body's askin' that. What we comin' to? Seems to me we don't never come to nothin'. Always on the way. Always goin' and goin'. Why don't folks think about that? They's movement now. People moving. We know why, an' we know how. Movin' 'cause they got to. That's why folks always move. Movin' 'cause they want somepin better'n what they got. An' that's the on'y way they'll ever git it. Wantin' it an' needin' it, they'll go out an' git it. It's bein' hurt that makes folks mad to fightin'. I been walkin' aroun' the country, an' hearin' folks talk like you."

The fat man pumped the gasoline and the needle turned on the pump dial, recording the amount. "Yeah, but what's it comin' to? That's what I want ta know."

Tom broke in irritably, "Well, you ain't never gonna know. Casy tries to tell ya an' you jest ast the same thing over. I seen fellas like you before. You ain't askin' nothin'; you're jus' singin' a kinda song. 'What we comin' to?' You don' wanta know. Country's movin' aroun', goin' places. They's folks dyin' all aroun'. Maybe you'll die pretty soon, but you won't know nothin'. I seen too many fellas like you. You don't want to know nothin'. Just sing yourself to sleep with a song—'What we comin' to?'" He looked at the gas pump, rusted and old, and at the shack behind it, built of old lumber, the nail holes of its first use still showing through the paint that had been brave, the brave yellow paint that had tried to imitate the big company stations in town. But the paint couldn't cover the old nail holes and the old cracks in the lumber, and the paint could not be renewed. The imitation was a failure and the owner had known it was a failure. And inside the open door of the shack Tom saw the oil barrels, only two of them, and the candy counter with stale candies and licorice whips turning brown with age, and cigarettes. He saw the broken chair and the fly screen with a rusted hole

10 in it. And the littered yard that should have been graveled, and behind, the corn field drying and dying in the sun. Beside the house the little stock of used tires and retreaded tires. And he saw for the first time the fat man's cheap washed pants and his cheap polo shirt and his paper hat. He said, "I didn' mean to sound off at ya, mister. It's the heat. You ain't got nothin'. Pretty soon you'll be on the road yourse'f. And it ain't tractors'll put you there. It's them pretty yella stations in town. Folks is movin'," he said ashamedly. "An'

20 you'll be movin', mister."

The fat man's hand slowed on the pump and stopped while Tom spoke. He looked worriedly at Tom. "How'd you know?" he asked helplessly. "How'd you know we was already talkin' about packin' up an' movin' west?"

Casy answered him. "It's ever'body," he said. "Here's me that used to give all my fight against the devil 'cause I figured the devil was the enemy. But they's somepin worse'n the devil got hold a the country, an' it ain't

30 gonna let go till it's chopped loose. Ever see one a them Gila monsters take hold, mister? Grabs hold, an' you chop him in two an' his head hangs on. Chop him at the neck an' his head hangs on. Got to take a screw-driver an' pry his head apart to git him loose. An' while he's layin' there, poison is drippin' an' drippin' into the hole he's made with his teeth." He stopped and looked sideways at Tom.

The fat man stared hopelessly straight ahead. His hand started turning the crank slowly. "I dunno what

40 we're comin' to," he said softly.

Over by the water hose, Connie and Rose of Sharon stood together, talking secretly. Connie washed the tin cup and felt the water with his finger before he filled the cup again. Rose of Sharon watched the cars go by on the highway. Connie held out the cup to her. "This water ain't cool, but it's wet," he said.

She looked at him and smiled secretly. She was all secrets now she was pregnant, secrets and little silences that seemed to have meanings. She was pleased with herself, and she complained about things that didn't 50 really matter. And she demanded services of Connie that were silly, and both of them knew they were silly. Connie was pleased with her too, and filled with wonder that she was pregnant. He liked to think he was in on the secrets she had. When she smiled slyly, he smiled slyly too, and they exchanged confidences in whispers. The world had drawn close around them, and they were in the center of it, or rather Rose of Sharon was in the center of it with Connie making a small orbit about her. Everything they said was a kind of secret. 60

She drew her eyes from the highway. "I ain't very thirsty," she said daintily. "But maybe I *ought* to drink."

And he nodded, for he knew well what she meant. She took the cup and rinsed her mouth and spat and then drank the cupful of tepid water. "Want another?" he asked.

"Jus' a half." And so he filled the cup just half, and gave it to her. A Lincoln Zephyr, silvery and low, whisked by. She turned to see where the others were and saw them clustered about the truck. Reassured, 70 she said, "How'd you like to be goin' along in that?"

Connie sighed, "Maybe—after." They both knew what he meant. "An' if they's plenty work in California, we'll git our own car. But them"—he indicated the disappearing Zephyr—"them kind costs as much as a good size house. I ruther have the house."

"I like to have the house *an'* one a them," she said. "But 'course the house would be first because—" And they both knew what she meant. They were terribly excited about the pregnancy. 80

"You feel awright?" he asked.

"Tar'd. Jus' tar'd ridin' in the sun."

"We *got* to do that or we won't never get to California."

"I know," she said.

The dog wandered, sniffing, past the truck, trotted to the puddle under the hose again and lapped at the muddy water. And then he moved away, nose down and ears hanging. He sniffed his way among the dusty weeds beside the road, to the edge of the pavement. 90 He raised his head and looked across, and then started over. Rose of Sharon screamed shrilly. A big swift car whisked near, tires squealed. The dog dodged help-lessly, and with a shriek, cut off in the middle, went under the wheels. The big car slowed for a moment and faces looked back, and then it gathered greater speed and disappeared. And the dog, a blot of blood and tangled, burst intestines, kicked slowly in the road.

Rose of Sharon's eyes were wide. "D'you think it'll hurt?" she begged. "Think it'll hurt?"

Connie put his arm around her. "Come set down," he said. "It wasn't nothin'."

"But I felt it hurt. I felt it kinda jar when I yelled."

"Come set down. It wasn't nothin'. It won't hurt." He led her to the side of the truck away from the dying dog and sat her down on the running board.

Tom and Uncle John walked out to the mess. The last quiver was going out of the crushed body. Tom took it by the legs and dragged it to the side of the road. Uncle John looked embarrassed, as though it were his fault. "I ought ta tied him up," he said.

Pa looked down at the dog for a moment and then he turned away. "Le's get outa here," he said, "I don' know how we was gonna feed 'im anyways. Just as well, maybe."

The fat man came from behind the truck. "I'm sorry, folks," he said. "A dog jus' don' last no time near a highway. I had three dogs run over in a year. Don't keep none, no more." And he said, "Don't you folks worry none about it. I'll take care of 'im. Bury 'im out in the corn field."

Ma walked over to Rose of Sharon, where she sat, still shuddering, on the running board. "You all right, Rosasharn?" she asked. "You feelin' poorly?"

"I seen that. Give me a start."

"I heard ya yip," said Ma. "Git yourself laced up now."

"You suppose it might of hurt?"

"No," said Ma. "'F you go to greasin' yourself an' feelin' sorry, an' tuckin' yourself in a swalla's nest, it might. Rise up now, an he'p me get Granma comf'table. Forget that baby for a minute. He'll take care a hisself."

"Where is Granma?" Rose of Sharon asked.

"I dunno. She's aroun' here somewheres. Maybe in the outhouse."

The girl went toward the toilet, and in a moment she came out, helping Granma along. "She went to sleep in there," said Rose of Sharon.

Granma grinned. "It's nice in there," she said. "They got a patent toilet in there an' the water comes down. I like it in there," she said contentedly. "Would of took a good nap if I wasn't woke up."

"It ain't a nice place to sleep," said Rose of Sharon, and she helped Granma into the car. Granma settled herself happily. "Maybe it ain't nice for purty, but it's nice for nice," she said.

Tom said, "Le's go. We got to make miles."

Pa whistled shrilly. "Now where'd them kids go?" He whistled again, putting his fingers in his mouth.

In a moment they broke from the corn field, Ruthie ahead and Winfield trailing her. "Eggs!" Ruthie cried. "Look!" A dozen soft, grayish-white eggs were in her grubby hand. And as she held up her hand, her eyes fell upon the dead dog beside the road. "Oh!" she said. Ruthie and Winfield walked slowly toward the dog. They inspected him.

Pa called to them, "Come on, you, 'less you want to git left."

They turned solemnly and walked to the truck. Ruthie looked once more at the gray reptile eggs in her hand, and then she threw them away. They climbed up the side of the truck. "His eyes was still open," said Ruthie in a hushed tone.

But Winfield gloried in the scene. He said boldly, "His guts was just strowed all over—all over"—he was silent for a moment—"strowed—all—over," he said, and then he rolled over quickly and vomited down the side of the truck. When he sat up again his eyes were watery and his nose running. "It ain't like killin' pigs," he said in explanation.

Al had the hood of the Hudson up, and he checked the oil level. He brought a gallon can from the floor of the front seat and poured a quantity of cheap black oil into the pipe and checked the level again.

Tom came beside him. "Want I should take her a piece?" he asked.

"I ain't tired," said Al.

"Well, you didn't get no sleep las' night. I took a snooze this morning. Get up there on top. I'll take her."

"Awright," Al said reluctantly. "But watch the oil gauge pretty close. Take her slow. An' I been watchin' for a short. Take a look a the needle now an' then. 'F she jumps to discharge it's a short. An' take her slow, Tom. She's overloaded."

Tom laughed. "I'll watch her," he said. "You can res' easy."

The family piled on top of the truck again. Ma settled herself beside Granma in the seat, and Tom took his place and started the motor. "Sure is loose," he said, and he put it in gear and pulled away down the highway.

The motor droned along steadily and the sun receded down the sky in front of them. Granma slept steadily, and even Ma dropped her head forward and dozed. Tom pulled his cap over his eyes to shut out the blinding sun.

Paden to Meeker is thirteen miles; Meeker to Harrah is fourteen miles; and then Oklahoma City—the big city. Tom drove straight on. Ma waked up and looked at the streets as they went through the city. And the family, on top of the truck, stared about at the stores, at the big houses, at the office buildings. And then the buildings grew smaller and the stores smaller. The wrecking yards and hot-dog stands, the out-city dance halls.

Ruthie and Winfield saw it all, and it embarrassed them with its bigness and its strangeness, and it frightened them with the fine-clothed people they saw. They did not speak of it to each other. Later—they would, but not now. They saw the oil derricks in the town, on the edge of the town; oil derricks black, and the smell of oil and gas in the air. But they didn't exclaim. It was so big and so strange it frightened them.

In the street Rose of Sharon saw a man in a light suit. He wore white shoes and a flat straw hat. She touched Connie and indicated the man with her eyes, and then Connie and Rose of Sharon giggled softly to themselves, and the giggles got the best of them. They covered their mouths. And it felt so good that they looked for other people to giggle at. Ruthie and Winfield saw them giggling and it looked such fun that they tried to do it too—but they couldn't. The giggles wouldn't come. But Connie and Rose of Sharon were breathless and red with stifling laughter before they could stop. It got so bad that they had only to look at each other to start over again.

The outskirts were wide spread. Tom drove slowly and carefully in the traffic, and then they were on 66—the great western road, and the sun was sinking on the line of the road. The windshield was bright with dust. Tom pulled his cap lower over his eyes, so low that he had to tilt his head back to see out at all. Granma slept on, the sun on her closed eyelids, and the veins on her temples were blue, and the little bright veins on her cheeks were wine-colored, and the old brown marks on her face turned darker.

Tom said, "We stay on this road right straight through."

Ma had been silent for a long time. "Maybe we better fin' a place to stop 'fore sunset," she said. "I got to get some pork a-boilin' an' some bread made. That takes time."

"Sure," Tom agreed. "We ain't gonna make this trip in one jump. Might's well stretch ourselves."

Oklahoma City to Bethany is fourteen miles.

Tom said, "I think we better stop 'fore the sun goes down. Al got to build that thing on the top. Sun'll kill the folks up there."

Ma had been dozing again. Her head jerked upright. "Got to get some supper a-cookin'," she said. And she said, "Tom, your pa tol' me about you crossin' the State line——"

He was a long time answering. "Yeah? What about it, Ma?"

"Well, I'm scairt about it. It'll make you kinda runnin' away. Maybe they'll catch ya."

Tom held his hand over his eyes to protect himself from the lowering sun. "Don't you worry," he said. "I figgered her out. They's lots a fellas out on parole an' they's more goin' in all the time. If I get caught for anything else out west, well, then they got my pitcher an' my prints in Washington. They'll sen' me back. But if I don't do no crimes, they won't give a damn."

"Well, I'm a-scairt about it. Sometimes you do a crime, an' you don't even know it's bad. Maybe they got crimes in California we don't even know about. Maybe you gonna do somepin an' it's all right, an' in California it ain't all right."

"Be jus' the same if I wasn't on parole," he said. "On'y if I get caught I get a bigger jolt'n other folks. Now you quit a-worryin'," he said. "We got plenty to worry about 'thout you figgerin' out things to worry about."

"I can't he'p it," she said. "Minute you cross the line you done a crime."

"Well, that's better'n stickin' aroun' Sallisaw an' starvin' to death," he said. "We better look out for a place to stop."

They went through Bethany and out on the other side. In a ditch, where a culvert went under the road, an old touring car was pulled off the highway and a little tent was pitched beside it, and smoke came out of a stove pipe through the tent. Tom pointed ahead. "There's some folks campin'. Looks like as good a place as we seen." He slowed his motor and pulled to a stop beside the road. The hood of the old touring car was up, and a middle-aged man stood looking down at the motor. He wore a cheap straw sombrero, a blue shirt, and a black, spotted vest, and his jeans were stiff and shiny with dirt. His face was lean, the deep cheek-lines great furrows down his face so that his cheek bones and chin stood out sharply. He looked up at the Joad truck and his eyes were puzzled and angry.

Tom leaned out of the window. "Any law 'gainst folks stoppin' here for the night?"

The man had seen only the truck. His eyes focused down on Tom. "I dunno," he said. "We on'y stopped here 'cause we couldn't git no further."

"Any water here?"

The man pointed to a service-station shack about a quarter of a mile ahead. "They's water there they'll let ya take a bucket of."

Tom hesitated. "Well, ya s'pose we could camp down 'longside?"

The lean man looked puzzled. "We don't own it," he said. "We on'y stopped here 'cause this goddamn ol' trap wouldn' go no further."

Tom insisted. "Anyways you're here an' we ain't. You got a right to say if you wan' neighbors or not."

The appeal to hospitality had an instant effect. The lean face broke into a smile. "Why, sure, come on off the road. Proud to have ya." And he called, "Sairy, there's some folks goin' ta stay with us. Come on out an' say how d'ya do. Sairy ain't well," he added. The tent flaps opened and a wizened woman came out— a face wrinkled as a dried leaf and eyes that seemed to flame in her face, black eyes that seemed to look out of a well of horror. She was small and shuddering. She held herself upright by a tent flap, and the hand holding onto the canvas was a skeleton covered with wrinkled skin.

When she spoke her voice had a beautiful low timbre, soft and modulated, and yet with ringing overtones. "Tell 'em welcome," she said. "Tell 'em good an' welcome."

Tom drove off the road and brought his truck into the field and lined it up with the touring car. And people boiled down from the truck; Ruthie and Winfield too quickly, so that their legs gave way and they shrieked at the pins and needles that ran through their limbs. Ma went quickly to work. She untied the three-gallon bucket from the back of the truck and approached the squealing children. "Now you go git water—right down there. Ask nice. Say, 'Please, kin we git a bucket of water?' and say, 'Thank you.' An' carry it back together helpin', an' don't spill none. An' if you see stick wood to burn, bring it on." The children stamped away toward the shack.

By the tent a little embarrassment had set in, and social intercourse had paused before it started. Pa said, "You ain't Oklahomy folks?"

And Al, who stood near the car, looked at the license plates. "Kansas," he said.

The lean man said, "Galena, or right about there. Wilson, Ivy Wilson."

"We're Joads," said Pa. "We come from right near Sallisaw."

"Well, we're proud to meet you folks," said Ivy Wilson. "Sairy, these is Joads."

"I knowed you wasn't Oklahomy folks. You talk queer kinda—that ain't no blame, you understan'."

"Ever'body says words different," said Ivy. "Arkansas folks says 'em different, and Oklahomy folks says 'em different. And we seen a lady from Massachusetts, an' she said 'em differentest of all. Couldn' hardly make out what she was sayin'."

Noah and Uncle John and the preacher began to unload the truck. They helped Grampa down and sat him on the ground and he sat limply, staring ahead of him. "You sick, Grampa?" Noah asked.

"You goddamn right," said Grampa weakly. "Sicker'n hell."

Sairy Wilson walked slowly and carefully toward him. "How'd you like ta come in our tent?" she asked. "You kin lay down on our mattress an' rest."

He looked up at her, drawn by her soft voice. "Come on now," she said. "You'll git some rest. We'll he'p you over."

Without warning Grampa began to cry. His chin wavered and his old lips tightened over his mouth and he sobbed hoarsely. Ma rushed over to him and put her arms around him. She lifted him to his feet, her broad back straining, and she half lifted, half helped him into the tent.

Uncle John said, "He must be good an' sick. He ain't never done that before. Never seen him blubberin' in my life." He jumped up on the truck and tossed a mattress down.

Ma came out of the tent and went to Casy. "You been aroun' sick people," she said. "Grampa's sick. Won't you go take a look at him?"

Casy walked quickly to the tent and went inside. A double mattress was on the ground, the blankets spread neatly; and a little tin stove stood on iron legs, and the fire in it burned unevenly. A bucket of water, a wooden box of supplies, and a box for a table, that was all. The light of the setting sun came pinkly through the tent walls. Sairy Wilson knelt on the ground, beside the mattress, and Grampa lay on his back. His eyes were open, staring upward, and his cheeks were flushed. He breathed heavily.

Casy took the skinny old wrist in his fingers. "Feeling kinda tired, Grampa?" he asked. The staring eyes moved toward his voice but did not find him. The lips practiced a speech but did not speak it. Casy felt the pulse and he dropped the wrist and put his hand on Grampa's forehead. A struggle began in the old man's body, his legs moved restlessly and his hands stirred. He said a whole string of blurred sounds that were not words, and his face was red under the spiky white whiskers.

Sairy Wilson spoke softly to Casy. "Know what's wrong?"

He looked up at the wrinkled face and the burning eyes. "Do you?"

"I—think so."

"What?" Casy asked.

"Might be wrong. I wouldn' like to say."

Casy looked back at the twitching red face. "Would you say—maybe—he's workin' up a stroke?"

"I'd say that," said Sairy. "I seen it three times before."

From outside came the sounds of camp-making, wood chopping, and the rattle of pans. Ma looked through the flaps. "Granma wants to come in. Would she better?"

The preacher said, "She'll just fret if she don't."

"Think he's awright?" Ma asked.

Casy shook his head slowly. Ma looked quickly down at the struggling old face with blood pounding through it. She drew outside and her voice came through. "He's awright, Granma. He's jus' takin' a little res'."

And Granma answered sulkily, "Well, I want ta see him. He's a tricky devil. He wouldn't never let ya know." And she came scurrying through the flaps. She stood over the mattresses and looked down. "What's the matter'th you?" she demanded of Grampa. And again his eyes reached toward her voice and his lips writhed. "He's sulkin'," said Granma. "I tol' you he was tricky. He was gonna sneak away this mornin' so he wouldn't have to come. An' then his hip got a-hurtin'," she said disgustedly. "He's jus' sulkin'. I seen him when he wouldn' talk to nobody before."

Casy said gently, "He ain't sulkin', Granma. He's sick."

"Oh!" She looked down at the old man again. "Sick bad, you think?"

"Purty bad, Granma."

For a moment she hesitated uncertainly. "Well," she said quickly, "why ain't you prayin'? You're a preacher, ain't you?"

Casy's strong fingers blundered over to Grampa's wrist and clasped around it. "I tol' you, Granma. I ain't a preacher no more."

"Pray anyway," she ordered. "You know all the stuff by heart."

"I can't," said Casy. "I don't know what to pray for or who to pray to."

Granma's eyes wandered away and came to rest on Sairy. "He won't pray," she said. "D'I ever tell ya how Ruthie prayed when she was a little skinner? Says, 'Now I lay me down to sleep. I pray the Lord my soul to keep. An' when she got there the cupboard was bare, an' so the poor dog got none. Amen.' That's jus' what she done." The shadow of someone walking between the tent and the sun crossed the canvas.

Grampa seemed to be struggling; all his muscles twitched. And suddenly he jarred as though under a heavy blow. He lay still and his breath was stopped.

Casy looked down at the old man's face and saw that it was turning a blackish purple. Sairy touched Casy's shoulder. She whispered, "His tongue, his tongue, his tongue."

Casy nodded. "Get in front a Granma." He pried the tight jaws apart and reached into the old man's throat for the tongue. And as he lifted it clear, a rattling breath came out, and a sobbing breath was indrawn. Casy found a stick on the ground and held down the tongue with it, and the uneven breath rattled in and out.

Granma hopped about like a chicken. "Pray," she said. "Pray, you. Pray, I tell ya." Sairy tried to hold her back. "Pray, goddamn you!" Granma cried.

Casy looked up at her for a moment. The rasping breath came louder and more unevenly. "Our Father which are in Heaven, hallowed be Thy name——"

"Glory!" shouted Granma.

"Thy kingdom come, Thy will be done—on earth—as it is in Heaven."

"Amen."

A long gasping sigh came from the open mouth, and then a crying release of air.

"Give us this day—our daily bread—and forgive us—" The breathing had stopped. Casy looked down into Grampa's eyes and they were clear and deep and penetrating, and there was a knowing serene look in them.

"Hallelujah!" said Granma. "Go on."

"Amen," said Casy.

Granma was still then. And outside the tent all the noise had stopped. A car whished by on the highway. Casy still knelt on the floor beside the mattress. The people outside were listening, standing quietly intent on the sounds of dying. Sairy took Granma by the arm and led her outside, and Granma moved with dignity and held her head high. She walked for the family and held her head straight for the family. Sairy took her to a mattress lying on the ground and sat her down on it. And Granma looked straight ahead, proudly, for she was on show now. The tent was still, and at last Casy spread the tent flaps with his hands and stepped out.

Pa asked softly, "What was it?"

"Stroke," said Casy. "A good quick stroke."

Life began to move again. The sun touched the horizon and flattened over it. And along the highway there came a long line of huge freight trucks with red sides. They rumbled along, putting a little earthquake in the ground, and the standing exhaust pipes sputtered blue smoke from the Diesel oil. One man drove each truck, and his relief man slept in a bunk high up against the ceiling. But the trucks never stopped; they thundered day and night and the ground shook under their heavy march.

The family became a unit. Pa squatted down on the ground, and Uncle John beside him. Pa was the head of the family now. Ma stood behind him. Noah and Tom and Al squatted, and the preacher sat down, and then reclined on his elbow. Connie and Rose of Sharon walked at a distance. Now Ruthie and Winfield, clattering up with a bucket of water held between them, felt the change, and they slowed up and set down the bucket and moved quietly to stand with Ma.

Granma sat proudly, coldly, until the group was formed, until no one looked at her, and then she lay down and covered her face with her arm. The red sun set and left a shining twilight on the land, so that faces were bright in the evening and eyes shone in reflection of the sky. The evening picked up light where it could.

Pa said, "It was in Mr. Wilson's tent."

Uncle John nodded. "He loaned his tent."

"Fine friendly folks," Pa said softly.

Wilson stood by his broken car, and Sairy had gone to the mattress to sit beside Granma, but Sairy was careful not to touch her.

Pa called, "Mr. Wilson!" The man scuffed near and squatted down, and Sairy came and stood beside him. Pa said, "We're thankful to you folks."

"We're proud to help," said Wilson.

"We're beholden to you," said Pa.

"There's no beholden in a time of dying," said Wilson, and Sairy echoed him, "Never no beholden."

Al said, "I'll fix your car—me an' Tom will." And Al looked proud that he could return the family's obligation.

"We could use some help." Wilson admitted the retiring of the obligation.

Pa said, "We got to figger what to do. They's laws. You got to report a death, an' when you do that, they either take forty dollars for the undertaker or they take him for a pauper."

Uncle John broke in, "We never did have no paupers."

The Grapes of Wrath 1159

Tom said, "Maybe we got to learn. We never got booted off no land before, neither."

"We done it clean," said Pa. "There can't no blame be laid on us. We never took nothin' we couldn' pay; we never suffered no man's charity. When Tom here got in trouble we could hold up our heads. He only done what any man would a done."

"Then what'll we do?" Uncle John asked.

"We go in like the laws says an' they'll come out for him. We on'y got a hundred an' fifty dollars. They take forty to bury Grampa an' we won't get to California—or else they'll bury him a pauper." The men stirred restively, and they studied the darkening ground in front of their knees.

Pa said softly, "Grampa buried his pa with his own hand, done it in dignity, an' shaped the grave nice with his own shovel. That was a time when a man had the right to be buried by his own son an' a son had the right to bury his own father."

"The law says different now," said Uncle John.

"Sometimes the law can't be foller'd no way," said Pa. "Not in decency, anyways. They's lots a times you can't. When Floyd was loose an' goin' wild, law said we got to give him up—an' nobody give him up. Sometimes a fella got to sift the law. I'm sayin' now I got the right to bury my own pa. Anybody got somepin to say?"

The preacher rose high on his elbow. "Law changes," he said, "but 'got to's' go on. You got the right to do what you got to do."

Pa turned to Uncle John. "It's your right too, John. You got any word against?"

"No word against," said Uncle John. "On'y it's like hidin' him in the night. Grampa's way was t'come out a-shootin'."

Pa said ashamedly, "We can't do like Grampa done. We got to get to California 'fore our money gives out."

Tom broke in, "Sometimes fellas workin' dig up a man an' then they raise hell an' figger he been killed. The gov'ment's got more interest in a dead man than a live one. They'll go hell-scrapin' tryin' to fin' out who he was and how he died. I offer we put a note of writin' in a bottle an' lay it with Grampa, tellin' who he is an' how he died, an' why he's buried here."

Pa nodded agreement. "That's good. Wrote out in a nice han'. Be not so lonesome too, knowin' his name is there with 'im, not jus' a old fella lonesome underground. Any more stuff to say?" The circle was silent.

Pa turned his head to Ma. "You'll lay 'im out?"

"I'll lay 'im out," said Ma. "But who's to get supper?"

Sairy Wilson said, "I'll get supper. You go right ahead. Me an' that big girl of yourn."

"We sure thank you," said Ma. "Noah, you get into them kegs an' bring out some nice pork. Salt won't be deep in it yet, but it'll be right nice eatin'."

"We got a half sack a potatoes," said Sairy.

Ma said, "Gimme two half-dollars." Pa dug in his pocket and gave her the silver. She found the basin, filled it full of water, and went into the tent. It was nearly dark in there. Sairy came in and lighted a candle and stuck it upright on a box and then she went out. For a moment Ma looked down at the dead old man. And then in pity she tore a strip from her own apron and tied up his jaw. She straightened his limbs, folded his hands over his chest. She held his eyelids down and laid a silver piece on each one. She buttoned his shirt and washed his face.

Sairy looked in, saying, "Can I give you any help?"

Ma looked slowly up. "Come in," she said. "I like to talk to ya."

"That's a good big girl you got," said Sairy. "She's right in peelin' potatoes. What can I do to help?"

"I was gonna wash Grampa all over," said Ma, "but he got no other clo'es to put on. An' 'course your quilt's spoilt. Can't never get the smell a death from a quilt. I seen a dog growl an' shake at a mattress my ma died on, an' that was two years later. We'll wrop 'im in your quilt. We'll make it up to you. We got a quilt for you."

Sairy said, "You shouldn' talk like that. We're proud to help. I ain't felt so—safe in a long time. People needs—to help."

Ma nodded. "They do," she said. She looked long into the old whiskery face, with its bound jaw and silver eyes shining in the candlelight. "He ain't gonna look natural. We'll wrop him up."

"The ol' lady took it good."

"Why, she's so old," said Ma, "maybe she don't even rightly know what happened. Maybe she won't really know for quite a while. Besides, us folks takes a pride holdin' in. My pa used to say, 'Anybody can break down. It takes a man not to.' We always try to hold in." She folded the quilt neatly about Grampa's legs and around his shoulders. She brought the corner of the quilt over his head like a cowl and pulled it down over his face. Sairy handed her half-a-dozen big safety pins, and she pinned the quilt neatly and tightly about the long package. And at last she stood up. "It won't be a bad burying," she said. "We got a preacher to see him in, an' his folks is all aroun'." Suddenly she swayed a little, and Sairy went to her and steadied her. "It's sleep—" Ma said in a shamed tone. "No, I'm awright. We been so busy gettin' ready, you see."

"Come out in the air," Sairy said.

"Yeah, I'm all done here." Sairy blew out the candle and the two went out.

A bright fire burned in the bottom of the little gulch. And Tom, with sticks and wire, had made supports from which two kettles hung and bubbled furiously, and good steam poured out under the lids. Rose of Sharon knelt on the ground out of range of the burning heat, and she had a long spoon in her hand. She saw Ma come out of the tent, and she stood up and went to her.

"Ma," she said, "I got to ask."

"Scared again?" Ma asked. "Why, you can't get through nine months without sorrow."

"But will it—hurt the baby?"

Ma said, "They used to be a sayin', 'A chile born outa sorrow'll be a happy chile.' Isn't that so, Mis' Wilson?"

"I heard it like that," said Sairy. "An' I heard the other: 'Born outa too much joy'll be a doleful boy.'"

"I'm all jumpy inside," said Rose of Sharon.

"Well, we ain't none of us jumpin' for fun," said Ma. "You jes' keep watchin' the pots."

On the edge of the ring of firelight the men had gathered. For tools they had a shovel and a mattock. Pa marked out the ground—eight feet long and three feet wide. The work went on in relays. Pa chopped the earth with the mattock and then Uncle John shoveled it out. Al chopped and Tom shoveled. Noah chopped and Connie shoveled. And the hole drove down, for the work never diminished in speed. The shovels of dirt flew out of the hole in quick spurts. When Tom was shoulder deep in the rectangular pit, he said, "How deep, Pa?"

"Good an' deep. A couple feet more. You get out now, Tom, and get that paper wrote."

Tom boosted himself out of the hole and Noah took his place. Tom went to Ma, where she tended the fire. "We got any paper an' pen, Ma?"

Ma shook her head slowly, "No-o. That's one thing we didn' bring." She looked toward Sairy. And the little woman walked quickly to her tent. She brought back a Bible and a half pencil. "Here," she said. "They's a clear page in front. Use that an' tear it out." She handed book and pencil to Tom.

Tom sat down in the firelight. He squinted his eyes in concentration, and at last wrote slowly and carefully on the end paper in big clear letters: "This here is William James Joad, dyed of a stroke, old old man. His fokes bured him becaws they got no money to pay for funerls. Nobody kilt him. Jus a stroke an he dyed." He stopped. "Ma, listen to this here." He read it slowly to her.

"Why, that soun's nice," she said. "Can't you stick on somepin from Scripture so it'll be religious? Open up an' git a sayin', somepin outa Scripture."

"Got to be short," said Tom. "I ain't got much room lef' on the page."

Sairy said, "How 'bout 'God have mercy on his soul'?"

"No," said Tom. "Sounds too much like he was hung. I'll copy somepin." He turned the pages and read, mumbling his lips, saying the words under his breath. "Here's a good short one," he said. "'An' Lot said unto them, Oh, not so, my Lord.'"

"Don't mean nothin'," said Ma. "Long's you're gonna put one down, it might's well mean somepin."

Sairy said, "Turn to Psalms, over further. You kin always get somepin outa Psalms."

Tom flipped the pages and looked down the verses. "Now here is one," he said. "This here's a nice one, just blowed full a religion: 'Blessed is he whose transgression is forgiven, whose sin is covered.' How's that?"

"That's real nice," said Ma. "Put that one in."

Tom wrote it carefully. Ma rinsed and wiped a fruit jar and Tom screwed the lid down tight on it. "Maybe the preacher ought to wrote it," he said.

Ma said, "No, the preacher wan't no kin." She took the jar from him and went into the dark tent. She unpinned the covering and slipped the fruit jar in under the thin cold hands and pinned the comforter tight again. And then she went back to the fire.

The men came from the grave, their faces shining

with perspiration. "Awright," said Pa. He and John and Noah and Al went into the tent, and they came out carrying the long, pinned bundle between them. They carried it to the grave. Pa leaped into the hole and received the bundle in his arms and laid it gently down. Uncle John put out a hand and helped Pa out of the hole. Pa asked, "How about Granma?"

"I'll see," Ma said. She walked to the mattress and looked down at the old woman for a moment. Then she went back to the grave. "Sleepin'," she said. "Maybe she'd hold it against me, but I ain't a-gonna wake her up. She's tar'd."

Pa said, "Where at's the preacher? We oughta have a prayer."

Tom said, "I seen him walkin' down the road. He don't like to pray no more."

"Don't like to pray?"

"No," said Tom. "He ain't a preacher no more. He figgers it ain't right to fool people actin' like a preacher when he ain't a preacher. I bet he went away so nobody wouldn' ast him."

Casy had come quietly near, and he heard Tom speaking. "I didn' run away," he said. "I'll he'p you folks, but I won't fool ya."

Pa said, "Won't you say a few words? Ain't none of our folks ever been buried without a few words."

"I'll say 'em," said the preacher.

Connie led Rose of Sharon to the graveside, she reluctant. "You got to," Connie said. "It ain't decent not to. It'll jus' be a little."

The firelight fell on the grouped people, showing their faces and their eyes, dwindling on their dark clothes. All the hats were off now. The light danced, jerking over the people.

Casy said, "It'll be a short one." He bowed his head, and the others followed his lead. Casy said solemnly, "This here ol' man jus' lived a life an' jus' died out of it. I don't know whether he was good or bad, but that don't matter much. He was alive, an' that's what matters. An' now he's dead, an' that don't matter. Heard a fella tell a poem one time, an' he says, 'All that lives is holy.' Got to thinkin', an' purty soon it means more than the words says. An' I wouldn' pray for a ol' fella that's dead. He's awright. He got a job to do, but it's all laid out for 'im an' there's on'y one way to do it. But us, we got a job to do, an' they's a thousan'

ways, an' we don't know which one to take. An' if I was to pray, it'd be for the folks that don' know which way to turn. Grampa here, he got the easy straight. An' now cover 'im up and let 'im get to his work." He raised his head.

Pa said, "Amen," and the others muttered, "A-men." Then Pa took the shovel, half filled it with dirt, and spread it gently into the black hole. He handed the shovel to Uncle John, and John dropped in a shovelful. Then the shovel went from hand to hand until every man had his turn. When all had taken their duty and their right, Pa attacked the mound of loose dirt and hurriedly filled the hole. The women moved back to the fire to see to supper. Ruthie and Winfield watched, absorbed.

Ruthie said solemnly, "Grampa's down under there." And Winfield looked at her with horrified eyes. And then he ran away to the fire and sat on the ground and sobbed to himself.

Pa half filled the hole, and then he stood panting with the effort while Uncle John finished it. And John was shaping up the mound when Tom stopped him. "Listen," Tom said. "'F we leave a grave, they'll have it open in no time. We got to hide it. Level her off an' we'll strew dry grass. We got to do that."

Pa said, "I didn' think a that. It ain't right to leave a grave unmounded."

"Can't he'p it," said Tom. "They'd dig 'im right up, an' we'd get it for breakin' the law. You know what I get if I break the law."

"Yeah," Pa said. "I forgot that." He took the shovel from John and leveled the grave. "She'll sink, come winter," he said.

"Can't he'p that," said Tom. "We'll be a long ways off by winter. Tromp her in good, an' we'll strew stuff over her."

When the pork and potatoes were done the families sat about on the ground and ate, and they were quiet, staring into the fire. Wilson, tearing a slab of meat with his teeth, sighed with contentment. "Nice eatin' pig," he said.

"Well," Pa explained, "we had a couple shoats, an' we thought we might's well eat 'em. Can't get nothin' for them. When we get kinda use' ta movin' an' Ma can set up bread, why, it'll be pretty nice, seein' the country an' two kags a' pork right in the truck. How long you folks been on the road?"

Wilson cleared his teeth with his tongue and swallowed. "We ain't been lucky," he said. "We been three weeks from home."

"Why, God Awmighty, we aim to be in California in ten days or less."

Al broke in, "I dunno, Pa. With that load we're packin', we maybe ain't never gonna get there. Not if they's mountains to go over."

They were silent about the fire. Their faces were turned downward and their hair and foreheads showed in the firelight. Above the little dome of the firelight the summer stars shone thinly, and the heat of the day was gradually withdrawing. On her mattress, away from the fire, Granma whimpered softly like a puppy. The heads of all turned in her direction.

Ma said, "Rosasharn, like a good girl go lay down with Granma. She needs somebody now. She's know-in', now."

Rose of Sharon got to her feet and walked to the mattress and lay beside the old woman, and the murmur of their soft voices drifted to the fire. Rose of Sharon and Granma whispered together on the mattress.

Noah said, "Funny thing is—losin' Grampa ain't made me feel no different than I done before. I ain't no sadder than I was."

"It's just the same thing," Casy said. "Grampa an' the old place, they was jus' the same thing."

Al said, "It's a goddamn shame. He been talkin' what he's gonna do, how he gonna squeeze grapes over his head an' let the juice run in his whiskers, an' all stuff like that."

Casy said, "He was foolin', all the time. I think he knowed it. An' Grampa didn' die tonight. He died the minute you took 'im off the place."

"You sure a that?" Pa cried.

"Why, no. Oh, he was breathin'," Casy went on, "but he was dead. He was that place, an' he knowed it."

Uncle John said, "Did you know he was a-dyin'?"

"Yeah," said Casy. "I knowed it."

John gazed at him, and a horror grew in his face. "An' you didn' tell nobody?"

"What good?" Casy asked.

"We—we might of did somepin."

"What?"

"I don' know, but——"

"No," Casy said, "you couldn' a done nothin'. Your way was fixed an' Grampa didn' have no part in it. He didn' suffer none. Not after fust thing this mornin'. He's jus' stayin' with the lan'. He couldn' leave it."

Uncle John sighed deeply.

Wilson said, "We hadda leave my brother Will." The heads turned toward him. "Him an' me had forties side by side. He's older'n me. Neither one ever drove a car. Well, we went in an' we sol' ever'thing. Will, he bought a car, an' they give him a kid to show 'im how to use it. So the afternoon 'fore we're gonna start, Will an' Aunt Minnie go a-practicin'. Will, he comes to a bend in the road an' he yells 'Whoa' an' yanks back, an' he goes through a fence. An' he yells 'Whoa, you bastard' an' tromps down on the gas an' goes over into a gulch. An' there he was. Didn't have nothin' more to sell an' didn't have no car. But it were his own damn fault, praise God. He's so damn mad he won't come along with us, jus' set there a-cussin' an' a-cussin'."

"What's he gonna do?"

"I dunno. He's too mad to figger. An' we couldn' wait. On'y had eighty-five dollars to go on. We couldn' set an' cut it up, but we et it up anyways. Didn' go a hundred mile when a tooth in the rear end bust, an' cost thirty dollars to get her fix', an' then we got to get a tire, an' then a spark plug cracked, an' Sairy got sick. Had ta stop ten days. An' now the goddamn car is bust again, an' money's gettin' low. I dunno when we'll ever get to California. 'F I could on'y fix a car, but I don't know nothin' about cars."

Al asked importantly, "What's the matter?"

"Well, she jus' won't run. Starts an' farts an' stops. In a minute she'll start again, an' then 'fore you can git her goin', she peters out again."

"Runs a minute an' then dies?"

"Yes, sir. An I can't keep her a-goin' no matter how much gas I give her. Got worse an' worse, an' now I cain't get her a-movin' a-tall."

Al was very proud and very mature, then. "I think you got a plugged gas line. I'll blow her out for ya."

And Pa was proud too. "He's a good hand with a car," Pa said.

"Well, I'll sure thank ya for a han'. I sure will. Makes a fella kinda feel—like a little kid, when he can't fix nothin'. When we get to California I aim to get me a nice car. Maybe she won't break down."

Pa said, "When we get there. Gettin' there's the trouble."

"Oh, but she's worth it," said Wilson. "Why, I seen han' bills how they need folks to pick fruit, an' good wages. Why, jus' think how it's gonna be, under them shady trees a-pickin' fruit an' takin' a bite ever' once in a while. Why, hell, they don't care how much you eat 'cause they got so much. An' with them good wages, maybe a fella can get hisself a little piece a land an' work out for extra cash. Why, hell, in a couple years I bet a fella could have a place of his own."

Pa said, "We seen them han'bills. I got one right here." He took out his purse and from it took a folded orange handbill. In black type it said, "Pea Pickers Wanted in California. Good Wages All Season. 800 Pickers Wanted."

Wilson looked at it curiously. "Why, that's the one I seen. The very same one. You s'pose—maybe they got all eight hunderd awready?"

Pa said, "This is jus' one little part a California. Why, that's the secon' biggest State we got. S'pose they did get all them eight hundred. They's plenty places else. I rather pick fruit anyways. Like you says, under them trees an' pickin' fruit—why, even the kids'd like to do that."

Suddenly Al got up and walked to the Wilsons' touring car. He looked in for a moment and then came back and sat down.

"You can't fix her tonight," Wilson said.

"I know. I'll get to her in the morning."

Tom had watched his young brother carefully. "I was thinkin' somepin like that myself," he said.

Noah asked, "What you two fellas talkin' about?"

Tom and Al went silent, each waiting for the other. "You tell 'em," Al said finally.

"Well, maybe it's no good, an' maybe it ain't the same thing Al's thinking. Here she is, anyways. We got a overload, but Mr. and Mis' Wilson ain't. If some of us folks could ride with them an' take some a their light stuff in the truck, we wouldn't break no springs an' we could git up hills. An' me an' Al both knows about a car, so we could keep that car a-rollin'. We'd keep together on the road an' it'd be good for ever'-body."

Wilson jumped up. "Why, sure. Why, we'd be proud. We certain'y would. You hear that, Sairy?"

"It's a nice thing," said Sairy. "Wouldn' be a burden on you folks?"

"No, by God," said Pa. "Wouldn't be no burden at all. You'd be helpin' us."

Wilson settled back uneasily. "Well, I dunno."

"What's a matter, don' you wanta?"

"Well, ya see—I on'y got 'bout thirty dollars lef', an' I won't be no burden."

Ma said, "You won't be no burden. Each'll help each, an' we'll all git to California. Sairy Wilson he'ped lay Grampa out," and she stopped. The relationship was plain.

Al cried, "That car'll take six easy. Say me to drive, an' Rosasharn an' Connie and Granma. Then we take the big light stuff an' pile her on the truck. An' we'll trade off ever' so often." He spoke loudly, for a load of worry was lifted from him.

They smiled shyly and looked down at the ground. Pa fingered the dusty earth with his fingertips. He said, "Ma favors a white house with oranges growin' around. They's a big pitcher on a calendar she seen."

Sairy said, "If I get sick again, you got to go on an' get there. We ain't a goin' to burden."

Ma looked carefully at Sairy, and she seemed to see for the first time the pain-tormented eyes and the face that was haunted and shrinking with pain. And Ma said, "We gonna see you get through. You said yourself, you can't let help go unwanted."

Sairy studied her wrinkled hands in the firelight. "We got to get some sleep tonight." She stood up.

"Grampa—it's like he's dead a year," Ma said.

The families moved lazily to their sleep, yawning luxuriously. Ma sloshed the tin plates off a little and rubbed the grease free with a flour sack. The fire died down and the stars descended. Few passenger cars went by on the highway now, but the transport trucks thundered by at intervals and put little earthquakes in the ground. In the ditch the cars were hardly visible under the starlight. A tied dog howled at the service station down the road. The families were quiet and sleeping, and the field mice grew bold and scampered about among the mattresses. Only Sairy Wilson was awake. She stared into the sky and braced her body firmly against pain.

CHAPTER FOURTEEN

The western land, nervous under the beginning change. The Western States, nervous as horses before a thunder storm. The great owners, nervous, sensing a change, knowing nothing of the nature of the change. The great owners, striking at the immediate thing, the widening government, the growing labor unity; striking at new taxes, at plans; not knowing these things are results, not causes. Results, not causes; results, not causes. The causes lie deep and simple—the causes are a hunger in a stom-10 ach, multiplied a million times; a hunger in a single soul, hunger for joy and some security, multiplied a million times; muscles and mind aching to grow, to work, to create, multiplied a million times. The last clear definite function of man—muscles aching to work, minds aching to create beyond the single need—this is man. To build a wall, to build a house, a dam, and in the wall and house and dam to put something of Manself, and to Manself take back something of the wall, the house, the dam; to take hard muscles from the lifting, to take the 20 clear lines and form from conceiving. For man, unlike any other thing organic or inorganic in the universe, grows beyond his work, walks up the stairs of his concepts, emerges ahead of his accomplishments. This you may say of man—when theories change and crash, when schools, philosophies, when narrow dark alleys of thought, national, religious, economic, grow and disintegrate, man reaches, stumbles forward, painfully, mistakenly sometimes. Having stepped forward, he may slip back, but only half a step, never the full step back. This you may 30 say and know it and know it. This you may know when the bombs plummet out of the black planes on the market place, when prisoners are stuck like pigs, when the crushed bodies drain filthily in the dust. You may know it in this way. If the step were not being taken, if the stumbling-forward ache were not alive, the bombs would not fall, the throats would not be cut. Fear the time when the bombs stop falling while the bombers live—for every bomb is proof that the spirit has not died. And fear the time when the strikes stop while the great owners live—40 for every little beaten strike is proof that the step is being taken. And this you can know—fear the time when Manself will not suffer and die for a concept, for this one quality is the foundation of Manself, and this one quality is man, distinctive in the universe.

The Western States nervous under the beginning change. Texas and Oklahoma, Kansas and Arkansas, New Mexico, Arizona, California. A single family moved from the land. Pa borrowed money from the bank, and now the bank wants the land. The land company—that's the bank when it has land—wants tractors, not families on 50 the land. Is a tractor bad? Is the power that turns the long furrows wrong? If this tractor were ours it would be good—not mine, but ours. If our tractor turned the long furrows of our land, it would be good. Not my land, but ours. We could love that tractor then as we have loved this land when it was ours. But this tractor does two things—it turns the land and turns us off the land. There is little difference between this tractor and a tank. The people are driven, intimidated, hurt by both. We must think about this. 60

One man, one family driven from the land; this rusty car creaking along the highway to the west. I lost my land, a single tractor took my land. I am alone and I am bewildered. And in the night one family camps in a ditch and another family pulls in and the tents come out. The two men squat on their hams and the women and children listen. Here is the node, you who hate change and fear revolution. Keep these two squatting men apart; make them hate, fear, suspect each other. Here is the anlage of the thing you fear. This is the zygote. For here "I lost my 70 land" is changed; a cell is split and from its splitting grows the thing you hate—"We lost *our* land." The danger is here, for two men are not as lonely and perplexed as one. And from this first "we" there grows a still more dangerous thing: "I have a little food" plus "I have none." If from this problem the sum is "We have a little food," the thing is on its way, the movement has direction. Only a little multiplication now, and this land, this tractor are ours. The two men squatting in a ditch, the little fire, the side-meat stewing in a single pot, the silent, 80 stone-eyed women; behind, the children listening with their souls to words their minds do not understand. The night draws down. The baby has a cold. Here, take this blanket. It's wool. It was my mother's blanket—take it for the baby. This is the thing to bomb. This is the beginning—from "I" to "we."

If you who own the things people must have could understand this, you might preserve yourself. If you could separate causes from results, if you could know that Paine, Marx, Jefferson, Lenin, were results, not causes, 90 you might survive. But that you cannot know. For the quality of owning freezes you forever into "I," and cuts you off forever from the "we."

The Western States are nervous under the beginning change. Need is the stimulus to concept, concept to action. A half-million people moving over the country; a million more restive, ready to move; ten million more feeling the first nervousness.

And tractors turning the multiple furrows in the vacant land.

CHAPTER FIFTEEN

Along 66 the hamburger stands—Al & Susy's Place—Carl's Lunch—Joe & Minnie—Will's Eats. Board-and-bat shacks. Two gasoline pumps in front, a screen door, a long bar, stools, and a foot rail. Near the door three slot machines, showing through glass the wealth of nickels three bars will bring. And beside them, the nickel phonograph with records piled up like pies, ready to swing out to the turntable and play dance music, "Ti-pi-ti-pi-tin," "Thanks for the Memory," Bing Crosby, Benny Goodman. At one end of the counter a covered case; candy cough drops, caffeine sulphate called Sleepless, No-Doze; candy, cigarettes, razor blades, aspirin, Bromo-Seltzer, Alka-Seltzer. The walls decorated with posters, bathing girls, blondes with big breasts and slender hips and waxen faces, in white bathing suits, and holding a bottle of Coca-Cola and smiling—see what you get with a Coca-Cola. Long bar, and salts, peppers, mustard pots, and paper napkins. Beer taps behind the counter, and in back the coffee urns, shiny and steaming, with glass gauges showing the coffee level. And pies in wire cages and oranges in pyramids of four. And little piles of Post Toasties, corn flakes, stacked up in designs.

The signs on cards, picked out with shining mica: Pies Like Mother Used to Make. Credit Makes Enemies. Let's Be Friends. Ladies May Smoke But Be Careful Where You Lay Your Butts. Eat Here and Keep Your Wife for a Pet. IITYWYBAD?

Down at one end the cooking plates, pots of stew, potatoes, pot roast, roast beef, gray roast pork waiting to be sliced.

Minnie or Susy or Mae, middle-aging behind the counter, hair curled and rouge and powder on a sweating face. Taking orders in a soft low voice, calling them to the cook with a screech like a peacock. Mopping the counter with circular strokes, polishing the big shining coffee urns. The cook is Joe or Carl or Al, hot in a white coat and apron, beady sweat on white forehead, below the white cook's cap; moody, rarely speaking, looking up for a moment at each new entry. Wiping the griddle, slapping down the hamburger. He repeats Mae's orders gently, scrapes the griddle, wipes it down with burlap. Moody and silent.

Mae is the contact, smiling, irritated, near to outbreak; smiling while her eyes look on past—unless for truck drivers. There's the backbone of the joint. Where the trucks stop, that's where the customers come. Can't fool truck drivers, they know. They bring the custom. They know. Give 'em a stale cup of coffee an' they're off the joint. Treat 'em right an' they come back. Mae really smiles with all her might at truck drivers. She bridles a little, fixes her back hair so that her breasts will lift with her raised arms, passes the time of day and indicates great things, great times, great jokes. Al never speaks. He is no contact. Sometimes he smiles a little at a joke, but he never laughs. Sometimes he looks up at the vivaciousness in Mae's voice, and then he scrapes the griddle with a spatula, scrapes the grease into an iron trough around the plate. He presses down a hissing hamburger with his spatula. He lays the split buns on the plate to toast and heat. He gathers up stray onions from the plate and heaps them on the meat and presses them in with the spatula. He puts half the bun on top of the meat, paints the other half with melted butter, with thin pickle relish. Holding the bun on the meat, he slips the spatula under the thin pad of meat, flips it over, lays the buttered half on top, and drops the hamburger on a small plate. Quarter of a dill pickle, two black olives beside the sandwich. Al skims the plate down the counter like a quoit. And he scrapes his griddle with the spatula and looks moodily at the stew kettle.

Cars whisking by on 66. License plates. Mass., Tenn., R.I., N.Y., Vt., Ohio. Going west. Fine cars, cruising at sixty-five.

There goes one of them Cords. Looks like a coffin on wheels.

But, Jesus, how they travel!

See that La Salle? Me for that. I ain't a hog. I go for a La Salle.

'F ya goin' big, what's a matter with a Cad'? Jus' a little bigger, little faster.

I'd take a Zephyr myself. You ain't ridin' no fortune, but you got class an' speed. Give me a Zephyr.

Well, sir, you may get a laugh outa this—I'll take a Buick-Puick. That's good enough.

But, hell, that costs in the Zephyr class an' it ain't got the sap.

I don't care. I don't want nothin' to do with nothing of Henry Ford's. I don't like 'im. Never did. Got a brother worked in the plant. Oughta hear him tell.

Well, a Zephyr got sap.

The big cars on the highway. Languid, heat-raddled ladies, small nucleuses about whom revolve a thousand accouterments: creams, ointments to grease themselves, coloring matter in phials—black, pink, red, white, green, silver—to change the color of hair, eyes, lips, nails, brows, lashes, lids. Oils, seeds, and pills to make the bowels move. A bag of bottles, syringes, pills, powders, fluids, jellies to make their sexual intercourse safe, odorless, and unproductive. And this apart from clothes. What a hell of a nuisance!

Lines of weariness around the eyes, lines of discontent down from the mouth, breasts lying heavily in little hammocks, stomach and thighs straining against cases of rubber. And the mouths panting, the eyes sullen, disliking sun and wind and earth, resenting food and weariness, hating time that rarely makes them beautiful and always makes them old.

Beside them, little pot-bellied men in light suits and panama hats; clean, pink men with puzzled, worried eyes, with restless eyes. Worried because formulas do not work out; hungry for security and yet sensing its disappearance from the earth. In their lapels the insignia of lodges and service clubs, places where they can go and, by a weight of numbers of little worried men, reassure themselves that business is noble and not the curious ritualized thievery they know it is; that business men are intelligent in spite of the records of their stupidity; that they are kind and charitable in spite of the principles of sound business; that their lives are rich instead of the thin tiresome routines they know; and that a time is coming when they will not be afraid any more.

And these two, going to California; going to sit in the lobby of the Beverly-Wilshire Hotel and watch people they envy go by, to look at mountains—mountains, mind you, and great trees—he with his worried eyes and she thinking how the sun will dry her skin. Going to look at the Pacific Ocean, and I'll bet a hundred thousand dollars to nothing at all, he will say, "It isn't as big as I thought it would be." And she will envy plump young bodies on the beach. Going to California really to go home again. To say, "So-and-So was at the table next to us at the Trocadero. She's really a mess, but she does wear nice clothes." And he, "I talked to good sound business men out there. They don't see a chance till we get rid of that fellow in the White House." And, "I got it from a man in the know—she has syphilis, you know. She was in that Warner picture. Man said she's slept her way into pictures. Well, she got what she was looking for." But the worried eyes are never calm, and the pouting mouth is never glad. The big car cruising along at sixty.

I want a cold drink.

Well, there's something up ahead. Want to stop?

Do you think it would be clean?

Clean as you're going to find in this God-forsaken country.

Well, maybe the bottled soda will be all right.

The great car squeals and pulls to a stop. The fat worried man helps his wife out.

Mae looks at and past them as they enter. Al looks up from his griddle, and down again. Mae knows. They'll drink a five-cent soda and crab that it ain't cold enough. The woman will use six paper napkins and drop them on the floor. The man will choke and try to put the blame on Mae. The woman will sniff as though she smelled rotting meat and they will go out again and tell forever afterward that the people in the West are sullen. And Mae, when she is alone with Al, has a name for them. She calls them shitheels.

Truck drivers. That's the stuff.

Here's a big transport comin'. Hope they stop; take away the taste of them shitheels. When I worked in that hotel in Albuquerque, Al, the way they steal—ever' darn thing. An' the bigger the car they got, the more they steal—towels, silver, soap dishes, I can't figger it.

And Al, morosely. Where ya think they get them big cars and stuff? Born with 'em? You won't never have nothin'.

The transport truck, a driver and relief. How 'bout stoppin' for a cup a Java? I know this dump.

How's the schedule?

Oh, we're ahead.

Pull up, then. They's a ol' war horse in here that's a kick. Good Java, too.

The truck pulls up. Two men in khaki riding trousers,

boots, short jackets, and shiny-visored military caps. Screen door—slam.

H'ya, Mae?

Well, if it ain't Big Bill the Rat! When'd you get back on this run?

Week ago.

The other man puts a nickel in the phonograph, watches the disk slip free and the turntable rise up under it. Bing Crosby's voice—golden. "Thanks for the mem-10 ory, of sunburn at the shore— You might have been a headache, but you never were a bore—" And the truck driver sings for Mae's ears, you might have been a haddock but you never was a whore—

Mae laughs. Who's ya frien', Bill? New on this run, ain't he?

The other puts a nickel in the slot machine, wins four slugs, and puts them back. Walks to the counter.

Well, what's it gonna be?

Oh, cup a Java. Kinda pie ya got?

20 Banana cream, pineapple cream, chocolate cream—an' apple.

Make it apple. Wait—Kind is that big thick one?

Mae lifts it out and sniffs it. Banana cream.

Cut off a hunk; make it a big hunk.

Man at the slot machine says, Two all around.

Two it is. Seen any new etchin's lately, Bill?

Well, here's one.

Now, you be careful front of a lady.

Oh, this ain't bad. Little kid comes in late ta school. 30 Teacher says, "Why ya late?" Kid says, "Had a take a heifer down—get 'er bred." Teacher says, "Couldn't your ol' man do it?" Kid says, "Sure he could, but not as good as the bull."

Mae squeaks with laughter, harsh screeching laughter. Al, slicing onions carefully on a board, looks up and smiles, and then looks down again. Truck drivers, that's the stuff. Gonna leave a quarter each for Mae. Fifteen cents for pie an' coffee an' a dime for Mae. An' they ain't tryin' to make her, neither.

40 Sitting together on the stools, spoons sticking up out of the coffee mugs. Passing the time of day. And Al, rubbing down his griddle, listening but making no comment. Bing Crosby's voice stops. The turntable drops down and the record swings into its place in the pile. The purple light goes off. The nickel, which has caused all this mechanism to work, has caused Crosby to sing and an orchestra to play—this nickel drops from be-

tween the contact points into the box where the profits go. The nickel, unlike most money, has actually done a job of work, has been physically responsible for a 50 reaction.

Steam spurts from the valve of the coffee urn. The compressor of the ice machine chugs softly for a time and then stops. The electric fan in the corner waves its head slowly back and forth, sweeping the room with a warm breeze. On the highway, on 66, the cars whiz by.

"They was a Massachusetts car stopped a while ago," said Mae.

Big Bill grasped his cup around the top so that the spoon stuck up between his first and second fingers. He 60 drew in a snort of air with the coffee, to cool it. "You ought to be out on 66. Cars from all over the country. All headin' west. Never seen so many before. Sure some honeys on the road."

"We seen a wreck this mornin'," his companion said. "Big car. Big Cad', a special job and a honey, low, cream-color, special job. Hit a truck. Folded the radiator right back into the driver. Must a been doin' ninety. Steerin' wheel went right on through the guy an' lef' him a-wig-glin' like a frog on a hook. Peach of a car. A honey. You 70 can have her for peanuts now. Drivin' alone, the guy was."

Al looked up from his work. "Hurt the truck?"

"Oh, Jesus Christ! Wasn't a truck. One of them cut-down cars full a stoves an' pans an' mattresses an' kids an' chickens. Goin' west, you know. This guy come by us doin' ninety—r'ared up on two wheels just to pass us, an' a car's comin' so he cuts in an' whangs this here truck. Drove like he's blin' drunk. Jesus, the air was full a bed clothes an' chickens an' kids. Killed one kid. Never seen 80 such a mess. We pulled up. Ol' man that's drivin' the truck, he jus' stan's there lookin' at that dead kid. Can't get a word out of 'im. Jus' rum-dumb. God Almighty, the road is full a them families goin' west. Never seen so many. Gets worse all a time. Wonder where the hell they all come from?"

"Wonder where they all go to," said Mae. "Come here for gas sometimes, but they don't hardly never buy nothin' else. People says they steal. We ain't got nothin' layin' around. They never stole nothin' from us." 90

Big Bill, munching his pie, looked up the road through the screened window. "Better tie your stuff down. I think you got some of 'em comin' now."

A 1926 Nash sedan pulled wearily off the highway.

The back seat was piled nearly to the ceiling with sacks, with pots and pans, and on the very top, right up against the ceiling, two boys rode. On the top of the car, a mattress and a folded tent; tent poles tied along the running board. The car pulled up to the gas pumps. A dark-haired, hatchet-faced man got slowly out. And the two boys slid down from the load and hit the ground.

Mae walked around the counter and stood in the door. The man was dressed in gray wool trousers and a blue shirt, dark blue with sweat on the back and under the arms. The boys in overalls and nothing else, ragged patched overalls. Their hair was light, and it stood up evenly all over their heads, for it had been roached. Their faces were streaked with dust. They went directly to the mud puddle under the hose and dug their toes into the mud.

The man asked, "Can we git some water, ma'am?"

A look of annoyance crossed Mae's face. "Sure, go ahead." She said softly over her shoulder, "I'll keep my eye on the hose." She watched while the man slowly unscrewed the radiator cap and ran the hose in.

A woman in the car, a flaxen-haired woman, said, "See if you can't git it here."

The man turned off the hose and screwed on the cap again. The little boys took the hose from him and they up-ended it and drank thirstily. The man took off his dark, stained hat and stood with a curious humility in front of the screen. "Could you see your way to sell us a loaf of bread, ma'am?"

Mae said, "This ain't a grocery store. We got bread to make san'widges."

"I know, ma'am." His humility was insistent. "We need bread and there ain't nothin' for quite a piece, they say."

" 'F we sell bread we gonna run out." Mae's tone was faltering.

"We're hungry," the man said.

"Whyn't you buy a san'widge? We got nice san'widges, hamburgs."

"We'd sure admire to do that, ma'am. But we can't. We got to make a dime do all of us." And he said embarrassedly, "We ain't got but a little."

Mae said, "You can't get no loaf of bread for a dime. We only got fifteen-cent loafs."

From behind her Al growled, "God Almighty, Mae, give 'em bread."

"We'll run out 'fore the bread truck comes."

John Steinbeck—photo from Theatre Arts Monthly, *June 1938*

"Run out, then, goddamn it," said Al. And he looked sullenly down at the potato salad he was mixing.

Mae shrugged her plump shoulders and looked to the truck drivers to show them what she was up against.

She held the screen door open and the man came in, bringing a smell of sweat with him. The boys edged in behind him and they went immediately to the candy case and stared in—not with craving or with hope or even with desire, but just with a kind of wonder that such things could be. They were alike in size and their faces were alike. One scratched his dusty ankle with the toe nails of his other foot. The other whispered some soft message and then they straightened their arms so that their clenched fists in the overall pockets showed through the thin blue cloth.

Mae opened a drawer and took out a long waxpaper-wrapped loaf. "This here is a fifteen-cent loaf."

The man put his hat back on his head. He answered with inflexible humility, "Won't you—can't you see your way to cut off ten cents' worth?"

Al said snarlingly, "Goddamn it, Mae. Give 'em the loaf."

The man turned toward Al. "No, we want ta buy ten

cents' worth of it. We got it figgered awful close, mister, to get to California."

Mae said resignedly, "You can have this for ten cents."

"That'd be robbin' you, ma'am."

"Go ahead—Al says to take it." She pushed the wax-papered loaf across the counter. The man took a deep leather pouch from his rear pocket, untied the strings, and spread it open. It was heavy with silver and with greasy bills.

"May soun' funny to be so tight," he apologized. "We got a thousan' miles to go, an' we don't know if we'll make it." He dug in the pouch with a forefinger, located a dime, and pinched in for it. When he put it down on the counter he had a penny with it. He was about to drop the penny back into the pouch when his eye fell on the boys frozen before the candy counter. He moved slowly down to them. He pointed in the case at big long sticks of striped peppermint. "Is them penny candy, ma'am?"

Mae moved down and looked in. "Which ones?"

"There, them stripy ones."

The little boys raised their eyes to her face and they stopped breathing; their mouths were partly opened, their half-naked bodies were rigid.

"Oh—them. Well, no—them's two for a penny."

"Well, gimme two then, ma'am." He placed the copper cent carefully on the counter. The boys expelled their held breath softly. Mae held the big sticks out.

"Take 'em," said the man.

They reached timidly, each took a stick, and they held them down at their sides and did not look at them. But they looked at each other, and their mouth corners smiled rigidly with embarrassment.

"Thank you, ma'am." The man picked up the bread and went out the door, and the little boys marched stiffly behind him, the red-striped sticks held tightly against their legs. They leaped like chipmunks over the front seat and onto the top of the load, and they burrowed back out of sight like chipmunks.

The man got in and started his car, and with a roaring motor and a cloud of blue oily smoke the ancient Nash climbed up on the highway and went on its way to the west.

From inside the restaurant the truck drivers and Mae and Al stared after them.

Big Bill wheeled back. "Them wasn't two-for-a-cent candy," he said.

"What's that to you?" Mae said fiercely.

"Them was a nickel apiece candy," said Bill.

"We got to get goin'," said the other man. "We're droppin' time." They reached in their pockets. Bill put a coin on the counter and the other man looked at it and reached again and put down a coin. They swung around and walked to the door.

"So long," said Bill.

Mae called, "Hey! Wait a minute. You got change."

"You go to hell," said Bill, and the screen door slammed.

Mae watched them get into the great truck, watched it lumber off in low gear, and heard them shift up the whining gears to cruising ratio. "Al—" she said softly.

He looked up from the hamburger he was patting thin and stacking between waxed papers. "What ya want?"

"Look there." She pointed at the coins beside the cups —two half-dollars. Al walked near and looked, and then he went back to his work.

"Truck drivers," Mae said reverently, "an' after them shitheels."

Flies struck the screen with little bumps and droned away. The compressor chugged for a time and then stopped. On 66 the traffic whizzed by, trucks and fine streamlined cars and jalopies; and they went by with a vicious whiz. Mae took down the plates and scraped the pie crusts into a bucket. She found her damp cloth and wiped the counter with circular sweeps. And her eyes were on the highway, where life whizzed by.

Al wiped his hands on his apron. He looked at a paper pinned to the wall over the griddle. Three lines of marks in columns on the paper. Al counted the longest line. He walked along the counter to the cash register, rang "No Sale," and took out a handful of nickels.

"What ya doin'?" Mae asked.

"Number three's ready to pay off," said Al. He went to the third slot machine and played his nickels in, and on the fifth spin of the wheels the three bars came up and the jackpot dumped out into the cup. Al gathered up the big handful of coins and went back of the counter. He dropped them in the drawer and slammed the cash register. Then he went back to his place and crossed out the line of dots. "Number three gets more play'n the others," he said. "Maybe I ought to shift 'em around." He lifted a lid and stirred the slowly simmering stew.

"I wonder what they'll do in California?" said Mae.

"Who?"

"Them folks that was just in."

"Christ knows," said Al.

"S'pose they'll get work?"

"How the hell would I know?" said Al.

She stared eastward along the highway. "Here comes a transport, double. Wonder if they stop? Hope they do." And as the huge truck came heavily down from the highway and parked, Mae seized her cloth and wiped the whole length of the counter. And she took a few swipes at the gleaming coffee urn too, and turned up the bottle-gas under the urn. Al brought out a handful of little
10 turnips and started to peel them. Mae's face was gay when the door opened and the two uniformed truck drivers entered.

"Hi, sister!"

"I won't be a sister to no man," said Mae. They laughed and Mae laughed. "What'll it be, boys?"

"Oh, a cup of Java. What kinda pie ya got?"

"Pineapple cream an' banana cream an' chocolate cream an' apple."

"Give me apple. No, wait—what's that big thick one?"

Mae picked up the pie and smelled it. "Pineapple 20 cream," she said.

"Well, chop out a hunk a that."

The cars whizzed viciously by on 66.

1939

Robert Penn Warren

1905 ·

Robert Penn Warren was born in Guthrie, Kentucky, and took his B.A. degree at Vanderbilt (in the class of 1925), his M.A. at the University of California, and his B. Litt. at Oxford. He has taught at Vanderbilt, Louisiana State University, the University of Minnesota, and, most recently, at Yale, where since 1951 he has been Professor of Dramatic Composition. At Vanderbilt, he was a member—along with John Crowe Ransom, Donald Davidson, Allen Tate, and others—of the now famous group of poets known as "Fugitives." At Louisiana State University, he was co-editor (with Cleanth Brooks) of the influential and important *Southern Review* (1935-1942), and co-author (also with Brooks) of a revolutionary textbook, *Understanding Poetry* (1938).

Few writers have been as versatile as Warren. His *Thirty-Six Poems* (1936) places him among the leading poets of our time. His *Rime of the Ancient Mariner by S. T. Coleridge* (1946) and other essays are significant contributions to literary criticism. His present fame, however, rests chiefly upon his prose fiction: upon his short stories, some of which were collected in *The Circus in the Attic* (1947), and even more, upon his novels,

Night Rider (1939), *At Heaven's Gate* (1943), *All the King's Men* (1946), and *World Enough and Time* (1950). *All the King's Men* was awarded a Pulitzer Prize.

Warren is sometimes regarded as a disciple of Faulkner. He is certainly an admirer of Faulkner, and his fiction doubtless resembles Faulkner's in some ways—in a vigorous, realistic handling of Southern subject-matter, in a philosophical and religious position rooted in Southern tradition, in technical virtuosity, in symbolical intensity. But Warren is no mere disciple. His background has been richly varied, much of his preparation has been formally academic, and he possesses certain advantages conveyed by a more academic and a more cosmopolitan experience. He is in a sense, therefore, less provincial than Faulkner, but his truest work, like Faulkner's, is at once Southern in its origins and universal in its meanings.

Norton R. Girault, "The Narrator's Mind as Symbol: An Analysis of All the King's Men," Accent, Summer 1947 • Eric Bentley, "The Meaning of Robert Penn Warren's Novels," Kenyon Review, Summer 1948 • Joseph Frank, "Romanticism and Reality in Robert Penn Warren," Hudson Review, Summer 1951

From

All the King's Men

All the King's Men tells the story of Willie Stark, whose career doubtless has some basic points of similarity with that of Huey Long: the time is the 1930's; the state, though unnamed in the novel, is obviously Louisiana; Stark, like Long, is a demagogue who rises to power on one suspender—in some respects a public benefactor, but ruthless in his methods; and Stark, again like Long, is assassinated in mid-career.

The story is told by Jack Burden (the book is perhaps as meaningfully his story as it is Stark's), who belongs to the conservative aristocracy. He is regarded as a traitor to his class by family and friends when, after graduating from the State University, and going into journalism instead of the law, he takes up with Stark, and later becomes his principal handyman.

When Willie Stark is told by Sadie Burke, a flamboyant young career woman in politics, that the city politicians are using him as a tool to split the country vote while ostensibly supporting him in the governor's race, Willie gets himself very drunk (for the first time, though not the last), and then proceeds out to the Fair Grounds, where—as seen in the following selection—he delivers a speech rather different from the written one prepared by his managers. Stark, needless to say, would be elected Governor at the next try.

FROM · CHAPTER TWO

The candidate could still stand, at least with one thigh propped against the table. He had begun to talk by this time, too. He had called them his friends in two or three ways and had said he was glad to be there. Now he stood there clutching the manuscript in both hands, with his head lowered like a dehorned cow beset by a couple of fierce dogs in the barnyard, while the sun beat on him and the sweat dropped. Then he took a grip on himself, and lifted his head.

"I have a speech here," he said. "It is a speech about what this state needs. But there's no use telling you what this state needs. You are the state. You know what you need. Look at your pants. Have they got holes in the knee? Listen to your belly. Did it ever rumble for emptiness? Look at your crop. Did it ever rot in the field because the road was so bad you couldn't get it to market? Look at your kids. Are they growing up ignorant as you and dirty because there isn't any school for them?"

Willie paused, and blinked around at the crowd. "No," he said, "I'm not going to read you any speech. You know what you need better'n I could tell you. But I'm going to tell you a story."

And he paused, steadied himself by the table, and took a deep breath while the sweat dripped.

I leaned toward Sadie. "What the hell's the bugger up to?" I asked.

"Shut up," she commanded, watching him.

He began again. "It's a funny story," he said. "Get ready to laugh. Get ready to bust your sides for it is sure a funny story. It's about a hick. It's about a red-neck, like you all, if you please. Yeah, like you. He grew up like any other mother's son on the dirt roads and gully washes of a north-state farm. He knew all about being a hick. He knew what it was to get up before day and get cow dung between his toes and feed and slop and milk before breakfast so he could set off by sunup to walk six miles to a one-room, slab-sided schoolhouse. He knew what it was to pay high taxes for that windy shack of a schoolhouse and those gully-washed red-clay roads to walk over—or to break his wagon axle or string-halt his mules on.

"Oh, he knew what it was to be a hick, summer and winter. He figured if he wanted to do anything he had to do it himself. So he sat up nights and studied books and studied law so maybe he could do something about changing things. He didn't study that law in any man's school or college. He studied it nights after a hard day's work in the field. So he could change things some. For himself and for folks like him. I am not lying to you. He didn't start out thinking about all the other hicks and how he was going to do wonderful things for them. He started out thinking of number one, but something came to him on the way. How he could not do something for himself and not for other folks or for himself without the help of other folks. It was going to be all together or none. That came to him.

"And it came to him with the powerful force of God's own lightning on a tragic time back in his own home county two years ago when the first brick schoolhouse ever built in his county collapsed because it was built of politics-rotten brick, and it killed and mangled a dozen poor little scholars. Oh, you know that story. He had fought the politics back of building that schoolhouse of rotten brick but he lost and it fell. But it started him thinking. Next time would be different.

"People were his friends because he had fought that rotten brick. And some of the public leaders down in the city knew that and they rode to his pappy's place in a big fine car and said how they wanted him to run for Governor."

I plucked Sadie's arm. "You think he's going to—"

"Shut up," she said savagely.

I looked toward Duffy up there on the platform back of Willie. Duffy's face was worried. It was red and round and sweating, and it was worried.

"Oh, they told him," Willie was saying, "and that hick swallowed it. He looked in his heart and thought he might try to change things. In all humility he thought how he might try. He was just a human, country boy, who believed like we have always believed back here in the hills that even the plainest, poorest fellow can be Governor if his fellow citizens find he has got the stuff and the character for the job.

"Those fellows in the striped pants saw the hick and they took him in. They said how MacMurfee was a limber-back and a dead-head and how Joe Harrison was the tool of the city machine, and how they wanted that hick to step in and try to give some honest government. They told him that. But—" Willie stopped, and lifted his right hand clutching the manuscript to high heaven —"do you know who they were? They were Joe Harrison's hired hands and lickspittles and they wanted to get a hick to run to split MacMurfee's hick vote. Did I guess this? I did not. No, for I heard their sweet talk. And I wouldn't know the truth this minute if that woman right there—" and he pointed down at Sadie— "if that woman right there—"

I nudged Sadie and said, "Sister, you are out of a job."

"—if that fine woman right there hadn't been honest enough and decent enough to tell the foul truth which stinks in the nostrils of the Most High!"

Duffy was on his feet, edging uncertainly toward the front of the platform. He kept looking desperately toward the band as though he might signal them to burst into music and then at the crowd as though he were trying to think of something to say. Then he edged toward Willie and said something to him.

But the words, whatever they were, were scarcely out of his mouth before Willie had turned on him. "There!" Willie roared. "There!" And he waved his right hand, the hand clutching the manuscript of his speech. "There is the Judas Iscariot, the lickspittle, the nose-wiper!"

And Willie waved his right arm at Duffy, clutching the manuscript which he had not read. Duffy was trying to say something to him, but Willie wasn't hearing it, for he was waving the manuscript under Duffy's retreating nose and shouting, "Look at him! Look at him!"

Duffy, still retreating, looked toward the band and waved his arms at them and shouted, "Play, play! Play the 'Star-Spangled Banner'!"

But the band didn't play. And just then as Duffy turned back to Willie, Willie made a more than usually energetic pass of the fluttering manuscript under Duffy's nose and shouted, "Look at him, Joe Harrison's dummy!"

Duffy shouted, "It's a lie!" and stepped back from the accusing arm.

I don't know whether Willie meant to do it. But anyway, he did it. He didn't exactly shove Duffy off the platform. He just started Duffy doing a dance along the edge, a kind of delicate, feather-toed, bemused, slow-motion adagio accompanied by arms pinwheeling around a face which was like a surprised custard pie with a hole scooped in the middle of the meringue, and the hole was Duffy's mouth, but no sound came out of it. There wasn't a sound over the five-acre tract of sweating humanity. They just watched Duffy do his dance.

Then he danced right off the platform. He broke his fall and half lay, half sat, propped against the bottom of the platform with his mouth still open. No sound came out of it now, for there wasn't any breath to make a sound.

All of that, and me without a camera.

Willie hadn't even bothered to look over the edge. "Let the hog lie!" he shouted. "Let the hog lie, and listen to me, you hicks. Yeah, you're hicks, too, and they've

All the King's Men 1173

fooled you, too, a thousand times, just like they fooled me. For that's what they think we're for. To fool. Well, this time I'm going to fool somebody. I'm getting out of this race. You know why?"

He paused and wiped the sweat off his face with his left hand, a flat scouring motion.

"Not because my little feelings are hurt. They aren't hurt, I never felt better in my life, because now I know the truth. What I ought to known long back. Whatever a hick wants he's got to do for himself. Nobody in a fine automobile and sweet-talking is going to do it for him. When I come back to run for Governor again, I'm coming on my own and I'm coming for blood. But I'm getting out now.

"I'm resigning in favor of MacMurfee. By God, everything I've said about MacMurfee stands and I'll say it again, but I'm going to stump this state for him. Me and the other hicks, we are going to kill Joe Harrison so dead he'll never even run for dogcatcher in this state. Then we'll see what MacMurfee does. This is his last chance. The time has come. The truth is going to be told and I'm going to tell it. I'm going to tell it over this state from one end to the other if I have to ride the rods or steal a mule to do it, and no man, Joe Harrison or any other man, can stop me. For I got me a gospel and I—"

I leaned to Sadie. "Listen," I said, "I've got to get on a telephone. I'm starting to town or the first telephone I hit. I got to telephone this in. You stay here and for God's sake remember what happens."

"All right," she said, not paying much mind to me.

"And nab Willie when it's over and bring him to town. It's a sure thing Duffy won't ask you to ride with him. You nab the sap, and—"

"Sap, hell," she said. And added, "You go on."

I went. I worked around the edge of the grandstand, through the crowd, with the sound of Willie's voice hammering on the eardrums and shaking dead leaves off the oak trees. As I rounded the end of the grandstand, I looked back and there was Willie flinging the sheets of his manuscript from him so they swirled about his feet and beating on his chest and shouting how the truth was there and didn't need writing down. There he was, with the papers about his feet and one arm up, the coat sleeve jammed elbow high, face red as a bruised beet and the sweat sluicing, hair over his forehead, eyes bugged out and shining, drunk as a hoot owl, and behind him the

bunting, red-white-and-blue, and over him God's bright, brassy, incandescent sky.

I walked down the gravel road a piece and hitched a ride on a truck to town.

That night when all was still and the train bearing Duffy back to the city (to report, no doubt, to Joe Harrison) was puffing across the sage country under the stars and Willie had been in bed for hours sleeping off the fumes, I reached for the bottle on the writing table in my room at the hotel in Upton and said to Sadie, "How about a little more of the stuff that let the bars down and kicked the boards loose?"

"What?" she asked.

"You would not understand that to which I so grammatically refer," I said, and poured the drink for her.

"Oh, I forgot," she said, "you're the fellow who went to college."

Yes, I was the fellow who had gone so grammatically to college where I had not learned, I decided, all there was to know.

Willie kept his word. He stumped the state for Mac-Murfee. He didn't ride the rods or buy him a mule or steal him one. But he drove the pants off his pretty good secondhand car over the washboard and through the hub-deep dust and got mired in the black gumbo when a rain came and sat in his car waiting for the span of mules to come and pull him out. He stood on schoolhouse steps, and on the top of boxes borrowed from the drygoods store and on the seats of farm wagons and on the porches of crossroads stores, and talked. "Friends, red-necks, suckers, and fellow hicks," he would say, leaning forward, leaning at them, looking at them. And he would pause, letting the words sink in. And in the quiet the crowd would be restless and resentful under these words they knew people called them but the words nobody ever got up and called them to their face. "Yeah," he would say, "yeah," and twist his mouth on the word, "that's what you are, and you needn't get mad at me for telling you. Well, get mad, but I'm telling you. That's what you are. And me—I'm one, too. Oh, I'm a red-neck, for the sun has beat down on me. Oh, I'm a sucker, for I fell for that sweet-talking fellow in the fine automobile. Oh, I took the sugar tit and hushed my crying. Oh, I'm a hick and I am the hick they were going to try to use and split the hick vote. But I'm standing here on my own hind legs, for even a dog can learn to do that, give him time. I learned. It took me a time but I learned, and here I am on my own hind legs." And he would lean at them. And demand, "Are you, are you on your hind legs? Have you learned that much yet? You think you can learn that much?"

He told them things they didn't like. He called them the names they didn't like to be called, but always, almost
10 always, the restlessness and resentment died and he leaned at them with his eyes bugging and his face glistening in the hot sunlight or the red light of a gasoline flare. They listened while he told them to stand on their own hind legs. Go and vote, he told them. Vote for MacMurfee this time, he told them, for he is all you have to vote for. But vote strong, strong enough to show what you can do. Vote him in and then if he doesn't deliver, nail up his hide. "Yeah," he would say, leaning, "yeah, nail him up if he don't deliver. Hand me the hammer and I'll nail
20 him." Vote, he told them. Put MacMurfee on the spot, he told them.

He leaned at them and said, "Listen to me, you hicks. Listen here and lift up your eyes and look on the God's blessed and unflyblown truth. If you've got the brain of a sapsucker left and can recognize the truth when you see it. This is the truth: you are a hick and nobody ever helped a hick but the hick himself. Up there in town they won't help you. It is up to you and God, and God helps those who help themselves!"

30 He gave them that, and they stood there in front of him, with a thumb hooked in the overall strap, and the eyes under the pulled down hat brim squinting at him as though he were something spied across a valley or cove, something they weren't quite easy in the mind about, too far away to make out good, or a sudden movement in the brush seen way off yonder across the valley or across the field and something might pop out of the brush, and under the eyes the jaw revolving worked the quid with a slow, punctilious, immitigable motion, like historical proc-
40 ess. And Time is nothing to a hog, or to History, either. They watched him, and if you watched close you might be able to see something beginning to happen. They stand so quiet, they don't even shift from one foot to the other—they've got a talent for being quiet, you can see them stand on the street corner when they come to town, not moving or talking, or see one of them squatting on

his heels by the road, just looking off where the road drops over the hill—and their squinched eyes don't flicker off the man up there in front of them. They've got a talent for being quiet. But sometimes the quietness stops.
50 It snaps all of a sudden, like a piece of string pulled tight. One of them sits quiet on the bench, at the brush-arbor revival, listening, and all of a sudden he jumps up and lifts up his arms and yells, "Oh Jesus! I have seen His name!" Or one of them presses his finger on the trigger, and the sound of the gun surprises even him.

Willie is up there. In the sun, or in the red light of the gasoline flare. "You ask me what my program is. Here it is, you hicks. And don't forget it. Nail 'em up! Nail up Joe Harrison. Nail up anybody who stands in
60 your way. Nail up MacMurfee if he don't deliver. Nail up anybody who stands in your way. You hand me the hammer and I'll do it with my own hand. Nail 'em up on the barn door! And don't fan away the bluebottles with any turkey wing!"

It was Willie, all right. It was the fellow with the same name.

MacMurfee was elected. Willie had something to do with it, for the biggest vote was polled in the sections Willie had worked that they had any record of. But all
70 the time MacMurfee didn't quite know what to make of Willie. He shied off him at first, for Willie had said some pretty hard things about him, and then when it did look as though Willie would make an impression, he shilly-shallied. And in the end Willie got up on his hind legs and said how the MacMurfee people were offering to pay his expenses but he was on his own, he wasn't Mac-Murfee's man, even if he was saying to vote for Mac-Murfee. He was paying his way, he said, even if he had to put another mortgage on his pappy's farm and the
80 last one it would hold. Yes, and if there was anybody who couldn't afford two dollars to pay his poll tax and came to him and said it straight out, he, Willie Stark, would pay that tax out of money he had got by mortgaging his pappy's farm. That was how much he believed in what he was saying. . . .

[Adam Stanton and his sister Anne were childhood friends and neighbors of the narrator, Jack Burden, at Burden's Landing on the Gulf Coast. Anne and Jack had been in love at one point, but had drifted apart, especially after Jack attached himself to Governor Stark. The little community at Burden's Landing epitomized the conservative hostility to Stark. Jack had undermined somewhat the attitude of Adam and Anne when he had dug up (at the Governor's behest, and for purposes of blackmail) a political scandal of twenty-five years earlier ("the truth" which he alludes to, below) pertaining to Governor Stanton, the father of Adam and Anne, and Judge Irwin, who is ironically revealed at the end of the story as Jack's own father.

Stark was a corrupt man: he was ruthless; he resorted to bullying and blackmail; two of the women in the story were his mistresses—Sadie Burke, and later, surprisingly enough, Anne Stanton. But he had a passionate vision of service to the underprivileged masses. He planned a magnificent hospital and selected Adam Stanton, the leading medical man in the state, to head it. When the opposition in the legislature attempted to impeach him, the hillbillies marched on the capitol and camped on the capitol grounds until the Governor sent them home. In the following selection, we see the Governor exercising his hypnotic power over the populace. We also see, in the scene with Dr. Stanton, his attempt to justify his career on ethical grounds, to formulate what might be called the "ethic" of the demagogue.]

FROM • CHAPTER SIX

The big black Cadillac, the hood glistening dully under the street lamps—as I could see even from the back seat —eased down the street, making its expensive whisper under the boughs which had new leaves on them, for it was early April now. Then we got to a street where there were not any nice trees arching over.

"Here," I said, "that place on the right, just beyond that grocery."

Sugar-Boy put the Cadillac up to the curb, like a 10 mother laying Little Precious down with a last kiss. Then he ran around to open the door for the Boss, but the Boss was already on the curb. I uncoiled myself and stood beside him. "This is the joint," I remarked, and started in.

For we were going to see Adam Stanton.

When I told the Boss that Adam Stanton would take the job and that he had sent me a message to arrange things, the Boss had said, "Well." Then he had looked at me from toe to crown, and said, "You must be Svengali."

20 "Yeah," I had said, "I am Svengali."

"I want to see him," the Boss had said.

"I'll try to get him up here."

"Get him up here?" the Boss had said. "I'll go there. Hell, he's doing me a favor."

"Well, you're the Governor, aren't you?"

"You're damned right I am," the Boss had said, "but he is Doc Stanton. When do we go?"

I had told him it would have to be at night, that you never could catch him except at night.

So here we were, at night, entering the door of the 30 crummy apartment house, climbing the dark stairs, stumbling over the kiddie car, inhaling the odor of cabbage and diapers. "He sure picked himself a place to live," the Boss said.

"Yeah," I agreed, "and lots of folks can't figure out why."

"I reckon I can," the Boss said.

And as I wondered whether he could or not, we reached the door, and I knocked, entered, and confronted the level eyes of Adam Stanton. 40

For a half moment, while Sugar-Boy was easing in, and I was shutting the door, Adam and the Boss simply took each other in, without a word. Then I turned and said, "Governor Stark, this is Dr. Stanton."

The Boss took a step forward and put out his right hand. Perhaps I imagined it, but I thought I noticed a shade of hesitation before Adam took it. And the Boss must have noticed it, too, for when Adam did put out his hand, the Boss, in the middle of the shake, before any other word had been spoken, grinned suddenly, and said, 50 "See, boy, it's not as bad as you thought, it won't kill you."

Then, by God, Adam grinned, too.

Then I said, "And this is Mr. O'Shean," and Sugar-Boy lurched forward and put out one of his stubby arms with a hand hanging on the end of it like a stuffed glove, and twisted his face and began, "I'm pl-pl-pl-pl—"

"I'm glad to know you," Adam said. Then I saw his glance pick up the bulge under Sugar-Boy's left armpit. He turned to the Boss. "So this is one of your gunmen I've heard about?" he said, definitely not grinning now. 60

"Hell," the Boss said, "Sugar-Boy just carries that for fun. Sugar-Boy is just a pal. Ain't anybody can drive a car like Sugar-Boy."

---

19 **Svengali**, an Austrian Jew, of marked hypnotic power and influence, in George du Maurier's novel, **Trilby**

Sugar-Boy was looking at him like a dog you've just scratched on the head.

Adam stood there, and didn't reply. For a second I thought the deal was about to blow up. Then Adam said, very formally, "Won't you gentlemen have seats?"

We did.

Sugar-Boy sneaked one of his lumps of sugar out of the side pocket of his coat, put it into his mouth, and began to suck it, with his fey Irish cheeks drawn in and his eyes blurred with bliss.

Adam waited, sitting straight up in his chair.

The Boss, leaning back in one of the overstuffed wrecks, didn't seem to be in any hurry. But he finally said, "Well, Doc, what do you think of it?"

"Of what?" Adam demanded.

"Of my hospital?"

"I think it will do the people of the state some good," he said. Then added, "And get you some votes."

"You can forget about the vote side of it," the Boss said. "There are lots of ways to get votes, son."

"So I understand," Adam said. Then he handed the Boss another big chunk of silence to admire.

The Boss admired it awhile, then said, "Yeah, it'll do some good. But not too much unless you take over."

"I won't stand any interference," Adam said, and bit the sentence off.

"Don't worry," the Boss laughed. "I might fire you, boy, but I won't interfere."

"If that is a threat," Adam said, and the pale-blue blaze flickered up in his eyes, "you have wasted your time by coming here. You know my opinions of this administration. They have been no secret. And they will be no secret in the future. You understand that?"

"Doc," the Boss said, "Doc, you just don't understand politics. I'll be frank with you. I could run this state and ten more like it with you howling on every street corner like a hound with a sore tail. No offense. But you just don't understand."

"I understand some things," Adam said grimly, and the jaw set.

"And some you don't, just like I don't, but one thing I understand and you don't is what makes the mare go. I can make the mare go. And one more thing, now we are taking down our hair—" The Boss suddenly stopped, cocked his head, leered at Adam, then demanded, "Or are we?"

"You said there was one more thing," Adam replied, ignoring the question, sitting straight in his chair.

"Yeah, one more thing. But look here, Doc—you know Hugh Miller?"

"Yes," Adam said, "yes, I know him."

"Well, he was in with me—yeah, Attorney General—and he resigned. And you know why?" But he went on without waiting for the answer. "He resigned because he wanted to keep his little hands clean. He wanted the bricks but he just didn't know somebody has to paddle in the mud to make 'em. He was like somebody that just loves beefsteak but just can't bear to go to a slaughter pen because there are some bad, rough men down there who aren't animal lovers and who ought to be reported to the S.P.C.A. Well, he resigned."

I watched Adam's face. It was white and stony, as though carved out of some slick stone. He was like a man braced to hear what the jury foreman was going to say. Or what the doctor was going to say. Adam must have seen a lot of faces like that in his time. He must have had to look into them and tell them what he had to tell.

"Yeah," the Boss said, "he resigned. He was one of those guys wants everything and wants everything two ways at once. You know the kind, Doc?"

He flicked a look over at Adam, like a man flicking a fly over by the willows in the trout stream. But there wasn't any strike.

"Yeah, old Hugh—he never learned that you can't have everything. That you can have mighty little. And you never have anything you don't make. Just because he inherited a little money and the name Miller he thought you could have everything. Yeah, and he wanted the one last damned thing you can't inherit. And you know what it is?" He stared at Adam's face.

"What?" Adam said, after a long pause.

"Goodness. Yeah, just plain, simple goodness. Well you can't inherit that from anybody. You got to make it, Doc. If you want it. And you got to make it out of badness. Badness. And you know why, Doc?" He raised his bulk up in the broken-down wreck of an overstuffed chair he was in, and leaned forward, his hands on his knees, his elbows cocked out, his head outthrust and the hair coming down to his eyes, and stared into Adam's face. "Out of badness," he repeated. "And you know why? Because there isn't anything else to make it out of." Then, sinking back into the wreck, he asked, softly, "Did you know that, Doc?"

Adam didn't say a word.

Then the Boss asked, softer still, almost whispering, "Did you know that, Doc?"

Adam wet his lips and said, "There is one question I should like to ask you. It is this. If, as you say, there is only the bad to start with, and the good must be made from the bad, then how do you ever know what the good
10 is? How do you even recognize the good? Assuming you have made it from the bad. Answer me that."

"Easy, Doc, easy," the Boss said.

"Well, answer it."

"You just make it up as you go along."

"Make up what?"

"The good," the Boss said. "What the hell else are we talking about? Good with a capital G."

"So you make it up as you go along?" Adam repeated gently.

20 "What the hell else you think folks been doing for a million years, Doc? When your great-great-grandpappy climbed down out of the tree, he didn't have any more notion of good or bad, or right and wrong, than the hoot owl that stayed up in the tree. Well, he climbed down and he began to make Good up as he went along. He made up what he needed to do business, Doc. And what he made up and got everybody to mirate on as good and right was always just a couple of jumps behind what he needed to do business on. That's why things change,
30 Doc. Because what folks claim is right is always just a couple of jumps short of what they need to do business. Now an individual, one fellow, he will stop doing business because he's got a notion of what is right, and he is a hero. But folks in general, which is society, Doc, is never going to stop doing business. Society is just going to cook up a new notion of what is right. Society is sure not ever going to commit suicide. At least, not that way and of a purpose. And that is a fact. Now ain't it?"

"It is?" Adam said.

40 "You're damned right it is, Doc. And right is a lid you put on something and some of the things under the lid look just like some of the things not under the lid, and there never was any notion of what was right if you put it down on folks in general that a lot of them didn't start squalling because they just couldn't do any human business under that kind of right. Hell, look at when folks couldn't get a divorce. Look at all the good women got beat and the good men got nagged and couldn't do any human damned thing about it. Then, all of a sudden, a divorce got to be right. What next, you don't know. 50 Nor me. But I do know this." He stopped, leaned forward again, the elbows again cocked out.

"What?" Adam demanded.

"This. I'm not denying there's got to be a notion of right to get business done, but by God, any particular notion at any particular time will sooner or later get to be just like a stopper put tight in a bottle of water and thrown in a hot stove the way we kids used to do at school to hear the bang. The steam that blows the bottle and scares the teacher to wet her drawers is just the 60 human business that is going to get done, and it will blow anything you put it in if you seal it tight, but, you put it in the right place and let it get out in a certain way and it will run a freight engine." He sank back again into the chair, his eyelids sagging now, but the eyes watchful, and the hair down over his forehead like an ambush.

Adam got up suddenly, and walked across the room. He stopped in front of the dead fireplace, with old ashes still in it, and some half-burned paper, though spring 70 was on us, and there hadn't been any fire for a time. The window was up, and the night air came into the room, with a smell different from the diaper-and-cabbage smell, a smell of damp grass and the leaves hanging down from the arched trees in the dark, a smell that definitely did not belong there in that room. And all of a sudden I remembered once how into a room where I was sitting one night, a big pale apple-green moth, big as a bullbat and soft and silent as a dream—a Luna moth, the name is, and it is a wonderful name—came flying in. Some- 80 body had left the screen door open, and the moth drifted in over the tables and chairs like a big pale-green, silky, live leaf, drifting and dancing along without any word under the electric light where a Luna moth certainly did not belong. The night air coming into the room now was like that.

Adam leaned an elbow on the wooden mantelpiece where you could write your name in the dust and the books were stacked and the old, dregs-crusted coffee cup sat. He stood there as though he were all by himself. 90

27 mirate, to wonder at, to admire, to be greatly pleased with

The Boss was watching him.

"Yeah," the Boss said, watchful, "it will run a freight engine and—"

But Adam broke in, "What are you trying to convince me of? You don't have to convince me of anything. I've told you I'd take the job. That's all!" He glared at the bulky man in the big chair, and said, "That's all! And my reasons are my own."

The Boss gave a slow smile, shifted his weight in the chair, and said, "Yeah, your reasons are your own, Doc. But I just thought you might want to know something about mine. Since we're going to do business together."

"I am going to run the hospital," Adam said, and added with curling lip, "if you call that doing business together."

The Boss laughed out loud. Then he got up from the chair. "Doc," he said, "just don't you worry. I'll keep your little mitts clean. I'll keep you clean all over, Doc. I'll put you in that beautiful, antiseptic, sterile, six-million-dollar hospital, and wrap you in cellophane, untouched by human hands." He stepped to Adam, and slapped him on the shoulder. "Don't you worry, Doc," he said.

"I can take care of myself," Adam affirmed, and looked down at the hand on his shoulder.

"Sure you can, Doc," the Boss said. He removed his hand from the shoulder. Then his tone changed, suddenly businesslike and calm. "You will no doubt want to see all the plans which have been drawn up. They are subject to your revision after you consult with the architects. Mr. Todd, of Todd and Waters, will come to see you about it. And you can start picking your staff. It is all your baby."

He turned away and picked up his hat from the piano top. He swung back toward Adam and gave him a summarizing look, from top to toe and back. "You're a great boy, Doc," he said, "and don't let 'em tell you different."

Then he wheeled to the door, and went out before Adam could say a word. If there was any word he had to say.

Sugar-Boy and I followed. We didn't stop to say good night and thanks for the hospitality. That just didn't seem to be in the cards. At the door, however, I looked back and said, "So long, boy," but Adam didn't answer.

Down in the street, the Boss hesitated on the curb, beside the car. Then he said, "You all go on. I'm walking." He turned up the street, toward town, past the crummy apartment house and the little grocery and the boarding houses and the shotgun bungalows.

Just as I climbed in beside Sugar-Boy, in the place the Boss always took, I heard the burst of music from the apartment house. The window was open and the music was very loud. Adam was beating the hell out of that expensive piano, and filling the night air with racket like Niagara Falls.

We rolled down the street, and passed the Boss, who, walking along with his head down, didn't pay us any mind. We pulled on into one of the good streets with the trees arching overhead and the new leaves looking black against the sky, or pale, almost whitish, where the rays of a street lamp struck them. We were beyond the sound of Adam's music now.

I lay back and closed my eyes and took the sway and dip of the car, which was soft and easy, and thought of the Boss and Adam Stanton facing each other across that room. I had never expected to see that. But it had happened.

I had found the truth, I had dug the truth up out of the ash pile, the garbage heap, the kitchen midden, the bone yard, and had sent that little piece of truth to Adam Stanton. I couldn't cut the truth to match his ideas. Well, he'd have to make his ideas match the truth. That is what all of us historical researchers believe. The truth shall make you free.

So I lay back and thought of Adam and the truth. And of the Boss and what he had said the truth was. The good was. The right was. And lying there, lulled in the Cadillac, I wondered if he believed what he had said. He had said that you have to make the good out of the bad because that is all you have got to make it out of. Well, he had made some good out of some bad. The hospital. The Willie Stark Hospital, which was going to be there when Willie Stark was dead and gone. As Willie Stark had said. Now if Willie Stark believed that you always had to make the good out of the bad, why did he get so excited when Tiny just wanted to make a logical little deal with the hospital contract? Why did he get so heated up just because Tiny's brand of Bad might get mixed in the raw materials from which he was going to make some Good? "Can't you understand?" the

73 The truth . . . free. See John 8:32

All the King's Men 1179

Boss had demanded of me, grabbing my lapel. "Can't you understand, either? I'm building that place, the best in the country, the best in the world, and a bugger like Tiny is not going to mess with it, and I'm going to call it the Willie Stark Hospital and it will be there a long time after I'm dead and gone and you are dead and gone and all those sons-of-bitches are dead and gone—" That was scarcely consistent. It was not at all consistent. I would have to ask the Boss about it sometime.

I had asked the Boss about something else once. The night after the impeachment blew up. The night when the great crowd that had poured into town stood on the lawn of the Capitol, trampling the flower beds beneath the great frock-coated and buckskin-clad and sword-bearing bronze statues which were History. When out of the tall dark doorway of the Capitol, under the blue glares of the spotlights Willie Stark walked out to stand at the top of the high steps, heavy and slow-looking, blinking in the light. He stood there, the only person up there on the wide expanse of stone, seeming to be lonely and lost against the mass of stone which reared behind him, standing there blinking. The long chant of "Willie—Willie—we want Willie," which had swelled up from the crowd, stopped as he came out. For an instant as he waited, there wasn't a sound. Then suddenly there was the great roar from the crowd, without any words. It was a long time before he lifted his hand to stop it. Then the roar died away as though under the pressure of his slowly descending hand.

Then he said, "They tried to ruin me, but they are ruined."

And the roar came again, and died away, under the hand.

He said, "They tried to ruin me because they did not like what I have done. Do you like what I have done?"

The roar came, and died.

He said, "I tell you what I am going to do. I am going to build a hospital. The biggest and the finest money can buy. It will belong to you. Any man or woman or child who is sick or in pain can go in those doors and know that all will be done that man can do. To heal sickness. To ease pain. Free. Not as charity. But as a right. It is your right. Do you hear? It is your right!"

The roar came.

He said, "And it is your right that every child shall have a complete education. That no person aged and infirm shall want or beg for bread. That the man who produces something shall be able to carry it to market without miring to the hub, without toll. That no poor man's house or land shall be taxed. That the rich men and the great companies that draw wealth from this state shall pay this state a fair share. That you shall not be deprived of hope!"

The roar came. As it died away, Anne Stanton, who had her arm through mine and was pressed close by the weight of the crowd, asked, "Does he mean that, Jack? Really?"

"He's done a great deal of it already," I said.

"Yes," Adam Stanton said, and his lips curled back with the words, "yes—that's his bribe."

I didn't answer—and I didn't know what my answer would have been—for Willie Stark, up there on the high steps, was saying, "I will do those things. So help me God. I shall live in your will and your right. And if any man tries to stop me in the fulfilling of that right and that will I'll break him. I'll break him like that!" He spread his arms far apart, shoulder-high, and crashed the right fist into the left palm. "Like that! I'll smite him. Hip and thigh, shinbone and neckbone, kidney punch, rabbit punch, uppercut, and solar plexus. And I don't care what I hit him with. Or how!"

Then, in the midst of the roar, I leaned toward Anne's ear and yelled, "He damned well means that."

I didn't know whether or not Anne heard me. She was watching the man up there on the steps, who was leaning forward toward the crowd, with bulging eyes, saying, "I'll hit him, I'll hit him with that meat ax!"

Then he suddenly stretched his arms above his head, the coat sleeves drawn tight to expose the shirt sleeves, the hands spread and clutching. He screamed, "Gimme that meat ax!"

And the crowd roared.

He brought both hands slowly down, for silence.

Then said, "Your will is my strength."

And after a moment of silence said, "Your need is my justice."

Then, "That is all."

He turned and walked slowly back into the tall door-

---

70 **hip and thigh,** from an account of Samson's treatment of the Philistines. See Judges 15:8: "And he smote them hip and thigh with a great slaughter"

way of the Capitol, into the darkness there, and disappeared. The roar was swelling and heaving in the air now, louder than ever, and I felt it inside of me, too, swelling like blood and victory. I stared into the darkness of the great doorway of the Capitol, where he had gone, while the roar kept on.

Anne Stanton was tugging at my arm. She asked me, "Does he mean that, Jack?"

"Hell," I said, and heard the savage tone in my own voice, "hell, how the hell do I know?"

Adam Stanton's lip curled and he said, "Justice! He used that word."

And suddenly, for the flicker of an instant, I hated Adam Stanton.

I told them I had to go, which was true, and worked my way around through the edge of the crowd, to the police cordon. Then I went around to the back of the Capitol, where I joined the Boss.

Late that night, back at the Mansion, after he had thrown Tiny and his rabble out of the study, I asked him the question. I asked, "Did you mean what you said?"

Propped back on the big leather couch, he stared at me, and demanded, "What?"

"What you said," I replied, "tonight. You said your strength was their will. You said your justice was their need. All of that."

He kept on staring at me, his eyes bulging, his stare grappling and probing into me.

"You said that," I said.

"God damn it," he exclaimed, violently, still staring at me, "God damn it—" he clenched his right fist and struck himself twice on the chest—"God damn it, there's something inside you—there's something inside you—"

He left the words hanging there. He turned his eyes from me and stared moodily into the fire. I didn't press my question. . . .

[Stark was assassinated in the state capitol building by Adam Stanton (who was in turn promptly riddled by Sugar-Boy) after Stanton had been told anonymously over the phone (his informant was Duffy, egged on by the cast-off Sadie Burke) that his sister Anne was Stark's mistress (which was true), and that she, in that capacity, had persuaded the Governor to give Adam the directorship of the big hospital (which was untrue). The book concludes with the narrator's speculations on the meaning of these catastrophic events. To Burden, Stanton was "the man of idea," and Stark, "the man of fact"; they were "doomed to destroy each other," "because each was incomplete with the terrible division of their age." The story, then, must be read as more than a history of political chicanery. It is essentially a richly symbolical account (to quote from Norton R. Girault's analytical essay, listed above) of "man's struggle toward integration in terms of his whole nature." The novel gives no pat, categorical answers to the questions which it raises. Human experience as portrayed by Warren is a tangled web of good and evil, and the phenomenon which was Willie Stark remains one of God's mysteries.]

1946

Acknowledgments

The editors are grateful to those who have given permission to reproduce the following materials:

Appleton-Century-Crofts, Inc.: "The Flower-Fed Buffaloes," from *Going to the Stars* by Vachel Lindsay; portrait of Henry Timrod from L. F. Tooker, "Timrod the Poet," *Century Magazine.* Copyright, 1898, Century Company. Reproduced by permission of the publishers Appleton-Century-Crofts, Inc.

Kenneth Burke: the essay "Psychology and Form," is reprinted from Kenneth Burke's *Counter-Statement,* a work originally published in 1931, and being reissued in 1953 under the imprint of Hermes Publications, Los Altos, California. Copyright, 1931, 1953, by Kenneth Burke

John Dos Passos: selections from *U.S.A.*

Doubleday, Doran and Company, Inc.: selections from Frank Norris' *The Octopus,* copyright 1901, and *The Responsibilities of the Novelist,* copyright 1903, by Doubleday, Doran and Company, Inc.; from *The Four Million* by O. Henry, copyright 1909 by Doubleday, Doran and Company, Inc.; and from *Europe Without Baedeker* by Edmund Wilson

Faber and Faber, Ltd.: Canadian rights for five poems from *The Collected Poems of T. S. Eliot*

Forum: "The Critic and American Life" by Irving Babbitt, which first appeared in *Forum,* February 1928

Harcourt, Brace and Company, Inc.: selections from *The Collected Poems of T. S. Eliot,* copyright 1936; from *Smoke and Steel* by Carl Sandburg, copyright 1920; from *Abraham Lincoln: The Prairie Years,* Volume I, by Carl Sandburg, copyright 1926; from *The People, Yes* by Carl Sandburg, copyright 1936; from *Main Street* by Sinclair Lewis, copyright 1920, by Harcourt, Brace and Company, Inc.; from *All the King's Men* by Robert Penn Warren, copyright, 1946, by Harcourt, Brace and Company, Inc.; "The Waste Land" from *Collected Poems 1909-1935* by T. S. Eliot, copyright, 1936, by Harcourt, Brace and Company, Inc.; and "Flowering Judas" from *Flowering Judas and Other Stories.* Reprinted by permission of Harcourt, Brace and Company, Inc.

Harper & Brothers: selections from *You Can't Go Home Again* by Thomas Wolfe; from *A New England Nun and Other Stories* by Mary E. Wilkins Freeman; from *Terminations* by Henry James; "The Character of Man" from *Mark Twain's Autobiography* by Samuel Clemens; from *Bolts of Melody, New Poems of Emily Dickinson,* edited by Mabel Loomis Todd and Millicent Todd Bingham; five poems from *Annie Allen* by Gwendolyn Brooks; and an illustration from *Mr. Dooley's Philosophy* by Finley Peter Dunne

The Harvard Theatre Collection: reproduction of a poster advertising a performance of *Uncle Tom's Cabin*

Henry Holt and Company, Inc.: selections from *Collected Poems* by Robert Frost; from *Chicago Poems* and *Cornhuskers* by Carl Sandburg; and a woodcut from *New Hampshire* by Robert Frost, copyright, 1923, by Henry Holt and Company, Inc., copyright, 1951, by Robert Frost. Used by permission of the publishers

Herbert C. Hoover: two public addresses

Houghton Mifflin Company: selections from *The Education of Henry Adams* by Henry Adams, and from *Poems* by William Vaughn Moody

John Mead Howells and Mildred Howells: selection from *Criticism and Fiction* by William Dean Howells, copyright 1891 by Harper & Brothers, copyright 1918 by William Dean Howells

Alfred A. Knopf, Inc.: "The Emperor of Ice-Cream" and "Sunday Morning" reprinted from *Harmonium* by Wallace Stevens, by permission of Alfred A. Knopf, Inc.; "Father and His Hard-Rocking Ship" reprinted from *Life with Father* by Clarence Day, by permission of Alfred A. Knopf, Inc.; and a drawing titled "Never say die!" reprinted from *Thoughts Without Words* by Clarence Day, by permission of Alfred A. Knopf, Inc. Copyright 1923, 1928 by Clarence Day

Lincoln Library of the University of Chicago: Lincoln silhouette

Little, Brown & Company: selections from *Poems by Emily Dickinson,* edited by Martha Dickinson Bianchi and Alfred Leete Hampson, by permission of Little, Brown & Company.

Liveright Publishing Corporation: "Proem: To Brooklyn Bridge," "The River," and "The Tunnel" from the *Collected Poems of Hart Crane,* edited with an introduction by Waldo Frank, published by Liveright Publishing Corporation, copyright 1933 by Liveright, Inc.

Isabel Garland Lord: selections from *Main-Travelled Roads* and *Crumbling Idols* by Hamlin Garland

The Macmillan Company: selections from *Adventures While Preaching the Gospel of Beauty* and *Collected Poems* by Vachel Lindsay; from *Collected Poems* by Edwin Arlington Robinson; and from *Partial Portraits* by Henry James

McGraw-Hill Book Company, Inc.: two quotations from *After the Lost Generation* by John W. Aldridge, 1951

The New York Public Library: poster advertising a lecture by Mark Twain; photograph of the kitchen set for the last act of *Shore Acres* from the Theatre Collection

G. P. Putnam's Sons: "The Second Choice," from *Free and Other Stories,* copyright 1918 by Boni and Liveright, Inc., copyright 1945 by Theodore Dreiser; "Narcissus as Narcissus," from *Reason in Madness: Critical Essays* by Allen Tate, copyright 1941 by Allen Tate

Random House, Inc.: *The Hairy Ape* by Eugene O'Neill; "A Rose for Emily," from *These 13* by William Faulkner; *Roan Stallion* by Robinson Jeffers; and "Progressive Government," from *The Public Papers and Addresses of Franklin D. Roosevelt,* Volume I

Simon and Schuster, Inc.: illustration from *A Treasury of the Blues,* copyright 1926, 1949, by W. C. Handy and Edward Abbe Niles, published by Charles Boni, distributed by Simon and Schuster, Inc.

Upton Sinclair: selection from *The Jungle*

The State University of Iowa: "Literature and the Modern World" by T. S. Eliot, from *American Prefaces,* Volume 5, No. 9, June 1940

The Viking Press, Inc.: selections from *Tortilla Flat* by John Steinbeck, copyright 1935 by the author, and from *The Grapes of Wrath* by John Steinbeck, copyright 1939 by the author

Mrs. Woodrow Wilson: two addresses by Woodrow Wilson

Ella Winter: "Philadelphia: Corrupt and Contented," from *The Shame of the Cities* by Lincoln Steffens

The editors are grateful to Ati Forberg for her drawings appearing on pp. 2, 218, and 754

Thanks are also due to *The South Atlantic Quarterly* for permission to reprint, with some additions, "Literature Between the Wars" by Randall Stewart, which first appeared in *The South Atlantic Quarterly,* Volume 44, No. 4, October 1945

Index of First Lines

General Index

Names of authors and titles of selections included in this volume are set in **boldface**. The **boldface numbers** refer to the pages on which the biographical sketch or selection appears.

Titles of works referred to but not included in this volume are set in medium bold.